The Hotel Guide 2005

C000203296

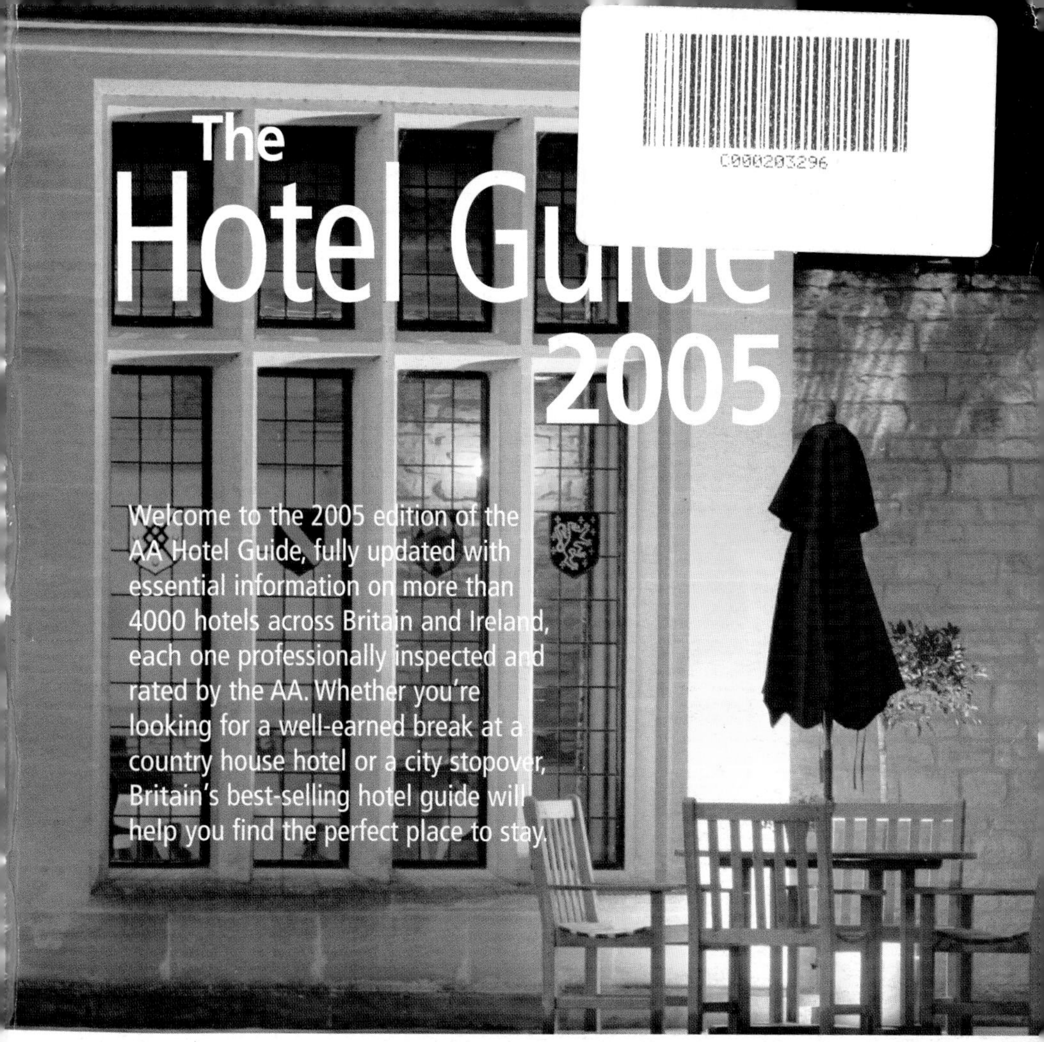

Welcome to the 2005 edition of the AA Hotel Guide, fully updated with essential information on more than 4000 hotels across Britain and Ireland, each one professionally inspected and rated by the AA. Whether you're looking for a well-earned break at a country house hotel or a city stopover, Britain's best-selling hotel guide will help you find the perfect place to stay.

38th edition September 2004

First published by the Automobile Association as the Hotel and Restaurant Guide, 1967

The information contained in this directory is sourced entirely from the AA's information resources.

Maps prepared by the Cartography Department of The Automobile Association.

Feature: Why do they do it? by Julia Hynard

The cover photographs courtesy of: Marriott Hotels (top left); Exclusive Hotels (bottom right), Exclusive Hotels (Lainston House, Winchester - top centre); Hotel du Vin Ltd/Georgia Glynn Smith (bottom left & centre); Red Cow Morans Hotel, Dublin (top right).

Typesetting and colour repro by Microset Graphics Ltd, Basingstoke, Hampshire

Printed and bound in Spain by Printer Industria Grafica S.A., Barcelona

Directory compiled by the AA Hotel Services Department and generated from the AA establishment database.

www.theAA.com

The contents of this publication are believed correct at the time of printing. Nevertheless, the publishers cannot be held responsible for any errors or omissions or for any changes in the details given in this guide or for the consequences of any reliance on the information provided by the same. This does not affect your statutory rights. Assessments of AA inspected establishments are based on the experience of the Hotel and Restaurant Inspectors on the occasion(s) of their visit(s) and therefore descriptions given in this guide necessarily contain an element of subjective opinion which may not reflect or dictate a reader's own opinion on another occasion. The AA strives to ensure accuracy of the information in this guide at the time of printing. Due to the constantly evolving nature of the subject matter the information is subject to change. The AA will gratefully receive any advice from our readers of any necessary updated information.
Please contact
Advertising Sales Department: advertisingsales@theAA.com
Editorial Department: lifestyleguides@theAA.com
AA Hotel Scheme Enquiries: 01256 844455

Published by AA Publishing, a trading name of Automobile Association Developments Limited, whose registered office is Millstream, Maidenhead Road, Windsor, Berkshire SL4 5GD. Registered number 1878835

A CIP catalogue record for this book is available from the British Library

ISBN 0 7495 4208 X

A02069

Contents

Welcome to the 2005 edition of the AA Hotel Guide

Fully updated for 2005, the AA Hotel Guide brings you the widest choice of accommodation across the length and breadth of Britain and Ireland. All the hotels featured have been assessed under quality standards agreed between the AA, VisitBritain and the RAC, enabling you to make your choice with confidence. Each hotel is given a classification that is based on an overnight 'mystery guest' visit by one of our own highly qualified inspectors. You can find out more about the AA's inspection procedures on page 9.

We know that people use the AA Hotel Guide for finding many different types of accommodation for many varied reasons, and as the AA inspects such a wide range of establishments it's no wonder that this guide proves an invaluable asset in finding just the right place.

Leisure...

The sporting and leisure facilities at many of the hotels featured is comprehensive and to find exactly what's on offer consult the FACILITIES section for each entry. Some hotels offer special leisure breaks too, indicated by LB in the guide.

Somewhere special...

If you're searching for somewhere really special take a look at the AA Top 200 Hotels in Britain & Ireland on pages 19-26. These hotels stand out as the very best in the country, regardless of size or type of operation. They range from large, luxury destination hotels to small country inns. Top 200 hotels are easily identified by their special highlighted entry and red star symbols.

Restaurants with Rooms

Food lovers will welcome the inclusion of the AA Restaurants with Rooms category. These are local or national dining destinations that also provide AA-rated accommodation. So now you can try a restaurant that's perhaps a little further afield without the hassle of a long drive home after your meal. For more information on Restaurants with Rooms and other categories of accommodation, turn to page 13.

AA Awards 2004-2005

Every year we present a range of awards to the finest AA-inspected and rated hotels from England, Scotland, Ireland and Wales. The Hotel of the Year Award is our ultimate accolade and is awarded to those hotels that are recognised as outstanding examples in their field. Often innovative, the winning hotels always set high standards in hotel keeping. The hotels nominated are listed on pages 28-29. The Courtesy and Care Award recognises establishments that offer exceptional standards of guest care, service and hospitality. Find out who this year's winners are on page 31.

AA Accessible Awards

The AA Accessible Hotel of the Year Award is presented to the hotel which has made the greatest effort in their accommodation for the independent disabled traveller. This year's winner and runners-up are listed on page 27.

Action for Blind People Hotels
Four hotels owned and managed by the charity Action for Blind People are included in our guide. They are run more in a normal hotel style than in an institutional manner. Most guests are unsighted or partially sighted, but sometimes sighted guests are welcome (as friends of guests or last minute bookers). These hotels are inspected annually by the AA in conjunction with the owning charity. Additionally they are working towards a national classification. The AA feels information about these hotels would be useful to many of its readers.

Hints on booking your stay
It's always worth booking as early as possible, particularly for the peak holiday period from the beginning of June to the end of September. Bear in mind that Easter and other public holidays may be busy too and in some parts of Scotland, the ski season is a peak holiday period. Some hotels will ask for a deposit or full payment in advance, especially for one-night bookings, and not all hotels will take advance bookings for bed and breakfast, overnight or short stays. Some will not make reservations from mid week. Some hotels charge half-board (bed, breakfast and dinner) whether you eat the meals or not, while others may only accept full-board bookings.

Once a booking is confirmed, let the hotel know at once if you are unable to keep your reservation. If the hotel cannot re-let your room you may be liable to pay about two-thirds of the room price (a deposit will count towards this payment). In Britain a legally binding contract is made when you accept an offer of accommodation, either in writing or by telephone, and illness is not accepted as a release from this contract. You are advised to take out insurance against possible cancellation, for example AA Single Trip Insurance (telephone 0800 085 7240 or consult the AA website www.theAA.com for details).

AA Hotel Booking Service
Booking a place to stay can be a time-consuming process. So why not search quickly and easily online for a place that best suits your needs. Whatever your preference we have the place for you. From a cosy farm cottage to a smart city centre hotel - we have them, all. Simply visit www.theAA.com/hotels to search from around 8,000 quality rated hotels and B&Bs in Great Britain and Ireland.

Latebeds
If you need a last-minute place to stay, visit Latebeds at www.theAA.com, the AA's late availability booking service. Latebeds offers last-minute deals at AA-approved hotels and B&Bs. Find the deal that meets your needs and then book it online in an instant. No booking fee is payable.

Feedback
We welcome your feedback about the hotels included and about the guide itself. You can write to us at AA Lifestyle Guides, Fanum House, Basingstoke RG21 4EA or e-mail us at: lifestyleguides@theAA.com. Please note, however, that if you have a complaint to make during a visit, we strongly recommend that you discuss the matter with the hotel management there and then so that they have a chance to put things right before your visit is spoilt. The AA does not undertake to arbitrate between you and the hotel management, or to obtain compensation or engage in correspondence.

How to Use the Guide

Explanation of entries and notes on abbreviations (see also the key opposite)

1 — ANYTOWN, Anyshire Map 4 SU46

2 — ★★★★ 71% **The Example Hotel**
Any Road XX1 11XX
☎ 0022 001122 0022 001122
e-mail: sendto@isp.co.uk www.theexamplehotel.co.uk

3 — ***Dir:*** *2m north of Any Town - Any Road signed turn left at Business Park.*

— 9

A purpose-built hotel with a well equipped leisure and conference centre in a separate, linked building. Bedrooms are generously planned to give working space and adequate power points and lighting. Reception rooms consist of a bar lounge and carvery-style dining room.

4 — **ROOMS:** 50 en suite (6 fmly) (5GF) s fr £68; d fr £125 (incl. bkfst) **LB**

5 — **FACILITIES: Spa** STV air con. Squash Snooker Gym Sauna **CONF:** BC Thtr 80 Class 30 Board 40 **PARKING:** 30 — 6

7 — **NOTES:** No children 14 yrs in restaurant Civ Wed 80

8 — **CARDS:**

1 Towns

These are listed alphabetically within each country section: England, Channel Islands, Isle of Man, Scotland, Wales, Ireland. The administrative county or region follows the town name. Towns on islands are listed under the island (e.g. Wight, Isle of). The map reference gives the map page number, then the National Grid Reference. Read the first figure horizontally and the second figure vertically within the lettered square.

2 Hotel name

This is preceded by the star rating, Quality Assessment Score (see page 9) and Rosette Award, followed by the address, phone/fax numbers and e-mail address where applicable. Please note that e-mail addresses are believed correct at the time of printing but may change during the currency of the guide. Hotels are listed in star and Quality Assessment Score order within each location. If the hotel name is in italic type the information that follows has not been confirmed by the hotel management. A company or consortium name or logo may appear (hotel groups are listed on pages 33-39); for those with a central reservation number, specify the name and location of your chosen hotel when booking.

Website Addresses

Web Site addresses are included where they have been supplied and specified by the respective establishment. Such Web Sites are not under the control of The Automobile Association Developments Limited and as such The Automobile Association Developments Limited has no control over them and will not accept any responsibility or liability in respect of any and all matters whatsoever relating to such Web Sites including access, content, material and functionality. By including the addresses of third party Web Sites the AA does not intend to solicit business or offer any security to any person in any country, directly or indirectly.

Country House Hotels

offer a relaxed, informal atmosphere, with an emphasis on personal welcome. They are usually, but not always, in a secluded or rural setting and should offer peace and quiet regardless of location.

3 Dir

Directions to the hotel.

4 Rooms

The first figure shows the number of en suite letting bedrooms, or total number of bedrooms, then the number with en suite or family facilities. Bedrooms in an annexe or extension are only noted if they are at least equivalent to those in the main building, but facilities and prices may differ. In some hotels all bedrooms are in an annexe or extension. **Prices** (per room per night) are provided by hoteliers in good faith and are indications not firm quotations. Some hotels only accept cheques if notice is given and a cheque card produced. Not all hotels take travellers cheques. **LB** indicates that the hotel offers special leisure breaks; these may be activity-based breaks or 'two nights for the price of one' type offers.

5 Facilities

Colour TV is provided in all bedrooms unless otherwise indicated. Where **entertainment** appears, weekly live entertainment should be available at least once a week all year. Some other hotels provide entertainment only in summer or on special occasions; check when booking. **Leisure facilities** are as stated. **Child facilities** may include: baby intercom, babysitting service, playroom, playground, laundry, drying/ironing facilities, cots, high chairs, special meals. In some hotels children can sleep in parents' rooms at no extra cost; check all details when booking.

6 **Parking**
Shows number of spaces available for guests' use. May include covered, charged spaces.

7 **Notes**
Although many hotels allow dogs, some breeds may be forbidden and dogs may be excluded from areas of the hotel, especially the dining room. It is essential to check when booking. However guide dogs for the blind and assist dogs should be accepted, but once again please check when booking.

No children A minimum age may be given, e.g. 'No children 4 yrs'. If neither 'ch fac' (see FACILITIES) nor 'no children' appears, the hotel accepts children but may not offer special facilities such as high chairs; check before booking if you have very young children. **RS** Some hotels have a restricted service during quieter months, when some of the listed facilities are not available; ask when booking. **Civ Wed 50** indicates that the hotel is licensed for civil weddings and can accommodate up to 50 guests for the ceremony

8 **Cards**
Credit cards may be subject to a surcharge; check when booking if this is how you intend to pay.

9 **Photograph**
Establishments may choose to include a photograph with their entry.

Symbols and Abbreviations

AA Rating & Awards

★ Star Classification (see page 11)

% Quality Assessment Score (see p9)

★ Red Stars indicate the AA's Top 200 Hotels in Britain & Ireland (see p9 and 19-26)

⊛ Rosette Award for quality of food (see p15)

Different accommodation categories

Country House Hotel (see explanation on opposite page)

See p13 for explanation of the following ...

Town House Accommodation

Restaurant with Rooms

Travel Accommodation

○ Hotel due to open during the currency of the guide

U Star rating not yet confirmed

A Associate Entries

Rooms

fmly – Family rooms (and number)

GF – Ground floor room (and number)

⊗ – No Smoking rooms (and number)

s – Single room

d – Double room

incl. bkfst – Breakfast included

LB – Special leisure breaks available

Bedroom restrictions are stated, e.g. no smoking in 15 bedrooms

Facilities

STV – Satellite television

air con – Air conditioning

– Indoor swimming pool

– Heated indoor swimming pool

– Outdoor swimming pool

– Heated outdoor swimming pool

♫ – Entertainment (see explanation on opposite page)

ch fac – Special facilities for children

Xmas – Special programme for Christmas/New Year

Leisure facilities are as stated, e.g. Squash, Snooker, Spa

– Tennis

– Croquet

– Golf Course

CONF – Conference facilities available

BC – Business centre available

Thtr – Seats theatre style (and number)

Class – Seats classroom style (and number)

Board – Seats boardroom style (and number)

Del – Typical overnight delegate rate

Notes

– No dogs allowed in bedrooms (guide dogs for the blind and assist dogs may be accepted)

No children – Indicates that children cannot be accommodated

RS – Restricted opening, e.g. RS Jan-Mar, Closed Xmas/New Year

Civ Wed – Licensed for civil weddings (and maximum number of guests for ceremony)

Other restrictions as stated, e.g. No smoking in restaurant

Cards

Cards accepted where symbols are shown

How does the AA Assess a Hotel?

Hotels applying for AA recognition are visited on a 'mystery guest' basis by one of the AA's team of qualified hotel and restaurant inspectors. The inspector stays overnight to make a thorough test of the accommodation, food and hospitality offered and as many of the hotel's facilities as possible. After settling the bill the following morning they declare their identity and ask to be shown round the entire premises. The inspector completes a full report, making a recommendation for the appropriate star classification and Quality Assessment Score.

Any hotel applying for AA recognition receives an annual unannounced visit to check standards. If the hotel changes hands, the new owners must reapply for classification as AA recognition is not transferable.

Hotels featured pay an annual fee for AA inspection, recognition and rating. The annual fee varies according to the star classification and the number of rooms. AA inspectors pay as a guest for their inspection visit. One of the benefits of such recognition is a text entry in the AA Hotel Guide. In addition to the text entry, hotels may purchase additional advertising such as a photograph or display advertisement.

Quality Assessment Score – making hotel choice easier

In addition to establishing the star classification, AA inspectors supplement their general report with an additional quality assessment of everything the hotel offers, including hospitality, based on what they experience as the 'mystery guest'. This enables them to award an overall Quality Assessment Score.

The Quality Assessment Score offers a comparison of quality within each star classification. So when using the guide, guests can see at a glance, for example, that a two star hotel with a percentage score of 69 offers a higher quality experience within its star classification than a two star hotel with a percentage score of 59. To gain AA recognition in the first place, a hotel must achieve a minimum quality score of 50 per cent.

AA Top 200 Hotels in Britain and Ireland

The AA's Top 200 Awards recognise the very best hotels in Britain and Ireland in each Star, Townhouse and Restaurant with Rooms catagory. A Top 200 hotel will offer outstanding levels of quality, comfort, cleanliness and customer care and (with the possible exception of town house properties) will serve food of at least one AA Rosette standard. Top 200 hotels can be easily identified in the guide by their Red Stars and highlighted 'Top 200' entry. The AA's Top 200 are assessed and announced annually.

The AA's Top 200 hotels are listed on pages 19-26

AA Star Classification

Quality standards you can expect from an AA recognised hotel

All hotels recognised by the AA should have the highest standards of cleanliness, proper records of booking, give prompt and professional service to guests, assist with luggage on request, accept and deliver messages, provide a designated area for breakfast and dinner with drinks available in a bar or lounge, provide an early morning call on request, good quality furniture and fittings, adequate heating and lighting and proper maintenance. A guide to some of the general expectations for each star classification is as follows:

What you can expect from a one star hotel ★

Polite, courteous staff providing a relatively informal yet competent style of service, available during the day and evening to receive guests. At least one designated eating area open to residents for breakfast. Dinner does not have to be offered. However if an establishment does offer dinner it should be on at least 5 days a week, last order should be no later than 6.30pm, there should be a reasonable choice of hot and cold dishes and a short range of wines should be available. Television in lounge or bedroom. Majority of rooms en suite, bath or shower room available at all times.

What you can expect from a two star hotel ★★

Smartly and professionally presented management and staff providing competent, often informal service, available throughout the day and evening to greet guests. At least one restaurant or dining room open to residents for breakfast (and for dinner at least five days a week). Last orders for dinner no earlier than 7pm, a choice of substantial hot and cold dishes and a short range of wines available. Television in bedroom. En suite or private bath or shower and WC.

What you can expect from a three star hotel ★★★

Management and staff smartly and professionally presented and usually uniformed. Technical and social skills of a good standard in responding to requests. A dedicated receptionist on duty at peak times, clear direction to rooms and some explanation of hotel facilities. At least one restaurant or dining room open to residents and non-residents for breakfast and dinner whenever the hotel is open. A wide selection of drinks served in a bar or lounge, available to residents and their guest throughout the day and evening. Last orders for dinner no earlier than 8pm, full dinner service provided. Remote-control television, direct-dial telephone. En suite bath or shower and WC.

What you can expect from a four star hotel ★★★★

A formal, professional staffing structure with smartly presented, uniformed staff, anticipating and responding to your needs or requests. Usually spacious, well-appointed public areas. Bedrooms offering superior quality and comfort than at three star. A strong emphasis on food and beverages and a serious approach to cuisine. Reception staffed 24 hours per day by well-trained staff. Express checkout facilities where appropriate. Porterage available on request and readily provided by uniformed staff. Night porter available. Newspapers can be ordered and delivered to your room, additional services and concierge as appropriate to the style and location of the hotel. At least one restaurant open to residents and non-residents for breakfast and dinner seven days per week, and lunch to be available in a designated eating area. Drinks available to residents and their guests throughout the day and evening, table service available. Last orders for dinner no earlier than 9pm, an extensive choice of hot and cold dishes and a comprehensive list of wines. Remote-control television, direct-dial telephone, a range of high-quality toiletries. En suite bath with fixed overhead shower, WC.

What you can expect from a five star hotel ★★★★★

Flawless guest services, professional, attentive staff, technical and social skills of the highest order. Spacious and luxurious accommodation and public areas with a range of extra facilities. As a minimum, first-time guests shown to their bedroom. Multilingual service consistent with the needs of the hotel's normal clientele. Guest accounts well explained and presented. Porterage offered and provided by uniformed staff. Luggage handling on arrival and departure. Doorman or means of greeting guests at the hotel entrance, full concierge service provided. At least one restaurant open to residents and non-residents for all meals seven days per week. Staff showing excellent knowledge of food and wine. A wide selection of drinks, including cocktails, available in a bar or lounge, table service provided. Last orders for dinner no earlier than 10pm. High-quality menu and wine list properly reflecting and complementing the style of cooking and providing exceptional quality. Evening turn-down service. Remote-control television, direct-dial telephone at bedside and desk, a range of luxury toiletries, bath sheets and robes. En suite bath with fixed overhead shower, WC.

Other Categories of Accommodation

🏘 Town House Accommodation

These individual, city or town-centre properties provide a high degree of personal service and privacy. They concentrate on luxuriously furnished bedrooms and suites, rather than the public rooms or formal dining rooms normally associated with hotels. Town house accommodation may have some restaurant provision but if not, a high standard of room service will be offered - in any case, they are usually in areas well served by restaurants. All fall within the four or five star classification, though no Quality Assessment Score is shown in the guide. Town house hotels have a special highlighted entry.

Restaurants with Rooms

A Restaurant with Rooms is usually a local (or national) destination for eating out which also offers accommodation, albeit on a smaller scale. Most have 12 bedrooms or less, and public areas may be limited to the restaurant itself. No star rating is shown in the guide but bedrooms reflect at least the level of quality normally associated with a two star hotel.

Travel Accommodation

This classification indicates budget or lodge accommodation, usually in purpose-built units close to main roads and motorways, (often forming part of motorway service areas) and in town and city centres. They provide consistent levels of accommodation and service.

U Hotels with an unconfirmed star classification

A small number of hotels in the guide have a U symbol instead of a star rating. These had not had their star classification confirmed at the time of going to print. Check the AA website **www.theAA.com** for current information.

○ Hotels with no star classification

Hotels preceded by a ○ symbol were not open at the time of going to print but are due to open during the year. Check the AA website **www.theAA.com** for current information.

A Associate Entries

These are establishments that have been inspected and rated by the RAC, VisitBritain, VisitScotland, Welsh Tourist Board or Northern Ireland Tourist Board. They are rated with stars ★ although VisitScotland, WTB and Northern Ireland Tourist Board use a slightly different set of criteria. The Associate Hotels shown have paid to belong to the AA Associate Hotels Scheme and therefore receive a limited entry in this guide. Descriptions of these establishments can be found on our website **www. theAA.com**.

AA Rosette Awards

Out of around 40,000 restaurants, the AA identifies, with its rosette awards, some 1,800 as the best in the UK. The following is an outline of what to expect from restaurants with AA Rosette Awards.

Excellent local restaurants serving food prepared with care, understanding and skill, using good quality ingredients. These restaurants stand out in their local area. The same expectations apply to hotel restaurants where guests should be able to eat in with confidence and a sense of anticipation. Of the total number of establishments with rosettes around 50% have one rosette.

The best local restaurants, which aim for and achieve higher standards, better consistency and where a greater precision is apparent in the cooking. There will be obvious attention to the selection of quality ingredients.

Outstanding restaurants that demand recognition well beyond their local area. The cooking will be underpinned by the selection and sympathetic treatment of the highest quality ingredients. Timing, seasoning and the judgement of flavour combinations will be consistently excellent, supported by other elements such as intelligent service and a well-chosen wine list. Around 10% of restaurants with rosettes have been awarded 3.

Amongst the very best restaurants in the British Isles where the cooking demands national recognition. These restaurants will exhibit intense ambition, a passion for excellence, superb technical skills and remarkable consistency. They will combine appreciation of culinary traditions with a passionate desire for further exploration and improvement. Around a dozen restaurants have four rosettes.

The finest restaurants in the British Isles, where the cooking stands comparison with the best in the world. These restaurants will have highly individual voices, exhibit breathtaking culinary skills and set the standards to which others aspire. Less than half a dozen restaurants have five rosettes.

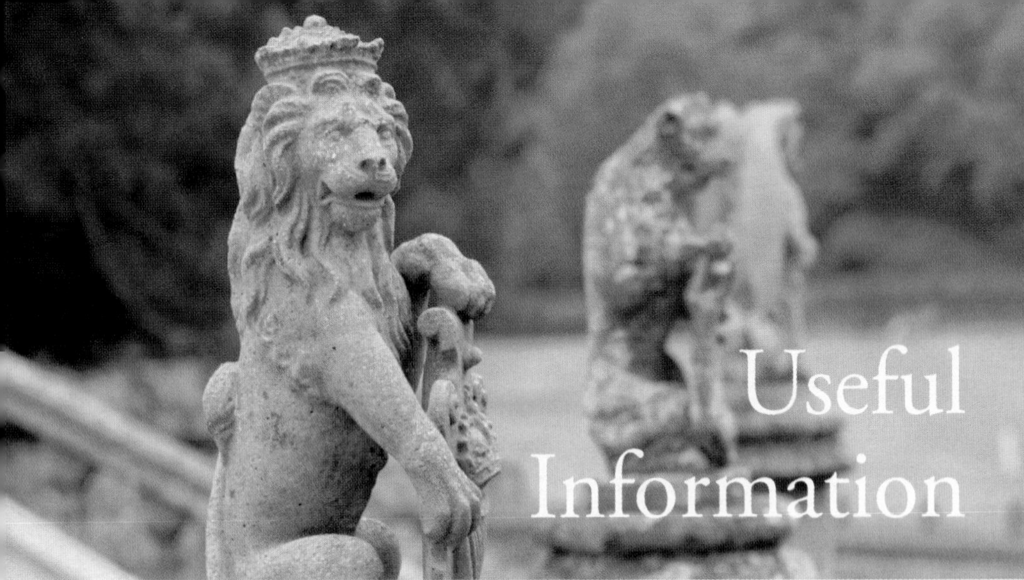

Useful Information

BRITAIN

The Fire Precautions Act does not apply to the Channel Islands, Republic of Ireland, or the Isle of Man, which have their own rules. As far as we are aware, all hotels listed in Great Britain have applied for and not been refused a fire certificate.

Licensing laws differ in England, Wales, Scotland, the Republic of Ireland, the Isle of Man, the Isles of Scilly and the Channel Islands. Public houses are generally open from mid morning to early afternoon, and from about 6 or 7pm until 11pm, although closing times may be earlier or later and some pubs are open all afternoon. Unless otherwise stated, establishments listed are licensed. Hotel residents can obtain alcoholic drinks at all times, if the licensee is prepared to serve them. Non-residents eating at the hotel restaurant can have drinks with meals. Children under 14 (or 18 in Scotland) may be excluded from bars where no food is served. Those under 18 may not purchase or consume alcoholic drinks. Club licence means that drinks are served to club members only, 48 hours must elapse between joining and ordering.

Prices The AA encourages the use of the Hotel Industry Voluntary Code of Booking Practice, which aims to ensure that guests know how much they will have to pay and what services and facilities that includes, before entering a financially binding agreement. If the price has not previously been confirmed in writing, guests should be given a card stipulating the total obligatory charge when they register at reception.

The Tourism (Sleeping Accommodation Price Display) **Order of 1977** compels hotels, travel accommodation, guest houses, farmhouses, inns and self-catering accommodation with four or more letting bedrooms, to display in entrance halls the minimum and maximum prices charged for each category of room. Tariffs shown are the minimum and maximum for one or two persons but they may vary without warning.

London Congestion Charging Scheme In 2003 Transport for London introduced a congestion charging scheme for most vehicles being used in a designated zone in Central London (roughly all the roads inside the Inner Ring Road). The charge is an area licence – vehicles used in the central London area must be registered. You pay £5 for the day (zone operates 7am-6.30pm weekdays) and can cross into and out of the zone as much as you want within the day. If your journey takes you into the charging zone you must either pre-pay the £5 charge or pay it before 10pm that day. Between 10pm and midnight the charge increases to £10 to encourage prompt payment. The system is controlled using a database of registered car registration numbers and a network of numberplate-reading cameras. At midnight each day all paid accounts are deleted from the system. Any vehicle recorded as having been in the zone during charging hours but with an unpaid account must pay a penalty charge. Payment can be made at any time, via the call centre - 0845 900 1234; via the congestion charging website www.cclondon.com or at paystations, selected petrol stations & retailers displaying the PayPoint logo.

For further details on London Congestion Charges see the AA website **www.TheAA.com**. The AA produces a Central Congestion

continued on next page

Charging Zone Map obtainable from bookshops or from the AA Travel Bookshop on 01256 491524.

NORTHERN IRELAND & REPUBLIC OF IRELAND

The Euro In 2002, Euro banknotes and coins came into circulation throughout the Republic of Ireland. Prices in the guide for hotels in the Republic of Ireland are therefore shown in Euros.

The Fire Services (NI) Order 1984 covers establishments accommodating more than six people, which must have a certificate from the Northern Ireland Fire Authority. Places accommodating fewer than six persons need adequate exits. AA officials inspect emergency notices, fire-fighting equipment and fire exits here. Republic of Ireland safety regulations are a matter for local authority regulations. For your own and others' safety, read the emergency notices and be sure you understand them.

Licensing Regulations

Northern Ireland: Public houses open Mon-Sat 11.30-23.00 and Sun 12.30-14.30 and 19.00-22.00. Hotels can serve residents without restriction. Non-residents can be served from 12.30-22.00 on Christmas Day. Children under 18 are not allowed in the bar area and may neither buy nor consume liquor in hotels.

Republic of Ireland: General licensing hours are Mon-Sat 10.30-23.00 (23.30 in summer). Sun and St Patrick's Day (17 March), 12.30-14.00 and 16.00-23.00. Hotels can serve residents without restriction. There is no service on Christmas Day (except for hotel residents) or Good Friday.

Telephone numbers Area codes for numbers in the Republic of Ireland apply only within the Republic. If dialling from outside check the telephone directory. Area codes for numbers in Britain and Northern Ireland cannot be used directly from the Republic.

For the latest travel information on Ireland, visit AA Ireland's website www.aaireland.ie

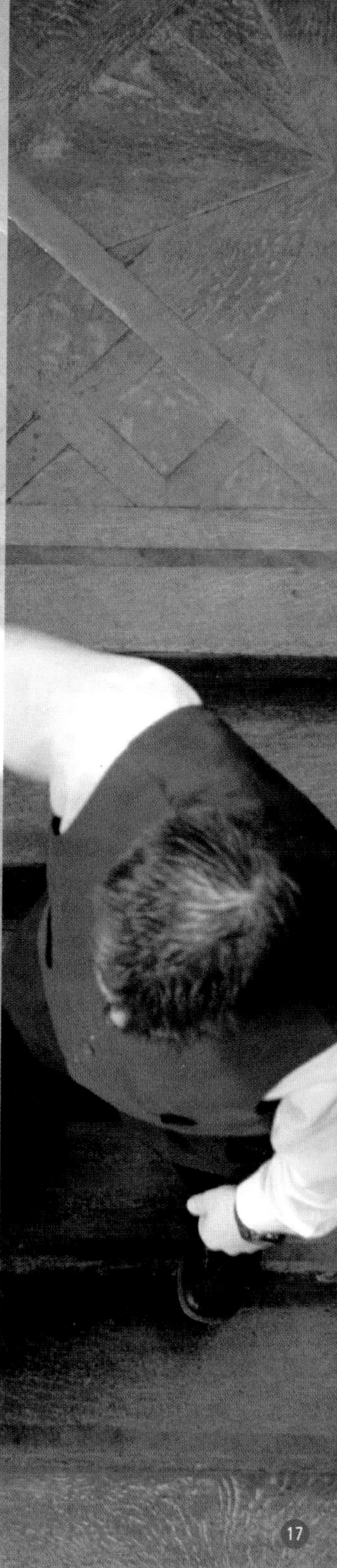

Bank and Public Holidays 2005

New Year's Day	1 January
Bank Holiday	2 January (SCOTLAND ONLY)
St Patrick's Day	17 March (N.I. & R.O.I. ONLY)
Good Friday	25 March
Easter Monday	28 March
May Day Bank Holiday	2 May
Spring Bank Holiday	30 May (EXCLUDING R.O.I.)
June Bank Holiday	6 June (R.O.I. ONLY)
Battle of the Boyne	12 July (N.I. ONLY)
Summer Bank Holiday	1 August (SCOTLAND & R.O.I. ONLY)
Late Summer Bank Holiday	31 August (EXCLUDING R.O.I.)
Bank Holiday	25 October (R.O.I. ONLY)
Christmas Day	25 December
Boxing Day	26 December (ST STEPHEN'S DAY IN R.O.I.)

Top 200

Hotels in Britain & Ireland

2004-2005

Assessed and announced annually, the AA's Top 200 Awards recognise the very best hotels in Britain and Ireland. A Top 200 hotel will offer consistently outstanding levels of quality, comfort, cleanliness and customer care.

Central London
Regent's Park
BLOOMSBURY
MARYLEBONE
STRAND
MAYFAIR
Hyde Park
KNIGHTS-BRIDGE
WESTMINSTER
LAMBETH
Thames
Inverness
Aberdeen
Fort William
Perth
Glasgow
Edinburgh
Stranraer
Carlisle
Newcastle upon Tyne
Middlesbrough
Belfast
Kendal
York
Leeds
Kingston upon Hull
Galway
Dublin
Liverpool
Manchester
Sheffield
Holyhead
Lincoln
Limerick
Nottingham
Rosslare
Norwich
Birmingham
Cork
Aberystwyth
Cambridge
Carmarthen
Gloucester
Oxford
Colchester
LONDON
Cardiff
Bristol
Maidstone
Guildford
Barnstaple
Dover
Southampton
Brighton
Exeter
Plymouth
Weymouth
Penzance
Isles of Scilly
The Channel Islands

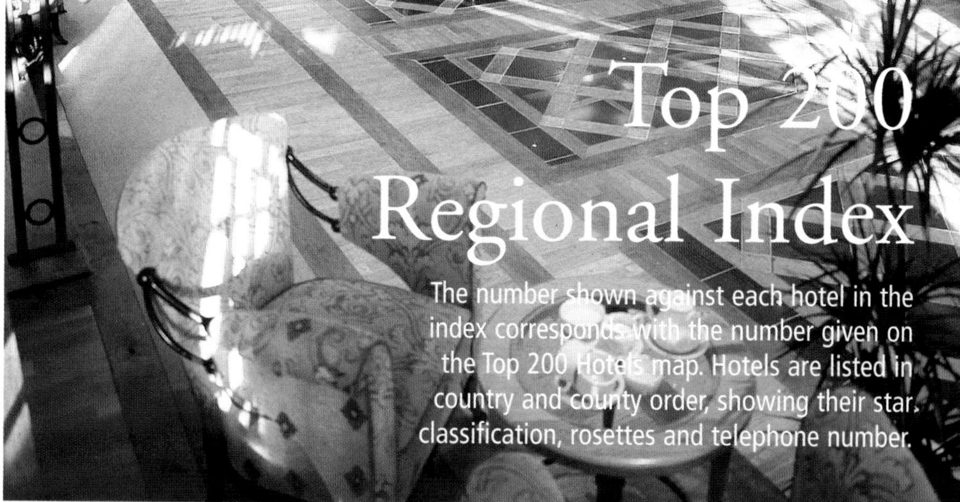

Top 200 Regional Index

The number shown against each hotel in the index corresponds with the number given on the Top 200 Hotels map. Hotels are listed in country and county order, showing their star classification, rosettes and telephone number.

ENGLAND

BEDFORDSHIRE

No.	Stars	Rosettes	Town	Hotel	Telephone
1	★★★	✿✿	FLITWICK	Menzies Flitwick Manor	☎ 01525 712242

BERKSHIRE

No.	Stars	Rosettes	Town	Hotel	Telephone
2	★★★★	✿✿✿	MAIDENHEAD	Fredrick's Hotel	☎ 01628 581000
3	★★★★★	✿✿✿✿	NEWBURY	The Vineyard at Stockcross	☎ 01635 528770

BUCKINGHAMSHIRE

No.	Stars	Rosettes	Town	Hotel	Telephone
4	★★★★	✿✿✿	AYLESBURY	Hartwell House	☎ 01296 747444
5	★★★★★	✿✿✿	TAPLOW	Cliveden	☎ 01628 668561

CHESHIRE

No.	Stars	Rosettes	Town	Hotel	Telephone
6	★★★★★	✿✿✿	CHESTER	The Chester Grosvenor	☎ 01244 324024
7	★★★★	✿✿	CHESTER	The Chester Crabwall Manor Hotel	☎ 01244 851666
8	★★★	✿✿	NANTWICH	Rookery Hall	☎ 01270 610016

CORNWALL & ISLES OF SCILLY

No.	Stars	Rosettes	Town	Hotel	Telephone
9	★★	✿✿	FOWEY	Marina Hotel	☎ 01726 833315
10	★★	✿	GILLAN	Tregildry Hotel	☎ 01326 231378
11	★★	✿✿✿	LISKEARD	Well House Hotel	☎ 01579 342001
12	★★★	✿✿	PORTSCATHO	Rosevine Hotel	☎ 01872 580206
13	★★★	✿✿✿	ST MARTIN'S	St Martin's on the Isle	☎ 01720 422090
14	★★★	✿✿	TRESCO	The Island	☎ 01720 422883

CUMBRIA

No.	Stars	Rosettes	Town	Hotel	Telephone
15	★★★	✿✿	BRAMPTON	Farlam Hall Hotel	☎ 016977 46234
16	★	✿	GRANGE-OVER-SANDS	Clare House	☎ 015395 33026
17	★	✿	GRASMERE	White Moss House	☎ 015394 35295
18	★★★	✿✿✿	HOWTOWN	Sharrow Bay Country House	☎ 017684 86301
19	★	✿✿	KESWICK	Swinside Lodge	☎ 017687 72948
20	★★★	✿✿✿	WATERMILLOCK	Rampsbeck Country House Hotel	☎ 017684 86442
21	★★★	✿✿✿	WINDERMERE	Gilpin Lodge Country House Hotel & Restaurant	☎ 015394 88818
22	★★★	✿✿✿	WINDERMERE	Holbeck Ghyll Country House Hotel	☎ 015394 32375
23	★★	✿	WINDERMERE	Lindeth Fell	☎ 015394 43286
24	★★★	✿✿	WINDERMERE	Linthwaite House Hotel	☎ 015394 88600
25	★★	✿✿	WINDERMERE	Miller Howe	☎ 015394 42536
26	★★★	✿✿✿	WINDERMERE	The Samling	☎ 015394 31922

DERBYSHIRE

No.	Stars	Rosettes	Town	Hotel	Telephone
27	★★	✿✿✿	BASLOW	Fischer's Baslow Hall	☎ 01246 583259

*(Hotels marked with an asterisk * had not had their Rosette rating confirmed at the time of going to press. See the AA website www.theAA.com for current information.)*

DEVON

No.	Rating	Rosettes	Location	Hotel	Telephone
28	★★	◎◎	ASHWATER	Blagdon Manor Hotel & Restaurant	☎ 01409 211224
29	★★★	◎◎	BURRINGTON	Northcote Manor	☎ 01769 560501
30	★★★	◎◎◎◎	CHAGFORD	Gidleigh Park	☎ 01647 432367
31	★★★	◎◎	HONITON	Combe House Hotel	☎ 01404 540400
32	★★★	◎◎	KINGSBRIDGE	Buckland-Tout-Saints	☎ 01548 853055
33	★★★	◎◎◎	LEWDOWN	Lewtrenchard Manor	☎ 01566 783256
34	★★★	◎◎	TORQUAY	Orestone Manor	☎ 01803 328098

DORSET

No.	Rating	Rosettes	Location	Hotel	Telephone
35	★★★		EVERSHOT	Summer Lodge *	☎ 01935 83424
36	★★★	◎◎◎	GILLINGHAM	Stock Hill Country House	☎ 01747 823626
37	★★★	◎◎	POOLE	Mansion House Hotel	☎ 01202 685666

CO DURHAM

No.	Rating	Rosettes	Location	Hotel	Telephone
38	★★	◎◎	ROMALDKIRK	Rose & Crown Hotel	☎ 01833 650213
39	★★★★	◎◎◎	SEAHAM	Seaham Hall Hotel	☎ 0191 516 1400

ESSEX

No.	Rating	Rosettes	Location	Hotel	Telephone
40	★★★	◎◎	DEDHAM	Maison Talbooth	☎ 01206 322367

GLOUCESTERSHIRE

No.	Rating	Rosettes	Location	Hotel	Telephone
41	★★★	◎◎◎	BUCKLAND	Buckland Manor	☎ 01386 852626
42	★★★	◎◎◎	CHELTENHAM	The Greenway	☎ 01242 862352
43	★★★	◎◎	CHELTENHAM	Hotel on the Park	☎ 01242 518898
44	★★★	◎◎	CHIPPING CAMPDEN	Cotswold House	☎ 01386 840330
45	★★	◎◎	COLN ST ALDWYNS	The New Inn At Coln	☎ 01285 750651
46	★★★	◎◎	CORSE LAWN	Corse Lawn	☎ 01452 780479
47	★★★	◎◎	LOWER SLAUGHTER	Lower Slaughter Manor	☎ 01451 820456
48	★★★	◎	TETBURY	Calcot Manor	☎ 01666 890391
49	★★★	◎◎	THORNBURY	Thornbury Castle	☎ 01454 281182
50	★★★		UPPER SLAUGHTER	Lords of the Manor *	☎ 01451 820243

HAMPSHIRE

No.	Rating	Rosettes	Location	Hotel	Telephone
51	★★★	◎◎	BEAULIEU	Montagu Arms	☎ 01590 612324
52	★★★	◎◎	MILFORD ON SEA	Westover Hall Hotel	☎ 01590 643044
53	★★★★★	◎◎◎	NEW MILTON	Chewton Glen Hotel	☎ 01425 275341
54	★★★★	◎◎	ROTHERWICK	Tylney Hall Hotel	☎ 01256 764881
55	★★★★	◎◎	WINCHESTER	Lainston House Hotel	☎ 01962 863588

HEREFORDSHIRE

No.	Rating	Rosettes	Location	Hotel	Telephone
56	★★★	◎◎◎	HEREFORD	Castle House Hotel	☎ 01432 356321

ISLE OF WIGHT

No.	Rating	Rosettes	Location	Hotel	Telephone
57	★★★	◎◎◎	YARMOUTH	George Hotel	☎ 01983 760331

KENT

No.	Rating	Rosettes	Location	Hotel	Telephone
58	★★★★	◎◎	ASHFORD	Eastwell Manor	☎ 01233 213000
59	★★★★	◎◎	LENHAM	Chilston Park	☎ 01622 859803

LEICESTERSHIRE

No.	Rating	Rosettes	Location	Hotel	Telephone
60	★★★★	◎◎	MELTON MOWBRAY	Stapleford Park	☎ 01572 787522

LINCOLNSHIRE

No.	Rating	Rosettes	Location	Hotel	Telephone
61	🏨	◎◎◎◎◎	WINTERINGHAM	Winteringham Fields	☎ 01724 733096

LONDON POSTAL DISTRICTS

62 ★★★★★ ◎ LONDON E14 — Four Seasons Hotel Canary Wharf ☎ 020 7510 1999

63 ★★★★★ ◎◎◎ LONDON EC2 — Great Eastern Hotel ☎ 020 7618 5000

64 ★★★★★ ◎ LONDON NW1 — Landmark London Hotel ☎ 020 7631 8000

65 ★★★★★ ◎◎◎◎◎ LONDON SW1 — The Berkeley ☎ 020 7235 6000

66 ★★★★★ ◎ LONDON SW1 — The Carlton Tower Hotel ☎ 020 7235 1234

67 ★★★★★ ◎◎ LONDON SW1 — The Goring ☎ 020 7396 9000

68 ★★★★ ◎◎◎ LONDON SW1 — The Halkin Hotel ☎ 020 7333 1000

69 ★★★★★ ◎◎ LONDON SW1 — The Lanesborough ☎ 020 7259 5599

70 ★★★★★ ◎◎◎◎◎ LONDON SW1 — Mandarin Oriental Hyde Park ☎ 020 7235 2000

71 ★★★★★ LONDON SW1 — No 41 ☎ 020 7300 0041

72 ★★★★ ◎◎ LONDON SW1 — The Stafford ☎ 020 7493 0111

73 ★★★★★ ◎◎◎◎ LONDON SW3 — The Capital ☎ 020 7589 5171

74 ★★★★★ ◎ LONDON W1 — Athenaeum Hotel & Apartments ☎ 020 7499 3464

75 ★★★★★ ◎◎◎ LONDON W1 — Claridge's ☎ 020 7629 8860

76 ★★★★★ ◎◎◎ LONDON W1 — The Connaught ☎ 020 7499 7070

77 ★★★★★ ◎◎◎ LONDON W1 — The Dorchester ☎ 020 7629 8888

78 ★★★★★ ◎ LONDON W1 — Four Seasons Hotel London ☎ 020 7499 0888

79 ★★★★★ ◎◎ LONDON W1 — The Ritz ☎ 020 7493 8181

80 ★★★★★ ◎◎◎ LONDON W8 — Royal Garden Hotel ☎ 020 7937 8000

81 ★★★★★ ◎ LONDON W8 — Milestone Hotel & Apartments ☎ 020 7917 1000

82 ★★★★★ ◎◎ LONDON WC2 — One Aldwych ☎ 020 7300 1000

83 ★★★★★ ◎◎◎ LONDON WC2 — The Savoy ☎ 020 7836 4343

NORFOLK

84 ★★ ◎◎◎ BLAKENEY — Morston Hall ☎ 01263 741041

85 ★★★ ◎◎ GRIMSTON — Congham Hall Country House Hotel ☎ 01485 600250

86 ★★ ◎◎ NORTH WALSHAM — Beechwood Hotel ☎ 01692 403231

87 ★★ ◎ NORWICH — The Old Rectory ☎ 01603 700772

NORTHAMPTONSHIRE

88 ★★★★ ◎◎ DAVENTRY — Fawsley Hall ☎ 01327 892000

NOTTINGHAMSHIRE

89 ◎◎◎ NOTTINGHAM — Hotel des Clos ☎ 0115 986 6566

OXFORDSHIRE

90 ★★★★ ◎◎◎◎◎ GREAT MILTON — Le Manoir Aux Quat' Saisons ☎ 01844 278881

RUTLAND

91 ★★★ ◎◎◎◎ OAKHAM — Hambleton Hall ☎ 01572 756991

SHROPSHIRE

92 ★★★ ◎◎◎ WORFIELD — Old Vicarage Hotel ☎ 01746 716497

SOMERSET

93 ★★★ ◎◎ BATH — The Queensberry Hotel ☎ 01225 447928

94 ★★ ◎ DULVERTON — Ashwick House Hotel ☎ 01398 323868

95 ★★ ◎ PORLOCK — The Oaks Hotel ☎ 01643 862265

96 ★★★ ◎◎◎ SHEPTON MALLET — Charlton House & Mulberry Restaurant ☎ 01749 342008

97 ★★★★ ◎◎ STON EASTON — Ston Easton Park ☎ 01761 241631

98 ★★★ ◎◎◎ TAUNTON — Castle Hotel ☎ 01823 272671

99 ★★★ ◎◎ WELLINGTON — Bindon Country House Hotel & Restaurant ☎ 01823 400070

100 ★ ◎◎◎ YEOVIL — Little Barwick House ☎ 01935 423902

SUFFOLK

No.	Stars	Rosettes	Location	Hotel	Telephone
101	★★★★	◎◎◎	HINTLESHAM	Hintlesham Hall Hotel	☎ 01473 652334

SURREY

No.	Stars	Rosettes	Location	Hotel	Telephone
102	★★★★★	◎◎◎	BAGSHOT	Pennyhill Park Hotel & Country Club	☎ 01276 471774
103	★★★	◎◎	HORLEY	Langshott Manor	☎ 01293 786680

SUSSEX EAST

No.	Stars	Rosettes	Location	Hotel	Telephone
104	★★★★	◎◎	FOREST ROW	Ashdown Park Hotel and Country Club	☎ 01342 824988
105	★★★	◎◎	NEWICK	Newick Park Hotel & Country Estate	☎ 01825 723633
106	★★★	◎◎	UCKFIELD	Horsted Place	☎ 01825 750581

SUSSEX WEST

No.	Stars	Rosettes	Location	Hotel	Telephone
107	★★★	◎◎	AMBERLEY	Amberley Castle	☎ 01798 831992
108	★★★	◎◎◎	CUCKFIELD	Ockenden Manor	☎ 01444 416111
109	★★★	◎◎◎	EAST GRINSTEAD	Gravetye Manor Hotel	☎ 01342 810567
110	★★★★	◎◎◎	LOWER BEEDING	South Lodge Hotel	☎ 01403 891711
111	★★★	◎◎	TURNERS HILL	Alexander House Hotel	☎ 01342 714914

WARWICKSHIRE

No.	Stars	Rosettes	Location	Hotel	Telephone
112	★★★	◎◎◎	ROYAL LEAMINGTON SPA	Mallory Court Hotel	☎ 01926 330214

WEST MIDLANDS

No.	Stars	Rosettes	Location	Hotel	Telephone
113	★★★	◎◎◎	HOCKLEY HEATH	Nuthurst Grange Country House & Restaurant	☎ 01564 783972

WILTSHIRE

No.	Stars	Rosettes	Location	Hotel	Telephone
114	★★★★	◎◎◎	CASTLE COMBE	Manor House Hotel	☎ 01249 782206
115	★★★★	◎◎◎	COLERNE	Lucknam Park	☎ 01225 742777
116	★★★★	◎◎◎	MALMESBURY	Whatley Manor	☎ 01666 822888

WORCESTERSHIRE

No.	Stars	Rosettes	Location	Hotel	Telephone
117	★★★	◎◎	CHADDESLEY CORBETT	Brockencote Hall Country House	☎ 01562 777876

YORKSHIRE NORTH

No.	Stars	Rosettes	Location	Hotel	Telephone
118	★★★	◎◎◎	BOLTON ABBEY	The Devonshire Arms Country House Hotel	☎ 01756 710441
119	★★★★	◎◎	CRATHORNE	Crathorne Hall Hotel	☎ 01642 700398
120	★★★★	◎◎	HARROGATE	Rudding Park Hotel & Golf	☎ 01423 871350
121	★★★★	◎◎	MASHAM	Swinton Park	☎ 01765 680900
122		◎◎◎	RAMSGILL	Yorke Arms	☎ 01423 755243
123	★★★	◎◎◎	YARM	Judges Country House Hotel	☎ 01642 789000
124	★★★	◎◎	YORK	The Grange Hotel	☎ 01904 644744
125	★★★	◎◎◎	YORK	Middlethorpe Hall Hotel	☎ 01904 641241

CHANNEL ISLANDS

JERSEY

No.	Stars	Rosettes	Location	Hotel	Telephone
126	★★★	◎◎	ROZEL BAY	Château la Chaire	☎ 01534 863354
127	★★★★	◎◎	ST BRELADE	The Atlantic Hotel	☎ 01534 744101
128	★★★★	◎◎◎	ST SAVIOUR	Longueville Manor Hotel	☎ 01534 725501

SCOTLAND

ABERDEENSHIRE

No.	Rating	Town	Hotel	Telephone
129	★★ ◎◎	BALLATER	Balgonie Country House Hotel	☎ 013397 55482
130	★★★ ◎◎◎	BALLATER	Darroch Learg Hotel	☎ 013397 55443

ANGUS

No.	Rating	Town	Hotel	Telephone
131	★★★ ◎◎◎	GLAMIS	Castleton House Hotel	☎ 01307 840340

ARGYLL & BUTE

No.	Rating	Town	Hotel	Telephone
132	★★★★ ◎◎◎	ERISKA	Isle of Eriska	☎ 01631 720371
133	★★★ ◎◎◎	PORT APPIN	Airds Hotel	☎ 01631 730236
134	★★ ◎◎	TOBERMORY	Highland Cottage	☎ 01688 302030

CITY OF EDINBURGH

No.	Rating	Town	Hotel	Telephone
135	★★★★ ⌂ ◎◎	EDINBURGH	The Bonham Hotel	☎ 0131 226 6050
136	★★★★ ◎◎	EDINBURGH	Channings	☎ 0131 332 3232
137	★★★★ ⌂	EDINBURGH	The Howard Hotel	☎ 0131 557 3500
138	★★★★ ◎◎	EDINBURGH	Prestonfield House	☎ 0131 225 7800
139	★★★★★ ⌂ ◎◎	EDINBURGH	The Scotsman	☎ 0131 556 5565

DUMFRIES & GALLOWAY

No.	Rating	Town	Hotel	Telephone
140	★ ◎◎	MOFFAT	Well View Hotel	☎ 01683 220184
141	★★★ ◎◎	NEWTON STEWART	Kirroughtree House	☎ 01671 402141
142	★★★ ◎◎◎	PORTPATRICK	Knockinaam Lodge	☎ 01776 810471

EAST LOTHIAN

No.	Rating	Town	Hotel	Telephone
143	★★★ ◎◎	GULLANE	Greywalls Hotel	☎ 01620 842144

FIFE

No.	Rating	Town	Hotel	Telephone
144	★★★★ ◎◎	MARKINCH	Balbirnie House	☎ 01592 610066
145	★★ ◎◎◎	PEAT INN	The Peat Inn	☎ 01334 840206
146	★★★★★ ◎◎◎	ST ANDREWS	The Old Course Hotel	☎ 01334 474371
147	★★★ ◎◎	ST ANDREWS	Rufflets Country House	☎ 01334 472594
148	★★★ ◎◎	ST ANDREWS	St Andrews Golf Hotel	☎ 01334 472611

CITY OF GLASGOW

No.	Rating	Town	Hotel	Telephone
149	★★★★ ⌂ ◎◎	GLASGOW	One Devonshire Gardens	☎ 0141 339 2001

HIGHLAND

No.	Rating	Town	Hotel	Telephone
150	⛫ ◎◎◎	COLBOST	The Three Chimneys & The House Over-By	☎ 01470 511258
151	★★★★ ◎◎◎	FORT WILLIAM	Inverlochy Castle Hotel	☎ 01397 702177
152	⛫ ◎◎	KINGUSSIE	The Cross	☎ 01540 661166
153	★★★ ◎	LOCHINVER	Inver Lodge Hotel	☎ 01571 844496
154	★ ◎◎	MUIR OF ORD	The Dower House	☎ 01463 870090
155	★★ ◎◎◎	NAIRN	Boath House	☎ 01667 454896
156	★★★ ◎◎	POOLEWE	Pool House Hotel	☎ 01445 781272
157	★ ◎◎	SHIELDAIG	Tigh an Eilean	☎ 01520 755251
158	★★ ◎◎	STRONTIAN	Kilcamb Lodge Hotel	☎ 01967 402257
159	★★ ◎◎	TAIN	The Glenmorangie Highland Home at Cadbole	☎ 01862 871671
160	★★★ ◎◎	TORRIDON	Loch Torridon Country House Hotel	☎ 01445 791242

NORTH AYRSHIRE

No.	Rating	Town	Hotel	Telephone
161	★★ ◎◎	BRODICK	Kilmichael Country House Hotel	☎ 01770 302219

PERTH & KINROSS

No.	Rating	Town	Hotel	Telephone
162	★★★★★ ◎◎◎◎	AUCHTERARDER	The Gleneagles Hotel	☎ 01764 662231
163	★★★ ◎◎	BLAIRGOWRIE	Kinloch House Hotel	☎ 01250 884237
164	★★★ ◎◎◎	DUNKELD	Kinnaird	☎ 01796 482440
165	★★★ ◎◎	KINCLAVEN	Ballathie House Hotel	☎ 01250 883268

SOUTH AYRSHIRE

No.	Rating	Town	Hotel	Telephone
166	★★★ ◎◎◎	BALLANTRAE	Glenapp Castle	☎ 01465 831212
167	★★ ◎	MAYBOLE	Ladyburn	☎ 01655 740585
168	★★★ ◎◎◎	TROON	Lochgreen House	☎ 01292 313343
169	★★★★★ ◎◎	TURNBERRY	Westin Turnberry Resort	☎ 01655 331000

STIRLING

No.	Rating	Town	Hotel	Telephone
170	★★★ ◎◎	DUNBLANE	Cromlix House Hotel	☎ 01786 822125
171	★ ◎◎	STRATHYRE	Creagan House	☎ 01877 384638

WALES

CEREDIGION

No.	Rating	Location	Hotel
172	★★★ ◎◎◎	EGLWYSFACH	Ynyshir Hall ☎ 01654 781209

CONWY

No.	Rating	Location	Hotel
173	★★ ◎◎◎	BETWS-Y-COED	Tan-y-Foel Country House ☎ 01690 710507
174	★★ ◎◎◎	CONWY	The Old Rectory Country House ☎ 01492 580611
175	★★★★ ◎◎	LLANDUDNO	Bodysgallen Hall Hotel ☎ 01492 584466
176	★★★★ 🏠 ◎	LLANDUDNO	Osborne House ☎ 01492 860330
177	★★ ◎◎◎	LLANDUDNO	St Tudno Hotel and Restaurant ☎ 01492 874411

GWYNEDD

No.	Rating	Location	Hotel
178	★★★ ◎◎	CAERNARFON	Seiont Manor ☎ 01286 673366
179	★★ ◎◎	TALSARNAU	Maes y Neuadd Country House Hotel ☎ 01766 780200

POWYS

No.	Rating	Location	Hotel
180	★★★ ◎◎	LLANGAMMARCH WELLS	Lake Country House Hotel ☎ 01591 620202

SWANSEA

No.	Rating	Location	Hotel
181	★★ ◎◎	REYNOLDSTON	Fairyhill ☎ 01792 390139
182	★★★★ ◎◎	SWANSEA	Morgans Hotel ☎ 01792 484848

IRELAND

CLARE

No.	Rating	Location	Hotel
183	★★★ ◎◎	BALLYVAUGHAN	Gregans Castle ☎ 065 7077005
184	★★★★★ ◎◎	NEWMARKET-ON-FERGUS	Dromoland Castle Hotel ☎ 061 368144

CORK

No.	Rating	Location	Hotel
185	★★★ ◎◎	BALLYLICKEY	Sea View House Hotel ☎ 027 50073
186	★★★★ ◎◎	CORK	Hayfield Manor ☎ 021 4845900
187	★★★ ◎◎◎	MALLOW	Longueville House Hotel ☎ 022 47156

DUBLIN

No.	Rating	Location	Hotel
188	★★★★ ◎◎	DUBLIN	The Clarence ☎ 01 4070800
189	★★★★★ ◎◎◎◎	DUBLIN	The Merrion Hotel ☎ 01 6030600
190	★★★★ ◎◎	PORTMARNOCK	Portmarnock Hotel & Golf Links ☎ 01 8460611

GALWAY

No.	Rating	Location	Hotel
191	★★★ ◎◎	CASHEL	Cashel House Hotel ☎ 095 31001

KERRY

No.	Rating	Location	Hotel
192	★★★★ ◎◎◎	KENMARE	Park Hotel Kenmare ☎ 064 41200
193	★★★★ ◎◎	KENMARE	Sheen Falls Lodge ☎ 064 41600
194	★★★★ ◎◎	KILLARNEY	Aghadoe Heights Hotel ☎ 064 31766
195	★★★★ ◎◎	KILLARNEY	Killarney Park Hotel ☎ 064 35555

KILDARE

No.	Rating	Location	Hotel
196	★★★★★ ◎◎◎	STRAFFAN	The Kildare Hotel & Golf Club ☎ 01 6017200

KILKENNY

No.	Rating	Location	Hotel
197	★★★★ ◎◎	THOMASTOWN	Mount Juliet Conrad Hotel ☎ 056 777 3000

WATERFORD

No.	Rating	Location	Hotel
198	★★★★ ◎◎	WATERFORD	Waterford Castle Hotel ☎ 051 878203

WEXFORD

No.	Rating	Location	Hotel
199	★★★ ◎◎◎	GOREY	Marlfield House Hotel ☎ 055 21124
200	★★★★ ◎◎	ROSSLARE	Kelly's Resort Hotel ☎ 053 32114

AA Accessible Hotel of the Year Award 2004-2005

These awards highlight establishments which are making particular progress in their welcome to disabled guests in the lead-up to the introduction of part 3 of the Disability Discrimination Act from 2004. From nearly 8000 establishments in the AA accommodation schemes, two Highly Commended and an outright Winner were chosen. The selection process involves assessment of accessible facilities against an 80 point checklist, mystery telephone enquiry, and an overnight visit by an independent judge.

Winner

De Vere Daresbury Park

Warrington, Cheshire

The De Vere Daresbury Park is very pro-active, with eight rooms for mobility-impaired guests. This year our independent judge is deaf. She praised the attention to detail, with staff being deaf-aware in all departments, from reception to the restaurant. She also commented that the management had given much thought to the needs of disabled guests throughout the hotel.

Highly Commended

Huntingdon Marriott Hotel

Huntingdon Cambridgeshire

Highly Commended

Meudon Hotel

Mawnan Smith, Cornwall

AA Awards 2004-2005
Hotel of the Year Award

Hotel of the Year is the AA's most prestigious award. One hotel from each of the country - England, Scotland, Wales and Ireland - is chosen as a winner. The winners will be anounced in the autumn of 2004 at the AA Hospitality Award events. Please visit the AA website (www.theAA.com) for further details. The hotels nominated for the 2004-5 awards are shown on these pages in order of their star rating.

England

★★★★ ❀❀❀

Whately Manor

Malmesbury, Wiltshire

★★★ ❀

Calcot Manor

Tetbury, Gloucestershire

★★★★★ 72% ❀❀❀

The Grove

Rickmansworth, Hertfordshire

Scotland

★★★★ ❀❀

Prestonfield

City of Edinburgh

★★★ ❀❀❀

Glenapp Castle

Ballantrae, South Ayrshire

★★★ ❀❀

Kinloch House Hotel

Blairgowrie, Perth & Kinross

Wales

★★★★

Osborne House

Llandudno, Conwy

★★★

Seiont Manor Hotel

Caernarfon, Gwynedd

★★★ 71%

Castle Hotel Conwy

Conwy, Conwy

Republic of Ireland

★★★★★

Dromoland Castle Hotel

Newmarket-on-Fergus, Co Clare

★★★★

The Clarence

Dublin, Co Dublin

★★★★

Killarney Park Hotel

Killarney, Co Kerry

Hotel Group of the Year Award

HandPICKED

This award reflects the hotel group which has demonstrated an outstanding commitment to improving and developing their portfolio of hotels, whilst maintaining a high level of consistency throughout the group.

AA Awards 2004-2005

Courtesy and Care Award

This award is made to hotels where staff offer exceptionally high standards of courtesy and care. National awards are made for England, Scotland & Northern Ireland, Wales and the Republic of Ireland. Members of staff receive a specially designed lapel badge to wear on duty. In addition, a large framed certificate is commissioned for display by the hotels and they have a highlighted entry in the guide. Awards for 2004-2005 are as follows:

England

★★★ 80%
The Westcliff Hotel
Sidmouth, Devon

Scotland

★★★ 80% ❀❀
The Dryfesdale Country House Hotel
Lockerbie, Dumfries & Galloway

Wales

★★ 80% ❀
Milebrook House Hotel
Knighton, Powys

Republic of Ireland

★★★★ ❀❀
Kelly's Resort Hotel
Rosslare, Co Wexford

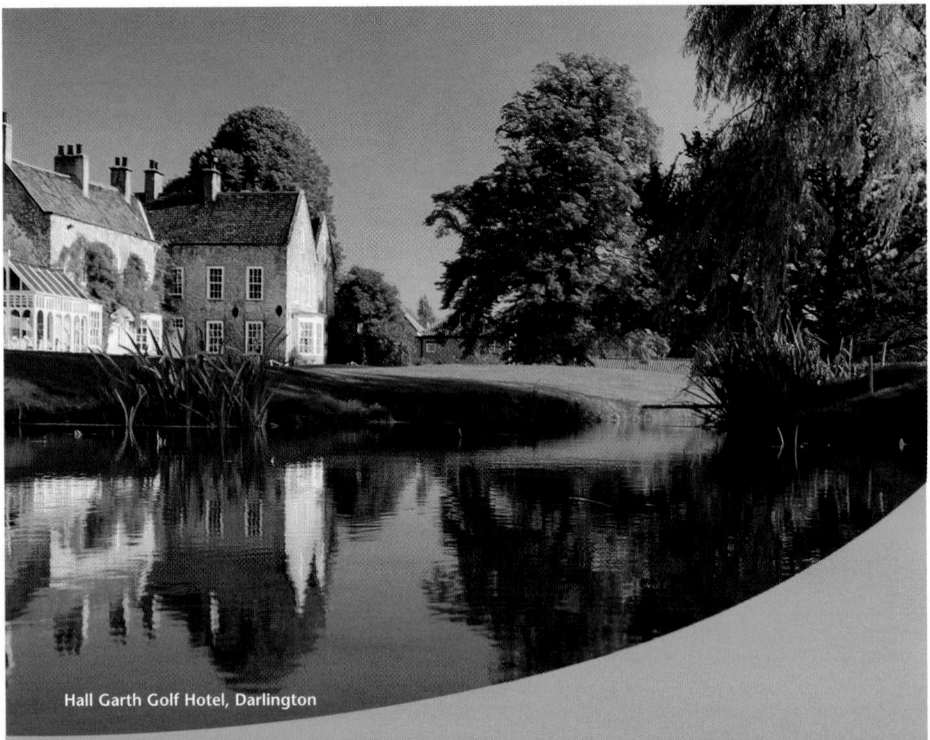

Hall Garth Golf Hotel, Darlington

Hotel Groups Information

The following hotel groups have at least four hotels and 400 rooms or are part of an internationally significant brand with a central reservations number.

Company Statement — **Central Reservations Contact Number**

Britain's largest group has around 350 independently owned and managed hotels, modern and traditional, in the two, three and four star markets. Many have leisure facilities and many have rosette awards

Best Western
08457 73 73 73

A privately owned group of 11 three and four star hotels in Devon and Cornwall

Brend
01271 34 44 96

A division of North British Trust Group, comprising of a selection of three star hotels, providing accommodation throughout Scotland and the north of England

Crearer
08700 507 711

Campanile offers modern accommodation for the budget market

Campanile
0208 326 1500

CHOICE HOTELS EUROPE

Choice offers mainly three brands in the UK: Quality Hotels in the three star market, Comfort Inns at two star and Sleep Inns in the travel accommodation market

Choice
0800 44 44 44

A consortium of independent hotels at the four star and high-quality three star level, categorised by quality and style, and marketed under the Classic British Hotels hallmark

Classic British
0845 0 70 70 90

Part of the Millennium and Copthorne group, comprising 11 four star hotels in primary provincial locations and London

Copthorne
0800 414741

A large group of three star hotels ranging from rural to city centre locations across the UK

Corus
0845 300 2000

There are 11 hotels in the UK, part of the international brand of modern three star hotels

Courtyard by Marriott
0800 221 222 or 0800 699 996

Good quality modern budget accommodation at motorway services. www.welcomebreak.co.uk

Days Inn
0800 02 80 400

De Vere comprises 21 four and five star hotels, which specialise in leisure, golf and conferences

De Vere
0870 606 3606

A small privately owned group of luxury five and four star hotels all located in the South of England

Exclusive
01276 471774

	Company Statement	Central Reservations Contact Number
Forestdale Hotels	A privately owned group of about a dozen three star hotels across the south of England	**Forestdale** **0808 1449494**
FOUR PILLARS HOTELS	Half a dozen three and four star hotels based in the Oxfordshire area	**Four Pillars** **01993 700100**
	A small group of personally managed three and four star hotels in leisure locations, with business facilities	**Furlong** **01225 867123** **(Head Office)**
	A collection of privately owned hotels, five located in central London and one in Bracknell, Berkshire	**Grange Hotels** **020 7233 7888**
GRESHAM HOTELS	Part of the Ryan Hotels group, Gresham is a collection of four star properties, conveniently located in city centre locations in the Republic of Ireland.	**Gresham Hotels** **00 353 1 7966** **(Head Office)**
	A group of 15 predominantly four star, high quality country house hotels, with a real emphasis on quality food	**Handpicked** **0800 9 177 877**
	A group of three and four star hotels located mainly in the central counties of England	**Hanover International** **01455 630000**
	Ibis is a growing chain of modern travel accommodation with properties across the UK	**Ibis** **0870 6090963**
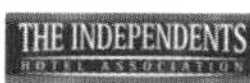	A consortium of independently owned, mainly two and three star hotels across Britain	**Independents** **0800 88 55 44**
	Travel accommodation from Bass Leisure Retail, featuring comfortable rooms and complimentary breakfast. www.innkeeperslodge.com	**Innkeepers Lodges** **0870 243 0500**
	This internationally renowned group is primarily represented in the UK with three five star hotels in central London	**Inter-Continental** **0800 0289 387**
	An association of owner-managed establishments across Ireland	**Ireland's Blue Book** **00 353 1 0462 3416**
	Friendly and informal in style, Irish Country Hotels is a collection of 30 individual family owned and run hotels, located throughout the country	**Irish Country Hotels** **00 353 1 295 8900**
JURYS DOYLE HOTELS	This Irish company has a range of three and four star hotels in the UK and the Republic of Ireland	**Jury's Doyle** **0870 9072222** **(Group Information)**
	A group of 14 two star hotels located in the 'Best of British' seaside resorts	**Leisureplex** **08451 305888 (Head Office)**
	A large group of predominantly four star hotels, traditional and modern in style, located across the UK	**Macdonald** **0870 400 90 90**
	A growing brand of three star city centre hotels, all rated over 70%	**Malmaison** **0207 479 9512 (Head Office)**

	Company Statement	Central Reservations Contact Number
	Located throughout Northern and Southern Ireland, Manor House Hotels is an independent group comprising Georgian manors, country houses, shooting lodges, castles and four star guest houses	**Manor House** **08705 300 200** **00 353 1 295 8900**
Marriott	This international brand offers four star hotels in primary locations. Most are modern and have leisure facilities; some have a focus on golf	**Marriott** **0800 221 222** **0800 699 996**
	A quality independent group of mainly four star hotels with leisure facilities in primary locations across England	**Marston** **0845 1300 700**
	Menzies hotels owns a portfolio of predominantly four star hotels located throughout the UK	**Menzies** **0870 600 3013**
	Part of the Millennium and Copthorne group, comprising six high-quality four star hotels, mainly in central London	**Millennium** **0800 41 47 41**
	Part of French group Accor, Novotel provides modern predominantly three star hotels in key locations throughout the UK	**Novotel** **020 8283 4500**
Old English Inns	A large collection of former coaching inns, mainly in the two and three star markets	**Old English Inns & Hotels** **0800 917 3085**
	A group of predominantly four star hotels, many with leisure facilities	**Paramount** **0500 342 543**
	A Europe based group increasing its presence within the UK through quality four star hotels in primary locations	**Park Plaza Hotels** **020 70344807**
	A Europe based group increasing its presence within the UK through quality four star hotels in primary locations	**Peel** **0800 1696128**
	High quality, modern, budget accommodation throughout the UK. Every Premier Lodge has an adjacent bar and family restaurant. For the best available rates, please visit www.premierlodge.com	**Premier Lodge** **08702 01 02 03**
	A consortium of privately owned British hotels, often in the country house style	**Pride of Britain** **01666 824666 (Head Office)**
	This high-quality London-based group offers mainly four star hotels in key locations throughout the capital	**Radisson Edwardian** **0800 374411**
	A recognised international brand increasing its presence in the UK, offering high-quality four star hotels in key locations	**Radisson SAS** **0800 37 44 11**
	A unique collection of prestigious four and five star central London hotels, providing luxurious surroundings and attentive service	**Red Carnation** **020 7514 5633** **(Head Office)**

	Company Statement	Central Reservations Contact Number
	An international consortium of rural, privately owned hotels, mainly in the country house style	**Relais et Chateaux** **00 33 1 457 296 50**
	One of the Marriott brands, Renaissance is a collection of individual hotels offering comfortable guest rooms, quality cuisine and good levels of service	**Renaissance** **0800 221 222** **0800 699 996**
	Small group of luxury hotels spread across Europe, owned by Sir Rocco Forte. Represented in the UK by 4 hotels all situated in major city locations	**Rocco Forte Hotels** **0870 460 6040**
	A prestigious group of four five star hotels in central London	**Savoy Group** **00800 7671 7671** **(General Enquiries)**
	A consortium of independent Scottish hotels, in the three and four star market	**Scotland's Hotels of Distinction** **01333 360 888**
	Sheraton is represented in the UK by a small number of four and five star hotels in London and Scotland	**Sheraton** **0800 35 35 35**
	A small group of mostly four star hotels many of which many feature spa facilities	**Shire** **01282 414141 (Head Office)**
	Part of an international consortium of mainly privately owned hotels, often in the country house style	**Small Luxury Hotels of the World** **00800 525 48000** **00 49 69 664 19601**
	A new brand from Choice Hotels representing a small group of hotels in the Midlands and Northern England.	**Stop Inn** **0800 44 44 44**
THE CIRCLE *Selected Individual Hotels* GREAT BRITAIN	A consortium of independently owned mainly two and three star hotels across Britain	**The Circle** **0845 345 1965**
	Good-quality, modern, budget accommodation across the UK. Almost every lodge has an adjacent family restaurant, often a Little Chef, Harry Ramsden's or Burger King	**Travelodge** **08700 850950**
	Good-quality, modern, budget accommodation. Every Travel Inn has an adjacent licensed family restaurant, often a Beefeater, Brewer's Fayre or TGI Fridays	**Travel Inn** **0870 242 8000**
	With over 90 properties across Europe, this brand is starting to grow its presence in the UK, currently represented by Tulip Inns in Manchester and Glasgow.	**Tulip Inn**
	A privately owned collection of country house hotels, all individual in style and based predominantly in the south of England	**Von Essen** **01761 241631**
	Good-quality, modern, budget accommodation at motorway services. www.welcomebreak.co.uk	**Welcome Break** **0800 731 4466**
	A small group of individual character hotels, located in countryside settings and in the historic towns of Windsor and Eton	**Wren's Hotels** **01753 442 455** **(Head Office)**

Seafood
- the ultimate dish when eating out

We're a nation of seafood lovers and that's not surprising considering we have access over 100 different species of fish and shellfish in the UK.

With such a wide range of seafood available, why not be adventurous and try something new from the menu next time you are dining out.From the meaty texture of tuna to the delicate flavour of Dover sole, there's an ocean of choice to choose from. Whether you fancy a light dish or a hearty meal, seafood is an excellent option when eating out. Seafood is incredibly versatile, you can choose poached, barbecued, fried, stir-fried, baked or steamed but seafood also tastes perfect lightly grilled with a squeeze of lemon. So go on, try something new next time you are in a restaurant and surprise yourself with how wonderful seafood can be.

A Passion for Seafood

We at Seafish (The Seafood Industry Authority), working closely with the AA, are keen to help you find the best seafood dishes in the country, created and served by these food loving establishments.

The AA Hotel Guide provides you with details of some of the best establishments that serve excellent seafood dishes. See page 914 for a list of these recognised establishments.

Look out for the blue fish symbol that stands for 'Good seafood served here', and enjoy!

Seafood, the food lovers' choice, is nutritious, delicious and offers oceans of variety when dining out.

Sea Fish Industry Authority,
18 Logie Mill, Logie Green Road, Edinburgh EH7 4HG
Tel: 0131 558 3331 Fax: 0131 558 1442
E-mail: marketing@seafish.co.uk Website: www.seafish.org.uk

Why do they do it?

By Julia Hynard

Why do we stay in hotels? There are many reasons, all of them fairly straightforward and easily understood. It might vary as an experience, from a practical stopover on a long journey to a luxurious weekend away or a comfortable holiday, but the basic concept remains the same. Somewhere to stay away from home for a limited amount of time, where someone else will make your breakfast and ensure your bed is made.

We all have our own reasons for staying at hotels, but have you ever wondered about the people who make your stay possible? What makes someone want to work in a hotel, or even own or run one? As a guest, maybe we take the staff for granted, unless they are very good (or very bad...) never wondering what brought them here, why they stay, why they like their jobs (or even if they do). At the same time, maybe you've toyed with the idea of running somewhere yourself, giving it all up to live in a Georgian manor house in a beautiful location, and throwing it open to the public.

Intrigued to know what response we'd get from our proprietors, we asked them some questions about their reasons for doing what they do. Some things were clear immediately. Owners, managers, chefs, receptionists, bar tenders, sales and marketing staff all love to work with people, and customer satisfaction is the biggest buzz of all. On the downside there are the long hours, 'hanging around late night bar bores' and then getting up to see to early morning breakfasts.

But why?

When asked what made them choose to do what they do, we found some interesting and diverse answers. For some it is a lifetime's ambition 'since watching Crossroads 20 years ago', and for others it's in the blood, growing up in a business that's been in the family three or four generations.

The Brooks family have been at **Ednam House**, Kelso since 1928, and Anne and Ralph Brooks are the fourth generation at the helm, as manager/chef/owners. So why do they do it? 'Pure passion' they say, and faith in the hotel's commitment – right from the beginning – to genuine hospitality. It's certainly working: around 70% of their guests are return visitors.

If 'the successful man is the one who is too stupid to give up', then Chris Robertson reckons he is pretty stupid, but after 26 years at the **Sefton Hotel**, Douglas (following priests' seminary and the army), he concludes that running a good hotel is the most fulfilling and satisfying career. Newer to the business is Nigel Schofield, who, with his wife, recently opted for a radical change of lifestyle. A director of a property consultancy in London, he took the chance to buy a hotel he'd known for many years – the **Loch Melfort** in Arduaine. He's really enjoying 'living in a wonderful location and having the time to talk to people'.

Kate Ewing may not have set out with any towering ambition, but has been at the **Woolacombe Bay Hotel** for 19 years – since she was 19. She commends the company for its positive approach to staff development. 'If you're worth it at Woolacombe Bay, you get it, irrespective of whether you are a man or a woman.' Kate didn't do 'degrees and gap years following years of college, learning hospitality, tourism, management etc.,' but in the course of time she's tried her hand as a kitchen porter, waitress, chambermaid, barmaid, receptionist and office worker and is now the manager, with a good working knowledge of all departments and happy to have 'the best job in the world'.

Top 5 reasons why I do this job

1 Passion – because I love it
2 Family business/in the blood
3 Working with people
4 Challenge
5 Change of lifestyle/quality of life

What did you do before?

So are hotels run by people who've been involved in the hospitality industry since they left school? It seems that for many this is the case. Sixty-four percent of our respondents have never done anything else, but what about the

remaining 36%? Of course there are many random listings – postman, panel-beater, petrol pump attendant and airline pilot – but a surprising number of occupations come up again and again. Are these careers that provide the ideal preparation for Teachers in particular it seems are abandoning their inhospitable classrooms in droves…

Top 10 previous occupations

1 Teaching
2 Secretarial
3 Accounting
4 HM Forces
5 Medical
6 Farming
7 Banking
8 IT
9 Legal
10 Sales

When it comes to professional inspiration, it seems it can be found in characters as diverse as Fanny Craddock and Basil Fawlty. For many who were born into the trade it was 'my father' or 'my mother', for others it has been elevating encounters at key points in their careers:

Gordon Ramsay
'The world thinks he's the devil but his staff know he is god'

My first general manager
'It was his lack of confidence in me that inspired me to achieve this goal'
(From a general manager)

George Goring
'A true gentleman'
Evangelo Brioni (aka Brian Evans, banqueting manager of The Savoy in the 70s)
'A wonderful leader, he was instrumental in teaching me to temper drive with humour and humility'

Jamie Oliver
'For his willingness to take on untrained, inexperienced young people and turn them into excellent representatives for the industry'

Anton Mosiman
'A true professional, great cook and a legend in his own lifetime. My years with him were truly inspirational'

A cleaner (in my first hotel who had been doing the same job for 50 years)
'On my first day she said, "No, I don't get bored doing this. The first person in will notice the shining brass and think 'wow – someone's gone to a lot of trouble' and I'll know that person was me."'

Top 10 people who have inspired me professionally

1 Richard Branson
2 Gordon Ramsay
3 Forte Family
4 Raymond Blanc
5 Rick Stein
6 Francis Coulson & Brian Sack
7 Jamie Oliver
8 George Goring/
Gary Rhodes/Roux Bros/
Marco Pierre White (tie)
9 Anton Mosiman
10 Keith Floyd/ Basil Fawlty (tie)

The best thing about your day?
It couldn't be clearer – satisfied customers make for satisfied staff – and as a guest, it's nice to know that staff feel the best thing about hotel life is meeting and chatting to guests, seeing them leave happy and, most importantly, coming back! Hotel personnel also get a real kick out of the variety of their work, being in a lovely place, and seeing colleagues learn and develop. There's a great sense of achievement, too, when it's busy, everything's going well and they've contributed to a really successful day or special event.

One of the perks of hotel life is proximity to great food and drink. **Three Ways House** at Chipping Campden is home to the world famous Pudding Club, and as owner of the hotel Simon Coombe has the enviable job of chief pudding taster. Another owner, Robert Cook from **The Abbey Hotel**, Tintern Parva, sees this as an occupational hazard. *'I tend to eat too much,'* is his wry observation.

The quality of the food is taken very seriously. For John Kelly, Head Chef of the **Bosville Hotel**, Portree the best bit of his day is the deliveries of produce arriving from all over the island. The worst bit is when it is stormy outside and he knows he won't get is usual delivery of fresh seafood.

Top 5 best things about my day

1 Satisfied customers
2 Meeting people
3 No two days the same
4 Getting up
5 Seeing improvement & development (particularly in staff)

Worst thing about your day?
Of course, there has to be a downside, or it wouldn't be fair and we'd all be running hotels. Long hours and piles of paperwork are attendant evils of day-to-day hotel life, and pretty much go with the territory, but complaints from customers are always gutting and certainly make their mark. Another headache is staffing, particularly when a member of staff doesn't show for a shift, or lets the hotel down in the service they provide.
Rude, thoughtless and awkward customers are a dispiriting aspect of our respondents' experience, including the 'drunkard who still demands alcohol' and 'clearing up after late night revellers'. Such behaviour can add stress to the working lives of hoteliers who may already be burning the candle at both ends. Another bugbear is phone calls from companies trying to sell things, which are described as 'a tedious waste of time'. Interestingly, 'getting up' figures in both the top 5 'best' and 'worst things about my day', perhaps it depends on how late your guests stay up in the bar, or how early they come down for breakfast?

Top 5 worst things about my day

1 Long hours
2 Paperwork/bureaucracy
3 Dissatisfied customers
4 Not enough hours in the day
5 Getting up

Running a hotel is not so much a job as a way of life, and this comes across clearly in the responses to our question What are you or your establishment trying to achieve? If your aim is to provide 'escapism and luxury' (Philippa Hughes, **Holne Chase Hotel,** Ashburton), then it is a dream that you and your family can share with the fortunate customer.

Often it means living in a fine property in a desirable location and spending the day with your nearest and dearest. The work may be challenging and the hours long, but for people who like people and are looking for a better quality of life and to be in charge of their own destiny and vision, it can be the answer.

Rhys Williams, a former journalist (principally with The Independent) and the creative and founding director of EMC Saatchi, decided a couple of years ago that 15 years in the London media was enough to last a lifetime. He bought the **Dunoon Hotel** in Llandudno with a view to establishing a completely new lifestyle with time to spend with his family. He writes: 'We want the hotel to be the best. We also want to take care of our staff – to create as many jobs as possible and pay as much as we can. We want to create an environment in which people can flourish, develop and take pride in their labours. We feel strongly that many people working in the hospitality sector have a pretty raw deal and we

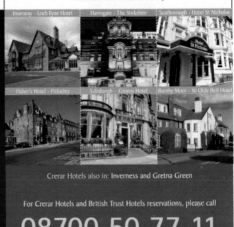

want to do something, however small in the great scheme of things, to correct that general wrong.'

It is both impressive and gratifying to see that to 'be the best' and to seek a higher AA rating are top of the top 10 ambitions, demonstrating a clear commitment to driving standards ever higher. This is not to say that every hotel should or needs to be the ultimate in opulence. To provide comfort, good food and good service is a laudable aim and all that most of us with modest means would ask. The most touching response is surely from the hotels, whatever their status, who aim to 'exceed the customer's expectations'.

Top 10 'what I want to achieve'

1 To be the best (in my area/of my type)
2 Higher AA rating
3 Quality, comfort, relaxation, good food & good service
4 Excellence/perfection
5 Customer satisfaction
6 Improved profitability
7 Value for money
8 To exceed guests' expectations
9 Consistency/maintainstandards
10 To raise standards, develop and improve

The hotels mentioned in this feature all appear in the 2005 Hotel Guide. Don't forget, however, that establishments may change hands during the currency of the Guide, and if you visit you may find the people who responded to our questions have moved on.

Nominations for

AA Hotel of the Year Award for England

2004-2005

★★★★ ®®®

Whately Manor

Malmesbury, Wiltshire

★★★ ®

Calcot Manor

Tetbury, Gloucestershire

★★★★★ 72% ®®®

The Grove

Rickmansworth, Hertfordshi

ABBERLEY, Worcestershire

Map 10 SO76

★★★ 73% Elms Hotel & Restaurant
Stockton Rd WR6 6AT
☎ 01299 896666 01299 896804
e-mail: management@theelmshotel.co.uk
web: www.theelmshotel.co.uk
Dir: *on A443 2m beyond Great Witley*

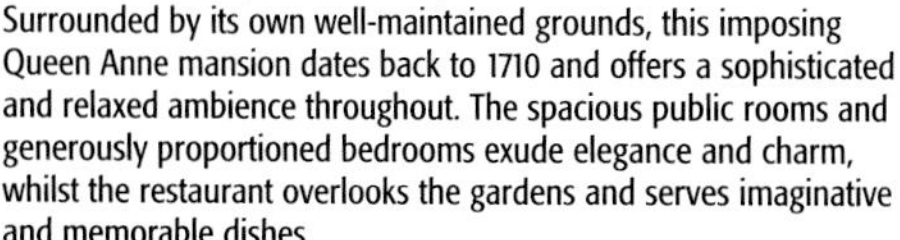

Surrounded by its own well-maintained grounds, this imposing Queen Anne mansion dates back to 1710 and offers a sophisticated and relaxed ambience throughout. The spacious public rooms and generously proportioned bedrooms exude elegance and charm, whilst the restaurant overlooks the gardens and serves imaginative and memorable dishes.
ROOMS: 16 en suite 5 annexe en suite (1 fmly) s £90-£110; d £120-£180 (incl. bkfst) **LB FACILITIES:** ch fac Xmas **CONF:** Thtr 70 Class 30 Board 30 Del from £140 **PARKING:** 100 **NOTES:** in restaurant Civ Wed 70
CARDS:

ABBOT'S SALFORD, Warwickshire

Map 10 SP05

★★★ 74% Salford Hall
WR11 5UT
☎ 01386 871300 01386 871301
e-mail: reception@salfordhall.co.uk
web: www.salfordhall.co.uk
Dir: *A46 take road signed Salford Priors, Abbot's Salford & Harvington. Hotel 1.5m on left*

Built in 1470 as a retreat for the Abbot of Evesham, this impressive building retains many original features. Bedrooms have their own individual character and most offer a view of the attractive gardens. Oak panelling, period tapestries, open fires and fresh flowers grace the public areas, while leisure facilities include a snooker room, tennis court, solarium and sauna.
ROOMS: 14 en suite 19 annexe en suite (4 GF) in 4 bedrooms s £60-£115; d £100-£150 (incl. bkfst) **LB FACILITIES:** STV Snooker Sauna Solarium **CONF:** Thtr 50 Class 35 Board 25 Del from £100 **PARKING:** 51 **NOTES:** in restaurant Closed 24-30 Dec Civ Wed 50 **CARDS:**

See advert under STRATFORD-UPON-AVON

ABINGDON, Oxfordshire

Map 05 SU49

★★★ 66% Abingdon Four Pillars Hotel
Marcham Rd OX14 1TZ
☎ 0800 374 692 01235 554117
e-mail: abingdon@four-pillars.co.uk
web: www.four-pillars.co.uk
Dir: *A34 at junct with A415, in Abingdon, turn right at rdbt, hotel on right*
Situated on the outskirts of Abingdon, this busy commercial hotel is well located for access to major road links. Bedrooms are comfortable and well equipped with extras such as satellite TV and trouser presses. All-day refreshments are offered in the lounge and conservatory.
ROOMS: 62 en suite (7 fmly) (31 GF) in 40 bedrooms s £73-£92; d £83-£105 **LB FACILITIES:** STV Xmas **CONF:** Thtr 140 Class 80 Board 48 Del £130 **PARKING:** 85 **NOTES:** in restaurant Civ Wed 100 **CARDS:**

★★ 64% Crown & Thistle
18 Bridge St OX14 3HS
☎ 01235 522556 01235 553281
e-mail: reception@crownandthistle.com
Dir: *follow A415 towards Dorchester into the centre of Abingdon*
This popular former coaching inn enjoys an enviable position close to the town centre and the river. Diners can choose between Stocks bar, which retains the air of a local pub, and the more formal but equally friendly restaurant. Bedrooms, located in the original building, are full of character and include some four-poster and family rooms.
ROOMS: 19 en suite (3 fmly) s fr £65; d £75-£100 **LB FACILITIES:** STV Snooker Xmas **CONF:** Thtr 12 Class 8 Board 12 Del from £100 **PARKING:** 35 **NOTES:** in restaurant
CARDS:

Travel Inn
Marcham Rd OX14 1AD
☎ 08701 977014 01235 554149
Dir: *On A415 0.5 m from Abingdon town centre. Approx. 0.5m from the A34 at the Abingdon South junct*
Travel Inn offers good-quality, value-for-money accommodation. Spacious, en suite rooms with bath and shower comfortably accommodate a family of up to two adults and two children (to age 15). The restaurant and bar offers a varied menu. For further details consult the Hotel Groups page.
ROOMS: 25 en suite s £45.95-£46.95; d £45.95-£46.95

ACCRINGTON, Lancashire

Map 18 SD72

★★★★ 62% *Dunkenhalgh*
Blackburn Rd, Clayton-le-Moors BB5 5JP
☎ 01254 398021 01254 872230
e-mail: dunkenhalgh@macdonald-hotels.co.uk
Dir: *adjacent to M65 junct 7*
This modern, smartly presented hotel stands in 17 acres of glorious parkland, just a few minutes from the motorway network. Features include a fully equipped indoor leisure centre and a brand new state-of-the-art conference centre. Bedrooms vary in size and style with a modern extension providing high standards of comfort and quality.
ROOMS: 53 en suite 69 annexe en suite (33 fmly) in 56 bedrooms **FACILITIES: Spa** STV Sauna Solarium Gym Jacuzzi Health & beauty spa, Dance studio **CONF:** Thtr 400 Class 200 Board 100 **SERVICES:** Lift **PARKING:** 400 **NOTES:** in restaurant Civ Wed 400
CARDS:

★★★ 66% Sparth House Hotel
Whalley Rd, Clayton Le Moors BB5 5RP
☎ 01254 872263 01254 872263
e-mail: mail.sparth@btinternet.com
Dir: *A6185 to Clitheroe along Dunkenhalgh Way, right at lights onto A678, left at next lights, A680 to Whalley. Hotel on left after 2 sets of lights*
This 18th-century listed building nestles in three acres of well-tended gardens close to the motorway. Bedrooms are individually styled and those in the original house are particularly spacious, including one with furnishings from one of the great

continued on p50

ACCRINGTON, continued

cruise liners. The panelled restaurant is a peaceful setting in which to enjoy a wide range of dishes.

Sparth House Hotel, Accrington

ROOMS: 16 en suite (3 fmly) ⊗ in 2 bedrooms s £62.50-£85; d £70-£99 (incl. bkfst) **LB** **FACILITIES:** ch fac **CONF:** Thtr 160 Class 50 Board 40 Del from £75 **PARKING:** 50 **NOTES:** ⊗ in restaurant Civ Wed 150 **CARDS:**

ACLE, Norfolk — Map 13 TG41

Travelodge Great Yarmouth

Travelodge

NR13 3BE
☎ 08700 850 950 📠 01493 751970
Dir: *junct of A47 & Acle by-pass*

Travelodge offers good quality, good value, modern accommodation. Ideal for families, the spacious, en suite bedrooms include remote-control TV, tea and coffee-making facilities and luxury beds. Meals can be taken at the nearby family restaurant. For further details consult the Hotel Groups page.

ROOMS: 40 en suite s fr £25; d fr £25

ALCESTER, Warwickshire — Map 10 SP05

★★★67% **Kings Court**

Kings Coughton B49 5QQ
☎ 01789 763111 📠 01789 400242
e-mail: info@kingscourthotel.co.uk
Dir: *1m N on A435*

This privately-owned hotel dates back to Tudor times and the bedrooms in the original house have oak beams. Most guests are accommodated in the well-appointed modern wings. The bar and restaurant have undergone complete refurbishment and offer very good cooking from interesting menus. The hotel is licensed to hold civil ceremonies and the pretty garden is ideal for summer weddings.

ROOMS: 4 en suite 37 annexe en suite (3 fmly) (22 GF) ⊗ in 15 bedrooms s £39-£70; d £66-£90 (incl. bkfst) **LB** **CONF:** Thtr 100 Class 60 Board 40 Del £92 **PARKING:** 120 **NOTES:** Closed 24-30 Dec Civ Wed 100 **CARDS:**

Travelodge Stratford Alcester

Travelodge

Oversley Mill Roundabout B49 6AA
☎ 08700 850 950 📠 01789 766987
Dir: *at junct A46/A435*

Travelodge offers good quality, good value, modern accommodation. Ideal for families, the spacious, en suite bedrooms include remote-control TV, tea and coffee-making facilities and luxury beds. Meals can be taken at the nearby family restaurant. For further details consult the Hotel Groups page.

ROOMS: 66 en suite s fr £25; d fr £25

ALDEBURGH, Suffolk — Map 13 TM45

★★★77% **The Brudenell**

The Parade IP15 5BU
☎ 01728 452071 📠 01728 454082
e-mail: info@brudenellhotel.co.uk
Dir: *A12/A1094, on reaching town, turn right at junct into High St. Hotel on seafront adjoining Fort Green car park*

Situated at the far end of the town centre just a step away from the beach. The hotel has a contemporary appearance, enhanced by subtle lighting and quality soft furnishings; many of the bedrooms have superb sea views. Deluxe rooms with king-sized beds and superior rooms suitable for families are available. Local seafood and grills are a speciality in the award-winning restaurant.

ROOMS: 42 en suite (15 fmly) ⊗ in all bedrooms s £63-£94; d £98-£192 (incl. bkfst) **LB** **FACILITIES:** STV Xmas **SERVICES:** Lift **PARKING:** 20 **NOTES:** ⊗ in restaurant **CARDS:**

★★★76% ***Wentworth***

Wentworth Rd IP15 5BD
☎ 01728 452312 📠 01728 454343
e-mail: stay@wentworth-aldeburgh.co.uk
web: www.wentworth-aldeburgh.com
Dir: *off A12 onto A1094, 6m to Aldeburgh, with church on left & left at bottom of hill*

A delightful privately owned hotel overlooking the beach and sea beyond. The attractive, well-maintained public rooms include three stylish lounges as well as a bar and elegant restaurant. Bedrooms are smartly decorated with co-ordinated fabrics and have many thoughtful touches; some rooms have superb sea views. Several very spacious Mediterranean-style rooms are located across the road.

ROOMS: 30 rms (28 en suite) 7 annexe en suite ⊗ in all bedrooms **FACILITIES:** STV **CONF:** Thtr 15 Class 12 Board 12 **PARKING:** 30 **NOTES:** ⊗ in restaurant Closed 28 Dec-9 Jan **CARDS:**

See advert on opposite page

★★★76% White Lion
Market Cross Place IP15 5BJ
☎ 01728 452720 📠 01728 452986
e-mail: whitelionaldeburgh@btinternet.com
web: www.whitelion.co.uk
Dir: *Follow signs to Aldeburgh & town centre. At x-rds left, hotel is in Market Cross Place*

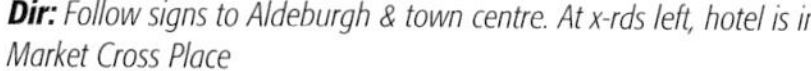

A popular 15th-century hotel situated at the quiet end of town overlooking the sea. Bedrooms are pleasantly decorated and thoughtfully equipped, many rooms have lovely sea views. Public areas include two lounges and an elegant restaurant where locally caught fish and seafood are served. There is also a modern brasserie.
ROOMS: 38 en suite (1 fmly) ⊘ in 19 bedrooms s £73.50-£102; d £114-£164 (incl. bkfst) **LB** **FACILITIES:** STV Xmas **CONF:** Thtr 120 Class 50 Board 50 Del from £90 **PARKING:** 15 **NOTES:** ⊘ in restaurant Civ Wed 100 **CARDS:**

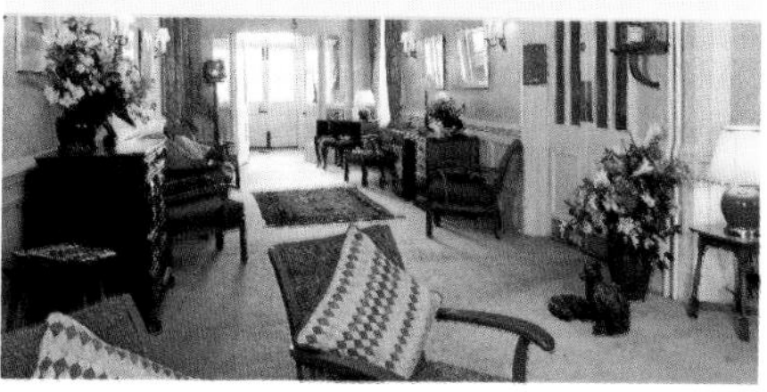

ALDERLEY EDGE, Cheshire — Map 16 SJ87

★★★77% ◎◎ Alderley Edge
Macclesfield Rd SK9 7BJ
☎ 01625 583033 📠 01625 586343
e-mail: sales@alderleyedgehotel.com
web: www.alderleyedgehotel.com
Dir: *off A34 in Alderley Edge onto B5087 towards Macclesfield. Hotel 200yds on right*

This well-furnished hotel, with its charming grounds, was originally a country house built for one of the region's cotton kings. The bedrooms and suites are attractively furnished, offering excellent quality and comfort. The welcoming bar and adjacent lounge lead into the split-level conservatory restaurant; imaginative, memorable food and friendly attentive service are highlights of any visit.
ROOMS: 52 en suite (6 GF) ⊘ in 19 bedrooms s £120-£400; d £140-£400 **LB** **FACILITIES:** STV ♫ Xmas **CONF:** Thtr 90 Class 40 Board 30 Del £165 **SERVICES:** Lift **PARKING:** 90 **NOTES:** ⊘ in restaurant Civ Wed 90 **CARDS:**

⌂ Innkeeper's Lodge Alderley Edge
5-9 Wilmslow Rd SK9 7NZ
☎ 01625 599959 📠 01625 599432
www.innkeeperslodge.com
Dir: *M56 junct 6, S on A538. Right at traffic lights towards Alderley Edge. Lodge on left, after 2nd rdbt*
Smart rooms meet essential business requirements but also have home comforts, and depending on location may well have meeting rooms and pub dining. Dining options generally include all-day menus plus the added advantage of breakfast.
ROOMS: 10 en suite s £48-£59.95; d £48-£59.95

⌂ Premier Lodge (Alderley Edge)
Congleton Rd, Alderley Edge SK9 7AA
☎ 0870 9906498 📠 0870 9906499
web: www.premierlodge.com
Dir: *From north, exit M56 junct 6 onto A538 towards Wilmslow then on A34 towards Alderley Edge. From south, exit M6 junct 17 and follow A534 to Congleton then A34 to Alderley Edge*
High quality, modern, budget accommodation, ideal for families and business travellers. All rooms feature bath, power shower and satellite TV, and most have telephones / modem points. The adjacent bar and restaurant offers a wide and varied menu.
ROOMS: 37 en suite s £50; d £50 **CONF:** Thtr 20

ALDERMINSTER, Warwickshire — Map 10 SP24

★★★★77% ◎◎ Ettington Park
CV37 8BU
☎ 01789 450123 📠 01789 450472
e-mail: ettington-cro@handpicked.co.uk
Dir: *off A3400, 5m S of Stratford just outside village of Alderminster*
Ettington Park offers the peaceful charm of Shakespeare country

continued on p52

ALDERMINSTER, continued

within easy access of the road network. Bedrooms have views over either the manicured parkland or the formal gardens and chapel. All are spacious and individually designed with comfort in mind. Public rooms include a period drawing room, oak-panelled dining room and contemporary meeting rooms and leisure centre. Hand Picked Hotels - AA Hotel Group of the Year 2004-5.

Ettington Park, Alderminster

ROOMS: 28 en suite 20 annexe en suite (5 fmly) s fr £137; d fr £158 (incl. bkfst) **FACILITIES: Spa** STV Fishing Sauna Spa bath, Clay pigeon shooting, Archery, Health & Beauty treatments Xmas **CONF:** Thtr 75 Class 40 Board 48 Del £195 **SERVICES:** Lift **PARKING:** 150 **NOTES:** in restaurant Civ Wed 96 **CARDS:**

See advert on opposite page

ALDERSHOT, Hampshire Map 05 SU85

★★★67% Potters International

1 Fleet Rd GU11 2ET
☎ 01252 344000 01252 311611
Dir: *access via A325 & A321 towards Fleet*

This modern hotel is located within easy reach of Aldershot. Extensive air-conditioned public areas include ample lounge areas, a pub and a more formal restaurant; there are also conference rooms and a very good leisure club. Bedrooms are mostly spacious, well equipped and have been attractively decorated and furnished.

ROOMS: 100 en suite (6 fmly) (8 GF) in 10 bedrooms **FACILITIES:** STV supervised Sauna Solarium Gym Jacuzzi **CONF:** Thtr 400 **SERVICES:** Lift **PARKING:** 120 **NOTES:** in restaurant **CARDS:**

Travel Inn

7 Wellington Av GU11 1SQ
☎ 08701 977015 01252 344073
Dir: *Exit M3 (J4), join A331 then A325 through Farnborough, past airfield, over roundabout. Travel Inn is ahead*

Travel Inn offers good-quality, value-for-money accommodation. Spacious, en suite rooms with bath and shower comfortably accommodate a family of up to two adults and two children (to age 15). The restaurant and bar offers a varied menu. For further details consult the Hotel Groups page.

ROOMS: 60 en suite s £45.95-£46.95; d £45.95-£46.95

Town House Hotel
Country House Hotel
Travel Accommodation

ALDWARK, North Yorkshire Map 19 SE46

★★★★77% Aldwark Manor

YO61 1UF
☎ 01347 838146 01347 838867
e-mail: aldwark@marstonhotels.com
web: www.marstonhotels.com
Dir: *A1/A59 towards Green Hammerton, then B6265 Little Ouseburn. Follow signs for Aldwark Bridge/Manor. A19 through Linton on Ouse*

Mature parkland forms the impressive backdrop for this rambling 19th-century mansion, with the River Ure flowing gently through its 18-hole golf course. Bedrooms vary and are traditional in the house and more modern in the extension. Public areas are a mix of period style and modern. Other features include impressive conference and banqueting facilities and a stylish, very well equipped leisure club.

ROOMS: 60 en suite (2 fmly) s £110-£135; d £156-£206 (incl. bkfst) **LB** **FACILITIES: Spa** STV 18 Fishing Sauna Solarium Gym Putt green Jacuzzi Health & beauty Xmas **CONF:** Thtr 240 Class 80 Board 50 Del from £154 **PARKING:** 150 **NOTES:** in restaurant Civ Wed 140 **CARDS:**

ALFRETON, Derbyshire Map 16 SK45

Travelodge

Old Swanwick Colliery Rd DE55 1HJ
☎ 08700 850 950 01773 520040
Dir: *3m from M1 junct 28 at A38/ A61 junct*

Travelodge offers good quality, good value, modern accommodation. Ideal for families, the spacious, en suite bedrooms include remote-control TV, tea and coffee-making facilities and luxury beds. Meals can be taken at the nearby family restaurant. For further details consult the Hotel Groups page.

ROOMS: 60 en suite s fr £25; d fr £25

ALFRISTON, East Sussex Map 06 TQ50

★★★70% Deans Place

Seaford Rd BN26 5TW
☎ 01323 870248 01323 870918
e-mail: mail@deansplacehotel.co.uk
Dir: *off A27 signed Alfriston & Drusillas Zoo Park. Continue S through village*

Situated on the southern fringe of the village, this friendly hotel is set in attractive gardens. Bedrooms vary in size and are well appointed with good facilities. A wide range of food is offered including an extensive bar menu and a fine dining option in Harcourt's Restaurant.

ROOMS: 36 en suite (2 fmly) (8 GF) in 16 bedrooms s £60-£100; d £100-£138 (incl. bkfst) **LB** **FACILITIES: Spa** STV Putt green Boules Xmas **CONF:** Thtr 200 Class 100 Board 60 Del from £115 **PARKING:** 100 **NOTES:** in restaurant Civ Wed 150 **CARDS:**

★★★69% **The Star Inn**
BN26 5TA
☎ 01323 870495 📠 01323 870922
web: www.star-inn-alfriston.com
Dir: *2m off A27 at Drusillas rdbt*
Located in a sleepy town on the edge of the South Downs this 14th-century inn provides smart accommodation. Whilst some rooms retain original features the majority are contemporary in style and design. Public areas have much charm and character including open fires and flagstones.
ROOMS: 37 en suite (12 GF) ⊗ in 18 bedrooms s £44-£64; d £88-£128 (incl. bkfst) **LB** **FACILITIES:** Xmas **CONF:** Thtr 30 Class 15 Del from £100 **PARKING:** 40 **NOTES:** ⊗ in restaurant
CARDS:

★★★68% **White Lodge Country House**
Sloe Ln BN26 5UR
☎ 01323 870265 📠 01323 870284
e-mail: sales@whitelodge-hotel.com
Dir: *on B2108 between A27 & A259*
An ideal retreat in peaceful surroundings, with views over the Cuckmere River Valley. Bedrooms are individually decorated with refurbishment on-going. Weekend breaks are well-planned and special themed events are very popular. Public areas include a choice of elegant lounges.
ROOMS: 20 en suite (1 fmly) (4 GF) ⊗ in 3 bedrooms s £47.50-£155; d £95-£155 (incl. bkfst) **LB** **FACILITIES:** STV Putt green Xmas **CONF:** Thtr 24 Class 16 Board 16 Del from £79 **SERVICES:** Lift **PARKING:** 40 **NOTES:** ⊗ in restaurant Civ Wed 50
CARDS:

ALMONDSBURY, Gloucestershire

Map 04 ST68

★★★★71% **Aztec**
Aztec West Business Park BS32 4TS
☎ 01454 201090 📠 01454 201593
e-mail: aztec@shirehotels.co.uk
(For full entry see Bristol)

SHIRE HOTELS

ALNWICK, Northumberland

Map 21 NU11

See also Embleton

★★★59% ***White Swan***
Bondgate Within NE66 1TD
☎ 01665 602109 📠 01665 510400
Dir: *A1 town centre signs. Hotel in town centre near Bondgate Tower*

This former coaching inn is situated in the centre of the town. Bedrooms are modern, while public areas include the Atlantic

continued on p54

ALNWICK, continued

Suite, which features original wooden panelling and fittings from the sister ship of the SS Titanic.
ROOMS: 56 en suite (5 fmly) (11 GF) ⊗ in 23 bedrooms **CONF:** Thtr 150 Class 50 Board 40 **PARKING:** 25 **NOTES:** ⊗ in restaurant Civ Wed 150 **CARDS:**

ALSAGER, Cheshire — Map 15 SJ75

★★★69% Manor House

Best Western

Audley Rd ST7 2QQ
☎ 01270 884000 🖹 01270 882483
e-mail: mhres@compasshotels.co.uk
***Dir:** M6 junct 16/A500 toward Stoke. After 0.5m take 1st slip road to Alsager. Left at top & continue, hotel on left approaching village*
Developed around an old farmhouse, the original oak beams are still very much a feature in the hotel bars and restaurant. Modernised and extended over the years, the hotel today is well geared towards the needs of the modern traveller. Some of the main features include a range of conference rooms, a lovely patio garden and an indoor swimming pool.
ROOMS: 57 en suite (4 fmly) (21 GF) ⊗ in 27 bedrooms s £95-£99; d £115-£145 (incl. bkfst) **LB** **FACILITIES:** STV CCTV Jacuzzi Xmas **CONF:** Thtr 200 Class 108 Board 82 Del £135 **PARKING:** 150 **NOTES:** ⊗ in restaurant RS Sat & Sun Civ Wed 150
CARDS:

ALSTON, Cumbria — Map 18 NY74

★★77% *Lovelady Shield Country House*

CA9 3LF
☎ 01434 381203 & 381305 🖹 01434 381515
e-mail: enquiries@lovelady.co.uk
***Dir:** 2m E, signed off A689 at junct with B6294*

Located in the heart of the Pennines close to England's highest market town, this delightful country house is set in three acres of landscaped gardens. Accommodation is provided in thoughtfully equipped bedrooms several of which have been attractively refurbished. Carefully prepared meals are served in the elegant dining room and there is a choice of appealing lounges.
ROOMS: 10 en suite (1 fmly) **CONF:** Class 12 Board 12 **PARKING:** 20 **NOTES:** ⊗ in restaurant Civ Wed 100 **CARDS:**

★★71% Lowbyer Manor Country House

CA9 3JX
☎ 01434 381230 🖹 01434 381425
e-mail: stay@lowbyer.com
***Dir:** on A686 edge of town towards Hexham*
This interesting 18th-century manor house is set in mature gardens on the edge of town, and very friendly and attentive services are a highlight here. There is an inviting lounge and an adjoining library, along with a traditional snug-style bar. Imaginative meals are served in the attractive dining room.
ROOMS: 9 en suite 2 annexe en suite ⊗ in all bedrooms s £67; d £82-£102 (incl. bkfst) **LB** **FACILITIES:** Xmas **CONF:** Board 10 Del £105 **PARKING:** 12 **NOTES:** ⊗ in restaurant
CARDS:

★★71% Nent Hall Country House Hotel

CA9 3LQ
☎ 01434 381584 🖹 01434 382668
e-mail: info@nenthallcountryhousehotel.co.uk
***Dir:** 2m SE of Alston, on A689 towards Nenthend, Stanhope & Durham*
Personally run by keen new owners this delightful old house has a wealth of charm and stands in extensive gardens. It provides warm and friendly hospitality and well-equipped accommodation, with ground floor and family bedded rooms available. There is a choice of bars and lounge areas, including one for non-smokers.
ROOMS: 7 en suite 9 annexe en suite (3 fmly) (9 GF) ⊗ in all bedrooms s £50-£70; d £70 (incl. bkfst) **LB** **PARKING:** 35 **NOTES:** ⊗ in restaurant Closed 24-30 Dec Civ Wed 60 **CARDS:**

ALTON, Hampshire — Map 05 SU73

★★★70% Alton Grange

London Rd GU34 4EG
☎ 01420 86565 🖹 01420 541346
e-mail: info@altongrange.co.uk
web: www.altongrange.co.uk
***Dir:** from A31 right at rdbt signed Alton/Holybourne/Bordon B3004. Hotel 300yds on left*
A friendly and family owned hotel, conveniently located on the outskirts of this market town and set in its own well-manicured grounds. The individually styled bedrooms include three suites and are thoughtfully equipped. Diners can choose between the more formal Truffles Restaurant or relaxed Muffins Brasserie. The attractive public areas also include a function suite.
ROOMS: 26 en suite 4 annexe en suite (4 fmly) (7 GF) ⊗ in 6 bedrooms s £81-£99; d £99-£115 (incl. bkfst) **FACILITIES:** STV Hot air ballooning **CONF:** BC Thtr 80 Class 30 Board 40 Del from £150 **PARKING:** 48 **NOTES:** No children 3yrs ⊗ in restaurant Closed 24 Dec-2 Jan Civ Wed 100 **CARDS:**

★★★66% Alton House

Normandy St GU34 1DW
☎ 01420 80033 🖹 01420 89222
e-mail: mail@altonhouse.com
web: www.altonhousehotel.com
***Dir:** off A31, close to railway station*
Conveniently located on the edge of the town, this popular hotel offers comfortably furnished and well-equipped bedrooms. The restaurant serves an extensive menu with daily specials with more informal meals served within the bar. Attractive rear gardens are a plus, along with an outdoor pool and tennis court.
ROOMS: 39 en suite (3 fmly) (3 GF) ⊗ in 2 bedrooms
FACILITIES: STV Snooker **CONF:** Thtr 170 Class 80 Board 50 Del from £99 **PARKING:** 94 **NOTES:** Closed 25-26 Dec RS 27-29 Dec Civ Wed 70 **CARDS:**

ALTRINCHAM, Greater Manchester — Map 15 SJ78

★★★67% Cresta Court

Best Western

Church St WA14 4DP
☎ 0161 927 7272 🖹 0161 929 6548
e-mail: stewart5738@btconnect.com
web: www.cresta-court.co.uk
This modern hotel enjoys a prime location on the A56, close to the

continued

station and town centre shops and amenities. Bedrooms vary in style from spacious four-posters to smaller, traditionally furnished rooms. Public areas include a choice of bars, a small gym, hair and beauty salon and extensive function and conference facilities.
ROOMS: 136 en suite (8 fmly) ⊗ in 80 bedrooms s £49-£69; d £49-£69 LB **FACILITIES:** STV Solarium Gym Putt green Beauty salon/fitness & cardiovascular training room ♫ ch fac Xmas **CONF:** BC Thtr 350 Class 200 Board 150 Del from £90 **SERVICES:** Lift **PARKING:** 200 **NOTES:** ⊗ in restaurant Civ Wed 300
CARDS:

★★★66% Quality Hotel Altrincham

Langham Rd, Bowdon WA14 2HT
☎ 0161 928 7121 🖹 0161 927 7560
e-mail: enquiries@hotels-altrincham.com
Dir: *M6 junct 19 to airport, join A556, over M56 rdbt onto A56, right at traffic lights onto B5161. Hotel 1m on right*
This popular hotel is located within easy reach of the motorways and airport. It provides comfortable and well-equipped bedrooms. The public areas consist of the modern Cafe Continental, the main restaurant which offers modern cuisine, and a leisure club. A range of conference rooms is also available.
ROOMS: 91 en suite (6 fmly) (13 GF) ⊗ in 19 bedrooms s £50-£99; d £75-£115 LB **FACILITIES:** STV supervised Sauna Solarium Gym Jacuzzi Beauty treatments Xmas **CONF:** Thtr 165 Class 60 Board 48 Del from £90 **PARKING:** 160 **NOTES:** Civ Wed 150
CARDS:

Premier Lodge (Altrincham North)

Manchester Rd, West Timperley WA14 5NH
☎ 0870 9906330 🖹 0870 9906631
web: www.premierlodge.com
Dir: *2 m from Altrincham off A56*
High quality, modern, budget accommodation, ideal for families and business travellers. All rooms feature bath, power shower and satellite TV, and most have telephones / modem points. The adjacent bar and restaurant offers a wide and varied menu.
ROOMS: 48 en suite s £48; d £48 **CONF:** Thtr 50

Premier Lodge (Altrincham South)

Manchester Rd WA14 4PH
☎ 0870 9906580 🖹 0870 9906581
web: www.premierlodge.com
Dir: *From north M60 junct 7 and follow A56 towards Altrincham. From south M6 junct 19. Follow A556 and continue onto A56 towards Sale*
High quality, modern, budget accommodation, ideal for families and business travellers. All rooms feature bath, power shower and satellite TV, and most have telephones / modem points. The adjacent bar and restaurant offers a wide and varied menu.
ROOMS: 46 en suite s £48; d £48

ALVELEY, Shropshire — Map 10 SO78

★★★★66% Mill Hotel & Restaurant

WV15 6HL
☎ 01746 780437 🖹 01746 780850
e-mail: enquiries@themillalveley.fsnet.co.uk
Dir: *Midway between Kidderminster & Bridgnorth, turn off A442 signposted Enville & Turley Green*
Built around a 17th-century water mill, with the original water wheel still on display, this extended and renovated hotel is set in eight acres of landscaped grounds. Bedrooms are pleasant and include some superior rooms, which have sitting areas, and some rooms with four-poster beds. The restaurant provides carefully prepared dishes. Twenty further bedrooms are due to be completed in 2004.

ROOMS: 41 en suite (3 fmly) ⊗ in 18 bedrooms s £88.50-£128.50; d £115-£152 (incl. bkfst) LB **FACILITIES:** STV Gym **CONF:** Thtr 220 Class 150 Board 80 Del from £120 **SERVICES:** Lift **PARKING:** 200 **NOTES:** ⊗ in restaurant Civ Wed 200
CARDS:

ALVESTON, Gloucestershire — Map 04 ST68

★★★75% Alveston House

Davids Ln BS35 2LA
☎ 01454 415050 🖹 01454 415425
e-mail: info@alvestonhousehotel.co.uk
web: www.alvestonhousehotel.co.uk
Dir: *M5 junct 14 from N or junct 16 from S, on A38*

In a quiet area with easy access to the city and a short drive from both the M4 and M5, this smartly presented hotel provides an impressive combination of good service, friendly hospitality and a relaxed atmosphere. Bedrooms are well-equipped and comfortable for business or leisure use. The restaurant offers carefully prepared fresh food, and a pleasant bar and conservatory are the newest additions.
ROOMS: 30 en suite (1 fmly) (6 GF) ⊗ in 24 bedrooms s £75-£99.50; d £104.50-£109.50 (incl. bkfst) LB **FACILITIES:** STV **CONF:** Thtr 85 Class 48 Board 50 Del from £135 **PARKING:** 75 **NOTES:** ⊗ in restaurant Civ Wed 75 **CARDS:**

See advert under BRISTOL

Premier Lodge (Bristol North)

Thornbury Rd BS35 3LL
☎ 0870 9906496 🖹 0870 9906497
web: www.premierlodge.com
Dir: *from north exit M5 at junct 14 onto A38 towards Bristol. From south exit M5 at junct 16 and take A38 towards Gloucester*
High quality, modern, budget accommodation, ideal for families and business travellers. All rooms feature bath, power shower and satellite TV, and most have telephones / modem points. The adjacent bar and restaurant offers a wide and varied menu.
ROOMS: 74 en suite s £50; d £50 **CONF:** Thtr 70 Class 40 Board 40

AMBERLEY, Gloucestershire — Map 04 SO80

★★69% The Amberley Inn
Culver Hill GL5 5AF
☎ 01453 872565 01453 872738
e-mail: theamberley@zoom.co.uk
Dir: *on A46*

Situated on a hillside, on the edge of the common, this traditional Cotswold inn provides an equally warm welcome to both visitors and locals alike. Most bedrooms have been upgraded and offer high standards of comfort and quality, with front facing rooms boasting wonderful panoramic views over the Woodchester Valley. Public areas include a choice of bars and the attractive restaurant where excellent local produce is used in the creation of impressive and innovative dishes.

ROOMS: 14 rms (9 en suite) (1 fmly) s £49-£52.50; d £67-£84 (incl. bkfst) **LB** **FACILITIES:** Xmas **CONF:** BC Thtr 20 Class 14 Board 14 Del from £119 **PARKING:** 14 **NOTES:** in restaurant
CARDS:

AMBERLEY, West Sussex — Map 06 TQ01

Top 200 – Hotel

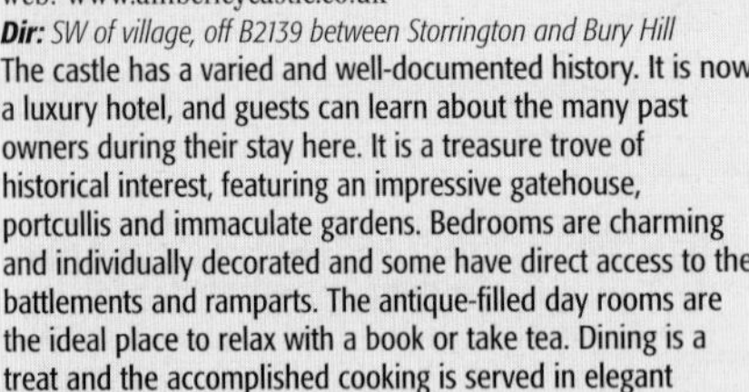

★★★ Amberley Castle
BN18 9ND
☎ 01798 831992 01798 831998
e-mail: info@amberleycastle.co.uk
web: www.amberleycastle.co.uk
Dir: *SW of village, off B2139 between Storrington and Bury Hill*

RELAIS & CHATEAUX

The castle has a varied and well-documented history. It is now a luxury hotel, and guests can learn about the many past owners during their stay here. It is a treasure trove of historical interest, featuring an impressive gatehouse, portcullis and immaculate gardens. Bedrooms are charming and individually decorated and some have direct access to the battlements and ramparts. The antique-filled day rooms are the ideal place to relax with a book or take tea. Dining is a treat and the accomplished cooking is served in elegant surroundings.

ROOMS: 14 en suite 5 annexe en suite (7 GF) d £155-£375 **LB** **FACILITIES:** 18 Putt green Jacuzzi Xmas **CONF:** Thtr 50 Class 24 Board 24 Del from £250 **PARKING:** 50 **NOTES:** No children 12yrs in restaurant Civ Wed 55
CARDS:

Packed in a hurry?
Ironing facilities should be available at all star levels, either in rooms or on request

AMBLESIDE, Cumbria — Map 18 NY30
See also Elterwater

Town House

★★★★ Waterhead
Lake Rd LA22 0ER
☎ 015394 32566 015394 31255
e-mail: waterhead@elhmail.co.uk
Dir: *A591 into Ambleside, hotel opposite Waterhead Pier*

With an enviable location opposite the bay, this well-established hotel offers contemporary and comfortable accommodation with some innovative features. There is a fine bar with a garden terrace overlooking the lake and a stylish restaurant serving classical cuisine with a modern twist. Staff are most attentive and friendly. Guests have full use of the Low Wood Hotel leisure facilities nearby.

ROOMS: 41 en suite (3 fmly) (7 GF) in 29 bedrooms s £78-£128; d £156-£206 (incl. bkfst) **LB** **FACILITIES:** STV Use of nearby sister hotel's leisure facilities Xmas **CONF:** BC Thtr 40 Class 30 Board 24 Del £129.95 **PARKING:** 43 **NOTES:** in restaurant
CARDS:

See advert under WINDERMERE

★★★78% Rothay Manor
Rothay Bridge LA22 0EH
☎ 015394 33605 015394 33607
e-mail: hotel@rothaymanor.co.uk
web: www.rothaymanor.co.uk
Dir: *In Ambleside follow signs for Coniston (A593). Hotel 0.25 mile SW of Ambleside opposite rugby pitch*

The former home of a Liverpool merchant, this attractive listed building, built in Regency style, is a short walk from both the town centre and Lake Windermere. Spacious bedrooms, including suites, family rooms and rooms with balconies, have been

continued

refurbished to a high standard. Public areas include a choice of lounges, a spacious restaurant and conference facilities.
ROOMS: 17 en suite 2 annexe en suite (7 fmly) (3 GF) ⊗ in all bedrooms s £70-£95; d £120-£180 (incl. bkfst) **LB** **FACILITIES:** Nearby leisure centre free to guests ch fac Xmas **CONF:** Thtr 22 Board 18 Del from £140 **PARKING:** 45 **NOTES:** ⊗ in restaurant Closed 3-28 Jan
CARDS:

See advert on this page

★★★75% Regent

Waterhead Bay LA22 0ES
☎ 01539 432254 01539 431474
e-mail: info@regentlakes.co.uk
Dir: *1m S on A591*

This attractive holiday hotel, situated close to Waterhead Bay, offers a warm welcome. Bedrooms come in a variety of styles, including three suites and five bedrooms in the garden wing. There is a modern swimming pool and the restaurant offers a fine dining experience in a contemporary setting.
ROOMS: 30 en suite (7 fmly) ⊗ in 4 bedrooms s £60-£80; d £90-£120 (incl. bkfst) **LB** **FACILITIES:** Xmas **PARKING:** 39 **NOTES:** ⊗ in restaurant **CARDS:**

★★★71% Ambleside Salutation Hotel

Best Western

Lake Rd LA22 9BX
☎ 015394 32244 015394 34157
e-mail: enquiries@hotelambleside.uk.com
web: www.hotelambleside.uk.com
Dir: *A591 to Ambleside, onto one-way system down Wansfell Rd into Compston Rd. Right at lights back into village*

A former coaching inn, this hotel has been welcoming guests since the 1600s. Bedrooms vary in size and all are tastefully appointed and thoughtfully equipped; many boast balconies and delightful views. Bright public areas include an attractive restaurant and there is also a choice of spacious lounges.
ROOMS: 38 en suite 4 annexe en suite (4 fmly) ⊗ in 9 bedrooms s £71.50-£100.50; d £93-£131 (incl. bkfst) **LB** **FACILITIES: Spa** STV Sauna Gym Jacuzzi Use of pool at sister hotel 4miles away Xmas **CONF:** Thtr 150 Class 40 Board 16 Del from £122.50 **PARKING:** 50 **NOTES:** ⊗ in restaurant **CARDS:**

★★★68% Skelwith Bridge

Skelwith Bridge LA22 9NJ
☎ 015394 32115 015394 34254
e-mail: skelwithbr@aol.com
web: www.skelwithbridgehotel.co.uk
Dir: *2.5m W on A593 at junct with B5343 to Langdale*

This delightful 17th-century inn is peacefully located at the heart of the Lake District National Park. It offers high standards of comfort and friendly service. Bedrooms include rooms with four-poster beds, and are tastefully appointed and thoughtfully equipped.

continued

Spacious public areas include a choice of lounges and bars and the elegant Bridge restaurant overlooks the stunning Lakeland fells.
ROOMS: 21 en suite 6 annexe en suite (2 fmly) ⊗ in 21 bedrooms s £40-£60; d £68-£150 (incl. bkfst) **LB** **FACILITIES:** Xmas **CONF:** Thtr 45 Class 25 Board 25 **PARKING:** 60 **NOTES:** ⊗ in restaurant
CARDS:

★★76% *Fisherbeck*

Lake Rd LA22 0DH
☎ 015394 33215 015394 33600
e-mail: email@fisherbeck.com
web: www.fisherbeck.com
Dir: *S of Ambleside on A591*

This friendly, family-owned and run hotel offers a high standard of service and memorable hospitality. Bedrooms, many of which offer modern décor, vary in size and include rooms with balconies affording lovely mountain views. Carefully prepared, creative food

continued on p58

AMBLESIDE, continued

is served in the elegant split-level restaurant, and impressive bar meals are also available.
ROOMS: 18 en suite (2 fmly) ⊗ in 6 bedrooms **FACILITIES:** Free use of nearby Leisure Complex **PARKING:** 24 **NOTES:** ⊗ in restaurant Closed 26 Dec-15 Jan **CARDS:**

★★67% Queens
Market Place LA22 9BU
☎ 015394 32206 015394 32721
e-mail: enquiries@queenshotelambleside.com
Dir: *A591 to Ambleside, follow town centre signs on one way system. Right lane at traffic lights, hotel on right.*
Situated in the heart of the village, this traditional Lakeland stone-clad hotel offers good tourist facilities. The bar meal operation, along with a good range of real ales, makes this a popular venue throughout the year. Bedrooms vary in size and have all the expected features.
ROOMS: 26 en suite (5 fmly) s £32-£47; d £64-£94 (incl. bkfst)
FACILITIES: STV Xmas **PARKING:** 11 **NOTES:** ⊗ in restaurant
CARDS:

Restaurant with Rooms

Log House Restaurant
Lake Rd LA22 0DN
☎ 015394 31077
e-mail: steve@loghouse.co.uk
Dir: *Approaching Ambleside from S A591. Hotel just past Hayes Garden Centre on the left.*
This Norwegian log house is a cosy restaurant and wine bar with three well appointed bedrooms on the first floor. The dining and lounge areas are on the two lower floors with comfortable settees views over the adjacent fields to the fells beyond. Available at both lunch and dinner, the carte and set menus provide a good range of dishes at attractive prices.
ROOMS: 3 en suite (3 fmly) ⊗ in all bedrooms s £60-£70; d £80-£100 (incl. bkfst) **LB** **FACILITIES:** Squash Sauna Solarium Gym Putt green Jacuzzi Xmas **NOTES:** No children 5yrs ⊗ in restaurant
CARDS:

AMERSHAM, Buckinghamshire Map 06 SU99

★★★69% The Crown
High St HP7 0DH
☎ 0870 400 8103 01494 431283
e-mail: crown@macdonald-hotels.co.uk
MACDONALD HOTELS
Combining the charm of a bygone era with the modern conveniences expected by today's traveller, this 16th-century coaching inn is a great base for antique shopping and walks in the Chilterns. One claim to fame is that the hotel was featured in the film *'Four Weddings and a Funeral'*. Bedrooms are a strength, all are individually styled and some feature original hand-painted murals.
ROOMS: 19 en suite 18 annexe en suite (10 GF) ⊗ in 21 bedrooms s £65-£170; d £130-£190 (incl. bkfst) **LB** **FACILITIES:** STV Xmas
CONF: Thtr 30 Board 18 Del from £145 **PARKING:** 30 **NOTES:** ⊗ in restaurant **CARDS:**

♫ Entertainment

AMESBURY, Wiltshire Map 05 SU14

★★63% Antrobus Arms
15 Church St SP4 7EU
☎ 01980 623163 01980 622112
e-mail: enquiries@antrobusarmshotel.co.uk
Dir: *A303 rdbt through one-way system. Turn left at t- junct & hotel on left*
Claiming to be the nearest hotel to Stonehenge, The Antrobus Arms offers individually furnished bedrooms, some of which overlook the walled Victorian garden at the rear of the property. With a history dating back to the 17th century, the establishment has much character, and public rooms reflect the elegance of the past. Bar meals are available as an alternative to dining in the main restaurant.
ROOMS: 16 en suite (2 fmly) **FACILITIES:** STV **CONF:** Thtr 40 Class 40 Board 20 **PARKING:** 15 **NOTES:** ⊗ in restaurant
CARDS:

Travelodge
Countess Services SP4 7AS
Travelodge
☎ 08700 850 950 01980 625273
Dir: *junct A345 & A303 eastbound*
Travelodge offers good quality, good value, modern accommodation. Ideal for families, the spacious, en suite bedrooms include remote-control TV, tea and coffee-making facilities and luxury beds. Meals can be taken at the nearby family restaurant. For further details consult the Hotel Groups page.
ROOMS: 48 en suite s fr £25; d fr £25

ANDOVER, Hampshire Map 05 SU34

★★★73% Esseborne Manor
SP11 0ER
☎ 01264 736444 01264 736725
e-mail: esseborne@aol.com
Dir: *halfway between Andover & Newbury on A343, just 1 mile N of Hurstbourne Tarrant*

Set in two acres of well-tended gardens, this attractive manor house is surrounded by the open countryside of the North Wessex Downs. Bedrooms are delightfully individual and are split between the main house, an adjoining courtyard and separate garden cottage. A wonderfully relaxed atmosphere pervades throughout, with public rooms combining elegance with comfort.
ROOMS: 6 en suite 9 annexe rms (8 en suite) (6 GF) s £95-£105; d £100-£180 (incl. bkfst) **LB** **FACILITIES:** STV **CONF:** Thtr 40 Class 35 Board 20 Del from £140 **PARKING:** 50 **NOTES:** ⊗ in restaurant Civ Wed 100 **CARDS:**

See advert on opposite page

★★★62% Quality Hotel Andover

Micheldever Rd SP11 6LA
☎ 01264 369111 📠 01264 369000
e-mail: andover@quality-hotels.co.uk

Dir: *off A303 at A3093. 1st rdbt take 1st exit, 2nd rdbt take 1st exit. Turn left immediately before BP petrol station, then left again*

Located on the outskirts of the town, this hotel is popular with business guests. Bedrooms offer some smart new rooms, and public areas consist of a cosy lounge, a hotel bar and a traditional style restaurant serving a range of meals. There is also a large conference suite available.

ROOMS: 13 en suite 36 annexe en suite (13 GF) ⊗ in 21 bedrooms s £39.95-£79; d £49.95-£89 (incl. bkfst) **LB** **FACILITIES:** STV Xmas **CONF:** Thtr 180 Class 60 Board 60 Del from £99 **PARKING:** 100 **NOTES:** ⊗ in restaurant Civ Wed 85
CARDS:

ANSTY, Warwickshire — Map 11 SP48

★★★★69% Ansty Hall

Main Rd CV7 9HZ
☎ 024 7661 2222 📠 024 7660 2155
e-mail: ansty@macdonald-hotels.co.uk

Dir: *M6 junct 2 onto B4065 signed 'Ansty'. Hotel 1.5m on left*

Dating back to 1678, this Grade II listed Georgian house is set within eight acres of attractive grounds and woodland. The hotel enjoys the best of both worlds with its central, yet tranquil, location. Spacious bedrooms feature a traditional decorative style and a range of extras. Rooms are divided between the main house and the more recently built annexe.

ROOMS: 23 en suite 39 annexe en suite (4 fmly) (22 GF) ⊗ in 24 bedrooms **CONF:** Thtr 200 Class 60 Board 60 **SERVICES:** Lift **PARKING:** 150 **NOTES:** ⊗ in restaurant Civ Wed 100
CARDS:

APPLEBY-IN-WESTMORLAND, Cumbria — Map 18 NY62

★★★78% Appleby Manor Country House

Roman Rd CA16 6JB
☎ 01768 351571 📠 017683 52888
e-mail: reception@applebymanor.co.uk
web: www.applebymanor.co.uk

Dir: *M6 junct 40/A66 towards Brough. Take Appleby turn, then immediately right. Continue 0.5m*

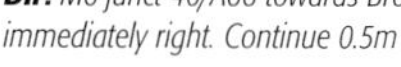

This imposing country mansion is set in extensive grounds amid fabulous Cumbrian scenery. The Dunbobbin family and their experienced staff ensure a warm welcome and attentive service. Bedrooms, including a number with patios, vary in style, with the

continued on p60

APPLEBY-IN-WESTMORLAND, continued

garden rooms now refurbished. The bar offers a wide range of malt whiskies and the restaurant serves carefully prepared meals.
ROOMS: 23 en suite 7 annexe en suite (9 fmly) ⊗ in 23 bedrooms s £84-£94; d £128-£148 (incl. bkfst) LB **FACILITIES:** STV Sauna Solarium Putt green Jacuzzi Steam room, Table tennis, Pool table **CONF:** Thtr 38 Class 25 Board 28 **PARKING:** 53 **NOTES:** ⊗ in restaurant Closed 24-26 Dec **CARDS:**

See advert on page 59

★★67% *Royal Oak Inn*

Bongate CA16 6UN
☎ 017683 51463 017683 52300
e-mail: RoyalOakInn@mortalmaninns.fsnet.co.uk
Dir: *M6 junct 38 follow B6260, hotel 0.5m from Appleby centre on A66 towards Scotch Corner*

This traditional 17th-century coaching inn, with exposed beams and open fires, offers a choice of bars where locals mingle with visitors. Meals can be taken in the lounge bar, and the wide-ranging menu is also served in the atmospheric restaurant. Bedrooms vary in size and style, the superior rooms offering greater comfort.
ROOMS: 9 rms (7 en suite) (1 fmly) **CONF:** Class 20 Board 15 **PARKING:** 13 **NOTES:** ⊗ in restaurant
CARDS:

ARNCLIFFE, North Yorkshire — Map 18 SD97

★★77% Amerdale House

BD23 5QE
☎ 01756 770250 01756 770266
Dir: *left at Threshfield-Kettlewell road 0.5m past Kilnsey Crag*

This former manor house enjoys a peaceful, idyllic location with wonderful views of the dale and fells from every room. Spacious, inviting public areas are tastefully furnished and have real fires in winter. A daily-changing imaginative menu and impressive wine list are offered in the elegant dining room. Bedrooms are beautifully decorated and elegantly furnished.
ROOMS: 10 en suite 1 annexe en suite (3 fmly) s £96-£100; d £162-£170 (incl. bkfst & dinner) LB **PARKING:** 30 **NOTES:** ⊗ in restaurant Closed mid Nov-mid Mar **CARDS:**

ARUNDEL, West Sussex — Map 06 TQ00

★★★67% Norfolk Arms

Forestdale Hotels

High St BN18 9AD
☎ 01903 882101 01903 884275
e-mail: norfolk.arms@forestdale.com
Built by the 10th Duke of Norfolk, this Georgian coaching inn enjoys a superb setting beneath the battlements of Arundel Castle. Bedrooms come in a variety of sizes and styles, all are well equipped. Public areas include two bars, a comfortable lounge, a traditional English restaurant and a range of meeting rooms.
ROOMS: 21 en suite 13 annexe en suite (4 fmly) (8 GF) ⊗ in 6 bedrooms s fr £75; d fr £120 (incl. bkfst) LB **FACILITIES:** Xmas **CONF:** Thtr 100 Class 40 Board 40 Del from £115 **PARKING:** 34 **NOTES:** ⊗ in restaurant Civ Wed 60
CARDS:

★★65% Comfort Inn

Crossbush BN17 7QQ
☎ 01903 840840 01903 849849
e-mail: admin@gb642.u-net.com
Dir: *A27/A284, 1st right into services*
This modern, purpose-built hotel provides a good base for exploring the nearby historic town. Good access to local road networks and a range of meeting rooms, all air conditioned, also make this an ideal venue for business guests. Bedrooms are spacious, smartly decorated and well-equipped.
ROOMS: 53 en suite (25 GF) ⊗ in 39 bedrooms s £55-£70; d £70-£80 (incl. bkfst) LB **FACILITIES:** STV Xmas **CONF:** Thtr 30 Class 30 Board 30 Del from £70 **PARKING:** 53 **NOTES:** ⊗ in restaurant
CARDS:

Travel Inn

Crossbush Ln BN18 9PQ
☎ 08701 977016 01903 884381
Dir: *1m E of Arundel at intersection of A27/A284*
Travel Inn offers good-quality, value-for-money accommodation. Spacious, en suite rooms with bath and shower comfortably accommodate a family of up to two adults and two children (to age 15). The restaurant and bar offers a varied menu. For further details consult the Hotel Groups page.
ROOMS: 30 en suite s £45.95-£46.95; d £45.95-£46.95 **CONF:** Thtr 50 Board 26

ASCOT, Berkshire — Map 06 SU96

★★★★70% The Royal Berkshire Ramada Plaza

London Rd, Sunninghill SL5 0PP
☎ 01344 623322 01344 627100
e-mail: sales.royalberkshire@ramadajarvis.co.uk
Dir: *A30 towards Bagshot, right opposite Wentworth Club onto A329, continue for 2m, hotel entrance on right*
Once occupied by the Churchill family, this delightful Queen Anne house is set in 14 acres of attractive gardens on the edge of Ascot. Public areas include a comfortable lounge bar, an attractive restaurant that overlooks the rear gardens and extensive

continued

conference facilities. The main house has been skilfully extended to offer smart, well-equipped bedrooms.

ROOMS: 63 en suite (1 fmly) in 34 bedrooms s £150-£225; d £150-£225 **LB** **FACILITIES:** STV Sauna Gym Putt green Jacuzzi Xmas **CONF:** BC Thtr 90 Class 60 Board 35 Del from £190 **PARKING:** 150 **NOTES:** in restaurant Civ Wed 100 **CARDS:**

★★★★66% The Berystede

MACDONALD HOTELS

Bagshot Rd, Sunninghill SL5 9JH
☎ 0870 400 8111 01344 872301
e-mail: berystede@macdonald-hotels.co.uk
Dir: *A30/B3020 (Windmill Pub). Continue 1.25m to hotel on left just before junct with A330*

This impressive Victorian mansion, close to Ascot Racecourse, is set in nine acres of wooded grounds. Spacious bedrooms have comfortable armchairs and internet facilities for guest use. There is a cosy bar and fine traditional restaurant, which overlooks the heated outdoor swimming pool and gardens. An excellent range of modern meeting rooms is available.
ROOMS: 90 en suite (26 fmly) (20 GF) in 58 bedrooms s £55-£170; d £108-£200 (incl. bkfst) **LB** **FACILITIES:** STV Putt green Full leisure complex from July 2005 Xmas **CONF:** BC Thtr 150 Class 90 Board 70 Del from £165 **SERVICES:** Lift **PARKING:** 240 **NOTES:** in restaurant Civ Wed 140 **CARDS:**

★★69% Highclere

19 Kings Rd, Sunninghill SL5 9AD
☎ 01344 625220 01344 872528
e-mail: info@highclerehotel.com
Dir: *opp Sunninghill Post Office*
This privately owned establishment is situated in a quiet residential area, not far from local attractions and road networks. Modest bedrooms are attractively decorated and well equipped. A cosy bar is available adjacent to the comfortable conservatory lounge. A range of home cooked meals is on offer in the restaurant.
ROOMS: 11 en suite (1 fmly) (2 GF) in 7 bedrooms s £70-£100; d £80-£110 (incl. bkfst) **FACILITIES:** Xmas **CONF:** Thtr 15 Class 15 Del from £120 **PARKING:** 11 **NOTES:** in restaurant **CARDS:**

★★66% *Brockenhurst*

Brockenhurst Rd SL5 9HA
☎ 01344 621912 01344 873252
Dir: *on A330*
Located within easy reach of the famous racecourse, Windsor Castle and other local attractions, this attractive Edwardian house offers comfortable accommodation. Bedrooms are mostly spacious with a range of thoughtful extras. Relaxed and friendly service is provided in the cosy bar and restaurant, both of which overlook the charming grounds.
ROOMS: 12 en suite 5 annexe en suite (2 fmly) (2 GF) **FACILITIES:** STV **CONF:** Thtr 50 Class 25 Board 30 **PARKING:** 32 **NOTES:** in restaurant **CARDS:**

Innkeeper's Lodge Ascot

Innkeeper's Lodge

London Rd SL5 7SB
☎ 01344 870931 01344 870932
www.innkeeperslodge.com
Dir: *M25 junct 13, at rdbt take A30 towards Sunningdale. Turn right onto A329 towards Ascot, continue for 1m and lodge on right*
Smart rooms meet essential business requirements but also have home comforts, and depending on location may well have meeting rooms and pub dining. Dining options generally include all-day menus plus the added advantage of breakfast.
ROOMS: 10 en suite s £49.95-£69.95; d £49.95-£69.95

ASHBOURNE, Derbyshire

Map 10 SK14

See also Thorpe

★★★74% Callow Hall

Mappleton Rd DE6 2AA
☎ 01335 300900 01335 300512
e-mail: reservations@callowhall.demon.co.uk
Dir: *A515 through Ashbourne towards Buxton, left at Bowling Green pub, then 1st right*
This delightful, creeper-clad, early Victorian house, set on a 44-acre estate, enjoys views over Bentley Brook and the Dove Valley. The atmosphere is relaxed and welcoming, and some of the spacious bedrooms in the main house have comfortable sitting areas. Public rooms feature high ceilings, ornate plasterwork and antique furniture. There is a good range of dishes available from both the fixed-price, daily changing menu and the carte.
ROOMS: 16 en suite (2 fmly) in 8 bedrooms s £90-£110; d £130-£195 (incl. bkfst) **LB** **FACILITIES:** Fishing Cycle hire nearby (Tissington Trail) **CONF:** Thtr 30 Board 16 Del from £144 **PARKING:** 21 **NOTES:** in restaurant Closed 25-26 Dec RS Sunday **CARDS:**

See advert on page 63

★★★67% Hanover International Hotel & Club

Derby Rd DE6 1XH
☎ 01335 346666 01335 346549
e-mail: rso@hanover-international.com
Dir: *A52 to Ashbourne, at rdbt turn right to Airfield Ind Est, hotel 400yds on right*
This modern, purpose-built hotel is just a short drive from the town on the Derby Road. It offers comfortable, well-equipped bedrooms, some of which are especially designed for visitors with disabilities. The indoor leisure facilities, which include a good-sized swimming pool and sauna, are an added attraction.
ROOMS: 50 en suite (5 fmly) in 10 bedrooms s £91-£101; d £106-£116 **LB** **FACILITIES:** STV supervised Sauna Steam room, Fitness room **CONF:** Thtr 200 Class 100 Board 80 Del from £115 **SERVICES:** Lift **PARKING:** 130 **NOTES:** in restaurant Civ Wed 200 **CARDS:**

ASHBOURNE, continued

★★64% The Dog & Partridge Country Inn

THE INDEPENDENTS

Swinscoe DE6 2HS
☎ 01335 343183 📠 01335 342742
e-mail: info@dogandpartridge.co.uk
web: www.dogandpartridge.co.uk
Dir: *A52 towards Leek, hotel 4m on left*

This 17th-century inn is situated in the hamlet of Swinscoe, within easy reach of Alton Towers. Bedroom vary in style, and are mainly sited within the grounds. Well-presented self-catering family suites are also available. Meals are served every evening until late and can be enjoyed either in the bar or the conservatory.

ROOMS: 25 en suite (15 fmly) s £45-£90; d £75-£100 (incl. bkfst) **LB** **FACILITIES:** Fishing ch fac Xmas **CONF:** Thtr 20 Class 15 Board 18 Del from £85 **PARKING:** 115 **NOTES:** ⊗ in restaurant **CARDS:**

ASHBURTON, Devon — Map 03 SX77

★★★74% @@ Holne Chase

Two Bridges Rd TQ13 7NS
☎ 01364 631471 📠 01364 631453
e-mail: info@holne-chase.co.uk
web: www.holne-chase.co.uk
Dir: *3m N on unclass Two Bridges/Tavistock road*

This former hunting lodge is peacefully situated in a secluded position, with sweeping lawns leading to the river and panoramic views of the moor. Bedrooms are attractively and individually furnished, and there are a number of split-level suites available. Good quality local produce features on the daily-changing menu.

ROOMS: 10 en suite 7 annexe en suite (9 fmly) (1 GF) s £95-£125; d £140-£230 (incl. bkfst) **LB** **FACILITIES:** Fishing Riding Putt green Fly fishing, Riding, Beauty treatments for people and dogs ch fac Xmas **CONF:** Thtr 40 Class 60 Board 60 Del from £150 **PARKING:** 40 **NOTES:** ⊗ in restaurant Civ Wed 60 **CARDS:**

ASHBY-DE-LA-ZOUCH, Leicestershire — Map 11 SK31

Travel Inn

travel inn

Flagstaff Island, Flagstaff Park LE65 1DS
☎ 08701 977281 📠 01530 561211
Dir: *Exit M1 (J23a), follow signs for A42 (M42) to Tamworth and Birmingham. Travel Inn is just off the roundabout at J13 of A42*

Travel Inn offers good-quality, value-for-money accommodation. Spacious, en suite rooms with bath and shower comfortably accommodate a family of up to two adults and two children (to age 15). The restaurant and bar offers a varied menu. For further details consult the Hotel Groups page.

ROOMS: 40 en suite s £45.95-£46.95; d £45.95-£46.95

ASHFORD, Kent — Map 07 TR04

Top 200 – Hotel

★★★★ @@ Eastwell Manor

PRIDE OF BRITAIN HOTELS

Eastwell Park, Boughton Lees TN25 4HR
☎ 01233 213000 📠 01233 635530
e-mail: enquiries@eastwellmanor.co.uk
Dir: *on A251, 200yds on left when entering Boughton Aluph*

Set in 62 acres of beautifully kept grounds, this lovely hotel dates back to the Norman conquest and boasts a number of interesting features, including carved wood panelled rooms and huge baronial stone fireplaces. Accommodation is divided between the manor house bedrooms and the courtyard apartments in the mews cottages.

ROOMS: 23 en suite 39 annexe en suite (2 fmly) ⊗ in 4 bedrooms **FACILITIES: Spa** STV Sauna Solarium Gym Putt green Jacuzzi Boules, Hairdressing salon & Beauty spa **CONF:** Thtr 200 Class 60 Board 48 **SERVICES:** Lift **PARKING:** 200 **NOTES:** ⊗ in restaurant Civ Wed 250 **CARDS:**

★★★★65% Ashford International

CLASSIC BRITISH

Simone Weil Av TN24 8UX
☎ 01233 219988 📠 01233 647743
e-mail: info@ashfordinthotel.com
Dir: *off M20 junct 9, 3rd exit for Ashford/Canterbury. Take L at 1st rdbt, hotel 200m on L.*

Ideally situated just off the M20 and its links to the channel tunnel and ferry terminal. Public areas feature a superb mall housing a range of boutiques and eating places, including a popular brasserie, the Alhambra Restaurant and Florentine Bar. The spacious bedrooms are pleasantly furnished and equipped with modern facilities.

ROOMS: 200 en suite (4 fmly) ⊗ in 57 bedrooms s £85-£110; d £95-£115 **LB** **FACILITIES:** Sauna Solarium Gym Jacuzzi **CONF:** BC Thtr 400 Class 160 Del from £131 **SERVICES:** Lift **PARKING:** 400 **NOTES:** ⊗ in restaurant Closed 24-27 Dec Civ Wed **CARDS:**

⌂ Travel Inn Ashford (North)

Maidstone Rd, Hothfield Common TN26 1AP
☎ 08701 977018 🖷 01233 713945
Dir: *on A20, between Ashford & Charing, close to M20 junct 8/9*
Travel Inn offers good-quality, value-for-money accommodation. Spacious, en suite rooms with bath and shower comfortably accommodate a family of up to two adults and two children (to age 15). The restaurant and bar offers a varied menu. For further details consult the Hotel Groups page.
ROOMS: 60 en suite s £45.95-£46.95; d £45.95-£46.95

⌂ Travel Inn (Ashford Central)

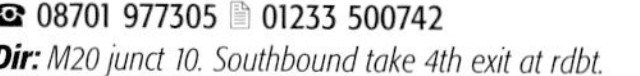

Hall Av, Orbital Park, Sevington TN24 0GN
☎ 08701 977305 🖷 01233 500742
Dir: *M20 junct 10. Southbound take 4th exit at rdbt. Northbound take 1st exit/ A2070 for Brenzett. Inn at next rdbt on right*
Travel Inn offers good-quality, value-for-money accommodation. Spacious, en suite rooms with bath and shower comfortably accommodate a family of up to two adults and two children (to age 15). The restaurant and bar offers a varied menu. For further details consult the Hotel Groups page.
ROOMS: 60 en suite s £45.95-£46.95; d £45.95-£46.95

⌂ Travelodge

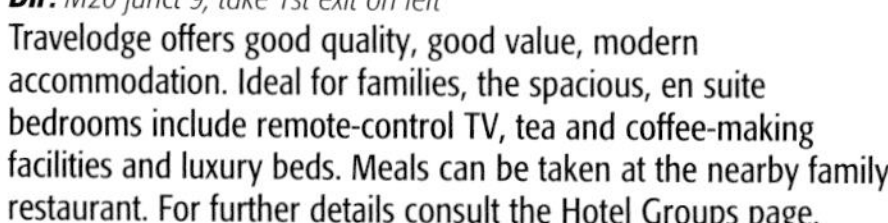

Eureka Leisure Park TN25 4BN
☎ 08700 850 950 🖷 01233 622676
Dir: *M20 junct 9, take 1st exit on left*
Travelodge offers good quality, good value, modern accommodation. Ideal for families, the spacious, en suite bedrooms include remote-control TV, tea and coffee-making facilities and luxury beds. Meals can be taken at the nearby family restaurant. For further details consult the Hotel Groups page.
ROOMS: 67 en suite s fr £25; d fr £25

ASHFORD-IN-THE-WATER, Derbyshire — Map 16 SK16

★★★79% ⊛⊛ Riverside House
Fennel St DE45 1QF
☎ 01629 814275 🖷 01629 812873
e-mail: riversidehouse@enta.net
Dir: *turn right off A6 Bakewell/Buxton road 2m from Bakewell, hotel at end of main street*
Partly dating back to 1630, this delightful hotel in the centre of the village is surrounded by gardens beside the River Wye. It offers individually decorated bedrooms, and public rooms include a conservatory, an oak-panelled lounge with inglenook fireplace, a drawing room and two dining rooms. Fine quality cuisine is served and service is very attentive.
ROOMS: 15 en suite (4 GF) ⊗ in all bedrooms s £100-£140; d £150-£250 (incl. bkfst & dinner) **LB** **FACILITIES:** STV Xmas
CONF: BC Thtr 15 Class 15 Board 15 Del from £150 **PARKING:** 40
NOTES: No children 16yrs ⊗ in restaurant Civ Wed 32
CARDS:

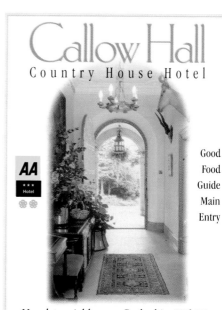

Looking for a last-minute weekend away?
Check out Latebeds,
the AA's late availability booking service, at www.theAA.com

Want to get away without the hassle
of finding a place to stay?
Let the AA Hotel Booking Service find the
place that best suits your needs. No fuss,
no worries and no booking fee.
Visit www.theAA.com

ASHWATER, Devon

Map 03 SX39

Top 200 – Hotel

★★ Blagdon Manor Hotel & Restaurant
EX21 5DF
☎ 01409 211224 01409 211634
e-mail: stay@blagdon.com
web: www.blagdon.com
Dir: *Take A388 N of Launceston towards Holsworthy. Approx 2m N of Chapman's Well take 2nd right for Ashwater. Next right beside Blagdon Lodge, hotel 0.25m*

Located on the borders of Devon and Cornwall, this small and friendly hotel offers a charming home-from-home atmosphere. The tranquillity of the secluded setting, the character and charm of the house and its unhurried pace ensures calm and relaxation. High levels of service, personal touches and thoughtful extras are all part of a stay here. Steve Morey cooks with passion and his dependence on only the finest of local ingredients speaks volumes.

ROOMS: 7 en suite in all bedrooms s fr £72; d fr £100 (incl. bkfst) **FACILITIES:** Boules, giant chess/draughts **CONF:** Board 14 Del from £120 **PARKING:** 10 **NOTES:** No children 12yrs in restaurant Closed 2wks Jan/Feb & 2wks Oct/Nov
CARDS:

ASPLEY GUISE, Bedfordshire

Map 11 SP93

★★★69% Moore Place
The Square MK17 8DW
☎ 01908 282000 01908 281888
e-mail: manager@mooreplace.com
web: www.mooreplace.co.uk
Dir: *M1 junct 13, take A507 signed Aspley Guise & Woburn Sands. Hotel on left side of village square*

This impressive Georgian house, set in delightful gardens in the village centre, is very conveniently located for the M1. Bedrooms do vary in size, but consideration has been given to guest comfort, with many thoughtful extras provided. There is a wide range of meeting rooms and private dining options.

ROOMS: 39 en suite 27 annexe en suite (16 GF) in 45 bedrooms s £55-£105; d £75-£200 (incl. bkfst) **LB** **FACILITIES:** Xmas **CONF:** Thtr 40 Class 24 Board 20 Del £160 **PARKING:** 70 **NOTES:** in restaurant Civ Wed 80 **CARDS:**

ASTON CLINTON, Buckinghamshire

Map 05 SP81

Innkeeper's Lodge Aylesbury East
London Rd HP22 5HP
☎ 01296 632777 01296 632685
www.innkeeperslodge.com

Dir: *on A41 in Aston Clinton, between Aylesbury & Tring*

Smart rooms meet essential business requirements but also have home comforts, and depending on location may well have meeting rooms and pub dining. Dining options generally include all-day menus plus the added advantage of breakfast.

ROOMS: 11 en suite s £48-£62; d £48-£62

AXMINSTER, Devon

Map 04 SY29

See also Colyford

★★★72% Fairwater Head
Hawkchurch EX13 5TX
☎ 01297 678349 01297 678459
e-mail: reception@fairwater.demon.co.uk
Dir: *off B3165, Crewkerne to Lyme Regis road. Hotel signposted to Hawkchurch*

Under new ownership, this well-managed hotel is peacefully located in the countryside and has attractive gardens. The proprietors and staff provide a friendly and attentive service in a relaxing environment. Bedrooms are individually decorated, spacious and comfortable, and guests can enjoy well-cooked dishes in the dining room.

ROOMS: 14 en suite 7 annexe en suite (9 GF) in all bedrooms s £93-£98; d £166-£196 (incl. bkfst) **LB** **FACILITIES:** Pianist twice weekly Xmas **CONF:** Thtr 12 Class 12 Board 12 **PARKING:** 25 **NOTES:** No children 6 yrs in restaurant **CARDS:**

AYLESBURY, Buckinghamshire

Map 11 SP81

Top 200 – Hotel

★★★★ Hartwell House Hotel, Restaurant & Spa
Oxford Rd HP17 8NL
☎ 01296 747444 01296 747450
e-mail: info@hartwell-house.com
web: www.hartwell-house.com
Dir: *from S - M40 junct 7, A329 to Thame, A418 towards Aylesbury. After 6m, through Stone, hotel on left. From N - M40 junct 9 for Bicester. A41 to Aylesbury, A418 to Oxford for 2m. Hotel on right*

This beautiful, historic house is set in 90 acres of unspoilt parkland. The grand public rooms are truly magnificent, and feature many fine works of art. Bedrooms are spacious and extremely comfortable, with high ceilings, sumptuous fabrics and many thoughtful extras. The elegant, award-winning restaurant serves an imaginative selection of seasonal dishes, created from quality local produce. Service is of a high standard.

ROOMS: 30 en suite 16 annexe en suite (10 GF) in 12 bedrooms s fr £155; d fr £260 (incl. cont bkfst) **LB** **FACILITIES: Spa** STV supervised Fishing Sauna Solarium Gym Jacuzzi Treatment rooms & Steam rooms Xmas **CONF:** BC Thtr 100 Class 40 Board 40 Del from £245 **SERVICES:** Lift **PARKING:** 91 **NOTES:** No children 8yrs in restaurant Civ Wed 60
CARDS:

continued

⌂ Innkeeper's Lodge Aylesbury South

40 Main St, Weston Turville HP22 5RW
☎ 01296 613131 & 0870 243 0500 Fax 01296 616902
www.innkeeperslodge.com
Dir: *M25 junct 20/A41(Hemel Hempstead). Continue for 12m to Aston Clinton. Left onto B4544 to Weston Turville, lodge on left*
Smart rooms meet essential business requirements but also have home comforts, and depending on location may well have meeting rooms and pub dining. Dining options generally include all-day menus plus the added advantage of breakfast.
ROOMS: 16 en suite s £48-£62; d £48-£62

⌂ Travel Inn

Buckingham Rd HP19 9QL
☎ 08701 977019 Fax 01206 330432
Dir: *N from Aylesbury centre on A413, Travel Inn 1m on left, adjacent to rdbt*

Travel Inn offers good-quality, value-for-money accommodation. Spacious, en suite rooms with bath and shower comfortably accommodate a family of up to two adults and two children (to age 15). The restaurant and bar offers a varied menu. For further details consult the Hotel Groups page.
ROOMS: 64 en suite s £45.95-£46.95; d £45.95-£46.95

AYSGARTH, North Yorkshire — Map 19 SE08

★★69% The George & Dragon Inn

DL8 3AD
☎ 01969 663358 Fax 01969 663773
e-mail: info@georgeanddragonaysgarth.co.uk
Now under new ownership, this 17th-century coaching inn offers spacious, comfortably appointed rooms. Popular with walkers, the cosy bar has a real fire and a good selection of local beers.
The beamed, tasteful restaurant serves interesting meals using fresh local produce and hearty breakfasts. Service is very friendly and attentive.
ROOMS: 7 en suite (2 fmly) s £36-£50.50; d £62-£71 (incl. bkfst) **LB**
FACILITIES: Xmas **PARKING:** 35 **NOTES:** ⊘ in restaurant
CARDS:

BABBACOMBE See Torquay

BAGINTON, Warwickshire — Map 11 SP37

★★71% Old Mill

Mill Hill CV8 3AH
☎ 024 7630 2241 Fax 024 7630 7070
Dir: *in village 0.25m from junct A45 & A46*
Enjoying a peaceful riverside location, yet within easy reach of the motorway networks, the Old Mill has been furnished to a high standard. Public areas include the popular Chef & Brewer bar and restaurant, with a pleasant patio for summer evenings. Spacious bedrooms are smartly appointed and well-equipped.

ROOMS: 28 en suite (6 fmly) s £60-£80; d £60-£80 **LB** **CONF:** Class 16 Board 20 **PARKING:** 200 **NOTES:**
CARDS:

BAGSHOT, Surrey — Map 06 SU96

Top 200 – Hotel

★★★★★ ⊛⊛⊛

Pennyhill Park Hotel & The Spa

London Rd GU19 5EU
☎ 01276 471774 Fax 01276 473217
e-mail: enquiries@pennyhillpark.co.uk
web: www.exclusivehotels.co.uk
Dir: *on A30 between Bagshot & Camberley opposite Texaco garage*
This delightful country house hotel set in 120 acres of grounds provides every modern comfort. Bedrooms are individually designed and stylish and have impressive bathrooms. The award-winning Latymer Restaurant is among the range of dining options and there is a choice of lounges and bars. Leisure facilities include a jogging trail, a golf course and a new state-of-the-art spa with a thermal sequencing experience, ozone treated swimming and hydrotherapy pools along with a comprehensive range of therapies and treatments.
ROOMS: 26 en suite 97 annexe en suite (6 fmly) (26 GF) ⊘ in 20 bedrooms s £211.50-£646.25; d £229-£646.25 **LB** **FACILITIES: Spa** STV 9 Fishing Snooker Sauna Gym Jacuzzi Archery, Clay pigeon shooting, Plunge pool, Turkish Steam Rm, Volleyball, ♫ ch fac Xmas **CONF:** BC Thtr 160 Class 80 Board 60 Del from £300 **SERVICES:** Lift **PARKING:** 500 **NOTES:** ⊘ in restaurant Civ Wed 160 **CARDS:**

See advert on page 67

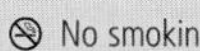

⊘ No smoking

BAGSHOT, continued

⌂ Travel Inn
1 London Rd GU19 5HR
☎ 08701 977021 📠 01276 451357
Dir: *on A30, 0.25m from Bagshot*
Travel Inn offers good-quality, value-for-money accommodation. Spacious, en suite rooms with bath and shower comfortably accommodate a family of up to two adults and two children (to age 15). The restaurant and bar offers a varied menu. For further details consult the Hotel Groups page.
ROOMS: 40 en suite s £45.95-£48.95; d £45.95-£48.95

BAINBRIDGE, North Yorkshire Map 18 SD99

★★67% ***Rose & Crown***
DL8 3EE
☎ 01969 650225 📠 01969 650735
e-mail: info@theprideofwensleydale.com
Dir: *on A684 between Hawes & Leyburn*

This old traditional coaching Inn overlooking the village green is full of character. Bedrooms are tastefully furnished and comfortably equipped. There are two well-stocked bars, one very popular with locals, both offering an interesting range of dishes. Finer dining is offered in the restaurant and a residents' lounge is also provided.
ROOMS: 12 rms (11 en suite) (1 fmly) ⊘ in 2 bedrooms **CONF:** Class 30 Board 30 **PARKING:** 65 **NOTES:** ⊘ in restaurant
CARDS:

BAKEWELL, Derbyshire Map 16 SK26

★★★67% **Rutland Arms**
The Square DE45 1BT
☎ 01629 812812 📠 01629 812309
e-mail: rutland@bakewell.demon.co.uk
Dir: *M1 junct 28 to Matlock, A6 to Bakewell. Hotel in town centre*

This 19th-century hotel lies at the very centre of Bakewell and offers a wide range of quality accommodation. The friendly staff are attentive and welcoming, and The Four Seasons candlelit restaurant offers interesting fine dining in elegant surroundings.
ROOMS: 18 en suite 17 annexe en suite (2 fmly) ⊘ in 12 bedrooms s £51-£69; d £81-£115 (incl. bkfst) **LB** **FACILITIES:** Xmas **CONF:** Thtr 100 Class 60 Board 40 Del £119 **PARKING:** 25 **NOTES:** ⊘ in restaurant
CARDS:

★★70% **Monsal Head Hotel**
Monsal Head DE45 1NL
☎ 01629 640250 📠 01629 640815
e-mail: christine@monsalhead.com
web: www.monsalhead.com
Dir: *A6 from Bakewell to Buxton. After 2m turn into Ashford-in-the-Water, take B6465 for 1m*
Popular with walkers, this friendly hotel commands one of the most splendid views in the Peak Park, overlooking Monsal Dale and the walking path along the disused railway line. Bedrooms are well equipped, and four have superb views down the valley. There is a comfortable lounge with an open fire and a wide selection of games. The hotel specialises in local foods, real ales and rare wines.
ROOMS: 7 en suite (1 fmly) s £45-£70; d £45-£100 (incl. bkfst) **LB** **CONF:** Thtr 60 Class 30 Board 30 **PARKING:** 20 **NOTES:** ⊘ in restaurant Closed 25 Dec RS Nov-Mar **CARDS:**

BALDOCK, Hertfordshire Map 12 TL23

⌂ Sleep Inn Baldock
Baldock Services (A1M/A507), Radwell SG7 5TR
☎ 01462 832900 📠 01462 832901
e-mail: enquiries@hotels-baldock.com
Dir: *400yds E of A1(M) junct 10 & A507*
This modern, purpose built accommodation offers smartly appointed, well-equipped bedrooms, with good power showers. There is a choice of adjacent food outlets where guests may enjoy breakfast, snacks and meals.
ROOMS: 62 en suite s £52.50-£59.50; d £52.50-£59.50

⌂ Travelodge
Great North Rd, Hinxworth SG7 5EX
☎ 08700 850 950 📠 01462 835329
Dir: *on A1, southbound*
Travelodge offers good quality, good value, modern accommodation. Ideal for families, the spacious, en suite bedrooms include remote-control TV, tea and coffee-making facilities and luxury beds. Meals can be taken at the nearby family restaurant. For further details consult the Hotel Groups page.
ROOMS: 40 en suite s fr £25; d fr £25

Early start?
Hotels at all star levels should provide in-room alarm clocks and/or alarm calls

BALSALL COMMON, West Midlands Map 10 SP27

★★★★66% **Nailcote Hall**
Nailcote Ln, Berkswell CV7 7DE
☎ 024 7646 6174 📠 024 7647 0720
e-mail: info@nailcotehall.co.uk
web: www.nailcotehall.co.uk
Dir: *on B4101*
This 17th-century house, set in 15 acres of grounds, boasts a 9-hole championship golf course and Roman bath style swimming pool amongst its many facilities. Rooms are spacious and elegantly

continued

furnished. Dinner may be taken in the fine dining restaurant (smart casual dress required) or the less formal Rick's Cafe & Bar.

ROOMS: 21 en suite 19 annexe en suite (2 fmly) (15 GF) in 30 bedrooms s £165-£275; d £175-£275 (incl. bkfst) LB **FACILITIES: Spa** supervised 9 Snooker Solarium Gym Putt green Jacuzzi Xmas **CONF:** Thtr 140 Class 80 Board 44 Del from £135 **SERVICES:** Lift **PARKING:** 200 **NOTES:** in restaurant Civ Wed 120 **CARDS:**

See advert under SOLIHULL

★★76% **Haigs**
Kenilworth Rd CV7 7EL
☎ 01676 533004 01676 535132
e-mail: haiinfo@mistral.co.uk
Dir: *on A452 4m N of Kenilworth & 6m S of M6 junct 4. 5m S of M42 junct 6. 8m N of M40 junct 15*

This hotel, set in residential surroundings, offers a warm welcome, highly attentive service and good food. The comfortable bedrooms

continued on p68

BALSALL COMMON, continued

are decorated in an attractive, homely style, and facilities include a lounge bar and a meeting room. It is well positioned for Birmingham NEC and just 5 miles from the M6.

Haigs, Balsall Common

ROOMS: 23 en suite (5 GF) ⊗ in 8 bedrooms s £65-£87.50; d £80-£107.50 (incl. bkfst) **LB** **CONF:** Thtr 25 Board 16 Del £150 **PARKING:** 23 **NOTES:** ⊗ in restaurant Closed 26 Dec-3 Jan & Etr RS Mon-Sat & Sun Lunch **CARDS:**

Travel Inn (Balsall Common Nr NEC)

Kenilworth Rd CV7 7EX
☎ 08701 977022 01676 535929
Dir: *M42 junct 6, A45 towards Coventry for 0.5m, then A452 towards Leamington, Travel Inn 3m on right*

travel inn

Travel Inn offers good-quality, value-for-money accommodation. Spacious, en suite rooms with bath and shower comfortably accommodate a family of up to two adults and two children (to age 15). The restaurant and bar offers a varied menu. For further details consult the Hotel Groups page.

ROOMS: 42 en suite s £45.95-£48.95; d £45.95-£48.95

BAMBURGH, Northumberland — Map 21 NU13

★★★71% Waren House

Waren Mill NE70 7EE
☎ 01668 214581 01668 214484
e-mail: enquiries@warenhousehotel.co.uk
web: www.warenhousehotel.co.uk
Dir: *2m E of A1 turn onto B1342 to Waren Mill, at t-junct turn right, hotel 100yds on right.*

This delightful Georgian mansion is set in six acres of woodland and offers views of the coastline. The individually designed bedrooms, including suites, are themed in differing styles, and many have large bathrooms. Good, home-cooked food is served in the elegant dining room. A comfortable lounge and library are also available.

ROOMS: 12 en suite (4 fmly) (1 GF) ⊗ in all bedrooms s £74-£110; d £90-£195 (incl. bkfst) **LB** **FACILITIES:** Xmas **CONF:** Class 24 Board 24 Del from £98 **PARKING:** 20 **NOTES:** No children 14yrs ⊗ in restaurant **CARDS:**

★★70% *Victoria*

Front St NE69 7BP
☎ 01668 214431 01668 214404
e-mail: enquiries@victoriahotel.net
web: www.victoriahotel.net
Dir: *off A1 N of Alnwick onto B1342, near Belford & follow signs to Bamburgh. Hotel in centre of Bamburgh opposite village green*

This hotel, which overlooks the village green, offers an interesting blend of traditional and modern. A Victorian-style bar is a relaxing venue throughout the day and evening, while the brasserie, with its conservatory roof, provides a contemporary dinner menu. Bedrooms come in a variety of styles and sizes.

ROOMS: 29 en suite (2 fmly) ⊗ in 18 bedrooms **FACILITIES:** Games room Childrens play den ch fac **CONF:** Thtr 50 Class 30 Board 20 **PARKING:** 12 **NOTES:** ⊗ in restaurant
CARDS:

★★69% The Lord Crewe

Front St NE69 7BL
☎ 01668 214243 01668 214273
e-mail: lordcrewebamburgh@tiscali.co.uk
Dir: *just below the castle*

Located in the heart of the village close to Bamburgh Castle, this hotel has been developed from an old inn. Bedrooms are generally spacious and offer good levels of comfort and facilities. Public areas include a choice of lounges, a comfortable bar and a smart modern restaurant.

ROOMS: 18 rms (17 en suite) s £47-£52; d £88-£98 (incl. bkfst) **PARKING:** 20 **NOTES:** No children 5yrs ⊗ in restaurant Closed Dec/Jan **CARDS:**

> Popped the question?
> Hotels with Civ Wed in their entry are licensed for civil wedding ceremonies. Maximum numbers for the ceremony only are shown, e.g. Civ Wed 120

★★65% *The Mizen Head*

Lucker Rd NE69 7BS
☎ 01668 214254 01668 214104
Dir: *off A1 onto B1341 for Bamburgh. Hotel 1st on left entering village*

A relaxed atmosphere prevails at this hotel, set in its own gardens on the western edge of the village. The dinner menu offers a good

continued

choice of dishes served either in the split-level dining room or in the bar.

ROOMS: 13 rms (12 en suite) (2 fmly) **FACILITIES:** Darts ch fac **CONF:** Class 45 **PARKING:** 30 **NOTES:** ⊗ in restaurant **CARDS:**

BAMFORD, Derbyshire — Map 16 SK28

★★72% Yorkshire Bridge Inn

Ashopton Rd, Hope Valley S33 0AZ
☎ 01433 651361 Fax 01433 651361
e-mail: mr@ybridge.force9.co.uk
web: www.yorkshire-bridge.co.uk
Dir: *A57 Sheffield/Glossop road, at Ladybower Reservoir take A6013 Bamford road, inn 1m on right*

A well-established country inn, ideally located beside Ladybower Dam and within reach of the Peak District's many beauty spots. The hotel offers a wide range of excellent dishes in both the bar and dining area, along with a good selection of real ales. Bedrooms are attractively furnished, comfortable and well equipped.
ROOMS: 14 en suite (3 fmly) (4 GF) ⊗ in 10 bedrooms s £47; d £64-£90 (incl. bkfst) LB **FACILITIES:** Xmas **CONF:** Class 12 **PARKING:** 40 **NOTES:** ⊗ in restaurant **CARDS:**

BANBURY, Oxfordshire — Map 11 SP44

★★★71% Banbury House

Oxford Rd OX16 9AH
☎ 01295 259361 Fax 01295 270954
e-mail: sales@banburyhouse.co.uk
web: www.banburyhouse.co.uk
Dir: *approx 200yds from Banbury Cross on A423 towards Oxford*
Situated very near the Banbury Cross, this attractive Georgian property is smartly presented and offers comfortable accommodation in individually decorated and furnished bedrooms. The public areas include a spacious foyer lounge, a contemporary bar and a restaurant which serves both fixed-price

continued

and carte menus. The friendly staff create a welcoming atmosphere.
ROOMS: 63 en suite (4 fmly) (8 GF) ⊗ in 24 bedrooms s fr £45; d fr £90 LB **FACILITIES:** STV **CONF:** Thtr 70 Class 35 Board 28 Del £140 **PARKING:** 60 **NOTES:** ✈ ⊗ in restaurant Closed 24 Dec-1 Jan **CARDS:**

★★★71% Whately Hall

Banbury Cross OX16 0AN
☎ 0870 400 8104 Fax 01295 271736
e-mail: whatelyhall@macdonald-hotels.co.uk
Dir: *M40 junct 11, straight over 2 rdbts, left at 3rd, 0.25m to Banbury Cross, hotel on right*
Dating back to 1677, this historic inn boasts many original features such as stone passages, priests' holes and a fine wooden staircase. The spacious public areas include the oak-panelled restaurant, which overlooks the attractive, well-tended gardens. Bedrooms vary in size and style; all have now been upgraded and have good facilities.
ROOMS: 69 en suite (3 fmly) ⊗ in 41 bedrooms **FACILITIES:** STV **CONF:** Thtr 150 Class 80 Board 40 Del from £135 **SERVICES:** Lift **PARKING:** 80 **NOTES:** ⊗ in restaurant Civ Wed 100 **CARDS:**

★★★69% Wroxton House

Wroxton St Mary OX15 6QB
☎ 01295 730777 Fax 01295 730800
e-mail: reservations@wroxtonhousehotel.com
Dir: *A422 from Banbury, 2.5m to Wroxton, hotel on right entering village*
Dating in parts from 1647, this partially thatched hotel is set just off the main road and is under new ownership. Bedrooms, which have either been created out of converted cottages or are situated in a more modern wing, are comfortable and well equipped. The public areas are open plan and consist of a reception lounge and a bar and the low-beamed Inglenook Restaurant which offers a peaceful atmosphere.
ROOMS: 32 en suite (1 fmly) (7 GF) ⊗ in 15 bedrooms s £85-£103; d £100-£120 (incl. bkfst) LB **FACILITIES:** Xmas **CONF:** Thtr 45 Class 20 Board 25 Del from £130 **NOTES:** ⊗ in restaurant Civ Wed 60 **CARDS:**

★★70% *Cromwell Lodge Hotel*

North Bar OX16 0TB
☎ 01295 259781 Fax (0295) 276619
Dir: *M40 junct 11, B4662 to Banbury, left at 3rd rdbt. Follow road to traffic lights, straight over, hotel on left.*
Enjoying a central location, this characteristic 17th-century property has been stylishly refurbished. Diners have a choice between the contemporary lounge bar leading on to the delightful walled garden and patio and the smart, modern restaurant. The comfortable bedrooms are furnished and equipped to a high standard and include a number of spacious suites.
ROOMS: 29 en suite (2 fmly) ⊗ in 21 bedrooms **FACILITIES:** STV **CONF:** Thtr 30 Class 20 Board 25 **PARKING:** 30 **NOTES:** ✈ ⊗ in restaurant **CARDS:**

⌂ Premier Lodge (Banbury)

Warwick Rd, Warmington OX17 1JJ
☎ 0870 9906512 Fax 0870 9906513
web: www.premierlodge.com
Dir: *5 miles from Banbury. From north M40 junct 12 onto B4100 towards Warmington. From south M40 junct 11 onto A423. Continue onto A442 and turn right onto B4100.*
High quality, modern, budget accommodation, ideal for families and business travellers. All rooms feature bath, power shower and satellite TV, and most have telephones / modem points. The adjacent bar and restaurant offers a wide and varied menu.
ROOMS: 39 en suite s £50; d £50

B

BARFORD, Warwickshire
Map 10 SP26

★★★68% The Glebe at Barford
Church St CV35 8BS
☎ 01926 624218 📠 01926 624625
e-mail: sales@glebehotel.co.uk
Dir: *M40 junct 15/A429 Barford/Wellesbourne. At mini island turn left, hotel 500mtrs on right*
The giant Lebanese cedar tree in front of this hotel was ancient even in 1820, when the original rectory was built. Public rooms within the house include a lounge bar and the aptly named Cedars Conservatory Restaurant which offers interesting cuisine. Individually appointed bedrooms are tastefully decorated in soft pastel fabrics, with coronet, tented ceiling or four-poster style beds.
ROOMS: 39 en suite (3 fmly) (4 GF) s £105; d £125 (incl. bkfst) **LB** **FACILITIES:** STV Sauna Solarium Gym Jacuzzi Beauty salon Xmas **CONF:** Thtr 120 Class 60 Board 60 Del £149 **SERVICES:** Lift **PARKING:** 60 **NOTES:** ⊗ in restaurant
CARDS:

BARKING, Greater London
See LONDON SECTION plan 1 H4

Hotel Ibis
Highbridge Rd IG11 7BA
☎ 020 8477 4100 📠 020 8477 4101
e-mail: H2042@accor-hotels.com
Dir: *exit Barking on A406*
Modern, budget hotel offering comfortable accommodation in bright and practical bedrooms. Breakfast is self-service and dinner is available in the restaurant. For further details, consult the Hotel Groups page.
ROOMS: 86 en suite s £50-£55; d £50-£55

Premier Lodge (Barking)
Highbridge Rd IG11 7BA
☎ 0870 9906318 📠 0870 9906319
web: www.premierlodge.com
Dir: *1.5m from Barking. From M25 junct 30 onto A13, signposted to London City and Docklands, onto A406 North Circular*
High quality, modern, budget accommodation, ideal for families and business travellers. All rooms feature bath, power shower and satellite TV, and most have telephones / modem points. The adjacent bar and restaurant offers a wide and varied menu.
ROOMS: 88 en suite s £58; d £58

BARLBOROUGH, Derbyshire
Map 16 SK47

Hotel Ibis Sheffield South
Tallys End, Chesterfield Rd S43 4TX
☎ 01246 813222 📠 01246 813444
e-mail: H3157@accor-hotels.com
Dir: *M1 junct 30. Towards A619, right at rdbt towards Chesterfield. Hotel immediately left*
Modern, budget hotel offering comfortable accommodation in bright and practical bedrooms. Breakfast is self-service and dinner is available in the restaurant. For further details, consult the Hotel Groups page.
ROOMS: 86 en suite s £31.95-£41.95; d £31.95-£41.95 **CONF:** Thtr 35 Class 18 Board 18

BARNARD CASTLE, Co Durham
Map 19 NZ01

★★★73% The Morritt Arms Hotel & Restaurant
Greta Bridge DL12 9SE
☎ 01833 627232 📠 01833 627392
e-mail: relax@themorritt.co.uk
Dir: *turn off A1 at Scotch Corner onto A66 towards Penrith. Greta Bridge 9m on left*
Set off the main road at Greta Bridge, this 17th-century coaching house provides comfortable public rooms full of character. The bar is focused on food and has an interesting Dickensian mural. A fine dining experience is offered in the oak-panelled restaurant. Bedrooms come in individual styles and varying sizes. The attentive service will leave a lasting impression.
ROOMS: 23 en suite (3 fmly) ⊗ in 17 bedrooms s £59.50-£75; d £87.50-£126.50 (incl. bkfst) **LB** **FACILITIES:** ch fac Xmas **CONF:** Thtr 200 Class 60 Board 50 Del from £90 **PARKING:** 40 **NOTES:** ⊗ in restaurant Civ Wed 200 **CARDS:**

A ★★★ Jersey Farm Country Hotel
Darlington Rd DL12 8TA
☎ 01833 638223 📠 01833 631988
e-mail: enquiries@jerseyfarm.co.uk
web: www.jerseyfarm.co.uk
Dir: *On A67 1m E of Barnard Castle*
ROOMS: 20 rms (11 en suite) (6 fmly) (9 GF) s £58.50-£80; d £80-£115 (incl. bkfst) **LB** **FACILITIES:** STV Pool table Xmas **CONF:** Thtr 200 Class 80 Board 60 Del from £80 **PARKING:** 202 **NOTES:** ⊗ in restaurant RS Mondays **CARDS:**

BARNBY MOOR, Nottinghamshire
Map 16 SK68

★★★67% Ye Olde Bell Hotel
CRERAR HOTELS
DN22 8QS
☎ 01777 705121 📠 01777 860424
e-mail: yeoldebell@crerarhotels.com
Dir: *on A638 midway between Retford and Bawtry*

Formerly a posting house on the London to York mail coach route, this charming inn has been welcoming guests for more than three centuries. Public rooms include the very smart, oak-panelled 1650 restaurant, a choice of lounges and an informal bar. Bedrooms vary in size and some overlook the attractive and well-kept gardens.
ROOMS: 51 en suite (12 fmly) ⊗ in 21 bedrooms s £45-£75; d £80-£125 (incl. bkfst) **LB** **FACILITIES:** Xmas **CONF:** Thtr 250 Class 50 Board 40 Del from £85 **PARKING:** 100 **NOTES:** ⊗ in restaurant Civ Wed 250 **CARDS:**

BARNHAM BROOM, Norfolk Map 13 TG00

★★★75% Barnham Broom Hotel, Golf & Country Club

CLASSIC BRITISH

NR9 4DD
☎ 01603 759393 759522 📠 01603 758224
e-mail: enquiry@barnhambroomhotel.co.uk
Dir: *From A11 onto A47 towards Swaffham, follow brown tourist signs*

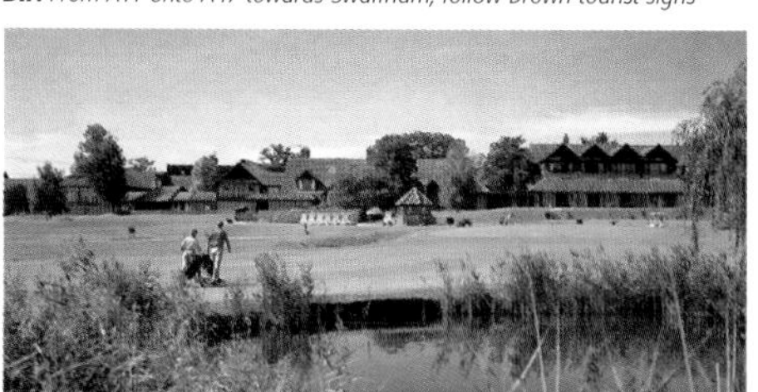

Situated in a peaceful rural location just a short drive from Norwich. Bedrooms are tastefully furnished in a contemporary style and equipped with a range of useful extras. The informal Sports bar serves a range of snacks and meals throughout the day, or guests may choose from the carte menu in the more formal Flints Restaurant. The hotel also has extensive leisure, conference and banqueting facilities.
ROOMS: 52 en suite (8 fmly) (6 GF) ⊗ in 37 bedrooms s £105-£165; d £130-£190 (incl. bkfst) **LB** **FACILITIES:** STV 36 Squash Sauna Solarium Gym Putt green Aerobics/yoga/pilates, pool table, 6ft projection screen Xmas **CONF:** Thtr 180 Class 90 Board 70 Del from £115 **PARKING:** 200 **NOTES:** ⊗ in restaurant Civ Wed 50
CARDS:

BARNSDALE BAR SERVICE AREA (A1), North Yorkshire Map 16 SE51

Travelodge Pontefract Barnsdale

Travelodge

Wentbridge WF8 3QQ
☎ 08700 850 950 📠 01977 620711
Dir: *on A1, southbound*
Travelodge offers good quality, good value, modern accommodation. Ideal for families, the spacious, en suite bedrooms include remote-control TV, tea and coffee-making facilities and luxury beds. Meals can be taken at the nearby family restaurant. For further details consult the Hotel Groups page.
ROOMS: 56 en suite s fr £25; d fr £25

BARNSLEY, South Yorkshire Map 16 SE30
See also Tankersley

★★★★71% Tankersley Manor

MARSTON HOTELS

Church Ln S75 3DQ
☎ 01226 744700 📠 01226 745405
e-mail: tankersley@marstonhotels.com
(For full entry see Tankersley)

> Late for dinner?
> Quality Standards mean that last orders for dinner vary according to star rating and should be no earlier than:
> ★★ 7.00pm ★★★ 8.00pm ★★★★ 9.00pm
> ★★★★★ 10.00pm

★★★73% Ardsley House

Forestdale Hotels

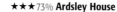

Doncaster Rd, Ardsley S71 5EH
☎ 01226 309955 📠 01226 205374
e-mail: ardsley.house@forestdale.com
Dir: *on A635, 0.75m from Stairfoot rdbt*
Quietly situated on the Barnsley to Doncaster Road, this hotel has many regular customers. Comfortable and well-equipped bedrooms, excellent leisure facilities including a gym and pool, and good conference facilities are just some of the attractions here. Public rooms include a choice of bars and a busy restaurant.
ROOMS: 75 en suite (12 fmly) (14 GF) ⊗ in 50 bedrooms s fr £100; d fr £120 (incl. bkfst) **LB** **FACILITIES:** STV supervised Sauna Solarium Gym Jacuzzi Beauty Spa ♫ Xmas **CONF:** Thtr 350 Class 250 Board 40 Del from £125 **PARKING:** 200 **NOTES:** Civ Wed
CARDS:

Travel Inn Barnsley

travel inn

Meadow Gate, Dearne Valley, Wombwell S73 0UN
☎ 08701 977024 📠 01226 273810
Dir: *M1 junct 36, eastbound. Take A6195 (A635) to Doncaster for 5 miles. Travel Inn is adjacent to rdbt*
Travel Inn offers good-quality, value-for-money accommodation. Spacious, en suite rooms with bath and shower comfortably accommodate a family of up to two adults and two children (to age 15). The restaurant and bar offers a varied menu. For further details consult the Hotel Groups page.
ROOMS: 41 en suite s £45.95-£46.95; d £45.95-£46.95

Travelodge

Travelodge

School St S70 3PE
☎ 08700 850 950 📠 01226 298799
Dir: *at Stairfoot rdbt A633/A635*
Travelodge offers good quality, good value, modern accommodation. Ideal for families, the spacious, en suite bedrooms include remote-control TV, tea and coffee-making facilities and luxury beds. Meals can be taken at the nearby family restaurant. For further details consult the Hotel Groups page.
ROOMS: 32 en suite s fr £25; d fr £25

BARNSTAPLE, Devon Map 03 SS53

★★★★72% The Imperial

Brend Hotels

Taw Vale Pde EX32 8NB
☎ 01271 345861 📠 01271 324448
e-mail: info@brend-imperial.co.uk
web: www.brend-imperial.co.uk
Dir: *M5 junct 27/A361 to Barnstaple. Follow town centre signs, passing Tesco. Straight on at next 2 rdbts. Hotel on right*

This smart and attractive hotel is pleasantly located at the centre of Barnstaple and overlooks the river. The staff are friendly and
continued on p72

BARNSTAPLE, continued

offer attentive service. The comfortable bedrooms are in a range of sizes, some with balconies and many overlooking the river. Afternoon tea is available in the refurbished lounge and the cuisine is appetising and freshly prepared.

ROOMS: 63 en suite (7 fmly) (4 GF) s £80-£130; d £85-£150 **LB** **FACILITIES:** STV leisure facilities at sister hotel ♫ ch fac Xmas **CONF:** Thtr 60 Class 40 Board 30 **SERVICES:** Lift **PARKING:** 80 **NOTES:** ⊗ in restaurant **CARDS:**

See advert on opposite page

★★★74% Barnstaple Hotel

Braunton Rd EX31 1LE
☎ 01271 376221 🖷 01271 324101
e-mail: info@barnstaplehotel.co.uk
web: www.barnstaplehotel.co.uk
Dir: *outskirts of Barnstaple on A361*

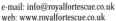

This well-established hotel enjoys a convenient location on the edge of town. Bedrooms are spacious and well equipped, many with access to a balcony overlooking the outdoor pool and garden. A wide choice is offered from various menus, all based on local produce, and there is an extensive range of leisure and conference facilities making this an ideal destination for either family leisure breaks, or as a business venue.

ROOMS: 60 en suite (3 fmly) (17 GF) s £57-£80; d £65-£90 **LB** **FACILITIES: Spa** STV supervised supervised Snooker Sauna Solarium Gym ch fac Xmas **CONF:** BC Thtr 250 **PARKING:** 250 **NOTES:** Civ Wed 100 **CARDS:**

★★★73% Royal & Fortescue

Boutport St EX31 1HG
☎ 01271 342289 🖷 01271 340102
e-mail: info@royalfortescue.co.uk
web: www.royalfortescue.co.uk
Dir: *A361 along Barbican Rd signed town centre, turn right into Queen St & left onto Boutport St, hotel on left*

Formerly a coaching inn, this friendly and convivial hotel is conveniently located in the centre of town. Bedrooms vary in size and all are decorated and furnished to a consistently high standard. In addition to the formal restaurant, guests can take snacks in the popular coffee shop or dine more informally in 'The Bank', a bistro and café bar.

ROOMS: 50 en suite (5 fmly) (3 GF) s £55-£65; d £65-£75 **LB** **FACILITIES:** STV ♫ ch fac Xmas **CONF:** Thtr 25 Class 25 Board 25 **SERVICES:** Lift **PARKING:** 40 **CARDS:**

★★★67% Park

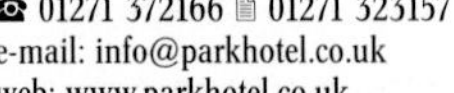

Taw Vale EX32 9AE
☎ 01271 372166 🖷 01271 323157
e-mail: info@parkhotel.co.uk
web: www.parkhotel.co.uk
Dir: *opposite Rock Park, 0.5m from town centre*

Enjoying views across the park and in easy walking distance of the town centre, this modern hotel offers a choice of bedrooms in both the main building and the Garden Court, just across the car park. Public rooms are open plan in style and the friendly staff offer attentive service in a relaxed atmosphere.

ROOMS: 25 en suite 17 annexe en suite (7 fmly) (5 GF) s £55-£65; d £65-£75 **LB** **FACILITIES:** STV ♫ ch fac Xmas **PARKING:** 80 **NOTES:** Civ Wed 100 **CARDS:**

Travel Inn

Eastern Av, Whiddon Dr EX32 8RY
☎ 08701 977025 🖷 01271 377710
Dir: *adjacent to North Devon Link Rd at junct with A39*

Travel Inn offers good-quality, value-for-money accommodation. Spacious, en suite rooms with bath and shower comfortably accommodate a family of up to two adults and two children (to age 15). The restaurant and bar offers a varied menu. For further details consult the Hotel Groups page.

ROOMS: 40 en suite s £45.95-£46.95; d £45.95-£46.95

BARROW-IN-FURNESS, Cumbria — Map 18 SD26

★★★69% *Clarke's Hotel & Brasserie*

Rampside LA13 0PX
☎ 01229 820303 🖷 01229 430594
e-mail: clarkeshotel@lineone.net
Dir: *A590 to Ulverston then A5087, take coast road for 8m, turn left at rdbt into Rampside*

This smart, well-maintained hotel enjoys a peaceful location on the south Cumbrian coastline, overlooking Morecambe Bay. The tastefully appointed bedrooms come in a variety of sizes and are thoughtfully equipped for the business guest. Inviting public areas include an open-plan bar and brasserie offering freshly prepared food throughout the day.

ROOMS: 14 en suite (1 fmly) ⊗ in 3 bedrooms **FACILITIES:** STV ♫ **PARKING:** 50 **NOTES:** ⊗ in restaurant **CARDS:**

★★64% Lisdoonie

307/309 Abbey Rd LA14 5LF
☎ 01229 827312 🖷 01229 820944
e-mail: lisdoonie@aol.com
Dir: *on A590, at 1st set of lights in town (Strawberry pub on left) continue for 100yds, hotel on right*

This friendly hotel is conveniently located for access to the centre of the town and is popular with commercial visitors. The comfortable bedrooms are well equipped, and vary in size and style. There are two comfortable lounges, one with a bar and restaurant adjacent. There is also a large function suite.

ROOMS: 12 en suite (2 fmly) s fr £49.50; d fr £60 (incl. bkfst) **LB** **CONF:** Class 255 **PARKING:** 30 **NOTES:** Closed Xmas & New Year Civ Wed **CARDS:**

BARTON, Lancashire — Map 18 SD53

★★★72% Barton Grange

Garstang Rd PR3 5AA
☎ 01772 862551 🖷 01772 861267
e-mail: stay@bartongrangehotel.com
web: www.bartongrangehotel.com
Dir: *M6 junct 32, follow signs to Garstang (A6) for 2.5 miles. Hotel on right*

Situated close to the M6, this modern, stylish hotel benefits from

continued

extensive public areas that include an award-winning garden centre, spa and leisure facilities. Comfortable, well-appointed bedrooms include four-poster and family rooms, as well as attractive rooms in an adjacent cottage. The unique Walled Garden restaurant offers all-day dining and refreshments.
ROOMS: 42 en suite 8 annexe en suite (4 fmly) (4 GF) ⊗ in 28 bedrooms s £84-£104; d £94-£104 **LB** **FACILITIES:** STV Sauna Gym Jacuzzi Garden Centre within the grounds, pool table, bar billiards ch fac Xmas **CONF:** BC Thtr 300 Class 100 Board 80 Del from £136.50 **SERVICES:** Lift **PARKING:** 250 **NOTES:** ⊗ in restaurant Civ Wed 120 **CARDS:**

BARTON MILLS, Suffolk Map 12 TL77

Travelodge
Fiveways IP28 6AE
☎ 08700 850 950 ⎙ 01638 717675
Dir: *on A11*
Travelodge offers good quality, good value, modern accommodation. Ideal for families, the spacious, en suite bedrooms include remote-control TV, tea and coffee-making facilities and luxury beds. Meals can be taken at the nearby family restaurant. For further details consult the Hotel Groups page.
ROOMS: 40 en suite s fr £25; d fr £25

BARTON STACEY, Hampshire Map 05 SU44

Travelodge
SO21 3NP
☎ 08700 850 950 ⎙ 01264 720260
Dir: *on A303*
Travelodge offers good quality, good value, modern accommodation. Ideal for families, the spacious, en suite bedrooms include remote-control TV, tea and coffee-making facilities and luxury beds. Meals can be taken at the nearby family restaurant. For further details consult the Hotel Groups page.
ROOMS: 20 en suite s fr £25; d fr £25

BARTON-UNDER-NEEDWOOD, Staffordshire Map 10 SK11

Travelodge Burton-upon-Trent
DE13 8EG
☎ 08700 850 950 ⎙ 01283 716343
Dir: *on A38, northbound*
Travelodge offers good quality, good value, modern accommodation. Ideal for families, the spacious, en suite bedrooms include remote-control TV, tea and coffee-making facilities and luxury beds. Meals can be taken at the nearby family restaurant. For further details consult the Hotel Groups page.
ROOMS: 20 en suite s fr £25; d fr £25

Travelodge Burton (South)
Rykneld St DE13 8EH
☎ 08700 850 950 ⎙ 01283 716784
Dir: *on A38, southbound*
Travelodge offers good quality, good value, modern accommodation. Ideal for families, the spacious, en suite bedrooms include remote-control TV, tea and coffee-making facilities and luxury beds. Meals can be taken at the nearby family restaurant. For further details consult the Hotel Groups page.
ROOMS: 40 en suite s fr £25; d fr £25

For central reservation numbers and more information on Hotel Groups, turn to pages 33-39

BARTON-UPON-HUMBER, Lincolnshire Map 17 TA02

★★★72% Reeds Hotel
Westfield Lakes, Far Ings Rd DN18 5RG
☎ 01652 632313 ⎙ 01652 636361
e-mail: info@reedshotel.co.uk
Dir: *A15 rdbt take 2nd exit (Humber Bridge) & leave road at Barton-upon-Humber, turn left at rdbt. In 200yds turn right at sign for hotel, down hill & hotel at junct*

This hotel is situated in a quiet wildlife sanctuary, with splendid views of the Humber Bridge. Public rooms include an attractive restaurant, an all-day brasserie and a foyer lounge. Bedroom sizes vary; all are well equipped and well presented, and service is both friendly and helpful.
ROOMS: 31 en suite (3 fmly) ⊗ in all bedrooms s £75; d £90 (incl. bkfst) **LB** **FACILITIES:** STV Xmas **CONF:** Thtr 300 Class 200 Board 70 Del £105 **SERVICES:** Lift **PARKING:** 100 **NOTES:** ⊗ in restaurant Civ Wed 300 **CARDS:**

BASILDON, Essex Map 06 TQ78

★★★67% Chichester
Old London Rd, Wickford SS11 8UE
☎ 01268 560555 📠 01268 560580
Dir: *off A129*
The same family has owned this friendly hotel, set in landscaped gardens and surrounded by farmland, for over 25 years. Spacious bedrooms are located around an attractive courtyard; each is pleasantly decorated and equipped with useful extras. A range of menus is offered in the smart restaurant with more informal fare served in the bar.
ROOMS: 2 en suite 32 annexe en suite (16 GF) s £59.75; d £71.75-£81.75 **LB FACILITIES:** STV **PARKING:** 150 **NOTES:** No children 5yrs in restaurant **CARDS:**

Campanile

Pipps Hill, Southend Arterial Rd SS14 3AE
☎ 01268 530810 📠 01268 286710
e-mail: basildon@envergure.co.uk
Dir: *M25 junct 29 Basildon exit., back under A127, then left at rdbt*

This modern building offers accommodation in smart, well-equipped bedrooms, all with en suite bathrooms. Refreshments may be taken at the informal Bistro. For further details consult the Hotel Groups page.
ROOMS: 97 annexe en suite s fr £44.95; d fr £44.95 **CONF:** Thtr 35 Class 18 Board 24

Premier Lodge (Basildon)
Festival Leisure Park, Pipps Hill Rd South, off Cranes Farm Rd SS14 3WB
☎ 0870 9906598 📠 0870 9906599
web: www.premierlodge.com
Dir: *from M25 junct 29 follow A127 towards Basildon. Lodge 4m from Basildon off A1235*
High quality, modern, budget accommodation, ideal for families and business travellers. All rooms feature bath, power shower and satellite TV, and most have telephones / modem points. The adjacent bar and restaurant offers a wide and varied menu.
ROOMS: 64 en suite s £52; d £52 **CONF:** Thtr 20 Class 20 Board 12

Travel Inn Basildon (East Mayne)
Felmores, East Mayne SS13 1BW
☎ 08701 977026 📠 01268 530092
Dir: *M25 junct 29/A127 towards Southend, then A132 towards Basildon*
Travel Inn offers good-quality, value-for-money accommodation. Spacious, en suite rooms with bath and shower comfortably accommodate a family of up to two adults and two children (to age 15). The restaurant and bar offers a varied menu. For further details consult the Hotel Groups page.
ROOMS: 32 en suite s £45.95-£48.95; d £45.95-£48.95

Travel Inn (Basildon South)
High Rd, Fobbing, Stanford le Hope SS17 9NR
☎ 08701 977027 📠 01268 581752
Dir: *From M25 (J30/31) take A13 towards Southend. Follow A13 for approx 10m, at Five Bells rbt turn right onto Fobbing High Rd, hotel on left*
Travel Inn offers good-quality, value-for-money accommodation. Spacious, en suite rooms with bath and shower comfortably accommodate a family of up to two adults and two children (to age 15). The restaurant and bar offers a varied menu. For further details consult the Hotel Groups page.
ROOMS: 60 en suite s £45.95-£48.95; d £45.95-£48.95 **CONF:** Thtr 40

Travelodge Basildon
Festival Leisure Park, Festival Way SS14 3WB
☎ 08700 850 950 📠 01268 186559
Dir: *M25 junct 29/A127, follow signs for Basildon centre to A176 and signs for Festival Park, lodge next to bowling alley*
Travelodge offers good quality, good value, modern accommodation. Ideal for families, the spacious, en suite bedrooms include remote-control TV, tea and coffee-making facilities and luxury beds. Meals can be taken at the nearby family restaurant. For further details consult the Hotel Groups page.
ROOMS: 60 en suite s fr £25; d fr £25

BASINGSTOKE, Hampshire Map 05 SU65
See also North Waltham, Odiham & Stratfield Turgis

★★★★ Tylney Hall Hotel
RG27 9AZ
☎ 01256 764881 📠 01256 768141
e-mail: sales@tylneyhall.com
web: www.tylneyhall.com
(For full entry see Rotherwick)

★★★★73% The Hampshire Centrecourt
Centre Dr, Chineham RG24 8FY
☎ 01256 816664 📠 01256 816727
e-mail: hampshirec@marstonhotels.com
Dir: *off A33 (Reading Road) behind the Chineham Shopping Centre via Great Binfields Rd*

Having completed a multi-million pound transformation, this hotel now boasts a range of smart new bedrooms and leisure facilities unrivalled locally. Facilities include indoor and outdoor tennis courts, two swimming pools, a gym and a number of treatment rooms. With further improvements planned, this hotel's reputation is certain to grow further.
ROOMS: 90 en suite (6 fmly) in 25 bedrooms s £137-£163; d £159-£209 (incl. bkfst) **LB FACILITIES: Spa** STV Sauna Solarium Gym Jacuzzi Steam room Beauty salon Xmas **CONF:** Thtr 220 Class 130 Board 60 Del from £159 **SERVICES:** Lift **PARKING:** 200
NOTES: in restaurant Civ Wed 220
CARDS:

★★★★69% Apollo

Aldermaston Roundabout RG24 9NU
☎ 01256 796700 01256 796701
e-mail: admin@apollo-hotels.co.uk
web: www.apollohotels.com
Dir: M3 junct 6. Follow ringroad N, exit A340 (Aldermaston). Hotel on rdbt, 5th exit into Popley Way for access

This modern hotel provides well-equipped accommodation and spacious public areas, appealing to both the leisure and business guest. Facilities include a smartly appointed leisure club, a business centre, along with a good choice of formal and informal dining within two restaurants – 'Vespers' is the fine dining option.

ROOMS: 125 en suite in 100 bedrooms **FACILITIES: Spa** STV supervised Sauna Solarium Gym Jacuzzi Xmas **CONF:** Thtr 255 Class 196 Board 30 **SERVICES:** Lift air con **PARKING:** 200 **NOTES:** Civ Wed **CARDS:**

Indoor Swimming Pool
Indoor Swimming Pool (heated)
Outdoor Swimming Pool
Outdoor Swimming Pool (heated)

★★★★69%
Hanover International Hotel & Club

Scures Hill, Nately Scures, Hook RG27 9JS
☎ 01256 764161 01256 768341
e-mail: reception.basingstoke@hanover-international.com
Dir: M3 junct 5, A287 towards Newnham. L at lights. Hotel 200mtrs on R

This modern hotel is popular with both business and leisure guests. Comfortable bedrooms are well equipped and include a number of spacious executive rooms. Guests have a choice of dining in the formal restaurant, or for lighter meals and snacks there is a relaxing café or a smart bar. Extensive conference and leisure facilities complete the picture.

ROOMS: 100 en suite (14 fmly) (26 GF) in 45 bedrooms s £47-£192.95; d £94-£205.90 (incl. bkfst) **FACILITIES:** STV supervised Sauna Solarium Gym Jacuzzi Xmas **CONF:** Thtr 220 Class 100 Board 80 Del from £145 **SERVICES:** Lift air con **PARKING:** 200 **NOTES:** in restaurant Civ Wed 90 **CARDS:**

★★★72% **Romans**

Little London Rd RG7 2PN
☎ 0118 970 0421 0118 970 0691
e-mail: romanhotel@hotmail.com
(For full entry see Silchester and advert below)

BASINGSTOKE, continued

★★★61% Red Lion

24 London St RG21 7NY
☎ 01256 328525 01256 844056
e-mail: redlion.enquiries@zolahotels.com
Dir: *M3 junct 6 to Black Dam rdbt. 2nd exit onto Ringway East (A339). Take slip road signed town centre onto Churchill Way East (A3010). At rdbt take 1st exit onto Timberlake Rd, leading into New Rd. After pedestrian traffic lights, right into Red Lion Lane*

Centrally located in Basingstoke, the Red Lion is an ideal choice for business guests. Bedrooms are mostly spacious and include non-smoking rooms, interconnecting rooms and rooms with four-poster beds. Public areas comprise an attractive lounge and restaurant, and a popular bar. Other facilities include a selection of function and conference rooms.

ROOMS: 59 en suite (2 fmly) ⊗ in 16 bedrooms s £45-£105; d £65-£140 (incl. bkfst) **LB** **FACILITIES:** STV ch fac Xmas **CONF:** Thtr 80 Class 40 Board 20 Del from £110 **SERVICES:** Lift **PARKING:** 62 **NOTES:** ⊗ in restaurant **CARDS:**

Travel Inn

Basingstoke Leisure Park, Worting Rd RG22 6PG
☎ 08701 977028 01256 819329
Dir: *M3 junct 6 follow signs for Leisure Park*

Travel Inn offers good-quality, value-for-money accommodation. Spacious, en suite rooms with bath and shower comfortably accommodate a family of up to two adults and two children (to age 15). The restaurant and bar offers a varied menu. For further details consult the Hotel Groups page.

ROOMS: 71 en suite s £45.95-£48.95; d £45.95-£48.95

Travelodge

Stag and Hounds, Winchester Rd RG22 6HN
☎ 08700 850 950 01256 843566
Dir: *off A30, S of town centre*

Travelodge offers good quality, good value, modern accommodation. Ideal for families, the spacious, en suite bedrooms include remote-control TV, tea and coffee-making facilities and luxury beds. Meals can be taken at the nearby family restaurant. For further details consult the Hotel Groups page.

ROOMS: 44 en suite s fr £25; d fr £25

BASLOW, Derbyshire

Map 16 SK27

★★★76% Cavendish

DE45 1SP
☎ 01246 582311 01246 582312
e-mail: info@cavendish-hotel.net
web: www.cavendish-hotel.net
Dir: *M1 junct 29/A617 W to Chesterfield & A619 to Baslow. Hotel in village centre, off main road*

This stylish property, dating back to the 18th century, is delightfully situated on the edge of the Chatsworth Estate. Elegantly appointed bedrooms offer a host of thoughtful amenities, while comfortable public areas are furnished with period pieces and paintings. Guests have a choice of dining in the informal conservatory Garden Room or the elegant Gallery Restaurant.

ROOMS: 24 en suite (3 fmly) (2 GF) ⊗ in 2 bedrooms s £103-£115; d £135-£148 **LB** **FACILITIES:** STV Fishing Putt green Xmas **CONF:** Thtr 25 Class 8 Board 18 Del from £190 **PARKING:** 50 **NOTES:** ⊗ in restaurant **CARDS:**

Top 200 – Hotel

★★ Fischer's Baslow Hall

Calver Rd DE45 1RR
☎ 01246 583259 01246 583818
e-mail: m.s@fischers-baslowhall.co.uk
web: www.fischers-baslowhall.co.uk
Dir: *on A623 between Baslow & Calver*

Located at the end of a chestnut tree-lined drive on the edge of the Chatsworth Estate, this beautiful Derbyshire manor house offers sumptuous accommodation and facilities. Staff provide very friendly and personally attentive hospitality and service. There are two styles of bedroom available: traditional, individually-themed rooms in the main house and spacious, more contemporary-styled rooms with Italian marble bathrooms in the Garden House. The cuisine is extremely memorable and a highlight of any stay.

ROOMS: 6 en suite 5 annexe en suite (4 GF) ⊗ in all bedrooms s £100-£120; d £120-£180 (incl. cont bkfst) **LB** **CONF:** Thtr 40 Board 18 Del from £160 **PARKING:** 40 **NOTES:** ⊗ in restaurant Closed 25-26 Dec Civ Wed 40
CARDS:

BASSENTHWAITE, Cumbria

Map 18 NY23

★★★★72% Armathwaite Hall

CA12 4RE
☎ 017687 76551 017687 76220
e-mail: reservations@armathwaite-hall.com
web: www.armathwaite-hall.com
Dir: *M6 junct 40/A66 to Keswick rdbt then A591 signed Carlisle. 8m to Castle Inn junct, turn left. Hotel 300yds*

Enjoying fine views over Bassenthwaite Lake, this impressive mansion, dating from the 17th century, is peacefully situated amid 400 acres of deer park. Comfortably furnished bedrooms are complemented by a choice of public rooms featuring splendid

continued

wood panelling and roaring log fires. The indoor and outdoor leisure facilities are an added attraction.
ROOMS: 43 en suite (4 fmly) (8 GF) s £119-£155; d £150-£290 (incl. bkfst) **LB** **FACILITIES: Spa** STV Fishing Snooker Sauna Solarium Gym Putt green Jacuzzi Archery, Beauty salon, Clayshooting, Quad bikes, Falconry, Mountain Bikes ch fac Xmas **CONF:** Thtr 80 Class 50 Board 60 Del from £139 **SERVICES:** Lift **PARKING:** 100 **NOTES:** in restaurant Civ Wed 80
CARDS:

See advert under KESWICK

★★★75% The Pheasant

CA13 9YE
☎ 01768 776234 01768 76002
e-mail: info@the-pheasant.co.uk
Dir: *Midway between Keswick & Cockermouth, signed from A66*

Enjoying a rural setting on the western side of Bassenthwaite Lake, this 500-year-old, friendly inn is steeped in tradition. The attractive oak-panelled bar has seen few changes in recent years and features log fires and a great selection of malt whisky. The individually decorated bedrooms are stylish and thoughtfully equipped.
ROOMS: 13 en suite 2 annexe en suite (2 GF) in 2 bedrooms s £80-£100; d £150-£200 (incl. bkfst) **LB** **PARKING:** 40 **NOTES:** No children 8yrs in restaurant Closed 25 Dec
CARDS:

★★★65% The Castle Inn Hotel

CA12 4RG
☎ 0870 609 6178 01768 776604
e-mail: reservations.castleinn@corushotels.com
Dir: *leave A66 at Keswick, onto A591 towards Carlisle, pass Bassenthwaite village on right & hotel 6m on left*

Located to the north of the lake and enjoying distant views of the hills, this hotel stands in extensive grounds and gardens. It has a wide range of indoor and outdoor leisure facilities, spacious public areas, and a selection of rooms for conferences and functions.

continued

Bedrooms are well equipped and come in a variety of styles and sizes.
ROOMS: 48 en suite (7 fmly) (4 GF) s £47-£82.50; d £64-£96.50 (incl. bkfst) **LB** **FACILITIES:** supervised Snooker Sauna Solarium Gym Putt green Jacuzzi Badminton, Table tennis Xmas **CONF:** BC Thtr 120 Class 60 Board 60 Del from £95 **PARKING:** 100 **NOTES:** in restaurant Civ Wed 120 **CARDS:**

★★70% *Ravenstone*

CA12 4QG
☎ 017687 76240 017687 76733
e-mail: info@ravenstone-hotel.co.uk
web: www.ravenstone-hotel.co.uk
Dir: *4.5m N of Keswick on A591 Carlisle road*

Set in terraced gardens and enjoying fine panoramic views across the valley, this delightful country house retains its original character and features oak panelling and artefacts. This is a relaxing and friendly hotel, run by a young family who make other families most welcome. The set menu features good, freshly prepared dishes.
ROOMS: 20 en suite (2 fmly) in all bedrooms **FACILITIES:** Snooker Table tennis **PARKING:** 25 **NOTES:** in restaurant
CARDS:

A ★★ Ouse Bridge

Dubwath CA13 9YD
☎ 017687 76322 017687 76350
e-mail: enquiries@ousebridge.com
web: www.ousebridge.com
Dir: *M6 junct 40/A66 westbound towards Keswick & Cockermouth. Approx. 8m from Keswick turn right at signposts for Dubwath for hotel 50yds on left*
ROOMS: 10 rms (8 en suite) (2 fmly) in all bedrooms s £23-£45; d £62-£70 (incl. bkfst) **LB** **PARKING:** 15 **NOTES:** No children 10yrs in restaurant Closed 23 Dec-31 Jan **CARDS:**

BATH, Somerset

Map 04 ST76

See also Colerne & Hinton Charterhouse

★★★★★72% The Royal Crescent

16 Royal Crescent BA1 2LS
☎ 01225 823333 01225 339401
e-mail: info@royalcrescent.co.uk
Dir: *along A4, right at traffic lights. 2nd left onto Bennett St. Continue into the Circus, 2nd exit onto Brock St (cobbled street)*

John Wood's masterpiece of fine Georgian architecture provides the setting for this elegant hotel in the centre of the world famous Royal Crescent. Spacious, air-conditioned bedrooms are individually designed and furnished with antiques. Delightful central grounds lead to a second house which is home to further rooms, Pimpernells restaurant and the Bath House, offering complementary therapies and treatments.
ROOMS: 45 en suite (8 fmly) in 8 bedrooms d £210-£840 (incl. bkfst) **LB** **FACILITIES:** STV Sauna Gym Hot air ballooning, 1920's river launch, Outdoor heated plunge pool Xmas **CONF:** Thtr 50 Class 25 Board 24 Del from £225 **SERVICES:** Lift air con **PARKING:** 27 **NOTES:** in restaurant Civ Wed 50
CARDS:

BATH, continued

★★★★★67% The Bath Spa

Sydney Rd BA2 6JF
☎ 0870 400 8222 01225 444006
e-mail: sales@bathspahotel.com
Dir: *M4 junct 18/A46 for Bath/A4 city centre. Left onto A36 at 1st traffic lights. Right at mini rdbt then left into Sydney Place. Hotel 200yds on right*

A delightful Georgian mansion set amidst seven acres of pretty landscaped grounds, just a short walk from the many and varied delights of the city centre. A timeless elegance pervades the gracious public areas and bedrooms. Facilities include a popular leisure club, a choice of dining options and a number of meeting rooms.
ROOMS: 104 en suite (3 fmly) (17 GF) in 76 bedrooms s £250-£280; d £250-£480 **LB** **FACILITIES:** STV supervised Sauna Gym Jacuzzi Beauty treatment, Hair salon Xmas **CONF:** Thtr 120 Class 100 Board 50 Del from £199 **SERVICES:** Lift **PARKING:** 156 **NOTES:** in restaurant Civ Wed 120 **CARDS:**

★★★★76% Bath Priory

Weston Rd BA1 2XT
☎ 01225 331922 01225 448276
e-mail: mail@thebathpriory.co.uk
web: www.thebathpriory.co.uk
Dir: *adjacent to Victoria Park*
Set in delightful walled gardens, this attractive Georgian house provides peace and tranquillity overlooking the city. In the sumptuously furnished public rooms an extensive display of pictures and fine art create a charming style. Cuisine is accomplished and there is an impressive wine list. Bedrooms, some are suites in an adjacent building, are well-proportioned and offer the many thoughtful touches.
ROOMS: 28 en suite (6 fmly) s £200-£245; d £245-£425 (incl. bkfst) **LB** **FACILITIES:** STV Sauna Solarium Gym Jacuzzi Holistic beauty therapy and treatments Xmas **CONF:** BC Thtr 60 Class 30 Board 30 Del from £190 **PARKING:** 40 **NOTES:** in restaurant Civ Wed 60 **CARDS:**

★★★★71% *Combe Grove Manor Hotel & Country Club*

FURLONG

Brassknocker Hill, Monkton Combe BA2 7HS
☎ 01225 834644 01225 834961
e-mail: info@combegrovemanor.com
Dir: *M4 junct 18/A46 to city centre, then signs for University & American Museum. Hotel 2m past University on left*
Set in over 80 acres of gardens, this Georgian mansion commands stunning views over Limpley Stoke Valley. Most bedrooms are in the Garden Lodge, a short walk from the main house. The superb range of indoor and outdoor leisure facilities includes a beauty clinic with holistic therapies, golf, tennis and two pools.

ROOMS: 9 en suite 31 annexe en suite (11 fmly) (9 GF) **FACILITIES: Spa** STV supervised supervised 5 Sauna Solarium Gym Putt green Jacuzzi Aerobics, Beauty salon, Jogging trail, Indoor tennis **CONF:** Thtr 120 Class 50 Board 40 **PARKING:** 150 **NOTES:** in restaurant Civ Wed 50
CARDS:

See advert on opposite page

Town House

★★★★ The Windsor Hotel

69 Great Pulteney St BA2 4DL
☎ 01225 422100 01225 422550
e-mail: sales@bathwindsorhotel.com
web: www.bathwindsorhotel.com
Dir: *M4 junct 18/A4. Turn left onto A36, after 500yds turn right at mini rdbt. 2nd left into Great Pulteney St*
This delightful Grade I listed, terraced Georgian town house is a short walk from the town centre. It has been refurbished to the highest standard and is sumptuously furnished with antique pieces. The restaurant has Japanese décor and offers a choice of either sukiyaki or shabu shabu where the fresh ingredients are cooked at the table. The Windsor is a non-smoking establishment.
ROOMS: 14 en suite (3 fmly) in all bedrooms s £85-£115; d £135-£275 (incl. bkfst) **LB** **FACILITIES:** STV **CONF:** Thtr 16 Class 14 Board 16 **PARKING:** 12 **NOTES:** No children 12yrs in restaurant Closed Xmas wk **CARDS:**

★★★★65% Menzies Waterside

MENZIES HOTELS

Rossiter Rd, Widcombe Basin BA2 4JP
☎ 01225 338855 01225 428941
e-mail: waterside@menzies-hotels.co.uk
Dir: *J18 M4, follow signs to Bath City centre. At 3rd set of lights turn left into A36 Widcombe Parade and turn right into Rossiter Rd.*
In a quiet location within walking distance of the main town and train station, this hotel is a popular leisure break destination. Now refurbished, the bedrooms are compact but well designed with comfortable seating and duvets on beds. The brasserie serves contemporary cuisine in air-conditioned surroundings overlooking the water.
ROOMS: 107 en suite 6 annexe en suite in 67 bedrooms s £130; d £130-£150 **LB** **FACILITIES:** Xmas **CONF:** Thtr 120 Class 70 Board 60 Del £150 **SERVICES:** Lift **PARKING:** 80 **NOTES:** in restaurant Civ Wed **CARDS:**

B

Top 200 – Hotel

★★★ Queensberry
Russel St BA1 2QF
☎ 01225 447928 01225 446065
e-mail: reservations@thequeensberry.co.uk
web: www.thequeensberry.co.uk
Dir: *100mtrs from the Assembly Rooms*

This charming family run hotel, situated in a quiet residential street near the centre of the city, consists of four delightful townhouses. The spacious bedrooms offer deep armchairs, marble bathrooms and a range of modern comforts. Sumptuously furnished sitting rooms add to The Queensberry's appeal and allow access to the very attractive and peaceful walled gardens. The Olive Tree is a stylish restaurant offering surroundings that combine Georgian opulence with contemporary simplicity. Innovative menus are based on best quality ingredients and competent cooking. Valet parking is a useful additional service.

ROOMS: 29 en suite s £100-£140; d £100-£140 **LB** **CONF:** Thtr 35 Board 25 Del £175 **SERVICES:** Lift **PARKING:** 9 **NOTES:** in restaurant **CARDS:**

★★★74% The Lansdown Grove
Lansdown Rd BA1 5EH
☎ 01225 483888 01225 483838
e-mail: lansdown@marstonhotels.com
Dir: *follow signs to Lansdown Park & Ride then towards town centre. Hotel on left*

MARSTON HOTELS

A short uphill walk from the city centre, this hotel offers a relaxed atmosphere and comfortable accommodation. Well-equipped, tastefully decorated bedrooms include a number of stylish executive rooms. There is a reception lounge, bar and peaceful drawing room. Innovative, award-winning cuisine using fresh ingredients is served in the elegant restaurant.

ROOMS: 60 en suite (3 fmly) in 9 bedrooms s £95.50-£120.50; d £127.50-£177.50 (incl. bkfst) **LB** **FACILITIES:** STV Xmas **CONF:** Thtr 100 Class 45 Board 40 Del from £131.50 **SERVICES:** Lift **PARKING:** 35 **NOTES:** in restaurant **CARDS:**

B

BATH, continued

★★★72% Cliffe

Cliffe Dr, Crowe Hill, Limpley Stoke BA2 7FY
☎ 01225 723226 📠 01225 723871
e-mail: cliffe@bestwestern.co.uk
Dir: *A36 S from Bath, at A36/B3108 lights left toward Bradford-on-Avon, 0.5m. Turn right before bridge through village, hotel on right*

Best Western

With stunning countryside views, this attractive country house is just a short drive from the City of Bath. Bedrooms vary in size and style and are well equipped; several are particularly spacious and a number of rooms are on the ground floor. The restaurant overlooks the well-tended garden and offers a tempting selection of carefully prepared dishes.
ROOMS: 8 en suite 3 annexe en suite (2 fmly) (4 GF) ⊗ in 4 bedrooms s £90-£100; d £110-£130 (incl. bkfst) **LB** **FACILITIES:** STV peaceful gardens ch fac Xmas **CONF:** Thtr 20 Class 15 Board 10 Del from £160 **PARKING:** 20 **NOTES:** ⊗ in restaurant
CARDS:

See advert on opposite page

★★★70% The Francis

Queen Square BA1 2HH
☎ 0870 400 8223 📠 01225 319715
e-mail: francis@macdonald-hotels.co.uk
Dir: *M4 junct 18/A46 to Bath junct. Take 3rd exit onto A4. Right fork into George St, sharp left into Gay St onto Queen Sq, hotel on left*

MACDONALD HOTELS

Overlooking Queen Square in the centre of the city, this elegant Georgian hotel is situated within walking distance of Bath's many attractions. Public rooms provide a variety of environments in which guests can eat, drink and relax, from the informal café-bar to the traditional lounge and more formal restaurant. Bedrooms now have air conditioning.
ROOMS: 95 en suite (16 fmly) ⊗ in 41 bedrooms s £120-£180; d £120-£180 **LB** **FACILITIES:** Xmas **CONF:** BC Thtr 80 Class 40 Board 30 Del from £100 **SERVICES:** Lift **PARKING:** 42 **NOTES:** ⊗ in restaurant **CARDS:**

★★★70% Pratts

South Pde BA2 4AB
☎ 01225 460441 📠 01225 448807
e-mail: pratts@forestdale.com
Dir: *A46 into city centre. Left at 1st lights (Curfew Pub), right at next rdbt. 2nd exit at next rdbt, right at lights, left at next rdbt, 1st left into South Pde*

Forestdale Hotels

Part of a Georgian terrace, this long-established and popular hotel stands close to the city centre. Public rooms and bedrooms have undergone a refurbishment programme and all decor has been chosen to complement the Georgian surroundings. The ground-floor day rooms include two lounges, a writing room and a very comfortable restaurant.
ROOMS: 46 en suite (2 fmly) ⊗ in 8 bedrooms s fr £95; d fr £130 (incl. bkfst) **LB** **FACILITIES:** Xmas **CONF:** Thtr 50 Class 12 Board 30 Del from £125 **SERVICES:** Lift **NOTES:** ⊗ in restaurant
CARDS:

★★★66% The Abbey Hotel

North Pde BA1 1LF
☎ 01225 461603 📠 01225 447758
e-mail: ahres@compasshotels.co.uk
Dir: *close to the Abbey in city centre*

Originally built for a wealthy merchant in the 1740s and forming part of a handsome Georgian terrace, this welcoming hotel is situated in the heart of the city. The thoughtfully equipped bedrooms vary in size and style. Public areas include a smart lounge bar and a refurbished restaurant offering a regularly changing menu.
ROOMS: 60 en suite (4 fmly) (2 GF) ⊗ in 22 bedrooms s £80-£90; d £110-£120 (incl. bkfst) **LB** **FACILITIES:** STV **SERVICES:** Lift
NOTES: ⊗ in restaurant Closed 23-27 Dec
CARDS:

★★75% Haringtons

Queen St BA1 1HE
☎ 01225 461728 📠 01225 444804
e-mail: post@haringtonshotel.co.uk
web: www.haringtonshotel.co.uk
Dir: *A4 to George St & turn into Milsom St. 1st right into Quiet St & 1st left into Queen St*

Dating back to the 18th century, this hotel has been completely refurbished to accommodate all modern facilities and comforts. The café-bar is open throughout the day for light meals and refreshments. A warm welcome is assured from the proprietors and their staff who create a delightful place to stay.
ROOMS: 13 en suite (3 fmly) ⊗ in all bedrooms s £68-£98; d £88-£128 (incl. bkfst) **LB** **FACILITIES:** STV **NOTES:** ⊗ in restaurant Closed 24-26 Dec **CARDS:**

GF Indicates the number of bedrooms at ground floor level.

B

★★70% Old Malt House
Radford, Timsbury BA2 0QF
☎ 01761 470106 01761 472726
e-mail: hotel@oldmalthouse.co.uk
web: www.oldmalthouse.co.uk
Dir: *A367 towards Radstock for 1m pass Park & Ride, right onto B3115 towards Tunley/Timsbury. At sharp bend straight ahead & hotel 2nd left*
This privately owned, personally run and friendly hotel provides an ideal base for exploring the many attractions the area has to offer. Formerly a brewery malt house, it is peacefully located within easy reach of Bath. Bedrooms, including two on the ground floor, are well equipped and include some thoughtful touches. A varied choice of home-cooked meals is served in the pleasant restaurant.
ROOMS: 10 en suite (1 fmly) (2 GF) in all bedrooms s fr £60; d £66-£78 (incl. bkfst) **LB** **PARKING:** 25 **NOTES:** in restaurant Closed Xmas/New Yr **CARDS:**

★★69% Avondale Hotel & Waterside Restaurant
London Rd East, Bathford BA1 7RB
☎ 01225 859847 & 852207 01225 859847
Dir: *A46/A4 junct follow signs Chippenham/Batheaston/Bathford. Continue through Batheaston, hotel on right just before large rdbt*
The peaceful riverside location of this hotel is convenient for the city, and easily accessible from all major transport links. Bedrooms are well-equipped and comfortable, and some have balconies overlooking the extensive gardens. The restaurant is memorable for its many interesting architectural features as well as its varied menu, which includes vegetarian options.
ROOMS: 15 rms (13 en suite) (3 fmly) s £49-£69; d fr £69 (incl. bkfst) **LB** **FACILITIES:** Fishing Boating, Fishing **CONF:** Thtr 90 Class 60 Board 40 **PARKING:** 60 **CARDS:**

★★69% Wentworth House Hotel
106 Bloomfield Rd BA2 2AP
☎ 01225 339193 01225 310460
e-mail: stay@wentworthhouse.co.uk
web: www.wentworthhouse.co.uk
Dir: *A367 Radstock/Shepton Mallet signs to small shopping area, 'The Bear' pub on right. Take 2nd turning past pub. Hotel on right*

This small personally managed hotel on the outskirts of Bath offers a delightful homely atmosphere, comfortable accommodation and delicious home-cooked dishes from a varied menu. The Wentworth has an outdoor swimming pool and a hot tub in the garden from where stunning views across the city can be enjoyed.
ROOMS: 18 en suite (2 fmly) (9 GF) in 5 bedrooms s £50-£70; d £50-£110 (incl. bkfst) **LB** **FACILITIES: Spa** Jacuzzi **PARKING:** 18 **NOTES:** No children 7yrs in restaurant
CARDS:

See advert on this page

BATH, continued

⌂ Travelodge Bath (Royal Oak)

York Buildings, George St BA1 2EB
☎ 08700 850 950 📠 01225 442061
Travelodge offers good quality, good value, modern accommodation. Ideal for families, the spacious, en suite bedrooms include remote-control TV, tea and coffee-making facilities and luxury beds. Meals can be taken at the nearby family restaurant. For further details consult the Hotel Groups page.
ROOMS: 66 en suite s fr £25; d fr £25

BATLEY, West Yorkshire Map 19 SE22

★★70% Alder House

Towngate Rd, Healey Ln WF17 7HR
☎ 01924 444777 📠 01924 442644
e-mail: info@alderhousehotel.co.uk
web: www.alderhousehotel.co.uk
Dir: *M62 junct 27/A62. After 2m turn left into Whitelee Rd, left at next junct. Left into Healey Ln & after 0.25m hotel on left*
An attractive Georgian house tucked away in leafy grounds. Bedrooms are pleasantly furnished and contain many comfortable extras. There is an intimate dining room offering a selection of interesting dishes, as well as a bar with a separate lounge area. The service and hospitality are both caring and friendly.
ROOMS: 20 en suite (1 fmly) (2 GF) ⊗ in 3 bedrooms s £39-£61; d £60-£72 (incl. bkfst) **LB FACILITIES:** STV **CONF:** BC Thtr 80 Class 40 Board 35 Del from £80 **PARKING:** 52 **NOTES:** ⊗ in restaurant Civ Wed 80 **CARDS:**

BATTLE, East Sussex Map 07 TQ71

★★★73% Powder Mills

Powdermill Ln TN33 0SP
☎ 01424 775511 📠 01424 774540
e-mail: powdc@aol.com
web: www.powdermillshotel.com
Dir: *pass Abbey on A2100. 1st right, hotel 1m on right*

A delightful 18th-century country house hotel set amidst 150 acres of landscaped grounds with lakes and woodland. The individually decorated bedrooms are tastefully furnished and thoughtfully equipped, some rooms have sun terraces with lovely views over the lake. Public rooms include a cosy lounge bar, music room, drawing room, library, restaurant and conservatory.
ROOMS: 30 en suite 10 annexe en suite (3 GF) s £90-£140; d £120-£190 (incl. bkfst) **LB FACILITIES:** STV Fishing Jogging trails & woodland walks ♫ Xmas **CONF:** Thtr 250 Class 50 Board 16 **PARKING:** 101 **NOTES:** ⊗ in restaurant Civ Wed 100
CARDS:

BEACONSFIELD, Buckinghamshire Map 06 SU99

★★★★68% De Vere Bellhouse

Oxford Rd HP9 2XE
☎ 01753 887211 📠 01753 888231
e-mail: bellhouse@devere-hotels.com
Dir: *M40 junct 2, exit signed Gerrards Cross/Beaconsfield. At rdbt take A40 to Gerrards Cross. Hotel 1m on right*

Surrounded by beautiful countryside, this distinctive, Mediterranean-style hotel is nevertheless conveniently located for access to major motorway networks. There is a range of conference and banqueting rooms, a smart restaurant and intimate cocktail bar. Guests also have the use of the indoor leisure club with its own bar and informal poolside brasserie.
ROOMS: 136 en suite (11 fmly) ⊗ in 86 bedrooms s £45-£160; d £90-£180 (incl. bkfst) **LB FACILITIES: Spa** STV Squash Snooker Sauna Solarium Gym Jacuzzi Beauty therapy room Xmas **CONF:** BC Thtr 350 Class 200 Board 80 **SERVICES:** Lift **PARKING:** 405 **NOTES:** ⊗ in restaurant Civ Wed 300
CARDS:

⌂ Innkeeper's Lodge

Aylesbury End HP9 1LW
☎ 01494 671211 📠 01494 685042
www.innkeeperslodge.com
Dir: *M40 junct 2 turn left at next two rdbts. Pub on rdbt*
Smart rooms meet essential business requirements but also have home comforts, and depending on location may well have meeting rooms and pub dining. Dining options generally include all-day menus plus the added advantage of breakfast.
ROOMS: 32 en suite s £49-£79.95; d £49-£79.95

BEAMINSTER, Dorset Map 04 ST40

★★★71% Bridge House

3 Prout Bridge DT8 3AY
☎ 01308 862200 📠 01308 863700
e-mail: enquiries@bridge-house.co.uk
web: www.bridge-house.co.uk
Dir: *off A3066, 100yds from Town Square*
Dating back to the 13th century, this family-owned property offers friendly and attentive service. Bedrooms are tastefully furnished and decorated; those in the main house are generally more spacious than those in the adjacent coach house. Smartly presented public areas include the Georgian dining room, cosy bar and adjacent lounge, together with a breakfast room overlooking the attractive garden.
ROOMS: 9 en suite 5 annexe en suite (1 fmly) (4 GF) ⊗ in all bedrooms s £55-£99; d £104-£138 (incl. bkfst) **LB FACILITIES:** Xmas **CONF:** Thtr 20 Class 16 Board 16 **PARKING:** 22 **NOTES:** ⊗ in restaurant Closed 27-30 Dec **CARDS:**

B

BEAMISH, Co Durham Map 19 NZ25

★★★69% Beamish Park

Beamish Burn Rd NE16 5EG
☎ 01207 230666 01207 281260
e-mail: reception@beamish-park-hotel.co.uk
web: www.beamish-park-hotel.co.uk
Dir: *A1(M)/A692 towards Consett, then A6076 towards Stanley. Hotel on left behind Causey Arch Inn*

The Metro Centre, Beamish Museum and South Tyneside are all within striking distance of this modern hotel, set in open countryside alongside its own golf course and floodlit range. Bedrooms, some with their own patios, provide a diverse mix of styles and sizes. The conservatory bistro offers a modern menu.
ROOMS: 47 en suite (7 fmly) in 20 bedrooms s £40-£59; d £50-£71 **LB** **FACILITIES:** STV 9 Putt green 20 bay floodlit golf driving range. Golf tuition by PGA professional ch fac **CONF:** Thtr 50 Class 20 Board 30 **PARKING:** 100 **CARDS:**

BEAULIEU, Hampshire Map 05 SU30

Top 200 – Hotel

★★★ Montagu Arms

Palace Ln SO42 7ZL
☎ 01590 612324 01590 612188
e-mail: reservations@montaguarmshotel.co.uk
web: www.montaguarmshotel.co.uk
Dir: *M27 junct 2, turn left at rdbt, follow signs for Beaulieu. Continue to Dibden Purlieu, then right at rdbt. Hotel on left*

Surrounded by the glorious scenery of the New Forest, this lovely hotel manages to achieve the impression of almost total seclusion, though it is within easy reach of the major towns and cities in the area. Bedrooms, all named after types of tree, are individually decorated and come with a range of thoughtful extras. Public rooms include a cosy lounge, an adjoining conservatory and a choice of two dining options, the informal Monty's, or the stylish Terrace Restaurant.
ROOMS: 23 en suite s £100-£125; d £160-£280 (incl. bkfst) **LB** **FACILITIES:** Use of health club in Brockenhurst Xmas **CONF:** Thtr 50 Class 16 Board 26 Del £165 **PARKING:** 86 **NOTES:** in restaurant Civ Wed 50 **CARDS:**

See advert on this page

★★★75% *Master Builders House Hotel*

SO42 7XB
☎ 01590 616253 01590 616297
e-mail: res@themasterbuilders.co.uk
web: www.themasterbuilders.co.uk
Dir: *M27 junct 2, follow Beaulieu signs. At t-junct left onto B3056, 1st left to Bucklers Hard. Hotel 2m on left before village entrance*

The name of the hotel is a testament to the master shipbuilder

continued

AA
★★★
JOHANSENS RECOMMENDED
The Montagu Arms Hotel
AT • BEAULIEU
Situated in the heart of Beaulieu village, the Montagu Arms Hotel enjoys an unrivaled reputation for providing outstanding levels of service, coupled with quality accommodation and award winning food.
24 unique and tastefully decorated rooms.
Terrace Restaurant - formal fine dining, overlooking beautiful terraced gardens. Alfresco dining late spring and summer. Monty's Bar & Brasserie, Oak panelled, home produced food, lively bar area.
Complimentary Leisure and Spa facilities nearby.
Montagu Arms Hotel, Beaulieu,
New Forest, Hampshire SO42 7ZL
Tel: 01590 612324 Fax: 01590 612188
Website: www.montaguarmshotel.co.uk
Email: enquiries@montagu-arms.co.uk

Henry Adams whose house this once was. A full list of the famous ships built within the village can be found in the Yachtsman's Bar. The Riverside Restaurant and many of the individually styled bedrooms enjoy views over the Beaulieu River. For those guests wishing to travel to the Isle of Wight, the hotel also has its own boat.
ROOMS: 8 en suite 17 annexe en suite (2 fmly) (8 GF) in 19 bedrooms **FACILITIES:** STV Fishing can sail from hotel on Beaulieu river **CONF:** Thtr 50 Board 25 **PARKING:** 70 **NOTES:** Civ Wed 60 **CARDS:**

★★★63% Beaulieu

Beaulieu Rd SO42 7YQ
☎ 023 8029 3344 023 8029 2729
e-mail: beaulieu@newforesthotels.co.uk
web: www.newforesthotels.co.uk
Dir: *M27 junct 1/A337 towards Lyndhurst. Left at lights in Lyndhurst, through village, turn right onto B3056, continue for 3m.*

Conveniently located in the heart of the New Forest and close to Beaulieu Road railway station, this popular, small hotel provides an ideal base for exploring this interesting area. Facilities include an indoor swimming pool, an outdoor children's play area and an adjoining pub. A daily changing menu is offered in the restaurant.
ROOMS: 15 en suite 3 annexe en suite (2 fmly) s £75-£82.50; d £120-£155 (incl. bkfst) **LB** **FACILITIES:** Steam room Xmas **CONF:** Thtr 60 Class 40 Board 30 Del from £90 **PARKING:** 60 **NOTES:** in restaurant Civ Wed 60 **CARDS:**

Late for dinner?
Quality Standards mean that last orders for dinner vary according to star rating and should be no earlier than:
★★ 7.00pm ★★★ 8.00pm ★★★★ 9.00pm
★★★★★ 10.00pm

BEBINGTON, Merseyside Map 15 SJ38

Travelodge Wirral
New Chester Rd CH62 9AQ
08700 850 950 0151 327 2489
Dir: *on A41, northbound off M53 junct 5*
Travelodge offers good quality, good value, modern accommodation. Ideal for families, the spacious, en suite bedrooms include remote-control TV, tea and coffee-making facilities and luxury beds. Meals can be taken at the nearby family restaurant. For further details consult the Hotel Groups page.
ROOMS: 31 en suite s fr £25; d fr £25

BECKENHAM, Greater London
See LONDON SECTION plan 1 G1

Innkeeper's Lodge
422 Upper Elmers End Rd BR3 3HQ
020 8650 2233
www.innkeeperslodge.com
Dir: *From M25 junct 6 Croydon, take A232 for Shirley. At West Wickham take A214 opposite Eden Park Station*
Smart rooms meet essential business requirements but also have home comforts, and depending on location may well have meeting rooms and pub dining. Dining options generally include all-day menus plus the added advantage of breakfast.
ROOMS: 24 en suite s £49-£62; d £49-£62

BECKINGTON, Somerset Map 04 ST85

★★68% *Woolpack Inn*
BA3 6SP
01373 831244 01373 831223
Dir: *on A36*
This charming coaching inn dates back to the 16th century and retains many original features including flagstone floors, open fireplaces and exposed beams. There is a cosy lounge and a choice of places to eat: the bar for light snacks and for more substantial meals the Oak Room or the Garden Room, which leads onto a pleasant inner courtyard.
ROOMS: 12 en suite in 1 bedroom **FACILITIES:** STV **CONF:** Thtr 30 Class 20 Board 20 **PARKING:** 16 **NOTES:** No children 5yrs
CARDS:

Travelodge
BA11 6SF
08700 850 950 01373 830251
Dir: *on A36*
Travelodge offers good quality, good value, modern accommodation. Ideal for families, the spacious, en suite bedrooms include remote-control TV, tea and coffee-making facilities and luxury beds. Meals can be taken at the nearby family restaurant. For further details consult the Hotel Groups page.
ROOMS: 40 en suite s fr £25; d fr £25

BEDFORD, Bedfordshire Map 12 TL04

★★★74% Woodlands Manor
Green Ln, Clapham MK41 6EP
0871 871 3248 0871 871 3249
e-mail: woodlands.manor@pageant.co.uk
web: www.pageant.co.uk/woodlands
Dir: *A6 towards Kettering. Clapham 1st village N of town centre. On entering village 1st right into Green Lane, Manor 200mtrs on right*
Sitting in acres of well-tended grounds, this Victorian manor offers a warm welcome. Bedrooms are spacious and well appointed providing a variety of thoughtful extras. Traditional public areas include a cosy bar and restaurant where award-winning food is served.

ROOMS: 30 en suite 3 annexe en suite (4 fmly) (10 GF) in 6 bedrooms s £85; d £105 (incl. bkfst) **LB** **FACILITIES:** STV Xmas **CONF:** Thtr 80 Class 40 Board 40 Del from £122.50 **PARKING:** 100 **NOTES:** in restaurant Civ Wed 90 **CARDS:**

★★★67% Corus Hotel Bedford
Cardington Rd MK44 3SA
0870 609 6108 01234 273102
e-mail: bedford@corushotels.com
Dir: *From M1 J13 follow A421 for approx 10m to A603 Sandy/Bedford exit, hotel on right at 2nd rdbt*

A tranquil location on the outskirts of Bedford, friendly staff and well-equipped bedrooms are the main attractions here. Cosy day rooms and two informal bars add to the appeal, while large windows in the restaurant make the most of the view over the river. The original barn now houses the conference and function suite.
ROOMS: 48 en suite (20 GF) in 16 bedrooms s £89; d £89 **LB** **FACILITIES:** STV Free use of local leisure centre (1mile) **CONF:** Thtr 120 Class 40 Board 40 Del from £90 **PARKING:** 90 **NOTES:** in restaurant Civ Wed 90 **CARDS:**

Innkeeper's Lodge Bedford
403 Goldington Rd MK41 0DS
0870 243 0500 & 01234 272707
01234 343926
www.innkeeperslodge.com
Dir: *on A428*
Smart rooms meet essential business requirements but also have home comforts, and depending on location may well have meeting rooms and pub dining. Dining options generally include all-day menus plus the added advantage of breakfast.
ROOMS: 47 en suite s £42-£49.95; d £42-£49.95 **CONF:** Thtr 25 Class 25 Board 20

Travel Inn
Priory Country Park, Barkers Ln MK41 9DJ
☎ 08701 977030 🖷 01234 325697
Dir: *M1 junct 13/A421/A6 towards Bedford then A428 signed Cambridge. Cross River Ouse & right at next rdbt, follow signs for Priory Country Park*
Travel Inn offers good-quality, value-for-money accommodation. Spacious, en suite rooms with bath and shower comfortably accommodate a family of up to two adults and two children (to age 15). The restaurant and bar offers a varied menu. For further details consult the Hotel Groups page.
ROOMS: 32 en suite s £45.95-£46.95; d £45.95-£46.95

Travelodge Bedford East
Black Cat Roundabout MK44 3OT
☎ 08700 850 950
Dir: *A1 North*
Travelodge offers good quality, good value, modern accommodation. Ideal for families, the spacious, en suite bedrooms include remote-control TV, tea and coffee-making facilities and luxury beds. Meals can be taken at the nearby family restaurant. For further details consult the Hotel Groups page.
ROOMS: 40 en suite s fr £25; d fr £25

BELFORD, Northumberland — Map 21 NU13

Blue Bell
Market Place NE70 7NE
☎ 01668 213543 🖷 01668 213787
e-mail: bluebel@globalnet.co.uk
web: www.bluebellhotel.com
Dir: *centre of village on left of St Mary's Church*
At the time of going to press, the star classification for this hotel was not confirmed. Please refer to the AA internet site www.theAA.com for current information.
ROOMS: 17 en suite (1 fmly) (1 GF) s £44-£49; d £44-£49 (incl. bkfst) LB **FACILITIES:** Riding Putt green Xmas **CONF:** Del from £60 **PARKING:** 16 **NOTES:** in restaurant
CARDS:

Purdy Lodge
Adderstone Services NE70 7JU
☎ 01668 213000 🖷 01668 213131
e-mail: james@purdylodge.co.uk
web: www.purdylodge.co.uk
Dir: *turn off A1 onto B1341 then immediately left*
Situated on the A1, this family-owned lodge provides convenient practical accommodation. All the bedrooms look out over fields towards Bamburgh Castle, and are quiet. Food is readily available in the attractive restaurant, the smart 24-hour café, or the cosy lounge bar.
ROOMS: 20 en suite **CONF:** Thtr 40 Class 30 Board 20

BELLINGHAM, Northumberland — Map 21 NY88

★★69% Riverdale Hall
NE48 2JT
☎ 01434 220254 🖷 01434 220457
e-mail: iben@riverdalehall.demon.co.uk
Dir: *turn off B6320, after bridge, hotel on left*
This hotel dates from 1866 and is located outside the village. It boasts its own cricket square and football pitch, and fishing on the Tyne. The well-equipped bedrooms are spacious and some have balconies. Meals are available in the bar or stylish restaurant, where local produce and Thai specialities feature on the menus.

ROOMS: 20 en suite (11 fmly) (3 GF) s £48-£54; d £88-£108 (incl. bkfst) LB **FACILITIES:** Fishing Sauna Putt green Cricket field ch fac Xmas **CONF:** Thtr 60 Class 40 Board 40 Del from £70
PARKING: 60 **NOTES:** in restaurant **CARDS:**

BELPER, Derbyshire — Map 11 SK34

★★★71% Makeney Hall Hotel
Makeney, Milford DE56 0RS
☎ 0870 609 6136 🖷 01332 842777
e-mail: makeneyhall@corushotels.com
Dir: *off A6 at Milford, signed Makeney. Hotel 0.25m on left*

This restored Victorian mansion stands in six acres of landscaped gardens and grounds above the River Derwent. Bedrooms vary in style and are generally very spacious. They are divided between the main house and the ground floor courtyard. Comfortable public rooms include a lounge, bar and spacious restaurant with views of the gardens.
ROOMS: 27 en suite 18 annexe en suite (8 fmly) in 15 bedrooms d fr £89 LB **FACILITIES:** STV Xmas **CONF:** Thtr 180 Class 80 Board 50 **SERVICES:** Lift **PARKING:** 150 **NOTES:** in restaurant Civ Wed 150
CARDS:

★★★62% The Lion Hotel & Restaurant
Bridge St DE56 1AX
☎ 01773 824033 🖷 01773 828393
e-mail: enquiries@lionhotel.uk.com
Dir: *8m NW of Derby, hotel on A6*
Situated in the centre of town and on the border of the Peak District, this 18th-century hotel provides an ideal base for exploring the many local attractions. The tastefully decorated bedrooms are well equipped and the public rooms include an

continued on p86

BELPER, continued

attractive restaurant and two cosy bars; a modern function suite also proves popular.

The Lion Hotel & Restaurant, Belper

ROOMS: 22 en suite (3 fmly) ⊗ in 7 bedrooms **FACILITIES:** STV Xmas **CONF:** Thtr 110 Class 60 Board 50 Del from £85 **PARKING:** 30 **NOTES:** ⊗ in restaurant Civ Wed 90 **CARDS:**

BELTON, Lincolnshire Map 11 SK93

★★★★75% De Vere Belton Woods

NG32 2LN

☎ 01476 593200 01476 574547

e-mail: belton.woods@devere-hotels.com

Dir: *A1 to Gonerby Moor services. Take B1174 towards Great Gonerby. At top of hill turn left towards Manthorpe/Belton. At T-junct left onto A607. Hotel 0.25m on left.*

Beautifully located amidst 475 acres of picturesque countryside, this is a destination venue for lovers of sport, and especially golf as well as being a relaxing executive retreat for seminars. Comfortable and well-equipped accommodation complements the elegant and spacious public areas, which provide a good choice of drinking and dining options. An onsite outdoor activity company is available.

ROOMS: 136 en suite (136 fmly) (68 GF) ⊗ in 117 bedrooms s £109-£135; d £125-£155 (incl. bkfst) **LB** **FACILITIES: Spa** STV 45 Fishing Squash Snooker Sauna Solarium Gym Putt green Jacuzzi Outdoor activity centre - quad biking, laser shooting etc ♫ ch fac Xmas **CONF:** Thtr 245 Class 180 Board 80 Del from £145 **SERVICES:** Lift **PARKING:** 350 **NOTES:** ⊗ in restaurant Civ Wed 80 **CARDS:**

BEMBRIDGE See Wight, Isle of

BERKELEY, Gloucestershire Map 04 ST69

★★66% The Old Schoolhouse Hotel & Restaurant

34 Canonbury St GL13 9BG

☎ 01453 811711 01453 511761

e-mail: oldschoolhouse@btopenworld.com

Dir: *0.5m off A38 next to Berkeley Castle. Follow tourist signs*

Situated just 10 minutes from the M5, this unique hotel is a conversion of a chapel and schoolhouse. Many original features have been retained. Bedrooms, all of a generous size, have extensive modern facilities, and public areas include a drawing room and dining room, both with crackling log fires in winter. The cooking is accomplished.

ROOMS: 10 rms (8 en suite) (1 fmly) (2 GF) ⊗ in all bedrooms s £60; d £72 (incl. bkfst) **LB** **CONF:** Class 12 Board 12 **PARKING:** 12 **NOTES:** ⊗ in restaurant **CARDS:**

★★61% The Malt House

22 Marybrook St GL13 9BA

☎ 01453 511177 01453 810257

e-mail: the-malthouse@btconnect.com

web: www.themalthouse.uk.com

Dir: *A38 into Berkeley, past Berkeley Castle on left. Into town & at town hall follow road to right. Hotel on right past hospital & opposite school.*

Conveniently located for both business and leisure travellers, this family-run inn offers a warm welcome and a convivial atmosphere. Soundly appointed bedrooms are equipped with contemporary comforts, while public areas include a choice of bars, a skittle alley and an attractive restaurant. Numerous local attractions are easily accessible, including Berkeley Castle and the Slimbridge Wildfowl and Wetlands Trust.

ROOMS: 9 en suite (2 fmly) ⊗ in 2 bedrooms s £58-£75; d £75-£85 (incl. bkfst) **FACILITIES:** Pool table Skittle Alley Dart board ♫ **PARKING:** 30 **NOTES:** **CARDS:**

BERKELEY ROAD, Gloucestershire Map 04 SO70

★★★65% *Prince of Wales*

Berkeley Rd GL13 9HD

☎ 01453 810474 01453 511370

e-mail: enquiries@theprinceofwaleshotel.com

Dir: *on A38, 6m S of M5 junct 13/6m N of junct 14*

Handily situated by the A38, this smartly presented hotel is convenient for major road networks. Bedrooms are generally a good size with a range of facilities. The public bar is popular with both residents and locals alike, whilst the restaurant menu features a selection of Italian dishes.

ROOMS: 43 en suite (2 fmly) ⊗ in 10 bedrooms **FACILITIES:** STV **CONF:** Thtr 200 Class 60 Board 60 **PARKING:** 150 **CARDS:**

BERWICK-UPON-TWEED, Northumberland Map 21 NT95

★★★70% Marshall Meadows Country House

TD15 1UT

☎ 01289 331133 01289 331438

e-mail: stay@marshallmeadows.co.uk

web: www.marshallmeadows.co.uk

Dir: *signed directly off A1, 300yds from Scottish Border*

This stylish Georgian mansion is set in wooded grounds flanked by farmland and has convenient access from the A1. A popular venue for weddings and conferences, it offers comfortable and well-equipped bedrooms. Public rooms include a cosy bar, a

continued

relaxing lounge and a two-tier restaurant, which serves imaginative dishes.

ROOMS: 19 en suite (2 fmly) ⊗ in 12 bedrooms s £80-£90; d £105-£150 (incl. bkfst) **LB** **FACILITIES:** Petanque Xmas **CONF:** Thtr 200 Class 120 Board 60 Del from £105 **PARKING:** 87 **NOTES:** ⊗ in restaurant Closed 15-27 Dec Civ Wed 200 **CARDS:**

See advert on this page

★★★64% King's Arms

43 Hide Hill TD15 1EJ
☎ 01289 307454 📠 01289 308867
e-mail: kingsarms.berwick@virgin.net
web: www.kings-arms-hotel.com
Dir: *follow town centre signs from A1. Hotel behind Guild Hall, on left of Hide Hill*

A hotel of contrasting styles, this former coaching inn boasts a bar and restaurant that are contemporary and trendy with menus to match. By contrast bedrooms are set on traditional lines but most are a good size.

ROOMS: 35 en suite (3 fmly) ⊗ in 20 bedrooms s £35-£79; d £60-£119 (incl. bkfst) **LB** **CONF:** Thtr 200 Class 100 Board 50 Del from £75 **NOTES:** ⊗ in restaurant Closed 24 Dec-14 Jan Civ Wed 150 **CARDS:**

★★64% Queens Head

Sandgate TD15 1EP
☎ 01289 307852 📠 01289 307858
e-mail: queensheadhotel@berwickontweed.fsbusiness.co.uk
Dir: *A1 towards centre & Town Hall, along High St. Turn right at bottom to Hide Hill, located next to cinema*

A small hotel, continuing to undergo a makeover, that is situated close to the old walls of this former garrison town. The cosy bar remains, but the reception lounge and restaurant have been transformed into modern stylish areas. Both provide an impressive choice of tasty freshly prepared dishes from a daily-changing blackboard menu. Bedrooms are being upgraded with pine furnishings.

ROOMS: 6 en suite (5 fmly) ⊗ in all bedrooms s £45; d £65 (incl. bkfst) **LB** **NOTES:** ⊗ in restaurant **CARDS:**

○ Travelodge (Berwick-upon-Tweed)

Travelodge

ROOMS: 40 en suite
NOTES: Due to open Nov 2004

Town House Hotel
Country House Hotel
Travel Accommodation

BEVERLEY, East Riding of Yorkshire

Map 17 TA03

★★★69% Tickton Grange

Tickton HU17 9SH
☎ 01964 543666 📠 01964 542556
e-mail: info@ticktongrange.co.uk
Dir: *3m NE on A1035*

A charming Georgian country house situated in four acres of private grounds and attractive gardens. Bedrooms are individual and decorated to a high specification. Pre-dinner drinks may be enjoyed in the comfortable library lounge, prior to enjoying fine, modern British cooking in the restaurant. The hotel has excellent facilities for both weddings and business conferences.

ROOMS: 17 en suite (2 fmly) (4 GF) in all bedrooms s £72; d £85 **LB** **CONF:** Thtr 200 Class 100 Board 80 Del from £120 **PARKING:** 65 **NOTES:** in restaurant RS 25-29 Dec Civ Wed 200 **CARDS:**

★★★67% The Beverley Arms Hotel

North Bar Within HU17 8DD
☎ 0870 609 6149 📠 01482 870907
e-mail: beverleyarms@corushotels.com
Dir: *opp St Marys Church. Left lane at lights just before North Bar. Hotel 100yds on left. Car park at rear*

This hotel has historic links to the highwayman Dick Turpin, and today features the spacious, flagstoned Shires Lounge, which includes the bar and several cosy sitting areas with a lounge menu. The attractively appointed restaurant also offers careful and friendly service. Bedrooms are all equipped with modern comforts and there are good parking facilities.

ROOMS: 56 en suite (4 fmly) in 41 bedrooms s £78-£90; d £78-£90 **LB** **FACILITIES:** Xmas **CONF:** Thtr 80 Class 40 Board 30 Del £112 **SERVICES:** Lift **PARKING:** 50 **NOTES:** in restaurant **CARDS:**

★★★67% Lairgate Hotel

30/32 Lairgate HU17 8EP
☎ 01482 882141 📠 01482 861067
e-mail: beverleylairgate@aol.com
Dir: *A63 towards town centre. Hotel 220yds on left (follow one-way system)*

Located just off the Market Square, this pleasing Georgian hotel has now been refurbished to offer stylish accommodation. Bedrooms are elegant and well equipped, and public rooms include a comfortable lounge, a lounge bar, and restaurant with a popular sun terrace.

ROOMS: 16 en suite (1 fmly) (2 GF) in 13 bedrooms s fr £65; d fr £90 (incl. bkfst) **LB** **CONF:** Thtr 50 Board 20 **PARKING:** 16 **NOTES:** in restaurant Civ Wed 80 **CARDS:**

★★74% Manor House

Northlands, Walkington HU17 8RT
☎ 01482 881645 📠 01482 866501
e-mail: info@walkingtonmanorhouse.co.uk
web: www.walkingtonmanorhouse.co.uk
Dir: *follow 'Walkington' signs from M62 junct 38. 4m SW off B1230. Through Walkington village, left at lights. Left at 1st x-roads. Approx 400yds on left*

This delightful country-house hotel is set in open country amid well-tended gardens. The spacious bedrooms have been attractively decorated and thoughtfully equipped. Public rooms include a conservatory restaurant and a very inviting lounge. A good range of dishes is available from two menus, with an emphasis on fresh and local produce.

ROOMS: 6 en suite 1 annexe en suite (1 fmly) (1 GF) s £75-£80; d £90-£110 **CONF:** Thtr 24 Class 16 Board 16 **PARKING:** 40 **NOTES:** in restaurant Closed 25 Dec-4 Jan RS Sun Civ Wed 40 **CARDS:**

BEWDLEY, Worcestershire

Map 10 SO77

★★67% *The George*

Load St DY12 2AW
☎ 01299 402117 📠 01299 401269
e-mail: enquiries@georgehotelbewdley.co.uk
Dir: *in town centre opposite town hall*

Situated in the heart of Bewdley, this friendly 16th-century inn features large oak beams, panelling, slate tiles and traditional fireplaces. Bedrooms are individually decorated and furnished to a good standard. Public areas include a coffee shop, function rooms, bars and a restaurant serving a wide-ranging menu.

ROOMS: 11 en suite **CONF:** Thtr 50 Class 50 Board 40 **PARKING:** 50 **NOTES:** in restaurant **CARDS:**

★★65% Black Boy

Kidderminster Rd DY12 1AG
☎ 01299 402119 📠 01299 402119
e-mail: rc@midnet.co.uk
web: www.blackboyhotel.co.uk
Dir: *follow town centre signs*

This privately-owned and personally-run 18th-century inn stands close to both the River Severn and the centre of this lovely old town. The Severn Valley Steam railway is also nearby. A good range of food is served in both the cosy restaurant and bar. The accommodation includes a two-bedroom unit, which is located in a separate house and is ideal for families.

ROOMS: 8 en suite (2 fmly) s £35-£45; d £50-£75 (incl. bkfst) **LB** **CONF:** Thtr 20 Class 20 Board 20 **PARKING:** 28 **NOTES:** in restaurant **CARDS:**

BEXLEY, Greater London

Map 06 TQ47

★★★★66% Bexleyheath Marriott Hotel

1 Broadway DA6 7JZ
☎ 0870 400 7245 📠 0870 400 7345
e-mail: bexleyheath@marriotthotels.co.uk
Dir: *M25 junct 2/A2 towards London. Exit at Black Prince junct onto A220, signed Bexleyheath. Left at 2nd set of lights into hotel*

Well-positioned for access to major road networks, this large, modern hotel offers spacious, air-conditioned bedrooms with a comprehensive range of extra facilities. Planters Bar is a popular venue for pre-dinner drinks and traditional English fare is served

continued

in the Copper Restaurant. The hotel also boasts a well-equipped leisure centre.
ROOMS: 142 en suite (16 fmly) ⊗ in 53 bedrooms s £99-£129; d £99-£149 **LB FACILITIES: Spa** STV supervised Solarium Gym Steam room, health & beauty Xmas **CONF:** Thtr 250 Class 120 Board 34 **SERVICES:** Lift air con **PARKING:** 77 **NOTES:** Civ Wed 40
CARDS:

BIBURY, Gloucestershire Map 05 SP10

★★★78% Swan

CLASSIC BRITISH

GL7 5NW
☎ 01285 740695 01285 740473
e-mail: info@swanhotel.co.uk
web: www.swanhotel.co.uk
Dir: *9m S of Burford A40 on B4425, 6M N of Cirencester A4179 on B4425*

The Swan Hotel, built in the 17th-century as a coaching inn, is set in peaceful, picturesque and beautiful surroundings. It now provides well-equipped and smartly presented accommodation, and public areas that are comfortable and elegant. There is a choice of dining options to suit all tastes.
ROOMS: 20 en suite (1 fmly) ⊗ in all bedrooms d £140-£220 (incl. bkfst) **LB FACILITIES:** Fishing Xmas **CONF:** Thtr 48 Class 10 Board 25 Del from £155 **SERVICES:** Lift **PARKING:** 22 **NOTES:** ⊗ in restaurant Civ Wed 48 **CARDS:**

See advert on this page

★★★74% Bibury Court

GL7 5NT
☎ 01285 740337 01285 740660
e-mail: info@biburycourt.com
web: www.biburycourt.com
Dir: *on B4425 beside the River Coln, behind St Marys Church*
Dating back to Tudor times, this elegant manor is the perfect antidote to the hustle and bustle of the modern world. Spacious public areas have abundant charm and character, while bedrooms offer solid quality and contemporary comfort. Seasonal produce is used to good effect in carefully prepared dishes served by a friendly team of helpful staff.
ROOMS: 18 en suite (3 fmly) (1 GF) s £115; d £135 (incl. cont bkfst) **LB FACILITIES:** Fishing **CONF:** Board 12 Del £200 **PARKING:** 100 **NOTES:** ⊗ in restaurant Civ Wed 32
CARDS:

See advert on this page

- Indoor Swimming Pool
- Indoor Swimming Pool (heated)
- Outdoor Swimming Pool
- Outdoor Swimming Pool (heated)

BICESTER, Oxfordshire — Map 11 SP52

★★★69%

Bignell Park Hotel & Restaurant

Chesterton OX26 1UE
☎ 01869 326550 📠 01869 322729
e-mail: enq@bignellparkhotel.co.uk
Dir: *M40 junct 9/A41 to Bicester, over 1st & 2nd rdbt, left at mini rdbt, follow signs to Witney A4095. Hotel 0.5m*

Situated in the pretty village of Chesterton, this friendly hotel offers a beamed restaurant, complete with gallery, in which an imaginative and varied menu is served. The spacious bedrooms are decorated in a contemporary style, each with a refurbished bathroom.

ROOMS: 23 en suite (1 fmly) (5 GF) s £70-£135; d £80-£145 (incl. bkfst) **FACILITIES:** STV Xmas **CONF:** Thtr 40 Class 16 Board 22 Del from £130 **PARKING:** 40 **NOTES:** ⊗ in restaurant Civ Wed 40
CARDS:

⌂ Travelodge (Cherwell Valley)

Moto Service Area, Northampton Rd, Ardley
OX6 9RD
☎ 08700 850 950 📠 01869 346390
Dir: *M40 junct 10*

Travelodge offers good quality, good value, modern accommodation. Ideal for families, the spacious, en suite bedrooms include remote-control TV, tea and coffee-making facilities and luxury beds. Meals can be taken at the nearby family restaurant. For further details consult the Hotel Groups page.

ROOMS: 98 en suite s fr £25; d fr £25 **CONF:** Thtr 40 Class 20 Board 20

BIDEFORD, Devon — Map 03 SS42

★★★69% **Royal**

Barnstaple St EX39 4AE
☎ 01237 472005 📠 01237 478957
e-mail: info@royalbideford.co.uk
web: www.royalbideford.co.uk
Dir: *at eastern end of Bideford Bridge*

A quiet and relaxing hotel, the Royal is set on the riverbank within five minutes' walk of the busy town centre and quay. Well-maintained public areas are bright and retain much of the charm and style of its 16th-century origins, particularly in the wood-panelled Kingsley Suite. Bedrooms are well equipped and comfortable. Dinner and lounge snacks are appetising.

ROOMS: 32 en suite (3 fmly) (2 GF) s £55-£75; d £65-£95 **LB** **FACILITIES:** STV ♫ ch fac Xmas **CONF:** Thtr 100 Class 100 Board 100 **SERVICES:** Lift **PARKING:** 70 **NOTES:** Civ Wed
CARDS:

★★74% **Yeoldon Country House**

Durrant Ln, Northam EX39 2RL
☎ 01237 474400 📠 01237 476618
e-mail: yeoldonhouse@aol.com
web: www.yeoldonhousehotel.co.uk
Dir: *A39 from Barnstaple over River Torridge Bridge. At rdbt turn right onto A386 towards Northam, then 3rd right into Durrant Lane*

In a tranquil location with superb views over the River Torridge and attractive grounds, the Yeoldon is a charming Victorian house. Bedrooms are individually decorated, some have balconies with breathtaking views and all are well equipped. The public rooms are full of character with many interesting features and artefacts.

continued

Dinner offers a daily-changing menu using fresh local produce in imaginative dishes.

ROOMS: 10 en suite ⊗ in all bedrooms s £65-£70; d £100-£115 (incl. bkfst) **LB** **PARKING:** 20 **NOTES:** ⊗ in restaurant Closed 24-27 Dec
CARDS:

BIDFORD-ON-AVON, Warwickshire — Map 10 SP15

★★★63% **Bidford Grange**

Stratford Rd B50 4LY
☎ 01789 490319 📠 01789 490998
e-mail: sales@bidfordgrange.com
Dir: *M42 junct 3 towards Studley & Alcester along bypass onto B439 through Bidford-on-Avon. Hotel on right.*

This pleasant hotel is situated by a golf course and is within easy driving distance of Stratford-upon-Avon. Staff are polite and friendly and there are two bars and a spacious dining room serving well-produced food.

ROOMS: 32 en suite 6 annexe en suite (10 GF) ⊗ in 10 bedrooms s fr £55; d fr £65 (incl. bkfst) **FACILITIES:** STV ⛳ 18 Fishing Snooker Putt green Xmas **CONF:** Del from £88 **PARKING:** 100 **NOTES:** Civ Wed **CARDS:**

BIGBURY-ON-SEA, Devon — Map 03 SX64

★★73% **Henley**

TQ7 4AR
☎ 01548 810240 📠 01548 810240
Dir: *through Bigbury, past Golf Centre into Bigbury-on-Sea. Hotel on left as road slopes towards shore*

Built in Edwardian times and complete with its own private cliff path to a sandy beach, this small hotel boasts stunning views from an elevated position. The Henley has an unhurried atmosphere which, when combined with its understated style, makes it a peaceful retreat and perfect for relaxation. The menu offers innovative dishes cooked with care using local produce.

ROOMS: 6 en suite (1 fmly) ⊗ in all bedrooms **PARKING:** 9 **NOTES:** ⊗ in restaurant Closed Nov-Mar
CARDS:

BILBROUGH, North Yorkshire — Map 16 SE54

⌂ Travel Inn (York South West)

Bilborough Top, Colton YO23 3PP
☎ 0870 238 3317 📠 01937 835934
Dir: *on A64 between Tadcaster & York*

Travel Inn offers good-quality, value-for-money accommodation. Spacious, en suite rooms with bath and shower comfortably accommodate a family of up to two adults and two children (to age 15). The restaurant and bar offers a varied menu. For further details consult the Hotel Groups page.

ROOMS: 59 en suite s £45.95-£46.95; d £45.95-£46.95
CONF: Thtr 20 Board 12

⌂ Travelodge York
Tadcaster LS24 8EG
☎ 08700 850 950 🖷 0870 1911685
Dir: *A64 eastbound*
Travelodge offers good quality, good value, modern accommodation. Ideal for families, the spacious, en suite bedrooms include remote-control TV, tea and coffee-making facilities and luxury beds. Meals can be taken at the nearby family restaurant. For further details consult the Hotel Groups page.
ROOMS: 62 en suite s fr £25; d fr £25

BILLINGHAM See Stockton-on-Tees

BILSBORROW, Lancashire — Map 18 SD53

⌂ Premier Lodge (Preston North)
Garstang Rd PR3 0RN
☎ 0870 9906410 🖷 0870 9906411
web: www.premierlodge.com
Dir: *M6 junct 32 on A6 towards Garstang*
High quality, modern, budget accommodation, ideal for families and business travellers. All rooms feature bath, power shower and satellite TV, and most have telephones / modem points. The adjacent bar and restaurant offers a wide and varied menu.
ROOMS: 40 en suite s £48; d £48

BINFIELD, Berkshire — Map 05 SU87

⌂ Travelodge Bracknell
London Rd RG12 4AA
☎ 08700 850 950 🖷 01344 485940
Dir: *M4 junct 10 (Bracknell) take 1st exit towards Binfield*
Travelodge offers good quality, good value, modern accommodation. Ideal for families, the spacious, en suite bedrooms include remote-control TV, tea and coffee-making facilities and luxury beds. Meals can be taken at the nearby family restaurant. For further details consult the Hotel Groups page.
ROOMS: 35 en suite s fr £25; d fr £25

BINGLEY, West Yorkshire — Map 19 SE13

⌂ Travel Inn (Bradford North)
Off Bradford Rd BD20 5NH
☎ 08701 977038 🖷 01274 551692
Dir: *M62 junct 27 follow signs for A650, then to Bingley Main Street. At next rdbt straight on 50mtrs on left*
Travel Inn offers good-quality, value-for-money accommodation. Spacious, en suite rooms with bath and shower comfortably accommodate a family of up to two adults and two children (to age 15). The restaurant and bar offers a varied menu. For further details consult the Hotel Groups page.
ROOMS: 40 en suite s £45.95-£46.95; d £45.95-£46.95

BIRCHANGER GREEN MOTORWAY SERVICE AREA (M11), Essex — Map 06 TL52

⌂ Days Inn Stansted
Birchanger Green, Bishop Stortford CM23 5QZ
☎ 01279 656477 🖷 01279 656590
e-mail: birchanger.hotel@welcomebreak.co.uk
web: www.welcomebreak.co.uk
Dir: *M11 junct 8*
This modern building offers accommodation in smart, spacious and well-equipped bedrooms, suitable for families and business

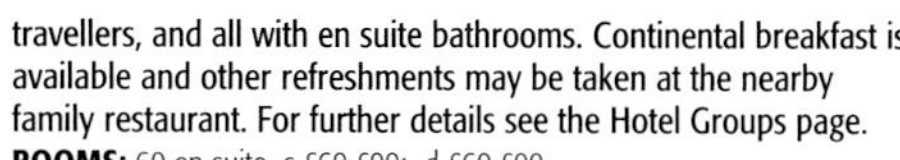

travellers, and all with en suite bathrooms. Continental breakfast is available and other refreshments may be taken at the nearby family restaurant. For further details see the Hotel Groups page.
ROOMS: 60 en suite s £69-£99; d £69-£99

BIRCH MOTORWAY SERVICE AREA (M62), Greater Manchester — Map 16 SD80

⌂ Travelodge Manchester North (Eastbound)
M62 Service Area East Bound OL10 2HQ
☎ 08700 850 950 🖷 0161 655 3716
Travelodge offers good quality, good value, modern accommodation. Ideal for families, the spacious, en suite bedrooms include remote-control TV, tea and coffee-making facilities and luxury beds. Meals can be taken at the nearby family restaurant. For further details consult the Hotel Groups page.
ROOMS: 55 en suite s fr £25; d fr £25

⌂ Travelodge Manchester North (Westbound)
M62 Service Area West Bound OL10 2HQ
☎ 08700 850 950 🖷 0161 655 6422
Travelodge offers good quality, good value, modern accommodation. Ideal for families, the spacious, en suite bedrooms include remote-control TV, tea and coffee-making facilities and luxury beds. Meals can be taken at the nearby family restaurant. For further details consult the Hotel Groups page.
ROOMS: 35 en suite s fr £25; d fr £25

BIRKENHEAD, Merseyside — Map 15 SJ38

★★★67% Riverhill
Talbot Rd, Prenton CH43 2HJ
☎ 0151 653 3773 🖷 0151 653 7162
e-mail: reception@theriverhill.co.uk
Dir: *1m from M53 junct 3, along A552. Turn left onto B5151 at lights hotel 0.5m on right*
Pretty lawns and gardens provide the setting for this friendly hotel, conveniently situated about a mile from the M53. Attractively furnished, well-equipped bedrooms include ground floor, family, and four-poster rooms. Business meetings and weddings can be catered for. A wide choice of dishes is available in the restaurant, overlooking the garden.
ROOMS: 15 en suite (1 fmly) **FACILITIES:** STV Free use of local leisure facilities **CONF:** Thtr 50 Class 30 Board 52 **PARKING:** 32 **NOTES:** Civ Wed 40 **CARDS:**

⌂ Premier Lodge (Wirral)
Greasby Rd CH49 2PP
☎ 0870 9906588 🖷 0870 9906589
web: www.premierlodge.com
Dir: *2m from M53 junct 2, just off B5139*
High quality, modern, budget accommodation, ideal for families and business travellers. All rooms feature bath, power shower and satellite TV, and most have telephones / modem points. The adjacent bar and restaurant offers a wide and varied menu.
ROOMS: 30 en suite s £50; d £50

continued

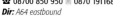

BIRMINGHAM, West Midlands Map 10 SP08
See also Bromsgrove, Lea Marston, Oldbury & Sutton Coldfield

Town House

★★★★ Hotel Du Vin & Bistro
25 Church St B3 2NR
☎ 0121 200 0600 0121 236 0889
e-mail: info@birmingham.hotelduvin.com
Dir: *M6 junct 6/A38(M) to city centre, over flyover. Keep left & exit at St Chads Circus signed Jewellery Quarter. At traffic lights & rdbt take 1st exit, follow signs for Colmore Row, opposite Cathedral. Right into Church St, across Berwick St. Hotel on right*
The former Birmingham Eye Hospital has undergone a dramatic transformation, with the Victorian structure now housing a chic, sophisticated hotel. Stylish, high-ceilinged rooms, all with a wine theme, are luxuriously appointed and feature stunning bathrooms, sumptuous duvets and Egyptian cotton sheets. The Bistro offers relaxed dining and a top-notch wine list, while other attractions include a champagne bar, a cigar and wine boutique and a health club.
ROOMS: 66 en suite s £120-£395; d £120-£395 **FACILITIES:** STV Snooker Sauna Solarium Gym Pool table Treatment rooms Xmas **CONF:** Thtr 80 Class 40 Board 40 Del from £190 **SERVICES:** Lift air con **NOTES:** in restaurant Civ Wed 60
CARDS:

★★★★71% Birmingham Marriott Hotel
Marriott HOTELS · RESORTS · SUITES
12 Hagley Rd, Five Ways B16 8SJ
☎ 0121 452 1144 0121 456 3442
e-mail: pascal.demarchi@whitbread.com
Situated in the suburb of Edgbaston, this Edwardian hotel is a prominent landmark on the outskirts of the city centre. Air-conditioned bedrooms are decorated in a comfortable, modern style and provide a comprehensive range of extra facilities. Public rooms include the contemporary, brasserie-style West 12 Bar and Restaurant.
ROOMS: 104 en suite in 60 bedrooms s fr £139; d fr £139 **LB** **FACILITIES: Spa** STV Solarium Gym Jacuzzi Beauty salon, Steam room Xmas **CONF:** Thtr 80 Board 35 Del from £140 **SERVICES:** Lift air con **PARKING:** 50 **NOTES:** Civ Wed 60
CARDS:

★★★★70% The Burlington
Burlington Arcade, 126 New St B2 4JQ
☎ 0121 643 9191 0121 628 5005
e-mail: mail@burlingtonhotel.com
web: www.burlingtonhotel.com
Dir: *M6 junct 6, follow signs for city centre, then onto A38*
The Burlington's original Victorian grandeur - marble and iron staircases, high ceilings - has been blended together with modern facilities. Bedrooms are equipped to a good standard and public areas include a stylish bar and coffee lounge. The Berlioz Restaurant specialises in innovative dishes using fresh produce.
ROOMS: 112 en suite (6 fmly) in 49 bedrooms **FACILITIES: Spa** STV Sauna Gym Jacuzzi Xmas **CONF:** Thtr 400 Class 175 **SERVICES:** Lift **NOTES:** Closed 25 Dec - 26 Dec Civ Wed
CARDS:

★★★★66% Copthorne Hotel Birmingham
COPTHORNE
Paradise Circus B3 3HJ
☎ 0121 200 2727 0121 200 1197
e-mail: reservations.birmingham@mill-cop.com
Dir: *M6/J6-City Centre A38(M). After Queensway tunnel emerge left, follow signs for International Convention Centre. Paradise Circus island - follow right lane - hotel in centre.*

This hotel is one of the few establishments in the city that benefits from its own car park. Bedrooms are spacious and come in a choice of styles, all with excellent facilities. Guests can enjoy a variety of dining options, including the contemporary menu in Goldies Brasserie.
ROOMS: 212 en suite in 108 bedrooms s £155; d £155-£195 **LB** **FACILITIES:** STV supervised Sauna Solarium Gym Jacuzzi Xmas **CONF:** Thtr 200 Class 120 Board 30 Del from £145 **SERVICES:** Lift **PARKING:** 88 **NOTES:** **CARDS:**

★★★79% Malmaison Birmingham
Malmaison
1 Wharfside St, The Mailbox B1 1RD
☎ 0121 246 5000 0121 246 5002
e-mail: birmingham@malmaison.com
Dir: *M6 junct 6, follow A38 towards B'ham, hotel within The Mailbox, signed from A38*
The 'Mailbox' development, of which this stylish and contemporary hotel is a part, incoporates the very best in fashionable shopping, an array of restaurants and ample car parking. Air-conditioned bedrooms are stylishly decorated and feature a great range of facilities. Public rooms include a stylish bar and brasserie which are already proving a hit with guests and locals alike.
ROOMS: 189 en suite in 132 bedrooms s £99-£129; d £99-£129 **FACILITIES: Spa** STV Sauna Gym Jacuzzi **CONF:** Thtr 40 Class 24 Board 24 Del £165 **SERVICES:** Lift air con
CARDS:

★★★70% The Westley
Best Western
80-90 Westley Rd, Acocks Green B27 7UJ
☎ 0121 706 4312 0121 706 2824
e-mail: reservations@westley-hotel.co.uk
web: www.westley-hotel.co.uk
Dir: *A41 signed Birmingham on Solihull by-pass, continue to Acocks Green. At rdbt, 2nd exit B4146 Westley Rd. Hotel 200yds on left*
Set in the city suburbs and conveniently located for the N.E.C and airport, this friendly hotel provides well-equipped, smartly

continued

B

presented bedrooms. In addition to the main restaurant, there is also a lively bar and brasserie together with a large function room.

ROOMS: 26 en suite 11 annexe en suite (1 fmly) ⊗ in 15 bedrooms s £71.50-£130; d £83.50-£180 (incl. bkfst) **LB** **FACILITIES:** STV Putt green ♫ **CONF:** Thtr 200 Class 80 Board 50 Del £129.50 **PARKING:** 150 **NOTES:** ⊗ in restaurant Civ Wed 200 **CARDS:**

See advert on this page

★★★67% Novotel Birmingham Centre

NOVOTEL

70 Broad St B1 2HT
☎ 0121 643 2000 ▤ 0121 643 9796
e-mail: h1077@accor-hotels.com

This large, modern, purpose-built hotel benefits from an excellent city centre location, with the bonus of secure car parking. Bedrooms are spacious, modern and well-equipped for business

continued

users. Four rooms have facilities for less able guests. Public areas include the Garden Brasserie, function rooms and a fitness room. **ROOMS:** 148 en suite (148 fmly) ⊗ in 98 bedrooms s £80-£145; d £155-£165 (incl. bkfst) **LB** **FACILITIES:** STV Sauna Gym Jacuzzi **CONF:** Thtr 300 Class 120 Board 90 Del from £85 **SERVICES:** Lift air con **PARKING:** 53 **CARDS:**

★★★66% *Corus hotel Birmingham South*

corus hotels

Redditch Rd, Hopwood B48 7AL
☎ 0870 609 6119 ▤ 0121 445 6163
e-mail: westmead@corushotels.com

Dir: *M42 junct 2 towards Birmingham on A441. At rdbt turn right and follow A441 for 1m. Hotel on right*

In a quiet location on the outskirts of the city, yet close to the M42, this hotel offers a number of meeting and conference rooms. The bedrooms are generally spacious, well equipped and

continued on p94

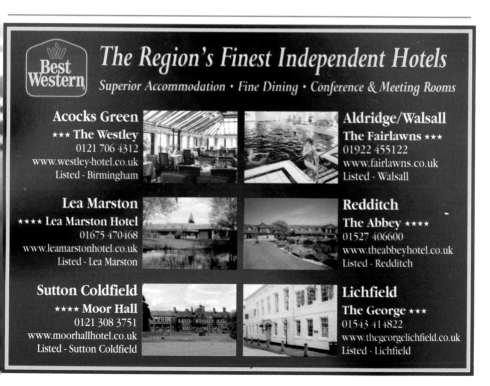

B

BIRMINGHAM, continued

comfortable. A bar offers carvery lunches, and dinner is served in the adjacent restaurant.
ROOMS: 58 en suite (2 fmly) ⊗ in 28 bedrooms **FACILITIES:** STV Sauna Solarium **CONF:** BC Thtr 220 Class 120 Board 80
PARKING: 155 **NOTES:** ⊗ in restaurant Civ Wed 120
CARDS:

★★★64% Jurys Inn Birmingham

JURYS DOYLE HOTELS

245 Broad St B1 2HQ
☎ 0121 626 0626 🖷 0121 626 0627
e-mail: jurysinn_birmingham@jurysdoyle.com
Dir: *on A456 (Broad St) in city centre.*
This large hotel is ideally located in the centre of the city and offers extensive conference facilities and is well equipped to cater for both leisure and business guests. Bedrooms are spacious and modern and the restaurant is designed for efficiency with a buffet-style operation.
ROOMS: 445 en suite (336 fmly) ⊗ in 325 bedrooms s £53-£125; d £53-£125 **FACILITIES:** STV **CONF:** Thtr 280 Board 44 Del from £120
SERVICES: Lift air con **PARKING:** 230 **NOTES:** ⊗ in restaurant Closed 24-26 Dec **CARDS:**

★★★64% The Plough & Harrow Hotel

corus hotels

135 Hagley Rd B16 8LS
☎ 0870 609 6118 🖷 0121 454 1868
e-mail: reservations@plough.co.uk
Dir: *from the city, A456 (Hagley Road). Hotel on right after rdbt*

This well-established hotel is approximately a mile west of the city centre, with a relaxed and friendly atmosphere. Bedrooms come in a variety of styles and sizes and the attractive garden restaurant offers a good selection of freshly prepared dishes. Free parking for residents is a bonus.
ROOMS: 44 en suite (5 fmly) (11 GF) ⊗ in 22 bedrooms s £99-£115; d £99-£135 **LB** **FACILITIES:** STV Xmas **CONF:** Thtr 70 Class 35 Board 35 Del from £105 **PARKING:** 90 **NOTES:** ⊗ in restaurant Civ Wed 100
CARDS:

★★★61% Great Barr Hotel & Conference Centre

Pear Tree Dr, Newton Rd, Great Barr B43 6HS
☎ 0121 357 1141 🖷 0121 357 7557
e-mail: sales@thegreatbarrhotel.co.uk
web: www.thegreatbarrhotel.co.uk
Dir: *M6 junct 7, at Scott Arms x-rds turn right towards West Bromwich (A4010) Newton Rd. Hotel 1m from Scotts Arms, on right*
This busy hotel, situated in a residential area, is particularly popular with business people. Bedrooms are well equipped and modern in style. There is a wide range of meeting rooms, a traditional oak-panelled bar and formal restaurant.

ROOMS: 105 en suite (6 fmly) ⊗ in 50 bedrooms **FACILITIES:** STV Xmas **CONF:** Thtr 200 Class 90 Board 60 Del from £105
PARKING: 200 **NOTES:** RS BH (restaurant may be closed) Civ Wed 200 **CARDS:**

★★72% Copperfield House

60 Upland Rd, Selly Park B29 7JS
☎ 0121 472 8344 🖷 0121 415 5655
e-mail: info@copperfieldhousehotel.fsnet.co.uk
Dir: *M6 junct 6/A38 through city centre. After tunnels, right at lights into Belgrave Middleway. Right at rdbt onto A441. At Selly Park Tavern, right into Upland Rd*
A delightful Victorian hotel, situated in a leafy suburb, close to the BBC's Pebble Mill Studios and within easy reach of the centre. Accommodation is smartly presented and well equipped; the executive rooms are particularly spacious. There is a lounge with honesty bar, and carefully prepared, seasonally-inspired food and a well-chosen wine list are offered.
ROOMS: 17 en suite (1 fmly) (2 GF) s £45-£75; d £60-£90 (incl. bkfst) **LB** **PARKING:** 11 **NOTES:** ⊗ in restaurant Closed 24 Dec - 2 Jan
CARDS:

★★68% Norwood

87-89 Bunbury Rd, Northfield B31 2ET
☎ 0121 411 2202 🖷 0121 477 7447
e-mail: norwoodhotel@aol.com
Dir: *left on A38 at Grosvenor shopping centre, 5m S of city centre*
This comfortable hotel provides well-equipped accommodation with several executive rooms. Pleasant public rooms enjoy an outlook over the pretty garden. Carefully prepared home-cooking is served in the attractive dining room.
ROOMS: 18 en suite s £50-£80; d £70-£80 (incl. bkfst) **LB**
FACILITIES: STV **CONF:** Thtr 40 Class 24 Board 20 **PARKING:** 11
NOTES: Closed 23 Dec-2 Jan **CARDS:**

★★66% Fountain Court

THE INDEPENDENTS

339-343 Fountain Court Hotel B17 8NH
☎ 0121 429 1754 🖷 0121 429 1209
e-mail: info@fountain-court.net
Dir: *on A456, towards Birmingham, 3 miles from M5 junct 3*
This family-owned hotel is on the A456, near to the M5 and a short drive from the city centre. Hospitality is excellent, the accommodation simple, and imaginative, home-cooked food is usually available.
ROOMS: 23 en suite (4 fmly) s £45-£48.50; d £65 (incl. bkfst)
PARKING: 20 **CARDS:**

★★63% Astoria
311 Hagley Rd B16 9LQ
☎ 0121 454 0795 ▤ 0121 456 3537
e-mail: anne@astoriahotel.uk.com
Dir: *on A456 2m from city centre*
This Victorian property stands between the city centre and the M5 motorway. Personally run, it provides simple yet spacious accommodation that includes some family and ground-floor rooms. There is a choice of lounges and a homely bar.
The traditionally furnished dining room serves a selection of grilled dishes.
ROOMS: 26 en suite (6 fmly) (5 GF) ⊘ in 2 bedrooms s £45-£49; d £55-£63 (incl. bkfst) **FACILITIES:** STV **CONF:** BC **PARKING:** 27 **NOTES:** ✗ ⊘ in restaurant **CARDS:**

★★63% *Comfort Inn Norfolk*

257/267 Hagley Rd, Edgbaston B16 9NA
☎ 0121 454 8071 ▤ 0121 455 6149
e-mail: admin@gb606.u-net.com
Dir: *M6 junct 8/A38 onto ringroad towards Kidderminster. After 4m right at rdbt, hotel on right*
Within easy access of the city centre, this large hotel is particularly popular with business travellers. The bedrooms vary both in size and style. Guests may use the leisure facilities at a nearby sister hotel. Evening meals are provided in the Headingley Restaurant.
ROOMS: 169 en suite (2 fmly) (30 GF) ⊘ in 45 bedrooms **FACILITIES:** STV **CONF:** Thtr 80 Class 50 Board 30 **SERVICES:** Lift **PARKING:** 90 **NOTES:** ✗ ⊘ in restaurant Civ Wed 80 **CARDS:**

⌂ Campanile

Aston Locks, Chester St B6 4BE
☎ 0121 359 3330 ▤ 0121 359 1223
e-mail: birmingham@envergure.co.uk
Dir: *next to rdbt at junct of A4540/A38*

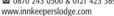

This modern building offers accommodation in smart, well-equipped bedrooms, all with en suite bathrooms. Refreshments may be taken at the informal Bistro. For further details consult the Hotel Groups page.
ROOMS: 109 en suite s fr £48.50; d fr £48.50 **CONF:** Thtr 150 Class 80 Board 55

⌂ *Hotel Ibis Birmingham Holloway*
55 Irving St B1 1DH
☎ 0121 622 4925 ▤ 0121 622 4195
e-mail: h2092@accor-hotels.com
Dir: *150yds from Dome Night Club, just off Bristol Street*
Modern, budget hotel offering comfortable accommodation in bright and practical bedrooms. Breakfast is self-service and dinner is available in the restaurant. For further details consult the Hotel Groups page.
ROOMS: 51 en suite

⌂ *Hotel Ibis Birmingham Bordesley*
1 Bordesley Park Rd, Bordesley B10 0PD
☎ 0121 506 2600 ▤ 0121 506 2610
e-mail: H2178@accor-hotels.com
Modern, budget hotel offering comfortable accommodation in bright and practical bedrooms. Breakfast is self-service and dinner is available in the restaurant. For further details consult the Hotel Groups page.
ROOMS: 87 en suite

⌂ Hotel Ibis Birmingham Centre

Arcadian Centre, Ladywell Walk B5 4ST
☎ 0121 622 6010 ▤ 0121 622 6020
e-mail: h1459@accor-hotels.com
Dir: *Follow signs to Birmingham city centre from all major motorways. Then follow signs for 'Markets Area' or 'Indoor Market', hotel next to market.*
Modern, budget hotel offering comfortable accommodation in bright and practical bedrooms. Breakfast is self-service and dinner is available in the restaurant. For further details consult the Hotel Groups page.
ROOMS: 159 en suite s £45.95-£59.95; d £45.95-£59.95 **CONF:** BC Thtr 100 Class 60 Board 40

⌂ Innkeeper's Lodge Birmingham West

563 Hagley Rd West, Quinton B32 1HP
☎ 0870 243 0500 & 0121 423 3895
www.innkeeperslodge.com

Dir: *M5 junct 3/A456 westbound. On opposite side of dual carriageway, accessed a short distance from rdbt*
Smart rooms meet essential business requirements but also have home comforts, and depending on location may well have meeting rooms and pub dining. Dining options generally include all-day menus plus the added advantage of breakfast.
ROOMS: 24 en suite s £45-£52.50; d £45-£52.50

⌂ Premier Lodge (Birmingham City Centre)
80 Broad St B15 1AU
☎ 0870 9906404 ▤ 0870 9906405

web: www.premierlodge.com
Dir: *M6 junct 6 onto A38 Aston Expressway and follow signs for the city centre, ICC and NIA then onto Broad St. T rt at lights and then take the 2nd lt at the rbt for Lodge on left*
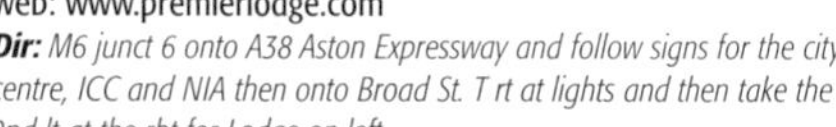
High quality, modern, budget accommodation, ideal for families and business travellers. All rooms feature bath, power shower and satellite TV, and most have telephones / modem points. The adjacent bar and restaurant offers a wide and varied menu.
ROOMS: 60 en suite s £56; d £56 **CONF:** Thtr 60

⌂ Premier Lodge (Birmingham South)

Birmingham Great Park, Ashbrook Drive, Parkway, Rubery B45 9PA
☎ 0870 9906538 ▤ 0870 9906539
web: www.premierlodge.com
Dir: *M5 junct 4 onto A38 towards Birmingham. Turn left into Birmingham Great Park, Lodge behind Safeway superstore*
High quality, modern, budget accommodation, ideal for families and business travellers. All rooms feature bath, power shower and satellite TV, and most have telephones / modem points. The adjacent bar and restaurant offers a wide and varied menu.
ROOMS: 62 en suite s £50; d £50 **CONF:** Board 12

> Packed in a hurry?
> Ironing facilities should be available at all star levels, either in rooms or on request

B

BIRMINGHAM, continued

⌂ Travel Inn (Birmingham Central East)

Richard St, Aston, Waterlinks B7 4AA
☎ 0870 238 3312 🖷 0121 333 6490
Dir: *On ring road A4540 at junct with A38(M). From M6 junct 6 take 2nd exit off A38(M), ring road, left at island, 1st left*
Travel Inn offers good-quality, value-for-money accommodation. Spacious, en suite rooms with bath and shower comfortably accommodate a family of up to two adults and two children (to age 15). The restaurant and bar offers a varied menu. For further details consult the Hotel Groups page.
ROOMS: 60 en suite s £45.95-£48.95; d £45.95-£48.95 **CONF:** Thtr 14

⌂ Travel Inn (Birmingham City Centre)

20 Bridge St B1 2JH
☎ 08701 977031 🖷 0121 633 4779
Dir: *From M6/M5/M42 follow signs for city centre. Bridge St off A456 (Broad Street). Turn left in front of Hyatt Hotel. Inn on right*

Travel Inn offers good-quality, value-for-money accommodation. Spacious, en suite rooms with bath and shower comfortably accommodate a family of up to two adults and two children (to age 15). The restaurant and bar offers a varied menu. For further details consult the Hotel Groups page.
ROOMS: 53 en suite s £52.95-£56.95; d £52.95-£56.95

⌂ Travelodge (Birmingham Central)

230 Broad St B15 1AY
☎ 08700 850 950 🖷 0121 644 5251
Travelodge offers good quality, good value, modern accommodation. Ideal for families, the spacious, en suite bedrooms include remote-control TV, tea and coffee-making facilities and luxury beds. Meals can be taken at the nearby family restaurant. For further details consult the Hotel Groups page.
ROOMS: 136 en suite s fr £25; d fr £25

⌂ Travelodge (Birmingham East)

A45 Coventry Rd, Acocks Green, Yardley B26 1DS
☎ 08700 850 950 🖷 0121 764 5882
Travelodge offers good quality, good value, modern accommodation. Ideal for families, the spacious, en suite bedrooms include remote-control TV, tea and coffee-making facilities and luxury beds. Meals can be taken at the nearby family restaurant. For further details consult the Hotel Groups page.
ROOMS: 40 en suite s fr £25; d fr £25

BIRMINGHAM AIRPORT, West Midlands Map 10 SP08

★★★ 67% Novotel Birmingham Airport

B26 3QL
☎ 0121 782 7000 🖷 0121 782 0445
e-mail: H1158@accor-hotels.com
Dir: *M42 junct 6/A45 to Birmingham, signed to airport. Hotel opposite main terminal*
This large, purpose-built hotel is located opposite the main passenger terminal. Bedrooms are spacious, modern in style and well equipped, including Playstations to keep the children busy. Two rooms have facilities for less able guests. The Garden Brasserie is open from noon until midnight and a full room service is available.
ROOMS: 195 en suite (31 fmly) ⊗ in 159 bedrooms s £125-£149; d £135-£159 (incl. bkfst) **FACILITIES:** STV **CONF:** BC Thtr 35 Class 20 Board 22 Del from £149 **SERVICES:** Lift air con
CARDS:

BIRMINGHAM (NATIONAL EXHIBITION CENTRE), West Midlands Map 10 SP18

★★★★ 73% ®
Crowne Plaza Birmingham NEC

National Exhibition Centre, Pendigo Way B40 1PS
☎ 0121 781 4000 🖷 0121 781 4321
e-mail: sales@cpbirminghamnec.com
Dir: *M42 junct 6, follow signs for NEC, take 2nd exit on left, South Way for hotel entrance 50mtrs on right*
Within walking distance of the NEC, this hotel has many attributes among which are the bar and restaurant facilities. The restaurant is run by celebrity chef Brian Turner and the bar is affiliated to the 606 jazz club in Chelsea. Bedrooms are air conditioned with duvet covered beds and well designed workstations. Leisure facilities include a gym and sauna.
ROOMS: 242 en suite ⊗ in 190 bedrooms **FACILITIES:** STV Sauna Solarium Gym ♫ **CONF:** BC Thtr 192 Class 114 Board 52 **SERVICES:** Lift air con **PARKING:** 180 **NOTES:** ✈ Civ Wed 70
CARDS:

★★★★ 68% Moor Hall

Moor Hall Dr, Four Oaks B75 6LN
☎ 0121 308 3751 🖷 0121 308 8974
e-mail: mail@moorhallhotel.co.uk
web: www.moorhallhotel.co.uk
(For full entry see Sutton Coldfield)

★★★★ 66% ®® Nailcote Hall

Nailcote Ln, Berkswell CV7 7DE
☎ 024 7646 6174 🖷 024 7647 0720
e-mail: info@nailcotehall.co.uk
web: www.nailcotehall.co.uk
(For full entry see Balsall Common)

> Early start?
> Hotels at all star levels should provide in-room alarm clocks and/or alarm calls

★★★68% **Arden Hotel & Leisure Club**
Coventry Rd, Bickenhill B92 0EH
THE INDEPENDENTS
☎ 01675 443221 ▯ 01675 445604
e-mail: enquiries@ardenhotel.co.uk
Dir: *M42 junct 6/A45 towards Birmingham. Hotel 0.25m on right, just off Birmingham International railway island*
This smart hotel neighbouring the NEC offers modern rooms and well-equipped leisure facilities. After dinner in the formal restaurant, the place to relax is the spacious lounge area. A buffet breakfast is served in the bright and airy Meeting Place.
ROOMS: 216 en suite (6 fmly) (6 GF) ⊘ in 105 bedrooms s fr £65; d fr £75 **FACILITIES:** STV supervised Snooker Sauna Solarium Gym Jacuzzi Steamroom ♫ Xmas **CONF:** Thtr 200 Class 40 Board 60 Del £150 **SERVICES:** Lift **PARKING:** 300 **NOTES:** ⊘ in restaurant Civ Wed 100 **CARDS:**
See advert on this page

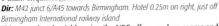

★★76% **Haigs**
Kenilworth Rd CV7 7EL
☎ 01676 533004 ▯ 01676 535132
e-mail: haiinfo@mistral.co.uk
(For full entry see Balsall Common)

★★67% **Heath Lodge**
117 Coleshill Rd, Marston Green B37 7HT
☎ 0121 779 2218 ▯ 0121 779 2218
e-mail: reception@heathlodgehotel.freeserve.co.uk
Dir: *M6 junct 4/A446 towards N Coleshill. After 0.5m turn left into Coleshill Heath Rd, signed to Marston Green. Hotel on right*
This privately-owned and personally-run hotel is ideally located for visitors to the NEC and Birmingham Airport. Hospitality and service standards are high and while some bedrooms are compact, all are well equipped and suitably comfortable. Public areas include a bar, a lounge and a dining room which overlooks the garden.
ROOMS: 17 rms (16 en suite) (1 fmly) s £49-£59; d £69-£77 (incl. bkfst) **CONF:** Thtr 20 Class 16 Board 14 **PARKING:** 22 **NOTES:** ⊘ in restaurant **CARDS:**

Premier Lodge (Birmingham NEC/Airport)
PREMIER LODGE.com
Bickenhill Parkway, Northway, National Exhibition Centre B40 3QE
☎ 0870 9906326 ▯ 0870 9906327
web: www.premierlodge.com
Dir: *M6 junct 4 follow A446 signed Warwick, exiting left after 0.5m signed NEC. At rbt take 2nd exit. At next rbt take 2nd exit onto Bickenhill Parkway and follow signs for Birmingham Airport then at the next rbt take 1st exit into Lodge*
High quality, modern, budget accommodation, ideal for families and business travellers. All rooms feature bath, power shower and satellite TV, and most have telephones / modem points. The adjacent bar and restaurant offers a wide and varied menu.
ROOMS: 199 en suite s £56; d £56 **CONF:** Class 12

Destination dining!
This symbol indicates a Restaurant with Rooms

BISHOP'S STORTFORD, Hertfordshire Map 06 TL42

★★★★71% **Down Hall Country House**
Hatfield Heath CM22 7AS
☎ 01279 731441 ▯ 01279 730416
e-mail: reservations@downhall.co.uk
Dir: *A1060, at Hatfield Heath keep left. Turn right into lane opposite Hunters Meet restaurant & left at end, follow sign*

This imposing Victorian country house hotel is set amidst 100 acres of mature grounds and is handy for Stansted Airport. Bedrooms are generally quite spacious; each one is pleasantly decorated, tastefully furnished and equipped with modern facilities. Public rooms include a choice of restaurants, a cocktail bar, two lounges and leisure facilities.
ROOMS: 99 en suite ⊘ in 81 bedrooms s fr £110; d fr £175 **LB**
FACILITIES: STV Snooker Sauna Putt green Jacuzzi Giant chess, Whirlpool Xmas **CONF:** Thtr 200 Class 140 Board 68 Del from £165 **SERVICES:** Lift **PARKING:** 150 **NOTES:** ⊘ in restaurant Civ Wed 120 **CARDS:**

BISHOPSTEIGNTON, Devon Map 03 SX97

★★65% Cockhaven Manor Hotel
Cockhaven Rd TQ14 9RF
☎ 01626 775252 01626 775572
e-mail: cockhaven.manor@virgin.net
Dir: *M5/A380, then A381 towards Teignmouth. Left at Metro Motors. Hotel 500yds on left*
A friendly, family run inn that dates back to the 16th century. Bedrooms are well equipped and many enjoy views across the beautiful Teign estuary. A choice of dining options is offered, and traditional and interesting dishes along with locally caught fish are popular with visitors and locals alike.
ROOMS: 12 en suite (2 fmly) ⊗ in 10 bedrooms s fr £35; d £55-£65 (incl. bkfst) **LB** **FACILITIES:** Petanque **CONF:** BC Thtr 50 Class 50 Board 30 **PARKING:** 50 **NOTES:** ⊗ in restaurant RS 26 Dec
CARDS:

BLACKBURN, Lancashire Map 18 SD62
See also Langho

★★★★65% Clarion Hotel & Suites Foxfields
Whalley Rd, Billington BB7 9HY
☎ 01254 822556 01254 824613
e-mail: enquiries@hotels-blackburn.com
Dir: *off A59 at signpost for Billington/Whalley & hotel 0.5m on right*
This modern, stylish hotel is easily accessible from major road networks. Bedrooms are comfortable and spacious, and include some suites and others with separate dressing areas. Facilities include a good-sized swimming pool, a small gym and conference suites. The traditional restaurant serves creative cuisine.
ROOMS: 44 en suite (27 fmly) (21 GF) ⊗ in 17 bedrooms s £89-£99; d £99-£112.50 (incl. bkfst) **LB** **FACILITIES:** STV Sauna Gym Steam room ♫ Xmas **CONF:** Thtr 180 Class 60 Board 60 Del £125
PARKING: 170 **NOTES:** ⊗ in restaurant Civ Wed 120
CARDS:

★★77% Millstone at Mellor
Church Ln, Mellor BB2 7JR
☎ 01254 813333 01254 812628
e-mail: info@millstonehotel.co.uk
Dir: *3m NW off A59*
Once a coaching inn, the Millstone is situated in a village just outside the town. The hotel provides a very high standard of accommodation, professional and friendly service and good food. Bedrooms, some in an adjacent house, are comfortable and generally spacious. All are very well equipped. A room for less able guests is available.
ROOMS: 18 en suite 6 annexe en suite (5 fmly) (8 GF) ⊗ in 10 bedrooms s £98-£108; d £98-£108 (incl. bkfst) **LB** **FACILITIES:** STV Xmas **CONF:** Thtr 25 Class 15 Board 16 **PARKING:** 40 **NOTES:** ⊗ in restaurant Civ Wed 60 **CARDS:**

Premier Lodge (Blackburn)
Myerscough Rd, Balderstone BB2 7LE
☎ 0870 9906388 0870 9906389
web: www.premierlodge.com
Dir: *M6 junct 31, A59 to Clitheroe opp British Aerospace*
High quality, modern, budget accommodation, ideal for families and business travellers. All rooms feature bath, power shower and satellite TV, and most have telephones / modem points. The adjacent bar and restaurant offers a wide and varied menu.
ROOMS: 20 en suite s £50; d £50 **CONF:** Board 12

BLACKPOOL, Lancashire Map 18 SD33

★★★★68% De Vere Herons' Reach
East Park Dr FY3 8LL
☎ 01253 838866 01253 798800
e-mail: reservations.herons@devere-hotels.com
Dir: *M6 junct 32/M55 junct 4/A583. At 4th traffic lights turn right into South Park Drive for 0.25m, right at mini-rdbt onto East Park Drive, hotel 0.25m on right*
Set in over 200 acres of grounds, this hotel is popular with both business and leisure guests. The pleasure beach is a few minutes' walk from the hotel, and the Lake District and Trough of Bowland are an hour away. Extensive indoor and outdoor leisure facilities include an 18-hole championship golf course. Bedrooms include a number of suites and smart, well-appointed clubrooms.
ROOMS: 172 en suite ⊗ in 70 bedrooms **FACILITIES:** STV supervised 18 Squash Snooker Sauna Solarium Gym Putt green Jacuzzi Aerobic studio, Beautyroom, Spinning Studio **CONF:** BC Thtr 650 Class 250 Board 70 **SERVICES:** Lift **PARKING:** 500 **NOTES:** ⊗ in restaurant Civ Wed 650 **CARDS:**

★★★★64% Imperial
North Promenade FY1 2HB
☎ 01253 623971 01253 751784
e-mail: imperialblackpool@paramount-hotels.co.uk
Dir: *M55 J2, take A583 North Shore, follow signs to North Promenade. Hotel on seafront, north of tower.*
Enjoying a prime seafront location, this grand Victorian hotel offers smartly appointed, well-equipped bedrooms and spacious, elegant public areas. Facilities include a smart leisure club; a comfortable lounge, the No.10 bar and an attractive split-level restaurant that overlooks the seafront. Conferences and functions are extremely well catered for.
ROOMS: 180 en suite (9 fmly) ⊗ in 80 bedrooms s £60-£130; d £120-£200 (incl. bkfst) **LB** **FACILITIES:** STV supervised Sauna Solarium Gym Jacuzzi Xmas **CONF:** Thtr 600 Class 240 Board 128 Del from £170 **SERVICES:** Lift **PARKING:** 150 **NOTES:** ⊗ in restaurant Civ Wed **CARDS:**

★★★70% Carousel
663-671 New South Prom FY4 1RN
☎ 01253 402642 01253 341100
e-mail: carousel@sleepwellhotels.com
Dir: *M55 follow signs to airport, pass airport to lights. Turn right, Hotel 100yds on right.*
This friendly seafront hotel, close to the Pleasure Beach, has undergone a complete refurbishment and offers smart, contemporary accommodation. Bedrooms are comfortably appointed and have a modern, stylish feel to them. An airy restaurant and a spacious bar/lounge both overlook the Promenade. The hotel boasts smart conference/meeting facilities and has its own car park.
ROOMS: 92 en suite (7 fmly) ⊗ in 28 bedrooms s £55-£65; d £75-£110 (incl. bkfst) **LB** **FACILITIES:** STV ♫ Xmas **CONF:** Thtr 80 Board 52 Del £110 **SERVICES:** Lift **PARKING:** 46 **NOTES:** ⊗ in restaurant Civ Wed 80 **CARDS:**

★★★67% Carlton
282-286 North Promenade FY1 2EZ
☎ 01253 628966 01253 752587
e-mail: reservations@carltonhotelblackpool.co.uk
web: www.carltonhotelblackpool.co.uk
Dir: *M6 junct 32/M55 follow signs for North Shore. Between Blackpool Tower and Gynn Sq*
Enjoying a prime seafront location, this hotel has been extensively

continued

refurbished throughout. Bedrooms are brightly appointed and modern in style. Public areas include an open-plan dining room and lounge bar, and a spacious additional bar where lunches are served. Ample parking is available.
ROOMS: 58 en suite ⊗ in 20 bedrooms s £55-£90; d £70-£110 (incl. bkfst) **LB** **FACILITIES:** STV Xmas **CONF:** Thtr 90 Class 40 Board 40 Del from £85 **SERVICES:** Lift **PARKING:** 43 **NOTES:** ⊗ in restaurant Civ Wed 80 **CARDS:**

★★★63% *Savoy*
Queens Promenade, North Shore FY2 9SJ
☎ 01253 352561 01253 595549
e-mail: events.savoy@macdonald-hotels.co.uk
Dir: *M6 junct 32, onto M55, cross rdbt on Yeadon Way follow signs to promenade, turn right, 2m to Gynn Sq, hotel on right*
This imposing hotel enjoys a prime seafront location on the North Promenade. Public areas are spacious and include a large, wood panelled, split-level dining room and open-plan lounge and bar area. The bedrooms vary in size and style. Conference and banqueting facilities are also available.
ROOMS: 131 en suite (17 fmly) ⊗ in 60 bedrooms **CONF:** Thtr 400 Class 100 Board 50 **SERVICES:** Lift **PARKING:** 46 **NOTES:** ⊗ in restaurant Civ Wed 250 **CARDS:**

★★70% Hotel Sheraton
54-62 Queens Promenade FY2 9RP
☎ 01253 352723 01253 595499
e-mail: email@hotelsheraton.co.uk
web: www.hotelsheraton.co.uk
Dir: *1m N from Blackpool Tower on promenade towards Fleetwood*
This family-owned and run hotel is situated at the quieter, northern end of the promenade. Public areas include a choice of spacious lounges with sea views, a large function suite where popular dancing and cabaret evenings are held, and a heated indoor swimming pool. The smartly appointed bedrooms come in a range of sizes and styles.
ROOMS: 104 en suite (45 fmly) s £25-£60; d £50-£120 (incl. bkfst & dinner) **LB** **FACILITIES:** Sauna Table tennis Darts ♫ Xmas **CONF:** Thtr 200 Class 100 Board 150 Del from £35 **SERVICES:** Lift **PARKING:** 20 **NOTES:** ⊗ in restaurant
CARDS:

See advert on this page

★★66% *Headlands*
611-613 South Promenade FY4 1NJ
☎ 01253 341179 01253 342657
e-mail: headlands@blackpool.net
Dir: *M55 & filter left, right at rdbt to Promenade, turn right & Hotel 0.5m on right*
This friendly, family owned hotel stands on the South Promenade, close to the Pleasure Beach and many of the town's major attractions. Bedrooms are traditionally furnished, many enjoying sea views. There is a choice of lounges and live entertainment is provided regularly. Home-cooked food is served in the panelled dining room.
ROOMS: 41 en suite (10 fmly) **FACILITIES:** Snooker Solarium Darts Games Room Pool Snooker ♫ **CONF:** Thtr 70 Class 70 **SERVICES:** Lift **PARKING:** 46 **NOTES:** ⊗ in restaurant Closed 2-15 Jan
CARDS:

★★65% *Belgrave Madison*
270-274 Queens Promenade FY2 9HD
☎ 01253 351570 01253 500698
This friendly, family-run hotel enjoys a seafront location at the quieter end of town. Thoughtfully equipped bedrooms vary in size and include family and four-poster rooms. Spacious public areas

continued

include a choice of lounges with views over the promenade, a bar lounge where guests can enjoy live entertainment and a bright restaurant.
ROOMS: 43 en suite (10 fmly) **FACILITIES:** **SERVICES:** Lift **PARKING:** 32 **NOTES:** ⊗ in restaurant **CARDS:**

★★60% Warwick
603-609 New South Promenade FY4 1NG
☎ 01253 342192 01253 405776
Dir: *M55 junct 4/A5230 for South Shore then right on A584, Promenade South*
This friendly hotel enjoys a seafront position close to the Pleasure Beach, making it particularly attractive to families. Traditionally furnished bedrooms are functional and offer economical accommodation for the cost conscious. Spacious public areas include a choice of lounges, a bar, restaurant and an indoor swimming pool.
ROOMS: 51 en suite (11 fmly) s £43-£80; d £86-£110 (incl. bkfst & dinner) **LB** **FACILITIES:** Pool ♫ Xmas **CONF:** Thtr 50 Class 24 Board 30 Del from £49 **SERVICES:** Lift **PARKING:** 24 **NOTES:** ⊗ in restaurant Closed Jan **CARDS:**

⌂ Premier Lodge (Blackpool)
Whitehills Park, Preston New Rd FY4 5NZ

☎ 0870 9906608 0870 9906609
web: www.premierlodge.com
Dir: *M55 junct 4, 1st left off rdbt, lodge on right*
High quality, modern, budget accommodation, ideal for families and business travellers. All rooms feature bath, power shower and satellite TV, and most have telephones / modem points. The adjacent bar and restaurant offers a wide and varied menu.
ROOMS: 81 en suite s £48; d £48

BLACKPOOL, continued

⌂ Travel Inn Blackpool (South)

Yeadon Way, South Shore FY1 6BF
☎ 08701 977032 ⎙ 01253 343805
Dir: *M55, follow signs for central car park/coach area. Located next to Total garage*
Travel Inn offers good-quality, value-for-money accommodation. Spacious, en suite rooms with bath and shower comfortably accommodate a family of up to two adults and two children (to age 15). The restaurant and bar offers a varied menu. For further details consult the Hotel Groups page.
ROOMS: 79 en suite s £45.95-£46.95; d £45.95-£46.95 **CONF:** Thtr 40

⌂ Travel Inn (Blackpool Airport)

Squires Gare Ln FY4 2QS
☎ 08701 977034 ⎙ 01253 362413
Dir: *M55 junct 4/A5230 & turn left at 1st rdbt towards airport. Travel Inn is just before Squires Gate railway station*
Travel Inn offers good-quality, value-for-money accommodation. Spacious, en suite rooms with bath and shower comfortably accommodate a family of up to two adults and two children (to age 15). The restaurant and bar offers a varied menu. For further details consult the Hotel Groups page.
ROOMS: 39 en suite s £45.95-£46.95; d £45.95-£46.95 **CONF:** Thtr 15 Board 8

⌂ Travel Inn (Blackpool Bispham)

Devonshire Rd, Bispham FY2 0AR
☎ 08701 977033 ⎙ 01253 590498
Dir: *M55 junct 4 right onto A583. At 5th set of lights turn right (Whitegate Drive) for approx 4-5 miles onto Devonshire Rd (A587)*
Travel Inn offers good-quality, value-for-money accommodation. Spacious, en suite rooms with bath and shower comfortably accommodate a family of up to two adults and two children (to age 15). The restaurant and bar offers a varied menu. For further details consult the Hotel Groups page.
ROOMS: 39 en suite s £45.95-£46.95; d £45.95-£46.95 **CONF:** Thtr 50 Board 20

BLAKENEY, Norfolk Map 13 TG04

★★★75% The Blakeney

The Quay NR25 7NE
☎ 01263 740797 ⎙ 01263 740795
e-mail: reception@blakeney-hotel.co.uk
web: www.blakeney-hotel.co.uk
Dir: *off A149 coast road, 8m W of Sheringham*
A traditional privately-owned hotel situated on the quayside with superb views across the estuary and the salt marshes to Blakeney Point. Public rooms feature an elegant restaurant, ground floor lounge, bar and a further first floor sun lounge overlooking the harbour. Bedrooms vary in size and style and all are smartly decorated and equipped with modern facilities, some have lovely sea views.
ROOMS: 49 en suite 10 annexe en suite (11 fmly) (10 GF) ⊘ in all bedrooms s £82-£132; d £164-£264 (incl. bkfst & dinner) **LB**
FACILITIES: Spa Snooker Sauna Gym Jacuzzi Table tennis Xmas
CONF: Thtr 100 Class 78 Board 112 Del from £108 **SERVICES:** Lift
PARKING: 60 **NOTES:** ⊘ in restaurant
CARDS:

For central reservation numbers and more information on Hotel Groups, turn to pages 33-39

Top 200 – Hotel

★★ Morston Hall

Morston, Holt NR25 7AA
☎ 01263 741041 ⎙ 01263 740419
e-mail: reception@morstonhall.com
web: www.morstonhall.com
Dir: *1m W of Blakeney on A149 Kings Lynn/Cromer Rd coastal road*
This delightful 17th-century country house hotel enjoys a tranquil setting amid well-tended gardens. The comfortable public rooms offer a choice of attractive lounges and a sunny conservatory, while the elegant dining room is a perfect setting to enjoy Galton Blackiston's award-winning cuisine. The spacious bedrooms are individually decorated and stylishly furnished with modern opulence.
ROOMS: 7 en suite (1 GF) s £130-£145; d £230-£240 (incl. bkfst & dinner) **LB FACILITIES:** ch fac **PARKING:** 40 **NOTES:** ⊘ in restaurant Closed 1 Jan-2 Feb
CARDS:

★★73% The Pheasant

Coast Rd, Kelling NR25 7EG
☎ 01263 588382 ⎙ 01263 588101
e-mail: enquiries@pheasanthotelnorfolk.co.uk
Dir: *on A419 coast road, mid-way between Sheringham & Blakeney*
Popular hotel ideally situated on the main road amidst landscaped grounds. Bedrooms are split between the main house and a modern wing of spacious rooms to the rear of the property. Public rooms include a busy lounge bar, a residents' lounge and a large restaurant where a wide-ranging selection of appetising dishes is served.
ROOMS: 30 rms (27 en suite) ⊘ in all bedrooms s £53; d £86-£96 (incl. bkfst) **LB FACILITIES:** Xmas **CONF:** Thtr 80 Class 50 Board 50
PARKING: 80 **NOTES:** ⊘ in restaurant **CARDS:**

★★68% Blakeney Manor

The Quay, Blakeney NR25 7ND
☎ 01263 740376 ⎙ 01263 741116
e-mail: reception@blakeneymanor.co.uk
Dir: *turn off A149 at Blakeney towards Blakeney Quay. Hotel at end of quay between Mariner's Hill & Friary Hills*
An attractive Norfolk-flint building overlooking Blakeney Marshes and within easy walking distance of the quayside. The bedrooms have been sympathetically converted from flint-faced barns and are located in courtyards adjacent to the main building. The spacious public rooms include a choice of lounges, a conservatory, popular bar and a large restaurant offering an interesting choice of dishes.
ROOMS: 8 en suite 29 annexe en suite (26 GF) **FACILITIES:** Xmas
PARKING: 40 **NOTES:** No children 14yrs ⊘ in restaurant Closed 4-25 Jan **CARDS:**

BLANCHLAND, Northumberland — Map 18 NY95

★★69% Lord Crewe Arms
DH8 9SP
☎ 01434 675251 Fax 01434 675337
e-mail: lord@crewearms.freeserve.co.uk
web: www.lordcrewehotel.com
Dir: *10m S of Hexham via B6306*

Adjacent to Blanchland Abbey, many rooms in this historic, monastic hotel date from medieval times. Public areas feature flagstone floors, vaulted ceilings and original inglenook fireplace. Bedrooms, some of which are housed in what was the village's second hotel, are well-equipped, and retain a period style. Bar meals are popular and there is an elegant restaurant.

ROOMS: 9 en suite 10 annexe en suite (2 fmly) **FACILITIES:** Xmas **CONF:** Thtr 20 Class 16 Board 16 **NOTES:** Civ Wed 65 **CARDS:**

BLANDFORD FORUM, Dorset — Map 04 ST80

★★★71% Crown

West St DT11 7AJ
☎ 01258 456626 Fax 01258 451084
Dir: *100mtrs from town bridge*

Efficient and friendly service is provided at this attractive, former coaching inn. The well-equipped, stylish bedrooms are very comfortable and have now been refurbished to a high standard. A choice of menus is offered in the panelled dining room, while in the bar an extensive range of meals is served in a less formal atmosphere.

ROOMS: 32 en suite (2 fmly) ⊗ in 27 bedrooms s £75; d £98 (incl. bkfst) **LB** **FACILITIES:** STV **CONF:** BC Thtr 250 Class 200 Board 60 Del from £100 **SERVICES:** Lift **PARKING:** 144 **NOTES:** Closed 25-28 Dec Civ Wed 150 **CARDS:**

BLOCKLEY, Gloucestershire — Map 10 SP13

A ★★★ Crown Inn & Hotel
High St GL56 9EX
☎ 01386 700245 Fax 01386 700247
e-mail: info@crown-inn-blockley.co.uk

ROOMS: 22 en suite 2 annexe en suite (7 fmly) (8 GF) s £54.95-£74.95; d £39.95-£59.95 (incl. bkfst) **LB** **FACILITIES:** Xmas **CONF:** Thtr 50 Class 36 Board 20 Del from £115 **PARKING:** 30 **NOTES:** ⊗ in restaurant **CARDS:**

> Popped the question?
> Hotels with Civ Wed in their entry are licensed for civil wedding ceremonies. Maximum numbers for the ceremony only are shown, e.g. Civ Wed 120

BLYTH, Nottinghamshire — Map 16 SK68

★★★70% Charnwood
Sheffield Rd S81 8HF
☎ 01909 591610 Fax 01909 591429
e-mail: reception@charnwood-hotel.com
web: www.bw-charnwoodhotel.com
Dir: *A614 into Blyth village, right past church onto A634 Sheffield road. Hotel 0.5m on right past humpback bridge*

This hotel enjoys a rural setting, surrounded by attractive gardens complete with a pond. Bedrooms are comfortably furnished and attractively decorated. A range of carefully prepared meals and snacks is offered in the restaurant, or in the comfortable lounge bar overlooking the gardens. Service is both friendly and attentive.

ROOMS: 34 en suite (1 fmly) ⊗ in 16 bedrooms s £65-£75; d £77-£85 (incl. bkfst) **LB** **FACILITIES:** STV Mini-gym **CONF:** Thtr 135 Class 60 Board 45 Del from £110.95 **PARKING:** 70 **NOTES:** ⊗ in restaurant Civ Wed 100 **CARDS:**

⌂ Travelodge
Hilltop Roundabout S81 8HG
☎ 08700 850 950 Fax 01909 591831
Dir: *at junct of A1M/A614*

Travelodge offers good quality, good value, modern accommodation. Ideal for families, the spacious, en suite bedrooms include remote-control TV, tea and coffee-making facilities and luxury beds. Meals can be taken at the nearby family restaurant. For further details consult the Hotel Groups page.

ROOMS: 38 en suite s fr £25; d fr £25

BODMIN, Cornwall & Isles of Scilly — Map 02 SX06

★★75% Trehellas House Hotel & Restaurant
Washaway PL30 3AD
☎ 01208 72700 & 74499 Fax 01208 73336
e-mail: christico@btinternet.com
web: www.trehellashouse.co.uk
Dir: *take A389 from Bodmin towards Wadebridge. Hotel on right 0.5m beyond turning for Camelford*

This 18th-century former posting inn retains many original features, with contemporary additions, and offers comfortable accommodation. Bedrooms are located in the main house and adjacent coach house; all provide the same high standards. An interesting choice of cuisine is offered in the impressive slate-floored restaurant, with an emphasis on locally sourced produce.

ROOMS: 4 en suite 7 annexe en suite (2 fmly) (5 GF) ⊗ in all bedrooms s £47.50-£90; d £87.50-£195 (incl. bkfst) **LB** **FACILITIES:** **CONF:** Thtr 12 Board 12 Del from £85 **PARKING:** 30 **NOTES:** No children 10yrs ⊗ in restaurant Closed 24 Dec-31 Dec **CARDS:**

BODMIN, continued

★★67% Westberry
Rhind St PL31 2EL
☎ 01208 72772 📠 01208 72212
e-mail: westberry@btconnect.com
web: www.westberryhotel.net
Dir: *on ring road off A30 & A38. St Petroc's Church on right, at mini rdbt turn right. Hotel on right*

This popular hotel is conveniently located for both Bodmin town centre and the A30. Bedrooms are comfortably furnished and well equipped and include a four-poster room. A spacious bar lounge and a billiard room are also provided. The restaurant serves a variety of dishes, ranging from bar snacks to a more extensive carte.
ROOMS: 14 en suite 12 annexe en suite (1 fmly) (4 GF) ⊗ in 11 bedrooms s £48-£58; d £68-£78 (incl. bkfst) **LB** **FACILITIES:** STV Snooker Gym Full sized snooker table **CONF:** BC Thtr 100 Class 80 Board 80 **PARKING:** 30 **NOTES:** ⊗ in restaurant
CARDS:

Travel Inn Bodmin
Launceston Rd PL31 2AR
☎ 08701 977107 📠 08701 977705
Dir: *1m N of town on A389. From A30 S/bound exit onto A389, lodge 0.5m on right. N/bound exit onto A38, follow A389 signs. At t-junct turn left*
Travel Inn offers good-quality, value-for-money accommodation. Spacious, en suite rooms with bath and shower comfortably accommodate a family of up to two adults and two children (to age 15). The restaurant and bar offers a varied menu. For further details consult the Hotel Groups page.
ROOMS: 44 en suite (incl. bkfst) s £45.95-£46.95; d £45.95-£46.95

Late for dinner?
Quality Standards mean that last orders for dinner vary according to star rating and should be no earlier than:
★★ 7.00pm ★★★ 8.00pm ★★★★ 9.00pm
★★★★★ 10.00pm

BOGNOR REGIS, West Sussex Map 06 SZ99

★★★64% The Inglenook
255 Pagham Rd, Nyetimber PO21 3QB
☎ 01243 262495 & 265411 📠 01243 262668
e-mail: reception@the-inglenook.com
Dir: *A27 to Vinnetrow Rd left at Walnut Tree 2.5m on right*
This 16th-century inn retains much of its original character, including exposed beams throughout. Bedrooms are individually decorated and vary in size. There is a cosy lounge, a well-kept garden and a bar (complete with a parrot and two cats) that offers a popular evening menu and convivial atmosphere. The restaurant, overlooking the garden, also serves enjoyable cuisine.

ROOMS: 18 en suite (1 fmly) (2 GF) ⊗ in all bedrooms s £50-£70; d £70-£200 (incl. bkfst) **LB** **FACILITIES:** STV Xmas **CONF:** BC Thtr 100 Class 50 Board 50 Del from £95 **PARKING:** 35 **NOTES:** ⊗ in restaurant Civ Wed 80 **CARDS:**

★★71% Beachcroft
Clyde Rd, Felpham Village PO22 7AH
☎ 01243 827142 📠 01243 863500
e-mail: reservations@beachcroft-hotel.co.uk
web: www.beachcroft-hotel.co.uk
Dir: *off A259 at Butlins rdbt into Felpham Village. In 800mtrs right into Sea Rd then 2nd left into Clyde Rd*
This popular family-run hotel overlooks a secluded part of the sea front. Bedrooms are bright and spacious with a good range of facilities, and leisure facilities include a heated indoor swimming pool. Diners may choose from the varied choice of the traditional restaurant menus or the more informal cosy bar.
ROOMS: 34 en suite (4 fmly) (6 GF) s £50-£68; d £60-£98 (incl. bkfst) **LB** **FACILITIES:** STV **CONF:** Thtr 60 Class 30 Board 30 Del from £84.25 **PARKING:** 27 **NOTES:** ⊗ in restaurant
CARDS:

A ★★ The Royal
The Esplanade PO21 1SZ
☎ 01243 864665 📠 863175
Dir: *opposite Bognor Pier, 300yds from town centre*
ROOMS: 22 en suite (3 fmly) s £35-£50; d £60-£80 (incl. bkfst) **LB** **FACILITIES:** Xmas **CONF:** Thtr 60 Class 30 Board 30 **SERVICES:** Lift
CARDS:

Action for Blind People Hotel

The Russell
King's Pde PO21 2QP
☎ 01243 871300
e-mail: russell_hotel@afbp.org
Dir: *A27 follow signs for town centre. Hotel on seafront*
In a pleasant location close to the seafront, the Russell Hotel offers large and well-appointed bedrooms, many with sea views. The hotel caters for the specific needs of blind and partially sighted people, their friends, relatives, carers and guide dogs as well as welcoming sighted guests. The hotel also provides entertainment on some evenings.
ROOMS: 41 rms (40 en suite) (4 fmly) ⊗ in all bedrooms **FACILITIES:** Gym Putt green ♫ **SERVICES:** Lift **PARKING:** 12 **NOTES:** ⊗ in restaurant **CARDS:**

Premier Lodge (Bognor Regis)
PREMIER LODGE.com
Shripney Rd PO22 9PA
☎ 0870 9906434 0870 9906435
web: www.premierlodge.com
Dir: *from the A27 take the Bognor Regis exit at the rbut with the junct of A29. Continue on the A29 for approx 4m and the Premier Lodge is on the left*
High quality, modern, budget accommodation, ideal for families and business travellers. All rooms feature bath, power shower and satellite TV, and most have telephones / modem points. The adjacent bar and restaurant offers a wide and varied menu.
ROOMS: 24 en suite s £50; d £50 **CONF:** Thtr 80 Class 40 Board 30

BOLTON, Greater Manchester — Map 15 SD70

★★★★71% *Last Drop Hotel*
MACDONALD HOTELS
The Last Drop Village & Hotel, Bromley Cross BL7 9PZ
☎ 01204 591131 01204 304122
e-mail: lastdrop@macdonald-hotels.co.uk
Dir: *3m N of Bolton off B5472*

Built along the lines of a small self-contained village, this resort complex includes a variety of shops, a pub, a steak house, a bakery and a tearoom. Bedrooms are varied, with some cottage-style accommodation located around a delightful courtyard.
A dazzling, fully equipped spa and extensive conference facilities make this an ideal business or leisure destination.
ROOMS: 118 en suite 10 annexe en suite (72 fmly) (36 GF) ⊗ in 60 bedrooms **FACILITIES:** STV Snooker Craft shops, Leisure facilities re-open Feb 2004 ♫ **CONF:** Thtr 700 Class 350 Board 95 **SERVICES:** Lift **PARKING:** 400 **NOTES:** ⊗ in restaurant Civ Wed 500 **CARDS:**

See advert under MANCHESTER

★★★71% Egerton House
Blackburn Rd, Egerton BL7 9PL
☎ 01204 307171 01204 593030
e-mail: reservation@egertonhouse-hotel.co.uk
Dir: *from M61 take A666 Bolton Rd continue beyond Asda on right. Hotel 500yds on right.*
Peace and relaxation come as standard at this popular hotel, nestling in acres of well-tended woodland gardens. The location offers the best of both worlds, close to the City of Manchester and also the natural beauty of the West Pennine Moors. Public rooms and many guest bedrooms enjoy delightful garden views.

ROOMS: 32 en suite (7 fmly) ⊗ in 20 bedrooms s £75-£95; d £98-£108 (incl. bkfst) **FACILITIES:** STV Complimentary use of nearby leisure club Xmas **CONF:** Thtr 150 Class 90 Board 60 Del from £120 **PARKING:** 120 **NOTES:** ⊗ in restaurant Civ Wed 150 **CARDS:**

Travel Inn
travel inn
991 Chorley New Rd, Horwich BL6 4BA
☎ 08701 977282 01204 692585
Dir: *M61junct 6 follow dual carriageway to Bolton/Horwich with Reebok Stadium on left, continue & Inn on 2nd rdbt*
Travel Inn offers good-quality, value-for-money accommodation. Spacious, en suite rooms with bath and shower comfortably accommodate a family of up to two adults and two children (to age 15). The restaurant and bar offers a varied menu. For further details consult the Hotel Groups page.
ROOMS: 40 en suite s £45.95-£46.95; d £45.95-£46.95

Travelodge Bolton West
Travelodge
Bolton West Service Area, Horwich BL6 5UZ
☎ 08700 850 950 01204 668585
Travelodge offers good quality, good value, modern accommodation. Ideal for families, the spacious, en suite bedrooms include remote-control TV, tea and coffee-making facilities and luxury beds. Meals can be taken at the nearby family restaurant. For further details consult the Hotel Groups page.
ROOMS: 32 en suite s fr £25; d fr £25 **CONF:** Thtr 60 Class 60 Board 30

B

BOLTON ABBEY, North Yorkshire Map 19 SE05

Top 200 – Hotel

★★★ The Devonshire Arms Country House
BD23 6AJ
☎ 01756 710441 01756 710564
e-mail: reservations@thedevonshirearms.co.uk
web: www.devonshirehotels.co.uk
Dir: *on B6160, 250yds N of junct with A59*
With stunning views of the Wharfedale countryside, this beautiful hotel, owned by the Duke and Duchess of Devonshire, dates back to the 17th century. Bedrooms are elegantly furnished; those in the old part of the house are particularly spacious, complete with four-posters and fine antiques. The sitting rooms are delightfully cosy with log fires and dedicated staff deliver service with a blend of friendliness and professionalism. The Burlington Restaurant offers highly accomplished dishes, while the brasserie provides a lighter alternative.
ROOMS: 41 en suite (18 GF) in 12 bedrooms s £160-£380; d £220-£380 (incl. bkfst) **LB FACILITIES:** supervised Fishing Sauna Solarium Gym Putt green Jacuzzi Laser pigeon shooting, Falconry ch fac Xmas **CONF:** Thtr 90 Class 80 Board 30 Del £185 **PARKING:** 150 **NOTES:** in restaurant Civ Wed 90
CARDS:

BONCHURCH See Wight, Isle of

BOOTLE, Merseyside Map 15 SJ39

Travel Inn (Liverpool North)
Northern Perimiter Rd, Bootle L30 7PT
☎ 08701 977158 0151 520 1842
Dir: *on A5207, off A5036, 0.25m from end of M58/M57*
Travel Inn offers good-quality, value-for-money accommodation. Spacious, en suite rooms with bath and shower comfortably accommodate a family of up to two adults and two children (to age 15). The restaurant and bar offers a varied menu. For further details consult the Hotel Groups page.
ROOMS: 63 en suite s £45.95-£46.95; d £45.95-£46.95 **CONF:** Thtr 50

BOREHAMWOOD, Hertfordshire Map 06 TQ19

Innkeeper's Lodge Borehamwood
Studio Way WD6 5JY
☎ 020 8905 1455 020 8236 9822
www.innkeeperslodge.com
Dir: *M25 junct 23/A1(M) signed to London. Follow signs to Borehamwood after double rdbt turn into Studio Way*
Smart rooms meet essential business requirements but also have home comforts, and depending on location may well have meeting rooms and pub dining. Dining options generally include all-day menus plus the added advantage of breakfast.
ROOMS: 55 en suite s £48-£62; d £48-£62 **CONF:** Thtr 38 Class 20 Board 20

BOROUGHBRIDGE, North Yorkshire Map 19 SE36

★★★71% *Crown*
Horsefair YO51 9LB
☎ 01423 322328 01423 324512
e-mail: sales@crownboroughbridge.co.uk
web: www.crownboroughbridge.co.uk
Dir: *A1(M) junct 48. Hotel 1m towards town centre at t-junct*

Situated in the centre of town but only a minute from the A1, The Crown provides modern well-appointed bedrooms and a range of comfortable public rooms, including a delightful restaurant, which serves a wide range of well-prepared food. Service is both relaxed and friendly. Several modern conference rooms are available, as well as a full leisure complex.
ROOMS: 37 en suite (3 fmly) in all bedrooms **FACILITIES:** STV supervised Sauna Solarium Gym Jacuzzi Beauty therapist **CONF:** Thtr 150 Class 80 Board 80 **SERVICES:** Lift **PARKING:** 60 **NOTES:** in restaurant Civ Wed 70 **CARDS:**

BORROWDALE, Cumbria Map 18 NY21
See also Keswick & Rosthwaite

★★★79% Borrowdale Gates Country House
CA12 5UQ
☎ 017687 77204 017687 77254
e-mail: hotel@borrowdale-gates.com
web: www.borrowdale-gates.com
Dir: *follow Borrowdale signs on B5289, after 4m right at sign for Grange. Hotel on right 0.25m through village*

This attractive, well-maintained and friendly hotel enjoys an idyllic, peaceful, woodland location in the middle of the Borrowdale

continued

Valley. Inviting public rooms include a choice of lounges and a smart restaurant, enjoying stunning views. Bedrooms come in a variety of styles and sizes, including superior rooms that are particularly thoughtfully equipped.
ROOMS: 31 en suite (1 fmly) s £80-£89; d £157-£180 (incl. bkfst & dinner) **LB** **FACILITIES:** STV Xmas **PARKING:** 40 **NOTES:** No children 12yrs in restaurant Closed 3-31 Jan
CARDS:

See advert under KESWICK

★★★70% Borrowdale
CA12 5UY
☎ 01768 777224 777338
e-mail: theborrowdalehotel@yahoo.com
Dir: *3 miles from Keswick, on B5289 at S end of Lake Derwentwater*
Situated in the beautiful Borrowdale Valley overlooking Derwent Water, this traditional hotel has been family-run for over 30 years. Extensive public areas include a choice of lounges, a stylish dining room, and a lounge bar, plus a conservatory. There are a wide variety of bedroom sizes and styles; some rooms are rather spacious, including two at the rear that are particularly suitable for a less able guest.
ROOMS: 34 en suite 2 annexe en suite (9 fmly) (2 GF) s £70-£90; d £130-£190 (incl. bkfst & dinner) **LB** **FACILITIES:** Free use of nearby Health Club ch fac Xmas **PARKING:** 100 **NOTES:** in restaurant
CARDS:

★69% Royal Oak
CA12 5XB
☎ 017687 77214 017687 77214
e-mail: info@royaloakhotel.co.uk
web: www.royaloakhotel.co.uk
Dir: *6m S of Keswick on B5289 in centre of Rosthwaite*
Set in a village in one of Lakeland's most picturesque valleys, this family-run hotel offers friendly and obliging service. There is a variety of accommodation styles, with particularly impressive rooms being located in a converted barn across the courtyard and backed by a stream. Family rooms are available. The cosy bar is for residents and diners only. A set home-cooked dinner is served at 7pm.
ROOMS: 11 rms (8 en suite) 4 annexe en suite (6 fmly) s £30-£34; d £60-£80 (incl. bkfst) **LB** **FACILITIES:** no TV in bdrms **PARKING:** 15 **NOTES:** in restaurant Closed 5-19 Jan & 7-27 Dec
CARDS:

BOSCASTLE, Cornwall & Isles of Scilly — Map 02 SX09

★★71% The Bottreaux Hotel and Restaurant
PL35 0BG
☎ 01840 250231 01840 250170
e-mail: info@boscastlecornwall.co.uk
web: www.boscastlecornwall.co.uk
Built some 200 years ago, this hotel is just a short walk from the picturesque harbour. Refurbishment has resulted in a stylish establishment where guests are genuinely welcomed. Bedrooms are light and airy, the doubles featuring wonderful 6ft teak beds. The bar is a convivial venue for a drink and perusal of the imaginative menu, which makes good use of local produce.
ROOMS: 9 en suite in all bedrooms s £50-£60; d £60-£80 (incl. bkfst) **LB** **FACILITIES:** Xmas **PARKING:** 10 **NOTES:** No children 10yrs in restaurant **CARDS:**

No smoking

Entertainment

★★68% The Wellington Hotel
The Harbour PL35 0AQ
☎ 01840 250202 01840 250621
e-mail: info@wellingtonboscastle.co.uk
web: www.wellingtonboscastle.co.uk
Dir: *A30/A395, right at Davidstow, signed to Boscastle*
Affectionately known as 'The Welly', this 16th-century coaching inn has an abundance of charm and character. The Long Bar is a popular watering hole for both visitors and locals alike. Bedrooms come in varying sizes, including the spacious Tower rooms; all are comfy and suitably equipped. There is a bar menu and, in the restaurant, a daily changing carte.
ROOMS: 15 en suite (1 fmly) s £35-£45; d £70-£130 (incl. bkfst) **LB** **FACILITIES:** ch fac Xmas **CONF:** Thtr 20 Class 6 Board 24 Del from £53 **PARKING:** 20 **NOTES:** in restaurant
CARDS:

BOSHAM, West Sussex — Map 05 SU80

★★★76% The Millstream
Bosham Ln PO18 8HL
☎ 01243 573234 01243 573459
e-mail: info@millstream-hotel.co.uk
Dir: *4m W of Chichester on A259, left at Bosham rdbt. After 1m right at t-junct signed to church & quay. Hotel 0.5m on right*

Lying in the idyllic village of Bosham, this attractive hotel provides comfortable, well-equipped and tastefully decorated bedrooms. Many guests regularly return here for the relaxed ambience created by the notably efficient and friendly staff. Public rooms include a cocktail bar, opening out onto the garden, and a pleasant restaurant where varied and freshly prepared cuisine can be enjoyed.
ROOMS: 33 en suite 2 annexe en suite (2 fmly) (9 GF) in all bedrooms s £85-£95; d £135-£149 (incl. bkfst) **LB** **FACILITIES:** Bridge breaks ch fac Xmas **CONF:** Thtr 45 Class 20 Board 20 Del from £99 **PARKING:** 44 **NOTES:** in restaurant Civ Wed 92
CARDS:

See advert under CHICHESTER

BOSTON, Lincolnshire — Map 12 TF34

★★65% *Comfort Inn*
Donnington Rd, Bicker Bar Roundabout
PE20 3AN
☎ 01205 820118 01205 820228
e-mail: admin@gb607.u-net.com
Dir: *towards A16 Spaking, on A17/A52 rdbt, 11m from Boston*
Public areas within this purpose-built hotel include an open-plan lounge bar and adjacent restaurant. Reasonably priced meals are available all day. Bedrooms are well equipped, offering good levels of comfort and value for money. Several meeting rooms are also available.
ROOMS: 55 en suite (15 fmly) in 25 bedrooms **FACILITIES:** STV **CONF:** Thtr 70 Class 30 Board 35 **PARKING:** 60 **NOTES:** in restaurant **CARDS:**

B

BOSTON, continued

⌂ Travel Inn

Wainfleet Rd PE21 9RW
☎ 08701 977035 ▯ 01205 310908
Dir: *A52, 300yds E of junct with A16 Boston/Grimsby road. (Nearest landmark is Pilgrim Hospital)*
Travel Inn offers good-quality, value-for-money accommodation. Spacious, en suite rooms with bath and shower comfortably accommodate a family of up to two adults and two children (to age 15). The restaurant and bar offers a varied menu. For further details consult the Hotel Groups page.
ROOMS: 34 en suite s £45.95-£46.95; d £45.95-£46.95 **CONF:** Thtr 12 Board 8

BOTLEY, Hampshire Map 05 SU51

★★★★69% Botley Park Hotel Golf & Country Club

MACDONALD HOTELS
Winchester Rd, Boorley Green SO32 2UA
☎ 01489 780888 ▯ 01489 789242
e-mail: botleypark@macdonald-hotels.co.uk
web: www.botleyparkhotel.co.uk
Dir: *A334 towards Botley, left at 1st rdbt past M&S, continue over next 4 mini-rdbts, at 3rd rdbt follow hotel signs*

This modern and spacious hotel sits peacefully in the midst of its own 176 acres parkland golf course. Bedrooms are comfortably appointed with a good range of extras and an extensive range of leisure facilities is on offer. Attractive public areas include a relaxing restaurant and the more informal Swing and Divot Bar.
ROOMS: 100 en suite (34 GF) ⊗ in 52 bedrooms **FACILITIES:** STV 18 Squash Sauna Solarium Gym Jacuzzi Aerobics studio, Beauty salon, Golf driving range ch fac **CONF:** Thtr 240 Class 100 Board 60 Del from £135 **PARKING:** 250 **NOTES:** ⊗ in restaurant Civ Wed 200
CARDS:

BOURNEMOUTH, Dorset Map 05 SZ19
See also Christchurch & Ferndown

★★★★75% Bournemouth Highcliff Marriott

Marriott HOTELS · RESORTS · SUITES
St Michaels Rd, West Cliff BH2 5DU
☎ 01202 557702 ▯ 01202 292734
e-mail: reservations.bournemouth@marriotthotels.co.uk
Dir: *A338 through Bournemouth. Follow BIC signs to West Cliff Rd. 2nd right into St Michaels Rd. Hotel at end of road on left*
Originally built as a row of coastguard cottages, this establishment has expanded over the years into a most elegant and charming hotel. Impeccably maintained throughout, many of the bedrooms have sea views. An excellent range of leisure, business and conference facilities are offered, as well as private dining and banqueting rooms. The hotel also has direct access to the Bournemouth International Centre.
ROOMS: 141 en suite 19 annexe en suite (26 fmly) ⊗ in 65 bedrooms s £110-£125; d £110-£125 **LB FACILITIES:** STV Sauna Solarium Gym Putt green Jacuzzi Beautician Xmas **CONF:** Thtr 350 Class 180 Board 90 **SERVICES:** Lift air con **PARKING:** 80 **NOTES:** ⊗ in restaurant Civ Wed 250 **CARDS:**

★★★★75% Menzies East Cliff Court

MENZIES HOTELS
East Overcliff Dr BH1 3AN
☎ 01202 554545 ▯ 01202 557456
e-mail: eastcliff@menzies-hotels.co.uk
Dir: *From M3/M27 approach Bournemouth on A338(which leads onto Wessex Way), follow signs to the East Cliff, hotel on seafront*
Enjoying panoramic views across the bay, extensive refurbishment at this popular hotel has had impressive results. Bedrooms, modern and contemporary in style, have been appointed to a very high standard, with many benefiting from balconies and sea views. Stylish public areas include a range of inviting lounges, a spacious restaurant and a selection of conference rooms.
ROOMS: 67 en suite (10 fmly) s £125-£150; d £150-£200 (incl. bkfst) **LB FACILITIES:** STV Leisure facilities at nearby hotel Xmas **CONF:** Thtr 200 Class 40 Board 45 Del £170 **SERVICES:** Lift **PARKING:** 70 **NOTES:** ⊗ in restaurant Civ Wed
CARDS:

★★★★70% De Vere Royal Bath

DE VERE HOTELS
Bath Rd BH1 2EW
☎ 01202 555555 ▯ 01202 554158
e-mail: royalbath@devere-hotels.com
Dir: *A338 follow signs for pier & beaches. Hotel on Bath Rd just before Lansdowne rdbt and Pier*
Overlooking the bay, this well-established seafront hotel is surrounded by beautifully kept gardens. Public rooms, which include lounges, a choice of restaurants and indoor leisure facilities, are of a scale and style befitting the golden era in which the hotel was built. Local attractions include the motor museum at Beaulieu and the Oceanarium. Valet parking is provided for a small charge.
ROOMS: 140 en suite (16 fmly) (5 GF) s fr £135; d fr £170 (incl. bkfst) **LB FACILITIES: Spa** STV supervised Sauna Solarium Gym Jacuzzi Beauty salon, Hairdressing Xmas **CONF:** Thtr 400 Class 220 Board 100 Del from £175 **SERVICES:** Lift **PARKING:** 70 **NOTES:** ⊗ in restaurant Civ Wed 200 **CARDS:**

Bad hair day?
Hairdryers in all rooms three stars and above

★★★★70% Menzies Carlton

MENZIES HOTELS
East Overcliff BH1 3DN
☎ 01202 552011 ▯ 01202 299573
e-mail: carlton@menzies-hotels.co.uk
Dir: *From M3/M27, approach Bournemouth on A338 (leads onto Wessex Way), follow signs to East Cliff, hotel on seafront*
Enjoying a prime location on the East Cliff, and with views of the Isle of Wight and Dorset coastline, the Carlton has attractive gardens and pool area. Conference and banqueting facilities are varied. Most of the spacious bedrooms enjoy sea views and all are

continued

well-equipped. Guests can enjoy an interesting range of carefully prepared dishes in Fredericks restaurant.
ROOMS: 73 en suite in 20 bedrooms s £125-£150; d £150-£200 (incl. bkfst) **LB** **FACILITIES:** STV Sauna Solarium Gym Jacuzzi Spa pool Xmas **CONF:** Thtr 140 Class 90 Board 45 Del £170 **SERVICES:** Lift **PARKING:** 90 **NOTES:** in restaurant Civ Wed
CARDS:

★★★77% Chine

Boscombe Spa Rd BH5 1AX
☎ 01202 396234 01202 391737
e-mail: reservations@chinehotel.co.uk
web: www.chinehotel.co.uk
Dir: *Follow BIC signs, A338/Wessex Way to St Pauls rdbt. 1st exit - St Pauls Rd to next rdbt, 2nd exit signed Eastcliff/Boscombe/Southbourne. Next rdbt, 1st exit into Christchurch Rd. After 2nd lights, right into Boscombe Spa Rd*

Best Western

Benefiting from superb views this popular hotel is set in delightful gardens with private access to the seafront and beach. The excellent range of facilities includes an indoor and outdoor pool, a small leisure centre and a selection of meeting rooms. The spacious bedrooms, some of which have balconies, are well appointed and thoughtfully equipped.
ROOMS: 65 en suite 22 annexe en suite (13 fmly) in 14 bedrooms s £70-£90; d £140-£180 (incl. bkfst) **LB** **FACILITIES: Spa** STV supervised supervised Sauna Solarium Gym Putt green Jacuzzi Games room, Outdoor & indoor childrens play area ch fac Xmas **CONF:** Thtr 140 Class 70 Board 40 Del £120 **SERVICES:** Lift **PARKING:** 50 **NOTES:** in restaurant Civ Wed 120
CARDS:

See advert on this page and hotels in POOLE

Early start?
Hotels at all star levels should provide in-room alarm clocks and/or alarm calls

★★★76% Langtry Manor - Lovenest of a King

Derby Rd, East Cliff BH1 3QB
☎ 01202 553887 01202 290115
e-mail: lillie@langtrymanor.com
web: www.langtrymanor.com
Dir: *A31/A338, 1st rdbt by rail station turn left. Over next rdbt, 1st left into Knyveton Rd. Hotel opposite*

Retaining a stately air, this property was originally built in 1877 by Edward VII for his mistress Lillie Langtry. The individually furnished and decorated bedrooms include several with four-poster beds. Enjoyable cuisine is served in the magnificent

continued on p108

BOURNEMOUTH, Dorset Map 05 SZ19

dining hall, complete with several large Tudor tapestries. There is an Edwardian banquet on Saturday evenings.

Langtry Manor, Bournemouth

ROOMS: 12 en suite 8 annexe en suite (2 fmly) (3 GF) ⊗ in 4 bedrooms s £89.75-£99.75; d £139.75-£239.50 (incl. bkfst) **LB** **FACILITIES:** STV Free use of local health club ♫ Xmas **CONF:** Thtr 100 Class 60 Board 40 Del from £120 **PARKING:** 30 **NOTES:** ⊗ in restaurant Civ Wed 100 **CARDS:**

★★★75% Elstead

Knyveton Rd BH1 3QP
☎ 01202 293071 📠 01202 293827
e-mail: info@the-elstead.co.uk
web: www.the-elstead.co.uk

Ideal as a base for both business and leisure travellers, this popular hotel is conveniently located for the town centre, seafront and BIC. An impressive range of facilities is offered, including meeting rooms, an indoor leisure centre and comfortable lounges. Most bedrooms have been refurbished to a high standard.
ROOMS: 50 en suite (15 fmly) ⊗ in 30 bedrooms s £43-£59; d £87-£97 (incl. bkfst) **LB** **FACILITIES: Spa** STV supervised Snooker Sauna Gym Steam room, Pool Table, Xmas **CONF:** BC Thtr 80 Class 60 Board 40 Del from £75 **SERVICES:** Lift **PARKING:** 40 **NOTES:** ⊗ in restaurant Closed 23 Dec-28 Dec **CARDS:**

★★★73% Hermitage

Exeter Rd BH2 5AH
☎ 01202 557363 📠 01202 559173
e-mail: info@hermitage-hotel.co.uk
Dir: *A338 Ringwood, left at St. Pauls rdbt, follow signs for BIC and pier. Across bridge Hotel entrance on right*
Occupying an impressive position overlooking the seafront, at the heart of Bournemouth's town centre, the Hermitage offers friendly and attentive service. The majority of the smart bedrooms are comfortably appointed and all are very well equipped; many rooms have sea views. The wood-panelled lounge provides an elegant and tranquil area as does the restaurant where well-prepared and interesting dishes are served.
ROOMS: 63 en suite 11 annexe en suite (9 fmly) (7 GF) ⊗ in 65 bedrooms s £54-£110; d £108-£144 (incl. bkfst) **LB** **FACILITIES:** Free swimming at Bournemouth International Centre Xmas **CONF:** Thtr 180 Class 60 Board 60 Del from £68 **SERVICES:** Lift **PARKING:** 58 **NOTES:** ⊗ in restaurant **CARDS:**

★★★72% Durley Hall

Durley Chine Rd, West Cliff BH2 5JS
☎ 01202 751000 📠 01202 757585
e-mail: Sales@durleyhall.co.uk
web: www.durleyhall.co.uk
Dir: *A338 follow signs to West Cliff & BIC*
This attractive, conveniently situated hotel offers a friendly atmosphere and attentive service. In addition to a diverse range of business and conference facilities, guests have access to extensive leisure, beauty and therapy treatments. The smart bedrooms are well designed, comfortable and suited to business and leisure guests alike. A candlelit dinner dance is normally held on Saturdays.
ROOMS: 66 en suite 11 annexe en suite (27 fmly) **FACILITIES: Spa** STV Sauna Solarium Gym Jacuzzi Beauty therapist Table tennis Hydro Therapy, aromatherapy ♫ Xmas **CONF:** Thtr 200 Class 80 Board 35 Del from £76 **SERVICES:** Lift **PARKING:** 150 **NOTES:** ⊗ in restaurant Civ Wed **CARDS:**

★★★71% East Anglia

Best Western

6 Poole Rd BH2 5QX
☎ 01202 765163 📠 01202 752949
e-mail: info@eastangliahotel.com
web: www.eastangliahotel.com
Dir: *A338 at Bournemouth West rdbt. Follow signs for BIC & West Cliff. At next rdbt right into Poole Rd. Hotel on right*
This privately owned and well-managed hotel provides modern accommodation, including ground floor bedrooms. The friendly team of staff offer a warm welcome and attentive service. Public areas include a number of function and conference rooms, ample lounges and an air-conditioned restaurant. There is also an outdoor swimming pool.
ROOMS: 45 en suite 25 annexe en suite (18 fmly) (10 GF) ⊗ in 23 bedrooms s £52-£58; d £104-£116 (incl. bkfst) **LB** **FACILITIES: Spa** STV Sauna American Pool Room Xmas **CONF:** Thtr 150 Class 75 Board 60 **SERVICES:** Lift **PARKING:** 70 **NOTES:** ⊗ in restaurant **CARDS:**

★★★71% Hotel Miramar

East Overcliff Dr, East Cliff BH1 3AL
☎ 01202 556581 📠 01202 291242
e-mail: sales@miramar-bournemouth.com
web: www.miramar-bournemouth.com
Dir: *Wessex Way rdbt turn into St Pauls Rd, right at next rdbt. 3rd exit at next rdbt, 2nd exit at next rdbt into Grove Rd. Hotel car park on right*
Conveniently located on the East Cliff, this Edwardian hotel enjoys glorious sea views. The Miramar was a favoured destination of Tolkien, who often stayed here. Friendly staff and a relaxing environment are keynotes, and the bedrooms are comfortable and

continued

well equipped. Spacious public areas and a choice of lounges complete the experience.

ROOMS: 43 en suite (6 fmly) ⊗ in 10 bedrooms s £60-£95; d £120-£155 (incl. bkfst) **LB** **FACILITIES:** STV ♫ Xmas **CONF:** Thtr 200 Class 50 Board 50 Del from £75 **SERVICES:** Lift **PARKING:** 80 **NOTES:** ⊗ in restaurant Civ Wed 110 **CARDS:**

★★★71% Piccadilly

Bath Rd BH1 2NN
☎ 01202 298024 ▯ 01202 298235
Dir: *From A338 take 1st exit on ASDA roundabout, sign posted East Cliff. Next roundabout take 3rd exit, signposted Lansdowne. Next roundabout take 3rd exit, Bath Road.*

This hotel offers a friendly welcome to guests, many of whom return on a regular basis, particularly for the superb ballroom dancing facilities and small breaks which are a feature here. Bedrooms are smartly decorated, well-maintained and comfortable. Dining in the attractive restaurant is always popular and dishes are freshly prepared and appetising.
ROOMS: 45 en suite (2 fmly) s £65; d £95-£105 (incl. bkfst) **LB** **FACILITIES:** Ballroom dancing Xmas **SERVICES:** Lift **PARKING:** 30 **NOTES:** ⊗ in restaurant **CARDS:**

★★★71% The Riviera

Burnaby Rd, Alum Chine BH4 8JF
☎ 01202 763653 ▯ 01202 768422
e-mail: info@rivierabournemouth.co.uk
Dir: *A338, follow signs to Alum Chine*
Part of the Calotels group, this refurbished hotel offers a range of comfortable, well-furnished bedrooms and bathrooms. Welcoming staff provide efficient service delivered in a friendly manner. In addition to a spacious lounge with regular entertainment there is an indoor and outdoor pool.
ROOMS: 69 en suite 4 annexe en suite (25 fmly) (11 GF) **FACILITIES:** Sauna Jacuzzi Games room ♫ Xmas **CONF:** Thtr 180 Class 120 Board 50 Del from £64 **SERVICES:** Lift **PARKING:** 70 **NOTES:** ⊗ in restaurant Civ Wed 100 **CARDS:**

★★★71% Suncliff

29 East Overcliff Dr BH1 3AG
☎ 01202 291711 ▯ 01202 293788
e-mail: info@suncliffbournemouth.co.uk
Dir: *A338 to Bmouth. 1st left at rdbt into St Pauls Rd, follow signs East Cliff*
Enjoying splendid views from the East Cliff, this friendly hotel provides a range of facilities and services. The hotel caters mainly for leisure guests; bedrooms are well equipped and comfortable and many have sea views. Public areas include a large conservatory, an attractive bar and pleasant lounges.
ROOMS: 94 en suite (29 fmly) (13 GF) s £40-£69; d £80-£138 (incl. bkfst) **LB** **FACILITIES:** Squash Snooker Sauna Gym Jacuzzi Table tennis ♫ Xmas **CONF:** Thtr 140 Class 96 Board 86 Del from £70 **SERVICES:** Lift **PARKING:** 60 **NOTES:** ⊗ in restaurant Civ Wed **CARDS:**

★★★71% Wessex

West Cliff Rd BH2 5EU
Forestdale Hotels
☎ 01202 551911 ▯ 01202 297354
e-mail: wessex@forestdale.com
Dir: *Follow M27/A35 or A338 from Dorchester & A347 N. Hotel on West Cliff side of town*
Centrally located and handy for the beach, the Wessex is a popular, relaxing hotel. Bedrooms vary in size and include premier rooms; all are comfortable, and equipped with a range of modern amenities. There are excellent leisure facilities, ample function rooms and an open-plan bar and lounge.
ROOMS: 109 en suite (22 fmly) ⊗ in 3 bedrooms s fr £75; d fr £120 (incl. bkfst) **LB** **FACILITIES:** STV Snooker Sauna Solarium Gym Table tennis Xmas **CONF:** Thtr 400 Class 160 Board 160 Del from £120 **SERVICES:** Lift **PARKING:** 160 **NOTES:** ⊗ in restaurant Civ Wed 100 **CARDS:**

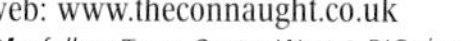

★★★70% The Connaught

West Hill Rd, West Cliff BH2 5PH
Best Western
☎ 01202 298020 ▯ 01202 298028
e-mail: sales@theconnaught.co.uk
web: www.theconnaught.co.uk
Dir: *follow Town Centre West & BIC signs*
Conveniently located on the West Cliff, close to the BIC, beaches and town centre, this attractive hotel offers well equipped, neatly decorated rooms, some with balconies. The hotel boasts a very well-equipped leisure complex with a large pool, snooker table and comprehensive gym facilities. Breakfast and dinner offer imaginative dishes made with quality local ingredients.
ROOMS: 56 en suite (15 fmly) ⊗ in 18 bedrooms s £43-£67; d £86-£134 (incl. bkfst) **LB** **FACILITIES:** **Spa** STV supervised supervised Snooker Sauna Solarium Gym Jacuzzi Cardio-vascular suite, Table tennis, Pool table Xmas **CONF:** Thtr 200 Class 60 Board 60 Del from £85 **SERVICES:** Lift **PARKING:** 45 **NOTES:** ⊗ in restaurant **CARDS:**

★★★70% Montague

Durley Rd South, West Cliff BH2 5JH
☎ 01202 551074 ▯ 01202 553948
e-mail: enquiries@montaguehotel.co.uk
web: www.montaguehotel.co.uk
Dir: *A31/A338 to Bournemouth turn left into Cambridge Rd at Bournemouth West rdbt, take 2nd exit at next rdbt into Durley Chine Rd. Next rdbt take 2nd exit. Hotel on right*
With its convenient location a short walk from the attractions of the town centre and beaches, this hotel has a busy leisure trade, especially at weekends. Bedrooms are especially attractive, having been refurbished, and all are well equipped. Guests can unwind

continued on p110

BOURNEMOUTH, Dorset Map 05 SZ19

on the terrace or in the relaxing bar. Dinner features appetising dishes made with fresh local produce.
ROOMS: 32 en suite (9 fmly) (10 GF) ⊘ in 6 bedrooms s £72-£82; d £110-£130 (incl. bkfst) **LB** **FACILITIES:** STV supervised ch fac Xmas **CONF:** Thtr 60 Board 30 Del from £70 **SERVICES:** Lift **PARKING:** 50 **NOTES:** ⊘ in restaurant
CARDS:

★★★69% Carrington House

31 Knyveton Rd BH1 3QQ
☎ 01202 369988 01202 292221
e-mail: carrington.house@forestdale.com

Forestdale Hotels

***Dir:** A338 at St Paul's rdbt, continue 200mtrs & turn left into Knyveton Rd. Hotel 400mtrs on right*

Carrington House occupies a prominent position on a tree-lined avenue and a short walk from the seafront. Bedrooms are generally spacious, comfortable and usefully equipped. In addition to the hotel's bar and restaurant there are extensive conference facilities and a leisure complex.
ROOMS: 145 en suite (42 fmly) ⊘ in 40 bedrooms s fr £75; d fr £120 (incl. bkfst) **FACILITIES:** STV Snooker Gym Purpose built children's play area Xmas **CONF:** Thtr 500 Class 260 Board 80 Del from £120 **SERVICES:** Lift **PARKING:** 100 **NOTES:** ⊘ in restaurant Civ Wed 350
CARDS:

★★★69% Hotel Collingwood

11 Priory Rd, West Cliff BH2 5DF
☎ 01202 557575 01202 293219
e-mail: info@hotel-collingwood.co.uk
web: www.hotel-collingwood.co.uk

***Dir:** A338 left at West Cliff sign, over 1st rdbt and left at 2nd rdbt. Hotel 500yds on left*

This privately owned and managed hotel is situated close to the BIC. Bedrooms are airy, with the emphasis on comfort. An excellent range of leisure facilities is available and the public areas are spacious and welcoming. Pinks Restaurant offers carefully prepared cuisine and a fixed-price, five-course dinner.
ROOMS: 53 en suite (16 fmly) (6 GF) ⊘ in 6 bedrooms s £59-£66; d £118-£132 (incl. bkfst & dinner) **LB** **FACILITIES:** STV Snooker Sauna Solarium Gym Jacuzzi Mini gym, Steam room, Games room ♫ Xmas **SERVICES:** Lift **PARKING:** 55 **NOTES:** ⊘ in restaurant Closed First 2 weeks of Jan. **CARDS:**

See advert on opposite page

★★★69% Queens

Meyrick Rd, East Cliff BH1 3DL
☎ 01202 554415 01202 294810
e-mail: queens@bluemermaidhotels.com

***Dir:** A338 St Paul's rdbt take Holdenhurst Rd. 2nd exit at Lansdown rdbt onto Meyrick Rd*

This attractive hotel enjoys a good location near to the seafront and is popular for conferences and functions. The public areas include a bar, lounge and a stunning restaurant. The Queensbury Leisure Club has much to offer guests. Bedrooms vary in size and style, and all are well-equipped and comfortable.
ROOMS: 109 en suite (15 fmly) s £59.50-£69.50; d £59.50-£69.50 (incl. bkfst) **LB** **FACILITIES: Spa** Snooker Sauna Solarium Gym Jacuzzi Beauty salon, Games Room, snooker table ♫ ch fac Xmas **CONF:** Thtr 220 Class 120 Board 50 Del from £82.50 **SERVICES:** Lift **PARKING:** 80 **NOTES:** ⊘ in restaurant **CARDS:**

★★★69% Trouville

Priory Rd BH2 5DH
☎ 01202 552262 01202 293324
e-mail: trouville@bluemermaidhotels.com

***Dir:** A338 onto A35, follow signs for BIC*

Located near Bournemouth International Centre and the seafront, this family-owned hotel is conveniently situated, whether staying for business or pleasure. The attractive bedrooms are modern and tastefully furnished and the inviting public areas include a comfortable bar, a separate lounge and a smart restaurant.
ROOMS: 77 en suite (21 fmly) s £47-£67; d £47-£67.50 (incl. bkfst) **LB** **FACILITIES:** Sauna Solarium Gym Jacuzzi ♫ ch fac Xmas **CONF:** Thtr 100 Class 45 Board 50 Del from £79 **SERVICES:** Lift **PARKING:** 55 **NOTES:** ⊘ in restaurant
CARDS:

★★★68% Hinton Firs

Manor Rd, East Cliff BH1 3ET
☎ 01202 555409 01202 299607
e-mail: reservations@hintonfirshotel.co.uk

***Dir:** A338 turn W at St Paul's rdbt, over next 2 rdbts then fork left to side of church. Hotel on next corner*

This efficient and friendly hotel is conveniently located on East Cliff. Guests are offered leisure facilities including indoor and outdoor pools and a games room. There is also a spacious lounge, bar and restaurant in which to relax. Bedrooms are light and airy, and six are situated in a separate wing.
ROOMS: 46 en suite 6 annexe en suite (12 fmly) (6 GF) s £45-£65; d £90-£105 (incl. bkfst) **LB** **FACILITIES: Spa** Sauna Games room ♫ ch fac Xmas **CONF:** Thtr 50 Class 40 Board 30 Del from £65 **SERVICES:** Lift **PARKING:** 40 **NOTES:** ⊘ in restaurant
CARDS:

TV dinner?
Room service at three stars and above

★★★68% *Royal Exeter*

Exeter Rd BH2 5AG
☎ 01202 438000 01202 297963
e-mail: royalexeterhotel@aol.com
web: www.royalexeterhotel.com

***Dir:** opposite Bournemouth International Centre*

Ideally located opposite the Bournemouth International Centre, and convenient for the beach and town centre, this busy hotel caters for both business and leisure guests. New and extensive refurbishment of the public areas has resulted in a smart, modern

continued

and open-plan lounge bar and restaurant together with an exciting adjoining bar complex.

ROOMS: 54 en suite (13 fmly) **FACILITIES:** STV **CONF:** Thtr 40 Class 20 Board 35 **SERVICES:** Lift **PARKING:** 50 **NOTES:**
CARDS:

★★★67% *Belvedere*

Bath Rd BH1 2EU
☎ 01202 297556 & 293336 ▯ 01202 294699
e-mail: enquiries@belvedere-hotel.co.uk
web: www.belvedere-hotel.co.uk
Dir: *from A338 with railway station and Asda on left. At rdbt 1st left then 3rd exit at next 2 rdbts. Hotel on Bath Hill after 4th rdbt*

Close to the town centre and the seafront, this friendly, family-run hotel offers spacious public areas and comfortable bedrooms. The lively bar and attractive restaurant are both popular with locals, *continued* and there are meeting rooms which provide an ideal location for both conferences and functions.

ROOMS: 61 en suite (12 fmly) **FACILITIES:** STV Beauty breaks with local natural spa ♫ **CONF:** Thtr 80 Class 30 Board 30 **SERVICES:** Lift **PARKING:** 55 **NOTES:** ⊘ in restaurant
CARDS:

★★★67% Cliffeside

East Overcliff Dr BH1 3AQ
☎ 01202 555724 ▯ 01202 314534
e-mail: hotels@arthuryoung.co.uk
Dir: *M27/A338 approx 7m, then 1st rdbt left into East Cliff*

A traditionally run and friendly hotel, benefiting from an elevated position on the seafront. Bedrooms and public areas are attractively appointed and many have sea views. The appealing Atlantic Restaurant offers guests a fixed-price menu and a relaxing atmosphere.

ROOMS: 62 en suite (10 fmly) s £45-£72.50; d £45-£72.50 (incl. bkfst) LB **FACILITIES:** Table tennis ch fac Xmas **CONF:** Thtr 180 Class 140 Board 60 Del from £75 **SERVICES:** Lift **PARKING:** 45 **NOTES:** ⊘ in restaurant **CARDS:**

★★★67% Heathlands Hotel

12 Grove Rd, East Cliff BH1 3AY
☎ 01202 553336 ▯ 01202 555937
e-mail: info@heathlandshotel.com
web: www.heathlandshotel.com
Dir: *A338 St Pauls rdbt 1st exit to East Cliff, 3rd exit at next rdbt to Holdenhurst Rd, 2nd exit off Lansdowne rdbt into Meyrick Rd. Left into Gervis Rd. Hotel on right*

This is a large hotel on the East Cliff with a newly refurbished leisure centre. The Heathlands is popular with many groups and

continued on p112

BOURNEMOUTH, Dorset Map 05 SZ19

conferences and the public areas are bright and spacious. There is a coffee shop, open all day, and regular live entertainment is provided for guests.
ROOMS: 115 en suite (16 fmly) (11 GF) ⊗ in 15 bedrooms s £66-£105; d £92-£190 (incl. bkfst) **LB** **FACILITIES:** STV Sauna Gym Jacuzzi Health suite ♫ Xmas **CONF:** Thtr 270 Class 102 Board 54 Del from £75 **SERVICES:** Lift **PARKING:** 100 **NOTES:** ⊗ in restaurant Civ Wed 90
CARDS:

★★★67% Marsham Court

Russell Cotes Rd, East Cliff BH1 3AB
☎ 01202 552111 📠 01202 294744
e-mail: reservations@marshamcourt.com
web: www.marshamcourt.com
Dir: From Wessex Way take Bournemouth East exit at St Pauls rdbt. Over station rdbt. Follow ringroad, over St Swithuns rdbt. Left with church on left over Meyrick rdbt. Left at St Peters rdbt. Hotel on left

This hotel is set in attractive gardens with splendid views over the sea and town, and is very accessible and convenient for the town and BIC. Bedrooms vary in size, are comfortably appointed and some have sea views. There is a well-stocked bar, lounge areas, terrace and pool, as well as impressive conference rooms.
ROOMS: 87 en suite (15 fmly) ⊗ in all bedrooms s £57-£66; d £94-£112 (incl. bkfst) **LB** **FACILITIES:** STV Pool table ch fac Xmas **CONF:** Thtr 200 Class 100 Board 80 Del from £89 **SERVICES:** Lift **PARKING:** 100 **NOTES:** ⊗ in restaurant Civ Wed 200
CARDS:

★★★66% Bay View Court

35 East Overcliff Dr BH1 3AH
☎ 01202 294449 📠 01202 292883
e-mail: enquiry@bayviewcourt.co.uk
Dir: on A338 left at St Pauls rdbt. Over St Swithuns rdbt. Bear left onto Manor Rd, 1st right, next right
This relaxed and friendly hotel enjoys far-reaching sea views from many of the public areas and bedrooms. Bedrooms vary in size and are attractively furnished. There is a choice of south-facing lounges and, for the more energetic, an indoor swimming pool. Live entertainment is provided during the evenings.
ROOMS: 64 en suite (11 fmly) (5 GF) s £56-£64; d £112-£128 (incl. bkfst & dinner) **LB** **FACILITIES: Spa** STV Snooker Sauna Gym Jacuzzi Steam room ♫ Xmas **CONF:** Thtr 170 Class 85 Board 50 Del from £70 **SERVICES:** Lift **PARKING:** 58 **NOTES:** ⊗ in restaurant
CARDS:

★★★66% Quality Hotel Bournemouth

47 Gervis Rd, East Cliff BH1 3DD
☎ 01202 316316 📠 01202 316999
e-mail: reservations@qualityhotelbournemouth.com
web: www.qualityhotelbournemouth.com
Dir: A338 left at rdbt, right at next rdbt. Take 2nd exit at next rdbt into Meyrick Rd. Then at next rdbt right into Gervis Rd. Hotel on left
The hotel was once the home of Tony Hancock and is situated a short walk form the East Cliff. Guests can enjoy the terrace, garden and the indoor heated swimming pool. A lounge menu is available through the day. Bedrooms are comfortable and well equipped; some are newly updated.
ROOMS: 57 en suite (11 fmly) (2 GF) ⊗ in 8 bedrooms s £38.50-£82.50; d £77-£110 (incl. bkfst) **LB** **FACILITIES:** Sauna Gym Gym privately run prebooking necessary Xmas **CONF:** Thtr 70 Class 60 Board 35 Del from £75 **SERVICES:** Lift **PARKING:** 36 **NOTES:** ⊗ in restaurant **CARDS:**

★★★65% Cumberland

East Overcliff Dr BH1 3AF
☎ 01202 290722 📠 01202 311394
e-mail: cumberland@bluemermaidhotels.com
Many of the well-equipped and attractively decorated bedrooms at this hotel benefit from sea views and balconies. The lounges and restaurant are spacious and comfortable. The restaurant offers a daily-changing, fixed price menu. Guests may use the leisure club at the sister hotel, The Queens.
ROOMS: 102 en suite (12 fmly) s £52.50-£70; d £52.50-£70 (incl. bkfst) **LB** **FACILITIES:** Free membership of nearby Leisure Club in sister hotel ch fac Xmas **CONF:** Thtr 120 Class 70 Board 45 Del from £79 **SERVICES:** Lift **PARKING:** 51 **NOTES:** ⊗ in restaurant Civ Wed 100
CARDS:

★★★64% New Durley Dean

West Cliff Rd BH2 5HE
☎ 01202 557711 📠 01202 292815
e-mail: enquiries@newdurleydeanhotel.co.uk
Dir: From A338 or A35 turn off at West Cliff and BIC exit. Hotel on West Cliff rdbt
Conveniently situated close to the BIC and attractions, this impressive period building has undergone major refurbishment in recent years. Bedrooms are well equipped and spacious. Public areas include comfortable lounges, a lively nightclub and quieter areas. Appetising cuisine is served in the bright and spacious dining room.
ROOMS: 123 en suite (27 fmly) s £30-£65; d £60-£130 (incl. bkfst) **LB** **FACILITIES:** Sauna Solarium Gym Table tennis Steam room pool table ♫ Xmas **CONF:** Thtr 120 Class 30 Board 30 Del from £80 **SERVICES:** Lift **PARKING:** 35 **NOTES:** ⊗ in restaurant
CARDS:

★★★63% Burley Court

Bath Rd BH1 2NP
☎ 01202 552824 & 556704 📠 01202 298514
e-mail: info@burleycourthotel.co.uk
Dir: leave A338 at St Pauls rdbt, take 3rd exit at next rdbt into Holdenhurst Rd. 3rd exit at next rdbt into Bath Rd, over crossing, 1st left
Located on Bournemouth's West Cliff, this well-established hotel is easily located and convenient for the town and beaches. Bedrooms, many now refurbished, are pleasantly furnished and decorated in bright colours. A daily-changing menu is served in the spacious dining room.
ROOMS: 38 en suite (8 fmly) ⊗ in 20 bedrooms s £33-£46; d £66-£92 (incl. bkfst) **LB** **FACILITIES:** Solarium Xmas **CONF:** Thtr 30 Class 15 Board 15 **SERVICES:** Lift **PARKING:** 35 **NOTES:** ⊗ in restaurant Closed 30 Dec-14 Jan **CARDS:**

B

★★★63% Ocean View Hotel

East Overcliff Dr BH1 3AR
☎ 01202 558057 📠 01202 556285
e-mail: enquiry@oceanview.uk.com

Splendid sea views can be enjoyed from all of the public rooms at this popular East Cliff hotel. Bedrooms vary in size, and all are light, airy and well equipped. A comfortable bar/lounge offers an informal alternative to the drawing room, whilst the spacious restaurant offers a fixed-price menu every evening.

ROOMS: 52 rms (51 en suite) (13 fmly) s £56-£64; d £112-£128 (incl. bkfst & dinner) **LB** **FACILITIES:** Indoor leisure suite at Bayview Court Hotel (sister hotel) ch fac Xmas **CONF:** Thtr 120 Class 100 Board 30 Del from £70 **SERVICES:** Lift **PARKING:** 39 **NOTES:** in restaurant Civ Wed 100 **CARDS:**

★★73% New Westcliff

27-29 Chine Crescent, West Cliff BH2 5LB
☎ 01202 551926 & 551062 📠 01202 315377
e-mail: reservations@newwestcliffhotel.co.uk

Dir: *off Wessex Way at signs for Westcliff and BIC. Over Poole Road rdbt, continue along Durley Chine Rd, hotel 0.5m right*

A warm welcome awaits guests at this privately owned hotel, which has now had a complete refurbishment. The bedrooms are of different sizes and are attractively decorated and well equipped. There is a lovely garden and a bowling green as well as three lounges. All-weather leisure facilities, including a small cinema, are a definite plus.

ROOMS: 55 en suite (16 fmly) (3 GF) in 45 bedrooms s £36-£50; d £72-£100 (incl. bkfst) **LB** **FACILITIES:** Sauna Solarium Jacuzzi Cinema, Bowling Green, Ballroom Xmas **SERVICES:** Lift **PARKING:** 70 **NOTES:** in restaurant **CARDS:**

★★71% Arlington

Exeter Park Rd BH2 5BD
☎ 01202 552879 & 553012 📠 01202 298317
e-mail: enquiries@arlingtonbournemouth.co.uk
web: www.arlingtonbournemouth.co.uk

Dir: *follow BIC signs through Priory Rd, onto rdbt and exit at Royal Exeter Hotel sign. Hotel along Exeter Park Rd*

Well-equipped bedrooms and comfortable accommodation along with friendly hospitality are offered at this privately owned and run hotel. Conveniently located, midway between the square and the pier and ideally situated for the BIC, the Arlington has direct access to the flower gardens, which are overlooked from the hotel's lounge and terrace bar.

ROOMS: 27 en suite 1 annexe en suite (6 fmly) s £40-£48.50; d £80-£97 (incl. bkfst & dinner) **LB** **FACILITIES:** STV Xmas **SERVICES:** Lift **PARKING:** 21 **NOTES:** No children 2yrs in restaurant Closed 4-15 Jan **CARDS:**

★★70% Durley Grange

6 Durley Rd, West Cliff BH2 5JL
☎ 01202 554473 📠 01202 293774
e-mail: durleygrangehotel@btopenworld.com

Dir: *A338/St Michaels rdbt. Over next rdbt, 1st left into Sommerville Rd & right into Durley Rd*

This family run hotel is a firm favourite with many of its guests and is often full. Located in a quiet area, with parking, the town and beaches are all in walking distance. Bedrooms are brightly decorated, comfortable and well equipped. The bar and dining room have now been refurbished. There is an indoor pool and sauna for year-round use.

ROOMS: 51 en suite (6 fmly) (4 GF) in 2 bedrooms s £40-£52; d £80-£104 (incl. bkfst & dinner) **LB** **FACILITIES: Spa** STV Sauna Solarium Xmas **SERVICES:** Lift **PARKING:** 35 **NOTES:** in restaurant Closed 2 Jan-1 Feb **CARDS:**

★★68% Sun Court

32 West Hill Rd BH2 5PH
☎ 01202 551343 📠 01202 316747
e-mail: sales@theconnaught.co.uk

Dir: *from A338 follow signs to West Cliff. First exit off St Michaels rdbt. 1st right into West Hill Road*

Located on the West Cliff, this hotel is well placed to offer convenient access to the town centre and seafront attractions. Bedrooms come in a range of sizes, some have sun lounges and there are also some family rooms. Public areas include an airy restaurant, a residents' lounge and a friendly bar where live entertainment is laid on for guests' enjoyment.

ROOMS: 33 en suite (7 fmly) s £30-£53; d £60-£106 (incl. bkfst) **FACILITIES:** STV Use of leisure facilities at nearby hotel Xmas **SERVICES:** Lift **PARKING:** 28 **NOTES:** in restaurant **CARDS:**

★★68% Whitehall

Exeter Park Rd BH2 5AX
☎ 01202 554682 📠 01202 292637
e-mail: reservations@thewhitehallhotel.co.uk
web: www.thewhitehallhotel.co.uk

Dir: *follow BIC signs then turn into Exeter Park Rd off Exeter Rd*

This friendly hotel enjoys an elevated position overlooking the park and is also close to the town centre and seafront. The spacious public areas include a choice of lounges, a cosy bar and a well-presented restaurant. The bedrooms are spread over three floors and are inviting and well equipped.

ROOMS: 46 en suite (5 fmly) (3 GF) in 20 bedrooms s £33-£55; d £66-£110 (incl. bkfst) **LB** **FACILITIES:** Xmas **CONF:** Thtr 70 Class 40 Board 32 Del from £50 **SERVICES:** Lift **PARKING:** 25 **NOTES:** in restaurant **CARDS:**

Late for dinner?
Quality Standards mean that last orders for dinner vary according to star rating and should be no earlier than:
★★ 7.00pm ★★★ 8.00pm ★★★★ 9.00pm
★★★★★ 10.00pm

Indoor Swimming Pool
Indoor Swimming Pool (heated)
Outdoor Swimming Pool
Outdoor Swimming Pool (heated)

B

BOURNEMOUTH, Dorset Map 05 SZ19

★★67% Mansfield
West Cliff Gardens BH2 5HL
☎ 01202 552659 01202 297115
e-mail: mail@bournemouthhotel.net
web: www.bournemouthhotel.net
Dir: *from A338 follow signs for West Cliff, over 2 rdbts via Cambridge & Durley Chine Rd*
This friendly and family-run hotel is located in a quiet crescent on the West Cliff and is convenient for access to the seafront and town centre. Bedrooms are comfortably furnished and many have four-poster beds. The inviting lounge is thoughtfully divided into smoking and non-smoking areas and generous portions of home cooking can be expected in the dining room.
ROOMS: 29 en suite (3 fmly) (2 GF) in 4 bedrooms
FACILITIES: Xmas **PARKING:** 12 **NOTES:** in restaurant
CARDS:

★★66% Bourne Hall Hotel
14 Priory Rd, West Cliff BH2 5DN
☎ 01202 299715 01202 552669
e-mail: info@bournehall.co.uk web: www.bournehall.co.uk
Dir: *M27/A31 from Ringwood into Bournemouth on A338, Wessex Way. Follow signs to BIC, onto West Cliff. Hotel on right*
A friendly, comfortable hotel conveniently located close to the BIC and seafront. Bedrooms are well equipped; some rooms are located on the ground floor and some have sea views. There is a spacious lounge, two bars and a meeting area provided.
ROOMS: 48 en suite (9 fmly) (5 GF) in all bedrooms s £35-£59; d £60-£90 (incl. bkfst) **LB** **FACILITIES:** STV ♫ Xmas **CONF:** Thtr 130 Class 60 Board 40 Del from £70 **SERVICES:** Lift **PARKING:** 35
NOTES: in restaurant **CARDS:**

★★66% Ullswater
West Cliff Gardens BH2 5HW
☎ 01202 555181 01202 317896
e-mail: enq@ullswater.uk.com web: www.ullswater.uk.com
Dir: *In Bournemouth follow signs to West Cliff. Hotel just off Westcliff Rd*
Conveniently situated close to the city centre and seafront, this pleasant hotel enjoys comfortable accommodation and attracts a loyal following. Bedrooms, many now refurbished, are generously equipped and offer a range of sizes, and the lounge and dining room are spacious and smartly appointed. Cuisine offers a good choice from the daily-changing menu.
ROOMS: 42 en suite (8 fmly) (2 GF) s £30-£38; d £60-£76 (incl. bkfst) **LB** **FACILITIES:** Snooker Table tennis ♫ Xmas **CONF:** Thtr 40 Class 30 Board 24 Del from £50 **SERVICES:** Lift **PARKING:** 10 **NOTES:** in restaurant **CARDS:**

★★65% Fircroft
4 Owls Rd BH5 1AE
☎ 01202 309771 01202 395644
e-mail: info@fircrofthotel.co.uk
web: www.fircrofthotel.co.uk
Dir: *off A338 signed Boscombe Pier. Hotel 400yds from pier close to Christchurch Rd*
This friendly hotel is pleasantly located close to Boscombe pier. Offering a range of comfortable lounges and meeting facilities, the hotel is popular with tour and dance groups. In addition, entertainment is provided most nights throughout the year. All of the bedrooms are comfortable and well equipped.
ROOMS: 51 en suite (20 fmly) s £30-£36; d £60-£72 (incl. bkfst) **LB**
FACILITIES: Sauna Solarium Gym Jacuzzi Sports at health club owned by hotel Xmas **CONF:** Thtr 200 Class 100 Board 40 Del £50
SERVICES: Lift **PARKING:** 50 **NOTES:** in restaurant
CARDS:

★★64% *Aaron Croham Hurst*
9 Durley Rd South, West Cliff BH2 5JH
☎ 01202 552353 01202 311484
e-mail: enquiries@crohamhurst.co.uk
This friendly hotel is popular with individuals and coach parties alike and is conveniently located for the beach and town centre. Bedrooms come in a variety of sizes and styles and all are well equipped. The lounge is also the venue for regular evening entertainment and the restaurant offers traditional home-cooked meals.
ROOMS: 41 en suite (11 fmly) (8 GF) **FACILITIES:** STV ♫
SERVICES: Lift **PARKING:** 28 **NOTES:** in restaurant
CARDS:

★★64% Bournemouth Sands
2 West Cliff Gardens BH2 5HR
☎ 01202 312314 01202 312315
e-mail: reservations@bournemouthsandshotel.com
Dir: *M27 -Five roads behind Bournemouth International Centre*
Conveniently located for the Bournemouth International Centre, beaches and other attractions, this friendly hotel offers a relaxed and informal atmosphere to guests. Bedrooms are simply furnished and comfortable. A choice of bars and lounges are available and entertainment is provided most evenings throughout the year.
ROOMS: 65 en suite (17 fmly) s £20-£38; d £40-£76 (incl. bkfst) **LB**
FACILITIES: Guests have use of leisure facilities at sister hotel Xmas
CONF: Thtr 120 Class 60 Board 30 **SERVICES:** Lift **PARKING:** 65
NOTES: in restaurant **CARDS:**

★★64% *Cliff Court*
15 Westcliff Rd BH2 5EX
☎ 01202 555994 01202 780954
e-mail: info@cliffcourthotel.com
Dir: *A338 Wessex Way into Cambridge Rd. Follow Durley Chine Rd into West Cliff Rd*
This friendly hotel enjoys easy access to the main approach roads and the seafront, which is only a few minutes' walk away. It is popular with tour groups, and boasts a spacious dining room, a bar and small lounge. The comfortable bedrooms make best use of the available space.
ROOMS: 40 en suite (4 fmly) **FACILITIES:** STV ♫ **SERVICES:** Lift
PARKING: 31 **NOTES:** in restaurant **CARDS:**

★★63% Devon Towers
58-62 St Michael's Rd, West Cliff BH2 5ED
☎ 01202 553863 01202 315265
e-mail: devontowers.bournemouth@alfatravel.co.uk

Leisureplex

Dir: *A338 into Bournemouth, follow signs for BIC. Left into St. Michaels Rd at top of hill. Hotel 100mtrs on left*
Located in a quiet road within walking distance of the West Cliff and central shops, this hotel appeals to the budget leisure market. The four-course menus offer plenty of choice and entertainment is featured on most evenings. The bar and lobby area offer plenty of space for relaxing.
ROOMS: 54 en suite (6 GF) s £30-£39; d £50-£68 (incl. bkfst) **LB**
FACILITIES: ♫ Xmas **SERVICES:** Lift **PARKING:** 6 **NOTES:** in restaurant Closed Jan-mid Feb ex Xmas RS Nov, Feb & Mar
CARDS:

Town House Hotel
Country House Hotel
Travel Accommodation

Pavilion
22 Bath Rd BH1 2NS
☎ 01202 291266 📠 01202 559264
e-mail: info@pavilion-hotel.com
Dir: *A388 left at St Paul's rdbt. 3rd exit at Bournemouth Station rdbt. Straight on at Lansdowne rdbt onto Bath Road. Hotel 150yds on left*
At the time of going to press, the star classification for this hotel was not confirmed. Please refer to the AA internet site www.theAA.com for current information.
ROOMS: 43 en suite (6 fmly) s £42-£54; d £84-£108 (incl. bkfst) **LB** **FACILITIES:** Special rates for International Centre Xmas **CONF:** Thtr 100 Class 50 Board 50 Del from £65 **SERVICES:** Lift **PARKING:** 40 **NOTES:** in restaurant **CARDS:**

Innkeeper's Lodge Bournemouth
Cooper Dean Roundabout, Castle Ln East BH7 7DP
☎ 01202 390837 📠 01202 390378
www.innkeeperslodge.com
Dir: *A338 Bournemouth spur road, follow until exit signed Bournemouth Hospital. Hotel on corner next to hospital*
Smart rooms meet essential business requirements but also have home comforts, and depending on location may well have meeting rooms and pub dining. Dining options generally include all-day menus plus the added advantage of breakfast.
ROOMS: 28 en suite s £59; d £59 **CONF:** Thtr 30 Class 22 Board 18

Travelodge (Bournemouth)
43 Christchurch Rd BH1 3NS
☎ 08700 850950
ROOMS: 107 en suite
NOTES: Due to open late Sept 2004

BOURTON-ON-THE-WATER, Gloucestershire
Map 10 SP12

★★77% **Dial House**
The Chestnuts, High St GL54 2AN
☎ 01451 822244 📠 01451 810126
e-mail: info@dialhousehotel.com
web: www.dialhousehotel.com
Dir: *off A429, 0.5m to village centre*

Tucked away in the centre of this beguiling village, this mellow, Cotswold-stone hotel dates back to 1698. In the summer guests can enjoy delightful gardens, and in winter log fires and comfy sofas ensure relaxation. Two intimate dining rooms provide the setting for quality cuisine, whilst bedrooms, including ones with four-posters, are comfortably furnished and well equipped.
ROOMS: 13 en suite (7 GF) in all bedrooms s £55-£114; d £110-£175 (incl. bkfst) **LB** **FACILITIES:** Putt green Xmas **CONF:** Class 15 Board 15 **PARKING:** 20 **NOTES:** No children 10 yrs in restaurant **CARDS:**

BOVEY TRACEY, Devon
Map 03 SX87

★★70% **Coombe Cross**
Coombe Ln TQ13 9EY
☎ 01626 832476 📠 01626 835298
e-mail: info@coombecross.co.uk
web: www.coombecross.co.uk
Dir: *A38 signed Bovey Tracey & town centre, along High St, up hill 400yds beyond Parish Church. Hotel on left*

With delightful views over Dartmoor, this peaceful hotel is set in well-tended gardens on the edge of the town. There are comfortable public areas and bedrooms and a range of leisure and fitness facilities is available. At dinner, carefully prepared dishes are served in the spacious dining room.
ROOMS: 22 en suite (1 fmly) (2 GF) in all bedrooms s £39-£44; d £58-£74 (incl. bkfst) **LB** **FACILITIES: Spa** Sauna Solarium Gym Table tennis **CONF:** Thtr 80 Class 30 Board 30 Del from £73.50 **PARKING:** 20 **NOTES:** in restaurant Closed 24 Dec-31 Jan **CARDS:**

BOWNESS ON WINDERMERE See Windermere

BOXWORTH, Cambridgeshire
Map 12 TL36

Sleep Inn Cambridge
Cambridge Services A14 CB3 8WU
☎ 01954 268400 📠 01954 268419
e-mail: enquiries@hotels-cambridge.com
Dir: *A14 junct 28 6m N of Cambridge. 8m S of Huntington*
This modern, purpose built accommodation offers smartly appointed, well-equipped bedrooms, with good power showers. There is a choice of adjacent food outlets where guests may enjoy breakfast, snacks and meals.
ROOMS: 82 en suite s £53.50-£59.95; d £53.50-£59.95

BRACKNELL, Berkshire
Map 05 SU86
See also Crowthorne & Wokingham

★★★★73% **Coppid Beech**
John Nike Way RG12 8TF
☎ 01344 303333 📠 01344 301200
e-mail: welcome@coppid-beech-hotel.co.uk
web: www.coppidbeech.com
Dir: *M4 junct 10 take Wokingham/Bracknell onto A329. In 2m take B3408 to Binfield at rdbt. Hotel 200yds on right*
This chalet-style complex offers extensive facilities and includes a ski-slope, ice rink, nightclub, health club and Bier Keller. Bedrooms offer a range of suites and standard rooms, all of which are impressively equipped. A choice of dining is offered and a full

continued on p116

BRACKNELL, continued

bistro menu is available in the Keller. For more formal dining Rowan's restaurant provides award-winning cuisine.
ROOMS: 205 en suite (6 fmly) ⊗ in 138 bedrooms s £110-£175; d £120-£195 (incl. bkfst) **LB** **FACILITIES: Spa** STV supervised Sauna Solarium Gym Jacuzzi Dry ski slope, Ice rink ♫ ch fac Xmas **CONF:** BC Thtr 400 Class 240 Board 24 Del from £185 **SERVICES:** Lift **PARKING:** 350 **NOTES:** Civ Wed 120 **CARDS:**

See advert on opposite page

★★★★67% Grange Bracknell
Charles Square RG12 1DF
☎ 01344 474000 01344 474125
e-mail: bracknell@grangehotels.co.uk

Just a few years ago the former Honeywell Offices opened their doors as an impressive Four Star hotel. Lighting is used to impressive effect both inside and outside to create a modern environment that is both comfortable and stylish. Public rooms include the Callela Bar, Ascot Green Restaurant, a fitness suite and a range of interconnecting conference and banqueting rooms. Air-conditioned bedrooms are spacious and come equipped with a host of extras.
ROOMS: 120 en suite (6 fmly) ⊗ in 60 bedrooms s £225; d £225 **LB** **FACILITIES:** STV Gym Xmas **CONF:** Thtr 200 Class 120 Board 80 Del from £220 **SERVICES:** Lift air con **PARKING:** 111 **NOTES:** **CARDS:**

★★★71% Stirrups Country House
Maidens Green RG42 6LD
☎ 01344 882284 01344 882300
e-mail: reception@stirrupshotel.co.uk
web: www.stirrupshotel.co.uk
Dir: *3m N on B3022 towards Windsor*
Situated in a peaceful location between Maidenhead, Bracknell and Windsor, this hotel has high standards of comfort in the bedrooms, with newer rooms boasting a small sitting room area. There is a popular bar, a refurbished restaurant, function rooms and the grounds are delightful.
ROOMS: 30 en suite (4 fmly) (2 GF) ⊗ in 20 bedrooms s £80-£135; d £100-£180 **LB** **FACILITIES:** STV **CONF:** Thtr 100 Class 50 Board 40 Del from £140 **SERVICES:** Lift **PARKING:** 100 **NOTES:** ⊗ in restaurant Civ Wed 100 **CARDS:**

Travel Inn
Arlington Square, Wokingham Rd RG42 1NA
☎ 08701 977036 01344 319526
Dir: *M4 (J10) A329(M) Bracknell to lights. 1st left, 3rd exit rdbt by Safeway to town centre. Left at rdbt, left at next rdbt. Travel Inn on left.*
Travel Inn offers good-quality, value-for-money accommodation. Spacious, en suite rooms with bath and shower comfortably accommodate a family of up to two adults and two children (to age 15). The restaurant and bar offers a varied menu. For further details consult the Hotel Groups page.
ROOMS: 60 en suite s £56.95; d £56.95

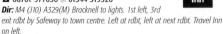

AA Rosette Award for culinary excellence

Popped the question?
Hotels with Civ Wed in their entry are licensed for civil wedding ceremonies. Maximum numbers for the ceremony only are shown, e.g. Civ Wed 120

BRADFORD, West Yorkshire Map 19 SE13
See also Gomersal & Shipley

★★★★63% Hanover International Hotel & Club
Mayo Av, Off Rooley Ln BD5 8HZ
☎ 01274 406606 & 406601 01274 406600
e-mail: enquiries.bradford@hanover-international.com
Dir: *M62 junct 26/M606. At end take 3rd exit off rdbt onto A6177 towards Bradford. Take 1st sharp right at lights*
This modern, attractive hotel is conveniently located just off the motorway and within easy access of the city centre and the airport. The hotel boasts extensive function and conference facilities, a well-equipped leisure club and an elegant restaurant. Bedrooms are comfortably appointed for both business and leisure guests.
ROOMS: 131 en suite (7 fmly) ⊗ in 75 bedrooms **FACILITIES:** STV Sauna Solarium Gym Jacuzzi Pool table **CONF:** BC Thtr 800 Class 300 Board 100 **SERVICES:** Lift **PARKING:** 300 **NOTES:** Civ Wed 600 **CARDS:**

★★★70% Midland Hotel
Forster Square BD1 4HU
☎ 01274 735735 01274 720003
e-mail: info@midland-hotel-bradford.com
Dir: *A6177/ A641/A6181. Past St Georges Hall to Eastbrook Well rdbt. Take 1st exit along Petergate to Forster Sq, left to Cheapside. Hotel on right*

Ideally situated in the heart of the city, this grand Victorian hotel provides modern, well-equipped accommodation and comfortable, spacious day rooms. Ample parking is available in what used to be the city's railway station, and a passage dating from Victorian times linking the hotel to the old platform can still be used today.
ROOMS: 90 en suite (4 fmly) ⊗ in 40 bedrooms s £94-£104; d £104-£118 **FACILITIES:** STV Free use of local health club ♫ ch fac Xmas **CONF:** BC Thtr 450 Class 150 Board 100 Del from £115 **SERVICES:** Lift **PARKING:** 50 **NOTES:** Civ Wed 400
CARDS:

★★★68% Courtyard by Marriott Leeds/Bradford
The Pastures, Tong Ln BD4 0RP
☎ 0870 400 7218 0870 400 7318
Dir: *M62 junct 27/A650 towards Bradford. 3rd rdbt, take 3rd exit to Tong Village & Pudsey. Left into Tong Lane. Hotel 0.5m on right*
Built onto an elegant, 19th-century former vicarage, this modern, stylish hotel has been sympathetically designed to complement its Victorian heritage. The hotel is particularly well located for both Leeds and Bradford and the local motorway networks. The well-equipped bedrooms are furnished and decorated to a high standard.
ROOMS: 53 en suite (8 fmly) (11 GF) ⊗ in 31 bedrooms s fr £91; d fr £91 **FACILITIES:** STV Gym **CONF:** Thtr 200 Class 150 Board 100 Del from £115 **SERVICES:** Lift **PARKING:** 230 **NOTES:** Civ Wed 100
CARDS:

B

★★★68% Guide Post Hotel

Common Rd, Low Moor BD12 0ST
☎ 01274 607866 📠 01274 671085
e-mail: sales@guideposthotel.net
web: www.guideposthotel.net
Dir: *take M606, then signed*

Situated south of the city, this hotel offers attractively furnished, comfortable bedrooms. The restaurant offers an extensive range of food using fresh, local produce; lighter snack meals are served in the bar. There is a choice of well-equipped meeting and function rooms.

ROOMS: 43 en suite (3 fmly) (14 GF) ⊘ in 8 bedrooms s £50-£95; d £60-£105 (incl. bkfst) **FACILITIES:** STV **CONF:** Thtr 120 Class 80 Board 60 Del £99.50 **PARKING:** 10 **NOTES:** ⊘ in restaurant Civ Wed 100 **CARDS:**

★★★63% Novotel Bradford

6 Roydsdale Way BD4 6SA
☎ 01274 683683 📠 01274 651342
e-mail: h0510@accor-hotels.com
Dir: *M606 junct 2, exit to Euroway Trading Estate turn right at traffic lights at bottom of slip road, take 2nd right onto Roydsdale Way*

This purpose-built hotel stands in an good location for access to the motorway. It provides spacious bedrooms that are comfortably equipped. Open-plan day rooms include a stylish bar, and a lounge that leads into the Garden Brasserie. Several function rooms are also available.

ROOMS: 119 en suite (37 fmly) (9 GF) ⊘ in 69 bedrooms s £60; d £60 **LB** **FACILITIES:** STV Xmas **CONF:** Thtr 200 Class 100 Board 100 Del £95 **SERVICES:** Lift **PARKING:** 200 **NOTES:** Civ Wed 200 **CARDS:**

BRADFORD, continued

Travel Inn (Leeds Bradford South)
Wakefield Rd, Drighlington BD11 1EA
08701 977152 0113 287 9115
Dir: *on Drighlington Bypass, adjacent to M62 J27. Follow A650 to Bradford then right to Drighlington, turn right and Inn on left*
Travel Inn offers good-quality, value-for-money accommodation. Spacious, en suite rooms with bath and shower comfortably accommodate a family of up to two adults and two children (to age 15). The restaurant and bar offers a varied menu. For further details consult the Hotel Groups page.
ROOMS: 42 en suite s £45.95-£46.95; d £45.95-£46.95

BRADFORD-ON-AVON, Wiltshire — Map 04 ST86

★★★73% Woolley Grange
Woolley Green BA15 1TX
01225 864705 01225 864059
e-mail: info@woolleygrange.com
web: www.luxuryfamilyhotels.com
Dir: *Turn off A4 onto B3109. Bradford Leigh, left at crossroads, hotel 0.5m on right at Woolley Green*

This splendid Cotswold manor house is set in beautiful countryside. Children are made especially welcome; there is a trained nanny on duty in the nursery. Bedrooms and public areas are charmingly furnished and decorated in true country-house style, with many thoughtful touches and luxurious extras. The hotel offers a varied and well-balanced menu selection, including ingredients from the hotel's own garden.
ROOMS: 14 en suite 12 annexe en suite (8 fmly) s £121-£157; d £160-£395 (incl. bkfst & dinner) **LB** **FACILITIES:** Putt green Badminton, Games room, beauty treatments ch fac Xmas **CONF:** Thtr 35 Class 12 Board 22 Del from £150 **PARKING:** 40 **NOTES:** in restaurant **CARDS:**

★★★70% Leigh Park Hotel
Leigh Park West BA15 2RA
01225 864885 01225 862315
e-mail: leighparkhotel@lineone.net
Dir: *A363 Bath/Frome road. Take B3105 signed Holt/Woolley Green. Hotel 0.25m on right on x-roads of B3105/B3109. N side of Bradford-on-Avon*

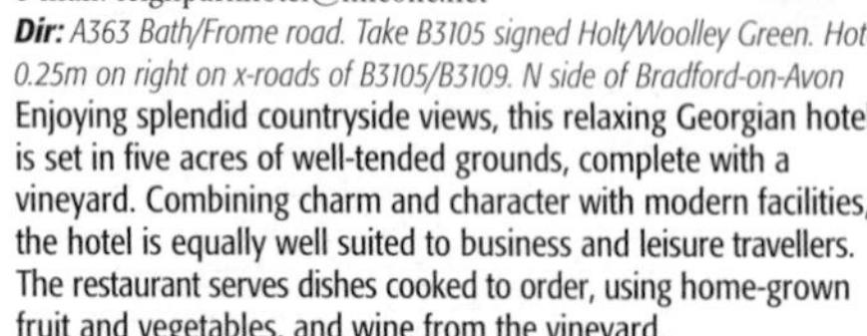

Enjoying splendid countryside views, this relaxing Georgian hotel is set in five acres of well-tended grounds, complete with a vineyard. Combining charm and character with modern facilities, the hotel is equally well suited to business and leisure travellers. The restaurant serves dishes cooked to order, using home-grown fruit and vegetables, and wine from the vineyard.
ROOMS: 22 en suite (4 fmly) (7 GF) in 14 bedrooms s £75-£78; d £110-£130 (incl. bkfst) **LB** **FACILITIES:** Xmas **CONF:** Thtr 120 Class 60 Board 60 Del from £105 **PARKING:** 80 **NOTES:** in restaurant Civ Wed 120 **CARDS:**

BRAINTREE, Essex — Map 07 TL72

★★★65% White Hart
Bocking End CM7 9AB
01376 321401 01376 552628
Dir: *off A120 towards town centre. Hotel at junct B1256 & Bocking Causeway*
This 18th-century former coaching inn is conveniently located in the heart of the bustling town centre. Now refurbished, public rooms include a large lounge bar, restaurant and meeting rooms. The pleasantly decorated, well-equipped bedrooms provide a good level of comfort throughout.
ROOMS: 31 en suite (8 fmly) in 21 bedrooms s £75; d £90 (incl. bkfst) **LB** **FACILITIES:** STV **CONF:** Thtr 40 Class 16 Board 24 Del from £100 **PARKING:** 52 **NOTES:** in restaurant **CARDS:**

Travel Inn
Cressing Rd, Galley's Corner CM7 8GG
08701 977039 01376 555087
Dir: *On A120 bypass at Braintree junction of Cressing Road & Galley's Corner*
Travel Inn offers good-quality, value-for-money accommodation. Spacious, en suite rooms with bath and shower comfortably accommodate a family of up to two adults and two children (to age 15). The restaurant and bar offers a varied menu. For further details consult the Hotel Groups page.
ROOMS: 40 en suite s £45.95-£48.95; d £45.95-£48.95

BRAITHWAITE, Cumbria — Map 18 NY22

★★74% The Cottage in the Wood
Whinlatter Pass CA12 5TW
017687 78409 017687 78064
e-mail: info@thecottageinthewood.co.uk
Dir: *A66 for Cockermouth & Keswick. After Keswick, turn off for Braithwaite & Lorton via Whinlatter Pass (B5292). Hotel at top of Whinlatter Pass*
Aptly named, this charming little hotel sits amid wooded hills with striking views of distant peaks, and is convenient for Keswick. Enthusiastic owners provide excellent hospitality in a friendly relaxed manner. Dinner is freshly prepared from a set menu and offers a vegetarian choice, and there is also a small residents' bar.
ROOMS: 10 en suite (1 fmly) (1 GF) in all bedrooms s £45-£50; d £70-£90 (incl. bkfst) **LB** **FACILITIES:** Xmas **PARKING:** 15 **NOTES:** No children 8yrs in restaurant Closed Jan-mid Feb RS Mon eve **CARDS:**

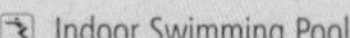

Indoor Swimming Pool
Indoor Swimming Pool (heated)
Outdoor Swimming Pool
Outdoor Swimming Pool (heated)

BRAMHALL, Greater Manchester Map 16 SJ88

★★★61% The County Hotel

Bramhall Ln South SK7 2EB
☎ 0870 609 6148 📠 0161 440 8071
Dir: *A34 by-pass to Bramhall. In Bramhall village at rdbt turn R, continue under bridge. Hotel 100yds on right.*

This hotel is situated in a quiet residential area on the edge of Bramhall, within easy reach of the airport and Cheadle shopping centre. Bedrooms are well equipped and include a number of ground floor rooms. Public areas include an open plan lounge restaurant and the traditional Shires Pub.
ROOMS: 65 en suite (3 fmly) (20 GF) ⊗ in 20 bedrooms s £80; d £80 **LB FACILITIES:** Xmas **CONF:** Thtr 200 Class 80 Board 60 Del from £84 **PARKING:** 120 **NOTES:** ⊗ in restaurant Civ Wed 100
CARDS:

BRAMPTON, Cambridgeshire Map 12 TL27

★★69% The Grange

115 High St PE28 4RA
☎ 01480 459516 📠 01480 459391
e-mail: nsteiger@grangehotelbrampton.com
web: www.grangehotelbrampton.com
Dir: *A1(M)/A14 towards Cambridge. After 0.5m take B1514 (racecourse) towards Huntingdon. After mini rdbt turn right into Grove Ln, hotel opp t-junct at bottom of road*
Located on the high street in the quiet village of Brampton, this historic building offers smartly appointed bedrooms; those newly refurbished are most attractively decorated. Imaginative cuisine is served in both the light and airy restaurant and in the more informal and inviting bar area. Guests have access to a comfortable lounge and service is both friendly and attentive.
ROOMS: 7 en suite ⊗ in all bedrooms s £60-£75; d £75-£90 (incl. bkfst) **CONF:** Thtr 30 Class 15 Board 36 **PARKING:** 20 **NOTES:** ⊗ in restaurant RS 29 Dec-5 Jan Civ Wed 40
CARDS:

Travel Inn (Huntingdon)

travel inn

Brampton Hut PE28 4NQ
☎ 08701 977139 📠 01480 811298
Dir: *junct of A1/A14. (From north do not use junct 14 but take next main exit for Huntingdon & Brampton). Access via services*
Travel Inn offers good-quality, value-for-money accommodation. Spacious, en suite rooms with bath and shower comfortably accommodate a family of up to two adults and two children (to age 15). The restaurant and bar offers a varied menu. For further details consult the Hotel Groups page.
ROOMS: 80 en suite s £45.95-£46.95; d £45.95-£46.95 **CONF:** Thtr 25

TV dinner?
Room service at three stars and above

BRAMPTON, Cumbria Map 21 NY56

Top 200 – Hotel

★★★ Farlam Hall

RELAIS & CHATEAUX

CA8 2NG
☎ 016977 46234 📠 016977 46683
e-mail: farlamhall@dial.pipex.com
web: www.farlamhall.co.uk
Dir: *On A689 (Brampton to Alston). Hotel 2m, not in Farlam*
This delightful family-run country house dates back to 1428. Steeped in history, the hotel is set in beautifully landscaped Victorian gardens complete with an ornamental lake and stream. Lovingly restored over many years, it now provides the highest standards of comfort and hospitality. Gracious public rooms invite relaxation, whilst every thought has gone into the beautiful bedrooms, many of which are simply stunning.
ROOMS: 11 en suite 1 annexe en suite (2 GF) ⊗ in all bedrooms s £135-£160; d £270-£300 (incl. bkfst & dinner) **LB FACILITIES:** **CONF:** Thtr 12 Class 12 Board 12 **PARKING:** 35 **NOTES:** No children 5yrs ⊗ in restaurant Closed 25-30 Dec **CARDS:**

BRANCASTER STAITHE, Norfolk Map 13 TF74

★★75% White Horse

PE31 8BY
☎ 01485 210262 📠 01485 210930
e-mail: reception@whitehorsebrancaster.co.uk
web: www.whitehorsebrancaster.co.uk
Dir: *on A149 between Hunstanton & Wells-next-the-Sea*

A charming hotel on the north Norfolk coast with stunning views over the tidal marshes to Scolt Head Island. The contemporary bedrooms, in two wings, are attractively decorated, some featuring an interesting cobbled fascia, and thoughtfully equipped. One even has a viewing telescope. There is a large bar and lounge area leading to the conservatory restaurant which has wide-sweeping views.
ROOMS: 7 en suite 8 annexe en suite (5 fmly) (8 GF) s £72-£90; d £104-£140 (incl. bkfst) **LB FACILITIES:** Bar billiards Xmas **PARKING:** 60 **NOTES:** ⊗ in restaurant **CARDS:**

BRANDESBURTON, East Riding of Yorkshire Map 17 TA14

★★68% Burton Lodge
YO25 8RU
☎ 01964 542847 01964 544771
e-mail: email@burtonlodge.fsnet.co.uk
Dir: *7m from Beverley off A165, adjoining Hainsworth Park Golf Club*
A tennis court, sports play area and extensive lawn are features of this friendly hotel, which is situated on a golf course. Rooms are modern and there is a comfortable lounge, while the spacious restaurant serves excellent home cooking.
ROOMS: 7 en suite 2 annexe en suite (3 fmly) (2 GF) in 5 bedrooms s £38-£42; d £58-£60 (incl. bkfst) **LB FACILITIES:** 18 Putt green Pitch and putt **CONF:** Class 20 **PARKING:** 15 **NOTES:** in restaurant **CARDS:**

BRANDON, Suffolk Map 13 TL78

★★66% *Brandon House*
High St IP27 0AX
☎ 01842 810171 01842 814859
Dir: *In town centre left at traffic lights into High St. Hotel 400yds on right after small bridge over River Ouse*
An 18th-century, red brick manor house set in landscaped gardens a short walk from the town centre. The pleasantly decorated, well-maintained bedrooms are thoughtfully equipped and come in a variety of styles. Public rooms include a comfortable lounge bar, the Conifers English Restaurant and a more relaxed bistro.
ROOMS: 15 en suite (3 fmly) **FACILITIES:** STV **CONF:** Thtr 70 Class 25 Board 20 **PARKING:** 40 **NOTES:** in restaurant Closed 25-26 Dec & 1 Jan **CARDS:**

BRANDON, Warwickshire Map 11 SP47

★★★66% Brandon Hall
Main St CV8 3FW
☎ 0870 400 8105 024 7654 4909
e-mail: general.brandonhall@macdonald-hotels.co.uk
MACDONALD HOTELS
Dir: *A45 towards Coventry S. After Peugeot-Citroen garage on left, at island take 5th exit to M1 South/London (back onto A45). After 200yds, immediately after Texaco garage, left into Brandon Ln, hotel after 2.5m*
Formerly a shooting lodge, the hotel is set in 17 acres of well-kept lawns and woodland and is located within easy reach of both Coventry and Rugby. Public rooms are stylish and modern, while bedrooms are more traditional in style. Leisure facilities include squash courts and a pitch-and-putt course on site.
ROOMS: 60 en suite (7 fmly) (20 GF) in 35 bedrooms s £85-£125; d £105-£145 (incl. bkfst) **LB FACILITIES:** STV Squash Putt green Xmas **CONF:** Thtr 120 Class 40 Board 36 Del from £120 **PARKING:** 100 **NOTES:** in restaurant Civ Wed 80
CARDS:

AA Rosette Award for culinary excellence

BRANDS HATCH, Kent Map 06 TQ56

★★★★74% Brandshatch Place
Brands Hatch Rd, Fawkham DA3 8NQ
HandPICKED
☎ 01474 875000 01474 879652
e-mail: brandshatchplace@handpicked.co.uk
Dir: *M25 junct 3/A20 West Kingsdown. Left at paddock entrance/Fawkham Green sign. 3rd left signed Fawkham Rd. Hotel 500mtrs on right*

This charming 18th-century Georgian country house close to the famous racing circuit has undergone an extensive refurbishment programme. Public areas have been completely transformed and include a range of stylish and elegant rooms. Bedrooms have also been upgraded to a very high standard, offering impressive facilities and levels of comfort and quality. The hotel also features a comprehensive leisure club with substantial crèche facilities. Hand Picked Hotels - AA Hotel Group of the Year 2004-5.
ROOMS: 26 en suite 12 annexe en suite (1 fmly) in 10 bedrooms **FACILITIES: Spa** STV Squash Snooker Sauna Solarium Gym Jacuzzi Use of health/leisure club Xmas **CONF:** Thtr 120 Class 60 Board 50 **PARKING:** 100 **NOTES:** in restaurant Civ Wed 80
CARDS:

See advert on opposite page

BRANKSOME See Poole

BRANSCOMBE, Devon Map 04 SY18

★★68% The Masons Arms
EX12 3DJ
☎ 01297 680300 01297 680500
e-mail: reception@masonsarms.co.uk
Dir: *off A3052 towards Branscombe, hotel in valley at bottom of hill*
This delightful 14th-century village inn is just half a mile from the sea. Bedrooms in the annexed thatched cottages tend to be more spacious and most have their own patio area with seating, whilst those in the inn enjoy the characters and charm of the period, as do the bars and public areas. An extensive selection of dishes, which includes many local specialities, is offered. The Waterfall Restaurant offers a more formal dining option.
ROOMS: 6 rms (4 en suite) 16 annexe en suite (2 fmly) (1 GF) s £25-£130; d £50-£150 (incl. bkfst) **LB FACILITIES:** Xmas **PARKING:** 43 **NOTES:** in restaurant **CARDS:**

BRAY, Berkshire Map 06 SU97

★★★★64% Monkey Island
Old Mill Ln SL6 2EE
☎ 01628 623400 01628 784732
e-mail: info@monkeyisland.co.uk
Dir: *M4 junct 8/9/A308 signed Windsor. 1st left into Bray, 1st right into Old Mill Lane, opp Crown pub*

This riverside hotel is charmingly set on an island in the Thames, within easy reach of major routes. Access is by footbridge or boat, but there is a large car park nearby. The hotel comprises two buildings, one for accommodation and the other for dining and drinking. The ample grounds are beautifully maintained and provide a peaceful haven for wildlife.
ROOMS: 26 en suite (1 fmly) (12 GF) **FACILITIES:** STV Fishing Boating Xmas **CONF:** Thtr 120 Class 70 Board 50 **PARKING:** 100 **NOTES:** in restaurant Civ Wed **CARDS:**

BREADSALL, Derbyshire Map 11 SK33

★★★★65% Marriott Breadsall Priory Hotel, Country Club
Moor Rd DE7 6DL
☎ 01332 832235 01332 833509
Dir: *A52 to Derby, then signs to Chesterfield. Right at 1st rdbt, left at next. Follow A608 to Heanor Rd, after 3m left then left again*
This extended mansion house is set in 400 acres of parkland and well-tended gardens. The smart bedrooms are mostly contained in the modern wing. There is a vibrant café-bar, a more formal restaurant and a large room-service menu. The extensive leisure facilities, including a golf course and swimming pool, are an asset. Dinner in the Priory Restaurant is a highlight.
ROOMS: 12 en suite 100 annexe en suite (35 fmly) in 69 bedrooms **FACILITIES:** STV 18 Sauna Solarium Gym Putt green Jacuzzi Health, beauty & hair salon, dance studio Xmas **CONF:** Thtr 120 Class 50 Board 36 Del from £150 **SERVICES:** Lift **PARKING:** 300 **NOTES:** in restaurant Civ Wed 100
CARDS:

GF Indicates the number of bedrooms at ground floor level.

Late for dinner?
Quality Standards mean that last orders for dinner vary according to star rating and should be no earlier than:
★★ 7.00pm ★★★ 8.00pm ★★★★ 9.00pm
★★★★★ 10.00pm

BRENTFORD, Greater London
See LONDON plan 1 C3

Travelodge (London Kew Bridge)

Travelodge

North Rd, High St TW8 0BO
☎ 08700 850 950 🖷 0208 758 1190
Dir: *M4 junct 2, Chiswick Roundabout turn right towards Kew, at traffic lights turn right in to Kew Bridge Road*
Travelodge offers good quality, good value, modern accommodation. Ideal for families, the spacious, en suite bedrooms include remote-control TV, tea and coffee-making facilities and luxury beds. Meals can be taken at the nearby family restaurant. For further details consult the Hotel Groups page.
ROOMS: 111 en suite s fr £25; d fr £25

BRENT KNOLL, Somerset Map 04 ST35

★★72% Woodlands Country House

Hill Ln TA9 4DF
☎ 01278 760232 🖷 01278 769090
e-mail: info@woodlands-hotel.co.uk
web: www.woodlands-hotel.co.uk
Dir: *A38 take 1st left into village, then 5th right & 1st left, follow brown tourist information signs*

With glorious countryside views, this family-run hotel is set in four acres of wooded parkland and offers a relaxed and peaceful environment. The attractively co-ordinated bedrooms are comfortable and very well equipped. Guests are welcome to use the outdoor pool and enjoy the terrace seating. Imaginative dishes make up the daily-changing dinner menu.
ROOMS: 9 en suite (1 fmly) (1 GF) ⊗ in all bedrooms s £69-£95; d £99-£135 (incl. bkfst) **LB FACILITIES:** Xmas **CONF:** Thtr 40 Class 25 Board 36 Del from £95 **PARKING:** 16 **NOTES:** ⊗ in restaurant RS Sun Civ Wed 60 **CARDS:**

See advert under WESTON-SUPER-MARE

Town House Hotel
Country House Hotel
Travel Accommodation

★★68% Battleborough Grange Country Hotel

Bristol Rd - A38 TA9 4HJ
☎ 01278 760208 🖷 01278 761950
e-mail: info@battleboroughgrangehotel.co.uk
Dir: *M5 J22, right at rdbt onto A38 past garden centre on right, hotel 500yds on left*

Conveniently located, this popular hotel is surrounded by mellow Somerset countryside. Bedrooms are well equipped and some have superb views of the Iron Age fort of Brent Knoll. In the conservatory restaurant, both fixed-price and carte menus are offered. Relax in the convivial bar after a busy day either working or exploring the area's many attractions. Extensive function facilities are also provided.
ROOMS: 15 en suite (1 fmly) s £57-£99; d £72-£139 (incl. bkfst)
FACILITIES: ch fac **CONF:** Thtr 85 Class 40 Board 40 Del from £80
PARKING: 50 **NOTES:** ⊗ in restaurant Closed 26 Dec - 1 Jan Civ Wed 90 **CARDS:**

BRENTWOOD, Essex Map 06 TQ59

★★★★72% Marygreen Manor

London Rd CM14 4NR
☎ 01277 225252 🖷 01277 262809
e-mail: info@marygreenmanor.co.uk
web: www.marygreenmanor.co.uk
Dir: *M25 J28, onto A1023 over 2 sets of lights, hotel on left*
16th-century house which was built in 1535 by Robert Wright, who named the house his 'Manor of Mary Green' after his young bride. Public rooms exude character and have a wealth of original features that include exposed beams, carved panelling and the impressive baronial restaurant. Bedrooms are located in courtyard-style buildings adjacent to the main property; each one is tastefully decorated and thoughtfully equipped.
ROOMS: 4 en suite 40 annexe en suite (35 GF) ⊗ in 24 bedrooms s £138-£205; d £155-£243 **FACILITIES:** STV **CONF:** Thtr 60 Class 20 Board 25 Del from £205 **PARKING:** 100 **NOTES:** ⊗ in restaurant Civ Wed 60 **CARDS:**

See advert on opposite page

★★★70% Weald Park Hotel, Golf & Country Club

Best Western

Coxtie Green Rd, South Weald CM14 5RJ
☎ 01277 375101 🖷 01277 374888
Dir: *M25 junct 28 Brentwood, at 1st set of t/lights turn left. Turn left at T-junct follow winding rd for 1.5m. 2nd right, 1m. Hotel on right.*
A friendly, family-run hotel ideally situated for the M25 and M11 with easy links to London or Stansted Airport. The spacious, tastefully appointed and well-equipped bedrooms are situated in attractive courtyard-style blocks adjacent to the main building.

continued

Public rooms include a first-floor bar, a residents' lounge and a stylish restaurant.
ROOMS: 32 annexe en suite (25 GF) **FACILITIES: Spa** 18 Fishing Putt green **PARKING:** 180 **NOTES:** No children 14yrs in restaurant **CARDS:**

BRIDGNORTH, Shropshire — Map 10 SO79
See also Alveley

★★★★66% Mill Hotel & Restaurant
WV15 6HL
01746 780437 01746 780850
e-mail: enquiries@themillalveley.fsnet.co.uk
(For full entry see Alveley)

★★★ Old Vicarage Hotel
Worfield WV15 5JZ
01746 716497 01746 716552
e-mail: admin@the-old-vicarage.demon.co.uk
web: www.oldvicarageworfield.com
(For full entry see Worfield)

★★67% Parlors Hall
Mill St WV15 5AL
01746 761931 01746 767058
e-mail: info@parlorshallhotel.co.uk
Dir: *from A454, right & right again in 200yds*
Parlors Hall has been a hotel since 1929 and retains many original features, such as oak panelling and magnificent fireplaces. Named after the family who lived here between 1419 and 1539, the property now features well-equipped bedrooms, some with four-poster beds, a restaurant and charming bar.
ROOMS: 15 en suite (2 fmly) **CONF:** Thtr 50 Class 25 Board 25 **PARKING:** 24 **NOTES:** **CARDS:**
See advert on this page

★★64% Falcon Hotel
Saint John St, Lowtown WV15 6AG
01746 763134 01746 765401
e-mail: enquiries@thefalconhotel.co.uk
web: www.thefalconhotel.co.uk
Dir: *A442 Telford to Kidderminster road. Follow Bridgnorth town centre signs. Hotel 100yds on left before bridge over River Severn*

This 17th-century former coaching inn stands near the River Severn in the Lowtown area of Bridgnorth, and offers comfortable bedrooms which are equipped to modern standards. A good selection of dishes is served in the open-plan bar with its beamed restaurant.
ROOMS: 12 en suite (4 fmly) in 5 bedrooms s £45; d £62 (incl. bkfst) **LB** **CONF:** Thtr 40 Class 20 Board 25 Del from £70 **PARKING:** 100 **CARDS:**

BRIDGWATER, Somerset Map 04 ST23
See also Holford

★★★72% ❀ Walnut Tree Hotel

North Petherton TA6 6QA
☎ 01278 662255 📠 01278 663946
e-mail: sales@walnuttreehotel.com
web: www.walnuttreehotel.com
Dir: *on A38, 1m S of M5 junct 24*

Popular with business and leisure guests, this 18th-century former coaching inn is located within easy reach of the M5. Smartly decorated bedrooms are well furnished and equipped with a range of facilities. An extensive selection of dishes is offered and guests can dine in either the restaurant, bistro area or bar.
ROOMS: 33 en suite (5 fmly) (13 GF) ⊗ in 7 bedrooms s £60-£100; d £90-£155 (incl. bkfst) **LB** **FACILITIES:** STV ♫ ch fac Xmas **CONF:** Thtr 120 Class 76 Board 70 Del from £125 **PARKING:** 70 **NOTES:** ✖ ⊗ in restaurant Civ Wed 50
CARDS:

★★71% Apple Tree

Keenthorne TA5 1HZ
☎ 01278 733238 📠 01278 732693
e-mail: reservations@appletreehotel.com
web: www.appletreehotel.com
(For full entry see Nether Stowey)

⌂ Travel Inn

Express Park, Bristol Rd TA6 4RR
☎ 0870 242 3344 📠 0870 241 9000
Travel Inn offers good-quality, value-for-money accommodation. Spacious, en suite rooms with bath and shower comfortably accommodate a family of up to two adults and two children (to age 15). The restaurant and bar offers a varied menu. For further details consult the Hotel Groups page.
ROOMS: 40 en suite s £45.95-£46.95; d £45.95-£46.95

BRIDLINGTON, East Riding of Yorkshire Map 17 TA16

★★★70% Revelstoke

1-3 Flamborough Rd YO15 2HU
☎ 01262 672362 📠 01262 672362
e-mail: info@revelstokehotel.co.uk
web: www.revelstokehotel.co.uk
Dir: *B1255 Flamborough Head Rd, 0.5m right at mini rdbt to junct of Promenade & Flamborough Rd. Hotel opp Holy Trinity Church*
Family owned and run, this friendly hotel is close to both the town centre and the North Bay seafront and is a popular choice. Bedrooms are well equipped and very comfortable. Lounges are well furnished, and in addition to the restaurant where a wide range of well-produced dishes is served, there is an extensive informal menu available in the bar.

ROOMS: 26 en suite (6 fmly) s £45-£55; d £70-£80 **LB**
FACILITIES: STV ♫ Xmas **CONF:** BC Thtr 250 Class 200 Board 100
PARKING: 14 **NOTES:** ✖ RS 25-28 Dec Civ Wed 200
CARDS:

See advert on opposite page

★★★67% Expanse

North Marine Dr YO15 2LS
☎ 01262 675347 📠 01262 604928
e-mail: expanse@brid.demon.co.uk
web: www.expanse.co.uk
Dir: *follow North Beach signs, pass under railway arch for North Marine Drive. Hotel at bottom of hill*

This traditional seaside hotel overlooks the bay and has been in the same family's ownership for many years. Service is relaxed and friendly and the modern bedrooms are well-equipped. Comfortable public areas include a conference suite, a large bar and an inviting lounge.
ROOMS: 48 en suite (4 fmly) ⊗ in 12 bedrooms s £38-£60; d £72-£120 (incl. bkfst) **LB** **FACILITIES:** STV ♫ Xmas **CONF:** Thtr 180 Class 50 Board 50 **SERVICES:** Lift **PARKING:** 23 **NOTES:** ✖ ⊗ in restaurant Civ Wed **CARDS:**

See advert on opposite page

★★65% Sewerby Grange

441 Sewerby Rd, Sewerby YO15 1ER
☎ 01262 673439 674535
Dir: *From NW edge of Bridlington take B1255 signed Flamborough. At 1st rdbt turn right then next left onto Sewerby Rd*
Built as a parsonage, this listed house stands in its own grounds overlooking the North Beach. The restaurant is popular with local residents and bedrooms are comfortable. Service is attentive and friendly.
ROOMS: 6 en suite ⊗ in all bedrooms s £37.50-£75; d £75 (incl. bkfst) **LB** **FACILITIES:** Xmas **PARKING:** 22 **NOTES:** ✖ ⊗ in restaurant
CARDS:

BRIDPORT, Dorset Map 04 SY49

★★★65% Haddon House

West Bay DT6 4EL
☎ 01308 423626 & 425323 📠 01308 427348
Dir: *At Crown Inn rdbt take B3157 West Bay Road, hotel 0.5m on R at mini-rdbt*

This attractive, creeper-clad hotel offers good standards of accommodation and is situated a few minutes' walk from the seafront and the quay. A friendly and relaxed style of service is provided. An extensive range of dishes, from lighter bar snacks to main meals, is on offer in the Tudor-style restaurant.
ROOMS: 12 en suite (2 fmly) (1 GF) ⊗ in 2 bedrooms
FACILITIES: STV Solarium ch fac Xmas **CONF:** Thtr 40 Class 20 Board 26 **PARKING:** 44 **NOTES:** ✈ ⊗ in restaurant
CARDS:

BRIDPORT, continued

★★64% Bridge House
115 East St DT6 3LB

☎ 01308 423371 📠 01308 459573
e-mail: info@bridgehousebridport.co.uk
Dir: *follow signs to town centre from A35 rdbt, hotel 200mtrs on right*
A short stroll from the town centre, this 18th-century Grade II listed property is undergoing a major refurbishment. The well-equipped bedrooms vary in size. In addition to the main lounge, there is a small bar-lounge and a separate breakfast room. An interesting range of home-cooked meals is provided in the restaurant.
ROOMS: 10 en suite (3 fmly) ⊘ in 5 bedrooms s £44-£50; d £65-£75 (incl. bkfst) **PARKING:** 13 **NOTES:** ⊘ in restaurant
CARDS:

BRIGG, Lincolnshire Map 17 TA00

★★66% The Red Lion Hotel
Main Rd, Redbourne DN21 4QR
☎ 01652 648302 📠 01652 648900
e-mail: enquiries@redlion.org
Dir: *from M180 junct 4 take A15. After 4m left at mini-rdbt, take signs left to Redbourne. Hotel 1st building on left in village*
Dating back to the 17th century, this former coaching inn overlooks the village green and holds a key to the historic fire station which is just next door. It offers pleasantly furnished bedrooms and a good range of food is available either in the bar or dining room. There is a friendly atmosphere and staff are very helpful.
ROOMS: 11 en suite (2 fmly) ⊘ in 2 bedrooms s £40-£45; d £55-£60 (incl. bkfst) **LB** **CONF:** Thtr 35 Class 35 Board 35 **PARKING:** 30 **NOTES:** ⊘ in restaurant **CARDS:**

BRIGHOUSE, West Yorkshire Map 16 SE12

Premier Lodge (Huddersfield North)
Wakefield Rd HD6 4HA
PREMIER LODGE.com
☎ 0870 9906360 📠 0870 9906361
web: www.premierlodge.com
Dir: *exit M62 junct 25 and at rbt signed A644 Huddersfield, Dewsbury and Wakefield. Lodge 500mtrs up hill on right*
High quality, modern, budget accommodation, ideal for families and business travellers. All rooms feature bath, power shower and satellite TV, and most have telephones / modem points. The adjacent bar and restaurant offers a wide and varied menu.
ROOMS: 71 en suite s £48; d £48

BRIGHTON & HOVE, East Sussex Map 06 TQ30

★★★★★67% De Vere Grand Brighton
King's Rd BN1 2FW
DE VERE HOTELS
☎ 01273 224300 📠 01273 224321
e-mail: reservations@grandbrighton.co.uk
Dir: *on seafront between piers, next to Brighton Centre*
Dating back to the mid 19th century, this landmark seafront hotel, with its eye-catching white façade and intricate balconies, is as grand as the name suggests. Bedrooms include a number of deluxe sea view rooms, some with balconies, and suites also with sea views. The hotel is perhaps best known for its extensive

continued

conference and banqueting facilities; there is also a well-equipped leisure centre and an impressive conservatory adjoining the bar.

ROOMS: 200 en suite (60 fmly) s fr £170; d £250-£360 (incl. bkfst) **LB**
FACILITIES: Spa STV supervised Sauna Solarium Gym Jacuzzi Hairdresser, Tropicarium, beauty salon & treatment rooms ♫ Xmas
CONF: Thtr 800 Class 420 Board 50 Del from £225 **SERVICES:** Lift
PARKING: 70 **NOTES:** Civ Wed 800
CARDS:

Town House

★★★★ Alias Hotel Seattle
The Strand, Brighton Marina BN2 5WA
☎ 01273 679799 📠 01273 679899
e-mail: info@aliasseattle.com
web: www.aliashotels.com
Dir: *Follow signs to Brighton seafront. Hotel in Brighton Marina, 1m E of main Palace Pier.*
This smart, modern hotel enjoys a prime position overlooking Brighton Marina and has much to offer guests whether on business or leisure. The chic saloon lounge and trendy Black and White bar both have balconies with sea views, while the spacious, atmospheric Café Paradis offers cuisine with a Mediterranean theme.
ROOMS: 71 en suite s £95-£160; d £95-£160 **FACILITIES:** STV Special rates for hotel guests at nearby David Lloyd Leisure Centre
CONF: Thtr 120 Class 50 Board 70 Del from £159 **SERVICES:** Lift
NOTES: ⊘ in restaurant Civ Wed 100
CARDS:

Town House

★★★★ Hotel Du Vin Brighton
2-6 Ship St BN1 1AD
☎ 01273 718588 📠 01273 718599
e-mail: info@brighton.hotelduvin.com
Dir: *A23 from London, signs to seafront/city centre. Right at seafront, right up Middle St follow road in U-shape to Ship St*
This tastefully converted mock-Tudor building occupies a convenient location in a quiet side street close to the sea front. The individual bedrooms all have a wine theme, are comprehensively equipped and include some suites. Public areas offer a spacious split-level bar, an atmospheric and locally popular restaurant and some useful private dining and meeting facilities.
ROOMS: 37 en suite s £119-£350; d £119-£350 **FACILITIES:** STV Snooker Xmas **CONF:** Thtr 30 Board 22 Del £185 **SERVICES:** air con **PARKING:** 10 **NOTES:** ⊘ in restaurant
CARDS:

Town House

★★★★ The Royal Pavilion Townhouse
12A Regency Square BN1 2FG
☎ 01273 722123 01273 722293
e-mail: info@rpthotel.co.uk
An elegant Regency townhouse on four floors enjoying close proximity to the West Pier and seafront. The spacious and individually themed bedrooms are comprehensively equipped and those on the front of the building offer views over the square. There is a comfortable bar and attractive Italian-style restaurant. Parking is available in the NCP car park opposite.
ROOMS: 8 en suite ⊗ in 3 bedrooms s £120-£150; d £150-£200 (incl. bkfst) **LB** **FACILITIES:** STV Xmas **CONF:** Thtr 12 Board 12 Del from £150 **NOTES:** No children 21yrs
CARDS:

★★★★65% Old Ship
King's Rd BN1 1NR
☎ 01273 329001 01273 820718
e-mail: oldship@paramount-hotels.co.uk
PARAMOUNT GROUP OF HOTELS
Dir: *A23 to seafront, right at rdbt along Kings Rd. Hotel 200yds on right*
The Old Ship enjoys a stunning seafront location and offers guests elegant surroundings in which to relax. Bedrooms are well-designed, with modern facilities ensuring guest comfort. Many original features have been retained, including the oak-panelled bar. Facilities include a variety of conference rooms and a car park.
ROOMS: 152 en suite (10 fmly) ⊗ in 15 bedrooms s £150-£175; d £205-£250 **LB** **FACILITIES:** STV Xmas **CONF:** Thtr 300 Class 100 Board 60 Del £175 **SERVICES:** Lift **PARKING:** 40 **NOTES:** Civ Wed
CARDS:

★★★68% The Courtlands
15-27 The Drive BN3 3JE
☎ 01273 731055 01273 328295
e-mail: courtlands@pavilion.co.uk
Dir: *At A23/ A27 Junct. 1st exit to Hove, 2nd exit at rdbt, right at 1st junct and left at shops. Straight on at junct. Hotel on left*
This hotel is within walking distance of the seafront and has its own small car park. The majority of bedrooms are newly decorated and have smart bathrooms. Guests have the use of a comfortable lounge, a light and spacious restaurant; service is both friendly and attentive.
ROOMS: 60 en suite 7 annexe en suite (8 fmly) ⊗ in 20 bedrooms s £45-£67.50; d £65-£97.50 (incl. bkfst) **LB** **FACILITIES:** Xmas **CONF:** Thtr 60 Class 20 Board 30 Del £80 **SERVICES:** Lift **PARKING:** 24 **NOTES:** ⊗ in restaurant
CARDS:

★★★68% Imperial
First Av BN3 2GU
☎ 01273 777320 01273 777310
e-mail: info@imperial-hove.com
web: www.imperial-hove.com
Dir: *M23 to Brighton seafront, right at rdbt to Hove, 1.5m to First Avenue turn right*
Located within minutes of the seafront, this Regency hotel is constantly being improved and upgraded. A good range of conference suites complement the comfortable public rooms, which include a lounge, a smart bar area and an attractive restaurant. Bedrooms are generally of comfortable proportions, well appointed and with a good range of facilities.

ROOMS: 76 en suite (4 fmly) ⊗ in 10 bedrooms s £45-£75; d £75-£115 (incl. bkfst) **LB** **FACILITIES:** Xmas **CONF:** BC Thtr 110 Class 30 Board 34 Del from £90 **SERVICES:** Lift **NOTES:** ⊗ in restaurant
CARDS:

★★★67% The Granville
124 King's Rd BN1 2FA
☎ 01273 326302 01273 728294
e-mail: granville@brighton.co.uk
web: www.granvillehotel.co.uk
Dir: *opposite West Pier*
This stylish hotel is located on Brighton's busy seafront. Bedrooms are carefully furnished and decorated with great style. A trendy cocktail bar and restaurant, 'DaDu', meaning big belly, serves a combination of Asian and British cuisine. Tasty traditional breakfasts are also available.
ROOMS: 24 en suite (2 fmly) (1 GF) ⊗ in all bedrooms s £55-£105; d £75-£185 (incl. bkfst) **LB** **FACILITIES:** Jacuzzi ch fac **CONF:** BC Thtr 50 Class 30 Board 30 Del from £70 **SERVICES:** Lift **PARKING:** 3
CARDS:

★★★66% Princes Marine
153 Kingsway BN3 4GR
☎ 01273 207660 01273 325913
e-mail: princesmarine@bestwestern.co.uk

Dir: *right at Brighton Pier, follow seafront for 2m. Hotel 200yds from King Alfred leisure centre*

This friendly hotel enjoys a seafront location and offers spacious, comfortable bedrooms equipped with a good range of facilities. There is a cosy restaurant, bar and useful meeting room and limited parking at the rear.
ROOMS: 48 en suite (4 fmly) ⊗ in 12 bedrooms s £50-£65; d £85-£135 (incl. bkfst) **LB** **FACILITIES:** Xmas **CONF:** BC Thtr 80 Class 40 Board 40 **SERVICES:** Lift **PARKING:** 30
CARDS:

BRIGHTON & HOVE, continued

★★★66% Queens Hotel
1 King's Rd BN1 1NS
☎ 01273 321222 📠 01273 203059
e-mail: res@queenshotelbrighton.com
Dir: *A23 to Brighton town centre - follow signs for seafront. At Brighton Pier right onto seafront, hotel 500mtrs*
Located on the seafront, this hotel has been refurbished to a high standard. All the bedrooms are richly decorated with warm colours, offer good facilities and many have wonderful sea views. A modern leisure centre and Atrium bar allow guests to relax, whilst the restaurant serves contemporary meals.
ROOMS: 97 en suite (12 fmly) ⊗ in 23 bedrooms s £60-£110; d £70-£300 (incl. cont bkfst) **LB** **FACILITIES:** STV supervised Sauna Solarium Gym ♫ **CONF:** BC Thtr 150 Class 50 Board 50 Del from £125 **SERVICES:** Lift **NOTES:** ⊗ in restaurant Civ Wed 100
CARDS:

★★★65% The Dudley
Lansdowne Place BN3 1HQ
THE INDEPENDENTS
☎ 01273 736266 📠 01273 729802
e-mail: admin@thedudleyhotel.co.uk
Dir: *M23 & A23 into Brighton. Right at seafront heading W, in Hove Lansdowne Place, 1st turn after Brunswick Sq*

This Regency-fronted hotel is located just a few metres from the seafront and dates from Victorian times. The Dudley offers traditional well-appointed public areas, including Marty's Bar and Restaurant, and an extensive range of function rooms.
ROOMS: 71 en suite (3 fmly) ⊗ in 40 bedrooms s £40-£85; d £80-£145 (incl. bkfst) **LB** **FACILITIES:** Xmas **CONF:** Thtr 150 Class 100 Board 90 Del from £80 **SERVICES:** Lift **PARKING:** 20 **NOTES:** ⊗ in restaurant **CARDS:**

See advert on opposite page

★★★64% Brighton Hotel
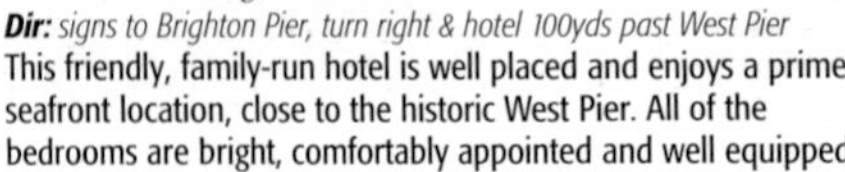
143/145 King's Rd BN1 2PQ
☎ 01273 820555 📠 01273 821555
e-mail: brighton.hotel@btconnect.com
web: www.bw-brightonhotel.co.uk
Dir: *signs to Brighton Pier, turn right & hotel 100yds past West Pier*
This friendly, family-run hotel is well placed and enjoys a prime seafront location, close to the historic West Pier. All of the bedrooms are bright, comfortably appointed and well equipped, and public rooms have been fully refurbished. The parking facilities, though limited, are a real bonus in Brighton.

ROOMS: 52 en suite s £78-£90; d £110-£240 (incl. bkfst) **LB** **FACILITIES:** STV **CONF:** Thtr 130 Class 35 Board 35 Del from £99 **SERVICES:** Lift **PARKING:** 12 **NOTES:** ⊗ in restaurant
CARDS:

★★★64% Quality Hotel Brighton
West St BN1 2RQ
☎ 01273 220033 📠 01273 778000
e-mail: enquiries@hotels-brighton.com
Dir: *A23 into Brighton, then town centre/seafront signs. A259 to Hove & Worthing. Hotel next to Brighton Centre*
Conveniently located for the seafront and close to the town centre, this purpose-built hotel offers newly refurbished, modern and well-equipped bedrooms. Public areas include a spacious, open-plan lounge bar area with a feature staircase. A choice of restaurants serves a wide selection of dishes.
ROOMS: 138 en suite (2 fmly) ⊗ in 60 bedrooms s £104-£135; d £115-£135 **LB** **FACILITIES:** Xmas **CONF:** Thtr 200 Class 80 Board 60 Del from £125 **SERVICES:** Lift **NOTES:** ⊗ in restaurant
CARDS:

Premier Lodge (Brighton City Centre)
144 North St BN1 1RE
PREMIER LODGE.com
☎ 0870 9906340 📠 0870 9906341
web: www.premierlodge.com
Dir: *from A23 follow signs city centre. At lights near Royal Pavilion, right, take road ahead on left which runs adjacent to Pavilion onto Church St, 1st left onto New Rd into North St*
High quality, modern, budget accommodation, ideal for families and business travellers. All rooms feature bath, power shower and satellite TV, and most have telephones / modem points. The adjacent bar and restaurant offers a wide and varied menu.
ROOMS: 160 en suite s £54; d £54

Travelodge Brighton Central
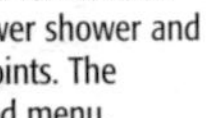

Preston Rd BN1 6AU
☎ 08700 850 950 📠 01273 554917
Travelodge offers good quality, good value, modern accommodation. Ideal for families, the spacious, en suite bedrooms include remote-control TV, tea and coffee-making facilities and luxury beds. Meals can be taken at the nearby family restaurant. For further details consult the Hotel Groups page.
ROOMS: 94 en suite s fr £25; d fr £25

BRISTOL, Bristol Map 04 ST57

★★★★74%

Bristol Marriott Royal Hotel
College Green BS1 5TA
☎ 0117 925 5100 0117 925 1515
e-mail: bristol.royal@marriotthotels.co.uk
Dir: *next to cathedral*
A truly stunning hotel located in the centre of the city, next to the cathedral. Public areas are particularly impressive with luxurious lounges and a leisure club. Dining options include the more informal Terrace and the newly opened Michael Caines restaurant, adjacent to the champagne bar. The spacious bedrooms have the benefit of air-conditioning, comfortable armchairs and marbled bathrooms.
ROOMS: 242 en suite (14 fmly) ⊘ in 163 bedrooms s £135-£145; d £155-£165 **LB** **FACILITIES:** STV Sauna Solarium Gym Jacuzzi **CONF:** BC Thtr 300 Class 80 Board 84 Del £180 **SERVICES:** Lift air con **PARKING:** 200 **NOTES:** ⊘ in restaurant Civ Wed 200
CARDS:

Town House

★★★★ **Hotel du Vin & Bistro**
The Sugar House, Narrow Lewins Mead BS1 2NU
☎ 0117 925 5577 0117 925 1199
e-mail: info@bristol.hotelduvin.com
Dir: *A4 follow city centre signs. After 400yds pass Rupert St NCP on right. Hotel on opp*
Another property in one of Britain's most innovative and now expanding hotel groups extends the high standards for which the chain is renowned. The hotel is housed in a Grade II listed, converted 18th-century sugar refinery. Bedrooms are exceptionally well-designed and the hotel provides great facilities with a modern minimalist feel. The bistro offers an excellent menu.
ROOMS: 40 en suite s £125-£325; d £125-£325 **FACILITIES:** STV Snooker Xmas **CONF:** Thtr 50 Class 25 Board 26 Del from £190 **SERVICES:** Lift **PARKING:** 33 **NOTES:** ⊘ in restaurant
CARDS:

★★★★71% **Aztec**
Aztec West Business Park BS32 4TS
☎ 01454 201090 01454 201593
e-mail: aztec@shirehotels.co.uk
Dir: *access via M5 junct 16 & M4*

Situated close to Cribbs Causeway shopping centre and major motorway links, this stylish hotel offers comfortable, very well-equipped bedrooms. Built in a Nordic style, public rooms

continued

boast log fires and vaulted ceilings. Leisure facilities include a very well-equipped gym and good sized pool. The new-look Quarterjacks restaurant offers relaxed informal dining with a focus on regional foods.
ROOMS: 128 en suite (6 fmly) (29 GF) ⊘ in 84 bedrooms s £159-£209; d £159-£209 (incl. bkfst) **LB** **FACILITIES: Spa** STV supervised Squash Sauna Solarium Gym Jacuzzi Steam room, Health & beauty, Childrens splash pool Xmas **CONF:** BC Thtr 200 Class 120 Board 36 Del £175 **SERVICES:** Lift air con **PARKING:** 240 **NOTES:** ⊘ in restaurant Civ Wed 120 **CARDS:**

See advert under BATH

★★★★67% **Bristol Marriott City Centre**
Lower Castle St BS1 3AD
☎ 0870 400 7210 0870 400 7310
Dir: *M32 follow signs to Broadmead, take slip road to large rdbt, take 3rd exit. Hotel on right*
Situated at the foot of the picturesque Castle Park, this mainly business-orientated hotel is well placed for the city centre. Free parking is available for residents along with complimentary membership of the hotel's leisure club. In addition to a coffee bar and lounge menu, the Mediterrano restaurant offers an interesting selection of well-prepared dishes.
ROOMS: 294 en suite (138 fmly) ⊘ in 221 bedrooms s fr £129; d fr £129 **LB** **FACILITIES: Spa** STV Sauna Solarium Gym Jacuzzi Steam room **CONF:** BC Thtr 600 Class 280 Board 40 Del from £145 **SERVICES:** Lift air con **NOTES:** ⊘ in restaurant Civ Wed
CARDS:

♫ Entertainment

B

BRISTOL, continued

★★★★66% The Brigstow
5-7 Welsh Back BS1 4SP
☎ 0117 929 1030 0117 929 2030
e-mail: brigstow@fullers.co.uk
Dir: *Follow signs to City Centre. Turn left into Baldwin St, 2nd right into Queen Charlotte St. NCP on left*

In a prime position, with its own riverside frontage, this handsome purpose-built structure is designed and finished with care in every detail. The shopping centre is within easy walking distance, as are the city's theatres. Bedrooms are stylish and extremely well equipped, even down to plasma television screens in bathrooms. There is an integrated state-of-the-art conference and meeting centre, and a smart restaurant and bar overlooking the quay.
ROOMS: 116 en suite ⊗ in 78 bedrooms s £89-£169; d £89-£169 **LB** **FACILITIES:** STV **CONF:** BC Thtr 60 Class 40 Board 36 Del £170 **SERVICES:** Lift air con **NOTES:** RS 24 Dec - 5 Jan Civ Wed 50 **CARDS:**

★★★★64% *Jurys Bristol Hotel*
JURYS DOYLE HOTELS
Prince St BS1 4QF
☎ 0117 923 0333 0117 923 0300
e-mail: bristol_hotel@jurysdoyle.com
Dir: *from Temple Meads right at 1st rdbt into Victoria St. At Bristol Bridge lights left into Baldwin St, 2nd left into Marsh St, right at rdbt*
This modern hotel enjoys an excellent location near Bristol's Millennium project. Bedrooms vary in size and are well-appointed with a range of facilities. There is a choice of eating options, including a Quayside restaurant and adjoining inn. Extensive conference facilities are also available.
ROOMS: 191 en suite (22 fmly) ⊗ in 53 bedrooms **FACILITIES:** STV Complimentary use of local gym ♫ **CONF:** Thtr 400 Class 160 Board 80 **SERVICES:** Lift **NOTES:** **CARDS:**

★★★70% Arno's Manor
Forestdale Hotels
470 Bath Rd, Arno's Vale BS4 3HQ
☎ 0117 971 1461 0117 971 5507
e-mail: arnos.manor@forestdale.com
Once the home of a wealthy merchant, this historic 18th-century building is now a comfortable hotel and offers spacious, well-appointed bedrooms with plenty of workspace. The lounge was once the chapel and has many original features, while meals are taken in the atmospheric, conservatory-style restaurant.
ROOMS: 73 en suite (1 fmly) (7 GF) s fr £95; d fr £120 (incl. bkfst) **LB** **FACILITIES:** STV Xmas **CONF:** Thtr 150 Class 60 Board 40 Del from £130 **SERVICES:** Lift **PARKING:** 200 **NOTES:** ⊗ in restaurant Civ Wed 100 **CARDS:**

★★★70% City Inn Bristol
Temple Way BS1 6BF
☎ 0117 925 1001 0117 907 4116
e-mail: bristol.reservations@cityinn.co.uk
The hotel offers spacious, contemporary public areas and bedrooms, and is situated within walking distance of the city centre and railway station. The young staff are well motivated and friendly. The City Café offers an interesting selection of carefully prepared, quality ingredients and the adjacent bar serves coffee and tea throughout the day.
ROOMS: 167 en suite (3 GF) ⊗ in 134 bedrooms s £70-£135; d £70-£135 **FACILITIES:** STV Gym **CONF:** Thtr 45 Class 22 Board 24 Del from £150 **SERVICES:** Lift air con **PARKING:** 45 **NOTES:** ⊗ in restaurant **CARDS:**

★★★69% Berkeley Square
Best Western
15 Berkeley Square, Clifton BS8 1HB
☎ 0117 925 4000 0117 925 2970
e-mail: berkeleysquare@bestwestern.co.uk
Dir: *M32 follow Clifton signs. 1st left at traffic lights by Nills Memorial Tower (University) into Berkeley Sq*
Set in a peaceful square close to the university, art gallery and Clifton village, this smart, elegant Georgian hotel has tastefully decorated bedrooms that include many welcome extras. There is a busy bar in the basement, and the restaurant features interesting dishes from a choice of menus.
ROOMS: 42 en suite ⊗ in 17 bedrooms s £54-£116; d £90-£127 (incl. bkfst) **LB** **FACILITIES:** STV complimentry use of local gym and swimming pool **CONF:** Thtr 40 Class 25 Board 25 **SERVICES:** Lift **PARKING:** 20 **NOTES:** ⊗ in restaurant **CARDS:**

★★★67% Corus hotel Bristol
corus hotels
Beggar Bush Ln, Failand BS8 3TG
☎ 0870 609 6144 01275 392104
e-mail: reservations.redwoodlodge@corushotels.com
Dir: *M5 junct 19, A369 for 3m then right at traffic lights. Hotel 1m on left*

Situated close to the suspension bridge, this popular hotel offers guests a peaceful location combined with excellent leisure facilities, including a cinema, gym, squash, badminton and tennis courts, plus indoor and outdoor pools. Bedrooms have plenty of amenities and are well-suited to the business guest.
ROOMS: 112 en suite (1 fmly) (52 GF) ⊗ in 81 bedrooms s £42-£99; d £84-£99 **LB** **FACILITIES:** STV Squash Sauna Solarium Gym 175 seater Cinema, Aerobics/Dance studios, Badminton courts Xmas **CONF:** BC Thtr 175 Class 80 Board 40 Del £155 **PARKING:** 1000 **NOTES:** ⊗ in restaurant Civ Wed 200 **CARDS:**

★★★67% Henbury Lodge

Station Rd, Henbury BS10 7QQ
☎ 0117 950 2615 📠 0117 950 9532
e-mail: jonathan.pearce@btconnect.co.uk
web: www.henburylodge.co.uk

Dir: *M5 junct 17/A4018 towards city centre, 3rd rdbt right into Crow Ln. At end turn right & hotel 200mtrs on right*

This comfortable 18th-century country house has a relaxed and welcoming atmosphere and is conveniently situated within easy access of the M5. Bedrooms are available both within the main house and in the adjoining stable conversion; all are attractively decorated and well equipped. The pleasant dining room offers a selection of carefully prepared dishes using fresh ingredients.

ROOMS: 12 en suite 9 annexe en suite (4 fmly) (3 GF) ⊘ in 8 bedrooms s £57-£96; d £94-£112 (incl. bkfst) **LB** **FACILITIES:** STV Sauna Solarium Xmas **CONF:** Thtr 32 Class 20 Board 20 Del from £120 **PARKING:** 24 **NOTES:** ⊘ in restaurant
CARDS:

★★★66% The Avon Gorge

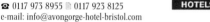

Sion Hill, Clifton BS8 4LD
☎ 0117 973 8955 📠 0117 923 8125
e-mail: info@avongorge-hotel-bristol.com

Dir: *M5 junct 19, follow signs for Clifton Toll, over suspension bridge, 1st right into Sion Hill*

Overlooking Avon Gorge and Brunel's famous suspension bridge, this popular hotel offers rooms with glorious views. Bedrooms are very well equipped and have extras such as ceiling fans. Public areas include a traditional restaurant and a popular modern bar and brasserie, both overlooking a large outdoor terraced area.

ROOMS: 76 en suite (6 fmly) ⊘ in 30 bedrooms s £120; d £130 (incl. bkfst) **LB** **FACILITIES:** STV Childrens activity play area Xmas **CONF:** Thtr 100 Class 50 Board 26 Del from £110 **SERVICES:** Lift **PARKING:** 20 **NOTES:** ⊘ in restaurant Civ Wed 100
CARDS:

★★71% Best Western Victoria Square

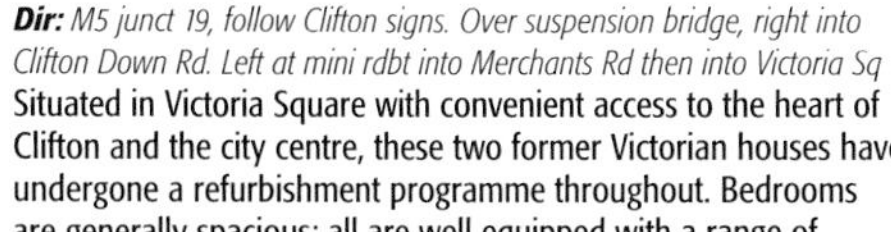

Victoria Square, Clifton BS8 4EW
☎ 0117 973 9058 📠 0117 970 6929
e-mail: victoriasquare@btopenworld.com
web: www.vicsquare.com

Dir: *M5 junct 19, follow Clifton signs. Over suspension bridge, right into Clifton Down Rd. Left at mini rdbt into Merchants Rd then into Victoria Sq*

Situated in Victoria Square with convenient access to the heart of Clifton and the city centre, these two former Victorian houses have undergone a refurbishment programme throughout. Bedrooms are generally spacious; all are well equipped with a range of

continued

useful extras such as modem points for internet access. A pleasant conference room and small rear car park are also on hand.

Best Western Victoria Square

ROOMS: 21 en suite 19 annexe en suite (6 fmly) (2 GF) ⊘ in 22 bedrooms s £65-£85; d £85-£95 (incl. bkfst) **FACILITIES:** STV **CONF:** Thtr 30 Class 20 Board 20 **PARKING:** 16 **NOTES:** Closed 22 Dec-2 Jan **CARDS:**

★★70% *Clifton*

St Pauls Rd, Clifton BS8 1LX
☎ 0117 973 6882 📠 0117 974 1082
e-mail: clifton@cliftonhotels.com
web: www.cliftonhotels.com/clifton

Dir: *M32 follow Bristol/Clifton signs, along Park St. Left at lights into St Pauls Rd*

This popular hotel offers very well-equipped bedrooms and relaxed, friendly service. There is a smart lounge at reception and during summer months drinks and meals can be taken on the

continued on p132

BRISTOL, continued

terrace. Racks Bar and Restaurant offers an interesting selection of modern dishes from an imaginative menu. Some street parking is possible although for a small charge, secure garage parking is available.
ROOMS: 59 en suite (2 fmly) ⊗ in 28 bedrooms **FACILITIES:** STV **SERVICES:** Lift **PARKING:** 20 **CARDS:**

★★68% The Bowl Inn

16 Church Rd, Lower Almondsbury BS32 4DT
☎ 01454 612757 01454 619910
e-mail: reception@thebowlinn.co.uk
web: www.thebowlinn.co.uk
Dir: *M5 junct 16 onto Gloucester road, N for 500yds. Turn left into Over Lane, turn right by Garden Centre. Hotel next to church on right*

With easy access to the motorway network, this village inn offers all the comforts of modern life in a charming 16th-century hostelry. Each bedroom has been individually furnished to complement the many original features. Dining options include an extensive bar menu with cask ales, or a more intimate restaurant.
ROOMS: 11 en suite 2 annexe en suite (1 GF) ⊗ in 4 bedrooms s £44.50-£95.45; d £71-£113.40 (incl. bkfst) **LB FACILITIES:** STV **CONF:** Thtr 30 Class 20 Board 24 Del from £90.45 **PARKING:** 30 **NOTES:** RS 25 Dec **CARDS:**

★★67% *Rodney Hotel*

4 Rodney Place, Clifton BS8 4HY
☎ 0117 973 5422 0117 946 7092
e-mail: rodney@cliftonhotels.com
Dir: *off Clifton Down Rd*
With easy access from the M5, this attractive, listed building in Clifton is conveniently close to the city centre. The individually decorated bedrooms provide a useful range of extra facilities for the business traveller. Snacks are served in the bar/lounge or via room service, and the more formal restaurant offers an appealing selection of dishes.
ROOMS: 31 en suite (2 GF) ⊗ in 10 bedrooms **FACILITIES:** STV **CONF:** Thtr 30 Class 20 Board 15 **NOTES:** Closed 22 Dec-3 Jan RS Sun **CARDS:**

★★64% *Westbourne*

THE INDEPENDENTS

40-44 St Pauls Rd, Clifton BS8 1LR
☎ 0117 973 4214 0117 974 3552
e-mail: westbournehotel@bristol8.fsworld.co.uk
web: www.westbournehotel-bristol.co.uk
Dir: *M32/A4018 along Park St to Triangle, then Whiteladies Rd. Turn left at 1st lights opp the BBC onto St Pauls Rd. Hotel 200yds on right*
This privately-owned hotel is situated in the heart of Clifton and is popular with business guests during the week. It offers comfortable, well-equipped bedrooms. Freddie's Bar and Restaurant provide a choice of eating options and during the summer guests can enjoy a drink on the rear terrace.

ROOMS: 29 en suite (7 fmly) (1 GF) ⊗ in 1 bedroom **PARKING:** 9 **NOTES:** **CARDS:**

Novotel Bristol Centre

NOVOTEL

Victoria St BS1 6HY
☎ 0117 976 9988 0117 976 9988
e-mail: h5622@accor-hotels.com
Dir: *at end of M32 follow signs for Temple Meads station to rdbt. Final exit, hotel immediately on right.*
At the time of going to press, the star classification for this hotel was not confirmed. Please refer to the AA internet site www.theAA.com for current information.
ROOMS: 128 en suite (6 fmly) ⊗ in 91 bedrooms s £50-£120; d £50-£120 **LB FACILITIES:** STV Solarium Gym **CONF:** Thtr 200 Class 70 Board 40 Del from £118 **SERVICES:** Lift **PARKING:** 120 **NOTES:** ⊗ in restaurant **CARDS:**

Premier Lodge (Bristol City Centre)

PREMIER LODGE.com

Llandoger Trow, Kings St BS1 4ER
☎ 0870 9906424 0870 9906425
web: www.premierlodge.com
Dir: *follow A38 into city centre. Turn left onto B4053 Baldwin St right into Queen Charlotte St. Follow one way system bearing right at river. Lodge on right*
High quality, modern, budget accommodation, ideal for families and business travellers. All rooms feature bath, power shower and satellite TV, and most have telephones / modem points. The adjacent bar and restaurant offers a wide and varied menu.
ROOMS: 60 en suite s £56; d £56

Premier Lodge (Bristol City East)

PREMIER LODGE.com

Shield Retail Park, Gloucester Rd North, Filton BS34 7BR
☎ 0870 9906456 0870 9906457
web: www.premierlodge.com
Dir: *exit M5 junct 16, towards A38 signed Filton & Patchway. Pass airport and Royal Mail on right. At 2nd rdt turn left and 1st left into retail park*
High quality, modern, budget accommodation, ideal for families and business travellers. All rooms feature bath, power shower and satellite TV, and most have telephones / modem points. The adjacent bar and restaurant offers a wide and varied menu.
ROOMS: 60 en suite s £50; d £50 **CONF:** Board 12

⊗ No smoking

For central reservation numbers and more information on Hotel Groups, turn to pages 33-39

continued

⌂ Premier Lodge (Bristol North West)

Cribbs Causeway, Catbrain Ln BS10 7TQ
☎ 0870 9906570 ▯ 0870 9906571
web: www.premierlodge.com
Dir: *M5 at junct 17 onto A4018. Take 1st left at rdt into Lysander Rd. Turn right into Catbrain Hill which follows into Catbrain Ln*
High quality, modern, budget accommodation, ideal for families and business travellers. All rooms feature bath, power shower and satellite TV, and most have telephones / modem points. The adjacent bar and restaurant offers a wide and varied menu.
ROOMS: 106 en suite s £52; d £52

⌂ Travel Inn (Bristol City Centre)

Haymarket BS1 3LR
☎ 0870 238 3307 ▯ 0117 910 0619
Dir: *M4 junct 19/M32 towards city centre. Through 2 sets of lights, at 3rd set, turn right. To rdbt, take 2nd exit. Travel Inn on left.*
Travel Inn offers good-quality, value-for-money accommodation. Spacious, en suite rooms with bath and shower comfortably accommodate a family of up to two adults and two children (to age 15). The restaurant and bar offers a varied menu. For further details consult the Hotel Groups page.
ROOMS: 224 en suite s £49.95-£56.95; d £49.95-£56.95

⌂ Travel Inn (Bristol City East)

200/202 Westerleigh Rd, Emersons Green
BS16 7AN
☎ 08701 977042 ▯ 0117 956 4644
Dir: *From M4 (J19) onto M32 (J1), turn left onto A4174 (Avon Ring Road). Travel Inn on 3rd rbt*

Travel Inn offers good-quality, value-for-money accommodation. Spacious, en suite rooms with bath and shower comfortably accommodate a family of up to two adults and two children (to age 15). The restaurant and bar offers a varied menu. For further details consult the Hotel Groups page.
ROOMS: 40 en suite s £45.95-£48.95; d £45.95-£48.95
CONF: Thtr 26 Board 17

⌂ Travel Inn (Bristol South)

Hengrove Leisure Park, Hengrove Way BS14 0HR
☎ 08701 977043 ▯ 01275 834721
Dir: *From City Centre take A37 to Wells and Shepton Mallet. Turn right onto A4174. The Travel Inn at 3rd lights*
Travel Inn offers good-quality, value-for-money accommodation. Spacious, en suite rooms with bath and shower comfortably accommodate a family of up to two adults and two children (to age 15). The restaurant and bar offers a varied menu. For further details consult the Hotel Groups page.
ROOMS: 40 en suite s £45.95-£46.95; d £45.95-£46.95

⌂ Travelodge (Bristol Central)

Anchor Rd, Harbourside BS1 5TT
☎ 08700 850 950 ▯ 0117 9255149
Travelodge offers good quality, good value, modern accommodation. Ideal for families, the spacious, en suite bedrooms include remote-control TV, tea and coffee-making facilities and luxury beds. Meals can be taken at the nearby family restaurant. For further details consult the Hotel Groups page.
ROOMS: 119 en suite (incl. bkfst) s fr £25; d fr £25

⌂ Travelodge (Bristol Cribbs Causeway)

Cribbs Causeway BS10 7TL
☎ 08700 850 950 ▯ 0117 950 1530
Dir: *A4018, off M5 junct 17*
Travelodge offers good quality, good value, modern accommodation. Ideal for families, the spacious, en suite bedrooms include remote-control TV, tea and coffee-making facilities and luxury beds. Meals can be taken at the nearby family restaurant. For further details consult the Hotel Groups page.
ROOMS: 56 en suite s fr £25; d fr £25

BRIXHAM, Devon

Map 03 SX95

★★★70% Quayside

41-49 King St TQ5 9TJ
☎ 01803 855751 ▯ 01803 882733
e-mail: reservations@quaysidehotel.co.uk
web: www.quaysidehotel.co.uk
Dir: *A380, at 2nd rdbt at Kinkerswell towards Brixham on A3022. Hotel overlooks harbour*

With views over the harbour and bay, this hotel was formerly six cottages. The owners and their team of local staff provide friendly and attentive service. Public rooms retain a certain cosiness and intimacy, and include the lounge, residents' bar and Ernie Lister's public bar. Freshly-landed fish features on menus in the well-appointed restaurant.
ROOMS: 29 en suite (2 fmly) ⊗ in 6 bedrooms s £55-£87; d £80-£120 (incl. bkfst) **LB** **FACILITIES:** ♫ Xmas **CONF:** Thtr 25 Class 18 Board 18
PARKING: 30 **NOTES:** ⊗ in restaurant
CARDS:

★★★68% Berryhead

Berryhead Rd TQ5 9AJ
☎ 01803 853225 ▯ 01803 882084
e-mail: stay@berryheadhotel.com
Dir: *Turn left at town hall to harbour. Right past statue, sharp left – leave marina, 1m, hotel on left*
From its stunning cliff-top location, this imposing property dating back to 1809 has spectacular views across Torbay. Public areas include two comfortable lounges, an outdoor terrace, a swimming

continued on p134

BRIXHAM, continued

pool, together with a bar serving a range of popular dishes. Many of the bedrooms have the benefit of the splendid sea views.
ROOMS: 32 en suite (7 fmly) s £48-£80; d £96-£160 (incl. bkfst) **LB** **FACILITIES: Spa** Jacuzzi Petanque Sailing Deep sea fishing ch fac Xmas **CONF:** BC Thtr 300 Class 250 Board 40 Del from £75 **PARKING:** 200 **NOTES:** in restaurant Civ Wed 200
CARDS:

See advert on opposite page

BROADSTAIRS, Kent Map 07 TR36

★★★65% Royal Albion

Albion St CT10 1AN
☎ 01843 868071 01843 861509
e-mail: enquiries@albionbroadstairs.co.uk
web: www.albionbroadstairs.co.uk
Dir: *follow signs for seafront and town centre*
This traditional seafront hotel enjoys delightful views from most bedrooms and the newly refurbished bar and lounge. The restaurant is two doors down the street in Marchesi's. Staff are friendly and the atmosphere is relaxed and informal.
ROOMS: 19 en suite (3 fmly) in 4 bedrooms s £65-£71; d £87-£115 (incl. bkfst) **LB** **FACILITIES:** STV Xmas **CONF:** Thtr 30 Class 20 Board 20 **PARKING:** 21 **NOTES:** in restaurant
CARDS:

BROADWAY, Worcestershire Map 10 SP03
See also Buckland

★★★★76% The Lygon Arms

FURLONG

High St WR12 7DU
☎ 01386 852255 01386 858611
e-mail: info@thelygonarms.co.uk
Dir: *Turn off A44, signed Broadway, hotel on High Street*

A hotel with a wealth of historic charm and character, the Lygon Arms is situated in the heart of Broadway. It dates back to the 16th century, and offers comfortable bedrooms with modern facilities and some fine antique furniture. Public rooms include a variety of lounge areas, some with open fires, and a choice of dining options - the Great Hall, with award-winning cuisine by Martin Blunos, or the more informal brasserie.
ROOMS: 69 rms (66 en suite) (3 fmly) (8 GF) **FACILITIES: Spa** STV Snooker Sauna Gym Beauty treatments, Steam Room, Bike Hire, Horse riding nearby, Walking **CONF:** BC Thtr 80 Class 48 Board 30 **PARKING:** 152 **NOTES:** in restaurant Civ Wed 80
CARDS:

See advert on opposite page

★★★78% Dormy House

Willersey Hill WR12 7LF
☎ 01386 852711 01386 858636
e-mail: reservations@dormyhouse.co.uk.
web: www.dormyhouse.co.uk
Dir: *2m E off A44, top of Fish Hill, turn for Saintbury/Picnic area. After 0.5m fork left and hotel on left*
A converted 17th-century farmhouse set in extensive grounds and with stunning views over Broadway. Some rooms are in a collection of honey-coloured stone cottages; some have four-poster beds. Furnishings are tasteful throughout, with some stylish contemporary touches. The best traditions have been retained - real fires, comfortable sofas and afternoon teas.
ROOMS: 25 en suite 23 annexe en suite (3 fmly) s £120-£130; d £160-£205 (incl. bkfst) **LB** **FACILITIES:** Sauna Gym Putt green Games room, nature & jogging trail **CONF:** Thtr 170 Class 100 Board 25 Del £185 **PARKING:** 80 **NOTES:** in restaurant Closed 25 & 26 Dec Civ Wed 170 **CARDS:**

See advert on page 137

★★★68% Broadway

CLASSIC BRITISH

The Green, High St WR12 7AA
☎ 01386 852401 01386 853879
e-mail: info@broadwayhotel.info
Dir: *From N take M5 J7, then A44. After Evesham follow signs to Broadway. From London M40 J8, A40 to A44. Follow signs to Evesham then Broadway.*
A half-timbered Cotswold stone property, built in the 15th century as a retreat for the Abbots of Pershore. Following refurbishment the hotel now combines modern, attractive décor with original charm and character. Bedrooms are tastefully furnished and well equipped while public rooms include a relaxing lounge, cosy bar and charming restaurant.
ROOMS: 20 en suite (1 fmly) in 4 bedrooms s £80-£115; d £130-£175 (incl. bkfst) **LB** **FACILITIES:** Xmas **CONF:** Thtr 20 Board 16 Del from £130 **PARKING:** 20 **NOTES:** in restaurant Civ Wed 50
CARDS:

BROCKENHURST, Hampshire Map 05 SU30

★★★★73% Rhinefield House

HandPICKED

Rhinefield Rd SO42 7QB
☎ 01590 622922 01590 622800
e-mail: rhinefieldhouse-cro@handpicked.co.uk
Dir: *A35 towards Chistchurch. 3m from Lyndhurst turn left to Rhinefield, 1.5m to hotel*

This splendid 19th-century, mock-Elizabethan mansion is set in 40 acres of beautifully landscaped gardens. Bedrooms are spacious and great consideration is given to guest comfort. The open-plan lounge and bar overlook an ornamental pond and the elegant

continued on p136

The Lygons Arms bears the stamp of the original Country House Hotel – inglenook fireplaces, snugs, and oak panels – alongside the comforts of the modern age, including an award-winning health spa. The Great Hall dining room is the perfect setting for Martin Blunos' celebrated cuisine. Set in the heart of the Cotswolds, the Lygon Arms, after 500 years as an Inn, remains a legend.

The Lygon Arms· Broadway · Worcestershire WR12 7DU
t 01386 852255 · f 01386 858611 · www.furlonghotels.co.uk
operated by FURLONG

The Berry Head Hotel

BERRY HEAD ROAD · BRIXHAM
SOUTH DEVON · TQ5 9AJ
Telephone 01803 853225/858583
Fax 01803 882084
Email: berryhd@aol.com
www.berryheadhotel.com

Nestling on the waters edge with panoramic views of Torbay. Steeped in history, set in six acres of private grounds surrounded by National Trust land, a short walk from the picturesque fishing port. A warm, comfortable and friendly hotel with atmosphere and an indoor heated swimming pool. The ideal base for watersports, rambling, and exploring Devon.

FAYRENESS HOTEL

Situated on the cliff top overlooking the English Channel, boasting beautiful panoramic views of the glorious surroundings on the East Kent coast. Having recently undergone a £1.3million refit, The Fayreness Hotel provides 29 luxurious rooms. All rooms have ensuite bathrooms, quality furniture and satellite TV. The hotel has double and twin rooms, a disabled room, Executive Double rooms, Junior Suites and the spacious Kingsgate & Fitzroy Suites. All Executive rooms and Suites have king size beds. The hotel bar serves a wide variety of draught and bottled drinks. The superb sea view restaurant offers an excellent choice of wines and the spacious function room has its own private bar.

The Fayreness Hotel, Marine Drive, Kingsgate, Kent CT10 3LG
Phone: +44 (0)1843 868641 Fax: +44 (0)1843 608750
Email: fayreness@thorleytaverns.com Web: www.thorleytaverns.com

BROCKENHURST, continued

restaurant is impressive with antique features. Hand Picked Hotels - AA Hotel Group of the Year 2004-5.
ROOMS: 34 en suite ⊗ in 16 bedrooms s £115-£190; d £125-£240 (incl. bkfst) **LB** **FACILITIES:** STV supervised new leisure facilities available from 2004/2005 Xmas **CONF:** Thtr 120 Class 50 Board 35 Del from £140 **PARKING:** 100 **NOTES:** ⊗ in restaurant Civ Wed 125
CARDS:

See advert on opposite page

★★★75% ***Balmer Lawn***
Lyndhurst Rd SO42 7ZB
☎ 01590 623116 01590 623864
e-mail: info@balmerlawnhotel.co.uk
Dir: *A337 towards Lymington, hotel on left behind village cricket green*

Situated in the heart of the New Forest, this imposing house provides comfortable public rooms and a good range of bedrooms. A selection of carefully prepared and enjoyable dishes are offered in the spacious restaurant whilst extensive function and leisure facilities make this a popular conference venue.
ROOMS: 55 en suite (9 fmly) ⊗ in 45 bedrooms **FACILITIES: Spa** Squash Sauna Gym Jacuzzi **CONF:** Thtr 150 Class 50 Board 50 **SERVICES:** Lift **PARKING:** 100 **NOTES:** ⊗ in restaurant Civ Wed 120
CARDS:

See advert on opposite page

★★★75% **Whitley Ridge Country House**
Beaulieu Rd SO42 7QL
☎ 01590 622354 01590 622856
e-mail: whitleyridge@brockenhurst.co.uk
web: www.newforest-hotels.co.uk/whitley-ridge/default.htm
Dir: *via B3055 towards Beaulieu*

This charming hotel enjoys a picturesque setting in the heart of the New Forest. Day rooms include two relaxing lounges and a large dining room, all with lovely views of the forest. Each bedroom has an individual style and bathrooms have been refurbished to a high standard. Enjoyable dining is strong feature of this hotel, with fresh local ingredients playing a key role.
ROOMS: 14 rms (13 en suite) (1 GF) ⊗ in all bedrooms s £65-£68; d £108-£140 (incl. bkfst) **LB** **FACILITIES:** STV Xmas **CONF:** Thtr 40 Class 40 Board 20 Del £130 **PARKING:** 32 **NOTES:** ⊗ in restaurant
CARDS:

★★★74% **New Park Manor**
Lyndhurst Rd SO42 7QH
☎ 01590 623467 Y 01590 622268
e-mail: info@newparkmanor.co.uk
Dir: *M27 junct 1, A337 to Lyndhurst & Brockenhurst. Hotel 1.5m on right*
Once the favoured hunting lodge of King Charles II, this well presented hotel enjoys a peaceful setting in extensive acreage of the New Forest and comes complete with an equestrian centre. Bedrooms have now been refurbished and are divided between the old house and a purpose-built wing. The smart public areas include a new mezzanine lounge.
ROOMS: 24 en suite (6 fmly) ⊗ in all bedrooms s £90-£130; d £120-£210 (incl. bkfst) **LB** **FACILITIES:** Riding Mountain biking Xmas **CONF:** Thtr 120 Class 52 Board 60 Del from £150 **PARKING:** 70 **NOTES:** ⊗ in restaurant Civ Wed 60
CARDS:

★★★73% **Careys Manor**
New Forest SO42 7RH
☎ 01590 623551 01590 622799
e-mail: stay@careysmanor.com web: www.careysmanor.com
Dir: *M27 J3, then M271, then A35 to Lyndhurst. Then A337 towards Brockenhurst. Hotel on left after 30mph sign.*

An imposing building on the outskirts of this New Forest town. The well-proportioned public areas include a spacious lounge, complete with inglenook fireplace, and an airy restaurant. Bedrooms are well equipped and of a generous size. Le Blaireau Café, within the grounds, offers an alternative dining option with a French flavour. A new spa facility is an exciting addition to the hotel.
ROOMS: 18 en suite 62 annexe en suite (32 GF) ⊗ in 28 bedrooms s £99-£139; d £159-£239 (incl. bkfst) **LB** **FACILITIES: Spa** STV supervised Sauna Gym Jacuzzi Steam room, Beauty therapists, treatment rooms, hydrotherapy pool Xmas **CONF:** Thtr 120 Class 70 Board 40 Del from £145 **PARKING:** 180 **NOTES:** ⊗ in restaurant Civ Wed 100 **CARDS:**

★★★67% **Forest Park**
Rhinefield Rd SO42 7ZG
Forestdale Hotels
☎ 01590 622844 01590 623948
e-mail: forest.park@forestdale.com
Dir: *A337 to Brockenhurst turn into Meerut Rd, follow road through Waters Green. Right at t-junct into Rhinefield Rd*
A friendly hotel offering good facilities for both adults and children. A heated pool, riding, children's meal times and a quiet location in the forest are just a few of the advantages here. The

continued on p138

75%

A traditional country house hotel with a contemporary touch, **set in the heart of the New Forest.** The Balmer Lawn offers the **very best in hotel accommodation,** the **finest cuisine and wines** in our **award winning restaurant**. A gym, indoor and outdoor pool, sauna, spa, tennis and squash courts complete our **excellent leisure facilities.** And with **six private function rooms** we know we can cater for **all your needs.**

Lyndhurst Road, Brockenhurst, Hampshire, SO42 7ZB
Tele: 01590 623116
Email: info@balmerlawnhotel.com
Web: www.balmerlawnhotel.com

Located between the Cotswold villages of Chipping Campden and Broadway, and only a few miles from Stratford-upon-Avon, you'll find the Dormy House Hotel.

Surrounded on three sides by Broadway Golf Course, enjoy the beautifully appointed rooms, superb restaurant and high standard of service.

Stay for one night, or take a Classic Dormy Break in the heart of the Cotswold.

Dormy House . . . a delightful discovery

WILLERSEY HILL, BROADWAY
WORCESTERSHIRE WR12 7LF
Tel: 01386 852711 Fax: 01386 858636
E-mail: reservations@dormyhouse.co.uk
www.dormyhouse.co.uk

A country house built for pleasure

RHINEFIELD HOUSE

New Forest, Hampshire

Known locally as the "Jewel in the Forest", this magnificent country mansion is hidden deep within an impressive forest of Canadian Redwood and Copper Beech trees. The Italian style ponds and ornamental gardens complete a fairytale setting where, in summer, you can relax and unwind while enjoying the sun and the outdoor pool.

Rhinefield House, Rhinefield Road, Brockenhurst, The New Forest, Hampshire Call 01590 622922
or email: rhinefieldhouse@handpicked.co.uk
www.handpicked.co.uk/rhinefieldhouse
Central Reservations: 0845 4580901
www.handpicked.co.uk

HOTEL GROUP OF THE YEAR 2004-2005

BROCKENHURST, continued

well-equipped, comfortable bedrooms vary in size and style, and a choice of lounge and bar areas is available.
ROOMS: 38 en suite (2 fmly) (7 GF) ⊗ in 2 bedrooms s fr £90; d fr £120 (incl. bkfst) **LB FACILITIES:** Riding Sauna Xmas **CONF:** Thtr 50 Class 20 Board 24 **PARKING:** 80 **NOTES:** ⊗ in restaurant Civ Wed 50 **CARDS:**

★★75% Cloud

Meerut Rd SO42 7TD
☎ 01590 622165 01590 622818
e-mail: enquiries@cloudhotel.co.uk web: www.cloudhotel.co.uk
Dir: *1st right off A337, follow tourist signs*
This charming hotel enjoys a peaceful location on the edge of the village. The bedrooms are bright and comfortable with pine furnishings and smart en suite facilities. Public rooms include a selection of cosy lounges, a delightful rear garden with outdoor seating and a restaurant specialising in home-cooked, wholesome English food.
ROOMS: 18 en suite (3 fmly) s fr £90; d fr £148 (incl. bkfst & dinner) **LB FACILITIES:** Xmas **CONF:** Thtr 40 Class 12 Board 12 Del from £105 **PARKING:** 20 **NOTES:** No children 8yrs ⊗ in restaurant Closed 28 Dec - 10 Jan **CARDS:**

★★67% *Watersplash*

The Rise SO42 7ZP
☎ 01590 622344 01590 624047
e-mail: bookings@watersplash.co.uk
web: www.watersplash.co.uk
Dir: *M3 junct 13/M27 junct 1/A337 S through Lyndhurst to Brockenhurst. Through Brockenhurst, The Rise on left, hotel on left*
This popular, welcoming Victorian hotel has been in the same family for 40 years. Upgraded bedrooms have co-ordinated décor and good facilities. The restaurant overlooks the neatly tended garden and there is also a comfortably furnished lounge, separate bar and an outdoor pool.
ROOMS: 23 en suite (6 fmly) **FACILITIES:** **CONF:** Thtr 80 Class 20 Board 20 **PARKING:** 29 **NOTES:** ⊗ in restaurant
CARDS:

BROMBOROUGH, Merseyside — Map 15 SJ38

⌂ Travel Inn (Wirral Bromborough)

travel inn

High St, Bromborough Cross CH62 7EZ
☎ 08701 977273 0151 344 0443
Dir: *on A41 New Chester Road, 2m from M53 junct 5*
Travel Inn offers good-quality, value-for-money accommodation. Spacious, en suite rooms with bath and shower comfortably accommodate a family of up to two adults and two children (to age 15). The restaurant and bar offers a varied menu. For further details consult the Hotel Groups page.
ROOMS: 32 en suite s £45.95-£46.95; d £45.95-£46.95
CONF: Thtr 80 Board 35

BROMLEY, Greater London
See LONDON SECTION plan 1 G1

★★★73% Bromley Court

Best Western

Bromley Hill BR1 4JD
☎ 020 8461 8600 020 8460 0899
e-mail: info@bromleycourthotel.co.uk
web: www.bw-bromleycourthotel.co.uk
Dir: *N of Bromley town centre, off A21 London road. Private drive opposite Volkswagen garage on Bromley Hill*
This grand mansion is set in three acres of grounds. Bedrooms are appointed to a good standard, each well designed and thoughtfully equipped. The contemporary-style restaurant offers a good choice of meals in comfortable surroundings. Extensive facilities include a leisure club and a good range of meeting rooms.
ROOMS: 114 en suite (4 fmly) ⊗ in 50 bedrooms s £85-£107; d £95-£120 (incl. bkfst) **LB FACILITIES: Spa** STV Sauna Gym Jacuzzi **CONF:** Thtr 150 Class 80 Board 45 Del from £130 **SERVICES:** Lift **PARKING:** 100 **NOTES:** ⊗ in restaurant Civ Wed 55
CARDS:

BROMSGROVE, Worcestershire — Map 10 SO97

★★★★66% Hanover International Hotel & Club

Hanover International Hotels & Clubs

Kidderminster Rd B61 9AB
☎ 01527 576600 01527 878981
e-mail: paul.wilkes@hanover-international.com
Dir: *on A448, 1m W of Bromsgrove town centre*
Public areas in this striking building have a Mediterranean theme with white-washed walls, a courtyard garden and plenty of natural light. Bedrooms are in a variety of styles; some are more compact than others and all offer an excellent working environment for the business guest. Leisure facilities include a steam room, sauna, pool and gym.
ROOMS: 114 en suite (17 fmly) (34 GF) ⊗ in 77 bedrooms s £38-£135; d £76-£155 **LB FACILITIES: Spa** STV Snooker Sauna Solarium Gym Jacuzzi Childrens play area Xmas **CONF:** BC Thtr 200 Class 140 Board 30 Del from £99 **SERVICES:** Lift **PARKING:** 250 **NOTES:** ⊗ in restaurant Civ Wed 200 **CARDS:**

⌂ Innkeeper's Lodge Bromsgrove

Innkeeper's Lodge

462 Birmingham Rd, Marlbrook B61 0HR
☎ 01527 878060
www.innkeeperslodge.com
Dir: *on the A38 0.5m between M5 & M42*
Smart rooms meet essential business requirements but also have home comforts, and depending on location may well have meeting rooms and pub dining. Dining options generally include all-day menus plus the added advantage of breakfast.
ROOMS: 29 en suite s £45-£49.95; d £45-£49.95

⌂ Premier Lodge (Bromsgrove)

PREMIER LODGE.com

Worcester Rd, Upton Warren B61 7ET
☎ 0870 9906408 0870 9906409
web: www.premierlodge.com
Dir: *1.5m from M5 junct 5 towards Bromsgrove on A38. From M42 junct 1 follow A38 south, over A448*
High quality, modern, budget accommodation, ideal for families and business travellers. All rooms feature bath, power shower and satellite TV, and most have telephones / modem points. The adjacent bar and restaurant offers a wide and varied menu.
ROOMS: 27 en suite s £50; d £50 **CONF:** Board 10

⌂ Travel Inn Bromsgrove

travel inn

Birmingham Rd B61 0BA
☎ 08701 977 044 01527 834719
Travel Inn offers good-quality, value-for-money accommodation. Spacious, en suite rooms with bath and shower comfortably accommodate a family of up to two adults and two children (to age 15). The restaurant and bar offers a varied menu. For further details consult the Hotel Groups page.
ROOMS: 74 en suite (incl. bkfst) s £45.95-£46.95; d £45.95-£46.95

BROOK (NEAR CADNAM), Hampshire Map 05 SU21

★★★67% Bell Inn
SO43 7HE
☎ 023 8081 2214 023 8081 3958
e-mail: bell@bramshaw.co.uk
web: www.bramshaw.co.uk
Dir: M27 junct 1 onto B3079, hotel 1.5m on right

The Inn is part of the Bramshaw Golf Club and has tailored its style to suit this market, but it is also an ideal base from which to visit the New Forest. Bedrooms are comfortable and attractively furnished, and the public areas, particularly the welcoming bar, have a cosy and friendly atmosphere.
ROOMS: 25 en suite (8 GF) in 11 bedrooms s £65-£90; d £90-£110 (incl. bkfst) **LB** **FACILITIES:** 54 Putt green Xmas **CONF:** Thtr 50 Class 20 Board 30 Del from £100 **PARKING:** 150 **NOTES:** in restaurant **CARDS:**

BROXTON, Cheshire Map 15 SJ45

★★★★74% De Vere Carden Park
Carden Park CH3 9DQ
DE VERE HOTELS
☎ 01829 731000 01829 731599
e-mail: reservations.carden@devere-hotels.com
web: www.devereonline.co.uk/cardenpark
Dir: M56 junct 15/M53 Chester. Take A41 for Whitchurch for approx 8m. At Broxton rdbt right onto A534 Wrexham. Hotel 1.5m on left
This impressive Cheshire estate dates back to the 17th century and consists of 750 acres of mature parkland. The hotel offers superb leisure facilities including challenging golf courses, a fully equipped gym, a swimming pool and popular spa. Traditionally furnished and decorated bedrooms are spacious and equipped with a comprehensive range of extras. Staff throughout are keen to please and there is a choice of dining options.
ROOMS: 113 en suite 79 annexe en suite (24 fmly) in 134 bedrooms s £130; d £150 **LB** **FACILITIES: Spa** STV supervised 45 Snooker Sauna Solarium Gym Putt green Jacuzzi Archery, Quadbikes, Off road driving, Mountain biking, Walking trails Xmas **CONF:** BC Thtr 400 Class 240 Board 125 Del £185 **SERVICES:** Lift **PARKING:** 500 **NOTES:** in restaurant Civ Wed 375
CARDS:

BRUTON, Somerset Map 04 ST63

Restaurant with Rooms

The Claire de Lune Restaurant with Rooms
2-4 HIgh St BA10 0AA
☎ 01749 813395 01749 813395
e-mail: enquiries@clairedelune.co.uk
Dir: in centre of Bruton at eastern end of High Street
This pleasant restaurant with rooms offers comfortable bedrooms

continued

and a delightful lounge and terrace. Fine dining in the restaurant presents interesting, well-prepared dishes, which use the freshest local produce and provides a memorable part to any visit.
The welcoming proprietors make every effort to ensure guests' comfort.
ROOMS: 3 en suite s £35; d £55 (incl. bkfst) **LB** **FACILITIES:** Xmas **NOTES:** No children 8yrs in restaurant Closed 1st 2 weeks Jan RS Oct-Nov & Feb-Mar **CARDS:**

BRYHER See Scilly, Isles of

BUCKDEN, North Yorkshire Map 18 SD97

★★69% Buck Inn
BD23 5JA
☎ 01756 760228 01756 760227
e-mail: info@thebuckinn.com
web: www.thebuckinn.com
Dir: A59/B6265 to Threshfield, then B6160 to Buckden through Kettlewell & Starbotton
This traditional Georgian inn is privately owned, personally run and provides warm, friendly hospitality. Fine views can be enjoyed from many of the smartly presented bedrooms. There is a cosy lounge area for guests and a wide range of interesting snacks and light meals are served in the lounge bar. The Courtyard restaurant provides a more formal menu using fresh, local, quality produce.
ROOMS: 14 en suite (2 fmly) (2 GF) s £44.50-£55; d £82-£99 (incl. bkfst) **LB** **FACILITIES:** Xmas **CONF:** Class 30 **PARKING:** 30 **NOTES:** in restaurant **CARDS:**

Bad hair day?
Hairdryers in all rooms three stars and above

BUCKINGHAM, Buckinghamshire

Map 11 SP63

★★★★69% *Villiers*

3 Castle St MK18 1BS
☎ 01280 822444 01280 822113
e-mail: villiers@villiers-hotels.demon.co.uk

Guests can enjoy a town centre location with a high degree of comfort at this 400-year-old former coaching inn. Relaxing public areas feature flagstone floors, oak panelling and real fires whilst bedrooms are modern, spacious and equipped to a high level. Diners can unwind in the atmospheric Swan and Castle bar before taking dinner in the award-winning Henry's restaurant.
ROOMS: 46 en suite (43 fmly) **FACILITIES:** STV Free membership of nearby private leisure club ♫ **CONF:** Thtr 250 Class 120 Board 80
SERVICES: Lift **PARKING:** 53 **NOTES:** Civ Wed 150
CARDS:

See advert on page 139

★★★64% Buckingham Beales

Buckingham Ring Rd MK18 1RY
☎ 01280 822622 01280 823074
e-mail: buckingham@bealeshotels.co.uk
Dir: *M1 junct 13/14 follow signs to Buckingham-A422/A421. M40 exit junct 9/10 follow signs Buckingham. Hotel on ring road*

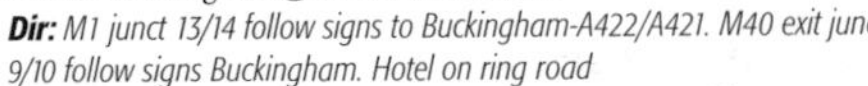

A purpose-built hotel which offers spacious rooms with well-designed working spaces for business travellers. There are also extensive conference facilities. The open-plan restaurant and bar offers a good range of dishes, and the well-equipped leisure suite is popular with guests.
ROOMS: 70 en suite (6 fmly) in 24 bedrooms s £80-£95; d £92-£115 (incl. bkfst) **LB** **FACILITIES:** STV Sauna Solarium Gym Jacuzzi ♫ Xmas **CONF:** BC Thtr 160 Class 90 Board 30 Del from £132
PARKING: 120 **NOTES:** in restaurant Civ Wed 120
CARDS:

Travel Inn Buckingham

13 High St MK18 1NT
☎ 08701 977286 08701 977709
Dir: *From A5 follow A422 or from A43 follow A413. Travel Inn in town centre*
Travel Inn offers good-quality, value-for-money accommodation. Spacious, en suite rooms with bath and shower comfortably accommodate a family of up to two adults and two children (to age 15). The restaurant and bar offers a varied menu. For further details consult the Hotel Groups page.
ROOMS: 41 en suite s £45.95-£46.96; d £45.95-£46.96

> Packed in a hurry?
> Ironing facilities should be available at all star levels, either in rooms or on request

BUCKLAND (NEAR BROADWAY), Gloucestershire

Map 10 SP03

Top 200 – Hotel

★★★ Buckland Manor

WR12 7LY
☎ 01386 852626 01386 853557
e-mail: buckland-manor-uk@msn.com
web: www.bucklandmanor.com
Dir: *off B4632 Broadway to Winchcombe Road*
A grand 13th-century manor house in extensive grounds with beautiful gardens where everything is geared to encourage rest and relaxation. Bedrooms and public areas are furnished with high quality pieces and decorated in keeping with the style of the manor. Crackling log fires warm the wonderful lounges. The cuisine continues to impress, with high quality produce skilfully used.
ROOMS: 13 en suite (2 fmly) (4 GF) s £225-£360; d £235-£370 (incl. bkfst) **LB** **FACILITIES:** STV Putt green Xmas
PARKING: 30 **NOTES:** No children 12yrs in restaurant
CARDS:

BUDE, Cornwall & Isles of Scilly

Map 02 SS20

★★★70% Falcon

Breakwater Rd EX23 8SD
☎ 01288 352005 01288 356359
e-mail: reception@falconhotel.com
Dir: *off A39 into Bude, follow road to Widemouth Bay. Hotel on right over canal bridge*

Dating back to 1798, this long-established hotel boasts delightful walled gardens, ideal for afternoon teas. Bedrooms all offer high standards of comfort and quality, with a four-poster room available complete with spa bath. A choice of menus is offered in

continued

the elegant restaurant or the friendly bar, and there is an impressive function room.
ROOMS: 27 en suite (7 fmly) s £51-£55; d £102-£110 (incl. bkfst) **LB** **FACILITIES:** STV Mini gym ch fac **CONF:** BC Thtr 200 Class 50 Board 50 **PARKING:** 40 **NOTES:** in restaurant RS 25 Dec Civ Wed 160 **CARDS:**

★★★69% *Hartland*

Hartland Ter EX23 8JY
☎ 01288 355661 01288 355664
e-mail: hartlandhotel@aol.com
Dir: *off A39 to Bude, follow town centre signs. Left into Hartland Terrace opp Boots the chemist. Hotel at seaward end of road*
Enjoying a pleasantly quiet, yet convenient location, the Hartland has excellent sea views. A popular stay for those wishing to tour the area and also with families, this hotel offers entertainment on many evenings throughout the year. Bedrooms are comfortable and offer a range of sizes. The public areas are smart, and in the dining room, a pleasant fixed-price menu is available.
ROOMS: 28 en suite (2 fmly) in 8 bedrooms **FACILITIES:** **SERVICES:** Lift **PARKING:** 30 **NOTES:** in restaurant Closed mid Nov-Etr (ex Xmas & New Year)

★★★68% Camelot

Downs View EX23 8RE
☎ 01288 352361 01288 355470
e-mail: stay@camelot-hotel.co.uk
web: www.camelot-hotel.co.uk
Dir: *off A39 into Bude town centre, join one-way system, left lane, bottom of hill on left*

This friendly and welcoming Edwardian property offers a range of facilities including a smart and comfortable conservatory bar and lounge, a games room and Hawkers restaurant, which offers skilful cooking using much local produce. Bedrooms are light and airy, with high standards of housekeeping and maintenance.
ROOMS: 24 en suite (2 fmly) (7 GF) in 21 bedrooms s £53-£57; d £82-£90 (incl. bkfst) **LB** **FACILITIES:** Darts Pool table Table tennis ch fac **PARKING:** 21 **NOTES:** in restaurant Closed Xmas & New Year **CARDS:**

★★69% Atlantic House

17-18 Summerleaze Crescent EX23 8HJ
☎ 01288 352451 01288 356666
e-mail: enq@atlantichousehotel.co.uk
web: www.atlantichousehotel.co.uk
Dir: *M5 junct 31, follow A30 to by-pass in Okehampton. Follow signs to Bude via Halwill & Holsworthy*
Facing south overlooking the beach, this relaxed and personally run hotel is set in a quiet area. Bedrooms vary in size and style; all

continued

are comfortable and well maintained. A well balanced, fixed-price meal is served is the charming dining room.

ROOMS: 16 en suite (2 fmly) in all bedrooms s £26.75-£31.80; d £53.50-£66.50 (incl. bkfst) **LB** **FACILITIES:** Games room Multi-activity outdoor sports ch fac **PARKING:** 10 **NOTES:** in restaurant Closed mid-Nov - mid-Feb **CARDS:**

★★68% Penarvor

Crooklets Beach EX23 8NE
☎ 01288 352036 01288 355027
e-mail: hotel.penarvor@boltblue.com
Dir: *From A39 towards Bude for 1.5m. At 2nd rdbt right, pass shops. Top of hill left signed Crooklets Beach*
Adjacent to the golf course and overlooking Crooklets Beach, this family owned hotel benefits from a relaxed and friendly atmosphere. Bedrooms vary in size and are all equipped to a similar standard. An interesting selection of dishes, using fresh local produce, is available in the restaurant; bar meals are also provided.
ROOMS: 16 en suite (6 fmly) in all bedrooms s £27-£45; d £54-£68 (incl. bkfst) **LB** **PARKING:** 20 **NOTES:** in restaurant
CARDS:

★★66% *Maer Lodge*

Maer Down Rd, Crooklets Beach EX23 8NG

☎ 01288 353306 01288 354005
e-mail: maerlodgehotel@btinternet.com
Dir: *exit A39 at Stratton. Right at mini rdbt into The Strand, up Belle Vue past shops. Left at Somerfield to Crooklets Beach, hotel on right*
With views over the Downs and countryside, this long established, family-run hotel is quietly located. Traditionally furnished public areas are comfortable and include a convivial bar and spacious lounge. A short fixed-price menu is offered in the dining room. Bedrooms are soundly furnished and well appointed, and some have lovely views.
ROOMS: 19 en suite (4 fmly) in all bedrooms **FACILITIES:** STV Putt green **CONF:** Thtr 60 Class 40 Board 15 **PARKING:** 15 **NOTES:** in restaurant **CARDS:**

BUNGAY, Suffolk

Map 13 TM38

★★65% Kings Head

2 Market Place NR35 1AW
☎ 01986 893583 01986 893583
e-mail: info@kingsheadhotel.biz
Dir: *Off A143 to town centre. Hotel located in town centre opposite The Three Tuns*
This 18th-century coaching inn is situated in the heart of town, amid a range of antique shops. The spacious bedrooms are furnished with pine pieces and have a good range of useful extras; one room has a superb four-poster bed. Public rooms include

continued on p142

BUNGAY, continued

Luciano's restaurant and the Duke of Wellington lounge bar; Oddfellows bar is being launched as a live music venue.
ROOMS: 12 en suite (1 fmly) ⊗ in 4 bedrooms s £35-£45; d £50-£59.50 (incl. bkfst) **LB FACILITIES:** ♫ **CONF:** Thtr 100 Class 50 Board 30 **PARKING:** 29 **NOTES:** ⊗ in restaurant
CARDS:

BURFORD, Oxfordshire Map 05 SP21

★★★74% The Lamb Inn
Sheep St OX18 4LR
☎ 01993 823155 01993 822228
e-mail: info@lambinn-burford.co.uk
Dir: *Turn off A40 into Burford, downhill, take 1st left into Sheep St, hotel last on right*

A stone's throw from the centre of this quintessential Cotswold town, this delightful old inn possesses an abundance of character and charm. The bedrooms retain many original features and there is a selection of comfortable lounges with flagstone floors and log fires together with an atmospheric bar in which to relax. In the elegant restaurant carefully cooked meals are served, using the best of ingredients.
ROOMS: 15 en suite (1 fmly) (3 GF) ⊗ in all bedrooms s £80-£100; d £130-£200 (incl. bkfst) **LB FACILITIES:** Xmas **NOTES:** ⊗ in restaurant
CARDS:

★★★73% The Bay Tree Hotel

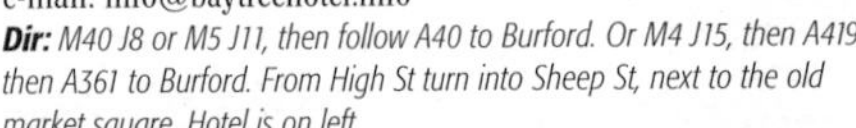

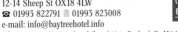

CLASSIC BRITISH

12-14 Sheep St OX18 4LW
☎ 01993 822791 01993 823008
e-mail: info@baytreehotel.info
Dir: *M40 J8 or M5 J11, then follow A40 to Burford. Or M4 J15, then A419 then A361 to Burford. From High St turn into Sheep St, next to the old market square. Hotel is on left.*
History and modern flair sit happily side by side at this delightful old inn, situated near the town centre. Bedrooms are tastefully furnished using the original features to good effect and some have four-poster and half-tester beds. Public areas consist of a character bar, a sophisticated airy restaurant, a selection of meeting rooms and an attractive walled garden.
ROOMS: 7 en suite 14 annexe en suite (2 fmly) s £119-£149; d £165-£205 (incl. bkfst) **LB FACILITIES:** Xmas **CONF:** Thtr 40 Class 12 Board 25 Del from £155 **PARKING:** 50 **NOTES:** ⊗ in restaurant Civ Wed 60 **CARDS:**

★★★68% Cotswold Gateway
Cheltenham Rd OX18 4HX
☎ 01993 822695 01993 823600
e-mail: cotswold.gateway@dial.pipex.com
web: www.cotswold-gateway.co.uk
Dir: *Hotel on rdbt at A40 Oxford/Cheltenham at junct with A361*

Ideally suited for both business and pleasure guests, The Cotswold Gateway Hotel is prominently situated on the A40 and yet only a short walk away from Burford. The tastefully decorated bedrooms include two four-poster rooms. Diners have an extensive choice of popular dishes and the option of eating in the character bar, the coffee shop or in the more formal restaurant.
ROOMS: 13 en suite 8 annexe en suite (2 fmly) ⊗ in all bedrooms
CONF: Thtr 40 Class 20 Board 24 **PARKING:** 60 **NOTES:** ⊗ in restaurant **CARDS:**

★★67% The Inn For All Seasons
THE INDEPENDENTS
The Barringtons OX18 4TN
☎ 01451 844324 01451 844375
e-mail: sharp@innforallseasons.com
web: www.innforallseasons.com
Dir: *3m W of Burford on A40 towards Cheltenham*

This 16th-century coaching inn is conveniently near to Burford. Bedrooms are comfortable and steadily being upgraded, public areas retain a feeling of period charm with original fireplaces and oak beams. A good selection of bar meals is available at lunchtime, whilst the evening menu includes an appetising selection of fresh fish.
ROOMS: 9 en suite 1 annexe en suite (2 fmly) (1 GF) s £46-£58; d £93-£97 (incl. bkfst) **LB FACILITIES:** STV Clay pigeon shooting Xmas **CONF:** Thtr 25 Class 30 Board 30 Del from £110 **PARKING:** 62
CARDS:

★★65% Golden Pheasant
91 High St OX18 4QA
☎ 01993 823223 📠 01993 822621
Dir: *M40 junct 8, follow signs A40 Cheltenham into Burford*
This attractive old inn is set on Burford's main street and dates, in part, back to the 16th century. Bedrooms can be compact and are well furnished with attractive fabrics, period furniture and many thoughtful extras. The bar and restaurant is full of character and serves a wide selection of meals.
ROOMS: 11 rms (10 en suite) (1 fmly) s £60-£75; d £85-£110 (incl. bkfst) **LB** **FACILITIES:** Xmas **PARKING:** 12 **NOTES:** ⊘ in restaurant
CARDS:

⌂ Travelodge (Cotswolds)
Bury Barn OX8 4JF
☎ 08700 850 950 📠 01993 822699
Dir: *A40*
Travelodge
Travelodge offers good quality, good value, modern accommodation. Ideal for families, the spacious, en suite bedrooms include remote-control TV, tea and coffee-making facilities and luxury beds. Meals can be taken at the nearby family restaurant. For further details consult the Hotel Groups page.
ROOMS: 40 en suite s fr £25; d fr £25

BURLEY, Hampshire
Map 05 SU20

★★★70% Burley Manor
Ringwood Rd BH24 4BS
☎ 01425 403522 📠 01425 403227
e-mail: burley.manor@forestdale.com
Dir: *leave A31 at Burley sign, hotel 3m on left*
Forestdale Hotels
Set in extensive grounds, this 18th-century former mansion enjoys a relaxed ambience and a peaceful setting. Half of the well-equipped, comfortable bedrooms, including several with four-posters, are located in the main house. The remainder, many of which have balconies, are in the adjacent converted stable block. Cosy public rooms benefit from log fires in winter.
ROOMS: 21 en suite 17 annexe en suite (3 fmly) (17 GF) ⊘ in 4 bedrooms s fr £115; d fr £130 (incl. bkfst) **LB** **FACILITIES:** Fishing Riding Xmas **CONF:** Thtr 60 Class 40 Board 40 Del from £140 **PARKING:** 60 **NOTES:** ⊘ in restaurant Civ Wed 70
CARDS:

★★★62% Moorhill House
BH24 4AH
☎ 01425 403285 📠 01425 403715
e-mail: moorhill@newforesthotels.co.uk
web: www.newforesthotels.co.uk
Dir: *M27, A31, follow signs to Burley village, through village, up hill, turn right opposite school and cricket grounds*
Situated deep in the heart of the New Forest and formerly a grand gentleman's residence, this charming hotel offers a relaxed and friendly environment. Bedrooms, of varying sizes, are smartly decorated. A range of facilities is provided and guests can relax by walking around the extensive grounds. Both dinner and breakfast offer a choice of interesting and freshly prepared dishes.
ROOMS: 31 en suite (13 fmly) (3 GF) s £75-£82.50; d £120-£135 (incl. bkfst) **LB** **FACILITIES:** Sauna Gym Putt green badminton (Apr-Sep) Xmas **CONF:** Thtr 120 Class 60 Board 65 Del from £90 **PARKING:** 50 **NOTES:** ⊘ in restaurant Civ Wed 80
CARDS:

TV dinner?
Room service at three stars and above

BURNHAM, Buckinghamshire
Map 06 SU98

★★★72% Grovefield
Taplow Common Rd SL1 8LP
☎ 01628 603131 📠 01628 668078
e-mail: grovefield@macdonald-hotels.co.uk
Dir: *From M4 left on A4 towards Maidenhead. Next rdbt turn right under railway bridge. Straight over mini rdbt, garage on right. Continue for 1.5m, hotel on right*

Set in its own spacious grounds, the Grovefield is conveniently located for Heathrow Airport as well as the industrial centres of Slough and Maidenhead. Accommodation is spacious and well presented and most have views over the attractive gardens. Public areas include a range of meeting rooms, comfortable bar/lounge area and Hamilton's restaurant.
ROOMS: 40 en suite (5 fmly) (7 GF) ⊘ in 24 bedrooms
FACILITIES: STV Fishing Putt green **CONF:** Thtr 180 Class 80 Board 80 **SERVICES:** Lift **PARKING:** 155 **NOTES:** ⊘ in restaurant Civ Wed 200 **CARDS:**

★★★64% Burnham Beeches Hotel
Grove Rd SL1 8DP
☎ 0870 609 6124 📠 01628 603994
e-mail: burnhambeeches@corushotels.com
Dir: *A355 towards Slough. R at 2 mini rdbts, left at next mini rdbt. Grove Rd 1st on right.*
corus hotels

Set in attractive mature grounds on the fringes of woodland, this extended Georgian manor house has spacious and comfortable bedrooms which are well equipped. Public rooms include a cosy lounge/bar offering all-day snacks and an elegant wood-panelled restaurant that serves interesting cuisine; there are also conference facilities, a fitness centre and pool.
ROOMS: 82 en suite (19 fmly) (9 GF) ⊘ in 30 bedrooms s £60-£100; d £120-£180 (incl. bkfst) **LB** **FACILITIES: Spa** STV Snooker Sauna Gym Jacuzzi Xmas **CONF:** Thtr 180 Class 100 Board 60 Del from £140 **SERVICES:** Lift **PARKING:** 200 **NOTES:** ⊘ in restaurant Civ Wed 120 **CARDS:**

B

BURNHAM MARKET, Norfolk
Map 13 TF84

★★77% Hoste Arms

The Green PE31 8HD
☎ 01328 738777 01328 730103
e-mail: reception@hostearms.co.uk

Dir: *signed on B1155, 5m W of Wells-next-the-Sea*

Stylish, privately owned inn situated in the heart of this bustling village close to the north Norfolk coast. The extensive public rooms feature a range of dining areas that include a conservatory with plush furniture, a sunny patio and a traditional pub. The tastefully furnished, thoughtfully equipped bedrooms are generally very spacious and offer a high degree of comfort.

ROOMS: 36 en suite (1 fmly) (7 GF) s £78-£168; d £108-£268 (incl. bkfst) **LB** **FACILITIES:** Xmas **CONF:** BC Thtr 25 Board 16 Del from £135 **PARKING:** 45 **CARDS:**

BURNLEY, Lancashire
Map 18 SD83

★★★74% Oaks

Colne Rd, Reedley BB10 2LF
☎ 01282 414141 01282 433401
e-mail: oaks@shirehotels.co.uk

Dir: *M65 junct 12. Follow signs to Burnley. At B&Q mini rdbt left, right at rdbt, right onto A682. Hotel 1m on left*

The friendly team here provide super hospitality in this former Victorian coffee merchant's house. The hotel offers traditional public areas and modern, well-equipped bedrooms. Gym, pool, sauna and steam rooms are all available in the leisure club on site.

ROOMS: 50 en suite (10 fmly) in 31 bedrooms s £99-£114; d £100-£130 (incl. bkfst) **LB** **FACILITIES:** STV supervised Sauna Solarium Gym Jacuzzi Steam room Xmas **CONF:** Thtr 120 Class 48 Board 60 Del £127 **PARKING:** 110 **NOTES:** in restaurant Civ Wed 100 **CARDS:**

★★★71% Sparrow Hawk

Church St BB11 2DN
☎ 01282 421551 01282 456506
e-mail: enquiries@sparrowhawkhotel.co.uk
web: www.sparrowhawkhotel.co.uk

Dir: *M65 junct 10, 5th exit at traffic island (Cavalry Way). Left at next island, right lane along Westway, right at lights. Take 2nd exit from rdbt , 2nd exit at next rdbt. Hotel 300yds on right*

This grand Victorian hotel is centrally located and is handy for key local attractions. Bedrooms vary in size and style and all are well equipped and have a host of thoughtful extras. Stylish public areas include the bright Mediterranean style Smithies Café Bar, Farriers Restaurant and a traditional bar serving speciality ale. Staffs throughout are particularly friendly.

ROOMS: 35 en suite (1 fmly) in 9 bedrooms s £46-£55; d £53-£62 (incl. bkfst) **LB** **FACILITIES:** STV ♫ Xmas **CONF:** BC Thtr 80 Class 50 Board 40 Del from £49 **PARKING:** 20 **NOTES:** **CARDS:**

★★★68% Rosehill House

Rosehill Av BB11 2PW
☎ 01282 453931 01282 455628
e-mail: rhhotel@provider.co.uk

Dir: *0.5m S of Burnley town centre, off A682*

This fine Grade II listed building stands its own leafy grounds in a quiet area of town. There are two restaurants (one a tapas bar) and a comfortable lounge bar. In addition to the standard accommodation, two loft conversions and a former coach house offer a range of stylish individual bedrooms.

ROOMS: 30 en suite (3 fmly) (4 GF) in 1 bedroom s £40-£70; d £55-£75 **LB** **FACILITIES:** STV Snooker Gym **CONF:** BC Thtr 50 Class 30 Board 30 **PARKING:** 52 **NOTES:** Civ Wed 90 **CARDS:**

Travel Inn

travel inn

Queen Victoria Rd BB10 3EF
☎ 08701 977045 01282 448431

Dir: *M65 junct 12 take 5th exit at rdbt, 1st exit at rdbt, keep in right lane at lights, next rdbt, 2nd exit then 3rd at next rdbt, under bridge turn left before football ground*

Travel Inn offers good-quality, value-for-money accommodation. Spacious, en suite rooms with bath and shower comfortably accommodate a family of up to two adults and two children (to age 15). The restaurant and bar offers a varied menu. For further details consult the Hotel Groups page.

ROOMS: 40 en suite s £45.95-£46.95; d £45.95-£46.95

Travelodge

Travelodge

Cavalry Barracks, Barracks Rd BB11 4AS
☎ 08700 850 950 01282 416039

Dir: *junct A671/A679*

Travelodge offers good quality, good value, modern accommodation. Ideal for families, the spacious, en suite bedrooms include remote-control TV, tea and coffee-making facilities and luxury beds. Meals can be taken at the nearby family restaurant. For further details consult the Hotel Groups page.

ROOMS: 32 en suite s fr £25; d fr £25

BURNSALL, North Yorkshire
Map 19 SE06

★★72% *Red Lion Hotel*

By the Bridge BD23 6BU
☎ 01756 720204 01756 720292
e-mail: redlion@daelnet.co.uk
web: www.redlion.co.uk

Dir: *on B6160 between Grassington and Bolton Abbey*

This delightful 16th-century Dales inn stands adjacent to a five-arch bridge over the scenic River Wharfe. Stylish, comfortable bedrooms are all individually decorated and well equipped. Public areas include a tasteful lounge and a traditional oak-panelled bar.

continued

The elegant restaurant makes good use of fresh local ingredients, and breakfasts are memorable. Guests are free to fish in the hotel's own stretch of water.
ROOMS: 7 en suite 4 annexe en suite (2 fmly) (2 GF)
FACILITIES: Fishing **CONF:** Thtr 30 Class 10 Board 20 **PARKING:** 80
NOTES: ⊗ in restaurant Civ Wed 50
CARDS:

BURRINGTON (NEAR PORTSMOUTH ARMS STATION), Devon Map 03 SS61

Top 200 – Hotel

★★★ ◎◎ **Northcote Manor**
EX37 9LZ
☎ 01769 560501 📠 01769 560770
e-mail: rest@northcotemanor.co.uk
web: www.northcotemanor.co.uk
Dir: *off A377 opp Portsmouth Arms, into hotel drive. Do not enter Burrington village*
A warm and friendly welcome is assured at this beautiful country house hotel. Built in 1716, the house sits in 20 acres of grounds and woodlands. Guests can enjoy wonderful views over the Taw River Valley whilst relaxing in the environment created by the attentive staff. An elegant restaurant is a highlight of any stay with the finest of local produce used in well-prepared dishes. Bedrooms, including some suites, are individually styled, spacious and well appointed.
ROOMS: 11 en suite s £99-£165; d £140-£240 (incl. bkfst) **LB**
FACILITIES: STV Xmas **CONF:** Thtr 20 Class 20 Board 20 Del from £155 **PARKING:** 30 **NOTES:** ⊗ in restaurant Civ Wed 80
CARDS:

BURTON MOTORWAY SERVICE AREA (M6), Cumbria Map 18 SD57

Travelodge
Burton in Kendal LA6 1JF
☎ 08700 850 950 📠 01524 784014
Dir: *between M6 junct 35/36 southbound*
Travelodge offers good quality, good value, modern accommodation. Ideal for families, the spacious, en suite bedrooms include remote-control TV, tea and coffee-making facilities and luxury beds. Meals can be taken at the nearby family restaurant. For further details consult the Hotel Groups page.
ROOMS: 47 en suite s fr £25; d fr £25

Popped the question?
Hotels with Civ Wed in their entry are licensed for civil wedding ceremonies. Maximum numbers for the ceremony only are shown, e.g. Civ Wed 120

B

BURTON UPON TRENT, Staffordshire Map 10 SK22

★★72% Riverside

Riverside Dr, Branston DE14 3EP
☎ 01283 511234 01283 511441
e-mail: riverside.branston@oldenglishinns.co.uk
Dir: *follow signs for Branston on A5121 until small humped bridge, over bridge and right turn into Warren Lane. Second left into Riverside Drive*
With its quiet residential location and well-kept terraced garden stretching down to the River Trent, this hotel has all the ingredients for a relaxing stay. Many of the tables in the Garden Room restaurant have views over the garden. Bedrooms are tastefully furnished and decorated and provide a good range of extras.
ROOMS: 22 en suite (10 GF) in all bedrooms s £60-£80; d £80-£90 (incl. bkfst) **LB** **FACILITIES:** STV Fishing ch fac Xmas **CONF:** Thtr 120 Class 60 Board 30 Del from £120 **PARKING:** 200 **NOTES:** in restaurant Civ Wed 120 **CARDS:**

BURTONWOOD MOTORWAY SERVICE AREA (M62), Cheshire Map 15 SJ59

Welome Lodge

Burtonwood Services (M62), Great Sankey WA5 3AX
☎ 01925 710376 01925 710378
e-mail: burtonwood.hotel@welcomebreak.co.uk
web: www.welcomebreak.co.uk
Dir: *between M62 junct 7-9*
This modern building offers accommodation in smart, spacious and well-equipped bedrooms, suitable for families and business travellers, and all with en suite bathrooms. Refreshments may be taken at the nearby family restaurant. For further details consult the Hotel Groups page.
ROOMS: 39 en suite s £35-£45; d £35-£45 **CONF:** Board 8 Del from £30

BURWARDSLEY, Cheshire Map 15 SJ55

★★72% Pheasant Inn

Higher Burwardsley CH3 9PF
☎ 01829 770434 01829 771097
e-mail: reception@thepheasant-burwardsley.com
web: www.thepheasant-burwardsley.com
Dir: *from A41, left to Tattenhall, right at 1st junct and left at 2nd to Higher Burwardsley. At post office left, hotel signed*
This delightful 300-year-old inn sits high on the Peckforton Hills and enjoys spectacular views over the Cheshire plain. Well-equipped, comfortable bedrooms are housed in an adjacent converted barn. Creative dishes are served either in the stylish restaurant or in the traditional, beamed bar. Fires are lit in the winter months.
ROOMS: 2 en suite 8 annexe en suite (2 fmly) (3 GF) in all bedrooms s £65; d £80-£90 **LB** **FACILITIES:** STV Xmas **CONF:** Thtr 16 **PARKING:** 40 **NOTES:** in restaurant
CARDS:

BURY, Greater Manchester Map 15 SD81

★★★66% *Bolholt Country Park*

Walshaw Rd BL8 1PU
☎ 0161 762 4000 0161 762 4100
e-mail: enquiries@bolholt.co.uk
Dir: *M60 junct 17 for Whitefield, A56 to Bury for 4m. Follow signs for A58 to Bolton. Take 3rd lane at car showroom signed Tottington. Left at pub, left again*
This former mill owner's house is located in attractive parkland and secluded gardens just a short walk from the town centre. The bedrooms are comfortable and modern and the newly extended leisure club includes a fashionable café-bar. Wide ranging conference and banqueting facilities are available and the setting is ideal for weddings.
ROOMS: 65 en suite (13 fmly) in 14 bedrooms **FACILITIES:** STV supervised Fishing Squash Sauna Solarium Gym Jacuzzi Fitness & leisure centre **CONF:** Thtr 300 Class 120 Board 40 **PARKING:** 300 **NOTES:** in restaurant Civ Wed 140
CARDS:

BURY ST EDMUNDS, Suffolk Map 13 TL86

★★★77% *Angel*

Angel Hill IP33 1LT
☎ 01284 714000 01284 714001
e-mail: sales@theangel.co.uk
Dir: *from A134, left at rdbt into Northgate St. Continue to t-junct with traffic lights, right into Mustow St, left into Angel Hill, hotel on right*
Impressive building situated just a short walk from the town centre. One of the Angel's more notable guests over the last 400 years was Charles Dickens who is reputed to have written part of the *Pickwick Papers* whilst in residence. The hotel offers a range of individually designed bedrooms that include a selection of four-poster rooms and a suite.
ROOMS: 64 en suite (4 fmly) in 6 bedrooms **FACILITIES:** STV **CONF:** Thtr 80 Class 20 Board 30 **SERVICES:** Lift **PARKING:** 54 **NOTES:** in restaurant Civ Wed 100
CARDS:

★★★75% Ravenwood Hall

Rougham IP30 9JA
☎ 01359 270345 01359 270788
e-mail: enquiries@ravenwoodhall.co.uk
Dir: *3m E off A14*
Delightful 15th-century property set in seven acres of woodland and landscaped gardens. The building has many original features including carved timbers and inglenook fireplaces. The spacious bedrooms are attractively decorated, tastefully furnished with well-chosen pieces and equipped with many thoughtful touches. Public rooms include an elegant restaurant and a smart lounge bar with an open fire.
ROOMS: 7 en suite 7 annexe en suite (5 GF) in all bedrooms s £81-£109; d £106-£149 (incl. bkfst) **LB** **FACILITIES:** supervised Riding Shooting & fishing ch fac Xmas **CONF:** Thtr 200 Class 80 Board 40 Del £132.40 **PARKING:** 150 **NOTES:** in restaurant Civ Wed 92 **CARDS:**

★★★74% The Priory

Tollgate IP32 6EH
☎ 01284 766181 01284 767604
e-mail: reservations@prioryhotel.co.uk
Dir: *from A14 take Bury St. Edmunds W sliproad. Follow signs to Brandon. At mini rdbt turn right. Hotel 0.5 m on left*
Delightful 18th-century Grade II listed building set in its own landscaped grounds on the outskirts of the town. Bedrooms are split between the main house and garden wings, which have their own patios. All rooms are attractively decorated, tastefully furnished and equipped with modern facilities. Public rooms feature a smart restaurant, two further conservatory-style dining areas and a lounge bar.
ROOMS: 9 en suite 30 annexe en suite (1 fmly) (30 GF) in 15 bedrooms s £75-£84; d £99-£125 (incl. bkfst) **LB** **FACILITIES:** Xmas **CONF:** Thtr 40 Class 20 Board 20 Del from £120 **PARKING:** 60 **NOTES:** in restaurant **CARDS:**

BUTTERMERE, Cumbria — Map 18 NY11

★★★70% **Bridge**
CA13 9UZ
☎ 017687 70252 ⎙ 017687 70215
e-mail: enquiries@bridge-hotel.com
web: www.bridge-hotel.com
Dir: *A66 around town centre, off at Braithwaite. Over Newlands Pass. Follow Buttermere signs. Hotel in village*

Enjoying a tranquil setting in a dramatic valley close to Buttermere, this long-established hotel has undergone impressive refurbishment. The bedrooms are tastefully appointed and have stylish bathrooms and the comfortable public areas include a delightful lounge, attractive dining room and lively bar, popular with walkers.

ROOMS: 21 en suite ⊗ in 15 bedrooms s £55-£79; d £110-£158 (incl. bkfst & dinner) **LB** **FACILITIES:** no TV in bdrms ch fac Xmas **CONF:** Board 10 Del from £75 **PARKING:** 40 **NOTES:** ⊗ in restaurant **CARDS:**

BUXTON, Derbyshire — Map 16 SK07

★★★★66% **Palace Hotel**
PARAMOUNT GROUP OF HOTELS
Palace Rd SK17 6AG
☎ 01298 22001 ⎙ 01298 72131
e-mail: palace@paramount-hotels.co.uk
Dir: *M6 junct 20, follow M56/M60 signs to Stockport then A6 to Buxton, hotel adjacent to railway station*

This impressive Victorian hotel is located on the hill overlooking the town. Public areas are traditional and elegant in style, including chandeliers and decorative ceilings. The bedrooms are spacious and equipped with modern facilities, and The Dovedale restaurant provides modern British cuisine.

ROOMS: 122 en suite (20 fmly) ⊗ in 80 bedrooms s fr £115; d £130-£140 (incl. bkfst) **LB** **FACILITIES:** STV supervised Sauna Solarium Gym Beauty and hairdressing facilities Xmas **CONF:** Thtr 300 Class 125 Board 80 Del from £144 **SERVICES:** Lift **PARKING:** 200 **NOTES:** ⊗ in restaurant Civ Wed **CARDS:**

★★★77% **Best Western Lee Wood**
Best Western
The Park SK17 6TQ
☎ 01298 23002 ⎙ 01298 23228
e-mail: leewoodhotel@btinternet.com
web: www.leewoodhotel.co.uk
Dir: *NE on A5004, 300mtrs beyond Devonshire Royal Hospital*

This elegant Georgian hotel offers high standards of comfort and hospitality. Individually furnished bedrooms are generally spacious, with all of the expected modern conveniences. There is a choice of two comfortable lounges and a conservatory restaurant. Quality cooking is a feature, as is good service and fine hospitality.

ROOMS: 35 en suite 5 annexe en suite (4 fmly) ⊗ in 25 bedrooms s £65-£90; d £95-£140 **LB** **FACILITIES:** STV Xmas **CONF:** Thtr 120 Class 65 Board 40 Del from £105 **SERVICES:** Lift **PARKING:** 50 **NOTES:** ⊗ in restaurant Civ Wed 120 **CARDS:**

★★★68% **Buckingham Hotel**
THE INDEPENDENTS
1 Burlington Rd SK17 9AS
☎ 01298 70481 ⎙ 01298 72186
e-mail: frontdesk@buckinghamhotel.co.uk
web: www.buckinghamhotel.co.uk
Dir: *follow signs for Pavilion Gardens Car Park. Hotel opp car park*

The Buckingham is close to the Pavilion Gardens and offers pleasant, modern public areas. These include Ramsay's Bar, serving bar meals and real ales, and the popular carvery, serving grills and other dishes. Bedrooms, many now refurbished, are spacious and comfortable; many overlook the Gardens. Walls throughout are adorned with photographs of film stars.

ROOMS: 37 en suite (13 fmly) ⊗ in 27 bedrooms s £50-£75; d £60-£99 (incl. bkfst) **LB** **FACILITIES:** STV **CONF:** Thtr 75 Class 20 Board 16 Del from £75 **SERVICES:** Lift **PARKING:** 35 **NOTES:** ⊗ in restaurant Closed Christmas Civ Wed 85 **CARDS:**

★★61% **Portland Hotel & Park Restaurant**
32 St John's Rd SK17 6XQ
☎ 01298 22462 ⎙ 01298 27464
e-mail: robert@portland-hotel.freeserve.co.uk
Dir: *on A53 opposite the Pavilion & Gardens*

This privately owned and personally run hotel is situated near the famous opera house and the Pavilion Gardens. Facilities include a comfortable lounge and an open plan bar & restaurant area with an adjacent conservatory. An extensive refurbishment is planned.

ROOMS: 22 en suite (3 fmly) ⊗ in 3 bedrooms **CONF:** Thtr 50 Class 30 Board 25 **PARKING:** 18 **NOTES:** ⊗ in restaurant **CARDS:**

CADNAM, Hampshire — Map 05 SU31

★★★69% ❁ **Bartley Lodge**
Lyndhurst Rd SO40 2NR
☎ 023 8081 2248 ⎙ 023 8081 2075
e-mail: bartley@newforesthotels.co.uk
web: www.newforesthotels.co.uk
Dir: *M27 junct 1 at 1st rdbt 1st exit, at 2nd rdbt 3rd exit onto A337.*

This 18th-century former hunting lodge is very quietly situated, yet is just minutes from the M27. Bedrooms vary in size and all are well equipped. There is a selection of small lounge areas, a cosy bar and an indoor pool, together with a small fitness suite. The Crystal dining room offers a tempting choice of well prepared dishes.

ROOMS: 31 en suite (12 fmly) (2 GF) s fr £60; d £120-£155 (incl. bkfst) **LB** **FACILITIES:** Sauna Gym Xmas **CONF:** Thtr 120 Class 60 Board 60 Del from £90 **PARKING:** 60 **NOTES:** ⊗ in restaurant Civ Wed 80 **CARDS:**

See advert on page 149

CALNE, Wiltshire — Map 04 ST97

★★★67% **Lansdowne Strand**
Best Western
The Strand SN11 0EH
☎ 01249 812488 ⎙ 01249 815323
e-mail: reservations@lansdownestrand.co.uk
web: www.lansdownestrand.co.uk
Dir: *off A4 in the centre of Calne*

In the town centre, this 16th-century, former coaching inn still retains many period features. Individually decorated bedrooms vary in size. There are two friendly bars; one offers a wide

continued on p148

CALNE, continued

selection of ales and a cosy fireplace. An interesting menu is available in the brasserie-style restaurant.
ROOMS: 21 en suite 5 annexe en suite (3 fmly) ⊗ in 9 bedrooms s £65-£85; d £75-£98 (incl. bkfst) **LB** **FACILITIES:** STV Complimentary use of nearby leisure centre ch fac Xmas **CONF:** Thtr 90 Class 28 Board 30 Del from £85 **PARKING:** 21 **CARDS:**

C

CAMBERLEY, Surrey — Map 06 SU86

★★★74% *Frimley Hall*

Lime Av GU15 2BG
☎ 0870 400 8224 📠 01276 691253
e-mail: general.frimleyhall@macdonald-hotels.co.uk
Dir: *M3 junct 3 follow Bagshot signs on A321. Over lights, left onto A30 signed Camberley, B'stoke. To rdbt, 2nd exit onto A325, 5th right*
Classic English elegance in the heart of rural Surrey, this ivy-clad Victorian manor house is set in two acres of immaculate grounds. With continued investment in the hotel, both bedrooms and public areas are looking particularly smart and feature a modern, yet timeless, decorative theme.
ROOMS: 86 en suite (2 fmly) ⊗ in 33 bedrooms **FACILITIES:** Putt green ♫ **CONF:** Thtr 60 Class 25 Board 25 **PARKING:** 100 **NOTES:** Civ Wed 100 **CARDS:**

★★★66% *Lakeside International*

Wharf Rd, Frimley Green GU16 6JR
☎ 01252 838000 📠 01252 837857
Dir: *off A321, at mini rdbt into Wharf Rd, lakeside complex on right*
This hotel, geared towards the business market, enjoys a lakeside location with noteworthy views. Bedrooms are modern, comfortable and with a range of facilities. Public areas are spacious and include a residents' lounge, bar and games room, a smart restaurant and an established health and leisure club. Bedrooms are modern, comfortable with a range of facilities.
ROOMS: 98 en suite (1 fmly) ⊗ in 18 bedrooms **FACILITIES:** STV Squash Snooker Sauna Solarium Gym Jacuzzi **CONF:** Thtr 120 Class 100 Board 40 **SERVICES:** Lift **PARKING:** 250 **NOTES:** ⊗ in restaurant Civ Wed 100 **CARDS:**

⌂ Travel Inn

221 Yorktown Rd, College Town LU6 3QP
☎ 08701 977047 📠 01582 842811
Dir: *M3 junct 4 A331 to Camberley. At large rdbt, exit to A321 towards Bracknell. At 3rd lights, Inn on left*
Travel Inn offers good-quality, value-for-money accommodation. Spacious, en suite rooms with bath and shower comfortably accommodate a family of up to two adults and two children (to age 15). The restaurant and bar offers a varied menu. For further details consult the Hotel Groups page.
ROOMS: 40 en suite s £45.95-£48.95; d £45.95-£48.95

CAMBORNE, Cornwall & Isles of Scilly — Map 02 SW64

★★★66% Tyacks

27 Commercial St TR14 8LD
☎ 01209 612424 📠 01209 612435
e-mail: tyacks@westcountryhotelrooms.co.uk
Dir: *W on A30 past A3047 junct & turn off at Camborne West junct. Left & left again at rdbt, follow town centre signs. Hotel on left*
This 18th-century former coaching inn has spacious, well-furnished public areas which include a smart lounge and bar, a popular bar and a restaurant serving fixed-price and carte menus. The comfortable bedrooms are attractively decorated and well equipped; two have separate sitting areas.
ROOMS: 15 en suite (2 fmly) ⊗ in 4 bedrooms s fr £49.50; d fr £75 (incl. bkfst) **LB** **FACILITIES:** STV 6x6 sports entertainment screen ♫ ch fac Xmas **CONF:** Class 35 **PARKING:** 27 **NOTES:** ⊗ in restaurant **CARDS:**

CAMBOURNE, Cambridgeshire — Map 12 TL35

★★★★74% The Cambridge Belfry

Back St CB3 6BW
☎ 01954 714995
e-mail: cambridge@marstonhotels.com
Dir: *M11 junct 13 take A428 to Bedford, follow signs to Cambourne. Leave at Cambourne keeping left. Left at rdbt, Hotel on the left.*

The latest addition to the Marston Hotels portfolio, this exciting new hotel is located at the gateway to Cambourne Village and Business Park. Contemporary in style throughout, the hotel boasts two eating options, state-of-the-art leisure facilities and extensive conference and banqueting rooms. Original artwork takes guests on a 'guided tour' of Cambridge, along the River Cam.
ROOMS: 120 en suite ⊗ in 105 bedrooms s £124-£224; d £158-£258 (incl. bkfst) **LB** **FACILITIES: Spa** STV supervised Sauna Solarium Gym Xmas **CONF:** Thtr 258 Class 104 Board 72 Del from £179 **SERVICES:** Lift **PARKING:** 260 **NOTES:** ⊗ in restaurant Civ Wed 260 **CARDS:**

CAMBRIDGE, Cambridgeshire — Map 12 TL45

★★★★76% Hotel Felix

Whitehouse Ln CB3 0LX
☎ 01223 277977 📠 01223 277973
e-mail: help@hotelfelix.co.uk web: www.hotelfelix.co.uk
Dir: *on A1307 turn R at The Travellers Rest into Whitehouse Lane.*

A beautiful Victorian mansion set amidst three acres of landscaped gardens, this property was originally built in 1852 for a surgeon from the famous Addenbrookes Hospital. The contemporary-style

continued

bedrooms have carefully chosen furniture and many thoughtful touches, whilst public rooms feature a large open-plan bar, the adjacent Graffiti restaurant and a small quiet lounge.
ROOMS: 52 en suite (5 fmly) (26 GF) ⊗ in 22 bedrooms s £128-£178; d £158-£265 (incl. cont bkfst) **LB** **FACILITIES:** STV Xmas **CONF:** Thtr 60 Class 36 Board 34 Del £180 **SERVICES:** Lift **PARKING:** 90 **NOTES:** ⊗ in restaurant Civ Wed 60 **CARDS:**

★★★★67% De Vere University Arms

DE VERE HOTELS

Regent St CB2 1AD
☎ 01223 351241 🖷 01223 273037
e-mail: dua.sales@devere-hotels.com
Dir: *M11 junct 11, follow city centre signs for 3m. Right at 2nd mini rdbt, left at lights into Regent St. Hotel 600yds on right*
Built as a post house in 1834, the University Arms has an enviable position in the very heart of the city, overlooking Parker's Piece. Public rooms include an elegant domed lounge, a smart restaurant with its own cocktail bar, separate bar/lounge area and extensive conference and banqueting rooms. Given the hotel's central location parking is a bonus.
ROOMS: 120 en suite (2 fmly) ⊗ in 83 bedrooms **FACILITIES:** STV Reduced rate at local fitness centre Play Stations and pay movies in all rooms **CONF:** Thtr 300 Class 150 Board 80 Del £195 **SERVICES:** Lift **PARKING:** 88 **NOTES:** ⊗ in restaurant Civ Wed 120
CARDS:

★★★74% Cambridge Quy Mill Hotel

Newmarket Rd CB5 9AG
☎ 01223 293383 🖷 01223 293770
e-mail: cambridgequy@bestwestern.co.uk
Dir: *off A14 at junct E of Cambridge onto B1102 for 50yds.*

This 19th-century former watermill is convenient for Cambridge. Bedroom styles differ, yet each room is smartly appointed and brightly decorated. Well-designed public areas include several spacious bar/lounges, with a choice of casual and formal eating areas; service is both friendly and helpful. A new leisure club with state-of-the-art equipment is impressive.
ROOMS: 23 en suite 18 annexe en suite (2 fmly) (18 GF) ⊗ in 18 bedrooms s £95-£140; d £98-£190 **LB** **FACILITIES:** STV supervised Sauna Gym Jacuzzi Clay pigeon shooting by prior booking subject to availability **CONF:** Thtr 80 Class 30 Board 24 Del from £135
PARKING: 90 **NOTES:** Closed 24-30 Dec RS 31 Dec Civ Wed 80
CARDS:

★★★71% Gonville

Best Western

Gonville Place CB1 1LY
☎ 01223 366611 & 221111 🖷 01223 315470
e-mail: all@gonvillehotel.co.uk
web: www.gonvillehotel.co.uk
Dir: *M11 junct 11, on A1309 follow city centre signs. At 2nd mini rdbt right into Lensfield Rd, over junct with traffic lights. Hotel 25yds on right*
This hotel is situated on the inner ring road, a short walk across

continued

the green from the city centre. Well established, with regular guests and very experienced staff, the Gonville is popular for its relaxing, informal atmosphere. The air-conditioned public areas are cheerfully furnished, now enhanced by the creation of a new lounge bar and brasserie; bedrooms are well-appointed and appealing.
ROOMS: 78 en suite (1 fmly) (5 GF) ⊗ in 38 bedrooms s £89-£120; d £99-£150 (incl. bkfst) **LB** **FACILITIES:** Arrangement with gym/swimming pool **CONF:** BC Thtr 200 Class 100 Board 50 Del from £129 **SERVICES:** Lift **PARKING:** 80 **NOTES:** ⊗ in restaurant
CARDS:

★★★68% Royal Cambridge

Forestdale Hotels

Trumpington St CB2 1PY
☎ 01223 351631 🖷 01223 352972
e-mail: royal.cambridge@forestdale.com
Dir: *M11 junct 11, signed city centre. 1st mini rdbt left into Fen Causeway. Hotel 1st right*
This impressive Georgian hotel enjoys a central location. Bedrooms are well equipped and comfortable and include new superior bedrooms/apartments. Public areas are traditionally decorated to a good standard: the elegant restaurant is a popular choice and the lounge/bar serves evening snacks. Parking and conferencing are added benefits.
ROOMS: 57 en suite (9 fmly) ⊗ in 28 bedrooms s fr £120; d fr £155 (incl. bkfst) **LB** **FACILITIES:** STV Xmas **CONF:** Thtr 120 Class 40 Board 40 Del from £140 **SERVICES:** Lift **PARKING:** 80 **NOTES:** ⊗ in restaurant Civ Wed 100 **CARDS:**

CAMBRIDGE, continued

★★★67% Sorrento

190-196 Cherry Hinton Rd CB1 7AN

☎ 01223 243533 📠 01223 213463

e-mail: info@sorrentohotel.com

web: www.sorrentohotel.com

THE INDEPENDENTS

C

Dir: *M11 junct 11 towards Cambridge on B1309, 2nd set lights right into Long Road. 1st set lights left into Hills Road. 1st set lights right into Cherry Hinton Rd*

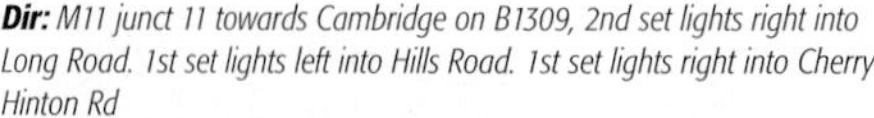

Friendly, family run hotel situated close to the city centre. Although the bedrooms vary in size and style, they are all are pleasantly decorated and equipped with many thoughtful extras. Public rooms have an Italian feel with superb marble flooring throughout; they include a smart lounge bar, attractive restaurant and a huge conservatory.

ROOMS: 30 en suite (4 fmly) (8 GF) ⊗ in 20 bedrooms s £69.50-£95; d £99-£139.50 (incl. bkfst) **LB** **FACILITIES:** STV Xmas **CONF:** Thtr 60 Class 35 Board 35 **PARKING:** 40 **NOTES:** ⊗ in restaurant

CARDS:

★★74% *Arundel House*

Chesterton Rd CB4 3AN

☎ 01223 367701 📠 01223 367721

e-mail: info@arundelhousehotels.co.uk

web: www.arundelhousehotels.co.uk

Dir: *city centre on A1303*

Overlooking the River Cam and enjoying views over open parkland, this popular hotel was originally a row of Victorian townhouses. Bedrooms are attractive and have a special character. The smart public areas feature a conservatory for informal snacks, a spacious bar and an elegant restaurant for serious dining; the restaurant is being redesigned in warm colour schemes to offer a modern dining experience.

ROOMS: 81 en suite 22 annexe en suite (7 fmly) ⊗ in all bedrooms **CONF:** Thtr 50 Class 34 Board 32 **PARKING:** 70 **NOTES:** ⊗ in restaurant Closed 25-26 Dec **CARDS:**

★★70% Centennial

63-71 Hills Rd CB2 1PG

☎ 01223 314652 📠 01223 315443

e-mail: reception@centennialhotel.co.uk

Dir: *M11 junct 11 take A1309 to Cambridge. Right onto Brooklands Ave to end. Left, hotel 100yds on right*

This friendly hotel is convenient for the railway station and town centre. Well-presented public areas include a welcoming lounge, and a relaxing bar and restaurant on the lower-ground level. Bedrooms are generally spacious, well-maintained and

continued

thoughtfully equipped with a good range of facilities; several rooms are available on the ground floor.

ROOMS: 39 en suite (1 fmly) (7 GF) ⊗ in 26 bedrooms s £70-£80; d £88-£96 (incl. bkfst) **LB** **CONF:** Thtr 25 Class 25 Board 25 **PARKING:** 30 **NOTES:** ⊗ in restaurant Closed 23 Dec-1 Jan

CARDS:

See advert on opposite page

⌂ Travelodge (Cambridge South)

Fourwentways CB8 6AP

☎ 08700 850 950 📠 01223 839479

Travelodge

Dir: *adjacent to Little Chef at junct A11/A1307, 5m S of Cambridge*

Travelodge offers good quality, good value, modern accommodation. Ideal for families, the spacious, en suite bedrooms include remote-control TV, tea and coffee-making facilities and luxury beds. Meals can be taken at the nearby family restaurant. For further details consult the Hotel Groups page.

ROOMS: 40 en suite s fr £25; d fr £25

CAMELFORD, Cornwall & Isles of Scilly — Map 02 SX18

★★★66% Bowood Park Hotel & Golf Course

Lanteglos PL32 9RF

☎ 01840 213017 📠 01840 212622

e-mail: golf@bowoodpark.com

web: www.bowoodpark.com

Dir: *A39 W through Camelford, 0.5m, turn right for Tintagel/Boscastle, 1st left after garage*

Situated in wonderfully picturesque countryside, this hotel provides much for golfers and non-golfers alike. Spacious bedrooms are comfortable and some have private patios and wonderful views over the course. Salmon and trout fishing is available on the River Camel and the hotel's treatment room is just the place for a relaxing massage or beauty treatment.

ROOMS: 31 en suite (3 fmly) ⊗ in 12 bedrooms **FACILITIES:** ⛳ 18 Fishing Putt green Massage, Sports therapy **CONF:** BC Thtr 160 Class 100 Board 100 **PARKING:** 100 **NOTES:** ⊗ in restaurant

CARDS:

See advert on opposite page

CANNOCK, Staffordshire — Map 10 SJ91

★★★67% The Whitehouse Hotel & Restaurant

Marquis Dr, Penkridge Bank Rd WS12 4PR

☎ 01543 422712 📠 01543 422639

e-mail: info@thewhitehouse-hotel.co.uk

Dir: *Turn off A34 at rdbt with wooden wigwam, towards Rugeley through Forest. Hotel approx 2m on right*

This privately owned and personally run hotel is quietly situated in the heart of Cannock Chase, only a short drive from Stafford and

continued

the motorway network. Bedrooms are modern and well-equipped. There is an attractive lounge bar and a pleasant restaurant where a good selection of grill dishes is available. The hotel also has a large function suite.
ROOMS: 6 en suite ⊗ in 1 bedroom d £65-£125 (incl. bkfst) **LB** **CONF:** Thtr 180 Class 140 Board 50 **PARKING:** 80 **NOTES:** Closed 26-2 Jan Civ Wed 100 **CARDS:**

★★★63% The Roman Way Hotel

Watling St, Hatherton WS11 1SH
☎ 0870 609 6125 01543 502749
e-mail: romanway@corushotels.com
Dir: *M6 junct 11 towards Cannock on A460. At rdbt take A5 to Telford. Hotel 100yds on left. Or M6 junct 12, then A5 towards Cannock. Hotel 2m on right*

Named after the Roman road on which it stands, this modern hotel provides a good standard of accommodation. Doric columns and marble floors feature in the reception area, and Nero's

continued on p152

CANNOCK, continued

Restaurant and Gilpin's Lounge provide options for formal or informal eating.
ROOMS: 56 en suite (17 fmly) (23 GF) ⊗ in 23 bedrooms s £85; d £85 (incl. bkfst) **LB** **FACILITIES:** STV Xmas **CONF:** BC Thtr 150 Class 100 Board 50 Del £110 **PARKING:** 150 **NOTES:** ⊗ in restaurant Civ Wed 150 **CARDS:**

Travel Inn
Watling St WS11 1SJ
☎ 08701 977048 01543 466130
Dir: *on at junct of A5/A460, 2m from M6 junct 11/12*
Travel Inn offers good-quality, value-for-money accommodation. Spacious, en suite rooms with bath and shower comfortably accommodate a family of up to two adults and two children (to age 15). The restaurant and bar offers a varied menu. For further details consult the Hotel Groups page.
ROOMS: 60 en suite s £45.95-£46.95; d £45.95-£46.95 **CONF:** Thtr 80 Board 40

CANTERBURY, Kent — Map 07 TR15

★★★★66% The County
High St CT1 2RX
☎ 01227 766266 01227 451512
e-mail: county@macdonald-hotels.co.uk
Dir: *M2, junct 7. Follow Canterbury signs onto ringroad. At Wincheap rdbt turn into city. Left into Rosemary Ln, into Stour St. Hotel at end*

This historic hotel has cellars dating back to the 12th century. It offers warm hospitality and comfortable accommodation in the heart of the city. Bedrooms are individually decorated and tastefully furnished, while public areas include tea rooms offering traditional cream teas and Sully's Restaurant, where the emphasis is on fine dining.
ROOMS: 74 en suite (9 fmly) ⊗ in 33 bedrooms s £80-£120; d £85-£130 (incl. bkfst) **LB** **FACILITIES:** STV Xmas **CONF:** BC Thtr 120 Class 80 Board 60 Del from £90 **SERVICES:** Lift **PARKING:** 62 **NOTES:** ⊗ in restaurant Civ Wed 100
CARDS:

★★★67% The Falstaff Hotel
8-10 St Dunstan's St CT2 8AF
☎ 0870 609 6102 01227 463525
e-mail: thefalstaff@corushotels.com
Dir: *In city take 2nd rdbt into St Peters Place, hotel is opposite Westgate, turn right then immediately left for car park*
Located next to the Westgate Tower, the hotel offers easy access to the city centre and motorway network. Many original 16th-century features are still present in this historic coaching inn, especially in the cosy lounge and bar. Bedrooms are split between the newer annexe and the rooms in the main building which have individual character.

ROOMS: 25 en suite 22 annexe en suite (1 fmly) (14 GF) ⊗ in 27 bedrooms s £92; d £92 **LB** **FACILITIES:** STV Xmas **PARKING:** 34 **NOTES:** ⊗ in restaurant **CARDS:**

★★75% Ebury
65/67 New Dover Rd CT1 3DX
☎ 01227 768433 01227 459187
e-mail: info@ebury-hotel.co.uk
web: www.ebury-hotel.co.uk
Dir: *A2 at Canterbury take ring road. Follow Dover signs, after 5th rdbt hotel 1m on left*
This Victorian property is set in two acres of attractive gardens and is only a short walk from the city centre. The elegant and spacious public rooms include a restaurant and lounge where the proprietor's collection of rare and unusual clocks tick away peacefully. Bedrooms are maintained to a high standard and contain a good range of useful facilities.
ROOMS: 15 en suite (2 fmly) s £60-£65; d £80-£95 (incl. bkfst) **LB** **FACILITIES:** Jacuzzi **PARKING:** 30 **NOTES:** ⊗ in restaurant Closed 21 Dec-13 Jan **CARDS:**

★★70% Bow Window Inn
50 High St, Littlebourne CT3 1ST
☎ 01227 721264 01227 721250
e-mail: sam@theimperial.fsnet.co.uk
Dir: *from Canterbury take A257 to Sandwich. From E of Canterbury to Littebourne, hotel at bottom of hill on left*
A country cottage offering friendly hospitality and comfortable accommodation, now under new ownership. Bedrooms are furnished to suit the style of the house and are all well equipped. Public areas are cosy with exposed beams providing character, especially in the restaurant, which offers an interesting menu.
ROOMS: 11 annexe en suite (1 fmly) (1 GF) s £40-£48; d £60-£68 (incl. bkfst) **LB** **PARKING:** 10 **NOTES:** ⊗ in restaurant
CARDS:

> Early start?
> Hotels at all star levels should provide in-room alarm clocks and/or alarm calls

★★64% *Victoria*
59 London Rd CT2 8JY
☎ 01227 459333 01227 781552
e-mail: manager@vichotel.fsnet.co.uk
Dir: *M2/A2 onto A2052, hotel on left off 1st rdbt*
Just 15 minutes' walk from the city, the hotel is away from the hustle and bustle of the centre, yet within sight of the cathedral. Bedrooms vary in size and shape, and all are attractively

continued

decorated with an excellent range of facilities. Public areas include a busy bar and carvery restaurant.

ROOMS: 34 en suite (12 fmly) ⊗ in 4 bedrooms **CONF:** Thtr 20 Class 20 Board 20 **PARKING:** 70 **NOTES:** ✈ **CARDS:**

Abbots Barton

New Dover Rd CT1 3DU
☎ 01227 760341 📠 01227 785442
e-mail: sales@abbotsbartonhotel.com
Dir: *Turn off A2 onto A2050 at bridge, S of Canterbury. Hotel is 0.75m past Old Gate Inn on left*

At the time of going to press, the star classification for this hotel was not confirmed. Please refer to the AA internet site www.theAA.com for current information.

ROOMS: 50 en suite (2 fmly) (6 GF) ⊗ in 27 bedrooms s £65-£110; d £80-£125 **LB** **FACILITIES:** STV Xmas **CONF:** Thtr 150 Class 80 Board 60 Del from £110 **SERVICES:** Lift **PARKING:** 80 **NOTES:** ⊗ in restaurant Civ Wed 100 **CARDS:**

Innkeeper's Lodge

162 New Dover Rd CT1 3EL
☎ 01227 829951 📠 01227 829952
www.innkeeperslodge.com
Dir: *M2 junct 7, A2 left at junct for Rough Common onto A2050. At 2nd rdbt follow signs for Dover (A2), lodge on right*

Smart rooms meet essential business requirements but also have home comforts, and depending on location may well have meeting rooms and pub dining. Dining options generally include all-day menus plus the added advantage of breakfast.

ROOMS: 9 en suite s £52; d £50

Travelodge (Canterbury West)

A2 Gate Services, Dunkirk ME13 9LN
☎ 08700 850 950 📠 01227 752781
Dir: *5m W on A2 northbound*

Travelodge offers good quality, good value, modern accommodation. Ideal for families, the spacious, en suite bedrooms include remote-control TV, tea and coffee-making facilities and luxury beds. Meals can be taken at the nearby family restaurant. For further details consult the Hotel Groups page.

ROOMS: 40 en suite s fr £25; d fr £25

CARBIS BAY See St Ives

Late for dinner?
Quality Standards mean that last orders for dinner vary according to star rating and should be no earlier than:
★★ 7.00pm ★★★ 8.00pm ★★★★ 9.00pm
★★★★★ 10.00pm

CARCROFT, South Yorkshire — Map 16 SE50

Travelodge Doncaster

Great North Rd DN6 9LF
☎ 08700 850 950 📠 0870 1911631
Dir: *on A1 northbound*

Travelodge offers good quality, good value, modern accommodation. Ideal for families, the spacious, en suite bedrooms include remote-control TV, tea and coffee-making facilities and luxury beds. Meals can be taken at the nearby family restaurant. For further details consult the Hotel Groups page.

ROOMS: 40 en suite s fr £25; d fr £25

CARLISLE, Cumbria — Map 18 NY35

See also Brampton

★★★71% *Crown*

Wetheral CA4 8ES
☎ 01228 561888 📠 01228 561637
e-mail: info@crownhotelwetheral.co.uk
Dir: *M6 junct 42 take B6263 to Wetheral, right at village shop, car park at rear of hotel*

Set in the attractive village of Wetheral and with landscaped gardens to the rear, this hotel is well suited to both business and leisure guests. Rooms vary in size and style and include two apartments in an adjacent house ideal for long stays. A choice of dining options is available, with the popular Waltons Bar an informal alternative to the main restaurant.

ROOMS: 49 en suite 2 annexe en suite (10 fmly) (3 GF) ⊗ in 30 bedrooms **FACILITIES: Spa** STV Squash Sauna Solarium Gym Jacuzzi Children's splash pool Steam room **CONF:** BC Thtr 175 Class 90 Board 50 **PARKING:** 80 **NOTES:** ⊗ in restaurant Civ Wed 120 **CARDS:**

★★★69% Cumbria Park

32 Scotland Rd, Stanwix CA3 9DG
☎ 01228 522887 📠 01228 514796
e-mail: enquiries@cumbriaparkhotel.co.uk
web: www.cumbriaparkhotel.co.uk
Dir: *M6 junct 44, 1.5 miles on main road into Carlisle on left*

Just minutes from the M6, this privately owned hotel, with its own feature garden, is also convenient for the city centre. Well-equipped bedrooms come in a variety of sizes, and several have four-poster or tester beds and whirlpool baths. Conferences and functions are well catered for with a wide choice of meeting rooms and suites.

ROOMS: 47 en suite (3 fmly) (7 GF) ⊗ in 13 bedrooms s £75.50-£90; d £98-£125 (incl. bkfst) **LB** **FACILITIES:** STV Sauna Solarium Gym Jacuzzi Steam room **CONF:** Thtr 120 Class 50 Board 35 Del from £105 **SERVICES:** Lift **PARKING:** 51 **NOTES:** ✈ Closed 25-26 Dec **CARDS:**

★★★66% Lakes Court

Court Square CA1 1QY
☎ 01228 531951 📠 01228 547799
e-mail: reservations@lakescourthotel.co.uk
Dir: *M6 junct 43, to city centre, then follow road to left & railway station*

This Victorian building is located in the heart of the city centre, adjacent to the railway station. The bedrooms, including a four-poster room, are modern in style and mostly spacious. There are extensive conference facilities and a secure car park. A comfortable bar serves light meals and a wide range of drinks.

ROOMS: 70 en suite (3 fmly) ⊗ in 19 bedrooms s £55-£70; d £65-£90 (incl. bkfst) **LB** **FACILITIES:** STV ♫ Xmas **CONF:** BC Thtr 175 Class 60 Board 60 Del from £99 **SERVICES:** Lift **PARKING:** 20 **NOTES:** ⊗ in restaurant Civ Wed 170 **CARDS:**

CARLISLE, continued

★★★61% The Crown & Mitre
4 English St CA3 8HZ
☎ 01228 525491 ▣ 01228 514553
e-mail: info@crownandmitre-hotel-carlisle.com
Dir: *A6 to city centre, pass station & Woolworths on left. Right into Blackfriars St. Rear entrance at end*
Located in the heart of the city, this Edwardian hotel is close to the cathedral and a few minutes' walk from the castle. Hotel bedrooms vary in size and style from smart executive rooms to more functional standard rooms. Public rooms include the lovely bar with its feature stained-glass windows and a comfortable lounge area.
ROOMS: 74 en suite 20 annexe en suite (4 fmly) ⊗ in 10 bedrooms s £85-£95; d £95-£110 (incl. bkfst) **LB** **FACILITIES:** STV Jacuzzi Xmas **CONF:** Thtr 400 Class 250 Board 50 Del from £95 **SERVICES:** Lift **PARKING:** 42 **CARDS:**

⇧ Hotel Ibis Carlisle

Portlands, Botchergate CA1 1RP
☎ 01228 518000 ▣ 01228 518010
e-mail: H3443@accor-hotels.com
Dir: *M6 junct 42/43 follow signs for city centre. Hotel on Botchergate.*
Modern, budget hotel offering comfortable accommodation in bright and practical bedrooms. Breakfast is self-service and dinner is available in the restaurant. For further details, consult the Hotel Groups page.
ROOMS: 102 en suite s £39.95-£42.95; d £39.95-£42.95

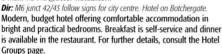

⇧ Premier Lodge (Carlisle)

Kingstown Rd CA3 0AT
☎ 0870 9906502 ▣ 0870 9906503
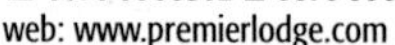
web: www.premierlodge.com
Dir: *1m from M6 junct 44 on the A7 towards Carlisle, on left*
High quality, modern, budget accommodation, ideal for families and business travellers. All rooms feature bath, power shower and satellite TV, and most have telephones / modem points. The adjacent bar and restaurant offers a wide and varied menu.
ROOMS: 49 en suite s £50; d £50 **CONF:** Board 12

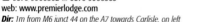

⇧ Travel Inn Carlisle (South)

Carleton CA4 0AD
☎ 08701 977054 ▣ 01228 633313
Dir: *just off J42 on M6 south of Carlisle*
Travel Inn offers good-quality, value-for-money accommodation. Spacious, en suite rooms with bath and shower comfortably accommodate a family of up to two adults and two children (to age 15). The restaurant and bar offers a varied menu. For further details consult the Hotel Groups page.
ROOMS: 40 en suite s £45.95-£46.95; d £45.95-£46.95
CONF: Thtr 50 Class 50

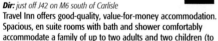

⇧ Travel Inn Carlisle (Central)

Warwick Rd CA1 2WF
☎ 08701 977053 ▣ 01228 534096
Dir: *M6 junct 43, on A69*
Travel Inn offers good-quality, value-for-money accommodation. Spacious, en suite rooms with bath and shower comfortably accommodate a family of up to two adults and two children (to age 15). The restaurant and bar offers a varied menu. For further details consult the Hotel Groups page.
ROOMS: 44 en suite s £45.95-£46.95; d £45.95-£46.95

⇧ Travelodge (Carlisle North)
A74 Southbound, Todhills CA6 4HA
☎ 08700 850 950 ▣ 01228 674335
Travelodge offers good quality, good value, modern accommodation. Ideal for families, the spacious, en suite bedrooms include remote-control TV, tea and coffee-making facilities and luxury beds. Meals can be taken at the nearby family restaurant. For further details consult the Hotel Groups page.
ROOMS: 40 en suite s fr £25; d fr £25

CARNFORTH, Lancashire — Map 18 SD47

★★65% Royal Station
Market St LA5 9BT
☎ 01524 732033 & 733636 ▣ 01524 720267
e-mail: royalstation@mitchellshotels.co.uk
Dir: *M6 junct 35 onto A6 signed Carnforth. After 1m at x-rds in town centre right into Market St. Hotel opposite railway station*
This commercial hotel enjoys a town centre location close to the railway station. Bedrooms are well equipped and comfortably furnished. A good range of tasty good value meals can be taken in either the bright attractive lounge bar or the restaurant.
ROOMS: 13 en suite (1 fmly) s £36-£41.50; d £44-£58 **LB**
FACILITIES: Xmas **CONF:** Thtr 150 Class 100 Board 100 **PARKING:** 4
NOTES: ⊗ in restaurant **CARDS:**

CARTMEL, Cumbria — Map 18 SD37

★★77% Aynsome Manor
LA11 6HH
☎ 015395 36653 ▣ 015395 36016
e-mail: info@aynsomemanorhotel.co.uk
Dir: *M6 junct 36, follow A590 signed Barrow-in-Furness towards Cartmel. Left at end of road, hotel before village*

Dating back to the early 16th century in parts, this manor house overlooks the fells and the nearby Priory. Spacious bedrooms, including some courtyard rooms, are comfortably furnished. Dinner in the elegant restaurant features local produce when possible and there is a choice of lounges to relax in afterwards.
ROOMS: 10 en suite 2 annexe en suite (2 fmly) s £72-£87.50; d £114-£155 (incl. bkfst & dinner) **LB** **PARKING:** 20 **NOTES:** ⊗ in restaurant Closed 2-31 Jan RS Sun **CARDS:**

Town House Hotel
Country House Hotel
⇧ Travel Accommodation

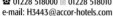

CASTLE ASHBY, Northamptonshire Map 11 SP85

★★74% **Falcon**
NN7 1LF
☎ 01604 696200 01604 696673
e-mail: falcon.castleashby@oldenglishinns.co.uk
Dir: *off A428*
Set in the heart of a peaceful village, this family-run hotel consists of a main house and two neighbouring cottages. Bedrooms are individually decorated and provide a wealth of thoughtful extras. Character public rooms, in the main house, include a first-floor sitting area, a choice of bars and a pretty restaurant serving good quality cuisine.
ROOMS: 5 en suite 11 annexe en suite (1 fmly) in 3 bedrooms
FACILITIES: STV **CONF:** Thtr 50 Class 30 Board 25 **PARKING:** 75
NOTES: Civ Wed 60 **CARDS:**

CASTLE COMBE, Wiltshire Map 04 ST87

Top 200 – Hotel

★★★★ **Manor House**
SN14 7HR
☎ 01249 782206 01249 782159
e-mail: enquiries@manor-housecc.co.uk
web: www.exclusivehotels.co.uk
Dir: *M4 junct 17 follow Chippenham signs onto A420 Bristol, then right onto B4039. Through village, right after crossing bridge*

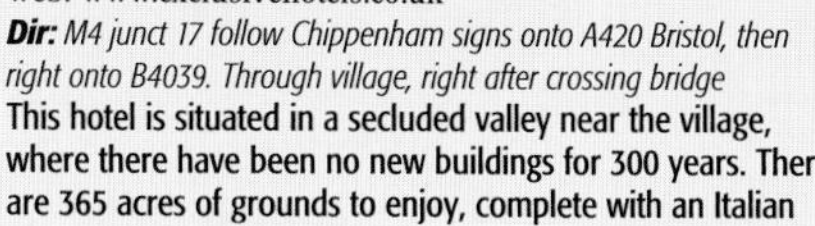

This hotel is situated in a secluded valley near the village, where there have been no new buildings for 300 years. There are 365 acres of grounds to enjoy, complete with an Italian garden and 18-hole golf course. Bedrooms, some in a row of stone cottages, have been superbly furnished, and public rooms include a number of cosy lounges with roaring fires. Service is a pleasing blend of professionalism and friendliness, while food focuses on top quality local produce.

Manor House

ROOMS: 22 en suite 26 annexe en suite (8 fmly) (12 GF) d £180-£600 (incl. bkfst) **LB** **FACILITIES:** STV 18 Fishing Snooker Sauna Gym Putt green Jogging track, croquet lawn ch fac Xmas **CONF:** BC Thtr 70 Class 70 Board 30 Del from £180 **PARKING:** 100 **NOTES:** in restaurant Civ Wed 110
CARDS:

See advert on this page

Early start?
Hotels at all star levels should provide in-room alarm clocks and/or alarm calls

CASTLE COMBE, continued

★★71% Castle Inn
SN14 7HN
☎ 01249 783030 ℻ 01249 782315
e-mail: enquiries@castle-inn.info
Dir: *M4 junct 17, follow signs to racing circuit, through Upper Castle Combe. Turn left into Lower Village. Hotel at bottom of hill on right*
This charming 12th-century hostelry is set in the market place of this historic village. Bedrooms, including many with old beams, are individually decorated and offer a host of thoughtful extras. Guests can choose from a varied and tempting menu focusing on fresh ingredients, served either in the smart restaurant or in the more informal surroundings of the bar.
ROOMS: 11 en suite ⊗ in all bedrooms s £75.50-£89; d £100-£125 (incl. bkfst) **LB** **FACILITIES:** Xmas **CONF:** Thtr 20 Class 20 Board 20 Del £130 **NOTES:** ⊗ in restaurant **CARDS:**

CASTLE DONINGTON
See Nottingham East Midlands Airport

CASTLEFORD, West Yorkshire — Map 16 SE42

Premier Lodge (Castleford)
Pioneer Way WF10 5TG
☎ 0870 9906592 ℻ 0870 9906593
web: www.premierlodge.com
Dir: *M62 junct 31 onto A655 to Castleford. At traffic lights right onto Commerce park. Lodge 2nd on left*
High quality, modern, budget accommodation, ideal for families and business travellers. All rooms feature bath, power shower and satellite TV, and most have telephones / modem points. The adjacent bar and restaurant offers a wide and varied menu.
ROOMS: 62 en suite s £50; d £50 **CONF:** Thtr 20 Class 8 Board 10

CASTLETON, Derbyshire — Map 16 SK18

Innkeeper's Lodge Castleton
Castle St S33 8WG
☎ 01433 620578 ℻ 01433 622902
www.innkeeperslodge.com
Dir: *on A6187, in the centre of the village*
Smart rooms meet essential business requirements but also have home comforts, and depending on location may well have meeting rooms and pub dining. Dining options generally include all-day menus plus the added advantage of breakfast.
ROOMS: 6 en suite 6 annexe en suite s £59.95-£69.95; d £59.95-£69.95

Packed in a hurry?
Ironing facilities should be available at all star levels, either in rooms or on request

CHADDESLEY CORBETT, Worcestershire — Map 10 SO87

Top 200 – Hotel

★★★ Brockencote Hall Country House
DY10 4PY
☎ 01562 777876 ℻ 01562 777872
e-mail: info@brockencotehall.com
web: www.brockencotehall.com
Dir: *0.5m W, off A448, opposite St Cassians Church*
Glorious countryside extends all around this magnificent mansion, and grazing sheep can be seen from the conservatory. Not surprisingly, relaxation comes high on the list of priorities here. Despite its very English location the hotel's owner actually hails from Alsace and the atmosphere is very much that of a provincial French château. The chef too is French (from Brittany) and the chandeliered dining room is a popular venue for the accomplished modern French cuisine.
ROOMS: 17 en suite (2 fmly) (5 GF) s £85-£96; d £116-£180 (incl. bkfst) **LB** **FACILITIES:** STV Reflexology /aromatherapy Xmas **CONF:** Thtr 30 Class 20 Board 20 Del from £155 **SERVICES:** Lift **PARKING:** 45 **NOTES:** ⊗ in restaurant
CARDS:

CHAGFORD, Devon Map 03 SX78

Top 200 – Hotel

★★★ ®®®® **Gidleigh Park**
TQ13 8HH
☎ 01647 432367 📠 01647 432574
e-mail: gidleighpark@gidleigh.co.uk
web: www.gidleigh.com
RELAIS & CHATEAUX
Dir: *from Chagford, right at Lloyds Bank into Mill St. After 150yds fork right, follow lane 2m to end*

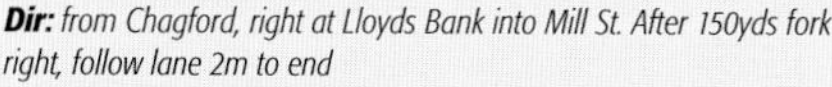

This delightful, globally acclaimed establishment, set in 45 acres of lovingly tended grounds and gardens, boasts its own putting course, along with bowling, croquet and tennis courts. Individually styled bedrooms are beautifully furnished, some with separate seating areas and many enjoying views across the gardens and valley beyond. Public rooms are spacious and inviting, featuring antique pieces and beautiful flower arrangements. Dinner is a highlight of any stay and the accompanying wine list reflects the proprietors' own enthusiasm for the subject.
ROOMS: 12 en suite 3 annexe en suite s £275-£500; d £440-£575 (incl. bkfst & dinner) **LB** **FACILITIES:** STV Fishing Putt green Bowls **CONF:** Board 22 Del from £300 **PARKING:** 25 **NOTES:** ⊗ in restaurant Closed 12 days Jan
CARDS:

★★★76% ®® **Mill End**
Dartmoor National Park, Sandy Park TQ13 8JN
☎ 01647 432282 📠 01647 433106
e-mail: info@millendhotel.com
Dir: *from A30 at Whiddon Down follow A382 to Moretonhampstead. After 3.5m hump back bridge at Sandy Park, hotel on right by river*

In a peaceful and attractive location, Mill End is set on the riverside and offers six miles of angling on the River Teign. Bedrooms are available in a range of sizes and all are stylishly decorated and thoughtfully equipped. Cuisine is a feature here and menus offer exciting dishes featuring local produce.
ROOMS: 15 en suite (3 GF) s £70-£100; d £100-£140 (incl. bkfst) **LB** **FACILITIES:** Fishing Xmas **CONF:** Thtr 40 Class 20 Board 30 **PARKING:** 21 **NOTES:** ⊗ in restaurant **CARDS:**

★★68% **Three Crowns Hotel**
High St TQ13 8AJ
☎ 01647 433444 📠 01647 433117
e-mail: threecrowns@msn.com
web: www.chagford-accom.co.uk
Dir: *A30 at Whiddon Down, in town centre opposite church*

This 13th-century inn is located in the heart of the village. Exposed beams, mullioned windows and open fires are part of the charm, which is well maintained here. There is a range of rooms; several with four-poster beds, all are comfortable and now upgraded. A choice of bars is available along with a pleasant lounge and separate dining room.
ROOMS: 17 en suite (1 fmly) ⊗ in 8 bedrooms s £55-£70; d £74 (incl. bkfst) **LB** **FACILITIES:** STV Xmas **CONF:** Board 90 **PARKING:** 20 **NOTES:** ⊗ in restaurant **CARDS:**

CHARD, Somerset Map 04 ST30

★★★70% **Lordleaze**
Henderson Dr, Forton Rd TA20 2HW
☎ 01460 61066 📠 01460 66468
e-mail: lordleaze@fsbdial.co.uk
web: www.lordleazehotel.co.uk
Dir: *from Chard take A358, at St Mary's Church turn left to Forton & Winsham on B3162. Follow signs to hotel*

The Lordleaze is an excellent base from which to explore the West Country. The comfortable bedrooms, some on the ground floor, are well equipped. A focal point is the relaxed and friendly lounge bar where a wood-burning stove adds to the character and

continued on p158

CHARD, continued

atmosphere. In addition to the carte menu offered in the restaurant, a tempting selection of bar meals is available.
ROOMS: 25 en suite (2 fmly) (7 GF) ⊗ in 21 bedrooms **FACILITIES:** **CONF:** Thtr 180 Class 60 Board 40 **PARKING:** 55 **NOTES:** ⊗ in restaurant Civ Wed **CARDS:**

C

CHARINGWORTH, Gloucestershire Map 10 SP13

★★★78% Charingworth Manor
GL55 6NS
☎ 01386 593555 01386 593353
e-mail: charingworthmanor@englishrosehotels.co.uk
web: www.englishrosehotels.co.uk/hotels/charingworth/index.html
Dir: *on B4035 3m E of Chipping Campden*
This 14th-century manor house retains many original features including flagstone floors, exposed beams and open fireplaces. The house has a beautiful setting in 50 acres of grounds and has been carefully extended to provide high quality accommodation and a delightful small leisure spa. Spacious bedrooms are furnished with period pieces and modern amenities.
ROOMS: 26 en suite (13 GF) s £125; d £170 (incl. bkfst) **LB**
FACILITIES: STV Sauna Solarium Gym Steam room Xmas
CONF: Thtr 60 Class 40 Board 40 **PARKING:** 50 **NOTES:** ⊗ in restaurant Civ Wed 60 **CARDS:**

See advert under CHIPPING CAMPDEN

CHARLBURY, Oxfordshire Map 11 SP31

★★65% The Bell
Church St OX7 3PP
☎ 01608 810278 01608 811447
e-mail: reservationsatthebell@msn.com
Dir: *from Oxford take A34 towards Woodstock, 2nd turn off B4437 towards Charlbury. In village, 2nd on left, hotel opposite St Mary's Church*
This mellow Cotswold stone inn dates back to the 16th century, when it was home to Customs and Excise, and sits close to the town centre. Popular with locals, the bar has an enjoyable and relaxed atmosphere and comes complete with flagstone floors and log fires. The well-equipped bedrooms are situated in the main building and the adjacent converted barn.
ROOMS: 7 en suite 4 annexe en suite (3 fmly) ⊗ in all bedrooms s fr £69; d fr £85 (incl. bkfst) **LB** **FACILITIES:** Xmas **CONF:** Thtr 60 Class 60 Board 30 Del from £100 **PARKING:** 40 **NOTES:** ⊗ in restaurant **CARDS:**

Popped the question?
Hotels with Civ Wed in their entry are licensed for civil wedding ceremonies. Maximum numbers for the ceremony only are shown, e.g. Civ Wed 120

CHARMOUTH, Dorset Map 04 SY39

★★74% White House
2 Hillside, The Street DT6 6PJ
☎ 01297 560411 01297 560702
e-mail: ian@whitehousehotel.com
Dir: *off A35 signed Charmouth. Hotel opposite church halfway up hill*
Famed for its fossils and cliff-top walks, the interesting beach at Charmouth is within walking distance of this charming Regency property. Comfortable accommodation is provided at this friendly, small hotel, where individually styled bedrooms are equipped with modern facilities. In the evening, imaginative cuisine is served in the attractive restaurant, cooked using fresh, local produce.

ROOMS: 6 en suite 2 annexe en suite (2 GF) ⊗ in all bedrooms s fr £15; d £110-£150 (incl. bkfst & dinner) **LB** **PARKING:** 9 **NOTES:** No children 14yrs ⊗ in restaurant Closed Jan RS Feb, Nov & Dec
CARDS:

CHARNOCK RICHARD MOTORWAY SERVICE AREA (M6), Lancashire Map 15 SD51

Welcome Lodge
Welcome Break Service Area PR7 5LR
☎ 01257 791746 01257 793596
e-mail: charnockhotel@welcomebreak.co.uk
web: www.welcomebreak.co.uk
Dir: *between junct 27 & 28 of M6 (N'bound). 500yds from Camelot Theme Park via Mill Lane*
This modern building offers accommodation in smart, spacious and well-equipped bedrooms, suitable for families and business travellers, and all with en suite bathrooms. Refreshments may be taken at the nearby family restaurant. For further details consult the Hotel Groups page.
ROOMS: 100 en suite s £35-£50; d £35-£50 **CONF:** Thtr 40 Class 16 Board 24

CHATHAM, Kent Map 07 TQ76

★★★★75%
Bridgewood Manor Hotel
Bridgewood Roundabout, Walderslade Woods ME5 9AX
☎ 01634 201333 01634 201330
e-mail: bridgewoodmanor@marstonhotels.com
Dir: *adjacent to Bridgewood rdbt on A229. Take 3rd exit signed Walderslade and Lordswood. Hotel 50mtrs on left*

A modern, purpose-built hotel situated on the outskirts of Rochester. Bedrooms are pleasantly decorated, comfortably furnished and equipped with many thoughtful touches. The hotel

continued

has an excellent range of leisure and conference facilities. Guests can dine in the informal Terrace Bistro or experience fine dining in the more formal Squires restaurant, where the service is both attentive and friendly.
ROOMS: 100 en suite (12 fmly) in 63 bedrooms s £124-£149; d £158-£208 (incl. bkfst) **LB FACILITIES: Spa** STV Snooker Sauna Solarium Gym Putt green Jacuzzi Beauty treatments Xmas **CONF:** Thtr 200 Class 110 Board 80 Del from £149 **SERVICES:** Lift **PARKING:** 170 **NOTES:** in restaurant Civ Wed 130 **CARDS:**

CHEADLE, Greater Manchester — Map 16 SJ88

Travel Inn (Manchester Cheadle)

Royal Crescent SK8 3FE
☎ 08701 977172 0161 491 5886
Dir: *off Cheadle Royal rdbt off A34 behind TGI Friday's*

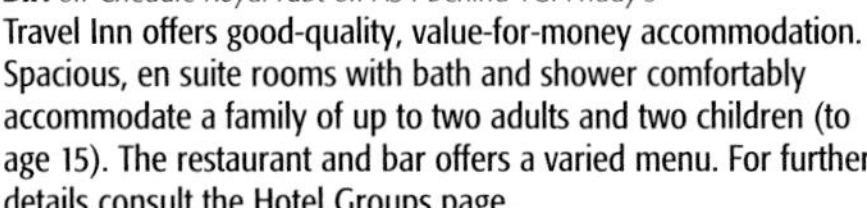

Travel Inn offers good-quality, value-for-money accommodation. Spacious, en suite rooms with bath and shower comfortably accommodate a family of up to two adults and two children (to age 15). The restaurant and bar offers a varied menu. For further details consult the Hotel Groups page.
ROOMS: 40 en suite s £45.95-£48.95; d £45.95-£48.95 **CONF:** Thtr 30

CHELMSFORD, Essex — Map 06 TL70

★★★72% Pontlands Park Country Hotel

West Hanningfield Rd, Great Baddow CM2 8HR
☎ 01245 476444 01245 478393
e-mail: sales@pontlandsparkhotel.co.uk
web: www.pontlandsparkhotel.co.uk
Dir: *A12/A130/A1114 to Chelmsford. 1st exit at rdbt, 1st slip road on left. Left towards Gt Baddow, 1st left into West Hanningfield Rd. Hotel 400yds on left*
A Victorian country house hotel in a peaceful rural setting amidst attractive landscaped grounds. The stylishly furnished bedrooms are generally quite spacious; each is individually decorated and equipped with modern facilities. The elegant public rooms include a tastefully furnished sitting room, a cosy lounge bar, smart conservatory restaurant and an intimate dining room.
ROOMS: 36 en suite (10 fmly) (12 GF) in 7 bedrooms s fr £105; d £140-£170 **LB FACILITIES:** STV Sauna Gym Jacuzzi Beauty salon **CONF:** Thtr 100 Class 20 Board 22 Del from £145 **PARKING:** 100 **NOTES:** in restaurant Closed 24 Dec-3 Jan (ex 31 Dec) Civ Wed 100 **CARDS:**

★★★70% Atlantic

New St CM1 1PP
☎ 01245 268168 01245 268169
e-mail: info@atlantichotel.co.uk
Ideally situated just a short walk from the railway station with its quick links to London, this purpose-built hotel has contemporary-style bedrooms equipped with modern facilities. The open-plan public areas include the popular New Street Brasserie, a lounge bar and a conservatory.
ROOMS: 59 en suite (3 fmly) (27 GF) in 49 bedrooms s £75-£109.95; d £85-£120.90 (incl. bkfst) **FACILITIES:** STV Sauna Solarium Gym Steam room ♫ **CONF:** Thtr 15 Board 10 Del from £120 **SERVICES:** air con **PARKING:** 60 **NOTES:** Closed 24 Dec-2 Jan **CARDS:**

★★★70% County

Rainsford Rd CM1 2PZ
☎ 01245 455700 01245 492762
e-mail: sales@countyhotel-essex.co.uk
web: www.countyhotel-essex.co.uk
Dir: *from town centre, past rail and bus station. Hotel 300yds*
Expect a friendly welcome at this popular hotel, which is ideally situated within easy walking distance of the railway station, bus depot and town centre. Public areas include a smart new restaurant and the plushly furnished wine bar. The hotel also has a range of meeting rooms and banqueting facilities.
ROOMS: 53 en suite 8 annexe en suite s £75-£95; d £100-£130 (incl. bkfst) **LB FACILITIES:** STV ch fac Xmas **CONF:** Thtr 200 Class 84 Board 64 **SERVICES:** Lift **PARKING:** 80 **NOTES:** in restaurant Closed 27-30 Dec Civ Wed 80 **CARDS:**

★★★67% Ivy Hill

Writtle Rd, Margaretting CM4 0EH
☎ 01277 353040 01277 355038
e-mail: sales@ivyhillhotel.co.uk
web: www.ivyhillhotel.co.uk
Dir: *at top of slip road off A12*
This smartly appointed hotel is ideally situated, just off the A12. The spacious bedrooms are tastefully decorated, have co-ordinated fabrics and all the usual facilities. Public rooms include a choice of lounges, a cosy bar, a smart conservatory and the Ivy restaurant as well as a range of conference and banqueting facilities.
ROOMS: 33 en suite (5 fmly) (11 GF) s £60-£110; d £80-£160 **FACILITIES:** STV **CONF:** BC Thtr 80 Class 60 Board 20 Del from £125 **PARKING:** 60 **NOTES:** in restaurant Civ Wed 100 **CARDS:**

Premier Lodge Chelmsford

Main Rd, Borham CM3 3HJ
☎ 0870 9906394 0870 9906395
web: www.premierlodge.com
Dir: *M25 junct 28, A12 to Colchester, then B1137 to Borham*
High quality, modern, budget accommodation, ideal for families and business travellers. All rooms feature bath, power shower and satellite TV, and most have telephones / modem points. The adjacent bar and restaurant offers a wide and varied menu.
ROOMS: 78 en suite s £50; d £50

Travel Inn

Chelmsford Service Area, Colchester Rd, Springfield CM2 5PY
☎ 0870 238 3310 01245 464010
Dir: *on A12 (J19), Chelmsford Bypass, signposted Chelmsford Service Area. 2nd service area from A12 on M25*
Travel Inn offers good-quality, value-for-money accommodation. Spacious, en suite rooms with bath and shower comfortably accommodate a family of up to two adults and two children (to age 15). The restaurant and bar offers a varied menu. For further details consult the Hotel Groups page.
ROOMS: 61 en suite s £45.95-£48.95; d £45.95-£48.95

♫ Entertainment

CHELTENHAM, Gloucestershire Map 10 SO92

Town House

★★★★ Alias Hotel Kandinsky
Bayshill Rd, Montpellier GL50 3AS
☎ 01242 527788 01242 226412
e-mail: info@aliaskandinsky.com
Dir: *M5 junct 11, A40 to town centre. Right at 2nd rdbt. 2nd exit at 3rd rdbt into Bayshill Rd. Hotel on corner of Bayshill/Parabola Rds*
A large Regency villa blending modern comfort with quirky eclectic decoration. Stylish bedrooms vary in size and have additional facilities such as CD/video players. There are several lounges, a conservatory, and the bright Café Paradiso restaurant. Hidden in the cellars is 'U-bahn', a wonderful 1950s'-style cocktail bar.
ROOMS: 48 en suite (3 fmly) (5 GF) in 4 bedrooms s £75; d £95 LB **FACILITIES:** STV Access to local pool & gym Xmas **CONF:** Board 20 Del from £140 **SERVICES:** Lift **PARKING:** 32 **NOTES:** in restaurant **CARDS:**

See advert on opposite page

★★★★69% The Queen's
The Promenade GL50 1NN
☎ 0870 400 8107 01242 224145
MACDONALD HOTELS
e-mail: general.queens@macdonald-hotels.co.uk
Dir: *follow town centre signs. Left at Montpellier Walk rdbt. Entrance 500mtrs right*
With its spectacular position at the top of the main promenade, this landmark hotel is an ideal base from which to explore the charms of this Regency spa town and the Cotswolds. An extensive bedroom refurbishment is being carried out, with early results being most impressive. Smart public rooms include the popular Gold Cup bar and a choice of dining options.
ROOMS: 79 en suite in 26 bedrooms s £65-£140; d £150-£210 (incl. bkfst) LB **FACILITIES:** STV Xmas **CONF:** Thtr 100 Class 60 Board 40 Del from £160 **SERVICES:** Lift **PARKING:** 80 **NOTES:** in restaurant Civ Wed **CARDS:**

★★★★65% Cheltenham Park
Cirencester Rd, Charlton Kings GL53 8EA
☎ 01242 222021 01242 254880
PARAMOUNT GROUP OF HOTELS
e-mail: cheltenhamparkreservations@paramount-hotels.co.uk
Dir: *on A435, 2m SE of Cheltenham near Lilley Brook Golf Course*
Located south of Cheltenham, this attractive Georgian hotel is set in its own landscaped gardens, adjacent to Lilley Brook Golf Course. All of the bedrooms are spacious and well equipped and the hotel has an impressive leisure club and extensive meeting facilities. The Lakeside restaurant serves carefully prepared cuisine.
ROOMS: 33 en suite 110 annexe en suite (2 fmly) in 67 bedrooms s £80-£240; d £100-£300 (incl. bkfst) LB **FACILITIES:** STV supervised Sauna Solarium Gym Jacuzzi Beauty treatment rooms Xmas **CONF:** BC Thtr 350 Class 180 Board 110 Del from £150 **SERVICES:** Lift **PARKING:** 170 **NOTES:** in restaurant Civ Wed
CARDS:

Top 200 – Hotel

★★★ The Greenway
Shurdington GL51 4UG
☎ 01242 862352 01242 862780
e-mail: greenway@btconnect.com
Dir: *2.5m SW on A46*
This hotel, with a wealth of history, is peacefully located in a delightful setting close to the A46 and the M5. Within easy reach of the many attractions of the Cotswolds as well as the interesting town of Cheltenham, The Greenway certainly offers something special. The attractive dining room overlooks the sunken garden and is the venue for exciting food, proudly served by dedicated and attentive staff.
ROOMS: 11 en suite 10 annexe en suite (1 fmly) (4 GF) in 10 bedrooms s £109-£159; d £150-£280 (incl. bkfst) LB **FACILITIES:** STV Clay pigeon shooting, Horse riding, Mountain biking, Beauty treatment Xmas **CONF:** Thtr 45 Class 25 Board 18 Del £205 **PARKING:** 50 **NOTES:** in restaurant Civ Wed 45
CARDS:

Top 200 – Hotel

★★★ Hotel on the Park
38 Evesham Rd GL52 2AH
☎ 01242 518898 01242 511526
e-mail: stay@hotelonthepark.com
web: www.hotelonthepark.com
Dir: *opposite Pittville Park. Join one-way system, off A435 towards Evesham*
The Hotel on the Park is a wonderfully different hotel with style, originality and flair throughout. Bedrooms have tremendous character, and exceptional comfort. Similar comments apply to public areas, comprising the elegant drawing room, library and the Bacchanalian Restaurant, the venue for accomplished and enjoyable cuisine. Look out for

continued

the two huge bears that sit dressed for dinner at one of the dining room tables.

ROOMS: 12 en suite ⊗ in all bedrooms s £86.50-£147; d £112-£162 LB **FACILITIES:** STV **CONF:** Board 18 **PARKING:** 8 **NOTES:** No children 8yrs ⊗ in restaurant **CARDS:**

★★★72% George Hotel

St Georges Rd GL50 3DZ
☎ 01242 235751 01242 224359
e-mail: hotel@stayatthegeorge.co.uk
web: www.stayatthegeorge.co.uk
Dir: *M5 junct 11 town centre signs. At 1st lights left into Gloucester Rd, past rail station over mini rdbt. At lights right into St Georges Rd. Hotel 0.75m on left*

Just a short stroll from the town centre, this genuinely friendly hotel is privately owned and occupies part of an elegant Regency terrace. Bedrooms are well equipped and tastefully furnished with additional features such as in-room safes and ironing facilities. There are two dining options - the modern and lively Monty's brasserie offering contemporary European cuisine and the elegant fine dining restaurant which has an intimate and relaxing atmosphere.

ROOMS: 38 en suite (1 GF) ⊗ in 30 bedrooms s £60-£85; d £95-£105 (incl. bkfst) LB **FACILITIES:** STV **CONF:** Thtr 40 Board 24 Del from £142.50 **PARKING:** 30 **NOTES:** ⊗ in restaurant RS 24-26 Dec
CARDS:

★★★70% Charlton Kings

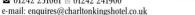

London Rd, Charlton Kings GL52 6UU
THE INDEPENDENTS
☎ 01242 231061 01242 241900
e-mail: enquires@charltonkingshotel.co.uk
web: www.charltonkingshotel.co.uk
Dir: *entering Cheltenham from Oxford on A40, 1st on left*

Conveniently located on the outskirts of Cheltenham, the Charlton Kings is an attractive and friendly hotel providing comfortable, modern accommodation. The neatly presented bedrooms are well equipped with tasteful furnishings and contemporary comforts. The popular and stylish restaurant serves a variety of dishes for all tastes from a menu based on quality ingredients.

Charlton Kings

ROOMS: 13 en suite (1 fmly) (4 GF) ⊗ in 12 bedrooms s £65-£85; d £95-£120 (incl. bkfst) LB **FACILITIES:** STV **CONF:** Thtr 20 Class 20 Board 20 **PARKING:** 26 **NOTES:** ⊗ in restaurant
CARDS:

★★★68% Carlton

Parabola Rd GL50 3AQ
☎ 01242 514453 01242 226487
e-mail: enquiries@thecarltonhotel.co.uk
Dir: *Follow signs to town centre, at Town Hall straight on through 2 sets of lights, turn left, then 1st right.*

This well-presented Regency property is conveniently situated within a short walk of the town centre. Family-owned and run, it provides comfortable accommodation with a relaxed and friendly atmosphere. Bedrooms are located both in the main hotel and

continued on p162

CHELTENHAM, continued

also within an annexe building, where rooms are larger and more luxurious. Other features include a choice of bars, lounge and conference facilities.
ROOMS: 62 en suite 13 annexe en suite (2 fmly) (4 GF) ⊗ in 15 bedrooms s £45-£72.50; d £90-£97 (incl. bkfst) **LB** **FACILITIES:** STV Xmas **CONF:** Thtr 200 Class 150 Board 100 Del £100 **SERVICES:** Lift **PARKING:** 85 **NOTES:** ⊗ in restaurant Civ Wed 170
CARDS:

★★★65% Royal George

Birdlip GL4 8JH
☎ 01452 862506 🖷 01452 862277
e-mail: 6503@greeneking.co.uk
Dir: *on B4070, off A417*
This attractive 18th-century Cotswold building has been sympathetically converted and extended into a pleasant hotel. Bedrooms are spacious and comfortably furnished with modern facilities. The public areas have been designed around a traditional English pub with the bar leading onto a terrace overlooking extensive lawns.
ROOMS: 34 en suite (2 fmly) (12 GF) ⊗ in 22 bedrooms s fr £70; d £90-£95 (incl. bkfst) **LB** **FACILITIES:** ♫ Xmas **CONF:** Thtr 90 Board 45 Del from £85 **PARKING:** 120 **NOTES:** ✗ ⊗ in restaurant Civ Wed 80 **CARDS:**

★★★64% The Prestbury House Hotel & Oaks Restaurant

The Burgage, Prestbury GL52 3DN
☎ 01242 529533 🖷 01242 227076
e-mail: enquiries@prestburyhouse.co.uk
web: www.prestburyhouse.co.uk
Dir: *1m NE of Cheltenham. Follow all signs for racecourse. From racecourse follow Prestbury signs. Hotel 2nd left, 500mtrs from racecourse*

This hotel retains much of its historical charm and is well situated for the town centre and racecourse. Well-equipped, spacious accommodation is offered in the main house and converted coach house. An interesting range of dishes is offered in 'Oaks', the hotel's elegant, oak-panelled restaurant. The owners also run a management training company, and team-building activities are sometimes held here.
ROOMS: 7 en suite 8 annexe en suite (3 GF) ⊗ in 16 bedrooms s £60-£78; d £65-£112 (incl. bkfst) **LB** **FACILITIES:** STV Riding Gym Putt green Clay pigeons, Archery, Bike hire, Trim Trail Hill Walking, Target golf, Petanque Xmas **CONF:** BC Thtr 65 Class 30 Board 25 Del from £95 **PARKING:** 40 **NOTES:** ✗ ⊗ in restaurant Civ Wed 100
CARDS:

GF Indicates the number of bedrooms at ground floor level.

★★★62% Hotel De La Bere

Southam GL52 3NH
☎ 01242 545454 🖷 01242 236016
e-mail: delabere@corushotels.com
Dir: *M5 junct 10 into Cheltenham, left at first rdbt on B-road for 3m crossing A435 to B4632. Turn right hotel on right.*

This elegant 15th-century building is situated to the north of town, overlooking the famous racecourse. There is a tangible sense of history here with many original features retained. Bedrooms are split between the main house and the courtyard, all of which offer ample comfort and plenty of character. Leisure facilities are also available, including a heated outdoor pool.
ROOMS: 33 en suite 24 annexe en suite (3 fmly) (10 GF) ⊗ in 28 bedrooms s £49-£99; d £99 **FACILITIES:** Squash Sauna Solarium Gym Xmas **CONF:** Thtr 100 Class 60 Board 40 Del £115 **PARKING:** 125 **NOTES:** ⊗ in restaurant Civ Wed 100
CARDS:

★★★59% White House

Gloucester Rd GL51 0ST
☎ 01452 713226 🖷 01452 857590
e-mail: stay@white-house-hotel.co.uk
Dir: *M5 junct 11 onto A40 to Cheltenham. Left at rdbt, hotel 0.5m on left*
This hotel is situated on the edge of town, and provides comfortable and modern accommodation. The lounge bar and the restaurant are attractively presented and function rooms are also available. Friendly service and helpful staff ensure a pleasant stay.
ROOMS: 49 en suite (4 fmly) ⊗ in 13 bedrooms s £40-£70; d £70-£95 (incl. bkfst) **LB** **FACILITIES:** STV pool table bar games ♫ **CONF:** Thtr 180 Class 80 Board 45 Del from £100 **PARKING:** 150 **NOTES:** ⊗ in restaurant RS 12-16 Mar & 10-12 Nov Civ Wed 150
CARDS:

★★68% Cotswold Grange

Pittville Circus Rd GL52 2QH
☎ 01242 515119 🖷 01242 241537
e-mail: paul@cotswoldgrange.co.uk
Dir: *from town centre, follow Prestbury signs. Right at 1st rdbt, hotel 200yds on left*
Built from Cotswold limestone, this attractive Georgian property retains many impressive architectural features. Situated conveniently close to the centre of Cheltenham, this long-established, family-run hotel offers well-equipped and comfortable accommodation. The convivial bar is a popular venue, and additional facilities include a spacious restaurant, cosy lounge and ample parking.
ROOMS: 25 en suite (4 fmly) s £55-£65; d £75-£85 (incl. bkfst) **FACILITIES:** ch fac **CONF:** Thtr 20 Class 15 Board 15 Del from £70 **PARKING:** 20 **NOTES:** ⊗ in restaurant Closed 24 Dec-5 Jan RS Sat & Sun evening (food by arrangement)
CARDS:

★★66% **North Hall**
Pittville Circus Rd GL52 2PZ
☎ 01242 520589 📠 01242 261953
e-mail: northhallhotel@btinternet.com
web: www.northhallhotel.co.uk
Dir: *from Cheltenham town centre, follow Pittville signs. At Pittville Circus take 1st left into Pittville Circus Rd. Hotel on right*

This three-storey Victorian house is conveniently located in a quiet residential area, within easy reach of the town centre and racecourse. Bedrooms are individually designed and offer ample comfort and quality with a range of extra facilities. A brasserie-style menu is served in the elegant surroundings of the restaurant, and there is also a bar/lounge with convivial atmosphere.
ROOMS: 20 en suite (2 fmly) ⊗ in 8 bedrooms s £45-£65; d £65-£90 (incl. bkfst) **LB** **FACILITIES:** STV Xmas **CONF:** Thtr 40 Class 25 Board 15 **PARKING:** 25 **NOTES:** ⊗ in restaurant
CARDS:

Travel Inn Cheltenham (West)
Tewkesbury Rd, Uckington GL51 9SL
☎ 08701 977055 📠 01242 244887
Dir: *opposite Sainsbury's & Homebase on A4019, 2 miles from J10 (southbound exit only) and 3 miles from J11 (both exits) of M5*
Travel Inn offers good-quality, value-for-money accommodation. Spacious, en suite rooms with bath and shower comfortably accommodate a family of up to two adults and two children (to age 15). The restaurant and bar offers a varied menu. For further details consult the Hotel Groups page.
ROOMS: 40 en suite s £45.95-£46.95; d £45.95-£46.95 **CONF:** Thtr 30 Class 30

Travel Inn (Cheltenham Central)
374 Gloucester Rd GL51 7AY
☎ 08701 977056 📠 01242 260042
Dir: *M5 junct 11 onto A40 (Cheltenham). Follow dual carriageway to end, straight at 1st rdbt, turn right at 2nd*
Travel Inn offers good-quality, value-for-money accommodation. Spacious, en suite rooms with bath and shower comfortably accommodate a family of up to two adults and two children (to age 15). The restaurant and bar offers a varied menu. For further details consult the Hotel Groups page.
ROOMS: 40 en suite s £45.95-£46.95; d £45.95-£46.95

CHENIES, Buckinghamshire — Map 06 TQ09

★★★71% **The Bedford Arms**
WD3 6EQ
☎ 01923 283301 📠 01923 284825
e-mail: contact@bedfordarms.co.uk
web: www.bedfordarms.co.uk
Dir: *M25 junct 18, then A404, follow signs for Amersham, approx 2.5m*
This attractive, 19th-century country inn enjoys a peaceful rural setting. Comfortable bedrooms are decorated in traditional style and feature a range of thoughtful extras. Each room is named after a relation of the Duke of Bedford, whose family has an historic association with the hotel. There are two bars, a lounge and a cosy, wood-panelled restaurant.
ROOMS: 10 en suite ⊗ in 3 bedrooms s £60-£110; d £95-£130 (incl. bkfst) **FACILITIES:** STV **CONF:** Thtr 25 Class 10 Board 15 Del from £115 **PARKING:** 60 **NOTES:** ⊗ in restaurant
CARDS:

CHESSINGTON, Greater London — Map 06 TQ16

Travel Inn
Leatherhead Rd KT9 2NE
☎ 08701 977057 📠 01372 720889
Dir: *From M25 (J9), towards Kingston on A243, for approx 2 miles. The Travel Inn is next to Chessington World of Adventures*
Travel Inn offers good-quality, value-for-money accommodation. Spacious, en suite rooms with bath and shower comfortably accommodate a family of up to two adults and two children (to age 15). The restaurant and bar offers a varied menu. For further details consult the Hotel Groups page.
ROOMS: 42 en suite s £56.95; d £56.95

CHESTER, Cheshire — Map 15 SJ46

See also Puddington

Top 200 – Hotel

★★★★★ ®®® **The Chester Grosvenor & Grosvenor Spa**
Eastgate CH1 1LT
☎ 01244 324024 📠 01244 313246
e-mail: chesgrov@chestergrosvenor.com
Dir: *off M56 for M53, then A56. Follow signs for city centre hotels*
Located within the Roman walls of the city, this Grade II listed, half-timbered building is the essence of Englishness. Furnished with fine fabrics and queen or king-size beds, the suites and bedrooms are of the highest standard, each designed with guest comfort as a priority. The brasserie is bustling, whilst the library has a discreet, club-like feel. In the Arkle Restaurant, guests are offered creative cuisine with flair and style. A luxury spa & small fitness centre are also available.
ROOMS: 80 en suite ⊗ in all bedrooms s £185-£217.38; d £185-£311.38 **LB** **FACILITIES: Spa** STV Sauna Solarium Gym Jacuzzi Membership of nearby Country Club ♫ **CONF:** BC Thtr 250 Class 120 Board 48 Del from £223.25 **SERVICES:** Lift air con **NOTES:** ⊗ in restaurant Closed 25-26 Dec RS 27-30 Dec & 1-20 Jan Civ Wed 100 **CARDS:**

continued

CHESTER, continued

Top 200 – Hotel

★★★★ ◎◎

The Chester Crabwall Manor Hotel

MARSTON HOTELS

Parkgate Rd, Mollington CH1 6NE
☎ 01244 851666 ▤ 01244 851400
e-mail: crabwallmanor@marstonhotels.com
Dir: NW off A540

A dwelling on this site was first recorded in the Domesday Book, although the present day manor dates from the mid-17th century. Today the hotel stands in 11 acres of immaculate mature gardens and woodland. Public rooms include a leisure club and indoor pool, a number of cosy lounges and a stylish conservatory restaurant. The individually designed bedrooms provide comfortable and well-equipped accommodation.

ROOMS: 48 en suite ⊗ in 2 bedrooms s £151-£251; d £181-£281 (incl. bkfst) **LB** **FACILITIES: Spa** STV Sauna Solarium Gym Jacuzzi Heli pad, beauty treatments Xmas **CONF:** Thtr 100 Class 60 Board 38 Del from £174 **PARKING:** 120 **NOTES:** ⊗ in restaurant Civ Wed 90 **CARDS:**

★★★★74% De Vere Carden Park

DE VERE HOTELS

Carden Park CH3 9DQ
☎ 01829 731000 ▤ 01829 731599
e-mail: reservations.carden@devere-hotels.com
web: www.devereonline.co.uk/cardenpark
(For full entry see Broxton)

★★★★70% *Mollington Banastre*

Best Western

Parkgate Rd CH1 6NN
☎ 01244 851471 ▤ 01244 851165
e-mail: events.mollington@arcadianhotels.co.uk
Dir: M56 junct 16 at rdbt left for Chester on A540. Hotel 2m on right

Set in its own attractive grounds, this hotel remains popular with both the business and the leisure markets. The bedrooms, which come in various styles, are well equipped and comfortable. Stylish, *continued* open-plan public areas include a comfortable bar and lounge, the Garden Room restaurant and a comprehensive leisure club.

ROOMS: 63 en suite (7 fmly) ⊗ in 40 bedrooms **FACILITIES:** STV Squash Sauna Solarium Gym Jacuzzi Hairdressing Health & beauty salon ♫ **CONF:** BC Thtr 260 Class 60 Board 50 **SERVICES:** Lift **PARKING:** 200 **NOTES:** ⊗ in restaurant Civ Wed 150 **CARDS:**

See advert on opposite page

★★★★66% The Queen Hotel

Best Western

City Rd CH1 3AH
☎ 01244 305000 ▤ 01244 318483
e-mail: queenhotel@feathers.uk.com
Dir: follow signs for railway station, hotel opposite

Now under new ownership, this hotel is ideally located opposite the railway station and just a couple minutes' walk from the city. Public areas have undergone an extensive refurbishment and include a new restaurant, small gym, waiting room bar, separate lounge and Roman themed gardens. Bedrooms are generally spacious, many of which have been also been upgraded.

ROOMS: 129 en suite (6 fmly) (10 GF) ⊗ in 66 bedrooms s £55-£130; d £75-£180 (incl. bkfst) **LB** **FACILITIES:** STV Gym Xmas **CONF:** BC Thtr 300 Class 100 Board 50 Del from £90 **SERVICES:** Lift **PARKING:** 100 **NOTES:** ⊗ in restaurant Civ Wed 250 **CARDS:**

★★★73% ◎ Rowton Hall Country House Hotel

Whitchurch Rd, Rowton CH3 6AD
☎ 01244 335262 ▤ 01244 335464
e-mail: rowtonhall@rowtonhall.co.uk
web: www.rowtonhallhotel.co.uk
Dir: 2m SE of Chester at Rowton off A41 towards Whitchurch

This delightful Georgian manor house set in mature grounds retains many original features such as a superb carved staircase and several eye-catching fireplaces. Bedrooms vary in style and all have been stylishly fitted and have impressive en suites. Public areas include a smart leisure centre, extensive function facilities and a striking restaurant that serves imaginative dishes.

ROOMS: 38 en suite (4 fmly) (8 GF) s £90-£400; d £90-£400 **LB** **FACILITIES:** STV Sauna Solarium Gym Jacuzzi ch fac Xmas **CONF:** Thtr 170 Class 48 Board 50 Del from £155 **PARKING:** 120 **NOTES:** ⊗ in restaurant Civ Wed 120 **CARDS:**

★★★72% Grosvenor Pulford

Wrexham Rd, Pulford CH4 9DG
☎ 01244 570560 ▤ 01244 570809
e-mail: enquiries@grosvenorpulfordhotel.co.uk
web: www.grosvenorpulfordhotel.co.uk
Dir: Leave M53/A55 at junct signposted A483 Chester, Wrexham and North Wales. Turn on to B5445, hotel 2m on right

Set in rural surroundings, this modern, stylish hotel features a magnificent leisure club with a large Roman-style swimming pool.

continued

Among the bedrooms available are several executive suites and others containing spiral staircases leading to the bedroom sections. A new brasserie restaurant and bar provide a wide range of imaginative dishes in a relaxed atmosphere.
ROOMS: 73 en suite (6 fmly) (21 GF) ⊗ in 10 bedrooms s £75-£105; d £100-£160 (incl. bkfst) **LB** **FACILITIES: Spa** STV Snooker Sauna Solarium Gym Jacuzzi Hairdressing & Beauty salon, coffee bar Xmas **CONF:** Thtr 200 Class 100 Board 50 Del £118 **PARKING:** 200
NOTES: ⊗ in restaurant Civ Wed 70
CARDS:

See advert on this page

★★★69% Westminster

City Rd CH1 3AF
☎ 01244 317341 01244 325369
Dir: *A56 3m to Chester city centre, left signed rail station. Hotel opp station, on right*

Best Western

Situated close to the railway station and city centre, the Westminster is an old-established hotel which has been extensively upgraded. It has an attractive Tudor-style exterior while bedrooms are brightly decorated with a modern theme. No smoking bedrooms and family rooms are both available. There is a choice of bars and lounges, and the large dining room serves a good range of dishes.
ROOMS: 75 en suite (5 fmly) (6 GF) ⊗ in 20 bedrooms s £45-£60; d £75-£110 (incl. bkfst) **LB** **FACILITIES:** STV ♫ Xmas **CONF:** Thtr 150 Class 60 Board 40 Del from £85 **SERVICES:** Lift **PARKING:** 50
NOTES: ⊗ in restaurant Civ Wed
CARDS:

★★★68% Mill

Milton St CH1 3NF
☎ 01244 350035 01244 345635
e-mail: reservations@millhotel.com
Dir: *M53 junct 12, turn right A56, at 2nd rdbt left (A5268), then 1st left & 2nd left*

This hotel is a stylish conversion of an old corn mill and enjoys an idyllic canalside location next to the inner ring road and close to the city centre. The bedrooms offer varying styles, and public rooms are spacious and comfortable. There are several dining options and dinner is often served on a large boat that cruises Chester's canal system between courses. A well-equipped leisure centre is also provided.
ROOMS: 80 en suite 49 annexe en suite (57 fmly) ⊗ in 51 bedrooms s £70-£95; d £85-£105 (incl. bkfst) **FACILITIES: Spa** STV supervised Sauna Solarium Gym Jacuzzi Steam room, hairdressing, nails, beauty treatments, fitness classes ♫ Xmas **CONF:** Thtr 40 Class 27 Board 28 Del from £110 **SERVICES:** Lift **PARKING:** 120 **NOTES:**
CARDS:

Destination dining!
This symbol indicates a Restaurant with Rooms

CHESTER, continued

★★★66% Blossoms
St John St CH1 1HL
☎ 0870 400 8108 📠 01244 346433
e-mail: general.blossoms@macdonald-hotels.co.uk
Dir: *in city centre, follow signs for Eastgate and City Centre Hotels, continue through pedestrianised zone, hotel on the left*
For those seeking to explore this charming, medieval walled city, the central location of this elegant hotel is ideal. The public areas retain much of their Victorian charm. Occasionally, piano music at dinner adds to the intimate atmosphere.
ROOMS: 64 en suite (3 fmly) ⊘ in 43 bedrooms s £65-£98; d £75-£118 (incl. bkfst) **LB** **FACILITIES:** STV Free use of local health club ♫ Xmas **CONF:** Thtr 80 Class 60 Board 60 Del from £98 **SERVICES:** Lift **NOTES:** ⊘ in restaurant Civ Wed
CARDS:

★★★66% *The Gateway To Wales*
Welsh Rd, Sealand, Deeside CH5 2HX
☎ 01244 830332 📠 01244 836190
e-mail: mikesudbury@gatewaytowaleshotel.co.uk
web: www.gatewaytowaleshotel.co.uk
Dir: *4m NW via A548 towards Sealand and Queensferry*
A modern hotel well located for exploring the area, with easy access to Chester. Public areas include The Louis XVI lounge bar, Regency Room restaurant and well-equipped leisure facilities. Bedrooms are a good size and well designed, and the Imperial Suite can cater for conferences, wedding and exhibitions.
ROOMS: 39 en suite (18 GF) ⊘ in 20 bedrooms **FACILITIES:** Sauna Solarium Gym Jacuzzi Use of Indoor Bowls & Snooker Club **CONF:** Thtr 150 Class 50 Board 50 **SERVICES:** Lift **PARKING:** 60 **NOTES:** ⊘ in restaurant **CARDS:**

★★★62% Hoole Hall Hotel
corus hotels
Warrington Rd, Hoole Village CH2 3PD
☎ 0870 609 6126 📠 01244 320251
e-mail: hoolehall@corushotels.com
Dir: *M53 junct 12, A56 for 0.5m towards city centre, hotel 500yds on left*

Situated in extensive gardens on the outskirts of the city, part of this hotel dates back to the 18th century. It is now much extended and modernised, with smart, well-equipped bedrooms. Meetings, banquets and conferences are well catered for and ample car parking space is available.
ROOMS: 97 en suite (4 fmly) (33 GF) ⊘ in 48 bedrooms s £75-£100; d £75-£100 **LB** **FACILITIES:** STV Xmas **CONF:** Thtr 150 Class 40 Board 50 Del from £95 **SERVICES:** Lift **PARKING:** 200 **NOTES:** ⊘ in restaurant Civ Wed 140 **CARDS:**

Bad hair day?
Hairdryers in all rooms three stars and above

★★70% Dene
95 Hoole Rd CH2 3ND
☎ 01244 321165 📠 01244 350277
e-mail: info@denehotel.com
web: www.denehotel.com
Dir: *M53 junct 12 take A56 towards Chester. Hotel 1m from M53 next to Alexander Park*
This friendly hotel is now part of a small privately owned group and is located close to both the city centre and M53. The bedrooms are very well equipped and many are on ground floor level. Family rooms and interconnecting rooms are both available. As well as bar meals, an interesting choice of dishes is offered in the welcoming Franc's Brasserie, which is also very popular with locals.
ROOMS: 44 en suite 8 annexe en suite (5 fmly) ⊘ in 16 bedrooms s £49.50-£85; d £60-£95 (incl. bkfst) **LB** **FACILITIES:** STV Pool table **CONF:** Thtr 30 Class 12 Board 16 **PARKING:** 55 **NOTES:** ⊘ in restaurant **CARDS:**

★★69% Curzon
52/54 Hough Green CH4 8JQ
☎ 01244 678581 📠 01244 680866
e-mail: curzon.chester@virgin.net
web: www.curzonhotel.co.uk
Dir: *on A5104*

This smart period property is located in a predominantly residential suburb, close to the racecourse and a short walk from the city centre. Spacious bedrooms are comfortable, well-equipped and include family and four-poster rooms. The atmosphere is friendly and the dinner menu offers a creative choice of freshly prepared dishes.
ROOMS: 16 en suite (7 fmly) (1 GF) ⊘ in 12 bedrooms s £55-£65; d £75-£100 (incl. bkfst) **LB** **PARKING:** 20 **NOTES:** ⊘ in restaurant Closed 20 Dec-6 Jan **CARDS:**
See advert on opposite page

★★67% Brookside
Brook Ln CH2 2AN
☎ 01244 381943 📠 01244 651910
e-mail: info@brookside-hotel.co.uk
web: www.brookside-hotel.co.uk
Dir: *From city centre, take A5116 towards of Birkenhead/Ellesmere Port. Right at mini-rdbt into Brook Ln, hotel 200yds on left. From M53, take A56 then A41, left into Plas Newton Ln, right into Brook Ln, hotel on right*
This friendly hotel is conveniently located in a residential area just north of the city centre. The attractive public areas consist of a foyer lounge, a small bar and a split-level restaurant. Bedrooms are modern and well-equipped. Facilities include a meeting room for up to 20 people.
ROOMS: 26 en suite (9 fmly) (4 GF) s £32-£40; d £50-£58 (incl. bkfst) **LB** **FACILITIES:** Xmas **CONF:** Class 20 Board 12 **PARKING:** 20 **NOTES:** ⊘ in restaurant **CARDS:**

⌂ Comfort Inn Chester

74 Hoole Rd, Hoole CH2 3NK
☎ 01244 327542 📠 01244 344889
e-mail: comfortinn@chestergb.u.net.com
Dir: *1m from town centre on A56 on right back from main road*
This former private house has been extended to provide modern and well-equipped accommodation, including bedrooms on ground-floor level, some of which are adapted for guests with disabilities. The hotel shares the bar and restaurant facilities of its sister hotel The Dene, which is located across the road. The M53 motorway and city centre are both within easy reach.
ROOMS: 26 en suite 5 annexe en suite s £49.50-£65; d £57-£72
CONF: Thtr 40 Class 18 Board 18 Del £95

⌂ Innkeeper's Lodge Chester

Whitchurch Rd CH3 6AE
☎ 01244 332200 📠 01244 336415
www.innkeeperslodge.com
Dir: *on A41. 1m outside Chester towards Whitchurch*
Smart rooms meet essential business requirements but also have home comforts, and depending on location may well have meeting rooms and pub dining. Dining options generally include all-day menus plus the added advantage of breakfast.
ROOMS: 5 en suite 9 annexe en suite s £55; d £55

⌂ Innkeeper's Lodge Chester Northeast

Warrington Rd, Mickle Trafford CH2 4EX
☎ 01244 301391 📠 01244 302002
www.innkeeperslodge.com
Dir: *M53 junct 12, onto A56 signed Helsby, hotel 0.25m on right*
Smart rooms meet essential business requirements but also have home comforts, and depending on location may well have meeting rooms and pub dining. Dining options generally include all-day menus plus the added advantage of breakfast.
ROOMS: 36 en suite s £49-£55; d £49-£55 **CONF:** Thtr 20 Class 12 Board 20

⌂ Premier Lodge (Chester)

76 Liverpool Rd CH2 1AU
☎ 0870 9906470 📠 0870 9906471
web: www.premierlodge.com
Dir: *M53 junct 12 and at 1st rbt right for A56. At 2nd rbt right signed A41/Chester Zoo. At 1st set of lights left into Heath Rd then into Mill Ln. Continue under small railway bridge for Lodge on right*
High quality, modern, budget accommodation, ideal for families and business travellers. All rooms feature bath, power shower and satellite TV, and most have telephones / modem points. The adjacent bar and restaurant offers a wide and varied menu.
ROOMS: 31 en suite s £50; d £50 **CONF:** Class 17

⌂ Travel Inn Chester (Central)

Caldy Valley Rd CH3 5QJ
☎ 08701 977058 📠 01244 403687
Dir: *Exit M53(J12) and at rbt 3rd exit onto A56 (signed Chester). At rdt take 1st exit onto A41 (signed Whitchurch) then at 2nd rbt take 3rd exit onto Caldy Valley Rd (signed Huntingdon) for The Travel Inn on right.*
Travel Inn offers good-quality, value-for-money accommodation. Spacious, en suite rooms with bath and shower comfortably accommodate a family of up to two adults and two children (to age 15). The restaurant and bar offers a varied menu. For further details consult the Hotel Groups page.
ROOMS: 70 en suite s £45.95-£46.95; d £45.95-£46.95 **CONF:** Class 20

⊘ No smoking

CHESTERFIELD, Derbyshire Map 16 SK37

See also Renishaw

★★★64% *Sandpiper*

Sheffield Rd, Sheepbridge S41 9EH
☎ 01246 450550 📠 01246 452805
e-mail: sales.sandpiper@virgin.net
web: www.sandpiperhotel.co.uk
Dir: *M1 junct 29, A617 to Chesterfield then A61 to Sheffield. 1st exit take Dronfield Rd. Hotel 0.5m on left*

Conveniently situated for both the A61 and M1 and providing a good touring base, being just three miles from Chesterfield, this modern hotel offers comfortable and well-furnished bedrooms. Public areas are situated in a separate building across the car park, and include a cosy bar and open plan restaurant, serving a range of interesting and popular dishes.

ROOMS: 46 en suite (8 fmly) (18 GF) ⊘ in 32 bedrooms **FACILITIES:** STV **CONF:** Thtr 100 Class 35 Board 35 **SERVICES:** Lift **PARKING:** 120 **NOTES:** ⊘ in restaurant Civ Wed 90 **CARDS:**

See advert on page 167

★★71% Abbeydale

Cross St S40 4TD
☎ 01246 277849 📠 01246 558223
e-mail: abbeydale1ef@aol.com
web: www.abbeydalehotel.co.uk
Dir: *M1 junct 29 onto A619 towards Buxton. At B&Q island turn by KFC into Flojambe Rd. Over lights into West St, right into Cross St*

Conveniently situated in a quiet residential area of the town, this friendly hotel is run personally by the proprietors and offers excellent service and warm hospitality. Bedrooms are bright, fresh and well equipped. A short selection of skilfully prepared dishes is served in the dining room, adjacent to the cosy lounge and bar.

ROOMS: 11 en suite (1 fmly) ⊘ in all bedrooms s £43-£45; d £58-£60 (incl. bkfst) **LB** **PARKING:** 14 **NOTES:** ✈ ⊘ in restaurant RS 23 Dec-1 Jan **CARDS:**

⌂ Hotel Ibis Chesterfield

Lordsmill St S41 7RW
☎ 01246 221333 📠 01246 221444
e-mail: H3160@accor-hotels.com
Dir: *M1 junct 29, take A617 to Chesterfield. 2nd exit at 1st rdbt. Hotel situated on right at 2nd rdbt.*

Modern, budget hotel offering comfortable accommodation in bright and practical bedrooms. Breakfast is self-service and dinner is available in the restaurant. For further details, consult the Hotel Groups page.

ROOMS: 86 en suite s £43-£47; d £43-£47 **CONF:** Thtr 30 Class 16 Board 20

⌂ Travel Inn

Tapton Lock Hill, Off Rotherway S41 7NJ
☎ 08701 977060 📠 01246 560707
Dir: *adjacent to Tesco, A61 and A619 rdbt, 1m N of city centre*

Travel Inn offers good-quality, value-for-money accommodation. Spacious, en suite rooms with bath and shower comfortably accommodate a family of up to two adults and two children (to age 15). The restaurant and bar offers a varied menu. For further details consult the Hotel Groups page.

ROOMS: 60 en suite s £45.95-£46.95; d £45.95-£46.95 **CONF:** Thtr 25

⌂ Travelodge

Brimmington Rd, Inner Ring Rd, Wittington Moor S41 9BE
☎ 08700 850 950 📠 01246 455411
Dir: *on A61, N of town centre*

Travelodge offers good quality, good value, modern accommodation. Ideal for families, the spacious, en suite bedrooms include remote-control TV, tea and coffee-making facilities and luxury beds. Meals can be taken at the nearby family restaurant. For further details consult the Hotel Groups page.

ROOMS: 20 en suite s fr £25; d fr £25

CHESTER-LE-STREET, Co Durham Map 19 NZ25

⌂ Innkeeper's Lodge Durham North

Church Mouse, Great North Rd, Chester Moor DH2 3RJ
☎ 0191 389 2628
www.innkeeperslodge.com
Dir: *A1(M) junct 63, take A167 S Durham/Chester-Le-Street. Straight on at 3 rdbts, Inn on left.*

Smart rooms meet essential business requirements but also have home comforts, and depending on location may well have meeting rooms and pub dining. Dining options generally include all-day menus plus the added advantage of breakfast.

ROOMS: 21 en suite s £47.50-£52.50; d £47.50-£52.50

CHESTER MOTORWAY SERVICE AREA (M56), Cheshire Map 15 SJ47

⌂ Travel Inn (Chester East)

Junction 14 M56, Chester East Service Area, Elton CH2 4QZ
☎ 08701 977059 📠 01928 726721
Dir: *M56 junct 14/A5117 interchange*

Travel Inn offers good-quality, value-for-money accommodation. Spacious, en suite rooms with bath and shower comfortably accommodate a family of up to two adults and two children (to age 15). The restaurant and bar offers a varied menu. For further details consult the Hotel Groups page.

ROOMS: 40 en suite s £45.95-£46.95; d £45.95-£46.95 **CONF:** Thtr 20

CHICHESTER, West Sussex Map 05 SU80

★★★★74% ®® Marriott Goodwood Park Hotel & Country Club

PO18 0QB
☎ 0870 400 7225 📠 0870 400 7325
e-mail: reservations.goodwood@marriotthotels.co.uk
(For full entry see Goodwood)

★★★76% ® The Millstream

Bosham Ln PO18 8HL
☎ 01243 573234 📠 01243 573459
e-mail: info@millstream-hotel.co.uk
(For full entry see Bosham & advert on opposite page)

Packed in a hurry?
Ironing facilities should be available at all star levels, either in rooms or on request

★★★70% Crouchers Country Hotel & Restaurant

Birdham Rd PO20 7EH
☎ 01243 784995 📠 01243 539797
e-mail: crouchers@btconnect.com
Dir: *off A27 to A286, 1.5m from Chichester centre opposite Black Horse pub*

This friendly, family run hotel is situated in open countryside and within a short drive from the harbour. The comfortable and well-equipped rooms include some in a separate barn and coachhouse and the open-plan public areas enjoy a spacious and attractive aspect.

ROOMS: 18 en suite (1 fmly) (12 GF) ⊘ in 9 bedrooms
FACILITIES: STV Xmas **CONF:** BC Thtr 80 Class 80 Board 50
PARKING: 70 **NOTES:** ⊘ in restaurant
CARDS:

See advert on this page

★★★63% The Ship Hotel

North St PO19 1NH
☎ 01243 778000 📠 01243 788000
e-mail: booking.shiphotel@eldridge-pope.co.uk
web: www.shiphotel.com
Dir: *from A27, onto inner ring road to Northgate. At large Northgate rdbt left into North St, hotel on left*

This well-presented former Georgian hotel has a prime position at the top of North Street. The bar and brasserie offer a contemporary lively venue for refreshments and meals, with cocktails and a wine list to tempt. The hotel is in a good location for the Festival Theatre, so pre- and post-performance dinner offers are popular.

ROOMS: 36 en suite (2 fmly) ⊘ in all bedrooms s £79; d £99-£148 (incl. bkfst) **FACILITIES:** STV ch fac Xmas **CONF:** Thtr 70 Class 35 Board 30 **SERVICES:** Lift **PARKING:** 35
CARDS:

★★62% Suffolk House

THE INDEPENDENTS HOTEL ASSOCIATION

3 East Row PO19 1PD
☎ 01243 778899 📠 01243 787282
e-mail: admin@suffolkhousehotel.co.uk
Dir: *right off East St into Little London, follow into East Row, hotel on left*

This former Georgian residence is situated in a quiet side street, yet only a few minutes' walk from the town centre. Bedrooms vary in shape and size and offer a good level of comfort and facilities. There is also a small bar area, a pleasant patio and a peaceful dining room. Telephone beforehand for advice on parking.

ROOMS: 11 en suite (2 fmly) (4 GF) ⊘ in 3 bedrooms s £59-£74; d £95-£125 (incl. bkfst) **LB** **CONF:** Thtr 25 Class 12 Board 16
NOTES: ⊘ in restaurant **CARDS:**

⌂ Premier Lodge (Chichester)

PREMIER LODGE.com

Chichester Gate Leisure Park, Terminus Rd PO19 8EL
☎ 0870 9906578 📠 0870 9906579
web: www.premierlodge.com
Dir: *Exit A27 at Stockbridge rbt, taking exit towards city centre. Follow signs for Terminus Rd Industrial Estate. At 1st set of lights turn left, then left again at next set of lights into Chichester Gate Leisure Park. Lodge across car park on right*

High quality, modern, budget accommodation, ideal for families and business travellers. All rooms feature bath, power shower and satellite TV, and most have telephones / modem points. The adjacent bar and restaurant offers a wide and varied menu.

ROOMS: 83 en suite s £50; d £50

TV dinner?
Room service at three stars and above

CHIDDINGFOLD, Surrey Map 06 SU93

Restaurant with Rooms

The Swan Inn

Petworth Rd GU8 4TY
☎ 01428 682073
This charming inn with deceptively traditionally façade has been lovingly renovated inside to a contemporary style. Spacious bedrooms are well appointed with extensive modern facilities. The bar and restaurant are highlights where a wide range of homemade fare is served. The wine list and guest ales are a feature.
ROOMS: 11 rms (10 en suite) (1 fmly) in 9 bedrooms s £70-£90; d £70-£160 (incl. cont bkfst) **FACILITIES:** Putt green **SERVICES:** air con **PARKING:** 25 **NOTES:** in restaurant **CARDS:**

CHIDEOCK, Dorset Map 04 SY49

★★71% Chideock House

Main St DT6 6JN
☎ 01297 489242 01297 489184
e-mail: aa@chideockhousehotel.com
web: www.chideockhousehotel.com
Dir: *on A35 between Lyme Regis and Bridport, in centre of Chideock*
This delightful, partly thatched, house dates back to the 15th century and retains many original features, such as the beams and fireplaces. Relaxed and quietly attentive, the service is genuinely friendly and welcoming. Lots of thoughtful extras are provided in the bedrooms. An interesting and innovative menu featuring local produce is served in the comfortable restaurant.
ROOMS: 9 rms (8 en suite) s £70-£85; d £75-£85 (incl. bkfst) **LB** **FACILITIES:** Xmas **PARKING:** 20 **NOTES:** No children 12yrs in restaurant RS 3 Jan-5 Feb **CARDS:**

CHIEVELEY, Berkshire Map 05 SU47

Restaurant with Rooms

The Crab at Chieveley

Wantage Rd RG20 8UE
☎ 01635 247550 01635 247440
e-mail: info@crabatchieveley.com
Dir: *M4 junct 13 N A34 to Oxford. 1st left to Chieveley after Red Lion. Left at school road. After 1.5m at T junct turn right. Hotel at the top of the hill.*
The individually themed bedrooms at this former pub have been appointed to a very high standard and include a full range of modern amenities. Ground-floor rooms have a small private patio area complete with a hot tub. The restaurant is divided into a modern brasserie area with a bar and a more formal dining area. Both offer an extensive and award-winning range of dishes and specialise in fish and seafood.
AA Seafish Restaurant of the Year 2004-5.
ROOMS: 10 en suite (6 GF) in all bedrooms s £100-£120; d £140-£150 (incl. bkfst) **LB** **FACILITIES:** STV Sauna Gym Jacuzzi Hot Tub Xmas **CONF:** Thtr 20 Class 20 Board 20 Del from £130 **PARKING:** 80 **NOTES:** in restaurant **CARDS:**

CHILDER THORNTON, Cheshire Map 15 SJ37

Travel Inn (Wirral South)

New Chester Rd CH66 1QW
☎ 08701 977275 0151 347 1401
Dir: *on A41, near M53 (J5), towards Chester. Travel Inn on right, same entrance as Burleydam Garden Centre*
Travel Inn offers good-quality, value-for-money accommodation. Spacious, en suite rooms with bath and shower comfortably accommodate a family of up to two adults and two children (to age 15). The restaurant and bar offers a varied menu. For further details consult the Hotel Groups page.
ROOMS: 31 en suite s £45.95-£46.95; d £45.95-£46.95 **CONF:** Thtr 20

CHIPPENHAM, Wiltshire Map 04 ST97

★★★72% Angel Hotel

Market Place SN15 3HD
☎ 01249 652615 01249 443210
e-mail: reception@angelhotelchippenham.co.uk
web: www.angelhotelchippenham.co.uk
Dir: *follow tourist signs for Bowood House. Under railway arch, follow 'Borough Parade Parking' signs. Hotel next to car park*
These impressive buildings make up a smart, comfortable hotel. The well-equipped bedrooms vary from the main house, where character is the key, to the smart executive-style, courtyard rooms. The lounge and restaurant are bright and modern where in addition to the imaginative carte, an all-day menu is served.
ROOMS: 15 en suite 35 annexe en suite (3 fmly) (12 GF) in 29 bedrooms s £70.50-£126; d £85.50-£147 **LB** **FACILITIES:** STV Gym **CONF:** Thtr 100 Class 50 Board 50 Del from £135 **PARKING:** 50 **CARDS:**

★★★72% Stanton Manor Country House Hotel

SN14 6DQ
☎ 01666 837552 01666 837022
e-mail: reception@stantonmanor.co.uk
(For full entry see Stanton St Quintin)

Travel Inn

Cepen Park, West Cepen Way SN14 6UZ
☎ 08701 977061 01249 461359
Dir: *M4 junct 17, take A350 towards Chippenham. Travel Inn is at 1st main rdbt at gateway to Chippenham*
Travel Inn offers good-quality, value-for-money accommodation. Spacious, en suite rooms with bath and shower comfortably accommodate a family of up to two adults and two children (to age 15). The restaurant and bar offers a varied menu. For further details consult the Hotel Groups page.
ROOMS: 79 en suite s £45.95-£46.95; d £45.95-£46.95

CHIPPERFIELD, Hertfordshire Map 06 TL00

★★72% The Two Brewers

The Common WD4 9BS
☎ 01923 265266 01923 261884
e-mail: twobrewers.hotel@spiritgroup.com
web: www.twobrewers.com
Dir: *left in centre of village overlooking common*
This 16th-century inn retains much of its old-world charm while providing modern comforts and amenities. The spacious bedrooms are tastefully furnished and decorated, offering a comprehensive range of in-room facilities. The bar, popular with

continued

locals, is the focal point of the hotel, which serves enjoyable pub-style meals.

ROOMS: 20 en suite ⊗ in 10 bedrooms s £70-£100; d £70-£100 (incl. bkfst) **LB** **FACILITIES:** STV **CONF:** Board 15 **PARKING:** 25 **NOTES:** ✗ **CARDS:**

CHIPPING CAMPDEN, Gloucestershire Map 10 SP13

Top 200 – Hotel

★★★ ◎◎ Cotswold House

The Square GL55 6AN
☎ 01386 840330 📠 01386 840310
e-mail: reception@cotswoldhouse.com
web: www.cotswoldhouse.com

Dir: *A44 take B4081 to Chipping Campden. Right at T-junct into High St. House in The Square*

Relaxation is inevitable at this mellow Cotswold stone house, set in the centre of the town. Bedrooms, including spacious suites in the courtyard, are impressively individual and offer a beguiling blend of style, quality and comfort. The newly refurbished Garden restaurant is a stunning venue to sample accomplished and imaginative cuisine, with local produce utilised wherever possible. Alternatively, Hicks Brasserie and Bar provides a more informal dining experience.

ROOMS: 20 en suite ⊗ in 18 bedrooms s fr £115; d fr £175 (incl. bkfst) **LB** **FACILITIES:** STV Gym Access to local Sports Centre ch fac Xmas **CONF:** BC Thtr 50 Class 30 Board 30 Del from £225 **PARKING:** 20 **NOTES:** ⊗ in restaurant Civ Wed 66 **CARDS:**

★★★72% *Seymour House*

High St GL55 6AH
☎ 01386 840429 📠 01386 840369
e-mail: enquiry@seymourhousehotel.com
web: www.seymourhousehotel.com

Dir: *Hotel in middle of High St opposite Lloyds Bank*

Centrally located in one of the most idyllic villages in England, this

continued

lovely Cotswold property dates back to the early 18th century. Bedrooms vary in size and style, and all offer good levels of comfort and individuality. Public rooms, including the elegant drawing room, the Vinery restaurant and separate bar, reflect the originality, charm and character that features throughout.

ROOMS: 11 en suite 5 annexe en suite **FACILITIES:** STV ♫ **CONF:** Thtr 65 Class 26 Board 30 **PARKING:** 28 **NOTES:** ✗ ⊗ in restaurant Civ Wed 65 **CARDS:**

★★★72% ◎ Three Ways House

Mickleton GL55 6SB
☎ 01386 438429 📠 01386 438118
e-mail: threeways@puddingclub.com

Dir: *in centre of Mickleton, on B4632 Stratford-upon-Avon to Broadway Rd*

Built in 1870, this charming hotel has welcomed guests for over 100 years and is home to the world famous Pudding Club, formed in 1985 to promote traditional English puddings. Individuality is a hallmark here, as reflected in a number of bedrooms which have

continued on p172

CHIPPING CAMPDEN, continued

been styled according to a pudding theme. Public areas are stylish and include the air-conditioned restaurant, lounges and meeting rooms.
ROOMS: 48 en suite (7 fmly) (14 GF) s £72-£85; d £99-£140 (incl. bkfst) **LB** **FACILITIES:** ♫ ch fac Xmas **CONF:** Thtr 100 Class 40 Board 35 Del £140 **SERVICES:** Lift **PARKING:** 37 **NOTES:** ⊗ in restaurant Civ Wed 65 **CARDS:**

★★★69% Noel Arms
High St GL55 6AT
☎ 01386 840317 📠 01386 841136
e-mail: info@noelarmshotel.info
Dir: *off A44 onto B4081 to Chipping Campden, 1st right down hill into town. Hotel on right opposite Market Hall*
This historic 14th-century hotel has a wealth of character and charm, and retains some original features. Bedrooms are very individual in style, but all have high levels of comfort and interesting interior design. Such distinctiveness is also evident throughout the public areas, which include the popular bar, conservatory lounge and attractive restaurant.
ROOMS: 26 en suite (1 fmly) s £90-£110; d £120-£159 (incl. bkfst) **LB** **FACILITIES:** Xmas **CONF:** Thtr 50 Class 10 Board 25 Del from £140 **PARKING:** 30 **NOTES:** ⊗ in restaurant Civ Wed 45
CARDS:

CHITTLEHAMHOLT, Devon — Map 03 SS62

★★★67% Highbullen
EX37 9HD
☎ 01769 540561 📠 01769 540492
e-mail: highbullen@sosi.net
Dir: *M5 junct 27 onto A361 to South Molton, then B3226 Crediton Rd. After 5.2m turn right to Chittlehamholt. Hotel 0.5m beyond village*
Set in magnificent parkland with extensive views and an 18-hole golf course, Highbullen also offers a magnificent new leisure complex with its own brasserie restaurant. The range of bedrooms, situated in the main house and in converted buildings, are all spacious and comfortable. A more formal dinner operation is served in the restaurant, which looks out over the impressive country views.
ROOMS: 12 en suite 25 annexe en suite s £78-£120; d £95-£110 (incl. cont bkfst & dinner) **LB** **FACILITIES:** 18 Fishing Squash Snooker Sauna Solarium Gym Putt green Hairdressing Beauty Massage **CONF:** Board 20 **PARKING:** 60 **NOTES:** No children 8yrs ⊗ in restaurant **CARDS:**

CHORLEY, Lancashire — Map 15 SD51

★★★69% Park Hall
Park Hall Rd, Charnock Richard PR7 5LP
☎ 01257 455000 📠 01257 451838
e-mail: conference@parkhall-hotel.co.uk
Dir: *between Preston & Wigan, signed from M6/J27 northbound and J28 southbound, or M61 J8.*
The popular Camelot Theme Park is just a short stroll across the grounds from this hotel, which provides a choice of well-equipped bedrooms ranging from contemporary rooms to themed cottage-style accommodation, including Cadbury-themed rooms. The Park View Restaurant has light modern décor; less formal eating is available in the lounge bar. Packages including entrance to the theme park are available.
ROOMS: 56 en suite 84 annexe en suite (52 fmly) (84 GF) ⊗ in 34 bedrooms s £89-£93; d £138-£146 (incl. bkfst & dinner) **LB** **FACILITIES:** **Spa** STV supervised Sauna Solarium Gym Jacuzzi Steam room, air-conditioned Gymnasium Xmas **CONF:** Thtr 700 Class 240 Board 40 Del from £93 **SERVICES:** Lift **PARKING:** 2600 **NOTES:** ⊗ in restaurant Civ Wed 150
CARDS:

See advert under PRESTON

Premier Lodge (Chorley)

Malthouse Farm, Moss Ln, Whittle le Woods PR6 8AB
☎ 0870 9906376 📠 0870 9906377
e-mail: malthousefarm20@hotmail.com
web: www.premierlodge.com
Dir: *M6 junct 29 join M65. Exit at junct 2, M61 (Manchester). Exit M61 at junct 8, take M674 (Wheelton), then 400yds on left into Moss Ln*
High quality, modern, budget accommodation, ideal for families and business travellers. All rooms feature bath, power shower and satellite TV, and most have telephones / modem points. The adjacent bar and restaurant offers a wide and varied menu.
ROOMS: 81 en suite s £44; d £44 **CONF:** Board 15

Premier Lodge (Chorley South)
Bolton Rd PR7 4AB
☎ 0870 9906604 📠 0870 9906605
web: www.premierlodge.com
Dir: *From north, exit M61 junct 8 onto A6 to Chorley. From south, exit M6 junct 27, follow signs for Standish. Turn left onto A5106 to Chorley then A6 towards Preston. The Lodge 0.5m on right*
High quality, modern, budget accommodation, ideal for families and business travellers. All rooms feature bath, power shower and satellite TV, and most have telephones / modem points. The adjacent bar and restaurant offers a wide and varied menu.
ROOMS: 29 en suite s £44; d £44 **CONF:** Board 12

Travelodge Preston Chorley

Preston Rd, Clayton-le-Woods PR6 7JB
☎ 08700 850 950 📠 01772 311963
Dir: *from M6 junct 28 take B5256 for 2m, next to Halfway House pub*
Travelodge offers good quality, good value, modern accommodation. Ideal for families, the spacious, en suite bedrooms include remote-control TV, tea and coffee-making facilities and luxury beds. Meals can be taken at the nearby family restaurant. For further details consult the Hotel Groups page.
ROOMS: 40 en suite s fr £25; d fr £25

CHRISTCHURCH, Dorset — Map 05 SZ19

★★★74% Waterford Lodge
87 Bure Ln, Friars Cliff BH23 4DN
☎ 01425 272948 & 278801 📠 01425 279130
e-mail: waterford@bestwestern.co.uk
web: www.waterfordlodge.com
Dir: *from A35 take A337 towards Highcliffe. Take right turn from rdbt signed Mudeford. Hotel 0.5m on left*
Peacefully located within easy reach of Christchurch, this welcoming hotel is popular with business guests as well as holidaymakers. It offers attractive, spacious and well-equipped bedrooms, a

continued

comfortable bar lounge overlooking the gardens and a pleasant restaurant serving carefully prepared, award-winning cuisine.

ROOMS: 18 en suite (2 fmly) (3 GF) ⊗ in 15 bedrooms s fr £79; d fr £108 (incl. bkfst) **LB** **FACILITIES:** STV Xmas **CONF:** Thtr 100 Class 48 Board 36 Del from £115 **PARKING:** 38 **NOTES:** No children 7yrs ⊗ in restaurant **CARDS:**

★★★69% The Avonmouth

95 Mudeford BH23 3NT
☎ 01202 483434 01202 479004
e-mail: info@avonmouth-hotel.co.uk
Dir: *A35 to Christchurch from Lyndhurst. Left at rdbt on A337 to Highcliffe. Right at rdbt, hotel 1.5m on left*

In a superb location alongside Mudeford Quay, this friendly hotel offers a variety of bedrooms including smart garden rooms with their own small patios. Several bedrooms in the main house overlook the quay and have private balconies. Modern facilities and décor enhance the overall comfort. Enjoyable cuisine is served in the pleasant restaurant.
ROOMS: 26 en suite 14 annexe en suite (7 fmly) (14 GF) ⊗ in 20 bedrooms s £79-£104; d £118-£168 (incl. bkfst & dinner) **LB** **FACILITIES:** STV Xmas **CONF:** Thtr 70 Class 20 Board 24 Del from £100 **PARKING:** 80 **NOTES:** ⊗ in restaurant Civ Wed 60 **CARDS:**

Travel Inn (Christchurch East)

Somerford Rd BH23 3QG
☎ 08701 977062 01202 474939
Dir: *from M27 take A337 to Lyndhurst, then A35 to Christchurch. On B3059 rdbt towards Somerford*
Travel Inn offers good-quality, value-for-money accommodation. Spacious, en suite rooms with bath and shower comfortably accommodate a family of up to two adults and two children (to age 15). The restaurant and bar offers a varied menu. For further details consult the Hotel Groups page.
ROOMS: 70 en suite s £45.95-£46.95; d £45.95-£46.95

Travel Inn (Christchurch West)

Barrack Rd BH23 2BN
☎ 08701 977063 01202 483453
Dir: *from A338 take A3060 towards Christchurch. Turn left onto A35 Travel Inn on right*
Travel Inn offers good-quality, value-for-money accommodation. Spacious, en suite rooms with bath and shower comfortably accommodate a family of up to two adults and two children (to age 15). The restaurant and bar offers a varied menu. For further details consult the Hotel Groups page.
ROOMS: 42 en suite s £45.95-£46.95; d £45.95-£46.95

CHURCHILL, Somerset — Map 04 ST46

★★71% Winston Manor

Bristol Rd BS25 5NL
☎ 01934 852348 01934 852033
Dir: *On A38 100yds N of junct with A368 (Bath to Weston-Super-Mare)*
Under new ownership this small hotel is run in a relaxed manner by resident proprietors. It is conveniently located for Bristol International Airport and many local attractions including Cheddar Caves and Gorge. Bedrooms, including several on the ground floor, are neatly decorated and well-equipped. Menus are based on an interesting selection of home cooked dishes.
ROOMS: 14 en suite (1 fmly) (4 GF) ⊗ in all bedrooms s fr £52; d £65-£85 (incl. bkfst) **LB** **CONF:** Class 20 Board 25 **PARKING:** 20 **NOTES:** ⊗ in restaurant **CARDS:**

CHURCH STRETTON, Shropshire — Map 15 SO49

★★★68% Stretton Hall Hotel

THE INDEPENDENTS

All Stretton SY6 6HG
☎ 01694 723224 01694 724365
e-mail: aa@strettonhall.co.uk
Dir: *from Shrewsbury, on A49, right onto B4370 signed All Stretton. Hotel 1m on left opposite The Yew Tree pub*
This fine 18th-century country house stands in spacious gardens. Original oak panelling features throughout the lounge bar, lounge and halls. Bedrooms are traditionally furnished and have modern facilities. Family and four-poster rooms are available and the restaurant has been tastefully refurbished.
ROOMS: 12 en suite (1 fmly) s £50-£115; d £80-£130 (incl. bkfst) **LB** **FACILITIES:** ch fac Xmas **CONF:** BC Thtr 70 Class 24 Board 18 Del from £90 **PARKING:** 70 **NOTES:** ⊗ in restaurant Civ Wed 60 **CARDS:**

★★70% Mynd House

Ludlow Rd, Little Stretton SY6 6RB
☎ 01694 722212
e-mail: info@myndhouse.co.uk
Dir: *A49 onto B4370, signed Little Stretton. Hotel 0.75m on left beyond Ragleth Inn*
This large Edwardian house is situated in the sleepy hamlet of Little Stretton, and is reached via a steep driveway. Privately owned and personally run, it provides well-equipped bedrooms which have many thoughtful extras. Public areas include a comfortable lounge, a pleasant bar and a traditional-style dining room.
ROOMS: 7 en suite (2 fmly) ⊗ in all bedrooms s £45-£50; d £60-£120 (incl. bkfst) **LB** **PARKING:** 8 **NOTES:** ⊗ in restaurant RS mid Nov-mid Feb **CARDS:**

AA Rosette Award for culinary excellence

CHURCH STRETTON, continued

★★65% *Longmynd Hotel*
Cunnery Rd SY6 6AG
☎ 01694 722244 📠 01694 722718
e-mail: info@longmynd.co.uk
Dir: *A49 into Church Stretton town centre along Sandford Ave, left at Lloyds TSB, over mini rdbt, 1st right into Cunnery Rd up hill, hotel at top on left.*
This family-run hotel overlooks this country town and the views from many of the rooms are breathtaking. Bedrooms are generally spacious and comfortable, and facilities include two restaurants, the Pavilion and the Alpine, as well as comfortable lounges. The hotel is set in attractive gardens.
ROOMS: 50 en suite (9 fmly) ⊗ in all bedrooms **FACILITIES:** Sauna Putt green Pitch and putt course **CONF:** Thtr 100 Class 50 Board 40 **SERVICES:** Lift **PARKING:** 100 **NOTES:** ⊗ in restaurant Civ Wed 100 **CARDS:**

CHURT, Surrey Map 05 SU83

★★★73% *Frensham Pond Hotel*
Best Western
Bacon Ln GU10 2QB
☎ 01252 795161 📠 01252 792631
e-mail: frenshampond@bestwestern.co.uk
web: www.frenshampondhotel.co.uk
Dir: *A3 onto A287. 4m left at 'Beware Horses' sign. Hotel 0.25m*

This 15th-century house occupies a superb location on the edge of Frensham Pond. Bedrooms are mostly spacious and there are also some pleasant garden suites available. Public areas are light and well-appointed and a good range of leisure facilities is offered, including a squash court.
ROOMS: 39 en suite 12 annexe en suite ⊗ in 15 bedrooms **FACILITIES:** STV Squash Sauna Solarium Gym Jacuzzi Steam room **CONF:** Thtr 120 Class 45 Board 40 **PARKING:** 120 **NOTES:** ⊗ in restaurant **CARDS:**

See advert under FARNHAM

Packed in a hurry?
Ironing facilities should be available at all star levels, either in rooms or on request

★★67% Pride of the Valley
THE INDEPENDENTS
Jumps Rd GU10 2LH
☎ 01428 605799 📠 01428 605875
e-mail: rpov@aol.com
Dir: *off A3 at Hindhead traffic lights for Farnham. Follow Tilford signs and in 0.5m turn right. Hotel 2m on left*
This delightful hotel is peacefully located in the Surrey countryside and boasts stylish, individually designed bedrooms. Some rooms are a little compact but all are well equipped and boast modern bathrooms. Guests have the choice of dining in the smart Dragon Bar or the more formal, panelled restaurant where imaginative modern French cuisine is a highlight.

ROOMS: 14 en suite (1 fmly) ⊗ in all bedrooms s fr £85; d fr £105 (incl. bkfst) **LB** **FACILITIES: Spa** Jacuzzi Xmas **PARKING:** 85 **NOTES:** **CARDS:**

CIRENCESTER, Gloucestershire Map 05 SP00

★★★70% Stratton House
Forestdale Hotels
Gloucester Rd GL7 2LE
☎ 01285 651761 📠 01285 640024
e-mail: stratton.house@forestdale.com
Dir: *M4 junct 15, A419 to Cirencester. Hotel on left on A417 or M5 junct 11 to Cheltenham onto B4070 to A417. Hotel on right*
This attractive 17th-century manor house is quietly situated about half a mile from the town centre. Bedrooms are well presented, and spacious premier rooms are available. The comfortable drawing rooms and restaurant have views over well-tended gardens: the perfect place to enjoy pre-dinner drinks on a summer evening.
ROOMS: 41 en suite (10 GF) ⊗ in 19 bedrooms s fr £110; d fr £125 (incl. bkfst) **LB** **FACILITIES:** Xmas **CONF:** Thtr 150 Class 50 Board 40 Del from £125 **PARKING:** 100 **NOTES:** ⊗ in restaurant Civ Wed **CARDS:**

★★★66% The Crown of Crucis
Ampney Crucis GL7 5RS
☎ 01285 851806 📠 01285 851735
e-mail: info@thecrownofcrucis.co.uk
web: www.thecrownofcrucis.co.uk
Dir: *A417 to Fairford, hotel 2.5m on left*
This delightful hotel consists of two buildings; one a 16th-century coaching inn, which now houses the bar and restaurant, and a more modern bedroom block which surrounds a courtyard. Rooms are attractively appointed and offer modern facilities; the restaurant serves a range of imaginative dishes.
ROOMS: 25 en suite (2 fmly) (13 GF) ⊗ in 10 bedrooms s fr £67; d £75-£95 (incl. bkfst) **LB** **FACILITIES:** Free membership of local leisure centre **CONF:** Thtr 80 Class 40 Board 25 Del from £115 **PARKING:** 82 **NOTES:** ⊗ in restaurant Closed 25-26 Dec & 1 Jan Civ Wed 50 **CARDS:**

★★★65% Fleece Hotel
THE INDEPENDENTS
Market Place GL7 2NZ
☎ 01285 658507 📠 01285 651017
e-mail: relax@fleecehotel.co.uk
web: www.fleecehotel.co.uk
Dir: *A417/A419 Burford Rd junct, follow signs for town centre. Right at lights into 'The Waterloo', hotel car park 250yds on left*
This old town-centre coaching inn, which dates back to the Tudor period, retains many original features such as flagstone floors and oak beams. Well-equipped bedrooms vary in size and shape, all

continued

offering good levels of comfort and plenty of character. The bar lounge is a popular venue for morning coffee, and the stylish restaurant offers a range of dishes in an informal and convivial atmosphere.
ROOMS: 28 en suite (3 fmly) (4 GF) ⊗ in 3 bedrooms s £49.50-£110; d £79-£119 (incl. bkfst) **LB** **FACILITIES:** Xmas **PARKING:** 10
NOTES: ⊗ in restaurant **CARDS:**

⌂ Travelodge
Hare Bushes, Burford Rd GL7 5DS
☎ 08700 850 950 ▤ 01285 655290
Travelodge offers good quality, good value, modern accommodation. Ideal for families, the spacious, en suite bedrooms include remote-control TV, tea and coffee-making facilities and luxury beds. Meals can be taken at the nearby family restaurant. For further details consult the Hotel Groups page.
ROOMS: 43 en suite s fr £25; d fr £25

CLACKET LANE MOTORWAY SERVICE AREA (M25), Surrey — Map 06 TQ45

⌂ Travel Inn (Westerham)
TN16 2ER
☎ 08701 977265 ▤ 01959 561311

Dir: M25 between junct 5 & 6
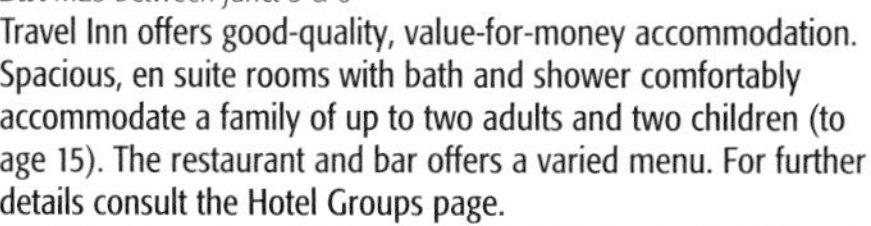
Travel Inn offers good-quality, value-for-money accommodation. Spacious, en suite rooms with bath and shower comfortably accommodate a family of up to two adults and two children (to age 15). The restaurant and bar offers a varied menu. For further details consult the Hotel Groups page.
ROOMS: 58 en suite s £49.95-£54.95; d £49.95-£54.95 **CONF:** Thtr 50 Board 30

CLACTON-ON-SEA, Essex — Map 07 TM11
See also Weeley

★★67% Esplanade Hotel
27-29 Marine Pde East CO15 1UU
☎ 01255 220450 ▤ 01255 221800
e-mail: mjs@esplanadehoteluk.com
web: www.esplanadehoteluk.com
Dir: from A133 to Clacton-on-Sea, follow seafront signs. At seafront turn right and hotel on right in 50yds
Situated in a prominent position on the seafront overlooking the pier and just a short walk from the town centre. Bedrooms vary in size and style and are pleasantly decorated and well equipped; some rooms have lovely sea views. Public rooms include a comfortable lounge bar and Coasters Restaurant.
ROOMS: 29 en suite (2 fmly) s £37-£57; d £65-£75 (incl. bkfst) **LB**
FACILITIES: Xmas **CONF:** BC Thtr 80 Class 50 Board 50 **PARKING:** 13
NOTES: ⊗ in restaurant Civ Wed 85
CARDS:

★73% Chudleigh
13 Agate Rd, Marine Pde West CO15 1RA
☎ 01255 425407 ▤ 01255 470280
e-mail: reception@chudleighhotel.com
Dir: follow town centre, seafront and pier signs. Right at seafront, right into Agate Rd after traffic lights at the pier
Expect a warm welcome from the caring hosts at this small, privately owned hotel. It is situated just off the seafront and within easy walking distance of the town centre and pier. Bedrooms are generally quite spacious; each is attractively decorated and equipped with many thoughtful touches. Public rooms include a

continued

cosy lounge and a smart dining room in which freshly prepared breakfasts are served.
ROOMS: 10 en suite (2 fmly) (2 GF) ⊗ in 3 bedrooms s £39.50; d £57 (incl. bkfst) **LB** **PARKING:** 7 **NOTES:** ⊗ in restaurant RS Oct-Mar
CARDS:

CLAVERDON, Warwickshire — Map 10 SP16

★★★★74% ◎◎ Ardencote Manor Hotel, Country Club & Spa
Lye Green Rd CV35 8LS
☎ 01926 843111 ▤ 01926 842646
e-mail: hotel@ardencote.com
web: www.ardencote.com
Dir: in centre of Claverdon, follow Shrewley signs off A4189. Hotel 0.5m on right

Originally built as a gentleman's residence around 1860, this hotel is set in 45 acres of landscaped grounds. Public rooms include a

continued on p176

CLAVERDON, continued

choice of lounge areas, a cocktail bar and conservatory breakfast room. Main meals are served in the Lodge, a separate building that sits on the lake. An extensive range of leisure and conference facilities is provided and bedrooms are smartly decorated and tastefully furnished.
ROOMS: 75 en suite (3 fmly) (11 GF) ⊗ in 49 bedrooms s fr £105; d fr £150 (incl. bkfst) **LB** **FACILITIES: Spa** STV ⛳ 9 Squash Sauna Solarium Gym Putt green Jacuzzi Ardencote Spa Xmas **CONF:** Thtr 250 Class 100 Board 50 Del from £115 **SERVICES:** Lift air con **PARKING:** 150 **NOTES:** ⊗ in restaurant Civ Wed 150 **CARDS:**

See advert under WARWICK

CLEARWELL, Gloucestershire — Map 04 SO50

★★★65% The Wyndham Arms
GL16 8JT
☎ 01594 833666 📠 01594 836450
e-mail: nigel@thewyndhamhotel.co.uk
Dir: *off B4228, in centre of village on B4231*

The history of this charming village inn can be traced back over 600 years. It has exposed stone walls, original beams and an impressive inglenook fireplace in the friendly bar. Most bedrooms are in a modern extension, whilst rooms in the main house are more traditional in style. A range of dishes is offered in the bar or restaurant.
ROOMS: 6 en suite 12 annexe en suite (3 fmly) (6 GF) ⊗ in 4 bedrooms s £35-£65; d £65-£110 (incl. bkfst) **LB** **FACILITIES:** ch fac Xmas **CONF:** Thtr 56 Class 30 Board 22 Del from £82.50 **PARKING:** 52 **NOTES:** ⊗ in restaurant Civ Wed 80 **CARDS:**

Town House Hotel
Country House Hotel
Travel Accommodation

★★74% Tudor Farmhouse Hotel & Restaurant
High St GL16 8JS
☎ 01594 833046 📠 01594 837093
e-mail: info@tudorfarmhousehotel.co.uk
web: www.tudorfarmhousehotel.co.uk
Dir: *off A4136 onto B4228, through Coleford, turn right into Clearwell, hotel on right just before War Memorial Cross*

Dating from the 13th century, this idyllic former farmhouse retains a host of original features including exposed stonework, oak beams, wall panelling and wonderful inglenook fireplaces. Bedrooms have great individuality and style and are located either within the main house, or in converted buildings within the grounds. Creative menus offer quality cuisine, served in the intimate, candlelit restaurant.

ROOMS: 6 en suite 16 annexe en suite (2 fmly) (7 GF) ⊗ in 19 bedrooms s £55; d £60-£80 (incl. bkfst) **LB** **FACILITIES:** STV **CONF:** Thtr 30 Class 20 Board 12 Del from £80 **PARKING:** 30 **NOTES:** ⊗ in restaurant Closed 24-27 Dec **CARDS:**

CLEATOR, Cumbria — Map 18 NY01

★★★76% Ennerdale Country House
CA23 3DT
☎ 01946 813907 📠 01946 815260
e-mail: ennerdale@bestwestern.co.uk
Dir: *A5086 to Egremont, approx 12m to Cleator Moor. A5086 for 1m to Cleator*

This fine Grade II listed building lies on the edge of the village and is backed by landscaped gardens. Impressive bedrooms, including split-level suites and four-poster rooms, are richly furnished, smartly decorated and offer an amazing array of facilities. Attractive public areas include an elegant restaurant, an inviting lounge and an American-theme bar which offers a good range of bar meals.
ROOMS: 30 en suite (4 fmly) ⊗ in 4 bedrooms s £99-£129; d £99-£129 (incl. bkfst) **LB** **FACILITIES:** STV Xmas **CONF:** Thtr 150 Class 100 Board 40 Del from £120 **PARKING:** 65 **NOTES:** ⊗ in restaurant Civ Wed **CARDS:**

CLECKHEATON, West Yorkshire — Map 19 SE12

★★★64% The Whitcliffe
Prospect Rd BD19 3HD
☎ 01274 873022 📠 01274 870376
e-mail: info@thewhitcliffehotel.co.uk
Dir: *M62 junct 26, follow A638 to Dewsbury, over 1st lights, right into Mount St, to T-junct, right then 1st left*

This popular commercial hotel offers comfortable, well-equipped accommodation. Spacious public areas provide a variety of amenities, including several meeting rooms, two attractive bars, and the popular Flickers Brasserie.
ROOMS: 34 en suite 6 annexe en suite (1 fmly) (6 GF) ⊗ in 17 bedrooms s £36-£49; d £49.50-£59.50 (incl. bkfst) **LB** **FACILITIES:** STV Xmas **CONF:** Thtr 100 Class 60 Board 30 Del from £49 **PARKING:** 150 **NOTES:** ⊗ in restaurant **CARDS:**

Travel Inn (Bradford South)

Whitehall Rd BD19 6HG
☎ 08701 977037 📠 01274 855901
Dir: *on A58 at junction with M62 & M606*

Travel Inn offers good-quality, value-for-money accommodation. Spacious, en suite rooms with bath and shower comfortably accommodate a family of up to two adults and two children (to age 15). The restaurant and bar offers a varied menu. For further details consult the Hotel Groups page.
ROOMS: 40 en suite s £45.95-£46.95; d £45.95-£46.95

CLEETHORPES, Lincolnshire Map 17 TA30

★★★69% Kingsway

Kingsway DN35 0AE
☎ 01472 601122 01472 601381
e-mail: reception@kingsway-hotel.com
web: www.kingsway-hotel.com
Dir: *leave A180 at Grimsby, to Cleethorpes seafront. Hotel at Kingsway and Queen Parade junct (A1098)*

This seafront hotel has been in the same family for four generations and continues to provide traditional comfort and friendly service. The lounges are comfortable and good food is served in the pleasant dining room. Most of the bedrooms are comfortably proportioned, and all are bright and pleasantly furnished.

ROOMS: 49 en suite in 10 bedrooms s £51-£78; d £86-£95 (incl. bkfst) **LB** **FACILITIES:** STV **CONF:** Thtr 22 Board 18 Del from £96 **SERVICES:** Lift **PARKING:** 50 **NOTES:** No children 5yrs Closed 25-26 Dec **CARDS:**

CLEVEDON, Somerset Map 04 ST47

★★★67% Walton Park

Best Western

Wellington Ter BS21 7BL
☎ 01275 874253 01275 343577
e-mail: waltonpark@aol.com
Dir: *M5 junct 20, signs for seafront. Stay on coast road, past pier into Wellington Terrace, hotel on left*

Quietly located with spectacular views across the Bristol Channel to Wales, this popular Victorian hotel offers a relaxed atmosphere. Bedrooms are well decorated and equipped to meet the demands of both business and leisure guests. In the comfortable restaurant, a high standard of home-cooked food is served and lighter meals are available in the convivial bar at lunchtime.

ROOMS: 40 en suite (4 fmly) in 12 bedrooms s £48-£79; d £83-£99 (incl. bkfst) **LB** **FACILITIES:** STV **CONF:** Thtr 120 Class 80 Board 80 **SERVICES:** Lift **PARKING:** 50 **NOTES:** Civ Wed 150 **CARDS:**

CLIMPING, West Sussex Map 06 SU90

★★★78% Bailiffscourt Hotel & Health Spa

Pride of Britain Hotels

Climping St BN17 5RW
☎ 01903 723511 01903 718987
e-mail: bailiffscourt@hshotels.co.uk
web: www.hshotels.co.uk
Dir: *turn off A259 at Climping follow signs for Climping Beach. Hotel 0.5m on right*

Dating from only the 1920s, this 'medieval manor' looks like it might have been there for centuries. Bedrooms are spacious and

continued

atmospheric in parts, whilst newer rooms provide an impressive contrast of style. There is a choice of cosy lounges, warmed by log fires in the cooler months, and carefully prepared meals are served. A well-equipped spa completes the package.

ROOMS: 9 en suite 30 annexe en suite (25 fmly) (16 GF) s £165-£270; d £185-£450 (incl. bkfst) **LB** **FACILITIES: Spa** STV supervised pool supervised Sauna Gym Jacuzzi ch fac Xmas **CONF:** Thtr 40 Class 20 Board 26 Del from £205 **PARKING:** 100 **NOTES:** in restaurant Civ Wed 50 **CARDS:**

See advert on this page

CLITHEROE, Lancashire Map 18 SD74

★★69% Shireburn Arms

Whalley Rd, Hurst Green BB7 9QJ
☎ 01254 826518 01254 826208
e-mail: sales@shireburnarmshotel.com
web: www.shireburnarmshotel.com
Dir: *A59 to Clitheroe, left at lights to Ribchester, follow Hurst Green signs. Hotel on B6243 at entrance to Hurst Green village*

This long established, family-owned hotel dates back to the 17th century and enjoys panoramic views over the Ribble Valley. Rooms are individually designed and thoughtfully equipped. The lounge bar offers a selection of real ales, and the spacious restaurant, opening onto an attractive patio and garden, offers home-cooked food.

ROOMS: 18 en suite (3 fmly) in 3 bedrooms s £48-£70; d £70-£90 (incl. bkfst) **LB** **FACILITIES:** ch fac Xmas **CONF:** Thtr 100 Class 50 Board 50 Del £80 **PARKING:** 71 **NOTES:** in restaurant Civ Wed 100 **CARDS:**

C

CLOVELLY, Devon

Map 03 SS32

★★70% New Inn

High St EX39 5TQ
☎ 01237 431303 🖷 01237 431636
e-mail: newinn@clovelly.co.uk
Dir: *at Clovelly Cross, off A39 onto B3237. Follow road down hill for 1.5m. Right at sign 'All vehicles for Clovelly'*

Famed for its cobbled descent to the harbour, this fascinating fishing village is a traffic-free zone. Consequently, luggage is conveyed by sledge or donkey to this much-photographed hotel. Carefully renovated bedrooms and public areas are smartly presented with quality, locally-made furnishings. Meals may be taken in the elegant restaurant or the popular Upalongs bar.
ROOMS: 8 en suite (2 fmly) s £38.25-£47; d £76.50-£94 (incl. bkfst) **LB**
FACILITIES: Xmas **NOTES:** ⊗ in restaurant
CARDS:

See advert on opposite page

★★70% Red Lion Hotel

The Quay EX39 5TF
☎ 01237 431237 🖷 01237 431044
e-mail: redlion@clovelly.co.uk
web: www.clovelly.co.uk
Dir: *turn off A39 at Clovelly Cross onto B3237. To bottom of hill and take 1st left by white rails to harbour*

Idyllic is the only way to describe the harbour-side setting of this charming 18th-century inn, where the historic fishing village forms a spectacular backdrop. Bedrooms are stylish and enjoy delightful views. The inn's relaxed atmosphere is conducive to switching off from the pressures of life, even if the harbour comes alive with the activities of the local fishermen during the day.
ROOMS: 11 en suite (2 fmly) s £46.75-£72.50; d £93.50-£115 (incl. bkfst) **LB** **FACILITIES:** Tennis can be arranged Xmas **PARKING:** 11
NOTES: ⊗ in restaurant **CARDS:**

See advert on opposite page

COBHAM, Surrey

Map 06 TQ16

Premier Lodge (Cobham)

PREMIER LODGE.com

Portsmouth Rd, Fairmile KT11 1BW
☎ 0870 9906358 🖷 0870 9906359
web: www.premierlodge.com
Dir: *10 mins from M25. At junct 10, follow A3 towards London. Exit A3 onto A245 towards Cobham. In town centre left onto A307 Portsmouth Rd for Lodge on left*
High quality, modern, budget accommodation, ideal for families and business travellers. All rooms feature bath, power shower and satellite TV, and most have telephones / modem points. The adjacent bar and restaurant offers a wide and varied menu.
ROOMS: 48 en suite s £58; d £58 **CONF:** Board 12

COCKERMOUTH, Cumbria

Map 18 NY13

★★★74% The Trout

Crown St CA13 0EJ
☎ 01900 823591 🖷 01900 827514
e-mail: enquiries@trouthotel.co.uk
web: www.trouthotel.co.uk
Dir: *next to Wordsworth House*
Dating back to 1670, this privately owned hotel has an enviable setting on the banks of the River Derwent. The well-equipped bedrooms vary in style and there is a well-stocked bar, a choice of comfortable lounges and an attractive, traditional style dining room offering a good choice of table d'hôte and carte dishes.
ROOMS: 43 en suite (4 fmly) (15 GF) ⊗ in 12 bedrooms s £59.95-£129; d £109-£149 (incl. bkfst) **LB** **FACILITIES:** STV Fishing ch fac Xmas **CONF:** Thtr 25 Class 20 Board 20 Del from £135 **PARKING:** 40
NOTES: ⊗ in restaurant Civ Wed 60 **CARDS:**

Shepherds Hotel

Lakeland Sheep & Wool Centre, Egremont Rd CA13 0QX
☎ 01900 822673 🖷 01900 822673
e-mail: reception@shepherdshotel.co.uk
web: www.shepherdshotel.co.uk
Dir: *At junct of A66 and A5086 S of Cockermouth, entrance off A5086 200mtrs off rdbt*
This hotel is modern in style and offers thoughtfully equipped accommodation. The property also houses the Lakeland Sheep and Wool Centre, with live sheep shows from Easter to mid November. A restaurant serving a wide variety of meals and snacks is open all day.
ROOMS: 13 en suite **CONF:** BC Thtr 200 Class 10 Board 10 Del from £65

COGGESHALL, Essex

Map 07 TL82

★★★70% White Hart

OLD ENGLISH INNS

Market End CO6 1NH
☎ 01376 561654 🖷 01376 561789
e-mail: 6529@greeneking.co.uk
Dir: *from A12 through Kelvedon & onto B1024 to Coggeshall*
This cosy inn, located in the centre of the town, has been completely refurbished. Bedrooms vary in size and all offer good quality and comfort with extras such as CD players, fruit and mineral water. Public areas are heavily beamed with a popular bar serving a varied menu, a large restaurant with an Italian menu and cosy residents' lounge.
ROOMS: 18 en suite (1 fmly) s £55-£75; d £75-£135 (incl. bkfst) **LB**
FACILITIES: STV ♫ ch fac Xmas **CONF:** Thtr 30 Class 10 Board 22 Del from £97.50 **PARKING:** 47 **CARDS:**

COLCHESTER, Essex
See also Earls Colne

Map 13 TL92

★★★★73% Five Lakes Resort
Colchester Rd CM9 8HX
☎ 01621 868888 01621 869696
e-mail: enquiries@fivelakes.co.uk
web: www.fivelakes.co.uk
(For full entry see Tolleshunt Knights)

★★★ Maison Talbooth

Stratford Rd CO7 6HN
☎ 01206 322367 01206 322752
e-mail: maison@milsomhotels.co.uk
web: www.maisonhotels.com
(For full entry see Dedham)

★★★71% George
116 High St CO1 1TD
☎ 01206 578494 01206 761732
e-mail: colcgeorge@aol.com
Dir: *200yds beyond Town Hall on High St*

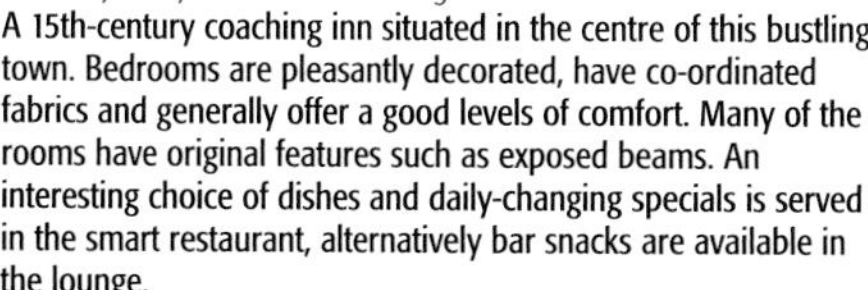

A 15th-century coaching inn situated in the centre of this bustling town. Bedrooms are pleasantly decorated, have co-ordinated fabrics and generally offer a good levels of comfort. Many of the rooms have original features such as exposed beams. An interesting choice of dishes and daily-changing specials is served in the smart restaurant, alternatively bar snacks are available in the lounge.
ROOMS: 47 en suite in 32 bedrooms s £59.95-£84.95; d £79.95-£109.95 **FACILITIES:** STV **CONF:** Thtr 70 Class 30 Board 30 Del from £129.95 **PARKING:** 40 **CARDS:**

★★★70% The Rose & Crown
East St CO1 2TZ
☎ 01206 866677 01206 866616
e-mail: info@rose-and-crown.com
web: www.rose-and-crown.com
Dir: *From A12 follow signs for "Rollerworld", hotel by level crossing*
This delightful coaching inn is situated close to the shops and is full of original charm. The character public areas feature a wealth of exposed beams and timbered walls and The Oak Room restaurant offers an interesting concept - French and Indian Fusion cuisine. Although the bedrooms vary in size and style they are pleasantly decorated and equipped with many thoughtful extras.
ROOMS: 31 en suite (3 fmly) (6 GF) in 5 bedrooms s £66-£80; d £76-£87 **FACILITIES:** STV Pay for Movie channels Internet/email each room **CONF:** Thtr 100 Class 50 Board 45 Del from £135 **PARKING:** 50 **NOTES:** in restaurant Civ Wed 120
CARDS:

★★★70% The Stoke by Nayland Club Hotel
Keepers Ln, Leavenheath CO6 4PZ
☎ 01206 262836 01206 263356
e-mail: sales@stokebynaylandclub.co.uk
web: www.stokebynaylandclub.co.uk
Dir: *off A134 at Leavenheath onto B1068, hotel 0.75m on right*
This hotel enjoys a delightful location on the edge of Dedham Vale, in 300 acres of undulating countryside, two golf courses and lakes. The spacious bedrooms are attractively decorated and equipped with modern facilities, including ISDN lines. Public rooms include the Spikes bar, a conservatory, a lounge, a smart restaurant, conference and banqueting suites and a superb leisure
continued
complex, which is being expanded to offer aerobics and spa beauty treatments.

The Stoke by Naland Club Hotel

ROOMS: 30 en suite (4 fmly) (15 GF) in 22 bedrooms s £80-£91; d £91-£114 (incl. bkfst) **LB** **FACILITIES: Spa** STV supervised 36 Fishing Squash Snooker Sauna Solarium Gym Putt green Jacuzzi Health/beauty salon, Driving range Xmas **CONF:** Thtr 500 Class 200 Board 36 Del from £125 **SERVICES:** Lift **PARKING:** 300 **NOTES:** in restaurant Civ Wed 200 **CARDS:**

★★★69% milsoms
Stratford Rd, Dedham CO7 6HW
☎ 01206 322795 01206 323689
e-mail: milsoms@milsomhotels.com
web: www.milsomhotels.com
(For full entry see Dedham)

COLCHESTER, continued

⌂ Travel Inn

Ipswich Rd CO4 9WP
☎ 08701 977065 📠 01206 751327
Dir: *take A120 (A1232) junct off A12, follow A1232 towards Colchester, Travel Inn on right*

Travel Inn offers good-quality, value-for-money accommodation. Spacious, en suite rooms with bath and shower comfortably accommodate a family of up to two adults and two children (to age 15). The restaurant and bar offers a varied menu. For further details consult the Hotel Groups page.
ROOMS: 40 en suite s £45.95-£48.95; d £45.95-£48.95

COLEFORD, Gloucestershire Map 04 SO51

★★★67% The Speech House

GL16 7EL
☎ 01594 822607 📠 01594 823658
e-mail: relax@thespeechhouse.co.uk
web: www.thespeechhouse.co.uk
Dir: *on B4226 between Cinderford and Coleford*

Dating back to 1676, this former hunting lodge is tucked away in the Forest of Dean. Bedrooms, some with impressive four-poster beds, combine modern amenities with period charm. The beamed restaurant serves good, imaginative food, whilst additional features include a mini gym, aqua spa and conference facilities.
ROOMS: 16 en suite 17 annexe rms (16 en suite) (4 fmly) (12 GF) ⊘ in 6 bedrooms s £50; d £86-£120 (incl. bkfst) **LB** **FACILITIES:** ⛳ 18 Sauna Solarium Gym Jacuzzi Beauty Salon Xmas **CONF:** BC Thtr 50 Class 30 Board 30 Del from £120 **PARKING:** 70 **NOTES:** ⊘ in restaurant Civ Wed 70 **CARDS:**

★★65% The Angel Hotel

Market Place GL16 8AE
☎ 01594 833113 📠 01594 832413
Dir: *access to hotel via A48 or A40*

This friendly 17th-century coaching inn is centrally located and provides an excellent base for exploring the area. All bedrooms are spacious, well equipped and suitable for both business and leisure guests. Additional features include a choice of bars, all with a relaxing atmosphere, a good range of real ales and wholesome cuisine.
ROOMS: 9 en suite (1 fmly) s £39-£45; d £65-£85 (incl. bkfst) **FACILITIES:** STV ♫ **PARKING:** 9 **CARDS:**

COLERNE, Wiltshire Map 04 ST87

Top 200 – Hotel

★★★★ ®®® Lucknam Park

SN14 8AZ
☎ 01225 742777 📠 01225 743536
e-mail: reservations@lucknampark.co.uk
web: www.lucknampark.co.uk
Dir: *M4 junct 17, A350 to Chippenham, then A420 to Bristol for 3m. At Ford village, left to Colerne, 3m right at x-rds. Entrance on right*

Guests may well feel a theatrical sense of arrival when approaching this Palladian mansion along its magnificent mile-long avenue of beech and lime trees. Surrounded by 500 acres of parkland and beautiful gardens, this fine hotel offers a wealth of choices ranging from enjoying pampering treatments to taking vigorous exercise. Elegant bedrooms and suites are split between the main building and adjacent courtyard. Dining options range from the informal Pavilion Restaurant, to the formal, and very accomplished, main restaurant.
ROOMS: 23 en suite 18 annexe en suite (16 GF) s fr £225; d £225-£770 **LB** **FACILITIES: Spa** STV Riding Snooker Sauna Solarium Gym Jacuzzi Whirlpool, Beauty & hair salon, Steam room, Cross country course, Mountain bikes ♫ ch fac Xmas **CONF:** BC Thtr 60 Class 24 Board 24 Del from £260 **PARKING:** 70 **NOTES:** ⊘ in restaurant Civ Wed 60 **CARDS:**

COLESHILL, Warwickshire Map 10 SP28

★★★66% Grimstock Country House

Gilson Rd, Gilson B46 1LJ
☎ 01675 462121 & 462161 📠 01675 467646
e-mail: enquiries@grimstockhotel.co.uk
Dir: *off A446 at rdbt onto B4117 to Gilson, hotel 100yds on right*

This privately owned hotel is convenient for Birmingham International Airport and the NEC, yet enjoys a peaceful rural setting. Bedrooms are spacious and comfortable. Public rooms include a choice of restaurants, a wood-panelled bar, good conference facilities and a gym featuring the latest cardiovascular equipment.
ROOMS: 44 en suite (1 fmly) (13 GF) s £95; d £109 (incl. bkfst) **LB** **FACILITIES:** STV Solarium Gym Xmas **CONF:** Thtr 100 Class 60 Board 50 Del £135 **PARKING:** 100 **NOTES:** ⊘ in restaurant Civ Wed 80 **CARDS:**

COLN ST ALDWYNS, Gloucestershire Map 05 SP10

Top 200 – Hotel

★★ 🏵🏵 **The New Inn At Coln**
GL7 5AN
☎ 01285 750651 📠 01285 750657
e-mail: stay@new-inn.co.uk
web: www.new-inn.co.uk
Dir: *8m E of Cirencester, between Bibury and Fairford*
Set in the heart of the Coln Valley, this quintessential Cotswold inn has been welcoming weary travellers since the reign of Elizabeth I. The bedrooms are very cosy, while crackling log fires, flagstone floors, wooden beams and genuine hospitality make for a beguiling atmosphere. An excellent bar menu is available. Apéritifs can be savoured in the lounge, whilst perusing the flavour-packed dishes from the restaurant menu.
ROOMS: 8 en suite 6 annexe en suite (1 GF) s £120-£132; d £186-£220 (incl. bkfst & dinner) **LB** **FACILITIES:** Fishing Xmas **CONF:** Thtr 20 Board 12 Del from £155 **PARKING:** 22 **NOTES:** No children 10 yrs ⊗ in restaurant **CARDS:**

COLSTERWORTH, Lincolnshire Map 11 SK92

⌂ **Travelodge Grantham Colsterworth**
NG35 5JR
☎ 08700 850 950 📠 01476 860680
Dir: *on A1/A151 southbound at junct with B151/B676*
Travelodge offers good quality, good value, modern accommodation. Ideal for families, the spacious, en suite bedrooms include remote-control TV, tea and coffee-making facilities and luxury beds. Meals can be taken at the nearby family restaurant. For further details consult the Hotel Groups page.
ROOMS: 31 en suite s fr £25; d fr £25

COLYFORD, Devon Map 04 SY29

★★77% 🏵 **Swallows Eaves**
EX24 6QJ
☎ 01297 553184 📠 01297 553574
e-mail: swallows.eaves@talk21.com
Dir: *on A3052 between Lyme Regis and Sidmouth, in village centre, opp post office store*
This delightful hotel has gained a well-deserved reputation for excellent standards of service, food and hospitality; many guests return year after year. Bedrooms combine comfort with quality,

continued

each individually styled and equipped with many thoughtful extras. The restaurant serves a daily menu of carefully prepared dishes, making good use of fresh local ingredients. Safe, on-site parking is an added bonus.
ROOMS: 8 en suite (1 GF) ⊗ in all bedrooms s £49-£55; d £74-£94 (incl. bkfst) **LB** **FACILITIES:** Free use of nearby Swimming Club **PARKING:** 10 **NOTES:** No dogs No children 14yrs ⊗ in restaurant RS Nov-Feb **CARDS:**

CONSETT, Co Durham Map 19 NZ15

★★★68% **Derwent Manor**
Allensford DH8 9BB
☎ 01207 592000 📠 01207 502472
e-mail: info@derwent-manor-hotel.com
Dir: *on A68 Darlington to Corbridge road. Access A68 from A1 junct 58 or A69. Hotel 1m on left*
This hotel, built in the style of a manor house, is set in open grounds overlooking the River Derwent. Spacious bedrooms, including a number of suites, are comfortably equipped. A popular wedding venue, there are also extensive conference facilities and a new impressive leisure suite. The 'Grouse & Claret' bar serves a wide range of drinks and light meals, and 'Guinevere's' restaurant offers fine dining.
ROOMS: 47 en suite (3 fmly) ⊗ in 10 bedrooms s £99-£149; d £109-£159 (incl. bkfst) **LB** **FACILITIES:** STV supervised Sauna Gym Jacuzzi Xmas **CONF:** BC Thtr 300 Class 200 Board 80 Del from £90 **SERVICES:** Lift **PARKING:** 150 **NOTES:** ⊗ in restaurant Civ Wed 300 **CARDS:**

★★★64% **The Raven Hotel**
Broomhill, Ebchester DH8 6RY
☎ 01207 562562 📠 01207 560262
Dir: *from A1 take A694 towards Consett to Ebchester, turn right after Chelford Arms, B6309, hotel on right*
This modern hotel stands on a hillside overlooking the village and countryside. Bedrooms, including some four-poster rooms, are spacious and many have stunning views. Well-prepared meals are served in the attractive conservatory restaurant and popular bar meals and cask ales are available in the bar area.
ROOMS: 29 en suite (29 fmly) (14 GF) ⊗ in 14 bedrooms s fr £45; d £55-£75 **LB** **FACILITIES:** STV Xmas **CONF:** Thtr 120 Class 80 Board 40 **PARKING:** 100 **NOTES:** No dogs ⊗ in restaurant Civ Wed 180 **CARDS:**

CONSTANTINE, Cornwall & Isles of Scilly Map 02 SW72

★★70% 🏵 **Trengilly Wartha Inn**
Nancenoy TR11 5RP
☎ 01326 340332 📠 01326 341121
e-mail: reception@trengilly.co.uk
Dir: *A39 to Falmouth. At rdbt by Asda in Penryn, signed to Constantine then Gweek. Hotel signed on left in 1m*
The charm and tranquillity of this character inn, which is located close to the Helford River, provides a welcoming environment. Interesting cuisine based on local produce, fine wines, hand-pulled ales and an impressive selection of malts are offered along with comfortable bedrooms and pleasant public rooms.
ROOMS: 6 en suite 2 annexe en suite (2 fmly) ⊗ in 2 bedrooms s fr £49; d £78-£96 (incl. bkfst) **LB** **PARKING:** 50 **NOTES:** ⊗ in restaurant RS 25 Dec (b'fast only) 31 Dec
CARDS:

C

CONSTANTINE BAY, Cornwall & Isles of Scilly Map 02 SW87

★★★79% Treglos

PL28 8JH
☎ 01841 520727 01841 521163
e-mail: enquiries@treglos-hotel.co.uk
web: www.tregloshotel.co.uk
Dir: *right at Constantine Bay stores, hotel 50yds on left*

Owned by the same family for over 30 years, this hotel has a tradition of high standards. The genuine welcome, choice of comfortable lounges, indoor pool and children's play facilities entice guests back year after year. Bedrooms vary in size; those with sea views are always popular. The restaurant continues to provide imaginative menus incorporating seasonal local produce.
ROOMS: 42 en suite (12 fmly) (1 GF) in all bedrooms **FACILITIES:** Snooker Jacuzzi Converted 'boat house' for table tennis ch fac **CONF:** Board 20 **SERVICES:** Lift **PARKING:** 58 **NOTES:** in restaurant Closed 17 Nov-5 Mar
CARDS:

COOKHAM DEAN, Berkshire Map 05 SU88

Restaurant with Rooms

The Inn on the Green Garry Holihead

The Old Cricket Common SL6 9NZ
☎ 01628 482638 01628 487474
e-mail: reception@theinnonthegreen.com
Dir: *A404 towards Marlow High St. Cross suspension bridge towards Bisham. 1st left into Quarry Wood Rd, right Hills Lane, right at Memorial Cross*
A traditional English country inn set in rural Berkshire where the bedrooms are individually decorated, spacious and comfortable. Now refurbished and modernised, the building retains many traditional features including a wood-panelled dining room and Old English bar with log fire. Food is imaginative and noteworthy.
ROOMS: 9 en suite (4 GF) s £120-£185; d £130-£195 (incl. bkfst) **LB** **FACILITIES: Spa** STV Jacuzzi Xmas **CONF:** BC Thtr 30 Class 30 Board 30 Del £195 **PARKING:** 50 **NOTES:** Civ Wed 150
CARDS:

COPTHORNE See Gatwick Airport

GF Indicates the number of bedrooms at ground floor level.

- Indoor Swimming Pool
- Indoor Swimming Pool (heated)
- Outdoor Swimming Pool
- Outdoor Swimming Pool (heated)

CORBRIDGE, Northumberland Map 21 NY96

Restaurant with Rooms

Angel of Corbridge

Main St NE45 5LA
☎ 01434 632119 01434 633496
e-mail: info@theangelofcorbridge.co.uk
Dir: *from A1 onto A69 (Hexham) for approx 10m, Corbridge exit, 2m to Corbridge, hotel 1st large building*
Corbridge's oldest inn is now a stylish gastro bar and restaurant, yet it successfully retains much of its original character. The intimate split-level restaurant and trendy modern bar are contrasting venues for carefully cooked contemporary dishes. The five stylish bedrooms are all very stylishly fitted.
ROOMS: 5 en suite (1 fmly) in all bedrooms s £55; d £79 (incl. bkfst) **FACILITIES:** Xmas **PARKING:** 25 **NOTES:** in restaurant
CARDS:

CORFE CASTLE, Dorset Map 04 SY98

★★★77% Mortons House

49 East St BH20 5EE
☎ 01929 480988 01929 480820
e-mail: stay@mortonshouse.co.uk
web: www.mortonshouse.co.uk
Dir: *on A351 between Wareham & Swanage*
Set in delightful gardens and grounds with excellent views of Corfe Castle, this impressive building dates back to Tudor times. The oak-panelled drawing room has a roaring log fire and an interesting range of enjoyable cuisine is available in the well-appointed dining room. Bedrooms, many with views of the castle, are comfortable and well equipped.
ROOMS: 14 en suite 5 annexe en suite (2 fmly) (5 GF) in all bedrooms s £75-£150; d £126-£145 (incl. bkfst) **LB** **FACILITIES:** Jacuzzi Xmas **CONF:** BC Thtr 45 Class 45 Board 20 Del from £115 **PARKING:** 40 **NOTES:** in restaurant Civ Wed 60
CARDS:

CORNHILL-ON-TWEED, Northumberland Map 21 NT83

★★★75% Tillmouth Park Country House

TD12 4UU
☎ 01890 882255 01890 882540
e-mail: reception@tillmouthpark.force9.co.uk
web: www.tillmouthpark.co.uk
Dir: *off A1(M) at East Ord rdbt at Berwick-upon-Tweed. Take A698 to Cornhill and Coldstream. Hotel 9m on left*

An imposing mansion set in landscaped grounds by the River Till. Gracious public rooms include a stunning galleried lounge with drawing room off. The quietly elegant dining room overlooks the gardens, whilst lunches and early dinners are available in the

continued

bistro. Bedrooms retain traditional character and include several magnificent master rooms.
ROOMS: 12 en suite 2 annexe en suite (1 fmly) s £60-£140; d £140-£180 (incl. bkfst) **LB** **FACILITIES:** STV Fishing 3/4 snooker table, Game shooting Xmas **CONF:** Thtr 50 Class 20 Board 20 Del from £125 **PARKING:** 50 **NOTES:** in restaurant Civ Wed 50
CARDS:

CORSE LAWN, Gloucestershire Map 10 SO83

Top 200 – Hotel

★★★ Corse Lawn House
GL19 4LZ
☎ 01452 780479 & 780771 01452 780840
e-mail: enquiries@corselawn.com
web: www.corselawn.com
Dir: *on B4211 5m SW of Tewkesbury*
This gracious Grade II listed Queen Anne house has been home to the Hine family since 1978. Aided by an enthusiastic and committed team, the family still presides over all aspects, creating a relaxed and wonderfully comforting environment. Bedrooms offer a reassuring mix of comfort and quality. Impressive cuisine is based upon excellent produce, much of it locally sourced.
ROOMS: 19 en suite (2 fmly) (5 GF) s £85; d £130-£165 (incl. bkfst) **LB** **FACILITIES:** STV Badminton Croquet Table tennis **CONF:** Thtr 50 Class 30 Board 25 Del £135 **PARKING:** 62 **NOTES:** in restaurant Closed 24-26 Dec Civ Wed 70
CARDS:

See advert under TEWKESBURY

COVENTRY, West Midlands Map 10 SP37
See also Brandon, Meriden & Nuneaton

★★★72% Brooklands Grange Hotel & Restaurant
Holyhead Rd CV5 8HX
☎ 024 7660 1601 024 7660 1277
e-mail: info@brooklands-grange.co.uk
web: www.brooklands-grange.co.uk
Dir: *leave A45 at city centre rdbt. At next rdbt take A4114. Hotel 100yds on left*
Behind the Jacobean façade of Brooklands Grange is a well run modern and comfortable business hotel. Well-appointed bedrooms are thoughtfully equipped for corporate guests and a smartly appointed four-poster bedroom has now been created. The food continues to be worthy of note, with the emphasis on contemporary, well-flavoured dishes.
ROOMS: 31 en suite (3 fmly) (11 GF) in 25 bedrooms s £55-£120; d £55-£155 (incl. bkfst) **LB** **CONF:** BC Thtr 20 Class 10 Board 18 Del from £100 **PARKING:** 52 **NOTES:** in restaurant Closed 26-28 Dec & 1-2 Jan **CARDS:**

★★★71% Menzies Leofric
Broadgate CV1 1LZ
☎ 024 7622 1371 024 7655 1352
e-mail: leofric@menzies-hotels.co.uk
Dir: *junct 9 off Coventry ring road, follow signs to West Orchards Car Park, situated to rear of hotel*
Right in the centre of the city, this refurbished hotel has the advantage of preferred parking rates in the nearby multi-storey car park, and most rooms have a quiet outlook. Bedrooms are well-lit and comfortable with good business facilities. Contemporary public areas include two bars, a brasserie, plus a hairdresser.
ROOMS: 94 en suite (5 fmly) in 20 bedrooms s £110-£120; d £120-£150 **LB** **FACILITIES:** STV Xmas **CONF:** Thtr 600 Class 200 Board 60 Del £145 **SERVICES:** Lift **NOTES:** in restaurant Civ Wed
CARDS:

★★★70% Courtyard by Marriott Coventry
London Rd, Ryton on Dunsmore CV8 3DY
☎ 0870 400 7216 0870 400 7316
e-mail: meetings.coventry@courtyardhotels.co.uk
Dir: *M6 junct 2, take A46 towards Warwick, then A45 London at Coventry Airport*
Located on the outskirts of the city, this modern hotel appeals to both business and leisure guests. A range of meeting rooms along with convenient access to the road networks makes this an ideal business venue, while the hotel's proximity to a number of attractions also makes it an excellent base for a weekend of sightseeing. The public areas and accommodation are smartly presented; the spacious bedrooms are particularly well equipped for corporate guests.
ROOMS: 51 en suite (2 fmly) (22 GF) in 25 bedrooms s £95-£125; d £103-£130 (incl. bkfst) **LB** **FACILITIES:** STV Gym Xmas **CONF:** Thtr 300 Class 100 Board 24 Del from £129 **PARKING:** 120 **NOTES:** in restaurant Civ Wed 116 **CARDS:**

★★★66% Best Western Hylands
Warwick Rd CV3 6AU
☎ 024 7650 1600 024 7650 1027
e-mail: hylands@bestwestern.co.uk
Dir: *on A429, 500yds from junct 6 of town centre ring road, opposite Memorial Park*
This hotel is convenient for the station and the city centre and overlooks an attractive park. Bedroom styles vary, yet each room is well-equipped; the most recent additions are smartly decorated and modern, with bold colour schemes. Public rooms offer an open-plan lounge bar and the Restaurant 153.
ROOMS: 61 en suite in 54 bedrooms s £45-£115; d £65-£135 (incl. bkfst) **LB** **FACILITIES:** STV Xmas **CONF:** Thtr 60 Class 40 Board 30 Del from £110 **PARKING:** 60 **NOTES:** **CARDS:**

★★★66% The Chace
London Rd, Toll Bar End CV3 4EQ
☎ 0870 609 6130 024 7630 1816
e-mail: chacehotel@corushotels.com
Dir: *A45 or A46 follow to Toll Bar Roundabout / Coventry Airport, take B4116 to Willenhall, over mini-rdbt, hotel on left*
A former doctor's mansion, the main building retains many of its original Victorian features, including public rooms with high ceilings, stained-glass windows, oak panelling and an impressive staircase; there is also a patio and well-kept gardens. Bedroom

continued on p184

COVENTRY, continued

styles and sizes vary somewhat; most are attractively appointed, bright and modern.

The Chace Hotel, Coventry

ROOMS: 66 en suite (23 fmly) (24 GF) ⊗ in 34 bedrooms s £82; d £82 **LB** **FACILITIES:** STV Pool Table, Free use of nearby leisure centre Xmas **CONF:** Thtr 65 Class 40 Board 36 Del from £80 **PARKING:** 120 **NOTES:** ⊗ in restaurant Civ Wed 60
CARDS:

★★★64% *Allesley*

Birmingham Rd, Allesley Village CV5 9GP
☎ 024 7640 3272 📠 024 7640 5190
e-mail: stay@allesley-hotel.co.uk
web: www.allesley-hotel.co.uk
Dir: *from A45 onto A4114 Brownshill Green and city centre road. 4th exit at rdbt , 1st exit next rdbt into Allesley Village. Hotel 150yds on left*
This purpose built hotel provides well-equipped bedrooms suited to the corporate guest. Public rooms are split over two levels and include a spacious reception foyer, a large restaurant and a lounge bar. Extensive conference and function facilities are available and prove popular.
ROOMS: 75 en suite 15 annexe en suite (2 fmly) ⊗ in 45 bedrooms **CONF:** BC Thtr 450 Class 150 Board 80 **SERVICES:** Lift **PARKING:** 500 **NOTES:** ⊗ in restaurant Civ Wed 350
CARDS:

★★★64% *Novotel Coventry*

Wilsons Ln CV6 6HL
☎ 024 7636 5000 📠 024 7636 2422
e-mail: h0506@accor-hotels.com
Dir: *M6 junct 3. Follow signs for B4113 towards Longford and Bedworth. 3rd exit on large rdbt*
A modern hotel, convenient for Birmingham, Coventry and the motorway network, offering spacious, well-equipped accommodation. The bright brasserie offers extended dining hours, or alternatively there is an extensive room-service menu. Family rooms and a play area make this a child-friendly hotel, and there is also a selection of meeting rooms.
ROOMS: 98 en suite (15 fmly) ⊗ in 70 bedrooms **FACILITIES:** Petanque, Pool table **CONF:** Thtr 200 Class 100 Board 40 **SERVICES:** Lift air con **PARKING:** 120
CARDS:

⌂ Hotel Campanile

4 Wigston Rd, Walsgrave CV2 2SD
☎ 024 7662 2311 📠 024 7660 2362
e-mail: coventry@envergure.co.uk
Dir: *M6 exit 2, 2nd rdbt turn right*
This modern building offers accommodation in smart, well-equipped bedrooms, all with en suite bathrooms. Refreshments may be taken at the informal Bistro. For further details consult the Hotel Groups page.

ROOMS: 47 en suite s fr £42.95; d fr £42.95 **CONF:** Thtr 35 Class 18 Board 24

⌂ Hotel Ibis Coventry Centre

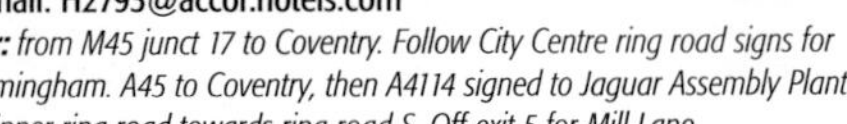

Mill Ln, St John's Ringway CV1 2LN
☎ 024 7625 0500 📠 024 7655 3548
e-mail: H2793@accor.hotels.com
Dir: *from M45 junct 17 to Coventry. Follow City Centre ring road signs for Birmingham. A45 to Coventry, then A4114 signed to Jaguar Assembly Plant. At inner ring road towards ring road S. Off exit 5 for Mill Lane*
Modern, budget hotel offering comfortable accommodation in bright and practical bedrooms. Breakfast is self-service and dinner is available in the restaurant. For further details, consult the Hotel Groups page.
ROOMS: 89 en suite (incl. bkfst) s £36.95-£47.95; d £36.95-£47.95

⌂ Hotel Ibis Coventry South

Abbey Rd, Whitley CV3 4BJ
☎ 024 7663 9922 📠 024 7630 6898
e-mail: H2094@accor-hotels.com
Dir: *signed from A46/A423 rdbt. Take A423 towards A45. Follow signs for Esporta Health Club and Jaguar Engineering Plant*
Modern, budget hotel offering comfortable accommodation in bright and practical bedrooms. Breakfast is self-service and dinner is available in the restaurant. For further details, consult the Hotel Groups page.
ROOMS: 51 en suite s £30.95-£53.95; d £43.95-£53.95
CONF: BC Thtr 20 Class 20

⌂ Innkeeper's Lodge Meriden

Main Rd, Meriden CV7 7NN
☎ 01676 523798 📠 01676 531922
www.innkeeperslodge.com
Dir: *in village of Meriden, just off main A45 between Coventry & Birmingham on B4102. Lodge on left down the hill from Meriden Village Green*
Smart rooms meet essential business requirements but also have home comforts, and depending on location may well have meeting rooms and pub dining. Dining options generally include all-day menus plus the added advantage of breakfast.
ROOMS: 13 rms (9 en suite) s £48-£59.95; d £48-£59.95

⌂ Premier Lodge (Coventry)

Combe Fields Rd, Ansty CV7 9JP
☎ 0870 9906472 📠 0870 9906473
web: www.premierlodge.com
Dir: *10 mins from Coventry on B4029. Exit M6 junct 2 onto B4065 towards Ansty. After village turn right onto B4029 signped Brinklow and right into Coombe Fields Rd for Lodge on right*
High quality, modern, budget accommodation, ideal for families and business travellers. All rooms feature bath, power shower and

continued

satellite TV, and most have telephones / modem points. The adjacent bar and restaurant offers a wide and varied menu.
ROOMS: 28 en suite s £50; d £50 **CONF:** Thtr 12 Class 14 Board 14

⇧ Travel Inn

Rugby Rd, Binley Woods CV3 2TA
☎ 08701 977066 🖹 024 7643 1178
Dir: from M6 (J2) follow signs Warwick (A46 & M40). Follow 'All traffic' signs, under bridge onto A46. Left at 1st rbt to Binley. Travel Inn on right at next rbt
Travel Inn offers good-quality, value-for-money accommodation. Spacious, en suite rooms with bath and shower comfortably accommodate a family of up to two adults and two children (to age 15). The restaurant and bar offers a varied menu. For further details consult the Hotel Groups page.
ROOMS: 75 en suite s £45.95-£46.95; d £45.95-£46.95
CONF: Thtr 25 Board 18

COWES See Wight, Isle of

CRAMLINGTON, Northumberland Map 21 NZ27

⇧ Innkeeper's Lodge Cramlington

Blagdon Ln NE23 8AU
☎ 01670 736111 🖹 01670 715709
www.innkeeperslodge.com
Dir: from A1, exit for A19. At rdbt, left onto A1068, lodge at junct of Blagdon Lane and Fisher Lane
Smart rooms meet essential business requirements but also have home comforts, and depending on location may well have meeting rooms and pub dining. Dining options generally include all-day menus plus the added advantage of breakfast.
ROOMS: 18 en suite s £48-£55; d £48-£55 **CONF:** Board 24

CRAMLINGTON, Northumberland Map 21 NZ27

⇧ Travel Inn (Newcastle-Upon-Tyne Cramlington)

Moor Farm Roundabout, off Front St NE23 7QA
☎ 08701 977188 📄 0191 250 2216
Dir: *at rdbt on junction of A19/A189 S of Cramlington*

Travel Inn offers good-quality, value-for-money accommodation. Spacious, en suite rooms with bath and shower comfortably accommodate a family of up to two adults and two children (to age 15). The restaurant and bar offers a varied menu. For further details consult the Hotel Groups page.

ROOMS: 40 en suite s £45.95-£46.95; d £45.95-£46.95

CRANBROOK, Kent Map 07 TQ73

★★69% *The George*

Stone St TN17 3HE
☎ 01580 713348 📄 01580 715532
Dir: *off A21 to Goudhurst & Cranbrook. At large rdbt, right into Cranbrook*

This delightful 13th-century coaching inn is located in the heart of the town centre. Bedrooms have a wealth of original features and include some with four-poster beds. There is a public bar, cosy wine bar and Brook's restaurant, where imaginative freshly prepared dishes are served.

ROOMS: 8 en suite (1 fmly) ⊗ in all bedrooms **FACILITIES:** STV Jacuzzi **CONF:** Thtr 75 Class 60 Board 50 **PARKING:** 10 **NOTES:** ⊗ in restaurant **CARDS:**

CRANTOCK, Cornwall & Isles of Scilly Map 02 SW76

★★★71% Crantock Bay

West Pentire TR8 5SE
☎ 01637 830229 📄 01637 831111
e-mail: stay@crantockbayhotel.co.uk
Dir: *at Newquay A3075 to Redruth. After 500yds right towards Crantock, follow signs to West Pentire*

This family-run hotel has spectacular sea views and a tradition of friendly and attentive service. With direct access to the beach from its four acres of grounds, and its extensive leisure facilities, the hotel is a great place for family guests. There are separate lounges, a spacious bar and enjoyable cuisine is served in the dining room.

ROOMS: 33 en suite (3 fmly) (10 GF) s £60-£90; d £120-£180 (incl. bkfst & dinner) **LB** **FACILITIES:** Sauna Gym Putt green Jacuzzi Hotel leads on to sandy beach ch fac Xmas **CONF:** Thtr 60 Class 30 Board 30 Del from £79 **PARKING:** 40 **NOTES:** ⊗ in restaurant Closed 2 wks Nov & Jan RS Dec & Feb
CARDS:

CRATHORNE, North Yorkshire Map 19 NZ40

Top 200 – Hotel

★★★★ Crathorne Hall

TS15 0AR
☎ 01642 700398 📄 01642 700814
e-mail: crathorne-cro@handpicked.co.uk
Dir: *off A19, take slip road signed Teesside Airport and Kirklevington, then right signed Crathorne to hotel*

This splendid Edwardian hall sits in its own landscaped grounds and enjoys fine views of the Leven Valley and rolling Cleveland Hills. Both the impressively equipped bedrooms and the delightful public areas offer sumptuous levels of comfort, with elegant antique furnishings that complement the hotel's architectural style. Conference and banqueting facilities are available.
Hand Picked Hotels - AA Hotel Group of the Year 2004-5.

ROOMS: 37 en suite (4 fmly) ⊗ in 15 bedrooms **FACILITIES:** STV Fishing Jogging track, Clay pigeon shooting Xmas **CONF:** Thtr 120 Class 80 Board 60 **PARKING:** 120 **NOTES:** ⊗ in restaurant Civ Wed 120 **CARDS:**

See advert on page 185

CRAWLEY See Gatwick Airport

CREWE, Cheshire Map 15 SJ75

★★★★75% Crewe Hall

Weston Rd CW1 6UZ
☎ 01270 253333 📄 01270 253322
e-mail: crewehall@marstonhotels.com
web: www.marstonhotels.com
Dir: *M6 junct 16 follow A500 to Crewe. Last exit at rdbt onto A5020. 1st exit next rdbt to Crewe. Crewe Hall 150yds on right*

Standing in 500 acres of mature grounds, this historic hall dates back to the 17th century. It retains an elaborate interior with Victorian-style architecture. Bedrooms are spacious, well equipped and comfortable – traditionally styled rooms in the main hall and modern suites in the west wing. Quality cooking is served in the elegant Ranulph restaurant.

ROOMS: 26 en suite 39 annexe en suite (5 fmly) (17 GF) ⊗ in 40 bedrooms s £135-£355; d £170-£390 (incl. bkfst) **LB** **FACILITIES:** STV Sauna Gym Jacuzzi Full size football pitch beauty, hydrotherapy pool Xmas **CONF:** Thtr 220 Class 110 Board 100 Del from £175 **SERVICES:** Lift **PARKING:** 140 **NOTES:** ⊗ in restaurant Civ Wed 180 **CARDS:**

★★★71% Hunters Lodge
Sydney Rd, Sydney CW1 5LU
☎ 01270 583440 01270 500553
e-mail: info@hunterslodge.co.uk
web: www.hunterslodge.co.uk
Dir: *1m from Crewe station, off A534*
Dating back to the 18th century, this family-run hotel has been extended and modernised. Accommodation, mainly located in adjacent well-equipped bedroom wings, includes family and four-poster rooms. Imaginative dishes are served in the spacious restaurant, and the popular bar also offers a choice of tempting meals. Service throughout is friendly.
ROOMS: 57 en suite (4 fmly) in 31 bedrooms s £73-£101; d £95-£119 (incl. bkfst) **FACILITIES:** STV Gym **CONF:** Thtr 160 Class 100 Board 80 Del from £110.15 **PARKING:** 240 **NOTES:** in restaurant RS Sunday Civ Wed 130
CARDS:

Travel Inn

Coppenhall Ln, Woolstanwood CW2 8SD
☎ 08701 977068 01270 256316
Dir: *at junct of A530 & A532, 9m from M6 junct 16 N'bound*
Travel Inn offers good-quality, value-for-money accommodation. Spacious, en suite rooms with bath and shower comfortably accommodate a family of up to two adults and two children (to age 15). The restaurant and bar offers a varied menu. For further details consult the Hotel Groups page.
ROOMS: 41 en suite s £45.95-£46.95; d £45.95-£46.95

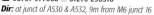

Travelodge

Alsager Rd, Barthomley CW2 5PT
☎ 08700 850 950 01270 883157
Dir: *5m E, at junct 16 M6/A500*
Travelodge offers good quality, good value, modern accommodation. Ideal for families, the spacious, en suite bedrooms include remote-control TV, tea and coffee-making facilities and luxury beds. Meals can be taken at the nearby family restaurant. For further details consult the Hotel Groups page.
ROOMS: 42 en suite s fr £25; d fr £25

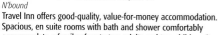

CRICK, Northamptonshire — Map 11 SP57

Hotel Ibis Rugby East
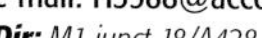
Parklands NN6 7EX
☎ 01788 824331 01788 824332
e-mail: H3588@accor-hotels.com
Dir: *M1 junct 18/A428*
Modern, budget hotel offering comfortable accommodation in bright and practical bedrooms. Breakfast is self-service and dinner is available in the restaurant. For further details, consult the Hotel Groups page.
ROOMS: 111 en suite s £34.95-£44.95; d £34.95-£44.95
CONF: BC Thtr 30 Class 16 Board 18

CRICKLADE, Wiltshire — Map 05 SU09

★★★71% Cricklade Hotel
Common Hill SN6 6HA
☎ 01793 750751 01793 751767
e-mail: info@crickladehotel.co.uk
web: www.crickladehotel.co.uk
Dir: *off A419 onto B4040. Turn left at clock tower. Right at rdbt. Hotel 0.5m up hill on left*
A haven of peace and tranquillity with spectacular views, this hotel is surrounded by over 30 acres of beautiful countryside. Bedrooms vary in size and style; those in the main building offer high levels of comfort and quality. There is an elegant lounge and dining room, and a Victorian-style conservatory runs the full length of the building.

ROOMS: 25 en suite 21 annexe en suite (1 fmly) in 34 bedrooms s £105-£110; d £140-£145 (incl. bkfst) **LB** **FACILITIES:** STV 9 Snooker Sauna Solarium Gym Jacuzzi Aromatherapy Beautician Xmas **CONF:** Thtr 80 Class 60 Board 30 Del £155 **PARKING:** 100 **NOTES:** No children 14yrs in restaurant Closed 25-26 Dec Civ Wed 120 **CARDS:**
See advert under SWINDON

CROMER, Norfolk — Map 13 TG24

★★★63% The Cliftonville
NR27 9AS
☎ 01263 512543 01263 515700
e-mail: reservations@cliftonvillehotel.co.uk
web: www.cliftonvillehotel.co.uk
Dir: *From A149 coastal road, 500yd from town centre, northbound*
An imposing Edwardian hotel situated on the main coast road with stunning views of the sea. Public rooms feature a magnificent staircase, Minstrels' gallery, coffee shop, lounge bar, a further residents' lounge, Boltons Bistro and an additional restaurant. The bedrooms, for the most part spacious, are pleasantly decorated and have lovely sea views.
ROOMS: 30 en suite (5 fmly) in 14 bedrooms s £40-£52; d £80-£104 (incl. bkfst) **LB** **FACILITIES:** ch fac Xmas **CONF:** Thtr 150 Class 100 Board 60 Del from £65 **SERVICES:** Lift **PARKING:** 20 **NOTES:** in restaurant **CARDS:**

★★72% Red Lion
Brook St NR27 9HD
☎ 01263 514964 01263 512834
e-mail: enquiries@yeolderedlionhotel.co.uk
web: www.yeolderedlionhotel.co.uk
Dir: *from town centre 1st left after church*
Well-maintained Victorian property situated in an elevated position overlooking the beach and sea beyond. The smartly appointed public areas include a billiard room, lounge bar, a popular restaurant, a sunny conservatory and a first-floor residents' lounge with superb views of the sea. The spacious bedrooms are tastefully decorated, with co-ordinated soft furnishings and many thoughtful touches.
ROOMS: 12 en suite (1 fmly) s fr £58; d fr £96 (incl. bkfst) **LB** **FACILITIES:** Snooker Sauna Solarium Discount for local leisure centre **CONF:** Thtr 100 Class 50 Board 60 **PARKING:** 12 **NOTES:** in restaurant Closed Xmas Day **CARDS:**

♫ Entertainment

CROMER, continued

★★62% Hotel de Paris

High St NR27 9HG
☎ 01263 513141 01263 515217
e-mail: deparis.cromer@alfatravel.co.uk

Leisureplex

***Dir:** enter Cromer on A140 Norwich Rd. Left at lights onto Mount St. 2nd traffic lights right into Prince of Wales Rd. 2nd right into New St leading into High St*

An imposing, traditional-style resort hotel, situated in a prominent position overlooking the pier and beach. The bedrooms are pleasantly decorated and equipped with a good range of useful extras; many rooms have lovely sea views. The spacious public areas include a large lounge bar, restaurant, games room and a further lounge.

ROOMS: 56 en suite (5 fmly) s £31-£41; d £52-£72 (incl. bkfst) **LB**
FACILITIES: Games room ♫ Xmas **SERVICES:** Lift **PARKING:** 14
NOTES: in restaurant Closed Dec-Feb RS Mar & Nov
CARDS:

CROOKLANDS, Cumbria

Map 18 SD58

★★★63% Crooklands

LA7 7NW
☎ 015395 67432 015395 67525
e-mail: reception@crooklands.com
web: www.crooklands.com

***Dir:** M6 junct 36 onto A65. Left at rdbt. Hotel 1.5m on right past garage*

Although only a short drive from the M6, this hotel enjoys a peaceful rural location. Housed in a converted 200-year-old farmhouse, the restaurant retains many original features such as beams and stone walls. Bedrooms are a mix of modern and traditional and vary in size.

ROOMS: 30 en suite in 15 bedrooms s £48-£60; d £48-£60 **LB**
FACILITIES: ch fac **CONF:** Thtr 80 Class 50 Board 40 Del from £105
PARKING: 80 **NOTES:** in restaurant Closed 24-26 Dec
CARDS:

CROSTHWAITE, Cumbria

Map 18 SD49

★★★61% Damson Dene

LA8 8JE
☎ 015395 68676 015395 68227
e-mail: info@damsondene.co.uk
web: www.damsondene.co.uk

***Dir:** M6 junct 36, follow A590 signed Barrow-in-Furness, after 5m turn right onto A5074. Hotel on right after 5m*

A short drive from Lake Windermere, this hotel enjoys a tranquil and scenic setting. Bedrooms, many now refurbished, include a number with four-poster beds and jacuzzi baths. The spacious restaurant serves a daily-changing menu,
with much of the produce coming from the hotel's own kitchen garden. Real fires warm the lounge and there is a games room and cosy bar.

ROOMS: 37 en suite (4 fmly) (9 GF) s £59-£79; d £78-£118 (incl. bkfst) **LB** **FACILITIES: Spa** Squash Sauna Solarium Gym Jacuzzi Beauty salon Xmas **CONF:** Thtr 140 Class 60 Board 40 Del from £67
PARKING: 45 **NOTES:** in restaurant Civ Wed 120
CARDS:

CROWTHORNE, Berkshire

Map 05 SU86

★★★68% Corus hotel Bracknell

Duke's Ride RG45 6DW
☎ 0870 609 6111 01344 778913
e-mail: reservations.bracknell@corushotels.com

corus hotels

***Dir:** M3 junct 4, A331 to Camberley, follow signs to Sandhurst/Crowthorne A3095, left B3348, hotel past 2nd rdbt*

Situated in a quiet location but convenient for both the M3 and M4, this hotel attracts a high proportion of business guests. The modern bedrooms, which include interconnecting pairs of rooms, are attractively appointed and well maintained. Public areas include a pleasant brasserie-style restaurant and a choice of bar areas.

ROOMS: 79 en suite in 43 bedrooms s £115; d £115 **LB**
FACILITIES: STV Discounts at local leisure facilities Xmas **CONF:** Thtr 50 Class 20 Board 24 Del £149 **PARKING:** 96 **NOTES:** in restaurant Civ Wed 40 **CARDS:**

★★70% Dial House

62 Dukes Ride RG45 6DL
☎ 01344 776941 01344 777191
e-mail: dhh@fardellhotels.com
web: www.fardellhotels.com/dialhouse/index.html

***Dir:** A3095/B3348 towards Crowthorne*

Located close to the station, this friendly hotel is particularly suitable for guests who require good connections into London. Bedrooms are comfortable - most have showers in the bathrooms. The welcoming bar and restaurant offers residents a home-from-home atmosphere together with interesting and competent cooking.

ROOMS: 19 en suite (2 fmly) (5 GF) in all bedrooms s £50-£108; d £65-£118 (incl. bkfst) **FACILITIES:** STV **CONF:** Thtr 16 Class 10 Board 12 Del from £114.95 **PARKING:** 20 **NOTES:** in restaurant Closed 22 Dec-3 Jan **CARDS:**

CROYDON, Greater London

Map 06 TQ36

★★★★77% Coulsdon Manor

Coulsdon Court Rd, Coulsdon CR5 2LL
☎ 020 8668 0414 020 8668 3118
e-mail: coulsdonmanor@marstonhotels.com

MARSTON HOTELS

***Dir:** A23 right into Stoats Nest Road. Hotel top of hill on left*

This delightful Victorian manor house is peacefully set amidst 140 acres of landscaped parkland, complete with its own professional 18-hole golf course. Bedrooms are spacious and comfortable, whilst public areas include a choice of lounges and an elegant

continued

restaurant serving carefully prepared, imaginative food. Excellent standards of hospitality and service are to be commended.

ROOMS: 35 en suite ⊗ in 13 bedrooms s £124-£134; d £158-£178 (incl. bkfst) **LB FACILITIES:** STV ⛳ 18 Squash Sauna Solarium Gym Putt green Racketball, aerobic studio **CONF:** Thtr 180 Class 90 Board 70 Del from £164 **SERVICES:** Lift **PARKING:** 200 **NOTES:** ⊗ in restaurant Civ Wed 60 **CARDS:**

★★★★69%

Selsdon Park Hotel & Golf Course

PRINCIPAL HOTELS

Addington Rd, Sanderstead CR2 8YA

☎ 020 8657 8811 020 8651 6171

e-mail: sales.selsdonpark@principal-hotels.com

web: www.principal-hotels.com

Dir: *3m SE of Croydon, off A2022*

Surrounded by 200 acres of mature parkland with its own 18-hole golf course, this imposing Jacobean mansion is less than 20 minutes from central London. The hotel's impressive range of conference rooms, along with spectacular views of the North Downs countryside, make this a popular venue for both weddings and meetings. The leisure facilities are impressive.

ROOMS: 204 en suite (12 fmly) (12 GF) s £75-£135; d £90-£165 (incl. bkfst) **LB FACILITIES: Spa** STV supervised ⛳ 18 Squash Sauna Solarium Gym Putt green Boules Jogging track, croquet ♫ Xmas **CONF:** BC Thtr 350 Class 220 Board 60 Del from £125 **SERVICES:** Lift **PARKING:** 300 **NOTES:** ⊗ in restaurant Civ Wed 120 **CARDS:**

★★★69% **Aerodrome**

CLASSIC BRITISH

Purley Way CR9 4LT

☎ 020 8710 9000 020 8681 6438

e-mail: info@aerodrome-hotel.co.uk

Dir: *Follow A23 Central London. Hotel on left next to Airport House*

This newly refurbished hotel is conveniently located on the edge of Croydon, next to what was London's first airport. Bedrooms vary in size and are furnished to a modern specification, including good business facilities and soundproofing. Two restaurants are available along with conference amenities.

ROOMS: 84 en suite ⊗ in 44 bedrooms s £70-£109; d £85-£129 (incl. bkfst) **LB FACILITIES:** Complimentary pass to nearby health club Xmas **CONF:** Thtr 100 Class 50 Board 40 Del from £125 **PARKING:** 200 **NOTES:** Civ Wed 100 **CARDS:**

★★★65% **Jurys Inn**

JURYS DOYLE HOTELS

Wellesley Rd CR0 9XY

☎ 020 8448 6000 020 8448 6111

e-mail: jurysinncroydon@jurysdoyle.com

Dir: *From A232 bear left, at top of road take right lane at large set of traffic lights & turn right into George St. At top of this road at lights turn left, continue until mini rdbt & turn left. Hotel is at top of the road*

This modern hotel, located in the town centre, has spacious bedrooms with air conditioning. The contemporary public areas include a choice of eating options and a busy state-of-the-art conference centre.

ROOMS: 240 en suite (168 fmly) ⊗ in 140 bedrooms s £63-£85; d £63-£85 **FACILITIES:** STV **CONF:** BC Thtr 100 Class 50 Board 40 Del from £100 **SERVICES:** Lift air con **NOTES:** Closed 24-28 Dec **CARDS:**

★★67% ***South Park Hotel***

3-5 South Park Hill Rd, South Croydon CR2 7DY

☎ 020 8688 5644 020 8760 0861

e-mail: reception@southparkhotel.co.uk

web: www.southparkhotel.co.uk

Dir: *M25 junct 11 onto M23 towards Croydon. At Purley Cross follow A235 to Croydon town centre. At Coombe Rd lights turn right (A212) towards Addington 0.5m to rdbt take 3rd exit into South Park Hill Rd, hotel on left*

This intimate hotel has easy access to rail and road networks with some off-street parking available. Attractively decorated bedrooms vary in size and offer a good range of in-room facilities. Public areas consist of an informal bar, a lounge with large sofas and a delightful back garden.

ROOMS: 21 en suite (2 fmly) ⊗ in 8 bedrooms **PARKING:** 15 **NOTES:** ⊗ in restaurant **CARDS:**

Innkeeper's Lodge Croydon South

Innkeeper's Lodge

415 Brighton Rd CR2 6EJ

☎ 020 8680 4559 020 8649 9802

www.innkeeperslodge.com

Dir: *M23 junct 7/ A23 or M25 junct 6/A22. At Purley take A235 Brighton Rd, N towards South Croydon, for 1m. Lodge on right.*

Smart rooms meet essential business requirements but also have home comforts, and depending on location may well have meeting rooms and pub dining. Dining options generally include all-day menus plus the added advantage of breakfast.

ROOMS: 30 en suite s £48-£62; d £48-£62

Premier Lodge (Croydon)

PREMIER LODGE.com

The Colonnades Leisure Park, 619 Purley Way CR0 4RQ

☎ 0870 9906554 0870 9906555

web: www.premierlodge.com

Dir: *from north, exit M1 onto M25, then follow A23 towards Croydon. From south, Lodge 8m from M25 junct 7 on A23 towards Purley Way, close to junction of Waddon Way*

High quality, modern, budget accommodation, ideal for families and business travellers. All rooms feature bath, power shower and satellite TV, and most have telephones / modem points. The adjacent bar and restaurant offers a wide and varied menu.

ROOMS: 82 en suite s £58; d £58 **CONF:** Thtr 120

Travel Inn

travel inn

104 Coombe Rd CR0 5RB

☎ 08701 977069 020 8686 6439

Dir: *M25 junct 7, A23 to Purley, then follow A235 to Croydon. Pass Tree House pub on left. Turn right at lights, onto A212*

Travel Inn offers good-quality, value-for-money accommodation. Spacious, en suite rooms with bath and shower comfortably accommodate a family of up to two adults and two children (to age 15). The restaurant and bar offers a varied menu. For further details consult the Hotel Groups page.

ROOMS: 39 en suite s £56.95; d £56.95

For central reservation numbers and more information on Hotel Groups, turn to pages 33-39

CUCKFIELD, West Sussex Map 06 TQ32

Top 200 – Hotel

★★★ Ockenden Manor

Ockenden Ln RH17 5LD
☎ 01444 416111 01444 415549
e-mail: ockenden@hshotels.co.uk

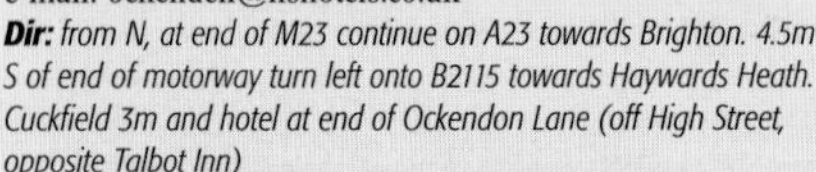

Dir: *from N, at end of M23 continue on A23 towards Brighton. 4.5m S of end of motorway turn left onto B2115 towards Haywards Heath. Cuckfield 3m and hotel at end of Ockendon Lane (off High Street, opposite Talbot Inn)*

This charming 16th-century hotel enjoys fine views of the South Downs. Bedrooms offer high standards of accommodation, some with historic features. Public rooms, retaining much of the original character, include an elegant sitting room with all the elements for a relaxing afternoon in front of the fire. Cuisine is impressive and a highlight to any stay.

ROOMS: 22 en suite (4 fmly) (4 GF) s £99-£175; d £155-£325 (incl. bkfst) **LB** **FACILITIES:** STV Xmas **CONF:** Thtr 50 Class 20 Board 26 Del £240.87 **PARKING:** 43 **NOTES:** in restaurant Civ Wed 75 **CARDS:**

★★72% Hilton Park Hotel

Tylers Green RH17 5EG
☎ 01444 454555 01444 457222
e-mail: hiltonpark@janus-systems.com

Dir: *halfway between Cuckfield and Haywards Heath on A272*

Situated between the delightful village of Cuckfield and Haywards Heath, this charming family-run, Victorian country house is set in three acres of landscaped grounds. The comfortable bedrooms are tastefully decorated and equipped with an excellent range of extra facilities. In addition to an elegant drawing room, the public rooms include a smartly presented dining room and a conservatory bar.

ROOMS: 11 en suite (2 fmly) s £75-£80; d £105-£115 (incl. bkfst) **LB** **FACILITIES:** ch fac **CONF:** Thtr 30 Board 12 Del from £135 **PARKING:** 50 **NOTES:** in restaurant **CARDS:**

DARLINGTON, Co Durham Map 19 NZ21
See also Tees-Side Airport

★★★74% Hall Garth Golf & Country Club

Coatham Mundeville DL1 3LU
☎ 01325 300400 01325 310083
e-mail: hallgarth@corushotels.com

Dir: *A1(M) junct 59, A167 towards Darlington. After 600yds left at top of hill, hotel on right*

This hotel, peacefully situated in its own grounds yet conveniently located for the motorway network, offers comfortable

continued

accommodation. Bedrooms are split between the original house, the converted water mill and the modern extension. Public areas display many original features, whilst the lounges and Hugo's restaurant provide views over the golf course.

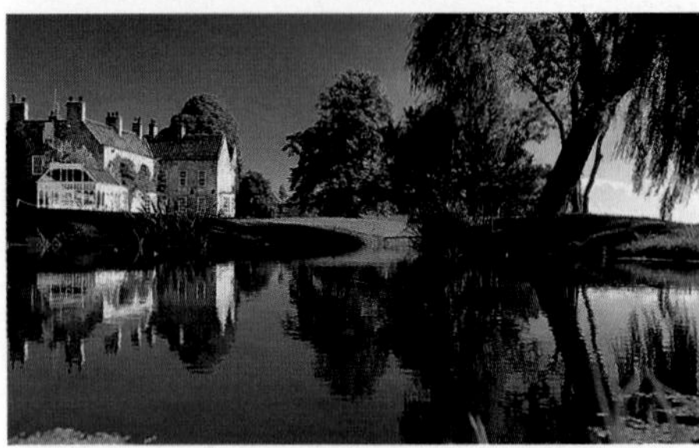

ROOMS: 40 en suite 11 annexe en suite (5 fmly) in 31 bedrooms **FACILITIES:** STV 9 Sauna Solarium Gym Putt green Jacuzzi Steam room Beauty Salon **CONF:** Thtr 300 Class 120 Board 80 **PARKING:** 150 **NOTES:** in restaurant Civ Wed 170 **CARDS:**

★★★73% Headlam Hall

Headlam, Gainford DL2 3HA
☎ 01325 730238 01325 730790
e-mail: admin@headlamhall.co.uk
web: www.headlamhall.co.uk

Dir: *2m N of A67 between Piercebridge and Gainford*

This impressive Jacobean hall lies in farmland north-east of Piercebridge. The main house retains many historical features, including flagstone floors and a pillared hall. Bedrooms are well-proportioned and traditionally styled. A converted coach house contains more modern rooms, as well as a conference and leisure centre.

ROOMS: 19 en suite 17 annexe en suite (4 fmly) (10 GF) in 25 bedrooms s £85-£125; d £100-£140 (incl. bkfst) **LB** **FACILITIES:** STV 9 Fishing Sauna Gym Putt green **CONF:** Thtr 150 Class 40 Board 40 Del from £120 **PARKING:** 60 **NOTES:** in restaurant Closed 24-25 Dec Civ Wed 150 **CARDS:**

★★★67% Walworth Castle Hotel

Walworth DL2 2LY
☎ 01325 485470 01325 462257
e-mail: enquiries@walworthcastle.co.uk
web: www.walworthcastle.co.uk

Dir: *A1(M) junct 58 follow signs to Corbridge. Left at rdbt, left at The Dog pub. Hotel on left after 1m*

This 12th-century castle is privately owned and has been tastefully converted. Accommodation is offered in a range of styles, including an impressive suite and more compact rooms in an adjoining wing. Dinner can be taken in the fine dining Hansards Restaurant or the more relaxed Farmer's Bar. A popular venue for conferences and weddings.

ROOMS: 20 en suite 14 annexe en suite (4 fmly) in 6 bedrooms s £65-£80; d £80-£195 (incl. bkfst) **LB** **FACILITIES:** Xmas **CONF:** BC Thtr 150 Class 100 Board 80 Del from £90 **PARKING:** 100 **NOTES:** in restaurant Civ Wed 120 **CARDS:**

Late for dinner?
Quality Standards mean that last orders for dinner vary according to star rating and should be no earlier than:
★★ 7.00pm ★★★ 8.00pm ★★★★ 9.00pm
★★★★★ 10.00pm

★★★66% The Blackwell Grange Hotel
Blackwell Grange DL3 8QH
☎ 0870 609 6121 01325 380899
e-mail: blackwellgrange@corushotels.com
Dir: *on A167, 1.5m from central ring road*
This hotel, peacefully situated in its own grounds yet conveniently located for the motorway network, offers comfortable accommodation. Rooms are split between the original house, modern extension and the courtyard. Public areas are spacious and display many original features, comfortable lounges and meeting rooms along with a stylish dining room.

ROOMS: 99 en suite 11 annexe en suite (3 fmly) (36 GF) in 51 bedrooms s £88-£108; d £108-£128 **LB FACILITIES: Spa** STV supervised Sauna Solarium Gym Jacuzzi Xmas **CONF:** Thtr 300 Class 110 Board 50 Del from £90 **SERVICES:** Lift **PARKING:** 250 **NOTES:** in restaurant Civ Wed 200 **CARDS:**

★★★65% Kings Head
9-12 Priestgate DL1 1NW
☎ 01325 380222 01325 382006
e-mail: admin@kingsheadhotel50.fsnet.co.uk
web: www.kingsheaddarlington.co.uk
Dir: *A1 northbound signed Darlington. 3rd exit off rdbt, 2nd off next rdbt. At 3rd rdbt 1st exit. 1st right, then 1st left. Hotel on right*
Adjacent to the Cornmill Shopping Centre, this town centre hotel provides a variety of bedroom styles. Public areas include an inviting foyer lounge and upstairs a comfortable bar and restaurant. The hotel has limited secure basement car parking.
ROOMS: 85 en suite (3 fmly) in 51 bedrooms s £60-£100; d £70-£100 (incl. bkfst) **LB FACILITIES:** Free use of nearby leisure complex Xmas **CONF:** Thtr 250 Class 100 Board 50 Del from £98 **SERVICES:** Lift **PARKING:** 28 **CARDS:**

U The Croft
Croft-on-Tees DL2 2ST
☎ 01325 720319 01325 721252
e-mail: enquiries@croft-hotel.co.uk
Dir: *from Darlington take A167 Northallerton road. Hotel 3m S*
At the time of going to press, the star classification for this hotel was not confirmed. Please refer to the AA internet site www.theAA.com for current information.
ROOMS: 20 en suite (2 fmly) in all bedrooms s £100-£170; d £100-£170 (incl. bkfst) **LB FACILITIES:** STV Snooker Sauna Gym Xmas **CONF:** Thtr 200 Class 120 Board 50 Del from £145 **PARKING:** 60 **NOTES:** in restaurant Civ Wed 200 **CARDS:**

Travel Inn
Morton Park Way, Morton Park DL1 4PJ
☎ 08701 977300 01325 373341
Travel Inn offers good-quality, value-for-money accommodation. Spacious, en suite rooms with bath and shower comfortably accommodate a family of up to two adults and two children (to age 15). The restaurant and bar offers a varied menu. For further details consult the Hotel Groups page.
ROOMS: (incl. bkfst) s £45.95-£46.95; d £45.95-£46.95

DARRINGTON, West Yorkshire — Map 16 SE42

Premier Lodge (Pontefract)
Great North Rd WF8 3BL
☎ 0870 9906386 0870 9906387
web: www.premierlodge.com
Dir: *just off A1, 2m south of the A1/M62 interchange*
High quality, modern, budget accommodation, ideal for families and business travellers. All rooms feature bath, power shower and satellite TV, and most have telephones / modem points. The adjacent bar and restaurant offers a wide and varied menu.
ROOMS: 28 en suite s £50; d £50 **CONF:** Thtr 10 Class 10 Board 10 Del from £77.50

DARTFORD, Kent — Map 06 TQ57

★★★★77% Rowhill Grange Hotel & Spa
DA2 7QH
☎ 01322 615136 01322 615137
e-mail: admin@rowhillgrange.co.uk
web: www.rowhillgrange.co.uk
Dir: *M25 junct 3 take B2173 to Swanley, then B258 to Hextable*

A country house hotel surrounded by nine acres of mature woodland and landscaped grounds that feature a walled Victorian garden. The stylish, individually decorated bedrooms offer a high degree of comfort. An imaginative menu is served in the conservatory restaurant and there is an informal brasserie.
ROOMS: 38 en suite (3 fmly) (3 GF) in all bedrooms s £155-£270; d £180-£330 (incl. bkfst) **LB FACILITIES: Spa** STV Sauna Solarium Gym Jacuzzi Beauty treatment, Hair salon, Aerobic studio, Japanese Therapy pool Xmas **CONF:** Thtr 160 Class 64 Board 34 Del from £150 **SERVICES:** Lift **PARKING:** 150 **NOTES:** in restaurant Civ Wed 150 **CARDS:**

Destination dining!
This symbol indicates a Restaurant with Rooms

DARTFORD, continued

⌂ Campanile
1 Clipper Boulevard West,
Crossways Business Park DA2 6QN
☎ 01322 278925 📠 01322 278948
e-mail: dartford@envergure.co.uk
Dir: *follow signs for Ferry Terminal from Dartford Bridge*

This modern building offers accommodation in smart, well-equipped bedrooms, all with en suite bathrooms. Refreshments may be taken at the informal Bistro. For further details consult the Hotel Groups page.
ROOMS: 125 en suite s fr £48.95; d fr £48.95 **CONF:** Thtr 50 Class 20 Board 40

⌂ Travelodge
Charles St, Greenhithe DA9 9AP
☎ 08700 850 950 📠 01322 387854
Travelodge offers good quality, good value, modern accommodation. Ideal for families, the spacious, en suite bedrooms include remote-control TV, tea and coffee-making facilities and luxury beds. Meals can be taken at the nearby family restaurant. For further details consult the Hotel Groups page.
ROOMS: 65 en suite s fr £25; d fr £25

DARTMOUTH, Devon — Map 03 SX85

★★★74% *Royal Castle*
11 The Quay TQ6 9PS
☎ 01803 833033 📠 01803 835445
e-mail: enquiry@royalcastle.co.uk
web: www.royalcastle.co.uk
Dir: *in centre of town, overlooking Inner Harbour*

At the edge of the harbour, this imposing 17th-century former coaching inn is filled with charm and character. Bedrooms are well equipped and comfortable; many have harbour views. A choice of quiet seating areas is offered in addition to both the traditional and contemporary bars. A variety of eating options is available, including the main restaurant which features accomplished cuisine and lovely views.
ROOMS: 25 en suite (4 fmly) ⊘ in all bedrooms **FACILITIES:** STV **CONF:** Thtr 70 Class 40 Board 40 **PARKING:** 17 **NOTES:** ⊘ in restaurant Civ Wed 60 **CARDS:**

★★★71% The Dart Marina
Sandquay TQ6 9PH
☎ 01803 832 580 📠 01803 835040
e-mail: info@dartmarinahotel.com
web: www.dartmarinahotel.com
Dir: *A3122 from Totnes to Dartmouth. Follow road which becomes College Way, before Higher Ferry. Hotel sharp left in Sandquay Rd*
This hotel is situated in an idyllic position by the marina, with direct access to the water and stunning views of the Dart Estuary. Bedrooms, or cabins as they are referred to, have a nautical theme and are named after famous ships, sailors and shipbuilders. Stylish and comfortable public areas enable guests to take full advantage of the waterside location.
ROOMS: 45 en suite 4 annexe en suite ⊘ in all bedrooms s £85-£136; d £149-£203 (incl. bkfst & dinner) **LB** **FACILITIES:** Use of hotel boat slipway, Sailing Canoeing Xmas **CONF:** Board 16 **SERVICES:** Lift **PARKING:** 50 **NOTES:** No children 14yrs ⊘ in restaurant Civ Wed 40 **CARDS:**

★★★68% Stoke Lodge
Stoke Fleming TQ6 0RA
☎ 01803 770523 📠 01803 770851
e-mail: mail@stokelodge.co.uk
web: www.stokelodge.co.uk
Dir: *2m S A379*
This family-run hotel continues to attract returning guests, and is set in three acres of gardens and grounds. There are views across the sea and a range of leisure facilities, along with a choice of comfortable lounges. Bedrooms are pleasantly appointed. The restaurant offers a choice of menus and an impressive wine list.
ROOMS: 25 en suite (5 fmly) s £57-£64; d £48-£114 (incl. bkfst) **LB** **FACILITIES: Spa** Snooker Sauna Putt green Table tennis, Pool table Xmas **CONF:** Thtr 80 Class 60 Board 30 **PARKING:** 50 **NOTES:** ⊘ in restaurant **CARDS:**

DARWEN, Lancashire — Map 15 SD62

⌂ Travel Inn Blackburn
Oakenhurst Farm, Eccleslink Rd BB3 0ST
☎ 08701 977 187 📠 08701 977701
Dir: *directly off M65 junction 4, near Blackburn*
Travel Inn offers good-quality, value-for-money accommodation. Spacious, en suite rooms with bath and shower comfortably accommodate a family of up to two adults and two children (to age 15). The restaurant and bar offers a varied menu. For further details consult the Hotel Groups page.
ROOMS: 41 en suite s £45.95-£46.95; d £45.95-£46.95

⌂ Travelodge Blackburn

Darwen Motorway services BB3 0AT
☎ 08700 850 950 📠 01254 776058
Dir: *off M65 junct 4 towards Blackburn*
Travelodge offers good quality, good value, modern accommodation. Ideal for families, the spacious, en suite bedrooms include remote-control TV, tea and coffee-making facilities and luxury beds. Meals can be taken at the nearby family restaurant. For further details consult the Hotel Groups page.
ROOMS: s fr £25; d fr £25

DAVENTRY, Northamptonshire Map 11 SP56

Top 200 – Hotel

★★★★ Fawsley Hall
Fawsley NN11 3BA
☎ 01327 892000 01327 892001
e-mail: reservations@fawsleyhall.com
web: www.fawsleyhall.com
Dir: *From A361 turn at 'Fawsley Hall' sign. Follow single track for 1.5m until reaching iron gates*
Dating back to the 15th century, this delightful hotel is peacefully located in beautiful gardens designed by 'Capability' Brown. Spacious, individually designed bedrooms and stylish public areas are beautifully furnished with antique and period pieces. Afternoon tea is served in the impressive Great Hall with its sumptuous deep cushioned sofas and real fires. Dinner in the Knightley Restaurant offers imaginative Enghlish cuisine with Mediterranean influences.
ROOMS: 43 en suite (2 GF) s fr £140; d £140-£390 (incl. cont bkfst) **LB** **FACILITIES: Spa** STV Sauna Gym Putt green Jacuzzi Health & Beauty treatment rooms Xmas **CONF:** Thtr 100 Class 45 Board 45 Del from £210 **PARKING:** 100 **NOTES:** in restaurant Civ Wed 100 **CARDS:**

★★★★62%
Hanover International Hotel & Club
Sedgemoor Way NN11 5SG
☎ 01327 307000 01327 706313
e-mail: rso@hanover-international.com
web: www.hanover-international.com
Dir: *N of Daventry on A361 Ring Road*
This modern, striking hotel overlooking Drayton Water boasts spacious public areas that include a good range of banqueting, meeting and leisure facilities. It is a popular venue for conferences. Bedrooms all have double beds and excellent showers.
ROOMS: 138 en suite in 100 bedrooms s fr £115; d fr £115 (incl. bkfst) **LB** **FACILITIES: Spa** STV Sauna Solarium Gym Steam room Health & beauty salon **CONF:** BC Thtr 600 Class 200 Board 30 Del £155 **SERVICES:** Lift **PARKING:** 350 **NOTES:** in restaurant RS 26-30 Dec Civ Wed 250 **CARDS:**

DAWLISH, Devon Map 03 SX97

★★★70% **Langstone Cliff**
Dawlish Warren EX7 0NA
☎ 01626 868000 01626 868006
e-mail: reception@langstone-hotel.co.uk
web: www.langstone-hotel.co.uk
Dir: *1.5m NE off A379 Exeter road to Dawlish Warren*
A family owned and run hotel, the Langstone Cliff offers a range of leisure, conference and function facilities. Bedrooms, many with sea views and balconies, are spacious, comfortable and well equipped. There are a number of attractive lounges and a well stocked bar. Dinner is served, often carvery style, in the restaurant.
ROOMS: 62 en suite 4 annexe en suite (52 fmly) (10 GF) s £62-£71; d £106-£154 (incl. bkfst) **LB** **FACILITIES:** STV Snooker Gym Table tennis, Golf practice area, Hair and beauty salon ch fac Xmas **CONF:** Thtr 400 Class 200 Board 80 Del from £90 **SERVICES:** Lift **PARKING:** 200 **NOTES:** Civ Wed 400
CARDS:

DEAL, Kent Map 07 TR35

★★★71% **Dunkerleys Hotel & Restaurant**
19 Beach St CT14 7AH
☎ 01304 375016 01304 380187
e-mail: dunkerleysofdeal@btinternet.com
web: www.dunkerleys.co.uk
Dir: *from M20 or M2 follow signs for A258 Deal. Hotel close to Pier*
This hotel is situated on the seafront and is centrally located. Bedrooms are furnished to a high standard with a good range of amenities. The restaurant and bar have been attractively refurbished and menus make the best use of local ingredients. Service throughout is friendly and attentive.
ROOMS: 16 en suite (2 fmly) s £65-£85; d £100-£170 (incl. bkfst) **LB** **FACILITIES:** STV Xmas **NOTES:** RS Mon
CARDS:

DEBENHAM, Suffolk Map 13 TM16

U **The Angel Inn**
5 High St IP14 6QL
☎ 01728 860954 01728 861854
Dir: *A14 junct 51, 2m A140 right Stonhams, follow signs to Debenham 3m.*
At the time of going to press, the star classification for this hotel was not confirmed. Please refer to the AA internet site www.theAA.com for current information.
ROOMS: 3 en suite (1 fmly) in all bedrooms s £40-£60; d £60-£90 (incl. bkfst) **FACILITIES:** Xmas **CONF:** Thtr 30 Class 30 Board 30 **PARKING:** 14 **NOTES:** in restaurant
CARDS:

DEDDINGTON, Oxfordshire Map 11 SP43

★★★70% **Deddington Arms**
Horsefair OX15 0SH
☎ 0800 3287031 01869 337010
e-mail: deddarms@oxfordshire-hotels.co.uk
web: www.deddington-arms-hotel.co.uk
Dir: *From S M40 junct 10 signed Northampton onto A43. 1st rdbt left to Aynho and left to Deddington. From N M40 junct 11 to Banbury. Through Banbury to hospital and Adderbury on A4260, then to Deddington*

This charming and friendly old inn is conveniently located off the

continued on p194

DEDDINGTON, continued

Market Square. The well-equipped bedrooms are comfortably appointed and either situated in the main building or a purpose built courtyard wing. The bar is full of character and the delightful restaurant enjoys well-deserved local popularity.
ROOMS: 27 en suite (4 fmly) (9 GF) ⊗ in 7 bedrooms s £85-£99; d £95-£120 (incl. bkfst) **LB** **FACILITIES:** STV Many facilities avaliable locally Xmas **CONF:** Thtr 40 Class 35 Board 35 Del from £110 **PARKING:** 36 **NOTES:** ⊗ in restaurant
CARDS:

D

★★★68% Holcombe Hotel & Restaurant

Best Western

High St OX15 0SL
☎ 01869 338274 01869 337010
e-mail: holcombe@oxfordshire-hotels.co.uk
web: www.holcombe-hotel.co.uk
Dir: *on A4260 Banbury to Oxford Road. From M40 J11 follow signs to Adderbury, then Deddington. From M40 J10 follow B4100 to Aynho then B4031 to Deddington.*

This hotel enjoys a convenient roadside location, within easy reach of the village centre. Public areas include the stylish Peppers bar and an eye-catching restaurant serving pasta, pizzas and other specialities; in the warmer months the gardens offer a peaceful place in which to relax. Bedrooms are traditional in design with many thoughtful touches.
ROOMS: 17 en suite (3 fmly) (1 GF) ⊗ in 4 bedrooms s £85-£95; d £95-£105 (incl. bkfst) **LB** **FACILITIES:** Xmas **CONF:** Thtr 25 Class 15 Board 18 Del from £110 **PARKING:** 40 **NOTES:** ⊗ in restaurant
CARDS:

DEDHAM, Essex — Map 13 TM03

Top 200 – Hotel

★★★ Maison Talbooth

PRIDE OF BRITAIN HOTELS

Stratford Rd CO7 6HN
☎ 01206 322367 01206 322752
e-mail: maison@milsomhotels.co.uk
web: www.maisonhotels.com
Dir: *A12 towards Ipswich, 1st turning signed Dedham, follow road until left bend, take right turn. Hotel 1m on right*
A Victorian country house hotel situated in a peaceful rural location amidst pretty landscaped grounds overlooking the Stour River valley. Public areas include a comfortable drawing room where guests may take afternoon tea or snacks. Residents are chauffeured to the popular Le Talbooth Restaurant, just a mile away, for dinner. The spacious bedrooms are individually decorated, tastefully furnished, have lovely co-ordinated fabrics and many thoughtful touches.
continued

Hospitality is warm and friendly and quality service is to be expected.

ROOMS: 10 en suite (1 fmly) (5 GF) s £120-£160; d £165-£225 (incl. bkfst) **LB** **FACILITIES:** Garden chess, croquet Xmas **CONF:** Thtr 30 Class 20 Board 16 Del from £150 **PARKING:** 20 **NOTES:** Civ Wed 50 **CARDS:**

★★★69% milsoms

Stratford Rd, Dedham CO7 6HW
☎ 01206 322795 01206 323689
e-mail: milsoms@milsomhotels.com
web: www.milsomhotels.com
Dir: *6m N of Colchester off A12, turn off to Stratford St Mary/Dedham. Turn right over A12, hotel on left*

Situated in the Dedham Vale, an Area of Outstanding Natural Beauty, this is the perfect base to explore the countryside on the Essex/Suffolk border. Milsom's is styled along the lines of a contemporary 'gastro bar' combining good food served in an informal atmosphere and stylish and well appointed accommodation.
ROOMS: 14 en suite (3 fmly) (4 GF) s £67.50-£87.50; d £95-£135 **FACILITIES:** STV **CONF:** Board 14 Del from £130 **PARKING:** 70 **NOTES:** **CARDS:**

DERBY, Derbyshire — Map 11 SK33

★★★★73% Menzies Mickleover Court

MENZIES HOTELS

Etwall Rd, Mickleover DE3 0XX
☎ 01332 521234 01332 521238
e-mail: mickleovercourt@menzies-hotels.co.uk
web: www.bookmenzies.com
Dir: *Take A50 towards Derby, leave at junct 5 and follow A516 towards Derby, take exit signed Mickleover*
Located close to Derby, this large, modern hotel is well suited for conference and leisure guests. Bedrooms are spacious, with some traditional rooms and some more contemporary in style. A choice
continued

of eating options, spacious seating and excellent conference and leisure facilities are all popular with residents and visitors.
ROOMS: 99 en suite (20 fmly) in 45 bedrooms s £145; d £145-£165 **LB** **FACILITIES:** STV Sauna Solarium Gym Jacuzzi Beauty salon, Steam room Xmas **CONF:** Thtr 200 Class 80 Board 40 Del £170 **SERVICES:** Lift air con **PARKING:** 270 **NOTES:** in restaurant Civ Wed **CARDS:**

★★★★65% Marriott Breadsall Priory Hotel, Country Club

Moor Rd DE7 6DL
☎ 01332 832235 01332 833509
(For full entry see Breadsall)

★★★76% Midland

Midland Rd DE1 2SQ
☎ 01332 345894 01332 293522
e-mail: sales@midland-derby.co.uk
web: www.midland-derby.co.uk
Dir: *opposite Derby railway station*

This early Victorian hotel situated opposite Derby Midland Station provides very comfortable accommodation. The executive rooms are ideal for business travellers, equipped with writing desks and fax/computer points. Public rooms include a comfortable lounge and a popular restaurant. Service is skilled, attentive and friendly. There is also a walled garden and private car parking.
ROOMS: 100 en suite in 75 bedrooms s £61.50-£116.50; d £61.50-£126.50 **LB** **FACILITIES:** **CONF:** Thtr 150 Class 50 Board 40 Del £145 **SERVICES:** Lift **PARKING:** 90 **NOTES:** in restaurant Closed 24-26 Dec & 1 Jan Civ Wed 150
CARDS:

See advert on this page

★★★68% Aston Court Hotel & Conference Centre
Midland Rd DE1 2SL
☎ 01332 342716 01332 293503
e-mail: astoncourtderby@hotelres.co.uk
Dir: *Midland Road opposite entrance of the Derby Railway Station*
Situated just a few minutes from the city centre and opposite the station. The hotel has recently undergone a massive refit programme which will be completed at the end of 2004. All bedrooms and public areas will have been refurbished, offering comfort and more contemporary surroundings.
ROOMS: 55 en suite (5 fmly) (6 GF) in 36 bedrooms s £30-£85; d £50-£125 **LB** **FACILITIES:** STV More facilities available at a nearby health club Xmas **CONF:** BC Thtr 250 Class 90 Board 65 Del from £124.50 **SERVICES:** Lift **PARKING:** 70 **NOTES:** in restaurant Civ Wed **CARDS:**

Early start?
Hotels at all star levels should provide in-room alarm clocks and/or alarm calls

DERBY, continued

★★★65% Littleover Lodge
222 Rykneld Rd, Littleover DE23 7AN
☎ 01332 510161 📠 01332 514010
e-mail: enquiries@littleoverlodge.co.uk
web: www.littleoverlodge.co.uk
Dir: *A38 towards Derby approx 1m on left slip lane signed Littleover/Mickleover/Findon, take 2nd exit off island marked Littleover 0.25m on right*

Situated in a rural location off the A5250 beside the A38, this friendly hotel offers modern bedrooms with direct access from the car park. Two styles of dining, an informal carvery operation which enjoys a high local demand, and a more formal restaurant experience are available at both lunch and dinner every day.

ROOMS: 16 en suite (3 fmly) (8 GF) s £55-£80; d £55-£90 (incl. bkfst) LB **FACILITIES:** STV ♫ Xmas **PARKING:** 75 **NOTES:** ⊗ in restaurant
CARDS:

See advert on page 195

★★★65% Hotel Ristorante La Gondola
THE INDEPENDENTS
220 Osmaston Rd DE23 8JX
☎ 01332 332895 📠 01332 384512
e-mail: service@la-gondola.co.uk
web: www.la-gondola.co.uk
Dir: *on A514 towards Melbourne*

Imaginatively designed and well-equipped bedrooms, including a spacious family suite, are offered at this conveniently located Georgian house. Situated between the inner and outer ring roads and close to the General Hospital. There are two small comfortable lounges, a well-established Italian restaurant and conference and banqueting rooms are available.

ROOMS: 20 rms (19 en suite) (7 fmly) **FACILITIES:** STV ♫ Xmas **CONF:** BC Thtr 80 Class 50 Board 80 **PARKING:** 70 **NOTES:**
CARDS:

★★★63% International
288 Burton Rd DE23 6AD
☎ 01332 369321 📠 01332 294430
e-mail: internationalhotel.derby@virgin.net
Dir: *0.5m from city centre on A5250*

Within easy reach of the city centre, this hotel offers comfortable, modern public rooms. An extensive range of dishes is served in the pleasant restaurant. There is a wide range of bedroom sizes and styles, and each room is very well equipped; some suites are also available, and parking is a bonus.

ROOMS: 41 en suite 21 annexe en suite (4 fmly) ⊗ in 28 bedrooms s £47.50-£81; d £54-£89.50 (incl. bkfst) LB **FACILITIES:** STV ♫ Xmas **CONF:** Thtr 100 Class 40 Board 40 Del from £97 **SERVICES:** Lift **PARKING:** 100 **NOTES:** Civ Wed 100
CARDS:

⌂ Days Hotel Derby
DAYS INN
Derbyshire C C Ground, Pentagon Roundabout, Nottingham Rd DE21 6DA
☎ 01332 363600 📠 01332 200630
e-mail: derby@kewgreen.co.uk
Dir: *M1 junct 25, take A52 towards Derby. At Pentagon rdbt take 4th exit and turn into cricket club*

This modern building offers accommodation in smart, spacious and well-equipped bedrooms, suitable for families and business travellers, and all with en suite bathrooms. Continental breakfast is available and other refreshments may be taken at the nearby family restaurant. For further details see the Hotel Groups page.

ROOMS: 100 en suite s £52.50-£74.95; d £52.50-£74.95 **CONF:** Thtr 50 Class 25 Board 18 Del £125

⌂ European Inn
Midland Rd DE1 2SL
☎ 01332 292000 📠 01332 293940
e-mail: admin@euro-derby.co.uk
web: www.euro-derby.co.uk
Dir: *City centre, 200yds from railway station*

Excellent value accommodation is provided at this modern lodge. Bedrooms are well-appointed and equipped with modern facilities. Shops form part of the complex and include an Italian pizza restaurant. A good choice of English breakfast is served buffet-style in the breakfast room; takeaway meals can also be eaten here.

ROOMS: 88 en suite s £55.50; d £55.50 **CONF:** Thtr 60 Class 30 Board 25 Del £100

⌂ Innkeeper's Lodge Derby

Nottingham Rd, Chaddesdon DE21 6LZ
☎ 0870 243 0500 & 01332 662504
📠 01332 673306
www.innkeeperslodge.com
Dir: *from M1 junct 25 take A52 towards Derby, take exit signed Spondon & Chaddesden, at rdbt take exit signed Chaddesden pass Asda store, 1m at lights right into car park*

Smart rooms meet essential business requirements but also have home comforts, and depending on location may well have meeting rooms and pub dining. Dining options generally include all-day menus plus the added advantage of breakfast.

ROOMS: 29 en suite s £45-£52; d £45-£52

⌂ Premier Lodge (Derby)

Foresters Leisure Park, Osmaston Park Rd DE23 8AG
☎ 0870 9906306 📠 0870 9906307
web: www.premierlodge.com
Dir: *exit M1 junct 24 A6 to Derby. Left onto A5111 ring road for 2m*

High quality, modern, budget accommodation, ideal for families and business travellers. All rooms feature bath, power shower and satellite TV, and most have telephones / modem points. The adjacent bar and restaurant offers a wide and varied menu.

ROOMS: 27 en suite s £50; d £50

⌂ Premier Lodge (Derby North)
PREMIER LODGE.com
95 Ashbourne Rd, Mackworth DE22 4LZ
☎ 0870 9906606 📠 0870 9906607
web: www.premierlodge.com
Dir: *exit M1 junct 25 A52 towards Derby. At Pentagon Island straight ahead towards city centre. Follow signs to A52 Ashbourne and follow road into Mackworth*

High quality, modern, budget accommodation, ideal for families and business travellers. All rooms feature bath, power shower and satellite TV, and most have telephones / modem points. The adjacent bar and restaurant offers a wide and varied menu.

ROOMS: 22 en suite s £50; d £50

⌂ Travel Inn (Derby East)

The Wyvern Business Park, Chaddesden Sidings DE21 6BF
☎ 0870 238 3313 📠 01332 667827
Dir: *From M1 junct 25 follow A52 to Derby. After 6.5m take exit for Wyvern/Pride Park. 1st exit at rdbt (A52 Nottingham), straight over next rdbt. Travel Inn on left*

Travel Inn offers good-quality, value-for-money accommodation. Spacious, en suite rooms with bath and shower comfortably accommodate a family of up to two adults and two children (to

continued

age 15). The restaurant and bar offers a varied menu. For further details consult the Hotel Groups page.

ROOMS: 82 en suite s £45.95-£48.95; d £45.95-£48.95

⌂ Travel Inn (Derby West)

Uttoxeter New Rd, Manor Park Way DE22 3HN
☎ 08701 977072 🖷 01332 207506

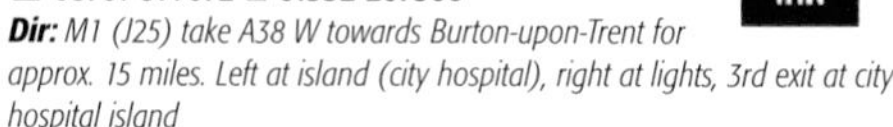

Dir: *M1 (J25) take A38 W towards Burton-upon-Trent for approx. 15 miles. Left at island (city hospital), right at lights, 3rd exit at city hospital island*

Travel Inn offers good-quality, value-for-money accommodation. Spacious, en suite rooms with bath and shower comfortably accommodate a family of up to two adults and two children (to age 15). The restaurant and bar offers a varied menu. For further details consult the Hotel Groups page.
ROOMS: 43 en suite s £45.95-£48.95; d £45.95-£48.95 **CONF:** Thtr 15

⌂ Travelodge

Kingsway, Rowditch DE22 3NN
☎ 08700 850 950 🖷 01332 367255

Travelodge offers good quality, good value, modern accommodation. Ideal for families, the spacious, en suite bedrooms include remote-control TV, tea and coffee-making facilities and luxury beds. Meals can be taken at the nearby family restaurant. For further details consult the Hotel Groups page.
ROOMS: 40 en suite s fr £25; d fr £25

DERBY SERVICE AREA (A50), Derbyshire — Map 11 SK42

⌂ Days Inn Donnington

Welcome Break Services DE72 2WW
☎ 01332 799666 🖷 01332 794166

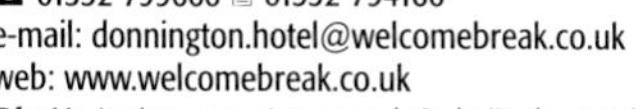

e-mail: donnington.hotel@welcomebreak.co.uk
web: www.welcomebreak.co.uk
Dir: *M1 J24/24a, onto A50 towards Stoke/Derby. Hotel between junct 1 & 2*

This modern building offers accommodation in smart, spacious and well-equipped bedrooms, suitable for families and business travellers, and all with en suite bathrooms. Continental breakfast is available and other refreshments may be taken at the nearby family restaurant. For further details see the Hotel Groups page.
ROOMS: 47 en suite s £49-£69; d £49-£69
CONF: Thtr 10 Class 10 Board 10

> Popped the question?
> Hotels with Civ Wed in their entry are licensed for civil wedding ceremonies. Maximum numbers for the ceremony only are shown, e.g. Civ Wed 120

DESBOROUGH, Northamptonshire — Map 11 SP88

⌂ Travelodge Market Harborough

Harborough Rd NN14 2UG
☎ 08700 850 950 🖷 01536 762034
Dir: *on A6, southbound*

Travelodge offers good quality, good value, modern accommodation. Ideal for families, the spacious, en suite bedrooms include remote-control TV, tea and coffee-making facilities and luxury beds. Meals can be taken at the nearby family restaurant. For further details consult the Hotel Groups page.
ROOMS: 32 en suite s fr £25; d fr £25

DEVIZES, Wiltshire — Map 04 SU06

★★★64% Bear

Market Place SN10 1HS
☎ 01380 722444 🖷 01380 722450
e-mail: info@thebearhotel.net
web: www.thebearhotel.net
Dir: *town centre*

Set in the market place of this small Wiltshire town, this attractive hotel has a popular local following. The individually furnished and decorated bedrooms vary in size. The attractive lounge offers a quiet area for residents to enjoy afternoon tea. Homemade cakes are available throughout the day and the restaurant serves enjoyable meals.
ROOMS: 24 en suite (5 fmly) ⊗ in all bedrooms s £50; d £75 (incl. bkfst) **LB** **FACILITIES:** Solarium **CONF:** Thtr 100 Class 60 Board 60 **SERVICES:** Lift **NOTES:** ⊗ in restaurant Closed 25-26 Dec
CARDS:

DEWSBURY, West Yorkshire — Map 16 SE22

★★★66% Heath Cottage Hotel & Restaurant

Wakefield Rd WF12 8ET
☎ 01924 465399 🖷 01924 459405
e-mail: bookings@heathcottage.co.uk
web: www.heathcottage.co.uk
Dir: *M1 junct 40/A638 for 2.5m towards Dewsbury. Hotel before traffic lights, opposite Earlsheaton Cemetery*

Standing in an acre of grounds, Heath Cottage is two and a half miles from the M1. It has extensive parking and the service is friendly and professional. The modern bedrooms are well appointed and some are in a converted stable building. The lounge bar and restaurant are both air conditioned.
ROOMS: 23 en suite 6 annexe en suite (3 fmly) ⊗ in 18 bedrooms s £52-£63; d £68-£74 (incl. bkfst) **LB** **FACILITIES:** Xmas **CONF:** Thtr 80 Class 50 Board 30 Del from £89 **PARKING:** 80 **NOTES:** ⊗ in restaurant Civ Wed 90 **CARDS:**

DEWSBURY, continued

★★★64% ® **Healds Hall**
Leeds Rd, Liversedge WF15 6JA
☎ 01924 409112 📠 01924 401895
e-mail: enquire@healdshall.co.uk
web: www.healdshall.co.uk
Dir: *on A62 between Leeds and Huddersfield. 50yds on left after Swan Pub traffic lights*

This 18th-century house in the heart of West Yorkshire offers comfortable and well-equipped accommodation and excellent hospitality. The hotel has earned a good local reputation for the quality of its food and offers a choice of casual or more formal dining styles, with a wide range of dishes on the various menus.
ROOMS: 24 en suite (3 fmly) (3 GF) ⊗ in 4 bedrooms s £45-£63; d £60-£75 (incl. bkfst) **LB** **CONF:** Thtr 100 Class 60 Board 80 Del from £90 **PARKING:** 90 **NOTES:** ✈ ⊗ in restaurant Closed New Years Day and BH Mondays **CARDS:**

DIDCOT, Oxfordshire Map 05 SU59

⌂ **Travel Inn**
Milton Interchange, Milton OX14 4DP
☎ 08701 977073 📠 01235 820465
Dir: *on A4130 at junct with A34*
Travel Inn offers good-quality, value-for-money accommodation. Spacious, en suite rooms with bath and shower comfortably accommodate a family of up to two adults and two children (to age 15). The restaurant and bar offers a varied menu. For further details consult the Hotel Groups page.
ROOMS: 60 en suite s £45.95-£46.95; d £45.95-£46.95

DIDSBURY, Greater Manchester Map 16 SJ89

⌂ **Travelodge Manchester South**
Kingsway M20 5PG
☎ 08700 850 950 📠 0161 448 0399
Travelodge offers good quality, good value, modern accommodation. Ideal for families, the spacious, en suite bedrooms include remote-control TV, tea and coffee-making facilities and luxury beds. Meals can be taken at the nearby family restaurant. For further details consult the Hotel Groups page.
ROOMS: 62 en suite s fr £25; d fr £25

DONCASTER, South Yorkshire Map 16 SE50

★★★★69% ® **Mount Pleasant**

Great North Rd DN11 0HW
☎ 01302 868696 & 868219 📠 01302 865130
e-mail: reception@mountpleasant.co.uk
web: www.bw-mountpleasant.co.uk
(For full entry see Rossington)

★★★68% **Regent**
Regent Square DN1 2DS
☎ 01302 364180 📠 01302 322331
e-mail: admin@theregenthotel.co.uk
web: www.theregenthotel.co.uk
Dir: *on corner of A630 & A638, 1m from racecourse*
This town centre hotel overlooks a delightful small square. Public rooms include a choice of bars and the restaurant, where an interesting range of dishes is offered. Service is friendly and attentive. Most bedrooms have been furnished in a modern style with contemporary colour schemes; a rolling programme of refurbishment ensures that standards are maintained.
ROOMS: 52 en suite (6 fmly) (8 GF) s £55-£90; d £70-£105 (incl. bkfst) **LB** **FACILITIES:** STV ♫ **CONF:** Thtr 100 Class 50 Board 40 Del from £99.50 **SERVICES:** Lift **PARKING:** 20 **NOTES:** ⊗ in restaurant Closed New Year's Day Xmas Day RS Bank Hols Civ Wed 100
CARDS:

★★★67% **Danum**
High St DN1 1DN
☎ 01302 342261 📠 01302 329034
e-mail: danum-hotel@btconnect.com
Dir: *M18 junct 3, A6182 to Doncaster. Over rdbt, right at next. Right at give way sign, left at mini rdbt, hotel ahead*
Situated in the centre of the town, this Edwardian hotel offers spacious public rooms together with soundly equipped accommodation. There has been major refurbishment to the popular ground-floor lounge and bedrooms. A pleasant restaurant on the first floor serves quality dinners, and especially negotiated rates at a local leisure centre are offered.
ROOMS: 66 en suite (5 fmly) ⊗ in 12 bedrooms **FACILITIES:** STV Jacuzzi special rates with Cannons health club ♫ **CONF:** Thtr 350 Class 160 Board 100 **SERVICES:** Lift **PARKING:** 36 **NOTES:** Civ Wed
CARDS:

★★★63% **Grand St Leger**
Bennetthorpe DN2 6AX
☎ 01302 364111 📠 01302 329865
e-mail: sales@grandstleger.com
web: www.grandstleger.com
Dir: *follow Doncaster Racecourse signs, at Racecourse rdbt hotel on corner*
This friendly hotel is located next to the racecourse and is only ten minutes' walk from the town centre. There is a cheerful bar-lounge and an elegant restaurant offering an extensive choice of dishes. The bedrooms are comfortable and thoughtfully equipped.
ROOMS: 20 en suite ⊗ in all bedrooms s £50-£100; d £80-£160 (incl. bkfst) **LB** **CONF:** Thtr 80 Class 50 Board 50 Del from £95
PARKING: 28 **NOTES:** ✈ ⊗ in restaurant RS Xmas Day (open for lunch only) Civ Wed 60 **CARDS:**

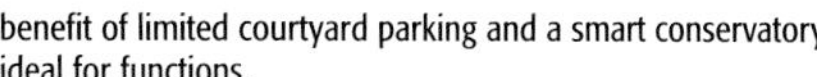

Campanile
Doncaster Leisure Park, Bawtry Rd DN4 7PD
☎ 01302 370770 📠 01302 370813
e-mail: doncaster@envergure.co.uk
Dir: *follow signs to Doncaster Leisure Centre, left at rdbt before Dome complex*

This modern building offers accommodation in smart, well-equipped bedrooms, all with en suite bathrooms. Refreshments may be taken at the informal Bistro. For further details consult the Hotel Groups page.
ROOMS: 50 en suite s fr £42.95; d fr £42.95 **CONF:** Thtr 35 Class 18 Board 24

Travel Inn (Doncaster Central)
Wilmington Dr, Doncaster Carr DN4 5PJ
☎ 08701 977074 📠 01302 364811
Dir: *off A6182 near junct with access road to M18 junct 3*
Travel Inn offers good-quality, value-for-money accommodation. Spacious, en suite rooms with bath and shower comfortably accommodate a family of up to two adults and two children (to age 15). The restaurant and bar offers a varied menu. For further details consult the Hotel Groups page.
ROOMS: 42 en suite s £45.95-£46.95; d £45.95-£46.95 **CONF:** Class 32

Travelodge (Doncaster North)
DN8 5GS
☎ 08700 850 950 📠 01302 845469
Dir: *M18 junct 5*
Travelodge offers good quality, good value, modern accommodation. Ideal for families, the spacious, en suite bedrooms include remote-control TV, tea and coffee-making facilities and luxury beds. Meals can be taken at the nearby family restaurant. For further details consult the Hotel Groups page.
ROOMS: 39 en suite s fr £25; d fr £25

DONNINGTON See Telford

DORCHESTER, Dorset — Map 04 SY69

★★★66% The Wessex Royale
High West St DT1 1UP
☎ 01305 262660 📠 01305 251941
e-mail: info@wessex-royale-hotel.com
web: www.wessex-royale-hotel.com
This centrally situated Georgian townhouse dates from 1756 but has been sympathetically refurbished to combine its historic charm with modern comforts. Durberville's Restaurant is a relaxed location for enjoying innovative food, and the hotel offers the

continued

benefit of limited courtyard parking and a smart conservatory ideal for functions.
ROOMS: 25 en suite 2 annexe en suite (2 fmly) ⊘ in 10 bedrooms s £69-£99; d £89-£139 (incl. bkfst) **FACILITIES:** STV **CONF:** Thtr 80 Class 40 Board 40 **PARKING:** 12 **NOTES:** ⊘ in restaurant
CARDS:

DORCHESTER (ON THAMES), Oxfordshire — Map 05 SU59

★★★68% White Hart
High St OX10 7HN
☎ 01865 340074 📠 01865 341082
e-mail: whitehartdorch@aol.com
web: www.oxford-restaurants-hotels.co.uk
Dir: *M40 junct 6, take B4009 through Watlington & Benson to A4074. Follow signs to Dorchester. Hotel on right*

Period charm and character are plentiful throughout this 17th-century coaching inn set on the picturesque high street. Bedrooms are individually appointed and well equipped, and the bar and atmospheric restaurant, complete with vaulted timber ceiling, are situated in a separate building across the courtyard.
ROOMS: 22 en suite 4 annexe en suite (2 fmly) (9 GF) ⊘ in 6 bedrooms s £65-£95; d £95-£120 (incl. bkfst) **LB FACILITIES:** STV Xmas **CONF:** BC Thtr 30 Class 20 Board 18 Del from £130
PARKING: 36 **CARDS:**

★★★67% *George*
25 High St OX10 7HH
☎ 01865 340404 📠 01865 341620
e-mail: thegeorgehotel@fsmail.net
Dir: *M40 junct 6 onto B4009 through Watlington & Benson. Take A4074 at BP petrol station, follow signposts to Dorchester. Hotel on left*

Full of character and charm, this quintessential coaching inn stands beside Dorchester Abbey and dates back to the 15th century. The bedrooms are decorated in keeping with the style of the building, and are divided between the main house and the

continued on p200

DORCHESTER (ON THAMES), continued

courtyard. Meals can be taken either in the lively, atmospheric bar or in the intimate restaurant.
ROOMS: 9 en suite 8 annexe en suite (1 fmly) ⊗ in 4 bedrooms **CONF:** Thtr 40 Class 36 Board 24 **PARKING:** 75 **NOTES:** ⊗ in restaurant **CARDS:**

DORKING, Surrey Map 06 TQ14

★★★★65% The Burford Bridge

MACDONALD HOTELS

Burford Bridge, Box Hill RH5 6BX
☎ 0870 400 8283 01306 880386
e-mail: burfordbridge@macdonald-hotels.co.uk
Dir: *M25 junct 9 follow Dorking signs on A24. Hotel on left*
Full of history, this hotel was reputedly the site of the final meeting between Lord Nelson and Lady Hamilton before the Battle of Trafalgar, and the landscape around the hotel has inspired poets. There are good transport links to major centres, including the capital, and local places of interest include Polesden Lacey and the RHS Gardens at Wisley.
ROOMS: 57 en suite (14 fmly) (8 GF) ⊗ in 37 bedrooms s £140-£160; d £150-£170 (incl. bkfst) **LB** **FACILITIES:** STV Putt green Xmas **CONF:** Thtr 300 Class 100 Board 60 Del from £150 **PARKING:** 100 **NOTES:** ⊗ in restaurant Civ Wed 200 **CARDS:**

★★★67% The White Horse

High St RH4 1BE
☎ 0870 400 8282 01306 887241
e-mail: whitehorsedorking@macdonald-hotels.co.uk
Dir: *M25 junct 9 take A24 S towards Dorking. Hotel in centre of town*
The hotel was first established as an inn in 1750, although parts of the building date back as far as the 15th century. Its town centre location and Dickensian charm have long made this a popular destination for travellers. Character features include beamed ceilings, open fires and four-poster beds.
ROOMS: 37 en suite 41 annexe en suite (2 fmly) (5 GF) ⊗ in 59 bedrooms **FACILITIES:** STV **CONF:** Thtr 50 Class 30 Board 30 Del from £145 **PARKING:** 73 **NOTES:** ⊗ in restaurant **CARDS:**

★★★63% Gatton Manor Hotel Golf & Country Club

Standon Ln RH5 5PQ
☎ 01306 627555 01306 627713
e-mail: gattonmanor@enterprise.net
web: www.gattonmanor.co.uk
(For full entry see Ockley)

Travelodge

Travelodge

Reigate Rd RH4 1QB
☎ 08700 850 950 01306 741673
Dir: *0.5m E, on A25*
Travelodge offers good quality, good value, modern accommodation. Ideal for families, the spacious, en suite bedrooms include remote-control TV, tea and coffee-making facilities and luxury beds. Meals can be taken at the nearby family restaurant. For further details consult the Hotel Groups page.
ROOMS: 55 en suite s fr £25; d fr £25

DORRIDGE, West Midlands Map 10 SP17

Restaurant with Rooms

The Forest

25 Station Approach B93 8JA
☎ 01564 772120 01564 732680
e-mail: info@forest-hotel.com
web: www.forest-hotel.com
Dir: *M42 junct 5, follow A4141 for 2m. After Knowle village turn right signed Dorridge in 1.5m. Left before rail bridge, hotel 200yds*

This well-established restaurant with rooms is situated in the heart of Dorridge village, 30 minutes from Stratford-upon-Avon and the Cotswolds. Rooms are very well equipped with modern facilities. Downstairs, a choice of bars serves meals; there is also a restaurant and a function room.
ROOMS: 12 en suite ⊗ in all bedrooms s £62.50-£87.50; d £72.50-£97.50 (incl. bkfst) **CONF:** Thtr 100 Class 60 Board 40 Del from £120 **PARKING:** 50 **NOTES:** ⊗ in restaurant RS Sun evenings Civ Wed 75 **CARDS:**

DOVER, Kent Map 07 TR34

★★★75% Wallett's Court Country House Hotel & Spa

West Cliffe, St Margarets-at-Cliffe CT15 6EW
☎ 01304 852424 & 0800 0351628 01304 853430
e-mail: wc@wallettscourt.com
Dir: *from Dover take A258 towards Deal. 1st right to St Margarets-at-Cliffe & West Cliffe, 1m on right opposite West Cliffe church*

This country house hotel has at its core a lovely Jacobean manor. Bedrooms in the original house are traditionally furnished and rooms in the courtyard buildings are more modern; all are equipped to a high standard. The restaurant offers cuisine that fuses traditional and modern approaches to largely British dishes,
continued

utilising local and some organic produce with great aplomb. A spa and gym are additional facilities.
ROOMS: 3 en suite 13 annexe en suite (2 fmly) (7 GF) s £79-£119; d £99-£159 (incl. bkfst) LB **FACILITIES: Spa** Sauna Solarium Gym Putt green Jacuzzi Treatment suite, aromatherapy massage, golf pitching range, beauty therapy ch fac **CONF:** BC Thtr 25 Class 25 Board 16 Del from £139 **PARKING:** 30 **NOTES:** in restaurant Closed 24-26 Dec **CARDS:**

★★★71% Best Western Churchill Hotel and Health Club

Dover Waterfront CT17 9BP
☎ 01304 203633 01304 216320
e-mail: enquiries@churchill-hotel.com
Dir: *A20 follow signs for Hoverport, left onto seafront, hotel 800yds along*

Attractive terraced waterfront hotel overlooking the harbour. The hotel offers a wide range of facilities including meeting rooms, health club, hairdressers and beauty treatments. Some of the tastefully decorated bedrooms have balconies and many of the rooms have superb sea views. Public rooms include a large, open-plan lounge bar and a smart Bistro restaurant.
ROOMS: 66 en suite (5 fmly) in 12 bedrooms s £60-£64; d £60-£84 LB **FACILITIES:** STV Sauna Solarium Gym Henley Health Club Hair & Beauty Salons Xmas **CONF:** Thtr 110 Class 60 Board 50 **SERVICES:** Lift **PARKING:** 32 **NOTES:** in restaurant Civ Wed 100
CARDS:

★★★69% The Mildmay

78 Folkestone Rd CT17 9SF
☎ 01304 204278 01304 215342
e-mail: themildmayhotel@btopenworld.com
Dir: *on B2011 Dover to London road, 300yds from Dover Priory Railway Station*

This friendly, family-run hotel has been completely refurbished by the present owners and is ideally placed for the town centre, railway station and ferry terminal. The spacious bedrooms are pleasantly decorated and thoughtfully equipped with modern facilities. Public rooms include a large open-plan lounge bar with plush seating and a smartly appointed restaurant.
ROOMS: 21 en suite (3 fmly) (2 GF) in 7 bedrooms s £50-£60; d £60-£80 (incl. cont bkfst) **PARKING:** 20 **NOTES:** in restaurant
CARDS:

★★★69% Ramada

Singledge Ln, Whitfield CT16 3EL
☎ 01304 821230 01304 825576
e-mail: reservations@ramadadover.co.uk
web: www.ramadainternational.com
Dir: *from M20 follow signs to A2 towards Canterbury. Turn right after Whitfield rdbt. From A2 towards Dover, turn left before Whitfield rdbt*

Modern purpose-built hotel situated in a quiet location between Dover and Canterbury, close to the ferry port and seaside. The open plan public areas are contemporary in style; they include a lounge, a bar and the Bleriot's restaurant. The stylish bedrooms are simply decorated, have co-ordinated soft furnishings and many thoughtful extras.

continued

ROOMS: 68 en suite (19 fmly) (68 GF) in 56 bedrooms s £69-£105; d £69-£105 **FACILITIES:** STV Gym Xmas **CONF:** Thtr 60 Class 18 Board 20 **PARKING:** 80 **NOTES:** in restaurant Civ Wed 45
CARDS:

Premier Lodge (Dover)

Marine Court, Marine Pde CT16 1LW
☎ 0870 9906516 0870 9906517
web: www.premierlodge.com
Dir: *adjacent to ferry terminal*

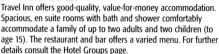

High quality, modern, budget accommodation, ideal for families and business travellers. All rooms feature bath, power shower and satellite TV, and most have telephones / modem points. The adjacent bar and restaurant offers a wide and varied menu.
ROOMS: 100 en suite s £50; d £50

Travel Inn Dover (East)

Jubilee Way, Guston Wood CT15 5FD
☎ 08701 977075 01304 240614
Dir: *on rdbt of A2 & A258*

Travel Inn offers good-quality, value-for-money accommodation. Spacious, en suite rooms with bath and shower comfortably accommodate a family of up to two adults and two children (to age 15). The restaurant and bar offers a varied menu. For further details consult the Hotel Groups page.
ROOMS: 40 en suite s £45.95-£46.95; d £45.95-£46.95

Travel Inn (Dover West)

Folkestone Rd CT15 7AB
☎ 08701 977076 01304 214504
Dir: *M20 then A20 to Dover. Through tunnel, take 2nd exit onto B2011. Take 1st left at rbt . Travel Inn is on the left, after 1 mile*

Travel Inn offers good-quality, value-for-money accommodation. Spacious, en suite rooms with bath and shower comfortably accommodate a family of up to two adults and two children (to age 15). The restaurant and bar offers a varied menu. For further details consult the Hotel Groups page.
ROOMS: 64 en suite s £45.95-£46.95; d £45.95-£46.95

DOWNHAM MARKET, Norfolk — Map 12 TF60

★★72% Castle

High St PE38 9HF
☎ 01366 384311 01366 384311
e-mail: howards@castle-hotel.com
Dir: *M11 take A10 for Ely into Downham Market, hotel opposite traffic lights, on corner of High St in town*

This popular coaching inn is situated close to the centre of town and has been welcoming guests for over 300 years. Well-maintained public areas include a cosy lounge bar and two smartly appointed restaurants. Inviting bedrooms, some with four-poster beds, are attractively decorated, thoughtfully equipped, and have bright, modern decor.
ROOMS: 12 en suite s £59-£65; d £79-£99 (incl. bkfst) LB **FACILITIES:** Xmas **CONF:** Thtr 60 Class 30 Board 40 **PARKING:** 26 **NOTES:** in restaurant **CARDS:**

D

DRIFFIELD (GREAT), East Riding of Yorkshire Map 17 TA05

★★★72% Bell

46 Market Place YO25 6AN
☎ 01377 256661 01377 253228
e-mail: bell@bestwestern.co.uk

Dir: *from A164, right at lights. Car park 50yds on left behind black railings*

This 250-year-old hotel now incorporates the old corn exchange and the old town hall. It is furnished with antique and period pieces, and contains many items of local historical interest. The bedrooms vary in size, but all offer modern facilities and some have their own sitting rooms. There is a good leisure club, and 300 whiskies on offer in the bar. The hotel has a relaxed and friendly atmosphere.

ROOMS: 16 en suite (3 GF) in 11 bedrooms s £72-£90; d £92-£120 (incl. bkfst) LB **FACILITIES: Spa** Squash Snooker Sauna Solarium Gym Jacuzzi Masseur, Hairdressing, Chiropody **CONF:** Thtr 150 Class 100 Board 40 **SERVICES:** Lift **PARKING:** 18 **NOTES:** No children 16yrs in restaurant Civ Wed **CARDS:**

DROITWICH, Worcestershire Map 10 SO86

★★★★67% *Château Impney*

WR9 0BN
☎ 01905 774411 01905 772371
e-mail: chateau@impney.demon.co.uk

Dir: *on A38, 1m from M5 junct 5 towards Droitwich/Worcester*

Overlooking 120 acres of beautiful parkland, this elegant and imposing French-style château dates back to the 1800s. All bedrooms are furnished and equipped to modern standards, and come in a variety of sizes. The hotel has excellent conference, function, exhibition and leisure facilities.

ROOMS: 67 en suite 53 annexe en suite (10 fmly) **FACILITIES:** Sauna Solarium Gym 55 acres of parkland **CONF:** Thtr 1000 Class 550 Board 160 **SERVICES:** Lift **PARKING:** 1000 **NOTES:** in restaurant Closed Xmas **CARDS:**

★★★★65% *Raven*

Victoria Square WR9 8DQ
☎ 01905 772224 01905 797100
e-mail: sales@ravenhotel.demon.co.uk

Dir: *in town centre on A38, 1.5m from M5 junct 5 towards Droitwich/Worcester*

Situated in the heart of the spa town, close to the Brine Baths, this timber-framed property dates back to the early 16th century. Considerably extended over the years, it provides comfortable, well-equipped accommodation. Public areas have a gentleman's club feel with leather sofas in the lounge and a relaxing bar, while the dessert trolley takes pride of place in the restaurant.

ROOMS: 72 en suite (1 fmly) **CONF:** Thtr 150 Class 70 Board 40 **SERVICES:** Lift **PARKING:** 250 **NOTES:** in restaurant Closed Xmas **CARDS:**

Travelodge

Rashwood Hill WR9 8DA
☎ 08700 850 950 01527 861807

Travelodge offers good quality, good value, modern accommodation. Ideal for families, the spacious, en suite bedrooms include remote-control TV, tea and coffee-making facilities and luxury beds. Meals can be taken at the nearby family restaurant. For further details consult the Hotel Groups page.

ROOMS: 32 en suite s fr £25; d fr £25

DUDLEY, West Midlands Map 10 SO99

See also Himley

★★★★68% Copthorne Hotel Merry Hill-Dudley

The Waterfront, Level St, Brierley Hill DY5 1UR
☎ 01384 482882 01384 482773
e-mail: apearson@mill-cop.com

Dir: *follow signs for Merry Hill Centre*

The hotel enjoys a waterfront aspect and is close to the Merry Hill shopping mall. Polished marble floors, rich fabrics and striking interior design are features of the stylish public areas. Bedrooms are spacious and some have Connoisseur status, which includes the use of a private lounge. A modern leisure centre with pool occupies the lower level.

ROOMS: 138 en suite (14 fmly) in 90 bedrooms s fr £140; d fr £150 LB **FACILITIES:** STV supervised Sauna Solarium Gym Jacuzzi Aerobics Beauty/massage therapists **CONF:** Thtr 570 Class 240 Board 60 Del £170 **SERVICES:** Lift **PARKING:** 100 **NOTES:** Civ Wed 400 **CARDS:**

★★★63% The Ward Arms Hotel

Birmingham Rd DY1 4RN
☎ 0870 609 6113 01384 457502
e-mail: wardarms@corushotels.com

Dir: *on A461. M5 junct 2 1st left at rdbt, 3rd exit at next rdbt. After 1.5m 1st exit at 3rd rdbt, hotel 500yds on left*

This busy and popular modern hotel is within easy reach of the M5, in the heart of the Black Country. The bedrooms are well equipped and some rooms on ground floor level are available. Public areas include the traditionally furnished conservatory restaurant and bar, where freshly prepared dishes are served.

ROOMS: 72 en suite (36 GF) in 14 bedrooms s £75; d £75 LB **FACILITIES:** STV Xmas **CONF:** Thtr 140 Class 50 Board 60 Del £105 **PARKING:** 150 **CARDS:**

⌂ Travelodge Birmingham Dudley

Dudley Rd, Brierley Hill DY5 1LQ
☎ 08700 850 950 📠 0870 1911563
Dir: *3m W, on A461*

Travelodge offers good quality, good value, modern accommodation. Ideal for families, the spacious, en suite bedrooms include remote-control TV, tea and coffee-making facilities and luxury beds. Meals can be taken at the nearby family restaurant. For further details consult the Hotel Groups page.

ROOMS: 32 en suite s fr £25; d fr £25

DULVERTON, Somerset — Map 03 SS92

Top 200 – Hotel

★★ ❀ Ashwick House

TA22 9QD
☎ 01398 323868 📠 01398 323868
e-mail: ashwickhouse@talk21.com
Dir: *left at post office, 3m NW on B3223, over 2 cattlegrids, signed on left*

A small yet inviting Edwardian hotel, set on the edge of Exmoor in six beautiful acres above the breathtaking valley of the River Barle. Exuding a quintessential country house ambience, the public areas include a galleried hall with welcoming log fire, and stylish lounges, which boast deep sofas. Bedrooms are spacious, comfortable and are equipped with a host of thoughtful touches. Each evening a set menu is served, with a choice of starter and pudding, using the finest local produce.

ROOMS: 6 en suite ⊗ in 1 bedroom s £68-£89; d £138-£155 (incl. bkfst & dinner) **LB FACILITIES:** Solarium Xmas **PARKING:** 27 **NOTES:** No children 8yrs ⊗ in restaurant

★★64% Lion

Bank Square TA22 9BU
☎ 01398 323444 📠 01398 323980
e-mail: jeffeveritt@tiscali.co.uk
Dir: *from A361 at Tiverton rdbt onto A396. Left at Exbridge onto B3223. Over bridge in Dulverton, hotel in Bank Sq*

Old-fashioned hospitality is always on offer at this charming, traditional inn in the centre of Dulverton, an ideal base from which to explore Exmoor National Park. The bar is popular with locals and visitors alike, offering a variety of local real ales and quality meals. A pleasant dining room provides a quieter, non-smoking option.

ROOMS: 13 en suite (2 fmly) ⊗ in 2 bedrooms s £38-£45; d fr £65 (incl. bkfst) **LB FACILITIES:** Xmas **PARKING:** 6 **NOTES:** ⊗ in restaurant **CARDS:**

DUMBLETON, Gloucestershire — Map 10 SP03

U Dumbleton Hall

WR11 7TS
☎ 01386 881240
Dir: *M5 junct 8 follow A46 for Evesham. 5m S of Evesham take right signed Dumbleton. Hotel is set back at S end of village.*

At the time of going to press, the star classification for this hotel was not confirmed. Please refer to the AA internet site www.theAA.com for current information.

ROOMS: 34 en suite (6 fmly) ⊗ in 20 bedrooms s £80; d £120-£160 (incl. bkfst) **LB FACILITIES:** Xmas **CONF:** Thtr 100 Del from £100 **SERVICES:** Lift **PARKING:** 60 **NOTES:** ⊗ in restaurant Civ Wed 100 **CARDS:**

DUNCHURCH, Warwickshire — Map 11 SP47

⌂ Travelodge Rugby

London Rd, Thurlaston CV23 9LG
☎ 08700 850 950 📠 01788 521538
Dir: *A45, westbound*

Travelodge offers good quality, good value, modern accommodation. Ideal for families, the spacious, en suite bedrooms include remote-control TV, tea and coffee-making facilities and luxury beds. Meals can be taken at the nearby family restaurant. For further details consult the Hotel Groups page.

ROOMS: 40 en suite s fr £25; d fr £25

DUNSTABLE, Bedfordshire — Map 11 TL02

★★★65% Hanover International Hotel

Church St LU5 4RT
☎ 01582 662201 📠 01582 696422
e-mail: gerard.virlombier@hanover-international.com
Dir: *M1 junct 11 and take A505. Hotel 2m on right opp Priory church*

Meeting the needs of a regular business trade, this hotel is ideally located close to the town centre and has ample private parking. Public areas include a comfortably furnished bar lounge and an attractive air-conditioned restaurant. Bedrooms are available in a variety of styles, club and executive rooms being the most plush.

ROOMS: 68 en suite (7 fmly) (21 GF) ⊗ in 36 bedrooms s £60-£109; d £119-£149 (incl. bkfst) **LB FACILITIES:** STV Xmas **CONF:** Thtr 40 Class 18 Board 26 Del from £99 **SERVICES:** Lift **PARKING:** 70 **NOTES:** ⊗ in restaurant Civ Wed 80 **CARDS:**

⌂ Travel Inn (Dunstable/Luton)

350 Luton Rd LU5 4LL
☎ 08701 977083 📠 01582 664114
Dir: *on A505. From M1 junct 11 follow signs to Dunstable. At first rdbt turn right. The Travel Inn on left*

Travel Inn offers good-quality, value-for-money accommodation. Spacious, en suite rooms with bath and shower comfortably accommodate a family of up to two adults and two children (to age 15). The restaurant and bar offers a varied menu. For further details consult the Hotel Groups page.

ROOMS: 42 en suite s £45.95-£48.95; d £45.95-£48.95

DUNSTABLE, continued

⌂ Travel Inn (Dunstable South)

Watling St, Kensworth LU6 3QP
☎ 08701 977082 ▯ 01582 842811
Dir: *M1 junct 9 towards Dunstable on A5, Travel Inn on right past Packhorse pub*
Travel Inn offers good-quality, value-for-money accommodation. Spacious, en suite rooms with bath and shower comfortably accommodate a family of up to two adults and two children (to age 15). The restaurant and bar offers a varied menu. For further details consult the Hotel Groups page.
ROOMS: 40 en suite s £45.95-£46.95; d £45.95-£46.95

⌂ Travelodge

Watling St LU7 9LZ
☎ 08700 850 950 ▯ 01525 211177
Dir: *3m N, on A5*
Travelodge offers good quality, good value, modern accommodation. Ideal for families, the spacious, en suite bedrooms include remote-control TV, tea and coffee-making facilities and luxury beds. Meals can be taken at the nearby family restaurant. For further details consult the Hotel Groups page.
ROOMS: 28 en suite s fr £25; d fr £25

DUNSTER, Somerset Map 03 SS94

★★★75% The Luttrell Arms Hotel

High St TA24 6SG
☎ 01643 821555 ▯ 01643 821567
e-mail: info@luttrellarms.fsnet.co.uk
Dir: *A39/A396 S toward Tiverton. Hotel on left opposite Yarn Market*
Occupying an enviable position in the high street, this 15th-century hotel looks up to the town's famous castle. Beautifully renovated and decorated in a contemporary style, high levels of comfort can be found throughout. The warm and friendly staff deliver attentive service in a relaxed atmosphere.
ROOMS: 28 en suite (3 fmly) ⊗ in all bedrooms s £85-£125; d £95-£140 (incl. bkfst) **LB** **FACILITIES:** Exmoor safaris, Historic tours, Walking tours Xmas **CONF:** Thtr 35 Class 20 Board 20 **NOTES:** ⊗ in restaurant **CARDS:**

DURHAM, Co Durham Map 19 NZ24
See also Rushyford

★★★★72% Durham Marriott Hotel, Royal County

Old Elvet DH1 3JN
☎ 0191 386 6821 ▯ 0191 386 0704
e-mail: durhamroyal.marriott@whitbread.com
Dir: *from A1(M) junct 62, then A690 to Durham, over 1st rdbt, left at 2nd rdbt left at lights, hotel on left*
In a wonderful position on the banks of the River Wear, the hotel's central location makes it ideal for visiting the attractions of this historic city. The building was developed from a series of Jacobean town houses (once owned by the Bowes-Lyon family, ancestors of the late Queen Mother). Today the hotel offers up-to-date, air-conditioned bedrooms; a choice of restaurants and lounge areas; gymnasium and swimming pool.
ROOMS: 142 en suite 8 annexe en suite (10 fmly) (15 GF) ⊗ in 111 bedrooms s £130-£145; d £140-£165 (incl. bkfst) **LB** **FACILITIES: Spa** STV Sauna Solarium Gym Jacuzzi Turkish steamroom Plungepool, sanarium, tropical fun shower **CONF:** Thtr 120 Class 50 Board 50 Del from £130 **SERVICES:** Lift **PARKING:** 76 **NOTES:** ⊗ in restaurant Civ Wed 70 **CARDS:**

★★★74% Whitworth Hall Country Park Hotel

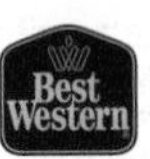

Stanners Ln DL16 7QX
☎ 01388 811772 ▯ 01388 818669
e-mail: enquiries@whitworthhall.co.uk
(For full entry see Spennymoor)

★★★71% Ramside Hall

Carrville DH1 1TD
☎ 0191 386 5282 ▯ 0191 386 0399
e-mail: mail@ramsidehallhotel.co.uk
web: www.ramsidehallhotel.co.uk
Dir: *A1(M) junct 62 A690 to Sunderland. After rail bridge turn right*
Close to the motorway, yet located in delightful parkland setting with its own golf course, this is the largest privately owned hotel in the north east. Bedrooms, all furnished to a high specification, include two presidential suites. There are a number of comfortable lounges and a choice of three dining venues.
ROOMS: 80 en suite (10 fmly) (28 GF) ⊗ in 36 bedrooms s £120-£140; d £140-£160 (incl. bkfst) **LB** **FACILITIES:** STV 27 Snooker Sauna Putt green Steam room Golf academy Driving Range ♫ ch fac **CONF:** BC Thtr 400 Class 160 Board 40 Del from £110 **SERVICES:** Lift **PARKING:** 500 **NOTES:** ⊗ in restaurant Civ Wed 400 **CARDS:**

★★★69% Kings Lodge Hotel & Restaurant

Flass Vale DH1 4BG
☎ 0191 370 9977 ▯ 0191 370 9988
e-mail: manager@kingslodge.info
Dir: *A1 junct 62, right at 4th rdbt. 1st left, 1st right. Hotel at end*
Benefiting from a city centre location, yet with the illusion of a secluded setting, this stylish modern hotel is popular with both business and leisure guests. Accommodation is provided in compact, well-designed rooms. Knights is a contemporary restaurant and Champagne bar; there is also a less formal bar and beer terrace and a bright and comfortable lounge.
ROOMS: 21 en suite (1 fmly) ⊗ in all bedrooms s £75-£80; d £85-£120 (incl. bkfst) **FACILITIES:** STV ♫ ch fac **CONF:** Thtr 25 Class 25 Board 18 Del £120 **SERVICES:** air con **PARKING:** 35 **NOTES:** ⊗ in restaurant Closed 26 Dec-1 Jan RS 25 Dec **CARDS:**

★★★66% Bowburn Hall

Bowburn DH6 5NH
☎ 0191 377 0311 ▯ 0191 377 3459
e-mail: onfo@bowburnhallhotel.co.uk
Dir: *towards Bowburn. Right at Cooperage Pub, then 0.5m to junct signed Durham. Hotel on left*
A former country mansion, this hotel lies in five acres of grounds in a residential area, but within easy reach of the A1. The spacious lounge bar and conservatory overlook the gardens and are comfortable venues for both bar and restaurant meals. Bedrooms are not large but are smartly presented and well equipped.
ROOMS: 19 en suite **FACILITIES:** STV **CONF:** Thtr 150 Class 80 Board 30 **PARKING:** 100 **NOTES:** RS 24-26 Dec & 1 Jan Civ Wed **CARDS:**

⌂ Travel Inn Durham (East)

Broomside Park, Belmont Industrial Estate DH1 1GG
☎ 08701 977084 ▯ 0191 370 6501
Dir: *from A1(M) junct 62 take A690 west towards Durham. 1st exit, after 1m turn left. Travel Inn on left*
Travel Inn offers good-quality, value-for-money accommodation. Spacious, en suite rooms with bath and shower comfortably accommodate a family of up to two adults and two children (to age 15). The restaurant and bar offers a varied menu. For further details consult the Hotel Groups page.
ROOMS: 40 en suite s £45.95-£46.95; d £45.95-£46.95

Travel Inn Durham (North)
Adj Arnison Retail Centre, Pity Me DH1 5GB
☎ 08701 977086 🖷 0191 383 1166
Dir: *A1(J63), then A167 to Durham. Over 5 rbts and turn left at 6th rbt. Travel Inn is on the right after 200yds*
Travel Inn offers good-quality, value-for-money accommodation. Spacious, en suite rooms with bath and shower comfortably accommodate a family of up to two adults and two children (to age 15). The restaurant and bar offers a varied menu. For further details consult the Hotel Groups page.
ROOMS: 60 en suite s £45.95-£46.95; d £45.95-£46.95

Travelodge Durham
Station Rd, Gilesgate DH1 1LJ
☎ 08700 850 950 🖷 0191 386 5461
Travelodge offers good quality, good value, modern accommodation. Ideal for families, the spacious, en suite bedrooms include remote-control TV, tea and coffee-making facilities and luxury beds. Meals can be taken at the nearby family restaurant. For further details consult the Hotel Groups page.
ROOMS: 57 en suite s fr £25; d fr £25

DURHAM SERVICE AREA (A1(M)), Co Durham Map 19 NZ33

Travel Inn (Durham South)
Motorway Service Area, Tursdale Rd, Bowburn DH6 5NP
☎ 08701 977087 🖷 0191 377 8722
Dir: *A1(M) junct 61& A177 Bowburn junction*
Travel Inn offers good-quality, value-for-money accommodation. Spacious, en suite rooms with bath and shower comfortably accommodate a family of up to two adults and two children (to age 15). The restaurant and bar offers a varied menu. For further details consult the Hotel Groups page.
ROOMS: 38 en suite s £45.95-£46.95; d £45.95-£46.95
CONF: Thtr 1 Board 10

DUXFORD, Cambridgeshire Map 12 TL44

★★★74% ❀❀ **Duxford Lodge**
Ickleton Rd CB2 4RT
☎ 01223 836444 🖷 01223 832271
e-mail: admin@duxfordlodgehotel.co.uk
web: www.duxfordlodgehotel.co.uk
Dir: *M11 junct 10, onto A505 to Duxford. 1st right at T- junct. Hotel on left*

A warm welcome is assured at this attractive red-brick hotel in the heart of a delightful village. Public areas include a cosy relaxing bar, separate lounge, and an attractive restaurant, where an excellent and imaginative menu is offered. The bedrooms are well-appointed, comfortable and smartly furnished.
ROOMS: 11 en suite 4 annexe en suite (2 fmly) s £60-£85; d £105-£115 (incl. bkfst) **LB** **FACILITIES:** ♫ Xmas **CONF:** Thtr 30 Class 20 Board 20 Del from £127 **PARKING:** 34 **NOTES:** in restaurant Closed 26-30 Dec
CARDS: *See advert on this page*

EARLS COLNE, Essex Map 13 TL82

★★★79% ❀❀ **de Vere Arms**
53 High St CO6 2PB
☎ 01787 223353 🖷 01787 223365
e-mail: dining@deverearms.com
web: www.deverearms.com

Situated in the heart of the Colne Valley, this former inn has been transformed into a very stylish restaurant with rooms. The open-plan reception/lounge and all the bedrooms have been enhanced in an energetic modern fashion with hand painted murals and original art, without compromising guest comfort. Cooking at dinner and breakfast shows care and skill.
ROOMS: 9 en suite (1 fmly) (1 GF) in all bedrooms s fr £92; d fr £135 (incl. bkfst & dinner) **FACILITIES:** Xmas **CONF:** Thtr 40 Board 20 **PARKING:** 12 **NOTES:** in restaurant **CARDS:**

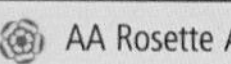

❀ AA Rosette Award for culinary excellence

EASINGWOLD, North Yorkshire Map 19 SE56

★★72% George

Market Place YO61 3AD
☎ 01347 821698 🖷 01347 823448
e-mail: info@the-george-hotel.co.uk
web: www.the-george-hotel.co.uk

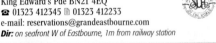

THE CIRCLE *Selected Individual Hotels* GREAT BRITAIN

Dir: *off A19 midway between York & Thirsk, in Market Place*

A friendly welcome awaits at the former coaching Inn facing the Georgian market square. Bedrooms are very comfortably furnished and well equipped, and the mews rooms have their own external access. An extensive range of well-produced food is available both in the bar and restaurant. There are two comfortable lounges and complimentary use of a local fitness centre.

ROOMS: 15 en suite (2 fmly) ⊗ in all bedrooms s £65; d £90 (incl. bkfst) **LB** **FACILITIES:** Complimentry use of local fitness centre Xmas **CONF:** Board 12 Del from £90 **PARKING:** 10 **NOTES:** ⊗ in restaurant **CARDS:**

EAST AYTON, North Yorkshire Map 17 SE98

★★★62% East Ayton Lodge

Moor Ln, Forge Valley YO13 9EW
☎ 01723 864227 🖷 01723 862680
e-mail: ealodge@cix.co.uk

Dir: *400yds off A170*

Set in three acres of grounds close to the River Derwent and discreetly situated in a quiet lane on the edge of the forest, this friendly, family-operated hotel is constructed around what was originally two cottages. Bedrooms are well equipped and those in the courtyard are particularly spacious. A good range of food is available.

ROOMS: 10 en suite 20 annexe en suite (5 fmly) (10 GF) **FACILITIES:** Xmas **CONF:** Thtr 46 Class 80 Board 32 **PARKING:** 50 **NOTES:** ⊗ in restaurant **CARDS:**

EASTBOURNE, East Sussex Map 06 TV69

See also Wilmington

★★★★★71% Grand

King Edward's Pde BN21 4EQ
☎ 01323 412345 🖷 01323 412233
e-mail: reservations@grandeastbourne.com

Dir: *on seafront W of Eastbourne, 1m from railway station*

This famous Victorian hotel offers high standards of service and hospitality. The extensive public rooms feature a magnificent Great Hall, with marble columns and high ceilings, where guests can relax and enjoy afternoon tea. The spacious bedrooms provide high levels of comfort and some rooms have balconies with stunning sea views. There is a choice of restaurants and bars as well as superb leisure facilities.

ROOMS: 152 en suite (20 fmly) s £135-£325; d £165-£385 (incl. bkfst) **LB** **FACILITIES:** **Spa** supervised supervised Snooker Sauna Solarium Gym Putt green Jacuzzi Hairdressing, Beauty therapy ♫ Xmas **CONF:** BC Thtr 350 Class 200 Board 40 Del from £245 **SERVICES:** Lift **PARKING:** 60 **NOTES:** ⊗ in restaurant Civ Wed 300 **CARDS:**

★★★73% Lansdowne

King Edward's Pde BN21 4EE
☎ 01323 725174 🖷 01323 739721
e-mail: reception@lansdowne-hotel.co.uk
web: www.bw-lansdownehotel.co.uk

Dir: *hotel at W end of seafront (B2103) facing Western Lawns*

Enjoying an enviable position at the quieter end of the parade, this hotel overlooks the Western Lawns and Wish Tower and is just a few minutes' walk from many of the city's attractions. Public rooms include a variety of lounges, a range of meeting rooms and games rooms. Bedrooms are attractively decorated and many offer sea views.

ROOMS: 101 en suite (9 fmly) ⊗ in 25 bedrooms s £47-£89; d £84-£162 (incl. bkfst) **LB** **FACILITIES:** STV Snooker Darts,Table tennis & Pool table ch fac Xmas **CONF:** Thtr 100 Class 40 Board 40 Del from £75 **SERVICES:** Lift **PARKING:** 22 **NOTES:** ⊗ in restaurant Closed 2-20 Jan Civ Wed 60 **CARDS:**

See advert on opposite page

★★★72% **Hydro**
Mount Rd BN20 7HZ
☎ 01323 720643 📠 01323 641167
e-mail: Sales@hydrohotel.com
Dir: *from pier/seafront, right along Grand Parade. At Grand Hotel follow Hydro Hotel sign. Up South Cliff 200yds*

This well-managed and popular hotel enjoys an elevated position with views of attractive gardens and the sea beyond. The refurbished, spacious bedrooms are attractive and well-equipped. In addition to the comfortable lounges, guests also have access to fitness facilities and a hairdressing salon. Service is both professional and efficient throughout.
ROOMS: 84 rms (83 en suite) (3 fmly) (3 GF) ⊗ in 1 bedroom s £45-£85; d £90-£170 (incl. bkfst & dinner) **LB** **FACILITIES:** STV Gym Putt green Beauty room, Hairdressing salon Xmas **CONF:** Thtr 140 Class 90 Board 40 Del from £84.50 **SERVICES:** Lift **PARKING:** 40
NOTES: ⊗ in restaurant RS 24-28 & 30-31 Dec Civ Wed 150
CARDS:

★★★67% **York House**
14/22 Royal Pde BN22 7AP
☎ 01323 412918 📠 01323 646238
e-mail: frontdesk@yorkhousehotel.co.uk
web: www.yorkhousehotel.co.uk
Dir: *A27 to Eastbourne. On seafront 0.25m E of pier*
Since 1896 and through five generations, this seafront hotel has been in the ownership of the Williamson family. Bedrooms vary in size; many have sea views. Public areas include a spacious lobby, cosy bar, non-smoking lounge, games room and indoor swimming pool. Limited street parking is available in front of the hotel.
ROOMS: 87 en suite (14 fmly) (5 GF) ⊗ in 30 bedrooms s £65-£71; d £100-£120 (incl. bkfst) **LB** **FACILITIES:** STV CCTV ch fac Xmas
CONF: Thtr 100 Class 30 Board 24 Del from £115 **SERVICES:** Lift
NOTES: ⊗ in restaurant Civ Wed 50
CARDS:

Looking for a last-minute weekend away?
Check out Latebeds,
the AA's late availability booking service, at www.theAA.com

★★★66% **Chatsworth**
Grand Pde BN21 3YR
☎ 01323 411016 📠 01323 643270
e-mail: stay@chatsworth-hotel.com
web: www.chatsworth-hotel.com
Dir: *M23 then A27 to Polegate. A2270 into Eastbourne, follow seafront & signs. Hotel is in centre of seafront near pier*
Within minutes of the town centre and pier, this attractive Edwardian hotel is located on the seafront. Service is friendly and helpful throughout the public areas, which consist of the Dukes Bar, a cosy lounge and the Devonshire Restaurant. Bedrooms,

continued on p208

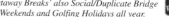

EASTBOURNE, continued

many with sea views, are traditional in style and have a range of facilities.

Chatsworth Hotel, Eastbourne

ROOMS: 47 en suite (2 fmly) ⊗ in 10 bedrooms s £55-£65; d £85-£125 (incl. bkfst) **LB** **FACILITIES:** STV ♫ ch fac Xmas **CONF:** Thtr 100 Class 60 Board 40 **SERVICES:** Lift **NOTES:** ⊗ in restaurant Civ Wed 140
CARDS:

See advert on page 207

★★★63% Quality Hotel Langham

Royal Pde BN22 7AH
☎ 01323 731451 📠 01323 646623
e-mail: info@langhamhotel.co.uk
web: www.langhamhotel.co.uk
Dir: *In Eastbourne, follow seafront signs. Hotel 0.5m E of pier*

This popular hotel is situated in a prominent position with superb views of the sea and pier. Bedrooms, most of which have been refurbished, are pleasantly decorated and equipped with modern facilities. The spacious public rooms include a terrace restaurant, business lounge area and Grand Parade bar.

ROOMS: 85 en suite (5 fmly) s £55-£65; d £85-£110 (incl. bkfst) **LB** **FACILITIES:** Temporary membership of Sovereign Club pools & gym Xmas **CONF:** Thtr 80 Class 40 Board 24 Del from £90 **SERVICES:** Lift **PARKING:** 4 **NOTES:** ⊗ in restaurant Civ Wed 110
CARDS:

★★70% New Wilmington

25 Compton St BN21 4DU
☎ 01323 721219 📠 01323 746255
e-mail: info@new-wilmington-hotel.co.uk
web: www.new-wilmington-hotel.co.uk
Dir: *A22 to Eastbourne along seafront. Right along promenade to Wish Tower. Right, then left at end of road, hotel 2nd on left*

This friendly, family-run hotel is conveniently located close to the sea front, the Congress Theatre and Winter Gardens. Public rooms are well presented and include a cosy bar, small comfortable non-smoking lounge and a spacious restaurant. Bedrooms are comfortably appointed and tastefully decorated; family and superior bedrooms are available.

ROOMS: 40 en suite (14 fmly) (3 GF) s £38-£45; d £66-£78 (incl. bkfst) **LB** **FACILITIES:** ♫ Xmas **SERVICES:** Lift **PARKING:** 2 **NOTES:** ⊗ in restaurant Closed 3 Jan - mid-Feb **CARDS:**

★★68% Ashley Grange Hotel

Lewes Rd BN21 2BY
☎ 01323 721550 📠 01323 721550
e-mail: ashleygrangehotel@hotmail.com
Dir: *from A22 follow signs for hospital A&E. At Rodmill Roundabout turn left, Kings Drive, Lewes Rd, Hotel on left*

THE CIRCLE
Selected Individual Hotels
GREAT BRITAIN

Located within easy reach of the town centre and local attractions, this small and friendly hotel provides a warm welcome. Bedrooms are comfortable with a range of facilities provided. A cosy bar and smart restaurant is on offer as well as an extensive and impressive garden.

ROOMS: 6 en suite s £35-£42; d £55-£68 (incl. bkfst) **LB** **FACILITIES:** outdoor pool under construction **PARKING:** 6 **NOTES:** No children 12yrs ⊗ in restaurant Closed 24-27 Dec
CARDS:

★★68% Farrar's Hotel

Wilmington Gardens BN21 4JN
☎ 01323 723737 📠 01323 732902
Dir: *off seafront by Wish Tower, hotel opposite Congress Theatre*

Situated opposite the Congress Theatre, this hotel is just a short walk from both the seafront and Devonshire Park. Bedrooms are comfortably furnished and pleasantly decorated. Public areas are smartly appointed and include a cosy bar, a separate lounge and an attractive downstairs dining room.

ROOMS: 45 en suite (4 fmly) **CONF:** Thtr 80 **SERVICES:** Lift **PARKING:** 35 **NOTES:** ⊗ in restaurant Closed Jan
CARDS:

★★68% West Rocks

Grand Pde BN21 4DL
☎ 01323 725217 📠 01323 720421
e-mail: westrockshotel@tiscali.co.uk
Dir: *western end if seafront*

Ideally located near to the pier and bandstand this hotel is only a short walk from the town centre. Bedrooms vary in size, with many offering a stunning sea view; all are furnished and decorated to a good standard. Guests have the choice of two comfortable lounges and a bar.

ROOMS: 47 rms (45 en suite) (8 fmly) (6 GF) s £48-£74; d £40-£74 (incl. bkfst & dinner) **LB** **FACILITIES:** ♫ Xmas **CONF:** BC Thtr 20 Class 12 Board 12 **SERVICES:** Lift **NOTES:** ⊗ in restaurant Closed 3 Jan -20 Feb **CARDS:**

★★64% Oban

King Edward's Pde BN21 4DS
☎ 01323 731581 📠 01323 721994
e-mail: info@oban-hotel.co.uk
Dir: *opposite Wish Tower on seafront*

Situated on the seafront overlooking the wishing tower this privately owned hotel provides a friendly welcome. Bedrooms vary in size and are pleasantly decorated. Public areas include a large open-plan lounge bar area with a small terrace. Enjoyable meals are served in the lower ground-floor dining room.

ROOMS: 31 en suite (2 fmly) (4 GF) s £25-£45; d £50-£90 (incl. bkfst) **LB** **FACILITIES:** ♫ Xmas **SERVICES:** Lift **NOTES:** ⊗ in restaurant Closed Jan & Feb **CARDS:**

★★64% Stanley House Hotel

9/10 Howard Square BN21 4BQ
☎ 01323 731393 📠 01323 738823
e-mail: stanleyhouseaa@aol.com
Dir: *From Eastbourne seafront drive W, Howard Sq is on R.*

Situated on a quiet square just of the main promenade this hotel is ideal for accessing the pier, bandstand and wishing tower. Bedrooms vary in size, and are well appointed and pleasantly decorated. A cosy bar and extensive lounges are on offer and the friendly and attentive team hosts occasional evening entertainment.

ROOMS: 26 rms (25 en suite) (3 fmly) s £30-£35; d £60-£70 (incl. bkfst) **FACILITIES:** ♫ Xmas **SERVICES:** Lift **NOTES:** ⊗ in restaurant Closed 3-31 Jan **CARDS:**

★★61% Queens Hotel
Marine Pde BN21 3DY
☎ 01323 722822 01323 731056
e-mail: queens.eastbourne@alfatravel.co.uk
Dir: *proceed to seafront, hotel opposite pier on left*
Popular with tour groups, this long-established hotel enjoys a central, prominent seafront location overlooking the pier. Spacious public areas include a choice of lounges, and regular entertainment is also provided. Bedrooms are suitably appointed and equipped.
ROOMS: 122 en suite (1 fmly) s £31-£41; d £52-£72 (incl. bkfst) **LB** **FACILITIES:** Snooker ♫ Xmas **CONF:** Thtr 100 Class 56 Board 40 **SERVICES:** Lift **PARKING:** 50 **NOTES:** in restaurant Closed Jan RS Nov, Feb-Mar **CARDS:**

Innkeeper's Lodge Eastbourne
Highfield Park, Willingdon Drove BN23 8AL
☎ 01323 507222
www.innkeeperslodge.com
Smart rooms meet essential business requirements but also have home comforts, and depending on location may well have meeting rooms and pub dining. Dining options generally include all-day menus plus the added advantage of breakfast.
ROOMS: 42 rms s £49.95; d £49.95

Travel Inn
Willingdon Dr BN23 8AL
☎ 08701 977089 01323 767379
Dir: *A22, towards Eastbourne. At next rbt left. Inn on the left*
Travel Inn offers good-quality, value-for-money accommodation. Spacious, en suite rooms with bath and shower comfortably accommodate a family of up to two adults and two children (to age 15). The restaurant and bar offers a varied menu. For further details consult the Hotel Groups page.
ROOMS: 47 en suite s £45.95-£46.95; d £45.95-£46.95

EAST GRINSTEAD, West Sussex — Map 06 TQ33

Top 200 – Hotel

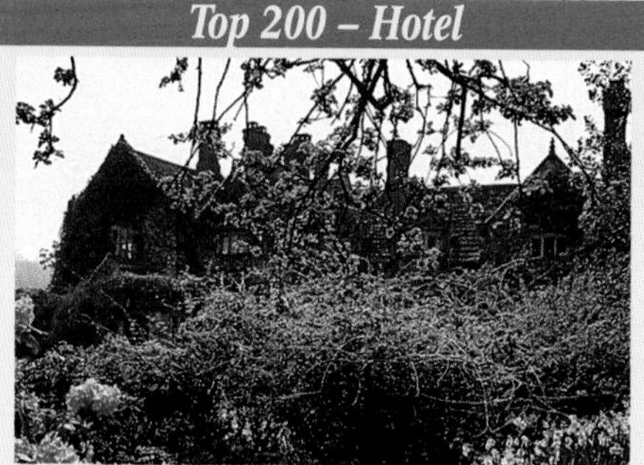

★★★ Gravetye Manor
RH19 4LJ
☎ 01342 810567 01342 810080
e-mail: info@gravetyemanor.co.uk
web: www.gravetyemanor.co.uk
Dir: *B2028 to Haywards Heath. 1m after Turners Hill fork left towards Sharpthorne, immediate 1st left into Vowels Lane*
This beautiful Elizabethan mansion was built in 1598 and enjoys a tranquil setting. It was one of the first country-house hotels and remains a shining example in its class. There are several day rooms, each with oak panelling, fresh flowers and open fires, that offer guests a relaxing atmosphere. Bedrooms are decorated in traditional English style, furnished with antiques and with many thoughtful extras. The cuisine is excellent and makes full use of home-grown fruit and vegetables. Guests should make a point of exploring the outstanding gardens.
ROOMS: 18 en suite s £100-£160; d £170-£325 **FACILITIES:** Fishing **CONF:** Del from £235 **PARKING:** 35 **NOTES:** No children 7yrs in restaurant RS 25 Dec Civ Wed 45
CARDS:

Travel Inn
London Rd, Felbridge RH19 2QR
☎ 08701 977088 01342 326187
Dir: *at junction of A22 & A264 south from M25 junct 6*
Travel Inn offers good-quality, value-for-money accommodation. Spacious, en suite rooms with bath and shower comfortably accommodate a family of up to two adults and two children (to age 15). The restaurant and bar offers a varied menu. For further details consult the Hotel Groups page.
ROOMS: 41 en suite s £45.95-£48.95; d £45.95-£48.95

EAST HORNDON, Essex — Map 06 TQ68

Travelodge Brentwood
CM13 3LL
☎ 08700 850 950 01277 810819
Dir: *on A127, eastbound 4m off M25 junct 29*
Travelodge offers good quality, good value, modern accommodation. Ideal for families, the spacious, en suite bedrooms include remote-control TV, tea and coffee-making facilities and luxury beds. Meals can be taken at the nearby family restaurant. For further details consult the Hotel Groups page.
ROOMS: 45 en suite s fr £25; d fr £25

EASTLEIGH, Hampshire — Map 05 SU41

★★★ Concorde Club & Hotel
Stoneham Ln SO50 9HQ
☎ 023 8065 1478 023 8065 1479
e-mail: hotel@theconcordeclub.com
web: www.theconcordeclub.com
Dir: *M27 junct 5, at rdbt take exit for Chandlers Ford, hotel 500yds on right*
ROOMS: 35 en suite (18 GF) in 26 bedrooms s £50-£95; d £60-£105 (incl. bkfst) **FACILITIES:** STV Fishing Fishing available with prior notice & chargeable daily ♫ **CONF:** Thtr 200 Class 50 Board 40 Del from £129 **SERVICES:** Lift air con **PARKING:** 250 **NOTES:** No children 18yrs in restaurant Closed 24-26 Dec **CARDS:**

Travel Inn
Leigh Rd SO50 9YX
☎ 08701 977090 023 8062 9048
Dir: *adjacent to M3 junct 13, near Eastleigh on A335*
Travel Inn offers good-quality, value-for-money accommodation. Spacious, en suite rooms with bath and shower comfortably accommodate a family of up to two adults and two children (to age 15). The restaurant and bar offers a varied menu. For further details consult the Hotel Groups page.
ROOMS: 60 en suite s £45.95-£48.95; d £45.95-£48.95

EASTLEIGH, continued

⌂ Travelodge Southampton Eastleigh

Twyford Rd SO50 4LF
☎ 08700 850 950 📠 023 8061 6813
Dir: *M3 junct 12 on A335*

Travelodge offers good quality, good value, modern accommodation. Ideal for families, the spacious, en suite bedrooms include remote-control TV, tea and coffee-making facilities and luxury beds. Meals can be taken at the nearby family restaurant. For further details consult the Hotel Groups page.
ROOMS: 32 en suite s fr £25; d fr £25

EAST MIDLANDS AIRPORT
now NOTTINGHAM EAST MIDLANDS AIRPORT see p443

EDGWARE, Greater London
See LONDON SECTION plan 1 C6

⌂ Premier Lodge (London Edgware)

435 Burnt Oak Broadway HA8 5AQ
☎ 0870 9906522 📠 0870 9906523
web: www.premierlodge.com
Dir: *on A5, 11m from Central London & 3m from M1 junct 4. From M1 take A41 & then A5 towards Edgware. Lodge on A5 opp Peugeot dealership*

High quality, modern, budget accommodation, ideal for families and business travellers. All rooms feature bath, power shower and satellite TV, and most have telephones / modem points. The adjacent bar and restaurant offers a wide and varied menu.
ROOMS: 111 en suite s £58; d £58

EGHAM, Surrey Map 06 TQ07

★★★★73% *Runnymede Hotel & Spa*

Windsor Rd TW20 0AG
☎ 01784 436171 📠 01784 436340
e-mail: info@runnymedehotel.com
web: www.runnymedehotel.com
Dir: *M25 junct 13, onto A308 towards Windsor*

Enjoying a peaceful location beside the River Thames, this large modern hotel attracts a largely business clientele during the week. Extensive function suites are available, together with spacious lounges and practically laid out bedrooms. At weekends, leisure visitors come to enjoy impressive spa facilities and regular dinner dances in the airy restaurant overlooking the river.
ROOMS: 180 en suite (19 fmly) ⊗ in 116 bedrooms **FACILITIES:** STV Snooker Sauna Solarium Gym Putt green Jacuzzi Beauty Salon Dance studio Hairdressers ♫ **CONF:** BC Thtr 300 Class 250 Board 76 **SERVICES:** Lift air con **PARKING:** 280 **NOTES:** RS Restaurant closed Sat lunch/Sun dinner Civ Wed 150
CARDS:

See advert under WINDSOR

ELLESMERE PORT, Cheshire Map 15 SJ47

★★★69% Quality Hotel Chester

Berwick Rd, Little Sutton CH66 4PS
☎ 0151 339 5121 📠 0151 339 3214
e-mail: enquiries@quality-hotels-chester.com
Dir: *M53 junct 5 left at rdbt. At 2nd lights right onto A550 over humpback bridge, left into Berwick Rd. Hotel 1m on left.*

This modern hotel has benefited from extensive improvements. The well-equipped accommodation includes bedrooms on ground floor level and no-smoking rooms. The hotel is conveniently located for access to Chester, the M53 and the many attractions of the area. Facilities include a leisure complex and versatile banqueting and conference suites. Staff are friendly and keen to please.
ROOMS: 75 en suite (20 fmly) (23 GF) ⊗ in 30 bedrooms s fr £95; d fr £110 **LB FACILITIES:** STV supervised Sauna Gym Steam room Exercise equipment ♫ **CONF:** Thtr 300 Class 150 Board 50 Del from £100 **PARKING:** 150 **NOTES:** ⊗ in restaurant Civ Wed 200
CARDS:

★★63% Woodcote Hotel & Restaurant

3 Hooton Rd CH66 1QU
☎ 0151 327 1542 📠 0151 328 1328
e-mail: thewoodcotehotel@lineone.net
Dir: *M53 junct 5, take A41 towards Chester, 1st lights right to Willaston. Hotel 300yds on left*

This popular commercial hotel offers generally spacious bedrooms, some of which are located in a separate building, adjacent to the pretty garden. Public areas include a bar and restaurant serving a range of popular, reasonably priced dishes and a separate breakfast room. Staff are friendly and helpful.
ROOMS: 10 en suite 11 annexe en suite (1 fmly) s £30-£40; d £35-£50 **FACILITIES:** ♫ **CONF:** Thtr 90 Class 50 Board 48 **PARKING:** 35 **NOTES:** RS Sun **CARDS:**

ELSTREE, Hertfordshire Map 06 TQ19

★★★72% Edgwarebury

Barnet Ln WD6 3RE
☎ 0870 609 6151 📠 020 8207 3668
e-mail: edgwarebury@corushotels.com
Dir: *M1 junct 5 follow A41 to Harrow, left onto A411 into Elstree. Through x-rds into Barnet Ln, hotel on right*

Sitting in 10 acres of landscaped gardens this hotel is full of charm and character, with a Tudor style façade and interiors of a traditional design. The oak-panelled bar, with two large fireplaces and the stately Cavendish restaurant enjoy wonderful views over the gardens and the city lights beyond.
ROOMS: 47 en suite (1 fmly) ⊗ in 19 bedrooms s £95-£99; d £105-£125 **LB FACILITIES:** STV Xmas **CONF:** Thtr 80 Class 50 Board 10 Del from £150 **PARKING:** 100 **NOTES:** ⊗ in restaurant Civ Wed 70
CARDS:

ELTERWATER, Cumbria

Map 18 NY30

★★★76% Langdale Hotel & Country Club

LA22 9JD
☎ 01539 437302 01539 437694
e-mail: info@langdale.co.uk
web: www.langdale.co.uk/accomm/frhotel.htm
Dir: *into Langdale, hotel part of private estate on left*
Founded on the site of an abandoned 19th-century gunpowder works, this modern hotel is set in 35 acres of woodland and waterways. Comfortable bedrooms, many with spa baths, vary in size. Extensive public areas include a choice of stylish restaurants, conference and leisure facilities and an elegant bar with an interesting selection of snuff. There is also a traditional pub in the grounds.
ROOMS: 5 en suite 52 annexe en suite (8 fmly) (17 GF) ⊗ in all bedrooms s £75-£130; d £100-£210 (incl. bkfst) **LB** **FACILITIES: Spa** STV supervised Fishing Squash Sauna Solarium Gym Jacuzzi Steam room Hair & beauty salon Cycle hire Xmas **CONF:** Thtr 80 Class 40 Board 35 Del from £110 **PARKING:** 65 **NOTES:** ⊗ in restaurant
CARDS:

★★70% New Dungeon Ghyll

Langdale LA22 9JX
☎ 015394 37213 015394 37666
e-mail: enquiries@dungeon-ghyll.com
web: www.dungeon-ghyll.com
Dir: *From Ambleside follow A593 towards Coniston for 3 miles, at Skelwith Bridge take right fork on B5343 towards The Langdales*

This friendly hotel enjoys a tranquil, idyllic position at the head of the valley. Bedrooms vary in size and style; the refurbished rooms are brightly decorated and smartly furnished. Bar meals are served all day, and dinner can be enjoyed in the restaurant overlooking the landscaped gardens; there is also a cosy lounge/bar.
ROOMS: 20 en suite **PARKING:** 30 **NOTES:** ⊗ in restaurant
CARDS:

ELY, Cambridgeshire

Map 12 TL58

★★★66% Lamb

2 Lynn Rd CB7 4EJ
☎ 01353 663574 01353 662023
e-mail: lamb.ely@oldenglishinns.co.uk
Dir: *from A10 into Ely, hotel in town centre on corner of Lynn Road & High Street*
Centrally located, this 15th-century former coaching inn is a focal point of this market town. Now fully refurbished, the hotel offers a combination of light, modern and traditional public rooms, whilst the bedrooms have all been upgraded to a good modern

continued

standard. Food is available throughout the hotel, the same menu provided within the bar and restaurant areas.
ROOMS: 31 en suite (6 fmly) ⊗ in 24 bedrooms s £50-£70; d £75-£95 (incl. bkfst) **LB** **FACILITIES:** STV Xmas **CONF:** Thtr 100 Class 40 Board 70 Del £95 **PARKING:** 20 **NOTES:** ⊗ in restaurant
CARDS:

Travelodge

Travelodge

Witchford Rd CB6 3NN
☎ 08700 850 950 01353 668499
Dir: *at rdbt A10/A142*
Travelodge offers good quality, good value, modern accommodation. Ideal for families, the spacious, en suite bedrooms include remote-control TV, tea and coffee-making facilities and luxury beds. Meals can be taken at the nearby family restaurant. For further details consult the Hotel Groups page.
ROOMS: 39 en suite s fr £25; d fr £25

EMBLETON, Northumberland

Map 21 NU22

★★71% Dunstanburgh Castle Hotel

NE66 3UN
☎ 01665 576111 01665 576203
e-mail: stay@dunstanburghcastlehotel.co.uk
web: www.dunstanburghcastlehotel.co.uk
Dir: *from A1, take B1340 to Denwick past Rennington & Masons Arms. Next right signed Embleton and into village*

The focal point of the village, this friendly family-run hotel has a dining room and grill room offering different menus. There is also a cosy bar and two lounges. In addition to the main bedrooms, a small courtyard conversion gives three stunning suites each with a lounge and galleried bedrooom above.
ROOMS: 20 en suite (4 fmly) s £32.50-£43.50; d £65-£87 (incl. bkfst) **LB** **PARKING:** 16 **NOTES:** ⊗ in restaurant Closed Nov-Feb
CARDS:

EMPINGHAM, Rutland

Map 11 SK90

★★69% The White Horse Inn

Main St LE15 8PS
☎ 01780 460221 & 460521 01780 460521
e-mail: info@whitehorserutland.co.uk
Dir: *on A606, Oakham to Stamford road*
This attractive stone-built inn, offering bright, comfortable accommodation, is conveniently located just minutes from the A1. Bedrooms in the main building are spacious and include a number of family rooms. Public areas include a well-stocked bar, a bistro and restaurant where a wide range of meals are served.
ROOMS: 4 en suite 9 annexe en suite (3 fmly) (5 GF) ⊗ in 1 bedroom s £50; d £65 (incl. bkfst) **LB** **FACILITIES:** Xmas **CONF:** Thtr 50 Class 40 Board 30 Del from £65 **PARKING:** 60 **NOTES:** ⊗ in restaurant
CARDS:

E

EMSWORTH, Hampshire Map 05 SU70

★★★69% Brookfield
Havant Rd PO10 7LF
☎ 01243 373363 📠 01243 376342
e-mail: bookings@brookfieldhotel.co.uk
Dir: *Emsworth junct off A27, onto A529. Hotel 0.5m on left*
This well-established family-run hotel has spacious public areas with popular conference and banqueting facilities. Bedrooms are in a modern style, and comfortably furnished. The popular Hermitage Restaurant offers a seasonally changing menu and an interesting wine list.
ROOMS: 40 en suite (4 fmly) (13 GF) in 20 bedrooms s £70-£75; d £90-£110 (incl. bkfst) **LB FACILITIES:** STV **CONF:** Thtr 100 Class 60 Board 40 Del from £110 **PARKING:** 80 **NOTES:** Closed 25 Dec-1 Jan
CARDS:

Restaurant with Rooms

36 on the Quay
47 South St PO10 7EG
☎ 01243 375592 372257
Occupying a prime position on the Quay with far reaching views over the estuary, this 16th-century house is the scene for the proprietor's accomplished and exciting cuisine. As would be expected the elegant restaurant occupies centre stage with peaceful pastel shades and crisp napery together with glimpses of the bustling harbour outside. The smart bedrooms offer style, comfort and thoughtful extras.
ROOMS: 4 en suite s £60-£85; d £85-£120 (incl. bkfst) **PARKING:** 6
NOTES: in restaurant Closed 3wks Jan, 1wk Oct
CARDS:

Travelodge Chichester (West)
Travelodge
PO10 7RB
☎ 08700 850 950 📠 01243 370877
Dir: *A27*
Travelodge offers good quality, good value, modern accommodation. Ideal for families, the spacious, en suite bedrooms include remote-control TV, tea and coffee-making facilities and luxury beds. Meals can be taken at the nearby family restaurant. For further details consult the Hotel Groups page.
ROOMS: 36 en suite s fr £25; d fr £25

ENFIELD, Greater London Map 06 TQ39

★★★75% Royal Chace
The Ridgeway EN2 8AR
☎ 020 8884 8181 📠 020 8884 8150
e-mail: enquiries@royalchacehotel.co.uk
Dir: *M25 junct 24 take A1005 towards Enfield. Hotel 3m on right*
This professionally run, privately owned hotel enjoys a peaceful location with open fields to the rear. Refurbished public rooms are smartly appointed; the first-floor Chace Brasserie is particularly appealing with its warm colour schemes, careful lighting, polished wood and friendly service. Bedrooms are well presented and thoughtfully equipped.
ROOMS: 92 en suite (2 fmly) (32 GF) in 34 bedrooms s fr £99; d fr £115 (incl. bkfst) **FACILITIES:** STV Free access to local leisure centre **CONF:** Thtr 250 Class 100 Board 40 **PARKING:** 200 **NOTES:** in restaurant Closed 24-30 Dec RS Restaurant closed lunchtime/Sun eve Civ Wed 220 **CARDS:**

> Destination dining!
> This symbol indicates a Restaurant with Rooms

★★62% Enfield
52 Rowantree Rd EN2 8PW
☎ 020 8366 3511 📠 020 8366 2432
e-mail: admin@enfieldhotel.com
Dir: *M25 junct 24, follow signs for A1005 towards Enfield. Hospital on L, across mini rdbt, 3rd L into Bycullah Rd, 2nd left into Rowantree Rd*
In a quiet residential area of town this hotel offers comfortable well-equipped bedrooms. Public areas include a Mediterranean-style restaurant serving a wide range of dishes, a small bar and cosy lounge. Conference rooms and ample parking are available.
ROOMS: 34 en suite (2 fmly) s £45-£70; d £55-£95 (incl. bkfst)
FACILITIES: STV **CONF:** Thtr 70 Class 20 Board 25 Del from £110
PARKING: 19 **NOTES:** in restaurant Civ Wed 65
CARDS:

Travel Inn
travel inn
Innova Park, Mollison Av EN3 7XY
☎ 0870 238 3306 📠 01992 707070
Dir: *M25 (J25), A10 to London, left onto Bullsmoor Lane/Mollison Avenue. Over rbt, right at lights into Innova Science Park.*

Travel Inn offers good-quality, value-for-money accommodation. Spacious, en suite rooms with bath and shower comfortably accommodate a family of up to two adults and two children (to age 15). The restaurant and bar offers a varied menu. For further details consult the Hotel Groups page.
ROOMS: 159 en suite s £52.95-£56.95; d £52.95-£56.95 **CONF:** Thtr 60 Board 26

EPSOM, Surrey Map 06 TQ26

★★★73% Chalk Lane Hotel
Chalk Ln, Woodcote End KT18 7BB
☎ 01372 721179 📠 01372 727878
e-mail: smcgregor@chalklanehotel.com
web: www.chalklanehotel.com
Dir: *from M25 junct 9 onto A24 to Epsom. Right at lights by BP garage. Left into Avenue Rd, right into Worple Rd. Left at T-junct & hotel on right*

This delightful, deceptively spacious, privately owned hotel is only
continued

a ten-minute walk from the racecourse. Staff are committed to providing a professional service and a warm and caring atmosphere. Bedrooms are mostly spacious, attractively furnished and thoughtfully equipped, while the smartly appointed restaurant offers an imaginative selection of dishes.
ROOMS: 22 en suite (1 fmly) s £85-£160; d £120-£160 (incl. bkfst) **FACILITIES:** STV Complimentary membership at local health club ch fac **CONF:** Thtr 140 Class 40 Board 30 Del £165 **PARKING:** 60 **NOTES:** ⊗ in restaurant **CARDS:**

Premier Lodge (Epsom)

272 Kingston Rd, Ewell KT19 0SH
☎ 0870 9906466 📠 0870 9906467
web: www.premierlodge.com
Dir: *exit M25 junct 8, A217 towards Sutton. Then A240 towards Ewell. At Beggars Hill rbt take 2nd exit onto Kingston Rd*
High quality, modern, budget accommodation, ideal for families and business travellers. All rooms feature bath, power shower and satellite TV, and most have telephones / modem points. The adjacent bar and restaurant offers a wide and varied menu.
ROOMS: 29 en suite s £58; d £58

Travel Inn

2-4 St Margarets Dr, Off Dorking Rd KT18 7LB
☎ 08701 977096 📠 01372 739761
Dir: *M25 junct 9, A24 towards Epsom, Travel Inn on left, just before town centre*
Travel Inn offers good-quality, value-for-money accommodation. Spacious, en suite rooms with bath and shower comfortably accommodate a family of up to two adults and two children (to age 15). The restaurant and bar offers a varied menu. For further details consult the Hotel Groups page.
ROOMS: 40 en suite s £56.95; d £56.95 **CONF:** Thtr 40

ERMINGTON, Devon — Map 03 SX65

★★★68% Plantation House

Totnes Rd PL21 9NS
☎ 01548 831100 📠 01548 831248
e-mail: enquiries@plantationhousehotel.com
Dir: *from A38 onto A3121 for 4.5m. Hotel on right past village of Ermington*

Transformed over recent years this comfortable Georgian house in the country offers a friendly atmosphere and comfortable accommodation. The cities of Plymouth and Exeter are easily accessible, as is all the beauty of the South Hams and Dartmoor. The restaurant Matisse is fast developing an enviable reputation for accomplished cuisine, thus dinner is a must for those who enjoy good food.
ROOMS: 10 en suite (2 fmly) ⊗ in all bedrooms **CONF:** Thtr 30 Class 20 Board 15 **PARKING:** 22 **NOTES:** ⊗ in restaurant
CARDS:

ESCRICK, North Yorkshire — Map 16 SE64

★★★73% Parsonage Country House

York Rd YO19 6LF
☎ 01904 728111 📠 01904 728151
e-mail: reservations@parsonagehotel.co.uk
web: www.parsonagehotel.co.uk
Dir: *From A64 take A19 Selby. Follow to Escrick village. Hotel on right of St Helens church.*

This 19th-century former parsonage has been lovingly restored and extended to provide delightful accommodation, set in well-tended gardens. Bedrooms are smartly appointed and well equipped both for business and leisure guests. Spacious public areas include an elegant restaurant, excellent meeting and conference facilities and a choice of attractive lounges.
ROOMS: 12 en suite 34 annexe en suite (4 fmly) (6 GF) ⊗ in 30 bedrooms s £75-£95; d £100-£120 (incl. bkfst) **LB** **FACILITIES:** STV Able to book tee times al local courses. Xmas **CONF:** Thtr 160 Class 80 Board 50 Del from £135 **SERVICES:** Lift **PARKING:** 100 **NOTES:** ⊗ in restaurant Civ Wed 100 **CARDS:**

ESKDALE GREEN, Cumbria — Map 18 NY10

★★67% Bower House Inn

CA19 1TD
☎ 019467 23244 📠 019467 23308
e-mail: Info@bowerhouseinn.freeserve.co.uk
web: www.bowerhouseinn.co.uk
Dir: *4m off A595 0.5m W of Eskdale Green*

This former farmhouse enjoys a countryside location with delightful mountain views and offers true peace and relaxation. The traditional bar and restaurant, where a good range of dishes are served, reflect the coaching inn origins of the house. The bedrooms in both the original house and the Garden Cottage have been refurbished and five attractive new bedrooms have been added.
ROOMS: 5 en suite 19 annexe en suite (3 fmly) (9 GF) s £45-£58; d £60-£80 (incl. bkfst) **LB** **FACILITIES:** STV ch fac Xmas **CONF:** Thtr 40 Class 20 Board 30 **PARKING:** 60 **NOTES:** ⊗ in restaurant Civ Wed 30 **CARDS:**

EVERSHOT, Dorset Map 04 ST50

Top 200 – Hotel

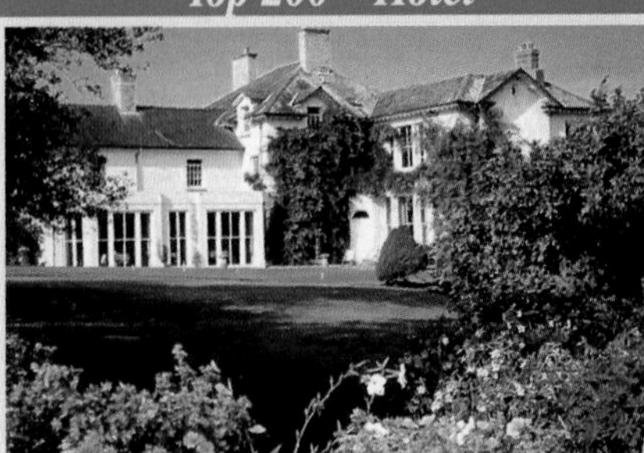

★★★ **Summer Lodge**
DT2 0JR
☎ 01935 83424 01935 83005
e-mail: enquiries@summerlodgehotel.com
Dir: 1m W of A37 halfway between Dorchester and Yeovil
This picturesque hotel is situated in the heart of Dorset and is the ideal retreat for getting away from it all. Try to arrive for afternoon tea or try out the new spa and swimming pool. Bedrooms have all now been refurbished to a very high standard, are individually designed and come with a wealth of facilities. Despite recent changes in the kitchen, early indications suggest the cuisine continues to be a high point of any stay.
ROOMS: 10 en suite 14 annexe en suite (6 fmly) (4 GF) in 10 bedrooms s fr £115; d £165-£360 (incl. bkfst) **FACILITIES: Spa** Sauna Gym Jacuzzi Xmas **CONF:** Thtr 20 Class 22 Board 16 Del from £195 **SERVICES:** air con **PARKING:** 40 **NOTES:** in restaurant Civ Wed 60 **CARDS:**

EVESHAM, Worcestershire Map 10 SP04

★★★★75% **Wood Norton Hall**
Wood Norton WR11 4YB
☎ 01386 425780 01386 425781
e-mail: info@wnhall.co.uk
Dir: 2m from Evesham on A44, after Chadbury

Formerly owned and run by the BBC, this impressive Grade II listed Victorian house stands in a 170-acre estate and provides excellent accommodation along with fine cuisine. The bedrooms have all been thoughtfully furnished and include a wealth of extras. Bathrooms are particularly stylish. Oak-panelled public areas include a bar and a billiards room, while original photographs and sketches from the BBC archive grace the corridors (the hotel once featured in an episode of Dr Who).
ROOMS: 15 en suite 30 annexe en suite (6 fmly) (14 GF) in 30 bedrooms s £80-£150; d £80-£225 (incl. bkfst) **FACILITIES:** STV Fishing Squash Gym Indoor sports hall - badminton, 5-a-side football etc Xmas **CONF:** BC Thtr 70 Class 30 Board 32 Del from £130 **PARKING:** 300 **NOTES:** in restaurant Civ Wed 72
CARDS:

See advert under WORCESTER

★★★75% **The Evesham**
Coopers Ln, Off Waterside WR11 1DA
☎ 01386 765566 & 0800 716969 (Res) 01386 765443
e-mail: reception@eveshamhotel.com
web: www.eveshamhotel.com
Dir: Coopers Ln is off-road by River Avon
Dating from 1540 and set in large grounds, this delightful hotel has well-equipped accommodation that includes a selection of quirkily themed rooms (Alice in Wonderland, Egyptian and Aquarium with a tropical fish tank in the bathroom). A reputation for food is well-deserved, with choice particularly strong for vegetarians. Children are especially welcome.
ROOMS: 39 en suite 1 annexe en suite (3 fmly) (11 GF) in 20 bedrooms s £74-£87; d £118 (incl. bkfst) **LB FACILITIES:** Putt green ch fac **CONF:** Thtr 12 Class 12 Board 12 **PARKING:** 50 **NOTES:** in restaurant Closed 25 & 26 Dec
CARDS:

★★★70% **Northwick Hotel**
Waterside WR11 1BT
☎ 01386 40322 01386 41070
e-mail: enquiries@northwickhotel.co.uk
Dir: off A46 onto A44 over traffic lights and right at next set onto B4035. Past hospital, hotel on right opposite river

Standing by the River Avon, this former coaching inn is within easy walking distance of the centre of Evesham. Bedrooms are tastefully decorated and well equipped, with one specially adapted for less able guests. The refurbished public areas offer a choice of bars, meeting rooms and a restaurant.
ROOMS: 31 en suite (4 fmly) in 15 bedrooms s £65-£81; d £90-£105 (incl. bkfst) **LB FACILITIES:** STV **CONF:** Thtr 240 Class 150 Board 80 Del £115 **PARKING:** 85 **NOTES:** in restaurant Civ Wed 60
CARDS:

★★73% **Riverside**
The Parks, Offenham Rd WR11 8JP
☎ 01386 446200 01386 40021
e-mail: info@theparksoffenham.freeserve.co.uk
Dir: A46 follow signs for Offenham, right onto B4510 (Offenham). Hotel 0.5m on left along private drive
This family owned and run hotel stands in three acres of gardens sloping down to the River Avon. The lounge, restaurant and many of the comfortable bedrooms overlook the river. Cooking remains

continued

one of the hotel's strong points, with a menu of imaginative dishes based on high-quality produce.
ROOMS: 10 rms (7 en suite) (5 GF) s £49-£59; d £98-£118 (incl. bkfst) **LB FACILITIES:** Fishing **PARKING:** 30 **NOTES:** ⊗ in restaurant Closed 1-15 Jan **CARDS:**

Dumbleton Hall

WR11 7TS
☎ 01386 881240
(For full entry see Dumbleton)

Travel Inn

Evesham Country Park, A46 Trunk Rd WR11 4TP
☎ 03701 977288 🖷 01386 444301

travel inn

Travel Inn offers good-quality, value-for-money accommodation. Spacious, en suite rooms with bath and shower comfortably accommodate a family of up to two adults and two children (to age 15). The restaurant and bar offers a varied menu. For further details consult the Hotel Groups page.
ROOMS: 40 en suite s £45.95-£46.95; d £45.95-£46.95

EWEN, Gloucestershire — Map 04 SU09

★★67% Wild Duck Inn

Drakes Island GL7 6BY
☎ 01285 770310 🖷 01285 770924
e-mail: wduckinn@aol.com
web: www.thewildduckinn.co.uk
Dir: *from Cirencester take A429. At Kemble left to Ewen*

This bustling, ever-popular inn dates back to the early 16th century and is full of character. Bedrooms vary in style and are well equipped and tastefully furnished. Open fires, old beams and rustic pine tables add to the charm in the bar and restaurant, where imaginative, robust cooking has earned a loyal following and well-deserved reputation.
ROOMS: 11 en suite s £60-£80; d £80-£130 (incl. cont bkfst)
FACILITIES: Discounted leisure facilities within 3m **PARKING:** 50
NOTES: RS 25 Dec **CARDS:**

See advert under CIRENCESTER

EXETER, Devon — Map 03 SX99

Town House

★★★★ Hotel Barcelona

Magdalen St EX2 4HY
☎ 01392 281000 🖷 01392 281001
e-mail: info@aliasbarcelona.com
web: www.aliasbarcelona.com
Dir: *from A30 Okehampton follow city centre signs. At Exe Bridges rdbt right for city centre, up hill, on at lights. Hotel on right*

Situated within walking distance of the city centre, Hotel Barcelona was formerly an eye hospital and has been totally transformed to provide stylish accommodation with a glamorous atmosphere. Public areas include Café Paradiso, an informal eatery with a varied menu, a night club, a range of meeting rooms and a delightful garden terrace ideal for al fresco dining.

Hotel Barcelona

ROOMS: 46 en suite ⊗ in 3 bedrooms s £85-£90; d £95-£120 **LB FACILITIES:** STV ♫ **CONF:** Thtr 65 Class 18 Board 22 Del from £135 **SERVICES:** Lift **PARKING:** 35 **NOTES:** ⊗ in restaurant
CARDS:

See advert on this page

Popped the question?
Hotels with Civ Wed in their entry are licensed for civil wedding ceremonies. Maximum numbers for the ceremony only are shown, e.g. Civ Wed 120

EXETER, continued

★★★★68% The Southgate

MACDONALD HOTELS

Southernhay East EX1 1QF
☎ 0870 400 8333 📠 01392 413549
e-mail: southgate@macdonald-hotels.co.uk
Dir: *M5 junct 30, 3rd exit (Exeter), 2nd left towards city centre, 3rd exit at next rdbt, hotel 2m on right*

Centrally located and with excellent parking, The Southgate offers a diverse range of leisure and business facilities. Public areas are smart and spacious with comfortable seating in the bar and lounge; there is also a pleasant terrace. A range of bedroom sizes is available and all are well equipped with modern facilities.
ROOMS: 110 en suite (6 fmly) (13 GF) ⊘ in 55 bedrooms s fr £127; d fr £138 (incl. bkfst) **LB FACILITIES: Spa** STV supervised Sauna Solarium Gym Xmas **CONF:** Thtr 150 Class 70 Board 50 Del from £135 **SERVICES:** Lift **PARKING:** 115 **NOTES:** ⊘ in restaurant RS Sat (restaurant closed for lunch) Civ Wed 80
CARDS:

★★★73% *Barton Cross Hotel & Restaurant*

Huxham, Stoke Canon EX5 4EJ
☎ 01392 841245 📠 01392 841942
e-mail: bartonxhuxham@aol.com
Dir: *0.5m off A396 at Stoke Canon, 3m N of Exeter*

17th-century charm combined with 21st-century luxury perfectly sums up the appeal of this lovely countryside hotel. The eight bedrooms are spacious, tastefully decorated and well maintained. Public areas include the cosy first-floor lounge and the lounge/bar with its warming log fire. The restaurant offers a seasonally changing menu and consistently enjoyable cuisine.
ROOMS: 9 en suite (2 fmly) (2 GF) ⊘ in 2 bedrooms **FACILITIES:** STV ch fac **CONF:** Thtr 20 Class 20 Board 20 **PARKING:** 35 **NOTES:** ⊘ in restaurant **CARDS:**

See advert on opposite page

★★★73% Devon

Exeter Bypass, Matford EX2 8XU
☎ 01392 259268 📠 01392 413142
e-mail: info@devonhotel.co.uk web: www.devonhotel.co.uk
Dir: *M5 junct 30, follow Marsh Barton Ind Est signs on A379, hotel on A38 rdbt*

Within easy access of the city centre, the M5 and the city's business parks, this smart Georgian hotel offers modern, comfortable accommodation. The 'Carriages' Bar and Brasserie is popular with guests and locals alike, offering a wide range of dishes as well as a carvery at both lunch and dinner. Service is friendly and attentive, and extensive meeting and business facilities are available.
ROOMS: 41 annexe en suite (3 fmly) (11 GF) s £59-£79; d £69-£79 **LB FACILITIES:** STV ♫ ch fac Xmas **CONF:** Thtr 150 Class 150 Board 150 **PARKING:** 250 **NOTES:** ⊘ in restaurant Civ Wed 100
CARDS:

★★★73%
Lord Haldon Country House

THE INDEPENDENTS

Dunchideock EX6 7YF
☎ 01392 832483 📠 01392 833765
e-mail: enquiries@lordhaldonhotel.co.uk
web: www.lordhaldonhotel.co.uk
Dir: *M5 junct 31or A30 signed to Ide, 2.5m through village. Left after phone box. 0.5m left after stone bridge*

Set amidst rural tranquillity, this attractive country house goes from strength to strength. Guests are assured of a warm welcome from the resident owners and the well-equipped bedrooms are comfortable, many with stunning views. Skilful cooking features on the daily-changing menu, with most of the produce sourced locally.
ROOMS: 19 en suite (3 fmly) ⊘ in 10 bedrooms s £48.50-£60; d £85-£105 (incl. bkfst) **LB FACILITIES:** Xmas **CONF:** Thtr 300 Class 150 Board 60 Del £105 **PARKING:** 90 **NOTES:** ⊘ in restaurant Civ Wed 120 **CARDS:**

See advert on opposite page

★★★72% St Olaves Court Restaurant & Hotel

Mary Arches St EX4 3AZ
☎ 01392 217736 📠 01392 413054
e-mail: info@olaves.co.uk
web: www.olaves.co.uk
Dir: *city centre, signed to Mary Arches Parking. Hotel entrance opposite car park entrance*

Only a short stroll from the cathedral and city centre and set in an attractive walled garden, St Olaves seems to be a country house in its almost hidden location. Bedrooms are comfortably furnished and full of character along with thoughtful extra touches. The daily-changing menus offer imaginative cuisine and feature West Country produce.
ROOMS: 15 en suite (2 fmly) (1 GF) ⊘ in all bedrooms s £105-£145; d £115-£155 (incl. cont bkfst) **LB FACILITIES:** STV Xmas **CONF:** Thtr 45 Class 35 Board 35 Del from £135 **PARKING:** 15 **NOTES:** ⊘ in restaurant Civ Wed 50 **CARDS:**

★★★68% ® **Queens Court**
Bystock Ter EX4 4HY
☎ 01392 272709 ⎙ 01392 491390
e-mail: sales@queenscourt-hotel.co.uk
web: www.queenscourt-hotel.co.uk
Dir: *M5 junct 30 to Middlemoor, follow sign for A377 Crediton. At clock tower rdbt exit to Crediton, 1st left, 1st left.*

Quietly located within walking distance of the city centre, this refurbished, privately owned hotel occupies listed early-Victorian premises and provides friendly hospitality. The smart public areas and bedrooms are tastefully furnished in contemporary style. Rooms are available for conferences, meetings and other functions. The bright and attractive Olive Tree restaurant offers an interesting selection of predominantly fish dishes.
ROOMS: 18 en suite (1 fmly) ⊗ in 9 bedrooms s £59-£59; d £66-£76 **LB FACILITIES:** Xmas **CONF:** Thtr 80 Class 30 Board 40 Del from £120 **SERVICES:** Lift **NOTES:** ⊗ in restaurant Closed Christmas & Boxing Day RS Restaurant closed Sunday lunch **CARDS:**

★★★68% ®® **The Royal Clarence Hotel**
Cathedral Yard EX1 1HD
☎ 01392 319955 ⎙ 01392 439423
e-mail: reservations@royalclarencehotel.co.uk
Dir: *M5 junct 30, towards A379. Follow signs to city centre and hotel opposite cathedral behind high street*

This historic, 14th-century building is a much-loved landmark in Exeter, situated opposite the magnificent cathedral. Bedrooms are full of character and range from compact to grand, some with views over the cathedral green. The hotel is known for its fine cuisine, served in the stylish surroundings of the Michael Caines restaurant, or for a more informal setting try the café bar or Well House Tavern.
ROOMS: 55 en suite (6 fmly) ⊗ in 28 bedrooms s £105-£140; d £130-£145 **LB FACILITIES:** ♫ Xmas **CONF:** Thtr 110 Class 50 Board 50 Del from £130 **SERVICES:** Lift **PARKING:** 15 **NOTES:** ⊗ in restaurant Civ Wed 50 **CARDS:**

⊗ No smoking

EXETER, continued

★★★66% Gipsy Hill
Gipsy Hill Ln, Monkerton EX1 3RN
☎ 01392 465252 🖷 01392 464302
e-mail: stay@gipsyhillhotel.co.uk
web: www.gipsyhillhotel.co.uk
Dir: *M5 junct 29 towards Exeter. Turn right at 1st rdbt and right again at next rdbt. Hotel 0.5m on right*
Located on the edge of the city, with easy access to the M5 and the airport, this popular hotel is set in attractive, well-tended gardens and boasts far-reaching country views. The hotel offers a range of conference and function rooms, comfortable bedrooms and modern facilities. An intimate bar and lounge are next to the elegant restaurant.
ROOMS: 20 en suite 17 annexe en suite (3 fmly) (12 GF) ⊗ in 11 bedrooms s £40-£70; d £40-£110 **LB** **FACILITIES:** Xmas **CONF:** Thtr 100 Class 40 Board 30 Del from £90 **PARKING:** 60 **NOTES:** ⊗ in restaurant Civ Wed 60 **CARDS:**

★★★64% *Buckerell Lodge Hotel*

Topsham Rd EX2 4SQ
☎ 01392 221111 🖷 01392 491111
Dir: *M5 junct 30 follow city centre signs, hotel on Topsham Rd, 0.5m from Exeter*

Although situated outside the city centre, this hotel is easily accessed by car or public transport. Accommodation is comfortable, fairly spacious and generally quiet. Public areas include a popular bar and restaurant and a variety of function rooms, and there is an attractive, extensive garden for guests to enjoy.
ROOMS: 53 en suite (2 fmly) ⊗ in 15 bedrooms **FACILITIES:** STV **CONF:** Thtr 80 Class 40 Board 40 **PARKING:** 60 **NOTES:** ⊗ in restaurant Civ Wed 50 **CARDS:**

⌂ Innkeeper's Lodge Exeter East
Clyst St George EX3 0QJ
☎ 01392 876121 🖷 01392 872022
www.innkeeperslodge.com
Dir: *M5 junct 30, A376 towards Exmouth. Right at 1st rdbt, straight over 2nd rdbt, at 3rd rdbt turn into Bridge Hill, lodge on right*
Smart rooms meet essential business requirements but also have home comforts, and depending on location may well have meeting rooms and pub dining. Dining options generally include all-day menus plus the added advantage of breakfast.
ROOMS: 13 en suite s £55; d £55 **CONF:** Thtr 75 Class 45 Board 30

⌂ Travel Inn
398 Topsham Rd EX2 6HE
☎ 08701 977097 🖷 01392 876174
Dir: *2m from M5 junct 30/A30 junct 29. Follow signs for Exeter & Dawlish (A379). On dual carriageway take 2nd slip road on left at Countess Wear rdbt. Travel Inn next to Beefeater*
Travel Inn offers good-quality, value-for-money accommodation. Spacious, en suite rooms with bath and shower comfortably accommodate a family of up to two adults and two children (to age 15). The restaurant and bar offers a varied menu. For further details consult the Hotel Groups page.
ROOMS: 44 en suite s £45.95-£48.95; d £45.95-£48.95

⌂ Travelodge
Moor Ln, Sandygate EX2 7HF
☎ 08700 850 950 🖷 01392 410406
Dir: *M5 junct 30*
Travelodge offers good quality, good value, modern accommodation. Ideal for families, the spacious, en suite bedrooms include remote-control TV, tea and coffee-making facilities and luxury beds. Meals can be taken at the nearby family restaurant. For further details consult the Hotel Groups page.
ROOMS: 102 en suite s fr £25; d fr £25 **CONF:** Thtr 80 Class 18 Board 25

EXFORD, Somerset — Map 03 SS83

★★★72% ◎◎ Crown
TA24 7PP
☎ 01643 831554 🖷 01643 831665
e-mail: info@crownhotelexmoor.co.uk
web: www.crownhotelexmoor.co.uk
Dir: *M5 junct 25, follow Taunton signs. Take A358 out of Taunton, then B3224 via Wheddon Cross into Exford*

Guest comfort is certainly a hallmark at the Crown Hotel. Afternoon tea is served in the lounge beside a roaring fire and tempting menus in the bar and restaurant are all part of the charm of this delightful old coaching inn that specialises in breaks for shooting and other country sports. Bedrooms retain a traditional style, yet offer a range of modern comforts and facilities, many with views of the pretty moorland village.
ROOMS: 17 en suite ⊗ in 3 bedrooms s £55-£65; d £95-£130 (incl. bkfst) **LB** **FACILITIES:** Fishing Riding Shooting, Riding Xmas **CONF:** BC **PARKING:** 30 **NOTES:** ⊗ in restaurant **CARDS:**

EXMOUTH, Devon Map 03 SY08

★★★71% Royal Beacon
The Beacon EX8 2AF
☎ 01395 264886 📠 01395 268890
e-mail: reception@royalbeaconhotel.co.uk
web: www.royalbeaconhotel.co.uk
Dir: *From M5 take A376 and Marine Way. Follow seafront signs. On Imperial Rd turn left at T-junct then 1st right. Hotel 100yds on left*

This elegant Georgian property sits in an elevated position overlooking the town and has fine views of the estuary towards the sea. Bedrooms are individually styled and many have sea views. Public areas include a well stocked bar, a cosy lounge, an impressive function suite and a restaurant where freshly prepared and enjoyable cuisine is offered.
ROOMS: 30 en suite (2 fmly) ⊗ in 10 bedrooms s £48-£80; d £85-£110 (incl. bkfst) **LB** **FACILITIES:** STV ♫ Xmas **CONF:** Thtr 160 Class 100 Board 60 Del from £105 **SERVICES:** Lift **PARKING:** 16 **NOTES:** ⊗ in restaurant Civ Wed 160 **CARDS:**

See advert on this page

★★73% Barn
Foxholes Hill, Marine Dr EX8 2DF
☎ 01395 224411 📠 01395 225445
e-mail: Info@barnhotel.co.uk
Dir: *M5 junct 30 take A376 to Exmouth, then signs to seafront. At rdbt last exit into Foxholes Hill. Hotel on right*
This unique Grade II listed property is quietly situated just a couple of minutes' walk from the beach. Views across the bay from the elegant public areas and most of the bedrooms are breathtaking. Akin to that of a country house hotel, the atmosphere here is relaxed and hospitable.
ROOMS: 11 en suite (4 fmly) ⊗ in all bedrooms s £30-£45; d £60-£90 (incl. bkfst) **LB** **FACILITIES:** Putt green **CONF:** Class 40 Board 20 **PARKING:** 24 **NOTES:** ⊗ in restaurant Closed 23 Dec-10 Jan
CARDS:

★★66% Manor Hotel
The Beacon EX8 2AG
☎ 01395 272549 & 274477 📠 01395 225519
e-mail: post@manorexmouth.co.uk
Dir: *M5 junct 30 take A376 to Exmouth. Hotel 300yds from seafront overlooking Manor Gardens*
Conveniently located for easy access to the town centre and with views overlooking the sea, this friendly hotel, now under new ownership, offers traditional values of hospitality and service, drawing guests back year after year. The well-equipped bedrooms vary in style and size; many have far-reaching views. The fixed price menu offers a varied selection of dishes.
ROOMS: 39 en suite (3 fmly) ⊗ in 6 bedrooms s £33-£40; d £56-£75 (incl. bkfst) **LB** **FACILITIES:** Xmas **CONF:** Thtr 100 Class 60 Board 60 **SERVICES:** Lift **PARKING:** 15 **NOTES:** ⊗ in restaurant
CARDS:

EXMOUTH, continued

★★63% Cavendish Hotel

11 Morton Crescent, The Esplanade EX8 1BE
☎ 01395 272528 01395 269361
e-mail: cavendish.exmouth@alfatravel.co.uk
Dir: *follow seafront signs, hotel in centre of large crescent*

Leisureplex

Situated on the seafront, this terraced hotel attracts many groups from around the country. With fine views out to sea, the hotel is within walking distance of the town centre. The bedrooms are neatly presented; front-facing rooms are always popular. Entertainment is provided on some evenings during the summer.
ROOMS: 72 en suite (3 fmly) (19 GF) s £30-£39; d £50-£68 (incl. bkfst) LB **FACILITIES:** Snooker ♫ Xmas **CONF:** Thtr 30 Board 12 **SERVICES:** Lift **PARKING:** 25 **NOTES:** ⊗ in restaurant Closed Dec-Jan ex Xmas RS Nov & Mar **CARDS:**

FAIRFORD, Gloucestershire Map 05 SP10

★★66% Bull Hotel

The Market Place GL7 4AA
☎ 01285 712535 & 712217 01285 713782
e-mail: info@thebullhotelfairford.co.uk
Dir: *on A417 in market square adjacent to post office*

Located in a picturesque Cotswold market town, this family-run inn's history dates back to the 15th century and still retains much period character and charm. A wide range of meals can be enjoyed within the popular bar or alternatively in the bistro restaurant. Bedrooms are all individual in style with a number overlooking the square.
ROOMS: 22 rms (20 en suite) 4 annexe en suite (4 fmly) **FACILITIES:** Fishing Cycle hire **CONF:** Thtr 60 Class 40 Board 40 **PARKING:** 10 **NOTES:** ⊗ in restaurant **CARDS:**

See advert on page 219

FAKENHAM, Norfolk Map 13 TF92

★★72% Crown

6 Market Place NR21 9BP
☎ 01328 851418 01328 862433
Dir: *A148, A1065 or A1065 to Fakenham town centre, follow signs to Market Place*

Friendly, family-run 17th-century coaching inn situated in the heart of this bustling town overlooking the market place. Bedrooms are attractively decorated with co-ordinated furnishings and many thoughtful touches. Public rooms include a comfortable lounge bar, an intimate restaurant and the smart new gallery bistro and function rooms.
ROOMS: 12 en suite (2 fmly) ⊗ in 1 bedroom s £50-£89; d £65-£105 (incl. bkfst) **FACILITIES:** Garage lock up for bicycles Xmas **CONF:** Class 35 Board 22 Del from £75 **PARKING:** 25 **NOTES:** ⊗ in restaurant Closed 25 Dec **CARDS:**

FALMOUTH, Cornwall & Isles of Scilly Map 02 SW83
See also Mawnan Smith

★★★★70% Royal Duchy

Cliff Rd TR11 4NX
☎ 01326 313042 01326 319420
e-mail: info@royalduchy.com
web: www.royalduchy.com
Dir: *on Cliff Rd, along Falmouth seafront*

Brend Hotels

Looking out over the sea and towards Pendennis Castle, this hotel provides a friendly environment. The comfortable lounge and cocktail bar are well appointed, and leisure facilities and meeting rooms are also available. The restaurant serves carefully prepared dishes and bedrooms vary in size but many have sea views.
ROOMS: 43 en suite (6 fmly) (1 GF) s £69-£93; d £130-£254 (incl. bkfst) LB **FACILITIES: Spa** STV Sauna Table tennis ♫ ch fac Xmas **CONF:** Thtr 50 Class 50 Board 50 **SERVICES:** Lift **PARKING:** 50 **NOTES:** ⊗ in restaurant Civ Wed 100 **CARDS:**

See advert on opposite page

★★★76% Penmere Manor

Mongleath Rd TR11 4PN
☎ 01326 211411 01326 317588
e-mail: reservations@penmere.co.uk
web: www.penmeremanorhotel.co.uk
Dir: *right off A39 at Hillhead rdbt, over double mini rdbt. After 0.75m left into Mongleath Rd*

Best Western

Set in five acres on the outskirts of Falmouth, this family-owned hotel provides friendly service and a range of facilities. A choice of freshly prepared dishes is served in either the bar or in the more formal Bolitho's Restaurant. A wide range of bedrooms is available - the spacious garden-wing rooms are furnished and equipped to a particularly high standard.
ROOMS: 37 en suite (12 fmly) (13 GF) ⊗ in all bedrooms s £68-£110; d £110-£158 (incl. bkfst) LB **FACILITIES: Spa** STV Sauna Gym Jacuzzi Beauty treatment room, Croquet **CONF:** Thtr 60 Class 20 Board 30 Del from £107 **PARKING:** 50 **NOTES:** ⊗ in restaurant Closed 23-26 Dec Civ Wed 70 **CARDS:**

See advert on opposite page

An oasis of gracious living in 5 acres of gardens and woodland offering the last word in comfort, friendliness and attentive service, a real home away from home.

Best Western

Penmere MANOR

FALMOUTH, CORNWALL UK

Mongleath Road, Falmouth,
Cornwall TR11 4PN

FREEPHONE 0800 980 4611

Web: www.penmeremanorhotel.co.uk

Email: reservations@penmere.co.uk

FALMOUTH'S FINEST

The Royal Duchy Hotel is the only 4 star hotel in Falmouth and has a reputation for luxurious accommodation, first class service and fine cuisine. It also sports excellent health and fitness facilities which include an indoor pool, sauna, solarium and spa bath as well as a family games room.

Enjoying panoramic views across Falmouth's famous bay, The Royal Duchy is the perfect base for exploring Cornwall. Discover the Eden Project, Tate St Ives, a beautiful cove or Falmouth's 300 years of maritime history.

Cliff Road, Falmouth, Cornwall, TR11 4NX
Tel: 01326 313042 Fax: 01326 319420
Web: www.royalduchy.co.uk

THE WESTCOUNTRY'S LEADING HOTEL GROUP

Green Lawns HOTEL

- AND THE -

Garras Restaurant

Western Terrace, Falmouth,
Cornwall TR11 4QJ
Tel: (01326) 312734 (3 lines)
Fax: (01326) 211427
E-mail: info@greenlawnshotel.com
www.greenlawnshotel.com

Chateau style hotel set in prize winning gardens, situated midway between the main sandy beaches and town. The hotel is privately owned and still retains and prides itself on the traditional standards.

Associated with first class cuisine, comfort and service. Hotel residents enjoy free membership of the Garras Leisure Club with indoor pool, sauna, jacuzzi and gymnasium. A solarium is also available.

A PLACE OF PEACE AND BEAUTY

...where the gardens sweep down to the sea

***Family run** Country House Hotel specialists in local seafood, traditional service, cosseted comforts, antiques, log fires and fresh flowers.*

Meudon

GOLF IS FREE

Please see full entry under Mawnan Smith

Tel 01 326 250541 • Fax 250543

www.meudon.co.uk

FALMOUTH, continued

★★★73% Green Lawns

Western Ter TR11 4QJ
☎ 01326 312734 🖹 01326 211427
e-mail: info@greenlawnshotel.com
web: www.greenlawnshotel.com
Dir: *on A39*

This attractive property enjoys a convenient location close to the town centre and within easy reach of the sea. Spacious public areas include inviting lounges, an elegant restaurant, conference and meeting facilities and a leisure centre. Bedrooms vary in size and style and all are well equipped and comfortable. The friendly service is noteworthy.
ROOMS: 39 en suite (8 fmly) (11 GF) ⊗ in 24 bedrooms s £60-£110; d £110-£170 (incl. bkfst) **LB** **FACILITIES:** Squash Sauna Solarium Gym Jacuzzi Swimming pool cameras **CONF:** Thtr 200 Class 80 Board 100 Del from £95 **PARKING:** 69 **NOTES:** ⊗ in restaurant Closed 24-30 Dec Civ Wed 50 **CARDS:**

See advert on page 221

★★★72% Falmouth Beach Resort Hotel

Gyllyngvase Beach, Seafront TR11 4NA
☎ 01326 310500 🖹 01326 319147
e-mail: info@falmouthbeachhotel.co.uk
web: www.falmouthbeachhotel.co.uk
Dir: *A39 to Falmouth, follow seafront signs.*

Enjoying wonderful views, this popular hotel is situated opposite the beach and within easy walking distance of Falmouth's attractions and port. A friendly atmosphere is maintained and guests have a good choice of leisure and fitness, entertainment and dining options. Bedrooms, many with balconies and sea views, are well equipped and comfortable.
ROOMS: 116 en suite 7 annexe en suite (20 fmly) (4 GF) ⊗ in 94 bedrooms s £51-£61; d £102-£122 (incl. bkfst) **LB** **FACILITIES: Spa** STV pool supervised Sauna Solarium Gym Jacuzzi Steam room ♫ Xmas **CONF:** Thtr 300 Class 200 Board 250 Del from £85 **SERVICES:** Lift **PARKING:** 88 **NOTES:** ⊗ in restaurant Civ Wed 120 **CARDS:**

See advert on opposite page

★★★72% The Greenbank

Harbourside TR11 2SR
☎ 01326 312440 🖹 01326 211362
e-mail: sales@greenbank-hotel.com
web: www.greenbank-hotel.com
Dir: *500yds past Falmouth Marina on Penryn River*

A strong maritime theme prevails at this smart hotel, located close to the marina and with its own private quay dating from the 17th century. Set at the water's edge, the lounge, restaurant and many bedrooms have harbour views. The restaurant provides a choice of interesting and enjoyable dishes.
ROOMS: 60 en suite (4 fmly) ⊗ in 30 bedrooms s £65-£90; d £100-£175 (incl. bkfst) **LB** **FACILITIES:** Private beach **CONF:** Thtr 60 Class 45 Board 20 Del from £97.50 **SERVICES:** Lift **PARKING:** 68 **NOTES:** ⊗ in restaurant Civ Wed 100 **CARDS:**

★★★69% Falmouth

Castle Beach TR11 4NZ
☎ 01326 312671 & 0800 0193121 🖹 01326 319533
e-mail: info@falmouthhotel.com
web: www.falmouthhotel.com
Dir: *take A30 to Truro then A390 to Falmouth. Follow signs for beaches, hotel on seafront near Pendennis Castle*

This spectacular beach-front Victorian property affords wonderful sea views from many of its comfortable bedrooms, some of which boast their own balconies. Spacious public areas include a number of inviting lounges, beautiful leafy grounds, a choice of dining options and an impressive range of leisure facilities.
ROOMS: 69 en suite 34 annexe en suite (13 fmly) ⊗ in 18 bedrooms s £45-£50; d £65-£135 **LB** **FACILITIES:** STV pool supervised Snooker Sauna Solarium Gym Putt green Jacuzzi Beauty Salon **CONF:** Thtr 250 Class 150 Board 100 Del from £62 **SERVICES:** Lift **PARKING:** 175 **NOTES:** ⊗ in restaurant Closed 24 Dec-2 Jan Civ Wed 250 **CARDS:**

See advert on opposite page

★★★68% *St Michaels of Falmouth*
Gyllyngvase Beach, Seafront TR11 4NB
☎ 01326 312707 🖷 01326 211772
e-mail: info@stmichaelshotel.co.uk
Dir: *A39 into Falmouth, follow beach signs, at 2nd mini-rdbt into Pennance Rd. Take 2nd left & 2nd left again*

Overlooking the bay, this establishment has an excellent location. The contemporary-style public areas include comfortable lounges, leisure facilities and attractive gardens. The Flying Fish bistro and the hotel's main restaurant, Oyster Bay, offer enjoyable dining. Bedrooms, currently undergoing refurbishment, are available in a range of sizes and all are well equipped.
ROOMS: 57 en suite 8 annexe en suite (7 fmly) ⊗ in 15 bedrooms **FACILITIES:** Sauna Solarium Gym Jacuzzi Concessionary golf rates **CONF:** Thtr 200 Class 150 Board 50 **PARKING:** 30 **NOTES:** ⊗ in restaurant Civ Wed 80 **CARDS:**

See advert on this page

The Falmouth Hotel commands an unrivalled seafront location with 100 quality rooms, serviced apartments and self-catering cottages with optional balcony and Jacuzzi.
Enjoy delightful views from ambient restaurants, bars and lounge. The Oasis leisure complex includes an indoor pool, sauna, Jacuzzi, solarium and gym.
The perfect venue for weddings, conferences and all functions.

CASTLE BEACH ROAD, FALMOUTH, CORNWALL TR11 4NZ

Please call for a brochure and tariffs.

FREEPHONE: 0800 019 3121 **Fax: 01326 319533**

Email: info@falmouthhotel.com **www.falmouthhotel.com**

FALMOUTH, continued

★★★66% Penmorvah Manor
Budock Water TR11 5ED
☎ 01326 250277 📠 01326 250509
e-mail: reception@penmorvah.co.uk
web: www.penmorvah.co.uk
Dir: *A39 to Hillhead rdbt, take 2nd exit. Right at Falmouth Football Club, through Budock and hotel opposite Penjerrick Gardens*

Situated within two miles of central Falmouth, this extended Victorian manor house is a peaceful hideaway, set in six acres of private woodland and gardens. Penmorvah is well positioned for visiting the local gardens, and offers many garden tour breaks. Dinner features locally sourced, quality ingredients such as Cornish cheeses, meat, fish and game.
ROOMS: 27 en suite (1 fmly) (10 GF) ⊗ in all bedrooms s £50-£60; d £90-£130 (incl. bkfst) **LB FACILITIES:** Pool table Xmas **CONF:** Thtr 250 Class 100 Board 56 Del from £95 **PARKING:** 150 **NOTES:** ⊗ in restaurant Closed 31 Dec - 31 Jan Civ Wed 120
CARDS:

★★75% Crill Manor
Maen Valley, Budock Water TR11 5BL
☎ 01326 211880 📠 01326 211229
e-mail: info@crillmanor.com
Dir: *A39 Truro towards Falmouth, then right for Mawnan Smith/ Budock Water. Over double mini rdbt. Through village to 40mph sign then left*
Set in a secluded Area of Outstanding Natural Beauty, this delightful hotel offers friendly and attentive service. Bedrooms are well equipped and attractively decorated. The open plan, split-level lounge and bar area overlooks the gardens. The Four Seasons Restaurant offers a daily-changing menu.
ROOMS: 14 en suite (2 GF) ⊗ in all bedrooms s £44-£61; d £88-£122 (incl. bkfst) **LB FACILITIES:** Xmas **PARKING:** 22 **NOTES:** No children 14yrs ⊗ in restaurant **CARDS:**

★★69% Hotel Anacapri
Gyllyngvase Rd TR11 4DJ
☎ 01326 311454 📠 01326 311454
e-mail: anacapri@btconnect.com
web: www.hotelanacapri.co.uk
Dir: *A39 Truro to Falmouth, straight on at lights, 2 rdbts straight on. 5th right into Gyllyngvase Road, hotel few mtrs on right*
In an elevated position, overlooking Gyllyngvase Beach and Falmouth Bay beyond, this family run establishment extends a warm welcome to all. Bedrooms all share similar standards of comfort and quality and the majority have sea views. Public areas include a convivial bar, a lounge and the smart restaurant, where carefully prepared and very enjoyable cuisine is on offer.
ROOMS: 16 en suite (1 fmly) ⊗ in 8 bedrooms s £25-£50; d £50-£100 (incl. bkfst) **LB PARKING:** 20 **NOTES:** No dogs No children 8yrs ⊗ in restaurant **CARDS:**

★★68% Park Grove
Kimberley Park Rd TR11 2DD
THE INDEPENDENTS
☎ 01326 313276 📠 01326 211926
e-mail: reception@parkgrovehotel.com
web: www.parkgrovehotel.com
Dir: *off A39 at lights by Riders Garage towards harbour. Hotel 400yds on left opp park*
Within walking distance of the town centre, this friendly family-run hotel is situated in a pleasant residential area opposite Kimberley Park. Comfortable accommodation is provided and public areas include a relaxing and stylish lounge and a well-spaced dining room and bar. Bedrooms, many now refurbished, are also comfortable and well equipped.
ROOMS: 17 en suite (6 fmly) s £33-£47; d £66-£74 (incl. bkfst) **LB PARKING:** 25 **NOTES:** No dogs ⊗ in restaurant Closed Dec-Feb
CARDS:

★★67% *Rosslyn*
110 Kimberley Park Rd TR11 2JJ
☎ 01326 312699 📠 01326 312699
e-mail: mail@rosslynhotel.co.uk
web: www.rosslynhotel.co.uk
Dir: *on A39 towards Falmouth, to Hillend rdbt, turn right and over next mini rdbt. At 2nd mini rdbt left into Trescobeas Rd. Hotel on left past hospital*
A relaxed and friendly atmosphere is maintained at this family run hotel. Situated on the northern edge of Falmouth, the Rosslyn is easily located and is suitable for both business and leisure guests. A comfortable lounge overlooks the well-tended garden, and enjoyable freshly prepared dinners are offered in the restaurant.
ROOMS: 27 rms (23 en suite) (2 fmly) (6 GF) ⊗ in all bedrooms **FACILITIES:** Putt green Table tennis Pool table **CONF:** Class 60 **PARKING:** 15 **NOTES:** ⊗ in restaurant **CARDS:**

★★65% Broadmead
66-68 Kimberley Park Rd TR11 2DD
THE CIRCLE Selected Individual Hotels GREAT BRITAIN
☎ 01326 315704 318036 📠 01326 311048
e-mail: mail@broadmeadhotel.fsnet.com
Dir: *turn off A39 at traffic lights by Riders Garage towards town centre. Hotel 150yds on left*
Conveniently located, with views across the park and within easy walking distance of the beaches and town centre, this pleasant hotel has smart and comfortable accommodation. Bedrooms are well equipped and attractively decorated. A choice of lounges is available and, in the dining room, menus offer home-cooked dishes.
ROOMS: 12 en suite (2 GF) ⊗ in 3 bedrooms s £25-£37; d £25-£42 (incl. bkfst) **LB PARKING:** 8 **NOTES:** No dogs ⊗ in restaurant
CARDS:

★★63% Madeira Hotel
Cliff Rd TR11 4NY
Leisureplex
☎ 01326 313531 📠 01326 319143
e-mail: madeira.falmouth@alfatravel.co.uk
Dir: *A39 Truro to Falmouth, follow tourist signs 'Hotels' to seafront*
This popular hotel offers splendid sea views and a pleasantly convenient location, which is close to the town. Extensive sun lounges are popular haunts in which to enjoy the views, whilst additional facilities include an oak-panelled cocktail bar. Bedrooms, many with sea views, are available in a range of sizes.
ROOMS: 50 en suite (8 fmly) (7 GF) s £31-£41; d £52-£72 (incl. bkfst) **LB FACILITIES:** ♫ Xmas **SERVICES:** Lift **PARKING:** 11 **NOTES:** No dogs ⊗ in restaurant Closed Dec-Feb RS Nov & Mar **CARDS:**

Bad hair day?
Hairdryers in all rooms three stars and above

★★63% Membly Hall

Sea Front, Cliff Rd TR11 4NT
☎ 01326 312869 & 311115 🖷 01326 211751
e-mail: memblyhallhotel@btopenworld.com
Dir: *A39 to Falmouth. Follow seafront and beaches sign.*

Located conveniently on the seafront and enjoying sea views, this family-run hotel offers friendly service. Bedrooms are pleasantly spacious and well-equipped. Carefully prepared and enjoyable meals are served in the spacious dining room. Live entertainment is provided on some evenings in the attractive lounge bar area and there is also a sun room.

ROOMS: 37 en suite (3 fmly) s fr £26; d fr £52 (incl. bkfst) **LB** **FACILITIES:** STV Putt green Indoor short bowls Table tennis Pool table ♫ **CONF:** Thtr 150 Class 130 Board 60 Del from £30 **SERVICES:** Lift **PARKING:** 30 **NOTES:** ⊘ in restaurant Closed Xmas week RS Dec-Jan

FAREHAM, Hampshire — Map 05 SU50

★★★★73% Solent

Rookery Av, Whiteley PO15 7AJ
☎ 01489 880000 🖷 01489 880007
e-mail: solent@shirehotels.co.uk
Dir: *M27 junct 9, hotel on Solent Business Park*

Although close to the M27, this smart, purpose-built hotel enjoys a peaceful location. Bedrooms are very spacious and well-appointed. The well-equipped leisure centre and spa has undergone a £1 million refurbishment, and the lounge, bar and restaurant feature beams and log fires throughout.

ROOMS: 111 en suite (9 fmly) (20 GF) ⊘ in 83 bedrooms s £140-£180; d £148-£180 (incl. bkfst) **LB** **FACILITIES: Spa** STV supervised Sauna Solarium Gym Steam room, Childrens splash pool, activity studio Xmas **CONF:** BC Thtr 250 Class 120 Board 80 Del £165 **SERVICES:** Lift **PARKING:** 200 **NOTES:** ⊘ in restaurant Civ Wed 160 **CARDS:**

See advert under SOUTHAMPTON

★★★66% Lysses House

51 High St PO16 7BQ
☎ 01329 822622 🖷 01329 822762
e-mail: lysses@lysses.co.uk
web: www.lysses.co.uk
Dir: *M27 junct 11 stay in left lane. At rdbt 3rd exit into East St & follow into High St. Hotel at top on right*

This attractive Georgian hotel is situated on the edge of the town in a quiet location and provides spacious and well-equipped accommodation. There are conference facilities and a lounge bar serving a range of snacks, whilst public areas have benefited from an extensive refurbishment. Cuisine in the Richmond Restaurant is both accomplished and imaginative.

ROOMS: 21 en suite (7 GF) s £55-£79; d £78-£99 (incl. bkfst) **CONF:** Thtr 95 Class 42 Board 28 Del from £98 **SERVICES:** Lift **PARKING:** 30 **NOTES:** ⊘ in restaurant Closed 25 Dec-1 Jan RS 24 Dec & BH's Civ Wed 100 **CARDS:**

⌂ Travel Inn

Southampton Rd, Park Gate SO31 6AF
☎ 08701 977100 🖷 01489 577238
Dir: *on 2nd rdbt off M27 junct 9, signed A27 Fareham*

Travel Inn offers good-quality, value-for-money accommodation. Spacious, en suite rooms with bath and shower comfortably accommodate a family of up to two adults and two children (to age 15). The restaurant and bar offers a varied menu. For further details consult the Hotel Groups page.

ROOMS: 41 en suite s £45.95-£48.95; d £45.95-£48.95

FARINGDON, Oxfordshire

Map 05 SU29

★★★71% Sudbury House Hotel & Conference Centre

London St SN7 8AA
☎ 01367 241272 🖷 01367 242346
e-mail: stay@sudburyhouse.co.uk
web: www.sudburyhouse.co.uk
Dir: *off A420, signposted Folly Hill*

Sudbury House lies between Oxford and Swindon. Bedrooms are attractive, decorated in warm colour schemes, spacious and well equipped. Dining options include the restaurant, bar and a comprehensive room service menu. In addition to pleasant grounds, conference facilities, a small fitness room and private dining rooms are also available.

ROOMS: 49 en suite (2 fmly) (10 GF) ⊗ in 22 bedrooms s £92; d £102 (incl. bkfst) **LB** **FACILITIES:** STV Gym Putt green Pitch & Putt, Badminton, Boules Xmas **CONF:** Thtr 90 Class 90 Board 40 Del £146 **SERVICES:** Lift **PARKING:** 100 **NOTES:** ⊗ in restaurant Civ Wed 160 **CARDS:**

See advert on page 225

FARNBOROUGH, Hampshire

Map 05 SU85

★★★65% Falcon

68 Farnborough Rd GU14 6TH
☎ 01252 545378 🖷 01252 522539
e-mail: hotel@falconfarnborough.com
web: www.falconfarnborough.com
Dir: *A325 off M3, pass Farnborough Gate Retail Park. Left at next rdbt & straight at next 2 rdbts. Hotel on left at junct of aircraft esplanade & A325*

This well-presented hotel is conveniently located for business guests. Modern bedrooms are practically furnished and equipped with a useful range of extras. Public areas include the conservatory restaurant offering a range of contemporary and traditional fare. Aircraft enthusiasts are well catered for as there is an aeronautical centre adjacent.

ROOMS: 30 en suite (1 fmly) (3 GF) s £55-£99; d £65-£110 (incl. bkfst) **FACILITIES:** STV Xmas **CONF:** Thtr 25 Class 8 Board 16 **PARKING:** 25 **NOTES:** ⊗ in restaurant RS 23 Dec - 4 Jan Civ Wed 50 **CARDS:**

Travel Inn

travel inn

Ively Rd, Southwood GU14 0JP
☎ 08701 977101 🖷 01252 546427
Dir: *From M3 (J4a), join A327 to Farnborough. Travel Inn on left hand side at 5th rbt (Monkey Puzzle roundabout)*

Travel Inn offers good-quality, value-for-money accommodation. Spacious, en suite rooms with bath and shower comfortably accommodate a family of up to two adults and two children (to age 15). The restaurant and bar offers a varied menu. For further details consult the Hotel Groups page.

ROOMS: 62 en suite s £45.95-£48.95; d £45.95-£48.95

FARNHAM, Surrey

Map 05 SU84

See also Churt

★★★72% Bishop's Table

27 West St GU9 7DR
☎ 01252 710222 🖷 01252 733494
e-mail: welcome@bishopstable.com
web: www.bishopstable.com
Dir: *from M3 junct 4 take A331 or from A3 take A31and follow town centre signs. Hotel next to library*

This family-run Georgian townhouse hotel is in the centre of Farnham and offers comfortable accommodation and friendly, attentive service. Each bedroom is individual in style and some are situated in a restored coach house. Public areas include a cosy bar and a refurbished, elegant restaurant.

ROOMS: 9 en suite 8 annexe en suite (6 GF) ⊗ in 5 bedrooms s £95-£165; d £95-£165 **LB** **FACILITIES:** free use of nearby gym **CONF:** BC Thtr 26 Class 10 Board 20 Del from £165 **NOTES:** No children 16yrs ⊗ in restaurant Closed 25 Dec-3 Jan RS Closed for lunch Mon **CARDS:**

★★★70% *Frensham Pond Hotel*

Bacon Ln GU10 2QB
☎ 01252 795161 🖷 01252 792631
e-mail: frenshampond@bestwestern.co.uk
web: www.frenshampondhotel.co.uk
(For full entry see Churt and advert on opposite page)

★★★68% The Bush

MACDONALD HOTELS

The Borough GU9 7NN
☎ 0870 400 8225 01252 715237
🖷 01252 733530
e-mail: gm.bush@macdonald-hotels.co.uk
Dir: *M3 J4 then join A31, follow signs for town centre. At East St traffic lights turn left, hotel on right.*

Dating back to the 17th century, this extended coaching inn is attractively presented and has a courtyard and an lawned garden. The bedrooms are well appointed, with quality fabrics and good facilities. The public areas include the panelled Oak Lounge, a smart cocktail bar and a new conference facility, developed in an adjoining building.

ROOMS: 83 en suite (3 fmly) (22 GF) ⊗ in 60 bedrooms s £90-£165; d £90-£165 (incl. bkfst) **LB** **FACILITIES:** Xmas **CONF:** Thtr 140 Class 80 Board 30 Del from £135 **PARKING:** 70 **NOTES:** ⊗ in restaurant Civ Wed 90 **CARDS:**

> Late for dinner?
> Quality Standards mean that last orders for dinner vary according to star rating and should be no earlier than:
> ★★ 7.00pm ★★★ 8.00pm ★★★★ 9.00pm
> ★★★★★ 10.00pm

★★★ 61% Farnham House

Alton Rd GU10 5ER
☎ 01252 716908 Fax 01252 722583
e-mail: mail@farnhamhousehotel.com
web: www.hollybournehotels.com
Dir: *1m from town, off A31 Alton road*

Popular for conferences and weddings, Farnham House is surrounded by five acres of grounds. The architecture is part Tudor, part baronial in style, and features an oak-panelled bar with an inglenook fireplace. Most bedrooms enjoy countryside views, and a tennis court and swimming pool are peacefully set in the tranquil gardens.

ROOMS: 25 en suite (1 fmly) ⊗ in 7 bedrooms s £64-£77; d £69-£87 **LB FACILITIES:** STV **CONF:** Thtr 55 Class 14 Board 25 Del from £99 **PARKING:** 75 **NOTES:** RS 25 & 26 Dec Civ Wed 74 **CARDS:**

FAVERSHAM, Kent — Map 07 TR06

Travelodge Canterbury North

Thanet Way ME13 9EL
☎ 08700 850 950 Fax 01227 281135
Dir: *from M2 junct 7, take A299*

Travelodge offers good quality, good value, modern accommodation. Ideal for families, the spacious, en suite bedrooms include remote-control TV, tea and coffee-making facilities and luxury beds. Meals can be taken at the nearby family restaurant. For further details consult the Hotel Groups page.

ROOMS: 40 en suite s fr £25; d fr £25

FEERING, Essex — Map 07 TL82

Travelodge (Colchester)

A12 London Rd Northbound CO5 9EL
☎ 08700 850 950 Fax 01376 572848

Travelodge offers good quality, good value, modern accommodation. Ideal for families, the spacious, en suite bedrooms include remote-control TV, tea and coffee-making facilities and luxury beds. Meals can be taken at the nearby family restaurant. For further details consult the Hotel Groups page.

ROOMS: 39 en suite s fr £25; d fr £25

FELIXSTOWE, Suffolk — Map 13 TM33

★★★ 72% Elizabeth Orwell

Hamilton Rd IP11 7DX
☎ 01394 285511 Fax 01394 670687
e-mail: elizabeth.orwell@elizabethhotels.co.uk
Dir: *from A14 over Dock rdbt and next rdbt. At 3rd rdbt 4th exit to Beatrice Avenue. At end of road hotel over rdbt*

Imposing Victorian building situated just a short walk from the town centre. The pleasantly decorated, well-equipped bedrooms come in a variety of styles and feature several large, superior rooms. The newly refurbished public areas are superbly appointed and offer a wealth of charm and character; they include two bars, a choice of lounges, an informal buttery and the spacious Westerfield's restaurant.

ROOMS: 60 en suite (8 fmly) s £85-£105; d £105-£170 (incl. bkfst) **LB FACILITIES:** STV Xmas **CONF:** Thtr 200 Class 100 Board 60 Del from £127 **SERVICES:** Lift **PARKING:** 70 **NOTES:** ⊗ in restaurant Civ Wed 200 **CARDS:**

★★ 64% Marlborough

Sea Front IP11 2BJ
☎ 01394 285621 Fax 01394 670724
e-mail: hsm@marlborough-hotel-felix.com
web: www.marlborough-hotel-felix.com
Dir: *from A14 follow Docks signs. Over Dock rdbt, railway crossing and traffic lights. Left at T-junct and hotel 400mtrs on left*

Situated on the seafront, overlooking the beach and just a short stroll from the pier and town centre. This traditional resort hotel offers a good range of facilities including the smart Rattan Restaurant, Flying Boat Bar and L'Aperitif lounge. The pleasantly decorated bedrooms come in a variety of styles; some have lovely sea views.

ROOMS: 49 en suite ⊗ in 3 bedrooms s £49-£70; d £62-£85 (incl. bkfst) **LB FACILITIES:** STV Pool table Xmas **CONF:** Thtr 80 Class 60 Board 40 **SERVICES:** Lift **PARKING:** 16 **NOTES:** ⊗ in restaurant **CARDS:**

> Early start?
> Hotels at all star levels should provide in-room alarm clocks and/or alarm calls

FENNY BENTLEY, Derbyshire Map 16 SK14

★★68% Bentley Brook Inn

DE6 1LF
☎ 01335 350278 01335 350422
e-mail: all@bentleybrookinn.co.uk
web: www.bentleybrookinn.co.uk
Dir: *2m N of Ashbourne at junct of A515 & B5056, entrance off B5056*

This popular family-owned inn is located within the Peak District National Park, just north of Ashbourne. It is a charming building with an attractive terrace, sweeping lawns, and nursery gardens. A well-appointed family restaurant dominates the ground floor, where a wide range of dishes is available all day. The character bar serves beer from its own micro-brewery. Bedrooms vary in styles and sizes, but all are well equipped.
ROOMS: 9 en suite 1 annexe rms in 1 bedroom s £50; d £72.50 (incl. bkfst) **LB** **FACILITIES:** Fishing Boules Skittles Brewery tour Xmas **CONF:** Thtr 28 Class 28 Board 18 Del £100 **PARKING:** 100 **NOTES:** in restaurant **CARDS:**

FENSTANTON, Cambridgeshire Map 12 TL36

Travelodge Huntingdon

Travelodge

PE18 9LP
☎ 08700 850 950 01954 230919
Dir: *4m SE of Huntingdon, on A14 eastbound*
Travelodge offers good quality, good value, modern accommodation. Ideal for families, the spacious, en suite bedrooms include remote-control TV, tea and coffee-making facilities and luxury beds. Meals can be taken at the nearby family restaurant. For further details consult the Hotel Groups page.
ROOMS: 40 en suite s fr £25; d fr £25

FERNDOWN, Dorset Map 05 SU00

★★★★73% *De Vere Dormy*

DE VERE HOTELS

New Rd BH22 8ES
☎ 01202 872121 01202 895388
e-mail: devere.dormy@devere-hotels.com
Dir: *town centre turn left at lights onto A347. Hotel 1 mile on left*
Set in spacious grounds, this well established hotel is conveniently located for Bournemouth's airport, the New Forest and the beaches. When it comes to dining, guests are spoiled for choice; options include the Garden Restaurant, the fine dining experience in Hennessy's and the informal Pavilion Brasserie. Bedrooms are located both in the main building and several nearby cottage wings.
ROOMS: 114 en suite **FACILITIES:** STV supervised Squash Snooker Sauna Solarium Gym Jacuzzi Beauty salon, Dance studio **CONF:** Thtr 300 Class 140 Board 50 **SERVICES:** Lift **PARKING:** 200 **NOTES:** in restaurant Civ Wed 150 **CARDS:**

Travel Inn Bournemouth/Ferndown

travel inn

Ringwood Rd, Tricketts Cross BH22 9BB
☎ 08701 977102 01202 897794
Dir: *off A348 just before Tricketts Cross rdbt*
Travel Inn offers good-quality, value-for-money accommodation. Spacious, en suite rooms with bath and shower comfortably accommodate a family of up to two adults and two children (to age 15). The restaurant and bar offers a varied menu. For further details consult the Hotel Groups page.
ROOMS: 32 en suite s £45.95-£48.95; d £45.95-£48.95 **CONF:** Thtr 20

FERRYBRIDGE SERVICE AREA (M62/A1), West Yorkshire Map 16 SE42

Travelodge Pontefract Ferrybridge

Travelodge

WF11 0AF
☎ 08700 850 950 01977 622509
Dir: *M62 junct 33*
Travelodge offers good quality, good value, modern accommodation. Ideal for families, the spacious, en suite bedrooms include remote-control TV, tea and coffee-making facilities and luxury beds. Meals can be taken at the nearby family restaurant. For further details consult the Hotel Groups page.
ROOMS: 36 en suite s fr £25; d fr £25

FILEY, North Yorkshire Map 17 TA18

★★74% Downcliffe House

6 The Beach YO14 9LA
☎ 01723 513310 01723 513773
e-mail: info@downcliffehouse.co.uk
Dir: *from A165 join A1039 into Filey, through town centre along Cargate Hill and turn right. Hotel 200yds along seafront*
The Downcliffe House Hotel is set right on the seafront. A friendly hotel, its inviting public areas include an attractive restaurant serving an excellent range of freshly prepared meals, and a bar. The hotel is furnished to a very high standard, and bedrooms are smart and suitably well equipped.
ROOMS: 11 en suite (2 fmly) in all bedrooms **FACILITIES:** Xmas **PARKING:** 3 **NOTES:** in restaurant Closed mid Dec-Jan **CARDS:**

FIR TREE, Co Durham Map 19 NZ13

★★★66% Helme Park Hall Hotel

DL13 4NW
☎ 01388 730970 01388 731799
e-mail: enquiries@helmeparkhotel.co.uk
web: www.helmeparkhotel.co.uk
Dir: *1m N of A689/A68 rdbt between Darlington & Corbridge*
Dating back to the 13th century, this welcoming hotel boasts superb panoramic views up the Wear Valley. The bedrooms are comfortably equipped and furnished. The cosy lounge bar is extremely popular for its comprehensive selection of bar meals, and the restaurant offers both table d'hote and carte menus.
ROOMS: 13 en suite (1 fmly) in 5 bedrooms s £52; d £85 (incl. bkfst) **LB** **FACILITIES:** STV Xmas **CONF:** BC Thtr 150 Class 80 Board 80 **PARKING:** 70 **NOTES:** in restaurant Civ Wed 100 **CARDS:**

FIVE OAKS, West Sussex — Map 06 TQ02

Travelodge Billingshurst

Staines St RH14 9AE
☎ 08700 850 950 ▯ 01403 782711
Dir: *on A29, northbound, 1m N of Billingshurst*
Travelodge offers good quality, good value, modern accommodation. Ideal for families, the spacious, en suite bedrooms include remote-control TV, tea and coffee-making facilities and luxury beds. Meals can be taken at the nearby family restaurant. For further details consult the Hotel Groups page.
ROOMS: 26 en suite s fr £25; d fr £25

FLAMBOROUGH, East Riding of Yorkshire — Map 17 TA27

★★72% North Star

North Marine Dr YO15 1BL
☎ 01262 850379 ▯ 01262 850379
web: www.puffinsatflamborough.co.uk
Dir: *follow signs for North Landing. Hotel 100yds from sea*
Standing close to the North Landing of Flamborough Head, this family-run hotel overlooks delightful countryside. The hotel has been refurbished and provides excellent accommodation together with a very popular bar. A good range of well-produced food is available in both the bar and the spacious dining room.
ROOMS: 7 en suite s £50-£60; d £70-£80 (incl. bkfst) **LB**
PARKING: 30 **NOTES:** ⊗ in restaurant Closed Xmas & 2wks Nov & Jan **CARDS:**

FLEET, Hampshire — Map 05 SU85

★★★63% Lismoyne

Church Rd GU51 4NE
☎ 01252 628555 ▯ 01252 811761
e-mail: info@lismoynehotel.com
Dir: *M3 junct 4a. B3013, over railway bridge to town centre. Through lights, take 4th right. Hotel 0.25m on left*
Set in extensive grounds, this attractive hotel is located close to the town centre. Public rooms include a comfortable lounge and pleasant bar with a conservatory overlooking the garden, and a traditional restaurant. Accommodation is divided between bedrooms in the original building and those in the modern extension; styles vary and all rooms are well equipped.
ROOMS: 62 en suite (3 fmly) (19 GF) ⊗ in 18 bedrooms s £55-£135; d £80-£155 (incl. bkfst) **LB** **FACILITIES:** STV mini-gym Xmas
CONF: Thtr 170 Class 92 Board 80 Del from £120 **PARKING:** 150
NOTES: ⊗ in restaurant Civ Wed
CARDS:

Innkeeper's Lodge

Cove Rd GU51 2SH
☎ 01252 774600
Dir: *M3, junct 4a*
www.innkeeperslodge.com
Smart rooms meet essential business requirements but also have home comforts, and depending on location may well have meeting rooms and pub dining. Dining options generally include all-day menus plus the added advantage of breakfast.
ROOMS: 40 en suite s £49-£65; d £49-£65

> Town House Hotel
> Country House Hotel
> Travel Accommodation

FLEET MOTORWAY SERVICE AREA (M3), Hampshire — Map 05 SU75

Days Inn

Fleet Services GU51 1AA
☎ 01252 815587 ▯ 01252 815587
e-mail: fleethotel@welcomebreak.co.uk
web: www.welcomebreak.co.uk
Dir: *Welcome Break Fleet Motorway Service area between junct 4a & 5 southbound on M3*
This modern building offers accommodation in smart, spacious and well-equipped bedrooms, suitable for families and business travellers, and all with en suite bathrooms. Continental breakfast is available and other refreshments may be taken at the nearby family restaurant. For further details see the Hotel Groups page.
ROOMS: 58 en suite s £45-£55; d £45-£65 **CONF:** Board 10

FLITWICK, Bedfordshire — Map 11 TL03

Top 200 – Hotel

★★★ ◎◎ Menzies Flitwick Manor

Church Rd MK45 1AE
☎ 01525 712242 ▯ 01525 718753
e-mail: flitwick@menzies-hotels.co.uk
Dir: *M1 J12, follow signs fro Flitwick, turn left into Church Rd, hotel on left.*
With its picturesque setting in acres of gardens and parkland, yet only minutes by car from the motorway, this lovely Georgian house combines the best of both worlds: peaceful and accessible. Bedrooms are individually decorated and furnished with period pieces; some are air conditioned. Cosy and intimate, the lounge and restaurant help give the hotel a home-from-home feel, which makes it popular with many guests.
ROOMS: 17 en suite s £140-£170; d £170-£200 **LB** **FACILITIES:** Putt green Xmas **CONF:** Thtr 40 Class 30 Board 24 Del £200
PARKING: 50 **NOTES:** ⊗ in restaurant Civ Wed
CARDS:

FLORE, Northamptonshire — Map 11 SP66

★★★72% Courtyard by Marriott Daventry

High St NN7 4LP
☎ 01327 349022 ▯ 01327 349017
e-mail: reservations.northamptonwest@whitbread.com
Dir: *M1 junct 16 onto A45 towards Daventry. Hotel 1m on right between Upper Heyford and Flore*
Just off the M1 motorway in rural surroundings, this modern hotel is particularly suited to the business guest. Professional staff provide a warm welcome and helpful service throughout the public areas, which comprise a lounge bar and restaurant.

continued on p230

FLORE, continued

Bedrooms provide smart décor, plenty of workspace and a good range of facilities.
ROOMS: 53 en suite (7 fmly) ⊗ in 34 bedrooms s £44-£87; d £58-£97 **LB FACILITIES:** STV Gym **CONF:** Thtr 80 Class 40 Board 48 Del from £105 **PARKING:** 120 **NOTES:** ✈ ⊗ in restaurant Civ Wed 100
CARDS:

FOLKESTONE, Kent Map 07 TR23

★★★70% Clifton

The Leas CT20 2EB
☎ 01303 851231 📠 01303 223949
e-mail: reservations@thecliftonhotel.com
Dir: *M20 junct 13, 0.25m W of town centre on A259*

This privately-owned Victorian-style hotel occupies a prime location, looking out across the English Channel. The bedrooms are all comfortably appointed and most have views of the sea. Public areas include a comfortable, traditionally furnished lounge, a popular bar serving a good range of beers and several well-appointed conference rooms.
ROOMS: 80 en suite (5 fmly) ⊗ in 31 bedrooms s £62.50-£77; d £85-£105 (incl. bkfst) **LB FACILITIES:** STV Games room Xmas **CONF:** Thtr 80 Class 36 Board 32 Del from £97.50 **SERVICES:** Lift **NOTES:** ✈ **CARDS:**

See advert on opposite page

⌂ Travel Inn

Cherry Garden Ln CT19 4AP
☎ 08701 977103 📠 01303 273641
Dir: *M20 junct 13. At 1st rdbt turn right, at 2nd rdbt turn right signed Folkestone A20. At traffic lights turn right, Inn on right.*
Travel Inn offers good-quality, value-for-money accommodation. Spacious, en suite rooms with bath and shower comfortably accommodate a family of up to two adults and two children (to age 15). The restaurant and bar offers a varied menu. For further details consult the Hotel Groups page.
ROOMS: 79 en suite s £45.95-£46.95; d £45.95-£46.95

FONTWELL, West Sussex Map 06 SU90

⌂ Travelodge Bognor Regis

BN18 0SB
☎ 08700 850 950 📠 01243 543973
Dir: *on A27/A29 rdbt*
Travelodge offers good quality, good value, modern accommodation. Ideal for families, the spacious, en suite bedrooms include remote-control TV, tea and coffee-making facilities and luxury beds. Meals can be taken at the nearby family restaurant. For further details consult the Hotel Groups page.
ROOMS: 63 en suite s fr £25; d fr £25

FORDINGBRIDGE, Hampshire Map 05 SU11

★★72% Ashburn Hotel & Restaurant

Station Rd SP6 1JP
☎ 01425 652060 📠 01425 652150
e-mail: ashburn@mistral.co.uk
web: www.ashburn.mistral.co.uk
Dir: *from Fordingbridge High St, follow Damerham signs. Pass police and fire stations, hotel 400yds on left*
This friendly family-run hotel, situated in an elevated position on the edge of the village, is surrounded by beautiful countryside. Bedrooms, some in the original house and others in a purpose built extension, are comfortable and well equipped. There is a smart function room, a spacious bar, a cosy lounge and a wonderful garden. A good choice is offered at dinner and dishes are carefully prepared.
ROOMS: 20 en suite (3 fmly) ⊗ in 10 bedrooms s £39.50-£69.50; d £80-£112 (incl. bkfst) **LB FACILITIES:** ch fac Xmas **CONF:** Thtr 130 Class 80 Board 40 Del from £70 **PARKING:** 60 **NOTES:** ⊗ in restaurant RS 24-29 Dec, 1-5 Jan Civ Wed 180
CARDS:

FOREST ROW, East Sussex Map 06 TQ43

Top 200 – Hotel

★★★★ Ashdown Park Hotel and Country Club

Wych Cross RH18 5JR
☎ 01342 824988 📠 01342 826206
e-mail: reservations@ashdownpark.com
web: www.ashdownpark.com
Dir: *A264 to East Grinstead, then A22 to Eastbourne, 2m S of Forest Row at Wych Cross traffic lights. Left to Hartfield, hotel on right 0.75m*
Magnificent country house hotel set in attractive landscaped grounds, overlooking 186 acres of parkland in the heart of Ashdown Forest. The stylish bedrooms are full of character; each one individually decorated and tastefully furnished to provide guests with an excellent degree of comfort. Public areas include a chapel, which has been converted into a conference room, a leisure club, a golf course and the Anderida Restaurant.
ROOMS: 106 en suite (15 GF) s £135-£325; d £165-£355 (incl. bkfst) **LB FACILITIES: Spa** STV 18 Snooker Sauna Solarium Gym Putt green Jacuzzi Beauty/Hair salon, Aerobics, Treatment room, Jogging trails, Mountain bike hire Xmas **CONF:** BC Thtr 170 Class 80 Board 60 **SERVICES:** Lift **PARKING:** 200 **NOTES:** ✈ ⊗ in restaurant Civ Wed 150
CARDS:

GF Indicates the number of bedrooms at ground floor level.

FORMBY, Merseyside

Map 15 SD30

★★★63% Tree Tops Country House Restaurant & Hotel
Southport Old Rd L37 0AB
☎ 01704 572430 📠 01704 572430
Dir: *off A565 Southport to Liverpool road*

This country house residence boasts an attractive restaurant where good food is served by an attentive staff. Rooms are in delightful lodges situated in five acres of wooded grounds. The hotel is adjacent to an excellent golf course, near to beaches and all the local amenities.

ROOMS: 11 annexe en suite (3 fmly) (11 GF) s £80-£150; d £100-£200 (incl. bkfst) **LB** **FACILITIES:** **CONF:** Thtr 200 Class 80 Board 40
PARKING: 100 **NOTES:** in restaurant Civ Wed 75
CARDS:

See advert under SOUTHPORT

FORTON MOTORWAY SERVICE AREA (M6), Lancashire

Map 18 SD55

Travelodge Lancaster Forton
White Carr Ln, Bay Horse LA2 9DU
☎ 08700 850 950 📠 01524 791703
Dir: *between junct 32 & 33 of M6*

Travelodge

Travelodge offers good quality, good value, modern accommodation. Ideal for families, the spacious, en suite bedrooms include remote-control TV, tea and coffee-making facilities and luxury beds. Meals can be taken at the nearby family restaurant. For further details consult the Hotel Groups page.

ROOMS: 53 en suite s fr £25; d fr £25

FOUR MARKS, Hampshire

Map 05 SU63

Travelodge Alton
156 Winchester Rd GU34 5HZ
☎ 08700 850 950 📠 01420 562659
Dir: *5m S of Alton on A31 northbound*

Travelodge

Travelodge offers good quality, good value, modern accommodation. Ideal for families, the spacious, en suite bedrooms include remote-control TV, tea and coffee-making facilities and luxury beds. Meals can be taken at the nearby family restaurant. For further details consult the Hotel Groups page.

ROOMS: 31 en suite s fr £25; d fr £25

- Indoor Swimming Pool
- Indoor Swimming Pool (heated)
- Outdoor Swimming Pool
- Outdoor Swimming Pool (heated)

FOWEY, Cornwall & Isles of Scilly Map 02 SX15

★★★78% Fowey Hall
Hanson Dr PL23 1ET
☎ 01726 833866 01726 834100
e-mail: info@foweyhall.com
Dir: *in Fowey, cross mini rdbt into town centre. Pass school on right, after 400mtrs right into Hanson Drive*

Built in 1899, this listed mansion looks out on to the English Channel. The imaginatively designed bedrooms offer charm, individuality and sumptuous comfort, while beautifully appointed public rooms include the wood-panelled dining room where accomplished cuisine is served. Enjoying glorious views, the well-kept grounds have a covered pool and sunbathing area.
ROOMS: 16 en suite 8 annexe en suite (18 fmly) s £144-£200; d £160-£395 (incl. bkfst & dinner) **LB FACILITIES:** STV supervised July & August Childrens play area, Table tennis, Bicycle hire ch fac Xmas **CONF:** Thtr 30 Class 20 Board 20 Del £150 **PARKING:** 40 **NOTES:** in restaurant Civ Wed 50 **CARDS:**

See advert on page 231

★★★72% *Fowey*
The Esplanade PL23 1HX
☎ 01726 832551 01726 832125
e-mail: fowey@richardsonhotels.co.uk
web: www.richardsonhotels.co.uk
Dir: *M5 take A30 to Okehampton, continue to Bodmin. Then B3269 to Fowey for 1m, on right bend left junct then right into Dagands Rd. Hotel 200mtrs on left*

Best Western

This attractive hotel stands proudly above the estuary, with marvellous views of the river from the public areas and the majority of the bedrooms. High standards are evident throughout, augmented by a relaxed and welcoming atmosphere. There is a spacious bar, elegant restaurant and smart drawing room. Imaginative dinners make good use of quality local ingredients.
ROOMS: 37 en suite (1 fmly) in 3 bedrooms **FACILITIES:** Fishing **CONF:** Thtr 100 Class 60 Board 20 **SERVICES:** Lift **PARKING:** 13 **NOTES:** in restaurant **CARDS:**

Top 200 – Hotel

★★ Marina
Esplanade PL23 1HY
☎ 01726 833315 01726 832779
e-mail: marina.hotel@dial.pipex.com
web: www.themarinahotel.co.uk
Dir: *into town down Lostwithiel St, near bottom of hill, right into Esplanade*
Built in 1815 as a seaside retreat, the Marina has much style, and from its setting on the water's edge has glorious views of the river and the sea. Bedrooms, some with balconies, are spacious and comfortable - not forgetting the addition of a host of thoughtful touches that are provided. Competent cooking, using the freshest local produce, including fish landed nearby, is the hallmark of the waterside restaurant.
ROOMS: 13 en suite (1 fmly) in all bedrooms s £90; d £130 (incl. bkfst) **LB FACILITIES:** Fishing Sailing Xmas **PARKING:** 13 **NOTES:** in restaurant Civ Wed 55
CARDS:

FRADDON, Cornwall & Isles of Scilly Map 02 SW95

Travel Inn Newquay (Fraddon)
Penhale TR9 6NA
☎ 08701 977194 01726 860641
Dir: *on A30 2m S of Indian Queens*
Travel Inn offers good-quality, value-for-money accommodation. Spacious, en suite rooms with bath and shower comfortably accommodate a family of up to two adults and two children (to age 15). The restaurant and bar offers a varied menu. For further details consult the Hotel Groups page.
ROOMS: 40 en suite s £45.95-£46.95; d £45.95-£46.95

travel inn

FRANKLEY MOTORWAY SERVICE AREA (M5), West Midlands Map 10 SO98

Travelodge Birmingham South
Illey Ln, Frankley Motorway Service Area, Frankley B32 4AR
☎ 08700 850 950 0121 501 2880
Dir: *between junct 3 and 4 on southbound carriageway of M5*
Travelodge offers good quality, good value, modern accommodation. Ideal for families, the spacious, en suite bedrooms include remote-control TV, tea and coffee-making facilities and luxury beds. Meals can be taken at the nearby family restaurant. For further details consult the Hotel Groups page.
ROOMS: 62 en suite s fr £25; d fr £25

Travelodge

FRESHWATER See Wight, Isle of

FRIMLEY, Surrey
Map 05 SU85

Innkeeper's Lodge Frimley

114 Portsmouth Rd GU15 1HS
☎ 01276 691939 01276 605900
www.innkeeperslodge.com
Dir: *M3 junct 4/ A321 for Frimley take A325 (towards A30 Bagshot), over 1st rdbt past Frimley Park Hospital, straight over 2nd rdbt into Portsmouth Rd. Lodge 500mtrs on left.*
Smart rooms meet essential business requirements but also have home comforts, and depending on location may well have meeting rooms and pub dining. Dining options generally include all-day menus plus the added advantage of breakfast.
ROOMS: 43 en suite s £49.95-£79.95; d £49.95-£79.95
CONF: Thtr 40 Class 20 Board 20

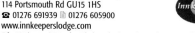

FRITTON, Norfolk
Map 13 TG40

★★★72% *Caldecott Hall Golf & Leisure*
Caldecott Hall, Beccles Rd NR31 9EY
☎ 01493 488488 01493 488561
e-mail: hotel@caldecotthall.co.uk
web: www.caldecotthall.com
Dir: *On A143 Beccles to Great Yarmouth road, 4m from Gt Yarmouth*
This hotel enjoys an ideal situation in its own attractive landscaped grounds that include an 18-hole golf course, fishing lakes and the Redwings Horse sanctuary. The individually decorated bedrooms are spacious, and equipped with many thoughtful touches. Public rooms include a smart sitting room, a lounge bar, restaurant, clubhouse and leisure facilities.
ROOMS: 8 en suite (6 fmly) in all bedrooms **FACILITIES:** 18 Fishing Putt green Driving range Pitch & Putt **CONF:** Thtr 100 Class 80 Board 20 **PARKING:** 100 **NOTES:** in restaurant
CARDS:

FRODSHAM, Cheshire
Map 15 SJ57

★★★70% Forest Hill Hotel & Leisure Complex
Overton Hill WA6 6HH
☎ 01928 735255 01928 735517
e-mail: info@foresthillshotel.com
Dir: *at Frodsham turn onto B5151. After 1m right into Manley Rd, right into Simons Ln after 0.5m. Hotel 0.5m past Frodsham golf course*
This modern, purpose-built hotel is set high up on Overton Hill, offering panoramic views. There is a range of spacious, well-equipped bedrooms, including executive rooms. Guests have a choice of bars and there is a tasteful split-level restaurant, as well as conference facilities and a very well equipped leisure suite and gymnasium.
ROOMS: 58 en suite (4 fmly) in 5 bedrooms s £65-£90; d £65-£90 (incl. bkfst) **LB** **FACILITIES:** STV Snooker Sauna Solarium Gym Jacuzzi Nightclub Xmas **CONF:** Thtr 200 Class 80 Board 70 Del from £130 **PARKING:** 350 **NOTES:** in restaurant Civ Wed 200
CARDS:

FROME, Somerset
Map 04 ST74

★★★66% Mendip House
Bath Rd BA11 2HP
☎ 01373 463223 01373 463990
e-mail: latonamlh@aol.com
Dir: *on Bath side of Frome, on B3090, opposite Frome College*
Conveniently located on the edge of town, this welcoming hotel is set in attractive grounds. The newly refurbished bedrooms include many located on the ground floor and most enjoy glorious country views over the Mendip Hills. Relaxed and friendly service can be enjoyed in the bar, on the outdoor terrace and in the comfortable restaurant.
ROOMS: 40 en suite (3 fmly) (20 GF) s £45-£55; d £55-£75 (incl. bkfst) **LB** **FACILITIES:** STV Xmas **CONF:** Thtr 80 Class 40 Board 40 Del from £95 **PARKING:** 80 **NOTES:** in restaurant Civ Wed 85
CARDS:

★★65% *The George at Nunney*
11 Church St BA11 4LW
☎ 01373 836458 01373 836565
e-mail: georgenunneyhotel@barbox.net
(For full entry see Nunney)

GARFORTH, West Yorkshire
Map 16 SE43

★★★73% Milford

A1 Great North Rd, Peckfield LS25 5LQ
☎ 01977 681800 01977 681245
e-mail: enquiries@mlh.co.uk
web: www.mlh.co.uk
Dir: *On A63, 1.5m W of A1 & 4.5m E of M1 junct 46*

This modern hotel provides comfortable bedrooms, which are air conditioned, particularly spacious and have been superbly insulated against traffic noise. The contemporary-style Watermill Restaurant and Bar, which features a working waterwheel, provides creative cuisine. Staff throughout are friendly and keen to please.
ROOMS: 47 en suite (10 fmly) (14 GF) in 19 bedrooms s £53-£63; d £53-£63 **LB** **FACILITIES:** STV Xmas **CONF:** Thtr 70 Class 35 Board 30 Del £105 **SERVICES:** air con **PARKING:** 80
CARDS:

See advert under LEEDS

GARSTANG, Lancashire
Map 18 SD44

★★★69% Pickerings
Garstang Rd, Catterall PR3 0HD
☎ 01995 600999 01995 602100
e-mail: info@pickeringshotel.com
Dir: *from S M6 junct 32 join M55, exit junct 1& take A6 N, after Esso garage right onto B6430 then right after bus shelter*
This appealing and welcoming hotel dates back to the 17th century and sits in carefully tended grounds that include a well-equipped children's play area. Bedrooms are spacious and include several smart four-poster rooms. Public areas include an inviting bar lounge, two elegant dining rooms and a purpose-built conference suite.
ROOMS: 12 en suite (1 fmly) s £50-£75; d £60-£115 (incl. bkfst) **LB** **FACILITIES:** STV ch fac Xmas **CONF:** Thtr 150 Class 80 Board 50 Del from £80 **PARKING:** 40 **NOTES:** in restaurant Civ Wed
CARDS:

GARSTANG, continued

★★★67% Garstang Country Hotel & Golf Club

Garstang Rd, Bowgreave PR3 1YE
☎ 01995 600100 01995 600950
e-mail: reception@garstanghotelandgolf.co.uk
web: www.garstanghotelandgolf.co.uk
Dir: *M6 junct 32 take 1st right after Rogers Esso garage on A6 onto B6430. Continue for 1m and hotel on left*

Conveniently situated for the M6, this smart, purpose-built hotel enjoys a peaceful location alongside its own 18-hole golf course. Modern, spacious bedrooms are well equipped for both business and leisure guests, whilst public areas include the informal Kingfisher Bar, a comfortable lounge bar and a choice of dining areas.
ROOMS: 32 en suite (16 GF) in 20 bedrooms s £60-£85; d £80-£95 (incl. bkfst) **LB FACILITIES:** STV 18 Golf driving range **CONF:** Thtr 200 Class 100 Board 80 Del from £85 **SERVICES:** Lift **PARKING:** 172 **NOTES:** in restaurant Civ Wed 250
CARDS:

GATESHEAD, Tyne & Wear Map 21 NZ26
See also Beamish & Whickham

★★★★68% Newcastle Marriott Hotel MetroCentre

Marriott HOTELS · RESORTS · SUITES

MetroCentre NE11 9XF
☎ 0191 493 2233 0191 493 2030
e-mail: reservations.newcastle@marriotthotels.co.uk
Dir: *from N leave A1 at MetroCentre exit, take 'Other Routes'. From S leave A1 at MetroCentre exit and turn right.*
Set in acres of woodland, this hotel was built in the 18th century. The public rooms have been sympathetically restored in keeping with the age of the building, yet have a contemporary twist. Four bedrooms are in the main house with others in a well-designed block to the side, accessed via a glazed link.
ROOMS: 150 en suite (145 fmly) in 90 bedrooms s fr £99; d fr £99 **LB FACILITIES:** STV Sauna Solarium Gym Jacuzzi Health & beauty clinic Dance studio, hairdressers Xmas **CONF:** BC Thtr 400 Class 147 Board 12 Del from £120 **SERVICES:** Lift air con **PARKING:** 300 **NOTES:** Civ Wed 100 **CARDS:**

★★★71% Eslington Villa

8 Station Rd, Low Fell NE9 6DR
☎ 0191 487 6017 & 420 0666 0191 420 0667
e-mail: admin@eslingtonvilla.fsnet.co.uk
Dir: *off A1 onto Team Valley Trading Est. Right at 2nd rdbt along Eastern Av then left past Belle Vue Motors, hotel on left*
Set in a residential area, this smart hotel marries a bright contemporary approach to the period style of a fine Victorian villa. The overall ambience is relaxed and inviting. Chunky sofas grace
continued

the cocktail lounge, while tempting dishes can be enjoyed in either the classical dining room or modern conservatory overlooking the Team Valley.
ROOMS: 17 en suite (2 fmly) (3 GF) s £59.50-£64.50; d £69.50-£74.50 (incl. bkfst) **CONF:** Thtr 36 Class 30 Board 25 Del from £103 **PARKING:** 15 **NOTES:** in restaurant Closed 25-26 Dec RS Sun/BHs (restricted restaurant service) **CARDS:**

Premier Lodge (Newcastle South)

PREMIER LODGE.com

Lobley Hill Rd NE11 9NA
☎ 0870 9906590 0870 9906591
web: www.premierlodge.com
Dir: *off A1 on A692, 2m from Angel of the North and 3m from Metro Centre*
High quality, modern, budget accommodation, ideal for families and business travellers. All rooms feature bath, power shower and satellite TV, and most have telephones / modem points. The adjacent bar and restaurant offers a wide and varied menu.
ROOMS: 40 en suite s £50; d £50

Travel Inn

travel inn

Derwent Haugh Rd, Swalwell NE16 3BL
☎ 08701 977283 0191 414 5032
Dir: *From A1/A694 junction. 1m north of Metro Centre*
Travel Inn offers good-quality, value-for-money accommodation. Spacious, en suite rooms with bath and shower comfortably accommodate a family of up to two adults and two children (to age 15). The restaurant and bar offers a varied menu. For further details consult the Hotel Groups page.
ROOMS: 40 en suite s £45.95-£46.95; d £45.95-£46.95

○ Travelodge (Gateshead)

Travelodge

ROOMS: 59 en suite
NOTES: Due to open Dec 2004

GATWICK AIRPORT (LONDON), West Sussex Map 06 TQ24
See also Dorking, East Grinstead & Reigate

★★★★70% Copthorne Hotel London Gatwick

COPTHORNE

Copthorne Way RH10 3PG
☎ 01342 348800 & 348888 01342 348833
e-mail: coplgw@mill-cop.com
Dir: *on A264, 2m E of A264/B2036 rdbt*

Situated in a tranquil position, the Copthorne is set in 100 acres of wooded, landscaped gardens containing jogging tracks, a putting green and even a petanque pit. The sprawling building is built around a 16th-century farmhouse and has comfortable, well-maintained bedrooms. In addition to the main restaurant,
continued

dining options include an inn or the more formal, award-winning restaurant.

ROOMS: 227 en suite (10 fmly) ⊗ in 136 bedrooms s £69-£145; d £69-£145 **LB** **FACILITIES: Spa** STV Squash Sauna Solarium Gym Putt green Jacuzzi Petanque pit Aerobic studio ch fac **CONF:** BC Thtr 135 Class 60 Board 40 Del from £155 **SERVICES:** Lift **PARKING:** 300 **NOTES:** Civ Wed 100 **CARDS:**

★★★★70% Le Meridien London Gatwick

North Terminal RH6 0PH
☎ 01293 567070 01293 567739
e-mail: reservations.gatwick@lemeridien.com
Dir: *M23 junct 9, follow to 2nd rdbt. Hotel large white building straight ahead*

One of the closest hotels to the airport, this modern, purpose-built hotel is located only minutes from the terminals. Bedrooms are contemporary and all are air conditioned. Guests have a choice of eating options including a French-style café, Brasserie and oriental restaurant.

ROOMS: 500 en suite (18 fmly) ⊗ in 283 bedrooms **FACILITIES:** STV Sauna Solarium Gym **CONF:** BC Thtr 300 Class 200 Board 120 Del from £155 **SERVICES:** Lift air con **PARKING:** 120 **NOTES:** Civ Wed **CARDS:**

★★★★66% Copthorne Hotel and Resort Effingham Park Gatwick

West Park Rd RH10 3EU
☎ 01342 714994 01342 716039
e-mail: sales.effingham@mill-cop.com
Dir: *M23 junct 10, take A264 towards East Grinstead. Over rdbt and at 2nd rdbt left onto B2028. Effingham Park on right*

A former stately home, set in 40 acres of grounds, this hotel is popular for conference and weekend functions. The main restaurant is an open-plan, Mediterranean-themed brasserie, and snacks are also available in the bar. Bedrooms are spacious and well cared for. Facilities include an 18-hole golf course and a leisure club.

ROOMS: 122 en suite (6 fmly) ⊗ in 48 bedrooms s £145-£255; d £145-£255 **LB** **FACILITIES:** STV 9 Sauna Solarium Gym Putt green Jacuzzi Aerobic studio Bowls Croquet **CONF:** BC Thtr 600 Class 250 Board 30 **SERVICES:** Lift **PARKING:** 500 **NOTES:** ⊗ in restaurant Closed 26-30 Dec Civ Wed **CARDS:**

Top 200 – Hotel

★★★ Langshott Manor

Langshott Ln RH6 9LN
☎ 01293 786680 01293 783905
e-mail: admin@langshottmanor.com
Dir: *from A23 take Ladbroke Rd, off Chequers rdbt to Langshott, after 0.75m hotel on right*

Charming timber-framed Tudor house set amidst beautifully landscaped grounds on the outskirts of town. The stylish public areas feature a choice of plushly furnished lounges with polished oak panelling, exposed beams and log fires. The individually decorated bedrooms combine the most up-to-date modern comforts with flair, individuality and traditional elegance. The Mulberry restaurant overlooks a picturesque pond and offers an imaginative menu.

Langshott Manor

ROOMS: 14 en suite 8 annexe en suite ⊗ in all bedrooms s £185-£220; d £220-£290 (incl. bkfst) **LB** **FACILITIES:** STV Xmas **CONF:** Thtr 40 Class 20 Board 22 Del from £159 **PARKING:** 25 **NOTES:** ⊗ in restaurant Civ Wed 60 **CARDS:**

Need a break without breaking the bank?
Latebeds offers last-minute deals with no nasty surprises at AA-approved hotels and B&Bs. Visit www.theAA.com to find out more

GATWICK AIRPORT (LONDON), continued

★★★75% Stanhill Court

Stanhill Rd, Charlwood RH6 0EP
☎ 01293 862166 01293 862773
e-mail: enquiries@stanhillcourthotel.co.uk
web: www.stanhillcourthotel.co.uk
Dir: *N of Charlwood towards Newdigate*

This hotel dates back to 1881 and enjoys a secluded location in 35 acres of well-tended grounds with views over the Downs. Bedrooms are individually furnished and decorated, and many have four-poster beds. Public areas include a library, a bright bar and a traditional wood-panelled restaurant.
ROOMS: 15 en suite (3 fmly) in 3 bedrooms s £75-£95; d £95-£125 (incl. bkfst) **LB** **FACILITIES:** STV Fishing Putt green ch fac
CONF: Thtr 250 Class 100 Board 60 Del from £139 **PARKING:** 110
NOTES: in restaurant Civ Wed 140
CARDS:

★★★63% Gatwick Worth Hotel

Crabbet Park, Turners Hill Rd, Worth RH10 4ST
☎ 01293 884806 01293 882444
e-mail: reception@gatwickworthhotel.com
web: www.gatwickworthhotel.com
Dir: *M23 junct 10, left to A264. At 1st rdbt right signed to Maidenbower. 1st left into Old Hollow Rd, follow to end. At T-junct right. Hotel 200yds right*
This purpose-built hotel is ideally placed for access to Gatwick Airport. The bedrooms are spacious and suitably appointed with good facilities. Public areas consist of a light and airy bar area and a brasserie-style restaurant offering good value meals. Guests have use of the superb leisure club next door.
ROOMS: 118 en suite (9 fmly) in 57 bedrooms s £38-£80; d £45-£100 **FACILITIES: Spa** pool supervised Riding Sauna Solarium Gym Jacuzzi Cannon's fitness centre adjacent to hotel. ch fac
CONF: Thtr 200 Class 100 Board 60 Del from £110 **PARKING:** 150
NOTES: in restaurant Civ Wed 150
CARDS:

Hotel Ibis London Gatwick

London Rd, County Oak RH11 0PF
☎ 01293 590300 01293 590310
e-mail: H1889@accor-hotels.com
Dir: *M23 junct 10, take A2011 to Crawley. At rdbt 3rd exit, at next rdbt A23 London Rd towards Gatwick. Adjacent to Manor Industrial Est*
Modern, budget hotel offering comfortable accommodation in bright and practical bedrooms. Breakfast is self-service and dinner is available in the restaurant. For further details, consult the Hotel Groups page.
ROOMS: 141 en suite

Premier Lodge (Gatwick Airport)

London Rd, Lowfield Heath RH10 9ST
☎ 0870 9906354 0870 9906355
web: www.premierlodge.com
Dir: *close to airport on A23, 2m from M23 junct 9a. Follow towards North Terminal rbt then signs for A23 Crawley*
High quality, modern, budget accommodation, ideal for families and business travellers. All rooms feature bath, power shower and satellite TV, and most have telephones / modem points. The adjacent bar and restaurant offers a wide and varied menu.
ROOMS: 102 en suite s £52; d £52 **CONF:** Thtr 200 Class 100 Board 80 Del from £105

Premier Lodge (Gatwick Crawley)

Goffs Park Rd RH11 8AX
☎ 0870 9906390 0870 9906391
web: www.premierlodge.com
Dir: *close to Gatwick Airport. Exit M23 at junct 11, follow A23 towards Crawley. At 2nd rbt take 3rd exit for town centre, then 2nd right into Goffs Park Rd*
High quality, modern, budget accommodation, ideal for families and business travellers. All rooms feature bath, power shower and satellite TV, and most have telephones / modem points. The adjacent bar and restaurant offers a wide and varied menu.
ROOMS: 57 en suite s £50; d £50 **CONF:** Thtr 120 Class 70 Board 40

Premier Lodge (Gatwick South)

Crawley Av, Gossops Green RH10 8BA
☎ 0870 9906546 0870 9906547
web: www.premierlodge.com
Dir: *2m from M23 and just under 5m from Gatwick Airport. Exit M23 at junct 11 and follow A23 towards Crawley and Gatwick Airport*
High quality, modern, budget accommodation, ideal for families and business travellers. All rooms feature bath, power shower and satellite TV, and most have telephones / modem points. The adjacent bar and restaurant offers a wide and varied menu.
ROOMS: 83 en suite s £50; d £50

Travel Inn

North Terminal, Longbridge Way RH6 0NX
☎ 0870 238 3305 01293 568278
Dir: *M23 junct 9/9A towards North Terminal, at rdbt take 3rd exit, hotel on right*

Travel Inn offers good-quality, value-for-money accommodation. Spacious, en suite rooms with bath and shower comfortably accommodate a family of up to two adults and two children (to age 15). The restaurant and bar offers a varied menu. For further details consult the Hotel Groups page.
ROOMS: 219 en suite s £49.95; d £49.95

⌂ Travel Inn (Crawley)
Balcombe Rd RH10 3NL
☎ 08701 977067 🖷 01293 873034
Dir: *On B2036 south towards Crawley from M23 junct 10*
Travel Inn offers good-quality, value-for-money accommodation. Spacious, en suite rooms with bath and shower comfortably accommodate a family of up to two adults and two children (to age 15). The restaurant and bar offers a varied menu. For further details consult the Hotel Groups page.
ROOMS: 41 en suite s £45.95-£48.95; d £45.95-£48.95

⌂ Travelodge Gatwick Airport
Church Rd, Lowfield Heath RH11 0PQ
☎ 08700 850 950 🖷 01293 535369
Dir: *M23 junct 10, 1m S off A23*
Travelodge offers good quality, good value, modern accommodation. Ideal for families, the spacious, en suite bedrooms include remote-control TV, tea and coffee-making facilities and luxury beds. Meals can be taken at the nearby family restaurant. For further details consult the Hotel Groups page.
ROOMS: 186 en suite s fr £25; d fr £25 **CONF:** Thtr 60 Class 25 Board 25

GERRARDS CROSS, Buckinghamshire — Map 06 TQ08

★★★69% Bull
Oxford Rd SL9 7PA
☎ 01753 885995 🖷 01753 885504
e-mail: bull@sarova.co.uk
web: www.sarova.co.uk/sarova/hotelcollection/bull
Dir: *M40 junct 2 follow Beaconsfield on A355. After 0.5m 2nd exit at rdbt signed A40 Gerrards Cross for 2m. The Bull on right*
This 17th-century inn has been sympathetically refurbished and extended. Public areas include the popular Jack Shrimpton bar offering bar meals in an informal atmosphere. There is also an attractive cocktail bar adjacent to the elegant restaurant and a good range of function rooms. Tastefully furnished, well-equipped bedrooms include a number of smart, spacious state rooms.
ROOMS: 123 en suite (3 fmly) (20 GF) ⊗ in 74 bedrooms s £170; d £180 LB **FACILITIES:** STV Leisure facilities available nearby Xmas **CONF:** Thtr 150 Class 60 Board 50 Del £190 **SERVICES:** Lift **PARKING:** 200 **NOTES:** ✈ ⊗ in restaurant Civ Wed
CARDS:

★★70% Ethorpe
Packhorse Rd SL9 8HY
☎ 01753 882039 🖷 01753 887012
e-mail: ethorpe.hotel@thespiritgroup.com
web: www.ethorpehotel.com
Dir: *M40 junct 2 for Beaconsfield. At island right onto A40 to Gerrards Cross. At lights left into Packhouse Rd. Hotel at end on left*
This attractive hotel is located in the centre of town, within easy reach of the motorway network and Heathrow Airport. A complete programme of refurbishment and alterations has resulted in modern, well-appointed and equipped bedrooms. Meals are taken in the popular informal 'Chef and Brewer' restaurant and bar.

continued

ROOMS: 32 en suite (3 fmly) (11 GF) ⊗ in 25 bedrooms
FACILITIES: STV Xmas **CONF:** Thtr 40 Class 30 Board 22
SERVICES: air con **PARKING:** 80 **NOTES:** ✈
CARDS:

GILLAN, Cornwall & Isles of Scilly — Map 02 SW72

Top 200 – Hotel

★★ Tregildry
TR12 6HG
☎ 01326 231378 🖷 01326 231561
e-mail: trgildry@globalnet.co.uk
web: www.tregildryhotel.co.uk
Dir: *From Helston take A3083 Lizard Rd. 1st left turn for St Keverne and follow signs for Manaccan & Gillan*
From its unspoilt and peaceful location Tregildry is blessed with both sea and river views. The tastefully furnished bedrooms and lounges are designed with comfort in mind and make the most of the wonderful views. Imaginative and innovative menus are served in the stylish dining room. There is direct access to the beach and adjacent coastal footpath.
ROOMS: 10 en suite ⊗ in all bedrooms s £80-£99; d £140-£198 (incl. bkfst & dinner) LB **FACILITIES:** Boat hire Windsurfing **PARKING:** 15 **NOTES:** No children 8yrs ⊗ in restaurant Closed Nov-Feb **CARDS:**

GILLINGHAM, Dorset

Map 04 ST82

Top 200 – Hotel

★★★ @@@

Stock Hill Country House

RELAIS & CHATEAUX

Stock Hill SP8 5NR
☎ 01747 823626 01747 825628
e-mail: reception@stockhillhouse.co.uk
web: www.stockhillhouse.co.uk
Dir: *3m E on B3081, off A303*

Set in eleven acres, Stockhill House has an impressive beech-lined driveway and beautiful gardens. The luxurious bedrooms, tastefully furnished with antiques, combine high standards of comfort with modern facilities. Public rooms are delightful in every way with sumptuous fabrics and furnishings. The complete peace makes the perfect setting for tea in front of the log fires. Accomplished cooking based on top-quality local ingredients shows strong Austrian influences. Nita and Peter Hauser and their team are clearly dedicated to their guests' enjoyment of this delightful small hotel.

ROOMS: 6 en suite 3 annexe en suite (3 GF) s £120-£165; d £240-£300 (incl. bkfst & dinner) LB **FACILITIES:** Sauna Bird watching, croquet Xmas **CONF:** Thtr 12 **PARKING:** 20 **NOTES:** No children 7yrs in restaurant **CARDS:**

GILLINGHAM, Kent

Map 07 TQ76

Travel Inn

travel inn

Will Adams Way ME8 6BY
☎ 08701 977105 01634 261232
Dir: *From M2 junct 4 onto A278 to A2. Left at Tesco & Travel Inn is left at next rdbt, 5 mins from Priestfield Football Ground*

Travel Inn offers good-quality, value-for-money accommodation. Spacious, en suite rooms with bath and shower comfortably accommodate a family of up to two adults and two children (to age 15). The restaurant and bar offers a varied menu. For further details consult the Hotel Groups page.

ROOMS: 45 en suite s £45.95-£46.95; d £45.95-£46.95 **CONF:** Thtr 20

Travelodge Medway

Travelodge

Medway Motorway Service Area, Rainham ME8 8PQ
☎ 08700 850 950 01634 263187
Dir: *between junct 4 & 5 of M2*

Travelodge offers good quality, good value, modern accommodation. Ideal for families, the spacious, en suite bedrooms include remote-control TV, tea and coffee-making facilities and luxury beds. Meals can be taken at the nearby family restaurant. For further details consult the Hotel Groups page.

ROOMS: 58 en suite s fr £25; d fr £25

GLENRIDDING, Cumbria

Map 18 NY31

★★★72% The Inn on the Lake

Lake Ullswater, Glenridding CA11 0PE
☎ 017684 82444 017684 82303
e-mail: info@innonthelakeullswater.co.uk
web: www.innonthelakeullswater.com
Dir: *M6 junct 40, then A66 to Keswick. At rdbt take A592 to Ullswater Lake. Along lake to Glenridding. Hotel on left on entering village*

In a picturesque lakeside setting, this restored Victorian hotel is a popular destination for weddings and conferences. Superb Lakeland views may be enjoyed from the bedrooms which face the open lake or towering fells, and afternoon teas are served on the garden terrace during warmer months. Moorings for yachts are available to guests and sailing tuition can be provided.

ROOMS: 46 en suite (6 fmly) (2 GF) in 15 bedrooms **FACILITIES:** STV 9 Fishing Sauna Solarium Gym Putt green Jacuzzi Sailing, 9 hole pitch and putt, Bowls **CONF:** BC Thtr 120 Class 60 Board 40 Del from £100 **SERVICES:** Lift **PARKING:** 200 **NOTES:** in restaurant Civ Wed 100 **CARDS:**

See advert on opposite page

★★★70% Glenridding

Best Western

CA11 0PB
☎ 017684 82228 017684 82555
e-mail: glenridding@bestwestern.co.uk
Dir: *Northbound M6 exit 36, A591 Windermere then A592 14 miles. Southbound M6 exit 40, A592 for 13 miles*

This friendly hotel benefits from a picturesque location in the centre of the village. Bedrooms, many with fine views of the lake and fells, include a number of newly upgraded rooms. Public areas are extensive and include a choice of restaurants and bars, a coffee shop including a cyber café, and smart leisure facilities.

ROOMS: 36 en suite (9 fmly) in all bedrooms s £70-£83; d £77-£145 (incl. bkfst) LB **FACILITIES:** STV Sauna Jacuzzi Billiards 3/4 Snooker table Table tennis Xmas **CONF:** Thtr 30 Class 30 Board 20 Del from £85 **SERVICES:** Lift **PARKING:** 38 **NOTES:** in restaurant Civ Wed 80 **CARDS:**

GLOSSOP, Derbyshire

Map 16 SK09

★★78% Wind in the Willows

Derbyshire Level SK13 7PT
☎ 01457 868001 01457 853354
e-mail: info@windinthewillows.co.uk
Dir: *1m E of Glossop on A57, turn right opp Royal Oak, hotel 400yds on right*

A warm and relaxed atmosphere prevails at this small and very comfortable hotel. The bedrooms are well furnished, each offering many thoughtful extras and some executive rooms are available.

continued on p240

Public areas include two comfortable lounges, a dining room, and a modern meeting room with views over the extensive grounds.

ROOMS: 12 en suite **FACILITIES:** Fishing **CONF:** Thtr 40 Class 12 Board 16 Del from £140 **PARKING:** 16 **NOTES:** No dogs No children 10yrs No smoking in restaurant **CARDS:**

GLOUCESTER, Gloucestershire Map 10 SO81

★★★72% Hatton Court

Upton Hill, Upton St Leonards GL4 8DE
☎ 01452 617412 Fax 01452 612945
e-mail: res@hatton-court.co.uk

Dir: *leave Gloucester on B4073 Painswick Rd. Hotel at top of hill on right*

This beautifully preserved 17th-century Cotswold manor house is set in seven acres of well-kept gardens and is popular with both business and leisure guests. It stands at the top of Upton Hill and commands truly spectacular views of the Severn Valley. Bedrooms are comfortable and tastefully furnished with many extra facilities provided. The elegant Carringtons Restaurant offers a varied choice of menus, and there is also a traditionally furnished bar and foyer lounge.

ROOMS: 17 en suite 28 annexe en suite No smoking in 11 bedrooms s £75-£175; d £90-£190 (incl. bkfst) **LB** **FACILITIES:** STV Sauna Gym Jacuzzi Xmas **CONF:** Thtr 60 Class 30 Board 30 Del from £139 **PARKING:** 80 **NOTES:** No dogs No smoking in restaurant Civ Wed 75 **CARDS:**

See advert on page 241

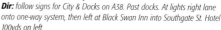

★★★65% *New County*

44 Southgate St GL1 2DU
☎ 01452 307000 Fax 01452 500487
e-mail: mail@thenewcounty.com
web: www.thenewcounty.com

Best Western

Dir: *follow signs for City & Docks on A38. Past docks. At lights right lane onto one-way system, then left at Black Swan Inn into Southgate St. Hotel 100yds on left*

In the heart of the city, this long-established hotel dates back to 1820 and offers a convenient base for business and leisure travellers. Whilst providing all the expected contemporary comforts, original features have been retained, thus ensuring character and atmosphere throughout. Public rooms include a bistro-style restaurant, a bar and a ballroom/function suite. Parking is available near the hotel.

ROOMS: 39 en suite (1 fmly) No smoking in 10 bedrooms **CONF:** **PARKING:** 5 **NOTES:** No smoking in restaurant **CARDS:**

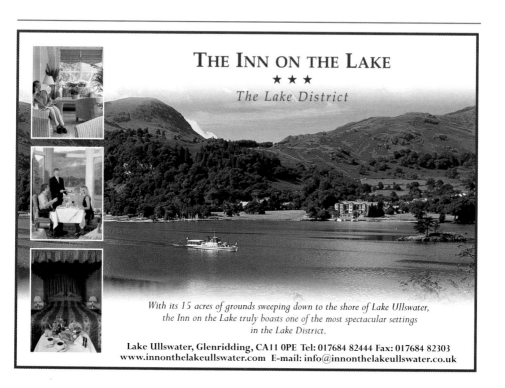

GLOUCESTER, continued

★★★62% Hatherley Manor

Down Hatherley Ln GL2 9QA
☎ 01452 730217 01452 731032
e-mail: hatherleymanor@countrytownhotels.co.uk
Dir: *off A38 onto Down Hatherley Lane, signposted. Hotel 600yds on left*

Within easy striking distance of the M5, Gloucester, Cheltenham and the Cotswolds, this stylish 17th-century manor remains popular with both business and leisure guests. Some bedrooms are in the original building, and some are purpose-built; all offer contemporary comforts. Meeting and function rooms are available.
ROOMS: 52 en suite in 20 bedrooms s £45-£85; d £50-£105 (incl. bkfst) **LB FACILITIES:** Xmas **CONF:** Thtr 300 Class 90 Board 75 Del from £90 **PARKING:** 250 **NOTES:** in restaurant Civ Wed 300
CARDS:

Premier Lodge (Gloucester East)

PREMIER LODGE.com

Barnwood GL4 3HR
☎ 0870 9906322 0870 9906323
web: www.premierlodge.com
Dir: *Exit M5 at junct 11. Follow A40 towards Gloucester, at 1st rbt take A417 towards Cirencester, at next rdbt take 4th exit*
High quality, modern, budget accommodation, ideal for families and business travellers. All rooms feature bath, power shower and satellite TV, and most have telephones / modem points. The adjacent bar and restaurant offers a wide and varied menu.
ROOMS: 83 en suite s £48; d £48

Premier Lodge (Gloucester North)

PREMIER LODGE.com

Tewkesbury Rd, Twigworth GL2 9PG
☎ 0870 9906560 0870 9906561
web: www.premierlodge.com

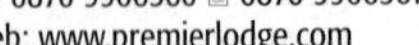

Dir: *2m from Gloucester. Exit M5 at junct 11, take A40 towards Gloucester and then A38 towards Tewkesbury*
High quality, modern, budget accommodation, ideal for families and business travellers. All rooms feature bath, power shower and satellite TV, and most have telephones / modem points. The adjacent bar and restaurant offers a wide and varied menu.
ROOMS: 52 en suite s £48; d £48

Travel Inn (Gloucester Longford)

travel inn

Tewkesbury Rd, Longford GL2 9BE
☎ 08701 977115 01452 300924
Dir: *10 minutes from M5 (J11), follow A40 to Gloucester, A40 to Ross, then Inn on A38 to Gloucester on Tewkesbury Rd*
Travel Inn offers good-quality, value-for-money accommodation. Spacious, en suite rooms with bath and shower comfortably accommodate a family of up to two adults and two children (to age 15). The restaurant and bar offers a varied menu. For further details consult the Hotel Groups page.
ROOMS: 60 en suite s £45.95-£46.95; d £45.95-£46.95 **CONF:** Thtr 40

Travel Inn (Gloucester Witcombe)

travel inn

Witcombe GL3 4SS
☎ 08701 977116 01452 864926
Dir: *M5 junct 11A follow A417 (Cirencester) at 1st exit turn right onto A46 towards Stroud/Witcombe. Left at next rdbt by Crosshands PH*
Travel Inn offers good-quality, value-for-money accommodation. Spacious, en suite rooms with bath and shower comfortably accommodate a family of up to two adults and two children (to age 15). The restaurant and bar offers a varied menu. For further details consult the Hotel Groups page.
ROOMS: 39 en suite s £45.95-£46.95; d £45.95-£46.95

GODALMING, Surrey — Map 06 SU94

Innkeeper's Lodge

Innkeeper's Lodge

Ockford Rd GU7 1RH
☎ 01483 419997 01483 410852
www.innkeeperslodge.com
Dir: *Turn off A3/Milford at petrol station turn left onto A3100 through Milford under railway bridge. Lodge on rdbt on right*
Smart rooms meet essential business requirements but also have home comforts, and depending on location may well have meeting rooms and pub dining. Dining options generally include all-day menus plus the added advantage of breakfast.
ROOMS: 19 rms s £49.95-£79.95; d £49.95-£79.95

GOMERSAL, West Yorkshire — Map 19 SE22

★★★73% Gomersal Park

CLASSIC BRITISH

Moor Ln BD19 4LJ
☎ 01274 869386 01274 861042
e-mail: enquiries@gomersalparkhotel.com
Dir: *A62 to Huddersfield. At junct with A65, by Greyhound Pub right, after 1m take 1st right after Oakwell Hall*

Constructed around a 19th-century house, this stylish, modern hotel enjoys a peaceful location and pleasant grounds. Deep sofas ensure comfort in the open-plan lounge and imaginative meals are served in the popular Brasserie 101. The well-equipped bedrooms have been refurbished to provide high quality and comfort. Extensive public areas include a well-equipped leisure complex and pool, and a wide variety of air-conditioned conference rooms.
ROOMS: 100 en suite (3 fmly) (32 GF) in 80 bedrooms s £95; d £95 (incl. bkfst) **LB FACILITIES:** STV supervised Sauna Solarium Gym Jacuzzi Xmas **CONF:** BC Thtr 250 Class 130 Board 60 **SERVICES:** Lift **PARKING:** 150 **NOTES:** in restaurant Closed 26-30 Dec Civ Wed 200 **CARDS:**

For central reservation numbers and more information on Hotel Groups, turn to pages 33-39

★★65% ***Gomersal Lodge***
Spen Ln BD19 4PJ
☎ 01274 861111 🖷 01274 861111
e-mail: enquiries@gomersallodge.co.uk
Dir: *M62 junct 27, A62 towards Huddersfield. Right at Greyhound Pub, hotel 1m on right*
This 19th-century house sits in five acres of landscaped grounds and attractive gardens and offers well-furnished bedrooms together with a cosy bar. The elegant restaurant is noted for its flexible, contemporary menu, and is popular as a venue for weddings.
ROOMS: 9 en suite (1 fmly) ⊗ in 4 bedrooms **CONF:** Thtr 20 Class 12 Board 12 **PARKING:** 70 **NOTES:** ✈ ⊗ in restaurant
CARDS:

GOODRICH, Herefordshire Map 10 SO51

★★71% ***Ye Hostelrie***
HR9 6HX
☎ 01600 890241 🖷 01600 890838
e-mail: info@ye-hostelrie.co.uk
Dir: *1m off A40, between Ross-on-Wye and Monmouth, 100yds from Goodrich Castle*
Parts of this unusual building are reputed to date back to 1625. It is privately owned and personally run, and considerable improvements to both the accommodation and the public areas have been made in recent years. Facilities include a function room, a pleasant garden and a patio area. The hotel is very popular for the extensive range of food on offer.
ROOMS: 7 en suite (1 fmly) **CONF:** Thtr 80 Class 60 Board 20 **PARKING:** 25 **NOTES:** ⊗ in restaurant **CARDS:**

GOODRINGTON See Paignton

GOODWOOD, West Sussex Map 06 SU81

★★★★74% ❀❀ **Marriott Goodwood Park Hotel & Country Club**
PO18 0QB
☎ 0870 400 7225 🖷 0870 400 7325
e-mail: reservations.goodwood@marriotthotels.co.uk
Dir: *off A285, 3m NE of Chichester*
Set in the middle of the 12,000-acre Goodwood Estate, this attractive hotel boasts extensive indoor and outdoor leisure facilities, along with a range of meeting rooms and conference and banqueting facilities. Bedrooms are furnished to a consistent high standard. Public rooms include the Richmond Restaurant and a smart cocktail bar, which recognises the Goodwood motor-racing heritage.
ROOMS: 94 en suite ⊗ in 54 bedrooms s £103-£114; d £146 (incl. bkfst) **LB** **FACILITIES:** STV supervised 18 Sauna Solarium Gym Putt green Jacuzzi Beauty salons Xmas **CONF:** BC Thtr 150 Class 60 Board 50 Del from £150 **PARKING:** 350 **NOTES:** ✈ ⊗ in restaurant Civ Wed 120 **CARDS:**

GOOLE, East Riding of Yorkshire Map 17 SE72

Travel Inn
Rawcliffe Rd, Airmyn DN14 8JS
☎ 08701 977177 🖷 01405 722661
Dir: *Leave M62 at junct 36, onto A614 signed Rawcliffe. Travel Inn immediately on left.*
Travel Inn offers good-quality, value-for-money accommodation. Spacious, en suite rooms with bath and shower comfortably accommodate a family of up to two adults and two children (to age 15). The restaurant and bar offers a varied menu. For further details consult the Hotel Groups page.
ROOMS: 41 en suite s £45.95-£46.95; d £45.95-£46.95 **CONF:** Board 12

GORDANO SERVICE AREA (M5), Somerset Map 04 ST57

Days Inn
BS20 7XG
☎ 01275 373709 & 373624 01275 374104
e-mail: gordano.hotel@welcomebreak.co.uk
web: www.welcomebreak.co.uk
Dir: *M5 junct 19, follow signs for Gordano services*
This modern building offers accommodation in smart, spacious and well-equipped bedrooms, suitable for families and business travellers, and all with en suite bathrooms. Continental breakfast is available and other refreshments may be taken at the nearby family restaurant. For further details see the Hotel Groups page.
ROOMS: 60 en suite s fr £49; d fr £49 **CONF:** Board 10

GORLESTON-ON-SEA See Great Yarmouth

G

GOSFORTH, Cumbria Map 18 NY00

★★72% *Westlakes*
CA20 1HP
☎ 01947 725221 01947 725099
Dir: *turn off A595 at x-rds for Gosforth & Searcale towards Seascale. Hotel entrance immediately on right*
This Georgian country house is set in tranquil, mature gardens just off the main road. Warm hospitality and honest wholesome food are trademarks of this hotel. Public areas include a comfortable lounge bar and an attractive dining room, comprising three rooms, one of which is ideal for private dining or meetings. Bedrooms vary in style and are all thoughtfully equipped.
ROOMS: 6 en suite 3 annexe en suite (1 fmly) **FACILITIES:** STV **PARKING:** 25 **NOTES:** in restaurant Closed short period over Xmas **CARDS:**

GRANGE-OVER-SANDS, Cumbria Map 18 SD47

★★★73% Netherwood
Lindale Rd LA11 6ET
☎ 015395 32552 015395 34121
e-mail: blawith@aol.com
Dir: *on B5277 before station*
This imposing hotel stands in terraced grounds and enjoys fine views of Morecambe Bay. Though a popular conference and wedding venue, good levels of hospitality and service ensure all guests are well looked after. Bedrooms vary in size but all are well furnished and decorated, and have smart modern bathrooms. Magnificent woodwork is a feature of the public areas.
ROOMS: 32 en suite (5 fmly) in 18 bedrooms s fr £65; d £140-£170 (incl. bkfst) **LB** **FACILITIES: Spa** supervised Solarium Gym Jacuzzi Beauty salon, Steam room **CONF:** BC Thtr 150 Class 30 Board 40 Del from £105 **SERVICES:** Lift **PARKING:** 100 **NOTES:** in restaurant Civ Wed 180 **CARDS:**

★★★65% Graythwaite Manor
Fernhill Rd LA11 7JE
☎ 015395 32001 & 33755 015395 35549
e-mail: enquiries@graythwaitemanor.co.uk
Dir: *B5277 through Grange, Fernhill Rd opposite fire station behind small traffic island, hotel 1st left*
This well established hotel is set in extensive gardens, complete with sub-tropical plants, and offers a delightful outlook over Morecambe Bay. Public areas include an Orangery, a number of comfortable lounges and an elegant restaurant. The comfortable bedrooms, which vary in size, are traditional in style.
ROOMS: 21 en suite (2 fmly) **FACILITIES:** Putt green Xmas **CONF:** Thtr 50 Class 30 Board 20 **SERVICES:** Lift **PARKING:** 32 **NOTES:** in restaurant **CARDS:**

★★70% Hampsfell House
Hampsfell Rd LA11 6BG
☎ 015395 32567 015395 35995
e-mail: hampsfellhotel@msn.com
web: www.hampsfellhotel.com
Dir: *M6 junct 36 take A590 signed Barrow-in-Furness. At junct with B5277, follow to Grange-over-Sands signs. Left at rdbt into Main St, 2nd rdbt right and right at x-rds. At Hampsfell Rd left*
Dating back to 1800, this family-run hotel is peacefully set in two acres of private grounds yet is just minutes' walk from the town centre. Bedrooms are smartly decorated and well maintained. The two cosy and comfortable lounges, where guests can enjoy pre-dinner drinks, share a central bar. Guests can enjoy very well-prepared meals in the refurbished, formal dining room.
ROOMS: 9 en suite (1 fmly) (1 GF) in 5 bedrooms s £41-£61; d £82-£102 (incl. bkfst) **LB** **FACILITIES:** Xmas **PARKING:** 12 **NOTES:** No children 5yrs in restaurant **CARDS:**

Top 200 – Hotel

★ Clare House
Park Rd LA11 7HQ
☎ 015395 33026 & 34253
e-mail: info@clarehousehotel.co.uk
web: www.clarehousehotel.co.uk
Dir: *off A590 onto B5277, through Lindale into Grange, keep left, hotel 0.5m on left past Crown Hill and St Paul's Church*
A warm, genuine welcome awaits guests at this delightful, family-run hotel. Sitting in its own secluded gardens, it provides a relaxed haven in which to enjoy the panoramic views across Morecambe Bay. Bedrooms and public areas are comfortable and attractively furnished. Skilfully prepared dinners and hearty breakfasts are served in the elegant dining room.
ROOMS: 17 rms (16 en suite) (1 fmly) (2 GF) s £58-£65; d £116-£130 (incl. bkfst & dinner) **LB** **FACILITIES:** Putt green **PARKING:** 18 **NOTES:** No children 5yrs in restaurant Closed Dec-Mar RS 10-30 Nov **CARDS:**

GRANTHAM, Lincolnshire Map 11 SK93

★★★74% *Angel & Royal*
High St NG31 6PN
☎ 01476 565816 01476 567149
e-mail: enquiries@angelandroyal.co.uk
web: www.angelandroyal.co.uk
Dir: *Follow signs to town centre. Hotel is on left, drive past taking 1st left after Marks & Spencers & 1st left again. Car Park is approx. 200yds on right*
This coaching inn, in the centre of town, claims to be one of the oldest in the country and retains many original features. Almost totally refurbished, the accommodation varies in size, yet is stylish and offers extensive comfort. The bar boasts over 200 whiskies,

continued

and a modern Brasserie offering a wide choice of dishes. Additionally the historic King's Room restaurant is open at weekends.
ROOMS: 30 en suite ⊗ in 10 bedrooms **FACILITIES:** STV **CONF:** Thtr 40 Board 30 **PARKING:** 70 **NOTES:** ✗ **CARDS:**

★★★71% Kings

North Pde NG31 8AU
☎ 01476 590800 ▯ 01476 577072
e-mail: kings@bestwestern.co.uk
Dir: *off A1 at rdbt N end of Grantham onto B1174, follow road for 2m. Hotel on left by bridge*
A friendly atmosphere exists within this extended Georgian house. Bedrooms are attractively decorated and furnished in modern light oak. Dining options include the formal Victorian restaurant and the popular Orangery, which also operates as a coffee shop and breakfast room; a lounge bar and a smart open-plan foyer lounge are also available.
ROOMS: 21 en suite (3 fmly) s £56-£66; d £66-£76 (incl. bkfst) **LB** **FACILITIES:** STV **CONF:** BC Thtr 100 Class 50 Board 40 Del from £89 **PARKING:** 36 **NOTES:** ⊗ in restaurant
CARDS:

★★★68% Grantham Marriott

Swingbridge Rd NG31 7XT
☎ 01476 593000 ▯ 01476 592592

e-mail: neil.shears@whitbread.com

Dir: *off A1 at junct Grantham/Melton Mowbray onto A607. From N 1st exit at mini rdbt, hotel on right. From S at T-junct, right to Grantham under A1. Left to hotel*
This smart, modern hotel is a convenient base from which to explore the countryside. Hotel bedrooms are spacious, tastefully decorated and have a range of extras. Public rooms, which extend into a pretty courtyard in the summer, include function rooms and a small leisure club with pool and fitness room.
ROOMS: 90 en suite ⊗ in 68 bedrooms s £99-£109; d £109-£119 (incl. bkfst) **LB** **FACILITIES: Spa** STV supervised Sauna Solarium Gym Jacuzzi Steam room Xmas **CONF:** Thtr 200 Class 90 Board 50 Del £150 **PARKING:** 150 **NOTES:** ✗ ⊗ in restaurant Civ Wed 80
CARDS:

⌂ Travelodge Grantham North

Grantham Service Area, Grantham North, Gonerby Moor NG32 2AB
☎ 08700 850 950 ▯ 01476 577500
Dir: *4m N on A1*
Travelodge offers good quality, good value, modern accommodation. Ideal for families, the spacious, en suite bedrooms include remote-control TV, tea and coffee-making facilities and luxury beds. Meals can be taken at the nearby family restaurant. For further details consult the Hotel Groups page.
ROOMS: 39 en suite s fr £25; d fr £25

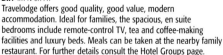

GRASMERE, Cumbria   Map 18 NY30

★★★★70% ❀❀ Wordsworth

LA22 9SW
☎ 015394 35592 ▯ 015394 35765
e-mail: enquiry@wordsworth-grasmere.co.uk
Dir: *centre of village adjacent to St Oswald's Church*
This traditional hotel, named after the poet who is buried in the adjacent churchyard, is set in well-tended gardens against a backdrop of towering fells. Bedrooms, varying in size and style, are complemented by a choice of comfortable lounge areas. To complete the package there are comprehensive leisure facilities,
continued

and diners have a choice between the popular pub and the more formal Prelude restaurant.

Wordsworth Hotel

ROOMS: 37 en suite (3 fmly) s £120-£200; d £190-£300 (incl. bkfst & dinner) **LB** **FACILITIES:** STV Sauna Solarium Gym Jacuzzi Xmas **CONF:** BC Thtr 100 Class 50 Board 40 Del from £142.50 **SERVICES:** Lift **PARKING:** 60 **NOTES:** ✗ ⊗ in restaurant Civ Wed 100
CARDS:

See advert on this page

★★★73% Gold Rill Country House

Red Bank Rd LA22 9PU
☎ 015394 35486 ▯ 015394 35486
e-mail: enquiries@gold-rill.com
web: www.gold-rill.com
Dir: *turn off A591 into village centre, then into road opposite St Oswald's Church. Hotel 300yds on left*
This popular hotel enjoys a peaceful location on the edge of the

continued on p244

GRASMERE, continued

village with spectacular views of the lake and surrounding fells. Spacious bedrooms, some with balconies, are tastefully decorated and many have separate, comfortable seating areas. The hotel boasts a private pier, an outdoor heated pool and a putting green. Public areas include a well-appointed restaurant and lounges complete with log fires.
ROOMS: 25 en suite 6 annexe en suite (2 fmly) s £49-£73; d £98-£162 (incl. bkfst & dinner) **LB** **FACILITIES:** STV Putt green Xmas **PARKING:** 35 **NOTES:** in restaurant Closed mid Dec-mid Jan (open New Year) **CARDS:**

★★★73% *Rothay Garden*

Broadgate LA22 9RJ
☎ 015394 35334 015394 35723
e-mail: stay@rothay-garden.com
web: www.rothay-garden.com
Dir: *off A591, opposite Swan Hotel, into Grasmere, 300yds on left*

Located on the northern approach to this unspoilt Cumbrian village, this hotel offers comfortable bedrooms, including some with four-posters and whirlpool baths. There is a choice of relaxing lounges, a cosy cocktail bar and an attractively refurbished conservatory restaurant, which looks out across the garden up into the fells.
ROOMS: 25 en suite (2 fmly) (6 GF) in 6 bedrooms **FACILITIES:** STV Fishing Jacuzzi use of local leisure club **PARKING:** 38 **NOTES:** in restaurant **CARDS:**

★★★72% Red Lion

Best Western

Red Lion Square LA22 9SS
☎ 015394 35456 015394 35579
e-mail: enquiries@hotelgrasmere.uk.com
web: www.hotelgrasmere.uk.com
Dir: *off A591, signed Grasmere Village, hotel in centre of village*
This modernised and extended 18th-century coaching inn, located in the heart of the village, offers spacious well-equipped rooms and a number of meeting and conference facilities. The Lamb Inn offers a range of pub meals to complement the more formal Courtyard restaurant. The comfortable lounge area is ideal for relaxing in with a drink after dinner.
ROOMS: 47 en suite (4 fmly) in 22 bedrooms s £46.50-£65.50; d £93-£131 (incl. bkfst) **FACILITIES:** STV Sauna Gym Jacuzzi Hairdressing ch fac Xmas **CONF:** Thtr 60 Class 30 Board 30 Del from £122.50 **SERVICES:** Lift **PARKING:** 38 **NOTES:** in restaurant **CARDS:**

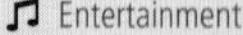
Entertainment

★★★72% Thistle Grasmere

Keswick Rd LA22 9PR
☎ 0870 333 9135 0870 333 9235
e-mail: grasmere@thistle.co.uk
Dir: *N - A51 Grasmere. 1st hotel on left opposite Dove Cottage. S - follow signs for Ambleside. Last hotel on right.*
This large hotel stands in its own gardens leading to the lake, and many of the bedrooms have fine views over the surrounding fells. Bedrooms are comfortably furnished and include a stylish suite, complete with a four-poster bed. Service is friendly and the choice of meals, from a selection of restaurant and bar menus, should suit most tastes.
ROOMS: 72 en suite (8 fmly) in 58 bedrooms s £59-£132; d fr £75 (incl. bkfst) **LB** **FACILITIES:** STV Fishing Xmas **CONF:** Thtr 110 Class 60 Board 40 Del from £75 **PARKING:** 60 **NOTES:** in restaurant Civ Wed 120 **CARDS:**

★★★71% The Swan

MACDONALD HOTELS

LA22 9RF
☎ 0870 400 8132 015394 35741
e-mail: swangrasmere@macdonald-hotels.co.uk
Dir: *M6 junct 36, A591 towards Kendal, A590 to Keswick through Ambleside. The Swan on right on entering the village*
Close to Dove Cottage and occupying a prominent position on the edge of the village, this 300-year-old inn is mentioned in Wordsworth's poem *'The Waggoner'*. Attractive public areas are spacious and comfortable, and bedrooms are equally stylish and have CD players. A good range of bar meals is available, while the elegant restaurant offers more formal dining.
ROOMS: 38 en suite (1 fmly) (28 GF) in 14 bedrooms s £50-£75; d £100-£150 (incl. bkfst) **LB** **FACILITIES:** Xmas **CONF:** Thtr 30 Class 24 Board 16 Del from £110 **PARKING:** 45 **NOTES:** in restaurant Civ Wed 58 **CARDS:**

★★74% Grasmere

Broadgate LA22 9TA
☎ 015394 35277 015394 35277
e-mail: enquiries@grasmerehotel.co.uk
web: www.grasmerehotel.co.uk
Dir: *A591 north from Ambleside, 2nd left into Grasmere town centre. Follow road over humpback bridge, past playing field. Hotel on left*
Attentive and hospitable service contribute to the atmosphere at this family-run hotel, set in secluded gardens by the River Rothay. There are two inviting lounges (one with residents' bar) and an attractive dining room looking onto the garden. The thoughtfully prepared dinner menu makes good use of fresh ingredients. Pine furniture is featured in most bedrooms, along with some welcome personal touches.
ROOMS: 13 en suite (2 GF) in all bedrooms s £50-£70; d £90-£140 (incl. bkfst & dinner) **LB** **FACILITIES:** Access to full leisure facilities at nearby country club Xmas **PARKING:** 14 **NOTES:** No children 9yrs in restaurant Closed 3 Jan-early Feb **CARDS:**

★★72% Oak Bank

Broadgate LA22 9TA
☎ 015394 35217 015394 35685
e-mail: info@lakedistricthotel.co.uk
Dir: *on right in village centre*
This privately owned and personally run hotel provides well-equipped accommodation, including a bedroom on ground floor level and a four-poster room. Public areas include a choice of comfortable lounges with welcoming log fires when the weather is

continued

cold. There is a pleasant bar and an attractive restaurant with a conservatory extension overlooking the garden.
ROOMS: 15 en suite (1 fmly) (1 GF) ⊗ in all bedrooms s £60-£65; d £50-£65 (incl. bkfst & dinner) **LB** **FACILITIES:** Jacuzzi Xmas **PARKING:** 11 **NOTES:** ⊗ in restaurant Closed 6-20 Jan
CARDS:

Top 200 – Hotel

★ White Moss House

Rydal Water LA22 9SE
☎ 015394 35295 015394 35516
e-mail: sue@whitemoss.com
web: www.whitemoss.com
Dir: *on A591, 1m S of Grasmere*

This traditional Lakeland house was once bought by Wordsworth for his son. It benefits from a central location and has a loyal following. The individually styled bedrooms are comfortable and thoughtfully equipped. There is also a two-room suite in a cottage on the hillside above the hotel. The five-course set dinner makes good use of the quality local ingredients. Afternoon tea and pre-dinner drinks are served in the inviting lounge.
ROOMS: 5 en suite 2 annexe en suite s £92-£97; d £154-£184 (incl. bkfst & dinner) **LB** **FACILITIES:** Free use local leisure club, Free fishing at local waters, walking **PARKING:** 10 **NOTES:** ⊗ in restaurant Closed Dec-Jan RS Sun **CARDS:**

GRASSINGTON, North Yorkshire — Map 19 SE06

★★65% *Grassington House*

5 The Square BD23 5AQ
☎ 01756 752406 01756 752135
web: www.grassingtonhousehotel.co.uk
Dir: *B6265 from Skipton, on right side of village square*

A warm welcome awaits guests at this conveniently located, central hotel in the main square. Comfortable accommodation is provided, with bedrooms of a good size. Public areas are spacious and pleasant to relax in. A good range of dishes is offered in both the informal bar and the modern well-appointed restaurant. Private parking is available.
ROOMS: 9 en suite (2 fmly) ⊗ in all bedrooms **PARKING:** 20
NOTES: ⊗ in restaurant **CARDS:**

Looking for a last-minute weekend away?
Check out Latebeds,
the AA's late availability booking service, at www.theAA.com

GRAVESEND, Kent
Map 06 TQ67

★★★72% Manor Hotel
Hever Court Rd DA12 5UQ
☎ 01474 353100 01474 354978
e-mail: manor@bestwestern.co.uk
Dir: *at junct of A2 Gravesend East turn off*
Conveniently located just off the A2, this hotel is ideal for the Bluewater shopping village. Attractively decorated bedrooms are spacious and fitted with numerous facilities. A newly refurbished bar and smart restaurant is available along with an impressive health club.
ROOMS: 52 en suite (3 fmly) in 37 bedrooms s £85-£95; d £95-£105 (incl. bkfst) **FACILITIES:** STV supervised Sauna Solarium Gym **CONF:** BC Thtr 200 Class 100 Board 25 Del from £120 **PARKING:** 100 **NOTES:** in restaurant **CARDS:**

G

Premier Lodge (Gravesend)

Hevercourt Rd, Singlewell DA12 5UQ
☎ 0870 9906352 0870 9906353
web: www.premierlodge.com
Dir: *off A2 towards Rochester and Channel Tunnel. Turn off at Singlewell Services Rd*
High quality, modern, budget accommodation, ideal for families and business travellers. All rooms feature bath, power shower and satellite TV, and most have telephones / modem points. The adjacent bar and restaurant offers a wide and varied menu.
ROOMS: 31 en suite s £50; d £50

Travel Inn
Wrotham Rd DA11 7LF
☎ 08701 977118 01474 323776

Dir: *1m from A2 on A227 towards Gravesend town centre*
Travel Inn offers good-quality, value-for-money accommodation. Spacious, en suite rooms with bath and shower comfortably accommodate a family of up to two adults and two children (to age 15). The restaurant and bar offers a varied menu. For further details consult the Hotel Groups page.
ROOMS: 36 en suite s £45.95-£48.95; d £45.95-£48.95
CONF: Thtr 40 Board 20

GREAT CHESTERFORD, Essex
Map 12 TL54

★★★67% The Crown House
CB10 1NY
☎ 01799 530515 01799 530683
e-mail: sales@thecrownhouse.com
web: www.thecrownhouse.com
Dir: *From north leave M11 at junct 9, from south junct 10, follow signs for Saffron Walden & then Great Chesterford (B1383)*
This Georgian coaching inn, situated in a peaceful village location close to the M11, has been sympathetically restored and retains much original character. The newly refurbished bedrooms are well equipped and individually decorated; some rooms have delightful four-poster beds. Public rooms include an attractive lounge bar, an elegant oak-panelled restaurant and an airy conservatory.
ROOMS: 8 en suite 10 annexe en suite (1 fmly) (5 GF) s £55-£69.50; d £79.50-£120 (incl. bkfst) **LB** **CONF:** Thtr 16 **PARKING:** 30 **NOTES:** in restaurant Civ Wed 60 **CARDS:**

See advert on page 245

Packed in a hurry?
Ironing facilities should be available at all star levels, either in rooms or on request

GREAT DUNMOW, Essex
Map 06 TL62

Restaurant with Rooms

Starr Restaurant with Rooms
Market Place CM6 1AX
☎ 01371 874321 01371 876337
e-mail: starrrestaurant@btinternet.com
Dir: *M11 junct 8, onto A120. After 7m, left into Great Dunmow, then left*

A 15th-century, former coaching inn situated in the heart of this charming Essex village. It is well known locally for its quality food, which is served in the elegantly appointed beamed restaurant and conservatory. The spacious bedrooms are in a converted stable block adjacent to the main building and each is individually decorated and tastefully furnished.
ROOMS: 8 annexe en suite s £75-£95; d £115-£134 (incl. bkfst)
CONF: Thtr 36 Board 16 **PARKING:** 16 **NOTES:** in restaurant
CARDS:

GREAT MILTON, Oxfordshire
Map 05 SP60

Top 200 – Hotel

★★★★ Le Manoir Aux Quat' Saisons
Church Rd OX44 7PD
☎ 01844 278881 01844 278847
e-mail: lemanoir@blanc.co.uk
web: www.manoir.com
Dir: *from A329 2nd right to Great Milton Manor, hotel 200yds on right*
Set in beautiful grounds and gardens that produce many of the organic ingredients for the kitchens, this renowned hotel epitomises luxury and truly memorable cooking. Bedrooms are individually styled and are either in the main house or in the garden courtyard. All offer the highest levels of comfort and quality, and are equipped with a host of thoughtful extra

continued

touches and benefit from magnificent marble bathrooms. Stylish public areas feature wonderful artwork and include the centrepiece of any visit to Le Manoir, the conservatory restaurant.
ROOMS: 9 en suite 23 annexe en suite **FACILITIES:** STV Cookery School, Water Gardens **CONF:** Thtr 24 Board 20 **PARKING:** 60 **NOTES:** in restaurant Civ Wed 50 **CARDS:**

GREAT YARMOUTH, Norfolk Map 13 TG50

★★★73% *Cliff*

Cliff Hill, Gorleston NR31 6DH
☎ 01493 662179 01493 653617
Dir: *M11 onto A11 to Norwich then A47 to Gt Yarmouth. At N end of Gorleston's Upper Marine Parade*

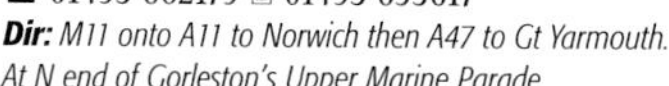

Overlooking the harbour just a short walk from the beach, promenade and Gorleston town centre. Public rooms include a choice of bars, an attractive lounge and a stylish restaurant where an interesting choice of dishes are served. Bedrooms are smartly decorated, with co-ordinated soft furnishings and have many thoughtful touches; some rooms have lovely sea views.
ROOMS: 39 en suite (2 fmly) in 2 bedrooms **FACILITIES:** STV **CONF:** Thtr 170 Class 150 Board 80 **PARKING:** 70 **NOTES:** Civ Wed 120 **CARDS:**

★★★71% Imperial

THE INDEPENDENTS

North Dr NR30 1EQ
☎ 01493 842000 01493 852229
e-mail: imperial@scs-datacom.co.uk
web: www.imperialhotel.co.uk
Dir: *follow signs to seafront and turn left. Hotel opposite tennis courts*
Friendly, family-run hotel situated at the quieter end of the seafront within easy walking distance of the town. Bedrooms are attractively decorated with co-ordinated soft furnishings and equipped with modern facilities; many rooms have superb sea views. Public areas offer a good level of comfort and include the smart Savoie Lounge Bar and the Rambouillet Restaurant.
ROOMS: 39 en suite (4 fmly) in 21 bedrooms s £50-£80; d £67-£90 (incl. bkfst) **LB** **FACILITIES:** STV Xmas **CONF:** Thtr 140 Class 40 Board 30 Del from £75 **SERVICES:** Lift **PARKING:** 50 **NOTES:** Civ Wed 140 **CARDS:**

★★★68% Regency Dolphin

Albert Square NR30 3JH
☎ 01493 855070 01493 853798
e-mail: regencydolphin@countrytown-hotels.co.uk
web: www.hotelselection.co.uk/regency-dolphin
Dir: *along seafront and right at Wellington Pier. Right into Kimberley Ter then left into Albert Sq, hotel on left*
Large privately owned hotel situated in the quieter end of town,

continued

just off the seafront and within easy walking distance of the town centre. The pleasantly decorated bedrooms are generally quite spacious and well equipped. Public rooms include a comfortable lounge, a bar and intimate restaurant. The hotel also has an outdoor swimming pool.
ROOMS: 47 en suite (5 fmly) (2 GF) in 9 bedrooms s £50-£70; d £60-£80 (incl. bkfst) **LB** **FACILITIES:** Xmas **CONF:** Thtr 140 Class 50 Board 30 Del from £75 **PARKING:** 19 **NOTES:** in restaurant Civ Wed 80 **CARDS:**

★★★66% Star

Hall Quay NR30 1HG
☎ 01493 842294 01493 330215
e-mail: star.hotel@elizabethhotels.co.uk
Dir: *from Norwich on A47 over 1st rdbt. At 2nd rdbt 3rd exit. Hotel on left*
The black and white façade of this 17th-century property makes it one of the town's most striking buildings. It overlooks the quay and is just a short walk from the town centre. Public rooms are smartly appointed and include a choice of bars, a restaurant and a tastefully furnished lounge. Bedrooms are pleasantly decorated and equipped with modern facilities.
ROOMS: 40 en suite (1 fmly) in 13 bedrooms s £55-£65; d £75-£90 (incl. bkfst) **LB** **FACILITIES:** STV Discount for the marina leisure centre pool, gym Xmas **CONF:** Thtr 75 Class 30 Board 30 Del from £60 **SERVICES:** Lift **PARKING:** 20 **NOTES:** in restaurant **CARDS:**

G

★★72% The Arden Court Hotel

93-94 North Denes Rd NR30 4LW
☎ 01493 855310 01493 843413
e-mail: barry@ardencourthotel.freeserve.co.uk
web: www.ardencourt-hotel.co.uk
Dir: *At seafront left along North Dr. At Boating lake left along Beaconsfield Rd. At mini rdbt right into North Denes Rd.*
Friendly, family-run hotel situated in a residential area just a short walk from the seafront. The individually decorated bedrooms are smartly furnished and equipped with a good range of useful extras. Public rooms are attractively presented; they include a smart lounge bar and a restaurant serving an interesting choice of dishes.
ROOMS: 14 en suite (5 fmly) (2 GF) in all bedrooms s £30-£34; d £60-£64 (incl. bkfst) **LB** **FACILITIES:** Xmas **PARKING:** 10 **NOTES:** in restaurant **CARDS:**

★★69% Furzedown

19-20 North Dr NR30 4EW
☎ 01493 844138 01493 844138
e-mail: Paul@furzedownhotel.co.uk
web: www.furzedownhotel.co.uk
Dir: *at end of A47 or A12 to seafront, left, hotel opposite Waterways*

Friendly family run hotel situated at the northern end of the seafront overlooking the beach and Venetian waterways.

continued on p248

GREAT YARMOUTH, continued

Bedrooms are pleasantly decorated and equipped with a good range of useful extras; many have superb sea views. The stylish public areas include a comfortable lounge bar, a smartly appointed restaurant and a cosy TV room.
ROOMS: 24 rms (20 en suite) (11 fmly) s £49-£54; d £64-£74 (incl. bkfst) **LB** **FACILITIES:** STV **CONF:** Thtr 75 Class 80 Board 40 Del from £68.50 **PARKING:** 15 **NOTES:** ⊗ in restaurant
CARDS:

★★63% New Beach Hotel

67 Marine Pde NR30 2EJ
☎ 01493 332300 📠 01493 331880
e-mail: newbeach.gtyarmouth@alfatravel.co.uk
Dir: *Follow signs to seafront, Hotel facing Britannia Pier*
This Victorian building is centrally located on the seafront, overlooking Britannia Pier and the sandy beach. Bedrooms are pleasantly decorated and equipped with modern facilities; many have lovely sea views. Dinner is taken in the restaurant which doubles as the ballroom, and guests can also relax in the bar or sunny lounge.
ROOMS: 75 en suite (3 fmly) s £28-£36; d £46-£62 (incl. bkfst) **LB** **FACILITIES:** ♫ Xmas **SERVICES:** Lift **NOTES:** ✗ ⊗ in restaurant Closed Dec-Feb RS Nov & Mar **CARDS:**

GREENFORD, Greater London
See LONDON SECTION plan 1 B4

★★★67% The Bridge

Western Av UB6 8ST
☎ 020 8566 6246 📠 020 8566 6140
e-mail: bridgehotel@youngs.co.uk
Dir: *Turn off A40 before flyover onto A4127 towards Greenford, hotel on roundabout*
A popular venue for business guests this hotel is ideally located, on the A40, for accessing central London. Spacious bedrooms offer good levels of comfort and a range of useful facilities. A popular public bar and bistro style restaurant are also on offer.
ROOMS: 68 en suite (4 fmly) ⊗ in 44 bedrooms **FACILITIES:** STV Arrangement with local leisure centre **CONF:** Thtr 120 Class 60 Board 60 **SERVICES:** Lift air con **PARKING:** 68 **NOTES:** ✗ ⊗ in restaurant Civ Wed **CARDS:**

⌂ Travel Inn

Western Av UB6 8TE
☎ 08701 977119 📠 020 8998 8823
Dir: *From the Western Avenue (A40), Eastbound, exit Perivale. Turn right, then at 2nd set of traffic lights turn left. Travel Inn is opposite the Hoover Building*
Travel Inn offers good-quality, value-for-money accommodation. Spacious, en suite rooms with bath and shower comfortably accommodate a family of up to two adults and two children (to age 15). The restaurant and bar offers a varied menu. For further details consult the Hotel Groups page.
ROOMS: 39 en suite s £58.95; d £58.95

GRIMSBY, Lincolnshire Map 17 TA21

★★★66% ⊛ Beeches

42 Waltham Rd, Scartho DN33 2LX
☎ 01472 278830 📠 01472 752880
e-mail: joeramsden@freeuk.com
web: www.thebeecheshotel.com
Located in the suburb of Scartho, not far from the town centre, this contemporary hotel offers good modern accommodation and pleasing public rooms. Bedrooms are inviting and well equipped with a thoughtful range of facilities. There is a popular brasserie and a comfortable lounge bar; food choices offer interest and quality.
ROOMS: 18 en suite (4 GF) ⊗ in all bedrooms s £48.50-£69.50; d £68.50-£84.50 (incl. bkfst) **LB** **CONF:** Class 40 **SERVICES:** Lift **PARKING:** 70 **NOTES:** ✗ ⊗ in restaurant Closed 25 Dec-1st wk Jan **CARDS:**

★★★66% Elizabeth

Littlecoates Rd DN34 4LX
☎ 01472 240024 📠 01472 241354
e-mail: elizabeth.grimsby@elizabethhotels.co.uk
web: www.elizabethhotels.co.uk
Dir: *A1136 signed Greatcoates, 1st rdbt left, 2nd rdbt right. Hotel on right*
Bedrooms at this pleasantly situated hotel are equipped with modern comforts and many have large windows and balconies overlooking the adjoining golf course. The popular restaurant shares the same tranquil view. There is a large banqueting suite, smaller meeting and conference rooms, and extensive parking which makes this an ideal business centre.
ROOMS: 52 en suite (4 fmly) ⊗ in 27 bedrooms s £60-£79; d £70-£89 (incl. bkfst) **LB** **FACILITIES:** STV Xmas **CONF:** Thtr 300 Class 100 Board 60 Del £89 **SERVICES:** Lift **PARKING:** 200 **NOTES:** ⊗ in restaurant Civ Wed 100 **CARDS:**

⌂ Travel Inn

Europa Park, Appian Way, Off Gilbey Rd DN31 2UT
☎ 08701 977121 📠 01472 241648
Dir: *From M180 (J5) A180 towards Grimsby centre. At 1st rbt 2nd exit. Take 1st left, then left at mini rbt*
Travel Inn offers good-quality, value-for-money accommodation. Spacious, en suite rooms with bath and shower comfortably accommodate a family of up to two adults and two children (to age 15). The restaurant and bar offers a varied menu. For further details consult the Hotel Groups page.
ROOMS: 40 en suite s £45.96-£46.95; d £45.95-£46.95

GRIMSTON, Norfolk Map 12 TF72

Top 200 – Hotel

★★★ ⊛⊛ Congham Hall Country House

Lynn Rd PE32 1AH
☎ 01485 600250 📠 01485 601191
e-mail: info@conghamhallhotel.co.uk
web: www.conghamhallhotel.co.uk
Dir: *A149/A148 junct NE of King's Lynn. A148 towards Fakenham for 100yds. Right to Grimston, hotel 2.5m on left*
This elegant 18th-century Georgian manor is set amid 30 acres of mature landscaped grounds and surrounded by parkland. The inviting public rooms provide a range of tastefully furnished areas in which to sit and relax. Imaginative cuisine is served in the Orangery Restaurant, which has an intimate atmosphere and panoramic views of the gardens.
continued

The bedrooms are tastefully furnished with period pieces and have modern facilities and many thoughtful touches.

ROOMS: 14 en suite ⊗ in all bedrooms s £115-£130; d £165-£230 (incl. bkfst & dinner) **LB** **FACILITIES:** Putt green ch fac Xmas **CONF:** Thtr 50 Class 20 Board 30 Del from £155 **PARKING:** 50 **NOTES:** ⊗ in restaurant Civ Wed 100 **CARDS:**

GRINDLEFORD, Derbyshire Map 16 SK27

★★★70% *Maynard Arms*

Main Rd S32 2HE
☎ 01433 630321 01433 630445
e-mail: info@maynardarms.co.uk
web: www.maynardarms.co.uk
Dir: *from Sheffield take A625 to Castleton. Left into Grindleford on B6521. After Fox House hotel on left*

A delightful country hotel set in attractive gardens with fine views. Bedrooms are very tastefully furnished and decorated; some have four-poster beds and two have separate sitting rooms. A residents' lounge is situated on the first floor, overlooking the garden, and the restaurant has similar views. Bar food is available at both lunch and dinner.

ROOMS: 10 en suite **FACILITIES:** STV **CONF:** BC Thtr 140 Class 80 Board 40 **PARKING:** 80 **NOTES:** ⊗ in restaurant Civ Wed 120 **CARDS:**

GUILDFORD, Surrey Map 06 SU94

★★★68% The Manor

Newlands Corner GU4 8SE
☎ 01483 222624 01483 211389
e-mail: mail@hollybournehotels.com
web: www.hollybournehotels.com
Dir: *3.5m on A25 to Dorking*

Set peacefully in its own grounds, this conveniently located hotel is a popular choice for weddings and conferences. The well-appointed public areas include a selection of meeting rooms, a spacious lounge, a choice of bars and an attractive restaurant whilst the bedrooms, which are mostly modern, are tastefully furnished and feature a good range of facilities.

ROOMS: 50 en suite (4 fmly) ⊗ in 4 bedrooms s fr £89; d fr £99 **LB** **FACILITIES:** Sauna Solarium Gym Jacuzzi Steam room, dance studio **CONF:** Thtr 150 Class 50 Board 50 Del from £150 **PARKING:** 100 **NOTES:** ⊗ in restaurant Civ Wed 120 **CARDS:**

Travel Inn

Parkway GU1 1UP
☎ 08701 977122 01483 450678
Dir: *From M25 (J10) follow signs to Portsmouth (A3). Turn off signed Guildford centre/Leisure Centre (JA322/A320/A25). Turn left and Travel Inn is on the left*

Travel Inn offers good-quality, value-for-money accommodation. Spacious, en suite rooms with bath and shower comfortably accommodate a family of up to two adults and two children (to age 15). The restaurant and bar offers a varied menu. For further details consult the Hotel Groups page.

ROOMS: 87 en suite s £56.95; d £56.95 **CONF:** Thtr 45 Board 25

GUISBOROUGH, North Yorkshire Map 19 NZ61

★★★★72% Gisborough Hall

MACDONALD HOTELS

Whitby Ln TS14 6PT
☎ 0870 400 8191 01287 610844
e-mail: general.gisboroughhall@macdonald-hotels.co.uk
Dir: *A171, follow signs for Whitby until Waterfall rdbt then into Whitby Lane, hotel 500yds on right*

Dating back to the mid-19th century, this elegant establishment has been carefully refurbished and extended to provide a pleasing combination of original features and modern facilities. Bedrooms, including four-poster and family rooms, are richly furnished, while there is a choice of welcoming lounges with log fires. Imaginative fare is served in Tockett's restaurant.

ROOMS: 71 en suite (2 fmly) (12 GF) ⊗ in 37 bedrooms s £99-£109; d £138-£158 (incl. bkfst) **FACILITIES:** STV Sauna Revival zone-2 beauty treatment zones Xmas **CONF:** BC Thtr 400 Class 150 Board 32 Del £165 **SERVICES:** Lift air con **PARKING:** 400 **NOTES:** ⊗ in restaurant Civ Wed **CARDS:**

Restaurant with Rooms

Pinchinthorpe Hall

Pinchinthorpe TS14 8HG
☎ 01287 630200 01287 632000
e-mail: nyb@pinchinthorpe.freeserve.co.uk
Dir: *Between Guisborough and Gt Ayton on A173.*

An elegant 17th-century country manor house that has stylish bedrooms, each very individually and tastefully decorated and with many thoughtful extras. The Brewhouse Bistro serves award-winning cuisine with flair and creativity, and the genuinely caring and attentive service is memorable.

ROOMS: 6 en suite ⊗ in all bedrooms s £80-£100; d £120-£160 **LB** **FACILITIES:** Fishing Putt green Xmas **CONF:** Thtr 50 Class 20 Board 24 **PARKING:** 110 **NOTES:** ⊗ in restaurant Civ Wed 80 **CARDS:**

Premier Lodge (Middlesbrough South)

Middlesbrough Rd, Upsall TS14 6RW
☎ 0870 9906540 0870 9906541
web: www.premierlodge.com
Dir: *from N A1 onto A19, A174 signed Teesport & Whitby A172. A1043 signed Whitby onto A171. From S, A1 junct 49 onto A168. A19 onto A172. At rbt take 3rd exit to Guisborough and at next rbt take 1st exit*

High quality, modern, budget accommodation, ideal for families and business travellers. All rooms feature bath, power shower and satellite TV, and most have telephones / modem points. The adjacent bar and restaurant offers a wide and varied menu.

ROOMS: 20 en suite s £48; d £48

GULWORTHY, Devon Map 03 SX47

★★★77% Horn of Plenty
PL19 8JD
☎ 01822 832528 Fax 01822 832528
e-mail: enquiries@thehornofplenty.co.uk
web: www.thehornofplenty.co.uk
Dir: *from Tavistock take A390 W for 3m. Right at Gulworthy Cross. After 400yds turn left and after 400yds hotel on right*

With memorable and stunning views over the Tamar Valley, The Horn of Plenty maintains its reputation as one of Britain's impressive country houses. The bedrooms are well equipped and have many thoughtful extras; some, more simply decorated, are in adjacent converted cottages. Cuisine here is also impressive and local produce provides interesting and memorable dining.
ROOMS: 4 en suite 6 annexe en suite (3 fmly) (4 GF) in all bedrooms s £105-£190; d £115-£200 (incl. bkfst) **LB FACILITIES:** Xmas **CONF:** BC Thtr 20 Class 20 Board 12 **PARKING:** 25 **NOTES:** in restaurant Closed 24-26 Dec Civ Wed **CARDS:**

GUNTHORPE, Nottinghamshire Map 11 SK64

★★66% *Unicorn*
Gunthorpe Bridge NG14 7FB
☎ 0115 966 3612 Fax 0115 966 4801
Dir: *on A6097, between Lowdham and Bingham*
Now under new ownership this popular riverside inn provides comfortable bedrooms, each thoughtfully equipped with many extra facilities. The spacious bars feature exposed timbers and brickwork and the all-day menus centre on home-cooked food.
ROOMS: 16 en suite (3 fmly) **FACILITIES:** STV Fishing **PARKING:** 200 **NOTES:** **CARDS:**

HACKNESS, North Yorkshire Map 17 SE99

★★★71% *Hackness Grange Country House*
Best Western
North York National Park YO13 0JW
☎ 01723 882345 Fax 01723 882391
e-mail: admin@englishrosehotels.co.uk
Dir: *A64 to Scarborough, then A171 to Whitby and Scalby. Follow Hackness and Forge Valley National Park signs, through Hackness village on left*
Close to Scarborough, and set in the North Yorkshire Moors National Park, Hackness Grange is surrounded by well-tended gardens. Comfortable bedrooms have views of the open countryside; those in the cottages are ideally suited to families, and the courtyard rooms include facilities for the less able. Lounges and the restaurant are spacious and relaxing.
ROOMS: 33 en suite (5 fmly) (8 GF) **FACILITIES:** Putt green 9 hole pitch & putt **CONF:** Thtr 20 Board 14 **PARKING:** 60 **NOTES:** in restaurant **CARDS:**

HADLEY WOOD, Greater London Map 06 TQ29

★★★★73% West Lodge Park
Cockfosters Rd EN4 0PY
☎ 020 8216 3900 Fax 020 8216 3937
e-mail: westlodgepark@bealeshotels.co.uk
Dir: *on A111, 1m S of M25 junct 24*
An impressive country house hotel set in mature parkland and gardens, yet only 12 miles from central London. Bedrooms are individually decorated and offer comprehensive in-room facilities; superior annexed rooms have air conditioning. The Cedar Restaurant provides a good choice of interesting dishes. Informal dining and afternoon teas are also readily available.
ROOMS: 46 en suite 13 annexe en suite (1 fmly) (11 GF) in 23 bedrooms s £108-£115; d £150-£170 **LB FACILITIES: Spa** STV Sauna Putt green Massage, Manicure, Free use of nearby leisure club Xmas **CONF:** BC Thtr 70 Class 30 Board 30 Del from £192 **SERVICES:** Lift **PARKING:** 200 **NOTES:** in restaurant RS Saturday Civ Wed **CARDS:**

HAGLEY, Worcestershire Map 10 SO98

Travel Inn
travel inn
Birmingham Rd DY9 9JS
☎ 08701 977123 Fax 01562 884416
Dir: *5m off M5 junct 3 on opposite side of A456 dual carriageway towards Kidderminster*
Travel Inn offers good-quality, value-for-money accommodation. Spacious, en suite rooms with bath and shower comfortably accommodate a family of up to two adults and two children (to age 15). The restaurant and bar offers a varied menu. For further details consult the Hotel Groups page.
ROOMS: 40 en suite s £45.95-£46.95; d £45.95-£46.95 **CONF:** Thtr 20 Board 18

HAILSHAM, East Sussex Map 06 TQ50

★★★66% Boship Farm
Forestdale Hotels
Lower Dicker BN27 4AT
☎ 01323 844826 Fax 01323 843945
e-mail: boship.farm@forestdale.com
Dir: *on A22 at Boship rdbt, junct of A22, A267 and A271*
Dating back to 1652, a lovely old farmhouse forms the hub of this hotel, which is set in 17 acres of well-tended grounds. Guests have the use of an all-weather tennis court, an outdoor pool and a croquet lawn. Bedrooms are smartly appointed and well-equipped; most have views across open fields and countryside.
ROOMS: 47 annexe en suite (5 fmly) (21 GF) in 17 bedrooms s fr £80; d fr £115 (incl. bkfst) **LB FACILITIES:** Sauna Jacuzzi Xmas **CONF:** Thtr 175 Class 40 Board 46 Del from £95 **PARKING:** 100 **NOTES:** in restaurant Civ Wed
CARDS:

> Late for dinner?
> Quality Standards mean that last orders for dinner vary according to star rating and should be no earlier than:
> ★★ 7.00pm ★★★ 8.00pm ★★★★ 9.00pm
> ★★★★★ 10.00pm

> Early start?
> Hotels at all star levels should provide in-room alarm clocks and/or alarm calls

★★71% The Olde Forge Hotel & Restaurant
Magham Down BN27 1PN
☎ 01323 842893 📠 01323 842893
e-mail: theoldeforgehotel@tesco.net
Dir: *off Boship rdbt on A271 to Bexhill & Herstmonceux. 3m on left*
In the heart of the countryside, this family-run hotel offers a friendly welcome and an informal atmosphere. The bedrooms are attractively decorated with thoughtful extras. The restaurant, a forge in the 16th century, has timbered beams and log fires and a good local reputation for its cuisine and service.
ROOMS: 7 en suite ⊗ in 4 bedrooms s fr £48; d fr £68 (incl. bkfst) **LB**
PARKING: 11 **NOTES:** ⊗ in restaurant **CARDS:**

⇧ Travelodge Hellingly Eastbourne
Travelodge
Boship Roundabout, Hellingly BN27 4DT
☎ 08700 850 950 📠 01323 844556
Dir: *on A22 at Boship rdbt*
Travelodge offers good quality, good value, modern accommodation. Ideal for families, the spacious, en suite bedrooms include remote-control TV, tea and coffee-making facilities and luxury beds. Meals can be taken at the nearby family restaurant. For further details consult the Hotel Groups page.
ROOMS: 58 en suite s fr £25; d fr £25

HALIFAX, West Yorkshire
Map 19 SE02

★★★77% ◎◎ Holdsworth House
Holdsworth HX2 9TG
☎ 01422 240024 📠 01422 245174
e-mail: info@holdsworthhouse.co.uk
web: www.holdsworthhouse.co.uk
Dir: *from town centre take A629 Keighley Road. Right at garage up Shay Ln after 1.5m. Hotel on right after 1m*

This delightful 17th-century Jacobean manor house is set in well-tended gardens and offers individually decorated, thoughtfully equipped bedrooms. Public rooms, adorned with beautiful paintings and antique pieces, include a choice of inviting lounges and superb conference and function facilities. Dinner provides the highlight of any stay and is served in the elegant restaurant, by friendly, attentive staff.
ROOMS: 40 en suite (2 fmly) ⊗ in 15 bedrooms s £95-£135; d £120-£160 (incl. cont bkfst) **LB** **FACILITIES:** STV **CONF:** Thtr 150 Class 75 Board 50 Del £135 **PARKING:** 60 **NOTES:** ⊗ in restaurant Civ Wed 100 **CARDS:**

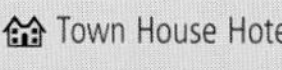
Town House Hotel
Country House Hotel
⇧ Travel Accommodation

★★★67% Rock Inn
Holywell Green HX4 9BS
☎ 01422 379721 📠 01422 379110
e-mail: reservations@rockinnhotel.com
web: www.rockinnhotel.com
Dir: *M62 junct 24, follow Blackley signs, left at x-rds 0.5m on left*
Situated in a quiet village between Huddersfield and Halifax, this hotel is popular with business guests and as a local dining venue. The newer bedrooms are particularly innovative with attractive design features, while the standard rooms - all with deep hip tubs - though more compact, are well laid out. A conservatory-style brasserie adjoins the bar.
ROOMS: 30 en suite (5 fmly) ⊗ in 15 bedrooms s £50-£65; d £64-£69 (incl. bkfst) **LB** **FACILITIES:** STV Xmas **CONF:** Thtr 200 Class 100 Board 100 **PARKING:** 122 **NOTES:** ⊗ in restaurant Civ Wed 200
CARDS:

★★★63% Imperial Crown Hotel
corus hotels
42/46 Horton St HX1 1QE
☎ 0870 609 6114 📠 01422 349866
e-mail: imperialcrown@corushotels.com
Dir: *opposite railway station & Eureka Children's Museum*

This friendly hotel is situated in the town centre and in addition to the main accommodation there are 15 smart contemporary bedrooms located above the hotel's American diner which is across the road. The Wallis Simpson Restaurant and Bar are in the main building, and complimentary use of a nearby gym is also available.
ROOMS: 41 en suite 15 annexe en suite (3 fmly) ⊗ in 22 bedrooms
FACILITIES: STV **CONF:** Thtr 150 Class 120 Board 70 Del from £95
PARKING: 63 **NOTES:** ⊗ in restaurant Civ Wed 150
CARDS:

⇧ Premier Lodge (Halifax)
PREMIER LODGE.com
Salterhebble Hill, Huddersfield Rd HX3 0QT
☎ 0870 9906308 📠 0870 9906309
web: www.premierlodge.com
Dir: *off M62 junct 24, on the A629 towards Halifax*
High quality, modern, budget accommodation, ideal for families and business travellers. All rooms feature bath, power shower and satellite TV, and most have telephones / modem points. The adjacent bar and restaurant offers a wide and varied menu.
ROOMS: 31 en suite s £48; d £48 **CONF:** Thtr 30

⇧ Travelodge (Halifax Central)
Travelodge
Dean Clough Park HX3 5AY
☎ 08700 850 950 📠 01422 362669
Travelodge offers good quality, good value, modern accommodation. Ideal for families, the spacious, en suite bedrooms include remote-control TV, tea and coffee-making facilities and luxury beds. Meals can be taken at the nearby family restaurant. For further details consult the Hotel Groups page.
ROOMS: 52 en suite s fr £25; d fr £25

HAMPTON COURT, Greater London
See LONDON SECTION plan 1 B1

★★★★62% The Carlton Mitre
Hampton Court Rd KT8 9BN
☎ 020 8979 9988 📠 020 8979 9777
e-mail: mitre@carltonhotels.co.uk
Dir: *M3 junct 1 follow signs to Sunbury & Hampton Court Palace. At Hampton Court Palace rdbt right and hotel on right*

This hotel, dating back in parts to 1655, enjoys an enviable setting on the banks of the River Thames opposite Hampton Court Palace. The riverside restaurant and Edge bar/brasserie command wonderful views. Bedrooms are generally spacious with excellent facilities. Parking is limited.
ROOMS: 36 en suite (2 fmly) ⊘ in 16 bedrooms **FACILITIES:** STV **CONF:** Thtr 120 Class 60 Board 40 Del from £205 **SERVICES:** Lift **PARKING:** 13 **NOTES:** ⊘ in restaurant Civ Wed 100
CARDS:

★★★66% Liongate
Hampton Court Rd KT8 9DD
☎ 020 8977 8121 📠 020 8943 4029
e-mail: events@dhillonhotels.co.uk
Dir: *M25 junct 12/M3 towards London. M3 junct 1, follow A308 at mini rdbt turn left. Hotel opposite gates for Hampton Court Palace*

Dating back to 1721 this hotel enjoys a wonderful location opposite the Lion Gate entrance to Hampton Court and beside the entrance to Bushy Park. Despite its history it boasts rooms with plenty of contemporary style and design. Public areas are all open plan and feature a modern European restaurant called Black Olive.
ROOMS: 14 en suite 18 annexe en suite (2 fmly) (12 GF) ⊘ in 5 bedrooms s £80-£89; d £90-£99 (incl. bkfst) **FACILITIES:** Xmas **CONF:** Thtr 60 Class 50 Board 35 Del from £175 **PARKING:** 30 **NOTES:** Civ Wed 150 **CARDS:**

HANDFORTH See Manchester Airport

HARLOW, Essex Map 06 TL41

★★★65% *The Green Man Hotel*
Mulberry Green, Old Harlow CM17 0ET
☎ 0870 609 6146 📠 01279 626113

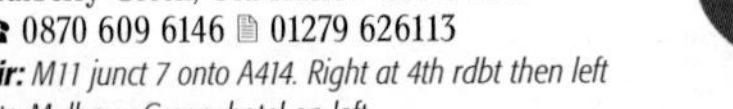

Dir: *M11 junct 7 onto A414. Right at 4th rdbt then left into Mulberry Green, hotel on left*

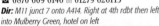

This popular coaching inn, dating back to the 14th century, is situated just a short drive from the town centre. The busy lounge bar is an enjoyable place for a drink, and there is also a trendy brasserie-style restaurant offering both carte and daily changing menus. Modern, well-equipped bedrooms are located at the rear of the property.
ROOMS: 55 annexe en suite (14 GF) ⊘ in 27 bedrooms **CONF:** Thtr 60 Class 26 Board 30 **PARKING:** 75 **NOTES:** ⊘ in restaurant
CARDS:

Travel Inn
Cambridge Rd CM20 2EP
☎ 08701 977125 📠 01279 452169
Dir: *M11(J7) onto A414 then A1184 Sawbridgeworth to Bishop's Stortford rd*

Travel Inn offers good-quality, value-for-money accommodation. Spacious, en suite rooms with bath and shower comfortably accommodate a family of up to two adults and two children (to age 15). The restaurant and bar offers a varied menu. For further details consult the Hotel Groups page.
ROOMS: 61 en suite s £45.95-£48.95; d £45.95-£48.95

Travelodge Harlow East (Stansted)
A414 Eastbound, Tylers Green, North Weald CM16 6BJ
☎ 08700 850 950 📠 01992 523276

Travelodge offers good quality, good value, modern accommodation. Ideal for families, the spacious, en suite bedrooms include remote-control TV, tea and coffee-making facilities and luxury beds. Meals can be taken at the nearby family restaurant. For further details consult the Hotel Groups page.
ROOMS: 60 en suite s fr £25; d fr £25

HAROME See Helmsley

HARPENDEN, Hertfordshire Map 06 TL11

★★★69% Corus hotel Harpenden
18 Southdown Rd AL5 1PE
☎ 01582 449955 📠 01582 769858
e-mail: harpendenhouse@corushotels.com
Dir: *M1 junct 10 left at rdbt. Next rdbt right onto A1081 to Harpenden. Over mini rdbt, through town centre and over next mini rdbt. Next rdbt left, hotel 200yds on left*

This attractive Grade II listed Georgian building overlooks East Common. The hotel gardens are particularly attractive and the public areas are stylishly decorated, including the restaurant that has an impressively decorated ceiling. Some of the bedrooms and a large suite are located in the original house but most of the accommodation is in the annexe.
ROOMS: 17 en suite 59 annexe en suite (13 fmly) (2 GF) ⊘ in 49 bedrooms s £35-£130; d £60-£150 **LB** **FACILITIES:** STV Complimentary use of local leisure centre **CONF:** BC Thtr 150 Class 60 Board 60 Del from £120 **PARKING:** 80 **NOTES:** ⊘ in restaurant RS wknds & BH's Civ Wed 120 **CARDS:**

> Popped the question?
> Hotels with Civ Wed in their entry are licensed for civil wedding ceremonies. Maximum numbers for the ceremony only are shown, e.g. Civ Wed 120

★★★66% **Hanover International Harpenden**
1 Luton Rd AL5 2PX
☎ 01582 760271 📠 01582 460819
e-mail: reception.harpenden@hanover-international.com
Dir: *M1 junct 10 to Luton Airport. At rdbt right for Harpenden on A1081 for 5m. Hotel on right beyond Oggelsby's Vauxhall garage*
Within easy reach of the M1, this hotel occupies a quiet location on the edge of town. Bedrooms are comfortable, providing guests with space and numerous facilities. A variety of well-appointed function rooms is also available for corporate or private use.
ROOMS: 60 en suite (12 fmly) (15 GF) ⊗ in 25 bedrooms s fr £110; d fr £130 **LB FACILITIES:** STV Free membership of local leisure club **CONF:** Thtr 150 Class 60 Board 44 **SERVICES:** Lift **PARKING:** 85 **NOTES:** Civ Wed 120 **CARDS:**

HARROGATE, North Yorkshire Map 19 SE35
See also Knaresborough

Top 200 – Hotel

★★★★ **Rudding Park Hotel & Golf**
Rudding Park, Follifoot HG3 1JH
☎ 01423 871350 📠 01423 872286
e-mail: sales@ruddingpark.com
web: www.ruddingpark.com
Dir: *from A61 at rdbt with A658 take York exit and follow signs to Rudding Park*
In the heart of 200-year-old landscaped parkland, this modern hotel is elegant and stylish. Bedrooms, including two luxurious suites, are smartly presented and thoughtfully equipped. Carefully prepared meals are served in the Clocktower, with its striking, contemporary decor. A spacious bar and comfortable lounges are also available. There is an adjoining 18-hole, par 72 golf course and an 18-bay floodlit, covered driving range.
ROOMS: 50 en suite (10 GF) ⊗ in 31 bedrooms s £135-£155; d £165-£178 (incl. bkfst) **LB FACILITIES:** STV 18 Putt green Driving range Jogging trail Membership of local gym Xmas **CONF:** BC Thtr 300 Class 150 Board 36 Del from £190 **SERVICES:** Lift **PARKING:** 150 **NOTES:** ⊗ in restaurant Civ Wed 300 **CARDS:**

Town House

★★★★ **Hotel du Vin & Bistro**
Prospect Place HG1 1LB
☎ 01423 856800 📠 01423 856801
e-mail: info@harrogate.hotelduvin.com
Dir: *Enter town centre & stay in right lane, pass West Park Church on right. Hotel on right*
The latest Hotel du Vin is a marvellous new town house overlooking the Stray. The spacious, open-plan lobby has seating, a bar and the reception desk. Hidden downstairs is a cosy snug cellar. The French-influenced Bistro offers high quality cooking and a great choice of wines. Bedrooms, including stunning loft suites, are smart and modern and have excellent showers.
ROOMS: 43 en suite (2 GF) s £95-£225; d £95-£225
FACILITIES: STV Snooker Gym Xmas **CONF:** Thtr 50 Board 20
SERVICES: Lift **PARKING:** 30 **NOTES:** Civ Wed 90
CARDS:

★★★★68% **The Majestic**
Ripon Rd HG1 2HU
☎ 01423 700300 📠 01423 521332
e-mail: majestic@paramount-hotels.co.uk
PARAMOUNT GROUP OF HOTELS
Dir: *from M1 onto A1(M) exit at Wetherby. Take A661 to Harrogate. Hotel in town centre adjacent to Royal Hall*
Popular for conferences and functions, this grand Victorian hotel is set in 12 acres of landscaped grounds and is centrally located within walking distance of the town centre. The bedrooms are comfortable, come in a variety of sizes and include several spacious suites.
ROOMS: 156 en suite (11 fmly) ⊗ in 86 bedrooms s £140-£150; d £212-£230 (incl. bkfst) **LB FACILITIES:** STV Squash Snooker Sauna Solarium Gym Jacuzzi Golf practice net Xmas **CONF:** BC Thtr 500 Class 250 Board 70 Del from £175 **SERVICES:** Lift **PARKING:** 250 **NOTES:** ⊗ in restaurant Civ Wed
CARDS:

AA Rosette Award for culinary excellence

HARROGATE, continued

★★★★65% Cedar Court

Queens Buildings, Park Pde HG1 5AH
☎ 01423 858585 & 858595(res)
01423 504950
e-mail: cedarcourt@bestwestern.co.uk
web: www.cedarcourthotels.co.uk/pages/cch/index.htm
Dir: *from A1(M) follow signs to Harrogate on A661 past Sainsburys. At rdbt left onto A6040. Hotel right after church*

Best Western

This Grade II listed building was Harrogate's first hotel and enjoys a peaceful location in landscaped grounds, close to the town centre. It has been carefully refurbished to provide spacious, well-equipped accommodation. Public areas include an elegant restaurant, a gymnasium and an open-plan lounge and bar. Functions and conferences are particularly well catered for.
ROOMS: 100 en suite (8 fmly) (7 GF) ⊗ in 75 bedrooms
FACILITIES: STV Gym **CONF:** BC Thtr 323 Class 90 Board 80 Del from £134 **SERVICES:** Lift **PARKING:** 150 **NOTES:** ⊗ in restaurant Civ Wed **CARDS:**

★★★79% The Boar's Head Hotel

Ripley Castle Estate HG3 3AY
☎ 01423 771888 01423 771509
e-mail: reservations@boarsheadripley.co.uk
Dir: *on A61 Harrogate to Ripon road. Hotel in centre of Ripley Village*

Situated in the private village of the Ripley Castle estate, this delightful and popular hotel is renowned for its warm hospitality and the restaurant, serving a mix of modern and traditional dishes. Bedrooms offer many comforts, and the luxurious day rooms feature works of art from the nearby castle.
ROOMS: 19 en suite 6 annexe en suite (2 fmly) ⊗ in 15 bedrooms s £105-£125; d £125-£150 (incl. bkfst) **LB** **FACILITIES:** Fishing Clay pigeon shooting ♫ ch fac Xmas **CONF:** Thtr 60 Class 35 Board 30 Del from £150 **PARKING:** 50 **NOTES:** ⊗ in restaurant Civ Wed 120
CARDS:

★★★74% Grants

3-13 Swan Rd HG1 2SS
☎ 01423 560666 01423 502550
e-mail: enquiries@grantshotel-harrogate.com
web: www.grantshotel-harrogate.com
Dir: *off A61*

A long established, family-run hotel with an attractive flower bedecked patio. The smartly presented, well-equipped bedrooms include some with four-poster beds. A comfortable lounge bar with plenty of interesting old photographs, and imaginative food in the colourful Chimney Pots Bistro, are just some of the features of this friendly hotel.
ROOMS: 42 en suite (2 fmly) s £75-£139; d £118.50-£174 (incl. bkfst)
LB **FACILITIES:** STV Use of local Health & Leisure Club Xmas
CONF: Thtr 70 Class 20 Board 30 **SERVICES:** Lift **PARKING:** 26
NOTES: ⊗ in restaurant **CARDS:**

★★★72% *Cutlers on the Stray*

19 West Park HG1 1BL
☎ 01423 524471 01423 506728
e-mail: info@cutlers-web.co.uk
Dir: *to Harrogate on A59 or A61 to Prince of Wales rdbt, follow signs for town centre, hotel 100yds right*

Enjoying a town centre location alongside one of the parks, this old coaching inn has been transformed into a trendy and stylish hotel and brasserie, offering contemporary-style accommodation. Taking its theme from its name, old cutlery adorns walls and reshaped spoons and forks become the room key-fobs and candle holders. Service is friendly and attentive and the versatile menus provide a great choice of dishes.
ROOMS: 19 en suite (1 fmly) (1 GF) ⊗ in 16 bedrooms
FACILITIES: Complimentary day pass available for local leisure & fitness centre **PARKING:** 10 **NOTES:** **CARDS:**

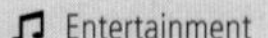
♫ Entertainment

★★★69% **The Yorkshire**
Prospect Place HG1 1LA
CRERAR HOTELS
☎ 01423 565071 📠 01423 500082
e-mail: theyorkshire@crerarhotels.com
web: www.crerarhotels.com
Dir: *follow A61 into town centre. Hotel opposite Betty's Tea Rooms*

Having undergone a major refurbishment of public areas, this town centre hotel has transformed itself into a smart, contemporary venue. It has two lounges, the fifth-floor Upstairs Restaurant and the modern HG1 Bar and Brasserie. All bedrooms are scheduled for a similar transformation.
ROOMS: 80 en suite (4 fmly) ⊗ in 52 bedrooms s £55-£90; d £85-£115 (incl. bkfst) **LB FACILITIES:** Xmas **CONF:** Thtr 150 Class 80 Board 80 Del from £110 **SERVICES:** Lift **PARKING:** 35 **NOTES:** ⊗ in restaurant **CARDS:**

★★★66% **Studley**
Swan Rd HG1 2SE
☎ 01423 560425 📠 01423 530967
e-mail: info@studleyhotel.co.uk web: www.studleyhotel.co.uk
Dir: *Swan Road adjacent to Valley Gardens, opp Mercer Gallery*
This friendly, well-established hotel, close to the town centre and Valley Gardens, is renowned for its Orchid Restaurant which provides a dynamic and authentic approach to Pacific Rim and Asian cuisine. Bedrooms come in a variety of styles and sizes, whilst the bar lounge provides a relaxing ambience.
ROOMS: 36 en suite (1 fmly) ⊗ in 6 bedrooms s £69-£100; d £89-£140 (incl. bkfst) **LB FACILITIES:** STV Free use of local Health & Spa Club Xmas **CONF:** Thtr 15 Class 15 Board 12 **SERVICES:** Lift **PARKING:** 15 **NOTES:** ⊗ in restaurant **CARDS:**

★★★59% **The Crown**
Crown Place HG1 2RZ
☎ 01423 567755 📠 01423 502284
e-mail: thecrown@corushotels.com
Dir: *A61 to Harrogate down Parliament St to traffic lights by Royal Hall. Left to Valley Gardens and 1st left to rdbt. Hotel on right*
Centrally situated, this hotel has been welcoming guests for the past 250 years. Bedrooms are mixed, both in standard and size but all have a movie channel and modem links. Public areas reflect a bygone era: tall ceilings and columns and plenty of space.
ROOMS: 121 en suite (8 fmly) ⊗ in 61 bedrooms s £92; d £92 **LB FACILITIES:** free use of local sports club Xmas **CONF:** Thtr 400 Class 200 Board 80 Del from £120 **SERVICES:** Lift **PARKING:** 25 **NOTES:** ⊗ in restaurant Civ Wed **CARDS:**

★★74% **Ascot House**
53 Kings Rd HG1 5HJ
☎ 01423 531005 📠 01423 503523
e-mail: admin@ascothouse.com
Dir: *follow town centre signs, Conference & Exhibition Centre into Kings Rd*
This late-Victorian house has been tastefully transformed into a

continued

friendly and meticulously maintained hotel. Near the International Conference Centre, it provides comfortable and extremely well-appointed bedrooms, an inviting lounge bar and a dining room offering an interesting choice at dinner.
ROOMS: 19 en suite (2 fmly) (5 GF) ⊗ in all bedrooms s £59-£71; d £87-£112 (incl. bkfst) **LB FACILITIES:** ch fac Xmas **CONF:** Thtr 80 Class 36 Board 36 Del from £99 **PARKING:** 14 **NOTES:** ⊗ in restaurant Closed 29 Dec-4 Jan & 23 Jan-6 Feb Civ Wed 80
CARDS:

Restaurant with Rooms

Harrogate Brasserie Hotel & Bar
28-30 Cheltenham Pde HG1 1DB
THE INDEPENDENTS HOTEL ASSOCIATION
☎ 01423 505041 📠 01423 722300
e-mail: info@brasserie.co.uk web: www.brasserie.co.uk
Dir: *on A61 town centre behind theatre*

This town centre hotel is distinctly continental in style and provides

continued on p256

HARROGATE, continued

individual, bold bedrooms. The popular brasserie features live jazz on Friday and Sunday nights, with a jazz pianist on Wednesday evenings. The menu offers popular dishes, including blackboard specials, makes good use of seasonal produce.
ROOMS: 17 en suite (3 fmly) s fr £52.50; d £75-£95 (incl. bkfst) **LB**
FACILITIES: ♫ Xmas **PARKING:** 12 **NOTES:** Closed 26 & 31 Dec
CARDS:

Innkeeper's Lodge Harrogate West
Otley Rd, Beckwith Knowle HG3 1PR
☎ 01423 533091 📠 01423 533092
www.innkeeperslodge.com
Dir: *from A1(M) junct 47, take A59 for Harrogate. Over 2 rdbts, at 3rd rdbt straight over onto B6162. Hotel on left opp church*
Smart rooms meet essential business requirements but also have home comforts, and depending on location may well have meeting rooms and pub dining. Dining options generally include all-day menus plus the added advantage of breakfast.
ROOMS: 11 en suite s £55; d £55 **CONF:** Thtr 30 Class 30 Board 30

Travel Inn Harrogate
Hornbeam Park Ave, Hornbeam Park HG2 8RA
☎ 08701 977 126 📠 01423 878581
Dir: *A1(M) junct 46 west then A661 to Harrogate. After 2m left at The Woodlands lights. Hornbeam Park Avenue 1.5m on left*
Travel Inn offers good-quality, value-for-money accommodation. Spacious, en suite rooms with bath and shower comfortably accommodate a family of up to two adults and two children (to age 15). The restaurant and bar offers a varied menu. For further details consult the Hotel Groups page.
ROOMS: 50 en suite s £45.95-£48.95; d £45.95-£48.95

Travelodge (Harrogate)
The Gubbel HG1 2RF
☎ 0870 1911737 📠 01423562734
Travelodge offers good quality, good value, modern accommodation. Ideal for families, the spacious, en suite bedrooms include remote-control TV, tea and coffee-making facilities and luxury beds. Meals can be taken at the nearby family restaurant. For further details consult the Hotel Groups page.
ROOMS: 46 en suite s fr £25; d fr £25

HARROW, Greater London
See LONDON SECTION plan 1 B5

★★★69% Best Western Cumberland
1 St Johns Rd HA1 2EF
☎ 020 8863 4111 📠 020 8861 5668
e-mail: reservatons@cumberlandhotel.co.uk
web: www.cumberlandhotel.co.uk
Dir: *from A404 or A409 into Gayton Rd, then into Lyon Rd. Hotel at end*
Situated within walking distance of the town centre, this hotel is ideally located for all local attractions and amenities. Bedrooms provide good levels of comfort and are practically equipped to meet the requirements of all travellers. Impressive public areas include a restaurant and newly refurbished bar, both serving a good variety of fresh food.

ROOMS: 31 en suite 53 annexe en suite (5 fmly) (15 GF) ⊗ in 51 bedrooms s £45-£98; d £55-£110 (incl. bkfst) **LB** **FACILITIES:** STV Sauna Gym Xmas **CONF:** Thtr 130 Class 70 Board 62 Del from £110
PARKING: 67 **NOTES:** ⊗ in restaurant
CARDS:

★★★68% Quality Harrow Hotel
12-22 Pinner Rd HA1 4HZ
☎ 020 8427 3435 📠 020 8861 1370
e-mail: info@harrowhotel.co.uk
web: www.harrowhotel.co.uk
Dir: *off rdbt on A404 at junct with A312*

This privately owned hotel offers a great variety of accommodation to suit all needs. At the top of the range are the new air-conditioned executive rooms and suites. These have hi-tech facilities including MD/CD, interactive TV and multiple phone lines. Public areas comprise a bar, conservatory lounge, meeting rooms and a smart restaurant.
ROOMS: 79 en suite 23 annexe en suite (2 fmly) ⊗ in 48 bedrooms s fr £98; d fr £113 (incl. bkfst) **FACILITIES:** STV **CONF:** Thtr 160 Class 60 Board 60 Del from £130 **SERVICES:** Lift **PARKING:** 70 **NOTES:** ⊗ in restaurant RS Xmas (limited service) Civ Wed 80
CARDS:

See advert on opposite page

★★59% The Lindal
2 Hindes Rd HA1 1SJ
☎ 020 8863 3164 020 8427 5435
Dir: *Turn off M40 or M1 towards Harrow, hotel is off A409, opposite Tesco*

This family-run hotel is conveniently located for the local shopping centre and provides good transport links to the centre of London. Bedrooms are modern and attractively furnished. Day rooms consist of a combined bar-lounge area and dining room.
ROOMS: 24 en suite (3 fmly) in 9 bedrooms **PARKING:** 21
NOTES: No children 6yrs in restaurant
CARDS:

HARROW WEALD, Greater London
LONDON SECTION plan 1 B6

★★★68% Grim's Dyke
Old Redding HA3 6SH
☎ 020 8385 3100 020 8954 4560
e-mail: enquiries@grimsdyke.com web: www.grimsdyke.com
Dir: *Turn off A410 onto A409 North towards Bushey, at top of hill traffic lights turn left into Old Redding*
Once home to Sir William Gilbert, this Grade II mansion contains many references to well-known Gilbert and Sullivan productions. The house is set in over 40 acres of beautiful parkland and gardens. Rooms in the main house are elegant and traditional, while those in the adjacent lodge are aimed more at the business guest.
ROOMS: 9 en suite 35 annexe en suite (15 GF) in 20 bedrooms s £125-£300; d £155-£300 (incl. bkfst) **LB** **FACILITIES:** STV Putt green Gilbert ans Sullivan opera dinner fortnightly. **CONF:** BC Thtr 100 Class 80 Board 32 Del from £160 **PARKING:** 97 **NOTES:** in restaurant RS 24-26 Dec Civ Wed 90 **CARDS:**

HARTINGTON, Derbyshire Map 16 SK16

A ★★ Biggin Hall
SK17 0DH
☎ 01298 84451 01298 84681
e-mail: enquiries@bigginhall.co.uk
web: www.bigginhall.co.uk
Dir: *0.5m off A515 midway between Ashbourne and Buxton*
ROOMS: 20 en suite (4 fmly) (4 GF) in 3 bedrooms s £58-£90; d £66-£116 (incl. bkfst) **LB** **FACILITIES:** Xmas **CONF:** Thtr 20 Class 20 Board 20 Del from £85 **PARKING:** 25 **NOTES:** No children 12yrs in restaurant **CARDS:**

See advert on this page

HARTLEBURY, Worcestershire Map 10 SO87

Travelodge

Shorthill Nurseries DY13 9SH
☎ 08700 850 950 01299 251774
Dir: A449 southbound
Travelodge offers good quality, good value, modern accommodation. Ideal for families, the spacious, en suite bedrooms include remote-control TV, tea and coffee-making facilities and luxury beds. Meals can be taken at the nearby family restaurant. For further details consult the Hotel Groups page.
ROOMS: 32 en suite s fr £25; d fr £25

HARTLEPOOL, Co Durham Map 19 NZ53

Travel Inn

Maritme Av, Hartlepool Marina TS24 0XZ
☎ 08701 977127 01429 233105
Dir: approx 1m from A689/A179 link road on marina
Travel Inn offers good-quality, value-for-money accommodation. Spacious, en suite rooms with bath and shower comfortably accommodate a family of up to two adults and two children (to age 15). The restaurant and bar offers a varied menu. For further details consult the Hotel Groups page.
ROOMS: 40 en suite s £45.95-£46.95; d £45.95-£46.95

HARTSHEAD MOOR MOTORWAY SERVICE AREA (M62), West Yorkshire Map 19 SE12

Days Inn

Hartshead Moor Service Area, Clifton HD6 4JX
☎ 01274 851706 01274 855169
e-mail: hartsheadmoor.hotel@welcomebreak.co.uk
web: www.welcomebreak.co.uk
Dir: M62 between junct 25 and 26
This modern building offers accommodation in smart, spacious and well-equipped bedrooms, suitable for families and business travellers, and all with en suite bathrooms. Continental breakfast is available and other refreshments may be taken at the nearby family restaurant. For further details see the Hotel Groups page.
ROOMS: 38 en suite s £45-£55; d £45-£55
CONF: Board 10 Del from £35

HARWICH, Essex Map 13 TM23

★★★74% The Pier at Harwich

The Quay CO12 3HH
☎ 01255 241212 01255 551922
e-mail: pier@milsomhotels.com
Dir: from A12, take A120 to Quay. Hotel opposite lifeboat station

This hotel is situated on the quay, overlooking the ports of Harwich and Felixstowe. The bedrooms are tastefully decorated, thoughtfully equipped, and furnished in a contemporary style; many rooms have superb sea views. Public rooms include an informal bistro, the Harbour restaurant, a smart lounge bar and a plush residents' lounge.
ROOMS: 7 en suite 7 annexe en suite (5 fmly) (1 GF) **FACILITIES:** STV Xmas **CONF:** Thtr 50 Class 50 Board 24 **PARKING:** 10 **NOTES:** in restaurant Civ Wed 50 **CARDS:**

★★68% Cliff

Marine Pde, Dovercourt CO12 3RE
☎ 01255 503345 & 507373 01255 240358
e-mail: reception@thecliffhotelharwich.fsnet.co.uk
web: www.thecliffhotelharwich.co.uk
Dir: A120 to Parkeston rdbt, take road to Dovercourt, on seafront after Dovercourt town centre

Conveniently situated on the seafront close to the railway station and ferry terminal. The newly refurbished public rooms are smartly appointed and include the Shade Bar, a comfortable lounge, a restaurant and the Marine Bar with views of Dovercourt Bay. The pleasantly decorated bedrooms have co-ordinated soft furnishings and modern facilities; many have sea views.
ROOMS: 26 en suite (3 fmly) in 1 bedroom s £55-£60; d £65-£70 (incl. bkfst) **LB** **FACILITIES:** STV Jacuzzi **CONF:** Thtr 200 Class 150 Board 40 Del from £85 **PARKING:** 50 **NOTES:** RS Xmas & New Year
CARDS:

★★68% *Hotel Continental*

28/29 Marine Pde, Dovercourt CO12 3RG
☎ 01255 551298 01255 551698
e-mail: hotconti@aol.com
web: www.hotelcontinental-harwich.co.uk
Dir: off A120 at Ramsay rdbt onto B1352 to pedestrian crossing and Co-op store on right, turn right into Fronks Rd
A privately owned hotel situated on the seafront within easy reach of the ferry terminals and town centre. Bedrooms are pleasantly decorated, well equipped and have many innovative features; some rooms also have lovely sea views. Public rooms include a popular lounge bar, a restaurant and a non-smoking lounge.
ROOMS: 14 en suite (2 fmly) in 1 bedroom **FACILITIES: Spa** STV
CONF: Thtr 10 **PARKING:** 4 **NOTES:** in restaurant
CARDS:

See advert on opposite page

HASLEMERE, Surrey Map 06 SU93

★★★★71% Lythe Hill Hotel and Spa
Petworth Rd GU27 3BQ
☎ 01428 651251 01428 644131
e-mail: lythe@lythehill.co.uk
web: www.lythehill.co.uk
Dir: *left from Haslemere High St onto B2131. Lythe Hill 1.25m on right*

This privately owned hotel sits in 30 acres of attractive parkland with lakes, complete with roaming geese. The hotel has been described as a hamlet of character buildings, each furnished in a style that complements the age of the property; the oldest one dating back to 1475. Cuisine in the adjacent 'Auberge de France' offers interesting, quality dishes, whilst breakfast is served in the hotel dining room. The bedrooms are split between a number of 15th-century buildings and vary in size. The stylish, new Spa includes a 16-metre swimming pool.
ROOMS: 41 en suite (8 fmly) (18 GF) **FACILITIES: Spa** STV Fishing Sauna Solarium Gym Boules Games Room ch fac Xmas **CONF:** Thtr 60 Class 40 Board 30 Del £209 **PARKING:** 200 **NOTES:** in restaurant Civ Wed 128 **CARDS:**

★★★67% Georgian House Hotel
High St GU27 2JY
☎ 01428 656644 01428 645600
e-mail: mail@georgianhousehotel.com
web: www.georgianhousehotel.com
Dir: *A3 onto A287 then A286. Past station, hotel on left on High St*
An attractive and imposing Georgian building, situated on the high street. Bedrooms in the old wing offer the most character with oak beams and four-poster beds, and all rooms are spacious and well-furnished. Public areas include a bar and restaurant, while the newly-opened leisure centre boasts an indoor pool and jacuzzi.
ROOMS: 51 en suite (7 GF) in 11 bedrooms s £74-£82.95; d £74-£111.90 (incl. bkfst) **LB** **FACILITIES:** STV supervised Sauna Solarium Gym Jacuzzi Beauty treatments **CONF:** Thtr 150 Class 50 Board 30 Del from £99 **SERVICES:** Lift **PARKING:** 50 **NOTES:** Civ Wed 60 **CARDS:**

HASTINGS & ST LEONARDS, East Sussex Map 07 TQ80

★★★70% Beauport Park
Battle Rd TN38 8EA
☎ 01424 851222 01424 852465
e-mail: reservations@beauportprkhotel.co.uk
web: www.beauportparkhotel.co.uk
Dir: *3m N off A2100*
Elegant Georgian manor house set in 40 acres of mature gardens on the outskirts of Hastings. The individually decorated bedrooms are tastefully furnished and thoughtfully equipped with modern facilities. Public rooms convey much of the original character and

continued on p260

HASTINGS & ST LEONARDS, continued

feature a large conservatory, a lounge bar, a restaurant and a further lounge, as well as conference and banqueting rooms.

Beauport Park, Hastings & St Leonards

ROOMS: 25 en suite (2 fmly) ⊗ in 11 bedrooms s £95; d £130 (incl. bkfst) **LB** **FACILITIES:** STV 18 Riding Putt green Country walks around estate ch fac Xmas **CONF:** Thtr 70 Class 25 Board 30 Del from £120 **PARKING:** 60 **NOTES:** ⊗ in restaurant Civ Wed 70
CARDS:

See advert on page 259

★★★67% *Cinque Ports Hotel*

Bohemia Rd TN34 1ET
☎ 01424 439222 01424 437277
e-mail: enquiries@cinqueports.co.uk
web: www.cinqueports.co.uk
Dir: *A21 into Hastings. Police HQ and courts on left, hotel next left before ambulance HQ*

THE CIRCLE
Selected Individual Hotels
GREAT BRITAIN

This modern hotel enjoys a central location and is close to the coast. Features of the public areas include old flagstone floors, oriental rugs, hanging tapestries, beams and open fireplaces. Bedrooms are well equipped and offer a good degree of comfort throughout.
ROOMS: 40 en suite (8 fmly) ⊗ in 6 bedrooms **FACILITIES:** STV free m/ship at next door leisure centre **CONF:** Thtr 250 Class 150 Board 120 **PARKING:** 80 **NOTES:** ⊗ in restaurant
CARDS:

★★★67% **High Beech**

Battle Rd TN37 7BS
☎ 01424 851383 01424 854265
e-mail: highbeech@barbox.net
Dir: *400yds from A2100 between Hastings and Battle*

A privately owned hotel situated between the historic towns of Hastings and Battle in a woodland setting. The generously proportioned bedrooms are pleasantly decorated and thoughtfully equipped. Public rooms include St. Patricks Bar, which also doubles as the lounge area, and the elegant Wedgwood Restaurant where an interesting and varied menu is served.

ROOMS: 17 en suite (4 fmly) ⊗ in all bedrooms s £65-£75; d £95-£125 (incl. bkfst) **LB** **FACILITIES:** STV ch fac **CONF:** Thtr 250 Class 60 Board 50 Del from £85 **PARKING:** 60 **NOTES:** ⊗ in restaurant
CARDS:

See advert on opposite page

★★★66% *Royal Victoria*

Marina, St Leonards-on-Sea TN38 0BD
☎ 01424 445544 01424 721995
e-mail: reception@royalvichotel.co.uk
web: www.royalvichotel.co.uk
Dir: *on A259 seafront road 1m W of Hastings pier*

This imposing 18th-century property is situated in a prominent position overlooking the sea. A superb marble staircase leads up from the lobby to the main public areas on the first floor, which has panoramic views of the sea. The spacious bedrooms are pleasantly decorated and well equipped, and include duplex and family suites.
ROOMS: 50 en suite (15 fmly) **CONF:** Thtr 100 Class 40 Board 40 **SERVICES:** Lift **PARKING:** 6 **NOTES:** ⊗ in restaurant Civ Wed 50
CARDS:

Bad hair day?
Hairdryers in all rooms three stars and above

★★69% **Chatsworth**

Carlisle Pde TN34 1JG
☎ 01424 720188 01424 445865
e-mail: mail@chatsworthhotel.com
Dir: *A21 to town centre. At seafront turn right before next set of lights.*

Enjoying a central position on the seafront, close to the pier, this much-improved hotel is a short walk from the old town and within easy reach of East Sussex's many attractions. Bedrooms are

continued

smartly decorated, equipped with a range of extras and many rooms enjoy splendid sea views.

ROOMS: 52 en suite (5 fmly) ⊗ in 10 bedrooms s fr £65; d fr £85 (incl. bkfst) **LB** **FACILITIES:** Xmas **CONF:** Thtr 40 Class 20 Board 20 Del from £65 **SERVICES:** Lift **PARKING:** 8 **NOTES:** ⊗ in restaurant **CARDS:** 

See advert on this page

Travel Inn
1 John Macadam Way, St Leonards on Sea
TN37 7DB
☎ 08701 977128 📠 01424 756911
Dir: *into Hastings on A21, Travel Inn on right after junct with A2100 Battle road*
Travel Inn offers good-quality, value-for-money accommodation. Spacious, en suite rooms with bath and shower comfortably accommodate a family of up to two adults and two children (to age 15). The restaurant and bar offers a varied menu. For further details consult the Hotel Groups page.
ROOMS: 44 en suite s £45.95-£46.95; d £45.95-£46.95

HATFIELD, Hertfordshire Map 06 TL20

★★★70% Bush Hall
Mill Green AL9 5NT
☎ 01707 271251 📠 01707 272289
e-mail: enquiries@bush-hall.com
Dir: *From A1(M) exit at junct 4. 2nd left at rdbt onto A414 signed Hertford & Welwyn Garden City. Turn left at rdbt onto A1000. Hotel on left.*

Standing in delightful grounds with a river running through it, this hotel boasts extensive facilities. Outdoor enthusiasts can enjoy a range of activities including go-karting and clay pigeon shooting. Bedrooms and public areas are comfortable and tastefully decorated. Kipling's restaurant continues to offer a wide range

continued on p262

HATFIELD, continued

freshly prepared dishes using quality produce; service is both professional and friendly.
ROOMS: 25 en suite (2 fmly) (8 GF) s £79.50-£125; d £99.50-£185 **FACILITIES:** Clay pigeon shooting, archery, quad bikes and karting - pre booked only **CONF:** Thtr 150 Class 70 Board 50 Del from £155 **PARKING:** 100 **NOTES:** Closed 26 Dec-3 Jan Civ Wed 160 **CARDS:**

★★★65% Quality Hotel Hatfield

Roehyde Way AL10 9AF
☎ 01707 275701 01707 266033
e-mail: enquiries@hotels-hatfield.com
Dir: *M25 junct 23 take A1(M) northbound to junct 2. At rdbt take exit left, hotel 0.5m on right*
The well-equipped rooms at this hotel feature extras such as trouser presses and modem access. Executive rooms are very spacious. Room service is 24 hour, or guests may dine in the bar or main restaurant, where service is informal and friendly.
ROOMS: 76 en suite (14 fmly) (39 GF) in 39 bedrooms s £105-£130; d £115-£140 **LB** **FACILITIES:** STV Xmas **CONF:** Thtr 120 Class 60 Board 50 **PARKING:** 120 **NOTES:** in restaurant **CARDS:**

Travel Inn

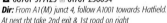

Comet Way, Lemsford Rd AL10 0DA
☎ 08701 977129 01707 256054
Dir: *From A1(M) junct 4, follow A1001 towards Hatfield. At next rbt take 2nd exit & 1st road on right*
Travel Inn offers good-quality, value-for-money accommodation. Spacious, en suite rooms with bath and shower comfortably accommodate a family of up to two adults and two children (to age 15). The restaurant and bar offers a varied menu. For further details consult the Hotel Groups page.
ROOMS: 40 en suite s £45.95-£48.95; d £45.95-£48.95

HATHERSAGE, Derbyshire — Map 16 SK28

★★★73% The George at Hathersage

Main Rd S32 1BB
☎ 01433 650436 01433 650099
e-mail: info@george-hotel.net
web: www.george-hotel.net
Dir: *in village centre on A6187 SW of Sheffield*
The George is a relaxing 500-year-old hostelry in the heart of this picturesque town. The beamed bar and lounge has great character, and the restaurant is full of antique charm. Upstairs the decor is simpler with lots of light hues; the split-level and four-poster rooms are especially appealing. Quality cooking is served in the modern restaurant.
ROOMS: 19 en suite (2 fmly) in 4 bedrooms s £69-£140; d £100-£162 (incl. bkfst) **LB** **FACILITIES:** Xmas **CONF:** Thtr 80 Class 20 Board 36 Del from £135 **PARKING:** 40 **NOTES:** in restaurant Civ Wed 50 **CARDS:**

HAVANT, Hampshire — Map 05 SU70

Travel Inn (Havant Portsmouth)

65 Bedhampton Hill, Bedhampton PO9 3JN
☎ 08701 977130 023 9245 3471
Dir: *on rdbt just off A3(M) to Bedhampton*
Travel Inn offers good-quality, value-for-money accommodation. Spacious, en suite rooms with bath and shower comfortably accommodate a family of up to two adults and two children (to age 15). The restaurant and bar offers a varied menu. For further details consult the Hotel Groups page.
ROOMS: 36 en suite s £45.95-£48.95; d £45.95-£48.95

HAWES, North Yorkshire — Map 18 SD88

★★73% Simonstone Hall

Simonstone DL8 3LY
☎ 01969 667255 01969 667741
e-mail: hotel@simonstonehall.demon.co.uk
web: www.simonstonehall.co.uk
Dir: *1.5m N on road signed to Muker and Buttertubs*
This former hunting lodge provides professional, friendly service and a relaxed atmosphere. There is an inviting drawing room, stylish fine dining restaurant and a bar and new conservatory. The generally spacious bedrooms are elegantly finished to reflect the style of the house, and many offer spectacular views of the countryside.
ROOMS: 18 en suite (10 fmly) (2 GF) in all bedrooms s £55-£120; d £110-£240 (incl. bkfst) **LB** **FACILITIES:** ch fac Xmas **CONF:** Thtr 50 Class 20 Board 20 Del from £165 **PARKING:** 40 **NOTES:** in restaurant Civ Wed **CARDS:**

★★72% Stone House

Sedbusk DL8 3PT
☎ 01969 667571 01969 667720
e-mail: daleshotel@aol.com
Dir: *from Hawes take road signed 'Muker & The Buttertubs' to T- junct then right to Sedbusk & Askrigg. Hotel 500yds on left*
Benefiting from a rural location with spectacular views of the unspoiled Wensleydale countryside, this elegant Georgian hotel is bursting with character. Bedrooms are comfortably furnished; many have luxurious bathrooms and some have their own private conservatories. Public rooms include a well-stocked library and several comfortable lounges.
ROOMS: 18 rms (17 en suite) 5 annexe en suite (1 fmly) (7 GF) in 22 bedrooms s £45-£103; d £77-£103 (incl. bkfst) **LB** **FACILITIES:** Billiards table ch fac Xmas **CONF:** Thtr 35 Class 35 Board 35 **PARKING:** 30 **NOTES:** in restaurant RS Dec & Jan **CARDS:**

HAWKSHEAD (NEAR AMBLESIDE), Cumbria — Map 18 SD39

★★70% Queen's Head

Main St LA22 0NS
☎ 015394 36271 015394 36722
e-mail: enquiries@queensheadhotel.co.uk
web: www.queensheadhotel.co.uk
Dir: *M6 junct 36, then A590 to Newby Bridge. Over rdbt, 1st right for 8m into Hawkshead*

This 16th-century inn features a wood-panelled bar with low,

continued

oak-beamed ceilings and an open log fire. Substantial, carefully prepared meals are served in the bar and in the pretty dining room. The bedrooms, three of which are in an adjacent cottage, are attractively furnished and include some four-poster rooms.
ROOMS: 11 rms (9 en suite) 3 annexe en suite (2 fmly) (2 GF) ⊗ in all bedrooms s £47.50; d £68 (incl. bkfst) **LB FACILITIES:** ch fac Xmas **NOTES:** ⊗ in restaurant **CARDS:**

See advert on this page

HAWORTH, West Yorkshire Map 19 SE03

★★71% Old White Lion

Main St BD22 8DU
☎ 01535 642313 01535 646222
e-mail: enquiries@oldwhitelionhotel.com
Dir: *turn off A629 onto B6142, hotel 0.5m past Haworth Station. Hotel at top of cobbled main street leading to Tourist Info Centre*

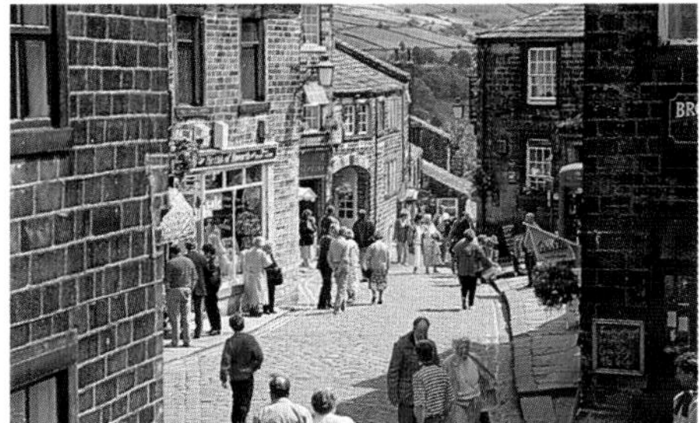

Prominently situated at the top of the old cobbled street in this popular village, this hotel is steeped in history. There is a small oak-panelled residents' lounge and a choice of cosy bars, serving a range of meals. Formal dining is available in the popular restaurant. Comfortably furnished bedrooms are well equipped and vary in size and style.
ROOMS: 15 en suite (3 fmly) s £48-£58; d £66.50-£76.50 (incl. bkfst) **LB FACILITIES:** STV Xmas **CONF:** Thtr 90 Class 20 Board 38 **PARKING:** 10 **NOTES:** **CARDS:**

See advert under BRADFORD

Restaurant with Rooms

Weavers Bar Restaurant with Rooms

13-17 West Ln BD22 8DU
☎ 01535 643822 01535 644832
e-mail: weaversinhaworth@amserve.net
web: www.weaversmallhotel.co.uk
Dir: *A629/B6142 towards Haworth, Stanbury and Colne. At top of village pass Brontë Weaving Shed on right. Left after 100yds to Parsonage car park*

Centrally located on the cobbled main street, this family-owned

continued

restaurant and bar provides well-equipped, stylish and comfortable bedrooms. Each of the three rooms is en suite and boast many thoughtful extras. The kitchen serves modern and traditional dishes with flair and creativity.
ROOMS: 3 en suite s fr £55; d fr £80 (incl. bkfst) **NOTES:** ⊗ in restaurant RS Sun/Mon **CARDS:**

HAYDOCK, Merseyside Map 15 SJ59

Travel Inn

Yew Tree Way, Golborne WA3 3JD
☎ 08701 977131 01942 296100
Dir: *M6 junct 23, take A580 towards Manchester. Then approx 2m passing over one major rdbt. Travel Inn on left*
Travel Inn offers good-quality, value-for-money accommodation. Spacious, en suite rooms with bath and shower comfortably accommodate a family of up to two adults and two children (to age 15). The restaurant and bar offers a varied menu. For further details consult the Hotel Groups page.
ROOMS: 60 en suite s £45.95-£46.95; d £45.95-£46.95

Travelodge

Travelodge

Piele Rd WA11 0JZ
☎ 08700 850 950 01942 272067
Dir: *2m W of junct 23 on M6, on A580 westbound*
Travelodge offers good quality, good value, modern accommodation. Ideal for families, the spacious, en suite bedrooms include remote-control TV, tea and coffee-making facilities and luxury beds. Meals can be taken at the nearby family restaurant. For further details consult the Hotel Groups page.
ROOMS: 62 en suite s fr £25; d fr £25

HAYLE, Cornwall & Isles of Scilly Map 02 SW53

Travel Inn
Carwin Rise TR27 4PN
☎ 08701 977133 01736 759514
Dir: *on A30 at Loggans Moor rdbt, take 1st exit on left, Carwin Rise, Travel Inn on right*
Travel Inn offers good-quality, value-for-money accommodation. Spacious, en suite rooms with bath and shower comfortably accommodate a family of up to two adults and two children (to age 15). The restaurant and bar offers a varied menu. For further details consult the Hotel Groups page.
ROOMS: 40 en suite s £45.95-£46.95; d £45.95-£46.95

HAYTOR VALE, Devon Map 03 SX77

★★75% Rock Inn
TQ13 9XP
☎ 01364 661305 & 661465 01364 661242
e-mail: inn@rock-inn.co.uk
Dir: *off A38 onto A382 to Bovey Tracey, after 0.5m turn left onto B3387 to Haytor*
Dating back to the 1750s, this former coaching inn is in a pretty hamlet on the edge of Dartmoor. Each named after a Grand National winner, the individually decorated bedrooms have some nice extra touches. Bars are full of character, with flagstone floors and old beams and offer a wide range of dishes, cooked with imagination and flair.
ROOMS: 9 en suite (2 fmly) in 2 bedrooms s £65.50; d £75.95-£85.95 (incl. bkfst) **LB** **FACILITIES:** STV **PARKING:** 20 **NOTES:** **CARDS:**

HAYWARDS HEATH, West Sussex Map 06 TQ32

★★★68% The Birch Hotel
Lewes Rd RH17 7SF
☎ 01444 451565 01444 440109
e-mail: info@birch-hotel.co.uk
Dir: *on A272 opposite Princess Royal Hospital and behind Shell Garage*
Originally the home of an eminent Harley Street surgeon, this attractive Victorian property has been extended to combine modern facilities with the charm of its original period. Public rooms include the conservatory-style Pavilion Restaurant, along with an open-plan lounge and brasserie-style bar serving a range of snacks.
ROOMS: 51 en suite (3 fmly) (12 GF) in 23 bedrooms s £63-£89; d £83-£99 (incl. bkfst) **FACILITIES:** STV **CONF:** Thtr 60 Class 30 Board 26 Del from £130 **PARKING:** 60 **NOTES:** in restaurant Civ Wed 60 **CARDS:**

HEATHROW AIRPORT (LONDON), Greater London
See LONDON SECTION plan 1 A3
See also Slough & Staines

★★★★76%
Crowne Plaza London - Heathrow
Stockley Rd UB7 9NA
☎ 0870 400 9140 01895 445122
e-mail: reservations.cplhr@ichotelsgroup.com
Dir: *M4 junct 4 follow signs to Uxbridge on A408, hotel 400yds on left*
This hotel is conveniently located for access to Heathrow Airport and the motorway network. It offers a very good range of facilities, including versatile conference and meeting rooms, golfing and a leisure complex. Guests have the choice of two bars, both serving food, and two restaurants. Air-conditioned bedrooms are furnished and decorated to a high standard and feature a comprehensive range of extra facilities.

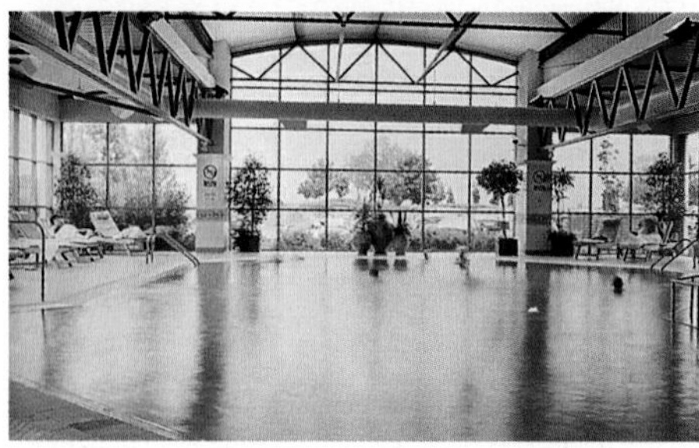

ROOMS: 458 en suite (237 fmly) (35 GF) in 370 bedrooms s £78-£250; d £78-£250 **LB** **FACILITIES:** STV supervised 9 Sauna Solarium Gym Jacuzzi Beauty room **CONF:** BC Thtr 200 Class 120 Board 75 Del from £170 **SERVICES:** Lift air con **PARKING:** 410 **NOTES:** **CARDS:**

★★★★73%
London Marriott Hotel Heathrow
Bath Rd UB3 5AN
☎ 020 8990 1100 020 8990 1110
Dir: *M4 junct 4, follow Terminal 1 2 & 3 signs via M4 and Heathrow Airport. Left at rdbt signed A4/London. Hotel 0.5m left through 2 sets of traffic lights*
This smart, modern hotel, with its striking design, meets all the expectations of a successful airport hotel. The light and airy atrium offers several eating and drinking options, each with a different theme. Spacious bedrooms are appointed to a good standard with an excellent range of facilities, and there are some indoor leisure facilities.
ROOMS: 390 en suite (140 fmly) in 327 bedrooms s fr £135; d fr £135 **FACILITIES: Spa** STV supervised Sauna Solarium Gym Steam Room Xmas **CONF:** BC Thtr 550 Class 220 Board 65 Del from £150 **SERVICES:** Lift air con **PARKING:** 220 **NOTES:** Civ Wed 112 **CARDS:**

★★★★72% Sheraton Skyline
Bath Rd UB3 5BP
☎ 020 8759 2535 020 8750 9150
e-mail: res268_skyline@sheraton.com
Dir: *M4 junct 4 for Heathrow, follow Terminal 1,2 & 3 signs. Before airport entrance take slip road to left for 0.25m signed A4 Central London*
Within easy reach of all terminals this hotel offers well appointed bedrooms featuring air conditioning. Newly refurbished rooms provide enhanced levels of quality and comfort. The extensive, contemporary public areas are light and spacious, and include a wide range of eating and drinking options, function rooms and a gym.
ROOMS: 350 en suite (12 fmly) in 212 bedrooms s £85-£225; d £85-£225 **LB** **FACILITIES:** STV Gym Pool table Xmas **CONF:** BC Thtr 500 Class 325 Board 100 Del from £150 **SERVICES:** Lift air con **PARKING:** 320 **NOTES:** RS Xmas Civ Wed 200 **CARDS:**

Indoor Swimming Pool
Indoor Swimming Pool (heated)
Outdoor Swimming Pool
Outdoor Swimming Pool (heated)

★★★★70%
Slough/Windsor Marriott Hotel

Ditton Rd, Langley SL3 8PT
☎ 0870 400 7244 🖹 0870 400 7344
e-mail: reservations.sloughwindsor@marriotthotels.co.uk
web: www.marriott.co.uk/LHRSL
Dir: *M4 junct 5, follow 'Langley' signs and left at lights into Ditton Rd*
Ideally located for access to Heathrow and the M4, this smart hotel offers a wide range of facilities. The well-appointed leisure centre includes a spa, gym and pool. Extensive conference facilities, a bar offering 24hr snacks and light meals and a restaurant offering a wide range of cuisine are also available. Spacious bedrooms are well equipped for both leisure and business guests.
ROOMS: 382 en suite (120 fmly) (96 GF) ⊗ in 267 bedrooms s fr £84; d fr £84 **FACILITIES:** STV supervised Sauna Solarium Gym **CONF:** Thtr 400 Class 220 Board 42 Del from £130 **SERVICES:** Lift air con **PARKING:** 550 **NOTES:** ⊗ in restaurant Civ Wed 250 **CARDS:**

★★★★66% **The Renaissance London Heathrow Hotel**
Bath Rd TW6 2AQ
☎ 020 8897 6363 🖹 020 8897 1113
e-mail: lhrrenaissance@aol.com
Dir: *M4 junct 4 follow spur road towards airport, take 2nd left. At rdbt take 2nd exit signposted 'Renaissance Hotel'. Hotel next to Customs House*
Located right on the perimeter of the airport, this hotel commands superb views over the runways. Smartly refurbished bedrooms are fully soundproofed and equipped with air conditioning, each room is well suited to meet the needs of today's business traveller. The hotel boasts extensive conference facilities, and is a very popular venue for air travellers and conference organisers.
ROOMS: 649 en suite (59 GF) ⊗ in 468 bedrooms s £80-£189; d £80-£189 **LB FACILITIES:** STV Sauna Solarium Gym Steam Room Fitness Studio Massage treatment Personal trainer, studio classes Xmas **CONF:** BC Thtr 400 Class 300 Board 110 Del from £169 **SERVICES:** Lift air con **PARKING:** 700 **NOTES:** Civ Wed 100 **CARDS:**

★★★69% **Novotel London Heathrow**
Junction 4 M4, Cherry Ln UB7 9HB
☎ 01895 431431 🖹 01895 431221
e-mail: H1551@accor-hotels.com
Dir: *M4 junct 4, follow Uxbridge signs on A408. Keep left and take 2nd exit off traffic island into Cherry Ln signed West Drayton. Hotel on left*
Conveniently located close to Heathrow and the motorway network, this modern hotel provides comfortable accommodation. The large, airy indoor atrium creates a good sense of space in the public areas, which include a bar, meeting rooms, fitness centre and swimming pool.
ROOMS: 178 en suite (34 fmly) (10 GF) ⊗ in 112 bedrooms s £115-£125; d £115-£125 **LB FACILITIES:** STV Gym **CONF:** Thtr 250 Class 100 Board 90 Del from £119 **SERVICES:** Lift **PARKING:** 100 **CARDS:**

★★★66% **Comfort Inn Heathrow**
Shepiston Ln UB3 1LP
☎ 020 8573 6162 🖹 020 8848 1057
e-mail: info@comfortheathrow.com
Dir: *M4 junct 4, follow directions to Hayes & Shepiston Lane, hotel approx 1m next to fire station*
This hotel is located a little way from the airport, and guests may prefer its quieter position. There is a frequent bus service, which

continued

runs to and from the hotel throughout the day. Bedrooms are well equipped and many have the benefit of air conditioning.
ROOMS: 184 en suite (7 fmly) (50 GF) ⊗ in 80 bedrooms s £49-£119; d £49-£119 **LB FACILITIES:** STV Gym **CONF:** Thtr 150 Class 72 Board 90 Del from £109 **SERVICES:** Lift **PARKING:** 120 **NOTES:** ⊗ in restaurant Civ Wed 90 **CARDS:**

★★★66% **Master Robert**
366 Great West Rd TW5 0BD
☎ 020 8570 6261 🖹 020 8569 4016
e-mail: stay@masterrobert.co.uk
web: www.masterrobert.co.uk
Dir: *M4 junct 3. A312 to Heathrow Airport. At rdbt take 1st exit to A4 Central London. At 2nd rdbt straight on 100yds left . Hotel on left*
A well-known landmark on the Great West Road, this hotel is conveniently located near to Heathrow and the area's business community. Bedrooms are set in motel-style buildings behind the main hotel; most are spacious with good facilities. There is residents' lounge bar, a restaurant and a popular pub.
ROOMS: 96 annexe en suite (22 fmly) (40 GF) ⊗ in 50 bedrooms s £40-£99; d £49.50-£114 **LB FACILITIES:** STV Putt green Local health club nearby **CONF:** Thtr 150 Class 60 Board 40 Del from £115 **PARKING:** 200 **NOTES:** ⊗ in restaurant Civ Wed 80 **CARDS:**

U ◎◎ **The Radisson Edwardian**
Bath Rd UB3 5AW
☎ 020 8759 6311 🖹 020 8759 4559
e-mail: resreh@radisson.com
At the time of going to press, the star classification for this hotel was not confirmed. Please refer to the AA internet site www.theAA.com for current information.
ROOMS: 459 en suite (83 GF) ⊗ in 132 bedrooms **FACILITIES: Spa** STV Sauna Solarium Gym Jacuzzi Massage, Hairdressing **CONF:** BC Thtr 700 Class 300 Board 60 **SERVICES:** Lift air con **PARKING:** 550 **NOTES:** **CARDS:**

⌂ **Hotel Ibis Heathrow**
112/114 Bath Rd UB3 5AL
☎ 020 8759 4888 🖹 020 8564 7894
e-mail: H0794@accor-hotels.com
Dir: *follow Heathrow Terminals 1, 2, 3 signs, onto the spur road, off at sign for A4 Central London. Hotel 0.5m on left*
Modern, budget hotel offering comfortable accommodation in bright and practical bedrooms. Breakfast is self-service and dinner is available in the restaurant. For further details, consult the Hotel Groups page.
ROOMS: 347 en suite s £44.95-£64.95; d £44.95-£64.95 **CONF:** BC

⌂ **Travel Inn**
362 Uxbridge Rd UB4 0HF
☎ 08701 977132 🖹 020 8569 1204
Dir: *M4 junct 3 A312 N, over at next rdbt onto dual carriageway, at A4020 junct left, Inn 100yds on right*
Travel Inn offers good-quality, value-for-money accommodation. Spacious, en suite rooms with bath and shower comfortably accommodate a family of up to two adults and two children (to age 15). The restaurant and bar offers a varied menu. For further details consult the Hotel Groups page.
ROOMS: 62 en suite s £49.95-£58.95; d £49.95-£58.95

⌂ **Travel Inn London Heathrow**

362 Uxbridge Rd UB4 0HF
☎ 08701 977132 🖹 020 8569 1204
Travel Inn offers good-quality, value-for-money accommodation. Spacious, en suite rooms with bath and shower

continued on p266

HEATHROW AIRPORT (LONDON), continued

comfortably accommodate a family of up to two adults and two children (to age 15). The restaurant and bar offers a varied menu. For further details consult the Hotel Groups page.
ROOMS: 590 en suite s £49.95-£58.95; d £49.95-£58.95

Travel Inn London Heathrow
Bath Rd TW6 2AB
☎ 0870 6075 075 🖷 0870 241 9000
Dir: *M4 junct 4 follow signs for Heathrow Terminals 1, 2 & 3. Left onto Bath Rd signed A4/London. Inn on right 0.5 mile*
Travel Inn offers good-quality, value-for-money accommodation. Spacious, en suite rooms with bath and shower comfortably accommodate a family of up to two adults and two children (to age 15). The restaurant and bar offers a varied menu. For further details consult the Hotel Groups page.
ROOMS: 590 en suite s £49.95-£72.95; d £49.95-£72.95

The Park Inn Heathrow
Bath Rd UB7 0DU
☎ 020 8759 6611
At the time of going to press, the star classification for this hotel was not confirmed. Please refer to the AA internet site www.theAA.com for current information.

Jury's Inn Heathrow
Hatton Cross
☎ 0870 907 2222
ROOMS: 340 en suite **NOTES:** Due to open Dec 2004

HELLIDON, Northamptonshire
Map 11 SP55

★★★★74% Hellidon Lakes
NN11 6GG
☎ 01327 262550 🖷 01327 262559
e-mail: hellidon@marstonhotels.com
Dir: *signed, off A361 between Daventry and Banbury*

Some 220 acres of beautiful countryside, which include 27 holes of golf and 12 lakes, combine to form a rather spectacular backdrop to this much improved and newly extended hotel. Bedroom styles vary, from new ultra smart rooms through to those in the original wing that offer superb views. The extensive facilities include ten-pin bowling and a golf simulator where golfers of all levels can try some of the world's most challenging courses.
ROOMS: 110 en suite s £124-£149; d £158-£208 (incl. bkfst) **LB** **FACILITIES: Spa** STV 27 Solarium Gym Putt green Beauty therapist, Indoor smartgolf (simulator), 4 lane ten pin bowling Xmas **CONF:** Thtr 300 Class 120 Board 60 Del from £174 **SERVICES:** Lift **PARKING:** 150 **NOTES:** in restaurant Civ Wed 220
CARDS:

HELMSLEY, North Yorkshire
Map 19 SE68

★★★77% Feversham Arms
1 High St YO62 5AG
☎ 01439 770766 🖷 01439 770346
e-mail: stay@fevershamarmshotel.com
Dir: *A168 'Thirsk' from A1 then A170 or A64 'York' from A1 to York North, then B1363 to Helmsley. Hotel 125mtrs from Market Place*
Now under new ownership a friendly welcome is guaranteed at this establishment. There is a snug bar and stylish but cosy lounges in which to relax. The bedrooms are comfortable and furnished to a high standard with many useful extras including DVDs and CDs. There is a comprehensively equipped leisure centre and pleasant grounds with a pool and tennis court.
ROOMS: 17 en suite (4 GF) in all bedrooms s fr £120; d fr £135 (incl. bkfst) **LB** **FACILITIES:** STV Gym Xmas **CONF:** Thtr 35 Class 20 Board 24 Del from £135 **PARKING:** 50 **NOTES:** in restaurant **CARDS:**

See advert on opposite page

★★★75% The Black Swan
Market Place YO62 5BJ
☎ 0870 400 8112 🖷 01439 770174
e-mail: blackswan@macdonald-hotels.co.uk
Dir: *follow A170 towards Scarborough into Helmsley. Hotel at top of Market Sq*
The face of this former coaching inn is a blend of Elizabethan, Georgian and Tudor and inside there are warm, welcoming interiors with candlelight, oak beams and open fireplaces. There are six guest lounges and plenty of cosy nooks for quiet conversation. The hotel has comfortable, individually decorated bedrooms and a popular restaurant.
ROOMS: 45 en suite (4 fmly) in 13 bedrooms s £65-£85; d £80-£105 (incl. bkfst) **LB** **FACILITIES:** STV ch fac Xmas **CONF:** Thtr 50 Class 16 Board 22 Del from £135 **PARKING:** 50 **NOTES:** in restaurant
CARDS:

★★★71% Pheasant
Harome YO62 5JG
☎ 01439 771241 🖷 01439 771744
Dir: *2.5m SE, leave A170 after 0.25m. Right signed Harome for further 2m*
Guests can expect a family welcome at this hotel, which has spacious, comfortable bedrooms and enjoys a delightful setting next to the village pond. The beamed, flag-stoned bar leads into the charming lounge and conservatory dining room, where very enjoyable English food is served. A separate building contains the swimming pool. The hotel offers dinner-inclusive tariffs, and has many regulars.
ROOMS: 12 en suite 2 annexe en suite s £72-£75; d £144-£150 (incl. bkfst & dinner) **LB** **FACILITIES:** STV **PARKING:** 20 **NOTES:** No children 12yrs in restaurant Closed Xmas & Jan-Feb
CARDS:

★★68% Crown
Market Square YO62 5BJ
☎ 01439 770297 🖷 01439 771595
Dir: *on A170*
A 16th-century inn with plenty of character standing in the market square. It is noted for its colourful flower arrangements, excellent morning coffee and home-made scones. Bedrooms are comfortable and thoughtfully equipped. Public areas are pleasantly traditional and include cosy bars and a dining room serving wholesome dishes in generous portions.
ROOMS: 12 en suite (1 fmly) (1 GF) **PARKING:** 20
CARDS:

HELSTON, Cornwall & Isles of Scilly Map 02 SW62

★★68% *The Gwealdues*

Falmouth Rd TR13 8JX
☎ 01326 572808 📠 01326 561388
e-mail: gwealdueshotel@btinternet.com

Dir: *from Truro/Falmouth on A394. Hotel on approach into Helston*

The family-run Gwealdues is a friendly establishment located just outside Helston. Bedrooms are comfortable and well maintained, and some have balconies. A major attraction here is the Thai restaurant (European dishes are also available) that has a great local following. For yachting enthusiasts, a 42-foot motor sailing yacht is available for hire.

ROOMS: 17 en suite (2 fmly) ⊗ in 5 bedrooms **FACILITIES:** Sailing on own yacht **CONF:** Thtr 70 Class 50 Board 50 **PARKING:** 50 **NOTES:** ⊗ in restaurant **CARDS:**

HEMEL HEMPSTEAD, Hertfordshire Map 06 TL00

★★★66% The Bobsleigh Inn

MACDONALD HOTELS

Hempstead Rd, Bovingdon HP3 0DS
☎ 01442 833276 📠 01442 832471
e-mail: bobsleigh@macdonald-hotels.co.uk

Dir: *turn left after Hemel Hempstead station onto B4505 towards Chesham and follow into Bovingdon, hotel on left*

Located just outside the town, the hotel enjoys a pleasant rural setting, yet is within easy reach of local transport links and the motorway network. Bedrooms vary in size; all are modern in style. There is an open-plan lobby and bar area and an attractive dining room with views over the garden.

ROOMS: 30 en suite 15 annexe en suite (8 fmly) (29 GF) ⊗ in 39 bedrooms s fr £110; d fr £130 (incl. bkfst) **LB** **FACILITIES:** STV Xmas **CONF:** Thtr 150 Class 50 Board 40 Del from £110 **PARKING:** 60 **NOTES:** ⊗ in restaurant Civ Wed 100 **CARDS:**

⌂ Travel Inn

travel inn

Stoney Ln, Bourne End Services HP1 2SB
☎ 0870 238 3309 📠 01442 879149

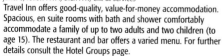

Dir: *from M25 junct 20 (A41) exit at services. From M1 junct 8, follow A414, then A41, exit at services*

Travel Inn offers good-quality, value-for-money accommodation. Spacious, en suite rooms with bath and shower comfortably accommodate a family of up to two adults and two children (to age 15). The restaurant and bar offers a varied menu. For further details consult the Hotel Groups page.

ROOMS: 61 en suite s £45.95-£48.95; d £45.95-£48.95

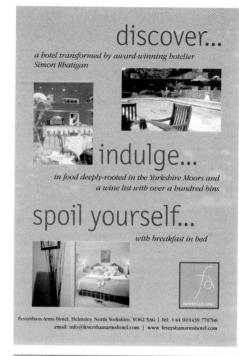

⌂ Travelodge

Travelodge

Wolsey House, Wolsey Rd HP2 4SS
☎ 08700 850 950 📠 01442 266887

Travelodge offers good quality, good value, modern accommodation. Ideal for families, the spacious, en suite bedrooms include remote-control TV, tea and coffee-making facilities and luxury beds. Meals can be taken at the nearby family restaurant. For further details consult the Hotel Groups page.

ROOMS: 53 en suite s fr £25; d fr £25

HENLEY-IN-ARDEN, Warwickshire Map 10 SP16

★★65% Henley

Tanworth Ln B95 5RA
☎ 01564 794551 📠 01564 795044
e-mail: reception@henleyhotel.co.uk

Dir: *Follow A3400 towards Henley-in-Arden*

This popular hotel is located just outside Henley-in-Arden and is well situated for access to major road networks. Bedrooms vary in style and all are thoughtfully equipped. Parking is an asset.

ROOMS: 32 en suite (2 fmly) (14 GF) ⊗ in 19 bedrooms s fr £49.50; d £59.50-£69.50 **LB** **FACILITIES:** STV **CONF:** BC Thtr 80 Class 50 Board 24 Del from £95 **PARKING:** 40 **NOTES:** ⊗ in restaurant Civ Wed 50 **CARDS:**

GF Indicates the number of bedrooms at ground floor level.

HENLEY-ON-THAMES, Oxfordshire Map 05 SU78

★★★71% Red Lion

Hart St RG9 2AR
☎ 01491 572161 01491 410039
e-mail: reservations@redlionhenley.co.uk
web: www.redlionhenley.co.uk
Dir: *adjacent to Henley Bridge*

The front rooms of this 16th-century, Thames-side hotel offer fabulous views of the river. Character bedrooms and public areas retain many of their original features, such as wood panelling, flagstone floors and beams. Bedrooms are comfortably appointed and decorated to a high standard; they feature period furniture and marble bathrooms.
ROOMS: 26 en suite (1 fmly) s £99; d £145 **LB** **FACILITIES:** STV **CONF:** Thtr 60 Class 20 Board 30 Del £185 **PARKING:** 25 **NOTES:**
CARDS:

Restaurant with Rooms

The White Hart Hotel

High St, Nettlebed RG9 5DD
☎ 01491 641245 01491 649018
e-mail: info@whitehartnettlebed.com
Dir: *on A4130 3.5m from Henley-on-Thames towards Oxford*
This pleasant restaurant with rooms is a popular venue. The combination of traditional and contemporary within such a relaxed atmosphere creates unique surroundings in which to enjoy the attentive service. Bedrooms, many of which have their own access from the inner courtyard, are equipped with a host of modern comforts and thoughtful extras. A wide selection of dishes, featuring carefully sourced, organic ingredients can be enjoyed in either the bar or the restaurant where cooking could be described as delightfully straightforward.
ROOMS: 6 en suite 6 annexe en suite (3 fmly) (3 GF) in all bedrooms d £105-£125 (incl. bkfst) **LB** **FACILITIES:** Xmas **CONF:** BC Thtr 30 Class 30 Board 20 **PARKING:** 50 **NOTES:**
CARDS:

HEREFORD, Herefordshire Map 10 SO54
See also Leominster & Much Birch

Top 200 – Hotel

★★★ Castle House

Castle St HR1 2NW
☎ 01432 356321 01432 365909
e-mail: info@castlehse.co.uk
web: www.castlehse.co.uk
Dir: *city centre; near cathedral. Follow signs to City Centre East. At junct of Commercial Rd and Union St, follow Castle House hotel signs.*
Enjoying a prime city centre location and overlooking the castle moat, this delightful Victorian mansion is the epitome of elegance and sophistication. The character bedrooms are equipped with every luxury to ensure a memorable stay and are complemented perfectly by the well-proportioned and restful lounge and bar. The experience is completed by award-winning cuisine in the topiary-themed restaurant.

ROOMS: 15 en suite s £100; d £175-£225 (incl. cont bkfst) **LB** **FACILITIES:** STV Xmas **SERVICES:** Lift **PARKING:** 15 **NOTES:** in restaurant **CARDS:**

See advert on opposite page

★★★69% Belmont Lodge & Golf Course

Belmont HR2 9SA
☎ 01432 352666 01432 358090
e-mail: info@belmont-hereford.co.uk
web: www.belmont-hereford.co.uk
Dir: *off A465 into Ruckhall Ln. Hotel on right in 0.5m*

This impressive complex is based around Belmont House, a Grade II listed building that dates back to 1788. It is surrounded by its own golf course and commands delightful views over the countryside and River Wye. Bedrooms, in a modern lodge, are comfortable and well equipped and the smart restaurant and bar are situated in the main house.
ROOMS: 30 en suite (4 fmly) (15 GF) in 15 bedrooms s £53-£68; d £61-£76 (incl. bkfst) **LB** **FACILITIES:** 18 Fishing Putt green Games room Xmas **CONF:** Thtr 60 Class 14 Board 25 Del from £69
PARKING: 150 **NOTES:** in restaurant
CARDS:

★★★67% Three Counties Hotel
Belmont Rd HR2 7BP
☎ 01432 299955 🖹 01432 275114
e-mail: enquiries@threecountieshotel.co.uk
web: www.threecountieshotel.co.uk
Dir: *on A465 Abergavenny Rd*
A mile west of the city centre, this large, privately owned, modern complex has well-equipped, spacious bedrooms, many of which are located in separate single-storey buildings around the extensive car park. There is a spacious, comfortable lounge, a traditional bar and an attractive restaurant.
ROOMS: 28 en suite 32 annexe en suite (4 fmly) (14 GF) ⊗ in 23 bedrooms s £35-£70; d £69-£87 (incl. bkfst) **LB FACILITIES:** STV **CONF:** Thtr 350 Class 154 Board 80 Del from £83 **PARKING:** 250 **NOTES:** Civ Wed 250 **CARDS:**

★★★60% Graftonbury Garden
Grafton Ln HR2 8BN
☎ 01432 268826 🖹 01432 354633
e-mail: sales@graftonbury.co.uk
Dir: *2m S of Hereford, 0.5m off A49 to Ross-on-Wye*
This hotel is set in a rural location to the south of the city. Public areas include an airy bar and a bright restaurant, both of which benefit from views over delightful rolling countryside. Bedrooms, some of which are in a single-storey annexe, are well proportioned and well equipped.
ROOMS: 15 en suite 11 annexe en suite (3 fmly) s £45-£55; d £70-£95 (incl. bkfst) **LB CONF:** Thtr 100 Class 50 Board 35 Del from £65 **PARKING:** 90 **NOTES:** ⊗ in restaurant Civ Wed 60
CARDS:

HEREFORD, continued

Restaurant with Rooms

Ancient Camp Inn
Ruckhall, Eaton Bishop HR2 9QX
☎ 01981 250449
e-mail: reservations@theancientcampinn.co.uk
Dir: *From A465 follow Ruckhall sign, after bridge follow Inn sign*
Named after the nearby Iron Age fort, this engaging establishment has all the right ingredients; great location, great food and great hosts. From its elevated position, it offers stunning views of the River Wye. Excellent seasonal produce is used to great effect in simple and memorable dishes. Bedrooms offer ample comfort, with those at the front benefiting from that wonderful view.
ROOMS: 5 en suite ⊗ in all bedrooms s £70-£100; d £80-£100 (incl. bkfst) **FACILITIES:** Fishing **PARKING:** 20 **NOTES:** No children 14yrs ⊗ in restaurant Closed 3 wks Feb **CARDS:**

Travel Inn
Holmer Rd, Holmer HR4 9RS
☎ 08701 977134 01432 343003
Dir: *from N M5 junct 7, follow A4103 to Worcester. M50 junct 4 take A49 Leominster road Travel Inn 800yds on left*
Travel Inn offers good-quality, value-for-money accommodation. Spacious, en suite rooms with bath and shower comfortably accommodate a family of up to two adults and two children (to age 15). The restaurant and bar offers a varied menu. For further details consult the Hotel Groups page.
ROOMS: 60 en suite s £45.95-£46.95; d £45.95-£46.95
CONF: Thtr 20 Board 24

HERTFORD, Hertfordshire — Map 06 TL31

★★★64% ***The White Horse***
MACDONALD HOTELS
Hertingfordbury SG14 2LB
☎ 01992 586791 01992 550809
e-mail: whitehorsehertingfordbury@macdonald-hotels.co.uk
Dir: *from A10 follow signs for A414. From Hertford under rail bridge over rdbt, left at next rdbt, hotel 300yds on right*
The Georgian façade of this former coaching inn belies an older interior with parts of the building dating back to the 17th century. Public rooms include a beamed bar with an open fire and a spacious conservatory restaurant overlooking rear gardens. Most of the bedrooms are located in a more modern extension of the property.
ROOMS: 42 en suite (4 fmly) ⊗ in 20 bedrooms **CONF:** Thtr 60 Class 30 Board 35 **PARKING:** 45 **NOTES:** ⊗ in restaurant Civ Wed 90
CARDS:

HESTON MOTORWAY SERVICE AREA (M4), Greater London
See LONDON SECTION plan 1 B3

Travelodge (Eastbound)
Phoenix Way TW5 9NB
☎ 08700 850 950 020 8580 2028
Dir: *M4 junct 2 & 3 westbound*
Travelodge offers good quality, good value, modern accommodation. Ideal for families, the spacious, en suite bedrooms include remote-control TV, tea and coffee-making facilities and luxury beds. Meals can be taken at the nearby family restaurant. For further details consult the Hotel Groups page.
ROOMS: 66 en suite s fr £25; d fr £25

Travelodge (Westbound)
Cranford Ln TW5 9NB
☎ 08700 850 950 0208 580 2006
Travelodge offers good quality, good value, modern accommodation. Ideal for families, the spacious, en suite bedrooms include remote-control TV, tea and coffee-making facilities and luxury beds. Meals can be taken at the nearby family restaurant. For further details consult the Hotel Groups page.
ROOMS: 145 en suite s fr £25; d fr £25

HESWALL, Merseyside — Map 15 SJ28

Travel Inn (Wirral North)
Chester Rd, Gayton CH60 3SD
☎ 08701 977274 0151 342 8983
Dir: *M53 junct 4 follow A5137 signed Heswall for 3m & turn left at next rdbt, Travel Inn on left*
Travel Inn offers good-quality, value-for-money accommodation. Spacious, en suite rooms with bath and shower comfortably accommodate a family of up to two adults and two children (to age 15). The restaurant and bar offers a varied menu. For further details consult the Hotel Groups page.
ROOMS: 37 en suite s £45.95-£46.95; d £45.95-£46.95

HETHERSETT, Norfolk — Map 13 TG10

★★★74% **Park Farm**
NR9 3DL
☎ 01603 810264 01603 812104
e-mail: enq@parkfarm-hotel.co.uk
web: www.parkfarm-hotel.co.uk
Dir: *5m S of Norwich, off A11 on B1172*

Set amid landscaped grounds and surrounded by open countryside, this elegant Georgian farmhouse has been owned and run by the Gowing family since 1958. The pleasantly decorated bedrooms are tastefully furnished and decorated, and some rooms have patio doors with a sun terrace. The extensive public rooms include a smart conservatory, a lounge, a bar and an intimate restaurant.
ROOMS: 5 en suite 42 annexe en suite (20 fmly) (20 GF) s £92-£125; d £118-£175 (incl. bkfst) **LB** **FACILITIES:** supervised Sauna Solarium Gym Jacuzzi Beauty salon, Hairdressing Xmas **CONF:** Thtr 120 Class 50 Board 50 Del from £135 **PARKING:** 150 **NOTES:** ⊗ in restaurant Civ Wed 100 **CARDS:**

See advert under NORWICH

For central reservation numbers and more information on Hotel Groups, turn to pages 33-39

HETTON, North Yorkshire Map 18 SD95

Restaurant with Rooms

The Angel Inn

BD23 6LT
☎ 01756 730263 01756 730363
e-mail: info@angelhetton.co.uk
web: www.angelhetton.co.uk
Dir: *Turn off A59 onto B6265 for Grassington. In Rylstone turn left at sign for Hetton*

These individually-furnished studios and suites bring together contemporary and traditional style in a tastefully converted Dale's Barn, opposite the inn. All are new, stylish, very comfortable and feature many thoughtful extras. The barn also houses a wine cave available to guests for private wine tasting. Tantalising dishes are served at the Angel Inn itself.

ROOMS: 5 annexe en suite (1 GF) in all bedrooms s £120-£140; d £120-£140 (incl. bkfst) **LB** **PARKING:** 40 **NOTES:** Civ Wed 40 **CARDS:**

HEXHAM, Northumberland Map 21 NY96

★★★★71% De Vere Slaley Hall

Slaley NE47 0BY
DE VERE HOTELS
☎ 01434 673350 01434 673962
e-mail: slaley.hall@devere-hotels.com
web: www.devereonline.co.uk
Dir: *A1 from S to A68 link road follow signs for Slaley Hall*

One thousand acres of Northumbrian forest and parkland, two championship golf courses and indoor leisure facilities all add up to a range of possibilities for guests, whatever their reason for visiting. Spacious bedrooms are fully air conditioned and equipped with a range of extras. Public rooms include a number of lounges, conference and banqueting rooms, the informal Golf Clubhouse restaurant and the impressive main restaurant.

ROOMS: 139 en suite (22 fmly) in 101 bedrooms s £85-£140; d £120-£190 (incl. bkfst) **LB** **FACILITIES: Spa** STV supervised 18 Sauna Solarium Gym Jacuzzi Quad bikes, Archery, Clay pigeon shoot, 4x4 driving, Creche Xmas **CONF:** Thtr 300 Class 220 Board 150 Del from £145 **SERVICES:** Lift air con **PARKING:** 500 **NOTES:** in restaurant Civ Wed 250 **CARDS:**

★★★★70% Langley Castle

Langley on Tyne NE47 5LU
☎ 01434 688888 01434 684019
e-mail: manager@langleycastle.com
web: www.langleycastle.com
Dir: *from A69 S on A686 for 2m. Castle on right*

Langley is a magnificent 14th-century fortified castle, set in ten acres of parkland. There is a restaurant, a comfortable drawing room and a cosy bar. Bedrooms are furnished with period pieces

continued

and most feature window seats; restored buildings in the grounds have been converted into very comfortable 'Castle View' bedrooms.

ROOMS: 8 en suite 10 annexe en suite (4 fmly) (5 GF) s £100-£170; d £109-£219 (incl. bkfst) **LB** **FACILITIES:** STV Xmas **CONF:** Thtr 120 Class 60 Board 40 Del from £125 **PARKING:** 70 **NOTES:** in restaurant Civ Wed 120 **CARDS:**

See advert on this page

★★★67% Beaumont

Beaumont St NE46 3LT
Best Western
☎ 01434 602331 01434 606184
e-mail: reservations@beaumonthotel.eclipse.co.uk
Dir: *A69 towards Hexham town centre*

In a region steeped in history, this hotel is located in the centre of the popular county town, overlooking the park and 6th-century abbey. The hotel has two bars, a comfortable reception lounge and a first-floor restaurant.

ROOMS: 25 en suite (3 fmly) in 18 bedrooms s £75-£85; d £105 (incl. bkfst) **LB** **FACILITIES:** STV Snooker Solarium **CONF:** Thtr 100 Class 60 Board 40 **SERVICES:** Lift **PARKING:** 16 **NOTES:** in restaurant Closed 25-26 Dec **CARDS:**

HICKSTEAD, West Sussex Map 06 TQ22

★★★62% *The Hickstead Hotel*

Jobs Ln, Bolney RH17 5NZ
☎ 01444 248023 01444 245280
e-mail: gm.hickstead@macdonald-hotels.co.uk
Dir: *M23 South, take A2300 exit (Burgess Hill), 1st left, next right, hotel is 100yds on left*

In the heart of West Sussex, this hotel is located not far from the

continued on p272

HICKSTEAD, continued

main London to Brighton road. The hotel's proximity to the local business park and its accessibility to a number of local attractions make it popular with both business and leisure guests who can make use of the indoor leisure centre.
ROOMS: 49 en suite (4 fmly) (24 GF) ⊗ in 34 bedrooms **FACILITIES: Spa** STV supervised Fishing Sauna Gym Jacuzzi **CONF:** BC Thtr 80 Class 60 Board 50 **PARKING:** 100 **NOTES:** ⊗ in restaurant Civ Wed 80 **CARDS:**

⌂ Travelodge

Travelodge

Jobs Ln RH17 5NX
☎ 08700 850 950 01444 881377
Dir: *A23 southbound*
Travelodge offers good quality, good value, modern accommodation. Ideal for families, the spacious, en suite bedrooms include remote-control TV, tea and coffee-making facilities and luxury beds. Meals can be taken at the nearby family restaurant. For further details consult the Hotel Groups page.
ROOMS: 55 en suite s fr £25; d fr £25

HIGHAM, Derbyshire — Map 16 SK35

★★★67% Santo's Higham Farm Hotel

Main Rd DE55 6EH
☎ 01773 833812 01773 520525
e-mail: reception@santoshighamfarm.demon.co.uk
web: www.santohighamfarm.demon.co.uk
Dir: *M1 junct 28 take A38 towards Derby, then A61 towards Chesterfield. Then onto B6013 towards Belper & hotel 300yds on right*
With panoramic views across the rolling Amber Valley, this 15th-century crook barn and farmhouse now have an Italian Wing and an International Wing of themed bedrooms. Freshly prepared dishes, especially fish, are available in Guiseppe's restaurant, and in summer barbecues are held in the Rose Garden. An ideal romantic hideaway.
ROOMS: 28 en suite (2 fmly) (7 GF) ⊗ in all bedrooms s fr £77; d fr £97 (incl. bkfst) **LB** **FACILITIES:** STV Xmas **CONF:** Thtr 100 Class 40 Board 34 Del from £96 **PARKING:** 100 **NOTES:** ⊗ in restaurant Civ Wed 100 **CARDS:**

HIGHBRIDGE, Somerset — Map 04 ST34

★★68% Sundowner

74 Main Rd, West Huntspill TA9 3QU
☎ 01278 784766 01278 794133
e-mail: runnalls@msn.com
Dir: *From M5 junct 23, 3m N on A38*
Friendly service and an informal atmosphere are just two of the highlights of this small hotel. The open-plan lounge/bar is a comfortable area in which to relax after a busy day exploring the area or working in the locality. An extensive menu, featuring freshly cooked, imaginative dishes, is offered in the popular restaurant.
ROOMS: 8 en suite (1 fmly) s £40-£45; d £55-£60 (incl. bkfst) **CONF:** Thtr 40 Board 24 Del £65 **PARKING:** 18 **NOTES:** ⊗ in restaurant Closed 26, 31 Dec & 1 Jan RS 25 Dec
CARDS:

> Packed in a hurry?
> Ironing facilities should be available at all star levels, either in rooms or on request

A ★★ Laburnum House Lodge

Sloway Ln, West Huntspill TA9 3RJ
☎ 01278 781830 01278 781612
e-mail: laburnumhh@aol.com
web: www.laburnumhh.co.uk
Dir: *M5 junct 22. Continue W on A38 for 5m, turn right at Crossways Inn. 300yds & left into Sloway Ln, follow lane for 300yds*
ROOMS: 60 annexe en suite (10 fmly) (60 GF) ⊗ in 30 bedrooms s £48-£64; d £64-£84 (incl. bkfst) **LB** **FACILITIES:** Fishing Sauna Solarium Clay pigeon shooting, Water-ski park, Go cart Xmas **CONF:** BC Thtr 140 Class 60 Board 40 Del from £72 **PARKING:** 100 **NOTES:** ⊗ in restaurant **CARDS:**

HIGH WYCOMBE, Buckinghamshire — Map 05 SU89
See also Stokenchurch

★★★70% Ambassador Court

145 West Wycombe Rd HP12 3AB
☎ 01494 461818 01494 461919
e-mail: ach@fardellhotels.com
Dir: *M4 junct 4/A404 to A40 west towards Aylesbury. Hotel 0.5m on left next to petrol station*
A small privately owned hotel handily situated close to the M40 midway between London and Oxford. Bedrooms are pleasantly decorated and suitably well equipped for business or leisure travellers. Public rooms are contemporary in style and include a lounge with leather sofas, a cosy bar and Fusions restaurant which is situated in the conservatory.
ROOMS: 18 en suite (1 GF) ⊗ in all bedrooms s £50-£109; d £60-£119 (incl. bkfst) **FACILITIES:** STV Xmas **CONF:** Thtr 20 Class 12 Board 16 Del from £125 **PARKING:** 18 **NOTES:** ⊗ in restaurant
CARDS:

⌂ Travel Inn

travel inn

Thanestead Farm, London Rd, Loudwater HP10 9YL
☎ 08701 977135 01494 446855
Dir: *On A40 near M40(J3), 3 miles from High Wycombe. If approaching from M40 (West), take J2. Follow signs to High Wycombe via Beaconsfield*
Travel Inn offers good-quality, value-for-money accommodation. Spacious, en suite rooms with bath and shower comfortably accommodate a family of up to two adults and two children (to age 15). The restaurant and bar offers a varied menu. For further details consult the Hotel Groups page.
ROOMS: 81 en suite s £45.95-£48.95; d £45.95-£48.95 **CONF:** Class 24 Board 24

HILLINGTON, Norfolk — Map 12 TF72

★★66% Ffolkes Arms

THE INDEPENDENTS

Lynn Rd PE31 6BJ
☎ 01485 600210 01485 601196
e-mail: ffolkespub@aol.com
Dir: *on A149 at Knights Hill rdbt, right onto A148 towards Cromer. Hotel 6m along A148 at Hillington*
A popular 17th-century former coaching inn, situated close to the Norfolk coastline and within easy reach of King's Lynn. Facilities include a bar, restaurant and lounge area. Bedrooms are in an annexe adjacent to the main building; each one is pleasantly appointed and well equipped. The hotel also has a function suite and social club.
ROOMS: 20 annexe en suite (2 fmly) ⊗ in all bedrooms s £40-£60; d £60-£80 (incl. bkfst) **LB** **FACILITIES:** Xmas **CONF:** BC Thtr 200 Class 60 Board 50 Del from £70 **PARKING:** 200 **NOTES:** ⊗ in restaurant
CARDS:

HILTON PARK MOTORWAY SERVICE AREA (M6), West Midlands — Map 10 SJ90

Travelodge Birmingham North

Hilton Park Services (M6), Essington WV11 2AT
☎ 08700 850 950 📠 01922 701967
Dir: *M6 between junct 10a & 11*

Travelodge offers good quality, good value, modern accommodation. Ideal for families, the spacious, en suite bedrooms include remote-control TV, tea and coffee-making facilities and luxury beds. Meals can be taken at the nearby family restaurant. For further details consult the Hotel Groups page.
ROOMS: 63 en suite s fr £25; d fr £25

HIMLEY, Staffordshire — Map 10 SO89

★★★63% The Himley Country Hotel

School Rd DY3 4LG
☎ 0870 609 6112 📠 01902 896668
e-mail: himleycountryhotel@corushotels.com
Dir: *leave A449 into School Rd at lights by Dudley Arms*

This modern hotel has been tastefully built around a 19th-century village schoolhouse. Bedrooms are well equipped and many are quite spacious. Day rooms include a stylish conservatory restaurant in which wide-ranging menus are accompanied by traditional buffet roasts.
ROOMS: 73 en suite (1 fmly) in 38 bedrooms s £55-£75; d £68-£75 **LB** **FACILITIES:** STV Xmas **CONF:** Thtr 150 Class 80 Board 50 **PARKING:** 100 **NOTES:** in restaurant Civ Wed 100
CARDS:

★★67% *Himley House Hotel*

Stourbridge Rd DY3 4LD
☎ 01902 892468 📠 01902 892604
e-mail: himleyhouse@hotmail.com
web: www.himleyhousehotel.com
Dir: *on A449 N of Stourbridge*

Dating back to the 17th century, and formerly the lodge for nearby Himley Hall, this hotel offers well-equipped and comfortable accommodation. The comfortable bedrooms of varying sizes are located both in the main house and separate buildings nearby, and the busy restaurant offers a wide selection of dishes.
ROOMS: 24 en suite (2 fmly) **FACILITIES:** ch fac **CONF:** Thtr 50 Class 30 Board 22 **PARKING:** 162 **NOTES:**
CARDS:

HINCKLEY, Leicestershire — Map 11 SP49

★★★★71% Sketchley Grange

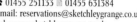

Sketchley Ln, Burbage LE10 3HU
☎ 01455 251133 📠 01455 631384
e-mail: reservations@sketchleygrange.co.uk
web: www.sketchleygrange.co.uk
Dir: *SE of town, off A5/M69 junct 1, take B4109 to Hinckley. Left at 2nd rdbt. 1st right onto Sketchley Ln*

Although close to motorway connections the hotel is peacefully set in its own grounds, and enjoys country views. Excellent facilities include the new and stylish Roman's Health and Leisure Spa, complete with a 'Little Romans' crèche, and a choice of bars and dining options. Bedrooms include many extras; many rooms have now been refurbished.
ROOMS: 52 en suite (9 fmly) (1 GF) in 15 bedrooms **FACILITIES: Spa** STV supervised Sauna Solarium Gym Steam room, Hairdressing, Creche, Beauty therapy **CONF:** BC Thtr 300 Class 150 Board 30 Del from £130 **SERVICES:** Lift **PARKING:** 200 **NOTES:** in restaurant Civ Wed 300 **CARDS:**

See advert under LEICESTER

★★★★61% Hanover International Hotel & Club

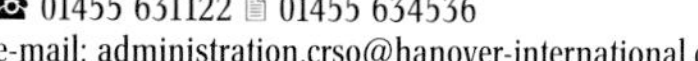

Watling St (A5) LE10 3JA
☎ 01455 631122 📠 01455 634536
e-mail: administration.crso@hanover-international.com
Dir: *on A5, S of junct 1 on M69*

A large hotel offering good facilities for conference and business guests. Bedrooms are spacious with the Club Floors providing high levels of comfort, such as leather seating at good-sized desks. The leisure centre has been refurbished, as have the new-look Brasserie and Conservatory restaurants.
ROOMS: 350 en suite (156 fmly) in 200 bedrooms s £80-£115; d £125 **LB** **FACILITIES: Spa** STV supervised Snooker Sauna Solarium Gym Putt green Jacuzzi Steam room **CONF:** Thtr 400 Class 180 Board 38 Del £160 **SERVICES:** Lift air con **PARKING:** 600 **NOTES:** in restaurant Civ Wed 350
CARDS:

HINCKLEY, continued

★★74% Kings Hotel & Restaurant
13/19 Mount Rd LE10 1AD
☎ 01455 637193 ▯ 01455 636201
e-mail: info@kings-hotel.net
Dir: *follow A447 signed to Hinckley. Under railway bridge, right at rdbt. 1st road left opposite railway station, then 3rd right*

A friendly atmosphere exists at this privately owned and managed hotel, which is situated in a quiet road within easy walking distance of the town centre and station. Bedrooms are tastefully decorated and have attractive furnishings and tiled bathrooms. The public rooms include a residents' lounge, a lounge-bar with striking Chinese-style wallpaper and a large restaurant with a baby grand piano and attractive Victorian fireplace.
ROOMS: 7 en suite ⊗ in all bedrooms s £65-£75; d £75-£85 (incl. bkfst) **LB FACILITIES: Spa** STV **CONF:** Thtr 30 Class 40 Board 20 Del from £110 **PARKING:** 20 **NOTES:** No children 10yrs ⊗ in restaurant
CARDS:

HINDON, Wiltshire Map 04 ST93

★★66% ◎◎ The Angel Inn
Angel Ln SP3 6DJ
☎ 01747 820696 ▯ 01747 820054
e-mail: theangelathindon@btconnect.com
Dir: *1m from both A350 & A303*

A welcoming 18th-century inn, under new management, which attracts locals and visitors from farther afield for its interesting range of carefully prepared dishes, augmented by a selection of well chosen wines. Bedrooms vary in size, while public rooms include a bar and a tree-lined patio area, ideal for al fresco dining.
ROOMS: 7 en suite (2 fmly) ⊗ in 6 bedrooms s £40-£60; d £60-£85 (incl. bkfst) **PARKING:** 24 **NOTES:** ⊗ in restaurant
CARDS:

HINTLESHAM, Suffolk Map 13 TM04

Top 200 - Hotel

★★★★ ◎◎◎ Hintlesham Hall
George St IP8 3NS
☎ 01473 652334 ▯ 01473 652463
e-mail: reservations@hintleshamhall.com
web: www.hintleshamhall.com
Dir: *4m W of Ipswich on B1071 to Hadleigh and Sudbury*
Hospitality and service are key features at this imposing Grade I listed country house hotel, situated in 175 acres of grounds and landscaped gardens. Individually decorated bedrooms offer a high degree of comfort; each one is tastefully furnished and equipped with many thoughtful touches. The spacious public rooms include an elegant restaurant, which serves fine classical cuisine.
ROOMS: 33 en suite (10 GF) s £98-£195; d £120-£220 (incl. cont bkfst) **LB FACILITIES:** 18 Sauna Gym Putt green Jacuzzi Xmas **CONF:** Thtr 80 Class 50 Board 32 Del from £195 **PARKING:** 60 **NOTES:** ⊗ in restaurant RS Sat Civ Wed 110
CARDS:

HINTON CHARTERHOUSE, Somerset Map 04 ST75

★★★77% ◎◎◎ Homewood Park
BA2 7TB
☎ 01225 723731 ▯ 01225 723820
e-mail: res@homewoodpark.com
web: www.homewoodpark.com
Dir: *6m SE of Bath on A36, turn left at 2nd sign for Freshford*

Homewood Park, an unassuming yet stylish Georgian house set in delightful grounds, offers relaxed surroundings and maintains high standards of quality and comfort throughout. Bedrooms, all individually decorated, include thoughtful extras to ensure a

continued

comfortable stay. The hotel has a reputation for excellent cuisine - offering an imaginative interpretation of classical dishes.
ROOMS: 19 en suite (1 fmly) ⊗ in 2 bedrooms s £120-£215; d £150-£270 (incl. bkfst) **LB** **FACILITIES:** STV Fishing, hunting & horseriding on request Xmas **CONF:** BC Thtr 40 Class 30 Board 25 Del from £165 **PARKING:** 30 **NOTES:** ⊗ in restaurant Civ Wed 50 **CARDS:**

HITCHIN, Hertfordshire Map 12 TL12

★★67% Firs

83 Bedford Rd SG5 2TY
☎ 01462 422322 01462 432051
e-mail: info@firshotel.co.uk
web: www.firshotel.co.uk
Dir: *from M1 junct 10 take A505 or A1 junct 8 onto A602 to Hitchin. Follow Bedford signs, on A600 hotel 1m on left, next to Shell petrol station*

THE INDEPENDENTS HOTEL ASSOCIATION

This family-run hotel is situated on the northern edge of town and caters for business as well as leisure guests. Well-equipped bedrooms vary in size and style, the majority have been tastefully refurbished boasting smartly appointed bathrooms. The restaurant offers a range of homemade Italian-style dishes.
ROOMS: 29 en suite (3 fmly) (9 GF) ⊗ in 16 bedrooms s £55-£60; d £68-£80 (incl. bkfst) **CONF:** Thtr 30 Class 24 Board 20 Del from £95 **PARKING:** 30 **NOTES:** ⊗ in restaurant
CARDS:

HOCKLEY HEATH, West Midlands Map 10 SP17

Top 200 – Hotel

★★★ Nuthurst Grange Country House & Restaurant

Nuthurst Grange Ln B94 5NL
☎ 01564 783972 01564 783919
e-mail: info@nuthurst-grange.com
web: www.nuthurst-grange.com
Dir: *off A3400, 0.5mile south of Hockley Heath. Turn at sign into Nuthurst Grange Lane*

The approach to this period country house is a stunning avenue drive, and the hotel benefits from several acres of well-tended gardens and mature grounds and views over rolling countryside. Public areas include restful lounges, meeting rooms and a sunny restaurant. The kitchen brigade produces highly imaginative British and French cuisine, complemented by very attentive, professional restaurant service. The spacious bedrooms and bathrooms offer considerable luxury and comfort.
ROOMS: 15 en suite (2 GF) s £129-£139; d £165-£195 (incl. bkfst) **LB** **FACILITIES:** STV Helipad **CONF:** BC Thtr 100 Class 50 Board 45 Del £179 **PARKING:** 86 **NOTES:** ⊗ in restaurant Closed 1 wk Xmas Civ Wed **CARDS:**

Travel Inn (Solihull Hockley Heath)

Stratford Rd, Hockley Heath B94 6NX
☎ 08701 977230 01564 783197
Dir: *on A3400, 2m S of M42 junct 4*

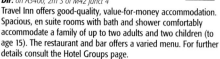

Travel Inn offers good-quality, value-for-money accommodation. Spacious, en suite rooms with bath and shower comfortably accommodate a family of up to two adults and two children (to age 15). The restaurant and bar offers a varied menu. For further details consult the Hotel Groups page.
ROOMS: 55 en suite s £45.95-£48.95; d £45.95-£48.95 **CONF:** Thtr 25

HODNET, Shropshire Map 15 SJ62

★★65% Bear

TF9 3NH
☎ 01630 685214 & 685788 01630 685787
e-mail: info@bearhotel.org
web: www.bearhotel.org.uk
Dir: *junct of A53 & A442 in village*

THE INDEPENDENTS HOTEL ASSOCIATION

This 16th-century former coaching inn provides bedrooms equipped with all modern comforts. The public areas have a wealth of charm and character, enhanced by features such as exposed beams. There is a large baronial-style function room; medieval banquets are something of a speciality here.
ROOMS: 6 en suite 2 annexe en suite (2 fmly) s £42.50-£45; d £60-£70 (incl. bkfst) **LB** **FACILITIES:** Xmas **CONF:** Thtr 100 Class 50 Board 40 **PARKING:** 70 **NOTES:** Civ Wed 70 **CARDS:**

HOLCOMBE, Somerset Map 04 ST64

★★71% *The Ring O' Roses*

Stratton Rd BA3 5EB
☎ 01761 232478 01761 233737
e-mail: ringorosesholcombe@tesco.net
Dir: *A367 to Stratton on The Fosse, look for hidden left turn opposite Downside Abbey, signposted Holcombe. Next right, hotel 1.5m on left*

With views of Downside Abbey in the distance, this inn dates back to the 16th century. The attentive owners and pleasant staff create a friendly and relaxed atmosphere. Bedrooms are individually furnished and very comfortable. Real ales are served in the bar while in the restaurant an imaginative menu is offered, using local ingredients wherever possible.
ROOMS: 8 en suite ⊗ in all bedrooms **CONF:** Thtr 40 Class 40 Board 14 **PARKING:** 35 **NOTES:** ⊗ in restaurant
CARDS:

Indoor Swimming Pool
Indoor Swimming Pool (heated)
Outdoor Swimming Pool
Outdoor Swimming Pool (heated)

HOLFORD, Somerset Map 04 ST14

★★76% Combe House

TA5 1RZ
☎ 01278 741382 📠 01278 741322
e-mail: enquiries@combehouse.co.uk
web: www.combehouse.co.uk
Dir: *from A39 W left in Holford then left at T-junct. Left at fork, 0.25m to Holford Combe*

Once a tannery, this 17th-century longhouse is peacefully situated in lovely grounds, and provides an ideal retreat for walking in the Quantock Hills. Bedrooms are traditional in style and the public rooms include a choice of sitting areas. There is a focus on home cooking in the dining room.
ROOMS: 17 rms (16 en suite) (3 fmly) (1 GF) ⊗ in 16 bedrooms s £45-£55; d £90-£110 (incl. bkfst) **LB** **FACILITIES:** STV Sauna Gym Xmas **PARKING:** 33 **NOTES:** ⊗ in restaurant
CARDS:

HOLKHAM, Norfolk Map 13 TF84

★★73% The Victoria at Holkham

Park Rd NR23 1RG
☎ 01328 711008 📠 01328 711009
e-mail: victoria@holkham.co.uk
web: www.victoriaatholkham.co.uk
Dir: *A149, 2m W of Wells-next-the-Sea*

A Grade II listed property is ideally situated on the North Norfolk coast road on the Holkham estate. Décor is influenced by the local landscape: the stylish bedrooms are individually decorated and tastefully furnished with pieces specially made for the hotel in India. The brasserie-style restaurant serves an interesting choice of dishes.
ROOMS: 9 en suite 1 annexe en suite (2 fmly) (1 GF) ⊗ in all bedrooms s £90-£110; d £110-£140 (incl. bkfst) **LB** **FACILITIES:** STV Fishing Shooting on Holkham Estate, Bird watching reserve nearby ch fac Xmas **CONF:** Thtr 12 Class 40 Board 30 **PARKING:** 30 **NOTES:** ⊗ in restaurant **CARDS:**

HOLMES CHAPEL, Cheshire Map 15 SJ76

★★★63% *Holly Lodge Hotel & "Truffles" Restaurant*

70 London Rd CW4 7AS
☎ 01477 537033 📠 01477 535823
e-mail: sales@hollylodgehotel.co.uk
web: www.hollylodgehotel.co.uk
Dir: *A50/A54 x-rds, 1m from M6 junct 18*
Situated close to the centre of Holmes Chapel, this hotel caters for both business and leisure guests. Accommodation varies in style, with particularly comfortable, bright modern bedrooms located in an adjacent cottage. A carefully prepared menu is served in Truffles restaurant, and there are also several function rooms available.
ROOMS: 17 en suite 25 annexe en suite (3 fmly) ⊗ in 17 bedrooms **FACILITIES:** STV Discounted rates with local gym **CONF:** Thtr 120 Class 60 Board 60 **PARKING:** 90 **NOTES:** ⊗ in restaurant Civ Wed 120
CARDS:

HOLMFIRTH, West Yorkshire Map 16 SE10

★★65% *Old Bridge*

HD9 7DA
☎ 01484 681212 📠 01484 687978
e-mail: oldbridgehotel@enterprise.net
web: www.oldbridgehotel.com
Dir: *at traffic lights on A6024/A635 in centre of Holmfirth, turn into Victoria St, left after bank and shops to hotel*
Located centrally in the town famous for the BBC's *The Last of the Summer Wine*, and with ample convenient parking, this stone-built hotel offers well-equipped bedrooms and a variety of spacious public rooms. There is a wide range of food available in both the attractive restaurant and the cosy bars.
ROOMS: 20 en suite **CONF:** Thtr 80 Class 50 Board 40 **PARKING:** 30
NOTES: **CARDS:**

HOLSWORTHY, Devon Map 03 SS30

★★73% *Court Barn Country House*

Clawton EX22 6PS
☎ 01409 271219 📠 01409 271309
e-mail: courtbarnhotel@talk21.com
web: www.hotels-devon.com
Dir: *2.5m S of Holsworthy off A388 Tamerton Rd next to Clawton Church*
This engaging, family-run Victorian country house is set in five acres of attractive grounds, including a nine-hole putting course and croquet lawn. Comfortable bedrooms are individually furnished, and there are two relaxing lounges. A four-course dinner featuring fresh, local produce is served in the spacious restaurant, and leisurely breakfasts are taken overlooking the garden.
ROOMS: 8 rms (7 en suite) (1 fmly) ⊗ in all bedrooms **FACILITIES:** Putt green Badminton **CONF:** Thtr 25 Board 8 **PARKING:** 13
NOTES: ⊗ in restaurant **CARDS:**

HONILEY, Warwickshire Map 10 SP27

★★★66% Corus hotel Warwick

corus hotels

Meer End Rd CV8 1NP
☎ 0870 609 6142 📠 01926 484474
e-mail: warwick@corushotels.com
Dir: *M40 junct 15, A46 then A4177 to Solihull. Right at 1st main rdbt, hotel 2m on left*
Incorporating an inn with 16th-century origins, this busy hotel provides brightly decorated and open-plan public areas. The spacious bedrooms are comfortably appointed and well equipped

continued

for both business and leisure guests. A good choice of meals and snacks is readily available in the contemporary Boot Inn and Bistro.

ROOMS: 62 en suite (2 fmly) (14 GF) ⊗ in 31 bedrooms **FACILITIES:** STV Xmas **CONF:** Thtr 200 Class 70 Board 30 **SERVICES:** Lift **PARKING:** 250 **NOTES:** ⊗ in restaurant Civ Wed **CARDS:**

HONITON, Devon

Map 04 ST10

Top 200 – Hotel

★★★ Combe House Hotel & Restaurant

Gittisham EX14 3AD
☎ 01404 540400 🖷 01404 46004
e-mail: stay@thishotel.com
web: www.thishotel.com
Dir: *off A30 1m S of Honiton, follow Gittisham Heathpark signs*

Standing proud in an elevated position, this Elizabethan mansion enjoys uninterrupted views over acres of its own woodland, meadow and pasture. Bedrooms are a blend of comfort and quality with relaxation being the ultimate objective. A range of atmospheric public rooms retain all the charm and history of the old house. Dining is equally impressive, a skilled kitchen brigade maximises the best of local and home-grown produce, augmented by excellent wines. Private dining is available in the magnificently restored old kitchen.

ROOMS: 15 en suite s £125-£165; d £140-£148 (incl. bkfst) **LB** **FACILITIES:** Fishing Jacuzzi ch fac Xmas **CONF:** BC Thtr 60 Class 40 Board 26 Del from £170 **PARKING:** 51 **NOTES:** ⊗ in restaurant Civ Wed 80 **CARDS:**

★★69% Home Farm

Wilmington EX14 9JR
☎ 01404 831278 🖷 01404 831411
e-mail: homefarmhotel@breathemail.net
web: www.homefarmhotel.co.uk
Dir: *3m E of Honiton on A35 in village of Wilmington*

Set in well-tended gardens, this thatched former farmhouse is now *continued* a comfortable hotel. Many of the original features have been retained with the cobbled courtyard and farm implements attractively displayed. A range of interesting dishes is offered either in the bar or in the more intimate restaurant. Bedrooms, some with private gardens, are well equipped and comfortably furnished.

ROOMS: 8 en suite 5 annexe en suite (4 fmly) (6 GF) ⊗ in all bedrooms s £48-£70; d £70-£100 (incl. bkfst) **LB** **FACILITIES:** Xmas **PARKING:** 20 **NOTES:** ⊗ in restaurant **CARDS:**

★★68% Monkton Court

Monkton EX14 9QH
☎ 01404 42309 🖷 01404 46861
e-mail: yeotelsmonkton@aol.com
Dir: *2m E of Honiton on A30 towards Ilminster, opposite Monkton Church*

Set in five acres of grounds, this attractive 17th-century manor house retains much of its historical character. Friendly staff provide attentive service, and many guests find the Monkton Court an ideal base for either business or leisure. A comfortable lounge and pleasant bar with crackling log fire are available. Cuisine offers a good choice of freshly cooked and imaginative dishes.

ROOMS: 6 en suite (1 fmly) s £45-£55; d £60-£75 (incl. bkfst) **LB** **CONF:** Thtr 50 Class 25 Board 25 **PARKING:** 40 **NOTES:** ⊗ in restaurant Closed Xmas & New Year **CARDS:**

HOOK, Hampshire

Map 05 SU75

★★74% Hook House

London Rd RG27 9EQ
☎ 01256 762630 🖷 01256 760232
e-mail: reception@hookhousehotel.co.uk
Dir: *1m E of Hook on A30*

Several acres of landscaped grounds and a relaxing environment are provided at this friendly, small hotel. Bedrooms are well equipped, and some are located in an adjacent building. Public areas have a comfortable atmosphere with two lounges and a dining room overlooking the gardens. The hotel is a popular wedding venue at weekends.

ROOMS: 13 en suite 9 annexe en suite (4 GF) s £79.50-£89.50; d £99.50 (incl. bkfst) **CONF:** Thtr 40 Class 20 Board 20 Del £130 **PARKING:** 20 **NOTES:** ⊗ in restaurant Closed Xmas Civ Wed 50 **CARDS:**

HOPE, Derbyshire

Map 16 SK18

★★★70% Losehill House

Edale Rd S33 6RF
☎ 01433 621219 🖷 01433 622501
e-mail: info@losehillhouse.co.uk
web: www.losehillhouse.co.uk
Dir: *From A6187 into Hope, take turn opposite church into Edale Rd. 0.5m, take left fork & follow hotel signs.*

Standing in a peaceful location in the heart of the Hope Valley, this newly refurbished hotel offers very well equipped bedrooms together with a delightfully comfortable lounge plus a leisure pool. Staff are friendly and helpful and quality cooking is served in the pleasant restaurant.

ROOMS: 18 en suite 4 annexe en suite (3 fmly) (4 GF) ⊗ in all bedrooms s £50-£65; d £100-£130 **FACILITIES:** **Spa** Sauna Jacuzzi Xmas **CONF:** Thtr 25 Class 25 Board 16 Del from £100 **SERVICES:** Lift **PARKING:** 25 **NOTES:** ⊗ in restaurant **CARDS:**

HOPE COVE, Devon Map 03 SX63

★★71% Lantern Lodge
TQ7 3HE
☎ 01548 561280 01548 561736
Dir: *right off A381 Kingsbridge to Salcombe road. 1st right after passing Hope Cove sign then 1st left along Grand View Rd*
This attractive hotel close to the South Devon coastal path benefits from a friendly team of loyal staff. Bedrooms are well furnished and some have balconies. An imaginative range of home-cooked meals is available. There is a choice of lounges and a pretty garden with putting green. The indoor pool has large doors opening directly on to the garden.
ROOMS: 14 en suite (1 fmly) (1 GF) s £62-£86; d £118-£144 (incl. bkfst & dinner) **LB FACILITIES:** Sauna Putt green Multi-gym **PARKING:** 15 **NOTES:** No children 12yrs in restaurant Closed Dec-Feb **CARDS:**

★★70% Cottage
TQ7 3HJ
☎ 01548 561555 01548 561455
e-mail: info@hopecove.com web: www.hopecove.com
Dir: *from Kingsbridge on A381 to Salcombe. 2nd right at Marlborough, left for Inner Hope*
Glorious sunsets can be seen over the attractive bay from this popular hotel. Friendly and attentive service from the staff and management mean many guests return here. Bedrooms, many with sea views and some with balconies, are well equipped. There are three lounges and particularly interesting is the cabin, built from shipwrecked timbers. The restaurant offers an enjoyable dining experience.
ROOMS: 35 rms (26 en suite) (5 fmly) (7 GF) s £52.75-£77.50; d £85.50-£135 (incl. bkfst & dinner) **LB FACILITIES:** Table Tennis ch fac Xmas **CONF:** Thtr 50 Class 20 Board 24 Del from £54.25 **PARKING:** 50 **NOTES:** in restaurant Closed Early Jan - Early Feb **CARDS:**

HORLEY Map 06 TQ24
Hotels are listed under Gatwick Airport

HORNBY, Lancashire Map 18 SD56

★★68% *Castle Hotel*
Main St LA2 8JT
☎ 015242 21204 015242 22258
e-mail: Info@CastleHotel.net
Dir: *M6 junct 34 onto A683, hotel just over bridge on left*
Dating back to the 17th century in parts, this traditional stone building is situated opposite the castle. Bedrooms vary in size and style, with family rooms and a split-level suite available. Extensive informal eating areas, including the atmospheric Stables, prove popular with locals and visitors alike, whilst the attractively furnished restaurant gives the opportunity to dine in style.
ROOMS: 8 en suite (2 fmly) in 6 bedrooms **FACILITIES:** Pool table, Darts, Games room **PARKING:** 20 **NOTES:** in restaurant RS 24-25 Dec **CARDS:**

HORNCASTLE, Lincolnshire Map 17 TF26

★★71% Admiral Rodney
Best Western
North St LN9 5DX
☎ 01507 523131 01507 523104
e-mail: reception@admiralrodney.com
web: www.admiralrodney.com
Dir: *off A153 - Louth to Horncastle*
Enjoying a prime location in the centre of town, this smart hotel offers a high standard of accommodation. Bedrooms are well appointed and thoughtfully equipped for both business and leisure guests. Public areas include the Rodney public bar, a selection of meeting and conference rooms and an open-plan restaurant and lounge bar.
ROOMS: 31 en suite (3 fmly) (7 GF) in 17 bedrooms s £50-£55; d £70-£80 (incl. bkfst) **LB FACILITIES:** STV Xmas **CONF:** Thtr 140 Class 60 Board 50 Del £77 **SERVICES:** Lift **PARKING:** 60 **NOTES:** **CARDS:**

HORNING, Norfolk Map 13 TG31
See also Wroxham

★★★68% Petersfield House
Lower St NR12 8PF
☎ 01692 630741 01692 630745
e-mail: reception@petersfieldhotel.co.uk
Dir: *from Wroxham take A1062 for 2.5m then right into Horning. Hotel in centre on left*
Charming property dating back to the 1920s situated amid pretty landscaped grounds in the heart of this delightful riverside village. Bedrooms vary in size and style, each one is comfortably furnished and thoughtfully equipped; many of the rooms have lovely views of the garden. Public areas include a large lounge, a bar and a restaurant.
ROOMS: 17 en suite (1 fmly) (3 GF) s £65-£75; d £90-£105 (incl. bkfst) **LB FACILITIES:** Fishing Putt green Private moorings Boating ♫ Xmas **CONF:** Thtr 100 Class 100 Board 50 Del from £1000 **PARKING:** 70 **NOTES:** in restaurant Closed Jan Civ Wed 90 **CARDS:**

HORNS CROSS, Devon Map 03 SS32

★★★67% Hoops
EX39 5DL
☎ 01237 451222 01237 451247
e-mail: sales@hoopsinn.co.uk
Dir: *M5 junct 27 follow signs for Barnstaple. Take A39 by-passing Bideford, towards Bude. Hotel in dip just outside Horns Cross.*
The Hoops has been welcoming guests for many centuries with its whitewashed walls, thatched roof and real fires. Bedrooms offer plenty of character and include a number that have four-poster or half-tester beds. Guests have the private use of a quiet lounge and a pleasant seating area in the delightful rear garden. A fine selection of home-cooked meals can be taken in the bar or restaurant.
ROOMS: 13 en suite (1 fmly) (1 GF) in 4 bedrooms s £60-£85; d £90-£140 (incl. bkfst) **LB CONF:** Thtr 40 Class 20 Board 20 Del from £90 **PARKING:** 100 **NOTES:** in restaurant Closed 25 Dec **CARDS:**

HORRINGER, Suffolk Map 13 TL86

★★★★77% The Ickworth
IP29 5QE
☎ 01284 735350 01284 736300
e-mail: info@ickworthhotel.com
Dir: *Follow brown signs for Ickworth House, take 4th exit at rdbt, follow to staggered x-rds. Straight onto t-junct, turn left into village & almost immediately turn right into Ickworth Estate*
This stunning property manages to combine a National Trust property with clever retro design and still be child friendly. The combination of friendly and easygoing staff, a children's den, horses and bikes to ride, and wonderful 'Capability' Brown

continued

gardens to roam is the winning formula. Quality produce and technical skill are behind the inspiring food here.

ROOMS: 27 en suite 11 annexe en suite (35 fmly) (4 GF) ⊗ in 35 bedrooms s £175.50-£486; d £195-£540 (incl. bkfst & dinner) **LB** **FACILITIES: Spa** STV Riding Childrens creche, massage, manicures, aromatherapy ch fac Xmas **CONF:** Thtr 35 Class 30 Board 20 Del from £165 **SERVICES:** Lift **PARKING:** 40 **NOTES:** ⊗ in restaurant Civ Wed 40 **CARDS:**

HORSHAM, West Sussex Map 06 TQ13

★★★★ South Lodge
Brighton Rd RH13 6PS
☎ 01403 891711 01403 891766
e-mail: enquiries@southlodgehotel.co.uk
web: www.exclusivehotels.co.uk
(For full entry see Lower Beeding)

★★68% Ye Olde King's Head
Carfax RH12 1EG
☎ 01403 253126 01403 242291
e-mail: info@kings-head-horsham.co.uk
Dir: *Opposite Barclays Bank, at junction of Carfax and East St.*
A 14th-century former coaching inn situated in the heart of this busy town centre. Bedrooms are pleasantly decorated, well maintained and equipped with a good range of useful facilities. The spacious public rooms retain much of their original character; they include a lounge bar, a restaurant and a popular coffee shop serving quality home-made cakes.
ROOMS: 42 rms (41 en suite) (1 fmly) (7 GF) ⊗ in 17 bedrooms s £85-£95; d £95-£125 (incl. bkfst) **FACILITIES:** STV Town leisure facilities nearby-within walking distance **CONF:** Thtr 40 Class 20 Board 20 Del from £119.50 **PARKING:** 30 **NOTES:** ⊗ in restaurant **CARDS:**

Travel Inn
57 North St RH12 1RB
☎ 08701 977136 01403 270797
Dir: *opposite railway station, 5m from M23 junct 11*
Travel Inn offers good-quality, value-for-money accommodation. Spacious, en suite rooms with bath and shower comfortably accommodate a family of up to two adults and two children (to age 15). The restaurant and bar offers a varied menu. For further details consult the Hotel Groups page.
ROOMS: 40 en suite s £45.95-£48.95; d £45.95-£48.95

Packed in a hurry?
Ironing facilities should be available at all star levels, either in rooms or on request

HORWICH, Greater Manchester Map 15 SD61

★★★★72% De Vere White's
De Havilland Way BL6 6SF
☎ 01204 667788 01204 673721
e-mail: whites@devere-hotels.com
Dir: *M61 junct 6. 3rd right from slip road rdbt onto A6027 Mansell Way. Follow visitors' car park A for Hotel*

DE VERE HOTELS

Fully integrated within the Reebock Football Stadium, home of Bolton Wanderers, this modern hotel is a popular venue for business and conferences. Bedrooms are contemporary in style and equipped with a range of extras and many offer views of the pitch. The hotel has two eating options: a fine dining restaurant and informal brasserie. It also boasts a fully equipped indoor leisure centre and spacious bar/lounge area.
ROOMS: 125 en suite (1 fmly) ⊗ in 99 bedrooms s £130-£190; d £145-£205 (incl. bkfst) **LB** **FACILITIES: Spa** STV Sauna Solarium Gym Jacuzzi Steam room, Beauty salon Xmas **CONF:** Thtr 1690 Class 1080 Board 72 Del from £130 **SERVICES:** Lift **PARKING:** 2750 **NOTES:** ⊗ in restaurant Civ Wed 1000 **CARDS:**

HOUGHTON-LE-SPRING, Tyne & Wear Map 19 NZ34

★★67% *Chilton Lodge*
Black Boy Rd, Chilton Moor, Fencehouses DH4 6LX
☎ 0191 385 2694 0191 385 6762
Dir: *A1(M) junct 62, onto A690 to Sunderland. Left at Rainton Bridge and Fencehouses sign, cross rdbt and 1st left*

This country pub and hotel has been extended from the original farm cottages. Bedrooms are modern and comfortable and some rooms are particularly spacious. This hotel is popular for local weddings and functions; there is also a well-stocked bar and a wide range of dishes is served in the Orangery and restaurant.
ROOMS: 25 en suite (7 fmly) ⊗ in 7 bedrooms **FACILITIES:** STV Horse riding **CONF:** Thtr 60 Class 50 Board 30 **PARKING:** 100 **NOTES:** **CARDS:**

HOUNSLOW Hotels are listed under Heathrow Airport

HOVE See Brighton & Hove

HOVINGHAM, North Yorkshire Map 19 SE67

★★★67% Worsley Arms
High St YO62 4LA
☎ 01653 628234 01653 628130
e-mail: worsleyarms@aol.com
Dir: *from S take A64, signed York. towards Malton. At dual carriageway left to Hovingham. At Slingsby left and Hovingham 2m. Hotel on main street*
Overlooking the village green, this hotel has relaxing and attractive lounges with welcoming open fires. Bedrooms are also comfortable and several are contained in cottages across the green. The restaurant provides interesting, quality cooking, plus less formal dining in the Cricketers' Bar and Bistro to the rear.
ROOMS: 12 en suite 8 annexe en suite (2 fmly) (4 GF) in all bedrooms s £60-£90; d £75-£150 (incl. bkfst) **LB** **FACILITIES:** Squash Shooting ch fac Xmas **CONF:** BC Thtr 40 Class 40 Board 20 Del from £100 **PARKING:** 25 **NOTES:** in restaurant Civ Wed 75 **CARDS:**

HOWTOWN (NEAR POOLEY BRIDGE), Cumbria Map 18 NY41

Top 200 – Hotel

★★★
Sharrow Bay Country House
Sharrow Bay CA10 2LZ
☎ 017684 86301 & 86483 017684 86349
e-mail: enquiries@sharrow-bay.com
web: www.sharrow-bay.com
Dir: *at Pooley Bridge right fork by church to Howtown. At x-rds right and follow Lakeside Rd for 2m*
Enjoying breathtaking views and an idyllic location on the shores of Lake Ullswater, Sharrow Bay is often described as the first country house hotel. Individually styled bedrooms, all with a host of thoughtful extras, are situated either in the main house, in delightful buildings in the hotel's grounds or at Bank House - an Elizabethan farmhouse complete with lounges and breakfast room. Opulently furnished public areas include a choice of inviting lounges and two elegant dining rooms.
ROOMS: 8 en suite 14 annexe en suite (5 GF) s £150; d £160-£235 (incl. bkfst & dinner) **LB** **FACILITIES:** Xmas **CONF:** Thtr 25 Board 20 Del £240 **PARKING:** 35 **NOTES:** No children 13yrs in restaurant Civ Wed 30 **CARDS:**

HOYLAKE, Merseyside Map 15 SJ28

★★★65% Kings Gap Court
CH47 1HE
☎ 0151 632 2073 0151 632 0247
e-mail: kingsgapcourt@aol.com
In the reign of William III 'Hoyle Lake' was an army staging post from where the invasion of Ireland was launched in 1690, and the 'Kings Gap' area commemorates this slice of history. The lake no longer exists but the hotel that has adopted the name enjoys a peaceful residential location just a short walk from glorious sandy beaches. Modern bedrooms are stylish and comfortable whilst the bright and spacious day rooms include a popular bar and a conservatory restaurant.
ROOMS: 30 en suite (4 fmly) (7 GF) in 15 bedrooms **CONF:** Thtr 150 Class 100 Board 32 **PARKING:** 60 **NOTES:** in restaurant **CARDS:**

HUCKNALL, Nottinghamshire Map 16 SK54

Premier Lodge (Nottingham North West)
PREMIER LODGE.com
Nottingham Rd NG15 7PY
☎ 0870 9906518 0870 9906519
web: www.premierlodge.com
Dir: *from N exit M1 junct 27, A608 for approx 4m, then follow signs for A611 South. From S, exit M1 junct 26 onto A610 for approx 0.5m then follow signs for A611 North*
High quality, modern, budget accommodation, ideal for families and business travellers. All rooms feature bath, power shower and satellite TV, and most have telephones / modem points. The adjacent bar and restaurant offers a wide and varied menu.
ROOMS: 35 en suite s £50; d £50 **CONF:** Thtr 80

HUDDERSFIELD, West Yorkshire Map 16 SE11

★★★★61% Cedar Court
Ainley Top HD3 3RH
☎ 01422 375431 01422 314050
e-mail: huddersfield@cedarcourthotels.co.uk
web: www.cedarcourthotels.co.uk
Dir: *500yds from M62 junct 24*
Sitting adjacent to the M62, this hotel is an ideal location for business travellers or for those touring West Yorkshire. Bedrooms are spacious and comfortable and there is a busy lounge with snacks available all day as well as a modern restaurant and a fully equipped leisure centre. There are extensive meeting and banqueting facilities.
ROOMS: 114 en suite (6 fmly) (10 GF) in 70 bedrooms s £60-£99; d £60-£99 **LB** **FACILITIES:** Sauna Solarium Gym Steam room **CONF:** Thtr 500 Class 150 Board 100 **SERVICES:** Lift **PARKING:** 250 **NOTES:** Civ Wed **CARDS:**

★★★67% Bagden Hall
Wakefield Rd, Scissett HD8 9LE
☎ 01484 865330 01484 861001
e-mail: info@bagdenhall.demon.co.uk
web: www.bagdenhall.demon.co.uk
Dir: *on A636, between Scissett and Denby Dale*
Set in forty acres of well-tended grounds, with a par three nine-hole golf course, this elegant mansion house is close to the village of Scissett. The traditional public rooms include a bright

continued

conservatory where light meals are served, and a versatile conference/function room. Bedrooms vary in size, and all are well equipped and pleasantly furnished.

ROOMS: 16 en suite (3 fmly) s fr £60; d fr £80 (incl. bkfst) **FACILITIES:** STV ⛳ 9 Putt green **CONF:** Thtr 180 Class 120 Board 50 Del from £110 **PARKING:** 96 **NOTES:** ✗ ⊗ in restaurant Civ Wed 150 **CARDS:**

★★★67% The Old Golf House Hotel

corus hotels

New Hey Rd, Outlane HD3 3YP
☎ 01422 379311 01422 372694
e-mail: oldgolfhouse@corushotels.com

Dir: *M62 junct 23 (eastbound only), or junct 24. Follow A640 to Rochdale. Hotel on A640*

Situated close to the M62, this traditional hotel offers bedrooms which are equipped to a high, modern standard. A wide choice of dishes is served in the restaurant, and lighter meals are available in the lounge bar. The hotel, with lovely grounds, is a popular venue for weddings.

ROOMS: 52 en suite (4 fmly) (19 GF) ⊗ in 30 bedrooms s £60-£65; d £65-£75 **LB** **FACILITIES:** STV Putt green 5 Hole pitch & putt Xmas **CONF:** Thtr 70 Class 35 Board 30 Del from £95 **PARKING:** 100 **NOTES:** ⊗ in restaurant Civ Wed 90 **CARDS:**

★★★66% Pennine Manor

Best Western

Nettleton Hill Rd, Scapegoat Hill HD7 4NH
☎ 01484 642368 01484 642866
e-mail: penninemanor@bestwestern.co.uk

Dir: *M62 junct 24, signed for Rochdale (A640) - Outlane Village, left after Highlander pub, hotel signposted from road*

Set high in The Pennines, this attractive stone-built hotel enjoys magnificent panoramic views. Bedrooms vary in size and all are thoughtfully equipped. There is a popular bar and restaurant

continued

offering a good selection of snacks and meals. The modern function facilities make this a popular venue for both weddings and business meetings.

ROOMS: 31 en suite (4 fmly) (15 GF) ⊗ in 23 bedrooms s £50-£65; d £62.50-£72.50 (incl. bkfst) **LB** **FACILITIES:** STV **CONF:** BC Thtr 132 Class 56 Board 40 Del from £100 **PARKING:** 115 **NOTES:** ✗ ⊗ in restaurant Civ Wed 100 **CARDS:**

★★71% Lodge

48 Birkby Lodge Rd, Birkby HD2 2BG
☎ 01484 431001 01484 421590
e-mail: contact@birkbylodgehotel.com

Dir: *M62 junct 24, exit A629 for Birkby. Left at 1st lights, right after Nuffield Hospital (Birkby Lodge Rd). Hotel 100yds on left*

This family-run hotel is in a quiet residential area close to the city centre, and provides a relaxed ambience. Smart public areas include two comfortable lounges and an inviting restaurant where carefully prepared meals are served. Bedrooms vary in size and style and are well equipped; one has a grand four-poster bed. Service is friendly and efficient.

ROOMS: 13 en suite (2 fmly) (3 GF) ⊗ in all bedrooms s £50-£60; d £60-£120 **CONF:** BC Thtr 40 Class 22 Board 22 Del from £110 **PARKING:** 41 **NOTES:** ⊗ in restaurant Closed 26-27 Dec Civ Wed 60 **CARDS:**

Premier Lodge (Huddersfield)

PREMIER LODGE.com

New Hey Rd, Ainley Top HD2 2EA
☎ 0870 9906488 0870 9906489
web: www.premierlodge.com

Dir: *from M62 junct 24, take Brighouse exit from rbt (A643), take 1st left into Grimescar Rd, turn right into New Hey Rd*

High quality, modern, budget accommodation, ideal for families and business travellers. All rooms feature bath, power shower and satellite TV, and most have telephones / modem points. The adjacent bar and restaurant offers a wide and varied menu.

ROOMS: 40 en suite s £48; d £48

Travelodge

Leeds Rd, Mirfield WF14 0BY
☎ 08700 850 950 01924 489921

Dir: *M62 junct 25, follow A62 across 2 rdbts. Lodge on right*

Travelodge offers good quality, good value, modern accommodation. Ideal for families, the spacious, en suite bedrooms include remote-control TV, tea and coffee-making facilities and luxury beds. Meals can be taken at the nearby family restaurant. For further details consult the Hotel Groups page.

ROOMS: 27 en suite s fr £25; d fr £25

HUNMANBY, North Yorkshire   Map 17 TA07

★★69% Wrangham House Hotel

10 Stonegate YO14 0NS
☎ 01723 891333 🖷 01723 892973
e-mail: mervynpoulter@lineone.net
web: www.wranghamhouse.co.uk
Dir: *A64 onto A1039 to Filey. Right onto Hunmanby Rd, hotel behind All Saints Church*

This former Georgian vicarage is only a few minutes' drive from lovely sandy beaches, and stands in beautiful wooded gardens next to the village church. The family-owned and well-furnished hotel features individually styled bedrooms, a comfortable sitting room and cosy bar. The spacious dining room offers a good selection of well-produced dishes.
ROOMS: 8 en suite 4 annexe en suite (1 fmly) (2 GF) ⊗ in all bedrooms s £45-£50; d £75-£90 (incl. bkfst) **LB** **FACILITIES:** Xmas **CONF:** Thtr 50 Class 20 Board 20 **PARKING:** 20 **NOTES:** ⊗ in restaurant Civ Wed 50 **CARDS:**

HUNSTANTON, Norfolk   Map 12 TF64

★★★69% Le Strange Arms

Best Western

Golf Course Rd, Old Hunstanton PE36 6JJ
☎ 01485 534411 🖷 01485 534724
e-mail: reception@lestrangearms.co.uk
Dir: *off A149 1m N of Hunstanton. Left at sharp right bend by pitch & putt course*

Impressive hotel with superb views from the wide lawns down to the sandy beach and across The Wash. Bedrooms come in a variety of styles, from original rooms in the main house with period furnishings to more contemporary rooms in the new wing. Public rooms include a comfortable lounge bar and an attractive restaurant, where an interesting choice of dishes is served.
ROOMS: 36 en suite (4 fmly) ⊗ in 6 bedrooms s £61-£75; d £90-£120 (incl. bkfst) **LB** **FACILITIES:** STV Snooker Xmas **CONF:** BC Thtr 180 Class 150 Board 50 Del from £104 **PARKING:** 80 **NOTES:** ⊗ in restaurant Civ Wed 70 **CARDS:**

★★72% The Lodge Hotel & Restaurant

Old Hunstanton Rd PE36 6HX
☎ 01485 532896 🖷 01485 535007
e-mail: reception@thelodge-hotel.co.uk
web: www.thelodge-hotel.co.uk
Dir: *1m E of Hunstanton on A149*
Expect a friendly welcome at this family-run hotel, situated in a large landscaped garden and within easy reach of the beach and town centre. The spacious bedrooms are smartly decorated, well maintained and offer a good range of facilities. Public areas include a large lounge bar and an attractive restaurant with a cosy seating area.
ROOMS: 16 en suite 6 annexe en suite (3 fmly) (4 GF) ⊗ in 6 bedrooms s £36-£59; d £72-£114 (incl. bkfst) **LB** **FACILITIES:** STV Darts room Pool table Xmas **PARKING:** 70 **NOTES:** ⊗ in restaurant **CARDS:**

See advert on opposite page

HUNSTRETE, Somerset   Map 04 ST66

★★★79% ◎◎ Hunstrete House

BS39 4NS
☎ 01761 490490 🖷 01761 490732
e-mail: user@hunstretehouse.co.uk
web: www.hunstretehouse.co.uk
Dir: *from Bath take A4 to Bristol. At Globe Inn rdbt 2nd left onto A368 to Wells. 1m after Marksbury turn right for Hunstrete village. Hotel next left*
This delightful Georgian house enjoys a stunning setting in 92 acres of deer park and woodland on the edge of the Mendip Hills. Elegant bedrooms in the main building and coach house are both spacious and comfortable. Public areas feature antiques, paintings and fine china. The restaurant enjoys a well-deserved reputation for fine food and utilises much home-grown produce.
ROOMS: 25 en suite (2 fmly) (8 GF) ⊗ in 14 bedrooms s £135-£145; d £170-£180 (incl. bkfst) **LB** **FACILITIES:** STV Xmas **CONF:** Thtr 50 Class 40 Board 30 Del from £175 **PARKING:** 50 **NOTES:** ⊗ in restaurant Civ Wed 50 **CARDS:**

HUNTINGDON, Cambridgeshire   Map 12 TL27

★★★★71% Huntingdon Marriott Hotel

Marriott HOTELS·RESORTS·SUITES

Kingfisher Way, Hinchingbrooke Business Park PE29 6FL
☎ 01480 446000 🖷 01480 451111
e-mail: reservations.huntingdon@whitbread.com
Dir: *1m from Huntington centre on A14, close to Brampton racecourse*
With its excellent road links, this modern, purpose-built hotel is a popular venue for conferences and business meetings, and is convenient for Huntingdon, Cambridge and racing at Newmarket. Bedrooms are spacious and offer every modern comfort, including air conditioning. This hotel has been Highly Commended in the AA Accessible Hotel of the Year Awards 2004-5.
ROOMS: 150 en suite (45 GF) ⊗ in 60 bedrooms s £72-£200; d £104-£250 (incl. bkfst) **LB** **FACILITIES:** **Spa** STV supervised Sauna Solarium Gym Jacuzzi ♫ Xmas **CONF:** Thtr 300 Class 150 Board 100 Del from £149 **SERVICES:** Lift air con **PARKING:** 250 **NOTES:** ⊗ in restaurant Civ Wed 300 **CARDS:**

★★★78% The Old Bridge
1 High St PE29 3TQ
☎ 01480 424300 01480 411017
e-mail: oldbridge@huntsbridge.co.uk
web: www.huntsbridge.com
Dir: *from A14 or A1 follow Huntingdon signs. Hotel visible from inner ring road*

An imposing 18th-century building on the ring road close to shops and amenities that offers superb accommodation with good modern facilities. Guests can choose from the same menu whether dining in the open-plan terrace or the more formal restaurant with its bold colour scheme. The stylish and individually decorated bedrooms include many useful extras. The hotel also has a particularly good business centre with secretarial services.
ROOMS: 24 en suite (2 fmly) (2 GF) s £95-£130; d £125-£190 (incl. bkfst) **LB FACILITIES:** STV Fishing Private mooring for boats Xmas **CONF:** BC Thtr 50 Class 20 Board 24 Del £170 **SERVICES:** air con **PARKING:** 50 **NOTES:** ⊗ in restaurant Civ Wed 100
CARDS:

HYDE, Cheshire
Map 16 SJ99

Premier Lodge (Manchester East)
Stockport Rd, Mottram SK14 3AU
☎ 0870 9906334 0870 9906335
web: www.premierlodge.com
Dir: *at end of M67, between A57 and A560*
PREMIER LODGE.com
High quality, modern, budget accommodation, ideal for families and business travellers. All rooms feature bath, power shower and satellite TV, and most have telephones / modem points. The adjacent bar and restaurant offers a wide and varied menu.
ROOMS: 83 en suite s £44; d £44

Destination dining!
This symbol indicates a Restaurant with Rooms

HYTHE, Kent
Map 07 TR13

★★★★76% The Hythe Imperial
Princes Pde CT21 6AE
☎ 01303 267441 01303 264610
e-mail: hytheimperial@marstonhotels.com
MARSTON HOTELS
Dir: *M20, junct 11 onto A261. In Hythe follow Folkestone signs. Right into Twiss Rd to hotel*
Enjoying a seafront setting in the historic town, this lovely hotel is surrounded by 50 acres of golf course and beautiful gardens. Well-kept bedrooms are spacious and many enjoy views of the grounds or sea. Guests have a whole host of facilities on hand

continued

during their stay, including indoor and outdoor leisure facilities, a beauty salon and a choice of informal and formal dining.

The Hythe Imperial

ROOMS: 100 en suite (5 fmly) ⊗ in 38 bedrooms s £108-£133; d £158-£208 (incl. bkfst & dinner) **LB FACILITIES:** STV 9 Squash Snooker Sauna Solarium Gym Putt green Jacuzzi Beauty salon Fitness assessments Xmas **CONF:** Thtr 220 Class 120 Board 80 Del from £159 **SERVICES:** Lift **PARKING:** 200 **NOTES:** ⊗ in restaurant Civ Wed **CARDS:**

★★★70% Stade Court
West Pde CT21 6DT
☎ 01303 268263 01303 261803
e-mail: stadecourt@marstonhotels.com
Best Western
Dir: *M20 junct 11 onto A261*
Now under new ownership, this hotel is built on the site of a landing place, or 'stade', and is located right on the seafront in this

continued on p284

HYTHE, Kent Map 07 TR13

historic Cinque Port. Many of its well-maintained bedrooms enjoy splendid sea views and some of these have additional seating areas.
ROOMS: 42 en suite (5 fmly) in 7 bedrooms **FACILITIES:** STV 9 Squash Snooker Sauna Solarium Gym Putt green Jacuzzi All leisure facilities at sister hotel 600 mtrs away **CONF:** Thtr 40 Class 20 Board 30 **SERVICES:** Lift **PARKING:** 11 **NOTES:** in restaurant
CARDS:

ILFORD, Greater London
See LONDON SECTION plan 1 H5

Travel Inn
Redbridge Ln East IG4 5BG
08701 977140 020 8550 6214
Dir: *M11 (signed London East/A12 Chelmsford) follow A12 Chelmsford signs, Travel Inn on left at bottom of slip road*
Travel Inn offers good-quality, value-for-money accommodation. Spacious, en suite rooms with bath and shower comfortably accommodate a family of up to two adults and two children (to age 15). The restaurant and bar offers a varied menu. For further details consult the Hotel Groups page.
ROOMS: 44 en suite s £58.95; d £58.95 **CONF:** Thtr 30

Travelodge London (Ilford Central)
Clements Rd IG1 1BA
08700 850 950 020 8553 2920
Travelodge offers good quality, good value, modern accommodation. Ideal for families, the spacious, en suite bedrooms include remote-control TV, tea and coffee-making facilities and luxury beds. Meals can be taken at the nearby family restaurant. For further details consult the Hotel Groups page.
ROOMS: 91 en suite s fr £25; d fr £25

Travelodge London (Ilford North)
Beehive Ln, Gants Hill IG4 5DR
08700 850 950 020 8551 1712
Travelodge offers good quality, good value, modern accommodation. Ideal for families, the spacious, en suite bedrooms include remote-control TV, tea and coffee-making facilities and luxury beds. Meals can be taken at the nearby family restaurant. For further details consult the Hotel Groups page.
ROOMS: 32 en suite s fr £25; d fr £25

ILFRACOMBE, Devon Map 03 SS54

★★71% Elmfield
Torrs Park EX34 8AZ
01271 863377 01271 866828
e-mail: ann@elmfieldhotelilfracombe.co.uk
web: www.elmfieldhotelilfracombe.co.uk
Dir: *A361 to Ilfracombe. Left at 1st lights, left at 2nd lights. After 10yds left, hotel near top of hill on left*
Set in attractive grounds and with good parking, this Victorian property maintains much charm and enjoys views over the town towards the sea. Bedrooms are well equipped and spacious. The friendly proprietor and staff provide attentive service and carefully prepared, home-cooked cuisine. Public areas include a cosy bar, a small games room and comfortable lounge.
ROOMS: 11 en suite 2 annexe en suite (3 GF) in 5 bedrooms s £40-£45; d £80-£90 (incl. bkfst) **LB** **FACILITIES:** Sauna Solarium Gym Jacuzzi Pool table Xmas **PARKING:** 14 **NOTES:** No children 8yrs in restaurant Closed Nov-Mar (ex Xmas)
CARDS:

See advert on opposite page

★★68% Ilfracombe Carlton
Runnacleave Rd EX34 8AR
01271 862446 & 863711 01271 865379
e-mail: enquiries@ilfracombecarlton.co.uk
web: www.ilfracombecarlton.co.uk
Dir: *A361 to Ilfracombe, left at traffic lights, left at lights. Follow signs 'Tunnels, Beaches'*

Situated in the town and just a short walk from the theatre and harbour, this well-maintained hotel has a loyal following. The public areas include two lounges and a bar with an entertainment area. The comfortable bedrooms are attractively decorated and well equipped. A short set-price menu is offered in the bright and airy dining room.
ROOMS: 48 en suite (8 fmly) (6 GF) in 24 bedrooms s £30-£35; d £60-£70 (incl. bkfst) **LB** **FACILITIES:** Xmas **SERVICES:** Lift **PARKING:** 25 **NOTES:** in restaurant Closed Jan RS Feb
CARDS:

★★66% St Helier
Hillsborough Rd EX34 9QQ
01271 864906 01271 864906
e-mail: st_helier_hotel@yahoo.co.uk
Dir: *M5 junct 27 onto A361 into Ilfracombe, take Combe Martin road through High St. Hotel opposite 'Old Thatched Inn'*
Within walking distance of the town centre and the harbour, this small hotel has been in the same family ownership for over 60 years. Some of the bedrooms have distant views of the sea. Public rooms include a comfortable lounge, a cellar bar and a separate dining room where the short fixed-price menu offers both imaginative and popular dishes.
ROOMS: 9 en suite (1 fmly) s £34-£36; d £60-£64 (incl. bkfst) **LB** **PARKING:** 18 **NOTES:** in restaurant Closed Oct-Mar RS Apr-May
CARDS:

★★64% Imperial Hotel
Wilder Rd EX34 9AL
01271 862536 01271 862571
e-mail: imperial.ilfracombe@alfatravel.co.uk
Dir: *hotel opposite Landmark Theatre*
This popular hotel is just a short walk from the shops and harbour, overlooking gardens and the sea. Public areas include the spacious sun lounge, where guests can relax and enjoy the excellent views. Comfortable bedrooms are well equipped with many having the added bonus of sea views.
ROOMS: 104 en suite (6 fmly) s £28-£36; d £46-£66 (incl. bkfst) **LB** **FACILITIES:** Xmas **SERVICES:** Lift **PARKING:** 10 **NOTES:** in restaurant Closed Dec-Feb RS Mar & Nov **CARDS:**

Early start?
Hotels at all star levels should provide in-room alarm clocks and/or alarm calls

★★59% **Palm Court**
Wilder Rd EX34 9AS
☎ 01271 866644 📠 01271 863581
e-mail: contactholiday@palmcourt-hotel.co.uk
Dir: *A361 to Ilfracombe, then follow signs to seafront*
This hotel is very popular with groups and is within level walking distance of the harbour. Bedrooms are neatly presented and are all of a similar standard. Entertainment is provided in the bar/ballroom on certain evenings during the season, and short mat bowls can be played in another large area.
ROOMS: 50 en suite (20 fmly) (3 GF) ⊗ in 25 bedrooms s £25-£27; d £50-£54 (incl. bkfst) **LB** **FACILITIES:** Pool table, Short mat bowls, Skittles ♫ Xmas **SERVICES:** Lift **PARKING:** 16 **NOTES:** ⊗ in restaurant Closed 3-26 Jan **CARDS:**

A ★★ **Westwell Hall Hotel**
Torrs Park EX34 8AZ
☎ 01271 862792 📠 01271 862792
e-mail: westwellh@llhotel.fsnet.co.uk
Dir: *along Ilfracombe High Street onto Northfield Rd at lights. Left up Torrs Park. Right into Upper Torrs. Hotel 3rd drive on left*
ROOMS: 10 en suite s £25; d £50-£54 (incl. bkfst) **PARKING:** 10
NOTES: ⊗ in restaurant Closed Nov-Etr
CARDS:

ILKLEY, West Yorkshire
Map 19 SE14

★★★76% ◎ **Rombalds**
11 West View, Wells Rd LS29 9JG
☎ 01943 603201 📠 01943 816586
e-mail: reception@rombalds.demon.co.uk
web: www.rombalds.co.uk
Dir: *A65 from Leeds. Left at 3rd main lights, follow Ilkley Moor signs. Right at HSBC Bank onto Wells Rd. Hotel 600yds on left*

Best Western

This elegantly furnished Georgian townhouse is located in a peaceful terrace between the town and the moors. Delightful day rooms include a choice of comfortable lounges and an attractive restaurant which provides a relaxed venue in which to sample the skilfully prepared, imaginative meals. The bedrooms are tastefully furnished, well-equipped and include several spacious suites.
ROOMS: 18 en suite (4 fmly) ⊗ in 12 bedrooms s £55-£99.50; d £80-£119 (incl. bkfst) **LB** **FACILITIES:** STV Xmas **CONF:** Thtr 70 Class 40 Board 25 Del from £112.50 **PARKING:** 28 **NOTES:** ⊗ in restaurant Closed 28 Dec-2 Jan Civ Wed 70 **CARDS:**

★★★66% ***The Crescent***
Brook St LS29 8DG
☎ 01943 600012 📠 01943 601513
e-mail: creschot@dialstart.net
Dir: *at junct of Leeds Rd (A65) & Brook St*
This modern hotel is located in the heart of Ilkley, yet is convenient for major travel networks and the stunning countryside in this area. Spacious bedrooms, including a honeymoon suite with a fabulous bathroom, offer pleasing décor and facilities. The restaurant serves a variety of interesting dishes.
ROOMS: 21 en suite (3 fmly) ⊗ in all bedrooms **FACILITIES:** STV ♫
CONF: Thtr 100 Class 60 Board 40 **SERVICES:** Lift **PARKING:** 10
NOTES: ⊗ in restaurant **CARDS:**

★★★63% ***The Craiglands***
Cowpasture Rd LS29 8RQ
☎ 01943 430001 📠 01943 430002
e-mail: reservations@craiglands.co.uk
web: www.craiglands.co.uk
Dir: *off A65 into Ilkley. Left at T-junct. Past railway station and fork right into Cowpasture Rd. Hotel opposite school*

This grand Victorian hotel is ideally situated close to the town centre. Spacious public areas and a good range of services are ideal for business or leisure. Extensive conference facilities are available along with an elegant restaurant and traditionally styled

continued on p286

ILKLEY, continued

bar and lounge. Bedrooms vary in size and style and are comfortably furnished and well equipped.
ROOMS: 60 en suite (6 fmly) ⊗ in 19 bedrooms
FACILITIES: Complimentary use of local fitness centre **CONF:** Thtr 500 Class 200 Board 100 **SERVICES:** Lift **PARKING:** 200 **NOTES:** Civ Wed 500 **CARDS:**

Innkeeper's Lodge Ilkley
Hangingstone Rd LS29 8BT
☎ 01943 607335 📠 01943 604712
www.innkeeperslodge.com
Dir: *from A65 towards Ilkley town centre and at station turn right into Cowpasture Rd. Lodge approx 0.75m on left*

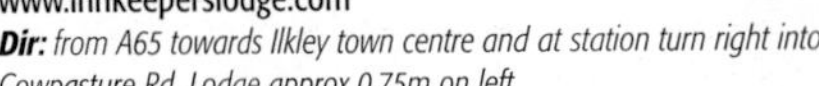

Smart rooms meet essential business requirements but also have home comforts, and depending on location may well have meeting rooms and pub dining. Dining options generally include all-day menus plus the added advantage of breakfast.
ROOMS: 16 en suite s £52-£55; d £52-£55

ILMINSTER, Somerset
Map 04 ST31

★★★67% Shrubbery
TA19 9AR
☎ 01460 52108 📠 01460 53660
e-mail: stuart@shrubberyhotel.com
Dir: *0.5m from A303 towards Ilminster town centre*
Set in attractive terraced gardens, this Victorian hotel offers well-equipped bedrooms of various sizes, including ground-floor rooms. Bar meals or full meals are available in the bar, lounges and restaurant. Additional facilities include a range of function rooms and a heated outdoor pool.
ROOMS: 16 en suite (3 fmly) s £65-£78; d £80-£98 (incl. bkfst) **LB**
FACILITIES: STV **CONF:** BC Thtr 250 Class 120 Board 80 Del from £120 **PARKING:** 100 **NOTES:** Civ Wed 200
CARDS:

Travelodge
Southfields Roundabout, Horton Cross TA19 9PT
☎ 08700 850 950 📠 01460 53748
Dir: *on A303*
Travelodge offers good quality, good value, modern accommodation. Ideal for families, the spacious, en suite bedrooms include remote-control TV, tea and coffee-making facilities and luxury beds. Meals can be taken at the nearby family restaurant. For further details consult the Hotel Groups page.
ROOMS: 32 en suite s fr £25; d fr £25

ILSINGTON, Devon
Map 03 SX77

★★★72%
The Ilsington Country House
Ilsington Village TQ13 9RR
☎ 01364 661452 📠 01364 661307
e-mail: hotel@ilsington.co.uk
web: www.ilsington.co.uk
Dir: *M5 onto A38 to Plymouth. Exit at Bovey Tracey. 3rd exit from rdbt to 'Ilsington', then 1st right. Hotel 5m by Post Office*
Peacefully situated with far-reaching views, this friendly hotel occupies an elevated position on the southern slopes of Dartmoor. Bedrooms, some of which are on the ground floor, are individually furnished. Local fish, meat and game feature on the daily-changing, innovative menus. On-site leisure facilities are available for hotel residents.

ROOMS: 25 en suite (2 fmly) (8 GF) ⊗ in 5 bedrooms s £76-£82; d £116-£120 (incl. bkfst) **LB** **FACILITIES: Spa** supervised Sauna Gym Jacuzzi Xmas **CONF:** Thtr 40 Class 30 Board 20 Del from £115 **SERVICES:** Lift **PARKING:** 100 **NOTES:** ⊗ in restaurant
CARDS:

INSTOW, Devon
Map 03 SS43

★★★74% Commodore
Marine Pde EX39 4JN
☎ 01271 860347 📠 01271 861233
e-mail: admin@the-commodore.co.uk
web: www.commodore-instow.co.uk
Dir: *M5 junct 27 follow N Devon link road to Bideford. Right before bridge, hotel 3m from bridge*

Maintaining its links with the local maritime and rural communities, The Commodore provides a comfortable and interesting place to stay. Situated at the mouth of the Tor and Torridge estuaries and overlooking the sandy beach, the hotel offers well equipped bedrooms, many with balconies and five new, ground floor suites especially suited to less able visitors. Guests have the option of eating in the restaurant, less formally in the Quarterdeck bar or on the terrace in the warmer months.
ROOMS: 20 en suite (2 fmly) (5 GF) ⊗ in 25 bedrooms s £60-£80; d £100-£180 (incl. bkfst & dinner) **LB** **FACILITIES:** Xmas **PARKING:** 200
NOTES: ⊗ in restaurant **CARDS:**

IPSWICH, Suffolk
Map 13 TM14

★★★★ Hintlesham Hall

George St IP8 3NS
☎ 01473 652334 📠 01473 652463
e-mail: reservations@hintleshamhall.com
web: www.hintleshamhall.com
(For full entry see Hintlesham)

Town House

★★★★ ◎◎ Salthouse Harbour
No 1 Neptune Quay IP4 1AS
☎ 01473 226789 📠 01473 226927
e-mail: staying@salthouseharbour.co.uk
Overlooking Ipswich quays this newly renovated hotel offers accommodation boasting a clever mix of contemporary style and original features. Spacious bedrooms provide luxurious comfort with good facilities. Two suites are available with stunning views and air conditioning. Award-winning food is served in the busy ground-floor brassiere.
ROOMS: 43 en suite (4 fmly) ⊗ in 35 bedrooms s £100-£190; d £130-£190 (incl. bkfst) **LB** **FACILITIES:** STV Xmas **SERVICES:** Lift **PARKING:** 30 **NOTES:** ⊗ in restaurant Civ Wed 70
CARDS:

★★★71% Courtyard by Marriott Ipswich

The Havens, Ransomes Europark IP3 9SJ
☎ 01473 272244 📠 01473 272484
e-mail: reservations.ipswich@whitbread.com
Dir: *off A14 Ipswich Bypass at 1st junct after Orwell Bridge signed Ransomes Europark. Hotel faces slip road*
Conveniently situated within easy striking distance of the town centre and major road networks, this modern and well-maintained hotel offers stylish accommodation with attractive, spacious bedrooms. The open-plan public rooms include a restaurant, a bar and a suite of conference rooms. Guests also have the use of a small fitness studio.
ROOMS: 60 en suite (28 fmly) (30 GF) ⊗ in 44 bedrooms s £52-£96; d £72-£105 (incl. bkfst) **LB** **FACILITIES:** STV Gym Guests may use nearby leisure club at special rate **CONF:** Thtr 160 Class 70 Board 55 Del £135 **SERVICES:** Lift **PARKING:** 150 **NOTES:** 🐕 Civ Wed 100
CARDS:

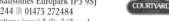

★★★68% Claydon Country House

16-18 Ipswich Rd, Claydon IP6 0AR
☎ 01473 830382 📠 01473 832476
e-mail: kayshotels@aol.com
Dir: *from A14, NW of Ipswich. After 4m take Great Blakenham Rd, B1113 to Claydon, hotel on left*

This delightful hotel is within easy driving distance of Ipswich town centre. The pleasantly decorated bedrooms are thoughtfully equipped; one room has a lovely four-poster bed. An interesting choice of freshly prepared dishes is available in the smart restaurant, and guests also have the use of a relaxing lounge bar.
ROOMS: 19 en suite (2 fmly) (5 GF) ⊗ in 10 bedrooms s £59-£79; d £69-£89 (incl. bkfst) **LB** **FACILITIES:** STV Xmas **CONF:** Thtr 120 Class 60 Board 55 Del from £110 **PARKING:** 60 **NOTES:** 🐕 ⊗ in restaurant Civ Wed 75 **CARDS:**

★★★65% Novotel Ipswich
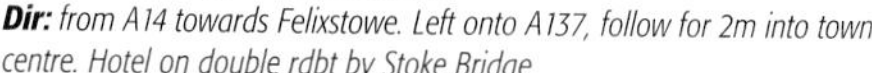
Greyfriars Rd IP1 1UP
☎ 01473 232400 📠 01473 232414
e-mail: h0995@accor-hotels.com
Dir: *from A14 towards Felixstowe. Left onto A137, follow for 2m into town centre. Hotel on double rdbt by Stoke Bridge*
Situated in the centre of town, this modern, red brick hotel is close to shops, bars and restaurants. The open-plan public areas include a Mediterranean-style restaurant and a bar with a small games area. Bedrooms are well-designed for most needs and simply decorated; three are suitable for less mobile guests.
ROOMS: 100 en suite (6 fmly) ⊗ in 76 bedrooms s £64-£98; d £75-£109 (incl. bkfst) **LB** **FACILITIES:** STV Pool table, Complimentary use of gym, sauna, jacuzzi **CONF:** Thtr 180 Class 75 Board 45 Del from £100 **SERVICES:** Lift air con **PARKING:** 50
CARDS:

★★★64% Hotel Elizabeth
London Rd, Copdock IP8 3JD
☎ 01473 209988 📠 01473 730801
e-mail: countyipswich@corushotels.com
Dir: *close to A12/A14 junct S of Ipswich. Exit A12 at Washbrook and Copdock sign. Hotel on A12, 1m on left*

A purpose-built hotel situated on the outskirts of the town centre, and close to the major road networks. The spacious bedrooms are pleasantly decorated and equipped with all the usual facilities. The open-plan public areas include a smart restaurant, a bar and a comfortable lounge, as well as leisure facilities.
ROOMS: 76 en suite (51 fmly) (23 GF) ⊗ in 60 bedrooms s £45-£110; d £45-£110 **LB** **FACILITIES:** Sauna Gym Jacuzzi Xmas **CONF:** BC Thtr 400 Class 200 Board 35 Del from £105 **SERVICES:** Lift **PARKING:** 360 **NOTES:** 🐕 ⊗ in restaurant Civ Wed
CARDS:

⌂ Travel Inn Ipswich (South)

Bourne Hill, Wherstead IP2 8ND
☎ 08701 977143 📠 01473 692283
Dir: *From A14 follow signs for Ipswich Central A137 and then Ipswich Central & Docks. At bottom of hill take 2nd exit off rdbt. Inn on right*
Travel Inn offers good-quality, value-for-money accommodation. Spacious, en suite rooms with bath and shower comfortably accommodate a family of up to two adults and two children (to age 15). The restaurant and bar offers a varied menu. For further details consult the Hotel Groups page.
ROOMS: 40 en suite s £45.95-£46.95; d £45.95-£46.95
CONF: Thtr 30 Board 20

 AA Rosette Award for culinary excellence

IPSWICH, continued

⌂ Travel Inn (Ipswich North)

Paper Mill Ln, Claydon IP6 0BE
☎ 0870 238 3311 📠 01473 833127
e-mail: ipswich.mti@whitbread.com
Dir: *on A14 NW of Ipswich at Great Blakenham/Claydon/RAF Wattisham junct, at rdbt take exit into Papermill Ln, Travel Inn on left*

travel inn

Travel Inn offers good-quality, value-for-money accommodation. Spacious, en suite rooms with bath and shower comfortably accommodate a family of up to two adults and two children (to age 15). The restaurant and bar offers a varied menu. For further details consult the Hotel Groups page.
ROOMS: 59 en suite s £45.95-£46.95; d £45.95-£46.95

⌂ Travelodge (Ipswich Capel)

Capel St Mary IP9 2JP
☎ 08700 850 950 📠 0870 1911542
Dir: *5m S on A12*

Travelodge

Travelodge offers good quality, good value, modern accommodation. Ideal for families, the spacious, en suite bedrooms include remote-control TV, tea and coffee-making facilities and luxury beds. Meals can be taken at the nearby family restaurant. For further details consult the Hotel Groups page.
ROOMS: 32 en suite s fr £25; d fr £25

ISLE OF Places incorporating the words 'Isle of' or 'Isle' will be found under the actual name - eg Isle of Wight is listed under Wight, Isle of.

IVYBRIDGE, Devon — Map 03 SX65

★★73% ❀ Glazebrook House Hotel & Restaurant

TQ10 9JE
☎ 01364 73322 📠 01364 72350
e-mail: enquiries@glazebrookhouse.com
Dir: *from Exeter take Marley Head exit to South Brent. 2nd turning on right after London Inn. From Plymouth take Woodpecker exit*

Enjoying a tranquil and convenient location next to the Dartmoor National Park and set within four acres of gardens, this 18th-century former gentleman's residence offers comfortable and friendly accommodation. Bedrooms are well appointed and public areas are spacious. Cuisine offers interesting combinations of fresh locally sourced produce.
ROOMS: 10 en suite ⊗ in all bedrooms s £50-£90; d £75-£145 (incl. bkfst) **LB** **CONF:** BC Thtr 100 Class 60 Board 40 Del from £65 **PARKING:** 40 **NOTES:** ✗ ⊗ in restaurant Closed 1st 2 weeks in Jan Civ Wed 80 **CARDS:**

★★66% *Sportsmans Inn Hotel & Restaurant*

Exeter Rd PL21 0BQ
☎ 01752 892280 📠 01752 690714
e-mail: info@thesportsmansinn.co.uk
Dir: *off A38 at Ivybridge. Through town, hotel on main road*

This deservedly popular and friendly inn continues to enjoy a healthy trade from both locals and visitors, attracted to the wide choice of good-value meals and snacks available in its open-plan bar and restaurant. Bedrooms are well-equipped and include both a ground-floor room and an impressive four-poster.
ROOMS: 14 en suite **FACILITIES:** ♫ **PARKING:** 50 **NOTES:** ✗ RS 25 Dec **CARDS:**

KEGWORTH See Nottingham East Midlands Airport

KEIGHLEY, West Yorkshire — Map 19 SE04

★★67% Dalesgate

406 Skipton Rd, Utley BD20 6HP
☎ 01535 664930 📠 01535 611253
e-mail: stephen.e.atha@btinternet.com
Dir: *In town centre follow A629 over rdbt. Right after 0.75m into St. John's Rd. 1st right into hotel car park*

Originally the residence of a local chapel minister, this modern, well-established hotel has been expanded with the addition of a new wing to provide well-equipped, comfortable bedrooms. The hotel also boasts a cosy bar and pleasant restaurant, serving an imaginative range of dishes. A large car park is provided to the rear.
ROOMS: 20 en suite (2 fmly) (3 GF) s £35-£42; d £50-£60 (incl. bkfst) **LB** **PARKING:** 25 **NOTES:** ⊗ in restaurant RS 22 Dec-4 Jan **CARDS:**

⌂ Innkeeper's Lodge

Bradford Rd BD21 4BB
☎ 01535 610611
www.innkeeperslodge.com
Dir: *From M606 rdbt take A6177, at next rdbt A641 & A650 towards Keighley. Lodge on 2nd rdbt*

Innkeeper's Lodge

Smart rooms meet essential business requirements but also have home comforts, and depending on location may well have meeting rooms and pub dining. Dining options generally include all-day menus plus the added advantage of breakfast.
ROOMS: 43 en suite s £42; d £42

KENDAL, Cumbria — Map 18 SD59

See also Crooklands

★★★75% ❀
The Castle Green Hotel in Kendal

LA9 6BH
☎ 01539 734000 📠 01539 735522
e-mail: reception@castlegreen.co.uk
web: www.castlegreen.co.uk
Dir: *M6 junct 36, towards Kendal. Right at 1st lights, left at rdbt to "K" Village then right for 0.75m to hotel at T- junct*

Best Western

This smart, modern hotel enjoys a peaceful location and is conveniently situated for access to both the town centre and the M6. Stylish bedrooms are thoughtfully equipped for both the business and leisure guest. The Greenhouse Restaurant provides imaginative dishes, alternatively Alexander's pub serves food all day. The hotel has a fully equipped business centre.
ROOMS: 100 en suite (3 fmly) (25 GF) ⊗ in 20 bedrooms s £69-£89; d £98-£118 (incl. bkfst) **LB** **FACILITIES:** STV Solarium Gym Steam Room, Aerobics, Yoga, Beauty Salon ♫ **CONF:** Thtr 350 Class 200 Board 120 Del from £135 **SERVICES:** Lift **PARKING:** 200 **NOTES:** ✗ ⊗ in restaurant Civ Wed 250 **CARDS:**

★★★60% *Riverside Hotel Kendal*
Beezon Rd, Stramongate Bridge LA9 4BZ
☎ 01539 734861 📠 01539 734863
e-mail: info@riversidekendal.co.uk
Dir: *M6 junct 36 Sedburgh, Kendal 7 miles, left at end of Ann St, 1st right onto Beelow Rd, hotel on left*

Centrally located in this market town, and enjoying a peaceful riverside location, this 17th-century former tannery provides an ideal base for both business travellers and tourists. The comfortable bedrooms are well equipped, and open-plan day rooms include the attractive restaurant and bar. Conference and leisure facilities are also available.

ROOMS: 47 en suite (18 fmly) (10 GF) ⊗ in 20 bedrooms **FACILITIES:** STV Squash Gym Badminton court **CONF:** Thtr 120 Class 90 Board 90 Del from £80 **SERVICES:** Lift **PARKING:** 60 **NOTES:** ⊗ in restaurant Civ Wed 120 **CARDS:**

KENILWORTH, Warwickshire — Map 10 SP27

★★★★63% Chesford Grange
Chesford Bridge CV8 2LD
☎ 01926 859331 📠 01926 859075
e-mail: chesfordgrange@paramount-hotels.co.uk
web: www.paramount-hotels.co.uk
Dir: *0.5m SE of junct A46/A452. At rdbt turn right signed Leamington Spa. After 250yds at x-rds turn right and hotel on left*

PARAMOUNT GROUP OF HOTELS

This much-extended hotel set in 17 acres of private grounds is well located for Birmingham International Airport, the NEC and major routes. Bedrooms range from traditional style to contemporary Art + Tech rooms featuring state-of-the-art technology. Public areas include a leisure club and extensive conference and banqueting facilities.

ROOMS: 210 en suite 9 annexe en suite (4 fmly) (50 GF) ⊗ in 80 bedrooms **FACILITIES:** STV Solarium Gym Jacuzzi Steam room Xmas **CONF:** BC Thtr 600 Class 400 Board 50 Del from £160 **SERVICES:** Lift **PARKING:** 600 **NOTES:** Civ Wed **CARDS:**

★★★★62% De Montfort
Abbey End CV8 1ED
☎ 01926 855944 📠 01926 857830
e-mail: demontfort@macdonald-hotels.co.uk
Dir: *from A46 take A452 towards Leamington. At rdbt left to Kenilworth town centre, along high street. Hotel at top opposite clock tower*

MACDONALD HOTELS

Situated in the centre of town, in the heart of Shakespeare country, this popular business hotel is well located for access to the major commercial centres of the Midlands. Public areas include a range of meeting and function rooms, a comfortable lounge/bar area and a traditional restaurant.

ROOMS: 108 en suite (15 fmly) ⊗ in 55 bedrooms s £40-£105; d £80-£125 (incl. bkfst) **LB** **FACILITIES:** STV Free use of nearby pool and gym Xmas **CONF:** Thtr 300 Class 100 Board 40 Del from £115 **SERVICES:** Lift **PARKING:** 65 **NOTES:** ⊗ in restaurant Civ Wed 116 **CARDS:**

★★★76% Peacock
149 Warwick Rd CV8 1HY
☎ 01926 851156 & 864500 📠 01926 864644
e-mail: reservations@peacockhotel.com
Dir: *A46/A452 signed to Kenilworth. Hotel in 0.25m on right after St John's Church*

Best Western

Conveniently located for the town centre, the Peacock offers a peaceful retreat and service is delivered in a most professional manner by friendly staff. Vibrant colour schemes run through pleasing public rooms and attractive accommodation are complemented by two dining options: the Malabar room, offering modern European dining, and the Coconut Lagoon serving Southern Indian dishes.

ROOMS: 23 en suite 6 annexe en suite (5 fmly) (10 GF) ⊗ in 18 bedrooms s £39-£100; d £49-£120 (incl. bkfst) **FACILITIES:** STV Xmas **CONF:** BC Thtr 90 Class 50 Board 50 Del from £90 **PARKING:** 30 **NOTES:** Civ Wed 90 **CARDS:**

KENTON, Greater London
See LONDON SECTION plan 1 C5

Travel Inn Harrow
Kenton Rd HA3 8AT
☎ 08701 977146 📠 020 8909 1604
Dir: *M1 junct 5 follow signs to Harrow & Kenton.*
Between Harrow & Wembley on A4006 opposite Kenton Railway Station

travel inn

Travel Inn offers good-quality, value-for-money accommodation. Spacious, en suite rooms with bath and shower comfortably accommodate a family of up to two adults and two children (to age 15). The restaurant and bar offers a varied menu. For further details consult the Hotel Groups page.

ROOMS: 70 en suite s £56.95; d £56.95 **CONF:** Class 50

KESWICK, Cumbria — Map 18 NY22

★★★75% Dale Head Hall Lakeside
Lake Thirlmere CA12 4TN
☎ 017687 72478 📠 017687 71070
e-mail: onthelakeside@daleheadhall.co.uk
web: www.daleheadhall.co.uk
Dir: *between Keswick and Grasmere. Off A591 onto private drive*

Formerly the summer residence of the Mayor of Manchester, the main house dates from the mid 16th century and has a spectacular lakeside location. Dinner is served in the atmospheric beamed restaurant and features the best local produce. Bedrooms, many newly upgraded, are spacious and feature high quality furniture, made by the proprietor.

ROOMS: 12 en suite (1 fmly) ⊗ in all bedrooms d £100-£120 (incl. bkfst) **LB** **FACILITIES:** no TV in bdrms Fishing ch fac Xmas **PARKING:** 31 **NOTES:** ⊗ in restaurant Closed 31 Dec-31 Jan **CARDS:**

See advert on page 291

K

KESWICK, continued

★★★75% Derwentwater

Portinscale CA12 5RE
☎ 017687 72538 📠 017687 71002
e-mail: info@derwentwater-hotel.co.uk
web: www.derwentwater-hotel.co.uk
Dir: *off A66 turn into Portinscale and through village then as road turns right take left turn as signed*

This is a popular and friendly holiday hotel with gardens that stretch down to the shores of Derwentwater. It offers a wide range of bedrooms, all thoughtfully equipped and some with good views of the lake. Inviting public areas include a conservatory lounge and shop.
ROOMS: 46 en suite (1 fmly) (2 GF) s £65-£85; d £130-£190 (incl. bkfst) **LB** **FACILITIES:** Fishing Putt green Access to local leisure facilities ♫ Xmas **CONF:** Thtr 20 Class 10 Board 14 Del from £80 **SERVICES:** Lift **PARKING:** 100 **NOTES:** ⊘ in restaurant
CARDS:

See advert on opposite page

★★★69% Keswick Country House

Station Rd CA12 4NQ
☎ 0845 458 4333 📠 01253 754222
e-mail: reservations@choice-hotels.co.uk
web: www.thekeswickhotel.co.uk
Dir: *M6 junct 40/A66 , 1st slip road into Keswick, then follow signs for leisure pool.*

This impressive Victorian hotel is set amid landscaped gardens. Eight superior bedrooms have been created in the Station Wing, which is accessed through the Victorian conservatory. Main house rooms, undergoing refurbishment, are comfortably modern in style and offer a good range of amenities. Public areas include a well-stocked bar, a spacious and relaxing lounge, and an attractive restaurant.
ROOMS: 74 en suite (6 fmly) s £42-£108; d £84-£216 (incl. bkfst & dinner) **FACILITIES:** STV Snooker Putt green Leisure facilities close by. ch fac Xmas **CONF:** Thtr 70 Class 40 Board 40 **SERVICES:** Lift **PARKING:** 70 **NOTES:** ⊘ in restaurant Civ Wed
CARDS:

★★★67% Skiddaw

Main St CA12 5BN
☎ 017687 72071 📠 017687 74850
e-mail: info@skiddawhotel.co.uk
web: www.skiddawhotel.co.uk
Dir: *A66 to Keswick follow signs for town centre. Hotel in Market Sq*

This privately owned hotel is centrally located overlooking Market Square. The smartly furnished bedrooms include some family suites and a room with a four-poster bed. Facilities include an

continued on p292

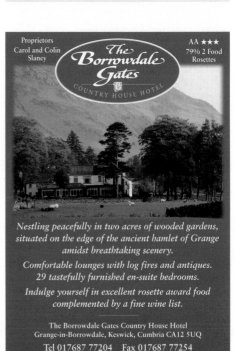

The Derwentwater Hotel

Privately owned, on the shore of Derwentwater one mile from Keswick.

48 bedrooms many with Lake and Borrowdale Valley view. 16 acres of conservation gardens and grounds down to the Lake. Magnificent Garden Room/Conservatory with views over putting green to the Lake.

Excellent 'Deer's Leap' restaurant with friendly staff, serving a wide variety of locally produced fare, all prepared with care by our Head Chef.

Guests have temporary membership of luxury health club and spa (no children under 16) at nearby Oxley's Health Club.

Well mannered dogs welcome, and full disabled facilities in two ground floor rooms.

Telephone 017687 72538
www.derwentwater-hotel.co.uk

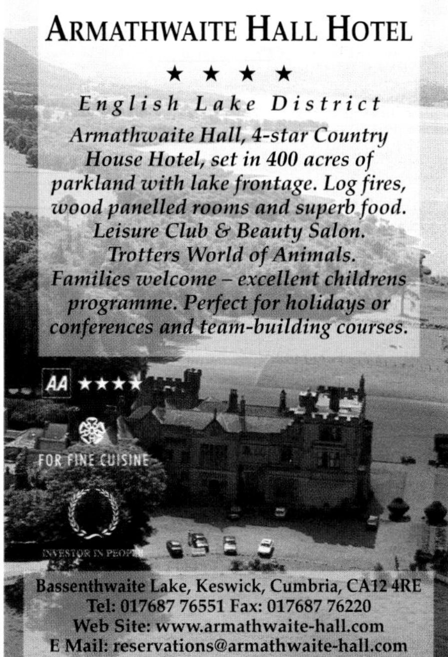

ARMATHWAITE HALL HOTEL
★ ★ ★ ★
English Lake District
Armathwaite Hall, 4-star Country House Hotel, set in 400 acres of parkland with lake frontage. Log fires, wood panelled rooms and superb food. Leisure Club & Beauty Salon. Trotters World of Animals. Families welcome – excellent childrens programme. Perfect for holidays or conferences and team-building courses.
AA ★★★★
FOR FINE CUISINE
Bassenthwaite Lake, Keswick, Cumbria, CA12 4RE
Tel: 017687 76551 Fax: 017687 76220
Web Site: www.armathwaite-hall.com
E Mail: reservations@armathwaite-hall.com

DALE HEAD HALL

on the lakeside

For those Special moments in your life

TEL: 017687 72478

Lake Thirlmere, Keswick CA12 4TN
email: onthelakeside@daleheadhall.co.uk
http://www.daleheadhall.co.uk
AA★★★ 75% - 2 Red Rosettes for Cuisine
ETC ★★★ - Gold Award for Excellence

ETC GOLD AWARD 2003

RECOMMENDED BY LEADING HOTEL GUIDES

K

KESWICK, continued

attractive and spacious restaurant, a lounge bar, a quiet lounge for residents and two conference/function rooms.

Skiddaw Hotel, Keswick

ROOMS: 40 en suite (7 fmly) ⊗ in 10 bedrooms **FACILITIES:** STV Sauna Free use of out of town leisure fac Xmas **CONF:** Thtr 70 Class 60 Board 40 **SERVICES:** Lift **PARKING:** 22 **NOTES:** ⊗ in restaurant Civ Wed **CARDS:**

See advert on opposite page

K

★★★63% *Kings Head Hotel & Inn*

Thirlspot, Thirlmere CA12 4TN
☎ 017687 72393 017687 72309
e-mail: stay@lakedistrictinns.co.uk
web: www.lakedistrictinns.co.uk
Dir: *M6 junct 40 onto A66 to Keswick, then A591 to Grasmere. Hotel in 4m*

This tastefully modernised 17th-century coaching inn enjoys a fabulous setting in a picturesque valley. Attractive bedrooms, some with outstanding views, vary in size. A smart lounge provides an alternative to the busy public bar, which serves a range of meals and snacks all day
ROOMS: 17 en suite (2 fmly) ⊗ in all bedrooms **FACILITIES:** STV Free use of local Leisure Centre **CONF:** Thtr 100 Class 40 Board 20 **PARKING:** 60 **NOTES:** ⊗ in restaurant Civ Wed 50
CARDS:

See advert on opposite page

★★76% Highfield

The Heads CA12 5ER
☎ 017687 72508 017687 80634
e-mail: info@highfieldkeswick.co.uk
Dir: *M6 junct 40, take A66 2nd exit at rdbt. Left following road to T- junct. Left again and right at mini rdbt. Then turn 4th right*
This friendly hotel close to the centre of town offers stunning views of Skiddaw, Cats Bells and Derwent Water. Elegant bedrooms, many of which are spacious, are thoughtfully equipped. Public areas include a choice of comfortable lounges, a small bar and a bright restaurant, where imaginative, modern cuisine is served.
ROOMS: 20 en suite (4 fmly) (2 GF) ⊗ in all bedrooms s £63-£80; d £100-£126 (incl. bkfst & dinner) **LB** **FACILITIES:** Xmas **PARKING:** 20 **NOTES:** ⊗ in restaurant Closed Jan **CARDS:**

★★75% Lyzzick Hall Country House

Under Skiddaw CA12 4PY
☎ 017687 72277 017687 72278
e-mail: lyzzickhall@btconnect.com
web: www.lyzzickhall.co.uk
Dir: *M6 junct 40 onto A66 to Keswick. Do not enter town, keep on Keswick by-pass. At rdbt 3rd exit onto A591 to Carlisle. Hotel 1.5m on right*
This privately-owned and personally run, delightful hotel stands in lovely landscaped gardens among the foothills of Skiddaw and enjoys fabulous views across the valley. Bedrooms are smartly appointed and thoughtfully equipped. Public areas include two spacious lounges, a small bar and an attractive restaurant offering a wide range of international cuisine.
ROOMS: 30 en suite 1 annexe en suite (3 fmly) s £51-£53; d £102-£106 (incl. bkfst) **LB** **FACILITIES:** Sauna Jacuzzi ch fac **CONF:** Board 15 **PARKING:** 40 **NOTES:** ⊗ in restaurant Closed 24-26 Dec & mid Jan-mid Feb **CARDS:**

★★74% Lairbeck

Vicarage Hill CA12 5QB
☎ 017687 73373 017687 73144
e-mail: aa@lairbeckhotel-keswick.co.uk
Dir: *A66 to rdbt with A591. Left then right onto Vicarage Hill, hotel 150yds on right*

This impeccably maintained, fine Victorian country house is situated close to the town in peacefully secluded, attractive gardens. There is a welcoming residents' bar and a comfortable dining room in which a range of freshly prepared dishes are served each day. Bedrooms, which include rooms on ground floor level, are individually styled and well equipped.
ROOMS: 14 en suite (1 fmly) (2 GF) ⊗ in all bedrooms s £40-£46; d £80-£86 (incl. bkfst) **LB** **PARKING:** 15 **NOTES:** No children 5yrs ⊗ in restaurant Closed 1st 2 wks Dec, Jan & Feb
CARDS:

★★67% Crow Park

The Heads CA12 5ER
☎ 017687 72208 017687 74776
e-mail: crowpark@marsh1.fsnet
Guests are warmly welcomed at this smartly presented hotel enjoying lovely views towards the lake and the Borrowdale Valley. Attractive day rooms include a lounge, a residents' bar and a dining room featuring photos of historic Lakeland scenes. Bedrooms come in a variety of sizes and offer a good range of amenities.
ROOMS: 26 en suite (1 fmly) ⊗ in 1 bedroom s £28.50-£35.50; d £57-£71 (incl. bkfst) **LB** **FACILITIES:** Xmas **PARKING:** 27 **NOTES:** ⊗ in restaurant **CARDS:**

K

KESWICK, continued

Top 200 – Hotel

★ Swinside Lodge
Grange Rd, Newlands CA12 5UE
☎ 017687 72948 017687 72948
e-mail: info@swinsidelodge-hotel.co.uk
Dir: *off A66 left at Portinscale. Follow road to Grange for 2m ignoring signs to Swinside & Newlands Valley*
No visit to the Lake District is complete without a stay at this delightful country house. Superb hospitality and skilful service mean that not only are new guests received like old friends, but the house party atmosphere that prevails means booking for dinner is increasingly necessary. Bedrooms are elegantly furnished and thoughtfully equipped. The lounges are cosy and comfortable, an ideal place to relax before dinner. The four-course set dinner menu is creative and well prepared and provides superb value for money.
ROOMS: 7 en suite in all bedrooms **FACILITIES:** Boules **CONF:** BC **PARKING:** 12 **NOTES:** No children 5yrs in restaurant **CARDS:**

K

KETTERING, Northamptonshire Map 11 SP87

★★★★74% Kettering Park
Kettering Parkway NN15 6XT
☎ 01536 416666 01536 416171
e-mail: kpark@shirehotels.co.uk
Dir: *off junct 9 A14, M1 to A1 link road, on Kettering Venture Park*

SHIRE HOTELS

A modern, stylish hotel providing a warm welcome and spacious, well-equipped and meticulously maintained bedrooms. Guests can choose from a menu of classical and contemporary dishes in the restaurant, alternatively light meals are served in the bar area.
continued

The wide-ranging leisure facilities are impressive and have been extended and refurbished.
ROOMS: 119 en suite (28 fmly) (20 GF) in 80 bedrooms s £144-£184; d £134-£204 (incl. bkfst) **LB** **FACILITIES: Spa** STV supervised Sauna Solarium Gym Steam rooms, Childrens splash pool, Activity studio Xmas **CONF:** BC Thtr 260 Class 120 Board 40 Del £179 **SERVICES:** Lift air con **PARKING:** 200 **NOTES:** in restaurant Civ Wed 150 **CARDS:**

See advert under NORTHAMPTON

Travel Inn
Rothwell Rd NN16 8XF
☎ 08701 977147 01536 415020
Dir: *on A14, off junct 7*

travel inn

Travel Inn offers good-quality, value-for-money accommodation. Spacious, en suite rooms with bath and shower comfortably accommodate a family of up to two adults and two children (to age 15). The restaurant and bar offers a varied menu. For further details consult the Hotel Groups page.
ROOMS: 39 en suite s £45.95-£46.95; d £45.95-£46.95 **CONF:** Thtr 15

Travelodge
On the A14 (Westbound) NN14 1WR
☎ 08700 850 950

Travelodge

Travelodge offers good quality, good value, modern accommodation. Ideal for families, the spacious, en suite bedrooms include remote-control TV, tea and coffee-making facilities and luxury beds. Meals can be taken at the nearby family restaurant. For further details consult the Hotel Groups page.
ROOMS: 40 en suite s fr £25; d fr £25

KIDDERMINSTER, Worcestershire Map 10 SO87
See also Stourport-on-Severn

★★★★68% Stone Manor
Stone DY10 4PJ
☎ 01562 777555 01562 777834
e-mail: enquiries@stonemanorhotel.co.uk
Dir: *2.5 miles from Kidderminster on A448, on right*
This converted, much extended former manor house stands in 25 acres of impressive grounds and gardens. The well-equipped accommodation includes rooms with four-poster beds and some more recently created, luxuriously appointed annexe bedrooms. The hotel is a popular venue for wedding receptions.
ROOMS: 52 en suite 5 annexe en suite (7 GF) in 11 bedrooms d £90-£150 **FACILITIES:** STV Putt green ch fac **CONF:** Thtr 150 Class 48 Board 60 Del £150 **PARKING:** 400 **NOTES:** in restaurant Civ Wed 150 **CARDS:**

★★★66% Gainsborough House
Bewdley Hill DY11 6BS
☎ 01562 820041 01562 66179
e-mail: reservations@gainsboroughhotel.co.uk
web: www.gainsborough-hotel.co.uk
Dir: *on A456. At hospital, over lights, hotel 200yds on right*
This listed Georgian property, situated on the edge of the town, has benefited from substantial improvements to public areas. The no-smoking bedrooms have also been extensively refurbished and are well equipped and comfortable. Additional features include a bar lounge, a restaurant with a carvery and also a carte menu, a lounge and attractive function rooms.
ROOMS: 43 en suite (8 fmly) in 12 bedrooms s £60-£75; d £80-£100 (incl. bkfst) **LB** **FACILITIES:** Solarium & beauty salon Xmas **CONF:** Thtr 250 Class 80 Board 60 Del from £110 **PARKING:** 130 **NOTES:** in restaurant Civ Wed 200 **CARDS:**

★★★66% The Granary Hotel & Restaurant

Heath Ln, Shenstone DY10 4BS
☎ 01562 777535 01562 777722
e-mail: info@granary-hotel.co.uk
web: www.granary-hotel.co.uk
Dir: *on A450, 0.5m from junct with A448*

This modern hotel offers spacious, well-equipped accommodation with many rooms enjoying views towards Great Witley and the Amberley Hills. There is an attractive modern restaurant and a carvery is available at weekends. There are also extensive conference facilities and the hotel is popular as a wedding venue.
ROOMS: 18 en suite (1 fmly) (18 GF) in 9 bedrooms s £65; d £75 (incl. bkfst) **LB** **CONF:** Thtr 200 Class 80 Board 70 Del from £100 **PARKING:** 96 **NOTES:** in restaurant Closed 24-26 Dec Civ Wed 199 **CARDS:**

KILLINGTON LAKE MOTORWAY SERVICE AREA (M6), Cumbria — Map 18 SD59

Travel Inn

Killington Lake, Motorway Service Area, Killington LA8 0NW
☎ 08701 977145 01539 621660
Dir: *From M6 southbound, Travel Inn 1 mile south of J37. From M6 northbound, exit J37 and rejoin southbound. Take access road to Travel Inn*
Travel Inn offers good-quality, value-for-money accommodation. Spacious, en suite rooms with bath and shower comfortably accommodate a family of up to two adults and two children (to age 15). The restaurant and bar offers a varied menu. For further details consult the Hotel Groups page.
ROOMS: 36 en suite s £45.95-£46.95; d £45.95-£46.95 **CONF:** Thtr 10

Town House Hotel
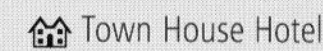
Country House Hotel
Travel Accommodation

KINGHAM, Oxfordshire — Map 10 SP22

★★★74% Mill House Hotel & Restaurant

OX7 6UH
☎ 01608 658188 01608 658492
e-mail: stay@millhousehotel.co.uk
Dir: *off A44 onto B4450. Hotel indicated by tourist sign*
This Cotswold-stone former mill house has been carefully converted into a comfortable and attractive hotel, and is set in well-kept grounds bordered by their own trout stream. Bedrooms are comfortable and provide thoughtfully equipped accommodation. There is a peaceful lounge and bar and an atmospheric restaurant where imaginative, skilful cooking is a highlight of any stay.

ROOMS: 21 en suite 2 annexe en suite (1 fmly) (7 GF) s £85-£95; d £120-£140 (incl. bkfst) **LB** **FACILITIES:** STV Fishing ch fac Xmas **CONF:** BC Thtr 70 Class 24 Board 20 **PARKING:** 62 **NOTES:** in restaurant **CARDS:**

KINGSBRIDGE, Devon — Map 03 SX74

Top 200 – Hotel

★★★ Buckland-Tout-Saints

Goveton TQ7 2DS
☎ 01548 853055 01548 856261
e-mail: buckland@tout-saints.co.uk
web: www.tout-saints.co.uk
Dir: *off A381 Totnes/Kingsbridge road to Goveton. Left into Goveton, up hill to St Peter's Church. Hotel 2nd right after church*
It's well worth navigating the winding country lanes to find this delightful Queen Anne manor house that has been host to many famous guests over the years. Set in seven acres of gardens and grounds the hotel is a peaceful retreat. Bedrooms are tastefully furnished and attractively decorated, most enjoying views of the gardens. Local produce is used with care and imagination in the restaurant. The large function room opens on to the terrace and is a popular choice for weddings.
ROOMS: 12 en suite (1 fmly) in 1 bedroom s £75-£140; d £150-£300 (incl. bkfst) **LB** **FACILITIES:** Putt green Petanque pitch Xmas **CONF:** Thtr 150 Class 100 Board 70 Del from £100 **PARKING:** 42 **NOTES:** in restaurant Closed 3 wks Jan Civ Wed 90 **CARDS:**

Popped the question?
Hotels with Civ Wed in their entry are licensed for civil wedding ceremonies. Maximum numbers for the ceremony only are shown, e.g. Civ Wed 120

KINGSGATE, Kent Map 07 TR37

★★★70% The Fayreness

Marine Dr CT10 3LG
☎ 01843 868641 🖷 01843 608750
e-mail: fayreness@thorleytaverns.com
Dir: *A28 onto B2051 which becomes B2052. Pass Holy Trinity Church on right and '19th Hole' public house. Next left, down Kingsgate Ave, hotel at end on left*

Situated on the cliff tops overlooking the English Channel, just a few steps from a sandy beach and adjacent to the North Foreland Golf Club. The spacious bedrooms are tastefully furnished with many thoughtful touches; some rooms have stunning sea views. Public rooms include a large open-plan lounge/bar, a function room, dining room and conservatory restaurant.

ROOMS: 29 en suite ⊘ in 17 bedrooms s £50-£140; d £65-£150 (incl. bkfst) **LB FACILITIES:** STV **CONF:** Thtr 50 Class 28 Board 36 **PARKING:** 70 **NOTES:** ⊘ in restaurant Civ Wed 80
CARDS:

See advert under BROADSTAIRS

KINGS LANGLEY, Hertfordshire Map 06 TL00

Premier Lodge (King's Langley)

PREMIER LODGE.com

Hempstead Rd WD4 8BR
☎ 0870 9906372 🖷 0870 9906373
web: www.premierlodge.com
Dir: *1m from M25 junct 20, on A4251 after Kings Langley*

High quality, modern, budget accommodation, ideal for families and business travellers. All rooms feature bath, power shower and satellite TV, and most have telephones / modem points. The adjacent bar and restaurant offers a wide and varied menu.

ROOMS: 60 en suite s £56; d £56

KING'S LYNN, Norfolk Map 12 TF62

★★★ Congham Hall Country House

Lynn Rd PE32 1AH
☎ 01485 600250 🖷 01485 601191
e-mail: info@conghamhallhotel.co.uk
web: www.conghamhallhotel.co.uk
(For full entry see Grimston)

★★★70% Knights Hill

Best Western

Knights Hill Village, South Wootton PE30 3HQ
☎ 01553 675566 🖷 01553 675568
e-mail: reception@knightshill.co.uk
Dir: *junct A148/A149*

Knights Hill is a hotel village complex, set on a 16th-century site, conveniently located for main road access on the outskirts of the town. Smartly decorated and well-equipped bedrooms are situated in extensions to the original hunting lodge. The main house is full of historic charm, combined with modern conference, banqueting and indoor leisure facilities. Public rooms also include a choice of dining options in the Garden Restaurant and the Farmers Arms pub.

ROOMS: 43 en suite 18 annexe en suite (33 GF) ⊘ in 39 bedrooms s £65-£120; d £85-£140 **LB FACILITIES:** STV Sauna Solarium Gym Jacuzzi Heli-pad Xmas **CONF:** Thtr 299 Class 150 Board 30 **PARKING:** 350 **NOTES:** ⊘ in restaurant Civ Wed 90
CARDS:

★★★62% *The Duke's Head Hotel*

Tuesday Market Place PE30 1JS
☎ 01553 774996 🖷 01553 763556
e-mail: dukeshead@corushotels.com
Dir: *on town centre one-way system left at road split then left at lights. Along St Anns St into Chapel St, hotel past car park on right*

Popular 16th-century coaching inn situated in a prominent position overlooking the market place. Bedrooms are pleasantly furnished and equipped with a good range of useful extras. Public areas include a spacious lounge, a non-smoking lounge-bar and a public bar. Dining options include the informal Griffins Brasserie or the more formal main restaurant.

ROOMS: 71 en suite (2 fmly) ⊘ in 33 bedrooms **CONF:** Thtr 240 Class 120 Board 60 **SERVICES:** Lift **PARKING:** 41 **NOTES:** ⊘ in restaurant Civ Wed 100 **CARDS:**

★★69% Stuart House

35 Goodwins Rd PE30 5QX
☎ 01553 772169 🖷 01553 774788
e-mail: reception@stuarthousehotel.co.uk
web: www.stuart-house-hotel.co.uk
Dir: *at A47/A10/A149 rdbt take signs to King's Lynn town centre. Under Southgate Arch, right into Guanock Ter and right Goodwins Rd*

This privately-owned hotel is situated in a peaceful residential area, yet is just a short walk from the town centre. Bedrooms come in a variety of styles and sizes; all rooms are pleasantly appointed and well equipped. A choice of dining options is available, with informal dining in the bar or a daily-changing menu in the elegant restaurant.

ROOMS: 18 en suite (2 fmly) ⊘ in 4 bedrooms s £58-£74; d £78-£130 **LB FACILITIES:** Jacuzzi ♫ **CONF:** BC Thtr 50 Class 30 Board 20 Del from £10.50 **PARKING:** 30 **NOTES:** ⊘ in restaurant RS 25-26 Dec & 1 Jan **CARDS:**

★★68% *Grange*

Willow Park, South Wootton Ln PE30 3BP
☎ 01553 673777 & 671222 🖷 01553 673777
e-mail: info@thegrangehotelkingslynn.co.uk
Dir: *A148 towards King's Lynn for 1.5m. At traffic lights left into Wootton Rd, 400yds on right South Wootton Ln. Hotel 1st on left*

Expect a warm welcome at this Edwardian house, which is situated in a quiet residential area amid its own grounds. Public rooms include an entrance hall, smart lounge bar and a cosy restaurant. The spacious bedrooms are pleasantly decorated, with some located in an adjacent wing, and are equipped with many thoughtful touches.

ROOMS: 5 en suite 4 annexe en suite (2 fmly) **CONF:** Thtr 20 Class 15 Board 12 **PARKING:** 15 **NOTES:** ⊘ in restaurant
CARDS:

★★65% *Russet House*
53 Goodwins Rd PE30 5PE
☎ 01553 773098 📠 01553 773098
e-mail: stewart@russethousehotel100.freeserve.co.uk
Dir: *follow town centre signs along Hardwick Rd. Right at rdbt before Southgates into Vancouver Av. Hotel on left*
A friendly and relaxed ambience exists within this detached property dating back to 1890 and situated just a short walk from the River Ouse and town centre. Public rooms offer a good choice of areas to relax in, including a cosy bar, restaurant and a lounge with an open fire. Bedrooms are pleasantly decorated with co-ordinated soft furnishings and many useful extras.
ROOMS: 13 en suite (2 fmly) ⊗ in 1 bedroom **PARKING:** 20
NOTES: ⊗ in restaurant **CARDS:**
See advert on this page

⌂ Travel Inn
Freebridge Farm PE34 3LJ
☎ 08701 977149 📠 01553 775827
Dir: *junct of A47 & A17*
Travel Inn offers good-quality, value-for-money accommodation. Spacious, en suite rooms with bath and shower comfortably accommodate a family of up to two adults and two children (to age 15). The restaurant and bar offers a varied menu. For further details consult the Hotel Groups page.
ROOMS: 40 en suite s £45.95-£46.95; d £45.95-£46.95

KINGSTON UPON HULL, East Riding of Yorkshire — Map 17 TA02
See also Little Weighton

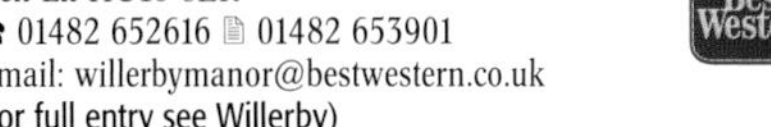

★★★73% Willerby Manor
Well Ln HU10 6ER
☎ 01482 652616 📠 01482 653901
e-mail: willerbymanor@bestwestern.co.uk
(For full entry see Willerby)

★★★68% Portland
Paragon St HU1 3JP
☎ 01482 326462 📠 01482 213460
e-mail: info@portland-hotel.co.uk
web: www.portland-hull.com
Dir: *M62 onto A63, to 1st main rdbt. Left at 2nd lights and over x-rds. Right at next junct onto Carr Ln, follow one-way system*
A modern hotel situated in the city centre providing a good range of accommodation. Most of the public rooms are on the first floor and include the Wilberforce Restaurant and the Humber Bar and Lounge. In addition, the Bay Tree Café, at street level, is open during the day and evening. The friendly staff are very helpful and even take care of car parking.
ROOMS: 126 en suite (4 fmly) ⊗ in 22 bedrooms s £42-£75; d £98
FACILITIES: STV Complimentary use of nearby health & fitness centre Xmas **CONF:** BC Thtr 220 Class 100 Board 50 Del from £135
SERVICES: Lift **PARKING:** 12 **CARDS:**

★★★67% Quality Hotel Royal Hull
170 Ferensway HU1 3UF
☎ 01482 325087 📠 01482 323172
e-mail: enquiries@hotel-hull.com
Dir: *From M62 join A63 to Hull. Over flyover, left at 2nd lights signed Railway Station. Hotel on left at 2nd lights*
A former Victorian railway hotel modernised in recent years. Bedrooms are well equipped and include a number of premier rooms. A spacious lounge provides an ideal setting for light meals,
continued

drinks and relaxation. There are extensive banqueting and conference facilities, as well as an adjacent leisure club.
ROOMS: 155 en suite (6 fmly) ⊗ in 85 bedrooms s £42-£98; d £50-£107 **LB** **FACILITIES:** Sauna Solarium Gym Jacuzzi Steamroom Xmas **CONF:** Thtr 450 Class 150 Board 105 Del from £70
SERVICES: Lift **PARKING:** 130 **NOTES:** Civ Wed 450
CARDS:

★★★65% Elizabeth Hotel Hull
Ferriby High Rd HU14 3LG
☎ 01482 645212 📠 01482 643332
e-mail: elizabeth.hull@elizabethhotels.co.uk
web: www.elizabethhotels.co.uk
(For full entry see North Ferriby)

★★68% The Rowley Manor
Rowley Rd HU20 3XR
☎ 01482 848248 📠 01482 849900
e-mail: info@rowleymanor.com
(For full entry see Little Weighton)

★★57% Stop Inn Hull
11 Anlaby Rd HU1 2PJ
☎ 01482 323299 📠 01482 214730
e-mail: hull@stop-inns.com
Dir: *M62 to A63, over flyover, left at lights, hotel 500yds on left*
An unpretentious hotel situated in the centre of the city with well-equipped and generally spacious bedrooms. Staff are friendly, and whilst there is no formal restaurant a limited range of dishes
continued on p298

KINGSTON UPON HULL, continued

is served in the lounge bar during the evening. Free parking is also available.
ROOMS: 59 en suite (5 fmly) ⊗ in 29 bedrooms s fr £35; d fr £35 **LB** **FACILITIES:** STV leisure facilities at sister hotel Xmas **CONF:** Thtr 140 Class 80 Board 45 Del £32 **SERVICES:** Lift **PARKING:** 100 **NOTES:** ⊗ in restaurant **CARDS:**

⌂ Campanile

Beverley Rd, Freetown Way HU2 9AN
☎ 01482 325530 ⎙ 01482 587538
e-mail: hull@envergure.co.uk
Dir: *From M62 join A63 to Hull, pass Humber Bridge on right. Over flyover, follow railway station signs onto A1079. Hotel at bottom of Ferensway*

This modern building offers accommodation in smart, well-equipped bedrooms, all with en suite bathrooms. Refreshments may be taken at the informal Bistro. For further details consult the Hotel Groups page.
ROOMS: 47 annexe en suite s fr £42.95; d fr £42.95 **CONF:** Thtr 35 Class 18 Board 24

⌂ Hotel Ibis Hull

Osborne St HU1 2NL

☎ 01482 387500 ⎙ 01482 385510
e-mail: h3479-gm@accor-hotels.com

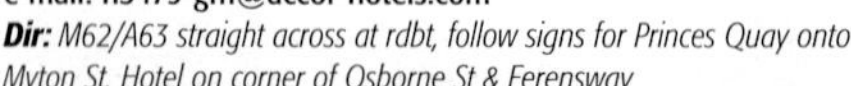

Dir: *M62/A63 straight across at rdbt, follow signs for Princes Quay onto Myton St. Hotel on corner of Osborne St & Ferensway*
Modern, budget hotel offering comfortable accommodation in bright and practical bedrooms. Breakfast is self-service and dinner is available in the restaurant. For further details, consult the Hotel Groups page.
ROOMS: 106 en suite s £39.95

⌂ Travel Inn (Hull North)

Kingswood Park, Ennerdale HU7 4HS
☎ 08701 977137 ⎙ 01482 820300
Dir: *N of Hull, Ennerdale link road in Kingswood Park. A63 to city centre, then A1079 north, right onto A1033, hotel on 2nd rdbt*

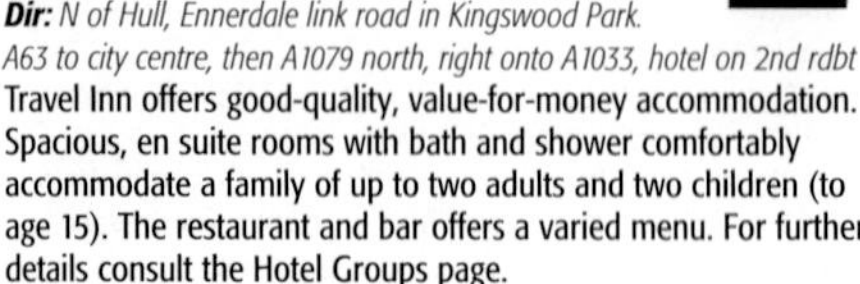

Travel Inn offers good-quality, value-for-money accommodation. Spacious, en suite rooms with bath and shower comfortably accommodate a family of up to two adults and two children (to age 15). The restaurant and bar offers a varied menu. For further details consult the Hotel Groups page.
ROOMS: 42 en suite s £45.95-£46.95; d £45.95-£46.95

⌂ Travel Inn (Hull West)

Ferriby Rd, Hessle HU13 0JA
☎ 08701 977138 ⎙ 01482 645285
Dir: *From A63 take exit for A164/A15 to Humber Bridge, Beverley & Hessle Viewpoint. Travel Inn on 1st rdbt*
Travel Inn offers good-quality, value-for-money accommodation. Spacious, en suite rooms with bath and shower comfortably accommodate a family of up to two adults and two children (to age 15). The restaurant and bar offers a varied menu. For further details consult the Hotel Groups page.
ROOMS: 40 en suite s £45.95-£46.95; d £45.95-£46.95

⌂ Travelodge Hull

Beacon Service Area HU15 1RZ
☎ 08700 850 950 ⎙ 01430 424455
(For full entry see South Cave)

KINGSTON UPON THAMES, Greater London
See LONDON SECTION plan 1 C1

⌂ Travelodge London Kingston

21-23 London Rd KT2 6ND
☎ 08700 850 950 ⎙ 020 8546 5904
Dir: *On Queen Elizabeth Road/London Road, opposite Rotunda complex*
Travelodge offers good quality, good value, modern accommodation. Ideal for families, the spacious, en suite bedrooms include remote-control TV, tea and coffee-making facilities and luxury beds. Meals can be taken at the nearby family restaurant. For further details consult the Hotel Groups page.
ROOMS: 72 en suite s fr £25; d fr £25

KINGSWINFORD, West Midlands Map 10 SO88

⌂ Innkeeper's Lodge

Swindon Rd DY6 9XA
☎ 01384 295254 & 270066 ⎙ 01384 287959
www.innkeeperslodge.com
Dir: *A491 into Kingswinford, at x-rds lights, turn onto A4101 towards Kidderminster along 'Summerhill'. At 1st set of lights, hotel on right*
Smart rooms meet essential business requirements but also have home comforts, and depending on location may well have meeting rooms and pub dining. Dining options generally include all-day menus plus the added advantage of breakfast.
ROOMS: 22 en suite s £45-£52.50; d £45-£52.50

⌂ Travel Inn (Dudley Kingswinford)

Dudley Rd DY6 8WT
☎ 08701 977303 ⎙ 01384 402736
Dir: *A4123 to Dudley, A461 following signs for Russell's Hall Hospital. On A4101 to Kingswinford, the Travel Inn is opposite Pensnett Trading Estate*
Travel Inn offers good-quality, value-for-money accommodation. Spacious, en suite rooms with bath and shower comfortably accommodate a family of up to two adults and two children (to age 15). The restaurant and bar offers a varied menu. For further details consult the Hotel Groups page.
ROOMS: 43 en suite s £45.95-£46.95; d £45.95-£46.95
CONF: Thtr 30 Board 20

KINGTON, Herefordshire Map 09 SO25

★★★67% Burton

Mill St HR5 3BQ
☎ 01544 230323 📠 01544 239023
e-mail: burton@hotelherefordshire.co.uk
Dir: *rdbt at A44/A411 junct take road signed Town Centre*
Situated in the town centre, this friendly, privately-owned hotel offers spacious, pleasantly proportioned and well equipped bedrooms. Smartly presented public areas include a lounge bar, a small lounge and an attractive restaurant where enjoyable, carefully prepared cuisine can be enjoyed. There are also function and meeting facilities in a purpose-built modern wing.
ROOMS: 16 en suite (5 fmly) ⊗ in 2 bedrooms s £42-£52; d £69-£75 (incl. bkfst) **LB** **FACILITIES:** Xmas **CONF:** Thtr 150 Class 100 Board 20 Del from £70 **PARKING:** 50 **NOTES:** Civ Wed **CARDS:**

KIRBY MUXLOE, Leicestershire Map 11 SK50

★★62% *Castle Hotel & Restaurant*

Main St LE9 2AP
☎ 0116 239 5337 📠 0116 238 7868
e-mail: thecastle.kirbymuxloe@snr.co.uk
Dir: *M1 junct 21A northbound, follow signs for Kirby Muxloe and enter village. Hotel on main road*

This attractive, creeper-clad former farmhouse dates back to the 16th century, when it was built using stone and timbers taken from the nearby castle. The property features inglenook fireplaces and exposed timbers and open-plan public rooms include a lounge bar and restaurant with a non-smoking area. Bedrooms vary in size and style, and all are pleasantly decorated.
ROOMS: 22 en suite (3 fmly) **CONF:** Thtr 150 Class 100 Board 100
NOTES: ✈ Civ Wed 100 **CARDS:**

KIRKBURTON, West Yorkshire Map 16 SE11

⌂ Innkeeper's Lodge Huddersfield

36a Penistone Rd HD8 0PQ
☎ 01484 602101 📠 01484 603938
www.innkeeperslodge.com
Dir: *from A62 Huddersfield ring road onto A629 towards Wakefield*
Smart rooms meet essential business requirements but also have home comforts, and depending on location may well have meeting rooms and pub dining. Dining options generally include all-day menus plus the added advantage of breakfast.
ROOMS: 20 en suite 3 annexe en suite s £45; d £45
CONF: Thtr 30 Board 20

> Popped the question?
> Hotels with Civ Wed in their entry are licensed for civil wedding ceremonies. Maximum numbers for the ceremony only are shown, e.g. Civ Wed 120

KIRKBY LONSDALE, Cumbria Map 18 SD67

★★67% *The Whoop Hall*

Burrow with Burrow LA6 2HP
☎ 015242 71284 📠 015242 72154
e-mail: info@whoophall.co.uk
Dir: *on A65 1m SE of Kirkby Lonsdale*
This popular inn combines traditional charm with modern facilities, which includes very well-equipped leisure facilities. Bedrooms, some with four-poster beds and some housed in converted barns, are attractively furnished. A fire warms the bar on chillier days and an interesting choice of dishes is available in the bar, bistro and galleried restaurant throughout the day and evening.
ROOMS: 22 en suite (3 fmly) (2 GF) ⊗ in 11 bedrooms
FACILITIES: Spa supervised Sauna Solarium Gym Jacuzzi Children's adventure playground, Steam/Treatment room ♫ **CONF:** Thtr 144 Class 60 Board 60 **PARKING:** 100 **NOTES:** Civ Wed 130
CARDS:

KIRKBYMOORSIDE, North Yorkshire Map 19 SE68

★★66% George & Dragon Hotel

17 Market Place YO62 6AA
☎ 01751 433334 📠 01751 432933
e-mail: georgeatkirkby@aol.com
Dir: *off A170 between Thirsk and Scarborough, in centre of market town*
Set in the market square, this coaching inn dates from the 1600s. With its blazing fire and sporting theme the pub offers a cosy, welcoming atmosphere. A wide range of hearty dishes is offered from both the menu and a blackboard. Spacious bedrooms are individually furnished and housed in two quiet buildings nearby.
ROOMS: 11 en suite 7 annexe en suite (2 fmly) (2 GF) s £49; d £79-£90 (incl. bkfst) **LB** **FACILITIES:** Gym Xmas **CONF:** Thtr 50 Class 20 Board 20 **PARKING:** 20 **NOTES:** ⊗ in restaurant
CARDS:

KIRKHAM, Lancashire Map 18 SD43

⌂ Premier Lodge (Blackpool East)

Fleetwood Rd, Greenhalgh PR4 3HE
☎ 0870 9906636 📠 0870 9906637
web: www.premierlodge.com
High quality, modern, budget accommodation, ideal for families and business travellers. All rooms feature bath, power shower and satellite TV, and most have telephones / modem points. The adjacent bar and restaurant offers a wide and varied menu.
ROOMS: 28 en suite s £48; d £48

KNARESBOROUGH, North Yorkshire Map 19 SE35

★★★70% Dower House

Bond End HG5 9AL
☎ 01423 863302 📠 01423 867665
e-mail: enquiries@bwdowerhouse.co.uk
Dir: *A1(M) onto A59 Harrogate road. Through Knaresborough, hotel on right after traffic lights at end of high street*
This attractive 15th-century house stands in pleasant gardens on the edge of the town. Features such as welcoming fires enhance its charm and character. The Terrace Restaurant has a relaxed and comfortable atmosphere and overlooks the garden. There is a cosy bar and comfortable non-smoking lounge. Other facilities include two function rooms and a popular health and leisure club, which has its own lounge bar.
ROOMS: 28 en suite 3 annexe en suite (2 fmly) (3 GF) ⊗ in 27 bedrooms s £89-£105; d £99-£115 (incl. bkfst) **LB** **FACILITIES:** supervised Sauna Gym Jacuzzi Xmas **CONF:** Thtr 65 Class 35 Board 36 Del from £99 **PARKING:** 100 **NOTES:** ✈ ⊗ in restaurant Civ Wed 70
CARDS: 

KNARESBOROUGH, continued

★★★68% General Tarleton Inn

Boroughbridge Rd, Ferrensby HG5 0PZ
☎ 01423 340284 01423 340288
e-mail: gti@generaltarleton.co.uk web: www.generaltarleton.co.uk
Dir: *A1 junct 48 at Boroughbridge, take A6055 to Knaresborough. Inn 4m on right*
Food is a real feature here with skilfully prepared meals served in the restaurant, traditional bar and modern conservatory. Accommodation is provided in brightly decorated and airy rooms, and the bathrooms are thoughtfully equipped. Enjoying a country location, yet close to the A1, ensures the hotel remains popular with both business and leisure guests.
ROOMS: 14 en suite (7 GF) in 9 bedrooms s fr £74.95; d fr £84.90 (incl. bkfst) **LB** **FACILITIES:** Xmas **CONF:** Thtr 40 Class 35 Board 20 Del £135 **PARKING:** 40 **NOTES:** in restaurant Civ Wed 40
CARDS:

Innkeeper's Lodge Harrogate East

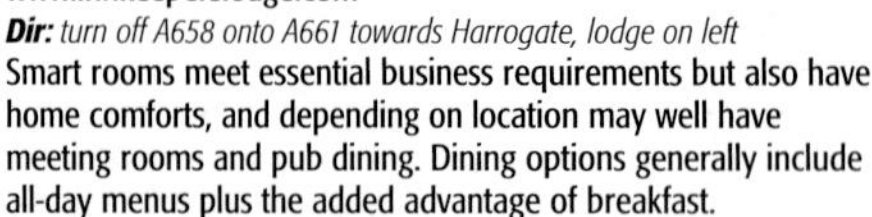

Wetherby Rd, Plompton HG5 8LY
☎ 01423 797979 01423 887276
www.innkeeperslodge.com
Dir: *turn off A658 onto A661 towards Harrogate, lodge on left*
Smart rooms meet essential business requirements but also have home comforts, and depending on location may well have meeting rooms and pub dining. Dining options generally include all-day menus plus the added advantage of breakfast.
ROOMS: 11 en suite s £55; d £55

K

KNOWLE, West Midlands Map 10 SP17

Innkeeper's Lodge Knowle

Warwick Rd, Knowle B93 0EE
☎ 01564 771177 01564 730862
Dir: *on A41*
A new concept in the travel accommodation market. Smart rooms meet essential business requirements but also have home comforts. Dining options include all-day menus plus the added advantage of breakfast, which is included in the room price. For further details, consult the Hotel Groups page.
ROOMS: 13 en suite s £48-£59; d £48-£59

KNUTSFORD, Cheshire Map 15 SJ77

★★★★71% Cottons Hotel & Spa

Manchester Rd WA16 0SU
☎ 01565 650333 01565 755351
e-mail: cottons@shirehotels.co.uk
Dir: *on A50 1m from M6 junct 19*

The superb leisure facilities and quiet location attract all types of guests to this hotel, just a short distance from Manchester Airport. Bedrooms are smartly appointed in a number of styles; executive rooms have very good working areas. The hotel has invested in more spacious lounge areas and extended the leisure centre.
ROOMS: 109 en suite (4 fmly) (38 GF) in 80 bedrooms s £135-£185; d £124-£184 (incl. bkfst) **LB** **FACILITIES: Spa** STV supervised Sauna Solarium Gym Jacuzzi Health & beauty treatment rooms, Steam room, Relaxation area Xmas **CONF:** BC Thtr 200 Class 120 Board 30 Del £170 **SERVICES:** Lift **PARKING:** 180 **NOTES:** in restaurant Civ Wed 120 **CARDS:**

See advert under MANCHESTER AIRPORT

★★★★70% Mere Court Hotel & Conference Centre

Warrington Rd, Mere WA16 0RW
☎ 01565 831000 01565 831001
e-mail: sales@merecourt.co.uk
web: www.merecourt.co.uk
Dir: *A50 Knutsford-Warrington road. 1 mile W of junct with A556 on right*

This is a smart and attractive hotel, set in well-tended gardens. The elegant and spacious bedrooms are all individually styled and offer a host of thoughtful extras. Conference facilities are particularly impressive. Dining is available in the fine dining Arboreum Restaurant or in the new modern conservatory dining area, which overlooks the lake and has a relaxed ambience.
ROOMS: 34 en suite (24 fmly) (12 GF) in 5 bedrooms s £110-£130; d £130-£160 (incl. bkfst) **FACILITIES:** STV **CONF:** Thtr 100 Class 60 Board 35 Del from £149 **SERVICES:** Lift **PARKING:** 150 **NOTES:** in restaurant Civ Wed 120 **CARDS:**

See advert on opposite page

★★75% The Longview Hotel & Restaurant

55 Manchester Rd WA16 0LX
☎ 01565 632119 01565 652402
e-mail: enquiries@longviewhotel.com
web: www.longviewhotel.com
Dir: *M6 junct 19 take A556 W towards Chester. Left at lights onto A5033, 1.5m to rdbt then left. Hotel 200yds on right*
This friendly Victorian hotel offers high standards of hospitality and service. Attractive public areas include a cellar bar and foyer lounge area. The restaurant has a traditional feel and offers an imaginative selection of dishes. Bedrooms are individually styled and offer a good range of thoughtful amenities, including broadband internet access.
ROOMS: 13 en suite 13 annexe en suite (1 fmly) (4 GF) s £52-£115; d £72-£137 (incl. bkfst) **LB** **FACILITIES:** ch fac **PARKING:** 20
CARDS:

For central reservation numbers and more information on Hotel Groups, turn to pages 33-39

U Cottage Restaurant & Lodge
London Rd, Allostock WA16 9LU
☎ 01565 722470 📠 01565 722749
web: www.thecottageknutsford.co.uk
Dir: *M6 junct 18/19 onto A50, Hotel between Holmes Chapel & Knutsford*
At the time of going to press, the star classification for this hotel was not confirmed. Please refer to the AA internet site www.theAA.com for current information.
ROOMS: 12 en suite (6 GF) ⊗ in 8 bedrooms s £45-£79; d £60-£95 (incl. bkfst) **FACILITIES:** STV **CONF:** Thtr 40 Class 20 Board 24 Del from £85 **NOTES:** ⊗ in restaurant Closed New Years Day
CARDS:

⇧ Premier Lodge (Knutsford North)
Bucklow Hill WA16 6RD
PREMIER LODGE.com
☎ 0870 9906428 📠 0870 9906429
web: www.premierlodge.com
Dir: *M56 junct 7, A556 towards Northwich & M6. Hotel 1m at lights on left*
High quality, modern, budget accommodation, ideal for families and business travellers. All rooms feature bath, power shower and satellite TV, and most have telephones / modem points. The adjacent bar and restaurant offers a wide and varied menu.
ROOMS: 66 en suite s £50; d £50 **CONF:** Thtr 60 Board 30

⇧ Premier Lodge (Knutsford North West)
Warrington Rd, Hoo Green, Mere WA16 0PZ
PREMIER LODGE.com
☎ 0870 9906482 📠 0870 9906483
web: www.premierlodge.com
Dir: *exit M6 junct 19 and follow the A556 Manchester signs. At 1st lights turn left onto A50 towards Warrington for hotel 1m on right*
High quality, modern, budget accommodation, ideal for families and business travellers. All rooms feature bath, power shower and satellite TV, and most have telephones / modem points. The adjacent bar and restaurant offers a wide and varied menu.
ROOMS: 28 en suite s £50; d £50

⇧ Travelodge
Chester Rd, Tabley WA16 0PP
Travelodge
☎ 08700 850 950 📠 01565 652187
Dir: *on A556, northbound just E of junct 19 on M6*
Travelodge offers good quality, good value, modern accommodation. Ideal for families, the spacious, en suite bedrooms include remote-control TV, tea and coffee-making facilities and luxury beds. Meals can be taken at the nearby family restaurant. For further details consult the Hotel Groups page.
ROOMS: 32 en suite s fr £25; d fr £25

KNUTSFORD MOTORWAY SERVICE AREA (M6), Cheshire — Map 15 SJ77

⇧ Travelodge
Granada Services, M6 junct 18/19 WA1 0TL
Travelodge
☎ 08700 850 950
Travelodge offers good quality, good value, modern accommodation. Ideal for families, the spacious, en suite bedrooms include remote-control TV, tea and coffee-making facilities and luxury beds. Meals can be taken at the nearby family restaurant. For further details consult the Hotel Groups page.
ROOMS: 54 en suite s fr £25; d fr £25

Late for dinner?
Quality Standards mean that last orders for dinner vary according to star rating and should be no earlier than:
★★ 7.00pm ★★★ 8.00pm ★★★★ 9.00pm
★★★★★ 10.00pm

L

LANCASTER, Lancashire — Map 18 SD46

★★★★ 71% ® Lancaster House
Green Ln, Ellel LA1 4GJ
Best Western
☎ 01524 844822 📠 01524 844766
e-mail: lancaster@elhmail.co.uk
Dir: *M6 junct 33 N towards Lancaster. Through Galgate and into Green Ln. Hotel before university on right*

This modern hotel enjoys a rural setting south of the city and close to the university. The attractive open-plan, balconied reception and lounge boasts traditional flagstone floors and a roaring log fire in colder months. Bedrooms are spacious and especially well equipped for business guests. The excellent business and leisure facilities make this hotel a popular conference venue. Staff are friendly and keen to please.
ROOMS: 80 en suite (10 fmly) (36 GF) ⊗ in 60 bedrooms s £89-£129; d £89-£129 **LB** **FACILITIES:** STV Sauna Solarium Gym Jacuzzi Beauty salon ♫ ch fac Xmas **CONF:** Thtr 120 Class 50 Board 48 Del from £94 **PARKING:** 100 **NOTES:** ⊗ in restaurant Civ Wed 80
CARDS:

LANCASTER, continued

★★★ *Thurnham Mill Hotel & Restaurant*

Thurnham Mill Ln, Conder Green LA2 0BD
☎ 01524 752852 01524 752477
e-mail: stay@thurnham-mill-hotel.fsnet.co.uk
Dir: *M6 junct 33, towards Lancaster. A6 to Galgate, left at lights. 1.75m. At bottom of road left over bridge, then left*
This converted cloth mill dates from the 16th century and lies only a few miles from the M6 on the Lancaster Canal. Spacious bedrooms are traditional in style and include a number of family rooms. Dinner can be enjoyed in the Canalside Restaurant, or on sunny days on a popular terrace.
ROOMS: 18 en suite (6 fmly) in 1 bedroom **FACILITIES:** ch fac **CONF:** Thtr 65 Class 30 Board 30 **PARKING:** 50 **NOTES:** in restaurant **CARDS:**

Travel Inn

Lancaster Business Park, Caton Rd LA1 3PE
☎ 0870 977 290 01524 384801
Travel Inn offers good-quality, value-for-money accommodation. Spacious, en suite rooms with bath and shower comfortably accommodate a family of up to two adults and two children (to age 15). The restaurant and bar offers a varied menu. For further details consult the Hotel Groups page.
ROOMS: 60 en suite s £45.95-£46.95; d £45.95-£46.95

LANDFORD, Wiltshire — Map 05 SU21

★★69% New Forest Lodge Hotel

Southampton Rd SP5 2ED
☎ 01794 390999 01794 390066
e-mail: reservations@newforestlodge.co.uk
web: www.newforestlodge.co.uk
Dir: *M27 junct 2, take A36 towards Salisbury, hotel 5m on left. From Salisbury A36 towards Southampton, hotel 9m on right.*
Set between Salisbury and Southampton, this is an ideal base either for business or leisure guests. Accommodation is self-contained and purpose built with bedrooms offering high standards of comfort and quality. Food is available in the adjacent Keepers Inn, where accomplished, contemporary cuisine is served in a convivial atmosphere.
ROOMS: 14 en suite (6 fmly) (6 GF) in all bedrooms s fr £59.50; d fr £69.50 (incl. bkfst) **LB** **CONF:** Thtr 20 Board 14 **PARKING:** 36 **NOTES:** in restaurant **CARDS:**

LAND'S END, Cornwall & Isles of Scilly — Map 02 SW32

See also Sennen

★★★65% *The Land's End Hotel*

TR19 7AA
☎ 01736 871844 01736 871599
e-mail: landsendhotel@madasafish.co.uk
web: www.landsendhotel.co.uk
Dir: *from Penzance take A30 and follow Land's End signs. After Sennen 1m to Land's End*
This famous location makes a very impressive setting for this attractive hotel. Bedrooms, many with stunning views of The Atlantic, are pleasantly decorated and comfortable. A relaxing lounge and attractive bar are provided and in the 'Longships' restaurant, fresh local produce and fish dishes are a speciality.
ROOMS: 33 en suite (2 fmly) **FACILITIES:** Free entry Lands End visitor centre ch fac **CONF:** Thtr 200 Class 100 Board 50 **PARKING:** 1000 **NOTES:** in restaurant Civ Wed 110 **CARDS:**

LANGAR, Nottinghamshire — Map 11 SK73

★★★73% Langar Hall

NG13 9HG
☎ 01949 860559 01949 861045
e-mail: langarhall-hotel@ndirect.co.uk
web: www.langarhall.com
Dir: *via Bingham from A52 or Cropwell Bishop from A46, both signed. Hotel behind church.*
This delightful hotel enjoys a picturesque rural location, yet is only a short drive from Nottingham. Individually styled bedrooms are furnished with fine period pieces and benefit from some thoughtful extras. There is a choice of lounges, warmed by real fires, and a snug little bar. Carefully prepared, imaginative food is served in the pillared dining room.
ROOMS: 12 en suite (1 fmly) in all bedrooms s £65-£97.50; d £130-£187.50 (incl. bkfst) **LB** **FACILITIES:** Fishing ch fac **CONF:** BC Thtr 20 Class 20 Board 20 **PARKING:** 20 **NOTES:** in restaurant Civ Wed **CARDS:**

LANGHO, Lancashire — Map 18 SD73

Restaurant with Rooms

Northcote Manor

Northcote Rd BB6 8BE
☎ 01254 240555 01254 246568
e-mail: sales@northcotemanor.com
web: www.northcotemanor.com
Dir: *M6 junct 31, 9m to Northcote. Follow Clitheroe (A59) signs, hotel on left before rdbt*
Northcote Manor is a gastronomic haven where many guests return to sample the delights of its famous kitchen, which has twice in the past produced the Young Chef of the Year. Excellent cooking includes much of Lancashire's finest fare. Drinks can be enjoyed in the comfortable, elegantly furnished lounges and bar. Bedrooms have been individually furnished and thoughtfully equipped.
ROOMS: 14 en suite (4 GF) s £110-£145; d £140-£175 (incl. bkfst) **LB** **FACILITIES:** STV Clay and game shooting, Blackburn Rovers tickets can be purchased by the hotel Xmas **CONF:** BC Thtr 40 Class 20 Board 26 Del from £142 **PARKING:** 50 **NOTES:** in restaurant Closed 25 Dec, 1 Jan & most BH Mondays Civ Wed 40
CARDS:

LANGTOFT, East Riding of Yorkshire — Map 17 TA06

★★71% *Old Mill Hotel & Restaurant*

Mill Ln YO25 3BQ
☎ 01377 267284 01377 267383
e-mail: oldmilllangtoft@btconnect.com
Dir: *6m N of Driffield, on B1249. Through Langtoft, approx 1m N, left at hotel sign*
Standing in the open countryside of the Wolds, this modern hotel has been very well furnished throughout. Bedrooms are thoughtfully equipped, and there is a popular bar/lounge where a good range of well produced food is available. There is also a charming restaurant that is a favourite haunt for locals.
ROOMS: 9 en suite (1 fmly) **CONF:** BC Thtr 40 Class 20 Board 20 **PARKING:** 30 **NOTES:** in restaurant
CARDS:

♫ Entertainment

LASTINGHAM, North Yorkshire Map 19 SE79

★★★74% Lastingham Grange

YO62 6TH
☎ 01751 417345 & 417402 ▯ 01751 417358
e-mail: lastinghamgrange@aol.com
Dir: *2m E on A170 to Scarborough, onto Lastingham. In village left uphill towards Moors. Hotel on right*

A warm welcome and sincere hospitality have been the hallmark of this hotel for over 50 years. Antique furniture abounds, and the lounge and the dining room both look out onto the terrace and sunken rose garden below. There is a large play area for older children and the moorland views are breathtaking.
ROOMS: 12 en suite (2 fmly) **FACILITIES:** Large adventure playground ch fac **PARKING:** 32 **NOTES:** in restaurant Closed Dec-Feb **CARDS:**

LAUNCESTON, Cornwall & Isles of Scilly Map 03 SX38
See also Lifton

★★65% Eagle House

Castle St PL15 8BA
☎ 01566 772036 ▯ 01566 772036
e-mail: eaglehousehotel@aol.com
Dir: *from Launceston on Holsworthy Rd follow brown signs for hotel*
Next to the castle, this elegant Georgian house dates back to 1767 and is within walking distance of all local amenities. Many of the bedrooms have wonderful views over the Cornish countryside. A fixed-price menu is served in the restaurant, and on Sunday evenings a more modest menu is available.
ROOMS: 14 en suite (1 fmly) **FACILITIES:** STV **CONF:** Thtr 190 Class 190 Board 190 **PARKING:** 100 **NOTES:** Civ Wed 190
CARDS:

LAVENHAM, Suffolk Map 13 TL94

★★★★75% The Swan

High St CO10 9QA
☎ 01787 247477 ▯ 01787 248286
e-mail: info@theswanatlavenham.co.uk
Dir: *join A134 from either A12 or A14, turn onto B1071 to Lavenham*
The Swan is a delightful collection of listed buildings dating back to the 14th century, lovingly restored to retain their original charm. Public rooms include comfortable lounge areas, a charming rustic bar, an informal brasserie and a fine-dining restaurant. Bedrooms are tastefully furnished and equipped with many thoughtful touches. The friendly staff are helpful, attentive and offer professional service.
ROOMS: 51 en suite (4 fmly) (12 GF) in 8 bedrooms
FACILITIES: STV **CONF:** Thtr 40 Class 18 Board 18 Del from £125
PARKING: 62 **NOTES:** in restaurant Civ Wed 110
CARDS:

★★72% Angel

Market Place CO10 9QZ
☎ 01787 247388 ▯ 01787 248344
e-mail: angellav@aol.com
web: www.lavenham.co.uk/angel
Dir: *from A14 take Bury East and Sudbury turn off onto A143. After 4m take A1141 to Lavenham, Angel off high street*
Delightful 15th-century inn situated in the heart of this historic medieval town overlooking the market place. The Angel is well known for its cuisine and offers an imaginative menu based on fresh ingredients, served throughout the ground floor bar and dining area, whilst the spacious first-floor lounge offers a comfortable area for guests. Bedrooms are tastefully furnished, attractively decorated and thoughtfully equipped.
ROOMS: 8 en suite (1 fmly) (1 GF) in all bedrooms s £50; d £75 (incl. bkfst) **LB** **FACILITIES:** Use of Lavenham Tennis Club facilities ♫
PARKING: 5 **NOTES:** in restaurant Closed 25-26 Dec
CARDS:

LEA MARSTON, Warwickshire Map 10 SP29

★★★★67% Lea Marston Hotel & Leisure Complex

Best Western

Haunch Ln B76 0BY
☎ 01675 470468 ▯ 01675 470871
e-mail: info@leamarstonhotel.co.uk
Dir: *M42 junct 9, take A4097 to Kingsbury. Hotel signposted 1.5m on right*

Excellent access to the motorway network and a good range of sports facilities make this hotel a popular choice for conferences and leisure breaks. Bedrooms are mostly set around an attractive quadrangle and are generously equipped. Diners can choose between the popular Sportsman's Lounge Bar and the elegant Adderley Restaurant.
ROOMS: 80 en suite (4 fmly) (46 GF) in 74 bedrooms s £120-£170; d £140-£190 (incl. bkfst) **LB** **FACILITIES: Spa** STV 9 Sauna Solarium Gym Putt green Jacuzzi Golf driving range, Beauty Salon, Childrens play area, Golf simulator Xmas **CONF:** Thtr 140 Class 50 Board 30 Del from £120 **SERVICES:** Lift **PARKING:** 220 **NOTES:** in restaurant Civ Wed 100 **CARDS:**

See advert under BIRMINGHAM

No smoking

L

LEAMINGTON SPA (ROYAL), Warwickshire Map 10 SP36

Top 200 – Hotel

★★★ ◎◎◎ **Mallory Court**
Harbury Ln, Bishop's Tachbrook CV33 9QB
☎ 01926 330214 🖷 01926 451714
e-mail: reception@mallory.co.uk
web: www.mallory.co.uk
Dir: *2m S off B4087 towards Harbury*
With its tranquil rural setting, this elegant Lutyens-style country house is an idyllic retreat. The hotel is set in ten acres of landscaped gardens and immaculate lawns. The two sumptuous lounges, drawing room, conservatory and elegant panelled restaurant provide ample opportunity for indulgence and relaxation. Bedrooms are nothing short of luxurious, each is individual in style, beautifully decorated and most have wonderful views.
ROOMS: 18 en suite (1 fmly) s £175-£195; d £185-£320 (incl. cont bkfst) **LB** **FACILITIES:** STV Use of nearby club facilities Xmas **CONF:** Thtr 120 Board 50 Del from £175 **SERVICES:** Lift **PARKING:** 50 **NOTES:** No children 9yrs ⊘ in restaurant Civ Wed **CARDS:**

★★★70% **Courtyard by Marriott Leamington Spa**
Olympus Av, Tachbrook Park CV34 6RJ
☎ 01926 425522 🖷 01926 881322
e-mail: reservations.leamingtonspa@whitbread.com
Dir: *From M40 J13 (northbound exit) or M40 J14 (southbound exit) follow signs for Leamington A452*
Just a short distance from both Warwick and Leamington Spa, this modern hotel is conveniently situated for local businesses and tourist attractions. Bedrooms are furnished and decorated to a high standard providing a comprehensive range of extras. A friendly and helpful team efficiently delivers a professional service.
ROOMS: 91 en suite (14 fmly) (13 GF) ⊘ in 48 bedrooms s £52-£129; d £74-£149 (incl. bkfst) **LB** **FACILITIES:** STV Gym Xmas **CONF:** Thtr 70 Class 30 Board 40 Del from £99 **SERVICES:** Lift **PARKING:** 150 **NOTES:** ⊘ in restaurant **CARDS:**

★★★66% **Falstaff**
16-20 Warwick New Rd CV32 5JQ
☎ 01926 312044 🖷 01926 450574
e-mail: falstaff@meridianleisure.com
web: www.meridianleisure.com
Dir: *M40 junct 13 or 14 follow signs for Leamington Spa. Over 4 rdbts then under bridge. Left into Princes Drive, then right at mini rdbt*
Bedrooms at this hotel come in a variety of sizes and styles and are well equipped, with many thoughtful extras. Snacks can be taken within the relaxing lounge bar and an interesting selection of English and continental dishes is offered in the restaurant; 24-hour room service is also available. Conference and banqueting facilities are extensive.

ROOMS: 63 en suite (2 fmly) (16 GF) ⊘ in 13 bedrooms s £70-£80; d £80-£90 (incl. bkfst) **LB** **FACILITIES:** Arrangement with local Health Club Xmas **CONF:** Thtr 70 Class 30 Board 30 Del from £90 **PARKING:** 50 **NOTES:** ⊘ in restaurant Civ Wed 60
CARDS:

See advert on opposite page

★★★65% **Angel**
143 Regent St CV32 4NZ
☎ 01926 881296 🖷 01926 313853
e-mail: angelhotel143@hotmail.com
web: www.angelhotelleamington.co.uk
Dir: *in town centre at junct of Regent St and Holly Walk*
This centrally-located hotel comes in two parts - the original inn and a more modern extension. Public rooms include a comfortable foyer lounge area, a smart restaurant and an informal bar. Bedrooms are individual in style, and, whether modern or traditional, have all the expected facilities.
ROOMS: 48 en suite (3 fmly) s £50-£70; d £70-£80 (incl. bkfst) **LB** **FACILITIES:** STV Xmas **CONF:** Thtr 70 Class 40 Board 40 Del from £90 **SERVICES:** Lift **PARKING:** 38 **NOTES:** ⊘ in restaurant
CARDS:

★★★65% **The Best Western Royal Leamington Hotel**
64 Upper Holly Walk CV32 4JL
☎ 01926 883777 🖷 01926 330467
e-mail: royal@meridianleisure.com
Dir: *off A46 onto A452, left onto Clarendon Ave, then right into Clarendon St, then left, hotel on left*

This Victorian town house is situated near the thriving shopping centre of Leamington Spa, yet retains the relaxed and peaceful feel of yesteryear. Bedrooms are individually appointed and well equipped; public areas are full of character and include a

continued

traditional residents' lounge. Guests can dine in the atmospheric brasserie, or choose from the room service menu.
ROOMS: 32 en suite (3 GF) ⊗ in 10 bedrooms s £80; d £90 (incl. cont bkfst) **LB** **FACILITIES:** STV Xmas **CONF:** Thtr 40 Class 20 Board 20 Del £125 **PARKING:** 20 **NOTES:** ⊗ in restaurant Civ Wed 50
CARDS:

See advert on this page

★★73% Adams

22 Avenue Rd CV31 3PQ
☎ 01926 450742 📠 01926 313110
e-mail: bookings@adams-hotel.co.uk
web: www.adams-hotel.co.uk
Dir: *near Library on A452*
This elegant Regency town house, originally built in 1827, is now a privately owned hotel offering high-quality accommodation, delicious home-cooked food and a relaxing setting. Public areas include a residents' bar with leather armchairs, and a pretty garden. Bedrooms are equipped with thoughtful extras, such as modem points and bathrobes.
ROOMS: 12 en suite (3 GF) **CONF:** BC Thtr 20 Class 14 Board 12 Del from £120 **PARKING:** 14 **NOTES:** ⊗ in restaurant
CARDS:

○ Travelodge (Leamington Spa)

Travelodge

CV32 4AT
☎ 08700 850950
ROOMS: 54 en suite **NOTES:** Due to open Winter 04

LEATHERHEAD, Surrey — Map 06 TQ15

★★65% Bookham Grange

THE INDEPENDENTS HOTEL ASSOCIATION

Little Bookham Common, Bookham KT23 3HS
☎ 01372 452742 📠 01372 450080
e-mail: bookhamgrange@easynet.co.uk
web: www.bookham-grange.co.uk
Dir: *off A246 at Bookham High Street onto Church Rd, 1st right after Bookham railway station*
This attractive family-run hotel is situated in over two acres of landscaped grounds with extensive parking. Spacious bedrooms are individually decorated and well equipped. Public areas include extensive banqueting facilities and a beamed bar. This is a popular wedding venue.
ROOMS: 27 en suite (5 fmly) s £75-£85; d £95-£95 (incl. bkfst) **LB** **FACILITIES:** Xmas **CONF:** Thtr 80 Class 24 Board 24 Del from £130 **PARKING:** 100 **NOTES:** ⊗ in restaurant Civ Wed 90
CARDS:

⇧ Travelodge (Leatherhead)

Travelodge

The Swan Centre, High St KT22 8AA
☎ 0870 191 1748 📠 01372 386577
Travelodge offers good quality, good value, modern accommodation. Ideal for families, the spacious, en suite bedrooms include remote-control TV, tea and coffee-making facilities and luxury beds. Meals can be taken at the nearby family restaurant. For further details consult the Hotel Groups page.
ROOMS: 91 en suite s fr £25; d fr £25

- Indoor Swimming Pool
- Indoor Swimming Pool (heated)
- Outdoor Swimming Pool
- Outdoor Swimming Pool (heated)

LEDBURY, Herefordshire

Map 10 SO73

★★★74% Feathers

High St HR8 1DS
☎ 01531 635266 01531 638955
e-mail: mary@feathers-ledbury.co.uk
web: www.feathersledbury.co.uk
Dir: *S from Worcester on A449, E from Hereford on A438, N from Gloucester on A417. Hotel in High St*

A wealth of old-fashioned charm greets the guest at this historic timber-framed hostelry, set in the High Street in the middle of town. The comfortably equipped bedrooms are authentically and tastefully decorated while well-prepared meals can be taken in Fuggles Brasserie with its adjoining bar. Facilities include a leisure centre and a function suite.

ROOMS: 19 en suite (2 fmly) in 2 bedrooms **FACILITIES:** STV Solarium Gym Jacuzzi Steam room **CONF:** Thtr 140 Class 80 Board 40 Del £130 **PARKING:** 30 **NOTES:** Civ Wed
CARDS:

★★72% Verzon Bar, Brasserie & Hotel

Hereford Rd, Trumpet HR8 2PZ
☎ 01531 670381 01531 670830
e-mail: info@theverzon.co.uk
web: www.theverzon.co.uk
Dir: *2m W of Ledbury on A438*

Dating back to 1790 this elegant establishment stands in extensive gardens, from which far-reaching views over the Malvern Hills can be enjoyed. Bedrooms are well-appointed and spacious; one of them has a four-poster bed. Stylish public areas include the popular bar and the brasserie restaurant which serves a range of well executed and flavour packed dishes.

ROOMS: 8 en suite (1 fmly) in all bedrooms s £55-£70; d £78-£98 (incl. bkfst) **LB** **FACILITIES:** STV ch fac **CONF:** Thtr 70 Class 40 Board 25 Del from £95 **PARKING:** 60 **NOTES:** in restaurant
CARDS:

A ★★ Leadon House

Ross Rd HR8 2LP
☎ 01531 631199 01531 631476
e-mail: leadon.house@amserve.net
Dir: *On A449, 500yds off by-pass on right*

ROOMS: 6 en suite (2 fmly) in all bedrooms s £42-£65; d £60-£85 (incl. bkfst) **LB** **PARKING:** 8 **NOTES:** in restaurant
CARDS:

LEEDS, West Yorkshire

Map 19 SE23

See also Gomersal & Shipley

★★★★★62% De Vere Oulton Hall

DE VERE HOTELS

Rothwell Ln, Oulton LS26 8HN
☎ 0113 282 1000 0113 282 8066
e-mail: oulton.hall@devere-hotels.com
Dir: *2m from M62 junct 30 on left, or 1m from M1 junct 44. Follow Castleford and Pontefract signs on A639*

Surrounded by the beautiful Yorkshire Dales, yet within 15 minutes of the city centre, this elegant 19th-century house really does offer the best of both worlds. Impressive features of the hotel include the formal gardens, which have been faithfully restored to their original design, and the galleried Great Hall. The hotel also offers a choice of dining options and golfers can book preferential tee times at the adjacent golf club.

ROOMS: 152 en suite in 144 bedrooms s £100-£150; d £120-£170 (incl. bkfst) **LB** **FACILITIES:** STV supervised Sauna Solarium Gym Jacuzzi Beauty therapy Aerobics, spa treatments Xmas **CONF:** Thtr 350 Class 150 Board 40 Del from £130 **SERVICES:** Lift **PARKING:** 260 **NOTES:** in restaurant **CARDS:**

★★★★77% The Thorpe Park Hotel

SHIRE HOTELS

Century Way, Thorpe Park LS15 8ZB
☎ 0113 264 1000 0113 264 1010
e-mail: thorpepark@shirehotels.co.uk
Dir: *M1 junct 46 left at top of slip road, then right at rdbt into Thorpe Park*

Conveniently close to the M1, bedrooms in this newly built property are modern in style and facilities. The terrace and courtyard offer all day casual dining and refreshments, and the restaurant features a Mediterranean-themed menu. There is also a state-of-the-art spa and leisure facility.

ROOMS: 123 en suite (31 GF) in 80 bedrooms s £140-£180; d £134-£184 (incl. bkfst) **LB** **FACILITIES: Spa** STV supervised Sauna Solarium Gym Jacuzzi Steam room, Health & beauty rooms, Activity studio Xmas **CONF:** BC Thtr 200 Class 100 Board 50 Del £175 **SERVICES:** Lift air con **PARKING:** 200 **NOTES:** in restaurant Civ Wed 150 **CARDS:**

See advert under YORK

Town House

★★★★ Haley's Hotel & Restaurant

Shire Oak Rd, Headingley LS6 2DE
☎ 0113 278 4446 0113 275 3342
e-mail: info@haleys.co.uk
web: www.haleys.co.uk
Dir: *from city centre follow signs to University on A660. After 1.5m right in Headingley between HSBC and Starbucks*

Although only ten minutes from the city centre, this hotel has

continued

a real country feel to it. The bedrooms offer tasteful decor, some with interesting period furnishings. The modern restaurant is decorated with contemporary works of art (all for sale) and is the setting for imaginative meals. There is a choice of comfortable lounges.
ROOMS: 22 en suite 6 annexe en suite (3 fmly) (2 GF) ⊗ in 10 bedrooms s £85-£125; d £110-£150 (incl. bkfst) **LB**
FACILITIES: STV **CONF:** Thtr 40 Class 20 Board 25 Del from £120
PARKING: 29 **NOTES:** ✈ ⊗ in restaurant Closed 26-30 Dec RS Sun evening & Mon-Sat lunch Civ Wed 100
CARDS:

See advert on this page

Town House

★★★★ ⌂ *Radisson SAS Leeds*
No 1 The Light, The Headrow LS1 8TL
☎ 0113 236 6000 📠 0113 236 6100
e-mail: deborah.heather@radissonsas.com
Dir: *follow city centre 'loop' up Park Row, straight at lights onto Cockeridge St, hotel on left*
Situated in the new shopping complex known as 'The Light', the hotel occupies a converted building that was formerly the headquarters of the Leeds Permanent Building Society. Three styles of décor have been used in the bedrooms: Art Deco, Hi Tech and Italian. All rooms are air conditioned, with excellent business facilities. The lobby bar area serves substantial meals and is ideal for relaxation. Public parking available, contact hotel for details.
ROOMS: 147 en suite ⊗ in 130 bedrooms **FACILITIES:** STV
CONF: Thtr 60 Class 35 Board 16 **SERVICES:** Lift air con
NOTES: ✈ **CARDS:**

★★★★71% Park Plaza Leeds
Boar Ln LS1 5NS
☎ 0113 380 4000 📠 0113 380 4100
e-mail: pplinfo@parkplazahotels.co.uk
Dir: *Follow signs for Leeds city centre*
Chic, stylish, ultra modern, city-centre hotel located just opposite City Square. 'Chino Latino', located on the first floor, is a fashionable bar and restaurant concept based on a fusion of Asian and Latin cooking. Stylish, air-conditioned bedrooms are spacious and boast a range of modern facilities, including high speed internet connection.
ROOMS: 187 en suite ⊗ in 96 bedrooms s £155-£250; d £155-£250 **LB**
FACILITIES: Gym Xmas **CONF:** BC Thtr 460 Class 120 Board 212 Del from £140 **SERVICES:** Lift air con **NOTES:** ✈ Civ Wed 150
CARDS:

★★★★68% Leeds Marriott Hotel

4 Trevelyan Square, Boar Ln LS1 6ET
☎ 0113 236 6366 📠 0113 236 6367
Dir: *M621/M1 junct 3. Follow signs for city centre on A653. Stay in right lane. Energis building on left, right and follow signs to hotel*
With a charming courtyard setting in the heart of the city, this modern, elegant hotel provides the perfect venue for shopping and sightseeing. Air-conditioned bedrooms are tastefully decorated and offer excellent workspace. Public areas include an informal bar, a restaurant and a smart leisure club with swimming pool and fitness room.
ROOMS: 244 en suite ⊗ in 194 bedrooms s £130; d £130 **LB**
FACILITIES: STV supervised Sauna Solarium Gym Jacuzzi Subsidised use of NCP car park **CONF:** BC Thtr 280 Class 120 Board 80
SERVICES: Lift air con **NOTES:** ✈ Civ Wed 240
CARDS:

★★★★68% The Queens
City Square LS1 1PL
☎ 0113 243 1323 📠 0113 242 5154
e-mail: queensreservations@paramount-hotels.co.uk
Dir: *M621 junct 3. Follow signs for City Centre, under railway bridge. After lights take slip road in front of the hotel.*
A legacy from the golden age of railways, this grand Victorian hotel has retained much of its original splendour and is located in the very heart of the city. Public rooms include the spacious bar, a range of function rooms and the restaurant.
ROOMS: 199 en suite (31 fmly) ⊗ in 121 bedrooms **FACILITIES:** STV
CONF: Thtr 600 Class 200 Board 80 Del from £168 **SERVICES:** Lift
PARKING: 80 **NOTES:** Civ Wed **CARDS:**

★★★★56% Hotel Metropole
King St LS1 2HQ
☎ 0113 245 0841 📠 0113 242 5156
e-mail: metropole.sales@principal-hotels.com
web: www.principal-hotels.com
Dir: *from M1, M62 and M621 follow city centre signs. Take A65 into Wellington St. At 1st traffic island right into King St, hotel on right*

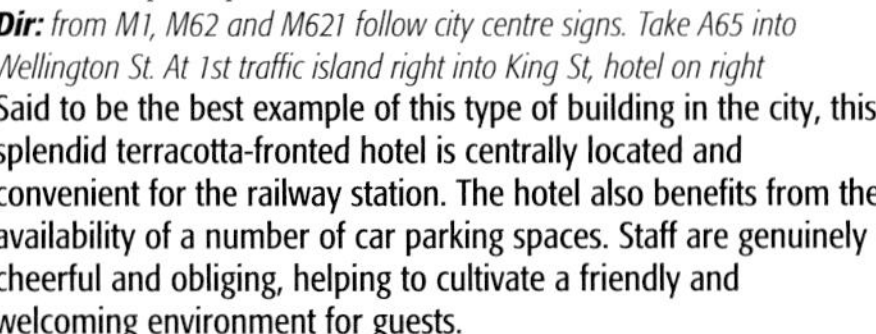

Said to be the best example of this type of building in the city, this splendid terracotta-fronted hotel is centrally located and convenient for the railway station. The hotel also benefits from the availability of a number of car parking spaces. Staff are genuinely cheerful and obliging, helping to cultivate a friendly and welcoming environment for guests.
ROOMS: 118 en suite ⊗ in 98 bedrooms s £110; d £120 **LB**
FACILITIES: STV **CONF:** BC Thtr 250 Class 100 Board 80 Del £150
SERVICES: Lift **PARKING:** 40 **NOTES:** ✈ ⊗ in restaurant RS 24 Dec-1 Jan Civ Wed 200 **CARDS:**

LEEDS, continued

★★★80% Hazlewood Castle
Paradise Ln, Hazlewood LS24 9NJ
☎ 01937 535353 Fax 01937 530630
e-mail: info@hazlewood-castle.co.uk
web: www.hazlewood-castle.co.uk
(For full entry see Tadcaster)

★★★77% Malmaison Hotel
Sovereign Quay LS1 1DQ
☎ 0113 398 1000 Fax 0113 398 1002
e-mail: leeds@malmaison.com
Dir: *M621/M1 junct 3, follow signs to city centre. At KPMG building, right into Sovereign St. Hotel at end of street on right.*
Close to the waterfront, this stylish property offers striking bedrooms with CD players and air conditioning. The popular bar and brasserie feature vaulted ceilings, intimate lighting and offer a choice of a three-course meal or a substantial snack. Service is both willing and friendly. A small fitness centre and impressive meeting rooms complete the package.
ROOMS: 100 en suite in 70 bedrooms s £79-£165; d £79-£165 **LB** **FACILITIES:** STV Gym Xmas **CONF:** Thtr 40 Class 20 Board 28 Del £165 **SERVICES:** Lift air con **NOTES:**
CARDS:

★★★73% Milford Hotel

A1 Great North Rd, Peckfield LS25 5LQ
☎ 01977 681800 Fax 01977 681245
e-mail: enquiries@mlh.co.uk
web: www.mlh.co.uk
(For full entry see Garforth and advert on opposite page)

★★★72% Novotel Leeds Centre
4 Whitehall, Whitehall Quay LS1 4HR
☎ 0113 242 6446 Fax 0113 242 6445
e-mail: H3270@accor-hotels.com
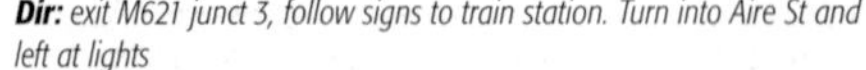
Dir: *exit M621 junct 3, follow signs to train station. Turn into Aire St and left at lights*
With minimalist flair and style, this contemporary hotel provides a quality, value-for-money experience close to the city centre. Spacious, air-conditioned bedrooms are provided, whilst public areas offer deep leather sofas and an eye-catching water feature in reception. Light snacks are provided in the airy bar and the restaurant doubles as a bistro.
ROOMS: 195 en suite (60 fmly) in 130 bedrooms s fr £105; d fr £105 **LB** **FACILITIES:** STV Sauna Gym Play station computers in rooms & play area Steam room Xmas **CONF:** Thtr 80 Class 50 Board 50 Del from £120 **SERVICES:** Lift air con **PARKING:** 70 **NOTES:** Civ Wed 70
CARDS:

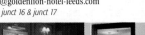

★★★70% The Merrion
Merrion Centre LS2 8NH
☎ 0113 243 9191 Fax 0113 242 3527
e-mail: info@merrion-hotel-leeds.com
Dir: *from M1, M62 and A61 onto city loop road to junct 7*
This smart modern hotel benefits from a city centre location. Bedrooms are smartly appointed and thoughtfully equipped for both business and leisure guests. Public areas include a comfortable lounge and an airy restaurant with an adjacent bar. There is direct access to a car park via a walkway.
ROOMS: 109 en suite in 48 bedrooms s £79-£95; d £85-£115 **LB** **FACILITIES:** STV Discount at local leisure club Xmas **CONF:** Thtr 80 Class 25 Board 25 Del from £85 **SERVICES:** Lift
CARDS:

★★★69% Chevin Country Park Hotel

Yorkgate LS21 3NU
☎ 01943 467818 Fax 01943 850335
e-mail: reception@chevinhotel.com
(For full entry see Otley)

★★★68% Golden Lion

2 Lower Briggate LS1 4AE
☎ 0113 243 6454 Fax 0113 242 9327
e-mail: info@goldenlion-hotel-leeds.com
Dir: *between junct 16 & junct 17*

This smartly presented hotel is set in a Victorian building on the south side of the city. The well-equipped bedrooms offer a choice of standard or executive grades. Staff are friendly and helpful, ensuring a warm and welcoming atmosphere. Free overnight parking is provided in a 24-hour car park by the hotel.
ROOMS: 89 en suite (5 fmly) in 46 bedrooms s £95-£110; d £110-£120 **LB** **FACILITIES:** STV Xmas **CONF:** Thtr 120 Class 65 Board 45 Del £140 **SERVICES:** Lift **PARKING:** 2
CARDS:

★★★68% Jurys Inn Leeds
Kendell St, Brewery Place, Brewery Wharf LS10 1NE
☎ 0113 283 8800 Fax 0113 283 8811
e-mail: info@jurysdoyle.com
This modern hotel is located near the Tetley Brewery, close to the centre of Leeds. Bedrooms provide good levels of comfort and in-room facilities are spot on for both the leisure and the business markets. Public areas include a number of meeting rooms, a restaurant and a popular bar.
ROOMS: 248 en suite in 200 bedrooms s £69-£73; d £69-£73 **FACILITIES:** STV **CONF:** Thtr 60 Class 50 Board 25 Del from £135 **SERVICES:** Lift air con **NOTES:** in restaurant Closed 24-26 Dec
CARDS:

Bewley's Hotel Leeds
City Walk, Sweet St LS11 9AT
☎ 0113 234 2340 📠 0113 234 2349
e-mail: leeds@BewleysHotels.com
web: www.bewleyshotels.com/leeds_index.htm
Dir: *M621 junct 3, at 2nd set of lights turn left, then right and right again. Hotel straight ahead.*

At the time of going to press, the star classification for this hotel was not confirmed. Please refer to the AA internet site www.theAA.com for current information.
ROOMS: 334 en suite (99 fmly) in 246 bedrooms s £59; d £59
FACILITIES: STV **CONF:** BC Board 18 Del £119 **SERVICES:** Lift
PARKING: 160 **NOTES:** Closed 24th-26th Dec
CARDS:

Hotel Ibis Leeds
Marlborough St LS1 4PB
☎ 0870 7809162
Dir: *M1 junct 43 signed Leeds, follow M621 to junct 2(A643), take 3rd exit at rdbt. At junct for A647 take 3rd exit signed A58M. Then left on slip road to Wellington St. Follw A58/West St then turn left onto Marlborough St*
Modern, budget hotel offering comfortable accommodation in bright and practical bedrooms. Breakfast is self-service and dinner is available in the restaurant. For further details, consult the Hotel Groups page.
ROOMS: 168 en suite s £42.95-£45.95; d £42.95-£45.95

Innkeeper's Lodge Leeds South
Bruntcliffe Rd, Morley LS27 0LY
☎ 0113 253 3115 📠 0113 253 9365
www.innkeeperslodge.com
Dir: *M62 junct 27 take A650 towards Morley. On junct of A650 and A643*
Smart rooms meet essential business requirements but also have home comforts, and depending on location may well have meeting rooms and pub dining. Dining options generally include all-day menus plus the added advantage of breakfast.
ROOMS: 32 en suite s £42-£55; d £42-£55

Premier Lodge (Leeds City West)
City West One Office Park, Gelderd Rd LS12 6LX
☎ 0870 9906448 📠 0870 9906449
web: www.premierlodge.com
Dir: *exit M621 junct 1 and take ring road towards Leeds. At 1st lights turn right onto Gelderd Rd then right at rbt*
High quality, modern, budget accommodation, ideal for families and business travellers. All rooms feature bath, power shower and satellite TV, and most have telephones / modem points. The adjacent bar and restaurant offers a wide and varied menu.
ROOMS: 126 en suite s £50; d £50 **CONF:** Thtr 12 Class 12 Board 12

AA Rosette Award for culinary excellence

Travel Inn (Leeds City Centre)
Citygate, Wellington St LS3 1LW
☎ 08701 977150 📠 0113 242 8105
Dir: *on junct of A65 & A58*
Travel Inn offers good-quality, value-for-money accommodation. Spacious, en suite rooms with bath and shower comfortably accommodate a family of up to two adults and two children (to age 15). The restaurant and bar offers a varied menu. For further details consult the Hotel Groups page.
ROOMS: 139 en suite s £52.95-£56.95; d £52.95-£56.95
CONF: Class 16 Board 16

Travel Inn Leeds (East)
Selby Rd, Whitkirk LS15 7AY
☎ 08701 977151 📠 0113 232 6195
Dir: *M1 junct 46 towards Leeds. At 2nd rdbt follow Temple Newsam signs. Inn 500mtrs on right.*

Travel Inn offers good-quality, value-for-money accommodation. Spacious, en suite rooms with bath and shower comfortably accommodate a family of up to two adults and two children (to age 15). The restaurant and bar offers a varied menu. For further details consult the Hotel Groups page.
ROOMS: 87 en suite s £45.95-£46.95; d £45.95-£46.95

Travelodge Leeds (Central)
Blaydes Court, Blaydes Yard, off Swinegate LS1 4AD
☎ 08700 850 950 📠 0113 246 0076
Travelodge offers good quality, good value, modern accommodation. Ideal for families, the spacious, en suite bedrooms include remote-control TV, tea and coffee-making facilities and luxury beds. Meals can be taken at the nearby family restaurant. For further details consult the Hotel Groups page.
ROOMS: 100 en suite s fr £25; d fr £25

LEEDS, continued

⌂ Travelodge Leeds (East)
Stile Hill Way, Colton LS15 9JA
☎ 08700 850 950 🖷 0113 264 8839
Travelodge offers good quality, good value, modern accommodation. Ideal for families, the spacious, en suite bedrooms include remote-control TV, tea and coffee-making facilities and luxury beds. Meals can be taken at the nearby family restaurant. For further details consult the Hotel Groups page.
ROOMS: 60 en suite s fr £25; d fr £25

○ Travelodge (Leeds Bradford Airport)
Whitehouse Ln LS19 7TZ
☎ 08700 850950
ROOMS: 56 en suite **NOTES:** Due to open Oct 04

LEEDS/BRADFORD AIRPORT, West Yorkshire Map 19 SE23

⌂ Travel Inn (Leeds Airport)
Victoria Av, Yeadon LS19 7AW
☎ 08701 977153 🖷 0113 202 9383
Dir: *on A658, near Leeds/Bradford Airport*
Travel Inn offers good-quality, value-for-money accommodation. Spacious, en suite rooms with bath and shower comfortably accommodate a family of up to two adults and two children (to age 15). The restaurant and bar offers a varied menu. For further details consult the Hotel Groups page.
ROOMS: 40 en suite s £45.95-£48.95; d £45.95-£48.95 **CONF:** Thtr 12

LEEK, Staffordshire Map 16 SJ95

★★★65% *Hotel Rudyard*
Lake Rd, Rudyard ST13 8RN
☎ 01538 306208 🖷 01538 306208
This large stone-built Victorian property is set in extensive wooded grounds in the centre of Rudyard village. It provides modern and well-equipped accommodation and a room with a four-poster bed is also available. There is a function room, a large carvery restaurant and a traditionally furnished bar.
ROOMS: 15 en suite (2 fmly) ⊘ in 2 bedrooms **CONF:** Thtr 80 Class 60 Board 40 **PARKING:** 100 **NOTES:** ⊘ in restaurant
CARDS:

★★69% ◎ Three Horseshoes Inn & Restaurant
Buxton Rd, Blackshaw Moor ST13 8TW
☎ 01538 300296 🖷 01538 300320
web: www.threeshoesinn.co.uk
Dir: *2m N of Leek on A53*

A family owned hostelry in spacious grounds, which include a beer garden and children's play area. The non-smoking bedrooms are tastefully appointed and furnished in keeping with the character of the hotel. The public areas include a choice of bars and eating options. The Bistro is open only at dinner.
ROOMS: 6 en suite ⊘ in all bedrooms **CONF:** Thtr 60 Class 50 Board 25 **PARKING:** 80 **NOTES:** ⊘ in restaurant Closed 24 Dec-1 Jan
CARDS:

Restaurant with Rooms

◎ Cottage Delight at Number 64
64 St Edwards St ST13 5DL
☎ 01538 381900 🖷 01538 370918
e-mail: enquiries@number64.com
web: www.number64.com
Dir: *in town centre near junct of A520/A53, at bottom of hill*

This listed Georgian building, located in the centre of the town, is devoted to food but also offers spacious and comfortably furnished bedrooms. There is also an evening wine bar, two speciality food shops and a coffee lounge, whilst an imaginative menu is offered in the main restaurant.
ROOMS: 3 en suite ⊘ in all bedrooms s £65-£85; d £75-£95 (incl. cont bkfst) **CONF:** Board 14 **NOTES:** ⊘ in restaurant Civ Wed 50
CARDS:

LEEMING BAR, North Yorkshire Map 19 SE28

★★61% The White Rose
Bedale Rd DL7 9AY
☎ 01677 422707 🖷 01677 425123
e-mail: john@whiterosehotel.co.uk
Dir: *turn off A1 onto A684 and turn left towards Northallerton. Hotel 0.25m on left*
Conveniently situated just minutes from the A1, this commercial hotel boasts pleasant, well-equipped bedrooms contained in a modern block to the rear. Good-value meals are offered in either the traditional bar or attractive dining room.
ROOMS: 18 en suite (2 fmly) (1 GF) s £49; d £63 (incl. bkfst)
FACILITIES: ♫ **CONF:** BC **PARKING:** 50 **NOTES:** ⊘ in restaurant
CARDS:

LEICESTER, Leicestershire Map 11 SK50
See also Rothley

★★★74% Belmont House
De Montfort St LE1 7GR
☎ 0116 254 4773 🖷 0116 247 0804
e-mail: info@belmonthotel.co.uk
web: www.belmonthotel.co.uk
Dir: *from A6, take 1st right after rail station. Hotel 200yds on left*
An attractive property situated within easy walking distance of the railway station and city centre. Extensive public rooms are smartly appointed and include a superb conservatory walkway, the

continued

informal Bowie's Bistro, formal dining within the Cherry Restaurant and a relaxed atmosphere in Jamie's Bar and Will's Lounge Bar. Bedrooms styles vary; each room is individually appointed and well equipped.

ROOMS: 77 en suite (7 fmly) ⊗ in 57 bedrooms s £105-£125; d £110-£135 **LB** **FACILITIES:** Gym **CONF:** Thtr 175 Class 75 Board 65 Del from £150 **SERVICES:** Lift **PARKING:** 75 **NOTES:** ⊗ in restaurant Closed 25-26 Dec Civ Wed 120 **CARDS:**

See advert on page 313

★★★68% Corus hotel Leicester

Enderby Rd, Blaby LE8 4GD
☎ 0116 278 7898 0870 609 6106
0116 278 1974
e-mail: corushotelleicester@corushotels.co.uk
Dir: *M1 junct 21, A5460 to Leicester. 4th exit at 1st rdbt, ahead at 2nd, left at 3rd. Follow signs to Blaby, over 4th rdbt. Hotel on left*

Situated in a quiet location on the outskirts of the city, yet remaining convenient for the adjacent link road. Public areas include a bar brasserie, Hunters Restaurant, various meeting rooms and an extensive gym and indoor pool. Bedrooms are comfortably appointed and generally quite spacious and many are decorated to very high standards.
ROOMS: 48 en suite (5 fmly) ⊗ in 30 bedrooms s fr £93; d fr £105 **LB** **FACILITIES: Spa** STV Sauna Solarium Gym Steam room Xmas **CONF:** Thtr 70 Class 30 Board 36 Del from £105 **PARKING:** 110 **NOTES:** ⊗ in restaurant Civ Wed 60
CARDS:

★★★68% Regency

360 London Rd LE2 2PL
☎ 0116 270 9634 0116 270 1375
e-mail: info@the-regency-hotel.com
web: www.the-regency-hotel.com
Dir: *on A6, 1.5m from city centre*
This friendly hotel is located on the edge of town and provides smart accommodation suitable for both business and leisure guests. The food options include, an airy conservatory brasserie and the formal restaurant; a relaxing lounge and bar are also

continued

available, along with good conference and banqueting facilities. Bedrooms vary in size and style and include some spacious and stylishly appointed rooms.

ROOMS: 32 en suite (4 fmly) s £38-£48; d £56-£62 **FACILITIES:** STV ♫ Xmas **CONF:** Thtr 50 Class 50 Board 25 Del from £92 **PARKING:** 40 **NOTES:** ⊗ in restaurant
CARDS:

★★★66% Leicester Stage Hotel

Leicester Rd, Wigston LE18 1JW
☎ 0116 288 6161 0116 257 3900
e-mail: reservations@stagehotel.co.uk
Dir: *M69/M1 junct 21 take ring road S to Leicester. Take Oadby and Wigston signs, right onto A5199 towards Northampton. Hotel on left*

This unusual, purpose-built, glass-fronted building is situated to the south of the city centre. Bedrooms come in a variety of styles and include executive rooms as well as four-poster bridal suites. Open-plan public areas include a lounge bar, restaurant and a further seating area in the entrance hall. Ample car parking and the swimming pool are an added bonus.
ROOMS: 75 en suite (10 fmly) (39 GF) ⊗ in 30 bedrooms s £69-£99; d £79-£109 (incl. bkfst) **LB** **FACILITIES:** STV Sauna Gym Jacuzzi Steam room Xmas **CONF:** Thtr 500 Class 320 Board 120 Del from £110 **PARKING:** 200 **NOTES:** Civ Wed 300
CARDS:

See advert on page 313

Campanile Leicester

St Matthew's Way, 1 Bedford St North LE1 3JE
☎ 0116 261 6600 0116 261 6601
e-mail: leicester@evergure.co.uk
Dir: *From M69/M1 exit J21, follow city centre along Narborough Rd (A5460). Right at end of road, left onto A594. Follow Vaughan Way, Burleys Way and St. Matthews Way. Hotel on left.*
This modern building offers accommodation in smart, well-equipped bedrooms, all with en suite bathrooms. Refreshments may be taken at the informal Bistro. For further details consult the Hotel Groups page.
ROOMS: 93 en suite s £41.95-£48.50; d £41.95-£48.50 **CONF:** Thtr 50 Class 30 Board 25 Del £75

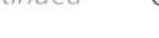

LEICESTER, continued

⌂ Hotel Ibis
St Georges Way, Constitution Hill LE1 1PL
☎ 0116 248 7200 📠 0116 262 0880
e-mail: H3061@accor-hotels.com
Dir: *From M1/M69 J21, follow town centre signs, central ring rd (A594)/railway station, hotel opposite the Leicester Mercury.*
Modern, budget hotel offering comfortable accommodation in bright and practical bedrooms. Breakfast is self-service and dinner is available in the restaurant. For further details, consult the Hotel Groups page.
ROOMS: 94 en suite s £44.95-£59.95; d £44.95-£59.95

⌂ Innkeeper's Lodge Leicester
Hinckley Rd LE3 3PG
☎ 0116 238 7878
www.innkeeperslodge.com
Smart rooms meet essential business requirements but also have home comforts, and depending on location may well have meeting rooms and pub dining. Dining options generally include all-day menus plus the added advantage of breakfast.
ROOMS: 31 rms s £48-£52; d £48-£52

⌂ Premier Lodge (Leciester West)
Leicester Rd, Glenfield LE3 8HB
☎ 0870 9906520 📠 0870 9906521
web: www.premierlodge.com
Dir: *exit M1 junct 21a onto A46 then onto A50 for Glenfield and County Hall. Turn off into County Hall, hotel on left. Or exit M1 junct 22 onto A50 for Leicester follow signs for County Hall*
High quality, modern, budget accommodation, ideal for families and business travellers. All rooms feature bath, power shower and satellite TV, and most have telephones / modem points. The adjacent bar and restaurant offers a wide and varied menu.
ROOMS: 43 en suite s £50; d £50 **CONF:** Thtr 25 Class 20 Board 20

⌂ Premier Lodge (Leicester Central)
Heathley Park, Groby Rd LE3 9QE
☎ 0870 9906398 📠 0870 9906399
web: www.premierlodge.com
Dir: *exit M1 junct 21a onto A46 then onto A50 towards Leicester city centre. 2m, hotel on left just past junct with A563. Or exit M1 at junct 22, A50 to Leicester. Straight over 5 rbts and turn left at lights*
High quality, modern, budget accommodation, ideal for families and business travellers. All rooms feature bath, power shower and satellite TV, and most have telephones / modem points. The adjacent bar and restaurant offers a wide and varied menu.
ROOMS: 72 en suite s £50; d £50 **CONF:** Thtr 10 Class 10 Board 10

⌂ Premier Lodge (Leicester South)
Glen Rise, Oadby LE2 4RG
☎ 0870 9906452 📠 0870 9906453
web: www.premierlodge.com
Dir: *from M1 junct 21 take A563 signed South. At Leicester racecourse rbt turn right. Follow signs for Market Harborough on dual carriageway. As it becomes single lane hotel on right*
High quality, modern, budget accommodation, ideal for families and business travellers. All rooms feature bath, power shower and satellite TV, and most have telephones / modem points. The adjacent bar and restaurant offers a wide and varied menu.
ROOMS: 30 en suite s £50; d £50 **CONF:** Thtr 10 Class 8 Board 10

> Packed in a hurry?
> Ironing facilities should be available at all star levels, either in rooms or on request

⌂ Travel Inn (Leicester South)
Hinckley Rd, Leicester Forest East LE3 3GD
☎ 08701 977155 📠 0116 239 3429
Dir: *M1 junct 21 onto A5460. At major junct (Holiday Inn on right), left into Braunstone Lane. After 2m, left onto A47 towards Hinkley. 400yds on left*
Travel Inn offers good-quality, value-for-money accommodation. Spacious, en suite rooms with bath and shower comfortably accommodate a family of up to two adults and two children (to age 15). The restaurant and bar offers a varied menu. For further details consult the Hotel Groups page.
ROOMS: 40 en suite s £45.95-£46.95; d £45.95-£46.95 **CONF:** Thtr 50 Board 25

⌂ Travel Inn Leicester (Thorpe Astley)
Meridian Business Park, Meridian Way, Braunstone LE19 1LU
☎ 08701 977154 📠 0116 282 7486
Dir: *M1 junct 21 follow signs for A563 (outer ring road) W to Thorpe Astley. Slip road past Texaco garage, Travel Inn on left.*
Travel Inn offers good-quality, value-for-money accommodation. Spacious, en suite rooms with bath and shower comfortably accommodate a family of up to two adults and two children (to age 15). The restaurant and bar offers a varied menu. For further details consult the Hotel Groups page.
ROOMS: 51 en suite s £45.95-£48.95; d £45.95-£48.95 **CONF:** Class 20 Board 20

⌂ Travelodge (Leicester)
Vaughan Way LE1 4NN
☎ 0870 1911755 📠 0116 251 0560
Travelodge offers good quality, good value, modern accommodation. Ideal for families, the spacious, en suite bedrooms include remote-control TV, tea and coffee-making facilities and luxury beds. Meals can be taken at the nearby family restaurant. For further details consult the Hotel Groups page.
ROOMS: 95 en suite s fr £25; d fr £25

LEICESTER FOREST MOTORWAY SERVICE AREA (M1), Leicestershire
Map 11 SK50

⌂ Days Inn
Leicester Forest East, Junction 21 M1 LE3 3GB
☎ 0116 239 0534 📠 0116 239 0546
e-mail: leicester.hotel@welcomebreak.co.uk
web: www.welcomebreak.co.uk
Dir: *on M1 northbound between junct 21 & 21A*
This modern building offers accommodation in smart, spacious and well-equipped bedrooms, suitable for families and business travellers, and all with en suite bathrooms. Continental breakfast is available and other refreshments may be taken at the nearby family restaurant. For further details see the Hotel Groups page.
ROOMS: 92 en suite s fr £45; d fr £45 **CONF:** Board 10

LEIGH DELAMERE MOTORWAY SERVICE AREA (M4), Wiltshire

Map 04 ST87

⌂ Travelodge Chippenham (Eastbound)
SN14 6LB
☎ 08700 850 950 📠 01666 837112
Dir: *Between junct 17 & 18 on M4*
Travelodge offers good quality, good value, modern accommodation. Ideal for families, the spacious, en suite bedrooms include remote-control TV, tea and coffee-making facilities and luxury beds. Meals can be taken at the nearby family restaurant. For further details consult the Hotel Groups page.
ROOMS: 69 en suite s fr £25; d fr £25

LEIGH DELAMERE MOTORWAY SERVICE AREA, continued

Travelodge Chippenham (Westbound)
Service Area SN14 6LB
☎ 08700 850 950 01666 838529
Dir: *Between J17 & J18 on M4*

Travelodge

Travelodge offers good quality, good value, modern accommodation. Ideal for families, the spacious, en suite bedrooms include remote-control TV, tea and coffee-making facilities and luxury beds. Meals can be taken at the nearby family restaurant. For further details consult the Hotel Groups page.
ROOMS: 31 en suite s fr £25; d fr £25

LENHAM, Kent Map 07 TQ85

Top 200 – Hotel

★★★★ **Chilston Park**
Sandway ME17 2BE
☎ 01622 859803 01622 858588
e-mail: chilstonpark-cro@handpicked.co.uk
Dir: *from A20 into Lenham village, turn right onto High St, pass railway station on right, 1st left, over crossroads, hotel 0.25 mile on left*

HandPICKED

This elegant Grade I listed country house is set in 23 acres of immaculately landscaped gardens and parkland. An impressive collection of original paintings and antiques creates a unique feel to the property. The sunken Venetian-style restaurant serves modern British food, with French influences. Bedrooms are individual in design; some have four-poster beds and many have garden views. Hand Picked Hotels - AA Hotel Group of the Year 2004-5.
ROOMS: 30 en suite 23 annexe en suite (2 fmly) (3 GF) s £130-£295; d £130-£295 LB **FACILITIES:** STV Fishing Xmas **CONF:** Thtr 100 Class 40 Board 40 Del from £195 **SERVICES:** Lift **PARKING:** 100 **NOTES:** in restaurant Civ Wed 80 **CARDS:**

See advert on page 313

LEOMINSTER, Herefordshire Map 10 SO45

★★★66% **Talbot**
West St HR6 8EP
☎ 01568 616347 01568 614880
e-mail: talbot@bestwestern.co.uk
Dir: *from A49, A44 or A4112, hotel in centre of town*

Best Western

This charming former coaching inn is located in the town centre and offers an ideal base from which to explore this delightful area. Public areas feature original beams and antique furniture, and include an atmospheric bar and elegant restaurant. Bedrooms are comfortably furnished and equipped and there are also facilities available for private functions and conferences.

continued

ROOMS: 20 en suite (3 fmly) in 15 bedrooms s £47-£52; d £68-£74 LB **FACILITIES:** Xmas **CONF:** Thtr 150 Class 25 Board 28 Del £90 **PARKING:** 20 **NOTES:** in restaurant RS 25 Dec **CARDS:**

LEWDOWN, Devon Map 03 SX48

Top 200 – Hotel

★★★ **Lewtrenchard Manor**
EX20 4PN
☎ 01566 783256 & 783222 01566 783332
e-mail: info@lewtrenchard.co.uk
web: www.lewtrenchard.co.uk
Dir: *A30 from Exeter to Plymouth/Tavistock road. At T-junct turn right, then left onto old A30 Lewdown road. After 6m left signed Lewtrenchard*

This Jacobean mansion was built in the 1600s, with many interesting architectural features, and is surrounded by its own idyllic grounds in a quiet valley close to the northern edge of Dartmoor. Public rooms include a fine gallery, as well as magnificent carvings and oak panelling. Meals can be taken in the dining room where imaginative and carefully prepared dishes are served. Bedrooms are comfortably furnished and spacious, many have had their bathrooms refurbished.
ROOMS: 9 en suite s £95-£120; d £135-£200 (incl. bkfst) LB **FACILITIES:** Fishing Clay pigeon shooting Xmas **CONF:** Thtr 50 Class 40 Board 20 Del from £175 **PARKING:** 50 **NOTES:** No children 8yrs in restaurant Civ Wed 100 **CARDS:**

LEWES, East Sussex Map 06 TQ41

★★★75% Shelleys Hotel
High St BN7 1XS
☎ 01273 472361 01273 483152
e-mail: info@shelleys-hotel-lewes.com
web: www.shelleys-hotel.com
Dir: *A23 to Brighton onto A27 to Lewes. At 1st rdbt left for town centre, after x-rds hotel on left*

This elegant hotel enjoys a central location and is steeped in history, with previous owners including the Earl of Dorset. Nowadays Shelleys boasts beautifully appointed bedrooms, furnished and decorated in a traditional style. The elegant restaurant overlooks the enclosed garden and serves good food using local produce.

ROOMS: 19 en suite (2 fmly) in 4 bedrooms s £95-£140; d £130-£185 **LB** **FACILITIES:** STV Xmas **CONF:** Thtr 50 Class 24 Board 28 Del from £165 **PARKING:** 25 **NOTES:** in restaurant Civ Wed 50 **CARDS:**

LEYBOURNE, Kent Map 06 TQ65

Travel Inn (Maidstone Leybourne)
Castle Way ME19 5TR
☎ 08701 977170 01732 844474
Dir: *M20 junct 4, take A228, Travel Inn on left*

Travel Inn offers good-quality, value-for-money accommodation. Spacious, en suite rooms with bath and shower comfortably accommodate a family of up to two adults and two children (to age 15). The restaurant and bar offers a varied menu. For further details consult the Hotel Groups page.

ROOMS: 40 en suite s £45.95-£46.95; d £45.95-£46.95

LEYBURN, North Yorkshire Map 19 SE19

★65% Golden Lion
Market Place DL8 5AS
☎ 01969 622161 01969 623836
e-mail: AnneGoldenLion@aol.com
Dir: *on A684 in market square*

Dating back to 1765, this traditional inn overlooks the cobbled market square where weekly markets still take place. Bedrooms, including some family rooms, offer appropriate levels of comfort. The restaurant features murals depicting scenes from the Dales and offers a good range of meals. Food can also be enjoyed in the cosy bar, a popular meeting place for local people.

ROOMS: 15 rms (14 en suite) (5 fmly) s £26-£34; d £52-£68 (incl. bkfst) **LB** **SERVICES:** Lift **NOTES:** Closed 25 & 26 Dec **CARDS:**

LICHFIELD, Staffordshire Map 10 SK10

★★★★77% Swinfen Hall
Swinfen WS14 9RE
☎ 01543 481494 01543 480341
e-mail: info@swinfenhallhotel.co.uk
web: www.swinfenhallhotel.co.uk
Dir: *set back from A38 2.5m outside Lichfield, towards Birmingham*

Dating from 1757, this lavishly decorated mansion has been painstakingly restored by the present owners. Public rooms are particularly stylish, with intricately carved ceilings and impressive oil portraits. Rooms on the first floor boast period features and tall sash windows; those on the second floor (the former servants' quarters) are smaller and more contemporary by comparison.

continued

Service in the award-winning restaurant is both professional and attentive.

Swinfen Hall

ROOMS: 19 en suite s £110-£125; d £125-£140 (incl. cont bkfst) **FACILITIES:** Fishing 100 acres of parkland **CONF:** Thtr 96 Class 50 Board 120 Del from £160 **PARKING:** 80 **NOTES:** in restaurant Civ Wed 120 **CARDS:**

★★★68% The George
12-14 Bird St WS13 6PR
☎ 01543 414822 01543 415817
e-mail: mail@thegeorgelichfield.co.uk
web: www.thegeorgelichfield.co.uk
Dir: *from Bowling Green Island on A461 take Lichfield exit. Left at next island into Swan Road and where road bears left, turn right for George Hotel straight ahead*

Situated in the city centre, this privately owned hotel has been extensively refurbished by the new owners to provide good

continued on p316

LICHFIELD, continued

quality, well-equipped accommodation, which includes a room with a four-poster bed. Facilities here include a large ballroom, plus several other rooms for meetings and functions.

The George, Lichfield

ROOMS: 36 en suite (6 fmly) ⊗ in 24 bedrooms s £47-£106; d £74-£120 (incl. bkfst) **LB** **CONF:** Thtr 110 Class 60 Board 40 Del from £125 **SERVICES:** Lift **PARKING:** 45 **NOTES:** ⊗ in restaurant Civ Wed 110 **CARDS:**

See advert under BIRMINGHAM

★★★68% Little Barrow

62 Beacon St WS13 7AR
☎ 01543 414500 01543 415734
e-mail: reservations@tlbh.co.uk
web: www.tlbh.co.uk

Conveniently situated for the cathedral and the city, this friendly hotel provides well-equipped accommodation. The cosy lounge bar, popular with locals and visitors alike, has a range of real ales and a choice of bar meals. More formal dining is offered in the pleasant restaurant. Service is relaxed and attentive.

ROOMS: 24 en suite (2 fmly) s £50-£69; d £68-£80 (incl. bkfst) **LB** **FACILITIES:** Xmas **CONF:** BC Thtr 100 Class 50 Board 50 Del £100 **PARKING:** 60 **NOTES:** ⊗ in restaurant Civ Wed 100 **CARDS:**

★★63% *Angel Croft*

Beacon St WS13 7AA
☎ 01543 258737 01543 415605

Dir: *opposite west gate entrance to Lichfield Cathedral*

This traditional, family-run Georgian hotel is close to the cathedral and city centre. A comfortable lounge leads into a pleasantly appointed dining room; there is also a cosy bar on the lower ground floor. Bedrooms vary but most are spacious, particularly those in the adjacent Westgate House.

ROOMS: 10 rms (8 en suite) 8 annexe en suite (1 fmly) **CONF:** Thtr 30 Board 20 **PARKING:** 60 **NOTES:** ⊗ in restaurant Closed 25 & 26 Dec RS Sun evenings **CARDS:**

Innkeeper's Lodge

Stafford Rd WS13 8JB
☎ 01543 415789 01543 420752
www.innkeeperslodge.com

Dir: *on A51, 0.75m outside city centre*

Smart rooms meet essential business requirements but also have home comforts, and depending on location may well have meeting rooms and pub dining. Dining options generally include all-day menus plus the added advantage of breakfast.

ROOMS: 10 en suite s £48-£59.95; d £48-£59.95

Premier Lodge (Lichfield)

Rykneld St, Fradley WS13 8RD
☎ 0870 9906438 0870 9906439
web: www.premierlodge.com

PREMIER LODGE.com

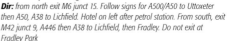

Dir: *from north exit M6 junct 15. Follow signs for A500/A50 to Uttoxeter then A50, A38 to Lichfield. Hotel on left after petrol station. From south, exit M42 junct 9, A446 then A38 to Lichfield, then Fradley. Do not exit at Fradley Park*

High quality, modern, budget accommodation, ideal for families and business travellers. All rooms feature bath, power shower and satellite TV, and most have telephones / modem points. The adjacent bar and restaurant offers a wide and varied menu.

ROOMS: 30 en suite s £50; d £50 **CONF:** Thtr 40

LIFTON, Devon — Map 03 SX38

★★★75% Arundell Arms

PL16 0AA
☎ 01566 784666 01566 784494
e-mail: reservations@arundellarms.com

Dir: *1m off A30 in Lifton*

This creeper clad, former coaching inn sits in the heart of a quiet Devon village. Internationally famous for its sporting facilities, the inn boasts a long history and continues to offer style, comfort and a relaxed atmosphere. Food is of major interest here and the cuisine is a celebration of the best of Devon's produce. Angling as well as winter shooting, golf and other country pursuits are offered.

ROOMS: 22 en suite 5 annexe en suite (4 GF) ⊗ in all bedrooms s £68-£89; d £104-£136 (incl. bkfst) **LB** **FACILITIES:** STV Fishing Skittle alley, 3 acre lake, Shooting in Winter **CONF:** Thtr 100 Class 30 Board 40 Del from £132 **PARKING:** 70 **NOTES:** ⊗ in restaurant Closed 3 days Xmas Civ Wed 80 **CARDS:**

See advert on opposite page

Early start?
Hotels at all star levels should provide in-room alarm clocks and/or alarm calls

★★75% Lifton Hall Country House

New Rd PL16 0DR
☎ 01566 784863 & 784263 01566 784770
e-mail: mail@liftonhall.co.uk
web: www.liftonhall.co.uk

THE INDEPENDENTS

Dir: *leave A30 at Liftondown junct, 2m E of Launceston. Right at T-junct signed Lifton, through village. Hotel on left 1m after T-junct*

This charming 350-year-old manor house is full of character. Dartmoor is on the doorstep and many of the north Cornish coastal resorts are within easy driving distance. Caring hospitality

continued

and accomplished cuisine are hallmarks of Lifton Hall, allied with high levels of comfort and quality throughout.

ROOMS: 9 en suite (2 fmly) ⊗ in all bedrooms s £58-£75; d £85-£99 (incl. bkfst) **LB** **FACILITIES:** Xmas **CONF:** Thtr 25 Class 25 Board 16 Del from £85 **PARKING:** 16 **NOTES:** No children 11yrs ⊗ in restaurant **CARDS:**

Restaurant with Rooms

Tinhay Mill Restaurant

Tinhay PL16 0AJ
☎ 01566 784201 01566 784201
e-mail: tinhay.mill@talk21.comweb: www.tinhaymillrestaurant.co.uk

Dir: *A30/A388, approach Lifton, restaurant at bottom of village on right*

Converted from 15th-century mill cottages, this delightful restaurant with rooms has a character and charm all of its own. Beams and open fireplaces set the scene, with everything geared to ensure a relaxed and comfortable stay. Bedrooms are spacious and well equipped with many thoughtful extras. Cuisine is taken seriously here, with the best of local produce used to create consistently impressive dishes.

ROOMS: 3 en suite **PARKING:** 18 **NOTES:** No children 12yrs ⊗ in restaurant **CARDS:**

LIMPLEY STOKE, Wiltshire — Map 04 ST76

★★★66% Limpley Stoke

BA2 7FZ
☎ 01225 723333 01225 722406
e-mail: latonalsh@aol.com

Best Western

Dir: *4.5m S of Bath on A36 turn left at lights on viaduct, take next right, just before bridge into Lower Stoke. Hotel opposite Hope Pole Inn*

Recently refurbished, this quietly located Georgian hotel is on the outskirts of Bath in a peaceful village setting; easily accessible from the M4. Attentive levels of service and friendly hospitality are to be found throughout the hotel. Bedrooms come in various shapes and sizes and all are well-equipped.

ROOMS: 60 en suite (8 fmly) ⊗ in 10 bedrooms s £59-£69; d £75-£95 (incl. bkfst) **LB** **FACILITIES:** ♫ Xmas **CONF:** Thtr 120 Class 40 Board 30 Del from £95 **SERVICES:** Lift **PARKING:** 90 **NOTES:** ⊗ in restaurant Civ Wed 120 **CARDS:**

LINCOLN, Lincolnshire — Map 17 SK97

★★★72% The Bentley Hotel & Leisure Club

Newark Rd, South Hykeham LN6 9NH
☎ 01522 878000 01522 878001
e-mail: info@thebentleyhotel.uk.com
web: www.thebentleyhotel.uk.com

Best Western

Dir: *from A1 take A46 E towards Lincoln for 10m. Over 1st rdbt on Lincoln Bypass to hotel 50yds on left*

This smart hotel offers bright, attractive accommodation. The

continued

bedrooms are spacious and well equipped with air conditioning. There is a stylish leisure suite and a large pool with access for the less able.

The Bentley Hotel & Leisure Club

ROOMS: 80 en suite (5 fmly) (26 GF) ⊗ in 50 bedrooms s £80-£90; d £95-£105 (incl. bkfst) **LB** **FACILITIES:** STV Sauna Gym Jacuzzi Beauty salon Xmas **CONF:** Thtr 300 Class 150 Board 30 Del £105 **SERVICES:** Lift **PARKING:** 140 **NOTES:** ⊗ in restaurant Civ Wed 120 **CARDS:**

★★★71% Branston Hall

Branston Park, Branston LN4 1PD
☎ 01522 793305 01522 790734
e-mail: info@branstonhall.com

Dir: *5 min drive from Lincoln on B1188*

Many original features have been retained in this country house, which sits in beautiful grounds complete with a lake. There is an elegant restaurant, a spacious bar and a beautiful lounge in addition to impressive conference and leisure facilities.

continued on p318

LINCOLN, continued

Individually styled bedrooms vary in size and include several with four-poster beds.

Branston Hall, Lincoln

ROOMS: 43 en suite 7 annexe en suite (3 fmly) (4 GF) ⊗ in 6 bedrooms s £70-£80; d £99-£164 (incl. bkfst) **LB** **FACILITIES: Spa** STV Sauna Gym Jacuzzi Xmas **CONF:** Thtr 200 Class 54 Board 40 Del £100 **SERVICES:** Lift **PARKING:** 100 **NOTES:** ⊗ in restaurant Civ Wed 160 **CARDS:**

★★★70% *Washingborough Hall*

Church Hill, Washingborough LN4 1BE
☎ 01522 790340 01522 792936
e-mail: enquiries@washingboroughhallhotel.com
Dir: *on B1190 signed Bardney. Right at mini island, hotel 200yds on left*

This Georgian manor stands on the edge of the quiet village of Washingborough among attractive gardens, with an outdoor swimming pool in the summer. Public rooms are pleasantly furnished and comfortable, whilst the restaurant offers interesting menus. Bedrooms are individually designed, and most have views out over the grounds and countryside.
ROOMS: 14 en suite (1 fmly) ⊗ in 2 bedrooms **FACILITIES:** ch fac **CONF:** Thtr 50 Class 20 Board 20 **PARKING:** 50 **NOTES:** ⊗ in restaurant Civ Wed 50 **CARDS:**

> Late for dinner?
> Quality Standards mean that last orders for dinner vary according to star rating and should be no earlier than:
> ★★ 7.00pm ★★★ 8.00pm ★★★★ 9.00pm
> ★★★★★ 10.00pm

★★★69% Courtyard by Marriott Lincoln

Brayford Wharf North LN1 1YW
☎ 01522 544244 01522 560805
e-mail: reservations.lincoln@whitbread.co.uk
Dir: *From A46 onto A57 to Lincoln Central. Left at lights, right, take next right onto Lucy Tower St then right onto Brayford Wharf North for hotel on right*

This smart hotel enjoys an idyllic waterfront location overlooking Brayford Pool, only a few minutes' walk from the city centre. Bedrooms are spacious and comfortably appointed, with many extra facilities. Public areas are focused around a galleried restaurant that overlooks the spacious lounge bar.
ROOMS: 97 en suite (9 GF) ⊗ in 47 bedrooms s £65-£94; d £90-£104 (incl. bkfst) **LB** **FACILITIES:** STV Fitness Room Xmas **CONF:** Thtr 30 Class 20 Board 20 Del from £115 **SERVICES:** Lift air con **PARKING:** 100 **NOTES:** ⊗ in restaurant
CARDS:

★★★68% The Lincoln

Eastgate LN2 1PN
☎ 0871 220 6070 0871 220 6071
e-mail: sales@thelincolnhotel.com
web: www.thelincolnhotel.com
Dir: *adjacent to cathedral*
This privately owned modern hotel enjoys superb uninterrupted views of Lincoln Cathedral. There are ruins of the Roman wall and Eastgate in the grounds. Bedrooms are undergoing refurbishment to have a contemporary style with up-to-the-minute facilities. An airy restaurant and bar, plus a comfortable lounge are provided, in addition to substantial conference and meeting facilities. Good hospitality is notable here.
ROOMS: 72 en suite (7 fmly) ⊗ in 46 bedrooms s £70-£89; d £70-£89 **LB** **CONF:** BC Thtr 100 Class 50 Board 40 Del from £100 **SERVICES:** Lift **PARKING:** 110 **NOTES:** ⊗ in restaurant Civ Wed 100
CARDS:

★★★67% *The White Hart*

Bailgate LN1 3AR
☎ 0870 400 8117 01522 531798
e-mail: info@whitehart-lincoln.co.uk
Dir: *A15 rdbt on N side of city follow Historic Lincoln signs, through Newport Arch, along Bailgate. Hotel on corner*
Lying in the shadow of Lincoln's magnificent cathedral, this hotel is perfectly positioned for exploring the shops and sights of this medieval city. The attractive bedrooms are furnished and decorated in a traditional style and many have views of the cathedral. Given the hotel's central location, parking is a bonus.
ROOMS: 48 en suite (4 fmly) ⊗ in 18 bedrooms **FACILITIES:** STV **CONF:** Thtr 90 Class 40 Board 30 **SERVICES:** Lift **PARKING:** 57 **NOTES:** ⊗ in restaurant Civ Wed 120 **CARDS:**

★★73% Hillcrest

15 Lindum Ter LN2 5RT
☎ 01522 510182 📠 01522 538009
e-mail: reservations@hillcrest-hotel.com
web: www.hillcrest-hotel.com
Dir: *from A15 Wragby Rd and Lindum Rd, turn into Upper Lindum St at sign. Left at bottom for hotel 200mtrs on right*

The hospitality offered by Jenny Bennett and her staff is one of the strengths of Hillcrest, which sits in a quiet residential location. Thoughtfully equipped bedrooms come in a variety of sizes and all are well presented and maintained. The cosy dining room and pleasant conservatory offer a good range of freshly prepared food with views out over the adjacent park. A computer room is available for residents.

ROOMS: 14 en suite (5 fmly) (6 GF) ⊗ in 6 bedrooms s £65; d £85-£95 (incl. bkfst) **LB** **FACILITIES:** ch fac **CONF:** Thtr 20 Class 16 Board 12 Del £108 **PARKING:** 8 **NOTES:** ⊗ in restaurant Closed 23 Dec-3 Jan **CARDS:**

See advert on this page

★★72% Castle

Westgate LN1 3AS
☎ 01522 538801 📠 01522 575457
e-mail: aa@castlehotel.net web: www.castlehotel.net
Dir: *follow signs for Historic Lincoln. Hotel at NE corner of castle*

Located in the heart of historic Lincoln, this privately owned and run hotel has been carefully restored to offer comfortable, attractive, well-appointed accommodation. Bedrooms are thoughtfully equipped, particularly the deluxe rooms and the spacious Lincoln Suite. Specialising in traditional fayre, Knights Restaurant has an interesting medieval theme.

ROOMS: 16 en suite 3 annexe en suite (5 GF) ⊗ in 12 bedrooms s £67-£150; d £89-£160 (incl. bkfst) **LB** **CONF:** Thtr 20 Class 40 Board 30 Del from £99 **PARKING:** 20 **NOTES:** No children 8yrs ⊗ in restaurant RS Evening of Dec 25 **CARDS:**

See advert on this page

★★66% Tower Hotel

38 Westgate LN1 3BD
☎ 01522 529999 📠 01522 560596
e-mail: tower.hotel@btclick.com
Dir: *from A46 follow signs to Lincoln N then to Bailgate area. Through arch and 2nd left*

This hotel stands facing the Norman castle wall and is in a very convenient location. The relaxed and friendly atmosphere is one of the strengths of this hotel. Public rooms are smartly appointed following a refurbishment programme which has seen the development of modern lounge bar, a separate, quieter lounge and a cosy brasserie dining area; food is also readily available in the bar.

ROOMS: 14 en suite (1 fmly) ⊗ in 2 bedrooms s £55-£67; d £80-£85 (incl. bkfst) **LB** **CONF:** Thtr 30 Class 30 Board 30 Del from £70 **PARKING:** 9 **NOTES:** ⊗ in restaurant Closed 24-26 Dec **CARDS:**

LINCOLN, continued

Hotel Ibis Lincoln
Runcorn Rd (A46), off Whisby Rd LN6 3QZ
☎ 01522 698333 01522 698444
e-mail: H3161@accor-hotels.com
Dir: off A46 ring road onto Whisby Rd. 1st turning on left
Modern, budget hotel offering comfortable accommodation in bright and practical bedrooms. Breakfast is self-service and dinner is available in the restaurant. For further details, consult the Hotel Groups page.
ROOMS: 86 en suite s fr £42.95; d fr £42.95
CONF: Thtr 35 Class 12 Board 20

Travel Inn
Lincoln Rd, Canwick Hill LN4 2RF
☎ 08701 977156 01522 542521
Dir: Approx 1 mile south of city centre at junct with B1188 to Branston and B1131 to Brakebridge Heath
Travel Inn offers good-quality, value-for-money accommodation. Spacious, en suite rooms with bath and shower comfortably accommodate a family of up to two adults and two children (to age 15). The restaurant and bar offers a varied menu. For further details consult the Hotel Groups page.
ROOMS: 40 en suite s £45.95-£46.95; d £45.95-£46.95

Travelodge
Thorpe on the Hill LN6 9AJ
☎ 08700 850 950 01522 697213
Dir: on A46
Travelodge offers good quality, good value, modern accommodation. Ideal for families, the spacious, en suite bedrooms include remote-control TV, tea and coffee-making facilities and luxury beds. Meals can be taken at the nearby family restaurant. For further details consult the Hotel Groups page.
ROOMS: 32 en suite s fr £25; d fr £25

LIPHOOK, Hampshire — Map 05 SU83

★★★75% Old Thorns Hotel, Golf & Country Club
Griggs Green GU30 7PE
☎ 01428 724555 01428 725036
e-mail: info@oldthorns.com web: www.oldthorns.com
Dir: A3 Guildford to Portsmouth road. Griggs Green exit S of Liphook

This smartly presented hotel offers a range of leisure facilities, including a golf course, indoor pool, sauna, solarium and fitness room. The refurbished bedrooms are spacious, and equipped with good facilities. There is a choice of eating options: the Japanese Nippon Kan Restaurant or the more informal Sands brasserie.
ROOMS: 29 en suite 4 annexe rms (3 en suite) (2 fmly) (14 GF) in 9 bedrooms s £140-£195; d £160-£205 (incl. bkfst) **LB** **FACILITIES:** STV 18 Sauna Solarium Gym Putt green Steam room, Beauty treatment rooms Xmas **CONF:** Thtr 100 Class 50 Board 30 Del from £160 **PARKING:** 80 **NOTES:** Civ Wed 77 **CARDS:**

Travelodge
GU30 7TT
☎ 08700 850 950 01428 727619
Dir: on northbound carriageway of A3, 1m from Griggs Green exit at Shell services
Travelodge offers good quality, good value, modern accommodation. Ideal for families, the spacious, en suite bedrooms include remote-control TV, tea and coffee-making facilities and luxury beds. Meals can be taken at the nearby family restaurant. For further details consult the Hotel Groups page.
ROOMS: 40 en suite s fr £25; d fr £25

LISKEARD, Cornwall & Isles of Scilly — Map 02 SX26

Top 200 – Hotel

★★ Well House
St Keyne PL14 4RN
☎ 01579 342001 01579 343891
e-mail: enquiries@wellhouse.co.uk
web: www.wellhouse.co.uk
Dir: from Liskeard on A38 take B3254 to St Keyne (3 miles). At church fork left and hotel 0.5m
Tucked away in an attractive valley and set in impressive grounds, Well House enjoys a tranquil setting. Friendly staff provide attentive yet relaxed service and add to the elegant atmosphere of the house. The comfortable lounge offers deep cushioned sofas and an open fire and in the intimate bar an extensive choice of wines and drinks is available. The accomplished cuisine features carefully sourced ingredients from local suppliers resulting in enjoyable dining.
ROOMS: 9 en suite (1 fmly) **FACILITIES:** Xmas
PARKING: 30 **NOTES:** in restaurant Closed 2 weeks in Jan
CARDS:

♫ Entertainment

LITTLE LANGDALE, Cumbria
Map 18 NY30

★★68% Three Shires Inn
LA22 9NZ
☎ 015394 37215 015394 37127
e-mail: enquiry@threeshiresinn.co.uk
web: www.threeshiresinn.co.uk
Dir: *off A593, 2.5m from Ambleside at 2nd junct signed Langdales & Wrynose Pass. 1st left for 0.5m, then hotel 1m up lane*
Enjoying an outstanding rural location, this family-run inn was built in 1872. The brightly decorated bedrooms are individual in style and many offer panoramic views. The attractive lounge features a roaring fire in the cooler months and there is a traditional style bar with a great selection of local ales. Meals can be taken in either the bar or cosy restaurant.
ROOMS: 10 en suite (1 fmly) in all bedrooms s £36-£47; d £72-£90 (incl. bkfst) **LB** **FACILITIES:** ch fac **PARKING:** 21 **NOTES:** in restaurant Closed Xmas RS Dec & Jan **CARDS:**

LITTLE WEIGHTON, East Riding of Yorkshire
Map 17 SE93

★★68% The Rowley Manor
Rowley Rd HU20 3XR
☎ 01482 848248 01482 849900
e-mail: info@rowleymanor.com
Dir: *leave A63 at South Cave/Market Weighton exit. Into South Cave, right into Beverley Rd at clock tower, and follow signs for Rowley*
A 17th-century former vicarage, Rowley Manor is a Georgian country house set in rural gardens and parkland. Bedrooms are traditionally decorated and furnished with period pieces; many rooms have panoramic views, and some are particularly spacious. The public rooms include a magnificent pine-panelled study, and the gardens feature a croquet lawn.
ROOMS: 16 en suite (2 fmly) s fr £60; d fr £80 (incl. bkfst) **LB** **FACILITIES:** ch fac Xmas **CONF:** Thtr 110 Class 48 Board 50 Del from £130 **PARKING:** 100 **NOTES:** in restaurant Civ Wed 110 **CARDS:**

LIVERPOOL, Merseyside
Map 15 SJ39

★★★★73%
Radisson SAS Hotel Liverpool
107 Old Hall St L3 9BD
☎ 0151 966 1500 0151 966 1501
e-mail: info.liverpool@radissonsas.com
Dir: *Follow signs for Liverpool City Centre & Albert Dock. Turn right onto Old Hall St. From the main Leeds St dual carriageway.*
This smart, new hotel enjoys an enviable location on the city's waterfront. The stylish bedrooms are designed in two eye-catching schemes, Ocean and Urban and are particularly well equipped; junior suites and business rooms offer additional amenities. Public areas include extensive conference and leisure facilities, the trendy White Bar and Filini Restaurant, serving imaginative, accomplished Italian cuisine.
ROOMS: 194 en suite in 131 bedrooms s £99-£130; d £99-£130 **FACILITIES:** STV Sauna Solarium Gym Jacuzzi **CONF:** BC Thtr 130 Class 70 Board 24 Del from £155 **SERVICES:** Lift air con **NOTES:** **CARDS:**

★★★★69%
Liverpool Marriott Hotel City Centre
1 Queen Square L1 1RH
☎ 0151 476 8000 0151 474 5000
e-mail: liverpool.city@marriotthotels.co.uk
Dir: *from city centre follow signs for Queen Sq Parking. Hotel adjacent*
An impressive modern hotel located in the heart of the city. The elegant public rooms include a café bar, cocktail bar and the stylish Oliver's Restaurant, the latter located on the first floor. The hotel also boasts a well-equipped, indoor leisure health club with pool. Bedrooms are stylishly appointed and benefit from a host of extra facilities.
ROOMS: 146 en suite (29 fmly) in 120 bedrooms s £98-£150; d £98-£150 **LB** **FACILITIES:** STV Sauna Solarium Gym Jacuzzi Xmas **CONF:** Thtr 300 Class 90 Board 30 Del £156 **SERVICES:** Lift air con **PARKING:** 158 **NOTES:** in restaurant Civ Wed 150 **CARDS:**

★★★★68%
Liverpool Marriott Hotel South
Speke Aerodrome L24 8QD
☎ 0151 494 5000 0151 494 5053
e-mail: liverpool.south@marriotthotels.co.uk
Dir: *M62 junct 6, take Knowsley Expressway towards Speke. At end of Expressway right onto A561 towards Liverpool. Continue for approx 4 miles, hotel on left just after Estuary Commerce Park*
Previously Liverpool airport, this hotel has a distinctive look, reflected by its art deco architecture and interior design. The spacious bedrooms are fully air conditioned and feature a comprehensive range of facilities. Feature rooms include the presidential suite in the base of the old control tower.
ROOMS: 164 en suite (50 fmly) (46 GF) in 100 bedrooms s £115-£125; d £115-£125 **FACILITIES:** STV supervised supervised Squash Sauna Solarium Gym Jacuzzi Selected use of David Lloyd Leisure Centre adjacent to hotel **CONF:** Thtr 280 Class 120 Board 24 Del from £115 **SERVICES:** Lift air con **PARKING:** 200 **NOTES:** Civ Wed 100 **CARDS:**

★★★★68% Thornton Hall

Neston Rd CH63 1JF
☎ 0151 336 3938 0151 336 7864
e-mail: reservations@thorntonhallhotel.com
web: www.thorntonhallhotel.com
(For full entry see Thornton Hough)

★★★67% Alicia
3 Aigburth Dr, Sefton Park L17 3AA
☎ 0151 727 4411 0151 727 6752
e-mail: aliciahotel@feathers.uk.com
This stylish and friendly hotel overlooks Sefton Park and is just a few minutes' drive from both the city centre and John Lennon Airport. Bedrooms are well equipped and comfortable. Day rooms include a striking modern restaurant and bar. Extensive, stylish function facilities make this a popular wedding venue.
ROOMS: 41 en suite (8 fmly) in 16 bedrooms s fr £55; d fr £80 (incl. bkfst) **LB** **FACILITIES:** STV Xmas **CONF:** Thtr 120 Class 80 Board 40 Del from £110 **SERVICES:** Lift **PARKING:** 40 **NOTES:** in restaurant Civ Wed 120 **CARDS:**

Late for dinner?
Quality Standards mean that last orders for dinner vary according to star rating and should be no earlier than:
★★ 7.00pm ★★★ 8.00pm ★★★★ 9.00pm
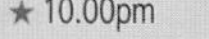 10.00pm

LIVERPOOL, continued

★★★67% *The Royal*

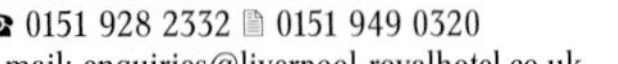

Marine Ter, Waterloo L22 5PR
☎ 0151 928 2332 📠 0151 949 0320
e-mail: enquiries@liverpool-royalhotel.co.uk
web: www.liverpool-royalhotel.co.uk
Dir: *6.5m NW of city centre, left off A565 Liverpool to Southport road at monument. Hotel at bottom of road*
Dating back to 1815, this Grade II listed hotel is situated on the outskirts of the city, beside the Marine Gardens. Bedrooms are smartly appointed and some feature four-poster beds and spa baths. Spacious public areas enjoy splendid views and include an elegant restaurant, an attractive bar lounge and a conservatory.
ROOMS: 25 en suite (5 fmly) ⊗ in 1 bedroom **FACILITIES:** STV **CONF:** Thtr 100 Class 70 Board 40 **PARKING:** 25 **NOTES:** ✈ **CARDS:**

⌂ Campanile

Chaloner St, Queens Dock L3 4AJ
☎ 0151 709 8104 📠 0151 709 8725
e-mail: liverpool@envergure.co.uk
Dir: *follow tourist signs marked Albert Dock. Hotel on waterfront*

This modern building offers accommodation in smart, well-equipped bedrooms, all with en suite bathrooms. Refreshments may be taken at the informal Bistro. For further details consult the Hotel Groups page.
ROOMS: 100 en suite s fr £46.50; d fr £46.50 **CONF:** Thtr 35 Class 20 Board 40

⌂ Hotel Ibis Liverpool

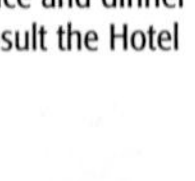

27 Wapping L1 8LY
☎ 0151 706 9800 📠 0151 706 9810
e-mail: H3140@accor-hotels.com
Dir: *from M62 follow signs for Albert Dock. Hotel opposite entrance to Albert Dock*
Modern, budget hotel offering comfortable accommodation in bright and practical bedrooms. Breakfast is self-service and dinner is available in the restaurant. For further details, consult the Hotel Groups page.
ROOMS: 127 en suite s £48; d £48

⌂ Innkeeper's Lodge

531 Aigburth Rd L19 9DN
☎ 0151 494 1032 📠 0151 494 3345
www.innkeeperslodge.com
Dir: *on A56, opposite Liverpool cricket ground*
Smart rooms meet essential business requirements but also have home comforts, and depending on location may well have meeting rooms and pub dining. Dining options generally include all-day menus plus the added advantage of breakfast.
ROOMS: 32 en suite s £48; d £48 **CONF:** Thtr 18 Class 20 Board 12

⌂ Innkeeper's Lodge Liverpool North

502 Queen's Dr, Stoneycroft L13 0AS
☎ 0151 254 2271 📠 0151 254 2394
www.innkeeperslodge.com
Dir: *from M62 take A5080 N towards Bootle Docks. Continue at lights at junct with A57. Hotel on left in Queens Drive*
Smart rooms meet essential business requirements but also have home comforts, and depending on location may well have meeting rooms and pub dining. Dining options generally include all-day menus plus the added advantage of breakfast.
ROOMS: 21 annexe en suite s £48; d £48

⌂ Premier Lodge (Liverpool Albert Dock)

East Britannia Building, Albert Dock L3 4AD
☎ 0870 9906432 📠 0870 9906433
web: www.premierlodge.com
Dir: *just off A5036. Once in city centre, follow brown tourist signs for Albert Dock/Beatles Story. When inside the dock, hotel beside Beatles Story*
High quality, modern, budget accommodation, ideal for families and business travellers. All rooms feature bath, power shower and satellite TV, and most have telephones / modem points. The adjacent bar and restaurant offers a wide and varied menu.
ROOMS: 130 en suite s £50; d £50

⌂ Premier Lodge (Liverpool City Centre)

45 Victoria St L1 6JB
☎ 0870 9906584 📠 0870 9906585
web: www.premierlodge.com
High quality, modern, budget accommodation, ideal for families and business travellers. All rooms feature bath, power shower and satellite TV, and most have telephones / modem points. The adjacent bar and restaurant offers a wide and varied menu.
ROOMS: 39 en suite s £50; d £50

⌂ Premier Lodge (Liverpool South East)

Roby Rd, Huyton L36 4HD
☎ 0870 9906596 📠 0870 9906597
web: www.premierlodge.com
Dir: *just off M62 junct 5, on A5080*
High quality, modern, budget accommodation, ideal for families and business travellers. All rooms feature bath, power shower and satellite TV, and most have telephones / modem points. The adjacent bar and restaurant offers a wide and varied menu.
ROOMS: 53 en suite s £48; d £48 **CONF:** Thtr 25 Class 15 Board 22

⌂ Travel Inn Liverpool City Centre

Vernon St L2 2AY
☎ 0870 238 3323 📠 0870 241 9000
Dir: *from M62 follow Liverpool City Centre and then Birkenhead Tunnel signs. At rbt take 3rd exit onto Dale St then right into Vernon St. The Travel Inn is on the left*
Travel Inn offers good-quality, value-for-money accommodation. Spacious, en suite rooms with bath and shower comfortably accommodate a family of up to two adults and two children (to age 15). The restaurant and bar offers a varied menu. For further details consult the Hotel Groups page.
ROOMS: 165 en suite s £49.95; d £49.95

⌂ Travel Inn (Liverpool Aintree)

1 Ormskirk Rd, Aintree L9 5AS
☎ 08701 977157 📠 0151 525 8696
Dir: *M58/57 then follow A59 to Liverpool. Past Aintree Retail Park, left at lights into Aintree Racecourse. Travel Inn on left*
Travel Inn offers good-quality, value-for-money accommodation.

continued

Spacious, en suite rooms with bath and shower comfortably accommodate a family of up to two adults and two children (to age 15). The restaurant and bar offers a varied menu. For further details consult the Hotel Groups page.
ROOMS: 40 en suite s £45.95-£46.95; d £45.95-£46.95 **CONF:** Thtr 10

Travel Inn (Liverpool Tarbock)
Wilson Rd, Tarbock L36 6AD
☎ 08701 977159 📠 0151 480 9361
Dir: *at junct M62/M57. M62 junct 6 take A5080 Huyton then 1st right into Wilson Rd*
Travel Inn offers good-quality, value-for-money accommodation. Spacious, en suite rooms with bath and shower comfortably accommodate a family of up to two adults and two children (to age 15). The restaurant and bar offers a varied menu. For further details consult the Hotel Groups page.
ROOMS: 40 en suite s £45.95-£46.95; d £45.95-£46.95

Travel Inn (Liverpool West Derby)
Queens Dr, West Derby L13 0DL
☎ 08701 977160 📠 0151 220 7610
Dir: *At end of M62 turn right under flyover onto A5058 (follow signs to football stadium). Travel Inn 1.5 m on left, just past Esso garage*
Travel Inn offers good-quality, value-for-money accommodation. Spacious, en suite rooms with bath and shower comfortably accommodate a family of up to two adults and two children (to age 15). The restaurant and bar offers a varied menu. For further details consult the Hotel Groups page.
ROOMS: 84 en suite s £45.95-£46.95; d £45.95-£46.95

Travelodge (Liverpool Central)
25 Haymarket L1 6ER
☎ 08700 850 950 📠 0151 227 5838
Dir: *Centre of Liverpool next to Birkenhead Tunnel.*
Travelodge offers good quality, good value, modern accommodation. Ideal for families, the spacious, en suite bedrooms include remote-control TV, tea and coffee-making facilities and luxury beds. Meals can be taken at the nearby family restaurant. For further details consult the Hotel Groups page.
ROOMS: 105 en suite s fr £25; d fr £25

Travelodge (Liverpool South)
Brunswick Dock, Sefton St L3 4BH
☎ 08700 850 950 📠 0151 707 7769
Dir: *Follow signs to City Centre & Docks, Travelodge 1m after Albert Docks, next to Royal Naval headquarters*
Travelodge offers good quality, good value, modern accommodation. Ideal for families, the spacious, en suite bedrooms include remote-control TV, tea and coffee-making facilities and luxury beds. Meals can be taken at the nearby family restaurant. For further details consult the Hotel Groups page.
ROOMS: 31 en suite s fr £25; d fr £25

LIZARD, THE, Cornwall & Isles of Scilly — Map 02 SW71

★★★68% Housel Bay
Housel Cove TR12 7PG
☎ 01326 290417 & 290917 📠 01326 290359
e-mail: info@houselbay.com
web: www.houselbay.com
Dir: *A39 or A394 to Helston, then A3083. At Lizard sign left, at school left and down lane to hotel*
This long-established hotel has stunning views across the Western Approaches, equally enjoyable from the lounge and many of the bedrooms. Most bedrooms have high standards of comfort with

continued

modern facilities. Enjoyable cuisine is available in the stylish, dining room, after which perhaps, take stroll to the end of the garden which leads directly onto the Cornwall coastal path.
ROOMS: 20 en suite (1 fmly) ⊗ in 10 bedrooms **FACILITIES:** STV **CONF:** Thtr 20 Class 16 Board 12 **SERVICES:** Lift **PARKING:** 37
NOTES: ⊗ in restaurant RS Winter
CARDS:

★★ Tregildry
TR12 6HG
☎ 01326 231378 📠 01326 231561
e-mail: trgildry@globalnet.co.uk
web: www.tregildryhotel.co.uk
(For full entry see Gillan)

LOCKINGTON Hotels are listed under Nottingham East Midlands Airport

LOLWORTH, Cambridgeshire — Map 12 TL36

Travelodge
Huntingdon Rd CB3 8DR
☎ 08700 850 950 📠 01954 781335
Dir: *on A14 northbound, 3m N of junct 14 on M11*
Travelodge offers good quality, good value, modern accommodation. Ideal for families, the spacious, en suite bedrooms include remote-control TV, tea and coffee-making facilities and luxury beds. Meals can be taken at the nearby family restaurant. For further details consult the Hotel Groups page.
ROOMS: 36 en suite s fr £25; d fr £25

GF Indicates the number of bedrooms at ground floor level.

Index of London Hotels

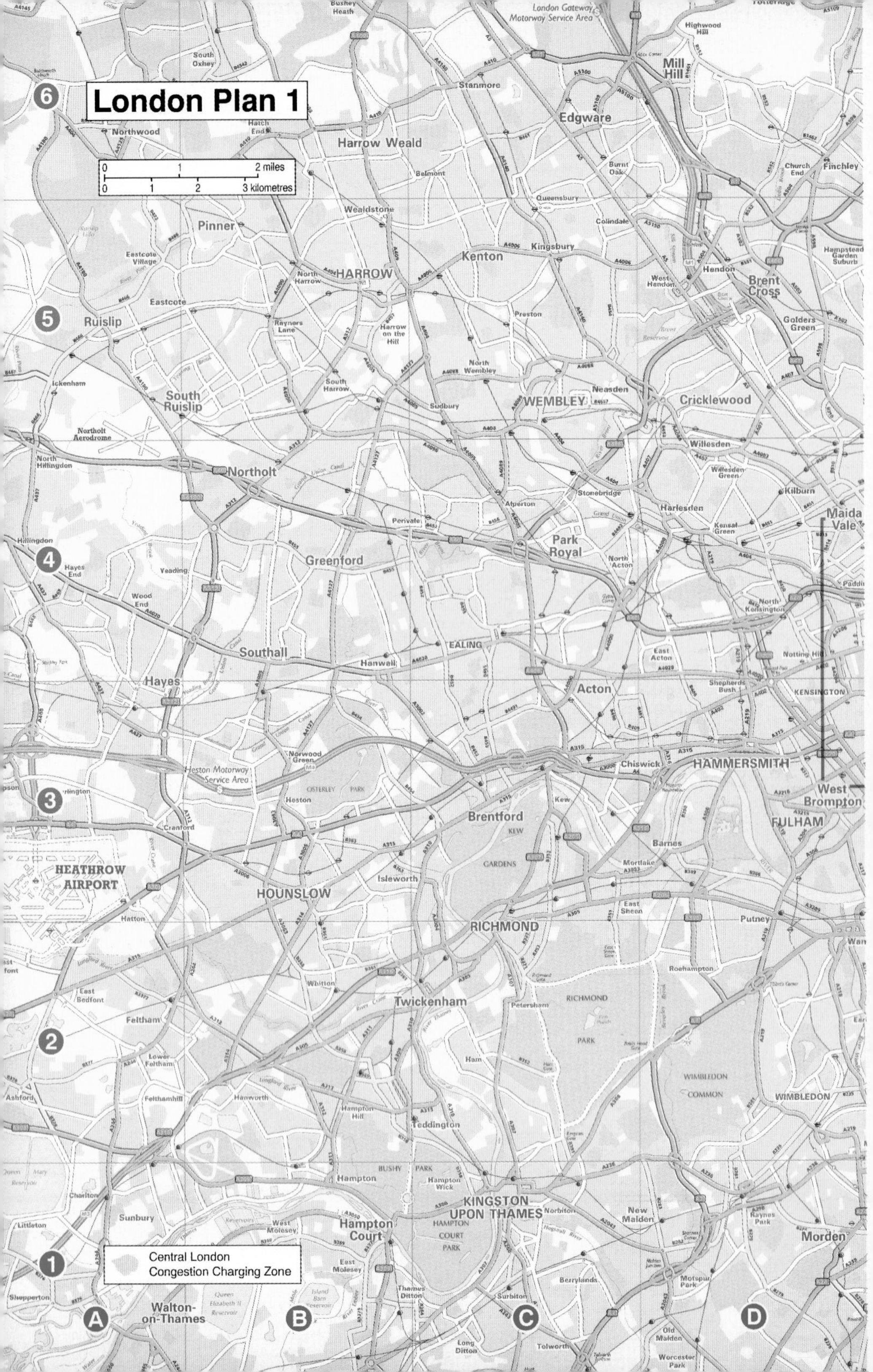
London Plan 1
0 1 2 miles
0 1 2 3 kilometres
Central London Congestion Charging Zone
London Gateway Motorway Service Area
Bushey Heath
South Oxhey
Northwood
Hatch End
Stanmore
Harrow Weald
Belmont
Edgware
Mill Hill
Highwood Hill
Burnt Oak
Queensbury
Colindale
Church End
Finchley
Pinner
Wealdstone
Eastcote Village
Eastcote
Ruislip
Kenton
Kingsbury
HARROW
North Harrow
Hendon
West Hendon
Brent Cross
Hampstead Garden Suburb
Golders Green
Rayners Lane
Harrow on the Hill
Preston
North Wembley
Ickenham
South Harrow
South Ruislip
Sudbury
WEMBLEY
Neasden
Cricklewood
Northolt Aerodrome
North Hillingdon
Northolt
Willesden
Willesden Green
Kilburn
Stonebridge
Alperton
Harlesden
Maida Vale
Perivale
Kensal Green
Hillingdon
Hayes End
Yeading
Greenford
Park Royal
North Acton
Wood End
North Kensington
Southall
Hanwell
EALING
East Acton
Notting Hill
Hayes
Acton
Shepherds Bush
KENSINGTON
Norwood Green
Heston Motorway Service Area
Chiswick
HAMMERSMITH
Heston
OSTERLEY PARK
Cranford
Brentford
Kew
KEW GARDENS
West Brompton
FULHAM
HEATHROW AIRPORT
Isleworth
Barnes
Mortlake
HOUNSLOW
Hatton
RICHMOND
East Sheen
Putney
East Bedfont
Whitton
Roehampton
Twickenham
Feltham
Petersham
RICHMOND PARK
Lower Feltham
Ham
Ashford
Felthamhill
Hanworth
WIMBLEDON COMMON
WIMBLEDON
Hampton Hill
Teddington
BUSHY PARK
Hampton
Hampton Wick
Charlton
Sunbury
KINGSTON UPON THAMES
Norbiton
New Malden
Raynes Park
Littleton
West Molesey
Hampton Court
HAMPTON COURT PARK
Morden
East Molesey
Berrylands
Motspur Park
Shepperton
Thames Ditton
Surbiton
Walton-on-Thames
Queen Elizabeth II Reservoir
Island Barn Reservoir
Long Ditton
Tolworth
Old Malden
Worcester Park
A B C D
1 2 3 4 5 6

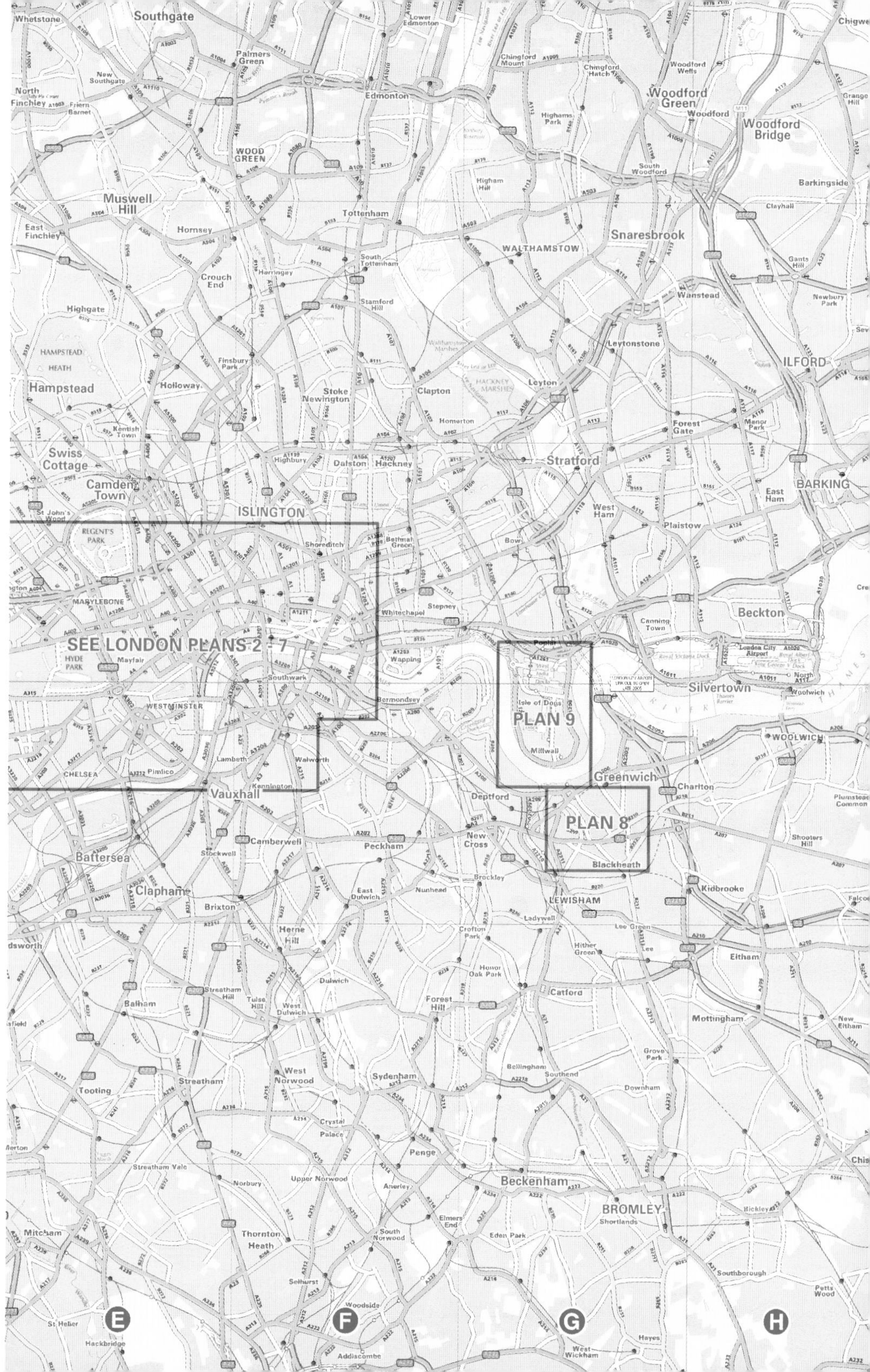

Whetstone
Southgate
Lower Edmonton
Chingford Mount
Chingford Hatch
Woodford Wells
Chigwell
New Southgate
Palmers Green
North Finchley
Friern Barnet
Edmonton
Woodford Green
Woodford
Grange Hill
Highams Park
Woodford Bridge
WOOD GREEN
South Woodford
Higham Hill
Barkingside
Muswell Hill
Tottenham
Clayhall
East Finchley
Hornsey
Snaresbrook
WALTHAMSTOW
South Tottenham
Gants Hill
Crouch End
Harringay
Stamford Hill
Wanstead
Newbury Park
Highgate
HAMPSTEAD HEATH
Finsbury Park
Leytonstone
ILFORD
Hampstead
Holloway
Stoke Newington
Clapton
HACKNEY MARSHES
Leyton
Kentish Town
Homerton
Forest Gate
Manor Park
Swiss Cottage
Highbury
Dalston
Hackney
Stratford
Camden Town
East Ham
BARKING
St John's Wood
ISLINGTON
West Ham
Plaistow
REGENT'S PARK
Shoreditch
Bethnal Green
Bow
MARYLEBONE
Stepney
Whitechapel
Canning Town
Beckton
SEE LONDON PLANS 2 - 7
HYDE PARK
Mayfair
Wapping
Poplar
London City Airport
Silvertown
Southwark
Isle of Dogs
PLAN 9
Thames Barrier
Woolwich
WESTMINSTER
Bermondsey
Millwall
WOOLWICH
Lambeth
Walworth
Greenwich
Charlton
CHELSEA
Pimlico
Kennington
Vauxhall
Deptford
Plumstead Common
PLAN 8
Camberwell
Peckham
New Cross
Shooters Hill
Battersea
Stockwell
Blackheath
Brockley
Clapham
Nunhead
East Dulwich
Kidbrooke
Brixton
LEWISHAM
Ladywell
Wandsworth
Herne Hill
Crofton Park
Lee Green
Lee
Hither Green
Eltham
Dulwich
Honor Oak Park
Balham
Streatham Hill
Tulse Hill
West Dulwich
Forest Hill
Catford
Mottingham
New Eltham
Grove Park
Bellingham
Southend
Streatham
West Norwood
Sydenham
Tooting
Downham
Crystal Palace
Merton
Penge
Streatham Vale
Norbury
Upper Norwood
Anerley
Beckenham
Bromley
Chislehurst
Mitcham
Thornton Heath
South Norwood
Elmers End
Eden Park
BROMLEY
Shortlands
Bickley
Selhurst
Southborough
Petts Wood
St Helier
Woodside
Hackbridge
Addiscombe
West Wickham
Hayes
E
F
G
H

London Plan 2
A
B
C
D
1
2
3
4
5
6
0 220 440 yards
0 100 200 300 400 metres
Maida Vale
Paddington Recreation Ground
Maida Vale Station
Middlesex CCC (Lord's Cricket Ground)
Lord's Tour & MCC Museum
Maida Vale Hospital
BBC Studios
Warwick Avenue Station
Royal Oak Station
PADDINGTON
Paddington Station
St Marys Hospital
Delmere Hotel
The Royal Park
Royal Lancaster Hotel
Lancaster Gate Station
Corus hotel Hyde Park
The Gresham Hyde Park
Bayswater
Berjaya Eden Park
Bayswater Stn
Queensway Station
Pembridge Court Hotel
The Abbey Court
Notting Hill Gate Stn
Kensington Gardens
Little Venice
Alma Square
Westbourne Green
KILBURN PARK ROAD
SHIRLAND ROAD
HARROW ROAD
CHIPPENHAM ROAD
MAIDA VALE
EDGWARE ROAD
GROVE END ROAD
ST JOHN'S WOOD ROAD
CLIFTON GARDENS
CLIFTON RD
WESTWAY
A40
BISHOP'S BRIDGE ROAD
WESTBOURNE GROVE
PORCHESTER RD
QUEENSWAY
CHEPSTOW ROAD
PEMBRIDGE VILLAS
PEMBRIDGE RD
NOTTING HL GATE
BAYSWATER ROAD
EASTBOURNE TERRACE
CRAVEN ROAD
PRAED
SUSSEX
KENSINGTON
PALACE GDNS TER
Warwick Avenue
Randolph Avenue
Elgin Avenue
Sutherland Avenue
Lauderdale Road
Castellain Road
Warrington Crescent
Blomfield Road
Delamere Terrace
Westbourne Park Villas
Westbourne Park Road
Westbourne Terrace
Gloucester Ter
Porchester Ter
Leinster Gardens
Lancaster Gate
Hamilton Terrace
Abercorn Pl
Grand Union Canal Wk
4

E
F
G
H
Regent's Park
London Central Mosque
London Business School
Clarence Gate
Cumberland Gate
Queen Mary's Garden
Inner Circle
Outer Circle
Chester Road
York Bridge
Royal Academy of Music
Park Square
Regent's Park Stn
Great Portland Street Stn
Madame Tussaud's
Planetarium
Baker Street Stn
Marylebone Station
Dorset Square Hotel
Lisson Grove
The Landmark London
Sherlock Holmes Hotel
MARYLEBONE
MARYLEBONE ROAD
PARK ROAD
BAKER ST
GLOUCESTER PL
DORSET SQ
PADDINGTON ST
YORK ST
EDGWARE ROAD
OLD MARYLEBONE RD
CHAPEL ST
Edgware Road Stn
W RD FLYOVER
PORTLAND PL
MARYLEBONE HIGH ST
WIGMORE STREET
CAVENDISH PL
OXFORD ST
NEW BOND STREET
PARK LANE
BAYSWATER ROAD
CUMBERLAND GATE
Speakers Corner
Marble Arch Station
Bond Street Stn
Oxford Circus Station
Jurys Clifton-Ford Hotel
The Mandeville
London Marriott Hotel Marble Arch
Radisson SAS Portman Hotel
PORTMAN SQUARE
Hyatt Regency London - The Churchill
Montcalm - Hotel Nikko London
Mostyn Hotel
Radisson Edwardian Sussex Hotel
Radisson Edwardian Berkshire Hotel
London Marriott Hotel Park Lane
London Marriott Hotel, Grosvenor Square
Claridge's
The Westbury Hotel
Millennium Hotel London - Mayfair
The Connaught
Le Meridien Grosvenor House
Emb of USA
Mayfair
Meliá White House Regents Park
Grange Fitzrovia
Hyde Park
The Chesterfield
The Dorchester
The Washington Mayfair Hotel
Radisson Edwardian May Fair
3
4
Congestion Charging Zone boundary

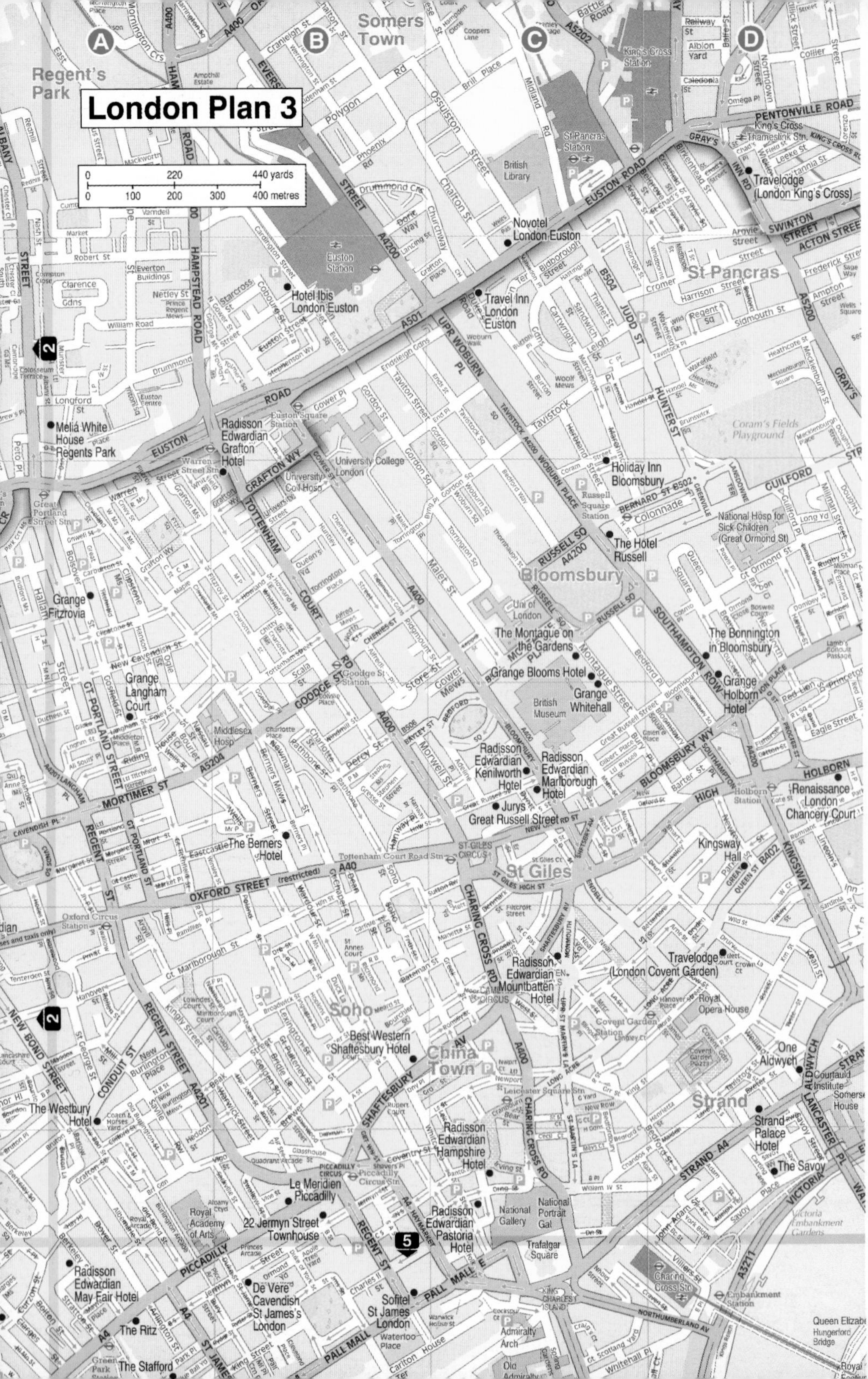
London Plan 3
0
220
440 yards
0
100
200
300
400 metres
A
B
C
D
Regent's Park
Somers Town
King's Cross Station
St Pancras Station
British Library
Euston Station
Novotel London Euston
Hotel Ibis London Euston
Travel Inn London Euston
Travelodge (London King's Cross)
St Pancras
Meliá White House Regents Park
Radisson Edwardian Grafton Hotel
University College London
Holiday Inn Bloomsbury
The Hotel Russell
Coram's Fields Playground
National Hosp for Sick Children (Great Ormond St)
Bloomsbury
Uni of London
The Montague on the Gardens
The Bonnington in Bloomsbury
Grange Blooms Hotel
Grange Whitehall
Grange Holborn Hotel
British Museum
Grange Fitzrovia
Grange Langham Court
Middlesex Hosp
Radisson Edwardian Kenilworth Hotel
Radisson Edwardian Marlborough Hotel
Jurys Great Russell Street
Renaissance London Chancery Court
The Berners Hotel
Kingsway Hall
St Giles
Oxford Circus Station
Radisson Edwardian Mountbatten Hotel
Travelodge (London Covent Garden)
Royal Opera House
Soho
Best Western Shaftesbury Hotel
China Town
One Aldwych
Courtauld Institute
Strand
The Westbury Hotel
Radisson Edwardian Hampshire Hotel
Strand Palace Hotel
The Savoy
Le Meridien Piccadilly
Royal Academy of Arts
22 Jermyn Street Townhouse
Radisson Edwardian Pastoria Hotel
National Gallery
National Portrait Gal
Trafalgar Square
Radisson Edwardian May Fair Hotel
De Vere Cavendish St James's London
Sofitel St James London
The Ritz
The Stafford
Admiralty Arch
Charing Cross Stn
Embankment Station
Victoria Embankment Gardens
EUSTON ROAD
PENTONVILLE ROAD
OXFORD STREET
REGENT STREET
PICCADILLY
CHARING CROSS RD
SHAFTESBURY AV
TOTTENHAM COURT RD
HOLBORN
KINGSWAY
STRAND
PALL MALL
NEW BOND STREET
GT PORTLAND STREET
HAMPSTEAD ROAD
BLOOMSBURY WY
SOUTHAMPTON ROW
RUSSELL SQ

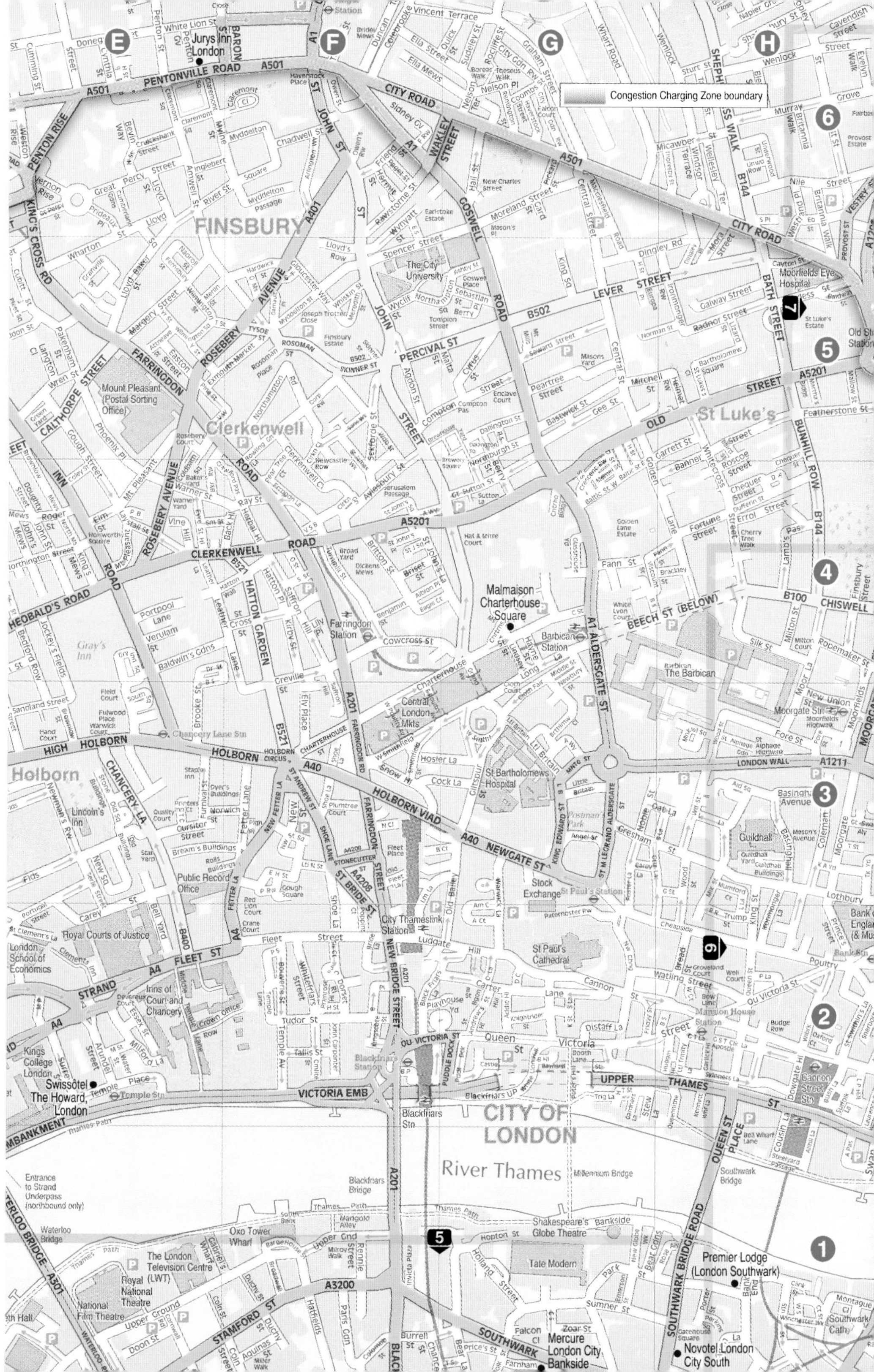

Congestion Charging Zone boundary
E
F
G
H
Jurys Inn London
PENTONVILLE ROAD
CITY ROAD
FINSBURY
The City University
GOSWELL ROAD
ST JOHN ST
LEVER STREET
OLD STREET
St Luke's
BUNHILL ROW
Moorfields Eye Hospital
Old St Station
CLERKENWELL ROAD
Clerkenwell
Mount Pleasant (Postal Sorting Office)
FARRINGDON ROAD
ROSEBERY AVENUE
KING'S CROSS RD
Malmaison Charterhouse Square
Farringdon Station
Barbican Station
The Barbican
A1 ALDERSGATE ST
CHISWELL
Central London Mkts
St Bartholomew's Hospital
HIGH HOLBORN
HOLBORN
Holborn
HOLBORN VIAD
NEWGATE ST
Lincoln's Inn
Public Record Office
Royal Courts of Justice
FLEET ST
STRAND
Inns of Court and Chancery
London School of Economics
Kings College London
Swissôtel The Howard, London
Temple Stn
VICTORIA EMB
City Thameslink Station
St Paul's Cathedral
St Paul's Station
Stock Exchange
Guildhall
Mansion House Station
Cannon Street Stn
UPPER THAMES ST
CITY OF LONDON
River Thames
Blackfriars Bridge
Blackfriars Stn
Millennium Bridge
Southwark Bridge
Shakespeare's Globe Theatre
Tate Modern
Oxo Tower Wharf
The London Television Centre (LWT)
Royal National Theatre
National Film Theatre
WATERLOO BRIDGE
SOUTHWARK BRIDGE ROAD
Premier Lodge (London Southwark)
Mercure London City Bankside
Novotel London City South
Southwark Cath
Entrance to Strand Underpass (northbound only)
STAMFORD ST
SOUTHWARK
1
2
3
4
5
6
7
9

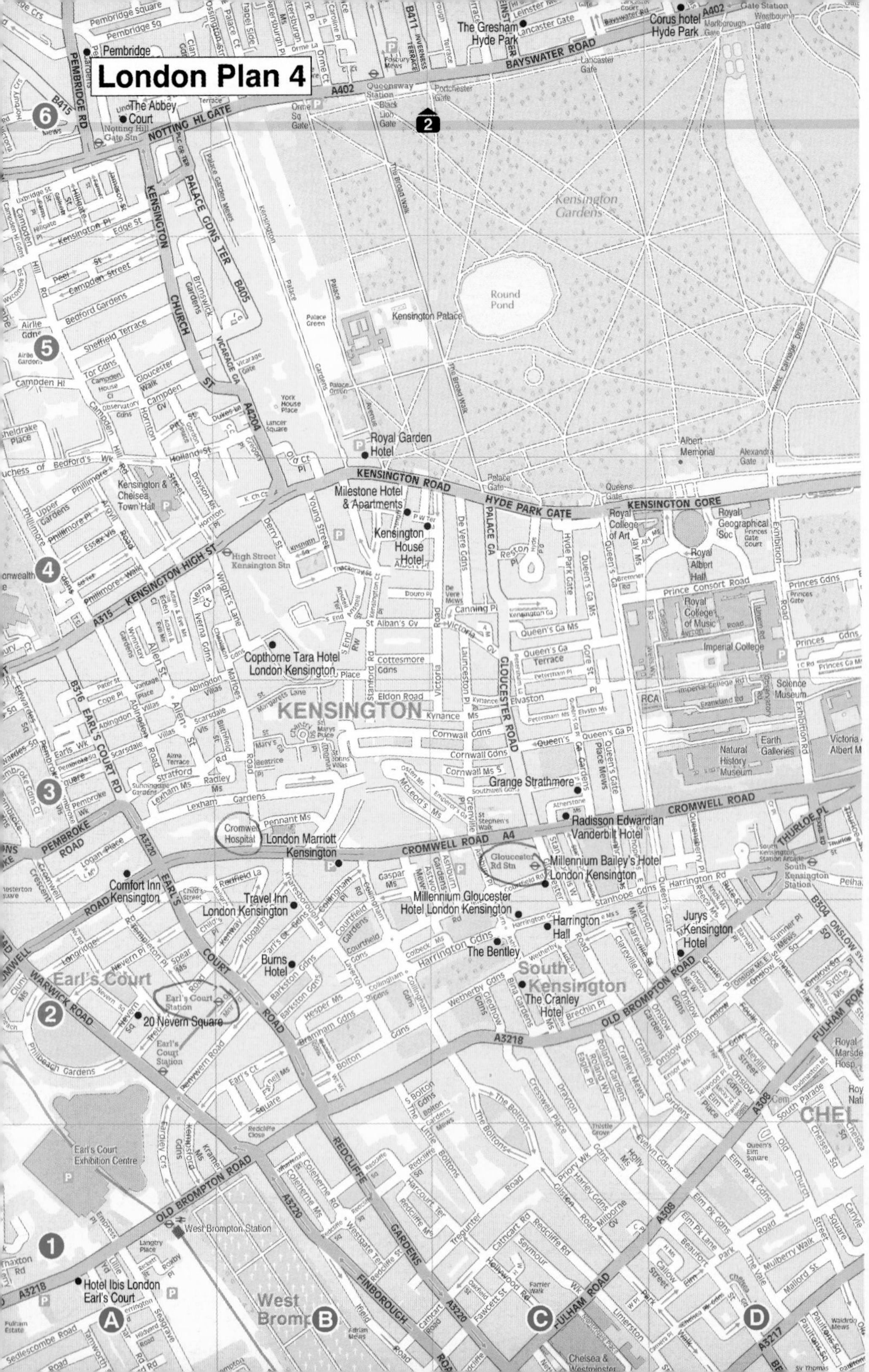
London Plan 4
Pembridge
The Abbey Court
The Gresham Hyde Park
Corus hotel Hyde Park
BAYSWATER ROAD
NOTTING HL GATE
Notting Hill Gate Stn
Queensway Station
Kensington Gardens
Round Pond
Kensington Palace
The Broad Walk
Royal Garden Hotel
Milestone Hotel & Apartments
Kensington House Hotel
KENSINGTON ROAD
HYDE PARK GATE
KENSINGTON GORE
Albert Memorial
Royal College of Art
Royal Geographical Soc
Royal Albert Hall
Royal College of Music
Imperial College
Science Museum
Natural History Museum
Victoria & Albert Museum
KENSINGTON HIGH ST
High Street Kensington Stn
Kensington & Chelsea Town Hall
KENSINGTON CHURCH ST
Copthorne Tara Hotel London Kensington
KENSINGTON
GLOUCESTER ROAD
Grange Strathmore
Radisson Edwardian Vanderbilt Hotel
CROMWELL ROAD
Cromwell Hospital
London Marriott Kensington
Millennium Bailey's Hotel London Kensington
Gloucester Rd Stn
Millennium Gloucester Hotel London Kensington
Harrington Hall
The Bentley
Jurys Kensington Hotel
South Kensington
South Kensington Station
The Cranley Hotel
Comfort Inn Kensington
Travel Inn London Kensington
Burns Hotel
EARL'S COURT RD
Earl's Court
Earl's Court Station
20 Nevern Square
WARWICK ROAD
OLD BROMPTON ROAD
Earl's Court Exhibition Centre
West Brompton Station
Hotel Ibis London Earl's Court
REDCLIFFE GARDENS
FINBOROUGH ROAD
FULHAM ROAD
West Brompton
Chelsea & Westminster
CHEL
1
2
3
4
5
6
A
B
C
D

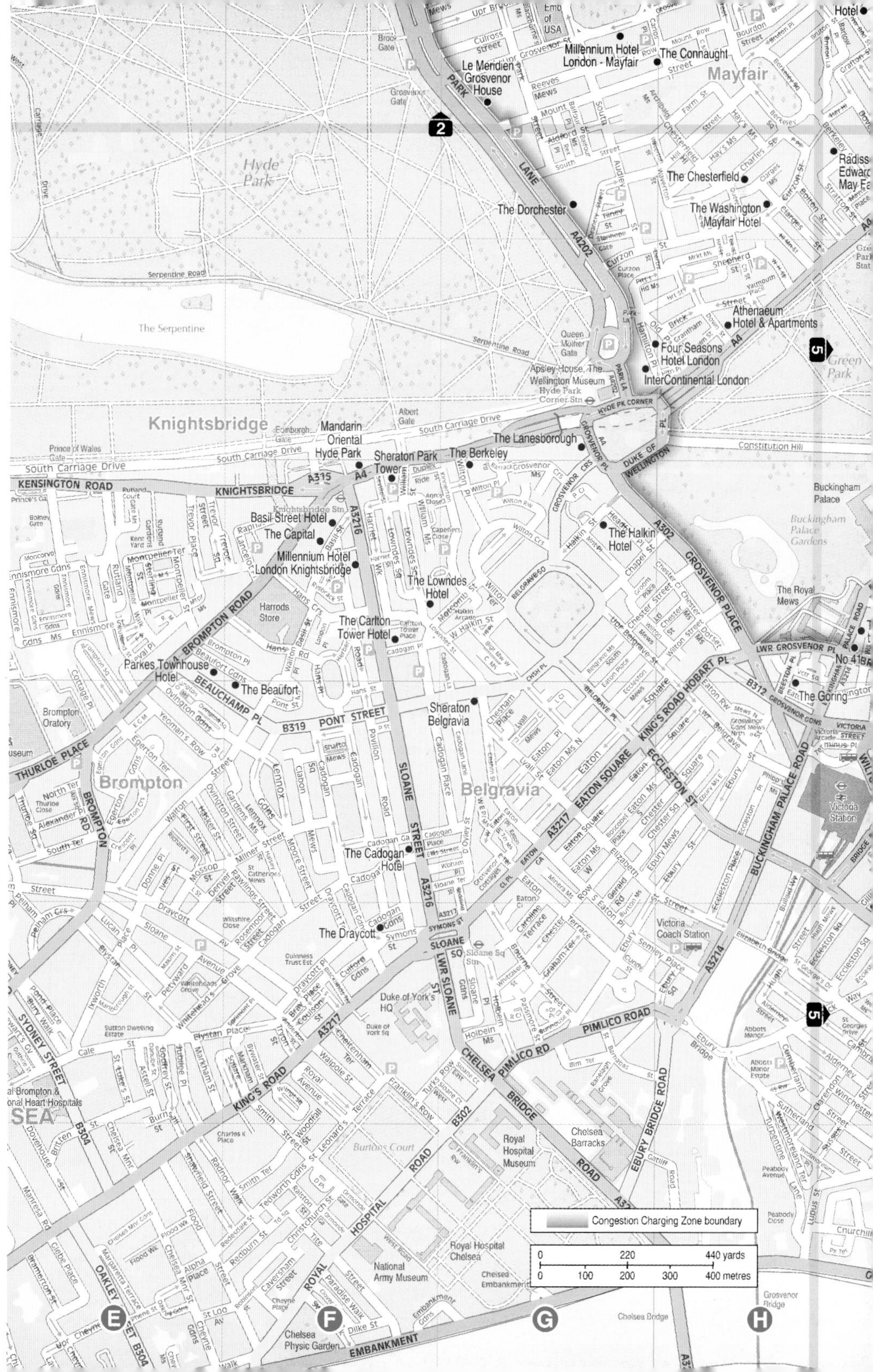
Mayfair
Millennium Hotel London - Mayfair
The Connaught
Le Meridien Grosvenor House
Hyde Park
The Dorchester
The Chesterfield
The Washington Mayfair Hotel
Radisson Edwardian May Fair
The Serpentine
Serpentine Road
Athenaeum Hotel & Apartments
Four Seasons Hotel London
InterContinental London
Apsley House, The Wellington Museum
Green Park
Knightsbridge
Mandarin Oriental Hyde Park
Sheraton Park Tower
The Berkeley
The Lanesborough
Constitution Hill
South Carriage Drive
KENSINGTON ROAD
KNIGHTSBRIDGE
Basil Street Hotel
The Capital
Millennium Hotel London Knightsbridge
The Halkin Hotel
Buckingham Palace
Buckingham Palace Gardens
The Royal Mews
Harrods Store
The Lowndes Hotel
The Carlton Tower Hotel
Parkes Townhouse Hotel
The Beaufort
No 41
The Goring
Sheraton Belgravia
Brompton Oratory
Brompton
Belgravia
GROSVENOR PLACE
PONT STREET
SLOANE STREET
EATON SQUARE
ECCLESTON ST
BUCKINGHAM PALACE ROAD
Victoria Station
The Cadogan Hotel
The Draycott
Victoria Coach Station
Duke of York's HQ
KING'S ROAD
PIMLICO ROAD
CHELSEA BRIDGE ROAD
EBURY BRIDGE ROAD
Chelsea Barracks
Royal Hospital Museum
Burtons Court
ROYAL HOSPITAL ROAD
Royal Hospital Chelsea
National Army Museum
Chelsea Physic Garden
EMBANKMENT
Chelsea Bridge
Grosvenor Bridge
SYDNEY STREET
OAKLEY STREET B304
Royal Brompton & National Heart Hospitals
Congestion Charging Zone boundary
0 220 440 yards
0 100 200 300 400 metres
2
5
5
E
F
G
H

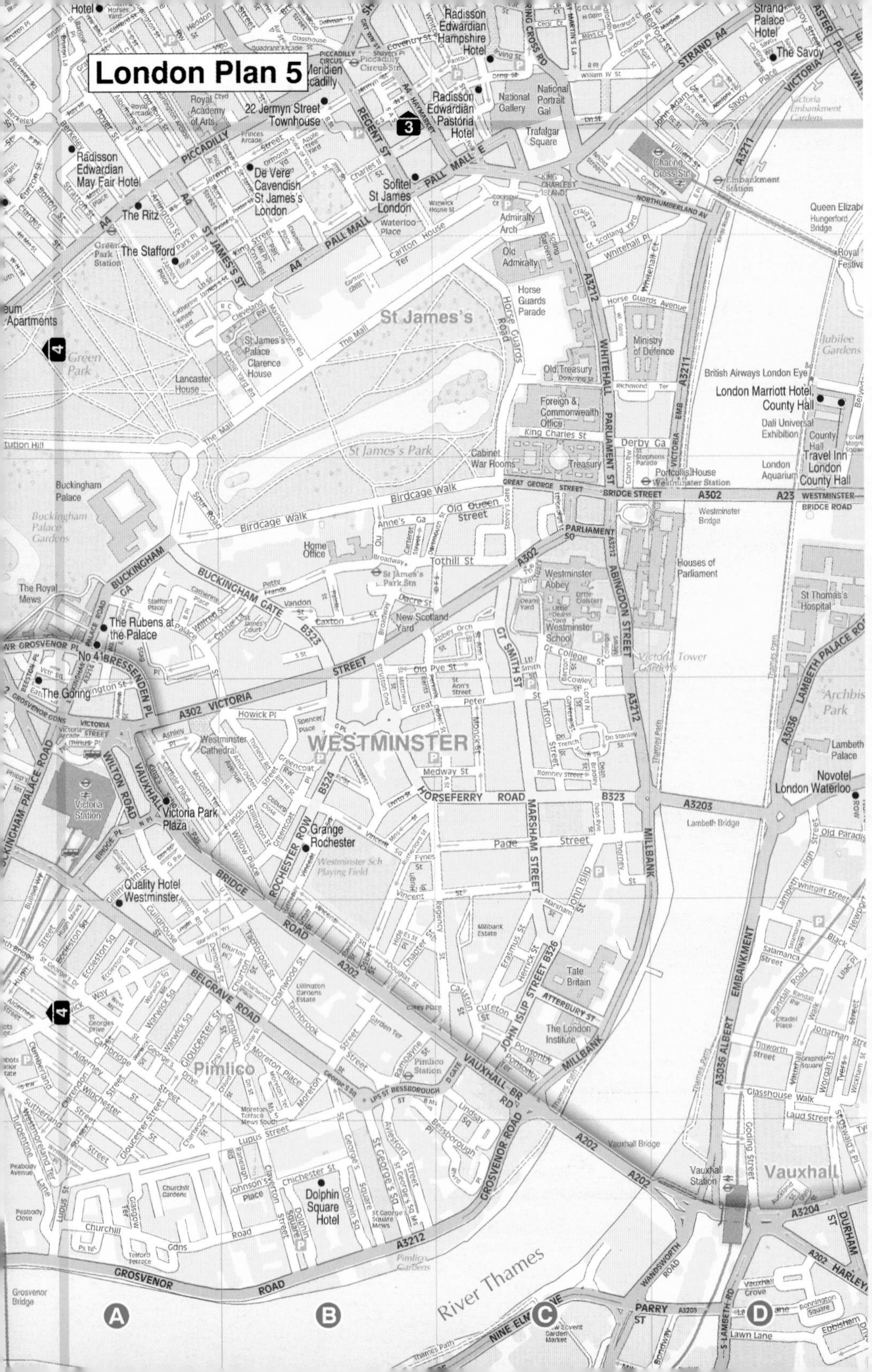

London Plan 5
WESTMINSTER
St James's
St James's Park
Green Park
Pimlico
Vauxhall
River Thames
Buckingham Palace
Buckingham Palace Gardens
Victoria Station
Westminster Abbey
Houses of Parliament
Tate Britain
The Ritz
The Stafford
The Goring
The Savoy
Strand Palace Hotel
Radisson Edwardian Hampshire Hotel
Radisson Edwardian Pastoria Hotel
Radisson Edwardian May Fair Hotel
22 Jermyn Street Townhouse
De Vere Cavendish St James's London
Sofitel St James London
The Rubens at the Palace
No 41
Victoria Park Plaza
Grange Rochester
Quality Hotel Westminster
Dolphin Square Hotel
London Marriott Hotel, County Hall
Travel Inn London County Hall
Novotel London Waterloo
National Gallery
National Portrait Gal
Trafalgar Square
Charing Cross Stn
Embankment Station
Westminster Station
St James's Park Stn
Pimlico Station
Vauxhall Station
Green Park Station
Westminster Bridge
Lambeth Bridge
Vauxhall Bridge
Grosvenor Bridge
Lambeth Palace
St Thomas's Hospital
British Airways London Eye
Ministry of Defence
Foreign & Commonwealth Office
Cabinet War Rooms
Treasury
New Scotland Yard
Home Office
Westminster Cathedral
Horse Guards Parade
Admiralty Arch
Old Admiralty
Lancaster House
St James's Palace
Clarence House
Royal Academy of Arts
The Royal Mews
Victoria Tower Gardens
Jubilee Gardens
Archbishop's Park
Victoria Embankment Gardens
PICCADILLY
PALL MALL
REGENT ST
STRAND
WHITEHALL
VICTORIA STREET
MILLBANK
GROSVENOR ROAD
VAUXHALL BRIDGE ROAD
BELGRAVE ROAD
HORSEFERRY ROAD
ALBERT EMBANKMENT

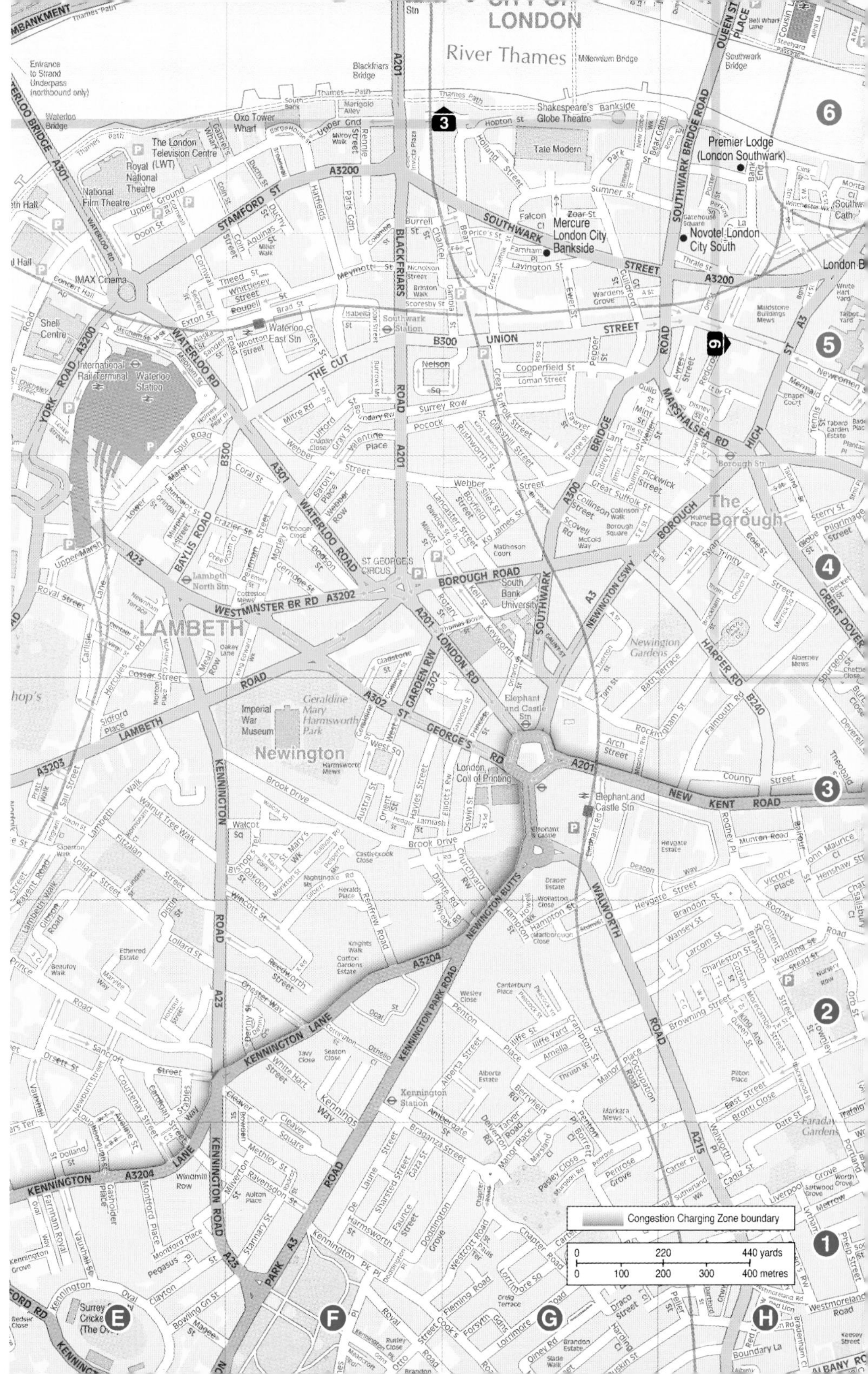

LONDON
River Thames
Millennium Bridge
Blackfriars Bridge
Entrance to Strand Underpass (northbound only)
Waterloo Bridge
Oxo Tower Wharf
Shakespeare's Globe Theatre
Tate Modern
Southwark Bridge
Premier Lodge (London Southwark)
The London Television Centre (LWT)
Royal National Theatre
National Film Theatre
Mercure London City Bankside
Novotel London City South
IMAX Cinema
Shell Centre
Waterloo East Stn
Southwark Station
International Rail Terminal
Waterloo Station
STAMFORD ST
SOUTHWARK STREET
A3200
BLACKFRIARS ROAD
A201
SOUTHWARK BRIDGE ROAD
WATERLOO RD
UNION STREET
B300
THE CUT
YORK ROAD
A301
WATERLOO ROAD
MARSHALSEA RD
BOROUGH HIGH ST
The Borough
BOROUGH ROAD
ST GEORGE'S CIRCUS
WESTMINSTER BR RD A3202
Lambeth North Stn
LAMBETH
BAYLIS ROAD
A23
South Bank University
LONDON RD
SOUTHWARK
NEWINGTON CSWY
A3
Newington Gardens
HARPER RD
GREAT DOVER
Imperial War Museum
Geraldine Mary Harmsworth Park
Newington
LAMBETH ROAD
ST GEORGE'S RD
A302
London Coll of Printing
Elephant and Castle Stn
NEW KENT ROAD
A201
County Street
KENNINGTON ROAD
NEWINGTON BUTTS
WALWORTH ROAD
A3204
KENNINGTON LANE
KENNINGTON PARK ROAD
Kennington Station
A215
Walworth Pl
KENNINGTON
Surrey Cricket (The Oval)
Congestion Charging Zone boundary
0 220 440 yards
0 100 200 300 400 metres
1
2
3
4
5
6
E
F
G
H

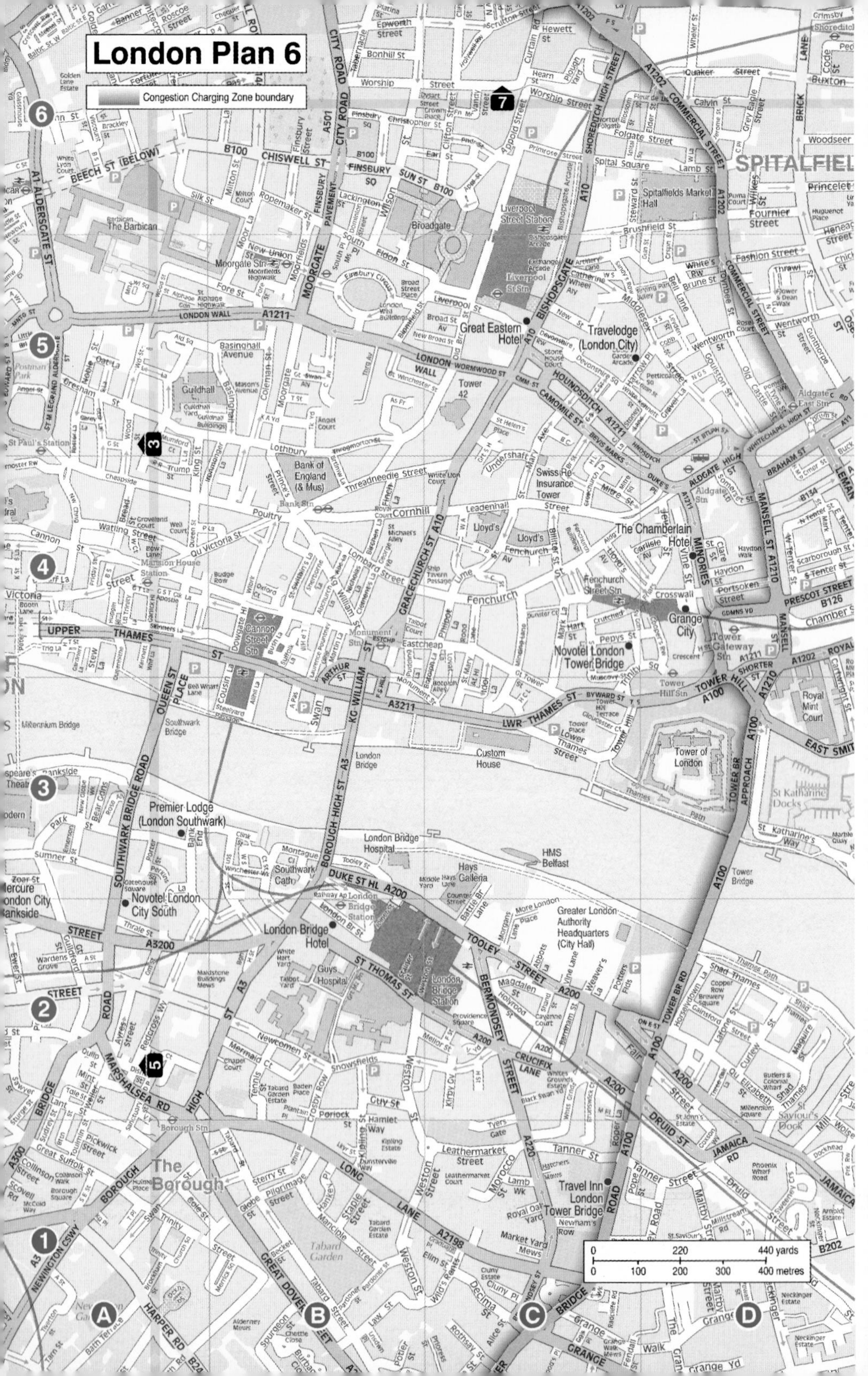
London Plan 6
Congestion Charging Zone boundary
0 220 440 yards
0 100 200 300 400 metres

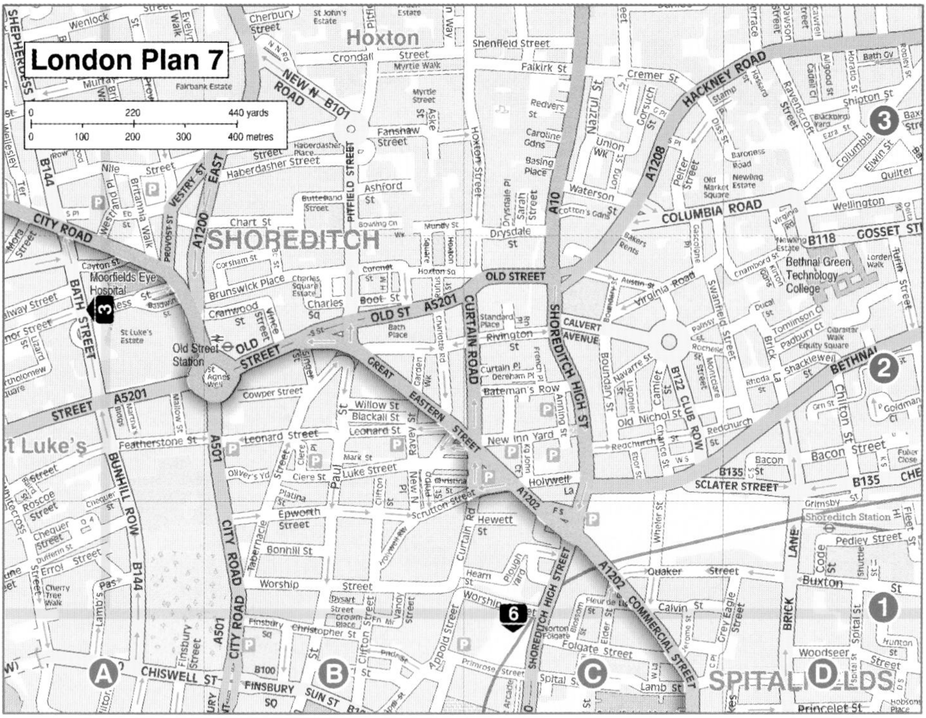

London Plan 7

0 220 440 yards

0 100 200 300 400 metres

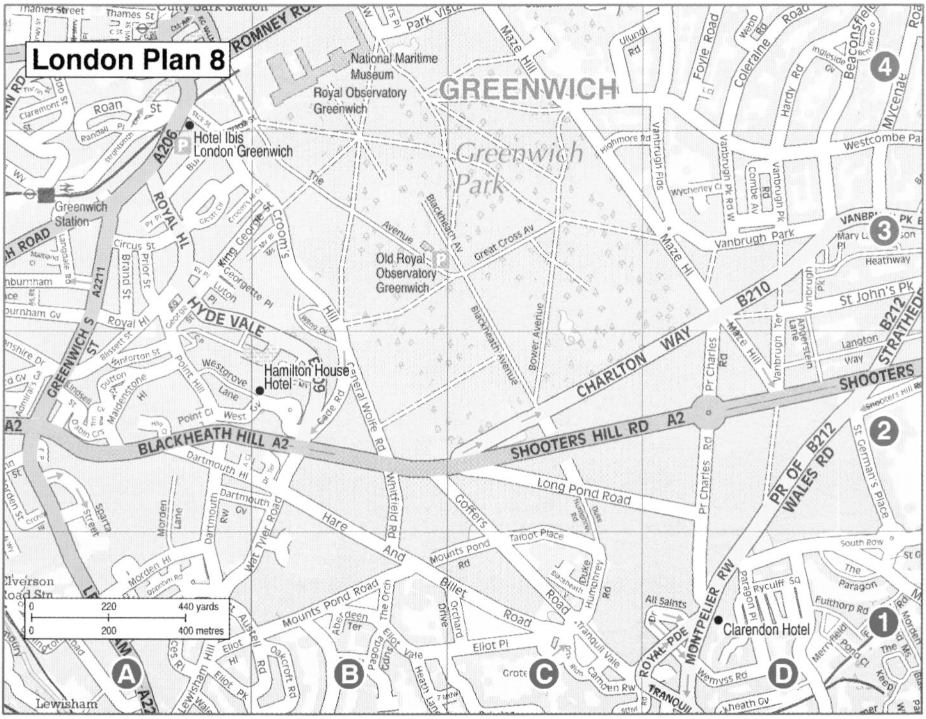

London Plan 8

0 220 440 yards

0 200 400 metres

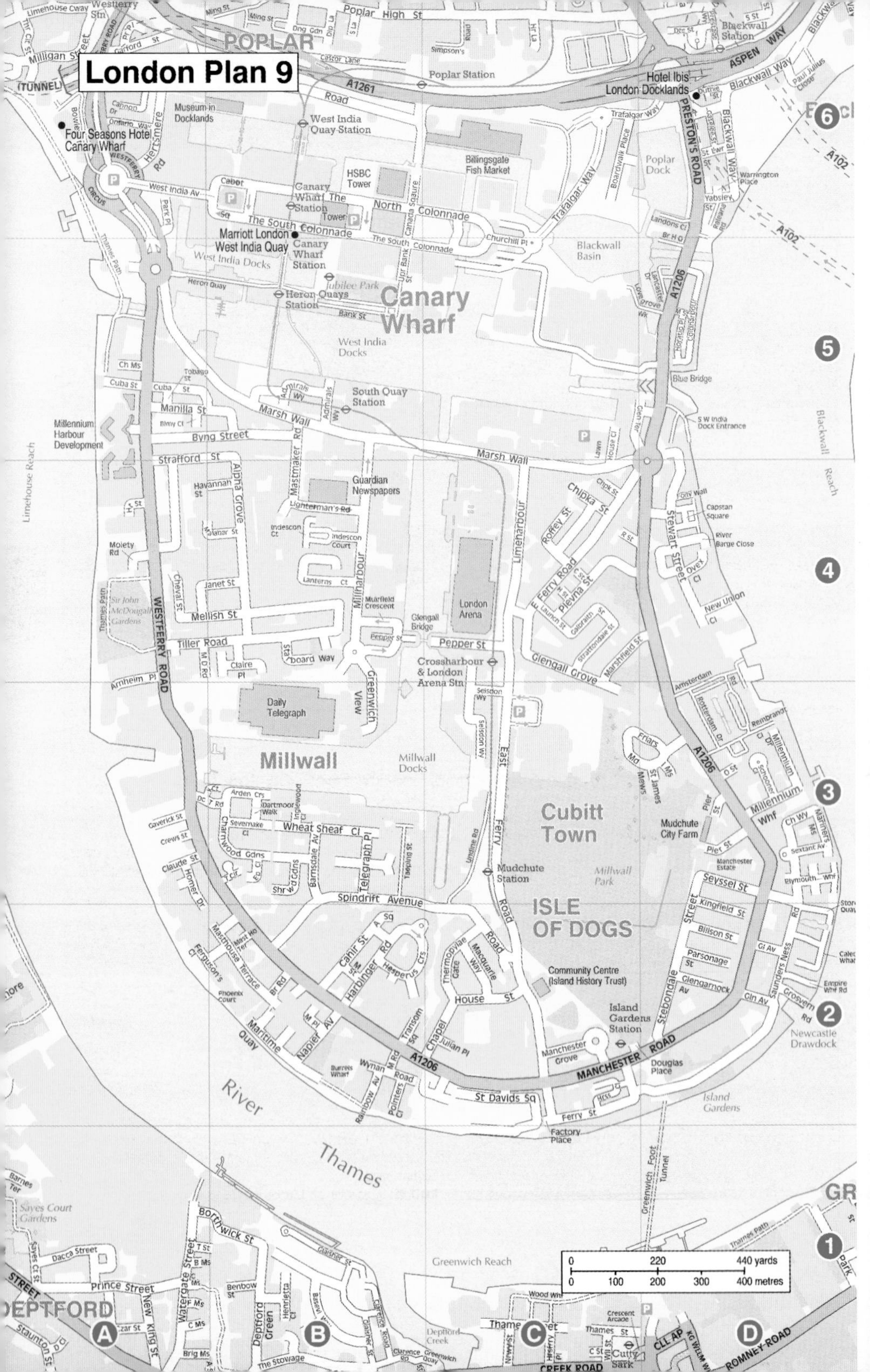
London Plan 9
POPLAR
Poplar High St
Poplar Station
Blackwall Station
ASPEN WAY
A1261
Hotel Ibis London Docklands
PRESTON'S ROAD
Four Seasons Hotel Canary Wharf
Museum in Docklands
West India Quay Station
Billingsgate Fish Market
Poplar Dock
HSBC Tower
Canary Wharf The Station
Tower
North Colonnade
The South Colonnade
Marriott London West India Quay
Canary Wharf Station
West India Docks
West India Av
Westferry Circus
Churchill Pl
Trafalgar Way
Blackwall Basin
Jubilee Park
Heron Quays Station
Canary Wharf
West India Docks
Bank St
Blue Bridge
South Quay Station
Marsh Wall
Millennium Harbour Development
Byng Street
Strafford St
Limehouse Reach
Guardian Newspapers
Chipka St
Blackwall Reach
Alpha Grove
Mastmaker Rd
Millharbour
Limeharbour
Stewart Street
London Arena
Glengall Bridge
Pepper St
Crossharbour & London Arena Stn
Glengall Grove
Ferry Road
Plevna St
Mellish St
Tiller Road
Sir John McDougall Gardens
Thames Path
WESTFERRY ROAD
Daily Telegraph
Greenwich View
Millwall
Millwall Docks
East Ferry Road
Cubitt Town
Mudchute City Farm
Millennium Whf
Wheat Sheaf Cl
Telegraph Pl
Spindrift Avenue
Mudchute Station
Millwall Park
ISLE OF DOGS
Seyssel St
Saunders Ness Rd
Community Centre (Island History Trust)
Island Gardens Station
Newcastle Drawdock
A1206
MANCHESTER ROAD
Douglas Place
Island Gardens
Ferry St
Factory Place
River Thames
Greenwich Foot Tunnel
Greenwich Reach
Deptford Creek
DEPTFORD
Prince Street
Borthwick St
Watergate Street
New King St
Deptford Green
Creek Road
Cutty Sark
ROMNEY ROAD
Thames Path
0 220 440 yards
0 100 200 300 400 metres
1
2
3
4
5
6
A
B
C
D

LONDON Greater London Plans 1-9, pages 328-340. (Small scale maps 6 & 7 at back of book.) Hotels are listed below in postal district order, commencing East, then North, South and West, with a brief indication of the area covered. Detailed plans 2-9 show the locations of AA-appointed hotels within the Central London postal districts. If you do not know the postal district of the hotel you want, please refer to the index preceding the street plans for the entry and map pages. The plan reference for each AA-appointed hotel also appears within its directory entry.

E1 STEPNEY AND EAST OF THE TOWER OF LONDON

Travelodge (London City)

1 Harrow Place E1 7DB plan 6 C5
☎ 08700 850 950 📠 020 7626 1105
Travelodge offers good quality, good value, modern accommodation. Ideal for families, the spacious, en suite bedrooms include remote-control TV, tea and coffee-making facilities and luxury beds. Meals can be taken at the nearby family restaurant. For further details consult the Hotel Groups page.
ROOMS: 142 en suite s fr £45; d fr £45

E6 BECKTON
See LONDON plan 1 H4

Travel Inn London Beckton

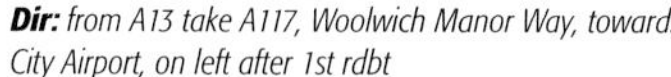

1 Woolwich Manor Way, Beckton E6 4NT
☎ 08701 977029 📠 020 7511 4214
Dir: *from A13 take A117, Woolwich Manor Way, towards City Airport, on left after 1st rdbt*
Travel Inn offers good-quality, value-for-money accommodation. Spacious, en suite rooms with bath and shower comfortably accommodate a family of up to two adults and two children (to age 15). The restaurant and bar offers a varied menu. For further details consult the Hotel Groups page.
ROOMS: 90 en suite s £49.95-£56.95; d £49.95-£56.95

E11 SNARESBROOK
See LONDON plan 1 G5

Innkeeper's Lodge Snaresbrook

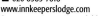

37 Hollybush Hill, Snaresbrook E11 1PE
☎ 020 8989 7618
www.innkeeperslodge.com
Smart rooms meet essential business requirements but also have home comforts, and depending on location may well have meeting rooms and pub dining. Dining options generally include all-day menus plus the added advantage of breakfast.
ROOMS: s £55; d £55

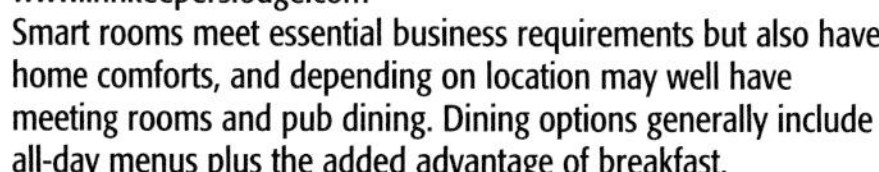

For central reservation numbers and more information on Hotel Groups, turn to pages 33-39

Town House Hotel
Country House Hotel
Travel Accommodation

E14 CANARY WHARF & LIMEHOUSE
See also LONDON plan 1 G3/4

Top 200 – Hotel

★★★★★ Four Seasons Hotel Canary Wharf
Westferry Circus, Canary Wharf E14 8RS plan 9 A6
☎ 020 7510 1999 📠 020 7510 1998
web: www.fourseasons.com/canarywharf
Dir: *From A13 follow signs to Canary Wharf, Isle of Dogs and Westferry Circus. Hotel off 3rd exit of Westferry Circus rdbt*
With superb views over the London skyline, this stylish modern hotel enjoys a delightful riverside location. Spacious contemporary bedrooms are particularly thoughtfully equipped. Public areas include the Italian Quadrato Bar and Restaurant, an impressive business centre and gymnasium. Guests also have complimentary use of the impressive Holmes Place health club and spa. Welcoming staff provide exemplary levels of service and hospitality.
ROOMS: 142 en suite ⊗ in 120 bedrooms s £353-£2115; d £376-£2115 **FACILITIES: Spa** STV supervised Sauna Solarium Gym Jacuzzi ♫ Xmas **CONF:** BC Thtr 200 Class 120 Board 56 **SERVICES:** Lift air con **PARKING:** 29 **NOTES:** Civ Wed 200 **CARDS:**

U Marriott London West India Quay

22 Hertzmere Rd, Canary Wharf E14 4ED plan 9 B6
☎ 020 7093 1000 📠 020 7093 1001
Dir: *Turn off Aspen Way at Hertmere Rd. Hotel adjacent to Canary Wharf*
At the time of going to press, the star classification for this hotel was not confirmed. Please refer to the AA internet site www.theAA.com for current information.
ROOMS: 301 en suite (21 fmly) ⊗ in 228 bedrooms s £193-£260; d £193-£260 **FACILITIES:** STV Sauna Solarium Gym Xmas **CONF:** BC Thtr 300 Class 120 Board 36 **SERVICES:** Lift air con **NOTES:** ⊗ in restaurant **CARDS:**

Hotel Ibis London Docklands

1 Baffin Way E14 9PE plan 9 D6
☎ 020 7517 1100 📠 020 7987 5916
e-mail: H2177@accor-hotels.com
Dir: *from Tower Bridge follow City Airport and Royal Docks signs,exit for 'Isle of Dogs'. Hotel on 1st left opposite McDonalds*
Modern, budget hotel offering comfortable accommodation in bright and practical bedrooms. Breakfast is self-service and dinner is available in the restaurant. For further details, consult the Hotel Groups page.
ROOMS: 87 en suite s fr £56.95; d fr £56.95

London

E14 CANARY WHARF & LIMEHOUSE, continued

Travelodge (London Dockland)

Coriander Av, East India Dock Rd E14 2AA
☎ 08700 850 950 📠 020 7515 9178
Dir: *fronts A13 at East India Dock Rd*
Travelodge offers good quality, good value, modern accommodation. Ideal for families, the spacious, en suite bedrooms include remote-control TV, tea and coffee-making facilities and luxury beds. Meals can be taken at the nearby family restaurant. For further details consult the Hotel Groups page.
ROOMS: 232 en suite s fr £25; d fr £25

E15 STRATFORD
See LONDON plan 1 G4

Hotel Ibis London Stratford

1A Romford Rd, Stratford E15 4LJ
☎ 020 8536 3700 📠 020 8519 5161
e-mail: H3099@accor-hotels.com
Modern, budget hotel offering comfortable accommodation in bright and practical bedrooms. Breakfast is self-service and dinner is available in the restaurant. For further details, consult the Hotel Groups page.
ROOMS: 108 en suite s £54.95-£64.95; d £54.95-£64.95

E16 SILVERTOWN
See LONDON plan 1 H3

★★★★70% Novotel London ExCel

7 Western Gateway, Royal Victoria Docks E16 1AA
☎ 020 7540 9700 📠 020 7540 9710
e-mail: H3656@accor-hotels.com
This new hotel is situated adjacent to the ExCel exhibition centre and overlooks the Royal Victoria Dock. Design throughout the hotel is contemporary and stylish. Public rooms include a range of meeting rooms, a modern coffee station, indoor leisure facilities and a smart bar and restaurant, both with a terrace overlooking the dock. Bedrooms feature modern decor, a bath and separate shower and an extensive range of extras.
ROOMS: 257 en suite (203 fmly) ⊗ in 183 bedrooms s £135-£148; d £155-£161 (incl. bkfst) **LB** **FACILITIES:** STV Sauna Gym Steam room Xmas **CONF:** Thtr 70 Class 55 Board 30 Del from £165 **SERVICES:** Lift air con **PARKING:** 80 **CARDS:**

Hotel Ibis London ExCel

9 Western Gateway, Royal Victoria Docks E16 1AB
☎ 020 7055 2300 📠 020 7055 2310
e-mail: H3655@accor-hotels.com
Dir: *M25 then A13 to London, City Airport, ExCel East*
Modern, budget hotel offering comfortable accommodation in bright and practical bedrooms. Breakfast is self-service and dinner is available in the restaurant. For further details, consult the Hotel Groups page.
ROOMS: 278 en suite s £49.95-£69.95; d £49.95-£69.95

Travel Inn London Docklands (ExCel)

Royal Victoria Dock E16 1SL
☎ 0870 238 3322 📠 020 7540 2250
Dir: *on ExCel East. A13 onto A1020. At Connaught rbt take 2nd exit into Connaught Rd. Inn on right.*
Travel Inn offers good-quality, value-for-money accommodation. Spacious, en suite rooms with bath and shower comfortably accommodate a family of up to two adults and two children (to age 15). The restaurant and bar offers a varied menu. For further details consult the Hotel Groups page.
ROOMS: 202 en suite s £54.95-£72.95; d £54.95-£72.95

EC1 CITY OF LONDON

★★★74% Malmaison Charterhouse Square

18-21 Charterhouse Square, Clerkenwell EC1M 6AH plan 3 G4
☎ 020 7012 3700 📠 020 7012 3702
e-mail: london@malmaison.com
Dir: *Exit Barbican Station turn left, take 1st left. Hotel on the far left corner of Charterhouse Square.*
Malmaison Charterhouse represents the new face of Malmaison, with the same focus on quality of service and food, but coupled with the peace found in this area of London, and the age of the building. The brasserie and bar form the centre of the hotel with a buzzing atmosphere and tradtional French cuisine.
ROOMS: 97 en suite (5 GF) ⊗ in 79 bedrooms s £99-£176.25; d £99-£193.88 **FACILITIES:** STV Gym **CONF:** Thtr 30 Board 16 **SERVICES:** Lift air con **NOTES:**
CARDS:

EC2

Top 200 – Hotel

★★★★★ Great Eastern Hotel

Liverpool St EC2M 7QN plan 6 C5
☎ 020 7618 5000 📠 020 7618 5001
e-mail: sales@great-eastern-hotel.co.uk
web: www.great-eastern-hotel.co.uk
The largest hotel in the city, the Great Eastern is adjacent to Liverpool Street station. Design-led bedrooms are stylish and come complete with all the extras you could need. The impressive array of restaurants includes the elegant Aurora offering fine dining, Fishmarket with its champagne bar, Terminus offering all-day meals and snacks and a Miyabi, a Japanese restaurant. The basement gym offers a range of treatments and personal trainers are available.
ROOMS: 267 en suite ⊗ in 74 bedrooms s fr £264; d fr £311 **LB** **FACILITIES:** STV Gym steam room **CONF:** Thtr 200 Class 120 **SERVICES:** Lift air con **NOTES:** Civ Wed
CARDS:

EC3 CHEAPSIDE

★★★★★68% The Grange City

Coopers Row EC3 2BQ plan 6 D4
☎ 020 7863 3700 📠 020 7863 3701
e-mail: city@grangehotels.com
Dir: *M4 E into A4 E, to Piccadilly, to Trafalgar Square, B308 to Victoria Embankment, follow river, just before Tower Hill. Coopers Row on left*
This modern hotel enjoys a prime city location overlooking the Tower of London and Tower Bridge. Spacious, air-conditioned

continued

bedrooms have been appointed to a high standard and are extensively equipped. Public areas include an impressive leisure club. Guests can choose from a variety of eating options, including the Forum, which offers Italian fare, a more informal brasserie, or Koto 2, a Japanese sushi and noodle bar.
ROOMS: 254 en suite ⊗ in 120 bedrooms s fr £280; d fr £280 **FACILITIES: Spa** STV Sauna Gym Jacuzzi Virtual golf simulator. Xmas **CONF:** BC Thtr 800 Class 400 Board 200 Del from £307 **SERVICES:** Lift air con **CARDS:**

Town House

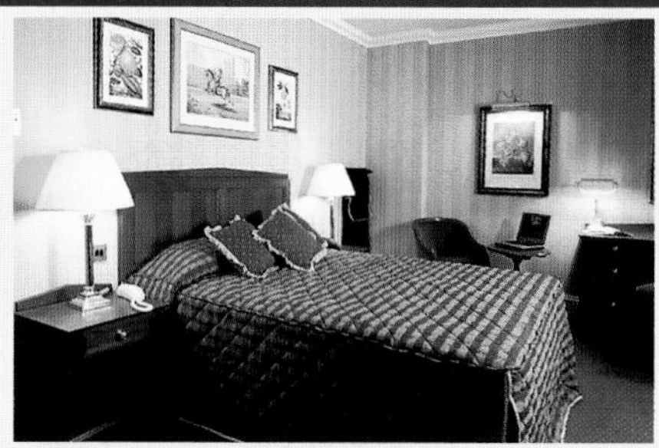

★★★★ The Chamberlain

130-135 Minories EC3N 1NU plan 6 D4
☎ 020 7680 1500 📠 020 7702 2500
e-mail: thechamberlain@fullers.co.uk
Dir: *M25 E J30. Then A13 W towards London. Follow into Aldgate, left after bus station. Hotel halfway down Minories.*
This smart hotel is ideally situated for the City, Tower Bridge, Aldgate and Tower Gateway tube stations. Impressive bedrooms are stylish, well-equipped and comfortable, while the modern bathrooms are fitted with TVs to watch while you soak in the bath. Informal day rooms include a popular pub and an attractive split-level dining room.
ROOMS: 64 en suite ⊗ in 49 bedrooms s fr £169; d fr £169 **LB** **FACILITIES:** STV Discounted leisure facilities for hotel guests nearby **CONF:** Thtr 50 Class 20 Board 25 **SERVICES:** Lift air con **NOTES:** Closed 24 Dec-2 Jan (TBC) **CARDS:**

★★★72% Novotel London Tower Bridge

10 Pepys St EC3N 2NR plan 6 C4
☎ 020 7265 6000 📠 020 7265 6060
e-mail: H3107@accor-hotels.com
Located near the Tower of London, this smart hotel is convenient for Docklands, the City, Heathrow and London City airports. Bedrooms are spacious, modern, and offer a great range of facilities, including air conditioning. There is a smart bar and restaurant, a small gym and extensive meeting and conference facilities.
ROOMS: 203 en suite (77 fmly) ⊗ in 145 bedrooms s £160-£270; d £180-£240 **LB** **FACILITIES:** STV Sauna Gym Steam Room **CONF:** Thtr 258 Class 146 Board 78 Del from £225 **SERVICES:** Lift air con **CARDS:**

○ Apex City of London

No 1 Seething Ln EC3N 4AX
☎ 0845 608 3456
ROOMS: 122 en suite **NOTES:** Due to open Spring 2005

N1 ISLINGTON

★★★63% Jurys Inn Islington

60 Pentonville Rd, Islington N1 9LA plan 3 E6
JURYS DOYLE HOTELS
☎ 020 7282 5500 📠 020 7282 5511
e-mail: london_inn@jurysdoyle.com
Dir: *from A1 right onto A501, right again onto Pentonville Rd*
This modern hotel offers spacious bedrooms with good facilities, and provides guests with a choice of comfortable public areas. There is an Irish pub serving snacks and a more formal restaurant with a daily changing menu.
ROOMS: 229 en suite (116 fmly) ⊗ in 135 bedrooms s £85-£104; d £85-£104 **FACILITIES:** STV **CONF:** Thtr 50 Class 24 Board 28 Del from £170 **SERVICES:** Lift air con **NOTES:** Closed 24-27 Dec **CARDS:**

N10 MUSWELL HILL
See LONDON plan 1 E5

★★★63% Raglan Hall

8-12 Queens Ave, Muswell Hill N10 3NR
Best Western
☎ 020 8883 9836 📠 020 8883 5002
e-mail: reservations@raglanhall.com
Dir: *A406 to Muswell Hill at B550 Colney Hatch Lane. At rdbt last exit to Queens Ave. Hotel 75yds on right*
Located on an elegant tree-lined avenue in North London, this hotel is well situated for access to major road and rail networks. Bedrooms vary in size and style, and some are suitable for families. Limited off-street parking is also available.
ROOMS: 48 en suite (8 fmly) (10 GF) ⊗ in 11 bedrooms s fr £89; d fr £99 (incl. cont bkfst) **LB** **CONF:** Thtr 120 Class 60 Board 30 Del from £165 **PARKING:** 6 **NOTES:** Civ Wed 120 **CARDS:**

N14 SOUTHGATE
See LONDON SECTION plan 1 E6

Innkeeper's Lodge Southgate

22 The Green, Southgate N14 6EN
Innkeeper's Lodge
☎ 020 8447 8022 📠 020 8447 8022
www.innkeeperslodge.com
Dir: *take A111 from J24, 3m to rdbt for A1004, turn right into High Street, hotel at next rdbt*
Smart rooms meet essential business requirements but also have home comforts, and depending on location may well have meeting rooms and pub dining. Dining options generally include all-day menus plus the added advantage of breakfast.
ROOMS: 19 en suite s £57.50-£69.95; d £57.50-£69.95

> Destination dining!
> This symbol indicates a Restaurant with Rooms

London

NW1 REGENT'S PARK
See LONDON plan 1 E4

Top 200 - Hotel

★★★★★ The Landmark London
222 Marylebone Rd NW1 6JQ plan 2 F4
☎ 020 7631 8000 020 7631 8080
e-mail: reservations@thelandmark.co.uk
web: www.landmarklondon.co.uk
Dir: *adjacent to Marylebone Station and near Paddington Station*
Said to be one of the last truly grand railway hotels, The Landmark boasts a number of stunning features, the most spectacular being the naturally lit central atrium. When it comes to eating and drinking there are plenty of options, including the Cellars for upmarket bar meals. The Winter Gardens make a beautiful venue for all-day dining, set in the central atrium. Air-conditioned bedrooms are spacious and have stunning marble bathrooms.
ROOMS: 299 en suite (60 fmly) in 179 bedrooms s £229.12-£388; d £258.50-£411 **LB FACILITIES: Spa** STV Sauna Gym Jacuzzi Beauty treatments and massages ♫ Xmas **CONF:** BC Thtr 380 Class 190 Board 50 Del from £365 **SERVICES:** Lift air con **PARKING:** 80 **NOTES:** Civ Wed 300 **CARDS:**

Town House

★★★★ Dorset Square Hotel
39-40 Dorset Square NW1 6QN plan 2 F4
☎ 020 7723 7874 020 7724 3328
e-mail: info@dorsetsquare.co.uk
Dir: *M40, A40 left lane off flyover. Turn left onto Gloucester Place. Hotel is 1st left.*
This delightfully restored Regency townhouse enjoys a prime location close to Hyde Park, Regent's Park and all of central London's attractions. Stylish bedrooms are individually themed and extremely well equipped both for business and leisure guests. Elegant public areas include the popular Potting Shed Restaurant and Bar as well as an inviting and sumptuous lounge. Service is personalised and attentive.
ROOMS: 37 en suite (2 fmly) (4 GF) s £164.50; d £235-£352.50 **FACILITIES:** STV ♫ Xmas **CONF:** Thtr 12 Board 10 **SERVICES:** Lift air con **NOTES:** **CARDS:**

★★★★73% *Meliá White House Regents Park*
Albany St, Regents Park NW1 3UP plan 3 A5
☎ 020 7391 3000 020 7388 0091
e-mail: melia.white.house@solmelia.com
Dir: *opposite Gt Portland St underground station*
This impressive Art Deco building, dating back to 1936, is conveniently located opposite Great Portland Street tube station. Public areas offer a high degree of comfort and include a fine dining restaurant and a more informal brasserie. Stylish bedrooms come in a variety of sizes, offer high levels of comfort, and are well equipped.
ROOMS: 582 en suite (1 fmly) in 166 bedrooms **FACILITIES:** STV Sauna Gym **CONF:** Thtr 120 Class 45 Board 40 **SERVICES:** Lift air con **PARKING:** 7 **NOTES:** **CARDS:**

★★★★69% Holiday Inn Camden Lock
30 Jamestown Rd, Camden Lock NW1 7BY
☎ 020 7485 4343 020 7485 4344
e-mail: info@holidayinncamden.co.uk
Dir: *From Camden underground station take left fork. Jamestown Rd 2nd on left*
In the heart of Camden this newly built hotel actually has rooms which overlook the Camden Lock. Bedrooms are spacious and well equipped, whilst the light and airy first-floor restaurant offers delicious and innovative Mediterranean dishes. A small but well equipped gym is located on the ground floor near the meeting rooms.
ROOMS: 130 en suite in 65 bedrooms **FACILITIES:** STV Gym **CONF:** Thtr 200 Class 80 Board 40 **SERVICES:** Lift air con **NOTES:** in restaurant **CARDS:**

★★★★67% Novotel London Euston
100-110 Euston Rd NW1 2AJ plan 3 C5
☎ 020 7666 9000 020 7766 9100
e-mail: H5309@accor-hotels.com
Dir: *between St Pancras & Euston stations*

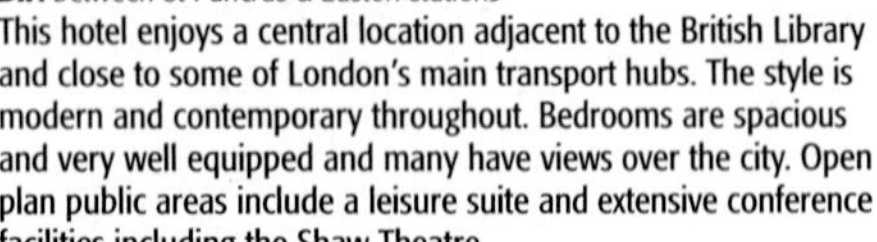

This hotel enjoys a central location adjacent to the British Library and close to some of London's main transport hubs. The style is modern and contemporary throughout. Bedrooms are spacious and very well equipped and many have views over the city. Open plan public areas include a leisure suite and extensive conference facilities including the Shaw Theatre.
ROOMS: 312 en suite (21 fmly) in 246 bedrooms s fr £160; d fr £160 **FACILITIES:** STV Sauna Gym Steam room Xmas **CONF:** Thtr 446 Class 220 Board 80 Del £252 **SERVICES:** Lift air con **NOTES:** **CARDS:**

Hotel Ibis London Euston
3 Cardington St NW1 2LW plan 3 B5
☎ 020 7388 7777 020 7388 0001
e-mail: H0921@accor-hotels.com
Dir: *from Euston Rd or station, right to Melton St leading to Cardington St*
Modern, budget hotel offering comfortable accommodation in bright and practical bedrooms. Breakfast is self-service and dinner is available in the restaurant. For further details, consult the Hotel Groups page.
ROOMS: 380 en suite s £69.95-£79.95; d £69.95-£79.95 **CONF:** BC Thtr 100 Class 40 Board 30

NW2 BRENT CROSS & CRICKLEWOOD
See LONDON plan 1 D5

★★★★72% Crown Moran
142-152 Cricklewood Broadway, Cricklewood NW2 3ED
☎ 020 8452 4175 020 8452 0952
e-mail: crowninfo@moranhotels.com
web: www.crownmoranhotel.co.uk
Dir: *M1 junct 1 follow signs onto North Circular (W) A406. Junct with A5 (Staples corner). At rdbt take 1st exit onto A5 to Cricklewood*
This striking hotel is a new addition to the north London scene and is joined by an impressive glass atrium to the popular Crown Pub. Features include excellent function and conference facilities, a leisure club, a choice of stylish lounges and bars and a

continued

contemporary restaurant. Air-conditioned bedrooms are appointed to a high standard and include a number of trendy suites.

ROOMS: 116 en suite (8 fmly) (20 GF) ⊗ in 60 bedrooms s £105-£180; d fr £125 (incl. bkfst) **LB** **FACILITIES:** STV Sauna Gym Jacuzzi ♫ **CONF:** Thtr 120 Class 50 Board 30 Del £220 **SERVICES:** Lift air con **PARKING:** 41 **NOTES:** Closed 25-26 Dec **CARDS:**

★★68% *The Garth Hotel*

64-76 Hendon Way NW2 2NL
☎ 020 8209 1511 Fax 020 8455 4744
e-mail: enquiry@garth-hotel.co.uk
Dir: *on S bound carriageway of A41 between The Vale & Cricklewood Lane.*
This hotel is something of a landmark in this part of north London, just minutes away from Brent Cross Shopping Centre and the North Circular. Bedrooms are spacious and simply appointed. The Italian theme is particularly obvious in the restaurant and bar, where home-cooked Italian dishes are the highlight.
ROOMS: 37 en suite (10 fmly) ⊗ in 15 bedrooms **FACILITIES:** STV **CONF:** BC Thtr 300 Class 250 Board 150 **PARKING:** 40 **NOTES:** ⊗ in restaurant **CARDS:**

NW3 HAMPSTEAD AND SWISS COTTAGE
See LONDON plan 1 E4

★★★★73% London Marriott Hotel Regents Park

128 King Henry's Rd NW3 3ST
☎ 0870 400 7240 Fax 0870 400 7340
Dir: *200yds off Finchley Rd on A41*
Situated in a quieter part of town and close to the tube station this hotel offers guests comfortably appointed, air-conditioned accommodation which meet the needs of today's business traveller. The open-plan ground floor contains all the main facilities including a well-equipped leisure centre with indoor pool.
ROOMS: 303 en suite ⊗ in 130 bedrooms s £85-£170; d £100-£170 **FACILITIES:** STV Sauna Solarium Gym Hair & Beauty salon, Steam room ♫ **CONF:** Thtr 440 Class 150 Board 175 Del from £180 **SERVICES:** Lift air con **PARKING:** 150 **NOTES:** Civ Wed 300 **CARDS:**

NW6 MAIDA VALE
See LONDON plan 1 D4

★★★★69% London Marriott Maida Vale

Plaza Pde, Maida Vale NW6 5RP
☎ 020 7543 6000 Fax 020 7543 2100
e-mail: marriottmaidavale@btinternet.com
Dir: *From M1, A406 W, A5 south, through Kilburn, hotel left*
This smart, modern hotel is conveniently located just north of central London. Air-conditioned bedrooms are tastefully decorated and provide a range of extras. The hotel also boasts extensive function facilities as well as a smart indoor leisure centre, which has a swimming pool, gymnasium and health and beauty salon.
ROOMS: 238 en suite (6 fmly) ⊗ in 110 bedrooms s £130-£180; d £130-£180 **LB** **FACILITIES:** STV supervised Sauna Solarium Gym Hair & beauty salons Xmas **CONF:** BC Thtr 200 Class 90 Board 40 Del from £165 **SERVICES:** Lift air con **PARKING:** 39 **NOTES:** **CARDS:**

SE1 SOUTHWARK AND WATERLOO

★★★★★67% London Marriott Hotel County Hall

Westminster Bridge Rd, County Hall SE1 7PB
plan 5 D5
☎ 020 7928 5200 Fax 020 7928 5300
e-mail: salesadmin.countyhall@marriotthotels.co.uk
Dir: *on The Thames, between Westminster Bridge and London Eye*
This impressive building enjoys an enviable position on the south bank of the Thames, adjacent to the London Eye. Public areas have a traditional elegance and the crescent-shaped restaurant offers fine views of Westminster. All bedrooms are smartly laid out and thoughtfully equipped with the business traveller in mind.
ROOMS: 200 en suite (60 fmly) ⊗ in 147 bedrooms s £205-£249; d £205-£249 **FACILITIES: Spa** STV Sauna Solarium Gym Jacuzzi Health & beauty spa ♫ ch fac Xmas **CONF:** BC Thtr 80 Class 40 Board 30 Del from £199 **SERVICES:** Lift air con **PARKING:** 70 **NOTES:** Civ Wed 80 **CARDS:**

★★★★68% Novotel London City South

Southwark Bridge Rd SE1 9HH plan 5 H5
☎ 020 7089 0400 Fax 020 7089 0410
e-mail: H3269@accor-hotels.com
Dir: *junct at Thrale St*
The first of a new generation of Novotels, this newly-built hotel is contemporary in design with smart, modern bedrooms and spacious public rooms. There are a number of options for guests wanting to unwind, including treatments such as reflexology and immersion therapy, while a gymnasium is available for the more energetic.
ROOMS: 182 en suite (139 fmly) ⊗ in 158 bedrooms s £150; d £170 **FACILITIES:** STV Gym **CONF:** Thtr 100 Class 40 Board 35 Del £225 **SERVICES:** Lift air con **PARKING:** 80 **CARDS:**

★★★★66% London Bridge Hotel

8-18 London Bridge St SE1 9SG plan 6 B2
☎ 020 7855 2200 Fax 020 7855 2233
e-mail: sales@london-bridge-hotel.co.uk
web: www.london-bridge-hotel.co.uk
Dir: *Access through London Bridge Station (bus/taxi yard), into London Bridge St (one-way). Hotel on left, 50yds from station*
This elegant independently owned hotel enjoys a prime location on the edge of the city, adjacent to London Bridge station. Smartly appointed, well-equipped bedrooms include a number of spacious deluxe rooms and suites. Compact yet sophisticated public areas include a selection of conference and meeting rooms, Georgetown Asian restaurant and a well-equipped gymnasium.
ROOMS: 138 en suite (12 fmly) ⊗ in 85 bedrooms s £99-£225; d £99-£225 **LB** **FACILITIES:** STV Sauna Solarium Gym Arrangement with local club **CONF:** Thtr 100 Class 40 Board 40 Del £266 **SERVICES:** Lift air con **NOTES:** **CARDS:**

> **GF** Indicates the number of bedrooms at ground floor level.

London

SE1 SOUTHWARK AND WATERLOO, continued

★★★71% Mercure London City Bankside
71-79 Southwark St SE1 0JA plan 5 G5
☎ 020 7902 0800 🖷 020 7902 0810
e-mail: H2814@accor-hotels.com

Dir: *A200 to London Bridge. Left into Southwark St. Hotel 2 mins by car from station*
This smart, contemporary hotel forms part of the rejuvenation of the South Bank. With the City of London just over the river and a number of tourist attractions within easy reach, the hotel is well located for business and leisure visitors alike. Facilities include spacious air-cooled bedrooms, a modern bar and the stylish Loft Restaurant.
ROOMS: 144 en suite (24 fmly) (5 GF) ⊗ in 88 bedrooms
FACILITIES: STV Gym **CONF:** Thtr 60 Class 40 Board 30 Del from £199
SERVICES: Lift air con **PARKING:** 3
CARDS:

★★★68% Novotel London Waterloo
113 Lambeth Rd SE1 7LS plan 5 D3
☎ 020 7793 1010 🖷 020 7793 0202
e-mail: h1785@accor-hotels.com
Dir: *opposite Houses of Parliament on S bank of River Thames, off Lambeth Bridge, opposite Lambeth Palace*
This hotel has an excellent location with Lambeth Palace, the Houses of Parliament and Waterloo Station all within a short walk. Bedrooms are spacious and air conditioned, a number of rooms have been designed for less able guests. The open-plan public areas include the Garden Brasserie, the Flag and Whistle Pub and children's play area.
ROOMS: 187 en suite (80 fmly) ⊗ in 158 bedrooms s £140-£155; d £160-£175 **LB** **FACILITIES:** Sauna Gym Steam room Fitness room **CONF:** Thtr 40 Class 24 Board 24 Del from £199 **SERVICES:** Lift **PARKING:** 40 **CARDS:**

⌂ Premier Lodge (London Southwark)
Anchor, Bankside, 34 Park St SE1 9EF plan 6 A3
☎ 0870 9906402 🖷 0870 9906403
web: www.premierlodge.com
Dir: *From A3200 north into Southwark Bridge Rd (A300), take left into Sumner St and follow into Park St. From south, take M3 and A3 and follow Central London signs*
High quality, modern, budget accommodation, ideal for families and business travellers. All rooms feature bath, power shower and satellite TV, and most have telephones / modem points. The adjacent bar and restaurant offers a wide and varied menu.
ROOMS: 56 en suite s £76; d £76 **CONF:** Thtr 22 Board 22

⌂ Travel Inn (London County Hall)
Belvedere Rd SE1 7PB plan 5 D5
☎ 0870 238 3300 🖷 020 7902 1619
Dir: *in County Hall building, next to London Eye*
Travel Inn offers good-quality, value-for-money accommodation. Spacious, en suite rooms with bath and shower comfortably accommodate a family of up to two adults and two children (to age 15). The restaurant and bar offers a varied menu. For further details and the Travel Inn phone number, consult the Hotel Groups page.

ROOMS: 313 en suite s £79.95-£84.95; d £79.95-£84.95

⌂ Travel Inn (London Tower Bridge)

Tower Bridge Rd SE1 3LP plan 6 C1
☎ 0870 238 3303 🖷 020 7940 3719
Dir: *South of Tower Bridge*

Travel Inn offers good-quality, value-for-money accommodation. Spacious, en suite rooms with bath and shower comfortably accommodate a family of up to two adults and two children (to age 15). The restaurant and bar offers a varied menu. For further details consult the Hotel Groups page.
ROOMS: 195 en suite s £69.95-£75.95; d £69.95-£75.95

○ Riverbank Park Plaza

Albert Embankment SE1 7SP
☎ 0207 769 9872
ROOMS: 462 en suite **NOTES:** Due to open mid 2005

SE3 BLACKHEATH

★★68% Clarendon
8-16 Montpelier Row, Blackheath SE3 0RW
plan 8 D1
☎ 020 8318 4321 🖷 020 8318 4378
e-mail: relax@clarendonhotel.com
web: www.clarendonhotel.com
Dir: *off A2 at Blackheath junct. Hotel on left before village*
Overlooking the heath, this impressive Georgian hotel offers well-equipped, attractive accommodation. A number of suites are also available. Spacious public areas include a choice of bars, a

continued

restaurant and meeting and conference facilities. The hotel has its own car park and guests have use of local leisure facilities.

ROOMS: 181 en suite (3 fmly) (5 GF) ⊗ in 22 bedrooms s £80-£95; d £90-£100 (incl. bkfst) **LB** **FACILITIES:** STV ♫ Xmas **CONF:** BC Thtr 120 Class 40 Board 50 Del from £115 **SERVICES:** Lift **PARKING:** 80 **NOTES:** ⊗ in restaurant Civ Wed 60
CARDS:

SE10 GREENWICH

★★70% Hamilton House

14 West Grove, Greenwich SE10 8QT plan 8 B2
☎ 020 8694 9899 020 8694 2370
e-mail: reception@hamiltonhousehotel.co.uk
web: www.hamiltonhousehotel.co.uk
Dir: *from Blackheath Common on A2 towards Central London, 2nd right after Blackheath Tea Hut into Hyde Vale. West Grove next left*

This small Georgian hotel boasts true style and character and some impressive views of the Docklands. Elegant bedrooms are individually designed and equipped with a host of thoughtful extras, including CD players. The restaurant is bright and offers creative cooking. The bar area opens out to an attractive garden with seating. This hotel is very popular as a wedding venue.
ROOMS: 9 en suite (8 fmly) (1 GF) ⊗ in 4 bedrooms s £100; d £120-£150 (incl. bkfst) **LB** **FACILITIES:** STV Xmas **CONF:** Thtr 50 Class 22 Board 22 **PARKING:** 8 **NOTES:** ⊗ in restaurant Civ Wed 104
CARDS:

Hotel Ibis London Greenwich

30 Stockwell St, Greenwich SE10 9JN plan 8 A4
☎ 020 8305 1177 020 8858 7139
e-mail: H0975@accor-hotels.com
Dir: *from Waterloo Bridge, Elephant & Castle, A2 to Greenwich.*

Modern, budget hotel offering comfortable accommodation in bright and practical bedrooms. Breakfast is self-service and dinner is available in the restaurant. For further details, consult the Hotel Groups page.
ROOMS: 82 en suite s £66.95-£74.95; d £66.95-£74.95

SW1 WESTMINSTER

Top 200 – Hotel

★★★★★ ⊛⊛⊛⊛⊛ The Berkeley

Wilton Place, Knightsbridge SW1X 7RL
plan 4 G4
The Savoy Group
☎ 020 7235 6000 020 7235 4330
e-mail: info@the-berkeley.co.uk
Dir: *300mtrs along Knightsbridge from Hyde Park Corner*

The Berkeley never fails to impress. Having undergone refurbishment there are an excellent range of bedrooms, each one furnished with care and attention to detail. The striking Blue Bar enhances the reception rooms, which are adorned with magnificent flower arrangements. The health spa offers a range of treatment rooms and includes a stunning open-air rooftop pool. The two restaurants provide a complete contrast of style: modern, snack-style at the Boxwood Café and stunning French cuisine at Pétrus.

ROOMS: 214 en suite ⊗ in 32 bedrooms **FACILITIES: Spa** STV supervised Sauna Solarium Gym Beauty/therapy treatments **CONF:** Thtr 250 Class 80 Board 52 **SERVICES:** Lift air con **PARKING:** 50 **NOTES:** Civ Wed 160
CARDS:

Top 200 – Hotel

★★★★★ ⊛⊛⊛⊛⊛ Mandarin Oriental Hyde Park

66 Knightsbridge SW1X 7LA plan 4 F4
☎ 020 7235 2000 020 7235 2001
e-mail: molon-reservations@mohg.com
Dir: *Harrods on right, hotel 0.5m on left opp Harvey Nichols*

This elegant hotel overlooks Hyde Park and Knightsbridge. Bedrooms and suites are appointed to the highest standard, many with unrivalled views; Irish linen sheets and goose down pillows add to the luxury. There is a good choice of dining options - The Park Restaurant offers light, brasserie-style dishes, the sophisticated Foliage restaurant, with its award-winning cuisine, and the fashionable Mandarin Bar that serves light snacks and cocktails. The stylish spa is a destination in its own right with booking essential.
ROOMS: 200 en suite ⊗ in 106 bedrooms s fr £425; d fr £425 **LB** **FACILITIES: Spa** STV Sauna Gym Jacuzzi Fitness centre, steam room, relaxation area, sanarium ♫ Xmas **CONF:** Thtr 250 Class 120 Board 60 **SERVICES:** Lift air con **PARKING:** 13 **NOTES:** Civ Wed 220 **CARDS:**

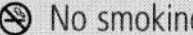

⊗ No smoking

SW1 WESTMINSTER, continued

Top 200 – Hotel

★★★★★ ◎◎ **The Goring**
Beeston Place, Grosvenor Gardens
SW1W 0JW plan 4 H3
☎ 020 7396 9000 020 7834 4393
e-mail: reception@goringhotel.co.uk
web: www.goringhotel.co.uk
Dir: *off Lower Grosvenor Place, just prior to Royal Mews*

Situated in central London, this icon of British hospitality is within walking distance of the Royal Parks and principal shopping areas. The well-equipped bedrooms are furnished in a traditional style and boast high levels of comfort and quality. Stylish reception rooms include the garden bar and the drawing room, both popular for afternoon tea and cocktails. The restaurant menu has a classic repertoire but also enjoys a well-deserved reputation for its contemporary British cuisine.

ROOMS: 73 en suite (9 fmly) s fr £235; d fr £300 LB **FACILITIES:** STV Free membership of nearby Health Club ♫ Xmas **CONF:** BC Thtr 60 Class 30 Board 30 **SERVICES:** Lift air con **PARKING:** 8 **NOTES:** Civ Wed 50 **CARDS:**

Top 200 – Hotel

★★★★★ ◎◎ **The Lanesborough**
Hyde Park Corner SW1X 7TA plan 4 G5
☎ 020 7259 5599 020 7259 5606
e-mail: info@lanesborough.co.uk
Dir: *follow signs to central London and Hyde Park Corner*

Occupying an enviable position on Hyde Park Corner, this elegant hotel has an ageless charm and engaging atmosphere, much appreciated by the loyal clientele. Quality is a hallmark here; bedrooms and public rooms reflect the highest levels of comfort. Service is equally impressive with a personal butler ensuring individual attention. The conservatory restaurant is a popular venue for accomplished international cuisine in a convivial setting.

ROOMS: 95 en suite in 24 bedrooms **FACILITIES: Spa** STV Gym Fitness studio ♫ **CONF:** Thtr 120 Class 60 Board 48 **SERVICES:** Lift air con **PARKING:** 38 **NOTES:** Civ Wed 100 **CARDS:**

Top 200 – Hotel

★★★★★ ◎ **The Carlton Tower**
Cadogan Place SW1X 9PY plan 4 F4
☎ 020 7235 1234 020 7235 9129
e-mail: contact@carltontower.com web: www.carltontower.com
Dir: *A4 towards Knightsbridge, turn right onto Sloane St. Hotel on left before Cadogan Place*

This impressive hotel enjoys an enviable position in the heart of Knightsbridge, overlooking Cadogan Gardens. Bedrooms vary in size and style and include a number of suites, many with wonderful views of the city. Leisure facilities include a glass-roofed swimming pool, a well-equipped gym and a number of treatment rooms. Dining options include Grissini London and the famous Rib Room and Oyster Bar.

ROOMS: 220 en suite (60 fmly) in 116 bedrooms s £325; d £325-£3750 **FACILITIES: Spa** STV supervised Sauna Gym Jacuzzi Massage and Spa treatments ♫ ch fac Xmas **CONF:** BC Thtr 400 Class 250 Board 30 **SERVICES:** Lift air con **PARKING:** 50 **NOTES:** Civ Wed 400 **CARDS:**

See advert on opposite page

Top 200 – Town House

★★★★★ **No 41**
41 Buckingham Palace Rd SW1W 0PS
plan 5 A4
☎ 020 7300 0041 020 7300 0141
e-mail: manager41@rchmail.com
Dir: *opp Buckingham Palace Mews entrance.*

Red Carnation HOTELS

Small, intimate and very private, this stunning town house is located opposite the Royal Mews and ideally positioned for London's theatres, shops and tourist attractions. Decorated in stylish black and white, bedrooms successfully combine comfort with state-of-the-art technology. Attentive personal

continued

London

service and a host of thoughtful extra touches make this town house really special.

ROOMS: 18 en suite d £220-£745 (incl. bkfst) **FACILITIES:** STV use of 2 health clubs **CONF:** BC Board 12 Del from £295 **SERVICES:** Lift air con **NOTES:** **CARDS:**

Town House

★★★★★ **22 Jermyn Street**
St James's SW1Y 6HL plan 3 B1
☎ 020 7734 2353 020 7734 0750
e-mail: office@22jermyn.com
web: www.22jermyn.com
Dir: *A4 into Piccadilly, right into Duke St and left into King St. Through St James' Sq to Charles II St. Left into Regent St and left again*
This attractive townhouse enjoys an enviable location close to Piccadilly, Regent Street and the fashionable St James's area. Smartly appointed accommodation mainly consists of spacious suites with a few smaller studios. All are thoughtfully equipped with mini-bar, satellite TV, video recorder and fax/modem lines. 24-hour room service is available and breakfast is served in guest bedrooms.
ROOMS: 18 en suite (13 fmly) s £246.75; d £246.75 **FACILITIES:** STV Membership of nearby Health Club ch fac **CONF:** BC Thtr 15 Class 15 Board 10 **SERVICES:** Lift air con **NOTES:** in restaurant **CARDS:**

★★★★★71%
Sheraton Park Tower

The Luxury Collection

101 Knightsbridge SW1X 7RN plan 4 F4
☎ 020 7235 8050 020 7235 8231
e-mail: anne.scott@luxurycollection.com
web: www.starwood.com
Dir: *next to Harvey Nichols*
Superbly located for some of London's most fashionable stores, this modern hotel offers some stunning views over the city. Bedrooms combine a high degree of comfort with up-to-date décor and a super range of extras. Suites are particularly impressive. Other features of the hotel include the intimate Knightsbridge lounge and the more formal Piano Bar. The hotel also boasts extensive conference and banqueting facilities. Restaurant One-O-One is renowned for its seafood.
ROOMS: 280 en suite (280 fmly) in 116 bedrooms **FACILITIES:** STV Gym Fitness room **CONF:** BC Thtr 70 Class 50 Board 26 **SERVICES:** Lift air con **PARKING:** 67 **NOTES:** **CARDS:**

★★★★★71%
Sofitel St James London

SOFITEL
ACCOR HOTELS & RESORTS

6 Waterloo Place SW1Y 4AN plan 5 B6
☎ 020 7747 2222 020 7747 2210
e-mail: H3144@accor-hotels.com
Dir: *On corner of Pall Mall & Waterloo Place*
Located in the exclusive area of St James's, this Grade II listed former bank is convenient for most of the city's attractions, theatres and the financial district. The design of the hotel is a happy marriage of modern and classical styles. The bedrooms are equipped to a high standard. Public areas include the Brasserie Roux, a small fitness room and the Rose Lounge.
ROOMS: 186 en suite in 97 bedrooms s £160-£320; d £160-£320 **LB** **FACILITIES:** STV Gym Steam rooms, Treatment rooms Xmas **CONF:** BC Thtr 180 Class 110 Board 60 Del from £310 **SERVICES:** Lift air con **NOTES:** Civ Wed 140 **CARDS:**

Late for dinner?
Quality Standards mean that last orders for dinner vary according to star rating and should be no earlier than:
★★ 7.00pm ★★★ 8.00pm ★★★★ 9.00pm
★★★★★ 10.00pm

London

SW1 WESTMINSTER, continued

Top 200 – Hotel

★★★★ The Halkin Hotel
Halkin St, Belgravia SW1X 7DJ plan 4 G4
☎ 020 7333 1000 020 7333 1100
e-mail: res@halkin.como.bz
Dir: *hotel between Belgrave Sq & Grosvenor Place. Via Chapel St into Headfort Place and left into Halkin St*
This smart, contemporary hotel enjoys an enviable and peaceful position just a short stroll from both Hyde Park and from the designer shops of Knightsbridge. Service is attentive, friendly and very personalised. The stylish bedrooms and suites are equipped to the highest standard with smart, marble bathrooms and every conceivable extra. Public areas include an airy bar lounge and the famous Thai restaurant, Nahm.
ROOMS: 41 en suite in 9 bedrooms s £175-£793; d £175-£793 LB **FACILITIES:** STV **CONF:** Thtr 36 Class 15 Board 22 **SERVICES:** Lift air con **NOTES:**
CARDS:

Top 200 – Hotel

★★★★ The Stafford
16-18 St James's Place SW1A 1NJ plan 5 A5
☎ 020 7493 0111 020 7493 7121
e-mail: info@thestaffordhotel.co.uk
Dir: *off Pall Mall into St James's St. 2nd left into St James's Place*
Tucked away in a quiet corner of exclusive St James's, this lovely boutique hotel retains an air of understated luxury. The American Bar is a fabulous venue in its own right, festooned with an eccentric array of celebrity photos, caps and ties.

continued

Afternoon tea is a long established tradition here. This is a traditional hotel keeping the highest standards, from the pristine, tastefully decorated and air-conditioned bedrooms, to the highly professional, yet friendly service.
ROOMS: 81 en suite (6 GF) in 73 bedrooms s fr £265; d fr £288 **FACILITIES:** STV Membership of Fitness Club available Xmas **CONF:** Thtr 40 Board 24 **SERVICES:** Lift air con **NOTES:** in restaurant Civ Wed 44 **CARDS:**

★★★★79% The Cadogan
75 Sloane St SW1X 9SG plan 4 F3
☎ 020 7235 7141 020 7245 0994
e-mail: info@cadogan.com
web: www.cadogan.com
Dir: *at Hyde Park rdbt follow signs for Knightsbridge, L at Harvey Nichols onto Sloane St. Hotel on R*
This delightful hotel, with an enviable location between Sloane Square and Knightsbridge, has undergone a major stylish refurbishment. Original features have been combined with contemporary, tasteful interior design. Airy public rooms include a comfortable drawing room, sophisticated bar and restaurant as well as elegant function rooms. All bedrooms boast air conditioning, well-appointed bathrooms and a host of thoughtful amenities.
ROOMS: 65 en suite (1 fmly) in 31 bedrooms s £188-£646.25; d £287.88-£646.25 LB **FACILITIES:** STV Xmas **CONF:** Thtr 30 Class 16 Board 20 **SERVICES:** Lift **NOTES:** Civ Wed 40
CARDS:

★★★★75% The Rubens at the Palace
Red Carnation Hotels
39 Buckingham Palace Rd SW1W 0PS plan 5 A4
☎ 020 7834 6600 020 7233 6037
e-mail: bookrb@rchmail.com
Dir: *opposite Royal Mews, 100mtrs away from Buckingham Palace*
This hotel enjoys an enviable location next to Buckingham Palace. Stylish, air-conditioned bedrooms include the pinstripe-walled Saville Row rooms, which follow a tailoring theme, and the opulent Royal rooms, named after different monarchs. Public rooms include the Library fine dining restaurant and a comfortable stylish cocktail bar and lounge. The team here pride themselves on their warmth and friendliness.
ROOMS: 173 en suite in 80 bedrooms s £180; d £245
FACILITIES: STV Health clubs locally ch fac Xmas **CONF:** Thtr 90 Class 40 Board 30 Del from £185 **SERVICES:** Lift air con **NOTES:** in restaurant **CARDS:**

★★★★74% Millennium Hotel London Knightsbridge

17 Sloane St, Knightsbridge SW1X 9NU plan 4 F4
☎ 020 7235 4377 020 7235 3705
e-mail: knightsbridge.reservations@mill.cop.com
Dir: *from Knightsbridge tube to Sloane St. Hotel 70mtrs on right*
This fashionable hotel boasts an enviable location in Knightsbridge's chic shopping district. Air-conditioned, thoughtfully equipped bedrooms are complemented by a popular lobby lounge and the much acclaimed Mju Restaurant and Bar. Cuisine has more than a touch of Pacific Rim about it with a tempting

continued

London

degustation menu proving a popular choice. Valet parking is available if pre-booked.

ROOMS: 222 en suite ⊗ in 86 bedrooms s £119-£317.25; d £129-£317.25 LB **FACILITIES:** STV **CONF:** BC Thtr 120 Class 80 Board 50 Del from £245 **SERVICES:** Lift air con **PARKING:** 7 **NOTES:** ✈
CARDS:

★★★★72% Dolphin Square Hotel

Dolphin Square, Chichester St SW1V 3LX plan 5 B1
☎ 020 7834 3800 020 7798 8735
e-mail: reservations@dolphinsquarehotel.co.uk
web: www.dolphinsquarehotel.co.uk
Dir: *Follow signs to Central London then Earls Court, after Chelsea Bridge take 2nd left, turn right into Chichester St, hotel on right*

Conveniently located close to the Embankment and Westminster, the Dolphin Square offers accommodation mainly in suites, which are smartly appointed, spacious and well equipped. A wealth of facilities includes a swimming pool, squash courts, a fully staffed business centre and on-site shops. Diners have the choice of an informal brasserie and celebrated chef Anton Edelmann's stylish Allium Restaurant.
ROOMS: 148 en suite (29 fmly) (17 GF) ⊗ in 43 bedrooms s £175-£450; d £175-£450 **FACILITIES:** STV supervised Squash Sauna Gym Jacuzzi Health & Fitness Spa (aerobics, yoga, therapeutic remedies, beauty treatments) **CONF:** Thtr 70 Class 20 Board 30 Del from £225 **SERVICES:** Lift **PARKING:** 18 **NOTES:** ✈ Civ Wed 60
CARDS:

★★★★71% De Vere Cavendish St James's London

DE VERE HOTELS

81 Jermyn St SW1Y 6JF plan 5 B6
☎ 020 7930 2111 020 7839 2125
e-mail: cavendish.reservations@devere-hotels.com
Dir: *from Marble Arch along Park Ln to Hyde Park Corner. Left to Piccadilly, past Ritz and right down Dukes St. Behind Fortnum and Mason*
This smart, stylish hotel enjoys an enviable location in the prestigious St James's area, minutes' walk from Green Park and Piccadilly. Bedrooms have a fresh, contemporary feel and include a number of spacious executive rooms, studios and suites. Elegant public areas include a spacious first-floor lounge, the popular Aslan Restaurant and well-appointed conference and function facilities.
ROOMS: 230 rms (229 en suite) ⊗ in 36 bedrooms s £235; d £245 LB **FACILITIES:** STV ch fac Xmas **CONF:** BC Thtr 80 Class 50 Board 35 Del £270 **SERVICES:** Lift air con **PARKING:** 60 **NOTES:** ✈
CARDS:

★★★★71% *Victoria Park Plaza*

Park Plaza

239 Vauxhall Bridge Rd SW1V 1EQ plan 5 A3
☎ 020 7769 9999 020 7769 9998
e-mail: info@victoriaparkplaza.com

This smart modern hotel close to Victoria station is well located for all of central London's major attractions. Air-conditioned bedrooms are tastefully appointed and thoughtfully equipped for both business and leisure guests. Airy, stylish public areas include an elegant bar and restaurant, a popular coffee bar and extensive conference facilities complete with a business centre.
ROOMS: 299 en suite ⊗ in 116 bedrooms **FACILITIES:** STV Sauna Gym ♫ **CONF:** Thtr 500 Class 240 Board 120 **SERVICES:** Lift air con **PARKING:** 50 **NOTES:** Civ Wed 1000 **CARDS:**

Town House

★★★★ *The Lowndes*

21 Lowndes St SW1X 9ES plan 4 F4
☎ 020 7823 1234 020 7235 1154
e-mail: contact@lowndeshotel.com
Dir: *M4 onto A4 into London. Left from Brompton Rd into Sloane St. Left into Pont St and Lowndes St next left. Hotel on right*
This friendly popular hotel enjoys an enviable location within walking distance of Harrods, Harvey Nichols and the designer shops of Sloane Street. Bedrooms are smartly appointed, well equipped and some boast spacious balconies; a number of junior suites are also available. Bijou public areas include a brasserie restaurant, lounge and meeting room.
ROOMS: 78 en suite ⊗ in 31 bedrooms **FACILITIES:** STV Use of facilities at Carlton Tower Hotel **CONF:** Thtr 25 Class 25 Board 18 **SERVICES:** Lift air con **NOTES:** ✈
CARDS:

★★★★68% Sheraton Belgravia

Sheraton HOTELS & RESORTS

20 Chesham Place SW1X 8HQ plan 4 G3
☎ 020 7235 6040 020 7259 6243
e-mail: judy-kent@sheraton.com
Dir: *A4 Brompton Rd into Central London. After Brompton Oratory right into Beauchamp Pl. Follow into Pont St, cross Sloane St & hotel on corner*
This modern hotel is situated in the heart of Belgravia, just a short walk from the shops of Knightsbridge, Kings Road and Sloane Street. Bedrooms are well-equipped for business and leisure guests and public areas are elegant. Light snacks are available

continued on p352

London

SW1 WESTMINSTER, continued

all day in the lounge, or Mulberry's restaurant offers a more formal option.
ROOMS: 89 en suite (16 fmly) ⊗ in 37 bedrooms **FACILITIES:** STV comp membership to local health spa ♫ **CONF:** BC Thtr 35 Class 14 Board 20 **SERVICES:** Lift air con **NOTES:** ✈
CARDS:

Town House

★★★★ Grange Rochester

69 Vincent Square SW1P 2PA plan 5 B3
☎ 020 7828 6611 020 7233 6724
e-mail: rochester@grangehotels.com
Overlooking leafy Vincent Square, this boutique-style hotel is well located for access to London's finest shopping, theatres and tourist attractions. Stylish bedrooms are quiet and well equipped, but do vary in size. Some rooms have balconies with views over the square. The compact public rooms are elegant and offer all day dining and drinking options.
ROOMS: 76 en suite (6 fmly) ⊗ in 30 bedrooms s fr £170; d fr £190 **FACILITIES:** STV **CONF:** Thtr 45 Class 35 Board 35 Del from £207 **SERVICES:** Lift **NOTES:** ✈
CARDS:

★★★64% Quality Hotel Westminster

82-83 Eccleston Square SW1V 1PS plan 5 A2
☎ 020 7834 8042 020 7630 8942
e-mail: enquiries@hotels-westminster.com
Dir: *Victoria Station into Wilton Rd, 3rd into Gillingham St, hotel 150mtrs*
Situated close to Victoria, this hotel provides a good base for exploring London. Bedrooms are all en suite but vary in size. Public areas include a seating area, and Connaughts Brasserie, offering a good range of meals.
ROOMS: 107 en suite (8 fmly) ⊗ in 62 bedrooms s £111-£145; d £125-£160 LB **FACILITIES:** STV **CONF:** Thtr 150 Class 60 Board 40 **SERVICES:** Lift **NOTES:** ✈ ⊗ in restaurant
CARDS:

SW3 CHELSEA, BROMPTON

Top 200 – Town House

★★★★★ ◎◎◎◎ Capital
Basil St, Knightsbridge SW3 1AT plan 4 F4
☎ 020 7589 5171 020 7225 0011
e-mail: reservations@capitalhotel.co.uk
Dir: *20yds from Harrods*
Personal service is assured at this small, family-owned hotel set in the heart of Knightsbridge. Beautifully designed bedrooms come in a number of styles and feature antique furniture and marble bathrooms. Dinner is a highlight of any visit. Eric Chavot and his committed brigade continue to cook to a consistently high standard. Cocktails are a speciality in the delightful, small bar.
ROOMS: 49 en suite ⊗ in 24 bedrooms s £170-£195; d £210-£275 LB **FACILITIES:** STV ch fac **CONF:** Thtr 30 Board 12 **SERVICES:** Lift air con **PARKING:** 15 **NOTES:** ✈
CARDS:

Town House

★★★★★ The Draycott
26 Cadogan Gardens SW3 2RP plan 4 F2
☎ 020 7730 6466 020 7730 0236
e-mail: reservations@draycotthotel.com
Dir: *From Sloane Sq station towards Peter Jones, keep to left. At Kings Rd take first right Cadogan Gdns, 2nd right, hotel on left.*
Enjoying a prime location just yards from Sloane Square, this town house provides an ideal base in one of the most fashionable areas of London. Many regular guests regard this as their London residence and staff pride themselves on their hospitality. Beautifully appointed bedrooms include a number of very spacious suites and all are equipped to a high standard. Attractive day rooms, furnished with antique and period pieces, include a choice of lounges, one with access to a lovely sheltered garden.
ROOMS: 35 en suite (9 fmly) (2 GF) ⊗ in 30 bedrooms s £141-£158; d £188-£425 **FACILITIES:** STV Beauty treatment, Massage **CONF:** Thtr 20 Class 12 Board 12 Del from £300 **SERVICES:** Lift air con **CARDS:**

Town House

★★★★ Parkes
41 Beaufort Gardens, Knightsbridge SW3 1PW plan 4 E4
☎ 020 7581 9944 020 7581 1999
e-mail: reception@parkeshotel.com
web: www.parkeshotel.com
Dir: *off Brompton Rd, 100yds from Harrods*
This sophisticated and friendly hotel is located in a tree-lined square in the heart of fashionable Knightsbridge. Stylish bedrooms and spacious suites with kitchens are beautifully appointed and equipped with every conceivable extra including UK/US modems and sockets, wireless ADSL and mini-bars. Whilst there is no hotel restaurant, a wide range of dishes from local eateries can be delivered to your room.
ROOMS: 33 en suite (16 fmly) (4 GF) s £230-£488; d £282-£488 **FACILITIES:** STV arrangement with nearby gym **CONF:** Board 12 **SERVICES:** Lift air con **NOTES:** ✈ ⊗ in restaurant
CARDS:

Town House

★★★★ The Beaufort
33 Beaufort Gardens SW3 1PP plan 4 F3
☎ 020 7584 5252 020 7589 2834
e-mail: reservations@thebeaufort.co.uk
web: www.thebeaufort.co.uk
Dir: *100yds past Harrods on left of Brompton Rd*
This friendly, attractive town house enjoys a peaceful location in a tree-lined cul-de-sac just minutes' walk from Knightsbridge. The tariff includes almost anything other than phone calls and laundry. Air-conditioned bedrooms are thoughtfully equipped with chocolates, fruit, fresh flowers, videos, CD players and free internet and movie channel access. Guests are offered complimentary drinks and afternoon tea, served in the attractive drawing room.
ROOMS: 29 en suite (3 GF) in 12 bedrooms s £185-£230; d fr £230 (incl. cont bkfst) **FACILITIES:** STV **SERVICES:** Lift air con **NOTES:** **CARDS:**

★★★73% Basil Street
Basil St, Knightsbridge SW3 1AH plan 4 F4
☎ 020 7581 3311 020 7581 3693
e-mail: info@TheBasil.com
web: www.TheBasil.com
Dir: *M4 & A4 Brompton Rd, right before Harrods. Left into Basil St and hotel on left*
An elegant, classic British hotel located in the heart of this shoppers' paradise. The public rooms are full of character with antiques, parquet floors, fine paintings and tapestries, and service is professional and efficient. Bedrooms are in keeping with the original style of the property with the addition of up-to-date facilities.
ROOMS: 80 en suite (4 fmly) in 40 bedrooms s fr £170.38; d fr £240.88 LB **FACILITIES:** STV Xmas **CONF:** Thtr 30 Class 16 Board 20 **SERVICES:** Lift **NOTES:**
CARDS:

SW4 CLAPHAM
See LONDON plan 1 E3

★★★68% The Windmill on The Common
Southside, Clapham Common SW4 9DE
☎ 020 8673 4578 020 8675 1486
e-mail: windmillhotel@youngs.co.uk
This popular hotel is located on the edge of Clapham Common and dates back to 1729. The lively pub bar, with its outdoor seating, makes it a favourite venue in the summer months. The *continued* smart air-conditioned bedrooms are spacious, comfortable and well equipped for business guests.
ROOMS: 29 en suite (12 GF) in 21 bedrooms s fr £99; d fr £115 (incl. bkfst) LB **FACILITIES:** STV **CONF:** Thtr 40 Class 25 Board 20 **SERVICES:** air con **PARKING:** 16 **NOTES:** in restaurant
CARDS:

SW5 EARLS COURT Map 06 TQ27

★★★★72%
London Marriott Kensington
Marriott HOTELS · RESORTS · SUITES
Cromwell Rd SW5 0TH plan 4 B3
☎ 020 7973 1000 020 7370 1685
e-mail: kensington.marriott@marriotthotels.co.uk
Dir: *on A4, opposite Cromwell Rd Hospital*
Now re-opened following extensive building and modernisation, this new Marriott features a stunning glass exterior and seven-storey atrium lobby. Fully air conditioned throughout, the hotel features elegant design combined with a great range of facilities, including indoor leisure, a range of conference rooms and parking. Smart bedrooms offer a host of extras including the very latest communications technology.
ROOMS: 216 en suite (39 fmly) s fr £159; d fr £159 LB **FACILITIES:** STV Sauna Gym Jacuzzi **CONF:** BC Thtr 200 Class 100 Board 60 Del from £240 **SERVICES:** Lift air con **PARKING:** 20 **NOTES:** in restaurant Civ Wed 50
CARDS:

Town House

★★★★ Twenty Nevern Square
20 Nevern Square, Earls Court SW5 9PD plan 4 A2
☎ 020 7565 9555 & 020 7370 4934 020 7565 9444
e-mail: hotel@twentynevernsquare.co.uk
web: www.twentynevernsquare.co.uk
Dir: *take Warwick Rd exit, right out of station, 2nd right into Nevern Square. Hotel 30yds on right*
This small, smart townhouse is discreetly located in Nevern Square and is ideally situated for both Earls Court and Olympia. Bedrooms, which vary in shape and size, are appointed to a high standard and well equipped. Public areas include a delightful lounge and Café Twenty where breakfast and dinner are served.
ROOMS: 20 en suite (3 GF) in 10 bedrooms s £89-£130; d £99-£165 (incl. cont bkfst) **FACILITIES:** STV arrangements for day membership at Cannons Leisure Centre ch fac **CONF:** BC **SERVICES:** Lift **PARKING:** 4 **NOTES:** in restaurant
CARDS:

London

SW5 EARLS COURT, continued

Town House

★★★★ The Cranley
10 Bina Gardens, South Kensington SW5 0LA plan 4 C2
☎ 020 7373 0123 020 7373 9497
e-mail: info@thecranley.com
web: www.thecranley.com
Dir: *down Gloucester Rd towards Old Brompton Rd. 3rd right after station into Hereford Sq, then 3rd left into Bina Gardens*
This elegant Victorian town house is set in a quiet residential area of South Kensington where a friendly welcome awaits guests. The bedrooms, including a number of suites, have all undergone a stylish refurbishment and feature antique pieces and many thoughtful extras. Complimentary afternoon tea is available, along with aperitifs and canapés in the evening.
ROOMS: 39 en suite (4 GF) s £118-£183; d £146-£224 **LB**
FACILITIES: STV **SERVICES:** Lift air con **NOTES:**
CARDS:

★★★66% *Burns*

18-26 Barkston Gardens, Kensingston SW5 0EN
plan 4 B2
☎ 020 7373 3151 020 7370 4090
e-mail: burnshotel@vienna-group.co.uk
Dir: *Off A4, right to Earls Court Rd (A3220), 2nd left. Hotel in Barkston Gardens, 2nd left past Earls Court underground station.*
This Victorian hotel overlooks a leafy garden in a quiet residential area not far from the Earls Court underground and exhibition centres. Bedrooms are attractively appointed and include modern facilities. Public areas, although not extensive, are stylish.
ROOMS: 105 en suite (10 fmly) in 38 bedrooms **FACILITIES:** STV
SERVICES: Lift **NOTES:** in restaurant
CARDS:

Comfort Inn Kensington

22-32 West Cromwell Rd, Kensington SW5 9QJ
plan 4 A3
☎ 020 7373 3300 020 7835 2040
e-mail: enquiries@hotels-kensington.com
Dir: *on N side of West Cromwell Rd, between juncts of Cromwell Rd, Earls Court Rd & Warwick Rd*
This modern building offers accommodation in smart, spacious and well equipped bedrooms, all with en suite bathrooms. Refreshments may be taken at the nearby family restaurant. For further details consult the Hotel Groups page under 'Choice'.
ROOMS: 125 en suite s £105-£125; d £125-£165 **CONF:** Thtr 80 Class 60 Board 30 Del from £100

Travel Inn (London Kensington)
11 Knaresborough Place, Kensington SW5 0TJ
plan 4 B2
☎ 0870 238 3304 020 7370 9292
Dir: *Just off A4 Cromwell Road, 2 minutes from Earls Court underground station*
Travel Inn offers good-quality, value-for-money accommodation. Spacious, en suite rooms with bath and shower comfortably accommodate a family of up to two adults and two children (to age 15). The restaurant and bar offers a varied menu. For further details consult the Hotel Groups page.
ROOMS: 183 en suite s £69.95-£75.95; d £69.95-£75.95

SW6 FULHAM
See LONDON plan 1 D3/E3

★★★★71% Chelsea Village
Stamford Bridge, Fulham Rd SW6 1HS
☎ 020 7565 1400 020 7565 1450
e-mail: reservation@chelseavillage.co.uk
This stylish, eye-catching hotel forms a part of the ambitious development of Chelsea Football Club and is situated adjacent to the ground. Public areas are extensive and feature a wide range of facilities including two restaurants and bars; the Chelsea Club is one of London's premier health and beauty spas. Air-conditioned bedrooms are spacious and well equipped.
ROOMS: 291 en suite (64 fmly) in 138 bedrooms s £105-£160; d £115-£180 **FACILITIES: Spa** STV supervised Sauna Solarium Gym Jacuzzi Xmas **CONF:** BC Thtr 300 Class 250 Board 50 Del from £195
SERVICES: Lift air con **PARKING:** 290 **NOTES:** Civ Wed 50
CARDS:

See advert on opposite page

★★★68% Jurys Inn Chelsea
Imperial Rd, Imperial Wharf SW6 2GA
JURYS DOYLE HOTELS
☎ 020 7411 2200 020 7411 2444
e-mail: info@jurysdoyle.com
This modern hotel is located in Chelesa close to the Wharf. Bedrooms provide good guest comfort and in-room facilities are ideal for both leisure and business markets. Public areas include a number of meeting rooms, a restaurant and a popular bar.
ROOMS: 172 en suite (172 fmly) in 29 bedrooms s £85; d £85
FACILITIES: STV **CONF:** Thtr 15 Board 10 Del £145 **SERVICES:** Lift air con **NOTES:** in restaurant Closed 24th-26th Dec
CARDS:

★★★66% Hotel Ibis London Earls Court

47 Lillie Rd SW6 1UD plan 4 A1
☎ 020 7610 0880 020 7381 4450
e-mail: h5623-gm@accor-hotels.com
web: www.ibishotels.com
Dir: *A4 to Central London. 0.5m after Hammersmith flyover turn right at traffic lights into North End Rd. After 0.5m left at mini rdbt into Lillie Rd*
Situated opposite the Earls Court Exhibition Centre, this large, modern hotel is popular with business and leisure guests. Bedrooms are comfortable and well equipped. Two restaurants offer a choice of light meals or a more formal, traditional menu and carvery. There are also extensive conference facilities and an underground car park.
ROOMS: 502 en suite (20 fmly) in 240 bedrooms s £69.95-£79.95; d £69.95-£79.95 **FACILITIES:** STV Health club and gym nearby
CONF: BC Thtr 1200 Class 700 Board 100 Del from £160
SERVICES: Lift **PARKING:** 130 **NOTES:** in restaurant
CARDS:

London

Travel Inn (London Putney Bridge)
3 Putney Bridge Approach SW6 3JD
☎ 0870 238 3302 Fax 020 7471 8315
Dir: *north bank of River Thames by Putney Bridge*
Travel Inn offers good-quality, value-for-money accommodation. Spacious, en suite rooms with bath and shower comfortably accommodate a family of up to two adults and two children (to age 15). The restaurant and bar offers a varied menu. For further details consult the Hotel Groups page.
ROOMS: 154 en suite s £69.95-£75.95; d £69.95-£75.95

SW7 SOUTH KENSINGTON

★★★★★75% The Bentley
27-33 Harrington Gardens SW7 4JX plan 4 C2
☎ 020 7244 5555 Fax 020 7244 5566
e-mail: info@thebentley-hotel.com
web: www.thebentley-hotel.com
Dir: *S of A4 into Knightsbridge at junct with Gloucester Rd, turn right, then right again at 2nd turn, hotel on left just after mini rdbt*
One of London's newest hotels, The Bentley is discreetly located in the heart of Kensington. The interior throughout is one of lavish opulence. Spacious air-conditioned bedrooms are equally luxurious featuring marble bathrooms with jacuzzi baths and walk-in showers. Public areas include the Perdiot where breakfast and lunch are served, a cosy cigar den and the cocktail bar Malachite. The fine-dining restaurant, 1880, which is open for dinner provides excellent contemporary cuisine and highly professional service.
ROOMS: 64 en suite in 11 bedrooms s £293.75-£2937.50; d £293.75-£2937.50 **FACILITIES: Spa** STV Sauna Gym Jacuzzi traditional Turkish Hanam ♫ Xmas **CONF:** Thtr 60 Class 35 Board 40 Del from £10 **SERVICES:** Lift air con
CARDS:

★★★★73% Millennium Gloucester Hotel London Kensington
MILLENNIUM HOTELS AND RESORTS
4-18 Harrington Gardens SW7 4LH plan 4 C2
☎ 020 7373 6030 Fax 020 7373 0409
e-mail: sales.gloucester@mill-cop.com
Dir: *opposite Gloucester Rd underground station*

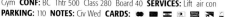

A popular choice for the international market, this hotel is located close to Gloucester Road tube station. Air conditioned bedrooms are furnished in a variety of contemporary styles. Additional amenities are provided in club rooms, which have a dedicated lounge. There is a wide range of eating options, including Singaporean cuisine and more formal Italian food.
ROOMS: 610 en suite (6 fmly) in 439 bedrooms **FACILITIES:** STV Gym **CONF:** BC Thtr 500 Class 280 Board 40 **SERVICES:** Lift air con **PARKING:** 110 **NOTES:** Civ Wed **CARDS:**

★★★★72% Harrington Hall
5-25 Harrington Gardens SW7 4JW plan 4 C2
☎ 020 7396 9696 Fax 020 7396 9090
e-mail: sales@harringtonhall.co.uk
web: www.harringtonhall.co.uk
Dir: *towards Knightsbridge into Gloucester Rd. 2nd right into Harrington Gdns and hotel on left*
This classic Victorian façade conceals a modern, elegant hotel. Bedrooms are spacious, comfortable, well equipped and air conditioned. Additional features include a multi-gym, extensive meeting rooms and a stylish restaurant, which serves a quality carvery at lunchtime and a creative carte menu at dinner.
ROOMS: 200 en suite in 132 bedrooms s £195 **LB FACILITIES:** STV Sauna Gym Xmas **CONF:** BC Thtr 200 Class 80 Board 25 Del £230 **SERVICES:** Lift air con **NOTES:**
CARDS:

★★★★71%
Radisson Edwardian Vanderbilt
Radisson EDWARDIAN
68-86 Cromwell Rd SW7 5BT plan 4 C3
☎ 020 7761 9000 Fax 020 7761 9001
e-mail: resvand@radisson.com
Dir: *A4 into central London on Cromwell Rd. Hotel on left at junct of Gloucester Rd & Cromwell Rd*
This hotel is an ideal base for visitors to the capital. The interior is both cheerful and contemporary. Room facilities are superb - all have air conditioning, modems, several telephone lines, safes and mini-bars. The bar and lounge are popular places to meet, take afternoon tea and just watch the world go by.
ROOMS: 215 en suite (18 fmly) (28 GF) in 113 bedrooms s £79-£195; d £89-£222 **LB FACILITIES:** Fitness room Business centre **CONF:** BC Thtr 100 Class 56 Board 40 **SERVICES:** Lift air con **NOTES:** **CARDS:**

SW7 SOUTH KENSINGTON, continued

★★★★70% Jurys Kensington Hotel
109-113 Queensgate, South Kensington
SW7 5LR plan 4 D2
☎ 020 7589 6300 📠 020 7581 1492
e-mail: Kensington@jurysdoyle.com
Dir: *From A4 take Cromwell Rd, turn right at V&A Museum onto Queensgate, hotel at end on left*
This beautiful building has been carefully refurbished and offers an excellent location for visitors to London. Smartly appointed public areas include an open-plan lobby/bar, Copplestones restaurant with adjoining library lounge and the lively Kavanagh's bar. Bedrooms vary in size and are well equipped with a modern colour theme.
ROOMS: 173 annexe en suite (10 fmly) in 130 bedrooms s £69-£215; d £69-£215 **FACILITIES:** STV Health Club facilities available locally at discounted rate Xmas **CONF:** Thtr 80 Class 45 Board 35 Del from £139 **SERVICES:** Lift air con **NOTES:**
CARDS:

★★★★69% Millennium Baileys Hotel London Kensington
140 Gloucester Rd SW7 4QH plan 4 C3
☎ 020 7373 6000 📠 020 7370 3760
e-mail: reservations@mill-cop.com
Dir: *A4, turn right at Cromwell Hospital into Knaresborough Place, follow to Courtfield Rd to corner of Gloucester Rd, hotel opposite underground*

This elegant hotel has a townhouse feel to it and enjoys a prime location opposite Gloucester Road tube station. Air-conditioned bedrooms are smartly appointed and thoughtfully equipped, particularly the club rooms which have DVD players. Public areas include a stylish, contemporary restaurant and bar. Guests may also use the facilities at its adjacent, larger sister hotel.
ROOMS: 212 en suite in 120 bedrooms s £155; d £250
FACILITIES: STV Gym **CONF:** Thtr 20 Class 18 Board 16
SERVICES: Lift air con **PARKING:** 70
CARDS:

★★★65% Grange Strathmore
41 Queens Gate Gardens SW7 5NB plan 4 C3
☎ 020 7584 0512 📠 020 7584 0246
e-mail: strathmore@grangehotels.com
Dir: *M4 E into Kensington, left into Queens Gate Gardens.*
Formerly the residence of the Earl of Strathmore, this elegant property retains many of its original features. Bedrooms, which vary in shape and size, are appointed to a high standard. Public areas include a selection of meeting rooms, Glamis lounge bar and the chandeliered Earls restaurant.
ROOMS: 77 en suite (10 fmly) in 40 bedrooms s £115-£145; d £130-£170 **LB** **FACILITIES:** STV Xmas **CONF:** Thtr 60 Class 25 Board 26 Del from £135 **SERVICES:** Lift
CARDS:

SW10 WEST BROMPTON
See LONDON plan 1 D/E3

★★★★★69% Conrad London
Chelsea Harbour SW10 0XG
☎ 020 7823 3000 📠 020 7351 6525
e-mail: londoninfo@conradhotels.com
web: www.conradhotels.com
Dir: *A4 to Earls Court Rd S towards river. Right into Kings Rd, left down Lots Rd. Chelsea Harbour in front*
Against the picturesque backdrop of Chelsea Harbour's small marina, this modern hotel offers spacious, comfortable accommodation. All rooms are suites which are superbly equipped, many enjoy splendid views of the marina. In addition, there are also several luxurious penthouse suites. Public areas include a modern bar and restaurant, excellent leisure facilities and extensive meeting and function rooms.
ROOMS: 160 en suite (39 fmly) in 110 bedrooms s £180-£330; d £200-£360 **LB** **FACILITIES:** STV Sauna Solarium Gym Conrad Health Club with beauty treatments Xmas **CONF:** Thtr 280 Class 120 Board 50 Del from £280 **SERVICES:** Lift air con **PARKING:** 17
NOTES: Civ Wed 200 **CARDS:**

SW11 BATTERSEA
See LONDON plan 1 E3

Travelodge (London Battersea)
200 York Rd, Battersea SW11 3SA
☎ 08700 850 950
Dir: *from Wandsworth Bridge southern rdbt, take York Rd A3205 towards Battersea. 0.5m on left*
Travelodge offers good quality, good value, modern accommodation. Ideal for families, the spacious, en suite bedrooms include remote-control TV, tea and coffee-making facilities and luxury beds. Meals can be taken at the nearby family restaurant. For further details consult the Hotel Groups page.
ROOMS: 87 en suite s fr £25; d fr £25

SW19 WIMBLEDON
See LONDON plan 1 D1

○ Premier Lodge (London Merton)
Merantum Way, Merton SW19 1DD

☎ 0870 9906342 📠 0870 9906343
web: www.premierlodge.com
Dir: *exit M25 junct 10 A3 towards Wimbledon. Right onto A295*
ROOMS: 132 en suite **NOTES:** Due to open Spring 2005

W1 WEST END

Top 200 – Town House

★★★★★ Athenaeum
116 Piccadilly W1J 7BJ plan 4 H5
☎ 020 7499 3464 📠 020 7493 1860
e-mail: info@athenaeumhotel.com
web: www.athenaeumhotel.com
Dir: *on Piccadilly, overlooking Green Park*
With a discreet address in the heart of Mayfair, this well-loved hotel has become a favourite with many guests over the years for its efficient service and excellent hospitality. Bedrooms are decorated to the highest standard and some have views over Green Park. A row of Edwardian town houses immediately adjacent to the hotel offer a range of spacious and

continued

well-appointed apartments. Public rooms include Bullochs Restaurant, the Windsor Lounge and a cosy cocktail bar specialising in malt whiskies.

ROOMS: 157 en suite ⊗ in 58 bedrooms s £265; d £285 **LB** **FACILITIES: Spa** STV Sauna Gym Jacuzzi Steam rooms, spa treatments ch fac Xmas **CONF:** BC Thtr 55 Class 35 Board 36 Del £225 **SERVICES:** Lift air con **NOTES:** Civ Wed 80 **CARDS:**

Top 200 – Hotel

★★★★★ ◎◎◎ **Claridge's**

Brook St W1A 2JQ plan 2 H2

☎ 020 7629 8860 📠 020 7499 2210

e-mail: info@claridges.co.uk

The Savoy Group

Dir: *Take 1st turn after Green Park underground station to Berkeley Sq & 4th exit into Davies St. Take 3rd turn right into Brook St*

Once renowned as the resort of kings and princes, Claridge's today continues to set the standards by which other hotels are judged. The sumptuous, air-conditioned bedrooms are elegantly themed to reflect the Victorian or Art Deco architecture of the building. Gordon Ramsay at Claridge's has fast become one of London's most popular dining venues, while the stylish cocktail bar is proving to be equally well supported by residents and non-residents alike. Service throughout is punctilious and thoroughly professional.

ROOMS: 203 en suite (144 fmly) ⊗ in 34 bedrooms **FACILITIES:** STV Gym Beauty & health treatments. Use of sister hotel swimming pool ♫ **CONF:** Thtr 250 Class 130 Board 60 **SERVICES:** Lift air con **NOTES:** Civ Wed 200 **CARDS:**

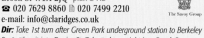

Town House Hotel

Country House Hotel

Travel Accommodation

Top 200 – Hotel

★★★★★ ◎◎◎ **Connaught**

Carlos Place W1K 2AL plan 2 G1

☎ 020 7499 7070 📠 020 7495 3262

e-mail: info@the-connaught.co.uk

The Savoy Group

Dir: *between Grosvenor Sq and Berkeley Sq in Mayfair*

Smaller than some of the major London hotels, The Connaught offers guests a more intimate atmosphere. Couple this with exemplary standards of service and its easy to see why people return time after time. To ensure that every guest is pampered, butlers and valets respond at the touch of a button and nothing is too much trouble. Dining is now in the hands of Angela Hartnett, a protégé of Gordon Ramsay, and the restaurant menu has more than a hint of Italian about it.

ROOMS: 92 en suite s £280-£300; d £390-£425 **LB** **FACILITIES:** STV Gym Fitness studio, Health club facilities at sister hotels **CONF:** Board 18 **SERVICES:** Lift air con **NOTES:** **CARDS:**

Top 200 – Hotel

★★★★★ ◎◎◎ **The Dorchester**

Park Ln W1A 2HJ plan 4 G6

☎ 020 7629 8888 📠 020 7409 0114

e-mail: reservations@dorchesterhotel.com

Dir: *halfway along Park Ln between Hyde Park Corner & Marble Arch*

One of London's finest hotels, The Dorchester is sumptuously decorated. The bedrooms, which have been refurbished, are beautifully appointed and feature huge, luxurious baths in marble bathrooms. Leading off from the foyer, The Promenade is the perfect setting for afternoon tea or drinks. In the evenings guests can relax to the sound of live jazz in the bar, and enjoy a cocktail or an Italian meal. Other dining options include the traditional Grill Restaurant and the award-winning Oriental, offering Cantonese cuisine.

ROOMS: 250 en suite ⊗ in 34 bedrooms s £323-£358.37; d £417.13-£546.38 **LB** **FACILITIES: Spa** STV Sauna Solarium Gym Jacuzzi The Dorchester Spa Health club ♫ ch fac Xmas **CONF:** Thtr 500 Class 300 Board 42 **SERVICES:** Lift air con **PARKING:** 21 **NOTES:** Civ Wed 500 **CARDS:**

London

W1 WEST END

Top 200 – Hotel

★★★★★ ◎◎ **The Ritz**
150 Piccadilly W1J 9BR plan 5 A6
☎ 020 7493 8181 📠 020 7493 2687
e-mail: enquire@theritzlondon.com
web: www.theritzlondon.com
Dir: *from Hyde Park Corner E on Piccadilly. Hotel on right after Green Park*

Synonymous with style, sophistication and attention to detail, The Ritz continues its stately progress into the third millennium, having recaptured much of its former glory. All bedrooms are comfortably furnished in Louis XVI style, with fine marble bathrooms and every imaginable comfort. Elegant reception rooms include the Palm Court with its legendary afternoon teas, the beautifully refurbished Rivoli Bar and the sumptuous Ritz Restaurant, complete with gold chandeliers and extraordinary trompe-l'oeil decoration.

ROOMS: 133 en suite ⊗ in 36 bedrooms s fr £353; d fr £429 LB **FACILITIES:** STV Gym ♫ ch fac Xmas **CONF:** Thtr 60 Class 25 Board 32 Del from £399 **SERVICES:** Lift air con **NOTES:** ✈ Civ Wed 70 **CARDS:**

Top 200 – Hotel

★★★★★ ◎ **Four Seasons Hotel London**
Hamilton Place, Park Ln W1A 1AZ plan 4 G5
☎ 020 7499 0888 📠 020 7493 1895
e-mail: fsh.london@fourseasons.com
Dir: *from Piccadilly into Old Park Ln. Then Hamilton Place*

This long-established popular hotel is discreetly located near Hyde Park Corner, in the heart of Mayfair. It successfully combines modern efficiencies with traditional luxury. Guest care is consistently of the highest order, even down to the smallest detail of the personalised wake-up call. The bedrooms are elegant and spacious, and the unique

continued

conservatory rooms are particularly special. Spacious public areas include extensive conference and banqueting facilities, Lane's bar and fine-dining restaurant and an elegant lounge where wonderful afternoon teas are served.

ROOMS: 220 en suite ⊗ in 96 bedrooms s £358.38-£1762.50; d £423-£2585 LB **FACILITIES:** STV Gym Fitness club ♫ ch fac Xmas **CONF:** BC Thtr 400 Class 200 Board 70 **SERVICES:** Lift air con **PARKING:** 72 **NOTES:** Civ Wed 400 **CARDS:**

★★★★★71% ◎◎◎
Hyatt Regency London - The Churchill
30 Portman Square W1A 4ZX plan 2 F2
☎ 020 7486 5800 📠 020 7486 1255
e-mail: churchill@interconti.com
Dir: *from Marble Arch rdbt, follow signs for Oxford Circus onto Oxford St. Left turn after 2nd lights onto Portman St. Hotel on left*

This smart hotel enjoys a central location overlooking Portman Square. Excellent conference, hairdressing and beauty facilities and a fitness room make this the ideal choice for both corporate and leisure guests. Two floors of executive club bedrooms benefit from a host of facilities and extras. The Terrace Restaurant offers a relaxed atmosphere, while Locanda Locatelli benefits from the enormous talents of Giorgio Locatelli and offers fine Italian cuisine.

ROOMS: 445 en suite ⊗ in 156 bedrooms **FACILITIES:** STV Sauna Gym ♫ Xmas **CONF:** BC Thtr 250 Class 160 Board 68 **SERVICES:** Lift air con **PARKING:** 48 **NOTES:** ✈ Civ Wed 300 **CARDS:**

★★★★★71% ◎◎
InterContinental London
1 Hamilton Place, Hyde Park Corner W1J 7QY plan 4 G5
☎ 020 7409 3131 📠 020 7493 3476
e-mail: london@interconti.com
Dir: *at Hyde Park Corner, on corner of Park Lane and Piccadilly*

INTER-CONTINENTAL. HOTELS AND RESORTS

A well-known and well-loved landmark on Hyde Park Corner, the hotel enjoys some of the best views in London from the upper floors and lounges. Bedrooms vary from inner courtyard rooms to spacious suites. The smart marbled foyer houses the Observatory lounge for light meals and afternoon teas, and the Coffee House for breakfast and all-day dining. The jewel in the hotel's crown is Le Soufflé Restaurant.

ROOMS: 458 en suite ⊗ in 312 bedrooms s fr £233; d fr £257 **FACILITIES:** STV Sauna Gym Jacuzzi Beauty treatments, Health Club, Horse riding, Crazy golf, Tennis courts nearby ♫ Xmas **CONF:** BC Thtr 750 Class 340 Board 62 **SERVICES:** Lift air con **PARKING:** 100 **NOTES:** ✈ Civ Wed 750 **CARDS:**

★★★★★70% ◎◎ **Le Meridien Piccadilly**
21 Piccadilly W1J 0BH plan 3 B1
☎ 0870 400 8400 📠 020 7437 3574
e-mail: lmpiccres@lemeridien.com
Dir: *100mtrs from Piccadilly Circus*

This elegant hotel enjoys a prime central location on the doorstep of Piccadilly, Regent Street, Soho and theatreland. Thoughtfully equipped bedrooms vary in size and style and include some elegant refurbished rooms and stylish, spacious suites. The hotel boasts the renowned Champneys health spa, the contemporary airy Terrace Restaurant and the palatial Oak Room lounge where a pianist accompanies afternoon teas.

ROOMS: 266 en suite (19 fmly) ⊗ in 87 bedrooms **FACILITIES:** STV Squash Sauna Solarium Gym Jacuzzi Beauty treatments Aerobics Massage **CONF:** BC Thtr 245 Class 160 Board 80 **SERVICES:** Lift air con **NOTES:** ✈ Civ Wed 120 **CARDS:**

London

★★★★★ 68%
London Marriott Hotel Park Lane
140 Park Ln W1K 7AA plan 2 F2
☎ 020 7493 7000 020 7493 8333
e-mail: mhrs.parklane@marriotthotels.com
Dir: *From Hyde Park Corner left on Park Ln onto A4202, 0.8m. At Marble Arch onto Park Ln. Take 1st left onto North Row. Hotel on left*
This modern and stylish hotel is situated in a prominent position in the heart of central London. Bedrooms are all superbly appointed and air conditioned. Public rooms include a popular lounge/bar, and there are wonderful leisure facilities and an executive lounge.
ROOMS: 157 en suite in 95 bedrooms s fr £265; d fr £265 **LB**
FACILITIES: STV Gym Steam Room Xmas **CONF:** BC Thtr 72 Class 33 Board 42 **SERVICES:** Lift air con **NOTES:** in restaurant
CARDS:

★★★★★ 65% ***Le Meridien Grosvenor House***
Park Ln W1A 3AA plan 2 G1
☎ 0870 400 8500 020 7493 3341
e-mail: grosvenor.enquiries@lemeridien.com
Dir: *Marble Arch, halfway down Park Ln*
Majestically positioned overlooking Hyde Park, this hotel enjoys a world-wide reputation. The property is appointed to a high standard with deluxe bedrooms, Royal Club Rooms and Suites offering an impressive range of facilities. The Park Room is ideal for refreshment at any time of day. This hotel excels at international award events and boasts some of the finest function facilities in London.
ROOMS: 453 en suite (140 fmly) in 154 bedrooms **FACILITIES: Spa** STV Sauna Solarium Gym Jacuzzi Health & Fitness centre/Beauty salon **CONF:** Thtr 110 Class 60 Board 36 **SERVICES:** Lift air con **PARKING:** 95 **NOTES:** Civ Wed 100
CARDS:

★★★★★ 63% ***Radisson Edwardian May Fair Hotel***
Stratton St W1J 8LL plan 5 A6
☎ 020 7629 7777 020 7629 1459
e-mail: mayfair@interconti.com
Dir: *from Hyde Park Corner or Piccadilly left onto Stratton St and hotel on left*
This well-established hotel with many return guests has an intimate atmosphere. Air-conditioned bedrooms are of varying sizes, including suites and business-dedicated rooms with a useful range of amenities. The choice of eating options includes the Opus 70 restaurant offering modern British cuisine. There is also a staffed business centre, leisure centre and a conference auditorium.
ROOMS: 289 en suite (14 fmly) in 148 bedrooms **FACILITIES:** STV Sauna Solarium Gym **CONF:** Thtr 292 Class 108 Board 60 **SERVICES:** Lift air con **NOTES:** Civ Wed 250
CARDS:

★★★★ 76% ***The Montcalm-Hotel Nikko London***
Great Cumberland Place W1H 7TW plan 2 F2
☎ 020 7402 4288 020 7724 9180
e-mail: reservations@montcalm.co.uk
Dir: *2 minutes' walk north from Marble Arch station*
Ideally located on a secluded crescent close to Marble Arch, this charming Georgian property is named after the Marquis de Montcalm. Japanese-owned, the hotel offers extremely comfortable accommodation, ranging from standard to duplex 'junior' and penthouse suites. Staff are thoughtful and the stylish restaurant has a reputation for creative, modern cooking. Lunch is particularly good value for money. Restaurant prices include a half bottle of wine per person.

ROOMS: 120 en suite in 58 bedrooms **FACILITIES:** STV **CONF:** Thtr 80 Class 36 Board 36 **SERVICES:** Lift air con **PARKING:** 10
NOTES: **CARDS:**

★★★★ 76% **The Westbury**
Bond St W1S 2YF plan 3 A2
☎ 020 7629 7755 020 7495 1163
e-mail: reservations@westburymayfair.com
Dir: *from Oxford Circus S down Regent St, right onto Conduit St, hotel at junct of Conduit St & Bond St*
A well-known favourite with an international clientele, The Westbury is located at the heart of London's finest shopping district and provides a calm atmosphere away from the hubbub of the city. The standards of accommodation are high throughout. Reception rooms offer a good choice for both relaxing and eating, including the Polo Bar for cocktails.
ROOMS: 247 en suite in 150 bedrooms s fr £240; d fr £240 **LB**
FACILITIES: STV Gym Fitness centre, Business centre Xmas
CONF: BC Thtr 120 Class 55 Board 35 Del from £267 **SERVICES:** Lift air con **NOTES:** **CARDS:**

★★★★ 75% **The Chesterfield**
35 Charles St, Mayfair W1J 5EB plan 4 H6
☎ 020 7491 2622 020 7491 4793
e-mail: bookch@rchmail.com
Dir: *From Hyde Park corner along Piccadilly, left into Half Moon St. At end left and 1st right into Queens St, then right into Charles St*
Quiet elegance and an atmosphere of exclusivity characterise this hotel, which has now completed an ambitious refurbishment programme. Bedrooms have been decorated in a variety of contemporary styles, some with fabric walls, and marble-clad bathrooms have heated floors and mirrors. Bedrooms and public areas are air conditioned.
ROOMS: 110 en suite (7 fmly) in 52 bedrooms s fr £160; d fr £175 **LB** **FACILITIES:** STV Xmas **CONF:** BC Thtr 120 Class 45 Board 45 Del from £195 **SERVICES:** Lift air con **NOTES:** Civ Wed 120
CARDS:

★★★★ 74%
London Marriott Hotel Grosvenor Square
Grosvenor Square W1K 6JP plan 2 G2
☎ 020 7493 1232 020 7491 3201
e-mail: businesscentre@londonmarriott.co.uk
web: www.marriott.com/LONDT
Dir: *M4 E to Cromwell Rd through Knightsbridge to Hyde Park Corner. Park Lane right at Brook Gate onto Upper Brook St to Grosvenor Sq*
Situated adjacent to Grosvenor Square in the heart of Mayfair, the hotel combines the best of a relatively peaceful setting with convenient access to the city, West End and some of the most

continued on p360

London

W1 WEST END

exclusive shopping in London. Bedrooms and public areas are furnished and decorated to a high standard and retain a traditional elegance for which the hotel is known.
ROOMS: 221 en suite (26 fmly) in 120 bedrooms **FACILITIES:** STV Gym Exercise & fitness centre Xmas **CONF:** BC Thtr 900 Class 500 Board 120 **SERVICES:** Lift air con **PARKING:** 80 **NOTES:** Civ Wed **CARDS:**

★★★★74% The Washington Mayfair Hotel
5-7 Curzon St, Mayfair W1J 5HE plan 4 H6
☎ 020 7499 7000 020 7495 6172
e-mail: sales@washington-mayfair.co.uk
Dir: *Green Park station take Piccadilly exit and turn right. Take 4th street on right into Curzon St.*
Situated in the heart of Mayfair, this stylish, independently owned hotel offers a very high standard of accommodation. Personalised, friendly service is a highlight. Bedrooms are attractively furnished and provide high levels of comfort. The hotel is also a popular venue for afternoon tea and refreshments, served in the marbled and wood-panelled public areas.
ROOMS: 171 en suite in 94 bedrooms **FACILITIES:** STV Gym ch fac Xmas **CONF:** BC Thtr 110 Class 40 Board 36 **SERVICES:** Lift air con **NOTES:** **CARDS:**

★★★★73%
Radisson Edwardian Berkshire
350 Oxford St W1N 0BY plan 2 H2
☎ 020 7629 7474 020 7629 8156
e-mail: resberk@radisson.com
Dir: *opposite Bond St underground. Entrance on Marylebone Lane.*
A friendly atmosphere prevails at this elegant hotel, centrally located behind Oxford Street's major department stores. Public areas have a boutique feel and include a contemporary bar, smart restaurant and a selection of meeting and conference rooms. Well-equipped bedrooms vary in size, though all have undergone a stylish refurbishment.
ROOMS: 148 en suite (10 fmly) in 78 bedrooms s £145-£290; d £175-£335 (incl. bkfst) **LB** **FACILITIES:** STV **CONF:** BC Thtr 40 Class 16 Board 16 Del from £280 **SERVICES:** Lift air con **NOTES:** **CARDS:**

★★★★72% Sherlock Holmes
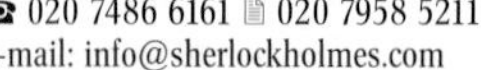

108 Baker St W1U 6LJ plan 2 F4
☎ 020 7486 6161 020 7958 5211
e-mail: info@sherlockholmes.com
Dir: *from Marylebone Flyover onto Marylebone Rd and at Baker St turn right for hotel on left*
Chic and modern, this boutique-style hotel is conveniently located close to a number of London underground lines and railway stations. Public rooms include a popular bar, sited just inside the main entrance, and Sherlock's Grill, where the mesquite wood-burning stove is a feature of the cooking. The hotel also features an indoor health suite and a relaxing lounge.
ROOMS: 119 en suite in 60 bedrooms s £186.82-£500; d £186.82-£500 **FACILITIES:** **Spa** STV Sauna Gym Xmas **CONF:** Thtr 50 Class 40 Board 30 **SERVICES:** Lift air con **NOTES:** in restaurant Civ Wed 50 **CARDS:**

Packed in a hurry?
Ironing facilities should be available at all star levels, either in rooms or on request

★★★★71%
Millennium Hotel London Mayfair
Grosvenor Square W1K 2HP plan 2 G1
☎ 020 7629 9400 020 7629 7736
e-mail: sales.mayfair@mill-cop.com
Dir: *on S side of Grosvenor Square - near Park Lane and Oxford St.*

This hotel benefits from a prestigious location in the heart of Mayfair, close to Bond Street. Smart bedrooms are generally spacious and club-floor rooms have use of their own lounge with complimentary refreshments. A choice of bars and dining options include the stylish Brian Turner Restaurant offering classic British food. Conference facilities along with a fitness room complete the picture.
ROOMS: 348 en suite in 265 bedrooms s £165-£265; d £185-£285 (incl. bkfst) **LB** **FACILITIES:** STV Gym ch fac Xmas **CONF:** BC Thtr 450 Class 250 Board 70 **SERVICES:** Lift air con **NOTES:** Civ Wed 250 **CARDS:**

Town House

★★★★ Grange Fitzrovia
20-28 Bolsover St W1W 5NB plan 3 A4
☎ 020 7467 7000 020 7636 5085
e-mail: fitzrovia@grangehotels.com
The Fitzrovia sits in a quiet street near the Tottenham Court Road and Regents Park. Bedrooms are richly decorated and feature polished wood furnishings and marbled bathrooms. Some also have air conditioning. The small lobby lounge is luxurious and comfortable.
ROOMS: 88 en suite in 40 bedrooms s £195-£220; d £195-£220 **FACILITIES:** STV Xmas **CONF:** Thtr 100 Class 45 Board 40 Del from £235 **SERVICES:** Lift **NOTES:** **CARDS:**

★★★★70% Jurys Clifton-Ford
47 Welbeck St W1M 8DN plan 2 G3
☎ 020 7486 6600 020 7486 7492
e-mail: cliftonford@jurysdoyle.com
Dir: *from Portland Place, turn into New Cavendish St. Welbeck St last turning on left*
This well kept hotel enjoys a central location just 5 minutes' walk from Oxford Street and fashionable Bond Street. Bedrooms vary in space and style and include a number of penthouse apartments with balconies. Public areas include an excellent leisure club with a good-sized swimming pool, extensive conference facilities and a spacious lounge, bar and restaurant.
ROOMS: 255 en suite (7 fmly) in 130 bedrooms s £101-£225; d £101-£220 **LB** **FACILITIES:** STV CCTV Sauna Solarium Gym Jacuzzi Leisure club Health/beauty treatments Dance studio **CONF:** Thtr 120 Class 70 Board 40 **SERVICES:** Lift air con **NOTES:** in restaurant **CARDS:**

★★★★70% **London Marriott Hotel Marble Arch**

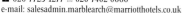

134 George St W1H 5DN plan 2 F3
☎ 020 7723 1277 020 7402 0666
e-mail: salesadmin.marblearch@marriotthotels.co.uk
Dir: *from Marble Arch turn into Edgware Rd, then 4th right into George St. Left into Forset St for entrance*

This modern hotel, conveniently situated just off the Edgware Road and close to Oxford Street shops, offers smart, well-equipped, air-conditioned bedrooms. Public areas are stylish but compact, and include a refurbished bar, a restaurant and a smart leisure club. A secure underground car park is available.

ROOMS: 240 en suite (100 fmly) in 120 bedrooms s fr £189 **LB** **FACILITIES:** STV supervised Sauna Solarium Gym Jacuzzi Xmas **CONF:** Thtr 150 Class 75 Board 80 **SERVICES:** Lift air con **PARKING:** 80 **NOTES:** **CARDS:**

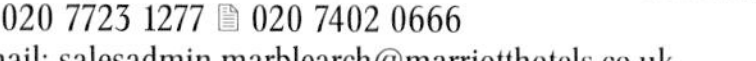

★★★★70% ***Radisson Edwardian Grafton Hotel***

130 Tottenham Court Rd W1T 5AY plan 3 B4
☎ 020 7388 4131 020 7387 7394
e-mail: resgraf@radisson.com
Dir: *Central London, along Euston Rd, onto Tottenham Court Rd. Past Warren St underground station*

Ongoing investment and a commitment to providing excellent levels of hospitality and service sees The Grafton going from strength to strength. Public areas are smart and a popular meeting venue. Bedrooms come in a variety of sizes; all have been fully refurbished to provide excellent comfort and facilities. The hotel is well placed next to Warren Street tube station.

ROOMS: 330 en suite (23 fmly) in 55 bedrooms **FACILITIES:** STV Gym Fitness room **CONF:** BC Thtr 100 Class 50 Board 30 **SERVICES:** Lift air con **NOTES:** **CARDS:**

★★★★70% **Radisson SAS Portman**

22 Portman Square W1H 7BG plan 2 F3
☎ 020 7208 6000 020 7208 6001
e-mail: sales.london@radissonsas.com
Dir: *100mtrs N of Oxford St and 500mtrs E of Edgware Rd*

This smart, popular hotel enjoys a prime location a short stroll from Oxford Street and close to all the city's major attractions. The spacious, well-equipped bedrooms are themed ranging from Oriental through to classical and contemporary Italian décor. Public areas include extensive conference facilities, a bar and a smart restaurant.

ROOMS: 272 en suite (93 fmly) in 129 bedrooms s £186.82; d £222.07 **LB** **FACILITIES:** STV Sauna Solarium Gym Xmas **CONF:** BC Thtr 600 Class 280 Board 70 **SERVICES:** Lift air con **PARKING:** 400 **NOTES:** Civ Wed **CARDS:**

★★★★67% ***The Berners Hotel***

Berners St W1A 3BE plan 3 B3
☎ 020 7666 2000 020 7666 2001
e-mail: berners@berners.co.uk
web: www.thebernershotel.co.uk

In the heart of London's West End, adjacent to Oxford Street, this traditional hotel has an elegant atmosphere. Marble columns and ornately carved ceilings are features of the luxurious lounge, a popular venue for afternoon tea. The elegant restaurant has an airy feel to it. Bedrooms are equipped with modern facilities and the clubrooms are particularly stylish.

ROOMS: 216 en suite in 100 bedrooms **FACILITIES:** STV **CONF:** BC Thtr 160 Class 80 Board 40 **SERVICES:** Lift **NOTES:** Civ Wed 70 **CARDS:**

Town House

★★★★ **Best Western Premier Shaftesbury**

65 - 73 Shaftesbury Av, Piccadilly W1V 6EX plan 3 B2
☎ 020 7871 6000
e-mail: reservations@shaftesburyhotel.co.uk
Dir: *from Piccadilly Circus 300yds up Shaftesbury Avenue, junction of Dean Street & Shaftesbury Avenue*

This smart town house enjoys a central location just minutes' walk from Covent Garden, in the heart of London's Theatreland. Bedrooms are stylishly appointed with a host of extra facilities and include a number of suites and four-poster rooms. A gym and small meeting room are available and guests may charge food taken in the adjacent Indian restaurant to their hotel bill.

ROOMS: 67 en suite (2 fmly) in 28 bedrooms s £155-£195; d £250-£275 **LB** **FACILITIES:** STV Gym **CONF:** BC Board 12 Del from £199 **SERVICES:** Lift air con **NOTES:** **CARDS:**

★★★66% **The Mandeville**

Mandeville Place W1U 2BE plan 2 G3
☎ 020 7935 5599 020 7935 9588
e-mail: info@mandeville.co.uk
web: www.mandeville.co.uk
Dir: *off Oxford Street and Wigmore St near Bond St underground station*

This elegant Edwardian building is situated only a short stroll from Oxford Street. Guests have a useful choice of eating and drinking options, and 24-hour room service is also available.

continued on p362

W1 WEST END

The owners are currently carrying out notable refurbishment, which includes a number of impressive new bedrooms with a stylish contemporary feel.
ROOMS: 155 en suite ⊗ in 30 bedrooms s £200; d £220 **LB**
FACILITIES: STV **CONF:** Thtr 35 Class 20 Board 20 Del from £200
SERVICES: Lift air con **NOTES:**
CARDS:

See advert on page 361

★★★66% Mostyn

4 Bryanston St W1H 7BY plan 2 F2
☎ 020 7935 2361 🖷 020 7487 2759
e-mail: info@mostynhotel.co.uk
web: www.mostynhotel.co.uk
Dir: *A40(M) Marylebone Rd, close to Marble Arch and Bond St underground*
The Mostyn enjoys an enviable location, just off Oxford Street, in the heart of the West End. Originally built as a residence for Lady Back, a lady-in-waiting at the court of George II, the hotel retains many original features. Well-equipped, modern bedrooms feature air conditioning and public rooms include a stylish open-plan lounge and cocktail bar.
ROOMS: 121 en suite (15 fmly) ⊗ in 54 bedrooms s £135-£145; d £145-£185 **FACILITIES:** STV **CONF:** Thtr 130 Class 70 Board 50
SERVICES: Lift air con **NOTES:**
CARDS:

London

★★★63% Grange Langham Court

31-35 Langham St W1W 6BU plan 3 A3
☎ 020 7436 6622 🖷 020 7436 2303
e-mail: langhamcourt@grangehotels.com
Dir: *west end of Central London. Just off Regents Street, near Oxford Street and Bond Street.*
Situated in a quiet, secluded street between Regents Park and Oxford Circus, this hotel has an elegant tiled façade. Formerly a nursing home, it now provides compact and well-equipped accommodation. Public areas include a wine bar serving snacks and light meals, a comfortable lounge and a basement dining room.
ROOMS: 58 en suite ⊗ in 20 bedrooms s £150-£210; d £165-£210
FACILITIES: STV Xmas **CONF:** Thtr 80 Class 35 Board 35 Del from £198 **SERVICES:** Lift **NOTES:**
CARDS:

U Radisson Edwardian Sussex

19-25 Granville Place W1H 6PE plan 2 G2
☎ 020 7408 0130 🖷 020 7493 2070
e-mail: ressuss@radisson.com
Dir: *off Oxford Street. Left to Portman St, right into Granville Place.*
At the time of going to press, the star classification for this hotel was not confirmed. Please refer to the AA internet site www.theAA.com for current information.
ROOMS: 101 en suite (12 fmly) ⊗ in 70 bedrooms s fr £203; d fr £254 **LB** **FACILITIES:** Gym **CONF:** BC Board 10 **SERVICES:** Lift air con **NOTES:** **CARDS:**

○ *Brown's*

Albemarle St, Mayfair W1S 4BP
☎ 020 7493 6020 🖷 020 7493 9381
e-mail: brownshotel@brownshotel.com
web: www.roccofortehotels.com
This landmark hotel is currently closed for a major refurbishment of bedrooms and public areas. The hotel is due to re-open in April 2005. Please see the AA website (www.theAA.com) for further information.
ROOMS: 118 en suite **NOTES:** Closed for refurbishment til Spring 2005

W2 BAYSWATER, PADDINGTON

Town House

★★★★ Royal Park

3 Westbourne Ter, Lancaster Gate, Hyde Park W2 3UL
plan 2 D2
☎ 020 7479 6600 🖷 020 7479 6601
e-mail: info@theroyalpark.com web: www.theroyalpark.com
Close to Lancaster Gate and minutes' walk from Hyde Park, this delightful hotel has been created from three Grade II listed town houses dating back to 1842. Stylish, comfortable bedrooms and suites are thoughtfully equipped for both leisure and business guests and most boast half-tester or four-poster beds. Complimentary afternoon tea, champagne and canapés are served in the elegant drawing rooms and 24-hour room service is available.
ROOMS: 48 en suite (7 GF) ⊗ in 15 bedrooms **FACILITIES:** STV
SERVICES: Lift air con **PARKING:** 10 **NOTES:**
CARDS:

★★★★75% ✿✿ *Royal Lancaster*

Lancaster Ter W2 2TY plan 2 D2
☎ 020 7262 6737 🖷 020 7724 3191
e-mail: book@royallancaster.com
Dir: *above Lancaster Gate Underground Station*
This smart hotel has an excellent range of public facilities, including impressive conference rooms, 24-hour business centre and car park. The rosette awarded Nipa Thai is among a choice of drinking and eating options; and more developments are planned. Bedrooms are modern and well equipped, with upper floors enjoying stunning views across London.
ROOMS: 416 en suite (11 fmly) ⊗ in 111 bedrooms **FACILITIES:** STV ♫ **CONF:** BC Thtr 1500 Class 650 Board 40 **SERVICES:** Lift air con
PARKING: 100 **NOTES:** **CARDS:**

Town House

★★★★ The Abbey Court

20 Pembridge Gardens, Kensington W2 4DU plan 2 A1
☎ 020 7221 7518 🖷 020 7792 0858
e-mail: info@abbeycourthotel.co.uk
web: www.abbeycourthotel.co.uk
Dir: *2mins from Notting Hill Gate underground station*
Situated in Notting Hill and close to Kensington, this five-storey Victorian town house stands in a quiet side road. Rooms are individually decorated and have marble bathrooms with jacuzzi baths. Room service is available for light snacks and full English breakfasts can be enjoyed in the conservatory.
ROOMS: 22 en suite (1 fmly) (3 GF) ⊗ in 10 bedrooms s £105-£159; d £135-£250 (incl. bkfst) **FACILITIES:** **Spa** STV ch fac
CONF: BC Board 10 **NOTES:**
CARDS:

Town House

★★★★ Pembridge Court

34 Pembridge Gardens W2 4DX plan 2 A1
☎ 020 7229 9977 🖷 020 7727 4982
e-mail: reservations@pemct.co.uk
web: www.pemct.co.uk
Dir: *off Bayswater Rd at Notting Hill Gate by underground station*
This attractive Victorian town house is in a residential street

continued

near the Portobello Market and Notting Hill Gate tube. Individually styled bedrooms are generally spacious and most are air conditioned. Public areas include two spacious lounges, a small conference room and an airy breakfast room. The hotel features a collection of antique clothing and fans.
ROOMS: 20 en suite (4 fmly) (5 GF) s £125-£165; d £160-£195 (incl. bkfst) **FACILITIES:** STV Membership of local Health Club **CONF:** BC Board 12 **SERVICES:** Lift air con **PARKING:** 2 **NOTES:** ⊗ in restaurant RS 24 Dec-1 Jan
CARDS:

★★★72% ***The Gresham Hyde Park***
66 Lancaster Gate W2 3NZ plan 2 C1
☎ 020 7262 5090 📠 020 7723 1244
e-mail: reservations@gresham-hydeparkhotel.com

Centrally located in Lancaster Gate, this landmark building with its historic stucco façade offers attractive public rooms and modern bedrooms that are air conditioned, of comfortable proportions and well equipped. Room service complements the availability of full restaurant and bar services. A modern meeting room and a fitness centre are also available.
ROOMS: 188 en suite (21 fmly) ⊗ in 77 bedrooms **FACILITIES:** STV Gym **CONF:** Thtr 35 Class 18 Board 18 **SERVICES:** Lift air con **NOTES:** ✈ **CARDS:**

★★★68% **Corus hotel Hyde Park**
1-7 Lancaster Gate W2 3LG plan 2 D2
☎ 0870 609 6161 📠 020 7724 8666
e-mail: londonhydepark@corushotels.com
Dir: *200yds from Lancaster Gate underground. 0.25m from Paddington Station*

This hotel has undergone a massive refurbishment programme. New bedrooms have been fitted out with modern colour schemes, good lighting and attention to detail. Some have air conditioning. Public areas include the popular Olio's restaurant, complete with pizza oven.
ROOMS: 401 en suite (10 fmly) ⊗ in 360 bedrooms s £119-£300; d £119-£300 **LB** **FACILITIES:** STV **CONF:** Thtr 60 Class 18 Board 24 Del from £140 **SERVICES:** Lift **NOTES:** ✈
CARDS:

★★★63% **Berjaya Eden Park Hotel**
35-39 Inverness Ter, Bayswater W2 3JS plan 2 B2
☎ 020 7221 2220 📠 020 7221 2286
e-mail: edenpark@dircon.co.uk
Dir: *from Marble Arch, over main rdbt onto Bayswater Rd. Right into Queensway, 1st left into Inverness Terrace*

Situated within easy reach of Oxford Street shops, West End attractions and minutes' walk from both Queensway and Bayswater underground stations, this is a well-located, friendly hotel. Bedrooms are attractively presented and a range of rooms is available. Public areas feature a spacious restaurant and a cosy bar.
ROOMS: 75 en suite 61 annexe en suite (8 fmly) ⊗ in 42 bedrooms s £86; d £129 **FACILITIES:** STV **CONF:** Thtr 50 Class 50 Board 25 **SERVICES:** Lift **NOTES:** ✈ **CARDS:**

★★71% **Delmere**
130 Sussex Gardens, Hyde Park W2 1UB plan 2 D2
☎ 020 7706 3344 📠 020 7262 1863
e-mail: delmerehotel@compuserve.com
Dir: *M25 take A40 to London, exit at Paddington. Along Westbourne Terrace and into Sussex Gdns*

This friendly, privately owned hotel is situated within walking distance of Paddington Station, Hyde Park and Marble Arch. The smartly presented bedrooms are extremely well equipped and include some ground-floor rooms. A small bar, a comfortable, elegant lounge and an Italian-style restaurant complete the picture.
ROOMS: 36 en suite (6 GF) ⊗ in 10 bedrooms s £88.20-£109; d £108.90-£121 (incl. cont bkfst) **LB** **FACILITIES:** STV **SERVICES:** Lift **PARKING:** 2 **NOTES:** ✈ **CARDS:**

W3 ACTON
See LONDON plan 1 C3

⇧ Travelodge (London Park Royal)
A40 Western Ave, Acton W3 0TE
☎ 08700 850 950 ▯ 020 8752 1134
Travelodge offers good quality, good value, modern accommodation. Ideal for families, the spacious, en suite bedrooms include remote-control TV, tea and coffee-making facilities and luxury beds. Meals can be taken at the nearby family restaurant. For further details consult the Hotel Groups page.
ROOMS: 64 en suite s fr £45; d fr £45

W6 HAMMERSMITH
See LONDON plan 1 D3

★★★72% *Novotel London West*
1 Shortlands W6 8DR
☎ 020 8741 1555 ▯ 020 8741 2120
e-mail: H0737@accor-hotels.com

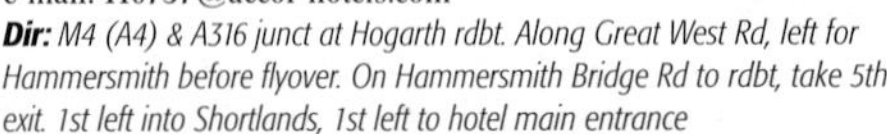

Dir: *M4 (A4) & A316 junct at Hogarth rdbt. Along Great West Rd, left for Hammersmith before flyover. On Hammersmith Bridge Rd to rdbt, take 5th exit. 1st left into Shortlands, 1st left to hotel main entrance*
Situated between Heathrow Airport and the West End, this substantial, purpose-built hotel is a popular base for both business and leisure travellers. Spacious, air-conditioned bedrooms boast a good range of extras and many have additional beds, making them suitable for families. The hotel also has its own paying car park and boasts one of the largest convention centres in Europe.
ROOMS: 629 en suite (148 fmly) ⊘ in 473 bedrooms **FACILITIES:** STV Snooker Gym **CONF:** BC Thtr 1000 Class 525 Board 200 **SERVICES:** Lift air con **PARKING:** 240 **NOTES:** Civ Wed 1400
CARDS:

★★★64% Vencourt
255 King St, Hammersmith W6 9LU
☎ 020 8563 8855 ▯ 020 8563 9988
Dir: *Central London on A4 to Hammersmith, follow A315 towards Chiswick*
This modern hotel provides good-value accommodation with city views from the higher floors. The hotel has open-plan public areas, including a lounge bar, where snacks are served all day, and an airy restaurant for more substantial meals. Smart, well-equipped conference and meeting facilities are also available.
ROOMS: 120 en suite (25 fmly) ⊘ in 18 bedrooms s £89-£109; d £99-£109 LB **FACILITIES:** STV Xmas **CONF:** BC Thtr 170 Class 86 Board 46 Del from £125 **SERVICES:** Lift **PARKING:** 27
CARDS:

W8 KENSINGTON

Top 200 – Hotel

★★★★★ ⊛⊛⊛ Royal Garden Hotel
2-24 Kensington High St W8 4PT plan 4 B5
☎ 020 7937 8000 ▯ 020 7361 1991
e-mail: sales@royalgardenhotel.co.uk
web: www.royalgardenhotel.co.uk
Dir: *next to Kensington Palace*
Situated in fashionable Kensington, this well-known landmark hotel is just a short walk from the Albert Hall and London's smart shops. Well-equipped, attractive bedrooms vary in size and overlook either Hyde Park or the Kensington rooftops. The hotel boasts a number of eating and drinking options; among these is their showcase restaurant, The Tenth, which offers fantastic views over the city and the park.

ROOMS: 396 en suite (19 fmly) ⊘ in 164 bedrooms s £288-£394; d £358-£429 **FACILITIES: Spa** STV Sauna Solarium Gym Health & fitness centre ♫ Xmas **CONF:** BC Thtr 550 Class 260 Board 80 **SERVICES:** Lift air con **PARKING:** 160 **NOTES:** ✗ Civ Wed 400
CARDS:

Top 200 – Town House

★★★★★ ⊛ Milestone Hotel & Apartments
1 Kensington Court W8 5DL plan 4 B4
☎ 020 7917 1000 ▯ 020 7917 1010
e-mail: guestservicesms@rchmail.com
Dir: *M4 into Central London. Into Warwick Rd, then right into Kensington High St. Hotel 400yds past Kensington underground*
This delightful, stylish town house enjoys a wonderful location opposite Kensington Palace; just minutes' walk from the elegant shops on Kensington High Street and Knightsbridge. Individually themed bedrooms include a selection of stunning suites and are equipped with every conceivable extra including DVDs and videos. Public areas include a luxurious lounge, where afternoon tea is served, a delightful panelled bar, a sumptuous restaurant and a small gym.
ROOMS: 57 en suite (3 fmly) (2 GF) ⊘ in 22 bedrooms s £305.50-£951.75; d £305.50-£951.75 LB **FACILITIES:** STV Sauna Gym Jacuzzi Health Club ♫ Xmas **CONF:** Thtr 30 Board 36 Del from £245 **SERVICES:** Lift air con **NOTES:** Civ Wed 30
CARDS:

Town House

★★★★ Kensington House
15-16 Prince of Wales Ter W8 5PQ plan 4 B4
☎ 020 7937 2345 📠 020 7368 6700
e-mail: sales@kenhouse.com
web: www.kenhouse.com
Dir: *off Kensington High St, opposite Kensington Palace*
This beautiful 19th-century property has been elegantly restored to provide contemporary, very comfortable and well-equipped accommodation in a quiet road just off Kensington High Street and the park. Tiger Bar provides an airy, informal setting for light snacks, meals and refreshments throughout the day. Bedrooms vary in size, some are air conditioned.
ROOMS: 41 en suite (3 GF) ⊗ in 30 bedrooms s £99-£150; d £99-£195 (incl. bkfst) LB **FACILITIES:** STV Arrangement with local health club **CONF:** BC **SERVICES:** Lift **NOTES:** ✈
CARDS:

★★★★64% Copthorne Tara Hotel London Kensington
COPTHORNE
Scarsdale Place, Wrights Ln W8 5SR plan 4 B4
☎ 020 7937 7211 📠 020 7937 7100
e-mail: sales.tara@mill-cop.com
Dir: *off Kensington High Street*

One of the city's larger hotels, the Tara is ideally located for Kensington High Street's stylish shops and tube station. Smart public areas include Café Mozart, a stylish Brasserie and bar and extensive conference and meeting facilities. Bedrooms include several well-equipped rooms for less mobile guests in addition to a number of Connoisseur rooms that include use of a club lounge with many complimentary facilities.
ROOMS: 834 en suite (3 fmly) ⊗ in 634 bedrooms s £89-£475; d £99-£475 LB **FACILITIES:** STV Xmas **CONF:** BC Thtr 280 Class 160 Board 90 Del £205 **SERVICES:** Lift air con **PARKING:** 65 **NOTES:** ✈
CARDS:

WC1 BLOOMSBURY, HOLBORN

★★★★★71% ◎◎ Renaissance Chancery Court London

RENAISSANCE HOTELS
252 High Holborn WC1V 7EN plan 3 D3
☎ 020 7829 9888 📠 020 7829 9889
e-mail: sales.chancerycourt@renaissancehotels.com
Dir: *A4 along Piccadilly onto Shaftesbury Av. Into High Holborn, hotel on right*
This is a grand place with splendid public areas, decorated from top to bottom in rare marble. Craftsmen have meticulously restored the sweeping staircases, archways and stately public rooms of the 1914 building. The result is a spacious, relaxed hotel offering everything from stylish, luxuriously appointed bedrooms to a health club and state-of-the-art meeting rooms. Pearl restaurant has an Art Deco feel and is becoming a destination in its own right.
ROOMS: 356 en suite ⊗ in 280 bedrooms s £282-£352.50; d £282-£352.50 LB **FACILITIES: Spa** STV Sauna Gym Jacuzzi Spa treatments by ESPA ch fac Xmas **CONF:** BC Thtr 435 Class 264 Board 60 **SERVICES:** Lift air con **PARKING:** 4 **NOTES:** ✈ Civ Wed 160
CARDS:

★★★★74% ◎ Jurys Great Russell Street
JURYS DOYLE HOTELS
16-22 Great Russell St WC1B 3NN plan 3 C3
☎ 020 7347 1000 📠 020 7347 1001
e-mail: great_russell@jurysdoyle.com
Dir: *A40 onto A400, Gower St then south to Bedford Sq. Turn right, then first left to end of road*
On the doorstep of Covent Garden, Oxford Street and the West End, this impressive building, designed by the renowned Sir Edwin Lutyens in the 1930s, retains many original features. Bedrooms are attractively appointed and benefit from an excellent range of facilities. Public areas include a grand reception lounge, an elegant bar and restaurant and extensive conference facilities.
ROOMS: 170 en suite (5 GF) ⊗ in 153 bedrooms s £225; d £225 LB **FACILITIES:** STV Xmas **CONF:** BC Thtr 300 Class 180 Board 60 Del £260 **SERVICES:** Lift air con **NOTES:** ✈ ⊗ in restaurant
CARDS:

★★★★72% ◎ The Montague on the Gardens
Red Carnation HOTELS
15 Montague St, Bloomsbury WC1B 5BJ plan 3 C4
☎ 020 7637 1001 📠 020 7637 2516
e-mail: bookmt@rchmail.com
Dir: *just off Russell Square.*
This stylish hotel is situated right next to the British Museum. A special feature is the alfresco terrace overlooking a delightful garden. Other public rooms include the Blue Door Bistro and Chef's Table, a bar, a lounge and a conservatory where traditional afternoon teas are served. The bedrooms are beautifully appointed and range from split-level suites to more compact rooms.
ROOMS: 104 en suite (18 GF) ⊗ in 47 bedrooms s £165-£220; d £195-£265 LB **FACILITIES:** STV Sauna Gym Jacuzzi ♫ ch fac Xmas **CONF:** Thtr 120 Class 50 Board 50 Del from £175 **SERVICES:** Lift air con **NOTES:** ⊗ in restaurant Civ Wed 90
CARDS:

★★★★71% Grange Holborn
50-60 Southampton Row WC1B 4AR plan 3 D4
☎ 020 7242 1800 📠 020 7242 0057
e-mail: holborn@grangehotels.co.uk
This smart hotel is centrally located, close to Oxford Street and Covent Garden. The elegantly furnished, spacious bedrooms offer high levels of comfort and are equipped with every conceivable extra. Public areas include a smart fitness centre, a choice of restaurants and extensive meeting and function facilities.
ROOMS: 200 en suite (10 fmly) ⊗ in 100 bedrooms s £280; d £320 **FACILITIES:** STV Sauna Gym Xmas **CONF:** Thtr 220 Class 120 Board 80 Del £275 **SERVICES:** Lift air con **NOTES:** ✈
CARDS:

★★★★71% ◎
Radisson Edwardian Kenilworth

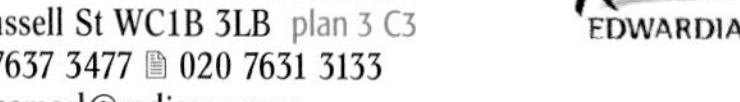

Radisson EDWARDIAN
Great Russell St WC1B 3LB plan 3 C3
☎ 020 7637 3477 📠 020 7631 3133
e-mail: resmarl@radisson.com
Dir: *past Oxford St and down New Oxford St. Turn into Bloomsbury St*
Ideally located for London's Theatreland, the City and the West End, this stylish hotel is popular with both business and leisure

continued on p366

WC1 BLOOMSBURY, HOLBORN, continued

travellers. Air-conditioned bedrooms feature elegant and modern décor, and come with a range of thoughtful extras. Public rooms include a range of meeting rooms, a small gym and an open-plan bar and restaurant.
ROOMS: 186 en suite (15 fmly) ⊗ in 139 bedrooms **FACILITIES:** STV Fitness room **CONF:** BC Thtr 120 Class 50 Board 40 **SERVICES:** Lift air con **NOTES:** ✈ **CARDS:**

★★★★70% Radisson Edwardian Marlborough
Bloomsbury St WC1B 3QD plan 3 C3
☎ 020 7636 5601 📠 020 7636 0532
e-mail: resmarl@radisson.com
Dir: past Oxford St, down New Oxford St and turn into Bloomsbury St
Within sight of the British Museum, this smart modern hotel is ideal for cultural visits to London. The theatre district is five minutes' walk away. Bedrooms are generally spacious with plenty of comfort, and public areas feature a number of interesting works of art. There are two bars and the modern Glass Restaurant. Guests can use the fitness room at the Radisson Edwardian Kenilworth Hotel located opposite.
ROOMS: 173 en suite (3 fmly) ⊗ in 82 bedrooms s £99-£195; d £99-£222 LB **FACILITIES:** Xmas **CONF:** BC Thtr 300 Class 150 Board 70 **SERVICES:** Lift **NOTES:** ✈ **CARDS:**

★★★★67% Holiday Inn Kings Cross/Bloomsbury
1 Kings Cross Rd WC1X 9HX plan 3 E5
☎ 020 7833 3900 📠 020 7917 6163
e-mail: sales@holidayinnlondon.com
Dir: 0.5m from Kings Cross Station on corner of King Cross Rd and Calthorpe St
Conveniently located for Kings Cross station and the City, this modern hotel offers smart, spacious air-conditioned accommodation with a wide range of facilities. The hotel has two restaurants (one is Indian), versatile meeting rooms, a bar and a well-equipped fitness centre.
ROOMS: 405 en suite (163 fmly) ⊗ in 160 bedrooms s £190; d £210 LB **FACILITIES:** STV supervised Sauna Solarium Gym Jacuzzi **CONF:** BC Thtr 220 Class 120 Board 30 Del £210 **SERVICES:** Lift air con **PARKING:** 12 **NOTES:** ✈ **CARDS:**

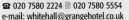

Town House

★★★★ Grange Whitehall

2-5 Montague St WC1B 5BP plan 3 C3
☎ 020 7580 2224 📠 020 7580 5554
e-mail: whitehall@grangehotel.co.uk
This elegant, small hotel is well located, close to the city's financial district and to the theatres of the West End. Smart bedrooms are decorated to a very high standard and many have views over the delightful landscaped rear gardens. Public areas include an elegant and cosy restaurant and a popular bar and lounge as well as conference facilities.
ROOMS: 56 en suite (2 fmly) (3 GF) ⊗ in 20 bedrooms s £155; d £220 **FACILITIES:** STV Xmas **CONF:** Thtr 90 Class 45 Board 45 Del £235 **SERVICES:** Lift air con
CARDS:

★★★★65% The Hotel Russell
Russell Square WC1B 5BE plan 3 C4
☎ 020 7837 6470 📠 020 7837 2857
web: www.principal-hotels.com
Dir: from A501 into Woburn Place. Hotel 500m on left.
This landmark Victorian hotel is located on Russell Square, within walking distance of the West End and theatre district. The property is in the middle of an ambitious refurbishment programme with many bedrooms having benefited from a stylish state-of-the-art transformation already. Spacious public areas include a choice of lounges and an elegant restaurant.
ROOMS: 371 rms (367 en suite) (7 fmly) ⊗ in 134 bedrooms s £79-£182; d £89-£212 **FACILITIES:** STV **CONF:** BC Thtr 1060 Class 470 Board 350 Del from £150 **SERVICES:** Lift **NOTES:** ✈
CARDS:

Town House

★★★★ Grange Blooms
7 Montague St WC1B 5BP plan 3 C4
☎ 020 7323 1717 📠 020 7636 6498
e-mail: blooms@grangehotels.com
Dir: off Russell Sq, behind the British Museum.
Part of an 18th-century terrace, this elegant town house is behind the British Museum. Bedrooms are furnished in Regency style; the rear ones are quieter. Day rooms include the lobby lounge, garden terrace, breakfast room and cocktail bar, all featuring antique pieces and paintings. Room service is available 24 hours a day.
ROOMS: 26 en suite ⊗ in 12 bedrooms s fr £155; d fr £195 LB **FACILITIES:** STV Patio garden Xmas **CONF:** Thtr 20 Class 10 Board 18 Del from £235 **SERVICES:** Lift **NOTES:** ✈ Civ Wed 20
CARDS:

★★★72% The Bonnington in Bloomsbury
92 Southampton Row WC1B 4BH plan 3 D4
☎ 020 7242 2828 📠 020 7831 9170
e-mail: sales@bonnington.com
web: www.bonnington.com
Dir: M40 Euston Rd. Opposite station turn S into Upper Woburn Place past Russell Sq into Southampton Row. Hotel on left

This smart hotel is centrally located close to the city, the British Museum and Covent Garden. Spacious public areas include the Malt Bar, Waterfalls Restaurant and a comfortable lobby lounge. Bedrooms are well equipped and include a number of superb new executive rooms and suites. A good range of conference and meeting rooms is available.
ROOMS: 247 en suite (4 fmly) ⊗ in 87 bedrooms s £85-£130; d £125-£164 (incl. bkfst) **FACILITIES:** STV Fitness room **CONF:** BC Thtr 250 Class 80 Board 50 Del from £155 **SERVICES:** Lift air con
NOTES: ✈ **CARDS:**

London

⌂ Travel Inn (London Euston)

1 Dukes Rd WC1H 9PJ plan 3 C5
☎ 0870 238 3301 🖷 020 7554 3419
Dir: *on corner of Euston Road (south side) and Duke's Road, between Kings Cross/St Pancras and Euston stations. Travel Inn is the blue building*

Travel Inn offers good-quality, value-for-money accommodation. Spacious, en suite rooms with bath and shower comfortably accommodate a family of up to two adults and two children (to age 15). The restaurant and bar offers a varied menu. For further details consult the Hotel Groups page.

ROOMS: 220 en suite s £74.95-£79.95; d £74.95-£79.95

⌂ Travelodge (London Kings Cross)

Willing House, Grays Inn Rd, Kings Cross WC1 8BH plan 3 D6
☎ 08700 850 950 🖷 020 7278 7396

Travelodge offers good quality, good value, modern accommodation. Ideal for families, the spacious, en suite bedrooms include remote-control TV, tea and coffee-making facilities and luxury beds. Meals can be taken at the nearby family restaurant. For further details consult the Hotel Groups page.

ROOMS: 140 en suite s fr £45; d fr £45

WC2 SOHO, STRAND

Top 200 – Hotel

★★★★★ The Savoy

Strand WC2R 0EU plan 3 D1
☎ 020 7836 4343 🖷 020 7240 6040
e-mail: info@the-savoy.co.uk
Dir: *halfway along The Strand between Trafalgar Sq and Aldwych*

There is a feeling of great anticipation as one arrives at this internationally renowned hotel. Services flow smoothly and bedrooms offer excellent levels of comfort; many have fine views along the river. The choice of dining areas presents a predicament - whether to opt for Marcus Wareing's menu at the Grill, the River Restaurant or the soon to open 'La Banquette'. No visit would be complete without experiencing afternoon tea in the Thames Foyer.

ROOMS: 263 en suite (6 fmly) in 55 bedrooms **FACILITIES:** STV Sauna Gym Health & beauty treatments ♫ **CONF:** Thtr 500 Class 200 Board 32 **SERVICES:** Lift air con **PARKING:** 65 **NOTES:** Civ Wed 300 **CARDS:**

> Popped the question?
> Hotels with Civ Wed in their entry are licensed for civil wedding ceremonies. Maximum numbers for the ceremony only are shown, e.g. Civ Wed 120

Top 200 – Hotel

★★★★★ One Aldwych

1 Aldwych WC2B 4RH plan 3 D2
☎ 020 7300 1000 🖷 020 7300 1001
e-mail: reservations@onealdwych.com
web: www.onealdwych.com
Dir: *at Aldwych & The Strand junct near Waterloo Bridge*

Still a relatively new hotel on the London scene, One Aldwych is already well known for its chic yet comfortable style and contemporary décor. There are many interesting features including a pool with underwater music in the health club, the dramatic 'amber city' mural in the double height Axis restaurant and the contemporary lobby bar where the Martini cocktail is a speciality. Bedrooms are no less stylish and feature giant pillows, down duvets and granite surfaces in bathrooms.

ROOMS: 105 en suite in 60 bedrooms s £229-£460; d £229-£503 (incl. bkfst) **LB** **FACILITIES:** STV Sauna Gym Steam room, 3 Treatment rooms ♫ Xmas **CONF:** BC Thtr 50 **SERVICES:** Lift air con **NOTES:** Civ Wed 50 **CARDS:**

★★★★★65% Swissôtel The Howard, London

Temple Place WC2R 2PR plan 3 E2
☎ 020 7836 3555 🖷 020 7379 4547
e-mail: emailus.london@swissotel.com
web: www.swissotel.com
Dir: *Turn off Aldwych, heading west, keep left of church in middle of rd. Left on Surrey St. Hotel at end.*

This smart hotel enjoys wonderful views across London's historic skyline from its riverside location. The Eurostar terminal, Covent Garden and Theatreland are all within easy reach. The air-conditioned bedrooms have been carefully refurbished and offer a host of extra facilities. The restaurant and bar open out onto a delightful garden offering al fresco dining when weather permits.

ROOMS: 189 en suite in 117 bedrooms s £295; d £320 **LB** **FACILITIES:** STV ♫ Xmas **CONF:** BC Thtr 150 Class 60 Board 60 **SERVICES:** Lift air con **PARKING:** 30 **NOTES:** Civ Wed 100 **CARDS:**

★★★★★64% Radisson Edwardian Hampshire Hotel

31 Leicester Square WC2H 7LH plan 3 C1
☎ 020 7839 9399 🖷 020 7930 8122
e-mail: reshamp@radisson.com
Dir: *from Charing Cross Rd turn into Cranbourn St at Leicester Sq. Left at end, hotel at bottom of square*

Located in the very heart of London's West End, most of the capital's top entertainment venues are within easy reach. The elegant public areas include the Apex Bar and Restaurant, with its beautiful wood panelling, and a small but smart gymnasium. The Crescent Bar, adjacent to the hotel, with its vaulted alcoves, is an

continued on p368

WC2 SOHO, STRAND, continued

intimate venue for drinks. Air-conditioned bedrooms are smartly decorated and feature triple glazing and thoughtful extras.
ROOMS: 124 en suite (5 fmly) ⊗ in 93 bedrooms d £386.58 **FACILITIES:** STV Gym Fitness room ch fac **CONF:** BC Thtr 100 Class 48 Board 35 **SERVICES:** Lift air con **NOTES:** ✗
CARDS:

★★★★74%
Radisson Edwardian Mountbatten
Radisson EDWARDIAN

Monmouth St, Seven Dials, Covent Garden WC2H 9HD plan 3 C2
☎ 020 7836 4300 🖷 020 7240 3540
e-mail: resmoun@radisson.com
Dir: *off Shaftesbury Av, on corner of Seven Dials rdbt*
Located in the heart of Theatreland and close to Covent Garden, this smart hotel is named after Lord Mountbatten. The air-conditioned, thoughtfully equipped and stylish bedrooms include a number of spacious suites. Public areas include the popular Dial Bar and Restaurant as well as conference and meeting facilities.
ROOMS: 151 en suite ⊗ in 104 bedrooms **FACILITIES:** STV Fitness room **CONF:** BC Thtr 90 Class 45 Board 32 **SERVICES:** Lift air con
CARDS:

★★★★72% Kingsway Hall
Great Queen St, Covent Garden WC2B 5BZ plan 3 D3
☎ 020 7309 0909 🖷 020 7309 9696
e-mail: enquiries@kingswayhall.co.uk
web: www.kingswayhall.co.uk
Dir: *from Holborn underground station follow Kingsway towards Aldwych. At 1st lights right. Hotel 50mtrs on left*
Conveniently situated close to Covent Garden, this stylish modern hotel offers very comfortable accommodation. Smart, air-conditioned bedrooms have been well designed and feature many extra facilities. The stylish compact lounge bar is available for drinks and lighter meals along with the Harlequin restaurant for more formal dining. There is a gym in the basement.
ROOMS: 170 en suite ⊗ in 125 bedrooms s £230-£270; d £230-£270 **FACILITIES:** STV Gym Jacuzzi Steam room **CONF:** BC Thtr 150 Class 90 Board 50 Del from £190 **SERVICES:** Lift air con **NOTES:** ✗
CARDS:

★★★69% Strand Palace
372 The Strand WC2R 0JJ plan 3 D2
☎ 020 7836 8080 🖷 020 7836 2077
e-mail: reservations@strandpalacehotel.co.uk
Dir: *From Trafalgar Square, on A4 to Charing Cross, 150mtrs, hotel on left.*

At the heart of Theatreland, this vast hotel is ideal for visiting many of the capital's attractions. The bedrooms vary in style and include Club rooms with enhanced facilities and exclusive use of

continued

the Club lounge as well as newly refurbished, bright contemporary rooms. The extensive public areas include four eateries and a popular cocktail bar.
ROOMS: 785 en suite ⊗ in 450 bedrooms s £89-£170; d £105-£185 **LB** **FACILITIES:** STV Xmas **CONF:** BC Thtr 200 Class 90 Board 40 Del from £150 **SERVICES:** Lift **NOTES:** ✗ ⊗ in restaurant
CARDS:

U Radisson Edwardian Pastoria Hotel
Radisson EDWARDIAN

3-6 Saint Martins St WC2H 7HL plan 3 C1
☎ 020 7930 8641 & 020 7451 0227(res)
🖷 020 7451 0191
e-mail: reshamp@radisson.com
Dir: *from Whitcomb St left to Panton St. St Martins St off Leicester Sq*
At the time of going to press, the star classification for this hotel was not confirmed. Please refer to the AA internet site www.theAA.com for current information.
ROOMS: 58 en suite ⊗ in 38 bedrooms s £238.53; d £271.42 **FACILITIES:** STV Gym **CONF:** BC **SERVICES:** Lift **NOTES:** ✗
CARDS:

⌂ Travelodge (London Covent Garden)
Travelodge

High Holborn WC2B 5RE plan 3 D2
☎ 08700 850 950 🖷 020 7831 1548
Travelodge offers good quality, good value, modern accommodation. Ideal for families, the spacious, en suite bedrooms include remote-control TV, tea and coffee-making facilities and luxury beds. Meals can be taken at the nearby family restaurant. For further details consult the Hotel Groups page.
ROOMS: s fr £45; d fr £45

LONDON AIRPORTS See under Gatwick & Heathrow

LONDON GATEWAY MOTORWAY SERVICE AREA (M1) See LONDON plan1 C6

★★★68% Days Hotel
DAYS INN

Welcome Break Service Area NW7 3HB
☎ 020 8906 7000 🖷 020 8906 7011
e-mail: lgw.hotel@welcomebreak.co.uk
web: www.welcomebreak.co.uk
Dir: *on M1 between junct 2/4 northbound & southbound*
This modern hotel is the flagship of the Days Inn brand and occupies a prime location on the outskirts of London at London Gateway Services. Bedrooms have a contemporary feel, are spacious and well equipped. Public rooms are airy and include an open-plan restaurant and bar/lounge and a range of meeting rooms. Ample parking is a bonus.
ROOMS: 200 en suite (190 fmly) (80 GF) ⊗ in 162 bedrooms s £54-£85; d £54-£85 **LB** **FACILITIES:** STV **CONF:** Thtr 70 Class 30 Board 50 Del from £95 **SERVICES:** Lift air con **PARKING:** 160 **NOTES:** ⊗ in restaurant **CARDS:**

LONDON COLNEY, Hertfordshire — Map 06 TL10

⌂ Innkeeper's Lodge
Innkeeper's Lodge

1 Barnet Rd AL2 1BL
☎ 01727 823698 🖷 01727 820902
www.innkeeperslodge.com
Dir: *clockwise from Heathrow on M25 towards Harlow, exit at junct 22 staying in left lane, at rdbt take 1st left to London Colney. Straight over rdbt The Colney Fox is 450 yds on right*
Smart rooms meet essential business requirements but also have home comforts, and depending on location may well have meeting rooms and pub dining. Dining options generally include all-day menus plus the added advantage of breakfast.
ROOMS: s £49-£59; d £49-£59

London

LONG EATON, Derbyshire Map 11 SK43

★★★66% Novotel Nottingham/Derby

Bostock Ln NG10 4EP
☎ 0115 946 5111 📠 0115 946 5900
e-mail: H0507@accor-hotels.com

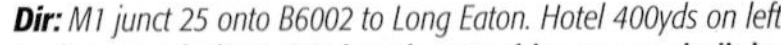

Dir: *M1 junct 25 onto B6002 to Long Eaton. Hotel 400yds on left*

In close proximity to M1 junction 25, this purpose-built hotel has much to offer. Bedrooms are spacious; many have sofa beds and all provide exceptional desk space. Public rooms include a bright brasserie, which is open all day and provides extended dining until midnight, and a comprehensive range of meeting rooms.

ROOMS: 108 en suite (40 fmly) ⊘ in 66 bedrooms s £49-£75; d £49-£75 **LB** **FACILITIES:** STV Outdoor Swimming Pool **CONF:** Thtr 220 Class 100 Board 100 Del from £110 **SERVICES:** Lift **PARKING:** 220 **CARDS:**

★★60% Europa

20-22 Derby Rd NG10 1LW
☎ 0115 972 8481 📠 0115 946 0229
e-mail: k.riley3@ntlworld.com

Dir: *on A6005, in centre of Long Eaton. 1.5m from M1 junct 25 & A52*

Convenient for the town centre and the M1, this commercial hotel offers suitably furnished bedrooms. In addition to the restaurant, where mainly Chinese cooking is provided, light refreshments are available throughout the day in the conservatory.

ROOMS: 15 en suite (2 fmly) ⊘ in 3 bedrooms s £40-£45; d £55 (incl. bkfst) **CONF:** Thtr 35 Class 35 Board 28 **PARKING:** 24 **NOTES:** ⊘ in restaurant Closed 25-28 Dec **CARDS:**

LONGHORSLEY, Northumberland Map 21 NZ19

★★★74% ◎◎ Linden Hall

MACDONALD HOTELS

NE65 8XF
☎ 01670 500000 📠 01670 500001
e-mail: stay@lindenhall.co.uk
web: www.lindenhall.co.uk

Dir: *Northbound A1 exit A697 towards Coldstream. 1 mile north of Longhorsley*

This impressive Georgian mansion lies in 400 acres of parkland and offers extensive indoor and outdoor leisure facilities including a golf course. Elegant public rooms include an imposing entrance hall, drawing room and cocktail bar. The Dobson restaurant provides a fine dining experience, or guests can eat in the more informal Linden Tree pub which is located in the grounds.

ROOMS: 50 en suite (4 fmly) (20 GF) ⊘ in 21 bedrooms s £84-£94; d fr £121 (incl. bkfst) **LB** **FACILITIES: Spa** STV Indoor Swimming Pool (heated) Snooker Sauna Solarium Gym Putt green Jacuzzi Own golf course Hard tennis court ch fac Xmas **CONF:** Thtr 300 Class 100 Board 30 **SERVICES:** Lift **PARKING:** 260 **NOTES:** ⊘ in restaurant Civ Wed 120 **CARDS:**

See advert on opposite page

LONG MELFORD, Suffolk Map 13 TL84

★★★75% ◎ The Black Lion

Church Walk, The Green CO10 9DN
☎ 01787 312356 📠 01787 374557
e-mail: enquiries@blacklionhotel.net

Dir: *at junct of A134/A1092, overlooking the green*

This charming 15th-century hotel is situated on the edge of this bustling town overlooking the green. Bedrooms are generally spacious and each is attractively decorated, tastefully furnished and equipped with useful extras. An interesting range of dishes is served in the lounge bar or guests may choose to dine in the more formal restaurant.

ROOMS: 10 en suite (3 fmly) ⊘ in all bedrooms s £85-£109; d £106-£146 (incl. bkfst) **LB** **FACILITIES:** Board games ch fac Xmas **CONF:** Thtr 50 Class 28 Board 28 Del £128.95 **PARKING:** 10 **NOTES:** ⊘ in restaurant **CARDS:**

★★★73% The Bull

OLD ENGLISH INNS

Hall St CO10 9JG
☎ 01787 378494 📠 01787 880307
e-mail: 6420@greeneking.co.uk

Dir: *3m N of Sudbury on A134*

The public areas of this delightful 14th-century property feature a wealth of charm and character, including exposed beams, carvings, heraldic markings and huge open fireplaces. Bedrooms are smartly decorated, thoughtfully equipped and retain many original features. Snacks or light lunches are served in the bar, or guests can choose to dine in the more formal restaurant.

ROOMS: 25 en suite (3 fmly) ⊘ in 11 bedrooms s £75-£100; d £110-£140 (incl. bkfst) **LB** **FACILITIES:** Xmas **CONF:** Thtr 60 Class 30 Board 35 Del from £120 **PARKING:** 30 **NOTES:** ⊘ in restaurant Civ Wed 100 **CARDS:**

LONG SUTTON, Lincolnshire Map 12 TF42

Travelodge Kings Lynn

Travelodge

Wisbech Rd PE12 9AG
☎ 08700 850 950 📠 01406 362230

Dir: *on junct A17/A1101 rdbt*

Travelodge offers good quality, good value, modern accommodation. Ideal for families, the spacious, en suite bedrooms include remote-control TV, tea and coffee-making facilities and luxury beds. Meals can be taken at the nearby family restaurant. For further details consult the Hotel Groups page.

ROOMS: 40 en suite s fr £25; d fr £25

LOOE, Cornwall & Isles of Scilly Map 02 SX25

See also Portwrinkle

★★★66% Hannafore Point

THE INDEPENDENTS

Marine Dr, West Looe PL13 2DG
☎ 01503 263273 📠 01503 263272
e-mail: stay@hannaforepointhotel.com

Dir: *A38, left onto A385 to Looe. Over bridge left. Hotel 0.5m on left*

With panoramic coastal views embracing St George's Island around to Rame Head, this popular hotel provides a warm welcome. The wonderful view is also a feature of the spacious restaurant and bar, a scenic backdrop for dinners and breakfasts. Additional facilities include a heated indoor pool, squash court and gymnasium.

ROOMS: 37 en suite (5 fmly) s fr £48; d fr £96 (incl. bkfst) **LB** **FACILITIES: Spa** Indoor Swimming Pool (heated) Squash Sauna Solarium Gym Jacuzzi Tennis/bowls 200yds away ♫ ch fac Xmas **CONF:** BC Thtr 120 Class 80 Board 40 **SERVICES:** Lift **PARKING:** 32 **NOTES:** ⊘ in restaurant Civ Wed 150 **CARDS:**

See advert on opposite page

Indoor Swimming Pool
Indoor Swimming Pool (heated)
Outdoor Swimming Pool
Outdoor Swimming Pool (heated)

★★76% Fieldhead
Portuan Rd, Hannafore PL13 2DR
☎ 01503 262689 📠 01503 264114
e-mail: enquiries@fieldheadhotel.co.uk
web: www.fieldheadhotel.co.uk
Dir: *in Looe over bridge & turn left, signposted 'Hannafore'. Past waterside church, up hill to seafront. 1st right then right again into Portuan Rd*

THE INDEPENDENTS

Overlooking the bay, this engaging hotel has a relaxing atmosphere. Bedrooms are furnished with care and many have sea views. Smartly presented public areas include a convivial bar and restaurant, and outside there is a palm-filled garden with a secluded patio and swimming pool. The fixed-price menu changes daily and features quality local produce.
ROOMS: 15 en suite (2 fmly) (2 GF) s £30-£45; d £60-£80 (incl. bkfst) **LB FACILITIES:** supervised ch fac **PARKING:** 15 **NOTES:** ⊗ in restaurant Closed Xmas **CARDS:**

See advert on this page

LOOE, continued

★★64% Rivercroft Hotel
Station Rd PL13 1HL
☎ 01503 262251 01503 265494
e-mail: rivercroft.hotel@virgin.net
web: www.rivercrofthotel.co.uk
Dir: *from A38 take B387 to Looe. Hotel on left near bridge*

Standing high above the river, this family-run hotel is conveniently located being just a short walk from the town centre and beach. Bedrooms are comfortably furnished and well-equipped, and many enjoy wonderful views. A carte menu is offered in the Croft Restaurant, or alternatively, meals can be enjoyed in the convivial atmosphere of the bar.
ROOMS: 15 en suite (8 fmly) s £27-£32; d £54-£76 (incl. bkfst) **LB**
FACILITIES: ch fac Xmas **NOTES:** in restaurant
CARDS:

L

LOSTWITHIEL, Cornwall & Isles of Scilly — Map 02 SX15

★★★69% Restormel
Castle Hill PL22 0DD
☎ 01208 872223 01208 873568

e-mail: restlodge@aol.com
web: www.restormelhotel.co.uk
Dir: *on A390 in Lostwithiel*

Best Western

A short drive from the Eden Project, this popular hotel offers a friendly welcome to all visitors and is ideally situated for exploring the area. The original building houses the bar, restaurant and lounges, with some original features adding to the character. Bedrooms are comfortably furnished, with a number overlooking the secluded outdoor pool.
ROOMS: 24 en suite 12 annexe en suite (2 fmly) in 30 bedrooms s fr £75; d £100-£120 (incl. bkfst) **LB** **FACILITIES:** STV Xmas **CONF:** Thtr 100 Board 10 Del from £117 **PARKING:** 40 **NOTES:** in restaurant **CARDS:**

★★★62% Lostwithiel Hotel Golf & Country Club
Lower Polscoe PL22 0HQ
☎ 01208 873550 01208 873479
e-mail: info@golf-hotel.co.uk
web: www.golf-hotel.co.uk
Dir: *off A38 at Dobwalls onto A390. In Lostwithiel right and hotel signed*

This rural hotel is based around its golf club and other leisure activities. The main building offers guests a choice of eating options, including all-day snacks in the popular Sports Bar. The bedrooms are in separate buildings.
ROOMS: 21 en suite (1 fmly) (14 GF) in 10 bedrooms s £30-£48; d £60-£96 (incl. bkfst) **LB** **FACILITIES:** 18 Snooker Gym Putt green Undercover floodlit driving range, Golf simulator Xmas **CONF:** Thtr 120 Class 60 Board 40 **PARKING:** 120 **NOTES:** Civ Wed 120
CARDS:

LOUGHBOROUGH, Leicestershire — Map 11 SK51

★★★★68% Quorn Country Hotel
Charnwood House, 66 Leicester Rd LE12 8BB
☎ 01509 415050 01509 415557
e-mail: reservations@quorncountryhotel.co.uk
(For full entry see Quorn)

★★★65% The Quality Hotel & Suites Loughborough
New Ashby Rd LE11 4EX
☎ 01509 211800 01509 211868
e-mail: enquiries@hotels-loughborough.com
Dir: *M1 junct 23 take A512 towards Loughborough. Hotel 1m on left*
Close to the motorway network, this popular, modern hotel offers comfortable, well-equipped accommodation. All bedrooms have a spacious work area, and some have small lounges and kitchenettes. It is an ideal hotel for a long stay or for families. Open-plan public rooms include a lounge area, bar and carvery restaurant.
ROOMS: 94 en suite (12 fmly) (47 GF) in 47 bedrooms s £54-£100; d £84-£120 **LB** **FACILITIES:** STV Sauna Solarium Gym Jacuzzi Xmas **CONF:** Thtr 225 Class 120 Board 80 Del from £85 **PARKING:** 160
NOTES: in restaurant Civ Wed 150
CARDS:

LOUTH, Lincolnshire — Map 17 TF38

★★★73% Brackenborough Arms Hotel
Cordeaux Corner, Brackenborough LN11 0SZ
☎ 01507 609169 01507 609413
e-mail: ashley@brackenborough.force9.co.uk
Dir: *off A16 2m N of Louth*
Set amid well tended gardens and patios, this hotel offers attractive bedrooms, each individually decorated with co-ordinated
continued

furnishings and many extras. Tippler's Retreat lounge bar offers informal dining; the more formal Signature Restaurant provides the best of local produce.
ROOMS: 24 en suite (1 fmly) (6 GF) ⊗ in 6 bedrooms s £58.95-£64; d £72-£77 (incl. bkfst) **LB FACILITIES:** STV **CONF:** Thtr 34 Class 24 Board 30 Del £110 **PARKING:** 91 **NOTES:** ⊗ in restaurant Closed 25-26 Dec Civ Wed 34 **CARDS:**

★★★70% **Kenwick Park**

Kenwick Park Estate LN11 8NR
☎ 01507 608806 01507 608027
e-mail: enquiries@kenwick-park.co.uk
web: www.kenwick-park.co.uk
Dir: *A16 from Grimsby, then A157. Hotel 400mtrs down hill on right*

This elegant Georgian house is situated on the 320-acre Kenwick Park estate, overlooking its own golf course. Bedrooms are spacious, comfortable and provide modern facilities. Public areas include a restaurant and a conservatory bar, which overlook the grounds. There is also an extensive leisure centre and state-of-the-art conference and banqueting facilities.
ROOMS: 29 en suite 5 annexe en suite (10 fmly) ⊗ in 11 bedrooms s £75-£105; d £100-£120 (incl. bkfst) **LB FACILITIES: Spa** STV supervised 18 Squash Sauna Solarium Gym Putt green Jacuzzi Health & Beauty Centre ch fac Xmas **CONF:** Thtr 250 Class 40 Board 90 Del from £120 **PARKING:** 100 **NOTES:** ⊗ in restaurant Civ Wed 200 **CARDS:**

★★★69% **Beaumont**

66 Victoria Rd LN11 0BX
☎ 01507 605005 01507 607768
e-mail: beaumonthotel@aol.com
This smart, family-run hotel enjoys a quiet location, within easy reach of the town centre. Bedrooms are spacious and individually designed. Public areas include a smart restaurant with a strong Italian influence and an inviting lounge bar with comfortable deep sofas and open fires. Weddings and functions are also catered for.
ROOMS: 16 en suite (2 fmly) (6 GF) s £55-£65; d £80-£120 (incl. bkfst) **FACILITIES:** ch fac **CONF:** Thtr 70 Class 50 Board 46 **SERVICES:** Lift **PARKING:** 70 **NOTES:** RS Sun **CARDS:**

Late for dinner?
Quality Standards mean that last orders for dinner vary according to star rating and should be no earlier than:
★★ 7.00pm ★★★ 8.00pm ★★★★ 9.00pm
★★★★★ 10.00pm

L

LOWER BEEDING, West Sussex Map 06 TQ22

Top 200 – Hotel

★★★★ South Lodge

Brighton Rd RH13 6PS

☎ 01403 891711 01403 891766

e-mail: enquiries@southlodgehotel.co.uk

web: www.exclusivehotels.co.uk

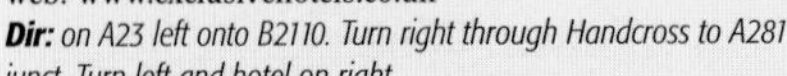

Dir: *on A23 left onto B2110. Turn right through Handcross to A281 junct. Turn left and hotel on right*

This impeccably presented 19th-century lodge is an ideal retreat for guests who wish to enjoy stunning views over the rolling South Downs. The traditional, award-winning restaurant offers memorable, seasonal dishes, and the elegant lounge is popular for afternoon teas. Bedrooms are individually designed with character and quality throughout. Leisure and conference facilities are impressive.

ROOMS: 45 en suite (4 fmly) (7 GF) **FACILITIES:** STV 18 Riding Snooker Gym Putt green Can organise riding, shooting, fishing & quad biking **CONF:** BC Thtr 160 Class 60 Board 50 Del from £240 **SERVICES:** Lift **PARKING:** 100 **NOTES:** in restaurant Civ Wed 120 **CARDS:**

See advert on page 373

★★★67% *Cisswood House*

Sandygate Ln RH13 6NF

☎ 0871 871 3242 0871 871 3243

e-mail: cisswood.house@pageant.co.uk

Dir: *Turn off A23 at Handcross, follow signs for Lower Beeding, turn right at Plough Pub. Hotel 0.5m on right*

Convenient for the M23, Cisswood House is set in beautifully maintained gardens. Bedrooms are spacious and well presented, some with whirlpool baths. Public areas include the Pageant Health Club with swimming pool, hairdresser, gym and treatment rooms. The attractive function rooms make this a popular venue for weddings and conferences.

ROOMS: 51 en suite in 6 bedrooms **FACILITIES:** STV supervised Sauna Solarium Gym Jacuzzi Health & beauty salon, Hairdressing **CONF:** Thtr 200 Class 70 Board 70 **PARKING:** 60 **NOTES:** in restaurant Civ Wed 160 **CARDS:**

LOWER SLAUGHTER, Gloucestershire Map 10 SP12

Top 200 – Hotel

★★★ Lower Slaughter Manor

GL54 2HP

☎ 01451 820456 01451 822150

e-mail: lowsmanor@aol.com

Dir: *off A429 signed "The Slaughters". Manor 0.5m on right on entering village*

There is a timeless elegance about this wonderful manor, which dates back to the 17th century. Its imposing presence makes it very much the centrepiece of this famous Cotswold village. Inside, the levels of comfort and quality are immediately evident, with crackling logs fires warming the many sumptuous lounges. The hotel's new dining room is an elegant creation that suitably complements the excellent cuisine on offer. Spacious and tastefully furnished bedrooms are either in the main building or in the adjacent coach house.

ROOMS: 11 en suite 5 annexe en suite s £175; d £220-£395 (incl. bkfst & dinner) **FACILITIES:** Xmas **CONF:** Thtr 36 Class 20 Board 18 Del from £160 **PARKING:** 30 **NOTES:** No children 12yrs in restaurant Civ Wed 60

CARDS:

★★★75% Washbourne Court

GL54 2HS

☎ 01451 822143 01451 821045

e-mail: info@washbournecourt.co.uk

Dir: *off A429 at signpost 'The Slaughters', between Stow-on-the-Wold and Bourton-on-the-Water. Hotel in centre of village*

Beamed ceilings, log fires and flagstone floors are some of the attractive features of this part 17th-century hotel, set in four acres of immaculate grounds beside the River Eye. Smartly decorated bedrooms are in the main house and self-contained cottages, many offering lovely views. The riverside terrace is popular during summer months, whilst the elegant dining room serves an interesting menu and a comprehensive wine list.

ROOMS: 15 en suite 13 annexe en suite s £80-£100; d £120-£130 (incl. bkfst) **LB** **FACILITIES:** Xmas **CONF:** Thtr 70 Class 40 Board 30 Del £130 **PARKING:** 40 **NOTES:** in restaurant Civ Wed 60

CARDS:

LOWESTOFT, Suffolk Map 13 TM59

★★★77% Ivy House Country Hotel

Ivy Ln, Beccles Rd, Oulton Broad NR33 8HY

☎ 01502 501353 & 588144 01502 501539

e-mail: aa@ivyhousefarm.co.uk

Dir: *on A146 SW of Oulton Broad turn into Ivy Ln beside Esso petrol station. Over railway bridge and follow private driveway*

A delightful, family-run hotel set in three acres of mature

continued

landscaped grounds just a short walk from Oulton Broad. Public rooms include an 18th-century thatched barn restaurant where an interesting choice of dishes is served. Service throughout is charming and attentive. The attractively decorated bedrooms are housed in garden wings, and many have lovely views of the garden and countryside.

ROOMS: 19 annexe en suite (1 fmly) (17 GF) ⊗ in 6 bedrooms s £84-£104; d £114-£149 (incl. bkfst) **LB** **FACILITIES:** Reduced rates at neighbouring leisure club **CONF:** Thtr 55 Board 22 Del from £135 **PARKING:** 50 **NOTES:** ⊗ in restaurant Closed 26 Dec-4 Jan **CARDS:**

★★★69% Hotel Victoria

Kirkley Cliff NR33 0BZ
☎ 01502 574433 01502 501529
e-mail: info@hotelvictoria.freeserve.co.uk
Dir: *A12 to seafront on one-way system signed A12 Ipswich. Hotel on seafront just beyond the Thatched Cottage*

This attractive Victorian building is on the esplanade overlooking the sea and has direct access to the beach. Bedrooms are pleasantly decorated and thoughtfully equipped, and many rooms have sea views. Public rooms include a choice of lounges, a comfortable bar and a restaurant, which overlooks the pretty garden. The hotel also offers modern conference and banqueting facilities.

ROOMS: 24 en suite (4 fmly) s £85-£100; d £115-£130 (incl. bkfst) **LB** **FACILITIES:** STV Xmas **CONF:** Thtr 200 Class 150 Board 50 Del from £115 **SERVICES:** Lift **PARKING:** 45 **NOTES:** Civ Wed 200 **CARDS:**

★★★68% *Hotel Hatfield*

The Esplanade NR33 0QP
☎ 01502 565337 01502 511885
e-mail: hotelhatfield@elizabethhotels.co.uk
Dir: *from town centre follow 'South Beach' signs on A12 Ipswich road. Hotel 200yds on left*

Ideally situated overlooking the sea, this hotel is in a prominent position on the esplanade. Bedrooms are pleasantly decorated and thoughtfully equipped and some have superb sea views. The spacious public rooms include a popular lounge bar, a cocktail bar and the Chaplins restaurant where an interesting choice of dishes is served.

continued

ROOMS: 33 en suite (1 fmly) ⊗ in 7 bedrooms **FACILITIES:** STV **CONF:** Thtr 100 Class 50 Board 40 **SERVICES:** Lift **PARKING:** 26 **NOTES:** Civ Wed 200 **CARDS:**

Travel Inn

249 Yarmouth Rd NR32 4AA
☎ 08701 977165 01502 581223
Dir: *on A12, 2m N of Lowestoft*

Travel Inn offers good-quality, value-for-money accommodation. Spacious, en suite rooms with bath and shower comfortably accommodate a family of up to two adults and two children (to age 15). The restaurant and bar offers a varied menu. For further details consult the Hotel Groups page.

ROOMS: 40 en suite s £45.95-£46.95; d £45.95-£46.95

LOWESWATER, Cumbria — Map 18 NY12

★★68% Grange Country House

CA13 0SU
☎ 01946 861211 & 861570
e-mail: gchloweswater@hotmail.com
Dir: *left off A5086 for Mockerkin, through village. After 2m left for Loweswater Lake. Hotel at bottom of hill on left*

This delightful country hotel is set in a quiet valley at the north-western end of Loweswater and continues to prove popular with guests seeking peace and quiet. It has a friendly and relaxed atmosphere, and the cosy public areas include a small bar, a residents' lounge, and an attractive dining room. The bedrooms are well equipped and comfortable.

ROOMS: 8 en suite (2 fmly) (1 GF) s £35-£45; d £66-£80 (incl. bkfst) **FACILITIES:** National Trust boats & fishing ch fac Xmas **CONF:** Thtr 25 Class 25 Board 25 **PARKING:** 22 **NOTES:** ⊗ in restaurant RS Jan-Feb

LOXTON, Somerset — Map 04 ST35

★★★66% Webbington

BS26 2XA
☎ 01934 750100 01934 750020
e-mail: webbington@latonahotels.co.uk

Despite being easily spotted from the M5 motorway, this popular hotel is situated in the countryside with splendid views from many bedrooms and public areas. Well suited to a wide range of guests from business to leisure to families, the hotel offers a warm welcome to all. Facilities include an indoor swimming pool, tennis courts, cardio gym and varied conference rooms.

ROOMS: 59 en suite (2 fmly) ⊗ in 10 bedrooms **FACILITIES:** Sauna Solarium Gym Beauty treatments Cardiovascular suite Steam Room Xmas **CONF:** Thtr 1000 Class 600 **PARKING:** 450 **NOTES:** ⊗ in restaurant Civ Wed 500 **CARDS:**

Indoor Swimming Pool
Indoor Swimming Pool (heated)
Outdoor Swimming Pool
Outdoor Swimming Pool (heated)

LUDLOW, Shropshire

Map 10 SO57

★★★75% Overton Grange Country House

Old Hereford Rd SY8 4AD
☎ 01584 873500 01584 873524
e-mail: info@overtongrangehotel.com
web: www.overtongrangehotel.com
Dir: *off A49 at B4361 to Ludlow. Hotel 200yds on left*

Overton Grange is a traditional country house offering superb views over the Shropshire countryside, comfortable bedrooms and a dedicated customer care team. The restaurant offers an exciting twist of good locally sourced food and a commitment to high culinary standards. Meeting and conference facilities are available.
ROOMS: 14 en suite (3 fmly) in all bedrooms s £75-£130; d £130-£190 (incl. bkfst) **LB** **FACILITIES:** Xmas **CONF:** BC Thtr 100 Class 40 Board 20 Del from £140 **PARKING:** 50 **NOTES:** in restaurant Civ Wed 30 **CARDS:**

L

★★★72% Dinham Hall

By the Castle SY8 1EJ
☎ 01584 876464 01584 876019
e-mail: info@dinhamhall.co.uk
web: www.dinhamhall.co.uk
Dir: *opposite the castle*

Built in 1792, this lovely house stands in attractive gardens opposite Ludlow Castle. It has a well-deserved reputation for warm hospitality and fine cuisine. Well-equipped bedrooms include two in a converted cottage and some with four-poster beds. The comfortable public rooms are elegantly appointed.
ROOMS: 11 en suite 2 annexe en suite (3 fmly) (1 GF) s £95-£250; d £130-£280 (incl. bkfst) **LB** **FACILITIES:** Xmas **CONF:** Thtr 28 Class 28 Board 24 Del from £135 **PARKING:** 16 **NOTES:** in restaurant Civ Wed 100 **CARDS:**

★★★67% Feathers

The Bull Ring SY8 1AA
☎ 01584 875261 01584 876030
e-mail: feathers.ludlow@btconnect.com
Dir: *from A49 and follow town centre signs to centre of Ludlow. Hotel on left*

Famous for the carved woodwork outside and in, this picturesque 17th-century hotel is one of the town's best-known landmarks and is in an excellent location. Bedrooms are traditional in style and décor. Public areas have retained much of the traditional charm; the first-floor lounge is particularly stunning.
ROOMS: 40 en suite (3 fmly) in 19 bedrooms s £60-£70; d £80-£90 (incl. bkfst) **LB** **FACILITIES:** Xmas **CONF:** Thtr 80 Class 40 Board 40 Del from £120 **SERVICES:** Lift **PARKING:** 33 **NOTES:** in restaurant Civ Wed 25 **CARDS:**

> Packed in a hurry?
> Ironing facilities should be available at all star levels, either in rooms or on request

★★68% Cliffe

Dinham SY8 2JE
☎ 01584 872063 01584 873991
e-mail: thecliffehotel@hotmail.com
Dir: *in town centre to Castle. Left at castle gates to Dinham, follow road over bridge. Take right fork, hotel 200yds on left*

Built in the 19th century and standing in extensive grounds and gardens, this privately owned and personally run hotel is quietly located close to the castle and the river. It provides well-equipped accommodation, and facilities include a lounge bar, a pleasant restaurant and a patio overlooking the garden.
ROOMS: 9 en suite (2 fmly) in all bedrooms s £40-£50; d £60-£80 (incl. bkfst) **LB** **PARKING:** 22 **NOTES:** in restaurant **CARDS:**

Travelodge

Travelodge

Woofferton SY8 4AL
☎ 08700 850 950 01584 711695
Dir: *on A49 at junct A456/B4362*

Travelodge offers good quality, good value, modern accommodation. Ideal for families, the spacious, en suite bedrooms include remote-control TV, tea and coffee-making facilities and luxury beds. Meals can be taken at the nearby family restaurant. For further details consult the Hotel Groups page.
ROOMS: 32 en suite s fr £25; d fr £25

LULWORTH COVE See West Lulworth

LUTON, Bedfordshire

Map 06 TL02

★★★66% Hotel St Lawrence

40 Guildford St LU1 2PA
☎ 01582 482119 01582 482818
e-mail: reservations@hotelstlawrence.co.uk
web: www.hotelstlawrence.co.uk
Dir: *M1 junct 10a & follow signs to town centre, after university take left fork at mini rdbt. Hotel 70yds on right*

This Victorian hotel enjoys a central location and smart public areas which include a modern restaurant and a welcoming bar. Bedrooms come in a variety of styles and sizes and are benefiting from ongoing refurbishment. Parking is available in the multi-storey opposite.
ROOMS: 28 en suite in 4 bedrooms s £65-£85; d £75-£85 (incl. bkfst) **FACILITIES:** Use of local fitness centre with pool & snooker club **NOTES:** in restaurant **CARDS:**

★★★60% The Chiltern Hotel

Waller Av LU4 9RU
☎ 0870 609 6120 01582 581859
e-mail: thechiltern@corushotels.com
Dir: *M1 junct 11, A505 to Luton past 2 sets of lights. Over rdbt, left at lights, hotel on right*

Conveniently close to the M1, this hotel is geared towards the

continued

business guest. It has a range of conference and meeting rooms. Bedrooms offer good levels of comfort. There is an air-conditioned restaurant and ample parking.

ROOMS: 91 en suite (6 fmly) ⊗ in 63 bedrooms **CONF:** Thtr 180 Class 120 Board 30 **SERVICES:** Lift **PARKING:** 150 **NOTES:** ⊗ in restaurant **CARDS:**

⌂ Travelodge

Travelodge

641 Dunstable Rd LU4 8RQ
☎ 08700 850 950 🖷 01582 490065
Dir: *M1 junct 11 towards Luton, hotel 100 yds on right*
Travelodge offers good quality, good value, modern accommodation. Ideal for families, the spacious, en suite bedrooms include remote-control TV, tea and coffee-making facilities and luxury beds. Meals can be taken at the nearby family restaurant. For further details consult the Hotel Groups page.
ROOMS: 140 en suite s fr £25; d fr £25 **CONF:** Thtr 80 Class 40 Board 30

LUTON AIRPORT, Bedfordshire — Map 06 TL12

⌂ Hotel Ibis Luton

ibis ACCOR hotels

Spittlesea Rd LU2 9NH
☎ 01582 424488 🖷 01582 455511
e-mail: H1040@accor-hotels.com
Dir: *From M1 junct 10 follow signs to airport*
Modern, budget hotel offering comfortable accommodation in bright and practical bedrooms. Breakfast is self-service and dinner is available in the restaurant. For further details, consult the Hotel Groups page.
ROOMS: 98 en suite s £49.95-£64.95; d £49.95-£64.95 **CONF:** Thtr 114 Class 64 Board 80

⌂ Travel Inn Luton Airport

travel inn

Osbourne Rd LU1 3HJ
☎ 08701 977166 🖷 01582 421900
Dir: *M1 junct 10 follow signs for Luton on A1081, at 3rd rdbt turn left onto Gypsy Lane, turn left at next rdbt*

Travel Inn offers good-quality, value-for-money accommodation.

continued

Spacious, en suite rooms with bath and shower comfortably accommodate a family of up to two adults and two children (to age 15). The restaurant and bar offers a varied menu. For further details consult the Hotel Groups page.
ROOMS: 129 en suite s £52.95-£58.95; d £52.95-£58.95 **CONF:** Thtr 70 Board 50

LYDFORD, Devon — Map 03 SX58

★★71% *Lydford House*

EX20 4AU
☎ 01822 820347 🖷 01822 820442
e-mail: relax@lydfordhouse.co.uk
web: www.lydfordhouse.co.uk
Dir: *off A386 halfway between Okehampton and Tavistock, signed Lydford, 0.25m on right*
Set in attractive grounds in a quiet location on the edge of Dartmoor, this friendly Victorian country house offers comfortable, well-equipped and attractively decorated accommodation. Public areas are spacious and offer a range of choices. The proprietors also run a livery stable which is adjacent to the property.
ROOMS: 12 rms (11 en suite) (4 fmly) **FACILITIES:** Riding **CONF:** Thtr 25 Class 25 Board 20 **PARKING:** 30 **NOTES:** ⊗ in restaurant Closed 25 Dec-Jan **CARDS:**

LYME REGIS, Dorset — Map 04 SY39

See also Colyford

★★★71% ® Alexandra

Pound St DT7 3HZ
☎ 01297 442010 🖷 01297 443229
e-mail: enquiries@hotelalexandra.co.uk
web: www.lymeregis.co.uk
Dir: *from A30 , A35, then onto A358, A3052 to Lyme Regis*
This welcoming, family-run hotel is Grade II listed and dates back to 1735. Public areas are spacious and comfortable, with ample seating areas to relax, unwind and enjoy the magnificent views. The elegant restaurant offers imaginative, innovative dishes. Bedrooms vary in size and shape, decorated with pretty chintz fabrics and attractive furniture.
ROOMS: 25 en suite 1 annexe en suite (8 fmly) (3 GF) s £50-£106; d £70-£136 (incl. bkfst) **LB** **PARKING:** 18 **NOTES:** ⊗ in restaurant Closed Xmas & Jan **CARDS:**

★★77% ® Swallows Eaves

EX24 6QJ
☎ 01297 553184 🖷 01297 553574
e-mail: swallows.eaves@talk21.com
(For full entry see Colyford)

Town House Hotel
Country House Hotel
⌂ Travel Accommodation

★★74% ® Mariners Hotel

Silver St DT7 3HS
☎ 01297 442753 🖷 01297 442431
e-mail: marinershotel@btopenworld.com
Dir: *W of town on A3052, right on B3070*
This small, friendly hotel has period character and charm and a relaxed atmosphere. The individually decorated bedrooms are comfortable; some rooms benefit from stunning views over the town to the sea. A beamed bar and choice of lounge is provided

continued on p378

LYME REGIS, continued

for guests, while in the restaurant carefully prepared meals use fresh ingredients, with local caught fish a highlight on the menus.

Mariners Hotel, Lyme Regis

ROOMS: 12 en suite ⊗ in 8 bedrooms s £55-£62; d £73-£86 (incl. bkfst) **FACILITIES:** Xmas **PARKING:** 20 **NOTES:** No children 7yrs ⊗ in restaurant Closed 27 Dec-31 Jan **CARDS:**

★★70% ***Buena Vista***
Pound St DT7 3HZ
☎ 01297 442494 📠 01297 444670
e-mail: buenavista@amserve.net
Dir: *W on A3052 out of town*
Set in an elevated position overlooking the Cobb, harbour and Dorset coastline, this family-run hotel provides friendly service. Bedrooms are individually styled with beds a particular feature, as is the collection of Victorian pictures and postcards. Guests can relax in the comfortable public areas and the award-winning gardens.
ROOMS: 18 rms (17 en suite) (1 fmly) **PARKING:** 18 **NOTES:** ⊗ in restaurant Closed Dec-Jan **CARDS:**

★★67% **Royal Lion**
Broad St DT7 3QF
☎ 01297 445622 📠 01297 445859
e-mail: reception@royallionhotel.fsnet.co.uk
web: www.royallionhotel.com
Dir: *From W on A35, take A3052 or from E take B3165 to Lyme Regis. Hotel in centre of town, opp The Fossil Shop. Car park at rear*
This 17th-century, former coaching inn is full of character and charm, and is situated a short walk from the seafront. Bedrooms vary in size; those in the newer wing are more spacious and some have balconies, sea views or a private terrace. In addition to the elegant dining room and guest lounges, a heated pool, small gym and snooker table are available.
ROOMS: 29 en suite (11 fmly) ⊗ in 12 bedrooms s £45-£50; d £86-£120 (incl. bkfst) **LB FACILITIES: Spa** Snooker Gym Jacuzzi Games room Pool table Table tennis Xmas **CONF:** Thtr 50 Class 20 Board 20 **PARKING:** 30 **NOTES:** ⊗ in restaurant
CARDS:

LYMINGTON, Hampshire — Map 05 SZ39

★★★75% **Passford House**
Mount Pleasant Ln SO41 8LS
☎ 01590 682398 📠 01590 683494
e-mail: sales@passfordhousehotel.co.uk
Dir: *from A337 at Lymington over mini rdbt. 1st right at Tollhouse pub, then after 1m right into Mount Pleasant Ln*
A peaceful hotel set in attractive grounds on the edge of town. Bedrooms vary in size but all are comfortably furnished and well-equipped. Extensive public areas include lounges, a smartly appointed restaurant and bar, and leisure facilities. A friendly and well-motivated team provides attentive service.
ROOMS: 49 en suite 2 annexe en suite (2 fmly) (10 GF) ⊗ in 10 bedrooms s £65-£120; d £80-£200 (incl. bkfst) **LB FACILITIES: Spa** Sauna Gym Putt green Petanque, Table tennis, Helipad, pool table Xmas **CONF:** Thtr 80 Class 30 Board 30 **PARKING:** 100
NOTES: No children 8yrs ⊗ in restaurant
CARDS:

★★★72% **Elmers Court**
South Baddesley Rd SO41 5ZB
☎ 01590 676011 📠 01590 679780
e-mail: elmerscourt@macdonald-hotels.co.uk
Dir: *M27 junct 1, through Lyndhurst, Brockenhurst & Lymington, hotel 200yds right after Lymington ferry terminal*

MACDONALD HOTELS

Originally known as The Elms, this Tudor-gabled manor house dates back to the 1820s. Ideally located at the edge of the New Forest and overlooking The Solent with views towards the Isle of Wight, the hotel offers suites and self-catering accommodation, along with well-appointed leisure facilities.
ROOMS: 42 annexe en suite (8 fmly) (22 GF) ⊗ in 16 bedrooms s £82-£105; d £144-£170 (incl. bkfst) **LB FACILITIES: Spa** supervised Squash Sauna Solarium Gym Putt green Jacuzzi Beauty treatment rooms,, Steam room, Aerobics classes ch fac Xmas
CONF: Thtr 100 Class 40 Board 40 Del from £110 **PARKING:** 100
NOTES: ⊗ in restaurant Civ Wed 100
CARDS:

★★★71% **Stanwell House**
14-15 High St SO41 9AA
☎ 01590 677123 📠 01590 677756
e-mail: sales@stanwellhousehotel.co.uk
web: www.stanwellhousehotel.co.uk
Dir: *A337 to town centre, on right of High St, before descent to quay*
Centrally situated, this stylish hotel offers friendly and attentive service. Bedrooms are comfortable and very well equipped; some rooms in the older part of the building are particularly interesting and some have four-poster beds. The award-winning cuisine provides interesting, freshly prepared dishes.
ROOMS: 29 en suite (1 fmly) ⊗ in 10 bedrooms s £85-£160; d £110-£160 (incl. bkfst) **LB CONF:** Thtr 30 Class 20 Board 22 Del from £125 **NOTES:** ⊗ in restaurant Civ Wed
CARDS:

★★★68% **String of Horses**
Mead End Rd SO41 6EH
☎ 01590 682631 📠 01590 682911
e-mail: relax@stringofhorses.co.uk
(For full entry see Sway)

★★70% The Mill at Gordleton
Silver St, Hordle SO41 6DJ
☎ 01590 682219 01590 683073
e-mail: gordletonmill@aol.com
Dir: *M27 junct 1 towards Lyndhurst to Lymington A337, turn right to Hordle at Tollhouse Inn, 1.5m to Mill*

A delightful 17th-century watermill located on the banks of the River Avon. The restaurant takes full advantage of the hotel's position and serves an extensive range of dishes at lunch and dinner. The picturesque gardens are popular for al fresco dining during the warmer months and the attractive bedrooms are equipped with whirlpool baths.
ROOMS: 9 en suite in 5 bedrooms s £85-£175; d £125-£175 (incl. bkfst) **FACILITIES:** Fishing **PARKING:** 60 **NOTES:** in restaurant RS Sun **CARDS:**

LYMM, Cheshire Map 15 SJ68

★★★68% Lymm Hotel
Whitbarrow Rd WA13 9AQ
☎ 01925 752233 01925 756035
e-mail: lymm@macdonald-hotels.co.uk
Dir: *take M6 to B5158 to Lymm. Left at junct, right at mini rdbt, left into Brookfield Rd and 3rd left into Whitbarrow Rd*

MACDONALD HOTELS

In a peaceful residential area, this hotel benefits from both its quiet setting and its convenient access to local motorway networks. The hotel offers comfortable bedrooms equipped for both the business and leisure guest. Public areas include an attractive bar and an elegant restaurant. There is also extensive parking.
ROOMS: 18 rms (15 en suite) 48 annexe en suite (5 fmly) (4 GF) in 34 bedrooms **FACILITIES:** STV Xmas **CONF:** BC Thtr 250 Class 140 Board 100 **PARKING:** 120 **NOTES:** in restaurant Civ Wed
CARDS:

Travelodge
Granada Services A50, Cliffe Ln WA13 0SP
☎ 08700 850 950 01925 759341

Travelodge

Travelodge offers good quality, good value, modern accommodation. Ideal for families, the spacious, en suite bedrooms include remote-control TV, tea and coffee-making facilities and luxury beds. Meals can be taken at the nearby family restaurant. For further details consult the Hotel Groups page.
ROOMS: 61 en suite s fr £25; d fr £25

LYMPSHAM, Somerset Map 04 ST35

★★69% *Batch Country Hotel*
Batch Ln BS24 0EX
☎ 01934 750371 01934 750501
web: www.batchcountryhotel.co.uk
Dir: *exit M5 junct 22, take last exit on rdbt signed A370 to Weston-S-Mare. After 3.5m turn left into Lympsham. After 1m sign at end of road*

THE CIRCLE Selected Individual Hotels GREAT BRITAIN

Rurally situated between Weston-Super-Mare and

continued on p380

LYMPSHAM, continued

Burnham-on-Sea, this former farmhouse offers a relaxed, friendly and peaceful environment. The comfortable bedrooms have views to the Mendip and Quantock Hills. Spacious lounges overlook the extensive gardens and the function room is very popular for wedding ceremonies. Meals are served in the beamed dining room.

Batch Country Hotel, Lympsham

ROOMS: 10 en suite (6 fmly) (1 GF) ⊗ in 2 bedrooms **FACILITIES:** Fishing **CONF:** Thtr 80 Class 60 Board 100 **PARKING:** 80 **NOTES:** ⊗ in restaurant Closed 25-26 Dec Civ Wed 120 **CARDS:**

See advert under WESTON-SUPER-MARE

LYNDHURST, Hampshire Map 05 SU30

★★★70% Crown

High St SO43 7NF
☎ 023 8028 2922 📠 023 8028 2751
e-mail: reception@crownhotel-lyndhurst.co.uk
web: www.crownhotel-lyndhurst.co.uk
***Dir:** in centre of village, opposite church*

Best Western

The Crown, with its stone mullioned windows, panelled rooms and elegant period decor evokes the style of an Edwardian English country house. Bedrooms are generally a good size and offer a useful range of facilities. Public areas have style and comfort and include a choice of function and meeting rooms. The pleasant garden and terrace are havens of peace and tranquillity.
ROOMS: 39 en suite (8 fmly) ⊗ in 23 bedrooms s £82-£87.50; d £115-£145 (incl. bkfst) **LB** **FACILITIES:** STV ch fac Xmas **CONF:** Thtr 70 Class 30 Board 45 Del from £115 **SERVICES:** Lift **PARKING:** 60 **NOTES:** ⊗ in restaurant Civ Wed 70 **CARDS:**

★★★69% Lyndhurst Park

High St SO43 7NL
☎ 023 8028 3923 📠 023 8028 3019
e-mail: lyndhurst.park@forestdale.com
***Dir:** M27 junct 1-3 to A35 to Lyndhurst. Hotel at bottom of High St*

Forestdale Hotels

Although it is only a short walk from the High Street, the hotel is offered some seclusion from the town by its five acres of mature grounds. The comfortable bedrooms include home-from-home touches such as ducks in the bath! There are two bars and an oak-panelled restaurant with a sunny conservatory.
ROOMS: 59 en suite (3 fmly) ⊗ in 10 bedrooms s fr £90; d fr £115 (incl. bkfst) **LB** **FACILITIES:** STV Snooker Sauna Table tennis Xmas **CONF:** Thtr 300 Class 120 Board 80 Del from £125 **SERVICES:** Lift **PARKING:** 100 **NOTES:** ⊗ in restaurant Civ Wed **CARDS:**

★★★67% Bell Inn

SO43 7HE
☎ 023 8081 2214 📠 023 8081 3958
e-mail: bell@bramshaw.co.uk
web: www.bramshaw.co.uk
(For full entry see Brook (Near Cadnam))

★★★66% Forest Lodge

Pikes Hill, Romsey Rd SO43 7AS
☎ 023 8028 3677 📠 023 8028 2940
e-mail: forest@newforesthotels.co.uk
web: www.newforesthotels.co.uk
***Dir:** M27 junct 1, A337 towards Lyndhurst. In village with police station and courts on right take 1st right into Pikes Hill*

Best Western

Situated on the edge of Lyndhurst, this hotel is set well back from the main road. Bedrooms are on different floors and a number are well suited for family use. The indoor pool, with delightful murals, is a real bonus.
ROOMS: 28 en suite (7 fmly) (6 GF) s fr £60; d £120-£165 (incl. bkfst) **LB** **FACILITIES:** Sauna Gym Xmas **CONF:** Thtr 100 Class 70 Board 50 Del from £90 **PARKING:** 50 **NOTES:** ⊗ in restaurant Civ Wed **CARDS:**

★★68% Ormonde House

Southampton Rd SO43 7BT
☎ 023 8028 2806 📠 023 8028 2004
e-mail: enquiries@ormondehouse.co.uk
***Dir:** 800yds E of Lyndhurst on A35 to Southampton*

Set back from the main road on the edge of Lyndhurst, this welcoming hotel combines an efficient mix of relaxed hospitality and attentive service. Bedrooms, including some on the ground floor, are well furnished and equipped. Larger suites with kitchen facilities are also available. Home-cooked dinners offer a range of carefully presented fresh ingredients.
ROOMS: 19 en suite 4 annexe en suite (1 fmly) (6 GF) ⊗ in all bedrooms s £35-£60; d £70-£120 (incl. bkfst) **LB** **FACILITIES:** **Spa** STV **PARKING:** 26 **NOTES:** ⊗ in restaurant Closed Xmas wk **CARDS:**

★71% Knightwood Lodge

Southampton Rd SO43 7BU
☎ 023 8028 2502 📠 023 8028 3730
e-mail: jackie4r@aol.com
web: www.knightwoodlodge.co.uk
***Dir:** exit M27 junct 1 follow A337 to Lyndhurst. Left at traffic lights in village onto A35 towards Southampton. Hotel 0.25m on left*

THE INDEPENDENTS

This friendly, family-run hotel is situated on the outskirts of Lyndhurst. Comfortable bedrooms are modern in style and well equipped with many useful extras. The hotel offers an excellent

continued

range of facilities including a swimming pool, a Jacuzzi and a small gym area.
ROOMS: 15 en suite 4 annexe en suite (2 fmly) s £45-£55; d £80-£110 (incl. bkfst) **LB** **FACILITIES:** STV Sauna Gym Jacuzzi Steam room **PARKING:** 15 **NOTES:** in restaurant
CARDS:

○ Le Poussin at Parkhill
Beaulieu Rd SO43 7FZ
☎ 023 8028 2944 023 8028 3268
e-mail: sales@lepoussin.co.uk
web: www.lepoussin.co.uk
Dir: *off A35 onto B3056 towards Beaulieu, hotel 1m on left*
Le Poussin at Parkhill is closing for 2 years for major refurbishment. In the meantime, the operation is moving to another establishment in the New Forest, Whitley Ridge Country House in Brockenhurst. Please see the AA website (www.theAA.com) for further information.

See advert on this page

Travelodge (New Forest)
A31 Westbound SO43 7GN
☎ 08700 850 950 02380 811544
Travelodge
Travelodge offers good quality, good value, modern accommodation. Ideal for families, the spacious, en suite bedrooms include remote-control TV, tea and coffee-making facilities and luxury beds. Meals can be taken at the nearby family restaurant. For further details consult the Hotel Groups page.
ROOMS: 32 en suite s fr £25; d fr £25

LYNMOUTH, Devon
Map 03 SS74
See also Lynton

★★★64% Tors
EX35 6NA
☎ 01598 753236 01598 752544
e-mail: torshotel@torslynmouth.co.uk
web: www.torslynmouth.co.uk
Dir: *adjacent to A39 on Countisbury Hill just before entering Lynmouth from Minehead*
In an elevated position overlooking Lynmouth Bay, this friendly hotel is set in five acres of woodland. The majority of the bedrooms benefit from the superb views, as do the public areas; which are generous and well presented. Both fixed-price and short carte menus are offered in the restaurant.
ROOMS: 31 en suite (6 fmly) s £68-£170; d £96-£200 (incl. bkfst) **LB** **FACILITIES:** Table tennis Pool table ch fac Xmas **CONF:** Thtr 60 Class 40 Board 25 **SERVICES:** Lift **PARKING:** 40 **NOTES:** in restaurant Closed 4-31 Jan RS Feb (wknds only)
CARDS:

Need a break without breaking the bank?
Latebeds offers last-minute deals with no nasty surprises at AA-approved hotels and B&Bs. Visit www.theAA.com to find out more

Popped the question?
Hotels with Civ Wed in their entry are licensed for civil wedding ceremonies. Maximum numbers for the ceremony only are shown, e.g. Civ Wed 120

★★73% Rising Sun
Harbourside EX35 6EG
☎ 01598 753223 01598 753480
e-mail: risingsunlynmouth@easynet.co.uk
web: www.risingsunlynmouth.co.uk
Dir: *M5 junct 23 to Minehead. A39 to Lynmouth, hotel on harbour*

This 'chocolate box' thatched inn that sits on the harbour front, was once a smugglers' inn. Popular with locals and hotel guests alike, there is the option of eating in either the convivial bar or the restaurant; a comfortable, quiet lounge is also available. Bedrooms, located in the inn or adjoining cottages, are all individually designed and have modern facilities.
ROOMS: 11 en suite 5 annexe en suite (1 GF) in 11 bedrooms **CONF:** Thtr 22 Class 18 Board 14 **NOTES:** No children 8yrs in restaurant **CARDS:**

LYNMOUTH, continued

★★68% Bath

Sea Front EX35 6EL
☎ 01598 752238 🖷 01598 753894
e-mail: bathhotel@torslynmouth.co.uk
Dir: *M5 junct 25, follow A39 to Minehead then Porlock and Lynmouth*
This well-established, friendly hotel is situated near the harbour and offers lovely views from the attractive, sea-facing bedrooms and an excellent starting point for scenic walks. There are two lounges and a sun lounge and the restaurant menu makes good use of fresh produce and locally caught fish.
ROOMS: 22 en suite (9 fmly) ⊗ in 1 bedroom s £40-£53; d £66-£116 (incl. bkfst) **LB** **FACILITIES:** ch fac **PARKING:** 12 **NOTES:** ⊗ in restaurant Closed Jan & Dec RS Feb-Mar and Nov
CARDS:

LYNTON, Devon

Map 03 SS74

See also Lynmouth

★★★68% Lynton Cottage

North Walk EX35 6ED
☎ 01598 752342 🖷 01598 752597
e-mail: enquiries@lynton-cottage.co.uk
web: www.lynton-cottage.co.uk
Dir: *M25 junct 23 A39 to Lynmouth then Lynton, hotel 100mtrs on right*

Magnificent views can be enjoyed from this peaceful hideaway, which stands some 500 feet above the sea. Bedrooms vary in size and most have scenic views, whilst public areas, such as the cosy Victorian-style bar, provide a relaxing environment. In Sanford's Restaurant, a short carte offers a balanced selection of tempting dishes.
ROOMS: 15 en suite (2 fmly) (1 GF) ⊗ in 3 bedrooms s £54-£105; d £78-£150 (incl. bkfst) **LB** **CONF:** Thtr 34 Class 24 Board 24 Del from £70 **PARKING:** 17 **NOTES:** ⊗ in restaurant Closed Dec-Jan
CARDS:

★★72% Seawood

North Walk EX35 6HJ
☎ 01598 752272 🖷 01598 752272
e-mail: GIInJnK@aol.com
Dir: *turn right at St. Mary's Church in Lynton High St for hotel, 2nd on left*
Tucked away in a quiet area and spectacularly situated 400 feet above the seashore, the Seawood enjoys magnificent views, and is set in delightful grounds. This is a friendly place where many guests return on a regular basis. Bedrooms, many with sea views and some with four-poster beds, are comfortable and well equipped. At dinner, the daily-changing menu provides freshly prepared and appetising dishes.
ROOMS: 12 en suite s £30-£34; d £60-£76 (incl. bkfst) **PARKING:** 12 **NOTES:** No children 10yrs ⊗ in restaurant Closed Dec-Feb
CARDS:

★★69% Chough's Nest

North Walk EX35 6HJ
☎ 01598 753315 🖷 01598 753315
e-mail: relax@choughsnesthotel.co.uk
web: www.choughsnesthotel.co.uk
Dir: *on Lynton High St. Turn at St. Marys Church, hotel 0.5m on left.*
Lying on the south-west coastal path, this charming hotel can claim to have one of the most spectacular views around. The resident owners work hard to ensure a relaxed and enjoyable stay. Bedrooms offer ample comfort and quality, the majority looking out across the sea. The dining room, also sharing the wonderful backdrop, is a lovely setting in which to enjoy tasty food in a convivial atmosphere.
ROOMS: 11 en suite (1 fmly) ⊗ in all bedrooms s £30-£35; d £48-£88 (incl. bkfst) **LB** **FACILITIES:** Xmas **PARKING:** 10 **NOTES:** No dogs No children 2yrs ⊗ in restaurant **CARDS:**

★★65% *Sandrock*

Longmead EX35 6DH
☎ 01598 753307 🖷 01598 752665
Dir: *follow signs to 'The Valley of the Rocks'*
On the edge of the village and at the head of the Valley of the Rocks, this long-established, family-run hotel offers light and airy, modern bedrooms. The public bar is popular with locals and residents alike and there is a first-floor lounge.
ROOMS: 8 en suite (3 fmly) **PARKING:** 9 **NOTES:** ⊗ in restaurant Closed Nov-Jan **CARDS:**

LYTHAM ST ANNES, Lancashire

Map 18 SD32

★★★★67% Clifton Arms

West Beach, Lytham FY8 5QJ
☎ 01253 739898 🖷 01253 730657
e-mail: welcome@cliftonarms-lytham.com
web: www.cliftonarm-lytham.com
Dir: *on A584 along seafront*

This well-established hotel occupies a prime position overlooking Lytham Green and the Ribble Estuary beyond. The bedrooms vary in size and style; front-facing rooms are particularly spacious and some of the side rooms are very stylish and contemporary. There is an elegant restaurant and an open-plan lounge and cocktail bar.
ROOMS: 48 en suite (2 fmly) ⊗ in 25 bedrooms s £60-£98; d £90-£120 (incl. bkfst) **LB** **FACILITIES:** STV ch fac Xmas **CONF:** Thtr 200 Class 100 Board 60 Del from £138 **SERVICES:** Lift **PARKING:** 50 **NOTES:** No dogs ⊗ in restaurant Civ Wed 100
CARDS:

See advert on opposite page

> Early start?
> Hotels at all star levels should provide in-room alarm clocks and/or alarm calls

★★★69% *Bedford*

307-311 Clifton Dr South FY8 1HN
☎ 01253 724636 📠 01253 729244
e-mail: reservations@bedford-hotel.com
web: www.bedford-hotel.com
Dir: *from M55 follow signs for airport to last lights. Left through 2 sets of lights. Hotel 300yds on left*

This popular family-run hotel, close to the town centre and the seafront, has been stylishly extended. Bedrooms vary in size and style and include family and four-poster rooms. New bedrooms are particularly elegant and tasteful. Spacious public areas include a choice of lounges and bars, a coffee shop, fitness facilities and an impressive function suite.

ROOMS: 46 en suite (7 fmly) ⊗ in 45 bedrooms **FACILITIES:** STV Solarium Gym Jacuzzi ♫ **CONF:** Thtr 200 Class 140 Board 60 **SERVICES:** Lift **PARKING:** 25 **NOTES:** ✈ ⊗ in restaurant Civ Wed 180
CARDS:

★★★67% Chadwick

South Promenade FY8 1NP
THE INDEPENDENTS
☎ 01253 720061 📠 01253 714455
e-mail: sales@thechadwickhotel.com
web: www.thechadwickhotel.com
Dir: *M6 junct 32 take M55 to Blackpool then A5230 to South Shore. Follow signs for St Annes*

This popular, comfortable and traditional hotel enjoys a seafront location. Bedrooms vary in size and style, but all are very thoughtfully equipped; those at the front boast panoramic sea views. Public rooms are spacious and comfortably furnished and the smart bar is stocked with 200 malt whiskies. The hotel has a well-equipped, air-conditioned gym and indoor pool.

ROOMS: 75 en suite (28 fmly) (13 GF) s £42-£50; d £62-£72 (incl. bkfst) **LB** **FACILITIES: Spa** STV Sauna Solarium Gym Jacuzzi Turkish bath Games room Soft play adventure area ♫ ch fac Xmas **CONF:** Thtr 72 Class 24 Board 28 Del from £66 **SERVICES:** Lift **PARKING:** 40 **NOTES:** ✈ ⊗ in restaurant
CARDS:

See advert on this page

★★★64% Glendower

North Promenade FY8 2NQ
Best Western
☎ 01253 723241 📠 01253 640069
e-mail: glendowerhotel@bestwestern.co.uk
web: www.theglendowerhotel.co.uk
Dir: *M55 follow airport signs. Left at Promenade to St Annes. Hotel 500yds from pier*

Located on the seafront and with easy access to the town centre, this popular, friendly hotel offers comfortably furnished, well-equipped accommodation. Bedrooms vary in size and style and include four-poster rooms and very popular family suites.

continued on p384

L

LYTHAM ST ANNES, continued

Public areas feature a choice of smart, comfortable lounges, a bright and modern leisure club and function facilities.
ROOMS: 60 en suite (17 fmly) ⊗ in 12 bedrooms s £52-£67; d £84-£114 (incl. bkfst) **LB** **FACILITIES: Spa** STV supervised Snooker Sauna Solarium Gym Jacuzzi Childrens playroom ch fac Xmas **CONF:** Thtr 150 Class 120 Board 40 Del from £82 **SERVICES:** Lift **PARKING:** 45 **NOTES:** ⊗ in restaurant **CARDS:**

★★69% Lindum

63-67 South Promenade FY8 1LZ
☎ 01253 721534 & 722516 01253 721364
e-mail: info@lindumhotel.co.uk
web: www.lindumhotel.co.uk
Dir: *from M55 follow A5230 & signs for Blackpool Airport. After airport, left at lights to St Annes, right at lights in town centre. 1st left onto seafront. Hotel 250yds on left*

The same family has run this friendly and popular seafront hotel for over 40 years. Well-equipped bedrooms are generally spacious and some enjoy superb coastal views. Extensive public areas include a games room, a choice of lounges and a popular health suite. The open-plan restaurant offers a good choice of well-cooked dishes at breakfast and dinner.
ROOMS: 76 en suite (25 fmly) ⊗ in all bedrooms s £30-£45; d £50-£79 (incl. bkfst) **LB** **FACILITIES:** Sauna Solarium Jacuzzi ♫ ch fac Xmas **CONF:** Thtr 80 Class 30 Board 25 Del from £55 **SERVICES:** Lift air con **PARKING:** 20 **NOTES:** ⊗ in restaurant **CARDS:**

Premier Lodge (Lytham St Annes)

PREMIER LODGE.com

Church Rd FY8 5LH
☎ 0870 9906548 0870 9906549
web: www.premierlodge.com
Dir: *exit M55 rbt signed Lytham St. Annes, left and over mini rdbt right at lights. Left into Ballam Rd. 1m right at T-junct. Right at next junct. Right then 2nd right*
High quality, modern, budget accommodation, ideal for families and business travellers. All rooms feature bath, power shower and satellite TV, and most have telephones / modem points. The adjacent bar and restaurant offers a wide and varied menu.
ROOMS: 22 en suite s £50; d £50

> Late for dinner?
> Quality Standards mean that last orders for dinner vary according to star rating and should be no earlier than:
> ★★ 7.00pm ★★★ 8.00pm ★★★★ 9.00pm
> ★★★★★ 10.00pm

MACCLESFIELD, Cheshire

Map 16 SJ97

★★★★68% Shrigley Hall Hotel Golf & Country Club

PARAMOUNT GROUP OF HOTELS

Shrigley Park, Pott Shrigley SK10 5SB
☎ 01625 575757 01625 573323
e-mail: shrigleyhall@paramount-hotels.co.uk
web: www.paramount-hotels.co.uk/shrigx.html
Dir: *off A523 at Legh Arms towards Pott Shrigley. Hotel 2m on left before village*
Originally built in 1825, Shrigley Hall is an impressive hotel set in 262 acres of mature parkland. Features include a championship golf course and stunning views of the countryside. There is a wide choice of bedroom size and style. The public areas are spacious, combining traditional and contemporary décor, and include a well-equipped gym.
ROOMS: 150 en suite (8 fmly) ⊗ in 28 bedrooms s £118-£131; d £142-£156 (incl. bkfst) **LB** **FACILITIES:** STV supervised 18 Fishing Sauna Solarium Gym Putt green Jacuzzi Beauty salon, tydro centre, Swimming pool supervised ♫ Xmas **CONF:** Thtr 280 Class 140 Board 50 Del from £149 **SERVICES:** Lift **PARKING:** 300 **NOTES:** ⊗ in restaurant Civ Wed **CARDS:**

★★★70% *Best Western Hollin Hall*

Best Western

Jackson Ln, Kerridge, Bollington SK10 5BG
☎ 01625 573246 01625 574791
e-mail: sales@hollinhallhotel.com
Dir: *off A523, 2m along B5090*
Set in the peaceful Cheshire countryside, this hotel is convenient for Manchester Airport (courtesy transport available). The main building has an impressive carved staircase, high ceilings and a bar lounge. Modern cooking is provided in the newly added Orangey conservatory and a gym and sauna is now available. Attractively furnished accommodation is situated in a modern extension.
ROOMS: 54 en suite (2 fmly) ⊗ in 36 bedrooms **FACILITIES:** STV Sauna Gym Free use neighbouring Leisure Club & Golf Course **CONF:** Thtr 120 Class 50 Board 50 **PARKING:** 200 **NOTES:** ⊗ in restaurant Civ Wed 100 **CARDS:**

Premier Lodge (Macclesfield)

PREMIER LODGE.com

Congleton Rd, Gawsworth SK11 7XD
☎ 0870 9906412 0870 9906413
web: www.premierlodge.com
Dir: *2m from Macclesfield. Exit M6 junct 17, A534 to Congleton, then A536 towards Macclesfield. Follow road to Gawsworth, hotel on left*
High quality, modern, budget accommodation, ideal for families and business travellers. All rooms feature bath, power shower and satellite TV, and most have telephones / modem points. The adjacent bar and restaurant offers a wide and varied menu.
ROOMS: 28 en suite s £50; d £50 **CONF:** Thtr 10 Board 10

Travel Inn

Tytherington Business Park, Springwood Way, Tytherington SK10 2XA
☎ 08701 977167 01625 422874
Dir: *on A523 Tytherington Business Park*
Travel Inn offers good-quality, value-for-money accommodation. Spacious, en suite rooms with bath and shower comfortably accommodate a family of up to two adults and two children (to age 15). The restaurant and bar offers a varied menu. For further details consult the Hotel Groups page.
ROOMS: 40 en suite s £45.95-£46.95; d £45.95-£46.95 **CONF:** Thtr 20

M

Travelodge Macclesfield

London Rd South SK12 4NA
☎ 08700 850 950 🖷 01625 875292
Dir: *on A523*
Travelodge offers good quality, good value, modern accommodation. Ideal for families, the spacious, en suite bedrooms include remote-control TV, tea and coffee-making facilities and luxury beds. Meals can be taken at the nearby family restaurant. For further details consult the Hotel Groups page.
ROOMS: 32 en suite s fr £25; d fr £25

MAIDENCOMBE See Torquay

MAIDENHEAD, Berkshire
Map 06 SU88
See also Bray

Top 200 – Hotel

★★★★ Fredrick's
Shoppenhangers Rd SL6 2PZ
☎ 01628 581000 🖷 01628 771054
e-mail: reservations@fredricks-hotel.co.uk
web: www.fredricks-hotel.co.uk
Dir: *M4 junct 8/9 onto A404(M) to Maidenhead West and Henley. 1st exit 9a to White Waltham. Left into Shoppenhangers Rd to Maidenhead, Fredrick's is on right*
This delightful hotel, in a quiet location, is in easy reach of the M4 and just 30 minutes from London. The spacious bedrooms are all comfortably furnished and very well equipped. An enthusiastic team of staff ensure friendly and efficient service. The highlight of any visit is a meal in the restaurant, where the focus is on high-quality ingredients. Wentworth and Sunningdale golf courses are both within 20 minutes' drive.
ROOMS: 37 en suite (11 GF) s £195-£215; d £260-£280 (incl. bkfst) **LB FACILITIES: Spa** STV supervised supervised Sauna Gym Jacuzzi Treatment rooms, hydrotherapy, Oriental steam room, Dead Sea flotation room **CONF:** BC Thtr 120 Class 80 Board 60 Del from £270 **SERVICES:** air con **PARKING:** 90 **NOTES:** Closed 24 Dec-3 Jan Civ Wed 120
CARDS:

★★68% Elva Lodge
Castle Hill SL6 4AD
☎ 01628 622948 🖷 01628 778954
e-mail: reservations@elvalodgehotel.co.uk
web: www.elvalodgehotel.co.uk
Dir: *A4 from Maidenhead towards Reading. Hotel at top of hill on left*
Within easy reach of the town centre, this family-run hotel offers a warm welcome and friendly service. Bedrooms are pleasantly decorated and equipped with thoughtful extras. Spacious public

continued

areas include a newly refurbished lounge, a bar and the Lion's Brassiere, which offers a wide range of popular dishes.

ROOMS: 26 rms (23 en suite) (1 fmly) (5 GF) in 6 bedrooms s £55-£95; d £70-£108 (incl. bkfst) **FACILITIES:** Reduced rates at local Leisure Centre **CONF:** Thtr 50 Class 30 Board 30 **PARKING:** 32 **NOTES:** in restaurant Closed 24-30 Dec Civ Wed 60
CARDS:

MAIDSTONE, Kent
Map 07 TQ75

★★★★70% Marriott Tudor Park Hotel & Country Club
Ashford Rd, Bearsted ME14 4NQ
☎ 01622 734334 🖷 01622 735360
e-mail: salesadmin.tudorpark@marriotthotels.co.uk
Dir: *M20 junct 8 to Lenham. Right at rdbt towards Bearsted and Maidstone on A20. Hotel 1m on left*
This fine country hotel provides good levels of comfort. Guests can dine in the main restaurant, Fairviews, which offers a range of modern, eclectic dishes, or in the more relaxed environment of the Long Weekend Brasserie. Take time to enjoy the excellent range of leisure options, such as playing golf, a workout, a swim, or pamper yourself in the beauty salon.
ROOMS: 120 en suite (48 fmly) (60 GF) in 65 bedrooms **FACILITIES: Spa** STV 18 Sauna Solarium Gym Putt green Driving range, Beauty salon, Steam room Xmas **CONF:** Thtr 250 Class 100 Board 60 **SERVICES:** Lift **PARKING:** 250 **NOTES:** in restaurant Civ Wed 180 **CARDS:**

★★★69% Russell

136 Boxley Rd ME14 2AE
☎ 01622 692221 🖷 01622 762084
e-mail: res@therussellhotel.com

Since its days as a Carmelite convent, this Victorian building has been extended and modernised. Set in attractive grounds and offering a range of function rooms, the hotel is a popular venue for weddings and conferences. The well-maintained bedrooms

continued on p386

MAIDSTONE, continued

feature pleasing, modern décor and the newly refurbished ground-floor public areas have considerable appeal.
ROOMS: 42 en suite (2 fmly) ⊗ in 8 bedrooms s £65-£95; d £85-£125 (incl. bkfst) **LB** **FACILITIES:** All residents allowed to use facilities at David Lloyd Health & Fitness Centre Xmas **CONF:** Thtr 300 Class 100 Board 70 Del from £100 **PARKING:** 100 **NOTES:** ⊗ in restaurant Civ Wed 250
CARDS:

★★★67% Larkfield Priory

London Rd, Larkfield ME20 6HJ
☎ 01732 846858 📠 01732 846786
e-mail: larkfieldpriory@corushotels.com
Dir: *M20 junct 4 take A228 to West Malling. At traffic lights left signed to Maidstone on A20, after 1m hotel on left*

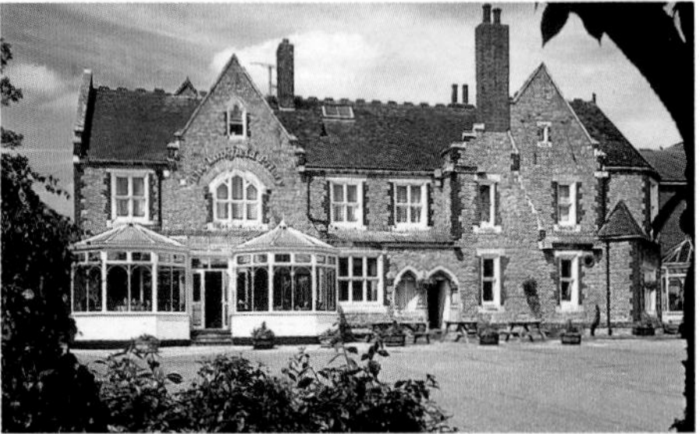

Conveniently located and close to the motorway links, this hotel, which dates from the 1890s, offers comfort and services to suit either the business or touring guest. Bedrooms are bright and smart. A spacious lounge and welcoming bar are available and in the dining room, choices can be made from the table d'hôte or carte menus.
ROOMS: 52 en suite (9 GF) ⊗ in 24 bedrooms s fr £69; d fr £69 **LB** **FACILITIES:** Xmas **CONF:** Thtr 80 Class 36 Board 30 Del from £130 **PARKING:** 80 **NOTES:** ⊗ in restaurant
CARDS:

★★69% Grange Moor

St Michael's Rd ME16 8BS
☎ 01622 677623 📠 01622 678246
e-mail: reservations@grangemoor.co.uk
Dir: *Town centre, towards A26 Tonbridge Rd. Hotel 0.25m on left, just after Church*
Expect a warm welcome at this friendly, family-run hotel, which is ideally situated, within easy walking distance of the town centre. Bedrooms, many of which have now been refurbished, are comfortable and well-appointed. Public areas include a popular bar, a smart restaurant and a small residents' lounge.
ROOMS: 39 en suite 12 annexe en suite (6 fmly) ⊗ in 21 bedrooms s £45-£49; d £58-£60 (incl. bkfst) **LB** **CONF:** Thtr 120 Class 60 Board 40 Del £85 **PARKING:** 60 **NOTES:** Closed 26-30 Dec Civ Wed 80
CARDS:

Innkeeper's Lodge Maidstone

Sandling Rd ME14 2RF
☎ 01622 692212 📠 01622 679265
www.innkeeperslodge.com
Dir: *M20 junct 6, S onto A229 towards Maidstone. At 3rd rdbt, turn left and left again*
Smart rooms meet essential business requirements but also have home comforts, and depending on location may well have meeting rooms and pub dining. Dining options generally include all-day menus plus the added advantage of breakfast.
ROOMS: 12 en suite s £52-£59.95; d £52-£59.95

Travel Inn (Maidstone Allington)

London Rd ME16 0HG
☎ 08701 977168 📠 01622 672469
Dir: *M20 junct 5, 0.5m on London Rd towards Maidstone*
Travel Inn offers good-quality, value-for-money accommodation. Spacious, en suite rooms with bath and shower comfortably accommodate a family of up to two adults and two children (to age 15). The restaurant and bar offers a varied menu. For further details consult the Hotel Groups page.
ROOMS: 40 en suite s £45.95-£46.95; d £45.95-£46.95
CONF: Thtr 45 Board 30

Travel Inn (Maidstone Sandling)

Allington Lock, Sandling ME14 3AS
☎ 08701 977308 📠 01622 715159
Dir: *M20 junct 6 follow sign for Museum of Kent Life*
Travel Inn offers good-quality, value-for-money accommodation. Spacious, en suite rooms with bath and shower comfortably accommodate a family of up to two adults and two children (to age 15). The restaurant and bar offers a varied menu. For further details consult the Hotel Groups page.
ROOMS: 40 en suite s £45.95-£46.95; d £45.95-£46.95

MAIDSTONE MOTORWAY SERVICE AREA (M20), Kent — Map 07 TQ85

Travel Inn (Maidstone Hollingbourne)

ME17 1SS
☎ 08701 977169 📠 01622 739535
Dir: *M20 junct 8*
Travel Inn offers good-quality, value-for-money accommodation. Spacious, en suite rooms with bath and shower comfortably accommodate a family of up to two adults and two children (to age 15). The restaurant and bar offers a varied menu. For further details consult the Hotel Groups page.
ROOMS: 58 en suite s £45.95-£46.95; d £45.95-£46.95
CONF: Thtr 30 Board 18

MALDON See Tolleshunt Knights

MALHAM, North Yorkshire — Map 18 SD96

★★65% The Buck Inn

BD23 4DA
☎ 01729 830317 📠 01729 830670
e-mail: thebuckinn@ukonline.co.uk
Dir: *from Skipton, take A65 to Gargrave, the 7m to Malham*
Situated at the centre of a popular village, this attractive inn is full of character. Bedrooms are all individual, some with four-poster beds; all are comfortable and well equipped. Imaginative menus offer a good choice of home-made dishes. A wide range of real ales and malt whiskies are served in the two cosy bars.
ROOMS: 10 en suite (3 fmly) s £30-£50; d £65-£90 (incl. bkfst) **LB** **FACILITIES:** Riding ch fac Xmas **CONF:** Class 1 Board 1 Del from £75 **PARKING:** 25 **NOTES:** ⊗ in restaurant
CARDS:

MALMESBURY, Wiltshire Map 04 ST98

Top 200 – Hotel

★★★★ Whatley Manor
Easton Grey SN16 0RB
☎ 01666 822888 01666 826120
e-mail: reservations@whatleymanor.com
web: www.whatleymanor.com
Dir: *M4 junct 17 to Malmesbury, left at t-junct, left at next t-junct onto B4040, hotel 2m on left*

This impressive country house has been lovingly renovated to provide the highest levels of luxury. Spacious bedrooms, mostly with views over the attractive gardens, are individually decorated with splendid features. Two restaurants are available: Mazo's brassiere and the fine dining option of The Dining Room. A magnificent spa with contemporary facilities is very inviting. Nominated for the AA Hotel of the Year Award for England 2004-5.

ROOMS: 23 en suite (4 GF) in 6 bedrooms s £275-£850; d £275-£850 (incl. bkfst) **LB** **FACILITIES: Spa** STV Fishing Sauna Solarium Gym Jacuzzi Cinema, hydro pool Xmas **CONF:** BC Thtr 40 Class 20 Board 25 Del from £295 **SERVICES:** Lift **PARKING:** 100 **NOTES:** No children 12yrs in restaurant Civ Wed **CARDS:**

★★★76% The Old Rectory Country House Hotel
SN16 9EP
☎ 01666 577194 01666 577853
e-mail: office@oldrectorycrudwell.co.uk
web: www.oldrectorycrudwell.co.uk
Dir: *M4 junct 17. Follow A429 to Cirencester, right opposite Plough pub in Crudwell. Hotel next to church*

A former rectory, this beautiful house, with its Victorian walled garden, offers a feeling of peace and seclusion. Individually decorated bedrooms offer comfort coupled with a host of thoughtful touches for guests' enjoyment. The highlight is the wood-panelled restaurant where local produce forms the basis of well-prepared dishes.

ROOMS: 12 en suite (1 fmly) in all bedrooms s £75-£108; d £98-£169 (incl. bkfst) **LB** **FACILITIES:** ch fac Xmas **CONF:** Thtr 40 Class 20 Board 20 Del from £125 **PARKING:** 50 **NOTES:** in restaurant Civ Wed 80 **CARDS:**

★★★75% Old Bell
CLASSIC BRITISH
Abbey Row SN16 0AG
☎ 01666 822344 01666 825145
e-mail: info@oldbellhotel.com
web: www.oldbellhotel.com
Dir: *M4 junct 11, follow A429 north. Left at first rdbt. Left at T-junction. Hotel next to Abbey*

Dating back to 1220, the Old Bell is reputed to be the oldest purpose-built hotel in England, and is now under new ownership. Bedrooms vary in size and style; those in the main house are traditionally furnished with antiques, while the newer bedrooms are modelled on a quasi-Japanese theme. Guests have a choice of comfortable sitting areas and dining options. Children are also well-catered for.

ROOMS: 16 en suite 15 annexe en suite (7 GF) in 12 bedrooms s fr £85; d fr £110 (incl. bkfst) **LB** **FACILITIES: Spa** STV Aromatherapy massages Xmas **CONF:** Thtr 50 Class 22 Board 28 Del from £130 **PARKING:** 31 **NOTES:** in restaurant Civ Wed 80 **CARDS:**

★★74% Mayfield House
Best Western
Crudwell SN16 9EW
☎ 01666 577409 01666 577977
e-mail: reception@mayfieldhousehotel.co.uk
web: www.mayfieldhousehotel.co.uk
Dir: *3m N on A429 from Malmesbury*

Guests are assured of a warm welcome at this charming hotel, on the edge of the Cotswolds. An imaginative menu is served in the renovated restaurant, overlooking the attractive gardens. Additionally, there is a foyer lounge and a bar offering a wide range of popular dishes. The bedrooms are all equipped with modern facilities.

ROOMS: 21 en suite 3 annexe en suite (2 fmly) in 6 bedrooms s £69; d £92 (incl. bkfst) **LB** **FACILITIES:** Xmas **CONF:** Thtr 40 Class 30 Board 25 Del from £105 **PARKING:** 50 **NOTES:** in restaurant **CARDS:**

See advert on this page

Packed in a hurry?
Ironing facilities should be available at all star levels, either in rooms or on request

M

MALTON, North Yorkshire Map 19 SE77

★★★72% Burythorpe House

Burythorpe YO17 9LB
☎ 01653 658200 01653 658204
e-mail: reception@burythorpehousehotel.com
web: www.burythorpehousehotel.com
Dir: *4m S of Malton, outside Burythorpe and 4m from A64 (York to Scarborough)*

This charming house offers spacious and individually furnished bedrooms. Five rooms are situated in a rear courtyard, two are equipped for less able guests, and all benefiting from small kitchen areas. Comfortable, spacious lounge areas are provided along with an impressive oak-panelled dining room where interesting, freshly prepared meals are served. Leisure facilities are available.

ROOMS: 11 en suite 5 annexe en suite (2 fmly) (5 GF) in all bedrooms s fr £55; d £72-£112 (incl. bkfst) **LB** **FACILITIES:** Snooker Sauna Solarium Gym Xmas **PARKING:** 40 **NOTES:** in restaurant Civ Wed **CARDS:**

★★65% Talbot

Yorkersgate YO17 7AJ
☎ 01653 694031 01653 693355
e-mail: sales@englishrosehotels.co.uk
Dir: *off A64 towards Malton. Hotel on right*

Situated close to the centre of town this long-established, creeper-covered hotel looks out towards the River Derwent and open countryside. Bedroom sizes vary, but all are comfortable. The public rooms are traditional and elegantly furnished and include a bar plus a separate lounge.

ROOMS: 31 en suite (3 fmly) s £39.50-£55; d £70-£120 (incl. bkfst) **LB** **FACILITIES:** Xmas **CONF:** Thtr 50 Board 20 Del from £75 **PARKING:** 30 **NOTES:** in restaurant **CARDS:**

See advert on opposite page

★★63% *Green Man*

15 Market St YO17 7LY
☎ 01653 600370 01653 696006
e-mail: greenman@englishrosehotels.co.uk
Dir: *from A64 follow signs to Malton town centre. Left into Market St, hotel on left*

This friendly hotel set in the centre of town includes an inviting reception lounge where a log fire burns in winter. There is also a cosy bar, and dining takes place in the traditional restaurant at the rear. Bedrooms vary in size and are thoughtfully equipped.

ROOMS: 24 en suite (4 fmly) **CONF:** Thtr 120 Class 20 Board 40 **PARKING:** 40 **NOTES:** in restaurant
CARDS:

MALVERN, Worcestershire Map 10 SO74

★★★75% Colwall Park

Walwyn Rd, Colwall WR13 6QG
☎ 01684 540000 01684 540847
e-mail: hotel@colwall.com
web: www.colwall.com
Dir: *Between Malvern & Ledbury in centre of Colwall on B4218*

Standing in extensive gardens, this hotel was purpose built in the early 20th century to serve the local racetrack. Today the proprietors and loyal staff provide high levels of hospitality and service, and the Seasons restaurant has a well-deserved reputation

continued

for its cuisine. Bedrooms have been tastefully refurbished and public areas help to create a fine country-house atmosphere.

ROOMS: 22 en suite (1 fmly) in 6 bedrooms s £65; d £110-£130 **LB** **FACILITIES:** STV Boules Xmas **CONF:** Thtr 150 Class 80 Board 50 Del £140 **PARKING:** 40 **NOTES:** in restaurant **CARDS:**

See advert on opposite page

★★★74% Cottage in the Wood

Holywell Rd, Malvern Wells WR14 4LG
☎ 01684 575859 01684 560662
e-mail: proprietor@cottageinthewood.co.uk
web: www.cottageinthewood.co.uk
Dir: *3m S of Great Malvern off A449, 500yds N of B4209 turning, on opposite side of road*

This delightful family-run hotel enjoys magnificent views across the Severn Valley. The cosy bedrooms are divided between the main house, Beech Cottage and the Pinnacles. All are well equipped and have many thoughtful extras. Public rooms are elegantly appointed and feature real fires, deep-cushioned sofas and fresh flowers.

ROOMS: 8 en suite 23 annexe en suite (10 GF) in 11 bedrooms s £79-£99; d £99-£170 (incl. bkfst) **LB** **FACILITIES:** STV Direct access to Malvern Hills Xmas **CONF:** Thtr 20 Board 14 Del £155 **PARKING:** 40 **NOTES:** in restaurant **CARDS:**

See advert on opposite page

★★★73% Foley Arms

Best Western

14 Worcester Rd WR14 4QS
☎ 01684 573397 01684 569665
e-mail: reservations@foleyarmshotel.com
web: www.foleyarmshotel.co.uk
Dir: *M5 junct 8 N or junct 7 S or M50 junct 1 to Great Malvern on A449*

With spectacular views of the Severn Valley, this hotel provides attentive, friendly service. Reputed to be the oldest hotel in Malvern, it is situated in the heart of town. The bedrooms are comfortable and tastefully decorated with period furnishings and

continued on p390

M

Colwall Park

Hotel, Bar & Restaurant

Winners of **the AA Courtesy & Care Award for England** we are situated on the sunny western side of the glorious Malvern Hills. Surrounded by lovely gardens with footpaths leading directly onto the hills.

Our Award Winning **Seasons Restaurant** serves gourmet food at reasonable prices. The friendly and popular **Lantern Bar**, is a meeting place for locals and residents, features a crackling log fire, real ales, great house wines and an exciting menu of home made meals and snacks.

T: 01684 540000 - F: 01684 540847
E: hotel@colwall.com - www.colwall.com

THE TALBOT HOTEL ★★

An elegant Georgian coaching inn.
31 pretty en-suite bedrooms.
Excellent food - smiling service.
Near to York, Castle Howard, Flamingo Land and the North Yorkshire Moors.

Yorkersgate, Malton, Nr York
North Yorkshire YO17 7AJ
Tel: 01653 694031 Fax: 01653 693355

THE FOLEY ARMS HOTEL
MALVERN

A historic Georgian hotel with the style and ambience of a country house – The Foley Arms is set on the slopes of the wonderful Malvern Hills and has far reaching views over the Severn Valley from the sun terrace and most of the 28 well appointed bedrooms. Malvern makes an ideal touring base for the Cotswolds and Wales.

AA rosetted terrace restaurant and cosy real ale bar with traditional bar food. Comfortable lounges, log fires, warm welcome.

Worcester Road, Malvern
Worcestershire WR14 4QS
Tel: 01684 573397
Fax: 01684 569665
reservations@foleyarms.com

AA ★★★

HOTEL & RESTAURANT

Need to unwind? 30 mile views await you at this beautifully situated country house hotel, together with a relaxing atmosphere, good food (2 AA Rosettes) and an award winning wine list.

Nineteen beautiful new bedrooms.

Check us out at www.cottageinthewood.co.uk or ring us for a brochure and full details.

Holywell Road, Malvern Wells, Worcestershire WR14 4LG
Tel: (01684) 575859 Fax: (01684) 560662

MALVERN, continued

modern facilities. Public areas include Elgar's Restaurant, a popular bar and a choice of comfortable lounges.

Foley Arms, Malvern

ROOMS: 28 en suite (2 fmly) ⊗ in 5 bedrooms s £78-£88; d £105-£145 (incl. bkfst) **LB** **FACILITIES:** STV Free use leisure centre pool, gym, solarium & sauna ch fac Xmas **CONF:** Thtr 150 Class 40 Board 45 Del from £118 **PARKING:** 64 **NOTES:** ⊗ in restaurant Civ Wed 100 **CARDS:**

See advert on page 389

★★★68% *Abbey*

Abbey Rd WR14 3ET
☎ 01684 892332 📠 01684 892662
e-mail: abbey@sarova.co.uk
web: www.sarova.co.uk/sarova/hotelcollection/abbey
Dir: *M5 junct 7 onto A449 to Malvern. Left by Barclays Bank into Church St. Right at traffic lights and 1st right into Abbey Rd*

This large, impressive, ivy-clad hotel stands in the centre of Great Malvern, next to the Abbey and close to the theatre. It provides well-equipped modern accommodation equally suitable for both business guests and tourists. Facilities include a good range of function rooms and the hotel is a popular venue for conferences.

ROOMS: 103 en suite (5 fmly) ⊗ in 24 bedrooms **FACILITIES:** STV Free entry to Malvern Leisure Complex **CONF:** Thtr 300 Class 180 Board 65 **SERVICES:** Lift **PARKING:** 90 **NOTES:** ⊗ in restaurant Civ Wed 100 **CARDS:**

★★74% Holdfast Cottage

Marlbank Rd, Little Malvern WR13 6NA
☎ 01684 310288 📠 01684 311117
e-mail: enquiries@holdfast-cottage.co.uk
web: www.holdfast-cottage.co.uk
Dir: *on A4104 midway between Welland and Upper Welland*

This charming, wisteria-covered hotel lies in attractive grounds at the foot of the Malvern Hills. The public areas offer all the comforts of a country retreat - log fire in the lounge, a cosy bar and an elegant dining room. The bedrooms include many thoughtful touches. The regularly changing menu features fresh local produce, and ice cream and breads are made on the premises.

ROOMS: 8 en suite (1 fmly) ⊗ in all bedrooms s £50-£70; d £84-£94 (incl. bkfst) **LB** **FACILITIES:** Walking, bird watching ch fac Xmas **CONF:** Class 30 Board 30 Del from £120 **PARKING:** 20 **NOTES:** ⊗ in restaurant **CARDS:**

See advert on opposite page

★★72% Cotford

51 Graham Rd WR14 2HU
☎ 01684 572427 📠 01684 572952
e-mail: reservations@cotfordhotel.co.uk
web: www.cotfordhotel.co.uk
Dir: *from Worcester follow signs to Malvern on A449. Left into Graham Rd signed town centre, hotel on right*

This delightful house, built in 1851, reputedly for the Bishop of Worcester, stands in attractive gardens with stunning views of the Malverns. Rooms have been sympathetically renovated, retaining many original features, and include all the expected comforts. Food, service and hospitality are major strengths.

ROOMS: 15 en suite (4 fmly) (1 GF) ⊗ in all bedrooms s £50-£55; d £75-£85 (incl. bkfst) **LB** **FACILITIES:** STV complimentary use of leisure centre in centre of Malvern **CONF:** Thtr 26 Class 26 Del from £75 **PARKING:** 18 **NOTES:** ⊗ in restaurant **CARDS:**

★★68% The Malvern Hills Hotel

Wynds Point WR13 6DW
☎ 01684 540690 📠 01684 540327
e-mail: malhilhotl@aol.com
web: www.malvernhillshotel.co.uk
Dir: *4m S, at junct of A449 with B4232*

This 19th-century hostelry is situated to the west of Malvern, opposite the British Camp, which was fortified and occupied by the Ancient Britons. Bedrooms are well equipped and facilities include a choice of bars and a sun terrace from which customers can view spectacular sunsets. The hotel is popular with walkers as well as business guests.

ROOMS: 14 en suite (1 fmly) (2 GF) ⊗ in 5 bedrooms s £35-£50; d £70-£90 (incl. bkfst) **CONF:** Thtr 40 Class 24 Board 30 **PARKING:** 30 **NOTES:** ⊗ in restaurant **CARDS:**

See advert on opposite page

★★67% Great Malvern
Graham Rd WR14 2HN
☎ 01684 563411 01684 560514
e-mail: sutton@great-malvern-hotel.co.uk
web: www.great-malvern-hotel.co.uk
Dir: *from Worcester on A449, left beyond fire station into Graham Rd. Hotel at end of road on right*

This is a privately-owned and personally-run town centre hotel, situated close to many cultural and scenic attractions. Popular with business people, theatregoers and leisure travellers, the hotel offers well-equipped and comfortable accommodation, a busy bar, a lounge and a meeting room.
ROOMS: 14 rms (13 en suite) (3 fmly) s fr £59.50; d fr £88 (incl. bkfst) LB **CONF:** Thtr 60 Class 20 Board 30 **SERVICES:** Lift **PARKING:** 9
NOTES: **CARDS:**

★★67% Mount Pleasant
Belle Vue Ter WR14 4PZ
☎ 01684 561837 01684 569968
e-mail: mountpleasanthotel@btinternet.com
web: www.mountpleasanthotel.co.uk
Dir: *on A449, in central Malvern by crossroads opposite Priory Church*

This is an attractive Georgian house in the centre of Great Malvern, that from its elevated position, overlooks the picturesque Severn Valley and Priory Church. Over the last few years there have been many changes to both the public areas and bedrooms including the creation of the smart Spring Bar & Brasserie
ROOMS: 14 en suite (1 fmly) s £45-£68; d £75-£98 (incl. bkfst) **LB**
FACILITIES: Xmas **CONF:** Thtr 90 Class 40 Board 50 Del from £80
PARKING: 20 **NOTES:** Closed 2-11 Jan
CARDS:

Town House Hotel
Country House Hotel
Travel Accommodation

M

MANCHESTER, Greater Manchester Map 16 SJ89
See also Manchester Airport & Sale

★★★★★72% The Lowry Hotel

50 Dearmans Place, Chapel Wharf, Salford M3 5LH
0161 827 4000 0161 827 4001
e-mail: enquiries@thelowryhotel.com
web: www.roccofortehotels.com

Dir: *M6 junct 19, A556 & M56 follow signs for Manchester. A5103 for 4.5m. At rdbt take A57(M) to lights & turn right onto Water St. Left to New Quay St/Trinity Way. At 1st lights turn right onto Chapel St to Hotel*

This modern hotel, set beside the River Irwell in the centre of the city, offers spacious bedrooms equipped to meet the needs of business and leisure visitors alike. Many of the rooms look out over the river, as do the sumptuous suites. The River Room restaurant produces good brasserie cooking. Extensive business and function facilities are available, together with a spa to provide extra pampering.

ROOMS: 165 en suite (7 fmly) in 90 bedrooms s fr £189; d fr £214 **LB FACILITIES:** STV Sauna Gym Spa facilities & swimming available offsite ch fac Xmas **CONF:** BC Thtr 350 Class 250 Board 60 Del from £240 **SERVICES:** Lift air con **PARKING:** 100 **NOTES:** Civ Wed **CARDS:**

★★★★71% Midland

Peter St M60 2DS
0161 236 3333 0161 932 4107
e-mail: midland@paramount-hotels.co.uk

Dir: *M602 junct 3 then follow signs for the G-Mex. Hotel is directly infront of the G-Mex*

Edwardian-style décor and friendly service are two of the attractions of this hotel. Bedrooms have loads of space; most are fairly quiet as they face into the centre of the hotel. The Octagon lounge and bar is a popular meeting spot for tea or pre-dinner drinks. The three restaurants comprise the newly refurbished, modern Trafford, the bright and simple Nico Central and the classical cuisine of the award-winning French.

ROOMS: 303 en suite (14 fmly) **FACILITIES: Spa** STV supervised Squash Sauna Solarium Gym Haird/beauty salon, dance studio, physiotherapist **CONF:** BC Thtr 450 Class 300 Board 120 Del from £195 **SERVICES:** Lift **NOTES:** in restaurant Civ Wed 500 **CARDS:**

Town House

★★★★ *Alias Hotel Rossetti*
107 Piccadilly M1 2DB
0161 247 7744 0161 247 7747
e-mail: info@aliashotels.com

Formerly a Victorian textile headquarters, this impressive building has been transformed to offer stylish accommodation. Bedrooms feature CD/DVD players and combine modern comfort with quirky eclectic décor. Unique 50's style diners are situated on each floor offering complimentary beverages, fresh fruit and cereals. Café Paradiso offers fresh Mediterranean food, while the basement has an exclusive club environment.

ROOMS: 61 en suite in 14 bedrooms **FACILITIES:** STV **CONF:** Thtr 50 Class 20 Board 20 **SERVICES:** Lift **NOTES:** in restaurant **CARDS:**

★★★★69% Marriott Worsley Park Hotel & Country Club

Marriott HOTELS · RESORTS · SUITES

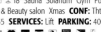

Worsley Park, Worsley M28 2QT
0161 975 2000 0161 799 6341
e-mail: salesadmin.worsleypark@marriotthotels.co.uk

Dir: *M60 junct 13, over 1st rdbt and take A575. Hotel 400yds on left*

This smart, modern hotel is set in impressive grounds that include a championship golf course. Bedrooms are comfortably appointed and well equipped for both leisure and business guests. Public areas include extensive leisure and conference facilities, an all day bistro and an elegant restaurant offering imaginative cuisine.

ROOMS: 158 en suite (5 fmly) (50 GF) in 116 bedrooms s fr £119; d fr £139 **LB FACILITIES:** STV 18 Sauna Solarium Gym Putt green Jacuzzi Steam room Health & Beauty salon Xmas **CONF:** Thtr 250 Class 150 Board 100 Del from £135 **SERVICES:** Lift **PARKING:** 400 **NOTES:** Civ Wed 200 **CARDS:**

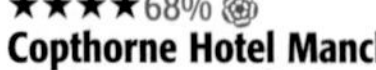

★★★★68%
Copthorne Hotel Manchester

COPTHORNE

Clippers Quay, Salford Quays M50 3SN
0161 873 7321 0161 873 7318
e-mail: manchester@mill-cop.com

Dir: *from M602 follow signs for Salford Quays and Trafford Park on A5063. Hotel 0.75m on right*

This smart hotel enjoys a convenient location on the redeveloped Salford Quays close to Old Trafford, The Lowry Centre and The Imperial War Museum. Bedrooms are comfortably appointed and well equipped for both business and leisure guests. A choice of dining options includes Chandlers Restaurant that serves accomplished food.

ROOMS: 166 en suite (6 fmly) in 118 bedrooms s £155-£215; d £165-£225 **LB FACILITIES:** STV **CONF:** Thtr 150 Class 70 Board 70 Del from £170 **SERVICES:** Lift **PARKING:** 120 **NOTES:** **CARDS:**

★★★★68% *The Palace*

PRINCIPAL HOTELS

Oxford St M60 7HA
0161 288 1111 0161 288 2222
web: www.principal-hotels.com

Dir: *opposite Oxford Rd Railway Station*

Formerly the offices of the Refuge Life Assurance Company, this impressive neo-Gothic building occupies a central location. There is a vast lobby, spacious open-plan bar-lounge and restaurant and extensive conference and function facilities. Bedrooms vary in size and style but are all spacious and well equipped.

ROOMS: 252 en suite (59 fmly) in 30 bedrooms **FACILITIES:** STV **CONF:** Thtr 1000 Class 450 Board 100 **SERVICES:** Lift **NOTES:** in restaurant Civ Wed 100 **CARDS:**

★★★★68% *The Victoria & Albert Hotel*

Water St M3 4JQ
☎ 0870 400 8585 📠 0161 834 2484
Dir: *M602 to A57 through lights on Regent Rd. Pass Sainsbury's, left at lights onto ring road, right at lights into Water St.*

This uniquely converted warehouse is located on the banks of the River Irwell, adjacent to the famous Granada Studios. Many of the hotel's individually styled and tastefully decorated bedrooms are themed around productions from the local studios. Interior features include original exposed brick walls and iron pillars. This establishment is become a Marriott hotel in Spring 2005.

ROOMS: 158 en suite (2 fmly) ⊘ in 90 bedrooms **FACILITIES:** STV Complimentary use of Livingwell Health Club **CONF:** BC Thtr 250 Class 120 Board 72 **SERVICES:** Lift air con **PARKING:** 120 **NOTES:** ✗ Civ Wed 200 **CARDS:**

★★★★67% Renaissance Manchester

Blackfriars St M3 2EQ
☎ 0161 831 6000 📠 0161 835 3077
e-mail: rhi.manbr.sales@renaissancehotels.com
Dir: *Follow signs to Deansgate, turn left onto Blackfriars St at 2nd set of lights after Kendals, hotel on right*

This smart hotel enjoys a central location just off Deansgate, within easy walking distance of The Arena and the city's many shops and attractions. Stylish, well-equipped bedrooms are extremely comfortable and those on higher floors offer wonderful views. Public areas include an elegant bar and restaurant and guests have use of a secure car park.

ROOMS: 200 en suite ⊘ in 153 bedrooms s £88-£141.50; d £98-£154 (incl. bkfst) **FACILITIES:** STV complimentary leisure facilities nearby **CONF:** BC Thtr 400 Class 300 Board 100 Del from £129 **SERVICES:** Lift air con **PARKING:** 80 **NOTES:** ✗ ⊘ in restaurant Civ Wed 100 **CARDS:**

★★★77% Malmaison

Piccadilly M1 3AQ
☎ 0161 278 1000 📠 0161 278 1002
e-mail: manchester@malmaison.com
Dir: *follow city centre signs, then signs to Piccadilly station. Hotel opposite station, at bottom of station approach*

Stylish and chic, the Malmaison offers the very best of contemporary hotel keeping in a relaxed and comfortable environment. The hotel offers a range of bright meeting rooms, health spa with gym and treatment rooms, as well as the ever popular bar and French-style brasserie. Air-conditioned bedrooms combine style and comfort and provide a range of extras.

ROOMS: 167 en suite s £129-£165; d £129-£165 **FACILITIES:** Spa STV Sauna Solarium Gym Jacuzzi **CONF:** Thtr 80 Class 48 Board 30 Del from £155 **SERVICES:** Lift air con **NOTES:** ✗ **CARDS:**

★★★73% ❀❀ Golden Tulip Manchester

Waters Reach, Trafford Park M17 1WS
☎ 0161 873 8899 📠 0161 872 6556
e-mail: info@goldentulipmanchester.com
Dir: *from A56 turn onto Sir Matt Busby Way past Manchester United Stadium to traffic lights. Hotel on right*

Situated opposite Old Trafford football stadium and within easy reach of the airport and motorway network, this modern establishment is the official hotel of Manchester United. The stylish rooms are spacious and comfortable and include mini-bars and CD players. The Waters Reach Restaurant and Bar is a fashionable and popular venue in which to enjoy modern British cooking.

ROOMS: 160 en suite (37 fmly) (8 GF) ⊘ in 70 bedrooms s £50-£105; d £50-£105 **LB** **FACILITIES:** STV Xmas **CONF:** BC Thtr 160 Class 100 Board 60 Del from £110 **SERVICES:** Lift **PARKING:** 160 **NOTES:** ✗ **CARDS:**

★★★69% Princess on Portland

101 Portland St M1 6DF
☎ 0161 236 5122 📠 0161 236 4468
e-mail: reception@princessonportland.co.uk
Dir: *From Piccadilly Station, along Piccadilly. Left on Portland St, hotel at junct to Princess St*

Situated in the heart of the city centre, this former Victorian silk warehouse has undergone extensive refurbishment under new ownership. Open-plan public areas are modern, contemporary in style and include a split-level brasserie offering an interesting selection of freshly prepared dishes. Smartly presented bedrooms are comfortably furnished and have modern facilities.

ROOMS: 85 en suite (7 fmly) ⊘ in 51 bedrooms s £118-£148; d £118-£158 (incl. bkfst) **FACILITIES:** STV **CONF:** Thtr 25 Class 15 Board 18 Del from £110 **SERVICES:** Lift **NOTES:** ✗ ⊘ in restaurant **CARDS:**

★★★68% Novotel Manchester Centre

21 Dickinson St M1 4LX
☎ 0161 235 2200 📠 0161 235 2210
e-mail: H3145@accor-hotels.com
Dir: *from Oxford St, into Portland St, left into Dickinson St. Hotel located on right*

This smart, modern property enjoys a central location convenient for theatres, shops and Manchester's business district. Spacious bedrooms are thoughtfully equipped and brightly decorated. Open plan, contemporary public areas include an all-day restaurant and a stylish bar. Extensive conference and meeting facilities are also available.

ROOMS: 164 en suite (60 fmly) ⊘ in 123 bedrooms s fr £103; d fr £103 **LB** **FACILITIES:** STV Sauna Gym Steam room **CONF:** Thtr 90 Class 50 Board 36 **SERVICES:** Lift air con **CARDS:**

MANCHESTER, continued

★★★68% ***Willow Bank Hotel***
340-342 Wilmslow Rd, Fallowfield M14 6AF
☎ 0161 224 0461 🖷 0161 257 2561
e-mail: willowbankhotel@feathers.uk.com
Dir: *From M60 junct 5 on to A5103, turn left on to B5093. Hotel 2.5m on left*
This popular hotel is conveniently located within three miles of the city centre and close to the universities. Bedrooms vary in style; some are traditionally furnished, others have been refurbished and are tastefully appointed. All are well equipped, and the newer rooms benefit from CD players and Playstations. Spacious, elegant public areas include a bar, restaurant, and meeting rooms.
ROOMS: 117 en suite (4 fmly) ⊗ in 30 bedrooms **FACILITIES:** STV **CONF:** Thtr 125 Class 60 Board 70 **PARKING:** 100 **NOTES:** ✗ Civ Wed 125 **CARDS:**

★★★66% **Manchester Conference Centre and Hotel**
Weston Building, Sackville St M1 3BB
☎ 0161 955 8000 🖷 0161 955 8050
e-mail: weston@umist.ac.uk
web: www.meeting.co.uk
Dir: *on Sackville St between Whitworth St & Mancunian Way*
This state-of-the-art conference centre is conveniently located at the heart of the UMIST university buildings. Bedrooms are comfortable and equipped with a range of business-friendly facilities, including a high-speed internet connection. Public areas comprise a stylish bar and a spacious restaurant, as well as flexible meeting room provision.
ROOMS: 117 en suite (2 fmly) ⊗ in 90 bedrooms s £35-£65; d £55-£100 **CONF:** Thtr 300 Class 100 Board 40 **SERVICES:** Lift **PARKING:** 700 **NOTES:** ✗ ⊗ in restaurant Closed 23 Dec-3 Jan **CARDS:**

★★★65% **Old Rectory Hotel**
Meadow Ln, Haughton Green, Denton M34 7GD
☎ 0161 336 7516 🖷 0161 320 3212
e-mail: reservations@oldrectoryhotelmanchester.co.uk

This former Victorian rectory, peacefully set around an enclosed garden, is only a short drive from Manchester city centre. Modern bedrooms are generally spacious and well appointed. Public rooms include a bar, an attractive and popular restaurant and a newly equipped mini-gym. Extensive banqueting facilities make this a popular wedding venue.
ROOMS: 30 en suite 6 annexe en suite (1 fmly) (12 GF) ⊗ in 12 bedrooms s £50-£55; d £60-£70 (incl. bkfst) **LB FACILITIES:** STV Gym Xmas **CONF:** Thtr 100 Class 45 Board 50 Del from £100 **PARKING:** 50 **NOTES:** ⊗ in restaurant Civ Wed 90
CARDS:

★★★63% **Jury's Inn Manchester**
56 Great Bridgewater St M1 5LE
☎ 0161 953 8888 🖷 0161 953 9090
e-mail: manchester_inn@jurysdoyle.com
Dir: *In city centre next to G-Mex centre and Bridgewater Hall*
Enjoying a prime city centre location, Jury's Inn offers good-value, air-conditioned accommodation, ideal for both business travellers and families. Public areas include a smart, spacious lobby, the Inn Pub and Arches Restaurant. There are several convenient car parks with special rates available.
ROOMS: 265 en suite (70 fmly) (16 GF) ⊗ in 230 bedrooms **FACILITIES:** STV **CONF:** Thtr 50 Class 25 Board 25 **SERVICES:** Lift air con **NOTES:** ✗ **CARDS:**

★★★63% **Novotel Manchester West**
Worsley Brow M28 2YA
☎ 0161 799 3535 🖷 0161 703 8207
e-mail: H0907@accor-hotels.com
(For full entry see Worsley)

★★62% **Monton House**
116-118 Monton Rd, Eccles M30 9HG
☎ 0161 789 7811 🖷 0161 787 7609
e-mail: hotel@montonhousehotel.co.uk
web: www.montonhousehotel.co.uk
Dir: *M602 junct. 2 & join A576, 2nd left onto B5229 (Half Edge Ln) right onto Monton Rd, pass garage on left, hotel 100yds on right*
A modern, purpose built hotel conveniently situated for the motorway network, airport and city centre. The bedrooms are well equipped and many have now been refurbished. The brightly furnished restaurant offers an imaginative choice at dinner and dishes served provide excellent value for money.
ROOMS: 62 en suite (2 fmly) (1 GF) ⊗ in 30 bedrooms s £35-£85; d £35-£95 **LB FACILITIES:** STV **CONF:** Thtr 150 Class 50 Board 50 Del from £75 **SERVICES:** Lift **PARKING:** 80 **NOTES:** ✗ Closed 25 Dec after 3pm-27 Dec Civ Wed 100 **CARDS:**

⌂ **Campanile**
55 Ordsall Ln, Salford M5 4RS
☎ 0161 833 1845 🖷 0161 833 1847
e-mail: manchester@envergure.co.uk
Dir: *M602 to Manchester, then A57. After large rdbt with Sainsbury's on left, left at next traffic lights. Hotel on right*

This modern building offers accommodation in smart, well-equipped bedrooms, all with en suite bathrooms. Refreshments may be taken at the informal Bistro. For further details consult the Hotel Groups page.
ROOMS: 104 en suite s fr £46.95; d fr £46.95 **CONF:** Thtr 50 Class 40 Board 30

⌂ Diamond Lodge
Hyde Rd, Belle Vue M18 7BA
☎ 0161 231 0770 0161 231 0660
web: www.diamondlodge.co uk
Dir: *On A57 Manchester E, 2.5m W of M60 junct 24, Manchester orbital*

Offering very good value for money, this modern lodge provides comfortable accommodation near the city centre, motorway networks and football stadiums. Bright and airy, open-plan day rooms include a lounge and a brasserie-style dining room where complimentary continental breakfasts are served. An evening menu is also available.
ROOMS: 85 en suite (incl. cont bkfst) s £42.50; d £42.50 **CONF:** Thtr 30 Class 15 Board 20 **NOTES:** Closed 24-26 Dec RS 31 Dec

See advert on this page

⌂ *Hotel Ibis Manchester (Charles Street)*

Charles St, Princess St M1 7DL
☎ 0161 272 5000 0161 272 5010
e-mail: H3143@accor-hotels.com
Dir: *M62, M602 towards Manchester Centre, follow signs to UMIST(A34)*
Modern, budget hotel offering comfortable accommodation in bright and practical bedrooms. Breakfast is self-service and dinner is available in the restaurant. For further details, consult the Hotel Groups page.
ROOMS: 126 en suite

⌂ Hotel Ibis Manchester City Centre
96 Portland St M1 4GY
☎ 0161 234 0600 0161 234 0610
e-mail: H3142@accor-hotels.com
Dir: *In city centre, between Princess St & Oxford St. 10min walk from Piccadilly*
Modern, budget hotel offering comfortable accommodation in bright and practical bedrooms. Breakfast is self-service and dinner is available in the restaurant. For further details, consult the Hotel Groups page.
ROOMS: 127 en suite s £45.95-£58.95; d £45.95-£58.95

⌂ Premier Lodge (City Centre GMEX 1)

Bishopsgate, 7-11 Lower Mosley St M2 3DW
☎ 0870 9906444 0870 9906445
web: www.premierlodge.com
Dir: *from M56 on A5103 towards Manchester City. Turn right at 2nd lights, at next turn left onto Oxford Rd then left at St Peters Sq junct. Hotel on left of Lower Mosley St*
High quality, modern, budget accommodation, ideal for families and business travellers. All rooms feature bath, power shower and satellite TV, and most have telephones / modem points. The adjacent bar and restaurant offers a wide and varied menu.
ROOMS: 147 en suite s £52; d £52 **CONF:** Thtr 60

⌂ Premier Lodge (City Centre GMEX 2)

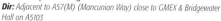

Gaythorne, River St M15 5FJ
☎ 0870 9906504 0870 9906505
web: www.premierlodge.com
Dir: *Adjacent to A57(M) (Mancunian Way) close to GMEX & Bridgewater Hall on A5103*
High quality, modern, budget accommodation, ideal for families and business travellers. All rooms feature bath, power shower and satellite TV, and most have telephones / modem points. The adjacent bar and restaurant offers a wide and varied menu.
ROOMS: 200 en suite s £52; d £52

⌂ Premier Lodge (Manchester City Centre)

North Tower, Victoria Bridge St, Salford M3 5AS
☎ 0870 9906366 0870 9906367
web: www.premierlodge.com
Dir: *M602 to Manchester city centre, then A57(M) towards GMEX. Take 2nd exit follow sign for A56 city centre. Turn left before MEN arena onto A6 and take 1st left*
High quality, modern, budget accommodation, ideal for families and business travellers. All rooms feature bath, power shower and satellite TV, and most have telephones / modem points. The adjacent bar and restaurant offers a wide and varied menu.
ROOMS: 170 en suite s £52; d £52

> Early start?
> Hotels at all star levels should provide in-room alarm clocks and/or alarm calls

M

MANCHESTER, continued

⌂ Travel Inn (Manchester City South)
Oxford St M1 4WB
☎ 0870 238 3315 ⎙ 01823 322054
Dir: *M6 junct 19 take 3rd exit onto A556. Join M56, exit junct 3 (A5103) to Medlock St, turn right into Whitworth St, then left into Oxford St & right into Portland St.*
Travel Inn offers good-quality, value-for-money accommodation. Spacious, en suite rooms with bath and shower comfortably accommodate a family of up to two adults and two children (to age 15). The restaurant and bar offers a varied menu. For further details consult the Hotel Groups page.
ROOMS: 226 en suite s £52.95; d £52.95

⌂ Travel Inn (Manchester Denton)

Alphington Dr, Manchester Rd South, Denton M34 3SH
☎ 08701 977173 ⎙ 0161 337 9652
Dir: *M60 junct 24 onto A57 signed Denton. 1st right at lights, right at next lights, Travel Inn on left*
Travel Inn offers good-quality, value-for-money accommodation. Spacious, en suite rooms with bath and shower comfortably accommodate a family of up to two adults and two children (to age 15). The restaurant and bar offers a varied menu. For further details consult the Hotel Groups page.
ROOMS: 40 en suite s £45.95-£48.95; d £45.95-£48.95

⌂ Travel Inn (Manchester Heaton Park)
Middleton Rd, Crumpsall M8 6NB
☎ 08701 977174 ⎙ 0161 740 9142
Dir: *off M60 junct 19, ring road east. Take A576 to Manchester through 2 sets of traffic lights. Travel Inn on left*

Travel Inn offers good-quality, value-for-money accommodation. Spacious, en suite rooms with bath and shower comfortably accommodate a family of up to two adults and two children (to age 15). The restaurant and bar offers a varied menu. For further details consult the Hotel Groups page.
ROOMS: 45 en suite s £45.95-£46.95; d £45.95-£46.95 **CONF:** Thtr 15

⌂ Travel Inn (Manchester Salford Quays)
Basin 8 The Quays, Salford Quays M50 3SQ
☎ 08701 977176 ⎙ 0161 876 0094
Dir: *From M602 (J3) take A5063 on Salford Quays, 1m from Manchester United's stadium.*

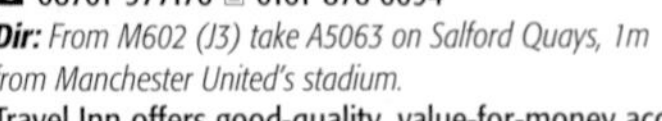

Travel Inn offers good-quality, value-for-money accommodation. Spacious, en suite rooms with bath and shower comfortably accommodate a family of up to two adults and two children (to age 15). The restaurant and bar offers a varied menu. For further details consult the Hotel Groups page.
ROOMS: 52 en suite s £45.95-£48.95; d £45.95-£48.95

⌂ Travel Inn (Manchester Trafford Centre)

Wilderspool Wood, Trafford Centre, Urmston M17 8WW
☎ 08701 977307 ⎙ 0161 747 4763
Dir: *M60 junct 10 on W side of Manchester*
Travel Inn offers good-quality, value-for-money accommodation. Spacious, en suite rooms with bath and shower comfortably accommodate a family of up to two adults and two children (to age 15). The restaurant and bar offers a varied menu. For further details consult the Hotel Groups page.
ROOMS: 60 en suite s £45.95-£48.95; d £45.95-£48.95 **CONF:** Thtr 12

⌂ Travel Inn Manchester (West Didsbury)
Princess Parkway, Chorlton
☎ 08701 977 309 ⎙ 08701 977703
Dir: *From M60 junct 5, to Manchester on A5103, Princess Parkway. Travel Inn is approx 1m on left*
Travel Inn offers good-quality, value-for-money accommodation. Spacious, en suite rooms with bath and shower comfortably accommodate a family of up to two adults and two children (to age 15). The restaurant and bar offers a varied menu. For further details consult the Hotel Groups page.
ROOMS: 78 en suite s £45.95-£46.95; d £45.95-£46.95

⌂ Travelodge (Manchester Central)
Townbury House, Blackfriars St M3 5AB
☎ 08700 850 950 ⎙ 0161 839 5181
Travelodge offers good quality, good value, modern accommodation. Ideal for families, the spacious, en suite bedrooms include remote-control TV, tea and coffee-making facilities and luxury beds. Meals can be taken at the nearby family restaurant. For further details consult the Hotel Groups page.
ROOMS: 181 en suite s fr £25; d fr £25

⌂ Tulip Inn
Old Park Ln M17 8PG
☎ 0161 755 3355 ⎙ 0161 755 3344
e-mail: info@tulipinnmanchester.co.uk
Dir: *From Manchester M60 Orbital, take junct 10 towards the Trafford Centre*
ROOMS: 121 en suite s £49.50-£69.50; d £49.50-£69.50
CONF: Thtr 30 Board 30

MANCHESTER AIRPORT, Greater Manchester Map 15 SJ88
See also Altrincham

★★★★ 70% ⊛⊛ Radisson SAS Hotel Manchester Airport
Chicago Av M90 3RA
☎ 0161 490 5000 ⎙ 0161 490 5095
e-mail: sales.airport.manchester@radissonsas.com
Dir: *M56 junct 5, follow signs for Terminal 2. At rdbt 2nd left and follow signs for railway station. Hotel next to station*
This modern hotel is strategically integrated into the airport's terminal system so all three terminals can be accessed quickly by covered, moving walkways. Facilities are excellent and include a well-equipped gym and indoor pool. Bedrooms are air-conditioned, thoughtfully equipped and come in a variety of decorative themes: Maritime, Oriental, Scandinavian and Italian. Super views of the runway can be enjoyed in the 'Phileas Fogg' restaurant where a creative international menu is carefully prepared with flair and skill.
ROOMS: 360 en suite (27 fmly) ⊗ in 280 bedrooms **FACILITIES:** STV supervised Sauna Solarium Gym Health & beauty treatments **CONF:** BC Thtr 350 Class 180 Board 50 Del from £189 **SERVICES:** Lift air con **PARKING:** 250 **NOTES:** ✈ Civ Wed 230
CARDS:

★★★★69% Manchester Airport Marriott
Hale Rd, Hale Barns WA15 8XW
☎ 0161 904 0301 Fax 0161 980 1787
e-mail: manchesterairportmarriott@whitbread.com

With good airport links and convenient access to the thriving city, this sprawling modern hotel is a popular destination. The hotel offers noteworthy leisure and business facilities, a choice of eating and drinking options and secure car parking. Bedrooms are situated around a courtyard and offer a comprehensive range of facilities.
ROOMS: 215 en suite (22 fmly) ⊗ in 160 bedrooms s £80-£129; d £84-£129 **LB** **FACILITIES: Spa** STV supervised Sauna Solarium Gym Jacuzzi **CONF:** BC Thtr 160 Class 70 Board 50 Del from £140 **SERVICES:** Lift **PARKING:** 400 **NOTES:** ⊗ in restaurant Civ Wed 110 **CARDS:**

★★★★68% Stanneylands
Stanneylands Rd SK9 4EY
☎ 01625 525225 Fax 01625 537282
e-mail: reservations@stanneylandshotel.co.uk
Dir: *from M56 for Airport turn off, follow signs to Wilmslow. Left into Station Rd, onto Stanneylands Rd. Hotel on right*

This traditional hotel is being tastefully transformed, thanks to the sympathetic refurbishment of the well-equipped bedrooms and delightful, comfortable day rooms. The cuisine on offer in the restaurant is of a high standard and ranges from traditional favourites to more imaginative contemporary dishes. Staff throughout are friendly and obliging.
ROOMS: 31 en suite (2 fmly) (10 GF) ⊗ in 10 bedrooms s £59-£98; d £82-£120 **LB** **FACILITIES:** STV **CONF:** BC Thtr 100 Class 50 Board 40 Del £140 **PARKING:** 80 **NOTES:** Civ Wed
CARDS:

See advert on this page

> Popped the question?
> Hotels with Civ Wed in their entry are licensed for civil wedding ceremonies. Maximum numbers for the ceremony only are shown, e.g. Civ Wed 120

★★★72% Etrop Grange
Thorley Ln M90 4EG
☎ 0870 609 6123 Fax 0161 499 0790
e-mail: etropgrange@corushotels.com
Dir: *M56 junct 5 follow signs for Terminal 2, on slip road to rdbt take 1st exit. Immediately left and hotel 400yds*
This Georgian country-house-style hotel is close to Terminal 2 but one would never know once inside. Stylish, comfortable bedrooms provide modern comforts and good business facilities. Comfortable, elegant day rooms include the Coach House Restaurant that serves creative, prepared dishes. A complimentary

continued on p398

MANCHESTER AIRPORT, continued

chauffeured limousine service is provided for guests wishing to connect with flights at the airport.

Etrop Grange, Manchester Airport

ROOMS: 64 en suite (10 GF) ⊗ in 25 bedrooms s £99-£149; d £99-£149 **LB** **FACILITIES:** STV **CONF:** Thtr 80 Class 35 Board 35 Del from £110 **PARKING:** 80 **NOTES:** ⊗ in restaurant RS 25-26 Dec Civ Wed 90 **CARDS:**

★★★67% Bewley's Hotel Manchester Airport

Outwood Ln M90 4HL
☎ 0161 498 0333 📠 0161 498 0222
e-mail: man@bewleyshotels.com
web: www.bewleyshotels.com/man_index.asp
Dir: *Follow signs to Manchester Airport Terminal 3. Hotel located on left on terminal 3 rdbt.*

Located adjacent to the airport this modern, stylish hotel provides an ideal stop-off for air travellers and business guests alike. All bedrooms are spacious and well equipped and include a wing of newly-built superior rooms. Open-plan day rooms continue the contemporary theme.
ROOMS: 226 en suite ⊗ in 158 bedrooms s £59; d £59 **FACILITIES:** STV **CONF:** Thtr 72 Class 40 Board 40 Del £120 **SERVICES:** Lift **PARKING:** 120 **NOTES:** 🐕 **CARDS:**

★★★66% *Belfry House*

Stanley Rd SK9 3LD
☎ 0161 437 0511 📠 0161 499 0597
e-mail: office@belfryhousehotel.co.uk
web: www.belfryhousehotel.co.uk
Dir: *off A34, 4m S of junct 3 M60*

This popular hotel, set in its own grounds, enjoys a convenient position close to Manchester Airport and the local motorway network. Extensive public areas include leisure and conference facilities and an elegant, contemporary restaurant. Bedrooms are traditionally furnished and overlook the attractive gardens.
ROOMS: 81 en suite (2 fmly) ⊗ in 40 bedrooms **FACILITIES:** STV Sauna Solarium Gym Jacuzzi ♫ **CONF:** Thtr 120 Class 70 Board 50 **SERVICES:** Lift **PARKING:** 150 **NOTES:** 🐕 ⊗ in restaurant **CARDS:**

⌂ Premier Lodge (Manchester Airport North)

PREMIER LODGE.com

30 Wilmslow Rd SK9 3EW
☎ 0870 9906602 📠 0870 9906603
web: www.premierlodge.com
Dir: *exit M56 junct 6 and follow A538 towards town centre. Approx 2m for hotel at top of hill on right, just after Wilmslow Garden Centre*

High quality, modern, budget accommodation, ideal for families and business travellers. All rooms feature bath, power shower and satellite TV, and most have telephones / modem points. The adjacent bar and restaurant offers a wide and varied menu.
ROOMS: 35 en suite s £50; d £50

⌂ Travel Inn

travel inn

Finney Ln, Heald Green SK8 3QH
☎ 08701 977178 📠 0161 437 4910
Dir: *M56 junct 5 follow signs to Terminal 1, at rdbt take 2nd exit, at next rdbt follow signs for Cheadle. At traffic lights turn left, then right at next lights*

Travel Inn offers good-quality, value-for-money accommodation. Spacious, en suite rooms with bath and shower comfortably accommodate a family of up to two adults and two children (to age 15). The restaurant and bar offers a varied menu. For further details consult the Hotel Groups page.
ROOMS: 66 en suite s £49.95-£54.95; d £49.95-£54.95

MANSFIELD, Nottinghamshire — Map 16 SK56

★★68% Pine Lodge

281-283 Nottingham Rd NG18 4SE
☎ 01623 622308 📠 01623 656819
e-mail: enquiries@pinelodge-hotel.co.uk
Dir: *on A60 Nottingham to Mansfield road, hotel is 1m S of Mansfield*

Located on the edge of Mansfield, this hotel offers welcoming and personal service to its guests, many of whom return time and again. The public rooms include a comfortable lounge bar, a cosy restaurant and a choice of meeting and function rooms. Bedrooms are thoughtfully equipped, the second floor bedrooms having been newly refurbished to a good standard; a bedroom suite is also available.
ROOMS: 20 en suite (2 fmly) ⊗ in all bedrooms s £40-£55; d £55-£70 (incl. bkfst) **LB** **FACILITIES:** STV Sauna **CONF:** Thtr 50 Class 30 Board 35 Del from £100 **PARKING:** 40 **NOTES:** 🐕 ⊗ in restaurant Closed 25-26 Dec **CARDS:**

★★65% Portland Hall

THE INDEPENDENTS

Carr Bank Park, Windmill Ln NG18 2AL
☎ 01623 452525 📠 01623 452550
e-mail: enquiries@portlandhallhotel.co.uk
web: www.portlandhallhotel.co.uk
Dir: *from town centre take A60 to Worksop for 100yds then right at pelican crossing into Nursery St, Carr Bank Park 50yds on right*

A former Georgian mansion, overlooking 15 acres of renovated parklands, the house retains some fine features, with original plasterwork and friezes displayed in the cosy lounge bar and around the domed skylight over the spiral stairs. The attractive restaurant

continued

proves to be a popular local venue, offering a flexible choice of carvery or menu options and service is skilled and attentive.
ROOMS: 10 en suite (1 fmly) ⊗ in 5 bedrooms s £47-£55; d £58.75-£65 (incl. bkfst) **FACILITIES:** Bowls Green Xmas **CONF:** Thtr 60 Class 30 Board 20 Del from £66.95 **PARKING:** 80 **NOTES:** ⊗ in restaurant Civ Wed 66 **CARDS:**

MARAZION, Cornwall & Isles of Scilly Map 02 SW53

★★77% Mount Haven Hotel & St Michaels Restaurant

Turnpike Rd TR17 0DQ
☎ 01736 710249 01736 711658
e-mail: reception@mounthaven.co.uk
web: www.mounthaven.co.uk
Dir: *From A30 towards Penzance. At rdbt take exit for Helston onto A394. Next rdbt right into Marazion, hotel on left*

Art and style abound at this delightfully located hotel where exceptional views can be enjoyed - sunsets and sunrises can be particularly splendid. Bedrooms, many with balconies, are comfortably appointed. Fresh seafood and local produce are simply treated to produce interesting menus. A range of holistic therapies is available. Service is attentive and friendly and a relaxing and enchanting environment has been created throughout.
ROOMS: 19 en suite (2 fmly) (6 GF) ⊗ in all bedrooms s £60-£80; d £84-£90 (incl. bkfst) **LB FACILITIES: Spa** Aromatherapy reflexology, massage & reiki ch fac **CONF:** Thtr 50 Class 30 **PARKING:** 30 **NOTES:** ⊗ in restaurant Closed 20 Dec-5 Feb **CARDS:**

★★70% Godolphin Arms

TR17 0EN
☎ 01736 710202 01736 710171
e-mail: enquiries@godolphinarms.co.uk
web: www.godolphinarms.co.uk
Dir: *from A30 follow Marazion signs for 1m to hotel. At end of the causeway to St Michael's Mount*

This 170-year-old waterside hotel is in a prime location. Stunning

continued

views of St Michael's Mount provide a backdrop for the restaurant and lounge bar. Bedrooms are colourful, comfortable and spacious. A choice of menu is offered in the main restaurant and the Gig Bar, all with an emphasis on local seafood.
ROOMS: 10 en suite (2 fmly) (2 GF) s £45-£69.50; d £70-£119 (incl. bkfst) **LB FACILITIES:** STV Direct access to large beach **PARKING:** 48 **NOTES:** ⊗ in restaurant Closed 24 & 25 Dec **CARDS:**

MARCH, Cambridgeshire Map 12 TL49

★★63% Olde Griffin

High St PE15 9JS
☎ 01354 652517 01354 650086
e-mail: griffhotel@aol.com
Dir: *on A141/142 N of Ely and off A47 E of Peterborough towards Norwich*

Overlooking the town square, this former coaching inn dates back to the 16th century, and retains many period features. Bedrooms vary in size and style and all are appropriately equipped and furnished. Meals are available in the lounge and bar areas, and there is a restaurant for more formal dining.
ROOMS: 21 rms (20 en suite) (1 fmly) s £45; d £59.50-£75 (incl. bkfst) **CONF:** Thtr 100 Class 50 Board 36 **PARKING:** 50 **NOTES:** ⊗ in restaurant **CARDS:**

MARGATE, Kent Map 07 TR37

★★★ Smiths Court

Eastern Esplanade, Cliftonville CT9 2HL
☎ 01843 222310 01843 222312
e-mail: info@courthotels.com
Dir: *from Clocktower on seafront take left fork on A28 for approx 1 mile, Hotel on Eastern Esplanade at junction with Godwin Rd.*
ROOMS: 40 en suite (6 fmly) (6 GF) ⊗ in 10 bedrooms s £39.50-£49.50; d £70-£80 (incl. bkfst) **LB FACILITIES:** Gym ♫ ch fac Xmas **CONF:** Thtr 80 Class 50 Board 80 Del from £89 **SERVICES:** Lift **PARKING:** 15 **NOTES:** ⊗ in restaurant **CARDS:**

Travel Inn

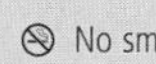

Station Green, Marine Ter CT9 5AF
☎ 08701 977182 01843 221101
Dir: *M2 follow A299 then A28 to Margate seafront. Travel Inn adjacent to Margate station, facing sea*
Travel Inn offers good-quality, value-for-money accommodation. Spacious, en suite rooms with bath and shower comfortably accommodate a family of up to two adults and two children (to age 15). The restaurant and bar offers a varied menu. For further details consult the Hotel Groups page.
ROOMS: 44 en suite s £45.95-£46.95; d £45.95-£46.95

⊗ No smoking

MARKET DRAYTON, Shropshire Map 15 SJ63

★★★70% Goldstone Hall
Goldstone TF9 2NA
☎ 01630 661202 01630 661585
e-mail: enquiries@goldstonehall.com
web: www.goldstonehall.com
Dir: *4m S of Market Drayton off A529 signed Goldstone Hall Gdns. 4m N of Newport signed from A41*

Situated in extensive grounds, this charming period property is a family-run hotel. It provides traditionally furnished, well-equipped accommodation, with some more contemporary artistic touches. Public rooms are extensive and include a choice of lounges, a snooker room and a conservatory. The hotel has a well-deserved reputation for good food.
ROOMS: 11 en suite (2 GF) s £75-£90; d £100-£125 (incl. bkfst) **LB** **FACILITIES:** STV Snooker **CONF:** BC Thtr 50 Class 30 Board 30 Del from £105 **PARKING:** 60 **NOTES:** ⊗ in restaurant Civ Wed 70
CARDS:

★★70% Rosehill Manor
Rosehill, Ternhill TF9 2JF
☎ 01630 638532 01630 637008
Dir: *from rdbt at Ternhill A53 S towards Newport. Hotel 2m on right*
Parts of this charming old house, which stands in mature gardens, date back to the 16th century. Privately owned and personally run, it provides well-equipped accommodation including family rooms. Public areas comprise a pleasant restaurant serving award-winning cuisine, a bar and a comfortable lounge. There is also a conservatory, which is available for functions.
ROOMS: 9 en suite (2 fmly) s fr £52.50 (incl. bkfst) **LB** **FACILITIES:** **CONF:** Thtr 100 Class 60 Board 40 Del from £75 **PARKING:** 80 **NOTES:** ⊗ in restaurant Civ Wed 100
CARDS:

MARKET HARBOROUGH, Leicestershire Map 11 SP78
See also Marston Trussell

★★★70% Three Swans
21 High St LE16 7NJ
☎ 01858 466644 01858 433101
e-mail: sales@threeswans.co.uk
web: www.threeswans.co.uk
Dir: *M1 junct 20 take A4304 to Market Harborough. Through town centre on A6 from Leicester, hotel on right*
Public areas in this former coaching inn include an elegant fine dining restaurant and cocktail bar, a smart foyer lounge and popular public bar areas. Bedroom styles and sizes vary, all are very well appointed and equipped and the most recently created wing of bedrooms is particularly impressive, offering high quality spacious accommodation.

ROOMS: 18 en suite 43 annexe en suite (8 fmly) (12 GF) ⊗ in 44 bedrooms s £55-£85; d £75-£135 (incl. bkfst) **LB** **FACILITIES:** STV ch fac Xmas **CONF:** Thtr 200 Class 120 Board 120 Del from £105 **SERVICES:** Lift **PARKING:** 100 **NOTES:** ⊗ in restaurant Civ Wed 140
CARDS:

See advert under LEICESTER

MARKFIELD, Leicestershire Map 11 SK40

Travelodge Leicester Markfield
Littleshaw Ln LE6 0PP
☎ 08700 850 950 01530 244580
Dir: *on A50 from M1 junct 22*
Travelodge offers good quality, good value, modern accommodation. Ideal for families, the spacious, en suite bedrooms include remote-control TV, tea and coffee-making facilities and luxury beds. Meals can be taken at the nearby family restaurant. For further details consult the Hotel Groups page.
ROOMS: 60 en suite s fr £25; d fr £25

MARKHAM MOOR, Nottinghamshire Map 17 SK77

Travelodge Retford
DN22 0QU
☎ 08700 850 950 01777 838091
Dir: *on A1 northbound*
Travelodge offers good quality, good value, modern accommodation. Ideal for families, the spacious, en suite bedrooms include remote-control TV, tea and coffee-making facilities and luxury beds. Meals can be taken at the nearby family restaurant. For further details consult the Hotel Groups page.
ROOMS: 40 en suite s fr £25; d fr £25

MARKINGTON, North Yorkshire Map 19 SE26

★★★79% Hob Green
HG3 3PJ
☎ 01423 770031 01423 771589
e-mail: info@hobgreen.com
web: www.hobgreen.com
Dir: *from A61, 4m N or Harrogate turn left at Wormald Green and follow hotel signs*
This hospitable country house sits in 800 acres of beautiful rolling countryside, not far from Harrogate and Ripon. Cosy lounges boast open fires in cooler months, whilst the extremely comfortable bedrooms come furnished with antiques and a host

continued

of thoughtful extras. The restaurant enjoys a fine reputation and features home-grown produce from its own gardens.

ROOMS: 12 en suite (1 fmly) ⊗ in all bedrooms s £98.50-£115; d £115-£125 (incl. bkfst) **LB** **FACILITIES:** STV ch fac Xmas **CONF:** Thtr 15 Class 10 Board 10 Del from £125 **PARKING:** 40 **NOTES:** ⊗ in restaurant Civ Wed 35 **CARDS:**

See advert under HARROGATE

MARLBOROUGH, Wiltshire Map 05 SU16

★★★66% *The Castle & Ball*

High St SN8 1LZ
☎ 01672 515201 📠 01672 515895
Dir: *A338 and A4 to Marlborough*

This traditional coaching inn in the town centre has now been upgraded. Bedrooms have been refurbished in a contemporary style and are very well-equipped. Open-plan public areas include a comfortable bar/lounge area and a smartly appointed restaurant, which serves food all day. Meeting rooms and parking are also available.

ROOMS: 34 en suite (1 fmly) ⊗ in 13 bedrooms **FACILITIES:** STV **CONF:** Thtr 45 Class 20 Board 30 **PARKING:** 48 **NOTES:** ⊗ in restaurant **CARDS:**

MARLOW, Buckinghamshire Map 05 SU88

★★★★76% **Danesfield House Hotel & Spa**

SLH

Henley Rd SL7 2EY
☎ 01628 891010 📠 01628 890408
e-mail: sales@danesfieldhouse.co.uk
web: www.danesfieldhouse.co.uk
Dir: *2m from Marlow on A4155 towards Henley*

Set in 65 acres of elevated grounds just 45 minutes from central London and 30 minutes from Heathrow, this hotel enjoys spectacular views across the River Thames. Impressive public rooms include the cathedral-like Great Hall, the panelled Oak

continued

Room Restaurant and The Orangery, a less formal option for dining. Some bedrooms have balconies and stunning views.

ROOMS: 87 en suite (3 fmly) (27 GF) ⊗ in 5 bedrooms s £155-£295; d £195-£315 (incl. bkfst) **LB** **FACILITIES:** **Spa** STV Snooker Sauna Solarium Gym Putt green Jacuzzi Jogging trail, Steam room, Hydrotherapy room, Treatment rooms ♫ Xmas **CONF:** Thtr 100 Class 60 Board 50 Del from £265 **SERVICES:** Lift **PARKING:** 100 **NOTES:** ⊗ in restaurant Civ Wed 100 **CARDS:**

See advert on this page

★★★★70% **The Compleat Angler**

MACDONALD HOTELS

Marlow Bridge SL7 1RG
☎ 0870 400 8100 📠 01628 486388
e-mail: compleatangler@macdonald-hotels.co.uk
Dir: *M4 J8/9, A404 to rdbt, Bisham exit, 1m to Marlow Bridge, hotel on right*

This well-established hotel enjoys a wonderful setting overlooking the River Thames and the Marlow weir. Bedrooms, which differ in size and style, are all individually decorated and comfortable.

continued on p402

MARLOW, continued

Dining choices include a cosy bar, informal brasserie-style restaurant and the award-winning Riverside restaurant.
ROOMS: 64 en suite (6 GF) ⊗ in 22 bedrooms s £220-£260; d £220-£150 **LB** **FACILITIES:** STV Fishing Boating, Fly fishing and course fishing ♫ Xmas **CONF:** Thtr 120 Class 65 Board 36 Del from £230 **SERVICES:** Lift **PARKING:** 60 **NOTES:** ⊗ in restaurant Civ Wed **CARDS:**

See advert on opposite page

MARSDEN, West Yorkshire — Map 16 SE01

★★73% *Hey Green Country House*

Waters Rd HD7 6NG
☎ 01484 844235 🖹 01484 847605
e-mail: info@heygreen.com
web: www.heygreen.com
Dir: *off A62 1m outside village, towards Manchester.*
This grand Victorian house is set in extensive landscaped gardens. Bedrooms are spacious and well equipped, public areas include many original features and a modern conservatory, and the brasserie serves a wide choice of carefully prepared dishes. The Standedge Visitor Centre and the restored Huddersfield Canal are close by.
ROOMS: 12 en suite ⊗ in 6 bedrooms **FACILITIES:** STV **CONF:** Thtr 100 Class 80 Board 50 **PARKING:** 70 **NOTES:** ⊗ in restaurant RS 2-3 Jan Civ Wed 150 **CARDS:**

MARSTON MORETAINE, Bedfordshire — Map 11 SP94

Travelodge Bedford South West

Travelodge

Beancroft Rd Junction MK43 0PZ
☎ 08700 850 950 🖹 01234 766755
Dir: *on A421, northbound*
Travelodge offers good quality, good value, modern accommodation. Ideal for families, the spacious, en suite bedrooms include remote-control TV, tea and coffee-making facilities and luxury beds. Meals can be taken at the nearby family restaurant. For further details consult the Hotel Groups page.
ROOMS: 54 en suite s fr £25; d fr £25

MARSTON TRUSSELL, Northamptonshire — Map 11 SP68

★★72% The Sun Inn

Main St LE16 9TY
☎ 01858 465531 🖹 01858 433155
e-mail: manager@suninn.com
Dir: *M1 junct 20 take A4304. After Theddingworth, right to Marston Trussell. Hotel on right of Main St*

This pleasant inn successfully combines a mixture of modern facilities and accommodation with the classical traditions of the rural English inn. Bedrooms are comfortably furnished and tastefully appointed and offer a host of thoughtful facilities. Public areas consist of two elegant dining areas and a bar, popular with locals. Service is both friendly and attentive.
ROOMS: 20 en suite (1 fmly) (10 GF) ⊗ in 10 bedrooms s £59; d £69 (incl. bkfst) **FACILITIES:** Rambling trails **CONF:** BC Thtr 60 Class 40 Board 28 Del from £85 **PARKING:** 60 **NOTES:** Closed 25 Dec-5 Jan RS Sun **CARDS:**

MARTINHOE, Devon — Map 03 SS64

★★75% The Old Rectory

EX31 4QT
☎ 01598 763368 🖹 01598 763567
e-mail: reception@oldrectoryhotel.co.uk
web: www.oldrectoryhotel.co.uk
Dir: *M5 junct 27 onto A361, right onto A399 Blackmoor Gate and right onto A39 bypass Parracombe. 2nd left to Martinhoe and follow signs*

Originally built in the 1800s for the local rector, this peaceful hideaway is an ideal base for exploring Exmoor and is just 500 yards from the coastal footpath. In addition to the comfortable lounges, guests can relax in the vinery, overlooking the delightful gardens. Interesting menus are served in the spacious dining room. The bedrooms are tastefully decorated and a self-catering cottage is also available.
ROOMS: 9 en suite (2 GF) ⊗ in all bedrooms s £77-£112; d £124-£214 (incl. bkfst & dinner) **LB** **PARKING:** 9 **NOTES:** No children 14yrs ⊗ in restaurant Closed Nov-Feb RS Mar **CARDS:**

MARTOCK, Somerset — Map 04 ST41

★★★72% The Hollies

Bower Hinton TA12 6LG
☎ 01935 822232 🖹 01935 822249
e-mail: info@theholllieshotel.com
Dir: *on B3165 S of town centre off A303, take Bower Hinton slip road & follow hotel signs*
Within easy access of the A303, the bar and restaurant of this popular venue are housed in an attractive 17th-century farmhouse. Bar meals are available in addition to the interesting main menu. The spacious, well-equipped bedrooms are located to the rear of the property in a purpose-built wing and include both suites and mini-suites.
ROOMS: 33 annexe en suite (2 fmly) (30 GF) ⊗ in 10 bedrooms s £73-£120; d fr £88 (incl. bkfst) **LB** **FACILITIES:** STV **CONF:** BC Thtr 150 Class 80 Board 60 Del from £98 **PARKING:** 80 **NOTES:** ⊗ in restaurant RS Xmas & New Year **CARDS:**

MASHAM, North Yorkshire Map 19 SE28

Top 200 – Hotel

★★★★ **Swinton Park**
HG4 4JH
☎ 01765 680900 01765 680901
e-mail: enquiries@swintonpark.com
web: www.swintonpark.com
Dir: *A1 onto B6267 to Masham. Follow signs through town centre & turn right onto Swinton Terrace. 1m past GC over bridge, up hill. Hotel is on right*

Extended during the Victorian and Edwardian eras, the original part of this welcoming castle dates from the 17th century. Bedrooms are luxuriously furnished and come with a host of thoughtful extras. Samuel's restaurant (built by the current owner's great-great-great grandfather) is very elegant and serves imaginative dishes which feature local produce, much being sourced from the Swinton estate.

ROOMS: 30 en suite in all bedrooms s £100-£350; d £120-£350 (incl. bkfst) **LB** **FACILITIES: Spa** STV 9 Fishing Riding Snooker Gym Putt green Jacuzzi Shooting, Falconry, Pony Trekking, cookery school ch fac Xmas **CONF:** Thtr 120 Class 60 Board 40 Del £170 **SERVICES:** Lift **PARKING:** 50 **NOTES:** in restaurant Civ Wed 120 **CARDS:**

★★67% ***The Kings Head***
Market Place HG4 4EF
☎ 01765 689295 01765 689070
Dir: *off A6108 Ripon to Leyburn road in centre of village*

This historic, stone-built hotel, with its uneven floors, beamed bars and attractive window boxes, looks out over the large Market Square. Bedrooms are elegantly furnished and thoughtfully equipped. Public areas are traditional and include a popular bar and smartly appointed restaurant.

ROOMS: 10 en suite **CONF:** Thtr 40 Class 20 Board 20 **NOTES:** **CARDS:**

MATFEN, Northumberland Map 21 NZ07

★★★★77% **Matfen Hall**
NE20 0RH
☎ 01661 886500 01661 886055
e-mail: info@matfenhall.com
web: www.matfenhall.com
Dir: *off A69 to B6318. Hotel just before village*

This fine mansion lies in landscaped parkland overlooking its own golf course. Additional contemporary bedrooms are now available along with the traditional ones in the main house; all are very comfortable and well equipped. Impressive public rooms include a splendid drawing room and the elegant Library and Print Room

continued

Restaurant, as well as a conservatory bar and the new addition of spa, leisure and conference facilities.

ROOMS: 53 en suite (11 fmly) in 42 bedrooms s £102-£147; d £140-£235 (incl. bkfst) **LB** **FACILITIES: Spa** STV 18 Sauna Solarium Gym Putt green Jacuzzi Xmas **CONF:** Thtr 120 Class 46 Board 40 Del from £155 **SERVICES:** Lift **PARKING:** 150 **NOTES:** in restaurant Civ Wed 120 **CARDS:**

See advert under NEWCASTLE UPON TYNE

MATLOCK, Derbyshire Map 16 SK35

★★★77% **Riber Hall**
DE4 5JU
☎ 01629 582795 01629 580475
e-mail: info@riber-hall.co.uk
web: www.riber-hall.co.uk
Dir: *1m off A615 at Tansley*

This beautiful Elizabethan manor house enjoys an idyllic location

continued on p404

MATLOCK, continued

in charming grounds overlooking Matlock. Beautifully furnished, thoughtfully equipped bedrooms, many with oak four-poster beds, are situated round a delightful courtyard with its own fountain. Tastefully appointed public rooms are furnished with period and antique pieces and an impressive wine list complements the imaginative and award-winning cuisine.

Riber Hall, Matlock

ROOMS: 3 en suite 11 annexe en suite in 4 bedrooms s £97-£112; d £136-£182 (incl. cont bkfst) **LB** **FACILITIES:** STV **CONF:** Thtr 20 Class 20 Board 20 Del from £148 **PARKING:** 50 **NOTES:** No children 10yrs in restaurant RS 25 Dec Civ Wed 50 **CARDS:**

★★★69% New Bath

New Bath Rd DE4 3PX
☎ 0870 400 8119 01629 580268
e-mail: general.newbath@macdonaldhotels.co.uk

MACDONALD HOTELS

***Dir:** M1 junct 28 to Alfreton, follow Matlock then Matlock Bath signs. Hotel on A6 just after Matlock Bath on right*

Set in five acres of grounds in the beautiful Derwent Gorge, the hotel has indoor and outdoor pools fed by natural thermal springs, the medicinal properties of which were first recognised in Regency times. Bedrooms are tastefully furnished and decorated, two rooms have four-poster beds, and some have balconies.

ROOMS: 55 en suite (5 fmly) in 45 bedrooms s £70-£100; d £90-£120 **LB** **FACILITIES:** STV supervised Sauna Solarium Xmas **CONF:** Thtr 180 Class 60 Board 50 Del from £100 **PARKING:** 200 **NOTES:** in restaurant Civ Wed **CARDS:**

★★74% The Red House Country Hotel

Old Rd, Darley Dale DE4 2ER
☎ 01629 734854 01629 734885
e-mail: enquiries@TheRedHouseCountryHotel.co.uk
web: www.theredhousecountryhotel.co.uk

***Dir:** off A6 onto Old Rd signed Carriage Museum, 2.5m N of Matlock*

A peaceful country hotel set in delightful Victorian gardens. Rich colour schemes are used to excellent effect throughout. The well-equipped bedrooms include three ground floor rooms in the adjacent coach house. A comfortable lounge with delightful rural views is available for refreshments and pre-dinner drinks; service is friendly and attentive.

ROOMS: 7 en suite 3 annexe en suite (3 GF) in all bedrooms s £60-£70; d fr £95 (incl. bkfst) **LB** **CONF:** Thtr 30 Class 24 Board 24 **PARKING:** 15 **NOTES:** No children 11 yrs in restaurant Closed 3-16 Jan **CARDS:**

MAWGAN PORTH, Cornwall & Isles of Scilly Map 02 SW86

★★72% Tredragon

TR8 4DQ
☎ 01637 860213 01637 860269
e-mail: tredragon@btinternet.com web: www.tredragon.co.uk

***Dir:** From Newquay Airport follow signs to Mawgan Porth, past beach, up hill & left turn at sign*

This hotel enjoys a glorious, unspoilt location with direct footpath access to the award-winning beach just below. Its new owners have made stylish improvements including the Sundowner Terrace. Both the restaurant's cuisine and views are delightful. The hotel attracts a large following of repeat custom and offers themed residential courses.

ROOMS: 26 en suite (12 fmly) (10 GF) in all bedrooms s £35-£80; d £65-£110 (incl. bkfst) **LB** **FACILITIES:** Sauna ch fac Xmas **CONF:** Thtr 50 Class 30 Board 25 **PARKING:** 30 **NOTES:** in restaurant **CARDS:**

MAWNAN SMITH, Cornwall & Isles of Scilly Map 02 SW72

★★★★73% Budock Vean-The Hotel on the River

TR11 5LG
☎ 01326 252100 & 0800 833927 01326 250892
e-mail: relax@budockvean.co.uk web: www.budockvean.co.uk

***Dir:** from A39 follow tourist signs to Trebah Gardens. 0.5m to hotel*

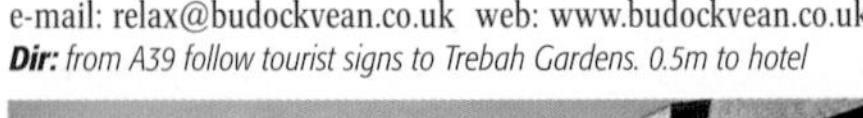

Set in 65 acres of attractive, well-tended grounds, this peaceful hotel offers an impressive range of facilities. Convenient for visiting

continued

the Helford River Estuary and many local gardens, or simply as a tranquil setting for a leisure break, The Budock Vean offers friendly and attentive service. Bedrooms are spacious and offer a choice of styles; some overlook the grounds and golf course.
ROOMS: 57 en suite (2 fmly) ⊗ in 6 bedrooms s £57-£96; d £114-£192 (incl. bkfst & dinner) **LB FACILITIES:** STV ⛳ 9 Fishing Snooker Putt green Natural health spa, private motor boat & foreshore ♫ ch fac Xmas **CONF:** Thtr 60 Class 40 Board 30 Del from £95 **SERVICES:** Lift **PARKING:** 100 **NOTES:** ⊗ in restaurant Closed 3 wks Jan Civ Wed 120
CARDS:

★★★ 78% Meudon
TR11 5HT
☎ 01326 250541 📠 01326 250543
e-mail: wecare@meudon.co.uk web: www.meudon.co.uk
Dir: from Truro A39 towards Falmouth at Hillhead rdbt, follow signs to Maenporth Beach. Hotel on left 1m after beach

This charming late Victorian mansion, with its friendly hospitality, attentive service and impressive nine acres of gardens leading down to a private beach, provides a relaxing place to stay. Bedrooms are comfortable and spacious and cuisine features the best of local Cornish produce served in the conservatory restaurant. This hotel has been Highly Commended in the AA Accessibility Awards for 2004-5.
ROOMS: 29 en suite (2 fmly) (15 GF) s £69-£125; d £138-£250 (incl. bkfst & dinner) **LB FACILITIES:** Fishing Riding Private beach, Hair salon, Yacht for skippered charter, sub-tropical gardens ch fac Xmas **CONF:** Thtr 30 Class 20 Board 15 Del from £80 **SERVICES:** Lift **PARKING:** 52 **NOTES:** ⊗ in restaurant Closed 3-31 Jan
CARDS:

See advert under FALMOUTH

★★★ 67% Trelawne
TR11 5HS
☎ 01326 250226 📠 01326 250909
e-mail: info@trelawnehotel.co.uk
Dir: A39 to Falmouth, right at Hillhead rdbt signed Maenporth. Past beach, up hill and hotel on left

The Trelawne is surrounded by attractive lawns and gardens, and
continued

enjoys superb coastal views. An informal atmosphere prevails, and many guests return year after year. Bedrooms, many with sea views, are of varying size. Dinner features quality local produce used in imaginative dishes.
ROOMS: 14 en suite (2 fmly) (4 GF) s £45-£60; d £90-£148 (incl. bkfst) **LB FACILITIES:** ch fac **PARKING:** 20 **NOTES:** ⊗ in restaurant Closed 23 Dec-12 Feb **CARDS:**

See advert on this page

MEDBOURNE, Leicestershire — Map 11 SP89

Restaurant with Rooms

The Horse & Trumpet
Old Green LE16 8DX
☎ 01858 565000 📠 01858 565551
Dir: In centre of village, opposaite church, at the back of the bowling green.
Tucked away behind the village bowling green, this carefully restored, thatched former farmhouse and pub now offers fine dining and quality accommodation. The golden stone building houses three intimate dining areas, where imaginative meals are offered. Smartly appointed and comfortably furnished bedrooms are located in a barn conversion to the rear of the main building.
ROOMS: 4 annexe en suite (2 GF) ⊗ in all bedrooms s fr £65; d fr £65 (incl. bkfst) **NOTES:** No children 5yrs
CARDS:

MELKSHAM, Wiltshire Map 04 ST96

★★71% Shaw Country
Bath Rd, Shaw SN12 8EF
☎ 01225 702836 & 790321 📠 01225 790275
e-mail: info@shawcountryhotel.co.uk
web: www.shawcountryhotel.co.uk
Dir: *1m from Melksham, 9m from Bath on A365*
Located within easy reach of both Bath and the M4, this hotel sits in wonderfully kept gardens. The house boasts some very well-appointed bedrooms, a comfortable lounge and bar and the Mulberry Restaurant, where a wide selection of well-cooked meals is available. A warm and friendly approach by the staff is offered throughout the stay.
ROOMS: 13 en suite (2 fmly) s £50; d £70-£90 (incl. bkfst) **LB** **FACILITIES:** Jacuzzi **CONF:** Thtr 30 Class 20 Board 15 **PARKING:** 30 **NOTES:** ⊗ in restaurant Closed 26-27 Dec & 1 Jan
CARDS:

Restaurant with Rooms

Conigre Farm Hotel
Semington Rd SN12 6BZ
☎ 01225 702229 📠 01225 707392
e-mail: enq@cfhotel.co.uk
Dir: *off A350 onto Semington Rd, hotel 0.5m on left after fire station*

This stone-built, 17th-century former farmhouse is a comfortable and friendly place to stay. Imaginative menus have a French influence and feature fresh and local produce, organic wherever possible. The well-furnished bedrooms are comfortable; one room boasts a four-poster bed.
ROOMS: 2 en suite 6 annexe en suite (1 fmly) ⊗ in 6 bedrooms s £43-£53; d £62-£72 (incl. bkfst) **LB** **FACILITIES:** STV **CONF:** Thtr 45 Board 25 **PARKING:** 15 **NOTES:** ⊗ in restaurant Closed 26 Dec-12 Jan
CARDS:

MELTON MOWBRAY, Leicestershire Map 11 SK71

Top 200 – Hotel

★★★★ Stapleford Park
Stapleford LE14 2EF
☎ 01572 787522 📠 01572 787651
e-mail: reservations@stapleford.co.uk
Dir: *1m SW of B676, 4m E of Melton Mowbray and 9m W of Colsterworth*
This stunning mansion, dating back to the 14th century, sits in over 500 acres of beautiful grounds. Spacious, sumptuous public rooms include a choice of lounges and an elegant restaurant; an additional brasserie-style restaurant is located in the new golf complex. The hotel also boasts a wonderful new spa with

continued

health and beauty treatments and gymnasium, a golf course, horse-riding and many other country pursuits. Bedrooms are individually styled and furnished to a high standard. Attentive service is delivered with a relaxed yet professional style, well suited to the house. Changes in the kitchen brigade, with Chef Wayne Vickerage at the helm, have introduced quality cuisine through an interesting, fixed-priced menu.

ROOMS: 44 en suite 8 annexe en suite ⊗ in 44 bedrooms s £175-£681; d £158-£681 (incl. bkfst) **LB** **FACILITIES:** STV 18 Fishing Riding Sauna Solarium Gym Putt green Jacuzzi Archery, Croquet, Falconry, Horse Riding, Petanque, Shooting ♫ Xmas **CONF:** BC Thtr 200 Class 140 Board 80 **SERVICES:** Lift **PARKING:** 120 **NOTES:** ⊗ in restaurant Civ Wed 200
CARDS:

★★★73% Sysonby Knoll
Asfordby Rd LE13 0HP
☎ 01664 563563 📠 01664 410364
e-mail: reception@sysonby.com web: www.sysonby.com
Dir: *0.5m from town centre beside A6006*
This well-established hotel is located towards the edge of town and is set within attractive gardens. A friendly and relaxed atmosphere prevails with the many return guests treated like old friends. Bedrooms, including superior rooms in an annexe, are generally spacious and thoughtfully equipped. Public areas include a cosy bar, choice of lounges and a smart and newly extended restaurant.
ROOMS: 23 en suite 7 annexe en suite (1 fmly) (7 GF) ⊗ in 6 bedrooms s £58.50-£75; d £71-£94 (incl. bkfst) **LB** **FACILITIES:** STV Fishing **CONF:** Thtr 50 Class 25 Board 34 Del £95 **PARKING:** 48 **NOTES:** ⊗ in restaurant Closed 25 Dec-1 Jan
CARDS:

See advert on opposite page

★★★68% Quorn Lodge
46 Asfordby Rd LE13 0HR
☎ 01664 566660 & 562590 📠 01664 480660
e-mail: quornlodge@aol.com web: www.quornlodge.co.uk
Dir: *from town centre take A6006. Hotel 300yds from junct of A606/A607 on right*
Centrally located, this smart privately owned and managed hotel offers a comfortable and welcoming atmosphere. Bedrooms are individually decorated and thoughtfully designed. The public rooms consist of a bright restaurant overlooking the garden, a cosy lounge bar and a modern function suite. High standards are maintained throughout and extensive parking is a bonus.
ROOMS: 19 en suite (2 fmly) (3 GF) ⊗ in 13 bedrooms s £59.50-£75; d £75-£95 (incl. bkfst) **LB** **FACILITIES:** STV **CONF:** Thtr 90 Class 60 Board 85 Del from £105 **PARKING:** 33 **NOTES:** ⊗ in restaurant Closed 26 Dec-2 Jan **CARDS:**

See advert on opposite page

Sysonby Knoll

Melton Mowbray, Leicestershire
Tel: +44 (0) 1664 563563
Email: reception@sysonby.co.uk
www.sysonby.co.uk

AA ★★★

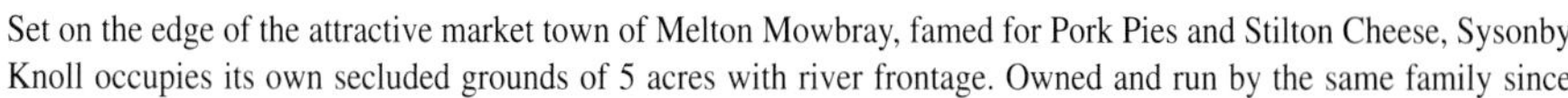

Set on the edge of the attractive market town of Melton Mowbray, famed for Pork Pies and Stilton Cheese, Sysonby Knoll occupies its own secluded grounds of 5 acres with river frontage. Owned and run by the same family since 1965, this Edwardian country house still retains much of it's original character, with period furnishings in the public areas.

Within easy reach are the cities of Nottingham and Leicester, the historic towns of Oakham and Stamford, any many other attractions such as Rutland Water and the National Space Centre.

Our restaurant is deservedly popular with hotel residents and local diners, providing a relaxed atmosphere in which to enjoy some of the creative dishes from our extensive menus.

Pets are genuinely welcome. See website for full details and menus.

Quorn Lodge Hotel

46 Asfordby Road LE13 0HR
Tel: 01664 566660 • Fax 01664 480660 • Email: quornlodge@aol.com

Directions: from town centre take A6006, hotel 300yds from junction of A606/A607 on right.

A warm welcome awaits you when you visit this Original Hunting Lodge situated on the edge of the bustling Market Town of Melton Mowbray renowned for its Pork Pies and Stilton Cheese. It is an ideal base for visiting the surrounding countryside and local attractions.

The Hotel is family owned and personally run by Julie Sturt and her professional and friendly staff which helps to give a home from home atmosphere the moment you step through the doors. Our aim is Luxury at affordable prices. The 19 bedrooms are all individually designed to the highest standard, there is a choice of Standard, Deluxe and Executive rooms as well as two magnificent Four Poster Rooms. The Hotel has recently been refurbished always being careful to keep the original charm of the building. The elegant Laurels Restaurant serves a variety of delicious food with a good selection of wine, so why not come and enjoy Good Food, Good Wine and Good Company? You can relax before and after your meal in the comfort of the Lounge Bar which overlooks a pretty garden. A modern function suite is available for business meetings, social functions and Weddings. Special weekend breaks are available.

MEMBURY MOTORWAY SERVICE AREA (M4), Berkshire — Map 05 SU37

Days Inn

Membury Service Area RG17 7TZ
01488 72336 01488 72336
e-mail: membury.hotel@welcomebreak.co.uk
web: www.welcomebreak.co.uk
Dir: M4 between junct 14 & 15

This modern building offers accommodation in smart, spacious and well-equipped bedrooms, suitable for families and business travellers, and all with en suite bathrooms. Continental breakfast is available and other refreshments may be taken at the nearby family restaurant. For further details see the Hotel Groups page.
ROOMS: 38 en suite s £40-£60; d £40-£60 **CONF:** BC Board 10

MERIDEN, West Midlands — Map 10 SP28

★★★★73% Marriott Forest of Arden Hotel & Country Club

Maxstoke Ln CV7 7HR
0870 400 7272 0870 400 7372
Dir: M42 junct 6 onto A45 towards Coventry, over Stonebridge flyover. After 0.75m left into Shepherds Ln. Hotel 1.5m on left

The ancient oaks, rolling hills and natural lakes of the 10,000 acre Forest of Arden estate provide an idyllic backdrop for this modern hotel and country club. The hotel boasts an excellent range of leisure facilities and is regarded as one of the finest golfing destinations in the UK. Bedrooms provide every modern convenience and a full range of facilities.
ROOMS: 214 en suite (4 fmly) (65 GF) in 135 bedrooms s fr £100; d fr £130 (incl. bkfst) **LB** **FACILITIES: Spa** STV supervised 18 Fishing Sauna Gym Putt green Jacuzzi Health & Beauty salon,Floodlit golf academy Xmas **CONF:** Thtr 300 Class 180 Board 40 Del from £150 **SERVICES:** Lift air con **PARKING:** 300 **NOTES:** in restaurant Civ Wed 160 **CARDS:**

★★★70% Manor

Main Rd CV7 7NH
01676 522735 01676 522186
e-mail: reservations@manorhotelmeriden.co.uk
web: www.manorhotelmeriden.co.uk
Dir: M42 junct 6 take A45 towards Coventry then A452, signed Leamington. At rbt join B4102, signed Meriden, for hotel on left.

A sympathetically extended Georgian manor in the heart of this sleepy village, a few minutes away from the M6, M42 and National Exhibition Centre. The Regency Restaurant offers modern dishes, while the Triumph Buttery serves lighter meals and snacks. Bedroom styles vary considerably; the Executive rooms and those in the Princess Diana wing are smart and well equipped.
ROOMS: 110 en suite (20 GF) in 54 bedrooms s £65-£145; d £80-£155 (incl. bkfst) **LB** **CONF:** Thtr 250 Class 150 Board 60 Del from £80 **SERVICES:** Lift **PARKING:** 200 **NOTES:** in restaurant RS 24 Dec-2 Jan Civ Wed 150 **CARDS:**

★★★64% Strawberry Bank

Main Rd CV7 7NF
01676 522117 01676 523804
e-mail: enquiries@strawberrybank.co.uk
Dir: M42 junct 6/A45 towards Coventry for approx 1.5m. Just prior to Little Chef turn left signed Meriden. Turn right over flyover to island, then turn left to Meriden Island, 3.5m from NEC, airport & railway station

This modern hotel enjoys a convenient position for both the airport and the exhibition centre. Bedrooms are well equipped and a good range of dishes is available in the spacious restaurant. Gardens are well kept and extensive.
ROOMS: 47 en suite in 35 bedrooms s £35-£95; d £70-£115 (incl. bkfst) **LB** **FACILITIES:** STV **CONF:** Thtr 180 Class 50 Board 60 Del from £110 **PARKING:** 200 **NOTES:** in restaurant RS Sun pm, Sat & Mon am Civ Wed 63 **CARDS:**

MEVAGISSEY, Cornwall & Isles of Scilly — Map 02 SX04

★★70% Tremarne

Polkirt PL26 6UL
01726 842213 01726 843420
e-mail: info@tremarne-hotel.co.uk
web: www.tremarne-hotel.co.uk
Dir: from A390 at St Austell take B3273 to Mevagissey. Follow Portmellon signs through Mevagissey, at top of Polkirt Hill turn right

A relaxing, family-run hotel ideal for those exploring this beautiful area or visiting the nearby Eden Project. Many of the bedrooms have views across the countryside to the sea beyond. The friendly team of staff makes every effort to ensure a comfortable and enjoyable stay. Public areas include a bar, a well-appointed restaurant and a spacious lounge.
ROOMS: 13 en suite (2 fmly) in all bedrooms s £40-£60; d £60-£100 (incl. bkfst) **LB** **FACILITIES:** Xmas **PARKING:** 13 **NOTES:** No children 5yrs in restaurant Closed Nov-Feb
CARDS:

★★65% Spa Hotel

Polkirt Hill PL26 6UY
01726 842244 01726 842244
e-mail: Alan@the-spa-hotel.fsnet.co.uk
web: www.spahotel.freeserve.co.uk
Dir: from St Austell follow Mevagissey then Portmellon signs. Sign for hotel on right

Quietly situated in an elevated position, this family-run hotel offers a friendly welcome with wonderful coastal and countryside views. A wide choice of bedrooms is available; all are light, airy and attractively decorated, and some have patio areas leading on to well-tended gardens. There is a comfortable, cane-furnished lounge and a cosy bar.
ROOMS: 11 en suite (5 fmly) in 7 bedrooms s £40-£50; d £64-£70 (incl. bkfst) **LB** **FACILITIES:** Putt green **PARKING:** 12 **NOTES:** in restaurant **CARDS:**

Indoor Swimming Pool
Indoor Swimming Pool (heated)
Outdoor Swimming Pool
Outdoor Swimming Pool (heated)

MEXBOROUGH, South Yorkshire Map 16 SE40

★★63% Pastures
Pastures Rd S64 0JJ
☎ 01709 577707 🖹 01709 577795
e-mail: sales@pastures-hotel.co.uk
web: www.pastures-hotel.co.uk
Dir: *0.5m from town centre on A6023, left by ATS Tyres, signed Denaby Ings & Cadeby. Hotel on right*
This hotel has a modern, purpose-built block of bedrooms and a separate lodge building where food is served. It is in a rural setting beside a working canal and convenient for the Earth Centre, Doncaster, or the Dearne Valley with its nature reserves and leisure centre. Bedrooms are quiet, comfortable and equipped with most modern facilities.
ROOMS: 29 en suite (6 fmly) (14 GF) ⊘ in 21 bedrooms s fr £45; d fr £45 **FACILITIES:** STV **CONF:** Thtr 250 Class 170 Board 100 Del from £79 **SERVICES:** Lift **PARKING:** 155 **NOTES:** ✈ Civ Wed 200
CARDS:

MICHAEL WOOD MOTORWAY SERVICE AREA (M5), Gloucestershire Map 04 ST79

⌂ Days Inn

Michaelwood Service Area, M5 Northbound, Lower Wick GL11 6DD
☎ 01454 261513 🖹 01454 269150
e-mail: michaelwood.hotel@welcomebreak.co.uk
web: www.welcomebreak.co.uk
Dir: *M5 northbound between junct 13 and 14*
This modern building offers accommodation in smart, spacious and well-equipped bedrooms, suitable for families and business travellers, and all with en suite bathrooms. Continental breakfast is available and other refreshments may be taken at the nearby family restaurant. For further details see the Hotel Groups page.
ROOMS: 38 en suite s £45-£55; d £45-£55 **CONF:** Board 10 Del from £35

MIDDLETON, Greater Manchester Map 16 SD80

⌂ Premier Lodge (Manchester North)

818 Manchester Old Rd, Rhodes M24 4RF
☎ 0870 9906406 🖹 0870 9906407
web: www.premierlodge.com
Dir: *M60/M62 junction 18 follow signs Manchester/Middleton. Leave M60 at junct 19, for A576 towards Middleton*
High quality, modern, budget accommodation, ideal for families and business travellers. All rooms feature bath, power shower and satellite TV, and most have telephones / modem points. The adjacent bar and restaurant offers a wide and varied menu.
ROOMS: 42 en suite s £50; d £50 **CONF:** Thtr 60 Class 60

MIDDLETON STONEY, Oxfordshire Map 11 SP52

★★70% Jersey Arms
OX25 4AD
☎ 01869 343234 🖹 01869 343565
e-mail: jerseyarms@bestwestern.co.uk
web: www.jerseyarms.co.uk
Dir: *on B430 10m N of Oxford, between junct 9 & 10 of M40*
With a history dating back to the 13th century, the Jersey Arms combines old-fashioned charm with contemporary style and elegance. The individually designed bedrooms are well-equipped and comfortable. The lounge has an open fire, and the spacious

continued

restaurant provides a calm atmosphere in which to enjoy the hotel's popular cuisine.
ROOMS: 6 en suite 14 annexe en suite (3 fmly) (9 GF) ⊘ in 6 bedrooms s £85-£108; d £96-£175 (incl. bkfst) **LB** **FACILITIES:** Xmas **CONF:** Board 20 Del £130 **PARKING:** 55 **NOTES:** ✈ ⊘ in restaurant
CARDS:

MIDDLEWICH, Cheshire Map 15 SJ76

⌂ Travelodge
M6 Junction 18, A54 CW10 0JB
☎ 08700 850 950 🖹 01606 738229
Travelodge offers good quality, good value, modern accommodation. Ideal for families, the spacious, en suite bedrooms include remote-control TV, tea and coffee-making facilities and luxury beds. Meals can be taken at the nearby family restaurant. For further details consult the Hotel Groups page.
ROOMS: 32 en suite s fr £25; d fr £25

MIDHURST, West Sussex Map 06 SU82

★★★73% ❀ The Angel
North St GU29 9DN
☎ 01730 812421 🖹 01730 815928
e-mail: info@theangelmidhurst.co.uk
web: www.theangelmidhurst.co.uk
Dir: *on S side of A272 in centre of Midhurst*
Dating back to the 15th century, this charming hotel offers a relaxed homely atmosphere. Bedrooms are individually decorated with some, including a room for less able guests, situated in an adjacent annexe. Public areas boast a cosy bar complete with log fire, Gabrial's, a fine-dining restaurant and Halo, a contemporary brassiere.
ROOMS: 24 en suite 4 annexe en suite (2 GF) ⊘ in all bedrooms s £80; d £110 (incl. bkfst) **LB** **FACILITIES:** STV ♫ Xmas **CONF:** Thtr 70 Class 40 Board 30 Del £125 **PARKING:** 75 **NOTES:** ⊘ in restaurant Civ Wed 100 **CARDS:**

★★★71% ❀ Spread Eagle Hotel and Health Spa
South St GU29 9NH
☎ 01730 816911 🖹 01730 815668
e-mail: spreadeagle@hshotels.co.uk
web: www.hshotels.co.uk/spread/spreadeagle-main.htm
Dir: *from M25 junct 10 follow A3 S, exit A3 at Milford and follow A286 to Midhurst. Hotel adjacent to Market Square on South Street*

Offering accommodation since 1430, this historic property has plenty of character, evident in its sloping floors and inglenook fireplaces. Individually decorated bedrooms provide modern comforts; those in

continued on p410

M

MIDHURST, continued

the main house have oak panelling. A spa with pool, gym and beauty treatments is an attraction, as is the restaurant.
ROOMS: 35 en suite 4 annexe en suite (8 GF) in 6 bedrooms s £85-£190; d £99-£225 (incl. bkfst) **LB** **FACILITIES: Spa** STV Sauna Gym Jacuzzi Health & beauty treatment rooms Steam room Fitness trainer Xmas **CONF:** Thtr 80 Class 40 Board 34 Del from £128 **PARKING:** 75 **NOTES:** in restaurant Civ Wed 80
CARDS:

★★★68% **Southdowns Country**
Dumpford Ln, Trotton GU31 5JN
01730 821521 01730 821790
e-mail: reception@southdownshotel.com
web: www.southdownshotel.com
Dir: *on A272, after town turn left at Keepers Arms*
Ideal for a relaxing break, this private hotel enjoys a secluded location with views over the Sussex countryside. It is a popular choice for weddings, due to its setting and spacious public areas. Some of the comfortable bedrooms overlook the grounds. Meals are available in the bar and in the more formal restaurant, which focuses on local produce.
ROOMS: 22 en suite (2 fmly) (2 GF) in 12 bedrooms s £50-£175; d £60-£180 (incl. bkfst) **LB** **FACILITIES:** Sauna Solarium Exercise equipment Xmas **CONF:** Thtr 100 Class 30 Board 30 Del from £95 **PARKING:** 70 **NOTES:** No children 10yrs in restaurant Civ Wed 100 **CARDS:**

See advert under PETERSFIELD

★★77% **Park House**
Bepton GU29 0JB
01730 819000 01730 819099
e-mail: reservations@parkhousehotel.com
web: www.parkhousehotel.com
Dir: *from centre of Midhurst, take B2226 to Bepton. Hotel 2m on left*
This charming country house hotel is set in attractive mature grounds in peaceful rural surroundings. Bedrooms are very comfortable and well equipped, and the smart public rooms include an elegant drawing room, honesty bar and dining room. A small team of staff provides attentive and friendly service.
ROOMS: 16 en suite (2 fmly) (1 GF) s £75-£150; d £110-£190 (incl. bkfst) **LB** **FACILITIES:** STV 9 Putt green ch fac Xmas **CONF:** Thtr 50 Class 50 Board 25 Del £145 **PARKING:** 35 **NOTES:** in restaurant Civ Wed 50 **CARDS:**

Bad hair day?
Hairdryers in all rooms three stars and above

MIDSOMER NORTON, Somerset — Map 04 ST65

★★★72% **Centurion**
Charlton Ln BA3 4BD
01761 417711 01761 418357
e-mail: enquiries@centurionhotel.co.uk
web: www.centurionhotel.com
Dir: *off A367, 10m S of Bath*
This privately owned, purpose-built hotel incorporates the adjacent Fosseway Country Club with its 9-hole golf course and other extensive leisure amenities. Bedrooms on ground floor level, including two for less able guests, are available, as are family bedded rooms. All bedrooms are non-smoking. Public areas include a choice of bars, an attractive lounge and a range of meeting/function rooms.

ROOMS: 44 en suite (4 fmly) (18 GF) in all bedrooms s £68-£73; d £90-£95 (incl. bkfst) **LB** **FACILITIES: Spa** STV 9 Sauna Gym Jacuzzi Bowling green Sports field **CONF:** Thtr 180 Class 70 Board 50 Del from £105 **PARKING:** 100 **NOTES:** in restaurant Closed 24 Dec-1 Jan Civ Wed 100 **CARDS:**

MILDENHALL, Suffolk — Map 12 TL77

★★★73% **Riverside**
Mill St IP28 7DP
01638 717274 01638 715997
e-mail: bookings@riverside-hotel.net
Dir: *from A11 at Fiveways rdbt take A1101 in Mildenhall Town. Left at mini rdbt along High St. Hotel last building on left before bridge*
An 18th-century red brick building situated in the heart of this charming town centre on the banks of the River Lark. Public rooms include a smart restaurant, which overlooks the river and the attractive gardens to the rear. The smartly decorated bedrooms have co-ordinated soft furnishings and many thoughtful touches.
ROOMS: 17 en suite 6 annexe en suite (4 fmly) (4 GF) s £69.50; d £95 (incl. bkfst) **LB** **FACILITIES:** Fishing Rowing boat hire Xmas **CONF:** Thtr 150 Class 60 Board 40 Del from £98 **SERVICES:** Lift **PARKING:** 80 **NOTES:** Civ Wed 120
CARDS:

★★★68% **The Smoke House**
Beck Row IP28 8DH
01638 713223 01638 712202
e-mail: enquiries@smoke-house.co.uk
web: www.smoke-house.co.uk
Dir: *A1101 into Mildenhall, follow Beck Row signs. Hotel after mini rdbt through Beck Row on right*

An extended 16th-century inn situated just a short drive from the town centre and ideally placed for touring the Suffolk countryside. Public areas have been sympathetically restored and retain much

continued

of their original character. The spacious bedrooms are attractively decorated and well equipped. Facilities include a shopping mall.
ROOMS: 94 en suite 2 annexe en suite (96 GF) s £97.50-£147.50; d £140-£195 (incl. bkfst) **LB FACILITIES:** ♫ Xmas **CONF:** Thtr 120 Class 80 Board 50 **PARKING:** 100 **NOTES:** ⊗ in restaurant
CARDS:

See advert on this page

MILFORD ON SEA, Hampshire

Map 05 SZ29

Top 200 – Hotel

★★★ Westover Hall
Park Ln SO41 0PT
☎ 01590 643044 01590 644490
e-mail: info@westoverhallhotel.com
web: www.westoverhallhotel.com
Dir: *M3 & M27 W onto A337 to Lymington. Follow signs to Milford-on-Sea onto B3058. Hotel outside village centre towards cliff*
Just a few moments' walk from the beach and boasting uninterrupted views across Christchurch Bay to the Isle of Wight in the distance, this late-Victorian mansion offers a relaxed, informal and friendly atmosphere together with efficient standards of hospitality and service. Each of the bedrooms has been decorated with flair and style. Architectural delights include dramatic stained-glass windows, extensive oak panelling and a galleried entrance hall. The cuisine is prepared with much care and attention to detail.
ROOMS: 12 en suite (1 fmly) ⊗ in all bedrooms s £100-£150; d £165-£230 (incl. bkfst) **LB FACILITIES:** Beach Hut Xmas **CONF:** Thtr 35 Class 20 Board 20 **PARKING:** 50 **NOTES:** No children 5 yrs ⊗ in restaurant Civ Wed 50
CARDS:

See advert under LYMINGTON

For central reservation numbers and more information on Hotel Groups, turn to pages 33-39

★★★73% *South Lawn*
Lymington Rd SO41 0RF
☎ 01590 643911 01590 644820
e-mail: enquiries@southlawn.co.uk
web: www.southlawn.co.uk
Dir: *left off A337 at Everton onto B3058. Hotel 0.5m on right*
Peacefully located, this former dower house offers attentive and friendly service. The hotel is situated close to the sea and is set in four acres of well-tended grounds. Bedrooms are spacious, include welcome extras and are attractively decorated; many enjoying

continued

delightful views over the garden. The bright dining room serves a varied range of carefully prepared local produce.

South Lawn Hotel

ROOMS: 24 en suite (3 GF) ⊗ in all bedrooms **PARKING:** 60
NOTES: No children 7yrs ⊗ in restaurant Closed 30 Dec-18 Jan
CARDS:

See advert under LYMINGTON

MILTON COMMON, Oxfordshire

Map 05 SP60

★★★★77% The Oxford Belfry
OX9 2JW
☎ 01844 279381 01844 279624
e-mail: oxfordbelfry@marstonhotels.com
Dir: *M40 junct 7 onto A329 to Thame. Left onto A40 by Three Pigeons pub. Hotel 300yds on right*
This modern hotel has a relatively rural location and enjoys lovely views of the countryside to the rear. The hotel is built around two

continued on p412

MILTON COMMON, continued

very attractive courtyards and has a number of lounges and conference rooms, as well as indoor leisure facilities and outdoor tennis courts. Bedrooms are large and feature a range of extras.

The Oxford Belfry, Milton Common

ROOMS: 130 en suite (10 fmly) ⊗ in 72 bedrooms s £124-£149; d £158-£208 (incl. bkfst) **LB FACILITIES:** STV Sauna Solarium Gym Xmas **CONF:** Thtr 350 Class 150 Del from £179 **SERVICES:** Lift **PARKING:** 250 **NOTES:** ⊗ in restaurant Civ Wed 110 **CARDS:**

MILTON KEYNES, Buckinghamshire Map 11 SP83
See also Aspley Guise & Flitwick

★★★70% Courtyard by Marriott Milton Keynes

London Rd, Newport Pagnell MK16 0JA
☎ 01908 613688 📠 01908 617335
e-mail: eventorganiser.miltonkeynes@whitbread.com
Dir: *M1 junct 14, follow signs for A509 (Newport Pagnell), hotel 0.5m on right*

Ideally situated for access to the motorway, town centre and local attractions, this once Georgian coach house enjoys a pleasant and peaceful rural location. Newly refurbished bedrooms are comfortable and well appointed. Public rooms include a modern bar and conservatory restaurant overlooking the courtyard.

ROOMS: 53 en suite (9 fmly) (22 GF) ⊗ in 36 bedrooms s £68-£117; d £76-£129 (incl. bkfst) **LB FACILITIES:** STV Gym **CONF:** Thtr 200 Class 90 Board 50 Del from £105 **PARKING:** 200 **NOTES:** ⊗ in restaurant Civ Wed 100 **CARDS:**

★★★70% Novotel Milton Keynes

Saxon St, Layburn Court, Heelands MK13 7RA
☎ 01908 322212 📠 01908 322235
e-mail: H3272@accor-hotels.com
Dir: *M1 junct 14, follow Childsway signs towards city centre. Turn right into Saxon Way, continue straight across all rdbts hotel on left*

Contemporary in style, this purpose-built hotel is situated on the outskirts of town, a few minutes' drive from the centre and mainline railway station. Bedrooms provide ample workspace and a good range of facilities for the modern traveller, and public rooms include a children's play area and indoor leisure centre.

ROOMS: 124 en suite (40 fmly) (40 GF) ⊗ in 105 bedrooms s £119; d £119 **LB FACILITIES:** STV Sauna Gym Steam bath **CONF:** Thtr 120 Class 75 Board 40 Del £155 **SERVICES:** Lift air con **PARKING:** 130 **NOTES:** Civ Wed 100 **CARDS:**

★★★70% Parkside

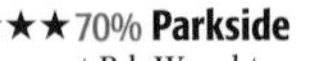

Newport Rd, Woughton on the Green MK6 3LR
☎ 01908 661919 📠 01908 676186
e-mail: parkside@macdonald-hotels.co.uk

Situated in five acres of landscaped grounds in a peaceful village setting, the Parkside is only five minutes' drive from the centre of Milton Keynes. Bedrooms are divided between executive rooms in the main house and standard rooms in the adjacent coach house. Public rooms include a range of meeting rooms, Lanes restaurant and Strollers bar.

ROOMS: 49 rms (38 en suite) (1 fmly) (19 GF) ⊗ in 15 bedrooms s £65-£135; d £80-£155 **FACILITIES:** STV Discounted entry to local health & fitness club Xmas **CONF:** Thtr 110 Class 60 Board 50 Del from £120 **PARKING:** 75 **NOTES:** ⊗ in restaurant Civ Wed 120 **CARDS:**

★★★65% Quality Hotel & Suites Milton Keynes

Monks Way, Two Mile Ash MK8 8LY
☎ 01908 561666 📠 01908 568303
e-mail: enquiries@hotels-milton-keynes.com
Dir: *junct of A5/A422*

Bedrooms at this purpose-built hotel are particularly well-equipped, having extra phones and mini-bars. There are also a number of suites with fax machines and kitchenettes. Eating options include an all-day room and lounge service in addition to the restaurant.

ROOMS: 88 en suite (15 fmly) ⊗ in 44 bedrooms s £40-£135; d £50-£145 **LB FACILITIES:** STV supervised Sauna Solarium Gym Jacuzzi Steam room, Whirlpool spa **CONF:** Thtr 120 Class 50 Board 50 Del from £90 **PARKING:** 200 **NOTES:** ⊗ in restaurant Civ Wed 100 **CARDS:**

★★70% Different Drummer

94 High St, Stony Stratford MK11 1AH
☎ 01908 564733 📠 01908 260646
e-mail: info@hoteldifferentdrummer.co.uk
web: www.hoteldifferentdrummer.co.uk

This attractive hotel located on the high street in historic Stony Stratford offers a genuine welcome to its guests. The oak-panelled restaurant is a popular dining venue and offers an Italian-style menu. Bedrooms are generally spacious and well equipped. A contemporary bar has now been added, and provides a further dining option.

ROOMS: 15 en suite 8 annexe en suite (2 fmly) (3 GF) ⊗ in 14 bedrooms s £49-£77; d £65-£87 (incl. bkfst) **FACILITIES:** STV **PARKING:** 6 **NOTES:** **CARDS:**

★★68% Swan Revived
High St, Newport Pagnell MK16 8AR
☎ 01908 610565 01908 210995
e-mail: swanrevived@btinternet.com
web: www.swanrevived.co.uk
Dir: *M1 junct 14 onto A509 then B526 into Newport Pagnell for 2m. Hotel on High St*

Once a coaching inn, this hotel dates from 17th century, occupying a prime location in the centre of town. Well-appointed bedrooms are spacious, individually styled and have good levels of comfort. Public areas include a popular bar and a restaurant offering a variety of freshly prepared dishes.
ROOMS: 42 en suite (2 fmly) s £49-£83.95; d £60-£90 (incl. bkfst) **LB** **FACILITIES:** STV **CONF:** Thtr 70 Class 30 Board 28 **SERVICES:** Lift **PARKING:** 18 **NOTES:** in restaurant RS 25 Dec-1 Jan Civ Wed
CARDS: 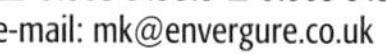

Campanile
40 Penn Rd, Fenny Stratford, Bletchley MK2 2AU
☎ 01908 649819 01908 649818
e-mail: mk@envergure.co.uk
Dir: *M1 junct 14, follow A4146 to A5. Southbound on A5. 4th exit at 1st rdbt to Fenny Stratford. Hotel 500yds on left*

This modern building offers accommodation in smart, well-equipped bedrooms, all with en suite bathrooms. Refreshments may be taken at the informal Bistro. For further details consult the Hotel Groups page.
ROOMS: 80 en suite s fr £45.95; d fr £45.95 **CONF:** Thtr 35 Class 40 Board 35

Premier Lodge (Central)
Shirwell Crescent, Furzton MK4 1GA

☎ 0870 9906396 0870 9906397
web: www.premierlodge.com
Dir: *M1 junct 14, onto A509 to Milton Keynes. At 9th 'North Grafton' rdbt left onto V6. Right at Leadenhall rdbt onto H7. Over 'The Bowl' rdbt*
High quality, modern, budget accommodation, ideal for families *continued* and business travellers. All rooms feature bath, power shower and satellite TV, and most have telephones / modem points. The adjacent bar and restaurant offers a wide and varied menu.
ROOMS: 120 en suite s £52; d £52 **CONF:** Thtr 10 Class 10 Board 10

Premier Lodge (Milton Keynes South)
Bletcham Way, Caldecotte MK7 8HP
☎ 0870 9906558 0870 9906559
web: www.premierlodge.com
Dir: *M1 junct 14, A509 to Milton Keynes. 1st rdbt take A4146, left at 2nd rdbt, over 3rd rdbt and right at 4th. Lodge over next rdbt on right*
High quality, modern, budget accommodation, ideal for families and business travellers. All rooms feature bath, power shower and satellite TV, and most have telephones / modem points. The adjacent bar and restaurant offers a wide and varied menu.
ROOMS: 40 en suite s £52; d £52 **CONF:** Board 10

Travel Inn Milton Keynes (Central)
Secklow Gate West MK9 3BZ
☎ 08701 977184 01908 607481
Dir: *from M1 junct 14 follow H6 route over 6 rdbts, at 7th (called Sth Secklow) turn right, Travel Inn on left*
Travel Inn offers good-quality, value-for-money accommodation. Spacious, en suite rooms with bath and shower comfortably accommodate a family of up to two adults and two children (to age 15). The restaurant and bar offers a varied menu. For further details consult the Hotel Groups page.
ROOMS: 38 en suite s £52.95-£54.95; d £52.95-£54.95 **CONF:** Thtr 16

Travel Inn (Milton Keynes East)
Willen Lake, Brickhill St MK15 9HQ
☎ 08701 977185 01908 678561
Dir: *M1 junct 14 follow H6 Childsway. Turn right at 3rd rdbt into Brickhill St. Right at 1st mini rdbt, Travel Inn 1st left*
Travel Inn offers good-quality, value-for-money accommodation. Spacious, en suite rooms with bath and shower comfortably accommodate a family of up to two adults and two children (to age 15). The restaurant and bar offers a varied menu. For further details consult the Hotel Groups page.
ROOMS: 41 en suite s £45.95-£46.95; d £45.95-£46.95

Travelodge
109 Grafton Gate MK9 1AL
☎ 08700 850 950
Travelodge offers good quality, good value, modern accommodation. Ideal for families, the spacious, en suite bedrooms include remote-control TV, tea and coffee-making facilities and luxury beds. Meals can be taken at the nearby family restaurant. For further details consult the Hotel Groups page.
ROOMS: 80 en suite s fr £25; d fr £25

Travelodge Milton Keynes North (Old Stratford)
Old Stratford Roundabout MK19 6AQ
☎ 08700 850 950 01908 260802
Dir: *On A5 towards Towcester, Travelodge on A508/A422 rdbt*
Travelodge offers good quality, good value, modern accommodation. Ideal for families, the spacious, en suite bedrooms include remote-control TV, tea and coffee-making facilities and luxury beds. Meals can be taken at the nearby family restaurant. For further details consult the Hotel Groups page.
ROOMS: 33 en suite s fr £25; d fr £25

Entertainment

M

MINEHEAD, Somerset Map 03 SS94

★★★67% Northfield

Northfield Rd TA24 5PU
☎ 01643 705155 01643 707715
e-mail: reservations@northfield-hotel.co.uk
web: www.northfield-hotel.co.uk
Dir: *M5 junct 23, follow A38 to Bridgwater and join A39 to Minehead*

Best Western

Located conveniently close to the town centre and the seafront, this hotel is set in delightfully maintained gardens and has a loyal, regular following. A range of comfortable sitting rooms and leisure facilities, including an indoor, heated pool are provided. A fixed price menu is served every evening in the oak-panelled dining room. The attractively co-ordinated bedrooms vary in size and are equipped to a good standard.

ROOMS: 28 en suite (7 fmly) s £53-£77; d £53-£69 (incl. bkfst & dinner) **LB** **FACILITIES:** STV Gym Putt green Jacuzzi Steam room Xmas **CONF:** BC Thtr 70 Class 45 Board 30 Del from £55 **SERVICES:** Lift **PARKING:** 44 **NOTES:** in restaurant **CARDS:**

★★78% Channel House

Church Path TA24 5QG
☎ 01643 703229 01643 708925
e-mail: channel.house@virgin.net web: www.channelhouse.co.uk
Dir: *from A39 right at rdbt to seafront, then left onto promenade. 1st right, 1st left to Blenheim Gdns and 1st right into Northfield Rd*

This charming, well-run hotel offers relaxing and tranquil surroundings, yet is only a short walk from the town centre, and is set in two acres of well tended gardens. Many of the exceptionally well-equipped bedrooms benefit from wonderful views. The dining room is the venue for imaginative menus using the best of local produce. The South West coastal path starts from the hotel garden. The hotel is totally no-smoking.

ROOMS: 8 en suite (1 fmly) in all bedrooms s £80-£93; d £130-£156 (incl. bkfst & dinner) **LB** **FACILITIES:** Xmas **SERVICES:** air con **PARKING:** 10 **NOTES:** No children 15yrs in restaurant Closed 2 Nov-15 Mar **CARDS:**

See advert on opposite page

★★74% Alcombe House

Bircham Rd, Alcombe TA24 6BG
☎ 01643 705130 01643 705130
e-mail: alcombe.house@virgin.net

Located mid way between Minehead and Dunster, this Grade II listed Georgian Hotel offers a delightful combination of efficient service delivered a friendly manner by the very welcoming resident proprietors. Public areas include a comfortable lounge and a candlelit dining room serving an enjoyable range of carefully prepared local produce.

ROOMS: 7 en suite in all bedrooms s £38; d £56 (incl. bkfst) **LB** **FACILITIES:** Xmas **PARKING:** 9 **NOTES:** No children 15yrs in restaurant 19 Mar-7 Nov **CARDS:**

MONK FRYSTON, North Yorkshire Map 16 SE52

★★★70% Monk Fryston Hall

LS25 5DU
☎ 01977 682369 01977 683544
e-mail: reception@monkfryston-hotel.co.uk
web: www.monkfrystonhotel.co.uk
Dir: *A1/A63 junct towards Selby. Left side in centre of Monk Fryston*

This delightful 16th-century mansion house enjoys a peaceful location in 30 acres of grounds, yet is only minutes' drive from the A1. Many original features have been retained and the public rooms are furnished with antique and period pieces. Bedrooms are individually styled and thoughtfully equipped for both business and leisure guests.

ROOMS: 29 en suite (2 fmly) (5 GF) in 20 bedrooms s £92-£102; d £116-£171 (incl. bkfst) **LB** **FACILITIES:** STV ch fac Xmas **CONF:** Thtr 50 Class 20 Board 20 Del from £137 **PARKING:** 80 **NOTES:** in restaurant Civ Wed 58 **CARDS:**

MORCOTT, Rutland Map 11 SK90

Travelodge Uppingham

Uppingham LE15 8SA
☎ 08700 850 950 01572 747719
Dir: *on A47, eastbound*

Travelodge

Travelodge offers good quality, good value, modern accommodation. Ideal for families, the spacious, en suite bedrooms include remote-control TV, tea and coffee-making facilities and luxury beds. Meals can be taken at the nearby family restaurant. For further details consult the Hotel Groups page.

ROOMS: 40 en suite s fr £25; d fr £25

MORDEN, Greater London
See LONDON SECTION plan 1 D1

Travelodge London Wimbledon

Epsom Rd SM4 5PH
☎ 08700 850 950 020 8640 8227
Dir: *on A24*

Travelodge

Travelodge offers good quality, good value, modern accommodation. Ideal for families, the spacious, en suite bedrooms include remote-control TV, tea and coffee-making facilities and luxury beds. Meals can be taken at the nearby family restaurant. For further details consult the Hotel Groups page.

ROOMS: 32 en suite s fr £25; d fr £25

MORECAMBE, Lancashire Map 18 SD46

★★★65% Clarendon

76 Marine Rd West, West End Promenade LA4 4EP
☎ 01524 410180 01524 421616
e-mail: clarendon@mitchellshotels.co.uk
Dir: *M6 junct 34 follow Morecambe signs. At rdbt with 'The Shrimp' on corner 1st exit to Westgate, follow to seafront. Right at traffic lights, hotel 3rd block along*

This seafront hotel was completely refurbished a few years ago. Well maintained throughout, it offers bright cheerful public areas and smartly appointed bedrooms all with fully tiled bathrooms.

ROOMS: 29 en suite (4 fmly) in 10 bedrooms s £60; d £90 (incl. bkfst) **LB** **FACILITIES:** Xmas **CONF:** Thtr 90 Class 40 Board 40 **SERVICES:** Lift **PARKING:** 22 **NOTES:** in restaurant **CARDS:**

Destination dining!
This symbol indicates a Restaurant with Rooms

★★★62% Elms
Bare Village LA4 6DD
☎ 01524 411501 🖷 01524 831979
Dir: *Exit M6 at J34. Follow signs to Morecambe to large rdbt. Take 4th exit into Hall Drive which becomes Bare Lane. Follow over railway crossing. Hotel is 200yds on R.*
This long-established hotel lies just off the North Promenade and is popular with business and leisure guests. Public rooms include a spacious lounge bar, a classical style restaurant, function facilities and a pub in the grounds. Many bedrooms have been upgraded.
ROOMS: 39 en suite (3 fmly) ⊗ in 180 bedrooms s fr £65; d fr £90 (incl. bkfst) **LB** **FACILITIES:** Xmas **CONF:** Thtr 200 Class 72 Board 60 Del from £75 **SERVICES:** Lift **PARKING:** 80 **NOTES:** ⊗ in restaurant Civ Wed 80 **CARDS:**

MORETON, Merseyside — Map 15 SJ28

★★★68% Leasowe Castle
Leasowe Rd CH46 3RF
☎ 0151 606 9191 🖷 0151 678 5551
e-mail: reservations@leasowecastle.com
web: www.leasowecastle.com
Dir: *M53 junct 1, 1st exit from rdbt, the take A551. Hotel 0.75m on right*

Located adjacent to Leasowe Golf Course and within easy reach of Liverpool, Chester and all of the Wirral's attractions, this historic hotel dates back to 1592. Bedrooms are smartly appointed and well-equipped, many enjoying ocean views. Public areas retain many original features. Weddings and functions are well catered for.
ROOMS: 47 en suite (3 fmly) ⊗ in 3 bedrooms s £50-£70; d £55-£85 (incl. bkfst) **LB** **FACILITIES:** STV Sauna Gym Water sports, Sea Fishing, Sailing, Health club (mid Apr 2004) Xmas **CONF:** Thtr 400 Class 200 Board 80 Del from £99 **SERVICES:** Lift **PARKING:** 200 **NOTES:** ⊗ in restaurant Civ Wed 250 **CARDS:**

See advert under LIVERPOOL

MORETONHAMPSTEAD, Devon — Map 03 SX78

U Bovey Castle
TQ13 8RE
☎ 01647 445000 🖷 01647 440961
e-mail: reception@boveycastle.com
web: www.boveycastle.com
Dir: *2m from Moretonhampstead towards Princetown on B3212*
The hotel has newly opened after extensive investment by Peter de Savary. It includes a championship golf course and excellent leisure facilities.
ROOMS: 60 en suite 5 annexe en suite (5 fmly) (2 GF) ⊗ in all bedrooms s £145-£550; d £145-£550 **FACILITIES: Spa** STV 18 Fishing Snooker Sauna Solarium Gym Putt green Jacuzzi clay pigeon shooting, archery, fly-fishing ch fac Xmas **CONF:** BC Thtr 100 Class 50 Board 40 Del from £240 **SERVICES:** Lift **PARKING:** 100 **NOTES:** ⊗ in restaurant Civ Wed 100 **CARDS:**

MORETON-IN-MARSH, Gloucestershire — Map 10 SP23

★★★78% Manor House
CLASSIC BRITISH
High St GL56 0LJ
☎ 01608 650501 🖷 01608 651481
e-mail: info@manorhousehotel.info
Dir: *off A429 at south end of the town. Take East St. Off the High St*
Dating back to the 16th century, this charming Cotswold coaching inn retains much of its original character with stone walls, impressive fireplaces and a relaxed, country-house atmosphere. Bedrooms vary in size and reflect the individuality of the building, all are well equipped and some are particularly opulent. Public rooms are comfortable and smartly presented.
ROOMS: 35 en suite 3 annexe en suite (3 fmly) ⊗ in 4 bedrooms s £115-£180; d £135-£220 (incl. bkfst) **LB** **FACILITIES: Spa** Putt green Jacuzzi Xmas **CONF:** Thtr 120 Class 50 Board 50 Del from £150 **SERVICES:** Lift **PARKING:** 24 **NOTES:** ⊗ in restaurant Civ Wed 120 **CARDS:**

★★★70% Redesdale Arms
High St GL56 0AW
☎ 01608 650308 🖷 01608 651843
e-mail: info@redesdalearms.co.uk
Dir: *on A429, 1km from train station*
This fine old inn has played a central role in this town for centuries. Extensive refurbishment has successfully combined traditional features with contemporary comforts. Bedrooms are split between the main building and the former stables, all have high standards of comfort. Guests can choose to dine either in the stylish restaurant or conservatory.
ROOMS: 9 en suite 7 annexe en suite (5 GF) ⊗ in 14 bedrooms s £60-£65; d £65-£85 (incl. bkfst) **FACILITIES:** STV Xmas **CONF:** Thtr 50 Class 65 Board 45 Del from £150 **PARKING:** 14 **NOTES:** ⊗ in restaurant **CARDS:**

MORETON-IN-MARSH, continued

★★63% *White Hart Royal*
High St GL56 0BA
☎ 01608 650731 📠 01608 650880
Dir: *on A429 in town centre*
This Cotswold coaching inn dates back to the 17th century and once provided a hiding place for Charles I. Much of the original character has been retained with flagstone floors, a cobbled entrance hall and a feature fireplace. Bedrooms are brightly decorated and comfortably appointed.
ROOMS: 19 en suite (2 fmly) **FACILITIES:** STV **CONF:** Thtr 80 **PARKING:** 20 **NOTES:** ⊘ in restaurant
CARDS:

MORLEY, West Yorkshire Map 19 SE22

★★67% The Old Vicarage
Bruntcliffe Rd LS27 0JZ
☎ 0113 253 2174 📠 0113 253 3549
e-mail: oldvicarage@btinternet.com
web: www.oldvicaragehotel.co.uk
Dir: *M62 junct 27, A650 towards Wakefield. Hotel on left adjacent to St Andrews Church*
A warm welcome awaits guests at this extended Victorian vicarage. The bedrooms are split between the main house and modern extension; all offer a range of extra facilities. There is a cosy lounge with honesty bar; hearty meals are served in the pleasant dining room. Private parking is provided.
ROOMS: 21 en suite (1 fmly) ⊘ in 14 bedrooms s £45-£49.50; d £50-£62 (incl. bkfst) **LB** **FACILITIES:** Access to park with football, tennis & basketball **CONF:** Board 15 **PARKING:** 21 **NOTES:** ⊘ in restaurant Closed 24-26 Dec RS 1 Jan
CARDS:

MORPETH, Northumberland Map 21 NZ18

★★★74% Linden Hall
NE65 8XF
☎ 01670 500000 📠 01670 500001
e-mail: stay@lindenhall.co.uk
web: www.lindenhall.co.uk
(For full entry see Longhorsley)

MORTEHOE, Devon Map 03 SS44

★★66% *Lundy House Hotel*
Chapel Hill EX34 7DZ
☎ 01271 870372 📠 01271 871001
e-mail: info@lundyhousehotel.co.uk
web: www.lundyhousehotel.co.uk
Dir: *A361 to Braunton and Ilfracombe. Woolacombe exit at rdbt. In village right along esplanade, up hill to Mortehoe, hotel on left*
Facing south across the rugged North Devon coastline to Lundy Island in the distance, this personally run hotel offers a warm, friendly welcome. In the dining room, honest home cooking is served; vegetarians are particularly well catered for. It is very much a dog-friendly hotel, and there is direct access to the coastal path from the hotel's terraced gardens.
ROOMS: 9 en suite (4 fmly) ⊘ in all bedrooms **PARKING:** 9
NOTES: ⊘ in restaurant Closed Nov-Mar **CARDS:**

MOUSEHOLE, Cornwall & Isles of Scilly Map 02 SW42

★★70% Old Coastguard Hotel
The Parade TR19 6PR
☎ 01736 731222 📠 01736 731720
e-mail: bookings@oldcoastguardhotel.co.uk
web: www.oldcoastguardhotel.co.uk
Dir: *A30 to Penzance, coast road to Newlyn then Mousehole. 1st building on left on entering village*

A place to relax and unwind. The views are magnificent and the staff are friendly and offer good service. Bedrooms are bright and stylish; some have sea views and balconies. Guests can dine in the restaurant, or in summer months, al fresco on the terrace, and fish is fresh from the nearby Newlyn markets.
ROOMS: 14 en suite 7 annexe en suite (2 fmly) s £35-£76; d £75-£110 (incl. bkfst) **LB** **FACILITIES:** Sub- tropical garden **PARKING:** 12
NOTES: ⊘ in restaurant Closed 25 Dec
CARDS:

Restaurant with Rooms

The Cornish Range Restaurant with Rooms
6 Chapel St TR19 6BD
☎ 01736 731488
e-mail: info@cornishrange.co.uk
Dir: *Follow coast road through Newlyn into Mousehole. Along harbour past Ship Inn, turn sharp right, then left and Restarant on right*

This charming restaurant with rooms is a memorable place to eat and stay. Comfortable, stylish rooms, with delightful Cornish handmade furnishings, and attentive, friendly service create a relaxing environment. Interesting and accurate cuisine relies heavily on local freshly landed fish and shellfish, as well as local meat and poultry and the freshest fruit and vegetables.
ROOMS: 3 en suite **NOTES:** Closed Mon & Tue in winter and 26 Dec & 1 Jan **CARDS:**

MUCH BIRCH, Herefordshire — Map 10 SO53

★★★66% Pilgrim

THE INDEPENDENTS HOTEL ASSOCIATION

Ross Rd HR2 8HJ
☎ 01981 540742 📠 01981 540620
e-mail: stay@pilgrimhotel.co.uk
web: www.pilgrimhotel.co.uk

Dir: *on A49 6m from Ross-on-Wye, 5m from Hereford*

This much-extended former rectory is set back from the A49 and has sweeping views over the surrounding countryside. The extensive grounds contain a pitch and putt course. Privately owned and personally run, it provides accommodation that includes ground floor and four-poster rooms. There is a restful lounge, a traditionally furnished restaurant and a pleasant bar.

ROOMS: 20 en suite (3 fmly) (8 GF) ⊗ in 12 bedrooms s £55-£75; d £75-£100 (incl. bkfst) **LB** **FACILITIES:** 3 Putt green Pitch & putt, Badminton Xmas **CONF:** Thtr 45 Class 45 Board 25 **PARKING:** 42 **NOTES:** ⊗ in restaurant **CARDS:**

See advert under HEREFORD

MUCH WENLOCK, Shropshire — Map 10 SO69

★★★72% Raven

Barrow St TF13 6EN
☎ 01952 727251 📠 01952 728416
e-mail: enquiry@ravenhotel.com
web: www.ravenhotel.com

Dir: *M54 junct 4 or 5, take A442 S, then A4169 to Much Wenlock*

This town centre hotel is spread across several historic buildings with a 17th-century coaching inn at its centre. Accommodation is well furnished and equipped to offer modern comfort, with some ground-floor rooms. Public areas feature an interesting collection of prints and memorabilia connected with the modern-day Olympic Games, the idea for which was, interestingly, born in Much Wenlock.

ROOMS: 8 en suite 7 annexe en suite s fr £65; d fr £85 (incl. bkfst) **LB** **FACILITIES:** STV Beauty salon **CONF:** Thtr 16 Board 16 **PARKING:** 30 **NOTES:** ⊗ in restaurant **CARDS:**

★★63% Gaskell Arms

Bourton Rd TF13 6AQ
☎ 01952 727212 📠 01952 728505
e-mail: maxine@gaskellarms.co.uk
web: www.gaskellarms.co.uk

Dir: *from M6 turn off at junct 10A onto M54. Take junct 4 off M54 follow signs for Ironbridge/ Much Wenlock*

This 17th-century former coaching inn has exposed beams and log fires in the public areas. In addition to the lounge bar and restaurant, featuring a wide range of meals and snacks, there is a small bar that proves popular with locals. Well-maintained

continued

bedrooms, which vary in size, are attractively furnished; family rooms are available.

ROOMS: 16 rms (14 en suite) (3 fmly) (6 GF) ⊗ in 5 bedrooms s £50-£65; d £70-£90 (incl. bkfst) **LB** **FACILITIES:** Walking, horse riding **CONF:** BC **PARKING:** 41 **NOTES:** ⊗ in restaurant **CARDS:**

MUDEFORD See Christchurch

MULLION, Cornwall & Isles of Scilly — Map 02 SW61

★★★71% Mullion Cove Hotel

TR12 7EP
☎ 01326 240328 📠 01326 240998
e-mail: mullion.cove@btinternet.com
web: www.mullioncove.com

Dir: *from Helston follow signs to The Lizard, right at Mullion Holiday Park. Through village, left for Cove. Then right and hotel on top of hill*

Built at the turn of the last century and set high above the working

continued on p418

MULLION, continued

harbour of Mullion, this hotel has spectacular views, and seaward facing rooms are always popular. The stylish restaurant offers some carefully prepared dishes using local produce. After dinner guests might like to relax in one of the elegant lounges.
ROOMS: 30 en suite (9 fmly) (3 GF) s £66-£212; d £84-£230 (incl. bkfst & dinner) **LB** **FACILITIES:** Sauna Solarium Beauty treatments Xmas **PARKING:** 60 **NOTES:** in restaurant
CARDS:

★★★71% Polurrian

TR12 7EN
THE INDEPENDENTS
☎ 01326 240421 01326 240083
e-mail: polurotel@aol.com
Dir: *A30 onto A3076 to Truro. Follow signs for Helston on A39 then A394 to The Lizard and Mullion*
This long-established hotel is set in 12 acres of landscaped gardens, 300 feet above the sea. The spectacular views over Polurrian Cove will remain long in the memory, along with the wonderful sunsets. Public areas are spacious and comfortable, and the bedrooms are individually styled. There is a well-equipped leisure centre.
ROOMS: 39 en suite (22 fmly) s £55-£120 (incl. bkfst & dinner) **LB** **FACILITIES:** STV Squash Snooker Sauna Solarium Gym Putt green Jacuzzi Cricket net Whirlpool Mountain bikes Surfing Body boarding ch fac Xmas **CONF:** BC Thtr 100 Class 60 Board 30 **PARKING:** 80 **NOTES:** in restaurant Civ Wed 100
CARDS:

See advert on page 417

MUNDESLEY, Norfolk — Map 13 TG33

★★68% Manor Hotel

Beach Rd NR11 8BG
☎ 01263 720309 01263 721731
e-mail: mundesleymanor@amserve.com
web: www.northnorfolk.co.uk/mundesleymanor
Dir: *B1150 Norwich-North Walsham, then follow coastal route & Mundesley signs*
An imposing Victorian property situated in an elevated position with superb views of the sea. The hotel has been owned and run by the same family for over 30 years. The spacious public rooms offer a choice of bars, two lounges, a conservatory, and traditional restaurant as well as the Bar Victoriana. The comfortable bedrooms are smartly decorated; some rooms have stunning sea views.
ROOMS: 22 en suite 4 annexe en suite (3 fmly) (1 GF) in 8 bedrooms s £50-£65; d £74-£90 (incl. bkfst) **LB** **FACILITIES:** Xmas **CONF:** Thtr 20 Class 20 Board 15 **PARKING:** 40 **NOTES:** in restaurant Closed 2-18 Jan **CARDS:**

MUNGRISDALE, Cumbria — Map 18 NY33

★77% The Mill

CA11 0XR
☎ 01768 779659 01768 779155
e-mail: quinlan@evemail.net
Dir: *M6 junct 40, 2m N of A66*
Formerly a mill cottage dating from 1651 and set in magnificent rural scenery, this charming hotel and restaurant lies beside the old millstream. Inside there are cosy lounges, low ceilings, books, antiques, paintings and period pieces. Excellent five-course dinners will satisfy the heartiest of appetites.
ROOMS: 7 rms (5 en suite) s £35-£50; d £60-£90 (incl. bkfst) **FACILITIES:** Fishing Games room **PARKING:** 15 **NOTES:** in restaurant Closed Nov-Feb

NAILSWORTH, Gloucestershire — Map 04 ST89

★★70% Egypt Mill

GL6 0AE
☎ 01453 833449 01453 836098
e-mail: ch@egypt-mill.co.uk
Dir: *on A46, midway between Cheltenham and Bath*

Millstones and working waterwheels have been incorporated in the innovative refurbishment of this 17th-century former corn mill. Well-equipped bedrooms are located in two adjacent buildings and are tastefully furnished. Facilities include a restaurant with adjoining bar, a stylish cellar bar and popular bistro. During the summer the riverside patios and gardens are great places to enjoy a drink.
ROOMS: 8 en suite 10 annexe en suite (2 fmly) **FACILITIES:** STV Boules pitch **CONF:** Thtr 100 Class 80 Board 80 **PARKING:** 120 **NOTES:** in restaurant **CARDS:**

NANTWICH, Cheshire — Map 15 SJ65

Top 200 – Hotel

★★★ Rookery Hall

Main Rd, Worleston CW5 6DQ
HandPICKED
☎ 01270 610016 01270 626027
e-mail: rookeryhall-cro@handpicked.co.uk
Dir: *B5074 off 4th rdbt, on Nantwich by-pass. Hotel 1.5m on right*
This fine 19th-century mansion is set in 38 acres of gardens, pasture and parkland. Bedrooms, some in an adjacent coach house, are spacious and luxuriously appointed. The public areas are particularly stylish and include a salon with enormous sofas and a mahogany-panelled dining room. Many of the refurbished bedrooms provide a dazzling array of extras that include wide screen plasma TVs and DVD players. The staff are notable for their professionalism and hospitality. Hand Picked Hotels - AA Hotel Group of the Year 2004-5.
ROOMS: 30 en suite 16 annexe en suite (6 GF) s £115-£130; d £150 (incl. bkfst) **LB** **FACILITIES:** STV Fishing Xmas **CONF:** Thtr 90 Class 40 Board 40 **SERVICES:** Lift **PARKING:** 100 **NOTES:** in restaurant Civ Wed 66 **CARDS:**

See advert on opposite page

★★70% Crown
High St CW5 5AS
☎ 01270 625283 🖷 01270 628047
e-mail: info@crown-hotel.net
Dir: *A52 to Nantwich, hotel in centre of town*
Ideally set in the heart of this historic and delightful market town, The Crown has been offering hospitality for centuries. It has an abundance of original features and the well-equipped bedrooms retain an old world charm. There is also a bar with live entertainment throughout the week and diners can enjoy Italian food in the atmospheric brasserie.
ROOMS: 18 en suite (2 fmly) ⊗ in 2 bedrooms s £60-£70; d £74-£80 **LB FACILITIES:** Putt green ♫ **CONF:** Thtr 200 Class 150 Board 70 **PARKING:** 18 **NOTES:** Civ Wed 140 **CARDS:**

⌂ Premier Lodge (Nantwich)
221 Crewe Rd CW5 6NE
☎ 0870 9906418 🖷 0870 9906419
web: www.premierlodge.com
Dir: *exit M6 junct 16 for A500 signed Nantwich and Chester. At 1st rbt take 2nd exit, approx 4m. At 3rd rbt, take 3rd exit signed A500 Chester, at 4th turn left onto A534 towards Nantwich. Hotel approx 100 yards on right*
High quality, modern, budget accommodation, ideal for families and business travellers. All rooms feature bath, power shower and satellite TV, and most have telephones / modem points. The adjacent bar and restaurant offers a wide and varied menu.
ROOMS: 37 en suite s £50; d £50

TV dinner?
Room service at three stars and above

NEEDHAM MARKET, Suffolk — Map 13 TM05

⌂ Travelodge Ipswich Beacon
Beacon Hill IP6 8LP
☎ 08700 850 950 🖷 01449 721640
Dir: *A14/A140*
Travelodge offers good quality, good value, modern accommodation. Ideal for families, the spacious, en suite bedrooms include remote-control TV, tea and coffee-making facilities and luxury beds. Meals can be taken at the nearby family restaurant. For further details consult the Hotel Groups page.
ROOMS: 40 en suite s fr £25; d fr £25

NETHER STOWEY, Somerset — Map 04 ST13

★★71% Apple Tree
Keenthorne TA5 1HZ
☎ 01278 733238 🖷 01278 732693
e-mail: reservations@appletreehotel.com
web: www.appletreehotel.com
Dir: *from Bridgwater follow A39 towards Minehead. Hotel on left 2m past Cannington*
Parts of this cottage-style property, convenient for the coast and the M5, date back some 340 years. Bedrooms vary in character and style; some are in an adjoining wing, overlooking the garden. The friendly resident owners and their small team of staff make every effort to ensure an enjoyable stay. Public areas include an attractive conservatory restaurant, a bar and a library lounge.
ROOMS: 14 en suite (2 fmly) (5 GF) ⊗ in 5 bedrooms s £54.50; d £68 (incl. bkfst) **LB FACILITIES:** ch fac **CONF:** BC Thtr 25 Class 12 Board 14 **PARKING:** 40 **NOTES:** ⊗ in restaurant **CARDS:**

N

NETHER WASDALE, Cumbria Map 18 NY10

★★76% Low Wood Hall Hotel & Restaurant

CA20 1ET
☎ 019467 26100 019467 26111
e-mail: reservations@lowwoodhall.co.uk
web: www.lowwoodhall.co.uk
Dir: *off A595 at Gosforth, bear left for Wasdale. After 3m right for Nether Wasdale*

This delightful country hotel is peacefully set in five acres of wooded gardens overlooking the village and valley. Personal service and a warm welcome are assured. There are two lovely lounges and both are stocked with plenty to read and have roaring fires in season. Stylish interior designs blend well with the classical architecture. The carefully prepared meals are a highlight.

ROOMS: 6 rms (5 en suite) 6 annexe en suite (4 GF) in all bedrooms s £75-£85; d £85-£160 (incl. bkfst) **CONF:** Thtr 30 Class 30 Board 20 **PARKING:** 15 **NOTES:** No children 12yrs in restaurant Closed Xmas, New Year Civ Wed 40 **CARDS:**

NEW ALRESFORD, Hampshire Map 05 SU53

★★61% Swan

11 West St SO24 9AD
☎ 01962 732302 & 734427 01962 735274
e-mail: swanhotel@btinternet.com
Dir: *off A31 onto B3047*

This former coaching inn dates back to the 18th century and remains a busy and popular destination for travellers and locals. Bedrooms are in the main building and the more modern wing. The lounge bar and adjacent restaurant are open all day; for more traditional dining there is another restaurant which overlooks the busy village street.

ROOMS: 11 rms (10 en suite) 12 annexe en suite (3 fmly) **CONF:** Thtr 90 Class 60 Board 40 Del from £70 **PARKING:** 75 **NOTES:** in restaurant RS 25-26 Dec **CARDS:**

See advert on opposite page

NEWARK-ON-TRENT, Nottinghamshire Map 17 SK75

★★★68% The Grange Hotel

73 London Rd NG24 1RZ
☎ 01636 703399 01636 702328
e-mail: info@grangenewark.co.uk
Dir: *from A1 follow signs to town centre. At castle rdbt follow signs to Balderton. Over 2 sets of lights. Hotel 0.25m on left*

Expect a warm welcome at this family-run hotel, situated just a short walk from the town. Bedrooms are attractively decorated with co-ordinated soft furnishings and equipped with many thoughtful extras. Public rooms include the Potters bar, Cutlers restaurant and a residents' lounge. In the summer guests may enjoy the pretty terrace garden.

ROOMS: 10 en suite 9 annexe en suite (1 fmly) in 14 bedrooms s £62-£69; d £84-£105 (incl. bkfst) **LB PARKING:** 17 **NOTES:** in restaurant **CARDS:**

Travel Inn

travel inn

Lincoln Rd NG24 2DB
☎ 08701 977186 01636 605135
Dir: *at intersection of A1/A46/A17, follow signs B6166*

Travel Inn offers good-quality, value-for-money accommodation. Spacious, en suite rooms with bath and shower comfortably accommodate a family of up to two adults and two children (to age 15). The restaurant and bar offers a varied menu. For further details consult the Hotel Groups page.

ROOMS: 40 en suite s £45.95-£46.95; d £45.95-£46.95

NEWBURY, Berkshire Map 05 SU46

Top 200 – Hotel

★★★★★ The Vineyard at Stockcross

RELAIS & CHATEAUX

Stockcross RG20 8JU
☎ 01635 528770 01635 528398
e-mail: general@the-vineyard.co.uk
web: www.the-vineyard.co.uk
Dir: *from M4 take A34 towards Newbury, exit at 3rd junct for Speen. Right at rdbt then right again at 2nd rdbt.*

A haven of style in the Berkshire countryside, this hotel prides itself on a superb art collection, which can be seen throughout the building. Bedrooms come in a variety of styles; many of them are newly built split-level suites that are exceptionally well equipped. Comfortable lounges lead into the stylish restaurant, which serves imaginative and precise cooking, complemented by an equally impressive selection of wines from California and around the world. The welcome is warm and sincere, the service professional yet relaxed.

ROOMS: 49 en suite (15 GF) in 10 bedrooms s £165-£635; d £245-£635 (incl. bkfst) **LB FACILITIES: Spa** STV Sauna Gym Jacuzzi Treatment rooms Xmas **CONF:** BC Thtr 60 Class 50 Board 48 Del from £320 **SERVICES:** Lift air con **PARKING:** 100 **NOTES:** Civ Wed 100 **CARDS:**

★★★★77% Donnington Valley

CLASSIC BRITISH

Old Oxford Rd, Donnington RG14 3AG
☎ 01635 551199 01635 551123
e-mail: general@donningtonvalley.co.uk
web: www.donningtonvalley.co.uk
Dir: *M4 junct 13, take A34 southbound, exit at Donnington Castle. Right over bridge then left hotel 1m on right*

This friendly hotel stands on its own 18-hole golf course and provides excellent accommodation. The striking modern building houses well-equipped meeting rooms and public areas that are furnished to a high standard. The WinePress restaurant offers

continued

imaginative food and a comprehensive choice of wines in comfortable surroundings; service is attentive and friendly.
ROOMS: 58 en suite (11 fmly) (18 GF) ⊗ in 30 bedrooms s £120-£160; d fr £160 **LB** **FACILITIES:** STV ⛳ 18 Putt green Leisure fac available at sister hotel, The Vineyard 2miles away ♫ Xmas **CONF:** BC Thtr 140 Class 60 Board 40 Del from £185 **SERVICES:** Lift **PARKING:** 160
NOTES: ✈ Civ Wed 90 **CARDS:**

★★★★75% Regency Park Hotel

Bowling Green Rd, Thatcham RG18 3RP
☎ 01635 871555 01635 871571
e-mail: info@regencyparkhotel.co.uk
web: www.regencyparkhotel.co.uk
Dir: *from Newbury take A4 signed Thatcham & Reading. 2nd rdbt exit signed Cold Ash. Hotel 1m on left*

Having completed a five-year redevelopment, this hotel now boasts roomy bedrooms, a state-of-the-art leisure club with beauty treatment salon and extensive business facilities. The smart, spacious, contemporary public areas are a relaxing environment to while away the day and the Watermark restaurant provides imaginative, award-winning cuisine.
ROOMS: 109 en suite (7 fmly) ⊗ in 52 bedrooms s £95-£359; d £115-£379 **LB** **FACILITIES: Spa** STV Sauna Solarium Gym Jacuzzi 4 Health & Beauty treatment rooms Xmas **CONF:** BC Thtr 200 Class 80 Board 70 Del from £165 **SERVICES:** Lift **PARKING:** 160
NOTES: ✈ ⊗ in restaurant Civ Wed 100
CARDS:

See advert on this page

★★★65% The Chequers Hotel

6-8 Oxford St RG14 1JB
☎ 01635 38000 01635 37170
e-mail: thechequers@corushotels.com
Dir: *off A34 at Newbury follow town centre signs. 2nd mini rdbt right, hotel on right*

corus hotels

In an enviable town centre location with parking, this hotel offers traditional public areas that include a lounge bar and pleasant restaurant. Bedrooms come in a variety sizes and outlook; most

continued on p422

N

NEWBURY, continued

are in the original buildings but some are in modern wings. All have good facilities and offer high levels of comfort.
ROOMS: 46 en suite 11 annexe en suite (3 fmly) (6 GF) ⊗ in 41 bedrooms s £85-£116; d £95-£116 **LB** **FACILITIES:** STV Xmas **CONF:** Thtr 100 Class 60 Board 40 Del from £130 **PARKING:** 60 **NOTES:** ⊗ in restaurant Civ Wed 70
CARDS:

Premier Lodge (Newbury)

Bath Rd, Midgham RG7 5UX
☎ 0870 9906556 📠 0870 9906557
web: www.premierlodge.com
Dir: *exit M4 junct 12 for A4 towards Newbury. Hotel 7m on the right*
High quality, modern, budget accommodation, ideal for families and business travellers. All rooms feature bath, power shower and satellite TV, and most have telephones / modem points. The adjacent bar and restaurant offers a wide and varied menu.
ROOMS: 49 en suite s £52; d £52 **CONF:** Thtr 10 Board 10

Travelodge (Newbury Chieveley)

Travelodge

Chieveley, Oxford Rd RG18 9XX
☎ 08700 850 950 📠 01635 247886
Dir: *on A34 off junct 13 of M4*
Travelodge offers good quality, good value, modern accommodation. Ideal for families, the spacious, en suite bedrooms include remote-control TV, tea and coffee-making facilities and luxury beds. Meals can be taken at the nearby family restaurant. For further details consult the Hotel Groups page.
ROOMS: 127 en suite s fr £25; d fr £25

Travelodge Newbury South

Travelodge

Tot Hill Services (A34), Newbury by-pass RG20 9ED
☎ 08700 850 950 📠 01635 278169
Dir: *Tot Hill Services on A34*
Travelodge offers good quality, good value, modern accommodation. Ideal for families, the spacious, en suite bedrooms include remote-control TV, tea and coffee-making facilities and luxury beds. Meals can be taken at the nearby family restaurant. For further details consult the Hotel Groups page.
ROOMS: 52 en suite s fr £25; d fr £25

NEWBY BRIDGE, Cumbria

Map 18 SD38

★★★★76% Lakeside

Lakeside LA12 8AT
☎ 015395 30001 📠 015395 31699
e-mail: sales@lakesidehotel.co.uk
web: www.lakesidehotel.co.uk
Dir: *M6 junct 36 join A590 to Barrow, take signs to Newby Bridge. Right over bridge, hotel 1m on right or follow Lakeside Steamers signs from junct 36*
This impressive hotel has an enviable location on the southern edge of Lake Windermere. Bedrooms are tastefully and individually styled, many with patios and wonderful lake views. Spacious lounges and a choice of restaurants are available. The addition of a luxury spa complex completes the picture.
ROOMS: 80 en suite (7 fmly) (8 GF) ⊗ in 34 bedrooms s £140-£320; d £190-£340 (incl. bkfst) **LB** **FACILITIES: Spa** STV Fishing Sauna Gym Jacuzzi Private jetty, Use of health club Xmas **CONF:** Thtr 100 Class 50 Board 40 Del from £140 **SERVICES:** Lift **PARKING:** 200 **NOTES:** ⊗ in restaurant Civ Wed 100
CARDS:

★★★★73% *Swan*

LA12 8NB
☎ 015395 31681 📠 015395 31917
e-mail: enquiries@swanhotel.com
web: www.swanhotel.com
Dir: *M6 junct 36 follow A590 signed Barrow for 16m. Hotel on right of old 5-arch bridge, at Newby Bridge*

Set among 14 acres of gardens and lakeside pathways with mooring for 80 boats, this hotel stands on the River Leven at the south end of Lake Windermere. Bedrooms are comfortable, spacious and thoughtfully equipped. Public areas include a choice of lounges and restaurants, a traditional bar and impressive spa facilities.
ROOMS: 55 en suite (4 fmly) (14 GF) ⊗ in 16 bedrooms **FACILITIES: Spa** STV supervised Fishing Sauna Solarium Gym Steam Room **CONF:** Thtr 120 Class 40 Board 40 **SERVICES:** Lift **PARKING:** 100 **NOTES:** ⊗ in restaurant Civ Wed 80
CARDS:

★★★67% Whitewater

The Lakeland Village LA12 8PX
☎ 015395 31133 📠 015395 31881
e-mail: enquiries@whitewater-hotel.co.uk
web: www.whitewater-hotel.co.uk
Dir: *M6 junct 36 follow signs for A590 Barrow, 1m through Newby Bridge. Right at sign for Lakeland Village, hotel on left*

This tasteful conversion of an old mill on the River Leven is close to the southern end of Lake Windermere. Bedrooms, many with lovely river views, are spacious and comfortable. Public areas include a luxurious, well-equipped spa, squash courts, and a choice of dining options. Mountain bikes are available. The Fisherman's bar hosts regular jazz nights that are popular with locals.
ROOMS: 35 en suite (10 fmly) (2 GF) ⊗ in 10 bedrooms s £92-£97; d £128-£195 (incl. bkfst) **LB** **FACILITIES: Spa** STV supervised Squash Sauna Solarium Gym Putt green Beauty treatment Table tennis Steam room Golf driving range Xmas **CONF:** Thtr 80 Class 32 Board 40 Del from £95 **SERVICES:** Lift **PARKING:** 50 **NOTES:** ⊗ in restaurant Civ Wed 110 **CARDS:**

NEWCASTLE-UNDER-LYME, Staffordshire Map 10 SJ84

★★62% Stop Inn Newcastle-under-Lyme
Liverpool Rd, Cross Heath ST5 9DX
☎ 01782 717000 📠 01782 713669
e-mail: enquiries@hotels-newcastle-under-lyme.com
Dir: *M6 junct 16 onto A500 to Stoke-on-Trent. Take A34 to Newcastle-under-Lyme, hotel on right after 1.5m*
Some of the well-equipped bedrooms at this purpose built hotel are in a separate block at the rear. There is a large lounge bar with a pool table and the restaurant offers a good range of food.
ROOMS: 43 rms (42 en suite) 24 annexe en suite (13 fmly) (23 GF) ⊗ in 31 bedrooms s £50-£64; d £50-£64 **LB FACILITIES:** STV Xmas **CONF:** Thtr 150 Class 80 Board 80 Del from £82 **PARKING:** 160 **NOTES:** ⊗ in restaurant **CARDS:**

Travel Inn
Talke Rd, Chesterton ST5 7AH
☎ 08701 977191 📠 01782 578901
Dir: *Exit M6 (J16) - follow A500 for approx. 3.5 miles. Take A34 towards Newcastle-under-Lyme. Travel Inn 0.5 mile on the right*
Travel Inn offers good-quality, value-for-money accommodation. Spacious, en suite rooms with bath and shower comfortably accommodate a family of up to two adults and two children (to age 15). The restaurant and bar offers a varied menu. For further details consult the Hotel Groups page.
ROOMS: 58 en suite s £45.95-£46.95; d £45.95-£46.95

NEWCASTLE UPON TYNE, Tyne & Wear Map 21 NZ26
See also Seaton Burn & Whickham

★★★★78% ⚘⚘
Newcastle Marriott Hotel Gosforth Park
High Gosforth Park, Gosforth NE3 5HN
☎ 0191 236 4111 📠 0191 236 8192
Dir: *onto A1056 to Killingworth and Wideopen. 3rd exit to Gosforth Park, hotel ahead*
Extensive conference, banqueting and leisure facilities are features of this hotel set in its own grounds and convenient for the by-pass, the racecourse and the airport. Bedrooms are well-equipped, with the executive rooms offering king-sized beds, CD players and the use of the executive lounge.
ROOMS: 178 en suite (30 fmly) ⊗ in 115 bedrooms s £99-£109; d £99-£119 **LB FACILITIES: Spa** STV supervised Squash Sauna Solarium Gym Jacuzzi Trim & jogging trail in hotel grounds ♫ **CONF:** BC Thtr 750 Class 280 Board 50 Del from £120 **SERVICES:** Lift **PARKING:** 340 **NOTES:** RS Xmas & New year Civ Wed 300 **CARDS:**

★★★★76% ⚘ Vermont
Castle Garth NE1 1RQ
☎ 0191 233 1010 📠 0191 233 1234
e-mail: info@vermont-hotel.co.uk
web: www.vermont-hotel.com
Dir: *city centre by high level bridge and Castle Keep*
Adjacent to the castle and close to the buzzing quayside area, this imposing hotel enjoys fine views of the Tyne Bridge. Thoughtfully equipped bedrooms offer a variety of styles, including grand suites. The elegant reception lounge and adjoining bar invite relaxation, while the Bridge restaurant is the focus for dining.
ROOMS: 101 en suite (12 fmly) ⊗ in 20 bedrooms s £120-£180; d £120-£180 **LB FACILITIES:** STV Solarium Gym ch fac Xmas **CONF:** BC Thtr 200 Class 60 Board 30 Del from £180 **SERVICES:** Lift **PARKING:** 100 **NOTES:** ⊗ in restaurant Civ Wed 120 **CARDS:**

★★★★71% Copthorne Hotel Newcastle
The Close, Quayside NE1 3RT
☎ 0191 222 0333 📠 0191 230 1111
e-mail: sales@newcastle.mill-cop.com
Dir: *follow signs to Newcastle city centre. Take B1600 Quayside exit, hotel on right*

Set on the banks of the River Tyne close to the city centre, this stylish purpose-built hotel provides modern amenities including a leisure centre, conference facilities and a choice of restaurants for dinner. Bedrooms overlook the river and there is a floor of 'Connoisseur' rooms with their exclusive lounge and business support services.
ROOMS: 156 en suite ⊗ in 85 bedrooms s £190-£220; d £190-£220 **FACILITIES: Spa** STV CCTV Sauna Solarium Gym Jacuzzi Steam room, Beauty treatment room, fitness studio Xmas **CONF:** Thtr 200 Class 85 Board 50 Del from £165 **SERVICES:** Lift air con **PARKING:** 180 **NOTES:** Civ Wed 150 **CARDS:**

NEWCASTLE UPON TYNE, continued

★★★★68% **Newcastle Marriott Hotel MetroCentre**
MetroCentre NE11 9XF
☎ 0191 493 2233 📠 0191 493 2030
e-mail: reservations.newcastle@marriotthotels.co.uk
(For full entry see Gateshead)

★★★★65% **Menzies Silverlink Park**
Silverlink, Coast Rd NE28 9HP
☎ 0191 202 9955 📠 0191 263 4172
e-mail: silverlinkpark@menzies-hotels.co.uk
Dir: *Through Tyne Tunnel follow signs for A19 Morpeth and then signs for Silverlink. At 1st rdbt 3rd exit and at 2nd rdbt take 1st exit.*
A purpose-built hotel located close to the Tyne Tunnel and major businesses in the area. Public areas are well proportioned and inviting, with pride of place going to the new Waves health and leisure club. Bedrooms meet the needs of the business guest, and it is worth asking for one of the larger Club rooms.
ROOMS: 122 en suite (4 fmly) ⊗ in 60 bedrooms s £110-£120; d £110-£130 **LB** **FACILITIES:** Sauna Solarium Gym Jacuzzi Xmas **CONF:** Thtr 400 Class 200 Board 40 Del from £130 **SERVICES:** Lift **PARKING:** 226 **NOTES:** ⊗ in restaurant Civ Wed
CARDS:

★★★77% ⊛ **Malmaison**
Quayside NE1 3DX
☎ 0191 245 5000 📠 0191 245 4545
e-mail: newcastle@malmaison.com
Dir: *follow signs for Newcastle City Centre, then for Quayside/Law Courts. Hotel 100yds past Law Courts*
Overlooking the river and the new Millennium Bridge, the hotel has a prime position in the up-and-coming redeveloped quayside district. Bedrooms have striking décor, CD players, mini-bars and a number of individual, welcoming touches. Food and drink are an integral part of the operation here, with a stylish brasserie-style restaurant and café bar.
ROOMS: 116 en suite (10 fmly) s fr £129; d fr £129 **LB** **FACILITIES:** STV Sauna Gym Xmas **CONF:** Thtr 50 Class 10 Board 24 Del £160 **SERVICES:** Lift air con **PARKING:** 50 **NOTES:**
CARDS:

★★★71% ⊛⊛ **Eslington Villa**
8 Station Rd, Low Fell NE9 6DR
☎ 0191 487 6017 & 420 0666 📠 0191 420 0667
e-mail: admin@eslingtonvilla.fsnet.co.uk
(For full entry see Gateshead)

⊛ AA Rosette Award for culinary excellence

★★★68% **The Caledonian Hotel, Newcastle**
64 Osborne Rd, Jesmond NE2 2AT
☎ 0191 281 7881 📠 0191 281 6241
e-mail: info@caledonian-hotel-newcastle.com
Dir: *from A1 follow signs to Newcastle City, cross Tyne Bridge to Tynemouth. Left at rdbt at Osborne Rd, hotel on right*
This hotel is located in the Jesmond area of the city, popular for its vibrant nightlife. Bedrooms are undergoing a modern revamp; all are comfortable and well-equipped for business guests. Public area include the trendy Billabong Bar and Bistro, which serves food all day, and also on the terrace where a cosmopolitan atmosphere prevails.

ROOMS: 89 en suite (6 fmly) (7 GF) ⊗ in 32 bedrooms s £79-£105; d £89-£122 **LB** **FACILITIES:** STV Xmas **CONF:** Thtr 100 Class 50 Board 50 Del from £105 **SERVICES:** Lift **PARKING:** 35 **NOTES:** Civ Wed 70 **CARDS:**

★★★68% **Jurys Inn Newcastle**
St James Gate, Scotswood Rd NE4 7JH
☎ 0191 201 4400 📠 0191 201 4411
e-mail: jurysinnnewcastle@jurysdoyle.com
Lying west of the city centre, this modern, stylish hotel is easily accessible from major road networks. Bedrooms provide good guest comfort and in-room facilities are suited for both leisure and business markets. Public areas include a number of meeting rooms and a popular bar and restaurant.
ROOMS: 274 en suite ⊗ in 172 bedrooms s £67-£75; d £67-£75 **CONF:** BC Thtr 90 Class 50 Board 45 Del from £105 **SERVICES:** Lift **NOTES:** **CARDS:**

★★★67% ***Novotel Newcastle***
Ponteland Rd, Kenton NE3 3HZ
☎ 0191 214 0303 📠 0191 214 0633
e-mail: H1118@accor-hotels.com
Dir: *off A1(M) airport junct onto A696, take Kingston Park exit*
This modern well proportioned hotel lies just off the bypass and is within easy reach of the airport and city centre. Bedrooms are spacious with a range of extras. The Garden Brasserie offers a flexible dining option and is open until late. There is also a small leisure centre for the more energetic.
ROOMS: 126 en suite (56 fmly) ⊗ in 82 bedrooms **FACILITIES:** STV Sauna Gym **CONF:** Thtr 200 Class 90 Board 40 **SERVICES:** Lift **PARKING:** 260 **NOTES:** Civ Wed 200
CARDS:

★★★66% **George Washington County Hotel**
Stone Cellar Rd, High Usworth NE37 1PH
☎ 0191 402 9988 📠 0191 415 1166
e-mail: reservations@georgewashington.co.uk
web: www.georgewashington.co.uk
(For full entry see Washington)

★★★66% **New Kent Hotel**
127 Osborne Rd NE2 2TB
☎ 0191 281 7711 📠 0191 281 3369
e-mail: newkenthotel@hotmail.com
Dir: *beside B1600, opposite St Georges Church*
This popular business hotel offers relaxed service and typical Geordie hospitality. Bedrooms, most of which are spacious, offer bright, modern décor. The smart bar is an ideal meeting point and

continued

a range of generous meals are served in the restaurant, which doubles as a wedding venue.
ROOMS: 32 en suite (4 fmly) s £50-£70; d fr £80 (incl. bkfst) **LB**
FACILITIES: STV Xmas **CONF:** Thtr 60 Class 30 Board 40 Del from £80
PARKING: 22 **NOTES:** ⊗ in restaurant Civ Wed 90
CARDS:

★★★63% Quality Hotel Newcastle upon Tyne

Newgate St NE1 5SX
☎ 0191 232 5025 🖷 0191 232 8428
e-mail: enquiries@hotels-newcastle-upon-tyne.com
Dir: *A1(M) take A184 Gateshead and Newcastle centre, follow A6082. Croos Redheugh Bridge take right lane, right at 3rd lights, then immediate right into Fenkle St. Car park behind Old Assembly Rooms*
Benefiting from a city centre location and a secure rooftop car park, this hotel is popular with business travellers. Accommodation is provided in compact yet thoughtfully equipped bedrooms. The rooftop restaurant and lounge have fine views over the city.
ROOMS: 93 en suite (4 fmly) ⊗ in 42 bedrooms s £96; d £110 **LB**
FACILITIES: STV Xmas **CONF:** Thtr 100 Class 40 Board 40 Del from £90 **SERVICES:** Lift **PARKING:** 120 **NOTES:** ⊗ in restaurant
CARDS:

★★63% Cairn

97/103 Osborne Rd, Jesmond NE2 2TJ
☎ 0191 281 1358 🖷 0191 281 9031
e-mail: cairnhotel@btconnect.com

A smart modern reception hall welcomes guests to this commercial hotel in the village suburb of Jesmond. Bedrooms are well equipped. There is a lively bar and a bright colourful restaurant.
ROOMS: 50 en suite (2 fmly) s £59-£65; d £80-£90 (incl. bkfst) **LB**
FACILITIES: STV Xmas **CONF:** Thtr 150 Class 110 Board 100 Del from £72.50 **PARKING:** 22 **CARDS:**

★★62% *Whites Hotel*

38-42 Osborne Rd, Jesmond NE2 2AL
☎ 0191 281 5126 🖷 0191 281 9953
Dir: *follow A1058 signs for coast, left into Osborne Rd at 1st rdbt*
Set in Jesmond, this commercial hotel has a contemporary bar that attracts a young trendy clientele. Its Indian restaurant provides hearty, good-value meals. Bedrooms vary in size, are well equipped, and most are furnished in a bright modern style.
ROOMS: 39 rms (38 en suite) (3 fmly) ⊗ in 3 bedrooms
FACILITIES: STV **CONF:** Thtr 75 Class 50 Board 40 **PARKING:** 40
CARDS:

> Popped the question?
> Hotels with Civ Wed in their entry are licensed for civil wedding ceremonies. Maximum numbers for the ceremony only are shown, e.g. Civ Wed 120

★66% Hadrian Lodge Hotel

Hadrian Rd, Wallsend NE28 6HH
☎ 0191 262 7733 & 08081 086892 🖷 0191 263 0714
e-mail: Claire.Stubbs@barbox.net
Dir: *from Newcastle city centre follow signs for Tyne Tunnel and Wallsend. Then follow A187 to Wallsend and Newcastle. Hotel opposite Hadrian Rd Metro station*
Mainly a business hotel, Hadrian Lodge lies on the north side of the River Tyne and takes its name from the nearby Roman remains. Situated only ten minutes away from Newcastle city centre, this hotel offers well-equipped and comfortable accommodation, many bedrooms being large. Home-cooked meals are served in the spacious bar and restaurant area.
ROOMS: 24 en suite (1 fmly) ⊗ in 8 bedrooms s £39.50-£46; d £55 (incl. bkfst) **FACILITIES:** Xmas **PARKING:** 60 **NOTES:** ✈ ⊗ in restaurant **CARDS:**

⌂ Innkeeper's Lodge Newcastle

Kenton Bank NE3 3TY
☎ 0191 214 0877 🖷 0191 214 1922
www.innkeeperslodge.com
Dir: *from A1(M), exit A696/B6918. At 1st rdbt, take B6918 (Kingston Park), 2nd rdbt turn right. Lodge located on left*
Smart rooms meet essential business requirements but also have home comforts, and depending on location may well have meeting rooms and pub dining. Dining options generally include all-day menus plus the added advantage of breakfast.
ROOMS: 30 en suite s £48-£55; d £48-£55 **CONF:** Thtr 40 Class 25 Board 20

⌂ Premier Lodge (Newcastle City Centre)

The Quayside NE1 3DW
☎ 0870 9906530 🖷 0870 9906531
web: www.premierlodge.com
Dir: *from north A1, A167, A186 Walker and Wallsend onto B1600 Quayside. From south A1, A184, A189 to city centre. First exit onto B1600 Quayside for hotel next to Tyne Bridge*
High quality, modern, budget accommodation, ideal for families and business travellers. All rooms feature bath, power shower and satellite TV, and most have telephones / modem points. The adjacent bar and restaurant offers a wide and varied menu.
ROOMS: 150 en suite s £56; d £56 **CONF:** Thtr 30 Class 30 Board 30 Del £99

⌂ Travel Inn (City Centre)

City Rd, Quayside NE1 2AN
☎ 0870 238 3318 🖷 0191 232 6557
Dir: *at corner of City Rd (A186) & Crawhall Rd*
Travel Inn offers good-quality, value-for-money accommodation. Spacious, en suite rooms with bath and shower comfortably accommodate a family of up to two adults and two children (to age 15). The restaurant and bar offers a varied menu. For further details consult the Hotel Groups page.
ROOMS: 81 en suite s £52.95-£54.95; d £52.95-£54.95
CONF: Thtr 15 Board 12

⌂ Travel Inn (Newcastle-Upon-Tyne Holystone)

Holystone Roundabout NE27 0DA
☎ 08701 977189 🖷 0191 259 9509
Dir: *3m N of Tyne Tunnel, adjacent to A19. Take A191 signed Gosforth/Whitley Bay*
Travel Inn offers good-quality, value-for-money accommodation. Spacious, en suite rooms with bath and shower comfortably accommodate a family of up to two adults and two children (to age 15). The restaurant and bar offers a varied menu. For further details consult the Hotel Groups page.
ROOMS: 40 en suite s £45.95-£46.95; d £45.95-£46.95

NEWCASTLE UPON TYNE, continued

⌂ Travelodge (Newcastle Central)

Forster St NE1 2NH
☎ 08700 850 950 🖷 0191 261 7105
Travelodge offers good quality, good value, modern accommodation. Ideal for families, the spacious, en suite bedrooms include remote-control TV, tea and coffee-making facilities and luxury beds. Meals can be taken at the nearby family restaurant. For further details consult the Hotel Groups page.
ROOMS: 120 en suite s fr £25; d fr £25

NEWCASTLE UPON TYNE AIRPORT, Tyne & Wear — Map 21 NZ17

⌂ Premier Lodge (Newcastle Airport)

Callerton Ln Ends, Woolsington NE13 8DF
☎ 0870 9906338 🖷 0870 9906339
web: www.premierlodge.com
Dir: *A1 onto A696 Jedburgh Rd to Newcastle airport. 2nd slip road signed Throckley and Woolsington. Right at top of road, over 2 rdbts and level crossing. Hotel on left*
High quality, modern, budget accommodation, ideal for families and business travellers. All rooms feature bath, power shower and satellite TV, and most have telephones / modem points. The adjacent bar and restaurant offers a wide and varied menu.
ROOMS: 42 en suite 10 annexe en suite s £50; d £50 **CONF:** Thtr 60 Class 20 Board 26 Del £77.50

⌂ Travel Inn

Newcastle Int. Airport, Ponteland Rd, Prestwick NE20 9DB
☎ 08701 977190 🖷 01661 824940
Dir: *immediately adjacent to main entrance to airport*
Travel Inn offers good-quality, value-for-money accommodation. Spacious, en suite rooms with bath and shower comfortably accommodate a family of up to two adults and two children (to age 15). The restaurant and bar offers a varied menu. For further details consult the Hotel Groups page.
ROOMS: 86 en suite s £49.95; d £49.95 **CONF:** Thtr 20

NEWENT, Gloucestershire — Map 10 SO72

Restaurant with Rooms

Three Choirs Vineyards

GL18 1LS
☎ 01531 890223 🖷 01531 890877
e-mail: info@threechoirs.com
web: www.threechoirs.com
Dir: *on B4215 North of Newent, follow brown tourist signs*
This thriving vineyard continues to go from strength to strength. The restaurant, which overlooks the 100-acre estate, enjoys a popular following. Spacious, high quality bedrooms are equipped with many extras and all have doors opening on to private patio areas, from which wonderful views can be enjoyed.
ROOMS: 8 annexe en suite (2 fmly) (8 GF) in all bedrooms s £65-£95; d £85-£105 (incl. bkfst) **LB** **FACILITIES:** Wine tasting, 75 acres of vineyards, guided & self guided tours **CONF:** Thtr 20 Class 15 Board 20 Del from £135 **PARKING:** 8 **NOTES:** in restaurant Closed 24-26 Dec Civ Wed 20 **CARDS:**

> Packed in a hurry?
> Ironing facilities should be available at all star levels, either in rooms or on request

NEWHAVEN, East Sussex — Map 06 TQ40

⌂ Travel Inn

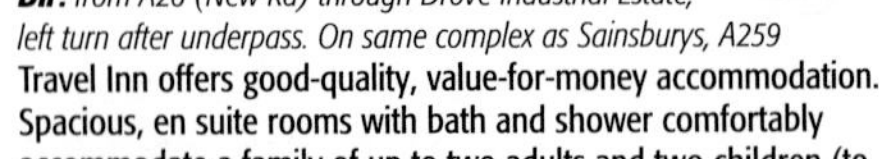

The Drove, Avis Rd BN9 0AG
☎ 08701 977192 🖷 01273 612359
Dir: *from A26 (New Rd) through Drove Industrial Estate, left turn after underpass. On same complex as Sainsburys, A259*
Travel Inn offers good-quality, value-for-money accommodation. Spacious, en suite rooms with bath and shower comfortably accommodate a family of up to two adults and two children (to age 15). The restaurant and bar offers a varied menu. For further details consult the Hotel Groups page.
ROOMS: 40 en suite s £45.95-£46.95; d £45.95-£46.95

NEWICK, East Sussex — Map 06 TQ42

Top 200 – Hotel

★★★ Newick Park Hotel & Country Estate

BN8 4SB
☎ 01825 723633 🖷 01825 723969
e-mail: bookings@newickpark.co.uk
web: www.newickpark.co.uk
Dir: *S off A272 in Newick between Haywards Heath and Uckfield. Pass church, left at junct and hotel 0.25m on right*
Delightful Grade II listed Georgian country house set amid 250 acres of Sussex parkland and landscaped gardens. The spacious, individually decorated bedrooms are tastefully furnished, thoughtfully equipped and have superb views of the grounds; many rooms have huge American king-size beds. The comfortable public rooms include a study, a sitting room, lounge bar and an elegant restaurant.
ROOMS: 13 en suite 3 annexe en suite (5 fmly) (1 GF) in all bedrooms s £110-£120; d £165-£285 (incl. bkfst) **LB**
FACILITIES: STV Fishing Badminton, Tank driving, Quad biking, Clay pigeon shooting Xmas **CONF:** Thtr 80 Class 80 Board 30 Del £185 **PARKING:** 52 **NOTES:** in restaurant Civ Wed 74
CARDS:

See advert under LEWES

NEWMARKET, Suffolk — Map 12 TL66

★★★★70% Bedford Lodge

Bury Rd CB8 7BX
☎ 01638 663175 🖷 01638 667391
e-mail: info@bedfordlodgehotel.co.uk
Dir: *from town centre take Bury St Edmunds road , hotel 0.5m on left*
This imposing 18th-century Georgian hunting lodge is set in three acres of secluded landscaped gardens. A new small lounge area is adjacent to the lounge bar, whilst interesting cuisine is offered in the elegant Orangery restaurant. The hotel also features superb leisure facilities and self-contained conference and banqueting

continued

suites. Contemporary bedrooms have a light, airy feel; each room tastefully furnished and well equipped.

ROOMS: 55 en suite (3 fmly) ⊗ in 33 bedrooms s £120-£250; d £155-£250 (incl. bkfst) **LB** **FACILITIES:** STV Sauna Solarium Gym Jacuzzi Steam room & beauty salon Xmas **CONF:** Thtr 200 Class 80 Board 60 Del from £135 **SERVICES:** Lift **PARKING:** 120 **NOTES:** ⊗ in restaurant Civ Wed 100 **CARDS:**

★★★72% Swynford Paddocks Hotel
CB8 0UE
☎ 01638 570234 01638 570283
e-mail: info@swynfordpaddocks.com
(For full entry see Six Mile Bottom)

★★★68% Heath Court
Moulton Rd CB8 8DY
☎ 01638 667171 01638 666533
e-mail: quality@heathcourthotel.com
Best Western
Dir: *leave A14 at Newmarket and Ely exit on A142. Follow town centre signs over mini rdbt. At clocktower left into Moulton Rd*
A modern red-brick hotel situated close to Newmarket Heath and perfectly placed for the town centre. Public rooms offer a choice of dining options; informal meals can be taken in the lounge bar or a modern carte is offered in the restaurant. Bedrooms are mostly spacious, each smartly presented and a number have air conditioning.
ROOMS: 41 en suite (2 fmly) ⊗ in 19 bedrooms s £91-£94; d £112-£167 (incl. bkfst) **LB** **FACILITIES:** STV **CONF:** Thtr 150 Class 40 Board 40 Del from £125 **SERVICES:** Lift **PARKING:** 60 **NOTES:** Civ Wed 50 **CARDS:**

NEW MILTON, Hampshire
Map 05 SZ29

Top 200 – Hotel

★★★★★ Chewton Glen
Christchurch Rd BH25 6QS
☎ 01425 275341 01425 272310
e-mail: reservations@chewtonglen.com
web: www.chewtonglen.com
Relais & Chateaux
Dir: *A35 from Lyndhurst for 10m, left at staggered junct. Follow tourist sign for hotel through Walkford, take 2nd left*
This outstanding hotel has been at the forefront of British hotel-keeping for many years. Once past the wrought iron entrance gates, guests are transported into a world of luxury. Log fires and afternoon tea are part of the tradition here, and lounges enjoy fine views over sweeping croquet lawns. Most bedrooms are very spacious, with private patios or balconies. Dining is a treat, and the extensive wine lists are essential reading for the enthusiast. The spa and leisure facilities are among the best in the country.

continued

ROOMS: 58 en suite (9 GF) s £199-£445; d £199-£780 **LB** **FACILITIES:** **Spa** STV 9 Snooker Sauna Gym Putt green Hairdresser, hydrotherapy spa, hot tub, dance studio Xmas **CONF:** BC Thtr 150 Class 70 Board 40 Del £330 **SERVICES:** air con **PARKING:** 100 **NOTES:** No children 5yrs ⊗ in restaurant Civ Wed 120 **CARDS:**

NEWPORT See Wight, Isle of

NEWPORT, Shropshire
Map 15 SJ71

★★66% *Royal Victoria*
St Mary's St TF10 7AB
☎ 01952 820331 01952 820209
e-mail: info@royal-victoria.co.uk
THE INDEPENDENTS
Dir: *off A41 at 2nd Newport by-pass rdbt towards town centre. Right at 1st traffic lights, hotel 150mtrs on left*
This town-centre hotel stands behind St Nicholas' Church. Dating from Georgian times, it derives its name from a visit made by Princess Victoria in 1832. The hotel provides well-equipped, modern accommodation. Facilities available to guests include an attractively appointed restaurant, a choice of bars and a large function/conference suite.
ROOMS: 24 rms (2 fmly) ⊗ in 6 bedrooms **CONF:** Thtr 150 Board 90 **PARKING:** 70 **NOTES:** ⊗ in restaurant **CARDS:**

NEWPORT PAGNELL MOTORWAY SERVICE AREA (M1), Buckinghamshire
Map 11 SP84

Welcome Lodge
Newport Pagnell MK16 8DS
☎ 01908 610878 01908 216539
e-mail: newport.hotel@welcomebreak.co.uk
web: www.welcomebreak.co.uk
Welcome Break
Dir: *M1 junct 14-15. In service area - follow signs to Barrier Lodge*
This modern building offers accommodation in smart, spacious and well-equipped bedrooms, suitable for families and business travellers, and all with en suite bathrooms. Refreshments may be taken at the nearby family restaurant. For further details consult the Hotel Groups page.
ROOMS: 90 en suite **CONF:** Thtr 40 Class 12 Board 16

N

NEWQUAY, Cornwall & Isles of Scilly Map 02 SW86

★★★★68% Headland
Fistral Beach TR7 1EW
☎ 01637 872211 01637 872212
e-mail: office@headlandhotel.co.uk
web: www.headlandhotel.co.uk
Dir: *off A30 onto A392 at Indian Queens, approaching Newquay follow signs for Fistral Beach, hotel adjacent*

This Victorian hotel enjoys a stunning location overlooking the sea on three sides - views can be enjoyed from most of the windows. Bedrooms are comfortable and spacious, with a number having now been refurbished. Grand public areas, with impressive floral displays, include various lounges and dining options.
ROOMS: 104 en suite (40 fmly) s £70-£123; d £110-£197 (incl. bkfst) **LB** **FACILITIES: Spa** STV 9 Snooker Sauna Gym Putt green Jacuzzi Children's outdoor play area, Harry Potter playroom ch fac Xmas **CONF:** Thtr 250 Class 120 Board 40 Del from £105 **SERVICES:** Lift **PARKING:** 400 **NOTES:** in restaurant Closed 23-27 Dec Civ Wed 250 **CARDS:**

★★★70% Hotel Bristol
Narrowcliff TR7 2PQ
☎ 01637 875181 01637 879347
e-mail: info@hotelbristol.co.uk
Dir: *off A30 onto A392, then onto A3058. Hotel 2.5m on left*

Best Western

This hotel is conveniently situated and many of the bedrooms enjoy fine sea views. Staff are friendly and provide a professional and attentive service. There is a range of comfortable lounges, ideal for relaxing prior to eating in the elegant dining room. There are also leisure and conference facilities.
ROOMS: 74 en suite (23 fmly) s £55-£80; d £90-£130 **LB** **FACILITIES:** STV Snooker Sauna Solarium Table tennis ch fac Xmas **CONF:** Thtr 200 Class 80 Board 20 Del from £80 **SERVICES:** Lift **PARKING:** 105 **NOTES:** in restaurant
CARDS:

See advert on opposite page

★★★70% Trebarwith
Trebarwith Crescent TR7 1BZ
☎ 01637 872288 01637 875431
e-mail: trebahotel@aol.com
web: www.trebarwith-hotel.co.uk
Dir: *from A3058 to Mount Wise Rd. 3rd right down Marcus Hill, across East St into Trebarwith Cres. Hotel at end*

With breathtaking views of the rugged coastline and a path leading to the beach, this friendly, family-run hotel is set in its own grounds close to the town centre. The public rooms include a lounge, ballroom, restaurant and cinema. The comfortable bedrooms include four-poster and family rooms, and many benefit from the sea views.
ROOMS: 41 en suite (8 fmly) (1 GF) s £35-£72; d £70-£144 (incl. bkfst & dinner) **LB** **FACILITIES: Spa** Fishing Snooker Sauna Solarium Jacuzzi Video theatre Games room ch fac **CONF:** Thtr 45 **PARKING:** 41 **NOTES:** in restaurant Closed Nov-5 Apr
CARDS:

See advert on opposite page

★★★69% Esplanade Hotel
Esplanade Rd, Pentire TR7 1PS
☎ 01637 873333 01637 851413
e-mail: info@newquay-hotels.co.uk
web: www.newquay-hotels.co.uk
Dir: *from A30 take A392 at Indian Queens towards Newquay, follow to rdbt and take left to Pentire, then right fork to beach*
Overlooking the rolling breakers at Fistral Beach, this family-owned hotel offers a friendly welcome. There is a choice of bedroom sizes; all have modern facilities and the most popular rooms benefit from stunning sea views. There are a number of bars, a continental-style coffee shop and the more formal Ocean View Restaurant.
ROOMS: 93 en suite (44 fmly) in 5 bedrooms s £28-£55; d £56-£110 (incl. bkfst & dinner) **LB** **FACILITIES: Spa** STV Sauna Solarium Jacuzzi Table tennis ch fac Xmas **CONF:** Thtr 300 Class 180 Board 150 **SERVICES:** Lift **PARKING:** 40 **NOTES:** in restaurant
CARDS:

★★★67% Barrowfield
Hilgrove Rd TR7 2QY
☎ 01637 878878 01637 879490
e-mail: booking@barrowfield.demon.co.uk
web: www.cranstar.co.uk
Dir: *A3058 to Newquay towards Quintrell Downs. Right at rdbt into town, left at Texaco garage*
Offering a pleasant range of facilities and spacious public rooms, this popular hotel is ideally situated and offers friendly and attentive service. Bedrooms, some with sea views and balconies, are well appointed and comfortable. Public areas include an and

continued

restaurant, spacious foyer lounge, attractive coffee shop and an intimate piano bar.

ROOMS: 81 en suite 2 annexe en suite (18 fmly) s £35-£42; d £70-£84 (incl. bkfst & dinner) **LB FACILITIES: Spa** STV Snooker Sauna Solarium Gym Jacuzzi Table tennis, Coffee shop, pool room, snooker room, trimnasium ♫ Xmas **CONF:** Thtr 250 Class 150 Board 90 **SERVICES:** Lift **PARKING:** 70 **NOTES:** in restaurant Civ Wed 60 **CARDS:**

★★★66% Hotel Riviera
Lusty Glaze Rd TR7 3AA
☎ 01637 874251 01637 850823
e-mail: hotelriviera@btconnect.com
Dir: *approaching Newquay from Porth right at The Barrowfields. Hotel on right*
This popular cliff-top hotel enjoys panoramic views across the gardens to the sea beyond. Bedrooms vary in size and style, and many have sea views. Comfortable lounges are provided for rest relaxation; the more energetic may wish to use the squash court

continued on p430

N

NEWQUAY, continued

or heated outdoor pool. There is also a range of conference and function facilities.
ROOMS: 48 en suite (6 fmly) s £91-£139; d £103-£152 (incl. bkfst) **FACILITIES:** supervised Squash Sauna Xmas **CONF:** Thtr 200 Class 150 Board 50 **SERVICES:** Lift **PARKING:** 80 **NOTES:** in restaurant Civ Wed **CARDS:**

See advert on page 429

★★★61% *Kilbirnie*

Narrowcliff TR7 2RS
☎ 01637 875155 01637 850769
e-mail: enquirykilbirnie@aol.com
web: www.connexions.co.uk/kilbirnie
Dir: *on A392*
With delightful views over the Barrowfields and the sea, this privately run hotel offers an impressive range of facilities. The reception rooms are spacious and comfortable, and during summer months feature a programme of entertainment. Bedrooms, many newly refurbished, vary in size and style and some enjoy fine sea views.
ROOMS: 66 en suite (3 fmly) (8 GF) **FACILITIES:** Snooker Sauna Solarium Gym Jacuzzi Table tennis **SERVICES:** Lift air con **PARKING:** 68 **NOTES:** in restaurant **CARDS:**

See advert on opposite page

★★72% Whipsiderry

Trevelgue Rd, Porth TR7 3LY
☎ 01637 874777 01637 874777
e-mail: info@whipsiderry.co.uk
Dir: *right onto Padstow road (B3276) out of Newquay, in 0.5m right at Trevelgue Rd*

Quietly located, overlooking Porth Beach, this friendly hotel offers bedrooms in a variety of sizes and styles, many with superb views. A daily-changing menu offers interesting and well-cooked dishes with the emphasis on fresh, local produce. An outdoor pool is available, and at dusk guests can enjoy badger-watching in the attractive grounds.
ROOMS: 20 rms (19 en suite) (5 fmly) (3 GF) in 8 bedrooms s £45-£54; d £90-£108 (incl. bkfst & dinner) **LB** **FACILITIES:** Sauna American pool ch fac Xmas **PARKING:** 30 **NOTES:** in restaurant Closed Nov-Etr (ex Xmas) **CARDS:**

★★71% Porth Veor Manor

Porth Way, Porth Bay TR7 3LW
☎ 01637 873274 01637 851690
e-mail: booking@porthveor.co.uk
Dir: *200yds from junct A3058/B3276, on B3276 towards Padstow*
A relaxed and friendly atmosphere is maintained at this pleasant, family-run hotel, which is set in a quiet area. The hotel overlooks Porth Beach to which it has direct access from its two-acre grounds. Bedrooms are decorated in different styles and all are pleasantly spacious. A daily-changing, set price menu is served in the dining room.
ROOMS: 22 en suite (7 fmly) (3 GF) in 6 bedrooms s £52.50-£61.50; d £100-£125 (incl. bkfst & dinner) **LB** **FACILITIES:** Sauna Gym Putt green Xmas **CONF:** BC Thtr 36 Class 24 Board 24 **PARKING:** 40 **NOTES:** in restaurant RS Nov-Feb **CARDS:**

★★69% Philema

1 Esplanade Rd, Pentire TR7 1PY
☎ 01637 872571 01637 873188
e-mail: info@philema.co.uk
Dir: *from A30 follow A392 then signs for Fistral Beach. Hotel on junction Esplanade Rd & Pentire Ave*
With excellent views over Fistral Beach, the Philema provides a relaxed and friendly family environment. Extensive leisure facilities are available, including the heated indoor pool, which overlooks the garden. Many rooms have wonderful views and all are comfortably furnished. The attractive dining room offers a range of home-cooked dishes.
ROOMS: 32 en suite (27 fmly) **FACILITIES: Spa** STV Snooker Sauna Solarium Jacuzzi pool table, games machine ch fac Xmas **PARKING:** 40 **NOTES:** in restaurant Closed 2 Jan-2 Feb **CARDS:**

★★64% *Trenance Hotel*

The Crescent TR7 1DF
☎ 01637 873159 01637 850008
e-mail: reception@trenancehotel.co.uk
Set close to the town's many attractions, yet quietly located, this popular and friendly hotel overlooks the harbour. Bedrooms, some with large bay windows and sea views, are well equipped and comfortable. Entertainment is provided most evenings and guests can relax in the lounge, bar or games room.
ROOMS: 57 en suite (4 fmly) **FACILITIES:** pool table **SERVICES:** Lift **PARKING:** 20 **NOTES:** in restaurant **CARDS:**

★★63% *Cedars*

Mount Wise TR7 2BA
☎ 01637 874225 01637 850421
e-mail: oakdon@btinternet.com
Dir: *enter Newquay via Narrowcliff into Berry Rd and Mount Wise. 500yds on right from Mount Wise car park*
Now under new ownership this hotel has views over the distant coast-line and the staff are friendly and efficient. Entertainment is provided in the spacious lounge/bar in season. Bedrooms vary in size, shape and style, and some are especially suitable for families.
ROOMS: 42 rms (31 en suite) (8 fmly) (6 GF) **FACILITIES:** Sauna Solarium Gym Jacuzzi **PARKING:** 42 **NOTES:** in restaurant Closed Dec-mid Mar **CARDS:**

★★63% Eliot

Leisureplex

Edgcumbe Av TR7 2NH
☎ 01637 878177 01637 852053
e-mail: eliot.newquay@alfatravel.co.uk
Dir: *A30 onto A392 towards Quintrell Downs. Right at rdbt onto A3058. 4m to Newquay, left at amusements onto Edgcumbe Av. Hotel on left*
Located in a quiet residential area just a short walk from the beaches and the varied attractions of the town, this long-established hotel offers comfortable accommodation. Entertainment is provided most nights throughout the season and guests can relax in the spacious public areas.
ROOMS: 76 en suite (10 fmly) s £28-£36; d £46-£62 (incl. bkfst) **LB** **FACILITIES:** Sauna Jacuzzi Pool table, Table tennis ch fac Xmas **SERVICES:** Lift **PARKING:** 20 **NOTES:** in restaurant Closed Dec-Jan RS Nov & Feb-Mar **CARDS:**

★★60% *Tremont*

Pentire Av TR7 1PB
☎ 01637 872984 01637 851984
Dir: *from A30 onto B3902 into Newquay and follow Pentire signs*
An impressive range of leisure facilities is on offer at this popular hotel, which has views of Fistral Beach and is just a short walk from the town. Entertainment is provided most nights in season and public areas are spacious. Bedrooms are available in a range of sizes and all are comfortably furnished.
ROOMS: 54 en suite (26 fmly) in all bedrooms **FACILITIES:** Sauna Solarium Gym Putt green Table tennis **SERVICES:** Lift **PARKING:** 60 **NOTES:** in restaurant **CARDS:**

NEWTON ABBOT, Devon

Map 03 SX87

See also Ilsington

★★★70% Passage House

Hackney Ln, Kingsteignton TQ12 3QH
☎ 01626 355515 Fax 01626 363336
e-mail: hotel@passagehousegroup.co.uk
Dir: *leave A380 for A381 and follow racecourse signs*

With memorable views of the Teign Estuary, this popular hotel provides spacious, well-equipped bedrooms. An impressive range of leisure and meeting facilities is offered and a new conservatory provides a pleasant extension to the bar and lounge. A choice of eating options is available, either in the main restaurant, or the adjacent Passage House Inn for less formal dining.

ROOMS: 38 en suite (32 fmly) (6 GF) ⊗ in 9 bedrooms s £69.50-£80; d £79.50-£90 (incl. bkfst) **LB FACILITIES: Spa** STV supervised Sauna Solarium Gym ch fac **CONF:** BC Thtr 120 Class 50 Board 40 Del £90 **SERVICES:** Lift **PARKING:** 300 **NOTES:** ⊗ in restaurant RS 24-27 Dec **CARDS:**

★★68% Queens

Queen St TQ12 2EZ
☎ 01626 363133 Fax 01626 354106
e-mail: queens@bestwestern.co.uk
Dir: *M5 onto A380, follow signs for railway station. Hotel opposite station*

Pleasantly and conveniently located close to the railway station and racecourse, this hotel continues to be a popular venue for both business people and tourists. Bedrooms are pleasantly appointed and well equipped. The lounge bar provides light meals

continued on p432

N

NEWTON ABBOT, continued

and specials, whilst a more extensive menu is available in the restaurant.
ROOMS: 20 en suite (3 fmly) in 8 bedrooms s £65-£70; d £84.50-£90 (incl. bkfst) **FACILITIES:** STV **CONF:** Thtr 130 Class 90 Board 40 **PARKING:** 7 **NOTES:** in restaurant
CARDS:

★★67% Hazelwood Hotel
33a Torquay Rd TQ12 2LW
☎ 01626 366130 01626 365021
Dir: *A380 to Newton Abbot. At main rdbt right past McDonalds. Left through 2 sets of lights. Hotel at top of hill on right*
Conveniently located a short stroll from the town centre, this smart hotel offers a friendly environment. An ideal base for either the business or leisure guest, many regularly return to the Hazelwood. Bedrooms are smartly decorated and well equipped with thoughtful extra touches and attractive fabrics. Freshly prepared home-cooked dishes are offered in the panelled dining room.
ROOMS: 8 en suite in all bedrooms s £40; d £56 (incl. bkfst)
CONF: Board 12 **PARKING:** 7 **NOTES:** in restaurant
CARDS:

NEWTON AYCLIFFE, Co Durham — Map 19 NZ22

Travel Inn Durham (Newton Aycliffe)
Great North Rd DL5 6JG
☎ 08701 977085 01325 324910
Dir: *on A167 east of Newton Aycliffe, 3 miles from A1(M)*
Travel Inn offers good-quality, value-for-money accommodation. Spacious, en suite rooms with bath and shower comfortably accommodate a family of up to two adults and two children (to age 15). The restaurant and bar offers a varied menu. For further details consult the Hotel Groups page.
ROOMS: 44 en suite s £45.95-£46.95; d £45.95-£46.95

NEWTON-LE-WILLOWS, Merseyside — Map 15 SJ59

★★66% *Kirkfield Hotel*
2/4 Church St WA12 9SU
☎ 01925 228196 01925 291540
e-mail: kirkfieldhotel@fsbdial.co.uk
Dir: *on A49 Newton-le-Willows opposite St Peter's Church*
A conveniently located hotel situated directly opposite the church, where car parking is also available. The hotel is family run and offers comfortable accommodation. A table d'hôte menu is available, or there are options for lighter dining in the bar area. Guests receive a friendly welcome and an informal atmosphere prevails.
ROOMS: 20 en suite (3 fmly) in 10 bedrooms **CONF:** Thtr 70 Class 60 Board 20 **PARKING:** 50 **CARDS:**

NORTHALLERTON, North Yorkshire — Map 19 SE39

★★★67% *Solberge Hall*
Newby Wiske DL7 9ER
☎ 01609 779191 01609 780472
e-mail: solberge@bestwestern.co.uk
Dir: *S of Northallerton on A167. Hotel on right passing through North Otterington*
This Grade II listed Georgian country house is set in 16 acres of parkland and commands panoramic views over open countryside. Spacious bedrooms, some with four poster beds, vary in style. Public areas include a comfortable bar and an elegant drawing room. The Garden Room restaurant offers a wide range of carefully prepared dishes.
ROOMS: 24 en suite (2 fmly) in 4 bedrooms **FACILITIES:** STV **CONF:** Thtr 100 Class 50 Board 40 **PARKING:** 100 **NOTES:** in restaurant Civ Wed 100 **CARDS:**

★★65% The Golden Lion
High St DL7 8PP
THE INDEPENDENTS
☎ 01609 777411 01609 773250
Dir: *A684 for 5m onto A167. Through built-up area, 3rd exit at next rdbt to town centre. 3rd rdbt left into High St*
This popular hotel has a convenient location in the heart of the town centre with private parking. Bedrooms and bathrooms are spacious and offer a good range of amenities. Public areas include a choice of dining options and a lively bar. The newly re-furbished drawing room and dining room are non-smoking.
ROOMS: 25 en suite (2 fmly) in 18 bedrooms s £55-£60; d £70-£85 (incl. bkfst) **FACILITIES:** ch fac **CONF:** Thtr 300 Class 150 Board 80 **PARKING:** 100 **NOTES:** in restaurant Civ Wed 200
CARDS:

Restaurant with Rooms

The Three Tuns
9 South End, Osmotherley DL6 3BN
☎ 01609 883301 01609 883988
Dir: *turn off A19 signed Northallerton/Osmotherley. Turn at junction signed Osmotherley at Kings Head Hotel. Follow road into village, inn straight ahead*
Situated in the popular village of Osmotherley, this restaurant with rooms is full of character. Bedrooms, set above the bar and in an adjoining building, vary in size but are stylishly furnished in pine and well equipped. The restaurant and cosy bar feature crafted hardwood furniture.
ROOMS: 7 en suite (1 fmly) (1 GF) in all bedrooms **PARKING:** 6
NOTES: in restaurant **CARDS:**

NORTHAMPTON, Northamptonshire — Map 11 SP76
See also Flore

★★★★70% Northampton Marriott Hotel
Eagle Dr NN4 7HW
Marriott HOTELS · RESORTS · SUITES
☎ 01604 768700 01604 769011
e-mail: northampton@marriotthotels.co.uk
Dir: *M1 junct 15, follow signs to Delapre Golf Course, hotel on right*
On the outskirts of town, this modern hotel has a great deal to offer to a wide cross section of guests. A self-contained management centre makes this a popular conference venue, and its spacious and well-designed bedrooms cater for business travellers especially well. The hotel's proximity to a number of attractions makes this a good base to explore the area.
ROOMS: 120 en suite (12 fmly) in 82 bedrooms s £55-£120; d £70-£140 (incl. bkfst) **LB** **FACILITIES:** **Spa** STV supervised Sauna Solarium Gym Jacuzzi Steam room, beauty treatment room Xmas
CONF: BC Thtr 220 Class 100 Board 36 Del from £145 **SERVICES:** air con **PARKING:** 187 **NOTES:** in restaurant Civ Wed 100
CARDS:

★★★72% Lime Trees

8 Langham Place, Barrack Rd NN2 6AA
☎ 01604 632188 📠 01604 233012
e-mail: info@limetreeshotel.co.uk
web: www.limetreeshotel.co.uk
Dir: *from city centre 0.5m N on A508 towards Leicester near racecourse park and cathedral*

A particularly well-presented hotel, popular with business travellers during the week and leisure guests at the weekend. Service is both efficient and friendly. Bedrooms are comfortable and in addition to all the usual facilities, many offer air conditioning. Notable features include an internal courtyard and a row of charming mews houses which have been converted into rooms.

ROOMS: 27 en suite (3 fmly) (5 GF) ⊗ in 8 bedrooms s £39-£79; d £69-£89 (incl. bkfst) **LB** **CONF:** Thtr 50 Class 30 Board 30 Del from £81 **PARKING:** 24 **NOTES:** ✈ ⊗ in restaurant Closed 25-26 Dec RS 27 Dec-New Year **CARDS:**

★★★69% Courtyard by Marriott Northampton

Bedford Rd NN4 7YF
☎ 0870 400 7214 📠 0870 400 7314
e-mail: reservations.northamptoncourtyard@whitbread.com
Dir: *M1 junct 15 onto A508 towards Northampton. Follow A45 towards Wellingborough for 2m then A428 towards Bedford, hotel on left*

With its convenient location on the eastern edge of town and easy access to transport links, this modern hotel is particularly popular with business travellers. Accommodation is spacious, practical, and includes a good range of extras. Open-plan public areas help to create an informal atmosphere and the staff are genuinely friendly.

ROOMS: 104 en suite (50 fmly) (27 GF) ⊗ in 91 bedrooms s £50-£89; d £50-£89 **LB** **FACILITIES:** STV Gym Xmas **CONF:** Thtr 60 Class 40 Board 40 Del from £120 **SERVICES:** Lift air con **PARKING:** 156 **NOTES:** ✈ ⊗ in restaurant **CARDS:**

★★★64% Quality Hotel Northampton

Ashley Way, Weston Favell NN3 3EA
☎ 01604 739955 📠 01604 415023
e-mail: enquiries@hotels-northampton.com
Dir: *leave A45 at junct with A43 towards Weston Favell. After 0.5m left to town centre. Left at top of slip road, hotel signed off A4500*

On the edge of town, this hotel offers well-equipped accommodation in an older-style building and a more modern block. Public rooms are attractive and include an air-conditioned lounge area, an attractively furnished flag-stoned conservatory restaurant and a number of versatile meeting rooms.

ROOMS: 33 en suite 38 annexe en suite (5 fmly) (19 GF) ⊗ in 45 bedrooms s £26-£155; d £31-£175 **LB** **FACILITIES:** STV Can purchase passes to use at nearby leisure centre Xmas **CONF:** Thtr 180 Class 160 Board 60 Del from £75 **SERVICES:** Lift **PARKING:** 120 **NOTES:** ⊗ in restaurant Civ Wed 140 **CARDS:**

⌂ Hotel Ibis Northampton

Sol Central, Marefair NN1 1SR
☎ 01604 608900 📠 01604 608910
e-mail: H3657@accor-hotels.com
Dir: *M1 junct 15/15a & head for city centre railway station*

Modern, budget hotel offering comfortable accommodation in bright and practical bedrooms. Breakfast is self-service and dinner is available in the restaurant. For further details, consult the Hotel Groups page.

ROOMS: 151 en suite s £37.95-£46.95; d £37.95-£46.95

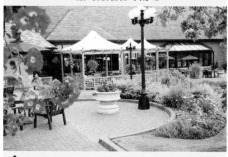

⌂ Innkeeper's Lodge Northampton East

Talavera Way, Round Spinney NN3 8RN
☎ 01604 494241 📠 01604 673701
www.innkeeperslodge.com
Dir: *M1 junct 15a, N on A43. Right at rdbt, pass 2 further rdbts. At 3rd rdbt, A45 N until exit for A43, continue to Round Spinney rdbt and Talavera Way*

Smart rooms meet essential business requirements but also have home comforts, and depending on location may well have meeting rooms and pub dining. Dining options generally include all-day menus plus the added advantage of breakfast.

ROOMS: 31 en suite s £42-£55; d £42-£55 **CONF:** Thtr 36 Class 24 Board 28

⌂ Innkeeper's Lodge Northampton South

London Rd, Wootton NN4 0TG
☎ 01604 769676 📠 01604 677981
www.innkeeperslodge.com
Dir: *M1 junct 15 take A508, towards Northampton. Pass under flyover, exit left immediately & turn right at rdbt into London Rd. Lodge on right.*

Smart rooms meet essential business requirements but also have home comforts, and depending on location may well have meeting rooms and pub dining. Dining options generally include all-day menus plus the added advantage of breakfast.

ROOMS: 51 en suite s £42-£55; d £42-£55 **CONF:** Thtr 100 Board 40

♫ Entertainment

NORTHAMPTON, continued

⇧ Premier Lodge (Northampton East)

Crow Ln, Great Billing NN3 9DA
☎ 0870 9906510 📠 0870 9906511
web: www.premierlodge.com
Dir: *5m from M1 junct 15. Take A508 to A45 then follow signs for Billing Aquadrome*
High quality, modern, budget accommodation, ideal for families and business travellers. All rooms feature bath, power shower and satellite TV, and most have telephones / modem points. The adjacent bar and restaurant offers a wide and varied menu.
ROOMS: 60 en suite s £50; d £50 **CONF:** Thtr 10 Board 10

⇧ Premier Lodge (Northampton South)

Newport Pagnell Rd West, Wootton NN4 7JJ
☎ 0870 9906426 📠 0870 9906427
web: www.premierlodge.com
Dir: *M1 junct 15 towards Northampton at A508/A45 junct. 5th exit off rdbt and lodge on right*
High quality, modern, budget accommodation, ideal for families and business travellers. All rooms feature bath, power shower and satellite TV, and most have telephones / modem points. The adjacent bar and restaurant offers a wide and varied menu.
ROOMS: 39 en suite s £50; d £50 **CONF:** Thtr 75 Class 48 Board 30 Del from £95

⇧ Travel Inn Northampdon (West)

Harpole Turn, Weedon Rd, Harpole NN7 4DD
☎ 08701 977195 📠 01604 831807
Dir: *From M1 (J16), take A45 to Northampton. After 1 mile turn left into Harpole Turn. Travel Inn is on the left*

Travel Inn offers good-quality, value-for-money accommodation. Spacious, en suite rooms with bath and shower comfortably accommodate a family of up to two adults and two children (to age 15). The restaurant and bar offers a varied menu. For further details consult the Hotel Groups page.
ROOMS: 51 en suite s £45.95-£46.95; d £45.95-£46.95 **CONF:** Thtr 40 Board 30

⇧ Travel Inn Northampton (East)

The Lakes, Bedford Rd NN4 7YD
☎ 08701 977196 📠 01604 621935
Dir: *M1 junct 15 follow A508 (A45) to Northampton.*

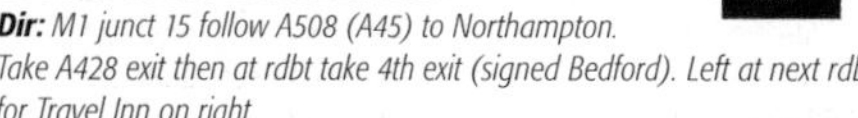

Take A428 exit then at rdbt take 4th exit (signed Bedford). Left at next rdbt for Travel Inn on right
Travel Inn offers good-quality, value-for-money accommodation. Spacious, en suite rooms with bath and shower comfortably accommodate a family of up to two adults and two children (to age 15). The restaurant and bar offers a varied menu. For further details consult the Hotel Groups page.
ROOMS: 44 en suite s £45.95-£46.95; d £45.95-£46.95

⇧ Travelodge

Upton Way NN5 6EG
☎ 08700 850 950 📠 01604 758395
Dir: *A45, towards M1 junct 16*
Travelodge offers good quality, good value, modern accommodation. Ideal for families, the spacious, en suite bedrooms include remote-control TV, tea and coffee-making facilities and luxury beds. Meals can be taken at the nearby family restaurant. For further details consult the Hotel Groups page.
ROOMS: 62 en suite s fr £25; d fr £25

○ Campanile Northampton

Off Junction 15 / M1, Grange Park
☎ 020 8572 3663
ROOMS: 80 en suite **NOTES:** Due to open Spring 2005

NORTH FERRIBY, East Riding of Yorkshire — Map 17 SE92

★★★65% Elizabeth Hotel Hull

Ferriby High Rd HU14 3LG
☎ 01482 645212 📠 01482 643332
e-mail: elizabeth.hull@elizabethhotels.co.uk
web: www.elizabethhotels.co.uk
Dir: *M62 onto A63 to Hull. Exit for Humber Bridge. At rdbt follow Leeds signs until signs for North Ferriby. Hotel 0.5m on left*
A modern, purpose built hotel that enjoys spectacular views of the Humber Bridge. Bedrooms are comfortable and well equipped. Public areas are spacious and both the restaurant and lounge bar look out over the river. There is ample car parking and also a children's play area at the rear. 24-hour room service is available.
ROOMS: 95 en suite (6 fmly) (17 GF) ⊗ in 77 bedrooms s £55-£75; d £65-£95 (incl. bkfst) **LB** **FACILITIES:** STV Nearly full size pool table Xmas **CONF:** Thtr 200 Class 85 Board 86 Del from £90 **PARKING:** 140 **NOTES:** Civ Wed 70 **CARDS:**

NORTH KILWORTH, Leicestershire — Map 11 SP68

★★★★73% ❀❀ Kilworth House

Lutterworth Rd LE17 6JE
☎ 01858 880058 📠 01858 880349
e-mail: info@kilworthhouse.co.uk
web: www.kilworthhouse.co.uk
Dir: *A4304 towards Market Harborough, after Walcote Village, hotel 1.5m on right*

A newly restored Victorian country house located in 38 acres of private grounds. The gracious public areas feature many period pieces and original artworks. Bedrooms are very comfortable and well equipped, and the large Orangery is now used for informal dining while an opulent restaurant has a more formal air.
ROOMS: 41 en suite (2 fmly) (13 GF) s fr £135; d £155-£195 **LB** **FACILITIES:** STV Fishing Gym Beauty therapy rooms Xmas **CONF:** Thtr 80 Class 30 Board 30 Del from £170 **SERVICES:** Lift **PARKING:** 98 **NOTES:** ⊗ in restaurant Civ Wed **CARDS:**

NORTH MUSKHAM, Nottinghamshire — Map 17 SK75

⇧ Travelodge (Newark)

NG23 6HT
☎ 08700 850 950 📠 01636 703635
Dir: *3m N, on A1 southbound*
Travelodge offers good quality, good value, modern accommodation. Ideal for families, the spacious, en suite

continued

bedrooms include remote-control TV, tea and coffee-making facilities and luxury beds. Meals can be taken at the nearby family restaurant. For further details consult the Hotel Groups page.
ROOMS: 30 en suite s fr £25; d fr £25

NORTHOLT, Greater London
See LONDON SECTION plan 1 B4

⌂ Innkeeper's Lodge

Mandeville Rd UB5 4LU
☎ 020 8422 2050
www.innkeeperslodge.com
Dir: *A40 at the Target roundabout*
Smart rooms meet essential business requirements but also have home comforts, and depending on location may well have meeting rooms and pub dining. Dining options generally include all-day menus plus the added advantage of breakfast.
ROOMS: 21 en suite s £57.50-£69; d £57.50-£69

NORTH WALSHAM, Norfolk — Map 13 TG23

Top 200 – Hotel

★★ Beechwood

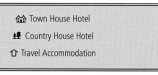

Cromer Rd NR28 0HD
☎ 01692 403231 🖷 01692 407284
e-mail: enquiries@beechwood-hotel.co.uk
web: www.beechwood-hotel.co.uk
Dir: *B1150 from Norwich. At North Walsham left at 1st traffic lights, then right at next*
Expect a warm welcome at this elegant 18th-century house, situated just a short walk from the town centre. The individually styled bedrooms are tastefully furnished with well-chosen antique pieces, attractive co-ordinated soft fabrics and many thoughtful touches. The spacious public areas include a lounge bar with plush furnishings, a further lounge and a smartly appointed restaurant.
ROOMS: 15 en suite (4 GF) ⊘ in 12 bedrooms **CONF:** Thtr 20 Class 20 Board 20 Del from £115 **PARKING:** 20 **NOTES:** No children 10yrs ⊘ in restaurant **CARDS:**

NORTH WALTHAM, Hampshire — Map 05 SU54

⌂ Premier Lodge (Basingstoke)

RG25 2BB
☎ 0870 9906476 🖷 0870 9906477
web: www.premierlodge.com
Dir: *on A30 just off M3 junct 7. Follow signs North Waltham, Popham and Kings Worthy. Lodge 2m on right, before A303*
High quality, modern, budget accommodation, ideal for families and business travellers. All rooms feature bath, power shower and satellite TV, and most have telephones / modem points. The adjacent bar and restaurant offers a wide and varied menu.
ROOMS: 28 en suite s £52; d £52
CONF: Thtr 80 Class 30 Board 35 Del from £85

NORTHWICH, Cheshire — Map 15 SJ67

★★★65% The Floatel, Northwich

London Rd CW9 5HD
☎ 01606 44443 🖷 01606 42596
e-mail: enquiries@hotels-northwich.com
Dir: *M6 junct 19, follow A556 for 4m, take right turn & follow signs for Town Centre*
A first in the UK - this floating hotel has been built over the river and a very successful concept has been created. The bedrooms are modern and well equipped, and there is a carvery style restaurant which overlooks the river.
ROOMS: 60 en suite (2 fmly) ⊘ in 30 bedrooms s £35-£75; d £45-£85 **LB** **FACILITIES:** STV Xmas **CONF:** Thtr 80 Class 40 Board 30 Del from £60 **SERVICES:** Lift **PARKING:** 110 **NOTES:** ⊘ in restaurant Civ Wed 80 **CARDS:**

★★62% *Hartford Hall*

School Ln, Hartford CW8 1PW
☎ 01606 780320 🖷 01606 782285
Dir: *in Hartford, between Northwich and Chester signed off A556*
Set in four acres of gardens and grounds on the edge of the village of Hartford, this 17th-century manor house offers well equipped accommodation. Public areas are characteristic of the period and include the heavily beamed Nunn's Room, where civil weddings and other functions are held.
ROOMS: 20 en suite (4 fmly) (8 GF) ⊘ in 13 bedrooms
FACILITIES: STV Games room **CONF:** Thtr 50 Class 50 Board 50
PARKING: 50 **NOTES:** ⊘ in restaurant RS 25 Dec Civ Wed 70
CARDS:

⌂ Premier Lodge (Northwich)

520 Chester Rd, Sandiway CW8 2DN
☎ 0870 9906494 🖷 0870 9906495
web: www.premierlodge.com
Dir: *1m from M6 junct 19 on A556 towards Chester*
High quality, modern, budget accommodation, ideal for families and business travellers. All rooms feature bath, power shower and satellite TV, and most have telephones / modem points. The adjacent bar and restaurant offers a wide and varied menu.
ROOMS: 52 en suite s £50; d £50 **CONF:** Thtr 65

⌂ Premier Lodge (Northwich South)

London Rd, Leftwich CW9 8EG
☎ 0870 9906362 🖷 0870 9906363
web: www.premierlodge.com
Dir: *off M6 junct 19, follow A556 to Chester. Turn right at the sign for Northwich and Davenham*
High quality, modern, budget accommodation, ideal for families and business travellers. All rooms feature bath, power shower and satellite TV, and most have telephones / modem points. The adjacent bar and restaurant offers a wide and varied menu.
ROOMS: 32 en suite s £50; d £50 **CONF:** Thtr 15 Class 15 Board 15

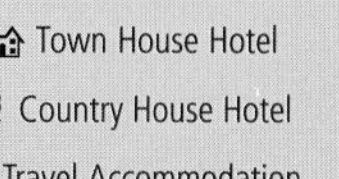

Town House Hotel
Country House Hotel
Travel Accommodation

N

NORTHWOLD, Norfolk
Map 13 TL79

★★66% Comfort Inn Thetford
Thetford Rd IP26 5LQ
☎ 01366 728888 🖷 01366 727121
e-mail: enquiries@hotels-thetford.com
Dir: W of Mundford on A134

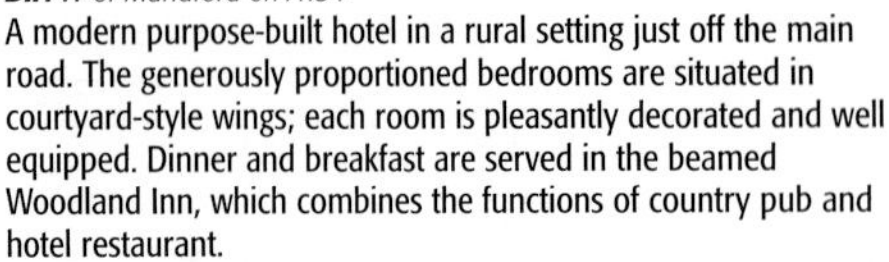

A modern purpose-built hotel in a rural setting just off the main road. The generously proportioned bedrooms are situated in courtyard-style wings; each room is pleasantly decorated and well equipped. Dinner and breakfast are served in the beamed Woodland Inn, which combines the functions of country pub and hotel restaurant.
ROOMS: 34 en suite (12 fmly) (18 GF) ⊘ in 17 bedrooms s £45-£85; d £55-£95 (incl. bkfst) **LB** **FACILITIES:** STV Xmas **CONF:** Thtr 150 Class 55 Board 60 Del from £85 **PARKING:** 250 **NOTES:** ⊘ in restaurant Civ Wed 95 **CARDS:**

NORTON, Shropshire
Map 10 SJ70

★★76% Hundred House Hotel
Bridgnorth Rd TF11 9EE
☎ 01952 730353 🖷 01952 730355
e-mail: reservations@hundredhouse.co.uk
web: www.hundredhouse.co.uk
Dir: midway between Telford and Bridgnorth on A442. In centre of Norton
Primarily Georgian, but with parts dating back to the 14th century, this friendly, family owned and run hotel offers individually styled, well-equipped bedrooms which have period furniture and attractive soft furnishings. Public areas include cosy bars and intimate dining areas where memorable meals are served. A conference centre is scheduled to open in the old barn.
ROOMS: 10 en suite (4 fmly) s £69-£85; d £99-£135 (incl. bkfst) **LB** **FACILITIES:** Xmas **CONF:** Thtr 80 Class 30 Board 32 Del from £115 **PARKING:** 45 **NOTES:** Closed Xmas night & Boxing Day Night RS Sunday evenings **CARDS:**

NORTON CANES MOTORWAY SERVICE AREA (M6 TOLL), Staffordshire
Map 10 SK00

Travel Inn Birmingham North (M6 Toll)
Norton Canes MSA, M6 Toll Rd, North Canes
WS11 9UX
☎ 08701 977070 🖷 08701 977 700

Dir: at motorway service area between J6/7 of M6 toll road. Access from both sides via barrier and from A5
Travel Inn offers good-quality, value-for-money accommodation. Spacious, en suite rooms with bath and shower comfortably accommodate a family of up to two adults and two children (to age 15). The restaurant and bar offers a varied menu. For further details consult the Hotel Groups page.
ROOMS: 40 en suite s £45.95-£46.95; d £45.95-£46.95

NORWICH, Norfolk
Map 13 TG20

★★★★75% Marriott Sprowston Manor Hotel & Country Club
Sprowston Park, Wroxham Rd, Sprowston NR7 8RP
☎ 01603 410871 🖷 01603 423911
e-mail: sprowston.manor@marriotthotels.co.uk
Dir: From A11/A47, 2m NE on A115 (Wroxham Rd). Follow signs to Sprowston Park
Surrounded by open parkland, this imposing property is set in attractively landscaped grounds and is just a short drive from the city centre. Bedrooms are spacious and feature a variety of decorative styles. The hotel also has extensive conference, banqueting and leisure facilities. Other public rooms include a variety of seating areas and the elegant Manor Restaurant.
ROOMS: 94 en suite (3 fmly) (5 GF) ⊘ in 61 bedrooms s fr £109; d £170 **LB** **FACILITIES: Spa** STV supervised 18 Sauna Solarium Gym Putt green Xmas **CONF:** Thtr 120 Class 50 Board 50 Del £145 **SERVICES:** Lift **PARKING:** 150 **NOTES:** ⊘ in restaurant Civ Wed 110 **CARDS:**

★★★★71% De Vere Dunston Hall
DE VERE HOTELS
Ipswich Rd NR14 8PQ
☎ 01508 470444 🖷 01508 471499
e-mail: dhreception@devere-hotels.com
Dir: from A47, take A140 Ipswich road, hotel off road on left after 0.25m
Imposing Grade II listed building set amidst 170 acres of landscaped grounds just a short drive from the city centre. The spacious bedrooms are smartly decorated, tastefully furnished and equipped to a high standard. The attractively appointed public rooms offer a wide choice of areas in which to relax and the hotel also boasts a superb range of leisure facilities including an 18-hole PGA golf course, floodlit tennis courts and a football pitch.
ROOMS: 130 en suite (15 fmly) (15 GF) ⊘ in 112 bedrooms s £90-£145; d £105-£220 (incl. bkfst) **LB** **FACILITIES: Spa** STV 18 Snooker Sauna Solarium Gym Putt green Jacuzzi Floodlit Driving Range Xmas **CONF:** Thtr 300 Class 140 Board 80 Del from £138 **SERVICES:** Lift **PARKING:** 500 **NOTES:** ⊘ in restaurant Civ Wed 90 **CARDS:**

★★★75% Annesley House

6 Newmarket Rd NR2 2LA
☎ 01603 624553 🖷 01603 621577
e-mail: annesleyhouse@bestwestern.co.uk
Dir: on A11, 0.5m before city centre

Delightful Georgian property situated amid three acres of landscaped gardens close to the city centre. Bedrooms are split between three separate houses, two of which are linked by a glass walkway; they are attractively decorated, tastefully furnished and equipped with many useful extras. Public rooms include a comfortable lounge/bar and a smart conservatory restaurant, which overlooks the gardens.
ROOMS: 18 en suite 8 annexe en suite (3 fmly) (7 GF) ⊘ in 22 bedrooms s £81.50-£96.50; d £96.50-£111.50 (incl. bkfst) **LB** **FACILITIES:** STV **CONF:** Thtr 16 Board 16 Del from £127.50 **PARKING:** 25 **NOTES:** ⊘ in restaurant Closed 24-27 & 30-31 Dec **CARDS:**

★★★75% Barnham Broom Hotel, Golf & Country Club

NR9 4DD
☎ 01603 759393 759522 🖷 01603 758224
e-mail: enquiry@barnhambroomhotel.co.uk
(For full entry see Barnham Broom)

★★★70% ❀
Beeches Hotel & Victorian Gardens

2-6 Earlham Rd NR2 3DB
☎ 01603 621167 📠 01603 620150
e-mail: reception@beeches.co.uk web: www.beeches.co.uk
Dir: *W of city centre on B1108, next to St Johns Cathedral, off inner ring road*

Ideally situated just a short walk from the city centre, and set amidst landscaped grounds that include a lovely sunken Victorian garden. The bedrooms are in three separate buildings; each room is tastefully decorated and equipped with many thoughtful touches. Public rooms include a smart lounge bar, a bistro-style restaurant and a residents' lounge.
ROOMS: 38 en suite ⊗ in 36 bedrooms s £69-£89; d £89-£110 (incl. bkfst) **FACILITIES:** Putt green **CONF:** BC Thtr 30 Class 20 Board 12 **PARKING:** 50 **NOTES:** No dogs No children 12yrs ⊗ in restaurant **CARDS:**

★★★70% ❀ **The Georgian House**
32-34 Unthank Rd NR2 2RB
☎ 01603 615655 📠 01603 765689
e-mail: reception@georgian-hotel.co.uk
web: www.georgian-hotel.co.uk
Dir: *from city centre follow Roman Catholic Cathedral signs, hotel off inner ring road*
This pair of Victorian houses has been carefully converted to create a comfortable hotel, which is situated just a short walk from the city centre. Public areas include a cosy bar, a TV lounge and an elegant restaurant offering a daily changing carte menu. The smartly refurbished bedrooms are well maintained and thoughtfully equipped.
ROOMS: 28 en suite (2 fmly) (10 GF) ⊗ in 20 bedrooms s £64-£81.50; d £90-£120 (incl. bkfst) **LB FACILITIES:** STV **CONF:** BC Thtr 25 Class 20 Board 20 Del from £95 **PARKING:** 40 **NOTES:** ⊗ in restaurant Closed 24 Dec-2 Jan **CARDS:**

See advert on this page

★★★70% **Quality Hotel Norwich**
2 Barnard Rd, Bowthorpe NR5 9JB
☎ 01603 741161 📠 01603 741500
e-mail: enquiries@hotels-norwich.com
web: www.choicehotelseurope.com
Dir: *A1074 to Norwich and Cromer. Hotel off A47 southern bypass 4m from city centre*
Modern hotel situated on the west side of the city, four miles from the centre. The spacious bedrooms are pleasantly decorated and equipped with up-to-date facilities. Public areas include a carvery restaurant, bar and lounge. The hotel offers conference and banqueting facilities, as well as a leisure centre.
ROOMS: 80 en suite (13 fmly) (40 GF) ⊗ in 40 bedrooms s £95; d £105 **LB FACILITIES:** STV Sauna Solarium Gym Jacuzzi Steamroom Xmas **CONF:** Thtr 200 Class 80 Board 60 Del from £95 **PARKING:** 200 **NOTES:** No dogs ⊗ in restaurant Civ Wed 75 **CARDS:**

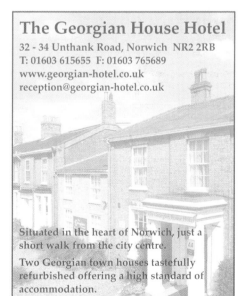

NORWICH, continued

★★★68% The George Hotel
10 Arlington Ln, Newmarket Rd NR2 2DA
☎ 01603 617841 📠 01603 663708
e-mail: reservations@georgehotel.co.uk
Dir: *on A11 follow city centre signs, Newmarket Rd towards centre. Hotel on left*

Within just 10 minutes' walk of the town centre, this friendly, family-run hotel is well placed for guests wishing to explore the many sights of this historic city. The hotel occupies three adjacent buildings, the restaurant, bar and most bedrooms are located in the main building, while the adjacent cottages have been converted into comfortable and modern guest bedrooms.
ROOMS: 38 en suite 5 annexe en suite (4 fmly) ⊗ in 9 bedrooms s £61-£75; d £85-£195 (incl. bkfst) **LB FACILITIES:** Xmas **CONF:** Thtr 70 Class 30 Board 30 Del from £99 **PARKING:** 40 **NOTES:** ✈ **CARDS:**

N

★★★68% Wensum Valley Hotel Golf & Country Club
Beech Av, Taverham NR8 6HP
☎ 01603 261012 📠 01603 261664
e-mail: enqs@wensumvalley.co.uk
Dir: *Turn left off A1067 Norwich to Fakenham road at Taverham into Beech Avenue. Hotel entrance on right next to High School*
Family run hotel set amid 240 acres of Norfolk countryside just a short distance from the city centre. The modern, purpose-built bedrooms are generally spacious and thoughtfully equipped. Public rooms include a choice of bars, a lounge and a large restaurant overlooking the green. The hotel has superb golf and leisure facilities.
ROOMS: 84 en suite (12 fmly) (32 GF) ⊗ in all bedrooms **FACILITIES:** ⛳ 36 Fishing Snooker Sauna Solarium Gym Putt green Jacuzzi Beauty therapy Golf driving range Hairdressing salon ♫ Xmas **CONF:** Thtr 200 Board 30 Del £80 **PARKING:** 250 **NOTES:** ✈ ⊗ in restaurant Civ Wed 100 **CARDS:**

★★★65% The Maids Head Hotel
Tombland NR3 1LB
☎ 0870 609 6110 📠 01603 613688
e-mail: maidshead@corushotels.com
Dir: *follow city centre signs past Norwich Castle. 3rd turning after castle into Upper King St, hotel opposite Norman Cathedral*
Imposing 13th-century building situated close to the impressive Norman cathedral and within easy walking distance of the city centre. The bedrooms are pleasantly decorated and thoughtfully equipped; some rooms have original oak beams. The spacious public rooms include a Jacobean bar, a range of seating areas and the Courtyard restaurant.

ROOMS: 84 en suite (7 fmly) ⊗ in 30 bedrooms s £94; d £109 **LB FACILITIES:** Xmas **CONF:** Thtr 300 Class 120 Board 40 Del from £115 **SERVICES:** Lift **PARKING:** 70 **NOTES:** ⊗ in restaurant Civ Wed 100 **CARDS:**

Top 200 – Hotel

★★ ® The Old Rectory
103 Yarmouth Rd, Thorpe St Andrew NR7 0HF
☎ 01603 700772 📠 01603 300772
e-mail: enquiries@oldrectorynorwich.com
web: www.oldrectorynorwich.com
Dir: *from A47 southern bypass onto A1042 towards Norwich N and E. Left at mini rdbt onto A1242. After 0.3m over traffic lights and hotel 100mtrs on right*
This delightful Grade II listed Georgian property is ideally located in a peaceful area overlooking the River Yare, just a few minutes' drive from the city centre. Spacious bedrooms are individually designed with carefully chosen soft fabrics, plush furniture and many thoughtful touches; many of the rooms overlook the swimming pool and landscaped gardens. An interesting daily-changing menu features skilfully prepared local produce served in the panelled dining room.
ROOMS: 5 en suite 3 annexe en suite ⊗ in all bedrooms s £68; d £88-£105 (incl. bkfst) **LB FACILITIES:** STV 🏊 **CONF:** Thtr 25 Class 18 Board 16 **PARKING:** 15 **NOTES:** ✈ ⊗ in restaurant Closed 21 Dec-4 Jan **CARDS:**

★★73% ® Stower Grange
School Rd, Drayton NR8 6EF
☎ 01603 860210 📠 01603 860464
e-mail: enquiries@stowergrange.co.uk
web: www.stowergrange.co.uk
Dir: *Norwich ring road N to Asda supermarket. Take A1067 Fakenham Rd at Drayton village, right at traffic lights along School Rd. Hotel 150yds on right*
A 17th-century ivy-clad property situated in a peaceful residential

continued

area just a short drive from the city centre and airport. The individually decorated bedrooms are generally quite spacious; each one is individually decorated, tastefully furnished and equipped with many thoughtful touches. Public rooms include a smart open-plan lounge bar and an elegant restaurant.

ROOMS: 11 en suite (1 fmly) s £67.50; d £89 (incl. bkfst)
FACILITIES: **CONF:** Thtr 100 Class 45 Board 30 Del £125
PARKING: 40 **NOTES:** in restaurant Civ Wed 100
CARDS:

★★70% The Old Rectory

North Walsham Rd, Crostwick NR12 7BG
☎ 01603 738513 01603 738712
e-mail: info@therectoryhotel.fsnet.co.uk
web: www.oldrectorycrostwick.com
Dir: *left off Norwich ring road onto B1150. Hotel 4m on left opposite St Peters church*

Attractive family-run hotel situated on the outskirts of Norwich city centre. Public rooms feature a superb hexagonal conservatory-style dining room, which overlooks the pretty gardens, and guests have the use of a smart lounge as well as a cosy bar and private dining room. Bedrooms are attractively decorated and well equipped.
ROOMS: 13 en suite (8 fmly) (13 GF) in 5 bedrooms s £46-£48; d £62.50-£65 (incl. bkfst) **FACILITIES:** ch fac **CONF:** Thtr 110 Class 80 Board 50 Del from £21.40 **PARKING:** 100 **NOTES:** in restaurant Civ Wed 150 **CARDS:**

★★64% Cumberland

212-216 Thorpe Rd NR1 1TJ
☎ 01603 434550 01603 433355
e-mail: cumberland@paston.co.uk
web: www.cumberlandhotel.com
Dir: *Hotel accessed from A47, then A1242 (past Norwich City FC)*

Now under new ownership this hotel is situated just a short drive from the railway station and city centre. Bedrooms are pleasantly decorated and thoughtfully equipped. An interesting choice of freshly prepared dishes is served in the Cape Dutch restaurant and guests also have the use of a smart lounge bar and cosy sitting room.
ROOMS: 22 en suite 4 annexe en suite (3 fmly) (6 GF) in 10 bedrooms s £45-£59; d £59-£89 (incl. bkfst) **LB** **FACILITIES:** ch fac **CONF:** Thtr 90 Class 30 Board 40 Del from £74.95 **PARKING:** 50 **NOTES:** in restaurant Closed 26-31 Dec
CARDS:

Travel Inn Norwich (Showground)

Longwater Interchange, Dereham Rd, New Costessey NR5 0TL
☎ 08701 977197 01603 741219
Dir: *Follow brown tourist signs for Royal Norfolk Showground on A47 and A1074. Travel Inn opp showground*

Travel Inn offers good-quality, value-for-money accommodation. Spacious, en suite rooms with bath and shower comfortably accommodate a family of up to two adults and two children (to age 15). The restaurant and bar offers a varied menu. For further details consult the Hotel Groups page.
ROOMS: 40 en suite s £45.95-£46.95; d £45.95-£46.95

Travel Inn Norwich Airport

Holt Rd, Norwich Airport NR6 6JA
☎ 08701 997 291 01603 428641

Travel Inn offers good-quality, value-for-money accommodation. Spacious, en suite rooms with bath and shower comfortably accommodate a family of up to two adults and two children (to age 15). The restaurant and bar offers a varied menu. For further details consult the Hotel Groups page.
ROOMS: 40 en suite s £45.95-£48.95; d £45.95-£48.95

Travel Inn (Norwich East)

Broadland Business Park, Old Chapel Way NR7 0WG
☎ 08701 977198 01603 307617
Dir: *A47 onto A1042, 3m E of city centre*

Travel Inn offers good-quality, value-for-money accommodation. Spacious, en suite rooms with bath and shower comfortably accommodate a family of up to two adults and two children (to age 15). The restaurant and bar offers a varied menu. For further details consult the Hotel Groups page.
ROOMS: 60 en suite s £45.95-£46.95; d £45.95-£46.95
CONF: Thtr 20 Board 14

Travelodge

Thickthorn Service Area, Norwich Southern Bypass NR9 3AU
☎ 08700 850 950 0870 191 1704
Dir: *A11/A47 junction*

Travelodge offers good quality, good value, modern accommodation. Ideal for families, the spacious, en suite bedrooms include remote-control TV, tea and coffee-making facilities and luxury beds. Meals can be taken at the nearby family restaurant. For further details consult the Hotel Groups page.
ROOMS: 62 en suite s fr £25; d fr £25

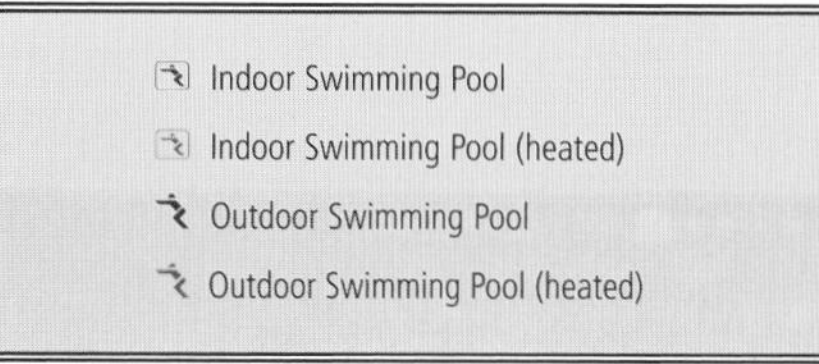

Indoor Swimming Pool
Indoor Swimming Pool (heated)
Outdoor Swimming Pool
Outdoor Swimming Pool (heated)

N

NOTTINGHAM, Nottinghamshire Map 11 SK53
See also Langar

Town House

★★★★ 🏠 Hart's
Standard Hill, Park Row NG1 6FN
☎ 0115 988 1900 📠 0115 947 7600
e-mail: ask@hartshotel.co.uk
web: www.hartsnottingham.co.uk
Dir: *At junct of Park Row & Rope Walk, close to city centre*
This outstanding modern building is on the site of the ramparts of the medieval castle, overlooking the city. Many of the bedrooms enjoy splendid views. Rooms are well appointed and stylish, while the Park Bar is the focal point of the public areas; service is professional and caring. Fine dining is offered at nearby Hart's Restaurant. Secure parking and private gardens are an added bonus.
ROOMS: 32 en suite ⊘ in all bedrooms s £115-£235; d £115-£235 **LB** **FACILITIES:** STV Gym Small, unsupervised exercise room Xmas **CONF:** Thtr 80 Class 75 Board 33 Del from £170 **SERVICES:** Lift **PARKING:** 21 **NOTES:** ⊘ in restaurant Civ Wed 80
CARDS:

Town House

★★★★ 🏠 Lace Market
29-31 High Pavement NG1 1HE
☎ 0115 852 3232 📠 0115 852 3223
e-mail: reservations@lacemarkethotel.co.uk
web: www.lacemarkethotel.co.uk
Dir: *follow tourist signs for Galleries of Justice which is opposite hotel*
This smart town house, a conversion of two Georgian houses, is located in the trendy Lace Market area of the city. Smart public areas, including the stylish and very popular Merchants Restaurant and Saints Bar, are complemented by the Cock and Hoop, a traditional pub offering real ales and fine wines.
continued

Accommodation is stylish and contemporary and bedrooms are all thoughtfully equipped.
ROOMS: 42 en suite ⊘ in all bedrooms s £90; d £110-£199 **LB** **FACILITIES:** STV Complimentary use of nearby health club. **CONF:** Thtr 35 Class 35 Board 20 Del from £150 **SERVICES:** Lift **NOTES:** ⊘ in restaurant **CARDS:**

★★★★66% *Park Plaza Nottingham*
41 Maid Marian Way NG1 6GD
☎ 0115 947 7200 📠 0115 947 7300
e-mail: info@parkplazanottingham.com
Park Plaza
This ultra modern hotel is located in the centre of the city within walking distance of retail, commercial and tourist attractions. Bedrooms are spacious and comfortable, with many extras, including laptop safes, high-speed telephone lines and air conditioning. Service is discreetly attentive in the Foyer lounge and the Chino Latino restaurant, where fusion cooking is a feature.
ROOMS: 178 en suite (10 fmly) ⊘ in 126 bedrooms **FACILITIES:** STV **CONF:** Thtr 175 Class 100 Board 54 **SERVICES:** Lift air con
CARDS:

★★★68% The Strathdon
Derby Rd, City Centre NG1 5FT
☎ 0115 941 8501 📠 0115 948 3725
e-mail: info@strathdon-hotel-nottingham.com
PEEL HOTELS
Dir: *follow city centre signs. Enter one-way system down Wollaton St, keep right and next right to hotel*
This city-centre hotel has modern facilities and is very convenient for all city attractions. A popular themed bar includes large-screen TV and serves an extensive range of popular fresh food, while more formal dining is available in Bobbins Restaurant. Bedrooms are modern and comprehensively equipped, and conference rooms are available.
ROOMS: 68 en suite (4 fmly) ⊘ in 46 bedrooms s fr £60; d fr £95 (incl. bkfst) **LB** **FACILITIES:** STV **CONF:** Thtr 150 Class 60 Board 40 Del from £90 **SERVICES:** Lift **CARDS:**

★★★67% Rutland Square Hotel
St James St NG1 6FJ
☎ 0115 941 1114 📠 0115 941 0014
e-mail: rutland.square@forestdale.com
Forestdale Hotels
Dir: *enter city and follow signs to castle. Hotel on right 50yds on from castle*
An enviable location in the heart of the city adjacent to the castle makes this hotel a popular choice. Behind its Regency façade the hotel is modern and comfortable with good business facilities. The well-equipped bedrooms are tastefully decorated. Public rooms include the informal Terrace Bar and Restaurant and Woods Restaurant.
ROOMS: 87 en suite (3 fmly) ⊘ in 38 bedrooms s fr £90; d fr £115 (incl. bkfst) **LB** **FACILITIES:** STV Discounted day passes to nearby gym Xmas **CONF:** Thtr 200 Class 70 Board 45 Del from £125 **SERVICES:** Lift **NOTES:** ⊘ in restaurant **CARDS:**

★★★67% Westminster Hotel
312 Mansfield Rd, Carrington NG5 2EF
☎ 0115 955 5000 📠 0115 955 5005
e-mail: mail@westminster-hotel.co.uk
web: www.westminster-hotel.co.uk
Best Western
Dir: *on A60 1m N of town centre*
This smart hotel is conveniently located close to the city centre, and offers well-appointed accommodation, suitably equipped for both business and leisure guests. Spacious superior rooms are
continued

particularly impressive. Public areas include a lounge bar, restaurant and range of meeting and function rooms.

ROOMS: 73 en suite (9 GF) ⊗ in 40 bedrooms s £37.50-£95; d £75-£110 **LB** **FACILITIES:** STV **CONF:** Thtr 60 Class 30 Board 30 Del from £95 **SERVICES:** Lift **PARKING:** 66 **NOTES:** ⊗ in restaurant Closed 25 Dec-2 Jan **CARDS:**

See advert on this page

★★★66% **Bestwood Lodge**

Bestwood Country Park, Arnold NG5 8NE
☎ 0115 920 3011 📠 0115 964 9678
e-mail: bestwoodlodge@btconnect.com

Dir: *3m N off A60. Left at traffic lights into Oxclose Ln, right at next lights into Queens Bower Rd. 1st right and keep right at fork in road*

A Victorian hunting lodge in 700 acres of parkland, providing modern bedrooms of varying styles and sizes. The interior architecture includes Gothic features and high vaulted ceilings in

continued on p442

NOTTINGHAM, continued

the lounge bar and the gallery. The newly refurbished banqueting suite is a popular venue for weddings and conferences.

Bestwood Lodge, Nottingham

ROOMS: 39 en suite (5 fmly) in 5 bedrooms s £45-£90; d £90-£150 (incl. bkfst) **LB** **FACILITIES:** Riding Guided walks Xmas **CONF:** Thtr 200 Class 65 Board 50 **PARKING:** 120 **NOTES:** in restaurant RS 25 Dec & 1 Jan **CARDS:**

See advert on page 441

★★★65% Comfort Hotel Nottingham

George St NG1 3BP
0115 947 5641 0115 948 3292
e-mail: enquiries@comfort-hotels-nottingham.com

Comfort Hotel BY CHOICE HOTELS

Dir: *M1 Jct24, follow signs for City Centre. George Street turn left and hotel at end of road on left.*

Situated in heart of the city, this hotel dates back to the late 17th century. Smartly appointed, compact public areas include a bar lounge, where all-day snacks are served, and a brightly decorated restaurant. Parking is available at a multi-storey a short walk from the hotel. More recently refurbished bedrooms are comfortable and thoughtfully equipped, well suited for both business and leisure guests.

ROOMS: 70 en suite (7 fmly) in 45 bedrooms s £40-£69; d £50-£79 **LB** **FACILITIES:** STV Xmas **CONF:** Thtr 150 Class 100 Board 60 Del from £90 **SERVICES:** Lift **NOTES:** in restaurant
CARDS:

★★★61% Swans Hotel & Restaurant

84-90 Radcliffe Rd, West Bridgford NG2 5HH
0115 981 4042 0115 945 5745
e-mail: enquiries@swanshotel.co.uk
web: www.swanshotel.co.uk

Dir: *on A6011, approached from A60 or A52 close to Trent Bridge*

This privately owned hotel is located on the outskirts of the city, conveniently placed for the various sports stadiums. Bedrooms, in various sizes, are equipped to meet the needs of both business and leisure visitors. An interesting range of dishes is served in either the cosy bar or, more formally, in the restaurant.

ROOMS: 30 en suite (3 fmly) (1 GF) in all bedrooms s £45-£65; d £60-£70 (incl. bkfst) **LB** **FACILITIES:** STV **CONF:** Thtr 50 Class 10 Board 24 **SERVICES:** Lift **PARKING:** 31 **NOTES:** in restaurant Closed 24-28 Dec **CARDS:**

> Late for dinner?
> Quality Standards mean that last orders for dinner vary according to star rating and should be no earlier than:
> ★★ 7.00pm ★★★ 8.00pm ★★★★ 9.00pm
> ★★★★★ 10.00pm

Top 200 – Restaurant with Rooms

Hotel des Clos

Old Lenton Ln NG7 2SA
0115 986 6566 0115 986 0343
e-mail: enquiries@hoteldesclos.com
web: www.hoteldesclos.com

Dir: *M1 junct 24 take A453 Nottingham S. Over River Trent in central lane to rdbt. Left then left again towards river. Hotel on left after bend*

This small hotel, a sympathetic conversion of Victorian farm buildings, is situated on the riverside. The bedrooms are attractively presented with quality soft furnishings and antique/period furniture; suites and four-poster bedrooms are available. Public rooms are cosy, and the delightful restaurant complements the excellent cuisine on offer.

ROOMS: 4 en suite 5 annexe en suite (1 fmly) (7 GF) in all bedrooms s £89.50-£109.50; d £99.50-£119.50 (incl. bkfst) **LB** **FACILITIES:** STV Fishing Facilities available at nearby David Lloyd club at subsidised rate Xmas **CONF:** Thtr 20 Class 10 Board 14 Del from £160 **PARKING:** 22 **NOTES:** in restaurant Closed 26-30 Dec, 1-7 Jan, Sun & BH's RS Mon
CARDS:

Citilodge

Wollaton St NG1 5FW
0115 912 8000 0115 912 8080
e-mail: mail@citilodge.co.uk
web: www.citilodge.co.uk

Dir: *From M1 junct 26, follow A610 into city centre. Hotel opposite Royal Centre on Wollaton St*

This city centre lodge offers superior accommodation along with a good range of bar and food options. Conferencing at the Citilodge is also a strength, with a comprehensive range of quality meeting rooms and an impressive 100-seater tiered lecture theatre. Bedrooms are spacious and light offering an excellent range of facilities that business guests will appreciate; each bedroom has air-conditioning and ISDN connections and a separate Citinet internet room is available.

ROOMS: 90 en suite s £58; d £58 **CONF:** Thtr 100 Class 25 Board 30 Del from £105

Innkeeper's Lodge Nottingham

Derby Rd, Wollaton Vale NG8 2NR
0115 922 1691
www.innkeeperslodge.com

Innkeeper's Lodge

Dir: *M1 junct 25, take A52 to Notttingham. At 3rd rdbt, left into Wollaton Vale, right across central reservation into car park*

Smart rooms meet essential business requirements but also have home comforts, and depending on location may well have meeting rooms and pub dining. Dining options generally include all-day menus plus the added advantage of breakfast.

ROOMS: 34 en suite s £57-£59; d £57-£59
CONF: Thtr 105 Class 62 Board 70

⌂ Premier Lodge (Nottingham City Centre)

PREMIER LODGE.com

Island Site, London Rd NG2 4UU
☎ 0870 9906574 📠 0870 9906575
web: www.premierlodge.com
Dir: *just off A6001, next to BBC building*
High quality, modern, budget accommodation, ideal for families and business travellers. All rooms feature bath, power shower and satellite TV, and most have telephones / modem points. The adjacent bar and restaurant offers a wide and varied menu.
ROOMS: 87 en suite s £54; d £54

⌂ Premier Lodge (Nottingham North)

PREMIER LODGE.com

101 Mansfield Rd, Daybrook NG5 6BH
☎ 0870 9906328 📠 0870 9906329
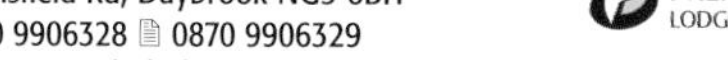
web: www.premierlodge.com
Dir: *M1 junct 27 onto A60. M1 junct 26 onto A610 & A6514 towards A60. Turn off A60 for Mansfield*
High quality, modern, budget accommodation, ideal for families and business travellers. All rooms feature bath, power shower and satellite TV, and most have telephones / modem points. The adjacent bar and restaurant offers a wide and varied menu.
ROOMS: 64 en suite s £50; d £50 **CONF:** Thtr 50 Class 50

⌂ Premier Lodge (Nottingham South)

PREMIER LODGE.com

Loughborough Rd, Ruddington NG11 6LS
☎ 0870 9906422 📠 0870 9906423
web: www.premierlodge.com
Dir: *exit M1 junct 24 and follow signs for A453 Nottingham, then A52 Grantham. Hotel at 1st rbt on left*
High quality, modern, budget accommodation, ideal for families and business travellers. All rooms feature bath, power shower and satellite TV, and most have telephones / modem points. The adjacent bar and restaurant offers a wide and varied menu.
ROOMS: 42 en suite s £50; d £50

⌂ Travel Inn Nottingham (City Centre)

travel inn

Goldsmith St NG1 5LT
☎ 0870 238 3314 📠 0115 908 1388
Dir: *Follow A610 to City Centre. Follow signs for Nottingham Trent University into Talbot Street. Take 1st left into Clarendon Street and at lights turn right for Travel Inn on right.*

Travel Inn offers good-quality, value-for-money accommodation. Spacious, en suite rooms with bath and shower comfortably accommodate a family of up to two adults and two children (to age 15). The restaurant and bar offers a varied menu. For further details consult the Hotel Groups page.
ROOMS: 161 en suite s £52.95-£54.95; d £52.95-£54.95

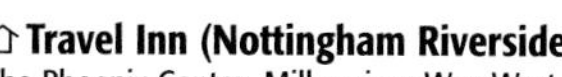

⌂ Travel Inn (Nottingham Riverside)

The Phoenix Centre, Millennium Way West
NG8 6AS
☎ 08701 977200 📠 0115 977 0113
Dir: *M1 junct 26, 1m on A610 towards Nottingham*
Travel Inn offers good-quality, value-for-money accommodation. Spacious, en suite rooms with bath and shower comfortably accommodate a family of up to two adults and two children (to age 15). The restaurant and bar offers a varied menu. For further details consult the Hotel Groups page.
ROOMS: 86 en suite s £45.95-£48.95; d £45.95-£48.95

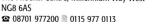

⌂ Travel Inn (Nottingham South)

Castle Marina Park, Castle Bridge Rd NG7 1GX
☎ 08701 977199 📠 0115 958 2362
Dir: *0.5m from Nottingham city centre, follow directions for Castle Marina*
Travel Inn offers good-quality, value-for-money accommodation. Spacious, en suite rooms with bath and shower comfortably accommodate a family of up to two adults and two children (to age 15). The restaurant and bar offers a varied menu. For further details consult the Hotel Groups page.
ROOMS: 38 en suite s £52.95-£54.95; d £52.95-£54.95

⌂ Travelodge (Nottingham Riverside)

Travelodge

Riverside Retail Park NG2 1RT
☎ 08700 850 950 📠 0115 986 0467
Dir: *on Riverside Retail Park*
Travelodge offers good quality, good value, modern accommodation. Ideal for families, the spacious, en suite bedrooms include remote-control TV, tea and coffee-making facilities and luxury beds. Meals can be taken at the nearby family restaurant. For further details consult the Hotel Groups page.
ROOMS: 61 en suite s fr £25; d fr £25

N

○ Jury's Inn Nottingham

JURYS DOYLE HOTELS

London Rd NG2
☎ 0870 907 2222
ROOMS: 250 en suite **NOTES:** Due to open Summer 2005

○ Nottingham Belfry

m MARSTON HOTELS

Woodhouse Way
☎ 0845 1300 700
ROOMS: 120 en suite
NOTES: Due to open Summer 2005

NOTTINGHAM EAST MIDLANDS AIRPORT, Leicestershire

Map 11 SK42

★★★★ 74% ◎◎
The Priest House on the River

HandPICKED

Kings Mills, Castle Donington DE74 2RR
☎ 01332 810649 📠 01332 811141
e-mail: thepriesthouse-cro@handpicked.co.uk
Dir: *M1 junct 24, onto A50, take 1st slip road signed Castle Donington right at traffic lights, hotel within 2m*
A historic hotel peacefully situated in a picturesque riverside setting. Public areas have been extensively refurbished and include a fine-dining restaurant, a modern brasserie and new conference rooms. Bedrooms are situated in both the main building and

continued on p444

NOTTINGHAM EAST MIDLANDS AIRPORT, continued

converted cottages, and newly designed executive rooms feature state-of-the-art technology.
Hand Picked Hotels - AA Hotel Group of the Year 2004-5.

The Priest House on the River, Nottingham East Midlands Airport

ROOMS: 24 en suite 18 annexe en suite (5 fmly) (16 GF) **FACILITIES: Spa** STV Fishing Archery Clay pigeon shooting **CONF:** Thtr 120 Class 40 Board 40 **PARKING:** 200 **NOTES:** in restaurant Civ Wed 70 **CARDS:**

See advert on opposite page

★★★75% Best Western Yew Lodge Hotel

Packington Hill, Kegworth DE74 2DF
☎ 01509 672518 01509 674730
e-mail: info@yewlodgehotel.co.uk
web: www.yewlodgehotel.co.uk
Dir: *M1 junct 24. Follow signs to Loughborough & Kegworth on A6. At bottom of hill, 1st right, after 400yds lodge on right*

This smart, family-owned hotel is close to both the motorway and airport, yet is peacefully located. Modern bedrooms and public areas are thoughtfully appointed offering modern comfort and facilities. The restaurant serves interesting dishes, while lounge service and extensive conference facilities are available.
ROOMS: 98 en suite (18 fmly) in 65 bedrooms s £50-£80; d £70-£100 (incl. bkfst) **FACILITIES: Spa** STV Sauna Solarium Gym Jacuzzi Beauty therapy suite, foot spa's Xmas **CONF:** Thtr 280 Class 60 Board 70 Del from £99 **SERVICES:** Lift **PARKING:** 180 **NOTES:** in restaurant Civ Wed 130 **CARDS:**

See advert under LEICESTER

Early start?
Hotels at all star levels should provide in-room alarm clocks and/or alarm calls

★★★70% Donington Manor

High St, Castle Donington DE74 2PP
☎ 01332 810253 01332 850330
e-mail: enquiries@doningtonmanorhotel.co.uk
web: www.doningtonmanorhotel.co.uk
Dir: *1m into village on B5430, left at traffic lights*
Near the village centre, this refined Georgian building offers high standards of hospitality and professional service. Many of the original architectural features have been preserved; the elegant dining room is particularly appealing. Bedrooms are individually designed, and the newer suites are especially comfortable and well equipped.
ROOMS: 26 en suite 6 annexe en suite (2 fmly) s £75-£100; d £95-£130 (incl. bkfst) **LB** **FACILITIES:** STV **CONF:** Thtr 120 Class 60 Board 40 **PARKING:** 40 **NOTES:** Closed 24-30 Dec Civ Wed 100 **CARDS:**

★★66% Tudor Hotel & Restaurant

Bond Gate DE74 2NR
☎ 01332 810875 01332 850883
e-mail: tudorinn@commodoreinternational.co.uk
web: www.commodoreinternational.co.uk/tudorhotel.htm
Dir: *M1 junct 24, A50 to Derby. Left to Long Eaton at rdbt, turning for Castle Donington*
This Tudor-style hotel is close to Donington race track and Nottingham East Midlands Airport. Bedrooms have been tastefully refurbished and are comfortable and very well equipped. Downstairs there is a large restaurant offering a wide range of dishes, a character bar and a beer garden.
ROOMS: 7 en suite (2 fmly) in all bedrooms s £43.50; d £43.50-£59.50 (incl. bkfst) **LB** **FACILITIES:** STV Xmas **CONF:** BC Thtr 30 Class 30 Board 30 Del £55 **PARKING:** 60 **NOTES:** **CARDS:**

Travelodge Donington Park

Castle Donington DE74 2TN
☎ 08700 850 950 01509 673494
Travelodge offers good quality, good value, modern accommodation. Ideal for families, the spacious, en suite bedrooms include remote-control TV, tea and coffee-making facilities and luxury beds. Meals can be taken at the nearby family restaurant. For further details consult the Hotel Groups page.
ROOMS: 80 en suite s fr £25; d fr £25

NUNEATON, Warwickshire — Map 11 SP39

★★★65% Weston Hall

Weston Ln, Bulkington CV12 9RU
☎ 024 7631 2989 024 7664 0846
e-mail: info@westonhallhotel.co.uk
Dir: *M6 junct 2 follow B4065 through Ansty. Left in Shilton, follow Nuneaton signs out of Bulkington, turn into Weston Ln at 30mph sign*

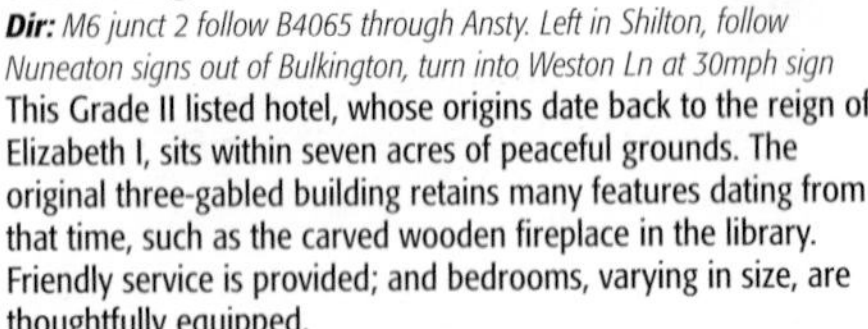

This Grade II listed hotel, whose origins date back to the reign of Elizabeth I, sits within seven acres of peaceful grounds. The original three-gabled building retains many features dating from that time, such as the carved wooden fireplace in the library. Friendly service is provided; and bedrooms, varying in size, are thoughtfully equipped.
ROOMS: 40 en suite (1 fmly) in 8 bedrooms s £70-£105; d £85-£105 (incl. bkfst) **LB** **FACILITIES: Spa** Fishing Sauna Gym Jacuzzi Steam room **CONF:** BC Thtr 200 Class 100 Board 60 Del from £125 **PARKING:** 300 **NOTES:** in restaurant Civ Wed 200 **CARDS:**

See advert under COVENTRY

Travel Inn

Coventry Rd CV10 7PJ
08701 977201 024 7632 7156

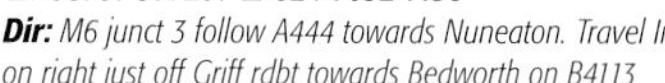

Dir: *M6 junct 3 follow A444 towards Nuneaton. Travel Inn on right just off Griff rdbt towards Bedworth on B4113*

Travel Inn offers good-quality, value-for-money accommodation. Spacious, en suite rooms with bath and shower comfortably accommodate a family of up to two adults and two children (to age 15). The restaurant and bar offers a varied menu. For further details consult the Hotel Groups page.

ROOMS: 48 en suite s £45.95-£46.95; d £45.95-£46.95 **CONF:** Thtr 25

Travelodge

St Nicholas Park Dr CV11 6EN
08700 850 950 0870 1911594

Dir: *on A47*

Travelodge offers good quality, good value, modern accommodation. Ideal for families, the spacious, en suite bedrooms include remote-control TV, tea and coffee-making facilities and luxury beds. Meals can be taken at the nearby family restaurant. For further details consult the Hotel Groups page.

ROOMS: 28 en suite s fr £25; d fr £25

No smoking

Travelodge Bedworth

Bedworth CV10 7TF
08700 850 950 024 7638 2541

Dir: *2m S, on A444*

Travelodge offers good quality, good value, modern accommodation. Ideal for families, the spacious, en suite bedrooms include remote-control TV, tea and coffee-making facilities and luxury beds. Meals can be taken at the nearby family restaurant. For further details consult the Hotel Groups page.

ROOMS: 40 en suite s fr £25; d fr £25

NUNNEY, Somerset

Map 04 ST74

★★65% *The George at Nunney*

11 Church St BA11 4LW
01373 836458 01373 836565
e-mail: georgenunneyhotel@barbox.net

Dir: *0.5m N off A361 Frome to Shepton Mallet road*

Situated in the centre of Nunney, opposite the castle, The George dates back to the 17th century. Guests may choose from an extensive range of bar meals or a selection of dishes offered in the more intimate restaurant. Bedrooms vary in size, have plenty of character and offer a very good selection of extras.

ROOMS: 9 rms (8 en suite) (2 fmly) in 2 bedrooms **PARKING:** 30
NOTES: **CARDS:**

OAKHAM, Rutland Map 11 SK80

Top 200 – Hotel

★★★ Hambleton Hall
Hambleton LE15 8TH
☎ 01572 756991 01572 724721
e-mail: hotel@hambletonhall.com
web: www.hambletonhall.com
Dir: *3m E off A606*

This delightful country house hotel enjoys a tranquil location amidst landscaped gardens overlooking Rutland Water. Stylish bedrooms are individually designed, tastefully decorated and thoughtfully equipped. Luxurious public areas include a cosy bar, a sumptuous drawing room and an elegant restaurant. Imaginative, skilfully prepared, award-winning cuisine, that features locally sourced and seasonal produce, is the highlight of any stay.

ROOMS: 15 en suite 2 annexe en suite in 1 bedroom s £160-£186; d £186-£355 (incl. cont bkfst) **FACILITIES:** STV CCTV Outdoor pool has CCTV, private access to lake Xmas **CONF:** Thtr 40 Board 24 Del from £220 **SERVICES:** Lift **PARKING:** 40 **NOTES:** in restaurant Civ Wed 64 **CARDS:**

★★★75% Barnsdale Lodge
The Avenue, Rutland Water, North Shore LE15 8AH
☎ 01572 724678 01572 724961
e-mail: enquiries@barnsdalelodge.co.uk
Dir: *off A1 onto A606. Hotel 5m on right, 2m E of Oakham*

A popular and interesting hotel converted from a farmstead and overlooking Rutland Water. The public areas are dominated by a very successful food operation with informal meals served in the brasserie, and a good range of appealing meals on offer in the more formal restaurant. Bedrooms are comfortably appointed with excellent beds and period furnishings, enhanced by contemporary soft furnishings and thoughtful extras.

ROOMS: 46 en suite (2 fmly) (15 GF) in 34 bedrooms s £75-£99.50; d £99.50-£120 (incl. bkfst) **LB** **FACILITIES:** STV Fishing Shooting Archery Golf Riding arranged Xmas **CONF:** BC Thtr 330 Class 120 Board 76 Del from £112.50 **PARKING:** 200 **NOTES:** in restaurant Civ Wed 200 **CARDS:**

★★★71% Barnsdale Hall
Barnsdale LE15 8AB
☎ 01572 757901 01572 756235
e-mail: reservations@barnsdalehotel.co.uk
web: www.barnsdalehotel.com
Dir: *from A1 take A606 to Oakham, through villages of Empingham and Whitwell. After 1m hotel on left overlooking Rutland Water*

Overlooking Rutland Water, this complex is set in attractive grounds leading to the water's edge. Public rooms offer a good choice of modern dining options and extensive leisure facilities; customer care is a particular strength. Spacious modern bedrooms have been refurbished and are equipped with many thoughtful extras; most are in adjacent buildings and many have a balcony.

ROOMS: 9 en suite 56 annexe en suite (9 fmly) (17 GF) in 61 bedrooms s £75; d £95 (incl. bkfst) **LB** **FACILITIES:** STV supervised Squash Snooker Sauna Solarium Gym Putt green Jacuzzi Boule, Bowls, Crazy Golf, Pitch & Putt, Soccer Pitch Xmas **CONF:** BC Thtr 200 Class 70 Board 42 Del from £112 **SERVICES:** Lift **PARKING:** 100 **NOTES:** in restaurant Civ Wed 110 **CARDS:**

See advert under LEICESTER

★★65% Admiral Hornblower
64 High St LE15 6AS
☎ 01572 723004 01572 722325
e-mail: enquiries@hornblowerhotel.co.uk
Dir: *town centre*

This sympathetically restored 17th-century farmhouse in the heart of Oakham is now an exceedingly popular small hotel offering tastefully appointed accommodation, good food and a lively bar. Bedrooms are individually appointed, furnished in country style and retain much of their original character. Public rooms are dominated by three dining areas with open fires and the main focal point is the bar.

ROOMS: 5 en suite 5 annexe en suite in all bedrooms s £59.50-£149; d £69.50-£149 (incl. bkfst) **PARKING:** 6 **NOTES:** in restaurant Closed 25 Dec, 1 Jan **CARDS:**

> Destination dining!
> This symbol indicates a Restaurant with Rooms

OCKLEY, Surrey — Map 06 TQ14

★★★63% Gatton Manor Hotel Golf & Country Club
Standon Ln RH5 5PQ
☎ 01306 627555 🖷 01306 627713
e-mail: gattonmanor@enterprise.net
web: www.gattonmanor.co.uk
Dir: *off A29 at Ockley turn into Cat Hill Ln. Hotel signed 2m on right*

This hotel enjoys a peaceful setting in its own grounds. A popular golf and country club, with an 18-hole professional course, it offers a range of comfortable, modern bedrooms. The public areas include the main club bar, a small restaurant and an attractive drawing room.

ROOMS: 18 en suite (2 fmly) ⊗ in 6 bedrooms s £74.50; d £115.50 (incl. bkfst) **LB** **FACILITIES:** STV ⛳ 18 Fishing Sauna Solarium Gym Putt green **CONF:** Thtr 50 Class 40 Board 30 Del from £99.50 **PARKING:** 250 **NOTES:** ⊗ in restaurant Civ Wed 50 **CARDS:**

ODIHAM, Hampshire — Map 05 SU75

★★74% George
High St RG29 1LP
☎ 01256 702081 🖷 01256 704213
e-mail: reception@georgehotelodiham.com
web: www.georgehotelodiham.com
Dir: *M3 junct 5 follow signs to Farnham and Odiham. In Odiham left at mini rdbt, hotel on left*

The George is over 450 years old and is a fine example of a typical English inn. Bedrooms come in a number of styles; the older part of the property has beams and period features, whilst new rooms have a contemporary feel. Guests can dine in the all-day café bar and bistro or the popular restaurant.

ROOMS: 19 en suite 9 annexe en suite (1 fmly) (6 GF) ⊗ in 14 bedrooms s £60-£115; d £80-£115 (incl. bkfst) **LB** **FACILITIES:** STV **CONF:** Thtr 30 Class 10 Board 26 Del from £135 **PARKING:** 20 **NOTES:** Closed 24-26 Dec **CARDS:**

OKEHAMPTON, Devon — Map 03 SX59

★★67% White Hart
Fore St EX20 1HD
☎ 01837 52730 & 54514 🖷 01837 53979
e-mail: whitehart.oke@btopenworld.com
Dir: *in town centre, adjacent to lights, car park at rear of hotel*

Dating back to the 17th century, the White Hart offers modern facilities. Bedrooms are well equipped and spacious and some have four-poster beds. A range of bar meals is offered or more

continued on p448

OKEHAMPTON, continued

relaxed dining may be taken in the Courtney restaurant. Guests can relax in the lounge or choice of bars, as well as a traditional skittles and games room.
ROOMS: 19 en suite (2 fmly) in 8 bedrooms **FACILITIES:** Games room Skittle alley Xmas **CONF:** Thtr 100 Class 80 Board 40 **PARKING:** 20 **NOTES:** **CARDS:**

See advert on opposite page

★★66% Ashbury
Higher Maddaford, Southcott EX20 4NL
☎ 01837 55453 01837 55468
Dir: *off A30 at Sourton Cross onto A386. Left onto A3079 to Bude at Fowley Cross. After 1m right to Ashbury. Hotel 0.5m on right*
Now boasting four courses and a clubhouse with lounge, bar and dining facilitites, The Ashbury is a golfer's paradise. In addition, guests can enjoy the many on-site leisure facilities or join the activities available at the adjacent sister hotel. The majority of the well-equipped bedrooms are located in the adjacent farmhouse and courtyard-style development around the putting green.
ROOMS: 61 en suite 30 annexe en suite (54 fmly) (29 GF) s £96-£156; d £182-£298 (incl. bkfst & dinner) **LB** **FACILITIES:** 63 Fishing Snooker Sauna Solarium Putt green Jacuzzi Driving range, Indoor bowls, Ten-pin bowling, table tennis,outdoor chess **PARKING:** 100 **NOTES:** in restaurant **CARDS:**

★★66% Manor House Hotel
Fowley Cross EX20 4NA
☎ 01837 53053 01837 55027
web: www.manorhousehotel.co.uk
Dir: *off A30 at Sourton Cross flyover, right onto A386. Hotel 1.5m on right*
Enjoying views to Dartmoor in the distance, this hotel is set in 17 acres of grounds close to the A30. An impressive range of facilities, including golf at their adjacent, sister hotel, is available at this friendly establishment which specialises in catering for short breaks. Bedrooms, many on the ground floor, are comfortable and well equipped.
ROOMS: 180 en suite (77 fmly) (96 GF) s £109-£171; d £208-£342 (incl. bkfst & dinner) **LB** **FACILITIES: Spa** Squash Snooker Sauna Gym Putt green Jacuzzi Craft centre Indoor bowls Shooting range Laser clay pigeon shooting Aerobics Xmas **PARKING:** 200 **NOTES:** in restaurant **CARDS:**

See advert on page 447

Travelodge (Okehampton East)
Whiddon Down EX20 2QT
☎ 08700 850 950 01647 231626
Dir: *at Merrymeet rdbt on A30/A382*
Travelodge offers good quality, good value, modern accommodation. Ideal for families, the spacious, en suite bedrooms include remote-control TV, tea and coffee-making facilities and luxury beds. Meals can be taken at the nearby family restaurant. For further details consult the Hotel Groups page.
ROOMS: 40 en suite s fr £25; d fr £25

OLDBURY, West Midlands — Map 10 SO98

Travel Inn
Wolverhampton Rd B69 2BH
☎ 08701 977202 0121 552 1012
Dir: *M5 junct 2, take A4123 towards Wolverhampton, hotel 0.75m on left*
Travel Inn offers good-quality, value-for-money accommodation. Spacious, en suite rooms with bath and shower comfortably accommodate a family of up to two adults and two children (to age 15). The restaurant and bar offers a varied menu. For further details consult the Hotel Groups page.
ROOMS: 40 en suite s £45.95-£46.95; d £45.95-£46.95

Travelodge
Wolverhampton Rd B69 2BH
☎ 08700 850 950 0121 552 2967
Dir: *on A4123, northbound off junct 2 of M5*
Travelodge offers good quality, good value, modern accommodation. Ideal for families, the spacious, en suite bedrooms include remote-control TV, tea and coffee-making facilities and luxury beds. Meals can be taken at the nearby family restaurant. For further details consult the Hotel Groups page.
ROOMS: 33 en suite s fr £25; d fr £25

OLDHAM, Greater Manchester — Map 16 SD90

★★★★66% Menzies Avant
Windsor Rd, Manchester St OL8 4AS
☎ 0161 627 5500 0161 627 5896
e-mail: avant@menzies-hotels.co.uk
Dir: *M60 junct 22, onto A62 into Oldham, right after petrol station.*
The Avant is a contemporary landmark building only a few minutes from the M60 and now features an excellent new leisure complex including fitness studios, a gym and a good-sized pool. Accommodation is smart, comfortable and spacious. A covered walkway leads to the public areas, which include the brasserie and bar area.
ROOMS: 103 en suite (2 fmly) in 16 bedrooms s £120; d £120-£140 **LB** **FACILITIES:** STV Sauna Solarium Gym Jacuzzi Xmas **CONF:** Thtr 250 Class 120 Board 60 Del £130 **SERVICES:** Lift **PARKING:** 120 **NOTES:** in restaurant Civ Wed **CARDS:**

★★★73% Hotel Smokies Park
Ashton Rd, Bardsley OL8 3HX
☎ 0161 785 5000 0161 785 5010
e-mail: sales@smokies.co.uk
web: www.smokies.co.uk
Dir: *on A627 between Oldham and Ashton-under-Lyne*

This modern, stylish hotel offers smart, comfortable bedrooms and suites. A wide range of Italian and English dishes is offered in the Mediterranean-style restaurant and there is a welcoming lounge bar with live entertainment at weekends. A small but well equipped fitness centre is for use by residents only. There is also a nightclub, to which guests can gain free admission.
ROOMS: 73 en suite (2 fmly) in 36 bedrooms s £60-£140; d £60-£140 (incl. bkfst) **LB** **FACILITIES:** STV Sauna Solarium Gym Night club Cabaret lounge **CONF:** BC Thtr 200 Class 100 Board 40 Del from £115 **SERVICES:** Lift **PARKING:** 120 **NOTES:** Civ Wed 120 **CARDS:**

★★★65% **La Pergola**

Rochdale Rd, Denshaw OL3 5UE
☎ 01457 871040 📠 01457 873804
e-mail: reception@lapergola.freeserve.co.uk
web: www.hotel-restaurant-uk.com
Dir: *M62 junct 21, right at rdbt onto A640, under motorway, left at Wagon & Horses public house. Hotel 500yds on left*
Situated in open moorland and convenient for the M62, this friendly, family-owned and run hotel offers comfortable and well-equipped bedrooms. There is a good range of food available in both the bar or restaurant, and there is a lounge in which to relax.
ROOMS: 26 en suite (4 fmly) ⊗ in 14 bedrooms s £43-£52.50; d £60.50-£65.50 (incl. bkfst) **LB** **FACILITIES:** Xmas **CONF:** Thtr 150 Board 25 Del £83.50 **PARKING:** 75 **NOTES:** ⊗ in restaurant Closed 26 Dec & 1 Jan RS BH Mondays Civ Wed 180
CARDS:

★★71% ***Old Bell Inn***
Huddersfield Rd, Delph OL3 5EG
☎ 01457 870130 📠 01457 876597
Dir: *on A62 Oldham-Huddersfield Rd, 100yds on left after crossroads*
Situated near the centre of Delph, this stone-built inn dates back to the 1770s, but has been extensively renovated by the present owners to provide well equipped and tastefully appointed accommodation. The pleasant public areas are very popular, particularly with customers wishing to enjoy the wide range of food, available in both the restaurant and the bar.
ROOMS: 14 en suite (3 fmly) **CONF:** Thtr 40 Class 24 Board 30
PARKING: 21 **NOTES:** ⊗ in restaurant
CARDS:

⌂ **Travel Inn Oldham (Central)**
Westwood Park, Chadderton Way
☎ 08701 977292 📠 08701 977702
Dir: *From M62 junct 20, take A627(M) to Oldham. Travel Inn on A627, opposite B&Q Depot*
Travel Inn offers good-quality, value-for-money accommodation. Spacious, en suite rooms with bath and shower comfortably accommodate a family of up to two adults and two children (to age 15). The restaurant and bar offers a varied menu. For further details consult the Hotel Groups page.
ROOMS: 40 en suite s £45.95-£46.95; d £45.95-£46.95

⌂ **Travel Inn (Oldham Chadderton)**
The Broadway OL9 8DW
☎ 08701 977203 📠 0161 682 7974
Dir: *M60 ringroad (anti clockwise) junct 21, signed Manchester City Centre. A663, 400yds on left*
Travel Inn offers good-quality, value-for-money accommodation. Spacious, en suite rooms with bath and shower comfortably accommodate a family of up to two adults and two children (to age 15). The restaurant and bar offers a varied menu. For further details consult the Hotel Groups page.
ROOMS: 40 en suite s £45.95-£46.95; d £45.95-£46.95

⌂ **Travelodge**
432 Broadway, Chadderton OL9 8AU
☎ 08700 850 950 📠 0161 681 9021
Travelodge offers good quality, good value, modern accommodation. Ideal for families, the spacious, en suite bedrooms include remote-control TV, tea and coffee-making facilities and luxury beds. Meals can be taken at the nearby family restaurant. For further details consult the Hotel Groups page.
ROOMS: 50 en suite s fr £25; d fr £25

ORFORD, Suffolk Map 13 TM45

★★74% ◎◎ **Crown & Castle Inn**
IP12 2LJ
☎ 01394 450205
e-mail: info@crownandcastle.co.uk
web: www.crownandcastle.co.uk
Dir: *turn right from B1084 on entering village, towards castle*
Adjacent to a Norman castle keep, this delightful inn has been transformed in recent years. Bedrooms, light, airy and contemporary, are in the main building (some with great views) and in a purpose-built garden wing; the latter are more spacious and have patios. The restaurant, with polished tables and local artwork, has an informal atmosphere and features a high quality menu.
ROOMS: 7 en suite 11 annexe en suite (1 fmly) (11 GF) ⊗ in all bedrooms s £72-£135; d £90-£135 (incl. bkfst) **LB** **FACILITIES:** ch fac **CONF:** Class 8 Board 14 Del from £130 **PARKING:** 25 **NOTES:** ⊗ in restaurant Closed 24-27 Dec, 4-8 Jan RS Nov-Etr
CARDS: 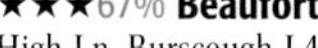

ORMSKIRK, Lancashire Map 15 SD40

★★★67% **Beaufort**
High Ln, Burscough L40 7SN
☎ 01704 892655 📠 01704 895135
e-mail: info@beaufort.uk.com
web: www.beaufort.uk.com
Dir: *M58 junct 3 follow signs for Ormskirk 7m. Hotel between Ormskirk and Burscough on A59*
This is a modern and privately owned hotel with pleasing public areas including an open-plan lounge bar and restaurant.
continued on p450

ORMSKIRK, continued

Conference and banqueting facilities are also available. There is a wide choice of food available that is served throughout the day.
ROOMS: 20 en suite s £70-£75; d £95-£105 (incl. bkfst) **LB**
FACILITIES: STV Free use of sister Hotel's (Stutelea Hotel, Southport) facilities **CONF:** Thtr 120 Class 32 Board 30 **PARKING:** 109 **NOTES:** ⊗ in restaurant Civ Wed 150 **CARDS:**

OSWESTRY, Shropshire

Map 15 SJ22

★★★75% Pen-y-Dyffryn Hall Country Hotel
Rhydycroesau SY10 7JD
☎ 01691 653700 01691 650066
e-mail: stay@peny.co.uk
Dir: *from A5 into Oswestry town centre. Follow signs to Llansilin on B4580, hotel 3m before Rhydycroesau village*
Peacefully situated in five acres of grounds, this charming old house dates back to around 1840, when it was built as a rectory. The tastefully appointed public rooms have real fires during cold weather, and accommodation includes several mini-cottages, each with their own patio. The hotel has a well deserved reputation for its food, that uses local and organic ingredients.
ROOMS: 8 en suite 4 annexe en suite (1 fmly) (1 GF) ⊗ in all bedrooms s £78-£79; d fr £106 (incl. bkfst) **LB** **FACILITIES: Spa** Jacuzzi Guided walks ch fac **PARKING:** 14 **NOTES:** No children 3yrs ⊗ in restaurant Closed 24 Dec-19 Jan **CARDS:**

★★★70% Wynnstay
Church St SY11 2SZ
☎ 01691 655261 01691 670606
e-mail: info@wynnstayhotel.com
web: www.wynnstayhotel.com
Dir: *B4083 to town, fork left at Honda Garage and right at traffic lights. Hotel opposite church*

This Georgian property was once a posting house and surrounds a unique 200-year-old Crown Bowling Green. Public areas include a health, leisure and beauty centre. Well-equipped bedrooms are individually styled and include several suites, four-poster rooms and a self-catering apartment. There is a traditional restaurant and bar food is also on offer.
ROOMS: 29 en suite (4 fmly) ⊗ in 14 bedrooms s £50-£95; d £68-£130 **LB** **FACILITIES: Spa** Sauna Solarium Gym Jacuzzi Crown green bowling Beauty suite ch fac **CONF:** Thtr 290 Class 150 Board 50 Del from £88.08 **PARKING:** 70 **NOTES:** ⊗ in restaurant Civ Wed 90
CARDS:

★★73% Sebastian's Hotel & Restaurant
45 Willow St SY11 1AQ
☎ 01691 655444 01691 653452
e-mail: sebastians.rest@virgin.net
web: www.sebastians-hotel.co.uk
Dir: *follow town centre signs. Junct with small pedestrian triangle take road towards Selattyn and Llansilin for 300yds into Willow St, hotel on left*
Parts of this privately owned and personally-run small hotel date back to 1640. It has a wealth of charm and character, enhanced by original features such as exposed beams and oak panelling in the cosy lounge, bar and popular bistro-style restaurant. Four newly constructed bedrooms are at the rear of the main building.
ROOMS: 7 en suite 1 annexe en suite (4 fmly) ⊗ in all bedrooms
FACILITIES: ch fac **CONF:** BC **PARKING:** 8 **NOTES:** ⊗ in restaurant Closed 25-26 Dec & 1 Jan **CARDS:**

Travelodge
Mile End Service Area SY11 4JA
☎ 08700 850 950 0870 191 1596
Dir: *junct A5/A483*
Travelodge offers good quality, good value, modern accommodation. Ideal for families, the spacious, en suite bedrooms include remote-control TV, tea and coffee-making facilities and luxury beds. Meals can be taken at the nearby family restaurant. For further details consult the Hotel Groups page.
ROOMS: 40 en suite s fr £25; d fr £25

OTLEY, West Yorkshire

Map 19 SE24

★★★69% Chevin Country Park Hotel
Yorkgate LS21 3NU
☎ 01943 467818 01943 850335
e-mail: reception@chevinhotel.com
Dir: *From Leeds/Bradford Airport rdbt take A658 N, towards Harrogate, for 0.75m to 1st traffic lights. Turn left, then 2nd left onto 'Yorkgate'. Hotel 0.5m on left*

This hotel, peacefully situated in its own woodlands yet conveniently located for major road links, offers comfortable accommodation. Rooms are split between the original main log building and chalet-style accommodation situated in the grounds. Public areas are spacious and well equipped. The split-level restaurant provides views over the small lake.
ROOMS: 19 en suite 30 annexe en suite (7 fmly) (45 GF) ⊗ in 10 bedrooms s £89-£121; d £96-£138 (incl. bkfst) **LB** **FACILITIES:** STV CCTV Fishing Sauna Solarium Gym Jacuzzi Mountain bikes, jogging trails, CCTV surveillance on indoor pool Xmas **CONF:** BC Thtr 120 Class 90 Board 50 Del from £129 **PARKING:** 100 **NOTES:** Civ Wed 120
CARDS:

OTTERBURN, Northumberland
Map 21 NY89

★★★64% The Otterburn Tower Hotel
NE19 1NS
☎ 01830 520620 🖷 01830 521504
e-mail: sales@otterburntower.com web: www.otterburntower.com
Dir: *in Otterburn, on A696 Newcastle to Edinburgh road*
Built by the cousin of William the Conqueror, this mansion is set in its own grounds and is steeped in history - Sir Walter Scott stayed here in 1812. Bedrooms come in a variety of sizes and some have huge ornamental fireplaces. Though furnished in period style, they are equipped with all modern amenities. The restaurant features 16th-century oak panelling.
ROOMS: 18 en suite (2 fmly) (2 GF) ⊗ in all bedrooms s £75-£90; d £120-£180 (incl. bkfst) **LB** **FACILITIES:** STV Fishing ch fac Xmas **CONF:** Thtr 90 Class 40 Board 30 Del from £125 **PARKING:** 70 **NOTES:** ⊗ in restaurant Civ Wed 250
CARDS:

★★68% Percy Arms
NE19 1NR
☎ 01830 520261 🖷 01830 520567
e-mail: percyarmshotel@yahoo.co.uk
Dir: *centre of Otterburn on A696*
This former coaching inn lies in the centre of the village, with good access to the Northumberland countryside. Real fires warm welcoming public areas in season and guests have a choice of mouth-watering dishes in either the restaurant or cosy bar/bistro. Bedrooms are cheerfully decorated and thoughtfully equipped.
ROOMS: 28 en suite (2 fmly) ⊗ in 2 bedrooms s £45-£68; d £80-£96 (incl. bkfst) **LB** **FACILITIES:** Fishing ch fac Xmas **CONF:** Thtr 70 Class 40 Board 50 Del from £75 **PARKING:** 74 **NOTES:** ⊗ in restaurant Civ Wed 80 **CARDS:**

OTTERSHAW, Surrey
Map 06 TQ06

★★★★71% Foxhills
Stonehill Rd KT16 0EL
☎ 01932 872050 🖷 01932 874762
e-mail: reservations@foxhills.co.uk
Dir: *A320 to Woking from M25. 2nd rdbt last exit into Chobham Rd. Right into Foxhills Rd, right at T junct, then left into Stonehill Rd*

This hotel enjoys a peaceful setting in extensive grounds, not far from the M25 and Heathrow. Spacious well-appointed bedrooms are provided in an annexe, a short walk from the main house. Golf, tennis, three pools and impressive indoor leisure facilities are available and there are two styles of restaurant.
ROOMS: 38 en suite (3 fmly) (25 GF) s £170-£300; d £170-£300 **LB** **FACILITIES:** STV 45 Squash Snooker Sauna Solarium Gym Putt green Boules, Childrens adventure playground, country pursuits, off-road course ch fac Xmas **CONF:** Thtr 100 Class 52 Board 56 Del from £180 **PARKING:** 500 **NOTES:** Civ Wed 75
CARDS:

OTTERY ST MARY, Devon
Map 03 SY19

★★70% Tumbling Weir Hotel
Canaan Way EX11 1AQ
☎ 01404 812752 🖷 01404 812752
e-mail: reception@tumblingweirhotel.com
web: www.tumblingweir-hotel.co.uk
Dir: *off A30 take B3177 into Ottery St Mary, hotel signed off Mill St, access through old mill*
Quietly located between the River Otter and its millstream and set in well-tended gardens, this family-run hotel offers friendly and attentive service. Bedrooms are attractively presented and equipped with modern comforts. In the dining room, where a selection of carefully prepared dishes makes up the carte menu, beams and subtle lighting help to create an intimate atmosphere.
ROOMS: 10 en suite (1 fmly) ⊗ in all bedrooms s £50-£53; d £80-£84 (incl. bkfst) **LB** **FACILITIES:** ch fac **CONF:** Thtr 90 Class 60 Board 50 Del from £80 **PARKING:** 10 **NOTES:** ⊗ in restaurant Closed 26 Dec - 10 Jan Civ Wed 80 **CARDS:**

OXFORD, Oxfordshire
Map 05 SP50
See also Milton Common

★★★★ Le Manoir Aux Quat' Saisons
RELAIS & CHATEAUX
Church Rd OX44 7PD
☎ 01844 278881 🖷 01844 278847
e-mail: lemanoir@blanc.co.uk web: www.manoir.com
(For full entry see Great Milton)

Town House

★★★★ The Old Bank Hotel
92-94 High St OX1 4BN
☎ 01865 799599 🖷 01865 799598
e-mail: info@oldbank-hotel.co.uk
web: www.oxford-hotels-restaurants.co.uk
Dir: *city centre to Magdalen Bridge, into High St, hotel 50yds on left*
This former bank has been converted into a very stylish and comfortable hotel. A wonderful collection of modern pictures and photographs livens the entire building. Bedrooms are smart and have CD players and air conditioning. Public areas are occupied mainly by the vibrant all-day Quod Bar and Restaurant, and there is a separate residents' bar. Parking and an outside courtyard are additional features.
ROOMS: 42 en suite (10 fmly) (1 GF) s £128-£140; d fr £160 **FACILITIES:** STV Discounts with various leisure facilities **CONF:** Thtr 20 Class 20 Board 14 **SERVICES:** Lift air con **PARKING:** 40 **NOTES:** Closed 25-27 Dec **CARDS:**

★★★★70% The Oxford Hotel
PARAMOUNT GROUP OF HOTELS
Godstow Rd, Wolvercote Roundabout OX2 8AL
☎ 01865 489952 🖷 01865 310259
e-mail: oxford@paramount-hotels.co.uk
Dir: *adjacent to A34/A40, 2m from city centre*
Conveniently located on the northern edge of the city centre, this purpose-built hotel offers bedrooms that are bright, modern and well equipped. Guests can eat in the 'Medio' restaurant or try the Cappuccino bar menu. The hotel has undergone substantial refurbishment and now offers impressive conference, business and leisure facilities.
ROOMS: 168 en suite ⊗ in 110 bedrooms s £149; d £159 (incl. bkfst) **LB** **FACILITIES:** STV Squash Sauna Solarium Gym Steam room Xmas **CONF:** BC Thtr 300 Class 150 Board 60 Del from £190 **SERVICES:** Lift **PARKING:** 250 **NOTES:** ⊗ in restaurant
CARDS:

O

OXFORD, continued

★★★★69% Cotswold Lodge
66a Banbury Rd OX2 6JP
☎ 01865 512121 01865 512490
e-mail: aa@cotswoldlodgehotel.co.uk
web: www.cotswoldlodgehotel.co.uk
Dir: *off A40 Oxford ring road onto A4165 Banbury Rd. Signed city centre and Summertown. Hotel 2m on left*

THE INDEPENDENTS HOTEL ASSOCIATION

This family-run Victorian property is located close to the centre of Oxford and offers smart, comfortable accommodation. Stylish bedrooms and suites are attractively presented and some have balconies. The public areas have an elegant country-house feel. The hotel is popular with business guests and caters for conferences and banquets.
ROOMS: 49 en suite in 40 bedrooms s £95-£125; d £125-£175 (incl. bkfst) **FACILITIES:** STV Discount at local gymnasium available to residents **CONF:** Thtr 80 Class 42 Board 24 **PARKING:** 40 **NOTES:** in restaurant **CARDS:**

★★★★69% The Randolph
Beaumont St OX1 2LN
☎ 0870 400 8200 01865 791678
e-mail: randolph@macdonald-hotels.co.uk
Dir: *M40 J8, A40 towards Oxford. Follow signs to City Centre, leads to St Giles, hotel on right*

MACDONALD HOTELS

Superbly located near the centre of town, The Randolph boasts impressive neo-Gothic architecture and tasteful décor. The restaurants with picture windows are ideal places to watch the world go by and delicious traditional teas may be enjoyed in the lounge. Refurbished bedrooms are classical in style and have a timeless elegance.
ROOMS: 150 en suite in 121 bedrooms s £120-£140; d £140-£190 **LB** **FACILITIES:** STV Xmas **CONF:** Thtr 300 Class 130 Board 60 Del from £150 **SERVICES:** Lift **PARKING:** 50 **NOTES:** in restaurant Civ Wed 120 **CARDS:**

Town House

★★★★ Old Parsonage
1 Banbury Rd OX2 6NN
☎ 01865 310210 01865 311262
e-mail: info@oldparsonage-hotel.co.uk
web: www.oxford-hotels-restaurants.co.uk/op.html
Dir: *from Oxford ring road to city centre via Summertown. Hotel last building on right next to St Giles Church before city centre*
Dating back in parts to the 16th century, this stylish town house hotel offers great character and charm and is conveniently located at the northern edge of the city centre. Bedrooms vary in size and are attractively furnished. The focal point is the all-day bar restaurant. Two small garden areas are available for residents.
ROOMS: 30 en suite (4 fmly) (10 GF) in all bedrooms s £125-£160; d £135-£195 **FACILITIES:** STV Complimentary use of punt and house bikes **SERVICES:** air con **PARKING:** 16 **NOTES:** in restaurant Closed 24-27 Dec **CARDS:**

★★★★66%
Oxford Spires Four Pillars Hotel
Abingdon Rd OX1 4PS
☎ 0800 374 692 01865 324325
e-mail: spires@four-pillars.co.uk
Dir: *M40 junct 8 towards Oxford. Left at rdbt towards Cowley. Straight over next 2 rdbts. At next rdbt follow signs for City Centre. Hotel 1m on right*

FOUR PILLARS HOTELS

This purpose-built hotel is surrounded by extensive parkland, yet is only a short walk from the city centre. Bedrooms are attractively furnished, well equipped and include several apartments. Smartly appointed public areas include a spacious restaurant, open-plan bar/lounge, leisure club and extensive conference facilities.
ROOMS: 115 en suite (8 fmly) in 44 bedrooms **FACILITIES:** STV Sauna Gym Jacuzzi Beauty, games, steam rooms ♫ **CONF:** BC Thtr 266 Class 96 Board 76 Del £169 **SERVICES:** Lift **PARKING:** 95 **NOTES:** Civ Wed 140 **CARDS:**

★★★★66%
Oxford Thames Four Pillars Hotel
Henley Rd, Sandford-on-Thames OX4 4GX
☎ 0800 374 692 01865 334400
e-mail: thames@four-pillars.co.uk
web: www.four-pillars.co.uk
Dir: *M40 junct 8. To Oxford follow ring road. Left at rdbt towards Cowley. At rdbt with lights take left exit to Littlemore, the hotel approx 1m on right*

FOUR PILLARS HOTELS

The main house of this hotel is built from local, yellow stone. The spacious and traditional River Restaurant has superb views over the hotel's own boat, moored on the river. The gardens can be enjoyed from the patios or balconies in the newer bedroom wings. Public rooms include a beamed bar and lounge area with minstrels' gallery.
ROOMS: 60 en suite (4 fmly) (24 GF) in 35 bedrooms s £75-£139; d £96-£172 **LB** **FACILITIES:** STV Sauna Gym Jacuzzi Steam room ♫ Xmas **CONF:** BC Thtr 160 Class 80 Board 60 Del £179 **PARKING:** 120 **NOTES:** Civ Wed 120
CARDS:

Late for dinner?
Quality Standards mean that last orders for dinner vary according to star rating and should be no earlier than:
★★ 7.00pm ★★★ 8.00pm ★★★★ 9.00pm
★★★★★ 10.00pm

★★★70% Fallowfields Country House Hotel
Faringdon Rd, Kingston Bagpuize, Southmoor OX13 5BH
☎ 01865 820416 📠 01865 821275
e-mail: stay@fallowfields.com
web: www.fallowfields.com
Dir: *from A420, take A415 towards Abingdon for 100yds. Right at mini rdbt, through Kingston Bagpuize, Southmoor and Longworth, follow signs*
With a history stretching back over 300 years, this spacious, comfortable hotel provides friendly, old-fashioned service. The thoughtfully equipped bedrooms are very much of this century and are decorated with skill. Public areas include an elegant drawing room and a charming conservatory restaurant in which the hotel's own seasonal produce is served.
ROOMS: 10 en suite (2 fmly) ⊗ in all bedrooms s £95-£115; d £145-£170 (incl. bkfst) **LB FACILITIES:** STV Falconry ch fac **CONF:** Thtr 60 Board 20 Del from £198.50 **PARKING:** 21 **NOTES:** ⊗ in restaurant Civ Wed 100 **CARDS:**

★★★70% Weston Manor Hotel
OX25 3QL
☎ 01869 350621 📠 01869 350901
e-mail: reception@westonmanor.co.uk
(For full entry see Weston-on-the-Green)

★★★69% Hawkwell House

Church Way, Iffley Village OX4 4DZ
☎ 01865 749988 📠 01865 748525
e-mail: info@hawkwellhouse.co.uk
Dir: *A34 follow signs to Cowley. At Littlemore rdbt take A4158 exit onto Iffley Rd. After traffic lights left to Iffley*

Set in a peaceful residential location, Hawkwell House is just a few minutes' drive from the Oxford ring road. The spacious rooms are modern, attractively decorated and well equipped. Public areas are tastefully appointed and the conservatory-style restaurant offers an interesting choice of dishes. The hotel also has a range of conference and function facilities.
ROOMS: 51 en suite (3 fmly) ⊗ in 13 bedrooms **FACILITIES:** STV **CONF:** Thtr 200 Class 100 Board 80 **SERVICES:** Lift **PARKING:** 85 **NOTES:** ⊗ in restaurant Civ Wed 200
CARDS:
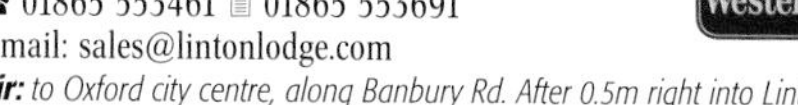

See advert on this page

★★★66% Linton Lodge
11-13 Linton Rd OX2 6UJ
☎ 01865 553461 📠 01865 553691
e-mail: sales@lintonlodge.com
Dir: *to Oxford city centre, along Banbury Rd. After 0.5m right into Linton Rd. Hotel opposite St Andrews Church*
Located in a residential area, this hotel is within walking distance of the town centre. Bedrooms are modern, well equipped and

continued on p454

OXFORD, continued

comfortable. The restaurant has a library theme, and the bar overlooks extensive lawned gardens to the rear of the hotel.

Linton Lodge Hotel, Oxford

ROOMS: 71 en suite (2 fmly) in 40 bedrooms s £115; d £135 (incl. bkfst) **LB** **FACILITIES:** STV Putt green **CONF:** Thtr 120 Class 50 Board 40 Del £155 **SERVICES:** Lift **PARKING:** 40 **NOTES:** in restaurant Civ Wed 120 **CARDS:**

See advert on page 453

★★★66% *Westwood Country*

Hinksey Hill, Boars Hill OX1 5BG
01865 735408 01865 736536
e-mail: reservations@westwoodhotel.co.uk
web: www.westwoodhotel.co.uk

THE CIRCLE Selected Individual Hotels GREAT BRITAIN

This Edwardian country house hotel is prominently set in terraced landscaped gardens and is within easy reach of the city centre by car. The hotel is modern in style, with very comfortable, well-equipped and tastefully decorated bedrooms. Public areas include a contemporary bar, a cosy lounge, and a newly extended restaurant looking out over the gardens.
ROOMS: 23 en suite (4 fmly) in 22 bedrooms **FACILITIES:** **CONF:** Thtr 60 Class 36 Board 35 **PARKING:** 60 **NOTES:** Civ Wed 85 **CARDS:**

★★★65% Eastgate

73 High St OX1 4BE
0870 400 8201 01865 791681
e-mail: sales.eastgate@macdonald-hotels.co.uk

MACDONALD HOTELS

Dir: *A40 follow signs to Headington & Oxford city centre, over Magdalen Bridge, stay in left lane, left into Merton St, entrance to car park on left*
Just a short stroll from the city centre, this hotel, as its name suggests, occupies the site of the city's medieval East Gate. The tastefully furnished and decorated bedrooms are situated on three floors, and the public areas include the popular Merton's bistro and bar.
ROOMS: 64 en suite (3 fmly) in 30 bedrooms s £85-£120; d £120-£140 (incl. bkfst) **LB** **FACILITIES:** STV Xmas **SERVICES:** Lift **PARKING:** 40 **NOTES:** in restaurant
CARDS:

★★67% *Victoria*

180 Abingdon Rd OX1 4RA
01865 724536 01865 794909
e-mail: victoriahotel@aol.com
Dir: *from M40/A40 take Eastern bypass and A4144 into city*
Located within easy reach of Oxford city centre and the motorway networks, this hotel offers a warm welcome. Bedrooms are comfortable, well maintained and furnished to a high standard. A conservatory bar and large dining room are ideal places to relax.
ROOMS: 15 en suite 5 annexe en suite (1 fmly) in 15 bedrooms **CONF:** Board 20 **PARKING:** 20 **NOTES:** in restaurant
CARDS:

★★65% The Balkan Lodge Hotel

315 Iffley Rd OX4 4AG
01865 244524 01865 251090
e-mail: balkanlodge@aol.co.uk
Dir: *from M40/A40 take eastern bypass, into city on A4158*
Conveniently located for the city centre and the ring road, this family operated hotel offers a comfortable stay. Bedrooms are attractive and well equipped; one has a four-poster bed and jacuzzi. Public areas include a lounge, bar and restaurant. A private car park is located to the rear of the building.
ROOMS: 13 en suite in all bedrooms **FACILITIES:** STV **NOTES:** in restaurant **CARDS:**

★★64% Manor House

250 Iffley Rd OX4 1SE
01865 727627 01865 200478
Dir: *on A4158 1m from city centre*
This conveniently situated hotel is easily accessible from the city centre and all major road links. The hotel is family run and provides informal but friendly and attentive service. Public areas are well maintained and presented. The comfortably furnished bedrooms are well equipped. Private parking is an asset.
ROOMS: 8 en suite (2 fmly) in all bedrooms s £69; d £80 (incl. bkfst) **LB** **PARKING:** 6 **NOTES:** Closed 20 Dec-20 Jan
CARDS:

Travel Inn

Oxford Business Park, Garsington Rd OX4 2JZ
08701 977204 01865 775887

travel inn

Dir: *on Oxford Business Park, just off A4142 junction with B480, opposite BMW Works, 3 miles from Oxford city centre*
Travel Inn offers good-quality, value-for-money accommodation. Spacious, en suite rooms with bath and shower comfortably accommodate a family of up to two adults and two children (to age 15). The restaurant and bar offers a varied menu. For further details consult the Hotel Groups page.
ROOMS: 120 en suite s £54.95-£58.95; d £54.95-£58.95

> Popped the question?
> Hotels with Civ Wed in their entry are licensed for civil wedding ceremonies. Maximum numbers for the ceremony only are shown, e.g. Civ Wed 120

Travelodge
Peartree Roundabout, Woodstock Rd OX2 8JZ
☎ 08700 850 950 01865 513474
Dir: *junct A34/A43*
Travelodge offers good quality, good value, modern accommodation. Ideal for families, the spacious, en suite bedrooms include remote-control TV, tea and coffee-making facilities and luxury beds. Meals can be taken at the nearby family restaurant. For further details consult the Hotel Groups page.
ROOMS: 150 en suite s fr £25; d fr £25 **CONF:** Thtr 300 Class 150 Board 60

Travelodge (Oxford East)
London Rd, Wheatley OX33 1JH
☎ 08700 850 950 01865 875905
Dir: *off A40 next to The Harvester on outskirts of Wheatley*
Travelodge offers good quality, good value, modern accommodation. Ideal for families, the spacious, en suite bedrooms include remote-control TV, tea and coffee-making facilities and luxury beds. Meals can be taken at the nearby family restaurant. For further details consult the Hotel Groups page.
ROOMS: 36 en suite s fr £25; d fr £25

OXFORD MOTORWAY SERVICE AREA (M40), Oxfordshire
Map 05 SP60

Days Inn
M40 junction 8A, Waterstock OX33 1LJ
☎ 01865 877000 01865 877016
e-mail: oxford.hotel@welcomebreak.co.uk
web: www.welcomebreak.co.uk
Dir: *M40 junct 8a, Welcome Break service area.*
This modern building offers accommodation in smart, spacious and well-equipped bedrooms, suitable for families and business travellers, and all with en suite bathrooms. Continental breakfast is available and other refreshments may be taken at the nearby family restaurant. For further details see the Hotel Groups page.
ROOMS: 59 en suite s £54-£60; d £54-£60

PADSTOW, Cornwall & Isles of Scilly
Map 02 SW97
See also Constantine Bay

★★★70% The Metropole
Station Rd PL28 8DB
☎ 01841 532486 01841 532867
e-mail: info@the-metropole.co.uk
web: www.richardsonhotels.co.uk
Dir: *M5/A30 pass Launceston, turn off & follow signs for Wadebridge & N Cornwall. Take A39 & follow signs for Padstow*

This long-established hotel first opened its doors to guests back in 1904 and there is still an air of the sophistication and elegance of
continued

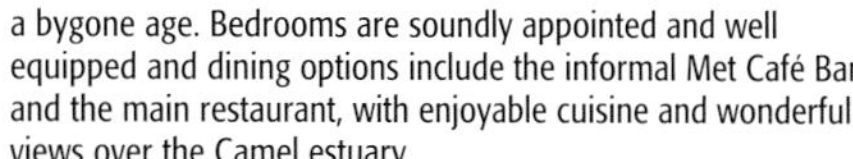

a bygone age. Bedrooms are soundly appointed and well equipped and dining options include the informal Met Café Bar and the main restaurant, with enjoyable cuisine and wonderful views over the Camel estuary.
ROOMS: 50 en suite (3 fmly) (2 GF) in 10 bedrooms s £69-£105; d £138-£170 (incl. bkfst & dinner) **LB** **FACILITIES:** Swimming pool open Jul & Aug only Xmas **SERVICES:** Lift **PARKING:** 36 **NOTES:** in restaurant **CARDS:**

★★★66% Old Custom House Inn
South Quay PL28 8BL
☎ 01841 532359 01841 533372
e-mail: oldcustomhouse@smallandfriendly.co.uk
Dir: *A359 from Wadebridge, take 2nd right. In Padstow follow road round bend to bottom of hill. Hotel on left*
Situated by the harbour, this charming inn continues to be a popular choice for locals and visitors alike. The lively bar serves real ales and good bar meals. Pescadou's restaurant provides a stylish and convivial venue for imaginative dishes that place the emphasis on locally caught fish. A wide selection of beauty treatments is available in the hotel's Lavender Room.
ROOMS: 24 en suite (8 fmly) in all bedrooms s £63-£95; d £82-£170 (incl. bkfst) **LB** **FACILITIES:** STV **NOTES:** in restaurant
CARDS:

★★67% The Old Ship Hotel
Mill Square PL28 8AE
☎ 01841 532357 01841 533211
e-mail: stay@oldshiphotel-padstow.co.uk
web: www.oldshiphotel-padstow.co.uk
Dir: *from M5 take A30 to Bodmin then A389 to Padstow, follow brown tourist signs to car park*
This attractive inn is situated in the heart of the old town's quaint and winding streets, just a short walk from the harbour. A warm welcome is assured, accommodation is pleasant and comfortable, and public areas have plenty of character. Freshly caught fish features on both the bar and restaurant menus.
ROOMS: 14 en suite (4 fmly) s £35-£45; d £70-£100 (incl. bkfst) **LB**
FACILITIES: STV Xmas **PARKING:** 20 **NOTES:** in restaurant
CARDS:

Indoor Swimming Pool
Indoor Swimming Pool (heated)
Outdoor Swimming Pool
Outdoor Swimming Pool (heated)

P

PADSTOW, continued

Restaurant with Rooms

The Seafood Restaurant

Riverside PL28 8BY
☎ 01841 532700 01841 532942
e-mail: reservations@rickstein.com
Dir: *A38 towards Newquay, then A389 towards Padstow. After 3m, right at t-junct, follow signs for Padstow town centre. Restaurant on left*
Rick Stein's Seafood Restaurant enjoys an enviable reputation for the freshness and quality of its cuisine, and it is no surprise to discover that such high standards are repeated in the accommodation here. Each of the bedrooms is spacious and comfortable, complete with fine quality fixtures and fittings. Additional rooms are housed close by in St. Edmunds, where refurbishment has resulted in luxurious standards with much style.
ROOMS: 13 en suite 19 annexe en suite (7 fmly) (3 GF)
FACILITIES: STV **PARKING:** 22 **NOTES:** Closed 1 May & 24-26 Dec
CARDS:

PAIGNTON, Devon Map 03 SX86

★★★71% Redcliffe

Marine Dr TQ3 2NL
THE INDEPENDENTS
☎ 01803 526397 01803 528030
e-mail: redclfe@aol.com
Dir: *Hotel on seafront at Torquay end of Paignton Green*
Set on the edge of the sea in three acres of well-tended grounds, this popular hotel enjoys uninterrupted views across Tor Bay. Offering a diverse range of facilities, including leisure, business and beauty treatments, the Redcliffe is suitable for leisure or business guests. Bedrooms are pleasantly appointed and comfortably furnished, whilst public areas offer ample space for rest and relaxation.
ROOMS: 67 en suite (8 fmly) (2 GF) s £52-£57; d £104-£114 (incl. bkfst) **FACILITIES: Spa** STV supervised Fishing Sauna Solarium Gym Putt green Jacuzzi Table tennis, Carpet Bowls ch fac Xmas **CONF:** Thtr 150 Class 50 Board 50 Del from £70 **SERVICES:** Lift **PARKING:** 80 **NOTES:** in restaurant Civ Wed 150 **CARDS:**

★★71% Dainton

95 Dartmouth Rd, Three Beaches, Goodrington TQ4 6NA
☎ 01803 550067 01803 666339
e-mail: enquiries@daintonhotel.com
Dir: *on A379 at Goodrington. Pass zoo entrance, right onto Penwill Way. At bottom of road right into Dartmouth Rd. Hotel 0.25m on left*
Located in a convenient position close to the beaches and Leisure Park, the Dainton provides a friendly and welcoming place to stay. Bedrooms are well-equipped and brightly decorated. Service is attentive, particularly in the new Christie's restaurant, which has an extensive menu with vegetarian options.
ROOMS: 10 en suite (3 fmly) (2 GF) in all bedrooms **PARKING:** 20 **NOTES:** in restaurant **CARDS:**

★★67% Sea Verge Hotel

21 Marine Dr TQ3 2NJ
☎ 01803 557795
Dir: *on seafront*
With the added benefit of dedicated owners, this family-run hotel is conveniently situated close to the seafront and Preston Green. Several of the light and airy bedrooms have balconies, with views over Torbay. Spacious public areas include a comfortable lounge with adjacent sunroom, a cosy bar and the soundly appointed dining room.
ROOMS: 10 en suite (1 fmly) in 4 bedrooms **PARKING:** 14 **NOTES:** No children 9yrs Closed Dec-Feb

★★67% *Torbay Holiday Motel*

Totnes Rd TQ4 7PP
☎ 01803 558226 01803 663375
e-mail: enquiries@thm.co.uk
Dir: *on A385 Totnes to Paignton road, 2.5m from Paignton*
Situated between Paignton and Totnes, this small complex offers purpose built leisure facilities, self-catering apartments and motel accommodation. The spacious bedrooms are comfortable and well co-ordinated. There are two restaurants and traditional dining is offered throughout.
ROOMS: 16 en suite **FACILITIES:** STV Sauna Solarium Gym Putt green Crazy golf, Adventure playground **PARKING:** 150 **NOTES:** RS 24-31 Dec **CARDS:**

See advert on opposite page

A ★★ Summerhill

Braeside Rd TQ4 6BX
☎ 01803 558101 01803 558101
e-mail: info@summerhillhotel.co.uk
web: www.summerhillhotel.co.uk
Dir: *with harbour on left, follow road for 600yds*
ROOMS: 26 en suite (9 fmly) (4 GF) in all bedrooms s £32-£45; d £64-£75 (incl. bkfst) **LB FACILITIES:** Free membership to nearby leisure centre. ch fac **SERVICES:** Lift **PARKING:** 40 **NOTES:** in restaurant **CARDS:**

★69% Britney

29 Esplanade Rd TQ4 6BL
☎ 01803 557820 01803 551285
Dir: *on seafront by pier*
In an impressive location on the seafront, this pleasant hotel offers comfortable accommodation. The hotel is family run and the proprietors are friendly and attentive. Bedrooms, some of which are sea facing and some with balconies, are available in a range of sizes. A lively bar is provided, as well as a quieter lounge and sunroom.
ROOMS: 20 en suite (2 fmly) in 3 bedrooms **FACILITIES:** Xmas **SERVICES:** Lift **PARKING:** 8 **NOTES:** in restaurant
CARDS:

★69% The Commodore Hotel

14 Esplanade Rd TQ4 6EB
☎ 01803 553107
e-mail: stay@commodorepaignton.co.uk
Dir: *follow A3022, left lane to seafront, just past multiplex cinema complex, hotel on right*
Enjoying a prime seafront position, this friendly, family-run hotel benefits from the added bonus of lovely views across the bay. Just a short walk from all the resort facilities, it is an excellent base from which to explore the area. Public areas are spacious and well presented, with ample seating in both the lounge and bar lounge. Bedrooms are comfortable and well equipped.
ROOMS: 11 en suite (4 fmly) (3 GF) in all bedrooms d £48-£54 (incl. bkfst) **FACILITIES:** Xmas **PARKING:** 11 **NOTES:** in restaurant **CARDS:**

PAINSWICK, Gloucestershire Map 04 SO81

★★★77% Painswick Hotel and Restaurant

Kemps Ln GL6 6YB
☎ 01452 812160 01452 814059
e-mail: reservations@painswickhotel.com
web: www.painswickhotel.com
Dir: *off A46 in centre of village by church. Hotel off 2nd road behind church off Tibbiwell Ln*
Dating back to 1790, this former rectory is situated in the heart of

continued

one of the Cotswolds' most enchanting villages. Attentive hospitality and service are key features. The day rooms house antiques and interesting artwork, contributing to a sense of timeless elegance. All bedrooms differ, while reflecting similar high standards. Accomplished cuisine and a serious choice of wine are served in the oak-panelled restaurant.

ROOMS: 19 en suite (2 fmly) (6 GF) s fr £85; d fr £140 (incl. bkfst) **LB**
FACILITIES: Xmas **CONF:** Thtr 50 Class 15 Board 26 Del from £150
PARKING: 20 **NOTES:** in restaurant Civ Wed 100
CARDS:

See advert on this page

PANGBOURNE, Berkshire Map 05 SU67

★★★75% The Copper Inn Hotel and Restaurant

Best Western

RG8 7AR
☎ 0118 984 2244 0118 984 5542
e-mail: reservations@copper-inn.co.uk
web: www.copper-inn.co.uk
Dir: *M4 junct 12 take A4 W then A340 to Pangbourne. Hotel next to church at junct of A329 & A340*

This 19th-century coaching inn is well known for its high standards of hotel keeping. Public rooms include a popular and lively bar, a quiet lounge and lovely restaurant where service is friendly and efficient. Well-equipped bedrooms, many of which overlook the secluded rear gardens, are comfortably appointed and individually decorated.
ROOMS: 14 en suite 8 annexe en suite (1 fmly) (4 GF) in all bedrooms s £50-£90; d £50-£110 **LB** **FACILITIES:** STV Xmas
CONF: BC Thtr 60 Class 24 Board 30 Del £145 **PARKING:** 20
NOTES: in restaurant Civ Wed 70
CARDS:

Early start?
Hotels at all star levels should provide in-room alarm clocks and/or alarm calls

P

PANGBOURNE, continued

★★★64% *George Hotel*

The Square RG8 7AJ
☎ 0118 984 2237 0118 984 4354
e-mail: info@georgehotelpangbourne.co.uk
Dir: *M4 junct 12 towards Newbury. Right at 2nd rdbt onto A340, 3m to Pangbourne. Right at rdbt, hotel 50yds on left*

Having undergone a transformation, this former coaching inn now offers modern facilities. Bedrooms are thoughtfully appointed and comfortable, a number are specially equipped for families. The 'Kidsden' rooms have computers and Playstations, and considering the hotel's location, just 20 minutes from Legoland, this is a popular venue for families. Dinner is available with an Italian theme in Mia Bene Restaurant.

ROOMS: 24 en suite (6 fmly) in 12 bedrooms **FACILITIES:** STV **CONF:** Thtr 60 Class 25 Board 20 **PARKING:** 30 **CARDS:**

PARKHAM, Devon — Map 03 SS32

★★★72% Penhaven Country House

Rectory Ln EX39 5PL
☎ 01237 451388 & 451711 01237 451878
e-mail: reservations@penhaven.co.uk
web: www.penhaven.co.uk
Dir: *off A39 at Horns Cross, follow signs to Parkham, 2nd left after church into Rectory Ln*

The countryside is very much at the heart of this establishment and lucky guests can spot tame badgers most evenings in the lovely grounds. The tranquillity of the location and the friendliness of the staff combine to create a truly relaxing place to stay. Bedrooms are spacious and well equipped; some are located in the cottage annexe and two are on the ground floor. Dinners feature fresh, local produce and vegetarians are especially welcome.

ROOMS: 12 en suite s £90-£100; d £180-£200 (incl. bkfst & dinner) **LB** **FACILITIES:** 9 acres of woodland trail Xmas **PARKING:** 50 **NOTES:** No children 10yrs in restaurant **CARDS:**

P

PATTERDALE, Cumbria — Map 18 NY31

★★64% Patterdale

CA11 0NN
☎ 0845 458 4333 & 017684 82231 01253 754222
e-mail: reservations@choice-hotels.co.uk
Dir: *M6 junct 40, take A592 towards Ullswater, then 10m up Lakeside Rd to Patterdale*

Patterdale is a real tourist destination and this hotel enjoys delightful views of the valley and fells, being located at the southern end of Ullswater. Bedrooms vary in style, with the refurbished ones brightly decorated with a modern feel. In busier periods accommodation is let for a minimum period of two nights.

ROOMS: 57 en suite (16 fmly) **FACILITIES:** Fishing Free bike hire ch fac Xmas **SERVICES:** Lift **PARKING:** 30 **NOTES:** in restaurant **CARDS:**

PATTINGHAM, Staffordshire — Map 10 SO89

★★★68% Patshull Park Hotel Golf & Country Club

Patshull Park WV6 7HR
☎ 01902 700100 01902 700874
e-mail: sales@patshull-park.co.uk
web: www.patshull-park.co.uk
Dir: *1.5m W of Pattingham, at Church into Patshull Rd, hotel 1.5m on right*

There has been a manor house here since before the Norman Conquest; the present house dates back to the 1730s and is now a comfortably appointed hotel. Sitting within 280 acres of parkland (with good golf and fishing) this hotel has a range of modern leisure and conference facilities. Public rooms include a lounge bar, coffee shop and restaurant with delightful views out over the lake. Bedrooms are well appointed and thoughtfully equipped; most have good views.

ROOMS: 49 en suite (15 fmly) (16 GF) in all bedrooms s £99-£114; d £109-£139 (incl. bkfst) **LB** **FACILITIES: Spa** STV 18 Fishing Sauna Solarium Gym Putt green Jacuzzi Beauty therapist, Pool table, Cardio suite Xmas **CONF:** BC Thtr 160 Class 75 Board 44 Del from £99 **PARKING:** 200 **NOTES:** in restaurant RS 25/26 Dec Civ Wed 100 **CARDS:**

See advert under WOLVERHAMPTON

PEASLAKE, Surrey — Map 06 TQ04

★★★69% Hurtwood Inn Hotel

Walking Bottom GU5 9RR
☎ 01306 730851 01306 731390
e-mail: sales@hurtwoodinnhotel.com
web: www.hurtwoodinnhotel.com
Dir: *off A25 at Gomshall opposite Jet Filling Station towards Peaslake. After 2.5m turn right at village shop, hotel in village centre*

With its tranquil location this hotel makes an ideal base for exploring the attractions of the area. The brightly decorated bedrooms are well appointed, and some have views over the gardens. Newly refurbished public areas include a restaurant, a private dining room and a bar/bistro where drinks by the open fire can be enjoyed. 'Oscars' is the setting to enjoy award-winning meals.

ROOMS: 15 en suite 6 annexe en suite (6 fmly) (6 GF) in 5 bedrooms s £65; d £75-£85 **CONF:** Thtr 40 Class 15 Board 20 Del £128 **PARKING:** 22 **NOTES:** in restaurant **CARDS:**

PEASMARSH, East Sussex Map 07 TQ82

★★★77% Flackley Ash

TN31 6YH
☎ 01797 230651 01797 230510
e-mail: enquiries@flackleyashhotel.co.uk
web: www.flackleyashhotel.co.uk
Dir: *3m from Rye, beside A268*

Five acres of beautifully kept grounds are the lovely backdrop to this elegant Georgian country house. The hotel is superbly situated for exploring the many local attractions, including the ancient Cinque Port of Rye, just a short drive away. Bedrooms are individually decorated and have a homely feel, and include added extras.
ROOMS: 45 en suite (3 fmly) s £87-£99; d £132-£156 (incl. bkfst) **LB** **FACILITIES: Spa** STV supervised Sauna Gym Putt green Beautician aromatherapy reflexology ch fac Xmas **CONF:** Thtr 100 Class 50 Board 40 Del from £110 **PARKING:** 70 **NOTES:** in restaurant Civ Wed 100 **CARDS:**

PENDLEBURY, Greater Manchester Map 15 SD70

Premier Lodge (Manchester North West)

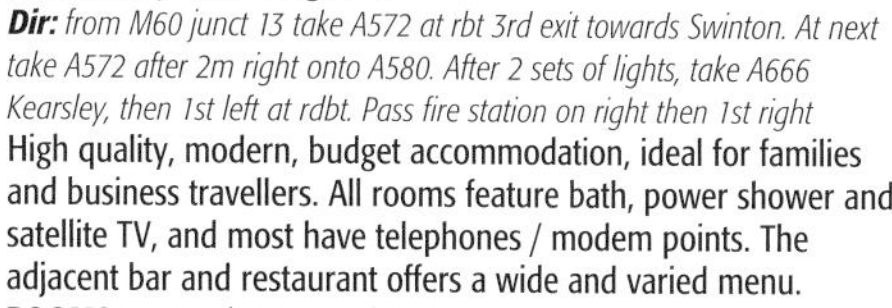

219 Bolton Rd M27 8TG
☎ 0870 9906528 0870 9906529
web: www.premierlodge.com
Dir: *from M60 junct 13 take A572 at rbt 3rd exit towards Swinton. At next take A572 after 2m right onto A580. After 2 sets of lights, take A666 Kearsley, then 1st left at rdbt. Pass fire station on right then 1st right*
High quality, modern, budget accommodation, ideal for families and business travellers. All rooms feature bath, power shower and satellite TV, and most have telephones / modem points. The adjacent bar and restaurant offers a wide and varied menu.
ROOMS: 31 en suite s £50; d £50

PENKRIDGE, Staffordshire Map 10 SJ91

★★★66% Quality Hotel Stafford

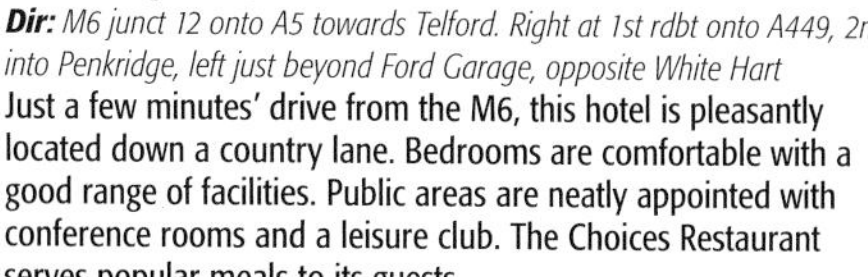

Pinfold Ln ST19 5QP
☎ 01785 712459 01785 715532
e-mail: enquiries@hotels-stafford.com
Dir: *M6 junct 12 onto A5 towards Telford. Right at 1st rdbt onto A449, 2m into Penkridge, left just beyond Ford Garage, opposite White Hart*
Just a few minutes' drive from the M6, this hotel is pleasantly located down a country lane. Bedrooms are comfortable with a good range of facilities. Public areas are neatly appointed with conference rooms and a leisure club. The Choices Restaurant serves popular meals to its guests.
ROOMS: 47 en suite (2 fmly) (6 GF) in 25 bedrooms s £90; d £99 **LB** **FACILITIES:** STV supervised Squash Sauna Solarium Gym Xmas **CONF:** Thtr 300 Class 120 Board 60 Del £120 **PARKING:** 175 **NOTES:** in restaurant Civ Wed 200 **CARDS:**

PENRITH, Cumbria Map 18 NY53

See also Shap & Temple Sowerby

★★★★72% North Lakes Hotel & Spa

Ullswater Rd CA11 8QT
☎ 01768 868111 01768 868291
e-mail: nlakes@shirehotels.co.uk
Dir: *M6 junct 40 at junct with A66*

With its great location, it is no wonder that this hotel enjoys a busy trade. Amenities include a good range of meeting and function rooms and excellent health and leisure facilities including full spa. Themed public areas have a contemporary Scandinavian country style and offer plenty of space and comfort.
ROOMS: 84 en suite (6 fmly) (22 GF) in 57 bedrooms s £108-£123; d £114-£134 (incl. bkfst) **LB** **FACILITIES: Spa** STV supervised Squash Sauna Solarium Gym Childrens pool, 5 Health & Beauty rooms, Steam room Xmas **CONF:** BC Thtr 200 Class 140 Board 24 Del £150 **SERVICES:** Lift **PARKING:** 150 **NOTES:** in restaurant Civ Wed 200 **CARDS:**

See advert under KESWICK

★★★77% Temple Sowerby House

CA10 1RZ
☎ 017683 61578 017683 61958
e-mail: stay@temple-sowerby.com
web: www.temple-sowerby.com
(For full entry see Temple Sowerby)

★★★72% Westmorland Hotel

Orton CA10 3SB
☎ 015396 24351 015396 24354
e-mail: sales@westmorlandhotel.com
web: www.westmorlandhotel.com
(For full entry see Tebay)

Town House Hotel
Country House Hotel
Travel Accommodation

★★★68% The George

Devonshire St CA11 7SU
☎ 01768 862696 01768 868223
e-mail: info@georgehotelpenrith.co.uk
web: www.georgehotelpenrith.co.uk
Dir: *M6 junct 40, 1m to town centre. From A6/A66 to Penrith*
Much of this long-established town centre hotel has been upgraded, including most of the well-equipped bedrooms. The spacious public areas retain their old-fashioned charm and include

continued on p460

PENRITH, continued

a choice of lounge areas, which are a popular venue for morning coffees and afternoon teas.

The George, Penrith

ROOMS: 32 en suite (3 fmly) ⊘ in 24 bedrooms s £49-£125; d £86-£170 (incl. bkfst) **LB** **FACILITIES:** STV Free use of local pool and gym ch fac Xmas **CONF:** Thtr 120 Class 60 Board 40 **PARKING:** 34 **NOTES:** ⊘ in restaurant Civ Wed 120 **CARDS:**

See advert on opposite page

★★70% Edenhall Country Hotel

Edenhall CA11 8SX
☎ 01768 881454 01768 881266
e-mail: info@edenhallhotel.co.uk
Dir: *take A686 from Penrith to Alston. Hotel signed on right in 3m*

Located in a peaceful hamlet yet convenient for the M6, this hotel is popular with business guests. Bedrooms and public areas are gradually being upgraded, with the comfortable lounge bar serving an attractive range of meals. Carefully prepared and well-presented dinners are served in the dining room that overlooks the well-tended gardens.

ROOMS: 17 en suite 8 annexe rms (7 en suite) (3 fmly) (7 GF) s £35-£50; d £65-£80 (incl. bkfst) **LB** **FACILITIES:** STV Jacuzzi Xmas **CONF:** Thtr 50 Class 30 Board 30 Del from £75 **PARKING:** 60 **NOTES:** ⊘ in restaurant Civ Wed 60 **CARDS:**

★★67% Brantwood Country Hotel

Stainton CA11 0EP
☎ 01768 862748 01768 890164
e-mail: brantwood2@aol.com
Dir: *M6 junct 40, A66. Left in 0.5m then right signed Stainton. Left at x-roads. On left*

Located in a peaceful village this family-run hotel enjoys an open outlook to the rear. The traditional bedrooms are individual and cheerful in colour; five rooms are in a converted courtyard building. Meals are served in both the bar and restaurant and there is a separate conservatory-style residents' lounge.

ROOMS: 7 en suite (3 fmly) ⊘ in 5 bedrooms s fr £45; d fr £66 (incl. bkfst) **LB** **FACILITIES:** Xmas **CONF:** Thtr 60 Class 30 Board 30 **PARKING:** 35 **NOTES:** ⊘ in restaurant **CARDS:**

Travelodge

Travelodge

Redhills CA11 0DT
☎ 08700 850 950 01768 866958
Dir: *on A66*

Travelodge offers good quality, good value, modern accommodation. Ideal for families, the spacious, en suite bedrooms include remote-control TV, tea and coffee-making facilities and luxury beds. Meals can be taken at the nearby family restaurant. For further details consult the Hotel Groups page.

ROOMS: 54 en suite s fr £25; d fr £25

PENSILVA, Cornwall & Isles of Scilly — Map 03 SX27

★★66% Wheal Tor Country Hotel

Caradon Hill PL14 5PJ
☎ 01579 362281 01579 363401
e-mail: enquiries@whealtorhotel.co.uk

Wheal Tor has splendid views over Bodmin Moor and is set well away from the road. The proprietors provide friendly hospitality. The hotel's 'Restaurant des Hauteurs' are proving increasingly popular with locals, offering attractive and accomplished cuisine.

ROOMS: 7 en suite (1 fmly) ⊘ in all bedrooms s £55-£72; d £65-£95 (incl. bkfst) **LB** **FACILITIES:** Xmas **CONF:** Del from £120 **PARKING:** 50 **NOTES:** ⊘ in restaurant **CARDS:**

PENZANCE, Cornwall & Isles of Scilly — Map 02 SW43

★★★76% Mount Prospect

THE CIRCLE
Selected Individual Hotels
GREAT BRITAIN

Britons Hill TR18 3AE
☎ 01736 363117 01736 350970
e-mail: enquiries@hotelpenzance.com
web: www.hotelpenzance.com
Dir: *from A30 pass heliport on right, left at next rdbt for town centre. 3rd right and hotel on right*

This Edwardian house has been tastefully redesigned, focusing on the contemporary Bay Restaurant. Style is not only limited to the rooms, but is also apparent in the cuisine based upon fresh Cornish produce. Bedrooms have also been appointed to modern standards and are particularly well-equipped; many rooms have views across Mounts Bay.

ROOMS: 24 en suite (2 fmly) (2 GF) ⊘ in 20 bedrooms s £58-£87.50; d £90-£125 (incl. bkfst) **LB** **FACILITIES:** STV ch fac Xmas **CONF:** Thtr 80 Class 50 Board 25 Del from £95 **PARKING:** 14 **NOTES:** ⊘ in restaurant RS Nov-Apr **CARDS:**

Indoor Swimming Pool
Indoor Swimming Pool (heated)
Outdoor Swimming Pool
Outdoor Swimming Pool (heated)

continued

★★★68% Queen's
The Promenade TR18 4HG
☎ 01736 362371 Fax 01736 350033
e-mail: enquiries@queens-hotel.com
web: www.queens-hotel.com
Dir: *A30 to Penzance, follow signs for seafront pass harbour and into promenade, hotel 0.5m on right*

With views across Mounts Bay towards Newlyn, this impressive Victorian hotel has a long and distinguished history. Comfortable public areas are filled with interesting pictures and artefacts, and in the dining room guests can choose from the daily-changing menu. Bedrooms, many with sea views, are of varying style and size.
ROOMS: 70 en suite (10 fmly) s £49-£69; d £94-£148 (incl. bkfst) **LB**
FACILITIES: STV Xmas **CONF:** Thtr 200 Class 100 Board 80
SERVICES: Lift **PARKING:** 50 **NOTES:** ⊗ in restaurant Civ Wed 180
CARDS:

See advert on this page

PETERBOROUGH, Cambridgeshire

Map 12 TL19

★★★★67% Peterborough Marriott

Peterborough Business Park, Lynchwood
PE2 6GB
☎ 01733 371111 🖷 01733 236725
e-mail: reservations.peterborough@marriotthotels.co.uk
Dir: *opposite East of England Showground. From A1 off at Alwalton Showground, Chesterton. Left at T-junct and hotel on left at next rdbt*

Just a few minutes' drive from the heart of the city, this modern hotel is located in the village of Alwalton, birthplace of Sir Frederick Henry Royce and the Rolls Royce motorcar. Air-conditioned bedrooms are spacious and well-designed for business use. Public rooms include the Garden Lounge, Cocktail Bar, Laurels Restaurant and leisure club.

ROOMS: 157 en suite (7 fmly) (68 GF) ⊗ in 119 bedrooms s £62-£97; d fr £97 **LB FACILITIES: Spa** STV Sauna Solarium Gym Putt green Jacuzzi Beauty therapist Hairdressing Xmas **CONF:** Thtr 300 Class 160 Board 45 Del from £135 **SERVICES:** air con **PARKING:** 175 **NOTES:** ⊗ in restaurant Civ Wed 80 **CARDS:**

★★★72% Bell Inn

Great North Rd PE7 3RA ☎ 01733 241066 🖷 01733 245173
e-mail: reception@thebellstilton.co.uk
(For full entry see Stilton)

★★★71% Bull

Westgate PE1 1RB
☎ 01733 561364 🖷 01733 557304
e-mail: info@bull-hotel-peterborough.com
Dir: *off A1, follow city centre signs. Hotel opp Queensgate shopping centre. Car park on Broadway next to Library*

This pleasant city-centre hotel offers well-equipped modern accommodation with new deluxe bedrooms, particularly well suited to corporate guests. Public rooms include a popular bar and a brasserie-style restaurant serving a flexible range of dishes, with further informal dining available in the lounge.

ROOMS: 118 en suite (3 fmly) ⊗ in 40 bedrooms **FACILITIES:** STV Xmas **CONF:** Thtr 200 Class 80 Board 60 Del from £12 **PARKING:** 100 **NOTES:** ⊗ in restaurant Civ Wed 200 **CARDS:**

★★★67% Orton Hall

Orton Longueville PE2 7DN
☎ 01733 391111 🖷 01733 231912
e-mail: reception@ortonhall.co.uk
Dir: *off A605 E opposite Orton Mere*

Set in 20 acres of woodland, this impressive country house has spacious and relaxing public areas. Original features include oak panelling in the Huntly Restaurant, in the Grand Hall, a popular banqueting venue, and 16th-century terracotta floors. The Ramblewood Inn, across a courtyard offers an alternative, informal dining option.

ROOMS: 65 en suite (2 fmly) (15 GF) ⊗ in 42 bedrooms
FACILITIES: STV Three quarter size snooker table **CONF:** Thtr 120 Class 48 Board 42 Del from £130 **PARKING:** 200 **NOTES:** ⊗ in restaurant Civ Wed 90 **CARDS:**

⌂ Sleep Inn Peterborough

Peterborough Services, Great North Rd, Haddon
PE7 3UQ ☎ 01733 396850 🖷 01733 396869
e-mail: enquiries@hotels-peterborough.co.uk
Dir: *At A1(M) J17 take A605 towards Northampton. Hotel 100mtrs*

This modern, purpose built accommodation offers smartly appointed, well-equipped bedrooms, with good power showers. There is a choice of adjacent food outlets where guests may enjoy breakfast, snacks and meals.

ROOMS: 82 en suite s £49-£60; d £53-£60

⌂ Travel Inn Peterborough (Ferry Meadows)

Ham Ln, Orton Meadows, Nene Park PE2 5UU
☎ 08701 977205 🖷 01733 391055
Dir: *From A1(M) S J16, A15 through Yaxley. Left at rdbt. From A1(M) N J17, A1139 J3 right to Yaxley. R at 2nd rdbt*

Travel Inn offers good-quality, value-for-money accommodation. Spacious, en suite rooms with bath and shower comfortably accommodate a family of up to two adults and two children (to age 15). The restaurant and bar offers a varied menu. For further details consult the Hotel Groups page.

ROOMS: 40 en suite s £45.95-£46.95; d £45.95-£46.95
CONF: Thtr 24 Board 24

⌂ Travel Inn Peterborough (Hampton)

4 Ashbourne Rd, Off London Rd, Hampton PE7 8BT
☎ 08701 977206 🖷 01733 391055
Dir: *S: A1(M) J16, A15 through Yaxley. Inn on left at 1st rdbt. N: A1(M) J17 A1139, 2nd exit J3 follow signs for Yaxley. Travel Inn on right.*

Travel Inn offers good-quality, value-for-money accommodation. Spacious, en suite rooms with bath and shower comfortably accommodate a family of up to two adults and two children (to age 15). The restaurant and bar offers a varied menu. For further details consult the Hotel Groups page.

ROOMS: 80 en suite s £45.95-£46.95; d £45.95-£46.95

⌂ Travelodge Alwalton

Great North Rd, Alwalton PE7 3UR
☎ 08700 850 950 🖷 01733 231109
Dir: *on A1, southbound*

Travelodge offers good quality, good value, modern accommodation. Ideal for families, the spacious, en suite bedrooms include remote-control TV, tea and coffee-making facilities and luxury beds. Meals can be taken at the nearby family restaurant. For further details consult the Hotel Groups page.

ROOMS: 32 en suite s fr £25; d fr £25

⌂ Travelodge Peterborough

Crowlands Rd PE6 7SZ
☎ 08700 850 950 🖷 01733 223199
Dir: *at junct of A47 & A1073*

Travelodge offers good quality, good value, modern accommodation. Ideal for families, the spacious, en suite bedrooms include remote-control TV, tea and coffee-making facilities and luxury beds. Meals can be taken at the nearby family restaurant. For further details consult the Hotel Groups page.

ROOMS: 42 en suite s fr £25; d fr £25

PETERLEE, Co Durham
Map 19 NZ44

★★69% Hardwicke Hall Manor
Hesleden TS27 4PA
☎ 01429 836326 📠 01429 837676
Dir: *NE on B1281, off A19 at sign for Durham and Blackhall*
This country mansion house nestles in pleasant gardens and is full of character, providing an ideal venue for secluded weddings or meetings. Bedrooms are all individual and each one is spacious, comfortable and very well equipped. Good value meals are presented in a variety of public areas.
ROOMS: 15 en suite (2 fmly) s £55-£65; d £65-£75 (incl. bkfst) **LB CONF:** Thtr 60 Board 20 **PARKING:** 100 **NOTES:** ⊗ in restaurant Civ Wed 100 **CARDS:**

PETERSFIELD, Hampshire
Map 05 SU72

★★69% Langrish House
Langrish GU32 1RN
☎ 01730 266941 📠 01730 260543
e-mail: frontdesk@langrishhouse.co.uk
web: www.langrishhouse.co.uk
Dir: *off A3 onto A272 towards Winchester. Hotel signed, 3m on left*
Located in a secluded spot just outside Petersfield, this family home dates back to the 17th century. Rooms offer good levels of comfort with beautiful views over the countryside. The public areas consist of a small cosy restaurant, a bar in the vaults, and conference and banqueting rooms that are popular for weddings.
ROOMS: 13 en suite (1 fmly) (3 GF) ⊗ in all bedrooms s £65.70-£73; d £104.40-£140 (incl. bkfst) **LB FACILITIES:** Fishing Xmas **CONF:** Thtr 60 Class 18 Board 25 Del £115 **PARKING:** 80 **NOTES:** ⊗ in restaurant Civ Wed 60 **CARDS:**

PICKERING, North Yorkshire
Map 19 SE78

★★★72% Forest & Vale
Best Western
Malton Rd YO18 7DL
☎ 01751 472722 📠 01751 472972
e-mail: forestvale@bestwestern.co.uk
web: www.bwforestandvalehotel.co.uk
Dir: *on A169 between York and Pickering at rdbt on outskirts of Pickering*

This lovely 18th-century hotel is an excellent base from which to explore the North Yorkshire Moors. A robust maintenance programme means that the hotel is particularly well kept, inside and out. Bedrooms vary in size and include some spacious 'superior' rooms, including one with a four-poster bed.
ROOMS: 13 en suite 5 annexe en suite (5 fmly) ⊗ in 6 bedrooms s £70-£90; d £96-£130 (incl. bkfst) **LB CONF:** Thtr 120 Class 50 Board 50 Del from £115 **PARKING:** 70 **NOTES:** ⊗ in restaurant Civ Wed 90 **CARDS:**

★★76% White Swan
Market Place YO18 7AA
☎ 01751 472288 📠 01751 475554
e-mail: welcome@white-swan.co.uk
web: www.white-swan.co.uk
Dir: *in Market Place between Church and Steam Railway Station*
This refurbished 16th-century coaching inn offers well-equipped, very comfortable bedrooms, including one suite. Service is friendly and attentive and the standard of cuisine high, in both the attractive restaurant and the cosy bars where log fires burn. A comprehensive wine list specialises in many fine vintages.
ROOMS: 12 en suite (3 fmly) ⊗ in all bedrooms s £80-£95; d £130-£180 (incl. bkfst) **LB FACILITIES:** Xmas **CONF:** Thtr 20 Class 14 Board 24 Del from £115 **PARKING:** 35 **NOTES:** ⊗ in restaurant **CARDS:**

Bad hair day?
Hairdryers in all rooms three stars and above

★★72% Fox & Hounds Country Inn
Main St, Sinnington YO62 6SQ
☎ 01751 431577 📠 01751 432791
e-mail: foxhoundsinn@easynet.co.uk
web: www.thefoxandhoundsinn.co.uk
Dir: *3m W of Pickering, off A170*
This attractive inn lies in the quiet village of Sinnington just off the main road. It offers attractive, well-equipped bedrooms together with a cosy residents' lounge. The restaurant provides a good

continued on p464

P

PICKERING, continued

selection of modern British dishes; there is also a good range of bar meals. Service throughout is friendly and attentive.

Fox & Hounds Country Inn, Pickering

ROOMS: 10 en suite (4 GF) ⊗ in all bedrooms s £49; d £80 (incl. bkfst) **LB** **PARKING:** 40 **NOTES:** ⊗ in restaurant
CARDS:

★★65% Old Manse

19 Middleton Rd YO18 8AL
☎ 01751 476484 🖷 01751 477124
e-mail: the_old_manse@btopenworld.com
Dir: *A169, left at rdbt. through lights, 1st right into Potter Hill. Follow road to left. From A170 left at 'local traffic only'*

A peacefully located house standing in mature grounds close to the town centre. It offers a combined dining room and lounge area and comfortable bedrooms that are also well equipped. Expect good hospitality from the resident owners.
ROOMS: 10 en suite (2 fmly) (2 GF) ⊗ in all bedrooms s £26-£30; d £52-£56 (incl. bkfst) **CONF:** Thtr 20 Class 12 Board 10 **PARKING:** 12
CARDS:

PICKHILL, North Yorkshire Map 19 SE38

★★70% Nags Head Country Inn

YO7 4JG
☎ 01845 567391 & 567570 🖷 01845 567212
e-mail: reservations@nagsheadpickhill.freeserve.co.uk
web: www.nagsheadpickhill.co.uk
Dir: *4m SE of Leeming Bar, 1.25m E of A1*

Convenient for the A1, this 200-year-old country inn offers superb hospitality, and an extensive range of food either in the bar or the attractive Library Restaurant. The bars offer an extensive range of handpicked wines and are full of character featuring country sport memorabilia in particular. Bedrooms are well-equipped with

continued

several having now been refurbished to a very high standard. Service is friendly.
ROOMS: 8 en suite 7 annexe en suite (1 fmly) s £45-£60; d fr £70 (incl. bkfst) **LB** **FACILITIES:** Putt green Quoits pitch **CONF:** Thtr 36 Class 18 Board 24 Del from £70 **PARKING:** 50 **NOTES:** ⊗ in restaurant
CARDS:

PINNER, Greater London
See LONDON SECTION plan 1 A5

★★69% Tudor Lodge

50 Field End Rd, Eastcote HA5 2QN
☎ 020 8429 0585 🖷 020 8429 0117
e-mail: tudorlodge@meridianleisure.com
web: www.meridianleisure.com
Dir: *off A40 at Swakeleys rdbt to Ickenham, onto A312 to Harrow. Left at Northholt Station to Eastcote*

This friendly hotel, set in its own grounds, is convenient for Heathrow Airport and the many local golf courses. Bedrooms vary in style and size but all are well equipped, with some suitable for families. A good range of bar snacks is offered as an alternative to the main restaurant.
ROOMS: 24 en suite 22 annexe en suite (9 fmly) (17 GF) ⊗ in 6 bedrooms s £65-£89; d £75-£94 (incl. bkfst) **LB** **FACILITIES:** STV Xmas **CONF:** Thtr 60 Class 20 Board 26 Del from £105 **PARKING:** 30 **NOTES:** ⊗ in restaurant **CARDS:**

See advert on opposite page

PLYMOUTH, Devon Map 03 SX45
See also St Mellion

★★★★63% Copthorne Hotel Plymouth

COPTHORNE

Armada Way PL1 1AR
☎ 01752 224161 🖷 01752 670688
e-mail: sales.plymouth@mill-cop.com
Dir: *from M5 follow A38 to Plymouth city centre. Follow ferryport signs over 3 rdbts. Hotel on 1st exit left before 4th rdbt*

Located right in the city centre, this hotel possesses plentiful

continued on p466

Discover Dartmoor and the historic City of Plymouth from the luxury of the Moorland Links Hotel. Superb views across the Tamar Valley this relaxing hotel offers comfort and service and is renowned locally for its excellent restaurant.

Yelverton,
near Plymouth,
South Devon
PL20 6DA

Tel: 01822 852245

AA ★★★

The Moorland Links
Hotel & Restaurant

TUDOR LODGE HOTEL

AA ★★

Meridian Leisure Hotels

50 Field End Road, Eastcote Pinner, Middx HA5 2QN
Tel: 020 8429 0585 Fax: 020 8429 0117
E-mail: tudorlodge@meridianleisure.com
www.meridianleisure.com

Brimming with old world character & set in two acres of landscaped gardens. The Tudor Lodge is ideally situated for visitors to London & nearby Heathrow. The hotel offers 46 fully refurbished bedrooms with satellite TV, blockbuster movies and all modern amenities. A perfect venue for weddings, conferences, anniversaries and celebrations.

Bed & Full English Breakfast daily from £55-£99.

Plymouth's largest independent hotel

- Traditional Victorian Hotel with modern facilities
- 99 individually decorated bedrooms
- Indoor leisure club
- Excellent Restaurant, Conference & Banqueting Facilities
- Free Coach & Car Parking

MILLBAY ROAD · PLYMOUTH · DEVON · PL1 3LD · Telephone: 01752 220782
Fax: 01752 227013 · Email: newconti@aol.com · Website: www.newcontinental.co.uk

PLYMOUTH, continued

conference facilities and parking. Suites, Connoisseur and Classic rooms are available; all are spacious and well-equipped. Public areas are spread over two floors and include Bentley's brasserie and bar and a small leisure centre with a pool and gym.
ROOMS: 135 en suite (29 fmly) in 93 bedrooms s £72-£135; d £72-£145 **LB** **FACILITIES:** STV supervised Gym Steam room ch fac Xmas **CONF:** Thtr 140 Class 60 Board 60 Del from £128 **SERVICES:** Lift **PARKING:** 50 **NOTES:** in restaurant Civ Wed 65
CARDS:

A ★★★★ Kitley House Hotel

Kitley Estate, Yealmpton PL8 2NW
☎ 01752 881555 01752 881667
e-mail: sales@kitleyhousehotel.com
web: www.kitleyhousehotel.com
Dir: *from Plymouth take A379 to Kingsbridge. Hotel on right after Brixton and before Yealmpton*
ROOMS: 19 en suite (9 fmly) (1 GF) in 12 bedrooms s £60-£99.50; d £75-£129 (incl. bkfst) **LB** **FACILITIES:** STV Fishing Beauty salon Xmas **CONF:** Thtr 70 Class 40 Board 35 Del from £94.50
PARKING: 100 **NOTES:** in restaurant
CARDS:

★★★70% Elfordleigh Hotel Golf Leisure

Colebrook, Plympton PL7 5EB
☎ 01752 336428 01752 344581
e-mail: reception@elfordleigh.co.uk
Dir: *Leave A38 at city centre exit, at Marsh Mills/Sainsbury's rdbt take Plympton road. At 4th lights left into Larkham Ln, at end right then left into Crossway. At end left into The Moors, hotel 1m*
Located in the beautiful Plym Valley, this well-established hotel is set in attractive wooded countryside. Bedrooms, many with lovely views, offer good levels of space and comfort, and there is an excellent range of leisure facilities including an 18-hole golf course. A choice of dining options is available, including the friendly brasserie or the more formal restaurant.
ROOMS: 34 en suite (2 fmly) (7 GF) s £79.50-£89.50; d £105-£115 (incl. bkfst) **LB** **FACILITIES: Spa** supervised 18 Fishing Squash Sauna Solarium Gym Putt green Jacuzzi Hairdresser, Beautician, Dance/Aerobics studio, 5 aside football pitch (hard) ch fac Xmas **CONF:** Thtr 200 Class 120 Board 50 Del £120 **SERVICES:** Lift **PARKING:** 200 **NOTES:** in restaurant Civ Wed 100
CARDS:

★★★69% New Continental

Millbay Rd PL1 3LD
☎ 01752 220782 01752 227013
e-mail: newconti@aol.com
web: www.newcontinental.co.uk
Dir: *A38, follow city centre signs for Continental Ferryport. Hotel before ferryport & next to Plymouth Pavilions Conference Centre*
Within easy reach of the city centre and The Hoe, this privately owned hotel continues to offer high standards of service and hospitality. A variety of bedroom sizes and styles are available, all with the same levels of equipment and comfort. The hotel is a popular choice for conferences and functions.
ROOMS: 99 en suite (20 fmly) in 28 bedrooms s £93-£98; d £103-£108 (incl. bkfst) **LB** **FACILITIES:** STV Sauna Solarium Gym Steam Room Beautician ch fac **CONF:** Thtr 400 Class 100 Board 70 Del from £115 **SERVICES:** Lift **PARKING:** 100 **NOTES:** Closed 24 Dec-2 Jan Civ Wed 110 **CARDS:**

See advert on page 465

★★★68% Duke of Cornwall

Best Western

Millbay Rd PL1 3LG
☎ 01752 275850 01752 275854
e-mail: duke@Bhere.co.uk
web: www.Bhere.co.uk
Dir: *follow city centre, then Plymouth Pavilions Conference & Leisure Centre signs past hotel*

An historic landmark, this city centre hotel is conveniently located. The spacious public areas include a popular bar, comfortable lounge and multi functional ballroom. Bedrooms, many with far reaching views, are individually styled and comfortably appointed. A range of dining options include bar meals, or the more formal atmosphere in the elegant dining room.
ROOMS: 71 en suite (6 fmly) in 20 bedrooms **CONF:** Thtr 300 Class 125 Board 84 **SERVICES:** Lift **PARKING:** 50 **NOTES:** in restaurant Civ Wed 120 **CARDS:**

★★★68% Invicta

11-12 Osborne Place, Lockyer St, The Hoe PL1 2PU
☎ 01752 664997 01752 664994
e-mail: info@invictahotel.co.uk
Dir: *A38 to Plymouth, follow city centre signs, then Hoe Park signs. Hotel opposite park entrance*
Just a short stroll from the city centre, this elegant Victorian establishment stands opposite the famous bowling green. The atmosphere is relaxed and friendly and bedrooms are neatly presented, well equipped and attractively decorated. Dining options include bar meals or the more formal setting of the dining room.
ROOMS: 23 en suite (6 fmly) **FACILITIES:** Xmas **CONF:** Board 45
PARKING: 14 **NOTES:** in restaurant
CARDS:

★★★65% Novotel Plymouth

NOVOTEL

Marsh Mills PL6 8NH
☎ 01752 221422 01752 223922
e-mail: H0508@accor-hotels.com
Dir: *Exit A38 at Marsh Mills, follow Plympton signs, hotel on left*
Conveniently located on the outskirts of the city, close to Marsh Mills roundabout, this modern hotel offers good value accommodation. All rooms are spacious and designed with flexibility for family use. Public areas are open-plan with meals available throughout the day in either the Garden Brasserie, the bar, or from room service.
ROOMS: 100 en suite (17 fmly) (18 GF) in 80 bedrooms s £50-£70; d £50-£85 **LB** **FACILITIES:** STV Xmas **CONF:** Thtr 300 Class 120 Board 100 Del £90 **SERVICES:** Lift **PARKING:** 140
CARDS:

★★71% Victoria Court
62/64 North Rd East PL4 6AL
☎ 01752 668133 📠 01752 668133
e-mail: victoria.court@btinternet.com
Dir: *from A38 follow city centre signs, past railway station. Follow North Road E for 200yds and hotel on left*
Situated within walking distance of the city centre and railway station, this long-established, family-run hotel offers impeccably presented accommodation. The public areas retain the Victorian character of the building and include a comfortable lounge, bar and dining area. The attractively decorated bedrooms are well maintained with modern facilities.
ROOMS: 13 en suite (4 fmly) s £39-£45; d £58-£65 (incl. bkfst) **LB**
PARKING: 6 **NOTES:** ✗ ⊘ in restaurant Closed 22 Dec-1 Jan
CARDS:

★★69% *Langdon Court*
Down Thomas PL9 0DY
☎ 01752 862358 📠 01752 863428
e-mail: enquiries@langdoncourt.co.uk
Dir: *follow HMS Cambridge signs from Elburton and tourist signs on A379*

This magnificent Grade II listed Tudor manor, set in seven acres of lush countryside, has a direct path leading to the beach at Wembury and coastal footpaths. Bedrooms all enjoy countryside views while public areas include a stylishly updated bar and brasserie restaurant, where the contemporary menu incorporates local produce with excellent seafood.
ROOMS: 18 en suite (4 fmly) ⊘ in 5 bedrooms **CONF:** Thtr 60 Board 20 **PARKING:** 100 **NOTES:** ⊘ in restaurant Closed 25 & 26 Dec Civ Wed 75 **CARDS:**

★★67% Drake
1 & 2 Windsor Villas, Lockyer St, The Hoe PL1 2QD
THE CIRCLE Selected Individual Hotels GREAT BRITAIN
☎ 01752 229730 📠 01752 255092
e-mail: reception@drakehotel.net
Dir: *follow city centre signs, left at Theatre Royal, last left and 1st right*

Handily placed for access to the city centre and the historic Hoe, this popular hotel was originally two adjoining Victorian houses. Bedrooms are neatly presented, and public areas include a lounge, bar and elegant dining room. The convenient location makes this an ideal choice for business and leisure guests alike.
ROOMS: 35 rms (3 fmly) s fr £48; d fr £58 (incl. bkfst) **LB**
PARKING: 26 **NOTES:** ✗ ⊘ in restaurant Closed 24 Dec-3 Jan
CARDS:

★★63% The Moorland
Wotter, Shaugh Prior PL7 5HP
☎ 01752 839228 📠 01752 839153
e-mail: reservations@moorlandhotel.com
Dir: *Take Lee Mill exit from A38. Through underpass turn right then left, follow road 6 miles through Cornwood and onto Wotter.*

Situated on the southern slopes of the Dartmoor National Park, this family-run hotel offers a warm welcome to visitors. Bedrooms are soundly appointed and all have pleasant views. The convivial bar is popular with both visitors and locals; the atmosphere always good-natured and entertaining. A range of menus is available in either the bar or attractive restaurant.
ROOMS: 18 en suite (2 fmly) ⊘ in 4 bedrooms s £32.30-£47.50; d £51-£60 (incl. bkfst) **LB** **FACILITIES:** Games room, secure field available for guests' horses. **CONF:** BC Thtr 70 Class 22 Board 30 Del from £60.50 **PARKING:** 40 **NOTES:** ⊘ in restaurant
CARDS:

★★61% Camelot
5 Elliot St, The Hoe PL1 2PP
☎ 01752 221255 & 669667 📠 01752 603660
e-mail: camelot@hotelplymouth.fsnet.co.uk
Dir: *from A38 follow city centre signs, then signs to The Hoe. Into Citadel Road, then onto Elliot Street*
Just a short walk from The Hoe, the Barbican and the city centre, this is a convenient choice for visitors to this historic naval city. The friendly, small hotel provides comfortable accommodation, with bedrooms varying in size and style. The convivial bar is a popular meeting point and additional facilities include a TV lounge and function room.
ROOMS: 18 en suite (5 fmly) ⊘ in 3 bedrooms s £43; d £55 (incl. bkfst) **NOTES:** ✗ ⊘ in restaurant
CARDS:

★62% Grosvenor Park
114-116 North Rd East PL4 6AH
☎ 01752 229312 📠 01752 252777
e-mail: gphotel@grosvenorparkhotel.co.uk
Dir: *turn off A380 onto A374, follow directions to railway station. Hotel is on next corner past the station road*
Conveniently located for the railway station and the city centre, this small hotel provides friendly and attentive service. Facilities include a small bar and a comfortable lounge. Dinner is availabe

continued on p468

P

PLYMOUTH, continued

for groups only, however a range of snacks is served in the lounge or bar. Traditional breakfasts provide a satisfying start to the day.
ROOMS: 15 rms (10 en suite) (1 GF) in all bedrooms s £22-£35; d £44-£50 (incl. bkfst) **PARKING:** 6 **NOTES:** No children 2yrs in restaurant Closed 19 Dec-5 Jan **CARDS:**

Hotel Ibis
Marsh Mills, Longbridge Rd, Forder Valley PL6 8LD
☎ 01752 601087 01752 223213
e-mail: H2093@accor-hotels.com
Dir: *A38 to Plymouth, 1st exit after flyover towards Estover, Leigham and Parkway Industrial Est. At rdbt, hotel on 4th exit*
Modern, budget hotel offering comfortable accommodation in bright and practical bedrooms. Breakfast is self-service and dinner is available in the restaurant. For further details, consult the Hotel Groups page.
ROOMS: 52 en suite

Travel Inn (Plymouth Centre)
Lockyers Quay, Coxside PL4 0DX
☎ 08701 977207 01752 663872
Dir: *A38 Marsh Mills rdbt then A374 into Plymouth. Follow signs for Coxside & National Marine Aquarium*
Travel Inn offers good-quality, value-for-money accommodation. Spacious, en suite rooms with bath and shower comfortably accommodate a family of up to two adults and two children (to age 15). The restaurant and bar offers a varied menu. For further details consult the Hotel Groups page.
ROOMS: 60 en suite s £54.95; d £54.95 **CONF:** Thtr 25 Board 20

Travel Inn (Plymouth East)
300 Plymouth Rd, Crabtree, Marsh Mills PL3 6RW
☎ 08701 977208 01752 600112
Dir: *From E: Exit A38 Marsh Mill junction. Straight across rbt, exit slip road 100mtrs on left. From W: Plympton junction A38, at rbt exit slip road next to A38 Liskeard*
Travel Inn offers good-quality, value-for-money accommodation. Spacious, en suite rooms with bath and shower comfortably accommodate a family of up to two adults and two children (to age 15). The restaurant and bar offers a varied menu. For further details consult the Hotel Groups page.
ROOMS: 40 en suite s £45.95-£46.95; d £45.95-£46.95
CONF: Thtr 50 Board 30

Travelodge
Derry's Cross PL1 2SW
☎ 08700 850 950
Travelodge offers good quality, good value, modern accommodation. Ideal for families, the spacious, en suite bedrooms include remote-control TV, tea and coffee-making facilities and luxury beds. Meals can be taken at the nearby family restaurant. For further details consult the Hotel Groups page.
ROOMS: 96 en suite s fr £25; d fr £25

POCKLINGTON, East Riding of Yorkshire — Map 17 SE84

★★63% Feathers
56 Market Place YO42 2AH
☎ 01759 303155 01759 304382
e-mail: info@thefeathers-hotel.co.uk
Dir: *from York, B1246 signed Pocklington. Hotel just off A1079*
This is busy, traditional inn has been sympathetically modernised to provide comfortable, well-equipped and spacious accommodation. Public areas are smartly presented and enjoyable meals are served in the bar and the conservatory restaurant. A wide choice of dishes makes excellent use of local and seasonal produce.
ROOMS: 6 en suite 6 annexe en suite (1 fmly) **CONF:** Thtr 20 Class 8 Board 12 **PARKING:** 46 **NOTES:**
CARDS:

PODIMORE, Somerset — Map 04 ST52

Travelodge Yeovil
BA22 8JG
☎ 08700 850 950 01935 840074
Dir: *on A303, near junct with A37*
Travelodge offers good quality, good value, modern accommodation. Ideal for families, the spacious, en suite bedrooms include remote-control TV, tea and coffee-making facilities and luxury beds. Meals can be taken at the nearby family restaurant. For further details consult the Hotel Groups page.
ROOMS: 41 en suite s fr £25; d fr £25

POLPERRO, Cornwall & Isles of Scilly — Map 02 SX25

★★★76% Talland Bay
PL13 2JB
☎ 01503 272667 01503 272940
e-mail: reception@tallandbayhotel.co.uk
web: www.tallandbayhotel.co.uk
Dir: *signed from x-rds on A387 Looe to Polperro road*
Midway between Looe and Polperro, this hotel overlooks the bay and has extensive gardens. The atmosphere is warm and friendly and staff are helpful. Quality and comfort is apparent in the bedrooms, with many different styles available; some rooms have sea views. After a day's exploration, the kitchen can be relied upon to provide good local Cornish fare.
ROOMS: 20 en suite 3 annexe en suite (4 fmly) (6 GF) in 3 bedrooms s £80-£170; d £90-£180 (incl. bkfst) **LB FACILITIES:** STV Putt green Xmas **PARKING:** 23 **NOTES:** in restaurant
CARDS:

POLZEATH, Cornwall & Isles of Scilly — Map 02 SW97

A ★★ Seascape
Dunder Hill PL27 6SX
☎ 01208 863638 01208 862940
e-mail: information@seascapehotel.co.uk
web: www.seascapehotel.co.uk
Dir: *M5 from Exeter/A30 towards Launceston. Onto A395 & A39. From A39 take B3314 to Polzeath & follow signs to hotel*
ROOMS: 12 en suite 3 annexe en suite (9 GF) in 2 bedrooms s £44-£110; d £68-£110 (incl. bkfst) **FACILITIES:** Xmas **CONF:** BC **PARKING:** 20 **NOTES:** No children 12yrs in restaurant Closed Nov-Feb **CARDS:**

PONTEFRACT, West Yorkshire — Map 16 SE42

★★★74% Wentbridge House
Wentbridge WF8 3JJ
☎ 01977 620444 01977 620148
e-mail: info@wentbridgehouse.co.uk
web: www.wentbridgehouse.co.uk
Dir: *0.5m off A1 & 4m S of M62 junct 33 onto A1 south*
This well-established hotel sits in 20 acres of landscaped gardens, offering spacious, well-equipped bedrooms and a choice of dining styles. Service in the Fleur de Lys restaurant is polished and

continued

friendly, and a varied menu offers a good choice of interesting dishes. The Brasserie offers a more relaxed style of dining.

ROOMS: 14 en suite 4 annexe en suite (4 GF) s £75-£110; d £95-£140 (incl. bkfst) **LB** **FACILITIES:** ch fac **CONF:** Thtr 130 Class 100 Board 60 Del from £96 **PARKING:** 100 **NOTES:** Closed 25 Dec-evening only Civ Wed 130 **CARDS:**

★★★65% Rogerthorpe Manor Hotel

Thorpe Ln, Badsworth WF9 1AB
☎ 01977 643839 01977 641571
e-mail: ops@rogerthorpemanor.co.uk
web: www.rogerthorpemanor.co.uk

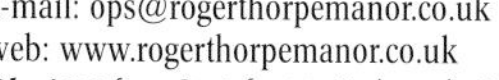

Dir: *A639 from Pontefract to Badsworth. Follow B6474 through Thorpe Audlin, hotel on left at end of Thorpe Audlin village*

This Jacobean manor house is situated in extensive grounds and lovely gardens in a delightful rural setting, with easy access to road networks. Bedrooms vary between those in the old house with their inherent charm, and the more modern rooms in new extensions. The range of function rooms available is popular for parties and conferences.

ROOMS: 23 en suite (3 fmly) ⊘ in 8 bedrooms s £65-£75; d £75-£120 (incl. bkfst) **FACILITIES:** STV Xmas **CONF:** BC Thtr 200 Class 150 Board 50 Del £124.95 **SERVICES:** air con **PARKING:** 90 **NOTES:** ⊘ in restaurant Civ Wed 300 **CARDS:**

Travel Inn

Pontefract Rd, Knottingley WF11 0BU
☎ 08701 977209 01977 607954

Dir: *From M62 (J33) onto A1 North. Take next junction (A645) Pontefract. Follow road to T-junct, right towards Pontefract. Travel Inn on right*

Travel Inn offers good-quality, value-for-money accommodation. Spacious, en suite rooms with bath and shower comfortably accommodate a family of up to two adults and two children (to age 15). The restaurant and bar offers a varied menu. For further details consult the Hotel Groups page.

ROOMS: 40 en suite s £45.95-£46.95; d £45.95-£46.95

POOLE, Dorset — Map 04 SZ09

★★★★76% Haven

Banks Rd, Sandbanks BH13 7QL
☎ 01202 707333 01202 708796
e-mail: reservations@havenhotel.co.uk
web: www.havenhotel.co.uk

Dir: *B3965 towards Poole Bay, left onto the Peninsula. Hotel 1.5m on left next to Swanage Toll Ferry point*

Enjoying an enviable location at the water's edge with views of Poole Bay, this well established hotel was also the site for the

continued

world's first wireless transmission. A friendly team of staff provide good levels of customer care through the range of stylish and comfortable lounge and bar areas. Bedrooms vary in size and style; many have balconies and wonderful sea views. Leisure facilities are noteworthy.

ROOMS: 78 en suite (4 fmly) s £90-£190; d £180-£350 (incl. bkfst) **LB** **FACILITIES:** **Spa** STV Sauna Solarium Gym Jacuzzi Steam room, Hair salon, Health & Beauty suite ch fac Xmas **CONF:** BC Thtr 160 Class 70 Board 50 Del from £145 **SERVICES:** Lift **PARKING:** 160 **NOTES:** ⊘ in restaurant Civ Wed 100
CARDS:

★★★★70% Harbour Heights

73 Haven Rd, Sandbanks BH13 7PS
☎ 01202 707272 01202 708594
e-mail: enquiries@harbourheights.net
web: www.fjbhotels.co.uk

Dir: *Follow signs for Sandbanks, hotel on left after Canford Cliffs*

The unassuming appearance of this hotel belies a wealth of innovation, quality and style. Following a four million pound refit, contemporary bedrooms now combine state-of-the-art facilities with traditional comforts. Throughout the smart public areas, which include a choice of dining options, popular bars and sitting areas, picture windows accentuate panoramic views of Poole Harbour. The sun deck, elevated above terraced gardens, is the perfect setting for watching the cross channel ferries come and go.

ROOMS: 38 en suite (2 fmly) ⊘ in all bedrooms s £105-£175; d fr £210 (incl. bkfst) **FACILITIES:** STV Spa bath in all rooms Xmas **CONF:** BC Thtr 70 Class 36 Board 22 Del from £145 **SERVICES:** Lift air con **PARKING:** 50 **NOTES:** ⊘ in restaurant Civ Wed 120
CARDS:

> Packed in a hurry?
> Ironing facilities should be available at all star levels, either in rooms or on request

POOLE, continued

Top 200 – Hotel

★★★ Mansion House

Thames St BH15 1JN
☎ 01202 685666 📠 01202 665709
e-mail: enquiries@themansionhouse.co.uk
web: www.themansionhouse.co.uk

Dir: *A31 to Poole, follow channel ferry signs. Left at Poole bridge onto Poole Quay, 1st left into Thames St. Hotel opposite St James Church*

This sophisticated hotel offers friendly hospitality and award-winning cuisine, equalled only by its relaxing charm and elegance. The comfortably furnished bedrooms are very well equipped with many thoughtful touches. Ideal for business or pleasure, the Mansion House is tucked away off the Old Quay, with the added bonus of parking.

ROOMS: 32 en suite (2 fmly) (2 GF) in 12 bedrooms s £75-£95; d £120-£140 (incl. bkfst) **LB** **FACILITIES:** STV facilities available locally Watersports, use of local fitness club ch fac Xmas **CONF:** Thtr 40 Class 18 Board 20 Del from £135 **PARKING:** 46 **NOTES:** in restaurant Civ Wed 35 **CARDS:**

★★★75% Sandbanks

15 Banks Rd, Sandbanks BH13 7PS
☎ 01202 707377 📠 01202 708885
e-mail: reservations@sandbankshotel.co.uk
web: www.sandbankshotel.co.uk

Dir: *A338 from Bournemouth onto Wessex Way, to Liverpool Victoria rdbt. Left and take 2nd exit onto B3965. Hotel on left*

Set on the delightful Sandbanks Peninsula, this large and popular hotel has direct access to a blue flag beach and stunning views across Poole Harbour. Most of the spacious bedrooms have sea views, and there is an extensive range of leisure facilities, which now include a state-of-the-art créche.

ROOMS: 110 en suite (31 fmly) (4 GF) in 40 bedrooms s £70-£128; d £140-£256 (incl. bkfst & dinner) **LB** **FACILITIES:** STV supervised Sauna Solarium Gym Jacuzzi Sailing, Mntn bikes, kids play area, massage room ♫ ch fac Xmas **CONF:** BC Thtr 150 Class 40 Board 25 Del from £115 **SERVICES:** Lift **PARKING:** 120 **NOTES:** in restaurant **CARDS:**

★★★65% Arndale Court

62/66 Wimborne Rd BH15 2BY
☎ 01202 683746 📠 01202 668838
e-mail: info@arndalecourthotel.com
web: www.arndalecourthotel.com

Dir: *on A349 close to town centre, opp Poole Stadium*

Ideally situated for the town centre and ferry terminal, this small, privately-owned hotel has now been extensively refurbished. Bedrooms are well equipped, pleasantly spacious and comfortable. Particularly well suited to business guests, the Arndale Court has a pleasant range of stylish public areas and good parking.

ROOMS: 39 en suite (7 fmly) (14 GF) in 12 bedrooms s £67; d £80-£100 (incl. bkfst) **FACILITIES:** STV **CONF:** Thtr 50 Class 35 Board 35 Del £80 **PARKING:** 40 **NOTES:** in restaurant **CARDS:**

★★★64% Salterns Harbourside

38 Salterns Way, Lilliput BH14 8JR
☎ 01202 707321 📠 01202 707488
e-mail: reception@salterns.co.uk
web: www.salternsharbourside.com

Dir: *in Poole follow B3369 Sandbanks road. 1m at Lilliput shops turn into Salterns Way by Barclays Bank*

Located next to the marina with superb views across to Brownsea Island, this modernised hotel used to be the headquarters for the flying boats in WW2 and was later a yacht club. Bedrooms are spacious and some have private balconies, whilst the busy bar and restaurant both share harbour views.

ROOMS: 20 en suite (4 fmly) in 3 bedrooms s £70-£110; d £80-£130 (incl. bkfst) **LB** **FACILITIES:** Xmas **CONF:** Thtr 100 Class 50 Board 50 Del from £130 **PARKING:** 80 **NOTES:** in restaurant Civ Wed 120 **CARDS:**

★★62% Norfolk Lodge

1 Flaghead Rd, Canford Cliffs BH13 7JL
☎ 01202 708614 📠 01202 708661
e-mail: allnmartin@aol.com

Dir: *between Poole and Bournemouth. Hotel on corner of Haven and Flaghead Rd*

This small, family-run hotel provides friendly and comfortable accommodation. Norfolk Lodge is convenient for the town and harbour, and only a few minutes' walk from the beaches.

continued

Bedrooms are well equipped and pleasantly spacious. The public areas offer choices of dining areas, with the dining room overlooking the attractive gardens.
ROOMS: 17 en suite (4 fmly) s £45-£55; d £58-£70 (incl. bkfst) **LB** **FACILITIES:** ch fac **PARKING:** 16 **NOTES:** ⊗ in restaurant
CARDS:

Premier Lodge (Poole)

Cabot Ln BH17 7DA
☎ 0870 9906332 0870 6606333
web: www.premierlodge.com
Dir: *from M27 onto A31 towards Bournemouth. Follow signs for Poole/Channel Ferries and at Darby's Corner rbt take 2nd exit. At 2nd set of lights turn right into Cabot Ln for hotel on right*
High quality, modern, budget accommodation, ideal for families and business travellers. All rooms feature bath, power shower and satellite TV, and most have telephones / modem points. The adjacent bar and restaurant offers a wide and varied menu.
ROOMS: 126 en suite s £52; d £52

Travel Inn

Holes Bay Rd BH15 2BD
☎ 08701 977210 01202 661497
Dir: *follow Poole Channel Ferry signs, hotel S of A35/A349 on A350 dual carriageway*
Travel Inn offers good-quality, value-for-money accommodation. Spacious, en suite rooms with bath and shower comfortably accommodate a family of up to two adults and two children (to age 15). The restaurant and bar offers a varied menu. For further details consult the Hotel Groups page.
ROOMS: 62 en suite s £54.95; d £54.95

PORLOCK, Somerset — Map 03 SS84

Top 200 – Hotel

★★ The Oaks

TA24 8ES
☎ 01643 862265 01643 863131
e-mail: info@oakshotel.co.uk
A relaxing atmosphere can be found at this charming Edwardian house, located near to the setting of *Lorna Doone*. Quietly located and set in attractive grounds, the hotel enjoys elevated views across the village towards the sea. Bedrooms are thoughtfully furnished and comfortable, and the public rooms include a charming bar and a peaceful drawing room. In the dining room, guests can choose from the daily changing menu, which features fresh, quality local produce.
ROOMS: 8 en suite ⊗ in all bedrooms s fr £100; d £160 (incl. bkfst & dinner) **LB** **FACILITIES:** Xmas **PARKING:** 12 **NOTES:** No children 8yrs ⊗ in restaurant Closed Nov-Mar (excl. Xmas & New Year) **CARDS:**

Restaurant with Rooms

Andrews on the Weir

Porlock Weir TA24 8PB
☎ 01643 863300 01643 863311
e-mail: information@andrewsontheweir.co.uk
web: www.andrewsontheweir.co.uk
Dir: *A39 from Minehead to Porlock, through village, 1st right signed Harbour (Porlock Weir) for 1.5m*

Enjoying a delightful location overlooking Porlock Bay, Andrews on the Weir is decorated in country-house style. Bedrooms are spacious and comfortable; one has a four-poster bed. During colder months, a log fire creates a cosy atmosphere in the sitting room/bar. There is a choice of imaginative, innovative dishes available in the award-winning restaurant - Andrew Dixon is an accomplished chef.
ROOMS: 5 en suite ⊗ in all bedrooms s £65-£100; d £75-£120 (incl. bkfst) **LB** **FACILITIES:** Xmas **PARKING:** 6 **NOTES:** No children 12yrs ⊗ in restaurant Closed Jan & Mon RS Sun night & Tue lunch
CARDS:

PORT GAVERNE, Cornwall & Isles of Scilly — Map 02 SX08

★★68% Port Gaverne

PL29 3SQ
☎ 01208 880244 01208 880151
e-mail: pghotel@telinco.co.uk
Dir: *signed from B3314*
In a quiet seaside port half a mile from the old fishing village of Port Isaac, this hotel has a romantic feel, retaining its flagstone floors, beamed ceilings and steep stairways. Bedrooms are available in a range of sizes. Local produce often features on the hotel menus, which include bar meals.
ROOMS: 14 en suite (4 fmly) s £37.50-£47.50; d £75-£90 (incl. bkfst) **LB** **FACILITIES:** ch fac **PARKING:** 30 **NOTES:** ⊗ in restaurant Closed 5 Jan-11 Feb **CARDS:**

PORTISHEAD, Somerset — Map 04 ST47

Travel Inn

Wyndham Way BS20 7GA
☎ 08701 977212 01275 846534
Dir: *From M5 (J19) follow A369 towards Portishead. Over first rbt and Inn is on next rbt, 0.25m from centre of Portsihead.*
Travel Inn offers good-quality, value-for-money accommodation. Spacious, en suite rooms with bath and shower comfortably accommodate a family of up to two adults and two children (to age 15). The restaurant and bar offers a varied menu. For further details consult the Hotel Groups page.
ROOMS: 40 en suite s £45.95-£46.95; d £45.95-£46.95

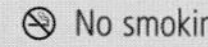

⊗ No smoking

PORTLOE, Cornwall & Isles of Scilly Map 02 SW93

★★★74% The Lugger

TR2 5RD
☎ 01872 501322 01872 501691
e-mail: office@luggerhotel.com
Dir: *M5/A30 or A38; turn off A390 St. Austell/Truro to Tregony B3287. A3078 St Mawes; 2m left Veryan; left Portloe.*

This delightful hotel has reopened its doors after a smart, stylish refurbishment. The hotel enjoys a superb location adjacent to the slipway of the harbour. Bedrooms are appealing and well equipped, while day rooms include a comfortable lounge and a contemporary-style restaurant that enjoys superb views. In warmer months a sun terrace overlooking the harbour proves a popular place to linger.

ROOMS: d £200-£310 (incl. bkfst & dinner) **LB** **FACILITIES:** STV Beauty treatments Xmas **PARKING:** 21 **NOTES:** No children 12 yrs in restaurant **CARDS:**

PORTSCATHO, Cornwall & Isles of Scilly Map 02 SW83

Top 200 – Hotel

★★★ Rosevine

TR2 5EW
☎ 01872 580206 01872 580230
e-mail: info@rosevinehotels.co.uk
web: www.rosevine.co.uk
Dir: *from St Austell take A390 for Truro. Left onto B3287 to Tregony. Take A3078 through Ruan High Lanes. Hotel 3rd left*

Set in secluded splendour, with views over beautifully tended gardens towards the sea, this Georgian country house has its own beach at the head of the Roseland peninsula. The proprietors and staff are attentive and friendly and create a relaxed atmosphere. Bedrooms are impressively equipped, with fresh fruit, flowers and up-to-date reading material - most enjoy the views and some have balconies. Cuisine features the local harvest of fresh fish and shellfish and the best of Cornish produce.

ROOMS: 11 en suite 6 annexe en suite (7 fmly) (3 GF) s £126-£178; d £168-£224 (incl. bkfst) **LB** **FACILITIES:** Table tennis Childrens playroom ch fac **PARKING:** 20 **NOTES:** in restaurant Closed Dec-8 Feb **CARDS:**

★★72% Driftwood

Rosevine TR2 5EW
☎ 01872 580644 01872 580801
e-mail: info@driftwoodhotel.co.uk

Perched overlooking Gerrans Bay, Driftwood is one of the new 'chic' Cornish hotels; contemporary in design and with a comfortably, relaxed and friendly atmosphere. The kitchen is at the heart of this hotel, producing a very short, simple evening menu of well conceived dishes, and at breakfast using the very best of local produce. Bedrooms are exceptionally well equipped; for those who want to get away from it all, book the cabin - even closer to the sea!

ROOMS: 10 en suite 1 annexe en suite (3 fmly) (1 GF) in all bedrooms s £112-£142; d £150-£190 (incl. bkfst) **FACILITIES:** Private Beach ch fac **PARKING:** 30 **NOTES:** in restaurant Closed 3-31Jan **CARDS:**

PORTSMOUTH, Hampshire Map 05 SU60

★★★★65% Portsmouth Marriott Hotel

Marriott HOTELS·RESORTS·SUITES

Southampton Rd PO6 4SH
☎ 0870 400 7285 0870 400 7385
e-mail: reservations.portsmouth@marriotthotels.com
Dir: *M27 junct 12 keep left and hotel on left*

Close to the motorway and ferry port, this hotel is well suited to business trade. The comfortable and well laid-out bedrooms provide a comprehensive range of facilities including up-to-date workstations. The leisure club offers a pool, a gym, and a health and beauty salon.

ROOMS: 174 en suite (77 fmly) in 130 bedrooms s £67-£155; d £84-£185 **FACILITIES:** STV supervised Sauna Solarium Gym Jacuzzi Exercise studio, Beauty salon Xmas **CONF:** Thtr 350 Class 180 Board 30 Del from £140 **SERVICES:** Lift air con **PARKING:** 250 **NOTES:** Civ Wed 100 **CARDS:**

★★★70% Royal Beach

South Pde, Southsea PO4 0RN
☎ 023 9273 1281 023 9281 7572
e-mail: enquiries@royalbeachhotel.co.uk
web: www.royalbeachhotel.co.uk
Dir: *M27 to M275, follow signs to seafront. Hotel on seafront*

A recent and ongoing refurbishment has transformed this former Victorian seafront hotel into a smart and comfortable venue suitable for leisure and business guests alike. Bedrooms are well-presented and generally spacious and there is an indoor golf simulator for those wishing to take some exercise after dinner!

ROOMS: 124 en suite (18 fmly) in 72 bedrooms s £75-£95; d £90-£105 (incl. bkfst) **LB** **FACILITIES:** STV Xmas **CONF:** Thtr 280 Class 180 Board 40 Del from £89.50 **SERVICES:** Lift **PARKING:** 50 **NOTES:** in restaurant **CARDS:**

★★★69% Westfield Hall

65 Festing Rd, Southsea PO4 0NQ
☎ 023 9282 6971 023 9287 0200
e-mail: enquirys@whhotel.info
Dir: *follow seafront signs, left at South Parade Pier then 3rd left*

This hotel is situated in a quiet side road close to the seafront and town centre. The accommodation is split between two identical houses; all rooms are smartly appointed and well-equipped. Public

continued

rooms are attractively decorated and include three lounges, a bar and a restaurant.
ROOMS: 15 en suite 11 annexe en suite (5 fmly) (6 GF) ⊘ in 18 bedrooms s £50-£58; d £65-£90 (incl. bkfst) **LB** **FACILITIES:** STV **PARKING:** 18 **NOTES:** ⊘ in restaurant
CARDS:

★★★67% Queen's Hotel

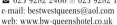

Clarence Pde, Southsea PO5 3LJ
☎ 023 9282 2466 023 9282 1901
e-mail: bestwestqueens@aol.com
web: www.bw-queenshotel.co.uk
Dir: *M27 junct 12 onto M275. Follow Southsea seafront signs. Hotel opposite hovercraft terminal*

This elegant Edwardian hotel has dominated the Southsea seafront for over 100 years and enjoys magnificent views. Bedrooms vary in size and style; there is a choice of room categories from family rooms to single rooms, and all are traditionally furnished and decorated. Public areas include a restaurant, garden, pool, and two comfortable bars.
ROOMS: 74 en suite (4 fmly) ⊘ in 43 bedrooms s £50-£140; d £88.50-£150 (incl. bkfst) **LB** **FACILITIES:** STV Private garden **CONF:** Thtr 150 Class 70 Board 50 Del from £100 **SERVICES:** Lift **PARKING:** 70 **NOTES:** **CARDS:**

★★73% The Beaufort

71 Festing Rd, Southsea PO4 0NQ
☎ 023 9282 3707 023 9287 0270
e-mail: enq@beauforthotel.co.uk
Dir: *follow seafront signs. Left at South Parade Pier, then 4th on left*
A warm welcome is guaranteed at this intimate hotel located within easy reach of the seafront and the city centre. Ideal for accessing both local attractions and amenities. Individually decorated bedrooms are generally spacious providing good levels of comfort. Public areas include a pleasant lounge and cosy bar.
ROOMS: 19 en suite (1 fmly) (6 GF) ⊘ in 10 bedrooms s £55-£60; d £60-£80 (incl. bkfst) **LB** **FACILITIES:** STV **PARKING:** 10 **NOTES:** ⊘ in restaurant **CARDS:**

★★72% Seacrest

11/12 South Pde, Southsea PO5 2JB
☎ 023 9273 3192 023 9283 2523
e-mail: seacrest@boltblue.com
web: www.seacresthotel.co.uk
Dir: *from M27/M275 follow signs for seafront, Pyramids and Sea Life Centre. Hotel opposite Rock Gardens and Pyramids*
In a premier seafront location, this smart hotel provides the ideal base for exploring the town. Bedrooms, many benefiting from sea views, are decorated to a high standard with good facilities. Guests can relax in either the south-facing lounge, furnished with large

continued

leather sofas, or the adjacent bar; there is also a cosy dining room popular with residents.

ROOMS: 28 en suite (3 fmly) ⊘ in 20 bedrooms s £45-£55; d £60-£89 (incl. bkfst) **LB** **FACILITIES:** STV **SERVICES:** Lift **PARKING:** 12 **NOTES:** ⊘ in restaurant **CARDS:**

⌂ Hotel Ibis

Winston Churchill Av PO1 2LX
☎ 023 9264 0000 023 9264 1000
e-mail: h1461@accor-hotels.com
Dir: *M27 junct 2 onto M275. Follow signs for city centre then Sealife Centre and then Guildhall. Right at rdbt into Winston Churchill Ave*
Modern, budget hotel offering comfortable accommodation in bright and practical bedrooms. Breakfast is self-service and dinner is available in the restaurant. For further details, consult the Hotel Groups page.
ROOMS: 144 en suite s £39.95-£44.95; d £39.95-£44.95 **CONF:** Thtr 45 Class 24 Board 24

⌂ Innkeeper's Lodge Portsmouth

Copnor Rd, Hilsea PO3 5HS
☎ 0870 243 0500 & 023 9265 4645
www.innkeeperslodge.com
Dir: *From A27 take A2030. Right at lights, over 3 rbdts into Norway Road. Inn on A288*
Smart rooms meet essential business requirements but also have home comforts, and depending on location may well have meeting rooms and pub dining. Dining options generally include all-day menus plus the added advantage of breakfast.
ROOMS: 33 en suite s £48-£55; d £48-£55

⌂ Travel Inn

Southampton Rd, North Harbour, Cosham PO6 4SA
☎ 08701 977213 023 9232 4895
Dir: *on A27, close to M27 junct 12*
Travel Inn offers good-quality, value-for-money accommodation. Spacious, en suite rooms with bath and shower comfortably accommodate a family of up to two adults and two children (to age 15). The restaurant and bar offers a varied menu. For further details consult the Hotel Groups page.
ROOMS: 64 en suite s £45.95-£48.95; d £45.95-£48.95 **CONF:** Thtr 25

⌂ Travel Inn (Southsea)

Long Curtain Rd, Clarence Pier, Southsea PO5 3AA
☎ 08701 977236 023 9273 3048
Dir: *Pier Rd leads to Clarence Pier. Travel Inn next to amusement park and Isle of Wight hovercraft*
Travel Inn offers good-quality, value-for-money accommodation. Spacious, en suite rooms with bath and shower comfortably accommodate a family of up to two adults and two children (to age 15). The restaurant and bar offers a varied menu. For further details consult the Hotel Groups page.
ROOMS: 40 en suite s £45.95-£48.95; d £45.95-£48.95

P

PORTSMOUTH, continued

Travelodge

Kingston Crescent, North End PO2 8AB
☎ 08700 850 950 📠 02392 639121

Travelodge offers good quality, good value, modern accommodation. Ideal for families, the spacious, en suite bedrooms include remote-control TV, tea and coffee-making facilities and luxury beds. Meals can be taken at the nearby family restaurant. For further details consult the Hotel Groups page.
ROOMS: 78 en suite s fr £25; d fr £25

PORTWRINKLE, Cornwall & Isles of Scilly — Map 03 SX45

★★★68% Whitsand Bay Hotel & Golf Club

PL11 3BU
☎ 01503 230276 📠 01503 230329
e-mail: whitsandbayhotel@btconnect.com
web: www.whitsandbayhotel.co.uk
Dir: *A38 from Exeter over Tamar, turn left at Trerulefoot rdbt onto A374 to Crafthole/Portwrinkle. Then follow signs for the hotel*

An imposing Victorian building with oak panelling, stained glass windows and a sweeping staircase. Bedrooms include family rooms and a suite with a balcony, and many have superb sea views. Facilities include an 18-hole, cliff-top golf course and indoor swimming pool. The fixed-price menu offers an interesting selection of dishes.
ROOMS: 32 en suite (7 fmly) in 10 bedrooms s £75; d £126-£146 (incl. bkfst & dinner) **LB FACILITIES:** 18 Sauna Solarium Gym Putt green ch fac Xmas **CONF:** BC Del from £90 **PARKING:** 60 **NOTES:** in restaurant **CARDS:**

PRESTBURY, Cheshire — Map 16 SJ87

Town House

★★★★ White House Manor

New Rd SK10 4HP
☎ 01625 829376 📠 01625 828627
e-mail: info@thewhitehouse.uk.com
web: www.thewhitehouse.uk.com
Dir: *on A538 Macclesfield road*

This elegant Georgian house, situated in attractive gardens on the edge of the village, offers charming, individually styled bedrooms, many with four-poster beds. Meals can be ordered from the room service menu and breakfast is served in the conservatory. The White House restaurant, under the same ownership, is just a short walk away but guests can be driven there if needed.
ROOMS: 11 en suite (2 GF) in all bedrooms s £45-£100; d £80-£130 **FACILITIES:** STV Jacuzzi Xmas **CONF:** Thtr 60 Class 40 Board 26 **PARKING:** 11 **NOTES:** No children 10yrs Closed 24-26 Dec **CARDS:**

★★★68% Bridge

The Village SK10 4DQ
☎ 01625 829326 📠 01625 827557
e-mail: reception@bridge-hotel.co.uk
web: www.bridge-hotel.co.uk
Dir: *off A538 through village. Hotel next to church*

Dating in parts from the 17th century, this delightful, stylish hotel stands between the River Bollin and the ancient church. The cocktail bar is the ideal place to relax before enjoying a meal in the newly refurbished Bridge Restaurant. A wide range of bedroom styles is available in the original building and in the modern extension.

ROOMS: 23 en suite (1 fmly) in 5 bedrooms s £50-£130; d £85-£130 **LB FACILITIES:** STV **CONF:** Thtr 100 Class 56 Board 48 Del from £115 **PARKING:** 52 **NOTES:** RS 25/26 Dec, 2/3 Jan Civ Wed 100 **CARDS:**

PRESTON, Lancashire — Map 18 SD52

See also Garstang

★★★★66% Preston Marriott Hotel

Garstang Rd, Broughton PR3 5JB
☎ 01772 864087 📠 01772 861728
e-mail: reservations.preston@marriotthotels.co.uk
Dir: *M6 junct 32 onto M55 junct 1, follow A6 towards Garstang. Hotel 0.5m on right*

With a country club feel, this hotel enjoys good links to both the city centre and motorway network. There are two dining options, and extensive leisure facilities ensure there is plenty to do in the hotel. The bedrooms are smartly decorated and equipped with a comprehensive range of extras.
ROOMS: 150 en suite (40 fmly) (63 GF) in 94 bedrooms s £77-£115; d £84-£125 (incl. bkfst) **LB FACILITIES: Spa** STV supervised Sauna Solarium Gym Jacuzzi Steam room, Beauty salon/hairdressing **CONF:** Thtr 220 Class 100 Board 70 Del from £145 **SERVICES:** Lift **PARKING:** 250 **NOTES:** in restaurant Civ Wed 180 **CARDS:**

★★★72% Barton Grange

Garstang Rd PR3 5AA
☎ 01772 862551 📠 01772 861267
e-mail: stay@bartongrangehotel.com
web: www.bartongrangehotel.com
(For full entry see Barton)

★★★70% Pines

570 Preston Rd, Clayton-Le-Woods PR6 7ED
☎ 01772 338551 📠 01772 629002
e-mail: mail@thepineshotel.co.uk
Dir: *on A6, 1m S of M6 junct 29*

This unique and stylish hotel sits in four acres of mature grounds just a short drive from the motorway network. Elegant bedrooms are individually designed and offer high levels of comfort and facilities. Day rooms include a smart bar and 'Haworths' brasserie, while extensive function rooms make this hotel a popular venue for weddings.
ROOMS: 37 en suite (12 fmly) (14 GF) in 21 bedrooms **FACILITIES:** STV Xmas **CONF:** BC Thtr 200 Class 150 Board 60 Del from £120 **PARKING:** 120 **NOTES:** Closed 26 Dec Civ Wed 150 **CARDS:**

★★★66% *Tickled Trout*

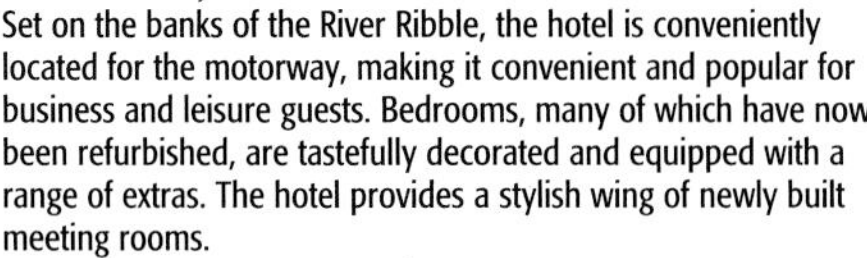

Preston New Rd, Samlesbury PR5 0UJ
☎ 01772 877671 🖷 01772 877463
e-mail: tickledtrout@macdonald-hotels.co.uk
Dir: *close to M6 junct 31*
Set on the banks of the River Ribble, the hotel is conveniently located for the motorway, making it convenient and popular for business and leisure guests. Bedrooms, many of which have now been refurbished, are tastefully decorated and equipped with a range of extras. The hotel provides a stylish wing of newly built meeting rooms.
ROOMS: 102 en suite (6 fmly) ⊗ in 43 bedrooms **FACILITIES:** STV Fishing ♫ **CONF:** BC Thtr 120 Class 60 Board 50 **SERVICES:** Lift **PARKING:** 240 **NOTES:** ⊗ in restaurant Civ Wed 100
CARDS:

★★★65% Novotel Preston

Reedfield Place, Walton Summit PR5 8AA
☎ 01772 313331 🖷 01772 627868
e-mail: H0838@accor-hotels.com
Dir: *M6 junct 29, M61 junct 9, then A6 Chorley Road. Hotel next to Bamber Bridge rdbt*
The hotel is ideally located just off main motorway networks. Bedrooms are spacious and feature ample desk area and additional bed space making them ideal for families or business travellers. Flexible dining is a feature with the Garden Brassiere, open throughout the day until midnight. The hotel also boasts an outdoor pool and children's play area.
ROOMS: 96 en suite (22 fmly) ⊗ in 49 bedrooms s fr £60; d fr £60 **LB** **FACILITIES:** STV supervised **CONF:** Thtr 180 Class 80 Board 52 Del from £95 **SERVICES:** Lift **PARKING:** 140 **NOTES:** ⊗ in restaurant
CARDS:

★★70% Haighton Manor

Haighton Green Ln, Haighton PR2 5SQ
☎ 01772 663170 🖷 01772 663171
e-mail: info@haightonmanor.net
Dir: *Off A6 onto Durton Rd, or from M6 junct 32 turn right at roundabout & right onto Durton Rd. Right at end of road onto Haighton Lane, Hotel 2 miles on left.*
Located in sleepy, rolling countryside just ten minutes to the east of city, this impressive hotel is ideally situated for both the business and leisure guest. External appearances are deceptive, for once inside, this 17th-century manor house has ultra-modern bedrooms and stylishly fashioned day rooms providing a wonderful fusion of ancient and modern. Wide-ranging creative menus can be sampled in the candlelit restaurant. This hotel is a popular wedding venue.
ROOMS: 8 en suite (1 fmly) ⊗ in all bedrooms s £50-£70; d £90-£120 (incl. bkfst) **LB** **FACILITIES:** STV **CONF:** Del from £89.90 **PARKING:** 45 **NOTES:** ✈ ⊗ in restaurant Civ Wed 55
CARDS:

★★66% *Claremont*

516 Blackpool Rd, Ashton-on-Ribble PR2 1HY
☎ 01772 729738 🖷 01772 726274
Dir: *M6 junct 31 onto A59 towards Preston. Right at hilltop rdbt onto A583. Hotel on right past pub and over bridge*
This friendly, family run hotel enjoys a convenient location for access to the town centre and the local motorway network. Bedrooms are traditionally furnished. Public areas include a cosy lounge, a bar lounge and adjacent restaurant that overlooks the rear garden. There is also a popular self-contained function room.
ROOMS: 10 en suite **CONF:** Thtr 85 Class 45 Board 50 **PARKING:** 27 **NOTES:** ✈ **CARDS:**

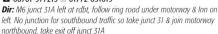

⌂ Hotel Ibis

Garstang Rd, Broughton PR3 5JE
☎ 01772 861800 🖷 01772 861900
e-mail: H3162@accor-hotels.com
Dir: *M6 junct 32, then M55 junct 1. Left lane onto A6. Left at slip road and left again at mini rdbt. 2nd turn and hotel on right past pub*
Modern, budget hotel offering comfortable accommodation in bright and practical bedrooms. Breakfast is self-service and dinner is available in the restaurant. For further details, consult the Hotel Groups page.
ROOMS: 82 en suite d £35.95-£43.95 **CONF:** Thtr 30 Class 20 Board 20

⌂ Premier Lodge (Preston)

Lostock Ln, Bamber Bridge PR5 6BA
☎ 0870 9906462 🖷 0870 9906463
web: www.premierlodge.com
Dir: *M65 junct 1, 0.5m from junct 29 of M6 close to rdbt of A582 and A6*
High quality, modern, budget accommodation, ideal for families and business travellers. All rooms feature bath, power shower and satellite TV, and most have telephones / modem points. The adjacent bar and restaurant offers a wide and varied menu.
ROOMS: 40 en suite s £48; d £48 **CONF:** Thtr 30 Board 30

⌂ Travel Inn (Preston East)

Bluebell Way, Preston East Link Rd, Fulwood PR2 5PZ
☎ 08701 977215 🖷 01772 651619
Dir: *M6 junct 31A left at rdbt, follow ring road under motorway & Inn on left. No junction for southbound traffic so take junct 31 & join motorway northbound, take exit off junct 31A*
Travel Inn offers good-quality, value-for-money accommodation. Spacious, en suite rooms with bath and shower comfortably

continued on p476

PRESTON, continued

accommodate a family of up to two adults and two children (to age 15). The restaurant and bar offers a varied menu. For further details consult the Hotel Groups page.
ROOMS: 65 en suite s £45.95-£46.95; d £45.95-£46.95 **CONF:** Thtr 20

Travel Inn Preston (West)
Blackpool Rd, Lea PR4 0XB
☎ 08701 977214 01772 729971
Dir: *off A583, opposite Texaco garage.*
Travel Inn offers good-quality, value-for-money accommodation. Spacious, en suite rooms with bath and shower comfortably accommodate a family of up to two adults and two children (to age 15). The restaurant and bar offers a varied menu. For further details consult the Hotel Groups page.
ROOMS: 38 en suite s £45.95-£46.95; d £45.95-£46.95

PRESTWICH, Greater Manchester — Map 15 SD80

Travel Inn (Manchester Prestwich)
Bury New Rd M25 3AJ
☎ 08701 977175 0161 773 8099
Dir: *M60 junct 17, on A56*
Travel Inn offers good-quality, value-for-money accommodation. Spacious, en suite rooms with bath and shower comfortably accommodate a family of up to two adults and two children (to age 15). The restaurant and bar offers a varied menu. For further details consult the Hotel Groups page.
ROOMS: 60 en suite s £45.95-£46.95; d £45.95-£46.95

PUDDINGTON, Cheshire — Map 15 SJ37

★★★★67% Craxton Wood
Parkgate Rd, Ledsham CH66 9PB
☎ 0151 347 4000 0151 347 4040
e-mail: craxtonwood@macdonald-hotels.co.uk
Dir: *from M6 take M56 towards N Wales, then A5117 then A540 to Hoylake. Hotel 200yds past lights*
Set in extensive grounds, this hotel offers a variety of bedroom styles; the modern rooms are particularly comfortable. The nicely furnished restaurant overlooks the grounds and offers a wide choice of dishes, whilst full leisure facilities and a choice of function suites completes the package.
ROOMS: 72 en suite (8 fmly) (30 GF) in all bedrooms s fr £60; d fr £100 (incl. bkfst) **LB** **FACILITIES:** STV Sauna Solarium Gym Beauty spa Xmas **CONF:** Thtr 400 Class 150 Board 60 Del from £120 **SERVICES:** Lift **PARKING:** 220 **NOTES:** in restaurant Civ Wed 350
CARDS:

Premier Lodge (Wirral South)

Parkgate Rd, Two Mills CH66 9PD
☎ 0870 9906564 0870 9906565
web: www.premierlodge.com
Dir: *5m from M56 junct 16 & junct 5 M53 on x-rds of A550 & A540*
High quality, modern, budget accommodation, ideal for families and business travellers. All rooms feature bath, power shower and satellite TV, and most have telephones / modem points. The adjacent bar and restaurant offers a wide and varied menu.
ROOMS: 31 en suite s £50; d £50

PUDSEY, West Yorkshire — Map 19 SE23

Travelodge Bradford
1 Mid Point, Dick Ln BD3 8QD
☎ 08700 850 950 01274 665436
Travelodge offers good quality, good value, modern accommodation. Ideal for families, the spacious, en suite bedrooms include remote-control TV, tea and coffee-making facilities and luxury beds. Meals can be taken at the nearby family restaurant. For further details consult the Hotel Groups page.
ROOMS: 48 en suite s fr £25; d fr £25

PULBOROUGH, West Sussex — Map 06 TQ01

★★66% Chequers
Old Rectory Ln RH20 1AD
☎ 01798 872486 01798 872715
e-mail: info@thechequershotel.com
Dir: *100mtrs N of junct of A283/A29 opposite church in Pulborough*
This Grade II listed building has been lovingly restored, offering a warm welcome and comfortable accommodation. Bedrooms vary in size and are all individually decorated; one with a four-poster bed is available. Traditionally appointed cosy lounges are adjacent to the restaurant where enjoyable meals are served.
ROOMS: 10 en suite (3 fmly) (4 GF) in all bedrooms s £55-£70; d £90-£120 (incl. bkfst) **LB** **FACILITIES:** Xmas **CONF:** Thtr 20 Class 20 Board 20 **PARKING:** 20 **NOTES:** in restaurant
CARDS:

PURFLEET, Essex — Map 06 TQ57

Travel Inn
High St RM19 1QA
☎ 08701 977216 01708 860852
Dir: *from Dartford Tunnel follow signs Dagenham (A13), at rdbt take 1st exit to Purfleet (A1090)*
Travel Inn offers good-quality, value-for-money accommodation. Spacious, en suite rooms with bath and shower comfortably accommodate a family of up to two adults and two children (to age 15). The restaurant and bar offers a varied menu. For further details consult the Hotel Groups page.
ROOMS: 30 en suite s £45.95-£46.95; d £45.95-£46.95

PURTON, Wiltshire — Map 05 SU08

★★★78% The Pear Tree at Purton
Church End SN5 4ED
☎ 01793 772100 01793 772369
e-mail: stay@peartreepurton.co.uk
Dir: *M4 junct 16 follow signs to Purton, at Spar shop turn right. Hotel 0.25m on left*
Set in attractive gardens and grounds, this 15th-century former vicarage offers a comfortable haven for guests. The resident proprietors and staff provide efficient, dedicated service and friendly hospitality. Individually styled bedrooms are spacious and feature thoughtful extra touches such as fresh flowers and sherry. Fresh ingredients feature on the menus at both lunch and dinner.
ROOMS: 17 en suite (2 fmly) (6 GF) s £115-£140; d £115-£140 (incl. bkfst) **LB** **FACILITIES:** **Spa** STV ch fac **CONF:** Thtr 70 Class 30 Board 30 Del £140 **PARKING:** 60 **NOTES:** in restaurant Closed 26-30 Dec Civ Wed 50 **CARDS:**

QUORN, Leicestershire Map 11 SK51

★★★★68% Quorn Country

Charnwood House, 66 Leicester Rd LE12 8BB
☎ 01509 415050 01509 415557
e-mail: reservations@quorncountryhotel.co.uk
Dir: *M1 junct 23 onto A512 into Loughborough. Follow A6 signs. At 1st rdbt towards Quorn, through lights, hotel 500yds from 2nd rdbt*

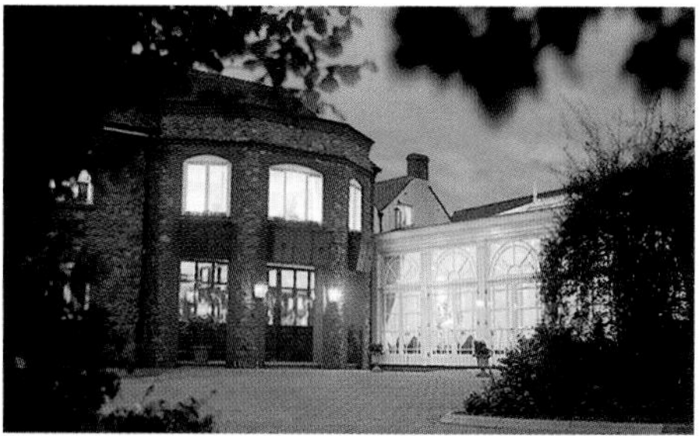

Professional service is one of the key strengths of this pleasing hotel, which sits beside the river in four acres of landscaped gardens and grounds. The smart modern conference centre and function suites has proved to be a great success for both corporate functions and weddings. Public rooms include a comfortable lounge and bar, whilst guests have the choice from two dining options: the formal Shires restaurant and the informal conservatory-style Orangery.
ROOMS: 30 en suite (1 fmly) (9 GF) in 13 bedrooms s £82-£140; d £95-£155 **LB** **FACILITIES:** STV Fishing **CONF:** BC Thtr 300 Class 162 Board 40 Del from £145 **SERVICES:** Lift **PARKING:** 100 **NOTES:** Civ Wed 200 **CARDS:**

See advert on this page

RADLETT, Hertfordshire Map 06 TL10

Travel Inn St Albans/Bricketwood

Smug Oak Ln AL2 3PN
☎ 08701 977040 01727 873289
Dir: *From M10 take A5183 towards Radlett. After bridge over M25 turn right. From M25 or M1, follow signs to Bricketwood then turn into Smug Oak Lane at The Gate pub*

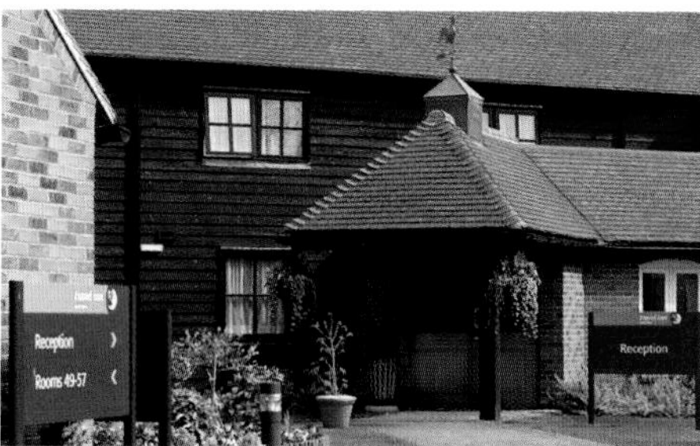

Travel Inn offers good-quality, value-for-money accommodation. Spacious, en suite rooms with bath and shower comfortably accommodate a family of up to two adults and two children (to age 15). The restaurant and bar offers a varied menu. For further details consult the Hotel Groups page.
ROOMS: 56 en suite s £54.95-£56.95; d £54.95-£56.95

RAINHAM, Greater London Map 06 TQ58

Travel Inn

New Rd, Wennington RM13 9ED
☎ 08701 977217 01708 634821
Dir: *M25 J30/31 - follow A13 for Dagenham/Rainham, then A1306 for Wennington, Aveley, Rainham. Inn 0.5 mile on right.*
Travel Inn offers good-quality, value-for-money accommodation. Spacious, en suite rooms with bath and shower comfortably accommodate a family of up to two adults and two children (to age 15). The restaurant and bar offers a varied menu. For further details consult the Hotel Groups page.
ROOMS: 60 en suite s £52.95-£56.95; d £52.95-£56.95

RAINHILL, Merseyside Map 15 SJ49

Premier Lodge (Liverpool East)

804 Warrington Rd, Rainhill L35 6PE
☎ 0870 9906446 0870 9906447
web: www.premierlodge.com
Dir: *off M62 junct 7, onto the A57 towards Rainhill*
High quality, modern, budget accommodation, ideal for families and business travellers. All rooms feature bath, power shower and satellite TV, and most have telephones / modem points. The adjacent bar and restaurant offers a wide and varied menu.
ROOMS: 34 en suite s £48; d £48 **CONF:** Thtr 20

 AA Rosette Award for culinary excellence

RAMSBOTTOM, Greater Manchester Map 15 SD71

★★★62% Old Mill

Springwood BL0 9DS
☎ 01706 822991 01706 822291
e-mail: reservations@oldmill-uk.com
Dir: *from M66 junct 4 follow A56 towards Rawtenstall. Take 1st left into Bridge Street. Continue over railway crossing and at traffic lights continue straight over into Carr Street. Take 2nd left into Springwood and continue to end of road and turn right to The Old Mill House*

Extended from an original water mill, this friendly hotel enjoys fine views over the town and Rossendale Valley. Refurbished bedrooms have attractive floral furnishings and inter-connecting family rooms are available. In addition to a comfortable bar and beamed restaurant, a well-equipped leisure centre is available to guests during their stay.

ROOMS: 28 en suite (5 fmly) s £59-£79; d £70-£89 (incl. bkfst) **LB** **FACILITIES:** STV Sauna Solarium Gym Jacuzzi Steam Room **CONF:** Thtr 70 Class 30 Board 20 Del from £89 **PARKING:** 50 **NOTES:** in restaurant **CARDS:**

RAMSGATE, Kent Map 07 TR36

★★★64% Comfort Inn Ramsgate

Victoria Pde, East Cliff CT11 8DT
☎ 01843 592345 01843 580157
e-mail: reservations@sancluhotel.co.uk
Dir: *From M2 take A299 signed Ramsgate, B2054 to Victoria Parade*

This Victorian hotel stands on the seafront, close to the ferry and the town. Bedrooms, some with balconies, are generously sized and well equipped. Meals are served both in the bar lounge and in the restaurant.

ROOMS: 44 en suite (5 fmly) in 22 bedrooms s £50-£80; d £80-£120 (incl. cont bkfst) **LB** **FACILITIES:** STV Xmas **CONF:** Thtr 50 Class 30 Board 70 Del from £80 **SERVICES:** Lift **PARKING:** 10 **NOTES:** in restaurant **CARDS:**

RAMSGILL, North Yorkshire Map 19 SE17

Top 200 – Restaurant with Rooms

Yorke Arms

HG3 5RL
☎ 01423 755243 01423 755330
e-mail: enquiries@yorke-arms.co.uk
web: www.yorke-arms.co.uk
Dir: *off B6265 at Pateley Bridge at Nidderdale filling station onto Low Wath road, signed to Ramsgill. Continue 4.5m*

Dominating the tiny hamlet, this ivy-clad former hunting lodge overlooks the village green in picturesque Nidderdale and a warm and welcoming ambience prevails throughout. Flagstone floors lead through to a cosy bar, and beams and open fires grace the two delightful dining rooms, where excellent cuisine is matched by caring and attentive service.

ROOMS: 13 en suite 1 annexe en suite (2 fmly) (5 GF) in 13 bedrooms s £105-£130; d £100-£170 (incl. bkfst & dinner) **LB** **FACILITIES:** shooting,mountain biking,walking, bird watching Xmas **CONF:** Class 20 Board 10 Del £180 **PARKING:** 20 **NOTES:** in restaurant RS Sun **CARDS:**

RANGEWORTHY, Gloucestershire Map 04 ST68

★★72% Rangeworthy Court

Church Ln, Wotton Rd BS37 7ND
☎ 01454 228347 01454 228945
e-mail: hotel@rangeworthy.demon.co.uk
web: www.rangeworthy.demon.co.uk
Dir: *signposted off B4058*

This welcoming manor house hotel is peacefully located within its own grounds, and is within easy reach of the motorway network. The character bedrooms come in a variety of sizes and there is a choice of comfortable lounges in which to relax. The candlelit restaurant offers a varied and interesting menu.

ROOMS: 13 en suite (4 fmly) in 3 bedrooms s £70; d £85 (incl. bkfst) **FACILITIES:** Boules **CONF:** BC Thtr 22 Class 14 Board 16 **PARKING:** 40 **NOTES:** in restaurant **CARDS:**

RAVENSCAR, North Yorkshire Map 19 NZ90

★★★67% *Raven Hall Country House*

YO13 OET
☎ 01723 870353 01723 870072
e-mail: enquiries@ravenhall.co.uk
Dir: *from Scarborough take A171 to Whitby Rd. Through Cloughton Village and right to Ravenscar*

Run by the Gridley family for over 40 years this impressive cliff top mansion enjoys breathtaking views over Robin Hood's Bay. Extensive well-kept grounds include tennis courts, putting green, swimming pools and historic battlements. The spacious bedrooms offer many thoughtful extras. Public rooms are extensive while the restaurant enjoys fine views over the bay.

ROOMS: 51 en suite (22 fmly) (5 GF) in 1 bedroom **FACILITIES:** supervised by CCTV 9 Snooker Sauna Putt green Crown green bowls Giant chess Table tennis ch fac **CONF:** Thtr 160 Class 100 Board 60 **SERVICES:** Lift **PARKING:** 200 **NOTES:** in restaurant Civ Wed 120 **CARDS:**

See advert under SCARBOROUGH

RAVENSTONEDALE, Cumbria Map 18 NY70

★★66% The Fat Lamb

Crossbank CA17 4LL
☎ 015396 23242 015396 23285
e-mail: fatlamb@cumbria.com
Dir: *on A683, between Kirkby Stephen and Sedbergh*

Open fires and solid stone walls are a feature of this 17th-century inn, set in its own nature reserve. There is a choice of dining options with an extensive menu available in the traditional bar or a more formal dining experience in the restaurant. Bedrooms are bright and cheerful and include family rooms and easily accessible rooms for guests with limited mobility.

ROOMS: 12 en suite (4 fmly) in all bedrooms s £48-£50; d £76-£80 (incl. bkfst) **LB** **FACILITIES:** Fishing Private 5 acre nature reserve ch fac Xmas **PARKING:** 60 **NOTES:** in restaurant **CARDS:**

Destination dining!
This symbol indicates a Restaurant with Rooms

READING, Berkshire Map 05 SU77
See also Swallowfield & Wokingham

★★★★74%
Millennium Madejski Hotel Reading
Madejski Stadium RG2 0FL
☎ 0118 925 3500 📠 0118 925 3501
e-mail: sales.reading@mill-cop.com
Dir: *M4 junct 11 onto A33, follow signs for Madejski Complex*

A stylish hotel, that features an atrium lobby with specially commissioned water sculpture, is part of the Madejski stadium complex, home to both Reading Football and London Irish Rugby teams. Bedrooms are appointed with spacious workstations and plenty of amenities; there is also a choice of suites and a club floor with its own lounge. The hotel also has an award-winning, fine dining restaurant.
ROOMS: 140 en suite (4 fmly) in 92 bedrooms s £195; d £195 **LB** **FACILITIES: Spa** STV supervised Sauna Solarium Gym Jacuzzi Stadium - home to Reading FC and London Irish RFC **CONF:** Board 12 **SERVICES:** Lift air con **PARKING:** 150 **NOTES:** RS Xmas & New Yr **CARDS:**

★★★★69% **Renaissance Hotel Reading**
Oxford Rd RG1 7RH
☎ 0118 958 6222 📠 0118 959 7842
e-mail: rhi.lhrlr.dos@renaissancehotels.com
Situated in the heart of the town, this long-established hotel is well positioned for both business travellers and shoppers. Air-conditioned bedrooms feature a host of extras that fulfil the needs of the business traveller including high speed internet access. Public areas include a fully equipped gymnasium, swimming pool, a variety of meeting rooms and a business centre. Free parking subject to availability.
ROOMS: 196 en suite (67 fmly) in 160 bedrooms s £132-£142; d £132-£142 **LB** **FACILITIES:** STV supervised Sauna Solarium Gym Jacuzzi **CONF:** BC Thtr 220 Class 130 Board 60 Del from £99 **SERVICES:** Lift air con **PARKING:** 70 **NOTES:** Civ Wed 140 **CARDS:**

★★★71% **Courtyard by Marriott Reading**
Bath Rd, Padworth RG7 5HT
☎ 0870 400 7234 📠 0870 400 7334
Dir: *M4 junct 12 onto A4 towards Newbury. Hotel 3.5m on left, after petrol station*
This purpose-built hotel combines the benefits of a peaceful rural location with the accessibility afforded by good road links. Modern comforts include air-conditioned bedrooms and rooms with easy access for less mobile guests. A feature of the hotel is its pretty courtyard garden, which can be seen from the restaurant.
ROOMS: 50 en suite (25 GF) in 45 bedrooms s £50-£110; d £50-£110 **LB** **FACILITIES:** STV Gym Fitness room Xmas **CONF:** Thtr 200 Class 70 Board 80 Del from £140 **SERVICES:** air con **PARKING:** 200 **NOTES:** in restaurant Civ Wed 100 **CARDS:**

★★★69% **Calcot Hotel**
98 Bath Rd, Calcot RG31 7QN
☎ 0118 941 6423 📠 0118 945 1223
e-mail: enquiries@calcothotel.co.uk
web: www.calcothotel.co.uk
Dir: *M4 junct 12 onto A4 towards Reading, hotel in 0.5m on N side of A4*
This hotel is conveniently located for both London and the motorway. Bedrooms are well equipped and tastefully decorated; bedroom styles vary slightly, newer bedrooms are particularly appealing. Attractive public rooms and function suites are additional features; the restaurant offers enjoyable food in welcoming surroundings.
ROOMS: 80 en suite (2 fmly) in 38 bedrooms s £46-£130; d £62-£140 **FACILITIES:** STV **CONF:** Thtr 120 Class 35 Board 35 Del from £130 **PARKING:** 130 **NOTES:** in restaurant Closed 25-27 Dec Civ Wed 60 **CARDS:**

★★★68%
Hanover International Hotel & Club
Pingewood RG30 3UN
☎ 0118 950 0885 📠 0118 939 1996
e-mail: reading@hanover-international.com
Dir: *A33 towards Basingstoke. At Three Mile Cross rdbt right signed Burghfield. After 300mtrs 2nd right, over M4, through lights, hotel on left*
Quietly located a short distance south of Reading, this modern hotel been built around a man-made lake which is occasionally used for water sports. Bedrooms are generally spacious with good facilities, and some have balconies overlooking the lake. Public areas include Brasserie 209 and a well-equipped leisure club with adjacent bar.
ROOMS: 81 en suite (23 fmly) in 57 bedrooms s £140; d £140 **LB** **FACILITIES:** STV Squash Snooker Sauna Gym Jacuzzi Watersports **CONF:** Thtr 110 Class 50 Board 45 Del £182 **SERVICES:** Lift **PARKING:** 250 **NOTES:** in restaurant Civ Wed 80 **CARDS:**

★★★63% **Quality Hotel Reading**
648-654 Oxford Rd RG30 1EH
☎ 0118 950 0541 📠 0118 956 7220
e-mail: info@qualityreading.co.uk
Dir: *M4 J11, follow A33 bypass towards town centre, then A329 towards Pangbourne, follow signs for Oxford Rd*
Close to the city centre this modern, purpose-built hotel is a popular choice with business guests. Bedrooms are generally spacious and offer a good range of facilities. Guests have a choice of eating lighter meals and snacks in the bar lounge or a more formal menu is offered in the spacious restaurant. The hotel benefits from conference facilities and ample car parking.
ROOMS: 96 rms (95 en suite) (15 fmly) in 39 bedrooms s £59-£99; d £59-£99 **LB** **FACILITIES:** STV **CONF:** BC Thtr 100 Class 50 Board 40 Del £125 **SERVICES:** Lift **PARKING:** 60 **NOTES:** in restaurant **CARDS:**

★★67% ***The Mill House***
Old Basingstoke Rd, Swallowfield RG7 1PY

☎ 0118 988 3124 📠 0118 988 5550
e-mail: info@themillhousehotel.co.uk
(For full entry see Swallowfield)

Premier Lodge
Grazeley Green Rd RG7 1LS
☎ 0870 9906454 📠 0870 9906455
web: www.premierlodge.com
Dir: *M4 junct 11 follow A33 towards Basingstoke, take Mortimer exit at 1st rdbt. 3rd right into Grazeley Rd, under railway bridge turn left. Lodge next to Old Bell Millers Kitchen*
High quality, modern, budget accommodation, ideal for families
continued on p480

R

READING, continued

and business travellers. All rooms feature bath, power shower and satellite TV, and most have telephones / modem points. The adjacent bar and restaurant offers a wide and varied menu.
ROOMS: 32 en suite s £52; d £52 **CONF:** Class 8 Board 8

Travelodge
387 Basingstoke Rd RG2 0JE
☎ 08700 850 950 0118 975 1303
Dir: *On A33, southbound.*
Travelodge offers good quality, good value, modern accommodation. Ideal for families, the spacious, en suite bedrooms include remote-control TV, tea and coffee-making facilities and luxury beds. Meals can be taken at the nearby family restaurant. For further details consult the Hotel Groups page.
ROOMS: 36 en suite s fr £25; d fr £25

Travelodge (Reading Central)
Oxford Rd RG1 7LT
☎ 08700 850 950 0118 950 3257
Travelodge offers good quality, good value, modern accommodation. Ideal for families, the spacious, en suite bedrooms include remote-control TV, tea and coffee-making facilities and luxury beds. Meals can be taken at the nearby family restaurant. For further details consult the Hotel Groups page.
ROOMS: 80 en suite s fr £25; d fr £25

Travelodge Reading M4 (Eastbound)
Burghfield RG30 3UQ
☎ 08700 850 950 0118 959 2045
Dir: *M4 between junct 11 and 12*
Travelodge offers good quality, good value, modern accommodation. Ideal for families, the spacious, en suite bedrooms include remote-control TV, tea and coffee-making facilities and luxury beds. Meals can be taken at the nearby family restaurant. For further details consult the Hotel Groups page.
ROOMS: 86 en suite s fr £25; d fr £25 **CONF:** Thtr 20 Class 20 Board 20

Travelodge Reading M4 (Westbound)
Burghfield RG30 3UQ
☎ 08700 850 950 0118 958 2350
Dir: *M4 between junct 11 & 12*
Travelodge offers good quality, good value, modern accommodation. Ideal for families, the spacious, en suite bedrooms include remote-control TV, tea and coffee-making facilities and luxury beds. Meals can be taken at the nearby family restaurant. For further details consult the Hotel Groups page.
ROOMS: 102 en suite s fr £25; d fr £25

REDDITCH, Worcestershire Map 10 SP06

★★★★67% The Abbey Hotel Golf & Country Club
Hither Green Ln, Dagnell End Rd, Bordesley B98 9BE
☎ 01527 406600 01527 406514
e-mail: info@theabbeyhotel.co.uk
Dir: *M42 junct 2 take A441 to Redditch. End of carriageway turn left (A441), Dagnell End Rd on left. Hotel 600yds on right*
With its convenient access to the motorway and its proximity to local attractions, this modern hotel is popular with both business and leisure travellers. Bedrooms are well equipped and attractively decorated; the executive corner rooms are especially spacious.
continued

Hotel facilities include an 18-hole golf course, pro shop, large indoor pool and extensive conference facilities.

ROOMS: 72 en suite (2 fmly) (30 GF) in 30 bedrooms s £120-£140; d £140-£180 (incl. bkfst) **LB** **FACILITIES:** STV 18 Fishing Sauna Solarium Gym Putt green Jacuzzi Beauty Salon,Golf driving range Xmas **CONF:** Thtr 150 Class 60 Board 30 Del from £120 **SERVICES:** Lift **PARKING:** 170 **NOTES:** in restaurant Civ Wed 100
CARDS:
See advert under BIRMINGHAM

★★★63% Quality Hotel Redditch
Pool Bank, Southcrest B97 4JS
☎ 01527 541511 01527 402600
e-mail: enquiries@hotels-redditch.com
Dir: *In Redditch follow signs for all other Redditch Districts until Southcrest signed, then follow signs for hotel*
Originally a manor house, this hotel enjoys a peaceful location in extensive wooded grounds. Bedrooms vary in size and style, and all are well appointed and equipped. Both the restaurant and bar/conservatory overlook the attractive, sloping gardens, with views stretching across to the Vale of Evesham.
ROOMS: 73 en suite (20 fmly) (22 GF) in 35 bedrooms s £50-£86; d £60-£99 **LB** **FACILITIES:** STV Xmas **CONF:** Thtr 100 Class 45 Board 50 Del from £85 **PARKING:** 100 **NOTES:** in restaurant Civ Wed 70
CARDS:

★★63% Montville
101 Mount Pleasant, Southcrest B97 4JE
☎ 01527 544411 01527 544341
e-mail: sales@montvillehotel.co.uk
web: www.montvillehotel.co.uk
Dir: *M42 junct 3, A435 follow Redditch centre signs, then signs towards Southcrest on A441*
Situated less than half a mile from the town centre, this is a small, friendly, privately owned hotel, suitable for both business and leisure guests. Rooms vary in size and style, and all have the necessary comforts. A well-stocked bar, a homely lounge and an interesting dining room complete the picture.
ROOMS: 14 en suite (2 fmly) (1 GF) in 5 bedrooms s £30-£50; d £55-£70 (incl. bkfst) **LB** **CONF:** Thtr 60 Class 30 Board 24 Del £75 **PARKING:** 12 **NOTES:** in restaurant
CARDS:

Campanile
Far Moor Ln, Winyates Green B98 0SD
☎ 01527 510710 01527 517269
e-mail: redditch@envergure.co.uk
Dir: *A435 towards Redditch, then A4023 to Redditch and Bromsgrove*
This modern building offers accommodation in smart, well-equipped bedrooms, all with en suite bathrooms.
continued

Refreshments may be taken at the informal Bistro. For further details consult the Hotel Groups page.

ROOMS: 46 annexe en suite s fr £42.95; d fr £42.95
CONF: Thtr 35 Class 18 Board 20

⌂ Premier Lodge (Redditch)

Birchfield Rd B97 6PX
☎ 0870 9906392 📠 0870 9906393
web: www.premierlodge.com
PREMIER LODGE.com
Dir: *A448 to Redditch & take 1st exit to Webheath, at rdbt take 3rd exit & 1st right*
High quality, modern, budget accommodation, ideal for families and business travellers. All rooms feature bath, power shower and satellite TV, and most have telephones / modem points. The adjacent bar and restaurant offers a wide and varied menu.
ROOMS: 33 en suite s £48; d £48 **CONF:** Thtr 150

REDHILL, Surrey

Map 06 TQ25

★★★★ 74% ®® Nutfield Priory

Nutfield RH1 4EL
HandPICKED
☎ 01737 824400 📠 01737 823321
e-mail: nutfieldpriory-cro@handpicked.co.uk
web: www.nutfield-priory.com
Dir: *M25 junct 6, follow Redhill signs via Godstone on A25. Hotel 1m on left after Nutfield Village or M25 junct 8 follow A25 through Reigate and Redhill, Godstone. Hotel on right 1.5m after railway bridge*

This Victorian country house dates back to 1872 and is set in 40 acres of grounds with stunning views over the Surrey countryside. Bedrooms are individually decorated and equipped with an excellent range of facilities. Public areas include the impressive

continued on p482

REDHILL, continued

grand hall, Cloisters restaurant, the library, and a cosy lounge bar area. Hand Picked Hotels - AA Hotel Group of the Year 2004-5.
ROOMS: 60 en suite (4 fmly) ⊗ in 24 bedrooms s £125-£165; d £145-£165 **LB** **FACILITIES: Spa** STV Squash Sauna Solarium Gym Jacuzzi Steam room Beauty therapy Aerobic & Step classes Xmas **CONF:** Thtr 80 Class 45 Board 40 Del from £189 **SERVICES:** Lift **PARKING:** 130 **NOTES:** ⊗ in restaurant Civ Wed 80
CARDS:

See advert on page 481

Innkeeper's Lodge Redhill
2 Redstone Hill RH1 4BL
☎ 01737 768434 01737 770742
www.innkeeperslodge.com
Dir: *M25 junct 8, follow signs for Redhill (A25). At railway station, left towards Godstone, located on right*
Smart rooms meet essential business requirements but also have home comforts, and depending on location may well have meeting rooms and pub dining. Dining options generally include all-day menus plus the added advantage of breakfast.
ROOMS: 37 en suite s £45-£69.95; d £45-£69.95 **CONF:** Thtr 50 Class 20 Board 24

Travel Inn
Brighton Rd, Salfords RH1 5BT
☎ 08701 977218 01737 778099
Dir: *on A23 , 2m south of Redhill and 3m north of Gatwick Airport*
Travel Inn offers good-quality, value-for-money accommodation. Spacious, en suite rooms with bath and shower comfortably accommodate a family of up to two adults and two children (to age 15). The restaurant and bar offers a varied menu. For further details consult the Hotel Groups page.
ROOMS: 48 en suite s £45.95-£48.95; d £45.95-£48.95 **CONF:** Thtr 35

REDRUTH, Cornwall & Isles of Scilly — Map 02 SW64

★★★70% Penventon Park
TR15 1TE
☎ 01209 203000 01209 203001
e-mail: hello@penventon.com
web: www.penventon.com
Dir: *off A30 at Redruth. Follow signs for Redruth West, hotel 1m S*

Set in attractive parkland, this Georgian mansion is ideal for either the business or leisure guest. Bedrooms are newly refurbished with 20 new Garden Suites. Cuisine offers a wide choice and specialises in Italian, French, British and Cornish dishes. Leisure facilities include a fitness suite and health spa as well as function rooms and bars.
ROOMS: 68 en suite (3 fmly) (25 GF) ⊗ in 6 bedrooms s £34-£84; d £58-£130 (incl. bkfst) **LB** **FACILITIES: Spa** supervised Sauna Solarium Gym Jacuzzi Leisure spa Masseuse Steam bath Pool table, beautician ♫ Xmas **CONF:** Thtr 200 Class 100 Board 60 Del from £49 **PARKING:** 100 **NOTES:** ⊗ in restaurant Civ Wed 150
CARDS:

★★65% Crossroads Lodge
Scorrier TR16 5BP
☎ 01209 820551 01209 820392
e-mail: crossroads@hotelstruro.com
web: www.hotelstruro.com/crossroads
Dir: *turn off A30 onto A3047 towards Scorrier*
Situated on an historic stanary site and conveniently located just off the A30, the Crossroads Lodge has a smart appearance with attractive flower baskets. Bedrooms are soundly furnished and include executive and family rooms. Public areas include an attractive dining room, a quiet lounge and a lively bar. Conference, banqueting and business facilities are also available.
ROOMS: 36 en suite (2 fmly) (8 GF) ⊗ in 8 bedrooms s £44-£54; d £60-£67.50 (incl. bkfst) **LB** **FACILITIES:** ch fac **CONF:** BC Thtr 150 Class 80 Board 60 **SERVICES:** Lift **PARKING:** 140 **NOTES:** ⊗ in restaurant **CARDS:**

REDWORTH, Co Durham — Map 19 NZ22

★★★★73% Redworth Hall Hotel
DL5 6NL
☎ 01388 770600 01388 770654
e-mail: redworthhall@paramount-hotels.co.uk
Dir: *from A1(M) junct 58 take A68 'Corbridge'. Follow hotel signs*

This imposing Georgian building has been enlarged and now includes a health club with state-of-the-art equipment. There are several spacious lounges and two restaurants: the relaxed Conservatory and the intimate 1744 fine-dining option. Bedrooms are thoughtfully equipped and impressive conference facilities make this a popular destination for business travellers.
ROOMS: 100 en suite (8 fmly) ⊗ in 45 bedrooms s £120; d £135-£165 (incl. bkfst) **LB** **FACILITIES:** STV Sauna Solarium Gym Jacuzzi Bodysense Health & Beauty Club ♫ Xmas **CONF:** Thtr 300 Class 150 Board 100 Del from £145 **SERVICES:** Lift **PARKING:** 300 **NOTES:** Civ Wed **CARDS:**

continued

REIGATE, Surrey Map 06 TQ25

★★★67% Reigate Manor Hotel

Reigate Hill RH2 9PF

☎ 01737 240125 📠 01737 223883

e-mail: hotel@reigatemanor.co.uk

web: www.reigatemanor.co.uk

Dir: *on A217, 1m S of junct 8 on M25*

On the slopes of Reigate Hill, the hotel is ideally located for access to the town and for motorway links. A range of public rooms is provided along with a variety of function rooms. Bedrooms are either traditional in style in the old house or of contemporary design in the newer wing.

ROOMS: 50 en suite (1 fmly) ⊘ in all bedrooms s £80-£90; d £90-£100 (incl. bkfst) **FACILITIES:** STV **CONF:** Thtr 200 Class 80 Board 50 Del from £130 **PARKING:** 130 **NOTES:** ⊘ in restaurant Civ Wed 200

CARDS:

★★★63% Bridge House

Reigate Hill RH2 9RP

☎ 01737 246801 & 244821 📠 01737 223756

Dir: *on A217 between M25 and Reigate*

Enjoying a prime position on top of Reigate Hill, this hotel offers some impressive views. Bedrooms are spacious and most have balconies. The Mediterranean-style restaurant is well established and is the venue for entertainment evenings. Parking and conference rooms are also available.

ROOMS: 39 en suite (3 fmly) (11 GF) **FACILITIES:** STV ♫ **CONF:** Thtr 100 Class 70 Board 60 **PARKING:** 110 **NOTES:**

CARDS:

RENISHAW, Derbyshire Map 16 SK47

★★★65% Sitwell Arms

Station Rd S21 3WF

☎ 01246 435226 📠 01246 433915

e-mail: sitwellarms@renishaw79.fsnet.co.uk

Dir: *on A6135 to Sheffield, W of M1 junct 30*

This stone-built hotel, parts of which date back to the 18th century, is conveniently situated close to the M1. The hotel is well maintained and offers good value accommodation. Bedrooms are of a comfortable size and include the expected range of facilities. There are extensive bars and a restaurant providing a wide range of dishes and grills.

ROOMS: 29 en suite (8 fmly) (9 GF) ⊘ in 10 bedrooms s £38-£61; d £60-£70 (incl. bkfst) **LB** **FACILITIES:** Planning permission for leisure centre end of 2004 Xmas **CONF:** Thtr 160 Class 60 Board 60 Del from £65.95 **PARKING:** 150 **NOTES:** ⊘ in restaurant Civ Wed 150

CARDS:

See advert on this page

RETFORD (EAST), Nottinghamshire Map 08 SK78

★★★65% The West Retford Hotel

24 North Rd DN22 7XG
☎ 0870 609 6162 🖷 01777 709951
Dir: *From A1 take A620 to Ranby/Retford. Left at rdbt into North Rd (A638). Hotel on right*

Set in attractive grounds close to the town centre, this 18th-century manor house offers a good range of well-equipped meeting facilities. The spacious, well laid out bedrooms and suites are located in separate buildings; the Garden Cottage rooms are particularly pleasing.
ROOMS: 62 annexe en suite (37 fmly) (34 GF) ⊗ in 36 bedrooms **FACILITIES:** STV **CONF:** Thtr 150 Class 40 Board 43 Del from £80 **PARKING:** 100 **NOTES:** ⊗ in restaurant Civ Wed 120
CARDS:

★★67% Frenchgate

59-61 Frenchgate DL10 7AE
☎ 01748 822087 🖷 01748 823596
e-mail: info@frenchgatehotel.com
web: www.frenchgatehotel.com
Dir: *from Scotch Corner take A6108. Through Richmond to New Queens Rd rdbt, left into Dundas St and left again into Frenchgate*

This elegant townhouse dates from the 16th and 17th Centuries. Bedrooms are brightly decorated and comfortably equipped. Public areas include an upstairs lounge with a low ceiling and original wooden beams. At dinner there is a good choice of freshly prepared dishes, and bar meals are also available.
ROOMS: 10 en suite 1 annexe en suite (1 fmly) (3 GF) ⊗ in all bedrooms **FACILITIES:** Award winning gardens ch fac **CONF:** BC **PARKING:** 9 **NOTES:** ⊗ in restaurant
CARDS:

RICHMOND, North Yorkshire Map 19 NZ10

★★★66% King's Head

Market Place DL10 4HS
☎ 01748 850220 🖷 01748 850635
e-mail: res@kingsheadrichmond.co.uk
web: www.kingsheadrichmond.co.uk
Dir: *leave A1 or A66 at Scotch Corner & take A6108 to Richmond. Follow signs to town centre*

Centrally located in the historic market square, this hotel is a converted coaching inn. Bedrooms are comfortable and tastefully furnished. The lounge, furnished with deep sofas, displays an interesting collection of antique clocks. Afternoon tea is served in the lounge/bar along with light meals and the stylish restaurant offers a varied choice of more formal yet relaxed dining with views over the square.
ROOMS: 26 en suite 4 annexe en suite (1 fmly) ⊗ in 11 bedrooms s £69; d £95 (incl. bkfst) **LB** **CONF:** Thtr 180 Class 80 Board 50 Del from £80 **PARKING:** 25 **NOTES:** ⊗ in restaurant
CARDS:

RICHMOND (UPON THAMES), Greater London
See LONDON SECTION plan 1 C2

★★★★72% ®® The Richmond Gate Hotel

corus hotels

Richmond Hill TW10 6RP
☎ 020 8940 0061 🖷 020 8332 0354
e-mail: richmondgate@corushotels.com
Dir: *from Richmond to top of Richmond Hill and hotel on left opposite Star & Garter home at Richmond Gate exit*

A stylish Georgian hotel, sitting at the top of Richmond Hill and opposite the gates to Richmond Park. Bedrooms are equipped to a very high standard and include luxury doubles and spacious suites. Dinner in the Park Restaurant features bold, contemporary cooking and is the highlight of any visit.
ROOMS: 68 en suite ⊗ in 35 bedrooms s £140-£170; d £150-£180 (incl. bkfst) **LB** **FACILITIES: Spa** STV Sauna Solarium Gym Jacuzzi Health & beauty suite Steam room Xmas **CONF:** Thtr 50 Class 20 Board 30 Del from £220 **PARKING:** 50 **NOTES:** ⊗ in restaurant Civ Wed 70 **CARDS:**

★★★★66% The Petersham
Nightingale Ln TW10 6UZ
☎ 020 8940 7471 020 8939 1098
e-mail: enq@petershamhotel.co.uk
Dir: *From Richmond Bridge rdbt (A316) follow signs to Ham and Petersham. Hotel in Nightingale Lane a small turning on the left off Petersham Rd.*
Managed by the same family for over 25 years, this attractive hotel is sited on a hill overlooking water meadows and a sweep of the River Thames. Bedrooms and suites are comfortably furnished, whilst public areas combine elegance and some fine architectural features. High quality produce is used to provide enjoyable meals in the newly refurbished restaurant that looks out over the river.
ROOMS: 61 en suite (4 fmly) (3 GF) s £135-£160; d £170-£295 (incl. bkfst) **LB** **FACILITIES:** STV Xmas **CONF:** Thtr 35 Class 20 Board 25 Del from £225 **SERVICES:** Lift **PARKING:** 61 **NOTES:** Civ Wed 40
CARDS:

★★★68% Richmond Hill

Richmond Hill TW10 6RW
☎ 020 8940 2247 020 8940 5424
e-mail: richmondhill@corushotels.com
Dir: *top of Richmond Hill on B321*

This attractive Georgian Manor built on Richmond Hill enjoys elevated views of the Thames. The town and the park are within easy walking distance. Bedrooms vary in size and style, all are comfortable and modern in design. The stylish, well-designed health club with large pool is shared with sister hotel the Richmond Gate.
ROOMS: 138 en suite (2 fmly) in 48 bedrooms **FACILITIES:** STV supervised Sauna Solarium Gym Jacuzzi Steam room Health & beauty suite **CONF:** Thtr 180 Class 100 Board 50 Del from £150 **SERVICES:** Lift **PARKING:** 150 **NOTES:** Civ Wed 150
CARDS:

★★★63% *Bingham Hotel*
61-63 Petersham Rd TW10 6UT
☎ 020 8940 0902 020 8948 8737
e-mail: reservations@binghamhotel.co.uk
Dir: *on A307*
This Georgian building overlooks the Thames and is within walking distance of the town centre. Bedrooms vary in size and style and comfortable public rooms enjoy views of the pretty garden and river. Diners can choose from a selection of meals from light snacks to three-course dinners.

continued

ROOMS: 23 en suite (2 fmly) **FACILITIES:** Gym **CONF:** Thtr 60 Class 40 Board 25 **PARKING:** 12 **NOTES:** Civ Wed 40
CARDS:

RICKMANSWORTH, Hertfordshire — Map 06 TQ09

★★★★★72% The Grove
Chandler's Cross WD3 4TG
☎ 01923 807807 01923 221008
e-mail: info@thegrove.co.uk
web: www.thegrove.co.uk
Dir: *From M25 follow signs for the A411 towards Watford, entrance to hotel is on the right. From M1 follow brown signs to The Grove.*

Set in 300 acres of grounds, this splendid new hotel combines historic character with marvellous modern design. The spacious bedrooms feature the latest in temperature control, flat-screen TV and lighting technology. Many have balconies and separate showers. Suites in the original mansion are particularly stunning. There is an impressive range of facilities including championship golf, a luxurious spa, three dining options and extensive conference facilities. Nominated for the AA Hotel of the Year Award for England 2004-5.
ROOMS: 227 en suite (31 fmly) (35 GF) in 144 bedrooms s fr £282 **FACILITIES: Spa** STV 18 Fishing Sauna Solarium Gym Putt green Jacuzzi 12 Treatment rooms, cycling, kids club ch fac Xmas **CONF:** BC Thtr 500 Class 300 Board 80 **SERVICES:** Lift air con **PARKING:** 400 **NOTES:** Civ Wed
CARDS:

R

RINGWOOD, Hampshire Map 05 SU10

★★★67% Tyrrells Ford Country House

Avon BH23 7BH
☎ 01425 672646 01425 672262
e-mail: tyrrellsford@aol.com
web: www.tyrrellsfordhotel.com
Dir: *off A31 to Ringwood. Follow B3347 and hotel 3m S on left at Avon*
Set in the New Forest, this delightful family-run hotel has much to offer. Most bedrooms have views over the open country. Diners may eat in the formal restaurant, or sample the wide range of bar meals, all prepared using fresh local produce. The gallery lounge offers guests a peaceful area in which to relax.
ROOMS: 16 en suite s £65-£80; d £50-£65 (incl. bkfst) **LB**
FACILITIES: arrangement with local David Lloyd Fitness Club. Xmas
CONF: Thtr 40 Class 20 Board 20 Del from £110 **PARKING:** 100
NOTES: in restaurant Civ Wed 60
CARDS:

★★64% *Candlesticks Inn*

136 Christchurch Rd BH24 3AP
☎ 01425 472587 01425 471600
e-mail: info@hotelnewforest.co.uk
web: www.hotelnewforest.co.uk
Dir: *from M27/A31, take B3347 to Christchurch. Hotel on right 0.5m from flyover*
This attractive, thatched 15th-century inn is close to the town centre. The cottage-style bedrooms are contained in a modern adjacent lodge and include ground floor rooms together with a bedroom equipped for less able guests. Snacks can be taken in a bright conservatory bar lounge and there is also an atmospheric restaurant for more formal meals.
ROOMS: 8 en suite (1 fmly) **PARKING:** 45 **NOTES:** No children 2yrs Closed 23 Dec-9 Jan **CARDS:**

Travelodge

Travelodge

St Leonards BH24 2NR
☎ 08700 850 950 01425 475941
Travelodge offers good quality, good value, modern accommodation. Ideal for families, the spacious, en suite bedrooms include remote-control TV, tea and coffee-making facilities and luxury beds. Meals can be taken at the nearby family restaurant. For further details consult the Hotel Groups page.
ROOMS: s fr £25; d fr £25

R

RIPLEY, Derbyshire Map 16 SK35

Moss Cottage

Nottingham Rd DE5 3JT
☎ 01773 742555 01773 741063
e-mail: edmundwarriner@btconnect.com
Dir: *10 mins from M1 junct 26, A610 to Ripley. Hotel approx 4m from motorway.*
At the time of going to press, the star classification for this hotel was not confirmed. Please refer to the AA internet site www.theAA.com for current information.
ROOMS: 14 en suite (4 fmly) s £55-£175; d £65-£175 (incl. bkfst) **LB**
FACILITIES: cycling, golf, outdoor pursuits. **PARKING:** 60 **NOTES:** in restaurant **CARDS:**

For central reservation numbers and more information on Hotel Groups, turn to pages 33-39

RIPON, North Yorkshire Map 19 SE37

★★★69% Ripon Spa

Best Western

Park St HG4 2BU
☎ 01765 602172 01765 690770
e-mail: spahotel@bronco.co.uk
web: www.riponspa.com
Dir: *From A61 follow signs for B6265 towards Fountains Abbey. Hotel on left after hospital*

This privately owned and personally run hotel is set in extensive and attractive gardens, yet is only a short walk from the city centre. It provides comfortable and traditional accommodation in a pleasant and relaxing environment. There are comfortable lounges, a terrace overlooking the gardens and the popular Turf Tavern. Traditional English cooking is served in the elegant main restaurant.
ROOMS: 40 en suite (5 fmly) (4 GF) in 8 bedrooms s £95-£100; d £105-£120 (incl. bkfst) **LB** **FACILITIES:** STV Xmas **CONF:** Thtr 150 Class 35 Board 40 Del from £100 **SERVICES:** Lift **PARKING:** 60
NOTES: in restaurant Civ Wed 150
CARDS:

See advert under HARROGATE

★★63% Unicorn

Market Place HG4 1BP
☎ 01765 602202 01765 690734
e-mail: info@unicorn-hotel.co.uk
web: www.unicorn-hotel.co.uk
Dir: *on SE corner of Market Place, 4m from A1 on A61*
Centrally located in Ripon's ancient market place, this traditional inn dates back 500 years to when it was a coaching house. The busy pub and attractive restaurant feature a wide selection of good-value dishes. Bedrooms are of mixed styles and all offer the expected amenities.
ROOMS: 33 en suite (4 fmly) s £53; d £75 (incl. bkfst) **LB**
FACILITIES: **CONF:** Thtr 60 Class 10 Board 26 Del £94.50
PARKING: 20 **NOTES:** in restaurant Closed 24-25 Dec
CARDS:

RISLEY, Derbyshire Map 11 SK43

★★★★68% *Risley Hall*

Derby Rd DE72 3SS
☎ 0115 939 9000 0115 939 7766
e-mail: info@risleyhallhotel.co.uk
Dir: *M1 junct 25, Sandiacre exit. Left at T-junct, hotel 0.5m on left*
This impressive 11th-century manor house is set in beautiful listed gardens. Relaxing public areas include a choice of bars, morning room, a new leisure pool suite, and a grand baronial hall. Many of the individually styled bedrooms in the main house boast antique

continued

furnishings, exposed beams and wall timbers, whilst the newly developed suites are exceptionally comfortable.
ROOMS: 16 en suite 18 annexe en suite (8 fmly) **FACILITIES:** STV Archery **CONF:** Thtr 150 Class 80 Board 60 **SERVICES:** Lift **PARKING:** 120 **NOTES:** in restaurant Civ Wed 120
CARDS:

See advert on this page

ROCHDALE, Greater Manchester — Map 16 SD81

★★★★62% Norton Grange

Manchester Rd, Castleton OL11 2XZ
☎ 01706 630788 01706 649313
e-mail: nortongrange@macdonald-hotels.co.uk
Dir: *M62 junct 20, follow signs for A664, left after "All-in-One" Garden centre*
Standing in nine acres of grounds and mature gardens, this Victorian house provides comfort in elegant surroundings. The well-equipped bedrooms have been refurbished to provide a host of extras for both the business and leisure guest. Public areas include the Pickwick bistro and bar and a smart restaurant, both offering a good choice of dishes.
ROOMS: 51 en suite in 40 bedrooms s £88-£105; d £103-£120 (incl. bkfst) **LB FACILITIES:** STV Complimentary use of leisure centre Xmas **CONF:** Thtr 220 Class 120 Board 70 Del £145 **SERVICES:** Lift **PARKING:** 150 **NOTES:** in restaurant Civ Wed 150
CARDS:

Travel Inn

Newhey Rd, Milnrow OL16 4JF
☎ 08701 977219 01706 299074
Dir: *M62 junct 21 at rdbt, right towards Shaw, under motorway bridge & take 1st left*
Travel Inn offers good-quality, value-for-money accommodation. Spacious, en suite rooms with bath and shower comfortably accommodate a family of up to two adults and two children (to age 15). The restaurant and bar offers a varied menu. For further details consult the Hotel Groups page.
ROOMS: 40 en suite s £45.95-£46.95; d £45.95-£46.95
CONF: Thtr 25 Board 12

ROMALDKIRK, Co Durham — Map 19 NY92

Top 200 – Hotel

★★ Rose & Crown

DL12 9EB
☎ 01833 650213 01833 650828
e-mail: hotel@rose-and-crown.co.uk
web: www.rose-and-crown.co.uk
Dir: *6m NW from Barnard Castle on B6277*
This charming country inn is located in the heart of the village, overlooking fine fell scenery. Attractively furnished bedrooms, including suites, are split between the main house and the rear courtyard. There is a cosy bar, warmed by log fires, and a welcoming restaurant. Good local produce features extensively on the menu. Service is both friendly and attentive.
ROOMS: 7 en suite 5 annexe en suite (1 fmly) in all bedrooms s £75-£90; d £110-£124 (incl. bkfst) **LB FACILITIES:** STV **PARKING:** 20 **NOTES:** in restaurant Closed 24-26 Dec
CARDS:

ROMFORD, Greater London — Map 06 TQ58

Premier Lodge (Romford)

Whalebone Ln North, Chadwell Heath RM6 6QU
☎ 0870 9906450 0870 9906451
web: www.premierlodge.com
Dir: *6m from M25 junc 28 on A12 at junction with A1112*
High quality, modern, budget accommodation, ideal for families and business travellers. All rooms feature bath, power shower and satellite TV, and most have telephones / modem points. The adjacent bar and restaurant offers a wide and varied menu.
ROOMS: 40 en suite s £58; d £58 **CONF:** Thtr 50

Travel Inn

Mercury Gardens RM1 3EN
☎ 08701 977220 01708 760456

Dir: *off M25(J28), take A12 to Gallows Corner. Take A118 to next rbt and turn left*
Travel Inn offers good-quality, value-for-money accommodation. Spacious, en suite rooms with bath and shower comfortably

continued on p488

ROMFORD, continued

accommodate a family of up to two adults and two children (to age 15). The restaurant and bar offers a varied menu. For further details consult the Hotel Groups page.
ROOMS: 40 en suite s £54.95-£56.95; d £54.95-£56.95

ROMSEY, Hampshire Map 05 SU32

★★★66% Corus hotel Romsey

Winchester Rd, Ampfield SO51 9ZF
☎ 0870 609 6155 📠 023 8025 1359
e-mail: pottersheron@corushotels.com
Dir: *M3 junct 12 follow Chandlers Ford signs. 2nd exit at 3rd rdbt and follow signs for Ampfield, over x-rds and hotel on left after 1m*

This distinctive thatched hotel retains many of its original features. Extensive refurbishment has taken place to offer modern, stylish accommodation and spacious public areas. The re-styled pub and restaurant offers an interesting range of dishes to suit a variety of tastes.
ROOMS: 54 en suite (29 GF) ⊗ in 40 bedrooms s £92; d £92 **LB**
FACILITIES: STV Xmas **CONF:** Thtr 120 Class 40 Board 40 Del £135
SERVICES: Lift **PARKING:** 150 **NOTES:** ⊗ in restaurant Civ Wed 100
CARDS:

★★★64% The White Horse

Market Place SO51 8ZJ
☎ 0870 400 8123 📠 01794 517485
e-mail: whitehorseromsey@macdonald-hotels.co.uk
MACDONALD HOTELS
Dir: *M27 junct 3, follow A3057 to Romsey, signs to town centre. Past hotel, take 1st left into Latimer St, then left again into car park.*
It is thought that the hotel was originally a guest house for Romsey Abbey in the 12th century, although the present structure dates back to the time of Henry VIII. Bedrooms vary in size; the majority have now been refurbished and all are equipped with a range of modern facilities. Public rooms include a cosy lounge, bar and restaurant.
ROOMS: 26 en suite 7 annexe en suite (7 fmly) (7 GF) ⊗ in 10 bedrooms s £70-£90; d £95-£130 **LB** **FACILITIES:** STV Xmas
CONF: Thtr 90 Class 60 Board 40 Del from £99 **PARKING:** 40
NOTES: ⊗ in restaurant **CARDS:**

⌂ Premier Lodge (Southampton)

Romsey Rd, Ower SO51 6ZJ
PREMIER LODGE.com
☎ 0870 9906350 📠 0870 9906351
web: www.premierlodge.com
Dir: *M27 junct 2, follow A36 towards Salisbury, follow brown tourist sign 'The Vine Inn'. 200yds on Romsey Rd on right*
High quality, modern, budget accommodation, ideal for families and business travellers. All rooms feature bath, power shower and satellite TV, and most have telephones / modem points. The adjacent bar and restaurant offers a wide and varied menu.
ROOMS: 67 en suite s £52; d £52 **CONF:** Thtr 150 Class 80 Board 60 Del from £85

ROSEDALE ABBEY, North Yorkshire Map 19 SE79

★★★69% *Blacksmith's Country Inn*

Hartoft End YO18 8EN
☎ 01751 417331 📠 01751 417167
Dir: *off A170 in village of Wrelton, N to Hartoft*

Set amongst the wooded valleys and hillsides of the Yorkshire Moors, this charming hotel, now under new ownership, offers a choice of popular bars and intimate, cosy lounges, and retains the friendly atmosphere of a country inn. Food is available either in the bars or the spacious restaurant, while bedrooms vary in size and are all equipped to comfortable modern standards.
ROOMS: 19 en suite (4 GF) ⊗ in all bedrooms **FACILITIES:** Fishing
PARKING: 100 **NOTES:** ⊗ in restaurant RS Oct-Mar
CARDS:

★★72% ® Milburn Arms

YO18 8RA
☎ 01751 417312 📠 01751 417541
e-mail: info@milburnarms.co.uk

This attractive inn dates back to the 16th century and enjoys an idyllic, peaceful location in this scenic village. Bedrooms, some located in an adjacent stone block, are spacious, comfortable and smartly appointed. Guests can enjoy carefully prepared food either in the traditional bar or in the elegant restaurant.
ROOMS: 3 en suite 8 annexe en suite (2 fmly) (4 GF) ⊗ in all bedrooms **FACILITIES:** Xmas **PARKING:** 10 **NOTES:** ⊗ in restaurant Civ Wed **CARDS:**

ROSSINGTON, South Yorkshire Map 16 SK69

★★★★69% Mount Pleasant

Great North Rd DN11 0HW
☎ 01302 868696 & 868219 📠 01302 865130
e-mail: reception@mountpleasant.co.uk
web: www.bw-mountpleasant.co.uk
Dir: *on A638 Great North Rd between Bawtry and Doncaster*

This charming 18th-century house stands in 100 acres of wooded parkland. The spacious bedrooms have been thoughtfully equipped and pleasantly furnished; the Premier bedrooms being particularly comfortable. Public rooms have been extended to include an elegant restaurant and a very comfortable bar lounge. The hotel has good meeting facilities and a licence for civil weddings.

ROOMS: 45 en suite (12 fmly) (22 GF) in 44 bedrooms s £94-£115; d £119-£140 (incl. bkfst) **LB** **FACILITIES:** STV **CONF:** Thtr 150 Class 60 Board 60 Del from £140 **PARKING:** 100 **NOTES:** in restaurant Closed 25 Dec RS 24 Dec Civ Wed 150
CARDS:

ROSS-ON-WYE, Herefordshire Map 10 SO52
See also Goodrich

★★★74% Pengethley Manor

Pengethley Park HR9 6LL
☎ 01989 730211 📠 01989 730238
e-mail: reservations@pengethleymanor.co.uk
web: www.pengethleymanor.co.uk
Dir: *4m N on A49 Hereford road, from Ross-on-Wye*

This fine Georgian mansion is set in extensive grounds with two vineyards and glorious views. The accommodation is tastefully appointed and there is a wide variety of bedroom styles, all similarly well equipped. The elegant public rooms are furnished in a style sympathetic to the character of the house.

ROOMS: 11 en suite 14 annexe en suite (3 fmly) (4 GF) s £75-£115; d £120-£180 (incl. bkfst) **LB** **FACILITIES:** 9 Fishing Golf improvement course, walks accessible from Hotel ch fac Xmas **CONF:** Thtr 70 Class 25 Board 28 Del from £105 **PARKING:** 70 **NOTES:** in restaurant Civ Wed 90
CARDS:

★★★70% Chase

Gloucester Rd HR9 5LH
☎ 01989 763161 📠 01989 768330
e-mail: info@chasehotel.co.uk
Dir: *M50 junct 4, 1st left exit towards rdbt, left at rdbt towards A40. Right at 2nd rdbt towards Ross-on-Wye town centre, hotel 0.5m on left*

This attractive Georgian mansion sits in its own landscaped grounds and is only a short walk from the town centre. Bedrooms, some now refurbished, vary in size and character and include two *continued* four-poster rooms. There is also a light and spacious bar and an elegant restaurant together with a large function suite.

ROOMS: 36 en suite (1 fmly) in 10 bedrooms s £79-£109; d £89-£159 (incl. bkfst) **LB** **FACILITIES:** STV Xmas **CONF:** Thtr 300 Class 100 Board 80 Del from £100 **PARKING:** 150 **NOTES:** in restaurant Closed 26-30 Dec Civ Wed 300
CARDS:

★★★68% Pencraig Court

Pencraig HR9 6HR
☎ 01989 770306 📠 01989 770040
e-mail: info@pencraig-court.co.uk
web: www.pencraig-court.co.uk
Dir: *off A40, into Pencraig 4m S of Ross-on-Wye*

Impressive views of the River Wye and Ross-on-Wye beyond set the scene for a relaxing stay at this former Georgian mansion. The proprietors are on hand to ensure personal attention and service, while the bedrooms evoke a traditional feel and include a room with a four-poster bed. The country house ambience is completed by a choice of lounges and an elegant restaurant.

ROOMS: 10 en suite (1 fmly) in 6 bedrooms s £49-£52.50; d £80-£88 (incl. bkfst) **LB** **FACILITIES:** Fishing **PARKING:** 20 **NOTES:** in restaurant **CARDS:**

★★★67% The Royal

Palace Pound HR9 5HZ
☎ 01989 565105 📠 01989 768058
e-mail: 6504@greeneking.co.uk
Dir: *at end of M50 take A40 'Monmouth'. At 3rd rdbt, left to Ross, over bridge and take road signed 'The Royal Hotel' after left bend*

Close to the town centre, this imposing hotel enjoys panoramic views from its prominent hilltop position. Reputedly visited by Charles Dickens in 1867, this establishment has been sympathetically furnished to create the ambience of a bygone era with the comforts of today. In addition to the lounge and elegant restaurant, there are function rooms and an attractive garden.

ROOMS: 42 en suite (1 fmly) in 18 bedrooms s £75-£100; d £100-£135 (incl. bkfst) **LB** **FACILITIES:** Xmas **CONF:** Thtr 85 Class 20 Board 28 Del £100 **PARKING:** 44 **NOTES:** in restaurant Civ Wed 75
CARDS:

★★75% *Glewstone Court*

Glewstone HR9 6AW
☎ 01989 770367 📠 01989 770282
e-mail: glewstone@aol.com
Dir: *from Ross Market Place take A40/A49 Monmouth/Hereford, over Wilton Bridge to rdbt, turn left onto A40 to Monmouth, after 1m turn right for Glewstone*

This charming hotel enjoys an elevated position with views over Ross-on-Wye, and is set in well-tended gardens. Informal service is delivered with great enthusiasm by Bill Reeve-Tucker, and the kitchen is the domain of Christine Reeve-Tucker who offers an

continued on p490

ROSS-ON-WYE, continued

extensive menu of well executed dishes. Bedrooms come in a variety of sizes and are tastefully furnished and well equipped.

Glewstone Court, Ross-on-Wye

ROOMS: 8 en suite (2 fmly) **FACILITIES:** ♫ **CONF:** Thtr 35 Board 16 **PARKING:** 25 **NOTES:** ⊗ in restaurant Closed 25-27 Dec **CARDS:**

★★74% ⊛ Wilton Court Hotel

Wilton Ln HR9 6AQ
☎ 01989 562569 📠 01989 768460
e-mail: info@wiltoncourthotel.com
web: www.wiltoncourthotel.com
Dir: *M50 junct 4 onto A40 towards Monmouth at 3rd rdbt turn left signed Ross then take 1st right, hotel on right facing river*

Dating back to the 16th century, this engaging hotel has great charm with a wealth of character. Standing on the banks of the River Wye and just a short walk from the town centre, there is a genuinely relaxed, friendly and unhurried atmosphere here. Bedrooms are tastefully furnished and well equipped, while public areas include a comfortable lounge, traditional bar and pleasant restaurant with a conservatory extension overlooking the garden.
ROOMS: 10 en suite (1 fmly) ⊗ in all bedrooms s £60-£85; d £80-£115 (incl. bkfst) **LB** **FACILITIES:** Fishing Boule Xmas **CONF:** Thtr 40 Class 25 Board 25 Del from £107.50 **PARKING:** 24 **NOTES:** ⊗ in restaurant **CARDS:**

★★71% Castle Lodge Hotel

Wilton HR9 6AD
☎ 01989 562234 📠 01989 768322
e-mail: info@castlelodge.co.uk
Dir: *on rdbt at junct of A40/A49, 0.5m from centre of Ross-on-Wye*
This friendly hotel dates back to the 16th century and offers a convenient base on the outskirts of the town. Bedrooms are well equipped and comfortably furnished, while diners can choose

continued

between a good selection of bar meals and a varied restaurant menu, which features a wide range of fresh seafood.
ROOMS: 10 en suite (3 fmly) s fr £42.95; d fr £49.95 **LB** **FACILITIES:** tennis courts(0.5m) **CONF:** Thtr 100 Class 80 Board 60 **PARKING:** 40 **CARDS:**

★★67% Orles Barn

Wilton HR9 6AE
☎ 01989 562155 📠 01989 768470
e-mail: orles.barn@clara.net
web: www.orles.barn.clara.net
Dir: *off junct A40/A49*

This privately owned and personally run hotel stands in extensive gardens. All of the bedrooms are well maintained and thoughtfully equipped. The owners' South African heritage is reflected in the restaurant menu. Extra facilities include an outdoor heated swimming pool.
ROOMS: 8 en suite (1 fmly) ⊗ in 2 bedrooms s £51; d £68 (incl. bkfst) **LB** **FACILITIES:** Fishing Golf chipping parctice facility Xmas **CONF:** Board 16 **PARKING:** 20 **NOTES:** ⊗ in restaurant RS Nov-Jan **CARDS:**

★★66% Chasedale

Walford Rd HR9 5PQ
☎ 01989 562423 📠 01989 567900
e-mail: chasedale@supanet.com
web: www.chasedale.co.uk
Dir: *from Ross-on-Wye town centre, S on B4234, hotel 0.5m on left*
This large, mid-Victorian property is situated on the south-west outskirts of the town. Privately owned and personally run, it provides spacious, well-proportioned public areas and extensive grounds. The accommodation is well equipped and includes ground floor and family rooms, whilst the restaurant offers a wide selection of wholesome food.
ROOMS: 10 en suite (2 fmly) (1 GF) ⊗ in 1 bedroom s £33.50-£37.50; d £67-£75 (incl. bkfst) **LB** **FACILITIES:** Xmas **CONF:** Thtr 40 Class 30 Board 25 **PARKING:** 14 **NOTES:** ⊗ in restaurant **CARDS:**

★★66% King's Head

THE INDEPENDENTS

8 High St HR9 5HL
☎ 01989 763174 📠 01989 769578
e-mail: reception@kingshead.co.uk
web: www.kingshead.co.uk
Dir: *in town centre*
The King's Head dates back to the 14th century and has a wealth of charm and character. Bedrooms are well equipped and include both four-poster and family rooms. The restaurant doubles as a

continued

coffee shop during the day and is a popular venue with locals. There is also a very pleasant bar and comfortable lounge.

ROOMS: 16 en suite s fr £53.50; d fr £100 (incl. bkfst) **LB** **FACILITIES:** Xmas **PARKING:** 24 **NOTES:** ⊗ in restaurant **CARDS:**

Travel Inn

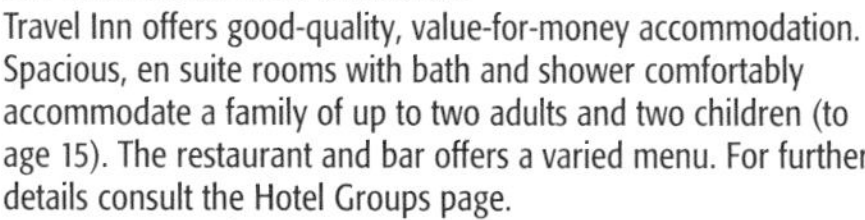

Ledbury Rd HR9 7QL
☎ 08701 977221 📠 01989 566124
Dir: *1m from town centre on M50 rdbt*

Travel Inn offers good-quality, value-for-money accommodation. Spacious, en suite rooms with bath and shower comfortably accommodate a family of up to two adults and two children (to age 15). The restaurant and bar offers a varied menu. For further details consult the Hotel Groups page.

ROOMS: 43 en suite s £45.95-£46.95; d £45.95-£46.95

ROSTHWAITE, Cumbria — Map 18 NY21

See also Borrowdale

★★64% Scafell

CA12 5XB
☎ 017687 77208 📠 017687 77280
e-mail: info@scafell.co.uk
Dir: *6m S of Keswick on B5289*

This friendly hotel is popular with walkers and enjoys a peaceful location. Bedrooms vary in style from traditional to modern, and are all well equipped and neatly decorated. Public areas include a residents' cocktail bar, lounge and spacious restaurant as well as the popular Riverside Inn pub, offering all day dining in summer months.

ROOMS: 24 en suite (2 fmly) (8 GF) s £68.50; d £137 (incl. bkfst & dinner) **LB** **FACILITIES:** Guided walks ch fac Xmas **PARKING:** 50 **NOTES:** ⊗ in restaurant Civ Wed 75 **CARDS:**

> Early start?
> Hotels at all star levels should provide in-room alarm clocks and/or alarm calls

ROTHERHAM, South Yorkshire — Map 16 SK49

★★★★64% Hellaby Hall

Old Hellaby Ln, Hellaby S66 8SN
☎ 01709 702701 📠 01709 700979
e-mail: reservations@hellabyhallhotel.co.uk
web: www.hellabyhallhotel.co.uk
Dir: *1m off M18 junct 1, onto A631 towards Maltby, in village of Hellaby*

This 17th-century house was built to a Flemish design with high, beamed ceilings, and staircases which lead off to private meeting rooms and a series of oak-panelled lounges. Bedrooms are elegant and well-equipped. Guests can dine in the formal Attic Restaurant, or Rizzio's informal pizzeria-restaurant/bar. There are extensive leisure facilities and conference areas, and the hotel holds a licence for civil weddings.

ROOMS: 90 en suite (4 fmly) ⊗ in 71 bedrooms s £45-£95; d £79-£105 **LB** **FACILITIES: Spa** STV supervised Sauna Solarium Gym Beauty room Xmas **CONF:** Thtr 500 Class 100 Board 100 Del from £99 **SERVICES:** Lift **PARKING:** 140 **NOTES:** ⊗ in restaurant Civ Wed 200 **CARDS:** *See advert on this page*

R

ROTHERHAM, continued

★★★74% ⊛ Consort
Brampton Rd, Thurcroft S66 9JA
☎ 01709 530022 📠 01709 531529
e-mail: info@consorthotel.com
web: www.consorthotel.com
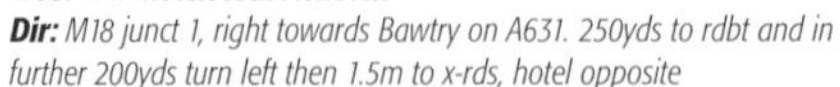
Dir: *M18 junct 1, right towards Bawtry on A631. 250yds to rdbt and in further 200yds turn left then 1.5m to x-rds, hotel opposite*
Bedrooms at this modern, friendly hotel are comfortable, attractive and air conditioned, and include ten superior rooms in a new wing. A wide range of dishes is served in the open-plan bar and restaurant, and there is a comfortable foyer lounge. There are good conference and function facilities, and entertainment evenings are often hosted here.
ROOMS: 27 en suite (2 fmly) (9 GF) ⊘ in 8 bedrooms s £50-£80; d £70-£90 (incl. bkfst) **LB** **FACILITIES:** STV ♫ **CONF:** Thtr 300 Class 120 Board 50 Del from £90 **SERVICES:** air con **PARKING:** 90 **NOTES:** ✈ ⊘ in restaurant Civ Wed 300
CARDS:

See advert on opposite page

★★★69% Best Western Elton
Main St, Bramley S66 2SF
☎ 01709 545681 📠 01709 549100
e-mail: bestwestern.eltonhotel@btinternet.com
Dir: *M18 junct 1 follow A631 Rotherham, turn right to Ravenfield, hotel at end of Bramley village, follow brown signs*
Within easy reach of the M18, this welcoming, stone-built hotel is set in well-tended gardens. Elton Hotel offers good modern accommodation, with larger rooms in the extension that are particularly comfortable and well equipped. The hotel has a civil wedding licence, and conference rooms are available.
ROOMS: 13 en suite 16 annexe en suite (4 fmly) (11 GF) ⊘ in 11 bedrooms s £49-£82; d £50-£90 (incl. bkfst) **LB** **FACILITIES:** STV **CONF:** Thtr 55 Class 24 Board 26 Del from £90 **PARKING:** 48 **NOTES:** ⊘ in restaurant Civ Wed 48
CARDS:

★★★68%
Courtyard by Marriott, Rotherham
West Bawtry Rd S60 4NA
☎ 0870 400 7235 📠 0870 400 7335
Dir: *M1 junct 33, A630 towards Rotherham, hotel 0.5m on right*
Stylish and contemporary, this modern hotel is well located just five minutes from the motorway. Bedrooms are spacious and boast an excellent range of facilities. Guests have the use of the newly refurbished leisure club with its swimming pool, spa bath and steam room.
ROOMS: 104 en suite (10 fmly) (22 GF) ⊘ in 76 bedrooms s £50-£120; d £70-£150 (incl. bkfst) **LB** **FACILITIES: Spa** STV supervised Solarium Gym Steam room, Childrens pool **CONF:** BC Thtr 300 Class 120 Board 40 Del from £125 **SERVICES:** Lift **PARKING:** 222 **NOTES:** ✈ Civ Wed 70 **CARDS:**

★★★65% *Carlton Park*
102/104 Moorgate Rd S60 2BG
☎ 01709 849955 📠 01709 368960
e-mail: reservations@carltonparkhotel.com
Dir: *M1 junct 33, onto A631, then A618. Hotel 800yds past Hospital*
This modern hotel is situated in a pleasant residential area of the town, close to the District General Hospital, yet within minutes of the M1. Bedrooms and bathrooms have been totally refurbished and offer very modern comfort and facilities. Three have separate sitting rooms. The restaurant and bar provide a lively atmosphere, and are popular with locals.
ROOMS: 80 en suite (14 fmly) (16 GF) ⊘ in 33 bedrooms **FACILITIES:** STV Sauna Solarium Gym Jacuzzi ♫ **CONF:** Thtr 250 Class 160 Board 60 **SERVICES:** Lift **PARKING:** 120 **NOTES:** ✈ ⊘ in restaurant Civ Wed 100 **CARDS:**

⌂ Hotel Ibis Rotherham
Moorhead Way, Bramley S66 1YY
☎ 01709 730333 📠 01709 730444
e-mail: H3163@accor-hotels.com
Dir: *M18 junct 1, left at rdbt & left at 1st lights. Hotel next to supermarket*
Modern, budget hotel offering comfortable accommodation in bright and practical bedrooms. Breakfast is self-service and dinner is available in the restaurant. For further details, consult the Hotel Groups page.
ROOMS: 86 en suite s fr £43.95; d fr £43.95 **CONF:** Thtr 40 Class 30 Board 30

⌂ Travel Inn
Bawtry Rd S65 3JB
☎ 08701 977222 📠 01709 531546
Dir: *on A631 towards Wickersley, between M18 junct 1 & M1 junct 33*
Travel Inn offers good-quality, value-for-money accommodation. Spacious, en suite rooms with bath and shower comfortably accommodate a family of up to two adults and two children (to age 15). The restaurant and bar offers a varied menu. For further details consult the Hotel Groups page.
ROOMS: 37 en suite s £45.95-£46.95; d £45.95-£46.95

ROTHERWICK, Hampshire — Map 05 SU75

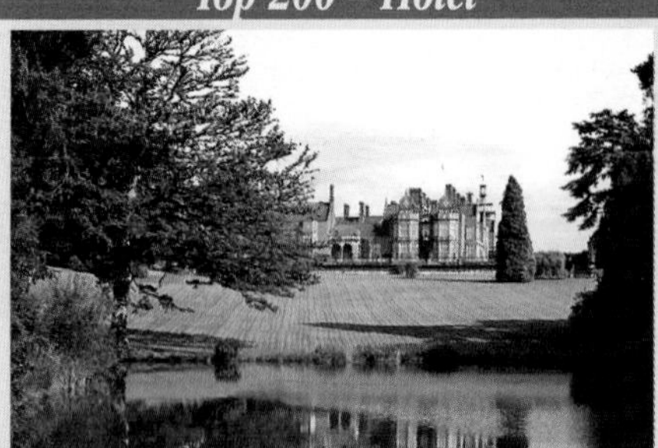

★★★★ ⊛⊛ Tylney Hall
RG27 9AZ
☎ 01256 764881 📠 01256 768141
e-mail: sales@tylneyhall.com
web: www.tylneyhall.com
Dir: *M3 junct 5, A287 to Basingstoke, over junct with A30, over railway bridge, towards Newnham. Right at Newnham Green. Hotel 1m on left*
A superb Grade II listed Victorian country house, set in 66 acres of beautiful parkland. The hotel offers very high standards of comfort in relaxed yet elegant surroundings, featuring magnificently restored water gardens, which were originally laid out by famous 19th-century gardener, Gertrude Jekyll. The spacious public rooms include the Wedgwood drawing room and panelled Oak Room, which are filled with fresh flowers and warmed by log fires. The spacious

continued

bedrooms are traditionally furnished and offer a high degree of comfort.
ROOMS: 35 en suite 77 annexe en suite (1 fmly) s £135-£400; d £165-£430 (incl. bkfst) **LB** **FACILITIES: Spa** STV Snooker Sauna Solarium Gym Clay pigeon shooting, Archery, Falconry, Balloon rides, Laser shooting ch fac Xmas **CONF:** BC Thtr 120 Class 70 Board 40 Del from £245 **PARKING:** 120 **NOTES:** in restaurant Civ Wed 100
CARDS:

ROTHLEY, Leicestershire — Map 11 SK51

★★★64% *Rothley Court*
Westfield Ln LE7 7LG
☎ 0116 237 4141 0116 237 4483
Dir: *on B5328*
Dating back to the 1500s and complete with its own chapel, this historic property sits in six acres of well-tended grounds. Public areas retain much of their original character and include an oak-panelled restaurant and a choice of function and meeting rooms. Bedrooms, some located in an adjacent stable block, are individually styled.
ROOMS: 13 en suite 21 annexe en suite in 14 bedrooms **CONF:** Thtr 100 Class 35 Board 35 **PARKING:** 100 **NOTES:** in restaurant
CARDS:

★★72% *The Limes*
35 Mountsorrel Ln LE7 7PS
☎ 0116 230 2531
Dir: *turn off old A6. Hotel off village green*
A relaxed and friendly environment prevails at The Limes. The well-maintained accommodation is equipped for the needs of its predominantly business clientele, with excellent facilities and comfortable executive swivel chairs. Public areas include a comfortable lounge bar and a smart restaurant. Good, secure car parking is a bonus.
ROOMS: 11 en suite **SERVICES:** air con **PARKING:** 15 **NOTES:** No children 14yrs Closed 23 Dec-2 Jan
CARDS:

ROUSDON, Devon — Map 04 SY29

★★★65% Dower House
Rousdon DT7 3RB
☎ 01297 21047 01297 24748
e-mail: info@dhhotel.com
Dir: *On A3052, 3m W of Lyme Regis*
Set in its own grounds, The Dower House Hotel offers attractively decorated bedrooms, each individually styled and well equipped with modern facilities. There is a comfortable bar/lounge and in the restaurant an imaginative, daily-changing menu is available.
ROOMS: 10 en suite (2 fmly) (1 GF) in all bedrooms s £60-£67.50; d £100-£110 (incl. bkfst) **LB** **FACILITIES:** Xmas **CONF:** Thtr 46 Class 30 Board 18 **PARKING:** 35 **NOTES:** in restaurant
CARDS:

ROWLAND'S CASTLE, Hampshire — Map 05 SU71

Innkeeper's Lodge Portsmouth North
Whichers Gate Rd PO9 6BB
☎ 0870 243 0500 & 023 9241 3761
www.innkeeperslodge.com
Dir: *M3 junct 2, at rdbt, right onto the B2149 (Rowlands Castle). After 2m, left onto B2148 Whichers Gate Rd, lodge on left*
Smart rooms meet essential business requirements but also have

continued

home comforts, and depending on location may well have meeting rooms and pub dining. Dining options generally include all-day menus plus the added advantage of breakfast.
ROOMS: 21 en suite s £48-£52.50; d £48-£52.50

ROWNHAMS MOTORWAY SERVICE AREA (M27), Hampshire — Map 05 SU31

Travel Inn (Southampton West)
Rownhams Service Area SO16 8AP
☎ 08701 977234 023 8074 0204
Dir: *M27 Westbound - between junctions 3 & 4. No access from eastbound services*
Travel Inn offers good-quality, value-for-money accommodation. Spacious, en suite rooms with bath and shower comfortably accommodate a family of up to two adults and two children (to age 15). The restaurant and bar offers a varied menu. For further details consult the Hotel Groups page.
ROOMS: 39 en suite s £45.95-£46.95; d £45.95-£46.95

ROWSLEY, Derbyshire — Map 16 SK26

★★★79% East Lodge Country House
DE4 2EF
☎ 01629 734474 01629 733949
e-mail: info@eastlodge.com
web: www.eastlodge.com
Dir: *A6, 3m from Bakewell, 5m from Matlock*
The hotel enjoys a romantic setting in ten acres of landscaped grounds and gardens. The newly refurbished stylish bedrooms are equipped with many extras such as TVs with DVD players. Most have lovely garden views. The restaurant has a popular local

continued on p494

ROWSLEY, continued

following and offers much locally sourced produce. The conservatory lounge, overlooking the gardens offers afternoon teas and light meals.

East Lodge Country House, Rowsley

ROOMS: 14 en suite (2 fmly) in all bedrooms s £80-£110; d £100-£110 (incl. bkfst) **LB** **FACILITIES:** Xmas **CONF:** Thtr 75 Class 20 Board 22 **PARKING:** 40 **NOTES:** No children 7yrs in restaurant Civ Wed 100 **CARDS:**

See advert under BAKEWELL

★★★76% The Peacock at Rowsley

Bakewell Rd DE4 2EB
☎ 01629 733518 01629 732671
e-mail: reception@thepeacockatrowsley.com
web: www.thepeacockatrowsley.com
Dir: *A6, 3m before Bakewell, 6m from Matlock towards Bakewell*

Now owned once again by the estate of Haddon Hall this hotel has undergone a massive transformation. It is now a smart contemporary destination; which still retains many original features and period pieces of furniture. Dry fly fishing is a great attraction here as the hotel owns fishing rights in the area.
ROOMS: 16 en suite (5 fmly) in 2 bedrooms s £65-£79; d £100 (incl. cont bkfst) **FACILITIES:** STV Fishing Woodlands Fitness Centre with concessions Xmas **CONF:** Thtr 20 Class 8 Board 20 Del from £135 **PARKING:** 27 **NOTES:** in restaurant Civ Wed 20
CARDS:

RUAN HIGH LANES, Cornwall & Isles of Scilly Map 02 SW93

★★74% *Hundred House*

TR2 5JR
☎ 01872 501336 01872 501151
e-mail: clarke@hundredhousehotel.co.uk
web: www.hundredhousehotel.co.uk
Dir: *from B3287 at Tregony, left onto A3078 to St Mawes, hotel 4m on right*

Set in attractive gardens, this Edwardian house offers good access to the Roseland Peninsula, and is an ideal base for a relaxing break or for touring the area. Bedrooms are comfortable and spacious. Both dinner and breakfast offer freshly cooked and appetising dishes. Staff are friendly and attentive.
ROOMS: 10 en suite in all bedrooms **FACILITIES:** **PARKING:** 15 **NOTES:** No children 12yrs in restaurant Closed 2 Nov-4 Mar
CARDS:

RUGBY, Warwickshire Map 11 SP57

★★★67% *Brownsover Hall*

corus hotels

Brownsover Ln, Old Brownsover CV21 1HU
☎ 0870 609 6104 01788 579241
e-mail: brownsoverhall@corushotels.com
Dir: *M6 junct 1, signs to Rugby A426. Dual-carriageway for 0.5m at rdbt signed "Ambulance & Brownsover Hall Hotel" turn right. Hotel 400mtrs on right*

A mock-Gothic hall designed by Sir Gilbert Scott, set in seven acres of wooded parkland. Bedrooms vary in size and style, including spacious and contemporary rooms in the converted stable block. The former chapel makes a stylish restaurant, and for a less formal meal or a relaxing drink, the rugby themed bar is popular.
ROOMS: 27 en suite 20 annexe en suite (3 fmly) (12 GF) in 31 bedrooms **FACILITIES:** STV Free use of Esparta Gym (0.5 mile away) **CONF:** Thtr 70 Class 36 Board 35 **PARKING:** 100 **NOTES:** in restaurant Civ Wed 56 **CARDS:**

★★★64% Grosvenor Hotel Rugby

81-87 Clifton Rd CV21 3QQ
☎ 01788 535686 01788 541297
e-mail: grosvenorrugby@btconnect.com
Dir: *M6 junct 1, turn right onto A426 towards Rugby centre, at 1st rdbt turn left, on to T-junct and turn right onto B5414, hotel 2m on right*

Close to the town centre, this family-owned hotel is popular with both business and leisure guests. The public rooms are cosy, inviting and pleasantly furnished, and service is both friendly and

continued

attentive. Bedrooms come in a variety of styles and sizes and include several newer rooms.
ROOMS: 26 en suite (3 fmly) ⊗ in 21 bedrooms s fr £77.50; d fr £88.50 (incl. bkfst) LB **CONF:** Thtr 100 Class 50 Board 60 **PARKING:** 50
NOTES: ⊗ in restaurant Civ Wed 100
CARDS:

★★69% Golden Lion Inn

Easenhall CV23 0JA
☎ 01788 832265 📠 01788 832878
e-mail: goldenlioninn@aol.com
web: www.goldenlion-easenhall.co.uk
Dir: *A426 Avon Mill rdbt turn to Newbold-upon-Avon B4112, approx 2m left at Harborough Parva sign, opposite agricultural showroom, then 1m to Easenhall*
This friendly, family-run 16th-century inn is situated between Rugby and Coventry, convenient for access to the M6. Bedrooms are all individually furnished and well equipped; one with a stunning Chinese-style bed. There is a traditional, welcoming bar and appealing restaurant, both offering a wide choice of interesting dishes.
ROOMS: 12 en suite (1 fmly) (4 GF) ⊗ in 8 bedrooms s £52-£74.50; d £71.50-£86.50 (incl. bkfst) **FACILITIES:** Jacuzzi ch fac **PARKING:** 80
NOTES: ⊗ in restaurant **CARDS:**

★★65% *Hillmorton Manor*

78 High St, Hillmorton CV21 4EE
☎ 01788 565533 & 572403 📠 01788 540027
Dir: *M1 junct 18, onto A428 to Rugby*
Formerly a Victorian manor house, this family-run hotel sits on the outskirts of Rugby, offering a delightful combination of home and hotel. Public rooms include an attractive, airy restaurant and a comfortable bar and lounge. The bedrooms vary in style and size, and each room is comfortable and well equipped.
ROOMS: 11 en suite (1 fmly) **CONF:** Class 30 Board 65 **PARKING:** 40
NOTES: ⊗ in restaurant **CARDS:**

Hotel Ibis Rugby East

Parklands NN6 7EX
☎ 01788 824331 📠 01788 824332
e-mail: H3588@accor-hotels.com
(For full entry see Crick)

Innkeeper's Lodge Rugby

The Green, Dunchurch CV22 6NJ
☎ 01788 810305 📠 01788 810931
www.innkeeperslodge.com
Dir: *M1 junct 17/M45/A45. Follow signs for Dunchurch B4429. Lodge in village centre on x-rds of A426 and B4429*
Smart rooms meet essential business requirements but also have home comforts, and depending on location may well have meeting rooms and pub dining. Dining options generally include all-day menus plus the added advantage of breakfast.
ROOMS: 16 en suite s £48-£59.95; d £48-£59.95

Travel Inn Rugby

Central Park Dr, Central Park CV23 0WE
☎ 08701 977 223 📠 01788 - 565949
Travel Inn offers good-quality, value-for-money accommodation. Spacious, en suite rooms with bath and shower comfortably accommodate a family of up to two adults and two children (to age 15). The restaurant and bar offers a varied menu. For further details consult the Hotel Groups page.
ROOMS: 60 en suite (incl. bkfst) s £45.95-£46.95; d £45.95-£46.95

RUGELEY, Staffordshire

Map 10 SK01

Travelodge

Travelodge

Western Springs Rd WS15 2AS
☎ 08700 850 950 📠 01889 570096
Dir: *on A51/B5013*
Travelodge offers good quality, good value, modern accommodation. Ideal for families, the spacious, en suite bedrooms include remote-control TV, tea and coffee-making facilities and luxury beds. Meals can be taken at the nearby family restaurant. For further details consult the Hotel Groups page.
ROOMS: 32 en suite s fr £25; d fr £25

RUISLIP, Greater London
See LONDON SECTION plan 1 A5

★★★71% Barn Hotel

West End Rd HA4 6JB
☎ 01895 636057 📠 01895 638379
e-mail: info@thebarnhotel.co.uk
web: www.thebarnhotel.co.uk
Dir: *take A4180 (Polish War Memorial) exit off A40 to Ruislip, 2m to hotel entrance off a mini-rdbt before Ruislip underground station*

Once a farm, with parts dating back to the 17th century, this impressive property sits in three acres of gardens. Bedrooms vary in style, from contemporary to traditional oak-beamed varieties. All are comfortable and well-appointed. The refurbished public areas provide a high level of quality and luxury.
ROOMS: 59 en suite (3 fmly) (24 GF) ⊗ in 10 bedrooms s £95-£130; d £125-£180 (incl. bkfst) LB **FACILITIES:** STV Xmas **CONF:** Thtr 80 Class 50 Board 30 **PARKING:** 42 **NOTES:** ⊗ in restaurant Civ Wed 74 **CARDS:**

See advert under UXBRIDGE

> Packed in a hurry?
> Ironing facilities should be available at all star levels, either in rooms or on request

RUNCORN, Cheshire

Map 15 SJ58

Campanile

Campanile

Lowlands Rd WA7 5TP
☎ 01928 581771 📠 01928 581730
e-mail: runcorn@envergure.co.uk
Dir: *M56 junct 12, take A557, then follow signs for Runcorn rail station*
This modern building offers accommodation in smart, well-equipped bedrooms, all with en suite bathrooms.

continued on p496

R

RUNCORN, continued

Refreshments may be taken at the informal Bistro. For further details consult the Hotel Groups page.

Campanile, Runcorn

ROOMS: 53 en suite s fr £41.95; d fr £41.95
CONF: Thtr 35 Class 18 Board 24

⌂ Travel Inn

Chester Rd, Preston Brook WA7 3BB
☎ 08701 977224 🖷 01928 719852
Dir: *1m from M56 junct 11, at Preston Brook*

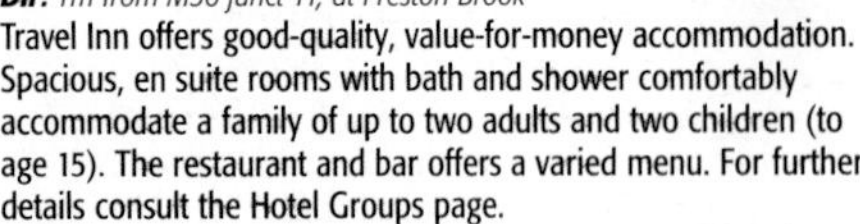

Travel Inn offers good-quality, value-for-money accommodation. Spacious, en suite rooms with bath and shower comfortably accommodate a family of up to two adults and two children (to age 15). The restaurant and bar offers a varied menu. For further details consult the Hotel Groups page.
ROOMS: 40 en suite s £45.95-£46.95; d £45.95-£46.95 **CONF:** Thtr 40

RUSHDEN, Northamptonshire — Map 11 SP96

⌂ Travelodge Wellingborough

Saunders Lodge NN10 9AP
☎ 08700 850 950 🖷 01933 57008
Dir: *on A45, eastbound*

Travelodge offers good quality, good value, modern accommodation. Ideal for families, the spacious, en suite bedrooms include remote-control TV, tea and coffee-making facilities and luxury beds. Meals can be taken at the nearby family restaurant. For further details consult the Hotel Groups page.
ROOMS: 40 en suite s fr £25; d fr £25

RUSTINGTON, West Sussex — Map 06 TQ00

⌂ Travelodge Littlehampton

Worthing Rd BN17 6LZ
☎ 08700 850 950 🖷 01903 733150
Dir: *on A259, 1m E of Littlehampton*

Travelodge offers good quality, good value, modern accommodation. Ideal for families, the spacious, en suite bedrooms include remote-control TV, tea and coffee-making facilities and luxury beds. Meals can be taken at the nearby family restaurant. For further details consult the Hotel Groups page.
ROOMS: 36 en suite s fr £25; d fr £25

RYDE See Wight, Isle of

RYE, East Sussex — Map 07 TQ92

★★★77% Flackley Ash

TN31 6YH
☎ 01797 230651 🖷 01797 230510
e-mail: enquiries@flackleyashhotel.co.uk
web: www.flackleyashhotel.co.uk
(For full entry see Peasmarsh)

★★★72% Rye Lodge

Hilder's Cliff TN31 7LD
☎ 01797 223838 🖷 01797 223585
e-mail: info@ryelodge.co.uk
web: www.ryelodge.co.uk
Dir: *one-way system in Rye, follow signs for town centre, through Landgate arch, hotel 100yds on right*

Standing in an elevated position, Rye Lodge has panoramic views across Romney Marshes and the Rother Estuary. Bedrooms come in a variety of sizes and styles; they are attractively decorated, tastefully furnished and thoughtfully equipped. Public rooms feature The Terrace Room Restaurant, where an interesting choice of home-made dishes is available, and indoor leisure facilities.
ROOMS: 18 en suite s £65-£120; d £90-£190 (incl. bkfst) **LB**
FACILITIES: Spa STV Sauna Aromatherapy Steam cabinet Xmas
PARKING: 20 **NOTES:** ⊗ in restaurant
CARDS:

See advert on opposite page

★★★71% ❀ Mermaid Inn

Mermaid St TN31 7EY
☎ 01797 223065 & 223788 🖷 01797 225069
e-mail: mermaidinnrye@btclick.com
web: www.mermaidinn .com
Dir: *A259, follow signs to town centre then into Mermaid St*

Situated near the top of a cobbled side street, this famous smugglers' inn is steeped in history. The charming interior has many architectural features such as attractive stone work. The bedrooms vary in size and style and are all tastefully furnished.

continued

Delightful public rooms include a choice of lounges, cosy bar and smart restaurant.
ROOMS: 31 en suite (5 fmly) s £80-£180; d £160-£200 (incl. bkfst) **LB**
FACILITIES: Xmas **CONF:** Thtr 50 Class 40 Board 30 Del from £135
PARKING: 25 **NOTES:** ⊗ in restaurant
CARDS:

★★★61% *The George*

High St TN31 7JP
☎ 01797 222114 📠 01797 224065
Situated in the centre of this popular town and surrounded by specialist shops, The George is full of character and offers comfortable public rooms including a bar, lounge and cosy restaurant, which reflect the period of the building. The bedrooms have been sympathetically modernised and each one is thoughtfully equipped.
ROOMS: 22 en suite ⊗ in 5 bedrooms **FACILITIES:** STV **CONF:** BC Thtr 100 Class 40 Board 40 **PARKING:** 7 **NOTES:** ⊗ in restaurant
CARDS:

★★71% Broomhill Lodge

Rye Foreign TN31 7UN
☎ 01797 280421 📠 01797 280402
Dir: *1.5m N on A268*
Built in the 1820s and set in its own three-acre grounds, this hotel is within easy reach of historic Rye, one of the Cinque Ports. Bedrooms are individually decorated, comfortably furnished and well-equipped. There are two lounges and an attractive restaurant.
ROOMS: 12 en suite s £68-£72; d £96-£160 (incl. bkfst) **LB**
FACILITIES: Sauna Mini gym Xmas **CONF:** Thtr 60 Class 60 Board 30
PARKING: 20 **NOTES:** ⊗ in restaurant
CARDS:

★★67% The Hope Anchor

Watchbell St TN31 7HA
☎ 01797 222216 📠 01797 223796
e-mail: info@thehopeanchor.co.uk
Dir: *from A268, Quayside, turn right into Wishard, up Mermaid St., right into West St., right into Watchbell St., hotel at end of street.*
This historic inn sits high above the town with enviable views out over the harbour and Romney Marsh, and is accessible via delightful cobbled streets. A relaxed and friendly atmosphere prevails within the cosy public rooms, while the attractively furnished bedrooms are well equipped and many enjoy good views over the marshes.
ROOMS: 11 en suite (1 fmly) ⊗ in all bedrooms s £55-£90; d £90-£140 (incl. bkfst) **LB** **FACILITIES:** Xmas **NOTES:** ⊗ in restaurant Closed 6 Jan-12 Jan **CARDS:**

SAFFRON WALDEN, Essex — Map 12 TL53

★★69% *Saffron*

10-12 High St CB10 1AZ
☎ 01799 522676 📠 01799 513979
e-mail: saffron.saffronwalden@oldenglishinns.co.uk
Dating back to the 16th century, this coaching inn retains much of its original character. The refurbished bedrooms are contemporary in style and boast numerous extra facilities. There is a popular public bar and conservatory restaurant where a wide range of freshly prepared dishes is served.
ROOMS: 16 en suite (1 fmly) ⊗ in all bedrooms **CONF:** Thtr 70 Class 50 Board 30 **PARKING:** 9 **NOTES:** ⊗ in restaurant
CARDS:

ST AGNES, Cornwall & Isles of Scilly — Map 02 SW75

★★★72% Rose in Vale Country House

Mithian TR5 0QD
☎ 01872 552202 📠 01872 552700
e-mail: reception@rose-in-vale-hotel.co.uk
Dir: *A30 through Cornwall, right onto B3277 signed St Agnus. Follow signs Rose-in-Vale in 500yds*

Peacefully located in a wooded valley this Georgian manor house has a wonderfully relaxed atmosphere and abundant charm and where guests are assured of a warm welcome. Accommodation varies in size and style; several rooms are situated on the ground floor. An imaginative fixed-price menu featuring local produce is served in the spacious restaurant.
ROOMS: 18 en suite (3 fmly) (3 GF) ⊗ in all bedrooms s £71-£80; d £126-£204 (incl. bkfst & dinner) **LB** **FACILITIES:** Sauna games room, table tennis, garden badminton Xmas **CONF:** Thtr 75 Class 50 Board 40 Del from £85 **PARKING:** 40 **NOTES:** ⊗ in restaurant Closed Jan-Feb Civ Wed 75 **CARDS:**

ST AGNES, continued

★★70% Rosemundy House

Rosemundy Hill TR5 0UF
☎ 01872 552101 🖹 01872 554000
e-mail: info@rosemundy.co.uk
Dir: *off A30 to St Agnes continue for approx 3m. On entering village take 1st right signed Rosemundy, hotel at foot of hill*

This elegant Queen Anne house has been carefully restored and extended to provide comfortable bedrooms and spacious, inviting public areas. The hotel is set in well-maintained gardens complete with an outdoor pool for warmer months. There is a choice of relaxing lounges, two restaurants and a cosy bar.

ROOMS: 46 en suite (3 fmly) (9 GF) ⊗ in 15 bedrooms s £33-£53; d £66-£106 (incl. bkfst & dinner) **LB** **FACILITIES:** Putt green Xmas **CONF:** Board 80 **PARKING:** 50 **NOTES:** No children 5 yrs ⊗ in restaurant **CARDS:**

★★70% Beacon Country House Hotel

Goonvrea Rd TR5 0NW
☎ 01872 552318 🖹 01872 552318
e-mail: info@beaconhotel.co.uk
web: www.beaconhotel.co.uk
Dir: *From A30 take B3277 to St Agnes. At rdbt left onto Goonvrea Rd. Hotel 0.75 miles on right.*

Set in a quiet and attractive area away from the busy village, this relaxed, family-run hotel has splendid views over the countryside towards the sea. Guests are assured of a friendly welcome, and many return for another stay. Bedrooms are comfortable and well equipped and many benefit from the good views.

ROOMS: 11 en suite (2 fmly) (2 GF) ⊗ in all bedrooms s £28-£41; d £56-£82 (incl. bkfst) **LB** **PARKING:** 14 **NOTES:** ⊗ in restaurant **CARDS:**

ST ALBANS, Hertfordshire — Map 06 TL10

★★★★72% Sopwell House Hotel, Country Club & Spa

Cottonmill Ln, Sopwell AL1 2HQ
☎ 01727 864477 🖹 01727 844741/845636
e-mail: enquiries@sopwellhouse.co.uk
web: www.sopwellhouse.co.uk
Dir: *M25 junct 22, follow A1081 St Albans. At traffic lights, turn left into Mile House Lane, over mini-rdbt into Cottonmill Lane*

This imposing Georgian house retains an exclusive ambience. Bedrooms vary in style and include a number of self-contained cottages within the Sopwell Mews. Meeting and function rooms are housed in a separate section and leisure and spa facilities are particularly impressive. Dining options include the brasserie and the fine-dining Magnolia restaurant.

ROOMS: 113 en suite 16 annexe en suite (12 fmly) ⊗ in 20 bedrooms s £129; d £169 **LB** **FACILITIES: Spa** STV supervised Sauna Solarium Gym Health & Beauty Spa, Hairdressing salon, 11 spa treatment room Xmas **CONF:** BC Thtr 400 Class 220 Board 120 Del from £185 **SERVICES:** Lift **PARKING:** 350 **NOTES:** ⊗ in restaurant Civ Wed 250 **CARDS:**

★★★78% St Michael's Manor

Fishpool St AL3 4RY
☎ 01727 864444 🖹 01727 848909
e-mail: reservations@stmichaelsmanor.com
Dir: *from St Albans Abbey follow Fishpool Street toward St Michael's village. Hotel 0.5m on left*

Adjacent to listed buildings, mills and ancient inns, this hotel is set in five acres of beautiful grounds, hidden from the street. Inside there is a real sense of luxury, encouraged by the high standard of décor and service. Award-winning food is served overlooking the immaculate gardens and the lake.

ROOMS: 22 en suite (1 fmly) ⊗ in 3 bedrooms s £140; d £175 (incl. bkfst) **LB** **FACILITIES:** STV ch fac Xmas **CONF:** Thtr 30 Class 20 Board 20 Del from £215 **PARKING:** 70 **NOTES:** ⊗ in restaurant Civ Wed 70 **CARDS:**

★★★63% Quality Hotel St Albans

232-236 London Rd AL1 1JQ
☎ 01727 857858 🖹 01727 855666
e-mail: st.albans@quality-hotels.net
Dir: *M25 junct 22 follow A1081 to St Albans, after 2.5m hotel on left, before bridge*

This hotel offers convenient access to and from the motorway network and the railway station in the town centre. The bedrooms are well equipped and there are also conference facilities. For relaxation, there is a comfortable bar which serves light snacks, and the Grapevine Restaurant serving more substantial meals.

ROOMS: 50 en suite (7 fmly) (12 GF) ⊗ in 28 bedrooms s £49-£85; d £69-£110 (incl. bkfst) **FACILITIES:** STV **CONF:** Thtr 220 Class 40 Board 50 Del from £100 **PARKING:** 70 **NOTES:** ⊗ in restaurant **CARDS:**

★★69% Comfort Hotel - Ryder House

Holywell Hill AL1 1HG
☎ 01727 848849 🖹 01727 812210
e-mail: adin@gb055.u-net.com

This listed building is ideally located in the centre of the town and provides smart, comfortable accommodation. Bedrooms are spacious, stylish and well equipped. Public areas include a restaurant/bar and several meeting rooms.

ROOMS: 60 en suite (18 fmly) ⊗ in 40 bedrooms s £75-£90; d £75-£90 **FACILITIES:** STV **CONF:** Thtr 45 Class 30 Board 25 Del from £120 **SERVICES:** Lift **PARKING:** 60 **NOTES:** ⊗ in restaurant **CARDS:**

ST ANNES See Lytham St Annes

ST AUSTELL, Cornwall & Isles of Scilly — Map 02 SX05

★★★★74% Carlyon Bay

Sea Rd, Carlyon Bay PL25 3RD
☎ 01726 812304 🖹 01726 814938
e-mail: reservations@carlyonbay.com
web: www.carlyonbay.com
Dir: *from St Austell, follow signs for Charlestown. Carlyon Bay signed on left, hotel at end of Sea Road*

Originally built in the 1920s, this long-established hotel lies on the clifftop in 250 acres of grounds, which include indoor and outdoor pools and a golf course. Bedrooms are well-maintained, many with marvellous views across St Austell Bay. A good choice of

continued

comfortable lounges is available, and facilities for families include kids clubs and entertainment.

ROOMS: 87 en suite (14 fmly) ⊗ in 14 bedrooms s £90-£106; d £170-£280 (incl. bkfst) **LB** **FACILITIES: Spa** STV 18 Snooker Sauna Solarium Putt green Table tennis 9-hole approach course, Health and beauty salon ♫ ch fac Xmas **SERVICES:** Lift **PARKING:** 100 **NOTES:** ⊗ in restaurant Civ Wed 100
CARDS:

See advert on this page

★★★72% Porth Avallen

Sea Rd, Carlyon Bay PL25 3SG
☎ 01726 812802 📠 01726 817097
e-mail: info@porthavallen.co.uk
Dir: *from A30 take A391 to St Austell. Turn right onto A390. Turn left at traffic lights and left at rdbt, then right into Sea Rd*

This traditional hotel boasts panoramic views over the rugged Cornish coastline. Refurbishment over recent years has resulted in smartly appointed public areas and well-presented bedrooms, many with sea views. There is an oak-panelled lounge and conservatory; both are ideal for relaxation. Both fixed-price and carte menus are offered in the elegant restaurant.

ROOMS: 27 en suite (2 fmly) ⊗ in 17 bedrooms s £65-£67; d £90-£156 (incl. bkfst) **LB** **FACILITIES:** ch fac Xmas **CONF:** Thtr 100 Class 40 Board 40 Del from £99 **PARKING:** 45 **NOTES:** ⊗ in restaurant
CARDS:

See advert on this page

★★★69% Cliff Head

Sea Rd, Carlyon Bay PL25 3RB
☎ 01726 812345 📠 01726 815511
e-mail: cliffheadhotel@btconnect.com
web: www.cliffheadhotel.com
Dir: *2m E off A390*

Set in extensive grounds and conveniently located for visiting the Eden Project, this hotel faces south and enjoys views over Carlyon Bay. A choice of lounges is provided, together with a swimming

continued on p500

S

ST AUSTELL, continued

pool and solarium. 'Expressions' restaurant offers a range of menus, which feature an interesting selection of dishes.
ROOMS: 60 rms (59 en suite) (2 fmly) s £55-£60; d £100-£110 (incl. bkfst) **LB** **FACILITIES:** Sauna Solarium Gym Xmas **CONF:** Thtr 150 Class 130 Board 70 Del from £75 **PARKING:** 60 **NOTES:** in restaurant Civ Wed 120 **CARDS:**

★★77% Boscundle Manor Country House

Tregrehan PL25 3RL
☎ 01726 813557 01726 814997
e-mail: stay@boscundlemanor.co.uk
Dir: *2m E on A390, 200yds on road signed Tregrehan*

Set in beautifully maintained gardens and grounds, this handsome 18th-century stone manor house is a short distance from the Eden Project. Quality and comfort are apparent in the public areas and spacious, well-equipped bedrooms. Equally suitable for both leisure and business travellers, Boscundle Manor boasts both indoor and outdoor pools.
ROOMS: 11 en suite 3 annexe en suite (4 fmly) (4 GF) in all bedrooms s £75-£80; d £130-£190 (incl. bkfst) **FACILITIES:** ch fac Xmas **CONF:** Thtr 40 Class 20 Board 20 Del from £45 **PARKING:** 15 **NOTES:** in restaurant Closed 2 Jan- 13 Feb Civ Wed 60 **CARDS:**

★★72% Pier House

Harbour Front, Charlestown PL25 3NJ
☎ 01726 67955 01726 69246
e-mail: pierhouse@btconnect.com
Dir: *follow A390 to St Austell, at Mt Charles rdbt left down Charlestown Rd*
This genuinely friendly hotel boasts a wonderful harbourside location. The unspoilt working port has been the setting for many film and television productions. Many bedrooms have sea views, and the convivial public bar is popular with locals and tourists alike. Locally caught fish features on the varied and interesting restaurant menu.
ROOMS: 26 en suite (4 fmly) in all bedrooms s £50-£55; d £82-£95 (incl. bkfst) **PARKING:** 50 **NOTES:** in restaurant Closed 24-25 Dec **CARDS:**

★★71% White Hart

Church St PL25 4AT
☎ 01726 72100 01726 74705
Situated in the town centre, this 18th-century, stone-built inn has been completely refurbished with impressive results. Bedrooms offer high standards of comfort and public areas are stylish and contemporary. The light and airy restaurant is the venue for a modern menu that makes good use of local produce.
ROOMS: 17 en suite (2 fmly) in all bedrooms s £55; d £80 (incl. bkfst) **LB** **FACILITIES:** Xmas **CONF:** Thtr 50 Board 20 **PARKING:** 13 **NOTES:** in restaurant
CARDS:

★★70% *Victoria Inn & Lodge*

Victoria, Roche PL26 8LQ
☎ 01726 890207 01726 891233
e-mail: victoriainn@talk21.com
Dir: *6m W of Bodmin on A30. 1st left after garage, Victoria Inn approx 500yds on right*
Situated midway between Bodmin and Newquay, this is a convenient choice for both the business and leisure traveller. The lodge-style bedrooms are purpose built and offer spacious, comfortable and well equipped accommodation. A wide choice of meals is available in the convivial surroundings of the inn.
ROOMS: 42 en suite (11 fmly) (20 GF) in all bedrooms
FACILITIES: STV **CONF:** Thtr 30 Class 18 Board 18 **PARKING:** 100
NOTES: RS 24-26 Dec **CARDS:**

ST HELENS, Merseyside — Map 15 SJ59

See also Rainhill

Premier Lodge (St Helens)

PREMIER LODGE.com

Garswood Old Rd, East Lancs Rd WA11 7LX
☎ 0870 9906374 0870 9906375
web: www.premierlodge.com
Dir: *3m from M6 junct 23, on A580 towards Liverpool*
High quality, modern, budget accommodation, ideal for families and business travellers. All rooms feature bath, power shower and satellite TV, and most have telephones / modem points. The adjacent bar and restaurant offers a wide and varied menu.
ROOMS: 43 en suite s £48; d £48 **CONF:** Thtr 85 Class 30 Board 40

Travel Inn

travel inn

Mickle Head Green, Eurolink, Lea Green WA9 4TT
☎ 08701 977237 01744 820531
Dir: *M62 junct 7, on A570 towards St Helens*
Travel Inn offers good-quality, value-for-money accommodation. Spacious, en suite rooms with bath and shower comfortably accommodate a family of up to two adults and two children (to age 15). The restaurant and bar offers a varied menu. For further details consult the Hotel Groups page.
ROOMS: 40 en suite s £45.95-£46.95; d £45.95-£46.95

ST IVES, Cambridgeshire — Map 12 TL37

★★★70% Slepe Hall

Ramsey Rd PE27 5RB
☎ 01480 463122 01480 300706
e-mail: mail@slepehall.co.uk
web: www.slepehall.co.uk
Dir: *from A14 on A1096 & follow by-pass signed Huntingdon towards St Ives, left into Ramsey Rd at lights by Toyota garage, hotel on left*

A welcoming and friendly atmosphere exists at Slepe Hall, which is located close to the town centre. Bedroom types vary, with traditional and modern styles both available. A choice of dining

continued

S

options is provided within the refurbished public rooms, with light meals served in the lounge and bar or more formal dining options in the restaurant.
ROOMS: 16 en suite (1 fmly) s £50-£80; d £75-£99 (incl. bkfst) **LB**
FACILITIES: STV Guests have free access to local private leisure club
CONF: Thtr 200 Class 80 Board 60 Del from £115 **PARKING:** 70
NOTES: in restaurant Closed 24-26 Dec & 1 Jan Civ Wed 60
CARDS:

★★★69% *Olivers Lodge*

Needingworth Rd PE27 5JP
☎ 01480 463252 01480 461150
e-mail: reception@oliverslodge.co.uk
web: www.oliverslodge.co.uk
Dir: *follow A14 towards Huntingdon/Cambridge, take B1040 to St Ives. Cross 1st rdbt, left at 2nd then 1st right. Hotel 500mtrs on right*

Olivers Lodge sits in a quiet residential area on the outskirts of the town. A popular and well-run hotel, the proprietors and staff providing a helpful and friendly service. Bedrooms are situated in the main house and adjoining wing, each room is well equipped with a good range of facilities. Public rooms include a conservatory dining area and a cosy lounge bar; function and meeting rooms are available.
ROOMS: 12 en suite 5 annexe en suite (3 fmly) in 16 bedrooms
FACILITIES: STV Free use of local health club **CONF:** Thtr 65 Class 35 Board 28 **PARKING:** 30 **NOTES:** in restaurant Civ Wed 85
CARDS:

★★★67% Dolphin

London Rd PE27 5EP
☎ 01480 466966 01480 495597
e-mail: enquiries@dolphinhotelcambs.co.uk
Dir: *from A14 between Huntingdon & Cambridge onto A1096 towards St Ives. Left at 1st rdbt & immediately right. Hotel on left after 0.5m*
This modern hotel sits in a delightful location beside water meadows on the banks of the River Ouse, beside the bridge leading into the town centre. Open-plan public rooms include a choice of bars and a pleasant restaurant offering enjoyable cuisine and views over the river. Modern bedrooms styles vary, all are of comfortable proportions, available in the hotel and an adjacent wing. Conference and function suites are available.
ROOMS: 30 en suite 37 annexe en suite (4 fmly) (22 GF) in 18 bedrooms s £80-£95; d £100-£120 (incl. bkfst) **LB** **FACILITIES:** STV Fishing Sauna Gym **CONF:** Thtr 150 Class 50 Board 50 Del from £98
PARKING: 400 **NOTES:** RS 24 Dec-2 Jan Civ Wed 60
CARDS:

> Popped the question?
> Hotels with Civ Wed in their entry are licensed for civil wedding ceremonies. Maximum numbers for the ceremony only are shown, e.g. Civ Wed 120

ST IVES, Cornwall & Isles of Scilly

Map 02 SW54

★★★74% *Carbis Bay*

Carbis Bay TR26 2NP
☎ 01736 795311 01736 797677
e-mail: carbisbayhotel@talk21.com
Dir: *M5 junct 31, take A30 then A3074. After 2m through Lelant, pass garage on right. Take next right (Porthreptor Rd), continue to sea*

A peaceful location with access to its own white-sand beach, this hotel offers comfortable accommodation. Attractive public areas feature a smart bar and lounge, and a sun lounge overlooking the sea. Bedrooms, many with fine views, are well equipped and spacious. Interesting cuisine and particularly enjoyable breakfasts are offered in the spacious dining room.
ROOMS: 35 en suite (9 fmly) in 5 bedrooms **FACILITIES:** Fishing Snooker Private beach **CONF:** Thtr 120 Class 80 Board 100
PARKING: 200 **NOTES:** in restaurant Closed Jan Civ Wed 140
CARDS:

See advert on this page

ST IVES, continued

★★★72% Porthminster

The Terrace TR26 2BN
☎ 01736 795221 01736 797043
e-mail: reception@porthminster-hotel.co.uk
web: www.porthminster-hotel.co.uk
Dir: on A3074
This friendly hotel enjoys an enviable location with spectacular views of St Ives Bay. Extensive leisure facilities, a versatile function suite and a number of lounges are available. Bedrooms are comfortable and well equipped and many rooms have sea views.
ROOMS: 43 en suite (14 fmly) **FACILITIES: Spa** Sauna Solarium Gym Xmas **CONF:** Thtr 130 Class 20 Board 35 **SERVICES:** Lift **PARKING:** 43 **NOTES:** Closed 2-13 Jan Civ Wed 130 **CARDS:**

See advert on opposite page

★★★68% Chy-an-Albany

Albany Ter TR26 2BS
☎ 01736 796759 01736 795584
e-mail: info@chyanalbanyhotel.com
Dir: from A30 onto A3074 signed St Ives, hotel on left just before junct
Conveniently located, this pleasant hotel enjoys splendid sea views. Comfortable bedrooms, some with balconies and sea views, come in a variety of sizes. Friendly staff and the relaxing environment mean that guests return on a regular basis. Freshly prepared and appetising cuisine is served in the dining room and a bar menu is also available.
ROOMS: 40 en suite (11 fmly) in all bedrooms **FACILITIES:** STV Xmas **CONF:** Thtr 80 Class 40 Board 30 Del from £80 **SERVICES:** Lift **PARKING:** 37 **NOTES:** in restaurant Civ Wed 80 **CARDS:**

★★★67% Garrack

Burthallan Ln, Higher Ayr TR26 3AA
☎ 01736 796199 01736 798955
e-mail: aa@garrack.com
Dir: turn off A30 for St Ives. Follow yellow holiday route signs on B3311. In St Ives, hotel is signed from 1st mini rdbt

Enjoying a peaceful, elevated position with splendid views across the harbour and Porthmeor Beach, the Garrack sits in its own delightful grounds and gardens. Bedrooms are comfortable and many have sea views. Public areas include a small leisure suite, a choice of lounges and an attractive restaurant.
ROOMS: 16 en suite 2 annexe en suite (2 fmly) s £70-£74; d £117-£175 (incl. bkfst) **LB FACILITIES:** Sauna Solarium Gym Jacuzzi ch fac Xmas **CONF:** Thtr 30 Board 12 **PARKING:** 30 **NOTES:** in restaurant **CARDS:**

★★★65% Tregenna Castle Hotel

TR26 2DE
☎ 01736 795254 01736 796066
e-mail: hotel@tregenna-castle.co.uk
Dir: A30 from Exeter to Penzance, at Lelant W of Hayle take A3074 to St Ives, through Carbis Bay, main entrance signed on left
Sitting at the top of town in beautiful landscaped gardens, this popular hotel boasts spectacular views of St Ives. Many leisure facilities are available, including indoor and outdoor pools, gymnasium and sauna. Families are particularly welcome. Bedrooms are generally spacious. A carte menu or carvery buffet are offered in the restaurant.
ROOMS: 83 en suite (12 fmly) (16 GF) in 49 bedrooms s £50-£95; d £80-£170 (incl. bkfst & dinner) **FACILITIES:** STV supervised 18 Squash Sauna Solarium Gym Putt green Jacuzzi Health spa Steam room ch fac Xmas **CONF:** Thtr 300 Class 150 Board 30 **SERVICES:** Lift **PARKING:** 200 **NOTES:** in restaurant Civ Wed 160 **CARDS:**

★★72% *Boskerris*

Boskerris Rd, Carbis Bay TR26 2NQ
☎ 01736 795295 01736 798632
e-mail: Boskerris.Hotel@btinternet.com
Dir: on entering Carbis Bay take 3rd right after petrol station
This hotel, now under new ownership, enjoys a peaceful location and great views, particularly from the terraced area, which looks out over Carbis Bay and St Ives harbour. The service is friendly and bedrooms are stylish and comfortable. Public areas provide a range of facilities including a swimming pool and attractive gardens.
ROOMS: 16 en suite (2 fmly) (2 GF) in 4 bedrooms **FACILITIES:** Table tennis **PARKING:** 20 **NOTES:** in restaurant Closed Nov-Etr **CARDS:**

★★72% *Pedn-Olva*

West Porthminster Beach TR26 2EA
☎ 01736 796222 01736 797710
e-mail: bookings@pednolva.freeserve.co.uk
Dir: A30 to Hayle, then A3074 to St Ives. In St Ives turn sharp right at bus station into railway station car park, down steps to hotel
Perched on the water's edge, this hotel is the closest thing to being aboard a ship, and the stylish public areas complement the unique location. Bedrooms combine comfort with quality and many have spectacular views across the bay. An imaginative, fixed-price menu is offered in the restaurant; during the summer, lighter meals are served on the terraces.
ROOMS: 30 en suite (5 fmly) in all bedrooms **FACILITIES:** STV **CONF:** Thtr 20 Class 20 Board 16 **PARKING:** 17 **NOTES:** in restaurant Civ Wed 60 **CARDS:**

★★67% Cottage Hotel

Boskerris Rd, Carbis Bay TR26 2PE
☎ 01736 795252 01736 798636
Leisureplex
e-mail: cottage.stives@alfatravel.co.uk
Dir: from A30 take A3074 to Carbis Bay. Right into Porthreptor Rd. Just before railway bridge, left through railway car park and into hotel car park
Set in quiet, lush gardens, this pleasant hotel offers friendly and attentive service. Smart bedrooms are pleasantly spacious and many rooms enjoy splendid views. Public areas are varied and include a snooker room, a comfortable lounge and a spacious dining room with sea views over the beach and Carbis Bay.
ROOMS: 80 en suite (7 fmly) (2 GF) s £28-£36; d £46-£62 (incl. bkfst) **LB FACILITIES:** Squash Snooker Sauna Gym Xmas **SERVICES:** Lift **PARKING:** 10 **NOTES:** in restaurant Closed Dec-Feb (ex Xmas) RS Nov & Mar **CARDS:**

S

★★67% Hotel St Eia
Trelyon Av TR26 2AA
☎ 01736 795531 📠 01736 793591
e-mail: hotelsteia@tinyonline.co.uk
Dir: *off A30 onto A3074, follow signs to St Ives, approaching town, hotel on right*
This smart hotel is conveniently located and enjoys spectacular views over St Ives, the harbour and Porthminster Beach. The friendly proprietors provide a relaxing environment and many guests return on a regular basis. Bedrooms are comfortable and well equipped, some with sea views. The spacious lounge-bar has a well-stocked bar and views can be enjoyed from the rooftop terrace.
ROOMS: 18 en suite (3 fmly) ⊗ in all bedrooms s £28.50-£40; d £57-£80 (incl. bkfst) **LB** **PARKING:** 16 **NOTES:** ⊗ in restaurant Closed Dec-Jan **CARDS:**

ST LEONARDS-ON-SEA See Hastings & St Leonards

ST MARTIN'S See Scilly, Isles of

ST MARY CHURCH See Torquay

ST MARY'S See Scilly, Isles of

ST MAWES, Cornwall & Isles of Scilly Map 02 SW83

★★★77% Idle Rocks
Harbour Side TR2 5AN
☎ 01326 270771 📠 01326 270062
e-mail: reception@idlerocks.co.uk
web: www.richardsonhotels.co.uk
Dir: *off A390 onto A3078, 14m to St Mawes. Hotel on left*

The Idle Rocks has splendid sea views overlooking the attractive fishing port. The lounge and bar also benefit from the views and in warmer months service is available on the terrace. Bedrooms are individually styled and tastefully furnished to a high standard. The daily-changing menu served in the new restaurant features fresh local produce and imaginative cooking.
ROOMS: 23 en suite 10 annexe en suite (1 GF) s £59-£179; d £118-£298 (incl. bkfst & dinner) **LB** **FACILITIES:** Xmas **PARKING:** 5 **NOTES:** ⊗ in restaurant **CARDS:**

See advert on this page

★★73% Rising Sun
TR2 5DJ
☎ 01326 270233 📠 01326 270198
e-mail: therisingsun@btclick.com
Dir: *from A39 take A3078 signed St Mawes, hotel in village centre*
Looking out across the harbour and the Fal estuary, this smart looking hotel is a popular venue. Bedrooms are stylish and many rooms have sea views. Menus feature seafood and local produce.

continued on p504

ST MAWES, continued

In the bar, which offers a large selection of ales, quality wines and malt whiskies, a range of dishes is offered. More casual dining is available in the brasserie.
ROOMS: 8 en suite (1 fmly) s £50-£65; d £100-£130 (incl. bkfst) **LB**
PARKING: 6 **NOTES:** ⊗ in restaurant **CARDS:**

ST MELLION, Cornwall & Isles of Scilly — Map 03 SX36

★★★68% St Mellion International
PL12 6SD
☎ 01579 351351 Fax 01579 350537
e-mail: stmellion@americangolf.uk.com
web: www.st-mellion.co.uk
Dir: *from M5/A38 towards Plymouth & Saltash. St Mellion off A38 on A388 towards Callington & Launceston*
This purpose-built hotel, golfing and leisure complex is surrounded by 450 acres of land with two highly regarded 18-hole golf courses. The bedrooms generally have views over the courses and public areas include a choice of bars and eating options. Function suites are also available.
ROOMS: 39 annexe en suite (15 fmly) (8 GF) s £75-£105; d £100-£160 (incl. bkfst) **LB** **FACILITIES: Spa** supervised 18 Squash Snooker Sauna Solarium Gym Putt green Jacuzzi Steam room Skincare Xmas **CONF:** Thtr 350 Class 140 Board 80 Del from £89.50
SERVICES: Lift **PARKING:** 400 **NOTES:** ⊗ in restaurant Civ Wed 120 **CARDS:**

ST NEOTS, Cambridgeshire — Map 12 TL16

★★63% Abbotsley Golf Hotel
Potton Rd, Eynesbury Hardwicke PE19 6XN
☎ 01480 474000 Fax 01480 471018
e-mail: abbotsley@americangolf.uk.com
Dir: *A1(M) onto A428 towards Cambridge, left at Tesco rdbt, 3rd exit at 4th rdbt then 1st right & follow signs*
This purpose-built hotel caters well for its many avid golfing guests, with a 250-acre estate encompassing two courses, a golf school and leisure complex. The bedrooms are generally spacious and surround a pleasing courtyard garden with a putting green. Public rooms overlook the adjacent greens.
ROOMS: 42 annexe en suite (2 fmly) (13 GF) ⊗ in 10 bedrooms s £54-£56; d £78-£85 (incl. bkfst) **LB** **FACILITIES:** 36 Squash Solarium Gym Putt green Holistic Health & Beauty Salon, pool tables
CONF: Thtr 60 Class 30 Board 30 Del from £90 **PARKING:** 80
NOTES: ⊗ in restaurant RS Closed Xmas Day
CARDS:

Premier Lodge (Eaton Socon)

Great North Rd, Eaton Socon PE19 8EN
☎ 0870 9906314 Fax 0870 9906315
web: www.premierlodge.com
Dir: *just off A1 at rdbt with A428 and B1428 before St. Neots, 1m from St. Neots train station*
High quality, modern, budget accommodation, ideal for families and business travellers. All rooms feature bath, power shower and satellite TV, and most have telephones / modem points. The adjacent bar and restaurant offers a wide and varied menu.
ROOMS: 63 en suite s £50; d £50

Travel Inn
Colmworth Business Park PE19 8YH
☎ 08701 977238 Fax 01480 408541
Dir: *from A1 at southern St Neots junct. Travel Inn at 1st rdbt (A428/B1428)*
Travel Inn offers good-quality, value-for-money accommodation. Spacious, en suite rooms with bath and shower comfortably accommodate a family of up to two adults and two children (to age 15). The restaurant and bar offers a varied menu. For further details consult the Hotel Groups page.
ROOMS: 41 en suite s £45.95-£46.95; d £45.95-£46.95

SALCOMBE, Devon — Map 03 SX73
See also Hope Cove, Kingsbridge & Thurlestone

★★★★73% Soar Mill Cove
Soar Mill Cove, Malborough TQ7 3DS
☎ 01548 561566 Fax 01548 561223
e-mail: info@soarmillcove.co.uk
web: www.soarmillcove.co.uk
Dir: *3m W of town off A381 at Malborough. Follow 'Soar' signs*
Situated amid spectacular scenery with dramatic sea views, this hotel provides a relaxing stay. Family-run, with a committed team, keen standards of hospitality and service are apparent. Bedrooms are well equipped and many rooms have private terraces. There are different seating areas where impressive cream teas are served, or, for the more active, a choice of swimming pools. Local produce is used to good effect in the restaurant.
ROOMS: 22 en suite (5 fmly) (21 GF) ⊗ in all bedrooms s £150-£180; d £180-£220 (incl. bkfst) **LB** **FACILITIES:** Sauna Putt green Table tennis, Games room, 9 hole Pitch n putt, Spa treatment suite ♫ ch fac Xmas **CONF:** BC **PARKING:** 30 **NOTES:** ⊗ in restaurant Closed 1 Nov-11 Feb **CARDS:**

★★★★72% Thurlestone Hotel
TQ7 3NN
☎ 01548 560382 Fax 01548 561069
e-mail: enquiries@thurlestone.co.uk
web: www.thurlestone.co.uk
(For full entry see Thurlestone)

★★★★68% Menzies Marine
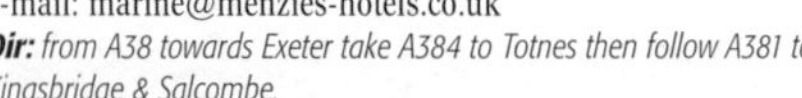
Cliff Rd TQ8 8JH
☎ 01548 844444 Fax 01548 843109
e-mail: marine@menzies-hotels.co.uk
Dir: *from A38 towards Exeter take A384 to Totnes then follow A381 to Kingsbridge & Salcombe.*

Enjoying a superb position overlooking the river and with views towards the sea, this hotel is an ideal base for those touring the area and for business guests. Bedrooms, many with balconies and
continued

sea views, are spacious and comfortable and most are located at the front of the hotel.
ROOMS: 53 en suite (10 fmly) s £125-£150; d £150-£200 (incl. bkfst) **LB FACILITIES:** STV Sauna Solarium Gym Jacuzzi Xmas **SERVICES:** Lift **PARKING:** 50 **NOTES:** in restaurant Civ Wed 70
CARDS:

★★★ Buckland-Tout-Saints

Goveton TQ7 2DS
☎ 01548 853055 01548 856261
e-mail: buckland@tout-saints.co.uk
web: www.tout-saints.co.uk
(For full entry see Kingsbridge)

★★★77% Tides Reach

South Sands TQ8 8LJ
☎ 01548 843466 01548 843954
e-mail: enquire@tidesreach.com
web: www.tidesreach.com
Dir: *off A38 at Buckfastleigh to Totnes. Then take A381 to Salcombe, follow signs to South Sands*

Superbly situated at the water's edge, this personally run, friendly hotel has splendid views of the estuary and beach. Bedrooms, many with balconies, are spacious and comfortable. In the bar and lounge attentive service can be enjoyed along with the view, and the Garden Room restaurant serves appetising and accomplished cuisine.

ROOMS: 35 en suite (7 fmly) in 2 bedrooms s £93-£128; d £158-£280 (incl. bkfst & dinner) **LB FACILITIES:** supervised Squash Snooker Sauna Solarium Gym Jacuzzi Windsurfing, dinghy sailing, kayaking, scuba diving ♫ **SERVICES:** Lift **PARKING:** 100 **NOTES:** No children 8yrs in restaurant Closed Dec-early Feb
CARDS:

See advert on this page

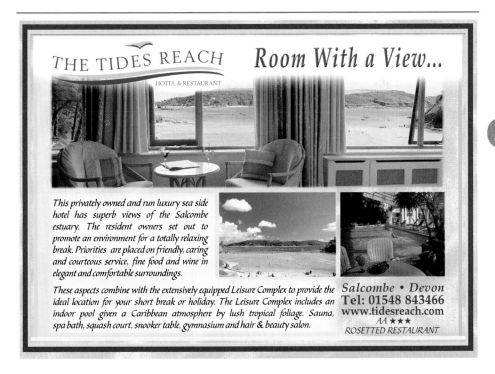

S

SALE, Greater Manchester Map 15 SJ79

★★★★ 68% Belmore Hotel

143 Brooklands Rd M33 3QN
☎ 0161 973 2538 🖷 0161 973 2665
e-mail: belmore_hotel@hotmail.com
Dir: *from A56 turn onto A6144. At traffic lights (Brooklands Station on right) turn right into Brooklands Rd*

This stylish, refurbished hotel is set in a quiet residential area. Public rooms include a choice of dining options: cooking in the fine-dining, classic restaurant is imaginative and prepared with skill, as is the more informal menu of the downstairs brasserie. Bedrooms are tastefully furnished, spacious and well equipped.
ROOMS: 23 en suite (2 fmly) ⊗ in 13 bedrooms s £100-£190; d £110-£200 **FACILITIES:** STV Free access to local Health Club Xmas **CONF:** Thtr 130 Class 70 Board 60 Del from £140 **PARKING:** 38 **NOTES:** ⊗ in restaurant Civ Wed 80
CARDS:

⌂ Travel Inn (Manchester South)

Carrington Ln, Ashton-Upon-Mersey M33 5BL
☎ 08701 977179 🖷 0161 905 1742
Dir: *M60 junct 8 take A6144(M) towards Carrington. Left at 1st lights, Inn on left*
Travel Inn offers good-quality, value-for-money accommodation. Spacious, en suite rooms with bath and shower comfortably accommodate a family of up to two adults and two children (to age 15). The restaurant and bar offers a varied menu. For further details consult the Hotel Groups page.

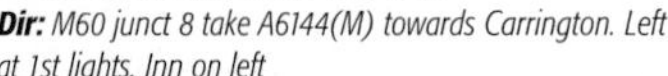

ROOMS: 40 en suite s £45.95-£48.95; d £45.95-£48.95 **CONF:** Thtr 25

SALISBURY, Wiltshire Map 05 SU12
See also Landford

★★★ 71% Milford Hall

206 Castle St SP1 3TE
☎ 01722 417411 🖷 01722 419444
e-mail: reception@milfordhallhotel.com
Dir: *few hundred yds from junct of Castle St, A36 ring road & A345 Amesbury Rd*
This hotel offers high standards of accommodation within easy walking distance of the city centre. There are two categories of bedroom; traditional rooms in the original Georgian house and spacious, modern rooms in a purpose built extension - all are extremely well equipped. Meals are served in the smart brasserie where a varied choice of dishes is provided.
ROOMS: 35 en suite (1 fmly) ⊗ in 6 bedrooms s £100-£140; d £110-£150 **LB** **FACILITIES:** STV Free facilities at local leisure centre **CONF:** Thtr 90 Class 70 Board 40 **PARKING:** 60 **NOTES:** ⊗ in restaurant Civ Wed **CARDS:**

★★★ 71% Red Lion

Milford St SP1 2AN
☎ 01722 323334 🖷 01722 325756
e-mail: reception@the-redlion.co.uk
web: www.the-redlion.co.uk
Dir: *in city centre close to Guildhall Square*

If you are looking for character, look no further than this 750-year-old hotel. The individual bedrooms combine contemporary comforts with historic features, including one room with a medieval fireplace dating back to 1220. Public areas are also distinctive with a bar, lounge and the elegant Vine Restaurant.
ROOMS: 51 en suite (2 fmly) ⊗ in 40 bedrooms s £94-£116; d £122-£152 (incl. bkfst) **LB** **FACILITIES:** STV Xmas **CONF:** Thtr 100 Class 50 Board 40 **SERVICES:** Lift **NOTES:** ⊗ in restaurant
CARDS:

See advert on opposite page

★★★ 71% The White Hart

St John St SP1 2SD
☎ 0870 400 8125 🖷 01722 412761
e-mail: whitehartsalisbury@macdonald-hotels.co.uk
Dir: *M3 junct 7/8 take A303 to A343 for Salisbury then A30. Follow signs for City Centre on ring rd, into Exeter St, leading into St. John Street. Car park at rear.*
There has been a hotel on this site since the 16th century. Bedrooms vary between the contemporary-style, newly refurbished rooms and those decorated in more traditional style, all of which boast a comprehensive range of facilities. The bar and lounge areas are popular with guests and locals for morning coffees and afternoon teas.
ROOMS: 68 en suite (6 fmly) ⊗ in 28 bedrooms s £75-£101; d £85-£111 (incl. bkfst & dinner) **LB** **FACILITIES:** STV Xmas **CONF:** Thtr 100 Class 40 Board 40 Del from £99 **PARKING:** 90 **NOTES:** ⊗ in restaurant Civ Wed **CARDS:**

GF Indicates the number of bedrooms at ground floor level.

★★★ 67% Grasmere House

Harnhan Rd SP2 8JN
☎ 01722 338388 🖷 01722 333710
e-mail: grasmerehotel@mistral.co.uk
web: www.grasmerehotel.com
Dir: *on A3094 on S side of Salisbury next to All Saints Church in Harnham*
This popular hotel dates from 1896 and has gardens overlooking the water meadows and the cathedral. The attractive bedrooms vary in size, with the 15 added most recently offering excellent quality and comfort. Some rooms are specially equipped for less

continued

mobile guests. In summer, guests have the option of dining on the pleasant outdoor terrace.

ROOMS: 4 en suite 31 annexe en suite (16 fmly) ⊗ in 30 bedrooms s £85.50-£95.50; d £115.50-£135.50 (incl. bkfst) **LB** **FACILITIES:** STV Fishing Jacuzzi Xmas **CONF:** Thtr 110 Class 45 Board 45 Del from £125 **PARKING:** 64 **NOTES:** Civ Wed 120
CARDS:

See advert on this page

★★★64% *The Rose & Crown Hotel*

Harnham Rd, Harnham SP2 8JQ
☎ 0870 6096163 01722 339816
Dir: *Just off A3094, on Harnham Rd, on S side of Salisbury*

This character hotel is situated on a quiet stretch of the River Avon, just five minutes from town. Most bedrooms are large and enjoy views of the cathedral and gardens, which reach down to the river. Public areas are spacious and there is plenty of parking.
ROOMS: 28 en suite (5 fmly) (3 GF) ⊗ in 10 bedrooms
FACILITIES: STV Fishing **CONF:** Thtr 80 Class 40 Board 40
PARKING: 42 **NOTES:** ⊗ in restaurant Civ Wed 90
CARDS:

U Kings Head Inn

1 Bridge St SP1 2ND
☎ 01722 342050 438400 01722 326743
e-mail: salisburylodge@jdwetherspoon.co.uk
Dir: *town centre*
At the time of going to press, the star classification for this hotel was not confirmed. Please refer to the AA internet site www.theAA.com for current information.
ROOMS: 32 en suite (3 fmly) ⊗ in all bedrooms s fr £59; d fr £59
SERVICES: Lift air con **NOTES:** Closed xmas
CARDS:

For central reservation numbers and more information on Hotel Groups, turn to pages 33-39

S

SALISBURY, continued

⌂ Travel Inn
Bishopdown Retail Park, Pearce Way SP1 3YU
☎ 08701 977225 ⎙ 01722 337889
Dir: *from Salisbury centre, follow A30 towards Marlborough for 1 mile. Travel Inn off Hampton Parkat rbt*
Travel Inn offers good-quality, value-for-money accommodation. Spacious, en suite rooms with bath and shower comfortably accommodate a family of up to two adults and two children (to age 15). The restaurant and bar offers a varied menu. For further details consult the Hotel Groups page.
ROOMS: 60 en suite s £45.95-£46.95; d £45.95-£46.95

SALTASH, Cornwall & Isles of Scilly — Map 03 SX45

★★★67% China Fleet Country Club
PL12 6LJ
☎ 01752 848668 ⎙ 01752 848456
e-mail: sales@china-fleet.co.uk
Dir: *A38 towards PLymouth/Saltash. Cross Tamar Bridge taking slip road before tunnel. Right at lights, 1st left follow signs 0.5m.*
In a convenient, quiet location, ideal for access to Plymouth and the countryside, this establishment offers an extensive range of sporting and leisure facilities including an impressive golf course. Bedrooms are located in annexe buildings and each is equipped with its own kitchen. There is a range of dining options, and the newly refurbished restaurant offers some interesting and imaginative choices.
ROOMS: 40 en suite (21 GF) in 30 bedrooms s £42-£72; d £42-£88 **FACILITIES: Spa** STV supervised 18 Squash Sauna Solarium Gym Putt green Jacuzzi 28 bay Floodlit driving range Health & beauty suite Hairdressers ch fac Xmas **CONF:** Thtr 80 Class 30 Board 34 **SERVICES:** Lift **PARKING:** 400 **NOTES:** in restaurant Civ Wed 80 **CARDS:**

⌂ Travelodge
Callington Rd, Carkeel PL12 6LF
☎ 08700 850 950 ⎙ 01752 841079
Dir: *on A38 Saltash by-pass - 1m from Tamar Bridge*
Travelodge offers good quality, good value, modern accommodation. Ideal for families, the spacious, en suite bedrooms include remote-control TV, tea and coffee-making facilities and luxury beds. Meals can be taken at the nearby family restaurant. For further details consult the Hotel Groups page.
ROOMS: 53 en suite s fr £25; d fr £25 **CONF:** Thtr 25 Class 15 Board 12

SALTBURN-BY-THE-SEA, North Yorkshire — Map 19 NZ62

★★★66% Rushpool Hall Hotel
Saltburn Ln TS12 1HD
☎ 01287 624111 ⎙ 01287 625255
A grand Victorian mansion situated in its own grounds and woodlands. Stylish, elegant bedrooms are well equipped and spacious; many enjoy excellent sea views. The interesting public rooms are filled with charm and character, and roaring fires welcome guests in cooler months. The hotel boasts an excellent reputation as a wedding venue thanks to its superb location and experienced event management.
ROOMS: 21 en suite s £70-£85; d £125-£150 (incl. bkfst) **LB** **FACILITIES:** STV Fishing Birdwatching ch fac Xmas **CONF:** Thtr 100 Class 75 Board 60 Del from £70 **PARKING:** 120 **NOTES:** in restaurant Civ Wed 120 **CARDS:**

★★66% Hunley Hall Golf Club & Hotel
Ings Ln, Brotton TS12 2QQ
☎ 01287 676216 ⎙ 01287 678250
e-mail: enquiries@hunleyhall.co.uk
web: www.hunleyhall.co.uk
Dir: *A174 bypass take left at rdbt with monument, at T-junct turn left, pass church, turn right. 50yds turn right through housing estate, approx 0.5m*
Spectacularly situated, this hotel overlooks a 27-hole golf course and beyond to the coastline. The members' bar is licensed and serves snacks all day, and the restaurant offers a wide choice of food. Bedrooms are being refurbished and all are comfortable and well equipped.
ROOMS: 8 en suite (1 fmly) (8 GF) in all bedrooms s £37.50-£42.50; d £65-£75 (incl. bkfst) **LB** **FACILITIES:** 27 Snooker Putt green **CONF:** Thtr 50 Class 40 Board 24 Del £59.95 **PARKING:** 100 **NOTES:** in restaurant **CARDS:**

SAMPFORD PEVERELL, Devon — Map 03 ST01

★★67% Parkway House Country Hotel
EX16 7BJ
☎ 01884 820255 ⎙ 01884 820780
e-mail: p-way@m-way.freeserve.co.uk
Dir: *M5 junct 27, follow signs for Tiverton Parkway Station. Hotel on right, entering village*
An ideal choice for both business and leisure travellers, this hotel is located within a mile of the M5 and benefits from extensive views across the Culm Valley. The well-equipped bedrooms are comfortable and smartly presented. A popular venue for conferences and day meetings.
ROOMS: 10 en suite (2 fmly) s £40-£50; d £60-£70 (incl. bkfst) **LB** **FACILITIES:** STV Childrens Play Area **CONF:** BC Thtr 100 Class 50 Board 40 Del from £75 **PARKING:** 100 **NOTES:** in restaurant **CARDS:**

⌂ Travelodge Tiverton
Sampford Peverell Service Area EX16 7HD
☎ 08700 850 950 ⎙ 01884 821087
Dir: *M5 junct 27*
Travelodge offers good quality, good value, modern accommodation. Ideal for families, the spacious, en suite bedrooms include remote-control TV, tea and coffee-making facilities and luxury beds. Meals can be taken at the nearby family restaurant. For further details consult the Hotel Groups page.
ROOMS: 40 en suite s fr £25; d fr £25

> Destination dining!
> This symbol indicates a Restaurant with Rooms

SANDBACH, Cheshire — Map 15 SJ76

★★★61% The Chimney House Hotel
Congleton Rd CW11 4ST
☎ 0870 609 6164 ⎙ 01270 768916
e-mail: chimneyhouse@corushotels.com
Dir: *on A534, 1m from M6 junct 17 towards Congleton*
This conveniently positioned Tudor-style building benefits from ease of access to major motorway networks. The hotel is ideal for business meetings and functions. Bedrooms are well planned and

continued

equipped. Relax in the spacious lounge areas, or enjoy a meal in the patio restaurant overlooking the hotel gardens.

ROOMS: 48 en suite (16 fmly) (18 GF) ⊗ in 33 bedrooms s £79-£99; d £79-£112 **LB** **FACILITIES:** STV Sauna Putt green **CONF:** Thtr 120 Class 40 Board 40 Del from £110 **PARKING:** 110 **NOTES:** ⊗ in restaurant RS Bank Holidays Civ Wed 70
CARDS:

Innkeeper's Lodge Sandbach

Bereton Green CW11 1RS
☎ 01477 544732
www.innkeeperslodge.com
Dir: *M6, junction 17, at roundabout bear left towards Holmes Chapel, follow road until Breton, lodge on left at Breton Green*
Smart rooms meet essential business requirements but also have home comforts, and depending on location may well have meeting rooms and pub dining. Dining options generally include all-day menus plus the added advantage of breakfast.
ROOMS: s £45-£49.95; d £45-£49.95

SANDBANKS See Poole

SANDOWN See Wight, Isle of

SANDWICH, Kent — Map 07 TR35

★★67% The Blazing Donkey Country Hotel & Inn

Hay Hill, Ham CT14 0ED
☎ 01304 617362 📠 01304 615264
e-mail: info@blazingdonkey.co.uk web: www.blazingdonkey.co.uk
Dir: *off A256 at Eastry into village, right at Five Bells public house, hotel 0.75m on left*
This former labourer's cottage and barn has been upgraded over the years and is now a distinctive inn of character. Set in the heart of peaceful Kentish farmland, the atmosphere is convivial and informal, with an open-plan bar and lounge and more formal dining area. Comfortably appointed bedrooms are spacious and arranged around a courtyard.
ROOMS: 19 en suite 3 annexe en suite (2 fmly) ⊗ in 15 bedrooms s £75-£85; d £99.50-£109.50 (incl. bkfst) **LB** **FACILITIES:** STV Putt green ch fac Xmas **CONF:** BC Thtr 200 Class 200 Board 200 **SERVICES:** air con **PARKING:** 108 **NOTES:** ⊗ in restaurant Civ Wed 250 **CARDS:**

SAUNDERTON, Buckinghamshire — Map 05 SP70

★★63% Rose & Crown

Wycombe Rd HP27 9NP
☎ 01844 345299 📠 01844 343140
e-mail: info@rosecrowninn.co.uk web: www.rosecrowninn.co.uk
Dir: *2m S of Princes Risborough on A4010, on right*
The Rose and Crown may have been offering hospitality to

continued

travellers for over a century, but the focal point of this hotel, a strikingly minimalist bar and restaurant, is resolutely modern. Rooms are comfortable and offer a range of extra facilities and the attractive patio is perfect for summer drinking.
ROOMS: 15 en suite ⊗ in all bedrooms s £70-£80; d £80-£99 (incl. bkfst) **LB** **FACILITIES:** STV Xmas **CONF:** Thtr 35 Class 20 Board 16 Del from £90 **PARKING:** 50 **NOTES:** ⊗ in restaurant
CARDS:

SAUNTON, Devon — Map 03 SS43

★★★★70% Saunton Sands

EX33 1LQ
☎ 01271 890212 📠 01271 890145
e-mail: info@sauntonsands.com
web: www.sauntonsands.com
Dir: *off A361 at Braunton, signed Croyde B3231, hotel 2m on left*

Stunning sea views and direct access to five miles of sandy beach

continued on p510

SAUNTON, continued

are just two of the features of this popular hotel. The majority of sea-facing rooms benefit from balconies, and splendid views can be enjoyed from all of the public areas, which include comfortable lounges. The Sands café/bar is a successful innovation and provides an informal eating option.
ROOMS: 92 en suite (39 fmly) s £73-£110; d £146-£320 (incl. bkfst) **LB**
FACILITIES: STV Squash Snooker Sauna Solarium Gym Putt green Table tennis, Sun Shower, Health and beauty salon ♫ ch fac Xmas
SERVICES: Lift **PARKING:** 142 **NOTES:** in restaurant Civ Wed
CARDS:

See advert on page 509

SAWBRIDGEWORTH, Hertfordshire Map 06 TL41

★★★72% Manor of Groves Hotel, Golf & Country Club

High Wych CM21 0JU
☎ 01279 600777 01279 600374
e-mail: info@manorofgroves.co.uk
Dir: *A1184 to Sawbridgeworth, left to High Wych, right at village green & hotel 200yds left*
This Georgian manor house is set in 150 acres of secluded grounds and gardens, with its own 18-hole championship golf course and superb leisure facilities. Public rooms include an imposing open-plan glass atrium that features a bar, lounge area and modern restaurant. The spacious bedrooms are smartly decorated and equipped with modern facilities.
ROOMS: 80 en suite (2 fmly) (17 GF) in 50 bedrooms s £95-£110; d £110-£141 (incl. bkfst) **LB** **FACILITIES: Spa** STV supervised 18 Sauna Solarium Gym Putt green Jacuzzi Dance studio, beauty salon Xmas **CONF:** Thtr 400 Class 250 Board 50 Del from £149
SERVICES: Lift **PARKING:** 200 **NOTES:** in restaurant RS 24/12/2004-02/01/2005 Civ Wed 300 **CARDS:**

SCARBOROUGH, North Yorkshire Map 17 TA08

★★★70% The Crescent

2 Belvoir Ter YO11 2PP
☎ 01723 360929 01723 354126
e-mail: reception@crescent-hotel.co.uk
Dir: *From A64 towards railway station, follow signs to Brunswick Pavilion, at lights turn into hotel entrance*
This smart hotel is a listed building, a short distance from the town centre. The comfortable accommodation is comprehensively equipped, and there are spacious bars and lounges. There is a choice of dining areas and bars: an elegant restaurant serves a set-price menu and carte, and a separate carvery offers a less formal option. Service is caring and attentive.
ROOMS: 20 en suite in 7 bedrooms s £60; d £105 (incl. bkfst) **LB**
CONF: Thtr 30 Class 25 Board 25 **SERVICES:** Lift **NOTES:** in restaurant Closed 25-26 Dec **CARDS:**

★★★70% Ox Pasture Hall

Lady Edith's Dr, Raincliffe Woods YO12 5TD
☎ 01723 365295 01723 355156
e-mail: oxpasturehall@btconnect.com
Dir: *Take Lady Edith's Drive from Scarborough to Scalby Rd*
Now under new ownership, this delightful family run country hotel is set in the quiet North Riding Forest Park and offers a very friendly atmosphere. Bedrooms are individual, stylish and comfortably equipped and are split between the main house, 'townhouse' and the delightful courtyard. Public areas include a split-level bar, quiet lounge, and attractive restaurant.

ROOMS: 17 en suite 6 annexe en suite (1 fmly) (14 GF) in 17 bedrooms s £50-£160; d £100-£160 (incl. bkfst) **LB** **FACILITIES:** Fishing Xmas **PARKING:** 50 **NOTES:** in restaurant
CARDS:

★★★69% Beiderbecke's Hotel

1-3 The Crescent YO11 2PW
☎ 01723 365766 01723 367433
e-mail: info@beiderbeckes.com
Dir: *in town centre, 200mtrs from railway station*

Situated in a Georgian Crescent this hotel is close to all the main attractions. Bedrooms are very smart, well equipped and offer plenty of space and comfort. Some rooms have views over the town to the sea. Marmalade's, the hotel restaurant, offers international cuisine with a modern twist and hosts live music acts at weekends, including the resident jazz band.
ROOMS: 27 en suite (1 fmly) in 10 bedrooms **FACILITIES:** Snooker ♫ **CONF:** Thtr 35 Class 35 Board 28 **SERVICES:** Lift **PARKING:** 18
NOTES: **CARDS:**

♫ Entertainment

★★★69% Crown

Esplanade YO11 2AG
☎ 01723 357400 01723 357404
e-mail: reservations@ScarboroughHotel.com
web: www.chariethotels.com
Dir: *on A64 follow town centre signs to lights opp railway station, turn right across Valley Bridge, then 1st left, right up Belmont Rd to cliff top*
Occupying a prime position on the South Cliff, this elegant hotel overlooks the sea and is only a short walk from the town centre. Several bedrooms enjoy spectacular views over Scarborough Bay.

continued on p512

ENGLISH ROSE HOTELS

WREA HEAD COUNTRY HOUSE HOTEL

Sample the delights of this beautifully restored Victorian Country House set in acres of glorious gardens and park lands at the edge of the North York Moors National Park. Twenty individually styled bedrooms. Award winning Four Seasons restaurant offers superb cuisine using fresh local produce. Ample free car parking. Situated three miles north of Scarborough – a perfect base for touring the heritage coast. Meeting facilities for up to 20 persons in privacy and seclusion.

For details ring 01723 378211
Barmoor Lane, Scalby
Scarborough YO13 0PB
Fax: 01723 355936

AA ★★★

HACKNESS GRANGE COUNTRY HOTEL

AA ★★★

North Yorkshire Moors National Park
nr Scarborough YO13 0JW

Situated on the outskirts of Scarborough, this gracious Country House is set in acres of beautiful gardens and grounds beside the River Derwent, within the North York Moors National Park. Excellent leisure choices - indoor heated swimming pool tennis court, croquet and nine hole pitch 'n putt. 33 delightful en-suite bedrooms, many with scenic country views, and award winning restaurant renowned for good food. Some ground floor rooms available. Perfect location for Board Meetings and available for exclusive use for corporated events and activities.

See entry under Hackness

Tel: 01723 882345 Fax: 01723 882391

THE Royal Hotel SCARBOROUGH

St. Nicholas Street, Scarborough
North Yorkshire YO11 2HE
Tel: 01723 364333 Fax: 01723 500618

AA ★★★

Centrally located above the South Bay with spectacular views of the picturesque harbour, marina and the wide sandy beach this completely refurbished 118 bed-roomed hotel now offers unrivalled comfort and excellent facilities for both leisure and discerning business clients alike. Contemporary ensuite accommodation at affordable rates and a leisure club that offers an indoor pool plus whirlpool, steam room and sauna. Two gyms for the more energetic or for relaxation try the spacious lounges, bars or the continental styled Café Bliss with an al fresco option.

ENGLISH ROSE HOTELS

SCARBOROUGH, continued

The hotel has comfortable lounges, extensive conference facilities, and an impressive leisure centre.

Crown Hotel, Scarborough

ROOMS: 83 en suite (7 fmly) ⊗ in 20 bedrooms **FACILITIES: Spa** Snooker Sauna Solarium Gym Fitness, Aqua & Retreat suites **CONF:** BC Thtr 200 Class 110 Board 100 **SERVICES:** Lift **PARKING:** 30 **NOTES:** ⊗ in restaurant Civ Wed 70 **CARDS:**

★★★69% Royal

St Nicholas St YO11 2HE
☎ 01723 364333 01723 371780
e-mail: royalhotel@englishrosehotels.co.uk
Dir: *from A1 turn off at junct for A64 signed York. Follow A64 signs for Scarborough. Follow town centre/South Bay signs. Hotel opp town hall*

This smart hotel enjoys a central location. Bedrooms are neatly appointed and offer a variety of styles from contemporary to traditional and include some suites. Public areas are elegant and include well-equipped conference and banqueting facilities, a leisure suite and the popular and modern Café Bliss where light snacks are served all day.

ROOMS: 118 en suite (14 fmly) ⊗ in 16 bedrooms s £60-£75; d £120-£275 (incl. bkfst) **LB FACILITIES:** Snooker Sauna Solarium Gym Jacuzzi ♫ Xmas **CONF:** Thtr 300 Class 125 Board 75 Del from £95 **SERVICES:** Lift **NOTES:** ⊗ in restaurant Civ Wed 150 **CARDS:**

★★★68% Wrea Head Country Hotel

Barmoor Ln, Scalby YO13 0PB
☎ 01723 378211 01723 371780
e-mail: wreahead@englishrosehotels.co.uk
web: www.englishrosehotels.co.uk
Dir: *from Scarborough follow A171 to hotel sign on left, turn into Barmoor Lane, follow road through ford & hotel entrance is immediately on left*

This elegant Victorian country house is situated in 14 acres of landscaped grounds and gardens amongst splendid scenery on the edge of the town. The comfortable bedrooms are individually furnished and decorated, many of them with fine views. Public rooms include the oak-panelled lounge with an inglenook fireplace and a beautiful library lounge, full of books and games. Staff are friendly, helpful and enthusiastic.

ROOMS: 20 en suite (2 fmly) (1 GF) s £60-£75; d £95-£190 (incl. bkfst) **LB FACILITIES:** STV Putt green Xmas **CONF:** Thtr 30 Class 16 Board 20 Del from £85 **PARKING:** 50 **NOTES:** ⊗ in restaurant Civ Wed 50 **CARDS:**

See advert on page 511

★★★66% Esplanade

Belmont Rd YO11 2AA
☎ 01723 360382 01723 376137
Dir: *from town centre over Valley Bridge, left then immediately right onto Belmont Rd, hotel 100mtrs on right*

This large hotel enjoys a superb position overlooking South Bay and the harbour. Both the terrace, leading from the lounge bar, and the restaurant, with its striking oriel window, benefit from magnificent views. Bedrooms are comfortably furnished to stylish, modern standards and are well equipped.

ROOMS: 73 en suite (9 fmly) s £50; d £94-£104 (incl. bkfst) **LB FACILITIES:** Table tennis Xmas **CONF:** Thtr 140 Class 100 Board 40 Del from £62 **SERVICES:** Lift **PARKING:** 20 **NOTES:** ⊗ in restaurant Closed 2 Jan-4 Feb **CARDS:**

★★★66% Hotel St Nicholas

St Nicholas Cliff YO11 2EU
☎ 01723 364101 01723 500538
e-mail: reservations.stnicholas@crerarhotels.com
web: www.crerarhotels.com
Dir: *in town centre, railway station on right, right at lights, left at next lights, across rdbt, next right*

This attractive Victorian hotel enjoys fine views over the South Bay and is just a short walk from the town. In recent years much of the hotel has been refurbished, and the public rooms and many of the bedrooms are now very smart. The hotel has a variety of seating areas, a traditional carvery restaurant and a street-side bar/bistro.

ROOMS: 138 en suite (17 fmly) ⊗ in 39 bedrooms s £70-£100; d £95-£160 (incl. bkfst) **LB FACILITIES:** STV supervised Sauna Solarium Gym ♫ ch fac Xmas **CONF:** Thtr 400 Class 150 Board 50 Del from £87.50 **SERVICES:** Lift **PARKING:** 15 **NOTES:** ⊗ in restaurant Civ Wed **CARDS:**

★★★64% Palm Court

St Nicholas Cliff YO11 2ES
☎ 01723 368161 01723 371547
e-mail: palmcourt@scarborough.co.uk
Dir: *follow signs for Town Centre & Town Hall, hotel before Town Hall on right*

The public rooms are spacious and comfortable at this modern, town centre hotel. Traditional cooking is provided in the attractive restaurant and staff are friendly and helpful. The bedrooms are comfortable and well equipped. Extra facilities include a swimming pool and free, covered parking.

ROOMS: 43 en suite (7 fmly) s £42-£52; d £78-£90 (incl. bkfst) **LB FACILITIES:** ♫ Xmas **CONF:** Thtr 200 Class 100 Board 60 Del £75 **SERVICES:** Lift **PARKING:** 80 **NOTES:** ⊗ in restaurant **CARDS:**

★★★63% Ambassador
Centre of the Esplanade YO11 2AY
☎ 01723 362841 🖷 01723 366166
e-mail: ask@ambassadorhotelscarborough.co.uk
web: www.ambassadorhotelscarborough.co.uk
Dir: *A64, right at 1st small rdbt opposite B&Q, right at next small rdbt, immediate left down Avenue Victoria to Cliff Top*

Standing on the South Cliff with excellent views over the bay, this friendly hotel offers well-equipped bedrooms, some of which are executive rooms. A large indoor swimming pool, sauna and solarium are available, and residents can also use the spa facilities at the Crown Hotel just along the road. Entertainment is provided during the summer season.
ROOMS: 59 en suite (10 fmly) ⊗ in 10 bedrooms s £24-£72; d £48-£144 (incl. bkfst & dinner) **LB FACILITIES: Spa** STV Sauna Solarium Steam room ♫ Xmas **CONF:** Thtr 140 Class 90 Board 60 Del from £55 **SERVICES:** Lift **NOTES:** ⊗ in restaurant
CARDS:

★★73% *The Mount*
Cliff Bridge Ter, Saint Nicholas Cliff YO11 2HA
☎ 01723 360961 🖷 01723 360961
Standing in a superb, elevated position and enjoying magnificent views of the South Bay, this elegant Regency hotel is personally owned and managed to a high standard. The richly furnished and comfortable public rooms are inviting, and the well-equipped bedrooms have been attractively decorated. The deluxe rooms are mini-suites and very comfortable.
ROOMS: 50 en suite (5 fmly) ⊗ in 2 bedrooms **FACILITIES: SERVICES:** Lift **NOTES:** Closed Jan-mid Mar **CARDS:**
See advert on this page

★★68% Park Manor
Northstead Manor Dr YO12 6BB
☎ 01723 372090 🖷 01723 500480
e-mail: info@parkmanor.co.uk web: www.parkmanor.co.uk
Dir: *off A165, next to Peasholm Park*

Enjoying a peaceful residential setting, this smartly presented,
continued on p514

S

SCARBOROUGH, continued

friendly hotel provides the seaside tourist with a wide range of facilities. Bedrooms vary in size and style but all are smartly furnished and well equipped. There is a spacious lounge, smart restaurant, games room and indoor pool and steam room for relaxation.
ROOMS: 42 en suite (6 fmly) s £36-£40; d £72-£120 (incl. bkfst) **LB** **FACILITIES: Spa** Jacuzzi Pool table Steam room Table tennis Xmas **CONF:** Thtr 25 Class 20 Board 20 Del from £59 **SERVICES:** Lift **PARKING:** 20 **NOTES:** No children 3yrs
CARDS:

★★67% Red Lea

Prince of Wales Ter YO11 2AJ
☎ 01723 362431 01723 371230
e-mail: redlea@globalnet.co.uk
web: www.redleahotel.co.uk
Dir: *follow signs for South Cliff, Prince of Wales Terrace leads off the esplanade opp the cliff lift*

This friendly, family-run hotel is situated close to the cliff lift. Bedrooms are well equipped and comfortably furnished, and many at the front have picturesque views of the coast. There are two large lounges and a spacious dining room in which good-value, traditional food is served.
ROOMS: 67 en suite (7 fmly) (2 GF) s £35-£39; d £70-£78 (incl. bkfst) **LB** **FACILITIES:** Sauna Solarium Gym Xmas **CONF:** Thtr 40 Class 25 Board 25 Del from £65 **SERVICES:** Lift **NOTES:** in restaurant
CARDS:

★★65% Bradley Court Hotel

Filey Rd, South Cliff YO11 2SE
☎ 01723 360476 01723 376661
e-mail: info@bradleycourthotel.co.uk
Dir: *from A64 into Scarborough, at 1st rdbt right signed Filey & South Cliff, left at next rdbt, hotel 50yds on left*
This popular hotel is only a short walk from both the town centre and the South Cliff promenade. Bedrooms are well equipped and there are spacious public rooms which include a bar lounge and a large, modern function room suitable for weddings and conferences.
ROOMS: 40 en suite (4 fmly) in 6 bedrooms s £45-£65; d £50-£80 (incl. bkfst) **LB** **FACILITIES:** ch fac Xmas **CONF:** Thtr 160 Class 100 Board 60 Del from £50 **SERVICES:** Lift **PARKING:** 20 **NOTES:** in restaurant **CARDS:**

★★65% *Clifton*

Queens Pde, North Cliff YO12 7HX
☎ 01723 375691 01723 364203
e-mail: clifton@englishrosehotels.co.uk
Dir: *on entering town centre, follow signs for North Bay*
Standing in an impressive position commanding fine views over the bay, this large holiday hotel is convenient for Peasholm Park and other local leisure attractions. Bedrooms are pleasant and entertainment is provided in the spacious public rooms during high season.
ROOMS: 71 en suite (11 fmly) **FACILITIES:** Sauna Solarium **CONF:** Thtr 120 Class 50 Board 50 **SERVICES:** Lift **PARKING:** 45 **NOTES:** in restaurant **CARDS:**

★★64% The New Southlands

15 West St, South Cliff YO11 2QW
☎ 01723 361461 01723 376035
e-mail: sales@southlandshotel.co.uk
web: www.southlandshotel.co.uk
Dir: *in Scarborough, follow town centre signs, right at railway station, left at 2nd lights, car park 200yds on left*
This hotel, popular with tour groups, is situated in a quiet area close to the South Cliff. Bedrooms are spacious and the refurbished public rooms are bright and modern. Friendly and attentive service is provided by a pleasant and well managed team.
ROOMS: 58 en suite (14 fmly) in 2 bedrooms s £30-£50; d £50-£112 (incl. bkfst) **LB** **FACILITIES:** ♫ Xmas **CONF:** Thtr 120 Class 30 Board 30 Del from £45 **SERVICES:** Lift **PARKING:** 35 **NOTES:** in restaurant
CARDS:

★★62% Delmont

18/19 Blenheim Ter YO12 7HE
☎ 01723 364500 01723 363554
e-mail: delmonthotelscar@aol.com
Dir: *Follow signs to North Bay. Then from seafront to top of cliff. Hotel near castle.*
A friendly welcome is found at this hotel on the North Bay. Bedrooms are comfortable, and many have picturesque sea views. There are two lounges and a bar and a spacious dining room in which good-value, traditional food is served - with entertainment on most evenings.
ROOMS: 50 en suite (17 fmly) (5 GF) s £20-£36; d £40-£72 (incl. bkfst) **LB** **FACILITIES:** Games Room with Pool Table, Table Tennis, Dart Board ♫ Xmas **SERVICES:** Lift **PARKING:** 2 **NOTES:** in restaurant
CARDS:

★★62% Manor Heath Hotel

67 Northstead Manor Dr YO12 6AF
☎ 01723 365720 01723 365720
e-mail: info@manorheath.co.uk
Dir: *follow signs for North Bay and Peasholm Park*
A warm welcome is offered at this pleasant, traditional private hotel, now under new ownership. Public areas include a comfortable lounge and a relaxing dining room. The bedrooms vary in size and style but all are modern and bright and offer all the expected comforts.
ROOMS: 14 en suite (6 fmly) in all bedrooms s £22-£26; d £44-£52 (incl. bkfst) **PARKING:** 11 **NOTES:** in restaurant Closed Nov-Jan
CARDS:

★★60% Brooklands

Esplanade Gardens, South Cliff YO11 2AW
☎ 01723 376576 01723 341093
Dir: *from A64 York, left at B&Q rdbt, right at next mini-rdbt, 1st left onto Victoria Av, at end turn left then 2nd left*
The Brooklands is a traditional, privately-owned and run seaside hotel. It often caters for tours and offers good value for money. The hotel stands on the South Cliff overlooking Esplanade

continued

Gardens, and is within easy access of the sea. There are ample lounges to relax in and wholesome home cooking to enjoy.

ROOMS: 55 en suite (11 fmly) (1 GF) ⊗ in 4 bedrooms s £25-£50; d £50-£100 (incl. bkfst) **LB FACILITIES:** ♫ Xmas **CONF:** Thtr 120 Class 80 Board 30 Del from £75 **SERVICES:** Lift **PARKING:** 1 **NOTES:** ⊗ in restaurant Closed Jan RS Feb **CARDS:**

★★59% The Bedford

The Crescent YO11 2PR
☎ 01723 360084 01723 507374
e-mail: reception@bedfordhotel.info
Dir: *Follow A64 to train station., turn right at lights, 1st left, 1st right, into The Crescent*

The Bedford is a traditional family-owned and run seaside hotel, ideally situated on the historic Crescent. The comfortable bedrooms vary in size; some are suitable for family occupancy, and several benefit from sea views. Public areas are spacious and comfortable, and service is informal and friendly.

ROOMS: 27 en suite (8 fmly) (1 GF) s £30-£43; d £50-£76 (incl. bkfst) **LB FACILITIES:** ♫ Xmas **CONF:** Thtr 60 Class 40 Board 25 **NOTES:** ⊗ in restaurant **CARDS:**

SCILLY, ISLES OF — Map 02

BRYHER — Map 02 SV81

★★★80% Hell Bay Hotel

TR23 0PR
☎ 01720 422947 01720 423004
e-mail: contactus@hellbay.co.uk
Dir: *Island location means it is only accessible by helicopter from Penzance, ship from Penzance or plane from Southampton, Bristol, Exeter, Plymouth or Land's End*

Located on the smallest of the inhabited Scilly Islands, this hotel provides a really special destination. Much of the hotel has been completely refurbished and bedrooms, many with garden access and stunning sea views, are stylish and very well equipped. Cuisine features fresh local produce and is a delight.

ROOMS: 12 en suite 11 annexe en suite (4 fmly) (18 GF) ⊗ in all bedrooms d £180-£400 (incl. bkfst & dinner) **LB FACILITIES:** STV 9 Sauna Gym Jacuzzi Boules Par 3 golf ch fac **CONF:** Thtr 36 Class 36 Board 36 **NOTES:** ⊗ in restaurant Closed Jan-Feb **CARDS:**

ST MARTIN'S — Map 02 SV91

Top 200 – Hotel

★★★ St Martin's on the Isle

Lower Town TR25 0QW
☎ 01720 422090 01720 422298
e-mail: stay@stmartinshotel.co.uk
web: www.stmartinshotel.co.uk
Dir: *20-minute helicopter flight to St Mary's, then 20-minute launch to St Martin's*

This attractive hotel, complete with its own sandy beach, enjoys an idyllic position on the waterfront overlooking Tresco and Tean. Bedrooms are brightly appointed, comfortably furnished and overlook the sea or the well-tended gardens. There is an elegant, award-winning restaurant and a split-level lounge bar where guests can relax and enjoy the memorable view. Locally caught fish features significantly on the daily-changing menus.

ROOMS: 30 en suite (10 fmly) (14 GF) s £125-£175; d £250-£350 (incl. bkfst & dinner) **LB FACILITIES:** Snooker Clay pigeon shooting Boating Bikes Diving Snorkelling ch fac **CONF:** Thtr 50 Class 50 Board 50 **NOTES:** ⊗ in restaurant Closed Nov-Feb Civ Wed 100 **CARDS:**

ST MARY'S — Map 02 SV91

★★★74% Tregarthens

Hugh Town TR21 0PP
☎ 01720 422540 01720 422089
e-mail: reception@tregarthens-hotel.co.uk
Dir: *100yds from quay*

Opened in 1848 by Captain Tregarthen this is now a well-established hotel. The impressively refurbished public areas provide wonderful views overlooking St Mary's harbour and some of the many islands, including Tresco and Bryher. The spacious bedrooms are well equipped and neatly furnished. Traditional cuisine is served in the restaurant.

ROOMS: 31 en suite 1 annexe en suite (5 fmly) ⊗ in 4 bedrooms s £85-£102; d £144-£224 (incl. bkfst & dinner) **LB NOTES:** ⊗ in restaurant Closed late Oct-mid Mar **CARDS:**

See advert on page 517

S

TRESCO Map 02 SV81

Top 200 – Hotel

★★★ The Island

TR24 0PU

☎ 01720 422883 01720 423008

e-mail: islandhotel@tresco.co.uk

web: www.tresco.co.uk/holidays/island_hotel.asp

Dir: *helicopter service Penzance to Tresco, hotel on NE of island*

This delightful colonial-style hotel enjoys a waterside location in its own attractive gardens. The spacious, comfortable lounges, airy restaurant and many of the bedrooms enjoy stunning sea views. All of the rooms are brightly furnished and many benefit from lounge areas, balconies or terraces. Carefully prepared, imaginative cuisine makes good use of locally caught fish.

ROOMS: 48 en suite (27 fmly) s £117-£283; d £117-£283 (incl. bkfst & dinner) **LB FACILITIES:** Fishing Boating Table tennis Bowls, boutique, internet access ch fac **CONF:** BC Thtr 80 Class 80 Board 80 **NOTES:** in restaurant Closed Nov-Feb **CARDS:**

★★76% **New Inn**

TR24 0QQ

☎ 01720 422844 01720 423200

e-mail: newinn@tresco.co.uk

web: www.tresco.co.uk/holidays/new_inn.asp

Dir: *by New Grimsby Quay*

This friendly, popular inn enjoys a central location and offers bright, attractive, well-equipped bedrooms, many with splendid sea views. The popular bar offering real ales, serves an interesting range of snacks and meals. In addition guests may choose to dine in the airy bistro-style Pavilion or the elegant restaurant complete with its own bar.

ROOMS: 16 en suite (2 GF) s £112.50-£172.50; d £150-£330 (incl. bkfst & dinner) **LB FACILITIES:** Sea fishing, bird watching ch fac Xmas **NOTES:** in restaurant **CARDS:**

SCOTCH CORNER (NEAR RICHMOND), North Yorkshire Map 19 NZ20

★★★64% **The Scotch Corner Hotel**

A1/A66 Great Noth Rd DL10 6NR

☎ 01748 850900 01748 825417

e-mail: enquiries@hotels-scotch-corner.com

Dir: *at A1/A66 junct turn off towards Penrith*

This hotel is ideally located for access to main road networks and offers excellent parking facilities. Bedrooms are generally spacious and are equipped with thoughtful extras. A popular venue for both

continued

conference and leisure guests, there are spacious lounges, meeting rooms and a particularly well equipped leisure club.

ROOMS: 90 en suite (5 fmly) (17 GF) in 36 bedrooms s £86; d £96 **LB FACILITIES: Spa** STV supervised Sauna Solarium Gym Jacuzzi Hair Salon, Beautician Xmas **CONF:** Thtr 300 Class 100 Board 80 Del £110 **SERVICES:** Lift **PARKING:** 200 **NOTES:** in restaurant Civ Wed 200 **CARDS:**

Travelodge

Middleton Tyas Ln DL10 6PQ

☎ 08700 850 950 01325 377616

Dir: *A1/A66*

Travelodge offers good quality, good value, modern accommodation. Ideal for families, the spacious, en suite bedrooms include remote-control TV, tea and coffee-making facilities and luxury beds. Meals can be taken at the nearby family restaurant. For further details consult the Hotel Groups page.

ROOMS: 50 en suite s fr £25; d fr £25

Travelodge Skeeby (Scotch Corner)

Skeeby DL10 5EQ

☎ 08700 850 950 0870 1911675

Dir: *0.5m S on A1*

Travelodge offers good quality, good value, modern accommodation. Ideal for families, the spacious, en suite bedrooms include remote-control TV, tea and coffee-making facilities and luxury beds. Meals can be taken at the nearby family restaurant. For further details consult the Hotel Groups page.

ROOMS: 40 en suite s fr £25; d fr £25

SCUNTHORPE, Lincolnshire Map 17 SE81

★★★★72% **Forest Pines Hotel**

Ermine St, Broughton DN20 0AQ

☎ 01652 650770 01652 650495

e-mail: enquiries@forestpines.co.uk

web: www.forestpines.co.uk

Dir: *200yds from M180 junct 4, on Brigg-Scunthorpe rdbt*

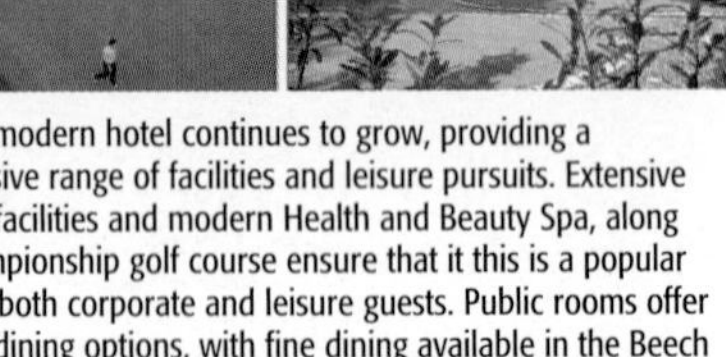

This smart, modern hotel continues to grow, providing a comprehensive range of facilities and leisure pursuits. Extensive conference facilities and modern Health and Beauty Spa, along with a Championship golf course ensure that it this is a popular choice with both corporate and leisure guests. Public rooms offer a choice of dining options, with fine dining available in the Beech Tree Restaurant or more informal eating in the Garden room or Mulligans bar. Bedrooms are mostly spacious and well equipped; ground-floor bedrooms and two suites are available.

ROOMS: 114 en suite (66 fmly) (41 GF) in 77 bedrooms s £79-£99; d £99-£109 (incl. bkfst) **LB FACILITIES: Spa** STV supervised 27 Sauna Gym Putt green Jacuzzi Mountain bikes Jogging track ch fac Xmas **CONF:** Thtr 375 Class 142 Board 134 Del from £135 **SERVICES:** Lift **PARKING:** 300 **NOTES:** in restaurant Civ Wed 200 **CARDS:**

★★★67% Wortley House
Rowland Rd DN16 1SU
☎ 01724 842223 📠 01724 280646
Dir: *M180 junct 3 take A18. Follow signs for Grimsby/Humberside airport, 2nd left into Brumby Wood Ln, over rdbt into Rowland Rd. Hotel 200yds on right*
A friendly hotel with good facilities for conferences, meetings, banquets and other functions. Bedrooms offer modern comfort and facilities. Popular bar meals are served in the cocktail lounge, while more formal meals are served in the pleasant restaurant.
ROOMS: 38 en suite (3 fmly) ⊗ in 28 bedrooms s £63-£84; d £67.50-£90 (incl. bkfst) **FACILITIES:** STV ch fac Xmas **CONF:** Thtr 300 Class 250 Board 50 **PARKING:** 100 **NOTES:** ⊗ in restaurant Civ Wed 200 **CARDS:**

⌂ Travel Inn
Lakeside Retail Park, Lakeside Parkway DN16 3UA
☎ 08701 977226 📠 01724 278651
Dir: *M180 junct 4, A18 towards Scunthorpe. At Morrisons rdbt left onto Lakeside Retail Park, Inn behind Morrisons petrol station*
Travel Inn offers good-quality, value-for-money accommodation. Spacious, en suite rooms with bath and shower comfortably accommodate a family of up to two adults and two children (to age 15). The restaurant and bar offers a varied menu. For further details consult the Hotel Groups page.
ROOMS: 40 en suite s £45.95-£46.95; d £45.95-£46.95

SEAHAM, Co Durham — Map 19 NZ44

Top 200 – Hotel

★★★★ ◎◎◎ Seaham Hall Hotel
Lord Byron's Walk SR7 7AG
☎ 0191 516 1400 📠 0191 516 1410
e-mail: reservations@seaham-hall.com
web: www.seaham-hall.com
Dir: *from A19 take B1404 to Seaham. At lights straight over level crossing. Hotel approx 0.25m on right*
This imposing house was the setting for the wedding of Lord Byron and has been restored with an opulence he would have appreciated. Bedrooms, including some stunning suites, offer cutting edge technology, contemporary artwork and a real sense of style. Bathrooms are particularly lavish, with two-person baths a feature. Public rooms are equally impressive and accomplished cooking is a hallmark. A stunning new Oriental Spa accessed via an underground walkway offers guests a wide range of treatments and a Thai brasserie.
ROOMS: 19 en suite (4 GF) ⊗ in all bedrooms s £195-£525; d £195-£525 (incl. bkfst) **LB** **FACILITIES: Spa** STV Sauna Gym Jacuzzi Full spa Xmas **CONF:** Thtr 120 Class 40 Board 40 **SERVICES:** Lift air con **PARKING:** 122 **NOTES:** ⊗ in restaurant Civ Wed 112 **CARDS:**

SEAHOUSES, Northumberland — Map 21 NU23

★★74% Olde Ship
NE68 7RD
☎ 01665 720200 📠 01665 721383
e-mail: theoldeship@seahouses.co.uk
Dir: *lower end of main street above harbour*

Under the same ownership since 1910, this friendly hotel overlooks the harbour. Its sense of history is evident by the amount of nautical memorabilia on display. Public areas include a character bar, cosy snug and restaurant. The individual bedrooms are well presented. A separate building contains four apartment rooms with stunning views.
ROOMS: 12 en suite 6 annexe en suite (3 GF) s £41-£48; d £82-£96 (incl. bkfst) **LB** **PARKING:** 19 **NOTES:** No children 10yrs ⊗ in restaurant Closed Dec-Jan **CARDS:**

⊗ No smoking

SEAHOUSES, continued

★★70% Bamburgh Castle

NE68 7SQ
☎ 01665 720283 🖷 01665 720848
e-mail: bamburghcastlehotel@btinternet.com
web: www.bamburghcastlehotel.co.uk
Dir: *from A1 follow signs for Seahouses, car park entrance on rdbt opposite Barclays Bank, automatic barrier will rise*

This hotel enjoys a seafront location overlooking the harbour. Bedrooms vary in size and style, yet all are well equipped, with superior rooms being spacious and attractively appointed. Front-facing rooms, plus the main lounge and restaurant all take advantage of the views.
ROOMS: 20 en suite (3 fmly) (3 GF) ⊘ in 10 bedrooms s £44.95-£56.95; d £89.90-£99.90 (incl. bkfst) **LB FACILITIES:** Putt green ch fac **CONF:** Thtr 40 Class 20 Board 25 **PARKING:** 30
NOTES: ⊘ in restaurant Closed 24-26 Dec & 2wks mid Jan
CARDS:

★★69% *Beach House*

Sea Front NE68 7SR
☎ 01665 720337 🖷 01665 720921
e-mail: enquiries@beachhousehotel.co.uk
web: www.beachhousehotel.co.uk
Dir: *follow signs from A1 between Alnwick & Berwick*
Enjoying a seafront location and views of the Farne Islands, this family-run hotel offers a relaxed and friendly atmosphere. Bedrooms come in a variety of sizes, but all are bright and airy. Dinner makes use of fresh produce and breakfast features local specialities. There is a well-stocked bar and comfortable lounge.
ROOMS: 14 en suite (5 fmly) ⊘ in all bedrooms **PARKING:** 16
NOTES: ⊘ in restaurant Closed Jan
CARDS:

> TV dinner?
> Room service at three stars and above

SEATON, Devon — Map 04 SY29

★★67% Seaton Heights Hotel

Seaton Down Hill EX12 2TF
☎ 01297 20932 🖷 01297 24839
e-mail: stay@seatonheightshotel.co.uk
web: www.seatonheightshotel.co.uk
Dir: *on A3052 at Tower Cross turn towards Seaton, hotel 200yds on left just past watertower*
Conveniently located, Seaton Heights overlooks the Axe Valley towards the sea. The restaurant and function suite have lovely views and the imaginative cuisine features freshly prepared dishes including a bar meal service. Bedrooms are modern in style and well-equipped. An extensive range of leisure facilities is provided along with spacious grounds.
ROOMS: 26 en suite (8 fmly) (11 GF) s £43-£66; d £66-£112 (incl. bkfst) **LB FACILITIES:** Squash Snooker Sauna Solarium Gym Badminton Basketball Table tennis Short mat bowls Aerobics Yoga Xmas
CONF: Thtr 500 Class 300 Board 150 Del from £80 **PARKING:** 128
NOTES: ⊘ in restaurant **CARDS:**

SEATON BURN, Tyne & Wear — Map 21 NZ27

⌂ Travelodge (Newcastle North)

Travelodge

Front St NE13 6ED
☎ 08700 850 950 🖷 0191 217 0107
Travelodge offers good quality, good value, modern accommodation. Ideal for families, the spacious, en suite bedrooms include remote-control TV, tea and coffee-making facilities and luxury beds. Meals can be taken at the nearby family restaurant. For further details consult the Hotel Groups page.
ROOMS: 40 en suite s fr £25; d fr £25

SEAVIEW See Wight, Isle of

SEDGEFIELD, Co Durham — Map 19 NZ32

★★★75% Hardwick Hall

Best Western

TS21 2EH
☎ 01740 620253 🖷 01740 622771
e-mail: info@hardwickhallhotel.co.uk
Dir: *off A1(M) junct 60 towards Sedgefield, left at 1st rdbt, hotel 400mtrs on left*
Set in extensive parkland, this 18th-century house has been transformed into a top conference and wedding venue. The hotel offers an impressive conference and banqueting complex, plus a new wing of stunning bedrooms to augment those in the original house. The atmospheric Cellar Bar and Bistro has a relaxed atmosphere.
ROOMS: 52 en suite (6 fmly) ⊘ in all bedrooms s £85-£155; d £110-£190 (incl. bkfst) **LB FACILITIES:** STV **CONF:** Thtr 700 Board 80
SERVICES: Lift **PARKING:** 200 **NOTES:** ⊘ in restaurant Civ Wed 500 **CARDS:**

⌂ Travelodge

Travelodge

TS21 2JX
☎ 08700 850 950 🖷 01740 623399
Dir: *on A689, 3m E of junct A1(M)*
Travelodge offers good quality, good value, modern accommodation. Ideal for families, the spacious, en suite bedrooms include remote-control TV, tea and coffee-making facilities and luxury beds. Meals can be taken at the nearby family restaurant. For further details consult the Hotel Groups page.
ROOMS: 40 en suite s fr £25; d fr £25

SEDGEMOOR MOTORWAY SERVICE AREA (M5), Somerset — Map 04 ST35

⌂ Days Inn

DAYS INN

M5 Northbound J22-21, Sedgemoor BS24 0JL
☎ 01934 750831 🖷 01934 750808
e-mail: sedgemoor.hotel@welcomebreak.co.uk
web: www.welcomebreak.co.uk
Dir: *M5 junct 21/22*
This modern building offers accommodation in smart, spacious and well-equipped bedrooms, suitable for families and business travellers, and all with en suite bathrooms. Continental breakfast is available and other refreshments may be taken at the nearby family restaurant. For further details see the Hotel Groups page.
ROOMS: 40 en suite s £45-£55; d £45-£55 **CONF:** BC

SEDLESCOMBE, East Sussex
Map 07 TQ71

★★★70% Brickwall
The Green TN33 0QA
☎ 01424 870253 🖷 01424 870785
e-mail: brickwallhotel@hotmail.com
Dir: *off A21 on B2244 at top of Sedlescombe Green*

A well-maintained Tudor house situated in the heart of this pretty village and overlooking the green. The spacious public rooms feature a lovely wood-panelled restaurant with a wealth of oak beams, a choice of lounges and a smart bar. Bedrooms are pleasantly decorated, have co-ordinated soft furnishings and all the usual facilities.

ROOMS: 26 en suite (2 fmly) (18 GF) ⊘ in 9 bedrooms s fr £55; d fr £80 (incl. bkfst) **LB FACILITIES:** STV Xmas **CONF:** Thtr 30 Class 40 Board 30 **PARKING:** 50 **NOTES:** ⊘ in restaurant
CARDS:

SENNEN, Cornwall & Isles of Scilly
Map 02 SW32

★★67% *Old Success Inn*
Sennen Cove TR19 7DG
☎ 01736 871232 🖷 01736 871457
e-mail: oldsuccess@sennencove.fsbusiness.co.uk
Dir: *turn right off A30 approx 1m before Land's End, signed Sennen Cove. Hotel on left at bottom of hill*

This inn is romantically located at the water's edge, with spectacular views of the cove and the Atlantic Ocean. Popular with locals and visitors alike, the inn offers friendly service and a choice of dining in either the restaurant and bar; there is always a selection of fresh fish dishes.

ROOMS: 12 en suite (1 fmly) **FACILITIES:** ♫ **PARKING:** 12
NOTES: ⊘ in restaurant **CARDS:**

SEVENOAKS, Kent
Map 06 TQ55

★★★71% Donnington Manor

London Rd, Dunton Green TN13 2TD
☎ 01732 462681 🖷 01732 458116
e-mail: reservations@donningtonmanorhotel.co.uk
web: www.donningtonmanorhotel.co.uk
Dir: *M25 junct 4, follow signs for Bromley/Orpington to rdbt. Left onto A224 (Dunton Green), left at 2nd rdbt. Left at Rose & Crown, hotel 300yds on right*

This extended 15th-century manor house is situated on the outskirts of Sevenoaks. Public rooms in the original part of the building have a wealth of character; they include an attractive oak-beamed restaurant, a comfortable lounge and a cosy bar. The purpose-built bedrooms are smartly decorated and well equipped.

ROOMS: 60 en suite (2 fmly) ⊘ in 20 bedrooms **FACILITIES:** STV supervised Squash Sauna Gym Jacuzzi Xmas **CONF:** Thtr 180 Class 60 Board 40 Del from £110 **PARKING:** 120 **NOTES:** ⊘ in restaurant Civ Wed 70 **CARDS:**

SEVERN VIEW MOTORWAY SERVICE AREA (M4), Gloucestershire
Map 04 ST58

⇧ Travelodge
Travelodge
M48 Motorway, Severn Bridge BS35 4BH
☎ 08700 850 950 🖷 01454 632482
Dir: *M48 junct 21*

Travelodge offers good quality, good value, modern accommodation. Ideal for families, the spacious, en suite bedrooms include remote-control TV, tea and coffee-making facilities and luxury beds. Meals can be taken at the nearby family restaurant. For further details consult the Hotel Groups page.

ROOMS: 50 en suite s fr £25; d fr £25

SHAFTESBURY, Dorset
Map 04 ST82

★★★66% Royal Chase
Best Western
Royal Chase Roundabout SP7 8DB
☎ 01747 853355 🖷 01747 851969
e-mail: royalchasehotel@btinternet.com
web: theroyalchasehotel.co.uk
Dir: *A303 to A350 signed Blandford Forum. Avoid town centre, follow road to 3rd rdbt*

Equally suitable for both leisure and business guests, this well-known local landmark is situated close to the famous Gold Hill. Bedrooms come in 'standard' and 'crown' and both types offer good levels of comfort and quality. In addition to the fixed price menu in the Byzant Restaurant, guests have the option of eating more informally in the convivial bar.

ROOMS: 33 en suite (13 fmly) (6 GF) ⊘ in 10 bedrooms s £95; d £110-£130 **LB FACILITIES: Spa** STV Turkish steam bath Xmas **CONF:** Thtr 180 Class 90 Board 50 Del from £110 **PARKING:** 100 **NOTES:** ⊘ in restaurant Civ Wed 76
CARDS:

Restaurant with Rooms

La Fleur de Lys Restaurant with Rooms
Bleke St SP7 8AW
☎ 01747 853717 🖷 01747 853130
e-mail: info@lafleurdelys.co.uk
Dir: *0.25m off the junct of A30 with A350 at Shaftesbury towards Town Centre*

Located just a 3 minute walk from the famous Gold Hill, this newly and totally refurbished restaurant with rooms combines efficient service standards with a relaxed and friendly atmosphere. Bedrooms vary in size, but all are well equipped, comfortable and include plenty of useful extras. A guest lounge and courtyard are available for afternoon tea or pre-dinner drinks.

ROOMS: 7 en suite (2 fmly) (1 GF) ⊘ in all bedrooms s £50-£55; d £75-£95 (incl. bkfst) **LB CONF:** Board 10 **PARKING:** 7 **NOTES:** ⊘ in restaurant **CARDS:**

SHALDON See Teignmouth

SHANKLIN See Wight, Isle of

SHAP, Cumbria
Map 18 NY51

★★★68% Shap Wells
CA10 3QU
☎ 01931 716628 🖷 01931 716377
e-mail: manager@shapwells.com
web: www.shapwells.com
Dir: *M6 junct 39, follow signs for Kendal, turn left at A6, after approx 1m turn left into drive. Hotel approx 1m*

This friendly, family-owned hotel occupies a wonderful secluded

continued on p520

S

SHAP, continued

position amid trees and waterfalls. Extensive public areas include function and meeting rooms, a well-stocked bar, a choice of lounges and a spacious restaurant. Bedrooms vary in size and style and all are equipped with the expected facilities.
ROOMS: 91 en suite 7 annexe en suite (10 fmly) s £55-£65; d £75-£95 (incl. bkfst) **LB** **FACILITIES:** Snooker Games room, walking in the 30 acre grounds **CONF:** Thtr 170 Class 80 Board 40 Del from £90 **SERVICES:** Lift **PARKING:** 200 **NOTES:** in restaurant Closed 23-28 Dec & 4-20 Jan RS 28 Dec-4 Jan Civ Wed 150
CARDS:

SHAPWICK, Somerset Map 04 ST43

★★76% Shapwick House
Monks Dr TA7 9NL
☎ 01458 210321 01458 210729
e-mail: keith@shapwickhouse.free-on-line.co.uk
Dir: *M5 junct 23 towards Glastonbury. Left onto A39 (Glastonbury). After 5m hotel signed on left*
Dating back to the 15th century, this fabulous stone manor house was originally built by Glastonbury Abbey. It is surrounded by lovely gardens and grounds and offers easy access to the M5. The main hall, with its splendid fireplace is the ideal place to relax after a busy day exploring. Bedrooms are spacious and well equipped with many thoughtful touches. The Georgian dining room offers an imaginative, fixed-price menu.
ROOMS: 13 en suite (1 fmly) (1 GF) in all bedrooms s £75-£150; d £100-£150 (incl. bkfst) **LB** **CONF:** Thtr 40 Class 25 Board 15 **PARKING:** 40 **NOTES:** No children 10yrs in restaurant RS 25 Dec-31 Jan Civ Wed 80 **CARDS:**

SHEDFIELD, Hampshire Map 05 SU51

★★★★67% Marriott Meon Valley Hotel & Country Club
Marriott HOTELS · RESORTS · SUITES
Sandy Ln SO32 2HQ
☎ 01329 833455 01329 834411
Dir: *from W, M27 junct 7 take A334 then towards Wickham and Botley. Sandy Lane is on left 2m from Botley*
This modern, smartly appointed hotel and country club has extensive indoor and outdoor leisure facilities, including two golf courses. Bedrooms are spacious and well equipped, and guests have a choice of eating and drinking options.
ROOMS: 113 en suite in 80 bedrooms **FACILITIES:** STV 18 Sauna Solarium Gym Putt green Jacuzzi Cardio-Vascular Aerobics Health & Beauty salon Xmas **CONF:** Thtr 80 Class 50 Board 32 Del from £135 **SERVICES:** Lift **PARKING:** 320 **NOTES:** in restaurant Civ Wed 96
CARDS:

SHEFFIELD, South Yorkshire Map 16 SK49

★★★★69% Sheffield Marriott Hotel
Marriott HOTELS · RESORTS · SUITES
Kenwood Rd S7 1NQ
☎ 0870 400 7261 0870 400 7361
e-mail: eventorganiser.sheffield@marriotthotels.co.uk
Dir: *follow A61 past Red Tape Studios on right , right at 2nd set of lights into St Marys Rd. At rdbt straight across, bear left into London Rd, right at lights, at top of hill straight across 1st and 2nd rdbt*
A smart, modern hotel peacefully located in a residential suburb a few miles from the city centre. Stylishly decorated bedrooms are spacious, quiet and provide very well equipped. The hotel also has an extensive range of leisure and meeting facilities. Drivers have the peace of mind of secure parking.
ROOMS: 114 en suite (14 fmly) (27 GF) in 90 bedrooms s £64-£120; d £78-£140 (incl. bkfst) **LB** **FACILITIES: Spa** STV Fishing Sauna Solarium Gym Jacuzzi Steam room, Health & beauty treatments **CONF:** Thtr 250 Class 100 Board 60 Del from £145 **SERVICES:** Lift **PARKING:** 200 **NOTES:** in restaurant Civ Wed 200
CARDS:

★★★74% Staindrop Lodge
CLASSIC BRITISH
Ln End, Chapeltown S35 3UH
☎ 0114 284 3111 0114 284 3110
e-mail: info@staindroplodge.co.uk
Dir: *M1 junct 35, take A629 for 1m straight over 1st rdbt, right at 2nd rdbt, hotel approx 0.5m on right*
Now fully refurbished and extended, this bar, brasserie and hotel offers smart modern public areas and accommodation. An Art Deco theme continues through the open-plan public rooms and the comfortably appointed, spacious bedrooms. Service is relaxed and friendly.
ROOMS: 31 en suite (6 fmly) in all bedrooms **FACILITIES:** STV Xmas **CONF:** Thtr 40 Class 60 Board 40 Del from £95.10 **SERVICES:** Lift air con **PARKING:** 80 **NOTES:** in restaurant
CARDS:

★★★72% *Whitley Hall*
Elliott Ln, Grenoside S35 8NR
☎ 0114 245 4444 0114 245 5414
e-mail: reservations@whitleyhall.com
Dir: *A61 past football ground and 2m further, turn right just before Norfolk Arms, turn left at bottom of hill. Hotel on left*
This 16th-century house stands in 30 acres of landscaped grounds and gardens. Public rooms are full of character and architectural features, and command the best views of the gardens. Bedrooms are individually furnished in a style in keeping with this country house setting, as are the oak-panelled restaurant and bar.
ROOMS: 19 en suite (1 fmly) **FACILITIES:** Putt green **CONF:** Thtr 70 Class 50 Board 40 **PARKING:** 100 **NOTES:** in restaurant RS Sat Civ Wed 80 **CARDS:**

★★★71% The Beauchief Hotel
corus hotels
161 Abbeydale Rd South S7 2QW
☎ 0114 262 0500 0114 235 0197
e-mail: beauchief@corushotels.com
Dir: *from city centre 2m on A621 signed Bakewell*

On the southern outskirts of the city, this busy property attracts both resident and local business. The popular restaurant and Merchant's bar have an excellent reputation in the area for good food and hospitality. Bedrooms are well proportioned with many extras such as movie channels on the TV. Ample parking is a bonus.
ROOMS: 50 en suite (3 fmly) (19 GF) in 39 bedrooms s £79; d £79 **LB** **FACILITIES:** STV **CONF:** Thtr 100 Class 50 Board 50 Del from £118 **PARKING:** 200 **NOTES:** in restaurant Civ Wed 95
CARDS:

★★★71% Charnwood
10 Sharrow Ln S11 8AA
☎ 0114 258 9411 📠 0114 255 5107
e-mail: reception@charnwoodhotel.co.uk
Dir: *Sharrow Lane is near London Rd/Abbeydale Rd junct, on A621, 1.5m SW of city centre*
A Georgian mansion house once owned by a Master Cutler, is within walking distance of the city centre, just off the London Road. The bedrooms are well equipped and the lounges and bars are well furnished and comfortable. Leo's Brasserie is a modern informal restaurant serving freshly cooked and interesting meals.
ROOMS: 22 en suite ⊗ in all bedrooms s £75-£93; d £83-£110 (incl. bkfst) **LB** **FACILITIES:** STV **CONF:** Thtr 90 Class 40 Board 35 Del from £124.50 **PARKING:** 22 **NOTES:** ✈ Civ Wed 100
CARDS:

★★★67% Aston Hall
Worksop Rd, Aston S26 2EE
☎ 0114 287 2309 📠 0114 287 3228
e-mail: reservations@astonhallhotel.co.uk
web: www.astonhallhotel.co.uk
Originally built as a manor house and set in spacious grounds with open views across the countryside to the south of the city, this hotel is well located for the M1, Meadowhall, the city or touring. Extensive conference and banqueting facilities, spacious bedrooms, and gracious service are all notable here.
ROOMS: 20 en suite (4 fmly) ⊗ in 10 bedrooms s £55-£70; d £65-£90 **FACILITIES:** STV **CONF:** Thtr 350 Class 200 Board 35 Del from £120 **SERVICES:** air con **PARKING:** 150 **NOTES:** Civ Wed 200
CARDS:

★★★67% Novotel Sheffield
50 Arundel Gate S1 2PR
☎ 0114 278 1781 📠 0114 278 7744
e-mail: h1348@accor-hotels.com
Dir: *between Registry Office and Crucible/Lyceum Theatres, follow signs to Town Hall/Theatres & Hallam University*
Located in the heart of the city centre, this modern hotel is popular with both business and leisure guests. Local theatres and shopping are within easy reach, while within the hotel, facilities include an indoor heated swimming pool and a range of meeting rooms. Spacious bedrooms are suitable for family occupation and yet manage to provide an equally ideal environment for business users.
ROOMS: 144 en suite (40 fmly) ⊗ in 108 bedrooms **FACILITIES:** STV Local gym facilities free for residents use **CONF:** Thtr 220 Class 180 Board 100 Del £130 **SERVICES:** Lift **PARKING:** 44 **NOTES:** RS 24 Dec-2 Jan Civ Wed 150 **CARDS:**

★★★66% *Mosborough Hall*
High St, Mosborough S20 5EA
☎ 0114 248 4353 📠 0114 247 9759
e-mail: hotel@mosboroughhall.co.uk
web: www.mosboroughhall.co.uk
Dir: *M1 J30, take A6135 towards Sheffield, hotel 0.5 mile after traffic lights, on right*
This 16th-century, Grade II listed manor house is set in gardens not far from the M1 and convenient for the city centre. Bedrooms vary in style, and some are very spacious. There is a galleried bar and conservatory lounge, and freshly prepared dishes are served in the brightly furnished dining room.
ROOMS: 52 en suite (1 fmly) (12 GF) ⊗ in 30 bedrooms **CONF:** Thtr 300 Class 125 Board 70 **PARKING:** 100 **NOTES:** ⊗ in restaurant Civ Wed 250 **CARDS:**

★★★65% The Garrison
Hillsborough Barracks, Penistone Rd S6 2GB
☎ 0114 249 9555 📠 0114 249 1900
e-mail: enquiries@garrisonhotel.com
web: www.garrisonhotel.com
This unique hotel close to Hillsborough football ground, the leisure centre and dry-ski slope, has been redeveloped from the former Hillsborough Barracks. The Jailhouse has become an interesting bar and restaurant serving fine meals, and the Armoury a meeting room. Bedrooms are comfortable and well equipped. The adjacent Supertram offers good access to the city centre.
ROOMS: 43 en suite (2 fmly) ⊗ in 34 bedrooms s £50-£60; d £50-£60 (incl. cont bkfst) **FACILITIES:** STV ♫ Xmas **CONF:** Thtr 30 Class 30 Board 30 Del £84 **PARKING:** 60 **NOTES:** ✈ ⊗ in restaurant Civ Wed 120 **CARDS:**

★★66% Cutlers Hotel
Theatreland George St S1 2PF
☎ 0114 273 9939 📠 0114 276 8332
e-mail: enquiries@cutlershotel.co.uk web: www.cutlershotel.co.uk
Dir: *In retail, commerce & academic centre, 50 metres from Crucible Theatre. Follow theatre signs.*
Situated close to the Crucible Theatre in the city centre, this boutique hotel offers accommodation in well-equipped bedrooms and extras including hairdryers, trouser presses and business facilities. Public areas include a lower ground floor bistro, and room service is available if required. Small meeting rooms are also available. Discounted overnight parking is provided in the nearby public car park.
ROOMS: 45 en suite (4 fmly) ⊗ in 18 bedrooms s £45-£62; d £47.50-£72 (incl. bkfst) **LB** **FACILITIES:** Xmas **CONF:** BC Thtr 90 Class 40 Board 30 Del from £60 **SERVICES:** Lift **NOTES:** ⊗ in restaurant Civ Wed 50 **CARDS:**

Hotel Ibis Sheffield City
Shude Hill S1 2AR
☎ 0114 241 9600 📠 0114 241 9610
e-mail: H2891@accor-hotels.com
Dir: *M1 junct 33, follow signs to Sheffield City Centre(A630/A57), at rdbt take 5th exit, signed Ponds Forge, for hotel*
Modern, budget hotel offering comfortable accommodation in bright and practical bedrooms. Breakfast is self-service and dinner is available in the restaurant. For further details, consult the Hotel Groups page.
ROOMS: 95 en suite s £42.95-£46.95; d £42.95-£46.95

Innkeeper's Lodge Sheffield South
Hathersage Rd, Longshaw S11 7TY
☎ 01433 630374 📠 01433 637102
www.innkeeperslodge.com
Dir: *8m from Sheffield city centre on A625 Sheffield Castleton Road at junction of A625 & B6051.*
Smart rooms meet essential business requirements but also have home comforts, and depending on location may well have meeting rooms and pub dining. Dining options generally include all-day menus plus the added advantage of breakfast.
ROOMS: 10 annexe en suite s £49.95; d £49.95

Premier Lodge (Sheffield)
Sheffield Rd, Meadowhall S9 2YL
☎ 0870 9906440 📠 0870 9906441
web: www.premierlodge.com
Dir: *1.5m from M1 junct 34 on A6178*
High quality, modern, budget accommodation, ideal for families and business travellers. All rooms feature bath, power shower and satellite TV, and most have telephones / modem points. The adjacent bar and restaurant offers a wide and varied menu.
ROOMS: 103 en suite s £50; d £50

SHEFFIELD, continued

Travel Inn Sheffield (Arena)

Attercliffe Common Rd S9 2LU
☎ 0870 238 3316 ▯ 0114 242 3703
Dir: *M1 junct 34, follow signs to city centre. Travel Inn opposite Arena*
Travel Inn offers good-quality, value-for-money accommodation. Spacious, en suite rooms with bath and shower comfortably accommodate a family of up to two adults and two children (to age 15). The restaurant and bar offers a varied menu. For further details consult the Hotel Groups page.
ROOMS: 61 en suite s £45.95-£46.95; d £45.95-£46.95

Travel Inn Sheffield City Centre

Angel St / Bank St Corner S3 8LN
☎ 0870 238 3324 ▯ 0870 241 9000
Dir: *from M1(J33), follow signs for Sheffield City Centre (A630 onto A57). At Park Square rdbt 4th exit (A61 Barnsley). Left at 4th set of lights into Snig Hill then right at lights into Bank Street*
Travel Inn offers good-quality, value-for-money accommodation. Spacious, en suite rooms with bath and shower comfortably accommodate a family of up to two adults and two children (to age 15). The restaurant and bar offers a varied menu. For further details consult the Hotel Groups page.
ROOMS: 160 en suite s £49.95; d £49.95

Travelodge

340 Prince of Wales Rd S2 1FF
☎ 08700 850 950 ▯ 0114 253 0935
Dir: *follow A630, take turn off for ring road & services*
Travelodge offers good quality, good value, modern accommodation. Ideal for families, the spacious, en suite bedrooms include remote-control TV, tea and coffee-making facilities and luxury beds. Meals can be taken at the nearby family restaurant. For further details consult the Hotel Groups page.
ROOMS: 67 en suite s fr £25; d fr £25 **CONF:** Thtr 30 Board 20

SHEPTON MALLET, Somerset Map 04 ST64

Top 200 – Hotel

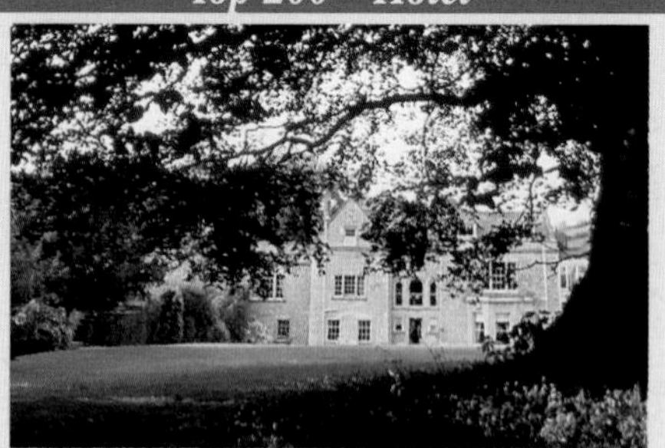

★★★ Charlton House & Mulberry Restaurant

Charlton Rd BA4 4PR
☎ 01749 342008 ▯ 01749 346362
e-mail: enquiry@charltonhouse.com
web: www.charltonhouse.com
Dir: *on A361 towards Frome, 1m from town centre*
A lifestyle destination where the design throughout the house is modelled on the furnishings and fabric company, Mulberry. Attention to detail is the order of the day with bedrooms decorated in individual style, all supremely comfortable. Monty's Spa, which is new this year, has hydrotherapy pools and two spa bedrooms for the ultimate pampering experience. Food remains a great attraction with Adam Fellow's accomplished menu winning accolades and praise.
ROOMS: 24 rms (21 en suite) 1 annexe en suite (1 fmly) **FACILITIES: Spa** STV Fishing Sauna Jacuzzi Archery Clay pigeon shooting Ballooning, Spa retreat programmes Xmas **CONF:** Thtr 120 Class 60 Board 40 Del £220 **PARKING:** 63 **NOTES:** in restaurant Civ Wed 100 **CARDS:**

★★71% Shrubbery

17 Commercial Rd BA4 5BU
☎ 01749 346671 ▯ 01749 346581
e-mail: reservations@shrubberyhotel17.fsnet.co.uk
Dir: *off A37 at Shepton Mallet onto A371 Wells Rd, hotel 50mtrs past lights in town centre*
This small hotel is located in the town centre and offers comfortable, well-equipped bedrooms, several of which are on the ground floor of a separate building. The atmosphere at this hotel is relaxed and informal, and the intimate restaurant, which overlooks a delightful award-winning garden, offers a varied choice of enjoyable and well-presented dishes.
ROOMS: 6 en suite 4 annexe en suite (3 fmly) (4 GF) in 4 bedrooms s fr £59; d fr £85 (incl. bkfst) **PARKING:** 30 **NOTES:** in restaurant **CARDS:**

SHERBORNE, Dorset Map 04 ST61

★★★72% Eastbury

Long St DT9 3BY
☎ 01935 813131 ▯ 01935 817296
e-mail: enquiries@theeastburyhotel.co.uk
web: www.theeastburyhotel.co.uk
Dir: *From A30 westbound, left into North Rd, then St Swithins, left at bottom, hotel 800yds on right*
Much of the original Georgian charm and elegance is maintained at this smart, comfortable hotel. Just five minutes' stroll from the abbey and close to the town centre, the Eastbury's friendly and attentive staff ensure a relaxed and enjoyable stay. The award-winning cuisine takes centre stage in the attractive dining room, which overlooks the walled garden.
ROOMS: 22 en suite (1 fmly) (3 GF) in 10 bedrooms s £50-£60; d £90-£125 (incl. bkfst) **LB FACILITIES:** STV Xmas **CONF:** Thtr 80 Class 40 Board 28 Del from £100 **PARKING:** 30 **NOTES:** in restaurant Civ Wed 80 **CARDS:**

★★★70% *The Grange Hotel & Restaurant*

Oborne DT9 4LA
☎ 01935 813463 ▯ 01935 817464
e-mail: reception@thegrange.co.uk
Dir: *In Oborne, turn off A30 & follow signs through village*
Set in beautiful gardens, in a quiet hamlet, this 200-year-old, family run, country house hotel has a wealth of charm and character. It offers warm and friendly hospitality together with attentive service. Bedrooms are comfortable and tastefully appointed. Half are in the main house and the other more contemporary rooms are on the ground and first floors of a separate building. Public areas are elegantly furnished and the

continued

popular restaurant offers a good choice and variety of dishes based on locally-sourced produce.
ROOMS: 4 en suite 6 annexe en suite (3 fmly) (4 GF) ⊗ in all bedrooms **CONF:** Thtr 30 Class 20 Board 18 **PARKING:** 45 **NOTES:** ⊗ in restaurant **CARDS:**

SHERINGHAM, Norfolk Map 13 TG14

★★★★69% Dales Country House Hotel
Lodge Hill, Upper Sheringham NR26 8TJ
☎ 01263 824555 01263 822647
e-mail: reservations@mackenziehotels.com
Dir: *on B1157 1m S of Sheringham, from A148 take turning at entrance to Sheringham Park continue for 0.5m hotel on left*

Superb Grade II listed building situated in extensive landscaped grounds on the edge of Sheringham Park. The attractive public rooms are full of original charm and character; they include a choice of lounges as well as an intimate restaurant and a cosy lounge bar. The spacious bedrooms are individually decorated, with co-ordinated soft furnishings and many thoughtful touches.
ROOMS: 17 en suite (1 fmly) (2 GF) ⊗ in all bedrooms s £97-£176; d £154-£176 (incl. bkfst & dinner) **LB** **FACILITIES:** Xmas **CONF:** Thtr 40 Class 20 Board 27 Del from £79 **SERVICES:** Lift **PARKING:** 50 **NOTES:** No children 14 ⊗ in restaurant Closed 2-16 Jan **CARDS:**

★★71% Roman Camp Inn
Holt Rd, Aylmerton NR11 8QD
☎ 01263 838291 01263 837071
e-mail: romancampinn@lineone.net
web: www.romancampinn.co.uk
Dir: *on A148 between Sheringham and Cromer, approx 1.5m from Cromer*
This hotel is ideally placed for touring the north Norfolk coastline, and provides spacious bedrooms, pleasantly decorated with a good range of useful extras. Public rooms include a smart conservatory-style restaurant, a comfortable lounge, a smart bar and a dining room.
ROOMS: 15 en suite ⊗ in 2 bedrooms s £54-£58; d £88-£96 (incl. bkfst) **LB** **CONF:** Thtr 25 Class 6 Board 12 **PARKING:** 50 **NOTES:** ⊗ in restaurant Closed 25 Dec **CARDS:**

★★70% Beaumaris
South St NR26 8LL
☎ 01263 822370 01263 821421
e-mail: beauhotel@aol.com
web: www.thebeaumarishotel.co.uk
Dir: *turn off A148, turn left at rdbt, 1st right over railway bridge, 1st left by church, 1st left into South St*
Ideally situated in a peaceful cul-de-sac just a short walk from the beach, town centre and golf course. This friendly hotel has been owned and run by the same family for over 50 years and continues to provide comfortable, thoughtfully equipped

continued

accommodation throughout. Public rooms feature a smart dining room, a cosy bar and two quiet lounges.

ROOMS: 21 en suite (5 fmly) s £45-£50; d £90-£100 (incl. bkfst) **LB** **FACILITIES:** ch fac **CONF:** Board 12 **PARKING:** 25 **NOTES:** ⊗ in restaurant Closed mid Dec-1 Mar **CARDS:**

★★70% Southlands
South St NR26 8LL
☎ 01263 822679 01263 822679
Dir: *from A1082, turn left at rdbt. Take 1st right & then 1st left at St Peters Church. Then 1st left again & hotel is on left*
Friendly, family-run hotel situated just a short walk from the town centre and seafront. The pleasantly decorated bedrooms are well maintained and equipped with many thoughtful touches. The open-plan public rooms provide a wide choice of areas in which to relax and include a choice of lounges, a smart bar and a large dining room.
ROOMS: 17 en suite (3 fmly) ⊗ in all bedrooms **FACILITIES:** ch fac **PARKING:** 20 **NOTES:** ⊗ in restaurant Closed Oct-Etr
CARDS:

SHIFNAL, Shropshire Map 10 SJ70

★★★★68% Park House
MACDONALD HOTELS
Park St TF11 9BA
☎ 01952 460128 01952 461658
e-mail: res.parkhouse@macdonald-hotels.co.uk
Dir: *M54 junct 4 follow A464 Wolverhampton Rd for approx 2m, under railway bridge and hotel is 100yds on left*
A major programme of expansion and redesign has created a hotel from what was originally two country homes of very different architectural styles. Located on the edge of the historic market town, the hotel offers guests easy access to motorway networks, a choice of banqueting and meeting rooms and leisure facilities.
ROOMS: 38 en suite 16 annexe en suite (4 fmly) (8 GF) ⊗ in 15 bedrooms s £55-£120; d £80-£180 (incl. bkfst) **LB** **FACILITIES:** STV Sauna Solarium Jacuzzi Xmas **CONF:** Thtr 180 Class 100 Board 40 Del from £110 **SERVICES:** Lift **PARKING:** 200 **NOTES:** ⊗ in restaurant Civ Wed 180 **CARDS:**

SHIPHAM, Somerset Map 04 ST45

★★★72% Daneswood House
Cuck Hill BS25 1RD
☎ 01934 843145 & 843945 01934 843824
e-mail: info@daneswoodhotel.co.uk
web: www.daneswoodhotel.co.uk
Dir: *turn off A38 towards Cheddar, through village, hotel on left*
With wonderful views over the countryside, to the Bristol Channel and Wales in the distance, this charming Edwardian hotel is set in its own carefully tended grounds. Each individually decorated

continued on p524

S

SHIPHAM, continued

bedroom is well equipped; the cottage suites have private lounges. Public rooms include a breakfast conservatory, comfortable lounge and inter-connecting dining areas.

Daneswood House Hotel, Shipham

ROOMS: 14 en suite 3 annexe en suite (3 fmly) in 5 bedrooms s £89.50-£99.50; d £105-£150 (incl. bkfst) **LB** **FACILITIES:** ch fac **CONF:** Thtr 40 Board 24 Del from £135 **PARKING:** 27 **NOTES:** in restaurant RS 24 Dec-6 Jan **CARDS:**

SHIPLEY, West Yorkshire Map 19 SE13

★★★★70% Marriott Hollins Hall Hotel & Country Club

Hollins Hill, Baildon BD17 7QW
0870 400 7227 0870 400 7327
e-mail: reservations.hollinshall@marriotthotels.co.uk

Dir: *from A650 follow signs to Salt Mill. At lights in Shipley take A6038. Hotel is 3m on left*

The hotel is located just to the north of Bradford and is easily accessible from national motorway networks. Built in the 19th-century this Elizabethan-style building is set within 200 acres of grounds and offers extensive leisure facilities, including a golf course and gymnasium. Bedrooms are attractively decorated and have a range of additional facilities.

ROOMS: 122 en suite (50 fmly) (25 GF) in 75 bedrooms s fr £115; d fr £125 (incl. bkfst) **LB** **FACILITIES:** STV supervised 18 Sauna Solarium Gym Putt green Jacuzzi Creche, Health Spa, Dance studio, Swimming lessons Xmas **CONF:** BC Thtr 175 Class 90 Board 80 Del from £125 **SERVICES:** Lift **PARKING:** 260 **NOTES:** in restaurant Civ Wed 120 **CARDS:**

Restaurant with Rooms

Beeties Gallery Restaurant

7 Victoria Rd, Saltaire Village BD18 3LA
01274 595988 581718 01274 582118
e-mail: jayne@beeties.co.uk

Beeties is located in the Saltaire model industrial village. The ground floor comprises a Tapas bar and bistro serving light meals and drinks at lunch and dinner, and on the first floor there is the elegant, contemporary restaurant serving imaginative, skilfully prepared dishes every evening. Bedrooms are smartly appointed and individually decorated.

ROOMS: 5 en suite (1 fmly) in all bedrooms s £47-£52; d £50-£60 **NOTES:** Closed 25 - 26 Dec, 1 Jan **CARDS:**

For central reservation numbers and more information on Hotel Groups, turn to pages 33-39

Hotel Ibis Bradford

Quayside, Salts Mill Rd BD18 3ST
01274 589333 01274 589444
e-mail: H3158@accor-hotels.com

Dir: *follow tourist signs for Salts Mill, then A650 signs through & out of Bradford for approx 5m to Shipley. Hotel on Salts Mill Rd*

Modern, budget hotel offering comfortable accommodation in bright and practical bedrooms. Breakfast is self-service and dinner is available in the restaurant. For further details, consult the Hotel Groups page.

ROOMS: 78 en suite s £36.95-£46.95; d £36.95-£46.95 **CONF:** Thtr 30 Class 18 Board 22

SHREWSBURY, Shropshire Map 15 SJ41
See also Church Stretton

★★★★66% Albrighton Hall

Albrighton SY4 3AG
01939 291000 01939 291123
e-mail: albrighton@macdonald-hotels.co.uk

Dir: *from S M6 junct 10a to M54 to end. From N M6 junct 12 to M5 then M54. Follow signs Harlescott & Ellesmere to A528*

Dating back to 1630, this former ancestral home is set within 15 acres of attractive gardens. Rooms are well kept and generally spacious, with attic rooms with their sloping beams, proving popular. Elegant public rooms have rich oak panelling and there is a modern, well-equipped health and fitness centre.

ROOMS: 29 en suite 42 annexe en suite (18 fmly) (11 GF) in 49 bedrooms s £50-£90; d £100-£140 (incl. bkfst) **LB** **FACILITIES: Spa** STV Squash Sauna Solarium Gym Jacuzzi Beauty treatment rooms Xmas **CONF:** Thtr 400 Class 120 Board 60 Del from £129 **SERVICES:** Lift **PARKING:** 200 **NOTES:** in restaurant Civ Wed 350 **CARDS:**

★★★77% Albright Hussey

Ellesmere Rd SY4 3AF
01939 290571 & 290523 01939 291143
e-mail: abhhotel@aol.com
web: www.albrighthussey.co.uk

Dir: *2.5m N of Shrewsbury on A528, follow signs for Ellesmere*

First mentioned in the Domesday Book, this enchanting medieval manor house is complete with a moat. Bedrooms are situated in either the sumptuously appointed main house or in the modern wing. The intimate restaurant displays an abundance of original features and there is also a comfortable cocktail bar and lounge.

ROOMS: 26 en suite (4 fmly) (8 GF) in 16 bedrooms s £79-£105; d £110-£180 (incl. bkfst) **LB** **FACILITIES:** Jacuzzi ch fac Xmas **CONF:** BC Thtr 250 Class 180 Board 80 Del from £110 **PARKING:** 85 **NOTES:** in restaurant Civ Wed 180 **CARDS:**

See advert on opposite page

Albright Hussey
Welcome to the family run Albright Hussey Hotel and Restaurant. Set in 4 acres of beautiful landscaped gardens and surrounded by an original moat, the Albright Hussey has an enviable reputation for offering some of the finest accommodation in the Midlands. Dating back to circa 1524 the hotel encompasses a wealth of history, whilst offering the very highest standard of modern comfort and cuisine.
F.P.V. Subbiani
Proprietors
Ellesmere Road Shrewsbury
Tel: 01939 291271 Fax: 01939 291143
www.albrighthussey.co.uk
e-mail: abhhotel@aol.com
77%
AA
★★★

The Prince Rupert Hotel
Shrewsbury
PRINCE RUPERT HOTEL
SITUATED IN THE HEART OF MEDIEVAL SHREWSBURY, THE PRINCE RUPERT HOTEL, ONCE HOME TO PRINCE RUPERT; GRANDSON OF KING JAMES I, IS A UNIQUE, STYLISH HOTEL FULL OF HISTORIC CHARM.
WITH 70 INDIVIDUAL ENSUITE BEDROOMS AND THREE FABULOUS RESTAURANTS TO CHOOSE FROM, THE PRINCE RUPERT IS THE PERFECT CHOICE WHEN EXPLORING SHREWSBURY.
BUTCHER ROW, SHREWSBURY
SHROPSHIRE, SY1 1UQ
Telephone: 01743 499955
Facsimile: 01743 357306
E Mail: post@prince-rupert-hotel.co.uk
www.prince-rupert-hotel.co.uk
ST JAMES TOWN HOUSE HOTELS
GSA 56
AA ★★★

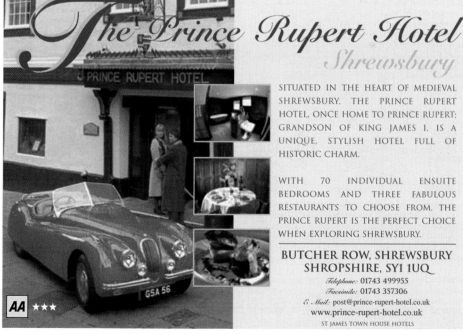

S

SHREWSBURY, continued

★★★75% Rowton Castle Hotel

Halfway House SY5 9EP
☎ 01743 884044 01743 884949
e-mail: post@rowtoncastle.com
web: www.rowtoncastle.com
Dir: *A5 near Shrewsbury take A458 to Welshpool, hotel 4 miles on right*

On the site of a Roman fort and dating back to 1696 this hotel stands in 17 acres of grounds which includes lovely formal gardens. Many original features remain in the building, including the oak panelling in the restaurant and a magnificent carved oak fireplace. Most bedrooms are spacious and all have modern facilities. Rooms with four-poster beds are available.
ROOMS: 19 en suite (3 fmly) s £74-£79; d £94 (incl. bkfst) **LB**
FACILITIES: **CONF:** Thtr 80 Class 30 Board 30 Del from £86.25
PARKING: 100 **NOTES:** in restaurant Civ Wed 110
CARDS:

★★★71% Prince Rupert

Butcher Row SY1 1UQ
☎ 01743 499955 01743 357306
e-mail: post@prince-rupert-hotel.co.uk
web: www.prince-rupert-hotel.co.uk
Dir: *follow signs to Town Centre, over English Bridge and Wyle Cop Hill. Turn right into Fish St, 200yds to hotel*

Parts of this popular town centre hotel date back to medieval times and many bedrooms have exposed beams and other original features. Luxury suites, family rooms and rooms with four-poster beds are all available. As an alternative to the main Royalist Restaurant, diners can eat in the less formal and popular Chambers bar-bistro. The hotel's car parking service comes recommended.
ROOMS: 70 en suite (4 fmly) s fr £83; d £103-£185 (incl. bkfst) **LB**
FACILITIES: Snooker Sauna Gym Jacuzzi Weight training room Beauty Salon Xmas **CONF:** Thtr 120 Class 80 Board 40 Del from £120
SERVICES: Lift **PARKING:** 70 **CARDS:**

See advert on page 525

★★★67% Mytton & Mermaid

Atcham SY5 6QG
☎ 01743 761220 01743 761292
e-mail: admin@myttonandmermaid.co.uk
web: www.myttonandmermaid.co.uk
Dir: *from Shrewsbury, over old bridge in Atcham. Hotel opposite main entrance to Attingham Park*

Convenient for Shrewsbury, this ivy-clad former coaching inn enjoys a pleasant location beside the River Severn. Some bedrooms, including family suites, are in a converted stable block adjacent to the hotel. The large lounge bar has been refurbished, and there is also a comfortable lounge and brasserie gaining a well-deserved local reputation for the quality of its food.
ROOMS: 11 en suite 7 annexe en suite (1 fmly) in 11 bedrooms s £60; d £80-£135 (incl. bkfst) **FACILITIES:** Fishing ♫ ch fac Xmas
CONF: BC Thtr 70 Class 24 Board 28 Del from £122.50 **PARKING:** 50
NOTES: in restaurant Civ Wed 80 **CARDS:**

★★★66% Lord Hill

Abbey Foregate SY2 6AX

THE INDEPENDENTS

☎ 01743 232601 01743 369734
e-mail: reservations@lordhill.u-net.com
web: www.lordhill.u-net.com
Dir: *from M54 take A5, at 1st rdbt left then 2nd rdbt take 4th exit into London Rd. At next rdbt (Lord Hill Column) take 3rd exit, hotel 300yds on left*

A pleasant, attractively appointed hotel located close to the town centre. Most of the bedrooms are set in a purpose-built separate property, but those in the main building include one with a four-poster and a newly created suite. There is also a conservatory restaurant and a large function suite.
ROOMS: 12 en suite 24 annexe en suite (2 fmly) (8 GF) in 12 bedrooms s £58-£66.50; d £77-£85.50 (incl. bkfst) **CONF:** Thtr 250 Class 180 Board 180 Del from £85 **PARKING:** 110 **NOTES:** in restaurant Civ Wed 70 **CARDS:**

★★★63% The Lion

Wyle Cop SY1 1UY
☎ 0870 609 6167 01743 352744
e-mail: thelion@corushotels.com
Dir: *from S cross English Bridge, take right fork, hotel at top of hill on left. From N to town centre, follow Castle St into Dogpole, hotel is ahead*

This 14th-century coaching inn, located in the town centre, boasts Charles Dickens amongst its earlier guests and is steeped in character. Bedrooms come in a variety of sizes, those at the rear

continued

being quieter. Public areas include the original ballroom and a bar and restaurant with oak beams and inglenook fireplace.

ROOMS: 59 en suite (3 fmly) ⊗ in 30 bedrooms s £79; d £79 **LB**
FACILITIES: use of local gym Xmas **CONF:** Thtr 200 Class 80 Board 60
SERVICES: Lift **PARKING:** 70 **NOTES:** ⊗ in restaurant Civ Wed 200
CARDS:

★★65% Lion & Pheasant

49-50 Wyle Cop SY1 1XJ
☎ 01743 236288 📠 01743 244475
e-mail: lionandpheasant@aol.com

This 16th-century coaching inn is privately owned, personally run and close to the town centre. The accommodation, which includes no-smoking rooms, is well equipped and the public areas are full of character, with exposed beams and wall timbers. An extensive choice of food is served in the bar/bistro.

ROOMS: 27 rms (25 en suite) (2 fmly) ⊗ in 8 bedrooms s £45-£50; d £50-£60 (incl. bkfst) **LB** **CONF:** Thtr 25 Class 25 Board 20
PARKING: 18 **NOTES:** ⊗ in restaurant Closed 24-25 Dec & 1 Jan
CARDS:

★★64% Abbots Mead

9 St Julian's Friars SY1 1XL
☎ 01743 235281 📠 01743 369133
e-mail: res@abbotsmeadhotel.co.uk
Dir: *first left after English Bridge coming into Shrewsbury from S*

This neatly maintained Georgian town house is located in a quiet cul-de-sac, near the English Bridge and close to the River Severn and town centre. Bedrooms are compact, neatly decorated and well equipped. The hotel also has a bright dining room, overlooking the garden, and a bar featuring horse racing pictures.

ROOMS: 15 en suite (1 fmly) s £45-£55; d £59-£65 (incl. bkfst) **LB**
PARKING: 10 **NOTES:** ⊗ in restaurant Closed Dec 24-26
CARDS:

⌂ The Shrewsbury Wetherlodge

Bridge Place SY1 1PU
☎ 01743 236203 📠 01743 236197
e-mail: shrewsburylodge@jdwetherspoon.uk
Dir: *from A49 right under rail bridge Hotel on Smithfield Rd opposite*

Overlooking the River Severn, opposite the Welsh Bridge, this popular hotel is just a short walk from the town centre. Bedrooms vary in size and provide stylish, modern accommodation. Downstairs the bar provides a wide choice of main dishes or snacks and there is a good selection of real ales and wines.

ROOMS: 22 en suite s £39-£44; d £39-£44 **CONF:** Thtr 10 Class 10 Board 10

> Packed in a hurry?
> Ironing facilities should be available at all star levels, either in rooms or on request

⌂ Travelodge

Travelodge

Bayston Hill Services SY3 0DA
☎ 08700 850 950 📠 01743 874256
Dir: *A5/A49 junct*

Travelodge offers good quality, good value, modern accommodation. Ideal for families, the spacious, en suite bedrooms include remote-control TV, tea and coffee-making facilities and luxury beds. Meals can be taken at the nearby family restaurant. For further details consult the Hotel Groups page.

ROOMS: 40 en suite s fr £25; d fr £25

SIDMOUTH, Devon — Map 03 SY18

★★★★75% ® Victoria

The Esplanade EX10 8RY
☎ 01395 512651 📠 01395 579154
e-mail: info@victoriahotel.co.uk web: www.victoriahotel.co.uk
Dir: *on Sidmouth seafront*

This imposing building, with manicured gardens, is situated overlooking the town. Wonderful sea views can be enjoyed from many of the comfortable bedrooms and elegant lounges. With indoor and outdoor leisure, the hotel caters to a year-round clientele. Carefully prepared meals are served in the refined atmosphere of the restaurant, with staff providing a professional and friendly service.

ROOMS: 61 en suite (18 fmly) s £100-£200; d £140-£250 **LB**
FACILITIES: **Spa** STV Snooker Sauna Solarium Gym Putt green ♫ ch fac Xmas **CONF:** Thtr 60 **SERVICES:** Lift **PARKING:** 104
NOTES: ⊗ in restaurant **CARDS:**

See advert on page 529

S

★★★★74% ® Riviera

The Esplanade EX10 8AY
☎ 01395 515201 📠 01395 577775
e-mail: enquiries@hotelriviera.co.uk web: www.hotelriviera.co.uk
Dir: *M5 junct 30 & follow A3052*

Overlooking the sea close to the town centre, the Riviera is a fine example of Regency architecture. High standards of both service

continued on p528

SIDMOUTH, continued

and hospitality are found here, with many of the guests regular visitors. The front-facing bedrooms benefit from wonderful sea views. The daily-changing menu places an emphasis upon fresh, local produce, served in an elegant dining room.

ROOMS: 27 en suite (6 fmly) s £109-£143; d £196-£264 (incl. bkfst & dinner) **LB** **FACILITIES:** STV ♫ Xmas **CONF:** Thtr 85 Class 60 Board 30 **SERVICES:** Lift **PARKING:** 26 **NOTES:** ⊗ in restaurant **CARDS:**

See advert on this page

★★★★ 71% Belmont

The Esplanade EX10 8RX
☎ 01395 512555 🖷 01395 579101
e-mail: reservations@belmont-hotel.co.uk
web: www.belmont-hotel.co.uk

Prominently positioned on the seafront just a few minutes' walk

continued on p530

AA ★★★★
Rosette ❄ for cuisine

The Belmont Hotel

AA ★★★★

The most luxurious choice in East Devon

Perfectly positioned on Sidmouth's famous esplanade, the Victoria is one of the resorts finest and most picturesque hotels. It's extensive leisure facilities include indoor and outdoor pools, sauna, solarium, spa bath, hairdressing salon, putting green, tennis court and snooker room.

Telephone : 01395 512651

www.victoriahotel.co.uk Email: info@victoriahotel.co.uk

The Belmont too commands spectacular views from the famous esplanade. As inviting in January as July, the Belmont offers fine cusine and superlative service that brings guests back year after year. With the indoor and outdoor leisure facilities of the adjacent Victoria Hotel at your disposal, the Belmont provides the perfect location for your holiday.

Telephone: 01395 512555

www.belmont-hotel.co.uk Email: info@belmont-hotel.co.uk

The Westcountry's Leading Hotel Group

SIDMOUTH, continued

from the town centre, this traditional hotel has a regular following. A choice of comfortable lounges provide ample space for relaxation, and the air-conditioned restaurant has a pianist accompanying at dinner. Bedrooms are attractively furnished and many have fine views over the esplanade. Leisure facilities are available at the adjacent sister hotel, the Victoria.
ROOMS: 50 en suite (4 fmly) (2 GF) s £80-£170; d £110-£170 **LB** **FACILITIES:** STV Putt green ♫ ch fac Xmas **CONF:** Thtr 50 **SERVICES:** Lift **PARKING:** 45 **NOTES:** in restaurant Civ Wed 110 **CARDS:**

See advert on page 529

Courtesy & Care Award

★★★80% Westcliff

Manor Rd EX10 8RU
☎ 01395 513252 01395 578203
e-mail: stay@westcliffhotel.co.uk
web: www.westcliffhotel.co.uk
Dir: *turn off A3052 to Sidmouth then to seafront and esplanade, turn right, hotel directly ahead*
This charming hotel, run by the same family for more than 35 years, is within walking distance of the promenade. Elegant lounges and the cocktail bar open onto a terrace, leading to the pool and croquet lawn. Bedrooms, several with balconies and glorious sea views, are spacious and comfortable, whilst the restaurant offers a choice of well-prepared dishes. Westcliff Hotel has been awarded the AA Courtesy & Care Award for England 2004-5.
ROOMS: 40 en suite (4 fmly) (5 GF) in 4 bedrooms s £65-£119; d £118-£254 (incl. bkfst & dinner) **LB** **FACILITIES:** STV Gym Putt green Jacuzzi Mini tennis, Pool table, Table tennis **SERVICES:** Lift **PARKING:** 40 **NOTES:** No children 6yrs in restaurant Closed Nov-Mar **CARDS:**

See advert on page 528

★★★73% Sid Valley Country House

Sidbury EX10 0QJ
☎ 01395 597274 & 597587
e-mail: sidvalleyhotel@totalise.co.uk
web: www.sidvalleyhotel.co.uk
Dir: *off A375, 2.5m from Sidmouth in village of Sidbury, hotel is clearly signposted*
Situated in an Area of Outstanding Natural Beauty, this family-run hotel has glorious views down the valley. Friendly, unobtrusive service is the key here. Bedrooms vary in size and are equipped with numerous thoughtful extras. Every evening an imaginative menu is served using the best of fresh, local produce. A selection of well-equipped, self-catering cottages is also available.

ROOMS: 10 en suite (2 fmly) (1 GF) in all bedrooms s £49.50-£65; d £99-£130 (incl. bkfst) **LB** **FACILITIES:** STV Riding ch fac Xmas **CONF:** BC Thtr 70 Class 70 Board 70 Del from £94.50 **PARKING:** 32 **NOTES:** in restaurant **CARDS:**

★★★66% Fortfield

EX10 8NU
☎ 01395 512403 01395 579366
e-mail: reservations@fortfield-hotel.co.uk
Offering good standards of hospitality and service, this long-established hotel overlooks the sea and cricket ground. A choice of comfortable lounges is available, and the 'Norske' bar is a relaxing venue for a pre-dinner drink. Bedrooms, some with sea views, are undergoing a programme of extensive upgrading. A new leisure complex completes the picture.
ROOMS: 52 en suite 3 annexe en suite (7 fmly) (4 GF) in all bedrooms s £56.50-£79.50; d £102-£148 (incl. bkfst & dinner) **LB** **FACILITIES:** Sauna Health & beauty salon ♫ ch fac Xmas **CONF:** Thtr 100 Class 70 Board 60 Del from £50 **SERVICES:** Lift **PARKING:** 60 **NOTES:** in restaurant **CARDS:**

★★★66% Royal Glen

Glen Rd EX10 8RW
☎ 01395 513221 & 513456 01395 514922
e-mail: sidmouthroyalglen.hotel@virgin.net
Dir: *take A303 to Honiton, A375 to Sidford, A175 to Sidmouth, follow seafront signs, right onto esplanade, right at end*

This historic 17th-century, 'cottage-orne' hotel has been owned by the same family for several generations. The connection is emphasised by the names of the comfortable bedrooms, which are furnished in period style. Guests have use of the well-maintained gardens and a heated indoor pool, and can enjoy well-prepared food in the dining room.
ROOMS: 32 en suite (4 fmly) s £35-£47 (incl. bkfst) **LB** **FACILITIES:** **PARKING:** 24 **NOTES:** in restaurant RS 2-31 Jan **CARDS:**

★★★66% *Salcombe Hill House*
Beatlands Rd EX10 8JQ
☎ 01395 514697 & 514398 📠 01395 578310
e-mail: salcombehillhousehotel@eclipse.co.uk
Dir: *At Radway Cinema in town centre turn left, over bridge, turn sharp right, left into Beatlands Rd. Hotel 50yds on left*
Set in an elevated position just a short walk from the seafront, this hotel is situated in a quiet location surrounded by attractive gardens. The south-facing aspect means the lounge and patio benefit from the best of the sunshine. Bedrooms are spacious, comfortable and appealing. The menu of freshly-prepared dishes on offer in the dining room changes daily.
ROOMS: 28 en suite (12 fmly) (2 GF) **FACILITIES:** Putt green Games room, Table Tennis, Darts **SERVICES:** Lift **PARKING:** 24 **NOTES:** ⊗ in restaurant **CARDS:**

★★76% Kingswood
The Esplanade EX10 8AX
☎ 01395 516367 📠 01395 513185
e-mail: enquiries@kingswood-hotel.co.uk
Dir: *in centre of Esplanade*
Super standards of hospitality are only surpassed by this hotel's prominent position on the esplanade. All bedrooms have modern facilities and some enjoy the stunning sea views. The two lounges offer comfort and space and the attractive dining room serves good traditional cooking.
ROOMS: 26 rms (25 en suite) (7 fmly) (2 GF) ⊗ in all bedrooms **FACILITIES:** guests receive vouchers for local swimming pool & spectating at cricket club **SERVICES:** Lift **PARKING:** 17 **NOTES:** ⊗ in restaurant Closed Dec-13 Feb **CARDS:**

★★74% Royal York & Faulkner
The Esplanade EX10 8AZ
☎ 01395 513043 & 0800 220714 (Freephone) 📠 01395 577472
e-mail: stay@royalyorkhotel.net
web: www.royalyorkhotel.net
Dir: *from M5 take A3052, 10m to Sidmouth, hotel in centre of esplanade*
This seafront hotel, owned and run by the same family for generations, maintains its Regency charm and grandeur, and offers well-equipped and comfortable accommodation. The attractive bedrooms vary in size and many have balconies and sea views. Staff are friendly and efficient. Public rooms are spacious, and traditional dining is provided in either the dining room overlooking Lyme Bay or in the more upbeat Blini's café-bar.
ROOMS: 68 en suite (8 fmly) (5 GF) s £40.50-£68.75; d £81-£137.50 (incl. bkfst & dinner) **LB** **FACILITIES:** STV Snooker Sauna Solarium Gym Jacuzzi Indoor short mat bowls Free swim at local indoor pool ♫ ch fac Xmas **SERVICES:** Lift **PARKING:** 20 **NOTES:** ⊗ in restaurant Closed Jan **CARDS:**

★★72% Mount Pleasant
Salcombe Rd EX10 8JA
☎ 01395 514694
Dir: *turn off A3052 at Sidford x-rds after 1.25m turn left into Salcombe Rd, hotel opposite Radway Cinema*
Quietly located within almost an acre of gardens, this sympathetically modernised Georgian hotel is minutes from the town centre and seafront. Bedrooms and public areas offer good levels of comfort and high quality furnishings. Guests return on a regular basis especially for the friendly, relaxed atmosphere. The daily-changing menu offers a choice of imaginative, yet traditional home-cooked dishes.
ROOMS: 16 en suite (2 fmly) s £42-£56; d £84-£112 (incl. bkfst & dinner) **LB** **FACILITIES:** Putt green **PARKING:** 20 **NOTES:** No children 8yrs ⊗ in restaurant Closed Dec-Jan **CARDS:**

★★71% Devoran
Esplanade EX10 8AU
☎ 01395 513151 📠 01395 579929
e-mail: devoran@cosmic.org.uk
Dir: *turn off B3052 at Bowd Inn follow Sidmouth sign for approx 2m turn left onto seafront, hotel 50yds at centre of Esplanade*

Known locally as the 'pink hotel on the seafront', the Devoran has comfortable and attractively decorated bedrooms, some with their own balconies and sea views. Well-maintained public rooms include a large dining room, where guests can enjoy a five-course dinner, and a comfortable lounge and bar.
ROOMS: 24 en suite (4 fmly) ⊗ in all bedrooms **SERVICES:** Lift **PARKING:** 4 **NOTES:** ⊗ in restaurant Closed mid Nov-mid Mar RS Dec-Mar **CARDS:**

★★70% Hunters Moon
Sid Rd EX10 9AA
☎ 01395 513380 📠 01395 514270
e-mail: huntersmoon.hotel@virgin.net
Dir: *from A3052 to Sidford, pass Blue Ball Pub, then next right at Fortescue, hotel 1m*

Set amid three acres of attractive and well-tended grounds, this friendly, family-run hotel is peacefully located in a quiet area within walking distance of the town and esplanade. Bedrooms are comfortable and well equipped and there is a spacious lounge. Dining provides a choice of well-cooked and imaginative dishes and tea may be taken on the lawn.
ROOMS: 21 en suite (6 fmly) (6 GF) ⊗ in all bedrooms s £62-£66; d £110-£128 (incl. bkfst & dinner) **LB** **FACILITIES:** Putt green outdoor bowling green Xmas **PARKING:** 26 **NOTES:** No children 2yrs ⊗ in restaurant Closed Jan-12 Feb RS Dec & Feb **CARDS:**

> Popped the question?
> Hotels with Civ Wed in their entry are licensed for civil wedding ceremonies. Maximum numbers for the ceremony only are shown, e.g. Civ Wed 120

S

SILCHESTER, Hampshire Map 05 SU66

★★★72% **Romans**

Little London Rd RG7 2PN
☎ 0118 970 0421 🖷 0118 970 0691
e-mail: romanhotel@hotmail.com
Dir: *A340 Basingstoke to Reading, hotel is signposted*

This Lutyens-style manor house is in a tranquil and attractive location. Bedrooms are smartly presented and well equipped, some located in an adjacent wing. The leisure club is proud of its outdoor swimming pool, which is kept heated year round.
ROOMS: 11 en suite 14 annexe en suite (1 fmly) (11 GF) ⊗ in 5 bedrooms **FACILITIES:** STV supervised Sauna Gym Jacuzzi Xmas **CONF:** Thtr 60 Class 30 Board 24 **PARKING:** 60 **NOTES:** ⊗ in restaurant Civ Wed 65 **CARDS:**

See advert under BASINGSTOKE

SILLOTH, Cumbria Map 18 NY15

★★★59% **The Skinburness**
CA7 4QY
☎ 016973 32332 🖷 016973 32549
Dir: *M6 junct 41, take B5305 to Wigton, then B5302 to Silloth. M74 junct 44, take A595 to Carlisle then on to Wigton, B5302 to Silloth*
Enviably located on the peaceful Solway Estuary, close to sandy beaches and coastal walks, this popular hotel provides traditionally furnished bedrooms with a host of modern facilities. There is also a leisure complex with a small pool, sauna and spa. Good meals are available in the Mediterranean-style bar and the pleasant hotel restaurant.
ROOMS: 33 en suite (3 fmly) (1 GF) ⊗ in 6 bedrooms **FACILITIES:** Sauna Solarium Gym Jacuzzi ♫ ch fac Xmas **CONF:** Thtr 120 Class 100 Board 60 **PARKING:** 120 **NOTES:** ⊗ in restaurant Closed 4-23 Jan
CARDS:

★★64% ***Golf Hotel***
Criffel St CA5 4AB
☎ 016973 31438 🖷 016973 32582
e-mail: golf.hotel@virgin.net
web: www.golfhotelsilloth.co.uk
Dir: *off B5302, in Silloth at T-junct turn left, hotel overlooks the green*
This friendly, family-run hotel occupies a prime position in the centre of the historic market town. Bedrooms are well equipped, generally modern in style and benefit from ongoing refurbishment. Public areas include a spacious bar, restaurant, lounge and games room. The varied menus offer a wide selection of dishes.
ROOMS: 22 en suite (4 fmly) **FACILITIES:** Snooker **CONF:** Thtr 100 Class 40 Board 40 **NOTES:** Closed 25 Dec
CARDS:

SILVERSTONE, Northamptonshire Map 11 SP64

⌂ **Premier Lodge (Silverstone)**
Brackley Hatch, Syresham NN13 5TX
☎ 0870 9906382 🖷 0870 9906383
web: www.premierlodge.com
Dir: *on A43 next to Green Man Chef & Brewer*

PREMIER LODGE.com

High quality, modern, budget accommodation, ideal for families and business travellers. All rooms feature bath, power shower and satellite TV, and most have telephones / modem points. The adjacent bar and restaurant offers a wide and varied menu.
ROOMS: 41 en suite s £50; d £50

SIMONSBATH, Somerset Map 03 SS73

★★73% **Simonsbath House**
TA24 7SH
☎ 01643 831259 & 831382 🖷 01643 831557
e-mail: hotel@simonsbathhouse.co.uk
web: www.simonsbathhouse.co.uk
Dir: *On the right of B3223 from Exford to Lynton, entrance just as you leave village*

This 17th-century house boasts a stunning rural location and a relaxed and friendly atmosphere ensures a memorable stay. Bedrooms have plenty of character, are equipped with modern facilities and offer good levels of comfort. Delightful public areas include a choice of lounges with original features such as wood panelling and ornate fireplaces.
ROOMS: 8 en suite (1 GF) ⊗ in all bedrooms s £42.50-£60; d £85-£95 (incl. bkfst) **LB** **FACILITIES:** Fishing Mountain biking, Archery, Orienteering trails, Nature walks Xmas **CONF:** BC Thtr 50 Class 35 Board 20 **PARKING:** 25 **NOTES:** No children 12yrs ⊗ in restaurant Closed 25-26 Dec **CARDS:**

SITTINGBOURNE, Kent Map 07 TQ96

★★★71% ◎ **Hempstead House Country Hotel**
London Rd, Bapchild ME9 9PP
☎ 01795 428020 🖷 01795 436362
e-mail: info@hempsteadhouse.co.uk
Dir: *1.5m from Sittingbourne town centre on A2 towards Canterbury*
Expect a warm welcome at this charming detached Victorian property, which is situated in three acres of mature landscaped gardens. Bedrooms are attractively decorated with lovely co-ordinated fabrics, tastefully furnished and equipped with many thoughtful touches. Public rooms feature a choice of beautifully furnished lounges as well as a superb conservatory dining room.
ROOMS: 27 en suite (7 fmly) (1 GF) ⊗ in all bedrooms s £75-£95; d £85-£105 (incl. bkfst) **LB** **FACILITIES:** STV ch fac Xmas **CONF:** BC Thtr 150 Class 150 Board 100 Del £145 **PARKING:** 100 **NOTES:** ⊗ in restaurant Civ Wed 150
CARDS:

S

⌂ Travel Inn

Bobbing Corner, Sheppy Way, Bobbing ME9 8PD
☎ 08701 977229 📠 01795 436748
Dir: *M2 junct 5 take A249 towards Sheerness approx 2m, 1st slip road after A2 underpass. Travel Inn on the left*

Travel Inn offers good-quality, value-for-money accommodation. Spacious, en suite rooms with bath and shower comfortably accommodate a family of up to two adults and two children (to age 15). The restaurant and bar offers a varied menu. For further details consult the Hotel Groups page.

ROOMS: 40 en suite s £45.95-£46.95; d £45.95-£46.95

> Late for dinner?
> Quality Standards mean that last orders for dinner vary according to star rating and should be no earlier than:
> ★★ 7.00pm ★★★ 8.00pm ★★★★ 9.00pm
> ★★★★★ 10.00pm

SIX MILE BOTTOM, Cambridgeshire — Map 12 TL55

★★★72% Swynford Paddocks

CB8 0UE
☎ 01638 570234 📠 01638 570283
e-mail: info@swynfordpaddocks.com
Dir: *M11 junct 9, take A11 towards Newmarket, turn onto A1304 to Newmarket, hotel 0.75m on left in Six Mile Bottom Village*

This smart country house is set in attractive grounds, within easy reach of Newmarket. Bedrooms are comfortably appointed, thoughtfully equipped and include some delightful four-poster rooms. Imaginative, carefully prepared food is served in the

continued

elegant restaurant, and meeting and conference facilities are available. Service is friendly and attentive.

ROOMS: 15 en suite (1 fmly) s £110-£140; d £135-£195 (incl. bkfst) **LB** **FACILITIES:** STV Putt green **CONF:** Thtr 60 Class 40 Board 40 Del from £145 **PARKING:** 180 **NOTES:** in restaurant Civ Wed 100
CARDS:

SKEGNESS, Lincolnshire — Map 17 TF56

★★★66% Vine

Vine Rd, Seacroft PE25 3DB
☎ 01754 763018 & 610611 📠 01754 769845
e-mail: info@thevinehotel.com
Dir: *A52 to Skegness, S towards Gibraltar Point, turn right on to Drummond Rd, after 0.5m turn right into Vine Rd*

Reputedly the second oldest building in Skegness, this traditional style hotel offers two character bars that serve excellent local beers. Freshly prepared dishes are served in both the bar and the

continued on p534

SKEGNESS, continued

restaurant; service is both friendly and helpful. The smartly refurbished bedrooms are well equipped and comfortably appointed.
ROOMS: 24 en suite (3 fmly) ⊗ in 6 bedrooms s £60-£70; d £80-£90 (incl. bkfst) **LB FACILITIES:** STV ⛳ 18 Putt green Xmas **CONF:** Thtr 100 Class 25 Board 30 Del £72 **PARKING:** 50 **NOTES:** ⊗ in restaurant Civ Wed 100 **CARDS:**

★★★64% *Crown*
Drummond Rd, Seacroft PE25 3AB
☎ 01754 610760 🖷 01754 610847
Dir: *take A52 to town centre, turn left onto Drummond Road, hotel 1m from clock tower*
The Crown is ideally situated just a short walk from the seafront and town centre, close to Seacroft Village golf course and bird sanctuary. Smart bedrooms are attractively decorated and thoughtfully equipped. Public areas include a spacious bar offering a wide selection of dishes, a formal restaurant, residents' TV lounge and indoor pool; ample car parking is provided.
ROOMS: 30 en suite (9 fmly) **FACILITIES:** STV **CONF:** Thtr 120 Class 130 Board 120 **SERVICES:** Lift **PARKING:** 90 **NOTES:** RS 25-26 Dec Civ Wed 80 **CARDS:**

See advert on page 533

★★67% North Shore
North Shore Rd PE25 1DN
☎ 01754 763298 🖷 01754 761902
e-mail: golf@north-shore.co.uk
web: www.north-shore.co.uk
Dir: *1m N of town centre on A52 Ingoldmells Rd, right opposite Fenland laundry*

This hotel enjoys an enviable position on the beach front, adjacent to its own championship golf course and only ten minutes from the town centre. Spacious public areas include a terrace bar serving informal meals and real ales, a formal restaurant and impressive function rooms. Bedrooms are smartly decorated and thoughtfully equipped.
ROOMS: 33 en suite 3 annexe en suite (4 fmly) s £32-£40; d £50-£64 (incl. bkfst) **LB FACILITIES:** ⛳ 18 Snooker Putt green Xmas **CONF:** Thtr 220 Class 60 Board 60 Del from £65 **PARKING:** 200 **NOTES:** ⊗ in restaurant Civ Wed 180 **CARDS:**

SKIPTON, North Yorkshire — Map 18 SD95

★★★73% The Coniston
Coniston Cold BD23 4EB
☎ 01756 748080 🖷 01756 749487
e-mail: info@theconistonhotel.com
Dir: *on A65, 6m NW of Skipton*
Privately owned and situated on a 1,200 acre estate centred around a beautiful 24-acre lake this hotel offers guests many exciting outdoor activities. The modern bedrooms are comfortable and most have king-size beds. McLeod's Bar and the main restaurant offer all-day meals and fine dining is available in the evening on both carte and fixed-price menus.

ROOMS: 40 en suite (4 fmly) (20 GF) s £82-£92; d £94-£104 (incl. bkfst) **LB FACILITIES:** STV Fishing Landrover driving, Clay pigeon shooting, Falconry, fishing ch fac Xmas **CONF:** Thtr 200 Class 80 Board 50 Del from £133.95 **PARKING:** 120 **NOTES:** ⊗ in restaurant Civ Wed 80 **CARDS:**

★★★65% Hanover International
Keighley Rd BD23 2TA
☎ 01756 700100 🖷 01756 700107
e-mail: hihskipton@totalise.co.uk
Dir: *on A629, 1m from town*
Located beside the canal just outside the town, the hotel has the advantage of plenty of parking and good amenities for the leisure guest. Bedrooms are well equipped and spacious, and have delightful views over the rolling countryside. Added attractions include the indoor pool and gym.
ROOMS: 75 en suite (10 fmly) (12 GF) ⊗ in 14 bedrooms **FACILITIES:** STV supervised Squash Sauna Solarium Gym Jacuzzi Whirlpool spa, Steam room Xmas **CONF:** Thtr 400 Class 180 Board 120 Del from £110 **SERVICES:** Lift **PARKING:** 150 **NOTES:** ⊗ in restaurant Closed 25-27 Dec Civ Wed 250 **CARDS:**

★★68% Herriots Hotel, Bar & Dining Rooms
Broughton Rd BD23 1RT
☎ 01756 792781 🖷 01756 793967
e-mail: herriots@mgrleisure.com
Dir: *off A59, opposite railway station*

Close to the centre of the market town, this friendly hotel offers tastefully decorated bedrooms which are well equipped and have now been re-furbished. The open-plan brasserie is a relaxing place in which to dine, and has a varied menu; meals and snacks are

continued

also available in the bar. The new extension includes modern well-equipped bedrooms and a stylish conservatory lounge.
ROOMS: 24 en suite (6 fmly) ⊗ in 10 bedrooms s £40-£65; d £50-£90 (incl. bkfst) **LB** **FACILITIES:** Xmas **CONF:** BC Thtr 100 Class 50 Board 52 Del from £99 **SERVICES:** Lift **PARKING:** 26 **NOTES:** ⊗ in restaurant **CARDS:**

Travelodge
Gargrave Rd BD23 1UD
☎ 08700 850 950 🖹 0870 1911676
Dir: *A65/A59 rdbt*
Travelodge offers good quality, good value, modern accommodation. Ideal for families, the spacious, en suite bedrooms include remote-control TV, tea and coffee-making facilities and luxury beds. Meals can be taken at the nearby family restaurant. For further details consult the Hotel Groups page.
ROOMS: 32 en suite s fr £25; d fr £25

SLEAFORD, Lincolnshire
Map 12 TF04

★★★64% **Carre Arms**
1 Mareham Ln NG34 7JP
☎ 01529 303156 🖹 01529 303139
e-mail: enquiries@carrearmshotel.co.uk
web: www.carrearmshotel.co.uk
Dir: *take A153 to Sleaford, hotel on right at level crossing*
This friendly, family-run hotel is located close to the station and offers suitably appointed accommodation. Public areas include two spacious bars where a good selection of bar meals is offered and a smart Brasserie. There is also a conservatory and an old stable housing a spacious, elegant function room.
ROOMS: 13 en suite (1 fmly) s £50-£60; d £70 (incl. bkfst) **CONF:** Thtr 120 Class 54 Board 40 Del from £65 **PARKING:** 100 **NOTES:** ⊗ in restaurant **CARDS:**

★★★64% **The Lincolnshire Oak**
East Rd NG34 7EH
THE INDEPENDENTS HOTEL ASSOCIATION
☎ 01529 413807 🖹 01529 413710
e-mail: reception@lincolnshire-oak.co.uk
web: www.lincolnshire-oak.co.uk
Dir: *From A17 (by-pass) exit on A153 into Sleaford. Hotel .75m on left*

Located on the edge of the town in well-tended grounds, this Victorian house hotel offers a relaxed and friendly environment throughout. A comfortable open-plan lounge bar is complemented by an intimate and cosy restaurant that looks out onto the rear garden; there are also several meeting rooms and the refurbished Acorn Suite. Bedroom styles differ; each room is well furnished and suitably equipped, although the 'superior' rooms are individually decorated and more comfortably appointed.
ROOMS: 17 en suite ⊗ in 12 bedrooms s £59-£72; d £72.50-£87.50 (incl. bkfst) **LB** **FACILITIES:** STV ch fac **CONF:** Thtr 140 Class 70 Board 50 Del £80 **PARKING:** 80 **NOTES:** ⊗ in restaurant Civ Wed 90
CARDS:

Travelodge
Holdingham NG34 8PN
☎ 08700 850 950 🖹 01529 414752
Dir: *1m N, at rdbt A17/A15*
Travelodge offers good quality, good value, modern accommodation. Ideal for families, the spacious, en suite bedrooms include remote-control TV, tea and coffee-making facilities and luxury beds. Meals can be taken at the nearby family restaurant. For further details consult the Hotel Groups page.
ROOMS: 40 en suite s fr £25; d fr £25

SLOUGH, Berkshire
Map 06 SU97

★★★★66%
Copthorne Hotel Slough-Windsor
COPTHORNE
400 Cippenham Ln SL1 2YE
☎ 01753 516222 🖹 01753 516237
e-mail: sales.slough@mill-cop.com
Dir: *M4 junct 6 & follow A355 to Slough at next rdbt turn left & left again for hotel entrance*

This is a modern property just off the M4 with views towards Heathrow and Windsor. Public areas include a good leisure centre and the Veranda restaurant. Bedrooms are spacious with excellent facilities including air conditioning. The hotel is popular for weekend breaks; special vouchers are issued offering discounts to various attractions in the area.
ROOMS: 219 en suite (47 fmly) ⊗ in 148 bedrooms s £80-£180; d £80-£180 **FACILITIES:** STV Sauna Gym Jacuzzi Xmas **CONF:** Thtr 250 Class 160 Board 60 **SERVICES:** Lift air con **PARKING:** 300 **NOTES:** ⊗ in restaurant **CARDS:**

S

★★★69% **Courtyard by Marriott Slough/Windsor**
COURTYARD
Church St SL1 2NH
☎ 0870 400 7215 🖹 0870 400 7315
Dir: *M4 junct 6, follow A355 to rdbt, turn right, hotel approx 50yds on right*
With Heathrow Airport and the motorway networks easily accessible by car this modern hotel is in an ideal location. Spacious bedrooms feature a comprehensive range of facilities. The public areas are lively, modern and have an informal atmosphere.
ROOMS: 150 en suite (64 fmly) (6 GF) ⊗ in 113 bedrooms
FACILITIES: STV Gym Xmas **CONF:** Thtr 80 Class 32 Board 40
SERVICES: Lift air con **PARKING:** 130 **NOTES:** ⊗ in restaurant
CARDS:

★★★66% ***Quality Hotel Heathrow***
QUALITY HOTEL BY CHOICE HOTELS
London Rd, Brands Hill SL3 8QB
☎ 01753 684001 🖹 01753 685767
e-mail: info@qualityheathrow.com
Dir: *M4 junct 5, follow signs for Colnbrook. Hotel approx 250mtrs on right*
This stylish, modern hotel is ideally located for Heathrow Airport,
continued on p536

SLOUGH, continued

and for commercial visitors to Slough. Bedrooms have good facilities, benefit from all-day room service and are smartly furnished. There is a bright and airy open-plan restaurant, bar and lounge. Transfers are available to and from the airport.
ROOMS: 128 en suite (23 fmly) (5 GF) ⊗ in 60 bedrooms
FACILITIES: STV Gym **CONF:** Thtr 120 Class 50 Board 40
SERVICES: Lift **PARKING:** 100 **NOTES:** ✖
CARDS:

⌂ Innkeeper's Lodge Slough/Windsor

399 London Rd, Langley SL3 8PS
☎ 01753 591212 🖷 01753 211362
www.innkeeperslodge.com
Dir: *M4 junct 5 onto London Rd, 100yds on right*
Smart rooms meet essential business requirements but also have home comforts, and depending on location may well have meeting rooms and pub dining. Dining options generally include all-day menus plus the added advantage of breakfast.
ROOMS: 57 en suite s £49.95-£69.95; d £49.95-£69.95 **CONF:** Board 15

⌂ Premier Lodge (Slough)

76 Uxbridge Rd SL1 1SU
☎ 0870 9906500 🖷 0870 9906501
web: www.premierlodge.com
Dir: *2m from M4 junct 5, just off A4*
High quality, modern, budget accommodation, ideal for families and business travellers. All rooms feature bath, power shower and satellite TV, and most have telephones / modem points. The adjacent bar and restaurant offers a wide and varied menu.
ROOMS: 84 en suite s £56; d £56

⌂ Travelodge

Landmark Place SL1 1BZ
☎ 08700 850 950 🖷 01753 - 516897
Travelodge offers good quality, good value, modern accommodation. Ideal for families, the spacious, en suite bedrooms include remote-control TV, tea and coffee-making facilities and luxury beds. Meals can be taken at the nearby family restaurant. For further details consult the Hotel Groups page.
ROOMS: 157 en suite s fr £25; d fr £25

SNETTISHAM, Norfolk — Map 12 TF63

★★70% Rose & Crown

Old Church Rd PE31 7LX
☎ 01485 541382 🖷 01485 543172
e-mail: info@roseandcrownsnettisham.co.uk
web: www.roseandcrownsnettisham.co.uk
Dir: *A149 N from Kings Lynn towards Hunstanton. Turn into Snettisham after approx. 10m, then turn into Old Church Rd. Hotel 100yds on L.*
This lovely village centre pub provides comfortable, well equipped bedrooms. A range of quality meals is served in the many dining areas, while a good variety of real ales and wines is on offer. Service is friendly and a delightful atmosphere prevails. A walled garden is available on sunny days, as is a children's play area.
ROOMS: 11 en suite (3 fmly) ⊗ in all bedrooms s £50-£65; d £70-£100 (incl. bkfst) **LB** **CONF:** Del from £50 **PARKING:** 70 **NOTES:** ⊗ in restaurant **CARDS:**

GF Indicates the number of bedrooms at ground floor level.

SOLIHULL, West Midlands — Map 10 SP17
See also Dorridge

★★★★70% Renaissance Solihull

651 Warwick Rd B91 1AT
☎ 0121 711 3000
🖷 0121 705 6629/0121 711 3963
e-mail: ed.schofield@whitbread.com
Dir: *M42 junct 5, follow signs for Solihull centre. 2nd left at rdbt (Warwick Rd). Straight over 3rd sets of lights. Barley Mow pub left on approaching large rdbt. Straight ahead, hotel on right.*
With its town centre location, this modern hotel is conveniently situated for the NEC, Birmingham and many local attractions. Bedrooms, many of which are air-conditoned, are attractively decorated and equipped with a comprehensive range of extras. The hotel boasts extensive conference facilities, an indoor leisure facility and extensive car parking.
ROOMS: 179 en suite (6 fmly) ⊗ in 87 bedrooms **FACILITIES:** STV Sauna Solarium Gym Jacuzzi Beauty therapist Large screen TV ♫ **CONF:** Thtr 700 Class 350 Board 60 **SERVICES:** Lift **PARKING:** 300 **NOTES:** Civ Wed 70 **CARDS:**

★★★67% Corus hotel Solihull

Stratford Rd, Shirley B90 4EB
☎ 0870 609 6133 🖷 0121 733 3801
e-mail: regency@corushotels.com
Dir: *M42 junct 4 onto A34 cross 1st 3 rdbts, double back along dual carriageway, hotel on left*

This popular business hotel offers its guests some extra facilities such as an indoor leisure club and newly refurbished bar. The bedrooms are well laid out, and some benefit from an attractive modern refurbishment.
ROOMS: 111 en suite (11 fmly) (13 GF) ⊗ in 64 bedrooms s £145; d £145 **LB** **FACILITIES: Spa** STV Sauna Solarium Gym Jacuzzi Beauty health salon, Steam room **CONF:** Thtr 180 Class 80 Board 60 Del from £90 **SERVICES:** Lift **PARKING:** 275 **NOTES:** ⊗ in restaurant
CARDS:

⌂ Travel Inn (Solihull North)

Stratford Rd, Shirley B90 3AG
☎ 08701 977231 🖷 0121 733 2762
Dir: *M42 junct 4 follow signs for Birmingham. Travel Inn in town centre, on A34*
Travel Inn offers good-quality, value-for-money accommodation. Spacious, en suite rooms with bath and shower comfortably accommodate a family of up to two adults and two children (to age 15). The restaurant and bar offers a varied menu. For further details consult the Hotel Groups page.
ROOMS: 44 en suite s £45.95-£46.95; d £45.95-£46.95

⇧ Travel Inn (Solihull Shirley)

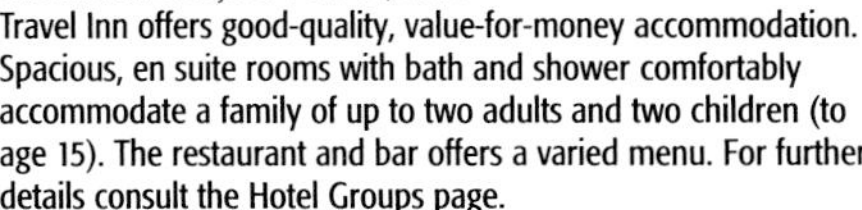

Stratford Rd, Shirley B90 4EP
☎ 08701 977232 📠 0121 733 7075
Dir: *1m from M42 junct 4 on A34, north*
Travel Inn offers good-quality, value-for-money accommodation. Spacious, en suite rooms with bath and shower comfortably accommodate a family of up to two adults and two children (to age 15). The restaurant and bar offers a varied menu. For further details consult the Hotel Groups page.
ROOMS: 51 en suite s £45.95-£48.95; d £45.95-£48.95

SONNING, Berkshire — Map 05 SU77

★★★78% French Horn
RG4 6TN
☎ 0118 969 2204 📠 0118 944 2210
e-mail: info@thefrenchhorn.co.uk
Dir: *From A4 into Sonning, follow B478 through village over bridge, hotel on right, car park on left*
This long established Thames-side restaurant with rooms has a lovely village setting and retains the traditions of classic hotel keeping. The restaurant is a particular attraction and provides attentive service. Bedrooms, including four cottage suites, are spacious and comfortable, many offering stunning views over the river. A private boardroom is available for corporate guests.
ROOMS: 13 en suite 8 annexe en suite (4 GF) s £110-£165; d £140-£205 (incl. bkfst) **FACILITIES:** STV Fishing Affiliation with Nirvana Spa, complimentary 10 minute journey **CONF:** Board 16 Del £235 **SERVICES:** air con **PARKING:** 40 **NOTES:** Closed 26 Dec-30 Jan RS 1st Jan **CARDS:**

★★★68% The Great House at Sonning
Thames St RG4 6UT
☎ 0118 969 2277 📠 0118 944 1296
e-mail: greathouse@btconnect.com
web: www.greathouseatsonning.co.uk
Dir: *exit A4 at rdbt with Texaco Garage & take B478 into Sonning (signed). Through village, over mini rdbt, down steep hill and bear right. Hotel on right, before bridge*
Enjoying a very attractive riverside setting, the Great House is a popular venue. Having a mile and a half of private moorings, a terrace and lawns that lead down to the river, this is an impressive and interesting setting. Bedrooms, many in the main house, enjoy the great views and others, situated in courtyard buildings, are attractive and comfortable. A number of function suites and conference rooms are available, and its riverside location provides a very popular wedding venue.
ROOMS: 12 en suite 37 annexe en suite (11 GF) s £129-£169; d £149-£199 (incl. bkfst) **LB** **FACILITIES:** STV ♫ ch fac **CONF:** Thtr 100 Class 50 Board 35 Del from £149 **PARKING:** 120 **NOTES:** RS 27 Dec -9 Jan Civ Wed 120 **CARDS:**

SOURTON, Devon — Map 03 SX59

★★75% Collaven Manor
EX20 4HH
☎ 01837 861522 📠 01837 861614
e-mail: collavenmanor@supanet.com
Dir: *off A30 onto A386 to Tavistock, hotel 2m on right*
This delightful 15th-century manor house is quietly located in five acres of well-tended grounds. The friendly proprietors provide attentive service and ensure a relaxing environment. Charming public rooms have old oak beams and granite fireplaces, and

continued

provide a range of comfortable lounges and a well stocked bar. In the restaurant, a daily-changing menu offers interesting dishes.

Collaven Manor

ROOMS: 9 en suite (1 fmly) s fr £58; d £92-£128 (incl. bkfst) **LB** **FACILITIES:** Bowls **CONF:** Thtr 30 Class 20 Board 16 Del from £85 **PARKING:** 50 **NOTES:** in restaurant Civ Wed 50 **CARDS:**

SOURTON CROSS, Devon — Map 03 SX59

⇧ Travelodge Okehampton West

Travelodge

EX20 4LY
☎ 08700 850 950 📠 0870 1911548
Dir: *4m W, at junct of A30/A386*
Travelodge offers good quality, good value, modern accommodation. Ideal for families, the spacious, en suite bedrooms include remote-control TV, tea and coffee-making facilities and luxury beds. Meals can be taken at the nearby family restaurant. For further details consult the Hotel Groups page.
ROOMS: 42 en suite s fr £25; d fr £25

SOUTHALL, Greater London
See LONDON SECTION plan 1 B4

U Three Tuns
45 The Green UB2 4AR
☎ 020 8606 8811 020 8606 8822
e-mail: threetunshotel@hotmail.com
Dir: *M4 junct 3/A312/A4020 rdbt turn right to Southall, follow A3005. Hotel on the green opposite St Anslem's Church*
At the time of going to press, the star classification for this hotel was not confirmed. Please refer to the AA internet site www.theAA.com for current information.
ROOMS: 31 en suite (9 fmly) in 25 bedrooms s £59-£89; d £69-£109 (incl. bkfst) **LB** **FACILITIES:** Xmas **CONF:** BC Thtr 180 Class 120 Board 120 Del from £110 **SERVICES:** Lift **PARKING:** 27 **NOTES:**
CARDS:

SOUTHAMPTON, Hampshire Map 05 SU41
See also Landford (Wilts) & Shedfield

★★★★★64% De Vere Grand Harbour
West Quay Rd SO15 1AG
☎ 023 8063 3033 023 8063 3066
e-mail: grandharbour@devere-hotels.com
Dir: *M27 junct 3 follow Waterfront signs keep in left lane of dual carriageway, then follow signs Heritage & Waterfront to old town & waterfront onto West Quay Rd*

Enjoying views of the harbour, this hotel stands alongside the medieval town walls and close to the West Quay centre. The modern design is impressive, with leisure facilities located in the dramatic glass pyramid. The spacious and thoughtfully equipped bedrooms have now undergone refurbishment. For dining, guests can choose between two bars as well as Allertons Restaurant and No 5 Brasserie.
ROOMS: 172 en suite (22 fmly) in 148 bedrooms s £170; d £190 (incl. bkfst) **LB** **FACILITIES: Spa** STV Snooker Sauna Solarium Gym Xmas **CONF:** BC Thtr 500 Class 200 Board 150 Del from £150 **SERVICES:** Lift **PARKING:** 190 **NOTES:** in restaurant Civ Wed 310 **CARDS:**

★★★★70% Botleigh Grange
Hedge End SO30 2GA
☎ 01489 787700 01489 788535
e-mail: enquiries@botleighgrangehotel.co.uk
Dir: *from M27 junct 7 follow A334 to Botley, hotel is 0.5m on left*
A recent upgrade of this impressive mansion has ensured good quality throughout. Many of the bedrooms are newly decorated and all are spacious with a good range of facilities. Public areas include a large conference room and a pleasant terrace with views overlooking the gardens and lake. The restaurant offers interesting menus using fresh, local produce.

ROOMS: 56 en suite (8 fmly) in 17 bedrooms s £75-£85; d £90-£115 (incl. bkfst) **LB** **FACILITIES:** STV Fishing Putt green Xmas **CONF:** Thtr 500 Class 175 Board 60 Del from £130 **SERVICES:** Lift **PARKING:** 200 **NOTES:** in restaurant Civ Wed 400
CARDS:

See advert on opposite page

★★★69% The Woodlands Lodge
Bartley Rd, Woodlands SO40 7GN
☎ 023 8029 2257 023 8029 3090
e-mail: reception@woodlands-lodge.co.uk
web: www.woodlands-lodge.co.uk
Dir: *A326 towards Fawley. 2nd rdbt turn right, left after 0.25m by White Horse PH. In 1.5m cross cattle grid, hotel is 70yds on left*
A hunting lodge in the 18th century, this hotel is set in four acres of impressive and well-tended grounds on the edge of the New Forest. Well-equipped bedrooms come in varying sizes and styles and all bathrooms have a jacuzzi bath. Public areas provide a pleasant lounge and intimate cocktail bar. The dining room, with its hand-painted ceiling, serves delicious award-winning cuisine.
ROOMS: 16 en suite (1 fmly) (3 GF) in 2 bedrooms s £72-£95; d £98-£142 (incl. bkfst) **LB** **FACILITIES:** STV Jacuzzi ch fac Xmas **CONF:** Thtr 55 Class 14 Board 20 Del from £116 **PARKING:** 31 **NOTES:** in restaurant Civ Wed 50 **CARDS:**

★★★66% Southampton Park
Cumberland Place SO15 2WY
☎ 023 8034 3343 023 8033 2538
e-mail: southampton.park@forestdale.com
Dir: *at northern end of Inner Ring Rd opp Watts Park & Civic Centre*
Located in the heart of the city opposite Watts Park, this modern hotel provides well-equipped, smartly appointed bedrooms with comfortable furnishings. The public areas include a good leisure centre, a spacious bar and lounge and the lively MJ's Brasserie. Parking is available in the multi-storey car park behind the hotel.
ROOMS: 72 en suite (10 fmly) in 20 bedrooms s fr £90; d fr £120 (incl. bkfst) **LB** **FACILITIES: Spa** STV Sauna Solarium Gym Jacuzzi **CONF:** Thtr 200 Class 60 Board 70 Del from £125 **SERVICES:** Lift **NOTES:** in restaurant Closed 25 & 26 Dec nights
CARDS:

Bad hair day?
Hairdryers in all rooms three stars and above

★★★65% **Chilworth Manor**

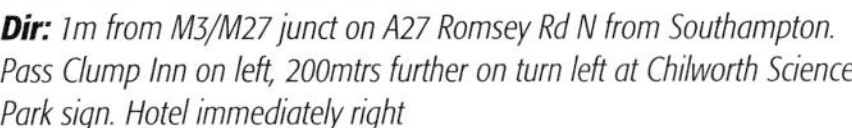

SO16 7PT
☎ 023 8076 7333 🖷 023 8076 6979
e-mail: general@chilworth-manor.co.uk
web: www.chilworth-manor.co.uk
Dir: *1m from M3/M27 junct on A27 Romsey Rd N from Southampton. Pass Clump Inn on left, 200mtrs further on turn left at Chilworth Science Park sign. Hotel immediately right*

This attractive Edwardian manor house is set in 12 acres of landscaped grounds where the rhododendrons in spring are spectacular. Bedrooms are located in the main house and an adjoining modern wing; rooms are peaceful, well equipped and well presented. This is a popular venue for conferences and wedding parties.

ROOMS: 95 en suite (6 fmly) ⊗ in 45 bedrooms s £50-£115; d £99-£145 (incl. bkfst) **LB FACILITIES:** STV Trim trail walking, Giant chess, Petanque **CONF:** Thtr 160 Class 50 Board 50 Del from £165 **SERVICES:** Lift **PARKING:** 200 **NOTES:** ⊗ in restaurant Civ Wed 80
CARDS:

★★★65% **Novotel Southampton**

1 West Quay Rd SO15 1RA
☎ 023 8033 0550 🖷 023 8022 2158
e-mail: H1073@accor-hotels.com
Dir: *M27 junct 3 & signs for City Centre (A33). After 1m take right lane for West Quay & Dock Gates 4-10. Hotel entrance on left. Turn at lights by McDonalds, left at rdbt, hotel straight ahead*

Modern purpose-built hotel situated close to the city centre, railway station, ferry terminal and major road networks. The brightly decorated bedrooms are ideal for families and business guests; four rooms have facilities for the less mobile. The open-plan public areas include the Garden brasserie, a bar and a leisure complex.

ROOMS: 121 en suite (50 fmly) ⊗ in 98 bedrooms s fr £89; d fr £89 **LB FACILITIES:** STV Sauna Gym **CONF:** Thtr 500 Class 300 Board 150 Del £130 **SERVICES:** Lift air con **PARKING:** 300
NOTES: Civ Wed 80 **CARDS:**

★★68% **Elizabeth House**
42-44 The Avenue SO17 1XP
☎ 023 8022 4327 🖷 023 8022 4327
e-mail: enquiries@elizabethhousehotel.com
web: www.elizabethhousehotel.com
Dir: *on A33, on left towards city centre, after Southampton Common, before main lights*

The Elizabeth House is conveniently situated on The Avenue, and as such provides an ideal base for both business and leisure guests. The bedrooms are well equipped and are attractively furnished with comfort in mind. There is also a relaxing and attractive restaurant and a cosy cellar bar.

ROOMS: 20 en suite 7 annexe en suite (8 fmly) (8 GF) s £52; d £62 (incl. bkfst) **CONF:** Thtr 40 Class 24 Board 24 Del £94.50
PARKING: 30 **NOTES:** ⊗ in restaurant
CARDS:

★★63% **Busketts Lawn**
174 Woodlands Rd, Woodlands SO40 7GL
☎ 023 8029 2272 & 8029 3417 🖷 023 8029 2487
e-mail: enquiries@buskettslawnhotel.co.uk
Dir: *A35 W of city through Ashurst, over railway bridge, sharp right into Woodlands Road*

A family run hotel on the edge of the New Forest. Bedrooms are traditionally furnished and well stocked with thoughtful additions. Leisure facilities comprise an outdoor swimming pool and croquet

continued

S

SOUTHAMPTON, continued

lawn, and a terrace overlooking the gardens. A small comfortable lounge and bar are also available.
ROOMS: 14 en suite (3 fmly) (1 GF) s £45-£70; d £70-£85 (incl. bkfst) **LB** **FACILITIES:** STV Putt green Mini Football pitch Xmas **CONF:** Thtr 100 Class 60 Board 40 Del from £87.50 **PARKING:** 50 **NOTES:** in restaurant Closed Xmas Civ Wed 100 **CARDS:**

Hotel Ibis
West Quay Rd, Western Esplanade SO15 1RA
☎ 023 8063 4463 023 8022 3273
e-mail: H1039@accor-hotels.com
Dir: *M27 junct 3/M271. Left to city centre (A35), follow Old Town Waterfront until 4th lights, left, then left again, hotel opposite station*
Modern, budget hotel offering comfortable accommodation in bright and practical bedrooms. Breakfast is self-service and dinner is available in the restaurant. For further details, consult the Hotel Groups page.
ROOMS: 93 en suite s £58.95

Travel Inn Southampton (City Centre)
New Rd SO14 0AB
☎ 0870 238 3308 023 8033 8395
Dir: *M27 junct 5/A335 towards city centre, at Charlotte Place rdbt take 2nd left into East Park Terrace, then 1st left onto New Rd. Travel Inn on right*

Travel Inn offers good-quality, value-for-money accommodation. Spacious, en suite rooms with bath and shower comfortably accommodate a family of up to two adults and two children (to age 15). The restaurant and bar offers a varied menu. For further details consult the Hotel Groups page.
ROOMS: 172 en suite s £52.95-£54.95; d £52.95-£54.95

Travel Inn (Southampton North)
Romsey Rd, Nursling SO16 0XJ
☎ 08701 977233 023 8074 0947
Dir: *M27 junct 3 take M271 towards Romsey. At next rdbt take 3rd exit towards Southampton (A3057) Travel Inn 1.5m on right*
Travel Inn offers good-quality, value-for-money accommodation. Spacious, en suite rooms with bath and shower comfortably accommodate a family of up to two adults and two children (to age 15). The restaurant and bar offers a varied menu. For further details consult the Hotel Groups page.
ROOMS: 32 en suite s £45.95-£48.95; d £45.95-£48.95

Travelodge
Lodge Rd SO14 6QR
☎ 08700 850 950 023 8033 4569
Travelodge offers good quality, good value, modern accommodation. Ideal for families, the spacious, en suite bedrooms include remote-control TV, tea and coffee-making facilities and luxury beds. Meals can be taken at the nearby family restaurant. For further details consult the Hotel Groups page.
ROOMS: 59 en suite s fr £25; d fr £25

○ Jury's Inn Southampton
Charlottle Place SO14
☎ 0870 907 2222
ROOMS: 257 en suite **NOTES:** Due to open Feb 2005

SOUTH CAVE, East Riding of Yorkshire Map 17 SE93

Travelodge Hull
Beacon Service Area HU15 1RZ
☎ 08700 850 950 01430 424455
Dir: *at services on A63 eastbound*
Travelodge offers good quality, good value, modern accommodation. Ideal for families, the spacious, en suite bedrooms include remote-control TV, tea and coffee-making facilities and luxury beds. Meals can be taken at the nearby family restaurant. For further details consult the Hotel Groups page.
ROOMS: 40 en suite s fr £25; d fr £25

SOUTHEND-ON-SEA, Essex Map 07 TQ88

★★★70% Camelia
178 Eastern Esplanade, Thorpe Bay SS1 3AA
☎ 01702 587917 01702 585704
e-mail: cameliahotel@fsbdial.co.uk
web: www.cameliahotel.com
Dir: *from A13 or A127 follow signs to Southend seafront. On seafront turn left, hotel 1m east of the pier*

A smartly presented, privately owned hotel, ideally situated at the quiet end of the seafront overlooking the beach. Bedrooms are pleasantly decorated and thoughtfully equipped; many rooms have superb sea views. The air-conditioned public areas include a cosy lounge bar, an informal restaurant and a coffee lounge.
ROOMS: 21 en suite 8 annexe en suite (7 fmly) (8 GF) in 19 bedrooms s £46-£65; d £60-£100 (incl. bkfst) **LB** **FACILITIES:** STV Cycle hire and tours arranged **PARKING:** 102 **NOTES:** in restaurant **CARDS:**

★★★68% Roslin Hotel

Thorpe Esplanade SS1 3BG
☎ 01702 586375 📠 01702 586663
e-mail: sales@roslinhotel.com
web: www.roslinhotel.com
Dir: *A127, follow signs for Southend-on-Sea. Hotel between Walton Road and Clieveden Road, on seafront*

This friendly, family-run hotel is situated at the quiet end of the esplanade, overlooking the beach and sea. The spacious bedrooms are pleasantly decorated and thoughtfully equipped; some rooms have superb sea views. Public rooms include a large lounge bar and the attractive Mulberry restaurant, which also overlooks the sea.
ROOMS: 39 rms (35 en suite) (4 fmly) (6 GF) s £40-£75; d £65-£90 (incl. bkfst) **LB** **FACILITIES:** STV Temp membership of local sports centre **CONF:** Thtr 40 Class 30 Board 30 **PARKING:** 34 **NOTES:** RS 26 Dec **CARDS:**

★★★68% Westcliff

Westcliff Pde, Westcliff-on-Sea SS0 7QW
☎ 01702 345247 📠 01702 431814
e-mail: westcliff@zolahotels.com
Dir: *M25 junct 29, A127 towards Southend, follow signs for Cliffs Pavillion when approaching town centre*
This impressive Grade II listed Victorian building is situated in an elevated position overlooking the cliffs, gardens and sea beyond. The spacious bedrooms are tastefully decorated and thoughtfully equipped; many have lovely sea views. Public rooms include a smart conservatory-style restaurant, a spacious lounge and a range of function rooms.
ROOMS: 55 en suite (2 fmly) in 32 bedrooms s £75-£85; d £95-£165 (incl. bkfst) **LB** **FACILITIES:** STV Jacuzzi Xmas **CONF:** Thtr 225 Class 90 Board 64 Del from £95 **SERVICES:** Lift **NOTES:** in restaurant Civ Wed 60 **CARDS:**

★★★65% *Erlsmere*

24/32 Pembury Rd, Westcliff-on-Sea SS0 8DS

☎ 01702 349025 📠 01702 337724
e-mail: erlsmerehotel@madasafish.com
Dir: *M25 junct 29 to A127 to Southend. Pass Kent Elms Corner exit at next lights to A1158 to Westbourne Grove signed seafront. At next main junct (A13) straight onto Chalkwell Ave, under rail bridge left, 4th right*
Situated in a peaceful side road, just a short walk from the seafront and shops. Bedrooms come in a variety of styles; each one is pleasantly decorated and well equipped. An interesting

continued

choice of dishes is served in the stylish new Restaurant 2432 and guests also have the use of the Patio Bar as well as a cosy lounge.

Erlsmere Hotel

ROOMS: 30 en suite 2 annexe en suite (2 fmly) **CONF:** Thtr 120 Class 40 Board 60 **PARKING:** 12 **NOTES:** **CARDS:**

★★70% Balmoral

34 Valkyrie Rd, Westcliff-on-Sea SS0 8BU
☎ 01702 342947 📠 01702 337828
e-mail: enq@balmoralsouthend.com
web: www.balmoralsouthend.com
Dir: *off A13*

A delightful hotel ideally situated just a short walk from the main shopping centre, railway station and seafront. The attractively decorated bedrooms are tastefully furnished and equipped with many thoughtful touches. Public rooms feature a smart open-plan bar/restaurant and further seating is provided in the reception area.
ROOMS: 29 en suite (4 fmly) (2 GF) **FACILITIES:** STV Arrangement with nearby health club **PARKING:** 23 **NOTES:** in restaurant Closed Xmas **CARDS:**

Premier Lodge (Southend-on-Sea)

213 Eastern Esplanade SS1 3AD

☎ 0870 9906370 📠 0870 9906371
web: www.premierlodge.com
Dir: *enter Southend follow signs for A1159 (A13) Shoeburyness onto dual carriageway, at rdbt follow signed Thorpe Bay seafront. At seafront turn right for hotel on right.*
High quality, modern, budget accommodation, ideal for families and business travellers. All rooms feature bath, power shower and satellite TV, and most have telephones / modem points. The adjacent bar and restaurant offers a wide and varied menu.
ROOMS: 42 en suite s £50; d £50

S

SOUTHEND-ON-SEA, continued

⌂ Travel Inn

Thanet Grange SS2 6GB
☎ 08701 977235 📠 01702 430838
***Dir:** on A127 at junct with B1013*
Travel Inn offers good-quality, value-for-money accommodation. Spacious, en suite rooms with bath and shower comfortably accommodate a family of up to two adults and two children (to age 15). The restaurant and bar offers a varied menu. For further details consult the Hotel Groups page.
ROOMS: 60 en suite s £45.95-£48.95; d £45.95-£48.95

○ Travelodge (Southend on Sea)

Chichester Rd SS1 2JY
☎ 08700 850950
ROOMS: 56 en suite **NOTES:** Due to open Oct 2004

SOUTH MIMMS SERVICE AREA (M25), Hertfordshire — Map 06 TL20

⌂ Days Inn

Bignells Corner EN6 3QQ
☎ 01707 665440 📠 01707 660189
e-mail: southmimmshotel@welcomebreak.co.uk
web: www.welcomebreak.co.uk
***Dir:** M25 junct 23, at rdbt follow signs*
This modern building offers accommodation in smart, spacious and well-equipped bedrooms, suitable for families and business travellers, and all with en suite bathrooms. Continental breakfast is available and other refreshments may be taken at the nearby family restaurant. For further details see the Hotel Groups page.
ROOMS: 74 en suite s £59-£74; d £59-£74 **CONF:** Board 10 Del from £35

SOUTH MOLTON, Devon — Map 03 SS72

★★68% The George Hotel

1 Broad St EX36 3AB
☎ 01769 572514 📠 01769 579218
e-mail: info@georgehotelsouthmolton.co.uk
web: www.georgehotelsouthmolton.co.uk
***Dir:** off A361 at rdbt signed South Molton, 1.5m to centre. Hotel in square*
Retaining many of its original features, this charming 17th-century hotel is situated in the centre of town. Providing comfortable accommodation, complemented by informal and friendly service, the property has undergone extensive refurbishment. Regularly changing menus, featuring local produce, are offered in the restaurant and bar.
ROOMS: 10 rms (9 en suite) (3 fmly) ⊘ in all bedrooms s £50-£60; d £75 (incl. bkfst) **LB** **FACILITIES:** Xmas **CONF:** Thtr 100 Class 30 Board 28 **PARKING:** 12 **NOTES:** ⊘ in restaurant RS Monday
CARDS:

SOUTH NORMANTON, Derbyshire — Map 16 SK45

★★★★70% Renaissance Derby/Nottingham Hotel

Carter Ln East DE55 2EH
☎ 01773 812000 📠 01773 580032
e-mail: derby@renaissancehotels.co.uk
***Dir:** M1 junct 28, E on A38 to Mansfield*
This hotel provides comfortable bedrooms, stylishly furnished and decorated with a comprehensive range of extras provided. Public rooms include a smart leisure centre, conference facilities and Chatterley's Restaurant.
ROOMS: 158 en suite (7 fmly) (61 GF) ⊘ in 100 bedrooms s £120-£132; d £140-£152 (incl. bkfst) **LB** **FACILITIES:** STV supervised Sauna Solarium Gym Jacuzzi Steam room, Whirlpool ch fac Xmas **CONF:** BC Thtr 220 Class 100 Board 60 Del from £10 **PARKING:** 220 **NOTES:** ⊘ in restaurant Civ Wed
CARDS:

⌂ Travel Inn (Mansfield)

Carter Ln East DE55 2EH
☎ 08701 977180 📠 01773 861155
***Dir:** just off M1 junct 28, on A38 signed Mansfield. Entrance 200yds on left*
Travel Inn offers good-quality, value-for-money accommodation. Spacious, en suite rooms with bath and shower comfortably accommodate a family of up to two adults and two children (to age 15). The restaurant and bar offers a varied menu. For further details consult the Hotel Groups page.
ROOMS: 80 en suite s £45.95-£46.95; d £45.95-£46.95

SOUTHPORT, Merseyside — Map 15 SD31

See also Formby

★★★71% *Scarisbrick*

Lord St PR8 1NZ
☎ 01704 543000 📠 01704 533335
e-mail: info@scarisbrickhotel.com
web: www.scarisbrickhotel.com
***Dir:** from S: M6 junct 26, M58 to Ormskirk then onto Southport; from N: A59 from Preston, well signed. Also M6 junct 26, then M58 junct A570*
Centrally located on Southport's famous Lord Street, this privately owned hotel offers a high standard of attractively furnished, thoughtfully equipped accommodation. A wide range of eating options is available, from the bistro style of Maloney's Kitchen to the more formal Knightsbridge restaurant. Extensive leisure and conference facilities are also available.
ROOMS: 88 en suite (5 fmly) **FACILITIES: Spa** STV Sauna Solarium Gym Jacuzzi Use of private leisure centre, Beauty & aromatherapy studio ♫ **CONF:** BC Thtr 200 Class 100 Board 80 **SERVICES:** Lift **PARKING:** 68 **NOTES:** ⊘ in restaurant Civ Wed 170
CARDS:

★★★69% Stutelea Hotel & Leisure Club

Alexandra Rd PR9 0NB
☎ 01704 544220 📠 01704 500232
e-mail: info@stutelea.co.uk
***Dir:** off the promenade near town & Hesketh Park*
This family owned and run hotel enjoys a quiet location in a residential area, a short walk from Lord Street and the Promenade. Bedrooms vary in size and style and include family suites and rooms with balconies overlooking the attractive gardens. The elegant restaurant has a cosmopolitan theme; alternatively the Garden Bar, located in the leisure centre, offers light snacks throughout the day.
ROOMS: 20 en suite (4 fmly) s £70-£75; d £99-£104 (incl. bkfst) **LB** **FACILITIES:** STV Sauna Solarium Gym Jacuzzi Games room Keep fit classes Steam room Xmas **SERVICES:** Lift **PARKING:** 10 **NOTES:** ⊘ in restaurant **CARDS:**

> Packed in a hurry?
> Ironing facilities should be available at all star levels, either in rooms or on request

★★★65% Royal Clifton

Promenade PR8 1RB
☎ 01704 533771 ▯ 01704 500657
e-mail: sales@royalclifton.co.uk
Dir: *hotel on Promenade adjacent to Marine Lake*
This grand, traditional hotel benefits from a prime location on the promenade. Bedrooms range in size and style, but all are comfortable and thoughtfully equipped. Public areas include the lively Bar C, the elegant Pavilion Restaurant and a modern, well-equipped leisure club. Extensive conference and banqueting facilities make this hotel a popular function venue.
ROOMS: 111 en suite (22 fmly) (6 GF) ⊗ in 30 bedrooms s £60-£83; d £90-£110 (incl. bkfst) **LB** **FACILITIES: Spa** STV Sauna Solarium Gym Jacuzzi Hair & beauty Steam room, Aromatherapy ♫ Xmas **CONF:** Thtr 250 Class 100 Board 65 Del from £95 **SERVICES:** Lift **PARKING:** 60 **NOTES:** ⊗ in restaurant Civ Wed 100
CARDS:

★★72% Balmoral Lodge
41 Queens Rd PR9 9EX
☎ 01704 544298 & 530751 ▯ 01704 501224
e-mail: balmorallg@aol.com
web: www.balmorallodge.co.uk
Dir: *edge of town on A565 Preston road*
Situated in a quiet residential area close to Lord Street, this friendly hotel is particularly popular with golfers. Smartly appointed bedrooms are extremely well equipped for both business and leisure guests; some benefit from private patios overlooking the attractive gardens. Stylish public areas include Oscar's restaurant and an attractive bar lounge.
ROOMS: 15 en suite (1 fmly) s £35-£55; d £70-£80 (incl. bkfst) **LB** **FACILITIES:** STV Sauna **PARKING:** 12 **NOTES:**
CARDS:

★★70% *Bold*
585 Lord St PR9 0BE
☎ 01704 532578 ▯ 01704 532528
e-mail: info@boldhotel.com
web: www.boldhotel.com
Dir: *M6 J26, onto M58, then take A570 to Southport, then follow signs to Lord St, hotel at north end of street, on corner of Seabank Rd*
Enjoying a central location, this family hotel is just a minute's walk from the promenade and local attractions. Thoughtfully equipped, spacious bedrooms are suitable for business or leisure guests as well as for families. Public areas include a spacious bar and bistro and a large carvery which is available for parties.
ROOMS: 23 en suite (4 fmly) **FACILITIES:** Special rates for local squash club **CONF:** Thtr 40 Class 40 Board 11 **SERVICES:** air con **PARKING:** 15 **NOTES:** **CARDS:**

★★65% Metropole
Portland St PR8 1LL
☎ 01704 536836 ▯ 01704 549041
e-mail: metropole.southport@btinternet.com
web: www.btinternet.com/~metropole.southport
Dir: *left off Lord St after Prince of Wales Hotel & Metropole is directly behind Prince of Wales*
This family-run hotel of long standing, popular with golfers, is ideally situated just 50 yards from the famous Lord Street. Accommodation is bright and modern with family rooms available. In addition to the restaurant that offers a selection of freshly prepared dishes, there is a choice of lounges including a popular bar-lounge.
ROOMS: 23 en suite (4 fmly) ⊗ in 6 bedrooms s £39; d £70 (incl. bkfst) **LB** **FACILITIES:** Snooker Golf can be arranged at 8 local courses Xmas **PARKING:** 12 **NOTES:** ⊗ in restaurant
CARDS:

⌂ Travel Inn Southport
Marine Dr PR8 1RY
☎ 08701 977071 ▯ 08701 977704
Dir: *in Southport follow signs for promenade and Marine Dr. Travel Inn at junction of Marine Pde and Marine Dr*
Travel Inn offers good-quality, value-for-money accommodation. Spacious, en suite rooms with bath and shower comfortably accommodate a family of up to two adults and two children (to age 15). The restaurant and bar offers a varied menu. For further details consult the Hotel Groups page.
ROOMS: 60 en suite s £45.95-£46.95; d £45.95-£46.95

Popped the question?
Hotels with Civ Wed in their entry are licensed for civil wedding ceremonies. Maximum numbers for the ceremony only are shown, e.g. Civ Wed 120

SOUTH RUISLIP, Greater London
See LONDON SECTION plan 1 B5

⌂ Days Hotel

Long Dr, Station Approach HA4 0HN
☎ 020 8845 8400 ▯ 020 8845 5500
e-mail: info@dayshotelheathrow.com
Dir: *turn off A40 at Polish War Memorial, follow signs to Ruislip and South Ruislip*
This modern building offers accommodation in smart, spacious and well-equipped bedrooms, suitable for families and business travellers, and all with en suite bathrooms. Continental breakfast is
continued on p544

S

SOUTH RUISLIP, continued

available and other refreshments may be taken at the nearby family restaurant. For further details see the Hotel Groups page.

Days Hotel, South Ruislip

ROOMS: 78 en suite **CONF:** BC Thtr 60 Class 40 Board 30

SOUTH SHIELDS, Tyne & Wear Map 21 NZ36

★★★65% Sea

Sea Rd NE33 2LD

☎ 0191 427 0999 📠 0191 454 0500

e-mail: sea@bestwestern.co.uk

Best Western

Dir: *A1(M) past Washington Services to A194. Continue along A194 and take A183 through South Shields town centre along Ocean Rd. Hotel on seafront*

A relaxed and friendly atmosphere prevails at this long-established business hotel, dating from the 1930s. Bedrooms, some overlooking the boating lake and the Tyne estuary, are generally spacious. A range of generously portioned meals is served in both the bar and restaurant. The extensive function rooms enable weddings to be catered for.

ROOMS: 32 en suite (5 fmly) ⊗ in 8 bedrooms s £57-£65; d £67-£75 (incl. bkfst) **FACILITIES:** STV **CONF:** Thtr 200 Class 100 Board 50 Del from £70 **PARKING:** 70 **NOTES:** RS 26 Dec

CARDS:

SOUTHWAITE MOTORWAY SERVICE AREA (M6), Cumbria Map 18 NY44

Travelodge Carlisle (Southwaite)

Broadfield Site CA4 0NT

☎ 08700 850 950 📠 016974 75354

Travelodge

Dir: *M6 junct 41/42*

Travelodge offers good quality, good value, modern accommodation. Ideal for families, the spacious, en suite bedrooms include remote-control TV, tea and coffee-making facilities and luxury beds. Meals can be taken at the nearby family restaurant. For further details consult the Hotel Groups page.

ROOMS: 38 en suite s fr £25; d fr £25

SOUTHWELL, Nottinghamshire Map 17 SK65

★★★67% Saracens Head

Market Place NG25 0HE

☎ 01636 812701 📠 01636 815408

Dir: *from A1 to Newark turn off & follow B6386 for approx 7m*

This half-timbered inn, rich in history, is set in the centre of town and close to the Minster. There is a relaxing atmosphere within the sumptuous public areas, which include a small bar, a comfortable lounge and a large restaurant. Bedroom styles vary; all are appealing, comfortable and well equipped.

ROOMS: 27 en suite (2 fmly) ⊗ in all bedrooms s £75; d £95-£150 (incl. bkfst) **LB** **FACILITIES:** STV ch fac Xmas **CONF:** BC Thtr 80 Class 60 Board 40 **PARKING:** 102 **NOTES:** ⊗ in restaurant Civ Wed 70

CARDS:

SOUTH WITHAM, Lincolnshire Map 11 SK91

Travelodge Grantham New Fox

New Fox NG33 5LN

☎ 08700 850 950 📠 0870 191 1576

Travelodge

Dir: *on A1, northbound*

Travelodge offers good quality, good value, modern accommodation. Ideal for families, the spacious, en suite bedrooms include remote-control TV, tea and coffee-making facilities and luxury beds. Meals can be taken at the nearby family restaurant. For further details consult the Hotel Groups page.

ROOMS: 32 en suite s fr £25; d fr £25

SOUTHWOLD, Suffolk Map 13 TM57

★★★74% Swan

Market Place IP18 6EG

☎ 01502 722186 📠 01502 724800

e-mail: swan.hotel@adnams.co.uk

Dir: *take A1095 to Southwold, hotel in town centre, parking via archway to left of hotel*

A charming 17th-century coaching inn situated in the heart of this bustling town centre overlooking the market place. Public rooms feature an elegant restaurant, a comfortable drawing room, a cosy bar and a lounge where guests can enjoy afternoon tea. The spacious bedrooms are attractively decorated, tastefully furnished and thoughtfully equipped.

ROOMS: 25 en suite 17 annexe en suite (17 GF) s £70-£75; d £130-£150 (incl. bkfst) **LB** **FACILITIES:** Xmas **CONF:** Thtr 40 Class 24 Board 12 Del from £175 **SERVICES:** Lift **PARKING:** 35 **NOTES:** ⊗ in restaurant Civ Wed 40 **CARDS:**

★★74% *The Crown*

90 High St IP18 6DP

☎ 01502 722275 📠 01502 727263

e-mail: crown.hotel@adnams.co.uk

Dir: *off A12 take A1095 to Southwold, into town centre, hotel on left in High St*

A delightful old posting inn situated in the heart of the town centre. The property combines a pub, wine bar and intimate restaurant with superb accommodation. The tastefully decorated bedrooms have attractive co-ordinated soft furnishings and many thoughtful touches. Public rooms feature a back room bar serving traditional Adnams ales as well as an elegant first-floor lounge.

ROOMS: 13 rms (12 en suite) (2 fmly) **PARKING:** 23 **NOTES:** ⊗ in restaurant Closed 1st or 2nd wk Jan

CARDS:

★★67% The Blyth Hotel

Station Rd IP18 6AY

☎ 01502 722632 📠 01502 724123

e-mail: accommodation@blythhotel.com

Dir: *A12 onto A1045, on entering town Mights Bridge & at the mini rdbt, hotel ahead*

Situated just a short walk from the centre of this delightful seaside town, this friendly, family-run hotel offers bedrooms that are thoughtfully equipped and individually decorated with co-ordinated soft furnishings and fabrics. Public rooms include a smart restaurant and two different bars serving the local Adnams ales.

ROOMS: 12 en suite (5 fmly) ⊗ in all bedrooms s £65-£75; d £85-£95 (incl. bkfst) **LB** **FACILITIES:** Boule pitch **PARKING:** 10 **NOTES:** ⊗ in restaurant **CARDS:**

Early start?
Hotels at all star levels should provide in-room alarm clocks and/or alarm calls

A ★★ Sutherland House Restaurant
56 High St IP18 6DN
☎ 01502 722260 01502 725270
e-mail: chefs@sutherlandhouse.co.uk
web: www.sutherlandhouse.co.uk
Dir: *In High Street, on left just past post office*
ROOMS: 4 en suite in all bedrooms s £90-£235; d £90-£235 (incl. bkfst) **LB FACILITIES:** Putt green Xmas **CONF:** Thtr 70 Class 45 Board 30 **NOTES:** No children 15yrs in restaurant
CARDS:

SOUTH ZEAL, Devon — Map 03 SX69

★★67% Oxenham Arms
EX20 2JT
☎ 01837 840244 & 840577 01837 840791
e-mail: theoxenhamarms@aol.com
Dir: *off A30, 4m E of Okehampton in centre of village*
Dating back to the 12th century this attractive inn features original stonework, an ancient standing stone, aged beams, flagstone floors and interesting nooks and crannies. Now equipped with modern facilities, the bedrooms are comfortable and spacious. A welcoming fire crackles in the lounge during colder months and dining options include bar meals and the relaxed dining room.
ROOMS: 8 rms (7 en suite) (3 fmly) s fr £45; d fr £70 (incl. bkfst)
FACILITIES: Xmas **PARKING:** 5 **NOTES:** in restaurant
CARDS:

SPALDING, Lincolnshire — Map 12 TF22

★★70% Cley Hall
22 High St PE11 1TX
☎ 01775 725157 01775 710785
e-mail: cleyhall@enterprise.net
web: www.cleyhallhotel.com
Dir: *from A16/A151 rdbt towards Spalding (with river on right) hotel 1.5m on left*
This Georgian house overlooks the River Welland, with landscaped gardens to the rear. Most bedrooms are in an adjacent building; all are smart and include modern amenities. Dining options are popular with residents and locals alike, particularly the fine dining menu offered within the smartly refurbished Garden Restaurant. A reception-based internet/PC workstation with language translation facility is available.
ROOMS: 4 en suite 8 annexe en suite (4 fmly) (1 GF) s £55-£85; d £80-£105 (incl. bkfst) **FACILITIES:** STV competition river fishing **CONF:** Thtr 35 Class 20 Board 18 **PARKING:** 20 **NOTES:** in restaurant Civ Wed 36 **CARDS:**

SPENNYMOOR, Co Durham — Map 19 NZ23

★★★74%
Whitworth Hall Country Park Hotel
Best Western
Stanners Ln DL16 7QX
☎ 01388 811772 01388 818669
e-mail: enquiries@whitworthhall.co.uk
This hotel, peacefully situated in its own grounds in the centre of the Deer Park, offers comfortable accommodation. Spacious bedrooms, some with excellent views over the lake, offer stylish and elegant décor. Public areas include a choice of restaurants and bars, a bright conservatory and well-equipped function and conference rooms.
ROOMS: 29 en suite (3 fmly) in 25 bedrooms s £115; d £130 (incl. bkfst) **LB FACILITIES:** Fishing Xmas **CONF:** Thtr 100 Class 30 Board 30 Del £135 **PARKING:** 100 **NOTES:** in restaurant Civ Wed 120
CARDS:

STADHAMPTON, Oxfordshire — Map 05 SU69

Restaurant with Rooms

The Crazy Bear
Bear Ln OX44 7UR
☎ 01865 890714 01865 400481
e-mail: sales@crazybearhotel.co.uk
Dir: *M40 junct 7 left at end of slip road, into Stadhampton village. Over mini rdbt left at petrol station. Hotel is 2nd left*
This popular and attractive restaurant successfully combines modern chic with old world character. Cuisine is extensive and varied with Thai and English restaurants under the same roof, and those choosing to make a night of it can enjoy the concept bedrooms, all presented and equipped to a very high standard.
ROOMS: 5 en suite 7 annexe en suite (3 fmly) (2 GF) s £65-£120; d £110-£290 (incl. bkfst) **FACILITIES:** STV Hairdressers, Beauty Treatments and Massages Xmas **CONF:** Thtr 30 Class 30 Board 2 Del £185 **PARKING:** 50 **NOTES:** Civ Wed 50
CARDS:

STAFFORD, Staffordshire — Map 10 SJ92

★★★★74% The Moat House
CLASSIC BRITISH
Lower Penkridge Rd, Acton Trussell ST17 0RJ
☎ 01785 712217 01785 715344
e-mail: info@moathouse.co.uk
web: www.moathouse.co.uk
Dir: *M6 junct 13 onto A449 through Acton Trussell. Hotel on right on exiting village*
This 17th-century timbered building, with a peaceful canal-side setting, has been skilfully extended. Bedrooms are stylishly

continued on p546

STAFFORD, continued

furnished, well equipped and comfortable. The refurbished bar offers a wide range of snacks and the restaurant boasts a popular fine dining option where the head chef displays his excellent skills using top quality produce.

The Moat House, Stafford

ROOMS: 32 en suite (4 fmly) (12 GF) ⊗ in 29 bedrooms **FACILITIES:** STV ch fac **CONF:** Thtr 200 Class 60 Board 50 **PARKING:** 200 **NOTES:** ⊗ in restaurant Closed 25-26 Dec & 1-2 Jan Civ Wed 130 **CARDS:**

See advert on page 545

★★★71% The Swan

CLASSIC BRITISH

46 Greengate St ST16 2JA
☎ 01785 258142 📠 01785 223372
e-mail: info@theswanstafford.co.uk
Dir: *from north follow A34 access via Mill Street in town centre. From south on A449*

This former coaching inn located in the centre of town has undergone a stylish refurbishment. Spacious, contemporary public areas include a popular brasserie, a choice of elegant bars, a coffee shop and conference facilities. Individually styled bedrooms, many with original period features, are tastefully appointed and include two four-poster suites.

ROOMS: 27 en suite (2 fmly) ⊗ in 25 bedrooms s £82-£112; d £100-£120 (incl. bkfst) **FACILITIES:** STV **CONF:** Thtr 40 Board 20 Del £120 **SERVICES:** Lift **PARKING:** 40 **NOTES:** Closed 25-26 Dec, 1 Jan **CARDS:**

★★★63% The Garth Hotel

Wolverhampton Rd, Moss Pit ST17 9JR
☎ 0870 609 6169 📠 01785 255152
e-mail: reservations@corushotels.com
Dir: *M6 junct 13 take A449*

With easy access to the M6, this is a pleasantly appointed hotel set within attractive gardens. The comfortable bedrooms have been equipped with thoughtful business traveller requirements and are well maintained. The bar offers light meals in a relaxed informal atmosphere or a full menu can be enjoyed in the modern restaurant.

ROOMS: 60 en suite (4 fmly) ⊗ in 42 bedrooms s £79; d £79 **LB** **FACILITIES:** STV Xmas **CONF:** Thtr 175 Class 50 Board 50 **PARKING:** 175 **NOTES:** ⊗ in restaurant Civ Wed 100 **CARDS:**

★★68% Abbey

THE INDEPENDENTS

65-68 Lichfield Rd ST17 4LW
☎ 01785 258531 📠 01785 246875
Dir: *M6 junct 13 towards Stafford. Turn right at Esso garage continue to mini-rdbt, then follow Silkmore Lane until 2nd rdbt, hotel 0.25m on right*

This privately owned and personally run hotel provides well-equipped accommodation and is particularly popular with commercial visitors. Family and ground floor rooms are both available. Facilities here include a choice of smoking and non-smoking lounges. Staff throughout are friendly and keen to please.

ROOMS: 17 en suite (3 fmly) s £45-£55; d £56-£70 (incl. bkfst) **LB** **PARKING:** 25 **NOTES:** ⊗ in restaurant Closed 22 Dec-7 Jan **CARDS:**

⌂ Premier Lodge (Stafford)

PREMIER LODGE.com

1 Hurricane Close ST16 1GZ
☎ 0870 9906478 📠 0870 9906479
web: www.premierlodge.com
Dir: *M6 junct 14. 2.5m NW of Stafford*

High quality, modern, budget accommodation, ideal for families and business travellers. All rooms feature bath, power shower and satellite TV, and most have telephones / modem points. The adjacent bar and restaurant offers a wide and varied menu.

ROOMS: 96 en suite s £50; d £50 **CONF:** Thtr 30

⌂ Travel Inn Stafford

travel inn

1 Spitfire Close ST16 1ST
☎ 08701 977310 📠 08701 977 707
Dir: *Exit M6 junct 14 and take A34 north. The Travel Inn 1m on left on approach to rdbt*

Travel Inn offers good-quality, value-for-money accommodation. Spacious, en suite rooms with bath and shower comfortably accommodate a family of up to two adults and two children (to age 15). The restaurant and bar offers a varied menu. For further details consult the Hotel Groups page.

ROOMS: 60 en suite s £45.95-£46.95; d £45.95-£46.95

STAFFORD MOTORWAY SERVICE AREA (M6), Staffordshire

Map 10 SJ82

⌂ Travel Inn Stafford (M6 Southbound)

travel inn

Stafford Motorway Service Area ST15 0EY
☎ 08701 977239 📠 01785 826303
Dir: *M6 southbound 8m S of junct 15*

Travel Inn offers good-quality, value-for-money accommodation. Spacious, en suite rooms with bath and shower comfortably accommodate a family of up to two adults and two children (to age 15). The restaurant and bar offers a varied menu. For further details consult the Hotel Groups page.

ROOMS: 40 en suite s £45.95-£46.95; d £45.95-£46.95 **CONF:** Thtr 25 Board 15

⌂ Travelodge (Northbound only)

Moto Service Area, Eccleshall Rd ST15 0EU
☎ 08700 850 950 🖷 01785 816107
Dir: *between M6 juncts 14 & 15 northbound only*
Travelodge offers good quality, good value, modern accommodation. Ideal for families, the spacious, en suite bedrooms include remote-control TV, tea and coffee-making facilities and luxury beds. Meals can be taken at the nearby family restaurant. For further details consult the Hotel Groups page.
ROOMS: 49 en suite s fr £25; d fr £25

STAINES, Surrey — Map 06 TQ07

★★★70% *The Thames Lodge*

MACDONALD HOTELS

Thames St TW18 4SF
☎ 0870 400 8121 🖷 01784 454858
e-mail: thameslodge@macdonald-hotels.co.uk
Dir: *follow signs A30 town centre, bus station on right, hotel straight ahead*
Enjoying an idyllic setting beside the river, and close to the town centre, this suave hotel offers well-equipped bedrooms, many now refurbished. The smart, contemporary style brasserie serves modern and imaginative food. There is a choice of function rooms.
ROOMS: 78 en suite (16 fmly) (28 GF) ⊗ in 48 bedrooms **FACILITIES:** STV Riverside tea garden with mooring, Use of facilities at local leisure centre **CONF:** Thtr 40 Class 20 Board 20 **PARKING:** 40 **NOTES:** ⊗ in restaurant **CARDS:**

⌂ Travelodge

Hale St, Two Rivers Retail Park TW18 4UW
☎ 08700 850 950 🖷 01784 491 026
Dir: *M25 junct 13, take B376 to Staines, Travelodge in Two Water Retail Park.*
Travelodge offers good quality, good value, modern accommodation. Ideal for families, the spacious, en suite bedrooms include remote-control TV, tea and coffee-making facilities and luxury beds. Meals can be taken at the nearby family restaurant. For further details consult the Hotel Groups page.
ROOMS: 65 en suite s fr £25; d fr £25

STALHAM, Norfolk — Map 13 TG32

★★66% Kingfisher

High St NR12 9AN
☎ 01692 581974 🖷 01692 582544
Dir: *from A149 between Gt Yarmouth & North Walsham, into village centre. Hotel just off High St at west end.*
Privately owned hotel situated in the centre of this busy little market town, in the heart of the Norfolk Broads. The spacious bedrooms are pleasantly decorated and thoughtfully equipped with a good range of useful facilities. Public rooms include a smart lounge bar and an intimate restaurant serving carte or fixed-price menus.
ROOMS: 18 en suite (2 fmly) s £40; d £55 (incl. bkfst) **LB** **FACILITIES:** Xmas **CONF:** Thtr 120 Class 50 Board 50 **PARKING:** 40 **NOTES:** ⊗ in restaurant **CARDS:**

STALLINGBOROUGH, Lincolnshire — Map 17 TA11

★★★65% Stallingborough Grange Hotel

Riby Rd DN41 8BU
☎ 01469 561302 🖷 01469 561338
e-mail: grange.hot@virgin.net
web: www.stallingborough-grange.com
Dir: *from A180 follow signs for Stallingborough Ind Est. Through the village, from rdbt take A1173 Caistor, hotel 1m on left just past windmill*
This 18th-century country house has been tastefully extended to provide spacious, well-equipped bedrooms. Popular with locals, this family-run hotel not far from the M180. A good range of food is offered in the Tavern, and there is also more formal dining in the restaurant: both have a friendly atmosphere.
ROOMS: 41 en suite (6 fmly) (9 GF) ⊗ in all bedrooms s £80-£100; d £95-£115 (incl. bkfst) **LB** **FACILITIES:** STV **CONF:** Thtr 60 Class 40 Board 28 **PARKING:** 100 **NOTES:** ⊗ in restaurant Civ Wed 65 **CARDS:**

STAMFORD, Lincolnshire — Map 11 TF00

★★★80% ⊛ The George of Stamford

71 St Martins PE9 2LB
☎ 01780 750750 & 750700 (Res) 🖷 01780 750701
e-mail: reservations@georgehotelofstamford.com
web: www.georgehotelofstamford.com
Dir: *turn off A1 15m north of Peterborough onto B1081, 1m on left*
Steeped in hundreds of years of history, this delightful coaching inn provides spacious public areas which include a choice of dining options, inviting, comfortable lounges, a business centre and a range of quality shops. A highlight is afternoon tea, taken in the colourful courtyard when weather permits. Bedrooms are stylishly appointed and range from traditional to contemporary in design.
ROOMS: 47 en suite (2 fmly) ⊗ in 3 bedrooms s £78-£110; d £110-£225 (incl. bkfst) **LB** **FACILITIES:** STV ch fac Xmas **CONF:** BC Thtr 50 Class 25 Board 25 Del from £145 **PARKING:** 120 **NOTES:** Civ Wed 50 **CARDS:**

★★★69% Garden House

High St, St Martin's PE9 2LP
☎ 01780 763359 🖷 01780 763339
e-mail: enquiries@gardenhousehotel.com
Dir: *A1 to South Stamford, B1081, signed Stamford & Burghley House. Hotel on left on entering town*
Situated within a few minutes' walk of the town centre, this sympathetically transformed 18th-century town house provides pleasant accommodation. Bedroom styles vary; all are well equipped and comfortably furnished. Public rooms include a charming lounge bar, conservatory restaurant and a smart breakfast room. Service is attentive and friendly throughout.
ROOMS: 20 en suite (2 fmly) (4 GF) ⊗ in 16 bedrooms s £65; d £89-£95 (incl. bkfst) **LB** **FACILITIES:** STV ch fac Xmas **CONF:** Thtr 40 Class 20 Board 20 Del from £100 **PARKING:** 22 **NOTES:** ⊗ in restaurant RS 1-12 Jan Civ Wed 46 **CARDS:**

★★69% Crown

All Saints Place PE9 2AG
☎ 01780 763136 🖷 01780 756111
e-mail: thecrownhotel@excite.com
web: www.thecrownhotelstamford.co.uk
Dir: *off A1 onto A43, straight through town until Red Lion Sq, hotel is behind All Saints church in the square*

This small, privately owned hotel is ideally situated in the town

continued on p548

STAMFORD, continued

centre. Unpretentious British food is served in the attractive restaurant and hospitality is spontaneous and sincere. The traditional bar is popular with locals. Bedrooms are mostly spacious and well equipped, some with four-poster beds; additional 'superior' rooms are located in a renovated Georgian Town House just a short walk up the street.
ROOMS: 17 rms (16 en suite) 6 annexe rms (5 en suite) (4 fmly) (1 GF) ⊗ in all bedrooms s £65-£95; d £80-£145 (incl. bkfst) **LB**
FACILITIES: STV Use of local health/gym club **CONF:** Thtr 20 Class 15 Board 15 Del from £120 **PARKING:** 21 **NOTES:** ⊗ in restaurant
CARDS:

STANDISH, Greater Manchester Map 15 SD51

Premier Lodge (Wigan North)

Almond Brook Rd WN6 0SS
☎ 0870 9906474 📠 0870 9906475
web: www.premierlodge.com

PREMIER LODGE.com

Dir: *M6 junct 27 follow signs for Standish. Turn left at t-junct, then 1st right*
High quality, modern, budget accommodation, ideal for families and business travellers. All rooms feature bath, power shower and satellite TV, and most have telephones / modem points. The adjacent bar and restaurant offers a wide and varied menu.
ROOMS: 36 en suite s £48; d £48

STANSTEAD ABBOTTS, Hertfordshire Map 06 TL31

★★★62% Briggens House

Stanstead Rd SG12 8LD
☎ 01279 829955 📠 01279 793685
e-mail: briggenshouse@corushotels.com
Dir: *M11 take A414 to Hertford, after 10th rdbt follow signs for Briggens Park*

Sitting in 80 acres of open countryside, this hotel was once a stately home and boasts a marvellous arboretum, 9-hole golf course, two all-weather tennis courts and a heated swimming pool. A number of meeting and conference rooms are available, and there is lounge seating in the traditional public rooms.
ROOMS: 54 en suite (3 fmly) (16 GF) ⊗ in 20 bedrooms s fr £75; d fr £105 (incl. bkfst) **LB** **FACILITIES:** ⛳ 9 Putt green Xmas **CONF:** Thtr 100 Class 50 Board 50 Del from £130 **SERVICES:** Lift **PARKING:** 100 **NOTES:** ⊗ in restaurant Civ Wed 100
CARDS:

STANSTED AIRPORT, Essex Map 06 TL52

See also see also Birchanger Green Motorway Service Area (M11)

★★★73% Whitehall

Church End CM6 2BZ
☎ 01279 850603 📠 01279 850385
e-mail: sales@whitehallhotel.co.uk
Dir: *M11 junct 8, follow signs to Stansted Airport, then hotel signs to Broxted village*
Situated just a stones' throw from Stansted Airport and the M25, this delightful Elizabethan manor house is set in pretty landscaped grounds surrounded by open countryside. The attractively decorated bedrooms are generally quite spacious, tastefully furnished and thoughtfully equipped. Public rooms feature a superb timber-vaulted restaurant, a cosy lounge, a residents' bar and a range of conference rooms as well as banqueting facilities.
ROOMS: 26 en suite (3 fmly) s fr £100; d fr £125 **LB**
FACILITIES: ch fac **CONF:** Thtr 120 Class 80 Board 48 Del from £150
PARKING: 35 **NOTES:** Closed 27-30 Dec RS Sat lunch & Sun evening Civ Wed 100 **CARDS:**

★★★71% The Stansted Manor

Birchanger Ln CM23 5ST
☎ 01279 859800 📠 01279 467245
e-mail: info@stanstedmanor-hotel.co.uk
web: www.stanstedmanor-hotel.co.uk

Best Western

Dir: *M11 junct 8 onto A120 towards Bishop's Stortford. Turn right at next major rdbt. Hotel on left in Birchanger Lane*
Located just of the M11, this modern hotel is conveniently located for Stansted Airport. The property is reached via a long drive and surrounded by landscaped grounds. Bedrooms feature clean, modern decor, tasteful furnishings and a thoughtful range of extras. Open-plan public rooms include a comfortable lobby lounge, a lounge/bar and a conservatory restaurant.
ROOMS: 70 en suite (8 fmly) (23 GF) ⊗ in 15 bedrooms
FACILITIES: STV **CONF:** Thtr 35 Class 14 Board 18 Del from £130
SERVICES: Lift **PARKING:** 100 **NOTES:** ⊗ in restaurant
CARDS:

STANTON ST QUINTIN, Wiltshire Map 04 ST97

★★★72% Stanton Manor Country House Hotel

SN14 6DQ
☎ 01666 837552 📠 01666 837022
e-mail: reception@stantonmanor.co.uk
Dir: *M4 junct 17 onto A429 Malmesbury/Cirencester, within 200yds turn 1st left signed Stanton St Quintin entrance to hotel on left just after church*
Set in seven acres of lovely gardens including a 9-hole golf course, this charming Cotswold stone manor house has easy access to the M4. Each bedroom and the delightful public areas have been totally refurbished with comfort in mind. In the restaurant, a short carte of imaginative dishes is supported by a selection of interesting wines.
ROOMS: 24 en suite (2 fmly) (8 GF) ⊗ in 8 bedrooms s £77.50-£99.50; d £99.50-£135 (incl. bkfst) **LB** **FACILITIES:** ⛳ 9 Putt green ch fac Xmas **CONF:** Thtr 60 Class 50 Board 40 Del from £125 **PARKING:** 40
NOTES: ⊗ in restaurant Closed 24-30 Dec
CARDS:

STAVERTON, Devon — Map 03 SX76

★★67% ® *Sea Trout Inn*
TQ9 6PA
☎ 01803 762274 🖷 01803 762506
e-mail: enquiries@seatroutinn.com
web: www.seatroutinn.com
Dir: *turn off A38 onto A384 at Buckfastleigh, follow signs to Staverton*
Set in a delightful location in the Dart Valley, this 15th-century inn has bags of character. Ideal for a relaxing break, and particularly suitable for anglers with the River Dart almost on the doorstep. A range of dining options is available and includes bar food and the conservatory restaurant, using local and some organic produce and offering excellent choices.
ROOMS: 10 en suite (1 fmly) **CONF:** Board 30 **PARKING:** 48
NOTES: ⊗ in restaurant **CARDS:**

STEEPLE ASTON, Oxfordshire — Map 11 SP42

★★★66% The Holt Hotel
Oxford Rd OX25 5QQ
☎ 01869 340259 🖷 01869 340865
e-mail: info@holthotel-oxford.co.uk
web: www.holthotel-oxford.co.uk
Dir: *junct of B4030/A4260*
This attractive former coaching inn has given hospitality to many over the centuries, not least Claude Duval a notorious 17th-century highwayman. Today guests are offered well-equipped, modern bedrooms and restful public areas which include a relaxing bar, attractive restaurant and a well appointed lounge. A selection of meeting rooms is also available.
ROOMS: 86 en suite (19 fmly) ⊗ in 16 bedrooms **FACILITIES:** STV Xmas **CONF:** Thtr 140 Class 70 Board 44 **PARKING:** 200 **NOTES:** ⊗ in restaurant Civ Wed 100 **CARDS:**

STEVENAGE, Hertfordshire — Map 12 TL22

★★★66% Novotel Stevenage
Knebworth Park SG1 2AX
☎ 01438 346100 🖷 01438 723872
e-mail: H0992@accor-hotels.com
Dir: *A1(M) junct 7, at entrance to Knebworth Park*
Located just off the A1(M), this hotel's accessible location and range of meeting rooms makes it a popular business and conference venue. There's plenty for leisure guests too: Knebworth Park is a noteworthy neighbour and the hotel's outdoor pool and children's play area will appeal to families.
ROOMS: 100 en suite (20 fmly) (30 GF) ⊗ in 85 bedrooms s £55-£95; d £55-£95 **LB** **FACILITIES:** STV supervised Special rates at local health club ♫ ch fac Xmas **CONF:** BC Thtr 200 Class 80 Board 70 Del from £68 **SERVICES:** Lift **PARKING:** 100
CARDS:

★★★65% The Cromwell Hotel
High St, Old Town SG1 3AZ
☎ 01438 779954 🖷 01438 742169
e-mail: cromwellhotel@corushotels.com
Dir: *A1(M) junct 8. Follow signs for town centre, over 2 rdbts. Join one-way system. Turn off into Old Town. Hotel is on the left after mini rdbt*
Easily accessible from the nearby A1(M) in the Old Town, this high street hotel has retained much of its historic charm. The bedroom styles vary between modern and traditional; each room is well equipped and comfortably appointed. Among the public areas, there is a bar/lounge and a smart modern business centre.

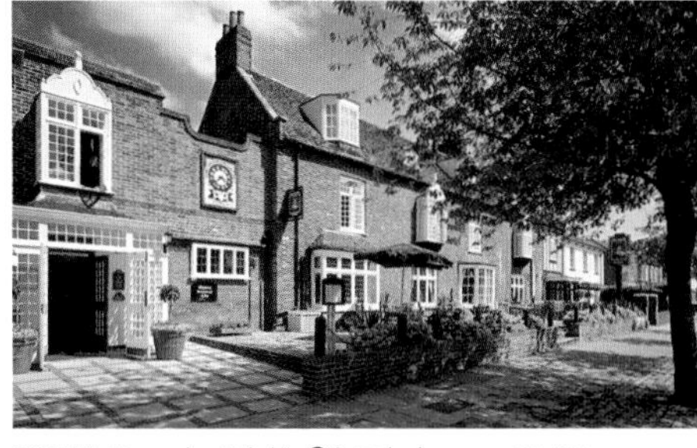

ROOMS: 76 en suite (2 fmly) ⊗ in 33 bedrooms s £93-£113; d £113-£133 **LB** **FACILITIES:** STV Access to David Lloyd Gym (£5) Xmas **CONF:** BC Thtr 200 Class 50 Board 54 Del from £99 **PARKING:** 70
NOTES: ⊗ in restaurant Civ Wed 180
CARDS:

★★★65% The Roebuck Inn
London Rd, Broadwater SG2 8DS
☎ 0870 011 9076 🖷 0870 011 9077
e-mail: hotel@roebuckinn.com
Dir: *from A1(M) junct 7, towards Stevenage. At 2nd rdbt take 2nd exit signed Roebuck-London/Knebworth B197, hotel 1.5m*
Suitable for both the business and leisure traveller, this hotel provides spacious contemporary accommodation in well equipped bedrooms. The older part of the building, where there is a restaurant and a cosy public bar with log fire and real ales, dates back to the 15th century.
ROOMS: 54 en suite (8 fmly) ⊗ in 27 bedrooms s £69-£99; d £79-£129 **LB** **FACILITIES:** Xmas **CONF:** Thtr 50 Class 20 Board 30 Del from £110
PARKING: 70 **NOTES:** ✈ **CARDS:**

⌂ Hotel Ibis Stevenage
Danestrete SG1 1EJ
☎ 01438 779955 🖷 01438 741880
e-mail: H2497@accor-hotels.com
Dir: *in town centre adjacent to Tesco & Westgate Multi-Store*
Modern, budget hotel offering comfortable accommodation in bright and practical bedrooms. Breakfast is self-service and dinner is available in the restaurant. For further details, consult the Hotel Groups page.
ROOMS: 98 en suite s £35-£47; d £35-£47

⌂ Travel Inn

Corey's Mill Ln SG1 4AA
☎ 08701 977240 🖷 01438 721609
Dir: *A1(M) junct 8, at junct with A602 Hitchin Rd & Corey's Mill Lane*
Travel Inn offers good-quality, value-for-money accommodation. Spacious, en suite rooms with bath and shower comfortably accommodate a family of up to two adults and two children (to age 15). The restaurant and bar offers a varied menu. For further details consult the Hotel Groups page.
ROOMS: 39 en suite s £45.95-£48.95; d £45.95-£48.95

○ Premier Lodge (Stevenage)
Six Hill Way, Horizon Technology Park SG1 2DA
web: www.premierlodge.com
ROOMS: 115 en suite **NOTES:** Due to open Winter 2004

STEYNING, West Sussex Map 06 TQ11

★★★69% The Old Tollgate

The Street BN44 3WE
☎ 01903 879494 📠 01903 813399
e-mail: info@oldtollgatehotel.com
web: www.oldtollgatehotel.com
Dir: *on A283 at Steyning rdbt, turn off to Bramber, hotel approx 200yds on right*

As its name suggests, this well-presented hotel is built on the site of the old tollhouse. The spacious bedrooms are smartly designed and are furnished to a high standard. Open for both lunch and dinner, the popular carvery-style restaurant offers an extensive choice of dishes. The hotel also has adaptable function rooms for weddings and conferences.
ROOMS: 11 en suite 20 annexe en suite (5 fmly) (10 GF) in 16 bedrooms s £77-£128; d £77-£128 **LB FACILITIES:** STV **CONF:** Thtr 50 Class 32 Board 26 Del £96.95 **SERVICES:** Lift **PARKING:** 60 **NOTES:** Civ Wed 60 **CARDS:**

STILTON, Cambridgeshire Map 12 TL18

★★★72% Bell Inn

Great North Rd PE7 3RA
☎ 01733 241066 📠 01733 245173
e-mail: reception@thebellstilton.co.uk
Dir: *A1(M) junct 16, follow signs for Stilton, hotel on main road in centre of village*

This delightful inn is steeped in history and retains many original features, with imaginative food served in both the village bar and the elegant beamed first-floor restaurant; refreshments can be enjoyed in the attractive courtyard and rear gardens when weather permits. Individually designed bedrooms are stylish and equipped to a high standard.
ROOMS: 19 en suite (1 fmly) in 17 bedrooms s £72.50-£89.50; d £96.50-£109.50 (incl. bkfst) **FACILITIES:** STV **CONF:** Thtr 100 Class 46 Board 50 Del from £115 **PARKING:** 30 **NOTES:** Closed 25 Dec RS 26 Dec Civ Wed 85 **CARDS:**

STOCK, Essex Map 06 TQ69

★★★★70% Greenwoods Estate Hotel Spa & Retreat

Stock Rd CM4 9BE
☎ 01277 829990 📠 01277 829899
e-mail: info@greenwoodsestate.com
Dir: *At junct 16 on A12 take B1007 signed Billericay. Hotel on right on entering village*

A 17th-century, Grade II listed manor house situated in the picturesque village of Stock amid landscaped grounds and surrounded by open countryside. The attractively decorated bedrooms are tastefully furnished and thoughtfully equipped, some rooms have lovely views of the gardens. Public rooms include a choice of elegant lounges, a smart restaurant and superb leisure facilities as well as meeting and conference rooms.
ROOMS: 39 en suite (6 GF) in all bedrooms s £150-£165; d £240-£260 (incl. bkfst) **LB FACILITIES: Spa** STV supervised Sauna Solarium Gym Jacuzzi Aerobic studio, therapy/relaxtion rooms ♫ Xmas **CONF:** Thtr 40 Class 20 Board 20 Del from £195 **PARKING:** 200 **NOTES:** No children 16yrs in restaurant Civ Wed 50
CARDS:

STOCKPORT, Greater Manchester Map 16 SJ89
See also Manchester Airport

★★★69% Bredbury Hall Hotel & Country Club

THE INDEPENDENTS

Goyt Valley SK6 2DH
☎ 0161 430 7421 📠 0161 430 5079
e-mail: reservations@bredburyhallhotel.co.uk
Dir: *M60 junct 25 signed Bredbury, right at traffic lights, left onto Osbourne St, hotel 500mtrs on right*

With views over open countryside, this large modern hotel is conveniently located for the M60. The stylish, well-equipped bedrooms offer space and comfort and the restaurant serves a very wide range of freshly prepared dishes. There is a popular nightclub next door to the hotel.
ROOMS: 150 en suite (2 fmly) (50 GF) s £54.50; d £74.50
FACILITIES: STV Fishing Snooker Night club(Fri&Sat eve) ♫ Xmas
CONF: Thtr 200 Class 120 Board 60 Del £95 **PARKING:** 400
NOTES: Civ Wed 100 **CARDS:**

★★★66% Alma Lodge Hotel

149 Buxton Rd SK2 6EL
☎ 0161 483 4431 📠 0161 483 1983
Dir: *M60 junct 1 at rdbt take 2nd exit under railway viaduct at traffic lights opp. Debenhams turn right onto A6, hotel approx 1.5m on left*

A large hotel, located on the main road close to the town, offering modern and well-equipped bedrooms. It is family owned and run and serves a good range of quality Italian cooking in Luigi's restaurant. Good function rooms are also provided.
ROOMS: 20 en suite 32 annexe en suite (2 fmly) in 22 bedrooms
CONF: Thtr 250 Class 100 Board 60 **PARKING:** 120 **NOTES:** RS Bank Hols Civ Wed 100 **CARDS:**

★★★61% The County Hotel

Bramhall Ln South SK7 2EB
☎ 0870 609 6148 📠 0161 440 8071
(For full entry see Bramhall)

★★69% Wycliffe

74 Edgeley Rd, Edgeley SK3 9NQ
☎ 0161 477 5395 📠 0161 476 3219
e-mail: wycliffe_hotel@yahoo.co.uk
Dir: *M60 junct 2 follow A560 for Stockport, at 1st lights turn right, hotel 0.5m on left*

This family-run, welcoming hotel provides immaculately maintained and well-equipped bedrooms. There is popular restaurant where the menu has an Italian bias, and a well stocked bar.
ROOMS: 18 en suite s fr £55; d fr £70 (incl. bkfst) **CONF:** Thtr 30 Class 20 Board 20 **PARKING:** 46 **NOTES:** Closed 25-27 Dec RS BH's
CARDS:

Town House Hotel
Country House Hotel
Travel Accommodation

S

⌂ Innkeeper's Lodge Stockport

271 Wellington Rd, North Heaton Chapel SK4 5BP
☎ 0161 432 2753
www.innkeeperslodge.com
Smart rooms meet essential business requirements but also have home comforts, and depending on location may well have meeting rooms and pub dining. Dining options generally include all-day menus plus the added advantage of breakfast.
ROOMS: s £45-£52; d £45-£52

⌂ Premier Lodge (Stockport)

Churchgate SK1 1YG
☎ 0870 9906544 📠 0870 9906545
web: www.premierlodge.com
***Dir:** M60 junct 27 onto A626 St Marys Way, turn right at Behhams BMW garage into Spring Gdns then 2nd right into car park*
High quality, modern, budget accommodation, ideal for families and business travellers. All rooms feature bath, power shower and satellite TV, and most have telephones / modem points. The adjacent bar and restaurant offers a wide and varied menu.
ROOMS: 46 en suite s £50; d £50 **CONF:** Thtr 20 Board 20

⌂ Travel Inn

Buxton Rd SK2 6NB
☎ 08701 977242 📠 0161 477 8320
***Dir:** on A6, 1.5m from town centre*
Travel Inn offers good-quality, value-for-money accommodation. Spacious, en suite rooms with bath and shower comfortably accommodate a family of up to two adults and two children (to age 15). The restaurant and bar offers a varied menu. For further details consult the Hotel Groups page.
ROOMS: 40 en suite s £45.95-£48.95; d £45.95-£48.95

STOCKTON-ON-TEES, Co Durham

Map 19 NZ41

★★★71% Parkmore

636 Yarm Rd, Eaglescliffe TS16 0DH
☎ 01642 786815 📠 01642 790485
e-mail: enquiries@parkmorehotel.co.uk
web: www.parkmorehotel.co.uk
***Dir:** off A19 at Crathorne, follow A67 to Yarm. Through Yarm bear right onto A135 to Stockton. Hotel 1m on left*
This modern, bustling hotel has grown from its Victorian house origins to provide stylish, comfortable bedrooms, extensive fitness and swimming facilities, and opulent public rooms. The 'Reeds at Six Three Six' restaurant boasts a reputation for flair and creativity. Staff throughout are friendly and nothing is too much trouble. Spacious function suites make this a popular venue for weddings.
ROOMS: 55 en suite (8 fmly) (9 GF) ⊘ in 30 bedrooms s £62.50-£66; d £72-£80 **LB FACILITIES: Spa** STV supervised Sauna Solarium Gym Jacuzzi Beauty salon Badminton Aerobics studio **CONF:** Thtr 140 Class 40 Board 40 Del from £105 **PARKING:** 90 **NOTES:** ⊘ in restaurant Civ Wed 150 **CARDS:**

★★68% Claireville

519 Yarm Rd, Eaglescliffe TS16 9BG
☎ 01642 780378 📠 01642 784109
e-mail: reception@clairevillehotel.com
***Dir:** on A135 adjacent to Eaglescliffe Golf Course, between Stockton-on-Tees and Yarm*
A family-run hotel with very comfortable bedrooms. There is a cosy bar/lounge and an attractive dining room that offers

continued on p552

STOCKTON-ON-TEES, continued

reasonably priced meals. A delightful conservatory to the rear provides a relaxing garden lounge area.
ROOMS: 18 en suite (2 fmly) in 4 bedrooms s £46-£50; d £58-£65 (incl. bkfst) **FACILITIES:** STV **CONF:** Thtr 40 Class 20 Board 25 **PARKING:** 30 **NOTES:** in restaurant RS Xmas & New Year **CARDS:**

Travel Inn

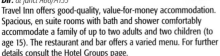

Yarm Rd TS18 3RT
☎ 08701 977244 01642 633339
Dir: *at junct A66/A135*
Travel Inn offers good-quality, value-for-money accommodation. Spacious, en suite rooms with bath and shower comfortably accommodate a family of up to two adults and two children (to age 15). The restaurant and bar offers a varied menu. For further details consult the Hotel Groups page.
ROOMS: 40 en suite s £45.95-£46.95; d £45.95-£46.95

Travel Inn Stockton-on-Tees/ Middlesbrough

Whitewater Way, Thornaby TS17 6QB
☎ 08701 977243 01642 671464
Dir: *A19 take A66 to Stockton/Darlington. Take 1st exit, Teeside Park/Teesdale. Right at lights over viaduct bridge rdbt & Tees Barrage*
Travel Inn offers good-quality, value-for-money accommodation. Spacious, en suite rooms with bath and shower comfortably accommodate a family of up to two adults and two children (to age 15). The restaurant and bar offers a varied menu. For further details consult the Hotel Groups page.
ROOMS: 62 en suite s £45.95-£46.95; d £45.95-£46.95

STOKE D'ABERNON, Surrey — Map 06 TQ15

★★★★75% Woodlands Park

Woodlands Ln KT11 3QB
☎ 01372 843933 01372 842704
e-mail: woodlandspark@handpicked.co.uk
web: www.handpicked.co.uk/woodlandspark
Dir: *from A3 towards London, exit at Cobham. Through town centre & Stoke D'Abernon, left at garden centre into Woodlands Ln, hotel 0.5m on right*

Originally built for the Bryant family, the matchmakers, this lovely Victorian mansion enjoys an attractive parkland setting. All bedrooms have been refurbished - rooms in the new wing are contemporary in style while those in the main house are more traditionally furnished and decorated. The hotel boasts two dining options, Quotes Bar & Brasserie and the Oak Room Restaurant. Hand Picked Hotels - AA Hotel Group of the Year 2004-5.
ROOMS: 57 en suite (4 fmly) in 47 bedrooms s £160; d £160 **LB** **FACILITIES:** STV Xmas **CONF:** Thtr 150 Class 40 Board 50 Del from £179 **SERVICES:** Lift **PARKING:** 150 **NOTES:** Civ Wed 200 **CARDS:**

See advert on page 551

STOKE GABRIEL, Devon — Map 03 SX85

★★★73% Gabriel Court

Stoke Hill TQ9 6SF
☎ 01803 782206 01803 782333
e-mail: reservations@gabrielcourthotel.co.uk
Dir: *off A38 at Buckfastleigh onto A384 (Totnes) then A385 (Paignton). Turn right at Parkers Arms to Stoke Gabriel*
Overlooking the pretty riverside village of Stoke Gabriel, this gracious manor house stands within terraced Elizabethan gardens, surrounded by three acres of grounds. Peace and tranquillity are in abundance and there are several secluded outdoor hideaways for relaxation, or there is an elegant lounge. Bedrooms offer ample space and comfort, and many also have lovely views. The 'Churchward' restaurant serves enjoyable cuisine.
ROOMS: 19 en suite (3 fmly) s £56-£64; d fr £92 (incl. bkfst) **LB** **FACILITIES:** ch fac Xmas **CONF:** Thtr 12 Class 12 Board 12 **PARKING:** 25 **NOTES:** in restaurant **CARDS:**

STOKENCHURCH, Buckinghamshire — Map 05 SU79

★★★68% The Kings Arms

Oxford Rd HP14 3TA
☎ 01494 609090 01494 484582
e-mail: kares@dhillonhotels.co.uk
Dir: *M40 junct 5, turn right over motorway bridge, hotel 600yds on left*
Located on the village green, this hotel blends traditional elegance with contemporary design. Rooms are attractively decorated and well equipped, particularly for the business guest. Public areas include a busy bar and a relaxed, informal restaurant serving a wide range of dishes throughout the day. The smart conference rooms are air conditioned.
ROOMS: 43 en suite (3 fmly) in 22 bedrooms s £89-£109; d £99-£129 (incl. bkfst) **LB** **FACILITIES:** STV Wycombe sports & leisure centre Xmas **CONF:** BC Thtr 200 Class 100 Board 70 Del from £135 **SERVICES:** Lift air con **PARKING:** 95 **NOTES:** Civ Wed 200 **CARDS:**

STOKE-ON-TRENT, Staffordshire — Map 10 SJ84

See also Newcastle-under-Lyme

★★★69% Manor House

Audley Rd ST7 2QQ
☎ 01270 884000 01270 882483
e-mail: mhres@compasshotels.co.uk
(For full entry see Alsager)

★★★66% Haydon House

Haydon St, Basford ST4 6JD
☎ 01782 711311 01782 717470
e-mail: enquiries@haydon-house-hotel.co.uk
Dir: *M6 junct 15, A500 to Stoke-on-Trent, onto A53 Hanley/Newcastle, at rdbt take 1st exit, up hill, take 2nd left at top of hill before traffic lights*
A Victorian property, within easy reach of Newcastle-under-Lyme. The public rooms are furnished in a style befitting the age and character of the house and bedrooms have modern furnishings; several rooms are located in a separate house across the road. The hotel has a good reputation for its food and is popular with locals.
ROOMS: 17 en suite 6 annexe en suite (4 fmly) s £65; d £85 (incl. bkfst) **CONF:** Thtr 80 Class 30 Board 24 **PARKING:** 52 **NOTES:** in restaurant Civ Wed 80 **CARDS:**

★★★65% Quality Hotel
66 Trinity St, Hanley ST1 5NB
☎ 01782 202361 📠 01782 286464
e-mail: info@grandhotel-stoke.co.uk

Dir: *M6 junct 15(S)/16(N) then A500 to city centre & Festival Park. A53 to Leek, keep in left lane, 3rd exit at rdbt for Hanley/city centre/Cultural Quarter. Hotel on left at top of hill*

This large town centre hotel offers well-equipped bedrooms and benefits from its own large car park. There is also a well-equipped leisure centre, together with good conference facilities.
ROOMS: 128 en suite 8 annexe en suite (54 fmly) (5 GF) ⊗ in 85 bedrooms s £40-£105; d £60-£115 **LB FACILITIES: Spa** STV Sauna Solarium Gym Jacuzzi **CONF:** Thtr 300 Class 125 Board 60 Del from £75 **SERVICES:** Lift **PARKING:** 150 **NOTES:** ⊗ in restaurant Civ Wed 250 **CARDS:**

Innkeeper's Lodge Stoke on Trent
Longton Rd ST4 8BU
☎ 01782 644448 📠 01782 644163
www.innkeeperslodge.com

Dir: *M6 junct 15, follow A500 until the slip road for A34 towards Stone. At roundabout turn left onto A5035, lodge is 0.5m on right*

Smart rooms meet essential business requirements but also have home comforts, and depending on location may well have meeting rooms and pub dining. Dining options generally include all-day menus plus the added advantage of breakfast.
ROOMS: 30 en suite s £49.95; d £49.95

STONE, Staffordshire
Map 10 SJ93

★★★68% Stone House
Stafford Rd ST15 0BQ
☎ 0870 609 6140 📠 01785 814764
Dir: *beside A34, 0.5m S of town centre*

corus hotels

This former country house, set in attractive grounds, is located within easy reach of the M6. Attractive comfortable bedrooms and tastefully appointed public areas complete with leisure and conference facilities make the hotel popular with corporate and leisure guests. A light menu is offered in the bar and lounge areas or guests can choose to dine in the stylish restaurant.
ROOMS: 50 en suite (1 fmly) ⊗ in 33 bedrooms s £79-£89; d £79-£89 **LB FACILITIES:** STV Sauna Solarium Gym **CONF:** Thtr 190 Class 60 Board 50 Del from £97.50 **PARKING:** 120 **NOTES:** ⊗ in restaurant RS Sat Civ Wed 60 **CARDS:**

> Destination dining!
> This symbol indicates a Restaurant with Rooms

★★★66% *Crown*
38 High St ST15 8AS
☎ 01785 813535 📠 01785 815942
web: www.stonehotels.co.uk
Dir: *M6 junct 14, A34 N to Stone. M6 junct 15, A34 S to Stone*

A traditional hotel in the centre of town with oak panelling and a glass-domed restaurant offering a choice of menus. The front lounge is delightfully furnished and staff are helpful and friendly.
ROOMS: 12 en suite 16 annexe en suite (2 fmly) (8 GF) ⊗ in 13 bedrooms **FACILITIES:** STV **CONF:** Thtr 150 Class 80 Board 60 **PARKING:** 100 **NOTES:** ⊗ in restaurant Civ Wed 100
CARDS:

STON EASTON, Somerset
Map 04 ST65

Top 200 – Hotel

★★★★ Ston Easton Park
BA3 4DF
☎ 01761 241631 📠 01761 241377
e-mail: info@stoneaston.co.uk
web: www.vonessenhotels.com
Dir: *on A37*

Dating back to 1740, this stunning Palladian mansion benefits from a tranquil location amidst parkland and landscaped gardens. Individually styled, spacious bedrooms include three rooms located in the charming Gardener's Cottage. The delightful and inviting public rooms retain much of their original character and are adorned with beautiful antiques and fine paintings. The imaginative cooking provided at dinner and breakfast is a highlight of any stay here.
ROOMS: 20 en suite 3 annexe en suite (2 fmly) (2 GF) ⊗ in all bedrooms s £120-£340; d £150-£395 (incl. bkfst) **LB**
FACILITIES: Fishing Snooker ch fac Xmas **CONF:** Thtr 120 Board 30 Del from £160 **PARKING:** 120 **NOTES:** ⊗ in restaurant Civ Wed 100 **CARDS:**

STONEHOUSE, Gloucestershire
Map 04 SO80

★★★68% Stonehouse Court
GL10 3RA
☎ 0871 871 3240 📠 0871 871 3241
e-mail: stonehouse.court@pageant.co.uk
Dir: *M5 junct 13, follow signs for Stonehouse, hotel on right 0.25m after 2nd rdbt*

Set in six acres of secluded gardens, this fine Grade II listed manor house dates back to 1601; since then it has been extended considerably. The individually decorated bedrooms offer all modern comforts, two of which have four-poster beds. Elegant

continued on p554

S

STONEHOUSE, continued

public rooms include a lounge, bar, restaurant and gymnasium. Extensive conference facilities are also available.

Stonehouse Court, Stonehouse

ROOMS: 9 en suite 27 annexe en suite (2 fmly) (2 GF) ⊗ in 6 bedrooms s £85-£90; d £95-£135 (incl. bkfst) **LB** **FACILITIES:** STV Fishing Gym Xmas **CONF:** Thtr 150 Class 75 Board 70 Del from £123 **PARKING:** 150 **NOTES:** ⊗ in restaurant Civ Wed 150 **CARDS:**

See advert under GLOUCESTER

Travelodge

A 419, Easington GL10 3SQ

☎ 08700 850 950 01453 828590

Travelodge

Travelodge offers good quality, good value, modern accommodation. Ideal for families, the spacious, en suite bedrooms include remote-control TV, tea and coffee-making facilities and luxury beds. Meals can be taken at the nearby family restaurant. For further details consult the Hotel Groups page.

ROOMS: 40 en suite s fr £25; d fr £25

STOURPORT-ON-SEVERN, Worcestershire Map 10 SO87

★★★★73% **Menzies Stourport Manor**

Hartlebury Rd DY13 9JA

☎ 01299 289955 01299 878520

MENZIES HOTELS

e-mail: stourport@menzies-hotels.co.uk

Dir: *M5 junct 6, follow A449 towards Kidderminster, take B4193 towards Stourport, hotel on right*

Once the home of Prime Minister Sir Stanley Baldwin, this much extended country house is set in attractive grounds. A number of bedrooms are located in the original building, although the majority are in a more modern, purpose-built section. Spacious public areas include a range of lounges, a popular brasserie, a leisure club and conference facilities.

ROOMS: 68 en suite (4 fmly) ⊗ in 25 bedrooms s £110-£120; d £120-£155 **LB** **FACILITIES:** STV Squash Sauna Solarium Gym Putt green Jacuzzi Xmas **CONF:** Thtr 420 Class 120 Board 80 Del £140 **PARKING:** 200 **NOTES:** ⊗ in restaurant Civ Wed **CARDS:**

S

STOWMARKET, Suffolk Map 13 TM05

★★68% **Cedars**

Needham Rd IP14 2AJ

☎ 01449 612668 01449 674704

THE INDEPENDENTS

e-mail: info@cedarshotel.co.uk

Dir: *A1308, 1m outside Stowmarket on road to Needham Market, close to junct with A1120*

Expect a friendly welcome at this privately owned hotel, which is situated just off the A14 and within easy reach of the town centre. Public rooms are full of charm and character with features such as exposed beams and open fireplaces. Bedrooms are pleasantly decorated and thoughtfully equipped with modern facilities.

ROOMS: 25 en suite (3 fmly) (9 GF) **CONF:** Thtr 150 Class 60 Board 40 **PARKING:** 75 **NOTES:** ⊗ in restaurant Closed 25 Dec-1 Jan Civ Wed 50 **CARDS:**

Travelodge Ipswich Stowmarket

IP14 3PY

☎ 08700 850 950 01449 615347

Travelodge

Dir: *on A14 westbound*

Travelodge offers good quality, good value, modern accommodation. Ideal for families, the spacious, en suite bedrooms include remote-control TV, tea and coffee-making facilities and luxury beds. Meals can be taken at the nearby family restaurant. For further details consult the Hotel Groups page.

ROOMS: 40 en suite s fr £25; d fr £25

STOW-ON-THE-WOLD, Gloucestershire Map 10 SP12

★★★★73% **Wyck Hill House**

Burford Rd GL54 1HY

☎ 01451 831936 01451 832243

e-mail: enquiries@wyckhillhouse.com

Dir: *turn off A429 Wyck Hill House is situated 1m on the right hand side*

This charming 18th-century house enjoys superb views across the Windrush Valley and is ideally positioned for a relaxing weekend exploring the Cotswolds. The spacious and thoughtfully equipped bedrooms provide high standards of comfort and quality and are located both in the main house and the original coach house. Elegant public rooms include the cosy bar, library and the magnificent front hall with crackling log fire. The imaginative cuisine makes effective use of local produce.

ROOMS: 16 en suite 16 annexe en suite (1 fmly) (10 GF) s £79-£118; d £79-£170 (incl. bkfst) **LB** **FACILITIES:** STV Archery Clay pigeon shooting Ballooning Honda pilots ch fac Xmas **CONF:** BC Thtr 60 Class 30 Board 24 Del from £149 **SERVICES:** Lift **PARKING:** 100 **NOTES:** ⊗ in restaurant Civ Wed 80 **CARDS:**

★★★75% **Fosse Manor**

GL54 1JX

☎ 01451 830354 01451 832486

e-mail: enquiries@fossemanor.co.uk

web: www.fossemanor.co.uk

Dir: *1m S on A429, 300yds past junct with A424*

Deriving its name from the historic Roman Fosse Way, this popular hotel is ideally located for exploring the many delights of this picturesque area. Bedrooms, located both in the main building and the adjacent coach house, offer high standards of comfort and quality. Public areas include a comfortable lounge, elegant

continued

restaurant and convivial bar. Classy cuisine completes the picture, with quality produce used in an imaginative range of dishes.
ROOMS: 11 en suite 10 annexe en suite (3 fmly) (5 GF) in 20 bedrooms s fr £75; d fr £125 (incl. bkfst) **LB** **FACILITIES:** STV Beautician Xmas **CONF:** Thtr 60 Class 20 Board 26 Del from £150 **PARKING:** 40 **NOTES:** in restaurant Civ Wed 60
CARDS:

See advert on this page

★★★73% *The Royalist*

Digbeth St GL54 1BN
☎ 01451 830670 01451 870048
e-mail: info@theroyalisthotel.co.uk
Dir: *M40 junct 8, follow A40 to Burford. Join A424 to Stow-on-the-Wold. Turn right onto A436, down hill, hotel on left of green*

Verified as the oldest inn in England, this charming hotel has a wealth of history and character. Bedrooms and public areas have been stylishly and sympathetically decorated to ensure high levels of comfort at every turn. There are two eating options: the 947AD restaurant offers high-quality cooking and the Eagle and Child provides a more informal alternative.
ROOMS: 8 en suite in all bedrooms **FACILITIES:** Jacuzzi Discounted rates at local private gym **CONF:** Thtr 46 Class 30 Board 46 Del from £125 **PARKING:** 8 **NOTES:** in restaurant
CARDS:

★★★72% Grapevine

Best Western

Sheep St GL54 1AU
☎ 01451 830344 01451 832278
e-mail: enquiries@vines.co.uk
web: www.vines.co.uk
Dir: *on A436 towards Chipping Norton. 150yds on right, facing green*

Situated in the heart of this unique market town, the Grapevine is a delightful 17th-century building with plenty of charm and character. Original features abound, such as stone-flagged floors, all adding a reassuring sense of solidity and tradition. Individually styled bedrooms combine comfort and quality, each being equipped with thoughtful extras. Canopied by the ancient vine, the Conservatory

continued

Restaurant is the civilised setting for accomplished cuisine. Alternatively, lighter meals can be enjoyed in the popular bar.
ROOMS: 12 en suite 10 annexe en suite (2 fmly) (5 GF) in all bedrooms s £70-£90; d £110-£150 (incl. bkfst) **LB** **FACILITIES:** Xmas **CONF:** Thtr 70 Class 45 Board 30 **PARKING:** 25 **NOTES:** in restaurant Civ Wed 70 **CARDS:**

★★★70% The Unicorn

Sheep St GL54 1HQ
☎ 01451 830257 01451 831090
e-mail: reception@birchhotels.co.uk
Dir: *situated at junct of A429 & A436*

This attractive limestone hotel dates back to the 17th century. Individually designed bedrooms are stylish and include some delightful four-poster rooms. Spacious public areas retain much character and include a choice of inviting lounges and a traditional bar offering a good selection of bar meals and ales, as well as an attractive restaurant.
ROOMS: 20 en suite in 8 bedrooms s £60-£65; d £78-£105 (incl. bkfst) **LB** **FACILITIES:** Xmas **CONF:** Thtr 50 Class 20 Board 28 Del from £95 **PARKING:** 40 **NOTES:** in restaurant Civ Wed 45
CARDS:

★★★69% Stow Lodge

The Square GL54 1AB
☎ 01451 830485 01451 831671
e-mail: enquiries@stowlodge.com
web: www.stowlodge.com
Dir: *in town centre*

Situated in smart grounds, this family-run hotel has direct access to the market square and provides a hospitable welcome to all. Bedrooms are offered both in the main building and in the

continued on p556

S

STOW-ON-THE-WOLD, continued

converted coach house, all of which provide similar standards of homely comfort. Extensive menus and an interesting wine list make for an enjoyable dining experience.
ROOMS: 11 en suite 10 annexe en suite (1 fmly) in all bedrooms s £60-£110; d £75-£140 (incl. bkfst) **LB** **PARKING:** 30 **NOTES:** No children 5yrs in restaurant Closed Xmas-end Jan
CARDS:

★★68% Old Stocks

The Square GL54 1AF
01451 830666 01451 870014
e-mail: aa@theoldstockshotel.co.uk
web: www.oldstockshotel.co.uk
Dir: *turn off A429 to town centre. Hotel is facing village green*

THE INDEPENDENTS

Overlooking the old market square, this Grade II listed, mellow Cotswold-stone building is a comfortable and friendly base from which to explore this picturesque area. There is a lot of character and atmosphere with bedrooms all offering individuality and charm. Facilities include guest lounge, restaurant and bar, whilst outside, the patio is a popular summer venue for refreshing drinks and good food.
ROOMS: 15 en suite 3 annexe en suite (5 fmly) (4 GF) in 10 bedrooms s £45-£60; d £90-£120 (incl. bkfst) **LB** **FACILITIES:** ch fac Xmas **PARKING:** 12 **NOTES:** in restaurant **CARDS:**

STRATFIELD TURGIS, Hampshire Map 05 SU65

★★★67% Wellington Arms

RG27 0AS
01256 882214 01256 882934
e-mail: Wellington.Arms@virgin.net
Dir: *A33 between Basingstoke & Reading*

Situated at one of the entrances to the ancestral home of the Duke of Wellington, the white Georgian façade is a familiar landmark on the A33. The majority of bedrooms are located in the Garden Wing and have now benefited from refurbishment, whereas rooms in the original building are more individual and have a period feel. Public rooms include a comfortable lounge bar with a log fire and a pleasant, formal restaurant; informal dining is available in the bar.
ROOMS: 35 en suite (2 fmly) in 3 bedrooms **CONF:** Thtr 160 Class 40 Board 50 **PARKING:** 150 **CARDS:**

For central reservation numbers and more information on Hotel Groups, turn to pages 33-39

STRATFORD-UPON-AVON, Warwickshire Map 10 SP25

★★★★72% Menzies Welcombe Hotel & Golf Course

Warwick Rd CV37 0NR
01789 295252 01789 266336
e-mail: welcombe@menzies-hotels.co.uk
web: www.bookmenzies.com
Dir: *M40 J15, follow A46 towards Stratford-upon-Avon, at rdbt follow signs for A439. Hotel 3 miles on right.*

MENZIES HOTELS

This privately-owned, Jacobean manor house is set in 157 acres of landscaped parkland. Public rooms are impressive, especially the lounge, with its wood panelling and ornate marble fireplace, and the gentleman's club-style bar. Bedrooms in the original building are the stylish and gracefully proportioned; those in the newer garden wing are comfortable and thoughtfully equipped.

ROOMS: 73 en suite (5 fmly) s £120-£150; d £150-£170 (incl. bkfst) **LB** **FACILITIES:** STV 18 Putt green Xmas **CONF:** Thtr 120 Class 75 Board 30 Del from £150 **PARKING:** 100 **NOTES:** in restaurant Civ Wed 120 **CARDS:**

★★★★71% *Billesley Manor*

Billesley, Alcester B49 6NF
01789 279955 01789 764145
e-mail: enquiries@billesleymanor.co.uk
Dir: *A46 in direction of Evesham. Over 3 rdbts, right turn for Billesley after 2m*

FURLONG

This 16th-century manor is set in peaceful grounds and parkland with a delightful yew topiary garden and fountain. The spacious bedrooms and suites, most in traditional country-house style, are thoughtfully designed and well equipped. The conference facilities and some bedrooms are in the new cedar barns. Public areas retain many original features, such as oak panelling, fireplaces and exposed stone.
ROOMS: 42 en suite 29 annexe en suite (8 fmly) (5 GF)
FACILITIES: STV Sauna Gym Putt green Steam room Beauty treatments **CONF:** Thtr 100 Class 60 Board 50 **PARKING:** 100
NOTES: in restaurant Civ Wed 75
CARDS:

See advert on opposite page

★★★★71% Stratford Manor

Warwick Rd CV37 0PY
01789 731173 01789 731131
e-mail: stratfordmanor@marstonhotels.com
Dir: *3m N of town centre on A439 towards Warwick, or exit M40 junct 15, take Stratford-upon-Avon road A439, hotel 2m on left*

MARSTON HOTELS

Just outside Stratford, this hotel is set against a rural backdrop with lovely gardens and ample parking. Public areas include a lounge bar and a busy split-level restaurant, while the leisure centre boasts a large indoor pool. Service is both professional and

continued

helpful. Bedrooms are spacious and have generously-proportioned beds and a range of useful facilities.

ROOMS: 104 en suite (8 fmly) in 52 bedrooms s £124-£134; d £158-£178 (incl. bkfst & dinner) **LB** **FACILITIES: Spa** STV Sauna Solarium Gym Beauty treatments ch fac Xmas **CONF:** Thtr 350 Class 200 Board 100 Del from £169 **SERVICES:** Lift **PARKING:** 250 **NOTES:** in restaurant Civ Wed 250 **CARDS:**

★★★★69% Stratford Victoria

Arden St CV37 6QQ
☎ 01789 271000 01789 271001
e-mail: stratfordvictoria@marstonhotels.com
Dir: *A439 into Stratford, in town follow A3400 Birmingham, at traffic lights turn left into Arden St, hotel 150yds on right*

MARSTON HOTELS

Situated adjacent to the hospital, this eye-catching modern hotel with its red-brick façade is within walking distance of the town centre. Bedrooms are spacious and feature framed embroideries. The open-plan public areas include a comfortable lounge, a small atmospheric bar and spacious restaurant with exposed beams and ornately carved furniture.
ROOMS: 100 en suite (35 fmly) in 40 bedrooms s £99-£199; d £149-£214 (incl. bkfst) **LB** **FACILITIES: Spa** STV Gym Xmas **CONF:** Thtr 160 Class 66 Board 54 Del £184 **SERVICES:** Lift **PARKING:** 100 **NOTES:** in restaurant Civ Wed 160 **CARDS:**

★★★★65% The Alveston Manor

Clopton Bridge CV37 7HP
☎ 0870 400 8181 01789 414095
e-mail: sales.alvestonmanor@macdonald-hotels.co.uk
Dir: *S of Clopton Bridge*

MACDONALD HOTELS

A striking red-brick and timbered façade, well-tended grounds, and a giant cedar tree all contribute to the charm of this well-established hotel, just five minutes from Stratford. The bedrooms vary in size and character - the coachhouse conversion offers an impressive mix of full and junior suites. The superb new

continued on p558

S

STRATFORD-UPON-AVON, continued

leisure complex offers a 20-metre swimming pool and steam sauna, a high-tech gym and a host of beauty treatments in modern surroundings.
ROOMS: 113 en suite (8 fmly) (45 GF) ⊗ in 46 bedrooms s £70-£160; d £140-£230 (incl. bkfst) **FACILITIES:** STV supervised Sauna Solarium Gym Leisure facilities - techno-gym etc, beauty treatments Xmas **CONF:** Thtr 140 Class 80 Board 40 Del from £120 **PARKING:** 150 **NOTES:** ⊗ in restaurant Civ Wed 110 **CARDS:**

★★★★61% The Shakespeare

Chapel St CV37 6ER
☎ 0870 400 8182 01789 415411
e-mail: shakespeare@macdonald-hotels.co.uk
***Dir:** M40 junct 15, take A46 then A439 into one-way system, left at rdbt opposite HSBC Bank, hotel on the left*

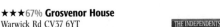

Dating back to the early 17th century, The Shakespeare is one of the oldest hotels in this historic town. The hotel name also represents one of the earliest exploitations of Stratford as the birthplace of one of the world's leading poets and playwrights. With exposed beams and open fires, the public rooms retain an ambience reminiscent of this bygone era.
ROOMS: 63 en suite 11 annexe en suite (3 GF) ⊗ in 18 bedrooms s £65-£150; d £130-£230 (incl. bkfst) **LB** **FACILITIES:** STV Use of swimming pool at sister hotel Xmas **CONF:** Thtr 80 Class 60 Board 40 Del from £120 **SERVICES:** Lift **PARKING:** 34 **NOTES:** ⊗ in restaurant Civ Wed 50 **CARDS:**

★★★74% Salford Hall

WR11 5UT
☎ 01386 871300 01386 871301
e-mail: reception@salfordhall.co.uk
web: www.salfordhall.co.uk
(For full entry see Abbot's Salford)

★★★67% Grosvenor House

Warwick Rd CV37 6YT
☎ 01789 269213 01789 266087
e-mail: info@groshotelstratford.co.uk
***Dir:** M40 junct 15, follow Stratford signs to A439 Warwick Rd, hotel is 7m from junct on town centre one-way system*

Grosvenor House is a short distance from the town centre and many of the historic attractions. Bedroom styles and sizes vary and the friendly staff offer an efficient service. Refreshments are served in the lounge all day, plus room service is available. The Garden Room restaurant offers a choice of dishes from set price and carte menus.
ROOMS: 73 en suite (12 fmly) (25 GF) ⊗ in 25 bedrooms s £65-£115; d £65-£125 **LB** **FACILITIES:** STV Xmas **CONF:** Thtr 100 Class 45 Board 50 Del from £110 **PARKING:** 48 **NOTES:** ⊗ in restaurant Civ Wed 40 **CARDS:**

★★★67% The Swan's Nest

Bridgefoot CV37 7LT
☎ 0870 400 8183 01789 414547
e-mail: swansnest@macdonald-hotels.co.uk
***Dir:** M40 junct 15, A46 for 2m, at 1st island turn left onto A439 towards Stratford. Follow one way system, left over river bridge, hotel on right by river*

Dating back to the 17th century, this hotel is said to be one of the earliest brick-built houses in the town. The hotel occupies a prime position on the banks of the River Avon and is ideally situated for exploring the town and the surrounding Warwickshire countryside.

continued

Bedrooms, all named after birds, have now been refurbished to a high standard.
ROOMS: 67 en suite (2 fmly) (25 GF) ⊗ in 45 bedrooms s £55-£135; d £110-£175 (incl. bkfst) **LB** **FACILITIES:** STV Use of facilities at sister hotel Xmas **CONF:** Thtr 150 Class 80 Board 40 Del from £100 **PARKING:** 80 **NOTES:** Civ Wed 110 **CARDS:**

★★★64% The Falcon

Chapel St CV37 6HA
☎ 01789 279953 01789 414260
e-mail: thefalcon@corushotels.com
***Dir:** town centre-opposite Guild Chapel and Nash House*

This 16th-century inn, situated in the heart of town, provides public rooms with much original character, including a choice of bars, a brasserie-style restaurant (with tables in the conservatory and garden), and a more formal dining option. Accommodation comes in a variety of styles; the older, beamed rooms in the original Tudor section retain much charm.
ROOMS: 73 en suite 11 annexe en suite (13 fmly) (3 GF) ⊗ in 38 bedrooms s £105; d £105 **LB** **FACILITIES:** Xmas **CONF:** Thtr 200 Class 110 Board 40 Del from £105 **SERVICES:** Lift **PARKING:** 124 **NOTES:** ⊗ in restaurant Civ Wed 160 **CARDS:**

★★★62% The Charlecote Pheasant Hotel

Charlecote CV35 9EW
☎ 01789 279954 01789 470222
e-mail: reservations@corushotels.com
***Dir:** M40 junct 15, take A429 towards Cirencester through Barford village after 2m turn right into Charlecote, hotel opposite Charlecote Manor Park*

Located just outside Stratford, this hotel is set in extensive grounds and is a popular conference venue. Various bedroom styles are available within the annexe wings, ranging from standard rooms to executive suites. The main building houses the restaurant and a lounge bar area.
ROOMS: 70 en suite (2 fmly) (20 GF) ⊗ in 26 bedrooms s £98-£118; d £98-£118 **LB** **FACILITIES:** Childrens Play area Xmas **CONF:** Thtr 160 Class 90 Board 50 **PARKING:** 100 **NOTES:** ⊗ in restaurant Civ Wed 176 **CARDS:**

★★66% **The New Inn Hotel & Restaurant**
Clifford Chambers CV37 8HR
☎ 01789 293402 01789 292716
e-mail: thenewinn65@aol.com
web: www.thenewinnhotel.co.uk
Dir: *off A3400 onto B4632 , follow signs to Shire Horse Centre, hotel 200yds on left*
This welcoming, family-run hotel is located in the pretty village of Clifford Chambers. The bar has an open log fire and, together with the restaurant, offers a choice of dining options. Bedrooms are appealing, both those in the new wing and the original six rooms which have been upgraded; rooms with four-poster beds and rooms suitable for less able guests are available.
ROOMS: 12 en suite (2 fmly) (3 GF) in all bedrooms s £49.50-£69.50; d £69.50-£75 (incl. bkfst) **LB** **FACILITIES:** **CONF:** Del from £82 **PARKING:** 40 **NOTES:** in restaurant Closed 23-28 Dec **CARDS:**

STREATLEY, Berkshire
Map 05 SU58

★★★★69% **The Swan at Streatley**
High St, Streatley on Thames RG8 9HR
☎ 01491 878800 01491 872554
e-mail: sales@swan-at-streatley.co.uk
Dir: *from S right at lights in Streatley, Swan on left before bridge*

A stunning location set beside the Thames, ideal on an English summer's day. Many bedrooms enjoy the views and rooms are well appointed. The hotel offers a range of facilities including meeting rooms, plus there's the 'Streatley Belle', moored beside the hotel, which makes an unusual venue. Cuisine is accomplished and dining here is not to be missed.
ROOMS: 46 en suite (13 GF) in 9 bedrooms s fr £99; d £138-£218 (incl. bkfst) **FACILITIES:** STV Fishing Sauna Solarium Gym Jacuzzi Electric motor launches for hire Xmas **CONF:** BC Thtr 140 Class 60 Board 40 Del from £175 **PARKING:** 170 **NOTES:** in restaurant Civ Wed 130 **CARDS:**

STREET, Somerset
Map 04 ST43

★★★64% ***Wessex***
High St BA16 0EF
☎ 01458 443383 01458 446589
e-mail: info@wessexhotel.com
Dir: *from A303, onto B3151 to Somerton. 7m, pass traffic lights by Millfield School. Left at mini-rdbt*
This purpose-built hotel in the centre of town has plenty of parking and is only a short walk from Clarks Village. Spacious bedrooms are equipped with modern facilities. Public areas include a range of function rooms, a cosy bar and a comfortable restaurant.
ROOMS: 49 en suite (4 fmly) in 24 bedrooms **FACILITIES:** STV **CONF:** BC Thtr 250 Class 120 Board 50 **SERVICES:** Lift **PARKING:** 70 **NOTES:** in restaurant Closed 27-29 Dec
CARDS:

STRENSHAM MOTORWAY SERVICE AREA (M5), Worcestershire
Map 10 SO84

Travel Inn (Tewkesbury)
WR8 0BZ
☎ 08701 977252 01684 273606
Dir: *M5 Northbound J8 M5/M50 Interchange (access available to southbound)*
Travel Inn offers good-quality, value-for-money accommodation. Spacious, en suite rooms with bath and shower comfortably accommodate a family of up to two adults and two children (to age 15). The restaurant and bar offers a varied menu. For further details consult the Hotel Groups page.
ROOMS: 49 en suite s £45.95-£46.95; d £45.95-£46.95 **CONF:** Thtr 22 Class 18 Board 24

STRETTON, Rutland
Map 11 SK91

★★72% **Ram Jam Inn**
Great North Rd LE15 7QX
☎ 01780 410776 01780 410361
e-mail: rji@rutnet.co.uk
Dir: *on N'bound carriageway of A1 past B668 turn off, through service station into hotel car park. S'bound take B668 - Oakham & follow signs under A1*
This delightful inn has an informal but stylish ambience, much like a café-bar and bistro with rooms. Warm colour schemes work well throughout the main public rooms, which are dominated by the popular restaurant. The spacious, high-quality bedrooms have cheerful soft furnishings and most overlook the orchard.
ROOMS: 7 en suite (1 fmly) s £47; d £57-£67 **CONF:** Thtr 60 Class 40 Board 40 Del £77.50 **PARKING:** 64 **NOTES:** in restaurant Closed 25 Dec **CARDS:**

STROUD, Gloucestershire
Map 04 SO80

★★★72% **Burleigh Court**
Burleigh, Minchinhampton GL5 2PF
☎ 01453 883804 01453 886870
e-mail: info@burleighcourthotel.co.uk
Dir: *From Stroud A419 towards Cirencester. Right after 2.5 miles signed Burleigh and Minchinhampton. Left after 500yds signposted Burleigh Court, hotel 300yds on right.*

Dating back to the 18th century, this former Gentleman's manor house is in a secluded yet accessible elevated position with some wonderful views over the countryside. Public rooms are elegantly styled and include a wonderful oak-panelled bar for pre-dinner drinks beside a crackling fire. Combining comfort and quality, no two bedrooms are the same and a number of rooms are in an adjoining coach house.
ROOMS: 18 en suite (2 fmly) (3 GF) s £80-£100; d £105-£145 (incl. bkfst) **LB** **FACILITIES:** ch fac **CONF:** Thtr 50 Class 30 Board 30 Del from £130 **PARKING:** 40 **NOTES:** in restaurant Civ Wed 50
CARDS:

S

STROUD, continued

★★★70% @@ The Bear of Rodborough

Rodborough Common GL5 5DE
☎ 01453 878522 📠 01453 872523
e-mail: info@bearofrodborough.info

Dir: *From M5 J13 take A419 to Stroud. Follow signs to Rodborough. Up hill, at top turn left at T-junct. Hotel on right. Or M4 J15, A419 signed Cirencester. Follow signs for Minchinhampton then Rodborough Common, hotel on left.*

This popular 17th-century coaching inn is situated high above Stroud in National Trust parkland. Character abounds in the lounges, cocktail bar and elegant Mulberry restaurant. Bedrooms offer equal measures of comfort and style with plenty of extra touches. There is also a traditional and well-patronised public bar. Food is of paramount importance here and uses local produce whenever possible.

ROOMS: 46 en suite (2 fmly) ⊗ in 13 bedrooms s £75-£99; d £120-£159 (incl. bkfst) LB **FACILITIES:** Putt green ch fac Xmas **CONF:** Thtr 75 Class 45 Board 30 Del from £115 **PARKING:** 70 **NOTES:** ⊗ in restaurant Civ Wed 60 **CARDS:**

★★66% The Bell

Wallbridge GL5 3JS
☎ 01453 763556 📠 01453 758611
e-mail: sarahclose@thebellhotel.demon.co.uk

Dir: *at junct of A419/A46, outside Stroud town centre*

This former coaching inn dates back to Victorian times and is conveniently situated close to the town centre. Small and friendly, there is an informal and relaxed atmosphere here and many guests return on a regular basis. Bedrooms are well equipped and comfortably furnished with a four-poster room available. Facilities include a meeting room, popular lounge bar and restaurant.

ROOMS: 12 en suite (2 fmly) s £30-£45; d £62.50-£115 (incl. bkfst) LB **FACILITIES:** Xmas **CONF:** Thtr 27 Class 20 Board 16 **PARKING:** 15 **NOTES:** ⊗ in restaurant **CARDS:**

Premier Lodge (Stroud)

Stratford Lodge, Stratford Rd GL5 4AF
☎ 0870 9906378 📠 0870 9906379
web: www.premierlodge.com

Dir: *M5 junct 13, follow A419 to Stroud town centre, then follow signs for leisure centre, the lodge is opposite, next to Tesco superstore*

High quality, modern, budget accommodation, ideal for families and business travellers. All rooms feature bath, power shower and satellite TV, and most have telephones / modem points. The adjacent bar and restaurant offers a wide and varied menu.

ROOMS: 32 en suite s £50; d £50

STUDLAND, Dorset — Map 05 SZ08

★★68% Manor House

BH19 3AU
☎ 01929 450288 📠 01929 450288
e-mail: themanorhousehotel@lineone.net
web: www.themanorhousehotel.com

Dir: *A338 from Bournemouth, follow signs to Sandbanks/Sandbanks ferry, cross on ferry, then 3m to Studland*

Set in 20 acres of attractive grounds and with delightful views overlooking Studland Bay, this elegant hotel provides an impressive range of facilities. Bedrooms, many with excellent sea views, are all well equipped and many retain charming features of the original Gothic house. In the oak-panelled dining room, carefully prepared meals offer an interesting choice of dishes from the daily-changing menu.

ROOMS: 18 en suite 3 annexe en suite (9 fmly) (4 GF) s £85-£100; d £70-£110 (incl. bkfst & dinner) LB **FACILITIES:** Xmas **PARKING:** 80 **NOTES:** No children 5yrs ⊗ in restaurant Closed 3 wks Jan **CARDS:**

STURMINSTER NEWTON, Dorset — Map 04 ST71

★★★70% @ Plumber Manor

Hazelbury Bryan Rd DT10 2AF
☎ 01258 472507 📠 01258 473370
e-mail: book@plumbermanor.com
web: www.plumbermanor.com

Dir: *Off A357, 1.5m SW towards Hazelbury Bryan. Follow brown tourist signs to Plumber Manor*

This 17th-century manor, set in extensive, lovingly tended grounds, is full of charm and character. Bedrooms, some set apart from the main house, are pleasantly spacious and modern in style. The public areas retain much of the style of the manor and guests can relax in the bar or lounge, or stroll in the grounds. Using fresh local produce, the restaurant is very much the focus of the hotel.

ROOMS: 6 en suite 10 annexe en suite ⊗ in all bedrooms s £90-£100; d fr £125 (incl. bkfst) LB **FACILITIES:** **CONF:** Thtr 25 Board 16 Del from £145 **PARKING:** 30 **NOTES:** ⊗ in restaurant Closed Feb **CARDS:**

SUDBURY, Derbyshire — Map 10 SK13

★★★69% *The Boars Head*

Lichfield Rd DE6 5GX
☎ 01283 820344 📠 01283 820075
e-mail: enquiries@boars-head-hotel.co.uk
web: www.boars-head-hotel.co.uk

Dir: *off A50 onto A515 towards Lichfield, hotel 1m on right*

This busy hotel offers comfortable accommodation in well-equipped bedrooms. There is a relaxed atmosphere in the

continued

public rooms, which offer a choice of bars and dining options. The refurbished beamed lounge bar provides informal dining while the restaurant and cocktail bar offer a more formal environment.
ROOMS: 22 en suite 1 annexe en suite (1 fmly) **FACILITIES:** STV **CONF:** Thtr 25 Class 16 Board 16 **PARKING:** 85 **NOTES:** ⊗ in restaurant **CARDS:**

See advert under BURTON-UPON-TRENT

SUDBURY, Suffolk — Map 13 TL84

★★★69% Mill
Walnut Tree Ln CO10 1BD
☎ 01787 375544 Fax 01787 373027
e-mail: reservations@millhotelsuffolk.fsnet.co.uk
Dir: *from Colchester take A134 to Sudbury, follow signs for Chelmsford, after town square take 2nd right*
Impressive building situated on the banks of the River Stour, overlooking open pastures on the edge of town. The hotel has its own mill pond and retains many charming features such as open fires, exposed beams and a working waterwheel. Bedrooms vary in size and style; each one is thoughtfully equipped and pleasantly furnished.
ROOMS: 52 en suite (2 fmly) (9 GF) ⊗ in 45 bedrooms s £59-£89; d £89-£129 **LB** **FACILITIES:** Xmas **CONF:** Thtr 70 Class 35 Board 35 Del £85 **PARKING:** 60 **NOTES:** ⊗ in restaurant
CARDS:

SUNDERLAND, Tyne & Wear — Map 19 NZ35

★★★★67% Sunderland Marriott
Queen's Pde, Seaburn SR6 8DB
☎ 0191 529 2041 Fax 0191 529 4227
e-mail: sunderland.marriott@whitbread.com
Dir: *A19, A184 (Boldon/Sunderland North), continue for 3m. At rdbt turn left, then right. At rdbt turn left, follow road to coast. Turn right, hotel on right*
Comfortable and spacious accommodation, some with fabulous views of the North Sea and vast expanses of sandy beach, is provided in this seafront hotel. Public rooms are bright and modern and a number of meeting rooms are available. The hotel is conveniently located for access to many visitor attractions.
ROOMS: 82 en suite (16 fmly) (4 GF) ⊗ in 55 bedrooms s £145; d £78-£145 (incl. bkfst) **LB** **FACILITIES:** STV supervised Sauna Solarium Gym Jacuzzi Xmas **CONF:** Thtr 300 Class 100 Board 70 Del from £125 **SERVICES:** Lift **PARKING:** 120 **NOTES:** ⊗ in restaurant Civ Wed **CARDS:**

★★★68% Quality Hotel Sunderland

Witney Way, Boldon NE35 9PE
☎ 0191 519 1999 Fax 0191 519 0655
e-mail: enquiries@hotels-sunderland.com
Dir: *From the Tyne Tunnel (A19) 2.5 miles south, take first exit to roundabout with A184*
This modern, purpose-built hotel is within easy reach of major business and tourism amenities and is well suited to the needs of both business and leisure travellers. The bedrooms are spacious and well equipped. Public areas include a leisure centre, a variety of meeting rooms and a spacious bar and restaurant.
ROOMS: 82 en suite (10 fmly) (41 GF) ⊗ in 42 bedrooms s £89-£99; d £99-£110 **LB** **FACILITIES:** STV supervised Sauna Solarium Gym Jacuzzi ch fac Xmas **CONF:** Thtr 230 Class 100 Board 75 Del from £99 **PARKING:** 150 **NOTES:** Civ Wed 200
CARDS:

Premier Lodge (Sunderland)
Timber Beach Rd, Off Wessington Way, Castletown SR5 3XG
☎ 0870 9906514 Fax 0870 9906515
web: www.premierlodge.com
Dir: *A1 junct 64 onto A1231 towards Sunderland, lodge on last rdbt on right*
High quality, modern, budget accommodation, ideal for families and business travellers. All rooms feature bath, power shower and satellite TV, and most have telephones / modem points. The adjacent bar and restaurant offers a wide and varied menu.
ROOMS: 63 en suite s £50; d £50 **CONF:** Thtr 12 Class 12 Board 12

Travel Inn
Wessington Way, Castletown SR5 3HR
☎ 08701 977245 Fax 0191 548 4044
Dir: *from A19 take A1231 towards Sunderland, Travel Inn 100yds from junction*
Travel Inn offers good-quality, value-for-money accommodation. Spacious, en suite rooms with bath and shower comfortably accommodate a family of up to two adults and two children (to age 15). The restaurant and bar offers a varied menu. For further details consult the Hotel Groups page.
ROOMS: 41 en suite s £45.95-£46.95; d £45.95-£46.95
CONF: Thtr 15 Board 10

Travelodge
Low Row SR1 3PT
☎ 08700 850 950 Fax 0191 514 3453
Travelodge offers good quality, good value, modern accommodation. Ideal for families, the spacious, en suite bedrooms include remote-control TV, tea and coffee-making facilities and luxury beds. Meals can be taken at the nearby family restaurant. For further details consult the Hotel Groups page.
ROOMS: 60 en suite s fr £25; d fr £25

SUTTON, Greater London — Map 06 TQ26

★★63% *Thatched House*
135 Cheam Rd SM1 2BN
☎ 020 8642 3131 Fax 020 8770 0684
e-mail: thatchedcottage@btconnect.com
Dir: *M25 junct 8, follow A217 towards London. Turn right onto A232, hotel 0.25m on right*
This family-run hotel is on a leafy road between Croydon and Epsom, within easy reach of the M25. Bedrooms are neatly presented with a good range of facilities, some of which overlook the attractive garden. Public areas include a cosy bar and a restaurant serving a good selection of dishes.
ROOMS: 32 rms (29 en suite) **CONF:** Thtr 50 Class 30 Board 26
PARKING: 25 **NOTES:** ⊗ in restaurant
CARDS:

SUTTON COLDFIELD, West Midlands — Map 10 SP19

★★★★74% *De Vere Belfry*
B76 9PR
☎ 01675 470301 Fax 01675 470178
e-mail: enquiries@thebelfry.com
(For full entry see Wishaw)

Entertainment

S

SUTTON COLDFIELD, continued

★★★★68% Moor Hall

Moor Hall Dr, Four Oaks B75 6LN
☎ 0121 308 3751 📠 0121 308 8974
e-mail: mail@moorhallhotel.co.uk
web: www.moorhallhotel.co.uk
Dir: *at junct of A38/A453 take A453 towards Sutton Coldfield, at traffic lights turn right into Weeford Rd, Moor Hall drive is 150yds on left*

Although only a short distance from the city centre this hotel enjoys a peaceful setting, overlooking extensive grounds and the adjacent golf course. Bedrooms are well equipped and executive rooms are particularly spacious. Public rooms include the formal Oak Room Restaurant, and the informal Country Kitchen, which offers carvery and blackboard specials.
ROOMS: 82 en suite (8 fmly) (9 GF) ⊗ in 53 bedrooms s £64-£120; d £84-£140 (incl. bkfst) **LB** **FACILITIES: Spa** STV Sauna Gym Jacuzzi Steam room, 3 Spa treatment rooms **CONF:** Thtr 250 Class 120 Board 45 Del £149 **SERVICES:** Lift **PARKING:** 170 **NOTES:** Civ Wed 180 **CARDS:**

See advert under BIRMINGHAM

Innkeeper's Lodge Birmingham East

Chester Rd, Streetley B73 6SP
☎ 0121 353 7785 📠 0121 352 1443
www.innkeeperslodge.com
Dir: *M6 junct 7 to A34 S & turn left onto A4041. At 4th rdbt turn right onto A452-Chester Road, lodge less 1m on right.*
Smart rooms meet essential business requirements but also have home comforts, and depending on location may well have meeting rooms and pub dining. Dining options generally include all-day menus plus the added advantage of breakfast.
ROOMS: 7 en suite 59 annexe en suite s £42-£49.95; d £42-£49.95
CONF: Thtr 40 Board 20

S

Innkeeper's Lodge Birmingham South

2225 Coventry Rd, Sheldon B26 3EH
☎ 0121 742 6201 📠 0121 722 2703
www.innkeeperslodge.com
Dir: *M42 junct 6/A45 towards Birmingham for 2m. Lodge on left approaching overhead traffic lights*
Smart rooms meet essential business requirements but also have home comforts, and depending on location may well have meeting rooms and pub dining. Dining options generally include all-day menus plus the added advantage of breakfast.
ROOMS: 85 en suite s £45-£59.95; d £45-£59.95

TV dinner?
Room service at three stars and above

Premier Lodge (Birmingham North)

Whitehouse Common Rd B75 6HD
☎ 0870 9906320 📠 0870 9906321
web: www.premierlodge.com
Dir: *M42 junct 9, follow A446 towards Lichfield, then A453 to Sutton Coldfield, and turn left into Whitehouse Common Rd for the hotel on left*
High quality, modern, budget accommodation, ideal for families and business travellers. All rooms feature bath, power shower and satellite TV, and most have telephones / modem points. The adjacent bar and restaurant offers a wide and varied menu.
ROOMS: 42 en suite s £50; d £50 **CONF:** Board 10

Travelodge

Boldmere Rd B73 5UP
☎ 08700 850 950 📠 0121 355 0017
Dir: *2m S, on B4142*
Travelodge offers good quality, good value, modern accommodation. Ideal for families, the spacious, en suite bedrooms include remote-control TV, tea and coffee-making facilities and luxury beds. Meals can be taken at the nearby family restaurant. For further details consult the Hotel Groups page.
ROOMS: 32 en suite s fr £25; d fr £25

SUTTON ON SEA, Lincolnshire — Map 17 TF58

★★★69% Grange & Links

Sea Ln, Sandilands LN12 2RA
☎ 01507 441334 📠 01507 443033
e-mail: grangelinks@ic24.net
Dir: *A1111 to Sutton-on-Sea, follow signs to Sandilands*
This friendly, family-run hotel sits in five acres of grounds with an 18-hole links golf course and close to the beach. Bedrooms are pleasantly appointed and are well equipped for both business and leisure guests. Public rooms include ample lounge areas, a formal restaurant and a traditional bar, serving a wide range of meals and snacks.
ROOMS: 23 en suite (10 fmly) (3 GF) ⊗ in 3 bedrooms s fr £78; d fr £85 (incl. bkfst) **LB** **FACILITIES:** 18 Snooker Gym Putt green Bowls Xmas **CONF:** Thtr 200 Board 100 Del from £75
PARKING: 60 **NOTES:** Civ Wed 150
CARDS:

SUTTON SCOTNEY, Hampshire — Map 05 SU43

Travelodge Winchester

SO21 3JY
☎ 08700 850 950 📠 01962 761096
Dir: *on A34 northbound*
Travelodge offers good quality, good value, modern accommodation. Ideal for families, the spacious, en suite bedrooms include remote-control TV, tea and coffee-making facilities and luxury beds. Meals can be taken at the nearby family restaurant. For further details consult the Hotel Groups page.
ROOMS: 30 en suite s fr £25; d fr £25

Travelodge Winchester

SO21 3JY
☎ 08700 850 950 📠 01962 761096
Dir: *on A34 southbound*
Travelodge offers good quality, good value, modern accommodation. Ideal for families, the spacious, en suite bedrooms include remote-control TV, tea and coffee-making facilities and luxury beds. Meals can be taken at the nearby family restaurant. For further details consult the Hotel Groups page.
ROOMS: 40 en suite s fr £25; d fr £25

SUTTON UPON DERWENT, East Riding of Yorkshire — Map 17 SE74

★★65% Old Rectory
Sandhill Ln YO41 4BX
☎ 01904 608548 Fax 01904 608548
web: www.oldrectoryhotel.freeserve.co.uk
Dir: *off A1079 at Grimston Bar rdbt onto B1228 for Howden, through Elvington to Sutton-upon-Derwent, hotel on left opposite tennis courts*
Dating from 1854, this large country rectory on the outskirts of York stands in the village centre overlooking the Derwent Valley. The hotel is handy for the Retail Outlet, the Yorkshire Air Museum and the city. Bedrooms and public areas are spacious and comfortable, and home cooking is a speciality in the dining room.
ROOMS: 6 rms (5 en suite) (2 fmly) s £35-£40; d £52-£56 (incl. bkfst) **LB PARKING:** 30 **NOTES:** ⊗ in restaurant Closed 2 wks Xmas
CARDS:

SWAFFHAM, Norfolk — Map 13 TF80

★★★67% George
Station Rd PE37 7LJ
☎ 01760 721238 Fax 01760 725333
e-mail: georgehotel@bestwestern.co.uk
Dir: *off A47 signed Swaffham, hotel opposite church of St Peter & St Paul*
Georgian hotel situated in the heart of this bustling market town, which is ideally placed for touring north Norfolk. Bedrooms vary in size and style; each one is pleasantly decorated and well equipped. Public rooms include a cosy restaurant, a lounge and a busy bar where a range of drinks and snacks is available.
ROOMS: 29 en suite (1 fmly) **FACILITIES:** STV **CONF:** Thtr 150 Class 70 Board 70 Del from £95 **PARKING:** 100 **NOTES:** ⊗ in restaurant
CARDS:

SWALLOWFIELD, Berkshire — Map 05 SU76

★★67% *The Mill House*

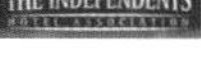

Old Basingstoke Rd, Swallowfield RG7 1PY
☎ 0118 988 3124 Fax 0118 988 5550
e-mail: info@themillhousehotel.co.uk
Dir: *M4 junct 11, S on A33, left at 1st rdbt onto B3349. Approx 1m after sign for Three Mile Cross & Spencer's Wood, hotel on right*
This smart Georgian house hotel enjoys a tranquil setting in its own delightful gardens, making it a popular wedding venue. Guests can enjoy fine dining in the conservatory-style restaurant or lighter meals in the cosy bar. Well-equipped bedrooms vary in size and style and include a number of spacious, well-appointed executive rooms.
ROOMS: 12 en suite (2 fmly) ⊗ in 2 bedrooms **FACILITIES:** **CONF:** Thtr 250 Class 100 Board 60 **PARKING:** 60 **NOTES:** ⊗ in restaurant Closed 24 Dec-4 Jan RS Sun evenings Civ Wed 125
CARDS:

SWANAGE, Dorset — Map 05 SZ07

★★★68% Purbeck House
91 High St BH19 2LZ
☎ 01929 422872 Fax 01929 421194
e-mail: purbeckhouse@easynet.co.uk
web: www.purbeckhousehotel.co.uk
Dir: *A351 to Swanage via Wareham, right into Shore Road, on into Institute Road, right into High Street*
Located close to the town centre, this former convent is set in well-tended grounds. The attractive bedrooms are located in the original building and also in a new annexe. In addition to a very pleasant and spacious conservatory, the smartly presented public areas have some stunning features, such as painted ceilings, wood panelling and fine tiled floors.
ROOMS: 18 en suite 20 annexe en suite (5 fmly) (10 GF) ⊗ in 10 bedrooms s £49-£68; d £98-£124 (incl. bkfst) **LB FACILITIES:** STV Xmas **CONF:** Thtr 100 Class 36 Board 25 **PARKING:** 50 **NOTES:** ⊗ in restaurant Civ Wed 100 **CARDS:**

See advert on this page

★★★67% Grand
Burlington Rd BH19 1LU
☎ 01929 423353 Fax 01929 427068
e-mail: reservations@grandhotelswanage.com
web: www.grandhotelswanage.co.uk
Dir: *via Sandbanks Toll Ferry from Bournemouth, follow signs to Swanage, at 2nd town centre sign 4th left into Burlington Rd*

Dating back to 1898, the Grand Hotel is located on the Isle of Purbeck and has spectacular views across Swanage Bay and

continued on p564

S

SWANAGE, continued

Peveril Point. Bedrooms are individually decorated and well equipped; public rooms offer a number of choices from relaxing lounges to extensive leisure facilities. The hotel also has its own private beach.
ROOMS: 30 en suite (2 fmly) in 8 bedrooms s £66-£78; d £132-£156 (incl. bkfst & dinner) **LB** **FACILITIES:** STV Fishing Sauna Solarium Gym Jacuzzi Table tennis Xmas **CONF:** Thtr 120 Class 40 Board 40 **SERVICES:** Lift **PARKING:** 15 **NOTES:** in restaurant Closed 10 days in Jan (dates on application) Civ Wed **CARDS:**

See advert on opposite page

★★★67% The Pines
Burlington Rd BH19 1LT
☎ 01929 425211 01929 422075
e-mail: reservations@pineshotel.co.uk
web: www.pineshotel.co.uk
Dir: *A351 to seafront, left then 2nd right. Hotel at end of road*

Enjoying a peaceful location with spectacular views over the cliffs and sea, The Pines is a pleasant place to stay. Bedrooms, many with sea views, are comfortable and some have now been refurbished. Guests can take tea in the lounge, enjoy appetising bar snacks in the attractive bar and interesting and accomplished cuisine in the restaurant.
ROOMS: 49 en suite (26 fmly) (6 GF) s £54.50-£72.50; d £109-£157 (incl. bkfst) **LB** **FACILITIES:** ch fac Xmas **CONF:** Thtr 80 Class 80 Board 80 Del from £82 **SERVICES:** Lift **PARKING:** 60 **NOTES:** in restaurant **CARDS:**

See advert on opposite page

SWANWICK See Alfreton

SWAVESEY, Cambridgeshire — Map 12 TL36

Travelodge Cambridge (West)
Cambridge Rd CB4 5QR
☎ 08700 850 950 01954 789113
Dir: *on eastbound carriageway of A14*

Travelodge

Travelodge offers good quality, good value, modern accommodation. Ideal for families, the spacious, en suite bedrooms include remote-control TV, tea and coffee-making facilities and luxury beds. Meals can be taken at the nearby family restaurant. For further details consult the Hotel Groups page.
ROOMS: 36 en suite s fr £25; d fr £25

Indoor Swimming Pool
Indoor Swimming Pool (heated)
Outdoor Swimming Pool
Outdoor Swimming Pool (heated)

SWAY, Hampshire — Map 05 SZ29

★★★68% String of Horses
Mead End Rd SO41 6EH
☎ 01590 682631 01590 682911
e-mail: relax@stringofhorses.co.uk
Dir: *M27 to A31, left at Burley, follow signs to Lymington & Sway, right over cattlegrid, 3rd right into Mead End Rd, hotel 350yds*
Having only eight rooms and tucked away from the main thoroughfares, the hotel has an exclusive feel to it. The majority of the well-presented bedrooms are equipped with large spa baths, and all feature thoughtful extras such as dressing gowns. There is a welcoming bar, separate breakfast room and comfortable lounge overlooking the pool and garden.
ROOMS: 8 en suite (6 GF) in all bedrooms s fr £77; d £114-£134 (incl. bkfst) **LB** **FACILITIES: Spa** STV Sauna Jacuzzi Health suite, steam room Xmas **CONF:** Thtr 40 Board 30 **PARKING:** 32 **NOTES:** No children 16yrs in restaurant Closed 1-27 Jan 2005 **CARDS:**

★★68% Sway Manor Restaurant & Hotel
Station Rd SO41 6BA
☎ 01590 682754 01590 682955
e-mail: info@swaymanor.com
web: www.swaymanor.com
Dir: *turn off B3055 Brockenhurst/New Milton road into Sway village centre*
Built at the turn of the 20th century, this attractive mansion is set in it own grounds, with an outdoor swimming pool, and is also conveniently located in the centre of the village. Bedrooms are well appointed and generously equipped whilst the bar and restaurant, which both have views over the gardens, are popular with locals.
ROOMS: 15 en suite (3 fmly) in 12 bedrooms s £43-£51; d £70-£102 (incl. bkfst) **LB** **FACILITIES:** Xmas **SERVICES:** Lift **PARKING:** 40 **NOTES:** in restaurant Civ Wed 50 **CARDS:**

SWINDON, Wiltshire — Map 05 SU18
See also Wootton Bassett

★★★★74% De Vere Swindon
Shaw Ridge Leisure Park, Whitehill Way SN5 7DW
☎ 01793 878785 01793 877822
e-mail: dvs.sales@devere-hotels.com
Dir: *M4 junct 16, signs for Swindon off 1st rdbt, 2nd rdbt follow signs for Link Centre over next 2 rdbts, 2nd left at 3rd rdbt, left onto slip road*

DE VERE HOTELS

This stylish, modern hotel is located close to the motorway network and the local business district. Day rooms are extensive and include a smart fitness centre, conference facilities and a popular restaurant. Bedrooms are very well equipped and come in a variety of sizes and styles. Staff throughout are friendly and willing to please.
ROOMS: 158 en suite (12 fmly) in 119 bedrooms s £125; d £125 **LB** **FACILITIES:** STV Sauna Solarium Gym Jacuzzi Health & beauty treatment rooms Xmas **CONF:** BC Thtr 300 Class 160 Board 80 Del from £120 **SERVICES:** Lift **PARKING:** 170 **NOTES:** in restaurant Civ Wed 300 **CARDS:**

★★★★71%
Blunsdon House Hotel & Leisure Club
Blunsdon SN26 7AS
☎ 01793 721701 01793 721056
e-mail: info@blunsdonhouse.co.uk
web: www.blunsdonhouse.co.uk
Dir: *200yds off A419 at Swindon, 1m N of Swindon*

Best Western

Located just to the north of Swindon, Blunsdon House is set in 30

continued on p566

Seaside paradise – fantastic coastal scenery and unspoilt countryside makes this an ideal choice for beach lovers, walkers and connoisseurs of fine scenery and places of historical interest.

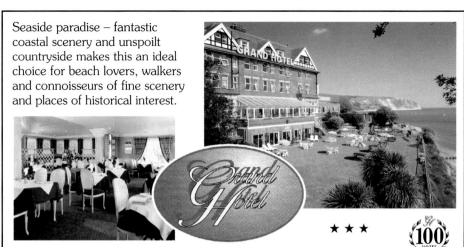

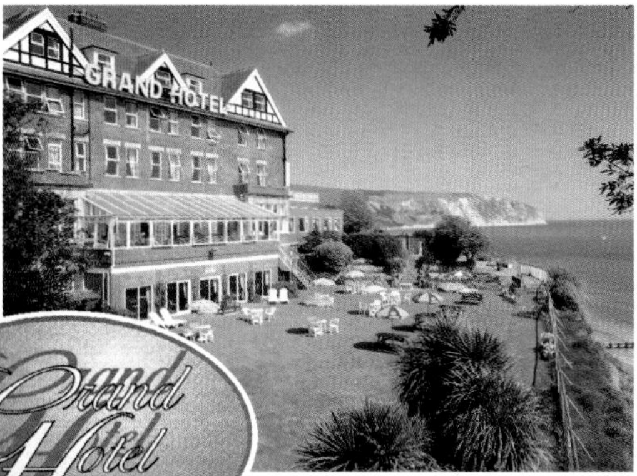

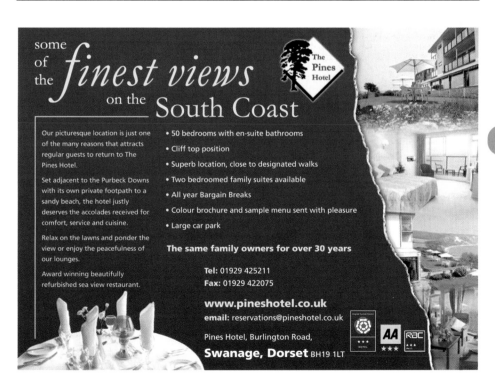

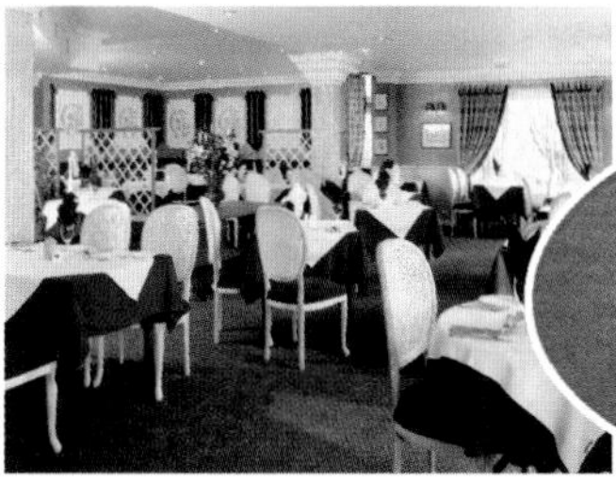

Grand Hotel

★ ★ ★

100 years of hospitality 1898 1998

The spacious lounges, bar and restaurant combine the best traditions of hospitality, comfort • A passenger lift serves all floors and steps lead down to the beach • Full leisure facilities including a heated plunge pool and spa bath.

View virtual tour on web site: **www.grandhotelswanage.co.uk · Tel: 01929 423353**

Fax: 01929 427068 · Email:reservations@grandhotelswanage.co.uk

SWANAGE · DORSET · BH19 1LU

some of the *finest views* on the South Coast

The Pines Hotel

Our picturesque location is just one of the many reasons that attracts regular guests to return to The Pines Hotel.

Set adjacent to the Purbeck Downs with its own private footpath to a sandy beach, the hotel justly deserves the accolades received for comfort, service and cuisine.

Relax on the lawns and ponder the view or enjoy the peacefulness of our lounges.

Award winning beautifully refurbished sea view restaurant.

- 50 bedrooms with en-suite bathrooms
- Cliff top position
- Superb location, close to designated walks
- Two bedroomed family suites available
- All year Bargain Breaks
- Colour brochure and sample menu sent with pleasure
- Large car park

The same family owners for over 30 years

Tel: 01929 425211
Fax: 01929 422075

www.pineshotel.co.uk
email: reservations@pineshotel.co.uk

Pines Hotel, Burlington Road,
Swanage, Dorset BH19 1LT

AA ★★★ RAC ★★★

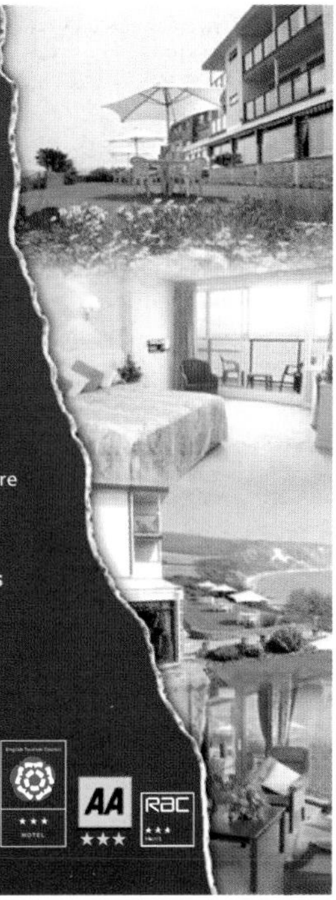

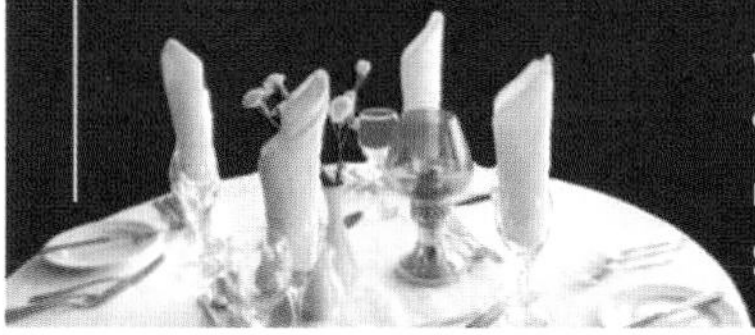

SWINDON, continued

acres of well-kept grounds and offers extensive leisure facilities and spacious day rooms. The hotel has a choice of eating and drinking options; there are three bars and two restaurants. Bedrooms are comfortably furnished, and the contemporary Pavilion rooms are especially spacious.

Blunsdon House Hotel & Leisure Club, Swindon

ROOMS: 118 en suite (14 fmly) (27 GF) ⊗ in 75 bedrooms **FACILITIES:** STV ⛆ ⛳ 9 Squash Sauna Solarium Gym Putt green Jacuzzi Beauty therapy, Woodland walk, 9 hole par 3 golf course ch fac Xmas **CONF:** Thtr 300 Class 200 Board 40 **SERVICES:** Lift **PARKING:** 300 **NOTES:** ⊗ in restaurant Civ Wed 200 **CARDS:**

★★★★64% Swindon Marriott Hotel

Pipers Way SN3 1SH
☎ 0870 400 7281 📠 0870 400 7381
Dir: *M4 junct 15, follow A419, then A4259 to Coate rdbt and B4006 signed 'Old Town'*

With convenient access to the motorway, this hotel is an easily accessible venue for meetings, and an ideal base from which to explore Wiltshire and the Cotswolds. The hotel offers a good range of public rooms, including a well-equipped leisure centre, Chats café bar and the informal, brasserie-style Mediterrano restaurant.
ROOMS: 156 en suite (42 fmly) ⊗ in 137 bedrooms s £50-£170; d £60-£170 **LB** **FACILITIES: Spa** STV ⛆ supervised Sauna Solarium Gym Jacuzzi Steam Room, Health & Beauty, Hair salon, Sports massage therapy **CONF:** Thtr 280 Class 100 Board 40 Del from £125 **SERVICES:** Lift air con **PARKING:** 185 **NOTES:** ⊗ in restaurant Civ Wed 280 **CARDS:**

★★★78% The Pear Tree at Purton

Church End SN5 4ED
☎ 01793 772100 📠 01793 772369
e-mail: stay@peartreepurton.co.uk
(For full entry see Purton)

★★★71% Marsh Farm

Coped Hall SN4 8ER
☎ 01793 848044 📠 01793 851528
e-mail: marshfarmhotel@btconnect.com
web: www.marshfarmhotel.co.uk
Dir: *from M4 take A3102, straight on at 1st rdbt, at next rdbt (with garage on left) turn right. Hotel 200yds on left*

Originally a Victorian farmhouse, this hotel combines character and elegance with modern facilities. Bedrooms, including superior rooms, are decorated to a high standard; some are self-contained in cottages adjacent to the main building. An enjoyable and varied selection of dishes is available at dinner, offered in the new conservatory dining room.
ROOMS: 11 en suite 39 annexe en suite (1 fmly) ⊗ in 23 bedrooms s £55-£110; d £70-£150 (incl. bkfst) **LB** **FACILITIES:** STV Putt green Clay pigeon shooting nearby **CONF:** Thtr 120 Class 60 Board 50 Del from £120 **PARKING:** 150 **NOTES:** ⊗ in restaurant RS 26-30 Dec Civ Wed 100 **CARDS:**

See advert on opposite page

★★★69% Chiseldon House

New Rd, Chiseldon SN4 0NE
☎ 01793 741010 📠 01793 741059
e-mail: chishoho@hotmail.com
web: www.chiseldonhousehotel.co.uk
Dir: *M4 junct 15, onto A346 signposted Marlborough, at brow of hill turn right by Esso garage onto B4005 into New Rd, hotel 200yds on right*

Chiseldon is a traditional country house near Swindon that is ideal for a peaceful and comfortable stay. Quiet and spacious bedrooms are tastefully decorated and include a number of thoughtful extras. A varied selection of tempting dishes is offered at dinner. Guests may also enjoy the comfortable lounge and well-kept gardens.
ROOMS: 21 en suite (4 fmly) ⊗ in 7 bedrooms s £85-£105; d £105-£125 (incl. bkfst) **FACILITIES:** STV ch fac **CONF:** Thtr 50 Class 30 Board 20 Del from £120 **PARKING:** 40 **NOTES:** Civ Wed 85 **CARDS:**

★★★69% Stanton House

The Avenue, Stanton Fitzwarren SN6 7SD
☎ 01793 861777 📠 01793 861857
e-mail: info@stantonhouse.co.uk
Dir: *off A419 onto A361 towards Highworth, pass Honda factory and turn left towards Stanton Fitzwarren about 600yds past business park, hotel on left*

Extensive grounds and superb gardens surround this Cotswold-stone manor house. Smart, well-maintained bedrooms have been equipped with modern comforts. Public areas include a games room, a lounge, a bar, conference facilities and an informal restaurant specialising in Japanese cuisine. Multi-lingual staff are friendly and a relaxed atmosphere prevails.
ROOMS: 86 en suite (31 GF) ⊗ in 35 bedrooms **FACILITIES:** STV Mah Jong Xmas **CONF:** Thtr 110 Class 70 Board 40 Del from £95 **SERVICES:** Lift **PARKING:** 110 **NOTES:** ⊗ in restaurant Civ Wed 110 **CARDS:**

See advert on opposite page

★★★66% Goddard Arms

Forestdale Hotels

High St, Old Town SN1 3EG
☎ 01793 692313 📠 01793 512984
e-mail: goddard.arms@forestdale.com
Dir: *M4 junct 15, take A4259 towards Swindon, onto B4006 to Old Town follow signs for PM Hospital. Hotel in High St opposite Wood St next to Lloyds Bank*

Situated in the attractive Old Town area, this ivy-clad coaching inn

continued

offers bedrooms in either the main building or in a modern annexe to the rear of the property. Public areas are tastefully decorated in a traditional style; there is a lounge, Vaults bar and a popular restaurant. The conference rooms are extensive and the car park secure.
ROOMS: 18 en suite 47 annexe en suite (3 fmly) (24 GF) ⊗ in 33 bedrooms s fr £95; d fr £120 (incl. bkfst) **LB** **FACILITIES:** STV **CONF:** Thtr 180 Class 100 Board 40 Del from £125 **PARKING:** 90 **NOTES:** ⊗ in restaurant Civ Wed 180
CARDS:

★★★65% **Corus hotel Swindon**
Oxford Rd, Stratton St Margaret SN3 4TL
☎ 0870 609 6150 01793 831401
e-mail: reservations.madisoninn@corushotels.com
Dir: *M4 junct 15, A419 to Cirencester. Over rdbt, then exit left (signed Oxford A420). Right at next 2 rdbts, hotel on left*

Conveniently located just off the M4, the hotel is ideal for touring

continued on p568

SWINDON, continued

the area. Bedrooms are large and well appointed, rooms to the rear being quieter. Facilities include four versatile conference rooms and the 'Olio' bar and restaurant.
ROOMS: 94 en suite (3 fmly) (45 GF) ⊗ in 73 bedrooms s £79; d £79 **LB FACILITIES:** STV Free use of nearby gym, pool and beauty parlour Xmas **CONF:** Thtr 100 Class 50 Board 40 Del from £112 **PARKING:** 150 **NOTES:** ⊗ in restaurant Civ Wed 70
CARDS:

★★★60% Villiers Inn

Moormead Rd, Wroughton SN4 9BY
☎ 01793 814744 01793 814119
e-mail: hotels@villiersinn.co.uk
Dir: *1m S of Swindon, on A4361, hotel 100mtrs on right*

Conveniently situated with easy access to the motorway and Swindon, this attractive period property provides well-equipped accommodation in the main building and in a purpose built extension. Public areas include a comfortable library lounge and a spacious bar. An interesting range of dishes is offered in the restaurant. Function facilities are also available.
ROOMS: 33 en suite ⊗ in 10 bedrooms s £55-£85; d £69-£99 (incl. bkfst) **LB FACILITIES:** STV ch fac Xmas **CONF:** Thtr 60 Class 30 Board 32 Del £125 **PARKING:** 60 **NOTES:** Civ Wed 120
CARDS:

See advert on opposite page

★★68% The School House

Hook St, Hook, Wootton Bassett SN4 8EF
☎ 01793 851198 01793 851025
e-mail: reservations@schoolhotel.com
web: www.schoolhotel.com
Dir: *from M4 junct 16 take exit for Swindon, follow signs for Hook. At 1st rbdt turn left, next rbdt turn left, 2-3m. Hotel at end of road on left*

This old school has been converted into a hotel full of character with an informal restaurant. A new extension provides ten spacious bedrooms, tastefully furnished and equipped with modern facilities, and many thoughtful extras. The restaurant is comfortable, and a good choice of dishes is offered on the well-balanced menu.
ROOMS: 10 en suite (5 GF) s £55-£99; d £55-£99 (incl. bkfst) **LB FACILITIES:** STV **CONF:** Thtr 60 Class 30 Board 30 Del from £99 **PARKING:** 30 **NOTES:** ⊗ in restaurant
CARDS:

See advert on opposite page

⌂ Hotel Ibis Swindon

Delta Business Park, Great Western Way SN5 7XG
☎ 01793 514777 01793 514570
e-mail: H1041@accor-hotels.com
Dir: *A3102 to Swindon, on at rdbt, slip road onto Business Park, turn left*
Modern, budget hotel offering comfortable accommodation in bright and practical bedrooms. Breakfast is self-service and dinner is available in the restaurant. For further details, consult the Hotel Groups page.
ROOMS: 120 en suite s £32-£44; d £32-£44 **CONF:** Thtr 80 Class 40 Board 40

⌂ Premier Lodge (Swindon)

Ermin St, Blunsdon SN26 8DJ
☎ 0870 9906356 0870 9906357
web: www.premierlodge.com
Dir: *N of Swindon, 5m M4 junct 15 on M4 at junct of A419 & B4019*
High quality, modern, budget accommodation, ideal for families and business travellers. All rooms feature bath, power shower and satellite TV, and most have telephones / modem points. The adjacent bar and restaurant offers a wide and varied menu.
ROOMS: 60 en suite s £50; d £50

⌂ Travel Inn

Lydiard Way, Great Western Way SN5 8UY
☎ 08701 977247 01793 886890
Dir: *M4 junct 16, 3m SW of Swindon, take left lane towards Swindon, A3102*
Travel Inn offers good-quality, value-for-money accommodation. Spacious, en suite rooms with bath and shower comfortably accommodate a family of up to two adults and two children (to age 15). The restaurant and bar offers a varied menu. For further details consult the Hotel Groups page.
ROOMS: 63 en suite s £45.95-£46.95; d £45.95-£46.95

⌂ Travel Inn Swindon (North)

Kembrey Business Park, Cricklade Rd
☎ 08701 977194 08701 977706
Dir: *M4 junct 15 follow A419 Swindon bypass towards Cheltenham. After 4m (Motorola Roundabout) take A4311 towards town. The Travel Inn is on left after 2m*
Travel Inn offers good-quality, value-for-money accommodation. Spacious, en suite rooms with bath and shower comfortably accommodate a family of up to two adults and two children (to age 15). The restaurant and bar offers a varied menu. For further details consult the Hotel Groups page.
ROOMS: 50 en suite s £45.95-£46.95; d £45.95-£46.95

SWINTON, Greater Manchester Map 15 SD70

Premier Lodge (Manchester West)

East Lancs Rd M27 0AA

0870 9906480 0870 9906481
web: www.premierlodge.com
Dir: *10 mins from Manchester city centre, off M60 junct 13 (Swinton/Leigh) on A580*

High quality, modern, budget accommodation, ideal for families and business travellers. All rooms feature bath, power shower and satellite TV, and most have telephones / modem points. The adjacent bar and restaurant offers a wide and varied menu.
ROOMS: 27 en suite s £50; d £50 **CONF:** Thtr 12 Board 12

TADCASTER, North Yorkshire Map 16 SE44

★★★80% Hazlewood Castle

Paradise Ln, Hazlewood LS24 9NJ
01937 535353 01937 530630
e-mail: info@hazlewood-castle.co.uk
web: www.hazlewood-castle.co.uk
Dir: *signed off A64, W of Tadcaster & before A1/M1 link road*

Mentioned in the Domesday Book, this castle is set in 77 acres of parkland. Hospitality and service are of the highest order and staff are only too happy to assist. Bedrooms, many of them with private sitting rooms, are split between the main house and other buildings in the courtyard. Dinner provides the highlight of any stay with eclectic, creative dishes.
ROOMS: 9 en suite 12 annexe en suite (6 fmly) (6 GF) in all bedrooms s £120-£160; d £140-£300 (incl. bkfst) **LB FACILITIES:** STV Clay pigeon shooting Xmas **CONF:** Thtr 150 Class 60 Board 36 Del £175 **PARKING:** 150 **NOTES:** in restaurant Civ Wed 120
CARDS:

TADWORTH, Surrey Map 06 TQ25

Premier Lodge (Epsom South)

Brighton Rd, Burgh Heath KT20 6BW

0870 9906442 0870 9906443
web: www.premierlodge.com
Dir: *just off junct 8 of M25, on A217 towards Sutton*

High quality, modern, budget accommodation, ideal for families and business travellers. All rooms feature bath, power shower and satellite TV, and most have telephones / modem points. The adjacent bar and restaurant offers a wide and varied menu.
ROOMS: 78 en suite s £58; d £58

TALKE, Staffordshire — Map 15 SJ85

Travelodge Stoke

Newcastle Rd ST7 1UP

☎ 08700 850 950 Fax 01782 777000

Dir: *at junct of A34/A500*

Travelodge offers good quality, good value, modern accommodation. Ideal for families, the spacious, en suite bedrooms include remote-control TV, tea and coffee-making facilities and luxury beds. Meals can be taken at the nearby family restaurant. For further details consult the Hotel Groups page.

ROOMS: 62 en suite s fr £25; d fr £25 **CONF:** Thtr 50 Class 25 Board 32

TAMWORTH, Staffordshire — Map 10 SK20

★★74% Drayton Court Hotel

65 Coleshill St, Fazeley B78 3RG

☎ 01827 285805 Fax 01827 284842

e-mail: draytoncthotel@yahoo.co.uk

web: www.draytoncourthotel.co.uk

Dir: *M42 junct 9 then A446 to Litchfield at next rdbt turn right onto A4091 after 2m Drayton Manor Park on left, hotel further on right*

Conveniently located close to the M42, this lovingly restored hotel has been considerably upgraded. The bedrooms are elegant and have been thoughtfully equipped to suit both business and leisure guests. Beds are particularly comfortable (a hand-made four poster is also available). Public areas include a panelled bar, a relaxing lounge and an attractive restaurant.

ROOMS: 19 en suite (3 fmly) s £60-£105; d £85-£135 (incl. bkfst) **LB** **CONF:** Board 14 **PARKING:** 23 **NOTES:** in restaurant Closed 24-27 Dec **CARDS:**

Travel Inn

Bonehill Rd, Bitterscote B78 3HQ

☎ 08701 977248 Fax 01827 310420

Dir: *M42 junct 10 follow A5 towards Tamworth. After 3m turn left onto A51. Straight over 1st rdbt, 3rd exit off next rdbt*

Travel Inn offers good-quality, value-for-money accommodation. Spacious, en suite rooms with bath and shower comfortably accommodate a family of up to two adults and two children (to age 15). The restaurant and bar offers a varied menu. For further details consult the Hotel Groups page.

ROOMS: 58 en suite s £45.95-£46.95; d £45.95-£46.95 **CONF:** Thtr 50 Board 20

Travelodge

Green Ln B77 5PS

☎ 08700 850 950/0800 850950 Fax 01827 260145

Dir: *A5/M42 junct 10*

Travelodge offers good quality, good value, modern accommodation. Ideal for families, the spacious, en suite

continued

bedrooms include remote-control TV, tea and coffee-making facilities and luxury beds. Meals can be taken at the nearby family restaurant. For further details consult the Hotel Groups page.

ROOMS: 62 en suite s fr £25; d fr £25

TANKERSLEY, South Yorkshire — Map 16 SK39

★★★★71% Tankersley Manor

Church Ln S75 3DQ

☎ 01226 744700 Fax 01226 745405

e-mail: tankersley@marstonhotels.com

Dir: *M1 junct 36 take A61 Sheffield road. Hotel 0.5m on left*

High on the moors with views over the countryside, this 17th-century residence is well located for major cities, tourist attractions and motorway links. Where appropriate, bedrooms retain original features such as exposed beams or Yorkshire stone windowsills. The hotel has its own traditional country pub, complete with old beams and open fires, alongside the more formal restaurant and bar.

ROOMS: 69 en suite (2 fmly) in 63 bedrooms s £110-£131; d £145-£185 (incl. bkfst) **LB** **FACILITIES: Spa** STV Sauna Gym Swimming lessons, beauty treatments Xmas **CONF:** Thtr 400 Class 200 Board 100 Del from £149 **PARKING:** 200 **NOTES:** in restaurant Civ Wed 90 **CARDS:**

Travel Inn (Sheffield Barnsley)

Maple Rd S75 3DL

☎ 08701 977228 Fax 01226 741524

Dir: *M1 junct 35A (northbound exit only) follow A616 for 2m. From junct 36 take A61 towards Sheffield*

Travel Inn offers good-quality, value-for-money accommodation. Spacious, en suite rooms with bath and shower comfortably accommodate a family of up to two adults and two children (to age 15). The restaurant and bar offers a varied menu. For further details consult the Hotel Groups page.

ROOMS: 42 en suite s £45.95-£46.95; d £45.95-£46.95

TAPLOW, Buckinghamshire — Map 06 SU98

Top 200 – Hotel

★★★★★ Cliveden

SL6 0JF

☎ 01628 668561 Fax 01628 661837

e-mail: reservations@clivedenhouse.co.uk

web: www.clivedenhouse.co.uk

Dir: *M4 junct 7, follow A4 towards Maidenhead for 1.5 miles, turn onto B476 towards Taplow, 2.5 miles, hotel on left*

This wonderful stately home stands at the top of a gravelled boulevard. Visitors are treated as house guests and staff recapture the tradition of fine hospitality. Bedrooms have

continued

individual quality and style, and reception rooms retain a timeless elegance. Both restaurants here are awarded AA rosettes – The Terrace with its delightful views has two rosettes, and Waldo's, offering innovative menus in discreet, luxurious surroundings, has three. Exceptional leisure facilities include cruises along Cliveden Reach and massages in the Pavilion.

ROOMS: 39 en suite (8 GF) ⊗ in 12 bedrooms d £225-£950 (incl. bkfst) **LB** **FACILITIES:** STV Squash Snooker Sauna Solarium Gym Jacuzzi Full range of beauty treatments at the Pavilion Spa, 3 vintage launches ♫ Xmas **CONF:** Thtr 40 Board 24 **SERVICES:** Lift **PARKING:** 60 **NOTES:** ⊗ in restaurant Civ Wed **CARDS:**

★★★70% Taplow House Hotel

Berry Hill SL6 0DA
☎ 01628 670056 ⎙ 01628 773625
e-mail: taplow@wrensgroup.com
web: www.taplowhouse.com.
Dir: *off A4 onto Berry Hill, hotel 0.5m on right*

WREN'S HOTELS

This elegant Georgian manor is set amid beautiful gardens and has been skilfully restored. Character public rooms are pleasing and include a number of air-conditioned conference rooms. Comfortable bedrooms are individually decorated and furnished to a high standard.

ROOMS: 32 en suite (4 fmly) ⊗ in all bedrooms **FACILITIES:** STV Putt green ch fac Xmas **CONF:** Thtr 100 Class 45 Board 40 Del from £155 **SERVICES:** air con **PARKING:** 100 **NOTES:** ⊗ in restaurant Civ Wed 80 **CARDS:**

> Packed in a hurry?
> Ironing facilities should be available at all star levels, either in rooms or on request

TARPORLEY, Cheshire

Map 15 SJ56

★★★70% Swan

50 High St CW6 0AG
☎ 01829 733838 ⎙ 01829 732932
Dir: *M56 junct 10, follow A49 signed Whitchurch*

Dating back to the 16th century, the Swan is situated in the heart of the village. Bedrooms, found in the main house and an adjacent converted coaching house, have been refurbished to a high standard. Public areas are full of charm and character and include a restaurant where guests can enjoy excellent cooking.

ROOMS: 10 en suite 6 annexe en suite (3 fmly) ⊗ in all bedrooms **CONF:** Thtr 65 Class 40 Board 25 **PARKING:** 26 **NOTES:** ⊗ in restaurant Closed 25 Dec evening **CARDS:**

★★★68% The Wild Boar

Whitchurch Rd, Beeston CW6 9NW
☎ 01829 260309 ⎙ 01829 261081
e-mail: wildboarpop@hotmail.com
Dir: *turn off A51 Nantwich/Chester road onto A49 to Whitchurch at Red Fox pub lights, hotel on left at brow of hill after about 1.5m*

This 17th-century, half-timbered former hunting lodge has been extended over the years to create a smart, spacious hotel with comfortable bedrooms and stylish public areas. Guests can choose between the elegant Tower Restaurant or the more informal Stables Grill. The hotel is a popular venue for meetings, functions and weddings, and offers impressive conference facilities.

ROOMS: 37 en suite (20 fmly) ⊗ in 23 bedrooms **FACILITIES:** 18 Putt green **CONF:** Thtr 100 Class 40 Board 40 **PARKING:** 70 **NOTES:** ⊗ in restaurant Civ Wed 100 **CARDS:**

★★★67% Willington Hall

Willington CW6 0NB
☎ 01829 752321 ⎙ 01829 752596
e-mail: enquiries@willingtonhall.co.uk
web: www.willingtonhall.co.uk
Dir: *3m NW off unclass road linking A51 & A54, at Clotton turn off A51 at Bulls Head, then follow signs*

Situated in 17 acres of parkland and built in 1829, this attractively furnished country house hotel offers spacious bedrooms, many with views over open countryside. Service is courteous and friendly, and freshly prepared meals are offered in the dining room or adjacent bar and drawing room. A smart new function suite confirms the popularity of this hotel as a premier venue for weddings and conferences.

ROOMS: 10 en suite s fr £70; d £110-£120 (incl. bkfst) **LB** **FACILITIES:** STV Fishing Riding **CONF:** Thtr 160 Class 80 Board 50 Del from £115 **PARKING:** 60 **NOTES:** Closed 25 & 26 Dec Civ Wed 100 **CARDS:**

T

TAUNTON, Somerset Map 04 ST22

Top 200 – Hotel

★★★ Castle
Castle Green TA1 1NF
☎ 01823 272671 01823 336066
e-mail: reception@the-castle-hotel.com
web: www.the-castle-hotel.com
Dir: *from M5 junct 25/26 follow signs to town centre and hotel*
The wisteria covered Castle has been owned and run by the same family for over half a century and, with its distinctive Norman keep, is a landmark in the centre of the town. Much thought has gone into furnishing the bedrooms and public areas, ensuring guest comfort while retaining the character and endearing charm of the original building. Renowned for its interpretation of classic British dishes in the elegant restaurant, this hotel also offers a lively, modern brasserie for less formal dining.
ROOMS: 44 en suite s fr £115; d fr £170 (incl. bkfst) **LB** **FACILITIES:** Xmas **CONF:** Thtr 100 Class 40 Board 40 Del from £155 **SERVICES:** Lift **PARKING:** 50 **NOTES:** in restaurant **CARDS:**

★★★73% The Mount Somerset
Lower Henlade TA3 5NB
☎ 01823 442500 01823 442900
e-mail: Info@mountsomersethotel.co.uk
web: www.mountsomersethotel.co.uk
Dir: *M5 junct 25, take A358 towards Chard/Ilminster, at Henlade right into Stoke Rd, left at T-junct at end Stoke Rd then right into drive*
From its elevated and rural position, this impressive Regency house has wonderful views over Taunton Vale. Some of the well-appointed bedrooms have feature bathrooms, and the elegant public rooms are stylish with an intimate atmosphere. In addition to the daily-changing, fixed-price menu, a carefully selected seasonal carte is available in the restaurant.
ROOMS: 11 en suite (1 fmly) s £95-£160; d £135-£200 (incl. bkfst) **LB** **FACILITIES:** ch fac Xmas **CONF:** Thtr 60 Class 30 Board 20 Del £155 **SERVICES:** Lift **PARKING:** 100 **NOTES:** Civ Wed 60 **CARDS:**

★★★73% Rumwell Manor
Rumwell TA4 1EL
☎ 01823 461902 01823 254861
e-mail: reception@rumwellmanor.co.uk
Dir: *M5 junct 26 follow signs to Wellington, turn right onto A38 to Taunton, hotel is 3m on right*
With easy access to Taunton and the M5, Rumwell Manor is situated in the countryside and surrounded by lovingly tended gardens. A selection of freshly prepared dishes is offered each evening in the candlelit restaurant. Bedrooms vary in size and style, with those in the main house offering greater space and character. In addition to the cosy bar and adjacent lounge, several meeting/conference rooms are available.

ROOMS: 10 en suite 10 annexe en suite (3 fmly) (6 GF) in 6 bedrooms s £68-£78; d £96-£116 **LB** **FACILITIES:** Xmas **CONF:** BC Thtr 40 Class 24 Board 26 Del from £114 **PARKING:** 40 **NOTES:** in restaurant Civ Wed 50 **CARDS:**

★★★71% Corner House Hotel
Park St TA1 4DQ
☎ 01823 284683 01823 323464
e-mail: res@corner-house.co.uk
Dir: *0.3m from centre of Taunton (5 mins walk). Hotel on junct of Park Street & A38 Wellington Road*

The unusual Victorian façade of the Corner House, with its turrets and stained glass windows, belies a wealth of innovation, quality and style. The contemporary bedrooms, newly refitted are equipped with state-of-the-art facilities and offer traditional comforts. Informality and exceptional value-for-money are the hallmark of the smart public areas, which include Bistro 4DQ - a relaxed place to eat good food.
ROOMS: 28 en suite (12 fmly) (1 GF) in 20 bedrooms s £57.50-£67.50; d £57.50-£67.50 **CONF:** Thtr 60 Class 10 Board 35 Del from £99.50 **PARKING:** 40 **NOTES:** **CARDS:**

★★78% Farthings Hotel & Restaurant
Hatch Beauchamp TA3 6SG
☎ 01823 480664 01823 481118
e-mail: farthing1@aol.com
web: www.farthingshotel.com
Dir: *from A358, between Taunton and Ilminster turn into Hatch Beauchamp for hotel in village centre*
This delightful family-run hotel, set in its own extensive gardens in a peaceful village location, offers comfortable accommodation combined with all the character and charm of a building dating

continued

back over 200 years. The atmosphere is relaxed and friendly and innovative menus feature best quality local ingredients.
ROOMS: 10 en suite (2 fmly) (1 GF) ⊘ in all bedrooms s £75-£90; d £105-£135 (incl. bkfst) **LB** **FACILITIES:** Xmas **CONF:** BC Thtr 30 Board 20 Del £130 **PARKING:** 22 **NOTES:** ⊘ in restaurant Civ Wed 50 **CARDS:**

Premier Lodge (Taunton)

Ilminster Rd, Ruishton TA3 5LU
☎ 0870 9906534 📠 0870 9906535
web: www.premierlodge.com
High quality, modern, budget accommodation, ideal for families and business travellers. All rooms feature bath, power shower and satellite TV, and most have telephones / modem points. The adjacent bar and restaurant offers a wide and varied menu.
ROOMS: 38 en suite s £50; d £50

Travel Inn Taunton (East)

81 Bridgwater Rd TA1 2DU
☎ 08701 977249 📠 01823 322054
Dir: *M5 junct 25 follow signs to Taunton over 1st rdbt & keep left at Creech Castle traffic lights, Travel Inn 200yds on right*
Travel Inn offers good-quality, value-for-money accommodation. Spacious, en suite rooms with bath and shower comfortably accommodate a family of up to two adults and two children (to age 15). The restaurant and bar offers a varied menu. For further details consult the Hotel Groups page.
ROOMS: 40 en suite s £45.95-£46.95; d £45.95-£46.95

Travel Inn Taunton (Central)

Massingham Park TA2 7RX
☎ 08701 977 293 📠 01823 422350
Travel Inn offers good-quality, value-for-money accommodation. Spacious, en suite rooms with bath and shower comfortably accommodate a family of up to two adults and two children (to age 15). The restaurant and bar offers a varied menu. For further details consult the Hotel Groups page.
ROOMS: 40 en suite s £45.95-£46.95; d £45.95-£46.95

Travelodge

Riverside Retail Park, Hankridge Farm TA1 2LR
☎ 08700 850 950 📠 01823 444704
Dir: *M5 junct 25*
Travelodge offers good quality, good value, modern accommodation. Ideal for families, the spacious, en suite bedrooms include remote-control TV, tea and coffee-making facilities and luxury beds. Meals can be taken at the nearby family restaurant. For further details consult the Hotel Groups page.
ROOMS: 48 en suite s fr £25; d fr £25

TAUNTON DEANE MOTORWAY SERVICE AREA (M5), Somerset

Map 04 ST12

Travel Inn

Trull TA3 7PF
☎ 08701 977250 📠 01823 338131
Dir: *M5 southbound between junct 25 & 26*
Travel Inn offers good-quality, value-for-money accommodation. Spacious, en suite rooms with bath and shower comfortably accommodate a family of up to two adults and two children (to age 15). The restaurant and bar offers a varied menu. For further details consult the Hotel Groups page.
ROOMS: 39 en suite s £45.95-£46.95; d £45.95-£46.95

TAVISTOCK, Devon

Map 03 SX47

★★★70% Bedford

1 Plymouth Rd PL19 8BB
☎ 01822 613221 📠 01822 618034
e-mail: jane@bedford-hotel.co.uk
web: www.bedford-hotel.co.uk
Dir: *M5 junct 31 - Launceston/Okehampton A30. Take A386 to Tavistock, follow town centre signs. Hotel opposite church*

Built on the site of a Benedictine abbey, this impressive castellated building has been welcoming visitors for over 200 years. Very much a local landmark, the hotel offers comfortable and relaxing public areas, all reflecting charm and character throughout. Bedrooms are traditionally styled with contemporary comforts, whilst the Woburn Restaurant provides a refined setting for enjoyable cuisine.
ROOMS: 30 en suite (1 fmly) ⊘ in 11 bedrooms s £55-£85; d £120-£130 (incl. bkfst) **LB** **FACILITIES:** Xmas **CONF:** Thtr 70 Class 45 Board 25 Del from £110 **PARKING:** 45 **NOTES:** ⊘ in restaurant
CARDS:

TEBAY, Cumbria

Map 18 NY60

★★★72% Westmorland Hotel & Bretherdale Restaurant

Orton CA10 3SB
☎ 015396 24351 📠 015396 24354
e-mail: sales@westmorlandhotel.com
web: www.westmorlandhotel.com
Dir: *M6 between junct 38 & 39 at northbound service area. Accessible from southbound service area*

This modern, friendly hotel has breathtaking views over the beautiful Cumbrian countryside. Bedrooms, varying in style, are all comfortably appointed and particularly well equipped. Spacious, open-plan public areas are visually appealing and include a

continued on p574

TEBAY, continued

split-level restaurant where local produce features highly. Meetings and conferences are well catered for.
ROOMS: 50 en suite (18 fmly) (13 GF) ⊗ in 30 bedrooms s £65-£89; d £83-£105 (incl. bkfst) LB **FACILITIES:** STV ch fac Xmas **CONF:** BC Thtr 75 Class 40 Board 30 Del from £103 **SERVICES:** Lift **PARKING:** 100 **NOTES:** ⊗ in restaurant Civ Wed 80
CARDS:

See advert on opposite page

TEES-SIDE AIRPORT, Co Durham — Map 19 NZ31

★★★64% The St George
Middleton St George DL2 1RH
☎ 01325 332631 01325 333851
e-mail: bookings@stgeorgehotel.net.
web: www.stgeorgehotel.net
Dir: *turn off A67 by-pass directly into Airport grounds*
This former wartime officers' mess is conveniently situated within walking distance of the airport terminal. Bedrooms, most of which are spacious, are located in two wings. Public areas include a well-stocked bar with games room, and a comfortable restaurant. Well-equipped conference and meeting rooms are also available.
ROOMS: 59 en suite ⊗ in 14 bedrooms s £57; d £67 (incl. bkfst) **FACILITIES:** STV Solarium Xmas **CONF:** BC Thtr 160 Class 60 Board 50 Del from £91 **PARKING:** 100 **NOTES:** ⊗ in restaurant Civ Wed 150
CARDS:

TEIGNMOUTH, Devon — Map 03 SX97

★★★70% Ness House
Ness Dr, Shaldon TQ14 0HP
☎ 01626 873480
e-mail: nesshouse@talk21.com
Dir: *M5 take A380 turn onto A381 to Teignmouth, cross bridge to Shaldon, hotel 0.5m on left on Torquay Rd*

Enjoying breathtaking views of the busy Teign Estuary, Ness House maintains much of its original charm. Friendly and attentive service is provided along with comfortable and well-equipped rooms; many boast balconies with sea views. A choice of dining in either the Terrace or Conservatory restaurants provides interesting dishes featuring fresh local produce and seafood.
ROOMS: 7 en suite 5 annexe en suite (2 fmly) ⊗ in all bedrooms s £60-£90; d £105-£140 (incl. bkfst) LB **PARKING:** 20 **NOTES:** ⊗ in restaurant Closed 24 & 25 Dec **CARDS:**

Popped the question?
Hotels with Civ Wed in their entry are licensed for civil wedding ceremonies. Maximum numbers for the ceremony only are shown, e.g. Civ Wed 120

Action for Blind People Hotel

U Cliffden
Dawlish Rd TQ14 8TE
☎ 01626 770052 01626 770594
e-mail: cliffden_hotel@afbp.org
Dir: *From M5 junct 31 follow signs Plymouth/Torquay, A31 then A380. Then B3192 to Teignmouth. Down hill on Exeter Rd to lights, turn left to rdbt (station on left). Turn left and follow Dawlish signs. Up hill and hotel next right*
Newly extended and refurbished, this welcoming hotel is a listed Victorian building set in six acres of delightful gardens overlooking a small valley. Bedrooms are comfortable, very spacious and thoughtfully equipped. The hotel caters for the specific needs of blind and partially sighted people, their friends, relatives, carers and guide dogs.
ROOMS: 48 en suite (4 fmly) (10 GF) ⊗ in all bedrooms s £217-£280; d £434-£560 (incl. bkfst & dinner) LB **FACILITIES:** STV supervised Putt green Outdoor chess, Pool table, Skittles ♫ ch fac Xmas **CONF:** Thtr 60 Class 45 Board 30 **SERVICES:** Lift **PARKING:** 40 **NOTES:** ⊗ in restaurant Closed 1st 3 wks of Jan
CARDS:

TELFORD, Shropshire — Map 10 SJ60
See also Worfield

★★★★65% *Buckatree Hall*
The Wrekin, Wellington TF6 5AL
☎ 01952 641821 01952 247540
e-mail: res.buckatree@macdonald-hotels.co.uk
Dir: *M54 junct 7, turn left, at T-junct turn left, hotel 0.25mile on left*
The name Buckatree means 'the well where deer drink'. Little wonder then that the hotel started life as a hunting lodge. The extensive wooded estates on the slopes of the Wrekin make for a peaceful retreat for business guests as well as a scenic wedding venue. Bedrooms are furnished and decorated in a traditional style and some have balconies.
ROOMS: 62 en suite (4 fmly) (12 GF) **FACILITIES:** STV **CONF:** Thtr 200 Class 100 Board 50 **SERVICES:** Lift **PARKING:** 80 **NOTES:** ⊗ in restaurant Civ Wed 200 **CARDS:**

★★★72% Valley
Best Western
TF8 7DW
☎ 01952 432247 01952 432308
e-mail: info@thevalleyhotel.co.uk
Dir: *M6, M54 junct 6 onto A5223 to Ironbridge*
This privately owned hotel is situated in attractive gardens, close to the famous Iron Bridge. It was once the home of the Maws family who manufactured ceramic tiles, and fine examples of their craft are found throughout the house. Bedrooms vary in size and are split between the main house and a mews development.
ROOMS: 35 en suite s £90-£110; d £110-£140 (incl. bkfst) LB **FACILITIES:** STV ch fac **CONF:** BC Thtr 200 Class 100 Board 60 Del from £120 **PARKING:** 100 **NOTES:** ⊗ in restaurant RS 24 Dec-1 Jan Civ Wed 200 **CARDS:**

★★★70%
Clarion Hotel Madeley Court, Telford
Clarion Hotel BY CHOICE HOTELS
Castlefields Way, Madeley TF7 5DW
☎ 01952 680068 01952 684275
e-mail: enquiries@hotels-telford.com
Dir: *M54 junct 4, A4169 Telford, A442 at 2nd rdbt signs for Kidderminster (ignore sign to Madeley & Kidderminster) 1st left off rdbt*
This beautifully restored 16th-century manor house is set in extensive grounds and gardens. Bedrooms vary between character

continued

T

rooms and the newer annexe rooms. There are two wood-panelled lounges and the restaurant features a mix of old stone walls and modern colour themes. Facilities include a large self-contained banqueting suite and a lakeside bar.
ROOMS: 29 en suite 18 annexe en suite (1 fmly) (21 GF) ⊗ in 16 bedrooms s £111; d £125 (incl. bkfst) **LB** **FACILITIES:** STV Archery,Horse riding arranged Xmas **CONF:** Thtr 175 Class 100 Board 45 Del £149.50 **PARKING:** 180 **NOTES:** ⊗ in restaurant Civ Wed 175
CARDS:

★★★68% Hadley Park House
Hadley Park TF1 6QJ
☎ 01952 677269 01952 676938
e-mail: info@hadleypark.co.uk
Located in Telford, but close to Ironbridge this elegant Georgian mansion is situated within three acres of it own grounds. Bedrooms are spacious and well equipped. There is a comfortable bar and lounge and meals are served in the attractive conservatory-style restaurant.
ROOMS: 10 en suite (3 fmly) ⊗ in 5 bedrooms s fr £80; d fr £90 (incl. bkfst) **LB** **FACILITIES:** STV **CONF:** Thtr 90 Class 60 Board 40 Del £145 **PARKING:** 40 **NOTES:** ⊗ in restaurant Closed 24-26 Dec 1-7 Jan Civ Wed 80 **CARDS:**

★★★64% Telford Golf & Country Club
Great Hay Dr, Sutton Heights TF7 4DT
☎ 01952 429977 01952 586602
e-mail: telfordcountryclub@corushotels.com
Dir: *M54 junct 4, A442 - Kidderminster, follow signs for Telford Golf Club*

A modern and much extended former farmhouse in an elevated situation. Comfortable bedrooms are located in several different wings, some have fine views of Ironbridge Gorge and others overlook the golf course. Guests can choose to dine in the brasserie or the more informal café. Extensive leisure facilities include the 18-hole golf course and large indoor swimming pool.
ROOMS: 96 en suite (16 fmly) (26 GF) ⊗ in 36 bedrooms s £55-£79; d £55-£79 **LB** **FACILITIES: Spa** 18 Squash Snooker Sauna Solarium Gym Putt green Jacuzzi Health & Beauty Golf driving range ♫ Xmas **CONF:** Thtr 250 Class 140 Board 60 Del from £95
PARKING: 200 **NOTES:** ⊗ in restaurant Civ Wed 100
CARDS:

★★68% *White House*
Wellington Rd, Muxton TF2 8NG
☎ 01952 604276 & 603603 01952 670336
e-mail: james@whhotel.co.uk
Dir: *off A518 Telford-Stafford road*
The White House is a friendly family-run hotel which provides well-equipped modern accommodation. The attractive public areas offer a choice of bars and a very pleasant restaurant, where a wide range of dishes is available. There is also a small lounge for residents, and a beer garden.
ROOMS: 31 en suite (3 fmly) **CONF:** Board 10 **PARKING:** 100
NOTES: ⊗ in restaurant **CARDS:**

Travel Inn
Euston Way TF3 4LY
☎ 08701 977251 01952 290742
Dir: *From M54 (J5) follow signs for Central Railway Station. Travel Inn on 2nd exit off rbt*
Travel Inn offers good-quality, value-for-money accommodation. Spacious, en suite rooms with bath and shower comfortably accommodate a family of up to two adults and two children (to age 15). The restaurant and bar offers a varied menu. For further details consult the Hotel Groups page.
ROOMS: 60 en suite s £45.95-£46.95; d £45.95-£46.95 **CONF:** Thtr 30 Board 20

Travelodge
Whitchurch Dr, Shawbirch TF1 3QA
☎ 08700 850 950 01952 246534
Dir: *1m NW, on A5223*
Travelodge offers good quality, good value, modern accommodation. Ideal for families, the spacious, en suite bedrooms include remote-control TV, tea and coffee-making facilities and luxury beds. Meals can be taken at the nearby family restaurant. For further details consult the Hotel Groups page.
ROOMS: 40 en suite s fr £25; d fr £25

TELFORD SERVICE AREA (M54), Shropshire Map 10 SJ70

Days Inn Telford
Telford Services, Priorslee Rd TF11 8TG
☎ 01952 238400 01952 238410
e-mail: telford.hotel@welcomebreak.co.uk
web: www.welcomebreak.co.uk
Dir: *M54 junct 4*
This modern building offers accommodation in smart, spacious

continued on p576

TELFORD SERVICE AREA (M54), continued

and well-equipped bedrooms, suitable for families and business travellers, and all with en suite bathrooms. Continental breakfast is available and other refreshments may be taken at the nearby family restaurant. For further details see the Hotel Groups page.
ROOMS: 48 en suite d £55-£75 **CONF:** Board 10

TEMPLE SOWERBY, Cumbria Map 18 NY62

★★★77% **Temple Sowerby House**
CA10 1RZ
☎ 017683 61578 017683 61958
e-mail: stay@temple-sowerby.com
web: www.temple-sowerby.com
Dir: *midway between Penrith and Appleby, 7m from M6 junct 40*
Set in the heart of the Eden Valley, this hotel is ideally placed for both the Pennines and Lake District. The original part of the building dates back to the 16th century and was the principal house of the village. Bedrooms are comfortable and stylish, and some include four-poster beds. There is a choice of lounges and a conservatory overlooking attractive landscaped gardens.
ROOMS: 8 en suite 4 annexe en suite (2 GF) in all bedrooms s £77; d £107-£130 (incl. bkfst) **LB** **FACILITIES:** **CONF:** Thtr 30 Class 20 Board 20 Del from £130 **PARKING:** 15 **NOTES:** in restaurant Closed 24-27 Dec Civ Wed 40 **CARDS:**

TENBURY WELLS, Worcestershire Map 10 SO56

★★67% **Cadmore Lodge**
Berrington Green, St Michaels WR15 8TQ
☎ 01584 810044 01584 810044
e-mail: info@cadmorelodge.co.uk
Dir: *Off A4112 for Berrington, hotel 0.75m on left*

Cadmore Lodge is situated in a secluded location on a 70-acre private estate that features a 9-hole golf course, two fishing lakes and indoor leisure facilities. The traditionally furnished bedrooms have modern amenities. A large function room with lake views is a popular venue for special occasions. The hotel is also earning itself a well-deserved reputation for its food.
ROOMS: 15 rms (14 en suite) (1 fmly) in all bedrooms s £54-£70; d £81-£123 (incl. bkfst) **LB** **FACILITIES:** 9 Fishing Gym Jacuzzi Bowling green Steam room Nature reserve Xmas **CONF:** BC Thtr 100 Class 40 Board 20 Del from £90 **PARKING:** 100 **NOTES:** in restaurant Civ Wed 160 **CARDS:**

See advert on opposite page

Town House Hotel
Country House Hotel
Travel Accommodation

Restaurant with Rooms

The Peacock Inn
Worcester Rd WR15 8LL
☎ 01584 810506 01584 811236
e-mail: jamesvidler@btconnect.com
web: www.thepeacockinn.com
Dir: *on A456 from Worcester follow A443 to Tenbury Wells. Inn 1.25m E of Tenbury Wells*
A warm welcome can be expected from resident proprietors at this 14th-century roadside inn, which has a wealth of original features such as wood panelling, beams and low ceilings. The atmospheric bar and restaurant are popular locally, and bedrooms are not only spacious and comfortable but are also usefully and thoughtfully equipped.
ROOMS: 6 en suite (1 GF) in all bedrooms s £47.50-£55; d £60-£85 (incl. bkfst) **LB** **PARKING:** 30 **NOTES:**
CARDS:

TENTERDEN, Kent Map 07 TQ83

★★★75%
London Beach Hotel & Golf Club
Ashford Rd TN30 6HX
☎ 01580 766279 01580 763884
e-mail: enquiries@londonbeach.com
web: www.londonbeach.net
Dir: *M20 junct 9, follow signs to Tenterden on A28, turn right after 0.5, hotel after 1m*
This purpose-built hotel is situated in mature grounds on the outskirts of Tenterden. The spacious bedrooms are smartly decorated, have co-ordinated soft furnishings and most rooms have balconies with superb views over the golf course. The open-plan public rooms feature a brasserie-style restaurant, where an interesting choice of dishes is served.
ROOMS: 26 en suite (2 fmly) in 22 bedrooms s £65-£105; d £65-£105 **LB** **FACILITIES:** 9 Fishing Putt green Own 9 hole golf course Driving range Pitch 'n' putt Xmas **CONF:** Thtr 100 Class 75 Board 40 Del from £95 **SERVICES:** Lift **PARKING:** 100 **NOTES:** in restaurant Civ Wed 100 **CARDS:**

TETBURY, Gloucestershire Map 04 ST89

Top 200 – Hotel

★★★ **Calcot Manor**
Calcot GL8 8YJ
☎ 01666 890391 01666 890394
e-mail: reception@calcotmanor.co.uk
web: www.calcotmanor.co.uk
Dir: *3m West of Tetbury at junct A4135/A46*
Cistercian monks built the ancient barns and stables around

continued

which this lovely English manor is set. No two rooms are the same, and each is beautifully decorated in country-house style and equipped with the comforts of home. Sumptuous sitting rooms, with crackling log fires in the winter, look out over well-kept gardens. There are two dining options: the elegant conservatory restaurant and the informal Gumstool Inn. A superb health and leisure spa includes an indoor pool, high-tech gym, massage tables, complementary therapies and much more. For children, a crèche and 'playzone' have been provided. Nominated for the AA Hotel of the Year Award for England 2004-5.
ROOMS: 9 en suite 21 annexe en suite (10 fmly) s £120-£150; d fr £190 (incl. bkfst) **LB** **FACILITIES: Spa** Sauna Solarium Gym Jacuzzi Clay pigeon shooting ch fac Xmas
CONF: BC Thtr 100 Class 24 Board 35 Del from £205
PARKING: 120 **NOTES:** in restaurant Civ Wed 100
CARDS:

★★★73% Close
8 Long St GL8 8AQ
☎ 01666 502272 01666 504401
e-mail: reception@theclosehotel.co.uk
Dir: *from M4 junct 17 onto A429 to Malmesbury, follow Tetbury signs. M5 junct 14 onto B4509 follow signs to Tetbury*

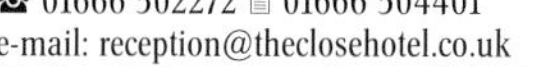

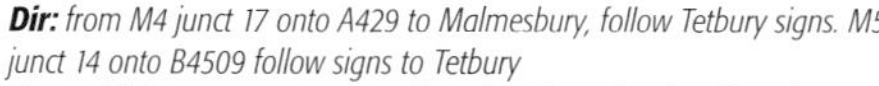

Even with its town centre location, this charming hotel retains a country-house feel that has made it a favourite with many for years. Bedrooms are traditional and feature thoughtful touches such as home-made biscuits, fresh fruit and bottled water. The public rooms provide a choice of relaxing areas in which to sit, with log fires in the winter. In the summer, guests can enjoy the terrace in the attractive walled garden.
ROOMS: 15 en suite **FACILITIES:** STV **CONF:** Thtr 50 Board 22
PARKING: 22 **NOTES:** in restaurant Civ Wed 50
CARDS:

★★★71% Snooty Fox
Market Place GL8 8DD
☎ 01666 502436 01666 503479
e-mail: res@snooty-fox.co.uk
Dir: *in the centre of the town*
Centrally situated, the Snooty Fox is a popular venue for weekend breaks, and retains many of the historic features associated with a 16th-century coaching inn. The atmosphere is relaxed and friendly, the accommodation of a high standard and the food offered in the bar and restaurant is another reason why many guests return.
ROOMS: 12 en suite in 2 bedrooms s £69-£125; d £89-£199 (incl. bkfst) **LB** **FACILITIES:** Xmas **CONF:** Thtr 30 Class 12 Board 15 Del from £112 **NOTES:** in restaurant
CARDS:

★★★70% Hare & Hounds
Westonbirt GL8 8QL
☎ 01666 880233 & 881000 01666 880241
e-mail: reception@hareandhoundshotel.com
web: www.hareandhoundshotel.com
Dir: *2.5m SW of Tetbury on A433*
This popular hotel, set in extensive grounds, is situated close to Westonbirt Arboretum and has been run by the same family for 50 years. Staff are keen to help and public areas are charming, with polished parquet flooring. Bedrooms are traditional in style

continued

and located in both the main house and adjacent coach house. Leisure facilities include squash and tennis courts.

Hare & Hounds

ROOMS: 24 en suite 7 annexe en suite (3 fmly) (5 GF) in 12 bedrooms s £75-£83; d £90-£105 (incl. bkfst) **LB** **FACILITIES:** STV Squash Putt green Table tennis Half size snooker table Xmas
CONF: Thtr 120 Class 80 Board 40 Del £150 **PARKING:** 85 **NOTES:** in restaurant Civ Wed 200 **CARDS:**

Early start?
Hotels at all star levels should provide in-room alarm clocks and/or alarm calls

TEWKESBURY, Gloucestershire Map 10 SO83

★★★67% The Tewkesbury Park Hotel Golf & Country Club
Lincoln Green Ln GL20 7DN
☎ 0870 609 6101 📠 01684 292386
e-mail: tewkesburypark@corushotels.com
Dir: *M5 junct 9/A438 through Tewkesbury, A38 passing Abbey on left, turn right into Lincoln Green Ln*

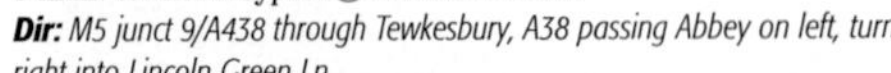

Only two miles from the M5, this extended 18th-century manor house boasts wonderful views across the Malvern Hills from its hilltop position. Bedrooms offer contemporary comforts and many have the added bonus of countryside views. In addition to the well-established golf course, an indoor pool, gym, sauna, squash and tennis courts are also available.
ROOMS: 80 en suite (8 fmly) ⊗ in 35 bedrooms d £78-£178 (incl. bkfst & dinner) **LB** **FACILITIES:** STV 18 Squash Sauna Solarium Gym Putt green Jacuzzi Activity field, 6 hole pitch & put Xmas
CONF: Thtr 150 Class 100 Board 50 Del from £125 **PARKING:** 250
NOTES: ⊗ in restaurant Civ Wed 100
CARDS:

TV dinner?
Room service at three stars and above

★★★60% Royal Hop Pole
Church St GL20 5RT
☎ 01684 293236 📠 01684 296680
e-mail: info@theroyalhoppolehotel.co.uk
Dir: *M5 junct 9 for Tewkesbury approx 1.5m. At War Memorial rdbt, straight across, hotel on right*

This former coaching inn is within walking distance of historic Tewkesbury Abbey and has been offering a warm welcome to weary travellers since the 14th century. There is character in abundance here with many original features including age darkened beams and sloping floors. Bedrooms have great individuality some being in the main house, others in a garden wing. Additional facilities include a popular bar, attractive restaurant and relaxing lounge.
ROOMS: 29 en suite (1 fmly) (5 GF) ⊗ in 20 bedrooms s £52-£75; d £90-£150 (incl. bkfst & dinner) **FACILITIES:** All guests have use of facilities at Tewkesbury Park Hotel Golf and Country Club Xmas
CONF: Board 34 Del £120 **PARKING:** 35 **NOTES:** ⊗ in restaurant
CARDS:

★★65% *Bell*
57 Church St GL20 5SA
☎ 01684 293293 📠 01684 295938
e-mail: 6408@greeneking.co.uk
Dir: *on A38 in town centre opposite Abbey*
This 14th-century former coaching house is situated on the edge of the town, opposite the Norman abbey. The bar and lounge are the focal point of this atmospheric and friendly establishment, with a large open fire providing warmth. Bedrooms have been refurbished and offer good levels of comfort and quality with many extra facilities provided, such as CD players.
ROOMS: 24 en suite (1 fmly) ⊗ in 5 bedrooms **CONF:** Thtr 50 Class 15 Board 20 **PARKING:** 35 **NOTES:** ⊗ in restaurant
CARDS:

THAME, Oxfordshire Map 05 SP70

★★★76% Spread Eagle
Cornmarket OX9 2BW
☎ 01844 213661 📠 01844 261380
e-mail: enquiries@spreadeaglethame.co.uk
web: www.spreadeaglethame.co.uk
Dir: *town centre on A418 Oxford to Aylesbury Road, M40 junct 6 S, junct 8 N*

This former coaching inn, which is privately owned, is set on the main thoroughfare of this delightful market town. Well-equipped bedrooms vary in size and style, with some located in a newly-built extension. Public areas include a comfortable bar and the informal Fothergills Restaurant, named after the diarist and raconteur who owned the hotel in the 1920s. The hotel offers an extensive range of banqueting facilities.
ROOMS: 33 en suite (1 fmly) s £97.95-£110.95; d £112.95-£120.95 (incl. bkfst) **LB** **FACILITIES:** Xmas **CONF:** Thtr 250 Class 100 Board 50
PARKING: 80 **NOTES:** Civ Wed 200
CARDS:

⌂ Travelodge
OX9 7XA
☎ 08700 850 950 📠 01844 218740
Dir: *A418/B4011*

Travelodge offers good quality, good value, modern accommodation. Ideal for families, the spacious, en suite bedrooms include remote-control TV, tea and coffee-making facilities and luxury beds. Meals can be taken at the nearby family restaurant. For further details consult the Hotel Groups page.
ROOMS: 31 en suite s fr £25; d fr £25

THAXTED, Essex Map 12 TL63

★★69% Thaxted Hall
CM6 2RE
☎ 01371 830129 📠 01371 830835
e-mail: reservations@thaxtedhall.co.uk
Dir: *B184/B1051 junct, 0.25m from town centre towards Saffron Walden*
Expect a warm welcome at this privately owned hotel set in two acres of attractive landscaped grounds and within easy driving distance of Stansted Airport. Bedrooms are pleasantly decorated with co-ordinated soft furnishings and have many thoughtful touches. Public rooms include a smart lounge and a cosy breakfast room with individual tables.
ROOMS: 8 en suite (3 fmly) ⊗ in all bedrooms s £59.50-£79.50; d £69.50-£89.50 **FACILITIES:** Xmas **CONF:** BC Thtr 150 Class 70 Board 40 **PARKING:** 50 **NOTES:** ⊗ in restaurant Civ Wed 150
CARDS:

THETFORD, Norfolk Map 13 TL88
See also Brandon (Suffolk)

★★66% The Thomas Paine Hotel
White Hart St IP24 1AA
THE INDEPENDENTS
☎ 01842 755631 📠 01842 766505
e-mail: bookings@thomaspainehotel.com
Dir: *N on A11, at rdbt before Thetford take A1075, hotel on right*
This Grade II listed building is believed to be the birthplace of Thomas Paine, who was a pioneer of democratic thinking. The property is situated close to the town centre and Thetford Forest Park is just a short drive away. Bedrooms vary in size and style; each one is pleasantly decorated and thoughtfully equipped.
ROOMS: 13 en suite (2 fmly) ⊗ in 5 bedrooms s £50-£55; d £60-£66 (incl. bkfst) **LB** **FACILITIES:** Xmas **CONF:** Thtr 70 Class 35 Board 30 **PARKING:** 30 **NOTES:** ⊗ in restaurant
CARDS:

THIRSK, North Yorkshire Map 19 SE48

★★73% Golden Fleece
42 Market Place YO7 1LL
Best Western
☎ 01845 523108 📠 01845 523996
e-mail: goldenfleece@bestwestern.co.uk
Dir: *off A19 at Thirsk to town centre*
This delightful hotel began life as a coaching inn, and enjoys a central location in the market square. Bedrooms are comfortably furnished, extremely well equipped and individually styled with beautiful soft furnishings. Guests can eat in the attractive bar, or choose more formal dining in the smart restaurant.
ROOMS: 23 en suite (3 fmly) ⊗ in 4 bedrooms s £65; d £85-£105 (incl. bkfst) **LB** **FACILITIES:** STV ch fac Xmas **CONF:** Thtr 75 Class 20 Board 30 Del from £95 **PARKING:** 35 **NOTES:** ⊗ in restaurant Civ Wed 70 **CARDS:**

THORNBURY, Gloucestershire Map 04 ST69

Top 200 – Hotel

★★★ Thornbury Castle
Castle St BS35 1HH
☎ 01454 281182 📠 01454 416188
e-mail: info@thornburycastle.co.uk
web: www.vonessenhotels.co.uk
Dir: *on A38 N from Bristol take 1st turn to Thornbury. At end High St left into Castle St, follow brown sign, entrance to Castle on left behind St Marys Church*
Henry VIII ordered the first owner of this castle to be beheaded! Guests today have the opportunity of sleeping in historical surroundings fitted out with all modern amenities. Most rooms have four-poster or coronet beds and real fires. Tranquil lounges enjoy views over the gardens, while elegant, wood-panelled dining rooms make a memorable setting for a leisurely, award-winning meal.

Thornbury Castle

ROOMS: 25 en suite (3 fmly) (2 GF) s £80-£110; d £130-£370 (incl. bkfst) **LB** **FACILITIES:** STV Snooker Hot air ballooning, archery, helicopter ride, clay pigeon shooting Xmas **CONF:** Thtr 70 Class 40 Board 30 Del £230 **PARKING:** 40 **NOTES:** ⊗ in restaurant Civ Wed 70 **CARDS:**

Looking for a last-minute weekend away?
Check out Latebeds,
the AA's late availability booking service, at www.theAA.com

THORNBURY, continued

★★66% *Thornbury Golf Lodge*
Bristol Rd BS35 3XL
☎ 01454 281144 📠 01454 281177
e-mail: info@thornburygc.co.uk web: www.thornburygc.co.uk
Dir: *M5 junct 16 take A38 Thornbury. At traffic lights (Berkeley Vale Motors) take left. Entrance 1m on left*

The old farmhouse exterior of this establishment disguises a completely refurbished interior with spacious and comfortable bedrooms, all well equipped and attractively decorated. Many have pleasant views over the centre's two golf courses or towards the Severn Estuary. The adjacent clubhouse, with a full bar, serves a range of hot and cold food all day.
ROOMS: 11 en suite (7 GF) **FACILITIES:** STV 18 Putt green **CONF:** Thtr 100 Class 40 Board 40 **PARKING:** 150 **NOTES:** No children 5yrs **CARDS:**

THORNE, South Yorkshire Map 17 SE61

★★★64% Belmont
Horsefair Green DN8 5EE
☎ 01405 812320 📠 01405 740508
e-mail: belmonthotel@aol.com
Dir: *M18 junct 6, A614 signed Thorne. Hotel on right of Market Place*
This privately owned, smartly appointed hotel enjoys a prime location in the centre of town. Bedrooms vary in size and style but are very well equipped for both business and leisure guests. There is a popular bar offering a good range of meals and snacks, and a more formal restaurant and cocktail bar.
ROOMS: 23 en suite (3 fmly) (5 GF) in 5 bedrooms s £74-£77; d £85-£99 (incl. bkfst) **LB** **FACILITIES:** STV Putt green ch fac **CONF:** Thtr 60 Class 20 Board 25 Del from £85 **PARKING:** 30 **NOTES:** Closed 24-28 Dec, 1 Jan **CARDS:**

THORNHAM, Norfolk Map 12 TF74

★★69% Lifeboat Inn
Ship Ln PE36 6LT
☎ 01485 512236 📠 01485 512323
e-mail: reception@lifeboatinn.co.uk web: www.lifeboatinn.co.uk
Dir: *follow A149 E from Hunstanton, 6m, 1st left after Thornham sign*
This 16th-century smugglers' alehouse enjoys superb views across open meadows to Thornham Harbour. The attractive bedrooms are furnished with pine pieces and have many thoughtful touches. The public rooms have a wealth of character and feature open fireplaces and oak beams. A range of bar meals is available or guests can choose from the carte menu in the smart restaurant.
ROOMS: 13 en suite (3 fmly) (1 GF) in all bedrooms s £59-£75; d £78-£110 (incl. bkfst) **LB** **FACILITIES:** Xmas **CONF:** Thtr 50 Class 30 Board 30 **PARKING:** 120 **NOTES:** in restaurant
CARDS:

THORNTON HOUGH, Merseyside Map 15 SJ38

★★★★68% Thornton Hall
CLASSIC BRITISH
Neston Rd CH63 1JF
☎ 0151 336 3938 📠 0151 336 7864
e-mail: reservations@thorntonhallhotel.com
web: www.thorntonhallhotel.com
Dir: *M53 junct 4 take B5151 Neston onto B5136 to Thornton Hough*

Built in the mid 1800s for a wealthy shipping merchant, this country house hotel lies on the edge of the village in well-kept mature grounds. Public rooms include the Italian Restaurant with ornate oak carvings, a leisure centre and a bar area with views over the garden. Bedrooms are divided between those in the original house and the more modern extension.
ROOMS: 63 en suite (6 fmly) (28 GF) in 36 bedrooms s £115-£140; d £115-£140 **LB** **FACILITIES: Spa** STV Sauna Solarium Gym Putt green Jacuzzi Hot tub Beauty Spa Hairdressing salon **CONF:** Thtr 200 Class 100 Board 60 Del £155 **PARKING:** 250 **NOTES:** in restaurant Civ Wed 140 **CARDS:**

THORNTON WATLASS, North Yorkshire Map 19 SE28

★69% Buck Inn
HG4 4AH
☎ 01677 422461 📠 01677 422447
e-mail: buckwatlass@btconnect.com
Dir: *A684 towards Bedale, B6268 towards Masham, after 2m turn right at x-roads to Thornton Watlass, hotel is by Cricket Green*
This traditional country inn is situated on the edge of the village green overlooking the cricket pitch. Cricket prints and old photographs are found throughout and an open fire in the bar adds to the warm and intimate atmosphere. Wholesome lunches and dinners are served in the bar or dining room from an extensive menu. Bedrooms are brightly decorated and well equipped.
ROOMS: 7 rms (5 en suite) (1 fmly) (1 GF) s £45-£50; d £60-£70 (incl. bkfst) **LB** **FACILITIES:** Fishing Quoits Childrens play area **CONF:** Thtr 70 Class 40 Board 30 Del from £65 **PARKING:** 10 **NOTES:** in restaurant Closed 24 & 25 Dec for accommodation
CARDS:

THORPE (DOVEDALE), Derbyshire Map 16 SK15

★★★76% Izaak Walton
Dovedale DE6 2AY
☎ 01335 350555 📠 01335 350539
e-mail: reception@izaakwaltonhotel.com
web: www.izaakwalton-hotel.com
Dir: *A515 on B5054, follow road to Thorpe village, continue straight over cattle grid & 2 small bridges, take 1st right & sharp left*
This hotel is peacefully situated, with magnificent views over the Valley of Dovedale to Thorpe Cloud. Many of the bedrooms have

continued

lovely views, and 'executive' rooms are particularly spacious. Meals are served in the bar area, with more formal dining in the Haddon restaurant. Staff are friendly and efficient. Fishing on the River Dove can be arranged.

ROOMS: 37 en suite (6 fmly) (7 GF) ⊘ in 31 bedrooms s £100-£110; d £130-£170 **LB** **FACILITIES:** STV Fly fishing on nearby River Dove Xmas **CONF:** Thtr 50 Class 40 Board 30 Del from £125 **PARKING:** 80 **NOTES:** ⊘ in restaurant Civ Wed 80 **CARDS:**

See advert under ASHBOURNE

★★★67% **The Peveril of the Peak**

DE6 2AW

☎ 01335 350396 🖹 01335 350507

e-mail: frontdesk@peverilofthepeak.co.uk

Dir: *Ashbourne A515 towards Buxton, after 1m turn left to Thorpe, approx. 4m on right just before Thorpe village.*

Situated in Dovedale's picture-book scenery, this hotel is named after one of Sir Walter Scott's heroic novels. Most bedrooms open onto the gardens, while the rest have individual patios. Some rooms have been adapted for less able guests. There is a cosy cocktail bar, a comfortable lounge and an attractive restaurant overlooking the extensive gardens. Conference and meeting rooms are also available.

ROOMS: 46 en suite (16 fmly) (6 GF) ⊘ in 30 bedrooms s £65-£75; d £95-£105 (incl. bkfst) **FACILITIES:** STV ch fac Xmas **CONF:** Thtr 70 Class 40 Board 30 Del from £97.50 **PARKING:** 80 **NOTES:** ⊘ in restaurant Civ Wed 60 **CARDS:**

See advert on this page

Late for dinner?
Quality Standards mean that last orders for dinner vary according to star rating and should be no earlier than:
★★ 7.00pm ★★★ 8.00pm ★★★★ 9.00pm
★★★★★ 10.00pm

THORPE MARKET, Norfolk
Map 13 TG23

★★74% ® Elderton Lodge Hotel & Langtry Restaurant
Gunton Park NR11 8TZ
☎ 01263 833547 📠 01263 834673
e-mail: enquiries@eldertonlodge.co.uk
web: www.eldertonlodge.co.uk
Dir: *at N Walsham take A149 towards Cromer, hotel is 3m out of North Walsham on left, just prior to entering Thorpe Market*

Ideally placed for touring the north Norfolk coastline, this delightful former shooting lodge is set amidst six acres of mature gardens adjacent to Gunton Hall estate. The individually decorated bedrooms are tastefully furnished and thoughtfully equipped. Public rooms include a smart lounge bar, an elegant restaurant and a sunny conservatory breakfast room.
ROOMS: 11 en suite (2 fmly) (2 GF) ⊗ in all bedrooms s fr £60; d fr £95 (incl. bkfst) **LB** **FACILITIES:** Xmas **CONF:** BC **PARKING:** 50 **NOTES:** No children 6yrs ⊗ in restaurant Civ Wed 55
CARDS:

★★64% Green Farm Restaurant & Hotel
North Walsham Rd NR11 8TH
☎ 01263 833602 📠 01263 833163
e-mail: grfarmh@aol.com
web: www.greenfarmhotel.co.uk
Dir: *Turn right off A140 Norwich to Cromer road at Roughton, beside fish and chip shop. Continue for 1.5m to 'Give Way' sign, turn right, hotel 200yds on left in centre, on village green*
Attractive flint-faced, 16th-century inn situated just a short drive from Cromer. Bedrooms are located in two courtyard-style wings adjacent to the main building; each one is tastefully furnished with pine pieces and has co-ordinated fabrics. Public rooms include a popular restaurant, a comfortable lounge bar, an informal dining area and a function suite.
ROOMS: 5 en suite 9 annexe en suite (1 fmly) s £55-£80; d £80-£120 (incl. bkfst) **LB** **FACILITIES:** Xmas **CONF:** Thtr 50 Class 40 Board 100 Del from £105 **PARKING:** 50 **NOTES:** ⊗ in restaurant Civ Wed 50
CARDS:

THORPENESS, Suffolk
Map 13 TM45

A ★★ Thorpeness Hotel & Golf Club
Lakeside Av IP16 4NH
☎ 01728 452176 📠 01728 453868
e-mail: info@thorpeness.co.uk
web: www.thorpeness.co.uk
Dir: *A12/A1094 signed to Snape/Aldeburgh. Onto B1069 towards Thorpeness. On entering village follow signs for golf club*
ROOMS: 30 annexe en suite (10 fmly) (10 GF) ⊗ in all bedrooms **FACILITIES:** 18 Fishing Snooker Putt green **CONF:** Thtr 50 Class 30 Board 24 **PARKING:** 60 **NOTES:** ⊗ in restaurant
CARDS:

THRAPSTON, Northamptonshire
Map 11 SP97

Travelodge
Thrapston Bypass NN14 4UR
☎ 08700 850 950 📠 01832 735199
Dir: *on A14 link road A1/M1*
Travelodge

Travelodge offers good quality, good value, modern accommodation. Ideal for families, the spacious, en suite bedrooms include remote-control TV, tea and coffee-making facilities and luxury beds. Meals can be taken at the nearby family restaurant. For further details consult the Hotel Groups page.
ROOMS: 40 en suite s fr £25; d fr £25

THRUSSINGTON, Leicestershire
Map 11 SK61

Travelodge Leicester North
LE7 8TF
☎ 08700 850 950 📠 0870 1911584
Dir: *on A46, southbound*
Travelodge

Travelodge offers good quality, good value, modern accommodation. Ideal for families, the spacious, en suite bedrooms include remote-control TV, tea and coffee-making facilities and luxury beds. Meals can be taken at the nearby family restaurant. For further details consult the Hotel Groups page.
ROOMS: 32 en suite s fr £25; d fr £25

THURLESTONE, Devon
Map 03 SX64

★★★★72% ® Thurlestone
TQ7 3NN
☎ 01548 560382 📠 01548 561069
e-mail: enquiries@thurlestone.co.uk web: www.thurlestone.co.uk
Dir: *A38 take A384 into Totnes, A381 towards Kingsbridge, onto A379 towards Churchstow, onto B3197 turn into lane signed to Thurlestone*
This perennially popular hotel has been in the same family-ownership since 1896. A range of indoor and outdoor leisure facilities provide something for everyone and wonderful views of the south Devon coast can be enjoyed from several vantage points, including many of the bedrooms, some of which have balconies. Elegant public rooms are styled to ensure rest and relaxation.
ROOMS: 64 en suite (23 fmly) s £60-£125; d £120-£250 (incl. bkfst & dinner) **LB** **FACILITIES: Spa** STV 9 Squash Snooker Sauna Solarium Gym Putt green Jacuzzi ch fac Xmas **CONF:** Thtr 140 Class 100 Board 40 Del from £120 **SERVICES:** Lift **PARKING:** 121 **NOTES:** ⊗ in restaurant Closed Jan
CARDS:

TIBSHELF MOTORWAY SERVICE AREA (M1), Derbyshire
Map 16 SK46

Travel Inn (Mansfield Tibshelf)
Tibshelf Motorway Service Area DE55 5TZ
☎ 08701 977181 📠 01773 876609
Dir: *M1 northbound between junct 28/29, access available southbound*
travel inn

Travel Inn offers good-quality, value-for-money accommodation. Spacious, en suite rooms with bath and shower comfortably accommodate a family of up to two adults and two children (to age 15). The restaurant and bar offers a varied menu. For further details consult the Hotel Groups page.
ROOMS: 40 en suite s £45.95-£46.95; d £45.95-£46.95

> Destination dining!
> This symbol indicates a Restaurant with Rooms

T

TICEHURST, East Sussex Map 06 TQ63

★★★★72% Dale Hill Hotel & Golf Club

TN5 7DQ
☎ 01580 200112 01580 201249
e-mail: info@dalehill.co.uk web: www.dalehill.co.uk
Dir: *M25 junct 5/A21. 5m after Lamberhurst turn right at traffic lights onto B2087 to Flimwell. Hotel 1m on the left*

This modern hotel is situated just a short drive from the village. Extensive public rooms include a lounge bar, a conservatory brasserie, a formal restaurant and the Spike Bar, which is mainly frequented by golf club members and has a lively atmosphere. The hotel also has a superb 18-hole golf course and swimming pool.
ROOMS: 35 en suite (8 fmly) (23 GF) in all bedrooms s £110-£130; d £120-£250 (incl. bkfst) **LB** **FACILITIES:** STV 36 Sauna Gym Putt green Covered driving range, putting green, Pool table Xmas **CONF:** Thtr 120 Class 50 Board 50 Del from £140 **SERVICES:** Lift **PARKING:** 220 **NOTES:** in restaurant Civ Wed
CARDS:

TINTAGEL, Cornwall & Isles of Scilly Map 02 SX08

★★66% Atlantic View

Treknow PL34 0EJ
☎ 01840 770221 01840 770995
e-mail: atlantic-view@eclipse.co.uk
Dir: *B3263 to Tregatta, turn left into Treknow, hotel on road to Trebarwith Strand Beach*

Conveniently located for all the attractions of Tintagel, this family-run hotel has a wonderfully relaxed and welcoming atmosphere. Public areas include a bar, comfortable lounge, TV/games room and heated swimming pool. Bedrooms are generally spacious and some have the added advantage of distant sea views.
ROOMS: 9 en suite (1 fmly) in all bedrooms s £32-£38; d £64-£76 (incl. bkfst) **LB** **FACILITIES:** Indoor pool heated Apr-Oct **PARKING:** 10 **NOTES:** in restaurant Closed Nov-Jan RS Feb-Mar
CARDS:

★★64% Bossiney House

Bossiney PL34 OAX
☎ 01840 770240 01840 770501
e-mail: bossineyhh@eclipse.co.uk web: www.bossineyhouse.co.uk
Dir: *from A39 take B3263 into Tintagel, then Boscastle Rd, 0.5m to hotel on left*

This personally-run, friendly hotel is located on the outskirts of the picturesque coastal village. Set in the grounds, an attractive Scandinavian-style log cabin houses the majority of the leisure facilities, including a swimming pool. Public areas include a comfortable lounge and the convivial bar, which is a popular venue for pre-dinner drinks and a chat.
ROOMS: 19 en suite (1 fmly) s £24-£35 (incl. bkfst) **LB** **FACILITIES:** Sauna Solarium Putt green **CONF:** BC **PARKING:** 17 **NOTES:** in restaurant Closed 25/26 Dec, 2-31 Jan **CARDS:**

TITCHWELL, Norfolk Map 13 TF74

★★78% Titchwell Manor

PE31 8BB
☎ 01485 210221 01485 210104
e-mail: margaret@titchwellmanor.com
web: www.titchwellmanor.com
Dir: *on A149 coast road between Brancaster and Thornham*

A popular venue for golfers, bird watchers and walkers, this family-run hotel is ideally placed for touring the north Norfolk coastline. Bedrooms are comfortable; some in the adjacent annexe have ground-floor access. Smart public rooms include a lounge area, relaxed informal bar and a delightful conservatory restaurant, overlooking the walled garden. Imaginative menus feature quality local produce and fresh fish.
ROOMS: 8 en suite 7 annexe en suite (2 fmly) (3 GF) in 9 bedrooms s £55-£100; d £84-£130 (incl. bkfst) **LB** **FACILITIES:** ch fac Xmas **PARKING:** 50 **NOTES:** in restaurant
CARDS:

See advert under BURNHAM MARKET

★★73% *Briarfields*

Main St PE31 8BB
☎ 01485 210742 01485 210933
e-mail: briarfields@norfolk-hotels.co.uk
Dir: *A149 coastal road towards Wells-next-the-Sea, Titchwell is 3rd village & 7m from Hunstanton, hotel on left of main road*

This delightful hotel is situated close to the RSPB reserve and ideally located for touring the region. Spacious bedrooms are attractively decorated and thoughtfully equipped; some rooms are located in an adjacent building. Ground-floor rooms have private terrace doors. The open-plan public rooms feature a lounge and a range of eating areas that include a conservatory extension and restaurant.
ROOMS: 4 en suite 17 annexe en suite (4 fmly) in 10 bedrooms **FACILITIES:** **CONF:** Thtr 40 Class 20 Board 20 **PARKING:** 50 **NOTES:** in restaurant **CARDS:**

TIVERTON, Devon Map 03 SS91

★★★68% Tiverton

Blundells Rd EX16 4DB
☎ 01884 256120 01884 258101
e-mail: sales@tivertonhotel.co.uk
web: www.tivertonhotel.co.uk
Dir: *M5 junct 27, onto dual carriageway A361 Devon link road, Tiverton exit 7m W. Hotel on Blundells Rd next to business park*

Best Western

Conveniently situated on the outskirts of the town, with easy access to the M5, this comfortable hotel has a relaxed atmosphere. The spacious bedrooms are well equipped and decorated in a contemporary style. A formal dining option is offered by the Gallery Restaurant, while lighter snacks are served

continued on p584

TIVERTON, continued

in the bar area. Room service is extensive, as is the range of conference facilities.
ROOMS: 69 en suite (10 fmly) ⊗ in 53 bedrooms s fr £65; d fr £92 (incl. bkfst) **LB** **FACILITIES:** STV ch fac Xmas **CONF:** Thtr 300 Class 140 Board 70 Del from £90 **PARKING:** 130 **NOTES:** ⊗ in restaurant Civ Wed 200 **CARDS:**

TIVETSHALL ST MARY, Norfolk — Map 13 TM18

★★75% The Old Ram Coaching Inn

Ipswich Rd NR15 2DE
☎ 01379 676794 📠 01379 608399
e-mail: theoldram@btinternet.com web: www.theoldram.com
Dir: *on A140 15m S of Norwich and A47 by-pass. 5m from Diss.*

This busy 17th-century coaching inn was once a staging post on the Norwich to London run. It has been sympathetically restored to retain many of its original features such as oak beams, fireplaces and exposed brickwork. The tastefully appointed bedrooms include two split-level suites and several modern executive rooms.
ROOMS: 11 en suite (1 fmly) s £52-£58; d £66-£77 **LB** **FACILITIES:** STV **CONF:** Thtr 20 Class 20 Board 20 Del £99.95 **PARKING:** 150 **NOTES:** Closed 25 & 26 Dec **CARDS:**

TODDINGTON MOTORWAY SERVICE AREA (M1), Bedfordshire — Map 11 TL02

Travelodge (Luton North)

Travelodge

LU5 6HR
☎ 08700 850 950 📠 01525 878452
Dir: *M1 between juncts 11 & 12*
Travelodge offers good quality, good value, modern accommodation. Ideal for families, the spacious, en suite bedrooms include remote-control TV, tea and coffee-making facilities and luxury beds. Meals can be taken at the nearby family restaurant. For further details consult the Hotel Groups page.
ROOMS: 66 en suite s fr £25; d fr £25

TOLLESHUNT KNIGHTS, Essex — Map 07 TL91

★★★★73% Five Lakes Country House

Colchester Rd CM9 8HX
☎ 01621 868888 📠 01621 869696
e-mail: enquiries@fivelakes.co.uk web: www.fivelakes.co.uk
Dir: *exit A12 at Kelvedon, then follow the brown tourist signs through Tiptree to Salcott and Five Lakes Resort*
This hotel is set amidst 320 acres of open countryside, featuring two golf courses. The spacious bedrooms are furnished to a high standard and have excellent facilities. The public rooms offer a high degree of comfort and include five bars, two restaurants and a large lounge. The property also boasts extensive leisure facilities.

ROOMS: 114 en suite 80 annexe en suite (4 fmly) (40 GF) ⊗ in 108 bedrooms s £110-£180; d £155-£225 **LB** **FACILITIES: Spa** STV 18 Squash Snooker Sauna Solarium Gym Putt green Jacuzzi Steam room, Health & Beauty Spa, Badminton, Aerobics Studio, Hairdresser Xmas **CONF:** Thtr 2000 Class 700 Board 60 Del £199 **SERVICES:** Lift **PARKING:** 500 **NOTES:** ⊗ in restaurant Civ Wed 250 **CARDS:**

TONBRIDGE, Kent — Map 06 TQ54

★★★66% The Langley

18-20 London Rd TN10 3DA
☎ 01732 353311 📠 01732 771471
e-mail: thelangley@btconnect.com
Dir: *from Tonbridge towards Hildenborough N*
Privately owned hotel just a short drive from Tonbridge centre. Bedrooms are generally quite spacious; each one is pleasantly decorated and equipped with modern facilities. The restaurant offers a varied menu of carefully prepared fresh produce and there is a popular bar.
ROOMS: 37 en suite (3 fmly) (10 GF) ⊗ in 27 bedrooms s £45-£85; d £55-£105 **LB** **FACILITIES:** STV Xmas **CONF:** Thtr 150 Class 100 Board 100 Del from £80 **SERVICES:** Lift **PARKING:** 40 **NOTES:** ⊗ in restaurant Civ Wed 150 **CARDS:**

★★★66% Rose & Crown

125 High St TN9 1DD
☎ 01732 357966 📠 01732 357194
e-mail: rose.crown@bestwestern.co.uk
Dir: *M25 J5 A21 to Hastings, then B245. Continue to Tonbridge. At 1st lights right, over next set. Hotel on left*

Charming 15th-century coaching inn situated in the town, adjacent to the ruins of the old Norman castle. The hotel still retains much of its original character such as oak beams and Jacobean

continued

panelling. The bedrooms are tastefully decorated and well-equipped. The bar is equally popular with locals and residents.
ROOMS: 54 en suite (2 fmly) (10 GF) ⊗ in 27 bedrooms s £95-£125; d £110-£155 **LB** **FACILITIES:** STV ch fac Xmas **CONF:** Thtr 80 Class 30 Board 35 Del from £90 **PARKING:** 39 **NOTES:** ⊗ in restaurant Civ Wed 50 **CARDS:**

Premier Lodge (Tonbridge)

Pembury Rd TN11 0NA
☎ 0870 9906552 📠 0870 9906553
web: www.premierlodge.com
Dir: *M25 junct 5. Follow A21 towards Hastings, pass junction for Tunbridge Wells (A26). Exit at the next junction & take 1st exit at rdbt*
High quality, modern, budget accommodation, ideal for families and business travellers. All rooms feature bath, power shower and satellite TV, and most have telephones / modem points. The adjacent bar and restaurant offers a wide and varied menu.
ROOMS: 38 en suite s £52; d £52 **CONF:** Class 14 Board 14

TOPCLIFFE, North Yorkshire — Map 19 SE37

★★69% *The Angel Inn*

Long St YO7 3RW
☎ 01845 577237 📠 01845 578000
e-mail: mail@angelinn.co.uk
Dir: *turn off (between A1(M) & A19). Inn in centre*

Located in the heart of Topcliffe, this attractive inn is popular for its country-style cooking using high quality local produce. Pleasant bars lead through to a fine pub water garden. The bedrooms are well equipped and comfortable. Staff are friendly, and wedding ceremonies can now be accommodated here.
ROOMS: 15 en suite (1 fmly) **FACILITIES:** STV **CONF:** Thtr 150 Class 60 Board 50 **PARKING:** 150 **NOTES:** ⊗ in restaurant Civ Wed 150 **CARDS:**

TORBAY See under Brixham, Paignton & Torquay

TORMARTON, Gloucestershire — Map 04 ST77

★★71% Compass Inn

GL9 1JB
☎ 01454 218242 & 218577 📠 01454 218741
e-mail: info@compass-inn.co.uk
web: www.compass-inn.co.uk
Dir: *0.5m from M4 junct 18*
Originally a coaching inn dating from the 18th century, this welcoming hostelry has grown considerably over the years. Bedrooms are spacious and well equipped, whilst public areas include a choice of bars and varied dining options. A range of conference rooms is also available, providing facilities for varied functions.
ROOMS: 26 en suite (5 fmly) (12 GF) ⊗ in 8 bedrooms s £83.50-£93.50; d £93.50-£103.50 **LB** **FACILITIES:** ch fac **CONF:** Thtr 100 Class 30 Board 34 Del from £107.50 **PARKING:** 160 **NOTES:** Closed 24-26 Dec Civ Wed 100 **CARDS:**

TORQUAY, Devon — Map 03 SX96

★★★★★68% The Imperial

Park Hill Rd TQ1 2DG
☎ 01803 294301 📠 01803 298293
e-mail: imperialtorquay@paramount-hotels.co.uk
Dir: *A380 towards the seafront. Turn left and follow road to harbour, at clocktower turn right. Hotel 300yds on right*
This hotel has an enviable location with extensive views over the coastline. Traditional in style, public areas are elegant with choice of dining including the informal TQ1 brasserie or the more formal Regatta Restaurant. Bedrooms are spacious, most with private balconies, and the hotel has an extensive range of indoor and outdoor leisure facilities.
ROOMS: 152 en suite (7 fmly) ⊗ in 26 bedrooms s £120-£130; d £210-£220 (incl. bkfst) **LB** **FACILITIES:** STV Squash Snooker Sauna Solarium Gym Jacuzzi Beauty salon Hairdresser ♫ Xmas **CONF:** Thtr 350 Class 200 Board 30 Del from £165 **SERVICES:** Lift **PARKING:** 140 **NOTES:** Civ Wed **CARDS:**

★★★★68% Palace

Babbacombe Rd TQ1 3TG
☎ 01803 200200 📠 01803 299899
e-mail: info@palacetorquay.co.uk
web: www.palacetorquay.co.uk
Dir: *towards harbour, left by clocktower into Babbacombe Rd, hotel on right after 1m*

Set in 25 acres of stunning, beautifully tended wooded grounds, the Palace offers a tranquil environment. Suitable for business or leisure, the hotel boasts a huge range of well-presented indoor and outdoor facilities. Much of the original charm and grandeur has been maintained, particularly in the newly refurbished dining room. Many of the bedrooms enjoy views of the gardens.
ROOMS: 141 en suite (7 fmly) ⊗ in 11 bedrooms s £71-£81; d £141-£240 (incl. bkfst) **LB** **FACILITIES:** STV supervised 9 Squash Snooker Sauna Gym Putt green Table tennis ch fac Xmas **CONF:** Thtr 1000 Class 800 Board 40 Del from £125 **SERVICES:** Lift **PARKING:** 140 **NOTES:** ⊗ in restaurant **CARDS:**

See advert on page 587

★★★★66% *Grand*

Sea Front TQ2 6NT
☎ 01803 296677 📠 01803 213462
e-mail: info@grandtorquay.co.uk
web: www.richardsonhotels.co.uk
Dir: *A380 to Torquay. At seafront turn right, then first right. Hotel is on corner, entrance 1st turning on left*
Within level walking distance of the town, this large Edwardian hotel overlooks the bay and offers modern facilities. Many of the bedrooms, some with balconies, enjoy the best of the views; all

continued on p586

TORQUAY, continued

are very well equipped. Boaters Bar also benefits from the hotel's stunning position and offer an informal alternative to the Gainsborough Restaurant.
ROOMS: 114 en suite (30 fmly) ⊗ in 20 bedrooms **FACILITIES:** STV ⚐ ⚐ ⚐ Snooker Sauna Solarium Gym Jacuzzi Hairdressers Beauty clinic ♫ ch fac **CONF:** Thtr 300 Class 130 Board 60 **SERVICES:** Lift **PARKING:** 45 **NOTES:** ⊗ in restaurant Civ Wed 250
CARDS:

See advert on opposite page

Top 200 – Hotel

★★★ ◎◎ Orestone Manor Hotel & Restaurant

Rockhouse Ln, Maidencombe TQ1 4SX
☎ 01803 328098 📠 01803 328336
e-mail: enquiries@orestone.co.uk
web: www.orestone.co.uk
Dir: *off A379 coast road,Torquay-Teignmouth road (formerly B3199)*
This country-house hotel is located on the fringe of Torbay and is set in a spectacular location overlooking Lyme Bay. There is a colonial theme throughout the public areas, which are very charming and comfortable. Bedrooms are individually styled and all are spacious; some have balconies. The hotel's cuisine is highly regarded and dishes, based on local ingredients, are skilfully prepared.
ROOMS: 12 en suite (3 fmly) (1 GF) s £89-£139; d £119-£199 (incl. bkfst) **LB** **FACILITIES:** STV ⚐ ch fac Xmas **CONF:** Thtr 30 Class 20 Board 15 Del from £169 **PARKING:** 40 **NOTES:** ⊗ in restaurant **CARDS:**

★★★74% ◎◎ Corbyn Head Hotel & Orchid Restaurant

Torquay Rd, Sea Front, Livermead TQ2 6RH
☎ 01803 213611 📠 01803 296152
e-mail: info@corbynhead.com
web: www.corbynhead.com
Dir: *follow signs to Torquay seafront, turn right on seafront. Hotel on right with green canopies*
The Corbyn Head occupies a prime position overlooking Torbay. Well-equipped bedrooms, many with sea views and some with balconies, come in a range of sizes. Staff are friendly and attentive, and a well-stocked bar and comfortable lounge are available. Guests can enjoy fine dining in the award-winning Orchid Restaurant or more traditional fare in the Harbour View restaurant.

ROOMS: 44 en suite (3 fmly) (9 GF) ⊗ in 15 bedrooms s £35-£140; d £70-£200 (incl. bkfst) **LB** **FACILITIES:** ⚐ Squash Snooker Sauna Solarium ♫ Xmas **CONF:** Thtr 30 Class 20 Board 20 Del from £60 **PARKING:** 50 **NOTES:** ⊗ in restaurant
CARDS:

See advert on page 589

★★★73% *Toorak Hotel*

Chestnut Av TQ2 5JS
☎ 01803 400400 📠 01803 400140
e-mail: toorak@tlh.co.uk
Dir: *opposite Riviera Conference Centre*
Forming part of a much larger complex, the Toorak Hotel offers excellent leisure facilities including indoor bowls, a cyber café and a magnificent indoor swimming pool. Bedrooms have modern facilities, and superior and standard rooms are available. The hotel also provides conference rooms and several relaxing lounges.
ROOMS: 92 en suite (29 fmly) (20 GF) ⊗ in 40 bedrooms **FACILITIES:** ⚐ ⚐ ⚐ Snooker Sauna Solarium ⚐ Jacuzzi Childrens play area, Indoor Games Arena, Swimming supervised, Internet Cafe ♫ ch fac **CONF:** Thtr 220 Class 150 Board 60 **SERVICES:** Lift **PARKING:** 90 **NOTES:** ⚐ ⊗ in restaurant **CARDS:**

★★★70% Lincombe Hall

Meadfoot Rd TQ1 2JX
☎ 01803 213361 📠 01803 211485
e-mail: lincombe.hall@lineone.net
web: www.lincombe-hall.co.uk
Dir: *From harbour into Torwood St, at traffic lights after 100yds, turn right into Meadfoot Rd. Hotel 200yds on left*
With views over Torquay, this hotel is conveniently close to the town centre and is set in five acres of gardens and grounds. Facilities include both indoor and outdoor swimming pools. The tastefully furnished bedrooms vary in size, and the Sutherland rooms are most spacious. There are comfortable lounges and Harleys restaurant offers a comprehensive choice of dishes and wines.
ROOMS: 25 en suite 19 annexe en suite (7 fmly) (2 GF) d £66-£120 (incl. bkfst & dinner) **LB** **FACILITIES:** STV ⚐ ⚐ ⚐ Putt green Jacuzzi Child's play area Crazy golf Pool table Table Tennis ♫ Xmas **CONF:** Thtr 30 Class 30 Board 30 **PARKING:** 44 **NOTES:** ⊗ in restaurant
CARDS:

continued

T

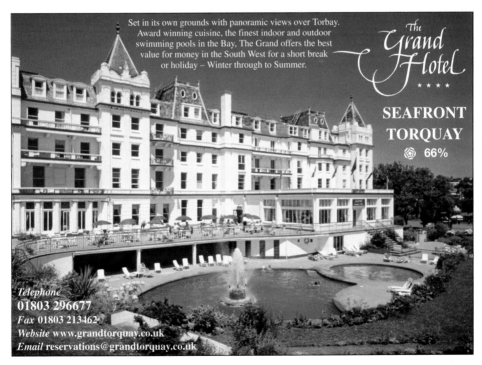

T

TORQUAY, continued

★★★ 70% Livermead House

Torbay Rd TQ2 6QJ
☎ 01803 294361 01803 200758
e-mail: info@livermead.com web: www.livermead.com
Dir: *from seafront turn right, follow A379 towards Paignton and Livermead, hotel opposite Institute Beach*

Having a splendid waterfront location, this hotel dates back to the 1820s and is where Charles Kingsley is said to have written '*The Water Babies*'. Bedrooms vary in size and style, excellent public rooms are popular for private parties and meetings and a range of leisure facilities is provided. Enjoyable cuisine is served in the impressively refurbished restaurant.
ROOMS: 67 en suite (6 fmly) (2 GF) in 12 bedrooms s £47-£84; d £94-£136 (incl. bkfst) **LB FACILITIES:** Squash Snooker Sauna Solarium Gym Xmas **CONF:** Thtr 320 Class 175 Board 80 Del from £51 **SERVICES:** Lift **PARKING:** 131 **NOTES:** in restaurant
CARDS:

See advert on page 591

★★★ 68% Livermead Cliff

Best Western

Torbay Rd TQ2 6RQ
☎ 01803 299666 01803 294496
e-mail: enquiries@livermeadcliff.co.uk
web: www.livermeadcliff.co.uk
Dir: *A379/A3022 to Torquay, through town centre, turn right for Paignton, hotel 600yds on seaward side*
Situated at the water's edge this long-established hotel offers friendly service. The splendid views can be enjoyed from the lounge, bar and dining room. Bedrooms, many with sea views and some with balconies, are comfortable and well equipped and a range of sizes is available.
ROOMS: 67 en suite (21 fmly) s £29.50-£82; d £69-£164 (incl. bkfst) **LB FACILITIES:** supervised only in the summer Fishing Solarium Sun terrace Xmas **CONF:** Thtr 80 Class 35 Board 35 Del £99 **SERVICES:** Lift **PARKING:** 92 **NOTES:** in restaurant
CARDS:

★★★ 67% Belgrave

Seafront TQ2 5HE
☎ 01803 296666 01803 211308
e-mail: info@belgrave-hotel.co.uk
web: www.belgrave-hotel.co.uk
Dir: *from Exeter A380 to Newton Abbot & Torquay. Continue to lights with Torre Station on right. Turn right into Avenue Rd continue to Kings Drive. Turn left at seafront , hotel at lights*
Enjoying an impressive position overlooking Torbay, the Belgrave offers a range of spacious and well-appointed public rooms, including comfortable lounges, the elegant restaurant and outdoor pool and patio areas. The Dickens bar is particularly stylish, and offers an innovative menu, featuring local produce. A variety of

continued

bedroom styles is available, many of which have the added bonus of stunning sea views.

ROOMS: 72 en suite (20 fmly) (18 GF) in 18 bedrooms s £49-£71; d £98 (incl. bkfst) **LB FACILITIES:** Xmas **CONF:** Thtr 200 Class 100 Board 60 Del £64 **SERVICES:** Lift **PARKING:** 90 **NOTES:** in restaurant **CARDS:**

★★★ 67% The Grosvenor

Belgrave Rd TQ2 5HG
☎ 01803 294373 01803 291032
e-mail: enquiries@grosvenor-torquay.co.uk
web: www.grosvenor-torquay.co.uk
Dir: *follow signs to seafront, then turn left, take 1st left into Belgrave Road, hotel is 1st on left*

Offering spacious and attractively furnished bedrooms, the Grosvenor Hotel is situated close to the seafront and the main attractions of the bay. Guests can choose to dine in the restaurant, coffee shop or Mima's Bistro. Many leisure facilities are available.
ROOMS: 44 en suite (8 fmly) in 10 bedrooms s £41-£92; d £82-£184 (incl. bkfst) **LB FACILITIES: Spa** STV Sauna Solarium Gym Jacuzzi Mini snooker table Library Xmas **CONF:** Thtr 150 Class 100 Board 40 Del from £65 **PARKING:** 50 **NOTES:** in restaurant Civ Wed 300 **CARDS:**

★★★ 61% Rainbow International

Belgrave Rd TQ2 5HJ
☎ 01803 213232 01803 212925
e-mail: enquiries@rainbow-hotel.co.uk
web: www.rainbow-hotel.co.uk
Dir: *Close to harbour and marina*
This large hotel is located within easy walking distance of the seafront. Bedrooms vary in size and shape; many family rooms are available and all rooms have the convenience of hairdryers and irons provided. Entertainment is provided every evening in the nightclub and the residents' ballroom.
ROOMS: 134 en suite (70 fmly) **FACILITIES:** Solarium Gym Table tennis Steam room ch fac **CONF:** Thtr 500 Class 250 Board 80 **SERVICES:** Lift **PARKING:** 100 **NOTES:** in restaurant
CARDS:

Corbyn Head Hotel ★★★

The Jewel in Torbay's Crown

- 3 STAR HOTEL & RESTAURANT WITH AA 2 ROSETTES
- SITUATED ON THE SEA FRONT
- REGENCY LOUNGE AND BAR WITH PANORAMIC SEA VIEWS
- 50 TASTEFULLY DECORATED EN SUITE ROOMS MANY WITH SEA VIEWS AND PRIVATE BALCONYS
- TEA AND COFFEE MAKING FACILITIES, TELEVISION, HAIR DRYERS, DIRECT DIAL TELEPHONES IN BEDROOMS
- OUTDOOR SWIMMING POOL AND SUN TERRACE
- SAUNA, SNOOKER TABLE AND SOLARIUM
- AMPLE FREE ON SITE PARKING

The Corbyn Head Hotel is the jewel in Torbay's crown. It has everything you could possibly wish for - the perfect hotel to compliment your holiday.

Our Gastronomic Orchid Restaurant holds a prestigious AA 2 Rosettes for culinary excellence.

This superb climate controlled restaurant is sure to leave a lasting impression providing you with a dining experience you will never forget.

TORQUAY, continued

★★★59% *Kistor Hotel*
Belgrave Rd TQ2 5HF
☎ 01803 212632 01803 293219
e-mail: kistorhotel@hotmail.com
Dir: *A380 to Torquay, hotel at junct of Belgrave Rd and promenade*
Within a short stroll of Torquay's many amenities and the promenade, the Kistor is conveniently located. Popular with groups, the hotel offers a relaxing and informal base for guests. Most bedrooms have sea views. In the restaurant, a fixed-price menu offers good, straightforward cooking.
ROOMS: 50 en suite (14 fmly) **FACILITIES:** Sauna Putt green Childrens play area ♫ **CONF:** Thtr 80 Class 30 Board 40 **SERVICES:** Lift **PARKING:** 40 **NOTES:** ⊗ in restaurant
CARDS:

★★74% Albaston House
27 St Marychurch Rd TQ1 3JF
☎ 01803 296758 01803 211509
Many guests return to this friendly, family run hotel where hospitality is genuine and welcoming. Situated close to the town centre and also for the more quieter attractions of Babbacombe, the Albaston also has some parking available. Standards are high throughout with both public areas and bedrooms reflecting a combination of comfort and quality.
ROOMS: 13 en suite (4 fmly) s £38-£40; d £76-£80 (incl. bkfst) **LB**
PARKING: 12 **NOTES:** ⊗ in restaurant Closed Jan
CARDS:

★★71% Bute Court
Belgrave Rd TQ2 5HQ
☎ 01803 293771 01803 213429
e-mail: stay@butecourthotel.co.uk
web: www.butecourthotel.co.uk
Dir: *take A380 to Torquay, continue to lights, bear right past police station, straight across at lights, hotel 200yds on right*
This popular hotel is only a short, level walk from the seafront and resort attractions. Now refurbished, it still retains many of its Victorian features. Comfortable bedrooms offer modern facilities and many have far-reaching views. Public areas include a bar and lounges, while the attractive dining room looks across secluded gardens to the sea. Entertainment is offered during busier periods.
ROOMS: 45 en suite (10 fmly) (13 GF) ⊗ in all bedrooms s £29-£52; d £58-£104 (incl. bkfst & dinner) **LB** **FACILITIES:** Snooker Darts billiards ♫ Xmas **SERVICES:** Lift **PARKING:** 37 **NOTES:** ⊗ in restaurant **CARDS:**

★★71% *Rawlyn House*
Rawlyn Rd, Chelston TQ2 6PL
☎ 01803 605208 01803 607040
e-mail: shirley@rawlynhousehotel.co.uk
web: www.rawlynhousehotel.co.uk
Dir: *A3022 at Newton Abbot to Torquay, follow sign for seafront, right at Halfords lights to Avenue Rd, at 2nd lights right to Walnut Rd, left to Old Mill Rd, Rawlyn Rd sharp right at top of hill*
Quietly located close to Cockington village and within easy reach of the centre, this friendly family-run hotel is set in well-tended grounds. Bedrooms are individual in style and offer all the expected facilities, with several rooms located on the ground floor. Dinner features freshly cooked dishes and residents can take a snack lunch around the pool or in the bar.
ROOMS: 12 rms (11 en suite) 2 annexe en suite (1 fmly) (2 GF) ⊗ in all bedrooms **FACILITIES:** Badminton Table tennis **PARKING:** 16
NOTES: ⊗ in restaurant Closed Nov-Apr
CARDS:

★★70% Ansteys Lea
Babbacombe Rd, Wellswood TQ1 2QJ
☎ 01803 294843 01803 214333
e-mail: stay@ansteys-lea.com
Dir: *from Torquay harbour take Babbacombe road, hotel approx 0.75m*
Taking its name from nearby Ansteys Cove, this friendly hotel is conveniently placed for both the town centre and seafront. The well-furnished bedrooms are comfortable and provide a good range of facilities. Public areas include an attractive lounge/TV room overlooking the garden with a heated outdoor pool. The fixed price, five-course dinner menu offers a choice of home-cooked dishes.
ROOMS: 24 en suite (4 fmly) ⊗ in all bedrooms s £26-£32; d £52-£64 (incl. bkfst) **LB** **FACILITIES:** Sauna ch fac Xmas **CONF:** Thtr 50 Class 40 Board 35 Del from £45 **PARKING:** 20 **NOTES:** ⊗ in restaurant
CARDS:

★★70% Red House
Rousdown Rd, Chelston TQ2 6PB
☎ 01803 607811 01803 200592
e-mail: stay@redhouse-hotel.co.uk
web: www.redhouse-hotel.co.uk
Dir: *towards seafront/Chelston, turn into Avenue Rd, 1st lights turn right. Follow road past shops and church, take next left. Hotel on right*

With views over Torbay, this pleasant and relaxing hotel enjoys a quiet location close to Cockington village. The comfortable bedrooms are well equipped and a good choice of bar meals are available in addition to the fixed-price menu for residents. Many guests return here on a regular basis for the excellent range of leisure facilities.
ROOMS: 10 en suite (5 fmly) s £25-£35; d £50-£70 (incl. bkfst)
FACILITIES: Spa Sauna Solarium Gym Games room Table tennis Beauty salon pool table Xmas **CONF:** Thtr 20 Class 20 Board 16
PARKING: 10 **NOTES:** ⊗ in restaurant **CARDS:**

★★70% Torcroft
Croft Rd TQ2 5UE
☎ 01803 298292 01803 291799
e-mail: enquiries@torcroft.co.uk
Dir: *from A390 take A3022 to Avenue Rd. Follow signs to seafront then turn left, cross lights and up Shedden Hill, 1st left into Croft Rd*
This well-maintained, Grade II listed Victorian property, now under new ownership, is pleasantly located in a quiet area, with well-tended gardens and a large patio. Bedrooms are individually furnished, and some rooms have views. Pleasant home-cooked meals are enthusiastically offered and provide enjoyable dining.
ROOMS: 15 en suite (2 fmly) ⊗ in all bedrooms s £25-£35; d £50-£70 (incl. bkfst) **LB** **FACILITIES:** ch fac Xmas **CONF:** Thtr 30 Class 20 Board 26 **PARKING:** 16 **NOTES:** ⊗ in restaurant
CARDS:

GF Indicates the number of bedrooms at ground floor level.

T

TORQUAY, continued

★★69% *Hotel Balmoral*
Meadfoot Sea Rd TQ1 2LQ
☎ 01803 293381 & 299224 01803 299224
e-mail: barry@hotel-balmoral.co.uk
Dir: *at Torquay harbour left at clock tower towards Babbacombe, after 100yds right at lights. Follow road to Meadfoot Beach. Hotel on right*
Situated a short walk from the beach, this friendly, privately-owned and personally run hotel has modern, well-equipped bedrooms including family rooms and a room at ground-floor level. The comfortable, spacious lounge has views over the well-tended gardens and the bar is an ideal venue for a drink before home-cooked dinners in the attractive dining room.
ROOMS: 24 en suite (7 fmly) **FACILITIES: PARKING:** 18 **NOTES:** in restaurant **CARDS:**

★★69% *Dunstone Hall*
Lower Warberry Rd TQ1 1QS
☎ 01803 293185 01803 201180
e-mail: info@dunstonehall.com
web: www.dunstonehall.co.uk
From its elevated position, this imposing Victorian mansion has panoramic views over the town to Torbay in the distance. Bedrooms are comfortable and equipped with modern facilities. Public areas include a choice of lounges, a magnificent wooden staircase and gallery and the Edwardian conservatory, which provides an intimate restaurant with lovely views.
ROOMS: 13 en suite (3 fmly) **FACILITIES:** Arrangement with nearby Health Club ch fac **CONF:** Thtr 30 Class 30 Board 24 **PARKING:** 18 **NOTES:** in restaurant **CARDS:**

★★69% Seascape
8-10 Tor Church Rd TQ2 5UT
☎ 01803 292617 01803 299260
e-mail: stay@seascapehoteltorquay.co.uk
Dir: *A380 Torquay, at Torre station turn right, left at 2nd lights. Through lights, hotel 100yds on right*
Enjoying a convenient location, just a short stroll from the town centre, this friendly, family run hotel prides itself on genuine hospitality. Bedrooms are comfortable and well equipped, some of which have the added bonus of views across the bay. Public rooms include the convivial bar with regular live entertainment, and a sauna and solarium.
ROOMS: 60 en suite (10 fmly) in 52 bedrooms **FACILITIES:** Sauna Solarium **SERVICES:** Lift **PARKING:** 13 **NOTES:** No children 12yrs in restaurant **CARDS:**

T

★★68% Gresham Court
Babbacombe Rd TQ1 1HG
☎ 01803 293007 01803 215951
e-mail: stay@gresham-court-hotel.co.uk
web: www.gresham-court-hotel.co.uk
Dir: *along seafront, left at clock tower, passing museum on left. Hotel immediately on left on corner of Braddons Hill Road West and Babbacombe Road*
This privately owned and personally run hotel is soundly maintained and provides modern accommodation, including bedrooms on the ground floor. There is a bright and pleasant dining room, a lounge bar where live entertainment is provided, a non-smoking lounge and a games room with pool table. The hotel is a popular venue for coach tour parties.
ROOMS: 30 en suite (6 fmly) (5 GF) **FACILITIES:** Snooker **SERVICES:** Lift **PARKING:** 4 **NOTES:** in restaurant
CARDS:

★★68% *Shelley Court*
29 Croft Rd TQ2 5UD
☎ 01803 295642 01803 215793
e-mail: shelleycourthotel@hotmail.com
Dir: *into Torquay on A380, approach seafront lights by footbridge, up Shedden Hill, 1st left after corner, hotel car park immediately left*
A popular family-run hotel with friendly staff, located in a pleasant and quiet area, which overlooks the town towards Torbay. Many guests return here time and again. Entertainment is provided most evenings in the season. Bedrooms offer a range of sizes and there is a large and comfortable lounge bar.
ROOMS: 27 en suite (3 fmly) **FACILITIES:** **PARKING:** 20
NOTES: in restaurant Closed 23 Dec-1 Feb
CARDS:

★★67% Elmington Hotel
St Agnes Ln, Chelston TQ2 6QE
☎ 01803 605192 01803 690488
e-mail: mail@elmington.co.uk
web: www.elmington.co.uk
Dir: *to the rear of Torquay Station*
Set in sub-tropical gardens with views over the bay, this splendid Victorian villa has been lovingly restored. The comfortable bedrooms are brightly decorated and vary in size and style. There is a spacious lounge, bar and dining room. Diners can choose from a menu of British dishes and an oriental buffet.
ROOMS: 22 rms (19 en suite) (5 fmly) (2 GF) in all bedrooms
FACILITIES: STV Pool table ch fac **CONF:** Thtr 40 Class 40 Board 30 **PARKING:** 22 **NOTES:** in restaurant
CARDS:

★★66% Anchorage Hotel
Cary Park, Aveland Rd TQ1 3PT
☎ 01803 326175 01803 316439
e-mail: enquiries@anchoragehotel.co.uk

This hotel is quietly located in a residential area. Providing a friendly welcome, this family-run establishment enjoys a great deal of repeat business. Bedrooms offer a range of sizes and all rooms are neatly presented. Evening entertainment is provided regularly in the large and comfortable lounge.
ROOMS: 56 en suite (5 fmly) in all bedrooms s £22.50-£31.50; d £45-£63 (incl. bkfst) **LB** **FACILITIES:** Xmas **SERVICES:** Lift
PARKING: 26 **NOTES:** in restaurant **CARDS:**

★★65% Ashley Court
107 Abbey Rd TQ2 5NP
☎ 01803 292417 01803 215035
e-mail: reception@ashleycourt.co.uk
Dir: *A380 onto seafront, left to Shedden Hill to lights, hotel opp*
Located close to the town centre and within easy strolling distance of the seafront, the Ashley Court offers a warm welcome to guests.

continued

Bedrooms are pleasantly appointed and some have sea views. The outdoor pool and patio are popular with guests wishing to soak up some sunshine. Live entertainment is provided regularly throughout the season.

ROOMS: 53 en suite (6 fmly) (8 GF) **FACILITIES:** Xmas **SERVICES:** Lift **PARKING:** 30 **NOTES:** in restaurant Closed 3 Jan-1 Feb **CARDS:**

★★65% Coppice

Babbacombe Rd TQ1 2QJ
☎ 01803 297786 01803 211085
e-mail: peter@coppicehotel.demon.co.uk
web: www.coppicehotel.co.uk
Dir: *From harbour left at clock tower for hotel 1m on left*

A friendly, comfortable and well-established hotel, The Coppice is a popular choice and provides a convenient location within walking distance of the beaches and shops. In addition to the indoor and outdoor swimming pools, evening entertainment is often provided in the spacious bar. Bedrooms are bright and airy with modern amenities.

ROOMS: 39 en suite (16 fmly) (22 GF) in all bedrooms s £20-£43; d £40-£86 (incl. bkfst & dinner) **LB** **FACILITIES: Spa** Sauna Solarium Gym Putt green **PARKING:** 36 **NOTES:** in restaurant Closed Dec-Jan **CARDS:**

★★64% *Burlington*

462-466 Babbacombe Rd TQ1 1HN
☎ 01803 210950 01803 200189
e-mail: info@burlingtontorquay.co.uk
web: www.burlingtontorquay.co.uk
Dir: *A380 follow signs to seafront, left at harbour, left at clock tower rdbt, hotel is 0.5m on right*

Popular with groups, this hotel is conveniently situated for the many attractions the area has to offer. A range of traditional dishes is served in the spacious dining room. Public areas include a games room, entertainment room, leisure facilities and a popular bar. Bedrooms are comfortable and available in a variety of sizes.

ROOMS: 55 en suite (7 fmly) **FACILITIES: Spa** Sauna Solarium Jacuzzi **PARKING:** 20 **NOTES:** in restaurant **CARDS:**

★★64% *Maycliffe*

St Lukes Rd North TQ2 5DP
☎ 01803 294964 01803 201167
web: www.maycliffehotel.co.uk
Dir: *left from Kings Dr, along seafront keep left lane, next lights (Belgrave Rd) up Shedden Hill, 2nd right into St Lukes Rd then 1st left*

Set in a quiet and elevated position which is convenient for the town centre and attractions, the Maycliffe is a popular venue for leisure breaks. Bedrooms are individually decorated and equipped with modern facilities, there are two rooms on the ground floor for less able guests. Visitors can relax in the quiet lounge and, in the bar, cabaret is offered on some nights during the season.

ROOMS: 28 en suite (1 fmly) in 9 bedrooms **FACILITIES:** **SERVICES:** Lift **PARKING:** 10 **NOTES:** No children 10yrs in restaurant Closed 2 Jan-12 Feb **CARDS:**

★★64% Norcliffe

7 Babbacombe Downs Rd, Babbacombe TQ1 3LF
☎ 01803 328456 01803 328023
e-mail: res@norcliffehotel.co.uk
Dir: *M5, take A380, after Sainsburys turn left at lights, across rdbt, next left at lights into Manor Rd, from Babbacombe Rd turn left*

With marvellous views across Lyme Bay, the Norcliffe is conveniently situated on the Babbacombe Downs and ideally located for visitors to St Marys Church or nearby Oddicombe Beach. Public areas are relaxing, take advantage of the views, and include an indoor swimming pool. All bedrooms are comfortable, varying in style and size.

ROOMS: 27 en suite (3 fmly) (1 GF) s £20-£35; d £40-£70 (incl. bkfst) **LB** **FACILITIES:** Sauna Table tennis, indoor pool has CCTV Xmas **SERVICES:** Lift **PARKING:** 20 **NOTES:** in restaurant **CARDS:**

★★62% Regina

Leisureplex

Victoria Pde TQ1 2BE
☎ 01803 292904 01803 290270
e-mail: regina.torquay@alfatravel.co.uk
Dir: *on entering Torquay, follow harbour signs, hotel on outer corner of harbour*

This hotel enjoys a pleasant and convenient location right on the harbour side, a short stroll from the town's attractions. Bedrooms, some with harbour views, vary in size. Entertainment is provided on most nights and there is a choice of bars.

ROOMS: 68 en suite (5 fmly) s £28-£36; d £46-£62 (incl. bkfst) **LB** **FACILITIES:** Xmas **SERVICES:** Lift **PARKING:** 6 **NOTES:** in restaurant Closed Jan& part Feb RS Nov-Dec (ex Xmas) & Feb-Mar **CARDS:**

★★61% Villa Marina

Cockington Ln, Livermead TQ2 6QU
☎ 01803 605440 & 606122 01803 606122
e-mail: stay@villa-marina.co.uk
Dir: *from main seafront towards Paignton, turn right towards Cockington. Hotel 70yds on left*

Convenient for the seafront and Cockington village, this establishment provides friendly service. Bedrooms are comfortable and some rooms have balconies with splendid views over Torbay. The views can also be enjoyed from the public rooms and the terrace swimming pool. Live entertainment is provided during the high season.

ROOMS: 26 en suite (5 fmly) (8 GF) in all bedrooms s £20-£30; d £40-£60 (incl. bkfst) **LB** **FACILITIES:** Xmas **PARKING:** 22 **NOTES:** in restaurant Closed Jan **CARDS:**

T

TORQUAY, continued

★62% Westwood
111 Abbey Rd TQ2 5NP
☎ 01803 293818 📠 01803 293818
e-mail: reception@westwoodhotel.co.uk
Dir: *on A380 follow signs for seafront. At lights facing sea turn left straight through next lights up Shedden Hill. At lights at top left into Abbey Rd, hotel on right*
An enthusiastic and friendly welcome is offered at this small, family-run hotel within walking distance of the town centre. Regular guests enjoy the informal atmosphere, particularly in the comfortable bar. Bedrooms are tastefully decorated and offer many modern facilities.
ROOMS: 25 en suite (6 fmly) **FACILITIES:** ♫ **PARKING:** 12
NOTES: ✈ ⊘ in restaurant **CARDS:**

TOTLAND BAY See Wight, Isle of

TOTNES, Devon Map 03 SX86
See also Staverton

★★65% Royal Seven Stars
The Plains TQ9 5DD
☎ 01803 862125 & 863241 📠 01803 867925
e-mail: royal7starshotel@aol.com
Dir: *A38 Devon Expressway, Buckfastleigh turn off onto A384, follow signs to Totnes town centre*
In a prominent position at the foot of the town and close to the river, this 17th-century hostelry is a popular place. Bedrooms are comfortable and well equipped, many retaining the original charm of the building. A central atrium offers a pleasant area adjacent to the busy bar, and the restaurant offers a large choice of freshly prepared dishes.
ROOMS: 16 rms (14 en suite) (2 fmly) s £52-£65; d £68-£84 (incl. bkfst) **LB** **CONF:** Thtr 70 Class 20 Board 20 **PARKING:** 20
CARDS:

TOWCESTER, Northamptonshire Map 11 SP64

⌂ Travelodge (Silverstone)
NN12 6TQ
☎ 08700 850 950 📠 01327 359105
Dir: *A43 East Towcester by-pass*
Travelodge offers good quality, good value, modern accommodation. Ideal for families, the spacious, en suite bedrooms include remote-control TV, tea and coffee-making facilities and luxury beds. Meals can be taken at the nearby family restaurant. For further details consult the Hotel Groups page.
ROOMS: 55 en suite s fr £25; d fr £25

TRESCO See Scilly, Isles of

TRING, Hertfordshire Map 06 SP91

★★★★66% ® Pendley Manor
Cow Ln HP23 5QY
☎ 01442 891891 📠 01442 890687
e-mail: info@pendley-manor.co.uk
web: www.pendley-manor.co.uk
Dir: *M25 junct 20. Take A41 leave at Tring exit. At rdbt take exit for Berkhamsted/London. Take 1st left signposted Tring Station & Pendley Manor*
This impressive Victorian mansion is set in extensive and mature landscaped grounds complete with peacocks. Bedrooms, situated in the manor house or in the new wing, offer a useful range of facilities and many have four-poster beds. Public areas include a cosy bar, a conservatory lounge and a leisure centre.
ROOMS: 74 en suite (6 fmly) ⊘ in 3 bedrooms **FACILITIES: Spa** STV supervised Snooker Sauna Gym Jacuzzi Steam room, Dance Studio, Internet coffee shop **CONF:** BC Thtr 230 Class 100 Board 50 **SERVICES:** Lift **PARKING:** 250 **NOTES:** ⊘ in restaurant Civ Wed 200
CARDS:

See advert on opposite page

★★★62% The Rose & Crown
High St HP23 5AH
☎ 01442 824071 📠 01442 890735
Dir: *just off A41 between Aylesbury/Hemel Hempstead, hotel in town centre*

This Tudor-style manor house offers a great deal of charm. Bedrooms vary in size, though all are comfortably equipped and have particularly smart bathrooms. The restaurant and bar form the centre of the hotel and are popular both with locals and residents.
ROOMS: 27 en suite (3 fmly) ⊘ in 3 bedrooms **FACILITIES:** STV Full indoor leisure facilities available at sister hotel Xmas **CONF:** Thtr 80 Class 30 Board 30 **PARKING:** 60 **NOTES:** ✈ Civ Wed 100
CARDS:

⌂ Travel Inn
Tring Hill HP23 4LD
☎ 08701 977254 📠 01442 890787
Dir: *M25 junct 20 take A41 towards Aylesbury, at end of Hemel Hempstead/Tring bypass straight over rdbt, Travel Inn on the right in approx 100yds*
Travel Inn offers good-quality, value-for-money accommodation. Spacious, en suite rooms with bath and shower comfortably accommodate a family of up to two adults and two children (to age 15). The restaurant and bar offers a varied menu. For further details consult the Hotel Groups page.
ROOMS: 30 en suite s £45.95-£46.95; d £45.95-£46.95

TROUTBECK (NEAR WINDERMERE), Cumbria Map 18 NY40

★★72% Mortal Man
LA23 1PL
☎ 015394 33193 📠 015394 31261
e-mail: enquiries@themortalman.co.uk
web: www.themortalman.co.uk
Dir: *2.5m N from junct of A591/A592, turn left before church into village, right at t-junct, hotel 800mtrs on right*
Dating from 1689, this traditional Lakeland inn enjoys a superb setting with stunning views towards Windermere. New owners are considerably improving the hotel, though the public areas, which include two bar areas and a cosy lounge, will retain their original features. A range of enjoyable meals can be served in either the bars, with real fires, outside on fine days, or in the formal

continued

restaurant. Bedrooms are particularly well equipped and include a four-poster room.
ROOMS: 12 en suite ⊗ in all bedrooms s £60-£65; d £100-£130 (incl. bkfst & dinner) **LB** **FACILITIES:** Fishing, Horse Riding, Sailing, Guided Walks, Watersports Xmas **CONF:** Thtr 30 **PARKING:** 20 **NOTES:** ⊗ in restaurant **CARDS:**

TROWBRIDGE, Wiltshire — Map 04 ST85

★★66% Fieldways Hotel & Health Club

Hilperton Rd BA14 7JP
☎ 01225 768336 📠 01225 753649
Dir: *last property on left when leaving Trowbridge on A361 towards Melksham/Chippenham/Devizes*
This establishment is quietly set in well-kept grounds and provides a pleasant combination of spacious, comfortably furnished bedrooms, an impressive wood-panelled dining room and a considerable range of indoor leisure facilities. 'Top to Toe' days are especially popular, and incorporate the wide range of beauty treatments on offer.
ROOMS: 8 en suite 5 annexe en suite (2 fmly) (2 GF) s £60; d £75-£85 (incl. bkfst) **LB** **FACILITIES: Spa** Sauna Solarium Gym Jacuzzi Range of beauty treatments/massage **CONF:** Thtr 40 Class 40 Board 8 **PARKING:** 70 **NOTES:** ⊗ in restaurant
CARDS:

TROWELL MOTORWAY SERVICE AREA (M1), Nottinghamshire — Map 11 SK43

Travelodge Nottingham Trowell

Travelodge

NG9 3PL
☎ 08700 850 950 📠 0115 944 7815
Dir: *M1 junct 25/26 northbound*
Travelodge offers good quality, good value, modern accommodation. Ideal for families, the spacious, en suite bedrooms include remote-control TV, tea and coffee-making facilities and luxury beds. Meals can be taken at the nearby family restaurant. For further details consult the Hotel Groups page.
ROOMS: 35 en suite s fr £25; d fr £25

TRURO, Cornwall & Isles of Scilly — Map 02 SW84

★★★73% Alverton Manor

Tregolls Rd TR1 1ZQ
☎ 01872 276633 📠 01872 222989
e-mail: reception@alvertonmanor.co.uk
Dir: *from Carland Cross take A39 to Truro*
Formerly a convent, this impressive sandstone property stands in six acres of grounds, within walking distance of the city centre. It has a wide range of smart bedrooms, combining comfort with character. Stylish public areas include the library and the former chapel, now a striking function room. An interesting range of dishes is offered in the elegant restaurant.
ROOMS: 32 en suite (3 GF) ⊗ in 10 bedrooms s £90-£130; d £115-£150 (incl. bkfst) **LB** **FACILITIES:** STV 18 Xmas **CONF:** Thtr 80 Class 60 Board 40 Del from £120 **SERVICES:** Lift **PARKING:** 120 **NOTES:** ⊗ in restaurant Civ Wed 80 **CARDS:**

★★★71% Royal

Lemon St TR1 2QB
☎ 01872 270345 📠 01872 242453
e-mail: reception@royalhotelcornwall.co.uk
web: www.royalhotelcornwall.co.uk
Dir: *follow A30 to Carland Cross then Truro. Follow brown tourists signs to hotel in city centre. To barrier & obtain pass from reception*
This popular hotel is located in the heart of Truro and is

continued on p596

TRURO, continued

redeveloping with a contemporary feel. Public areas offer a stylish atmosphere; the new bar and restaurant proving popular with locals and residents alike. A wide choice of appetising dishes is available, which feature ethnic, classical and vegetarian as well as daily specials. Bedrooms are pleasantly appointed.
ROOMS: 35 en suite 9 annexe en suite (4 fmly) (3 GF) in 31 bedrooms s £59-£150; d £85-£150 (incl. bkfst) **LB** **FACILITIES:** STV **PARKING:** 44 **NOTES:** Closed 25 & 26 Dec
CARDS:

See advert on page 595

★★★62% Brookdale

Tregolls Rd TR1 1JZ
☎ 01872 273513 01872 272400
e-mail: brookdale@hotelstruro.com
Dir: *from A30 onto A39, at A390 junct turn right into city centre. Hotel 600mtrs down hill*

THE INDEPENDENTS

Pleasantly situated in an elevated position close to the city centre, the Brookdale provides a range of accommodation options; all rooms are pleasantly spacious and well equipped, with some located in an adjacent annexe. Meals can be served in guests' rooms, and in the dining room a pleasant selection of dishes is available.
ROOMS: 30 en suite (2 fmly) in 11 bedrooms s £55-£63.50; d £79.50-£150 (incl. bkfst) **LB** **FACILITIES:** STV ch fac Xmas **CONF:** Thtr 85 Class 65 Board 25 **PARKING:** 45 **NOTES:** in restaurant **CARDS:**

★★68% Carlton

Falmouth Rd TR1 2HL
☎ 01872 272450 01872 223938
e-mail: reception@carltonhotel.co.uk
Dir: *on A39 straight across 1st & 2nd rdbts onto bypass (Morlaix Avenue). At top of sweeping bend/hill turn right at mini rdbt into Falmouth Rd. Hotel is 100mtrs on right*

This family-run hotel is pleasantly located a short stroll from the city centre. A friendly welcome is assured and both business and leisure guests choose the Carlton on a regular basis. A smart, comfortable lounge is available, along with leisure facilities. A wide selection of home-cooked dishes is offered in the dining room.
ROOMS: 29 en suite (4 fmly) in 15 bedrooms s £42-£48; d £58-£68 (incl. bkfst) **FACILITIES:** STV Sauna Jacuzzi **CONF:** Thtr 60 Class 24 Board 36 **PARKING:** 31 **NOTES:** in restaurant Closed 23 Dec-6 Jan
CARDS:

Travel Inn

Old Carnon Hill, Carnon Downs TR3 6JT
☎ 08701 977255 01872 865620
Dir: *on A39 (Truro to Falmouth road), 3 miles of Truro*

travel inn

Travel Inn offers good-quality, value-for-money accommodation. Spacious, en suite rooms with bath and shower comfortably accommodate a family of up to two adults and two children (to age 15). The restaurant and bar offers a varied menu. For further details consult the Hotel Groups page.
ROOMS: 40 en suite s £45.95-£46.95; d £45.95-£46.95

TUNBRIDGE WELLS (ROYAL), Kent

Map 06 TQ53

Town House

★★★★ Hotel Du Vin & Bistro

Crescent Rd TN1 2LY
☎ 01892 526455 01892 512044
e-mail: reception@tunbridgewells.hotelduvin.com
web: www.hotelduvin.com
Dir: *follow town centre to main junct of Mount Pleasant Rd & Crescent Rd/Church Rd. Hotel 150yds on Crescent Rd on right just past Phillips House*

This impressive Grade II listed building dates from 1762. As a princess, Queen Victoria often stayed here. The spacious bedrooms are available in a range of sizes, beautifully and individually appointed, and equipped with a host of thoughtful extras. Public rooms include a bistro-style restaurant, two elegant lounges and a small bar. Outside, there are delightful gardens and a terrace.
ROOMS: 31 en suite 4 annexe en suite s £89-£250; d £89-£250 **FACILITIES:** STV Snooker Boules court in garden **CONF:** Thtr 40 Class 30 Board 25 Del £165 **SERVICES:** Lift **PARKING:** 30 **NOTES:** in restaurant **CARDS:**

★★★★71% *The Spa*

Mount Ephraim TN4 8XJ
☎ 01892 520331 01892 510575
e-mail: info@spahotel.co.uk
web: www.spahotel.co.uk
Dir: *off A21 to A26, follow signs to A264 East Grinstead, hotel on right*

This imposing 18th-century country house is set in 14 acres of attractive landscaped grounds overlooking the town. The spacious bedrooms are individually decorated, tastefully furnished and thoughtfully equipped; many rooms overlook the pretty gardens. Public rooms include a comfortable lounge, a large bar, the Chandelier restaurant and excellent leisure facilities.
ROOMS: 69 en suite (10 fmly) (2 GF) **FACILITIES:** STV supervised Riding Sauna Gym Steam room Beauty Salon Jogging trail ch fac **CONF:** BC Thtr 300 Class 93 Board 90 **SERVICES:** Lift **PARKING:** 120 **NOTES:** in restaurant Civ Wed 250
CARDS:

See advert on opposite page

For central reservation numbers and more information on Hotel Groups, turn to pages 33-39

T

★★★ 69% The Royal Wells Inn

Mount Ephraim TN4 8BE
☎ 01892 511188 📠 01892 511908
e-mail: info@royalwells.co.uk
web: www.royalwells.co.uk

Dir: *from London on A21 onto A264 to Tunbridge Wells. On entering town take right turn at 1st mini rdbt. At 2nd mini rdbt, Mount Ephraim and hotel 150yds on right*

A delightful family-run hotel situated in an elevated position with stunning views of the town centre. The accommodation is being continually upgraded to provide stylish, tastefully furnished and well-equipped bedrooms throughout. There is a choice of two restaurants and dishes are interesting and carefully prepared from fresh local produce. The wine list is well chosen and reasonably priced.

ROOMS: 22 en suite (2 fmly) s £75-£80; d £99-£119 (incl. bkfst) **LB** **FACILITIES:** STV ♫ **CONF:** BC Thtr 80 Class 30 Board 40 Del from £104 **SERVICES:** Lift **PARKING:** 35 **NOTES:** Civ Wed 80
CARDS:

See advert on this page

★★ 65% Russell

80 London Rd TN1 1DZ
THE INDEPENDENTS
☎ 01892 544833 📠 01892 515846
e-mail: Sales@russell-hotel.com
web: www.russell-hotel.com

Dir: *at junct A26/A264 uphill onto A26, hotel on right*

This detached Victorian property is situated just a short walk from the centre of town. The generously proportioned bedrooms in the main house are pleasantly decorated and well equipped. In addition, there are several smartly appointed, self-contained suites in an adjacent building. The public rooms include a lounge, a cosy bar and a restaurant.

ROOMS: 19 en suite 5 annexe en suite (5 fmly) (1 GF) ⊘ in 10 bedrooms s £55-£70; d £68-£85 (incl. bkfst) **LB** **FACILITIES:** ch fac **CONF:** Thtr 35 Class 35 Board 35 **PARKING:** 15 **NOTES:** ✗
CARDS:

⌂ Innkeeper's Lodge Tunbridge

21 London Rd, Southborough TN4 0RL
☎ 01892 529292 📠 01892 510620
www.innkeeperslodge.com

Dir: *Off M25 onto A21, take A26 Tonbridge/Southborough turn off. Lodge in Southborough on A26, opposite the cricket green on Church Road.*

Smart rooms meet essential business requirements but also have home comforts, and depending on location may well have meeting rooms and pub dining. Dining options generally include all-day menus plus the added advantage of breakfast.

ROOMS: 15 en suite s £52-£57

⊘ No smoking

TURNERS HILL, West Sussex Map 06 TQ33

Top 200 – Hotel

★★★ Alexander House Hotel

East St RH10 4QD
☎ 01342 714914 01342 717328
e-mail: info@alexanderhouse.co.uk
web: www.alexanderhouse.co.uk
Dir: *on B2110 between Turners Hill and East Grinstead, 6m from M23 junct 10*

Set in 175 acres of parklands and landscaped gardens, this delightful country house hotel dates back to the 17th century. Comfortable, stylish bedrooms have been individually refurbished to a high standard; all are thoughtfully equipped and benefit from superbly appointed bathrooms. Spacious, elegant public areas, furnished with antique pieces and paintings, include a choice of comfortable lounges and a stylish restaurant.

ROOMS: 18 en suite (3 fmly) (1 GF) in all bedrooms s £125-£370; d £155-£370 **LB** **FACILITIES:** STV Clay Shooting, Archery by arrangement. Xmas **CONF:** Thtr 24 Board 18 Del from £215 **SERVICES:** Lift **PARKING:** 50 **NOTES:** No children 7yrs in restaurant Civ Wed 50 **CARDS:**

See advert under GATWICK AIRPORT (LONDON)

TWICKENHAM, Greater London
See LONDON SECTION plan 1 B2

Premier Lodge (Twickenham)

Chertsey Rd, Whitton TW2 6LS
☎ 0870 9906416 0870 9906417
web: www.premierlodge.com
Dir: *M25 junct 12/M3 & follow signs for Central London. At end of M3 onto A316. In Richmond, 100 yards further straight over rdbt. Lodge 500 yards on left*

High quality, modern, budget accommodation, ideal for families and business travellers. All rooms feature bath, power shower and satellite TV, and most have telephones / modem points. The adjacent bar and restaurant offers a wide and varied menu.

ROOMS: 31 en suite s £60; d £60

TWO BRIDGES, Devon Map 03 SX67

★★76% Prince Hall

PL20 6SA
☎ 01822 890403 01822 890676
e-mail: bookings@princehall.co.uk
web: www.princehall.co.uk
Dir: *on B3357 1m E of Two Bridges road junct*

Charm, peace and relaxed informality pervade at this small hotel, which has a stunning location at the heart of Dartmoor. Bedrooms, each named after a Dartmoor tor, have been equipped with thoughtful extras. The history of the house and its location are reflected throughout the comfortable public areas. The accomplished cooking is memorable.

ROOMS: 8 en suite (1 fmly) s £84-£125; d £148-£230 (incl. bkfst & dinner) **LB** **FACILITIES:** Fishing Riding Guided Dartmoor Walks, Fly fishing, Garden tours **CONF:** Class 25 Del £115 **PARKING:** 13 **NOTES:** No children 10yrs in restaurant Closed 16 Dec-10 Feb **CARDS:**

★★72% Two Bridges Hotel

PL20 6SW
THE INDEPENDENTS
☎ 01822 890581 01822 890575
e-mail: enquiries@warm-welcome-hotels.co.uk
web: www.twobridges.co.uk
Dir: *junct of B3212 & B3357*

This wonderfully relaxing hotel is set in the heart of the Dartmoor National Park, in a beautiful riverside location. Three standards of comfortable rooms provide every modern convenience. There is a choice of lounges and fine dining is available in the restaurant, with menus featuring local game and seasonal produce.

ROOMS: 33 en suite (2 fmly) (6 GF) in 25 bedrooms **FACILITIES:** STV Fishing **CONF:** Thtr 110 Class 60 Board 40 **PARKING:** 100 **NOTES:** in restaurant Civ Wed 130 **CARDS:**

See advert on opposite page

TYNEMOUTH, Tyne & Wear Map 21 NZ36

★★★68% Grand

Grand Pde NE30 4ER
☎ 0191 293 6666 0191 293 6665
e-mail: info@grandhotel-uk.com
web: www.grandhotel-uk.com
Dir: *A1058 for Tynemouth, at coast rdbt turn right. Hotel on right 0.5m*

Completely refurbished some years ago and attracting a wide customer base, this grand Victorian building offers stunning views of the coastline. In addition to the restaurant there are two bars and an elegant and imposing staircase is the focal point. Bedrooms come in a variety of styles and are well equipped, tastefully decorated and have impressive bathrooms.

ROOMS: 40 en suite 4 annexe en suite (12 fmly) s £60-£150; d £65-£160 (incl. bkfst) **FACILITIES:** STV Xmas **CONF:** Thtr 130 Class 40 Board 40 **SERVICES:** Lift **PARKING:** 16 **NOTES:** in restaurant RS Sun evening Civ Wed 120 **CARDS:**

- Indoor Swimming Pool
- Indoor Swimming Pool (heated)
- Outdoor Swimming Pool
- Outdoor Swimming Pool (heated)

TYWARDREATH, Cornwall & Isles of Scilly Map 02 SX05

★★★74% Trenython Manor

Castle Dore Rd PL24 2TS
☎ 01726 814797 01726 817030
e-mail: hotel@trenython.co.uk
web: www.trenython.co.uk
Dir: *A390/B3269 towards Fowey, 2m, right into Castledore. Hotel 100mtrs*

Dating from the 1800s, there is something distinctly different about Trenython, an English manor house designed by an Italian architect. Peacefully situated in extensive grounds, public areas have grace and elegance with many original features and many of

continued

the bedrooms have wonderful views. The splendour of the panelled restaurant is the venue for contemporary cuisine.

ROOMS: 24 en suite (2 fmly) ⊗ in all bedrooms s £90-£180; d £125-£225 (incl. bkfst) **LB** **FACILITIES: Spa** supervised Sauna Solarium Gym Jacuzzi Woodland walks, health & beauty centre ch fac Xmas **CONF:** BC Thtr 100 Class 60 Board 40 Del from £125 **PARKING:** 50 **NOTES:** ⊗ in restaurant Civ Wed 85
CARDS:

UCKFIELD, East Sussex

Map 06 TQ42

★★★★74%

Buxted Park Country House Hotel

HandPICKED

Buxted TN22 4AY
☎ 01825 733 333 01825 732 990
e-mail: buxtedpark@handpicked.co.uk
Dir: *From A26 (Uckfield Bypass) take A272 signposted Buxted. Through traffic lights, hotel 1 mile on right*

An attractive Grade II listed Georgian mansion dating back to the 17th century and set amidst 300 acres of beautiful countryside and landscaped gardens. The stylish, thoughtfully equipped bedrooms are split between the main house and the modern Garden Wing. An interesting choice of dishes is served in the original Victorian Orangery. Hand Picked Hotels - AA Hotel Group of the Year 2004-5.

ROOMS: 44 en suite (6 fmly) (16 GF) in 22 bedrooms s £120-£370; d £140-£370 (incl. bkfst) **LB** **FACILITIES:** STV Fishing Snooker Sauna Solarium Gym Putt green Beauty salon, clay pigeon shoot, archery, fishing, mountain biking, orienteering ch fac Xmas **CONF:** Thtr 130 Class 70 Board 60 Del from £185 **PARKING:** 150 **NOTES:** in restaurant Civ Wed 130 **CARDS:**

See advert on page 599

Top 200 – Hotel

★★★

Horsted Place

Little Horsted TN22 5TS
☎ 01825 750581 01825 750459
e-mail: hotel@horstedplace.co.uk
Dir: *2m S on A26 towards Lewes*

This 17th-century property is one of Britain's finest examples of Gothic revivalist architecture. It is situated in extensive landscaped grounds, with a tennis court and croquet lawn, and is adjacent to the East Sussex National Golf Club. The spacious bedrooms are attractively decorated, tastefully furnished and equipped with many thoughtful touches such

continued

as flowers and books. Most rooms also have a separate sitting area.

ROOMS: 17 en suite 3 annexe en suite (5 fmly) (2 GF) s £130-£340; d £130-£340 (incl. bkfst) **LB** **FACILITIES:** STV 36 Xmas **CONF:** Thtr 80 Class 50 Board 40 Del from £160 **SERVICES:** Lift **PARKING:** 32 **NOTES:** No children 7yrs in restaurant Civ Wed 100 **CARDS:**

ULLESTHORPE, Leicestershire

Map 11 SP58

★★★68% Ullesthorpe Court Hotel & Golf Club

Frolesworth Rd LE17 5BZ
☎ 01455 209023 01455 202537
e-mail: bookings@ullesthorpecourt.co.uk
web: www.ullesthorpecourt.co.uk
Dir: *M1 junct 20 towards Lutterworth, then follow brown tourist signs*

Complete with its own golf club, this impressively equipped hotel is within easy reach of the motorway network, the NEC and Birmingham Airport. Public areas include a choice of restaurants, conference and leisure facilities. Bedrooms are mostly spacious and thoughtfully equipped for both the corporate and leisure guests and a four-poster room is available.

ROOMS: 38 en suite (1 fmly) in 20 bedrooms s fr £90; d fr £115 (incl. bkfst) **LB** **FACILITIES:** STV supervised 18 Snooker Sauna Solarium Gym Putt green Jacuzzi Beauty room, Steam Room **CONF:** Thtr 80 Class 48 Board 30 Del from £110 **PARKING:** 500 **NOTES:** in restaurant RS 25 & 26 Dec Civ Wed 120 **CARDS:**

ULLSWATER See Glenridding, Patterdale & Watermillock

ULVERSTON, Cumbria

Map 18 SD27

★★70% Lonsdale House Hotel

11 Daltongate LA12 7BD
☎ 01229 582598 01229 581260
e-mail: info@lonsdalehousehotel.co.uk
web: www.lonsdalehousehotel.co.uk
Dir: *In Ulverston take right at 2nd rdbt, follow one-way system to mini-rdbt. Turn left pass zebra crossing then right & 1st right.*

Enjoying a town centre location, this family-run hotel was once a coaching inn. Bedrooms vary in style and size but all are extremely well equipped, and refurbished rooms benefit from stylish furniture and soft furnishings. Public areas include an attractive bar and restaurant, an inviting lounge and a delightful rear garden.

ROOMS: 20 en suite (2 fmly) in 16 bedrooms s £55-£72.50; d £75-£110 (incl. bkfst) **LB** **FACILITIES:** STV Xmas **NOTES:** in restaurant **CARDS:**

UMBERLEIGH, Devon Map 03 SS62

★★69% Rising Sun Inn

EX37 9DU
☎ 01769 560447 🖹 01769 560764
e-mail: risingsuninn@btinternet.com
web: www.risingsuninn.com
Dir: *on A377, Exeter/Barnstaple Rd, at junct of B3227*

Overlooking the Taw River Valley, this 13th-century inn has retained much of its charm and character and offers comfortable modern facilities. Local musicians, fishing memorabilia and an inglenook fireplace set the style in the bar, where a good choice of interesting dishes, many featuring fresh fish, is offered.

ROOMS: 6 en suite 3 annexe en suite (1 fmly) ⊗ in all bedrooms s fr £49; d fr £89 (incl. bkfst) **LB** **FACILITIES:** STV Fishing ♫ Xmas **CONF:** Thtr 60 **PARKING:** 20 **NOTES:** ⊗ in restaurant **CARDS:**

UPHOLLAND, Lancashire Map 15 SD50

★★★64% Lancashire Manor

StopInn

Prescott Rd WN8 9PU
☎ 01695 720401 🖹 01695 50953
e-mail: enquiries@hotels-skelmersdale.com
Dir: *M6 junct 26 to M58. Leave at junct 5 for 'Pimbo' & turn left at rdbt follow into Prescott Road. Hotel on right*

Conveniently situated, this friendly hotel has attractive grounds and a magnificent Great Hall, dating back to 1580, now used primarily for banquets and weddings. The modern bedrooms are well equipped, and include facilities for less mobile guests. The bare stone walls in the bar and restaurant give character to the public areas.

ROOMS: 55 en suite (3 fmly) (21 GF) ⊗ in 35 bedrooms s £48-£95; d £75-£105 (incl. bkfst) **LB** **FACILITIES:** STV ch fac Xmas **CONF:** Thtr 200 Class 125 Board 70 Del from £89 **SERVICES:** air con **PARKING:** 250 **NOTES:** ⊗ in restaurant Civ Wed 150 **CARDS:**

UPPER SLAUGHTER, Gloucestershire Map 10 SP12

Top 200 – Hotel

★★★ Lords of the Manor

FURLONG

GL54 2JD
☎ 01451 820243 🖹 01451 820696
e-mail: enquiries@lordsofthemanor.com
web: www.lordsofthemanor.com
Dir: *2m W of A429. Turn off A40 onto A429, take 'The Slaughters' turning. Continue through Lower Slaughter for 1m Upper Slaughter. Hotel on right*

This wonderfully welcoming 17th-century manor-house hotel sits in eight acres of gardens and parkland surrounded by *continued* beautiful Cotswold countryside. A relaxed atmosphere, underpinned by professional and attentive service, is the hallmark here with guests often reluctant to leave! The public rooms are elegant and comfortable and the restaurant is the venue for consistently impressive cuisine. Bedrooms enjoy all the character and charm of the old building, combined with the extra touches expected of a hotel of this stature.

ROOMS: 27 en suite (9 GF) s fr £100; d £160-£310 (incl. bkfst) **LB** **FACILITIES:** STV Fishing Xmas **CONF:** Thtr 30 Class 20 Board 20 Del from £170 **PARKING:** 40 **NOTES:** ⊗ in restaurant Civ Wed 50 **CARDS:**

UPPINGHAM, Rutland Map 11 SP89

★★★67% Falcon

The Market Place LE15 9PY
☎ 01572 823535 🖹 01572 821620
e-mail: sales@thefalconhotel.com web: www.thefalconhotel.com
Dir: *turn off A47 onto A6003, left at lights, hotel on right*

An attractive, 16th-century coaching inn situated in the heart of this bustling market town. Public areas feature a superb, open-plan lounge bar, with a relaxing atmosphere and comfortable sofas. The brasserie offers a cosmopolitan-style snack menu and more formal meals are provided in the Garden Terrace Restaurant. Conference and functions rooms are also available.

ROOMS: 25 en suite (4 fmly) (3 GF) s £60; d £90-£125 (incl. bkfst) **LB** **FACILITIES:** STV Snooker ♫ ch fac Xmas **CONF:** Thtr 60 Class 40 Board 34 Del from £98 **PARKING:** 33 **NOTES:** ⊗ in restaurant Civ Wed 150 **CARDS:**

★★72% The Lake Isle Restaurant & Town House Hotel

16 High St East LE15 9PZ
☎ 01572 822951 🖹 01572 824400
e-mail: info@lakeislehotel.com
web: www.lakeislehotel.com
Dir: *in the centre of Uppingham via Queen Street*

This attractive, town-house hotel centres round a delightful restaurant and small, elegant bar. There is also an inviting and comfortable first-floor guest lounge. Bedrooms are extremely well-appointed and thoughtfully equipped and include some spacious split-level cottage suites situated across a quiet courtyard. Imaginative cooking and an extremely impressive list of wines are a highlight.

ROOMS: 9 en suite 3 annexe en suite (1 fmly) ⊗ in all bedrooms s £55-£65; d £70-£85 (incl. bkfst) **LB** **FACILITIES:** ch fac Xmas **CONF:** Board 10 **PARKING:** 7 **NOTES:** ⊗ in restaurant **CARDS:**

Bad hair day?
Hairdryers in all rooms three stars and above

U

UPTON UPON SEVERN, Worcestershire Map 10 SO84

★★★69% White Lion
21 High St WR8 0HJ
☎ 01684 592551 01684 593333
e-mail: reservations@whitelionhotel.biz
Dir: *A422, A38 towards Tewkesbury. In 8m take B4104, after 1m cross bridge, turn left to hotel, past bend on left*
Famed for being the inn depicted in Henry Fielding's novel *Tom Jones*, this 16th-century hotel brings old England to the fore with exposed beams, wall timbers, and traditional furniture with lace table cloths and vases of fresh flowers. The White Lion has a well-deserved reputation for the quality of its food, which is complemented by friendly, attentive service.
ROOMS: 13 rms (11 en suite) (2 GF) s £67.50; d £92.50 (incl. bkfst) **LB**
CONF: Thtr 24 Class 12 Board 12 **PARKING:** 18 **NOTES:** in restaurant Closed 1 Jan RS 25 Dec & 1 Jan
CARDS:

URMSTON, Greater Manchester Map 15 SJ79

Premier Lodge (Manchester Trafford Centre)
PREMIER LODGE.com
Trafford Boulevard M41 7JE
☎ 0870 9906310 0870 9906311
web: www.premierlodge.com
Dir: *from M6, onto M62 at junct 21a towards Manchester. Exit at junct 1, onto M60 south to junct 10, then B5214. Hotel on left just before Ellesmere Circle*
High quality, modern, budget accommodation, ideal for families and business travellers. All rooms feature bath, power shower and satellite TV, and most have telephones / modem points. The adjacent bar and restaurant offers a wide and varied menu.
ROOMS: 42 en suite s £50; d £50

UTTOXETER, Staffordshire Map 10 SK03

U The Riversholme Hotel & Restaurant
High St, Rocester ST14 5JU
☎ 01889 590900 01889 591960
e-mail: info@riversholme.co.uk
web: www.riversholme.co.uk
Dir: *A50 exit B5030 signed Rocester. Follow to JCB Headquarters, turn right into village. Hotel stands back off High Street.*
At the time of going to press, the star classification for this hotel was not confirmed. Please refer to the AA internet site www.theAA.com for current information.
ROOMS: 8 en suite (3 fmly) (4 GF) in all bedrooms s £75; d £85 (incl. bkfst) **PARKING:** 20 **NOTES:** in restaurant Closed 25 Dec-2 Jan **CARDS:**

U

Travel Inn
travel inn
Derby Rd, (A518/A50) ST14 5AA
☎ 08701 977256 01889 561801
Dir: *at junction of A50/A518, 1m north of Uttoxeter town centre*
Travel Inn offers good-quality, value-for-money accommodation. Spacious, en suite rooms with bath and shower comfortably accommodate a family of up to two adults and two children (to age 15). The restaurant and bar offers a varied menu. For further details consult the Hotel Groups page.
ROOMS: 41 en suite s £45.95-£46.95; d £45.95-£46.95

Travelodge
Travelodge
Ashbourne Rd ST14 5AA
☎ 08700 850 950 01889 562043
Dir: *on A50/A5030*
Travelodge offers good quality, good value, modern accommodation. Ideal for families, the spacious, en suite bedrooms include remote-control TV, tea and coffee-making facilities and luxury beds. Meals can be taken at the nearby family restaurant. For further details consult the Hotel Groups page.
ROOMS: 32 en suite s fr £25; d fr £25

UXBRIDGE See advert on opposite page

VENTNOR See Wight, Isle of

VERYAN, Cornwall & Isles of Scilly Map 02 SW93

★★★★77% Nare
Carne Beach TR2 5PF
☎ 01872 501111 01872 501856
e-mail: office@narehotel.co.uk
web: www.narehotel.co.uk
Dir: *from Tregony follow A3078 for approx 1.5m turn left at Veryan sign, through village towards sea and hotel*
This delightful hotel offers a relaxed, country-house atmosphere in a spectacular coastal setting. Many of the bedrooms have balconies, and fresh flowers, carefully chosen artwork and antiques all contribute to the engaging individuality. A choice of dining options is available, from light snacks to superb local seafood.
ROOMS: 38 en suite (4 fmly) s £80-£180; d £210-£360 (incl. bkfst) **LB**
FACILITIES: Spa STV Snooker Sauna Gym Jacuzzi Health & Beauty clinic Hotel Boat Shooting, steam room ch fac Xmas
SERVICES: Lift **PARKING:** 80 **NOTES:** in restaurant
CARDS:

VIRGINIA WATER, Surrey Map 06 TQ06

★★72% *The Wheatsheaf*
London Rd GU25 4QF
☎ 01344 842057 01344 842932
e-mail: sales@wheatsheafhotel.com
web: www.wheatsheafhotel.com
Dir: *M25 junct 13/A30 towards Camberley, follow A30 for approx 3m. From M3 junct 3/A30 towards London & Staines, through Sunningdale, continue for 3m, pass Wentworth Golf Course. Hotel on left at traffic lights*

This 19th-century inn is in a prime location overlooking the lake in Great Windsor Park. Bedrooms are well proportioned and

continued

comfortable, with stylish décor and a good range of facilities. The public rooms consist of a country-style bar and restaurant which offers a substantial lunch and dinner menu. Secure car parking is provided.
ROOMS: 17 en suite (2 fmly) ⊗ in 10 bedrooms **FACILITIES:** STV **CONF:** Thtr 50 Class 30 Board 25 **SERVICES:** air con **PARKING:** 100 **NOTES:** Civ Wed 60 **CARDS:**

WADEBRIDGE, Cornwall & Isles of Scilly — Map 02 SW97

★★★★ 71% Hustyns

St Breock Downs PL27 7LG
☎ 01208 893700 01208 893701
e-mail: reception@hustyns.com
web: www.hustyns.com
Dir: *take A39 to Town Centre. Follow brown heritage signs to Hustyns*

There is literally something for everyone at Hustyns, a secluded haven in 180 acres. Bedrooms are lavishly equipped and reflect contemporary expectations of comfort and quality; a number have the added bonus of decked balconies. A multitude of leisure facilities is offered for all ages, including an excellent indoor swimming pool and fitness suite. There is an informal brasserie and a fine dining restaurant to choose from.
ROOMS: 37 en suite (2 fmly) (13 GF) ⊗ in 23 bedrooms **FACILITIES:** STV Sauna Gym Putt green Jacuzzi All weather running track Steam room Spa opening 2004 Xmas **CONF:** Thtr 50 Class 25 Board 20 **SERVICES:** Lift air con **NOTES:** ⊗ in restaurant Civ Wed **CARDS:**

★★ 66% Molesworth Arms

Molesworth St PL27 7DP
☎ 01208 812055 01208 814254
e-mail: info@moleswortharms.co.uk
web: www.moleswortharms.co.uk
Dir: *A30 to & through Bodmin, then A389 into Wadebridge. Over old bridge, turn right at rdbt, then 1st left*

Situated in a pedestrian area of the town, this 16th-century former coaching inn is a popular base for exploring the area. The comfortable bedrooms retain their original character and charm and are suitable for both business and leisure travellers. In addition to the wide range of snacks and meals served in the lively bar, the Courtyard Restaurant offers a comprehensive carte with daily specials.
ROOMS: 16 rms (14 en suite) (2 fmly) s £57.50; d £90 (incl. bkfst & dinner) **LB** **FACILITIES:** STV **CONF:** Thtr 60 Class 50 Board 40 **PARKING:** 16 **NOTES:** ⊗ in restaurant **CARDS:**

WAKEFIELD, West Yorkshire — Map 16 SE32

★★★★ 64% Cedar Court

Denby Dale Rd WF4 3QZ
☎ 01924 276310 01924 280221
e-mail: sales@cedarcourthotels.co.uk
web: www.cedarcourthotels.co.uk
Dir: *adjacent to M1 junct 39*

This hotel enjoys a convenient location just off the M1. Traditionally styled bedrooms offer a good range of facilities while open-plan public areas include a busy bar and restaurant operation. Conferences and functions are extremely well catered for and a brand new leisure club completes the picture.
ROOMS: 151 en suite (2 fmly) (74 GF) ⊗ in 100 bedrooms s £65-£130; d £75-£140 **LB** **FACILITIES:** **Spa** STV supervised Sauna Solarium Gym Jacuzzi Xmas **CONF:** BC Thtr 400 Class 140 Board 80 Del £160 **SERVICES:** Lift **PARKING:** 350 **NOTES:** ⊗ in restaurant Civ Wed 250 **CARDS:**

★★★ 74% Waterton Park

Walton Hall, The Balk, Walton WF2 6PW
☎ 01924 257911 & 249800 01924 259686
e-mail: watertonpark@bestwestern.co.uk
Dir: *3m SE off B6378 - off M1 junct 39 towards Wakefield. At 3rd rdbt take right for Crofton. At the 2nd set of traffic lights turn right follow signs*

Best Western

A stately private house, built on an island in the centre of a lake in an idyllic setting. The main house contains many feature bedrooms, and the new annexe houses more spacious rooms, all equally well equipped with modern facilities. The delightful beamed restaurant, two bars and leisure centre are located in the old hall, and there is a licence for civil weddings.
ROOMS: 25 en suite 36 annexe en suite (16 GF) ⊗ in 12 bedrooms s fr £75; d fr £120 (incl. bkfst) **LB** **FACILITIES:** **Spa** STV 18 Fishing Sauna Solarium Gym Jacuzzi Steam room **CONF:** Thtr 150 Class 80 Board 80 Del from £130 **PARKING:** 200 **NOTES:** ⊗ in restaurant Civ Wed 80 **CARDS:**

WAKEFIELD, continued

★★★69% Hotel St Pierre

Barnsley Rd, Newmillerdam WF2 6QG
☎ 01924 255596 🖷 01924 252746
e-mail: sales@hotelstpierre.co.uk
***Dir:** M1 junct 39 take A636 to Wakefield, turn right at rdbt, on to Asdale Road to traffic lights. Turn right onto A61 towards Barnsley. Hotel just after lake*

This well-furnished hotel lies south of Wakefield, close to Newmiller Dam. The interior of the modern building has comfortable and thoughtfully equipped bedrooms and smart public rooms. A good selection of conference rooms, a small gymnasium and an intimate restaurant are all provided for guests' use.

ROOMS: 54 en suite (3 fmly) (4 GF) ⊗ in 33 bedrooms s £55-£80; d £65-£90 **LB** **FACILITIES:** STV Gym Xmas **CONF:** Thtr 120 Class 60 Board 60 Del from £79 **SERVICES:** Lift **PARKING:** 70 **NOTES:** Civ Wed 120 **CARDS:**

★★★64% Chasley Hotel

Queen St WF1 1JU
☎ 01924 372111 🖷 01924 383648
e-mail: anybody@chasleywakefield.supanet.com
web: chasleywakfield.supanet.com
***Dir:** leave M1 junct 39 & follow signs for town centre. Queen St is on the left*

Situated in the city centre and close to the cathedral, this modern commercial hotel offers well-equipped and pleasantly furnished bedrooms. There is a comfortable bar lounge next to the spacious restaurant, where a set-price menu is offered. Conference and gymnasium facilities are also available.

ROOMS: 64 en suite (4 fmly) ⊗ in 16 bedrooms s £39.95-£49.95; d £44.95-£54.95 (incl. bkfst) **FACILITIES:** Sunbeds, Fitness Room ch fac Xmas **CONF:** Thtr 250 Class 90 Board 54 **SERVICES:** Lift **PARKING:** 30 **NOTES:** ⊗ in restaurant Civ Wed 250
CARDS:

⌂ Campanile

Monckton Rd WF2 7AL
☎ 01924 201054 🖷 01924 201055
e-mail: wakefield@envergure.co.uk
***Dir:** M1 junct 39, A636 1m towards Wakefield, left onto Monckton Rd, hotel on left*

This modern building offers accommodation in smart, well-equipped bedrooms, all with en suite bathrooms. Refreshments may be taken at the informal Bistro. For further details consult the Hotel Groups page.

ROOMS: 76 annexe en suite s fr £42.50; d fr £42.50
CONF: Thtr 35 Class 18 Board 24

⌂ Days Inn Hotel Wakefield

Fryers Way, Silkwood Park, Ossett WF5 9TJ
☎ 01924 274200 🖷 01924 274246
e-mail: wakefield@dayshotel.co.uk
***Dir:** M1 junct 40 onto A638 to Wakefield. Take 1st left into Silkwood Park and hotel is on right*

This modern building offers accommodation in smart, spacious and well-equipped bedrooms, suitable for families and business travellers, and all with en suite bathrooms. Continental breakfast is available and other refreshments may be taken at the nearby family restaurant. For further details see the Hotel Groups page.

ROOMS: 100 en suite s £52.50-£69.45; d £52.50-£76.40 **CONF:** BC Thtr 40 Class 14 Board 20 Del from £70

⌂ Travel Inn

Thornes Park, Denby Dale Rd WF2 8DY
☎ 08701 977257 🖷 01924 373620
***Dir:** From the M1 (J39) take A636 towards Wakefield town centre. Travel Inn on left at 3rd rbt.*

Travel Inn offers good-quality, value-for-money accommodation. Spacious, en suite rooms with bath and shower comfortably accommodate a family of up to two adults and two children (to age 15). The restaurant and bar offers a varied menu. For further details consult the Hotel Groups page.

ROOMS: 42 en suite s £45.95-£46.95; d £45.95-£46.95 **CONF:** Thtr 54 Board 24

⌂ Travelodge Wakefield (Northbound)

M1 Service Area, West Bretton WF4 4LQ
☎ 08700 850 950 🖷 01924 830609
(For full entry see Woolley Edge)

WALLASEY, Merseyside — Map 15 SJ29

★★★70% Grove House

Grove Rd CH45 3HF
☎ 0151 639 3947 & 0151 630 4558 🖷 0151 639 0028
e-mail: reception@thegrovehouse.fsnet.co.uk
***Dir:** M53 J1, A554 Wallasey New Brighton, right after church onto Harrison Drive, left after Windsors Garage onto Grove Rd.*

This is an immaculately maintained, family-owned hotel. Many of the bedrooms enjoy a view over the attractive gardens to the rear of the hotel; all are comfortably furnished and particularly well-equipped. The bar lounge provides a venue to relax with drinks before dinner in the tastefully appointed oak-panelled restaurant.

ROOMS: 14 en suite (7 fmly) s £54.50-£59.75; d £59.75-£69.75 **LB**
FACILITIES: STV **CONF:** Thtr 50 Class 30 Board 50 Del £94.95
PARKING: 28 **NOTES:** RS Bank holidays Civ Wed 50
CARDS:

WALLINGFORD, Oxfordshire — Map 05 SU68

★★★75% ® Springs Hotel & Golf Club

Wallingford Rd, North Stoke OX10 6BE
☎ 01491 836687 🖷 01491 836877
e-mail: info@thespringshotel.com
web: www.thespringshotel.com
***Dir:** off A4074 Oxford-Reading Rd onto B4009 - Goring. Hotel approx 1m on right*

Set on its own golf course, this Victorian mansion has a timeless and peaceful atmosphere. Bedrooms vary in size; many are spacious, and all are generously equipped. The elegant restaurant enjoys splendid views over the spring-fed lake. There is also a

continued

comfortable lounge with original features, and a cosy bar in which to relax.

ROOMS: 31 en suite (3 fmly) (8 GF) ⊘ in 6 bedrooms s £95-£120; d £110-£135 (incl. bkfst) **LB** **FACILITIES:** STV 18 Fishing Sauna Putt green Clay pigeon shooting ch fac Xmas **CONF:** BC Thtr 60 Class 16 Board 26 Del from £140 **PARKING:** 150 **NOTES:** ⊘ in restaurant Civ Wed 90 **CARDS:**

★★★68% The George

High St OX10 0BS
☎ 01491 836665 01491 825359
e-mail: info@george-hotel-wallingford.com
Dir: *E side of A329 on N entry to town*

Old-world charm and modern facilities merge seamlessly in this former coaching inn. Bedrooms in the main house have charm and character in abundance. Those in the new wing have a more contemporary style, but all are well equipped and attractively decorated. Diners can choose between the restaurant and bistro, or relax in the cosy bar.
ROOMS: 39 en suite (1 fmly) ⊘ in 21 bedrooms s £110-£125; d £115-£140 **LB** **FACILITIES:** STV Xmas **CONF:** Thtr 120 Class 60 Board 40 Del from £135 **PARKING:** 60 **NOTES:** ⊘ in restaurant Civ Wed 100
CARDS:

★★★68% Shillingford Bridge

Forestdale Hotels

Shillingford OX10 8LZ
☎ 01865 858567 01865 858636
e-mail: shillingford.bridge@forestdale.com
Dir: *M4 junct 10 follow A329 through Wallingford towards Thame, then B4009 through Watlington turn right on A4074 at Benson, then left at Shillingford rdbt (unclass road) Wallingford Rd*
This hotel enjoys a superb position right on the banks of the River Thames, and benefits from private moorings and a waterside open-air swimming pool. The public areas have large picture windows making the best use of the view. Bedrooms are well equipped and furnished with comfort in mind.
ROOMS: 34 en suite 8 annexe en suite (6 fmly) ⊘ in 8 bedrooms s fr £70; d fr £120 (incl. bkfst) **LB** **FACILITIES:** supervised Fishing Squash Xmas **CONF:** Thtr 80 Class 36 Board 26 Del from £125 **PARKING:** 100 **NOTES:** ⊘ in restaurant Civ Wed
CARDS:

WALSALL, West Midlands — Map 10 SP09

★★★★65% Menzies Baron's Court

Walsall Rd, Walsall Wood WS9 9AH
☎ 01543 452020 01543 361276
e-mail: barons@menzies-hotels.co.uk
Dir: *M6 junct 7, take A34 towards Walsall, follow A4148 ring road, at rdbt turn right onto A461 towards Lichfield, hotel 3 miles on right*
This hotel prides itself on warm hospitality and is conveniently situated for business guests to this area. The lounge, bar and restaurant are modern and thoughtfully designed following refurbishment. Additional features include a small leisure complex and conference facilities.
ROOMS: 94 en suite (2 fmly) ⊘ in 19 bedrooms s £99; d £99-£119 **LB**
FACILITIES: STV Sauna Solarium Gym Jacuzzi Xmas
CONF: Thtr 200 Class 100 Board 100 Del from £135 **SERVICES:** Lift
PARKING: 200 **NOTES:** ⊘ in restaurant Civ Wed
CARDS:

★★★76% The Fairlawns at Aldridge

Best Western

178 Little Aston Rd, Aldridge WS9 0NU
☎ 01922 455122 01922 743210
e-mail: welcome@fairlawns.co.uk
web: www.fairlawns.co.uk
Dir: *off A452 towards Aldridge at x-roads with A454. Hotel 600yds on right*

In a rural location, this friendly hotel offers a wide range of facilities and modern, comfortable bedrooms. Family rooms, one with a four-poster bed, suites and even budget rooms are available. The Fairlawns Restaurant serves a wide range of award-winning seasonal dishes. The extensive leisure complex is predominantly for adult use as there is restricted availability to young people.
ROOMS: 50 en suite (8 fmly) (1 GF) ⊘ in 34 bedrooms s £72.50-£150; d £84.50-£172.50 (incl. bkfst) **LB** **FACILITIES:** **Spa** STV Sauna Solarium Gym Jacuzzi Dance studio Beauty Salon, Indoor supervised
CONF: BC Thtr 80 Class 40 Board 30 Del from £117.50 **PARKING:** 150
NOTES: ⊘ in restaurant Civ Wed 100
CARDS:

See advert under BIRMINGHAM

WALSALL, continued

★★★68% Beverley
58 Lichfield Rd WS4 2DJ
☎ 01922 614967 & 622999 01922 724187
e-mail: beverleyhotel@aol.com
Dir: *1m N of Walsall town centre on A461 to Lichfield*
This privately-owned hotel dates back to 1880. Bedrooms are comfortably appointed and equipped with thoughtful extras. The tastefully decorated public areas include a relaxing guest lounge and a spacious bar combined with a conservatory. The Gallery Restaurant offers a choice of carefully prepared, appetising dishes.
ROOMS: 40 en suite (2 fmly) (4 GF) ⊗ in 6 bedrooms s £70-£80; d £80-£100 (incl. bkfst) **LB** **FACILITIES:** Games room **CONF:** BC Thtr 60 Class 30 Board 30 Del from £100 **PARKING:** 68 **NOTES:** ⊗ in restaurant RS 24 Dec-2 Jan Civ Wed 50
CARDS:

★★★66% Quality Hotel & Suites Walsall
20 Wolverhampton Rd West, Bentley WS2 0BS
☎ 01922 724444 01922 723148
e-mail: enquiries@hotels-walsall.com
Dir: *on rdbt at M6 junct 10*
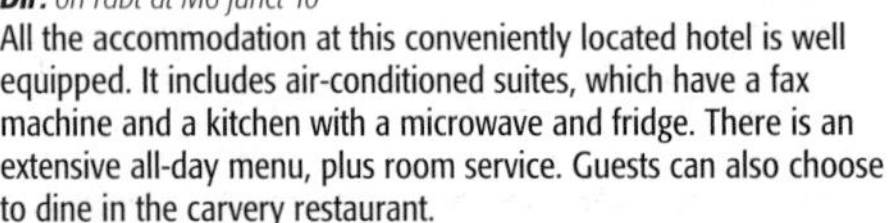
All the accommodation at this conveniently located hotel is well equipped. It includes air-conditioned suites, which have a fax machine and a kitchen with a microwave and fridge. There is an extensive all-day menu, plus room service. Guests can also choose to dine in the carvery restaurant.
ROOMS: 154 en suite (120 fmly) (78 GF) ⊗ in 64 bedrooms s £45-£115; d £55-£135 (incl. bkfst) **LB** **FACILITIES: Spa** STV supervised Sauna Gym Jacuzzi Xmas **CONF:** Thtr 180 Class 70 Board 80 Del from £70 **PARKING:** 160 **NOTES:** ⊗ in restaurant Civ Wed 150
CARDS:

★★★64% Quality Hotel Birmingham North
Birmingham Rd WS5 3AB
☎ 01922 633609 01922 635727
e-mail: info@boundaryhotel.com
Dir: *M6 junct 7, A34 to Walsall. Hotel 1.5m on left*
Bedrooms at this purpose-built hotel, including some on the ground floor, are soundly furnished and well equipped. Public areas include a pleasantly appointed main restaurant (more informal meals are served in the public bar) and a cellar bar which occasionally features live music. Hotel guests also have the use of a well-maintained tennis court.
ROOMS: 96 en suite (3 fmly) (4 GF) ⊗ in 50 bedrooms s £105; d £105 **LB** **FACILITIES:** STV Pool table Xmas **CONF:** Thtr 60 Class 30 Board 30 Del £140 **SERVICES:** Lift **PARKING:** 250 **NOTES:** ⊗ in restaurant Civ Wed 60 **CARDS:**

★★63% Bescot
83-89 Bescot Rd WS2 9DG
☎ 01922 622447 01922 630256
e-mail: enquiries@bescothotel.com
Dir: *M6 junct 9 at rdbt take Walsall turning. Hotel on right*
The Bescot is a business-focused hotel. Public rooms are comfortable and freshly furnished, and include a lounge bar, a restaurant and large function suite. Bedrooms have a good range of facilities and the annexe rooms are spacious, especially the two ground-floor courtyard rooms.
ROOMS: 22 en suite 11 annexe en suite (2 fmly) ⊗ in 4 bedrooms s £44.50; d £54.50 (incl. bkfst) **FACILITIES:** STV Xmas **CONF:** Thtr 100 Class 100 Del from £61.50 **PARKING:** 60 **NOTES:**
CARDS:

Travel Inn
Bentley Green, Bentley Rd North WS2 0WB
☎ 08701 977258 01922 724098
Dir: *M6 junct 10, A454 signed Wolverhampton & then 2nd exit (Ansons junct). Left at rdbt, 1st left at next rdbt, Travel Inn on right*
Travel Inn offers good-quality, value-for-money accommodation. Spacious, en suite rooms with bath and shower comfortably accommodate a family of up to two adults and two children (to age 15). The restaurant and bar offers a varied menu. For further details consult the Hotel Groups page.
ROOMS: 40 en suite s £45.95-£46.95; d £45.95-£46.95

WALTERSTONE, Herefordshire — Map 09 SO32

★★★68% *Allt-yr-Ynys Country House Hotel*
HR2 0DU
☎ 01873 890307 01873 890539
e-mail: allthotel@compuserve.com
(For full entry see Abergavenny (Wales))

WALTHAM ABBEY, Essex — Map 06 TL30

★★★★69% Waltham Abbey Marriott
Old Shire Ln EN9 3LX
☎ 01992 717170 01992 711841
Dir: *M25 junct 26*
This hotel benefits from convenient access to London and the major road networks. Air-conditioned bedrooms are spacious, tastefully decorated and offer a range of facilities for the modern business traveller. The hotel also has a range of meeting rooms, substantial car parking and a well-equipped indoor leisure centre.
ROOMS: 162 en suite (16 fmly) (80 GF) ⊗ in 132 bedrooms s £109-£119; d £109-£119 **LB** **FACILITIES:** STV Sauna Solarium Gym Jacuzzi Steam room, Beauty Salon ch fac Xmas **CONF:** BC Thtr 280 Class 120 Board 50 Del £185 **SERVICES:** air con **PARKING:** 250 **NOTES:** ⊗ in restaurant Civ Wed 200
CARDS:

Premier Lodge (Waltham Abbey)
The Grange, Sewardstone Rd EN9 3QF
☎ 0870 9906568 0870 9906569
web: www.premierlodge.com
Dir: *M25 junct 26 & follow A121 towards Waltham Abbey. Turn left onto A112, lodge 0.5m on left*

High quality, modern, budget accommodation, ideal for families and business travellers. All rooms feature bath, power shower and satellite TV, and most have telephones / modem points. The adjacent bar and restaurant offers a wide and varied menu.
ROOMS: 93 en suite s £58; d £58

WALTON-ON-THAMES, Surrey
See LONDON SECTION plan 1 A1

Innkeeper's Lodge Walton-on-Thames
Ashley Park Rd KT12 1JP
☎ 01932 220196 01932 220660
www.innkeeperslodge.com
Dir: *M25 junct 11 E towards A317 & Weybridge, at B365 rdbt for Ashley Park, turn left then right into Station Av, left opposite station*
Smart rooms meet essential business requirements but also have home comforts, and depending on location may well have meeting rooms and pub dining. Dining options generally include all-day menus plus the added advantage of breakfast.
ROOMS: 32 en suite s £49.95-£79.95; d £49.95-£79.95
CONF: Thtr 60 Class 24 Board 24

WARDLEY, Tyne & Wear — Map 21 NZ36

Travelodge Newcastle East

Leam Ln, Whitemare Pool NE10 8YB
☎ 08700 850 950 📠 0191 438 3333
Dir: *at junc of A194(M)/A184*
Travelodge offers good quality, good value, modern accommodation. Ideal for families, the spacious, en suite bedrooms include remote-control TV, tea and coffee-making facilities and luxury beds. Meals can be taken at the nearby family restaurant. For further details consult the Hotel Groups page.
ROOMS: 71 en suite s fr £25; d fr £25

WARE, Hertfordshire — Map 06 TL31

★★★★★71% Marriott Hanbury Manor Hotel & Country Club

SG12 0SD
☎ 01920 487722 & 0870 400 7222
📠 01920 487692
e-mail: guestrelations.hanburymanor@marriotthotels.co.uk
Dir: *M25 junct 25, take A10 north for 12m, hotel is on the left*
Set in 200 acres of landscaped grounds, this impressive Jacobean-style mansion boasts an enviable range of leisure facilities, including an excellent health club and championship golf course. Bedrooms are traditionally and comfortably furnished in the country-house style and have lovely marbled bathrooms. There are a number of food and drink options, including the renowned Zodiac and Oakes restaurants.
ROOMS: 134 en suite 27 annexe en suite (3 GF) ⊘ in 96 bedrooms s £138-£178; d £138-£178 (incl. bkfst) **LB FACILITIES: Spa** STV supervised 18 Snooker Sauna Solarium Gym Putt green Jacuzzi Health & beauty treatments, Aerobics, Yoga Dance class Xmas **CONF:** BC Thtr 120 Class 76 Board 36 **SERVICES:** Lift **PARKING:** 200 **NOTES:** Civ Wed 120 **CARDS:**

★★★68% Roebuck

Baldock St SG12 9DR
☎ 01920 409955 📠 01920 468016
e-mail: roebuck@forestdale.com
Dir: *turn off A10 onto B1001, turn left at rdbt first left behind Fire Station*
Formerly a private mansion, this conveniently located hotel has been extended and modernised over the years to produce a popular venue for business guests in particular. Bedrooms are mostly spacious and a few are suitable for less mobile guests, whilst the smart public areas include a range of conference rooms, a bar and an airy restaurant.
ROOMS: 50 en suite (1 fmly) (16 GF) ⊘ in 16 bedrooms s fr £95; d fr £120 (incl. bkfst) **LB FACILITIES:** STV **CONF:** Thtr 200 Class 75 Board 60 Del from £125 **SERVICES:** Lift **PARKING:** 64 **NOTES:** ⊘ in restaurant Civ Wed 80 **CARDS:**

WAREHAM, Dorset — Map 04 SY98

★★★68% *Springfield Country Hotel & Leisure Club*

Grange Rd BH20 5AL
☎ 01929 552177 📠 01929 551862
Dir: *from Wareham take Stoborough road then 1st right in village to join by-pass. Then left, and immediately right*
Suitable for a touring base, this attractive hotel is well located in the heart of Purbeck. Extensive grounds and leisure facilities attract the leisure guest; the hotel boasts both indoor and outdoor pools. Conference and business facilities are well patronised. Bedrooms are a good size; many have now been refurbished.
ROOMS: 48 en suite (7 fmly) **FACILITIES:** Squash Snooker Sauna Gym Jacuzzi Steam room Table tennis Beauty treatment ch fac **CONF:** Thtr 200 Class 50 Board 60 **SERVICES:** Lift **PARKING:** 150 **NOTES:** ⊘ in restaurant **CARDS:**

★★★65% Worgret Manor

Worgret Rd BH20 6AB
☎ 01929 552957 📠 01929 554804
e-mail: admin@worgretmanorhotel.co.uk
web: www.worgretmanorhotel.co.uk
Dir: *on A352 from Wareham to Wool, 0.5m from Wareham rdbt*
On the edge of Wareham, with easy access to major routes, this privately owned Georgian manor house offers a friendly, cheerful ambience. The bedrooms come in a variety of sizes. Public rooms are well presented and comprise a popular bar, a quiet lounge and an airy restaurant.
ROOMS: 12 en suite (1 fmly) (3 GF) ⊘ in 8 bedrooms s £55-£60; d £80-£90 (incl. bkfst) **LB FACILITIES:** Free use of local sports centre **CONF:** Thtr 50 **PARKING:** 25 **NOTES:** ⊘ in restaurant **CARDS:**

★★67% *Kemps Country House*

East Stoke BH20 6AL
☎ 01929 462563 📠 01929 405287
e-mail: kemps.hotel@lineone.net
Dir: *midway between Wareham & Wool on A352*
A relaxing family-owned hotel with views over the Purbeck Hills in the distance. Bedrooms are spacious and include modern garden rooms, and there are two comfortable lounges and an adjoining bar. An extensive choice is offered from the imaginative set and carte menus; bar meals are available at lunchtime.
ROOMS: 5 rms (4 en suite) 10 annexe en suite (4 fmly) **FACILITIES:** Jacuzzi **CONF:** Thtr 100 Class 50 Board 24 **PARKING:** 50 **NOTES:** ⊘ in restaurant **CARDS:**

WARMINSTER, Wiltshire — Map 04 ST84

★★★★74% Bishopstrow House

BA12 9HH
☎ 01985 212312 📠 01985 216769
e-mail: info@bishopstrow.co.uk
Dir: *A303, A36, B3414, hotel 2m on right*
This is a fine example of a Georgian country home, situated in 27 acres of grounds. Public areas are traditional in style and feature antiques and open fires. All bedrooms offer DVD players. A spa, a tennis court and several country walks ensure there is something for all guests. The restaurant serves quality contemporary cuisine.
ROOMS: 32 en suite (3 fmly) (4 GF) ⊘ in 1 bedroom s fr £99; d £199-£330 (incl. bkfst) **LB FACILITIES: Spa** STV Fishing Sauna Gym Clay pigeon shooting Archery Cycling ch fac Xmas **CONF:** Thtr 65 Class 32 Board 36 Del from £175 **PARKING:** 100 **NOTES:** ⊘ in restaurant Civ Wed 70 **CARDS:**

Travelodge

A36 Bath Rd BA12 7RU
☎ 08700 850 950 📠 01985 214380
Dir: *junct A350/A36*
Travelodge offers good quality, good value, modern accommodation. Ideal for families, the spacious, en suite bedrooms include remote-control TV, tea and coffee-making facilities and luxury beds. Meals can be taken at the nearby family restaurant. For further details consult the Hotel Groups page.
ROOMS: 31 en suite s fr £25; d fr £25

WARRINGTON, Cheshire Map 15 SJ68

Accessible Hotel of the Year

★★★★75% **De Vere Daresbury Park**
Chester Rd, Daresbury WA4 4BB
☎ 01925 267331 📠 01925 265615
e-mail: reservations.daresbury@devere-hotels.com
Dir: *M56 junct 11, take 'Daresbury Park' exit at rdbt. Hotel in 100mtrs*
Close to the local motorway networks and many tourist attractions, this modern hotel is a very popular venue for both business and leisure travellers. Public areas are themed around 'Alice in Wonderland' in tribute to local author Lewis Carroll. These include a range of eating and drinking options, leisure facilities and extensive conference facilities. AA Accessible Hotel of the Year 2004-5.
ROOMS: 181 en suite (14 fmly) (62 GF) ⊗ in 128 bedrooms s £70-£129; d £80-£139 **LB** **FACILITIES: Spa** STV supervised Squash Snooker Sauna Solarium Gym Jacuzzi Steam Room, Beauty salon ch fac Xmas **CONF:** BC Thtr 300 Class 200 Board 100 Del from £120 **SERVICES:** Lift **PARKING:** 400 **NOTES:** Civ Wed 220 **CARDS:**

★★★★72%
Hanover International Hotel & Club

Stretton Rd, Stretton WA4 4NS
☎ 01925 730706 📠 01925 730740
e-mail: reception@hanover-international.com
Dir: *M56 junct 10, A49 to Warrington, at lights turn right to Appleton Thorn, hotel 200yds on right*
This modern hotel enjoys a peaceful setting, yet is conveniently located minutes from the M56. Comfortable bedrooms are smartly appointed and thoughtfully equipped. Spacious, attractive public areas include extensive conference and function facilities, and a comprehensive leisure centre complete with outdoor tennis courts and an impressive beauty centre.
ROOMS: 142 en suite (15 fmly) (31 GF) ⊗ in 54 bedrooms s £115-£180; d £125-£180 **LB** **FACILITIES:** STV Sauna Solarium Gym Jacuzzi Retreat Beauty centre, Dance studio, Steam room ch fac Xmas **CONF:** BC Thtr 400 Class 200 Board 90 Del from £135 **SERVICES:** Lift **PARKING:** 400 **NOTES:** ⊗ in restaurant Civ Wed 400
CARDS:

★★★72% **Fir Grove**
Knutsford Old Rd WA4 2LD
☎ 01925 267471 📠 01925 601092
e-mail: firgrove@bestwestern.co.uk
Dir: *M6 junct 20, follow signs for A50 to Warrington for 2.4m, before swing bridge over canal, turn right, and right again*
Situated in a quiet residential area, this hotel is convenient for both the town centre and the motorway network. Comfortable, smart bedrooms, including new spacious executive rooms, offer some excellent extra facilities such as Playstations and CD players. Public areas include a smart lounge/bar, a neatly appointed restaurant and excellent function and meeting facilities.
ROOMS: 52 en suite (3 fmly) (20 GF) ⊗ in 20 bedrooms s £70-£94; d £70-£104 (incl. bkfst) **FACILITIES:** STV Xmas **CONF:** Thtr 200 Class 150 Board 50 Del from £99 **PARKING:** 100 **NOTES:** ⊗ in restaurant Civ Wed 200 **CARDS:**

★★68% **Paddington House**
514 Old Manchester Rd WA1 3TZ
☎ 01925 816767 📠 01925 816651
e-mail: hotel@paddingtonhouse.co.uk
web: www.paddingtonhouse.co.uk
Dir: *1m from M6 junct 21, off A57, 2m from town centre*
This busy, friendly hotel is conveniently situated just over a mile from the M6. Bedrooms are attractively furnished, and include four-poster and ground-floor rooms. Guests can dine in the wood-panelled Padgate restaurant or in the cosy bar. Conference and function facilities are also available.
ROOMS: 37 en suite (9 fmly) (6 GF) ⊗ in 17 bedrooms s £57.50; d £63 (incl. bkfst) **LB** **CONF:** Thtr 180 Class 100 Board 40 Del £90 **SERVICES:** Lift **PARKING:** 50 **NOTES:** ⊗ in restaurant Civ Wed 150
CARDS:

Innkeeper's Lodge Warrington

322 Newton Rd, Lowton Village WA3 1HD
☎ 0870 243 0500 & 01942 671421 📠 01942 269692
www.innkeeperslodge.com
Dir: *A580 via M56 junct 23 towards Manchester, follow signs for Toby Carvery*
Smart rooms meet essential business requirements but also have home comforts, and depending on location may well have meeting rooms and pub dining. Dining options generally include all-day menus plus the added advantage of breakfast.
ROOMS: 58 en suite s £45; d £45

Premier Lodge (Warrington Central)

Manchester Rd, Woolston WA1 4GB
☎ 0870 9906524 📠 0870 9906525
web: www.premierlodge.com
High quality, modern, budget accommodation, ideal for families and business travellers. All rooms feature bath, power shower and satellite TV, and most have telephones / modem points. The adjacent bar and restaurant offers a wide and varied menu.
ROOMS: 105 en suite s £48; d £48

Premier Lodge (Warrington North)

Golborne Rd, Winwick WA2 8LF
☎ 0870 9906600 📠 0870 9906601
web: www.premierlodge.com
Dir: *M6 junct 22. Follow signs for A573 towards Newton-le-Willows. Follow dual carriageway to end & take 3rd exit at rdbt. Church facing lodge to right of church*
High quality, modern, budget accommodation, ideal for families and business travellers. All rooms feature bath, power shower and satellite TV, and most have telephones / modem points. The adjacent bar and restaurant offers a wide and varied menu.
ROOMS: 42 en suite s £50; d £50
CONF: Thtr 30 Class 20 Board 25 Del £85

⌂ Premier Lodge (Warrington South)

Tarporley Rd, Stretton WA4 4NB
☎ 0870 9906526 📠 0870 9906527
web: www.premierlodge.com
Dir: *Just off M56 junct 10. Follow A49 to Warrington & turn left at 1st set of traffic lights*
High quality, modern, budget accommodation, ideal for families and business travellers. All rooms feature bath, power shower and satellite TV, and most have telephones / modem points. The adjacent bar and restaurant offers a wide and varied menu.
ROOMS: 29 en suite s £50; d £50

⌂ Travel Inn (Warrington East)
1430 Centre Park, Park Boulevard WA1 1QR
☎ 08701 977259 📠 01925 244259
Dir: *at Bridgefoot junct of A49/A50/A56 in centre of Warrington*
Travel Inn offers good-quality, value-for-money accommodation. Spacious, en suite rooms with bath and shower comfortably accommodate a family of up to two adults and two children (to age 15). The restaurant and bar offers a varied menu. For further details consult the Hotel Groups page.
ROOMS: 42 en suite s £45.95-£46.95; d £45.95-£46.95

⌂ Travel Inn (Warrington North)
Woburn Rd WA2 8RN
☎ 08701 977260 📠 01925 414544
Dir: *M62 junct 9 towards Warrington, 100yds from junct*
Travel Inn offers good-quality, value-for-money accommodation. Spacious, en suite rooms with bath and shower comfortably accommodate a family of up to two adults and two children (to age 15). The restaurant and bar offers a varied menu. For further details consult the Hotel Groups page.
ROOMS: 40 en suite s £45.95-£46.95; d £45.95-£46.95

⌂ Travelodge
Kendrick/Leigh St WA1 1UZ
☎ 08700 850 950 📠 01925 639432
Dir: *M6 junct 21, follow A57 towards Liverpool & Widnes to Warrington town centre, through Asda rdbt, lodge next left at lights*
Travelodge offers good quality, good value, modern accommodation. Ideal for families, the spacious, en suite bedrooms include remote-control TV, tea and coffee-making facilities and luxury beds. Meals can be taken at the nearby family restaurant. For further details consult the Hotel Groups page.
ROOMS: 63 en suite s fr £25; d fr £25

WARWICK, Warwickshire
Map 10 SP26
See also Honiley & Leamington Spa (Royal)

★★★★74% ⊛⊛ Ardencote Manor Hotel, Country Club & Spa
Lye Green Rd CV35 8LS
☎ 01926 843111 📠 01926 842646
e-mail: hotel@ardencote.com web: www.ardencote.com
(For full entry see Claverdon)

★★★64% Lord Leycester
Jury St CV34 4EJ
☎ 01926 491481 📠 01926 491561
e-mail: reception@lord-leycester.co.uk
web: www.lord-leycester.co.uk
Dir: *M40 junct 15/A429. Follow road into town centre, past West Gate onto High St & Jury St.*
This historic Grade II listed property is just a short walk from the famous castle. Upgraded bedrooms and public rooms provide

continued

comfortable accommodation. A choice of eating options is available in either the informal Squires Buttery or the Knights Restaurant.

Lord Leycester

ROOMS: 48 en suite (3 fmly) ⊘ in 25 bedrooms s £62.50-£85; d £80-£95 (incl. bkfst) **LB** **FACILITIES:** Xmas **CONF:** Thtr 120 Class 50 Board 40 Del from £105 **SERVICES:** Lift **PARKING:** 40 **NOTES:** ✈ ⊘ in restaurant **CARDS:**

★★63% Warwick Arms
17 High St CV34 4AT
☎ 01926 492759 📠 01926 410587
e-mail: warwickarms@ukonline.co.uk
Dir: *M40 junct 15, main rd into Warwick, hotel 100yds past Lord Leycester Hospital*
A relaxed hotel in the heart of Warwick, close to the castle walls. Typical in an older building, bedrooms vary in size and style but have a good range of facilities. Bar meals are very popular, and

continued on p610

W

WARWICK, continued

thanks to the work of some local art students, the restaurant is stylishly decorated and well worth a look too.
ROOMS: 35 en suite (4 fmly) s £55; d £65 (incl. bkfst)
FACILITIES: Xmas **CONF:** Thtr 100 Class 30 Board 30 **PARKING:** 21
CARDS:

WARWICK MOTORWAY SERVICE AREA (M40), Warwickshire — Map 10 SP35

Days Inn Stratford upon Avon

DAYS INN

Warwick Services, M40 Northbound junction 12-13, Banbury Rd CV35 0AA
☎ 01926 651681 📠 01926 651634
e-mail: warwick.north.hotel@welcomebreak.co.uk
web: www.welcomebreak.co.uk
Dir: *M40 northbound between junct 12 & 13*
This modern building offers accommodation in smart, spacious and well-equipped bedrooms, suitable for families and business travellers, and all with en suite bathrooms. Continental breakfast is available and other refreshments may be taken at the nearby family restaurant. For further details see the Hotel Groups page.
ROOMS: 54 en suite **CONF:** Board 10

Days Inn Stratford Upon Avon

Warwick Services, M40 Southbound, Banbury Rd CV35 0AA
☎ 01926 650168 📠 01926 651601
web: www.welcomebreak.co.uk
Dir: *M40 southbound between junct 14 & 12*
This modern building offers accommodation in smart, spacious and well-equipped bedrooms, suitable for families and business travellers, and all with en suite bathrooms. Continental breakfast is available and other refreshments may be taken at the nearby family restaurant. For further details see the Hotel Groups page.
ROOMS: 40 en suite

WASHINGTON, Tyne & Wear — Map 19 NZ35

★★★66% George Washington Golf & Country Club

Stone Cellar Rd, High Usworth NE37 1PH
☎ 0191 402 9988 📠 0191 415 1166
e-mail: reservations@georgewashington.co.uk
web: www.georgewashington.co.uk
Dir: *turn off A1(M) junct 65 onto A194(M). Take A195 signed Washington North. Take last exit from rdbt for Washington then right at mini rdbt. Hotel 0.5m on right*
Popular with business and leisure guests, this purpose-built hotel boasts two golf courses and a driving range. Bedrooms are generally spacious and comfortably equipped. Public areas include extensive conference facilities, a business centre and fitness club.
ROOMS: 103 en suite (9 fmly) (41 GF) ⊗ in 44 bedrooms s £79; d £89 **LB** **FACILITIES: Spa** supervised 18 Squash Sauna Solarium Gym Putt green Jacuzzi Golf driving range, Pitch & Putt, Pool table, Beauty salon Xmas **CONF:** Thtr 200 Class 80 Board 80 Del £115
PARKING: 180 **NOTES:** ⊗ in restaurant Civ Wed 180
CARDS:

Campanile

Campanile

Emerson Rd, District 5 NE37 1LE
☎ 0191 416 5010 📠 0191 416 5023
e-mail: washington@envergure.co.uk
Dir: *A1 junct 64, A195 to Washington, 1st left at rdbt into Emerson Road, Hotel 800yds on left*
This modern building offers accommodation in smart, well-equipped bedrooms, all with en suite bathrooms. Refreshments may be taken at the informal Bistro. For further details consult the Hotel Groups page.

ROOMS: 79 annexe en suite s fr £42.95; d fr £42.95 **CONF:** Thtr 35 Class 18 Board 24

WASHINGTON SERVICE AREA (A1(M)), Tyne & Wear — Map 19 NZ25

Travelodge (North)

Travelodge

Motorway Service Area, Portobello DH3 2SJ
☎ 08700 850 950 📠 0191 410 9258
Dir: *northbound carriageway of A1(M)*
Travelodge offers good quality, good value, modern accommodation. Ideal for families, the spacious, en suite bedrooms include remote-control TV, tea and coffee-making facilities and luxury beds. Meals can be taken at the nearby family restaurant. For further details consult the Hotel Groups page.
ROOMS: 31 en suite s fr £25; d fr £25

Travelodge (South)

Travelodge

Portobello DH3 2SJ
☎ 08700 850 950 📠 0191 410 0057
Dir: *A1(M)*
Travelodge offers good quality, good value, modern accommodation. Ideal for families, the spacious, en suite bedrooms include remote-control TV, tea and coffee-making facilities and luxury beds. Meals can be taken at the nearby family restaurant. For further details consult the Hotel Groups page.
ROOMS: 36 en suite s fr £25; d fr £25

WATERGATE BAY, Cornwall & Isles of Scilly — Map 02 SW86

★67% Tregurrian

TR8 4AB
☎ 01637 860280 📠 01637 860540
e-mail: tregurrian@holidaysincornwall.net
Dir: *Leave A30 onto A3059 towards airport, 2nd exit at rdbt, right onto B3276, left to Watergate Bay*
Located almost on the beach at this increasingly popular destination, this hotel makes a friendly and convenient place to stay. Bedrooms are comfortable and attractively presented, and some have sea views. In the dining room, both breakfast and dinner are served buffet-style with good use of fresh ingredients.
ROOMS: 26 en suite (8 fmly) ⊗ in all bedrooms s £24-£100; d £48-£100 (incl. bkfst) **LB** **FACILITIES:** Sauna Jacuzzi Games room
PARKING: 24 **NOTES:** ⊗ in restaurant Closed Nov-Feb RS Mar
CARDS:

See advert under NEWQUAY

For central reservation numbers and more information on Hotel Groups, turn to pages 33-39

continued

WATERINGBURY, Kent
Map 06 TQ65

Premier Lodge (Maidstone)

103 Tonbridge Rd ME18 5NS
☎ 0870 9906346 📠 0870 9906347
web: www.premierlodge.com

Dir: *exit M25 junct 3 onto M20. Exit at junct 4 onto A228 towards West Malling. Follow A26 towards Maidstone for approximately 3m*

High quality, modern, budget accommodation, ideal for families and business travellers. All rooms feature bath, power shower and satellite TV, and most have telephones / modem points. The adjacent bar and restaurant offers a wide and varied menu.

ROOMS: 40 en suite s £52; d £52 **CONF:** Thtr 30

WATERMILLOCK, Cumbria
Map 18 NY42

★★★★ 70% Leeming House

CA11 0JJ
☎ 0870 400 8131 📠 017684 86443
e-mail: leeminghouse@macdonald-hotels.co.uk

Dir: *M6 junct 40, take A66 to Keswick. Turn left after 1m onto A592 (to Ullswater). Continue for 5m until T-junct and turn right. Hotel on left (3m)*

This hotel enjoys a superb location set in 20 acres of mature wooded gardens in the Lake District National Park, overlooking Ullswater. Many rooms offer views of the lake and the rugged fells beyond, with more than half having their own balcony. Public rooms include three sumptuous lounges, a cosy bar and library.

ROOMS: 41 en suite ⊗ in 11 bedrooms **FACILITIES:** STV Fishing ♫ **CONF:** Thtr 30 Board 24 Del from £140 **PARKING:** 50 **NOTES:** ⊗ in restaurant Civ Wed 65 **CARDS:**

Top 200 – Hotel

★★★ ®®® Rampsbeck Country House

CA11 0LP
☎ 017684 86442 & 86688 📠 017684 86688
e-mail: enquiries@rampsbeck.fsnet.co.uk
web: www.rampsbeck.fsnet.co.uk

Dir: *M6 junct 40, signs for A592 to Ullswater, at T-junct with lake in front, turn right, hotel is 1.5m along lake's edge*

This fine country house lies in 18 acres of parkland on the shores of Lake Ullswater and is furnished with many period and antique pieces. There are three delightful lounges, an elegant restaurant and a traditional, and re-furbished, bar. Bedrooms come in three grades. Overlooking the lake, the most spacious rooms are spectacular. Service is attentive and the cuisine a real highlight.

ROOMS: 19 en suite (1 GF) ⊗ in 3 bedrooms s £65-£195; d £110-£230 (incl. bkfst) **LB** **FACILITIES:** Fishing ♫ Xmas **CONF:** Board 15 Del from £125 **PARKING:** 30 **NOTES:** ⊗ in restaurant Closed early Jan-early Feb **CARDS:**

WATFORD, Hertfordshire
Map 06 TQ19

★★★ 67% The White House

Best Western

Upton Rd WD18 0JF
☎ 01923 237316 📠 01923 233109
e-mail: info@whitehousehotel.co.uk
web: www.whitehousehotel.co.uk

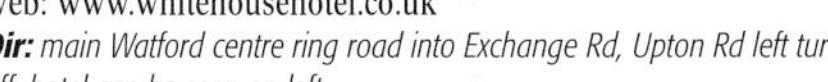

Dir: *main Watford centre ring road into Exchange Rd, Upton Rd left turn off, hotel can be seen on left*

This is a well located and popular commercial hotel. Bedrooms are practically furnished and decorated, and offer a good range of in-room facilities including interactive TV. The public areas are open plan in style and comprise a lounge/bar and an attractive conservatory restaurant. Functions suites are also available.

ROOMS: 57 en suite (8 GF) ⊗ in 45 bedrooms s £55-£149; d £79-£164 (incl. bkfst) **LB** **FACILITIES:** STV **CONF:** Thtr 200 Class 80 Board 50 **SERVICES:** Lift **PARKING:** 55 **NOTES:** ⊗ in restaurant
CARDS:

See advert on this page

WATFORD, continued

⌂ Premier Lodge (Watford)

Timms Meadow, Water Ln WD17 2NJ
☎ 0870 9906620 📠 0870 9906621
web: www.premierlodge.com
Dir: *M1 junct 5/A41 into town centre. At rdbt take 3rd exit & stay in left lane through traffic lights. Take 1st left into Water Ln lodge on left*
High quality, modern, budget accommodation, ideal for families and business travellers. All rooms feature bath, power shower and satellite TV, and most have telephones / modem points. The adjacent bar and restaurant offers a wide and varied menu.
ROOMS: 105 en suite s £58; d £58

⌂ Travel Inn

859 St Albans Rd, Garston WD25 0LH
☎ 08701 977261 📠 01923 682164

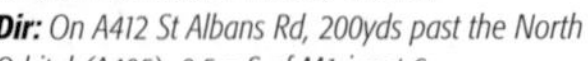

Dir: *On A412 St Albans Rd, 200yds past the North Orbital (A405), 0.5m S of M1 junct 6*

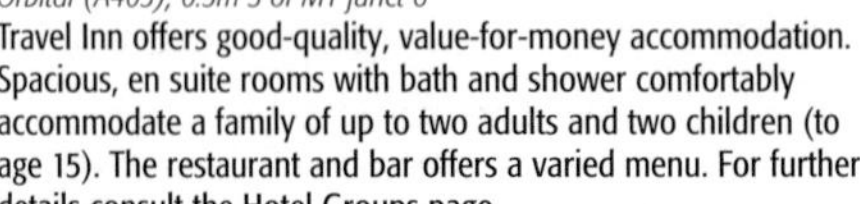

Travel Inn offers good-quality, value-for-money accommodation. Spacious, en suite rooms with bath and shower comfortably accommodate a family of up to two adults and two children (to age 15). The restaurant and bar offers a varied menu. For further details consult the Hotel Groups page.
ROOMS: 45 en suite s £56.95; d £56.95

WATFORD GAP MOTORWAY SERVICE AREA (M1), Northamptonshire — Map 11 SP66

⌂ Travel Inn (Daventry)

NN6 7UZ
☎ 08701 977301 📠 01327 871333
Dir: *M1 southbound between J16 & 17. (Access from northbound via barrier)*
Travel Inn offers good-quality, value-for-money accommodation. Spacious, en suite rooms with bath and shower comfortably accommodate a family of up to two adults and two children (to age 15). The restaurant and bar offers a varied menu. For further details consult the Hotel Groups page.
ROOMS: 36 en suite s £45.95-£46.95; d £45.95-£46.95

WATTON, Norfolk — Map 13 TF90

★★ Broom Hall Country Hotel

Richmond Rd, Saham Toney IP25 7EX
☎ 01953 882125 📠 01953 885325
e-mail: enquiries@broomhallhotel.co.uk
web: www.broomhallhotel.co.uk
Dir: *leave A11 at Thetford onto A1075 to Watton (12m) B1108 towards Swaffham, in 0.5m at rdbt take B1077 to Saham Toney, hotel 0.5m on the left*
ROOMS: 10 en suite 5 annexe en suite (3 fmly) (5 GF) ⊘ in all bedrooms s £60-£75; d £85-£130 (incl. bkfst) **LB** **FACILITIES:** **CONF:** Thtr 30 Class 30 Board 25 **PARKING:** 30 **NOTES:** ⊘ in restaurant Closed 24 Dec-4 Jan **CARDS:**

W

WEEDON, Northamptonshire — Map 11 SP64

⌂ Premier Lodge (Daventry)

High St NN7 4PX
☎ 0870 9906364 📠 0870 9906365
web: www.premierlodge.com
Dir: *exit M1 at junct 16 and follow A45 towards Daventry. Through villages of Upper Heyford and Flore and on approach to Weedon. Lodge on left before A5 junct*
High quality, modern, budget accommodation, ideal for families and business travellers. All rooms feature bath, power shower and satellite TV, and most have telephones / modem points. The adjacent bar and restaurant offers a wide and varied menu.
ROOMS: 46 en suite s £50; d £50 **CONF:** Thtr 70 Class 25 Board 24

WEELEY, Essex — Map 07 TM12

⌂ Travel Inn (Clacton-on-Sea)

Crown Green Roundabout, Colchester Rd, Weeley CO16 9AA
☎ 08701 977064 📠 01255 833106
Dir: *take A120 off A12 towards Harwich. After 4m, A133 to Clacton-on-Sea. Located on Weeley rdbt*
Travel Inn offers good-quality, value-for-money accommodation. Spacious, en suite rooms with bath and shower comfortably accommodate a family of up to two adults and two children (to age 15). The restaurant and bar offers a varied menu. For further details consult the Hotel Groups page.
ROOMS: 40 en suite s £45.95-£46.95; d £45.95-£46.95

WELLESBOURNE, Warwickshire — Map 10 SP25

⌂ Innkeeper's Lodge Stratford-upon-Avon East

Warwick Rd CV35 9LX
☎ 01789 840206 📠 01789 472902
www.innkeeperslodge.com
Dir: *M40 junct 15 S onto A429 towards Wellesbourne. Turn left at rdbt onto B4086 & lodge 300yds on right.*
Smart rooms meet essential business requirements but also have home comforts, and depending on location may well have meeting rooms and pub dining. Dining options generally include all-day menus plus the added advantage of breakfast.
ROOMS: 9 en suite s £58; d £58

WELLINGBOROUGH, Northamptonshire — Map 11 SP86

★★★ 65% The Hind

Sheep St NN8 1BY
☎ 01933 222827 📠 01933 441921
e-mail: enquiries@thehind.co.uk
Dir: *on A509 in town centre*
Dating back to Jacobean times, this centrally located hotel provides a good base for business and leisure guests visiting the town. A good choice of dishes is available in the restaurant; alternatively the all-day coffee shop offers light snacks. Bedrooms come in a variety of styles, mostly of spacious dimensions.
ROOMS: 34 en suite (2 fmly) (5 GF) ⊘ in 20 bedrooms s £45-£65; d £60-£90 (incl. bkfst) **LB** **FACILITIES:** Pool table in public bar Xmas **CONF:** Thtr 70 Class 40 Board 40 Del from £90 **PARKING:** 17 **NOTES:** ⊘ in restaurant RS 24 Dec-2 Jan Civ Wed 70 **CARDS:**

★★ High View

156 Midland Rd NN8 1NG
☎ 01933 278733 📠 01933 225948
e-mail: hotelhighview@hotmail.com
Dir: *turn off A45 onto B573, follow sign to rail station, at Midland Road t-junct turn left towards town centre, hotel approx 100yds on left*
ROOMS: 14 en suite (2 fmly) s £29-£39; d £45-£49 (incl. bkfst) **PARKING:** 8 **NOTES:** No children 3yrs ⊘ in restaurant Closed 25 Dec-1 Jan **CARDS:**

 AA Rosette Award for culinary excellence

⌂ Hotel Ibis Wellingborough

Enstone Court NN8 2DR
☎ 01933 228333 📠 01933 228444
e-mail: H3164@accor-hotels.com
Dir: *at junct of A45 & A509 towards Kettering on SW edge of Wellingborough*

Modern, budget hotel offering comfortable accommodation in bright and practical bedrooms. Breakfast is self-service and dinner is available in the restaurant. For further details, consult the Hotel Groups page.

ROOMS: 78 en suite s fr £51.95; d fr £51.95 **CONF:** Thtr 20 Board 14

⌂ Travel Inn

London Rd NN8 2DP
☎ 08701 977262 📠 01933 275947
Dir: *0.5m from Wellingborough town centre on A5193 near Dennington Industrial Estate*

Travel Inn offers good-quality, value-for-money accommodation. Spacious, en suite rooms with bath and shower comfortably accommodate a family of up to two adults and two children (to age 15). The restaurant and bar offers a varied menu. For further details consult the Hotel Groups page.

ROOMS: 40 en suite s £45.95-£46.95; d £45.95-£46.95

WELLINGTON See Telford (Shropshire)

WELLINGTON, Somerset Map 03 ST12

Top 200 – Hotel

★★★ Bindon Country House Hotel & Restaurant

Langford Budville TA21 0RU
☎ 01823 400070 📠 01823 400071
e-mail: stay@bindon.com
web: www.bindon.com
Dir: *from Wellington B3187 to Langford Budville, through village, right towards Wiveliscombe, right at junct, pass Bindon Farm, right after 450yds*

This delightful country retreat is set in seven acres of formal woodland gardens. Mentioned in the Domesday Book, it offers peace and tranquillity, the perfect antidote to stress. Bedrooms are named after battles fought by the Duke of Wellington and each is individually decorated with sumptuous fabrics and equipped with useful extras. Elegance, style and comfort can all be found within the public rooms, and the dining room is the venue for impressive and accomplished cuisine.

ROOMS: 12 en suite (2 fmly) (1 GF) in all bedrooms s fr £95; d £115-£215 (incl. bkfst) **FACILITIES:** ch fac Xmas **CONF:** Thtr 50 Class 25 Board 25 Del from £135 **PARKING:** 30 **NOTES:** in restaurant Civ Wed 50

CARDS: 

See advert on this page

★★★67% The Cleve Hotel & Country Club

Mantle St TA21 8SN
☎ 01823 662033 📠 01823 660874
e-mail: reception@clevehotel.com
Dir: *M5 junct 26 follow signs to Wellington, then left before Total petrol station on leaving town*

Offering comfortable bedrooms and public areas, this hotel is quietly located in an elevated position above the town. The atmosphere is relaxed and guests can enjoy Mediterranean-influenced cuisine in the stylish restaurant. Extensive leisure facilities are available including a heated indoor pool, well-equipped gym, sauna, and snooker table.

ROOMS: 20 en suite (5 fmly) (3 GF) in all bedrooms s £55-£79.50; d £70-£95.50 (incl. bkfst) **LB FACILITIES: Spa** supervised Snooker Sauna Solarium Gym **CONF:** Thtr 300 Class 100 Board 50 Del from £79.50 **PARKING:** 60 **NOTES:** in restaurant Civ Wed 150

CARDS:

WELLS, Somerset Map 04 ST54

★★★72% Swan

Sadler St BA5 2RX
☎ 01749 836300 📠 01749 836301
e-mail: swan@bhere.co.uk
web: www.bhere.co.uk
Dir: *A39, A371, opp cathedral*

The Swan is a former coaching inn and has a wonderful view of the west front of Wells Cathedral. The individually decorated bedrooms vary in size and style from the newly completed rooms in an adjacent wing to the more traditionally furnished rooms

continued on p614

WELLS, continued

including many with four-poster beds. Dinner includes a varied selection of carefully prepared dishes.

Swan Hotel, Wells

ROOMS: 50 en suite (4 fmly) (4 GF) ⊗ in 25 bedrooms s fr £89; d fr £125 **LB** **FACILITIES:** Xmas **CONF:** Thtr 100 Class 45 Board 40 Del £127.50 **PARKING:** 30 **NOTES:** ⊗ in restaurant Civ Wed 70 **CARDS:**

★★72% White Hart

Sadler St BA5 2RR

THE INDEPENDENTS HOTEL ASSOCIATION

☎ 01749 672056 01749 671074
e-mail: info@whitehart-wells.co.uk
web: www.whitehart-wells.co.uk
Dir: *Sadler St is at start of the one-way system. Hotel opp cathedral*

This former coaching inn dates back to the 15th century. The bedrooms, some in an adjoining former stable block, offer comfortable, modern accommodation. Public areas include a refurbished guest lounge, together with a popular restaurant and cosy bar. The newly styled restaurant serves mainly fish, plus daily specials and meat and vegetarian dishes.
ROOMS: 15 en suite (3 fmly) (2 GF) ⊗ in 5 bedrooms s £72.50-£77.50; d £92.50-£102.50 (incl. bkfst) **LB** **FACILITIES:** ch fac Xmas **CONF:** Thtr 150 Class 50 Board 35 Del from £99.50 **PARKING:** 17 **NOTES:** ⊗ in restaurant Civ Wed 100 **CARDS:**

W

★★71% Ancient Gate House

20 Sadler St BA5 2SE
☎ 01749 672029 01749 670319
e-mail: info@ancientgatehouse.co.uk
Dir: *1st hotel on left on Cathedral Green, overlooking the West Front of Cathedral*
Guests are treated to good old-fashioned hospitality in a friendly informal atmosphere at this charming hotel. Bedrooms, many of which boast unrivalled cathedral views and four-poster beds, are well equipped and furnished in keeping with the age and character of the building. The hotel's Rugantino Restaurant remains popular, offering typically Italian specialities and some traditional English dishes.

ROOMS: 9 en suite ⊗ in 2 bedrooms s £67.50-£72.50; d £82.50 (incl. bkfst) **LB** **FACILITIES:** Xmas **NOTES:** ⊗ in restaurant **CARDS:**

★★67% Crown at Wells

Market Place BA5 2RP
☎ 01749 673457 01749 679792
e-mail: reception@crownatwells.co.uk
web: www.crownatwells.co.uk
Dir: *in Market Place, follow signs for Hotels/Deliveries*

Retaining its original features and period charm, this historic inn is situated in the heart of Wells, just a short stroll from the cathedral. Bedrooms vary in size and style and have modern facilities. Public areas focus around Anton's, the popular bistro, with its bold paintings and relaxed atmosphere, and the Penn Bar, an alternative eating option.
ROOMS: 15 en suite (1 fmly) ⊗ in all bedrooms s £50-£80; d £80-£95 (incl. bkfst) **LB** **PARKING:** 15 **NOTES:** ⊗ in restaurant RS 25 Dec food not available in the evening **CARDS:**

U Coxley Vineyard

Coxley BA5 1RQ
☎ 01749 670285 01749 679708
e-mail: max@orofino.freeserve.co.uk
Dir: *A39 from Wells signed Coxley. Village halfway between Wells & Glastonbury. Hotel off main road at end of village.*
At the time of going to press, the star classification for this hotel was not confirmed. Please refer to the AA internet site www.theAA.com for current information.
ROOMS: 9 en suite (5 fmly) ⊗ in 5 bedrooms s £49.50-£69.50; d £69.50-£89.50 (incl. bkfst) **LB** **FACILITIES:** **CONF:** Thtr 90 Class 50 Board 40 Del from £89.50 **PARKING:** 50 **NOTES:** ⊗ in restaurant **CARDS:**

WELWYN, Hertfordshire — Map 06 TL21

★★★61% Quality Hotel Welwyn

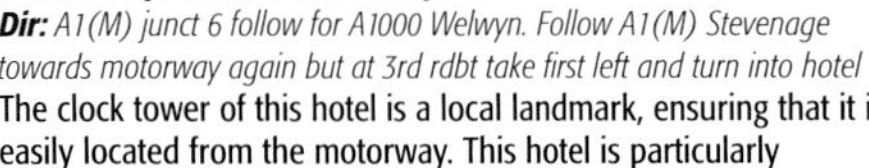

The Link AL6 9XA
☎ 01438 716911 / 01438 714065
e-mail: enquiries@hotels-welwyn.com

Dir: *A1(M) junct 6 follow for A1000 Welwyn. Follow A1(M) Stevenage towards motorway again but at 3rd rdbt take first left and turn into hotel*

The clock tower of this hotel is a local landmark, ensuring that it is easily located from the motorway. This hotel is particularly popular with business guests for the range of conference and meeting rooms provided. Bedrooms are suitably appointed and feature extras such as satellite TV and Playstation games.

ROOMS: 96 en suite (3 fmly) (28 GF) 🚭 in 47 bedrooms s fr £91; d fr £113 **LB FACILITIES:** STV Gym Xmas **CONF:** Thtr 250 Class 60 Board 50 Del from £90 **PARKING:** 150 **NOTES:** 🚭 in restaurant Civ Wed 100 **CARDS:**

WELWYN GARDEN CITY, Hertfordshire — Map 06 TL21

★★★67% The Homestead Court Hotel

Homestead Ln AL7 4LX
☎ 01707 324336 / 01707 326447
e-mail: enquiries@homesteadcourt.co.uk
web: www.bw-homesteadcourt.co.uk

Dir: *off A1000, left at traffic lights at Bushall Hotel. Right at rdbt into Howlands, 2nd left at Hollybush public house into Hollybush Lane. 2nd right at War Memorial into Homestead Lane*

Less than two miles from the city centre, this friendly hotel is set in a tranquil location, next to parkland. It boasts stylish, brightly decorated public areas, comfortable bedrooms and ample parking. Conference facilities are popular with local businesses.

ROOMS: 58 en suite 🚭 in 40 bedrooms s £45-£105; d £55-£115 (incl. bkfst) **LB FACILITIES:** STV Xmas **CONF:** BC Thtr 80 Class 40 Board 30 Del from £99 **SERVICES:** Lift **PARKING:** 60 **NOTES:** 🚭 in restaurant Civ Wed 80 **CARDS:**

⌂ Travel Inn

Gosling Park AL8 6DQ
☎ 08701 977263 / 01707 393789

Dir: *on A6129 off A1(M) junct 4*

Travel Inn offers good-quality, value-for-money accommodation. Spacious, en suite rooms with bath and shower comfortably accommodate a family of up to two adults and two children (to age 15). The restaurant and bar offers a varied menu. For further details consult the Hotel Groups page.

ROOMS: 60 en suite s £45.95-£48.95; d £45.95-£48.95

> Popped the question?
> Hotels with Civ Wed in their entry are licensed for civil wedding ceremonies. Maximum numbers for the ceremony only are shown, e.g. Civ Wed 120

WEMBLEY, Greater London
See LONDON SECTION plan 1 C5

★★★65% Quality Hotel, Wembley

Empire Way HA9 0NN
☎ 020 8733 9000 / 020 8733 9001
e-mail: gm@hotels-wembley.com

Conveniently situated within walking distance of both the Arena and conference centres this modern hotel offers smart spacious bedrooms that are well equipped and provide good levels of comfort. Air-conditioned public areas include a large restaurant serving a wide range of contemporary dishes.

ROOMS: 165 en suite (10 fmly) (3 GF) 🚭 in 95 bedrooms s fr £95; d fr £105 (incl. bkfst) **LB FACILITIES:** STV Xmas **CONF:** Thtr 150 Class 70 Board 70 Del £99 **SERVICES:** Lift **PARKING:** 85 **NOTES:** Civ Wed 220 **CARDS:**

⌂ Hotel Ibis Wembley

Southway HA9 6BA
☎ 0870 609 0963
e-mail: H3141@accor-hotels.com

Dir: *From Hanger Lane on A40, follow A406 north, exit at Wembley. Follow A404 to traffic lights with Wembley Hill Rd, turn right then 1st right into Southway. Hotel is 75mtrs on left.*

Modern, budget hotel offering comfortable accommodation in bright and practical bedrooms. Breakfast is self-service and dinner is available in the restaurant. For further details, consult the Hotel Groups page.

ROOMS: 210 en suite s £50-£60; d £50-£60

⌂ Premier Lodge (London Wembley)

151 Wembley Park Dr HA9 8HQ
☎ 0870 9906484 / 0870 9906485
web: www.premierlodge.com

Dir: *from A406 North Circular take A404 towards Wembley. Approx 2m turn right into Wembley Hill Rd, keep right into Empire Way (B4565) passing Wembley Arena on right, and keep right around the petrol station. Hotel 200yds on left*

High quality, modern, budget accommodation, ideal for families and business travellers. All rooms feature bath, power shower and satellite TV, and most have telephones / modem points. The adjacent bar and restaurant offers a wide and varied menu.

ROOMS: 154 en suite s £58; d £58

⌂ Travel Inn Wembley

Dagmar Av, Wembley Hill Rd HA9 8DF
☎ 08701 9770294 / 08701 241900

Dir: *From A406, follow signs for Wembley. Continue to Wembley Triangle (The Clock). Right into Wembley Hill Rd for 0.25m. The Travel Inn is on left*

Travel Inn offers good-quality, value-for-money accommodation. Spacious, en suite rooms with bath and shower comfortably accommodate a family of up to two adults and two children (to age 15). The restaurant and bar offers a varied menu. For further details consult the Hotel Groups page.

ROOMS: 56 en suite s £45.95-£46.95; d £45.95-£46.95

WEST AUCKLAND, Co Durham — Map 19 NZ12

★★★70% The Manor House Hotel & Country Club

The Green DL14 9HW
☎ 01388 834834 / 01388 833566
e-mail: enquiries@manorhousehotel.net
web: www.manorhousehotel.net

Dir: *A1(M) junct 58, then A68 to West Auckland. At T-junct turn left, hotel 150yds on right*

This historic manor house, dating back to the 14th century, is full

continued on p616

WEST AUCKLAND, continued

of character. Welcoming log fires await guests on cooler evenings. Comfortable bedrooms are individual, tastefully furnished and well equipped. The brasserie and 'Juniper's' restaurant both offer an interesting selection of freshly prepared dishes. Well-equipped leisure facilities are also available.

The Manor House Hotel & Country Club, West Auckland

ROOMS: 24 en suite 11 annexe en suite (6 fmly) (2 GF) s £36.50-£68; d £73-£99 (incl. bkfst) **LB** **FACILITIES:** Sauna Solarium Gym Jacuzzi ch fac Xmas **CONF:** Thtr 100 Class 80 Board 50 Del from £80 **PARKING:** 200 **NOTES:** in restaurant Civ Wed 120
CARDS:

WEST BAY See Bridport

WEST BEXINGTON, Dorset — Map 04 SY58

★★69% The Manor

Beach Rd DT2 9DF
☎ 01308 897616 & 897785 01308 897035
e-mail: themanorhotel@btconnect.com
Dir: *B3157 Weymouth/Bridport coast road, turn at Swyre, towards West Bexington*

Surrounded by scenic splendour and tranquillity, this south-facing hotel enjoys sea views. Each bedroom has its own charm and a number of thoughtful extras. The Cellar Bar provides a range of meals, and an imaginative selection of dishes is offered in the totally refurbished, delightful restaurant.

ROOMS: 13 en suite (3 fmly) s £70-£75; d £110-£120 (incl. bkfst) **LB** **CONF:** Thtr 40 Class 20 Board 20 **PARKING:** 40 **NOTES:** in restaurant Civ Wed 58 **CARDS:**

WEST BROMWICH, West Midlands — Map 10 SP09

Travel Inn

New Gas St B70 0NP
☎ 08701 977264 0121 500 5670
Dir: *From M5 junct 1 take A41 Expressway towards Wolverhampton. At 3rd rdt, Travel Inn on right*

Travel Inn offers good-quality, value-for-money accommodation. Spacious, en suite rooms with bath and shower comfortably accommodate a family of up to two adults and two children (to age 15). The restaurant and bar offers a varied menu. For further details consult the Hotel Groups page.

ROOMS: 40 en suite s £45.95-£46.95; d £45.95-£46.95

WESTBURY, Wiltshire — Map 04 ST85

★★65% The Cedar

THE INDEPENDENTS

Warminster Rd BA13 3PR
☎ 01373 822753 01373 858423
e-mail: cedarwestbury@aol.com
Dir: *on A350, 0.5m S of town towards Warminster*

This 18th-century hotel offers attractive accommodation in well-equipped, individually decorated bedrooms. The hotel is an ideal base for exploring Bath and the surrounding area. An interesting selection of meals is available in both the bar lounge and conservatory; the Regency restaurant is popular for more formal dining.

ROOMS: 8 en suite 8 annexe en suite (2 fmly) (8 GF) s £50-£65; d £60-£72 (incl. bkfst) **FACILITIES:** STV **CONF:** Thtr 35 Class 20 Board 20 **PARKING:** 30 **NOTES:** in restaurant
CARDS:

★★65% Westbury

The Market Place BA13 3DQ
☎ 01373 822500 01373 824144
e-mail: stay@thewestburyhotel.co.uk
Dir: *turn into Market Place off main road & hotel on the corner*

Centrally located in the market place of this historic town, parts of this hotel date back to 1545. Bedrooms come in a variety of shapes and sizes but all are well equipped. Dinner is a highlight here with a considerable range of carefully prepared options. Guests may use the popular bar in which to relax or the quieter surroundings of the restaurant and small guest lounge.

ROOMS: 7 en suite 4 annexe en suite (2 fmly) in 3 bedrooms s £65; d £85 (incl. bkfst) **CONF:** Thtr 30 Class 30 Board 30 **PARKING:** 20 **NOTES:** in restaurant Closed 25 Dec-5 Jan
CARDS:

WEST CHILTINGTON, West Sussex — Map 06 TQ01

★★★69% Best Western Roundabout

Best Western

Monkmead Ln RH20 2PF
☎ 01798 813838 01798 812962
e-mail: roundabouthotelltd@btinternet.com
web: www.bw-roundabouthotel.co.uk
Dir: *A24 onto A283, right at mini rdbt in Storrington, left at hill top. Left after 1m*

Enjoying a most peaceful setting, surrounded by gardens, this well-established hotel is located deep in the Sussex countryside. Mock-Tudor in style, the hotel has plenty of character. The comfortably furnished bedrooms are well equipped, and public

continued

areas offer a spacious lounge and bar, as well as a neatly appointed restaurant serving an extensive range of dishes.
ROOMS: 23 en suite (4 fmly) (5 GF) ⊗ in 5 bedrooms s £68.95-£74.95; d £112-£118 (incl. bkfst) **LB FACILITIES:** STV Xmas **CONF:** Thtr 60 Class 20 Board 26 Del from £94.50 **PARKING:** 46 **NOTES:** No children 3yrs ⊗ in restaurant Civ Wed 49
CARDS:

See advert on this page

WEST DRAYTON Hotels are listed under Heathrow Airport

WESTLETON, Suffolk Map 13 TM46

★★75% Westleton Crown

IP17 3AD
☎ 0800 328 6001 🖷 01728 648239
e-mail: reception@westletoncrown.com
web: www.westletoncrown.com
Dir: *N on A12, turn just beyond Yoxford, follow AA signs for 2m*

A charming coaching inn situated in a peaceful village location just a few minutes from the A12. Public rooms include a smart, award-winning restaurant, comfortable lounge, and a busy bar with exposed beams and open fireplaces. The bedrooms are individually decorated and have many thoughtful little extras.
ROOMS: 10 en suite 9 annexe en suite (2 fmly) (4 GF) ⊗ in all bedrooms s fr £64; d fr £79 (incl. bkfst) **LB FACILITIES:** Xmas **CONF:** Thtr 60 Class 40 Board 30 **PARKING:** 40 **NOTES:** ⊗ in restaurant RS Wknds Dinner B&B only, 24-26 Dec
CARDS:

Late for dinner?
Quality Standards mean that last orders for dinner vary according to star rating and should be no earlier than:
★★ 7.00pm ★★★ 8.00pm ★★★★ 9.00pm
★★★★★ 10.00pm

WEST LULWORTH, Dorset Map 04 SY88

★★66% Cromwell House

Lulworth Cove BH20 5RJ
☎ 01929 400253 & 400332 🖷 01929 400566
e-mail: catriona@lulworthcove.co.uk
web: www.lulworthcove.co.uk
Dir: *200yds beyond end of West Lulworth village, left onto high slip road, hotel 100yds on left opposite beach car park*
Built in 1881 by the Mayor of Weymouth, specifically as a guest house, this family-run hotel now provides guests with an ideal base for touring the area and for exploring the beaches and coast. Cromwell House enjoys spectacular views across the sea and

continued

countryside. Bedrooms, many with sea views, are comfortable and some have been specifically designed for family use.

Cromwell House

ROOMS: 17 en suite (3 fmly) (17 GF) s £37.50-£55.50; d £70-£80 (incl. bkfst) **LB FACILITIES:** Access to Dorset Coastal footpath & Jurassic Coast ch fac **PARKING:** 15 **NOTES:** ⊗ in restaurant Closed 22 Dec-3 Jan **CARDS:**

WESTON-ON-THE-GREEN, Oxfordshire Map 11 SP51

★★★70% Weston Manor

OX25 3QL
☎ 01869 350621 🖷 01869 350901
e-mail: reception@westonmanor.co.uk
Dir: *M40 junct 9 towards Oxford on A34, turn right at rdbt (B4030), hotel 100yds on left*
Character, charm and sophistication blend effortlessly in this friendly hotel set in well-tended grounds. Bedrooms are

continued on p618

WESTON-ON-THE-GREEN, continued

well-equipped and are located in the main house, coach house and a cottage annexe. Award-winning food can be enjoyed in the impressive vaulted restaurant, complete with original oak panelling and minstrels' gallery; other public areas include an atmospheric foyer lounge, a bar and meeting facilities.
ROOMS: 15 en suite 20 annexe en suite (5 fmly) (6 GF) ⊗ in 6 bedrooms s £90-£115; d £121-£154 (incl. bkfst) **LB** **FACILITIES:** Xmas **CONF:** Thtr 60 Class 20 Board 25 Del from £145 **PARKING:** 100
NOTES: ⊗ in restaurant Civ Wed 90
CARDS:

WESTON-SUPER-MARE, Somerset Map 04 ST36

★★★65% Beachlands

17 Uphill Rd North BS23 4NG
☎ 01934 621401 01934 621966
e-mail: info@beachlandshotel.com
web: www.beachlandshotel.com
Dir: *M5 junct 21, follow signs for Hospital. At Hospital rdbt follow signs for beach, hotel 300yds before beach*

This popular hotel has the bonus of a 10-metre indoor pool and sauna. It is very close to the 18-hole links course and a short walk from the seafront. Elegant public areas include a bar, a choice of lounges and a bright dining room. Bedrooms vary slightly in size, but all are well-equipped for both the business and leisure guest.
ROOMS: 23 en suite (6 fmly) (11 GF) ⊗ in all bedrooms s £49.75-£72.50; d £79.50-£102.50 (incl. bkfst) **LB** **FACILITIES:** Sauna ch fac **CONF:** Thtr 60 Class 20 Board 30 Del from £93.50
PARKING: 28 **NOTES:** ⊗ in restaurant Closed 23 Dec-2 Jan Civ Wed 80 **CARDS:**

★★★64% Commodore

Beach Rd, Sand Bay, Kewstoke BS22 9UZ
☎ 01934 415778 01934 750020
e-mail: latonacom@aol.com
Dir: *From Weston-Super-Mare take Kewstoke road through Weston Woods*

Located in the pleasant village of Kewstoke by unspoilt Sand Bay, this popular hotel has direct access to the beach. There is a range of dining options, from the relaxed carvery and two-for-one specials in the beamed bar, to the more formal menu of Alice's Restaurant. Bedrooms vary in size and are split between the main hotel and two adjacent buildings.
ROOMS: 19 en suite ⊗ in 6 bedrooms s £54-£60; d £80-£90 (incl. bkfst) **LB** **FACILITIES:** Putt green Xmas **CONF:** Thtr 90 Class 50 Board 40 **PARKING:** 70 **NOTES:** ⊗ in restaurant Civ Wed 100
CARDS:

★★★61% Royal Hotel

1 South Pde BS23 1JP
☎ 01934 423100 01934 415135
e-mail: royalwsm@btopenworld.com

The Royal, which opened in 1810, was the first hotel in Weston and occupies a prime seafront position. Bedrooms are soundly appointed and include both four-poster and family rooms, many having sea views. Public areas include a choice of bars and the refurbished restaurant, offering a range of dishes to meet all tastes. Entertainment is provided during the season with a regular jazz slot on Sundays.
ROOMS: 37 en suite (5 fmly) ⊗ in 9 bedrooms s £56-£62; d £79-£83 (incl. bkfst) **FACILITIES:** STV ♫ **CONF:** Thtr 200 Class 100 Board 80 Del from £93 **SERVICES:** Lift **PARKING:** 152 **NOTES:** Civ Wed 200
CARDS:

★★72% Woodlands Country House

Hill Ln TA9 4DF
☎ 01278 760232 01278 769090
e-mail: info@woodlands-hotel.co.uk
web: www.woodlands-hotel.co.uk
(For full entry see Brent Knoll)

★★68% Battleborough Grange Country Hotel

Bristol Rd - A38 TA9 4HJ
☎ 01278 760208 01278 761950
e-mail: info@battleboroughgrangehotel.co.uk
(For full entry see Brent Knoll)

★★68% Madeira Cove Hotel

32-34 Birnbeck Rd BS23 2BX
☎ 01934 626707 01934 624882
e-mail: madeiracove@telco4u.net
Dir: *signs to Western Seafront, follow Madeira Cove sign, north towards Kewstoke and Sand Bay, pass Grand Pier, hotel on right*
Within easy walking distance of the town centre, this popular and friendly hotel enjoys an ideal location overlooking the sea. It provides comfortable and well-equipped accommodation. A good range of food is offered in the spacious restaurant and in addition to the bar, a separate upper floor lounge is available to guests.
ROOMS: 22 rms (21 en suite) 4 annexe en suite (2 fmly) ⊗ in 3 bedrooms s £30-£45; d £60-£80 (incl. bkfst) **LB** **FACILITIES:** Xmas
CONF: Thtr 20 **SERVICES:** Lift **NOTES:** ⊗ in restaurant
CARDS:

Destination dining!
This symbol indicates a Restaurant with Rooms

★★63% Anchorhead
19 Claremont Crescent, Birnbeck Rd BS23 2EE
☎ 01934 620880 📠 01934 621767
e-mail: anchor.weston@alfatravel.co.uk

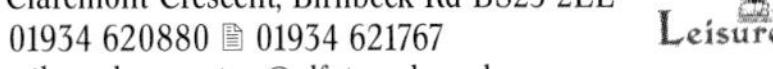

Dir: *M5 junct 21/ A370 to Weston seafront, turn right towards northern end of resort past Grand Pier towards Brimbeck Pier. Hotel at end of terrace on left.*

Enjoying a very pleasant location with views across the bay, the Anchorhead offers a varied choice of comfortable lounges and a relaxing outdoor patio area. Bedrooms and bathrooms are traditionally furnished and include several ground-floor rooms. Dinner and breakfast are served in the spacious dining room that also benefits from sea views.

ROOMS: 52 en suite (1 fmly) (5 GF) s £28-£36; d £46-£62 (incl. bkfst) **LB FACILITIES:** ♫ Xmas **SERVICES:** Lift **NOTES:** No dogs ⊗ in restaurant Closed Dec-Feb RS Mar & Nov **CARDS:**

★★63% New Ocean
Madeira Cove BS23 2BS
☎ 01934 621839 📠 01934 626474
e-mail: info@newoceanhotel.co.uk
web: www.newoceanhotel.co.uk

Dir: *on seafront*

Ideally positioned on the seafront, opposite the Marine Lake, several bedrooms at this family-run hotel enjoy pleasant views over Weston Bay. In the downstairs restaurant, dinner offers traditional home cooking using fresh ingredients. The smart public areas include a well-furnished bar and lounge, where entertainment is regularly provided.

ROOMS: 53 en suite (2 fmly) **FACILITIES:** ♫ Xmas **SERVICES:** Lift **PARKING:** 6 **NOTES:** No dogs ⊗ in restaurant RS Jan **CARDS:**

★69% Timbertop Aparthotel
8 Victoria Park BS23 2HZ
☎ 01934 631178 & 01934 424348 📠 01934 414716
e-mail: stay@aparthoteltimbertop.com

Dir: *follow signs to pier, then 1st right after Winter Gardens, 1st left (Lower Church Rd). Left, then right to hotel*

Located in a leafy cul-de-sac, close to the seafront and Winter Gardens, this homely hotel offers a warm and personal welcome. Bedrooms are bright and fresh with pine furnishings and in addition to a small bar, there is a relaxing lounge. Substantial home-cooked dinners are provided with the emphasis on fresh ingredients.

ROOMS: 8 rms (7 en suite) 4 annexe en suite (2 fmly) s £27.50-£40; d £53-£80 (incl. bkfst) **LB CONF:** BC Thtr 10 Class 10 Board 10 **PARKING:** 15 **NOTES:** No dogs ⊗ in restaurant **CARDS:**

Looking for a last-minute weekend away?
Check out Latebeds,
the AA's late availability booking service, at www.theAA.com

W

WESTON-SUPER-MARE, continued

Action for Blind People Hotel

Lauriston
6-12 Knightstone Rd BS23 2AN
☎ 01934 620758 📠 01934 621154
e-mail: lauriston_hotel@afbp.org
Dir: *1st right after Winter Gardens, hotel entrance opposite Cabot public house*
A friendly welcome is assured at this pleasant hotel, located right on the seafront, just a few minutes' stroll from the pier. Bedrooms and bathrooms are neatly decorated and well equipped, and there is a choice of comfortable lounges in which to relax. The hotel caters for the specific needs of blind and partially sighted people, their friends, relatives, carers and guide dogs.
ROOMS: 37 en suite **FACILITIES:** ♫ **SERVICES:** Lift **PARKING:** 25 **NOTES:** ⊗ in restaurant **CARDS:**

Travel Inn
Hutton Moor Rd BS22 8LY
☎ 08701 977266 📠 01934 627401
Dir: *From M25 (J21), follow A370 to Weston-Super-Ware. After 3rd rbt turn right at traffic lights into Hutton Moor Leisure Centre. Turn left and follow road into car park*
Travel Inn offers good-quality, value-for-money accommodation. Spacious, en suite rooms with bath and shower comfortably accommodate a family of up to two adults and two children (to age 15). The restaurant and bar offers a varied menu. For further details consult the Hotel Groups page.
ROOMS: 60 en suite s £45.95-£46.95; d £45.95-£46.95

WEST THURROCK, Essex — Map 06 TQ57

Hotel Ibis London Thurrock
Weston Av RM20 3JQ
☎ 01708 686000 📠 01708 680525
e-mail: H2176@accor-hotels.com
Dir: *M25 junct 31 to West Thurrock Services, right at 1st and 2nd rdbts then left at 3rd rdbt. Hotel on right after 500yds*
Modern, budget hotel offering comfortable accommodation in bright and practical bedrooms. Breakfast is self-service and dinner is available in the restaurant. For further details, consult the Hotel Groups page.
ROOMS: 102 en suite s £37.95-£48.95; d £37.95-£48.95

Premier Lodge (Thurrock)
Stonehouse Ln RM19 1NS
☎ 0870 9906490 📠 0870 9906491
web: www.premierlodge.com

Dir: *From N, M25 junct 31 & follow signs for A1090 to Purfleet. Do not cross Dartford Bridge & do not follow signs for Lakeside. From S, M25 junct 31. On approach to Dartford Tunnel, bear far left signed Dagenham. Out of tunnel, lodge at top of slip road*
High quality, modern, budget accommodation, ideal for families and business travellers. All rooms feature bath, power shower and satellite TV, and most have telephones / modem points. The adjacent bar and restaurant offers a wide and varied menu.
ROOMS: 161 en suite s £56; d £56

Travel Inn (Thurrock)
Fleming Rd, Unicorn Estate, Chafford Hundred RM16 6YJ
☎ 08701 977253 📠 01375 481876
Dir: *from A13 follow signs for Lakeside Shopping Centre. Turn right at 1st rdbt, straight over next rdbt then 1st slip road. Turn left at next rdbt*
Travel Inn offers good-quality, value-for-money accommodation. Spacious, en suite rooms with bath and shower comfortably accommodate a family of up to two adults and two children (to age 15). The restaurant and bar offers a varied menu. For further details consult the Hotel Groups page.
ROOMS: 62 en suite s £52.95-£56.95; d £52.95-£56.95

Travelodge Thurrock
Arterial Rd RM16 3BG
☎ 08700 850 950 & 0800 850950 📠 01708 860971
Dir: *off A1306*
Travelodge offers good quality, good value, modern accommodation. Ideal for families, the spacious, en suite bedrooms include remote-control TV, tea and coffee-making facilities and luxury beds. Meals can be taken at the nearby family restaurant. For further details consult the Hotel Groups page.
ROOMS: 48 en suite s fr £25; d fr £25

WEST WITTON, North Yorkshire — Map 19 SE08

★★72% Wensleydale Heifer Inn
DL8 4LS
☎ 01969 622322 📠 01969 624183
e-mail: info@wensleydaleheifer.co.uk
web: www.wensleydaleheifer.co.uk
Dir: *A1 to Leeming Bar junct, A684 towards Bedale for approx 10m to Leyburn, then towards Hawes 3.5m to West Witton*
Originally a 17th-century coaching inn, this sympathetically restored hotel retains much of its character. Bedrooms are all individual, comfortable and well equipped. Welcoming log fires await guests on chilly evenings. The beamed bar serves real ales and meals can be taken in the cosy bistro or the more formal restaurant.
ROOMS: 9 en suite (2 fmly) ⊗ in all bedrooms s £60-£80; d £72-£98 (incl. bkfst) **LB FACILITIES:** Xmas **CONF:** BC Thtr 50 Class 40 Board 20 Del from £85 **PARKING:** 40 **NOTES:** No children 12 yrs ⊗ in restaurant **CARDS:**

WETHERBY, West Yorkshire — Map 16 SE44

★★★★76% *Wood Hall*
Trip Ln, Linton LS22 4JA
HandPICKED
☎ 01937 587271 📠 01937 584353
e-mail: woodhall-cro@handpicked.co.uk
Dir: *from Wetherby take Harrogate Rd N (A661) for 0.5m, left to Sicklinghall & Linton. Cross bridge, left to Linton & Woodhall. Turn right opposite Windmill Inn, 1.25m to hotel*
A striking Georgian hall located in 100 acres of parkland, this hotel has been extensively upgraded throughout. Spacious bedrooms have been refurbished to an impressive standard, and feature comprehensive facilities including large plasma screen TVs. Elegant public rooms have been given the same attention and include a smart drawing room and dining room, both enjoying

continued

the fantastic views. Hand Picked Hotels - AA Hotel Group of the Year 2004-5.

ROOMS: 14 en suite 30 annexe en suite (7 fmly) **FACILITIES: Spa** STV supervised Fishing Gym Beauty spa **CONF:** Thtr 140 Class 70 Board 40 **SERVICES:** Lift **PARKING:** 200 **NOTES:** in restaurant Civ Wed 110 **CARDS:**

See advert on this page

★★★66% The Bridge Hotel

Walshford LS22 5HS

☎ 01937 580115 01937 580556
e-mail: info@bridgeinn-bridgehotel.co.uk
web: www.bridgeinn-bridgehotel.co.uk

Dir: *A1 Southbound - leave A1(M) at junct 47 (York), 1st left Walshford and follow brown tourist signs*

A very conveniently located hotel close to the A1 with spacious public areas and a good range of services making this an ideal venue for business or leisure. Bedrooms are comfortable and well appointed. The Bridge offers a choice of bars and a large open-plan restaurant. Conference and banqueting suites are also available.

ROOMS: 30 en suite (1 fmly) s £65-£75; d £85-£125 (incl. bkfst) **LB**
FACILITIES: Gym Xmas **CONF:** Thtr 150 Class 50 Board 50
NOTES: Civ Wed **CARDS:**

WEYBRIDGE, Surrey Map 06 TQ06
See LONDON SECTION plan 1 A1

★★★★70% Oatlands Park

146 Oatlands Dr KT13 9HB
☎ 01932 847242 01932 842252
e-mail: info@oatlandsparkhotel.com
web: www.oatlandsparkhotel.com

Dir: *through Weybridge High Street to top of Monument Hill. Hotel on left*

Once a palace for Henry VIII, this impressive building sits in extensive grounds encompassing tennis courts, a gym and a

continued on p622

WEYBRIDGE, continued

9-hole golf course. The spacious lounge and bar create a wonderful first impression with tall marble pillars and plush comfortable seating. Most of the bedrooms, now refurbished, are very spacious.
ROOMS: 144 en suite (5 fmly) (31 GF) ⊗ in 68 bedrooms s £100-£171; d £113-£192 **LB** **FACILITIES:** STV ⛳ 9 Gym Putt green Jogging course Fitness suite, board games ♫ Xmas **CONF:** BC Thtr 300 Class 150 Board 80 Del from £140 **SERVICES:** Lift **PARKING:** 140
NOTES: Civ Wed 220 **CARDS:**

★★★67% The Ship

Monument Green KT13 8BQ
☎ 01932 848364 🖷 01932 857153
e-mail: recship@desbroughhotels.com
Dir: *M25 junct 11, at 3rd rdbt left into High St. Hotel on left 300yds*
A former coaching inn, The Ship retains its period charm and is now a spacious and comfortable hotel. Bedrooms, some of which overlook a delightful courtyard, are spacious and cheerfully decorated. Public areas include a lounge and cocktail bar, restaurant and a popular pub. The high street location and private car parking prove a bonus.
ROOMS: 39 en suite ⊗ in 10 bedrooms s £130-£140; d £160-£170 **LB**
FACILITIES: STV **CONF:** Thtr 140 Class 70 Board 60 Del from £121.80
PARKING: 65 **NOTES:** ⊗ in restaurant
CARDS:

Innkeeper's Lodge

25 Oatlands Chase KT13 9RW
☎ 01932 253277 🖷 01932 252412
e-mail: badgers.rest@bass.com
www.innkeeperslodge.com
Dir: *M25 junct 11, A317 towards Weybridge, at 3rd rdbt take A3050, left 1m. Turn into Oatlands Chase, lodge on right*
Smart rooms meet essential business requirements but also have home comforts, and depending on location may well have meeting rooms and pub dining. Dining options generally include all-day menus plus the added advantage of breakfast.
ROOMS: 18 en suite s £52-£79.95; d £52-£79.95

WEYMOUTH, Dorset — Map 04 SY67

★★★73% *Moonfleet Manor*

Fleet DT3 4ED
☎ 01305 786948 🖷 01305 774395
Dir: *A354 to Weymouth; right on B3157 to Bridport. At Chickerell left at mini rdbt to Fleet*

This enchanting hideaway, peacefully located at the end of the village of Fleet, enjoys a wonderful sea-facing position. Children are especially welcomed throughout the hotel. Many of the well-equipped bedrooms overlook Chesil Beach and the hotel is furnished with style and panache, particularly the sumptuous lounges. Accomplished cuisine is served in the beautiful restaurant.
ROOMS: 33 en suite 6 annexe en suite (26 fmly) **FACILITIES:** STV Squash Snooker Sauna Solarium Childrens nursery ch fac
CONF: Thtr 50 Class 18 Board 26 **SERVICES:** Lift **PARKING:** 50
NOTES: ⊗ in restaurant **CARDS:**

★★★66% *Hotel Prince Regent*

139 The Esplanade DT4 7NR
☎ 01305 771313 🖷 01305 778100
e-mail: info@princeregentweymouth.co.uk
Dir: *from A354 follow seafront signs. Left at Jubilee Clock, 0.25m on seafront*
Dating back to 1855, this welcoming resort hotel boasts splendid views over Weymouth Bay from the majority of public rooms and front-facing bedrooms. Conveniently close to the town centre, harbour and opposite the beach, the hotel has now undergone extensive refurbishment. The restaurant offers a choice of menus, and entertainment is regularly provided in the ballroom during the season.
ROOMS: 63 en suite (14 fmly) (2 GF) ⊗ in 35 bedrooms
FACILITIES: Use of leisure facilities at sister hotel **CONF:** Thtr 180 Class 150 Board 150 **SERVICES:** Lift **PARKING:** 26 **NOTES:** ⊗ in restaurant **CARDS:**

★★★64% Hotel Rex

29 The Esplanade DT4 8DN
☎ 01305 760400 🖷 01305 760500
e-mail: rex@kingshotels.co.uk
web: www.kingshotels.co.uk
Dir: *on seafront opp Alexandra Gardens*

Originally built as the summer residence for the Duke of Clarence, this hotel benefits from its seafront location with stunning views across Weymouth Bay. Bedrooms include several sea-facing rooms and are all well equipped. A wide range of imaginative dishes is served in the popular vaulted restaurant.
ROOMS: 31 en suite (5 fmly) s £54-£62; d £76-£108 (incl. bkfst) **LB**
FACILITIES: STV **CONF:** Thtr 40 Class 30 Board 25 **SERVICES:** Lift
PARKING: 6 **NOTES:** Closed Xmas
CARDS:

★★★62% Hotel Rembrandt

12-18 Dorchester Rd DT4 7JU
☎ 01305 764000 🖷 01305 764022
e-mail: reception@hotelrembrandt.co.uk
web: www.hotelrembrandt.co.uk
Dir: *0.75m on left after Manor rdbt on A354 from Dorchester*
Only a short distance from the seafront and town centre, this hotel is ideal for visiting local attractions. Facilities include indoor leisure, a bar and extensive meeting rooms. The hotel restaurant is

continued

W

open for lunch and dinner, offering an impressive carvery and carte menu.
ROOMS: 74 en suite (5 fmly) in 30 bedrooms s £58.50-£82; d £98-£108 (incl. bkfst) **LB** **FACILITIES:** STV Sauna Solarium Gym Jacuzzi Steam room, table tennis Xmas **CONF:** Thtr 200 Class 100 Board 50 Del £90 **SERVICES:** Lift **PARKING:** 80 **NOTES:** in restaurant Civ Wed 100 **CARDS:**

★★71% Glenburn

42 Preston Rd DT3 6PZ
☎ 01305 832353 01305 835610
e-mail: info@glenburnhotel.com
Dir: *on A353 1.5m E of town centre*

This small family-run hotel is located close to the seafront. Offering good parking and attractive gardens, including a pleasant play area, the Glenburn is ideal for either business or leisure guests. Bedrooms are comfortable and well equipped. Good use is made of fresh local produce to create the dishes on the daily changing menu.
ROOMS: 13 en suite (2 fmly) in 8 bedrooms s £35-£49; d £58-£75 (incl. bkfst) **LB** **FACILITIES:** Jacuzzi **CONF:** Thtr 20 Class 20 Board 15 **PARKING:** 15 **NOTES:** in restaurant
CARDS:

★★70% *Acropolis*

53-55 Dorchester Rd DT4 7JT
☎ 01305 784282 01305 767172
e-mail: acropolishotel@plantours.fsnet.co.uk
This friendly hotel offering comfortable, stylishly decorated and well-equipped rooms has now undergone refurbishment. A pleasant lounge and bar is provided and guests can relax around the pool in warmer months, where vines and olive trees provide a Mediterranean feel. Appetising, authentic Greek cuisine and wines are served in the restaurant.
ROOMS: 11 en suite (4 fmly) in 6 bedrooms **FACILITIES:**
PARKING: 17 **CARDS:**

★★69% *Russell*

135-13 The Esplanade DT4 7NG
☎ 01305 786059 01305 775723
This hotel is newly refurbished throughout and offers comfortable and spacious accommodation. It is situated on the seafront and so many rooms benefit from magnificent views. With a sister hotel next door, the hotel can also offer banqueting facilities in a superb ballroom. Live music and entertainment are also provided for guests during their stay.
ROOMS: 80 en suite (23 GF) **FACILITIES:** **SERVICES:** Lift **PARKING:** 20 **NOTES:** in restaurant **CARDS:**

> TV dinner?
> Room service at three stars and above

★★66% Crown

51-53 St Thomas St DT4 8EQ
☎ 01305 760800 01305 760300
e-mail: crown@kingshotels.co.uk
web: www.kingshotels.co.uk
Dir: *From Dorchester A354 to Weymouth. Follow Back Water on left & cross second bridge*
This popular hotel is conveniently located adjacent to the old harbour and is ideal for shopping, local attractions or transportation links, including the ferry. Public areas include an extensive bar, ballroom and comfortable residents' lounge on the first floor. Themed events, such as mock cruises, are a speciality.
ROOMS: 86 en suite (11 fmly) s £39-£43; d £72-£80 (incl. bkfst) **LB** **FACILITIES:** STV **CONF:** Class 140 Board 80 **SERVICES:** Lift **PARKING:** 14 **NOTES:** Closed 25-26 Dec **CARDS:**

Travel Inn

Green Hill DT4 7SX
☎ 08701 977267 01305 760589
Dir: *Follow signs to Weymouth, then brown signs to Lodmoor Country Park*
Travel Inn offers good-quality, value-for-money accommodation. Spacious, en suite rooms with bath and shower comfortably accommodate a family of up to two adults and two children (to age 15). The restaurant and bar offers a varied menu. For further details consult the Hotel Groups page.
ROOMS: 40 en suite s £45.95-£46.95; d £45.95-£46.95

WHICKHAM, Tyne & Wear — Map 21 NZ26

★★★69% Gibside Arms

Front St NE16 4JG
☎ 0191 488 9292 0191 488 8000
e-mail: reception@gibside-hotel.co.uk
web: www.gibside-hotel.co.uk
Dir: *off A1(M) towards Whickham on B6317, onto Front Street, 2m on right*
Conveniently located in the village centre, this hotel is close to the Newcastle by-pass and its elevated position affords views over the Tyne Valley. Bedrooms come in two styles, classical and contemporary. Public rooms include the Egyptian-themed Sphinx bar and a more formal restaurant. Secure garage parking is available.
ROOMS: 45 en suite (2 fmly) (13 GF) in 10 bedrooms s £45-£59.50; d £60-£71 **LB** **FACILITIES:** STV Golf Academy at The Beamish Park ch fac Xmas **CONF:** Thtr 100 Class 50 Board 50 Del from £74 **SERVICES:** Lift **PARKING:** 28 **CARDS:**

WHITBY, North Yorkshire — Map 19 NZ81

★★★71% Dunsley Hall

Dunsley YO21 3TL
☎ 01947 893437 01947 893505
e-mail: reception@dunsleyhall.com
web: www.dunsleyhall.com
Dir: *3m N of Whitby, signed off A171*
Friendly hospitality and fine cooking are strong features of this country house, situated in four acres of well-tended gardens. Oak panelling, carved fireplaces and mullion windows all add to the character of the house, which offers a well-appointed restaurant and a popular bar. Spacious bedrooms are bright, comfortable and beautifully furnished, and many have sea views.
ROOMS: 18 en suite (2 fmly) (2 GF) in all bedrooms s £80-£105; d £130-£174 (incl. bkfst) **LB** **FACILITIES:** Sauna Solarium Gym Putt green Xmas **CONF:** Thtr 95 Class 50 Board 40 Del from £90 **PARKING:** 60 **NOTES:** in restaurant Civ Wed 60
CARDS:

WHITBY, continued

★★★67% Saxonville

Ladysmith Av, Argyle Rd YO21 3HX
☎ 01947 602631 01947 820523
e-mail: newtons@saxonville.co.uk
web: www.saxonville.co.uk
Dir: *A174 on to North Promenade. Turn inland at large four towered building visible on West Cliff into Argyle Road, then 1st turning on right*

This comfortable holiday hotel provides very well presented modern bedrooms. Public areas include a choice of lounges, a newly created and enlarged bar, and an attractive restaurant where an extensive range of carefully prepared English dishes is offered. Operated by the same family for several generations, friendly hospitality is a key factor.

ROOMS: 23 en suite (2 fmly) (1 GF) in all bedrooms s £55-£60; d £110-£120 (incl. bkfst) **LB** **FACILITIES:** STV **CONF:** Thtr 100 Class 64 Board 48 **PARKING:** 20 **NOTES:** in restaurant Closed Dec-Jan RS Feb-Mar & Nov **CARDS:**

★★72% Stakesby Manor

Manor Close, High Stakesby YO21 1HL
☎ 01947 602773 01947 602140
e-mail: relax@stakesby-manor.co.uk
web: www.stakesby-manor.co.uk
Dir: *at rdbt junct of A171/B1416 take road for West Cliff. 3rd turning on right*

Situated in a residential area, this Georgian mansion's friendly and relaxed atmosphere attracts many regulars, both business people and tourists. Inviting public areas include a comfortable bar lounge and attractive oak-panelled dining room. The bedrooms are impressively furnished and thoughtfully equipped, and the management very professional.

ROOMS: 13 en suite (2 fmly) in 6 bedrooms s £62-£65; d £88-£92 (incl. bkfst) **LB** **CONF:** Thtr 100 Class 46 Board 40 **PARKING:** 40 **NOTES:** in restaurant Closed 24-30 Dec
CARDS:

★★70% Cliffemount

Runswick Bay TS13 5HU
☎ 01947 840103 01947 841025
e-mail: cliffemount@runswickbay.fsnet.co.uk
web: www.cliffemounthotel.co.uk
Dir: *turn off A174 8m N of Whitby, follow road 1m to end. Hotel on clifftop*

Standing in a delightful elevated position, overlooking the pretty cliff-side village and with splendid views across the bay, a warm welcome awaits guests here. The cosy bar leads to the stylish restaurant where locally caught fish features strongly on the interesting, extensive menus and special boards. The bedrooms, many with sea-view balconies, are well equipped and comfortably furnished.

ROOMS: 19 en suite (5 GF) s £31.50-£51; d £66-£100 (incl. bkfst) **LB** **PARKING:** 30 **NOTES:** in restaurant Closed 25-26 Dec
CARDS:

★★67% *White House*

Upgang Ln, West Cliff YO21 3JJ
☎ 01947 600469 01947 821600
Dir: *turn off A171 onto High Stakesby road, follow signs for West Cliff and Sandsend. Hotel adjacent to golf course*

This pleasant hotel is on the cliff top overlooking the golf course and Sandsend Bay. Attractively appointed bedrooms vary in size, and there is a choice of two bars where locals and visitors mingle. Both the bars and the dining room offer a varied selection of dishes including fresh local fish.

ROOMS: 10 en suite (3 fmly) **PARKING:** 30 **NOTES:** in restaurant
CARDS:

★★64% Old West Cliff Hotel

42 Crescent Av YO21 3EQ
☎ 01947 603292 01947 821716
e-mail: oldwestcliff@telinco.co.uk
web: www.oldwestcliff.telinco.co.uk
Dir: *from A171 follow signs for West Cliff, approach spa complex. Hotel 100yds from centre off Crescent Gardens*

This family owned and run hotel is close to the sea and convenient for the town centre. It provides well-equipped bedrooms, a cosy lounge and separate bar. A wide range of food is served in the cosy basement restaurant.

ROOMS: 12 en suite (6 fmly) s £50; d £60 (incl. bkfst) **NOTES:** in restaurant Closed 24 Dec-31 Jan **CARDS:**

U Estbek House

East Row, Sandsend YO21 3SU
☎ 01947 893424
e-mail: reservations@estbekhouse.co.uk
Dir: *on Cleveland Way, within Sandsend, next to East Beck.*

At the time of going to press, the star classification for this hotel was not confirmed. Please refer to the AA internet site www.theAA.com for current information.

ROOMS: 5 rms (4 en suite) (1 fmly) in all bedrooms s £40-£50; d £30-£45 (incl. bkfst) **LB** **FACILITIES:** Xmas **NOTES:** in restaurant **CARDS:**

See advert on opposite page

WHITEHAVEN, Cumbria — Map 18 NX91

Travel Inn

Howgate CA28 6PL
☎ 08701 977268 01946 590106
Dir: *On outskirts of Whitehaven on A595 towards Workington*

Travel Inn offers good-quality, value-for-money accommodation. Spacious, en suite rooms with bath and shower comfortably accommodate a family of up to two adults and two children (to age 15). The restaurant and bar offers a varied menu. For further details consult the Hotel Groups page.

ROOMS: 38 en suite s £45.95-£46.95; d £45.95-£46.95

WHITEWELL, Lancashire — Map 18 SD64

Restaurant with Rooms

The Inn at Whitewell

Forest of Bowland, Clitheroe BB7 3AT
☎ 01200 448222 01200 448298

This long-established culinary destination hides away in quintessential Lancashire countryside just 20 minutes from the M6. The fine dining restaurant is complemented by two historic,

continued

cosy bars, and roaring fires, real ales and slick service make an irresistible combination. Bedrooms are richly furnished with antiques and eye-catching bijouterie, while many of the bathrooms have voluminous Victorian brass showers.
ROOMS: 13 en suite 4 annexe en suite (1 fmly) (1 GF) s £69-£110; d £94-£140 (incl. bkfst) **FACILITIES:** STV Fishing Xmas **CONF:** Class 60 Board 35 **PARKING:** 60 **NOTES:** Civ Wed 80
CARDS:

WHITLEY, Wiltshire Map 04 ST86

Restaurant with Rooms

The Pear Tree Inn
Top Ln SN12 8QX
☎ 01225 709131 01225 702276
Many accolades have been handed to Martin and Debbie Still who have run the property for several years. The eight very superior bedrooms have luxurious bathrooms and state-of-the-art TVs and DVDs. The Restaurant draws customers from a wide area to experience both the excellent food and the friendliness of the professional team. AA Pub of the Year for England 2004-5.
ROOMS: 4 en suite 4 annexe en suite (2 fmly) (4 GF) in all bedrooms s £65-£75; d £90-£110 (incl. bkfst) **FACILITIES:** boules pitch **PARKING:** 60 **NOTES:** in restaurant Closed 25-26 Dec
CARDS:

WHITLEY BAY, Tyne & Wear Map 21 NZ37

★★★72% Windsor
South Pde NE26 2RF
☎ 0191 251 8888 0191 297 0272
e-mail: info@windsorhotel-uk.com
web: www.windsorhotel-uk.com
Dir: *from A19 Tyne Tunnel take A1058 to Tynemouth. At coast rdbt turn left to Whitley Bay. After 2m turn left at Rex Hotel. Hotel on left*

This tastefully modernised hotel is conveniently located between the town centre and the seafront, where lively bars transform Thursday to Sunday nights with a carnival atmosphere. Most bedrooms boast superior bathrooms with bath and separate shower cubicle. Public areas are smartly presented and include Bazil, a smart and stylish brasserie.
ROOMS: 69 en suite (24 fmly) (4 GF) s £59-£69; d £65-£80 (incl. bkfst) **LB** **FACILITIES:** STV **CONF:** Thtr 80 Class 60 Board 40 Del from £69 **SERVICES:** Lift **PARKING:** 46 **NOTES:**
CARDS:

Packed in a hurry?
Ironing facilities should be available at all star levels, either in rooms or on request

WHITNEY-ON-WYE, Herefordshire Map 09 SO24

★★72% The Rhydspence Inn
HR3 6EU
☎ 01497 831262 01497 831751
e-mail: info@rhydspence-inn.co.uk
Dir: *1m W of Whitney-on-Wye on A438, Hereford to Brecon road*

With a history as an inn stretching back 600 years, this hotel offers the charm of yesteryear with the comforts of today and is personally run by the proprietors. Guests can expect well-equipped bedrooms and public areas with exposed beams and timber-framed walls. There is an extensive menu in the elegant restaurant and the atmospheric bar also has a blackboard menu.
ROOMS: 7 en suite s £37.50-£42.50; d £75 (incl. bkfst) **LB**
PARKING: 30 **NOTES:** in restaurant Closed 2wks (varies)
CARDS:

W

WHITSTABLE, Kent
Map 07 TR16

Travel Inn
Thanet Way CT5 3DB
☎ 08701 977269 01227 263151
Dir: *2m W of town centre on B2205*
Travel Inn offers good-quality, value-for-money accommodation. Spacious, en suite rooms with bath and shower comfortably accommodate a family of up to two adults and two children (to age 15). The restaurant and bar offers a varied menu. For further details consult the Hotel Groups page.
ROOMS: 40 en suite s £45.95-£46.95; d £45.95-£46.95 **CONF:** Thtr 30 Board 20

WHITTLEBURY, Northamptonshire
Map 11 SP64

★★★★79% Whittlebury Hall
NN12 8QH
☎ 01327 857857 01237 857867
e-mail: sales@whittleburyhall.co.uk
web: www.whittleburyhall.co.uk
Dir: *A43/A413 towards Buckingham, through Whittlebury village, turning for Whittlebury Hall on right (signed)*
A purpose-built, Georgian-style country-house hotel with excellent spa and leisure facilities and pedestrian access to the Silverstone circuit. Grand public areas include F1 car racing memorabilia and the accommodation includes some lavishly appointed suites. Food is a strength, with a choice of various dining options. Particularly good are the afternoon teas in the spacious, comfortable lounge and the fine dining in Murray's Restaurant.
ROOMS: 210 en suite in 160 bedrooms **FACILITIES: Spa** STV Sauna Solarium Gym Jacuzzi Beauty treatments, Relaxation Room, Aerobic Studio, Hair Studio **CONF:** Thtr 600 Class 175 Board 40 **SERVICES:** Lift **PARKING:** 250 **NOTES:** in restaurant Civ Wed 200 **CARDS:**

WICKFORD, Essex
Map 06 TQ79

Innkeeper's Lodge Basildon/Wickford
Runwell Rd SS11 7QJ
☎ 01268 769671 01268 578012
www.innkeeperslodge.com
Dir: *M25 junct 29/A127 Southend, exit at Basildon/Wickford, left at rdbt towards Wickford. Straight over next 2 rdbts, at 3rd rdbt take 2nd exit*
Smart rooms meet essential business requirements but also have home comforts, and depending on location may well have meeting rooms and pub dining. Dining options generally include all-day menus plus the added advantage of breakfast.
ROOMS: 24 en suite s £48-£58; d £48-£58

WICKHAM, Hampshire
Map 05 SU51

★★70% Old House Hotel & Restaurant
The Square PO17 5JG
☎ 01329 833049 01329 833672
e-mail: oldhousehotel@aol.com
Dir: *M27 junct 10, N on A32 for 2m towards Alton.*
This creeper-clad former Georgian residence occupies a prime position in a charming square in the centre of town. Ongoing refurbishment is resulting in smart and comfortable public areas that include a choice of eating areas and an inviting bar and

continued

lounge. Bedrooms are well equipped although some are larger than others.

ROOMS: 8 en suite 4 annexe en suite in all bedrooms s fr £70; d £85-£120 (incl. cont bkfst) **LB** **FACILITIES:** ch fac **CONF:** Board 1 Del from £120 **PARKING:** 8 **NOTES:** in restaurant
CARDS:

WIDNES, Cheshire
Map 15 SJ58

★★★62% The Hillcrest Hotel
75 Cronton Ln WA8 9AR
☎ 0151 424 1616 0151 495 1348
e-mail: thehillcrest@corushotels.com
Dir: *A5080 Cronton to lights turn right for 0.75m, right at T-junct, follow A5080 for 500yds. Hotel on right*

This comfortable hotel is located within easy reach of the motorway network. All bedrooms are comfortable and well equipped, particularly the executive rooms, and suites with four-poster or canopy beds and spa baths are also available. Public areas include extensive conference facilities, Palms restaurant and bar, as well as Nelsons public bar.
ROOMS: 50 en suite (5 fmly) in 25 bedrooms s £45-£59; d £64-£75 **LB** **FACILITIES:** STV Xmas **CONF:** Thtr 140 Class 80 Board 40 Del from £77 **SERVICES:** Lift **PARKING:** 150 **NOTES:** Civ Wed 100
CARDS:

Travelodge
Fiddlers Ferry Rd WA8 2NR
☎ 08700 850 950 0151 424 8930
Dir: *on A562*
Travelodge offers good quality, good value, modern accommodation. Ideal for families, the spacious, en suite bedrooms include remote-control TV, tea and coffee-making facilities and luxury beds. Meals can be taken at the nearby family restaurant. For further details consult the Hotel Groups page.
ROOMS: 32 en suite s fr £25; d fr £25

WIGAN, Greater Manchester Map 15 SD50

★★★★63% Kilhey Court
Chorley Rd, Standish WN1 2XN
☎ 01257 472100 01257 422401
e-mail: kilheycourt@macdonald-hotels.co.uk
Dir: *M6 J27, A5209 Standish, straight over at lights, past church on right, left at T-junct, hotel on right 350yds, or M61 J6, signed Wigan & Haigh Hall. Right at t-junct after 3 miles. Hotel 0.5 miles on right.*

MACDONALD HOTELS

This hotel, peacefully situated in its own grounds yet conveniently located for the motorway network, offers comfortable accommodation. Rooms are split between the original Victorian house and a modern extension. Public areas display many original features and the split-level restaurant offers views over the Worthington lakes. This hotel is an especially popular venue for weddings.
ROOMS: 62 en suite (3 fmly) (8 GF) in 33 bedrooms s £110; d £130 LB **FACILITIES: Spa** STV Sauna Solarium Gym Jacuzzi Aerobics and yoga classes, private fishing arranged Xmas **CONF:** BC Thtr 400 Class 180 Board 60 Del from £100 **SERVICES:** Lift **PARKING:** 200 **NOTES:** in restaurant Civ Wed 300
CARDS:

★★★74%
Wrightington Hotel & Country Club
Moss Ln, Wrightington WN6 9PB
☎ 01257 425803 01257 425830
e-mail: info@wrightingtonhotel.co.uk
Dir: *M6 junct 27, 0.25m W, hotel on right after church*

Situated in open countryside close to the M6 motorway, this privately owned hotel offers friendly hospitality. Accommodation is well equipped and spacious and public areas include an extensive leisure complex, Blazers Restaurant, two bars and air-conditioned function and banqueting facilities, along with the new and impressive fine dining restaurant, Heathcotes.
ROOMS: 74 en suite (6 fmly) (36 GF) in 59 bedrooms s £70-£95; d £80-£110 (incl. bkfst) LB **FACILITIES:** STV Squash Sauna Solarium Gym Jacuzzi Sprt Inj clinic,Hlth&Bty clinic,H'drsr **CONF:** Thtr 200 Class 120 Board 40 Del from £110 **SERVICES:** Lift **PARKING:** 240 **NOTES:** in restaurant RS 24 Dec-3 Jan Civ Wed 100
CARDS:

★★★65% Quality Hotel Wigan
Riverway WN1 3SS
☎ 01942 826888 01942 825800
e-mail: enquiries@hotels-wigan.com
Dir: *from A49 take B5238 from rdbt, continue for 1.5m through lights, through 3 more sets of lights, right at 4th set, 1st left*

QUALITY HOTEL BY CHOICE HOTELS

Close to the centre of the town this modern hotel offers spacious and well-equipped bedrooms. The open plan public areas include a

continued

comfortable lounge bar adjacent to the popular restaurant, which serves a good range of dishes. Secure car parking is a bonus.
ROOMS: 88 en suite (16 GF) in 42 bedrooms s £47-£99; d £55-£119 (incl. bkfst) LB **CONF:** Thtr 240 Class 90 Board 50 **SERVICES:** Lift **PARKING:** 100 **NOTES:** in restaurant Civ Wed 60
CARDS:

★★65% Bel-Air
236 Wigan Ln WN1 2NU
☎ 01942 241410 01942 243967
e-mail: belair@hotelwigan.freeserve.co.uk
web: www.belairhotel.co.uk
Dir: *M6 junct 27, follow signs for Standish. In Standish turn right at lights towards A49. Hotel 1.5m on right, towards Wigan*
This friendly, family-owned and run hotel is located just to the north of town. Accommodation varies in size and style but all rooms are well equipped. An extensive range of freshly prepared dishes is offered in the restaurant.
ROOMS: 11 en suite (1 fmly) s £35-£39.50; d £45-£49.50 (incl. bkfst) **CONF:** Thtr 20 Board 8 **PARKING:** 10 **NOTES:** in restaurant
CARDS:

⌂ Premier Lodge (Wigan South)
53 Warrington Rd, Ashton-in-Makerfield WN4 9PJ
☎ 0870 9906582 0870 9906583
web: www.premierlodge.com
Dir: *M6 junct 23, onto A49 towards Ashton. Hotel 0.5m on left*

PREMIER LODGE.com

High quality, modern, budget accommodation, ideal for families and business travellers. All rooms feature bath, power shower and satellite TV, and most have telephones / modem points. The adjacent bar and restaurant offers a wide and varied menu.
ROOMS: 28 en suite s £48; d £48

⌂ Travel Inn (Wigan South)
Warrington Rd, Marus Bridge WN3 6XB
☎ 08701 977270 01942 498679
Dir: *M6 junct 25 (N'bound) slip road to rdbt turn left, Travel Inn on left*

travel inn

Travel Inn offers good-quality, value-for-money accommodation. Spacious, en suite rooms with bath and shower comfortably accommodate a family of up to two adults and two children (to age 15). The restaurant and bar offers a varied menu. For further details consult the Hotel Groups page.
ROOMS: 40 en suite s £45.95-£46.95; d £45.95-£46.95

⌂ Travel Inn (Wigan West)
Orrell Rd, Orrell WN5 8HQ
☎ 08701 977271 01942 215002
Dir: *From M6 junct 26 follow signs for Upholland & Orrell. At first lights turn left. Inn on right behind Priory Wood Beefeater*

travel inn

Travel Inn offers good-quality, value-for-money accommodation. Spacious, en suite rooms with bath and shower comfortably accommodate a family of up to two adults and two children (to age 15). The restaurant and bar offers a varied menu. For further details consult the Hotel Groups page.
ROOMS: 40 en suite s £45.95-£46.95; d £45.95-£46.95
CONF: Thtr 75 Board 40

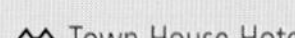
Town House Hotel
Country House Hotel
⌂ Travel Accommodation

WIGHT, ISLE OF — Map 05

BEMBRIDGE — Map 05 SZ68

★★★66% The Windmill Inn Hotel & Restaurant
1 Steyne Rd PO35 5UH
☎ 01983 872875 01983 874760
e-mail: info@thewindmillhotel.co.uk
web: www.windmill-inn.com
Dir: *0.5m from town centre, towards lifeboat station*

This newly refurbished hotel offers a range of comfortably furnished public rooms where an excellent choice of freshly prepared food is available to suit virtually all tastes. Bedrooms are well presented and thoughtfully equipped, while service is both attentive and friendly. There is an attractive garden to the rear.
ROOMS: 14 en suite (2 fmly) in 3 bedrooms s fr £60; d £70-£100 (incl. bkfst) **LB** **FACILITIES:** **CONF:** Thtr 100 Class 100 Board 100 **PARKING:** 50 **NOTES:** in restaurant Civ Wed 100
CARDS:

BONCHURCH See Ventnor

COWES — Map 05 SZ49

★★★68% New Holmwood
Queens Rd, Egypt Point PO31 8BW
☎ 01983 292508 01983 295020
e-mail: nholmwdh@aol.com
Dir: *from A3020 at Northwood Garage lights, left & follow road to rdbt. 1st left then sharp right into Baring Rd, 4th left into Egypt Hill. At bottom turn right, hotel on right*

Best Western

Just metres from the Esplanade, this hotel has an enviable outlook. Bedrooms are comfortable and very well equipped. The glass-fronted restaurant looking out to sea serves a range of interesting meals and the sun terrace is delightful in the summer. There is a small pool area and a conference room.
ROOMS: 26 en suite (1 fmly) (9 GF) in all bedrooms s £75-£120; d £90-£120 (incl. bkfst) **LB** **FACILITIES: Spa** STV Xmas **CONF:** Thtr 130 Class 60 Board 50 Del £98 **PARKING:** 20 **NOTES:** in restaurant
CARDS:

See advert on opposite page

★62% Duke of York
Mill Hill Rd PO31 7BT
☎ 01983 295171 01983 295047
This family-run inn is quietly situated close to the town centre. Bedrooms are divided between the main building and a nearby annexe and are neatly appointed. There is a well-stocked bar and a pleasant restaurant offering a good range of popular dishes, many featuring fish and seafood. The inn has a nautical theme enhanced by an abundance of maritime memorabilia.
ROOMS: 7 en suite 5 annexe rms (1 fmly) in 4 bedrooms
PARKING: 12 **CARDS:**

FRESHWATER — Map 05 SZ38

★★★68% Farringford
Bedbury Ln PO40 9TQ
☎ 01983 752500 01983 756515
web: www.farringford.co.uk
Dir: *A3054, left to Norton Green down Pixlie Hill. Left to Freshwater Bay. At bay turn right into Bedbury Ln, hotel on left*
Upon seeing Farringford, Alfred Lord Tennyson is said to have remarked 'we will go no further, this must be our home' and so it was for some forty years. Now, some 150 years later, the hotel provides bedrooms ranging in style and size, from large rooms in the main house to adjoining chalet-style rooms. The atmosphere is relaxed and dinner features fresh local produce.
ROOMS: 14 en suite 4 annexe en suite (5 fmly) (4 GF) s £37-£53; d £74-£120 (incl. bkfst) **LB** **FACILITIES:** 9 Putt green Bowling green ch fac Xmas **CONF:** BC Thtr 120 Class 50 Board 50 Del from £55 **PARKING:** 55 **NOTES:** Civ Wed 130
CARDS:

NEWPORT — Map 05 SZ58

Travel Inn Isle of Wight (Newport)
Seaclose, Fairlee Rd PO30 2DN
☎ 08701 977144 0870 241 9000
Dir: *From town centre take A3054 signed Ryde. After 0.75m at Seaclose lights, turn left. Inn adjacent to council offices*

travel inn

Travel Inn offers good-quality, value-for-money accommodation. Spacious, en suite rooms with bath and shower comfortably accommodate a family of up to two adults and two children (to age 15). The restaurant and bar offers a varied menu. For further details consult the Hotel Groups page.
ROOMS: 42 en suite s £45.95-£46.95; d £45.95-£46.95

W

RYDE

Map 05 SZ59

★★★ 61% Appley Manor

Appley Rd PO33 1PH
☎ 01983 564777 01983 564704
e-mail: appleymanor@lineone.net
Dir: *A3055 onto B3330. Hotel 0.25m on left*

Located only five minutes from the town centre this property, which sits in peaceful surroundings, was once a Victorian manor house. The spacious bedrooms are well furnished and have now been redecorated. Dinner can be taken in the intimate dining room or more informally at the adjacent Manor Inn.

ROOMS: 12 en suite (2 fmly) ⊗ in 3 bedrooms **CONF:** Thtr 40 Class 40 Board 30 **PARKING:** 60 **NOTES:** ✈ **CARDS:**

★★ 67% Yelf's

Union St PO33 2LG
☎ 01983 564062 01983 563937
e-mail: manager@yelfshotel.com
web: www.yelfshotel.com
Dir: *from Ryde Esplanande, turn into Union St. Hotel on right*

This former coaching inn has smart public areas including a busy bar, a separate lounge and an attractive dining room. Bedrooms are comfortably furnished and well equipped and some are located in an adjoining wing. A new conservatory lounge bar and stylish terrace have been added.

ROOMS: 30 en suite (2 fmly) ⊗ in 5 bedrooms s £51-£57; d £68-£72 (incl. bkfst) **LB** **FACILITIES:** STV ch fac **CONF:** Thtr 70 Class 30 Board 50 **NOTES:** ⊗ in restaurant Civ Wed 100 **CARDS:**

SANDOWN

Map 05 SZ58

★★ 68% Riviera

2 Royal St PO36 8LP
☎ 01983 402518 01983 402518
e-mail: enquiries@rivierahotel.org.uk
Dir: *pass Heights Leisure Centre and church on left. Turn 2nd right (Melville St), then 2nd right again into Royal St*

Regular guests return year after year to this friendly and welcoming family-run hotel. It is located near to the High Street and just a short stroll from the beach, pier and shops. Bedrooms, including several at ground floor level, are very well furnished and comfortably equipped. Enjoyable home-cooked meals are served in the spacious dining room.

ROOMS: 41 en suite (6 fmly) (10 GF) s £38-£44; d £76-£88 (incl. bkfst & dinner) **LB** **FACILITIES:** ♫ ch fac **PARKING:** 20 **NOTES:** ⊗ in restaurant Closed Nov-Mar **CARDS:**

★★ 66% Cygnet Hotel

58 Carter St PO36 8DQ
☎ 01983 402930 01983 405112
e-mail: info@cygnethotel.com
web: www.cygnethotel.com
Dir: *on corner of Broadway and Carter St*

Popular with tour groups, this family-run hotel offers bedrooms that are generally spacious, comfortably furnished and well equipped. Extensive public areas include an indoor swimming pool, two lounge areas and a bar where live entertainment is regularly staged.

ROOMS: 46 rms (45 en suite) (8 fmly) (21 GF) s £30-£40; d £60-£80 (incl. bkfst & dinner) **LB** **FACILITIES:** **Spa** Sauna Solarium pool table ♫ Xmas **SERVICES:** Lift **PARKING:** 25 **NOTES:** ✈ ⊗ in restaurant Closed Jan **CARDS:**

SANDOWN, continued

★★61% Bayshore
12 - 16 Pier St PO36 8JX
☎ 01983 403154 📠 01983 406574
e-mail: bayshore.sandown@alfatravel.co.uk

Dir: *from Broadway into Melville St, signed to Tourist Information Office. Across High St and bear right opposite pier. Hotel on right*

This large hotel is located on the seafront opposite the pier and offers extensive public rooms where live entertainment is provided in season. The bedrooms are well equipped and staff very friendly and helpful.

ROOMS: 78 en suite (19 fmly) s £28-£36; d £46-£62 (incl. bkfst) **LB** **FACILITIES:** Sauna ♫ Xmas **SERVICES:** Lift **NOTES:** in restaurant Closed Dec-Feb RS Mar & Nov **CARDS:**

★★61% Sandringham
Esplanade PO36 8AH
☎ 01983 406655 📠 01983 404395
e-mail: info@sandringhamhotel.co.uk

With a prime seafront location and splendid views, this is one of the largest hotels on the island. Comfortable public areas include a spacious lounge and a heated indoor swimming pool and Jacuzzi. Bedrooms vary in size and many sea-facing rooms have a balcony. Regular entertainment is provided in the ballroom.

ROOMS: 110 en suite (39 fmly) (6 GF) in 3 bedrooms s £33-£49; d £66-£98 (incl. bkfst & dinner) **LB** **FACILITIES:** Snooker Sauna Jacuzzi ♫ Xmas **SERVICES:** Lift **PARKING:** 82 **NOTES:** in restaurant **CARDS:**

SEAVIEW Map 05 SZ69

★★★77% Priory Bay
Priory Dr PO34 5BU
☎ 01983 613146 📠 01983 616539
e-mail: enquiries@priorybay.co.uk
web: www.priorybay.co.uk

Dir: *B3330 towards Seaview, through Nettlestone. Do not take Seaview turning, but continue 0.5m until sign for Hotel*

This peacefully located hotel has its own stretch of beach and a range of outdoor leisure facilities. Public areas are especially comfortable, as are the well-equipped and mostly spacious bedrooms. The kitchen creates interesting and imaginative dishes, using local produce as much as possible.

ROOMS: 19 en suite 12 annexe en suite (13 fmly) (2 GF) s £65-£220; d £110-£260 (incl. bkfst) **LB** **FACILITIES:** STV 9 Private beach, 70 Acres of woodland lawns and formal gardens. ♫ Xmas **CONF:** Thtr 80 Class 60 Board 40 **PARKING:** 100 **NOTES:** in restaurant Civ Wed 100 **CARDS:**

★★66% *Springvale Hotel & Restaurant*
Springvale PO34 5AN
☎ 01983 612533 📠 01983 812905
e-mail: reception@springvalehotel.com
web: www.springvalehotel.com

Dir: *towards Ryde, follow A3055 onto A3330 towards Bembridge. Left at signs to Seaview, follow brown tourist signs for hotel*

A friendly hotel in a quiet beach-front location with views across the Solent. Bedrooms, which differ in shape and size, are attractive and well equipped. Public areas are traditionally furnished and include a cosy bar, dining room and small separate lounge.

ROOMS: 13 en suite (2 fmly) **FACILITIES:** Jacuzzi Sailing dinghy hire & tuition, Cruiser Charter ♫ ch fac **CONF:** Class 30 Board 20 **PARKING:** 1 **NOTES:** in restaurant **CARDS:**

SHANKLIN Map 05 SZ58

★★★67% Keats Green
3 Queens Rd PO37 6AN
☎ 01983 862742 📠 01983 868572
e-mail: enquiries@keatsgreenhoteliow.co.uk

Dir: *on A3055 follow signs Old Village/Ventnor, avoiding town centre, hotel on left past St Saviours Church*

This well-established hotel enjoys a super location overlooking Keats Green and Sandown Bay. Bedrooms are attractively decorated and furnished with pine. Public rooms include a comfortable bar/lounge and a smartly appointed dining room, both affording lovely sea views.

ROOMS: 33 en suite (7 fmly) **FACILITIES:** **SERVICES:** Lift **PARKING:** 34 **NOTES:** in restaurant Closed Jan-Mar **CARDS:**

★★★65% Luccombe Hall
8 Luccombe Rd PO37 6RL
☎ 01983 869000 📠 01983 863082
e-mail: enquiries@luccombehall.co.uk

Dir: *take A3055 to Shanklin, through old village then 1st left into Priory Rd, left into Popham Rd, 1st right into Luccombe Rd. Hotel on right*

Appropriately described as 'the view with the hotel', this property was originally built in 1870 as a summer home for the Bishop of Portsmouth. Enjoying an impressive cliff-top location, the hotel benefits from wonderful sea views, delightful gardens and direct access to the beach. Well-equipped bedrooms are comfortably furnished and there is a range of leisure facilities.

ROOMS: 30 en suite (15 fmly) (7 GF) s £35-£55; d £70-£110 (incl. bkfst) **FACILITIES:** Squash Sauna Solarium Gym Putt green Jacuzzi Games room, Treatment room ♫ ch fac Xmas **PARKING:** 20 **NOTES:** in restaurant **CARDS:**

See advert on opposite page

W

★★70% Channel View
Hope Rd PO37 6EH
☎ 01983 862309 01983 868400
e-mail: enquiries@channelviewhotel.co.uk
Dir: *off A3055 at sign for esplanade & beach, hotel 250mtrs on left*

With an elevated cliff-top location overlooking Shanklin Bay, several rooms at this hotel enjoy pleasant views and all are very well decorated and furnished. The hotel is family run, and guests can enjoy efficient service, regular evening entertainment, a heated indoor swimming pool and holistic therapy.
ROOMS: 56 en suite (15 fmly) s £29-£46; d £58-£92 (incl. bkfst) **LB**
FACILITIES: Spa Sauna Solarium ♫ **SERVICES:** Lift **PARKING:** 22
NOTES: in restaurant Closed Jan-Feb **CARDS:**

★★65% Cliff Hall
16 Crescent Rd PO37 6DJ
☎ 01983 862828 01983 861476
e-mail: cliffhallhotel@tiscali.co.uk
Dir: *From Lake to Shanklin take Ventnor Rd at traffic lights, left to esplanade*
A privately owned hotel situated close to the beach lift and town centre. The pleasantly decorated bedrooms are generally quite spacious and have all the usual facilities; most rooms also have stunning sea views. Public areas include a lounge, bar, restaurant, coffee shop and a superb terrace with an outdoor swimming pool.
ROOMS: 28 en suite (16 fmly) (8 GF) s £37-£45; d £74-£90 (incl. bkfst & dinner) **LB** **FACILITIES:** Snooker Pool Table Table Tennis ♫ Xmas
CONF: Del from £60 **NOTES:** in restaurant Closed 1 Jan-13 Feb
CARDS:

★★64% Curraghmore
22 Hope Rd PO37 6EA
☎ 01983 862605 01983 867431
e-mail: curraghmore@ukgateway.net
Dir: *from Sandown towards Shanklin along Arthurs Hill. L before lights into Beatrice Ave, 100mtrs to hotel car park*
This hotel has a pleasant location, close to the beach and just a short stroll from the shops and Shanklin village. Bedrooms include several with sea views. Entertainment is provided three or four nights of the week with dancing in the lounge and a separate adjoining bar.
ROOMS: 24 en suite (8 fmly) s £22-£26; d £44-£52 (incl. bkfst)
FACILITIES: ♫ **PARKING:** 20 **NOTES:** in restaurant Closed Nov-Feb

Early start?
Hotels at all star levels should provide in-room alarm clocks and/or alarm calls

★★64% Malton House
8 Park Rd PO37 6AY
☎ 01983 865007 01983 865576
e-mail: christos@excite.co.uk
web: maltonhouse.co.uk
Dir: *from Hope Road lights up hill then left into 3rd road*
A well-kept Victorian hotel set in its own gardens in a quiet area, conveniently located for cliff-top walks and the public lift down to the promenade. The bedrooms are comfortable and public rooms include a small lounge, a separate bar and a dining room where traditional homemade meals are served.
ROOMS: 15 en suite (3 fmly) d £50-£56 (incl. bkfst) **PARKING:** 12
NOTES: in restaurant **CARDS:**

★★64% Villa Mentone
11 Park Rd PO37 6AY
☎ 01983 862346 01983 862130
e-mail: enquiry@villa-mentone.co.uk
Built in 1860, the Villa Mentone enjoys an excellent cliff-top position close to the town centre. Bedrooms vary in size but are all well equipped, and a smart new conservatory extension offers views over Shanklin Bay. Enjoyable home cooking is served in the pleasant dining room, and entertainment is regularly provided in the bar.
ROOMS: 30 en suite (3 fmly) (7 GF) s £25-£45; d £40-£60 (incl. bkfst)
LB **FACILITIES:** STV ♫ Xmas **CONF:** Thtr 45 Class 25 Board 10
PARKING: 10 **NOTES:** in restaurant
CARDS:

W

SHANKLIN, continued

★★62% Melbourne Ardenlea
Queen's Rd PO37 6AP
☎ 01983 862283 01983 862865
Dir: *turn left at Fiveways crossroads, off A3055, hotel on right 150yds past church with tall spire*
This quietly located hotel is within easy walking distance of the town centre and the lift down to the promenade and successfully caters for the needs of holidaymakers. Bedrooms are traditionally furnished and guests can enjoy the various spacious public areas including a welcoming bar and a large heated indoor swimming pool.
ROOMS: 50 en suite (14 fmly) (6 GF) s £34-£50; d £68-£100 (incl. bkfst & dinner) LB **FACILITIES: Spa** Sauna Table tennis, Pool table, Football table ♫ ch fac **SERVICES:** Lift **PARKING:** 28 **NOTES:** in restaurant Closed mid Dec-mid Feb RS Nov-mid Dec & mid Feb-Mar
CARDS:

TOTLAND BAY Map 05 SZ38

★★★68% Sentry Mead
Madeira Rd PO39 0BJ
☎ 01983 753212 01983 753212
e-mail: julie@sentry-mead.co.uk
Dir: *off A3054 at Totland war memorial rdbt, 300yds on right*
Just two minutes' walk from the sea at Totland Bay, this well-kept Victorian villa has a comfortable lounge and separate bar, as well as a conservatory that looks out over the delightful garden. Bedrooms feature co-ordinated soft furnishings and welcome extras such as mineral water and biscuits.
ROOMS: 14 en suite (4 fmly) **PARKING:** 10 **NOTES:** in restaurant Closed 20 Dec-4 Jan **CARDS:**

VENTNOR Map 05 SZ57

★★★★67% The Royal Hotel
Belgrave Rd PO38 1JJ
☎ 01983 852186 01983 855395
e-mail: enquiries@royalhoteliow.co.uk
web: www.royalhoteliow.co.uk
Dir: *A3055 into Ventnor follow one-way system, after lights left into Belgrave Road. Hotel on right*
This hotel provides good quality accommodation and the staff deliver professional service in a relaxed manner. Public areas include a sunny conservatory and restful lounge, and there is also an outdoor pool. The restaurant provides traditional surroundings in which to enjoy modern British cuisine.
ROOMS: 55 en suite (7 fmly) in all bedrooms s £70-£106; d £115-£175 (incl. bkfst) LB **FACILITIES:** STV Xmas **CONF:** Thtr 100 Class 80 Board 50 Del from £100 **SERVICES:** Lift **PARKING:** 56 **NOTES:** in restaurant Closed 1'st 2 wks Jan Civ Wed 150
CARDS:

See advert on opposite page

★★★69% Burlington
Bellevue Rd PO38 1DB
☎ 01983 852113 01983 853862
e-mail: patmctoldrige@burlingtonhotel.freeserve.co.uk
Eight of the attractively decorated bedrooms at this establishment benefit from balconies, and the three ground floor rooms have French doors that lead onto the garden. There is a cosy bar, a comfortable lounge and a dining room where home-made bread rolls accompany the five-course dinners. Service is friendly and attentive.
ROOMS: 24 en suite (8 fmly) (3 GF) in all bedrooms s £42-£53; d £84-£106 (incl. bkfst & dinner) LB **FACILITIES:** **PARKING:** 20 **NOTES:** No children 3yrs in restaurant Closed Nov-Etr
CARDS:

★★★68% Ventnor Towers
Madeira Rd PO38 1QT
☎ 01983 852277 01983 855536
e-mail: reservations@ventnortowers.com
web: www.ventnortowers.com
Dir: *1st left after Trinity church, follow road for 0.25m*

This mid-Victorian hotel set in spacious grounds - from where a path leads down to the shore - is high above the bay and enjoys splendid sea views. Many potted plants and fresh flowers grace the day rooms, which include two lounges and a spacious bar. Bedrooms include two four-poster rooms and some that have their own balconies.
ROOMS: 27 en suite (4 fmly) in 14 bedrooms **FACILITIES:** Putt green Games room with table tennis & pool table ♫ **CONF:** Thtr 80 Class 50 Board 35 **PARKING:** 26 **NOTES:** in restaurant Closed 21-27 Dec **CARDS:**

★★★66% Eversley
Park Av PO38 1LB
☎ 01983 852244 & 852462 01983 856534
e-mail: eversleyhotel@yahoo.co.uk
web: www.eversleyhotel.com
Dir: *on A3055 W of Ventnor, next to Ventnor Park*
Located west of Ventnor, this hotel enjoys a quiet location with some rooms offering garden and pool views. The spacious restaurant is also used for local functions and there is a bar, television room, lounge area and a card room as well as a new jacuzzi and gym. Bedrooms are generally a good size.
ROOMS: 30 en suite (8 fmly) (2 GF) s £30-£55; d £59-£99 (incl. bkfst) LB **FACILITIES:** Gym Jacuzzi Childrens play equipment Pool table ch fac Xmas **CONF:** Class 40 Board 20 Del from £65 **PARKING:** 23 **NOTES:** in restaurant Closed 31 Nov-22 Dec & 2 Jan-8 Feb
CARDS:

★★68% Hillside Hotel
Mitchell Av PO38 1DR
☎ 01983 852271 01983 852271
e-mail: aa@hillside-hotel.co.uk
Dir: *off A3055 onto B3327. Hotel 0.5m on right behind tennis courts*
Dating back to the 19th century and enjoying a superb location overlooking Ventnor and the sea beyond. Public areas consist of a

continued

traditional lounge, a cosy bar area with an adjoining conservatory and a light, airy dining room. Bedrooms have been refurbished with quality fabrics. A welcoming and homely atmosphere is assured.
ROOMS: 12 en suite (1 fmly) (1 GF) ⊗ in all bedrooms s £29; d £58 (incl. bkfst) **LB** **FACILITIES:** **PARKING:** 12 **NOTES:** No children 5yrs ⊗ in restaurant Closed Xmas **CARDS:**

★★67% St Maur Hotel
Castle Rd PO38 1LG
☎ 01983 852570 & 853645 01983 852306
e-mail: sales@stmaur.co.uk
Dir: *W of Ventnor off A3055. Right at end of Park Avenue*
Guests will find a warm welcome awaits them at this hotel, which is pleasantly and quietly located overlooking the bay. The well-equipped bedrooms are traditionally decorated. In addition to a spacious lounge, the hotel benefits from a cosy residents' bar. The gardens here are a delight.
ROOMS: 12 en suite (2 fmly) ⊗ in all bedrooms s £34-£42; d £68-£84 (incl. bkfst) **LB** **FACILITIES:** STV **PARKING:** 12 **NOTES:** No children 5yrs ⊗ in restaurant Closed Dec **CARDS:**

YARMOUTH

Map 05 SZ38

Top 200 – Hotel

★★★ George Hotel
Quay St PO41 0PE
☎ 01983 760331 01983 760425
e-mail: res@thegeorge.co.uk
Dir: *between the castle and the pier*
This delightful 17th-century hotel enjoys a wonderful location at the water's edge, adjacent to the castle and the quay. Public areas include an elegant fine dining restaurant and a bright brasserie as a more informal eating option. In addition, guests can also relax in either the cosy bar or an inviting lounge. Individually styled bedrooms, with many thoughtful extras, are beautifully appointed and some benefit from spacious balconies. The hotel's motor yacht is available for hire by guests.
ROOMS: 17 en suite ⊗ in 4 bedrooms **FACILITIES:** STV Sailing from Yarmouth **CONF:** Thtr 30 Class 10 Board 18 **NOTES:** No children 10yrs Civ Wed 50 **CARDS:**

Bad hair day?
Hairdryers in all rooms three stars and above

★★65% *Bugle Coaching Inn*
The Square PO41 0NS
☎ 01983 760272 01983 760883
Dir: *200yds from Yarmouth Wightlink Ferry Terminal, in town square*

Taking pride of place in the market square, this listed 17th-century building is close to the ferry and has ample car parking. Spacious, well-furnished bedrooms are available. A selection of bars and lounges offer contemporary style and comfort. A varied range of delicious home-cooked meals is offered including daily specials.
ROOMS: 7 en suite (1 fmly) ⊗ in all bedrooms **FACILITIES:** ♫
PARKING: 15 **NOTES:** ⊗ in restaurant
CARDS:

WILLERBY, East Riding of Yorkshire — Map 17 TA03

★★★73% ❀ Willerby Manor

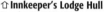

Well Ln HU10 6ER
☎ 01482 652616 ▯ 01482 653901
e-mail: willerbymanor@bestwestern.co.uk
Dir: *off A63, signed Humber Bridge. Follow road, right at rdbt by Safeway. At next rdbt hotel is signed*

Set in a quiet residential area, amid well-tended gardens, this hotel was originally a private mansion; it has now been thoughtfully extended to provide very comfortable bedrooms, equipped with many useful extras. The extensive public areas include a choice of eating options in various styles, including the smart Icon Restaurant. Extensive leisure facilities and a retail wine store are features of the hotel.

ROOMS: 51 en suite (6 fmly) (16 GF) ⊗ in 38 bedrooms s £81; d £99 **LB FACILITIES:** STV supervised Sauna Solarium Gym Jacuzzi Steam room Beauty therapist Aerobic classes ♫ **CONF:** Thtr 500 Class 200 Board 100 Del from £99 **PARKING:** 300 **NOTES:** Closed 24-26 Dec RS 24-26 Dec Civ Wed 150 **CARDS:**

Innkeeper's Lodge Hull

Beverley Rd HU10 6NT
☎ 01482 651518 ▯ 01482 658380
www.innkeeperslodge.com
Dir: *M62/A63, Humber Bridge exit off A63, follow signs for A164. Lodge 3m on left opp Willerby shopping centre*

Smart rooms meet essential business requirements but also have home comforts, and depending on location may well have meeting rooms and pub dining. Dining options generally include all-day menus plus the added advantage of breakfast.

ROOMS: 32 en suite s £48; d £48

WILLITON, Somerset — Map 03 ST04

★★73% ❀❀ White House

Long St TA4 4QW
☎ 01984 632306 & 632777
Dir: *on A39 in village centre*

A relaxed and easy-going atmosphere is the hallmark of this charming little Georgian hotel. Bedrooms in the main building are more spacious, and well-equipped with extra touches that make the White House a home-from-home. Delicious award-winning cooking and an impressive wine list can be found in the dining room.

ROOMS: 6 rms (5 en suite) 4 annexe en suite (1 fmly) s £55-£72; d £92-£120 (incl. bkfst) **LB PARKING:** 12 **NOTES:** ⊗ in restaurant Closed 28 Oct -mid May

WILMINGTON, East Sussex — Map 06 TQ50

Restaurant with Rooms

❀❀ *Crossways*

Lewes Rd BN26 5SG
☎ 01323 482455 ▯ 01323 487811
e-mail: stay@crosswayshotel.co.uk
Dir: *On A27 between Lewes & Polegate, 2m E of Alfriston rdbt.*

A well-established restaurant with a good local reputation is the focus for this attractive property. Bedrooms are all individually decorated with taste and style and superior rooms are available. Guest comfort is paramount, and there are excellent facilities and levels of hospitality that ensure guests return frequently.

ROOMS: 7 en suite **PARKING:** 30 **NOTES:** No children 12yrs Closed 24 Dec-23 Jan **CARDS:**

WILMSLOW, Cheshire — Map 16 SJ88

See also Manchester Airport

★★★★69% De Vere Mottram Hall

Wilmslow Rd, Mottram St Andrew, Prestbury SK10 4QT
☎ 01625 828135 ▯ 01625 828950
e-mail: dmh.sales@devere-hotels.com
Dir: *M6 junct 18 from S, M6 junct 20 from N, M56 junct 6, A538 Prestbury*

Set in 272 acres of some of Cheshire's most beautiful parkland, this 18th-century Georgian house is certainly an idyllic retreat. The hotel boasts extensive leisure facilities, including a championship golf course, a swimming pool and gymnasium. Bedrooms are well-equipped and elegantly furnished, and include a number of four-poster rooms and suites.

ROOMS: 132 en suite (44 GF) ⊗ in 64 bedrooms s fr £180 (incl. bkfst) **LB FACILITIES:** STV supervised at certain times 18 Squash Snooker Sauna Solarium Gym Putt green Jacuzzi Childrens play ground ♫ Xmas **CONF:** Thtr 275 Class 140 Board 60 Del from £140 **SERVICES:** Lift **PARKING:** 300 **NOTES:** ⊗ in restaurant Civ Wed 160 **CARDS:**

Premier Lodge (Manchester Airport South)

Racecourse Rd SK9 5LR
☎ 0870 9906506 ▯ 0870 9906507
web: www.premierlodge.com
Dir: *M6 junct 19, through Knutsford and follow Wilmslow signs. Left at 1st lights and turn left. Through Mobberley at next left just before Bird in Hand pub. At T-junction, turn right, hotel 150yds on right*

High quality, modern, budget accommodation, ideal for families and business travellers. All rooms feature bath, power shower and satellite TV, and most have telephones / modem points. The adjacent bar and restaurant offers a wide and varied menu.

ROOMS: 37 en suite s £50; d £50

Indoor Swimming Pool
Indoor Swimming Pool (heated)
Outdoor Swimming Pool
Outdoor Swimming Pool (heated)

WINCANTON, Somerset Map 04 ST72

★★★78% ֍֍ **Holbrook House**
Holbrook BA9 8BS
☎ 01963 824466 🖹 01963 32681
e-mail: reception@holbrookhouse.co.uk
Dir: *from A303 at Wincanton, turn left on A371 towards Castle Cary and Shepton Mallet*

This handsome country house offers a unique blend of quality and comfort combined with a friendly atmosphere. Set in peaceful gardens and wooded grounds, Holbrook House is the perfect retreat. The restaurant provides a selection of innovative dishes prepared with enthusiasm and served by a team of caring staff.
ROOMS: 16 en suite 5 annexe en suite (2 fmly) s £135-£275; d £135-£275 (incl. bkfst) **LB** **FACILITIES:** STV Sauna Solarium Gym Jacuzzi Beauty treatment ♫ ch fac Xmas **CONF:** Thtr 200 Class 50 Board 55 Del from £150 **PARKING:** 100 **NOTES:** ⊗ in restaurant Civ Wed 90 **CARDS:**

WINCHCOMBE, Gloucestershire Map 10 SP02

Restaurant with Rooms

֍֍ **Wesley House**
High St GL54 5LJ
☎ 01242 602366 🖹 01242 609046
e-mail: enquiries@wesleyhouse.co.uk
web: www.wesleyhouse.co.uk
Dir: *on High St - B4632 between Cheltenham and Broadway*
This engaging property dates back to the 15th century and is situated in the heart of bustling Winchcombe. There are a number of original features, such as open fires and exposed beams. The comfortable bedrooms offer plenty of character and individuality. The elegant restaurant is the setting for accomplished cuisine served by friendly, attentive staff.
ROOMS: 6 en suite ⊗ in all bedrooms s £90-£120; d £150-£180 (incl. bkfst & dinner) **LB** **NOTES:** ⊗ in restaurant Closed 25-26 Dec RS Sunday nights **CARDS:**

Destination dining!
This symbol indicates a Restaurant with Rooms

Want to get away without the hassle
of finding a place to stay?
Let the AA Hotel Booking Service find the
place that best suits your needs. No fuss,
no worries and no booking fee.
Visit www.theAA.com

WINCHESTER, Hampshire Map 05 SU42

Top 200 – Hotel

★★★★ @@ **Lainston House**
Sparsholt SO21 2LT
☎ 01962 863588 📠 01962 776672
e-mail: enquiries@lainstonhouse.com
web: www.exclusivehotels.co.uk

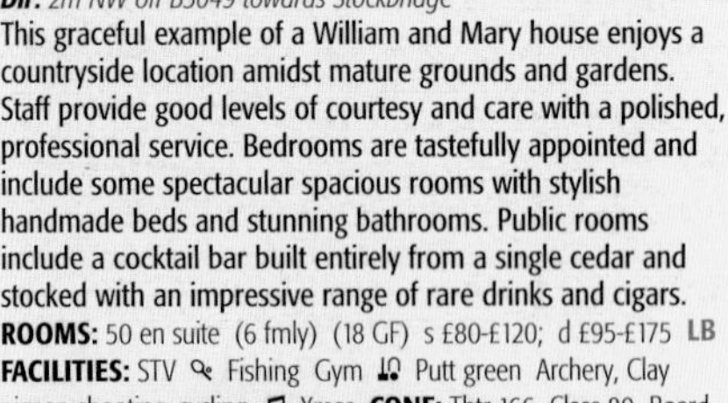

***Dir:** 2m NW off B3049 towards Stockbridge*

This graceful example of a William and Mary house enjoys a countryside location amidst mature grounds and gardens. Staff provide good levels of courtesy and care with a polished, professional service. Bedrooms are tastefully appointed and include some spectacular spacious rooms with stylish handmade beds and stunning bathrooms. Public rooms include a cocktail bar built entirely from a single cedar and stocked with an impressive range of rare drinks and cigars.

ROOMS: 50 en suite (6 fmly) (18 GF) s £80-£120; d £95-£175 **LB** **FACILITIES:** STV Fishing Gym Putt green Archery, Clay pigeon shooting, cycling Xmas **CONF:** Thtr 166 Class 80 Board 40 Del from £200 **PARKING:** 150 **NOTES:** ⊗ in restaurant Civ Wed 200 **CARDS:**

See advert on page 635

Town House

★★★★ @@ **Hotel du Vin & Bistro**
Southgate St SO23 9EF
☎ 01962 841414 📠 01962 842458
e-mail: info@winchester.hotelduvin.com
web: www.hotelduvin.com
***Dir:** M3 junct 11 towards Winchester, follow signs. Hotel approx 2m from junct 11 on left side just past cinema*

Continuing to set high standards, this inviting hotel is best known for its high profile bistro. The individually decorated bedrooms, each sponsored by a different wine house, show considerable originality of style, and are very well equipped. The bistro serves imaginative yet simply cooked dishes from a seasonal, daily-changing menu.

ROOMS: 23 en suite (4 GF) s £105-£225; d £105-£225 **FACILITIES:** STV Xmas **CONF:** Thtr 40 Class 30 Board 20 Del from £175 **PARKING:** 35 **NOTES:** Civ Wed 60 **CARDS:**

★★★★63% **The Wessex**
Paternoster Row SO23 9LQ
☎ 0870 400 8126 📠 01962 841503
e-mail: wessex@macdonald-hotels.co.uk
***Dir:** M3, follow signs for town centre, at rdbt by King Alfred's statue past Guildhall, next left, hotel on right*

MACDONALD HOTELS

A modern hotel occupying an enviable location in the centre of this historic city and adjacent to the spectacular cathedral, yet quietly situated on a side street. Inside, the ambience is modern, restful and welcoming, with many public areas and bedrooms enjoying unrivalled views of the hotel's centuries-old neighbour.

ROOMS: 94 en suite (6 fmly) ⊗ in 61 bedrooms s £65-£160; d £110-£250 (incl. bkfst) **LB** **FACILITIES:** STV Solarium Gym Free use of local leisure centre, beauty therapy Xmas **CONF:** Thtr 200 Class 60 Board 60 Del from £115 **SERVICES:** Lift **PARKING:** 60 **NOTES:** ⊗ in restaurant Civ Wed 200 **CARDS:**

★★★73% **The Winchester Royal**
Saint Peter St SO23 8BS
☎ 01962 840840 📠 01962 841582
e-mail: royal@marstonhotels.com
web: www.marstonhotels.com
***Dir:** M3 junct 9 to Winnal Trading Estate. Follow road to city centre, cross river, left, 1st right. Onto one-way system and 2nd right. Hotel immediately on right*

MARSTON HOTELS

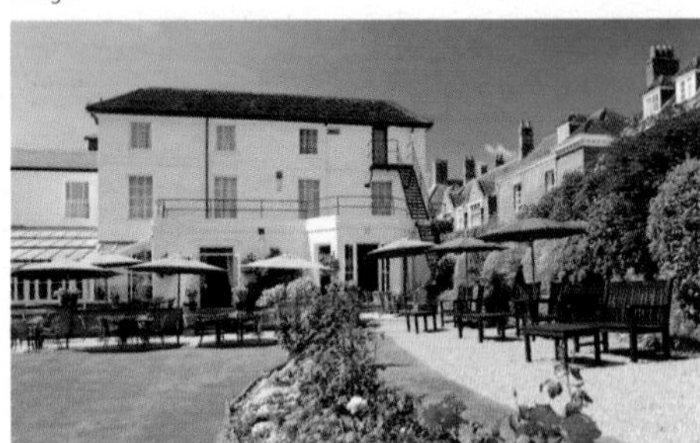

Situated in the heart of the former capital of England, this friendly hotel dates back in parts to the 16th century. The hotel has undergone improvements to ground floor areas. The variety of bedrooms are split between the main house and the modern annexe, which overlook the attractive gardens.

ROOMS: 75 en suite ⊗ in 48 bedrooms s £115-£140; d £138-£188 (incl. bkfst) **LB** **FACILITIES:** STV Xmas **CONF:** Thtr 120 Class 50 Board 40 Del from £145 **PARKING:** 50 **NOTES:** ⊗ in restaurant Civ Wed 110 **CARDS:**

★★★67% ***Marwell***
Thompsons Ln, Colden Common, Marwell SO21 1JY
☎ 01962 777681 📠 01962 777625
e-mail: info@marwellhotel.co.uk
***Dir:** Follow brown signs for Marwell Zoological Park, hotel adjacent*

FURLONG

Taking its theme from the adjacent zoo, this unusual hotel is based on the famous TreeTops safari lodge in Kenya. Bedrooms are being refurbished and are well appointed and equipped, while the smart public areas include an airy lobby bar and an 'Out of Africa'

continued

style restaurant. There is also a selection of meeting and leisure facilities.
ROOMS: 68 en suite (10 fmly) in 40 bedrooms **FACILITIES: Spa** STV Fishing Sauna Solarium Gym **CONF:** BC Thtr 150 Class 60 Board 60 **PARKING:** 120 **NOTES:** in restaurant Civ Wed 100
CARDS:

See advert on this page

WINCHESTER MOTORWAY SERVICE AREA (M3), Hampshire — Map 05 SU53

Travel Inn (Winchester)

SO21 1PP
☎ 08701 977272 🖹 01962 791137
***Dir:** M3 S'bound - between juncts 8 & 9. (please note that distance to Travel Inn from Winchester is approx 26m due to location on motorway)*
Travel Inn offers good-quality, value-for-money accommodation. Spacious, en suite rooms with bath and shower comfortably accommodate a family of up to two adults and two children (to age 15). The restaurant and bar offers a varied menu. For further details consult the Hotel Groups page.
ROOMS: 40 en suite s £45.95-£46.95; d £45.95-£46.95

WINDERMERE, Cumbria — Map 18 SD49

★★★★66% Low Wood

LA23 1LP
☎ 015394 33338 🖹 015394 34072
e-mail: lowwood@elhmail.co.uk
***Dir:** M6 junct 36, follow A590 then A591 to Windermere, then 3m towards Ambleside, hotel on right*

Benefiting from a lakeside location, this hotel offers an excellent range of leisure and conference facilities. Bedrooms, many with panoramic lake views, are attractively furnished, and include a number of larger executive rooms and suites. There is a choice of bars, a spacious restaurant and the more informal Café del Lago. The Poolside bar offers internet and e-mail access.
ROOMS: 110 en suite (13 fmly) in 55 bedrooms s £103-£120; d £150-£190 (incl. bkfst) **LB FACILITIES: Spa** STV Fishing Squash Snooker Sauna Solarium Gym Jacuzzi Water skiing Sub aqua diving Windsurfing Canoeing Laser clay pigeon shooting ch fac Xmas
CONF: Thtr 340 Class 180 Board 150 Del from £113 **SERVICES:** Lift
PARKING: 200 **NOTES:** in restaurant Civ Wed 200
CARDS:

Town House Hotel
Country House Hotel
Travel Accommodation

WINDERMERE, continued

Top 200 – Hotel

★★★ ◎◎◎ **Gilpin Lodge Country House Hotel & Restaurant**
Crook Rd LA23 3NE
☎ 015394 88818 ▯ 015394 88058
e-mail: hotel@gilpinlodge.com
web: www.gilpinlodge.com
Dir: *M6 junct 36, take A590/A591 to rdbt north of Kendal, take B5284, hotel 5m on right*

This smart Victorian residence is set amidst delightful gardens leading to the fells, and is just a short drive from the lake. Bedrooms are stylish and very individual. A number benefit from private terraces but all are spacious and thoughtfully equipped. The welcoming atmosphere is a real plus and the attractive day rooms are perfect for relaxing in front of a real fire. Vibrant, exciting cuisine is served in one of four intimate dining rooms.

ROOMS: 14 en suite ⊗ in all bedrooms s £150; d £220-£290 (incl. bkfst & dinner) **LB** **FACILITIES:** Free membership at local Leisure Club Xmas **PARKING:** 30 **NOTES:** No children 7yrs ⊗ in restaurant **CARDS:**

Top 200 – Hotel

★★★ ◎◎◎
Holbeck Ghyll Country House
Holbeck Ln LA23 1LU
☎ 015394 32375 ▯ 015394 34743
e-mail: stay@holbeckghyll.com
Dir: *3m N on A591, right into Holbeck Lane (signed Troutbeck), hotel 0.5m on left*

With a peaceful setting in extensive grounds, this beautifully maintained hotel enjoys breathtaking views over Lake Windermere and the Langdale Fells. Public rooms include luxurious, comfortable lounges and two elegant dining rooms, *continued*

where memorable meals are served. Bedrooms are individually styled, beautifully furnished and many have balconies or patios. Some in an adjacent, more private lodge are less traditional in design and have superb views. The professionalism and attentiveness of the staff is exemplary.

ROOMS: 14 en suite 6 annexe en suite (3 fmly) (3 GF) ⊗ in 6 bedrooms s £125-£280; d £190-£340 (incl. bkfst & dinner) **LB** **FACILITIES: Spa** STV Sauna Gym Putt green Jacuzzi Beautician Steam room ch fac Xmas **CONF:** BC Thtr 45 Class 25 Board 25 Del from £135 **PARKING:** 28 **NOTES:** ⊗ in restaurant Civ Wed 65 **CARDS:**

Top 200 – Hotel

★★★ ◎◎◎ **The Samling**
Ambleside Rd LA23 1LR
☎ 015394 31922 ▯ 015394 30400
e-mail: info@thesamling.com
web: www.thesamling.com
Dir: *turn right off A591, 300mtrs after Low Wood Hotel*

This stylish house built in the late 1700s, is situated in 67 acres of grounds and enjoys an elevated position overlooking Lake Windermere. The spacious, beautifully furnished bedrooms and suites, some in adjacent buildings, are thoughtfully equipped and all have superb bathrooms. Public rooms include a sumptuous drawing room, a small library and an elegant dining room where imaginative, skilfully prepared food is served.

ROOMS: 5 en suite 6 annexe en suite s £175-£405; d £175-£405 (incl. bkfst) **FACILITIES:** STV Jacuzzi Xmas **CONF:** Thtr 60 Class 14 Board 14 Del £260 **PARKING:** 15 **NOTES:** ⊗ in restaurant Civ Wed 100 **CARDS:**

Top 200 – Hotel

★★★ ◎◎ **Linthwaite House Hotel**
Crook Rd LA23 3JA
☎ 015394 88600 ▯ 015394 88601
e-mail: admin@linthwaite.com
web: www.linthwaite.com
Dir: *A591 towards The Lakes for 8m to large rdbt, take 1st exit (B5284), 6m, hotel on left , 1m past Windermere golf club*

Linthwaite House is set in 14 acres of hilltop grounds and enjoys stunning views over Lake Windermere. Inviting public rooms include an attractive conservatory and adjoining lounge, a smokers' bar and an elegant restaurant serving cutting-edge cuisine. Bedrooms, which are individually decorated, combine contemporary furnishings with classical *continued*

styles. All are thoughtfully equipped and include CD players. Service and hospitality at this delightful hotel are first class.

ROOMS: 26 en suite (1 fmly) (7 GF) ⊗ in all bedrooms s £99-£149; d £170-£270 (incl. bkfst & dinner) **LB** **FACILITIES:** STV Fishing Putt green Free use of nearby leisure spa, Practice golf hole Xmas **CONF:** Thtr 47 Class 19 Board 25 Del from £120 **PARKING:** 40 **NOTES:** ⊗ in restaurant Civ Wed 52 **CARDS:**

See advert on this page

★★★79% Storrs Hall
Storrs Park LA23 3LG
☎ 015394 47111 015394 47555
e-mail: storrshall@ELHmail.co.uk
web: www.elh.co.uk/hotels/storrs-contact.htm
Dir: *on A592 2m S of Bowness, on Newby Bridge road*

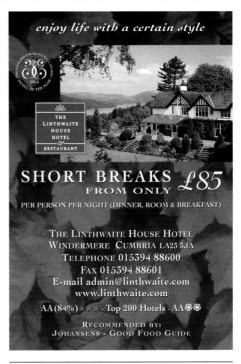

Set in 17 acres of landscaped grounds by the lakeside, this imposing Georgian mansion is a delight. There are numerous lounges to relax in, furnished with fine art and antiques. Bedrooms are mostly well-proportioned and boast impressive bathrooms. The restaurant enjoys fine views across the lawn to the lake and fells beyond.
ROOMS: 29 en suite ⊗ in 10 bedrooms s fr £125; d fr £185 (incl. bkfst) **LB** **FACILITIES:** Fishing Sailing Water skiing Water sports Xmas **CONF:** Thtr 36 Board 24 Del £145 **PARKING:** 50 **NOTES:** No children 12yrs ⊗ in restaurant Civ Wed 64 **CARDS:**

★★★79%
Lindeth Howe Country House
CLASSIC BRITISH
Lindeth Dr, Longtail Hill LA23 3JF
☎ 015394 45759 015394 46368
e-mail: hotel@lindeth-howe.co.uk
web: www.lindeth-howe.co.uk
Dir: *turn off A592, 1m S of Bowness onto B5284 (Longtail Hill) signed Kendal & Lancaster, hotel last driveway on right*
Old photographs commemorate the fact that this delightful house was once the family home of Beatrix Potter. Secluded in landscaped

continued

grounds, it enjoys views across the valley and Lake Windermere. Public rooms are plentiful and inviting, with the restaurant a perfect setting for modern country-house cooking. Deluxe and superior bedrooms are spacious and smartly appointed.

Lindeth Howe Country House

ROOMS: 36 en suite (3 fmly) (2 GF) ⊗ in 30 bedrooms d £108-£188 (incl. bkfst) **LB** **FACILITIES:** STV Sauna Solarium Gym ch fac Xmas **CONF:** Thtr 30 Class 20 Board 18 Del from £115 **PARKING:** 50 **NOTES:** ⊗ in restaurant **CARDS:**

★★★73% Fayrer Garden Hotel
Lyth Valley Rd, Bowness on Windermere LA23 3JP
☎ 015394 88195 015394 45986
e-mail: lakescene@fayrergarden.com
web: www.fayrergarden.com
Dir: *on A5074 1m from Bowness Bay*
Sitting in lovely landscaped gardens, this elegant hotel enjoys spectacular views over the lake. Bedrooms come in a variety of

continued on p640

WINDERMERE, continued

styles and sizes, some with bathrooms of a high specification, and all are comfortably appointed. There is a choice of lounges and a stylish, conservatory restaurant. The attentive, hospitable staff ensure a relaxing stay.

Fayrer Garden Hotel, Windermere

ROOMS: 18 en suite 5 annexe rms (3 fmly) (11 GF) ⊗ in 6 bedrooms s £65-£150; d £120-£250 (incl. bkfst & dinner) **LB FACILITIES:** STV Fishing Free membership of leisure club Xmas **PARKING:** 40 **NOTES:** ⊗ in restaurant Civ Wed 60 **CARDS:**

★★★73%

Burn How Garden House Hotel

Back Belsfield Rd, Bowness LA23 3HH
☎ 015394 46226 015394 47000
e-mail: info@burnhow.co.uk web: www.burnhow.co.uk
Dir: *Exit A591 at Windermere, following signs to Bowness. Pass Lake Piers on right, take 1st left to hotel entrance*

Set in its own leafy grounds, this hotel is only minutes' walk from both the lakeside and the town centre. Attractive, spacious rooms, some with four-poster beds, are situated in modern chalets or in an adjacent Victorian house. Many have private patios or terraces. Coffee can be enjoyed in the comfortable open-plan lounge after taking dinner in the formal restaurant.

ROOMS: 28 annexe en suite (10 fmly) (6 GF) ⊗ in 8 bedrooms s £60-£95; d £70-£120 (incl. bkfst) **LB FACILITIES:** ch fac Xmas **PARKING:** 30 **NOTES:** ⊗ in restaurant **CARDS:**

★★★72% **Langdale Chase**

Langdale Chase LA23 1LW
☎ 015394 32201 015394 32604
e-mail: sales@langdalechase.co.uk
web: www.langdalechase.co.uk
Dir: *2m S of Ambleside and 3m N of Windermere, on A591*

Enjoying unrivalled views of Lake Windermere, this imposing country manor has been trading as a hotel for over 70 years. Public areas feature carved fireplaces, oak panelling and a galleried staircase. Bedrooms, many now refurbished, have stylish, spacious bathrooms and outstanding views.

ROOMS: 20 en suite 7 annexe en suite (2 fmly) (1 GF) s £65-£99 (incl. bkfst) **LB FACILITIES:** Fishing Putt green Sailing boats ch fac Xmas **CONF:** Thtr 30 Class 30 Board 28 Del from £120 **PARKING:** 50 **NOTES:** ⊗ in restaurant Civ Wed 100 **CARDS:**

★★★71% **Beech Hill**

Newby Bridge Rd LA23 3LR
☎ 015394 42137 015394 43745
e-mail: reservations@beechhillhotel.co.uk
web: www.beechhillhotel.co.uk
Dir: *A592 towards Bowness, hotel on left, 4m S from Bowness*

This stylish, terraced hotel is set on high ground leading to the shore of Lake Windermere and has a spacious, open-plan lounge which, like the restaurant, affords splendid views across the lake. The well-equipped bedrooms come in a range of styles; some have four-poster beds. Leisure facilities and a choice of conference rooms complete the package.

ROOMS: 58 en suite (4 fmly) (4 GF) ⊗ in 10 bedrooms s £50-£85; d £100-£170 (incl. bkfst) **LB FACILITIES:** Fishing Sauna Solarium ♫ Xmas **CONF:** Thtr 180 Class 110 Board 94 Del from £95 **PARKING:** 70 **NOTES:** ⊗ in restaurant Civ Wed 130 **CARDS:**

See advert on opposite page

★★★68% ***Famous Wild Boar***

Crook LA23 3NF
☎ 015394 45225 015394 42498
e-mail: wildboar@elhmail.co.uk
Dir: *2.5m S of Windermere on B5284. From Crook 3.5m, hotel on right*

This historic former coaching inn enjoys a peaceful rural location close to Windermere. Public areas include a cosy bar where an extensive range of wines is served by the glass, a character restaurant serving wholesome food and a welcoming lounge. Bedrooms, some with four-poster beds, vary in style and size.

ROOMS: 36 en suite (3 fmly) ⊗ in 6 bedrooms **FACILITIES:** STV Use of leisure facilities at sister hotel whilst in residence. ♫ **CONF:** Thtr 40 Class 20 Board 26 **PARKING:** 60 **NOTES:** ⊗ in restaurant **CARDS:**

Late for dinner?
Quality Standards mean that last orders for dinner vary according to star rating and should be no earlier than:
★★ 7.00pm ★★★ 8.00pm ★★★★ 9.00pm
★★★★★ 10.00pm

★★★64% The Belsfield Hotel

Kendal Rd, Bowness LA23 3EL
☎ 0870 609 6109 🖷 015394 46397
e-mail: belsfield@corushotels.com
Dir: *In Bowness take 1st left after Royal Hotel*

This hotel stands in six acres of gardens and has one of the best locations in the area. Bedrooms are generally spacious and well equipped, and come in a variety of styles. Views from public areas are outstanding. Main meals are taken in the spacious dining room overlooking the lake.
ROOMS: 64 en suite (6 fmly) (6 GF) ⊗ in 50 bedrooms s fr £99; d fr £99 **LB** **FACILITIES:** Snooker Sauna Putt green Mini golf - Pitch & Putt 9 holes Xmas **CONF:** Thtr 130 Class 60 Board 50 Del from £115 **SERVICES:** Lift **PARKING:** 64 **NOTES:** ⊗ in restaurant Civ Wed 100
CARDS:

★★★62% The Old England

MACDONALD HOTELS

Church St, Bowness LA23 3DF
☎ 0870 400 8130 🖷 015394 43432
e-mail: oldengland@macdonald-hotels.co.uk
Dir: *Through Windermere to Bowness. Hotel behind church*

Occupying arguably one of the best positions on Lake Windermere, this elegant Victorian mansion is tastefully furnished with period and antique pieces. Many of the stylish bedrooms have wonderful lake views, as do the restaurant, bar and lounge. The hotel benefits from an outdoor heated swimming pool and a private jetty. Stylish conference facilities are impressive.
ROOMS: 76 en suite (8 fmly) (6 GF) ⊗ in 26 bedrooms s £55-£80; d £120-£160 (incl. bkfst) **LB** **FACILITIES:** Snooker Xmas **CONF:** BC Thtr 100 Class 40 Board 26 Del from £110 **SERVICES:** Lift **PARKING:** 82 **NOTES:** ⊗ in restaurant Civ Wed 80
CARDS:

★★★61% Craig Manor

Lake Rd LA23 2JF
☎ 015394 88877 🖷 015394 88878
e-mail: info@craigmanor.co.uk
Dir: *A590, then A591 into Windermere, left at Windermere Hotel, through village, pass Magistrates' Court, hotel on left*
There are fine views to be had across the lake towards the fells from this family-run hotel. Traditionally furnished bedrooms, including family rooms and some with four-poster beds, are complemented by spacious public areas. There is a choice of comfortable lounges and a wide selection of dishes is served in the refurbished restaurant overlooking the lake.
ROOMS: 16 en suite s £45-£90; d £80-£150 (incl. bkfst) **LB** **FACILITIES:** Use of Parklands Leisure Club Xmas **PARKING:** 70 **NOTES:** ⊗ in restaurant **CARDS:**

Indoor Swimming Pool
Indoor Swimming Pool (heated)
Outdoor Swimming Pool
Outdoor Swimming Pool (heated)

W

WINDERMERE, continued

Top 200 – Hotel

★★ ◎◎ Miller Howe
Rayrigg Rd LA23 1EY
☎ 015394 42536 ⎙ 015394 45664
e-mail: lakeview@millerhowe.com
web: www.millerhowe.com
Dir: *on A592 between Bowness & Windermere*

This long established hotel of much character enjoys a lakeside setting amidst delightful landscaped gardens. Day rooms are bright and welcoming and include sumptuous lounges, a conservatory and an opulently decorated restaurant. Imaginative dinners, served promptly at 8pm, make use of fresh, local produce where possible and there is an extensive, well-balanced wine list. Stylish bedrooms, many with fabulous lake views, include well-equipped cottage rooms and a number with whirlpool baths.

ROOMS: 12 en suite 3 annexe en suite **FACILITIES:** ♫ **PARKING:** 40 **NOTES:** No children 8yrs ⊘ in restaurant Civ Wed 60 **CARDS:**

Top 200 – Hotel

★★ ◎ Lindeth Fell
Lyth Valley Rd, Bowness-on-Windermere LA23 3JP
☎ 015394 43286 & 44287 ⎙ 015394 47455
e-mail: kennedy@lindethfell.co.uk
web: www.lindethfell.co.uk
Dir: *1m S of Bowness on A5074*

Enjoying delightful views, this smart Edwardian residence stands in seven acres of glorious, landscaped gardens. Bedrooms, which vary in size and style, are comfortably equipped. Skilfully prepared dinners are served in the spacious dining room, which also provides fine views. The resident owners and their attentive, friendly staff provide high levels of hospitality and service.

continued

ROOMS: 14 en suite (2 fmly) (1 GF) s £40-£55; d £80-£110 (incl. bkfst) **LB** **FACILITIES:** Fishing Putt green Bowling Pitch&Putt Xmas **CONF:** Board 12 Del from £100 **PARKING:** 20 **NOTES:** ⊘ in restaurant Closed 6-31 Jan **CARDS:**

★★71% Glenburn
New Rd LA23 2EE
☎ 015394 42649 ⎙ 015394 88998
e-mail: glen.burn@virgin.net
web: www.glenburn.uk.com
Dir: *M6 junct 36, A591, through Windermere, hotel 500yds on left*

This friendly, family-run hotel enjoys a convenient location between Bowness and Windermere. Smartly presented and well maintained throughout, it offers stylish, well-equipped accommodation in a variety of sizes and styles. Bedrooms include both family and four-poster rooms. There is a spacious bar and lounge and an attractive restaurant, where carefully prepared meals are served.

ROOMS: 16 en suite (2 fmly) ⊘ in all bedrooms s £47.50-£49.50; d £65-£93 (incl. bkfst) **LB** **FACILITIES:** Fishing Free use of nearby country club Xmas **PARKING:** 17 **NOTES:** No children 5yrs ⊘ in restaurant Closed 20-28 Dec **CARDS:**

★★70% Crag Brow Hotel & Coco's Restaurant
Helm Rd LA23 3BU
☎ 015394 44080 ⎙ 015394 46003
e-mail: rooms@cragbrow.com
web: www.cragbrow.com
Dir: *Leave A591 at Windermere. Follow signs for Bowness. Crag Row is on the left on Helm Rd, approx 1m*

A warm welcome awaits at this family-run, conveniently located guest house with private parking. The house has been sympathetically renovated to provide very comfortable accommodation. Bedrooms are of a good size and feature both practical and homely extras; many have views to the lake. There is an attractive lounge with views over the garden; dinner, is available in the stylish restaurant.

ROOMS: 11 en suite (2 fmly) ⊘ in all bedrooms s £35-£70; d £50-£115 (incl. bkfst) **LB** **FACILITIES:** Xmas **PARKING:** 20 **NOTES:** ⊘ in restaurant Closed 24-26 Dec **CARDS:**

> Popped the question?
> Hotels with Civ Wed in their entry are licensed for civil wedding ceremonies. Maximum numbers for the ceremony only are shown, e.g. Civ Wed 120

W

★★70% **Hideaway**
Phoenix Way LA23 1DB
☎ 015394 43070 015394 48664
e-mail: enquiries@hideaway-hotel.co.uk
web: www.hideaway-hotel co.uk
Dir: *off A591 at Ravensworth Hotel. Hotel 100yds on right*

Enjoying a secluded location, yet near the centre of town, hospitality is a real feature at this family-run hotel. Bedrooms, some in a separate building across the courtyard, are smartly appointed and individually furnished. Four-poster and family rooms are available. Dinner features tasty, home-made food.
ROOMS: 10 en suite 5 annexe en suite (3 fmly) s £40-£60; d £70-£130 (incl. bkfst) **LB** **FACILITIES:** Free use of nearby leisure facilities Xmas **PARKING:** 16 **NOTES:** in restaurant Closed 3-31 Jan
CARDS:

See advert on this page

★★67% **Cranleigh**
Kendal Rd, Bowness on Windermere LA23 3EW
☎ 015394 43293 015394 47283
e-mail: mike@thecranleigh.com
Dir: *off Lake Rd opp St Martin's Church, along Kendal Rd for 150mtrs*
This friendly hotel is located minutes' walk from the centre of town. Comfortable bedrooms, including a number with four-poster beds, vary in style. Guests have a choice of lounges, one with a real fire, a small bar that offers a wide range of drinks and freshly prepared meals are served in the attractive dining room.
ROOMS: 9 en suite 6 annexe en suite (3 fmly) s £43-£77; d £52-£120 (incl. bkfst) **LB** **FACILITIES:** Free membership of leisure club **PARKING:** 15 **NOTES:** in restaurant
CARDS:

Action for Blind People Hotel

U Windermere Manor
Rayrigg Rd LA23 1ES
☎ 01539 445801 01539 448397
e-mail: windermere@afbp.org
Dir: *A591 towards Ambleside. At mini-rdbt, turn left, hotel 1st left*
Set above the shores of Lake Windermere, this former manor house has been restored to its original splendour. The attractive dining room has an unusual barrel-vaulted wooden roof and serves delicious home cooking. There are pleasant landscaped gardens with natural woodland. The hotel caters for the specific needs of blind and partially sighted people, their friends, relatives, carers and guide dogs.
ROOMS: 28 en suite (2 fmly) (5 GF) in all bedrooms s £34-£40; d £68-£80 (incl. bkfst & dinner) **LB** **FACILITIES:** STV supervised Sauna Solarium Gym Various activities available Xmas **SERVICES:** Lift **PARKING:** 20 **NOTES:** in restaurant
CARDS:

WINDSOR, Berkshire — Map 06 SU97

★★★★72% **Oakley Court**
Windsor Rd, Water Oakley SL4 5UR
☎ 01753 609988 01628 637011
e-mail: reservations.oakleycourt@moathousehotels.com
Dir: *M4 junct 6, towards Windsor, then right onto A308 Maidenhead. Pass racecourse & hotel is 2.5m on right*

Built in 1859 this splendid Victorian Gothic mansion is enviably situated in extensive grounds that lead down to The Thames. All rooms are spacious, beautifully furnished and many enjoy river views. Extensive public areas include a range of comfortable lounges, the Oakleaf restaurant and comprehensive facilities, which also features a small 9-hole golf course.
ROOMS: 69 en suite 49 annexe en suite (15 fmly) (43 GF) in 75 bedrooms s £192-£425; d £229-£425 **FACILITIES: Spa** STV 9 Fishing Snooker Sauna Solarium Gym Jacuzzi Boating **CONF:** BC Thtr 170 Class 190 Board 50 Del from £199 **SERVICES:** air con **PARKING:** 140 **NOTES:** in restaurant Civ Wed 120
CARDS:

WINDSOR, continued

★★★★69% Sir Christopher Wren's House Hotel & Spa

WREN'S HOTELS

Thames St SL4 1PX
☎ 01753 861354 01753 860172
e-mail: reservations@wrensgroup.com
Dir: *M4 junct 6, 1st exit from relief road, follow signs to Windsor, 1st major exit on left, turn left at lights*

This hotel has an enviable location right on the edge of the River Thames overlooking Eton Bridge. Diners in Strokes, the award-winning restaurant, enjoy the best views. A variety of well appointed bedrooms is available, including several in adjacent annexes. There is also a luxury health and leisure spa.
ROOMS: 57 en suite 33 annexe en suite (11 fmly) (3 GF) in 22 bedrooms s £100-£155; d £155-£205 (incl. bkfst) **LB FACILITIES: Spa** STV Sauna Solarium Gym Jacuzzi Health & beauty club Xmas **CONF:** Thtr 120 Class 70 Board 50 Del from £200 **PARKING:** 15 **NOTES:** in restaurant Civ Wed 90
CARDS:

★★★74% The Castle

MACDONALD HOTELS

18 High St SL4 1LJ
☎ 0870 400 8300 01753 830244
e-mail: castle@macdonald-hotels.co.uk
Dir: *M4 junct 6/M25 junct 15 - follow signs to Windsor town centre and castle. Hotel at top of hill by castle opp Guildhall*
The Castle Hotel is one of the oldest hotels in Windsor, beginning life as a coaching inn in the middle of the 16th century. Located opposite the Castle itself, it is an ideal base from which to explore the town. Bedrooms are traditional in style and include four-poster and executive rooms. Guests have a choice of formal and informal dining options and an all-day lounge menu.
ROOMS: 41 en suite 70 annexe en suite (18 fmly) in 50 bedrooms s fr £175; d fr £175 (incl. bkfst) **LB FACILITIES:** STV Xmas **CONF:** BC Thtr 370 Class 155 Board 80 Del from £195 **SERVICES:** Lift air con **PARKING:** 100 **NOTES:** in restaurant Civ Wed 85
CARDS:

★★★70% Christopher Hotel

WREN'S HOTELS

110 High St, Eton SL4 6AN
☎ 01753 852359 01753 830914
e-mail: sales@christopher-hotel.co.uk
web: www.christopher-hotel.co.uk
Dir: *M4 junct 5 (Slough E), Colnbrook Datchet Eton (B470). At rdbt 2nd exit for Datchet. Right at mini rdbt (Eton), left into Eton Rd (3rd rdbt). Left, hotel on right*
Centrally located on Eton High Street, this former coaching inn is ideal for visiting Windsor and other local attractions. Comfortable bedrooms in the main house or in a separate wing vary in size; some have been stylishly refurbished. Award-winning cuisine is served in Renata's, the hotel's contemporary restaurant.

ROOMS: 11 en suite 22 annexe en suite (3 fmly) (17 GF) in 17 bedrooms s £74-£105; d £81-£145 **LB FACILITIES:** STV Use of Health & beauty centre at nearby sister hotel (3 mins walk) Xmas **PARKING:** 23 **NOTES:** in restaurant **CARDS:**

★★★69% Royal Adelaide

46 Kings Rd SL4 2AG
☎ 01753 863916 01753 830682
e-mail: royaladelaide@meridianleisure.com
web: www.meridianleisure.com
Dir: *M4 junct 6, A322 to Windsor. 1st left off rdbt into Clarence Rd. At 4th lights right into Sheet St and into Kings Rd. Hotel on right*

This attractive Georgian-style hotel has seen much renovation and enhancement. Close to the town centre and with parking, it offers tastefully furnished and well-equipped bedrooms. Public areas include a range of meeting rooms, a bar and an elegant restaurant.
ROOMS: 38 en suite 4 annexe en suite (5 fmly) in 12 bedrooms s £60-£99; d £79-£119 (incl. bkfst) **LB FACILITIES:** STV Xmas **CONF:** Thtr 120 Class 80 Board 60 Del from £135 **SERVICES:** air con **PARKING:** 22 **NOTES:** in restaurant Civ Wed 120
CARDS:

See advert on opposite page

★★★66% Ye Harte & Garter

High St SL4 1PH
☎ 01753 863426 01753 830527
e-mail: harteandgarter.windsor@thespiritgroup.com
Dir: *in town centre opposite front entrance to Windsor Castle*
Situated on the High Street, this hotel combines traditional style with modern comforts. Bedrooms vary in size and offer a useful range of facilities. Many have exceptional views of the castle courtyards opposite. Popular public areas include a café bar, two restaurants and a traditional pub.
ROOMS: 39 en suite 19 annexe en suite (6 fmly) in 30 bedrooms s £70-£190; d £105-£190 (incl. bkfst) **LB FACILITIES:** STV ch fac **CONF:** Thtr 300 Class 150 Board 80 Del from £150 **SERVICES:** Lift **NOTES:** Civ Wed 180 **CARDS:**

See advert on opposite page

Royal Adelaide

AA ★★★  ETC ★★★

Windsor Town Centre
46 Kings Road, Windsor, Berks SL4 2AG
Tel: 01753 863916 Fax: 01753 830682
E-mail: royaladelaide@meridianleisure.com
www.meridianleisure.com

Ideally situated in the heart of Windsor town centre and within walking distance of Windsor Castle. This beautiful Georgian property offers 42 fully refurbished en-suite bedrooms with air-conditioning, satellite TV, courtesy tray, modem telephone, ironing board, hairdryer & safe. A perfect venue for weddings, anniversaries & conferences for up to 140, benefiting from complimentary car parking. Special Leisure Break & Legoland packages available.

Bed & Full English Breakfast daily from £60-£119.

THE BEST RIVERSIDE ADDRESS IN THE THAMES VALLEY

★ ★ ★ ★

Windsor Road · Egham · Surrey · TW20 0AG
Tel: 01784 436171 · Fax: 01784 436340
Internet: http://www.runnymedehotel·com
Email: info@runnymedehotel.com

Privately owned hotel on the banks of the River Thames. Just seven miles from Heathrow and five miles from Royal Windsor.
Our dramatic waterfront restaurant **Left Bank** offers a Mediterranean inspired menu and **Charlie Bell's** is a popular café bar with a riverside terrace.
State of the art Health & Fitness Spa including indoor pool, tennis courts, gym, saunas and steam room.
Extensive conference and banqueting facilities.

YE HARTE & GARTER HOTEL

High Street • Windsor • Berkshire SL4 1PH
Tel: 01753 863426 Fax: 01753 830527
www.harteandgarter.com

Situated in the centre of Windsor, Ye Harte & Garter is superbly appointed with many rooms overlooking the courtyards of Windsor Castle. The existing building dates back to mid 19th Century but the site has long been associated with traditional English Inns. The original Garter Inn was frequented by theatrical circles as far back as the 17th Century, and was the setting for a scene in Shakespeare's 'Merry Wives of Windsor'. Public areas include a Victorian Restaurant & Carvery which serves traditional freshly carved roast meals and à la carte menu, the Continental Cafe Bar open all day for coffee, snacks and light meals, or why not enjoy with a group of friends our Medieval Banquet in the Dungeons of Windsor which are adjoined to the hotel.

WINDSOR, continued

★★75% Aurora Garden
Bolton Av SL4 3JF
☎ 01753 868686 📠 01753 831394
e-mail: aurora@auroragarden.co.uk
web: www.auroragarden.co.uk
Dir: *M4 junct 6 onto A332 (Windsor). At 1st rdbt, 2nd exit towards Staines. At 3rd rdbt, 3rd exit for 500yds. Hotel on right*
A warm welcome is assured at this privately run hotel, located in a quiet residential area near the town. The highlights include a beautiful garden with terrace and water features, spacious rooms with extra facilities for a comfortable stay and a delightful conservatory restaurant serving a wide variety of dishes.
ROOMS: 19 en suite (7 fmly) (4 GF) s £85-£95; d £100-£115 (incl. bkfst) **LB** **FACILITIES:** STV **CONF:** Thtr 90 Class 30 Board 25 Del from £135 **PARKING:** 25 **NOTES:** ⊗ in restaurant Closed 25 Dec Civ Wed 70 **CARDS:**

Innkeeper's Lodge Old Windsor
14 Straight Rd, Old Windsor SL4 2RR
☎ 01753 860769 📠 01753 851649
www.innkeeperslodge.com
Smart rooms meet essential business requirements but also have home comforts, and depending on location may well have meeting rooms and pub dining. Dining options generally include all-day menus plus the added advantage of breakfast.
ROOMS: 15 en suite s £55-£79.95; d £55-£49.95

WINSCOMBE, Somerset — Map 04 ST45

Premier Lodge (Bristol Airport)
Bridgwater Rd BS25 1NN
☎ 0870 9906302 📠 0870 9906303
web: www.premierlodge.com
Dir: *M5 between junct 21 and 22, 9m from Bristol Airport. Exit onto A371 to Banwell, Winscombe to A38. At lights turn right for Lodge 300yds on left*
High quality, modern, budget accommodation, ideal for families and business travellers. All rooms feature bath, power shower and satellite TV, and most have telephones / modem points. The adjacent bar and restaurant offers a wide and varied menu.
ROOMS: 31 en suite s £50; d £50

WINTERINGHAM, Lincolnshire — Map 17 SE92

Top 200 - Restaurant with Rooms

Winteringham Fields
DN15 9PF
☎ 01724 733096 📠 01724 733898
e-mail: wintfields@aol.com
web: www.winteringhamfields.com
Dir: *in the centre of the village at the crossroads*
This highly regarded restaurant with rooms, located deep in the countryside, yet only six miles west of the Humber Bridge. Chef Germain Schwab has a hand in every skilfully crafted dish that leaves his kitchen, whilst Anne Schwab admirably leads a superb front of house team. Public rooms and bedrooms, some of which are housed in renovated barns and cottages, are delightfully cosseting, but it is the inspired and highly acclaimed cooking that remains the main draw.

ROOMS: 4 en suite 6 annexe en suite ⊗ in all bedrooms s £95-£135; d £125-£195 (incl. cont bkfst) **PARKING:** 17 **NOTES:** ⊗ in restaurant Closed Sun, Mon & BH/2wks Xmas/1wk Aug/1wk Mar **CARDS:**

WISBECH, Cambridgeshire — Map 12 TF40

★★★68% Elme Hall
Elm High Rd PE14 0DQ
☎ 01945 475566 📠 01945 475666
e-mail: elme@paktel.co.uk
web: www.paktel.co.uk
Dir: *off A47 onto A1101 towards Wisbech. Hotel on right*
An imposing, Georgian-style property conveniently situated on the outskirts of the town centre just off the A47. The spacious, individually decorated bedrooms are tastefully furnished with quality reproduction pieces and equipped to a high standard. Public rooms include a choice of attractive lounges, as well as two bars, meeting rooms and a banqueting suite.
ROOMS: 7 en suite (3 fmly) ⊗ in all bedrooms d £68-£210 (incl. bkfst) **CONF:** Thtr 350 Class 200 Board 20 **PARKING:** 200 **NOTES:** ⊗ in restaurant Civ Wed 350 **CARDS:**

★★73% Crown Lodge
Downham Rd, Outwell PE14 8SE
☎ 01945 773391 & 772206 📠 01945 772668
e-mail: crownlodgehotel@hotmail.com
Dir: *on A1122/A1101 approx 5m from Wisbech and 7m from Downham Market*

This friendly, privately owned hotel enjoys a peaceful location on the banks of Well Creek in the village of Outwell, a short drive from Wisbech. The property has been carefully extended and both bedrooms and public areas are smartly appointed and

continued

well-equipped. Hotel facilities include squash courts and a popular restaurant and bar.
ROOMS: 10 en suite (10 GF) ⊗ in 8 bedrooms s £57.50; d £75 (incl. bkfst) **LB** **FACILITIES:** Squash Snooker Solarium **CONF:** Thtr 40 Class 30 Board 20 **PARKING:** 57 **NOTES:** ⊗ in restaurant
CARDS:

WISHAW, Warwickshire Map 10 SP19

★★★★74% De Vere Belfry

DE VERE HOTELS

B76 9PR
☎ 01675 470301 📠 01675 470178
e-mail: enquiries@thebelfry.com
Dir: *M42 junct 9, A446 towards Lichfield, hotel 1m on right*
Well known as a venue for the Ryder Cup, The Belfry offers three championship golf courses along with many other leisure facilities. There is a sophisticated French restaurant and cocktail bar and the spa centre boasts an impressive range of health and beauty treatments. Bedrooms vary in size, style and location; many have spectacular views.
ROOMS: 324 en suite (109 fmly) ⊗ in 187 bedrooms **FACILITIES: Spa** STV supervised 18 Squash Snooker Sauna Solarium Gym Putt green Jacuzzi Night club in grounds, Driving range, Aqua spa ♫ ch fac **CONF:** Thtr 400 Class 220 Board 40 **SERVICES:** Lift **PARKING:** 1000 **NOTES:** ⊗ in restaurant Civ Wed 200
CARDS:

WITHYPOOL, Somerset Map 03 SS83

★★75% Royal Oak Inn

TA24 7QP
☎ 01643 831506 📠 01643 831659
e-mail: enquiries@royaloakwithypool.co.uk
Dir: *7m N of Dulverton, off B3223*

For centuries this old inn has provided travellers with food, drink and shelter. Lovers of the great outdoors will find this an ideal base for exploration. Bedrooms are comfortable and each displays individuality and charm. Public areas include a choice of bars, complete with beams and crackling log fires, and the Acorn Restaurant is the venue for accomplished cuisine with an emphasis on local produce.
ROOMS: 8 rms (7 en suite) s £50-£55; d £100-£110 (incl. bkfst) **FACILITIES:** Riding Shooting Safaris arranged Xmas **PARKING:** 20 **NOTES:** ⊗ in restaurant **CARDS:**

Packed in a hurry?
Ironing facilities should be available at all star levels, either in rooms or on request

WITNEY, Oxfordshire Map 05 SP31

★★★70% Witney Four Pillars Hotel

FOUR PILLARS HOTELS

Ducklington Ln OX28 4TJ
☎ 0800 374 692 📠 01993 703467
e-mail: witney@four-pillars.co.uk
web: www.four-pillars.co.uk
Dir: *M40 junct 9, A34 to A40, exit A415 Witney/Abingdon. Hotel on left, 2nd exit for Witney*

This attractive modern hotel is close to Oxford and Burford and offers spacious, well-equipped bedrooms. The cosy Spinners Bar has comfortable seating areas and the popular Weavers Restaurant offers a good range of dishes. Other facilities include a swimming pool, gym, spa, sauna and live entertainment every Saturday.
ROOMS: 83 en suite (16 fmly) ⊗ in 30 bedrooms s £73-£92; d £83-£105 **LB** **FACILITIES: Spa** STV Sauna Gym Whirlpool spa, steam room ♫ Xmas **CONF:** Thtr 160 Class 80 Board 46 Del £140 **SERVICES:** air con **PARKING:** 170 **NOTES:** ⊗ in restaurant Civ Wed 120 **CARDS:**

WOBURN, Bedfordshire Map 11 SP93

★★★73% The Inn at Woburn

George St MK17 9PX
☎ 01525 290441 📠 01525 290432
e-mail: enquiries@theinnatwoburn.com
Dir: *M1 junct 13, left to Woburn, at Woburn left at T-junct, hotel in village*
This inn has been substantially refurbished and provides a high standard of accommodation. Bedrooms are divided between the original house, a modern extension and some stunning cottage suites. Public areas include the beamed, club-style Tavistock Bar, a range of meeting rooms and an attractive restaurant with interesting dishes on offer.
ROOMS: 50 en suite 7 annexe en suite (4 fmly) (21 GF) ⊗ in 19 bedrooms s £105-£125; d £120-£180 **LB** **FACILITIES:** STV 54 Access to Woburn Safari Park and Woburn Abbey Xmas **CONF:** Thtr 60 Class 40 Board 40 Del from £135 **PARKING:** 80 **NOTES:** No children ⊗ in restaurant **CARDS:**

WOKING, Surrey Map 06 TQ05

Innkeeper's Lodge Woking

Innkeeper's Lodge

Chobham Rd, Horsell GU21 4AL
☎ 01483 733047
www.innkeeperslodge.com
Smart rooms meet essential business requirements but also have home comforts, and depending on location may well have meeting rooms and pub dining. Dining options generally include all-day menus plus the added advantage of breakfast.
ROOMS: s £52-£79.95; d £52-£79.95

W

WOKING, continued

⌂ Travel Inn

Bridge Barn Ln GU21 6NL
☎ 08701 977276 ▤ 01483 771735
Dir: *M25 (J11) follow A320. Turn right at traffic lights by Toys R Us. Take 3rd mini rbt 0.75m down Goldsworth Rd. Turn right into Bridge Barn Ln, Travel Inn on left*

Travel Inn offers good-quality, value-for-money accommodation. Spacious, en suite rooms with bath and shower comfortably accommodate a family of up to two adults and two children (to age 15). The restaurant and bar offers a varied menu. For further details consult the Hotel Groups page.

ROOMS: 34 en suite s £52.95-£56.95; d £52.95-£56.95

WOKINGHAM, Berkshire — Map 05 SU86

★★★64% Edward Court Hotel

Wellington Rd RG40 2AN
☎ 0118 977 5886 ▤ 0118 977 2018
e-mail: edward_court@hotmail.com
Dir: *from Wokingham follow A329 towards Reading. Left at mini-rdbt signed Railway Station/Arborfield. Next left before level crossing. Hotel on right*

The hotel is located next to Wokingham Station, and is popular with business visitors. Most bedrooms are quite spacious and provide plenty of desk space. The bar and restaurant, with comfortable seating and a friendly atmosphere, offer a good selection of well prepared dishes.

ROOMS: 27 en suite (4 GF) ⊘ in 16 bedrooms s £48-£95; d £60-£120 (incl. bkfst) **FACILITIES:** Xmas **CONF:** Thtr 55 Class 38 Board 24 **PARKING:** 45 **NOTES:** ⊘ in restaurant **CARDS:**

WOLVERHAMPTON, West Midlands — Map 10 SO99
See also Himley & Worfield

★★★68% Ely House

53 Tettenhall Rd WV3 9NB
☎ 01902 311311 ▤ 01902 421098
e-mail: elyhousehotel@btconnect.com
Dir: *A41 towards Whitchurch from town centre ring road. 200yds on left after lights*

This delightful property dates back to 1742 and has been tastefully converted into a charming hotel. Privately owned and personally run in a warm and friendly manner, it provides spacious, comfortably furnished bedrooms, some on ground-floor level. There is also an attractive dining room and a spacious, elegant lounge containing a bar.

ROOMS: 18 en suite (4 GF) ⊘ in 6 bedrooms s £65-£85; d £79-£109 (incl. bkfst) **FACILITIES:** Xmas **CONF:** Thtr 20 Class 20 Board 20 **PARKING:** 22 **NOTES:** ⊘ in restaurant Closed 25-31 Dec **CARDS:**

★★★67% Park Hall Hotel

Park Dr, Goldthorn Park WV4 5AJ
☎ 01902 349500
e-mail: enquiries@parkhallhotel.co.uk
Dir: *off A4039 towards Penn and Wombourne, 2nd left (Ednam Rd), hotel at end of road*

Now under new ownership, this 18th-century house stands in extensive grounds and gardens, a short drive from the town centre. Bedrooms vary in style, but all are well equipped. Meals can be taken in the Terrace restaurant, which offers a carvery buffet. Conference facilities are available.

ROOMS: 57 en suite ⊘ in 37 bedrooms s £35-£70; d £40-£80 **LB** **FACILITIES:** STV Xmas **CONF:** BC Thtr 450 Class 250 Board 100 Del from £80 **PARKING:** 250 **NOTES:** ⊘ in restaurant Civ Wed 400 **CARDS:**

★★★66% Novotel Wolverhampton

Union St WV1 3JN
☎ 01902 871100 ▤ 01902 870054
e-mail: H1188@accor-hotels.com
Dir: *6m from M6 junct 10. A454 to Wolverhampton. Hotel on main ring road*

This large, modern, purpose-built hotel stands close to the town centre and ring road. It provides spacious, smartly presented and well-equipped bedrooms, all of which contain convertible bed settees for family occupancy. In addition to the open-plan lounge and bar area, there is an attractive brasserie-style restaurant, which overlooks the small outdoor swimming pool.

ROOMS: 132 en suite (10 fmly) ⊘ in 88 bedrooms s £65-£105; d £75-£115 (incl. bkfst) **LB** **FACILITIES:** STV **CONF:** Thtr 200 Class 100 Board 80 Del from £95 **SERVICES:** Lift **PARKING:** 120 **NOTES:** Civ Wed 200 **CARDS:**

★★★66% Quality Hotel Wolverhampton

Penn Rd WV3 0ER
☎ 01902 429216 ▤ 01902 710419
e-mail: enquiries@hotels-wolverhampton.com
Dir: *on A449, Wolverhampton to Kidderminster, 0.25m from ring road on right, turn onto Oaklands Rd at 1st lights*

The original Victorian house here has been considerably extended to create a large, busy and popular hotel. Ornately carved woodwork and ceilings still remain in the original building. All the bedrooms are well equipped. The pleasant public areas have a lot of character and offer a choice of bars.

ROOMS: 66 en suite 26 annexe en suite (6 fmly) (21 GF) ⊘ in 32 bedrooms s £47-£95; d £64-£119 **LB** **FACILITIES: Spa** STV supervised Sauna Gym Steam room, Playstation, Pay movies Xmas **CONF:** BC Thtr 140 Class 60 Board 40 Del from £75 **PARKING:** 124 **NOTES:** ⊘ in restaurant Civ Wed 100 **CARDS:**

⌂ Travel Inn

Wolverhampton Business Park, Stafford Rd WV10 6TA
☎ 08701 977277 ▤ 01902 785260
Dir: *approx 100 yds off M54 junct 2 at traffic lights*

Travel Inn offers good-quality, value-for-money accommodation. Spacious, en suite rooms with bath and shower comfortably accommodate a family of up to two adults and two children (to age 15). The restaurant and bar offers a varied menu. For further details consult the Hotel Groups page.

ROOMS: 54 en suite s £45.95-£46.95; d £45.95-£46.95
CONF: Thtr 20 Board 10

For central reservation numbers and more information on Hotel Groups, turn to pages 33-39

WOOBURN COMMON, Buckinghamshire Map 06 SU98

★★69% Chequers Inn
Kiln Ln, Wooburn HP10 0JQ
☎ 01628 529575 01628 850124
e-mail: info@chequers-inn.com
web: www.chequers-inn.com
Dir: *M40 junct 2 take A40 through Beaconsfield Old Town towards High Wycombe. 2m from town turn left into Broad Lane. Hotel 2.5m*

This 17th-century inn enjoys a peaceful, rural location beside the common. Bedrooms feature stripped-pine furniture, co-ordinated fabrics and an excellent range of extra facilities. The bar, with its massive oak post, beams and flagstone floor, and the restaurant, which overlooks a pretty patio, are very much focal points here.
ROOMS: 17 en suite (8 GF) s £72.50-£99.50; d £77.50-£107.50 (incl. bkfst) **LB FACILITIES:** STV **CONF:** Thtr 50 Class 30 Board 20 Del from £150 **PARKING:** 60 **NOTES:** **CARDS:**

WOODALL MOTORWAY SERVICE AREA (M1), South Yorkshire Map 16 SK48

Days Inn
Woodall Service Area S26 7XR
☎ 0114 248 7992 0114 248 5634
e-mail: woodall.hotel@welcomebreak.co.uk
web: www.welcomebreak.co.uk
Dir: *M1 S'bound - Woodall Services - between juncts 30 & 31*
This modern building offers accommodation in smart, spacious and well-equipped bedrooms, suitable for families and business travellers, and all with en suite bathrooms. Continental breakfast is available and other refreshments may be taken at the nearby family restaurant. For further details see the Hotel Groups page.
ROOMS: 38 en suite s £45-£55; d £45-£55 **CONF:** Board 10 Del from £35

Looking for a last-minute weekend away?
Check out Latebeds,
the AA's late availability booking service, at www.theAA.com

WOODBRIDGE, Suffolk Map 13 TM24

★★★76% Seckford Hall
IP13 6NU
☎ 01394 385678 01394 380610
e-mail: reception@seckford.co.uk
web: www.seckford.co.uk
Dir: *signed on A12. Do not follow signs for town centre*
This superb Tudor manor house is set amid lovely landscaped grounds just off the A12. The property is reputed to have been visited by Queen Elizabeth I, and retains much of its original charm and character. Public rooms include a superb panelled lounge, a cosy bar and an intimate restaurant. Bedrooms are spacious, attractively decorated, tastefully furnished and equipped with many thoughtful touches.
ROOMS: 22 en suite 10 annexe en suite (4 fmly) s £85-£130; d £130-£200 (incl. bkfst) **LB FACILITIES: Spa** 18 Fishing Gym Putt green Beauty Salon **CONF:** Thtr 100 Class 46 Board 40 Del from £150 **PARKING:** 200 **NOTES:** in restaurant Closed 25 Dec Civ Wed 120 **CARDS:**

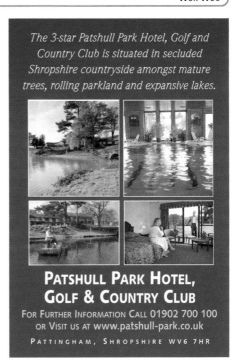

★★★72% Best Western Ufford Park Hotel Golf & Leisure
Yarmouth Rd, Ufford IP12 1QW
☎ 01394 383555 01394 383582
e-mail: mail@uffordpark.co.uk
web: www.uffordpark.co.uk
Dir: *A12 N to A1152, in Melton turn left at lights, premises 1m on right*

Modern, purpose-built hotel set in open countryside and boasting superb leisure facilities, including a challenging golf course. The spacious public rooms provide a wide choice of areas in which to

continued on p650

WOODBRIDGE, continued

relax and include a busy lounge bar, a carvery restaurant and the Vista restaurant. Bedrooms are pleasantly decorated and thoughtfully equipped; many rooms overlook the golf course.
ROOMS: 84 en suite 6 annexe en suite (8 fmly) (24 GF) ⊗ in 30 bedrooms s £90-£120; d £110-£140 (incl. bkfst) **LB** **FACILITIES: Spa** supervised 18 Fishing Sauna Solarium Gym Putt green Jacuzzi Steam room, Golf Academy with PGA tuition, Beauty salon Xmas
CONF: Thtr 200 Class 80 Board 80 Del from £99 **SERVICES:** Lift
PARKING: 200 **NOTES:** ⊗ in restaurant Civ Wed 120
CARDS:

WOODBURY, Devon Map 03 SY08

★★★★67% *Woodbury Park Hotel Golf & Country Club*

Woodbury Castle EX5 1JJ
☎ 01395 233382 01395 233384
e-mail: enquiries@woodburypark.co.uk
web: www.woodburypark.co.uk
Dir: *M5 junct 30, A376 then A302 towards Sidmouth, onto B3180, hotel signed*
Situated in 500 acres of beautiful and unspoilt countryside, just a short drive from the M5, this hotel offers smart, well-equipped and immaculately presented accommodation with a host of leisure, sporting and banqueting facilities. Re-live the thrills and drama of Nigel Mansell's career in 'The Nigel Mansell World of Racing', enjoy a game of golf on one of the two parkland courses or be pampered in the new bodyzone beauty centre.
ROOMS: 57 en suite (4 fmly) ⊗ in all bedrooms **FACILITIES: Spa** STV 27 Fishing Squash Snooker Sauna Gym Putt green Jacuzzi beauty salon, football pitch, driving range, 2 golf courses, hydrotherapy spa
CONF: Thtr 250 Class 100 Board 50 **SERVICES:** Lift **PARKING:** 400
NOTES: ⊗ in restaurant Civ Wed 150 **CARDS:**

WOODFORD BRIDGE, Greater London
See LONDON SECTION plan 1 H6

★★★★66% Menzies Prince Regent

Manor Rd IG8 8AE
☎ 020 8505 9966 020 8506 0807
e-mail: princeregent@menzies-hotels.co.uk
Dir: *M25 junct 26, to Loughton and Chigwell, hotel on Manor Rd*
Situated on the edge of Woodford Bridge and Chigwell, this hotel offers easy access into London and the M11 & M25. There is a good range of spacious, well-equipped bedrooms, most with a quiet aspect. The six conference and banqueting rooms have good facilities and are well suited to weddings and business events.
ROOMS: 61 en suite ⊗ in 10 bedrooms s £99; d £99-£119 **LB**
FACILITIES: STV Xmas **CONF:** Thtr 500 Class 150 Board 120 Del £155
SERVICES: Lift **PARKING:** 60 **NOTES:** ⊗ in restaurant Civ Wed
CARDS:

W

WOODFORD GREEN, Greater London
See LONDON SECTION plan 1 G6

★★★59% County

30 Oak Hill IG8 9NY
☎ 0870 609 6156 020 8506 0941
e-mail: countyepping@corushotels.com
Dir: *A406 onto A104 towards Woodford. At rdbt right, then take 3rd exit A104. At filling station left into Oak Hill, hotel 200yds on right*
In a residential area on the edge of Epping Forest, this modern hotel is convenient for both the North Circular and M11. Bedrooms have been decorated and equipped to a sound standard. Public areas include an informal brasserie and extensive meeting rooms.

ROOMS: 99 en suite (16 fmly) (24 GF) ⊗ in 50 bedrooms s £79-£89; d £79-£89 **LB** **FACILITIES:** Forest around hotel for walking **CONF:** BC Thtr 150 Class 80 Board 40 Del from £85 **SERVICES:** Lift
PARKING: 100 **NOTES:** ⊗ in restaurant Civ Wed 150
CARDS:

WOODHALL SPA, Lincolnshire Map 17 TF16

★★★68% Petwood

Stixwould Rd LN10 6QF
☎ 01526 352411 01526 353473
e-mail: reception@petwood.co.uk
web: www.petwood.co.uk
Dir: *from Sleaford take A153 (signed Skegness). At Tattershall turn left on B1192. Hotel is signed from village*

This lovely Edwardian house, set in 30 acres of gardens and woodlands, is steeped in history. Built in 1905, the house was used by the famous 'Dambusters' as an officers' mess during World War II. Bedrooms and public areas are spacious, comfortable and retain many original period features. Weddings and conferences are well catered for with brand new facilities.
ROOMS: 53 en suite (3 GF) ⊗ in 17 bedrooms s £90-£110; d £130-£180 (incl. bkfst) **LB** **FACILITIES:** Snooker Putt green Complimentary pass to leisure centre ♫ Xmas **CONF:** Thtr 250 Class 100 Board 50 Del £90
SERVICES: Lift **PARKING:** 140 **NOTES:** ⊗ in restaurant Civ Wed 100
CARDS:

★★★63% Golf Hotel

The Broadway LN10 6SG
☎ 01526 353535 01526 353096
Dir: *from Lincoln take B1189 to Metheringham onto B1191 towards Woodhall Spa. Hotel on left approx 500yds along from rdbt*
Located near the centre of the village, this traditional hotel is ideally situated to explore the Lincolnshire countryside and coast. The adjacent golf course makes this a popular venue for golfers and

continued

gives rise to the hotel's name and much of its decorative theme. Bedrooms vary in size and include several 'Club' style rooms.
ROOMS: 50 en suite (4 fmly) (8 GF) ⊗ in 21 bedrooms s £70-£84; d £90-£118 (incl. bkfst & dinner) **LB FACILITIES:** STV Guests have use of private leisure centre 1m from hotel Xmas **CONF:** Thtr 150 Class 45 Board 50 Del from £80 **PARKING:** 100 **NOTES:** ⊗ in restaurant Civ Wed 150 **CARDS:**

★★65% Eagle Lodge

The Broadway LN10 6ST
☎ 01526 353231 01526 352797
e-mail: user@eaglelodge.fsbusiness.co.uk
Dir: *in the centre of Woodhall Spa*

This family owned hotel is located in the centre of town, close to local shops and golf courses. Spacious bedrooms are well equipped for both business and leisure guests. Public areas include a bar and brasserie in addition to a formal restaurant offering a good range of dishes to suit all tastes. Conference and meeting facilities are also available.
ROOMS: 23 en suite (2 fmly) **FACILITIES:** STV ♫ **CONF:** Thtr 100 Class 50 Board 50 **PARKING:** 70 **NOTES:** ⊗ in restaurant **CARDS:**

WOODSTOCK, Oxfordshire — Map 11 SP41

★★★73% Feathers

FURLONG

Market St OX20 1SX
☎ 01993 812291 01993 813158
e-mail: enquiries@feathers.co.uk
Dir: *from Oxford take A44 to Woodstock, 1st left after lights. Hotel on left*

This small and individual hotel enjoys a town centre location with easy access to nearby Blenheim Palace. Public areas are elegant and full of traditional character from the cosy drawing room to the atmospheric restaurant. Individually styled bedrooms are appointed to a high standard and are furnished with attractive period and reproduction furniture.
ROOMS: 20 en suite (4 fmly) (2 GF) ⊗ in 1 bedroom s £99-£185; d £135-£225 (incl. bkfst) **LB FACILITIES:** STV 1 suite has steam room Xmas **CONF:** Thtr 25 Class 10 Board 16 Del £176.25 **NOTES:** ⊗ in restaurant **CARDS:**

★★★69% The Bear

MACDONALD HOTELS

Park St OX20 1SZ
☎ 0870 400 8202 01993 813380
e-mail: bear@macdonald-hotels.co.uk
Dir: *M40 junct 8 onto A40 to Oxford/M40 junct 9 onto A34 S to Oxford. Take A44 into Woodstock. Left to town centre hotel on left opp town hall*

With its ivy-clad façade, oak beams and open fireplaces, this 13th-century coaching inn exudes charm and cosiness. The hotel boasts bedrooms decorated in a modern style that is sympathetic to their original character. Public rooms include a variety of function rooms, an intimate bar area and an attractive restaurant.

ROOMS: 34 en suite 18 annexe en suite (1 fmly) (9 GF) ⊗ in 20 bedrooms s £85-£140; d £110-£178 (incl. bkfst) **LB FACILITIES:** STV Xmas **CONF:** Thtr 60 Class 14 Board 26 Del from £150 **PARKING:** 40 **NOTES:** ⊗ in restaurant RS 1 Jan **CARDS:**

★★★67% Kings Arms

19 Market St OX20 1SU
☎ 01993 813636 01993 813737
e-mail: enquiries@kings-woodstock.fsnet.co.uk
web: www.kings-hotel-woodstock.co.uk
Dir: *on corner of Market St and A44 Oxford Rd in town centre*

This appealing and contemporary hotel is situated in the centre of town just a short walk from Blenheim Palace. Public areas include an attractive bistro-style restaurant and a smart bar. Bedrooms and bathrooms are comfortably furnished and equipped, having been totally refurbished to a high standard.
ROOMS: 15 en suite ⊗ in all bedrooms s £70-£100; d £130-£150 (incl. bkfst) **NOTES:** No children 12 ⊗ in restaurant
CARDS:

A ★★ *Marlborough Arms*

26 Oxford St OX20 1TS
☎ 01993 811227 01993 811657
e-mail: themarlborough@ic24.net
Dir: *200mtrs from Blenheim Palace*
ROOMS: 10 en suite (2 fmly) **CONF:** Board 14 **PARKING:** 11
NOTES: ⊗ in restaurant **CARDS:**

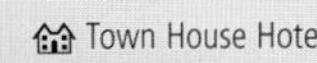
Town House Hotel

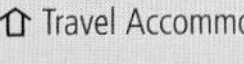
Country House Hotel

Travel Accommodation

W

WOODY BAY, Devon Map 03 SS64

★★65% *Woody Bay Hotel*

EX31 4QX
☎ 01598 763264 & 763563
Dir: *Signed off A39 between Blackmoor Gate & Lynton*
Popular with walkers, this hotel is perfectly situated to enjoy sweeping views over Woody Bay. Bedrooms vary in style and size; the majority have stunning views. Guests have a choice of dining options, either from the imaginative fixed-price menu in the restaurant or the simple bar menu.
ROOMS: 10 rms (8 en suite) (1 fmly) **PARKING:** 10 **NOTES:** in restaurant Closed Jan RS Nov, Dec & Feb **CARDS:**

WOOLACOMBE, Devon Map 03 SS44
See also Mortehoe

★★★79% Watersmeet

Mortehoe EX34 7EB
☎ 01271 870333 01271 870890
e-mail: info@watersmeethotel.co.uk
web: www.watersmeethotel.co.uk
Dir: *follow B3343 into Woolacombe, turn right onto esplanade, hotel 0.75m on left*
Offering attentive service, this popular hotel boasts magnificent views over the bay. Bedrooms benefit from wonderful sea views and some have the added bonus of private balconies. The public areas, now upgraded, all benefit from the hotel's stunning position, especially the attractive tiered restaurant. An imaginative and innovative range of dishes is offered each evening from a fixed-price menu.
ROOMS: 25 en suite (4 fmly) (3 GF) s £125-£185; d £170-£290 (incl. bkfst & dinner) **LB** **FACILITIES:** STV Jacuzzi Steam room, hot tub Xmas **PARKING:** 38 **NOTES:** in restaurant
CARDS:

See advert on opposite page

★★★74% Woolacombe Bay

South St EX34 7BN
☎ 01271 870388 01271 870613
e-mail: woolacombe.bayhotel@btinternet.com
web: www.woolacombe-bay-hotel.co.uk
Dir: *from A361 take B3343 to Woolacombe. Hotel in centre on left*

This family-friendly hotel is adjacent to the beach and the village centre, and has a welcoming and friendly environment. The public areas are spacious and comfortable, and many of the well-equipped bedrooms have balconies with splendid views over

continued

the bay. In addition to the fixed-price menu served in the stylish restaurant, Maxwell's bistro offers an informal alternative.
ROOMS: 64 en suite (27 fmly) (2 GF) in all bedrooms s £53-£147; d £106-£294 (incl. bkfst & dinner) **LB** **FACILITIES: Spa** STV 9 Squash Snooker Sauna Solarium Gym Jacuzzi Beauty salon, Creche, Childrens club, Table Tennis, Hairdresser ch fac Xmas **CONF:** Thtr 200 Class 150 Board 150 Del from £67.50 **SERVICES:** Lift **PARKING:** 150 **NOTES:** in restaurant Closed 3 Jan-mid Feb
CARDS:

WOOLER, Northumberland Map 21 NT92

★★69% Tankerville Arms

Cottage Rd NE71 6AD
☎ 01668 281581 01668 281387
e-mail: enquiries@tankervillehotel.co.uk
web: www.tankervillehotel.co.uk
Dir: *on A697*
Dating from the 17th century, this popular inn is ideally placed for the many local attractions. The comfortable and thoughtfully equipped bedrooms come in a variety of styles and sizes. The traditional bar has an adjacent brasserie and there is a spacious restaurant. Wide-ranging menus provide a choice to suit all.
ROOMS: 16 en suite (2 fmly) s £34-£51; d £68-£96 (incl. bkfst) **LB** **CONF:** Thtr 60 Class 60 Board 30 **PARKING:** 100 **NOTES:** in restaurant Closed 22-28 Dec Civ Wed **CARDS:**

WOOLLEY EDGE MOTORWAY SERVICE AREA (M1), West Yorkshire Map 16 SE31

Travelodge Wakefield (Northbound)

Travelodge

M1 Service Area, West Bretton WF4 4LQ
☎ 08700 850 950 01924 830609
Dir: *between junct 38/39, adj to service area*
Travelodge offers good quality, good value, modern accommodation. Ideal for families, the spacious, en suite bedrooms include remote-control TV, tea and coffee-making facilities and luxury beds. Meals can be taken at the nearby family restaurant. For further details consult the Hotel Groups page.
ROOMS: 32 en suite s fr £25; d fr £25

Travelodge Wakefield (Southbound)

Travelodge

M1 Service Area Southbound, West Bretton WF4 4LQ
☎ 08700 850 950 01924 830174
Travelodge offers good quality, good value, modern accommodation. Ideal for families, the spacious, en suite bedrooms include remote-control TV, tea and coffee-making facilities and luxury beds. Meals can be taken at the nearby family restaurant. For further details consult the Hotel Groups page.
ROOMS: 41 en suite s fr £25; d fr £25

WORCESTER, Worcestershire Map 10 SO85

★★★74% Pear Tree Inn & Country Hotel

Smite WR3 8SY
☎ 01905 756565 01905 756777
e-mail: thepeartreeuk@aol.com
web: www.thepeartree.co.uk
Dir: *M5 junct 6 take Droitwich road after 300yds take 1st right into small country lane over canal bridge, up a hill, hotel on left*
This traditional English inn and country hotel has spacious bedrooms with attractive colour schemes and good facilities. Ground-floor bedrooms are available, as are suites. Guests can

continued

enjoy good food and a drink in warm and relaxed surroundings; there is also an excellent range of conference/function rooms.

ROOMS: 24 en suite (2 fmly) (12 GF) ⊗ in 12 bedrooms s £65-£84.95; d £85-£105.95 (incl. bkfst) **LB** **FACILITIES:** STV **CONF:** BC Thtr 300 Class 150 Board 30 Del from £135 **SERVICES:** Lift air con **PARKING:** 200 **NOTES:** ⊗ in restaurant Civ Wed 120 **CARDS:**

★★★70% Bank House Hotel Golf & Country Club

Best Western

Bransford WR6 5JD
☎ 01886 833551 01886 832461
e-mail: info@bankhousehotel.co.uk
web: www.bw-bankhouse.co.uk
Dir: *M5 junct 7 follow signs to Worcester West, then Hereford on A4440, & A4103. Turn left, hotel approx 2m on left*

Partly dating back to the 17th century, Bank House is set in 123 acres overlooking the Malvern Hills, three miles west of Worcester. There is a good choice of function and conference suites, and the bedrooms are traditionally appointed. Facilities here include a leisure and fitness suite and an 18-hole golf course with pro shop and clubhouse.

ROOMS: 68 en suite (20 fmly) (12 GF) ⊗ in 15 bedrooms s £92; d £120 (incl. bkfst) **LB** **FACILITIES: Spa** 18 Sauna Solarium Gym Putt green Jacuzzi Xmas **CONF:** Thtr 400 Class 150 Board 70 Del £150 **PARKING:** 350 **NOTES:** ⊗ in restaurant Civ Wed 200 **CARDS:**

★★★64% Fownes

City Walls Rd WR1 2AP
☎ 01905 613151 01905 23742
e-mail: reservations@fowneshotel.co.uk
Dir: *M5 junct 7 take A44 for Worcester city centre. Turn right at 4th set of traffic lights into City Walls Rd*

On the Birmingham Canal and located close to the city centre this former Victorian glove factory has been converted into an interesting-looking, modern hotel with well proportioned bedrooms. Snacks are available in the lounge bar and the King's

continued on p654

W

WORCESTER, continued

restaurant offers an interesting carte menu. Conference and meeting facilities are available.
ROOMS: 61 en suite (10 GF) ⊗ in 28 bedrooms s £98.50; d £79-£104.50 (incl. bkfst) **LB** **FACILITIES:** ch fac Xmas **CONF:** Thtr 100 Class 35 Board 25 Del from £110 **SERVICES:** Lift **PARKING:** 82 **NOTES:** ⊗ in restaurant Civ Wed 80 **CARDS:**

Travel Inn

Wainwright Way, Warndon WR4 9FA
☎ 08701 977278 🖷 01905 756601
Dir: *M5 junct 6, at entrance of Warndon commercial development area*
Travel Inn offers good-quality, value-for-money accommodation. Spacious, en suite rooms with bath and shower comfortably accommodate a family of up to two adults and two children (to age 15). The restaurant and bar offers a varied menu. For further details consult the Hotel Groups page.
ROOMS: 60 en suite s £45.95-£46.95; d £45.95-£46.95 **CONF:** Thtr 8

WORFIELD, Shropshire — Map 10 SO79

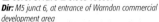

Top 200 – Hotel

★★★ ®®® Old Vicarage

Worfield WV15 5JZ
☎ 01746 716497 🖷 01746 716552
e-mail: admin@the-old-vicarage.demon.co.uk
web: www.oldvicarageworfield.com
Dir: *off A454 between Bridgnorth & Wolverhampton, 5m S of Telford's southern business area*
This delightful property is set in acres of farm and woodland in a quiet and peaceful area of Shropshire and was originally an elegant Edwardian vicarage. Service is friendly and helpful, and customer care is one the many strengths of this charming small hotel. The restaurant is a joy, serving award-winning modern British cuisine in elegant surroundings. The lounge and conservatory are the perfect places to enjoy a pre-dinner drink or the complimentary afternoon tea. Bedrooms, meanwhile, are individually appointed, thoughtfully and luxuriously furnished and well equipped.
ROOMS: 10 en suite 4 annexe en suite (1 fmly) (2 GF) ⊗ in all bedrooms s £80-£110; d £135-£175 (incl. bkfst) **LB**
FACILITIES: **Spa** ch fac **CONF:** Thtr 30 Class 30 Board 20 Del £140 **PARKING:** 30 **NOTES:** ⊗ in restaurant
CARDS:

WORKINGTON, Cumbria — Map 18 NY02

★★★82% ® Washington Central

Washington St CA14 3AY
☎ 01900 65772 🖷 01900 68770
e-mail: kawildwchotel@aol.com
web: www.washingtoncentralhotelworkington.com
Dir: *M6 junct 40 towards Keswick, follow to Workington. At lights at bottom of Ramsey Brow, turn right and follow signs for hotel*

Enjoying a prominent town centre location, this modern hotel boasts memorably hospitable staff. The well-maintained and comfortable bedrooms are equipped with a range of thoughtful extras. Public areas include numerous lounges, a spacious bar, Ceasars leisure club, a smart restaurant and a popular coffee shop. The comprehensive conference facilities are ideal for meetings and weddings.
ROOMS: 46 en suite (4 fmly) ⊗ in 37 bedrooms s £77-£89.95; d £109.95-£159.95 (incl. bkfst) **LB** **FACILITIES:** STV supervised Sauna Solarium Gym Jacuzzi Free bike hire, Nightclub ♫ ch fac **CONF:** BC Thtr 300 Class 250 Board 150 Del from £104.95 **SERVICES:** Lift **PARKING:** 16 **NOTES:** ⊗ in restaurant RS 25 Dec Civ Wed 300 **CARDS:**

★★★67% Hunday Manor Country House

Hunday, Winscales CA14 4JF
☎ 01900 61798 🖷 01900 601202
e-mail: info@hunday-manor-hotel.co.uk
Dir: *off A66 onto A595 towards Whitehaven, hotel is 3m on right, signed*
Delightfully situated and enjoying distant views of the Solway Firth, this charming hotel has comfortable, well-furnished rooms. The open-plan bar and foyer lounge boast welcoming open fires, and the attractive restaurant overlooks the woodland gardens. The function suite has ensured that the hotel makes an excellent wedding venue.
ROOMS: 24 en suite s £55-£69; d £69-£89 (incl. bkfst) **LB** **FACILITIES:** Xmas **CONF:** Thtr 200 Class 200 Board 200 Del £90 **PARKING:** 50 **NOTES:** ⊗ in restaurant Civ Wed 250
CARDS:

WORKSOP, Nottinghamshire — Map 16 SK57

★★★67% *Lion*

112 Bridge St S80 1HT
☎ 01909 477925 🖷 01909 479038
e-mail: reservations@the-lionhotel.co.uk
Dir: *A57 to town centre, turn at Walkers Garage on right and follow road to Norfolk Arms and turn left*
This former coaching inn has been extended to offer modern and spacious accommodation, including a number of suites. It is conveniently situated on the edge of the main shopping and

continued

business area of Worksop; many locals join visitors in enjoying the wide range of dishes offered in the bar and restaurant.

ROOMS: 45 en suite (3 fmly) (5 GF) ⊗ in 7 bedrooms **FACILITIES:** STV **CONF:** Thtr 160 Class 80 Board 70 **SERVICES:** Lift **PARKING:** 50 **NOTES:** ⊗ in restaurant Civ Wed 75
CARDS:

★★★65% Clumber Park
Clumber Park S80 3PA
☎ 01623 835333 🖷 01623 835525
e-mail: reservations@clumberparkhotel
Dir: *M1 junct 30/31 follow signs for Worksop. A1 Fiveways rdbt onto A614, 5m NE*

Beside the A614, this hotel is situated in open countryside, edging on to Sherwood Forest and Clumber Park. Bedrooms are comfortably furnished and well-equipped and public areas include a choice of formal and informal eating options. The refurbished Dukes Tavern is lively and casual, while the restaurant offers a more traditional style of service.
ROOMS: 48 en suite (6 fmly) (16 GF) ⊗ in 31 bedrooms s £65; d £65 **LB FACILITIES:** STV Xmas **CONF:** Thtr 250 Class 150 Board 90 Del £115 **PARKING:** 200 **NOTES:** ⊗ in restaurant Civ Wed 100
CARDS:

⌂ Travelodge
St Anne's Dr, Dukeries Dr S80 3QD
☎ 08700 850 950 🖷 0870 191 1684
Dir: *on rdbt junct of A60/A57*

Travelodge

Travelodge offers good quality, good value, modern accommodation. Ideal for families, the spacious, en suite bedrooms include remote-control TV, tea and coffee-making facilities and luxury beds. Meals can be taken at the nearby family restaurant. For further details consult the Hotel Groups page.
ROOMS: 40 en suite s fr £25; d fr £25

WORSLEY, Greater Manchester — Map 15 SD70

★★★63% Novotel Manchester West
Worsley Brow M28 2YA
☎ 0161 799 3535 🖷 0161 703 8207
e-mail: H0907@accor-hotels.com
Dir: *adjacent to M60 junct 13*

NOVOTEL

Well-placed for access to the Peak and Lake Districts, as well as the thriving city of Manchester, this modern hotel successfully caters for both families and business guests. Spacious bedrooms all have sofa beds and a large work area, and the hotel also boasts an outdoor swimming pool and children's play area.
ROOMS: 119 en suite (4 fmly) **FACILITIES:** STV **CONF:** Thtr 230 Class 140 Board 20 **SERVICES:** Lift **PARKING:** 140 **NOTES:** Civ Wed
CARDS:

WORTHING, West Sussex — Map 06 TQ10

★★★71% Ardington
Steyne Gardens BN11 3DZ
☎ 01903 230451 🖷 01903 526526
Dir: *A27 to Lancing, then to seafront. Follow signs for Worthing. Left at 1st Church into Steyne Gardens*

Overlooking the Steyne Gardens next to the seafront, this popular hotel offers well-appointed bedrooms with a good range of facilities. An elegant lounge/bar area caters for guests throughout the day and has ample seating. The restaurant has been designed in a contemporary style, and offers good standards of cuisine.
ROOMS: 45 en suite (4 fmly) ⊗ in 10 bedrooms s £60-£95; d £95-£110 (incl. bkfst) **LB FACILITIES:** STV ch fac Xmas **CONF:** Thtr 140 Class 60 Board 35 Del from £75 **NOTES:** Closed 25 Dec-4 Jan
CARDS:

★★★70% Berkeley
86-95 Marine Pde BN11 3QD
☎ 01903 820000 🖷 01903 821333
e-mail: berkbn@aol.com
Dir: *follow signs to Worthing seafront; hotel 0.5m W from pier*

Best Western

This hotel occupies a prime location on the seafront just a short walk from the high street. Bedrooms are modern in style and equipped with a good range of facilities; many have superb sea views. The public areas are tastefully decorated, and include a comfortable cocktail bar and a spacious restaurant.
ROOMS: 80 en suite (3 fmly) ⊗ in 29 bedrooms s £82-£87; d £105-£112 (incl. bkfst) **LB FACILITIES:** STV Xmas **CONF:** Thtr 100 Class 50 Board 50 Del from £99 **SERVICES:** Lift **PARKING:** 35 **NOTES:** Civ Wed 50 **CARDS:**

WORTHING, continued

★★★70% Windsor
14/20 Windsor Rd BN11 2LX
☎ 01903 239655 & 0800 9804442 01903 210763
e-mail: reception@thewindsor.co.uk
web: www.thewindsor.co.uk
Dir: *From A27, A259. Follow Hotels signs through town centre to seafront towards Brighton.*
Located on a quiet road near to the seafront, this well-established hotel is popular with both business and leisure guests. Public areas include a smart lounge bar, an appealing conservatory reception and lounge area, and a popular restaurant. A choice of tastefully furnished bedrooms is available, each with a good range of facilities.
ROOMS: 30 en suite (4 fmly) (5 GF) in 15 bedrooms s £80-£99; d £95-£125 (incl. bkfst) **LB** **FACILITIES:** STV **CONF:** Thtr 120 Class 48 Board 40 Del from £105 **SERVICES:** air con **PARKING:** 28 **NOTES:** in restaurant Closed 23-31 Dec Civ Wed 100
CARDS:

★★★68% Beach
Marine Pde BN11 3QJ
☎ 01903 234001 01903 234567
e-mail: thebeachhotel@btinternet.com
web: www.thebeachhotel.co.uk
Dir: *W of town centre, approx 0.3m from pier*
With an impressive 1930's façade this well-established hotel is extremely popular with both leisure and business guests. Bedrooms, some with sea views and balconies, are comfortable and well equipped. Spacious public areas incorporate a busy restaurant serving a wide range of popular dishes. Secure parking is available.
ROOMS: 79 en suite (8 fmly) in 24 bedrooms s £56-£82; d £87-£105 (incl. bkfst) **LB** **FACILITIES:** STV Xmas **CONF:** Thtr 250 Class 60 Board 60 Del from £83 **SERVICES:** Lift **PARKING:** 55 **NOTES:** in restaurant **CARDS:**

★★★65% Kingsway
Marine Pde BN11 3QQ
☎ 01903 237542 01903 204173
e-mail: thekingsway@totalise.co.uk
Dir: *A27 follow signs to Worthing, then at seafront follow signs 'Hotel West'. Hotel 0.75m west of pier*
THE CIRCLE Selected Individual Hotels GREAT BRITAIN
Ideally located on the seafront and close to the town centre, the Kingsway continues to provide warm hospitality to guests. Bedrooms, which are gradually being upgraded, are comfortably furnished and equipped with modern facilities. Day rooms include two comfortable lounge areas, a bar serving snacks and a well-appointed restaurant.
ROOMS: 29 en suite 7 annexe en suite (2 fmly) (3 GF) in 13 bedrooms s £65-£76; d £106-£132 (incl. bkfst) **LB** **FACILITIES:** STV Xmas **CONF:** Thtr 50 Class 20 Board 30 Del from £96 **SERVICES:** Lift **PARKING:** 9 **NOTES:** in restaurant
CARDS:

★★★62% Findon Manor
High St, Findon BN14 0TA
☎ 01903 872733 01903 877473
e-mail: hotel@findonmanor.com
Dir: *500yds off A24 between Worthing & Horsham, at the sign for Findon follow signs to Findon Manor into village*
Located in the centre of the village, Findon Manor was built as a rectory and has a beamed lounge, which doubles as the reception area. Bedrooms, several with four-poster beds, are attractively decorated in a traditional style. The cosy bar offers a very good range of bar food, and is popular with locals, while the restaurant overlooks a garden and offers modern and traditional dishes.
ROOMS: 11 en suite (2 fmly) s £63-£73; d £93-£140 (incl. bkfst) **LB** **FACILITIES:** Boule Xmas **CONF:** Thtr 50 Class 18 Board 25 **PARKING:** 25 **NOTES:** No children 12yrs in restaurant RS 24-30 Dec Civ Wed 60 **CARDS:**

★★65% Cavendish
115 Marine Pde BN11 3QG
☎ 01903 236767 01903 823840
e-mail: cavendishworthing@btinternet.com
web: www.cavendishworthing.co.uk
Dir: *on seafront 600yds W of pier*
THE INDEPENDENTS
This popular, family-run hotel enjoys a prominent seafront location. Bedrooms are well-equipped and soundly decorated. Guests have an extensive choice of meal options, with a varied bar menu, and carte and daily menus offered in the restaurant. Limited car parking is available at the rear of the hotel.
ROOMS: 17 en suite (4 fmly) in 3 bedrooms s £39.50-£45; d £65-£80 (incl. bkfst) **LB** **FACILITIES:** STV **SERVICES:** air con **PARKING:** 5 **CARDS:**

WOTTON-UNDER-EDGE, Gloucestershire — Map 04 ST79

★★★★66% Tortworth Court Four Pillars
Tortworth GL12 8HH
☎ 0800 374 692 01454 263001
e-mail: bristol@four-pillars.co.uk
Dir: *M5 junct 14, B4509 pass Tortworth Visitors Centre take next right, hotel 0.5m on right*
FOUR PILLARS HOTELS
Set within 30 acres of parkland, this Gothic mansion displays original features cleverly combined with contemporary additions. Elegant public rooms include a choice of dining options, one housed within the library, another in the atrium and the third in the orangery. Bedrooms are well equipped, and additional facilities include a host of conference rooms and a leisure centre.
ROOMS: 189 en suite in 95 bedrooms s £75-£139; d £96-£172 **LB** **FACILITIES:** STV Sauna Gym Jacuzzi Beauty suite, Steam room Xmas **CONF:** BC Thtr 400 Class 200 Board 80 Del £179 **SERVICES:** Lift **PARKING:** 350 **NOTES:** Closed 27-29 Dec Civ Wed 100
CARDS:

WREA GREEN, Lancashire — Map 18 SD33

★★★69% Manor House
Ribby Hall Village, Ribby Rd PR4 2PR
☎ 01772 688000 01772 688036
e-mail: themanorhousehotel@ribbyhall.co.uk
web: ww.mhhotel.co.uk
Dir: *M55 junct 33 follow A585 towards Kirkham & brown tourist signs for manor house. Straight across 3 rdbts. Ribby Hall Village 200yds on left*
THE INDEPENDENTS

This smart hotel, located in the Ribby Hall Holiday Village, overlooks

continued

an ornamental lake, complete with 50ft fountain. Accommodation consists of modern one and two-bedroom suites, some with spacious balconies. Two opulent penthouses are particularly impressive. Meals are served in the nearby restaurant. Hotel guests can make use of the extensive leisure and conference facilities.
ROOMS: 29 en suite (6 fmly) (13 GF) ⊗ in all bedrooms s £75-£115; d £100-£160 (incl. cont bkfst) **LB** **FACILITIES: Spa** STV supervised 9 Fishing Squash Riding Snooker Sauna Solarium Gym Jacuzzi Various other facilities available ♫ Xmas **CONF:** Thtr 350 Class 200 **SERVICES:** Lift **PARKING:** 100 **NOTES:** ⊗ in restaurant Civ Wed **CARDS:**

WROTHAM, Kent Map 06 TQ65

Travel Inn (Sevenoaks/Maidstone)
London Rd, Wrotham Heath TN15 7RX
☎ 08701 977227 01732 870368
Dir: *10 minutes from J2 M20 and 5 minutes from J2a of M26. Follow A20 to Wrotham Heath and West Malling. The Travel Inn is past lights on right*
Travel Inn offers good-quality, value-for-money accommodation. Spacious, en suite rooms with bath and shower comfortably accommodate a family of up to two adults and two children (to age 15). The restaurant and bar offers a varied menu. For further details consult the Hotel Groups page.
ROOMS: 40 en suite s £45.95-£46.95; d £45.95-£46.95 **CONF:** Thtr 18

WROXHAM, Norfolk Map 13 TG31

★★66% **Hotel Wroxham**
The Bridge NR12 8AJ
☎ 01603 782061 01603 784279
e-mail: reservations@hotelwroxham.co.uk
Dir: *From Norwich, A1151 signed Wroxham & The Broads for approx 7m. Over bridge at Wroxham take 1st right, & sharp right again. Hotel car park on right*

Overlooking the Norfolk Broads in the heart of this bustling town centre. Bedrooms are pleasantly decorated and well equipped; some rooms have balconies with lovely views of the busy waterways. The open-plan public rooms include the lively riverside bar, a lounge, a large sun terrace and a smart restaurant serving an interesting choice of dishes.
ROOMS: 18 en suite s £50-£72; d £75-£95 (incl. bkfst) **LB** **FACILITIES:** Fishing Boating facilities (by arrangement) ♫ Xmas **CONF:** Thtr 200 Class 50 Board 20 Del from £85 **PARKING:** 45 **NOTES:** ⊗ in restaurant **CARDS:**

★★62% **Kings Head**
Station Rd NR12 8UR
☎ 01603 782429 01603 784622
Dir: *in centre of village*

In the heart of the bustling town centre and on the edge of the Norfolk Broads, this hotel has spacious public rooms leading out onto the river frontage and gardens. There is a popular carvery restaurant and a conservatory that overlooks the busy waterways. The well-equipped bedrooms are pleasantly furnished and simply decorated.
ROOMS: 8 en suite (2 fmly) ⊗ in all bedrooms s fr £41.50; d fr £41.50 **FACILITIES:** Fishing **PARKING:** 45 **NOTES:** ⊗ in restaurant **CARDS:**

WYMONDHAM, Norfolk Map 13 TG10

★★★70% **Abbey**
10 Church St NR18 0PH
☎ 01953 602148 01953 606247
e-mail: info@abbeyhotels.co.uk
web: www.abbeyhotels.co.uk
Dir: *from A11 follow Wymondham sign. At lights left and 1st left into one-way system. Left into Church St*

Charming 16th-century hotel situated close to the abbey just off the main high street of this delightful market town. The spacious bedrooms are pleasantly decorated, tastefully furnished and thoughtfully equipped. Public rooms include a cosy lounge bar, the Benims restaurant and a further sitting room.
ROOMS: 27 en suite 1 annexe en suite (3 fmly) (6 GF) ⊗ in all bedrooms s £49-£49; d £65-£69 (incl. bkfst) **LB** **FACILITIES:** STV Xmas **SERVICES:** Lift **PARKING:** 3 **NOTES:** ⊗ in restaurant **CARDS:**

WYMONDHAM, continued

★★73% *Wymondham Consort Hotel*

Best Western

28 Market St NR18 0BB
☎ 01953 606721 Fax 01953 601361
e-mail: wymondham@bestwestern.co.uk
Dir: *off A11 (M11) Thetford to Norwich road, left at lights and left again*

Privately-owned hotel situated in the centre of this bustling market town. The individually decorated bedrooms come in a variety of sizes; each one is pleasantly decorated and thoughtfully equipped. Public rooms include a cosy bar, a separate lounge, a coffee shop and an intimate restaurant, which overlooks the busy high street.
ROOMS: 20 en suite (1 fmly) (3 GF) ⊘ in all bedrooms **CONF:** Thtr 20 Board 20 **PARKING:** 16 **NOTES:** ⊘ in restaurant
CARDS:

YARM, North Yorkshire — Map 19 NZ41

Top 200 – Hotel

★★★ ◎◎◎

Judges Country House Hotel

Pride of Britain Hotels

Kirklevington Hall TS15 9LW
☎ 01642 789000 Fax 01642 782878
e-mail: enquiries@judgeshotel.co.uk
web: www.judgeshotel.co.uk
Dir: *1.5m from A19. At A67 junct, follow Yarm road, hotel on left*
Formerly a lodging for local circuit judges, this gracious mansion lies in landscaped grounds through which a stream runs. Stylish bedrooms are individually decorated and come with 101 extras, including a pet goldfish. The Conservatory restaurant serves award-winning cuisine, and the genuinely caring and attentive service is equally memorable.
ROOMS: 21 en suite (3 fmly) (5 GF) ⊘ in 10 bedrooms s £134-£148; d £159-£174 (incl. bkfst) **LB FACILITIES:** STV Gym Boating, 4x4 hire, mountain bikes, nature trails Xmas **CONF:** BC Thtr 200 Class 120 Board 80 Del from £175 **PARKING:** 102 **NOTES:** ⊘ in restaurant Civ Wed 200
CARDS:

YARMOUTH See Wight, Isle of

YATELEY, Hampshire — Map 05 SU86

U Casa dei Cesari Restaurant & Hotel
Handford Ln GU46 6BT
☎ 01252 873275 Fax 01252 870614
e-mail: casareservations@aol.com
Dir: *M3 junct 4a, follow signs for Yateley town centre. Hotel is signed approx 1.5m from M3*
At the time of going to press, the star classification for this hotel was not confirmed. Please refer to the AA internet site www.theAA.com for current information.
ROOMS: 44 en suite (2 fmly) (11 GF) ⊘ in 11 bedrooms s £80-£93.50; d £100-£108.50 (incl. bkfst) **LB FACILITIES:** STV Riding Xmas **CONF:** Thtr 35 Class 30 Board 25 Del from £140 **PARKING:** 80 **NOTES:** ⊘ in restaurant Closed 26-30 Dec Civ Wed 50
CARDS:

YATTENDON, Berkshire

★★72% ◎◎ Royal Oak
The Square RG18 0UG
☎ 01635 201325 Fax 01635 201926
e-mail: oakyattendon@aol.com
Dir: *M4 junct 13, N on A34, 1st slip road right to Hermitage, left at t-junct, 2nd right signed Yattendon*
This smart country inn dates back to the 16th century and is located in a charming Berkshire village within easy reach of the M4. Bedrooms are equipped to a high standard and bathrooms are well appointed. The kitchen offers interesting dishes, available in the bar or the more formal restaurant.
ROOMS: 5 en suite ⊘ in all bedrooms s £75-£105; d £95-£130 **LB FACILITIES:** Xmas **CONF:** Thtr 30 Class 18 Board 22 Del £190 **NOTES:** No children 6yrs ⊘ in restaurant
CARDS:

YELVERTON, Devon — Map 03 SX56

★★★72% Moorland Links

Forestdale Hotels

PL20 6DA
☎ 01822 852245 Fax 01822 855004
e-mail: moorland.links@forestdale.com
Dir: *A38 from Exeter to Plymouth, then A386 towards Tavistock. 5m onto open moorland, hotel 1m on left*

In Dartmoor National Park, set in nine acres of well-tended grounds, Moorland Links has spectacular views from many of the rooms across open moorland and the Tamar Valley. Bedrooms are well equipped and comfortably furnished, and some rooms have

continued

open balconies. An ideal hotel for weddings and which also has ample, quiet meeting room facilities for business guests.
ROOMS: 45 en suite (4 fmly) (17 GF) ⊗ in 2 bedrooms s fr £95; d fr £120 (incl. bkfst) **LB** **FACILITIES:** STV Xmas **CONF:** Thtr 120 Class 60 Board 40 Del from £125 **PARKING:** 120 **NOTES:** ⊗ in restaurant Civ Wed **CARDS:**

See advert under PLYMOUTH

YEOVIL, Somerset — Map 04 ST51

See also Martock

★★★74% Yeovil Court

West Coker Rd BA20 2HE
☎ 01935 863746 🖷 01935 863990
e-mail: unwind@yeovilhotel.com web: www.yeovilhotel.com
Dir: *2.5m W of town centre on A30*

This comfortable, family-run hotel benefits from a very relaxed and caring atmosphere. Bedrooms are well equipped and neatly presented; some are located in a new adjacent building. Public areas consist of a smart lounge, a popular bar and an attractive restaurant. Menus combine an interesting selection including lighter options and dishes more suited to special occasion dining.
ROOMS: 18 en suite 12 annexe en suite (3 fmly) (11 GF) ⊗ in 8 bedrooms s £57-£74; d £85-£105 (incl. bkfst) **LB** **CONF:** Thtr 50 Class 18 Board 22 **PARKING:** 65 **NOTES:** ⊗ in restaurant RS Sat lunch, 25 Dec eve **CARDS:**

See advert on this page

★★62% Preston

64 Preston Rd BA20 2DL
☎ 01935 474400 🖷 01935 410142
e-mail: prestonhotelyeo@aol.co.uk
Dir: *A303 onto A3088, left at 1st rdbt, over 2nd rdbt & turn right at 3rd rdbt*

A relaxed and friendly atmosphere has been maintained at this popular hotel, which has undergone upgrading throughout. Well suited to both business and leisure guests, a spacious bar and cosy restaurant are available where home-cooked meals satisfy the heartiest of appetites.
ROOMS: 6 en suite 7 annexe en suite (1 fmly) (7 GF) s fr £45; d fr £55 (incl. bkfst) **CONF:** BC Class 40 Board 15 **PARKING:** 22 **NOTES:** ⊗ in restaurant **CARDS:**

Top 200 – Hotel

★ Little Barwick House

Barwick Village BA22 9TD
☎ 01935 423902 🖷 01935 420908
e-mail: littlebarwick@hotmail.com
Dir: *from Yeovil on A37 towards Dorchester, left at 1st rdbt. 1st left, hotel 0.25m on left*

Situated in a quiet hamlet this delightful, listed Georgian dower house is an ideal retreat for those seeking peaceful surroundings and good food. Just one of the highlights of a stay here is a meal in the restaurant. Each of the bedrooms have their own character, charm and range of thoughtful extras such as fresh flowers and magazines. The informal atmosphere of a private home, coupled with the facilities and comforts of a modern hotel, result in a very special combination.

Little Barwick House

ROOMS: 6 en suite **PARKING:** 30 **NOTES:** ⊗ in restaurant
CARDS:

YORK, North Yorkshire — Map 16 SE65

See also Aldwark, Escrick, Pocklington & Sutton upon Derwent

★★★★68% York Marriott

Marriott HOTELS · RESORTS · SUITES

Tadcaster Rd YO24 1QQ
☎ 01904 701000 📠 01904 702308
e-mail: york@marriotthotels.co.uk
Dir: *from A64 at York 'West' onto A1036, follow signs to city centre. Approx 1.5m, hotel on right after church and lights*

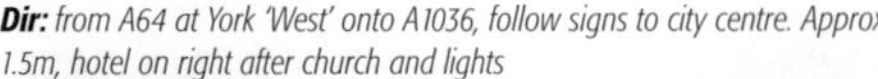

Overlooking the racecourse and Knavesmire Parkland, the hotel offers modern accommodation, including family rooms, all with a comfort cooling system. Within the hotel, guests can make use of extensive leisure facilities including indoor pool, putting green and tennis court. For those wishing to explore the historic and cultural attractions of the city there is a daily courtesy mini-bus service to the city centre, less than a mile from the hotel.
ROOMS: 108 en suite (14 fmly) (16 GF) ⊗ in 60 bedrooms
FACILITIES: Spa STV Sauna Solarium Gym Putt green Jacuzzi Beauty treatment Xmas **CONF:** BC Thtr 170 Class 90 Board 40
SERVICES: Lift air con **PARKING:** 200 **NOTES:** ⊗ in restaurant Civ Wed 140 **CARDS:**

★★★★65% The Royal York

PRINCIPAL HOTELS

Station Rd YO24 2AA
☎ 01904 653681 📠 01904 623503
e-mail: reservation.centreuk@lemeridien.com
web: www.principal-hotels.com
Dir: *adjacent to railway station*

Situated in three acres of landscaped grounds in the very heart of the city, this Victorian railway hotel has views over the city and York Minster. Contemporary bedrooms are divided between those in the main hotel and the air-conditioned garden mews. There is also a leisure complex and state-of-the-art conference centre.
ROOMS: 165 en suite (10 fmly) s £69-£130; d £90-£150 **LB**
FACILITIES: STV supervised Sauna Solarium Gym Jacuzzi Steam room Xmas **CONF:** BC Thtr 450 Class 250 Board 80 Del from £130
SERVICES: Lift **PARKING:** 80 **NOTES:** ⊗ in restaurant Civ Wed 400
CARDS:

Top 200 – Hotel

★★★ ◎◎◎ Middlethorpe Hall Hotel, Restaurant & Spa

RELAIS & CHÂTEAUX

Bishopthorpe Rd, Middlethorpe YO23 2GB
☎ 01904 641241 📠 01904 620176
e-mail: info@middlethorpe.com
Dir: *from A1036 signed York (west), follow signs to Bishopthorpe and racecourse. Hotel on right just before racecourse*

This fine Georgian house, convenient for town and the racecourse, sits in acres of beautifully landscaped gardens. The bedrooms are all comfortably furnished and are split *continued* between the main house and converted stables set around an attractive courtyard. Public areas, in keeping with the style of the house, include a stately drawing room and an oak-panelled dining room, where carefully prepared seasonal fare is served. There is also a small spa facility adjacent to the hotel.

ROOMS: 29 en suite s £109-£155; d £165-£370 **LB**
FACILITIES: Spa STV Sauna Solarium Gym Jacuzzi Leisure Spa Xmas **CONF:** Thtr 56 Class 30 Board 25 Del from £170.38
SERVICES: Lift **PARKING:** 70 **NOTES:** No children 8yrs ⊗ in restaurant RS 25 & 31 Dec **CARDS:**

Top 200 – Hotel

★★★ ◎◎ The Grange

1 Clifton YO30 6AA
☎ 01904 644744 📠 01904 612453
e-mail: info@grangehotel.co.uk
web: www.grangehotel.co.uk
Dir: *on A19 York/Thirsk road, approx 500yds from city centre*

This bustling Regency town house is just a few minutes' walk from the centre of York. A professional service is efficiently delivered by caring staff in a very friendly and helpful manner. Public rooms are comfortable and have been stylishly furnished; these include two dining options, the popular and informal cellar brasserie and The Ivy that offers fine dining in a lavishly decorated environment. The individually designed bedrooms are comfortably appointed and have been thoughtfully equipped.
ROOMS: 30 en suite (6 GF) s £110-£190; d £115-£250 (incl. bkfst) **LB** **FACILITIES:** STV Discount at local health spa Xmas **CONF:** Thtr 50 Class 20 Board 24 Del from £153 **PARKING:** 26 **NOTES:** ⊗ in restaurant Civ Wed 90 **CARDS:**

> Popped the question?
> Hotels with Civ Wed in their entry are licensed for civil wedding ceremonies. Maximum numbers for the ceremony only are shown, e.g. Civ Wed 120

★★★77% Dean Court

Duncombe Place YO1 7EF
☎ 01904 625082 01904 620305
e-mail: info@deancourt-york.co.uk
web: www.deancourt-york.co.uk
Dir: *city centre opposite York Minster*

This smart hotel enjoys a central location overlooking the Minster. Public areas have been re-furbished in an elegant, contemporary style and include the popular D.C.H. restaurant which enjoys wonderful views of the cathedral. Bedrooms are smartly appointed. Service is particularly friendly and efficient and light snacks are served all day in Terry's conservatory café. Valet parking is offered.
ROOMS: 39 en suite (4 fmly) in 14 bedrooms s £75-£110; d £110-£190 (incl. bkfst) **LB** **FACILITIES:** ch fac Xmas **CONF:** Thtr 50 Class 24 Board 32 Del from £125 **SERVICES:** Lift **PARKING:** 30
NOTES: in restaurant Civ Wed 50
CARDS:

★★★73% Mount Royale
The Mount YO24 1GU
☎ 01904 628856 01904 611171
e-mail: reservations@mountroyale.co.uk
Dir: *W on A1036, 0.5 mile after racecourse. Hotel on right after lights*
This friendly hotel offers comfortable bedrooms in a variety of styles, several leading onto the delightful gardens. Public rooms include a lounge, a meeting room and a cosy bar. There is a separate restaurant and cocktail lounge, also overlooking the gardens, called Sous le Mont where all meals and drinks can be charged to your room account. A beauty therapist is available by appointment.
ROOMS: 24 en suite (2 fmly) (6 GF) s £85-£115; d £97.50-£150 (incl. bkfst) **LB** **FACILITIES:** STV supervised Solarium Beauty treatment centre, Outdoor Hot-tub Xmas **CONF:** Thtr 35 Board 22 Del from £135
PARKING: 24 **NOTES:** Closed 1-6 Jan
CARDS:

★★★73% Parsonage Country House
York Rd YO19 6LF
☎ 01904 728111 01904 728151
e-mail: reservations@parsonagehotel.co.uk
web: www.parsonagehotel.co.uk
(For full entry see Escrick)

★★★73% York Pavilion
45 Main St, Fulford YO10 4PJ
☎ 01904 622099 01904 626939
e-mail: reservations@yorkpavilionhotel.com
web: www.yorkpavilionhotel.com
Dir: *off A64 York ringroad at A19 junct towards York. Hotel 0.5m on right opposite filling station*
An attractive Georgian hotel situated in its own grounds. All the

continued on p662

YORK, continued

bedrooms are individually designed to a high specification; some are in the old house and some in the converted stables set around a garden terrace. There is a comfortable lounge, a conference centre and an inviting brasserie-style restaurant with a regularly changing menu.

York Pavilion, York

ROOMS: 57 en suite (4 fmly) (11 GF) ⊗ in 23 bedrooms s £90-£105; d £120-£150 (incl. bkfst) **LB** **FACILITIES:** STV Xmas **CONF:** Thtr 150 Class 60 Board 45 Del from £120 **PARKING:** 40 **NOTES:** ⊗ in restaurant Civ Wed 120 **CARDS:**

See advert onpage 661

★★★71% Kilima Hotel

129 Holgate Rd YO24 4AZ
☎ 01904 625787 📠 01904 612083
e-mail: sales@kilima.co.uk
web: www.kilima.co.uk
Dir: *on A59, on W outskirts*

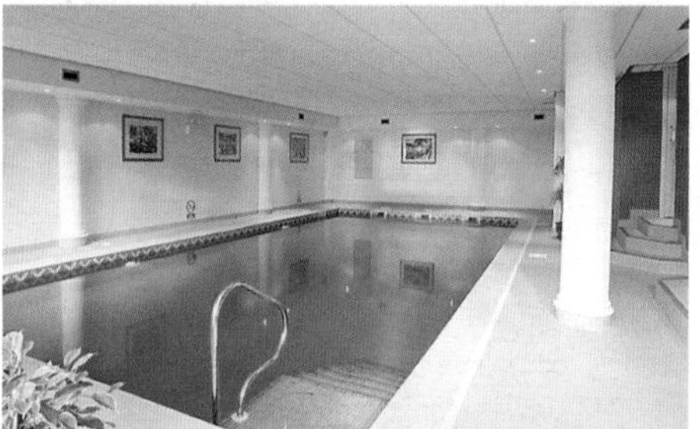

Kilima is conveniently situated within easy walking distance of the city centre. There is a relaxed and friendly atmosphere in the hotel, with professional, friendly staff providing attentive service. Bedrooms are comfortable and well equipped. The hotel benefits from private parking and leisure facilities.
ROOMS: 26 en suite (2 fmly) (10 GF) ⊗ in all bedrooms s £71.50; d £101-£131.50 (incl. bkfst) **LB** **FACILITIES:** STV Gym Leisure complex, Steam room, Fitness Suite ch fac Xmas **CONF:** Board 14 Del from £115 **PARKING:** 26 **NOTES:** ⊗ in restaurant
CARDS:

★★★70% Monkbar

Monkbar YO31 7JA
☎ 01904 638086 📠 01904 629195
e-mail: june@monkbarhotel.co.uk
Dir: *From A64 take A1079 to City, turn right at city wall, take middle lane at lights. Hotel on right*
This smart hotel enjoys a prominent position adjacent to the city walls, minutes' walk from the cathedral. Individually styled bedrooms are well equipped for both business and leisure guests. Spacious public areas include comfortable lounges, an American-style bar, an airy restaurant and impressive meeting and training facilities.

ROOMS: 99 en suite (3 fmly) ⊗ in 45 bedrooms s £98-£108; d £140-£175 (incl. bkfst) **LB** **FACILITIES:** STV ch fac Xmas **CONF:** Thtr 140 Class 80 Board 50 Del from £140 **SERVICES:** Lift **PARKING:** 70 **NOTES:** ⊗ in restaurant Civ Wed 65
CARDS:

★★★69% *The Gateway to York*

Hull Rd, Kexby YO4 5LD
☎ 01759 388223 📠 01759 388822
e-mail: enquiry@thegatewaytoyorkhotel.co.uk
web: www.thegatewaytoyorkhotel.co.uk
Dir: *off A64 onto A1079, 3m from York, hotel on left*

Close to York's 'Park & Ride' and the retail shopping outlet, this hotel is set in eight acres of gardens that has private fishing available for residents. Its spacious bedrooms are very comfortable and well equipped. There is a pleasant bar/lounge and a re-furbished restaurant serving interesting and enjoyable dishes.
ROOMS: 30 en suite (9 fmly) ⊗ in 23 bedrooms **FACILITIES:** STV Fishing **CONF:** Thtr 50 Class 30 Board 30 **PARKING:** 60 **NOTES:** ⊗ in restaurant Closed Jan **CARDS:**

★★★66% Minster Hotel

60 Bootham YO30 7BZ
☎ 01904 621267 📠 01904 654719
e-mail: info@yorkminsterhotel.co.uk
Dir: *from York outer ringroad A1237 exit A19 N into York Centre, hotel on right 150yds from Bootham Bar*
Now under new ownership this hotel is within easy walking distance of the Minster and the city centre. It is a careful conversion of two large Victorian houses refurbished to provide stylish, comfortable and well-equipped bedrooms. There is a cosy

continued

bar and a bistro serving imaginative dishes, and conference facilities are also available along with secure parking.
ROOMS: 31 en suite 3 annexe en suite (1 fmly) (5 GF) ⊗ in 31 bedrooms s £65-£85; d £75-£160 (incl. bkfst) **LB** **FACILITIES: Spa** STV Jacuzzi **CONF:** Thtr 65 Class 45 Board 30 Del from £125 **SERVICES:** Lift **PARKING:** 35 **NOTES:** ⊗ in restaurant
CARDS:

★★★66% Novotel York

Fishergate YO10 4FD
☎ 01904 611660 01904 610925
e-mail: H0949@accor-hotels.com
Dir: *A19 north to city centre, hotel set back on left*
Set just outside the ancient city walls, this modern, family-friendly hotel is conveniently located for visitors to the city. Bedrooms feature bathrooms with separate toilet, plus excellent desk space and sofa beds. Four rooms are equipped for less able guests. The hotel's facilities include indoor and outdoor children's play areas and an indoor pool.
ROOMS: 124 en suite (124 fmly) ⊗ in 91 bedrooms s fr £108; d fr £108 **LB** **FACILITIES:** STV **CONF:** Thtr 220 Class 100 Board 120 **SERVICES:** Lift **PARKING:** 150 **CARDS:**

★★71% Clifton Bridge

Water End YO30 6LL
☎ 01904 610510 01904 640208
e-mail: enq@cliftonbridgehotel.co.uk
web: www.cliftonbridgehotel.co.uk
Dir: *turn off A1237 onto A19 towards city centre. Right at lights by church, hotel 50yds on left*
Standing between Clifton Green and the River Ouse and within walking distance of the city, this hotel offers good hospitality and attentive service. The house is well furnished and features oak panelling in the public rooms. Bedrooms are attractively decorated and thoughtfully equipped. Good home cooking is served in the cosy dining room.
ROOMS: 14 en suite (1 fmly) (3 GF) ⊗ in 2 bedrooms s £45-£60; d £74-£95 (incl. bkfst) **LB** **CONF:** Board 12 Del from £50 **PARKING:** 16 **NOTES:** ⊗ in restaurant Closed 24-26 Dec **CARDS:**

★★71% Heworth Court

Heworth Green YO31 7TQ
☎ 01904 425156 01904 415290
e-mail: hotel@heworth.co.uk
web: www.visityork.com
Dir: *outer ring road towards Scarborough rdbt on NE side of York, exit onto A1036 Malton Rd, hotel on left*

Friendly and attentive service is provided at this family-owned hotel, conveniently located within walking distance of the city. Public rooms are comfortable and bedrooms are thoughtfully

continued

equipped. An extensive range of freshly prepared food is served in the Lamp Light Restaurant. Parking facilities are good.
ROOMS: 17 en suite 11 annexe en suite (2 fmly) (9 GF) ⊗ in 21 bedrooms s £52-£89.50; d £66-£124 (incl. bkfst) **LB** **FACILITIES:** STV Whisky bar Xmas **CONF:** Thtr 50 Class 24 Board 28 **PARKING:** 29 **NOTES:** ⊗ in restaurant **CARDS:**

See advert on inside back cover

★★71% Knavesmire Manor

302 Tadcaster Rd YO24 1HE
☎ 01904 702941 01904 709274
e-mail: knavesmire@tiscali.co.uk
web: www.knavesmire.co.uk
Dir: *A1036 into city centre. Hotel on right, overlooking racecourse*

Commanding superb views across York's famous racecourse, this former manor house offers comfortable, well-equipped bedrooms, either in the main house or the garden rooms to the rear. Comfortable day rooms are stylishly furnished, whilst the heated indoor pool provides a popular addition.
ROOMS: 11 en suite 9 annexe en suite (3 fmly) **FACILITIES:** Sauna Xmas **CONF:** Thtr 40 Class 36 Board 30 **SERVICES:** Lift **PARKING:** 28 **NOTES:** ⊗ in restaurant Civ Wed 60
CARDS:

★★70% Beechwood Close

19 Shipton Rd, Clifton YO30 5RE
☎ 01904 658378 01904 647124
e-mail: bch@selcom.co.uk
web: www.beechwood-close.co.uk
Dir: *on A19 (Thirsk Road, between ring road and city centre) on right entering 30mph zone*
This long-established, comfortable hotel, personally managed by the owners, is situated just a mile north of the city centre. It offers spacious, well-equipped and well-maintained bedrooms. There is a cosy bar-lounge, and wide-ranging menus in the dining room.
ROOMS: 14 en suite (2 fmly) s £45-£49; d £68-£80 (incl. bkfst) **LB** **FACILITIES:** STV **CONF:** Thtr 50 Class 40 Board 30 **PARKING:** 36 **NOTES:** Closed 25 Dec **CARDS:**

★★69% Alhambra Court

31 St Mary's, Bootham YO30 7DD
☎ 01904 628474 01904 610690
e-mail: enq@alhambracourthotel.co.uk
web: www.alhambracourthotel.co.uk
Dir: *off Bootham A19*
In a quiet side road within easy walking distance of the Minster, this attractive Georgian building is pleasantly furnished and the

continued on p664

Y

YORK, continued

bedrooms are well equipped. Service is cheerful and attentive, and good home cooking is a feature.

Alhambra Court, York

ROOMS: 24 en suite (4 fmly) (4 GF) ⊗ in 14 bedrooms s £39-£55; d £55-£90 (incl. bkfst) **LB FACILITIES:** ch fac **SERVICES:** Lift **PARKING:** 25 **NOTES:** ⊗ in restaurant Closed 24-31 Dec & 1-7 Jan **CARDS:**

★★68% The Groves

8 St Peters Grove, Clifton YO30 6AQ
☎ 01904 559777 📠 01904 627729
e-mail: groves@ecsyork.co.uk
web: www.ecsyork.co.uk
Dir: *off A19 at Clifton*

This hotel is peacefully situated on both sides of a quiet side road within easy walking distance of the city and the Minster. Bedrooms offer comfortable, well-equipped accommodation and are available in the main buildings or courtyard. Public areas are split between the two main buildings; dinner is served in the Acorn and Oak restaurant.

ROOMS: 17 en suite 27 annexe en suite (11 fmly) (13 GF) ⊗ in 10 bedrooms s £42; d £84 (incl. bkfst) **LB FACILITIES:** STV **CONF:** Thtr 25 Class 24 Board 26 Del £89 **PARKING:** 39 **NOTES:** ⊗ in restaurant RS 19 Dec-3 Jan **CARDS:**

★★67% Jacobean Lodge

Plainville Ln, Wigginton YO32 2RG
☎ 01904 762749 📠 01904 768403
Dir: *from M1/A1 take A64 York Rd, then A1237 and onto B1363 signed to Wigginton. Past sign for Wigginton & Haxby. Left at next major junct into Corban Lane & in 0.5m turn right at x-rds into Plainville Lane. Hotel 0.5m on right*

Now under new ownership, this comfortable inn stands in extensive lawned gardens amid open farmland along a quiet lane. The hotel provides comfortable well-equipped bedrooms. Home-cooked meals are available in the pleasant bars or the restaurant, which are well patronised by locals. Small conferences are also catered for.

ROOMS: 8 en suite s £40; d £65 (incl. bkfst) **LB FACILITIES:** Xmas **CONF:** Thtr 35 Class 20 Board 35 **PARKING:** 40 **NOTES:** ⊗ in restaurant **CARDS:**

★★66% Blue Bridge

Fishergate YO10 4AP
☎ 01904 621193 📠 01904 671571
e-mail: book@bluebridgehotel.co.uk
Dir: *from A64 outer ring road take A19 (York/Selby) south exit into York. Follow road for approx 2m, hotel on right.*

Convenient for the Barbican Centre and within walking distance of the city centre, this hotel provides pine-furnished bedrooms which include three spacious apartment rooms across the courtyard. Good value breakfast and dinner will satisfy the heartiest of appetites. Residents and diners have their own bar.

ROOMS: 18 rms (14 en suite) (1 fmly) ⊗ in all bedrooms s £45-£50; d £60-£95 (incl. bkfst) **LB FACILITIES:** STV ch fac Xmas **PARKING:** 15 **NOTES:** **CARDS:**

★★65% Lady Anne Middletons Hotel

Skeldergate YO1 6DS
☎ 01904 611570 📠 01904 613043
e-mail: bookings@ladyannes.co.uk
web: www.ladyannes.co.uk
Dir: *from A1036 towards city centre. Right at City Walls lights, keep left, 1st left before bridge, then 1st left into Cromwell Rd. Hotel on right*

This well furnished city-centre hotel has been created from several listed buildings and is very well located in the centre of York. Among its amenities are a bar-lounge and a dining room where a satisfying range of food is served, and an extensive fitness club.

ROOMS: 37 en suite 15 annexe en suite (3 fmly) ⊗ in 15 bedrooms s £80; d £115 (incl. bkfst) **LB FACILITIES:** supervised Sauna Solarium Gym No leisure facilities for under 16yrs ch fac **CONF:** Thtr 100 Class 30 Board 30 **PARKING:** 40 **NOTES:** ⊗ in restaurant Closed 24-29 Dec Civ Wed 30 **CARDS:**

Premier Lodge (York City Centre)

PREMIER LODGE.com

20 Blossom St YO24 1AJ
☎ 0870 9906594 📠 0870 9906595
web: www.premierlodge.com
Dir: *Just off A59*

High quality, modern, budget accommodation, ideal for families and business travellers. All rooms feature bath, power shower and satellite TV, and most have telephones / modem points. The adjacent bar and restaurant offers a wide and varied menu.

ROOMS: 86 en suite s £56; d £56

Travel Inn (York North West)

travel inn

White Rose Close, York Business Park, Nether Poppleton YO26 6RL
☎ 08701 977280 📠 01904 787633
Dir: *on A1237 between A19 Thirsk road & A59 Harrogate road*

Travel Inn offers good-quality, value-for-money accommodation. Spacious, en suite rooms with bath and shower comfortably accommodate a family of up to two adults and two children (to

continued

age 15). The restaurant and bar offers a varied menu. For further details consult the Hotel Groups page.

ROOMS: 44 en suite s £45.95-£48.95; d £45.95-£48.95

Travelodge (York Central)

Travelodge

90 Piccadilly YO1 9NX
☎ 08700 850 950 📠 01904 652171

Travelodge offers good quality, good value, modern accommodation. Ideal for families, the spacious, en suite bedrooms include remote-control TV, tea and coffee-making facilities and luxury beds. Meals can be taken at the nearby family restaurant. For further details consult the Hotel Groups page.
ROOMS: 90 en suite s fr £25; d fr £25

YOXFORD, Suffolk — Map 13 TM36

★★75% Satis House

IP17 3EX
☎ 01728 668418 📠 01728 668640
e-mail: yblackmore@aol.com
Dir: *off A12 between Ipswich & Lowestoft. 9m E Alderburgh & Snape*

A charming, privately owned hotel set in landscaped grounds just off the A12. The property was once frequented by Charles Dickens, and the name Satis House features in his novel *Great Expectations.* The spacious, individually decorated bedrooms are tastefully furnished and equipped with many thoughtful touches. Public areas include an elegant lounge, smart bar and a choice of dining rooms.
ROOMS: 8 en suite (1 GF) in 1 bedroom **FACILITIES:** Sauna Jacuzzi **CONF:** Thtr 22 Class 20 Board 14 **PARKING:** 30 **NOTES:** No children 7yrs in restaurant Closed 26-27 Dec, 2 wks Jan RS 25 Dec
CARDS:

Channel Islands

Directory of establishments in alphabetical order of location.

CHANNEL ISLANDS Map 24

GUERNSEY Map 24

CATEL Map 24

★★★70% Hotel Hougue du Pommier

Hougue du Pommier Rd GY5 7FQ
☎ 01481 256531 01481 256260
e-mail: hotel@houguedupommier.guernsey.net
web: www.hotelhouguedupommier.com
Dir: *turn inland from Cobo Village (coast road). Turn left at first junct. Hotel 50yds on right*

Retaining much of its original 18th-century character and charm, this hotel combines modern comforts with friendly yet efficient service. Bedrooms vary in size and standard, with exceptionally well-appointed and spacious deluxe rooms. An informal eating option is available in the beamed bar and the restaurant offers a carefully cooked, fixed-price menu.
ROOMS: 37 en suite 6 annexe en suite (5 fmly) in all bedrooms
FACILITIES: STV 6 Sauna **PARKING:** 50 **NOTES:** in restaurant **CARDS:**

See advert on opposite page

COBO Map 24

★★★74% Cobo Bay

Coast Rd GY5 7HB
☎ 01481 257102 01481 254542
e-mail: reservations@cobobayhotel.com
web: www.cobobayhotel.com
Dir: *from airport turn right, follow road to W coast at L'Eree. Turn right onto coast road for 3m to Cobo Bay. Hotel on right*

This very popular hotel, overlooking Cobo Bay, offers modern, well-equipped and tastefully decorated accommodation. Bedrooms at the front have balconies and there is a secluded sun terrace. Guests can enjoy the candle-lit restaurant and the Chesterfield bar with its leather sofas and armchairs. The Cobo Suite is available for private parties. Hospitality is a great strength here.
ROOMS: 36 en suite (4 fmly) s £44-£89; d £68-£118 (incl. bkfst) **LB**
FACILITIES: STV Snooker Sauna Jacuzzi **CONF:** Thtr 50 Class 30 Board 20 Del from £79 **SERVICES:** Lift **PARKING:** 60 **NOTES:** in restaurant Closed Jan-Feb **CARDS:**

FERMAIN BAY Map 24

★★★69% Le Chalet

GY4 6SD
☎ 01481 235716 01481 235718
e-mail: chalet@sarniahotels.com
Dir: *from airport left towards St Martins village. Right at filter to Sausmarez Rd, follow sign for Fermain Bay & Le Chalet Hotel*

Nestling in the wooded valley above the Fermain Bay, this family-run hotel is popular, and many guests return on a regular basis. Bedrooms vary in size and are tastefully furnished and decorated. The public areas include a panelled lounge, bar area, restaurant and a stunning sun terrace adjoining the small indoor leisure facility.
ROOMS: 40 en suite (5 fmly) s £50-£80; d £80-£110 (incl. bkfst) **LB**
FACILITIES: Sauna Solarium Jacuzzi Spa pool **PARKING:** 35
NOTES: in restaurant Closed mid Oct-mid Apr
CARDS:

FOREST Map 24

★★71% Le Chene

Forest Rd GY8 0AH
☎ 01481 235566 01481 239456
e-mail: info@lechene.co.uk
web: www.lechene.co.uk
Dir: *on south coast near airport.*

Within easy reach of the coast, this Victorian manor house is well located for guests wishing to explore Guernsey's spectacular south coast. The building has been skilfully extended to house a range of well-equipped, modern bedrooms. There is a swimming pool, a cosy cellar bar and a varied range of enjoyable freshly cooked dishes at dinner.
ROOMS: 26 en suite (2 fmly) s £28-£41; d £56-£82 (incl. bkfst) **LB**
FACILITIES: Xmas **PARKING:** 20 **NOTES:** No children 12yrs in restaurant **CARDS:**

PERELLE Map 24

★★★73% L'Atlantique

Perelle Bay GY7 9NA
☎ 01481 264056 01481 263800
e-mail: enquiries@perellebay.com
web: www.perellebay.com
Dir: *from airport, turn right and continue to sea. Turn right and follow coast road for 1.5m*

This modern seaside hotel, now under new ownership offers spectacular views of the sea and often, memorable sunsets. Bedrooms vary; those with sea views have balconies, and there are suites suitable for families. L'Atlantique Restaurant has an enviable reputation on the island, and the Victorian bar offers a less formal dining option.
ROOMS: 23 rms (21 en suite) (4 fmly) in 12 bedrooms s £40-£60; d £70-£120 (incl. bkfst) **LB** **FACILITIES:** STV **PARKING:** 80
NOTES: in restaurant Closed Nov-Mar
CARDS:

ST MARTIN Map 24

★★★75% La Barbarie
Saints Rd, Saints Bay GY4 6ES
☎ 01481 235217 01481 235208
e-mail: reservations@labarbariehotel.com
web: www.labarbariehotel.com

This former priory dates back to the 17th century and retains much of its charm and style. Staff provide a very friendly and attentive environment, and the modern facilities offer guests a relaxing stay. Menus provide excellent choices and fresh, local ingredients form the basis of the interesting dishes offered in the attractive restaurant and bar.
ROOMS: 22 en suite (4 fmly) (8 GF) in all bedrooms s £43-£59; d £58-£90 (incl. bkfst) **LB** **FACILITIES:** ch fac **PARKING:** 50
NOTES: in restaurant Closed 1 Nov- 25 Feb **CARDS:**

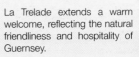

S

ST MARTIN, continued

★★★72% La Trelade

Forest Rd GY4 6UB
☎ 01481 235454 01481 237855
e-mail: latrelade@guernsey.net
web: www.latrelade.co.uk
Dir: *3m from St Peter Port, 1m from airport*
Having now undergone extensive refurbishment, this hotel offers a stylish and versatile range of public areas and an impressive leisure suite. Located close to the airport, La Trelade is an ideal base from which to explore the island, or equally suitable for business guests. Bedrooms and bathrooms are tastefully decorated and equipped to high standards with modern comforts.
ROOMS: 45 en suite (3 fmly) s £55-£57; d £90-£110 (incl. bkfst) **LB** **FACILITIES:** STV Sauna Gym **CONF:** Thtr 120 Class 48 Board 40 Del from £147 **SERVICES:** Lift **PARKING:** 80 **NOTES:** in restaurant
CARDS:

See advert on page 667

★★★71% *Bella Luce Hotel & Restaurant*

La Fosse GY4 6EB
☎ 01481 238764 01481 239561
e-mail: info@bellalucehotel.guernsey.net
web: www.bellalucehotel.guernsey.net
Dir: *from airport, turn left to St Martin. At 3rd set of lights continue 30yds, turn right, straight on to hotel*
This hotel dates back to the 12th century and much of its original charm and character remains. Located in an attractive area and set amidst well-tended gardens, this is a tranquil setting. Bedrooms are comfortable and individually styled, and public rooms are bright and tastefully decorated. Local produce features on the bar menu and also in the more formal dining room.
ROOMS: 31 en suite (5 fmly) **FACILITIES:** STV Sauna Solarium Gym equipment is available **PARKING:** 60 **NOTES:** in restaurant
CARDS:

See advert on page 667

★★★70% Hotel Jerbourg

Jerbourg Point GY4 6BJ
☎ 01481 238826 01481 238238
e-mail: hoteljerbourg@aol.com
Dir: *from airport turn left and follow road to St Martin village, right onto filter road, straight on at lights, hotel at end of road on right*
Situated at the end of a quiet lane, this hotel boasts excellent sea views, from its cliff-top location. The public areas are extensive and smartly appointed and include an extensive bar/lounge and bright conservatory-style restaurant. In addition to the fairly extensive carte, a daily-changing, fixed-price menu is available. Bedrooms are all well presented and comfortable, the newer luxury Bay rooms being generally more spacious.
ROOMS: 32 en suite (4 fmly) (5 GF) in all bedrooms s £45-£75; d £70-£145 (incl. bkfst) **LB** **FACILITIES:** STV **PARKING:** 50 **NOTES:** in restaurant Closed 27 Oct-25 Mar
CARDS:

★★★69% Green Acres

Les Hubits GY4 6LS
☎ 01481 235711 01481 235978
e-mail: greenacres@guernsey.net
Dir: *from airport, take road to St Martin. Turn off road leading to parish church, continue to hotel*
Quietly located in the leafy lanes of St Martin, this pleasant hotel is ideal as a base for a relaxing break. Bedrooms are comfortable and well equipped, and staff are friendly and attentive. The public areas include a stylish lounge which opens out onto the terrace pool area. Cuisine offers a choice of menus in different dining areas.
ROOMS: 43 en suite (3 fmly) s £30-£58; d £44-£92 (incl. bkfst) **LB** **FACILITIES:** Xmas **CONF:** Thtr 60 Class 35 Board 25 Del from £50 **PARKING:** 75 **NOTES:** in restaurant **CARDS:**

★★★68% La Villette

GY4 6QG
☎ 01481 235292 01481 237699
e-mail: reservations@lavillettehotel.co.uk
Dir: *turn left out of airport. Follow road past La Trelade Hotel. Take next right, hotel on left*
Set in spacious grounds, this peacefully located, family-run hotel has a friendly atmosphere. The well-equipped, refurbished bedrooms are spacious and comfortable. Live music is a regular feature in the large bar, while in the separate restaurant a fixed-price menu is provided. Residents have use of the excellent indoor leisure facilities.
ROOMS: 37 en suite (7 fmly) (14 GF) in all bedrooms s £38-£51.50; d £65-£90 (incl. bkfst) **FACILITIES:** Solarium Gym Jacuzzi Steam room Petanque Leisure suite Beauty salon hair dressers Xmas **CONF:** Thtr 80 Board 40 **PARKING:** 50 **NOTES:** in restaurant
CARDS:

★★74% Hotel La Michele

Les Hubits GY4 6NB
☎ 01481 238065 01481 239492
e-mail: info@lamichelehotel.com
Dir: *approx 1.5m from St Peter Port*
This family-run hotel provides a friendly environment and many guests return on a regular basis to this quiet and relaxing location. Bedrooms are particularly well equipped and comfortable. Public areas include a conservatory and cosy bar, and guests can relax in the well-tended gardens around the pool.
ROOMS: 16 en suite (3 fmly) (6 GF) s £39-£52; d £78-£104 (incl. bkfst & dinner) **LB** **FACILITIES:** **PARKING:** 16 **NOTES:** No children 10yrs in restaurant Closed Nov-Mar **CARDS:**

★★67% *Carlton*

Les Caches, Forest Rd GY4 6PR
☎ 01481 235678 01481 236590
e-mail: carltonhotel@cwgsy.net
Dir: *on road from airport to St Peter Port*

Conveniently located in St Martin, this newly upgraded hotel is within minutes of many of the island's superb cliff walks. The public areas are smart and inviting, particularly the new swimming pool and health centre. Meals can be taken in the main dining room or in a traditional-style pub, now all part of the hotel itself.
ROOMS: 41 en suite 2 annexe en suite (8 fmly) **FACILITIES:** Snooker Sauna Gym **CONF:** Thtr 150 Class 100 Board 30 **PARKING:** 40 **NOTES:** in restaurant Closed Nov-Etr wknd RS groups only in winter **CARDS:**

See advert on opposite page

ST PETER PORT Map 24

★★★★71% ◎ Old Government House Hotel
Ann's Place GY1 4AZ
☎ 01481 724921 📠 01481 724429
e-mail: ogh@guernsey.net
Dir: *at junction of St. Julians Avenue and College St.*

The affectionately known OGH is one of the island's leading hotels. Bedrooms vary in size but are comfortable and offer high-quality accommodation. The restaurant overlooks the town and neighbouring islands, and offers fine dining, while snacks are available in the Centenary bar. The varied leisure facilities, 'Beauty and The East', are well worth a visit.
ROOMS: 68 en suite (3 fmly) (1 GF) ⊗ in 30 bedrooms s £105-£235; d £140-£235 (incl. bkfst) **LB FACILITIES: Spa** STV Sauna Solarium Gym Jacuzzi Steam room, Eastern treatments, aerobics studio ch fac Xmas **CONF:** Thtr 300 Class 180 Board 90 Del from £145
SERVICES: Lift **PARKING:** 28 **NOTES:** Closed 2-9 Jan
CARDS:

★★★★66% ◎◎ St Pierre Park
Rohais GY1 1FD
☎ 01481 728282 📠 01481 712041
e-mail: info@stpierreparkhotel.com
Dir: *10 mins from airport. From harbour straight over rdbt, up hill through 3 sets of lights. Right at filter and continue to lights. Straight ahead, hotel 100mtrs on left*

Peacefully located in 45 acres of gardens and grounds on the outskirts of St Peter Port, this attractive hotel has its own golf course. Bedrooms include many that overlook the pleasant grounds and all have either balcony or terrace. Guests have a choice of two dining options. The lounge bar opens onto a spacious terrace, which overlooks an elegant water feature.
ROOMS: 131 en suite (4 fmly) ⊗ in 17 bedrooms s £130; d £170 (incl. bkfst) **LB FACILITIES:** STV 9 Snooker Sauna Solarium Gym Putt green Jacuzzi Bird watching, Childrens playground, Crazy golf ch fac Xmas **CONF:** Thtr 300 Class 120 Board 30 **SERVICES:** Lift
PARKING: 150 **NOTES:** **CARDS:**

★★★74% ◎◎ La Fregate
Les Cotils GY1 1UT
☎ 01481 724624 📠 01481 720443
e-mail: c.sharp@lafregatehotel.com
web: www.lafregatehotel.com
Ask for directions to this charming small hotel, which enjoys splendid views over the town and harbour from its elevated position. Bedrooms are comfortably furnished and well equipped; many have private balconies. The restaurant is popular with both residents and locals for its carefully cooked meals and formal yet efficient service.
ROOMS: 13 en suite s £85-£160; d £135-£180 (incl. bkfst) **LB**
CONF: BC Thtr 40 Class 24 Board 22 **PARKING:** 25 **NOTES:**
CARDS:

★★★73% Hotel de Havelet
Best Western
Havelet GY1 1BA
☎ 01481 722199 📠 01481 714057
e-mail: havelet@sarniahotels.com
web: www.havelet.sarniahotels.com
Dir: *from airport follow signs for St Peter Port through St. Martins. At bottom of 'Val de Terres' hill turn left into Havelet*
This extended Georgian hotel looks over the harbour to Castle Cornet. Many of the well-equipped bedrooms are set around a pretty colonial-style courtyard. Day rooms in the original building have period elegance; the restaurant and bar are on the other side of the car park in converted stables.
ROOMS: 34 en suite (4 fmly) ⊗ in 8 bedrooms s £65-£100; d £80-£130 (incl. bkfst) **LB FACILITIES:** STV Sauna Jacuzzi Xmas **CONF:** Thtr 40 Class 24 Board 26 Del from £90 **PARKING:** 40 **NOTES:**
CARDS:

S

ST PETER PORT, continued

★★★70% The Duke of Richmond

Cambridge Park GY1 1UY
☎ 01481 726221 🖷 01481 728945
e-mail: duke@guernsey.net
web: www.dukesofrichmond.com
Dir: *hotel on corner of Cambridge Park Rd and L'Hyvreuse Ave, opposite leisure centre*

Peacefully located in a predominantly residential area overlooking Cambridge Park, this hotel has comfortable, well-appointed bedrooms that vary in size. Public areas include a spacious lounge, a terrace and the unique Sausmarez Bar, with its nautical theme. The smartly uniformed team of staff provide professional standards of service.
ROOMS: 75 en suite (16 fmly) ⊗ in 35 bedrooms s £58-£150; d £90-£200 (incl. bkfst) **LB** **FACILITIES:** STV Leisure centre close to hotel Xmas **CONF:** BC Thtr 150 Class 50 Board 36 **SERVICES:** Lift **PARKING:** 7 **NOTES:** ⊗ in restaurant
CARDS:

★★★70% Moore's

Pollet GY1 1WH
☎ 01481 724452 🖷 01481 714037
e-mail: moores@sarniahotels.com

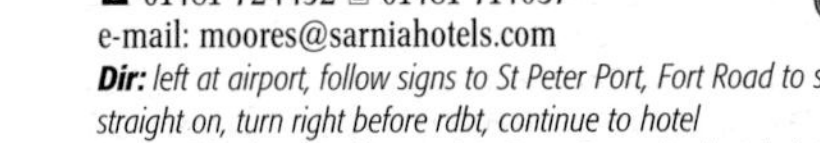

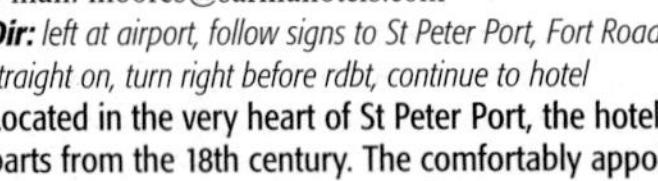

Best Western

Dir: *left at airport, follow signs to St Peter Port, Fort Road to seafront, straight on, turn right before rdbt, continue to hotel*
Located in the very heart of St Peter Port, the hotel dates back in parts from the 18th century. The comfortably appointed bedrooms vary in size and are priced accordingly. Attractive public areas include an Austrian patisserie, conservatory restaurant, library bar, health suite and carvery. Service is both attentive and friendly.
ROOMS: 46 en suite 3 annexe en suite (8 fmly) ⊗ in 12 bedrooms s £56-£95; d £74-£115 (incl. bkfst) **LB** **FACILITIES:** STV Sauna Solarium Gym Jacuzzi Xmas **CONF:** Thtr 40 Class 20 Board 18 Del from £85 **SERVICES:** Lift **NOTES:** **CARDS:**

★★62% Duke of Normandie

Lefebvre St GY1 2JP
☎ 01481 721431 🖷 01481 711763
e-mail: dukeofnormandie@cwgsy.net
web: www.dukeofnormandie-hotel-guernsey.com
Dir: *from harbour rdbt St Julians Ave, 3rd left into Anns Place, continue to right, up hill, then left into Lefebvre St, archway entrance on right*
Dating back to the 18th century, this hotel is perfectly located just a short stroll from the harbour and high street. Bedrooms tend to vary in size and comfort. The rooms surround a courtyard that also provides guest parking. Public areas include the very busy bar, now restored with beams and an open fireplace.
ROOMS: 20 en suite 17 annexe en suite (1 fmly) ⊗ in 13 bedrooms s £30-£45; d £60-£90 (incl. bkfst) **LB** **FACILITIES:** STV Xmas **CONF:** BC **PARKING:** 15 **NOTES:** ⊗ in restaurant
CARDS:

VALE Map 24

★★★63% Peninsula

Les Dicqs GY6 8JP
☎ 01481 248400 🖷 01481 248706
e-mail: peninsula@guernsey.net
Dir: *Coast Rd, Grand Havre Bay*
Adjacent to a sandy beach and set in five acres of grounds, this modern hotel provides comfortable accommodation. Bedrooms have additional sofa beds to suit families and good workspace for the business traveller. Both fixed-price and carte menus are served in the restaurant, or guests may eat more informally in the bar.
ROOMS: 99 en suite (99 fmly) (25 GF) ⊗ in 38 bedrooms s £52.50-£66; d £85-£112 (incl. bkfst) **LB** **FACILITIES:** STV Putt green Petanque Playground ♫ Xmas **CONF:** Thtr 250 Class 140 Board 105 Del from £94 **SERVICES:** Lift **PARKING:** 120 **NOTES:** ⊗ in restaurant **CARDS:**

HERM

★★76% White House

GY1 3HR
☎ 01481 722159 🖷 01481 710066
e-mail: hotel@herm-island.com
web: www.herm-island.com
Dir: *close to harbour*

Enjoying a unique island setting, this attractive hotel is just a twenty-minute boat trip from Guernsey. Set in well-tended gardens, it offers neatly decorated bedrooms, located in either the main house or adjacent cottages; the majority of rooms benefit from sea views. Guests can relax in one of several comfortable lounges, enjoy a drink in one of two bars and choose from the imaginative and ambitious dishes served in the Conservatory Restaurant or more informally from the Captain's Table menu in the Ship Inn.
ROOMS: 17 en suite 23 annexe en suite (23 fmly) (7 GF) s £67-£78; d £134-£198 (incl. bkfst & dinner) **LB** **FACILITIES:** no TV in bdrms Fishing trips, Yacht & Motor boat charters **CONF:** Board 10 **NOTES:** ⊗ in restaurant 2 Apr-2 Oct
CARDS:

> Packed in a hurry?
> Ironing facilities should be available at all star levels, either in rooms or on request

> Late for dinner?
> Quality Standards mean that last orders for dinner vary according to star rating and should be no earlier than:
> ★★ 7.00pm ★★★ 8.00pm ★★★★ 9.00pm
> ★★★★★ 10.00pm

S

JERSEY Map 24

GOREY Map 24

★★★68% *Old Court House*

JE3 9FS
☎ 01534 854444 01534 853587
e-mail: ochhotel@itl.net

Situated on the east of the island, a short walk from the beach, this long established hotel continues to have a loyal following for its relaxed atmosphere and friendly staff. Bedrooms are of similar standard throughout and some have balconies overlooking the gardens. Spacious public areas include a restaurant, a large bar with a dance floor and a comfortable, quiet lounge.

ROOMS: 58 en suite (4 fmly) (9 GF) **FACILITIES:** STV Sauna ♫ **SERVICES:** Lift **PARKING:** 40 **NOTES:** Closed Nov-Mar
CARDS:

★★★67% The Moorings

Gorey Pier JE3 6EW
☎ 01534 853633 01534 857618
e-mail: reservations@themooringshotel.com
web: www.themooringshotel.com
Dir: *at foot of Mont Orgueil Castle*

Enjoying an enviable position by the harbour, the heart of this hotel is the restaurant where a selection of menus offers an extensive choice of dishes. Other public areas include two bars and a comfortable first-floor residents' lounge. Bedrooms at the front have a fine view of the harbour; three of which have access to a balcony. A small sun terrace at the back of the hotel is also available for guests.

ROOMS: 15 en suite s £47-£62; d £94-£124 (incl. bkfst) **LB**
FACILITIES: STV ch fac Xmas **CONF:** Thtr 20 Class 20 Board 20
NOTES: **CARDS:**

ROZEL Map 24

Top 200 – Hotel

★★★ **Château la Chaire**

Rozel Bay JE3 6AJ
☎ 01534 863354 01534 865137
e-mail: res@chateau-la-chaire.co.uk

***Dir:** from St Helier on B38 turn left in village by the Rozel Bay Inn, hotel 100yds on right*

Built as a gentleman's residence in 1843, Château La Chaire is a haven of peace and tranquillity, set in a secluded wooded valley. Picturesque Rozel Harbour is within easy walking distance and the house is surrounded by terraced gardens. There is a wonderful atmosphere here and the helpful staff delivers high standards of guest care. Imaginative menus, making best use of local produce, are served in the oak-panelled dining room. Bedrooms are purposely varied, with a range of different sizes and styles available.

ROOMS: 14 en suite (1 fmly) s £99-£121; d £132-£251 (incl. bkfst) **LB** **FACILITIES:** STV Xmas **CONF:** Thtr 20 Class 20 Board 20 Del from £145 **PARKING:** 30 **NOTES:** No children 7yrs in restaurant Civ Wed 30 **CARDS:**

ST AUBIN Map 24

★★★74% **Somerville**

Mont du Boulevard JE3 8AD
☎ 01534 741226 01534 746621
e-mail: somerville@dolanhotels.com
web: www.dolanhotels.com

***Dir:** from village, follow harbour then take Mont du Boulevard and 2nd right bend*

Enjoying spectacular views of St Aubin's Bay, this friendly, long established hotel is popular with both leisure and business guests. Bedrooms vary in style with a number of superior rooms offering higher levels of luxury and wonderful views. Public areas are smartly presented and include a spacious bar lounge and elegant dining room, both of which take full advantage of the hotel's enviable position.

ROOMS: 59 en suite (7 fmly) (4 GF) s £41-£111; d £82-£148 (incl. bkfst) **FACILITIES:** STV Xmas **CONF:** Thtr 40 Class 25 Board 30 Del from £76 **SERVICES:** Lift **PARKING:** 26 **NOTES:** No children 4yrs in restaurant **CARDS:**

See advert on page 671

ST BRELADE Map 24

Top 200 – Hotel

★★★★ **The Atlantic**

Le Mont de la Pulente JE3 8HE
☎ 01534 744101 01534 744102
e-mail: info@theatlantichotel.com

***Dir:** from Petit Port, right into Rue de la Sergente & right*

Adjoining the manicured fairways of La Moye championship golf course, The Atlantic Hotel enjoys a peaceful setting with breathtaking views over St Ouen's Bay. Stylish bedrooms look out over golf course or sea and offer a blend of high quality and reassuring comfort. An air of understated luxury is apparent throughout, and the attentive service achieves the perfect balance of friendliness and professionalism. Lunch and drinks are available around the pool or on the terrace, and award-winning cuisine awaits at dinner.

ROOMS: 50 en suite (8 GF) s £145-£160; d £190-£220 (incl. bkfst) **LB** **FACILITIES:** STV Sauna Solarium Gym Jacuzzi Xmas **CONF:** Thtr 60 Class 40 Board 20 **SERVICES:** Lift **PARKING:** 60 **NOTES:** in restaurant Closed 5 Jan-5 Feb Civ Wed **CARDS:**

★★★★77% **Hotel L'Horizon**

St Brelade's Bay JE3 8EF HandPICKED
☎ 01534 743101 01534 746269
e-mail: lhorizon@handpicked.co.uk

***Dir:** 3m from airport. 6m from harbour*

A combination of a truly wonderful setting on the golden sands of

continued

St Brelade's Bay, a relaxed atmosphere and excellent facilities is the winning formula here. The bedrooms have all been stylishly decorated and are equipped with modern comforts and many thoughtful touches. Public areas are spacious and bright and include a leisure club and a choice of eating options, including the more formal Grill. Hand Picked Hotels - AA Hotel Group of the Year 2004-5.
ROOMS: 106 en suite (7 fmly) (15 GF) s £100-£115; d £200-£230 (incl. bkfst) **LB** **FACILITIES:** STV Sauna Gym Jacuzzi Windsurfing Water skiing Treatment rooms Xmas **CONF:** Thtr 250 Class 100 Board 50 Del from £110 **SERVICES:** Lift **PARKING:** 125 **NOTES:** Civ Wed **CARDS:**

See advert on this page

Town House Hotel
Country House Hotel
Travel Accommodation

★★★★71% Hotel La Place
Route du Coin, La Haule JE3 8BT
☎ 01534 744261 01534 745164
e-mail: reservations@hotellaplacejersey.com
web: www.hotellaplacejersey.com
Dir: *off main St Helier/St Aubin coast road at La Haule Manor (B25). Up hill, 2nd left (to Redhouses), 1st right. Hotel is 100mtrs on right*
Developed around a 17th-century farmhouse, this friendly hotel is well placed for exploration of the island. A range of bedroom types is provided, some rooms have private patios and direct access to the sheltered pool area. The stylish cocktail bar is popular for pre-dinner drinks and a more traditional lounge is available. An interesting menu is offered, making good use of local produce.

Hotel La Place

ROOMS: 42 en suite (1 fmly) in 25 bedrooms s £86-£118; d £130-£232 (incl. bkfst) **LB** **FACILITIES:** STV Sauna Discount at Les Ormes Country Club, including golf, gym & indoor tennis Xmas **CONF:** Thtr 120 Class 40 Board 40 **PARKING:** 100 **NOTES:** in restaurant Civ Wed 100 **CARDS:**

See advert on page 671

★★★★70% St Brelade's Bay Hotel
JE3 8EF
☎ 01534 746141 01534 747278
e-mail: info@stbreladesbayhotel.com
web: www.stbreladesbayhotel.com
Dir: *SW corner of the island*
Set adjacent to one of the most beautiful beaches on the island this newly refurbished family hotel offers a warm welcome.

continued on p674

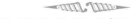

ST BRELADE, continued

Extensive facilities include a range of dining options, a heated outdoor pool set in impressive gardens, a tennis court and a croquet lawn. Many of the comfortable rooms feature king-size beds and stunning views across the bay.

St Brelade's Bay Hotel, St Brelade

ROOMS: 72 en suite (50 fmly) s £70-£105; d £100-£170 (incl. bkfst) **FACILITIES:** STV supervised Snooker Sauna Gym Putt green Petanque, Mini-gym, Games room, Table tennis ch fac **CONF:** Thtr 20 Board 12 Del from £125 **SERVICES:** Lift **PARKING:** 60 **NOTES:** in restaurant Closed 3 Oct-21 Apr **CARDS:**

★★★70% Golden Sands

St Brelade's Bay JE3 8EF
☎ 01534 741241 01534 499366
e-mail: goldensands@dolanhotels.com
web: www.dolanhotels.com
Dir: *follow signs to St Brelade's Bay. Hotel on coast side of road*

With direct access to the beach, this popular holiday hotel is centrally located overlooking the wonderful sandy expanse of St Brelade's Bay. Fortunately many of the comfortable bedrooms are sea-facing with balconies, thus many hours can be spent relaxing, breathing in the fresh air and looking out across the sands to the sea beyond! Public areas include a lounge, bar and restaurant, all of which look out over the bay.
ROOMS: 62 en suite (5 fmly) s £36-£78; d £72-£104 (incl. bkfst) **FACILITIES:** STV Childrens play room **SERVICES:** Lift **NOTES:** in restaurant Closed Nov-mid Apr **CARDS:**

See advert on page 671

★★71% Beau Rivage

St Brelade's Bay JE3 8EF
☎ 01534 745983 01534 747127
e-mail: beau@jerseyweb.demon.co.uk
web: www.jersey.co.uk/hotels/beau
Dir: *sea side of coast road in centre of St Brelades Bay, 1.5m S of airport*

With direct access to one of Jersey's most popular beaches, residents and non-residents are welcome to this hotel's bar and terrace. Most of the well-equipped bedrooms have wonderful sea views, some the bonus of balconies. Residents have a choice of lounges, plus a sun deck exclusively for their use. Between daily set menus and an extensive carte, a range of dishes featuring English and Continental cuisine is available each evening.
ROOMS: 27 en suite (9 fmly) in 1 bedroom s £48-£83; d £64-£134 (incl. bkfst) **LB** **FACILITIES:** STV Sunbathing terrace ch fac **SERVICES:** Lift **PARKING:** 16 **NOTES:** in restaurant RS Nov-Mar Civ Wed 80 **CARDS:**

ST HELIER

Map 24

★★★★69% De Vere Grand Jersey

The Esplanade JE4 8WD
☎ 01534 722301 01534 737815
e-mail: grand.jersey@devere-hotels.com

DE VERE HOTELS

An imposing Victorian building located on The Esplanade with bustling streets of St Helier to the rear and pleasant views across St Aubin's Bay to the front. Guests can enjoy interesting cuisine in the delightful Regency Restaurant with views of Elizabeth Castle. A full range of indoor leisure is available including pool, sauna, steam room, gym and many health and beauty treatments.
ROOMS: 118 en suite (7 GF) in 22 bedrooms **FACILITIES: Spa** STV supervised Snooker Sauna Solarium Gym Jacuzzi Beauty therapy, Hairdressing Xmas **CONF:** Thtr 200 Class 100 Board 80 Del from £140 **SERVICES:** Lift **PARKING:** 27 **NOTES:** in restaurant Civ Wed **CARDS:**

★★★70% Pomme d'Or

Liberation Square JE1 3UF
☎ 01534 880110 01534 737781
e-mail: enquiries@pommedorhotel.com
Dir: *opposite harbour*

This historic hotel overlooks Liberation Square and the marina, and offers comfortably furnished, well-equipped bedrooms. Popular with commercial guests, a range of conference facilities and meeting rooms are available. Dining options include the

continued

traditional fine dining of the 'Petite Pomme', the smart carvery restaurant or the informal coffee shop.
ROOMS: 143 en suite (3 fmly) in 72 bedrooms s £72-£102; d £104-£164 (incl. bkfst) **LB** **FACILITIES:** STV Use of Aquadome at Merton Hotel ch fac Xmas **CONF:** Thtr 220 Class 100 Board 50 Del from £125 **SERVICES:** Lift air con **NOTES:**
CARDS:

★★★67% Apollo

St Saviours Rd JE2 4GJ
☎ 01534 725441 01534 722120
e-mail: reservations@huggler.com
web: www.huggler.com
Dir: *on St Saviours Road at its junct with La Motte Street*

Centrally located, this popular hotel has a relaxed, informal atmosphere. Bedrooms are comfortably furnished and include useful extras. Many guests return regularly to enjoy the variety of leisure facilities including an outdoor pool with water slide and indoor pool with separate jacuzzi. The elegant cocktail bar is an ideal place for a pre-dinner drink.
ROOMS: 85 en suite (5 fmly) s £69-£79; d £92-£112 (incl. bkfst) **LB** **FACILITIES:** supervised supervised Sauna Solarium Gym Jacuzzi ch fac Xmas **CONF:** Thtr 150 Class 100 Board 80 **SERVICES:** Lift **PARKING:** 50 **NOTES:** **CARDS:**

★★★66% Beaufort

Green St JE2 4UH
☎ 01534 732471 01534 720371
e-mail: reservations@huggler.com
web: www.huggler.com
Dir: *5 mins walk from main shopping centre*

Within walking distance of the main business and shopping areas, the Beaufort is ideally located for all travellers. Every bedroom is spacious, with excellent facilities. Refurbishment of public areas has included the creation of 'Bohemia', a stylish bar/restaurant promoting the highly regarded cooking skills of Shaun Rankin,

continued

whilst steam and sauna rooms are now available in addition to the indoor and outdoor pools.
ROOMS: 54 en suite (4 fmly) s £96-£100; d £122-£138 (incl. bkfst) **LB** **FACILITIES:** supervised supervised Sauna Jacuzzi Steam room ch fac Xmas **CONF:** Thtr 30 Class 24 Board 14 Del from £150 **SERVICES:** Lift **PARKING:** 20 **NOTES:**
CARDS:

★★★66% Royal Yacht

The Weighbridge JE2 3NF
☎ 01534 720511 01534 767729
e-mail: theroyalyacht@mail.com
Dir: *in town centre, opp the Marina and harbour, 0.5m from beach*
Overlooking the marina and steam clock, the Royal Yacht is thought to be the oldest established hotel on the island. Bedrooms are generally spacious, soundproofed and thoughtfully equipped. There is something for everyone in the choice of dining options, with the traditional grill room, bar carvery and the first-floor restaurant which has views over the harbour.
ROOMS: 45 en suite s fr £67; d £89-£137 (incl. bkfst) **LB** **FACILITIES:** STV Xmas **CONF:** Thtr 80 Class 20 Board 20 **SERVICES:** Lift **NOTES:** Civ Wed 100
CARDS:

★★★62% Royal

Best Western

David Place JE2 4TD
☎ 01534 726521 01534 811046
e-mail: royal@bestwestern.co.uk
Dir: *follow signs for Ring Rd, pass Queen Victoria rdbt keep left, left at lights, left into Piersons Rd. Follow one-way system to Cheapside, Rouge Bouillon, at A14 turn to Midvale Rd, hotel on left*
This long established hotel is located in the centre of town and is within easy walking distance of the business district and shops. It provides individual bedrooms and a range of public areas. Dining choices include the No 27 Bar and Brasserie and the Henry VIII restaurant. The hotel also boasts extensive conference facilities.
ROOMS: 88 en suite (39 fmly) in 16 bedrooms d £85-£138 (incl. bkfst) **LB** **FACILITIES:** Xmas **CONF:** BC Thtr 400 Class 120 Board 80 Del from £125 **SERVICES:** Lift **PARKING:** 15 **NOTES:** Civ Wed 80 **CARDS:**

★★70% *Uplands*

St John's Rd JE2 3LE
☎ 01534 730151 01534 639899
e-mail: uplands@morvanhotels.com
web: www.morvanhotels.com/pages/uplands.html
Dir: *off main esplanade (A1) onto Pierson Rd by Grand Hotel, follow ring road for 200mtrs, 3rd on left into St John's Rd, hotel in 0.5m*
This hotel is set on twelve acres of farmland just one mile from the centre of St Helier. Bedrooms are modern, spacious and comfortable; some overlook the swimming pool while others having country views. Plenty of parking and spacious public areas add to the attraction of this friendly and popular hotel. Twelve self-catering cottages are also available.
ROOMS: 43 en suite (3 fmly) **FACILITIES:** STV **PARKING:** 44 **NOTES:** in restaurant **CARDS:**

ST LAWRENCE

Map 24

★★★69% Hotel Cristina

Mont Feland JE3 1JA
☎ 01534 758024 01534 758028
e-mail: cristina@dolanhotels.com
Dir: *turn off A10 onto Mont Felard, hotel on left*
From its hillside location, this hotel has impressive views of the bay, which can be enjoyed from most of the stylish bedrooms. Public

continued on p676

S

ST LAWRENCE, continued

areas reflect the contemporary style that makes this a refreshingly different hotel, with the modern restaurant serving a range of fresh produce in bistro-like atmosphere. The terrace is adorned with flowers and is a popular place for soaking up the sun.

Hotel Cristina, St Lawrence

ROOMS: 63 en suite (3 fmly) s £36-£77; d £72-£102 (incl. bkfst) **LB** **FACILITIES:** STV Off peak membership to Les Ormes Golf/Leisure Club **CONF:** Thtr 100 Class 70 **PARKING:** 60 **NOTES:** No children 4yrs in restaurant Closed Nov-Mar
CARDS:

See advert on page 671

ST MARY — Map 24

★★66% West View

La Grande Rue JE3 3BD
☎ 01534 481643 01534 483283
e-mail: westview@jerseymail.co.uk
web: www.westviewhoteljersey.com
Dir: *N of island, at junct of B33 & C103, rear of St Mary village*
Located in the quiet parish of St. Mary and close to the delightful walks and cycle routes of the north coast. Bedrooms here are well equipped especially the larger, superior rooms. Entertainment is provided in the lounge bar during the summer months when guests can also enjoy a swim in the heated outdoor pool.
ROOMS: 42 en suite (3 fmly) (18 GF) s £30-£44.50; d £54-£89 (incl. bkfst & dinner) **FACILITIES:** Xmas **PARKING:** 38 **NOTES:** in restaurant Closed 2 Jan-13 Mar **CARDS:**

ST SAVIOUR — Map 24

Top 200 – Hotel

★★★★ Longueville Manor

JE2 7WF
☎ 01534 725501 01534 731613
e-mail: info@longuevillemanor.com
web: www.longuevillemanor.com
Dir: *A3 E from St Helier towards Gorey. Hotel 1m on left*
Dating back to the 13th century, there is something very special about Longueville, which is why so many guests return here. It is set in 17 acres of grounds, including woodland walks, a spectacular rose garden and a lake. Bedrooms have great style and individuality, with fresh flowers, fine embroidered bed linen and plenty of extras. The committed staff create a welcoming atmosphere and every effort is made to ensure a memorable stay. The accomplished cuisine is a real delight.

ROOMS: 29 en suite 1 annexe en suite (7 GF) s £170-£180; d £210-£230 (incl. bkfst) **LB** **FACILITIES:** STV Xmas **CONF:** Thtr 45 Class 30 Board 30 Del from £247.50 **SERVICES:** Lift **PARKING:** 40 **NOTES:** Civ Wed 40
CARDS:

TRINITY — Map 24

★★★70% Highfield Country

Route d'Ebenezer JE3 5DT
☎ 01534 862194 01534 865342
e-mail: reservations@highfieldjersey.com
web: www.highfieldjersey.com
Dir: *on A8 next to Ebenezer Chapel*
Rurally located in landscaped gardens, this family-friendly hotel offers comfortable bedrooms and a relaxed atmosphere. Public areas are light and attractively styled, with the conservatory a popular venue for pre-dinner drinks. Leisure facilities include an indoor pool and sauna, and an outdoor pool with waterslide. A varied menu is provided at dinner, and breakfast is a self-service buffet.
ROOMS: 38 en suite (32 fmly) (1 GF) in all bedrooms s £62-£71; d £94-£112 (incl. bkfst) **LB** **FACILITIES: Spa** Sauna Gym Petanque ch fac **SERVICES:** Lift **PARKING:** 41 **NOTES:** in restaurant Closed Dec-Mar **CARDS:**

★★★70% Water's Edge

Bouley Bay JE3 5AS
☎ 01534 862777 01534 863645
e-mail: mail@watersedgehotel.co.je
Set in the tranquil surroundings of Bouley Bay on Jersey's north coast, this hotel is exactly as its name conveys and offers breathtaking views. Many of the bedrooms here have now been upgraded to offer high standards of quality and comfort. Dining options include the relaxed atmosphere of the adjoining Black Dog bar or the more formal award-winning restaurant.
ROOMS: 51 en suite (3 fmly) in 10 bedrooms **FACILITIES:** Sauna Solarium **CONF:** Thtr 30 Class 25 Board 20 **SERVICES:** Lift **PARKING:** 20 **NOTES:** in restaurant Closed 11 Oct-6 Apr Civ Wed **CARDS:**

Isle of Man

Directory of establishments in alphabetical order of location.

MAN, ISLE OF — Map 24

DOUGLAS — Map 24 SC37

★★★★72% Sefton
Harris Promenade IM1 2RW
☎ 01624 645500 Fax 01624 676004
e-mail: info@seftonhotel.co.im
web: www.seftonhotel.co.im
Dir: *500yds from Ferry Dock on Douglas promenade*

This Victorian hotel has been sympathetically extended and upgraded over recent years. Many of the spacious and comfortably furnished bedrooms have balconies overlooking the atrium water garden, whilst other boast sweeping views across the bay. A choice of comfortable lounges is available and freshly prepared dishes are served in the informal Gallery restaurant.
ROOMS: 100 en suite in 36 bedrooms s £63-£89; d £80-£106 (incl. bkfst) **LB** **FACILITIES: Spa** STV Sauna Solarium Gym Jacuzzi Cycle hire, Steam room, Atrium water garden, Library with free internet access. **CONF:** BC Thtr 100 Class 30 Board 20 Del from £140
SERVICES: Lift **PARKING:** 44 **NOTES:** No children
CARDS:

★★★★70% Mount Murray
Santon IM4 2HT
☎ 01624 661111 Fax 01624 611116
e-mail: hotel@mountmurray.com
web: www.mountmurray.com
Dir: *4m from Douglas towards airport. Hotel signed at Santon*

This large, modern hotel and country club offers a wide range of sporting and leisure facilities, and a health and beauty salon. The attractively appointed public areas give a choice of bars and eating options. The spacious bedrooms are well equipped and many enjoy fine views over the 200-acre grounds and golf course. There is a very large function suite.
ROOMS: 90 en suite (4 fmly) (28 GF) in 12 bedrooms s £60.50-£121; d £81.50-£240 (incl. bkfst) **FACILITIES: Spa** STV 18 Squash Sauna Solarium Gym Putt green Jacuzzi Bowling green, Driving range, Sports hall, Squash courts Xmas **CONF:** Thtr 300 Class 260 Board 100 Del from £125 **SERVICES:** Lift **PARKING:** 400 **NOTES:** in restaurant **CARDS:**

★★★69% Welbeck Hotel
13/15 Mona Dr IM2 4LF
☎ 01624 675663 Fax 01624 661545
e-mail: mail@welbeck.com
Dir: *at crossroads of Mona & Empress Drive off Central Promenade*
The Welbeck is a privately owned and personally run hotel situated within easy reach of the seafront. It offers guests a friendly welcome and a choice of attractive accommodation, ranging from well-equipped bedrooms to six newly constructed luxury apartments, each with its own lounge and small kitchen. Other facilities include two rooms for meetings and functions, plus a mini-gym and steam room.
ROOMS: 27 en suite (7 fmly) s £49-£65; d £66-£87 (incl. bkfst)
FACILITIES: STV Gym Steam room ch fac **CONF:** BC Thtr 50 Class 30 Board 30 Del from £74.50 **SERVICES:** Lift **NOTES:** Closed 19 Dec-5 Jan **CARDS:**

D

DOUGLAS, continued

★★★68% *Empress*

Central Promenade IM2 4RA
☎ 01624 661155 🖹 01624 673554
e-mail: empresshotel@manx.net
web: www.theempresshotel.net

This hotel is a large Victorian building on the central promenade, overlooking Douglas Bay. Well-equipped, modern bedrooms include suites, and rooms with sea views. A pianist entertains in the lounge bar most evenings. Other facilities available include a lounge, a sun lounge and a brasserie-style restaurant.
ROOMS: 102 en suite ⊗ in 6 bedrooms **FACILITIES:** STV Sauna Solarium Gym Jacuzzi ♫ **CONF:** BC Thtr 200 Class 150 Board 50 **SERVICES:** Lift **NOTES:** **CARDS:**

See advert on page 677

PEEL Map 24 SC28

★★70% *Ballacallin House*

THE INDEPENDENTS

Dalby Village, Patrick IM5 3BT
☎ 01624 841100 🖹 01624 845055
e-mail: ballacallin@advsys.co.uk
web: www.ballacallin.com
Dir: *A27 Peel to Port Erin Rd at S end of Dalby Village*
This small, privately owned hotel situated in Dalby village is personally run and offers well-equipped, modern accommodation of a very good standard. Bedrooms with four-posters and a two-bedroom suite are available. Sea views can be enjoyed from some of the bedrooms, the bright restaurant and the spacious lounge bar.
ROOMS: 10 en suite (1 fmly) ⊗ in all bedrooms **CONF:** Thtr 30 Class 24 Board 24 **PARKING:** 70 **NOTES:** ⊗ in restaurant Closed 5-25 Jan **CARDS:**

PORT ERIN Map 24 SC16

★★★67% Ocean Castle

The Promenade IM9 6LH
☎ 01624 836399 🖹 01624 836537
e-mail: oceancastle@btinternet.com
web: www.oceancastle.co.uk
This hotel is set overlooking the harbour, with spacious bedrooms enjoying views over the bay. It offers a choice of restaurants at weekends, with a combination of local menus with a French twist. A large function room is ideal for conference guests as well as those enjoying a family party.
ROOMS: 40 en suite (2 fmly) s £35; d £70 (incl. bkfst) **LB** **FACILITIES:** STV Ballroom ♫ **CONF:** Thtr 200 Class 150 Board 100 **SERVICES:** Lift **NOTES:** ⊗ in restaurant Closed Nov - before Easter **CARDS:**

★★65% Falcon's Nest

The Promenade IM9 6AF
☎ 01624 834077 🖹 01624 835370
e-mail: falconsnest@enterprise.net
web: www.falconsnesthotel.co.uk
Dir: *follow coastal road, S from airport or ferry. Hotel on seafront, immediately after steam railway station*
Situated overlooking the bay and harbour, this Victorian hotel offers generally spacious bedrooms. There is a choice of bars, one of which attracts many locals, and of dining options also. Meals can be taken in the lounge bar or in the attractively decorated main restaurant.
ROOMS: 35 en suite (9 fmly) ⊗ in 3 bedrooms s £43-£49; d £70-£85 (incl. bkfst) **LB** **FACILITIES:** STV ch fac **CONF:** Thtr 50 Class 50 Board 50 **PARKING:** 40 **CARDS:**

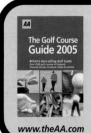

Nominations for
AA Hotel of the Year Award for Scotland
2004-2005

★★★★ 🏵🏵

Prestonfield

City of Edinburgh

★★★ 🏵🏵🏵

Glenapp Castle

Ballantrae, South Ayrshire

★★★ 🏵🏵

Kinloch House Hotel

Blairgowrie, Perth & Kinross

ABERDEEN, Aberdeen City Map 23 NJ90
See also Aberdeen Airport

★★★★78% The Marcliffe at Pitfodels

SLH

North Deeside Rd AB15 9YA
☎ 01224 861000 🖷 01224 868860
e-mail: enquiries@marcliffe.com
web: www.marcliffe.com
Dir: *turn off A90 onto A93 signed Braemar. 1m on right after turn at lights*

Set in attractive landscaped grounds west of the city, this impressive hotel presents a blend of styles backed by caring and attentive service. A split-level conservatory restaurant, terraces and courtyards all give a sense of the Mediterranean, whilst the elegant and sophisticated cocktail lounge is classical in style. Bedrooms are well-proportioned and thoughtfully equipped.
ROOMS: 40 en suite (2 fmly) (12 GF) ⊗ in 16 bedrooms s £115-£295; d £130-£295 (incl. bkfst) **LB** **FACILITIES:** STV Snooker Putt green Xmas **CONF:** Thtr 500 Class 300 Board 84 Del £210 **SERVICES:** Lift **PARKING:** 220 **NOTES:** ⊗ in restaurant Civ Wed 450
CARDS:

★★★★74% ❁❁ Ardoe House

South Deeside Rd, Blairs AB12 5YP
☎ 01224 860600 🖷 01224 861283
e-mail: ardoe@macdonald-hotels.co.uk
Dir: *4m W of city off B9077*

From its elevated position on the banks of the River Dee, this baronial-style mansion commands excellent countryside views. Tastefully decorated bedrooms are located in the main house, or more modern extension. Public rooms include an impressive leisure club, cosy lounge and cocktail bar with over 180 different malt whiskies.
ROOMS: 117 en suite (4 fmly) ⊗ in 86 bedrooms s fr £75; d fr £110 (incl. bkfst) **LB** **FACILITIES:** STV supervised Sauna Solarium Gym Jacuzzi Petanque Xmas **CONF:** Thtr 500 Class 200 Board 150 **SERVICES:** Lift **PARKING:** 250 **NOTES:** ⊗ in restaurant Civ Wed
CARDS:

★★★★67% Aberdeen Patio

Beach Boulevard AB24 5EF
☎ 01224 633339 & 380000 🖷 01224 638833
e-mail: patioab@globalnet.co.uk
web: www.patiohotels.com
Dir: *from A90 follow signs for city centre, then for sea. On Beach Blvd, turn left at lights, hotel on right*

Popular with both business and leisure guests, this modern, purpose-built hotel is close to the seafront and its many attractions. Bedrooms come in two different styles with the spacious Premier Club rooms particularly appealing. The conservatory-style restaurant holds regular themed dining nights and there is also a striking Atrium bar.
ROOMS: 124 en suite (8 fmly) (10 GF) ⊗ in 93 bedrooms s £45-£125; d £60-£135 (incl. bkfst) **LB** **FACILITIES:** STV supervised Sauna Solarium Gym Jacuzzi Steam room, Treatment Room Xmas **CONF:** Thtr 150 Class 80 Board 50 Del from £70 **SERVICES:** Lift **PARKING:** 196
NOTES: ⊗ in restaurant **CARDS:**

★★★★65% ❁❁
Copthorne Hotel Aberdeen

COPTHORNE

122 Huntly St AB10 1SU
☎ 01224 630404 🖷 01224 640573
e-mail: reservations.aberdeen@mill-cop.com
Dir: *W of city centre, off Union Street, up Rose Street, hotel 0.25m on right on corner with Huntly Street*

Set just out of the city centre, this hotel offers friendly, attentive service. The smart bedrooms are well proportioned and guests will appreciate the added quality of the Connoisseur rooms. Mac's bar provides a relaxed atmosphere in which to enjoy a drink or to dine informally, whilst Poachers Restaurant offers a fine dining experience.
ROOMS: 89 en suite (15 fmly) ⊗ in 37 bedrooms s £85-£170; d £85-£170 **LB** **FACILITIES:** STV **CONF:** Thtr 200 Class 100 Board 70 **SERVICES:** Lift **PARKING:** 20 **NOTES:** RS 25-26 Dec Civ Wed
CARDS:

A

★★★74% Atholl

54 Kings Gate AB15 4YN
☎ 01224 323505 📠 01224 321555
e-mail: info@atholl-aberdeen.co.uk
web: www.atholl-aberdeen.com
Dir: *in West End 400yds from Anderson Drive, the main ring road*

A high level of hospitality and guest care are features of this hotel, set in the suburbs within easy reach of central amenities and the ring road. The stylish modern bedrooms include Broadband internet access. Guests can choose between the restaurant and bar to enjoy the dinner menu.
ROOMS: 34 en suite (1 fmly) ⊗ in all bedrooms s £75-£95; d £100-£110 (incl. bkfst) **LB** **FACILITIES:** STV **CONF:** Thtr 60 Class 25 Board 25 Del from £125 **PARKING:** 60 **NOTES:** ⊗ in restaurant Closed 1 Jan **CARDS:**

★★★71% Norwood Hall

Best Western

Garthdee Rd, Cults AB15 9FX
☎ 01224 868951 📠 01224 869868
e-mail: info@norwood-hall.co.uk
web: www.norwood-hall.co.uk
Dir: *off A90, at 1st rdbt cross Bridge of Dee and turn left at rdbt onto Garthdee Rd (B&Q and Sainsbury on left) continue to hotel sign*

This imposing Victorian mansion has retained many of its features, most notably the fine oak staircase, stained glass and ornately decorated walls and ceilings. Accommodation comes in different styles with a major bedroom extension being undertaken. The extensive grounds ensure the hotel is a popular wedding venue.
ROOMS: 37 en suite (3 fmly) ⊗ in 15 bedrooms s £115-£155; d £115-£155 (incl. bkfst) **LB** **FACILITIES:** STV Xmas **CONF:** Thtr 200 Class 100 Board 70 Del from £165 **SERVICES:** Lift **PARKING:** 100 **NOTES:** ⊗ in restaurant Civ Wed 150
CARDS:

Bad hair day?
Hairdryers in all rooms three stars and above

★★★71% Queens Hotel

51-53 Queens Rd AB15 4YP
☎ 01224 209999 📠 01224 209009
e-mail: enquiries@the-queens-hotel.com
web: www.the-queens-hotel.com
Dir: *Turn off A90 from Anderson Drive at Queens Road, hotel is 400yds on right. From city centre take West End exit*

This well-established hotel, located a short drive from the city centre, is popular with both business travellers and for functions. Public areas include a welcoming lounge and a traditionally styled bar, where the restaurant menu is also available. Bedrooms, many of which are spacious and well equipped, are in the original house and a newly acquired wing.
ROOMS: 32 en suite 2 annexe en suite (6 fmly) (10 GF) ⊗ in 12 bedrooms s £50-£95; d £60-£105 (incl. bkfst) **FACILITIES:** STV **CONF:** Thtr 400 Class 150 Board 60 Del from £120.50 **PARKING:** 80 **NOTES:** ⊗ in restaurant Closed 25-26 Dec & 1-2 Jan Civ Wed 120
CARDS:

★★★70% The Craighaar

Waterton Rd, Bucksburn AB21 9HS
☎ 01224 712275 📠 01224 716362
e-mail: info@craighaar.co.uk
Dir: *turn off A96 (Airport/Inverness) onto A947, hotel signed*
Conveniently located for the airport, this welcoming hotel is a popular base for business people. Guests can make use of a quiet library/lounge, and enjoy meals in the bar or restaurant. Bedrooms are well equipped and a wing of galleried suites offer a lounge with an upstairs bedroom.
ROOMS: 55 en suite (6 fmly) (18 GF) ⊗ in 12 bedrooms s £45-£115; d £55-£125 (incl. bkfst) **LB** **FACILITIES:** STV Hotel Library **CONF:** BC Thtr 90 Class 33 Board 30 Del £110 **PARKING:** 80 **NOTES:** Closed 26 Dec & 1-2 Jan Civ Wed 50 **CARDS:**

★★★70% Westhill

Westhill AB32 6TT
☎ 01224 740388 📠 01224 744354
e-mail: info@westhillhotel.co.uk
web: www.westhillhotel.co.uk
Dir: *follow A944 W of city towards Alford. Hotel 6m on right*
Just a short drive from the city centre and airport, this comfortable business hotel has inviting public areas that include a choice of three contrasting bars and a smart fitness centre. Meals are available in both the lounge bar and the split-level brasserie. Bedrooms are modern in appointment and offer a good range of amenities.
ROOMS: 38 en suite (2 fmly) ⊗ in 8 bedrooms s £38-£75; d £46-£95 (incl. bkfst) **LB** **FACILITIES:** STV Sauna Solarium Gym ♫ Xmas **CONF:** Thtr 300 Class 200 Board 200 Del from £90 **SERVICES:** Lift **PARKING:** 150 **NOTES:** ⊗ in restaurant Civ Wed 100
CARDS:

A

ABERDEEN, continued

★★★68% ⊛ Maryculter House Hotel

South Deeside Rd, Maryculter AB12 5GB
☎ 01224 732124 📠 01224 733510
e-mail: info@maryculterhousehotel.com
web: www.maryculterhousehotel.com
Dir: *off A90 on S side of Aberdeen, onto B9077. Hotel 8m on right, 0.5m beyond Lower Deeside Caravan Park*

Set in grounds on the banks of the River Dee, this charming Scottish mansion dates back to medieval times and is now a popular wedding and conference venue. Exposed stonework and open fires feature in the oldest parts, which house the cocktail bar and Priory Restaurant. Lunch and breakfast are taken overlooking the river and bedrooms are equipped especially with business travellers in mind.
ROOMS: 23 en suite (1 fmly) (12 GF) ⊘ in 17 bedrooms s £45-£75; d £70-£95 (incl. bkfst) **LB** **FACILITIES:** STV Fishing Clay pigeon shooting, Archery Xmas **CONF:** BC Thtr 220 Class 100 Board 50 Del from £130 **PARKING:** 150 **NOTES:** ⊘ in restaurant Civ Wed 150
CARDS:

★★★65% Mariner

349 Great Western Rd AB10 6NW
☎ 01224 588901 📠 01224 571621
e-mail: marinerhotel@vagabond-hotels.com
Dir: *E off Anderson Drive at Great Western Road. Hotel on right on corner of Gray Street*
A good range of tasty meals is served in both the conservatory restaurant and lounge bar of this friendly family-run hotel, located near the town centre and airport. Smart modern bedrooms are well equipped, and there are four apartment-style rooms complete with kitchenettes, ideal for the long-stay guest.
ROOMS: 17 en suite 8 annexe en suite ⊘ in 18 bedrooms s fr £65; d fr £90 (incl. bkfst) **FACILITIES:** STV Xmas **PARKING:** 51 **NOTES:** ✈
CARDS:

> Early start?
> Hotels at all star levels should provide in-room alarm clocks and/or alarm calls

★★★64% *Grampian*

Stirling St AB11 6JU
☎ 01224 589101 📠 01224 574288
e-mail: gm.grampian@countrytown-hotels.co.uk
Dir: *From S follow signs to Centre, continue along riverside, left at rdbt onto South Market St, through 1st lights, left at next set then left onto Guild St and 1st right onto Stirling St, hotel on left*
The Grampian Hotel is set in the heart of the city, located close to the railway station. This hotel provides modern, well equipped accommodation, a library-style lounge and a bar and brasserie.

ROOMS: 49 en suite (3 fmly) **CONF:** Thtr 120 Class 60 Board 40
SERVICES: Lift **NOTES:** ⊘ in restaurant RS 25 Dec-3 Jan
CARDS:

★★69% *Dunavon House*

THE INDEPENDENTS

60 Victoria St, Dyce AB21 7EE
☎ 01224 722483 📠 01224 772721
e-mail: info@dunavonhousehotel.co.uk
Dir: *from A96 north to Inverness follow A947 into Victoria St, Dyce. Hotel 500yds on right*
Within easy reach of the airport, this hotel is housed in a sympathetically converted Victorian villa and is now under new ownership. Bedrooms, many of which have now been refurbished, are generally spacious and well laid out. An extensive range of meals is served in both the lounge bar and the restaurant.
ROOMS: 18 en suite (5 GF) ⊘ in 6 bedrooms **PARKING:** 23
NOTES: ✈ ⊘ in restaurant **CARDS:**

⌂ Premier Lodge (Aberdeen City Centre)

PREMIER LODGE.com

Inverlair House, West North St AB24 5AR
☎ 0870 9906300 📠 0870 9906301
web: www.premierlodge.com
Dir: *From A90, follow A9013 into Aberdeen city centre. Turn onto A966 towards King St and take the 1st left*
High quality, modern, budget accommodation, ideal for families and business travellers. All rooms feature bath, power shower and satellite TV, and most have telephones / modem points. The adjacent bar and restaurant offers a wide and varied menu.
ROOMS: 162 en suite s £52; d £52 **CONF:** Thtr 60

⌂ Premier Lodge (Aberdeen South West)

PREMIER LODGE.com

Straik Rd, Westhill AB32 6HF
☎ 0870 9906348 📠 0870 9906349
web: www.premierlodge.com
Dir: *6 miles from city centre on A944*
High quality, modern, budget accommodation, ideal for families and business travellers. All rooms feature bath, power shower and satellite TV, and most have telephones / modem points. The adjacent bar and restaurant offers a wide and varied menu.
ROOMS: 61 en suite s £46; d £46

⌂ Premier Lodge (Aberdeen West)

PREMIER LODGE.com

North Anderson Dr AB15 6DW
☎ 0870 9906430 📠 0870 9906431
web: www.premierlodge.com
Dir: *3m from city centre (5m from Aberdeen airport). From south, follow signs for airport. Lodge 1st left after fire station*
High quality, modern, budget accommodation, ideal for families

continued

and business travellers. All rooms feature bath, power shower and satellite TV, and most have telephones / modem points. The adjacent bar and restaurant offers a wide and varied menu.
ROOMS: 60 en suite s £46; d £46

Travel Inn (Aberdeen North)
Ellon Rd, Murcar, Bridge of Don AB23 8BP
☎ 08701 977012 📠 01224 706869
Dir: *From City Centre take A90 north. At roundabout, 1m past Exhibition Centre, turn left onto B999. Travel Inn is on the right*
Travel Inn offers good-quality, value-for-money accommodation. Spacious, en suite rooms with bath and shower comfortably accommodate a family of up to two adults and two children (to age 15). The restaurant and bar offers a varied menu. For further details consult the Hotel Groups page.
ROOMS: 40 en suite s £45.95-£46.95; d £45.95-£46.95

Travel Inn (Aberdeen South West)
Mains of Balquharn, Portlethen AB12 4QS
☎ 08701 977013 📠 01224 783836
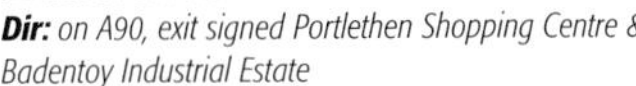
Dir: *on A90, exit signed Portlethen Shopping Centre & Badentoy Industrial Estate*
Travel Inn offers good-quality, value-for-money accommodation. Spacious, en suite rooms with bath and shower comfortably accommodate a family of up to two adults and two children (to age 15). The restaurant and bar offers a varied menu. For further details consult the Hotel Groups page.
ROOMS: 40 en suite s £45.95-£46.95; d £45.95-£46.95

Travelodge
9 Bridge St AB11 6JL
☎ 08700 850 950 📠 01224 584587
Travelodge offers good quality, good value, modern accommodation. Ideal for families, the spacious, en suite bedrooms include remote-control TV, tea and coffee-making facilities and luxury beds. Meals can be taken at the nearby family restaurant. For further details consult the Hotel Groups page.
ROOMS: 97 en suite s fr £25; d fr £25

Travelodge (Aberdeen West)
Inverurie Rd, Bucksburn AB21 9BB
☎ 08700 850 950 📠 01224 715609
Travelodge offers good quality, good value, modern accommodation. Ideal for families, the spacious, en suite bedrooms include remote-control TV, tea and coffee-making facilities and luxury beds. Meals can be taken at the nearby family restaurant. For further details consult the Hotel Groups page.
ROOMS: 48 en suite s fr £25; d fr £25

AA Rosette Award for culinary excellence

ABERDEEN AIRPORT, Aberdeen City — Map 23 NJ81

★★★★67% Aberdeen Marriott Hotel
Overton Circle, Dyce AB21 7AZ
☎ 01224 770011 📠 01224 722347
e-mail: reservations.aberdeen@marriotthotels.co.uk
Dir: *follow A96 to Bucksburn village, turn right at rdbt onto A947. Hotel after 2m at 2nd rdbt*
Close to the airport and conveniently located for the business district, this purpose-built hotel is a popular conference venue. The well-proportioned bedrooms come with many thoughtful extras. Public areas include an informal bar and lounge, a split-level restaurant and a leisure centre that can be accessed directly from a number of bedrooms.
ROOMS: 155 en suite (68 fmly) (61 GF) in 88 bedrooms s £110-£135; d £110-£135 **LB** **FACILITIES: Spa** STV supervised Sauna Solarium Gym Jacuzzi Xmas **CONF:** BC Thtr 400 Class 200 Board 60 Del from £120 **SERVICES:** air con **PARKING:** 180 **NOTES:** Civ Wed 120 **CARDS:**

Travel Inn (Aberdeen Dyce)

Burnside Dr, off Riverside Dr, Dyce AB21 0HW
☎ 08701 977304 📠 01224 772968
Dir: *from Aberdeen A96 towards Inverness, turn right at rdbt onto A947, at 2nd rdbt turn right then 2nd right*

Travel Inn offers good-quality, value-for-money accommodation. Spacious, en suite rooms with bath and shower comfortably accommodate a family of up to two adults and two children (to age 15). The restaurant and bar offers a varied menu. For further details consult the Hotel Groups page.
ROOMS: 40 en suite s £45.95-£46.95; d £45.95-£46.95

ABERDOUR, Fife Map 21 NT18

★★★65% Woodside

High St KY3 0SW
☎ 01383 860328 01383 860920
e-mail: reception@thewoodsidehotel.co.uk
Dir: *M90 junct 1, E on A291 for 5m, hotel on left on entering village*

This well-established hotel is popular with business travellers and enjoys a convenient location in the centre of the village. The Clipper Bar restaurant features a stained glass ceiling and wood panelling from the vessel 'Orontes', which sailed for the Orient Line in the early 1900s. Bedrooms, all named after Scottish clans, vary in size and style.
ROOMS: 20 en suite (1 fmly) s fr £58; d fr £75 (incl. bkfst) **LB**
FACILITIES: Xmas **CONF:** Thtr 80 Class 40 Board 40 Del from £102
PARKING: 40 **NOTES:** in restaurant Civ Wed 50
CARDS:

See advert on opposite page

★★65% The Aberdour Hotel

THE CIRCLE
Selected Individual Hotels
GREAT BRITAIN

38 High St KY3 0SW
☎ 01383 860325 01383 860808
e-mail: reception@aberdourhotel.co.uk
web: www.aberdourhotel.co.uk
Dir: *M90 junct 1, E on A921 for 5m. Hotel in centre of village opp post office*
This small hotel has a relaxed and welcoming atmosphere. Real ales are featured in the cosy bar where good value, home-cooked meals are available, as they are in the beamed dining room. Though all are well equipped, bedrooms vary in size and style, and those in the stable block are particularly comfortable. The hotel is in easy reach of Edinburgh by train.
ROOMS: 12 en suite 4 annexe en suite (4 fmly) (2 GF) s £40-£48; d £50-£65 (incl. bkfst) **LB** **FACILITIES:** STV **PARKING:** 8 **NOTES:** in restaurant **CARDS:**

ABERFELDY, Perth & Kinross Map 23 NN84

★★★63% Moness House Hotel & Country Club

Crieff Rd PH15 2DY
☎ 0870 443 1460 0870 443 1461
e-mail: info@moness.com
web: www.moness.com
Dir: *from A9, off at A827 to Aberfeldy. In village go through main square, left at lights onto A826 for hotel on left after 0.25m*
Part of a holiday ownership resort, this small hotel is set in extensive grounds. Accommodation is provided in generally spacious bedrooms a short walk away from the public rooms and leisure facilities. There is a choice of bars where meals are served in addition to the restaurant.

ROOMS: 12 en suite (1 fmly) s £41-£65; d £52-£100 (incl. bkfst) **LB**
FACILITIES: Squash Snooker Solarium Putt green Jacuzzi Badminton Indoor Bowls Pool Table Tennis Steam room ch fac Xmas
CONF: Thtr 120 Class 120 Board 50 Del from £67.50 **PARKING:** 12
NOTES: in restaurant Closed 2-9 Dec 2005 Civ Wed 120
CARDS:

See advert on opposite page

U Farleyer Restaurant & Rooms

Farleyer House PH15 2JE
☎ 01887 820332 01887 829879
e-mail: info@farleyer.com
Dir: *W on B846 beyond Castle Menzies*
At the time of going to press, the star classification for this hotel was not confirmed. Please refer to the AA internet site www.theAA.com for current information.
ROOMS: 6 en suite (1 fmly) (6 GF) in 5 bedrooms s £52-£65; d £85-£120 (incl. bkfst) **LB** **FACILITIES:** 6 Fishing Putt green rough shooting ch fac Xmas **PARKING:** 20 **NOTES:** in restaurant Civ Wed 200 **CARDS:**

ABERFOYLE, Stirling Map 20 NN50

★★★★65% Forest Hills

MACDONALD
HOTELS

Kinlochard FK8 3TL
☎ 01877 387277 01877 387307
e-mail: forest_hills@macdonald-hotels.co.uk
Dir: *3m W on B829*

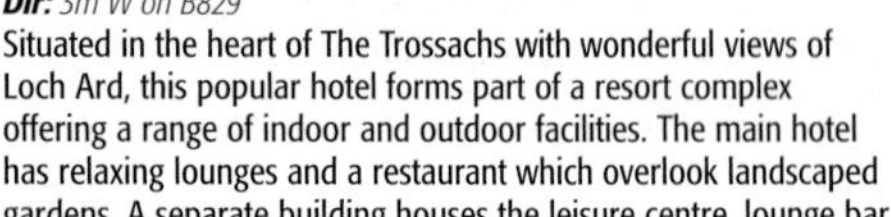

Situated in the heart of The Trossachs with wonderful views of Loch Ard, this popular hotel forms part of a resort complex offering a range of indoor and outdoor facilities. The main hotel has relaxing lounges and a restaurant which overlook landscaped gardens. A separate building houses the leisure centre, lounge bar and bistro.
ROOMS: 54 en suite (16 fmly) (12 GF) in 26 bedrooms s £80-£105; d £120-£170 (incl. bkfst & dinner) **LB** **FACILITIES:** Fishing Snooker Sauna Solarium Gym Putt green Jacuzzi Quad biking, Sailing, Canoeing, Abseiling, Archery, Mountain bikes, Guided walks ch fac Xmas
CONF: Thtr 150 Class 60 Board 45 Del from £125 **SERVICES:** Lift
PARKING: 80 **NOTES:** in restaurant Civ Wed 80
CARDS:

U Inchrie Castle Inn

FK8 3XD
☎ 01877 382347
e-mail: enquiries@inchriecastle.co.uk
At the time of going to press, the star classification for this hotel was not confirmed. Please refer to the AA internet site www.theAA.com for current information.

ABERLOUR See Archiestown

ABINGTON, South Lanarkshire Map 21 NS92

★★66% Abington Hotel

Abington By Biggar ML12 6SD

THE INDEPENDENTS

☎ 01864 502467 🖷 01864 502223
e-mail: info@ab-hotel.com
web: www.ab-hotel.com

Dir: *M74 junct 13 & follow signs into village or A702 S of Edinburgh at junct for M74 follow signs into Abington*

This family-run hotel is situated in the quiet village of Abington, close to Biggar and just off the M74 motorway. It makes a convenient stop-off and its central position makes it ideal for small meetings. Guests will find friendly attention, good comfortable accommodation, and wholesome meals at affordable prices.

ROOMS: 28 en suite (6 fmly) ⊗ in 19 bedrooms s £45-£55; d £65-£85 (incl. bkfst) **LB** **FACILITIES:** STV ♫ Xmas **CONF:** Thtr 60 Class 50 Board 50 Del from £70 **PARKING:** 30 **NOTES:** ⊗ in restaurant **CARDS:**

ABINGTON MOTORWAY SERVICE AREA (M74), South Lanarkshire Map 21 NS92

⇧ Days Inn

ML12 6RG
☎ 01864 502782 🖷 01864 502759
e-mail: abington.hotel@welcomebreak.co.uk
web: www.welcomebreak.co.uk

Dir: *M74 junct 13, accessible from N'bound and S'bound carriageways*

This modern building offers accommodation in smart, spacious and well-equipped bedrooms, suitable for families and business travellers, and all with en suite bathrooms. Continental breakfast is available and other refreshments may be taken at the nearby family restaurant. For further details see the Hotel Groups page.

ROOMS: 52 en suite s £35-£55; d £35-£55 **CONF:** Board 10 Del from £35

ALLOWAY, South Ayrshire Map 20 NS31

★★★76% Ivy House

KA7 4NL
☎ 01292 442336 🖷 01292 445572
e-mail: enquiries@theivyhouse.uk.com

Dir: *M74 junct 8, A71/A77 S, for approx 2m & follow signs for Burns National Heritage Park. Right along Doonholm Rd to T-junct. Right past Burns Cottage, hotel 300mtrs on left*

Situated almost next door to Burns' Cottage and overlooking the Bellisle Golf Course, this small boutique-style hotel provides friendly, personal service. A series of conservatories and lounge areas, plus a patio, give a feel of the Mediterranean and this

continued on p686

ALLOWAY, continued

A

influence extends to the food. Bedrooms are all individual and thoughtfully equipped.
ROOMS: 5 en suite in all bedrooms s £95-£125; d £110-£150 (incl. bkfst) **FACILITIES:** STV Xmas **CONF:** Thtr 50 Class 30 Board 24 **PARKING:** 48 **NOTES:** in restaurant Civ Wed 60
CARDS:

ALYTH, Perth & Kinross Map 23 NO24

Drumnacree House
St Ninian's Rd PH11 8AP
01828 632194 01828 632194
e-mail: derek@drumnacreehouse.co.uk
web: www.drumnacreehouse.co.uk
Dir: *take A926 from Blairgowrie, turn left into Alyth & left again at St Ninian's Rd at the church*
ROOMS: 6 en suite (2 fmly) in all bedrooms s £30-£40; d £60-£80 (incl. bkfst) **LB** **FACILITIES:** Xmas **PARKING:** 20 **NOTES:** YYYY in restaurant **CARDS:**

ANNANDALE WATER MOTORWAY SERVICE AREA (M74), Dumfries & Galloway Map 21 NY19

Travel Inn (Lockerbie Annandale Water)
Johnstonbridge DG11 1HD
08701 977163 01576 470644
Dir: *A74(M) - adjacent to J16. Accessible north and southbound*
Travel Inn offers good-quality, value-for-money accommodation. Spacious, en suite rooms with bath and shower comfortably accommodate a family of up to two adults and two children (to age 15). The restaurant and bar offers a varied menu. For further details consult the Hotel Groups page.
ROOMS: 42 en suite s £45.95-£46.95; d £45.95-£46.95

ARBROATH, Angus Map 21 NO64

★★65% ***Hotel Seaforth***
Dundee Rd DD11 1QF
01241 872232 01241 877473
e-mail: hotelseaforth@ukonline.co.uk
Dir: *on southern outskirts, on A92*

This long-established commercial hotel enjoys a seafront location close to many local amenities. Family-run, a welcoming and friendly atmosphere prevails. Spacious, thoughtfully equipped bedrooms all have smart, refurbished bedrooms. Public areas include a popular bar and restaurant that serves a range of good value meals.
ROOMS: 19 en suite (4 fmly) **FACILITIES:** Snooker Sauna Gym Jacuzzi Steam room ch fac **CONF:** Thtr 120 Class 60 Board 40 **PARKING:** 60 **NOTES:** in restaurant Civ Wed 120
CARDS:

ARCHIESTOWN, Moray Map 23 NJ24

★★78% **Archiestown**
AB38 7QL
01340 810218 01340 810239
e-mail: rml@archiestownhotel.co.uk
web: www.archiestownhotel.co.uk
Dir: *from A95 Grantown to Elgin road, at Craigellachie onto B9102. Archiestown is 4m from main road, hotel in village square*
This small, smart hotel is set in the heart of this attractive Speyside village, and is very popular with anglers. The owners are now promoting its charm and character to a broader market, with particular emphasis on food. The newly refurbished bedrooms and bathrooms are comfortable and well equipped.
ROOMS: 11 en suite s £30-£49; d £60-£98 (incl. bkfst) **LB**
PARKING: 18 **NOTES:** in restaurant Closed 24-27 Dec, 3 wks in Jan
CARDS:

ARDUAINE, Argyll & Bute Map 20 NM71

★★★76% **Loch Melfort**
PA34 4XG
01852 200233 01852 200214
e-mail: reception@lochmelfort.co.uk
web: www.lochmelfort.co.uk
Dir: *on A816, midway between Oban and Lochgilphead*

Enjoying one of the finest locations on the West Coast, this popular, family-run hotel has outstanding views across Asknish Bay towards the Islands of Jura, Scarba and Shuna. Accommodation is provided in either the balconied rooms of the Cedar wing or the more traditional rooms in the main hotel. Dinner can be enjoyed in both the informal Skerry Bistro and the restaurant.
ROOMS: 7 en suite 20 annexe en suite (2 fmly) in 11 bedrooms s £49-£79; d £78-£158 (incl. bkfst) **LB** **FACILITIES:** ch fac Xmas **CONF:** Thtr 50 Class 35 Board 24 Del from £80 **PARKING:** 65 **NOTES:** in restaurant **CARDS:**

ARDVASAR See Skye, Isle of

ARISAIG, Highland Map 22 NM68

★★72% **Arisaig**
PH39 4NH
01687 450210 01687 450310
e-mail: arisaighotel@dial.pipex.com
web: www.arisaighotel.co.uk
Dir: *on A830 opposite the harbour*
In the heart of a scenic highland village this hotel has super views towards the islands of Rhum, Eigg, Muck and Skye. Public rooms include a choice of bars, a traditional restaurant, lounge and a

continued

well-equipped children's playroom. Bedrooms vary in size but all are smartly appointed.
ROOMS: 13 en suite (2 fmly) ⊗ in all bedrooms s £35-£45; d £70-£90 (incl. bkfst) **LB** **PARKING:** 30 **NOTES:** ⊗ in restaurant Closed 24-26 Dec **CARDS:**

ARRAN, ISLE OF, North Ayrshire Map 20

BLACKWATERFOOT Map 20 NR92

★★★68% Kinloch

KA27 8ET
☎ 01770 860444 01770 860447
e-mail: reservations@kinlochhotel.eclipse.co.uk
Dir: *Ferry from Ardrossan to Brodick, follow signs for Blackwaterfoot, hotel in centre of village*

This family-run hotel overlooks the Mull of Kintyre. Spacious public areas include a choice of lounges, bars and good leisure facilities. Bedrooms offer mixed modern appointments and are gradually being upgraded. The main dining room offers a well-prepared and innovative four-course dinner menu, in addition to meals served in the bars.
ROOMS: 43 en suite (7 fmly) (7 GF) ⊗ in 24 bedrooms s £35-£51.50; d £70-£103 (incl. bkfst) **LB** **FACILITIES:** STV Squash Snooker Sauna Gym Beauty therapy ♫ ch fac Xmas **CONF:** Thtr 120 Class 20 Board 40 **SERVICES:** Lift **PARKING:** 2 **NOTES:** ⊗ in restaurant Civ Wed 60 **CARDS:**

BRODICK Map 20 NS03

★★★76% *Auchrannie Country House*

KA27 8BZ
☎ 01770 302234 01770 302812
e-mail: info@auchrannie.co.uk
Dir: *turn right from Brodick Ferry terminal, through Brodick village, 2nd left after Brodick Golf Course clubhouse, 300yds to hotel*
This Victorian mansion lies in landscaped grounds and provides well-equipped bedrooms. Dine in the 'Garden Restaurant' or the bistro, while a brasserie is also available in the extensive spa centre, which itself offers excellent family accommodation. Residents have their own leisure facilities but will be attracted to the superb spa set in the grounds.
ROOMS: 28 en suite (3 fmly) (4 GF) **FACILITIES: Spa** STV supervised Snooker Sauna Solarium Gym Hair salon Aromatherapy Shiatsu Hockey Badminton ch fac **CONF:** Thtr 120 Class 80 Board 50 **PARKING:** 50 **NOTES:** ⊗ in restaurant Civ Wed 120 **CARDS:**

For central reservation numbers and more information on Hotel Groups, turn to pages 33-39

Top 200 – Hotel

★★ Kilmichael Country House

Glen Cloy KA27 8BY
☎ 01770 302219 01770 302068
e-mail: enquiries@kilmichael.com web: www.kilmichael.com
Dir: *from Brodick ferry terminal follow N'bound (Lochranza) road for 1m. Left at golf course, inland between sports field & church, follow signs*
Reputed to be the oldest on the island, this lovely house lies in attractive gardens in a quiet glen less than five minutes' drive from the ferry terminal. It has been lovingly restored to create a stylish, elegant country house, adorned with ornaments from around the world. There are two inviting drawing rooms and a bright dining room, serving award-winning contemporary cuisine. The delightful bedrooms are furnished in classical style; some are contained in a pretty courtyard conversion.
ROOMS: 4 en suite 3 annexe en suite (6 GF) ⊗ in all bedrooms s fr £85; d £150-£190 (incl. bkfst) **LB** **FACILITIES:** STV Jacuzzi **PARKING:** 12 **NOTES:** No children 12yrs ⊗ in restaurant Closed Nov-Feb (ex for prior bookings) **CARDS:**

AUCHENCAIRN, Dumfries & Galloway Map 21 NX75

★★★76% Balcary Bay

DG7 1QZ
☎ 01556 640217 & 640311 01556 640272
e-mail: reservations@balcary-bay-hotel.co.uk
web: www.balcary-bay-hotel.co.uk
Dir: *on the A711 between Dalbeattie and Kirkcudbright, hotel on Shore road, 2m from village*

Taking its name from the bay on which it lies, this hotel has lawns running down to the shore. The larger bedrooms enjoy stunning views over the bay, whilst others overlook the gardens. Comfortable public areas invite relaxation. Imaginative dishes feature at dinner, accompanied by a good wine list.
ROOMS: 20 en suite (1 fmly) (3 GF) s £64; d £114-£138 (incl. bkfst) **LB** **PARKING:** 50 **NOTES:** ⊗ in restaurant Closed Dec-Jan **CARDS:**

AUCHTERARDER, Perth & Kinross Map 21 NN91

Top 200 – Hotel

★★★★★ The Gleneagles Hotel
PH3 1NF
01764 662231 01764 662134
e-mail: resort.sales@gleneagles.com
Dir: *off A9 at exit for A823 follow signs for Gleneagles Hotel*

With its international reputation for high standards, this grand hotel provides something for everyone. Set in a delightful location, Gleneagles offers a peaceful retreat, as well as many sporting activities, including the famous championship golf courses. Afternoon tea is a feature, and cocktails are prepared with flair and skill at the bar. Amongst the dining options is Strathearn, with two AA rosettes, as well as some inspired cooking at Andrew Fairlie at Gleneagles, a restaurant with four rosettes. Service is always professional, staff are friendly and nothing is too much trouble.

ROOMS: 270 en suite (115 fmly) (11 GF) in 149 bedrooms d £330-£465 (incl. bkfst) **LB** **FACILITIES: Spa** STV supervised 18 Fishing Squash Riding Snooker Sauna Solarium Gym Putt green Jacuzzi Falconry, Equestrian, Off roading, Golf range, Archery, Clay target shooting ch fac Xmas **CONF:** BC Thtr 360 Class 240 Board 60 Del from £355 **SERVICES:** Lift **PARKING:** 200 **NOTES:** Civ Wed 360 **CARDS:**

★★76% Cairn Lodge
Orchil Rd PH3 1LX
01764 662634 01764 662866
e-mail: info@cairnlodge.co.uk
web: www.cairnlodge.co.uk
Dir: *leave A9 at Gleneagles exit. Turn left on A823, pass entrance to Gleneagles Hotel and take 2nd turning towards Auchterarder on Orchil Rd*

This twin-turreted hotel stands in large grounds on the edge of the town. Bedrooms differ in style and size, with the newer rooms offering superb levels of quality and comfort. Public areas are smartly appointed and food can be enjoyed in either the informal atmosphere of the bar or the Capercaillie restaurant.

ROOMS: 10 en suite (6 fmly) (2 GF) **PARKING:** 30 **NOTES:** Civ Wed 30 **CARDS:**

AYR, South Ayrshire Map 20 NS32

★★★★71% Fairfield House
12 Fairfield Rd KA7 2AR
01292 267461 01292 261456
e-mail: reservations@fairfieldhotel.co.uk
Dir: *from A77 towards Ayr South (A30). Follow signs for town centre, down Miller Road and turn left then right into Fairfield Road*

Lying in a quiet street close to the esplanade, this hotel enjoys sea views towards to the Isle of Arran. Bedrooms offer either modern or classical styles, the latter featuring impressive bathrooms. Public rooms provide country house style. Enjoyable meals are served in either the brasserie or elegant restaurant.

ROOMS: 40 en suite 4 annexe en suite (3 fmly) in 7 bedrooms **FACILITIES:** STV supervised Sauna Solarium Gym Jacuzzi Xmas **CONF:** Thtr 80 Class 50 Board 40 **SERVICES:** Lift **PARKING:** 52 **NOTES:** in restaurant Civ Wed **CARDS:**

★★★76% Enterkine House
Annbank KA6 5AL
01292 521608 520580 01292 521582
e-mail: mail@enterkine.com
web: www.enterkine.com
Dir: *follow A77 to Ayr, then B743 Mossblown/Mauchline for hotel on Coylton Rd on outskirts of Annbank*

This gracious country mansion dates from the 1930s and retains many original features, notably the luxurious bathroom suites. The focus is very much on dining and in keeping with country-house tradition there is no bar, drinks being served in the elegant lounge and library. The well-proportioned bedrooms are furnished and equipped to high standards, many with lovely views over the countryside.

ROOMS: 6 en suite (1 fmly) s £75-£110; d £130-£150 (incl. bkfst) **LB** **FACILITIES:** STV Fishing Sauna Beauty treatments, golf, fishing, hunting ch fac Xmas **CONF:** BC Thtr 50 Class 30 Board 12 Del from £93.50 **SERVICES:** Lift **PARKING:** 20 **NOTES:** in restaurant Civ Wed 80 **CARDS:**

★★★72% Savoy Park
16 Racecourse Rd KA7 2UT
THE INDEPENDENTS
01292 266112 01292 611488
e-mail: mail@savoypark.com
Dir: *from A77 follow Holmston Road(A70) for 2m, through Parkhouse Street, turn left into Beresford Terrace, 1st right into Bellevue Rd*

This well-established hotel retains many of its traditional values. Public rooms feature impressive panelled walls, ornate ceilings and open fires. The restaurant is reminiscent of a Highland

continued

shooting lodge and offers a good-value menu to suit all tastes. The large superior bedrooms retain a classical elegance while others are smart and modern; all have lovely bathrooms.

ROOMS: 15 en suite (3 fmly) ⊗ in all bedrooms s £75-£85; d £95-£115 (incl. bkfst) **LB** **FACILITIES:** STV ch fac Xmas **CONF:** Thtr 50 Class 40 Board 30 Del from £100 **PARKING:** 60 **NOTES:** ⊗ in restaurant Civ Wed 100 **CARDS:**

See advert on this page

★★ Ladyburn
KA19 7SG
☎ 01655 740585 01655 740580
e-mail: jh@ladyburn.co.uk
(For full entry see Maybole)

Travel Inn
Kilmarnock Rd, Monkton KA9 2RJ
☎ 08701 977020 01292 678248
Dir: *on A77/A78 rdbt at Monkton, approx 2m from Prestwick Airport*

Travel Inn offers good-quality, value-for-money accommodation. Spacious, en suite rooms with bath and shower comfortably accommodate a family of up to two adults and two children (to age 15). The restaurant and bar offers a varied menu. For further details consult the Hotel Groups page.

ROOMS: 40 en suite s £45.95-£46.95; d £45.95-£46.95 **CONF:** Thtr 50 Board 20

BALLACHULISH, Highland — Map 22 NN05

★★★70% Ballachulish Hotel
PH49 4JY
☎ 0871 222 3415 0871 222 3416
e-mail: reservations@freedomglen.co.uk
web: www.freedomglen.co.uk
Dir: *on A828, Fort William-Oban road, 3m N of Glencoe*

A relaxed and welcoming atmosphere prevails at this long-established holiday hotel which overlooks Loch Linnhe. Bedrooms vary in size and in style and all are comfortably appointed. Inviting public areas include a spacious and comfortable lounge, the informal Ferry Bar and a cocktail bar adjacent to the bold and attractive restaurant.

Ballachulish Hotel

ROOMS: 54 en suite (4 fmly) s £52.50-£150; d £110-£280 (incl. bkfst & dinner) **LB** **FACILITIES:** Complimentary Membership of Leisure Club at nearby sister hotel ♫ ch fac Xmas **CONF:** Thtr 100 Class 50 Board 30 Del from £59.50 **PARKING:** 50 **NOTES:** ⊗ in restaurant Closed 9-23 Dec & 5-27 Jan **CARDS:**

BALLANTRAE, South Ayrshire Map 20 NX08

Top 200 – Hotel

★★★ ◎◎◎ Glenapp Castle
KA26 0NZ
☎ 01465 831212 📠 01465 831000
e-mail: enquiries@glenappcastle.com
web: www.glenappcastle.com
Dir: *1m from A77 near Ballantrae village*

RELAIS & CHATEAUX

This stunning Victorian castle is set in extensive, private grounds to the south of the village. The all-inclusive price covers a skilfully prepared five-course dinner with carefully selected wines, afternoon tea, and aperitifs and liqueurs. Impeccably furnished bedrooms are graced with antiques and period pieces and there are a number of spacious, luxurious suites. Breathtaking views of Arran and Ailsa Craig can be enjoyed from the bedrooms and the delightful day rooms. Nominated for the AA Hotel of the Year Award for Scotland 2004-5.

ROOMS: 17 en suite (2 fmly) (7 GF) ⊗ in all bedrooms s £255-£395; d £365-£515 (incl. bkfst & dinner) **FACILITIES:** 30 acres of beautifully tended gardens ch fac Xmas **CONF:** Thtr 17 Class 12 Board 17 Del from £293 **SERVICES:** Lift **PARKING:** 20 **NOTES:** ⊗ in restaurant Closed Nov-Mar (Open New Year) Civ Wed 34 **CARDS:**

Indoor Swimming Pool
Indoor Swimming Pool (heated)
Outdoor Swimming Pool
Outdoor Swimming Pool (heated)

BALLATER, Aberdeenshire Map 23 NO39

Top 200 – Hotel

★★★ ◎◎◎ Darroch Learg
Braemar Rd AB35 5UX
☎ 013397 55443 📠 013397 55252
e-mail: nigel@darrochlearg.co.uk
Dir: *on A93, at western side of Ballater*

Set high above the road in extensive wooded grounds, this hotel offers fine views over Royal Deeside. Bedrooms, some with four-poster beds, are individually styled, bright and spacious, especially the newly created suite. Food is a highlight of any visit, whether it is a freshly prepared breakfast, a light lunch or the award-winning Scottish cuisine served in the delightful conservatory restaurant.

ROOMS: 12 en suite 5 annexe en suite (1 GF) ⊗ in all bedrooms s £97.50-£135; d £155-£230 (incl. bkfst & dinner) **LB** **FACILITIES:** Xmas **CONF:** Thtr 25 Board 12 Del from £127.50 **PARKING:** 25 **NOTES:** ⊗ in restaurant Closed Xmas & Jan (ex New Year) **CARDS:**

Top 200 – Hotel

★★ ◎◎ Balgonie Country House
Braemar Place AB35 5NQ
☎ 013397 55482 📠 013397 55497
e-mail: balgoniech@aol.com
Dir: *off A93 on west outskirts of Ballater, hotel signed*

SCOTLAND'S HOTELS OF DISTINCTION

Genuinely warm hospitality is a feature of this delightful Edwardian house, set in well-tended gardens adjacent to the river and golf course. Accommodation is provided in thoughtfully equipped, well-maintained bedrooms. The cosy bar offers a wide selection of malt whiskies and there is a comfortable sitting room. Carefully prepared and interesting meals are prepared with skill.

ROOMS: 9 en suite s £65-£80; d £100-£140 (incl. bkfst) **LB** **FACILITIES:** Xmas **PARKING:** 12 **NOTES:** ⊗ in restaurant Closed 6 Jan-Feb **CARDS:**

★★73% ❀ Loch Kinord

THE CIRCLE *Selected Individual Hotels* GREAT BRITAIN

Ballater Rd, Dinnet AB34 5JY
☎ 013398 85229 🖷 013398 87007
e-mail: ask@kinord.com

Dir: *Between Aboyne & Ballater, on A93, in village of Dinnet*

Family-run, this roadside hotel lies between Aboyne and Ballater and is well-located for leisure and sporting pursuits. It has lots of character and a friendly atmosphere. There are two bars, one outside and a cosy one inside, plus a dining room in bold, stylish colour schemes. Food is well-promoted throughout the hotel.

ROOMS: 21 rms (19 en suite) (3 fmly) (4 GF) ⊗ in 5 bedrooms s £35-£55; d £50-£85 (incl. bkfst) **LB** **FACILITIES:** Sauna Jacuzzi Pool table Xmas **CONF:** Thtr 40 Class 30 Board 30 **PARKING:** 20 **NOTES:** ⊗ in restaurant Civ Wed 50 **CARDS:**

For central reservation numbers and more information on Hotel Groups, turn to pages 33-39

🅰 Cambus O'May

AB35 5SE ☎ 013397 55428 🖷 013397 55428
e-mail: mckechnie@cambusomay.freeserve.co.uk
web: www.cambusomayhotel.co.uk

Dir: *from Ballater follow A93 for 4m towards Aberdeen, hotel on left*

ROOMS: 12 en suite (1 fmly) s £32-£35; d £64-£70 (incl. bkfst) **LB** **PARKING:** 12 **NOTES:** ★★★ ⊗ in restaurant

BALLOCH, West Dunbartonshire — Map 20 NS38

★★★★★69% ❀❀❀

De Vere Cameron House

DE VERE HOTELS

G83 8QZ
☎ 01389 755565 🖷 01389 759522
e-mail: reservations@cameronhouse.co.uk
web: www.devereonline.co.uk/cameronhouse

Dir: *M8 (W) junct 30 for Erskine Bridge. Then A82 for Crainlarich. After 14m, at rdbt signed Luss straight on towards Luss, hotel on right*

Enjoying an idyllic location on the banks of Loch Lomond, this leisure-orientated hotel offers spacious, well-equipped accommodation. Bedrooms vary in size and style and many boast wonderful views of the loch. A choice of restaurants, bars and lounges, a host of indoor and outdoor sporting activities and a smart spa are just some of the facilities available. Dinner in the Georgian room is a highlight of any stay.

ROOMS: 96 en suite (9 fmly) ⊗ in all bedrooms s £150-£200; d £200-£495 (incl. bkfst) **LB** **FACILITIES: Spa** STV ⛳ 9 Fishing Squash Snooker Sauna Solarium Gym Jacuzzi Whole range of outdoor sports, Motor boat on Loch Lomond, Hair dressers ch fac Xmas **CONF:** Thtr 300 Class 80 Board 80 Del from £170 **SERVICES:** Lift **PARKING:** 200 **NOTES:** Civ Wed 200 **CARDS:**

See advert on this page

BALLOCH, continued

⌂ Innkeeper's Lodge Loch Lomond

Balloch Rd G83 8LQ
☎ 0870 243 0500 01389 752579
www.innkeeperslodge.com
Dir: *M8 junct 30 onto M898. Left at Duntocher rdbt onto A82, right at rdbt (A811), left into Daluart Rd, lodge opposite*
Smart rooms meet essential business requirements but also have home comforts, and depending on location may well have meeting rooms and pub dining. Dining options generally include all-day menus plus the added advantage of breakfast.
ROOMS: 14 rms (12 en suite) s £57.50-£59; d £57.50-£59

BALQUHIDDER, Stirling — Map 20 NN52

★★74% Monachyle Mhor

FK19 8PQ
☎ 01877 384622 📠 01877 384305
e-mail: info@monachylemhor.com
web: www.monachylemhor.com
Dir: *11m N of Callander on A84, turn right at Kingshouse Hotel and under A84 towards Balquhidder, hotel 6m on right*
A warm welcome and delicious food are assured at this country hotel, set in a 2000-acre estate and reached by a single-track road alongside Loch Voil. Bedrooms, including those in the rear courtyard, combine traditional furnishings with cutting-edge fixtures and fittings. The conservatory-style restaurant gives fine views across the glen, an ideal setting for the imaginative fixed-price menu.
ROOMS: 6 en suite 5 annexe en suite (2 GF) ⊗ in all bedrooms s £55-£150; d £95-£200 (incl. bkfst) **FACILITIES:** Fishing Grouse shooting, Hill walking, Deer Stalking, Petanque Pitch Xmas **CONF:** Board 10 Del from £142 **PARKING:** 20 **NOTES:** No children 12yrs ⊗ in restaurant Closed January Civ Wed 40 **CARDS:**

BANCHORY, Aberdeenshire — Map 23 NO69

★★★78% Raemoir House

Raemoir AB31 4ED
☎ 01330 824884 📠 01330 822171
e-mail: relax@raemoir.com
web: www.raemoir.com
Dir: *A93 to Banchory right onto A980, to Torphins, 2m at T-junct*

This country mansion dates from the mid-18th century and retains many period features. Individually designed bedrooms vary in size and layout, though all are well-equipped. Gracious public rooms include a choice of sitting rooms, a cocktail bar and a Georgian dining room. These rooms have tapestry-covered walls, open fires, and fine antiques.
ROOMS: 14 en suite 6 annexe en suite (1 fmly) s £60-£90; d £100-£130 (incl. bkfst) **LB** **FACILITIES:** 9 Putt green Shooting Stalking **CONF:** Thtr 45 Class 25 Board 30 **PARKING:** 100 **NOTES:** ⊗ in restaurant Civ Wed 40 **CARDS:**

★★★78% Tor-na-Coille

AB31 4AB
☎ 01330 822242 📠 01330 824012
e-mail: tornacoille@btinternet.com
web: www.tornacoille.com
Dir: *on A93 Aberdeen/Braemar road, opposite golf course.*

This fine granite-stone house sits in tree-studded grounds on the west side of the town. Bedrooms come in a variety of styles and sizes, many mirroring the period charm of the house. Inviting public areas include a lovely sitting room and an elegant restaurant.
ROOMS: 22 en suite (4 fmly) ⊗ in 17 bedrooms s £70-£80; d £100-£130 (incl. bkfst) **LB** **FACILITIES:** Squash ch fac **CONF:** Thtr 90 Class 60 Board 30 Del from £95 **SERVICES:** Lift **PARKING:** 130 **NOTES:** ⊗ in restaurant Closed 24-28 Dec Civ Wed 96 **CARDS:**

★★★75% *Banchory Lodge*

AB31 5HS
☎ 01330 822625 📠 01330 825019
e-mail: enquiries@banchorylodge.co.uk
Dir: *off A93, 13m W of Aberdeen, hotel is off Dee St*

This hotel enjoys a scenic setting in grounds by the River Dee. Inviting public areas include a choice of lounges, a cosy bar and a restaurant with views of the river. Bedrooms come in two distinct styles; those in the original part of the house contrasting with the newer wing rooms, which are particularly spacious.
ROOMS: 22 en suite (11 fmly) ⊗ in 10 bedrooms **FACILITIES:** Fishing Pool room **CONF:** Thtr 30 Class 30 Board 28 **PARKING:** 50 **NOTES:** ⊗ in restaurant Civ Wed 70 **CARDS:**

★★70% Burnett Arms

25 High St AB31 5TD
☎ 01330 824944 📠 01330 825553
e-mail: theburnett@totalise.co.uk
Dir: *town centre on N side of A93, 18m from centre of Aberdeen*
This popular hotel is located in the heart of the town centre and gives easy access to the many attractions of Royal Deeside. Public

continued

areas include a choice of eating and drinking options, with food served in the restaurant, bar and foyer lounge. Bedrooms are thoughtfully equipped and comfortably modern.

ROOMS: 16 en suite ⊗ in 5 bedrooms s £48-£65; d £65-£90 (incl. bkfst) **LB** **FACILITIES:** STV ch fac Xmas **CONF:** Thtr 100 Class 50 Board 50 Del from £89.50 **PARKING:** 40 **NOTES:** ⊗ in restaurant **CARDS:**

See advert under ABERDEEN

BANFF, Aberdeenshire Map 23 NJ66

★★★68% *Banff Springs*

Golden Knowes Rd AB45 2JE
☎ 01261 812881 01261 815546
e-mail: info@banffspringshotel.co.uk
Dir: *western outskirts of town on A98 Banff to Inverness road*

Attentive service by cheerful staff is a feature of this comfortable business and tourist hotel, which enjoys lovely sea views. Public areas include a smart foyer lounge and a popular bar/bistro, which provides an informal dining alternative to the restaurant. The bedrooms are spacious and comfortable.

ROOMS: 31 en suite **FACILITIES:** STV Gym **CONF:** Thtr 400 Class 100 Board 40 **PARKING:** 200 **NOTES:** ⊗ in restaurant Closed 25 Dec **CARDS:**

BARRA, ISLE OF, Western Isles Map 22

TANGASDALE Map 22 NF60

★★68% Isle of Barra

Tangasdale Beach HS9 5XW
☎ 01871 810383 01871 810385
e-mail: barrahotel@aol.com
Dir: *left from ferry terminal onto A888, hotel 2m on left*

Overlooking the white sands of Halaman Bay and the Atlantic Ocean beyond, this modern hotel enjoys a stunning location. Public areas, including a comfortable lounge and light and airy restaurant, make the most of the views, as do most of the bedrooms. The restaurant features superb local shellfish. Service is both friendly and attentive.

ROOMS: 30 en suite (2 fmly) (7 GF) s £42-£49; d £68-£84 (incl. bkfst) **LB** **FACILITIES:** STV Beach ch fac **CONF:** BC Thtr 70 Class 70 Board 60 Del from £57 **PARKING:** 50 **NOTES:** ⊗ in restaurant Closed mid Oct-Mar **CARDS:**

BEARSDEN, East Dunbartonshire Map 20 NS57

Premier Lodge (Glasgow North)

PREMIER LODGE.com

Milngavie Rd G61 3TA
☎ 0870 9906532 0870 9906533
web: www.premierlodge.com
Dir: *6m from the city centre. From east, exit M8 at junct 16. From west, exit at junct 17. Follow A81 signposted to Milngavie for Lodge on left*

High quality, modern, budget accommodation, ideal for families and business travellers. All rooms feature bath, power shower and satellite TV, and most have telephones / modem points. The adjacent bar and restaurant offers a wide and varied menu.

ROOMS: 61 en suite s £46; d £46

BEAULY, Highland Map 23 NH54

★★★72% Priory

The Square IV4 7BX
☎ 01463 782309 01463 782531
e-mail: reservations@priory-hotel.com
web: www.priory-hotel.com
Dir: *signed from A832, into Beauly, hotel in square on left*

This popular hotel occupies an enviable location in the town square. There are two standards of accommodation offered, with the executive rooms providing very high standards of comfort and facilities. A wide range of meals is served throughout the day in the open-plan public areas.

ROOMS: 34 en suite (3 fmly) ⊗ in 9 bedrooms s £42.50-£52.50; d £65-£85 (incl. bkfst) **LB** **FACILITIES:** STV Snooker ch fac Xmas **CONF:** BC Thtr 40 Class 40 Board 30 Del from £75 **SERVICES:** Lift **PARKING:** 20 **NOTES:** ⊗ in restaurant **CARDS:**

BIGGAR, South Lanarkshire Map 21 NT03

★★★73% Shieldhill Castle

Quothquan ML12 6NA
☎ 01899 220035 01899 221092
e-mail: enquiries@shieldhill.co.uk
web: www.shieldhill.co.uk
Dir: *off A702 onto B7016 Biggar to Carnwath Rd, after 2m turn left into Shieldhill Rd. Hotel 1.5m on right*

This imposing castle is set in rolling countryside and dates back almost 800 years. Public areas are atmospheric and include the high ceilinged Chancellor's restaurant and oak-panelled lounge. Bedrooms, many with oversized baths, are spacious. A friendly welcome is assured from both the enthusiastic staff and even the proprietor's dogs! Food is a highlight of any stay and uses local produce where possible.

ROOMS: 16 en suite ⊗ in all bedrooms s £95-£248; d £118-£190 (incl. bkfst) **LB** **FACILITIES:** Jacuzzi Cycling, Clay shoot, Hot air ballooning, laser shooting Xmas **CONF:** Thtr 500 Class 200 Board 250 Del from £150 **PARKING:** 50 **NOTES:** ⊗ in restaurant Civ Wed 200 **CARDS:**

BLACKWATERFOOT See Arran, Isle of

BLAIR ATHOLL, Perth & Kinross Map 23 NN86

★★71% Atholl Arms
Old North Rd PH18 5SG
☎ 01796 481205 🖷 01796 481550
e-mail: hotel@athollarms.u-net.com
web: www.athollarmshotel.co.uk
Dir: *off A9 to B8079, 1m into Blair Atholl, hotel near entrance to Blair Castle*
Set close to Blair Castle, this stylish hotel has welcoming public rooms that include a choice of bars, with the Bothy offering an extensive menu as an alternative to dinner served in the splendid baronial-style dining room. Bedrooms come in a range of sizes and styles; all have a good range of amenities.
ROOMS: 30 en suite (3 fmly) **FACILITIES:** Fishing Rough shooting **CONF:** BC Thtr 120 Class 80 Board 60 **PARKING:** 130 **NOTES:** ⊗ in restaurant **CARDS:**

★★62% Bridge of Tilt
Bridge of Tilt PH18 5SU
☎ 01796 481333 🖷 01796 481335
e-mail: hotels@theholidaygroup.com
Dir: *turn off A9 onto B8079, hotel 0.75m on left with wishing well in front*
Frequented by tour groups, this friendly hotel is situated close to Blair Castle. Bedrooms come in a variety of styles, with the chalet rooms being particularly popular. Public areas include a lounge, dining areas and a bar which offers live entertainment three times a week in season.
ROOMS: 20 en suite 7 annexe en suite (7 fmly) (7 GF) s £30-£35; d £40-£80 (incl. bkfst) **LB** **FACILITIES:** Jacuzzi ♫ Xmas **PARKING:** 40 **NOTES:** ⊗ in restaurant Closed Jan-Feb **CARDS:**

BLAIRGOWRIE, Perth & Kinross Map 21 NO14

Top 200 – Hotel

★★★ ◎◎ Kinloch House
PH10 6SG
☎ 01250 884237 🖷 01250 884303
e-mail: reception@kinlochhouse.com
Dir: *2m W of Blairgowrie on A923*
RELAIS & CHATEAUX.
The Allen family (formerly of Airds Hotel) has invested considerably in this idyllically located hotel. The result is elegantly furnished and inviting public areas that include a choice of lounges, a conservatory bar with an impressive range of malt whiskies and a beauty and fitness centre. Spacious bedrooms are stylishly appointed and many boast opulent bathrooms. Carefully prepared meals feature high quality, local produce. Nominated for the AA Hotel of the Year Award for Scotland 2004-5.
ROOMS: 18 en suite (1 fmly) (4 GF) s £95-£200; d £250-£330 (incl. bkfst & dinner) **LB** **FACILITIES:** Fishing Sauna Gym ch fac Xmas **CONF:** Thtr 16 Class 14 Board 20 Del from £151.50 **PARKING:** 36 **NOTES:** ⊗ in restaurant Closed 18 -29 Dec **CARDS:**

★★★62% Angus
Wellmeadow PH10 6NH
☎ 01250 872455 🖷 01250 875615
e-mail: reservations@theangushotel.com
Dir: *20 mins north of Perth. On A93 Perth/Blairgowrie Rd overlooking Wellmeadow in town centre*
Inside this traditional town centre building is an attractive modern hotel which is popular with visiting tour groups. Bedrooms are smartly furnished and come in a variety of sizes. There is a spacious bar lounge and a restaurant offering good value meals.
ROOMS: 81 en suite (4 fmly) s £35-£45; d £70-£90 (incl. bkfst) **LB** **FACILITIES: Spa** Sauna Solarium Table tennis, playstations ♫ ch fac Xmas **CONF:** Thtr 200 Class 100 Board 50 Del from £42 **SERVICES:** Lift **PARKING:** 62 **NOTES:** ⊗ in restaurant Civ Wed 180 **CARDS:**

BOAT OF GARTEN, Highland Map 23 NH91

★★★72% ◎◎ Boat
PH24 3BH
☎ 01479 831258 🖷 01479 831414
e-mail: info@boathotel.co.uk
web: www.boathotel.co.uk
Dir: *off A9 N of Aviemore onto A95, follow signs to Boat of Garten*
THE CIRCLE Selected Individual Hotels GREAT BRITAIN

In the heart of the Spey Valley, this Victorian station hotel is adjacent to the Strathspey Steam Railway. Bedrooms, all individually decorated, have been tastefully upgraded and comfortably appointed. The Capercaille Restaurant offers classic cuisine with a Scottish twist, whilst the warm cocktail bar has a selection of meals and specialises in a wide range of malt whisky.
ROOMS: 28 en suite (2 fmly) ⊗ in 22 bedrooms s £69.50-£155; d £109-£155 (incl. bkfst) **LB** **FACILITIES:** Snooker Golf course adjacent Xmas **CONF:** Thtr 50 Class 35 Board 25 Del from £105 **PARKING:** 36 **NOTES:** ⊗ in restaurant RS 3 wks Jan Civ Wed 60
CARDS:

BOTHWELL, South Lanarkshire Map 20 NS75

★★★67% Bothwell Bridge
89 Main St G71 8EU
☎ 01698 852246 🖷 01698 854686
e-mail: enquiries@bothwellbridge-hotel.com
web: www.bothwellbridge-hotel.com
Dir: *M74 junct 5 & follow signs to Uddingston, right at mini-rdbt. Hotel just past shops on left*
This red-sandstone mansion house is a popular business, function and conference hotel conveniently placed for the motorway. Most bedrooms are spacious and all are well equipped. The conservatory is now a bright and comfortable restaurant serving an interesting variety of meals with an Italian influence. The

continued

lounge bar offers a comfortable seating area and is popular as a local venue for coffee.
ROOMS: 90 en suite (14 fmly) (26 GF) in 53 bedrooms s £60-£68; d £70-£90 (incl. bkfst) **LB** **FACILITIES:** STV Xmas **CONF:** BC Thtr 200 Class 80 Board 50 Del from £82 **SERVICES:** Lift **PARKING:** 125 **NOTES:** Civ Wed 180 **CARDS:**

BRAE See Shetland

BRIDGEND OF LINTRATHEN, Angus Map 23 NO25

Restaurant with Rooms

Lochside Lodge & Roundhouse Restaurant

DD8 5JJ
☎ 01575 560340 01575 560202
e-mail: enquiries@lochsidelodge.com
web: www.lochsidelodge.com
Dir: *B951 from Kirriemuir towards Glenisla for 7m & take left turn to Lintrathen. Follow road over top of loch & into village. Hotel on left*

This converted farmstead enjoys a rural location in the heart of Angus. The comfortable bedrooms, which offer private facilities, are in the former hayloft and the original windows have been retained. Accomplished modern cuisine is served in the atmospheric Roundhouse restaurant. A spacious bar bedecked with agricultural implements and church pews features a wide range of drinks including local beers.
ROOMS: 4 en suite (1 fmly) s £45-£55; d £65-£75 (incl. bkfst) **CONF:** BC Class 20 Board 25 Del from £120 **PARKING:** 40 **NOTES:** in restaurant Closed 1-24 Jan RS Sun, Mon
CARDS:

BRIDGE OF ALLAN, Stirling Map 21 NS79

★★★71% Royal

Best Western

Henderson St FK9 4HG
☎ 01786 832284 01786 834377
e-mail: stay@royal-stirling.co.uk
web: www.royal-stirling.co.uk
Dir: *M9 junct 11, turn right at rdbt for Bridge of Allan. Hotel in centre on left*

This impressive Victorian building is a smart hotel offering a welcoming atmosphere and a fine dining experience. The bedrooms are comfortably modern in style and offer a good range of amenities. Public areas include an elegant restaurant serving innovative dishes and a bar providing a good range of bar meals.
ROOMS: 32 en suite (4 fmly) in 10 bedrooms s £55-£95; d £110-£140 (incl. bkfst) **LB** **FACILITIES:** STV Xmas **CONF:** Thtr 150 Class 60 Board 50 **SERVICES:** Lift **PARKING:** 40 **NOTES:** in restaurant Civ Wed 80 **CARDS:**

BRODICK See Arran, Isle of

BRORA, Highland Map 23 NC90

★★★72% Royal Marine

CLASSIC BRITISH

Golf Rd KW9 6QS
☎ 01408 621252 01408 621181
e-mail: info@highlandescape.com
web: www.highlandescape.com
Dir: *off A9 in village toward beach and golf course*

A distinctive Edwardian residence sympathetically extended, the Royal Marine attracts a mixed market. Its leisure centre is popular, and the restaurant, Hunters Lounge and café bar offer three contrasting eating options. A modern bedroom wing complements the original bedrooms, which retain their period style.
ROOMS: 22 en suite (1 fmly) s £75-£95; d £120-£150 (incl. bkfst) **LB** **FACILITIES:** 18 Fishing Snooker Sauna Solarium Gym Putt green Jacuzzi Ice curling rink in season Xmas **CONF:** Thtr 70 Class 40 Board 40 Del £125 **PARKING:** 40 **NOTES:** in restaurant
CARDS:

BROUGHTY FERRY, Dundee City Map 21 NO43

Premier Lodge (Dundee East)

PREMIER LODGE.com

115-117 Lawers Dr, Panmurefield Village DD5 3UP
☎ 0870 9906324 0870 9906325
web: www.premierlodge.com
Dir: *from north follow A92 Dundee to Arbroath. The Lodge is 1.5m past the group of 32 traffic lights, on right. From south, follow signs for A90 Perth to Dundee. At end of the dual carriageway follow signs for Dundee to Arbroath*

High quality, modern, budget accommodation, ideal for families and business travellers. All rooms feature bath, power shower and satellite TV, and most have telephones / modem points. The adjacent bar and restaurant offers a wide and varied menu.
ROOMS: 60 en suite s £44; d £44

BURNTISLAND, Fife Map 21 NT28

★★★63% Kingswood

Kinghorn Rd KY3 9LL
☎ 01592 872329 01592 873123
e-mail: rankin@kingswoodhotel.co.uk
web: www.kingswoodhotel.co.uk
Dir: *A921 coastal road at Burntisland, right at rdbt, left at T-junct, at bottom of hill to Kingshorn road, hotel 0.5m on left*

Lying in sheltered grounds east of the town, this hotel has views across the Firth of Forth to Edinburgh. Bedrooms are housed in a modern extension on the first floor. Public areas include a newly completed function suite, lounge bar and extended restaurant where good-value meals are served.
ROOMS: 13 en suite (3 fmly) (1 GF) in 2 bedrooms s £47-£66; d £76-£105 (incl. bkfst) **LB** **FACILITIES:** ch fac **CONF:** Thtr 150 Class 20 Board 40 Del from £80 **PARKING:** 50 **NOTES:** Closed 26 Dec & 1 Jan
CARDS:

BURNTISLAND, continued

★★68% Inchview Hotel
69 Kinghorn Rd KY3 9EB
☎ 01592 872239 01592 874866
e-mail: reception@inchview.co.uk
Dir: *on A921, adjacent to links and beach.*
A welcoming atmosphere prevails at this family-run hotel, a listed Georgian terraced house, which looks out over the links to the Firth of Forth. Bedrooms include two newly added family rooms housed in an adjacent building. A range of meals can be enjoyed in both the popular bar and elegant restaurant.
ROOMS: 12 en suite (1 fmly) ⊗ in 8 bedrooms s £42.50-£52.50; d £72.50-£82.50 (incl. bkfst) **LB** **FACILITIES:** ch fac Xmas **CONF:** Thtr 60 Class 20 Board 20 Del from £75 **PARKING:** 15
CARDS:

CAIRNDOW, Argyll & Bute — Map 20 NN11

★★65% Cairndow Stagecoach Inn
PA26 8BN
☎ 01499 600286 & 600252 01499 600220
e-mail: cairndowinn@aol.com

Dir: *from North, either A82 to Tarbet, then A83 to Cairndown or A85 to Palmally, A819 to Inveraray and A83 to Cairndown.*

A relaxed, friendly atmosphere prevails at this 18th-century inn, overlooking the beautiful Loch Fyne. Bedrooms offer individual décor and thoughtful extras. Traditional public areas include a comfortable beamed lounge, a well-stocked bar where food is served throughout the day, and a spacious restaurant with conservatory extension.
ROOMS: 13 en suite (2 fmly) ⊗ in 3 bedrooms s £35-£60; d £30-£70 (incl. bkfst) **LB** **FACILITIES:** Sauna Solarium Gym Xmas **PARKING:** 32
CARDS:

CALLANDER, Stirling — Map 20 NN60

★★★76% @@@ Roman Camp Country House
FK17 8BG
☎ 01877 330003 01877 331533
e-mail: mail@roman-camp-hotel.co.uk
Dir: *N on A84, turn left at east end of Callander High Street, then 300yd driveway into hotel grounds*
Originally a shooting lodge, this charming country house has a rich history. 20 acres of gardens and grounds lead down to the River Teith and the town centre and its attractions are only a short walk away. Food is a highlight of any stay and menus are dominated by high-quality Scottish produce that is sympathetically treated by the talented kitchen team. Real fires warm the atmospheric public areas and service is friendly yet professional.
ROOMS: 14 en suite (3 fmly) **FACILITIES:** Fishing **CONF:** Thtr 100 Class 40 Board 20 **PARKING:** 80 **NOTES:** ⊗ in restaurant
CARDS:

CANONBIE, Dumfries & Galloway — Map 21 NY37

★★65% Cross Keys
DG14 0SY
☎ 013873 71205 013873 71878
e-mail: sg.laverack@ukonline.co.uk web: www.crosskeys.biz
Located in the quiet village of Canonbie, this former 17th-century coaching inn is full of character. The hotel is family run, and guests will experience a welcoming and friendly atmosphere. Bedrooms are all individually appointed, comfortable and well equipped. The restaurant and public bar retain many original features and offer an interesting selection of freshly prepared dishes.
ROOMS: 10 rms (9 en suite) (1 fmly) s £35-£38; d £55-£58 (incl. bkfst) **PARKING:** 30 **NOTES:** ⊗ in restaurant **CARDS:**

CARNOUSTIE, Angus — Map 21 NO53

Kinloch Arms
27-29 High St DD7 6AN
☎ 01241 853127 01241 855183
Dir: *A92 towards Arbroath, take 1st sign for Carnoustie to main street. Hotel next to library*
ROOMS: 7 en suite (1 fmly) s fr £29.50; d fr £49 (incl. bkfst) **LB**
FACILITIES: STV Putt green **PARKING:** 28 **NOTES:** ★★
CARDS:

CARRBRIDGE, Highland — Map 23 NH92

★★★68% Dalrachney Lodge
PH23 3AT
☎ 01479 841252 01479 841383
e-mail: dalrachney@aol.com web: www.dalrachney.co.uk
Dir: *follow Carrbridge signs off A9. At the N end of the village on A938*
A traditional Highland lodge, Dalrachney lies in grounds by the River Dulnain on the edge of the village. Spotlessly maintained public areas include a comfortable and relaxing sitting room and a cosy well-stocked bar, which has a popular menu providing an alternative to the dining room. Bedrooms are generally spacious and furnished in period style.
ROOMS: 11 en suite (3 fmly) ⊗ in 7 bedrooms s £50-£75; d £90-£150 (incl. bkfst) **LB** **FACILITIES:** STV Fishing Xmas **PARKING:** 40
NOTES: ⊗ in restaurant **CARDS:**

CARRUTHERSTOWN, Dumfries & Galloway — Map 21 NY17

★★★68% Hetland Hall
DG1 4JX

☎ 01387 840201 01387 840211
e-mail: info@hetlandhallhotel.co.uk
web: www.hetlandhallhotel.co.uk
Dir: *midway between Annan & Dumfries on A75*

This well-established hotel is set in extensive parkland and is

continued

conveniently located just off the A75. Hetland Hall appeals to a wide market, including weddings and conferences. It offers well-equipped bedrooms in a variety of styles and sizes, all enhanced by attractive fabrics and furnishings.
ROOMS: 14 en suite 15 annexe en suite (5 fmly) (1 GF) ⊗ in 5 bedrooms s £65-£75; d £90-£105 (incl. bkfst) **LB** **FACILITIES:** STV Sauna Gym Putt green Mini Pitch & putt, Toning tables ch fac Xmas **CONF:** Thtr 200 Class 100 Board 100 Del from £85 **PARKING:** 60 **NOTES:** ⊗ in restaurant Civ Wed 150 **CARDS:**

CASTLECARY, Falkirk — Map 21 NS77

★★66% Castlecary House
Castlecary Rd G68 0HD
☎ 01324 840233 📠 01324 841608
e-mail: enquiries@castlecaryhotel.com
web: www.castlecaryhotel.com
Dir: *off A80 onto B816 between Glasgow and Stirling*
Close to the Forth Clyde Canal and convenient for the M80, this popular hotel provides a versatile range of accommodation, within purpose-built units in the grounds and also in an extension to the original house. The attractive and spacious restaurant serves a short carte menu and enjoyable meals are also served in the busy bars.
ROOMS: 60 rms (55 en suite) (2 fmly) s £60-£75; d £60-£75 (incl. bkfst) **CONF:** BC Thtr 60 **SERVICES:** Lift **PARKING:** 100 **NOTES:** Civ Wed 60 **CARDS:**

CASTLE DOUGLAS, Dumfries & Galloway — Map 21 NX76

★★67% Imperial
35 King St DG7 1AA
☎ 01556 502086 📠 01556 503009
e-mail: david@thegolfhotel.co.uk
web: www.thegolfhotel.co.uk
Dir: *off A75 at sign for Castle Douglas, hotel opp town library.*
Situated in the main street, this former coaching inn, popular with golfers, offers guests well-equipped and cheerfully decorated bedrooms. There is a choice of bars and good-value meals are served either in the foyer bar or the upstairs dining room.
ROOMS: 12 en suite (1 fmly) ⊗ in 6 bedrooms s £40-£50; d £62-£70 (incl. bkfst) **LB** **FACILITIES:** local pool and sauna/gym 75 yds away ch fac **CONF:** Thtr 40 Class 20 Board 20 **PARKING:** 29 **NOTES:** ⊗ in restaurant Closed 23-26 Dec & 1-3 Jan **CARDS:**

★★67% King's Arms
St Andrew's St DG7 1EL
☎ 01556 502626 📠 01556 502097
e-mail: david@galloway-golf.co.uk
Dir: *through main street, left at town clock, hotel on corner*
The King's Arms Hotel is a former coaching inn and boasts a traditional and comfortable interior. Cosy day rooms include a choice of bar areas and a restaurant overlooking an ivy-clad courtyard. Creative menus are offered in both the bar and the restaurant.
ROOMS: 10 rms (9 en suite) (2 fmly) ⊗ in 3 bedrooms s £40-£50; d £62-£68 (incl. bkfst) **LB** **CONF:** Thtr 35 Class 20 Board 25 **PARKING:** 15 **NOTES:** ⊗ in restaurant Closed 25-26 Dec & 1-2 Jan **CARDS:**

CASTLE KENNEDY, Dumfries & Galloway — Map 20 NX15

★★65% The Plantings Inn
DG9 8SQ
☎ 01581 400633 📠 01581 400637
e-mail: info@plantings.com
Convenient for Stranraer and the Irish ferries, this small hotel focuses on an pleasantly informal eating operation with a

continued

wide-ranging menu that offers hearty good-value dishes. Bedrooms are smartly furnished.
ROOMS: 5 en suite ⊗ in all bedrooms s £35; d £60 (incl. bkfst) **LB** **FACILITIES:** Xmas **CONF:** Thtr 30 Class 16 Board 16 **PARKING:** 30 **NOTES:** Civ Wed 40 **CARDS:**

CHIRNSIDE, Scottish Borders — Map 21 NT85

★★★68% Chirnside Hall
TD11 3LD
☎ 01890 818219 📠 01890 818231
e-mail: chirnsidehall@globalnet.co.uk
Dir: *on A6105 Berwick on Tweed/Duns road approx 3m after Foulden. Hotel sign on right*
At the end of a tree-lined drive this hotel is ideal for guests wishing to get away from the hustle and bustle of life. Bedrooms are spacious, many with views of the rolling Borders countryside. Real fires warm the elegantly styled lounges and fresh local produce features on the restaurant menus.
ROOMS: 10 en suite (2 fmly) s £85-£140; d £140-£155 (incl. bkfst) **LB** **FACILITIES:** Fishing Snooker Gym Putt green Shooting ch fac Xmas **CONF:** Board 16 **PARKING:** 20 **NOTES:** ⊗ in restaurant Civ Wed 40 **CARDS:**

CLACHAN, Argyll & Bute — Map 20 NR75

A Balinakill Country House
PA29 6XL
☎ 01880 740206 📠 01880 740298
e-mail: info@balinakill.com
Dir: *access from A83, 50mtrs beyond the Thames Garage in Clachan*
ROOMS: 10 en suite (2 GF) ⊗ in all bedrooms s £42; d £80-£90 (incl. bkfst) **LB** **FACILITIES:** Fishing Aromatherapy, Reflexology, Relaxing health treatments Xmas **PARKING:** 20 **NOTES:** ★★★ ⊗ in restaurant Closed mid Nov-mid Dec **CARDS:**

CLACHAN-SEIL, Argyll & Bute — Map 20 NM71

★★76% Willowburn
PA34 4TJ
☎ 01852 300276 📠 01852 300597
e-mail: willowburn.hotel@virgin.net
web: www.willowburn.co.uk
Dir: *0.5m from Atlantic Bridge, on left*

This welcoming small hotel enjoys a peaceful setting, with grounds stretching down to the shores of Clachan Sound. Friendly unassuming service, a relaxed atmosphere and fine food are keys to its success. Watch the wildlife from the dining room, lounge or cosy bar. Bedrooms are bright, cheerful and thoughtfully equipped.
ROOMS: 7 en suite (1 GF) ⊗ in all bedrooms s £72-£74; d £144-£148 (incl. bkfst & dinner) **LB** **PARKING:** 20 **NOTES:** No children 8 yrs ⊗ in restaurant Closed Dec-Feb **CARDS:**

CLUANIE INN, Highland
Map 22 NH01

★★63% Cluanie Inn
Glenmoriston IV63 7YW
☎ 01320 340238 📠 01320 340293
e-mail: cluanie@ecosse.net
web: www.cluanie.co.uk
Dir: *On A87 mid-way between Loch Ness & Isle of Skye*

THE CIRCLE
Selected Individual Hotels
GREAT BRITAIN

Set at the western end of Loch Cluanie this traditional roadside inn is surrounded by some spectacular Highland scenery. It is an ideal base for climbers and perfectly placed for travelling to or from the Isle of Skye. Public areas have been given a facelift and bedrooms are spacious and smartly furnished.
ROOMS: 13 en suite (2 fmly) (10 GF) s £40-£55; d £90-£110 (incl. bkfst) **LB** **FACILITIES:** Fishing Xmas **PARKING:** 20 **NOTES:** ⊗ in restaurant RS Xmas **CARDS:**

CLYDEBANK, West Dunbartonshire
Map 20 NS47

★★★★71% ⊛⊛ Beardmore
Beardmore St G81 4SA
☎ 0141 951 6000 📠 0141 951 6018
e-mail: info@beardmore.scot.nhs.uk
Dir: *M8 junct 19/A814 towards Dumbarton then follow tourist signs. Turn left onto Beardmore St & follow signs*

Best Western

Attracting business and conference custom, this impressive modern hotel lies beside the River Clyde and shares a building with a hospital (but the latter does not intrude). Spacious and imposing public areas include a stylish restaurant providing innovative contemporary cooking. The café bar offers a more extensive choice of equally tempting dishes.
ROOMS: 168 en suite ⊗ in 92 bedrooms s fr £97; d fr £97 **FACILITIES:** **Spa** STV supervised Sauna Solarium Gym Complimentary therapies Xmas **CONF:** BC Thtr 170 Class 24 Board 26 Del from £120 **SERVICES:** Lift air con **PARKING:** 400 **NOTES:** ⊗ in restaurant **CARDS:**

COATBRIDGE, North Lanarkshire
Map 20 NS76

Georgian Hotel
26 Lefroy St ML5 1LZ
☎ 01236 421888 📠 01236 421173
Dir: *Follow brown tourist signs for Time Capsule, hotel signed on A89*
ROOMS: 8 rms (6 en suite) s £25-£50; d £40-£60 (incl. bkfst) **CONF:** BC Thtr 120 Class 70 Board 60 **PARKING:** 16 **NOTES:** ★★ Closed 26 Dec & 1 Jan **CARDS:**

COLBOST See Skye, Isle of

COLVEND, Dumfries & Galloway
Map 21 NX85

★★69% Clonyard House
DG5 4QW
☎ 01556 630372 📠 01556 630422
e-mail: nickthompson@clara.net
Dir: *through Dalbeattie, left onto A710 for about 4m, hotel on left*
This long-established and popular family-run hotel is set in seven acres of woodland gardens, which include a children's play area and an 'enchanted tree'. Most of the spacious, comfortable bedrooms are housed in a purpose-built extension. Creative menus are served in the bar lounge or in the restaurant.
ROOMS: 15 en suite (3 fmly) (12 GF) s £35-£45; d £55-£70 (incl. bkfst) **LB** **CONF:** Class 35 Board 20 Del £55 **PARKING:** 40 **CARDS:**

COMRIE, Perth & Kinross
Map 21 NN72

★★★74% ⊛ Royal
Melville Square PH6 2DN
☎ 01764 679200 📠 01764 679219
e-mail: reception@royalhotel.co.uk
web: www.royalhotel.co.uk
Dir: *off A9 on A822 to Crieff, then B827 to Comrie. Hotel in main square of village on A85*

A traditional façade gives little indication of the total refurbishment that has brought much style and elegance to this long-established hotel in the village centre. Public areas include a bar and library, a bright modern restaurant and a conservatory-style brasserie. Bedrooms are tastefully appointed and furnished with smart reproduction antiques.
ROOMS: 11 en suite s fr £70; d fr £110 (incl. bkfst) **LB** **FACILITIES:** STV Fishing Pool table, Fishing/shooting arranged Xmas **CONF:** Thtr 20 Class 10 Board 20 Del from £110 **PARKING:** 22 **NOTES:** ⊗ in restaurant **CARDS:**

CONNEL, Argyll & Bute
Map 20 NM93

★★72% Falls of Lora
PA37 1PB
☎ 01631 710483 📠 01631 710694
Dir: *hotel set back from A85 from Glasgow, 0.5 mile past Connel sign*
Personally run and welcoming, this long-established holiday hotel enjoys fine views over Loch Etive. The pleasant public areas include a comfortable, traditional lounge and a well-stocked bar with a popular bistro and there is a separate breakfast room.

continued

Bedrooms come in a variety of styles, ranging from the standard cabin rooms to high quality, luxury rooms.

ROOMS: 30 en suite (4 fmly) (4 GF) s £39-£49; d £43-£119 (incl. bkfst) **LB** **FACILITIES:** ch fac **CONF:** Thtr 45 Class 20 Board 15 **PARKING:** 40 **NOTES:** Closed mid Dec & Jan **CARDS:**

See advert under OBAN

CONTIN, Highland — Map 23 NH45

★★★71% Coul House
IV14 9ES
☎ 01997 421487 📠 01997 421945
e-mail: coulhouse@bestloved.com
Dir: *Turn off A9 north onto A835 Ullapool road. Hotel drive on right in Contin just beyond filling station*

This imposing mansion house is set back from the road in extensive grounds. A number of the generally spacious bedrooms have superb views of the distant mountains and all are thoughtfully equipped. There is a choice of dining options available, with international cuisine served in both the dining room and the less formal bistro.
ROOMS: 20 en suite (3 fmly) (4 GF) ⊗ in 7 bedrooms s £55-£75; d £78-£163 (incl. bkfst) **LB** **FACILITIES:** STV Putt green 9 hole pitch & putt Xmas **CONF:** Thtr 50 Class 30 Board 30 Del from £67.50 **PARKING:** 36 **NOTES:** ⊗ in restaurant **CARDS:**

★★★67% Achilty
IV14 9EG
☎ 01997 421355 📠 01997 421923
e-mail: info@achilityhotel.co.uk
web: www.achiltyhotel.co.uk
Dir: *A9 over Kessock bridge then 2nd road on left at Tor rdbt onto A835, hotel on right through Contin*
Friendly owners contribute to great hospitality and a relaxed atmosphere at this roadside hotel. Public areas are full of interest; the lounges have books and games and the breakfast room has a musical theme. The Steading bar features exposed stone walls and offers a good selection of tasty home-cooked meals. Bedrooms are smartly furnished and well equipped.
ROOMS: 9 en suite 2 annexe en suite (3 GF) ⊗ in 9 bedrooms s £40.50-£66; d £62.50-£92.50 (incl. bkfst) **LB** **FACILITIES:** Xmas **CONF:** Thtr 50 Class 50 Board 20 Del from £26.90 **PARKING:** 100 **NOTES:** ⊗ in restaurant **CARDS:**

CRAIGELLACHIE, Moray — Map 23 NJ24

★★★78% Craigellachie
AB38 9SR
☎ 01340 881204 📠 01340 881253
e-mail: info@craigellachie.com
web: www.craigellachie.com
Dir: *on A95 in Craigellachie, 300yds from A95/A941 junct*
This impressive hotel is located in the heart of Speyside, so it is no surprise that malt whisky is a real feature. The Quaich bar boasts one of the largest collections of malts in the world and the enthusiasm for them is infectious! Bedrooms come in a various sizes, all are tastefully decorated and bathrooms are of a high specification.
ROOMS: 25 en suite ⊗ in all bedrooms s £100-£135; d £125-£160 (incl. bkfst) **LB** **FACILITIES:** STV Gym Xmas **CONF:** Thtr 60 Class 36 Board 26 Del from £117.50 **PARKING:** 50 **NOTES:** ⊗ in restaurant Civ Wed 50 **CARDS:**

CRAIGNURE See Mull, Isle of

CRAIL, Fife — Map 21 NO60

★★65% Balcomie Links
Balcomie Rd KY10 3TN
☎ 01333 450237 📠 01333 450540
e-mail: mikekadir@balcomie.fsnet.co.uk
web: www.balcomie.co.uk
Dir: *follow road to village shops, at junct of High St & Market Gate turn right. This road becomes Balcomie Rd, hotel on left*
Especially popular with visiting golfers, this family-run hotel on the east side of the village represents good value for money and has a relaxing atmosphere. Bedrooms come in a variety of sizes and styles and offer all the expected amenities. Food is served from midday in the attractive lounge bar, and in the evening also in the bright, cheerful dining room.
ROOMS: 15 rms (13 en suite) (2 fmly) ⊗ in 3 bedrooms s £55-£65; d £85 (incl. bkfst) **LB** **FACILITIES:** STV Games room ♫ ch fac Xmas **PARKING:** 25 **NOTES:** ⊗ in restaurant Civ Wed 45 **CARDS:**

CROCKETFORD, Dumfries & Galloway — Map 21 NX87

A *Galloway Arms*
DG2 8RA
☎ 01556 690248 📠 01556 690266
e-mail: info@gallowayarmshotel.co.uk
ROOMS: 12 rms (8 en suite) **CONF:** **PARKING:** 20 **NOTES:** ★★ ⊗ in restaurant **CARDS:**

CRUDEN BAY, Aberdeenshire — Map 23 NK03

★★69% Kilmarnock Arms
Bridge St AB42 0HD
☎ 01779 812213 📠 01779 812153
e-mail: reception@kilmarnockarms.com
web: www.kilmarnockarms.com
Dir: *off A90 onto A975 N of Ellon, or 8m S of Peterhead. Hotel in village centre*
Lying by the riverside at the northern end of the village close to the

continued on p700

CRUDEN BAY, continued

golf course and beach, this family-run hotel offers smart modern accommodation. There is also an inviting reception lounge, plus a bar and restaurant offering a good range of popular dishes.

Kilmarnock Arms Hotel, Cruden Bay

ROOMS: 14 en suite (1 fmly) ⊗ in all bedrooms s £50; d £70 (incl. bkfst) **LB** **FACILITIES:** Xmas **PARKING:** 6 **NOTES:** ⊗ in restaurant Civ Wed **CARDS:**

CULLEN, Moray Map 23 NJ56

★★★66% Cullen Bay Hotel

A98 AB56 4XA

☎ 01542 840432 🖹 01542 840900

e-mail: stay@cullenbayhotel.com

web: www.cullenbayhotel.com

Dir: *on A98, 1m west of Cullen*

This family-run hotel sits on the hillside west of the town and gives lovely views of the golf course, beach and Moray Firth. The spacious restaurant, which offers a selection of fine dishes, makes the most of the view, as do many of the well-equipped bedrooms. There is a comfortable modern bar, a homely lounge and a second dining room.

ROOMS: 14 en suite (3 fmly) ⊗ in all bedrooms s £45-£48; d £65-£82 (incl. bkfst) **LB** **FACILITIES:** Xmas **CONF:** Thtr 200 Class 80 Board 80 Del from £90 **PARKING:** 100 **NOTES:** ⊗ in restaurant Civ Wed 200 **CARDS:**

★★★65% The Seafield Hotel

Seafield St AB56 4SG

☎ 01542 840791 🖹 01542 840736

e-mail: accom@theseafieldhotel.com

web: www.theseafieldhotel.com

Dir: *in centre of town on A950*

Originally built by the Earl of Seafield as a coaching inn, this hotel was modernised in the early 1970s to provide individually designed, comfortable bedrooms and is now gradually being refurbished. One of the features here is a lovely, carved wooden fireplace in the spacious lounge bar. Service is friendly and attentive with good-value and enjoyable meals served in the restaurant.

ROOMS: 19 en suite (2 fmly) s £45-£60; d £75-£85 (incl. bkfst) **LB** **FACILITIES:** STV Snooker Clay pigeon shooting, Cycling, Quads, 4x4 driving, Archery ch fac Xmas **CONF:** Thtr 140 Class 90 Board 30 **PARKING:** 28 **NOTES:** ⊗ in restaurant **CARDS:**

CUMBERNAULD, North Lanarkshire Map 21 NS77

★★★★69% Westerwood Hotel Golf & Country Club

1 St Andrews Dr, Westerwood G68 0EW

☎ 01236 457171 🖹 01236 738478

e-mail: westerwood@morton-hotels.com

Dir: *A80 exit after passing Oki factory signed Wardpark/Castlecary, 2nd left at Old Inns rdbt and right at mini-rdbt*

This stylish, contemporary hotel enjoys an elevated position within 400 acres at the foot of the Campsie Hills. Accommodation is provided in spacious, bright bedrooms, many with super bathrooms, and day rooms include sumptuous lounges, an airy restaurant and extensive golf, fitness and conference facilities.

ROOMS: 100 en suite (13 fmly) ⊗ in 51 bedrooms s £95-£118; d £110-£133 (incl. bkfst) **LB** **FACILITIES: Spa** STV 18 Sauna Solarium Gym Putt green Jacuzzi Beauty salon Hairdresser Xmas **CONF:** Thtr 200 Class 120 Board 60 Del from £135 **SERVICES:** Lift air con **PARKING:** 204 **NOTES:** ⊗ in restaurant Civ Wed 166 **CARDS:**

Travel Inn Glasgow (Cumbernauld)

travel inn

4 South Muirhead Rd G67 1AX

☎ 08701 977108 🖹 01236 736380

Dir: *From A80, A8011 following signs to Cumbernauld and town centre. Travel Inn opposite Asda/McDonalds. Turn at rdbt towards Esso garage. Turn right at mini-rdbt*

Travel Inn offers good-quality, value-for-money accommodation. Spacious, en suite rooms with bath and shower comfortably accommodate a family of up to two adults and two children (to age 15). The restaurant and bar offers a varied menu. For further details consult the Hotel Groups page.

ROOMS: 37 en suite s £45.95-£46.95; d £45.95-£46.95

CUPAR, Fife Map 21 NO31

★★★72% Craigsanquhar House

KY15 4PZ

☎ 01334 653426 🖹 01334 653457

e-mail: info@craigsanquhar.com

With views over the surrounding countryside, this house of much character enjoys a tranquil setting. Elegantly traditional public rooms and master bedrooms are graced with rich fabrics and period pieces. The bedrooms on the second floor are individually

continued

styled and in various sizes. Private functions and weddings are well catered for.
ROOMS: 13 en suite (3 fmly) ⊗ in all bedrooms **FACILITIES:** STV Xmas **CONF:** Thtr 200 Class 80 **PARKING:** 50 **NOTES:** ⊗ in restaurant **CARDS:**

★★60% Eden House

2 Pitscottie Rd KY15 4HF
☎ 01334 652510 01334 652277
e-mail: info@edenhousehotel.com
web: www.edenhousehotel.com
Dir: *on A91 on eastern side of Cupar, opposite Haugh Park*

Enjoying a location on the outskirts of town, this small hotel is convenient for the many golf courses and attractions in both Fife and neighbouring Perth & Kinross. Bedrooms, which vary in size and style, include a number in an adjacent cottage. Meals can be taken in either the conservatory restaurant or newly refurbished bar.
ROOMS: 9 en suite 2 annexe en suite (2 GF) s fr £50; d fr £75 (incl. bkfst) **LB** **FACILITIES:** STV **PARKING:** 20 **NOTES:** ⊗ in restaurant
CARDS:

DALWHINNIE, Highland — Map 23 NN68

The Inn at Loch Ericht

PH19 1AG
☎ 01528 522257 01528 522270
e-mail: reservations@priory-hotel.com
Dir: *off A9 onto A886. 1m on right opposite filling station*
ROOMS: 27 en suite (2 fmly) (14 GF) ⊗ in 4 bedrooms s £27.50-£35; d £51-£59 (incl. bkfst) **LB** **FACILITIES:** Fishing **CONF:** Thtr 50 Class 30 Board 30 Del from £45 **PARKING:** 60 **NOTES:** ★ ⊗ in restaurant
CARDS:

DERVAIG See Mull, Isle of

DIRLETON, East Lothian — Map 21 NT58

★★★70% *The Open Arms*

EH39 5EG
☎ 01620 850241 01620 850570
e-mail: openarms@clara.co.uk
web: www.openarmshotel.com
Dir: *from A1, follow signs for North Berwick, through Gullane, 2m on left*
Across from the picturesque village green and Dirleton Castle this long established hotel is popular with both business and leisure guests. Inviting public areas include a choice of lounges and a cosy bar. A variety of carefully prepared meals can be enjoyed in both

continued

the informal setting of Deveau's brasserie or the more intimate Library restaurant.

ROOMS: 10 en suite (1 fmly) **CONF:** Thtr 200 Class 150 Board 100
PARKING: 30 **NOTES:** ⊗ in restaurant Closed 4-15 Jan
CARDS:

DOLLAR, Clackmannanshire — Map 21 NS99

★★71% Castle Campbell Hotel

11 Bridge St FK14 7DE
☎ 01259 742519 01259 743742
e-mail: bookings@castle-campbell.co.uk
web: www.castle-campbell.co.uk
Dir: *on A91 Stirling to St Andrews Rd, in the centre of Dollar, by bridge overlooking Dollar Burn & Clock Tower*
Set in the centre of a delightful country town, this hotel is popular with both local people and tourists. Accommodation ranges in size, though all rooms are thoughtfully equipped. Inviting public rooms feature a delightful lounge with real fire, a well-stocked whisky bar and a stylish restaurant.
ROOMS: 8 en suite (2 fmly) ⊗ in all bedrooms s fr £55; d fr £80 (incl. bkfst) **LB** **FACILITIES:** Xmas **CONF:** Thtr 80 Class 60 Board 40
PARKING: 8 **NOTES:** ⊗ in restaurant Civ Wed 80
CARDS:

DORNOCH, Highland — Map 23 NH78

★★★70% Royal Golf Hotel

The 1st Tee IV25 3LG
☎ 01862 810283 01862 810923
e-mail: royalgolf@morton-hotels.com
Dir: *from A9, right to Dornoch and continue through main street. Straight ahead at crossroads, hotel 200yds on right*

This stylish hotel benefits from a super location adjacent to the Royal Dornoch Golf Club, and has glorious views over the Dornoch Firth. Bedrooms are spacious and modern and include two stunning suites. A split-level conservatory restaurant gives

continued on p702

DORNOCH, continued

sweeping views of the golf course and there is also a smart cocktail lounge.
ROOMS: 25 en suite (2 fmly) s £92-£113; d £139-£216 (incl. bkfst) **LB** **FACILITIES:** Xmas **PARKING:** 20 **NOTES:** in restaurant
CARDS:

★★67% *Burghfield House*
IV25 3HN
01862 810212 01862 810404
e-mail: burghfield@cali.co.uk
Dir: *off A9 at Evelix junct, 1m into Dornoch. Just before War Memorial turn left and follow road up hill to tower in the trees*
Set in gardens above the town this extended Victorian mansion provides a friendly and relaxing atmosphere. Public areas, including a delightful lounge, are enhanced with antiques, fresh flowers and real fires. Bedrooms are generally well proportioned and split between the main house and the adjacent garden wing.
ROOMS: 13 en suite 15 annexe en suite **FACILITIES:** Sauna Putt green ch fac **CONF:** Thtr 100 Board 80 **PARKING:** 62 **NOTES:** in restaurant Closed Jan - Feb Civ Wed 50 **CARDS:**

DRUMNADROCHIT, Highland
Map 23 NH53

★★★68% Polmaily House Hotel
IV63 6XT
01456 450343 01456 450813
e-mail: polmaily@btinternet.com
Dir: *in Drumnadrochit, next to the Monster Exhibition, turn onto A831(signed Cannich), hotel 2m on right. 1.5m from Loch Ness*
Run by a family, this relaxing country house is geared for children, with a pets' corner and well-stocked play areas. The 18 acres of lawns and woods also include good leisure facilities, such as a swimming pool, horse riding and tennis. Good home-cooked dinners are also on offer.
ROOMS: 10 en suite (6 fmly) (1 GF) in all bedrooms s £40-£72; d £80-£144 (incl. bkfst) **LB** **FACILITIES:** Fishing Riding Solarium Indoor/outdoor childs play area, Boating, Pony rides, Beauty massage, bicycles ch fac Xmas **CONF:** BC Thtr 25 Class 8 Board 14 **PARKING:** 20 **NOTES:** in restaurant Civ Wed 60
CARDS:

Loch Ness Lodge
IV63 6TU
01456 450342 01456 450429
e-mail: info@lochness-hotel.com
Dir: *off A82 onto A831 Cannich Rd, hotel above junction, 1m from Loch Ness*
ROOMS: 50 rms (7 en suite) (4 fmly) (10 GF) in 10 bedrooms s £50-£75; d £90-£120 (incl. bkfst) **LB** **FACILITIES:** ch fac Xmas **CONF:** Thtr 50 Class 40 Board 40 **PARKING:** 80 **NOTES:** ★★★ RS Mid-Jan to Mid-Feb **CARDS:**

DRYMEN, Stirling
Map 20 NS48

★★★70% Buchanan Arms Hotel and Leisure Club
23 Main St G63 0BQ
01360 660588 01360 660943
e-mail: enquiries@buchananarms.co.uk
Dir: *N from Glasgow on A81 take A811, hotel at S end of Main Street*
This former coaching inn offers comfortable bedrooms in a variety of styles, with spacious public areas that include an intimate bar, a formal dining room and good function and meeting facilities as well as a fully equipped leisure centre. Teas and light meals can be

continued

served in the conservatory lounge which overlooks the gardens towards the Campsie Fells.
ROOMS: 52 en suite (3 fmly) (13 GF) in 20 bedrooms s £75-£95; d £75 (incl. bkfst & dinner) **LB** **FACILITIES:** supervised Fishing Squash Sauna Solarium Gym Putt green Jacuzzi Bowling Green Xmas **CONF:** Thtr 150 Class 60 Board 60 Del £117.50 **PARKING:** 120 **NOTES:** in restaurant Civ Wed 120
CARDS:

★★★68% Winnock
The Square G63 0BL
01360 660245 01360 660267
e-mail: info@winnockhotel.com
Dir: *from S follow M74 onto M8 through Glasgow. Exit junct 16B, follow A809 to Aberfoyle*

Best Western

Occupying a prominent position overlooking the village green, this is a popular hotel offering well-equipped bedrooms of various sizes and styles. The public rooms have undergone a total refurbishment, including the relocation of the bar and the creation of a new lounge and attractive formal dining room that serves good, locally-produced food.
ROOMS: 48 en suite (12 fmly) in 17 bedrooms s fr £71; d fr £92 (incl. bkfst) **LB** **FACILITIES:** Petanque Xmas **CONF:** Thtr 140 Class 60 Board 70 Del from £55 **PARKING:** 60 **NOTES:** in restaurant Civ Wed **CARDS:**

DUMBARTON, West Dunbartonshire
Map 20 NS37

Travelodge
Milton G82 2TZ
08700 850 950 01389 765202
Dir: *1m E, on A82 westbound*

Travelodge

Travelodge offers good quality, good value, modern accommodation. Ideal for families, the spacious, en suite bedrooms include remote-control TV, tea and coffee-making facilities and luxury beds. Meals can be taken at the nearby family restaurant. For further details consult the Hotel Groups page.
ROOMS: 32 en suite s fr £25; d fr £25

DUMFRIES, Dumfries & Galloway
Map 21 NX97
See also Carrutherstown

★★★71% Cairndale Hotel & Leisure Club
English St DG1 2DF
01387 254111 01387 250555
e-mail: sales@cairndale.fsnet.co.uk
web: www.cairndalehotel.co.uk
Dir: *from S turn off M6 onto A75 to Dumfries, left at 1st rdbt, cross railway bridge, continue to traffic lights, hotel 1st building on left*
Within walking distance of the town centre, this hotel provides a wide range of amenities, including leisure facilities and an impressive conference and entertainment centre. Bedrooms range

continued

from stylish suites to cosy singles. There's a choice of eating options in the evening. The Reivers Restaurant is smartly modern with food to match.

ROOMS: 91 en suite (22 fmly) (5 GF) ⊗ in 45 bedrooms s £49-£109; d £69-£149 (incl. bkfst) **LB** **FACILITIES: Spa** STV Sauna Solarium Gym Jacuzzi Steam room, air conditioned gymnasium ♫ ch fac Xmas **CONF:** Thtr 300 Class 150 Board 50 Del from £95 **SERVICES:** Lift **PARKING:** 120 **NOTES:** ⊗ in restaurant Civ Wed 200 **CARDS:**

See advert on this page

★★★69% *Station*

49 Lovers Walk DG1 1LT
☎ 01387 254316 01387 250388
e-mail: info@stationhotel.co.uk
web: www.stationhotel.co.uk
Dir: *A75, follow signs to Dumfries town centre, hotel opp railway station*

Best Western

This hotel, sympathetically modernised in harmony with its fine Victorian characteristics, offers well-equipped bedrooms. The Courtyard Bistro serves an extensive menu in an informal atmosphere during the evening, and good value meals can also be served in the lounge bar and conservatory.
ROOMS: 32 en suite (2 fmly) ⊗ in 12 bedrooms **FACILITIES: Spa** STV **CONF:** Thtr 60 Class 35 Board 30 **SERVICES:** Lift **PARKING:** 34 **NOTES:** Civ Wed 60 **CARDS:**

⌂ Travel Inn

Annan Rd, Collin DG1 3JX
☎ 08701 977078 01387 266475
Dir: *on main central rdbt junct of Euroroute bypass (A75)*

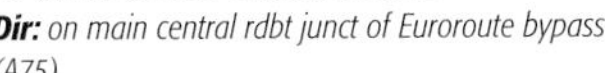

travel inn

Travel Inn offers good-quality, value-for-money accommodation. Spacious, en suite rooms with bath and shower comfortably accommodate a family of up to two adults and two children (to age 15). The restaurant and bar offers a varied menu. For further details consult the Hotel Groups page.
ROOMS: 40 en suite s £45.95-£46.95; d £45.95-£46.95

⌂ Travelodge

Annan Rd, Collin DG1 3SE
☎ 08700 850 950 01387 750658
Dir: *on A75*

Travelodge

Travelodge offers good quality, good value, modern accommodation. Ideal for families, the spacious, en suite bedrooms include remote-control TV, tea and coffee-making facilities and luxury beds. Meals can be taken at the nearby family restaurant. For further details consult the Hotel Groups page.
ROOMS: 40 en suite s fr £25; d fr £25

DUNBLANE, Stirling Map 21 NN70

Top 200 – Hotel

★★★ ◎◎ **Cromlix House**
Kinbuck FK15 9JT
☎ 01786 822125 🖷 01786 825450
e-mail: reservations@cromlixhouse.com
web: www.cromlixhouse.com
Dir: *off A9 N of Dunblane. Exit B8033 to Kinbuck Village then after village cross narrow bridge drive 200yds on left*

Situated in sweeping gardens and surrounded by a 2000-acre estate, Cromlix House is an imposing Victorian mansion, boasting gracious and inviting public areas. Well-appointed bedrooms, the majority of which are suites, are spacious and elegant. The two dining rooms offer contrasting décor but both ideal in which to enjoy the skilfully prepared food.

ROOMS: 14 en suite s £140-£210; d £235-£385 (incl. bkfst) **LB** **FACILITIES:** Fishing Clay pigeon shooting, Falconry, Archery ch fac Xmas **CONF:** Thtr 40 Class 24 Board 24 Del from £175 **PARKING:** 51 **NOTES:** in restaurant Closed 2-29 Jan RS Oct-Apr Civ Wed 50 **CARDS:**

DUNDEE, Dundee City Map 21 NO43

★★★★76% **Apex City Quay Hotel & Spa**
1 West Victoria Dock Rd DD1 3JP
☎ 01382 202404 & 0845 608 3456 🖷 01382 201401
e-mail: cityquay@apexhotels.co.uk
Dir: *A85 Riverside Drive to Discovery Quay. Exit rdbt for City Quay.*

This stylish, purpose-built, modern hotel occupies an enviable position at the heart of Dundee's regenerated centre. Bedrooms, including a number of smart suites, feature the very latest in design. Warm hospitality and professional service are an integral

continued

part of the appeal. Open-plan public areas with panoramic windows and contemporary food options complete the package.

ROOMS: 153 en suite (16 fmly) in 122 bedrooms s £80-£220; d £80-£220 **LB** **FACILITIES: Spa** STV supervised Sauna Gym Jacuzzi Elemis treatment rooms, steam room Xmas **CONF:** BC Thtr 400 Class 180 Board 120 Del from £125 **SERVICES:** Lift **PARKING:** 150 **NOTES:** in restaurant **CARDS:**

See advert under EDINBURGH

★★★72% **The Woodlands Hotel**
13 Panmure Ter, Barnhill, Broughty Ferry DD5 2QL
☎ 01382 480033 🖷 01382 480126
e-mail: woodlands@bestwestern.co.uk

Dir: *from Perth A85 to Dundee, then take A930 to Broughty Ferry; from Tay Bridge A930 East to Broughty Ferry*

This popular business and tourist hotel stands in mature wooded grounds and has a welcoming atmosphere. Inviting public areas include a choice of relaxing lounges, a well stocked bar, an attractive restaurant with both carte and fixed price menus. Good leisure and banqueting facilities are offered. Bedrooms in the new wing are appointed to a high standard while those in the original house tend to be more individual in style.

ROOMS: 38 en suite (1 fmly) (10 GF) in 8 bedrooms **FACILITIES:** STV Sauna Solarium Gym Jacuzzi Steam room and beauty therapy **CONF:** Thtr 200 Class 140 Board 80 **PARKING:** 120 **NOTES:** in restaurant Closed 24-26 Dec & 31 Dec-3 Jan Civ Wed 180 **CARDS:**

★★★67% ◎ **Sandford Country House Hotel**
Newton Hill, Wormit DD6 8RG
☎ 01382 541802 🖷 01382 542136
e-mail: sandford.hotel@btinternet.com
web: www.sandfordhotelfife.com
Dir: *off A92 at junct B946, hotel entrance 100yds from junct on left*

Built around the turn of the last century, this hotel lies in wooded grounds well off the main road. Set around a small terraced courtyard, it is a popular venue for meals, which are served in the bar or restaurant. Bedrooms come in a variety of sizes and have been refurbished in a smart, modern style.

ROOMS: 16 en suite (2 fmly) in 15 bedrooms s £70-£90; d £110-£130 (incl. bkfst) **LB** **FACILITIES:** STV Adj to sports club, Cycle hire Xmas **CONF:** Thtr 45 Class 25 Board 25 Del from £75 **PARKING:** 30 **NOTES:** in restaurant Civ Wed 40 **CARDS:**

★★73% **The Shaftesbury**
1 Hyndford St DD2 1HQ
☎ 01382 669216 🖷 01382 641598
e-mail: reservations@shaftesbury-hotel.co.uk
web: www.shaftesbury-hotel.co.uk

THE CIRCLE
Selected Individual Hotels
GREAT BRITAIN

Dir: *from Perth signed to Airport, take 1st left at circle, turn right, follow Perth Rd, turn right*

A comfortable, welcoming hotel situated in the west end where the owners and their staff are friendly and willing to please. Spotlessly maintained, this impressive Victorian house has been sympathetically converted, offering inviting public areas including a cosy lounge, bar and restaurant. Bedrooms are individually decorated.

ROOMS: 12 en suite (2 fmly) s £49.50-£52; d £56-£96 (incl. bkfst & dinner) **LB** **NOTES:** in restaurant RS Sun-Mon **CARDS:**

⌂ Days Inn

296a Strathmore Av DD3 6SH
☎ 01382 826000 ▤ 01382 825839
e-mail: dundee@daysinn.co.uk
Dir: *leave A90 Kingsway at Ardler rdbt signed City Centre B960, Cledington Road. On Cledington Road 1st right into Johnston Avenue. Continue to end of avenue until reaching rdbt. Turn left into Strathmole Avenue and hotel on left*
This modern building offers accommodation in smart, spacious and well-equipped bedrooms, suitable for families and business travellers, and all with en suite bathrooms. Continental breakfast is available and other refreshments may be taken at the nearby family restaurant. For further details see the Hotel Groups page.
ROOMS: 67 en suite **CONF:** BC Board 10

⌂ Premier Lodge (Dundee North)

Dayton Dr, Camperdown Leisure Park, Kingsway DD2 3SQ
☎ 0870 9906420 ▤ 0870 9906421
web: www.premierlodge.com
Dir: *off A90 into Coupar Angus Rd, hotel visible from dual-carriageway, exit by slip road for Camperdown Leisure Park*
High quality, modern, budget accommodation, ideal for families and business travellers. All rooms feature bath, power shower and satellite TV, and most have telephones / modem points. The adjacent bar and restaurant offers a wide and varied menu.
ROOMS: 78 en suite s £44; d £44

⌂ Travel Inn Dundee (Centre)

Discovery Quay, Riverside Dr DD1 4XA
☎ 08701 977079 ▤ 01382 203237

Dir: *follow signs for Discovery Quay, on waterfront*

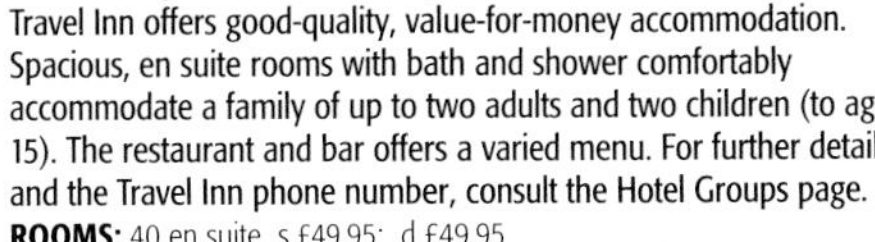

Travel Inn offers good-quality, value-for-money accommodation. Spacious, en suite rooms with bath and shower comfortably accommodate a family of up to two adults and two children (to age 15). The restaurant and bar offers a varied menu. For further details and the Travel Inn phone number, consult the Hotel Groups page.
ROOMS: 40 en suite s £49.95; d £49.95

⌂ Travel Inn (Dundee East)

Ethiebeaton Park, Arbroath Rd, Monifieth DD5 4HB
☎ 08701 977080 ▤ 01382 530468
Dir: *From A90 Kingsway Road follow signs for Carnoustie/Arbroath (A92)*
Travel Inn offers good-quality, value-for-money accommodation. Spacious, en suite rooms with bath and shower comfortably accommodate a family of up to two adults and two children (to age 15). The restaurant and bar offers a varied menu. For further details consult the Hotel Groups page.
ROOMS: 40 en suite s £45.95-£46.95; d £45.95-£46.95 **CONF:** Board 8

⌂ Travel Inn (Dundee West)

Kingsway West, Invergowrie DD2 5JU
☎ 08701 977081 ▤ 01382 568431
Dir: *approaching Swallow rdbt next to Technology Park rdbt take A90 towards Aberdeen, Travel Inn on left after 250yds*
Travel Inn offers good-quality, value-for-money accommodation. Spacious, en suite rooms with bath and shower comfortably accommodate a family of up to two adults and two children (to age 15). The restaurant and bar offers a varied menu. For further details consult the Hotel Groups page.
ROOMS: 64 en suite s £45.95-£46.95; d £45.95-£46.95

⌂ Travelodge

A90 Kingsway DD2 4TD
☎ 08700 850 950 ▤ 01382 610488
Dir: *on A90*
Travelodge offers good quality, good value, modern accommodation. Ideal for families, the spacious, en suite bedrooms include remote-control TV, tea and coffee-making facilities and luxury beds. Meals can be taken at the nearby family restaurant. For further details consult the Hotel Groups page.
ROOMS: 32 en suite s fr £25; d fr £25

D

DUNDONNELL, Highland — Map 22 NH08

★★★70% Dundonnell

IV23 2QR
☎ 01854 633204 ▤ 01854 633366
e-mail: enquiries@dundonnellhotel.co.uk
web: www.dundonnellhotel.com
Dir: *Turn off A835 at Braemore Junction onto A832. Hotel 14 miles.*
A beautiful, isolated location at the head of Little Loch Broom is perhaps an unlikely spot for such a smart and extensively developed hotel as this. A haven of relaxation and good food, it offers a range of attractive and comfortable public areas and a choice of eating options and bars. Many of the bedrooms enjoy fine views.
ROOMS: 29 en suite 3 annexe en suite (2 fmly) (3 GF) s £45-£75; d £90-£120 (incl. bkfst) **LB** **FACILITIES:** Xmas **CONF:** Thtr 70 Class 50 Board 40 Del from £95 **PARKING:** 60 **NOTES:** ⊗ in restaurant
CARDS:

DUNFERMLINE, Fife — Map 21 NT08

★★★75% *Garvock House Hotel*

St John's Dr, Transy KY12 7TU
☎ 01383 621067 ▤ 01383 621168
e-mail: sales@garvock.co.uk
Dir: *M90 junct 3/A907 (Dunfermline). Left after football stadium (Garvock Hill), 1st right (St John's Drive), hotel on right*

A warm welcome is assured at this impeccably presented Georgian house which stands in its own beautifully landscaped gardens. Modern stylish bedrooms set high standards of quality and have been refurbished to include DVD players. A spacious modern function suite makes this a popular venue for weddings and conferences. Contemporary cuisine is served in the restaurant.
ROOMS: 12 en suite (1 fmly) ⊗ in all bedrooms **CONF:** Thtr 70 Class 50 Board 30 **PARKING:** 70 **NOTES:** ⊗ in restaurant Civ Wed
CARDS:

DUNFERMLINE, continued

★★★74% Keavil House

Crossford KY12 8QW
☎ 01383 736258 📠 01383 621600
e-mail: sales@keavilhouse.co.uk
web: www.keavilhouse.co.uk
Dir: *2m W of Dunfermline on A994*

Dating from the 16th century, this former manor house is set in gardens and parkland. With a modern leisure centre and conference rooms it is suited to business and leisure guests. Bedrooms come in a variety of sizes and occupy the original house and a modern wing. A conservatory restaurant is the focal point of public rooms.

ROOMS: 47 en suite (6 fmly) (17 GF) in 28 bedrooms s £55-£115; d £90-£175 (incl. bkfst) **LB** **FACILITIES: Spa** STV supervised Sauna Solarium Gym Jacuzzi Aerobics studio, Steam room, Beautician ch fac Xmas **CONF:** Thtr 200 Class 60 Board 50 Del from £125 **PARKING:** 150 **NOTES:** in restaurant Civ Wed 200 **CARDS:**

★★★70% Pitbauchlie House

Aberdour Rd KY11 4PB
☎ 01383 722282 📠 01383 620738
e-mail: info@pitbauchlie.com
web: www.pitbauchlie.com
Dir: *M90 junct 2, onto A823, then B916. Hotel 0.5m on right*

This family hotel is set in landscaped gardens a mile south of the town centre. A stylish foyer, cocktail lounge, restaurant, bar and bistro all overlook the garden. The modern bedrooms are well equipped, the deluxe rooms having CD players and videos.

ROOMS: 50 en suite (2 fmly) (19 GF) in 19 bedrooms s £85-£95; d £103-£113 (incl. bkfst) **LB** **FACILITIES:** STV Gym **CONF:** BC Thtr 150 Class 80 Board 60 Del from £122 **PARKING:** 80 **NOTES:** in restaurant Civ Wed 120 **CARDS:**

★★★65% King Malcolm

Queensferry Rd KY11 8DS
☎ 01383 722611 📠 01383 730865
e-mail: info@kingmalcolm-hotel-dunfermline.com
Dir: *on A823, S of town*

Located to the south of the city, this purpose-built hotel remains popular with business clientele and is convenient for access to both Edinburgh and Fife. Public rooms include a smart foyer lounge and a conservatory bar, as well as a restaurant. Bedrooms, although not large, are well laid out and well equipped.

ROOMS: 48 en suite (2 fmly) in 36 bedrooms s £90-£100; d £110-£130 **LB** **FACILITIES:** STV Xmas **CONF:** Thtr 150 Class 60 Board 50 Del from £99 **PARKING:** 60 **CARDS:**

DUNKELD, Perth & Kinross Map 21 NO04

Top 200 – Hotel

★★★ Kinnaird

Kinnaird Estate PH8 0LB
☎ 01796 482440 📠 01796 482289
e-mail: enquiry@kinnairdestate.com
Dir: *from Perth, A9 towards Inverness towards Dunkeld but do not enter town, continue N for 2m then B898 on left*

An imposing Edwardian mansion set in 9000 acres of beautiful countryside on the west bank of the River Tay. Sitting rooms are warm and inviting with deep-cushioned sofas and open fires. Bedrooms are furnished with rich, soft, luxurious fabrics, and have marble bathrooms. Food is creative and imaginative, with abundant local produce featuring on all menus. While jacket and tie are required at dinner, the atmosphere overall is tranquil and relaxed.

ROOMS: 9 en suite (1 GF) s £225-£425; d £275-£425 (incl. bkfst & dinner) **LB** **FACILITIES: Spa** STV Fishing Snooker Shooting **CONF:** Thtr 25 Class 10 Board 15 Del from £225 **SERVICES:** Lift **PARKING:** 22 **NOTES:** No children 12yrs in restaurant Civ Wed 36 **CARDS:**

DUNOON, Argyll & Bute Map 20 NS17

★★78% Enmore

Marine Pde, Hunters Quay PA23 8HH
☎ 01369 702230 📠 01369 702148
e-mail: enmorehotel@btinternet.com
Dir: *on coastal route between two ferries, 1m N of Dunoon*

This seafront hotel, built in 1875 by a Glasgow merchant, has super views over the Firth of Clyde. Elegant public areas include a peaceful lounge, a dining room that features high quality, local ingredients and two squash courts to work off the calories. Bedrooms are individual and a number have stunning bathrooms.

ROOMS: 9 en suite (1 fmly) in all bedrooms s £59-£95; d £90-£150 (incl. bkfst) **LB** **FACILITIES:** Squash Jacuzzi ch fac **CONF:** Thtr 25 Class 20 Board 12 Del from £75 **PARKING:** 10 **NOTES:** in restaurant Closed 12 Dec-12 Feb RS Nov-Mar Civ Wed **CARDS:**

★★73% Royal Marine

Hunters Quay PA23 8HJ
☎ 01369 705810 📠 01369 702329
e-mail: rmhotel@sol.co.uk
web: www.rmhotel.co.uk
Dir: *on A815 opposite Western Ferries terminal*

This welcoming family-run hotel commands impressive views over the Firth of Clyde. The bedrooms vary in size and are modern in appointment, offering a good range of amenities. Public areas include a formal dining room where a fixed-price menu is

continued

available, a well-stocked bar and the popular Ghillies café-bar with its attractive garden area.

ROOMS: 31 en suite 10 annexe en suite (3 fmly) (5 GF) s £49-£51; d £73-£79 (incl. bkfst) **LB** **FACILITIES:** ♫ Xmas **CONF:** Thtr 90 Class 40 Board 30 Del from £65 **PARKING:** 40 **NOTES:** ⊗ in restaurant **CARDS:**

★★66% Selborne

Clyde St, West Bay PA23 7HU
☎ 01369 702761 Fax 01369 704032
e-mail: selborne.dunoon@alfatravel.co.uk
Dir: *from Caledonian Macbrayne pier. Follow road past castle, left into Jane St and then right into Clyde St*

This holiday hotel is situated overlooking the West Bay and provides unrestricted views of the Clyde Estuary towards the Isles of Cumbrae. Tour groups are especially well catered for in this good-value establishment which offers entertainment most nights. Bedrooms offer good facilities, many having sea views.
ROOMS: 98 en suite (14 GF) s £28-£36; d £44-£62 (incl. bkfst) **LB** **FACILITIES:** Pool table, Table tennis ♫ Xmas **SERVICES:** Lift **PARKING:** 30 **NOTES:** ⊗ in restaurant Closed Dec-Feb ex Xmas RS Nov & Mar **CARDS:**

★★64% *Esplanade Hotel*

West Bay PA23 7HU
☎ 01369 704070 Fax 01369 702129
e-mail: relax@ehd.co.uk
Dir: *100mtrs from Dunoon pier, 1st left after Castle House Museum*

This family-run hotel enjoys a prime location and views over the Firth of Clyde. Public areas include relaxing lounges on both the first and ground floors and a large dining room. Thoughtfully equipped bedrooms, many of which are spacious, come in a variety of styles.
ROOMS: 60 en suite 5 annexe en suite (5 fmly) (17 GF) ⊗ in 30 bedrooms **FACILITIES:** STV Putt green ♫ **CONF:** Thtr 50 Class 50 Board 40 **SERVICES:** Lift **PARKING:** 23 **NOTES:** ⊗ in restaurant Closed 2 Jan-9 Apr **CARDS:**

EAST KILBRIDE, South Lanarkshire — Map 20 NS65

★★★★70%
Crutherland Country House Hotel

MACDONALD HOTELS

Strathaven Rd G75 0QZ
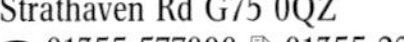

☎ 01355 577000 Fax 01355 220855
e-mail: crutherland@macdonald-hotels.co.uk
Dir: *Follow A726 signed Strathaven, straight over Torrance rdbt, hotel on left after 250yds*

Extensively renovated, this mansion is set in 37 acres of landscaped grounds two miles from the town centre. Behind its Georgian façade is a very relaxing hotel with elegant public areas plus extensive banqueting and leisure facilities. The bedrooms are spacious and comfortable. Staff provide good levels of attention and enjoyable meals are served in the restaurant.

ROOMS: 75 en suite (16 fmly) (16 GF) ⊗ in 65 bedrooms s £95-£135; d £105-£155 (incl. bkfst) **FACILITIES:** STV Sauna Solarium Gym Xmas **CONF:** Thtr 500 Class 100 Board 50 Del from £135 **SERVICES:** Lift **PARKING:** 200 **NOTES:** ⊗ in restaurant Civ Wed 300 **CARDS:**

★★★65% Bruce Hotel

Cornwall St G74 1AF
☎ 01355 229771 Fax 01355 242216
e-mail: enquiries@thebrucehotel.com
web: www.thebrucehotel.com
Dir: *M74 junct 5, onto A725, follow to East Kilbride town centre, turn right (Cornwall St), hotel 200yds on left*

Purpose-built in the 1960s, this hotel is centrally located and forms part of the main shopping centre. The smart lounge bar now serves light meals in addition to meals in the elegant restaurant. Secure underground car parking is available.
ROOMS: 65 en suite (5 fmly) ⊗ in 5 bedrooms s fr £49.50; d fr £89 **LB** **FACILITIES:** STV ♫ Xmas **CONF:** BC Thtr 300 Class 100 Board 50 Del £95 **SERVICES:** Lift **PARKING:** 30 **NOTES:** ⊗ in restaurant Civ Wed 150 **CARDS:**

Premier Lodge (East Kilbride)

PREMIER LODGE.com

Eaglesham Rd G75 8LW
☎ 0870 9906542 Fax 0870 9906543
web: www.premierlodge.com
Dir: *8m from M74 junct 5, on A726 at rdbt of B764*

High quality, modern, budget accommodation, ideal for families and business travellers. All rooms feature bath, power shower and satellite TV, and most have telephones / modem points. The adjacent bar and restaurant offers a wide and varied menu.
ROOMS: 40 en suite s £48; d £48

Travel Inn (Glasgow East Kilbride)

travel inn

Brunel Way, The Murray G75 0JD
☎ 08701 977110 Fax 01355 230517
Dir: *M74 junct 5, follow signs for East Kilbride A725, then signs Paisley A726, turn left at Murray rdbt and left into Brunel Way*

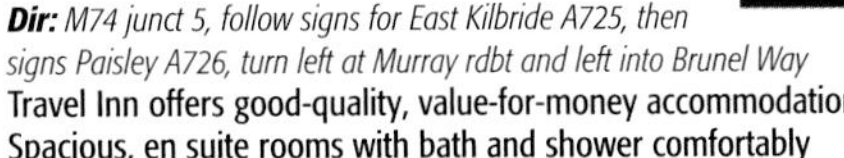

Travel Inn offers good-quality, value-for-money accommodation. Spacious, en suite rooms with bath and shower comfortably accommodate a family of up to two adults and two children (to age 15). The restaurant and bar offers a varied menu. For further details consult the Hotel Groups page.
ROOMS: 40 en suite s £45.95-£46.95; d £45.95-£46.95

> Popped the question?
> Hotels with Civ Wed in their entry are licensed for civil wedding ceremonies. Maximum numbers for the ceremony only are shown, e.g. Civ Wed 120

continued

EDINBURGH, City of Edinburgh Map 21 NT27

Top 200 – Town House

★★★★★ **The Scotsman**
20 North Bridge EH1 1YT
☎ 0131 556 5565 0131 652 3652
e-mail: reservations@thescotsmanhotelgroup.co.uk
Dir: *A8 to city centre, left onto Charlotte St. Right into Queen St, right at rdbt onto Leith Street. Straight on, left onto North Bridge, hotel on right*

This stunning conversion was formerly the headquarters of The Scotsman newspaper. The classical elegance of the public areas, complete with a marble staircase, blends seamlessly with the contemporary bedrooms and their state-of-the-art technology. The superbly equipped leisure club includes a stainless steel swimming pool and large gym. Dining arrangements can be made in the funky North Bridge Brasserie, or in the opulent Vermilion restaurant.

ROOMS: 69 en suite (4 GF) in 25 bedrooms s £250-£295; d £250-£750 **FACILITIES: Spa** STV supervised Sauna Solarium Gym Jacuzzi Beauty treatments **CONF:** Thtr 100 Class 50 Board 40 Del from £190 **SERVICES:** Lift **NOTES:** Civ Wed 70 **CARDS:**

★★★★★71% **Sheraton Grand Hotel & Spa**
1 Festival Square EH3 9SR
☎ 0131 229 9131 0131 228 4510
e-mail: grandedinburgh.sheraton@sheraton.com
Dir: *follow City Centre signs(A8). Through Shandwick, right at lights into Lothian Rd. Right at next lights. Hotel on left at next lights*

Sheraton HOTELS & RESORTS

This modern hotel has one of the best leisure centre and spas in the city - the pool is well worth a look. The spacious bedrooms are available in a variety of styles, and the suites prove very popular. There are a wide range of eating options - The Terrace, Santini's and the Grillroom that all have a loyal local following.

ROOMS: 260 en suite (25 fmly) in 204 bedrooms s £139-£290; d £139-£330 **LB FACILITIES: Spa** STV Sauna Gym Jacuzzi Indoor/Outdoor hydropool ♫ ch fac Xmas **CONF:** BC Thtr 485 Class 350 Board 120 Del from £200 **SERVICES:** Lift air con **PARKING:** 150 **NOTES:** Civ Wed 485 **CARDS:**

★★★★★69% **Balmoral**
1 Princes St EH2 2EQ
☎ 0131 556 2414 0131 622 8806
0131 557 3747
e-mail: reservations@thebalmoralhotel.com
web: www.roccofortehotels.com
Dir: *follow signs to City Centre. Hotel at the east end of Princes Street, adjacent to Wavereley Station*

ROCCO FORTE HOTELS

Built in the tradition of the great Victorian transport hotels, this grand city centre hotel first opened its doors in 1902. Even today, the clock in the tower is kept two minutes fast so that people don't miss their trains. Many of the elegantly furnished bedrooms enjoy fine views of the city and the castle. Indulge yourself with treatments at the Roman-style health spa or cream teas in the Palm Court bar; and choose from two very different dining options - Number One offers fine dining, while Hadrians is a bustling, informal brasserie.

ROOMS: 188 en suite (23 fmly) in 145 bedrooms s £220-£270; d £250-£370 **LB FACILITIES: Spa** STV supervised Sauna Solarium Gym ESPA treatment rooms, steam room, exercise studio ♫ Xmas **CONF:** BC Thtr 350 Class 180 Board 60 Del £265 **SERVICES:** Lift air con **PARKING:** 100 **NOTES:** **CARDS:**

Top 200 – Town House

★★★★ **The Bonham**
35 Drumsheugh Gardens EH3 7RN
☎ 0131 226 6050 & 0131 623 9116 0131 226 6080
e-mail: reserve@thebonham.com
web: www.thebonham.com
Dir: *located close to West End & Princes St*

This stylish hotel is located in a quiet, tree lined street, a few minutes' walk from Princes Street and from the city's major shops and attractions. Inviting day rooms and eye-catching bedrooms combine Victorian architecture with 21st-century technology, and there is a refreshing contemporary atmosphere throughout. Imaginative dinners highlight the chef's commitment to accuracy and good use is made of local fresh produce.

ROOMS: 48 en suite (1 GF) in 24 bedrooms s £108-£145; d £145-£195 (incl. bkfst) **LB FACILITIES:** STV Xmas **CONF:** Thtr 50 Board 26 Del £185 **SERVICES:** Lift **PARKING:** 20 **NOTES:** in restaurant **CARDS:**

Top 200 – Town House

★★★★ **Channings**
15 South Learmonth Gardens EH4 1EZ
☎ 0131 332 3232 & 315 2226 0131 332 9631
e-mail: reserve@channings.co.uk
web: www.channings.co.uk
Dir: *from A90 and Forth Road Bridge, follow signs for city centre*

CLASSIC BRITISH

Minutes from the city centre, this stylish town house occupies five Edwardian terraced houses. Public areas have undergone a stylish refurbishment and include sumptuous, inviting lounges and a choice of dining options: The popular Ochre Vita wine bar or the elegant Channings Restaurant where accomplished, imaginative food is served. Individually

continued

designed bedrooms are well equipped and attractively appointed. Service is attentive and friendly.

ROOMS: 46 en suite (4 GF) ⊗ in 30 bedrooms s £105-£140; d £138-£185 (incl. bkfst) **LB** **FACILITIES:** STV Xmas **CONF:** Thtr 35 Board 18 Del £185 **SERVICES:** Lift **NOTES:** ⊗ in restaurant Civ Wed 80 **CARDS:**

Top 200 – Town House

★★★★ **The Howard**
34 Great King St EH3 6QH
☎ 0131 557 3500 📠 0131 557 6515
e-mail: reserve@thehoward.com web: www.thehoward.com
Dir: *E on Queen St, take 2nd left, Dundas St. Continue through 3 sets of lights, turn right & hotel on left*

Quietly elegant, The Howard is made up of three linked Georgian houses and is situated just a short walk from Princes Street. There are some splendid suites and well-proportioned rooms, with equally impressive bathrooms featuring claw-foot baths and separate power showers. Ornate chandeliers and lavish drapes adorn the drawing room, while the Atholl Dining Room contains some unique hand-painted murals dating from the 1800s. Room service provides an extensive choice.

continued

ROOMS: 18 en suite s £108-£145; d £206-£275 (incl. bkfst) **LB** **FACILITIES:** STV Xmas **CONF:** Thtr 16 Board 14 **SERVICES:** Lift **PARKING:** 10 **NOTES:** ⊗ in restaurant **CARDS:**

Town House Hotel
Country House Hotel
Travel Accommodation

EDINBURGH, continued

Top 200 – Hotel

★★★★ Prestonfield
Priestfield Rd EH16 5UT
☎ 0131 225 7800 0131 220 4392
e-mail: info@prestonfield.com web: www.prestonfield.com
Dir: *200mtrs from R. Commonwealth Pool, into Priestfield Rd.*
This centuries-old landmark has been lovingly restored and enhanced to provide deeply comfortable and dramatically furnished bedrooms. The building demands to be explored: from the tapestry lounge to the whisky room and to the restaurant, where the walls are adorned with pictures of former owners. Facilities and services are up to the minute, and carefully prepared meals are served in Rhubarb restaurant. Nominated for the AA Hotel of the Year Award for Scotland 2004-5.
ROOMS: 26 en suite (6 GF) s £150-£250; d £150-£250 (incl. bkfst) **LB** **FACILITIES:** STV 18 Xmas **CONF:** Thtr 700 Class 500 Board 40 **SERVICES:** Lift **PARKING:** 250 **NOTES:** Civ Wed 350
CARDS:

★★★★74% Norton House
Ingliston EH28 8LX
HandPICKED
☎ 0131 333 1275 0131 333 5305
e-mail: nortonhouse-cro@handpicked.co.uk
Dir: *off A8, 5m W of city centre*

Situated close to the airport, this extended Victorian mansion lies in 55 acres of parkland. Public rooms adopt a mainly contemporary style with a conservatory bar lounge, adjoining brasserie and intimate fine dining restaurant. Elegant bedrooms are in the main house and the trendy boutique-style ones in the wing. Hand Picked Hotels - AA Hotel Group of the Year 2004-5.
ROOMS: 47 en suite (2 fmly) (10 GF) in 27 bedrooms s £150-£190; d £150-£190 **LB** **FACILITIES:** STV Archery, Laser, Clay pigeon shooting, Quad biking Xmas **CONF:** Thtr 300 Class 100 Board 60 Del from £140 **PARKING:** 200 **NOTES:** in restaurant Civ Wed 150
CARDS:

See advert on page 709

★★★★71% *Holyrood Hotel*

Holyrood Rd EH8 8AU
☎ 0131 550 4500 0131 550 4545
MACDONALD HOTELS
e-mail: holyrood@macdonald-hotels.co.uk
Dir: *parallel to Royal Mile, near Holyrood Palace & Dynamic Earth*
Situated just a short walk from Holyrood Palace, this impressive new hotel lies next to the new Scottish Parliament building. Air-conditioned bedrooms are comfortably furnished, whilst the Club floor boasts a private lounge. Full business services complement the extensive conference suites and the spa provides an opportunity for relaxation.
ROOMS: 157 en suite (10 fmly) in 140 bedrooms **FACILITIES:** STV Sauna Solarium Gym Beauty treatment rooms **CONF:** BC Thtr 300 Class 80 Board 80 **SERVICES:** Lift air con **PARKING:** 70 **NOTES:** Civ Wed 60 **CARDS:**

★★★★71% Marriott Dalmahoy Hotel & Country Club
Marriott HOTELS·RESORTS·SUITES
Kirknewton EH27 8EB
☎ 0870 400 7299 0870 400 7399
e-mail: reservations.dalmahoy@marriotthotels.co.uk
Dir: *Edinburgh City Bypass (A720) turn onto A71, on left*
The rolling Pentland Hills and beautifully kept parkland provide a stunning backdrop for this imposing Georgian mansion. With two championship golf courses and a health and beauty club, there is plenty here to occupy guests. Bedrooms are spacious and most have fine views, while public rooms offer a choice of formal and informal drinking and dining options.
ROOMS: 43 en suite 172 annexe en suite (59 fmly) in 136 bedrooms s £105-£118; d £110-£136 (incl. bkfst) **LB** **FACILITIES:** STV 18 Sauna Solarium Gym Putt green Jacuzzi Health & beauty treatments, Steam room, Dance studio, Driving range, Hair salon ch fac Xmas **CONF:** Thtr 300 Class 200 Board 120 Del from £140 **SERVICES:** Lift **PARKING:** 350 **NOTES:** in restaurant Civ Wed 250
CARDS:

★★★★71% Novotel Edinburgh Centre
NOVOTEL
Lauriston Place, Lady Lawson St EH3 9DE
☎ 0131 656 3500 0131 656 3510
e-mail: H3271@accor-hotels.com
Dir: *from Edinburgh Castle right onto George IV Bridge from Royal Mile. Follow to junct, then right onto Lauriston Pl for hotel 700mtrs on right.*
One of the new generation of Novotels, this modern hotel is located in the centre of the city, close to Edinburgh Castle and five minutes from Princes Street. Public areas are contemporary in style and include a smart bar, brasserie style restaurant and indoor leisure facilities. The air-conditioned bedrooms feature a comprehensive range of extras and bathrooms with baths and separate shower cabinets.
ROOMS: 180 en suite (146 fmly) in 135 bedrooms s £109-£129; d £109-£129 **LB** **FACILITIES:** STV Sauna Solarium Gym Jacuzzi ch fac Xmas **CONF:** BC Thtr 80 Class 50 Board 32 Del from £120 **SERVICES:** Lift air con **PARKING:** 17 **CARDS:**

★★★★70% Apex International
31/35 Grassmarket EH1 2HS
☎ 0131 300 3456 & 0845 608 3456 0131 220 5345
e-mail: international@apexhotels.co.uk
web: www.apexhotels.co.uk
Dir: *into Lothian Rd at west end of Princes Street, turn 1st left along King Stables Rd. This leads into the Grassmarket*
A sister to the Apex City Hotel close by, the International enjoys a superb city centre location, lying in a historic square in the shadow of Edinburgh Castle. It has a versatile business and conference centre, and the bedrooms are contemporary in style

continued on p712

EDINBURGH, continued

and well equipped. The fifth floor restaurant boasts stunning views of the castle.

Apex International, Edinburgh

ROOMS: 175 en suite (99 fmly) ⊗ in 100 bedrooms s £80-£220; d £80-£220 **LB FACILITIES:** STV Xmas **CONF:** Thtr 200 Class 80 Board 40 Del from £160 **SERVICES:** Lift **PARKING:** 60 **NOTES:** Civ Wed 200 **CARDS:**

See advert on page 711

★★★★70% Carlton

North Bridge EH1 1SD
☎ 0131 472 3000 0131 556 2691
e-mail: carlton@paramount-hotels.co.uk
Dir: *on North Bridge which links Princes St to the Royal Mile*

The Carlton occupies a city centre location just off the Royal Mile, and has been extensively upgraded to a modern and stylish design. Public areas include an impressive open-plan reception/lobby, modern first-floor bar and restaurant and basement leisure club. Bedrooms, many air-conditioned, are generally spacious, with an excellent range of facilities.

ROOMS: 189 en suite (20 fmly) ⊗ in 140 bedrooms s £210-£230; d £225-£245 (incl. bkfst) **LB FACILITIES: Spa** STV Squash Sauna Solarium Gym Jacuzzi Table tennis, Dance studio, Creche, Exercise classes ♫ Xmas **CONF:** BC Thtr 240 Class 100 Board 60 Del from £175 **SERVICES:** Lift **NOTES:** ⊗ in restaurant Civ Wed **CARDS:**

★★★★70% Menzies Belford

69 Belford Rd EH4 3DG
☎ 0131 332 2545 0131 332 3805
e-mail: belford@menzies-hotels.co.uk
Dir: *Belford Rd off Queensferry Rd, close to city centre. Opposite the Dean Gallery.*

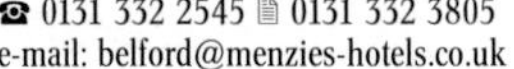

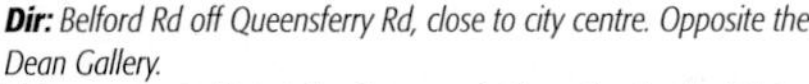

This purpose-built hotel enjoys a quiet location by the Water of Leith. The majority of the bedrooms have been stylishly refurbished. Bright, airy public areas include a comfortable reception lounge and spacious open-plan bar and restaurant overlooking the river, as does the separate Granary bar which focuses on pub food. There is a manned business centre.

ROOMS: 146 en suite (1 fmly) ⊗ in 56 bedrooms s £135; d £135-£165 **LB FACILITIES:** Xmas **CONF:** BC Thtr 120 Class 50 Board 45 Del £155 **SERVICES:** Lift **PARKING:** 57 **NOTES:** ⊗ in restaurant Civ Wed **CARDS:**

★★★★70% Roxburghe

38 Charlotte Square EH2 4HG
☎ 0131 240 5500 0131 240 5555
e-mail: roxburghe@csmm.co.uk
Dir: *on corner of Charlotte St & George St*

This long-established hotel lies in the heart of the city overlooking Charlotte Square Gardens. Public areas are inviting and include relaxing lounges, a choice of bars (in the evening) and an inner concourse that looks onto a small lawn area. Smart bedrooms come in classic or contemporary style. There is a secure underground car park.

ROOMS: 197 en suite (4 fmly) ⊗ in 167 bedrooms s £79-£210; d £99-£230 **LB FACILITIES:** STV Sauna Solarium Gym Dance studio, Spa treatment rooms, steam room ♫ Xmas **CONF:** Thtr 300 Class 120 Board 80 Del from £120 **SERVICES:** Lift **PARKING:** 20 **NOTES:** ⊗ in restaurant Civ Wed 280 **CARDS:**

★★★★69% Edinburgh Marriott Hotel

111 Glasgow Rd EH12 8NF
☎ 0870 400 7293 0870 400 7393
e-mail: edinburgh@marriotthotels.co.uk
Dir: *M8 junct 1 for Gogar, at rdbt turn right for city centre, hotel on right*

This purpose-built hotel is sited on the city's western fringe, close to the bypass and convenient for the airport, showground and business park, and attracts an international clientele. The public areas radiate from the attractive marbled foyer and include two bars, a restaurant providing a choice of modern dishes, and an inviting carvery.

ROOMS: 245 en suite (131 fmly) (64 GF) ⊗ in 89 bedrooms s £76-£90; d £82-£110 (incl. bkfst) **LB FACILITIES:** STV Sauna Solarium Gym Jacuzzi Steam room, Massage and beauty treatment room Xmas **CONF:** BC Thtr 300 Class 120 Board 45 Del from £130 **SERVICES:** Lift air con **PARKING:** 300 **NOTES:** ⊗ in restaurant Civ Wed 80 **CARDS:**

★★★★68% George Inter-Continental

19-21 George St EH2 2PB
☎ 0131 225 1251 0131 226 5644
e-mail: edinburgh@interconti.com
Dir: *Charlotte Sq, follow signs to Leith, along Queen St. Take 2nd turning on right, Hanover St, to rdbt. Left onto George St, hotel 50mtrs on right*

This hotel enjoys an enviable location in the city. The splendid public areas consist of many original features, such as intricate plasterwork, marble-floored foyer and chandeliers. Bedrooms vary in size and are comfortable, some offer city views. There are two restaurants, the formal, elegant Chambertin or the more informal Carvers.

ROOMS: 195 en suite ⊗ in 73 bedrooms s £180-£220; d £205-£240 **LB FACILITIES:** STV Complimentary fitness club nearby ♫ ch fac Xmas **CONF:** BC Thtr 200 Class 80 Board 80 Del from £160 **SERVICES:** Lift **PARKING:** 20 **NOTES:** Civ Wed 200 **CARDS:**

★★★★65% Apex City

61 Grassmarket EH1 2JF
☎ 0131 243 3456 & 0845 608 3456 0131 225 6346
e-mail: city@apexhotels.co.uk
Dir: *turn into Lothian Rd at the west end of Princes Street, then turn 1st left along King Stables Rd. This leads into Grassmarket*

This modern, stylish hotel is located in the heart of the city, within

continued

easy walking distance of many of Edinburgh's attractions. The spacious, design-led bedrooms are fresh and contemporary and all come with artwork by Richard Dimarco. Agua bar and restaurant is a smart open-plan area in dark wood and chrome that serves a range of meals and cocktails.
ROOMS: 119 en suite ⊗ in 84 bedrooms s £80-£220; d £80-£220 **LB** **FACILITIES:** STV Xmas **CONF:** Thtr 70 Class 24 Board 34 Del from £170 **SERVICES:** Lift **PARKING:** 10 **NOTES:** ⊗ in restaurant **CARDS:**

See advert on page 711

★★★★60% The Royal Terrace

18 Royal Ter EH7 5AQ
☎ 0131 557 3222 & 524 5000 📠 0131 557 5334
e-mail: sales@royalterracehotel.co.uk
web: www.royalterracehotel.co.uk
Dir: *A71 to city centre, follow one-way system and turn left into Charlotte Sq. At end of the road turn right onto Queens St. then take left at rdbt. At next island turn right into London Rd and right again into Royal Ter*

With the atmosphere of a town house, this hotel forms part of a quiet Georgian terrace and is now under new ownership. Bedrooms are in a variety of styles, some lofty and spacious with four-poster beds, others more compact. The upper rooms look out either over the city to the north, or onto terraced gardens at the rear.
ROOMS: 108 en suite (6 fmly) (5 GF) ⊗ in 30 bedrooms s £115; d £175 **FACILITIES:** STV Sauna Solarium Gym Jacuzzi Steam room Xmas **CONF:** BC Thtr 90 Class 60 Board 40 **SERVICES:** Lift **NOTES:** ⊗ in restaurant Civ Wed 80 **CARDS:**

See advert on this page

★★★76% Best Western Bruntsfield

69/74 Bruntsfield Place EH10 4HH
☎ 0131 229 1393 📠 0131 229 5634
e-mail: sales@thebruntsfield.co.uk
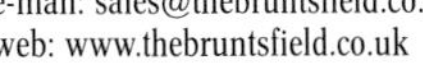
web: www.thebruntsfield.co.uk
Dir: *from S into Edinburgh on A702. Hotel 1m S of Princes Street*

Overlooking Bruntsfield Links, this smart hotel has stylish public rooms including relaxing lounge areas and a lively pub. Bedrooms come in a variety of sizes and styles and are well equipped. Imaginative dinner menus and hearty Scottish breakfasts are served in the bright and modern Cardoon conservatory restaurant. Smart staff provide good levels of service and attention.
ROOMS: 73 en suite (5 fmly) ⊗ in 49 bedrooms s £75-£150; d £125-£275 (incl. bkfst) **LB** **FACILITIES:** STV Xmas **CONF:** Thtr 75 Class 30 Board 30 Del from £125 **SERVICES:** Lift **PARKING:** 25 **NOTES:** ⊗ in restaurant Closed 25 Dec Civ Wed 85 **CARDS:**

★★★76% *Malmaison*

One Tower Place EH6 7DB
☎ 0131 468 5000 📠 0131 468 5002
e-mail: edinburgh@malmaison.com
Dir: *A900 from city centre towards Leith, at end of Leith Walk continue over lights through 2 more sets of lights, left into Tower St, hotel on right at the end of road*

Overlooking the port of Leith, this former seamen's mission is now home to the stylish Malmaison. Bedrooms have striking décor, CD players, mini-bars and a number of individual, welcoming touches. Food and drink are equally important here, with brasserie-style dining and a café bar, both of which are popular with the local clientele.
ROOMS: 101 en suite (18 fmly) ⊗ in 12 bedrooms **FACILITIES:** STV Gym **CONF:** Thtr 55 Class 30 Board 26 **SERVICES:** Lift **PARKING:** 50 **CARDS:**

Looking for a last-minute weekend away?
Check out Latebeds,
the AA's late availability booking service, at www.theAA.com

EDINBURGH, continued

★★★75%

Dalhousie Castle & Aqueous Spa

Bonnyrigg EH19 3JB
☎ 01875 820153 🖹 01875 821936
e-mail: info@dalhousiecastle.co.uk
web: www.dalhousiecastle.co.uk
Dir: *A7 S from Edinburgh through Lasswade/Newtongrange, right at Shell Garage (B704), hotel 0.5m from junct*

A popular wedding venue, this imposing medieval castle sits amid lawns and parkland and even has a falconry. Bedrooms offer a mix of styles and sizes, including richly decorated themed rooms named after various historical figures. The Dungeon restaurant provides an atmospheric setting for dinner, and the less formal Orangery serves food all day.

ROOMS: 27 en suite 6 annexe en suite (3 fmly) ⊗ in all bedrooms s £120-£140; d £165-£325 (incl. bkfst) **LB** **FACILITIES: Spa** STV Fishing Sauna Solarium Jacuzzi Falconry, Clay pigeon shooting, Archery, Loch fishing Xmas **CONF:** Thtr 120 Class 60 Board 40 Del £185 **PARKING:** 110 **NOTES:** ⊗ in restaurant Civ Wed 100 **CARDS:**

★★★71%

Best Western Edinburgh City

79 Laurieston Place EH3 9HZ
☎ 0131 622 7979 🖹 0131 622 7900
e-mail: reservations@bestwesternedinburghcity.co.uk
Dir: *follow signs for city centre A8. Onto A702, 3rd exit on left, hotel on right*

Occupying a site that was once the old maternity hospital, this tasteful conversion is located close to the city centre. Spacious bedrooms are smartly modern and well equipped to include fridges. Meals can be enjoyed in the bright contemporary restaurant and guests can relax in the cosy bar and reception lounge. Staff are friendly and obliging.

ROOMS: 52 en suite (12 fmly) (5 GF) ⊗ in 37 bedrooms s £75-£130; d £85-£190 **LB** **FACILITIES:** STV **SERVICES:** Lift **NOTES:** ⊗ in restaurant **CARDS:**

★★★71%

Melville Castle

Melville Gate, Gilmerton Rd EH18 1AP
☎ 0131 654 0088 🖹 0131 654 4666
e-mail: reception@melvillecastle.com web: www.melvillecastle.com
Dir: *from S on Bypass, exit at Gilmerton junct onto A7. Pass Dobbies Garden Centre, straight over rdbt for hotel next on right. From N on Bypass, take exit for Galashiels off Sheriff Hall rdbt. Turn left at next rdbt for hotel next on right.*

A castellated mansion set in wooded grounds close to the bypass near the city's southern boundary. Impressively refurbished, it focuses on receptions, small conferences and corporate events. The business and leisure guest will appreciate the lovely bedrooms, including galleried suites. Meals are served in the vaulted cellar bar and brasserie.

ROOMS: 30 en suite (1 fmly) (10 GF) ⊗ in all bedrooms s £115-£130; d £145-£175 (incl. bkfst) **FACILITIES:** STV Fishing Xmas **CONF:** Thtr 100 Class 70 Board 40 Del from £160 **SERVICES:** Lift **PARKING:** 70 **NOTES:** ⊗ in restaurant Civ Wed 120 **CARDS:**

★★★70%

Braid Hills

134 Braid Rd EH10 6JD
☎ 0131 447 8888 🖹 0131 452 8477
e-mail: bookings@braidhillshotel.co.uk
web: www.braidhillshotel.co.uk
Dir: *2.5m S A702, opposite Braid Burn Park*

From its elevated position on the south side, this long-established hotel enjoys splendid panoramic views of the city and castle. Bedrooms are smart, stylish and well equipped. The public areas are comfortable and inviting, and guests can dine in either the restaurant or popular bistro/bar.

ROOMS: 67 en suite (6 fmly) ⊗ in 8 bedrooms s £70-£90; d £90-£145 (incl. bkfst) **LB** **FACILITIES:** STV Xmas **CONF:** Thtr 100 Class 50 Board 30 Del from £120 **PARKING:** 38 **NOTES:** ⊗ in restaurant Civ Wed 100 **CARDS:**

See advert on opposite page

★★★68%

Kings Manor

100 Milton Rd East EH15 2NP
☎ 0131 669 0444 🖹 0131 669 6650
e-mail: info@kingsmanor.com
web: www.kingsmanor.com
Dir: *A720 E until Old Craighall junct, left into city, turn right at junct of A1/A199, hotel 200mtrs on right*

Lying on the eastern side of the city and convenient for the bypass, this hotel is popular with business guests, tour groups and for conferences. It boasts a fine leisure complex and a bright modern bistro, which complements the more traditional restaurant.

ROOMS: 67 en suite (2 fmly) (5 GF) ⊗ in 31 bedrooms s £60-£83; d £90-£135 (incl. bkfst) **LB** **FACILITIES:** STV supervised Sauna Solarium Gym Jacuzzi Health & beauty salon Xmas **CONF:** BC Thtr 140 Class 70 Board 50 Del from £125 **SERVICES:** Lift **PARKING:** 100 **NOTES:** Civ Wed 100 **CARDS:**

★★★67%

Apex European

90 Haymarket Ter EH12 5LQ
☎ 0131 474 3456 & 0845 608 3456 🖹 0131 474 3400
e-mail: european@apexhotels.co.uk
web: www.apexhotels.co.uk
Dir: *A8 to city centre, hotel at Haymarket just after Donaldsons School for Deaf.*

Ideally located for the financial district, conference centre and Haymarket Station, this modern hotel is popular with business travellers. Compact bedrooms offer an excellent range of facilities

continued

and have been designed with work in mind. Public areas include Metro, an informal bistro.

ROOMS: 66 en suite (3 GF) ⊗ in 51 bedrooms s £80-£220; d £80-£220 **LB FACILITIES:** STV **CONF:** Thtr 80 Class 30 Board 36 Del from £140 **SERVICES:** Lift **PARKING:** 17 **NOTES:** ⊗ in restaurant Closed 24-27 Dec **CARDS:**

See advert on page 711

★★★66% Old Waverley
43 Princes St EH2 2BY
☎ 0131 556 4648 0131 557 6316
e-mail: reservations@oldwaverley.co.uk
Dir: *in city centre, opposite Scott Monument, Waverley Station & Jenners*
Occupying a commanding position opposite Sir Walter Scott's famous monument on Princes Street, this hotel is convenient for the station and the city centre. Public rooms are all on first-floor level and along with front-facing bedrooms enjoy the fine views.
ROOMS: 66 en suite (3 fmly) ⊗ in 53 bedrooms s £45-£129; d £55-£169 (incl. bkfst) **LB FACILITIES:** STV leisure facilities at sister hotel Xmas **SERVICES:** Lift **NOTES:** ⊗ in restaurant
CARDS:

★★★66% *Quality Hotel*

Edinburgh Airport, Ingliston EH28 8NF
☎ 0131 333 4331 0131 333 4124
Dir: *from M8 take turn for airport. At rdbt before Airport terminal turn left, then 2nd left then 1st right*
Located adjacent to the Royal Highland Showground at Ingliston, this modern hotel is also convenient for the airport. The spacious executive bedrooms are the pick of the accommodation, and there is a café/restaurant offering a range of contemporary dishes.
ROOMS: 95 en suite ⊗ in 64 bedrooms **FACILITIES:** STV **CONF:** Thtr 70 Class 24 Board 24 **SERVICES:** Lift **PARKING:** 100 **NOTES:** ⊗ in restaurant **CARDS:**

★★★65% *Agenda*
92-98 St Johns Rd EH12 8AT
☎ 0131 316 4466 0131 334 9174
e-mail: info@agenda-edinburgh.co.uk
web: www.agenda-edinburgh.co.uk
Dir: *on A8 road into Edinburgh*
Set in the western village suburb of Corstophine this contemporary hotel is a popular venue for the young trendy bar goers, but also attracts a mixed market. A brasserie menu is available in the minimalist style all-day café bar as well as in the restaurant. Service is friendly and attentive.
ROOMS: 28 en suite **FACILITIES:** STV ♫ **PARKING:** 27 **NOTES:**
CARDS:

♫ Entertainment

★★★65% Greens Hotel

24 Eglinton Crescent, Haymarket EH12 5BY
☎ 0131 337 1565 0131 337 9405
e-mail: greens@crerarhotels.com
web: www.crerarhotels.com
Dir: *close to Haymarket Station in west of city, at head of Coates Gdns off Haymarket Ter*

Four Georgian houses have been converted to create this friendly hotel in the West End. Bedrooms are well equipped and superior rooms are particularly spacious. There is a choice of dining options that includes the Garden Restaurant and a more relaxed bar and brasserie; smart conference and meeting facilities are also available.
ROOMS: 55 en suite (6 fmly) ⊗ in 20 bedrooms s £45-£85; d £75-£140 (incl. bkfst) **LB FACILITIES:** Xmas **CONF:** Thtr 50 Class 24 Board 30 Del from £80 **SERVICES:** Lift **NOTES:** ⊗ in restaurant Civ Wed 50
CARDS:

EDINBURGH, continued

★★★64% Edinburgh Capital
187 Clermiston Rd EH12 6UG
☎ 0131 535 9988 📠 0131 334 9712
e-mail: manager@edinburghcapitalhotel.co.uk
Dir: *from A8 turn left into Clermiston Rd at the National Tyre Garage. Hotel is at the top of the hill.*
Attracting business, conference and leisure markets, this purpose-built hotel lies on the west side of the city and is convenient for the airport and the north. The conservatory restaurant provides fine views along with friendly service and good value meals.
ROOMS: 111 en suite (6 fmly) (14 GF) ⊘ in 68 bedrooms s £63-£127; d £63-£155 (incl. bkfst) **LB FACILITIES: Spa** STV supervised Sauna Solarium Gym Jacuzzi Beautician and sunbeds Xmas **CONF:** Thtr 300 Class 150 Board 80 Del from £90 **SERVICES:** Lift **PARKING:** 106 **NOTES:** ⊘ in restaurant Civ Wed 200
CARDS:

★★★63% Jurys Inn Edinburgh
43 Jeffrey St EH1 1DH
☎ 0131 200 3300 📠 0131 200 0400
e-mail: jurysinnedinburgh@jurysdoyle.com
Dir: *A8/M8 to City Centre, follow one-way system, across Waverley Bridge, 1st left, hotel on right.*
A smart, elegant reception lounge greets guests at this modern hotel set in the heart of the city close to Waverley Station and the Royal Mile. There is a pub and an informal restaurant serving a wide range of dishes, including a canteen-style breakfast. Bedrooms are bright and spacious.
ROOMS: 186 en suite (68 fmly) ⊘ in 121 bedrooms s £75-£150; d £75-£150 **FACILITIES:** STV Discounted leisure facilities at nearby hotel. ♫ **CONF:** Thtr 50 Class 35 Board 30 Del from £120 **SERVICES:** Lift **NOTES:** Closed 24-25 Dec **CARDS:**

Restaurant with Rooms

The Witchery by the Castle
352 Castlehill, Royal Mile EH1 2NF
☎ 0131 225 5613 📠 0131 220 4392
e-mail: mail@thewitchery.com
web: www.thewitchery.com
Dir: *near Edinburgh Castle gate*

Whether staying or dining, the Witchery is one of the most romantic and memorable of destinations. It occupies 16th-century buildings right by Edinburgh Castle. Two suites are located above the restaurant, with others across the cobbled street. All are breathtakingly furnished in lavish Gothic style and superbly equipped.
ROOMS: 2 en suite 5 annexe en suite (1 GF) d £250 (incl. bkfst) **FACILITIES:** STV **NOTES:** No children 10yrs
CARDS:

Christopher North House
6 Gloucester Place EH3 6EF
☎ 0131 225 2720 📠 0131 220 4706
e-mail: reservations@christophernorth.co.uk
web: www.hoteledinburgh.co.uk
Dir: *In city centre, just off Queen St*
ROOMS: 15 en suite (5 fmly) ⊘ in 10 bedrooms **FACILITIES:** STV Guests may use leisure facilities at the Caledonian Hotel **NOTES:** ★★★
CARDS:

Dukes of Windsor Street
17 Windsor St EH7 5LA
☎ 0131 556 6046
e-mail: info@dukesofwindsor.com
Dir: *E end of Princess St onto Leith St. Pass Playhouse Theatre, right onto London Rd, Windsor St is 1st left.*
ROOMS: 8 en suite (1 fmly) (1 GF) ⊘ in all bedrooms s £35-£70; d £60-£140 (incl. bkfst) **LB NOTES:** ★★★ ⊘ in restaurant Closed 22nd-27th Dec **CARDS:**

Hotel Ibis

6 Hunter Square, (off The Royal Mile) EH1 1QW
☎ 0131 240 7000 📠 0131 240 7007
e-mail: H2039@accor-hotels.com
Dir: *from Queen St (M8/M9) or Waterloo Pl (A1) over North Bridge (A7) & High St, take 1st right off South Bridge, into Hunter Sq*
Modern, budget hotel offering comfortable accommodation in bright and practical bedrooms. Breakfast is self-service and dinner is available in the restaurant. For further details, consult the Hotel Groups page.
ROOMS: 99 en suite

Innkeeper's Lodge Edinburgh West
114-116 St John's Rd, Corstophine EH12 8AX
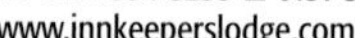
☎ 0131 334 8235 📠 0131 316 5012
www.innkeeperslodge.com
Dir: *M8 junct 1, N on A720. At Gogar rdbt, right onto A8, straight over next rdbt, hotel on left just past church at St John's Rd*
Smart rooms meet essential business requirements but also have home comforts, and depending on location may well have meeting rooms and pub dining. Dining options generally include all-day menus plus the added advantage of breakfast.
ROOMS: 28 en suite s £62; d £62

Premier Lodge (Edinburgh City Centre South)
Lauriston Place, Lady Lawson St EH3 9HZ
☎ 0870 9906610 📠 0870 9906611
web: www.premierlodge.com
Dir: *from A8, right onto A702 Lothian Rd and continue to Tollcross. Turn left into Lauriston Pl and Lodge at junction with Lauriston St, on left*
High quality, modern, budget accommodation, ideal for families and business travellers. All rooms feature bath, power shower and satellite TV, and most have telephones / modem points. The adjacent bar and restaurant offers a wide and varied menu.
ROOMS: 112 en suite s £54; d £54

Premier Lodge (Edinburgh East)

91 Newcraighall Rd, Newcraighall EH21 8RX
☎ 0870 9906336 📠 0870 9906337
web: www.premierlodge.com
Dir: *close to city centre at junct of A1 and A6095 towards Musselburgh*
High quality, modern, budget accommodation, ideal for families and business travellers. All rooms feature bath, power shower and satellite TV, and most have telephones / modem points. The adjacent bar and restaurant offers a wide and varied menu.
ROOMS: 42 en suite s £50; d £50

⌂ Travel Inn (Edinburgh City Centre)
1 Morrison Link EH3 8DN
☎ 0870 238 3319 📠 0131 228 9836
Dir: *next to Edinburgh International Conference Centre*

Travel Inn offers good-quality, value-for-money accommodation. Spacious, en suite rooms with bath and shower comfortably accommodate a family of up to two adults and two children (to age 15). The restaurant and bar offers a varied menu. For further details consult the Hotel Groups page.
ROOMS: 281 en suite s £58.95; d £58.95

⌂ Travel Inn (Edinburgh East)
228 Willowbrae Rd EH8 7NG
☎ 08701 977091 📠 0131 652 2789
Dir: *M8(J1) follow A720 (south for 12 miles). Take turn for A1. At rdbt after ASDA turn left. Follow for 2 miles. Travel Inn on left side before Esso garage*
Travel Inn offers good-quality, value-for-money accommodation. Spacious, en suite rooms with bath and shower comfortably accommodate a family of up to two adults and two children (to age 15). The restaurant and bar offers a varied menu. For further details consult the Hotel Groups page.
ROOMS: 39 en suite s £45.95-£48.95; d £45.95-£48.95

⌂ Travel Inn (Edinburgh Inveresk)
Carberry Rd, Inveresk, Musselburgh EH21 8PT
☎ 08701 977092 📠 0131 653 2270
Dir: *from A1, take exit signed Dalkeith (A6094). Follow signs until rdbt, turn right, Travel Inn 300yds on right*
Travel Inn offers good-quality, value-for-money accommodation. Spacious, en suite rooms with bath and shower comfortably accommodate a family of up to two adults and two children (to age 15). The restaurant and bar offers a varied menu. For further details consult the Hotel Groups page.
ROOMS: 40 en suite s £45.95-£46.95; d £45.95-£46.95 **CONF:** Thtr 80

⌂ Travel Inn (Edinburgh Leith)
Pier Place, Newhaven Dicks EH6 4TX
☎ 08701 977093 📠 0131 554 5994
Dir: *From A1 follow coast road through Leith. Pass Ocean Terminal, straight ahead at mini -rdbt, take 2nd exit marked Harry Ramsden's car park*
Travel Inn offers good-quality, value-for-money accommodation. Spacious, en suite rooms with bath and shower comfortably accommodate a family of up to two adults and two children (to age 15). The restaurant and bar offers a varied menu. For further details consult the Hotel Groups page.
ROOMS: 60 en suite s £45.95-£48.95; d £45.95-£48.95
CONF: Thtr 35 Board 25

⌂ Travelodge (Edinburgh Central)
33 Saint Marys St EH1 1TA
☎ 08700 850 950 📠 0131 557 3681
Travelodge offers good quality, good value, modern accommodation. Ideal for families, the spacious, en suite bedrooms include remote-control TV, tea and coffee-making facilities and luxury beds. Meals can be taken at the nearby family restaurant. For further details consult the Hotel Groups page.
ROOMS: 193 en suite s fr £25; d fr £25

⌂ Travelodge (Edinburgh East)
Old Craighall EH21 8RE
☎ 08700 850 950 📠 0131 653 6106
Dir: *off A1, 2m from E outskirts*
Travelodge offers good quality, good value, modern accommodation. Ideal for families, the spacious, en suite bedrooms include remote-control TV, tea and coffee-making facilities and luxury beds. Meals can be taken at the nearby family restaurant. For further details consult the Hotel Groups page.
ROOMS: 45 en suite s fr £25; d fr £25

⌂ Travelodge (Edinburgh South)
46 Dreghorn Link EH13 9QR
☎ 08700 850 950 📠 0131 441 4296
Dir: *6m S, A720 Ring Rd S*
Travelodge offers good quality, good value, modern accommodation. Ideal for families, the spacious, en suite bedrooms include remote-control TV, tea and coffee-making facilities and luxury beds. Meals can be taken at the nearby family restaurant. For further details consult the Hotel Groups page.
ROOMS: 72 en suite s fr £25; d fr £25

EDZELL, Angus
Map 23 NO66

★★★65% *Glenesk*
High St DD9 7TF
☎ 01356 648319 📠 01356 647333
e-mail: gleneskhotel@btconnect.com
Dir: *off A90 just after Brechin Bypass*
Set in gardens by the golf course, this long established hotel is popular with both leisure and business guests. Public areas are comfortable and include a leisure club with a swimming pool.
ROOMS: 24 en suite (5 fmly) **FACILITIES:** Snooker Sauna Solarium Gym Jacuzzi **CONF:** Thtr 120 Class 60 Board 30 **PARKING:** 81 **NOTES:** in restaurant Civ Wed 60 **CARDS:**

ELGIN, Moray
Map 23 NJ26

★★★74% Mansion House
The Haugh IV30 1AW
☎ 01343 548811 📠 01343 547916
e-mail: reception@mhelgin.co.uk
Dir: *turn off A96 into Haugh Rd, then1st left*
This popular hotel is located close to the centre of town on the River Lossie. Bedrooms, many now stylishly upgraded, are spacious with a number enjoying views of the surrounding area. Extensive public areas include a choice of restaurants with the informality of the bistro contrasting well with the traditional restaurant.
ROOMS: 23 en suite s £85-£98; d £135-£165 (incl. bkfst) **LB**
FACILITIES: Spa STV supervised Fishing Snooker Sauna Solarium Gym Jacuzzi Xmas **CONF:** BC Thtr 200 **PARKING:** 50 **NOTES:** in restaurant Civ Wed 160 **CARDS:**

See advert on page 719

ELGIN, continued

★★★71% Laichmoray
Maisondieu Rd IV30 1QR
☎ 01343 540045 01343 540055
e-mail: enquiries@laichmorayhotel.co.uk
web: www.laichmorayhotel.co.uk
Dir: *opposite the railway station*

This popular business hotel is located close to the city centre and railway station. Warm hospitality and an informal atmosphere are real features. Bedrooms come in a variety of styles and sizes. An impressive range of meals is served in the bar, conservatory and restaurant and there is a choice of over 170 malt whiskies.
ROOMS: 35 rms (34 en suite) (4 fmly) in 8 bedrooms
FACILITIES: Pool **CONF:** Thtr 200 Class 160 Board 40 **PARKING:** 60
NOTES: Closed 24-26 Dec & 31 Dec - 3 Jan Civ Wed
CARDS:

Travel Inn
1 Linkwood Way IV30 1HY
☎ 08701 977095 01343 540635
Dir: *on A96, 1.5m E of city centre*

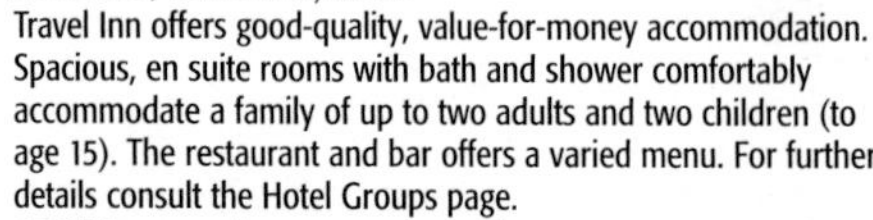

Travel Inn offers good-quality, value-for-money accommodation. Spacious, en suite rooms with bath and shower comfortably accommodate a family of up to two adults and two children (to age 15). The restaurant and bar offers a varied menu. For further details consult the Hotel Groups page.
ROOMS: 40 en suite s £45.95-£46.95; d £45.95-£46.95 **CONF:** Thtr 24

ERISKA, Argyll & Bute Map 20 NM94

Top 200 – Hotel

★★★★ Isle of Eriska
Eriska, Ledaig PA37 1SD
☎ 01631 720371 01631 720531
e-mail: office@eriska-hotel.co.uk
Dir: *leave A85 at Connel, onto A828, follow for 4m, then follow signs from N of Benderloch*
Situated on its own private island with delightful beaches and walking trails, this hotel offers a tranquil, private setting for total relaxation. Spacious bedrooms are comfortable and boast some fine antique pieces. Local seafood, meats and game feature prominently on the award-winning menu, as do vegetables and herbs grown in the hotel's kitchen garden.
continued

Leisure facilities include an indoor swimming pool, gym, spa treatment rooms and a small golf course.

ROOMS: 17 en suite s £195; d £250 (incl. bkfst) **LB**
FACILITIES: Spa supervised 6 Fishing Sauna Gym Putt green Jacuzzi Steam room, Skeet shooting, Nature trails Xmas
CONF: Thtr 30 Class 30 Board 30 **PARKING:** 40 **NOTES:** in restaurant Closed Jan Civ Wed **CARDS:**

ERSKINE, Renfrewshire Map 20 NS47

★★68% *The Erskine Bridge Hotel*
North Barr PA8 6AN
☎ 0141 812 0123 0141 812 7642
e-mail: erskineres@cosmopolitan-hotels.com
Dir: *M8 junct 30, A726 to Erskine. At 1st rdbt turn right, 2nd straight on, 3rd turn left*
Close to Erskine Bridge and the M8, this popular business hotel offers a good range of conference and banqueting facilities. Bedrooms, many with fine views over the River Clyde, come in two contrasting styles, with the newer rooms particularly appealing. Facilities include an indoor golf range and a children's play area.
ROOMS: 177 en suite (26 fmly) in 88 bedrooms **FACILITIES:** Sauna Solarium Gym Jacuzzi **CONF:** Thtr 600 Class 400 Board 50
SERVICES: Lift **PARKING:** 350 **NOTES:** Civ Wed 200
CARDS:

FALKIRK, Falkirk Map 21 NS88

★★★68% Park
Camelon Rd FK1 5RY
☎ 01324 628331 01324 611593
e-mail: info@parkhotelfalkirk.co.uk
web: www.parkhotelfalkirk.co.uk
Dir: *from M8 take A803 into Falkirk, hotel 1m beyond Mariner Leisure Centre, opposite Dollar Park. From M9, A803 through Falkirk, follow signs for Dollar Park*
This purpose-built, well-established hotel is popular with business travellers and easily accessible from all major transport routes. Smart contemporary public areas feature a spacious and inviting lounge and restaurant with a bar. Well-equipped bedrooms come in a variety of sizes.
ROOMS: 55 en suite (3 fmly) in 32 bedrooms s £50-£79; d £60-£89 (incl. bkfst) **LB** **FACILITIES:** STV **CONF:** BC Thtr 300 Class 140 Board 80 Del from £95 **SERVICES:** Lift **PARKING:** 160 **NOTES:** in restaurant Civ Wed 120 **CARDS:**

★★★66% Radisson SAS Airth Castle & Hotel

FK2 8JF
☎ 01324 831411 ▯ 01324 831184/831419
e-mail: reservations.stirlingshire@radissonsas.com
Dir: *M9 junct 7, M876 take 1st left A905 towards Airth. Hotel 0.5m on left*

Accommodation is provided in spacious rooms, housed in two separate buildings, one of which is an imposing castle. A popular choice for weddings, this hotel boasts excellent conference and leisure facilities. A choice of restaurants is provided, with a fine dining restaurant in the castle and a bistro-style eatery in the main building.

ROOMS: 99 en suite 23 annexe en suite (36 fmly) (33 GF) ⊗ in 65 bedrooms s £80-£120; d £80-£130 **FACILITIES:** STV Sauna Solarium Gym Jacuzzi Steam room Xmas **CONF:** Thtr 300 Class 180 Board 80 Del from £110 **SERVICES:** Lift **PARKING:** 150 **NOTES:** ⊗ in restaurant Civ Wed 120 **CARDS:**

Premier Lodge (Falkirk)

Glenbervie Business Park, Bellsdyke Rd, Larbert
FK5 4EG
☎ 0870 9906550 ▯ 0870 9906551
web: www.premierlodge.com
Dir: *just off A88, less than 1m from M876 junct 2 (4m from town centre)*

High quality, modern, budget accommodation, ideal for families and business travellers. All rooms feature bath, power shower and satellite TV, and most have telephones / modem points. The adjacent bar and restaurant offers a wide and varied menu.

ROOMS: 60 en suite s £46; d £46

FINTRY, Stirling — Map 20 NS68

★★★66% Culcreuch Castle

Kippen Rd G63 0LW
☎ 01360 860555 & 860228 ▯ 01360 860556
e-mail: info@culcreuch.com
web: www.culcreuch.com
Dir: *on B822 (17m W of Stirling & 20 miles N of Glasgow)*

Peacefully located in 1600 acres of parkland, this ancient castle dates back to 1296. Tastefully restored accommodation is in a mixture of individually themed castle rooms, some with four-poster beds and more modern courtyard rooms, which are suitable for families. Period-style public rooms include a bar, serving light meals, a wood-panelled dining room and an elegant lounge.

ROOMS: 10 en suite 4 annexe en suite (3 fmly) (4 GF) s £67-£110; d £84-£170 (incl. bkfst) **LB FACILITIES:** Fishing ch fac Xmas **CONF:** BC Thtr 140 Class 70 Del from £87.50 **PARKING:** 100 **NOTES:** ⊗ in restaurant Civ Wed 110 **CARDS:**

Packed in a hurry?
Ironing facilities should be available at all star levels, either in rooms or on request

- Indoor Swimming Pool
- Indoor Swimming Pool (heated)
- Outdoor Swimming Pool
- Outdoor Swimming Pool (heated)

FORRES, Moray — Map 23 NJ05

★★★67% *Ramnee*

Victoria Rd IV36 3BN
☎ 01309 672410 ▯ 01309 673392
e-mail: ramneehotel@btconnect.com
Dir: *off A96 at rdbt on E side of Forres, hotel 200yds on right*

Genuinely friendly staff ensure this well-established hotel remains popular with business travellers. Accommodation, including a family suite, varies in size, although all rooms are well-presented. Hearty bar food provides a less formal dining option to the imaginative restaurant menu.

ROOMS: 20 en suite (4 fmly) **FACILITIES:** STV use of leisure facilities at sister hotel ch fac **CONF:** Thtr 100 Class 30 Board 45 **PARKING:** 50 **NOTES:** ⊗ in restaurant Closed 25 Dec & 1-3 Jan Civ Wed 100 **CARDS:**

FORT WILLIAM, Highland Map 22 NN17

Top 200 – Hotel

★★★★ ⓇⓇⓇ **Inverlochy Castle**
Torlundy PH33 6SN
☎ 01397 702177 📠 01397 702953
e-mail: info@inverlochy.co.uk
Dir: *accessible from either A82 Glasgow-Fort William or A9 Edinburgh-Dalwhinnie. Hotel 3m N of Fort William on A82, in Torlundy*
With a backdrop of Ben Nevis, this imposing and gracious castle sits amidst extensive gardens and grounds overlooking the hotel's own loch to the valley of the Lochy. Lavishly appointed in classic country-house style, bedrooms are well proportioned and extremely comfortable. Luxurious public rooms include the main hall and lounge, both inviting quiet relaxation. Meals are taken in one of three dining rooms. A snooker room and a private video library are available if the weather is inclement.
ROOMS: 17 en suite s £205-£290; d £290-£550 (incl. bkfst) **LB** **FACILITIES:** STV Fishing Snooker Loch available for fishing ch fac Xmas **CONF:** Thtr 50 Class 20 Board 20 Del from £250 **PARKING:** 18 **NOTES:** in restaurant Closed 6 Jan-12 Feb Civ Wed 50 **CARDS:**

RELAIS & CHATEAUX

★★★75% Ⓡ **Moorings**
Banavie PH33 7LY
☎ 01397 772797 📠 01397 772441
e-mail: reservations@moorings-fortwilliam.co.uk
web: www.moorings-fortwilliam.co.uk
Dir: *3m N, off A830. Take A830 for 1m, cross the Caledonian Canal, 1st right*

Located on the Caledonian Canal next to a series of locks known as Neptune's Staircase, and close to Thomas Telford's house, this hotel offers friendly service from a dedicated, young team. Accommodation comes in two distinct styles with the newer

continued

rooms particularly appealing. Meals can be taken in a choice of bars and the spacious dining room.
ROOMS: 28 en suite (1 fmly) (1 GF) in 9 bedrooms s £62-£66; d £82-£110 (incl. bkfst) **LB** **FACILITIES:** STV Xmas **CONF:** Thtr 120 Class 40 Board 40 **PARKING:** 60 **NOTES:** in restaurant Civ Wed 120 **CARDS:**

See advert on opposite page

★★★66% **Grand**
Gordon Square PH33 6DX
☎ 01397 702928 📠 01397 702928
e-mail: enquiries@grandhotel-scotland.co.uk
Dir: *on A82 at W end of High St*
A relaxed and welcoming atmosphere is provided at this long-established, family-run hotel, at the south end of the high street. The bedrooms are smart and modern, and there is a choice of lounges. A good range of innovative dishes is served in both the restaurant and bar.
ROOMS: 30 en suite (4 fmly) in 15 bedrooms s £37.50-£47.50; d £55-£75 (incl. bkfst) **LB** **FACILITIES:** ch fac **CONF:** Thtr 110 Class 60 Board 20 **PARKING:** 20 **NOTES:** in restaurant Closed 30 Dec-11 Feb Civ Wed **CARDS:**

★★71% **Imperial**
Fraser's Square PH33 6DW
☎ 01397 702040 & 703921 📠 01397 706277
e-mail: imperial@bestwestern.co.uk
Dir: *from town centre, along Middle St, approx 400mtrs from junct with A82*
Benefiting from a town centre location this hotel is popular with both business and leisure guests and is ideally placed for the many local attractions. Public areas include a newly upgraded bar, a smart restaurant and lounge. Generally spacious bedrooms are comfortably appointed.
ROOMS: 34 en suite (2 fmly) in 6 bedrooms s £53-£90; d £90-£108 (incl. bkfst) **LB** **FACILITIES:** Xmas **CONF:** Thtr 60 Class 12 Board 16 **PARKING:** 15 **NOTES:** in restaurant
CARDS:

Best Western

★★70% **Nevis Bank**
Belford Rd PH33 6BY
☎ 01397 705721 📠 01397 706275
e-mail: info@nevisbankhotel.co.uk
web: www.nevisbankhotel.co.uk
Dir: *on A82, at junct to Glen Nevis*

A warm welcome is assured at this long-established hotel. It enjoys a fine location on the outskirts of the town close to the access road for the West Highland Way and Glen Nevis. Accommodation is provided in thoughtfully equipped bedrooms that vary in size. There is a choice of bars and dining options.
ROOMS: 31 en suite (3 fmly) (2 GF) s £25-£50; d £50-£85 (incl. bkfst) **LB** **FACILITIES:** Xmas **CONF:** BC Thtr 50 Class 30 Board 25 **PARKING:** 50 **NOTES:** in restaurant **CARDS:**

See advert on opposite page

NEVIS BANK HOTEL

Belford Road PH33 6BY
Tel: 01397 705721 Fax: 01397 706275
e-mail: info@nevisbankhotel.co.uk
web: www.nevisbankhotel.co.uk

Ideally situated close to the centre of Fort William, this privately owned hotel offers the very best in Highland hospitality, with the welcoming staff being both attentive and friendly. Bedrooms are equipped with all modern amenities, and the hotel's two bars and "Lower Falls" restaurant offer the very best in food, drink and atmosphere, capturing the true spirit of the Highlands.

Moorings Hotel, Banavie, Fort William
Inverness-shire, Scotland PH33 7LY
Tel: 01397 772797 Fax: 01397 772441
www.moorings-fortwilliam.co.uk
Email: reservations@moorings-fortwilliam.co.uk

Set in a peaceful countryside location beside the Caledonian Canal with panoramic views of Ben Nevis, yet just a five minute drive to the town of Fort William. The Moorings offers a warm friendly welcome with a relaxing ambience and superb cuisine. Dine in the award winning restaurant or enjoy a freshly prepared bar meal in the Upper Deck Bar.

F

• CORRIEGOUR LODGE • • HOTEL •

Loch Lochy, By Spean Bridge PH34 4EB
Tel: 01397 712685
www.corriegour-lodge-hotel.com

"BETTER FOOD THAN THE TOP LONDON RESTAURANTS, AND A VIEW TO DIE FOR" THE MIRROR

Dine by Candlelight and Crystal, enjoying panoramic views and seriously good food. King Scallops, Mouth-watering Beef, Puddings to die for, Fish fresh from the sea. Ambience, location, comfort and décor. Relax in front of a roaring log fire, big comfy sofas. Our emphasis is on guests' total relaxation and comfort. Enjoy the best of Scottish Produce, and watch the world go by in this Magical setting. Fishing, Walking, History Scenery. We have it all.
Dinner reservations telephone 01397 712 685

AA
★★★

Allt-nan-Ros Hotel

FOR BEN NEVIS AND GLENCOE
Onich, by Fort William
Inverness-shire PH33 6RY
Tel: 01855 821210/250 Fax: 01855 821462

Set in four acres with truly panoramic views from all bedrooms, restaurant and lounge across the garden and over Loch Linnhe to the hills of Appin and Morvern, it is no wonder that the MacLeod family's celebrated hotel is endorsed by so many leading authorities. Superb "Taste of Scotland" cuisine, log fire and malt whiskies — indeed, everything a Scottish West Highland Hotel should be!

For Special Offers check
Email: aa@allt-nan-ros.co.uk
Web: www.allt-nan-ros.co.uk

FORT WILLIAM, continued

★★63% Croit Anna
Achaintore Rd, Drimarben PH33 6RR
☎ 01397 702268 01397 704099
Leisureplex
e-mail: croitanna.fortwilliam@alfatravel.co.uk
Dir: *entering Fort William on A82 from Glencoe hotel 1st on right*
Located on the edge of Loch Linnhe, just two miles out of town, this hotel offers some spacious bedrooms, many of which have fine views over the loch. There is a choice of two lounges and a large airy restaurant. The hotel appeals to coach parties and independent travellers alike.
ROOMS: 89 rms (79 en suite) s £31-£41; d £52-£72 (incl. bkfst) **LB**
FACILITIES: ♫ ch fac Xmas **PARKING:** 25 **NOTES:** ⊗ in restaurant Closed Dec-Jan RS Nov, Feb, Mar **CARDS:**

F

Travel Inn
Loch Iall, An Aird PH33 6AN
☎ 08701 977104 01397 703618
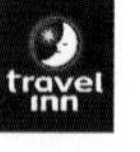

Dir: *N end of Fort William Shopping Centre, just off A82 ring road*
Travel Inn offers good-quality, value-for-money accommodation. Spacious, en suite rooms with bath and shower comfortably accommodate a family of up to two adults and two children (to age 15). The restaurant and bar offers a varied menu. For further details consult the Hotel Groups page.
ROOMS: 40 en suite s £45.95-£46.95; d £45.95-£46.95

FREUCHIE, Fife Map 21 NO20

★★67% *Lomond Hills*
Parliament Square KY15 7EY
THE INDEPENDENTS HOTEL ASSOCIATION
☎ 01337 857329 & 857498 01337 858180
e-mail: reception@lomondhillshotel.net
web: www.lomondhillshotel.net
Dir: *in centre of village off A92, 2m N of Glenrothes*
This long-established former coaching inn has been extended to create a welcoming tourist and business hotel in the centre of the village. Bedrooms come in varying sizes and styles, all offering a good range of facilities. Public areas include a cosy bar, a range of dining areas providing good value meals, and a small leisure centre.
ROOMS: 24 en suite (3 fmly) ⊗ in 3 bedrooms **FACILITIES:** STV Sauna Solarium Gym Jacuzzi **CONF:** Thtr 200 Class 100 Board 80
PARKING: 21 **NOTES:** ⊗ in restaurant Civ Wed 100
CARDS:

GAIRLOCH, Highland Map 22 NG87

★★69% Myrtle Bank
Low Rd IV21 2BS
☎ 01445 712004 01445 712214
e-mail: myrtlebank@msn.com
web: www.myrtlebankhotel.co.uk
Dir: *turn onto A832 to Gairloch. Straight through village, at Mace store turn left at T-junction. Hotel 2nd on Left*
A seafront location and views to the Isle of Skye are key factors at this friendly, family-run hotel. The spacious bedrooms are comfortably equipped. The public areas include a smart conservatory lounge, a well-stocked bar and the sea-facing restaurant, where guests can enjoy the breathtaking sunsets of Wester Ross.
ROOMS: 12 en suite (2 fmly) s £36-£44; d £72-£88 (incl. bkfst)
PARKING: 20 **NOTES:** ⊗ in restaurant **CARDS:**

GALASHIELS, Scottish Borders Map 21 NT43

★★★67% Kingsknowes
Selkirk Rd TD1 3HY
☎ 01896 758375 01896 750377
e-mail: enq@kingsknowes.co.uk
web: www.kingsknowes.co.uk
Dir: *off A7 at Galashiels/Selkirk rdbt*
Now under new ownership friendly service is the trademark of this hotel. It is set in attractive gardens overlooking the River Tweed on the outskirts of town. A turreted mansion, it boasts elegant public areas and many spacious bedrooms, some with excellent views. There is a choice of bars, one with a popular menu to supplement the restaurant.
ROOMS: 12 en suite (2 fmly) s fr £59; d fr £89 (incl. bkfst) **LB**
FACILITIES: STV **CONF:** Thtr 60 Class 40 Board 30 Del from £85
PARKING: 50 **NOTES:** ⊗ in restaurant Civ Wed 50
CARDS:

★★★67% Woodlands House Hotel & Restaurants
Windyknowe Rd TD1 1RG
☎ 01896 754722 01896 754892
e-mail: woodlands.uk@virgin.net
Dir: *A7 into Galashiels*
Quietly situated in two acres of grounds, this fine Victorian Gothic mansion is sited high above the town centre. Bedrooms come in a variety of sizes; some are very spacious, with many having views over the gardens. Both the bar and restaurant feature fine period architecture. Meals offered in both are well worth trying.
ROOMS: 10 en suite (1 fmly) **CONF:** Thtr 40 Class 40 Board 20
PARKING: 35 **NOTES:** ⊗ in restaurant Civ Wed 50
CARDS:

★★65% King's
56 Market St TD1 3AN
☎ 01896 755497 01896 755497
e-mail: kingshotel@talk21.com
Dir: *take A7 from Carlisle into Galashiels and follow one-way system. Turn left into Market St for hotel on right*
A welcoming atmosphere prevails at this friendly hotel, located just off the town centre. The bedrooms are sensibly furnished and have a good range of amenities. Freshly prepared meals are provided in the dining room and bar, both bright and cheerful rooms.
ROOMS: 7 en suite (2 fmly) ⊗ in all bedrooms s £40-£46; d £62-£72 (incl. bkfst) **FACILITIES:** Xmas **CONF:** Thtr 80 Class 50 Board 20
NOTES: ⊗ in restaurant **CARDS:**

★★64% Abbotsford Arms
63 Stirling St TD1 1BY
☎ 01896 752517 01896 750744
e-mail: roberts750@aol.com
Dir: *off A7 down Ladhope Vale, turn left opposite bus station*
A friendly and informal hotel handy for the town centre and bus station. Food is served throughout the day, with a range of generous dishes served mainly in the lounge bar. Bedrooms are cheerfully decorated and well equipped.
ROOMS: 14 en suite (3 fmly) s £40-£45; d £60-£72 (incl. bkfst) **LB**
FACILITIES: STV **CONF:** Thtr 100 Class 25 Board 40 Del from £85
NOTES: RS 25 Dec& 01 Jan Civ Wed 100 **CARDS:**

TV dinner?
Room service at three stars and above

GATEHOUSE OF FLEET, Dumfries & Galloway Map 20 NX55

★★★★71% **Cally Palace**
DG7 2DL
☎ 01557 814341 01557 814522
e-mail: info@callypalace.co.uk web: www.callypalace.co.uk
Dir: *M6 & A74, signed A75 Dumfries then Stranraer. At Gatehouse-of-Fleet turn right onto B727, left at Cally*

Now a resort hotel with extensive leisure facilities, this grand 18th-century building is set in 500 acres of forest and parkland, that incorporates a private golf course. Bedrooms are spacious and well equipped. The short dinner menu focuses on freshly prepared dishes; jacket and tie are the preferred attire in the evening.
ROOMS: 55 en suite (7 fmly) s £91-£135; d £172-£196 (incl. bkfst & dinner) **LB** **FACILITIES:** STV 18 Fishing Snooker Sauna Putt green Jacuzzi Table tennis Practice fairway ch fac Xmas **CONF:** Thtr 40 Class 40 Board 25 **SERVICES:** Lift **PARKING:** 100 **NOTES:** in restaurant Closed Jan-early Feb **CARDS:**

See advert on this page

★★★67% **Murray Arms**
DG7 2HY
☎ 01557 814207 01557 814370
e-mail: murrayarmshotel@ukonline.co.uk
web: www.murrayarms.com
Dir: *off A75, hotel at edge of town, near clock tower*
A relaxed and welcoming atmosphere prevails at this family-run hotel, a former coaching inn at the north end of the main street. Public areas retain a comfortable, traditional feel and include a choice of lounges, a snug bar and an all-day restaurant. Bedrooms are comfortable and well presented.
ROOMS: 12 en suite (3 fmly) s £50-£60; d £95-£110 (incl. bkfst) **LB** **FACILITIES:** Xmas **CONF:** Thtr 120 Class 50 Board 30 **PARKING:** 50 **CARDS:**

Early start?
Hotels at all star levels should provide in-room alarm clocks and/or alarm calls

GIFFORD, East Lothian Map 21 NT56

★★69% **Tweeddale Arms**
High St EH41 4QU
☎ 01620 810240 01620 810488
web: www.tweeddalearmshotel.co.uk
Dir: *A1 S from Edinburgh, turn off at Haddington, 4m to hotel*
In a picturesque setting by the village green, this hotel is enjoying a renaissance under new family ownership. Refurbishment is ongoing, though the original character is being retained. An

continued on p724

GIFFORD, continued

inviting lounge leads to a small but elegant dining room and the lounge bar is popular for bar meals.

Tweedale Arms Hotel, Gifford

ROOMS: 14 en suite (2 fmly) ⊗ in 10 bedrooms s £49-£65; d £65-£75 (incl. bkfst) **LB** **FACILITIES:** Putt green ch fac Xmas **CONF:** Thtr 80 Class 40 Board 30 Del from £65 **NOTES:** ⊗ in restaurant Civ Wed 200 **CARDS:**

GLAMIS, Angus Map 21 NO34

Top 200 – Hotel

★★★ Castleton House

Castleton of Eassie DD8 1SJ
☎ 01307 840340 01307 840506
e-mail: hotel@castletonglamis.co.uk
web: www.castletonglamis.co.uk
Dir: *on A94 midway between Forfar/Cupar Angus, 3m W of Glamis*

Set in its own grounds and with a moat, this impressive Victorian house has a relaxed and friendly atmosphere. Accommodation is provided in individually designed, spacious bedrooms. Personal service from the enthusiastic proprietors is a real feature and many guests return time and again. Accomplished cooking, utilising the best local produce, is served in the conservatory restaurant.

ROOMS: 6 en suite (2 fmly) ⊗ in 1 bedroom s £100-£120; d £140-£180 (incl. bkfst) **LB** **FACILITIES:** Putt green ch fac Xmas **CONF:** Thtr 30 Class 20 Board 20 Del from £100 **PARKING:** 50 **NOTES:** Civ Wed 50 **CARDS:**

GLASGOW, City of Glasgow Map 20 NS66
See also Clydebank & Uplawmoor

Top 200 – Town House

★★★★ One Devonshire Gardens

1 Devonshire Gardens G12 0UX
☎ 0141 339 2001 0141 337 1663
e-mail: reservations@onedevonshiregardens.com
web: www.onedevonshiregardens.com
Dir: *M8 junct 17, follow signs for A82, after 1.5m turn left into Hyndland Rd, 1st right, right at mini rdbt, right at end, continue to end*

This renowned townhouse occupies four houses of a Victorian terrace in a residential area. Bedrooms, including a number of suites and four-poster rooms, are stylish, individually designed and thoughtfully equipped to a high standard. Public rooms include a choice of inviting drawing rooms, meeting and conference facilities and a smart restaurant offering imaginative cooking. Personal, attentive service is a highlight.

ROOMS: 36 en suite (4 GF) s £145-£485; d £145-£485 **FACILITIES:** STV Squash Gym Tennis facilities at nearby club ch fac **CONF:** BC Thtr 40 Class 30 Board 30 Del from £250 **NOTES:** ⊗ in restaurant Civ Wed 48 **CARDS:**

★★★★73% Radisson SAS Glasgow

301 Argyle St G2 8DL
☎ 0141 204 3333 0141 204 3344
e-mail: reservations.glasgow@radissonsas.com
Dir: *M8 junct 19 take 1st right, continue to Argyle St. 1st left, hotel is on left opposite central station*

This new hotel offers contemporary design as well as comfort and style. The huge glass and wood atrium forms the central core of the hotel, leading to the lobby, bar, restaurants and the leisure centre. Bedrooms feature the best in design with the focus on comfort, facilities and quality.

ROOMS: 246 en suite ⊗ in 200 bedrooms s £85-£180; d £95-£180 **LB** **FACILITIES:** STV supervised CCTV Sauna Solarium Gym Jacuzzi ch fac **CONF:** BC Thtr 800 Class 360 Board 40 Del £164 **SERVICES:** Lift air con **NOTES:** **CARDS:**

★★★★71% Beardmore

Beardmore St G81 4SA
☎ 0141 951 6000 0141 951 6018
e-mail: info@beardmore.scot.nhs.uk
(For full entry see Clydebank)

★★★★71% Millennium Hotel Glasgow

George Square G2 1DS
☎ 0141 332 6711 🖷 0141 332 4264
e-mail: reservations.glasgow@mill-cop.com
Dir: *M8 junct 15 follow road through 4 sets of lights, at 5th set turn left into Hanover Street. George Square directly ahead, hotel on right*

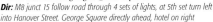

Right in the heart of the city, the Millennium has pride of place overlooking George Square. Inside, the property has a contemporary air, with a spacious reception concourse and a glass veranda overlooking the square. There is a stylish brasserie and separate wine bar, and bedrooms come in a variety of sizes.
ROOMS: 117 en suite ⊗ in 54 bedrooms s £105-£165; d £165-£225 **FACILITIES:** STV Xmas **CONF:** Thtr 40 Class 24 Board 32 Del from £125 **SERVICES:** Lift air con **NOTES:** ✗ **CARDS:**

★★★★69% Glasgow Moat House

Congress Rd G3 8QT
☎ 0141 306 9988 🖷 0141 221 2022
e-mail: reservations.glasgow@moathousehotels.com
Dir: *M8 junct 19, follow signs for SECC, hotel adjacent to centre*
This modern building, instantly recognisable from its mirrored glass exterior, has a convenient location alongside the River Clyde. A feature of the public rooms is a huge wall mural, depicting the city's history, which looks down over the informal No 1 Dockhouse restaurant and the stylish Mariners Restaurant. Bedrooms are comfortable and well-appointed and most enjoy splendid panoramic views.
ROOMS: 283 en suite (10 fmly) ⊗ in 171 bedrooms s £75-£165; d £80-£165 (incl. bkfst) **LB** **FACILITIES:** STV Sauna Solarium Gym Xmas **CONF:** Thtr 800 Class 462 Board 68 **SERVICES:** Lift air con **PARKING:** 300 **NOTES:** Closed 25-26 Dec, 1 Jan Civ Wed **CARDS:**

★★★★69% Milton Hotel & Spa

27 Washington St G3 8AZ
☎ 0141 222 2929 🖷 0141 222 2626
e-mail: sales@miltonhotels.com
Dir: *M8 junct 19 for SECC & follow signs for Broomielaw. Turn left at lights*
Centrally located, this modern hotel is a short drive from the airport and an even shorter walk from the centre of the city. Bedrooms are generally spacious and boast a range of facilities, including high-speed internet access. Public rooms include the Tuscan-themed Medici Grill and an impressive indoor leisure facility.
ROOMS: 141 en suite (49 fmly) ⊗ in 121 bedrooms s £84.50-£169; d £84.50-£169 **LB** **FACILITIES: Spa** STV Sauna Solarium Gym Jacuzzi Xmas **CONF:** Thtr 150 Class 50 Board 50 Del £159 **SERVICES:** Lift air con **PARKING:** 80 **NOTES:** ⊗ in restaurant Civ Wed 160 **CARDS:**

★★★★68% Langs Hotel

2 Port Dundas Place G2 3LD
☎ 0141 333 1500 & 352 2452 🖷 0141 333 5700
e-mail: reservations@langshotels.co.uk
Dir: *M8 junct 16, follow signs for George Square. Hotel immediately left after Concert Square Car Park.*
A contemporary-style, city centre hotel offering a choice of restaurants for dinner. Oshi has an eastern slant, whilst Las Brisas has been awarded an AA rosette. Bedrooms offer various designs, all with a retro style. Some feature stunning suites with a gallery bedroom above the lounge. All have Playstations and CD players.
ROOMS: 100 en suite (4 fmly) ⊗ in 60 bedrooms s £90-£155; d £100-£165 (incl. bkfst) **FACILITIES: Spa** STV Sauna Gym **CONF:** Thtr 60 Class 10 Board 12 **SERVICES:** Lift **NOTES:** ⊗ in restaurant Civ Wed 120 **CARDS:**

★★★★67% Glasgow Marriott Hotel

500 Argyle St, Anderston G3 8RR
☎ 0870 400 7230 🖷 0870 400 7330
Dir: *M8 junct 19, turn left at lights, then left into hotel*
Conveniently located for all major transport links and the city centre, this hotel benefits from extensive conference and banqueting facilities and a spacious car park. Public areas include an open-plan lounge/bar and a Mediterranean restaurant. High quality, well-equipped bedrooms benefit from air conditioning and generously sized beds; the suites are particularly comfortable.
ROOMS: 300 en suite (89 fmly) ⊗ in 212 bedrooms s £69-£145; d £88-£145 (incl. bkfst) **LB** **FACILITIES:** STV Sauna Solarium Gym Beautician, poolside steam room **CONF:** BC Thtr 700 Class 300 Board 50 Del from £135 **SERVICES:** Lift air con **PARKING:** 180 **NOTES:** ✗ Civ Wed 700 **CARDS:**

★★★76% Malmaison

278 West George St G2 4LL
☎ 0141 572 1000 🖷 0141 572 1002
e-mail: glasgow@malmaison.com
Dir: *from S & E - M8 junct 18 (Charing Cross), from W & N - M8 City Centre Glasgow*
Built around a former church in the historic Charing Cross area, Malmaison is a smart, contemporary hotel offering impressive levels of service and hospitality. Bedrooms are spacious and feature a host of modern facilities, such as CD players and mini bars. Dining is a treat, with French brasserie-style cuisine served in the original crypt.
ROOMS: 72 en suite (4 fmly) ⊗ in 30 bedrooms s £129-£165; d £129-£165 **LB** **FACILITIES:** STV Gym Cardiovascular gym **CONF:** Thtr 25 Class 20 Board 20 Del £155 **SERVICES:** Lift **NOTES:** ✗ **CARDS:**

★★★71% Holiday Inn

161 West Nile St G1 2RL
☎ 0141 352 8300 🖷 0141 332 7447
e-mail: info@higlasgow.com
Dir: *M8 junct 16, follow signs for Royal Concert Hall, hotel is opposite*
Built on a corner site close to the Theatre Royal Concert Hall and the main shopping areas, this contemporary hotel features the popular Bonne Auberge French restaurant, a bar area and conservatory. Bedrooms are well-equipped and comfortable with suites available. Staff are friendly and attentive.
ROOMS: 113 en suite (6 fmly) ⊗ in 79 bedrooms s £75-£165; d £85-£165 **FACILITIES:** STV Mini Gym Xmas **CONF:** Thtr 120 Class 80 Board 80 Del from £120 **SERVICES:** Lift air con **NOTES:** ✗ Civ Wed 100 **CARDS:**

GLASGOW, continued

★★★71% Novotel Glasgow Centre

181 Pitt St G2 4DT
☎ 0141 222 2775 🖷 0141 204 5438
e-mail: H3136@accor-hotels.com
Dir: *next to Strathclyde Police HQ. Close to the SECC, just off Sauchiehall St*
Enjoying a convenient city centre location and with limited car park spaces, this hotel is ideal for both business and leisure travellers. Well equipped bedrooms are brightly decorated and offer functional design. Modern public areas include a brasserie serving a range of meals all day and a small fitness club.
ROOMS: 139 en suite (139 fmly) ⊘ in 90 bedrooms s £65-£99; d £65-£119 **LB** **FACILITIES:** STV Sauna Gym Pool table, play station Xmas **CONF:** Thtr 40 Class 20 Board 20 Del from £110 **SERVICES:** Lift air con **PARKING:** 19 **CARDS:**

★★★68% Jurys Inn Glasgow

80 Jamaica St G1 4QE
☎ 0141 314 4800 🖷 0141 314 4888
e-mail: bookings@jurysdoyle.com
Dir: *M8 junct 19 westbound. Left onto A814 Stobcross Street, then left onto Oswald Street, right into Midland Street and right into Jamaica Street. Hotel 200yds on right*
This modern, stylish hotel is easily accessible from major road networks and occupies a prominent location in the city, close to the river. Bedrooms provide good guest comfort and in-room facilities are suited to both leisure and business markets. Public areas include a number of meeting rooms, a popular bar and restaurant.
ROOMS: 321 en suite (321 fmly) ⊘ in 249 bedrooms s £99; d £99 **FACILITIES:** STV Xmas **CONF:** BC Thtr 100 Class 35 Board 40 Del £110 **SERVICES:** Lift air con **NOTES:** ⊘ in restaurant Closed 25 Dec & 26 Dec **CARDS:**

★★★67% Corus hotel Glasgow

377 Argyle St G2 8LL
☎ 0870 609 6166 🖷 0141 221 1014
Dir: *from S, M8 junct 19, at pedestrian lights turn left onto Argyle St. Hotel 200yds on right*

At the west end of one of the city's best-known streets, this refurbished hotel is ideal for business guests. The compact and well-equipped bedrooms are contemporary in style and have all the essential facilities. There is a bright restaurant, lounge bar and a number of meeting rooms, and free overnight parking is available nearby.
ROOMS: 121 en suite ⊘ in 79 bedrooms s £89 **LB** **FACILITIES:** STV Xmas **CONF:** Thtr 70 Class 15 Board 20 **SERVICES:** Lift **NOTES:** ⊘ in restaurant **CARDS:**

★★★66% Ewington

Balmoral Ter, 132 Queens Dr, Queens Park G42 8QW
☎ 0141 423 1152 🖷 0141 422 2030
e-mail: ewington.info@countryhotels.net
web: www.countryhotels.net/ewington
Dir: *M8 junct 20, A77, through 8 sets of lights, left (Allison St), right (Victoria Rd) to Park Gates. Turn right, hotel 500yds on right*

Quietly located on the south side of the city, this townhouse-style hotel forms part of a Victorian terrace opposite Queens Park. Public areas include a foyer lounge, restaurant and comfortable cocktail lounge. It's worth asking for one of the larger bedrooms that overlook the park.
ROOMS: 43 en suite (5 fmly) ⊘ in 8 bedrooms s £50-£79; d £60-£99 **LB** **FACILITIES:** STV Xmas **CONF:** Thtr 70 Class 20 Board 30 Del from £95 **SERVICES:** Lift **PARKING:** 10 **NOTES:** ⊘ in restaurant Civ Wed 50 **CARDS:**

★★★64% Campanile Glasgow

10 Tunnel St G3 8HL
☎ 0141 287 7700 🖷 0141 287 7701
e-mail: glasgow@envergure.co.uk
Dir: *M8 junct 19, follow signs to SECC. Hotel next to SECC and Rotunda Casino*
This modern building offers accommodation in smart well-equipped bedrooms, all with en suite bathrooms. Refreshments can be taken at the informal Bistro. For further details consult the Hotel Groups page.
ROOMS: 106 en suite (2 fmly) (21 GF) ⊘ in 76 bedrooms s fr £55; d fr £55 **FACILITIES:** STV Xmas **CONF:** Thtr 150 Class 60 Board 90 Del £75 **SERVICES:** Lift air con **PARKING:** 36 **NOTES:** ⊘ in restaurant **CARDS:**

★★★64% *Jurys Glasgow*

Great Western Rd G12 0XP
☎ 0141 334 8161 🖷 0141 334 3846
e-mail: glasgow_hotel@jurys.com
Dir: *M8 junct 17, onto Great Western Road (A82), through 2 sets of lights, left by Gartnavel Hospital & just before Safeway. Sharp right into Shelley Rd*
This purpose-built hotel is situated on the west side of the city. Most single occupancy bedrooms provide a double bed and sofa, whilst others cater for the family/leisure market. Public areas include an Irish bar, an attractive split-level restaurant, a well-equipped leisure club and conference and banqueting facilities.
ROOMS: 137 en suite (12 fmly) ⊘ in 100 bedrooms **FACILITIES:** STV supervised Sauna Solarium Gym Jacuzzi **CONF:** Thtr 140 Class 80 Board 40 **SERVICES:** Lift **PARKING:** 300 **NOTES:** ⊘ in restaurant Civ Wed 120 **CARDS:**

★★★63% Bewley's Hotel Glasgow
110 Bath St G2 2EN
☎ 0141 353 0800 🖹 0141 353 0900
e-mail: gla@bewleyshotels.com
web: www.bewleyshotels.com
Dir: *M8 junct 18, left to Sauchiehall St & right to Birthwood St then left to West Regent St & left into Bath St.*

In the heart of the city, this modern hotel is ideally suited for business and for leisure breaks. Bedrooms are comfortable and well equipped, with several enjoying impressive views over the Glasgow skyline. Loop restaurant and bar serves cosmopolitan food all day in a relaxed informal setting.
ROOMS: 103 en suite (47 fmly) ⊗ in 64 bedrooms **FACILITIES:** STV
SERVICES: Lift **NOTES:** Closed 24-26 Dec
CARDS:

★★★62% Quality Hotel Glasgow
99 Gordon St G1 3SF
☎ 0141 221 9680 🖹 0141 226 3948
e-mail: enquiries@quality-hotels-glasgow.com
Dir: *M8 junct 19, left into Argyle St and left into Hope St*
A splendid Victorian railway hotel, forming part of Central Station. It retains much original charm combined with modern facilities. Public rooms are impressive and include a newly transformed bar area and a modernised reception. Bedrooms continue to be upgraded and are generally spacious and well laid out.
ROOMS: 222 en suite (8 fmly) ⊗ in 70 bedrooms **FACILITIES:** **Spa** STV Sauna Solarium Gym Jacuzzi Hair & beauty salon, Steam room, Sports therapist Xmas **CONF:** Thtr 600 Class 160 Board 40
SERVICES: Lift **NOTES:** ⊗ in restaurant Civ Wed 250
CARDS:

★★76% Uplawmoor

Neilston Rd G78 4AF
☎ 01505 850565 🖹 01505 850689
e-mail: enquiries@uplawmoor.co.uk
web: www.uplawmoor.co.uk
(For full entry see Uplawmoor)

Hotel Ibis Glasgow City Centre
220 West Regent St G2 4DQ
☎ 0141 225 6000 🖹 0141 225 6010
e-mail: H3139@accor-hotels.com
Modern, budget hotel offering comfortable accommodation in bright and practical bedrooms. Breakfast is self-service and dinner is available in the restaurant. For further details, consult the Hotel Groups page.
ROOMS: 141 en suite s £45.95-£55.95; d £45.95-£55.95

Premier Lodge (Glasgow City Centre)

10 Elmbank Gardens G2 4PP
☎ 0870 9906312 🖹 0870 9906313
e-mail: glasgow@premierlodge.co.uk
web: www.premierlodge.com
Dir: *from south, exit M8 junct 18 (right junct), through 2 sets of lights and turn left into Elmbank Cres. From north, exit M8 junct 18. Follow signs City Centre. Turn left at lights and left again at next lights then right at lights into Elmbank St and left at BP petrol station*
High quality, modern, budget accommodation, ideal for families and business travellers. All rooms feature bath, power shower and satellite TV, and most have telephones / modem points. The adjacent bar and restaurant offers a wide and varied menu.
ROOMS: 278 en suite s £46; d £46 **CONF:** Thtr 50 Class 25 Board 20

Premier Lodge (Glasgow North East)
Cumbernauld Rd, Muirhead, Chryston G69 9BS
☎ 0870 9906508 🖹 0870 9906509
web: www.premierlodge.com
Dir: *off M8 junct 13, follow M80 and A80 to Stepps bypass. Turn left onto A80. The Lodge 400 yards from bypass on left*
High quality, modern, budget accommodation, ideal for families and business travellers. All rooms feature bath, power shower and satellite TV, and most have telephones / modem points. The adjacent bar and restaurant offers a wide and varied menu.
ROOMS: 38 en suite s £44; d £44 **CONF:** Thtr 85 Class 25 Board 30

GLASGOW, continued

Travel Inn (Glasgow Cambuslang)

Cambuslang G32 8EY
☎ 08701 977306 Fax 0141 778 1703
Dir: *on rdbt at end of M74, turn right at rdbt, at traffic lights turn right & Travel Inn on right*
Travel Inn offers good-quality, value-for-money accommodation. Spacious, en suite rooms with bath and shower comfortably accommodate a family of up to two adults and two children (to age 15). The restaurant and bar offers a varied menu. For further details consult the Hotel Groups page.
ROOMS: 40 en suite s £45.95-£46.95; d £45.95-£46.95

Travel Inn (Glasgow City Centre)

Montrose House, 187 George St G1 1YU
☎ 0870 238 3320 Fax 0141 553 2719
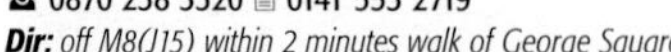
Dir: *off M8(J15) within 2 minutes walk of George Square*

Travel Inn offers good-quality, value-for-money accommodation. Spacious, en suite rooms with bath and shower comfortably accommodate a family of up to two adults and two children (to age 15). The restaurant and bar offers a varied menu. For further details consult the Hotel Groups page.
ROOMS: 254 en suite s £49.95; d £49.95 **CONF:** Thtr 20 Board 10

Travel Inn (Glasgow East)

601 Hamilton Rd G71 7SA
☎ 08701 977109 Fax 0141 773 8554
Dir: *From J4 follow signs to Uddingston Mt. Vernon and then Zoo Park. Situated at entrance to Glasgow Zoo, J4 of M73 & M74*
Travel Inn offers good-quality, value-for-money accommodation. Spacious, en suite rooms with bath and shower comfortably accommodate a family of up to two adults and two children (to age 15). The restaurant and bar offers a varied menu. For further details consult the Hotel Groups page.
ROOMS: 66 en suite s £45.95-£46.95; d £45.95-£46.95

Travelodge (Glasgow Central)

9 Hill St G3 6PR
☎ 08700 850 950 Fax 0141 333 1221
Travelodge offers good quality, good value, modern accommodation. Ideal for families, the spacious, en suite bedrooms include remote-control TV, tea and coffee-making facilities and luxury beds. Meals can be taken at the nearby family restaurant. For further details consult the Hotel Groups page.
ROOMS: 95 en suite s fr £25; d fr £25

> Late for dinner?
> Quality Standards mean that last orders for dinner vary according to star rating and should be no earlier than:
> ★★ 7.00pm ★★★ 8.00pm ★★★★ 9.00pm
> ★★★★★ 10.00pm

Travelodge Glagow Paisley Road

251 Paisley Rd G5 8RA
☎ 08700 850 950 Fax 0141 420 3884
Dir: *0.5m from city centre just off M8 junct 20 from S, M8 junct 21 from N. Behind Harry Ramsden's*
Travelodge offers good quality, good value, modern accommodation. Ideal for families, the spacious, en suite bedrooms include remote-control TV, tea and coffee-making facilities and luxury beds. Meals can be taken at the nearby family restaurant. For further details consult the Hotel Groups page.
ROOMS: 75 en suite s fr £25; d fr £25

Tulip Inn Glasgow

80 Ballater St G5 0TW
☎ 0141 429 4233 Fax 0141 429 4244
e-mail: info@tulipinnglasgow.co.uk
Dir: *From Glasgow Airport M8 junct 21 follow signs for East Kilbride, right onto A8 along Kingston St. Right onto South Portland St, left onto Norfolk St, straight through Gorbals St & onto Ballater St.*
A modern budget hotel suitable for business travellers, families and tourists. Bedrooms are bright, well-proportioned and comprehensively equipped. There is a bistro and bar.
ROOMS: 114 en suite s £45-£74.50; d £45-£74.50 **CONF:** BC Thtr 180 Class 100 Board 60 Del from £95

GLASGOW AIRPORT, Renfrewshire — Map 20 NS46

★★★70% Glynhill Hotel & Leisure Club

Paisley Rd PA4 8XB
☎ 0141 886 5555 Fax 0141 885 2838
e-mail: glynhillleisurehotel@msn.com
Dir: *M8 junct 27, take A741 towards Renfrew cross, small rdbt - approx 300yds from motorway exit, hotel on right*
A smart and welcoming hotel with bedrooms ranging from spacious executive rooms to smaller standard rooms. All are tastefully appointed and have a good range of amenities. The hotel boasts a luxurious leisure complex and extensive conference facilities. The choice of contrasting bars and restaurants should suit most tastes and budgets.
ROOMS: 145 en suite (25 fmly) in 72 bedrooms **FACILITIES:** STV supervised Sauna Solarium Gym Jacuzzi ♫ Xmas **CONF:** Thtr 450 Class 240 Del from £115 **PARKING:** 230 **NOTES:** Civ Wed 450
CARDS:

★★★70% *Lynnhurst*

Park Rd PA5 8LS
☎ 01505 324331 & 324600 Fax 01505 324219
e-mail: enquiries@lynnhurst.co.uk web: www.lynnhurst.co.uk
Dir: *past airport, take slip road (A737). Continue 2m, take B789 then left into Johnstone and at 1st main lights right, then 1st left and 2nd right*
Genuine hospitality together with high standards of guest care are the hallmarks of this family-run hotel, set in a quiet residential area. Refurbished bedrooms are thoughtfully equipped for both business and leisure guests. Public areas include a smart conservatory, spacious lounge bar and an impressive wood-panelled dining room.
ROOMS: 21 en suite (2 fmly) **FACILITIES:** STV Arrangement with local leisure centre **CONF:** Thtr 160 Class 160 Board 20 **PARKING:** 100 **NOTES:** Closed 1-3 Jan **CARDS:**

★★★64% *Dean Park*

91 Glasgow Rd PA4 8YB
☎ 0141 886 3771 Fax 0141 885 0681
e-mail: deanparkres@cosmopolitan-hotels.com
Dir: *off M8 junct 26 onto A8 for Renfrew, 600yds, hotel on left*
Situated close to the airport, this modern purpose-built and

continued

refurbished hotel attracts both the business and leisure traveller and is also a popular venue for local functions. Although not expansive, bedrooms are comfortable and well equipped.
ROOMS: 118 en suite (6 fmly) (50 GF) **FACILITIES:** STV Snooker Beautician & arrangement with leisure club **CONF:** BC Thtr 350 Class 150 Board 100 **PARKING:** 200 **NOTES:** Civ Wed 200
CARDS:

Travel Inn Glasgow Airport
Whitecart Rd PA3 2TH
☎ 0870 238 3321 0141 842 1570
Dir: *close to airport terminal, follow signs*

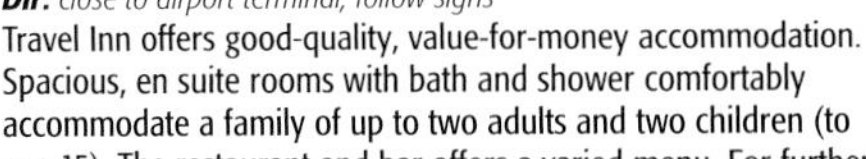

Travel Inn offers good-quality, value-for-money accommodation. Spacious, en suite rooms with bath and shower comfortably accommodate a family of up to two adults and two children (to age 15). The restaurant and bar offers a varied menu. For further details consult the Hotel Groups page.
ROOMS: 104 en suite s £45.95-£46.95; d £45.95-£46.95 **CONF:** Thtr 30

Travel Inn (Glasgow Paisley)
Phoenix Retail Park PA1 2BH
☎ 08701 977113 0141 887 2799
Dir: *M8 junct 28A St James Interchange take A737 signed Irvine, take 1st exit signed Linwood & turn left at 1st rdbt to Phoenix Park*

Travel Inn offers good-quality, value-for-money accommodation. Spacious, en suite rooms with bath and shower comfortably accommodate a family of up to two adults and two children (to age 15). The restaurant and bar offers a varied menu. For further details consult the Hotel Groups page.
ROOMS: 40 en suite s £45.95-£46.95; d £45.95-£46.95 **CONF:** Thtr 20 Board 15

Travelodge (Glasgow Airport)
Marchburn Dr, Glasgow Airport Business Park, Paisley PA3 2AR
☎ 08700 850 950 0141 889 0583
Travelodge offers good quality, good value, modern accommodation. Ideal for families, the spacious, en suite bedrooms include remote-control TV, tea and coffee-making facilities and luxury beds. Meals can be taken at the nearby family restaurant. For further details consult the Hotel Groups page.
ROOMS: 98 en suite (incl. bkfst) s fr £25; d fr £25

GLENEAGLES See Auchterarder

GLENFINNAN, Highland — Map 22 NM98

★★75% The Prince's House
PH37 4LT
☎ 01397 722246 01397 722323
e-mail: princeshouse@glenfinnan.co.uk
web: www.glenfinnan.co.uk
Dir: *on A830, 0.5m on right past Glenfinnan Monument. 200mtrs from Glenfinnan Railway Sta*
A welcoming atmosphere is provided at this delightful hotel that is close to the site where Bonnie Prince Charlie raised the Jacobite standard. Comfortably appointed bedrooms offer pleasing décor and bathrooms and have now been upgraded. Meals can be taken in either Flora's restaurant or the spacious bar.
ROOMS: 9 en suite (1 fmly) ⊗ in all bedrooms s £42-£48; d £70-£80 (incl. bkfst) **LB** **FACILITIES:** Fishing Xmas **CONF:** Thtr 40 Class 20 **PARKING:** 18 **NOTES:** ⊗ in restaurant Closed Christmas & Jan-early Feb
CARDS:

GLENLUCE, Dumfries & Galloway — Map 20 NX15

★★67% Kelvin House Hotel
53 Main St DG8 0PP
☎ 01581 300303 01581 300303
e-mail: kelvinhouse@lineone.net
Dir: *midway between Newton Stewart & Stranraer, just off A75*
This small, privately run hotel lies in the centre of a village. The bedrooms are bright and spacious and there is a comfortable residents' lounge. Wholesome, good-value meals are served either in the popular bar or separate restaurant overlooking the garden. Special golf packages are worth enquiring about.
ROOMS: 6 rms (5 en suite) (3 fmly) ⊗ in 3 bedrooms s £30-£35; d £50-£60 (incl. bkfst) **LB** **FACILITIES:** Xmas **CONF:** Thtr 50 Class 20 Board 20 **CARDS:**

GLENROTHES, Fife — Map 21 NO20

★★77% Rescobie House Hotel & Restaurant
6 Valley Dr, Leslie KY6 3BQ
☎ 01592 749555 01592 620231
e-mail: rescobiehotel@compuserve.com
web: www.rescobie-hotel.co.uk
Dir: *off A92 at Glenrothes onto A911, through Leslie. End of High St follow straight ahead. Take 1st left, hotel entrance 2nd left*
Hospitality and guest care are second to none at this relaxing country house, which lies secluded in gardens on the fringe of Leslie. Period architecture is enhanced by a combination of contemporary and Art Deco styling, a theme carried through to the bright airy bedrooms. There is an inviting lounge and an intimate restaurant serving memorable meals.
ROOMS: 10 en suite s £49-£68; d £72-£98 (incl. bkfst) **PARKING:** 12 **NOTES:** ⊗ in restaurant Civ Wed 24 **CARDS:**

Travel Inn
Beaufort Dr KY7 4UJ
☎ 08701 977114 01592 773453
Dir: *From M90 (J2a), northbound, take A92 to Glenrothes. At 2nd rbt (Bankhead), take 3rd exit. Travel Inn on left*
Travel Inn offers good-quality, value-for-money accommodation. Spacious, en suite rooms with bath and shower comfortably accommodate a family of up to two adults and two children (to age 15). The restaurant and bar offers a varied menu. For further details consult the Hotel Groups page.
ROOMS: 40 en suite s £45.95-£46.95; d £45.95-£46.95

GLENSHEE (SPITTAL OF), Perth & Kinross — Map 21 NO17

★★72% ® Dalmunzie House
PH10 7QG
☎ 01250 885224 ▯ 01250 885225
e-mail: reservations@dalmunzie.com
web: www.dalmunzie.com
Dir: *on A93 at Spittal of Glenshee, follow signs to hotel*

This turreted mansion house enjoys a remote setting in the heart of a 6,500 acre estate, yet is within easy reach of the ski slopes of Glenshee. Accommodation ranges in style from large rooms with period furnishings to more compact rooms with modern décor. Public areas include a traditional bar, a spacious restaurant and a choice of lounges.
ROOMS: 19 rms (16 en suite) s £50-£65; d £70-£130 (incl. bkfst) **LB** **FACILITIES:** 9 Fishing Clay pigeon shooting, Mountain bikes, Estate tours, Grouse shooting, Stalking Xmas **CONF:** Thtr 20 Class 20 Board 20 **SERVICES:** Lift **PARKING:** 33 **NOTES:** ⊗ in restaurant Closed 24-27 Dec **CARDS:**

GRANGEMOUTH, Falkirk — Map 21 NS98

★★★76% ®® The Grange Manor
Glensburgh FK3 8XJ
☎ 01324 474836 ▯ 01324 665861
e-mail: info@grangemanor.co.uk
web: www.grangemanor.co.uk
Dir: *E; off M9 junct 6, hotel 200m to right. W; off M9 junct 5, A905 for 2m*
Located south of town close to the M9, this stylish hotel, popular with business and corporate clientele, benefits from hands-on family ownership. It offers high-quality, spacious accommodation with superb bathrooms. Public areas include a comfortable foyer area, lounge bar and smart restaurant and there is also a bar/bistro in the grounds. Staff throughout the hotel are especially friendly.
ROOMS: 6 en suite 30 annexe en suite (6 fmly) (15 GF) ⊗ in 22 bedrooms s £55-£89; d £89-£125 (incl. bkfst) **LB** **FACILITIES:** STV Xmas **CONF:** Thtr 190 Class 68 Board 40 Del from £120 **SERVICES:** Lift **PARKING:** 154 **NOTES:** Civ Wed 160
CARDS:

GRANTOWN-ON-SPEY, Highland — Map 23 NJ03

★★★71% ®® *Muckrach Lodge*
Dulnain Bridge PH26 3LY
☎ 01479 851257 ▯ 01479 851325
e-mail: info@muckrach.co.uk
Dir: *from A95 Dulnain Bridge exit follow A938 towards Carrbridge. Hotel 500mtrs on right*
This former sporting lodge is set in ten acres of landscaped grounds, at the foot of the Cairngorm Mountains. Bedrooms come in a variety of sizes and styles; the larger ones are particularly well appointed. The cosy bar is popular with the sporting clientele and features a roaring log fire. Dinner can be taken in either the bistro or award-winning Finlarig restaurant.

ROOMS: 9 en suite 4 annexe en suite (3 fmly) ⊗ in all bedrooms **FACILITIES:** Beauty & aroma therapy **CONF:** Thtr 30 Class 20 Board 16 **PARKING:** 53 **NOTES:** ⊗ in restaurant Closed 5-20 Jan RS Nov-Mar Civ Wed 50 **CARDS:**

★★77% ® Culdearn House
Woodlands Ter PH26 3JU
☎ 01479 872106 ▯ 01479 873641
e-mail: enquiries@culdearn.com
web: www.culdearn.com
Dir: *enter Grantown on A95 from SW and turn left at 30mph sign. Hotel opposite*

Enjoying fresh input from new proprietors, this immaculately maintained small hotel sits in gardens on the edge of town. Hospitality is excellent and every effort is made to make guests feel at home. The hotel has the atmosphere of a relaxed country house.
ROOMS: 7 en suite (1 GF) ⊗ in all bedrooms s £85; d £170 (incl. bkfst & dinner) **LB** **PARKING:** 12 **NOTES:** No children 10yrs ⊗ in restaurant Closed Jan-Feb **CARDS:**

★★76% The Pines
Woodside Av PH26 3JR
☎ 01479 872092 ▯ 01479 872092
e-mail: info@thepinesgrantown.co.uk
Dir: *at traffic lights turn onto A939, first right*
This impressive Victorian house is set in well-tended gardens, a short walk from the centre of town. The delightful public areas include a choice of two lounges, both furnished with some fine period pieces and many original works of art, a library and an elegant dining room. The thoughtfully equipped bedrooms are individually styled and generally spacious; many have fine views of the lovely Speyside scenery.
ROOMS: 8 en suite (1 GF) ⊗ in all bedrooms s £50-£70; d £100-£130 (incl. bkfst) **PARKING:** 8 **NOTES:** No children 12yrs ⊗ in restaurant Closed Nov-Feb **CARDS:**

GREENOCK, Inverclyde — Map 20 NS27

Travel Inn

1-3 James Watt Way PA15 2AJ
☎ 08701 977120 Fax 01475 730890
Dir: *Follow M8 until it becomes A8 at Langbank, straight ahead through rdbt to Greenock, turn right off A8 at 3rd rdbt, next to McDonalds*
Travel Inn offers good-quality, value-for-money accommodation. Spacious, en suite rooms with bath and shower comfortably accommodate a family of up to two adults and two children (to age 15). The restaurant and bar offers a varied menu. For further details consult the Hotel Groups page.
ROOMS: 40 en suite s £45.95-£46.95; d £45.95-£46.95

GRETNA (WITH GRETNA GREEN), Dumfries & Galloway — Map 21 NY36

★★★68% Gretna Chase

DG16 5JB
☎ 01461 337517 Fax 01461 337766
e-mail: enquiries@gretnachase.co.uk
Dir: *off M74 onto B7076, left at top of slip road, hotel 400yds on right*
With its colourful landscaped gardens, this hotel is a favourite venue for wedding parties. Bedrooms range from the comfortable standard rooms to the impressively spacious superior and honeymoon rooms; all are well equipped. There is a foyer lounge, a spacious dining room that can accommodate functions, and a popular lounge bar serving food.
ROOMS: 19 en suite (9 fmly) non-smoking in 6 bedrooms s £70-£95; d £89-£175 (incl. bkfst) **LB** **FACILITIES:** Jacuzzi **CONF:** Thtr 50 Class 30 Board 20 Del from £75 **PARKING:** 40 **NOTES:** No dogs Closed First 2 wks of Jan
CARDS:

★★★67% *Garden House*

Sarkfoot Rd DG16 5EP
☎ 01461 337621 Fax 01461 337692
e-mail: info@gardenhouse.co.uk
Dir: *just off M6 junct 45 at Gretna*

This purpose-built modern hotel lies on the edge of the village. With a focus on weddings its landscaped gardens are a feature, while inside corridor walls are adorned with photographs portraying that 'special day'. Accommodation is well presented and there is a new wing of spacious and comfortable bedrooms, many overlooking the Japanese water gardens.
ROOMS: 38 en suite (10 fmly) (14 GF) **FACILITIES: Spa** STV Indoor pool supervised Sauna Jacuzzi Entertainment **CONF:** BC Thtr 150 Class 80 Board 40 **SERVICES:** Lift **PARKING:** 105 **NOTES:** No dogs Civ Wed 150
CARDS:

See advert on this page

GRETNA SERVICE AREA (A74(M)), Dumfries & Galloway — Map 21 NY36

Days Inn

Welcome Break Service Area DG16 5HQ
☎ 01461 337566 Fax 01461 337823
e-mail: gretna.hotel@welcomebreak.co.uk
web: www.daysinn.com
Dir: *between junct 21 & 22 on M74 - accessible from both N'bound & S'bound carriageways*
This modern building offers accommodation in smart, spacious and well-equipped bedrooms, suitable for families and business travellers, and all with en suite bathrooms. Continental breakfast is available and other refreshments may be taken at the nearby family restaurant. For further details see the Hotel Groups page.
ROOMS: 64 en suite s £45-£55; d £45-£55 **CONF:** Thtr 40 Board 20

GULLANE, East Lothian
Map 21 NT48

Top 200 – Hotel

★★★ ◎◎ **Greywalls**
Muirfield EH31 2EG
☎ 01620 842144 ▯ 01620 842241
e-mail: hotel@greywalls.co.uk
web: www.greywalls.co.uk
Dir: *A198, hotel signposted at E end of village*

A dignified but relaxing Edwardian country house designed by Sir Edwin Lutyens; Greywalls overlooks the famous Muirfield Golf Course and is ideally placed just a half hours' drive from Edinburgh. Delightful public rooms look onto beautiful gardens and freshly prepared cuisine may be enjoyed in the restaurant. Bedrooms, whether cosy singles or spacious master rooms, are mostly furnished in period style and many command views of the course. A gatehouse lodge is ideal for golfing parties.

ROOMS: 17 en suite 5 annexe en suite (5 GF) s £130-£245; d £220-£260 (incl. bkfst) **LB** **FACILITIES:** STV Putt green Extensive gardens **CONF:** Thtr 30 Class 20 Board 20 Del £215 **PARKING:** 40 **NOTES:** ⊗ in restaurant Closed Nov-Mar **CARDS:**

HADDINGTON, East Lothian
Map 21 NT57

★★★62% **Maitlandfield House**
24 Sidegate EH41 4BZ
☎ 01620 826513 ▯ 01620 826713
e-mail: reception@maitlandfieldhouse.co.uk
web: www.maitlandfieldhouse.co.uk
Dir: *in Haddington follow signs to St Mary's church/Lennoxlove House on B6369 (road to Gifford)*

This popular hotel lies in attractive gardens looking across to the historic St Mary's Church. Public areas include an inviting lounge and a conservatory brasserie serving a range of Portuguese and Scottish cuisine. There are superior bedrooms and smaller standard ones but all are well equipped and comfortable.

ROOMS: 25 en suite (3 GF) ⊗ in all bedrooms s £60-£98; d £98-£150 (incl. bkfst) **LB** **FACILITIES:** Xmas **CONF:** BC Thtr 180 Class 100 Board 98 Del from £55 **PARKING:** 80 **NOTES:** No children 12yrs ⊗ in restaurant Civ Wed 50 **CARDS:**

Indoor Swimming Pool
Indoor Swimming Pool (heated)
Outdoor Swimming Pool
Outdoor Swimming Pool (heated)

HALKIRK, Highland
Map 23 ND15

★★62% ***Ulbster Arms***
Bridge St KW12 6XY
☎ 01847 831206 & 831641 ▯ 01847 831206
e-mail: ulbster-arms@ecosse.net
Dir: *from A9, 3m after village of Spittal turn left*

This small hotel is located in the centre of the small village of Halkirk, close to Thurso. Attracting a mainly sporting clientele there is good fishing and shooting nearby. Bedrooms vary in size and style and public areas include a choice of eating options.

ROOMS: 10 en suite 16 annexe en suite **FACILITIES:** Fishing Shooting ♫ **CONF:** Thtr 30 Class 25 Board 20 **PARKING:** 36 **NOTES:** ⊗ in restaurant **CARDS:**

HAMILTON MOTORWAY SERVICE AREA (M74), South Lanarkshire
Map 20 NS75

Travel Inn Glasgow (Hamilton)
Hamilton Motorway Service Area ML3 6JW
☎ 08701 977124 ▯ 01698 891682
Dir: *M74 northbound, 1m N of junct 6. For southbound access exit junct 6 onto A723, double back at rdbt & join M74 Glasgow exit*

travel inn

Travel Inn offers good-quality, value-for-money accommodation. Spacious, en suite rooms with bath and shower comfortably accommodate a family of up to two adults and two children (to age 15). The restaurant and bar offers a varied menu. For further details consult the Hotel Groups page.

ROOMS: 36 en suite s £45.95-£46.95; d £45.95-£46.95 **CONF:** Thtr 30 Board 20

HARRIS, ISLE OF, Western Isles
Map 22

SCARISTA
Map 22 NG09

Restaurant with Rooms

◎◎ **Scarista House**
HS3 3HX
☎ 01859 550238 ▯ 01859 550277
e-mail: timandpatricia@scaristahouse.com
Dir: *on A859, 15 miles south of Tarbert*

A former manse, Scarista lies in an idyllic position with a panoramic view of the Atlantic and just a short walk to miles of sandy beach. The house is run in a relaxed country house manner by the friendly hosts. Expect wellies in the hall and masses of books and CDs in one of two lounges. Bedrooms are cosy and delicious set dinners and memorable breakfasts are provided.

ROOMS: 3 en suite 2 annexe en suite (2 GF) ⊗ in all bedrooms s £83-£88; d £130-£140 (incl. bkfst) **LB** **FACILITIES:** no TV in bdrms **CONF:** Thtr 20 Class 16 Board 16 **PARKING:** 12 **NOTES:** ⊗ in restaurant Closed Xmas RS Nov-Mar Civ Wed 40 **CARDS:**

HOWWOOD, Renfrewshire Map 20 NS36

★★★70% Bowfield Hotel & Country Club

PA9 1DB
☎ 01505 705225 01505 705230
e-mail: enquiries@bowfieldcountryclub.co.uk
Dir: *M8, A737 for 6m, left onto B787, right after 2m, follow road for 1m to hotel*

This former textile mill is now a popular hotel which has become a convenient stopover for travellers using Glasgow Airport. The leisure club has been considerably expanded and offers very good facilities. Public areas have beamed ceilings and welcoming open fires. Bedrooms are housed in a separate wing and offer good modern comforts and facilities.

ROOMS: 23 en suite (3 fmly) (7 GF) s £80-£85; d £60-£65 (incl. bkfst) **FACILITIES: Spa** Squash Snooker Sauna Solarium Gym Jacuzzi Childrens soft play, aerobics studio inc classes Xmas **CONF:** Thtr 150 Class 120 Board 120 Del £105 **PARKING:** 100 **NOTES:** in restaurant **CARDS:**

HUNTLY, Aberdeenshire Map 23 NJ53

★★63% Gordon Arms Hotel

THE INDEPENDENTS

The Square AB54 8AF
☎ 01466 792288 01466 794556
e-mail: reception@gordonarms.demon.co.uk
Dir: *off A96 Aberdeen to Inverness road at Huntly. Hotel immediately on left after entering town square*

This friendly family-run hotel is located in the town square and offers a good selection of tasty, well-portioned dishes served in the bar (or in the restaurant at weekends or midweek by appointment). Bedrooms come in a variety of sizes, and all are cheerfully decorated.

ROOMS: 13 en suite (3 fmly) s £35-£45; d £48.50-£58.50 (incl. bkfst) LB **FACILITIES:** Xmas **CONF:** Thtr 160 Class 80 Board 60 Del from £50 **CARDS:**

INVERARAY, Argyll & Bute Map 20 NN00

★★★68% The Argyll

Best Western

Front St PA32 8XB
☎ 01499 302466 01499 302389
e-mail: reception@the-argyll-hotel.co.uk
web: www.the-argyll-hotel.co.uk
Dir: *from Glasgow A82 then A83 from Tarbet to Inverary. Hotel is 1st building facing loch on entering Inveraray*

Located beside The Arch and enjoying views of Loch Fyne, this hotel offers smartly furnished bedrooms that are comfortable and well equipped. Facilities include a choice of bars, foyer lounge and conservatory. The attractive restaurant features freshly prepared meals based on quality Scottish ingredients.

ROOMS: 35 en suite (7 fmly) in 4 bedrooms **FACILITIES:** ch fac Xmas **CONF:** Thtr 150 Class 80 Board 70 **PARKING:** 50 **NOTES:** in restaurant Closed 25-26 Dec Civ Wed 120
CARDS:

> Late for dinner?
> Quality Standards mean that last orders for dinner vary according to star rating and should be no earlier than:
> ★★ 7.00pm ★★★ 8.00pm ★★★★ 9.00pm
> ★★★★★ 10.00pm

★★★68% Loch Fyne Hotel & Leisure Club

CRERAR HOTELS

PA32 8XT
☎ 01499 302148 01499 302348
e-mail: lochfyne@crerarhotels.com
web: www.crerarhotels.com
Dir: *from A83 Loch Lomond, through town centre on A80 to Lochgilphead. Hotel 0.5m*

This popular holiday hotel overlooks Loch Fyne. Bedrooms are mainly spacious and offer comfortable modern appointments. Guests can relax in the well-stocked bar and enjoy views over the Loch, or enjoy a meal in the contemporary-style bistro or more formal restaurant. There is also a well-equipped leisure centre.

ROOMS: 80 en suite s £45-£75; d £65-£125 (incl. bkfst) LB **FACILITIES: Spa** supervised Riding Sauna Jacuzzi Steam Room Xmas **CONF:** Thtr 50 Class 30 Board 20 Del from £95 **SERVICES:** Lift **PARKING:** 50 **NOTES:** in restaurant **CARDS:**

INVERGARRY, Highland Map 22 NH30

★★★74% Glengarry Castle

PH35 4HW
☎ 01809 501254 01809 501207
e-mail: castle@glengarry.net
web: www.glengarry.net
Dir: *on A82 beside Loch Oich, 0.5m from A82/A87 junct*

This charming country-house hotel is set in 50 acres of grounds on the shores of Loch Oich. Inviting public areas include a choice of comfortable sitting rooms with lots to read, and the classical dining room has an innovative menu. Bedrooms are mainly well proportioned; some have four-poster or half-tester beds.

ROOMS: 26 en suite (2 fmly) in 8 bedrooms s £56-£88; d £84-£156 (incl. bkfst) **FACILITIES:** Fishing **PARKING:** 32 **NOTES:** in restaurant Closed early Nov-mid Mar **CARDS:**

See advert on page 735

INVERGORDON, Highland
Map 23 NH76

★★★67% Kincraig House
IV18 0LF
☎ 01349 852587 01349 852193
e-mail: kingcraighousehotel@btopenworld.com
Dir: *off A9 for Invergordon & Alness. Hotel entrance on left 0.25m past Rosleen Church*

This mansion house is set within well-tended grounds in an elevated position, providing views over the Cromarty Firth. Bedrooms are comfortable, with the front-facing premier rooms offering greater facilities. The elegant restaurant is a fitting venue for fine dining from a short innovative menu, while the lounge invites relaxation. The friendly staff provide attentive service.

ROOMS: 14 en suite (1 fmly) (2 GF) in 4 bedrooms s £45-£68; d £90-£104 (incl. bkfst) **LB** **FACILITIES:** Snooker ch fac Xmas **PARKING:** 30 **NOTES:** in restaurant **CARDS:**

INVERKEITHING, Fife
Map 21 NT18

★★★63% Corus hotel Edinburgh North
St Margaret's Head, North Queensferry
KY11 1HP
☎ 01383 410000 0870 609 6160
01383 419708
e-mail: edinburghnorth@corushotels.com
Dir: *from N take exit after M90 junct 1 signed Park & Ride, follow signs for Deep Sea World, hotel on left. From S over Forth Road Bridge, take 1st exit then 1st left, hotel in 0.5m on left*

From its position on the north side of the river this smart, modern hotel enjoys fine views of the famous road and rail bridges. Bright, modern public areas include a comfortable foyer lounge and bar, a smart restaurant, and a good range of banqueting facilities. Bedrooms are comfortable and offer a good range of amenities.

ROOMS: 77 en suite (4 fmly) (15 GF) in 46 bedrooms s fr £95; d fr £105 **LB** **FACILITIES:** STV Xmas **CONF:** Thtr 150 Class 60 Board 45 Del £115 **SERVICES:** Lift **PARKING:** 180 **NOTES:** in restaurant Civ Wed 100 **CARDS:**

INVERMORISTON, Highland
Map 23 NH41

★★77% Glenmoriston Arms Hotel & Restaurant
IV63 7YA
☎ 01320 351206 01320 351308
e-mail: reception@glenmoristonarms.co.uk
web: www.glenmoristonarms.co.uk
Dir: *on junct of A82 & A887 road to the Isle of Skye*

Now under enthusiastic new ownership this charming, well-maintained, small hotel, which is steeped in history, offers a warm welcome. Inviting public areas include a cosy bar and attractive formal restaurant where fine dinners, prepared and cooked with care and dedication, are served. An alternative is offered by the Tavern bar/bistro in the grounds. The well-equipped bedrooms reflect the individuality of the house.

ROOMS: 8 en suite (1 fmly) in 2 bedrooms s £45-£70; d £30-£120 (incl. bkfst) **LB** **FACILITIES:** Fishing ch fac Xmas **CONF:** BC Board 8 **PARKING:** 24 **NOTES:** in restaurant Closed 5 Jan-end Feb **CARDS:**

INVERNESS, Highland
Map 23 NH64

See also Kirkhill

★★★★71% Culloden House
Culloden IV2 7BZ
☎ 01463 790461 01463 792181
e-mail: reserv@cullodenhouse.co.uk
web: www.cullodenhouse.co.uk
Dir: *take A96 from town and turn right for Culloden. After 1m, turn left at White Church after 2nd traffic lights*

Dating from the late 1700s this impressive mansion is set in extensive grounds close to the famous Culloden battlefield. High ceilings and intricate cornices are particular features of the public rooms, including the elegant Adam dining room. Bedrooms come in a range of sizes and styles, with a number housed in a separate building.

ROOMS: 23 en suite 5 annexe en suite (1 fmly) in 8 bedrooms s £85-£155; d £130-£199 (incl. bkfst) **LB** **FACILITIES:** STV Sauna Boules, Badminton, Golf Driving Nets, Putting Green ch fac **CONF:** Thtr 60 Class 40 Board 30 Del from £210 **PARKING:** 50 **NOTES:** No children 10yrs in restaurant Civ Wed 65 **CARDS:**

★★★★71% *Inverness Marriott Hotel*
Culcabock Rd IV2 3LP
☎ 01463 237166 01463 225208
e-mail: events@marriotthotels.co.uk
Dir: *from A9 S, exit Culduthel/Kingsmills 5th exit at rdbt, follow road 0.5m, over mini-rdbt past golf club, hotel on left after lights*

Located on the south side of the city, this smart hotel is popular with both business and leisure guests. Accommodation is provided in spacious, thoughtfully equipped rooms, with those in the newer wing particularly impressive. Well-proportioned public areas include a choice of restaurants and lounges and conference facilities.

ROOMS: 76 en suite 6 annexe en suite (11 fmly) (26 GF) in 29 bedrooms **FACILITIES:** **Spa** STV Sauna Solarium Gym Putt green Hair & beauty salon Steam room **CONF:** Thtr 100 Class 35 Board 36 **SERVICES:** Lift **PARKING:** 120 **NOTES:** in restaurant **CARDS:**

Town House Hotel
Country House Hotel
Travel Accommodation

★★★79% Glenmoriston Town House Hotel
20 Ness Bank IV2 4SF
☎ 01463 223777 01463 712378
e-mail: glenmoriston@cali.co.uk
web: www.glenmoriston.com
Dir: *on riverside opposite theatre, 5 mins from town centre*

Bold, contemporary designs blend seamlessly with the classical architecture of this stylish hotel, situated on the banks of the River Ness. Delightful day rooms include a cosy cocktail bar and a sophisticated restaurant offering a tempting range of Mediterranean influenced dishes. The smart, modern bedrooms

continued

have many facilities, including CD players. Service is very friendly and attentive.

ROOMS: 30 en suite (1 fmly) (3 GF) ⊗ in 15 bedrooms s £95-£115; d £130-£150 (incl. bkfst) **LB** **FACILITIES:** STV Xmas **CONF:** Thtr 100 Class 50 Board 30 Del from £140 **PARKING:** 40 **NOTES:** ⊗ in restaurant **CARDS:**

★★★75% *Craigmonie*

9 Annfield Rd IV2 3HX
☎ 01463 231649 01463 233720
e-mail: info@craigmoniehotel.eu.com
Dir: *off A9/A96 follow signs to Hilton & Culcabock. Pass golf course to traffic lights, 1st right after lights*

Set in a leafy suburb of the city, this hotel that is full of character, dates from the 18th century. Extensive public areas include a choice of restaurants, conference facilities and a popular bar. Accommodation comes in a variety of styles, including a number of poolside suites and spacious rooms with spa baths and balconies.
ROOMS: 35 en suite **FACILITIES:** Sauna Gym Jacuzzi **CONF:** Thtr 160 Class 70 Board 50 **SERVICES:** Lift **PARKING:** 60 **NOTES:** ⊗ in restaurant **CARDS:**

★★★74% Bunchrew House

Bunchrew IV3 8TA
☎ 01463 234917 01463 710620
e-mail: welcome@bunchrew-inverness.co.uk
web: www.bunchrew-inverness.co.uk
Dir: *W on A862 along shore of Beauly Firth. Hotel on right 2m after crossing canal*

Overlooking the Beauly Firth this impressive mansion house dates from the 17th century and retains much original character. Individually styled bedrooms are spacious and tastefully furnished. A wood-panelled restaurant is the setting for artfully constructed cooking and there is a choice of comfortable lounges complete with real fires.
ROOMS: 14 en suite (3 fmly) s £90-£127.50; d £130-£155 (incl. bkfst) **LB** **FACILITIES:** Fishing **CONF:** Thtr 80 Class 30 Board 30 Del from £92 **PARKING:** 40 **NOTES:** ⊗ in restaurant Closed 24 Dec-27 Dec Civ Wed 92 **CARDS:**

★★★68% Lochardil House

Best Western

Stratherrick Rd IV2 4LF
☎ 01463 235995 01463 713394
e-mail: lochardil@ukonline.co.uk
Dir: *follow Island Bank Road for 1m, fork left into Drummond Crescent, into Stratherrick Road, 0.5m hotel on left*

A fine Victorian mansion set in extensive gardens in a residential area south of the city centre. Though not large, bedrooms are smartly furnished and boast attractive bathrooms. Meals in the conservatory restaurant will satisfy the heartiest of appetites.
ROOMS: 12 en suite ⊗ in 3 bedrooms s £74-£95; d £95-£112 (incl. bkfst) **LB** **FACILITIES:** STV **CONF:** Thtr 200 Class 100 Board 60 Del from £105 **PARKING:** 123 **NOTES:** Civ Wed 150
CARDS:

★★★68% Royal Highland

Station Square, Academy St IV1 1LG
☎ 01463 231926 01463 710705
e-mail: info@royalhighlandhotel.co.uk
web: www.royalhighlandhotel.co.uk

Built in 1858, this hotel has the typically grand foyer of the Victorian era with comfortable seating. Adjacent to this is the new ASH brasserie and bar, which offers a refreshing style for both eating and drinking throughout the day. The generally spacious bedrooms are comfortably equipped for the business traveller, with the railway station nearby.
ROOMS: 70 en suite (12 fmly) ⊗ in 40 bedrooms s £39.95-£79.95; d £59.95-£119.95 (incl. bkfst) **LB** **FACILITIES:** STV Putt green Jacuzzi Xmas **CONF:** Thtr 200 Class 80 Board 80 Del from £95 **SERVICES:** Lift **PARKING:** 8 **NOTES:** ⊗ in restaurant
CARDS:

INVERNESS, continued

★★★66% The Palace Milton Hotel & Leisure Club
8 Ness Walk IV3 5NG
☎ 01463 223243 01463 236865
e-mail: palace@miltonhotels.com
Dir: *A82 Glenurquhart Rd onto Ness Walk. Hotel 300yds on right opposite Inverness Castle*
Set on the north side of the River Ness close to the Eden Court theatre and a short walk from the town, this hotel has seen a significant refurbishment. Bedrooms offer good levels of comfort and equipment, and a smart leisure centre proves popular.
ROOMS: 40 en suite 48 annexe en suite (4 fmly) ⊗ in 51 bedrooms s £50-£79; d £70-£109 (incl. bkfst) **FACILITIES: Spa** STV supervised Sauna Gym Jacuzzi Beautician, steam room, classes ch fac Xmas **CONF:** Thtr 80 Class 40 Board 30 Del from £99 **SERVICES:** Lift **PARKING:** 18 **NOTES:** ⊗ in restaurant
CARDS:

★★★63% Loch Ness House
THE INDEPENDENTS
Glenurquhart Rd IV3 8JL
☎ 01463 231248 01463 239327
e-mail: lnhhchris@aol.com
Dir: *1.5m from town centre, overlooking Tomnahurich Bridge on canal. From A9, left at Longman rdbt, follow signs for A82 for 2.5m*
This is a family-run hotel, lying close to the canal, which offers friendly and attentive service. Tasty meals can be chosen from a good range of dishes, available in the restaurant or the bar.
ROOMS: 21 en suite (3 fmly) ⊗ in 6 bedrooms s £60-£80; d £110-£130 (incl. bkfst) **LB** **FACILITIES:** STV Xmas **CONF:** Thtr 150 Class 60 Board 40 Del from £85 **PARKING:** 60 **NOTES:** ⊗ in restaurant Civ Wed 75
CARDS:

★★70% The Maple Court
12 Ness Walk IV3 5SQ
☎ 01463 230330 01463 237700
e-mail: maplecourt@macleodhotels.co.uk
Dir: *off A9 into City Centre, follow one-way system. Over Tomnachurich St Bridge, 1st right onto Ness Walk*
Set in gardens on the banks of the River Ness and close to the Eden Court Theatre, this hotel is within a short stroll of the city centre. It has been substantially upgraded and provides smart ground-floor bedrooms and a restaurant serving good-value meals. The friendliness of staff leaves a lasting impression.
ROOMS: 9 en suite (2 fmly) (9 GF) ⊗ in 5 bedrooms s £60-£65; d £80-£90 (incl. bkfst) **LB** **FACILITIES:** ♫ ch fac Xmas **CONF:** BC Thtr 450 Class 200 Board 40 Del from £90 **PARKING:** 32 **NOTES:** ⊗ in restaurant Civ Wed 200 **CARDS:**

⌂ Travel Inn
travel inn
Millburn Rd IV2 3QX
☎ 08701 977141 01463 717826
Dir: *at A9 junct with A96 (Raigmore Interchange, signed Airport/Aberdeen), follow B865 towards town centre, hotel 100yds past next rdbt*
Travel Inn offers good-quality, value-for-money accommodation. Spacious, en suite rooms with bath and shower comfortably accommodate a family of up to two adults and two children (to age 15). The restaurant and bar offers a varied menu. For further details consult the Hotel Groups page.
ROOMS: 39 en suite s £52.95; d £52.95

Packed in a hurry?
Ironing facilities should be available at all star levels, either in rooms or on request

⌂ Travel Inn (Inverness East)
travel inn
Beechwood Business Park IV2 3BW
☎ 08701 977142 01463 225233
Dir: *on A9, turn left sigposted Raigmore Hospital, Police HQ & Inshes Retail Park*
Travel Inn offers good-quality, value-for-money accommodation. Spacious, en suite rooms with bath and shower comfortably accommodate a family of up to two adults and two children (to age 15). The restaurant and bar offers a varied menu. For further details consult the Hotel Groups page.
ROOMS: 60 en suite s £45.95-£46.95; d £45.95-£46.95

⌂ Travelodge
Travelodge
Stoneyfield, A96 Inverness Rd IV2 7PA
☎ 08700 850 950 01463 718152
Dir: *Junction of A9 / A96*
Travelodge offers good quality, good value, modern accommodation. Ideal for families, the spacious, en suite bedrooms include remote-control TV, tea and coffee-making facilities and luxury beds. Meals can be taken at the nearby family restaurant. For further details consult the Hotel Groups page.
ROOMS: s fr £25; d fr £25

INVERURIE, Aberdeenshire — Map 23 NJ72

★★★68% Strathburn
Burghmuir Dr AB51 4GY
☎ 01467 624422 01467 625133
e-mail: strathburn@btconnect.com
web: www.strathburn-hotel.co.uk
Dir: *at Blackhall rbt into Blackhall Rd for 100yds then into Burghmuir Drive*
Located on the western side of town, this friendly, family run hotel provides accommodation in tastefully appointed, newly refurbished bedrooms. Public areas include a spacious lounge with conservatory and a range of meals can be enjoyed in both the bar and more formal restaurant.
ROOMS: 25 en suite (2 fmly) (13 GF) ⊗ in 22 bedrooms s £50-£80; d £85-£95 (incl. bkfst) **LB** **FACILITIES:** STV **CONF:** Thtr 30 Class 24 Board 18 Del from £105 **PARKING:** 40 **NOTES:** ⊗ in restaurant Closed 25-26 Dec & 1-2 Jan **CARDS:**

★★★67% Pittodrie House
Chapel of Garioch, Pitcaple AB51 5HS
☎ 01467 681444 01467 681648
e-mail: pittodrie@macdonald-hotels.co.uk
Dir: *A96, Chapel of Garioch turn off*
This house dates from the 15th century and retains many original features. Bedrooms come in two distinct styles; those in the original house are full of character and the newer wing has been refurbished to provide more modern comfort. Public areas include a striking drawing room, restaurant and a cosy bar.
ROOMS: 27 en suite (6 fmly) ⊗ in 13 bedrooms s £68-£95; d £90-£140 (incl. bkfst) **LB** **FACILITIES:** STV Squash Snooker Clay pigeon shooting Quad biking Archery etc on estate Xmas **CONF:** Thtr 100 Class 70 Board 40 Del from £125 **PARKING:** 150 **NOTES:** ⊗ in restaurant Civ Wed 120 **CARDS:**

IRVINE, North Ayrshire — Map 20 NS33

⌂ Gailes Lodge Restaurant and Hotel
Marine Dr, Gailes KA11 5AE
☎ 01294 204040 01294 204047
e-mail: info@gaileshotel.com
web: www.gaileshotel.com
With several golf courses on its doorstep and within easy reach of Prestwick Airport, Gailes Lodge offers comfortable bedrooms

continued

furnished in contemporary style. A bright attractive café bar/restaurant provides food throughout the day until late.
ROOMS: 41 en suite (incl. bkfst) s £75; d £90 **CONF:** BC Thtr 430 Class 100 Board 80 Del from £115

ISLE OF Placenames incorporating the words 'Isle' or 'Isle of' will be found under the actual name, eg Isle of Arran is under Arran, Isle of.

ISLAY, ISLE OF, Argyll & Bute — Map 20

PORT ASKAIG — Map 20 NR46

★★63% Port Askaig

PA46 7RD
☎ 01496 840245 Fax 01496 840295
e-mail: hotel@portaskaig.co.uk
Dir: *at Ferry Terminal*

This family-run hotel, set in an 18th-century building, offers comfortable bedrooms. The lounge provides fine views over to nearby Jura and there is a choice of bars, popular with locals. Traditional dinners are served in the bright restaurant and a full range of bar snacks and meals is also available.
ROOMS: 8 rms (6 en suite) (1 fmly) s £35-£55; d £60-£78 (incl. bkfst) LB **PARKING:** 21 **NOTES:** No children 5yrs ⊗ in restaurant
CARDS:

ISLE ORNSAY See Skye, Isle of

JEDBURGH, Scottish Borders — Map 21 NT62

★★★77% ®® Jedforest Hotel

Camptown TD8 6PJ
☎ 01835 840222 Fax 01835 840226
e-mail: info@jedforesthotel.com
web: www.jedforesthotel.com
Dir: *on the A68 4m S of Jedburgh*

The phrase 'small is beautiful' is nowhere more aptly applied than to this friendly and immaculately maintained country hotel. Bedrooms are extremely smart, and the larger ones are particularly impressive. Inviting public rooms include a choice of dining options, with the fine dining room having earned our 2 rosette award.
ROOMS: 8 en suite 4 annexe en suite (1 fmly) (4 GF) ⊗ in all bedrooms s £60-£110; d £140-£180 (incl. bkfst & dinner) LB
FACILITIES: Fishing Xmas **PARKING:** 25 **NOTES:** No children 12yrs ⊗ in restaurant **CARDS:**

> Early start?
> Hotels at all star levels should provide in-room alarm clocks and/or alarm calls

KELSO, Scottish Borders — Map 21 NT73

★★★76% ®® The Roxburghe Hotel & Golf Course

Heiton TD5 8JZ
☎ 01573 450331 Fax 01573 450611
e-mail: hotel@roxburghe.net
web: www.roxburghe.net
Dir: *from A68 Jedburgh join A698 to Heiton, 3m SW of Kelso*

Outdoor sporting pursuits are popular at this impressive Jacobean mansion owned by the Duke of Roxburghe and set in 500 acres of woods and parkland. Gracious public areas are the perfect settings for afternoon teas and carefully prepared meals. Bedrooms are individually designed, with some of the superior rooms having their own fires.
ROOMS: 16 en suite 6 annexe en suite (3 fmly) (3 GF) ⊗ in 1 bedroom s £125-£225; d £140-£280 (incl. bkfst) LB **FACILITIES:** STV 18 Fishing Putt green Clay shooting Health & Beauty Salon Mountain bike hire, riding stables nearby ch fac Xmas **CONF:** BC Thtr 50 Class 20 Board 20 Del from £99 **PARKING:** 150 **NOTES:** ⊗ in restaurant Civ Wed 60 **CARDS:**

★★★71% Ednam House

Bridge St TD5 7HT
☎ 01573 224168 Fax 01573 226319
e-mail: contact@ednamhouse.com
Dir: *50mtrs from Town Sq on Bridge St leading to Abbey and Kelso Old Bridge*

Overlooking a wide expanse of the River Tweed, this fine Georgian mansion has now been under the Brooks family ownership for over 75 years. Accommodation styles range from standard to grand, with a house in the grounds converted into a gracious two-bedroom apartment. Public areas include a choice of lounges and an elegant dining room, which has views of the gardens.
ROOMS: 30 en suite (4 fmly) ⊗ in 3 bedrooms s £75-£110; d £93-£130 (incl. bkfst) LB **FACILITIES:** Free access to Abbey Fitness Centre
CONF: Thtr 250 Board 200 **PARKING:** 60 **NOTES:** Closed 24 Dec-06 Jan Civ Wed 100 **CARDS:**

★★★66% *Cross Keys*

36-37 The Square TD5 7HL
☎ 01573 223303 Fax 01573 225792
e-mail: cross-keys-hotel@easynet.co.uk
web: www.cross-keys-hotel.co.uk
Dir: *on approaching Kelso, follow signs for town centre. Hotel in main square*

Originally a coaching inn, but now tastefully modernised, this family-run hotel overlooks Kelso's fine cobbled square. Bedrooms are either superior or standard level, and the spacious lounge bar and restaurant are supplemented by the Oak Room bar/bistro.
ROOMS: 27 en suite (5 fmly) ⊗ in 12 bedrooms **FACILITIES:** STV
CONF: BC Thtr 220 Class 160 Board 60 **SERVICES:** Lift air con
NOTES: Civ Wed 100 **CARDS:**

KENMORE, Perth & Kinross Map 21 NN74

★★★64% Kenmore Hotel
The Square PH15 2NU
☎ 01887 830205 📠 01887 830262
e-mail: reception@kenmorehotel.co.uk
Dir: *off A9 at Ballinluig onto A827, through Aberfeldy to Kenmore for hotel in village centre*
Dating back to 1572, this riverside hotel is Scotland's oldest inn and has a rich and interesting history. Bedrooms have been upgraded and modernised, with tasteful décor. Dinner can be enjoyed in the restaurant with its panoramic views of the River Tay. The choice of bars includes one with real fires.
ROOMS: 27 en suite 13 annexe en suite (4 fmly) (7 GF) s £43-£66; d £70-£102 (incl. bkfst) **LB** **FACILITIES:** STV Fishing Jacuzzi Discounted salmon fishing on River Tay Xmas **CONF:** Thtr 80 Class 60 Board 50 Del from £82 **SERVICES:** Lift **PARKING:** 30 **NOTES:** ⊗ in restaurant **CARDS:**

KILCHRENAN, Argyll & Bute Map 20 NN02

★★★77% Taychreggan
PA35 1HQ
☎ 01866 833211 & 833366 📠 01866 833244
e-mail: info@taychregganhotel.co.uk
Dir: *W from Crianlarich on A85 to Taynuilt, S for 7m on B845 to Kilchrenan and Taychreggan*

Surrounded by some stunning highland scenery this romantic hotel enjoys an idyllic setting, in 40 acres of grounds, on the shores of Loch Awe. Public areas include a smart bar with adjacent Orangery and a choice of quiet lounges. Carefully prepared meals are served in an elegant dining room.
ROOMS: 19 en suite ⊗ in 3 bedrooms s fr £99; d fr £127 (incl. bkfst) **LB** **FACILITIES:** no TV in bdrms Fishing Snooker Jacuzzi **CONF:** Class 15 Board 20 Del from £155 **PARKING:** 40 **NOTES:** No children 14yrs ⊗ in restaurant Civ Wed 70 **CARDS:**

For central reservation numbers and more information on Hotel Groups, turn to pages 33-39

★★★72% The Ardanaiseig
by Loch Awe PA35 1HE
☎ 01866 833333 📠 01866 833222
e-mail: ardanaiseig@clara.net
Dir: *turn S off A85 at Taynuilt onto B845 to Kilchrenan. Left in front of pub (road very narrow) signed Ardanaiseig Hotel and No Through Road*
Set amid lovely gardens and breathtaking scenery beside the shore of Loch Awe, this peaceful country-house hotel was built in the Scottish baronial style in 1834. Many fine pieces of furniture are evident in the bedrooms and charming day rooms, which include a drawing room, a library bar, and an elegant dining room.

ROOMS: 16 en suite (4 fmly) s £133-£168; d £103-£138 (incl. bkfst) **LB** **FACILITIES:** STV Fishing Snooker Boating, Clay pigeon shooting, Bikes for hire ch fac Xmas **PARKING:** 20 **NOTES:** ⊗ in restaurant Closed 2 Jan-14 Feb Civ Wed 50 **CARDS:**

KILLIECRANKIE, Perth & Kinross Map 23 NN96

★★77% Killiecrankie House
PH16 5LG
☎ 01796 473220 📠 01796 472451
e-mail: enquiries@killiecrankiehotel.co.uk
web: www.killiecrankiehotel.co.uk
Dir: *off A9 at Killiecrankie, hotel 3m along B8079 on right*

A long-established hotel set in mature grounds close to the historic Pass of Killiecrankie. The owners Tim and Maillie Waters and their charming staff provide friendly and attentive service. Accomplished cooking can be enjoyed in the atmospheric restaurant, and a healthy and tasty selection of dishes can be found in the bar.
ROOMS: 10 en suite (2 fmly) (2 GF) ⊗ in all bedrooms s £79-£99; d £158-£198 (incl. bkfst & dinner) **LB** **FACILITIES:** Putt green Xmas **PARKING:** 20 **NOTES:** ⊗ in restaurant Closed 3 Jan - 14 Feb RS Nov, Dec, Feb & Mar **CARDS:**

KILMARNOCK, East Ayrshire Map 20 NS43

★★★68% *Fenwick*
Ayr Rd, Fenwick KA3 6AU
☎ 01560 600478 📠 01560 600334
e-mail: fenwick@bestwestern.co.uk
Dir: *approx 4m N of Kilmarnock, adjacent to A77 & B751*
Conveniently situated between Glasgow and the Ayrshire coast, this hotel is popular for its food with creative, innovative menus forming the basis for its own dining club. Bedrooms are suited to the business traveller. Comfortable public rooms include a cosy

continued

fireside lounge, a bright restaurant and informal bar offering an impressive pub menu.
ROOMS: 31 en suite (2 fmly) (10 GF) ⊗ in 4 bedrooms
FACILITIES: STV Clay pigeon Quad bike ch fac **CONF:** Thtr 160 Class 60 Board 50 **PARKING:** 80 **NOTES:** ⊗ in restaurant Civ Wed 100
CARDS:

Travel Inn
Annadale KA1 2RS
☎ 08701 977148 01563 570536
Dir: *from M74(J8) signed Kilmarnock (A71). From M77 join A71 to Irvine. At next rbt turn right onto B7064 signed Crosshouse Hospital. Travel Inn is on the right*
Travel Inn offers good-quality, value-for-money accommodation. Spacious, en suite rooms with bath and shower comfortably accommodate a family of up to two adults and two children (to age 15). The restaurant and bar offers a varied menu. For further details consult the Hotel Groups page.
ROOMS: 40 en suite s £45.95-£46.95; d £45.95-£46.95

Travelodge
Kilmarnock By Pass KA1 5LQ
☎ 08700 850 950 01563 573810
Dir: *at Bellfield Interchange just off A77*
Travelodge offers good quality, good value, modern accommodation. Ideal for families, the spacious, en suite bedrooms include remote-control TV, tea and coffee-making facilities and luxury beds. Meals can be taken at the nearby family restaurant. For further details consult the Hotel Groups page.
ROOMS: 40 en suite s fr £25; d fr £25

KILWINNING, North Ayrshire — Map 20 NS34

★★★72% Montgreenan Mansion House
Montgreenan Estate KA13 7QZ
☎ 01294 557733 01294 850397
e-mail: enquiries@montgreenhotel.com
web: www.montgreenanhotel.com
Dir: *signs for hotel 4m north of Irvine on A736 and from Kilwinning on A737*
In a peaceful setting of 48 acres of parkland and woods, this 19th-century mansion retains many of its original features. Public areas include a splendid drawing room, a library, a club-style bar and a restaurant. Accommodation ranges from compact modern rooms to the well-proportioned classical rooms of the original house. Service is friendly and attentive.
ROOMS: 21 en suite (1 fmly) ⊗ in 16 bedrooms s £79.50-£139.50; d £159-£219 (incl. bkfst & dinner) **LB** **FACILITIES:** STV 5 Snooker Putt green Jacuzzi in honeymoon suite, woodland walks ch fac Xmas **CONF:** Thtr 100 Class 60 Board 40 Del from £115 **PARKING:** 50 **NOTES:** ⊗ in restaurant Civ Wed 140
CARDS:

KINCARDINE, Fife — Map 21 NS98

Travel Inn (Falkirk North)
Bowtrees Farm FK2 8PJ
☎ 08701 977099 01324 831934
Dir: *From north M9 junct 7 towards Kincardine Bridge, from south M876 for Kincardine Bridge. On rdbt at end of slip road*
Travel Inn offers good-quality, value-for-money accommodation. Spacious, en suite rooms with bath and shower comfortably accommodate a family of up to two adults and two children (to age 15). The restaurant and bar offers a varied menu. For further details consult the Hotel Groups page.
ROOMS: 40 en suite s £45.95-£46.95; d £45.95-£46.95

KINCLAVEN, Perth & Kinross — Map 21 NO13

Top 200 – Hotel

★★★ Ballathie House
PH1 4QN
☎ 01250 883268 01250 883396
e-mail: email@ballathiehousehotel.com
web: www.ballathiehousehotel.com
Dir: *from A9 2m N of Perth, B9099 through Stanley & signposted or off A93 at Beech Hedge follow signs for Ballathie 2.5m*
Set in delightful grounds, this splendid Scottish mansion house combines classical grandeur with modern comfort. Bedrooms range from well-proportioned master rooms to modern standard rooms and many boast antique furniture and Art Deco bathrooms. For the ultimate in quality, request one of the Riverside Rooms, a purpose-built development right on the banks of the river, complete with balconies and terraces. The elegant restaurant has views over the River Tay.
ROOMS: 26 en suite 16 annexe en suite (2 fmly) s £79-£110; d £158-£220 (incl. bkfst) **LB** **FACILITIES:** STV Fishing Putt green Xmas **CONF:** Thtr 50 Class 20 Board 30 Del from £150 **SERVICES:** Lift **PARKING:** 50 **NOTES:** ⊗ in restaurant Civ Wed 90
CARDS:

KINGUSSIE, Highland — Map 23 NH70

★★71% The Scot House
Newtonmore Rd PH21 1HE
☎ 01540 661351 01540 661111
e-mail: enquiries@scothouse.com
web: www.scothouse.com
Dir: *A9, take Kingussie exit, hotel approx 0.50m at S end of village Main St*
This long established hotel offers comfortable accommodation in thoughtfully equipped, generally spacious rooms. The young enthusiastic team provides warm hospitality. A popular bar and restaurant are the setting for a wide range of carefully prepared meals and an excellent range of malt whiskies.
ROOMS: 9 en suite (1 fmly) ⊗ in all bedrooms s £42-£50; d £68-£84 (incl. bkfst) **LB** **FACILITIES:** Xmas **PARKING:** 50 **NOTES:** ⊗ in restaurant Closed 10-31 Jan **CARDS:**

KINGUSSIE, continued

Top 200 – Hotel

The Cross

Tweed Mill Brae, Ardbroilach Rd PH21 1LB
☎ 01540 661166 01540 661080
e-mail: relax@thecross.co.uk
web: www.thecross.co.uk
Dir: *from traffic lights in centre of Kingussie, along Ardbroilach Rd for 300mtrs, turn left into Tweed Mill Brae*

This converted tweed mill in a wooded riverside setting offers comfortable bedrooms in a mix of traditional and quality pine styles. Lounges are also inviting, but it is the light and airy restaurant that forms the highlight of any visit. Refreshingly and deceptively simple in concept, dinner displays fine local ingredients sympathetically cooked to draw out the natural flavours. Service is attentive, backed up by a genuine feeling that guests are very welcome indeed.

ROOMS: 8 en suite (1 fmly) in all bedrooms s £95-£140; d £150-£240 (incl. bkfst & dinner) **LB CONF:** Thtr 20 Class 20 Board 20 Del from £120 **PARKING:** 12 **NOTES:** in restaurant Closed Xmas, New Year & Jan RS Sun & Mon
CARDS:

KINROSS, Perth & Kinross — Map 21 NO10

★★★75% Green

2 The Muirs KY13 8AS
☎ 01577 863467 01577 863180
e-mail: reservations@green-hotel.com
web: www.green-hotel.com
Dir: *M90 junct 6 follow signs for Kinross, onto A922, hotel on this road*

A long-established hotel offering a wide range of indoor and outdoor activities. Public areas include a classical restaurant, a choice of bars and a well-stocked gift shop. The comfortable, well-equipped bedrooms, most of which are generously proportioned, boast attractive colour schemes and smart modern furnishings.

ROOMS: 46 en suite (4 fmly) (14 GF) in 12 bedrooms s £85-£105; d £150-£170 (incl. bkfst) **LB FACILITIES:** STV supervised 36 Fishing Squash Sauna Solarium Gym Putt green Curling in season, Petanque (French boules) ch fac Xmas **CONF:** BC Thtr 130 Class 75 Board 60 Del from £105 **PARKING:** 60 **NOTES:** in restaurant Closed 23-28 Dec excluding Xmas day RS 25 Dec
CARDS:

★★★69% *Windlestrae Hotel and Leisure Club*

The Muirs KY13 8AS
☎ 0870 609 6153 01577 864733
e-mail: windlestrae@corushotels.com
Dir: *M90 junct 6 turn E into Kinross, stop at 2nd mini rdbt turn left in approx 350yds, hotel on right*

This hotel is set in landscaped gardens back from the main road, yet conveniently placed for access to the town centre and many local attractions. There are impressive leisure and conference facilities and accommodation is provided in well-proportioned bedrooms. Comfortable public areas include a lounge, bar and roomy restaurant.

ROOMS: 45 en suite (5 fmly) (14 GF) in 15 bedrooms
FACILITIES: STV Snooker Sauna Solarium Gym Jacuzzi Beautician, Steam room, Toning tables **CONF:** Thtr 250 Class 100 Board 80 **SERVICES:** air con **PARKING:** 80 **NOTES:** in restaurant Civ Wed 100
CARDS:

Travelodge

Travelodge

Kincardine Rd KY13 7NQ
☎ 08700 850 950 01577 861641
Dir: *on A977, M90 junct 6 Turthills Tourist Centre*

Travelodge offers good quality, good value, modern accommodation. Ideal for families, the spacious, en suite bedrooms include remote-control TV, tea and coffee-making facilities and luxury beds. Meals can be taken at the nearby family restaurant. For further details consult the Hotel Groups page.

ROOMS: 35 en suite s fr £25; d fr £25

KIRKBEAN, Dumfries & Galloway — Map 21 NX95

★★77% Cavens

DG2 8AA
☎ 01387 880234 01387 880467
e-mail: enquiries@cavens.com
web: www.cavens.com
Dir: *on entering village of Kirkbean on A710, hotel signed*

Set in parkland gardens, Cavens encapsulates all the virtues of an intimate country-house hotel. Quality is the keynote, and Angus and Jane Fordyce have spared no effort in completing a fine renovation of the house. Bedrooms - some with their own sun

continued

lounge - are delightfully individual, whilst lounges invite peaceful relaxation. A set dinner offers the best of local produce.

ROOMS: 6 en suite ⊗ in all bedrooms s £70-£100; d £90-£115 (incl. bkfst) **LB** **FACILITIES:** Shooting, Fishing, Horse Riding Xmas **CONF:** Thtr 20 Class 20 Board 20 Del from £150 **PARKING:** 12 **NOTES:** ⊗ in restaurant Civ Wed 100 **CARDS:**

KIRKCALDY, Fife — Map 21 NT29

★★★68% Dunnikier House Hotel

Dunnikier Park KY1 3LP
☎ 01592 268393 01592 642340
e-mail: recp@dunnikier-house-hotel.co.uk
web: www.dunnikier-house-hotel.co.uk
Dir: *off A92 at Kirkcaldy West, then 3rd exit on rdbt signed 'Hospital/Crematorium'. 1st left past school*

This imposing 18th-century manor house is set in parkland adjacent to Dunnikier Golf Course. Public areas contain many original features. Views over the park can be enjoyed from the lounge, and the bar offers a wide selection of whiskies as well as a comprehensive food menu. The Oswald restaurant provides fine meals featuring fresh, carefully prepared local produce.

ROOMS: 15 en suite (1 fmly) s £60-£67.50; d £75-£95 (incl. bkfst) **CONF:** Thtr 60 Class 20 Board 30 **PARKING:** 100 **NOTES:** ⊗ in restaurant **CARDS:**

★★★67% Dean Park

Chapel Level KY2 6QW
☎ 01592 261635 01592 261371
e-mail: reception@deanparkhotel.co.uk
Dir: *signed from A92, Kirkcaldy West junct*

Popular with both business and leisure guests, this smart hotel has extensive conference and meeting facilities and ample car parking. Executive bedrooms are spacious and comfortable, and all are well equipped with modern decor and amenities. Twelve direct-access, chalet-style rooms are also available. Public areas include a choice of bars and a popular dining room.

ROOMS: 34 en suite 12 annexe en suite (2 fmly) (5 GF) ⊗ in 10 bedrooms **FACILITIES:** STV ch fac **CONF:** Thtr 250 Class 125 Board 54 **SERVICES:** Lift **PARKING:** 250 **NOTES:** Civ Wed 250 **CARDS:**

★★68% *The Belvedere*

Coxstool, West Wemyss KY1 4SL
☎ 01592 654167 01592 655279
e-mail: info@thebelvederehotel.com
web: www.thebelvederehotel.com
Dir: *A92 from M90 junct 2A, at Kirkcaldy East take A915, 1m NE turn right to Coaltown, at T-junct turn right then left, hotel 1st building in village*

This welcoming hotel enjoys a lovely location in the small village of Coxstool and scenic views over the Firth of Forth. The bright airy bedrooms are attractively decorated and feature comfortable modern furnishings. Public areas include a small bar and a stylish restaurant.

ROOMS: 5 en suite 15 annexe en suite (2 fmly) **FACILITIES:** STV **CONF:** Thtr 40 Class 12 Board 20 **PARKING:** 50 **NOTES:** ⊗ in restaurant Civ Wed 40 **CARDS:**

KIRKCUDBRIGHT, Dumfries & Galloway — Map 20 NX65

★★66% Arden House Hotel

Tongland Rd DG6 4UU
☎ 01557 330544 01557 330742
Dir: *off A57 Euro route (Stranraer), 4m W of Castle Douglas onto A711. Signed for Kirkcudbright, crossing Telford Bridge. Hotel 400mtrs on left*

Set well back from the main road in extensive grounds on the north-east side of town, this well-maintained hotel offers attractive bedrooms, a lounge bar and adjoining conservatory serving a range of popular dishes, which are also available in the dining room. It boasts an impressive function suite in its grounds.

ROOMS: 9 rms (8 en suite) (7 fmly) s £35; d £60 (incl. bkfst) **CONF:** Thtr 175 Class 175 **PARKING:** 70

★★64% Royal

St Cuthbert St DG6 4DY
THE INDEPENDENTS
☎ 01557 331213 01557 331513
e-mail: reception@theroyalhotel.net
Dir: *off A75 onto A711, hotel in town centre at crossroads*

Lying right in the town centre this hotel has colourfully decorated bedrooms with good facilities. Good value meals are provided throughout the day and evening in either the coffee lounge, bar or dining room. Residents have a comfortable upstairs lounge in which to relax.

ROOMS: 17 en suite (7 fmly) **FACILITIES:** ♫ **CONF:** Thtr 120 Class 60 Board 60 **NOTES:** ⊗ in restaurant Civ Wed 100 **CARDS:**

KIRRIEMUIR, Angus — Map 23 NO35

Airlie Arms

4 St Malcolms Wynd DD8 4HB
☎ 01575 572847 01575 573055
e-mail: info@airliearms-hotel.co.uk

ROOMS: 10 en suite (2 fmly) (5 GF) ⊗ in 2 bedrooms s £35-£45; d £60-£80 (incl. bkfst) **LB** **FACILITIES:** STV Xmas **CONF:** Thtr 90 Class 70 Board 50 **PARKING:** 5 **NOTES:** ★★ ⊗ in restaurant **CARDS:**

KYLE OF LOCHALSH, Highland — Map 22 NG72

★★★62% Lochalsh

Ferry Rd IV40 8AF
☎ 01599 534202 01599 534881
e-mail: mdmacrae@lochalsh-hotel.demon.co.uk
Dir: *turn off A82 onto A87*

Benefiting from lovely views over to the Isle of Skye, this hotel is set in the heart of the town close to the old ferry slip. Many of the bedrooms overlook the harbour and the modern Skye Bridge. Meals can be enjoyed in either the relaxed atmosphere of the lounge and bar or the spacious restaurant.

ROOMS: 38 en suite (8 fmly) s £40-£75; d £75-£140 (incl. bkfst) **LB** **FACILITIES:** STV Xmas **CONF:** Thtr 20 Class 20 Board 20 **SERVICES:** Lift **PARKING:** 50 **NOTES:** ⊗ in restaurant **CARDS:**

See advert on page 743

LADYBANK, Fife — Map 21 NO30

★★★61% Fernie Castle
Letham KY15 7RU
☎ 01337 810381 📠 01337 810422
e-mail: mail@ferniecastle.demon.co.uk
Dir: *M90 junct 8 take A91E (Tay Bridge/St Andrews) to Melville Lodges rdbt. Left onto A92 signed Tay Bridge. Hotel 1.2m on right*

This turreted castle is set amid 17 acres of wooded grounds in the heart of Fife. Bedrooms range from King and Queen rooms, to the more standard-sized Squire and Lady rooms. The elegant Auld Alliance Restaurant presents a formal setting, whilst guests can also dine in the keep bar with its impressive vaulted walls and ceiling.
ROOMS: 20 en suite (2 fmly) ⊗ in 15 bedrooms s £70-£99; d £70-£99 (incl. bkfst & dinner) LB **FACILITIES:** ch fac Xmas **CONF:** Thtr 180 Class 120 Board 25 Del from £140 **PARKING:** 80 **NOTES:** ⊗ in restaurant Civ Wed 200 **CARDS:**

LAIRG, Highland — Map 23 NC50

★★68% Overscaig
Loch Shin IV27 4NY
☎ 01549 431203
Dir: *on A838*
Now under new ownership this Highland hotel enjoys a lochside location amid unspoilt scenery and is popular with fishermen and birdwatchers. The dining room overlooks Loch Shin and there is a choice of bars plus a coffee lounge. Bedrooms are modern in style and comfortably appointed. Fishing excursions can be arranged.
ROOMS: 9 en suite (2 fmly) ⊗ in all bedrooms **FACILITIES:** Fishing Snooker **PARKING:** 10 **NOTES:** ⊗ in restaurant

LANARK, South Lanarkshire — Map 21 NS84
See also Biggar

★★★66% Cartland Bridge
Glasgow Rd ML11 9UF
☎ 01555 664426 📠 01555 663773
e-mail: sales@cartlandbridge.co.uk
Dir: *follow A73 through Lanark towards Carluke. Hotel 1.25m on right*
Situated in wooded grounds on the edge of the town, this Grade I listed mansion continues to be popular with both business and leisure guests. Public areas feature wood panelling and a gallery staircase. In addition to the restaurant, food is available in the bar. Well-equipped bedrooms vary in size and style.
ROOMS: 20 rms (18 en suite) (2 fmly) ⊗ in 9 bedrooms s £49-£55; d £70-£79 (incl. bkfst) **FACILITIES:** STV Xmas **CONF:** Thtr 250 Class 180 Board 30 Del from £109 **PARKING:** 120 **NOTES:** ⊗ in restaurant Civ Wed 200 **CARDS:**

⊗ No smoking

LANGBANK, Renfrewshire — Map 20 NS37

U Gleddoch House
PA14 6YE
☎ 01475 540711 📠 01475 540201
e-mail: info@gleddochhouse.com
Dir: *signed from B789 at Langbank rdbt*
At the time of going to press, the star classification for this hotel was not confirmed. Please refer to the AA internet site www.theAA.com for current information.
ROOMS: 39 en suite (8 fmly) (5 GF) ⊗ in 6 bedrooms
FACILITIES: STV supervised 18 Fishing Riding Sauna Gym Putt green Clay pigeon shooting, Offroad driving **CONF:** Thtr 150 Class 60 Board 52 **PARKING:** 200 **CARDS:**

LARGS, North Ayrshire — Map 20 NS25

★★69% Willowbank
96 Greenock Rd KA30 8PG
☎ 01475 672311 & 675435 📠 01475 689027
e-mail: iaincsmith@btconnect.com
Dir: *on A78*
A relaxed, friendly atmosphere prevails at this well-maintained hotel. The well-decorated bedrooms tend to be spacious and offer comfortable modern appointments, while public areas include a large, well-stocked bar, a lounge and a dining room. Attractive hanging baskets are a feature in the summer.
ROOMS: 30 en suite (4 fmly) **FACILITIES:** ♫ Xmas **CONF:** Thtr 200 Class 100 Board 40 Del from £80 **PARKING:** 40 **NOTES:** ⊗ in restaurant **CARDS:**

LAUDER, Scottish Borders — Map 21 NT54

★★67% Lauderdale
1 Edinburgh Rd TD2 6TW
☎ 01578 722231 📠 01578 718642
e-mail: enquiries@lauderdale-hotel.co.uk
web: www.lauderdale-hotel.co.uk
Dir: *from S on A68, through town centre, hotel on right. From Edinburgh, hotel on left at 1st bend after passing sign for Lauder*
Lying on the north side of the village with spacious gardens to the side and rear, this friendly hotel is ideally placed for those wishing to stay outside of Edinburgh itself. A good range of meals is served in both the bar and the restaurant. The well-equipped bedrooms come in a variety of sizes.
ROOMS: 10 en suite (1 fmly) ⊗ in all bedrooms s £42; d £70-£80 (incl. bkfst) **FACILITIES:** STV ch fac Xmas **PARKING:** 200 **NOTES:** ⊗ in restaurant **CARDS:**

LERWICK See Shetland

LETTERFINLAY, Highland — Map 22 NN29

★★67% Letterfinlay Lodge
PH34 4DZ
☎ 01397 712622
e-mail: info@letterfinlaylodgehotel.com
Dir: *7m N of Spean Bridge, on A82 beside Loch Lochy*
This comfortable, family-run hotel stands in grounds beside the A82, overlooking Loch Lochy. There is a cosy bar, a choice of lounges - one of which has stunning lochside views and is popular for its bar food - and an attractive dining room. Bedrooms come in a variety of sizes, some being particularly spacious.
ROOMS: 13 rms (11 en suite) (5 fmly) s £30-£45; d £60-£80 (incl. bkfst) LB **FACILITIES:** Fishing **PARKING:** 100 **NOTES:** ⊗ in restaurant Closed Nov-Feb **CARDS:**

LIVINGSTON, West Lothian Map 21 NT06

Travel Inn (Livingston Nr Edinburgh)
Deer Park Av, Knightsridge EH54 8AD
☎ 08701 977161 📠 01506 438912
Dir: *on M8 (J3). Follow road to rdbt and Travel Inn opposite rdbt*
Travel Inn offers good-quality, value-for-money accommodation. Spacious, en suite rooms with bath and shower comfortably accommodate a family of up to two adults and two children (to age 15). The restaurant and bar offers a varied menu. For further details consult the Hotel Groups page.
ROOMS: 83 en suite s £45.95-£46.95; d £45.95-£46.95

○ Travelodge (Livingston)
Almondvale Cresent EH
ROOMS: 60 en suite
NOTES: Due to open Dec 2004

LOCHGILPHEAD, Argyll & Bute Map 20 NR88

★★★72% *Cairnbaan*
Crinan Canal, Cairnbaan PA31 8SJ
☎ 01546 603668 📠 01546 606045
e-mail: cairnbaanhotel@virgin.net
web: www.cairnbaan.com
Dir: *2m N, A816 from Lochgilphead, hotel off B841*
Located on the Crinan Canal, this small hotel offers relaxed hospitality in a delightful setting. Bedrooms are thoughtfully equipped, generally spacious and benefit from bright décor. Fresh seafood is a real feature in both the formal restaurant and the comfortable bar area and al fresco dining is popular in the warmer months.
ROOMS: 12 en suite ⊗ in all bedrooms **CONF:** Thtr 160 Class 100 Board 80 **PARKING:** 53 **NOTES:** ⊗ in restaurant Civ Wed 120
CARDS:

★★62% Stag
Argyll St PA31 8NE
☎ 01546 602496 📠 01546 603549
e-mail: reservatiosn@staghotel.com
Dir: *on entering Lochgilphead at main mini-rdbt into Argyll Street for hotel at junct of Lorne Street & Argyll Street*
This long-established hotel benefits from a central location in this popular tourist destination. The refurbished restaurant offers a range of popular dishes at reasonable prices. The thoughtfully equipped bedrooms offer good value accommodation.
ROOMS: 18 en suite s fr £44.95; d fr £59.95 (incl. bkfst)
FACILITIES: Xmas **CONF:** Thtr 40 Class 50 Board 40 **NOTES:**
CARDS:

LOCHINVER, Highland Map 22 NC02

Top 200 – Hotel

★★★ Inver Lodge
IV27 4LU
☎ 01571 844496 📠 01571 844395
e-mail: stay@inverlodge.com
web: www.inverlodge.com
Dir: *A835 to Lochinver continue through village and turn left after village hall, follow private rod for 0.5m*
Genuine hospitality is notable at this delightful, modern hotel set high on the hillside above the village. Stunning views can be enjoyed throughout, and public areas include a choice of lounges, a well-stocked bar and a restaurant where skilful chefs make use of the abundant local produce. Accommodation is spacious, stylish and of high quality.

ROOMS: 20 en suite s fr £80; d fr £150 (incl. bkfst) LB
FACILITIES: STV Fishing Snooker Sauna Solarium **CONF:** Thtr 30 Board 20 **PARKING:** 30 **NOTES:** ⊗ in restaurant Closed Nov-Etr
CARDS:

Albannach
Baddidarrach IV27 4LP
☎ 01571 844407 📠 01571 844285
e-mail: thealbannach@virgin.net
Dir: *from Ullapool turn right over old stone bridge at foot of hill, signed Baddidarrach & Highland Stoneware Pottery. After 0.5m over cattle grid & turn left*
At the time of going to press, the star classification for this hotel

continued on p744

LOCHINVER, continued

was not confirmed. Please refer to the AA internet site www.theAA.com for current information.
ROOMS: 4 en suite 1 annexe en suite (1 GF) ⊗ in all bedrooms s £102-£140; d £204-£234 (incl. bkfst) **FACILITIES:** STV **PARKING:** 8 **NOTES:** No children 12yrs ⊗ in restaurant Closed Dec-Feb **CARDS:**

LOCH LOMOND See Balloch Drymen & Luss

LOCKERBIE, Dumfries & Galloway Map 21 NY18

Courtesy & Care Award

★★★80% Dryfesdale
Dryfebridge DG11 2SF
☎ 01576 202427 01576 204187
e-mail: reception@dryfesdalehotel.co.uk
web: www.dryfesdalehotel.co.uk
Dir: *from M74 take 'Lockerbie North' junct 17, 3rd left at 1st rdbt, 1st exit left at 2nd rdbt, hotel is 200yds on left*
Conveniently situated for the M74, yet discreetly screened from it, this friendly hotel provides memorable service from a team of thoughtful, enthusiastic staff. Bedrooms, some with access to patio areas, vary in size and style, offer good levels of comfort and are well equipped. Creative, good value dinners make excellent use of local produce and are served in the airy restaurant overlooking the manicured gardens and rolling countryside. This hotel has been awarded the AA Courtesy & Care Award for Scotland 2004-5.
ROOMS: 16 en suite (2 fmly) (7 GF) ⊗ in 4 bedrooms s fr £65; d fr £105 (incl. bkfst) LB **FACILITIES:** STV 9 Fishing Putt green Clay pigeon shooting,Fishing ♫ Xmas **CONF:** BC Thtr 100 Class 80 Board 45 Del from £100 **PARKING:** 40 **NOTES:** ⊗ in restaurant Civ Wed 100 **CARDS:**

★★73% Somerton House
35 Carlisle Rd DG11 2DR
☎ 01576 202583 & 202384 01576 204218
e-mail: somerton@somertonhotel.co.uk
Dir: *off A74*
This friendly, family-run Victorian mansion has been sympathetically preserved and features beautiful woodwork, particularly in the dining room. Two attractive conservatories add a new dimension and are popular for bar meals and functions. The bedrooms are particularly stylish and well equipped.
ROOMS: 7 en suite 4 annexe en suite (1 fmly) ⊗ in 7 bedrooms s £46; d £60-£75 (incl. bkfst) LB **FACILITIES:** Xmas **CONF:** Thtr 60 Class 25 Board 25 **PARKING:** 100 **NOTES:** ⊗ in restaurant **CARDS:**

★★70% Kings Arms Hotel
High St DG11 2JL
☎ 01576 202410 01576 202410
e-mail: reception@kingsarmshotel.co.uk
web: www.kingsarmshotel.co.uk
Dir: *A74(M), 0.5m into town centre, hotel is opposite Town Hall*
Dating from the 17th century this former inn lies right in the town centre. Now a family-run hotel, it provides attractive well-equipped bedrooms. During lunch and dinner a menu ranging from snacks to full meals is served in the two cosy bars.
ROOMS: 13 en suite (2 fmly) ⊗ in 1 bedroom s £37.50; d £65 (incl. bkfst) **FACILITIES:** ch fac Xmas **CONF:** Thtr 80 Class 40 Board 30 **PARKING:** 8 **NOTES:** ⊗ in restaurant **CARDS:**

★★65% Ravenshill House
12 Dumfries Rd DG11 2EF
☎ 01576 202882 01576 202882
e-mail: aaenquiries@ravenshillhotellockerbie.co.uk
web: www.ravenshillhotellockerbie.co.uk
Dir: *from A74(M) Lockerbie junct onto A709. Hotel is 0.5m on right*
This friendly, family-run hotel is located close to the town and is set in its own tidy gardens. The bright bedrooms are very well-equipped and comfortable. Ravenshill House boasts cheerful service and features good value, home-cooked meals.
ROOMS: 8 rms (7 en suite) (2 fmly) ⊗ in 5 bedrooms s £40-£60; d £60-£70 (incl. bkfst) LB **CONF:** Thtr 30 Class 20 Board 12 **PARKING:** 35 **NOTES:** ⊗ in restaurant **CARDS:**

LUNDIN LINKS, Fife Map 21 NO40

★★★78% Old Manor
Leven Rd KY8 6AJ
☎ 01333 320368 01333 320911
e-mail: enquiries@oldmanorhotel.co.uk
web: www.oldmanorhotel.co.uk
Dir: *1m E of Leven on A915 Kirkcaldy-St Andrews Rd for hotel on right*
This long-established hotel lies on the edge of the village and overlooks the golf course to the Firth of Forth. Enthusiastically run, high standards are maintained throughout. Bedrooms come in a variety of styles and there is a choice of restaurants - the new conservatory Terrace Brasserie and Grill with outstanding views or the more informal Coachman's Bistro within the well-tended grounds.
ROOMS: 24 en suite (2 fmly) (8 GF) ⊗ in 4 bedrooms s £75-£100; d £67.50-£135 (incl. bkfst) LB **FACILITIES:** Complimentary membership of Lundin Sports Club ch fac Xmas **CONF:** Thtr 140 Class 70 Board 50 Del from £133 **PARKING:** 100 **NOTES:** ⊗ in restaurant Civ Wed 100 **CARDS:**

♫ Entertainment

LUSS, Argyll & Bute Map 20 NS39

★★★73% The Lodge on Loch Lomond
G83 8PA
☎ 01436 860201 01436 860203
e-mail: res@loch-lomond.co.uk
web: www.loch-lomond.co.uk
Dir: *off A82, follow sign for hotel*
This hotel is idyllically set on the shores of Loch Lomond. Public areas consist of an open-plan, split-level bar and fine dining restaurant overlooking the loch. The pine finished bedrooms also enjoy the views and are comfortable, spacious and well equipped,

continued

some with DVDs/internet access and all with saunas. A stunning new state-of-the-art leisure suite has now opened.

ROOMS: 29 en suite 17 annexe en suite (20 fmly) (13 GF) ⊗ in all bedrooms s fr £79.95; d fr £99 (incl. bkfst) **LB** **FACILITIES: Spa** STV Sauna Jacuzzi Resident only state-of-the-art health suite & spa., fishing, boating Xmas **CONF:** Thtr 150 Class 80 Board 60 Del from £120 **PARKING:** 120 **NOTES:** ⊗ in restaurant Civ Wed 100 **CARDS:**

MALLAIG, Highland

Map 22 NM69

★★67% West Highland

PH41 4QZ
☎ 01687 462210 01687 462130
e-mail: westhighland.hotel@virgin.net
Dir: *from Fort William turn right at rdbt then 1st right up hill, from ferry left at rdbt then 1st right uphill*

Originally the town's station hotel the original building was destroyed by fire and the current hotel built on the same site in the early 20th century. There are fine views over to Skye from the public rooms, whilst bedrooms are thoughtfully equipped and generally spacious.

ROOMS: 34 en suite (6 fmly) ⊗ in 6 bedrooms s £35-£40; d £70-£74 (incl. bkfst) **LB** **FACILITIES:** ♫ **CONF:** Thtr 100 Class 80 Board 100 **PARKING:** 40 **NOTES:** ⊗ in restaurant Closed 16 Oct-15 Mar RS 16 Mar-1 Apr **CARDS:**

★★65% Marine

PH41 4PY
☎ 01687 462217 01687 462821
e-mail: marinehotel@btinternet.com
web: www.marinehotel-mallaig.co.uk
Dir: *1st Hotel on right entering Mallaig off A830*

This town-centre hotel sits beside the railway station and close to the ferry terminal and harbour. All amenities are found on the first-floor level, where a bright spacious lounge bar and attractive restaurant feature seafood on their menus. Bedrooms are smartly appointed.

ROOMS: 19 rms (18 en suite) (2 fmly) (4 GF) ⊗ in 5 bedrooms s £35-£45; d £60-£80 (incl. bkfst) **LB** **FACILITIES:** ♫ Xmas **PARKING:** 6 **CARDS:**

MARKINCH, Fife

Map 21 NO20

Top 200 – Hotel

★★★★ Balbirnie House

Balbirnie Park KY7 6NE
☎ 01592 610066 01592 610529
e-mail: info@balbirnie.co.uk
web: www.balbirnie.co.uk
Dir: *off A92 onto B9130, entrance 0.5m on left*

Set in the midst of the scenic Balbirnie Park, this listed

continued

Georgian building overlooks the challenging golf course. Bedrooms, many of which are spacious, offer tasteful décor and high quality furnishings. There are a number of comfortable lounges, of which the Long Gallery is the most striking. A visit to the award-winning Orangery restaurant is a highlight of any visit.

ROOMS: 30 en suite (9 fmly) (7 GF) s £130-£160; d £190-£250 (incl. bkfst) **LB** **FACILITIES:** STV 18 Putt green Woodland walks Jogging trails Xmas **CONF:** Thtr 220 Class 100 Board 60 Del £162 **PARKING:** 120 **NOTES:** ⊗ in restaurant Civ Wed 150 **CARDS:**

MAYBOLE, South Ayrshire

Map 20 NS20

Top 200 – Hotel

★★ Ladyburn

KA19 7SG
☎ 01655 740585 01655 740580
e-mail: jh@ladyburn.co.uk
Dir: *A77 (Glasgow/Stranraer) at Maybole turn to B7023 to Crosshill and right at War Memorial. In 2m turn left for hotel approx 1m on right*

This charming country house is the home of the Hepburn family, who take great pride in their warmth of welcome. Sitting in open countryside with attractive gardens, it's a great place to come to relax. Classically styled bedrooms, two with four-poster beds, offer every comfort and are complemented by the library and the drawing room. Dinner comprises a carefully cooked three-course set menu, and is served in a gracious candlelit setting.

ROOMS: 5 en suite ⊗ in all bedrooms s £65-£85; d £130-£170 (incl. bkfst) **LB** **FACILITIES:** Boules **PARKING:** 12 **NOTES:** No children 16yrs ⊗ in restaurant RS 2 wks Nov-Dec, 4 wks Jan/Mar Civ Wed 50 **CARDS:**

M

MELROSE, Scottish Borders Map 21 NT53

★★★71% Burt's
Market Square TD6 9PL
☎ 01896 822285 01896 822870
e-mail: burtshotel@aol.com
web: www.burtshotel.co.uk
Dir: *A6091, 2m from A68 3m S of Earlston*

Enjoying a super location in the heart of this small market town, this hotel has been under the same family ownership for over 30 years and where the genuine warmth of hospitality is notable. Food is important at Burt's and the elegant restaurant is well complemented by the range of tasty meals in the bar. Burt's Hotel has received the AA Pub of the Year Award for Scotland & Northern Ireland 2004-5.
ROOMS: 20 en suite in all bedrooms s £54; d £98 (incl. bkfst) **LB**
FACILITIES: STV Shooting Salmon Fishing ch fac **CONF:** Thtr 38 Class 20 Board 20 **PARKING:** 40 **NOTES:** in restaurant Closed 24-26 Dec
CARDS:

★★★66% The Townhouse Hotel
3 Market Square TD6 9PQ
☎ 01896 822645 01896 822870
e-mail: info@thetownhousemelrose.co.uk
Dir: *from A68 into Melrose, hotel in market square*
Built as the town house for a local dignitary, this comfortable hotel has now changed owners and has been upgraded. Bedrooms vary in size but all are well equipped and comfortable. The service is caring and friendly, and the restaurant and brasserie are popular with locals.
ROOMS: 11 en suite (1 fmly) (1 GF) in all bedrooms s £65-£85; d £88-£130 (incl. bkfst) **LB** **CONF:** Thtr 60 Class 30 Board 40
NOTES: in restaurant Closed 26th-27th Dec
CARDS:

MILNGAVIE, East Dunbartonshire Map 20 NS57

Travel Inn (Glasgow North)
103 Main St G62 6BJ
☎ 08701 977112 0141 956 7839
Dir: *on A81 6 miles north of Glasgow city centre. From M8 (J16) follow signs A879 to Milngavie*
Travel Inn offers good-quality, value-for-money accommodation. Spacious, en suite rooms with bath and shower comfortably accommodate a family of up to two adults and two children (to age 15). The restaurant and bar offers a varied menu. For further details consult the Hotel Groups page.
ROOMS: 60 en suite s £45.95-£46.95; d £45.95-£46.95 **CONF:** Class 16 Board 16

MOFFAT, Dumfries & Galloway Map 21 NT00

★★★71% *Moffat House*

High St DG10 9HL
☎ 01683 220039 01683 221288
e-mail: moffat@talk21.com
web: www.moffathouse.co.uk
Dir: *M74 junct 15, Beattock, take A701 hotel in 1m at end of High St*

Moffat House is a fine Adam mansion set back from the main road in the centre of this popular country town. Inviting public areas include a quiet sun lounge to the rear, a comfortable lounge bar serving tasty meals and an attractive restaurant for the more formal occasion. Bedrooms present a mix of classical and modern styles.
ROOMS: 21 en suite (2 fmly) in 6 bedrooms **CONF:** Thtr 100 Class 80 Board 60 **PARKING:** 61 **NOTES:** Civ Wed 110
CARDS:

★★★70% *Auchen Castle*
Beattock DG10 9SH
☎ 01683 300407 01683 300667
e-mail: reception@auchencastle.com
web: www.auchencastle.com
Dir: *M74 junct 15, 1m on B7076 Abington road*
Despite sharing a valley with the motorway, this imposing mansion is separated from it by its extensive grounds, including terraced gardens and a lake. Public rooms include a comfortable drawing room and an elegant restaurant overlooking the valley. Bedrooms are classical in style, come in a variety of sizes and include some superior four-poster rooms with DVD players and mini-bars.
ROOMS: 15 en suite 10 annexe en suite (12 fmly) in 10 bedrooms
FACILITIES: STV Fishing **CONF:** Thtr 40 Board 20 **PARKING:** 50
NOTES: in restaurant Civ Wed 95
CARDS:

★★78% Beechwood Country House
Harthope Place DG10 9HX
☎ 01683 220210 01683 220889
e-mail: enquiries@beechwoodcountryhousehotel.co.uk
web: www.beechwoodcountryhousehotel.co.uk
Dir: *at north end of town turn right at St Marys Church into Harthope Place and follow sign to hotel*
This delightful hotel stands in landscaped gardens just a short walk from the town centre. Individually styled bedrooms are complemented by a choice of welcoming lounges, one of which

continued

has a small bar. Ever-present owners ensure prompt service in a relaxed environment.

ROOMS: 7 en suite (1 fmly) ⊗ in all bedrooms s £50-£62; d £79-£96 (incl. bkfst) LB **FACILITIES:** Childrens' swings **CONF:** Class 20 Board 20 **PARKING:** 15 **NOTES:** ⊗ in restaurant Closed Jan-mid Feb Civ Wed 25 **CARDS:**

★★68% The Star

44 High St DG10 9EF
☎ 01683 220156 01683 221524
e-mail: tim@famousstarhotel.com
Dir: *M74 junct 15 signed Moffat, hotel 2m from junct, 1st hotel on right in High Street*

Smart, modern and well-equipped bedrooms plus a good range of food, served either in the bar or the restaurant, are just some of the virtues of this friendly hotel. Its claim to be the world's narrowest hotel is a novel talking point.

ROOMS: 8 en suite (1 fmly) s £40; d £56-£65 (incl. bkfst) LB **FACILITIES:** STV Large screen in bar for sport **NOTES:** ⊗ in restaurant **CARDS:**

Top 200 – Hotel

★ Well View

Ballplay Rd DG10 9JU
☎ 01683 220184 01683 220088
e-mail: info@wellview.co.uk
web: www.wellview.co.uk
Dir: *on A708 from Moffat, pass fire station & 1st left*

THE CIRCLE Selected Individual Hotels GREAT BRITAIN

Well View is situated on a quiet road within walking distance of the small town of Moffat and retains many of its original Victorian features. Individually furnished bedrooms are very comfortable and thoughtfully equipped. Dinner is certainly the highlight of a stay in this small family-run hotel; the six-course menu emphasises fine ingredients, many of which are locally sourced whenever possible.

ROOMS: 6 en suite ⊗ in all bedrooms s £65-£75; d £80-£120 (incl. bkfst) LB **FACILITIES:** Xmas **CONF:** Thtr 12 Board 8 Del from £100 **PARKING:** 8 **NOTES:** ⊗ in restaurant Closed 2wks Feb & 2wks Oct **CARDS:**

MONTROSE, Angus — Map 23 NO75

★★★73% Links Hotel

Mid Links DD10 8RL
☎ 01674 671000 01674 672698
e-mail: reception@linkshotel.com
Dir: *A935 to Montrose then right at Lochside junct, left at swimming pool and right by tennis courts for hotel 200yds*

Best Western

This former Edwardian town house has been fully refurbished and restored. Bedrooms offer a choice of attractive modern styles and are extremely well equipped to cater for business guests. Public areas include a bar, a restaurant, and a popular coffee shop where food is available all day.

ROOMS: 25 en suite (1 GF) ⊗ in 15 bedrooms s £54-£80; d £68-£88 (incl. bkfst) LB **FACILITIES:** STV ♫ Xmas **CONF:** Thtr 220 Class 70 Board 70 Del from £99 **PARKING:** 45 **NOTES:** ⊗ in restaurant Civ Wed 120 **CARDS:**

MOTHERWELL, North Lanarkshire — Map 21 NS75

Travel Inn (Glasgow Bellshill)

Belziehill Farm, New Edinburgh Rd ML4 3HH
☎ 08701 977106 01698 845969
Dir: *M74 junct 5 follow signs towards Coatbridge & Bellshill on A725. At 2nd exit off A725 Travel Inn on left of rdbt*

travel inn

Travel Inn offers good-quality, value-for-money accommodation. Spacious, en suite rooms with bath and shower comfortably accommodate a family of up to two adults and two children (to age 15). The restaurant and bar offers a varied menu. For further details consult the Hotel Groups page.

ROOMS: 40 en suite s £45.95-£46.95; d £45.95-£46.95

Travel Inn Glasgow (near Motherwell)

Edinburgh Rd, Newhouse ML3 6JW
☎ 08701 977164 01698 861353
Dir: *From south M74 junct 5 onto A725 towards Coatbridge. Take A8 towards Edinburgh & leave at junct 6, follow signs for Lanark. Travel Inn 400yds on right*

travel inn

Travel Inn offers good-quality, value-for-money accommodation. Spacious, en suite rooms with bath and shower comfortably accommodate a family of up to two adults and two children (to age 15). The restaurant and bar offers a varied menu. For further details consult the Hotel Groups page.

ROOMS: 40 en suite s £45.95-£46.95; d £45.95-£46.95 **CONF:** Thtr 40

Popped the question?
Hotels with Civ Wed in their entry are licensed for civil wedding ceremonies. Maximum numbers for the ceremony only are shown, e.g. Civ Wed 120

MUIR OF ORD, Highland Map 23 NH55

★★67% Ord House
IV6 7UH
☎ 01463 870492 Fax 01463 870492
e-mail: eliza@ord-house.com

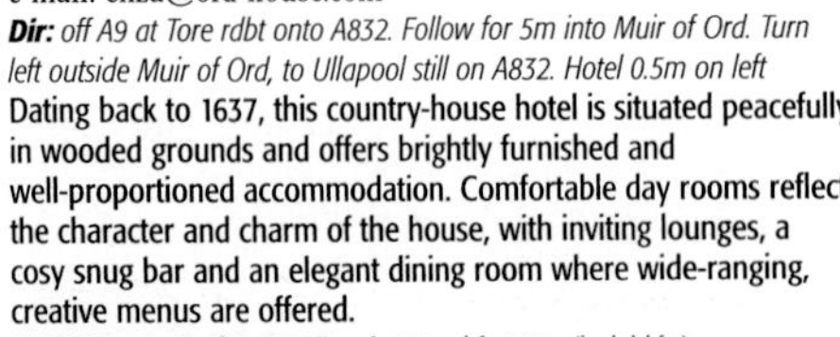

***Dir:** off A9 at Tore rdbt onto A832. Follow for 5m into Muir of Ord. Turn left outside Muir of Ord, to Ullapool still on A832. Hotel 0.5m on left*

Dating back to 1637, this country-house hotel is situated peacefully in wooded grounds and offers brightly furnished and well-proportioned accommodation. Comfortable day rooms reflect the character and charm of the house, with inviting lounges, a cosy snug bar and an elegant dining room where wide-ranging, creative menus are offered.

ROOMS: 11 en suite (2 GF) s fr £50; d fr £100 (incl. bkfst) **FACILITIES:** no TV in bdrms Putt green Clay pigeon shooting **PARKING:** 30 **NOTES:** in restaurant Closed Nov-Apr **CARDS:**

Top 200 – Hotel

★ The Dower House
Highfield IV6 7XN
☎ 01463 870090 Fax 01463 870090
e-mail: aa@thedowerhouse.co.uk
web: www.thedowerhouse.co.uk

***Dir:** on Dingwall road A862, 1m from Muir of Ord, on left*

This enchanting house enjoys a secluded location on the northern edge of the village. The relaxed, friendly atmosphere and attentive service are key features of the hotel and guests are made to feel that this is a real home-from-home. The cosy sitting room is full of books, whilst the dining room has quiet elegance and antique furniture. The charming bedrooms come in various sizes; one has its own sitting room.

ROOMS: 5 en suite 2 annexe en suite (1 fmly) (5 GF) in all bedrooms s £65-£105; d £110-£150 (incl. bkfst) **LB** **FACILITIES:** Bird watching ch fac **PARKING:** 20 **NOTES:** in restaurant Closed 25 Dec & 2wks Nov Civ Wed 16 **CARDS:**

MULL, ISLE OF, Argyll & Bute Map 20

CRAIGNURE Map 20 NM73

★★★63% Isle Of Mull Hotel
PA65 6BB
☎ 01680 812351 Fax 01680 812462
e-mail: isleofmull@british-trust-hotels.com

***Dir:** ferry from Oban. Turn right on main road, then right again*

This purpose-built hotel sits on the western shore of Craignure Bay, only half a mile from the ferry pier. Popular with coach tours, it has fine views across the bay to the mainland. The hotel is well appointed, with spacious lounges and bedrooms that are attractively furnished with all the expected facilities.

ROOMS: 85 en suite (6 fmly) in 55 bedrooms s £33-£53; d £66-£106 (incl. bkfst & dinner) **LB** **FACILITIES:** STV Xmas **CONF:** Thtr 150 Class 85 Board 60 Del from £53 **PARKING:** 36 **NOTES:** in restaurant **CARDS:**

DERVAIG Map 22 NM45

★★78% Druimard Country House
PA75 6QW
☎ 01688 400345 & 400291 Fax 01688 400345
e-mail: druimard.hotel@virgin.net

***Dir:** from Craignure ferry terminal turn right towards Tobermory, through Salen Village, after 1.5m turn left to Dervaig, hotel on right before village*

A charming Victorian country house, on the edge of the village beside the Mull Little Theatre. Attractive colour schemes feature in the bedrooms, which are comfortably furnished and thoughtfully equipped. There is a relaxing lounge and conservatory bar, but the focal point is the newly refurbished dining room, where tempting five-course dinners attract much praise.

ROOMS: 5 en suite 2 annexe en suite (2 fmly) (2 GF) s £90-£110; d £130-£170 (incl. bkfst & dinner) **LB** **FACILITIES:** Mull Little Theatre within grounds **PARKING:** 20 **NOTES:** in restaurant Closed Nov-Mar **CARDS:**

TOBERMORY Map 22 NM55

★★★73% Western Isles
PA75 6PR
☎ 01688 302012 Fax 01688 302297
e-mail: wihotel@aol.com
web: www.mullhotel.com

***Dir:** from ferry follow signs to Tobermory. Over 1st mini-rdbt in Tobermory then over small bridge and immediate right & follow road to T-junct. Right again then keep left and take 1st left for hotel at top of hill on right*

Built in 1883 and standing high above the village, this hotel enjoys spectacular views over Tobermory's harbour and the Sound of Mull. Public rooms range from the classical drawing room and restaurant to the bright modern conservatory bar/bistro. Bedrooms come in a variety of styles; the impressive superior rooms include a suite complete with its own piano.

ROOMS: 28 en suite s £45-£114; d £99-£124 (incl. bkfst) **LB** **FACILITIES:** ch fac Xmas **CONF:** Thtr 35 Class 20 Board 20 Del from £85 **PARKING:** 28 **NOTES:** in restaurant Closed 17-27 Dec Civ Wed 70 **CARDS:**

Bad hair day?
Hairdryers in all rooms three stars and above

Top 200 – Hotel

★★ Highland Cottage
Breadalbane St PA75 6PD
☎ 01688 302030
e-mail: davidandjo@highlandcottage.co.uk
web: www.highlandcottage.co.uk
Dir: *A848 Craignure/Fishnish ferry terminal, pass Tobermory signs, ahead at mini rdbt across narrow bridge, turn right. Hotel on right opposite Fire Station*
Providing the highest level of natural and unassuming hospitality, this delightful little gem lies high above the island's capital. There are two inviting lounges in which to relax, one with an honesty bar and both adorned with books and magazines. The cosy dining room offers memorable dinners and splendid breakfasts. Bedrooms are all individual; some have four-posters and all are comprehensively equipped to include video TVs and music centres.
ROOMS: 6 en suite (1 GF) in all bedrooms s £95-£120; d £120-£150 (incl. bkfst) **LB** **FACILITIES:** STV **PARKING:** 6 **NOTES:** No children 10yrs in restaurant Closed 4 wks mid Oct/mid Nov RS 6 Jan -6 Mar **CARDS:**

★★69% Tobermory
53 Main St PA75 6NT
☎ 01688 302091 01688 302254
e-mail: tobhotel@tinyworld.co.uk
web: www.thetobermoryhotel.com
Dir: *on waterfront, overlooking Tobermory Bay*
This friendly hotel, with its pretty pink frontage, sits on the seafront amid other brightly coloured buildings. There is a comfortable lounge where drinks are served (there is no bar) prior to dining in the cosy restaurant. Bedrooms come in a variety of sizes; all are bright and vibrant with the superiors having video TVs.
ROOMS: 16 rms (15 en suite) (3 fmly) (2 GF) in all bedrooms s £41-£102; d £82-£102 (incl. bkfst) **LB** **FACILITIES:** ch fac Xmas **NOTES:** in restaurant Closed Xmas **CARDS:**

NAIRN, Highland — Map 23 NH85

★★★★71% Golf View
The Seafront IV12 4HD
☎ 01667 452301 01667 455267
e-mail: golfview@morton-hotels.com
web: www.morton-hotels.com/golfview/index.html
Dir: *off A96 into Seabank Rd, follow road to end, hotel on right*
Adjacent to both the beach and Nairn Golf Club, this hotel has benefited from recent investment. Thoughtfully equipped bedrooms are spacious and include a number of lovely suites. Public areas include an attractive leisure club. Freshly prepared meals can be enjoyed in both the informal conservatory and restaurant.

continued

ROOMS: 42 en suite (7 fmly) in 7 bedrooms s £92-£113; d £139-£236 (incl. bkfst) **LB** **FACILITIES:** STV Sauna Solarium Gym Putt green Jacuzzi Cycle hire, Swimming supervised ch fac Xmas **CONF:** Thtr 120 Class 80 Board 55 Del £139 **SERVICES:** Lift **PARKING:** 65 **NOTES:** in restaurant Civ Wed 120 **CARDS:**

★★★★70% Newton
Inverness Rd IV12 4RX
☎ 01667 453144 01667 454026
e-mail: info@morton-hotels.com
Dir: *15m from Inverness on A96, turn left into tree-lined driveway*

The original part of this hotel dates from 1650, while a stylish, modern extension houses a large conference centre and some super bedrooms. Public rooms include spacious lounges, a well-stocked, a refurbished bar and an elegant restaurant, where much use is made of the abundant local produce.
ROOMS: 56 en suite (2 fmly) in 15 bedrooms s £92-£113; d £114-£196 (incl. bkfst) **LB** **FACILITIES:** STV Fishing Use of leisure club at sister hotel ch fac Xmas **CONF:** BC Thtr 400 Class 150 Board 50 Del £139 **SERVICES:** Lift **PARKING:** 200 **NOTES:** in restaurant Closed 23-27 Dec **CARDS:**

> Late for dinner?
> Quality Standards mean that last orders for dinner vary according to star rating and should be no earlier than:
> ★★ 7.00pm ★★★ 8.00pm ★★★★ 9.00pm
> ★★★★★ 10.00pm

N

NAIRN, continued

Top 200 – Hotel

★★ @@@ **Boath House**
Auldearn IV12 5TE
☎ 01667 454896 01667 455469
e-mail: wendy@boath-house.com
web: www.boath-house.com
Dir: *2m past Nairn on A96 E towards Forres, signed on main road*
Standing in its own grounds, this splendid Georgian mansion has been lovingly restored. Hospitality is first class. Owners Don and Wendy Matheson are passionate about what they do, and have an ability to establish a special relationship with their guests that will be particularly remembered. The food is also memorable at Boath House; the five-course dinners are a culinary adventure, matched only by the excellence of breakfasts. The house itself is delightful, with inviting lounges and a dining room overlooking a trout loch. Bedrooms are striking, comfortable and include many fine antique pieces.
ROOMS: 6 en suite (1 fmly) (1 GF) in all bedrooms s fr £110; d £110-£220 (incl. bkfst) **LB** **FACILITIES: Spa** STV Fishing Sauna Gym Jacuzzi Beauty salon ch fac **CONF:** Board 10 **PARKING:** 20 **NOTES:** in restaurant Closed Xmas Civ Wed **CARDS:**

★★64% ***Alton Burn***
Alton Burn Rd IV12 5ND
☎ 01667 452051 & 453325 01667 456697
e-mail: enquiries@altonburn.co.uk
Dir: *follow signs from A96 at western boundary of Nairn*
This long-established, family-run hotel is located on the western edge of town with views over the Moray Firth. The friendly, relaxed atmosphere is a major strength here, and bedrooms are both practical and simple in style. There is a cosy bar, spacious lounges and a dining room.
ROOMS: 23 en suite (7 GF) **FACILITIES:** Putt green Table tennis ch fac **CONF:** Thtr 100 Class 50 Board 40 **PARKING:** 40 **NOTES:** Closed Nov-Mar **CARDS:**

NETHY BRIDGE, Highland — Map 23 NJ02

★★71% @ **The Mountview Hotel**
Grantown Rd PH25 3EB
☎ 01479 821248 01479 821515
e-mail: mviewhotel@aol.com
Dir: *from Aviemore follow signs through Boat of Garten to Nethy Bridge, through village and hotel on right, 100mtrs beyond Nethy Bridge Hotel.*
Aptly named, this country-house hotel enjoys stunning panoramic views from its elevated position on the edge of the village. It specialises in guided holidays and is a favoured base for bird-watching and walking groups. Public rooms include inviting lounges, while imaginative, well-prepared dinners are served in a bright and modern restaurant extension.
ROOMS: 12 rms (11 en suite) (1 GF) s fr £37.50; d fr £70 (incl. bkfst) **PARKING:** 20 **NOTES:** in restaurant **CARDS:**

NEWBURGH, Aberdeenshire — Map 23 NJ92

★★72% @ **Udny Arms**
Main St AB41 6BL
☎ 01358 789444 01358 789012
e-mail: enquiry@udny.demon.co.uk
web: www.udny.co.uk
Dir: *off A92 at signed Newburgh, hotel 2m, in village centre on right*
Enjoying a superb location with fine views over the golf course and Ythan estuary, this friendly, family-run hotel is popular with both business travellers and golfers. Accommodation is provided in traditionally styled bedrooms. A comfortable lounge, split-level bistro and a choice of bars offer a variety of eating and drinking options.
ROOMS: 26 en suite (1 fmly) in all bedrooms **FACILITIES:** Fishing Petanque ch fac **CONF:** Thtr 100 Class 30 Board 30 Del from £120 **PARKING:** 100 **NOTES:** in restaurant **CARDS:**

NEW LANARK, South Lanarkshire — Map 21 NS84

★★★71% **New Lanark Mill Hotel**
Mill One, New Lanark Mills ML11 9DB
☎ 01555 667200 01555 667222
e-mail: hotel@newlanark.org
web: www.newlanark.org
Dir: *signed from all major roads, M74 junct 7 and from M8*

Originally a cotton mill in the 18th century, this hotel forms part of a fully restored village, now a World Heritage Site. There's a bright modern style throughout which contrasts nicely with features from the original mill. The hotel enjoys stunning views over the River Clyde and there is a comfortable foyer-lounge with a gallery restaurant above.
ROOMS: 38 en suite (2 fmly) in 28 bedrooms s £64.50; d £99 (incl. bkfst) **LB** **FACILITIES:** Fishing Xmas **CONF:** Thtr 180 Class 60 Board 40 Del from £99 **SERVICES:** Lift **PARKING:** 75 **NOTES:** in restaurant Civ Wed 110 **CARDS:**

NEWTON STEWART, Dumfries & Galloway Map 20 NX46

Top 200 – Hotel

★★★ **Kirroughtree House**
Minnigaff DG8 6AN
☎ 01671 402141 🖹 01671 402425
e-mail: info@kirroughtreehouse.co.uk
web: www.kirroughtreehouse.co.uk
Dir: *from A75 take A712, New Galloway road, entrance to hotel 300yds on left*
This imposing mansion enjoys a peaceful location in eight acres of landscaped gardens near Galloway Forest Park. The inviting day rooms comprise a choice of lounges and two elegant dining rooms. Well-proportioned, individually styled bedrooms include some suites and mini-suites and many rooms enjoy fine views. Service is very friendly and attentive.
ROOMS: 17 en suite s £78-£103; d £136-£192 (incl. bkfst) **LB**
FACILITIES: STV 9 hole pitch and putt Xmas **CONF:** Thtr 30 Class 20 Board 20 Del from £105 **PARKING:** 50 **NOTES:** No children 10yrs in restaurant Closed 4 Jan-16 Feb
CARDS:

NORTH BERWICK, East Lothian Map 21 NT58

★★★67% ***The Marine***
Cromwell Rd EH39 4LZ
☎ 0870 400 8129 🖹 01620 894480
e-mail: marine@macdonald-hotels.co.uk
Dir: *from A198 turn into Hamilton Rd at lights then take 2nd right*
This imposing leisure, conference and golfing hotel commands stunning views across the golf course to the Firth of Forth. A good range of leisure facilities accompanies well-proportioned public areas. Bedrooms come in a variety of sizes, some being impressively large.
ROOMS: 83 en suite (4 fmly) (4 GF) in 20 bedrooms
FACILITIES: STV Snooker Sauna Solarium Putt green Childrens playground **CONF:** Thtr 300 Class 150 Board 100 **SERVICES:** Lift
PARKING: 50 **NOTES:** in restaurant Civ Wed 200
CARDS:

★★64% **Nether Abbey**
20 Dirleton Av EH39 4BQ
☎ 01620 892802 🖹 01620 895298
e-mail: bookings@netherabbey.co.uk
web: www.netherabbey.co.uk
Dir: *at junct with A198, leave A1 and continue S to rdbt, take B6371 to N Berwick, hotel is 2nd on left when entering town*
Popular with golfers this hotel boasts stylish well-equipped bedrooms, the two junior suites having CD/video players.

continued

Downstairs the focus is on a lively bar/bistro where tasty home cooked dishes are on offer.
ROOMS: 13 en suite (4 fmly) s £35-£65; d £70-£90 (incl. bkfst) **LB**
FACILITIES: Xmas **CONF:** Thtr 80 Class 50 Board 30 **PARKING:** 40
NOTES: Civ Wed 50 **CARDS:**

OBAN, Argyll & Bute Map 20 NM93

★★★74% **The Oban Caledonian Hotel & Spa**

Station Square PA34 5RT
☎ 01855 821582 🖹 01855 821463
e-mail: reservations@freedomglen.co.uk
web: www.freedomglen.co.uk
Dir: *at head of main pier, close to rail terminal*

This Victorian hotel, overlooking the bay, has undergone a transformation in recent years. Public areas are modern and stylish and include a smart restaurant, spacious lounges and an informal dining option in Café Caledonian. Attractive bedrooms come in a number of different styles and grades, some with comfortable seating areas, feature bathrooms and fine sea views. Valet parking is available.
ROOMS: 59 en suite (4 fmly) in 10 bedrooms s £52.50-£100; d £52.50-£240 (incl. bkfst) **LB** **FACILITIES:** Discounted entry to local leisure centre Xmas **CONF:** Del from £59.50 **SERVICES:** Lift
PARKING: 6 **NOTES:** in restaurant **CARDS:**

★★★72% **Manor House**
Gallanach Rd PA34 4LS
☎ 01631 562087 🖹 01631 563053
e-mail: manorhouse@aol.com
Dir: *follow signs MacBrayne Ferries and pass ferry entrance for hotel on right*

An elegant Georgian residence, this historic building was built for the Duke of Argyll and enjoys fine views over the harbour. Bedrooms now offer stylish design. Public rooms include a

continued on p752

O

OBAN, continued

well-stocked bar, a choice of lounges and a smart restaurant, where carefully prepared dinners are served.
ROOMS: 11 en suite ⊗ in all bedrooms s £98-£130; d £134-£180 (incl. bkfst & dinner) **LB FACILITIES:** STV **PARKING:** 20 **NOTES:** No children 12yrs ⊗ in restaurant Closed 25-26 Dec **CARDS:**

★★★59% *Columba*
North Pier PA34 5QD
☎ 01631 562183 🖹 01631 564683
Dir: *A85 to Oban, 1st set of lights in town and turn right.*
This popular tourist hotel is located on the North Pier and many of the bedrooms overlook the bay. Public areas include a restaurant, breakfast room and a choice of contrasting bars. Guests are welcome to use the leisure facilities at the sister hotel, The Alexandra.
ROOMS: 48 en suite (6 fmly) **CONF:** Thtr 70 Class 30 Board 20 **SERVICES:** Lift **PARKING:** 8 **NOTES:** ⊗ in restaurant
CARDS:

★★76% Willowburn
PA34 4TJ
☎ 01852 300276 🖹 01852 300597
e-mail: willowburn.hotel@virgin.net
web: www.willowburn.co.uk
(For full entry see Clachan-Seil)

★★72% Falls of Lora
PA37 1PB
☎ 01631 710483 🖹 01631 710694
(For full entry see Connel)

★★61% Lancaster
Corran Esplanade PA34 5AD
☎ 01631 562587 🖹 01631 562587
e-mail: john@lancasteroban.com
Dir: *on seafront next to St Columba's Cathedral*
Lovely views over the bay towards the Isle of Mull can be enjoyed from this welcoming family-run hotel on the Esplanade. Comfortable bedrooms vary in size and style and offer a good range of amenities. Public areas include a choice of contrasting lounges and bars.
ROOMS: 27 rms (24 en suite) (3 fmly) s £27.50-£33; d £60-£64 (incl. bkfst) **LB FACILITIES: Spa** STV Sauna Steam room **CONF:** Thtr 30 Class 20 Board 12 **PARKING:** 20 **CARDS:**

O

OLDMELDRUM, Aberdeenshire — Map 23 NJ82

★★65% Meldrum Arms
The Square AB51 0DS
☎ 01651 872238 🖹 01651 872238
Dir: *off the B947, in centre of village*
Located in the centre of the village, the Meldrum Arms Hotel combines a cosy and welcoming atmosphere with a good range of tasty dishes available in both the bar and comfortable restaurant. Try their popular high tea, which is a main course, tea and toast plus scones and cakes.
ROOMS: 7 en suite (1 fmly) s £39.50; d £60 (incl. bkfst) **FACILITIES:** STV **CONF:** Thtr 80 Board 40 **PARKING:** 25 **NOTES:** ⊗ in restaurant **CARDS:**

ONICH, Highland — Map 22 NN06

★★★76% Onich
PH33 6RY
☎ 01855 821214 🖹 01855 821484
e-mail: enquiries@onich-fortwilliam.co.uk
web: www.onich-fortwilliam.co.uk
Dir: *beside A82, 2m N of Ballachulish Bridge*

Genuine hospitality is part of the appeal of this hotel, which has gardens extending to the shore of picturesque Loch Linnhe. Nicely presented public areas include a choice of inviting lounges and contrasting bars, and views of the loch can be enjoyed from the attractive restaurant. Bedrooms, with pleasing colour schemes, are comfortably modern in appointment.
ROOMS: 25 en suite (6 fmly) ⊗ in 6 bedrooms d £82-£125 (incl. bkfst) **LB FACILITIES:** STV Jacuzzi Games room Xmas **CONF:** Thtr 30 Class 20 Board 20 Del from £90 **PARKING:** 50 **NOTES:** ⊗ in restaurant
CARDS:

★★★72% Lodge on the Loch
PH33 6RY
☎ 0871 222 3462 🖹 0871 222 3416
e-mail: reservations@freedomglen.co.uk
web: www.freedomglen.co.uk/ll
Dir: *beside A82 in village of Onich - 5m N of Glencoe, 10m S of Fort William*

Warm, Highland hospitality is a real feature of this stunningly located, holiday hotel. Fine views over Loch Linnhe can be enjoyed from the public areas and many of the individually styled bedrooms. A real fire warms the cosy lounge in the cooler months and accomplished cooking features on the dinner menus.
ROOMS: 16 en suite (1 GF) ⊗ in all bedrooms s £80-£300; d £160-£300 (incl. bkfst & dinner) **LB FACILITIES:** Free use of leisure facilities at sister hotel Xmas **CONF:** Thtr 40 Class 30 Board 30 Del from £59.50 **PARKING:** 25 **NOTES:** No children 16yrs ⊗ in restaurant Closed Jan-14 Feb & Nov-23 Dec RS 14 Feb - 4 April **CARDS:**

★★★69% ⊛ **Allt-nan-Ros**
PH33 6RY
☎ 01855 821210 📠 01855 821462
e-mail: AA@allt-nan-ros.co.uk
Dir: *1.5m N of Ballachulish Bridge on A82*

THE CIRCLE
Selected Individual Hotels
GREAT BRITAIN

Highland hospitality and good food are just part of the appeal of this comfortable hotel set in attractive gardens overlooking Loch Linnhe. Bedrooms vary in size and are modern in style. Inviting public areas include a pleasant lounge and a bright spacious dining room, both enjoying splendid views.
ROOMS: 20 en suite (2 fmly) s £85-£95; d £170-£190 (incl. bkfst & dinner) **LB** **FACILITIES:** ch fac **PARKING:** 30 **NOTES:** ⊗ in restaurant Closed 21 Nov-5 Dec **CARDS:**

See advert under FORT WILLIAM

PEAT INN, Fife Map 21 NO40

Top 200 – Hotel

★★ ⊛⊛⊛ **Peat Inn**
KY15 5LH
☎ 01334 840206 📠 01334 840530
e-mail: reception@thepeatinn.co.uk
web: www.thepeatinn.co.uk
Dir: *6m SW of St Andrews at junct of B940 & B941*
This 300-year-old former coaching inn enjoys a rural location yet is close to St Andrews. Accommodation, luxuriously appointed, is provided in an adjacent building and comprises split-level suites with a comfortable lounge upstairs. Food is a highlight of any visit with high quality, local produce utilised by David Wilson and his talented kitchen team.
ROOMS: 8 en suite (2 fmly) s £80-£95; d £165-£175 (incl. bkfst) **LB** **PARKING:** 24 **NOTES:** ⊗ in restaurant Closed Sun, Mon, 25 Dec & 1 Jan **CARDS:**

PEEBLES, Scottish Borders Map 21 NT24

★★★★74%
Cardrona Hotel Golf & Country Club
Cardrona Mains EH45 6LZ
☎ 01896 831144 📠 01896 831166
e-mail: general.cardrona@macdonald-hotels.co.uk
Dir: *20m S of Edinburgh on A72, 3m S of Peebles.*

MACDONALD HOTELS

The rolling hills of the Scottish Borders are a stunning backdrop for this modern, purpose-built hotel. Spacious bedrooms are traditional in style, equipped with a range of extras, and most enjoy fantastic views of the countryside. The hotel features some

continued

impressive leisure facilities, including an 18-hole golf course, 18-metre indoor pool and state-of-the-art gymnasium.
ROOMS: 100 en suite (23 fmly) (17 GF) ⊗ in all bedrooms s £65-£150; d £85-£200 **LB** **FACILITIES:** **Spa** STV 18 Fishing Sauna Solarium Gym Putt green Quad biking, Kayaking, Shooting, Archery, Horse riding, Bike Trail. **CONF:** Thtr 300 Class 120 Board 90 Del from £120 **SERVICES:** Lift **PARKING:** 200 **NOTES:** ⊗ in restaurant Civ Wed 250 **CARDS:**

★★★★69% **Peebles Hotel Hydro**
EH45 8LX
☎ 01721 720602 📠 01721 722999
e-mail: info@peebleshydro.com
web: www.peebleshydro.com
Dir: *on A702, 0.3m from town*
This privately owned resort hotel benefits from an elevated location with striking views across the valley. Accommodation comes in a range of styles and includes a number of family rooms. A super range of leisure activities is available and the hotel is popular with both families and conference delegates.
ROOMS: 128 en suite (25 fmly) (15 GF) s £114-£125; d £182-£298 (incl. bkfst & dinner) **LB** **FACILITIES:** **Spa** STV Riding Snooker Sauna Solarium Gym Putt green Badminton, Beautician, Hairdressing, Giant Chess & Draughts, Pitch & Putt ch fac Xmas **CONF:** Thtr 450 Class 200 Board 74 Del £147 **SERVICES:** Lift **PARKING:** 200 **NOTES:** ⊗ in restaurant Civ Wed 200 **CARDS:**

P

PEEBLES, continued

★★★80% Cringletie House

Edinburgh Rd EH45 8PL
☎ 01721 725750 01721 725751
e-mail: enquiries@cringletie.com
web: www.cringletie.com
Dir: *2m N on A703*

This long-established and now refurbished hotel is a romantic baronial mansion set in 28 acres of gardens and woodland with stunning views from all rooms. Delightful public rooms include a cocktail lounge with adjoining conservatory, whilst the first-floor restaurant is graced by a magnificent hand-painted ceiling. Bedrooms come in a variety of sizes, and all areas have wheelchair access.

ROOMS: 14 en suite (2 GF) in all bedrooms s £95-£120; d £115-£160 (incl. bkfst) **LB** **FACILITIES:** STV Putt green Xmas **CONF:** BC Thtr 45 Class 20 Board 24 Del from £120 **SERVICES:** Lift **PARKING:** 30 **NOTES:** in restaurant Closed Early Jan-Early Feb Civ Wed 45 **CARDS:**

★★★73% Castle Venlaw

Edinburgh Rd EH45 8QG
☎ 01721 720384 01721 724066
e-mail: stay@venlaw.co.uk
web: www.venlaw.co.uk
Dir: *off A703 Peebles/Edinburgh road, 0.75m from Peebles*

This 18th-century castle is set in four acres of landscaped gardens, set high above the town. Bedrooms, many with delightful views, are named after malt whiskies and include three in turrets. Well-prepared meals are served in the formal restaurant, while light meals are served in the wood-panelled library bar.

ROOMS: 13 en suite (3 fmly) in 12 bedrooms s £72-£92; d £120-£170 (incl. bkfst) **LB** **FACILITIES:** STV Xmas **CONF:** BC Thtr 30 Class 20 Board 20 Del from £120 **PARKING:** 30 **NOTES:** in restaurant Civ Wed 35 **CARDS:**

★★★71% Park

Innerleithen Rd EH45 8BA
☎ 01721 720451 01721 723510
e-mail: reserve@parkpeebles.co.uk
Dir: *in centre of Peebles opposite filling station*

The Park Hotel offers pleasant, well-equipped bedrooms of various sizes; those in the original house are particularly spacious. Public areas enjoy views of the gardens and include a tartan-clad bar, a relaxing lounge and a spacious wood-panelled restaurant. Guests can use the extensive leisure facilities on offer at the sister hotel, The Hydro.

ROOMS: 24 en suite in 6 bedrooms s £75-£89; d £136-£195 (incl. bkfst & dinner) **LB** **FACILITIES:** Putt green Use of facilities of Peebles Hotel Hydro ♫ Xmas **SERVICES:** Lift **PARKING:** 50 **CARDS:**

★★★70% Tontine

High St EH45 8AJ
☎ 01721 720892 01721 729732
e-mail: info@tontinehotel.com
web: www.tontinehotel.com
Dir: *In town centre.*

Conveniently situated in the main street, this long-established hotel has undergone extensive refurbishment. Public rooms include an elegant Adam restaurant, inviting lounge and 'clubby' bar. Bedrooms, contained in the original house and the river-facing wing, offer a smart, classical style of accommodation. The lasting impression however, will be of the excellent level of hospitality and guest care.

ROOMS: 36 en suite (3 fmly) in 20 bedrooms **FACILITIES:** ch fac **CONF:** Thtr 40 Class 24 Board 24 Del from £95 **PARKING:** 24 **NOTES:** in restaurant **CARDS:**

TV dinner?
Room service at three stars and above

PERTH, Perth & Kinross Map 21 NO12

Top 200 – Hotel

★★★ ◎◎ **Kinfauns Ca**
CLOSED
Kinfauns PH2 7JZ
☎ 01738 620777
e-mail: emai ... o.uk
web: www.k ... e.co.uk
Dir: *2m beyond ... on the A90 Perth/Dundee road*

This imposing castle dates from 1827 and lies in extensive landscaped grounds high above the road. A magnificent oak staircase is a feature, as are ornately decorated ceilings and large marble fireplaces. The bar is made from a striking oriental dragon boat, whilst the restaurant provides a gracious setting for carefully prepared cuisine; a jacket and tie code applies for dinner. Bedrooms are spacious and impressively individual, with suites and mini-suites available.

ROOMS: 16 en suite s £130-£190; d £200-£320 (incl. bkfst) **FACILITIES: Spa** STV Fishing Clay pigeon shooting, Archery, Falconry available with prior notice Xmas **CONF:** Thtr 50 Class 40 Board 26 Del from £160 **PARKING:** 40 **NOTES:** No children 8yrs in restaurant Closed 4-24 Jan **CARDS:**

See advert on this page

★★★74% ◎ **Huntingtower**
Crieff Rd PH1 3JT
☎ 01738 583771 01738 583777
e-mail: reservations@huntingtowerhotel.co.uk
web: www.huntingtowerhotel.co.uk
Dir: *3m W off A85*

Enjoying an idyllic country setting, this Edwardian house has been extended to offer smart, comfortable public areas and a high

continued on p756

PERTH, continued

standard of accommodation. Comfortable lounges lead to a conservatory where lunches are served, whilst the elegant Oak Room restaurant offers skilfully prepared dinners. Bedrooms are generally spacious and provide a host of modern facilities.
ROOMS: 31 en suite 3 annexe en suite (2 fmly) (8 GF) s £70-£110; d £100-£160 (incl. bkfst) **LB** **FACILITIES:** STV ch fac Xmas **CONF:** BC Thtr 200 Class 140 Board 30 Del from £90 **SERVICES:** Lift **PARKING:** 150 **NOTES:** ⊗ in restaurant Civ Wed 100
CARDS:

★★★74% Murrayshall Country House Hotel & Golf Course

New Scone PH2 7PH
☎ 01738 551171 01738 552595
e-mail: lin.murrayshall@virgin.net
Dir: *from Perth take A94 (Coupar Angus), 1m from Perth, right to Murrayshall just before New Scone*
This imposing country house is set in 350 acres of grounds, which include two golf courses, one of which is of championship standard. Bedrooms come in two distinct styles: modern suites in a purpose-built building contrast with more traditional rooms in the main building. The Clubhouse bar serves a range of meals all day, whilst more accomplished cooking can be enjoyed in the Old Masters Restaurant.
ROOMS: 27 en suite 14 annexe en suite (17 fmly) (4 GF) ⊗ in 1 bedroom s £80-£110; d £110-£150 (incl. bkfst & dinner) **LB** **FACILITIES: Spa** STV 36 Sauna Gym Putt green Jacuzzi Driving range ch fac Xmas **CONF:** Thtr 180 Class 60 Board 30 Del from £95 **PARKING:** 80 **NOTES:** ⊗ in restaurant Civ Wed 130
CARDS:

★★★72% Parklands Hotel

2 St Leonards Bank PH2 8EB
☎ 01738 622451 01738 622046
e-mail: info@theparklandshotel.com
web: www.theparklandshotel.com
Dir: *exit M90 junct 10, after 1m turn left at end of park area at traffic lights, hotel on left*
This hotel has an excellent location with views over the South Inch. Enthusiastic new proprietors are investing heavily in the business and have given bedrooms a smart contemporary feel. Public areas include a choice of restaurants with a fine dining experience offered in Acanthus.
ROOMS: 14 en suite (1 fmly) (4 GF) ⊗ in 4 bedrooms s £69-£99; d £99-£149 (incl. bkfst) **LB** **FACILITIES:** STV **CONF:** BC Thtr 24 Class 18 Board 18 Del from £99 **PARKING:** 30 **NOTES:** ⊗ in restaurant RS 25-26 Dec & 31 Dec-3 Jan Civ Wed 30 **CARDS:**

★★★69% Lovat

90 Glasgow Rd PH2 0LT
☎ 01738 636555 01738 643123
e-mail: e-mail@lovat.co.uk
Dir: *from M90 follow signs for Stirling to rdbt, then turn right into Glasgow Rd, hotel 1.5m on right*
This popular, long-established hotel on the Glasgow road offers excellent function facilities and largely attracts a business clientele. Public areas include a conservatory lounge and a well-stocked bar where the Bistro menu provides an informal eating alternative to the restaurant. Bedrooms are smartly appointed and thoughtfully equipped.
ROOMS: 30 en suite (1 fmly) (9 GF) ⊗ in 12 bedrooms s £45-£97; d £60-£120 (incl. bkfst) **LB** **FACILITIES:** STV Use of facilities at nearby sister hotel (indoor pool, gym, steam room, jacuzzi) Xmas **CONF:** Thtr 200 Class 70 Board 70 Del from £112.50 **PARKING:** 40 **NOTES:** ⊗ in restaurant Civ Wed 220 **CARDS:**

★★★66% Queens Hotel

Leonard St PH2 8HB
☎ 01738 442222 01738 638496
e-mail: email@queensperth.co.uk
Dir: *from M90 follow road to 2nd lights, turn left. Hotel on right, opposite railway station*
This popular hotel benefits from a central location close to both the bus and rail stations. Bedrooms vary in size, though all are well equipped. Public rooms include a smart leisure centre and versatile conference space. A range of meals is served in both the bar and restaurant.
ROOMS: 50 en suite (7 fmly) ⊗ in 20 bedrooms s £45-£100; d £60-£120 (incl. bkfst) **LB** **FACILITIES: Spa** STV Sauna Gym Jacuzzi Steam room Xmas **CONF:** Thtr 200 Class 120 Board 70 Del from £112.50 **SERVICES:** Lift **PARKING:** 50 **NOTES:** ⊗ in restaurant Civ Wed 220 **CARDS:**

Travelodge

PH2 0PL
☎ 08700 850 950 01738 444783
Travelodge offers good quality, good value, modern accommodation. Ideal for families, the spacious, en suite bedrooms include remote-control TV, tea and coffee-making facilities and luxury beds. Meals can be taken at the nearby family restaurant. For further details consult the Hotel Groups page.
ROOMS: s fr £25; d fr £25

PETERHEAD, Aberdeenshire Map 23 NK14

★★★66% Palace

Prince St AB42 1PL
☎ 01779 474821 01779 476119
e-mail: info@palacehotel.co.uk
Dir: *from Aberdeen, take A90 and follow signs to Peterhead, on entering town turn into Prince St, then right into main car park*
This town centre hotel is a popular venue both for business travellers and social functions. Bedrooms come in two styles, with the newly refurbished executive rooms being particularly spacious and well equipped. Public areas include a themed bar, an informal diner reached via a spiral staircase, and a brasserie restaurant.
ROOMS: 64 en suite (2 fmly) (14 GF) ⊗ in 44 bedrooms s £35-£50; d £45-£60 (incl. bkfst) **LB** **FACILITIES:** STV Snooker pool table, snooker room & live entertainment ♫ Xmas **CONF:** Thtr 250 Class 120 Board 250 **SERVICES:** Lift **PARKING:** 90 **NOTES:** Civ Wed
CARDS:

Town House Hotel
Country House Hotel
Travel Accommodation

PITLOCHRY, Perth & Kinross Map 23 NN95

★★★76% Green Park

Clunie Bridge Rd PH16 5JY
☎ 01796 473248 01796 473520
e-mail: bookings@thegreenpark.co.uk
web: www.thegreenpark.co.uk
Dir: *turn off A9 at Pitlochry, follow signs 0.25m through town, hotel on banks of Loch Faskally*
Benefiting from a stunning setting on the shores of Loch Faskally, this lovely hotel has lovely landscaped gardens, complete with interesting works of art. Thoughtfully designed bedrooms, many

continued

with fine views, are spacious and offer bright décor. Dinner utilises fresh produce, much of it grown in the kitchen garden.

ROOMS: 39 en suite (10 GF) ⊗ in all bedrooms s £49-£79; d £98-£142 (incl. bkfst & dinner) LB **FACILITIES:** Putt green Xmas **PARKING:** 45 **NOTES:** ⊗ in restaurant **CARDS:**

See advert on this page

★★★72% Pine Trees

Strathview Ter PH16 5QR
☎ 01796 472121 📠 01796 472460
e-mail: info@pinetreeshotel.co.uk
web: www.pinetreeshotel.co.uk
Dir: *along main street (Atholl Rd), into Larchwood Rd, follow signs for hotel*

Set in ten acres of tree-studded grounds high above the town, this fine Victorian mansion retains many fine features including wood panelling, ornate ceilings and a wonderful marble staircase. The atmosphere is refined and relaxing, with public rooms looking onto the lawns. Bedrooms come in a variety of sizes and many are well proportioned.

ROOMS: 20 en suite (3 fmly) ⊗ in all bedrooms s £62-£86; d £108-£152 (incl. bkfst & dinner) LB **FACILITIES:** ch fac Xmas **PARKING:** 20 **NOTES:** ⊗ in restaurant Civ Wed 70 **CARDS:**

★★★71% Dundarach

Perth Rd PH16 5DJ
☎ 01796 472862 📠 01796 473024
e-mail: mail@pitlochryhotel.co.uk
web: www.dundarach.co.uk
Dir: *S of town centre on main route*

This welcoming, family-run hotel stands in mature grounds at the south end of town. Bedrooms offer a variety of styles, including a block of large purpose-built rooms that will appeal to business guests. Well-proportioned public areas feature inviting lounges and a conservatory restaurant giving fine views of the Tummel Valley.

ROOMS: 20 en suite 19 annexe en suite (7 fmly) ⊗ in 11 bedrooms s £30-£60; d fr £60 (incl. bkfst) LB **FACILITIES:** STV Sauna **CONF:** Thtr 60 Class 40 Board 40 Del £95 **PARKING:** 39 **NOTES:** ⊗ in restaurant Closed Jan RS Dec-early Feb **CARDS:**

★★★68% Scotland's

Best Western

40 Bonnethill Rd PH16 5BT
☎ 01796 472292 📠 01796 473284
e-mail: stay@scotlandshotel.co.uk
web: www.scotlandshotel.co.uk
Dir: *follow A924 Perth road into town until War Memorial then take next right for hotel 200mtrs on right*

Enjoying a convenient town centre location, this long-established hotel is a popular base for tourists. Bedrooms, including family rooms and some with four-poster beds, vary in size and style. A

continued

choice of restaurants and bars are offered and guests can relax in the comfortable lounges.

ROOMS: 57 en suite 15 annexe en suite (21 fmly) s £45-£75; d £70-£120 (incl. bkfst) LB **FACILITIES:** Sauna Solarium Gym Jacuzzi Therapy treatments ♫ Xmas **CONF:** Thtr 200 Class 75 Board 30 Del from £95 **SERVICES:** Lift **PARKING:** 100 **NOTES:** ⊗ in restaurant **CARDS:**

★★★66% Fisher's

CRERAR HOTELS

75-79 Atholl Rd PH16 5BN
☎ 01796 472000 📠 01796 473949
e-mail: fishers@crerarhotels.com
Dir: *N on A9 turn off to Pitlochry, 3m after Ballinluig. Or S on A9 turn left to Pitlochry 10m after Bruar*

This traditional town centre hotel is convenient for the station and an ideal base for visiting local attractions. There are several styles of bedrooms, some overlook the main street, whilst others overlook the attractive gardens and many have views of the

continued on p758

PITLOCHRY, continued

surrounding hills. Public areas are extensive, with several dining options and two bars, including the popular Kingfisher Bar.
ROOMS: 80 en suite 51 annexe en suite (8 fmly) (22 GF) s £31.50-£45; d £63-£90 (incl. bkfst) **LB** **FACILITIES:** Putt green ♫ Xmas **CONF:** BC Thtr 230 Class 100 Board 100 Del from £85 **SERVICES:** Lift **PARKING:** 45 **NOTES:** ⊘ in restaurant **CARDS:**

★★77% Knockendarroch House

Higher Oakfield PH16 5HT
☎ 01796 473473 01796 474068
e-mail: info@knockendarroch.co.uk
web: www.knockendarroch.co.uk
Dir: *off A9 going N at Pitlochry sign. After railway bridge, take 1st right, then 2nd left*

An immaculate Victorian mansion overlooking the town and Tummel Valley. There is no bar, but guests can enjoy a drink in the delightful lounge while studying the daily menu of freshly prepared and enjoyable dishes. Bedrooms are tastefully furnished, comfortable and well equipped. Those on the top floor are smaller but are not without character and appeal.
ROOMS: 12 en suite ⊘ in all bedrooms s £65-£94; d £104-£146 (incl. bkfst & dinner) **LB** **FACILITIES:** Leisure facilities at nearby hotel **PARKING:** 30 **NOTES:** No children 10yrs ⊘ in restaurant Closed 2nd wk Nov-mid Feb **CARDS:**

★★72% Donavourd House

PH16 5JS
☎ 01796 472100 01796 474455
e-mail: reservations@donavourdhousehotel.co.uk
Dir: *from A9 slip road take immediate right under railway, continue 0.5m, then left up hill. At junct take left for hotel 0.5m on left*
This attractive country house sits in its own gardens in a quiet, elevated location overlooking Strathtummel. Bedrooms are spacious and well appointed with attractive colour schemes. The public areas are in period style where the dining room has crisp linen and fine glassware that complements the sound cooking skills of chef-patron Nicole McKechnie.
ROOMS: 9 en suite (1 fmly) (1 GF) ⊘ in all bedrooms s £65-£75; d £130-£150 (incl. bkfst & dinner) **LB** **FACILITIES:** Xmas **PARKING:** 15 **NOTES:** ⊘ in restaurant Closed 25 Dec, 5 Jan-Feb Civ Wed 100
CARDS:

★★72% Moulin Hotel

11-13 Kirkmichael Rd, Moulin PH16 5EW
☎ 01796 472196 01796 474098
e-mail: sales@moulinhotel.co.uk
web: www.moulinhotel.co.uk
Dir: *off A9 into Pitlochry in centre of town take A924 signed Braemar. Moulin village 0.75m outside Pitlochry*
Steeped in history, original parts of this friendly hotel date back to 1695. One of them, the Moulin bar, serves an excellent choice of bar meals as well as real ales from the hotel's own microbrewery. Alternatively, the comfortable restaurant overlooks the Moulin Burn. Bedrooms are well -quipped, with many having been refurbished.

ROOMS: 15 en suite (3 fmly) s £45-£60; d £50-£75 (incl. bkfst) **LB** **FACILITIES:** Xmas **CONF:** Thtr 15 Class 12 Board 10 **PARKING:** 30 **NOTES:** ⊘ in restaurant **CARDS:**

★★71% Birchwood

THE CIRCLE Selected Individual Hotels GREAT BRITAIN

2 East Moulin Rd PH16 5DW
☎ 01796 472477 01796 473951
e-mail: viv@birchwoodhotel.co.uk
Dir: *signposted from Atholl Rd on S side of town*
This Victorian house is peacefully situated at the southern side of town and is within walking distance of the town's many attractions. The refurbished bedrooms blend contemporary style with traditional architecture to provide comfortable, well-equipped accommodation. Day rooms are elegantly furnished and creative dinners can be enjoyed in the dining room. The hotel operates a no-smoking policy.
ROOMS: 12 en suite (1 GF) ⊘ in all bedrooms s £33-£42; d £66-£88 (incl. bkfst) **LB** **PARKING:** 25 **NOTES:** ⊘ in restaurant Closed Nov-Mar **CARDS:**

★★70% Balrobin

THE CIRCLE Selected Individual Hotels GREAT BRITAIN

Higher Oakfield PH16 5HT
☎ 01796 472901 01796 474200
e-mail: info@balrobin.co.uk
web: www.balrobin.co.uk
Dir: *leave A9 at Pitlochry junct, continue to town centre and follow brown tourists signs to hotel*
A welcoming atmosphere prevails at this family-run hotel which, from its position above the town, enjoys delightful countryside views. Public rooms include a relaxing lounge, a well-stocked bar and an attractive restaurant offering traditional home-cooked fare. The bedrooms are comfortable and many enjoy the fine views.
ROOMS: 14 en suite (2 fmly) ⊘ in all bedrooms s £38-£49.50; d £61-£86 (incl. bkfst) **LB** **PARKING:** 15 **NOTES:** No children 5yrs ⊘ in restaurant Closed Nov-Feb **CARDS:**

★★70% *Craigvrack*

West Moulin Rd PH16 5EQ
☎ 01796 472399 01796 473990
e-mail: info@craigvrack-hotel.demon.co.uk
web: www.craigvrack-hotel.demon.co.uk
Dir: *from Main St, turn into West Moulin Rd*
Situated above the town, this comfortable hotel has well-presented public areas, including an attractive restaurant and comfortable bar serving a varied menu. The bedrooms come in a variety of

continued

P

sizes and are smartly furnished, with several enjoying fine views of the countryside.

ROOMS: 16 en suite (2 fmly) (3 GF) ⊗ in 7 bedrooms **CONF:** Thtr 30 Class 32 Board 16 **PARKING:** 26 **NOTES:** ⊗ in restaurant **CARDS:**

PLOCKTON, Highland Map 22 NG83

★★75% *Haven*

Innes St IV52 8TW
☎ 01599 544334 & 544223 01599 544467
e-mail: thehavenhotel@aol.com
Dir: *off A87 just before Kyle of Lochalsh, after Balmacara signed to Plockton, hotel on main road just before lochside*

A delightful hotel in the picturesque west Highland village of Plockton that indeed lives up to its name. Comfortable public areas include a choice of lounges, a snug bar for residents and diners only, and an attractive restaurant which offers an imaginative dinner menu. Smart modern bedrooms include two delightful and very spacious suites.
ROOMS: 15 en suite **PARKING:** 7 **NOTES:** No children 7yrs ⊗ in restaurant Closed 20 Dec-1 Feb **CARDS:**

Indoor Swimming Pool
Indoor Swimming Pool (heated)
Outdoor Swimming Pool
Outdoor Swimming Pool (heated)

★★71% The Plockton

41 Harbour St IV52 8TN
☎ 01599 544274 01599 544475
e-mail: info@plocktonhotel.co.uk
Dir: *6 miles from Kyle of Lochalsh or 6 miles from Balmacara*
This small hotel occupies an idyllic position on the waterfront of Loch Carron. Bedrooms offer individual, pleasing décor and many have spacious balconies or panoramic views. There is a choice of three dining areas offering different atmospheres in which seafood is very much a speciality. The staff and owners provide a relaxed and informal style of attentive service.
ROOMS: 11 en suite 4 annexe en suite (1 fmly) (1 GF) ⊗ in all bedrooms s £45-£55; d £60-£90 (incl. bkfst) **LB** **FACILITIES:** STV Pool table ch fac Xmas **NOTES:** ⊗ in restaurant Civ Wed 45
CARDS:

POLMONT, Falkirk Map 21 NS97

★★★★69% *The Inchyra*

MACDONALD HOTELS

Grange Rd FK2 0YB
☎ 01324 711911 01324 716134
e-mail: inchyra@macdonald-hotels.co.uk
web: www.macdonaldhotels.co.uk/inchyra-grange-hotel/index.html
Dir: *just beyond BP Social Club*

Well placed for the M9 and Grangemouth terminal, this former manor house has been tastefully extended. It provides extensive conference facilities and a choice of eating options: the relaxed atmosphere of the Steakhouse or the Priory Restaurant, which provides a more formal dining experience. Bedrooms are mostly spacious and comfortable.
ROOMS: 109 en suite (5 fmly) ⊗ in 57 bedrooms **FACILITIES:** STV Sauna Solarium Gym Jacuzzi Steam room, Beauty therapy salons, Aromatherapist ch fac **CONF:** Thtr 700 Class 250 Board 80 **SERVICES:** Lift **PARKING:** 400 **NOTES:** ⊗ in restaurant Civ Wed 500
CARDS:

Travel Inn (Falkirk East)

travel inn

Beancross Rd FK2 0YS
☎ 08701 977098 01324 720777
Dir: *M9 junct5 at rdbt take exit signed Polmont A9. Travel Inn on left*
Travel Inn offers good-quality, value-for-money accommodation. Spacious, en suite rooms with bath and shower comfortably accommodate a family of up to two adults and two children (to age 15). The restaurant and bar offers a varied menu. For further details consult the Hotel Groups page.
ROOMS: 40 en suite s £45.95-£46.95; d £45.95-£46.95

POOLEWE, Highland Map 22 NG88

Top 200 – Hotel

★★★ ◎◎ **Pool House Hotel**

IV22 2LD

☎ 01445 781272 🖷 01445 781403

e-mail: enquiries@poolhousehotel.co.uk

Dir: *6m N of Gairloch on A832. Village centre*

Set on the shores of Loch Ewe where the river meets the bay, this hotel's unassuming façade gives little hint of its splendid interior. Extensively upgraded a few years ago it offers delightful public rooms and magnificent suites named after World War II ships, reflecting the building's former use as a military base. Delightful views are to be found everywhere. The hotel is run very much as a country house; service and hospitality by the Harrison Family are second to none, which together with the excellent food, will leave a lasting impression.

ROOMS: 5 en suite (1 fmly) ⊗ in all bedrooms **FACILITIES:** Snooker Sea fishing from jetty in front of hotel **PARKING:** 20 **NOTES:** No children 8yrs ⊗ in restaurant Closed Jan-Feb RS Nov & Dec **CARDS:**

P

PORT APPIN, Argyll & Bute Map 20 NM94

Top 200 – Hotel

★★★ ◎◎◎ **Airds**

PA38 4DF

☎ 01631 730236 🖷 01631 730535

e-mail: airds@airds-hotel.com

web: www.airds-hotel.com

Dir: *from A828, turn at Appin signed Port Appin. Hotel 2.5m on left.*

Stunning views are to be had from this delightful small hotel on the shores of Loch Linnhe. Finely prepared meals that utilise first-rate, mostly locally sourced ingredients, are served in the dining room. The bedrooms offer tasteful décor and bathrooms of a high specification. Lounges are quiet and inviting, with real fires and attractive artwork. The ever attentive staff can recommend many walks to guests.

ROOMS: 12 en suite (2 fmly) (2 GF) ⊗ in all bedrooms s £160-£255; d £230-£360 (incl. bkfst & dinner) LB **FACILITIES:** ch fac Xmas **CONF:** Thtr 16 Class 16 Board 16 Del from £117.50 **PARKING:** 21 **NOTES:** ⊗ in restaurant Closed 5-26 Jan RS Nov - Feb Civ Wed 30 **CARDS:**

PORT ASKAIG See Islay, Isle of

PORT OF MENTEITH, Stirling Map 20 NN50

★★70% ◎ **Lake**

FK8 3RA

☎ 01877 385258 🖷 01877 385671

e-mail: enquiries@lake-of-menteith-hotel.com

Dir: *M9 junct 10, take either A84/A873/A81 to Port of Menteith. Hotel beside village church*

Art déco styling and a stunning setting on the shores of Scotland's only lake make this hotel unique. The conservatory-style restaurant has fantastic views over the lake and there is a spacious lounge and bar. Individually styled bedrooms come in a range of sizes and offer co-ordinated decor.

ROOMS: 16 en suite (5 GF) ⊗ in all bedrooms s £60-£88; d £120-£156 (incl. bkfst & dinner) LB **FACILITIES:** Fishing Xmas **CONF:** Thtr 25 Class 25 Board 25 Del from £87 **PARKING:** 50 **NOTES:** No children 8yrs ⊗ in restaurant Closed 1 Jan RS Jan & Feb Civ Wed 50 **CARDS:**

PORTPATRICK, Dumfries & Galloway Map 20 NW95

Top 200 – Hotel

★★★ ◎◎◎ **Knockinaam Lodge**

DG9 9AD

☎ 01776 810471 🖷 01776 810435

e-mail: reservations@knockinaamlodge.com

Dir: *from A77 or A75 follow signs to Portpatrick. Through Lochans. After 2m turn left at signs for Knockinaam Lodge and follow hotel signs*

This relaxing hotel has a stunning cliff top location with views over the sea to Ireland. A warm welcome is assured from the proprietors and their committed team. Bedrooms are equipped with many extra touches, most are spacious and all have great bathrooms. Dinner in the restaurant makes use of the best quality produce and breakfasts are memorable.

ROOMS: 9 en suite ⊗ in 2 bedrooms s £125-£145; d £210-£270 (incl. bkfst & dinner) LB **FACILITIES:** Fishing Shooting, Walking, Sea fishing ch fac Xmas **CONF:** Thtr 30 Class 10 Board 16 Del from £125 **PARKING:** 20 **NOTES:** ⊗ in restaurant Civ Wed 40 **CARDS:**

★★★74% Fernhill
Heugh Rd DG9 8TD
☎ 01776 810220 01776 810596
e-mail: info@fernhillhotel.co.uk
web: www.fernhillhotel.co.uk
Dir: *from Stranraer A77 to Portpatrick, 100yds past Portpatrick village sign, turn right before war memorial. Hotel is 1st on left*

Set high above the village, this hotel looks out over the harbour and Irish Sea. A smart conservatory restaurant and some of the bedrooms take advantage of the views. A modern wing offers particularly spacious and well-appointed rooms - some have balconies.
ROOMS: 27 en suite 9 annexe en suite (3 fmly) (8 GF) ⊗ in 10 bedrooms s £50-£87; d £100-£124 (incl. bkfst) **LB** **FACILITIES:** STV Leisure facilities available at sister hotel in Stranraer ch fac Xmas **CONF:** Thtr 24 Class 12 Board 12 **PARKING:** 45 **NOTES:** ⊗ in restaurant Closed mid-Jan - mid-Feb Civ Wed 40
CARDS:

PORTREE See Skye, Isle of

POWFOOT, Dumfries & Galloway Map 21 NY16

A Powfoot Golf Hotel
Links Av DG12 5PN
☎ 01461 700254 01461 700288
e-mail: rooms@powfootgolfhotel.co.uk
web: www.powfootgolfhotel.co.uk
Dir: *leave A75 & travel through Annan on B721. Then take B724 for approx 3m & turn left onto local road*
ROOMS: 15 en suite (4 fmly) s £45-£50; d £65-£75 (incl. bkfst) **LB**
FACILITIES: Xmas **CONF:** Thtr 120 Class 60 Board 40 **PARKING:** 40
NOTES: ★★ ⊗ in restaurant Closed 25-26 Dec
CARDS:

PRESTWICK, South Ayrshire — Map 20 NS32

★★★69% ◎ Parkstone
Esplanade KA9 1QN
☎ 01292 477286 📠 01292 477671
e-mail: info@parkstonehotel.co.uk
web: www.parkstonehotel.co.uk
Dir: *from Prestwick Main St (A79) turn W to seafront - hotel 600yds*

Situated on the seafront in a quiet residential area, this family-run hotel caters for business visitors as well as golfers. Bedrooms come in a variety of sizes, all being furnished in a smart contemporary style. The attractive, modern look of the bar and restaurant is matched by an equally up-to-date menu.
ROOMS: 22 en suite (2 fmly) ⊗ in all bedrooms s £45-£58; d £75-£86 (incl. bkfst) **LB** **FACILITIES:** Xmas **CONF:** Thtr 100 **PARKING:** 34 **NOTES:** ✗ ⊗ in restaurant Civ Wed 100
CARDS:

RENFREW For hotels see Glasgow Airport

ROSEBANK, South Lanarkshire — Map 21 NS84

★★★71% Popinjay
Lanark Rd ML8 5QB
☎ 01555 860441 📠 01555 860204
e-mail: popinjayhotel@attglobal.net
web: www.popinjayhotel.co.uk
Dir: *on A72 between Hamilton & Lanark*
This attractive Tudor-style hotel is set in landscaped grounds leading down to the River Clyde. There is a panelled bar and a light and airy restaurant where a wide choice of dishes is offered. Well-equipped bedrooms come in a variety of sizes. Stylish function suites attract weddings and conferences.
ROOMS: 38 en suite (2 fmly) ⊗ in 19 bedrooms s £65-£75; d fr £75 (incl. bkfst) **LB** **FACILITIES:** STV Fishing ch fac Xmas **CONF:** Thtr 250 Class 120 Board 60 Del from £95 **PARKING:** 300 **NOTES:** ⊗ in restaurant Civ Wed **CARDS:**

See advert on page 761

ROY BRIDGE, Highland — Map 22 NN28

★★★71% Glenspean Lodge Hotel
Best Western
PH31 4AW
☎ 01397 712223 📠 01397 712660
e-mail: reservations@glenspeanlodge.co.uk
web: www.glenspeanlodge.co.uk
Dir: *2m E of Roy Bridge, right off A82 at Spean Bridge onto A86*
Originally a Victorian hunting lodge, this hotel has been impressively extended and enjoys stunning views from its elevated position in the Spean Valley. Accommodation is provided in well laid out bedrooms, some suitable for families. Meals can be enjoyed in either the smart restaurant or less formal bar area.

ROOMS: 15 en suite (3 fmly) ⊗ in 10 bedrooms s £45-£95; d £90-£200 (incl. bkfst) **LB** **FACILITIES:** STV Sauna Gym Jacuzzi snooker room, small children's play room Xmas **CONF:** Thtr 50 Class 25 Board 25 **PARKING:** 50 **NOTES:** ⊗ in restaurant Civ Wed 80
CARDS:

★★68% *The Stronlossit Inn*
PH31 4AG
☎ 01397 712253 & 0800 015 5321 📠 01397 712641
e-mail: stay@stronlossit.co.uk
web: www.stronlossit.co.uk
Dir: *off A82 at Spean Bridge onto A86, signed Roy Bridge. Hotel on left*
A relaxed, informal atmosphere prevails at this family-run holiday hotel. The spacious bar is the focal point and a favourite with both resident and non-resident diners. Alternatively one can eat in the attractive restaurant. Bedrooms come in a mix of sizes and styles, most being smartly modern.
ROOMS: 10 en suite (5 GF) ⊗ in all bedrooms **FACILITIES:** Pool table, Internet Cafe **CONF:** Thtr 30 Class 18 Board 12 **PARKING:** 30 **NOTES:** ✗ No children ⊗ in restaurant Closed 10 Nov-10 Dec & 6-31 Jan Civ Wed 30 **CARDS:**

ST ANDREWS, Fife — Map 21 NO51

Top 200 – Hotel

★★★★★ ◎◎◎ The Old Course Hotel, Golf Resort & Spa
KY16 9SP
☎ 01334 474371 📠 01334 477668
e-mail: reservations@oldcoursehotel.co.uk
Dir: *close to A91 on outskirts of the city*
A haven for golfers, this internationally renowned hotel sits adjacent to the 17th hole of the championship course. Bedrooms vary in size and range from the traditional to the

continued

contemporary and stylish fairway rooms, complete with course facing balconies. Day rooms include intimate lounges, a bright conservatory, a well-equipped spa and a range of golf shops. The fine dining 'Grill', the seafood bar 'Sands' or the informal Jigger Inn pub prove popular eating venues.
ROOMS: 134 en suite (6 fmly) in 118 bedrooms s £230-£580; d £295-£595 (incl. bkfst) LB **FACILITIES: Spa** STV 18 Sauna Solarium Gym Putt green Jacuzzi Health spa Steam room ch fac Xmas **CONF:** BC Thtr 300 Class 150 Board 60 **SERVICES:** Lift **PARKING:** 150 **NOTES:** in restaurant Closed 24-28 Dec Civ Wed 180 **CARDS:**

★★★★74% **Rusacks**

Pilmour Links KY16 9JQ
☎ 0870 400 8128 01334 477896
e-mail: rusacks@macdonald-hotels.co.uk
web: www.heritage-hotels.com/discover/info/hotels/38.htm
Dir: *from W on A91 past golf course, through an old viaduct, hotel 200mtrs on left before rdbt*

This long-established hotel enjoys an almost unrivalled location with superb views across the famous golf course. Bedrooms are generally spacious and all are comfortably appointed and well equipped. Public rooms include a smart restaurant - the perfect place to watch golfers - plus a choice of bars and roomy lounges.
ROOMS: 68 en suite **FACILITIES:** STV Sauna Golf Mgr to organise golf **CONF:** Thtr 90 Class 40 Board 20 **SERVICES:** Lift **PARKING:** 21 **NOTES:** in restaurant Civ Wed 60
CARDS:

Top 200 – Hotel

★★★ **Rufflets Country House**
Strathkinness Low Rd KY16 9TX
☎ 01334 472594 01334 478703
e-mail: reservations@rufflets.co.uk
web: www.rufflets.co.uk
Dir: *1.5m W on B939*

This charming property is set in extensive award-winning gardens, a few minutes' drive from the town centre. Stylish, spacious bedrooms are individually decorated and most benefit from impressive bathrooms. Public rooms include a well-stocked bar, a choice of inviting lounges and the delightful Garden Room restaurant; imaginative, carefully prepared cooking utilises produce from the hotel's own gardens whenever possible.
ROOMS: 19 en suite 5 annexe en suite (2 fmly) in 13 bedrooms s £110; d £190 (incl. bkfst) LB **FACILITIES: Spa** STV Putt green Golf driving net Xmas **CONF:** Thtr 50 Class 30 Board 25 Del from £135 **PARKING:** 52 **NOTES:** in restaurant Civ Wed 60
CARDS:

Top 200 – Hotel

★★★ **St Andrews Golf**
40 The Scores KY16 9AS
☎ 01334 472611 01334 472188
e-mail: reception@standrews-golf.co.uk
web: www.standrews-golf.co.uk
Dir: *follow signs 'Golf Course' into Golf Place and in 200yds turn right into The Scores*

A genuinely warm approach to guest care is found at this delightful, family-run hotel. In a stunning location the views of the beach, golf links and coastline can be enjoyed from the inviting day rooms. There is a choice of bars and an informal atmosphere in Ma Bell's. Bedrooms come in two distinct styles with those on the higher floors offering stylish, modern design and comfort.
ROOMS: 21 en suite (9 fmly) s £115-£170; d £170-£215 (incl. bkfst) LB **FACILITIES:** STV ch fac Xmas **CONF:** Thtr 200 Class 80 Board 20 **SERVICES:** Lift **PARKING:** 6 **NOTES:** in restaurant
CARDS:

★★★67% ***Scores***
76 The Scores KY16 9BB
☎ 01334 472451 01334 473947
e-mail: office@scoreshotel.co.uk
Dir: *on entering St Andrews follow signs to West Sands and Sea Life Centre, hotel diagonally opposite Royal & Ancient Clubhouse*

Best Western

This elegant hotel enjoys views over St Andrews Bay and is situated only a few yards from the first tee of the famous Old Course. Public areas include a choice of bars, an all-day coffee shop, and an attractive restaurant. Bedrooms are well equipped and come in various sizes, many quite spacious.
ROOMS: 30 en suite (1 fmly) in 9 bedrooms **FACILITIES:** STV **CONF:** Thtr 150 Class 60 Board 40 **SERVICES:** Lift **PARKING:** 10 **NOTES:** in restaurant **CARDS:**

S

ST ANDREWS, continued

★★74% The Inn at Lathones

Largoward KY9 1JE

THE INDEPENDENTS

☎ 01334 840494 01334 840694

e-mail: lathones@theinn.co.uk

Dir: *5m S of St Andrews on A915, 0.5m before village of Largoward on left just after hidden dip*

A lovely little country inn, full of character and individuality, parts of which date back 400 years. The friendly staff help to create a relaxed atmosphere. Bedrooms are in two separate wings, both accessed from outside. The colourful, cosy restaurant is the main focus, the menu reflects a modern style in Scottish and European dishes.

ROOMS: 13 annexe en suite (2 fmly) (11 GF) s £100-£130; d £140-£200 (incl. bkfst) **LB** **FACILITIES:** STV ch fac **CONF:** Thtr 40 Class 10 Board 20 Del from £155 **PARKING:** 35 **NOTES:** ⊘ in restaurant Closed 25-26 Dec & 3-23 Jan RS 24 Dec Civ Wed 45 **CARDS:**

★★70% *Russell Hotel*

26 The Scores KY16 9AS

☎ 01334 473447 01334 478279

e-mail: russellhotel@talk21.com

Dir: *A91-St Andrews turn left at 2nd rdbt into Golf Place, turn right after 200yds into The Scores, hotel in 300yds on the left*

This family-run hotel enjoys lovely views over the east bay, especially from its upper sea-facing bedrooms. The town centre and famous Old Course are nearby and well-appointed bedrooms come in a variety of sizes. A good range of dishes is available in the bar, but it's worth experiencing dinner in the cosy little restaurant.

ROOMS: 10 en suite (3 fmly) **FACILITIES:** STV **NOTES:** ⊘ in restaurant Civ Wed 40 **CARDS:**

St Andrews Bay Golf Resort & Spa

KY16 8PN

☎ 01334 837000 01334 471115

e-mail: info@standrewsbay.com

At the time of going to press, the star classification for this hotel was not confirmed. Please refer to the AA internet site www.theAA.com for current information.

ROOMS: 209 en suite 8 annexe en suite (86 fmly) (57 GF) ⊘ in 195 bedrooms s £120-£270; d £120-£270 (incl. bkfst & dinner) **LB** **FACILITIES: Spa** STV 36 Sauna Gym Putt green Jacuzzi Clay pigeon shooting etc can be organised Xmas **CONF:** BC Thtr 500 Class 450 Board 168 **SERVICES:** Lift air con **NOTES:** ⊘ in restaurant Civ Wed 600 **CARDS:**

ST BOSWELLS, Scottish Borders — Map 21 NT53

★★★73% Dryburgh Abbey

TD6 0RQ

SCOTLAND'S HOTELS OF DISTINCTION

☎ 01835 822261 01835 823945

e-mail: enquiries@dryburgh.co.uk

Dir: *from A68 at St Boswells turn onto B6404, through village. Continue 2m, turn left B6356 Scott's View. Through Clintmains village, hotel 1.8m*

This long-established hotel has a super setting close to the river Tweed. The red-sandstone baronial mansion enjoys fine views of Dryburgh Abbey. Public areas include a choice of lounges and a traditionally styled restaurant. Bedrooms are generally spacious and there are a number of suites.

ROOMS: 37 en suite 1 annexe en suite (5 fmly) s £48-£152; d £96-£166 (incl. bkfst) **LB** **FACILITIES:** Fishing Putt green ch fac Xmas **CONF:** Thtr 150 Class 90 Board 70 Del from £125 **SERVICES:** Lift **PARKING:** 103 **NOTES:** ⊘ in restaurant Civ Wed 110 **CARDS:**

★★71% Buccleuch Arms

The Green TD6 0EW

☎ 01835 822243 01835 823965

e-mail: bucchotel@aol.com

web: www.buccleucharmshotel.co.uk

Dir: *on A68, 8m N of Jedburgh*

Formerly a coaching inn, this long-established hotel stands opposite the village green. The lounge bar is a popular eating venue and complements the restaurant. Morning coffees and afternoon teas are served in the attractive lounge with its open fire. The well-equipped bedrooms come in a variety of sizes.

ROOMS: 19 en suite (2 fmly) ⊘ in all bedrooms s £46-£49; d £77-£82 (incl. bkfst) **LB** **FACILITIES:** Putt green Xmas **CONF:** Thtr 100 Class 40 Board 30 Del from £70 **PARKING:** 50 **NOTES:** ⊘ in restaurant Closed 25 Dec **CARDS:**

S

ST FILLANS, Perth & Kinross — Map 20 NN62

★★★68% The Four Seasons Hotel
Loch Earn PH6 2NF
☎ 01764 685333 01764 685444
e-mail: info@thefourseasonshotel.co.uk
Dir: *on A85, towards W of village facing Loch*

Set on the edge of Loch Earn, this welcoming hotel and many of its bedrooms benefit from fine views. There is a choice of lounges, including a library, warmed by log fires during winter. Local produce is used to good effect in both the Meall Reamhar restaurant and the more informal Tarken Room.
ROOMS: 12 en suite 6 annexe en suite (7 fmly) in 3 bedrooms s £40-£78; d £80-£106 (incl. bkfst) **LB** **FACILITIES:** ch fac Xmas **CONF:** Thtr 95 Class 45 Board 38 **PARKING:** 40 **NOTES:** in restaurant Closed 5 Jan-end of Feb RS Nov, Dec, Mar Civ Wed 80
CARDS:

★★72% Achray House
PH6 2NF
☎ 01764 685231 01764 685320
e-mail: info@achray-house.co.uk
Dir: *follow A85 towards Crainlarich, from Stirling follow A9 then B822 at Braco, B827 to Comrie. Turn left onto A85 to St Fillans*

A friendly holiday hotel set in gardens overlooking picturesque Loch Earn, Achray House offers smart, attractive and well-equipped bedrooms. An interesting range of freshly prepared dishes is served both in the conservatory and in the adjoining dining rooms.
ROOMS: 9 rms (8 en suite) 1 annexe en suite (2 fmly) (3 GF) in 5 bedrooms s £50-£55; d £70-£80 (incl. bkfst) **LB** **FACILITIES:** Xmas **CONF:** Class 20 Board 20 **PARKING:** 30 **NOTES:** in restaurant
CARDS:

SANQUHAR, Dumfries & Galloway — Map 21 NS70

★★66% Blackaddie House
Blackaddie Rd DG4 6JJ
☎ 01659 50270 01659 50900
e-mail: enquiries@blackaddiehotel.co.uk
Dir: *off A76 just N of Sanquhar at Burnside Service Station. Private road to hotel 300mtrs on right*
This charming house, a former rectory, is quietly situated on the edge of the village beside the river. As well as an inviting lounge, public areas include a cosy bar, adorned with angling memorabilia, and a conservatory restaurant giving a very fine view over the neat garden to the River Nith.
ROOMS: 9 en suite (2 fmly) s £40; d £70 (incl. bkfst)
FACILITIES: Riding **CONF:** Thtr 50 Class 20 Board 20 **PARKING:** 25
NOTES: in restaurant **CARDS:**

SCARISTA See Harris, Isle of

SCOURIE, Highland — Map 22 NC14

★★72% Eddrachilles
Badcall Bay IV27 4TH
☎ 01971 502080 01971 502477
e-mail: enq@eddrachilles.com web: www.eddrachilles.com
Dir: *2m S, on A894, 7m N of Kylesku Bridge*

This appealing holiday hotel is in an idyllic woodland setting beside the Badcall Bay and enjoys stunning sea and island views. There are inviting lounges and a popular conservatory overlooking the bay. The dining room offers both fixed-price and carte menus and the well-equipped bedrooms are pleasantly decorated and furnished.
ROOMS: 11 en suite (1 fmly) (4 GF) s £51.90-£54.90; d £83.80-£89.90 (incl. bkfst) **LB** **FACILITIES:** Fishing Boats for hire **PARKING:** 25
NOTES: No children 3yrs in restaurant Closed Nov-Feb
CARDS:

★★70% Scourie
IV27 4SX
☎ 01971 502396 01971 502423
e-mail: patrick@scourie-hotel.co.uk
Dir: *on A894 in village, on left*
This well-established hotel is an angler's paradise with extensive fishing rights available on a 25,000-acre estate. Public areas include a choice of comfortable lounges, a cosy bar and a smart dining room offering wholesome fare. The bedrooms are comfortable and generally spacious and the resident proprietors and their staff create a relaxed and friendly atmosphere.
ROOMS: 18 rms (17 en suite) 2 annexe en suite (2 fmly) (5 GF) in all bedrooms s £35-£46; d £60-£80 (incl. bkfst) **LB** **FACILITIES:** no TV in bdrms Fishing Trout and Salmon fishing, Hill walking, Sea fishing
PARKING: 30 **NOTES:** in restaurant Closed mid Oct-end Mar
CARDS:

S

SHETLAND Map 24

BRAE Map 24 HU36

★★★69% Busta House
ZE2 9QN
☎ 01806 522506 01806 522588
e-mail: reservations@bustahouse.com

THE CIRCLE
Selected Individual Hotels
GREAT BRITAIN

Dir: *take A970 north through village, at north end follow signs to Busta House, 0.5m*

Dating back to 1724, this popular hotel boasts the reputation of being Britain's most northerly country-house hotel. Bedrooms vary in size and style but are well equipped, comfortable, and many have excellent sea views. Day rooms include the comfortable "long room" lounge; and wide-ranging menus are to be found in the Pitcairn restaurant and popular, traditional bar. The staff are friendly and keen to please.

ROOMS: 20 en suite (1 fmly) in 6 bedrooms s £75; d £100-£140 (incl. bkfst) LB **CONF:** Thtr 30 Class 24 Board 24 Del from £120 **PARKING:** 40 **NOTES:** in restaurant Closed 23 Dec-5 Jan Civ Wed 59 **CARDS:**

LERWICK Map 24 HU44

★★★69% Shetland
Holmsgarth Rd ZE1 0PW
☎ 01595 695515 01595 695828
e-mail: reception@shetlandhotel.co.uk

Dir: *opposite ferry terminal, on main route N from town centre*

This purpose built hotel, situated opposite the main ferry terminal, offers spacious and comfortable bedrooms on three floors. Two dining options are available, including the informal Oasis bistro and Ninians Restaurant. Service is prompt and friendly.

ROOMS: 64 en suite (4 fmly) in 14 bedrooms s £75; d £95 (incl. bkfst) LB **FACILITIES:** STV **CONF:** Thtr 300 Class 75 Board 50 **SERVICES:** Lift **PARKING:** 150 **NOTES:** Civ Wed 200 **CARDS:**

★★★68% Lerwick
15 South Rd ZE1 0RB
☎ 01595 692166 01595 694419
e-mail: reception@lerwickhotel.co.uk
web: www.shetlandhotels.com

Dir: *near town centre, on main road to/from airport. (25m from main airport)*

Enjoying fine views across Breiwick Bay from the restaurant and some of the bedrooms, this purpose-built hotel appeals to tourists and business guests alike. Bedrooms, which vary in size and aspect, are attractively furnished and family accommodation is available. The Breiwick restaurant has fine sea views, and there is also a more informal brasserie.

ROOMS: 34 en suite (3 fmly) s fr £73; d fr £90 (incl. bkfst) LB **FACILITIES:** STV **CONF:** BC Thtr 100 Class 40 Board 26 **PARKING:** 50 **NOTES:** Civ Wed 100 **CARDS:**

UNST Map 24 HP60

★★65% *The Baltasound*
ZE2 9DS
☎ 01957 711334 01957 711358
e-mail: balta.hotel@zetnet.co.uk

Dir: *from ferry from Lerwick, follow the main road N. Hotel is in Baltasound close to the pier.*

A visit to the Shetlands is not complete without staying at Britain's most northerly-located hotel. Set amid sea lochs, an abundance of rare wildlife and stunning scenery, this welcoming hotel offers a variety of accommodation styles. Most rooms are located in well-maintained log cabins in the grounds. The comfortable lounge leads into an open-plan bar and dining area, with a separate bright and airy room used for breakfast.

ROOMS: 8 rms (6 en suite) 17 annexe en suite (17 fmly) in 17 bedrooms **FACILITIES:** Pool table **CONF:** Board 20 **PARKING:** 20 **NOTES:** in restaurant **CARDS:**

SHIELDAIG, Highland Map 22 NG85

Top 200 – Hotel

★ Tigh an Eilean
IV54 8XN
☎ 01520 755251 01520 755321
e-mail: tighaneileanhotel@shieldaig.fsnet.co.uk

Dir: *off A896 onto village road signped Shieldaig, hotel in centre of village on loch front*

A superb location on the seafront with views over the bay is the icing on the cake for this delightful small hotel. Genuine hospitality and well-developed customer-care skills ensure that many guests return time and time again. The brightly decorated bedrooms vary in size. Dinner features carefully prepared local produce served in the lovely front-facing dining room.

ROOMS: 11 en suite (1 fmly) s fr £55; d fr £120 (incl. bkfst) LB **FACILITIES:** no TV in bdrms Bird watching, Boat available, Kayaks, Astronomy ch fac **PARKING:** 15 **NOTES:** in restaurant Closed late Oct-end Mar Civ Wed 40 **CARDS:**

SKEABOST BRIDGE, Highland

U Skeabost Country House
IV51 9NP
☎ 01470 532202 01470 532215 01470 532454
e-mail: reception@skeabostcountryhouse.com

Dir: *on A87 north of Portree, left onto A850. Hotel 1.5 miles on right, just beyond Snizort river bridge*

At the time of going to press, the star classification for this hotel was not confirmed. Please refer to the AA internet site www.theAA.com for current information.

ROOMS: 17 en suite 4 annexe en suite (1 fmly) (9 GF) in all bedrooms s £80-£90; d £100-£110 (incl. bkfst) LB **FACILITIES:** STV 9 Fishing Snooker ch fac Xmas **CONF:** BC Thtr 60 Class 30 Board 30 Del from £170 **PARKING:** 100 **NOTES:** in restaurant **CARDS:**

Popped the question?
Hotels with Civ Wed in their entry are licensed for civil wedding ceremonies. Maximum numbers for the ceremony only are shown, e.g. Civ Wed 120

SKYE, ISLE OF, Highland — Map 22

ARDVASAR — Map 22 NG60

★★67% *Ardvasar Hotel*
Sleat IV45 8RS
☎ 01471 844223 📠 01471 844495
e-mail: richard@ardvasar-hotel.demon.co.uk
web: www.ardvasarhotel.com
Dir: *from ferry 500mtrs turn left*

Less than five minutes' drive from the Mallaig ferry, this well maintained hotel is the hub of the community. Bedrooms are smartly furnished and well equipped and public areas include a cosy lounge for residents. Seafood is prominent on menus, and meals can be enjoyed in either the popular bar or the attractive dining room.
ROOMS: 10 en suite (4 fmly) ⊗ in 6 bedrooms **CONF:** Thtr 50 Board 24 **PARKING:** 30 **NOTES:** ⊗ in restaurant
CARDS:

COLBOST — Map 22 NG24

Top 200 – Restaurant with Rooms

Three Chimneys Restaurant & The House Over-By
IV55 8ZT
☎ 01470 511258 📠 01470 511358
e-mail: eatandstay@threechimneys.co.uk
web: www.threechimneys.co.uk
Dir: *4m W of Dunvegan village on B884 signed Glendale*
This delightful property and memorable restaurant make a trip to Skye a necessity. Shirley Spear's stunning food is the highlight of any visit. Her skilful and deft approach to cooking utilises quality local ingredients that shine through. Stylish, thoughtfully equipped bedrooms in the 'House Over-By' enjoy wonderful views across Loch Dunvegan and boast spacious well appointed en suite facilities. Breakfast is an impressive event with an array of locally smoked fish and meats, local
continued
cheeses, freshly made bakery items and home-made preserves. AA Wine Award Winner for Scotland 2004-5.
ROOMS: 6 en suite (1 fmly) (6 GF) ⊗ in all bedrooms
PARKING: 8 **NOTES:** ⊗ in restaurant Closed 13-19 Dec, 9-28 Jan RS Sun & Nov-Mar **CARDS:**

ISLE ORNSAY — Map 22 NG71

★★★74% Duisdale Country House
IV43 8QW
☎ 01471 833202 📠 01471 833404
e-mail: john.duisdalehotel@tiscali.co.uk
web: www.duisdale.com
Dir: *on A851 Armadale to Broadford road, just N of village*

Warm hospitality is a real feature at this delightfully situated country house. Set in landscaped grounds a short walk from a lovely beach the location offers fine views of the Sound of Sleat
continued on p768

S

ISLE ORNSAY, continued

and distant hills. Bedrooms come in a range of sizes and styles, all being comfortably equipped. Fresh local produce is utilised on the classically inspired menus.
ROOMS: 17 en suite (3 fmly) ⊗ in all bedrooms s £65-£90; d £90-£160 **LB** **FACILITIES:** STV Putt green Clay shooting **PARKING:** 20 **NOTES:** No children 6yrs ⊗ in restaurant Closed 30 Nov-28 Feb
CARDS:

★★74% **Hotel Eilean Iarmain**
IV43 8QR
☎ 01471 833332 01471 833275
e-mail: hotel@eilean-iarmain.co.uk
Dir: *A851, A852, right to Isle Ornsay Harbour front*

A hotel of charm and character, this 19th-century former inn lies by the pier and enjoys fine views across the sea lochs. Bedrooms are individual and retain a traditional style (not all have TVs), and a stable block has been converted into four delightful suites. Public rooms are cosy and inviting.
ROOMS: 6 en suite 10 annexe en suite (6 fmly) ⊗ in 10 bedrooms **FACILITIES:** Fishing Shooting Exibitions Whisky tasting ♫ **CONF:** Thtr 50 Class 30 Board 25 **PARKING:** 35 **NOTES:** ⊗ in restaurant
CARDS:

See advert on page 767

PORTREE Map 22 NG44

★★★77% **Cuillin Hills**
IV51 9QU
☎ 01478 612003 01478 613092
e-mail: info@cuillinhills-hotel-skye.co.uk
web: www.cuillinhills-hotel-skye.co.uk
Dir: *turn right 0.25m N of Portree off A855 and follow signs for hotel*

This imposing building enjoys a superb location overlooking Portree Bay and the Cuillin Hills. Accommodation is provided in smart, well-equipped rooms that are generally spacious. Some

continued

bedrooms are found in an adjacent building. Public areas include a split-level restaurant that takes advantage of the views. Service is particularly attentive.
ROOMS: 21 en suite 7 annexe en suite (4 fmly) (8 GF) ⊘ in 14 bedrooms s £60-£150; d £120-£170 (incl. bkfst) **LB** **FACILITIES:** STV Xmas **CONF:** Thtr 160 Class 70 Board 40 Del from £70 **PARKING:** 56 **NOTES:** ⊘ in restaurant Civ Wed 70 **CARDS:**

See advert on opposite page

★★★75% Bosville
Bosville Ter IV51 9DG
☎ 01478 612846 01478 613434
e-mail: bosville@macleodhotels.co.uk
web: www.macleodhotels.co.uk
Dir: *A87 signed Portree, then A855 into town*

This stylish, popular hotel has now been extended and enjoys fine views over the harbour. Bedrooms are furnished to a high specification and have a fresh, contemporary feel. Public areas include a smart new bar, bistro and the Chandlery restaurant where fantastic local produce is treated with respect and refreshing restraint.
ROOMS: 25 en suite (2 fmly) ⊘ in 10 bedrooms s £65-£75; d £80-£150 (incl. bkfst) **LB** **FACILITIES:** Use of nearby leisure club Xmas **CONF:** Thtr 20 Class 20 Board 20 Del from £99 **PARKING:** 10 **NOTES:** ⊘ in restaurant Civ Wed 80
CARDS:

See advert on this page

★★73% Rosedale
Beaumont Crescent IV51 9DB
☎ 01478 613131 01478 612531
e-mail: rosedalehotelsky@aol.com
web: www.rosedalehotelskye.co.uk
Dir: *follow directions to village centre & harbour, hotel on harbour*

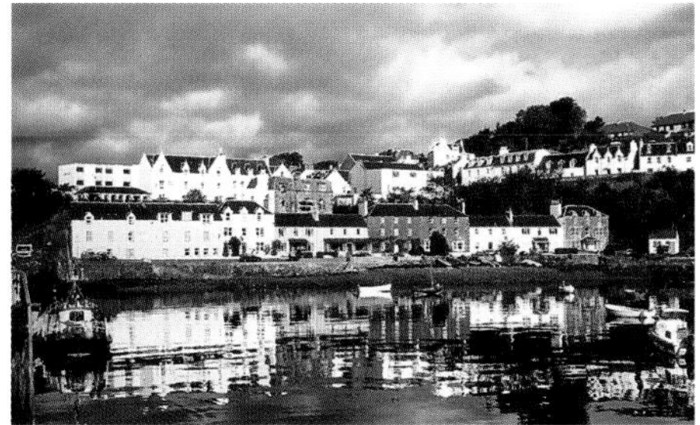

The atmosphere is wonderfully warm at this delightful family-run waterfront hotel. A labyrinth of stairs and corridors connects the comfortable lounges, bar and charming restaurant, which are set on different levels. The restaurant offers fine views of the bay. Modern bedrooms offer a good range of amenities.
ROOMS: 18 en suite (1 fmly) ⊘ in all bedrooms s £35-£50; d £60-£116 (incl. bkfst) **LB** **PARKING:** 2 **NOTES:** ⊘ in restaurant Closed mid Nov-Mar **CARDS:**

SORN, East Ayrshire Map 20 NS52

Restaurant with Rooms

The Sorn Inn
35 Main St KA5 6HU
☎ 01290 551305 01290 553470
e-mail: craig@sorninn.com
Dir: *A70 from S or A76 from N onto B743 to Sorn*
Centrally situated within this rural village, which is convenient for many of Ayrshire's attractions, this renovated inn is now a fine dining restaurant with a cosy lounge area. There is also a popular chop house within a more pub-like environment. Bedrooms are freshly decorated, have comfortable beds and good facilities.
ROOMS: 4 en suite (1 fmly) in all bedrooms s £35-£50; d £45-£90 (incl. bkfst) **LB** **FACILITIES:** Fishing Shooting Xmas **PARKING:** 9 **NOTES:** in restaurant **CARDS:**

SOUTH QUEENSFERRY, City of Edinburgh Map 21 NT17

Innkeeper's Lodge South Queensferry
7 Newhalls Rd EH30 9TA
☎ 0131 331 1990 0131 331 3168
www.innkeeperslodge.com
Dir: *M8 follow signs for Forth Road Bridge exit at junct 2 onto M9/A8000. At rdbt take B907 follow to junction with B249. Turn right and lodge close to Forth Railway Bridge in Newhalls Rd*
Smart rooms meet essential business requirements but also have home comforts, and depending on location may well have meeting rooms and pub dining. Dining options generally include all-day menus plus the added advantage of breakfast.
ROOMS: s £57.50; d £57.50 **CONF:** Class 18 Board 18

Travel Inn (Edinburgh Queensferry)
Builyeon Rd EH30 9YJ
☎ 08701 977094 0131 319 1156
Dir: *M8 junct 2 follow signs M9 Stirling, leave at junct 1A take A8000 towards Forth Road Bridge, at 3rd rdbt take 2nd exit into Builyeon Road (do not go onto Forth Road Bridge)*
Travel Inn offers good-quality, value-for-money accommodation. Spacious, en suite rooms with bath and shower comfortably accommodate a family of up to two adults and two children (to age 15). The restaurant and bar offers a varied menu. For further details consult the Hotel Groups page.
ROOMS: 46 en suite s £45.95-£48.95; d £45.95-£48.95

SPEAN BRIDGE, Highland Map 22 NN28

Corriegour Lodge
Loch Lochy PH34 4EB
☎ 01397 712685 01397 712696
e-mail: info@corriegour-lodge-hotel.com
web: www.corriegour-lodge-hotel.com
Dir: *N of Fort William on A82 (south side of Loch Lochy). Between Spean Bridge & Invergarry*
ROOMS: 9 en suite (3 fmly) in all bedrooms s £55.50-£69.50; d £111-£139 (incl. bkfst) **LB** **FACILITIES:** Xmas **PARKING:** 20 **NOTES:** ★★★★ No children 8yrs in restaurant Closed Dec-Jan ex New Year RS Nov-Feb wknds only **CARDS:**

See advert under FORT WILLIAM

STEPPS, North Lanarkshire Map 20 NS66

★★★68% *Garfield House Hotel*
Cumbernauld Rd G33 6HW
☎ 0141 779 2111 0141 779 9799
e-mail: rooms@garfieldhotel.co.uk
Dir: *M8 J11 exit at Stepps/Queenslie, follow signs for Stepps – A80*

Situated close to the A80, this considerably extended business hotel is a popular venue for local conferences and functions. Public areas include a welcoming reception lounge and the popular Distillery Bar/Restaurant, an all-day eatery providing good value meals in an informal setting. Smart, well-presented bedrooms come in a range of sizes.
ROOMS: 45 en suite (10 fmly) (8 GF) in 31 bedrooms **CONF:** Thtr 150 Class 40 Board 36 **PARKING:** 90 **NOTES:** Closed 1-2 Jan **CARDS:**

Travel Inn Glasgow (North East)
Crowood Roundabout, Cumbernauld Rd G33 6LE
☎ 08701 977111 0141 779 8060
Dir: *M8 junct 13 signed M80. Exit M80 at Crowwood rdbt, take 3rd exit signed A80 west. Travel Inn is 1st left*
Travel Inn offers good-quality, value-for-money accommodation. Spacious, en suite rooms with bath and shower comfortably accommodate a family of up to two adults and two children (to age 15). The restaurant and bar offers a varied menu. For further details consult the Hotel Groups page.
ROOMS: 80 en suite s £45.95-£46.95; d £45.95-£46.95

STIRLING, Stirling Map 21 NS79

★★★★66% Stirling Highland
Spittal St FK8 1DU
☎ 01786 272727 01786 272829
e-mail: stirling@paramount-hotels.co.uk
web: www.paramount-hotels.co.uk
Dir: *take A84 into Stirling and follow signs for Stirling Castle as far as Albert Hall. Turn left and left again, following signs to Castle*
Enjoying a location close to the castle and historic old town, this atmospheric hotel was previously the High School. Public rooms have been converted from the original classrooms and retain many interesting features. Bedrooms are more modern in style and comfortably equipped.
ROOMS: 96 en suite (4 fmly) in 67 bedrooms **FACILITIES:** STV Squash Sauna Solarium Gym Jacuzzi Steam room Dance Studio Beauty therapist **CONF:** Thtr 100 Class 80 Board 45 Del from £155 **SERVICES:** Lift **PARKING:** 96 **NOTES:** in restaurant Civ Wed
CARDS:

★★68% ***Terraces***
4 Melville Ter FK8 2ND
☎ 01786 472268 📠 01786 450314
e-mail: sales@terraceshotel.com
Dir: *A872 1st left at 2nd rdbt, at lights onto Melville Terrace (inside lane) parallel to main road on left. Hotel at bottom*
Popular with both business and leisure guests, this hotel has an excellent location close to the town centre and its attractions. The comfortable bedrooms are modern in style and thoughtfully equipped. Public areas include a bar, a steakhouse style restaurant and a newly refurbished function suite.
ROOMS: 17 en suite (3 fmly) ⊘ in 2 bedrooms **FACILITIES:** STV **CONF:** Thtr 100 Class 35 Board 38 **PARKING:** 23 **NOTES:** ⊘ in restaurant **CARDS:**

Travel Inn
Whins of Milton, Glasgow Rd FK7 8EX
☎ 08701 977241 📠 01786 816415
Dir: *on A872, 0.25m from M9/M80 junct 9 intersection*
Travel Inn offers good-quality, value-for-money accommodation. Spacious, en suite rooms with bath and shower comfortably accommodate a family of up to two adults and two children (to age 15). The restaurant and bar offers a varied menu. For further details consult the Hotel Groups page.
ROOMS: 60 en suite s £45.95-£46.95; d £45.95-£46.95

Travelodge
Pirnhall Roundabout, Snabhead FK7 8EU
☎ 08700 850 950 📠 01786 817646
Dir: *junct M9/M80*
Travelodge offers good quality, good value, modern accommodation. Ideal for families, the spacious, en suite bedrooms include remote-control TV, tea and coffee-making facilities and luxury beds. Meals can be taken at the nearby family restaurant. For further details consult the Hotel Groups page.
ROOMS: 37 en suite s fr £25; d fr £25

STONEHAVEN, Aberdeenshire — Map 23 NO88

★★66% **County Hotel & Squash Club**
Arduthie Rd AB39 2EH
☎ 01569 764386 📠 01569 762214
Dir: *off A90, opposite railway station*
This small hotel is family-owned and operated. It is situated close to the railway station. Generally spacious bedrooms are traditionally decorated. It is popular for its good-value meals featuring a wide-ranging selection, served in a choice of dining rooms. The breakfast room displays a fascinating collection of photographs and posters of a theatrical nature.
ROOMS: 14 en suite (1 fmly) s £40-£46; d £50-£60 (incl. bkfst) **LB** **FACILITIES:** Squash Sauna Gym Table tennis **CONF:** Thtr 150 Class 60 Board 32 **PARKING:** 40 **NOTES:** **CARDS:**

STRACHUR, Argyll & Bute — Map 20 NN00

★★★67% **Creggans Inn**
PA27 8BX
☎ 01369 860279 📠 01369 860637
e-mail: info@creggans-inn.co.uk
web: www.creggans-inn.co.uk
Dir: *follow A82/A83 Loch Lomond road to Arrochar. Continue on A83 then take A815 Strachur*
Benefiting from a super location on the shores of Loch Fyne, this well-established hotel is well placed for both tourists and business travellers. Many of the bedrooms have fine views and a number have high quality bathrooms. There is a choice of spacious lounges and freshly prepared meals can be enjoyed in either the popular bar or stylish restaurant.
ROOMS: 14 en suite s £60-£100; d £100-£160 (incl. bkfst) **LB** **FACILITIES:** Fishing ch fac **CONF:** Thtr 25 Class 25 Board 25 Del from £95 **PARKING:** 50 **NOTES:** ⊘ in restaurant **CARDS:**

STRANRAER, Dumfries & Galloway — Map 20 NX06

See also Castle Kennedy

★★★★68% **North West Castle**
DG9 8EH
☎ 01776 704413 📠 01776 702646
e-mail: info@northwestcastle.co.uk
web: www.northwestcastle.co.uk
Dir: *on seafront, close to Stena ferry terminal*

This is long-established hotel, overlooks the bay and the ferry terminal which will eventually be relocated to Cairn Ryan. The public areas include a classical dining room where a pianist plays during dinner and an adjoining lounge with large leather armchairs and blazing fire in season. There is a shop, leisure centre, and a curling rink which is the focus in winter. Bedrooms are comfortable and spacious.
ROOMS: 70 en suite 2 annexe en suite (22 fmly) ⊘ in 26 bedrooms s £78-£88; d £92-£102 (incl. bkfst & dinner) **LB** **FACILITIES:** STV supervised Snooker Sauna Solarium Gym Jacuzzi Curling (Oct-Apr) Games room ch fac Xmas **CONF:** Thtr 150 Class 60 Board 40 Del from £65 **SERVICES:** Lift **PARKING:** 100 **NOTES:** ⊘ in restaurant Civ Wed 130 **CARDS:**

★★★69% **Corsewall Lighthouse Hotel**
Corsewall Point, Kirkcolm DG9 0QG
☎ 01776 853220 📠 01776 854231
e-mail: lighthousehotel@btinternet.com
web: www.lighthousehotel.co.uk
Dir: *A718 from Stranraer to Kirkcolm (approx 8m) then follow signs to hotel for a further 4m*

Looking for something completely different? A unique hotel

continued on p772

STRANRAER, Dumfries & Galloway Map 20 NX06

converted from buildings that adjoin a listed 19th-century lighthouse set on a rocky coastline. Bedrooms come in a variety of sizes, some reached by a spiral staircase, and as with the public areas, are cosy and atmospheric. Three cottage suites in the grounds offer greater space.
ROOMS: 6 en suite 3 annexe en suite (2 fmly) (5 GF) ⊗ in 6 bedrooms s £110-£260; d £130-£280 (incl. bkfst & dinner) LB **CONF:** Thtr 20 **PARKING:** 20 **NOTES:** ⊗ in restaurant Civ Wed 28 **CARDS:**

STRATHAVEN, South Lanarkshire Map 20 NS74

★★★74% Strathaven

Hamilton Rd ML10 6SZ
☎ 01357 521778 01357 520789
e-mail: info@strathavenhotel.com
web: www.strathavenhotel.com

Best Western

This imposing mansion house on the edge of town has been extended with a wing of modern, stylish bedrooms, which are all well equipped. Public areas include a comfortable lounge, Lauders restaurant and a popular bar that serves a range of freshly prepared meals.
ROOMS: 22 en suite ⊗ in 12 bedrooms s £56-£72; d £80-£90 (incl. bkfst) LB **FACILITIES:** STV **CONF:** Thtr 180 Class 120 Board 40 Del from £80 **PARKING:** 80 **NOTES:** ⊗ in restaurant Civ Wed 120 **CARDS:**

STRATHDON, Aberdeenshire Map 23 NJ31

A The Colquhonnie

AB36 8UN
☎ 01975 651210 019756 51398
e-mail: mail@colquhonnie.co.uk
Dir: *on A944 Alford to Tomintoul Rd, 1 mile east of Bellabeg shop and post office*
ROOMS: 9 en suite (1 fmly) ⊗ in 8 bedrooms s £40; d £65-£70 (incl. bkfst) LB **FACILITIES:** Fishing Xmas **CONF:** Class 60 Board 20 **PARKING:** 12 **NOTES:** ★★ ⊗ in restaurant Closed 25-26 Dec **CARDS:**

STRATHYRE, Stirling Map 20 NN51

Top 200 – Hotel

★ Creagan House

FK18 8ND
☎ 01877 384638 01877 384319
e-mail: eatandstay@creaganhouse.co.uk
Dir: *0.25m N of Strathyre on A84*
This delightful property dates back to the 17th century and *continued* has been sympathetically restored and upgraded to provide comfortable accommodation. Attractive bedrooms are thoughtfully equipped with CD players, mineral water and bathrobes, and TVs and videos are available on request. The baronial-style dining room provides a wonderful backdrop for imaginative cooking. Warm hospitality and attentive service are the highlight of any stay.
ROOMS: 5 en suite (1 fmly) (1 GF) ⊗ in all bedrooms s £60; d £100 (incl. bkfst) LB **FACILITIES:** Xmas **CONF:** Thtr 35 Class 12 Board 35 **PARKING:** 26 **NOTES:** ⊗ in restaurant Closed 23 Jan-5 Mar, 6-25 Nov RS Thurs **CARDS:**

STRONTIAN, Highland Map 22 NM86

Top 200 – Hotel

★★ Kilcamb Lodge

PH36 4HY
☎ 01967 402257 01967 402041
e-mail: enquiries@kilcamblodge.co.uk
Dir: *off A861, via Corran Ferry*
This historic house on the shores of Loch Sunart was one of the first stone buildings in the area and was used as military barracks around the time of the Jacobite uprising. Accommodation is provided in tastefully decorated rooms with high quality fabrics. Accomplished cooking, utilising much local produce, can be enjoyed in the stylish dining room. Warm hospitality is assured.
ROOMS: 11 en suite ⊗ in all bedrooms s £75; d £110-£170 (incl. bkfst) LB **FACILITIES:** Fishing Boating Xmas **CONF:** BC **PARKING:** 18 **NOTES:** No children 12yrs ⊗ in restaurant Closed 2 Jan-11 Feb Civ Wed 60 **CARDS:**

Packed in a hurry?
Ironing facilities should be available at all star levels, either in rooms or on request

SWINTON, Scottish Borders Map 21 NT84

Restaurant with Rooms

The Wheatsheaf

Main St TD11 3JJ
☎ 01890 860257 01890 860688
e-mail: reception@wheatsheaf-swinton.co.uk
Dir: *from Edinburgh turn off A697 onto B6461. From East Lothian, turn off A1 onto B6461*
Overlooking the village green, The Wheatsheaf has a country pub atmosphere. It's the food that is the main focus however, served in a bright pine-furnished sun lounge, and when times are busy also

continued

S

in the cosy traditional dining room. Bedrooms offer a mix of sizes, but all are well equipped, the larger ones having luxury bathrooms.

ROOMS: 7 en suite ⊗ in all bedrooms s £62-£90; d £95-£120 (incl. bkfst) **LB** **FACILITIES:** Xmas **CONF:** BC Thtr 18 Class 18 Board 12 **PARKING:** 7 **NOTES:** ⊗ in restaurant Closed 24-26 Dec RS 1 Dec-31 Jan **CARDS:**

TAIN, Highland Map 23 NH88

★★★74% Morangie House

Morangie Rd IV19 1PY
☎ 01862 892281 01862 892872
e-mail: wynne@morangiehotel.com
web: www.morangiehotel.com
Dir: *turn right off A9 northwards*

This welcoming family-run hotel has fine views of the Dornoch Firth. Spacious bedrooms in the newer wing are comfortable and modern, and those in the main house are more traditional; all are well equipped with useful accessories. A wide range of dishes is available in the smart Garden Restaurant.
ROOMS: 26 en suite (1 fmly) (6 GF) ⊗ in 6 bedrooms s £65-£75; d £100-£130 (incl. bkfst) **LB** **FACILITIES:** STV **CONF:** Thtr 40 Class 40 Board 24 Del from £75 **PARKING:** 40 **NOTES:** Civ Wed 40 **CARDS:**

★★★67% Mansfield House

Scotsburn Rd IV19 1PR
☎ 01862 892052 01862 892260
e-mail: info@mansfieldhouse.eu.com
web: www.mansfieldhouse.eu.com
Dir: *A9 from S, ignore 1st exit signed Tain and take the 2nd exit signed police station*
Built in the 1870s, this impressive baronial-style mansion is set in pretty, landscaped grounds. The comfortably equipped bedrooms come in two distinct styles with those in the original part of the house full of character. Meals are served in both the bar and one of two stylish dining rooms.
ROOMS: 9 en suite 10 annexe en suite (3 fmly) (6 GF) ⊗ in all bedrooms s £70-£100; d £120-£180 (incl. bkfst) **LB** **FACILITIES:** STV Jacuzzi Beauty salon Xmas **CONF:** Thtr 40 Board 40 Del from £85 **PARKING:** 40 **NOTES:** ⊗ in restaurant **CARDS:**

Top 200 – Hotel

★★ Glenmorangie Highland Home at Cadboll

Cadboll, Fearn IV20 1XP
☎ 01862 871671 01862 871625
e-mail: relax@glenmorangieplc.co.uk
Dir: *from A9 turn onto B9175 towards Nigg and follow tourist signs*
A warm welcome is assured at this historic house that has been converted into a very individual hotel by the famous whisky distillers. Stylish accommodation is provided in both the main house and a row of converted cottages. A relaxed atmosphere prevails with dinner taken house-party style in the impressive dining room. Enjoy a walk on the nearby beach before tucking in to a hearty breakfast.
ROOMS: 6 en suite 3 annexe en suite (4 fmly) (3 GF) ⊗ in all bedrooms s £140-£185; d £280-£370 (incl. bkfst & dinner) **LB** **FACILITIES:** STV Fishing Putt green Falconry, Clay pigeon shooting, Beauty treatments, Husky Sledding, Archery ♫ Xmas **CONF:** Thtr 12 Class 12 Board 12 Del from £150 **PARKING:** 20 **NOTES:** No children 14yrs ⊗ in restaurant Closed 3-31 Jan RS Feb&Mar Civ Wed 24 **CARDS:**

TANGASDALE See Barra, Isle of

TARBERT LOCH FYNE, Argyll & Bute Map 20 NN30

★★★71% *Stonefield Castle*

PA29 6YJ
☎ 01880 820836
e-mail: enquiries@stonefieldcastle.co.uk
Dir: *off A83, 2m N of Tarbert, hotel approx 0.25m down driveway*
This fine baronial castle commands a superb lochside setting amidst beautiful woodland gardens renowned for their rhododendrons - visit in late spring to see them at their best. Elegant public rooms are a feature, and the picture-windowed restaurant offers unrivalled views across Loch Fyne. Bedrooms are split between the main house and a purpose-built wing.
ROOMS: 33 rms **FACILITIES:** Fishing Snooker **CONF:** Thtr 150 Class 100 Board 60 **NOTES:** ⊗ in restaurant

TARBERT LOCH FYNE, continued

★★69% *The Columba Hotel*

East Pier Rd PA29 6UF
☎ 01880 820808 🖷 01880 820808
e-mail: info@columbahotel.com
Dir: *off A82 into village, hotel 0.25m on right*

Overlooking the approach to the busy harbour, this Victorian hotel is a short walk from the village centre. Accommodation, including upgraded rooms, is generally spacious and offers appropriate levels of comfort. Meals can be taken in either the atmospheric bar or the restaurant with its fine views.

ROOMS: 10 en suite (2 fmly) **CONF:** Thtr 30 Class 30 Board 18
PARKING: 11 **NOTES:** ⊘ in restaurant **CARDS:**

TAYNUILT, Argyll & Bute — Map 20 NN03

★★60% *Polfearn*

PA35 1JQ
☎ 01866 822251 🖷 01866 822251
Dir: *turn N off A85, continue 1.5m through village down to Loch Shore*

A relaxed and friendly atmosphere prevails at this homely family-run hotel which overlooks Loch Etive. Public areas include a well-stocked bar with open fire and separate dining room. A good range of home-cooked food is available in both areas. Bedrooms vary in size and in style.

ROOMS: 14 en suite (2 fmly) **FACILITIES:** Fishing, Boating, Walking
PARKING: 21 **NOTES:** ⊘ in restaurant Closed 26 Dec RS Nov-Apr
CARDS:

THORNHILL, Dumfries & Galloway — Map 21 NX89

★★74% *Trigony House*

Closeburn DG3 5EZ
☎ 01848 331211 🖷 01848 331303
e-mail: info@trigonyhotel.co.uk
web: www.trigonyhotel.co.uk
Dir: *off A76 between Thornhill & Closeburn on left, clearly signed*

A friendly and relaxed atmosphere prevails at this family-run, Edwardian hunting lodge, set in four acres of gardens and grounds south of the village. Bedrooms come in a variety of sizes and some are quite spacious. Food, which can be enjoyed either in the cosy bar or formal dining room, is refreshingly simple and honest and features fresh produce, organically grown whenever available.

ROOMS: 8 en suite **FACILITIES:** Fishing Bicycle loan free of charge **CONF:** Thtr 30 Class 30 Board 30 **PARKING:** 20 **NOTES:** ⊘ in restaurant **CARDS:**

> Early start?
> Hotels at all star levels should provide in-room alarm clocks and/or alarm calls

---

THURSO, Highland — Map 23 ND16
See also Halkirk

★★★60% Royal

Traill St KW14 8EH
☎ 01847 893191 🖷 01847 895338
e-mail: royal@british-trust-hotels.com
web: www.british-trust-hotels.com
Dir: *A9 to Thurso, cross Thurso Bridge and at 1st set of traffic lights turn right. Hotel on right*

BRITISH TRUST HOTELS

Located in the heart of the town centre this traditional hotel attracts a mixed market, being popular with both business guests and tour groups. Spacious public areas include a large bar and comfortable lounges where entertainment is a feature. High ceilinged bedrooms are generally well proportioned.

ROOMS: 102 en suite (4 fmly) s £39-£49; d £78-£88 (incl. bkfst) **LB**
FACILITIES: ♫ **SERVICES:** Lift **NOTES:** ⊘ in restaurant
CARDS:

★★62% *Ulbster Arms*

Bridge St KW12 6XY
☎ 01847 831206 & 831641 🖷 01847 831206
e-mail: ulbster-arms@ecosse.net
(For full entry see Halkirk)

A Station House & Apartments

54-58 Princes St KW14 7DH
☎ 01847 892003 🖷 01847 891820
e-mail: stationhotel@lineone.net web: www.stationthurso.co.uk
Dir: *from A9, in Thurso at 2nd set of lights turn left. Hotel at end of Sinclair St, next to library. 2m from ferry terminal for Orkney*

ROOMS: 21 en suite 9 annexe en suite (8 fmly) (8 GF) ⊘ in 5 bedrooms s £38-£58; d £60-£80 (incl. bkfst) **LB** **FACILITIES:** STV ch fac Xmas
PARKING: 35 **NOTES:** ★★★ ⊘ in restaurant
CARDS: *See advert on opposite page*

TIGHNABRUAICH, Argyll & Bute — Map 20 NR97

★★79% The Royal at Tighnabruaich

Shore Rd PA21 2BE
☎ 01700 811239 🖷 01700 811300
e-mail: info@royalhotel.org.uk
web: www.royalhotel.org.uk
Dir: *from Strachur on A886 turn right onto A8003 to Tighnabruaich. Hotel on right at bottom of hill, at T-junct*

This outstanding family-run hotel continues to go from strength to strength. Set just yards from the loch shore, stunning views are guaranteed from many rooms, including the elegant restaurant and informal brasserie bar where fresh seafood and game are served. The comfortable bedrooms vary in size and style.

ROOMS: 11 en suite (2 fmly) ⊘ in all bedrooms d £70-£150 (incl. bkfst) **LB** **FACILITIES:** sailing, fishing, windsurfing, riding, walking, bird watching **CONF:** Class 20 Board 10 **PARKING:** 20 **NOTES:** ⊘ in restaurant Closed 25-26 Dec **CARDS:**

TOBERMORY See Mull, Isle of

TONGUE, Highland Map 23 NC55

★★71% Ben Loyal
Main St IV27 4XE
☎ 01847 611216 01847 611336
e-mail: benloyalhotel@btinternet.com
web: www.benloyal.co.uk
Dir: *at junct of A838/A836, hotel in centre of village, next to Royal Bank of Scotland*

Enjoying a super location close to Ben Loyal and with views of the Kyle of Tongue, a welcoming atmosphere is the hallmark of this family-run hotel. Bedrooms are thoughtfully equipped and brightly decorated. Five-course dinners are available in the restaurant and a wide-ranging menu is provided in the bar.

ROOMS: 11 en suite in all bedrooms s £32; d £50-£64 (incl. bkfst) LB **FACILITIES:** Fishing Fly fishing tuition and equipment **PARKING:** 20 **NOTES:** in restaurant RS Nov-Mar **CARDS:**

U Borgie Lodge Hotel
Skerray KW14 7TH
☎ 01641 521332 01641 521332
e-mail: info@borgielodgehotel.co.uk
web: www.borgielodgehotel.co.uk

At the time of going to press, the star classification for this hotel was not confirmed. Please refer to the AA internet site www.theAA.com for current information.

ROOMS: 8 rms (7 en suite) (1 GF) in all bedrooms **FACILITIES:** Fishing Mountain bikes, Shooting, Stalking, Boating ch fac **PARKING:** 20 **NOTES:** in restaurant Closed Nov - Feb **CARDS:**

TORRIDON, Highland Map 22 NG95

Top 200 – Hotel

★★★
Loch Torridon Country House Hotel
By Achnasheen, Wester Ross IV22 2EY
☎ 01445 791242 01445 791296
e-mail: stay@lochtorridonhotel.com
web: www.lochtorridonhotel.com
Dir: *from A832 at Kinlochewe, take A896 towards Torridon, do not turn into village but continue 1m, hotel on right*

Delightfully set amidst inspiring loch and mountain scenery, this elegant Victorian shooting lodge has been beautifully restored to make the most of its many original features. The attractive bedrooms are all individually furnished and most enjoy stunning Highland views. Comfortable day rooms feature fine wood panelling and roaring fires in cooler

continued

months. The whisky bar is aptly named, boasting over 300 malts and in-depth tasting notes. Outdoor activities include shooting, cycling and walking.

Loch Torridon Country House Hotel

ROOMS: 19 en suite (2 GF) in all bedrooms s £64-£110; d £101-£331 (incl. bkfst) LB **FACILITIES:** STV Fishing Pony trekking, Mountain biking, Archery, Clay pigeon shooting, Falconry ch fac Xmas **CONF:** Board 16 Del from £142 **SERVICES:** Lift **PARKING:** 20 **NOTES:** in restaurant Closed 3-27 Jan **CARDS:**

Late for dinner?
Quality Standards mean that last orders for dinner vary according to star rating and should be no earlier than:
★★ 7.00pm ★★★ 8.00pm ★★★★ 9.00pm
★★★★★ 10.00pm

TROON, South Ayrshire Map 20 NS33

★★★★64% Marine
Crosbie Rd KA10 6HE
☎ 01292 314444 01292 316922
e-mail: marine@paramount-hotels.co.uk
web: www.paramount-hotels.co.uk/marine
Dir: *from A77 to A78, then A79 onto B749. Hotel on left beyond Golf Course*

PARAMOUNT GROUP OF HOTELS

A favourite with conference and leisure guests, this hotel overlooks Royal Troon's 18th fairway. The cocktail lounge and split-level restaurant enjoy panoramic views of the Firth of Clyde across to the Isle of Arran. Bedrooms have undergone an impressive upgrade.
ROOMS: 90 en suite (6 fmly) in 58 bedrooms s £125-£136; d £190-£206 (incl. bkfst) **LB** **FACILITIES:** STV supervised Squash Sauna Solarium Gym Jacuzzi Steam room, Beauty room Xmas **CONF:** BC Thtr 220 Class 120 Board 60 Del from £180 **SERVICES:** Lift **PARKING:** 200 **NOTES:** in restaurant
CARDS:

Top 200 – Hotel

★★★ Lochgreen House
Monktonhill Rd, Southwood KA10 7EN
☎ 01292 313343 01292 318661
e-mail: lochgreen@costley-hotels.co.uk
web: www.lochgreenhouse.co.uk
Dir: *from A77 follow signs for Prestwick airport, 0.5m before airport take B749 to Troon. Hotel 1m on left*

Set in immaculately maintained grounds, Lochgreen House is graced by tasteful extensions which have created stunning public rooms and spacious, comfortable and elegantly furnished bedrooms. The main lounge boasts a gift boutique, whilst the modern brasserie is where lunch and breakfast are served. The magnificent Tapestry Restaurant provides the ideal setting for dinners that are immaculately presented.
ROOMS: 32 en suite 8 annexe en suite (18 GF) **FACILITIES:** Xmas **CONF:** BC Thtr 100 Class 50 Board 50 **SERVICES:** Lift **PARKING:** 50 **NOTES:** in restaurant Civ Wed
CARDS:

★★★74% Piersland House
Craigend Rd KA10 6HD
☎ 01292 314747 01292 315613
e-mail: reservations@piersland.co.uk
web: www.piersland.co.uk
Dir: *just off A77 on B749 opposite Royal Troon Golf Club*

A Grade I listed building, this well presented hotel is located opposite to the famous championship golf course. Public areas retain delightful oak panelling. Bedrooms are thoughtfully equipped and include a row of 15 'cottages' each with a lounge and its own entrance, ideal for golfers. The hotel is popular both for its bar and for the good food in the restaurant.
ROOMS: 15 en suite 15 annexe en suite (15 fmly) (15 GF) s £82.50; d £124-£170 (incl. bkfst) **LB** **FACILITIES:** STV Xmas **CONF:** Thtr 100 Class 60 Board 30 Del £105 **PARKING:** 150 **NOTES:** in restaurant Civ Wed 85 **CARDS:**

See advert on opposite page

TURNBERRY, South Ayrshire Map 20 NS20

Top 200 – Hotel

★★★★★ Westin Turnberry Resort
KA26 9LT
☎ 01655 331000 01655 331706
e-mail: turnberry@westin.com
Dir: *from Glasgow take A77/M77 S towards Stranraer, 2m past Kirkoswald, follow signs for A719 Turnberry, hotel 500mtrs on right*

WESTIN HOTELS & RESORTS

This famous hotel enjoys magnificent views to Arran, Ailsa Craig and the Mull of Kintyre. Facilities include a world-renowned golf course, the excellent Colin Montgomerie Golf Academy, a luxurious spa and a host of outdoor and country pursuits. Elegant bedrooms and suites are located in the main hotel, while adjacent lodges provide spacious, well-equipped accommodation. The Ailsa lounge is a very welcoming area since its refurbishment. As well as the elegant main restaurant for dining, there is a Mediterranean Terrace Brasserie, or the relaxed Clubhouse.
ROOMS: 132 en suite 89 annexe en suite (9 fmly) in 28 bedrooms s £115-£735; d £149-£790 (incl. bkfst) **LB** **FACILITIES: Spa** STV supervised 36 Fishing Riding Snooker Sauna Gym Putt green Jacuzzi Health Spa & Leisure Club,Outdoor activity centre,Colin Montgomerie Golf Academy Xmas **CONF:** BC Thtr 275 Class 145 Board 100 **SERVICES:** Lift **PARKING:** 200 **NOTES:** in restaurant Closed 12 - 27Dec
CARDS:

★★★76% Malin Court
KA26 9PB
☎ 01655 331457 01655 331072
e-mail: info@malincourt.co.uk
web: www.malincourt.co.uk
Dir: *A74 take Ayr exit. From Ayr take A719 to Turnberry & Maidens*

Forming part of the Malin Court Residential and Nursing Home Complex, this friendly and comfortable hotel enjoys delightful views over the Firth of Clyde and Turnberry golf courses. Standard and

continued

executive rooms are available; all are well-equipped. Public areas are plentiful, with the restaurant serving dinners and light lunches.

ROOMS: 18 en suite (9 fmly) ⊗ in 9 bedrooms s £72-£82; d £104-£124 (incl. bkfst) **LB** **FACILITIES:** STV Putt green Pitch & putt Xmas **CONF:** Thtr 200 Class 60 Board 30 Del from £65.50 **SERVICES:** Lift **PARKING:** 110 **NOTES:** ⊗ in restaurant RS Oct - Mar Civ Wed 120 **CARDS:**

See advert on this page

UNST See Shetland

UPHALL, West Lothian Map 21 NT07

★★★★68% ***Houstoun House***

MACDONALD HOTELS

EH52 6JS
☎ 01506 853831 01506 854220
e-mail: houstoun@macdonald-hotels.co.uk

Dir: *M8 junct 3 follow signs for Broxburn, straight over rdbt then at mini-rdbt turn right towards Uphall, hotel is 1m on right*

This historic 17th-century tower house lies in beautifully landscaped grounds and gardens and features a leisure club and Spa, a choice of dining options, a vaulted cocktail bar and extensive conference and meeting facilities. Stylish bedrooms, some located around a courtyard, are comfortably furnished and well equipped.

ROOMS: 24 en suite 47 annexe en suite (30 fmly) ⊗ in 63 bedrooms **FACILITIES:** STV Sauna Solarium Gym Steam room, Dance studio, Beauty therapy room **CONF:** Thtr 350 Class 120 Board 70 **PARKING:** 200 **NOTES:** ⊗ in restaurant Civ Wed 80 **CARDS:**

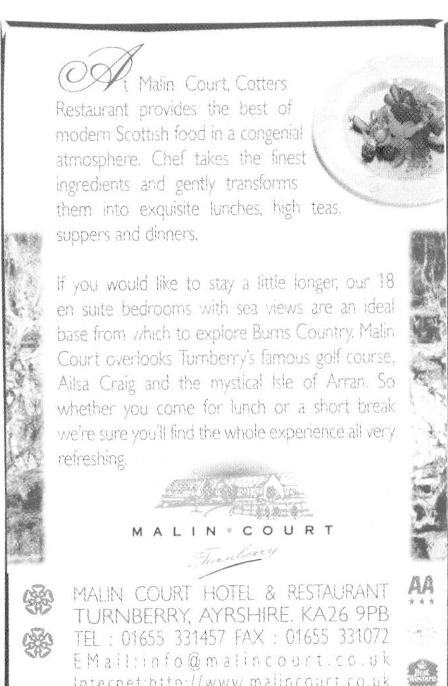

U

UPLAWMOOR, East Renfrewshire Map 20 NS45

★★76% Uplawmoor Hotel
Neilston Rd G78 4AF
☎ 01505 850565 📠 01505 850689
e-mail: enquiries@uplawmoor.co.uk
web: www.uplawmoor.co.uk
Dir: *M77 junct 2, take A736 signed to Barrhead and Irvine. Hotel 4m beyond Barrhead*

Originally a coaching inn, this friendly hotel is set in a village off the Glasgow to Irvine road. The comfortable restaurant (with cocktail lounge adjacent) features imaginative dishes, whilst the separate lounge bar is popular for freshly prepared bar meals. The modern bedrooms are both comfortable and well equipped.
ROOMS: 14 en suite (1 fmly) ⊗ in 8 bedrooms **FACILITIES:** STV **CONF:** BC Thtr 40 Class 12 Board 12 Del from £65 **PARKING:** 40 **NOTES:** ⊗ in restaurant **CARDS:**

See advert under GLASGOW

WHITBURN, West Lothian Map 21 NS96

★★★68% The Hilcroft
East Main St EH47 0JU
☎ 01501 740818 📠 01501 744013
e-mail: hilcroft@bestwestern.co.uk
Dir: *M8 junct 4 follow signs for Whitburn, hotel 0.5m on left from junct*

This modern hotel features a split-level bar and restaurant offering an extensive menu throughout the day. The attractive bedrooms are well equipped, and the executive rooms are particularly spacious.
ROOMS: 32 en suite (7 fmly) (5 GF) ⊗ in 17 bedrooms s £55-£75; d £55-£90 (incl. bkfst) **LB FACILITIES:** STV Free use of Balbardie Sports Centre Xmas **CONF:** Thtr 200 Class 50 Board 30 Del from £80 **PARKING:** 80 **NOTES:** ⊗ in restaurant Civ Wed 180 **CARDS:**

WHITEBRIDGE, Highland Map 23 NH41

★★66% Whitebridge
IV2 6UN
☎ 01456 486226 & 486272 📠 01456 486413
e-mail: info@whitebridgehotel.co.uk
web: www.whitebridgehotel.co.uk
Dir: *off A9 onto B851, follow signs to Fort Augustus. Off A82 onto B862 at Fort Augustus.*

Close to Loch Ness and set amid rugged mountain and moorland scenery this hotel is popular with tourists, fishermen and deer stalkers. The cosy bar is the hub of the village and the ideal place to enjoy a chat with local people. Bedrooms are appropriately equipped and simply furnished.
ROOMS: 12 rms (11 en suite) (3 fmly) s £35-£38; d £50-£58 (incl. bkfst) **LB FACILITIES:** Fishing **CONF:** Class 30 Board 25 **PARKING:** 32 **NOTES:** ⊗ in restaurant Closed 21 Dec-Feb **CARDS:**

WICK, Highland Map 23 ND35

★★69% *Mackay's*
Union St KW1 5ED
☎ 01955 602323 📠 01955 605930
e-mail: res@mackayshotel.co.uk
Dir: *opposite Caithness General Hospital*

This well-established hotel is situated just off the town centre and overlooks the River Wick. Mackay's provides first-class accommodation especially suited to the business traveller. There is an attractive restaurant and a choice of bars that also offer food.
ROOMS: 27 rms (19 en suite) (4 fmly) **FACILITIES:** STV ♫ **CONF:** Thtr 100 Class 100 Board 60 **SERVICES:** Lift **NOTES:** ⊗ in restaurant Closed 1-2 Jan **CARDS:**

Nominations for
AA Hotel of the Year Award for Wales
2004-2005

★★★★ ⊛ ⌂

Osborne House

Llandudno, Conwy

★★★ ⊛⊛

Seiont Manor Hotel

Caernarfon, Gwynedd

★★★ 71% ⊛⊛

Castle Hotel Conwy

Conwy, Conwy

A

ABERDYFI, Gwynedd Map 14 SN69

★★★74% Trefeddian

LL35 0SB
☎ 01654 767213 01654 767777
e-mail: info@trefwales.com
web: www.trefwales.com
Dir: *0.5m N of Aberdyfi off A493*

This privately-owned hotel overlooks Cardigan Bay and is surrounded by grounds and gardens. It provides sound modern accommodation with well-equipped bedrooms and bathrooms, plus some luxury rooms with balconies and sea views. Public areas include elegantly furnished lounges, a beauty salon and indoor pool. Children are welcome and recreation areas are provided. The hotel has been owned and run by the Cave family for 100 years.

ROOMS: 59 en suite (13 fmly) in all bedrooms s £73-£93; d £146-£186 (incl. bkfst & dinner) **LB** **FACILITIES:** Snooker Solarium Putt green Table tennis, Play area, Beauty salon ch fac Xmas **CONF:** Class 25 **SERVICES:** Lift **PARKING:** 68 **NOTES:** in restaurant **CARDS:**

See advert on opposite page

★★74% Penhelig Arms Hotel & Restaurant

LL35 0LT
☎ 01654 767215 01654 767690
e-mail: info@penheligarms.com
web: www.penheligarms.com
Dir: *take A493 coastal road, hotel faces Penhelig harbour*

Situated opposite the old harbour, this delightful 18th-century hotel overlooks the Dyfi estuary. The well-maintained bedrooms have good quality furnishings and modern facilities. The public bar retains its original character and is much loved by locals who enjoy the real ale selections and the food with its emphasis on seafood. AA Seafish Pub of the Year for Wales 2004-5.

ROOMS: 10 en suite 5 annexe en suite (4 fmly) in all bedrooms s fr £45; d £78-£98 (incl. bkfst) **LB** **FACILITIES:** ch fac **PARKING:** 14 **NOTES:** in restaurant Closed 25 & 26 Dec **CARDS:**

★★66% *Dovey Inn*

Seaview Ter LL35 0EF
☎ 01654 767332 01654 767996
e-mail: info@doveyinn.com
web: www.doveyinn.com
Dir: *In village centre on A493, on R. Dovey, 9m from Machynlleth*

In the heart of Aberdyfi, this inn offers attractive refurbished rooms which are comfortable and very well equipped; most have sea views. Downstairs there are four bars where a wide range of dishes, featuring local produce, is available. Breakfast is served in a separate upstairs dining room.

ROOMS: 8 en suite (2 fmly) in all bedrooms **FACILITIES:** STV Guest may use facilities at Plas Talgarth Country Club **NOTES:** in restaurant **CARDS:**

ABERGAVENNY, Monmouthshire Map 09 SO21

★★★70% Llansantffraed Court

Llanvihangel Gobion NP7 9BA
☎ 01873 840678 01873 840674
e-mail: reception@llch.co.uk
web: www.llch.co.uk
Dir: *at A465/A40 Abergavenny junct take B4598 signed to Usk (do not join A40). Continue towards Raglan and hotel on left after 4.5m*

In a commanding position and in its own grounds this red brick country hotel has enviable views of the Brecon Beacons. Extensive public areas are complemented by a spacious restaurant, where imaginative and enjoyable dishes are served. Bedrooms are comfortably furnished and have modern facilities.

ROOMS: 21 en suite (3 fmly) in 7 bedrooms s £86-£110; d £110-£160 (incl. bkfst) **LB** **FACILITIES:** STV Fishing Putt green Ornamental trout lake, Salmon fishing on River Usk ch fac **CONF:** BC Thtr 220 Class 120 Board 100 Del from £150 **SERVICES:** Lift **PARKING:** 250 **NOTES:** in restaurant Civ Wed 150 **CARDS:**

★★★68% *Allt-yr-Ynys Country House Hotel*

HR2 0DU
☎ 01873 890307 01873 890539
e-mail: allthotel@compuserve.com
Dir: *take A465 N of Abergavenny. After 5m turn left at Old Pandy Inn in Pandy. After 300yds turn right, hotel on right*

Set in rolling countryside, the main house of this charming hotel dates back to 1550 and Elizabeth I is reputed to have stayed here. Most of the comfortable bedrooms are contained in separate, purpose-built buildings, located within the extensive grounds. Homely lounges, a bar with a cider mill, and an adjoining

continued

swimming pool complete the experience, together with the charming restaurant.

ROOMS: 3 en suite 18 annexe en suite (2 fmly) (18 GF) ⊗ in 6 bedrooms **FACILITIES: Spa** Fishing Sauna Clay pigeon range **CONF:** BC Thtr 100 Class 30 Board 40 **PARKING:** 100 **NOTES:** ⊗ in restaurant Civ Wed 80 **CARDS:**

★★★67% Angel

15 Cross St NP7 5EN
☎ 01873 857121 01873 858059
e-mail: mail@angelhotelabergavenny.com
web: www.angelhotelabergavenny.com

Dir: *follow town centre signs from rdbt south of Abergavenny, past railway and bus stations. Turn left by hotel*

The Angel Hotel has long been a popular venue for both local people and visitors to the area. Two traditional function rooms and a ballroom are in regular use. However, those not having called for a while may be surprised to note the changes with a major refurbishment programme now well underway, resulting in a comfortable lounge, relaxed bar and award-winning restaurant.

ROOMS: 29 en suite (1 fmly) ⊗ in 14 bedrooms s fr £60; d fr £85 (incl. bkfst) **FACILITIES:** STV ♫ ch fac Xmas **CONF:** Thtr 200 Class 120 Board 60 Del from £115.40 **PARKING:** 30 **NOTES:** ⊗ in restaurant Closed 25 Dec RS 24-26 Dec Civ Wed 200
CARDS:

★★69% Llanwenarth

Brecon Rd NP8 1EP
☎ 01873 810550 01873 811880
e-mail: mto@llanwenarthhotel.com
web: www.llanwenarthhotel.com

Dir: *take A40 from Abergavenny towards Brecon. Hotel 3m past hospital on left*

Dating from the 16th century and set in magnificent scenery, this delightful hotel, now under new ownership, offers guests the chance to relax and unwind in style. Bedrooms are in a detached wing, with most enjoying views over the river and beyond. Many have private balconies. The airy conservatory lounge and restaurant also have lovely views.

ROOMS: 18 en suite (2 fmly) (6 GF) ⊗ in 16 bedrooms s fr £48; d fr £65 (incl. bkfst) **PARKING:** 30 **NOTES:** ⊗ in restaurant
CARDS:

Indoor Swimming Pool
Indoor Swimming Pool (heated)
Outdoor Swimming Pool
Outdoor Swimming Pool (heated)

A

ABERGELE, Conwy Map 14 SH97

★★★66% Kinmel Manor
St George's Rd LL22 9AS
☎ 01745 832014 01745 832014
e-mail: kinmelmanor@virgin.net
Dir: *exit A55 at junct 24, hotel entrance on rndbt*
Parts of this hotel complex date back to the 16th century and some original features are still in evidence. Set in extensive grounds, it provides well-equipped rooms and extensive leisure facilities.
ROOMS: 51 en suite (3 fmly) in 12 bedrooms s £55-£59.50; d £75-£79.50 (incl. bkfst) **LB** **FACILITIES: Spa** STV Sauna Solarium Gym Steam room ch fac Xmas **CONF:** Thtr 250 Class 100 Board 100 Del from £75 **PARKING:** 120 **NOTES:** Civ Wed 250
CARDS:

ABERPORTH, Ceredigion Map 08 SN25

★★★71% Hotel Penrallt
SA43 2BS
☎ 01239 810227 01239 811375
e-mail: info@hotelpenrallt.co.uk
Dir: *take B4333 signed Aberporth. Hotel 1m on right*
This magnificent Edwardian mansion is peacefully located in extensive grounds and offers spacious accommodation. The well-maintained public areas feature original carved ceiling beams, an impressive staircase and an eye-catching stained glass window. Guests can enjoy the relaxing atmosphere in the comfortable lounge, the popular bar and elegant restaurant. The leisure & fitness centre offers a choice of swimming pools.
ROOMS: 15 en suite (2 fmly) s £65-£75; d £100-£125 (incl. bkfst) **LB** **FACILITIES:** supervised supervised Sauna Gym Putt green Jacuzzi Pool table, Golf Driving net, Table Tennis, Childrens Play Area ch fac Xmas **CONF:** Class 24 Board 20 **PARKING:** 100 **NOTES:** in restaurant **CARDS:**

★★73% Penbontbren Farm
Glynarthen, Llandysul SA44 6PE
☎ 01239 810248 01239 811129
e-mail: welcome@penbontbren.com
Dir: *N on A487, 2nd right after Tan-y-Groes, signed. From south, 1st left after Salnau, signed*
Set in rolling countryside this charming hotel has been sympathetically converted from farm buildings. Bedrooms are furnished in a cottage style, are thoughtfully and extensively equipped and include one that is suitable for use by less able guests. There is an atmospheric restaurant, with an adjoining bar and a comfortable lounge. There is also a very pleasant garden.
ROOMS: 10 annexe en suite (6 GF) s £63; d £96 (incl. bkfst) **LB** **FACILITIES:** Museum of farming ch fac **CONF:** Thtr 25 Class 25 Board 25 **PARKING:** 50 **NOTES:** in restaurant Closed Xmas
CARDS:

★★63% Morlan
SA43 2EN
☎ 01239 810611
e-mail: richardcalebs@aol.com
web: www.morlanhotel.co.uk
Dir: *on B4333 2m off A487 in centre of village*
This former motel is now a small, privately owned and personally run hotel. The accommodation has benefited from refurbishment work and the bedrooms are attractively appointed. Public areas include a bar, which is popular with locals, and a games room.

ROOMS: 6 en suite (1 fmly) in all bedrooms s £35-£45; d £60-£80 (incl. bkfst) **LB** **FACILITIES:** Jacuzzi in all bedrooms **PARKING:** 11 **NOTES:** in restaurant **CARDS:**

ABERSOCH, Gwynedd Map 14 SH32

★★★75% Porth Tocyn
Bwlch Tocyn LL53 7BU
☎ 01758 713303 01758 713538
e-mail: bookings@porthtocyn.fsnet.co.uk
web: www.porth-tocyn-hotel.co.uk
Dir: *2.5m S follow signs 'Porth Tocyn', after passing through hamlet of Sarnbach*

Located above Cardigan Bay with fine views over the area, Porth Tocyn is set in attractive gardens. Several elegantly sitting rooms are provided and bedrooms are comfortably furnished. Children are especially welcome and have a play room. Award-winning food is served in the restaurant.
ROOMS: 17 en suite (1 fmly) (3 GF) in all bedrooms s £60-£79; d £81-£149 (incl. cont bkfst) **LB** **FACILITIES:** **PARKING:** 50 **NOTES:** in restaurant Closed mid Nov-wk before Etr
CARDS:

See advert on opposite page

★★77% Neigwl
Lon Sarn Bach LL53 7DY
☎ 01758 712363 01758 712544
e-mail: relax@neigwl.com web: www.neigwl.com
Dir: *on A499, drive through Abersoch, hotel on left*
This delightful, small, family-run hotel is conveniently located for access to the town, harbour and beach. It has a deservedly excellent reputation for its food and warm hospitality. Both the attractive restaurant and the pleasant lounge bar overlook the sea, as do several of the tastefully appointed bedrooms.
ROOMS: 7 en suite 2 annexe en suite (3 fmly) s £65-£100; d £112-£173 (incl. bkfst & dinner) **LB** **FACILITIES:** ch fac **PARKING:** 30 **NOTES:** Closed January **CARDS:**

A

★★66% **Deucoch**
LL53 7LD
☎ 01758 712680 01758 712670
e-mail: deucoch@supanet.com
web: www.deucochhotel.co.uk
Dir: *through Abersoch village following signs for Sarn Bach. At crossroads in Sarn Bach (approx 1m from village centre) turn right, hotel on top of hill on left*
This hotel sits in an elevated position above the village and enjoys lovely views. There is a choice of bars and food options; the regular carvery is excellent value and has a large following, so booking is essential. Pretty bedrooms are equipped with modern amenities and the hotel specialises in golfing packages.
ROOMS: 10 rms (9 en suite) (2 fmly) s £35-£39; d £70-£78 (incl. bkfst) LB **FACILITIES:** Xmas **PARKING:** 30 **NOTES:** in restaurant
CARDS:

ABERYSTWYTH, Ceredigion Map 08 SN58

★★★75% **Conrah**
Ffosrhydygaled, Chancery SY23 4DF
☎ 01970 617941 01970 624546
e-mail: enquiries@conrah.co.uk
web: www.conrah.co.uk
Dir: *on A487, 3.5m S of Aberystwyth*

This privately owned and personally run country-house hotel stands in 22 acres of mature grounds. The elegant public rooms include a choice of comfortable lounges with welcoming open fires. Bedrooms are located in both the main house and a nearby wing. The cuisine, which is French with modern influences, achieves very high standards. Conference and leisure facilities are available.
ROOMS: 11 en suite 6 annexe en suite (1 fmly) (3 GF) s £78-£88; d £120-£150 (incl. bkfst) LB **FACILITIES:** Sauna Table tennis **CONF:** Thtr 40 Class 20 Board 20 Del from £125 **SERVICES:** Lift **PARKING:** 50 **NOTES:** No children 5yrs in restaurant Closed 22-30 Dec Civ Wed 50 **CARDS:**

★★★66% **Belle Vue Royal**
Marine Ter SY23 2BA
☎ 01970 617558 01970 612190
e-mail: reception@bellevueroyalhotel.co.uk
Dir: *on seafront, 200yds from the pier*
This large hotel dates back more than 170 years and stands on the promenade, a short walk from the shops. Family and sea-view rooms are available and all are well equipped. Public areas include extensive function rooms and a choice of bars, and for

continued

dining there are bar meals or a more formal restaurant with a well deserved reputation for its cuisine.

ROOMS: 37 rms (34 en suite) (6 fmly) (1 GF) in 10 bedrooms s fr £63; d £93-£106 (incl. bkfst) LB **FACILITIES:** STV ch fac Xmas **CONF:** Thtr 100 Class 30 Board 30 Del from £82 **PARKING:** 14 **NOTES:** in restaurant **CARDS:**

★★69% ***Richmond***
44-45 Marine Ter SY23 2BX
☎ 01970 612201 01970 626706
e-mail: reservations@richmondhotel.uk.com
web: www.richmondhotel.uk.com
Dir: *on entering town follow signs for Promenade*
This hotel has good sea views from its day rooms and many of the bedrooms. The public areas and bedrooms are comfortably

continued on p784

ABERYSTWYTH, Ceredigion Map 08 SN58

furnished. An attractive dining room and a comfortable lounge and bar are provided.

Richmond Hotel, Aberystwyth

ROOMS: 15 en suite (6 fmly) **FACILITIES:** STV **CONF:** Thtr 60 Class 22 Board 28 **PARKING:** 24 **NOTES:** ⊗ in restaurant Closed 20 Dec-3 Jan **CARDS:**

★★68% Four Seasons
50-54 Portland St SY23 2DX
☎ 01970 612120 01970 627458
e-mail: reservations@fourseasonshotel.demon.co.uk
web: www.fourseasonshotel.uk.com
Dir: *From railway station, turn left onto Terrace Rd by traffic lights, into North Pde & left onto Queens Rd & 2nd left into Portland St. Hotel on right*
This privately owned hotel is well-maintained and friendly. Bedrooms are well equipped. A cosy lounge is provided, plus a separate bar. A wide choice of food is available.
ROOMS: 16 rms (15 en suite) (2 fmly) ⊗ in 14 bedrooms s £45-£55; d £60-£75 (incl. bkfst) **LB** **FACILITIES:** ch fac **CONF:** Thtr 15 Class 15 Board 12 **PARKING:** 8 **NOTES:** ⊗ in restaurant
CARDS:

★★65% Harry's
40-46 North Pde SY23 2NF
☎ 01970 612647 01970 627068
e-mail: info@harrysaberystwyth.com
Dir: *N on A487, in town centre*
Conveniently located for the shopping area and seafront, this is a friendly and popular hotel. The main attraction is the popular Harry's restaurant with its wide selection of dishes and specialising in local produce. Bedrooms are well equipped with modern facilities.
ROOMS: 24 en suite (2 fmly) ⊗ in 6 bedrooms s fr £45; d fr £70 (incl. bkfst) **LB** **CONF:** Thtr 24 Class 24 Board 40 **PARKING:** 6
NOTES: Closed 25-26 Dec **CARDS:**

★★65% Marine Hotel
The Promenade SY23 2BX
☎ 01970 612444 01970 617435
e-mail: marinehotel1@btconnect.com
web: www.marinehotelaberystwyth.co.uk
Dir: *from W on A44. From N or S Wales on A487. On seafront west of pier*
The Marine is a privately owned hotel situated on the promenade overlooking Cardigan Bay. Bedrooms have been tastefully decorated, some have four-poster beds and many have sea views. The refurbished reception rooms are comfortable and relaxing, and meals are served in the elegant dining room or the bar.
ROOMS: 44 rms (43 en suite) (7 fmly) ⊗ in 1 bedroom s £45-£60; d £60-£95 (incl. bkfst) **LB** **FACILITIES: Spa** Sauna Solarium Gym Jacuzzi ch fac Xmas **CONF:** BC Thtr 220 Class 150 Board 60 Del from £75 **SERVICES:** Lift **PARKING:** 15 **NOTES:** ⊗ in restaurant Civ Wed 200 **CARDS:**

AMLWCH See Anglesey, Isle of

AMMANFORD, Carmarthenshire Map 08 SN61

★★67% *Mill at Glynhir*
Glynhir Rd, Llandybie SA18 2TE
☎ 01269 850672 01269 850672
e-mail: millatglynhir@aol.com
web: www.glynhir.co.uk
Dir: *off A483 at Llandybie signposted Golf Course*
This former flourmill is set peacefully on a hillside with a river at the end of the garden. There is an indoor swimming pool and a golf driving range in the grounds. The bedrooms are all a good size, well-equipped and most have private balconies, whilst public areas consist of a comfortable lounge bar and a cheerful dining room.
ROOMS: 7 en suite 3 annexe en suite **FACILITIES: Spa** 18 Fishing Jacuzzi **PARKING:** 15 **NOTES:** No children 11yrs ⊗ in restaurant RS 23-29 Dec **CARDS:**

ANGLESEY, ISLE OF, Isle of Anglesey Map 14

AMLWCH Map 14 SH49

★★70% Lastra Farm
Penrhyd LL68 9TF
☎ 01407 830906 01407 832522
e-mail: booking@lastra-hotel.com
web: www.lastra-hotel.com
Dir: *after 'Welcome to Amlwch' sign turn left. Straight across main road, left at T-junct on to Rhosgoch Rd*
This 17th-century farmhouse offers pine-furnished, colourfully decorated bedrooms. There is also a comfortable lounge and a cosy bar. A wide range of good-value food is available either in the restaurant or Granary's Bistro. The hotel can cater for functions in a separate, purpose-built suite.
ROOMS: 5 en suite 3 annexe en suite (1 fmly) s £39.50-£44.50; d £60-£68 (incl. bkfst) **LB** **CONF:** Thtr 100 Class 80 Board 30 **PARKING:** 40 **NOTES:** ⊗ in restaurant Civ Wed 100
CARDS:

BEAUMARIS Map 14 SH67

★★★64% The Bulkeley Hotel
Castle St LL58 8AW
☎ 01248 810415 01248 810146
e-mail: bulkeley@bestwestern.co.uk
Dir: *from M56 & M6 take A5 or A55 coast road*
A Grade I listed hotel built in 1831, the Bulkeley has fine views from many rooms. Well-equipped bedrooms are generally spacious, with pretty fabrics and wallpapers. There is a choice of bars, an all-day coffee lounge and a health club. Regular jazz evenings, a resident pianist and a friendly staff create a relaxed atmosphere.
ROOMS: 43 en suite (6 fmly) ⊗ in 10 bedrooms s fr £74.50; d fr £107 (incl. bkfst) **LB** **FACILITIES: Spa** Sauna Solarium Gym Jacuzzi Hair & Beauty Salon Xmas **CONF:** Thtr 180 Class 120 Board 36 **SERVICES:** Lift **PARKING:** 30 **NOTES:** ⊗ in restaurant Civ Wed 140
CARDS:

★★75% Ye Olde Bulls Head Inn
Castle St LL58 8AP
☎ 01248 810329 01248 811294
e-mail: info@bullsheadinn.co.uk
Dir: *from Britannia road bridge follow A545, located in town centre*
Charles Dickens and Samuel Johnson were regular visitors to this

continued

inn where features include exposed beams, fireplaces and antique weaponry. Richly decorated bedrooms are well equipped and there is a spacious lounge. Meetings and small functions are catered for and food continues to attract praise in the restaurant and brasserie.
ROOMS: 12 en suite 1 annexe en suite (2 GF) ⊗ in all bedrooms s fr £67; d fr £95 (incl. bkfst) **LB** **FACILITIES:** Leisure centre nearby **CONF:** Thtr 25 Board 16 **PARKING:** 10 **NOTES:** ⊗ in restaurant Closed 25-26 Dec & 1 Jan **CARDS:**

★★73% *Bishopsgate House*

54 Castle St LL58 8BB
☎ 01248 810302 01248 810166
e-mail: hazel@johnson-ollier.freeserve.co.uk
Dir: *turn off in Menai Bridge onto A545. Follow the only road into Beaumaris, hotel on left in the main street*
This immaculately maintained, privately owned and personally run small hotel dates back to 1760. It features fine examples of wood panelling and a Chinese Chippendale staircase. Well-equipped bedrooms are attractively decorated and two have four-poster beds. Quality cooking is served in the elegant restaurant and guests have a comfortable lounge and cosy bar in which to relax.
ROOMS: 9 en suite **PARKING:** 8 **NOTES:** ⊗ in restaurant
CARDS:

HOLYHEAD

Map 14 SH28

★★66% Boathouse

Newry Promenade, Newry Beach LL65 1YF
☎ 01407 762094 01407 764898
e-mail: boathousehotel@supanet.com
Dir: *follow expressway into Holyhead continue through yellow box & follow signs for Marina. From ferry terminal turn right at 1st set of traffic lights and right at 2nd set and follow signs for Marina. Hotel at bottom of hill on seafront*
Situated in a prominent position overlooking the harbour, this hotel makes an ideal stop for ferry travellers. Bedrooms are attractively decorated to a high standard and are well equipped. The attractive lounge bar offers a wide range of home-cooked food; there is also a separate dining room.
ROOMS: 17 en suite (1 fmly) (5 GF) ⊗ in 15 bedrooms s £40-£55; d £70-£80 (incl. bkfst) **LB** **FACILITIES:** Painting & sketching guidance available **CONF:** Thtr 40 Class 30 Board 30 **PARKING:** 40 **NOTES:** ⊗ in restaurant **CARDS:**

LLANFAIRPWLLGWYNGYLL

Map 14 SH57

★★61% *Carreg Bran Country Hotel*

Church Ln LL61 5YH
☎ 01248 714224 01248 716516
e-mail: info@carregbran.uk.com
Dir: *from Holyhead 1st junct for Llanfairpwll. Through village then 1st right before dual carriageway and bridge*
This privately owned and personally run hotel is situated close to the banks of the Menai Strait. Rooms are spacious and well equipped. The restaurant is attractive and the food is locally inspired. There is a choice of bars and a large function room, popular for weddings and business meetings.
ROOMS: 20 en suite (2 fmly) ⊗ in 5 bedrooms **CONF:** Thtr 120 Class 60 Board 30 **PARKING:** 150 **NOTES:** ⊗ in restaurant Civ Wed 100
CARDS:

> Popped the question?
> Hotels with Civ Wed in their entry are licensed for civil wedding ceremonies. Maximum numbers for the ceremony only are shown, e.g. Civ Wed 120

LLANGEFNI

Map 14 SH47

★★★76% Tre-Ysgawen Hall Country House & Spa

Capel Coch LL77 7UR
☎ 01248 750750 01248 750035
e-mail: enquiries@treysgawen-hall.co.uk
web: www.treysgawen-hall.co.uk
Dir: *From junct 6, North Wales Expressway, take B5111 from Llangefni for Amlwch/Llanerchymedd. After Rhosmeich, turn right to Capel Coch. Hotel 1 mile on left at end of long drive*
Quietly located in extensive wooded grounds, this charming mansion was built in 1882 and has been extended over time. It offers a range of delightful bedrooms, with many personal touches. Public areas are elegant, spacious and comfortable. The restaurant offers an interesting choice of dishes. There is a bar/bistro, a coffee shop and extensive leisure facilities.
ROOMS: 19 en suite 10 annexe en suite (2 fmly) (8 GF) ⊗ in 15 bedrooms s fr £95; d fr £150 (incl. bkfst) **LB** **FACILITIES: Spa** STV Sauna Solarium Gym Jacuzzi Steam Room, Beauty Therapy Suite **CONF:** Thtr 200 Class 75 Board 50 Del from £130 **PARKING:** 140 **NOTES:** ⊗ in restaurant Closed 25 Dec-2 Jan Civ Wed 200
CARDS:

See advert on this page

★★68% Bull Hotel

Bulkley Square LL77 7LR
☎ 01248 722119 01248 750488
e-mail: bull@welsh-historic-inns.com
web: www.hotelbull.co.uk
Dir: *leave A55 at Llangefni follow signs for town centre, hotel on right on entering town through one-way system*
This town centre hostelry was built in 1817. Now completely

continued on p786

LLANGEFNI, continued

refurbished, it provides well-equipped, tastefully furnished accommodation both in the main building and the annexe, including a room with a four-poster bed and a family room. Public areas offer a choice of bars, a spacious and traditional restaurant together with a comfortable, relaxing lounge.

Bull Hotel, Llangefni

ROOMS: 20 en suite (2 fmly) ⊗ in all bedrooms s £55-£75; d £69.50-£85 (incl. bkfst) **LB FACILITIES:** STV Xmas **CONF:** Thtr 60 Class 40 Board 30 **PARKING:** 18 **NOTES:** ⊗ in restaurant **CARDS:**

MENAI BRIDGE — Map 14 SH57

★★67% *Anglesey Arms*

LL59 5EA
☎ 01248 712305 01248 712076
e-mail: bookings@theangleseyarmshotel.co.uk
Dir: *First slip road off Britannia Bridge, follow signs to Menai Bridge, hotel on rdbt at end of Menai Bridge*

This popular hotel sits next to the Menai suspension bridge and lies in well-maintained gardens. The hotel provides smart, well equipped accommodation. Bedrooms are attractively furnished in pine and have many thoughtful extras. There is a choice of bars and an excellent selection of meals.

ROOMS: 16 en suite (2 fmly) **CONF:** Thtr 60 Class 40 Board 40 **PARKING:** 60 **NOTES:** Civ Wed 60 **CARDS:**

★★63% Victoria Hotel

Telford Rd LL59 5DR
☎ 01248 712309 01248 716774
e-mail: vicmenai@barbox.net
Dir: *over Menai Suspension Bridge, take 2nd exit from rdbt on Anglesey side, continue 100yds, hotel on right*

This family-run hotel is situated in Menai Bridge and has panoramic views of the Menai Straits and Britannia Bridge. Many bedrooms have their own balconies. There are two character bars where meals are available, and also a more formal conservatory dining room.

ROOMS: 14 en suite 3 annexe en suite (4 fmly) (1 GF) s fr £39; d fr £49.50 (incl. bkfst) **LB FACILITIES:** Childrens playground Xmas **CONF:** Thtr 80 Class 80 Board 50 Del from £65 **PARKING:** 40 **NOTES:** ⊗ in restaurant RS 25 Dec Civ Wed 85 **CARDS:**

TREARDDUR BAY — Map 14 SH27

★★★72% Trearddur Bay

LL65 2UN
☎ 01407 860301 01407 861181
e-mail: enquiries@trearddurbayhotel.co.uk
Dir: *leave A55 at junct signed Caergeiliog. Through Caergeiliog and continue on A5. Left at lights in Valley onto B4545 towards Trearddur Bay, with Power garage on right, left opp garage, hotel on right*

Facilities at this fine modern hotel include extensive function and conference rooms, an indoor swimming pool and a games room. Bedrooms are well equipped, many have sea views, and suites are available. An all-day bar serves a wide range of snacks and lighter meals, supplemented by a cocktail bar and the more formal hotel restaurant.

ROOMS: 36 en suite (7 fmly) ⊗ in 15 bedrooms s £85-£115; d £124-£156 (incl. bkfst) **LB FACILITIES:** STV Sailing, Shooting, Horse riding, Fishing, Diving, Golf packages ♫ Xmas **CONF:** Thtr 190 Class 100 Board 78 Del from £85 **PARKING:** 300 **NOTES:** ⊗ in restaurant Civ Wed 65 **CARDS:**

BALA, Gwynedd — Map 14 SH93

★★★78% Palé Hall Country House

Palé Estate, Llandderfel LL23 7PS
☎ 01678 530285 01678 530220
e-mail: enquiries@palehall.co.uk
web: www.palehall.co.uk
Dir: *off B4401 Corwen/Bala road 4m from Llandrillo*

This enchanting mansion was built in 1870 and overlooks extensive grounds and beautiful woodland. The fine entrance hall, with its stained-glass lantern ceiling and galleried oak staircase, leads off to the library bar, two elegant lounges and the smart dining room. The standard of cooking remains high and is complemented by fine wines. The spacious bedrooms are furnished to the highest standards with many thoughtful extras.

ROOMS: 17 en suite (1 fmly) ⊗ in all bedrooms s £80-£140; d £105-£200 (incl. bkfst) **LB FACILITIES:** Fishing Clay pigeon/Game shooting Xmas **CONF:** Board 22 **PARKING:** 40 **NOTES:** No children ⊗ in restaurant Civ Wed **CARDS:**

See advert on opposite page

★★66% Plas Coch

High St LL23 7AB
☎ 01678 520309 01678 521135
e-mail: plascoch@tiscali.co.uk
Dir: *on A494, located in centre of Bala*

A focal point in a bustling town, this 18th-century former coaching inn is popular with locals and resident guests alike. The public areas are very attractive and bedrooms are spacious.

ROOMS: 10 en suite (4 fmly) ⊗ in all bedrooms **FACILITIES:** Windsurfing, Canoeing, Sailing, Whitewater Rafting, **CONF:** Thtr 30 Class 20 Board 20 **PARKING:** 12 **NOTES:** **CARDS:**

BANGOR, Gwynedd — Map 14 SH57

★★66% Garden Hotel

1 High St LL57 1DQ
☎ 01248 362189 01248 371328
e-mail: reception@gardenhotelbangor.co.uk
Dir: *before railway station take 1st left, past Plaza cinema, car park on right*

This city hotel is located close to the university, hospital and railway station and makes a good base for touring Snowdonia and North Wales. The modern bedrooms are spacious and very well

continued

B

equipped, and the hotel also has a renowned Cantonese restaurant. A function suite is also available.
ROOMS: 11 rms (10 en suite) (1 fmly) ⊗ in all bedrooms s £45; d £70 (incl. bkfst) **FACILITIES:** STV Xmas **PARKING:** 6 **NOTES:** No children 10yrs **CARDS:**

Eryl Mor
2 Upper Garth Rd LL57 2SR
☎ 01248 353789 01248 354042
e-mail: erylmorhotel@aol.com
Dir: *Turn off A55 to Bangor, turn right after boatyard, hotel overlooking the pier*
ROOMS: 22 rms (9 en suite) (3 fmly) (3 GF) ⊗ in 11 bedrooms s £30-£50; d £44-£70 (incl. bkfst) **LB** **CONF:** Del from £49.95 **PARKING:** 11 **NOTES:** ★★ ⊗ in restaurant
CARDS:

Travel Inn
Menai Business Park LL57 4FA
☎ 08701 977023 01248 679214
Dir: *From A55 take 3rd Bangor turn off signed Caernarfon A487, Bangor & hospital. Take 3rd exit at 1st rdbt*
Travel Inn offers good-quality, value-for-money accommodation. Spacious, en suite rooms with bath and shower comfortably accommodate a family of up to two adults and two children (to age 15). The restaurant and bar offers a varied menu. For further details consult the Hotel Groups page.
ROOMS: 40 en suite s £45.95-£46.95; d £45.95-£46.95

Travelodge
Llys-y-Gwynt LL57 4BG
☎ 08700 850 950 0870 1911561
Dir: *junct A5/A55*
Travelodge offers good quality, good value, modern accommodation. Ideal for families, the spacious, en suite bedrooms include remote-control TV, tea and coffee-making facilities and luxury beds. Meals can be taken at the nearby family restaurant. For further details consult the Hotel Groups page.
ROOMS: 62 en suite s fr £25; d fr £25

BARMOUTH, Gwynedd — Map 14 SH61

★★★68% Bae Abermaw
Panorama Hill LL42 1DQ
☎ 01341 280550 01341 280346
e-mail: enquiries@baeabermaw.com
web: www.baeabermaw.com
This large stone-built Victorian house, now a privately owned and personally run hotel, stands in its own wooded grounds on a hillside with stunning views across the Mawddach estuary. It is decorated and furnished throughout in a striking contemporary style and provides spacious, well-equipped accommodation. Facilities include a room for conferences and other functions.
ROOMS: 14 en suite (4 fmly) ⊗ in all bedrooms s £86-£103; d £126-£152 (incl. bkfst) **LB** **FACILITIES:** Xmas **CONF:** Thtr 100 Class 40 Board 40 **PARKING:** 40 **NOTES:** ⊗ in restaurant RS Mon Civ Wed 100 **CARDS:**

★★71% *Wavecrest Hotel*
8 Marine Pde LL42 1NA
☎ 01341 280330 01341 280330
e-mail: thewavecrest@talk21.com
Dir: *left over level-crossing, then immediately right onto Marine Parade*
There are superb views over Cardigan Bay towards the Cader Idris Mountains from many of the attractive rooms at this delightful hotel on the promenade. There is an open-plan bar and restaurant

continued

serving excellent cuisine using local produce, complemented by an impressive wine list and extensive collection of malt whiskies.
ROOMS: 9 en suite (3 fmly) ⊗ in all bedrooms **NOTES:** ⊗ in restaurant Closed Nov-Mar **CARDS:**

★★70% Ty'r Graig Castle Hotel
Llanaber Rd LL42 1YN
☎ 01341 280470 01341 281260
e-mail: reservations@tyr-graig-castle.co.uk
Dir: *0.75m from Barmouth on the Harlech road, seaward side*
This impressive and unusual house was designed and built by the famous Birmingham gunsmith WW Greener. Victorian and Gothic charm are combined, and original features include some magnificent stained-glass windows and wood panelling. Bedrooms are well equipped and many have views of Cardigan Bay. Dishes range from authentic Welsh to globally inspired choices.
ROOMS: 11 en suite ⊗ in all bedrooms s £55; d £88 (incl. bkfst) **LB** **PARKING:** 15 **NOTES:** ⊗ in restaurant Closed 25 Dec-6 Feb
CARDS:

BARRY, Vale of Glamorgan — Map 09 ST16

★★★73% Egerton Grey Country House
Porthkerry CF62 3BZ
☎ 01446 711666 01446 711690
e-mail: info@egertongrey.co.uk
web: www.egertongrey.co.uk
Dir: *M4 junct 33 follow signs for airport, left at rdbt for Porthkerry, after 500yds turn left down lane between thatched cottages*
This former rectory enjoys a peaceful setting and views over delightful countryside with distant glimpses of the sea. The non-smoking bedrooms are spacious and individually furnished.

continued on p788

B

BARRY, continued

Public areas offer charm and elegance, and include an airy lounge and restaurant, which has been sympathetically converted from the billiards room.
ROOMS: 10 en suite (4 fmly) s £89.50-£95; d £100-£130 (incl. bkfst) **LB FACILITIES:** STV Putt green 9 hole golf course 200 yds away. ch fac Xmas **CONF:** BC Thtr 30 Class 30 Board 22 Del from £240 **PARKING:** 41 **NOTES:** in restaurant Civ Wed 40
CARDS:

★★★69% Mount Sorrel

Best Western

Porthkerry Rd CF62 7XY
☎ 01446 740069 01446 746600
e-mail: reservations@mountsorrel.co.uk
Dir: M4 J33 on A4232. Follow signs for A4050 through Barry. Upon reaching mini rdbt with church opposite turn L, hotel 300mtrs on L.
Situated in an elevated position above the town centre, this extended Victorian property is ideally placed for exploring the nearby coast and Cardiff, and offers comfortable accommodation. The public areas include a choice of conference rooms, a restaurant and a bar, together with leisure facilities.
ROOMS: 42 en suite (3 fmly) (5 GF) in 8 bedrooms s £65-£130; d £90-£130 (incl. bkfst) **LB FACILITIES:** STV supervised Sauna Gym Xmas **CONF:** Thtr 150 Class 100 Board 50 Del from £95 **PARKING:** 17 **NOTES:** in restaurant Civ Wed 150
CARDS:

A Aberthaw House

28 Porthkerry Rd CF67 7AX
☎ 01446 737314 01446 732376
Dir: turn off A4050 Park Crescent onto Porthkerry Rd, hotel on right
ROOMS: 8 en suite (2 fmly) s £39.50; d £59.50 (incl. bkfst)
NOTES: ★★ in restaurant **CARDS:**

BEAUMARIS See Anglesey, Isle of

BEDDGELERT, Gwynedd Map 14 SH54

★★★67% The Royal Goat

THE CIRCLE Selected Individual Hotels GREAT BRITAIN

LL55 4YE
☎ 01766 890224 01766 890422
e-mail: info@royalgoathotel.co.uk
Dir: On A498 at Beddgelert
An impressive building steeped in history, the Royal Goat provides well-equipped accommodation. Public areas include a choice of bars and restaurants, a residents' lounge and function rooms.
ROOMS: 32 en suite (3 fmly) in 10 bedrooms s £50-£64; d £86-£116 (incl. bkfst) **LB FACILITIES:** STV Fishing Xmas **CONF:** Thtr 80 Class 70 Board 70 **SERVICES:** Lift **PARKING:** 100 **NOTES:** in restaurant Closed 1 Jan-1 Mar **CARDS:**

★★72% Tanronnen Inn

LL55 4YB
☎ 01766 890347 01766 890606
Dir: in the centre of village
This delightful small hotel offers comfortable, well equipped and attractively appointed accommodation, including a family room. There is also a selection of pleasant and relaxing public areas. The wide range of bar food is popular with tourists, and more formal meals are served in the restaurant.
ROOMS: 7 en suite (3 fmly) in all bedrooms s £50; d £90 (incl. bkfst) **LB FACILITIES:** STV Xmas **PARKING:** 15 **NOTES:**
CARDS:

BETWS-Y-COED, Conwy Map 14 SH75
See also Llanrwst

★★★71% Royal Oak

Holyhead Rd LL24 0AY
☎ 01690 710219 01690 710603
e-mail: royaloakmail@btopenworld.com
web: www.royaloakhotel.net
Dir: on A5 in centre of town, next to St Mary's church
This fine, privately owned hotel started life as a coaching inn and now provides smart bedrooms and a wide range of public areas. The choice of eating options includes the Grill Bar and the main dining room, which provides a more formal dinner option from Wednesdays to Saturdays.
ROOMS: 27 en suite (3 fmly) in 6 bedrooms s £60-£70; d £80 (incl. bkfst) **LB FACILITIES:** STV ch fac **CONF:** BC Thtr 20 Class 20 Board 20 Del from £75 **PARKING:** 90 **NOTES:** in restaurant Closed 25-26 Dec Civ Wed 35 **CARDS:**

See advert on opposite page

★★★70% Craig-y-Dderwen Riverside Hotel

THE INDEPENDENTS HOTEL ASSOCIATION

LL24 0AS
☎ 01690 710293 01690 710362
e-mail: craig-y-dderwen@betws-y-coed.co.uk
web: www.snowdonia-hotel.com
Dir: A5 to town, cross Waterloo Bridge and take 1st left
This Victorian country-house hotel is set in well-maintained grounds alongside the River Conwy, at the end of a tree-lined drive. Very pleasant views can be enjoyed from many rooms, and two of the bedrooms have four-poster beds. There are comfortable lounges and the atmosphere is tranquil and relaxing.
ROOMS: 16 en suite (2 fmly) (1 GF) s £60-£100; d £70-£110 (incl. bkfst) **LB FACILITIES: Spa** Badminton, Volleyball ch fac **CONF:** Thtr 50 Class 25 Board 20 Del from £62 **PARKING:** 50 **NOTES:** in restaurant Closed 23-26 Dec & 30 Dec-1 Feb
CARDS:

See advert on opposite page

★★★68% Best Western Waterloo

Best Western

LL24 0AR
☎ 01690 710411 01690 710666
e-mail: reservations@waterloo-hotel.info
web: www.waterloo-hotel.info
Dir: A5 London-Holyhead near Waterloo Bridge

This long-established hotel, named after the nearby Waterloo Bridge, is ideally located for Snowdonia. Accommodation is split between rooms in the main hotel and modern, cottage-style rooms located in buildings to the rear. The attractive Garden

continued

Room Restaurant serves traditional Welsh specialities, and the Wellington Bar offers light meals and snacks.
ROOMS: 10 en suite 30 annexe en suite (2 fmly) (30 GF) ⊗ in 14 bedrooms s £55-£70; d £90-£120 (incl. bkfst) **LB FACILITIES: Spa** supervised Sauna Solarium Gym Jacuzzi Steam room ch fac
CONF: Thtr 50 Class 16 Board 20 Del £95 **PARKING:** 180 **NOTES:** ⊗ in restaurant Closed 25 Dec **CARDS:**

Top 200 – Hotel

★★ Tan-y-Foel Country House
Capel Garmon LL26 0RE
☎ 01690 710507 01690 710681
e-mail: enquiries@tyfhotel.co.uk web: www.tyfhotel.co.uk
Dir: *off A5 at Betws-y-Coed onto A470, 2m N to sign marked Capel Garmon on right, turn towards Capel Garmon for 1.5m, hotel sign on left*
In an idyllic hillside location with stunning views of Conwy Valley, this stylish, sophisticated hotel is a must for travellers seeking a modern, eclectic hotel. The traditional exterior reflects the hotel's 16th-century origins, while inside the design and furnishings are cutting edge. Dinner, using local organic produce whenever possible, is a highlight of any stay. Individually furnished bedrooms, which include an imaginatively converted hayloft, are designed for comfort and relaxation.
ROOMS: 4 en suite 2 annexe en suite (1 GF) ⊗ in all bedrooms
PARKING: 16 **NOTES:** No children 7yrs ⊗ in restaurant Closed Dec RS Jan **CARDS:**

★★68% Fairy Glen
LL24 0SH
☎ 01690 710269
e-mail: hotelfairyglen@amserve.com
web: www.fairyglenhotel.co.uk
Dir: *off A5 onto A470 Southbound (Dolwyddelan Road). Hotel 0.5m on left by Beaver Bridge*

This privately owned and personally run former coaching inn is over 300 years old. It is located near the Fairy Glen beauty spot,

continued on p790

B

BETWS-Y-COED, continued

south of Betws-y-Coed. The modern accommodation is well equipped and service is willing, friendly and attentive. Facilities include a cosy bar and a separate comfortable lounge.
ROOMS: 8 rms (6 en suite) (2 fmly) s £23-£37; d £46-£50 (incl. bkfst) **LB** **PARKING:** 10 **NOTES:** in restaurant Closed Nov-Jan RS Feb
CARDS:

★★68% Park Hill
Llanrwst Rd LL24 0HD
☎ 01690 710540 01690 710540
e-mail: welcome@park-hill-hotel.co.uk
web: www.park-hill-hotel.co.uk
Dir: *0.5m N of Betws-y-Coed on A470 Llanrwst road*
This friendly hotel benefits from a peaceful location overlooking the village. Comfortable bedrooms come in a wide range of sizes and are well equipped. A room with a four-poster bed and family rooms are available. There is a choice of lounges, a heated swimming pool, sauna and whirlpool bath available to residents.
ROOMS: 9 en suite (2 fmly) s £48; d £56-£80 (incl. bkfst) **LB**
FACILITIES: Sauna Jacuzzi Xmas **PARKING:** 11 **NOTES:** No children 6yrs in restaurant **CARDS:**

BLACKWOOD, Caerphilly — Map 09 ST19

★★★67% Maes Manor
NP12 0AG
☎ 01495 224551 & 220011 01495 228217
e-mail: maesmanor@lineone.net
Dir: *A4048 to Tredega. At Pontllanfraith left at rdbt, through Blackwood High St. After 1.25m left at Rack Inn. Hotel 400yds on left*

Standing high above the town, this 19th-century manor house is set in nine acres of gardens and woodland. Bedrooms are attractively decorated with co-ordinated furnishings. As well as the restaurant, public rooms include a choice of bars, a lounge/lobby area and a large function room.
ROOMS: 8 en suite 14 annexe en suite (6 fmly) s £50-£62; d £72-£80 (incl. bkfst) **CONF:** Thtr 200 Class 200 **PARKING:** 100 **NOTES:** in restaurant Closed 24-25 Dec Civ Wed 200
CARDS:

See advert on opposite page

BLAENAU FFESTINIOG, Gwynedd — Map 14 SH74

★★69% Queens Hotel
1 High St LL41 3ES
☎ 01766 830055 01766 830046
e-mail: cathy@queensffestiniog.freeserve.co.uk
Dir: *on A470 adjacent to Ffestiniog Railway, between Betws-y-Coed & Dolgellau*
This flourishing hotel has an all-day bistro serving meals and snacks. Bedrooms are well equipped and attractive. The hotel lies at the northern end of the famous Ffestiniog Railway, and the bedrooms are named after locomotives which have operated on the line.
ROOMS: 12 en suite (4 fmly) s £40-£60; d £55-£80 (incl. bkfst) **LB**
FACILITIES: **CONF:** Thtr 80 Class 30 Board 30 **NOTES:** in restaurant Closed 25 Dec **CARDS:**

BRECON, Powys — Map 09 SO02

★★★75% Nant Ddu Lodge, Bistro & Spa
Cwm Taf, Nant Ddu CF48 2HY
☎ 01685 379111 01685 377088
e-mail: enquiries@nant-ddu-lodge.co.uk
web: www.nant-ddu-lodge.co.uk
(For full entry see Nant-Ddu)

★★★71% Peterstone Court
Llanhamlach LD3 7YB
☎ 01874 665387 01874 665376
e-mail: info@peterstone-court.com
web: www.peterstone-court.com
Dir: *from Brecon take A40 towards Abergavenny, hotel in approx 4m, on right*

This location provides stunning views, standing on the edge of the Brecon Beacons and overlooking the River Usk. The style is friendly and informal, without any unnecessary fuss! No two bedrooms are alike, but all share comparable levels of comfort, quality and elegance. Public areas reflect similar standards, eclectically styled with a blend of contemporary and traditional. Quality produce is cooked with care in simple and successful dishes in the 'Bistro' restaurant.
ROOMS: 8 en suite 4 annexe en suite (4 fmly) in 4 bedrooms
FACILITIES: Sauna Gym Jacuzzi **CONF:** Thtr 150 Class 150 Board 100 **PARKING:** 50 **NOTES:** in restaurant Civ Wed 100
CARDS:

★★70% Lansdowne Hotel & Restaurant
The Watton LD3 7EG
☎ 01874 623321 01874 610438
e-mail: reception@lansdownehotel.co.uk
Dir: *off A40/A470 onto the B4601, hotel in town centre*
Now a privately owned and personally run hotel, this Georgian house is conveniently located close to the town centre. The accommodation is well equipped and includes family rooms and a bedroom on ground floor level. There is a comfortable lounge and an attractive split-level dining room containing a bar.
ROOMS: 9 en suite (2 fmly) (1 GF) s £30-£35; d £50-£55 (incl. bkfst) **LB** **NOTES:** No children 5yrs in restaurant
CARDS:

Bad hair day?
Hairdryers in all rooms three stars and above

B

★★67% *The Castle of Brecon*

Castle Square LD3 9DB
☎ 01874 624611 📠 01874 623737
e-mail: hotel@breconcastle.co.uk
web: www.breconcastle.co.uk
Dir: *A40 to Brecon, follow town centre for 2kms, left at traffic lights, right towards Cradoc, right into Castle Sq*

This former coaching inn occupies an elevated position overlooking the town and River Usk. This view is shared by the restaurant and some of the bedrooms, whilst the remaining public areas are roomy and relaxed. Function and meeting rooms are available and incorporate one of the castle walls.
ROOMS: 31 en suite 12 annexe en suite (8 fmly) (2 GF) ⊗ in 12 bedrooms **FACILITIES:** STV **CONF:** Thtr 160 Class 60 Board 80 **PARKING:** 30 **NOTES:** ⊗ in restaurant Civ Wed 120
CARDS:

🅰 The Felin Fach Griffin

Felin Fach LD3 0UB
☎ 01874 620111 📠 01874 620120
e-mail: enquiries@eatdrinksleep.ltd.uk
web: www.eatdrinksleep.ltd.uk
Dir: *A470 NW from Brecon towards Leominster then left following signs Felin Fach. Hotel is the large terracotta building just off the road*
ROOMS: 7 en suite ⊗ in all bedrooms s £60-£67.50; d £92.50-£115 (incl. bkfst) **LB FACILITIES:** no TV in bdrms ♫ **PARKING:** 60 **NOTES:** ★★★★ ⊗ in restaurant Closed last wk Jan, 1st wk Feb
CARDS:

Town House Hotel
Country House Hotel
Travel Accommodation

BRIDGEND, Bridgend

Map 09 SS97

See also Porthcawl

★★★★76% Coed-y-Mwstwr

Coychurch CF35 6AF
☎ 01656 860621 📠 01656 863122
e-mail: enquiries@coed-y-mwstwr.com
Dir: *leave A473 at Coychurch right at petrol station. Follow signs at top of hill*
This former Victorian mansion, set in 17 acres of grounds a few miles from Bridgend, is an inviting retreat for both business people and leisure guests. An original oak-panelled billiards room houses the elegant restaurant and bedrooms; these have been refurbished in individual styles with a good range of facilities, and include two full suites. There are also meeting rooms and a large

continued on p792

BRIDGEND, continued

and attractive function suite. A gymnasium and other fitness facilities including an outdoor swimming pool are also available.

B

Coed-Y-Mwstwr Hotel, Bridgend

ROOMS: 28 en suite (2 fmly) ⊗ in 20 bedrooms s £85-£98; d £110-£140 (incl. bkfst) **LB** **FACILITIES:** STV 12 Sauna Solarium Gym Xmas **CONF:** Thtr 180 Class 120 Board 50 Del from £125 **SERVICES:** Lift **PARKING:** 100 **NOTES:** ⊗ in restaurant Civ Wed 150 **CARDS:**

★★★76% The Great House Restaurant & Hotel
Laleston CF32 0HP
☎ 01656 657644 01656 668892
e-mail: enquiries@great-house-laleston.co.uk
web: www.great-house-laleston.co.uk
Dir: *on A473, 400yds from junct with A48*
A delightful Grade II listed building, dating back to 1550. Traditional features throughout the house add plenty of character. Leicester's restaurant offers a wide range of freshly prepared dishes; lighter snacks can be taken in the more informal bistro. The stylish, well-equipped bedrooms are located in the original building and a separate wing.
ROOMS: 8 en suite 8 annexe en suite (8 GF) ⊗ in 4 bedrooms s £60-£85; d £85-£140 (incl. bkfst) **LB** **FACILITIES:** STV Sauna Gym Jacuzzi Health suite with sauna ch fac **CONF:** Thtr 40 Class 25 Board 20 Del from £100 **PARKING:** 40 **NOTES:** ⊗ in restaurant Closed 25 Dec-2 Jan Civ Wed 50 **CARDS:**

★★★69% Heronston
Ewenny Rd CF35 5AW
☎ 01656 668811 01656 767391
e-mail: reservations@heronston-hotel.demon.co.uk
Dir: *M4 junct 35, follow signs for Porthcawl, at 4th rdbt turn left towards Ogmore-by-Sea (B4265) hotel 200yds on left*
Situated within easy reach of the town centre and the M4, this large modern hotel offers spacious well-equipped accommodation, including no-smoking bedrooms and ground floor rooms. Public areas include an open-plan lounge/bar, attractive restaurant and a smart leisure & fitness club. The hotel also has a choice of function/conference rooms.

ROOMS: 69 en suite 6 annexe en suite (4 fmly) (37 GF) ⊗ in 21 bedrooms s fr £39.50; d fr £59 (incl. bkfst) **LB** **FACILITIES:** STV Sauna Solarium Gym Jacuzzi Steamroom ch fac Xmas **CONF:** Thtr 200 Class 80 Board 60 Del from £99.50 **SERVICES:** Lift **PARKING:** 250 **NOTES:** ⊗ in restaurant Civ Wed 150
CARDS:

BUILTH WELLS, Powys — Map 09 SO05

★★★70% Caer Beris Manor
LD2 3NP
☎ 01982 552601 01982 552586
e-mail: caerberismanor@btinternet.com
web: www.caerberis.co.uk
Dir: *from town centre follow signs for A483 Llandovery. Hotel on left*
With extensive landscaped grounds, guests can expect a relaxing stay at this friendly and privately owned hotel. Bedrooms are individually decorated and furnished and retain a feel of a bygone era. A spacious and comfortable lounge and a lounge bar enhance this atmosphere together with the elegant restaurant, complete with 16th-century panelling.
ROOMS: 23 en suite (1 fmly) (3 GF) s £57.50-£67.50; d £95-£105 (incl. bkfst) **LB** **FACILITIES:** STV Fishing Riding Sauna Gym Clay pigeon shooting ch fac Xmas **CONF:** BC Thtr 100 Class 75 Board 50 Del from £62.95 **PARKING:** 32 **NOTES:** ⊗ in restaurant Civ Wed 100
CARDS:

Pencerrig Gardens
Llandrindod Wells Rd LD2 3TF
☎ 01982 553226 01982 552347
e-mail: invoices@pencerrig.co.uk
web: www.pencerrig.co.uk
Dir: *2m N on A483 towards Llandrindod Wells*
ROOMS: 10 en suite 10 annexe en suite (4 fmly) (5 GF) s £40-£55; d £70 (incl. bkfst) **LB** **FACILITIES:** **Spa** **CONF:** Thtr 60 Class 30 Board 35 **PARKING:** 50 **NOTES:** ★★ ⊗ in restaurant
CARDS:

C

CAERNARFON, Gwynedd
Map 14 SH46

Top 200 – Hotel

★★★ ®® Seiont Manor
Llanrug LL55 2AQ
HandPICKED
☎ 01286 673366 📠 01286 672840
e-mail: seiontmanor-cro@handpicked.co.uk
Dir: *E on A4086, 2.5m from Caernarfon*
A splendid hotel created from authentic rural buildings, set in the tranquil countryside near Snowdonia. Bedrooms are individually decorated and well equipped, with luxurious extra touches. Public rooms are cosy and comfortable and furnished in country-house style. The kitchen team use the best of local produce to provide exciting takes on traditional dishes. Hand Picked Hotels - AA Hotel Group of the Year 2004-5 and Seiont Manor Hotel has also been nominated for the AA Hotel of the Year Award for Wales 2004-5.
ROOMS: 28 en suite (10 fmly) (14 GF) ⊗ in 8 bedrooms s £100-£160; d £130-£210 (incl. bkfst & dinner) **LB** **FACILITIES: Spa** STV Fishing Sauna Gym Xmas **CONF:** Thtr 100 Class 40 Board 40 **PARKING:** 100 **NOTES:** ⊗ in restaurant Civ Wed 90
CARDS:

See advert on page 793

★★★71% Celtic Royal Hotel
Bangor St LL55 1AY
☎ 01286 674477 📠 01286 674139
e-mail: admin@celtic-royal.co.uk
web: www.celtic-royal.co.uk
Dir: *7m off A55 Expressway at Bangor. Follow A487 towards Caernarfon*

This large, impressive, privately owned hotel is situated in the town centre. It provides attractively appointed accommodation, which includes non-smoking rooms, bedrooms for less able guests and family rooms. The spacious public areas include a bar, a choice of lounges and a pleasant split-level restaurant. Guests also have the use of the impressive health club.
ROOMS: 110 en suite s £60-£65; d £90-£100 (incl. bkfst) **LB**
FACILITIES: STV Sauna Solarium Gym Jacuzzi Sun shower ♫ Xmas **CONF:** BC Thtr 300 Class 120 Del from £95 **SERVICES:** Lift
PARKING: 180 **NOTES:** ⊗ in restaurant Civ Wed 200
CARDS:

★★75% Ty'n Rhos Country Hotel & Restaurant
Llanddeiniolen LL55 3AE
☎ 01248 670489 📠 01248 670079
e-mail: enquiries@tynrhos.co.uk
web: www.tynrhos.co.uk
Dir: *in hamlet of Seion between B4366 and B4547*
Ty'n Rhos is a converted farmhouse, set in lovely countryside between Snowdon and the Menai Straits. The lounge, with its slate inglenook fireplace, is elegantly furnished and there is a small bar for pre-dinner drinks. The conservatory offers a comfortable vantage point from which to enjoy the gardens and the views beyond. The bedrooms are well equipped and have modern facilities. There is now a separate and self-contained conference centre.
ROOMS: 11 en suite 3 annexe en suite ⊗ in all bedrooms s £55-£65; d £86-£120 (incl. bkfst) **LB** **FACILITIES:** **CONF:** Thtr 40 Class 30 Board 20 **PARKING:** 20 **NOTES:** No children 6yrs ⊗ in restaurant Closed 22-30 Dec RS Sun evening (rest closed to non-res)
CARDS:

★★67% *Stables*
Llanwnda LL54 5SD
☎ 01286 830711 📠 01286 830413
Dir: *3m S of Caernarfon, on A499*
This privately owned and personally run hotel is set in 15 acres of its own land, south of Caernarfon. The bar and restaurant are located in converted stables. The bedrooms are all situated in two purpose-built, motel-style wings.
ROOMS: 22 annexe en suite (8 fmly) **FACILITIES:** Guests may bring own horse to stables **CONF:** Thtr 50 Class 30 Board 30 **PARKING:** 40
CARDS:

CAERPHILLY, Caerphilly
Map 09 ST18

⌂ Premier Lodge (Caerphilly)
Corbetts Ln CF83 3HX
PREMIER LODGE.com
☎ 0870 9906368 📠 0870 9906369
web: www.premierlodge.com
Dir: *4m from M4 junct 32. Follow A470 then 2nd left signed Caerphilly. At rdbt take 4th exit and at next rdbt take 2nd exit. Over next rdbt and at Pwllypant rdbt Lodge on left*
High quality, modern, budget accommodation, ideal for families and business travellers. All rooms feature bath, power shower and satellite TV, and most have telephones / modem points. The adjacent bar and restaurant offers a wide and varied menu.
ROOMS: 40 en suite s £50; d £50

⌂ Travel Inn
Crossways Business Park, Pontypandy CF83 3NL
travel inn
☎ 08701 977046 📠 029 2086 5546
Dir: *M4(J32) take A470 towards Merthyr Tydfil. J4 take A458 to Caerphilly. Stay on ring rd until Crossways Business Park (5th roundabout). Travel Inn on the right of McDonald's rbt.*
Travel Inn offers good-quality, value-for-money accommodation. Spacious, en suite rooms with bath and shower comfortably accommodate a family of up to two adults and two children (to age 15). The restaurant and bar offers a varied menu. For further details consult the Hotel Groups page.
ROOMS: 40 en suite s £45.95-£46.95; d £45.95-£46.95 **CONF:** Class 30

CAPEL CURIG, Conwy

Map 14 SH75

★★66% *Cobdens*

LL24 0EE
☎ 01690 720243 📠 01690 720354
e-mail: info@cobdens.co.uk
Dir: *on A5, 4m N of Betws-y-Coed*

For 200 years this hotel in the heart of Snowdonia, has been a centre for mountaineering and other outdoor pursuits. The bedrooms are modern and well equipped, and many enjoy lovely views. There is a bar and a wide range of meals, using local produce, is served in the restaurant. A small conference room is also available.

ROOMS: 16 en suite (3 fmly) **FACILITIES:** Fishing **CONF:** Thtr 50 **PARKING:** 40 **NOTES:** ⊘ in restaurant Closed Jan RS 25 & 31 Dec **CARDS:**

CARDIFF, Cardiff

Map 09 ST17

See also Barry

★★★★★73% ⊛ St David's Hotel & Spa

ROCCO FORTE HOTELS

Havannah St CF10 5SD
☎ 029 2045 4045 📠 029 2048 7056
e-mail: reservations@thestdavidshotel.com
web: www.roccofortehotels.com

Dir: *M4 junct 33/A4232 for 9m, for Techniquest, at top exit slip road, 1st left at rdbt, 1st right*

This imposing contemporary building sits in a prime position on Cardiff Bay. A seven-storey atrium provides a dramatic first impression and leading off from this are the practically laid out and comfortable bedrooms. Tides restaurant, adjacent to the stylish cocktail bar, has views across the water to Penarth, and there is a quiet first-floor lounge for guests seeking a peaceful environment. A well-equipped spa and extensive business areas complete the package.

ROOMS: 132 en suite (6 fmly) ⊘ in 108 bedrooms **FACILITIES:** **Spa** STV Sauna Gym Jacuzzi Fitness studio, 14 treatment rooms ♫ Xmas **CONF:** BC Thtr 270 Class 110 Board 60 **SERVICES:** Lift air con **PARKING:** 80 **NOTES:** ⊘ in restaurant Civ Wed **CARDS:**

★★★★74% ⊛ Holland House

MACDONALD HOTELS

24/26 Newport Rd CF24 0DD
☎ 0870 122 0020 📠 029 2048 8894

Conveniently located just a few minutes' walk from the centre, this exciting new hotel combines contemporary styling with a genuinely friendly welcome. Bedrooms, including five luxurious suites, are spacious and include many welcome extras. A state-of-the-art leisure club and spa is available in addition to a large function room. An eclectic menu provides a varied range of freshly prepared, quality dishes.

ROOMS: 165 en suite ⊘ in all bedrooms s £154-£210; d £164-£285 (incl. bkfst) **LB** **FACILITIES:** STV Gym full leisure facilities & 14 treatment rooms ♫ **CONF:** Thtr 710 Class 400 Board 50 **SERVICES:** Lift air con **NOTES:** ⊘ in restaurant **CARDS:**

★★★★70% ⊛ Copthorne Hotel Cardiff-Caerdydd

COPTHORNE

Copthorne Way, Culverhouse Cross CF5 6DH
☎ 029 2059 9100 📠 029 2059 9080
e-mail: sales.cardiff@mill-cop.com
Dir: *M4 junct 33, take A4232 for 2.5m towards Cardiff West and then A48 W to Cowbridge*

A comfortable, popular and modern hotel, conveniently located for the airport and city. Bedrooms are a good size and some have a private lounge. Public areas are smartly presented with features

continued on p796

C

CARDIFF, continued

including a gym, pool, meeting rooms and a restaurant which overlooks the lake.

Copthorne Hotel Cardiff-Caerdydd, Cardiff

ROOMS: 135 en suite (14 fmly) (27 GF) in 97 bedrooms s £85-£195; d £95-£205 (incl. bkfst) **LB FACILITIES:** STV Sauna Gym Jacuzzi Steam room ch fac Xmas **CONF:** Thtr 300 Class 140 Board 80 Del £175 **SERVICES:** Lift **PARKING:** 225 **NOTES:** Civ Wed 200 **CARDS:**

★★★★68% Cardiff Marriott Hotel

Marriott HOTELS·RESORTS·SUITES

Mill Ln CF10 1EZ
☎ 029 2039 9944 029 2039 5578
e-mail: sara.nurse@marriotthotels.co.uk
Dir: *M4 junct 29 follow signs City Centre. Turn left into High Street opposite Castle, then 2nd left, at bottom of High St into Mill Lane*

A centrally located modern hotel, with spacious public areas and a good range of services, is ideal for business or leisure. Eating options include the informal Chats café bar and the contemporary Mediterrano restaurant. Well-equipped bedrooms are comfortable and air conditioned. The leisure suite includes a gym and good sized pool.

ROOMS: 182 en suite (58 fmly) in 127 bedrooms s fr £131; d fr £143 (incl. bkfst) **LB FACILITIES:** STV Sauna Solarium Gym Jacuzzi Steam room Xmas **CONF:** Thtr 400 Class 200 Board 100 **SERVICES:** Lift air con **PARKING:** 110 **NOTES:** in restaurant Civ Wed 100 **CARDS:**

★★★★65% Angel Hotel

PARAMOUNT GROUP OF HOTELS

Castle St CF10 1SZ
☎ 029 2064 9200 029 2039 6212
e-mail: angelreservations@paramount-hotels.co.uk
Dir: *opposite Cardiff Castle*

This well-established hotel is in the heart of the city overlooking the castle. All bedrooms offer air conditioning and are decorated and furnished to a high standard. Public areas include an impressive lobby, a modern restaurant and a selection of conference rooms. There is limited parking at the rear of the hotel.

ROOMS: 102 en suite (4 fmly) in 62 bedrooms s £85-£170; d £108-£220 (incl. bkfst) **LB FACILITIES:** Xmas **CONF:** Thtr 300 Class 180 Board 80 Del £150 **SERVICES:** Lift air con **PARKING:** 60 **NOTES:** in restaurant Civ Wed **CARDS:**

★★★★64% Jurys Cardiff

JURYS DOYLE HOTELS

Mary Ann St CF10 2JH
☎ 029 2034 1441 029 2022 3742
e-mail: info@jurysdoyle.com
Dir: *next to Ice Rink, opposite Cardiff International Arena*

This modern hotel is situated opposite the Cardiff International Arena. Bedrooms are largely set around an impressive atrium which houses the reception and offers access to Dylan's restaurant and Kavanagh's Irish bar, whilst those rooms on the executive floor are particularly well appointed. Conference and function facilities are offered, together with a business centre.

ROOMS: 146 en suite (6 fmly) in 48 bedrooms s £68-£240; d £78-£260 (incl. bkfst) **LB FACILITIES:** STV **CONF:** Thtr 300 Class 120 Board 50 Del from £130 **SERVICES:** Lift **PARKING:** 55 **NOTES:** Civ Wed 150 **CARDS:**

★★★★61% Hanover International Hotel & Club

Schooner Way, Atlantic Wharf CF10 4RT
☎ 029 2047 5000 029 2048 1491
Dir: *M4 junct 33/A4232 follow Cardiff Bay signs, to Atlantic Wharf & Hanover International Hotel*

Situated in the heart of the city's new development area, this hotel is equally convenient for the centre and Cardiff Bay. Bedrooms vary between standard rooms in the original wing and deluxe rooms in the more modern extension. The hotel offers good seating space in public rooms, a galleried bar and a popular leisure club.

ROOMS: 156 en suite (6 fmly) in 50 bedrooms **FACILITIES:** STV Sauna Solarium Gym Jacuzzi Xmas **CONF:** Thtr 250 Class 90 Board 40 **SERVICES:** Lift **PARKING:** 150 **NOTES:** in restaurant Civ Wed 250 **CARDS:**

★★★74% Manor Parc Country Hotel & Restaurant

Thornhill Rd, Thornhill CF14 9UA
☎ 029 2069 3723 029 2061 4624
e-mail: reception@manorparchotel.fnet
Dir: *on A469*

Set in open countryside on the outskirts of Cardiff, this delightful hotel retains traditional values of hospitality and service. Bedrooms, including a suite, are spacious and attractive, whilst public areas comprise a comfortable lounge and a restaurant with a magnificent lantern ceiling overlooking the well-tended grounds.

ROOMS: 21 en suite (4 fmly) in all bedrooms s £47.50-£65; d £95-£130 (incl. bkfst) **LB FACILITIES:** STV **CONF:** Thtr 120 Class 80 Board 50 Del from £95 **PARKING:** 70 **NOTES:** in restaurant Closed 24-26 Dec & 1 Jan Civ Wed 100 **CARDS:**

★★★72% St Mellons Hotel & Country Club

Best Western

Castleton CF3 2XR
☎ 01633 680355 01633 680399
e-mail: stmellons@bestwestern.co.uk
web: www.stmellonshotel.com
Dir: *M4 junct 28 follow signs into Castleton. Through village, then sharp left at brow of hill following hotel sign into driveway*

This former Regency mansion has been tastefully converted into an elegant hotel and has an adjoining leisure complex with a strong local following. Bedrooms are spacious and smart; some are in purpose-built wings. The public areas retain their pleasing former proportions and include relaxing lounges and a restaurant.

ROOMS: 21 en suite 20 annexe en suite (9 fmly) in 18 bedrooms s £105-£115; d £115-£125 (incl. bkfst) **LB FACILITIES:** STV Squash Sauna Solarium Gym Jacuzzi Beauty salon Xmas **CONF:** Thtr 220 Class 70 Board 40 Del from £130 **PARKING:** 90 **NOTES:** in restaurant Civ Wed **CARDS:**

Early start?
Hotels at all star levels should provide in-room alarm clocks and/or alarm calls

continued

★★★71% New House Country Hotel
Thornhill CF14 9UA
☎ 029 2052 0280 029 2052 0324
e-mail: enquiries@newhousehotel.com
Dir: *M4 J32, A470 towards Cardiff, then A469 to Caerphilly, pass Thornhill Crematorium, 1m on left*
Enjoying an elevated, hilltop position, the New House enjoys unrivalled views of the city and, on clear days, across the channel to the coast of Somerset. The public areas comprise a lounge and bar, an elegant restaurant and various function suites. Accommodation is spacious and comfortable, in attractive, well-equipped rooms, many of which boast their own balcony or terrace.
ROOMS: 36 en suite (5 fmly) (10 GF) ⊘ in 18 bedrooms s £95-£130; d £120-£150 (incl. bkfst) **LB FACILITIES: Spa** STV Sauna Gym Jacuzzi Xmas **CONF:** BC Thtr 200 Class 150 Board 200 Del £135.12
PARKING: 100 **NOTES:** ⊘ in restaurant Civ Wed
CARDS:

★★★65% Quality Hotel & Suites Cardiff
Merthyr Rd, Tongwynlais CF15 7LD
☎ 029 2052 9988 029 2052 9977
e-mail: enquiries@quality-hotels-cardiff.com
web: www.choicehotelseurope.com
Dir: *M4 junct 32, take exit for Tongwynlais A4054 off large rdbt, hotel on right*
This modern hotel is conveniently located off the M4 with easy access to Cardiff. Guests can enjoy the spacious open-plan public areas and impressive leisure facilities and relax in the well-proportioned and equipped bedrooms, which include some suites. A good range of meeting rooms make this hotel a popular conference venue.
ROOMS: 95 en suite (12 fmly) (19 GF) ⊘ in 38 bedrooms s £57-£96; d £75-£135 **LB FACILITIES:** STV supervised Sauna Solarium Gym Jacuzzi ch fac Xmas **CONF:** Thtr 200 Class 140 Board 60 Del from £80
SERVICES: Lift **PARKING:** 130 **NOTES:** ⊘ in restaurant Civ Wed 180 **CARDS:**

★★66% Sandringham
21 St Mary St CF10 1PL
☎ 029 2023 2161 029 2038 3998
e-mail: hotel@sandringham21.fsnet.co.uk
Dir: *M4 junct 29 follow 'City Centre' signs. Opposite the castle turn into High Street which leads to Saint Mary St*
This friendly, privately owned and personally run hotel is near to the Millennium Stadium and offers a convenient base for access to the city centre. Bedrooms are well equipped, and diners can relax in Café Jazz, the hotel's adjoining restaurant, where live music is provided most weeknights. There is also a separate lounge/bar for residents, and an airy breakfast room.
ROOMS: 28 en suite (1 fmly) ⊘ in 14 bedrooms s £35-£100; d £45-£130 (incl. bkfst) **LB FACILITIES:** ♫ **CONF:** Thtr 100 Class 70 Board 60 Del from £70 **PARKING:** 10 **NOTES:**
CARDS:

Restaurant with Rooms

The Old Post Office
Greenwood Ln, St Fagans CF5 6EL
☎ 029 2056 5400 029 2056 3400
e-mail: heiditheoldpost@aol.com
Dir: *M4 junct 33 onto A4232. Take Culverhouse Cross exit then 1st exit onto Michaelston Rd. Over rdbt and level crossing, then left at Castle Hill*
Located just five miles from Cardiff in the historic village of St.Fagans, this establishment offers contemporary style based on New England design. Bedrooms, like the dining room, feature striking white walls

continued

with spotlights offering a fresh, clean feel. Delicious meals include a carefully prepared selection of local produce.
ROOMS: 6 en suite (2 fmly) (6 GF) ⊘ in all bedrooms s fr £65; d fr £75 (incl. bkfst) **LB PARKING:** 40 **NOTES:** ⊘ in restaurant
CARDS:

Campanile
Caxton Place, Pentwyn CF23 8HA
☎ 029 2054 9044 029 2054 9900
e-mail: cardiff@envergure.co.uk
Dir: *take Pentwyn exit from A48, follow signs for Pentwyn Industrial Estate*

This modern building offers accommodation in smart, well-equipped bedrooms, all with en suite bathrooms. Refreshments may be taken at the informal Bistro. For further details consult the Hotel Groups page.
ROOMS: 47 annexe en suite s fr £42.95; d fr £42.95 **CONF:** Thtr 35 Class 18 Board 24

Hotel Ibis Cardiff
Churchill Way CF10 2HA
☎ 029 2064 9250 029 2920 9260
e-mail: H2936@accor-hotels.com
Dir: *M4, then A48 2nd exit A4232. Follow signs to City Centre on Newport Rd, left after railway bridge, left after Queen St station.*
Modern, budget hotel offering comfortable accommodation in bright and practical bedrooms. Breakfast is self-service and dinner is available in the restaurant. For further details, consult the Hotel Groups page.
ROOMS: 102 en suite s fr £47; d £47-£52

Hotel Ibis Cardiff Gate
Malthouse Av, Cardiff Gate Business Park, Pontprennau CF23 8RA
☎ 029 2073 3222 029 2073 4222
e-mail: H3159@accor-hotels.com
Dir: *M4 junct 30, take slip rd signed Cardiff Service Station. Hotel on left.*
Modern, budget hotel offering comfortable accommodation in bright and practical bedrooms. Breakfast is self-service and dinner is available in the restaurant. For further details, consult the Hotel Groups page.
ROOMS: 78 en suite s £38.95-£43.95; d £38.95-£43.95 **CONF:** Thtr 18 Class 12 Board 14

Innkeeper's Lodge Cardiff
Tyn-y-Parc Rd, Whitchurch CF14 6BG
☎ 029 2069 2554 029 2052 7052
www.innkeeperslodge.com
Dir: *M4 junct 32, southbound on A470. At 3rd set of T-lights, turn left , opposite Safeway supermarket*
Smart rooms meet essential business requirements but also have home comforts, and depending on location may well have meeting rooms and pub dining. Dining options generally include all-day menus plus the added advantage of breakfast.
ROOMS: 52 en suite s £49; d £49 **CONF:** Thtr 40 Class 40 Board 20

CARDIFF, continued

⌂ Travel Inn (Cardiff Bay)
Keen Rd CF24 5JT
☎ 08701 977050 029 2049 0403
Dir: *Cardiff Docks & Bay signs from A48(M), over flyover & next 4 rdbts. At 5th rdbt, take 3rd exit. Travel Inn 1st right & 1st right again*
Travel Inn offers good-quality, value-for-money accommodation. Spacious, en suite rooms with bath and shower comfortably accommodate a family of up to two adults and two children (to age 15). The restaurant and bar offers a varied menu. For further details consult the Hotel Groups page.
ROOMS: 73 en suite s £45.95-£46.95; d £45.95-£46.95 **CONF:** Thtr 15

⌂ Travel Inn Cardiff (Roath)
David Lloyd Leisure Club, Ipswich Rd, Roath CF23 9AQ
☎ 08701 977049 029 2046 2482
Dir: *M4 (J30) take A4232 to A48. 2nd exit off A48 to Cardiff East and Docks, (A4161). Follow signs for David Lloyd Leisure Club.*
Travel Inn offers good-quality, value-for-money accommodation. Spacious, en suite rooms with bath and shower comfortably accommodate a family of up to two adults and two children (to age 15). The restaurant and bar offers a varied menu. For further details consult the Hotel Groups page.
ROOMS: 70 en suite s £45.95-£46.95; d £45.95-£46.95 **CONF:** Thtr 300

⌂ Travel Inn (Cardiff West)
The Walston Castle, Port Road, Nantisaf, Wenvoe CF5 6DD
☎ 08701 977052 029 2059 1436
Dir: *From M4 (J33) south on A4232. Take 2nd exit (signed Airport), then 3rd exit at Culverhouse Cross rdt. Travel Inn 0.5m on Barry Rd (A4050)*
Travel Inn offers good-quality, value-for-money accommodation. Spacious, en suite rooms with bath and shower comfortably accommodate a family of up to two adults and two children (to age 15). The restaurant and bar offers a varied menu. For further details consult the Hotel Groups page.
ROOMS: 39 en suite s £45.95-£46.95; d £45.95-£46.95 **CONF:** Thtr 12

⌂ Travelodge (Cardiff Central)
Imperial Gate, Saint Marys St CF10 1FA
☎ 08700 850 950 029 2039 8737
Travelodge offers good quality, good value, modern accommodation. Ideal for families, the spacious, en suite bedrooms include remote-control TV, tea and coffee-making facilities and luxury beds. Meals can be taken at the nearby family restaurant. For further details consult the Hotel Groups page.
ROOMS: 100 en suite s fr £25; d fr £25

⌂ Travelodge (Cardiff East)
Circle Way East, Llanedeyrn CF23 9PD
☎ 08700 850 950 029 2054 9564
Dir: *M4 junct 30, take A4232 to North Pentwyn junct. A48 & signs for Cardiff East & Docks. 3rd exit at Llanedeyrn junct, follow Circle Way East*
Travelodge offers good quality, good value, modern accommodation. Ideal for families, the spacious, en suite bedrooms include remote-control TV, tea and coffee-making facilities and luxury beds. Meals can be taken at the nearby family restaurant. For further details consult the Hotel Groups page.
ROOMS: 32 en suite s fr £25; d fr £25

⌂ Travelodge (Cardiff West)
Granada Service Area M4, Pontyclun CF72 8SA
☎ 08700 850 950 029 2089 9412
Dir: *M4, junct 33/A4232*
Travelodge offers good quality, good value, modern accommodation. Ideal for families, the spacious, en suite bedrooms include remote-control TV, tea and coffee-making facilities and luxury beds. Meals can be taken at the nearby family restaurant. For further details consult the Hotel Groups page.
ROOMS: 50 en suite s fr £25; d fr £25 **CONF:** Thtr 45 Board 34

○ Park Plaza Cardiff
Greyfriars Rd CF10 5AB
☎ 020 7776 99872
ROOMS: 129 en suite **NOTES:** Due to open mid 2005

CARDIGAN See Gwbert-on-Sea

CARMARTHEN, Carmarthenshire — Map 08 SN42

★★70% Falcon
Lammas St SA31 3AP
☎ 01267 234959 & 237152 01267 221277
e-mail: reception@falconcarmarthen.co.uk
web: www.falconcarmarthen.co.uk
Dir: *in town centre pass bus station turn left, hotel 200yds on left*

This friendly hotel has been owned by the Exton family for 45 years. Personally run, it is well placed in the centre of the town. Bedrooms, some with four-poster beds, are tastefully decorated with good facilities. There is an comfortable lounge with adjacent bar and the restaurant, open for lunch and dinner, has a varied selection of dishes on the carte menu.
ROOMS: 14 en suite (1 fmly) **CONF:** Thtr 80 Class 50 Board 40
PARKING: 38 **NOTES:** Closed 25-26 Dec RS Sun
CARDS:

CASTLETON, Newport — Map 09 ST28

⌂ Travel Inn (Cardiff East)
Newport Rd CF3 2UQ
☎ 08701 977051 01633 681143
Dir: *M4 junct 8, at rdbt take 2nd exit A48 Castleton and follow for 3m, Travel Inn on right*
Travel Inn offers good-quality, value-for-money accommodation. Spacious, en suite rooms with bath and shower comfortably accommodate a family of up to two adults and two children (to age 15). The restaurant and bar offers a varied menu. For further details consult the Hotel Groups page.
ROOMS: 49 en suite s £45.95-£46.95; d £45.95-£46.95

CHEPSTOW, Monmouthshire Map 04 ST59

★★★★71% Marriott St Pierre Hotel & Country Club
St Pierre Park NP16 6YA
☎ 01291 625261 01291 629975
Dir: *M48 junct 2. At rdbt on slip road take A466 Chepstow. At next rdbt take 1st exit Caerwent A48. Hotel approx 2m on left*
This 14th-century property offers an extensive range of leisure and conference facilities. Bedrooms are well equipped, comfortable and located either in adjacent wings or in a lakeside cottage complex. The main bar, popular with golfers, overlooks the 18th green, whilst diners can choose between a traditional elegant restaurant and modern brasserie.
ROOMS: 148 en suite (16 fmly) (75 GF) ⊗ in 74 bedrooms s fr £108; d fr £156 (incl. bkfst) **LB** **FACILITIES: Spa** STV 36 Fishing Sauna Solarium Gym Putt green Jacuzzi Health spa, Floodlit driving range, Chipping green, Short game area Xmas **CONF:** Thtr 220 Class 120 Board 90 **PARKING:** 430 **NOTES:** ⊗ in restaurant Civ Wed 200 **CARDS:**

★★★66% Chepstow
Newport Rd NP16 5PR
☎ 01291 626261 01291 626263
e-mail: info@chepstowhotel.com
web: www.chepstowhotel.com
Dir: *M48 junct 2, follow signs to Chepstow, A466 & A48 into town, hotel on left*
This privately owned hotel is conveniently situated on the main road into town with easy access for the M4 and M48. Bedrooms vary in size and style, but all have modern equipment and facilities. The majority have been refurbished, as have the pleasant and attractively appointed public areas. Facilities here include an air-conditioned conference room and a large ballroom.
ROOMS: 31 en suite (4 fmly) ⊗ in 14 bedrooms s fr £57; d fr £69 **LB** **FACILITIES:** ch fac Xmas **CONF:** Thtr 200 Class 70 Board 50 Del from £92.50 **SERVICES:** Lift **PARKING:** 180 **NOTES:** ⊗ in restaurant Civ Wed 150 **CARDS:**

See advert on this page

★★66% Beaufort
Beaufort Square NP16 5EP
☎ 01291 622497 01291 627389
e-mail: info@thebeauforthotel.co.uk
web: www.beauforthotelchepstow.com
Dir: *off A48, at St Mary's church turn left and left again at end of public car park (Nelson St). Hotel car park 100yds on right*
Privately owned and personally run, this 16th-century coaching inn is centrally located in town. The bedrooms vary in style and size and include two rooms on ground-floor level with direct access from the car park. The inviting and popular public areas have plenty of charm and character. They include a friendly bar and a pleasant restaurant where well-prepared meals are served. There is also a large meeting and function room available.
ROOMS: 22 en suite (2 fmly) s £35-£46; d £59 **LB** **FACILITIES:** STV ch fac **CONF:** Thtr 140 Class 70 Board 40 **PARKING:** 14 **NOTES:** ⊗ in restaurant Civ Wed 140 **CARDS:**

★★66% Castle View
16 Bridge St NP6 5EZ
☎ 01291 620349 01291 627397
e-mail: dave@castview.demon.co.uk
Dir: *M48 junct 2 for Wye Valley on A466 at 1st rdbt turn right onto A48 towards Gloucester. Follow 2nd sign to town centre & follow directions to Chepstow Castle, hotel directly opposite*
This privately owned inn is situated opposite the Norman castle.

continued on p800

CHEPSTOW, continued

Bedrooms vary in size, and all are similarly furnished and well equipped, with some rooms situated in separate buildings. Several family rooms are available. Public areas include a comfortable lounge, a pleasant lounge bar and a cosy restaurant offering freshly prepared cuisine.
ROOMS: 9 en suite 4 annexe en suite (7 fmly) s £50; d fr £71 (incl. cont bkfst) **LB** **FACILITIES:** Xmas **NOTES:** ⊗ in restaurant
CARDS:

See advert on page 799

CHIRK, Wrexham Map 15 SJ23

★★★66% Moreton Park Lodge

Moreton Park, Gledrid LL14 5DG
☎ 01691 776666 📠 01691 776655
e-mail: reservations@moretonpark.com
web: www.moretonpark.com
Dir: *200yds from rdbt of A5 and B5070*
This privately-owned and purpose-built modern hotel is on the outskirts of Chirk. It offers well-equipped accommodation, which includes bedrooms suitable for less able guests. Some rooms have separate lounge areas. Meals are available in the Lord Moreton pub/restaurant, and there is an indoor play area for children.
ROOMS: 46 en suite (20 fmly) ⊗ in 26 bedrooms s £65-£75; d £65-£75 **LB** **FACILITIES:** STV Xmas **PARKING:** 400 **NOTES:** 🐕
CARDS:

COLWYN BAY, Conwy Map 14 SH87

★★★68% *Hopeside*

63-67 Prince's Dr, West End LL29 8PW
☎ 01492 533244 📠 01492 532850
e-mail: hopesidejd@aol.com
Dir: *off A55 at Rhos-on-Sea exit, turn left at lights, hotel 50yds on right*
The promenade and town centre are within easy walking distance of this friendly hotel. The restaurant offers a good choice, and bar food and blackboard specials are also available. The bedrooms are mostly pine-furnished and all are attractively decorated. The hotel also holds a licence for civil marriage ceremonies.
ROOMS: 18 en suite (2 fmly) ⊗ in 9 bedrooms **FACILITIES:** STV Sauna Gym **CONF:** Thtr 50 Class 50 Board 34 **PARKING:** 14
NOTES: ⊗ in restaurant **CARDS:**

★★★66% *Norfolk House*

39 Princes Dr LL29 8PF
☎ 01492 531757 & 536466 📠 01492 533781
e-mail: timbucknall@aol.com
web: www.norfolkhousehotel.co.uk
Dir: *A55 at Colwyn Bay, into right lane of slip road, right at traffic lights, pass station, hotel almost opposite filling station*
Norfolk House is a privately owned and personally run hotel with a warm, friendly atmosphere. It is within easy walking distance of the seafront, town centre and railway station. The accommodation is well equipped, comfortable and relaxing. Bedrooms are prettily decorated with family suites available. There are several lounges, a popular bar and conference facilities.
ROOMS: 22 en suite (4 fmly) (5 GF) **CONF:** Thtr 60 Board 30
SERVICES: Lift **PARKING:** 25 **NOTES:** ⊗ in restaurant
CARDS:

★★64% Lyndale

410 Abergele Rd, Old Colwyn LL29 9AB
THE INDEPENDENTS
☎ 01492 515429 📠 01492 518805
e-mail: lyndale@tinyworld.co.uk
Dir: *A55 junct 22 Old Colwyn, turn left. At rdbt through village continue for 1m on A547*
A range of accommodation is available at this friendly, family-run hotel, including suites that are suitable for family use and a four-poster bedroom. There is a cosy bar and a comfortable foyer lounge, and weddings and other functions can be catered for.
ROOMS: 14 en suite (3 fmly) ⊗ in 3 bedrooms s £25-£39; d £45-£59 (incl. bkfst) **LB** **FACILITIES:** ch fac **CONF:** Thtr 40 Class 20 Board 20
PARKING: 20 **CARDS:**

★★64% Marine

West Promenade LL28 4BP
☎ 01492 530295 📠 0870 168 9400
e-mail: reservations@marinehotel.co.uk
Dir: *off A55 at Old Colwyn to seafront. Turn left, after pier left before lights, car park on corner*
This privately owned and personally run hotel stands on the promenade, overlooking the sea. The accommodation is soundly maintained and equipped to suit both commercial visitors and holidaymakers. Facilities include a small bar and a lounge.
ROOMS: 14 rms (12 en suite) (4 fmly) ⊗ in 9 bedrooms s £27-£32; d fr £54 (incl. bkfst) **LB** **PARKING:** 11 **NOTES:** ⊗ in restaurant Closed mid Oct-Apr **CARDS:**

CONWY, Conwy Map 14 SH77

★★★73% ⊛ Groes Inn

Tyn-y-Groes LL32 8TN
☎ 01492 650545 📠 01492 650855
web: www.groesinn.com
Dir: *A55, over Old Conwy Bridge, 1st left through Castle Walls on B5106 (Trefriw road), hotel 2m on right.*

This inn dates back in part to the 16th century and has charming features. It offers a choice of bars and has a beautifully appointed restaurant, with a conservatory extension opening on to the lovely rear garden. The comfortable, well-equipped bedrooms are contained in a separate building; some have balconies or private terraces.
ROOMS: 14 en suite (1 fmly) (4 GF) ⊗ in 6 bedrooms **CONF:** Thtr 22 Class 20 Board 20 **PARKING:** 100 **NOTES:** ⊗ in restaurant Closed Xmas
CARDS:

★★★71% Castle Hotel Conwy

High St LL32 8DB
☎ 01492 582800 📠 01492 582300
e-mail: mail@castlewales.co.uk web: www.castlewales.co.uk
Dir: *A55 junct 18, follow signs for town centre and cross estuary with castle on left. Right then left at mini rdbts onto one-way system. Right at Town Wall Gate, right onto Berry St then along High St, hotel on left*

This family-run, 16th-century hotel is one of Conwy's most distinguished buildings and offers a relaxed and friendly atmosphere. Bedrooms have been extensively refurbished to an impressive standard including a stunning new suite. Public areas have also been upgraded and include a popular modern bar and the award-winning Shakespeare's restaurant. Nominated for the AA Hotel of the Year Award for Wales 2004-5.
ROOMS: 28 en suite (2 fmly) ⊗ in 20 bedrooms s £60-£79; d £90-£250 (incl. bkfst) **LB** **FACILITIES:** ch fac Xmas **CONF:** Thtr 30 Class 20 Board 20 Del from £89.95 **PARKING:** 34 **NOTES:** ⊗ in restaurant **CARDS:**

See advert on this page

Top 200 – Hotel

★★ ®®® The Old Rectory Country House

Llanrwst Rd, Llansanffraid Glan Conwy LL28 5LF
☎ 01492 580611 📠 01492 584555
e-mail: info@oldrectorycountryhouse.co.uk
web: www.oldrectorycountryhouse.co.uk
Dir: *0.5m S from A470/A55 junct on left side, by 30mph sign*

This friendly and welcoming hotel enjoys elevated views of the Conwy Estuary and Snowdonia. Traditionally-styled day rooms are luxurious and elegant and home-baked afternoon teas can be taken in the elegant lounge. Dinner is the highlight of any stay and the daily changing set menu makes excellent use of fresh and seasonal local produce. Bedrooms make the most of the views and are furnished with thought and care. Super hospitality sustains a real 'home-from-home' ambience.
ROOMS: 4 en suite 2 annexe en suite ⊗ in all bedrooms **PARKING:** 10 **NOTES:** No children 5yrs ⊗ in restaurant Closed 14 Dec-15 Jan **CARDS:**

★★70% Tir-y-Coed Country House

Rowen LL32 8TP
☎ 01492 650219 📠 01492 650219
e-mail: info@tirycoedhotel.co.uk
web: www.tirycoedhotel.co.uk
Dir: *off B5106 into unclassified road signed Rowen, hotel approx 60mtrs N of Post Office*

This small hotel is a haven of peace and relaxation. Standing in its own extensive and delightful garden, the house is located in the picturesque Conwy Valley. It is convenient for access to Snowdonia and the coast. The accommodation is well maintained and equipped, and the hospitality warm and friendly.
ROOMS: 7 en suite 1 annexe en suite (1 fmly) s £32-£36; d £59-£67 (incl. bkfst) **LB** **FACILITIES:** ch fac **PARKING:** 8 **NOTES:** ⊗ in restaurant Closed Xmas & New Year RS Nov-Feb **CARDS:**

GF Indicates the number of bedrooms at ground floor level.

C

COWBRIDGE, Vale of Glamorgan — Map 09 SS97

★★★69% The Bear Hotel
63 High St CF71 7AF
☎ 01446 774814 01446 775425
e-mail: enquiries@bearhotel.com
web: www.bearhotel.com
Dir: *in town centre*
Guests receive a genuinely friendly welcome at this famous coaching inn. It is infused with character throughout and features oak beams, real fires and a vaulted bear pit where Napoleon's troops were apparently held captive. It is now a delightful restaurant serving enjoyable cuisine. Rooms vary in size and style and are individually decorated. The hotel is a popular wedding venue.
ROOMS: 19 en suite 16 annexe en suite (2 fmly) (4 GF) in 14 bedrooms s £50-£55; d £70-£80 (incl. bkfst) **LB** **FACILITIES:** STV Xmas **CONF:** Thtr 100 Class 60 Board 50 Del £89.95 **PARKING:** 70 **NOTES:** in restaurant Civ Wed 90 **CARDS:**

CRICCIETH, Gwynedd — Map 14 SH43

★★★75% Bron Eifion Country House
LL52 0SA
☎ 01766 522385 01766 522003
e-mail: stay@broneifion.co.uk
web: www.broneifion.co.uk
Dir: *0.5m outside Criccieth on A497 towards Pwllheli*

This delightful country house is set in extensive grounds to the west of Criccieth. Most of the tasteful bedrooms have period and antique furniture, and some have four-poster beds or attractive canopies. The central hall features a minstrels' gallery, and there is a choice of comfortable lounges. The restaurant overlooks the gardens.
ROOMS: 19 en suite (1 fmly) (1 GF) in 4 bedrooms s £69-£76; d £100-£120 (incl. bkfst) **LB** **FACILITIES:** Xmas **CONF:** Thtr 30 Class 25 Board 25 **PARKING:** 80 **NOTES:** in restaurant
CARDS:

★★70% Caerwylan
LL52 0HW
☎ 01766 522547
e-mail: caerwylan_hotel@plevy.fsbusiness.co.uk
Dir: *near lifeboat station*
Privately owned and personally run, this long established holiday hotel commands panoramic sea views of Cardigan Bay and the castle. Comfortably furnished lounges are available for residents and the five-course menu changes daily. Bedrooms, including family rooms, are smart and modern, and several have their own private sitting areas. The friendly atmosphere ensures that many guests return year after year.
ROOMS: 25 en suite (3 fmly) s £25-£30; d £50-£60 (incl. bkfst) **LB** **SERVICES:** Lift **PARKING:** 9 **NOTES:** in restaurant Closed Nov-Etr
CARDS:

★★67% Gwyndy
Llanystumdwy LL52 0SP
☎ 01766 522720 01766 522720
e-mail: gwyndy@lineone.net
Dir: *A497 into village of Llanystumdwy follow road for 0.25m, hotel is next to church*
This popular hotel comprises a 17th-century cottage and a nearby purpose-built bedroom complex. The original cottage contains the lounge, bar and restaurant, all comfortably furnished. Exposed timbers and several stone fireplaces are attractive features, and bedrooms are spacious and relaxing.
ROOMS: 10 annexe en suite (5 fmly) (6 GF) s £26.50-£31.50; d £53 (incl. bkfst) **FACILITIES:** Fishing Xmas **PARKING:** 20 **NOTES:** in restaurant Closed Nov-Mar **CARDS:**

★★66% Lion
Y Maes LL52 0AA
☎ 01766 522460 01766 523075
e-mail: info@lionhotelcriccieth.co.uk
Dir: *A497 on to village green north, hotel on green*
This hotel lies just a short walk from Criccieth castle and seafront, with fine views from many rooms. The bars enjoy a good local following and staff are friendly and welcoming. Bedrooms are well-decorated and furnished, divided between the main building and a nearby annexe. Regular live entertainment is provided during the summer.
ROOMS: 34 en suite 12 annexe en suite (8 fmly) s £36-£40; d £60-£68 (incl. bkfst) **LB** **FACILITIES:** STV ♫ Xmas **SERVICES:** Lift **PARKING:** 30 **NOTES:** in restaurant
CARDS:

CRICKHOWELL, Powys — Map 09 SO21

★★★71% Bear
NP8 1BW
☎ 01873 810408 01873 811696
e-mail: bearhotel@aol.com
Dir: *on A40 between Abergavenny and Breen*
A favourite with locals as well as visitors, the character and friendliness of this 15th-century coaching inn are renowned. The bar and restaurant areas are furnished in keeping with the style and character of the building and provide a comfortable area in which to enjoy some of the finest locally-sourced ingredients. The hotel has very popular and extensive bar food.
ROOMS: 13 en suite 13 annexe en suite (6 fmly) s £59-£110; d £78-£145 (incl. bkfst) **CONF:** Thtr 60 Class 30 Board 20 **PARKING:** 45 **CARDS:**
See advert on opposite page

Packed in a hurry?
Ironing facilities should be available at all star levels, either in rooms or on request

★★★71% Gliffaes Country House Hotel
NP8 1RH
☎ 01874 730371 & 0800 146719 (Freephone) 01874 730463
e-mail: calls@gliffaeshotel.com
web: www.gliffaeshotel.com
Dir: *1m off A40, 2.5m W of Crickhowell*
This impressive Victorian mansion, standing in 33 acres of its own gardens and wooded grounds by the River Usk, is a privately owned and personally run hotel. Public rooms retain elegance and generous proportions and include a balcony and conservatory
continued

from which to enjoy the views. Bedrooms are furnished to a high standard and offer high levels of comfort.

ROOMS: 19 en suite 3 annexe en suite in all bedrooms s £65-£168; d £78-£180 (incl. bkfst) **LB** **FACILITIES:** Fishing Snooker Putt green Cycling, Birdwatching, Walking, Fishing, Falconry ch fac Xmas **CONF:** Thtr 40 Class 16 Board 16 **PARKING:** 34 **NOTES:** in restaurant Closed 2-18 Jan Civ Wed 50 **CARDS:**

★★★68% **Manor**
Brecon Rd NP8 1SE
01873 810212 01873 811938
e-mail: info@manorhotel.co.uk
web: www.manorhotel.co.uk
Dir: *on A40, Crickhowell/Brecon, 0.5m from Crickhowell*
This impressive manor house set in a stunning location was the birthplace of Sir George Everest. The bedrooms and public areas are elegant, and there are extensive leisure facilities. The restaurant has panoramic views and is the setting for exciting

continued

modern cooking. Guests can also dine informally at the nearby Nantyffin Cider Mill, a sister operation of the hotel.

Manor Hotel

ROOMS: 22 en suite (1 fmly) in 8 bedrooms s £45-£65; d £70-£95 (incl. bkfst) **LB** **FACILITIES:** STV Sauna Solarium Gym Jacuzzi Fitness assessment Sunbed ch fac Xmas **CONF:** Thtr 400 Class 300 Board 300 Del from £90 **PARKING:** 200 **NOTES:** in restaurant Civ Wed 100 **CARDS:**

★★74% **Ty Croeso**
The Dardy, Llangattock NP8 1PU
01873 810573 01873 810573
e-mail: info@ty-croeso.co.uk

Dir: *A40 at Shell garage take opposite road, down hill over river bridge. Turn right, after 0.5m turn left, up hill over canal, hotel signed*
Ty Croeso, meaning 'House of Welcome' lives up to its name. The restaurant has an interesting carte and set-price menu. Glamorgan sausages and laverbread are available at breakfast. Public areas

continued on p804

CRICKHOWELL, continued

are comfortable and feature log fires. Bedrooms are decorated with pretty fabrics and all have good facilities.
ROOMS: 8 en suite (1 fmly) ⊘ in 4 bedrooms **PARKING:** 20
NOTES: ⊘ in restaurant RS 24-26 Dec **CARDS:**

C

CROSS HANDS, Carmarthenshire Map 08 SN51

Travelodge Llanelli

Travelodge

SA14 6NW
☎ 08700 850 950 0870 191 1729
Dir: *on A48, westbound*
Travelodge offers good quality, good value, modern accommodation. Ideal for families, the spacious, en suite bedrooms include remote-control TV, tea and coffee-making facilities and luxury beds. Meals can be taken at the nearby family restaurant. For further details consult the Hotel Groups page.
ROOMS: 32 en suite s fr £25; d fr £25

CWMBRAN, Torfaen Map 09 ST29

★★★★66% Parkway

Best Western

Cwmbran Dr NP44 3UW
☎ 01633 871199 01633 869160
e-mail: enquiries@parkwayhotel.co.uk
web: www.bw-parkwayhotel.co.uk
Dir: *M4 junct 25A/26/A4051 follow signs Cwmbran-Llantarnam Park. Turn right at rdbt then right for hotel*
This hotel is purpose-built and offers comfortable bedrooms and public areas for a wide range of guests. There is a sports centre and a range of conference and meeting facilities. The coffee shop offers an informal eating option during the day and there is fine dining in Ravello's Restaurant.
ROOMS: 70 en suite (4 fmly) (34 GF) ⊘ in 34 bedrooms s £75-£95; d £85-£110 **LB** **FACILITIES:** STV Sauna Solarium Gym Jacuzzi Steam room, Private sun bathing terrace, Sports shop, solaria, relaxation area ♫ ch fac Xmas **CONF:** Thtr 500 Class 240 Board 100 Del from £104 **PARKING:** 300 **NOTES:** ⊘ in restaurant Civ Wed 100
CARDS:

DEVIL'S BRIDGE, Ceredigion Map 09 SN77

★★69% *Hafod Arms*

SY23 3JL
☎ 01970 890232 01970 890394
e-mail: enquiries@hafodarms.co.uk
Dir: *leave A44 at Ponterwyd. Hotel 5m along A4120, 11m E of Aberystwyth*
This former hunting lodge dates back to the 17th century and is now a family-owned and run hotel, providing accommodation suitable for both business people and tourists. Family rooms and a four-poster room are available. In addition to the dining area and lounge, there are tea rooms and six acres of grounds.
ROOMS: 15 rms (11 en suite) (1 fmly) **CONF:** Board 25 **PARKING:** 70
NOTES: No children 12yrs ⊘ in restaurant Closed 15 Dec-Jan
CARDS:

DOLGELLAU, Gwynedd Map 14 SH71

★★★80% Penmaenuchaf Hall

Penmaenpool LL40 1YB
☎ 01341 422129 01341 422787
e-mail: relax@penhall.co.uk
web: www.penhall.co.uk
Dir: *off A470 onto A493 to Tywyn. Hotel approx 1m on left*
Built in 1860, this impressive hall stands in 20 acres of formal gardens, grounds and woodland and enjoys magnificent views across the River Mawddach. Careful restoration has created a comfortable and welcoming hotel. Fresh produce cooked in modern British style is served in the panelled restaurant.

Penmaenuchaf Hall

ROOMS: 14 en suite (2 fmly) (1 GF) ⊘ in 5 bedrooms s £75-£135; d £120-£180 (incl. bkfst) **LB** **FACILITIES:** Fishing Snooker Complimentary salmon & trout fishing ch fac Xmas **CONF:** BC Thtr 50 Class 30 Board 22 Del from £140 **PARKING:** 30 **NOTES:** No children 6yrs ⊘ in restaurant Civ Wed 50 **CARDS:**

★★★74% Plas Dolmelynllyn

Ganllwyd LL40 2HP
☎ 01341 440273 01341 440640
e-mail: info@dolly-hotel.co.uk
web: www.dolly-hotel.co.uk
Dir: *5m N of Dolgellau on A470*
Surrounded by three acres of mature gardens and National Trust land, this fine house dates back to the 16th century. Spacious bedrooms are attractive and offer many thoughtful extras. Carefully prepared meals are served in the comfortable dining room, adjacent to the conservatory bar.
ROOMS: 10 en suite (2 fmly) ⊘ in all bedrooms **FACILITIES:** STV Fishing Mountain walking Mountain Bike riding Xmas **CONF:** Class 15 Board 15 Del from £100 **PARKING:** 16 **NOTES:** ⊘ in restaurant Closed Jan **CARDS:**

⊘ No smoking

★★★73% Dolserau Hall

LL40 2AG
☎ 01341 422522 01341 422400
e-mail: aa@dhh.co.uk
web: www.dhh.co.uk
Dir: *1.5m outside town between A494 to Bala and A470 to Dinas Mawddwy*

This privately-owned, friendly hotel lies in attractive grounds extending to the river and is surrounded by green fields. Several

continued

comfortable lounges are provided and welcoming log fires are lit during cold weather. The smart bedrooms are well equipped and comfortable. A varied menu offers very competently prepared dishes.
ROOMS: 15 en suite (3 fmly) s £45-£70; d £85-£135 (incl. bkfst & dinner) **LB FACILITIES:** STV Xmas **SERVICES:** Lift **PARKING:** 40 **NOTES:** No children 6yrs ⊗ in restaurant Closed mid Nov-Jan (ex Xmas & New Year) **CARDS:**

See advert on this page

★★67% Fronoleu Country Hotel
Tabor LL40 2PS
☎ 01341 422361 & 422197 ⎙ 01341 422023
e-mail: fronoleu@fronoleu.co.uk
web: www.fronoleu.co.uk
Dir: *A487/A470 junct, towards Tabor opposite Cross Foxes & continue for 1.25m. From Dolgellau take road for hospital & continue 1.25m up the hill*

This 16th-century farmhouse lies in the shadow of Cader Idris. Carefully extended, it retains many original features. The bar and lounge are located in the old building where there are exposed timbers and open fires. Most of the bedrooms are in a modern extension. The restaurant attracts a large local following.
ROOMS: 11 en suite (3 fmly) ⊗ in 6 bedrooms s £36.50-£39; d £63-£68 (incl. bkfst) **LB FACILITIES:** Fishing Pool table, Childrens play area ♫ ch fac **CONF:** BC Thtr 150 Class 100 Board 50 Del from £60 **PARKING:** 60 **NOTES:** ⊗ in restaurant Civ Wed 150
CARDS:

★★67% Royal Ship
Queens Square LL40 1AR
☎ 01341 422209 ⎙ 01341 421027
Dir: *in town centre*
The Royal Ship dates from 1813 when it was a coaching inn. There are three bars and several lounges, all most comfortably furnished and appointed. It is very much the centre of local activities and a wide range of food is available. Bedrooms are tastefully decorated.
ROOMS: 24 en suite (4 fmly) s £47.50-£50; d £70-£87.50 (incl. bkfst) **LB FACILITIES:** Fishing arrangements available Xmas **CONF:** Thtr 80 Class 60 Board 60 **PARKING:** 12 **NOTES:** ⊗ in restaurant
CARDS:

See advert on this page

DOLWYDDELAN, Conwy — Map 14 SH75

★★64% *Elen's Castle*
LL25 0EJ
☎ 01690 750207 ⎙ 01690 750207
e-mail: info@elenscastlehotel.co.uk
Dir: *on A470, 5m S of Betws-y-Coed*
This small hotel is very friendly and was operated as a beer house in the 18th century. The original bar, complete with a slab floor and potbelly stove, remains, and there are two cosy sitting rooms

continued on p806

DOLWYDDELAN, continued

with open fires and exposed timbers. Two of the bedrooms have four-poster beds and families can be accommodated. A good range of bar and restaurant food is provided.
ROOMS: 9 rms (8 en suite) (2 fmly) ⊗ in 2 bedrooms
FACILITIES: Coarse & fly fishing ch fac **CONF:** Thtr 30 Class 20 Board 15 **PARKING:** 40 **NOTES:** ⊗ in restaurant **CARDS:**

EGLWYSFACH, Ceredigion Map 14 SN69

Top 200 – Hotel

★★★ **Ynyshir Hall**
SY20 8TA
☎ 01654 781209 01654 781366
e-mail: info@ynyshir-hall.co.uk
web: www.ynyshir-hall.co.uk
Dir: *off A487, 5.5m S of Machynlleth, signed from main road*
Set in beautifully landscaped grounds and surrounded by an RSBP reserve, Ynyshir Hall is a haven of calm. The hotel dates to the 16th century and was once a retreat for Queen Victoria. Lavishly styled bedrooms, each of which is individually themed around a great painter, offer high standards of luxury. Flair and skill are evident in the preparation of meals, which are served in the stylish dining room overlooking the garden.
ROOMS: 7 en suite 2 annexe en suite ⊗ in all bedrooms s £95-£220; d £180-£250 (incl. bkfst) **LB** **FACILITIES:** Xmas
CONF: Thtr 25 Class 20 Board 18 Del from £185 **PARKING:** 20
NOTES: No children 9yrs ⊗ in restaurant Closed 5-29 Jan Civ Wed 40 **CARDS:**

RELAIS & CHATEAUX.

EWLOE, Flintshire Map 15 SJ36

★★★★70% **De Vere St David's Park**
St Davids Park CH5 3YB
☎ 01244 520800 01244 520930
e-mail: reservations.stdavids@devere-hotels.com
Dir: *A494 Queensferry to Mold for 4m, then left slip road B5127 signed Buckley, hotel visible at rdbt*
This modern hotel is conveniently situated and offers a range of rooms, including four-poster suites and family rooms. Public areas include leisure and spa facilities, an all-day café, and, nearby, the hotel's own golf course. Younger guests are not forgotten either and can have fun in the Dai the Dove Club.

DE VERE HOTELS

De Vere, St David's Park

ROOMS: 145 en suite (24 fmly) (43 GF) ⊗ in 54 bedrooms
FACILITIES: STV supervised Snooker Sauna Solarium Gym Putt green Jacuzzi Steam bath, Beauty Therapist, Playroom Xmas **CONF:** BC Thtr 300 Class 150 Board 40 **SERVICES:** Lift **PARKING:** 240
NOTES: ⊗ in restaurant Civ Wed 60
CARDS:

FISHGUARD, Pembrokeshire Map 08 SM93

★★69% ***Cartref***
15-19 High St SA65 9AW
☎ 01348 872430 01348 873664
e-mail: cartref@themail.co.uk
Dir: *on A40 in town centre*
Personally run by the proprietor, this friendly hotel offers convenient access to the town centre and ferry terminal. Bedrooms are well maintained and include some family bedded rooms. There is also a cosy lounge bar and a welcoming restaurant, which looks out over the High Street.
ROOMS: 10 en suite (2 fmly) **PARKING:** 4 **NOTES:** ⊗ in restaurant
CARDS:

FLINT, Flintshire Map 15 SJ27

★★★59% ***Mountain Park Hotel***
Northop Rd, Flint Mountain CH6 5QG
☎ 01352 736000 & 730972 01352 736010
Dir: *off A55 for Flint onto A5119, hotel 1 mile on left*
This former farmhouse has modern, well-equipped bedrooms and is conveniently situated close to the motorway. Facilities include the Sevens Brasserie Restaurant serving modern cuisine; a comfortable lounge bar offering a range of bar meals; and an attractively designed function/conference room. There is also a 9-hole golf course.
ROOMS: 21 annexe en suite (1 fmly) ⊗ in 11 bedrooms
FACILITIES: 9 Jacuzzi ch fac **CONF:** Thtr 80 Class 80 Board 60
SERVICES: air con **PARKING:** 94 **NOTES:** ⊗ in restaurant
CARDS:

GLYN CEIRIOG, Wrexham Map 15 SJ23

★★★66% **Golden Pheasant**
LL20 7BB
☎ 01691 718281 01691 718479
e-mail: goldenpheasant@micro-plus-web.net
web: www.goldenpheasanthotel.co.uk
Dir: *A5/B4500 at Chirk, continue for 5m to Pontfadog & follow signs for hotel, 1st left after Cheshire Home, follow to top of small hill to hotel*
This 18th-century hostelry is quietly situated in open countryside

continued

surrounded by rolling hills. The bedrooms include four-poster and family rooms and there is a choice of bars, as well as a lounge and a restaurant. To the rear is an attractive courtyard with shrubs and flowerbeds.
ROOMS: 19 en suite (5 fmly) s £40-£88; d £80-£100 (incl. bkfst) LB **FACILITIES:** Xmas **CONF:** Thtr 60 Board 10 **PARKING:** 45 **NOTES:** ⊗ in restaurant RS Closed 25 Dec pm **CARDS:**

GWBERT-ON-SEA, Ceredigion Map 08 SN15

★★★67% Cliff
SA43 1PP
☎ 01239 613241 📠 01239 615391
e-mail: reservations@cliffhotel.com
Dir: *off A487 into Cardigan, follow signs to Gwbert, 3m to hotel*

Set in 30 acres of grounds that include a 9-hole golf course, and enjoying a cliff-top location overlooking Cardigan Bay, this hotel offers superb sea views. Bedrooms come in a variety of sizes, with some overlooking the bay. Public areas are spacious and offer a choice of bars.
ROOMS: 72 en suite (5 fmly) ⊗ in 10 bedrooms **FACILITIES:** STV 9 Fishing Snooker Sauna Gym Putt green ♫ **CONF:** BC Thtr 350 Class 100 Board 70 Del from £85 **SERVICES:** Lift **PARKING:** 95 **NOTES:** ⊗ in restaurant Civ Wed 220
CARDS:

See advert on this page

HALKYN, Flintshire Map 15 SJ27

Travelodge
CH8 8RF
☎ 08700 850 950 📠 01352 781966
Dir: *on A55, westbound*

Travelodge

Travelodge offers good quality, good value, modern accommodation. Ideal for families, the spacious, en suite bedrooms include remote-control TV, tea and coffee-making facilities and luxury beds. Meals can be taken at the nearby family restaurant. For further details consult the Hotel Groups page.
ROOMS: 31 en suite s fr £25; d fr £25

Indoor Swimming Pool
Indoor Swimming Pool (heated)
Outdoor Swimming Pool
Outdoor Swimming Pool (heated)

HARLECH, Gwynedd

Top 200 – Hotel

★★

Maes y Neuadd Country House

LL47 6YA
☎ 01766 780200 01766 780211
e-mail: maes@neuadd.com
web: www.neuadd.com
Dir: *3m NE of Harlech, signed on an unclassed road off B4573*

This 14th-century hotel enjoys fine views over the mountains and across the bay to the Lleyn Peninsula. The team here is committed to highlighting and restoring some of the hidden features of the house. Bedrooms, some in an adjacent coach house, are individually furnished and many boast fine antique pieces. Public areas display a similar welcoming charm, including the restaurant, which serves many home-grown and locally-sourced ingredients.

ROOMS: 16 en suite (3 GF) ⊗ in all bedrooms s £75-£95; d £179-£270 (incl. bkfst & dinner) **LB** **FACILITIES:** clay pigeon,cooking tuition Xmas **CONF:** Thtr 20 Class 10 Board 12 Del from £185 **PARKING:** 50 **NOTES:** ⊗ in restaurant Civ Wed 65 **CARDS:**

★★67% Estuary Motel

Stryd Fawr LL47 6TA
☎ 01766 771155 01766 771393
e-mail: enquiries@the-estuary.fsnet.co.uk
Dir: *from Barmouth take A496 to Porthmadog. Talsarnau is approximately 4m N of Harlech. Motel on right*

This single storey, purpose-built small hotel is conveniently located for visiting Snowdonia, Harlech Castle and the many coastal attractions of the area. Privately owned and personally run, it provides friendly hospitality and well equipped, motel-style accommodation.

ROOMS: 10 annexe en suite (3 fmly) (10 GF) ⊗ in 9 bedrooms s £35-£41; d £50-£62 (incl. bkfst) **LB** **PARKING:** 20 **NOTES:** ⊗ in restaurant **CARDS:**

The Castle

Castle Square LL46 2YH
☎ 01766 780529 01766 780499
Dir: *directly opposite entrance to Harlech Castle*

ROOMS: 7 en suite (1 fmly) s £26-£36; d £52-£72 (incl. bkfst) **PARKING:** 30 **NOTES:** ★★ ⊗ in restaurant **CARDS:**

HAVERFORDWEST, Pembrokeshire Map 08 SM91

★★68% Hotel Mariners

THE INDEPENDENTS

Mariners Square SA61 2DU
☎ 01437 763353 01437 764258
Dir: *follow town centre signs, over bridge, up High St, 1st turning on right, hotel at the end*

Located just out of the town centre, this privately owned and friendly hotel is reputed to date back to 1625. The bedrooms are equipped with modern facilities and are soundly maintained. A good range of food is offered in the popular bar, which is a focus for the town. The restaurant offers a more formal dining option. Facilities include a choice of meeting rooms.

ROOMS: 28 en suite (5 fmly) ⊗ in 11 bedrooms s £56.50-£65.50; d £75.50-£85 (incl. bkfst) **LB** **FACILITIES:** STV Short mat bowls **CONF:** Thtr 50 Class 20 Board 20 **PARKING:** 50 **NOTES:** Closed 25-27 Dec & 1 Jan **CARDS:**

★★65% Wilton House Hotel

6 Quay St SA61 1BG
☎ 01437 760033 01437 760297
e-mail: wad99@hotmail.com
Dir: *M4 junct 49/A48 to Carmarthen & A40 to Haverfordwest. Follow signs into town centre & take 1st left into Quay St. Hotel 50mtrs on left*

This hotel is under new ownership. Formerly a saddlery, it is situated in a quiet side street close to the town centre and the River Cleddau. The well-proportioned bedrooms are tastefully decorated and well equipped. Public areas consist of a lounge and a bistro-style restaurant serving home-made food.

ROOMS: 11 en suite (3 fmly) (2 GF) s fr £45; d fr £60 (incl. bkfst) **FACILITIES:** **PARKING:** 5 **NOTES:** **CARDS:**

★★64% Castle Hotel

Castle Square SA61 2AA
☎ 01437 769322 01437 768806
Dir: *from main rdbt into Haverfordwest follow town centre signs, approx 200yds, hotel on right*

This 19th-century inn is centrally located off the High Street of this bustling town. Bedrooms are tastefully decorated and thoughtfully equipped and the spacious bar, which fronts Castle Square, is popular with locals for its evening entertainment. Relaxed dining is offered in Turrets Restaurant where enjoyable home-cooked meals can be enjoyed.

ROOMS: 9 en suite (1 fmly) s fr £42.50; d fr £57.50 (incl. bkfst) **LB** **NOTES:** ⊗ in restaurant Closed 24-25 & 31 Dec **CARDS:**

HAY-ON-WYE, Powys Map 09 SO24

★★★70% The Swan-at-Hay

Church St HR3 5DQ
☎ 01497 821188 01497 821424
e-mail: info@swanathay.co.uk
Dir: *on B4350 from Brecon, hotel on left. From any other route follow signs for Brecon & just before leaving town hotel on right*

This former coaching inn dates back to the 1800s and is only a short walk from the town centre. Bedrooms are well equipped and some are located in converted cottages across the courtyard. Spacious, relaxing public areas include a comfortable lounge, a choice of bars and a more formal restaurant. There is also a large function room and a smaller meeting room.

ROOMS: 15 en suite 4 annexe en suite (1 fmly) s £65-£115; d £85-£125 (incl. bkfst) **LB** **FACILITIES:** Fishing Xmas **CONF:** Thtr 140 Class 60 Board 50 Del from £110 **PARKING:** 18 **NOTES:** ⊗ in restaurant Civ Wed 50 **CARDS:**

★★72% Old Black Lion
26 Lion St HR3 5AD
☎ 01497 820841 01497 822960
e-mail: info@oldblacklion.co.uk
web: www.oldblacklion.co.uk
Dir: *from Tourist Information car park turn right along Oxford Rd, pass Nat West bank, next left (Lion St), hotel 20yds on right*
This fine old coaching inn, with a history stretching back several centuries, has a wealth of charm and character. It was occupied by Oliver Cromwell during the siege of Hay Castle. Privately owned and personally run, it provides cosy and well-equipped bedrooms, some of which are located in an adjacent building. A wide range of competently prepared food is provided and service is friendly.
ROOMS: 6 rms (5 en suite) 4 annexe en suite (2 GF) s £42.50-£50; d £80-£110 (incl. bkfst) **LB** **FACILITIES:** Xmas **PARKING:** 16 **NOTES:** No children 5yrs in restaurant **CARDS:**

★★69% Baskerville Arms
Clyro HR3 5RZ
☎ 01497 820670 01497 821609
e-mail: lyn@baskervillearms.co.uk
Dir: *from Hereford follow Brecon A438 into Clyro. Hotel signed*
Situated near Hay-on-Wye in the peaceful village of Clyro, this former Georgian coaching inn is personally run by its friendly and enthusiastic owners. Bedrooms are well equipped with comfort in mind, while public areas include a bar with a village inn atmosphere, a separate restaurant and a comfortable residents' lounge. There is also a large function room, plus a meeting room.
ROOMS: 12 rms (10 en suite) (1 fmly) in 4 bedrooms s £35-£45; d £60-£80 (incl. bkfst) **LB** **FACILITIES:** Fishing ch fac **CONF:** Thtr 65 Class 40 Board 36 **PARKING:** 12 **NOTES:** in restaurant **CARDS:**

★★67% Kilverts Hotel
The Bull Ring HR3 5AG
☎ 01497 821042 01497 821580
e-mail: info@kilverts.co.uk
Dir: *from Brecon on B4350, on entering Hay-on-Wye take 1st right after Cinema Bookshop. Then 1st left and hotel is on right after 40yds*
Situated in the centre of this fascinating town, Kilverts is a genuinely friendly and welcoming hotel. The committed staff provide attentive hospitality within a convivial atmosphere. Well-equipped bedrooms are cosy, with plenty of character. Food has an international influence, available in either the bar or stylish restaurant. The extensive gardens are ideal in the summer months.
ROOMS: 11 en suite (1 fmly) s fr £50; d £70-£90 (incl. bkfst) **LB** **CONF:** Thtr 30 Class 10 **PARKING:** 13 **NOTES:** in restaurant Closed 25 Dec **CARDS:**

 AA Rosette Award for culinary excellence

HENSOL, Vale of Glamorgan
Map 09 ST07

★★★★71% Vale Hotel Golf & Spa Resort
Hensol Park CF72 8JY
☎ 01443 667800 01443 665850
e-mail: reservations@vale-hotel.com
web: www.vale-hotel.com
Dir: *M4 junct 34, towards Pendoylan, hotel is signposted,approx 3 mins drive from junct.*
A wealth of leisure facilities are offered at this large and modern, purpose-built complex, including two golf courses and a driving range, extensive health spa, gym, swimming pool, squash courts and an orthopaedic clinic. Public areas are spacious and attractive,

continued

whilst bedrooms, many of which have balconies, are well appointed. Meeting and conference facilities are also available.
ROOMS: 29 en suite 114 annexe en suite (17 fmly) (36 GF) in 71 bedrooms s £80-£160; d £90-£180 **LB** **FACILITIES:** **Spa** STV 36 Fishing Squash Riding Sauna Solarium Gym Putt green Jacuzzi Beauty & Hydrotherapy treatments, Childrens club, Indoor training arena ch fac **CONF:** Thtr 300 Class 180 Board 60 Del from £145 **SERVICES:** Lift air con **PARKING:** 300 **NOTES:** in restaurant Civ Wed 200 **CARDS:** VISA

See advert under CARDIFF

HOLYHEAD See Anglesey, Isle of

HOLYWELL, Flintshire
Map 15 SJ17

★★70% Stamford Gate
Halkyn Rd CH8 7SJ
☎ 01352 712942 01352 713309
e-mail: hotel@stamfordgate.freeserve.co.uk
Dir: *take Holywell turn off A55 onto A5026, hotel 1m on right*
This popular, friendly hotel enjoys impressive views across the Dee Estuary from its elevated position. It provides well-equipped accommodation, including a number of ground-floor bedrooms. Public areas include a smart nautical themed restaurant, a stylish, spacious bar and there are meeting and function facilities.
ROOMS: 12 en suite (6 GF) **FACILITIES:** STV **CONF:** Thtr 100 Class 50 Board 30 **PARKING:** 100 **NOTES:** **CARDS:**

ISLE OF Placenames incorporating the words 'Isle' or 'Isle of' will be found under the actual name, eg Isle of Anglesey is under Anglesey, Isle of.

KNIGHTON, Powys
Map 09 SO27

Courtesy & Care Award

★★80% Milebrook House
Milebrook LD7 1LT
☎ 01547 528632 01547 520509
e-mail: hotel@milebrook.kc3ltd.co.uk
Dir: *2m E of Knighton, on A4113*
Set in three acres of grounds and gardens in the Teme Valley, this charming house dates back to 1760. Since it was converted into a hotel in 1987, it has acquired a well-deserved reputation for its warm hospitality, comfortable accommodation and the quality of its food, using local produce and home-grown vegetables. Milebrook House Hotel has been awarded the AA Courtesy & Care Award for Wales 2004-5.
ROOMS: 10 en suite (2 fmly) (2 GF) in all bedrooms s £58-£62; d £89-£95 (incl. bkfst) **LB** **FACILITIES:** Fishing Badminton,Trout Fly Fishing Xmas **CONF:** Class 30 **PARKING:** 21 **NOTES:** No children 8yrs in restaurant RS Mon **CARDS:**

LAMPETER, Ceredigion — Map 08 SN54

★★★71% Falcondale Mansion

SA48 7RX
☎ 01570 422910 📠 01570 423559
e-mail: info@falcondalehotel.com
Dir: *800yds W of High St A475 or 1.5m NW of Lampeter A482*

Built in the Italianate style, this charming Victorian property is set in extensive grounds and beautiful parkland. Bedrooms are generally spacious, well equipped and, following a refurbishment programme, are individually and tastefully decorated. Bars and lounges are similarly well appointed with additional facilities including a conservatory and function room.

ROOMS: 20 en suite (2 fmly) in 8 bedrooms s £80-£150; d £120-£180 (incl. bkfst) **LB** **FACILITIES:** Xmas **CONF:** Thtr 60 Class 30 Board 25 Del from £110 **SERVICES:** Lift **PARKING:** 60 **NOTES:** in restaurant Civ Wed 60 **CARDS:**

LAMPHEY See Pembroke

LLANARMON DYFFRYN CEIRIOG, Wrexham — Map 15 SJ13

★★74% West Arms

LL20 7LD
☎ 01691 600665 & 600612 📠 01691 600622
e-mail: gowestarms@aol.com
Dir: *off A483/A5 at Chirk, take B4500 to Ceiriog Valley, Llanarmon is 11m at end of B4500*

Set in the beautiful Ceiriog Valley, this delightful hotel has a wealth of charm and character. There is a comfortable lounge, a room for private dining and two bars, as well as a pleasant restaurant offering a fixed-price menu of freshly cooked dishes. The attractive bedrooms have a mixture of modern and period furnishings.

ROOMS: 15 en suite (2 fmly) (3 GF) s £52.50-£94; d £85-£174 (incl. bkfst) **LB** **FACILITIES:** Fishing ch fac Xmas **CONF:** BC Thtr 60 Class 50 Board 50 Del from £120 **PARKING:** 22 **NOTES:** in restaurant Civ Wed 50 **CARDS:**

LLANBEDR, Gwynedd — Map 14 SH52

★★64% Ty Mawr

LL45 2NH
☎ 01341 241440 📠 01341 241440
e-mail: tymawrhotel@onetel.com
Dir: *from Barmouth A496 Harlech road and at Llanbedr turn right after bridge in the village, hotel 50yds on left, brown tourist signs on junct*

Located in a picturesque village, this family-run hotel has a relaxed, friendly atmosphere. The pleasant grounds opposite the River Artro make a popular beer garden during fine weather. The attractive, cane-furnished bar offers a blackboard selection and a good choice of real ales. A more formal menu is available in the restaurant. Bedrooms are smart and brightly decorated.

ROOMS: 10 en suite (2 fmly) in all bedrooms s £40-£45; d £60-£70 (incl. bkfst) **LB** **FACILITIES:** STV ch fac **CONF:** Class 25 **PARKING:** 30 **NOTES:** in restaurant Closed 24-26 Dec **CARDS:**

LLANBERIS, Gwynedd — Map 14 SH56

★★★68% Quality Hotel Snowdonia

LL55 4TY
☎ 01286 870253 📠 01286 870149
e-mail: enquiries@hotels-snowdonia.com
web: www.hotels-snowdonia.com
Dir: *on A4086 Caernarfon to Llanberis road, directly opposite Snowdon Mountain railway*

This well-established hotel sits near the foot of Snowdon, between the Peris and Padarn Lakes. Pretty gardens and grounds make an attractive backdrop for the many weddings held here. Bedrooms have been refurbished and are well equipped. There are spacious lounges and bars, and a large dining room with conservatory overlooks the lakes.

ROOMS: 106 en suite (7 fmly) in 30 bedrooms s £69; d £100 (incl. bkfst) **LB** **FACILITIES:** STV Mountaineering, Cycling, Walking ♫ Xmas **CONF:** Thtr 100 Class 60 Board 50 Del £90 **SERVICES:** Lift **PARKING:** 300 **NOTES:** in restaurant RS 24-28 Dec Civ Wed 100 **CARDS:**

See advert on opposite page

Lake View Hotel & Restaurant

Tan-y-Pant LL55 4EL
☎ 01286 870422 📠 01286 872591
e-mail: reception@lakeviewhotel.co.uk
Dir: *1m from Llanberis on A4086 towards Caernarfon half-way along Lake Padarn*

ROOMS: 10 rms (9 en suite) (2 fmly) in all bedrooms s £30-£35; d £48-£62 (incl. bkfst) **LB** **FACILITIES:** 2 footpaths adjacent to hotel **PARKING:** 20 **NOTES:** ★★ in restaurant RS Jan-Feb **CARDS:**

LLANDEGLA, Denbighshire Map 15 SJ25

★★★72% Bodidris Hall
LL11 3AL
☎ 0870 7292292 01978 790335
e-mail: ceri@bodidrishall.com
Dir: *in village take A5104 towards Chester. Hotel 2m on left, signed*
This impressive manor house is in a quiet location surrounded by ornamental gardens and mature woodlands. It has an interesting history and a wealth of charm and character, with original features such as oak beams and inglenook fireplaces. Bedrooms are furnished with antique pieces and some have four-poster beds. Dining here is an enjoyable experience; the food is cooked with flair and stylishly presented.
ROOMS: 9 en suite ⊗ in 3 bedrooms **FACILITIES:** Fishing Shooting **CONF:** Thtr 65 Class 20 Board 20 **PARKING:** 60 **NOTES:** ⊗ in restaurant Civ Wed 65 **CARDS:**

LLANDEILO, Carmarthenshire Map 08 SN62

★★★70% The Plough Inn
Rhosmaen SA19 6NP
☎ 01558 823431 01558 823969
e-mail: enquiries@ploughrhosmaen.co.uk
web: www.ploughrhosmaen.co.uk
Dir: *0.5m N of Llandeilo on A40*

This privately owned hotel has memorable views over the Towy Valley and the Black Mountains. Bedrooms, situated in a separate wing, are tastefully furnished, spacious and comfortable. The public lounge bar is popular with locals, as is the spacious restaurant where freshly prepared food can be enjoyed. Additional facilities include a sauna, gym and conference facilities.
ROOMS: 14 en suite (5 GF) ⊗ in 10 bedrooms s £55-£65; d £70-£80 (incl. bkfst) **FACILITIES:** STV Sauna Gym Xmas **CONF:** Thtr 45 Class 24 Board 24 Del from £42.50 **PARKING:** 70 **NOTES:** ⊗ in restaurant Civ Wed 90 **CARDS:**

★★67% White Hart Inn
36 Carmarthen Rd SA19 6RS
☎ 01558 823419 01558 823089
e-mail: therese@whitehartinn.fsnet.co.uk
web: www.whitehartinn.fsnet.co.uk
Dir: *off A40 onto A483, hotel 200yds on left*
This privately owned, 19th-century roadside hostelry is on the outskirts of town. The modern bedrooms are well equipped and tastefully furnished. Family rooms are available. Public areas include a choice of bars and both smoking and non-smoking dining areas, where a wide range of grill type dishes is available. There are several function rooms, including a large self-contained suite.
ROOMS: 11 en suite (2 fmly) s fr £40; d fr £60 (incl. bkfst) **FACILITIES:** STV **PARKING:** 50 **NOTES:** Civ Wed 70
CARDS:

LLANDOVERY, Carmarthenshire Map 09 SN73

★★★63% Castle
King's Rd SA20 0AP
☎ 01550 720343 01550 720673
e-mail: castlehotelllandovery@hotmail.com
Dir: *on A40 in town centre, between Brecon & Carmarthen*
Overlooked by the original Norman keep, the Castle Hotel is in the heart of this market town. There is a warm atmosphere, enhanced by the roaring log fires lit in the winter. There is a wide variety of bedroom styles and sizes and many have benefited from refurbishment, including rooms once occupied by George Borrow and Lord Nelson.
ROOMS: 23 en suite (4 fmly) ⊗ in 21 bedrooms s £35-£45; d £60-£75 (incl. bkfst) **FACILITIES:** STV Fishing Xmas **CONF:** BC Thtr 150 Class 150 Board 100 Del from £50 **PARKING:** 30 **NOTES:** ⊗ in restaurant
CARDS:

LLANDRINDOD WELLS, Powys Map 09 SO06

★★★71% Hotel Metropole
Temple St LD1 5DY
☎ 01597 823700 01597 824828
e-mail: info@metropole.co.uk
web: www.metropole.co.uk
Dir: *on A483 in centre of town*
The centre of this famous spa town is dominated by this Victorian hotel, which has been personally run by the same family for over 100 years. The lobby leads to a choice of bars and an elegant lounge. Bedrooms, the many of which are non-smoking, vary in

continued on p812

LLANDRINDOD WELLS, continued

style and all are quite spacious and well-equipped. Facilities here include conference and function rooms as well as a leisure centre.

Hotel Metropole, Llandrindod Wells

ROOMS: 120 en suite (7 fmly) ⊗ in 57 bedrooms s fr £75; d £98-£118 (incl. bkfst) **LB** **FACILITIES:** Sauna Solarium Gym Jacuzzi Mini-gym, Beauty and holistic treatments Xmas **CONF:** Thtr 300 Class 200 Board 80 Del from £104 **SERVICES:** Lift **PARKING:** 150 **NOTES:** ⊗ in restaurant Civ Wed 300 **CARDS:**

See advert on opposite page

LLANDUDNO, Conwy Map 14 SH78

Top 200 – Hotel

★★★★ Bodysgallen Hall

LL30 1RS

☎ 01492 584466 01492 582519

e-mail: info@bodysgallen.com

web: www.bodysgallen.com

RELAIS & CHATEAUX.

Dir: *A55 to intersection, exit at junct 19, then follow A470 towards Llandudno. Hotel 1m on right*

Situated in fairytale surroundings of its own parkland and formal gardens, this 17th-century house is in an elevated position, allowing views towards Snowdonia and across to Conwy Castle. Accommodation is provided in the house and in converted cottages in the grounds. The cottage accommodation is more contemporary with some having their own small kitchens. The main house lounges and dining room show off fine antiques and have great character. Friendly and attentive service is discreetly offered, whilst the restaurant features fine local produce, carefully prepared.

ROOMS: 19 en suite 16 annexe en suite (3 fmly) (4 GF) ⊗ in 19 bedrooms s £120-£165; d £165-£290 (incl. cont bkfst) **LB** **FACILITIES:** STV Sauna Solarium Gym Jacuzzi Beauty salons Steam room Club room Xmas **CONF:** Thtr 50 Class 30 Board 24 Del £145 **PARKING:** 50 **NOTES:** No children 8yrs ⊗ in restaurant Civ Wed 45 **CARDS:**

Town House

★★★★ **Osborne House**

17 North House LL30 2LP

☎ 01492 860330 01492 860791

e-mail: sales@osbornehouse.com

web: www.osbornehouse.co.uk

Dir: *exit A55 junct 19. Follow signs for Llandudno then Promenade. Continue until junction, turn right. Hotel on left opposite pier entrance*

Originally built in 1832, this Victorian house has been restored and converted into a luxurious townhouse by the Maddocks family. Spacious suites offer unrivalled comfort and luxury, combining antique furnishings with state-of-the-art technology and facilities. Each suite provides super views over the pier and bay. Osborne's café grill is open throughout the day and offers high quality food whilst the bar blends elegance with plasma screens, dazzling chandeliers and guilt-edged mirrors. Nominated for the AA Hotel of the Year Award for Wales 2004-5.

ROOMS: 6 en suite s £130-£200; d £130-£200 (incl. cont bkfst) **FACILITIES:** STV use of swimming pool/sauna/jacuzzi at Empire Hotel (100 yds) **SERVICES:** air con **PARKING:** 6 **NOTES:** No children 11yrs Closed 19-29 Dec

CARDS:

★★★75% **Empire**

Church Walks LL30 2HE

☎ 01492 860555 01492 860791

e-mail: reservations@empirehotel.co.uk

web: www.empirehotel.co.uk

Dir: *A55 from Chester - leave at intersection for Llandudno (junct 19). Follow signs for town centre - Hotel is at end & facing main street*

Run by the same family for over almost 60 years, the Empire offers luxuriously appointed bedrooms with every modern facility. The 'Number 72' rooms in an adjacent house are particularly sumptuous. The indoor pool is overlooked by a lounge area where snacks are served all day, and in summer an outdoor pool and

continued

roof garden are available. The Watkins restaurant offers an interesting fixed-price menu.
ROOMS: 51 en suite 8 annexe en suite (3 fmly) (2 GF) s £60-£75; d £90-£120 (incl. bkfst) **LB FACILITIES: Spa** STV Sauna Full range of beauty treatments **CONF:** Thtr 36 Class 20 Board 20 Del from £85 **SERVICES:** Lift **PARKING:** 40 **NOTES:** Closed 10 days Xmas
CARDS:

See advert on this page

★★★73% Imperial
The Promenade LL30 1AP
☎ 01492 877466 01492 878043
e-mail: imphotel@btinternet.com
web: www.theimperial.co.uk
Dir: *A470 to Llandudno*

The Imperial is a large and impressive hotel, situated on the promenade, within easy reach of the town centre and other

continued on p814

TEMPLE ST. LLANDRINDOD WELLS
POWYS LD1 5DY
Tel: 01597 823700 Fax: 01597 824828
E-mail: info@metropole.co.uk
www.metropole.co.uk

Wonderful countryside complements the splendour of our family-owned, Victorian style Hotel with 120 ensuite, fully appointed bedrooms and extensive conference facilities in the centre of the beautiful Spa Town of Llandrindod Wells. Guests enjoy our superb indoor Leisure Complex with 54' indoor pool, sauna, steamroom, jacuzzi, mini gym and games room and an imaginative range of traditional cuisine prepared by our award-winning Chef.

One of Llandudno's largest hotels, set proudly on the Promenade with 98 en-suite bedrooms, 2 bars and a health & fitness centre

★★★

The Promenade, Llandudno
North Wales LL30 1AP
Telephone: (01492) 877466/9
Facsimile: (01492) 878043
Email: imphotel@btinternet.com
www.theimperial.co.uk

CHURCH WALKS
LLANDUDNO
CONWY
LL30 2HE

A popular long standing family run hotel with a central location. Beautifully furnished with antiques a special feature are artist's proofs by Sir William Russel Flint. The bedrooms all have original cast iron beds and have a romantic style but with all modern amenities.

There is an award winning Restaurant, Poolside Coffee Shop also Cocktail Bar. The Indoor Pool has a Sauna, steam room, whirlpool and there is a small outdoor pool and sun terraces. Beauty treatments. Car Parks. Ideal base from which to tour Snowdonia.

***Tel:* (01492) 860555 *Fax:* (01492) 860791**
Email: Reservations@empirehotel.co.uk
www.empirehotel.co.uk

L

LLANDUDNO, continued

amenities. Many of the bedrooms have views over the bay and there are also several suites available. The elegant Chantrey restaurant offers a fixed-price menu which changes monthly and dishes take full advantage of local produce.
ROOMS: 100 en suite (10 fmly) s £70-£120; d £100-£150 (incl. bkfst) **LB** **FACILITIES:** STV Sauna Solarium Gym Jacuzzi Beauty therapist Hairdressing ♫ Xmas **CONF:** Thtr 150 Class 50 Board 50 Del from £110 **SERVICES:** Lift **PARKING:** 25 **NOTES:** in restaurant Civ Wed 150 **CARDS:**

See advert on page 813

★★★69% Dunoon
Gloddaeth St LL30 2DW
☎ 01492 860787 01492 860031
e-mail: reservations@dunoonhotel.co.uk
web: www.dunoonhotel.co.uk
Dir: *exit Promenade at War Memorial by pier onto wide avenue. 200yds from Promenade on right*

This hotel is centrally located in the town and is smart and with a choice of attractive well-equipped accommodation. The restaurant offers freshly prepared tasty meals, whilst lighter snacks and afternoon tea may be taken in one of the lounges or bar.
ROOMS: 50 en suite (7 fmly) s £55-£65; d £96-£130 (incl. bkfst & dinner) **LB** **FACILITIES:** STV ♫ ch fac Xmas **CONF:** BC **SERVICES:** Lift **PARKING:** 24 **NOTES:** in restaurant Closed 28 Dec - mid-Mar **CARDS:**

★★★64% St George's
The Promenade LL30 2LG
☎ 01492 877544 01492 877788
e-mail: stgeorges@countrytown-hotels.co.uk
Dir: *A55-A470, follow road to the promenade, 0.25m, hotel on corner*

This popular and friendly seafront hotel was the first to be built in the town. Its many Victorian features include the splendid, ornate Wedgwood Room. The main lounges overlook the bay, are comfortable, and hot and cold snacks are available all day. Several bedrooms have views over the sea, and some have balconies.
ROOMS: 86 en suite (6 fmly) in 12 bedrooms s £72-£112; d £110-£150 (incl. bkfst) **LB** **FACILITIES:** STV Sauna Solarium Jacuzzi Hairdressing Health & beauty salon ch fac Xmas **CONF:** Thtr 250 Class 200 Board 45 Del from £94 **SERVICES:** Lift **PARKING:** 50 **NOTES:** in restaurant Civ Wed 200 **CARDS:**

★★★63% *Chatsworth House*
Central Promenade LL30 2XS
☎ 01492 860788 01492 871417
e-mail: manager@chatsworth-hotel.co.uk
web: www.chatsworth-hotel.co.uk
This traditional family-run Victorian hotel occupies a central position on the promenade and caters for many families and groups. There is an indoor swimming pool, a sauna and a solarium. Public areas are well maintained, and bathrooms are modern, some of them quite spacious.
ROOMS: 72 en suite (19 fmly) **FACILITIES:** Sauna Jacuzzi **SERVICES:** Lift **PARKING:** 9 **CARDS:**

★★★63% *Risboro*
Clement Av LL30 2ED
☎ 01492 876343 01492 879881
e-mail: risborohotel@ukonline.co.uk
Dir: *A55 to Llandudno, follow A470 into town centre, left at large rdbt, then take 3rd right*
This hotel is now under new ownership. Situated close to the foot of the Great Orme and convenient for the seafront and town centre, this popular family establishment provides agreeable bedrooms. Amongst the extensive public areas there is a comfortable lounge with a small terrace and a large restaurant overlooking the pool.
ROOMS: 65 en suite (7 fmly) **FACILITIES: Spa** Sauna Solarium Gym Jacuzzi Swimming supervised ♫ **CONF:** BC Thtr 150 Class 100 Board 80 **SERVICES:** Lift **PARKING:** 40 **NOTES:** in restaurant **CARDS:**

Top 200 – Hotel

★★ St Tudno Hotel and Restaurant
The Promenade LL30 2LP
☎ 01492 874411 01492 860407
e-mail: sttudnohotel@btinternet.com
web: www.st-tudno.co.uk
Dir: *on reaching Promenade towards pier, hotel opposite pier entrance & gardens*
A high quality family-owned hotel with friendly, attentive staff, and enjoying fine sea views. The stylish bedrooms are well equipped with mini-bars, robes, satellite TVs with videos and many other thoughtful extras. Public rooms include a lounge, a welcoming bar and a small indoor pool. The Terrace

continued

Restaurant, where seasonal and daily-changing menus are offered, has a delightful Mediterranean atmosphere. Afternoon tea is a real highlight. AA Wine Award Winner for Wales 2004-5.
ROOMS: 19 en suite (4 fmly) ⊗ in 3 bedrooms s £72.50-£82.50; d £105-£210 (incl. bkfst) **LB** **FACILITIES:** STV supervised ♫ ch fac Xmas **CONF:** Thtr 40 Class 25 Board 20 Del from £140 **SERVICES:** Lift **PARKING:** 12 **NOTES:** ⊗ in restaurant **CARDS:**

★★73% Epperstone
15 Abbey Rd LL30 2EE
☎ 01492 878746 01492 871223
e-mail: epperstonehotel@btconnect.com
Dir: *A55-A470 to Mostyn Street. Left at rdbt, 4th right into York Rd. Hotel on junct of York Rd & Abbey Rd*
This delightful hotel is located in wonderful gardens in a residential part of town, within easy walking distance of the seafront and shopping area. Bedrooms are attractively decorated and thoughtfully equipped. Two lounges, a comfortable non-smoking room and a Victorian-style conservatory are available. A daily changing menu is offered in the bright dining room.
ROOMS: 8 en suite (5 fmly) (1 GF) ⊗ in all bedrooms s £25-£33; d £50-£66 (incl. bkfst) **LB** **FACILITIES:** STV Xmas **PARKING:** 8 **NOTES:** No children 5yrs ⊗ in restaurant **CARDS:**

★★72% Sunnymede
West Pde LL30 2BD
☎ 01492 877130 01492 871824
Dir: *from A55 follow signs for Llandudno & Deganwy. At 1st rdbt after Deganwy take 1st exit towards sea. At corner left & follow road for 400yds*
Sunnymede is a friendly family-run hotel located on Llandudno's West Shore. Many rooms have views over the Conwy Estuary and Snowdonia. Modern bedrooms are attractively decorated and well equipped. Bar and lounge areas are particularly comfortable and attractive. All areas of the hotel have benefited from refurbishment.
ROOMS: 15 en suite (3 fmly) (4 GF) ⊗ in all bedrooms s £43-£86; d £86-£98 (incl. bkfst & dinner) **LB** **FACILITIES:** Xmas **PARKING:** 18 **NOTES:** No children 3yrs ⊗ in restaurant Closed Jan-Feb & Nov RS Xmas period **CARDS:**

★★72% Tan Lan
Great Orme's Rd, West Shore LL30 2AR
☎ 01492 860221 01492 870219
e-mail: info@tanlanhotel.co.uk
Dir: *off A55 junct 18 onto A546 signed Deganwy. Approx 3m from A55, straight over mini-rdbt and hotel 50 metres on left*
Warm and friendly hospitality is one of the many strengths at this small, well-maintained, privately owned and personally run hotel. It is located on Llandudno's West Shore, close to the Great Orme. The newly refurbished bedrooms, some on the ground floor, are modern and well equipped. Facilities include a pleasant dining room, lounge and bar. This is a totally no-smoking establishment.
ROOMS: 17 en suite (3 fmly) (6 GF) ⊗ in all bedrooms d fr £52 (incl. bkfst) **LB** **PARKING:** 12 **NOTES:** ⊗ in restaurant Closed Nov - mid Mar **CARDS:**

★★72% Tynedale
Central Promenade LL30 2XS
☎ 01492 877426 01492 871213
e-mail: enquiries@tynedalehotel.co.uk
web: www.tynedalehotel.co.uk
Dir: *on promenade opposite bandstand*
Tour groups are well catered for at this privately owned and personally run hotel, and regular live entertainment is a feature. Public areas include good lounge facilities and an attractive patio overlooking the bay. The well maintained, no-smoking bedrooms are fresh and well equipped. Many have good views over the sea front and the Great Orme.
ROOMS: 54 en suite (4 fmly) ⊗ in all bedrooms s £28-£50; d £56-£100 (incl. bkfst) **LB** **FACILITIES:** ♫ Xmas **SERVICES:** Lift **PARKING:** 30 **NOTES:** ⊗ in restaurant **CARDS:**

★★68% *Oak Alyn*
2 Deganwy Av LL30 2YB
☎ 01492 860320
Dir: *in town centre, 200yds from Town Hall, opposite Catholic Church*
This private hotel has been much improved by the present owners. It is close to the town centre and within a few minutes' walk of the promenade. Bedrooms have modern facilities. There is a bright and pleasant dining room with a conservatory extension, and a lounge bar.
ROOMS: 12 en suite (2 fmly) **CONF:** Thtr 26 Class 30 **PARKING:** 16 **NOTES:** ⊗ in restaurant Closed 22-31 Dec **CARDS:**

★★68% Somerset
St Georges Crescent, Promenade LL30 2LF
☎ 01492 876540 01492 863700
e-mail: somerset@favroy.freeserve.co.uk
Dir: *on the Promenade*
With its sister hotel, The Wavecrest, this cheerful holiday hotel occupies an ideal location on the central promenade and affords superb views over the bay from many rooms. Regular entertainment is provided as well as a range of bar and lounge areas. Bedrooms are well decorated and modern facilities are provided.
ROOMS: 37 en suite (4 fmly) **FACILITIES:** Games room ♫ Xmas **CONF:** Thtr 70 Class 70 Board 30 **SERVICES:** Lift **PARKING:** 20 **NOTES:** ⊗ in restaurant Closed Jan-Feb **CARDS:**

★★68% Wavecrest
St Georges Crescent, Central Promenade LL30 2LF
☎ 01492 860615 01492 863700
e-mail: somerset@favroy.freeserve.co.uk
Dir: *on promenade behind Marks & Spencer*
The Wavecrest is the sister hotel of the adjoining Somerset, and public areas are shared. It lies on the central promenade and most bedrooms have lovely sea views. Lounge and bar areas are comfortably furnished and a games room is available. Staff are friendly and regular entertainment is staged.
ROOMS: 41 en suite (7 fmly) **FACILITIES:** Games room, Patio garden ♫ Xmas **CONF:** Class 70 **SERVICES:** Lift **PARKING:** 12 **NOTES:** ⊗ in restaurant Closed Jan-Feb **CARDS:**

★★67% *Ravenhurst*
West Pde LL30 2BB
☎ 01492 875525 01248 681143
e-mail: ravenhursthotel@aol.co.uk
web: ravenhurst-hotel.co.uk
Dir: *on West Shore, opposite boating pool*
This privately owned and comfortable hotel lies on the quieter West Shore of the town and enjoys lovely views over the Conwy Estuary towards Snowdonia. The traditionally styled accommodation includes bedrooms on ground-floor level. There is a choice of lounges and a bar, and a daily changing, fixed-price menu is provided in the dining room.
ROOMS: 25 en suite (3 fmly) (6 GF) **PARKING:** 15 **NOTES:** ⊗ in restaurant Closed Dec-Feb **CARDS:**

L

LLANDUDNO, continued

★★66% Esplanade
Glan-y-Mor Pde, Promenade LL30 2LL
☎ 0800 318688 (freephone) & 01492 860300 ▯ 01492 860418
e-mail: info@esplanadehotel.co.uk
web: www.esplanadehotel.co.uk
Dir: *off A55 at Llandudno junct, onto A470, follow signs to promenade, turn left towards Great Orme. Hotel 500yds left*
This family owned and run hotel stands on the promenade, conveniently close to the town centre and with views of the bay. Bedrooms vary in size and style, but all have modern equipment and facilities. Public areas are bright and attractively appointed, and include a room for functions and conferences.
ROOMS: 59 en suite (17 fmly) ⊗ in 36 bedrooms s £14.50-£48; d £29-£96 (incl. bkfst) **LB** **FACILITIES:** ♫ Xmas **CONF:** Thtr 80 Class 40 Board 40 Del from £69 **SERVICES:** Lift **PARKING:** 30 **NOTES:** ✗ ⊗ in restaurant Closed 3 Jan-1 Feb
CARDS:

★★66% Hydro Hotel
Neville Crescent LL30 1AT
☎ 01492 870101 ▯ 01492 870992
Leisureplex
e-mail: hydro.llandudno@alfatravel.co.uk
Dir: *follow signs for theatre to seafront, towards pier. Hotel short distance after theatre on left facing North Bay*
This large hotel is situated on the promenade overlooking the sea, and offers good value-for-money, modern accommodation. Public areas are quite extensive and include a choice of lounges, a games/snooker room and a ballroom, where entertainment is provided every night. The hotel is a popular venue for coach tour parties.
ROOMS: 112 en suite (4 fmly) (8 GF) s £28-£36; d £46-£62 (incl. bkfst) **LB** **FACILITIES:** Snooker Sauna Gym Table tennis ♫ Xmas **CONF:** Thtr 260 Class 40 **SERVICES:** Lift **PARKING:** 10 **NOTES:** ✗ ⊗ in restaurant Closed Jan-mid Feb RS Nov -Dec & mid Feb-Mar
CARDS:

★★65% Ambassador Hotel
Grand Promenade LL30 2NR

☎ 01492 876886 ▯ 01492 876347
e-mail: reception@ambasshotel.demon.co.uk
Dir: *off A55 onto A470. Take turn to Promenade, then left towards pier*
This friendly, family-run hotel is located on the seafront, close to the town centre. Bedrooms are tasteful and many have sea views. There is a choice of lounges, a patisserie, bar and restaurant.
ROOMS: 57 en suite (8 fmly) s £33-£50; d £60-£110 (incl. bkfst) **LB** **FACILITIES:** ♫ Xmas **CONF:** Thtr 45 Class 14 Board 20 Del £51.50 **SERVICES:** Lift **PARKING:** 11 **NOTES:** ✗ ⊗ in restaurant
CARDS:

★★65% Evans
Charlton St LL30 2AA
☎ 01492 860784 ▯ 01492 860784
Dir: *from A470 to Llandudno pass Asda, stay in left lane, turn left, hotel on 1st right corner*
This is a privately owned and friendly hotel, which provides well-maintained accommodation, including family bedrooms. The spacious public areas include a well-equipped games room and a comfortable lounge bar, where regular live evening entertainment is held. The hotel is particularly popular with coach tour groups.
ROOMS: 50 en suite (4 fmly) s £39-£41; d £66-£72 (incl. bkfst) **LB** **FACILITIES:** STV Snooker Solarium ♫ Xmas **SERVICES:** Lift **NOTES:** ✗ ⊗ in restaurant Closed Jan

★★65% *Ormescliffe*
East Pde LL30 1BE
☎ 01492 877191 ▯ 01492 860311
e-mail: ormescliffe@clara.net
Dir: *M6, M56, A55 exit Llandudno. A470 promenade near theatre and conference centre*
A family-run hotel at the eastern end of the promenade. Bedrooms are modern and well equipped; most have superb views over the seafront and Great Orme. Comfortable bars and lounges are provided and there is a ballroom with regular entertainment.
ROOMS: 61 en suite (7 fmly) ⊗ in 6 bedrooms **FACILITIES:** Snooker Table tennis **CONF:** Thtr 120 Class 120 Board 80 **SERVICES:** Lift **PARKING:** 15 **NOTES:** ⊗ in restaurant Closed 2 Jan-2 Feb
CARDS:

★★62% *Royal*
Church Walks LL30 2HW
☎ 01492 876476 ▯ 01492 870210
e-mail: royalllandudno@aol.com
Dir: *exit A55 for A470 to Llandudno. Follow through town to T-junct, then left into Church Walks. Hotel 200yds on left, almost opposite Great Orme tram station*
Reputed to be the first hotel in Llandudno, the Royal is located on the eastern side of the Great Orme, close to the town centre and seafront. The well-equipped accommodation is particularly popular with golfers and coach tour groups.
ROOMS: 38 rms (36 en suite) (7 fmly) **FACILITIES:** Putt green **SERVICES:** Lift **PARKING:** 20 **NOTES:** ✗ ⊗ in restaurant
CARDS:

★63% *Min-y-Don*
North Pde LL30 2LP
☎ 01492 876511 ▯ 01492 878169
Dir: *leave A55 Expressway Llandudno junct onto A470. Through Martyn St, turn right at rdbt then left into North Parade*
This cheerful family-run hotel is located under the Great Orme, opposite the pier. Bedrooms include several suitable for families and many have lovely views over the bay. Regular entertainment is held and there are comfortable lounge and bar areas.
ROOMS: 28 rms (19 en suite) (12 fmly) **FACILITIES:** **SERVICES:** air con **PARKING:** 7 **NOTES:** ✗ ⊗ in restaurant Closed Jan-Feb
CARDS:

Packed in a hurry?
Ironing facilities should be available at all star levels, either in rooms or on request

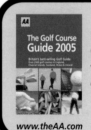

LLANDUDNO JUNCTION, Conwy Map 14 SH77

Travel Inn

Afon Conway, Llandudno Junction LL28 5LB
☎ 08701 977162 📠 01492 583614
Dir: *at J19 off A55. Exit roundabout at A470 Betws-y-Coed. Travel Inn immediately on left, opposite petrol station*

Travel Inn offers good-quality, value-for-money accommodation. Spacious, en suite rooms with bath and shower comfortably accommodate a family of up to two adults and two children (to age 15). The restaurant and bar offers a varied menu. For further details consult the Hotel Groups page.

ROOMS: 40 en suite s £45.95-£46.95; d £45.95-£46.95

LLANELLI, Carmarthenshire Map 08 SN50

★★★67% Diplomat Hotel

Felinfoel SA15 3PJ
☎ 01554 756156 📠 01554 751649

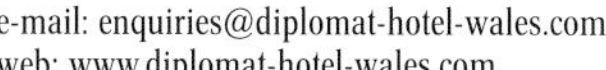

e-mail: enquiries@diplomat-hotel-wales.com
web: www.diplomat-hotel-wales.com

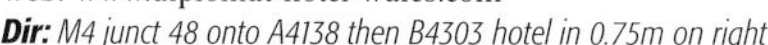

Dir: *M4 junct 48 onto A4138 then B4303 hotel in 0.75m on right*

This Victorian mansion, set in mature grounds, has been extended over the years to provide a comfortable and relaxing hotel. The well-appointed bedrooms are located in the main house and the nearby coach house. Public areas include Trubshaw's restaurant, a large function suite and a modern leisure centre.

ROOMS: 23 en suite 8 annexe en suite (2 fmly) ⊘ in 6 bedrooms s £65-£75; d £85-£95 (incl. bkfst) **LB** **FACILITIES: Spa** supervised Sauna Solarium Gym Jacuzzi ♫ Xmas **CONF:** Thtr 450 Class 150 Board 100 Del from £85 **SERVICES:** Lift **PARKING:** 250 **NOTES:** Civ Wed 300 **CARDS:**

See advert on this page

★★★67% Stradey Park

Furnace SA15 4HA
☎ 01554 758171 📠 01554 777974
e-mail: reservations@stradeyparkhotel.com
web: www.stradeyparkhotel.com
Dir: *M4 junct 48/A484 to B4309*

The present owners have extensively upgraded this large, modern complex. It provides a good range of accommodation, including full suites, no-smoking bedrooms and bedrooms on ground-floor level. The spacious and attractively appointed public areas include a choice of comfortable lounges, a pleasant lounge bar and a bright brasserie-style restaurant.

ROOMS: 84 en suite (3 fmly) (19 GF) ⊘ in 40 bedrooms s £75-£95; d £95-£150 (incl. bkfst) **LB** **FACILITIES:** Xmas **CONF:** Thtr 300 Class 300 Board 240 Del from £95.45 **SERVICES:** Lift **PARKING:** 100 **NOTES:** ⊘ in restaurant Civ Wed 200 **CARDS:**

★★70% Ashburnham

Ashburnham Rd, Pembrey SA16 0TH
☎ 01554 834343 & 834455 📠 01554 834483
e-mail: ashpembrey@btopenworld.com
Dir: *M4 junct 48, A4138 to Llanelli, A484 West to Pembrey, follow sign as entering village*

Amelia Earhart stayed at this friendly hotel after finishing her historic trans-Atlantic flight of 1928. Public areas include a bright bar and restaurant offering a good choice of menus, extensive function facilities and a children's outdoor play area. Bedrooms have modern furnishings and facilities. The hotel is licensed for civil wedding ceremonies and proves a popular venue.

ROOMS: 13 en suite (2 fmly) s £45-£60; d £60-£70 (incl. bkfst) **LB** **FACILITIES:** various within 1 mile of hotel ch fac **CONF:** Thtr 150 Class 150 Board 80 Del £65 **PARKING:** 100 **NOTES:** ⊘ in restaurant RS 25 Dec Civ Wed 130 **CARDS:**

★★66% Miramar

158 Station Rd SA15 1YU
☎ 01554 754726 📠 01554 772454
e-mail: miramar2002d@aol.com
Dir: *M4 junct 48. Follow road to Llanelli, then follow railway station signs. Hotel adjacent to station*

This privately owned hotel is conveniently located near to the railway station and is within walking distance of the town centre. Bedrooms are well maintained and generously equipped, whilst public areas include a cheerful bar providing a good range of bar meals and a pleasantly appointed restaurant where a good choice is also available.

ROOMS: 12 en suite (2 fmly) (2 GF) s fr £29; d fr £48 (incl. bkfst) **FACILITIES:** Golf course and racing course nearby **PARKING:** 10 **NOTES:** ⊘ in restaurant **CARDS:**

LLANFAIRPWLLGWYNGYLL See Anglesey, Isle of

LLANFYLLIN, Powys — Map 15 SJ11

★★67% Cain Valley
High St SY22 5AQ
☎ 01691 648366 📠 01691 648307
e-mail: info@cainvalleyhotel.co.uk
Dir: *at end of A490 - Llanfyllin, 12m from Welshpool. Hotel in centre of town on square, car park at rear*

An unpretentious, privately-owned, Grade II listed coaching inn with exposed beams and a Jacobean staircase. The comfortable accommodation includes family rooms and food is available in a choice of bars (the public bar is popular with locals) or in the restaurant, which has a well-deserved reputation for its locally-sourced steaks.

ROOMS: 13 en suite (3 fmly) s £42; d £69 (incl. bkfst) **LB**
PARKING: 12 **NOTES:** ⊗ in restaurant RS 24-25 Dec
CARDS:

LLANGAMMARCH WELLS, Powys — Map 09 SN94

Top 200 – Hotel

★★★ ◎◎ Lake Country House
LD4 4BS
☎ 01591 620202 & 620474
📠 01591 620457
e-mail: info@lakecountryhouse.co.uk
web: www.lakecountryhouse.co.uk
Dir: *W from Builth Wells on A483 to Garth (approx 6m). Left for Llangammarch Wells, follow hotel signs*

Expect good old fashioned values of service and hospitality at this Victorian country-house hotel, which comes complete with a 9-hole, par 3 golf course, 50 acres of wooded grounds and a river. Bedrooms, including many suites, are individually decorated and have many extra comforts as standard. Traditional afternoon teas are served in the lounge in front of a log fire, and award-winning cuisine is provided in the spacious and elegant restaurant.

ROOMS: 19 en suite (2 GF) ⊗ in 6 bedrooms s £105-£170; d £140-£240 (incl. bkfst) **LB** **FACILITIES:** ⛳ 9 Fishing Snooker Putt green Clay pigeon shooting, horse riding, mountain biking, quad biking, archery Xmas **CONF:** Thtr 80 Class 30 Board 25 Del from £120 **PARKING:** 72 **NOTES:** ⊗ in restaurant Civ Wed 95
CARDS:

LLANGEFNI See Anglesey, Isle of

LLANGOLLEN, Denbighshire — Map 15 SJ24

See also Glyn Ceiriog

★★★75% ◎ The Wild Pheasant Hotel & Restaurant
Berwyn Rd LL20 8AD
☎ 01978 860629 📠 01978 861837
e-mail: wild.pheasant@talk21.com
Dir: *hotel 0.5m from town centre on left side of A5 towards Betws-y-Coed & Holyhead*

This professionally-run hotel provides friendly hospitality and smart accommodation, including ground-floor, four-poster and no-smoking rooms. There is also a new extension that offers a range of superior rooms and suites, as well as a swimming pool and beauty facilities. There is the popular Cinnamon restaurant, and snacks are available in the Bistro and Chef's Bar. The hotel is a popular venue for weddings and conferences.

ROOMS: 46 en suite (4 fmly) (12 GF) ⊗ in 9 bedrooms
FACILITIES: Spa Sauna Jacuzzi Xmas **CONF:** BC Thtr 200 Class 70 Board 50 **SERVICES:** Lift **PARKING:** 100 **NOTES:** Civ Wed 60
CARDS:

★★★66% Bryn Howel Hotel & Restaurant
LL20 7UW
☎ 01978 860331 📠 01978 860119
e-mail: hotel@brynhowel.co.uk
Dir: *A483 bypassing Wrexham. At Ruabon follow A539 to Llangollen. Continue through Acrefair & Trefor. Hotel signed on left*

Bryn Howel occupies an enviable position in the beautiful Vale of Llangollen, with views directly over extensive formal gardens, the canal and mountains. The comfortably furnished bedrooms vary in size and style and are divided between the original main house and the newer wing. The hotel has a choice of function rooms including a large suite, and is understandably a popular venue for weddings.

ROOMS: 36 en suite (8 GF) ⊗ in 13 bedrooms s £65-£81; d £99-£108 (incl. bkfst) **LB** **FACILITIES:** STV Sauna Solarium Jacuzzi Xmas **CONF:** Thtr 380 Class 96 Board 86 Del from £117 **SERVICES:** Lift **PARKING:** 250 **NOTES:** ⊗ in restaurant Civ Wed 250
CARDS:

★★67% *Chain Bridge Hotel*
Berwyn LL20 8BS
☎ 01978 860215 📠 01978 861841
e-mail: chainbridgehotel@aol.com
Dir: *1.5m A539 W of Llangollen, signed Horseshoe Pass. Left to B5103 500yds, signed entrance left, over narrow bridge, along canal towpath to hotel*

Chain Bridge is situated in an idyllic location between the River Dee and the Shropshire Union Canal. It takes its name from the footbridge, which spans the river at this point. Several of the comfortably furnished bedrooms have balconies and some are

continued

suitable for families. The restaurant overlooks the river and meals are also available in the Tudor bar.
ROOMS: 29 en suite 4 annexe en suite (2 fmly) ⊗ in 5 bedrooms **FACILITIES:** STV Fishing ♫ **CONF:** Thtr 80 Class 80 Board 50 **PARKING:** 40 **NOTES:** ⊗ in restaurant Civ Wed 120
CARDS:

★★63% *Abbey Grange Hotel*

LL20 8DD
☎ 01978 860753 📠 01978 869070
e-mail: enquiries@abbey-grange-hotel.co.uk
web: www.abbey-grange-hotel.co.uk
Dir: *A542 signed Ruthin Abbey Grange. Hotel approx 2m on left*

This hotel, situated close to Llangollen, is a good base for exploring Offa's Dyke and the lovely countryside. Rooms are spacious and well equipped, and some are suitable for families. Guests can dine in the restaurant or the bar, and outside is a sun patio and a large children's play area.
ROOMS: 8 en suite (3 fmly) **PARKING:** 40
CARDS:

LLANRHIDIAN, Swansea — Map 08 SS49

★★66% *North Gower*

SA3 1EE
☎ 01792 390042 📠 01792 391401
e-mail: enquiries@northgowerhotel.co.uk
web: www.northgowerhotel.co.uk
Dir: *on B4295, turn left at Llanrhidian Esso Service Station*

Situated on the Gower Peninsula with delightful views over the sea, this family-owned hotel offers guests a relaxing and comfortable stay. Bedrooms are spacious and airy, whilst public areas consist of a bar full of character, a pleasant restaurant and a choice of meeting and function rooms.
ROOMS: 18 en suite (10 fmly) (7 GF) ⊗ in 8 bedrooms **CONF:** BC Thtr 250 Class 170 Board 60 **PARKING:** 100 **NOTES:** ⊗ in restaurant
CARDS:

See advert on this page

LLANRWST, Conwy — Map 14 SH86

See also Betws-y-Coed

★★★66% Maenan Abbey

Maenan LL26 0UL
☎ 01492 660247 📠 01492 660734
e-mail: reservations@manab.co.uk
Dir: *3m N on A470*
This personally run private hotel was built as an abbey in 1850 on the site of a 13th-century monastery. It is now a popular venue for weddings as the grounds and magnificent galleried staircase make an ideal backdrop for photographs. Bedrooms include a large suite and are equipped with modern facilities. Meals are served in the bar and restaurant.
ROOMS: 14 en suite (2 fmly) s £45; d £80 (incl. bkfst) **LB** **FACILITIES:** Fishing guided mountain walks Xmas **CONF:** BC Thtr 50 Class 30 Board 30 **PARKING:** 60 **NOTES:** ⊗ in restaurant Civ Wed 55
CARDS:

LLANTRISANT, Monmouthshire — Map 09 ST39

A Greyhound Inn

NP15 1LE
☎ 01291 673447 672505 📠 01291 673255
e-mail: enquiry@greyhound-inn.com
web: www.greyhound-inn.com
Dir: *M4 junct 24, onto A449, 1st exit for Usk, 2.5m from town square following signs to Llantrisant*
ROOMS: 10 en suite (2 fmly) (5 GF) ⊗ in 8 bedrooms s fr £51; d fr £70 (incl. bkfst) **LB** **FACILITIES:** ch fac **PARKING:** 60 **NOTES:** ★★★ ⊗ in restaurant Closed 25-26 Dec RS Sunday eve no food **CARDS:**

LLANWDDYN, Powys — Map 15 SJ01

★★★73% ◎◎ Lake Vyrnwy
Lake Vyrnwy SY10 0LY
☎ 01691 870692 01691 870259
e-mail: res@lakevyrnwy.com
web: www.lakevyrnwy.com
Dir: *on A4393, 200yds past dam*

This fine country-house hotel lies in 26,000 acres of woodland above Lake Vyrnwy. It provides a wide range of bedrooms, most with superb views and many with four-poster beds and balconies. The extensive public rooms are elegantly furnished and include a terrace, a choice of bars serving meals and the more formal dining in the restaurant.

ROOMS: 35 en suite (4 fmly) s £90-£135; d £120-£190 (incl. bkfst) **LB** **FACILITIES:** STV Fishing Riding Game/Clay shooting, Sailing, Cycling, Archery, Quad trekking, Fly fishing ch fac Xmas **CONF:** Thtr 120 Class 50 Board 45 Del from £135 **PARKING:** 70 **NOTES:** in restaurant Civ Wed 120 **CARDS:**

See advert on opposite page

LLANWRTYD WELLS, Powys — Map 09 SN84

★★71% ◎ Lasswade Country House Hotel
Station Rd LD5 4RW
☎ 01591 610515 01591 610611
e-mail: info@lasswadehotel.co.uk
web: www.lasswadehotel.co.uk
Dir: *off A483 into Ifron Terrace, right into Station Rd, hotel 350yds on right*

This friendly hotel on the edge of the town has impressive views over the countryside. Bedrooms are comfortably furnished and well equipped, while the public areas consist of a tastefully decorated lounge, an elegant restaurant and an airy conservatory which looks out on to the neighbouring hills. The hotel is non-smoking throughout and utilises fresh, local produce to provide an enjoyable dining experience.

ROOMS: 8 en suite in all bedrooms s £45-£55; d £75 (incl. bkfst) **LB** **FACILITIES:** Sauna Xmas **CONF:** Thtr 20 Class 20 Board 16 **PARKING:** 8 **NOTES:** in restaurant **CARDS:**

Restaurant with Rooms

◎◎◎ Carlton House
Dolycoed Rd LD5 4RA
☎ 01591 610248 01591 610242
e-mail: info@carltonrestaurant.co.uk
web: www.carltonrestaurant.co.uk
Dir: *centre of town*

Guests are made to feel like one of the family at this house, set amidst stunning countryside in what is reputedly the smallest rural town in Britain. Carlton House offers award-winning cuisine, complemented by a well-chosen wine list and served in an atmospheric restaurant. The themed bedrooms, like the public areas, have period furniture and are decorated in warm colours.

ROOMS: 6 rms (5 en suite) (2 fmly) s £45; d £60-£80 (incl. bkfst) **LB** **FACILITIES:** Pony trekking Mountain biking **NOTES:** in restaurant Closed 15-30 Dec RS All year **CARDS:**

LLYSWEN, Powys — Map 09 SO13

★★★★74% ◎◎ Llangoed Hall
LD3 0YP
☎ 01874 754525 01874 754545
e-mail: enquiries@llangoedhall.com web: www.llangoedhall.com
Dir: *A470 through village for 2m. Hotel drive on right*

Set against the stunning backdrop of the Black Mountains and the Wye Valley, this imposing country house is a haven of peace and quiet. The interior no less impressive, with a noteworthy art collection complementing the many antiques featured in day rooms and bedrooms. Comfortable, spacious bedrooms and suites are matched by equally inviting lounges.

ROOMS: 23 en suite s £140-£320; d £180-£360 (incl. bkfst) **LB** **FACILITIES:** STV Fishing Snooker Maze, Clay pigeon shooting Xmas **CONF:** Thtr 60 Class 30 Board 28 Del £187 **PARKING:** 80 **NOTES:** No children 8yrs in restaurant Civ Wed 80 **CARDS:**

MACHYNLLETH, Powys — Map 14 SH70

See also Eglwysfach

★★67% ◎ Wynnstay
Maengwyn St SY20 8AE
☎ 01654 702941 01654 703884
e-mail: info@wynnstay-hotel.com
web: www.wynnstay-hotel.com
Dir: *at junct of A487/A489, in the town centre, 25yds from the clock tower*

Long established, this former posting house lies in the centre of historic Machynlleth. Bedrooms, which include no-smoking rooms and family bedded rooms, have modern facilities. The bars are popular with locals and a good range of food is available. The restaurant offers more formal dining and guests can choose from a fixed-price menu.

ROOMS: 23 en suite (3 fmly) in all bedrooms s £50-£65; d £80-£100 (incl. bkfst) **LB** **FACILITIES:** STV Fishing Clay shooting, Game shooting, Mountain biking Xmas **CONF:** Thtr 40 Class 12 Board 16 **PARKING:** 40 **NOTES:** in restaurant RS New Years Day **CARDS:**

See advert on opposite page

MAGOR SERVICE AREA (M4), Monmouthshire — Map 09 ST48

Travelodge
Magor Service Area NP26 3YL
☎ 08700 850 950 01633 881896
Dir: *M4 junct 23A*

Travelodge offers good quality, good value, modern accommodation. Ideal for families, the spacious, en suite bedrooms include remote-control TV, tea and coffee-making facilities and luxury beds. Meals can be taken at the nearby family restaurant. For further details consult the Hotel Groups page.

ROOMS: 43 en suite s fr £25; d fr £25

MANORBIER, Pembrokeshire — Map 08 SS09

★★67% Castle Mead
SA70 7TA
☎ 01834 871358 01834 871358
e-mail: castlemeadhotel@aol.com
web: www.castlemeadhotel.com
Dir: *A4139 towards Pembroke, turn onto B4585 into village & follow signs to beach & castle. Hotel on left above beach*

Benefiting from a superb location with spectacular views of the bay, the Norman church and Manorbier Castle, this family-run establishment is friendly and welcoming. Bedrooms are generally quite spacious and offer modern facilities throughout. Public areas include a sea view restaurant, bar and residents' lounge and an extensive garden.

ROOMS: 5 en suite 3 annexe en suite (2 fmly) (3 GF) in 2 bedrooms s fr £40; d fr £78 (incl. bkfst) **LB** **PARKING:** 20 **NOTES:** in restaurant Closed Jan-Feb RS Nov/Dec/Feb **CARDS:**

continued

MENAI BRIDGE See Anglesey, Isle of

MERTHYR TYDFIL, Merthyr Tydfil Map 09 SO00
See also Nant-Ddu

★★★62% Bessemer
Hermon Close, Dowlais CF48 3DP
☎ 01685 350780 📠 01685 352874
e-mail: information@bessemerhotel.co.uk
A modern hotel, with a friendly and relaxed atmosphere, that has newly completed, high quality bedrooms and bathrooms. Business guests will appreciate the spacious work desks and modem points. Dinner includes the popular option of a self-service carvery, and there are three bars including one in a large function room catering for up to 160 guests.
ROOMS: 17 en suite ⊗ in 12 bedrooms s £55-£60; d £60-£69 (incl. bkfst) **FACILITIES:** STV Jacuzzi **CONF:** Del from £65 **SERVICES:** Lift **PARKING:** 30 **NOTES:** ⊗ in restaurant
CARDS:

Travel Inn
Pentrebach CF48 4BD
☎ 08701 977183 📠 01443 699171
Dir: *M4 junct 32 follow A470 to Merthyr Tydfil. At 2nd rdbt turn right to Pentrebach, follow signs to Ind Estate*
Travel Inn offers good-quality, value-for-money accommodation. Spacious, en suite rooms with bath and shower comfortably accommodate a family of up to two adults and two children (to age 15). The restaurant and bar offers a varied menu. For further details consult the Hotel Groups page.
ROOMS: 40 en suite s £45.95-£46.95; d £45.95-£46.95
CONF: Thtr 65 Board 30

M

MISKIN, Rhondda Cynon Taff Map 09 ST08

★★★★69%
Miskin Manor Hotel & Health Club
Groes Faen, Pontyclun CF72 8ND
☎ 01443 224204 🖷 01443 237606
e-mail: info@miskin-manor.co.uk
web: www.miskin-manor.co.uk
Dir: *M4 junct 34, exit onto A4119, signed Llantrisant, hotel is 300yds on left*
This manor house is set in 20 acres of grounds, only minutes' away from the M4. Bedrooms are furnished to a high standard and include some located in converted stables and cottages. Public areas are spacious and comfortable and include a variety of function rooms. Frederick's health club has leisure facilities and a bar/bistro.
ROOMS: 34 en suite 9 annexe en suite (6 fmly) (6 GF) ⊗ in 11 bedrooms s £80-£94; d £100-£126 (incl. bkfst) **LB** **FACILITIES:** STV supervised Squash Sauna Solarium Gym Jacuzzi ch fac Xmas **CONF:** Thtr 160 Class 80 Board 65 Del from £135 **PARKING:** 200 **NOTES:** ⊗ in restaurant Civ Wed 120 **CARDS:**
See advert under CARDIFF

MOLD, Flintshire Map 15 SJ26
See also Northop Hall

★★★67% **Beaufort Park Hotel**
Alltami Rd, New Brighton CH7 6RQ
☎ 01352 758646 🖷 01352 757132
e-mail: bph@beaufortparkhotel.co.uk
web: www.beaufortparkhotel.co.uk
Dir: *A55/A494. Through Alltami lights, over mini rdbt by petrol station towards Mold, A5119. Hotel 100yds on right*
This large, modern hotel is conveniently located a short drive from the North Wales Expressway and offers various styles of spacious accommodation. There are extensive public areas, and several meeting and function rooms are available. There is a wide choice of meals in the formal restaurant and in the popular Arches bar.
ROOMS: 106 en suite (4 fmly) (33 GF) ⊗ in 25 bedrooms s £70-£95; d £120 (incl. bkfst) **LB** **FACILITIES:** Squash Jacuzzi Games Room,Darts ♫ ch fac Xmas **CONF:** Thtr 250 Class 120 Board 50 Del £120 **PARKING:** 200 **NOTES:** Civ Wed 250
CARDS:

MONMOUTH, Monmouthshire Map 10 SO51
See also Whitebrook

★★65% **Riverside**
Cinderhill St NP25 5EY
☎ 01600 715577 & 713236 🖷 01600 712668
e-mail: info@riversidehotelmonmouth.co.uk
Dir: *leave A40 signposted Rockfield & Monmouth hotel on left beyond garage & before rdbt*
Just a short walk from the famous 13th-century bridge, this hotel, now under new ownership offers accommodation in a relaxed and informal atmosphere. Bedrooms are well equipped and soundly decorated. Public areas include a separate restaurant, a popular bar and a conservatory lounge at the rear of the property.
ROOMS: 17 en suite (2 fmly) ⊗ in 2 bedrooms s £43-£49.95; d £50-£59.95 **LB** **FACILITIES:** STV ch fac Xmas **CONF:** Thtr 150 Class 60 Board 40 Del from £85 **PARKING:** 30 **NOTES:** ⊗ in restaurant
CARDS:

Popped the question?
Hotels with Civ Wed in their entry are licensed for civil wedding ceremonies. Maximum numbers for the ceremony only are shown, e.g. Civ Wed 120

MONTGOMERY, Powys Map 15 SO29

★★71% **Dragon**
SY15 6PA
THE INDEPENDENTS
☎ 01686 668359 🖷 01686 668287
e-mail: reception@dragonhotel.com
web: www.dragonhotel.com
Dir: *behind the Town Hall*
This fine 17th-century coaching inn stands in the centre of Montgomery. Beams and timbers from the nearby castle, which was destroyed by Cromwell, are visible in the lounge and bar. A wide choice of soundly prepared, wholesome food is available in both the restaurant and bar. Bedrooms are well equipped and family rooms are available.
ROOMS: 20 en suite (6 fmly) ⊗ in 16 bedrooms s £47-£57; d £79.50 (incl. bkfst) **LB** **FACILITIES:** Sauna ♫ ch fac Xmas **CONF:** Thtr 40 Class 30 Board 25 **PARKING:** 21 **NOTES:** ⊗ in restaurant
CARDS:

MUMBLES (NEAR SWANSEA), Swansea Map 08 SS68

★★★65% ***St Anne's***
Western Ln SA3 4EY
☎ 01792 369147 🖷 01792 360537
e-mail: info@stanneshotel-mumbles.com
web: www.stanneshotel-mumbles.com
Dir: *A483/A4067 along coastal road to Mumbles. In village straight over mini rdbt and Western Ln is 3rd right*
This privately owned hotel stands on a steep hillside close to the town centre, and enjoys some superb views over the Swansea Bay. The accommodation is modern and the bedrooms are well equipped. No-smoking bedrooms, family rooms, interconnecting rooms and bedrooms on ground-floor level are all available. The bright and pleasant public areas include a spacious lounge.
ROOMS: 33 en suite (3 fmly) ⊗ in 7 bedrooms **FACILITIES:** STV **CONF:** Thtr 100 Class 50 Board 50 **PARKING:** 50 **NOTES:** ⊗ in restaurant **CARDS:**

Restaurant with Rooms

Patricks with Rooms
638 Mumbles Rd SA3 4EA
☎ 01792 360199 🖷 01792 369926
web: www.patrickswithrooms.com
Dir: *M4 junct 42 (sea on left) through Swansea to Mumbles. Over mini rdbt at White Rose pub. 0.25m hotel opposite children's park on right.*
A popular restaurant located on the front at Mumbles with a lively atmosphere and friendly, efficient service. Bedrooms are a real highlight here offering a choice of modern styles in a range of vibrant colours. The colonial-style lounge is the perfect place to unwind with a pre or post-dinner drink.
ROOMS: 8 en suite ⊗ in 18 bedrooms s fr £105; d fr £105 (incl. bkfst) **PARKING:** 60 **NOTES:** ⊗ in restaurant Closed 3 wks Sep & 1 wk Jan
CARDS:

NANT-DDU (NEAR MERTHYR TYDFIL), Powys Map 09 SO01

★★★75% **Nant Ddu Lodge**
Cwm Taf, Nant Ddu CF48 2HY
☎ 01685 379111 🖷 01685 377088
e-mail: enquiries@nant-ddu-lodge.co.uk
web: www.nant-ddu-lodge.co.uk
Dir: *6m N of Merthyr Tydfil & 12m S of Brecon on A470*
Close to the Brecon Beacons and stretching back 200 years, this delightful hotel has seen many improvements in the hands of the present owners. Décor throughout is contemporary and the

continued

bedrooms are thoughtfully furnished and well equipped. Meals can be taken in the modern bistro and there is a bar with a more traditional 'village inn' atmosphere. There is also a well-equipped health, beauty, leisure and fitness centre and spa.
ROOMS: 12 en suite 16 annexe en suite (3 fmly) ⊗ in 6 bedrooms s £65-£75; d £79.50-£99.50 (incl. bkfst) **FACILITIES: Spa** STV supervised Sauna Solarium Gym Jacuzzi **CONF:** BC Thtr 20 Class 20 Board 20 Del from £110 **PARKING:** 60 **NOTES:** ⊗ in restaurant RS 24-26 Dec **CARDS:**

See advert under BRECON and on this page

NEATH, Neath Port Talbot Map 09 SS79

★★★66% Castle Hotel

The Parade SA11 1RB
☎ 01639 641119 & 643581 01639 641624
e-mail: info@castlehotelneath.co.uk
web: www.castlehotelneath.co.uk
Dir: *M4 junct 43, follow signs for Neath, 500yds past railway station, hotel on right. Car park 50yds further on left*
Situated in the town centre, this Georgian former coaching inn has a wealth of history and character. Lord Nelson and Lady Hamilton are reputed to have stayed here and the Welsh Rugby Union was founded here in 1881. More recently, all areas have been extensively upgraded to provide well-equipped accommodation and pleasant public areas. Bedrooms include one with a four-poster bed, non-smoking rooms and family bedded rooms. Facilities include functions and meeting rooms.
ROOMS: 29 en suite (3 fmly) ⊗ in 4 bedrooms s £45-£60; d £60-£80 (incl. bkfst) **LB FACILITIES:** STV ch fac **CONF:** Thtr 160 Class 75 Board 50 **PARKING:** 26 **NOTES:** **CARDS:**

NEVERN, Pembrokeshire Map 08 SN04

★★69% Trewern Arms

SA42 0NB
☎ 01239 820395 01239 820173
e-mail: trevor.wood4@virgin.net
Dir: *off A487 coast road - midway between Cardigan and Fishguard*
Set in a peaceful and picturesque village, this charming 16th-century inn is well positioned to offer a relaxing stay. There are many original features to be seen in the two character bars and attractive restaurant, and the spacious bedrooms are appointed to a high standard and include some family rooms.
ROOMS: 10 en suite (4 fmly) s £35; d £50-£60 (incl. bkfst) **FACILITIES:** Fishing Riding Xmas **PARKING:** 100 **NOTES:** **CARDS:**

NEWPORT, Newport Map 09 ST38

★★★★★70% *The Celtic Manor Resort*

Coldra Woods NP18 1HQ
☎ 01633 413000 01633 412910
e-mail: postbox@celtic-manor.com
Dir: *M4 junct 24, take A48 towards Newport. Hotel 1st right past Alcatel*
This luxurious resort offers a whole host of facilities to suit any guest, whether they are conference delegates, business users or leisure guests. Three golf courses are complemented by superb leisure facilities, whilst the convention centre can accommodate 1500 delegates. There is also a wide choice of dining options to tempt

continued on p824

N

NEWPORT, continued

guests out of the deeply comfortable bedrooms and suites, some of which are located in the original Grade II listed manor house.
ROOMS: 400 en suite (28 fmly) ⊘ in 167 bedrooms **FACILITIES: Spa** STV supervised 18 Snooker Sauna Solarium Gym Putt green Jacuzzi Golf school, Spa with beauty treatments ♫ ch fac **CONF:** BC Thtr 1500 Class 300 Board 50 **SERVICES:** Lift air con **PARKING:** 1300 **NOTES:** Civ Wed 100 **CARDS:**

★★★68% Newport Lodge

Bryn Bevan, Brynglas Rd NP20 5QN
☎ 01633 821818 01633 856360
e-mail: info@newportlodgehotel.co.uk
web: www.newportlodgehotel.co.uk
Dir: *M4 junct 26 follow signs Newport. Turn left after 0.5m onto Malpal Rd, up hill for 0.5m to hotel*
On the edge of the town centre and convenient for the M4, this purpose-built, friendly hotel provides comfortable and well-maintained bedrooms, with modern facilities. A room with a four-poster bed is available, as are ground floor bedrooms and no smoking rooms. The bistro-style restaurant offers a wide range of freshly prepared dishes, often using local ingredients.
ROOMS: 27 en suite ⊘ in 8 bedrooms **CONF:** Thtr 25 Class 20 Board 20 **PARKING:** 63 **NOTES:** No children 14yrs ⊘ in restaurant **CARDS:**

★★★66% *Kings*

High St NP20 1QU
☎ 01633 842020 01633 244667
e-mail: kingshotelswales@netscapeonline.co.uk
Dir: *from town centre, take left road (not flyover) right lane to next rdbt, 3rd exit, pass front of hotel then left for car park*
This large, imposing property is situated right in the town centre and helpfully has its own car park. Privately owned, it offers comfortable bedrooms including non-smoking and family rooms, and bright spacious public areas. Facilities include a choice of function rooms and a large ballroom.
ROOMS: 61 en suite (15 fmly) ⊘ in 20 bedrooms **FACILITIES:** STV ♫ **CONF:** Thtr 150 Class 70 Board 50 **SERVICES:** Lift **PARKING:** 50 **NOTES:** Closed 26 Dec-4 Jan Civ Wed **CARDS:**

See advert on page 823

Travel Inn

Coldra Junction, Chepstow Rd NP18 2NX
☎ 08701 977193 01633 411376
Dir: *Just off M4 J24. Take A48 to Langstone, at next rdbt return towards J24. The Travel Inn 50 metres on left (only 20 minute drive from Millennium Stadium).*
Travel Inn offers good-quality, value-for-money accommodation. Spacious, en suite rooms with bath and shower comfortably accommodate a family of up to two adults and two children (to age 15). The restaurant and bar offers a varied menu. For further details consult the Hotel Groups page.
ROOMS: 63 en suite s £45.95-£46.95; d £45.95-£46.95

NEWPORT, Pembrokeshire Map 08 SN03

Salutation Inn

Felindre Farcnog SA41 3UY
☎ 01239 820564 01239 820355
e-mail: johndenley@aol.com
web: www.salutationcountryhotel.co.uk
Dir: *on A487 between Cardigan & Fishguard. 3m N of Newport*
ROOMS: 8 en suite (2 fmly) (8 GF) ⊘ in all bedrooms **PARKING:** 60 **NOTES:** ★★★ ⊘ in restaurant **CARDS:**

NEWTOWN, Powys Map 15 SO19

Elephant & Castle

Broad St SY16 2BQ
☎ 01686 626271 01686 622123
e-mail: enquire@elephanthotel.fsnet.co.uk
web: www.watb.net/elephant
Dir: *A483 to town on T-junct of town centre*
At the time of going to press, the star classification for this hotel was not confirmed. Please refer to the AA internet site www.theAA.com for current information.
ROOMS: 24 en suite 11 annexe en suite (3 fmly) (4 GF) ⊘ in all bedrooms **FACILITIES: Spa** STV Fishing ♫ **CONF:** Thtr 250 Class 175 Board 175 **PARKING:** 60 **NOTES:** ⊘ in restaurant Civ Wed 40 **CARDS:**

NORTHOP, Flintshire Map 15 SJ26

★★★75% *Soughton Hall*

CH7 6AB
☎ 01352 840811 01352 840382
e-mail: info@soughtonhall.co.uk
Dir: *A55/B5126, after 500mtrs turn left for Northop, left at traffic lights (A5119-Mold). After 0.5m follow signs*
Built as a bishop's palace in 1714, this elegant country house has magnificent grounds. Bedrooms are individually decorated and furnished with fine antiques and rich fabrics. There are several spacious day rooms furnished in keeping with the style of the house. The trendy bar and restaurant offer a good range of dishes at both lunch and dinner. Understandably, the hotel is a very popular venue for weddings.
ROOMS: 14 en suite (2 fmly) (2 GF) ⊘ in all bedrooms **FACILITIES: Spa** Riding Jacuzzi Riding stables nearby **CONF:** BC Thtr 40 Class 40 Board 20 **PARKING:** 100 **NOTES:** ⊘ in restaurant Civ Wed 120 **CARDS:**

NORTHOP HALL, Flintshire Map 15 SJ26

★★★ Northop Hall Country House

Chester Rd CH7 6HJ
☎ 01244 816181 01244 814661
e-mail: northop@hotel-chester.com
web: www.hotel-chester.com
Dir: *M56/A5117/A494. Exit Buckley/St David's Park. At rdbt, 3rd exit then 1st right to Northop Hall. After 2m, bear left at mini rdbt. Hotel entrance 200yds on left*
ROOMS: 39 en suite (16 fmly) ⊘ in 12 bedrooms s £50-£80; d £54-£110 **LB** **FACILITIES:** Childrens Play Area ch fac Xmas **CONF:** Thtr 120 Class 80 Board 70 Del from £89.50 **PARKING:** 100 **NOTES:** ⊘ in restaurant **CARDS:**

Travelodge

CH7 6HB
☎ 08700 850 950 01244 816473
Dir: *on A55, eastbound*
Travelodge offers good quality, good value, modern accommodation. Ideal for families, the spacious, en suite bedrooms include remote-control TV, tea and coffee-making facilities and luxury beds. Meals can be taken at the nearby family restaurant. For further details consult the Hotel Groups page.
ROOMS: 40 en suite s fr £25; d fr £25

Early start?
Hotels at all star levels should provide in-room alarm clocks and/or alarm calls

PEMBROKE, Pembrokeshire Map 08 SM90

★★★72% Lamphey Court

Lamphey SA71 5NT
☎ 01646 672273 🖷 01646 672480
e-mail: info@lampheycourt.co.uk
web: www.lampheycourt.co.uk
Dir: *A477 to Pembroke. Turn left for Milton village. In Lamphey hotel on right*

Best Western

This former Georgian mansion is set in attractive countryside and well situated for exploring the stunning Pembrokeshire coast and beaches. Bedrooms are well appointed and family suites are situated in a converted coach house in the grounds. The elegant public areas include a leisure spa with treatment rooms, and formal and informal dining rooms that both feature dishes inspired by the local produce.
ROOMS: 26 en suite 12 annexe en suite (7 fmly) (6 GF) in 10 bedrooms s £74-£85; d £105-£145 (incl. bkfst) **LB** **FACILITIES:** STV Sauna Solarium Gym Jacuzzi Yacht charter Xmas **CONF:** Thtr 60 Class 40 Board 30 **PARKING:** 50 **NOTES:** in restaurant Civ Wed 60 **CARDS:**

See advert under TENBY

★★★70% Beggars Reach

SA73 1PD
☎ 01646 600700 🖷 01646 600560
e-mail: stay@beggars-reach.com web: www.beggars-reach.com
Dir: *8m S of Haverfordwest, 6m N of Pembroke, off A477*

This privately owned and personally run hotel was once a Georgian rectory. Having undergone much refurbishment in recent years it stands in four acres of grounds and is peacefully located close to the village of Burton. Milford Haven and the ferry terminal at Pembroke Dock are both within easy reach. It provides modern, well-equipped accommodation and two of the bedrooms are located in former stables, which date back to the 14th century.
ROOMS: 15 en suite 2 annexe en suite (4 fmly) (2 GF) in 8 bedrooms s £59.50-£79.50; d £75-£110 (incl. bkfst) **LB** **FACILITIES:** STV **CONF:** Thtr 100 Class 60 Board 60 Del from £80 **PARKING:** 50 **NOTES:** in restaurant **CARDS:**

See advert on this page

★★75% Bethwaite's Lamphey Hall

Lamphey SA71 5NR
☎ 01646 672394 🖷 01646 672369
e-mail: george@bethwaite.freeserve.co.uk
Dir: *from M4 follow signs for A48 towards Carmarthen, then A40 to St Clears. Follow signs for A477 & turn left at Milton Village*

Set in a delightful village, this very friendly, family-owned and run hotel offers an ideal base from which to explore the surrounding countryside. Bedrooms are well equipped, comfortably furnished and include family rooms as well as rooms on the ground floor. Diners have an extensive choice of dishes and a choice of restaurants. There is also a lounge, a bar and attractive gardens.
ROOMS: 10 en suite (1 fmly) (2 GF) in all bedrooms s £50-£60; d £75-£80 (incl. bkfst) **PARKING:** 32 **NOTES:** in restaurant **CARDS:**

★★66% Highgate Inn

Hundleton SA71 5RD
☎ 01646 685904 🖷 01646 681888
e-mail: windy.gail@virgin.net
Dir: *B4320 signed Angle, follow signs to Highgate in Hundleton, hotel opposite playing fields*

The hotel is a popular village meeting place, with the bar and games room offering interesting views of the Pembroke Docks and surrounding countryside. Bedrooms are modern, comfortable and equipped with lots of useful extras. Staff are friendly in the restaurant at dinner, or over a Welsh breakfast.
ROOMS: 6 rms (5 en suite) (2 fmly) in all bedrooms s fr £55; d fr £65 (incl. bkfst) **LB** **FACILITIES:** Riding Pool table & games bar ch fac Xmas **CONF:** BC Thtr 30 Class 30 Board 30 **PARKING:** 65 **NOTES:** in restaurant **CARDS:**

P

PEMBROKE, continued

★★65% Old Kings Arms
Main St SA71 4JS
☎ 01646 683611 📠 01646 682335
e-mail: reception@oldkingsarmshotel.freeserve.co.uk
Dir: *M4/A477 to Pembroke. Turn left for Pembroke, at rdbt follow town centre sign. Turn right onto the parade, car park is signed*
At the centre of the bustling town, this former coaching inn is very much at the heart of local activities and is a favourite with locals. The restaurant and bar have traditional stone walls, flagstone floors and roaring log fires. Both areas offer good, wholesome food.
ROOMS: 18 en suite s £40-£50; d £60 (incl. bkfst) **FACILITIES:** STV ch fac **PARKING:** 21 **NOTES:** Closed 25-26 Dec & 1 Jan
CARDS:

PEMBROKE DOCK, Pembrokeshire — Map 08 SM90

★★★67% Cleddau Bridge
Essex Rd SA72 6EG
☎ 01646 685961 📠 01646 685746
e-mail: information@cleddaubridgehotel.co.uk
Dir: *M4/A40 to St Clears A477 to Pembroke Dock at rdbt 2nd exit for Haverfordwest via toll bridge, then left before the toll bridge*
This modern, purpose-built hotel, now under new ownership, is sited adjacent to the Cleddau Bridge and overlooks the river. The well-equipped bedrooms are all on the ground floor, while the comfortable public areas consist of an attractive bar and restaurant, both with impressive views.
ROOMS: 24 en suite (2 fmly) ⊗ in 12 bedrooms **FACILITIES:** STV Xmas **CONF:** Thtr 160 Class 60 Board 60 **PARKING:** 140 **NOTES:** ⊗ in restaurant Closed 25-26 Dec RS Xmas Eve and New Years Day Civ Wed 150 **CARDS:**

PENCOED, Bridgend — Map 09 SS98

★★★73%
St Mary's Hotel & Country Club
St Marys Golf Club CF35 5EA
☎ 01656 861100 & 860280 📠 01656 863400
e-mail: stmarysgolfhotel@btinternet.com
Dir: *M4 junct 35, on A473*

Best Western

This charming 16th-century farmhouse has been converted and extended into a modern and restful hotel, surrounded by its own two golf courses. Bedrooms are generously appointed, well-equipped and most feature whirlpool baths. Guests are offered a choice of bars, which are popular with club members, and may dine in the Rafters Restaurant.
ROOMS: 24 en suite (19 fmly) **FACILITIES:** STV ⛳ 18 Putt green Floodlit driving range Xmas **CONF:** Thtr 120 Class 60 Board 40 **PARKING:** 140 **NOTES:** ✗ Civ Wed 120 **CARDS:**

See advert under BRIDGEND

⌂ Travel Inn (Bridgend)
Pantruthyn Farm, Pencoed CF35 5HY
☎ 08701 977041 📠 01656 864792
Dir: *M4 junct 35 off roundabout, behind the petrol station and McDonalds.*

travel inn

Travel Inn offers good-quality, value-for-money accommodation. Spacious, en suite rooms with bath and shower comfortably accommodate a family of up to two adults and two children (to age 15). The restaurant and bar offers a varied menu. For further details consult the Hotel Groups page.
ROOMS: 40 en suite s £45.95-£46.95; d £45.95-£46.95

⌂ Travelodge
Old Mill, Felindre Rd CF3 5HU
☎ 08700 850 950 📠 01656 864404
Dir: *on A473*

Travelodge

Travelodge offers good quality, good value, modern accommodation. Ideal for families, the spacious, en suite bedrooms include remote-control TV, tea and coffee-making facilities and luxury beds. Meals can be taken at the nearby family restaurant. For further details consult the Hotel Groups page.
ROOMS: 39 en suite s fr £25; d fr £25

PONTERWYD, Ceredigion — Map 09 SN78

★★65% The George Borrow Hotel
SY23 3AD
☎ 01970 890230 📠 01970 890587
e-mail: georgeborrow@lycos.co.uk
Dir: *on A44 Aberystwyth-Llangurig road. Aberystwyth side of village*

THE CIRCLE
Selected Individual Hotels
GREAT BRITAIN

This friendly hotel nestles in the foothills of the Cambrian Mountains, about 12 miles from the university town of Aberystwyth. The hotel provides an ideal base for walking, fishing and bird watching (look out for red kites). Bedrooms which include family rooms, are comfortable and well equipped. There are two character bars and a restaurant. An extensive choice of food is available.
ROOMS: 9 en suite (2 fmly) ⊗ in all bedrooms s £30-£35; d £60-£70 **LB** **PARKING:** 30 **NOTES:** ✗ ⊗ in restaurant
CARDS:

PONTYPRIDD, Rhondda Cynon Taff — Map 09 ST08

★★★70% Llechwen Hall
Llanfabon CF37 4HP
☎ 01443 742050 & 743020 📠 01443 742189
e-mail: llechwen@aol.com
web: www.llechwen.com
Dir: *A470 N towards Merthyr Tydfil, then A472, then onto A4054 for Cilfynydd. After 0.25m, turn left at hotel sign & follow to top of hill*

Set on top of a hill with a stunning approach, this hotel has served a variety of uses in its 200-year history, including as a private

continued

school and as a magistrates' court. Bedrooms are individually decorated and well equipped and some are situated in the comfortable coach house nearby. The Victorian-style public areas are attractively appointed and the hotel is a popular venue for weddings.
ROOMS: 12 en suite 8 annexe en suite (11 fmly) (4 GF) ⊗ in 8 bedrooms s £54.50-£65.45; d £70-£106.90 (incl. bkfst) **LB**
FACILITIES: ch fac Xmas **CONF:** Thtr 80 Class 30 Board 30 Del from £80 **PARKING:** 100 **NOTES:** ⊗ in restaurant Closed 25-28 Dec Civ Wed 60 **CARDS:**

★★★67% Heritage Park
Coed Cae Rd, Trehafod CF37 2NP
☎ 01443 687057 01443 687060
e-mail: heritageparkhotel@talk21.com
web: www.heritageparkhotel.co.uk
Dir: *off A4058, follow signs to the Rhondda Heritage Park*
This privately owned, modern hotel is suitable for all types of guest. The spacious bedrooms include ground-floor and interconnecting rooms, and a room equipped for less mobile guests. Meals can be taken in the attractive, wood-beamed Loft Restaurant. Facilities include a large function suite, a choice of meeting rooms and a leisure/fitness centre.
ROOMS: 44 en suite (4 fmly) ⊗ in 19 bedrooms s £69.50-£82; d £87.50-£92 (incl. bkfst) **LB FACILITIES:** STV Sauna Solarium Gym Jacuzzi Xmas **CONF:** Thtr 220 Class 40 Board 30 Del from £70
PARKING: 150 **NOTES:** ⊗ in restaurant Civ Wed 100
CARDS:

PORTHCAWL, Bridgend — Map 09 SS87

★★★68% Atlantic
West Dr CF36 3LT

THE INDEPENDENTS HOTEL ASSOCIATION

☎ 01656 785011 01656 771877
e-mail: enquiries@atlantichotelporthcawl.co.uk
Dir: *M4 junct 35/37, follow Porthcawl signs. In Porthcawl follow signs for Seafront/Promenade*
This friendly hotel is privately owned and located on the seafront, a short walk from the town centre. Guests can enjoy sea views from the sun terrace, bright conservatory and some of the bedrooms, which are well equipped, well maintained, and tastefully decorated.
ROOMS: 18 en suite (2 fmly) s £64-£74; d £85-£95 (incl. bkfst)
FACILITIES: STV Xmas **CONF:** Thtr 50 Class 50 Board 25
SERVICES: Lift **PARKING:** 20 **NOTES:**
CARDS:

★★★65% Seabank
The Promenade CF36 3LU
☎ 01656 782261 01656 785363
e-mail: info@seabankhotel.co.uk
Dir: *M4 junct 37, follow A4229 to seafront, hotel on the promenade*

This large, privately owned hotel stands on the promenade. The majority of the well-equipped bedrooms enjoy panoramic sea views and several have four-poster beds. There is a spacious restaurant, a lounge bar and a choice of lounges. The hotel is a popular venue for coach tour parties, as well as weddings and conferences.
ROOMS: 67 en suite (2 fmly) ⊗ in 14 bedrooms s £39-£65; d £58-£85 (incl. bkfst) **LB FACILITIES: Spa** STV Sauna Gym Jacuzzi ♫ Xmas
CONF: Thtr 250 Class 150 Board 70 **SERVICES:** Lift **PARKING:** 140
NOTES: Civ Wed 100 **CARDS:**

PORTHMADOG, Gwynedd — Map 14 SH53

★★69% Royal Sportsman
131 High St LL49 9HB
☎ 01766 512015 01766 512490
e-mail: enquiries@royalsportsman.co.uk
Dir: *by rdbt, at junct of A497 & A487*
Ideally located in the centre of Porthmadog, this former Victorian coaching inn dates from 1862 and has been restored into a friendly, family-run hotel. Rooms are tastefully decorated and well equipped. Some are in an annexe close to the hotel. There is a large comfortable lounge and a wide range of meals is served in the bar or restaurant.
ROOMS: 19 en suite 9 annexe en suite (7 fmly) (9 GF) ⊗ in all bedrooms s £42; d £65-£75 (incl. bkfst) **LB FACILITIES:** ♫ Xmas
CONF: Thtr 50 Class 50 Board 30 **PARKING:** 18 **NOTES:** ⊗ in restaurant **CARDS:**

PORTMEIRION, Gwynedd — Map 14 SH53

★★★78% Castell Deudraeth
LL48 6EN
☎ 01766 772400 01766 771771
e-mail: castell@portmeirion-village.com
Dir: *A4212 for Trawsfynydd/Porthmadog. 1.5m beyond Penrhyndeudraeth, hotel on right*
A refurbished castellated mansion that overlooks Snowdonia and the famous Italianate village featured in the 1960's cult series *'The Prisoner'.* A unique concept, Castell Deudraeth combines traditional materials, such as oak and slate, with state-of-the-art technology and design. Dynamically styled bedrooms boast underfloor heating, real-flame gas fires and wide-screen TVs with DVDs and cinema surround sound. The brasserie-themed dining room provides an informal option at dinner.
ROOMS: 11 en suite (5 fmly) s fr £150; d fr £175 **LB FACILITIES: Spa** STV ♫ Xmas **CONF:** Thtr 30 Class 18 Board 25 **SERVICES:** Lift air con
PARKING: 30 **NOTES:** Civ Wed
CARDS:

★★★77% The Hotel Portmeirion
LL48 6ET
☎ 01766 770000 01766 771331
e-mail: hotel@portmeirion-village.com
web: www.portmeirion-village.com
Dir: *2m W, Portmeirion village is S off A487*
Saved from dereliction in the 1920s by Clough Williams-Ellis, the elegant Hotel Portmeirion enjoys one of the finest settings in Wales, located beneath the wooded slopes of the village, overlooking the sandy estuary towards Snowdonia. Many rooms have private sitting rooms and balconies with spectacular views. The mostly Welsh-speaking staff offer warm hospitality.
ROOMS: 25 en suite 26 annexe en suite (4 fmly) s fr £110; d fr £175
LB FACILITIES: STV Beauty Salon Xmas **CONF:** Thtr 100
PARKING: 40 **NOTES:** ⊗ in restaurant Civ Wed
CARDS:

P

PORT TALBOT, Neath Port Talbot — Map 09 SS78

★★★ 68% Aberavon Beach

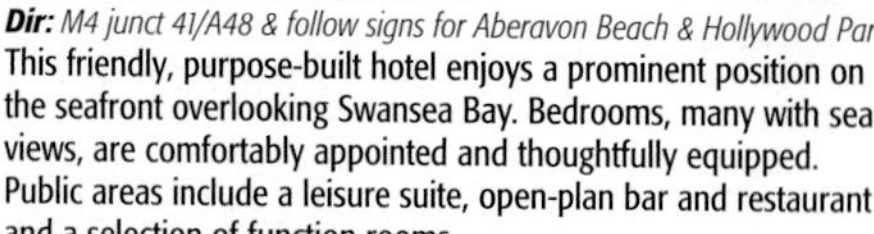

SA12 6QP
☎ 01639 884949 📠 01639 897885
e-mail: sales@aberavonbeach.com
Dir: *M4 junct 41/A48 & follow signs for Aberavon Beach & Hollywood Park*

This friendly, purpose-built hotel enjoys a prominent position on the seafront overlooking Swansea Bay. Bedrooms, many with sea views, are comfortably appointed and thoughtfully equipped. Public areas include a leisure suite, open-plan bar and restaurant and a selection of function rooms.

ROOMS: 52 en suite (6 fmly) ⊗ in 26 bedrooms s £74-£79; d £84-£89 (incl. bkfst) LB **FACILITIES:** Sauna Jacuzzi All weather leisure centre ♫ ch fac Xmas **CONF:** Thtr 300 Class 200 Board 100 Del from £105 **SERVICES:** Lift **PARKING:** 150 **NOTES:** ⊗ in restaurant Civ Wed 300 **CARDS:**

See advert under SWANSEA

Travel Inn

Baglan Rd, Baglan SA12 8ES
☎ 08701 977211 📠 01639 823096
Dir: *Exit M4 (J41 westbound) to rbt. Travel Inn just off 4th exit. J42 eastbound, left turn for Port Talbot. 2nd exit off 2nd rbt.*

Travel Inn offers good-quality, value-for-money accommodation. Spacious, en suite rooms with bath and shower comfortably accommodate a family of up to two adults and two children (to age 15). The restaurant and bar offers a varied menu. For further details consult the Hotel Groups page.

ROOMS: 42 en suite s £45.95-£46.95; d £45.95-£46.95

RAGLAN, Monmouthshire — Map 09 SO40

★★ 70% The Beaufort Arms Coaching Inn & Restaurant

High St NP15 2DY
☎ 01291 690412 📠 01291 690935
e-mail: thebeauforthotel@hotmail.com
Dir: *Opposite church in Raglan village. 1 min from junction of A40 Monmouth and A449 Abergavenny-Newport.*

A friendly, family-run village inn dating back to the 15th century. It has historic links with nearby Raglan Castle. The bright and newly refurbished bedrooms are suitably equipped both for tourists and for business guests. Food is served in either the restaurant or traditional lounge and both offer friendly, relaxed service and an enjoyable selection of carefully prepared food.

ROOMS: 15 rms (10 en suite) (5 GF) ⊗ in 6 bedrooms s fr £50; d £55-£75 (incl. bkfst) **FACILITIES:** Xmas **CONF:** Thtr 120 Class 60 Board 30 Del from £75 **PARKING:** 30 **NOTES:** ⊗ in restaurant **CARDS:**

Travelodge Monmouth

Granada Services A40, Nr Monmouth NP5 4BG
☎ 08700 850 950 📠 01600 740329
Dir: *on A40 near junct with A449*

Travelodge offers good quality, good value, modern accommodation. Ideal for families, the spacious, en suite bedrooms include remote-control TV, tea and coffee-making facilities and luxury beds. Meals can be taken at the nearby family restaurant. For further details consult the Hotel Groups page.

ROOMS: 43 en suite s fr £25; d fr £25

For central reservation numbers and more information on Hotel Groups, turn to pages 33-39

REYNOLDSTON, Swansea — Map 08 SS48

Top 200 – Hotel

★★ Fairyhill

SA3 1BS
☎ 01792 390139 📠 01792 391358
e-mail: postbox@fairyhill.net
web: www.fairyhill.net
Dir: *just outside Reynoldston off A4118*

Peace and tranquillity are never far away at this charming Georgian mansion set in the heart of the beautiful Gower Peninsula. Bedrooms are furnished with care individuality and are filled with many thoughtful extras. There are also a range of comfortable seating areas with crackling log fires to choose from and a smartly appointed, award-winning restaurant featuring local produce. The hotel sometimes has special wine events so do ask when you book.

ROOMS: 8 en suite s £120-£225; d £140-£245 (incl. bkfst) LB **FACILITIES:** STV mountain bikes available **CONF:** Thtr 40 Class 20 Board 26 **PARKING:** 50 **NOTES:** No children 8yrs ⊗ in restaurant Closed 24-26 Dec & 3-21 Jan **CARDS:**

RHAYADER, Powys — Map 09 SN96

★★ 68% Brynafon Country House

South St LD6 5BL
☎ 01597 810735 📠 01597 810111
e-mail: info@brynafon.co.uk
web: www.brynafon.co.uk
Dir: *0.5m from Rhayader on A470*

This imposing stone-built, former workhouse dates back to 1878 and stands in its own pleasant gardens, half a mile south of the town. Now a privately owned and personally run hotel, it provides well-equipped accommodation including four-poster beds and no

continued

smoking bedrooms. Public areas have lots of charm and character and include a no smoking lounge and a choice of conference rooms.
ROOMS: 20 en suite (2 fmly) in 15 bedrooms s £35-£50; d £55-£80 (incl. bkfst) **LB** **CONF:** Thtr 30 Class 30 Board 20 Del from £95 **PARKING:** 40 **NOTES:** in restaurant Closed 18-27 Dec **CARDS:**

A Elan
West St LD6 5AF
☎ 01597 810109 📠 01597 810524
e-mail: davemackie@elanhotel.fsnet.co.uk
web: www.elanhotel.co.uk
Dir: *600mtrs from junct of A44/A470 Rhayader*
ROOMS: 10 en suite (1 fmly) in all bedrooms **FACILITIES:** Xmas **PARKING:** 16 **NOTES:** ★★ in restaurant **CARDS:**

ROSSETT, Wrexham
Map 15 SJ35

★★★73% Rossett Hall
Chester Rd LL12 0DE
☎ 01244 571000 📠 01244 571505
e-mail: reservations@rossetthallhotel.co.uk
web: www.rossetthallhotel.co.uk
Dir: *M56/M53/A55. Take Wrexham/Chester exit towards Wrexham. Onto B5445, hotel entrance in Rossett village*
This hotel lies in several acres of mature gardens in lovely Welsh border country. Pretty bedrooms are generally spacious and well equipped, and include ground-floor rooms and a full suite. A comfortable foyer lounge is provided and Oscar's bistro serves a wide range of skilfully prepared dishes.
ROOMS: 30 en suite (2 fmly) (10 GF) in 15 bedrooms **FACILITIES:** STV Xmas **CONF:** Thtr 120 Class 50 Board 50 Del from £85 **PARKING:** 120 **NOTES:** Civ Wed **CARDS:**

★★★71% *Llyndir Hall*
Llyndir Ln LL12 0AY
☎ 01244 571648 📠 01244 571258
e-mail: llyndir.hall@pageant.co.uk
Dir: *5m S of Chester on B5445 follow Pulford signs. Hotel is set back off road*
Located on the English/Welsh border within easy reach of Chester and Wrexham, this charming manor house lies in several acres of mature grounds. The well-equipped accommodation is popular with leisure and business guests. Facilities include conference rooms, the Business Training Centre, an impressive leisure centre, a choice of comfortable lounges and a brasserie-style restaurant.
ROOMS: 48 en suite (3 fmly) in 12 bedrooms **FACILITIES:** STV Solarium Gym Jacuzzi Steam room ch fac **CONF:** Thtr 140 Class 60 Board 40 **PARKING:** 80 **NOTES:** in restaurant Civ Wed 120 **CARDS:**

Late for dinner?
Quality Standards mean that last orders for dinner vary according to star rating and should be no earlier than:
★★ 7.00pm ★★★ 8.00pm ★★★★ 9.00pm
★★★★★ 10.00pm

RUTHIN, Denbighshire
Map 15 SJ15

★★★69% Ruthin Castle
LL15 2NU
☎ 01824 702664 📠 01824 705978
e-mail: reservations@ruthincastle.co.uk
web: www.ruthincastle.co.uk
Dir: *A550 to Mold, A494 to Ruthin, hotel at end of Castle St just off Town Square*

The main part of this impressive castle was built in the early 19th century, but many of the ruins found in the impressive grounds date back much further. The elegantly panelled public areas include a restaurant and bar along with a medieval banqueting hall and a tea shop. Many of the modernly equipped bedrooms are spacious and furnished with fine period pieces.
ROOMS: 58 en suite (6 fmly) in 10 bedrooms s £62-£72; d £99-£116 (incl. bkfst) **LB** **FACILITIES:** Fishing Snooker **CONF:** Thtr 150 Class 100 Board 80 Del from £106.50 **SERVICES:** Lift **PARKING:** 200 **NOTES:** Civ Wed 140 **CARDS:**

★★68% Ye Olde Anchor Inn
2 Rhos St LL15 1DY
☎ 01824 702813 📠 01824 703050
e-mail: reception@anchorinn.co.uk
Dir: *A55 turn off at Mold A494 into Ruthin. Hotel on junct of A494 and A525.*
This well-equipped accommodation, situated in the town centre, is suitable for both tourists and commercial visitors. Family rooms and interconnecting bedrooms are available. A wide choice of food is available in either the traditionally furnished restaurant, or from the bar. The lounge bar is attractively appointed and features a wood-burning stove. The hotel also has a conservatory function room.
ROOMS: 21 en suite 4 annexe en suite (5 fmly) (4 GF) s £40; d £70 (incl. bkfst) **LB** **FACILITIES:** STV Xmas **CONF:** Thtr 40 Class 40 Board 30 **PARKING:** 10 **NOTES:** in restaurant **CARDS:**

★★65% Castle
St Peters Square LL15 1AA
☎ 01824 702479 📠 01824 703488
e-mail: reception@castle-hotel-ruthin.co.uk
This hotel is located in the centre of this attractive market town and is an ideal base for touring North Wales and the surrounding areas. Bedrooms are tastefully decorated and well equipped. There is a choice of bars and restaurants and functions are also catered for.
ROOMS: 18 en suite (5 fmly) (1 GF) s £49.95; d £79.95 (incl. bkfst) **FACILITIES:** Xmas **PARKING:** 20 **NOTES:** in restaurant **CARDS:**

R

ST ASAPH, Denbighshire

Map 15 SJ07

★★★70% Oriel House

Upper Denbigh Rd LL17 0LW
☎ 01745 582716 ▤ 01745 585208
e-mail: bookings@orielhousehotel
web: www.orielhousehotel.co.uk
Dir: *A55/A525, left at cathedral 1m along A525 on right*

Set in several acres of mature grounds south of St Asaph, Oriel House offers generally spacious, well-equipped bedrooms and has a friendly and hospitable staff. The Terrace restaurant serves imaginative food with an emphasis on local produce. Extensive function facilities cater for business meetings and weddings, and the leisure club is available to guests.

ROOMS: 31 en suite (3 fmly) (9 GF) ⊗ in 26 bedrooms **FACILITIES:** STV Fishing Sauna Solarium Gym Xmas **CONF:** Thtr 250 Class 100 Board 50 Del from £99 **PARKING:** 200 **NOTES:** ⊗ in restaurant Civ Wed 120 **CARDS:**

★★67% Plas Elwy Hotel & Restaurant

The Roe LL17 0LT
☎ 01745 582263 & 582089 ▤ 01745 583864
e-mail: plaselwy@gtleisure.co.uk
Dir: *off A55 junct 27, A525 signed Rhyl/St Asaph. On left opposite Total petrol station*

This hotel, which dates back to 1850, has retained much of its original character. Bedrooms in the purpose-built extension are spacious, and one has a four-poster bed; those in the main building are equally well equipped. Public rooms are smart and comfortably furnished and a range of food options is provided in the attractive restaurant.

ROOMS: 7 en suite 6 annexe en suite (3 fmly) (2 GF) ⊗ in 6 bedrooms s £40-£48; d £58-£70 (incl. bkfst) **PARKING:** 25 **NOTES:** ⊗ in restaurant Closed 25 Dec-4 Jan **CARDS:**

U Talardy

The Roe LL17 0HY
☎ 01745 584957 ▤ 01745 584385
e-mail: info@talardy.co.uk
web: www.talardy.co.uk
Dir: *Leave A55 at junct 27. Take A525 to Rhuddlan; hotel on left*

At the time of going to press, the star classification for this hotel was not confirmed. Please refer to the AA internet site www.theAA.com for current information.

ROOMS: 16 en suite (6 fmly) ⊗ in all bedrooms s £70-£130; d £95-£160 (incl. bkfst) **LB** **FACILITIES:** ch fac Xmas **CONF:** Thtr 120 Class 120 Board 30 Del from £130 **PARKING:** 120 **NOTES:** Civ Wed 100 **CARDS:**

ST CLEARS, Carmarthenshire

Map 08 SN21

⌂ Travelodge (Carmarthen)

Travelodge

Tenby Rd SA33 4JN
☎ 08700 850 950 ▤ 01994 231227

Travelodge offers good quality, good value, modern accommodation. Ideal for families, the spacious, en suite bedrooms include remote-control TV, tea and coffee-making facilities and luxury beds. Meals can be taken at the nearby family restaurant. For further details consult the Hotel Groups page.

ROOMS: 32 en suite s fr £25; d fr £25

Bad hair day?
Hairdryers in all rooms three stars and above

ST DAVID'S, Pembrokeshire

Map 08 SM72

★★★77% Warpool Court

SA62 6BN
☎ 01437 720300 ▤ 01437 720676
e-mail: warpool@enterprise.net
web: www.warpoolcourthotel.com
Dir: *At Cross Square bear left beside Cartref Restaurant (Goat St). Pass Farmers Arms Pub, after 400mtrs take left and follow hotel signs, entrance on right*

Originally the cathedral choir school, Warpool Court Hotel is set in landscaped gardens looking out to sea and is within easy walking distance of the Pembrokeshire coastal path. The lounges are spacious and comfortable and bedrooms are well furnished and equipped with modern facilities. The restaurant offers delightful cuisine.

ROOMS: 25 en suite (3 fmly) s £65-£100; d £130-£200 (incl. bkfst) **LB** **FACILITIES:** Gym ch fac Xmas **CONF:** Thtr 40 Class 25 Board 25 Del from £95 **PARKING:** 100 **NOTES:** ⊗ in restaurant Closed Jan Civ Wed 80 **CARDS:**

★★69% Old Cross

Cross Square SA62 6SP
☎ 01437 720387 ▤ 01437 720394
e-mail: enquiries@oldcrosshotel.co.uk
web: www.oldcrosshotel.co.uk
Dir: *in centre of St David's*

This friendly and comfortable hotel is situated in the centre of the town, just a short walk from the famous cathedral. Bedrooms are generally spacious and have a good range of facilities with some being suitable for families. Public areas include comfortable lounges, a popular bar and an airy restaurant where good wholesome food is offered.

ROOMS: 17 rms (16 en suite) 1 annexe en suite (2 fmly) ⊗ in 8 bedrooms s £38-£75; d £68-£100 (incl. bkfst) **PARKING:** 17 **NOTES:** ⊗ in restaurant Closed end Dec-last week Jan **CARDS:**

SARN PARK MOTORWAY SERVICE AREA (M4), Bridgend

Map 09 SS98

⌂ Welcome Lodge

Welcome Break

Sarn Park Services CF32 9RW
☎ 01656 659218 ▤ 01656 768665
e-mail: sarnpark.hotel@welcomebreak.co.uk
web: www.welcomebreak.co.uk
Dir: *M4 junct 36*

This modern building offers accommodation in smart, spacious and well-equipped bedrooms, suitable for families and business travellers, and all with en suite bathrooms. Refreshments may be taken at the nearby family restaurant. For further details consult the Hotel Groups page.

ROOMS: 40 en suite s £35-£55; d £35-£55

SAUNDERSFOOT, Pembrokeshire Map 08 SN10

★★★67% St Brides
St Brides Hill SA69 9NH
☎ 01834 812304 🖹 01834 811766
e-mail: reservations@stbrideshotel.com
web: www.stbrideshotel.com
Dir: *Exit A478 at Twycross rdbt, signed Saundersfoot. Hotel at bottom of hill on right.*

This privately owned hotel is situated above the village and has stunning views of the harbour and coastline. The refurbished public areas are spacious and tastefully decorated, and feature exhibitions of Welsh artists' work. Bedrooms, many of which have sea views, vary in size and style.

ROOMS: 43 en suite (2 fmly) (5 GF) ⊗ in 6 bedrooms s £65-£95; d £80-£140 (incl. bkfst) **LB** **FACILITIES:** Art gallery exhibiting Welsh modern art Xmas **CONF:** Thtr 150 Class 80 Board 60 Del from £110 **PARKING:** 70 **NOTES:** ⊗ in restaurant Civ Wed 100 **CARDS:**

★★69% Rhodewood House
St Brides Hill SA69 9NU
☎ 01834 812200 🖹 01834 815005
e-mail: relax@rhodewood.co.uk
web: www.rhodewood.co.uk
Dir: *from St Clears, take A477 to Kilgetty, then A478 to Tenby, turn left onto B4316 signed Saundersfoot*

Personally run by the owners, this busy hotel is situated on the outskirts of the village and is popular with coach tour groups. Live entertainment is a regular feature and the public areas include two restaurants, a comfortable bar and a reception lounge. The bedrooms are well equipped and some are on the ground floor.

ROOMS: 45 en suite (14 fmly) (10 GF) ⊗ in 6 bedrooms s £38-£47; d £56-£74 (incl. bkfst) **LB** **FACILITIES:** STV ♫ ch fac Xmas **CONF:** Thtr 100 Board 100 **PARKING:** 70 **NOTES:** Closed 3 Jan-1Feb **CARDS:**

★★66% Merlewood
St Brides Hill SA69 9NP
☎ 01834 812421 🖹 01834 814886
Dir: *A477/A4316, hotel on other side of village on St Brides Hill*

Possessing delightful views over the village and bay and with regular live entertainment, this hotel is a popular destination for coach parties. Bedrooms include ground floor and family rooms and there is a comfortable dining room and a large lounge bar. A pleasant outdoor swimming pool is also available for guests' use.

ROOMS: 29 en suite (8 fmly) (11 GF) ⊗ in 28 bedrooms s £29.50-£33.50; d £59-£67 (incl. bkfst) **LB** **FACILITIES:** Putt green Children's swings, Table tennis ♫ ch fac Xmas **CONF:** Thtr 60 Class 100 Board 40 **PARKING:** 34 **NOTES:** ⊗ in restaurant Closed Nov-Mar RS Xmas & New Year **CARDS:**

SKENFRITH, Monmouthshire Map 09 SO42

Restaurant with Rooms

The Bell at Skenfrith
NP7 8UH
☎ 01600 750235 🖹 01600 750525
e-mail: enquiries@skenfrith.co.uk
web: www.skenfrith.co.uk
Dir: *A40/ A466 N towards Hereford. 4m turn left onto B4521, hotel 2m on left*

The Bell is a beautifully restored, 17th-century former coaching inn which still retains much of its charm and character. Natural materials have been used throughout, while the bedrooms, which

continued

include full suites and rooms with four-poster beds, are stylish, luxurious and equipped with DVDs.

ROOMS: 8 en suite ⊗ in all bedrooms s £85-£120; d £100-£165 (incl. bkfst) **FACILITIES:** Xmas **CONF:** Thtr 20 Board 16 Del from £170 **PARKING:** 36 **NOTES:** ⊗ in restaurant RS end Oct-Etr **CARDS:**

SWANSEA, Swansea Map 09 SS69
See also Port Talbot

Top 200 – Hotel

★★★★ Morgans
Somerset Place SA1 1RR
☎ 01792 484848 🖹 01792 484849
e-mail: info@morganshotel.co.uk

This new and stunning hotel has been imaginatively developed from the Port's Authority building near the harbour side. The bedrooms are modern in design with much attention given to guest comfort. Features include big beds, best linen, large screen TV, high ceilings, and DVDs. Public areas enjoy wonderful period elements and guests have a choice of eating and drinking options.

ROOMS: 20 en suite (4 fmly) ⊗ in all bedrooms **FACILITIES:** STV **SERVICES:** Lift air con **PARKING:** 27 **NOTES:** ⊗ in restaurant Civ Wed 100 **CARDS:**

★★★★68% Swansea Marriott Hotel
The Maritime Quarter SA1 3SS
☎ 0870 400 7282 🖹 0870 400 7382
Dir: *M4 junct 42, A483 to city centre past Leisure Centre, then follow signs to Maritime Quarter*

Just opposite City Hall, this busy hotel enjoys fantastic views over the bay and marina. Bedrooms are spacious and equipped with a range of extras. Public rooms include a popular leisure club and

continued on p832

S

SWANSEA, continued

Abernethy's restaurant, which overlooks the marina. It is worth noting, however, that lounge seating is limited.
ROOMS: 122 en suite (50 fmly) (11 GF) ⊗ in 90 bedrooms s £75-£125; d £100-£155 (incl. bkfst) **LB** **FACILITIES:** STV Sauna Gym Jacuzzi **CONF:** Thtr 250 Class 120 Board 30 Del from £135 **SERVICES:** Lift air con **PARKING:** 122 **NOTES:** ⊗ in restaurant Civ Wed 200
CARDS:

★★★70% The Towers Hotel
Jersey Marine, Swansea Bay SA10 6JL
☎ 01792 814155 01792 324414
e-mail: reception2@towershotel.co.uk
Dir: *M4 junct 42 towards Swansea. Join A483 & turn right at 1st rdbt. Take 1st turning left onto B4290*
The Towers is a smart, modern, purpose-built hotel. It takes its name from the tower which is all that remains of the original 1860's hotel. Bedrooms vary; some are suites, some have balconies, access to patio areas or facilities for less able guests. In addition to the bright and pleasant restaurant and bars, the hotel has extensive conference and function rooms and is licensed for civil wedding ceremonies.
ROOMS: 44 en suite 3 annexe en suite (2 fmly) (12 GF) ⊗ in 40 bedrooms s fr £60; d fr £75 (incl. bkfst) **FACILITIES:** STV Use of Glamorgan Health Club (pool, gym, spa, jacuzzi) ♫ Xmas **CONF:** BC Thtr 240 Class 120 Board 60 **SERVICES:** Lift air con **PARKING:** 100 **NOTES:** Civ Wed 150 **CARDS:**

★★ Fairyhill
SA3 1BS
☎ 01792 390139 01792 391358
e-mail: postbox@fairyhill.net
web: www.fairyhill.net
(For full entry see Reynoldston)

★★72% *Beaumont*
72-73 Walter Rd SA1 4QA
☎ 01792 643956 01792 643044
e-mail: info@beaumonthotel.co.uk
web: www.beaumonthotel.co.uk
Dir: *M4, towards city centre. Follow Uplands & Sketty signs. 0.5m from centre along Walter Rd, hotel on left opposite St James Church*

Situated within walking distance of the city centre, this family owned hotel offers a high level of comfort and stylish décor. Bedrooms are well equipped and thoughtfully furnished. There is a relaxing lounge bar where guests can enjoy a drink before sampling good home cooking in the Conservatory Restaurant. There is a secure car park, which is locked each evening.
ROOMS: 16 en suite (3 fmly) **CONF:** BC Class 50 Board 30 **PARKING:** 12 **NOTES:** ⊗ in restaurant Closed 25-26 Dec & 31 Dec-1 Jan
CARDS:

See advert on opposite page

★★71% Windsor Lodge
Mount Pleasant SA1 6EG
☎ 01792 642158 & 652744 01792 648996
e-mail: reservations@windsor-lodge.co.uk
web: www.windsor-lodge.co.uk
Dir: *M4 junct 42, A483, right at lights past Sainsburys, left at station, right immediately after 2nd set of lights*
This privately owned and personally run hotel is just a short walk from the city centre. Bedrooms vary in size, but all are similarly well equipped. There is a choice of lounge areas and a deservedly popular restaurant.
ROOMS: 19 en suite (2 fmly) s £50-£65; d £65-£75 (incl. bkfst) **LB** **CONF:** Thtr 30 Class 15 Board 24 **PARKING:** 25 **NOTES:** ⊗ in restaurant Closed 25-26 Dec RS Sun & BH's
CARDS:

Travel Inn
Upper Fforest Way, Morriston SA6 8WB
☎ 08701 977246 01792 311929
Dir: *M4 junct 45/A4067 towards Swansea. At 2nd exit, after 0.5m, turn left onto Clase Rd. Travel Inn 400yds on the left*
Travel Inn offers good-quality, value-for-money accommodation. Spacious, en suite rooms with bath and shower comfortably accommodate a family of up to two adults and two children (to age 15). The restaurant and bar offers a varied menu. For further details consult the Hotel Groups page.
ROOMS: 40 en suite s £45.95-£46.95; d £45.95-£46.95

Travelodge
Penllergaer SA4 1GT
☎ 08700 850 950 01792 898972
Dir: *M4 junct 47*
Travelodge offers good quality, good value, modern accommodation. Ideal for families, the spacious, en suite bedrooms include remote-control TV, tea and coffee-making facilities and luxury beds. Meals can be taken at the nearby family restaurant. For further details consult the Hotel Groups page.
ROOMS: 50 en suite s fr £25; d fr £25 **CONF:** Thtr 25 Class 32 Board 20

○ Premier Lodge (Swansea City Central)
Salubrious Place, Salubrious Quarter, Wind St SA1 1DP
ROOMS: 116 en suite
NOTES: Due to open Spring 2005

TALSARNAU See Harlech

TENBY, Pembrokeshire Map 08 SN10

★★★76% *Penally Abbey Country House*
Penally SA70 7PY
☎ 01834 843033 01834 844714
e-mail: penally.abbey@btinternet.com
web: www.penally-abbey.com
Dir: *1.5m from Tenby, off A4139, Penally village green*
With monastic origins, this delightful country house stands in five acres of grounds with views over Carmarthen Bay. The drawing room, bar and restaurant are tastefully decorated and attractively furnished and set the scene for a relaxing stay. The bedrooms are

continued

similarly appointed; some are situated in the stylish coach house annexe.

ROOMS: 8 en suite 4 annexe en suite (3 fmly) **FACILITIES:** Snooker **CONF:** Board 14 **PARKING:** 17 **NOTES:** in restaurant Civ Wed 50 **CARDS:**

★★★ 75% Atlantic

The Esplanade SA70 7DU
☎ 01834 842881 & 844176 01834 842881 ex 256
e-mail: enquiries@atlantic-hotel.uk.com
Dir: *A478 into Tenby & follow town centre signs, keep town walls on left then turn right at Esplanade, hotel half way along on right*

This privately owned and personally run, friendly hotel has an enviable position looking out over South Beach towards Caldy Island. Bedrooms vary in size and style, and are well equipped and tastefully appointed. The comfortable public areas include a

continued on p834

T

TEN

TENBY, continued

choice of restaurants and in fine weather guests can also enjoy the cliff-top gardens.
ROOMS: 42 en suite (11 fmly) (4 GF) ⊗ in 4 bedrooms s £70-£74; d £94-£156 (incl. bkfst) **FACILITIES: Spa** STV Solarium Steam room ch fac **CONF:** Board 10 **SERVICES:** Lift **PARKING:** 25 **NOTES:** Closed 14-29 Dec **CARDS:**

★★★71% Heywood Mount
Heywood Ln SA70 8DA
☎ 01834 842087 01834 842113
e-mail: reception@heywoodmount.co.uk
web: www.heywoodmount.co.uk
Dir: *A478 into Tenby, follow Heywood Mount signs then right into Serpentine Rd, turn right at T-junct into Heywood Lane, 3rd hotel on left*
This privately owned hotel is situated in a peaceful residential area, close to Tenby's beaches and town centre. The well-maintained house is surrounded by extensive gardens, and public areas include a comfortable lounge, bar, restaurant and health & fitness spa. Several of the well-appointed and equipped bedrooms are on the ground floor.
ROOMS: 30 en suite (6 fmly) (10 GF) ⊗ in all bedrooms s £42-£85; d £84-£170 (incl. bkfst) **LB** **FACILITIES: Spa** supervised Sauna Solarium Gym Jacuzzi ♫ ch fac Xmas **CONF:** BC Thtr 80 Class 50 Board 25 Del from £74 **PARKING:** 25 **NOTES:** No children 3yrs ⊗ in restaurant Civ Wed 90 **CARDS:**

★★★69% Fourcroft
North Beach SA70 8AP
☎ 01834 842886 01834 842888
e-mail: staying@fourcroft-hotel.co.uk
web: www.fourcroft-hotel.co.uk
Dir: *A478, after 'Welcome to Tenby' sign left towards North Beach & walled town. At seafront turn sharp left. Hotel on left*
This friendly, family-run hotel offers a beach-front location, together with a number of extra facilities that make it particularly suitable for guests with children. There is direct access to the beach through the hotel's clifftop gardens. Bedrooms are of a good size, with modern facilities.
ROOMS: 40 en suite (12 fmly) ⊗ in 10 bedrooms s £39-£59; d £78-£118 (incl. bkfst) **LB** **FACILITIES:** STV Sauna Jacuzzi Table tennis Giant chess Human Gyroscope Snooker Pool Xmas **CONF:** BC Thtr 90 Class 40 Board 50 Del from £95 **SERVICES:** Lift **PARKING:** 12 **NOTES:** ⊗ in restaurant Civ Wed 90
CARDS:

★★73% Panorama Hotel & Restaurant
The Esplanade SA70 7DU
☎ 01834 844976 01834 844976
e-mail: mail@panoramahotel.f9.co.uk
web: www.panoramahotel.force9.co.uk
Dir: *A478 follow 'South Beach' & 'Town Centre' signs. Sharp left under railway arches, up Greenhill Rd, onto South Pde then Esplanade*
This charming little hotel is part of a Victorian terrace, overlooking the South Beach and Caldy Island. It provides a variety of non-smoking bedrooms, all of which are well equipped. Facilities include a cosy bar and an elegant restaurant, where a good choice of skilfully prepared dishes is available.
ROOMS: 7 en suite (2 fmly) ⊗ in all bedrooms s £42.50-£45; d £60-£85 (incl. bkfst) **LB** **NOTES:** No children 5yrs ⊗ in restaurant
CARDS:

♫ Entertainment

★★67% *Hammonds Park*
Narberth Rd SA70 8HT
☎ 01834 842696 01834 844295
e-mail: info@hoteltenby.com
Dir: *left off A478 into Narberth Rd, hotel 200yds on left*
This friendly and privately owned hotel is situated within walking distance of North Beach and the town centre. There are some four-poster and ground-floor rooms and all are thoughtfully equipped. Homely and wholesome cooking can be enjoyed in the bright conservatory restaurant and there is also a cosy lounge in which to relax, as well as a pleasant bar.
ROOMS: 13 en suite (6 fmly) (5 GF) ⊗ in all bedrooms
FACILITIES: Gym **PARKING:** 15 **NOTES:** ⊗ in restaurant
CARDS:

THREE COCKS, Powys — Map 09 SO13

★★74% Three Cocks
LD3 0SL
☎ 01497 847215 01497 847339
e-mail: info@threecockshotel.com
web: www.threecockshotel.com
Dir: *on A438, in centre of Three Cocks Village*
This charming old country hostelry dates back to the 15th century. It is set in the glorious countryside of the Beacons National Park. There is a wealth of original features and wooden beams in the comfortable lounges, whilst the elegant restaurant overlooks the garden. Bedrooms are tastefully decorated and a television lounge is available to guests.
ROOMS: 7 en suite (2 fmly) s £45-£75; d £70-£130 (incl. bkfst) **LB** **FACILITIES:** no TV in bdrms Xmas **PARKING:** 40 **NOTES:** ⊗ in restaurant **CARDS:**

TINTERN PARVA, Monmouthshire — Map 04 SO50

★★★71% The Abbey Hotel
NP16 6SF

THE INDEPENDENTS

☎ 01291 689777 01291 689727
e-mail: info@theabbeyhoteltintern.com
web: www.theabbeyhoteltintern.com
Dir: *M48 junct 2/A466, hotel opposite the abbey ruins*

Now refurbished to a high standard and possessing stunning views of nearby Tintern Abbey, this friendly hotel provides modern bedrooms, including a family suite. Diners are spoilt for choice between the brasserie with its daytime carvery, the formal carte service for dinner, and the pleasant hotel bar where lighter meal options are on offer.
ROOMS: 23 en suite ⊗ in 7 bedrooms s £70-£75; d £99-£140 (incl. bkfst) **LB** **FACILITIES: Spa** STV Fishing Jacuzzi ♫ ch fac Xmas **CONF:** Thtr 150 Class 60 Board 30 Del from £100 **PARKING:** 60 **NOTES:** ⊗ in restaurant Civ Wed 140 **CARDS:**

★★★67% Royal George

NP16 6SF
☎ 01291 689205 01291 689448
e-mail: royalgeorgetintern@hotmail.com
Dir: *off M48/A466, 4m into Tintern 2nd on left*

This privately owned and personally run hotel provides comfortable, spacious accommodation, including bedrooms with balconies overlooking the well-tended garden. There are some ground floor rooms. The public areas include a choice of bars, and a large function room.

ROOMS: 2 en suite 14 annexe en suite (13 fmly) (10 GF) in 11 bedrooms s £65-£70; d £92-£102 (incl. bkfst) **LB** **FACILITIES:** Xmas **CONF:** Thtr 120 Class 40 Board 50 Del from £90 **PARKING:** 50 **NOTES:** in restaurant Civ Wed 120
CARDS:

★★73% Parva Farmhouse Hotel & Restaurant

NP16 6SQ
☎ 01291 689411 & 689511 01291 689557
e-mail: parva_hotelintern@hotmail.com
Dir: *From S leave M48 junct 2, N edge of village on A466. From N, 10m S of Monmouth town & M50*

This relaxed and friendly hotel is situated on a sweep of the River Wye with far reaching views of the valley. Originally a farmhouse dating from the 17th century, many of the original features have been retained to provide a lounge full of character, which has a fire in colder months, and an atmospheric restaurant with a popular local following. Bedrooms are tastefully decorated and thoughtfully equipped.

ROOMS: 9 en suite (3 fmly) (1 GF) s £55-£76; d £76-£80 (incl. bkfst) **LB** **FACILITIES:** Cycle hire ch fac **CONF:** Thtr 12 Board 12 Del from £70 **PARKING:** 10 **NOTES:** in restaurant
CARDS:

TREARDDUR BAY See Anglesey, Isle of

TREFRIW, Conwy — Map 14 SH76

★★73% Hafod Country Hotel

LL27 0RQ
☎ 01492 640029 01492 641351
e-mail: hafod@breathemail.net
web: www.hafodhouse.co.uk
Dir: *on B5106 between A5 at Betws-y-Coed & A55 at Conwy. 2nd entrance on right entering Trefriw village from S.*

This former farmhouse is a personally run and friendly hotel with a wealth of charm and character. The tasteful bedrooms feature period furnishings and thoughtful extras such as fresh fruit. There is a comfortable sitting room and a cosy bar. The fixed-price menu is imaginative and makes good use of fresh, local produce while the breakfast menu offers a wide choice.

ROOMS: 6 en suite in all bedrooms s £35-£43; d £60-£75 (incl. bkfst) **LB** **FACILITIES:** Xmas **PARKING:** 14 **NOTES:** No children 11yrs in restaurant Closed early Jan-mid Feb
CARDS:

★★70% *Princes Arms*

LL27 0JP
☎ 01492 640592 01492 640559
e-mail: enquiries@princes-arms.co.uk
web: www.princes-arms.co.uk
Dir: *A470 to Llanrwst left onto B5106 over bridge & follow to Trefriw, hotel just through village on left*

Located in the Conwy Valley, this privately-owned and personally-run hotel offers superb views from many bedrooms. The two-bedroomed apartments are ideal for families. Excellent food can be enjoyed in the attractive restaurant, and there is also a comfortable brasserie with log fires.

ROOMS: 14 en suite (5 fmly) **FACILITIES:** STV **CONF:** Thtr 80 Class 40 Board 20 **PARKING:** 40 **NOTES:** in restaurant
CARDS:

USK, Monmouthshire — Map 09 SO30

★★★70% *Glen-yr-Afon House*

Pontypool Rd NP15 1SY
☎ 01291 672302 & 673202 01291 672597
e-mail: enquiries@glen-yr-afon.co.uk
web: www.glen-yr-afon.co.uk
Dir: *A472 through Usk High St, over river bridge following main road to right, hotel is 200yds on left*

In the same private ownership for nearly 30 years, this friendly hotel bears the marks of proprietors' care and style throughout. The elegant and well-proportioned public areas consist of a restful lounge, bar and wood-panelled restaurant. Bedrooms, situated in

continued on p836

USK, continued

both the original building and a new wing, are well equipped and individually furnished.
ROOMS: 28 en suite (2 fmly) ⊗ in 14 bedrooms **FACILITIES:** STV **CONF:** Thtr 100 Class 200 Board 30 **SERVICES:** Lift **PARKING:** 101 **NOTES:** ⊗ in restaurant Civ Wed 200
CARDS:

★★★70% Three Salmons

Porthycarne St NP15 1RY
☎ 01291 672133 01291 673979
e-mail: threesalmons.hotel@talk21.com
web: www.3-salmons-usk.co.uk
Dir: *off A449, 1m into Usk, hotel on corner of Porthycarne St, B4598*
This 17th-century coaching inn in the heart of Usk offers spacious bedrooms that are comfortably furnished and well maintained. Both the restaurant and bar offer a wide range of carefully prepared dishes. The function room and meeting room overlook the pretty garden and courtyard to the rear.
ROOMS: 10 en suite 14 annexe en suite (2 fmly) s fr £72; d fr £105 (incl. bkfst) **LB** **FACILITIES:** STV Xmas **CONF:** Thtr 100 Class 40 Board 50 Del from £99.95 **PARKING:** 38 **NOTES:** ✈ ⊗ in restaurant Civ Wed 100 **CARDS:**

See advert on opposite page

Restaurant with Rooms

The Newbridge

Tredunnock NP15 1LY
☎ 01633 451000 01633 451001
e-mail: thenewbridge@tinyonline.co.uk
web: www.thenewbridge.co.uk
Dir: *Turn off B4236 between Usk & Caerleon at Tredunnock sign*
This 200-year-old inn stands alongside the River Usk at Tredunnock, just four miles south of Usk. It has been renovated and converted into a spacious, traditionally furnished restaurant occupying the ground and first-floor levels. Six smart, modern and well-equipped bedrooms are located in a stone-clad, purpose-built unit adjacent to the restaurant. AA Restaurant of the Year for Wales 2004-5.
ROOMS: 6 en suite (2 fmly) (4 GF) ⊗ in all bedrooms s £85-£105; d £95-£125 (incl. bkfst) **LB** **FACILITIES:** STV Fishing Xmas **CONF:** Thtr 20 Class 10 Board 14 **PARKING:** 65 **NOTES:** ✈ Civ Wed 60
CARDS:

WELSHPOOL, Powys — Map 15 SJ20

★★★68% Royal Oak

Best Western

The Cross SY21 7DG
☎ 01938 552217 01938 556652
e-mail: oakwpool@aol.com
web: www.royaloakhotel.info
Dir: *by traffic lights at junct of A483/A458*
This traditional market town hotel dates back over 350 years. It provides well-equipped bedrooms, a choice of bars and extensive function and conference facilities. The attractively appointed restaurant is a popular venue for dining out and there is also a busy coffee shop open throughout the day.
ROOMS: 24 en suite (2 fmly) ⊗ in 10 bedrooms s £50-£69; d £75-£94 (incl. bkfst) **LB** **FACILITIES:** STV **CONF:** Thtr 150 Class 60 Board 80 Del from £85 **PARKING:** 40 **CARDS:**

> Destination dining!
> This symbol indicates a Restaurant with Rooms

★★66% Golfa Hall

Llanfair Rd SY21 9AF
☎ 01938 553399 01938 554777
e-mail: golfahall@welshpool.sagehost.co.uk
Dir: *1.5m W of Welshpool on A458 to Dolgellau*
Set on the Powys Castle estate, this privately owned and personally run hotel was originally a Georgian farmhouse. Some of the well-equipped bedrooms are contained in a separate stone built cottage. Elegant public rooms include a meeting room and a comfortable non-smoking lounge.
ROOMS: 10 en suite 4 annexe en suite (4 fmly) **CONF:** Thtr 120 Class 16 Board 16 **PARKING:** 26 **NOTES:** ✈ ⊗ in restaurant Civ Wed 50
CARDS:

WHITEBROOK, Monmouthshire — Map 04 SO50

Restaurant with Rooms

Crown at Whitebrook

NP25 4TX
☎ 01600 860254 01600 860607
e-mail: crown@whitebrook.demon.co.uk
web: www.crownatwhitebrook.co.uk
Dir: *turn off A449, hotel 2m on right.*
Now under new ownership and set in a delightful wooded valley, this former drover's inn dates back to the 17th century. The lounge bar and restaurant are furnished with relaxation and comfort in mind and make an ideal partner for the cuisine, which uses quality local ingredients skilfully prepared to offer a most impressive and memorable culinary experience.
ROOMS: 10 en suite s £70-£80; d £120-£140 (incl. bkfst & dinner) **CONF:** Board 10 **PARKING:** 20 **NOTES:** ✈ No children 12yrs ⊗ in restaurant **CARDS:**

WOLF'S CASTLE, Pembrokeshire — Map 08 SM92

★★73% Wolfscastle Country Hotel

SA62 5LZ
☎ 01437 741688 & 741225 01437 741383
e-mail: enquiries@wolfscastle.com
web: www.wolfscastle.com
Dir: *on A40 in the village of Wolf's Castle, at top of hill left, 6m N of Haverfordwest*

This large stone house dates back to the mid-19th century and has stunning views of the village. Now a friendly, privately owned and personally run hotel, it provides modern, well-maintained and equipped bedrooms. There is a pleasant bar and an attractive restaurant, which has a well-deserved, high reputation for its food.
ROOMS: 20 en suite 4 annexe en suite (2 fmly) ⊗ in 21 bedrooms s £55-£75; d £79-£107 (incl. bkfst) **LB** **FACILITIES:** STV **CONF:** Thtr 100 Class 100 Board 30 Del from £85 **PARKING:** 60 **NOTES:** ⊗ in restaurant Closed 24-26 Dec RS Sun nights Civ Wed 60
CARDS:

WREXHAM, Wrexham Map 15 SJ35

★★★ 68%

Cross Lanes Hotel & Restaurant

Cross Lanes, Bangor Rd, Marchwiel LL13 0TF
☎ 01978 780555 🖷 01978 780568
e-mail: guestservices@crosslanes.co.uk
Dir: *3m SE of Wrexham, on A525*

This hotel was built as a private house in 1890 and stands in over six acres of beautiful grounds. Bedrooms include two with four-poster beds. Kagan's Brasserie offers a good selection of food and fine dining is available in Reflections Restaurant at the weekends.
ROOMS: 16 en suite (1 fmly) **FACILITIES:** Putt green Fishing rights **CONF:** Thtr 120 Class 60 Board 40 **PARKING:** 80 **NOTES:** in restaurant Closed 25 Dec (night) & 26 Dec Civ Wed 120
CARDS:

See advert on this page

★★★ 66% **Llwyn Onn Hall**

THE INDEPENDENTS

Cefn Rd LL13 0NY
☎ 01978 261225 🖷 01978 363233
e-mail: llwynonnhallhotel@breathemail.net
Dir: *Easy access Wrexham Ind Estate, 2m off Wrexham-Chester A483*
Surrounded by open countryside, this fine 17th-century manor house is set in several acres of mature grounds. Exposed timbers remain and the original oak staircase is still in use. Bedrooms are equipped with modern facilities and one room has a four-poster bed which Bonnie Prince Charlie is reputed to have slept in.
ROOMS: 13 en suite (1 fmly) in 7 bedrooms s £64-£74; d £84-£99 (incl. bkfst) **LB** **CONF:** Thtr 60 Class 40 Board 12 Del £90 **PARKING:** 40 **NOTES:** in restaurant Civ Wed 60
CARDS:

Travel Inn

travel inn

Chester Rd, Gresford LL12 8PW
☎ 08701 977279 🖷 01978 856838
Dir: *on B5445 just off A483 dual carriageway*
Travel Inn offers good-quality, value-for-money accommodation. Spacious, en suite rooms with bath and shower comfortably accommodate a family of up to two adults and two children (to age 15). The restaurant and bar offers a varied menu. For further details consult the Hotel Groups page.
ROOMS: 36 en suite s £45.95-£46.95; d £45.95-£46.95

Travelodge

Travelodge

Wrexham By Pass, Rhostyllen LL14 4EJ
☎ 08700 850 950 🖷 01978 365705
Dir: *2m S, A483/A5152 rdbt*
Travelodge offers good quality, good value, modern accommodation. Ideal for families, the spacious, en suite bedrooms include remote-control TV, tea and coffee-making facilities and luxury beds. Meals can be taken at the nearby family restaurant. For further details consult the Hotel Groups page.
ROOMS: 32 en suite s fr £25; d fr £25

Nominations for
AA Hotel of the Year Award for Republic of Ireland
2004-2005

★★★★★ ❀❀
Dromoland Castle Hotel
Newmarket-on-Fergus, Co Cla

★★★★ ❀❀
The Clarence
Dublin, Co Dublin

★★★★ ❀❀
Killarney Park Hotel
Killarney, Co Kerry

A

ABBEYLEIX, Co Laois
Map 01 C3

★★★61% Abbeyleix Manor Hotel
☎ 0502 30111 🖷 0502 30220
e-mail: info@abbeyleixmanorhotel.com
Dir: *on N8 (main Dublin-Cork road) just S of Abbeyleix*

This modern hotel is situated on the outskirts of Abbeyleix town, on the N8 and ideal for those travelling on the National Route. Bedrooms are spacious and well appointed to a high standard. Public areas are comfortable with a cosy lobby and conservatory and a themed bar where food is served all day. There is off street car parking.
ROOMS: 23 en suite (2 fmly) **SERVICES:** air con **PARKING:** 270 **NOTES:** in restaurant Closed 25-26 Dec
CARDS:

ACHILL ISLAND, Co Mayo
Map 01 A4

★★★61% Achill Cliff House
Keel
☎ 098 43400 🖷 098 43007
e-mail: info@achillcliff.com
Dir: *From Castlebar take Newport Rd, then onto Mulranny and R319 to Achill Sound. Hotel on right, in the village of Keel.*
This family run hotel is situated on Achill Island, an unspoilt place made famous by painter Paul Henry and has a lot to offer those seeking relaxation, dramatic scenery, hill walking and historic interest. Bedrooms are comfortable and the popular restaurant serves local fish and lamb dishes at reasonable prices.
ROOMS: 10 en suite (4 fmly) (2 GF) in all bedrooms s €35-€100; d €60-€120 (incl. bkfst) **LB** **FACILITIES:** Sauna photography, painting, walking trails **PARKING:** 20 **NOTES:** No children 10yrs in restaurant Closed 23-26 Dec **CARDS:**

ADARE, Co Limerick
Map 01 B3

★★★★70% *Dunraven Arms*
☎ 061 396633 🖷 061 396541
e-mail: dunraven@iol.ie

MANOR HOUSE

This charming hotel was established in 1792 in the heart of one of Ireland's prettiest villages. It is a traditional country inn both in style and atmosphere. Comfortable lounges and bedrooms, attractive gardens, leisure and beauty facilities and good cuisine all add to an enjoyable visit at the hotel. Golf and equestrian activities are specialities in Adare.
ROOMS: 75 en suite (1 fmly) **FACILITIES:** STV Fishing Riding Sauna Gym Jacuzzi Beauty salon ♫ **CONF:** Thtr 180 Class 60 **SERVICES:** Lift **PARKING:** 90 **CARDS:**

AGHADOWEY, Co Londonderry
Map 01 C6

★★70% Brown Trout Golf & Country Inn
209 Agivey Rd BT51 4AD
☎ 028 7086 8209 🖷 028 7086 8878
e-mail: bill@browntroutinn.com
Dir: *at junct of A54 & B66 on road to Coleraine*
Set alongside the Agivey River and featuring its own 9-hole golf course, this welcoming inn offers a choice of spacious accommodation. Comfortable and attractively furnished bedrooms are situated around a courtyard area whilst the cottage suites also have lounge areas. Home-cooked meals are served in the restaurant; lighter fare is available in the charming lounge bar.
ROOMS: 15 en suite (11 fmly) **FACILITIES:** 9 Fishing Gym Putt green Game fishing ♫ Xmas **CONF:** Thtr 40 Class 24 Board 28 Del from £65 **PARKING:** 80 **NOTES:** in restaurant
CARDS:

ARDMORE, Co Waterford
Map 01 C2

★62% *Round Tower*
☎ 024 94494 & 94382 🖷 024 94254
e-mail: rth@eircom.net
Dir: *N25 Rosslare-Cork route, onto R673. Hotel in centre of village*
A large country house set in its own grounds in a pretty fishing village, boasting a blue flag beach, lovely, marked cliff walks and much early monastic history. The atmosphere is friendly and there is a comfortable lounge, panelled bar and a conservatory, where bar food is served. A carte menu is available in the restaurant, featuring 'catch of the day' seafood.
ROOMS: 12 en suite (4 fmly) **CONF:** Thtr 50 Class 25 Board 30 **PARKING:** 40 **NOTES:** RS Oct-Apr **CARDS:**

ARKLOW, Co Wicklow
Map 01 D3

★★★67% *Arklow Bay*
Ferrybank
☎ 0402 32309 🖷 0402 32300
e-mail: arklowbay@eircom.net
Dir: *off N11 at by-pass for Arklow. After 1m turn left, 200yds on left*

This hotel enjoys panoramic views of Arklow Bay and many of the well-appointed bedrooms take full advantage of this. The public areas are decorated in a contemporary style, and include a spacious lobby lounge and a comfortable bar where casual dining is available. For more formal dining, Howard's restaurant opens for dinner.
ROOMS: 92 en suite (3 fmly) (27 GF) in 20 bedrooms
FACILITIES: STV supervised Sauna Solarium Gym Jacuzzi ♫
CONF: Thtr 500 Class 200 Board 60 **SERVICES:** Lift **PARKING:** 100
NOTES: **CARDS:**

A

ARMAGH, Co Armagh

Map 01 C5

★★★61% Charlemont Arms Hotel

57/65 English St BT61 7LB
☎ 028 3752 2028 📠 028 3752 6979
e-mail: info@charlemontarmshotel.com

Dir: *A3 from Partadown or A28 from Newry, into Armagh. Follow signs for Tourist Information. Hotel is 100yds on right after Information office.*

Centrally located for all of this historic city's principal attractions, this hotel has been under the same family ownership for almost 70 years and offers a choice of dining styles and bars. The mostly spacious bedrooms have all been refurbished in a contemporary style and provide all of the expected facilities.

ROOMS: 30 en suite (2 fmly) ⊘ in all bedrooms s fr £50; d £65-£70 (incl. bkfst) **LB** **FACILITIES:** ♫ Xmas **CONF:** Thtr 150 Class 100 Board 80 Del from £88 **SERVICES:** Lift **PARKING:** 30 **NOTES:** ✈ Closed 25-26 Dec **CARDS:**

ATHLONE, Co Westmeath

Map 01 C4

★★★70% ® Hodson Bay

Hodson Bay
☎ 090 6442000 📠 090 6442020
e-mail: info@hodsonbayhotel.com

Dir: *from N6 take N61 to Roscommon. Take right turn - hotel 1km on Lough Rea*

On the shores of Lough Rea and close to the River Shannon this hotel has its own marina and is surrounded by Athlone Golf course. Public areas include comfortable lounges, carvery bar, an attractive restaurant and excellent banqueting and leisure facilities. The spacious bedrooms have been designed to capture the magnificent lake views.

ROOMS: 133 en suite (23 fmly) ⊘ in 3 bedrooms s €75-€180; d €55-€240 (incl. bkfst) **LB** **FACILITIES:** STV supervised 18 Fishing Sauna Gym Steam room, play room, beauty salon ♫ ch fac Xmas **CONF:** Thtr 700 Class 250 Board 200 **SERVICES:** Lift **PARKING:** 300 **NOTES:** ✈ ⊘ in restaurant **CARDS:**

See advert on this page

★★68% *Royal Hoey*

Mardyke St
☎ 090 647 2924 & 647 5395 📠 090 647 5194

Upholding a tradition of warm hospitality is the priority at this family-run hotel. Located in the centre of town, it has a comfortable foyer lounge bar and restaurant and the coffee shop serves snacks all day. Bedrooms are carefully maintained and well appointed.

ROOMS: 38 en suite (8 fmly) ⊘ in 10 bedrooms **FACILITIES:** STV ♫ **CONF:** Thtr 250 Class 130 Board 40 **SERVICES:** Lift air con **PARKING:** 50 **NOTES:** ✈ Closed 25-27 Dec **CARDS:**

Restaurant with Rooms

® Wineport Lodge

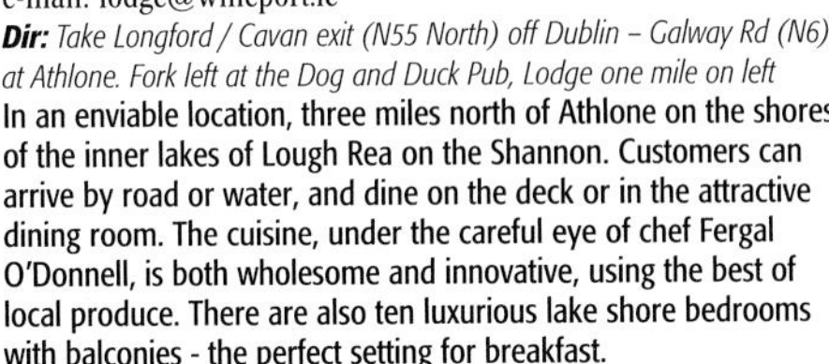

Glasson
☎ 090 643 9010 📠 090 648 5471
e-mail: lodge@wineport.ie

Dir: *Take Longford / Cavan exit (N55 North) off Dublin – Galway Rd (N6) at Athlone. Fork left at the Dog and Duck Pub, Lodge one mile on left*

In an enviable location, three miles north of Athlone on the shores of the inner lakes of Lough Rea on the Shannon. Customers can arrive by road or water, and dine on the deck or in the attractive dining room. The cuisine, under the careful eye of chef Fergal O'Donnell, is both wholesome and innovative, using the best of local produce. There are also ten luxurious lake shore bedrooms with balconies - the perfect setting for breakfast.

ROOMS: 10 en suite ⊘ in all bedrooms s €165-€275; d €220-€275 (incl. bkfst) **LB** **FACILITIES:** STV Massage, boat hire ch fac **CONF:** Thtr 50 Class 30 Board 20 Del from €250 **SERVICES:** air con **PARKING:** 60 **NOTES:** ✈ ⊘ in restaurant Closed 24-26 Dec

CARDS:

ATHLONE, continued

A

Glasson Golf Hotel & Country Club
Glasson
☎ 090 6485120 090 6485444
e-mail: info@glassongolf.ie
Dir: 6m N of Athlone on N55
At the time of going to press, the star classification for this hotel was not confirmed. Please refer to the AA internet site www.theAA.com for current information.
ROOMS: 29 en suite (13 fmly) **FACILITIES:** STV 21 Putt green **CONF:** Thtr 120 Class 50 Board 30 Del from €140.50 **SERVICES:** Lift **PARKING:** 150 **NOTES:** **CARDS:**

BALLINA, Co Mayo Map 01 B4

★★★69% Teach Iorrais
Geesala
☎ 097 86888 097 86855
e-mail: teachior@iol.ie
Located in the heart of the Erris Peninsula, in north-west Mayo, this is a warm friendly hotel offering spacious well appointed bedrooms. The public areas include a relaxing bar and a restaurant on the first-floor where quality cuisine is served. A good base for golfers and anglers.
ROOMS: 31 en suite (2 fmly) (15 GF) s €42-€59; d €84-€118 (incl. bkfst) LB **FACILITIES:** STV ch fac Xmas **CONF:** BC Thtr 300 Class 150 Board 60 **SERVICES:** air con **PARKING:** 85 **NOTES:** in restaurant **CARDS:**

BALLYBOFEY, Co Donegal Map 01 C5

★★★70% *Kee's*
Stranorlar
☎ 074 913 1018 074 913 1917
e-mail: info@keeshotel.ie
Dir: 2km NE on N15, in Stranorlar village
This long established hotel is now in the fourth generation of the Kee family. Warm hospitality is one of the many features of the establishment, which enjoys a steady local custom at the Gallery Bistro, while fine dining is available in the Looking Glass restaurant at weekends and during the holiday season.
ROOMS: 53 en suite (10 fmly) **FACILITIES: Spa** STV supervised Sauna Solarium Gym Jacuzzi **CONF:** Thtr 250 Class 100 Board 30 **SERVICES:** Lift **PARKING:** 90 **NOTES:** **CARDS:**

Town House Hotel
Country House Hotel
Travel Accommodation

BALLYCONNELL, Co Cavan Map 01 C4

★★★★70% *Slieve Russell Hotel Golf & Country Club*
☎ 049 9526444 049 9526474
e-mail: slieve-russell@quinn-hotels.com
Dir: N3 towards Cavan. At rdbt before Cavan follow Enniskillen sign and to Belturbet. Then towards Ballyconnell, hotel approx 6m on left.
This imposing hotel stands on 300 acres, encompassing a championship golf course and a 9-hole par three course. The spacious public areas include relaxing lounges, three restaurants and extensive leisure and banqueting facilities. Bedrooms are comfortable and tastefully furnished.
ROOMS: 157 en suite (87 fmly) **FACILITIES:** STV supervised 18 Snooker Sauna Solarium Gym Putt green Jacuzzi Hair & Beauty salon, Floodlit driving range **CONF:** BC Thtr 800 Class 400 Board 40 **SERVICES:** Lift **PARKING:** 600 **NOTES:**
CARDS:

BALLYCOTTON, Co Cork Map 01 C2

★★★74% Bay View
☎ 021 4646746 021 4646075
e-mail: bayhotel@iol.ie
Dir: N25 Castlemartyr, turn right through Ladysbridge, Garryvoe and onto Ballycotton.
MANOR HOUSE HOTELS
Situated with panoramic views of the harbour and Ballycotton Bay, the Bay View has a particularly pleasant atmosphere. Bedrooms and public areas are all positioned to make the most of the views. Locally caught seafood is a feature of the menu in the award-winning restaurant.
ROOMS: 35 en suite (5 GF) in 25 bedrooms s €112-€129; d €160-€194 (incl. bkfst) LB **FACILITIES:** STV Fishing, Pitch and putt, Sea angling ch fac **CONF:** Thtr 60 Class 30 Board 24 Del from €135 **SERVICES:** Lift air con **PARKING:** 40 **NOTES:** Closed Nov-Apr
CARDS:

BALLYHEIGE, Co Kerry Map 01 A2

★★★66% *The White Sands*
☎ 066 7133102 066 7133357
e-mail: whitesands@eircom.net
Dir: 18km from Tralee on coast road in North Kerry, hotel on left on main street.
IRISH COUNTRY HOTELS
Friendly staff welcome guests to this family run hotel, situated beside the beach and close to golf clubs. Attractively decorated throughout, facilities include a lounge bar, traditional pub, good restaurant and comfortable bedrooms.
ROOMS: 81 en suite **FACILITIES:** STV **SERVICES:** Lift air con **PARKING:** 40 **NOTES:** Closed Nov-Feb RS Mar-Apr & Oct
CARDS:

BALLYLICKEY, Co Cork Map 01 B2

Top 200 – Hotel

★★★ Sea View House Hotel
☎ 027 50073 & 50462 027 51555
e-mail: info@seaviewhousehotel.com
Dir: 5km from Bantry, 11km from Glengarriff on N71
MANOR HOUSE HOTELS
This delightful country house is framed by colourful gardens, and wonderful glimpses of the sea at Bantry Bay can be seen through the mature trees. Personally run by owner, Kathleen O'Sullivan whose team of staff are exceptionally welcoming. Comfort and good cuisine are the top priorities. Bedrooms are

continued

spacious and individually styled, some are on the ground floor and fitted to facilitate the less able.
ROOMS: 25 en suite (3 fmly) (5 GF) s €90-€100; d €150-€185 (incl. bkfst) LB **FACILITIES:** STV ch fac **PARKING:** 32 **NOTES:** ⊗ in restaurant Closed mid Nov-mid Mar
CARDS:

BALLYMENA, Co Antrim Map 01 D5

★★★★58% **Galgorm Manor**
BT42 1EA
☎ 028 2588 1001 🖷 028 2588 0080
e-mail: mail@galgorm.com
Dir: *1m outside Ballymena on A42, between Galgorm & Cullybackey*
Standing in 85 acres of private woodland and sweeping lawns beside the River Maine, this 19th-century mansion offers spacious comfortable bedrooms. Public areas include a welcoming cocktail bar and elegant restaurant, as well as Gillies, a lively and atmospheric locals' bar. Also on the estate is an equestrian centre and a conference hall and the hotel is a popular venue for weddings.
ROOMS: 24 en suite (6 fmly) s £75-£99; d £90-£119 (incl. bkfst) LB **FACILITIES:** STV Fishing Riding Clay pigeon shooting,Archery,Waterskiing ♫ Xmas **CONF:** Thtr 500 Class 200 Board 12 Del from £100 **PARKING:** 170 **NOTES:** RS 25-26 Dec Civ Wed 250
CARDS:

BALLYVAUGHAN, Co Clare Map 01 B3

Top 200 – Hotel

★★★ **Gregans Castle**
☎ 065 7077005 🖷 065 7077111
e-mail: res@gregans.ie
Dir: *3.5m S of village of Ballyvaughan on N67*

Situated in an oasis at the foot of Corkscrew Hill in the heart of the Burren, this hotel enjoys splendid views towards Galway Bay. The area is rich in archaeological, geological and botanical interest. The Hayden family and welcoming staff offer a high level of personal service, where hospitality, good food and relaxation are the themes. Bedrooms are individually decorated, superior rooms and suites are particularly comfortable, and some of these are at ground-floor level.
ROOMS: 22 en suite **FACILITIES:** no TV in bdrms **CONF:** Thtr 25 Class 25 Board 25 **PARKING:** 25 **NOTES:** ⊗ in restaurant Closed 23 Dec-14 Feb **CARDS:**

BALTIMORE, Co Cork Map 01 B1

★★★67% ***Baltimore Harbour Resort Hotel & Leisure Centre***
☎ 028 20361 🖷 028 20466
e-mail: info@bhrhotel.ie
Dir: *S from Cork N71 to Skibbereen, continue on R595 13km to Baltimore*

Overlooking the natural harbour of Baltimore, this family orientated leisure hotel is perfect for a relaxing break. Bedrooms are well appointed and most have a sea view. The popular bar and sun room open out onto the patio and gardens.
ROOMS: 64 en suite (30 fmly) **FACILITIES:** supervised Sauna Gym Jacuzzi Table Tennis, In-house video channel, Indoor bowls ♫ ch fac **CONF:** Thtr 120 Class 100 Board 30 **SERVICES:** Lift **PARKING:** 80 **NOTES:** ⊗ in restaurant Closed Jan RS Nov-Dec & Feb-mid Mar
CARDS:

★★★64% **Casey's of Baltimore**
☎ 028 20197 🖷 028 20509
e-mail: info@caseysofbaltimore.com
Dir: *take N71 from Cork to Skibbereen, then follow R595*

IRISH COUNTRY HOTELS

This relaxed family run hotel is situated in the sailing and fishing village of Baltimore. There are comfortable bedrooms, a cosy bar with open fires and traditional music. The Casey's ensure that the freshest of seafood is served in the restaurant and organise trips to the Islands.
ROOMS: 14 en suite (1 fmly) s €89-€103; d €129-€155 (incl. bkfst) LB **FACILITIES:** STV ♫ ch fac **CONF:** Thtr 45 Class 30 Board 25 Del from €115 **PARKING:** 50 **NOTES:** ⊗ in restaurant Closed 21-27 Dec
CARDS:

⊗ No smoking

B

BANGOR, Co Down Map 01 D5

★★★78% Old Inn
15 Main St BT19 1JH
☎ 028 9185 3255 028 9185 2775
e-mail: info@theoldinn.com
Dir: *A2, passing Belfast Airport and Holywood, 3m past Holywood sign for The Old Inn, 100yds turn left at lights, follow into village, hotel on left*

This delightful hotel enjoys a peaceful rural setting just a short drive from Belfast. Dating from 1614, many of the day rooms exude charm and character. Individually styled bedrooms, many with feature beds, offer comfort and modern facilities. The popular bar and intimate restaurant offer a variety of creative menus and staff throughout are keen to please.
ROOMS: 31 en suite 1 annexe en suite (7 fmly) (7 GF) in 6 bedrooms s £75-£120; d £75-£200 (incl. bkfst) **LB FACILITIES:** STV Xmas **CONF:** Thtr 120 Class 27 Board 40 Del from £120 **PARKING:** 105 **NOTES:** in restaurant RS 25 Dec Civ Wed
CARDS:

★★★77% Clandeboye Lodge
10 Estate Rd, Clandeboye BT19 1UR
☎ 028 9185 2500 028 9185 2772
e-mail: info@clandeboyelodge.com
Dir: *from Belfast on A2 turn right at sign for Blackwood Golf Centre & Hotel. 500yds down Ballysallagh Road turn left and take Crawfordsburn road. Hotel 200yds on left.*

This hotel is located three miles west of Bangor, and nestles in delightful landscaped and wooded grounds. It provides high quality accommodation as well as extensive conference, banqueting and wedding facilities. Public areas also include a bright open-plan foyer bar and attractive lounge.
ROOMS: 43 en suite (2 fmly) (13 GF) in 20 bedrooms s £70-£90; d £90-£100 (incl. bkfst) **LB FACILITIES:** STV **CONF:** Thtr 450 Class 150 Board 50 **SERVICES:** Lift **PARKING:** 250 **NOTES:** in restaurant Closed 24-26 Dec Civ Wed 250 **CARDS:**

★★★69% Marine Court
The Marina BT20 5ED
☎ 028 9145 1100 028 9145 1200
e-mail: admin@marinecourt.fsnet.co.uk
Dir: *pass Belfast city airport, follow A2 through Holywood to Bangor, down main street follow road to left for seafront*
Enjoying a delightful location overlooking the marina, this hotel offers a good range of conference and leisure facilities suited to both the business and leisure guest. Extensive public areas include the first-floor restaurant and cocktail bar. Alternatively, the popular Lord Nelson's Bistro/Bar is more relaxed and there is also the lively restyled Bar Mocha.
ROOMS: 52 en suite (11 fmly) in 16 bedrooms s £80-£90; d £90-£100 (incl. bkfst) **LB FACILITIES: Spa** STV supervised Solarium Gym Steam room Xmas **CONF:** Thtr 350 Class 150 **SERVICES:** Lift **PARKING:** 30 **NOTES:** Closed 25 Dec Civ Wed 250
CARDS:

★★★66% Royal
Seafront BT20 5ED
☎ 028 9127 1866 028 9146 7810
e-mail: royalhotelbangor@aol.com
web: www.royalhotelbangor.com
Dir: *take A2 from Belfast. Through Bangor town centre to seafront. Turn right, hotel 300yds overlooking Marina*

This substantial Victorian hotel enjoys a prime seafront location and overlooks the marina. Bedrooms are comfortable and practical in style. Public areas are traditional and include a choice of contrasting bars whilst traditional Irish cooking can be sampled in a popular brasserie venue.
ROOMS: 50 en suite (5 fmly) in 10 bedrooms s £50-£68; d £60-£75 (incl. bkfst) **LB FACILITIES:** STV ch fac **CONF:** Thtr 120 Class 90 Board 80 Del from £95 **SERVICES:** Lift **NOTES:** Closed 25 Dec
CARDS:

BANTRY, Co Cork Map 01 B2

★★★ 64% *Westlodge*

☎ 027 50360 📠 027 50438
e-mail: reservations@westlodgehotel.ie
Dir: *N71 to West Cork*
A superb leisure centre and good children's facilities makes this hotel very popular with families. Its situation on the outskirts of the town also makes it an ideal base for touring west Cork and south Kerry. All the staff are friendly and hospitable.
ROOMS: 90 en suite (20 fmly) (20 GF) in 15 bedrooms **FACILITIES:** STV Squash Snooker Sauna Solarium Gym Putt green Jacuzzi Pitch & Putt, wooded walks ch fac **CONF:** Thtr 400 Class 200 Board 24 **SERVICES:** Lift air con **PARKING:** 400 **NOTES:** Closed 23-27 Dec **CARDS:**

BELFAST Map 01 D5

★★★★ 67% Ramada Belfast

117 Milltown Rd, Shaws Bridge BT8 7XP
☎ 028 9092 3500 📠 028 9092 3600
e-mail: mail@ramadabelfast.com
web: www.ramadabelfast.com
Dir: *S from city centre, follow Malone Rd to rdbt and signs for Barnett Demense. Left into Milltown Rd, hotel on left, 400mtrs from rdbt*
Set within the Laggan Valley Regional Park, this modern conference and leisure hotel caters well for all markets. Bedrooms are stylish and furnished in eye-catching designs. The LA Fitness Club is very well equipped, and the Grand Ballroom attracts many top national events. The Belfast Bar and Grill serves innovative Irish cuisine, whilst the trendy Suburbia bar offers a lighter alternative.
ROOMS: 120 en suite (43 GF) in 88 bedrooms s fr £69.95; d fr £69.95 (incl. bkfst) **FACILITIES: Spa** STV supervised Sauna Solarium Gym Jacuzzi Xmas **CONF:** Thtr 900 Class 450 Board 40 **SERVICES:** Lift air con **PARKING:** 150 **NOTES:** **CARDS:**

★★★ 71% Malone Lodge

60 Eglantine Av BT9 6DY
☎ 028 9038 8000 📠 028 9038 8088
e-mail: info@malonelodgehotel.com
web: www.malonelodgehotel.com
Dir: *at hospital rdbt exit towards Bouchar Rd, left at 1st rdbt, right at lights at top, 1st left is Eglantine Ave*
Situated in the leafy suburbs of the university area of south Belfast, this stylish hotel forms the centrepiece of an attractive row of Victorian terraced properties. The unassuming exterior belies an attractive and spacious interior with a smart lounge, popular bar and stylish Green Door restaurant. The hotel also has a small, well-equipped fitness room.
ROOMS: 51 en suite (5 fmly) (1 GF) s £59-£95; d £79-£115 (incl. bkfst) LB **FACILITIES:** STV Sauna Gym **CONF:** BC Thtr 150 Class 90 Board 40 Del from £80 **SERVICES:** Lift **PARKING:** 35 **NOTES:** **CARDS:**

★★★ 70% *The Crescent Townhouse*

13 Lower Crescent BT7 1NR
☎ 028 9032 3349 📠 028 9032 0646
e-mail: info@crescenttownhouse.com
Dir: *S towards Queens University, hotel on Botanic Avenue opposite Botanic Train Station*
This stylish, smartly presented Regency town house enjoys a central location close to the botanic gardens and railway station. The popular Bar Twelve and Metro Brasserie are found on the

continued

ground floor whilst the reception and well-equipped bedrooms are situated on the upper floors.

ROOMS: 11 en suite in 2 bedrooms **FACILITIES:** **NOTES:** Closed 25-27 Dec & part of Jul **CARDS:**

★★★ 66% Jurys Belfast Inn

Fisherwick Place, Great Victoria St BT2 7AP
JURYS DOYLE HOTELS
☎ 028 9053 3500 📠 028 9053 3511
e-mail: info@jurys.com
Dir: *junct of Grosvenor Rd & Great Victoria St, beside Opera House*
Enjoying a central location, this modern hotel is well equipped for business guests. Public areas are contemporary in style and include a foyer lounge, a bar and a smart restaurant. Spacious bedrooms provide modern facilities.
ROOMS: 190 en suite in 76 bedrooms **FACILITIES:** STV **CONF:** Thtr 30 Class 16 Board 16 **SERVICES:** Lift **NOTES:** Closed 24-26 Dec **CARDS:**

Travelodge

15 Brunswick St BT2 7GE
Travelodge
☎ 08700 850 950 📠 028 9023 2999
Dir: *from M2 follow city centre signs to Oxford St turn right to May St, Brunswick St is 4th on left*
Travelodge offers good quality, good value, modern accommodation. Ideal for families, the spacious, en suite bedrooms include remote-control TV, tea and coffee-making facilities and luxury beds. Meals can be taken at the nearby family restaurant. For further details consult the Hotel Groups page.
ROOMS: 90 en suite s fr £25; d fr £25 **CONF:** Thtr 65 Class 50 Board 34

○ Malmaison Belfast

34 - 38 Victoria St BT1 3GH
Malmaison
☎ 020 7479 9512
ROOMS: 62 en suite **NOTES:** Due to open Nov 2004

BETTYSTOWN, Co Meath Map 01 D4

★★★★ 59% *Neptune Beach Hotel & Leisure Club*

☎ 041 9827107 📠 041 9827412
e-mail: info@neptunebeach.ie
Dir: *just off Dublin/Belfast road N1*
This hotel, overlooking the sea, has access to a sandy beach. Public areas include an inviting lounge and an attractive Winter Garden. Many bedrooms enjoy sea views.
ROOMS: 38 en suite in 14 bedrooms **FACILITIES:** STV Sauna Solarium Gym Jacuzzi Steam room Kiddies pool **CONF:** Thtr 250 Class 150 **SERVICES:** Lift **PARKING:** 60 **NOTES:** in restaurant **CARDS:**

€ Don't forget, the Euro is now the unit of currency in the Republic of Ireland

B

BIRR, Co Offaly Map 01 C3

★★★63% *County Arms*
☎ 0509 20791 🖹 0509 21234
e-mail: countyarmshotel@eircom.net
***Dir:** take N7 from Dublin to Roscrea, N62 to Birr, hotel on right before the church*
This fine Georgian House (c1810) has been run by the Loughnane family for four generations. Authentic décor and architectural features combine well with modern comforts. Public areas include comfortable lounges, a traditional bar and conservatory, and first-floor restaurant – all with views of the meticulously kept Victorian walled gardens, which supply the fruit, vegetables and herbs to the hotel kitchen. Bedroom are well appointed and decorated to a high standard.
ROOMS: 24 en suite (4 fmly) ⊗ in 2 bedrooms **FACILITIES:** STV Gym ♫ **CONF:** Thtr 250 Class 250 Board 25 **PARKING:** 150 **NOTES:** ✖ RS 25 Dec **CARDS:**

BLARNEY, Co Cork Map 01 B2

★★★69% Blarney Castle
The Village Green
☎ 021 4385116 🖹 021 4385542
e-mail: info@blarneycastlehotel.com
***Dir:** Take N20 (Cork to Limerick road) and turn off onto R617 for Blarney, hotel in centre of village*
Situated in the centre of the town within walking distance of the famous Blarney Stone, this friendly hotel has been in the same family since 1873. Many of the bedrooms are spacious and all are newly decorated to a very comfortable standard. The popular bar serves good food throughout most of the day.
ROOMS: ⊗ in 13 bedrooms s €60-€85; d €110-€130 (incl. bkfst) **LB** **FACILITIES:** STV **CONF:** Thtr 120 **SERVICES:** air con **PARKING:** 5 **NOTES:** ✖ ⊗ in restaurant Closed 25 Dec **CARDS:**

BLESSINGTON, Co Wicklow Map 01 D3

★★★66% ⊛ *Downshire House*
☎ 045 865199 🖹 045 865335
e-mail: info@downshirehouse.com
***Dir:** on N81*
This family-run Georgian house is renowned for its friendly atmosphere, comfortable lounges with open log fires and country-house style cooking. Bedrooms are very attractively decorated and well appointed. The hotel is near to Blessington Lake, the Wicklow Hills, golf clubs and racecourses.
ROOMS: 14 en suite 11 annexe en suite **FACILITIES:** Table tennis **CONF:** Thtr 40 Class 20 Board 20 **PARKING:** 30 **NOTES:** ✖ Closed 22 Dec-6 Jan **CARDS:**

BRAY, Co Wicklow Map 01 D4

★★★62% *Royal*
Main St
☎ 01 2862935 🖹 01 2867373
e-mail: royal@regencyhotels.com
***Dir:** from N11, 1st exit for Bray, 2nd exit from rdbt, through 2 sets of traffic lights across bridge, hotel on left*
The Royal Hotel stands on the main street, close to the seafront, and within easy reach of the Dun Laoighaire ferry port. Public areas offer comfortable lounges, traditional bar and The Heritage Restaurant. Bedrooms vary in size and are well appointed. There is

continued

a well-equipped leisure centre and a supervised car park is available at the rear.
ROOMS: 91 en suite (10 fmly) ⊗ in 14 bedrooms **FACILITIES:** Sauna Solarium Gym Jacuzzi Massage and beauty clinic Therapy room Whirlpool spa,madhatters creche ♫ ch fac **CONF:** Thtr 300 Class 200 Board 100 **SERVICES:** Lift **PARKING:** 60 **NOTES:** ✖ Civ Wed 225 **CARDS:**

BUNCLODY, Co Wexford

○ The Millrace
☎ 054 75100
ROOMS: 60 rms **NOTES:** Open Sept 2004

BUNRATTY, Co Clare Map 01 B3

★★★69% *Fitzpatrick Bunratty*
☎ 061 361177 🖹 061 471252
e-mail: reservations@bunratty.fitzpatricks.com
***Dir:** take Bunratty by-pass, exit off Limerick/Shannon dual carriageway*
Situated in the picturesque village of Bunratty, and in the shadow of the famous Bunratty Medieval Castle, this modern hotel is surrounded by well-maintained lawns and colourful flowerbeds. Bedrooms and public areas are spacious and comfortable, and there are extensive indoor leisure facilities plus an impressive conference and banqueting centre.
ROOMS: 115 en suite 4 annexe en suite (12 fmly) ⊗ in 10 bedrooms **FACILITIES:** STV Sauna Solarium Gym Jacuzzi ♫ **CONF:** Thtr 1000 Class 650 Board 300 **PARKING:** 300 **NOTES:** ✖ Closed 24-26 Dec **CARDS:**

CAHERDANIEL, Co Kerry Map 01 A2

★★★66% ⊛ Derrynane
☎ 066 9475136 🖹 066 9475160
e-mail: info@derrynane.com
***Dir:** just off main road*

Super clifftop location overlooking Derrynane Bay with spectacular views adding a stunning dimension to this well run hotel where pleasant, efficient staff contributes to the very relaxed atmosphere. Public areas include spacious lounges, bar and restaurant, an outdoor heated pool in the garden. Bedrooms are well appointed and most enjoy the views.
ROOMS: 73 en suite (30 fmly) ⊗ in 40 bedrooms s €95-€120; d €150-€180 (incl. bkfst) **LB** **FACILITIES:** STV supervised Sauna Solarium Gym Steam room, seaweed therapy room ♫ ch fac **SERVICES:** air con **PARKING:** 60 **NOTES:** ✖ ⊗ in restaurant Closed 4 Oct-15 Apr **CARDS:**

CAHIR, Co Tipperary — Map 01 C3

★★★64% Cahir House

The Square
☎ 052 43000 📠 052 42728
e-mail: info@cahirhousehotel.ie
Dir: *S on N8 turn off at Cahir by-pass follow N24 to town, hotel on square in centre of town, car park at rear*

Situated in the centre of the town, this hotel has been extending hospitality to visitors since the days of the Bianconi horse-drawn coaches. It offers modern comforts in well-equipped and tastefully furnished rooms and maintains traditional standards in terms of both the welcome and the cuisine.

ROOMS: 42 en suite (3 fmly) ⊘ in 17 bedrooms **FACILITIES:** STV Sauna Gym Newly built health & beauty spa ♫ ch fac **CONF:** Thtr 400 Class 200 Board 50 Del from €90 **PARKING:** 80 **NOTES:** ✈ ⊘ in restaurant Closed 25 Dec RS 24-26 Dec & Good Fri
CARDS:

CARLOW, Co Carlow — Map 01 C3

★★★70% Seven Oaks

Athy Rd
☎ 059 913 1308 📠 059 913 2155
e-mail: info@sevenoakshotel.com

Conveniently situated within walking distance of the town centre this newly refurbished hotel offers comfortable lounges, a traditional style bar and restaurant. Bedrooms are spacious and very well appointed. There are extensive leisure and banqueting facilities and a secure car park.

ROOMS: 59 en suite (5 fmly) s €76-€85; d €120-€140 (incl. bkfst) **LB**
FACILITIES: STV supervised Sauna Gym Jacuzzi Aerobic studio, Steam room ♫ **CONF:** Thtr 400 Class 150 Board 80 Del from €110 **SERVICES:** Lift air con **PARKING:** 200 **NOTES:** ✈ ⊘ in restaurant Closed 25-26 Dec RS Good Fri **CARDS:**

★★★68% *Dolmen*

Kilkenny Rd
☎ 059 914 2002 📠 059 914 2375
e-mail: reservations@dolmenhotel.ie
Dir: *approx 1m outside Carlow on Kilkenny-Waterford road. Approx 0.5m on right past The Institute of Technology*

In 20 acres of landscaped grounds, this hotel nestles in a peaceful riverside location. Guests can relax in the grounds or take advantage of the free coarse fishing. There is a spacious reception and foyer, a large bar and restaurant, and a luxurious boardroom, which doubles as an additional lounge, overlooking the river. Bedrooms are all well equipped and comfortable.

ROOMS: 40 en suite 12 annexe en suite (1 fmly) **FACILITIES:** STV Fishing **CONF:** Thtr 1000 Class 300 Board 50 **SERVICES:** air con **PARKING:** 300 **NOTES:** ✈ **CARDS:**

CARNA, Co Galway — Map 01 A4

★★★61% *Carna Bay Hotel*

IRISH COUNTRY HOTELS

☎ 095 32255 📠 095 32530
e-mail: carnaby@iol.ie
Dir: *from Galway take N59 to Recess, then left onto R340 for approx 9m*

This family owned and run hotel overlooks Carna Bay on the Connemara coastline and has a very friendly and relaxed atmosphere. Public areas are bright and spacious with casual meals served in the bar at lunch and in the evenings. A more formal dinner is available in the restaurant where there is an *continued* emphasis on good quality local ingredients. Many of the comfortable rooms have sea views.

ROOMS: 26 en suite (1 fmly) (11 GF) ⊘ in 10 bedrooms
PARKING: 60 **NOTES:** ⊘ in restaurant Closed 23-26 Dec
CARDS:

CARNLOUGH, Co Antrim — Map 01 D6

★★★68% ® *Londonderry Arms*

20 Harbour Rd BT44 0EU
☎ 028 2888 5255 📠 028 2888 5263
e-mail: lda@glensofantrim.com
Dir: *14m N from Larne on the coast road, A2*

This delightful hotel was built in the mid-19th century by Lady Londonderry, whose grandson, Winston Churchill, also owned it at one time. Today the hotel's Georgian architecture and rooms are still evident, and spacious bedrooms can be found in the modern extension. The hotel enjoys a prime location in this pretty fishing village overlooking the Antrim coast.

ROOMS: 35 en suite (5 fmly) **FACILITIES:** Fishing ♫ **CONF:** Thtr 120 Class 60 Board 40 **SERVICES:** Lift **PARKING:** 50 **NOTES:** ✈ Closed Xmas **CARDS:**

CARRICKFERGUS, Co Antrim — Map 01 D5

★★67% Dobbins Inn

6-8 High St BT38 7AP
☎ 028 9335 1905 📠 028 9335 1905
e-mail: info@dobbinsinnhotel.co.uk
Dir: *at Belfast take M2, keep right at rdbt, follow A2 to Carrickfergus, turn left opposite castle*

Colourful window boxes adorn the front of this popular inn near the ancient castle and seafront. Public areas are furnished to a modern standard without compromising the inn's interesting, historic character. Bedrooms vary in size and style and all provide modern comforts. Staff throughout are very friendly.

ROOMS: 15 en suite (2 fmly) s £38-£48; d £58-£68 (incl. bkfst) **LB**
FACILITIES: ♫ ch fac **NOTES:** Closed 25-26 Dec & 1 Jan RS Good Fri
CARDS:

CARRICKMACROSS, Co Monaghan — Map 01 C4

★★★★72% ®® Nuremore

☎ 042 9661438 📠 042 9661853
e-mail: info@nuremore.com
Dir: *3km S of Carrickmacross, on N2 Dublin/Derry road*

Overlooking its own golf course and lakes, the Nuremore is a quiet retreat with excellent facilities. Public areas are spacious and include an indoor pool and new gym. Ray McArdle's food in the restaurant continues to impress, with an imaginative range of dishes on offer.

ROOMS: 72 en suite (4 fmly) ⊘ in 30 bedrooms s €140-€220; d €230-€295 (incl. bkfst) **LB** **FACILITIES: Spa** STV 18 Fishing Snooker Sauna Solarium Gym Putt green Beauty treatments, Aromatherapy, Massage ♫ Xmas **CONF:** BC Thtr 250 Class 100 Board 30 Del from €190 **SERVICES:** Lift **PARKING:** 200 **NOTES:** ✈ ⊘ in restaurant **CARDS:**

CARRICK-ON-SHANNON, Co Leitrim — Map 01 C4

★★★★60% The Landmark

☎ 071 962 2222 📠 071 962 2233
e-mail: landmarkhotel@eircom.net
Dir: *N4 approaching Carrick-on-Shannon from Dublin, take first exit off roundabout, hotel on right*

Overlooking the River Shannon, close to the Marina, this hotel offers luxurious public areas including a choice of bars and

continued on p848

C

CARRICK-ON-SHANNON, continued

restaurants, lounges, a fitness club and ballroom. Pleasant staff will be pleased to arrange cruising, horse riding, golf and angling. CJ's restaurant is open on Fridays and Saturdays.

The Landmark, Carrick-on-Shannon

ROOMS: 50 en suite (4 fmly) s €125-€140; d €190-€220 (incl. bkfst) LB **FACILITIES:** STV Gym ♫ Xmas **CONF:** Thtr 500 Class 170 **SERVICES:** Lift **PARKING:** 100 **NOTES:** in restaurant Closed 24-25 Dec RS 26 Dec **CARDS:**

CARRIGALINE, Co Cork — Map 01 B2

Carrigaline Court Hotel

☎ 021 4852100 021 4371103

e-mail: reception@carrigcourt.com

Dir: *Take exit for Carrigaline off South Link road east from airport or west from Dublin/Lee Tunnel. Keep in right lane, follow to Carrigaline.*

At the time of going to press, the star classification for this hotel was not confirmed. Please refer to the AA internet site www.theAA.com for current information.

ROOMS: 91 en suite (3 fmly) in 39 bedrooms s £99-£120; d £150-£180 (incl. bkfst) LB **FACILITIES:** STV Sauna Solarium Gym Jacuzzi Beauty salon & massage treatment rooms ♫ **CONF:** BC Thtr 400 Class 300 Board 150 Del from £163 **SERVICES:** Lift **PARKING:** 220 **NOTES:** **CARDS:**

CASHEL, Co Galway — Map 01 A4

Top 200 – Hotel

★★★ Cashel House

☎ 095 31001 095 31077

e-mail: info@cashel-house-hotel.com

Dir: *turn S off N59, 1.5km W of Recess, well signed*

RELAIS & CHATEAUX

Cashel House is a mid-19th century house standing at the head of Cashel Bay, in the heart of Connemara. Quietly secluded in award-winning gardens and woodland walks.

continued

Attentive service comes with the perfect balance of friendliness and professionalism from McEvilly family and their staff. The comfortable lounges have turf fires and antique furnishings. The restaurant offers local produce as the famous Connemara Lamb and fish from the nearby coast.

ROOMS: 32 en suite (4 fmly) (6 GF) in 10 bedrooms s €90-€135; d €180-€270 (incl. bkfst) LB **FACILITIES:** Xmas **PARKING:** 40 **NOTES:** No children 5yrs in restaurant Closed 4 Jan-4 Feb **CARDS:**

★★★76% *Zetland Country House*

MANOR HOUSE HOTELS

Cashel Bay

☎ 095 31111 095 31117

e-mail: zetland@iol.ie

Dir: *N59 from Galway towards Clifden, right after Recess onto R340, left after 4m (R341), hotel 1m on right*

Standing on the edge of Cashel Bay, this former sporting lodge is a cosy and relaxing family run hotel that exudes charm. Many of the comfortable rooms have sea views, as has the restaurant where very good cuisine is served.

ROOMS: 19 en suite (10 fmly) **FACILITIES:** STV Snooker **CONF:** Board 20 **PARKING:** 32 **NOTES:** in restaurant Closed Nov-9 Apr **CARDS:**

CASHEL, Co Tipperary — Map 01 C3

★★★★68% *Cashel Palace Hotel*

☎ 062 62707 062 61521

e-mail: reception@cashel-palace.ie

Dir: *On N8 through centre of Cashel, hotel on main street near traffic lights, car park at front*

The Rock of Cashel, floodlit at night, forms a dramatic backdrop to this fine 18th-century house. A former Archbishop's Palace, it is elegantly furnished with antiques and fine art. The drawing room has garden access and luxurious bedrooms in the main house are most comfortable. Those in the adjacent mews are ideal for families or groups.

ROOMS: 13 en suite 10 annexe en suite (8 fmly) in 5 bedrooms **FACILITIES:** STV Fishing Private path walk to the Rock of Cashel ♫ **CONF:** Thtr 80 Class 45 Board 40 **SERVICES:** Lift **PARKING:** 35 **NOTES:** Closed 2 weeks in Xmas - Jan **CARDS:**

Restaurant with Rooms

Legends Townhouse & Restaurant

The Kiln

☎ 062 61292

e-mail: info@legendsguesthouse.com

Dir: *turn off N8 onto R660 towards Holycross, establishment 30yds on left, signed*

Sitting underneath the Rock of Cashel this distinctive house has been purpose built to blend in with the dramatic location. An interesting menu featuring local produce and skilful cooking by Chef/Proprietor Michael O'Neill is served in the restaurant that enjoys mystical flood lit views and diners will experience an atmosphere of almost eerie magic in the evenings. A cosy guest lounge and very comfortable bedrooms complete the picture.

ROOMS: 7 en suite (2 fmly) (3 GF) in all bedrooms s €45-€60; d €90-€124 (incl. bkfst) LB **FACILITIES:** STV **PARKING:** 7 **NOTES:** in restaurant Closed 23-26 Dec, 14 Feb-10 Mar, 6-20 Nov **CARDS:**

€ Don't forget, the Euro is now the unit of currency in the Republic of Ireland

CASTLEBAR, Co Mayo
Map 01 B4

★★64% *Welcome Inn*
094 902 2288 & 902 2054 094 902 1766
e-mail: welcomeinn@eircom.net
Dir: *take N5 to Castlebar. Inn near town centre via ring road & rdbts past Church of the Holy Rosary*
This town centre hotel offers a range of modern facilities behind its Tudor frontage, including a banqueting/conference centre. Bedrooms are comfortable and well equipped. Enjoyable food is served in Reynards Restaurant and there is a traditional style bar and a nightclub with disco at weekends.
ROOMS: 40 en suite (5 fmly) **FACILITIES:** STV **CONF:** Thtr 500 Class 350 **SERVICES:** Lift **PARKING:** 100 **NOTES:** Closed 23-25 Dec **CARDS:**

CAVAN, Co Cavan
Map 01 C4

★★★67% Kilmore
Dublin Rd
049 4332288 049 4332458
e-mail: kilmore@quinn-hotels.com
Dir: *approx 3km from Cavan on N3.*
Located on the outskirts of Cavan, easily accessible from the main N3 route, this comfortable hotel features spacious and welcoming public areas. Good food is served in the Annalee Restaurant, which is always appreciated by guests returning from nearby fishing or golf.
ROOMS: 39 en suite (17 fmly) (19 GF) s €75-€85; d €115-€125 (incl. bkfst) **LB** **FACILITIES:** STV free use of facilities at Slieve Russell Golf & Country Club Xmas **CONF:** BC Thtr 500 Class 200 Board 60 Del from €109.25 **SERVICES:** air con **PARKING:** 450 **NOTES:** in restaurant Closed 25 Dec **CARDS:**

CLIFDEN, Co Galway
Map 01 A4

★★★77% *Rock Glen Country House Hotel*
MANOR HOUSE HOTELS
095 21035 & 21393 095 21737
e-mail: rockglen@iol.ie
Dir: *N6 from Dublin to Galway, N57 from Galway to Clifden, hotel 1.5m from Clifden*
The inviting clematis and creeper-framed façade of this house is but an introduction to the comfort that lies inside. The hospitality of the Roche family and their staff makes a visit to this hotel relaxing and very pleasant. Well-appointed bedrooms and comfortable lounges here have lovely views of the gardens and bay.
ROOMS: 26 en suite (2 fmly) (18 GF) **FACILITIES:** Snooker Putt green **PARKING:** 50 **NOTES:** in restaurant Closed mid Nov-mid Feb (ex New Year) **CARDS:**

★★★76% *Abbeyglen Castle*
MANOR HOUSE HOTELS
Sky Rd
095 21201 095 21797
e-mail: info@abbeyglen.ie
Dir: *take N59 from Galway to Clifden. Hotel 1km from Clifden*
The tranquil setting overlooking Clifden, matched with the dedication of the Hughes father and son team and their attentive staff, combine to create a magical atmosphere here at Abbeyglen Castle. Well-appointed rooms and very comfortable suites are available, together with a range of relaxing lounge areas.
ROOMS: 38 en suite (9 GF) in 10 bedrooms **FACILITIES:** STV Snooker Sauna Putt green Jacuzzi **CONF:** Thtr 100 Class 50 Board 40 **SERVICES:** Lift **PARKING:** 40 **NOTES:** No children Closed 5 Jan-1 Feb **CARDS:**

★★★73% Ardagh
IRISH COUNTRY HOTELS
Ballyconneely Rd
095 21384 095 21314
e-mail: ardaghhotel@eircom.net
Dir: *N59 Galway to Clifden, signed for Ballyconneely*
Situated at the head of Ardbear Bay, this family-run hotel makes full use of the spectacular scenery in the area. The restaurant is renowned for its cuisine, which is complemented by friendly and knowledgeable service. Bedrooms have large picture windows and plenty of comfort.
ROOMS: 19 en suite (2 fmly) in all bedrooms s €105-€118; d €150-€196 (incl. bkfst) **LB** **FACILITIES:** Pool room **PARKING:** 35 **NOTES:** in restaurant Closed Nov-Mar **CARDS:**

★★★66% Alcock & Brown Hotel
095 21206 & 21086 095 21842
e-mail: alcockandbrown@eircom.net
Dir: *take N59 from Galway via Oughterard, hotel in centre of town*
This comfortable family owned hotel is situated in the town centre. There is a cosy bar and lounge with open fire and the restaurant is attractively decorated where the dinner menu offers good food with many fresh local fish specialities. Bedrooms are well appointed. The friendly and attentive staff offers good service.
ROOMS: 19 annexe en suite in 9 bedrooms s €68-€83; d €100-€130 (incl. bkfst) **LB** **FACILITIES:** STV Xmas **NOTES:** in restaurant Closed 23-25 Dec **CARDS:**

CLONAKILTY, Co Cork
Map 01 B2

★★★★75% *The Lodge & Spa at Inchydoney Island*
023 33143 023 35229
e-mail: reservations@inchydoneyisland.com
Dir: *follow N71 West Cork road to Clonakilty, at entry rdbt in Clonakilty take 2nd exit and follow signs to Lodge*
This modern hotel is stunningly located on the coastline with steps down to two long sandy beaches. Bedrooms are decorated in warm colours and are well appointed. Diners have a choice of the third-floor Gulfstream restaurant or the more casual Dunes bar and bistro.
ROOMS: 67 en suite (24 fmly) in 17 bedrooms **FACILITIES: Spa** STV supervised Fishing Riding Snooker Sauna Gym Jacuzzi Thalassotherapy spa **CONF:** Thtr 300 Class 150 Board 100 **SERVICES:** Lift **PARKING:** 200 **NOTES:** in restaurant Closed 25-26 Dec **CARDS:**

CLONMEL, Co Tipperary
Map 01 C2

★★★73% Minella
052 22388 052 24381
e-mail: hotelminella@eircom.net
Dir: *south of River Suir*
This family-run hotel is set on 9 acres of well-tended gardens on the banks of the Suir River. Facilities include a cocktail bar and a range of lounge areas. The leisure centre in the grounds is particularly noteworthy. Two bedroom holiday homes are also available on the site.
ROOMS: 70 en suite (8 fmly) (14 GF) in 16 bedrooms s fr €110; d fr €160 (incl. bkfst) **LB** **FACILITIES:** STV Fishing Sauna Gym Jacuzzi Aerobics room **CONF:** Thtr 500 Class 300 Board 20 Del from €150 **SERVICES:** Lift **PARKING:** 100 **NOTES:** in restaurant Closed 24-28 Dec **CARDS:**

> **GF** Indicates the number of bedrooms at ground floor level.

C

COBH, Co Cork Map 01 B2

★★★70% *WatersEdge*

Yacht Club Quay
☎ 021 4815566 ▣ 021 4812011
e-mail: info@watersedgehotel.ie
Dir: *follow road signs for Cobh Heritage Centre & Fota Golf Club*

This smart hotel is situated on the waterfront beside the Heritage Centre and railway station. Spectacular views of Cork Harbour can be enjoyed while dining in Jacob's Ladder Restaurant. The bedrooms are furnished to a high standard and some have private balconies. Secure underground car parking is available.

ROOMS: 19 en suite (5 fmly) (5 GF) ⊗ in 6 bedrooms **PARKING:** 25 **NOTES:** Closed 1-4 Jan & 23-28 Dec **CARDS:**

CORK, Co Cork Map 01 B2

Top 200 – Hotel

★★★★ Hayfield Manor

Perrott Av, College Rd
☎ 021 4845900 ▣ 021 4316839
e-mail: enquiries@hayfieldmanor.ie
Dir: *1m W of Cork city centre-head for N22 to Killarney, turn left at University Gates off Western Rd. Turn right into College Rd, left into Perrott Ave*

As part of a grand two-acre estate with lovely walled gardens, Hayfield Manor offers luxury and seclusion, just a short distance from UCC. This fine hotel has every modern comfort and maintains an atmosphere of tranquillity, with real fires in the public areas where elegant architecture and fine furnishings are carefully combined. Bedrooms offer very high levels of comfort with many thoughtful extras. There are beauty treatments and leisure facilities available for resident guests.

ROOMS: 88 en suite ⊗ in 25 bedrooms **FACILITIES:** STV Gym Jacuzzi Steam room ♫ **CONF:** Thtr 100 Class 60 Board 40 **SERVICES:** Lift air con **PARKING:** 100 **NOTES:** ⊗ in restaurant **CARDS:**

Packed in a hurry?
Ironing facilities should be available at all star levels, either in rooms or on request

★★★★76% *The Kingsley Hotel*

Victoria Cross
☎ 021 4800500 ▣ 021 4800527
e-mail: resv@kingsleyhotel.com
Dir: *off N22 opposite the Cork County Hall, beside River Lee*

Situated on the banks of the River Lee, directly opposite County Hall, Ireland's tallest building, this luxurious hotel has good facilities. The bedrooms are spacious and feature thoughtful additional touches. The bar and restaurant are informal and contemporary, while both the lounge and library are elegant and relaxing,

ROOMS: 69 en suite (4 fmly) ⊗ in 36 bedrooms **FACILITIES:** STV supervised Fishing Sauna Solarium Gym Jacuzzi Treatment rooms & Beautician **CONF:** Thtr 95 Class 50 Board 32 **SERVICES:** Lift air con **PARKING:** 250 **NOTES:** **CARDS:**

See advert on opposite page

★★★★72% Rochestown Park Hotel

Rochestown Rd, Douglas
☎ 021 4890800 ▣ 021 4892178
e-mail: info@rochestownpark.com
Dir: *from Lee Tunnel, 2nd exit left off dual carriageway. Continue for 400mtrs, then 1st left and right at small rdbt. Hotel 600mtrs on right*

This modern hotel is situated in mature gardens on the south side of Cork City. Various bedroom styles, including suites, are available; most rooms are air conditioned and overlook Mahon Golf Club. Public areas include a traditional bar and Gallery Restaurant. There are extensive leisure, conference and exhibition facilities. Convenient for both the airport and the ferries.

ROOMS: 160 en suite (17 fmly) (23 GF) s fr €75; d fr €120 (incl. bkfst) **LB** **FACILITIES: Spa** STV supervised Sauna Solarium Gym Jacuzzi Thalasso therapy & beauty centre ch fac Xmas **CONF:** BC Thtr 800 Class 360 Board 100 **SERVICES:** Lift **PARKING:** 300 **NOTES:** ⊗ in restaurant Closed 25-26 Dec **CARDS:**

★★★★69% Jurys

Western Rd
JURYS DOYLE HOTELS
☎ 021 4276622 & 4252700 ▣ 021 4274477
e-mail: info@jurysdoyle.com
Dir: *close to city centre, on main Killarney road (past court house on right side), hotel 500yds on left*

This hotel enjoys a riverside setting near to the university and within walking distance of the city centre. The public areas have a fresh outlook, with a comfortable library lounge, in addition to leisure and conference facilities. Bedrooms are well equipped.

ROOMS: 185 en suite (23 fmly) (83 GF) ⊗ in 48 bedrooms s €170-€190; d €220-€320 (incl. bkfst) **LB** **FACILITIES:** STV supervised supervised Squash Sauna Gym Jacuzzi ♫ **CONF:** Thtr 700 Class 400 Board 150 **SERVICES:** Lift **PARKING:** 231 **NOTES:** Closed 25-26 Dec **CARDS:**

★★★★68% Maryborough House

Maryborough Hill
☎ 021 4365555 ▣ 021 4365662
e-mail: maryboro@indigo.ie
Dir: *From Jack Lynch Tunnel take 2nd exit & slip road, signed Douglas. Turn right at 1st rdbt & follow Rochestown Rd to next 'fingerpost' rdbt. Turn left, hotel on left 0.5m up hill*

Dating from 1715, Maryborough house has been renovated and extended to a fine hotel set in beautifully landscaped grounds. The suites in the main house, and the bedrooms in the new modern

continued

wing are well appointed and comfortable. The extensive lounge is very popular with Corkonians for the range of food served throughout the day.

ROOMS: 79 en suite (6 fmly) ⊗ in 23 bedrooms s €145-€250; d €198-€350 (incl. bkfst) **LB** **FACILITIES:** STV supervised Snooker Sauna Gym Jacuzzi Aromatherapy Beauty therapy Massage Reiki ch fac **CONF:** Thtr 500 Class 250 Board 60 Del from €225 **SERVICES:** Lift **PARKING:** 300 **NOTES:** ⊗ in restaurant **CARDS:**

★★★★ 65% Silver Springs Moran

Tivoli
☎ 021 4507533 021 4507641
e-mail: silverspringsinfo@morangroup.ie
Dir: *N8 south Silver Springs exit and right on overpass then right for hotel on left*

Under new ownership, this hotel offers a choice of bedrooms including the refurbished Tower Rooms and the larger Club Rooms. There is a spacious lounge, a bar and restaurant, excellent conference facilities and a helipad. Guests have use of a nearby leisure centre.

ROOMS: 109 en suite (29 fmly) ⊗ in 17 bedrooms s €98-€140; d €130-€180 (incl. bkfst) **LB** **FACILITIES:** STV Squash Snooker Sauna Gym Jacuzzi Aerobics classes ch fac Xmas **CONF:** Thtr 700 Class 400 Board 30 **SERVICES:** Lift **PARKING:** 325 **NOTES:** ⊗ in restaurant Closed 24-26 Dec **CARDS:**

★★★ 69% *Ambassador*

Military Hill, St Lukes
☎ 021 4551996 021 4551997
e-mail: reservations@ambassadorhotel.ie
Dir: *city centre, just off Wellington Rd*

Many pleasing features distinguish this sandstone and granite building which dates from the 19th century and has commanding views over the city. There is a feeling of space and comfort throughout the public areas which include a cocktail lounge, bar and restaurant. There are balconies attached to some bedrooms, all are very well appointed.

ROOMS: 60 en suite (8 fmly) ⊗ in 8 bedrooms **FACILITIES:** STV ♫ **CONF:** Thtr 80 Class 40 Board 35 **SERVICES:** Lift **PARKING:** 60 **NOTES:** Closed 24-26 Dec **CARDS:**

★★★ 69% Gresham Metropole

MacCurtain St
GRESHAM HOTELS
☎ 021 4508122 021 4506450
e-mail: info@gresham-metropolehotel.com
Dir: *in city centre, opposite Merchant Quay Shopping Centre.*

This long-established property has undergone a major refurbishment in the last few years, resulting in a very comfortable city-centre hotel. Bedrooms vary in size and are well equipped.

continued

Public areas include the popular Met bar and a good leisure centre. Enquire on reservation about car parking.

ROOMS: 113 en suite (3 fmly) ⊗ in 90 bedrooms s €95-€260; d €95-€260 **LB** **FACILITIES:** STV supervised Sauna Solarium Gym Jacuzzi Aerobic studio & Steam room ♫ Xmas **CONF:** Thtr 500 Class 180 Board 60 **SERVICES:** Lift **PARKING:** 240 **NOTES:** ⊗ in restaurant **CARDS:**

See advert on page 839

★★★ 69% Imperial Hotel

South Mall
☎ 021 4274040 021 4275375
e-mail: info@imperialhotelcork.ie
Dir: *in city centre business area*

This fine, long established hotel has a hospitable and welcoming atmosphere. The reception rooms are on a grand scale, especially the foyer and coffee shop. Bedrooms are of a high standard and are soon to be augmented by others in a refurbishment programme, adding 30 new bedrooms. Parking, about five minutes away, is available by prior arrangement.

ROOMS: 90 en suite (4 fmly) ⊗ in 50 bedrooms s €94-€160; d €94-€160 **LB** **FACILITIES:** STV ♫ ch fac **CONF:** Thtr 400 Class 200 Board 60 **SERVICES:** Lift **NOTES:** ⊗ in restaurant Closed 24-27 Dec **CARDS:**

★★★ 59% *Jurys Inn*

Anderson's Quay
JURYS DOYLE HOTELS
☎ 021 4276444 021 4276144
e-mail: enquiry@jurys.com
Dir: *in city centre, on river beside eastern approach to the city from Dublin and south link road to airport*

This hotel overlooks the River Lee and is just a short walk from the

continued on p852

CORK, continued

main street and shopping area. Attractively decorated in a modern style. Rooms are spacious and can accommodate families. The restaurant is informal and there is also a lively pub.
ROOMS: 133 en suite ⊗ in 32 bedrooms **FACILITIES:** STV ♫
CONF: Thtr 35 Class 20 Board 20 **SERVICES:** Lift **PARKING:** 22
NOTES: Closed 24-26 Dec **CARDS:**

C

★★60% Ashley
Coburg St
☎ 021 4501518 021 4501178
e-mail: info@ashleyhotel.com
Dir: *From N8 to 4th bridge (do not cross any bridges) & turn right then right at next junct*
This hotel is centrally located near the railway station and much of Cork's nightlife. Bedrooms vary in size, but are warm and comfortable. The bar is welcoming and serves food at lunch and dinner. Secure car parking is available to the rear of the hotel.
ROOMS: 27 en suite (1 fmly) ⊗ in 15 bedrooms s €80; d €75
FACILITIES: STV **PARKING:** 8 **NOTES:** ⊗ in restaurant Closed 22 Dec-5 Jan **CARDS:**

Travelodge
Blackash
☎ 08700 850 950 021 4310723
Dir: *at rdbt junct of South Ring Road/Kinsale Rd R600*

Travelodge

Travelodge offers good quality, good value, modern accommodation. Ideal for families, the spacious, en suite bedrooms include remote-control TV, tea and coffee-making facilities and luxury beds. Meals can be taken at the nearby family restaurant. For further details consult the Hotel Groups page.
ROOMS: 60 en suite

COURTOWN HARBOUR, Co Wexford Map 01 D3

★★★60% *Bay View*
☎ 055 25307 055 25576
e-mail: bayview@iol.ie
Dir: *clearly signed to Courtown, turn left before Gorey off N11, hotel in main square*
This long-establshed comfortable hotel overlooks the marina and the Irish Sea. The McGarry family are attentive hosts as are their friendly staff. Good cuisine is served in both the restaurant and the popular bar.
ROOMS: 17 en suite (12 fmly) **FACILITIES:** Squash **PARKING:** 30
NOTES: ⊗ in restaurant Closed 30 Nov-14 Mar
CARDS:

★★★60% Courtown
☎ 055 25210 & 25108 055 25304
e-mail: info@courtownhotel.com
Dir: *Turn left on approach to Gorey, 5km on left*
Situated in the town centre, near to the beach and an 18-hole golf course, this refurbished family run hotel offers relaxing public areas. There is a comfortable lounge, spacious bar and an attractive restaurant and the leisure centre includes a swimming pool, gym and solarium.
ROOMS: 21 en suite (4 fmly) s €70-€90; d €120-€150 (incl. bkfst) **LB**
FACILITIES: supervised Squash Sauna Solarium Gym Jacuzzi Steam room, Massage, Crazy golf ♫ **PARKING:** 10 **NOTES:** Closed mid Nov - early Mar **CARDS:**

DELGANY, Co Wicklow Map 01 D3

★★★★62% *Glenview*
Glen O' the Downs
☎ 01 2873399 01 2877511
e-mail: glenview@iol.ie
Dir: *from Dublin city centre follow signs for N11, past Bray on southbound N11*
In a lovely hillside location overlooking terraced gardens this hotel boasts an excellent range of leisure and conference facilities. Impressive public areas provide a conservatory bar, lounge and choice of dining options. Bedrooms are spacious and some enjoy excellent views over the valley. Championship golf, horse riding and many tourist amenities are available nearby.
ROOMS: 70 en suite (11 fmly) (16 GF) ⊗ in 11 bedrooms
FACILITIES: Spa STV supervised Snooker Sauna Solarium Gym Jacuzzi Aerobics studio, Massage, Beauty treatment room ♫ ch fac
CONF: Thtr 220 Class 120 Board 50 **SERVICES:** Lift **PARKING:** 200
NOTES: ⊗ in restaurant **CARDS:**

DONEGAL, Co Donegal Map 01 B5

★★★75% *Harvey's Point Country*
Lough Eske
☎ 074 972 2208 074 972 2352
e-mail: reservations@harveyspoint.com
Dir: *from Donegal, take N56 then 1st right (Loch Eske/Harvey's Point). Hotel is approx 10 mins drive*
Nestled in a clearing by the lakeshore, this is a distinctive hotel where comfort and attentive care are priorities. High quality cuisine is served at dinner in the breathtaking dining room. A very popular buffet lunch is served every Sunday. Comfortable bedrooms are located in a nearby building.
ROOMS: 20 en suite **FACILITIES:** STV ♫ **CONF:** Thtr 200 Class 200 Board 50 **PARKING:** 300 **NOTES:** No children 10yrs ⊗ in restaurant
CARDS:

DOOLIN, Co Clare Map 01 B3

★★★64% *Aran View House*
Coast Rd
☎ 065 7074061 & 7074420 065 7074540
e-mail: bookings@aranview.com
Situated in 100 acres of rolling farmland and commanding panoramic views of the Cliffs of Moher and the Aran Islands, this family-run hotel offers comfortable accommodation. With welcoming staff and a convivial atmosphere, guests are assured of a relaxing stay. Seafood is a feature of the menu served in the attractive restaurant.
ROOMS: 13 en suite 6 annexe en suite (1 fmly) **FACILITIES:** ♫
PARKING: 40 **NOTES:** Closed Nov-1 Apr **CARDS:**

See advert on opposite page

DROGHEDA, Co Louth Map 01 D4

★★★65% *Boyne Valley Hotel & Country Club*
Stameen, Dublin Rd
☎ 041 9837737 041 9839188
e-mail: admin@boyne-valley-hotel.ie
Dir: *M1 towards Belfast, N of Dublin Airport on right - up Avenue before town of Drogheda*
This historic mansion stands in 16 acres of gardens and woodlands on the outskirts of Drogheda. The new bedrooms are very smart and provide high standards of comfort. Public areas include

continued

relaxing lounges, Terrace bar, Cellars Bistro, extensive banqueting facilities and a leisure centre and hard tennis courts.
ROOMS: 73 en suite (4 fmly) (26 GF) in 35 bedrooms
FACILITIES: STV supervised Sauna Solarium Gym Jacuzzi
CONF: BC Thtr 500 Class 350 Board 25 **SERVICES:** Lift **PARKING:** 200
NOTES: **CARDS:**

DUBLIN, Co Dublin Map 01 D4
See also Portmarnock

Top 200 – Hotel

★★★★★ **The Merrion Hotel**
Upper Merrion St
01 6030600 01 6030700
e-mail: info@merrionhotel.com
Dir: *at top of Upper Merrion St on left, beyond Government buildings on right*
This terrace of gracious Georgian buildings, reputed to have been the birthplace of the Duke of Wellington, embraces the character of the many changes of use through over 200 years. Bedrooms and suites are spacious, offering great comfort and a wide range of extra facilities. The lounges retain the charm and opulence of days gone by while the Cellar bar area is ideal for a relaxing drink. There is also a choice of dining options. Irish favourites focus on fresh and simply prepared ingredients in the Cellar Restaurant and, for that very special occasion, award-winning Restaurant Patrick Guilbaud is Dublin's finest.
ROOMS: 145 en suite in 65 bedrooms s €350-€1100; d €370-€1100 **LB** **FACILITIES:** STV Gym Steam room
CONF: BC Thtr 60 Class 25 Board 25 **SERVICES:** Lift air con
PARKING: 60 **NOTES:** **CARDS:**

★★★★★65% **Berkeley Court**
Lansdowne Rd JURYS DOYLE HOTELS
01 665 3200 01 6617238
e-mail: berkeley_court@jurysdoyle.com
Dir: *from N11 turn right at Donnybrook Church, 1st left over bridge, turn right immediately then take 1st left, hotel is 1st on left*
Situated in the leafy suburb of Ballsbridge, near the Lansdowne road stadium, this modern hotel is well positioned for business and leisure visitors alike. A refurbishment programme has been completed, and each of the guest rooms and suites is comfortably appointed with all the facilities expected by today's traveller.
ROOMS: 186 en suite in 126 bedrooms s €365; d €365 **LB**
FACILITIES: STV Hair & Beauty salon, Weirs Boutique Xmas
CONF: BC Thtr 450 Class 210 Board 50 Del €351 **SERVICES:** Lift air con **PARKING:** 130 **NOTES:** in restaurant
CARDS:

DUBLIN, continued

Top 200 – Hotel

★★★★ The Clarence

6-8 Wellington Quay D2
☎ 01 4070800 📠 01 4070820
e-mail: reservations@theclarence.ie
Dir: *from O'Connell Bridge, W along quays, through 1st set of traffic lights (at the Ha'penny Bridge) hotel 500mtrs further on*

Located on the banks of the River Liffey in the city centre, The Clarence is within walking distance of the shops and visitor attractions. This is a very distinctive property, where the character of the 1850 building has been successfully combined with contemporary design of the bedrooms and suites. The friendly staff provide unobtrusive professional service. Nominated for the AA Hotel of the Year Award for the Republic of Ireland 2004-5.

ROOMS: 50 en suite ⊗ in 4 bedrooms s €315-€2100; d €315-€2100 **FACILITIES:** STV Gym Treatment and massage room **CONF:** Thtr 50 Class 24 Board 35 **SERVICES:** Lift **PARKING:** 15 **NOTES:** ⊗ in restaurant Closed 24-27 Dec **CARDS:**

See advert on page 853

★★★★78% The Fitzwilliam

St Stephen's Green
☎ 01 4787000 📠 01 4787878
e-mail: enq@fitzwilliamhotel.com
Dir: *in city centre on St Stephen's Green, adjacent to the top of Grafton Street*

In a central position on St Stephen's Green, this friendly hotel is a pleasant blend of contemporary style with all the traditions of good hotel keeping. Bedrooms, many of which overlook an internal rooftop garden, have been equipped with a wide range of thoughtful extras. There is plenty to tempt the palate - Citron offers an informal eating option while Thornton's provides a fine dining alternative.

ROOMS: 140 en suite ⊗ in 90 bedrooms s €300-€380; d €340-€420 **LB** **FACILITIES:** STV Xmas **CONF:** Thtr 80 Class 50 Board 35 Del from €295 **SERVICES:** Lift **PARKING:** 85 **NOTES:** ⊗ in restaurant **CARDS:**

★★★★77% The Herbert Park Hotel

Ballsbridge
☎ 01 6672200 📠 01 6672595
e-mail: reservations@herbertparkhotel.ie
Dir: *2m from city centre along Nassau St, Mount St over canal bridge along Northumberland Rd. Cross bridge in Ballsbridge, 1st right*

In an enviable location adjoining the lovely park of the same name and close to the US Embassy, RDS and convenient to the city centre. Herbert Park Hotel has spacious, lightfilled and very comfortable public areas. Staff are professional and very friendly. Views of the park from the Pavilion restaurant and many of the

continued

contemporary-style bedrooms are delightful in any season. Secure underground car parking is available.

ROOMS: 153 en suite (4 fmly) ⊗ in 60 bedrooms s €230-€350; d €275-€350 **LB** **FACILITIES:** STV Gym **CONF:** BC Thtr 120 Class 70 Board 50 Del €275 **SERVICES:** Lift air con **PARKING:** 80 **NOTES:** ⊗ in restaurant **CARDS:**

★★★★73% Clarion Hotel Dublin IFSC

I.F.S.C.
☎ 01 4338800 📠 01 4338801
e-mail: info@clarionhotelifsc.com
Dir: *N1 to city centre, at Dorset St turn left onto North Circular Rd, down to 5 Lamps-Portland Row. Right into Amiens St, then left after IFSC Building/Custom House, onto North Wall Quay. Continue through 2 sets of lights, hotel on left.*

Whether staying here for business or leisure, or eating in the restaurant, this hotel is totally focussed on providing a professional service to its guests. Located at the heart of the International Financial Services Centre, this well designed hotel has stylish décor, comfortable bedrooms and the staff are pleasant and attentive.

ROOMS: 147 en suite (5 fmly) ⊗ in 73 bedrooms s €255-€280; d €255-€280 **LB** **FACILITIES:** STV supervised Sauna Solarium Gym Jacuzzi Spinning room, treatment room, aerobics area, gym with CV equipment. Xmas **CONF:** Thtr 110 Class 42 Board 34 Del from €90 **SERVICES:** Lift air con **PARKING:** 55 **NOTES:** ⊗ in restaurant **CARDS:**

★★★★73% *The Shelbourne*

27 St Stephen's Green
☎ 01 6634500 📠 01 6616006
e-mail: shelbourneinfo@lemeridien.com
Dir: *M1 to city centre, along Parnell St to O'Connell St towards Trinity College, take 3rd right along Kildare St, hotel on left*

This Georgian hotel has been a Dublin landmark since 1824 and has a rare and timeless elegance, and strong literary and historical connections. It boasts gracious reception rooms, a choice of restaurants, a leisure centre and popular bars. Bedrooms are smart, well appointed and comfortable and many offer truly beautiful views of the gardens of St. Stephen's Green.

ROOMS: 190 en suite (5 GF) ⊗ in 110 bedrooms **FACILITIES: Spa** STV Sauna Gym Jacuzzi Beauty salon, Hairdresser, Barber shop **CONF:** BC Thtr 380 Class 180 Board 60 **SERVICES:** Lift **PARKING:** 45 **CARDS:**

★★★★72% *Jurys Hotel and Towers*

Pembroke Rd, Ballsbridge
JURYS DOYLE HOTELS
☎ 01 660 5000 📠 01 667 5276
e-mail: ballsbridge@jurysdoyle.com
Dir: *from Dun Laoghaire, follow signs for city to Merrion Rd, Ballsbridge & Pembroke Rd, hotel at junct of Pembroke Rd and Northumberland Rd*

This establishment has two identities: Jurys Hotel, and the more recently opened Towers building. A wide choice of bars and restaurants along with a dedicated boardroom centre make up the spacious public areas. Bedrooms and suites are well appointed in the main hotel, while the Towers offers discreet luxury together with a separate entrance.

ROOMS: 303 en suite (13 fmly) ⊗ in 140 bedrooms **FACILITIES:** Sauna Gym Jacuzzi Hairdresser, Beauty Salon with Masseuse **CONF:** Thtr 850 Class 450 Board 40 **SERVICES:** Lift **PARKING:** 200 **NOTES:** **CARDS:**

★★★★71% Gresham
O'Connell St
☎ 01 8746881 01 8787175
e-mail: info@thegresham.com
Dir: *on O'Connell St, just off M1 close to the GPO*

This elegant hotel enjoys a prime centre city location close to theatres, shops and museums. Excellent conference, the choice of restaurants and bars made this the ideal choice for both corporate and leisure guests. A variety of bedroom options is available. Friendly staff has always been strength here. The hotel has a multi-storey car park.
ROOMS: 289 en suite (4 fmly) in 200 bedrooms s €144-€348.75; d €160-€360 **LB** **FACILITIES:** STV Gym Xmas **CONF:** BC Thtr 350 Class 150 Board 80 Del from €265 **SERVICES:** Lift air con **PARKING:** 150 **NOTES:** in restaurant **CARDS:**

See advert on page 839

★★★★70% *The Morrison*
Lower Ormond Quay
☎ 01 8872400 01 8783185
e-mail: info@morrisonhotel.ie
This newly built hotel was designed by the renowned John Rocha. Inside, wood, stone and natural fabrics are combined with vibrant colours to create a relaxing environment. There is a lobby lounge, café bar and the Halo Restaurant. Bedrooms and suites have a contemporary style and a dedicated, hospitable team ensures a pleasant stay. A popular club operates at weekends.
ROOMS: 94 en suite in 40 bedrooms **FACILITIES:** STV **CONF:** Thtr 90 Class 10 **SERVICES:** Lift air con **NOTES:** Closed Xmas **CARDS:**

★★★★67% Burlington
Upper Leeson St
☎ 01 660 5222 01 660 8496
Dir: *From airport take M1 into City Centre, follow signs for St. Stephens Green, up Leeson St., into Upper Leeson St.*
Close to the city, this bustling hotel features comfortable bedrooms that are well-appointed, many have been renovated. An executive floor offers additional services and a lounge area. Smart public areas include the popular Buck Mulligan pub, spacious lounges, the Sussex Room and Diplomat restaurants, where good food is served.
ROOMS: 500 en suite in 245 bedrooms s fr €272; d fr €305 **LB** **FACILITIES:** STV Gym Night club Use of facilities at fitness club Xmas **CONF:** BC Thtr 1500 Class 650 Board 40 Del €327 **SERVICES:** Lift **PARKING:** 700 **NOTES:** in restaurant **CARDS:**

★★★★66% Stillorgan Park
Stillorgan Rd
☎ 01 2881621 01 2831610
e-mail: sales@stillorganpark.com
Dir: *on N11 follow signs for Wexford, pass RTE studios on left, through 5 sets of lights, hotel on left*
This modern hotel is attractively decorated and is situated on the southern outskirts of the city. Comfortable public areas include a spacious lobby, contemporary restaurant and inviting bar. A new air-conditioned banqueting and conference centre has all the latest communication technology. Bedrooms are smartly appointed. The hotel benefits from a good-sized car park.

ROOMS: 125 en suite (12 fmly) in 25 bedrooms s €125-€145; d €145-€170 (incl. bkfst) **LB** **FACILITIES:** STV Special rates for residents at Westwood Leisure Centre & local golf courses Xmas **CONF:** BC Thtr 500 Class 220 Board 130 Del from €175 **SERVICES:** Lift air con **PARKING:** 350 **NOTES:** Civ Wed 300 **CARDS:**

★★★★64% *Red Cow Morans*
Red Cow Complex, Naas Rd
☎ 01 4593650 01 4591588
e-mail: reservations@morangroup.ie
Dir: *at junct of M50 & N7 Naas road on the city side of the motorway*

Located near the M50 and regional access routes, the Red Cow Morans is an ideal meeting place. Bedrooms are well equipped and comfortable, while public areas and conference rooms are spacious. Staff show a genuine willingness to help make your stay memorable.
ROOMS: 123 en suite (21 fmly) in 44 bedrooms **FACILITIES:** STV **CONF:** Thtr 700 Class 350 Board 150 **SERVICES:** Lift air con **PARKING:** 700 **NOTES:** Closed 24-26 Dec **CARDS:**

★★★★62% The Plaza Hotel
Belgard Rd, Tallaght
☎ 01 4624200 01 4624600
e-mail: reservations@plazahotel.ie web: www.plazahotel.ie
Dir: *6m from city centre, at S end of M50*
A contemporary hotel conveniently situated just off the M50 and beside The Square Shopping Centre. Public areas are spacious and there are good corporate facilities and secure underground car parking. Bedrooms are comfortable and well equipped. The Vista Café and Olive Restaurant are on the first-floor mezzanine and enjoy views of the Dublin Mountains.
ROOMS: 122 en suite (2 fmly) in 61 bedrooms **FACILITIES:** STV **CONF:** BC Thtr 200 Class 150 Board 50 **SERVICES:** Lift air con **PARKING:** 520 **NOTES:** in restaurant Closed 24-30 Dec **CARDS:**

DUBLIN, continued

★★★70% Finnstown Country House Hotel & Golf Course

Newcastle Rd, Lucan
☎ 01 6010700 01 6281088
e-mail: manager@finnstown-hotel.ie
Dir: from M1 take 1st exit onto M50 S/bound. 1st exit after Toll Bridge. At rdbt take 3rd left (N4 W). Left at traffic lights. Over next 2 rdbts. Hotel on right

Set in 45 acres of wooded grounds, Finnstown is a calm and peaceful country house. There is a wide choice of bedrooms available, with the garden suites being particularly comfortable. Lounge areas are numerous with games facilities provided. The staff are very guest focussed.
ROOMS: 25 en suite 28 annexe en suite (6 fmly) (9 GF) in 27 bedrooms s €130-€195; d €190-€270 (incl. bkfst) **LB FACILITIES:** STV Solarium Gym Putt green Turkish bath, Table tennis, Massage, Pool Table, Games Room Xmas **CONF:** BC Thtr 300 Class 60 Board 40 Del from €220 **PARKING:** 90 **CARDS:**

★★★70% Marine

Sutton Cross
☎ 01 8390000 01 8390442
e-mail: sales@marinehotel.ie
Dir: From O'Connell Bridge (Dublin City Centre) right into The Quays then left at Liberty Hall into Amien St. Follow through Fairview (R105) to Sutton Cross for hotel on right
On the north shore of Dublin Bay, this hotel is situated in attractive gardens. Bedrooms are spacious and well appointed, most enjoying the spectacular views. Public areas offer comfortable lounges, an inviting restaurant, conference rooms and a leisure centre.
ROOMS: 48 en suite (5 fmly) in 12 bedrooms s €95-€145; d €165-€235 (incl. bkfst) **LB FACILITIES:** STV Sauna Steam Room **CONF:** Thtr 220 Class 140 Board 40 Del from €180 **SERVICES:** Lift **PARKING:** 150 **NOTES:** in restaurant Closed 25-27 Dec
CARDS:

★★★68% *Buswells*

23-25 Molesworth St
☎ 01 6146500 01 6762090
e-mail: buswells@quinn-hotels.com
Dir: on corner of Molesworth St & Kildare St opposite Dail Eireann (Government Buildings)
Originally a number of Georgian townhouses, Buswells is a popular meeting place for the parliamentarians from the Dail opposite. Bedrooms are comfortable and attractively decorated. Public areas include an elegant lounge where friendly staff are at hand to serve drinks and snacks. Further meeting rooms are currently being developed.
ROOMS: 69 en suite (17 fmly) in 18 bedrooms **FACILITIES:** Gym Leisure suite **CONF:** BC Thtr 85 Class 30 Board 24 **SERVICES:** Lift **NOTES:** Closed 25 & 26 Dec RS 24 Dec
CARDS:

★★★68% *Jurys Green Isle*

Naas Rd
☎ 01 4593406 01 4592178
Dir: on N7, 10km SW of the city centre
This hotel lies on the southern outskirts of Dublin just off the M50. Both standard and executive bedrooms are generously proportioned and stylishly furnished. Public areas include Sorrells Restaurant, a spacious lobby, Rosie O'Gradys Bar and extensive banqueting and conference facilities.
ROOMS: 90 en suite **FACILITIES:** STV **CONF:** Thtr 300 Class 100 Board 100 **SERVICES:** Lift **PARKING:** 250 **NOTES:**
CARDS:

★★★67% Bewley's Hotel Ballsbridge

Merrion Rd, Ballsbridge
☎ 01 6681111 01 6681999
e-mail: bb@bewleyshotels.com

This stylish hotel is conveniently situated near the RDS Showgrounds. It offers comfortable, good value accommodation. Lunch and dinner are available in O'Connell's Restaurant and food is available all day in the spacious lounge café, which is a popular meeting place. Secure underground car parking is available at a nominal fee.
ROOMS: 220 en suite (25 fmly) in 140 bedrooms s €99; d €99 **CONF:** Class 30 Board 14 **SERVICES:** Lift **PARKING:** 240 **NOTES:** in restaurant Closed 24-26 Dec **CARDS:**

★★★67% The Carnegie Court

North St, Swords
☎ 01 8404384 01 8404505
e-mail: info@carnegiecourt.com
Dir: from Dublin airport take N1 towards Belfast. At 5th rdbt take 1st exit for Swords, than a sharp left for hotel
This modern hotel has been tastefully built and is conveniently located close to Dublin Airport just off the N1 in Swords village. The air-conditioned bedrooms are well appointed, and many are particularly spacious. Public areas include a select residents' lounge, contemporary Courtyard Restaurant, a dramatically designed Harp Bar and modern conference and banqueting facilities. Extensive parking is provided.
ROOMS: 36 en suite (4 fmly) in 7 bedrooms **FACILITIES:** STV **CONF:** Thtr 280 Class 50 Board 40 **SERVICES:** Lift air con **PARKING:** 150 **NOTES:** in restaurant Closed 25-26 Dec
CARDS:

★★★67% *Jurys Montrose*

Stillorgan Rd
☎ 01 2693311 01 2691164
e-mail: montrose@jurysdoyle.com
Dir: From city centre follow signs for N11 motorway
Close to the University campus, this hotel offers comfortable bedrooms and smart lounges with a choice of bars and dedicated

continued

meeting rooms. Casual dining is available throughout the day, with a more formal service in the restaurant at both lunch and dinner.
ROOMS: 178 en suite ⊗ in 30 bedrooms **FACILITIES:** STV **CONF:** Thtr 80 Class 30 Board 30 **SERVICES:** Lift **PARKING:** 100 **NOTES:**
CARDS:

★★★67% *Longfield's Hotel*

Fitzwilliam St Lower
☎ 01 6761367 01 6761542
e-mail: info@longfields.ie
Dir: *take Shelbourne Hotel exit from St Stephens Green, continue down Baggot St for 400mtrs, turn left at Fitzwilliam St junct and hotel on left*

MANOR HOUSE

Longfield's, a series of Georgian houses, has a very warm hospitable feel to it. Staff are all focused on guest care in an informal yet professional manner. Drinks are available in the comfortable lounge. Rooms vary in size but are well appointed and comfortable.
ROOMS: 26 en suite **FACILITIES:** STV **CONF:** Thtr 20 Board 20 **SERVICES:** Lift **NOTES:** ⊗ in restaurant RS 23-27 Dec
CARDS:

★★★66% *Camden Court*

Camden St
☎ 01 4759666 01 4759677
e-mail: reservations@camdencourthotel.ie
Dir: *off Camden St close to St Stephens Green & Grafton St*
This hotel has a number of fine features in addition to its convenient location. These include spacious public areas, a leisure centre, well-equipped bedrooms, a summer beer garden and the bonus of a car park in the city centre.
ROOMS: 246 en suite (33 fmly) ⊗ in 13 bedrooms **FACILITIES:** Sauna Solarium Gym Jacuzzi **CONF:** Thtr 40 Class 40 Board 20 **SERVICES:** Lift **PARKING:** 96 **NOTES:** Closed Xmas/New Year
CARDS:

★★★66% *McEniff Grand Canal Hotel*

Grand Canal St
☎ 01 646 1000 01 645 1001
This newly built hotel is situated on the banks of the Grand Canal in Ballsbridge, close to Lansdowne Road Stadium, RDS and the city centre. Bedrooms are well appointed. The public areas have a contemporary design, are spacious and include a comfortable lounge, restaurant, Kitty O'Shea's pub and extensive conference rooms. Secure underground parking is available.
ROOMS: 142 rms

> € Don't forget, the Euro is now the unit of currency in the Republic of Ireland

★★★65% *Bewleys Hotel Leopardstown*

Central Park, Leopardstown Rd
☎ 01 2935 000 021 2935 099
e-mail: leop@bewleyshotel.com
This newly built hotel is conveniently situated for the Central Business Park and Leopardstown Racecourse. Contemporary in style, the open-plan public areas include a spacious lounge bar, Brasserie and a selection of conference rooms. Bedrooms are well appointed. There is free underground parking.
ROOMS: 306 rms

★★★65% Bewley's Hotel Newlands Cross

Newlands Cross, Naas Rd
☎ 01 4640140 01 4640900
e-mail: res@bewleyshotels.com
Dir: *M50 junct 9 take N7 Naas road, hotel is short distance from junct of N7 with Belgard Rd at Newlands Cross*

This modern hotel is situated on the outskirts of Dublin off the N7 and close to M50. Bedrooms are well furnished and prices are competitive. The restaurant is open for casual dining all day and serves more formal meals in the evening. There is a comfortable lounge and bar and ample car parking.
ROOMS: 258 en suite ⊗ in 183 bedrooms s €79; d €79
FACILITIES: STV **CONF:** Board 12 **SERVICES:** Lift **PARKING:** 200
NOTES: ⊗ in restaurant Closed 24-26 Dec
CARDS:

★★★65% *Jurys Tara Hotel*

Merrion Rd
☎ 01 2694666 01 2691027
e-mail: tara@jurysdoyle.com
Dir: *N11/University College follow road towards Montrose Hotel & take 1st left before hotel. Along Woodbine Rd & turn left at traffic lights*
The well-equipped bedrooms of this hotel enjoy spectacular views of Dublin Bay and Howth Head. Attractively decorated public areas include a comfortable and relaxing foyer lounge, PJ Branagans Pub and a split-level conservatory restaurant.
ROOMS: 113 en suite (2 fmly) ⊗ in 20 bedrooms **FACILITIES:** STV **CONF:** Thtr 300 Class 100 Board 40 **SERVICES:** Lift **PARKING:** 100
NOTES: **CARDS:**

★★★64% Cassidys

Cavendish Row, O'Connell St Upper
☎ 01 8780555 01 8780687
e-mail: stay@cassidyshotel.com
Dir: *in city centre. At north end of O'Connell St opposite Gate Theatre.*
This family run hotel is located at the top of O'Connell Street, on a terrace of red-brick Georgian townhouses. The warm and welcoming atmosphere of Grooms Bar lends a traditional air to Cassidy's and Restaurant 6 is contemporary and stylish. The

continued on p858

DUBLIN, continued

modern bedrooms are well appointed. Limited parking for guests and conference facilities available.

Cassidys, Dublin

ROOMS: 88 en suite (3 fmly) (12 GF) ⊗ in 23 bedrooms s €85-€175; d €95-€195 (incl. bkfst) LB **FACILITIES:** STV ♫ **CONF:** Thtr 80 Class 45 Board 45 **SERVICES:** Lift **PARKING:** 15 **NOTES:** ✈ ⊗ in restaurant Closed 24-26 Dec **CARDS:**

★★★ 64% *Mount Herbert Hotel*

Herbert Rd, Lansdowne Rd
☎ 01 6684321 🖹 01 6607077
e-mail: info@mountherberthotel.ie
Dir: *close to Lansdowne Road Rugby Stadium, 200mtrs from Dart Rail Station*
Located in the leafy suburb of Ballsbridge, this family-run hotel is an oasis of calm, offering true hospitality. Bedrooms are comfortable, as are the lounge areas. Good value cuisine is served in the restful restaurant overlooking the floodlit gardens.
ROOMS: 185 en suite (15 fmly) **FACILITIES:** STV Sauna Childrens playground, Badminton court **CONF:** Thtr 80 Class 60 Board 40 **SERVICES:** Lift **PARKING:** 90 **NOTES:** ✈ Closed 21-27 Dec
CARDS:

★★★ 64% Royal Dublin

O'Connell St
☎ 01 8733666 🖹 01 8733120
e-mail: eng@royaldublin.com
Located in the heart of the city on O'Connell Street convenient to shops, theatres, museums and galleries this hotel is undergoing major refurbishment. Spacious public areas include the Georgian Room Lounge, Raffles Bar and Café Royale Brassiere. Bedrooms offer modern comforts and are well appointed. Secure car parking available.
ROOMS: 117 en suite ⊗ in 36 bedrooms s €120-€190; d €140-€270 **FACILITIES:** Xmas **CONF:** Thtr 220 Class 120 Board 60 Del from €250 **SERVICES:** Lift **PARKING:** 20 **NOTES:** ✈ ⊗ in restaurant Closed 24-25 Dec **CARDS:**

★★★ 63% *McEniff Skylon*

Drumcondra Rd
☎ 01 8379121 🖹 01 8372778
e-mail: skylon_hotel@jurysdoyle.com
Dir: *from Airport take M1 towards city centre. Hotel 3m on right*
In a convenient location, with easy access to the city centre and the airport, this hotel has a spacious, comfortable lobby lounge and bar where food is available all day, with more formal dining in the attractive restaurant. Bedrooms are well appointed and there is ample car parking available.
ROOMS: 88 en suite (8 fmly) ⊗ in 22 bedrooms **FACILITIES:** STV **CONF:** Thtr 35 Class 20 Board 20 **SERVICES:** Lift **NOTES:** ✈
CARDS:

★★★ 63% The Mercer Hotel

Mercer St Lower
☎ 01 4782179 🖹 01 4780328
e-mail: stay@mercerhotel.ie
Dir: *St Stephens Green before shopping centre turn left down York St, then right at end of road, hotel on right*
This modern hotel is situated in the city centre close to Grafton Street. Bedrooms are attractively decorated and well equipped with fridges and CD players, as well as the usual facilities. Public areas include an open-plan lounge with cocktail bar and a restaurant. Parking is available in car park next door.
ROOMS: 41 en suite ⊗ in 4 bedrooms s €145-€179; d €185-€240 LB **FACILITIES:** STV **CONF:** Thtr 100 Class 80 Board 60 **SERVICES:** Lift air con **PARKING:** 41 **NOTES:** ✈ Closed 24-26 Dec Civ Wed
CARDS:

★★★ 63% Temple Bar

Fleet St, Temple Bar
☎ 01 6773333 🖹 01 6773088
e-mail: reservations@tbh.ie
Dir: *from Trinity College, towards O'Connell Bridge & take 1st left onto Fleet St & hotel on right*
This hotel is situated in the heart of Dublin's Temple Bar, and in close to the shops, restaurants and cultural life of the city. Bedrooms are comfortable and well equipped. Food is served throughout the day in Buskers theme bar. There is a multi-storey car park nearby.
ROOMS: 129 en suite (6 fmly) ⊗ in 60 bedrooms s €100-€150; d €120-€195 (incl. bkfst) LB **FACILITIES:** STV Guest reduced rates at nearby leisure facilities **CONF:** Thtr 70 Class 40 Board 40 Del €140 **SERVICES:** Lift **NOTES:** ✈ ⊗ in restaurant Closed 23-25 Dec RS Good Friday **CARDS:**

★★★ 62% *Abberley Court*

Belgard Rd, Tallaght
☎ 01 4596000 🖹 01 4621000
e-mail: abberley@iol.ie
Dir: *opposite The Square in town centre at junct of Belgard Rd and Tallaght by-pass (N81)*
Located beside an excellent complex of shops, restaurants and cinema, this hotel offers comfortable well-appointed bedrooms, the choice of two bars, a carvery and a Chinese restaurant. There are sports facilities available nearby.
ROOMS: 40 en suite (34 fmly) ⊗ in 8 bedrooms **CONF:** Thtr 40 Class 25 Board 20 **SERVICES:** Lift **PARKING:** 450 **NOTES:** ✈ Closed 25 Dec
CARDS:

★★★ 60% The Ormond Quay

7-11 Upper Ormond Quay
☎ 01 8721811 🖹 01 8721362
e-mail: ormondqh@indigo.ie.
Dir: *From M50, exit N4 towards city centre onto Quays. Hotel approx 1 mile from Heuston train station, on left.*
Conveniently located across the river from the Temple Bar district, this hotel has now been refurbished. Public areas include a popular bar, restaurant and some well-equipped conference rooms. Staff are friendly and very attentive.
ROOMS: 62 en suite (12 fmly) ⊗ in 10 bedrooms s €80-€160; d €100-€300 (incl. bkfst) LB **FACILITIES:** STV ♫ Xmas **CONF:** BC Thtr 340 Class 170 Board 175 **SERVICES:** Lift **NOTES:** ✈ ⊗ in restaurant Closed 24-25 Dec **CARDS:**

For central reservation numbers and more information on Hotel Groups, turn to pages 33-39

★★★59% Jurys Christchurch Inn

Christchurch Place

JURYS DOYLE HOTELS

☎ 01 4540000 📠 01 4540012
e-mail: info@jurysdoyle.com

Dir: *N7 onto Naas Rd, follow signs for city centre to O'Connell St, continue past Trinity College, turn right onto Dame St up to Lord Edward St, hotel on left*

Centrally located opposite the 12th-century Christchurch Cathedral, this hotel is close to the Temple Bar and all the city amenities. The foyer lounge and pub are popular meeting places and there is also an informal restaurant. The bedrooms are well appointed and can accommodate families. The adjoining car park is a bonus in the city centre.

ROOMS: 182 en suite ⊗ in 114 bedrooms s €108-€117; d €108-€117 **SERVICES:** Lift **NOTES:** ⊗ in restaurant Closed 24-26 Dec **CARDS:**

★★★59% *Jurys Custom House Inn*

Custom House Quay

JURYS DOYLE HOTELS

☎ 01 6075000 📠 01 8290400

Overlooking the River Liffey, this hotel is situated less than ten minutes' walk away from the city's main shopping and tourist areas. Family rooms offer good value for money and facilities for business guests are excellent.

ROOMS: 239 en suite ⊗ in 140 bedrooms **FACILITIES:** STV **CONF:** BC Thtr 80 Class 30 Board 30 **SERVICES:** Lift **NOTES:** Closed 25-26 Dec **CARDS:**

★★★58% The Parliament Hotel

Lord Edward St

☎ 01 6708777 📠 01 6708787
e-mail: parl@regencyhotels.com

Dir: *adjacent to Dublin Castle in the Temple Bar area*

An attractive hotel, near to the Temple Bar area and Dublin Castle, offering a friendly welcome to all its guests. It provides well-furnished bedrooms, decorated in a modern style. There is also a popular bar and a separate restaurant.

ROOMS: 63 en suite (8 fmly) ⊗ in 22 bedrooms s €160; d €220 (incl. bkfst) **LB** **FACILITIES:** STV **CONF:** Thtr 20 Board 10 **SERVICES:** Lift **NOTES:** ⊗ in restaurant **CARDS:**

U The Westin

College Green

☎ 01 635 1000 📠 01 645 1234

At the time of going to press, the star classification for this hotel was not confirmed. Please refer to the AA internet site www.theAA.com for current information.

ROOMS: 163 rms

Travelodge Dublin Airport

Swords By Pass

Travelodge

☎ 08700 850 950 📠 01 8409235

Dir: *on N1 Dublin/Belfast road*

Travelodge offers good quality, good value, modern accommodation. Ideal for families, the spacious, en suite bedrooms include remote-control TV, tea and coffee-making facilities and luxury beds. Meals can be taken at the nearby family restaurant. For further details consult the Hotel Groups page.

ROOMS: 100 en suite

Indoor Swimming Pool
Indoor Swimming Pool (heated)
Outdoor Swimming Pool
Outdoor Swimming Pool (heated)

Travelodge Dublin (Navan Road)

Auburn Av Roundabout, Navan Rd

Travelodge

☎ 08700 850 950

Travelodge offers good quality, good value, modern accommodation. Ideal for families, the spacious, en suite bedrooms include remote-control TV, tea and coffee-making facilities and luxury beds. Meals can be taken at the nearby family restaurant. For further details consult the Hotel Groups page.

ROOMS: 100 en suite

DUNDALK, Co Louth — Map 01 D4

★★★73% Ballymascanlon House

Best Western

☎ 042 9358200 📠 042 9371598
e-mail: info@ballymascanlon.com

Dir: *N of Dundalk take T62 to Carlingford. Hotel approx 1km*

This Victorian mansion is set in 130 acres of woodland at the foot of the Cooley Mountains. New additions have been sympathetically designed to fit with the original house, resulting in a very comfortable hotel with some really stylish bedrooms. Public areas include an elegant restaurant and spacious lounge and bar, and a well-equipped leisure centre.

ROOMS: 90 en suite (11 fmly) (5 GF) ⊗ in 28 bedrooms s €105-€190; d €155-€250 (incl. bkfst) **LB** **FACILITIES:** STV supervised 18 Sauna Gym Putt green Jacuzzi ♫ Xmas **CONF:** Thtr 300 Class 160 Board 75 Del from €160 **SERVICES:** Lift **PARKING:** 250 **NOTES:** **CARDS:**

★★★65% Fairways Hotel

Dublin Rd

☎ 042 9321500 📠 042 9321511
e-mail: info@fairways.ie

Dir: *on N1 3km S of Dundalk*

Situated south of Dundalk on the Castlebellingham road, this modern hotel has now been refurbished to a high standard. A wide range of food is available in the carvery/grill all day, with a more formal dinner served in Modi's restaurant. Golf can be arranged by the hotel on a choice of nearby courses.

ROOMS: 101 en suite (2 fmly) (30 GF) ⊗ in 30 bedrooms s €85-€110; d €130-€150 (incl. bkfst) **LB** **FACILITIES:** **Spa** STV supervised Sauna Gym Jacuzzi ♫ **CONF:** BC Thtr 1000 Class 500 **SERVICES:** Lift **PARKING:** 700 **NOTES:** ⊗ in restaurant Closed 25 Dec **CARDS:**

★★60% *Imperial*

Park St

☎ 042 9332241 📠 042 9337909
e-mail: info@imperialhoteldundalk.com

Dir: *past Heinz Factory 2nd set of lights turn left. Follow signs to town centre*

This hotel in the centre of the town enjoys a very strong local business. Many of the rooms have now been refurbished. Music is a nightly feature in the bar, and Sgt Peppers, the hotel nightclub, operates at weekends.

ROOMS: 47 en suite (47 fmly) **FACILITIES:** STV Free use of facilities at sister hotel 3m away ♫ **CONF:** Thtr 400 Class 125 Board 50 **SERVICES:** Lift **PARKING:** 75 **NOTES:** Closed 25 Dec **CARDS:**

DUNFANAGHY, Co Donegal — Map 01 C6

★★★67% Arnold's

IRISH COUNTRY HOTELS

☎ 074 913 6208 📠 074 913 6352
e-mail: arnoldshotel@eircom.net

Dir: *on N56 from Letterkenny, hotel on left on entering village*

This family run hotel is noted for its warm welcome and good

continued on p860

DUNFANAGHY, continued

food. Situated in a coastal village with sandy beaches, links golf courses and beautiful scenery. Public areas and bedrooms are comfortable, there is a traditional bar, choice of two restaurants, delightful garden, riding stables and outdoor activities available.

Arnold's, Dunfanaghy

ROOMS: 30 en suite (10 fmly) s €95-€120; d €130-€180 (incl. bkfst) **LB FACILITIES:** STV Fishing Riding Putt green **PARKING:** 60 **NOTES:** in restaurant Closed Nov-mid March **CARDS:**

DUNGANNON, Co Tyrone Map 01 C5

Cohannon Inn

212 Ballynakilly Rd BT71 6HJ
☎ 028 8772 4488 028 8775 2217
e-mail: enquiries@cohannon-inn.com
Dir: *400yds from M1 junct 14*

Handy for the M1, The Cohannon Inn offers competitive prices and well-maintained bedrooms, located behind the inn complex in a smart purpose-built wing. Public areas are smartly furnished and wide-ranging menus are served throughout the day.

ROOMS: 42 en suite **CONF:** Thtr 100 Class 50 Board 50

DUNGARVAN, Co Waterford Map 01 C2

★★★61% Lawlors

☎ 058 41122 & 41056 058 41000
e-mail: info@lawlors-hotel.ie
Dir: *off N25*

This town centre hotel enjoys a busy local trade especially in the bar where good food is served throughout the day. The restaurant offers a particularly wide choice of menu. Many of the bedrooms are very spacious. Conference and meeting rooms are also available.

ROOMS: 89 en suite (8 fmly) **FACILITIES:** Xmas **CONF:** Thtr 420 Class 215 Board 420 **SERVICES:** Lift **NOTES:** Closed 25 Dec **CARDS:**

ENFIELD, Co Meath Map 01 C4

★★★★69% Johnstown House

☎ 046 9540000 046 9540001
e-mail: info@johnstownhouse.com

Built around a Georgian listed mansion on 80 acres of parkland and landscaped gardens, this fine hotel offers hi-tech conference facilities, comfortable bedrooms and suites, two restaurants and bars. The reception hall and library reflect the elegance of 18th-century design.

ROOMS: 126 en suite (8 fmly) (41 GF) in 40 bedrooms s €210; d €240 (incl. bkfst) **LB FACILITIES: Spa** STV supervised Fishing Sauna Gym Jacuzzi New spa opening Jan 2005 Xmas **CONF:** BC Thtr 900 Class 900 Board 16 Del €190 **SERVICES:** Lift **PARKING:** 350 **NOTES:** in restaurant Closed 24-25 Dec **CARDS:**

ENNIS, Co Clare Map 01 B3

★★★65% Temple Gate

The Square
☎ 065 682 3300 065 682 3322
e-mail: info@templegatehotel.com
Dir: *on Limerick side of Ennis, turn off N18 and continue on Tulla Rd for 0.25m, hotel on the left*

This smart hotel is located in the very centre of the town with private car parking. Incorporating an 19th-century Gothic style building the public areas are well planned and include a comfortable lounge, popular pub and Le Bistro restaurant. Bedrooms are attractive and well equipped.

ROOMS: 70 en suite (3 fmly) (25 GF) in 11 bedrooms s €100-€120; d €140-€170 (incl. bkfst) **LB FACILITIES:** STV **CONF:** Thtr 220 Class 100 Board 80 Del from €149.50 **SERVICES:** Lift **PARKING:** 52 **NOTES:** in restaurant Closed 25 Dec RS 26 Dec Civ Wed 150 **CARDS:**

★★65% *Magowna House*

Inch
☎ 065 6839009 065 6839258
e-mail: info@magowna.com
Dir: *on R474 off N18 pass Ennis golf course, and after approx 5km, hotel signed to right, 300mtrs from junct*

Just a few kilometres from Ennis, just past the village of Inch, this family operated hotel offers a true reflection of Irish hospitality. Some rooms are compact but are comfortable. Enjoyable meals are served in both the restaurant and the bar. Fishing and golf are the local attractions.

ROOMS: 10 en suite (3 fmly) in 4 bedrooms **FACILITIES:** 3 Boats for hire, Golf driving net **CONF:** Thtr 350 Class 200 Board 20 **PARKING:** 60 **NOTES:** Closed 24-26 Dec **CARDS:**

ENNISCORTHY, Co Wexford Map 01 D3

★★★70% *Riverside Park Hotel*

The Promenade
☎ 054 37800 054 37900
e-mail: info@riversideparkhotel.com
Dir: *0.5km from New Bridge, centre of Enniscorthy, N11 Dublin/Rosslare Rd*

Situated in a picturesque position beside the River Slaney, this hotel is easily distinguished by its terracotta and blue colour scheme. The foyer is equally dramatic and the public areas all take full advantage of the riverside views, including the Mill House pub. The spacious, attractively decorated bedrooms have every modern comfort.

ROOMS: 60 en suite (15 fmly) in 10 bedrooms **FACILITIES:** STV Sauna Solarium Gym Jacuzzi ch fac **CONF:** Thtr 750 Class 350 Board 300 **SERVICES:** Lift **PARKING:** 250 **NOTES:** **CARDS:**

★★★64% *Treacys*

Templeshannon
☎ 054 37798 054 37733
e-mail: info@treacyshotel.com
Dir: *Follow N11 into Enniscorthy, over bridge in left lane and up street, hotel on right*

This modern hotel is family run and conveniently located in the town centre where guests can use of the Waterfront Leisure facilities. There is a choice of dining options in the Chang Thai and Begenal Harvey, there is music nightly in the bar, and Benedict's super-pub is open at weekends. Bedrooms are comfortable and well appointed.

ROOMS: 59 rms (2 fmly) in 11 bedrooms **FACILITIES:** STV Discount at adjacent leisure complex **SERVICES:** Lift **NOTES:** Closed 23 - 25 Dec **CARDS:**

ENNISKILLEN, Co Fermanagh

Map 01 C5

★★★★ 72% Killyhevlin
BT74 6RW
☎ 028 6632 3481 Fax 028 6632 4726
e-mail: info@killyhevlin.com web: www.killyhevlin.com
Dir: *2m S, off A4*

A modern, stylish hotel located on the shores of Lough Erne, just south of the town. Bedrooms are particularly spacious, well equipped, and many enjoy fine views. An open-plan restaurant and informal bar complement the comfortable lounges. Staff throughout are friendly and helpful.

ROOMS: 43 en suite (32 fmly) (9 GF) in 12 bedrooms s £67.50-£80; d £95-£120 (incl. bkfst) **LB** **FACILITIES:** STV Fishing Leisure club due to open early 2005 ch fac Xmas **CONF:** BC Thtr 600 Class 350 Board 150 Del from £110 **PARKING:** 500 **NOTES:** Closed 25 Dec **CARDS:**

FERMOY, Co Cork

Map 01 B2

★★★ 71% *Castlehyde Hotel*
Castlehyde
☎ 025 31865 Fax 025 31485
e-mail: cashyde@iol.ie
Dir: *off N8 just outside Fermoy onto N72 Fermoy-Mallow. Hotel in 2m*

Carefully restored 18th-century courtyard buildings. Individual, attractive bedrooms include five cottage suites. The welcoming lobby lounge features an open fire and there is a stylish restaurant overlooking the gardens and woodland.

ROOMS: 24 en suite (5 fmly) in 10 bedrooms **FACILITIES:** STV **CONF:** Thtr 30 Class 18 Board 14 **PARKING:** 35 **NOTES:** in restaurant RS Feb **CARDS:**

FOXFORD, Co Mayo

Map 01 B4

★★ 64% Healys Restaurant & Country House Hotel
Pontoon
☎ 094 9256443 Fax 094 9256572
e-mail: info@healyspontoon.com

This attractive creeper-clad former shooting lodge is now a comfortable and friendly hotel with a great view of Lough Cullen. Both the bar and restaurant serve enjoyable meals. Bedrooms are cosy and comfortable.

ROOMS: 14 en suite (1 fmly) s €59-€79; d €98-€138 (incl. bkfst) **FACILITIES:** Fishing Xmas **PARKING:** 300 **NOTES:** in restaurant Closed 25 Dec **CARDS:**

GALWAY, Co Galway

Map 01 B3

★★★★ 77% Glenlo Abbey
Bushypark
☎ 091 526666 Fax 091 527800
e-mail: info@glennabbey.ie
Dir: *4km from Galway city centre on N59*

This cut-stone Abbey was built in 1740 and has been lovingly restored to its original glory and features sculpted cornices and fine antique furniture. There is an elegant drawing room, a cocktail bar, a library, the delightful River Room restaurant and a cellar bar. The unique Orient Express Pullman Restaurant provides a second dining option. Bedrooms are in the modern wing and are spacious and well appointed.

ROOMS: 46 en suite in all bedrooms s €145-€250; d €195-€370 **LB** **FACILITIES:** STV 18 Fishing Putt green Boating, Clay pigeon shooting, Archery ch fac Xmas **CONF:** BC Thtr 220 Class 100 Board 50 Del from €250 **SERVICES:** Lift **PARKING:** 150 **NOTES:** in restaurant **CARDS:**

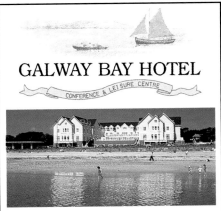

★★★★ 72% Radisson SAS Hotel
Lough Atalia Rd
☎ 091 538300 Fax 091 538380
e-mail: sales.galway@radissonsas.com
Dir: *take N6 into Galway City. At Hunstman Inn rdbt turn 1st left. At next traffic lights take left side of fork. Continue for 0.5m, hotel at next right junct*

In a prime position on the waterfront at Lough Atalia, striking interior design and excellent levels of quality and comfort are the keynotes of this hotel. Bedrooms come in a range of styles and are all well equipped. The leisure and corporate facilities are particularly good, with complimentary underground car parking available.

ROOMS: 217 en suite (7 fmly) in 132 bedrooms s €130-€180; d €150-€200 **FACILITIES: Spa** STV supervised Sauna Solarium Gym Putt green Jacuzzi Outdoor Canadian Hot-tub ch fac Xmas **CONF:** BC Thtr 750 Class 540 Board 40 Del from €250 **SERVICES:** Lift air con **PARKING:** 260 **NOTES:** in restaurant **CARDS:**

★★★★ 69% Ardilaun Conference & Leisure Centre
Taylor's Hill
☎ 091 521433 Fax 091 521546
e-mail: info@ardilaunhousehotel.ie
Dir: *Take N6 to Galway City West, then follow signs for N59 Clifden and then N6 towards Salthill*

Located in five acres of private grounds and landscaped gardens, the original Ardilaun House was built in 1840 and converted to a hotel in 1962. The bedrooms have been thoughtfully equipped and pleasantly furnished. Public areas include an elegant

continued on p862

GALWAY, continued

restaurant overlooking the garden, comfortable lounges and bar and there are extensive banqueting and leisure facilities.
ROOMS: 89 en suite (7 fmly) ⊘ in 20 bedrooms s €110-€145; d €180-€260 (incl. bkfst) **LB** **FACILITIES: Spa** STV supervised Snooker Sauna Solarium Gym Jacuzzi Treatment & Analysis Rooms, beauty salon ♫ Xmas **CONF:** Thtr 400 Class 200 Board 60 Del from €170 **SERVICES:** Lift **PARKING:** 240 **NOTES:** ⊘ in restaurant Closed 22-27 Dec **CARDS:**

★★★★69% Galway Bay Hotel Conference & Leisure Centre

The Promenade, Salthill
☎ 091 520520 091 520530
e-mail: info@galwaybayhotel.net
Dir: *on coast road to Connemara. Follow signs to Salthill from all major routes*

This smart modern hotel enjoys a most spectacular location overlooking Galway Bay and most bedrooms, lounges and the restaurant enjoy these views. There are two dining options, fine dining in the Lobster Pot and the less formal Café Lido. Conference/banqueting and leisure facilities are impressive.
ROOMS: 153 en suite (10 fmly) (8 GF) ⊘ in 24 bedrooms s €75-€175; d €110-€240 (incl. bkfst) **LB** **FACILITIES:** STV Sauna Gym Steam room, beauty salon ♫ Xmas **CONF:** BC Thtr 1100 Class 325 **SERVICES:** Lift air con **PARKING:** 300 **NOTES:**
CARDS:

See advert on page 861

★★★★65% *Park House Hotel & Park Room Restaurant*

Forster St, Eyre Square
☎ 091 564924 091 569219
e-mail: parkhousehotel@eircom.net
Dir: *in city centre*

This centre-city property offers well decorated and comfortable bedrooms which vary in size. The spacious restaurant has been a popular spot for the people of Galway for many years.
ROOMS: 57 en suite **FACILITIES:** STV ♫ **CONF:** Thtr 50 Class 30 Board 30 **SERVICES:** Lift **PARKING:** 26 **NOTES:** Closed 24-26 Dec
CARDS:

★★★★65% Westwood House Hotel

Dangan, Upper Newcastle
☎ 091 521442 091 521400
e-mail: reservations@westwoodhousehotel.com
Dir: *from N6 enter Galway, continue on N6 following signs for Clifden (N59). Hotel is on left*

Close to the university, this modern hotel is luxuriously appointed. The public areas include a themed bar popular with locals, a comfortable restaurant and conference suites. A range of bedroom options is available, well decorated in rich colours.
ROOMS: 58 en suite (44 fmly) ⊘ in 17 bedrooms s €110-€140; d €150-€199 (incl. bkfst) **LB** **FACILITIES:** STV Arrangement with local health and leisure club **CONF:** Thtr 350 Class 200 Board 70 **SERVICES:** Lift air con **PARKING:** 130 **NOTES:** ⊘ in restaurant Closed 24-25 Dec Civ Wed 275 **CARDS:**

★★★66% The Harbour

The Harbour
☎ 091 569466 091 569455
e-mail: stay@harbour.ie
Dir: *follow signs for Galway City East, at rdbt take 1st exit to Galway City, follow signs to docks, hotel approx 1m from rdbt on left*

This hotel is situated on the newly developed Galway Harbour in the heart of the city. Contemporary in style, with a large lobby lounge with generous seating and open fires. Krusoes café bar and restaurant offers modern cuisine. Bedrooms are smartly furnished, comfortable and well equipped. Guests have the benefit of complimentary secure car parking at the rear.
ROOMS: 96 en suite ⊘ in 34 bedrooms s €99-€220; d €118-€350 (incl. bkfst) **LB** **FACILITIES: Spa** STV Gym Jacuzzi ♫ Xmas **CONF:** Thtr 80 Class 35 Board 25 **SERVICES:** Lift **PARKING:** 64 **NOTES:** ⊘ in restaurant Closed 23-27 Dec **CARDS:**

★★★65% *Menlo Park Hotel*

THE INDEPENDENTS

Terryland
☎ 091 761122 091 761222
e-mail: menlopkh@iol.ie
web: www.menloparkhotel.com
Dir: *at Terryland rdbt off N6 and N84 (Castlebar Rd)*

This hotel's location on the outskirts of the city makes it equally well suited to both tourists and business guests. Bedrooms are spacious, well appointed and offer a choice of standard and executive rooms. The restaurant, bar and lounge are comfortably furnished. Conference facilities and ample car parking available.
ROOMS: 64 en suite (6 fmly) ⊘ in 10 bedrooms **FACILITIES:** STV ♫ **CONF:** Thtr 350 Class 190 Board 40 **SERVICES:** Lift air con **PARKING:** 100 **NOTES:** Closed 24-25 Dec **CARDS:**

★★★65% *Oranmore Lodge*

Oranmore
☎ 091 794400 091 790227
e-mail: orlodge@eircom.net

This long-established hotel is well positioned for travellers on business in the greater Galway City area. Staff provide a warm welcome, and the bar and restaurant are popular with the local population. The bedrooms, which have been refurbished, are well appointed, and residents at the hotel are able to use the adjoining leisure centre.
ROOMS: 56 en suite (50 fmly) **FACILITIES: Spa** STV Sauna Solarium Gym Jacuzzi ♫ **CONF:** Thtr 200 Class 100 Board 50 **PARKING:** 150 **NOTES:** Closed 22-27 Dec **CARDS:**

★★★ 61% **Brennans Yard**
Lower Merchants Rd
☎ 091 568166 Fax 091 568262
e-mail: info@brennansyardhotel.com
This friendly hotel is situated in the city centre close to the shops and business districts. All the bedrooms are individually furnished with antique pine furniture. Terry's restaurant has a wide range of options including Japanese dishes on some nights. The Spanish Bar offers an intimate, warm and lively atmosphere.
ROOMS: 45 en suite s €79-€127; d €99-€177 (incl. bkfst) LB
FACILITIES: STV ♫ **SERVICES:** Lift **NOTES:** in restaurant Closed 21-28 Dec **CARDS:**
See advert on this page

★★★ 60% **Lochlurgain**
22 Monksfield, Upper Salthill
☎ 091 529595 Fax 091 522399
e-mail: lochlurgain@eircom.net
Dir: *off R336 behind Bank of Ireland beside RC church*
This small family-run hotel stands in a quiet street, at Salthill, beside the Roman Catholic church. Service is of a very good standard and the bedrooms are comfortable, extras include electric blankets in colder months. Public rooms are attractively decorated.
ROOMS: 13 en suite (3 fmly) s €50-€95; d €90-€160 (incl. bkfst) LB
FACILITIES: STV **PARKING:** 8 **NOTES:** in restaurant Closed 26 Oct-13 Mar **CARDS:**

★★★ 59% ***Jurys Galway Inn***
JURYS DOYLE HOTELS
Quay St
☎ 091 566444 Fax 091 568415
e-mail: enquiry@jurys.com
Dir: *N6 follow signs for Docks. Then follow Salthill Rd for 2-3mins*
This modern hotel stands in the heart of the city, opposite the famous Spanish Arch. The hotel has an attractive patio by the river and a popular bar and restaurant. The room-only rate is ideal for families and budget travellers.
ROOMS: 128 en suite (6 fmly) in 39 bedrooms **FACILITIES:** STV ♫
CONF: Thtr 40 Class 40 Board 40 **SERVICES:** Lift **NOTES:** Closed 24-26 Dec **CARDS:**

★★★ 59% ***Victoria***
Victoria Place, Eyre Square
☎ 091 567433 Fax 091 565880
e-mail: bookings@victoriahotel.ie
Dir: *off Eyre Sq on Victoria Place, beside the rail station*
This city centre hotel lies off Eyre Square and very close to the railway station and the shopping area. Bedrooms are well equipped and other facilities include a good bar and pleasant restaurant. The atmosphere is relaxing and staff are friendly and attentive.
ROOMS: 57 en suite (20 fmly) in 1 bedroom **FACILITIES:** STV
CONF: Thtr 50 Class 30 Board 25 **SERVICES:** Lift **NOTES:** Closed 25 Dec **CARDS:**

⌂ **Travelodge**
Travelodge
Tuam Rd
☎ 08700 850 950
Travelodge offers good quality, good value, modern accommodation. Ideal for families, the spacious, en suite bedrooms include remote-control TV, tea and coffee-making facilities and luxury beds. Meals can be taken at the nearby family restaurant. For further details consult the Hotel Groups page.

Bad hair day?
Hairdryers in all rooms three stars and above

GARRYVOE, Co Cork
Map 01 C2

★★ 67% **Garryvoe**
IRISH COUNTRY HOTELS
☎ 021 4646718 Fax 021 4646824
e-mail: garryvoehotel@eircom.net
Dir: *off N25 onto L72 at Castlemartyr between Midleton and Youghal and continue for 6km*
A comfortable, family-run hotel with caring staff, the Garryvoe has been upgraded. It stands in a delightful position facing a sandy beach and the first-floor lounge overlooks the sea. There is a hotel bar and also a public bar.
ROOMS: 38 en suite (6 fmly) in 30 bedrooms s €82-€87; d €114-€124 (incl. bkfst) LB **FACILITIES:** STV Putt green ♫ ch fac
CONF: Thtr 300 Class 150 Board 12 Del from €100 **SERVICES:** Lift
PARKING: 40 **NOTES:** in restaurant Closed 25 Dec
CARDS:

GLENDALOUGH, Co Wicklow
Map 01 D3

★★★ 63% ***The Glendalough***
☎ 0404 45135 Fax 0404 45142
e-mail: info@glendaloughhotel.ie
Dir: *N11 to Kilmacongue, right onto R755, straight on at Caragh then right onto R756*
Mountains and forest provide the setting for this long-established hotel at the edge of the famed monastic site. Refurbishment has now been carried out and many of the well-appointed bedrooms have superb views. Bar food is served daily in the very popular bar while relaxing dinners are served in the charming restaurant that overlooks the river and forest.
ROOMS: 44 en suite (3 fmly) **FACILITIES:** STV Fishing ♫ **CONF:** Thtr 200 Class 150 Board 50 **SERVICES:** Lift **PARKING:** 100 **NOTES:** Closed Dec-Jan **CARDS:**

GOREY, Co Wexford
Map 01 D3

★★★★66% Ashdown Park Hotel
The Coach Rd
☎ 055 80500 055 80777
e-mail: info@ashdownparkhotel.com
Dir: *from N11, towards Gorey, 1st left before railway bridge, hotel on left*
Situated on an elevated position overlooking the town, this modern hotel has excellent health, leisure and banqueting facilities. There are comfortable lounges and two dining options - the popular carvery bar and first-floor, fine dining restaurant. Bedrooms are spacious and well equipped. Close to golf courses, beaches and hill walking.
ROOMS: 60 en suite (12 fmly) (20 GF) s €115-€130; d €160-€200 (incl. bkfst) **LB FACILITIES:** supervised Sauna Solarium Gym Jacuzzi Steam & Therapy rooms, Beauty salon **CONF:** Thtr 800 Class 315 Board 100 **SERVICES:** Lift **PARKING:** 150 **NOTES:** in restaurant Closed 24-25 Dec **CARDS:**

G

Top 200 – Hotel

★★★ Marlfield House
☎ 055 21124 055 21572
e-mail: info@marlfieldhouse.ie
Dir: *off N11, 1 mile outside Gorey on the Courtown Road*
RELAIS & CHATEAUX
This Regency-style building has been sympathetically extended and developed into an excellent hotel. An atmosphere of elegance and luxury permeates every corner of the house, underpinned by truly friendly yet professional service led by the Bowe family who are always in evidence. The bedrooms are decorated in keeping with the style of the house, with some really spacious rooms and suites on the ground floor. Dinner in the restaurant is always a highlight of a stay at Marlfield.
ROOMS: 20 en suite (3 fmly) (6 GF) in all bedrooms **FACILITIES:** STV Sauna **CONF:** Thtr 60 Board 20 **PARKING:** 50 **NOTES:** in restaurant Closed 15 Dec-30 Jan **CARDS:**

GOUGANE BARRA, Co Cork
Map 01 B2

★★66% *Gougane Barra*
☎ 026 47069 026 47226
e-mail: gouganbarrahotel@tinet.ie
Dir: *off N22*
IRISH COUNTRY HOTELS
Right on the shore of the lake, this hotel is very popular. Refurbishments have improved the restaurant, bedrooms and bathrooms, all of which have lovely views. Guests can be met from their train, boat or plane by prior arrangement.
ROOMS: 27 en suite **FACILITIES:** STV Fishing **PARKING:** 25 **NOTES:** in restaurant Closed 13 Oct-13 Apr **CARDS:**

HOWTH, Co Dublin
Map 01 D4

★★★67% Deer Park Hotel & Golf Courses
☎ 01 8322624 01 8392405
e-mail: sales@deerpark.iol.ie
IRISH COUNTRY HOTELS
Dir: *follow coast road from Dublin via Clontarf. Through Sutton Cross pass Offington Park. Hotel 0.5m after traffic lights on right*
This modern hotel is situated in 400 acres overlooking Dublin Bay and within easy reach of Dublin City and Airport. The spacious well-equipped bedrooms have spectacular views, the Four Earls Restaurant is famous for fresh fish from Howth Harbour and there a lively bar and bistro. Guests can enjoy the leisure centre, all-weather tennis courts and have a choice of golf courses right on their door step.
ROOMS: 80 en suite (4 fmly) (36 GF) s €70-€114; d €120-€176 (incl. bkfst) **LB FACILITIES: Spa** supervised 18 Sauna Putt green **CONF:** Thtr 95 Class 60 Board 25 **PARKING:** 200 **NOTES:** in restaurant Closed 23-26 Dec **CARDS:**

INNISHANNON, Co Cork
Map 01 B2

★★★65% *Innishannon House*
☎ 021 4775121 021 4775609
e-mail: info@innishannon-hotel.ie
MANOR HOUSE HOTELS
Dir: *off N71 at eastern end of village, left onto Kinsale road, hotel right about 1m along this route*
This charming country house was built in 1720 in a beautiful location in lovely gardens that run down to the banks of the River Bandon close to Kinsale. Public areas are comfortable and there is a relaxed atmosphere. Bedrooms range from cosy and charming to large and gracious.
ROOMS: 12 en suite (4 fmly) **FACILITIES:** STV Fishing **CONF:** BC Thtr 200 Class 80 Board 50 **PARKING:** 100 **NOTES:** in restaurant Closed 22-26 Dec **CARDS:**

IRVINESTOWN, Co Fermanagh
Map 01 C5

★★63% Mahons
Mill St BT94 1GS
☎ 028 6862 1656 028 6862 8344
e-mail: info@mahonshotel.co.uk
Dir: *on A32 midway between Enniskillen and Omagh - beside town clock in town centre*
This family-run hotel has been in the same ownership and offering friendly hospitality for well over 100 years. Public areas, especially the bar, have a wealth of charm and character. In the restaurant, the extensive menu offers a wide range of dishes. The prettily decorated bedrooms come in a variety of sizes.
ROOMS: 24 en suite (10 fmly) (1 GF) in 2 bedrooms s £35-£37.50; d £60-£70 (incl. bkfst) **LB FACILITIES:** STV Riding Solarium ch fac **CONF:** Thtr 400 Class 250 Board 100 Del from £45 **SERVICES:** air con **PARKING:** 40 **NOTES:** Closed 25 Dec **CARDS:**

KENMARE, Co Kerry
Map 01 B2

Top 200 – Hotel

★★★★ Park Hotel Kenmare
☎ 064 41200 064 41402
e-mail: info@parkkenmare.com
Dir: *on R569 beside golf course at top of town*
The Park Hotel Kenmare is a luxurious house, on the famed Ring of Kerry, that has been welcoming guests for over 100

continued

years. Warm hospitality and professional service come naturally to all the team, who endeavor to make you feel pampered. The suites and bedrooms are all spacious and very well appointed, and many of them have sea views. The elegant Restaurant serves fine wines and excellent cuisine, much of which is locally sourced.

ROOMS: 49 en suite (2 fmly) in 5 bedrooms s €185-€230; d €295-€410 (incl. bkfst) **LB** **FACILITIES: Spa** STV 18 Snooker Sauna Solarium Gym Putt green Jacuzzi Beauty Suite, Tai Chi Pavilion Xmas **CONF:** Thtr 60 Class 40 Board 28 **SERVICES:** Lift **PARKING:** 60 **NOTES:** in restaurant Closed 1-23 Dec & 2 Jan-14 Feb Civ Wed 120 **CARDS:**

Top 200 – Hotel

★★★★ Sheen Falls Lodge

☎ 064 41600 064 41386
e-mail: info@sheenfallslodge.ie
Dir: *from Kenmare take N71 to Glengarriff over suspension bridge, take 1st turn left*

This former fishing lodge has been developed into a beautiful hotel run by an amenable team of staff. The cascading Sheen Falls are floodlit at night, forming a romantic backdrop to the enjoyment of award-winning cuisine in La Cascade restaurant. Bedrooms are very comfortably appointed, many of the suites are particularly spacious. The leisure centre and beauty therapy facilities offer a number of exclusive treatments.
ROOMS: 66 en suite (14 fmly) (14 GF) in 10 bedrooms d €275-€415 **LB** **FACILITIES:** STV Fishing Riding Snooker Sauna Solarium Gym Jacuzzi Table tennis,steam room,clay pigeon shooting,cycling,vintage car rides,library ch fac Xmas **CONF:** BC Thtr 120 Class 65 Board 50 **SERVICES:** Lift **PARKING:** 76 **NOTES:** in restaurant Closed 2 Jan-1 Feb RS December **CARDS:**

KILKEE, Co Clare — Map 01 B3

★★64% Halpin's

Erin St
☎ 065 9056032 065 9056317
e-mail: halpinstownhouse@iol.ie
Dir: *in centre of town*

The finest tradition of hotel service is offered at this family-run hotel which has a commanding view over the old Victorian town. The attractive bedrooms are comfortable.
ROOMS: 12 en suite (6 fmly) in 4 bedrooms **FACILITIES:** STV **CONF:** Thtr 60 Class 36 Board 30 **SERVICES:** air con **PARKING:** 3 **NOTES:** Closed 16 Nov-14 Mar **CARDS:**

KILKENNY, Co Kilkenny — Map 01 C3

★★★★70% Kilkenny River Court Hotel

The Bridge, John St
☎ 056 772 3388 056 772 3389
e-mail: reservations@kilrivercourt.com
Dir: *at bridge in town centre, opposite Kilkenny Castle, on River Nore side of castle*

Once through the entrance archway, this superb establishment really is a revelation. The restaurant, bar and many of the well-equipped bedrooms command great views of the River Nore and Kilkenny Castle. Attentive, friendly staff ensure good service in all areas. Excellent corporate and leisure facilities are provided.
ROOMS: 90 en suite (4 fmly) in 20 bedrooms **FACILITIES:** STV supervised Sauna Gym Jacuzzi Beauty Salon **CONF:** Thtr 260 Class 110 Board 45 **SERVICES:** Lift **PARKING:** 84 **NOTES:** in restaurant Closed 24-26 Dec **CARDS:**

★★★73% Newpark

☎ 056 776 0500 056 776 0555
e-mail: info@newparkhotel.com

Following a major investment programme, this hotel offers a range of well appointed rooms, to match the impressive foyer lounge, leisure club and other public areas. Renowned for the friendliness of the staff, there is also a choice of two dining rooms, The Bistro and Gulliver's, a more formal option.
ROOMS: 111 en suite (42 fmly) in 8 bedrooms **FACILITIES:** STV Sauna Solarium Gym Jacuzzi Plunge pool **CONF:** Thtr 600 Class 300 Board 50 **PARKING:** 350 **NOTES:** in restaurant **CARDS:**

★★★64% Langtons

69 John St
☎ 056 776 5133 056 776 3693
e-mail: reservations@langtons.ie
Dir: *take N9 & N10 from Dublin follow signs for city centre at outskirts of Kilkenny turn to left Langtons 500mtrs on left after 1st set of lights*

Langton's has a long and well founded reputation as an entertainment venue and bar. These facilities are now complemented by a range of accommodation, all very comfortably decorated and well appointed. The busy restaurant is popular with visitors and locals alike.
ROOMS: 14 en suite 16 annexe en suite (4 fmly) (8 GF) s €65-€80; d €160-€220 (incl. bkfst) **LB** **FACILITIES:** STV **CONF:** Thtr 600 Class 300 Board 50 **PARKING:** 60 **NOTES:** Closed Good Fri, 25 Dec **CARDS:**

Entertainment

K

KILKENNY, continued

Restaurant with Rooms

Lacken House & Restaurant

Dublin Rd
056 7761085 056 7762435
e-mail: info@lackenhouse.ie
Dir: *In city at start of N10 Dublin/Carlow road*

Located just five minutes' walk from the city, this fine Victorian house offers comfortable accommodation in a friendly and relaxing atmosphere. The restaurant, open from Tuesday to Saturday, has an interesting menu using carefully chosen local produce. An ideal base to explore the historic sites of Kilkenny, and Mount Juliet Golf course is nearby.

ROOMS: 11 en suite (2 fmly) (4 GF) s €75-€200; d €120-€250 (incl. bkfst) LB **FACILITIES: Spa** STV **CONF:** Thtr 25 Class 20 Board 12 Del from €125 **PARKING:** 25 **NOTES:** Closed 24-26 Dec
CARDS:

KILL, Co Kildare — Map 01 D4

★★★59% *Ambassador*

045 877064 045 877515
e-mail: ambassador-sales@quinn-hotels.com
Dir: *close to Dublin centre on N7 S*

Immediately south of Kill village, close to Goffs Sales Complex, racecourse and Mondello Park this hotel offers an all-day lounge carvery. The Restaurant is closed Mondays and Tuesdays but dinner is served in the grill room. Bedrooms are well equipped and comfortable and there are conference and syndicate rooms available.

ROOMS: 36 en suite (36 fmly) **FACILITIES:** STV **CONF:** Thtr 260 Class 140 Board 60 **PARKING:** 150 **NOTES:**
CARDS:

KILLARNEY, Co Kerry — Map 01 B2

Top 200 – Hotel

★★★★ Aghadoe Heights

064 31766 064 31345
e-mail: info@aghadoeheights.com
Dir: *16km S of Kerry Airport and 5km N of Killarney. Signed off N22 Tralee road*

Superbly positioned overlooking Loch Lein with spectacular views of the Kerry Mountains, this hotel has been refurbished and extended to a very high standard. The warmth of the professional staff makes for a very relaxing stay. Many of the bedrooms also have sun decks that make the most of the panoramic scene. A health spa has now been added.

ROOMS: 75 en suite (6 fmly) in 10 bedrooms s €200-€280; d €200-€280 (incl. bkfst) LB **FACILITIES: Spa** STV Fishing Sauna Solarium Gym Jacuzzi The Heights spa, treatment rooms, thermal suites Xmas **CONF:** BC Thtr 120 Class 60 Board 40 **SERVICES:** Lift **PARKING:** 120 **NOTES:** in restaurant
CARDS:

Top 200 – Hotel

★★★★ Killarney Park

Kenmare Place
064 35555 064 35266
e-mail: info@killarneyparkhotel.ie
Dir: *N22 from Cork to Killarney. At 1st rdbt take 1st exit to town centre and at 2nd rdbt take 2nd exit, 3rd rdbt take 1st exit. Hotel 2nd entrance left*

This charming hotel on the edge of the town combines elegance with comfort. It has a warm atmosphere with open fires, restful colours and friendly caring staff who ensure your stay is an enjoyable one. Bedrooms and suites are spacious and many have air conditioning and open fires. A health spa has been developed to further enhance the leisure facilities. Nominated for the AA Hotel of the Year Award for the Republic of Ireland 2004-5.

ROOMS: 72 en suite (4 fmly) in 49 bedrooms s €250-€370; d €250-€370 (incl. bkfst) LB **FACILITIES: Spa** STV Snooker Sauna Gym Jacuzzi Outdoor Canadian hot-tub Plunge pool, Caldarium, Relaxation room Xmas **CONF:** BC Thtr 150 Class 70 Board 35 **SERVICES:** Lift air con **PARKING:** 70 **NOTES:** in restaurant Closed 24-26 Dec **CARDS:**

★★★★70% *Randles Court*

Muckross Rd
064 35333 064 35206
e-mail: info@randlescourt.com
Dir: *N22 towards Muckross, turn tight at T-junct on right. From N72 take 3rd exit on 1st rdbt into town & follow signs for Muckross, hotel on left*

This comfortable family-run hotel is conveniently situated close to all the town's attractions. The emphasis is on friendliness and guest care. The relaxing public areas include a drawing room, leisure centre and a choice of two dining options. Bedrooms range in size and are all well appointed. Facilities for pets can be made with advance notice.

ROOMS: 52 en suite **FACILITIES:** STV Sauna Gym Putt green **CONF:** Thtr 80 Class 60 Board 40 **SERVICES:** Lift **PARKING:** 39 **NOTES:** Closed 23-27 Dec **CARDS:**

★★★★ 69% Cahernane House

Muckross Rd
☎ 064 31895 Fax 064 34340
e-mail: cahernane@eircom.net
web: www.cahernane.com

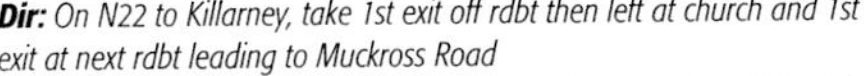

Dir: *On N22 to Killarney, take 1st exit off rdbt then left at church and 1st exit at next rdbt leading to Muckross Road*

This fine country mansion, former home of the Earls of Pembroke, has a magnificent mountain backdrop and panoramic views from its lakeside setting. Elegant period furniture is complemented by more modern pieces to create a comfortable hotel with a warm atmosphere. The staff are friendly.

ROOMS: 12 en suite 26 annexe en suite s €105-€130; d €145-€205 (incl. bkfst) LB **FACILITIES:** Fishing ch fac **CONF:** Thtr 15 Class 10 Board 10 **SERVICES:** Lift air con **PARKING:** 50 **NOTES:** in restaurant Closed 21 Dec-31 Jan **CARDS:**

★★★★ 69% Muckross Park Hotel

Muckross Village
☎ 064 31938 Fax 064 31965
e-mail: muckrossparkhotel@eircom.net

Dir: *from Killarney take road to Kenmare, hotel 4km on left, adjacent to National Park, Muckross House & Gardens*

Offering hospitality since 1795, this comfortable hotel is located a few kilometres from the centre of the town amid well-tended gardens. Spacious bedrooms are individually designed. Informal dining is available in the popular Molly Drake's pub throughout the day, with dinner served in GB Shaw's Restaurant.

ROOMS: 27 en suite (2 fmly) in 2 bedrooms s €120; d €170 (incl. bkfst) LB **FACILITIES:** STV Jacuzzi **CONF:** Thtr 200 Class 80 Board 40 Del from €145 **PARKING:** 250 **NOTES:** in restaurant Closed Dec-Feb Civ Wed 170 **CARDS:**

★★★ 70% *Gleneagle*

☎ 064 36000 Fax 064 32646
e-mail: info@gleneaglehotel.com

Dir: *1m outside Killarney town on the Kenmare Road - N71*

The facilities at this large hotel are excellent and numerous. Family entertainment is a strong element of the Gleneagle experience, popular with the Irish market for almost 50 years. Comfortable rooms are matched with a range lounges, leisure centre and INEC, one of Ireland's largest events' centres.

ROOMS: 250 en suite (57 fmly) in 20 bedrooms **FACILITIES:** STV Squash Snooker Sauna Gym Jacuzzi Pitch & Putt Table tennis Steam room **CONF:** Thtr 2500 Class 1000 Board 50 **SERVICES:** Lift **PARKING:** 500 **CARDS:**

★★★ 69% Lake

Muckross Rd
☎ 064 31035 Fax 064 31902
e-mail: lakehotel@eircom.net

Dir: *on Kenmare road out of Killarney*

Set on Killarney's lakeshore this family run hotel offers a relaxed and friendly atmosphere with views of the mountains, a former mansion it is approached by a wooded drive. Bedrooms are well appointed, some with four-poster beds and Jacuzzis. The comfortable lounges and bar have open log fires and guests can enjoy the stunning views from the attractive restaurant.

ROOMS: 69 rms (65 en suite) (6 fmly) (9 GF) s €45-€220; d €90-€240 (incl. bkfst) LB **FACILITIES: Spa** STV Fishing Sauna Gym Putt green Jacuzzi out door hot tub ch fac **CONF:** Thtr 80 Class 60 Board 40 **SERVICES:** Lift air con **PARKING:** 140 **NOTES:** in restaurant Closed 18 Dec-10 Feb **CARDS:**

See advert on this page

★★★ 68% Castlerosse

☎ 064 31144 Fax 064 31031
e-mail: castler@iol.ie

Dir: *from Killarney town take R562 for Killorglin and The Ring of Kerry, hotel 1.5km from town on left*

Located on 6,000 acres overlooking the Lakes of Killarney and the golf course, this hotel can offer some rooms with breathtaking views. Leisure guests find the Castleross very welcoming and relaxing. The newly refurbished restaurant also enjoys the panoramic view.

ROOMS: 121 en suite (27 fmly) in 4 bedrooms s €60-€110; d €90-€170 (incl. bkfst) LB **FACILITIES:** supervised 9 Sauna Gym Jacuzzi Golfing & riding arranged **CONF:** Thtr 200 Class 100 Board 40 **SERVICES:** Lift **PARKING:** 100 **NOTES:** in restaurant Closed Dec-Feb **CARDS:**

KILLARNEY, continued

★★★68% International

East Avenue Rd
☎ 064 31816 ▯ 064 31837
e-mail: inter@iol.ie
Dir: *take N21 from Limerick to Farranfore, N22 from Farranfore to Killarney, turn right at 1st rdbt entering Killarney follow town bypass road*
Quality bedrooms with modern comforts are on offer at this warm and friendly hotel. Hannigan's bar and brasserie serves food throughout the day, with an inviting mahogany-panelled room open in the evenings. Relaxing lounge areas include a snooker room and a library.
ROOMS: 80 en suite (6 fmly) ⊘ in 30 bedrooms s €65-€95; d €95-€150 (incl. bkfst) **LB** **FACILITIES:** STV Billiards ♫ ch fac **CONF:** Thtr 200 Class 100 Board 25 **SERVICES:** Lift **NOTES:** ⊘ in restaurant Closed 23-27 Dec **CARDS:**

★★★66% *Killarney Royal*

College St
☎ 064 318543 ▯ 064 34001
This charming hotel is situated in the heart of Killarney and has been run by the Scally family for three generations. Bedrooms and junior suites are individually decorated with antique furniture and many thoughtful extras. Comfortable public areas include a lounge, spacious restaurant and a cosy bar.
ROOMS: 29 rms

K

★★★66% *Killarney Ryan*

Cork Rd
☎ 064 31555 ▯ 064 32438
e-mail: info@killarneyryan.com

On the outskirts of Killarney, this hotel offers good standards of comfort. Public rooms include a large lounge, a restaurant and lounge bar opening on to the gardens. Many of the bedrooms can accommodate families, and the Ryan Group offer an all-inclusive summer holiday rate which can be good value.
ROOMS: 168 en suite (164 fmly) ⊘ in 60 bedrooms **FACILITIES:** Snooker Sauna Jacuzzi Steam room Crazy golf Games room ♫ **SERVICES:** Lift **NOTES:** Closed Dec & Jan **CARDS:**

★★★64% *Arbutus*

College St
☎ 064 31037 ▯ 064 34033
e-mail: arbutushotel@eircom.net
Situated in the centre of the town, the Buckley family have run this smart hotel since 1926. Public areas include a comfortable foyer lounge, guest sitting room, traditional-style bar and restaurant. Staff are friendly and helpful.

ROOMS: 35 en suite (4 fmly) **FACILITIES:** STV **NOTES:** Closed 12 Dec-30 Jan **CARDS:**

See advert on opposite page

★★★64% White Gates

Muckross Rd
☎ 064 31164 ▯ 064 34850
e-mail: whitegates@iol.ie
Dir: *1km from Killarney town on Muckross road on left*
One's eye is drawn to this hotel with its ochre and blue painted frontage. The same flair with colour is in evidence throughout the interior where bedrooms of mixed sizes are well decorated and very comfortable. There is also a light filled restaurant, with casual dining in the bar, which has a popular local trade.
ROOMS: 27 en suite s €70-€90; d €120-€140 (incl. bkfst) **FACILITIES:** STV ♫ ch fac **CONF:** Class 50 **PARKING:** 50 **NOTES:** Closed 21-29 Dec **CARDS:**

★★★61% Darby O'Gills

Lissivigeen, Mallow Rd
☎ 064 34168 & 34919 ▯ 064 36794
e-mail: darbyogill@eircom.net
Dir: *turn off N22 (Cork road) to N72(Mallow)*

This modern hotel is situated just five minute's drive from the town centre it is an ideal location for touring the Ring of Kerry. Accommodation includes well-equipped bedrooms, Cluricaunes restaurant and traditional music is played in Darby's bar during the season.
ROOMS: 25 en suite (7 fmly) **FACILITIES:** STV ♫ Xmas **CONF:** Thtr 200 Board 100 **SERVICES:** air con **PARKING:** 150 **NOTES:** **CARDS:**

★★★ 59% *Scotts Garden Hotel*
College St
☎ 064 31060 📠 064 36656
e-mail: scottskill@eircom.net
Dir: *N20/N22 to town, at Friary go left. 500mtrs along on East Avenue Rd entrance to car park*

Located in the town centre, this hotel offers pleasant bedrooms, a bar and a patio garden. Special concessions are available at the leisure facilities in the sister hotel, Gleneagles.
ROOMS: 52 en suite (4 fmly) **FACILITIES:** ♫ **SERVICES:** Lift **PARKING:** 60 **NOTES:** ✈ ⊗ in restaurant Closed 24-25 Dec **CARDS:**

U The Brehon
Muckross Rd
☎ 064 30700 📠 064 30701
e-mail: info@thebrehon.com
Dir: *1m outside Killarney on N71*
At the time of going to press, the star classification for this hotel was not confirmed. Please refer to the AA internet site www.theAA.com for current information.
ROOMS: 125 en suite (3 fmly) ⊗ in 100 bedrooms s €110-€155; d €170-€260 (incl. bkfst) LB **FACILITIES: Spa** STV supervised Sauna Putt green Jacuzzi Thai Spa inc treatments and massages. ♫ **CONF:** BC Thtr 200 Class 60 Board 60 **SERVICES:** Lift air con **PARKING:** 126 **NOTES:** ✈ ⊗ in restaurant **CARDS:**

KILLINEY, Co Dublin — Map 01 D4

★★★★ 68% Fitzpatrick Castle
☎ 01 2305400 📠 01 2305430
e-mail: reservations@fitzpatricks.com
Dir: *from Dun Laoghaire port turn left, continue on coast road, turn right at lights, left at next lights. Follow road to Dalkey village, right at McDonaghs pub, immediate left, continue up hill, hotel at the top*
Situated on Killiney Hill, this converted castle has been extensively refurbished. Bedrooms are comfortable, many with stunning views of Dublin city and bay. Facilities include a large lounge, excellent leisure centre and a choice of restaurants. A range of conference and banqueting rooms are also available.
ROOMS: 113 en suite (42 fmly) ⊗ in 50 bedrooms s €180-€205; d €220-€245 LB **FACILITIES:** STV supervised Sauna Solarium Gym Jacuzzi Beauty/hairdressing salon, Steam room ♫ ch fac **CONF:** BC Thtr 400 Class 250 Board 80 Del from €216 **SERVICES:** Lift **PARKING:** 300 **NOTES:** ✈ ⊗ in restaurant **CARDS:**

AA Rosette Award for culinary excellence

KILMESSAN, Co Meath — Map 01 C/D4

★★★ 65% The Station House Hotel
☎ 046 9025239 📠 046 9025588
e-mail: info@thestationhousehotel.com
Dir: *M50, N3 towards Navan, to Dunshaughlin and turn left at end of village, follow signs*
The Station House saw its last train pass by in 1963, and is now a comfortable, family-run hotel with a popular restaurant. The Carriage House has been refurbished and new bedrooms added; the Signal Box houses a suite. There is a sun terrace and conference/banqueting suite.
ROOMS: 6 en suite 14 annexe en suite (3 fmly) (5 GF) ⊗ in 15 bedrooms s €85-€115; d €140-€190 (incl. bkfst) LB **FACILITIES:** ♫ Xmas **CONF:** BC Thtr 400 Class 300 Board 100 Del from €120 **PARKING:** 200 **NOTES:** ✈ **CARDS:**

KINSALE, Co Cork — Map 01 B2

★★★ 73% ® Actons
Pier Rd
☎ 021 4772135 📠 021 4772231
e-mail: info@actonshotelkinsale.com
Dir: *in town centre 500yds from Yacht Club Marina*
Located on a site overlooking the harbour, Actons is a well established hotel with a good reputation for its friendly and courteous staff. Bedrooms are well appointed and many of them

continued on p870

KINSALE, continued

enjoy sea views, as does the restaurant where enjoyable dinner is served. The adjoining leisure centre is well equipped.

Actons Hotel, Kinsale

ROOMS: 76 en suite (20 fmly) s €100-€140; d €140-€230 (incl. bkfst) **LB** **FACILITIES: Spa** STV supervised Sauna Solarium Gym Jacuzzi Aerobics studio, Outdoor hot tub, Steam room ♫ **CONF:** Thtr 300 Class 200 Board 100 Del from €145 **SERVICES:** Lift **PARKING:** 70 **NOTES:** in restaurant Closed 24-27 Dec
CARDS:

K

★★★69% Trident
Worlds End
☎ 021 4772301 021 4774173
e-mail: info@tridenthotel.com
Dir: *take R600 from Cork city to Kinsale, along Kinsale waterfront, hotel just beyond pier*

Located at the harbour's edge, the Trident Hotel has its own marina with boats for hire. Many of the bedrooms have superb views and two have balconies. The restaurant and lounge both overlook the harbour and pleasant staff provide hospitable service.
ROOMS: 58 en suite (2 fmly) **FACILITIES:** Sauna Gym Jacuzzi Steam room, Deep sea angling **CONF:** Thtr 220 Class 130 Board 40 **SERVICES:** Lift **PARKING:** 60 **NOTES:** Closed 24-26 Dec
CARDS:

★★★63% Blue Haven Hotel & Restaurant
3 Pearse St
☎ 021 4772209 021 4774268
e-mail: bluhaven@iol.ie
Dir: *in town centre*
Situated in the centre of this thriving town, the Blue Haven enjoys a busy food trade in the popular Fish Market Tavern, with more formal dinners in the restaurant that opens at weekends and at peak times. Compact bedrooms are cosily decorated and well equipped. The hotel provides very good customer care.

ROOMS: 17 en suite (2 fmly) in all bedrooms s €95-€178; d €140-€220 (incl. bkfst) **LB** **FACILITIES:** ♫ ch fac Xmas **CONF:** Thtr 50 Class 35 Board 25 **NOTES:** in restaurant
CARDS:

KNOCK, Co Mayo — Map 01 B4

★★★66% Knock House
Ballyhaunis Rd
☎ 094 938 8088 094 938 8044
e-mail: info@knockhousehotel.ie
Dir: *0.5km from Knock village*
Adjacent to the Marian Shrine and Basilica, this creatively designed limestone-clad building is surrounded by landscaped gardens. Facilities include comfortable lounges and bedrooms, a dispense bar, conference rooms and an attractive restaurant where lunch and dinner is served. There are six rooms adapted to facilitate wheelchair users.
ROOMS: 68 en suite (12 fmly) (40 GF) s €70-€89; d €104-€136 (incl. bkfst) **LB** **FACILITIES:** Xmas **CONF:** Thtr 150 Class 90 Board 45 **SERVICES:** Lift **PARKING:** 150 **NOTES:** **CARDS:**

★★★63% Belmont
☎ 094 938 8122 094 938 8532
e-mail: reception@belmonthotel.ie
Dir: *on N17, Galway side of Knock village. Turn right at Burke's supermarket & pub. Hotel 150yds on right*
This hotel, close to the Marian Shrine and the Basilica, has an Old World charm and offers lounges, a traditional bar and An Bialann Restaurant. Bedroom standards vary, but all are well appointed and comfortable. There is a specially adapted room for less able guests. A natural health and fitness club offers a range of therapies.
ROOMS: 63 en suite (6 fmly) in 3 bedrooms **FACILITIES:** Solarium Gym Jacuzzi Steamroom Natural health therapies ♫ **CONF:** Thtr 500 Class 100 Board 20 **SERVICES:** Lift air con **PARKING:** 110 **NOTES:** in restaurant Closed 25 & 26 Dec **CARDS:**

LEIXLIP, Co Kildare — Map 01 D4

★★★75% Leixlip House
Captains Hill
☎ 01 6242268 01 6244177
e-mail: info@leixliphouse.com
Dir: *from Leixlip motorway junct continue into village. Turn right at lights and continue up hill*
This Georgian house dates back to 1772 and retains many of its original features. Overlooking the village, the hotel is just eight miles from Dublin city centre. Bedrooms and public areas are

continued

furnished and decorated to a high standard. The Bradaun Restaurant offers a wide range of interesting dishes.
ROOMS: 19 en suite (2 fmly) s €135-€165; d €150-€190 (incl. bkfst) **LB** **FACILITIES:** STV **CONF:** Thtr 130 Class 60 Board 40 **PARKING:** 64 **NOTES:** ✈ ⊗ in restaurant **CARDS:**

LETTERKENNY, Co Donegal — Map 01 C5

★★★67% Castle Grove Country House

Castlegrove, Ballymaleel
☎ 074 915 1118 074 915 1384
e-mail: enquiries@castlegrove.com

This elegant Georgian house, set in a sheltered position and reached by a long avenue through parkland, enjoys spectacular views of Lough Swilly. Family-owned and friendly, true Irish hospitality is offered. The dining room serves dishes based on local produce. Bedrooms are spacious, equipped with modern necessities and furnished with fine antique pieces. Ideal for touring the north west.
ROOMS: 15 en suite ⊗ in 3 bedrooms **CONF:** Thtr 28 Class 12 Board 16 **PARKING:** 400 **NOTES:** ✈ No children 14yrs ⊗ in restaurant Closed Xmas/New Year RS Jan-May (closed Sun)
CARDS:

LIMAVADY, Co Londonderry — Map 01 C6

★★★★70% Radisson SAS Row Park Resort

Radisson SAS Hotels & Resorts

BT49 9LB
☎ 028 7772 2222 028 7772 2313
e-mail: reservations@radissonroepark.com
Dir: *on A2 Londonderry/Limavady road, 16m from Londonderry, 1m from Limavady*
This impressive, popular hotel sits centrally on its own modern golf resort. The spacious, up-to-date bedrooms are well equipped and many have excellent views of the fairways and estate. Greens Restaurant provides a refreshing dining experience and the Coach House brasserie offers a lighter menu. The leisure options are extensive.
ROOMS: 118 en suite (15 fmly) ⊗ in 76 bedrooms **FACILITIES:** STV supervised 18 Fishing Sauna Solarium Gym Putt green Jacuzzi Floodlit driving range, Outside tees, Golf training academy, Bicycle hire ♫ ch fac Xmas **CONF:** Thtr 450 Class 190 Board 140 Del from £90 **SERVICES:** Lift **PARKING:** 300 **NOTES:** ✈ Civ Wed 400
CARDS:

★★★68% Gorteen House

Deerpark, Roemill Rd BT49 9EX
☎ 028 7772 2333 028 7772 2333
e-mail: info@gorteen.com
Dir: *A2 Londonderry/Coleraine, 16m from Londonderry and 12m from Coleraine. 0.5m from town centre on Ballyquinn Road*
Situated on the outskirts of the town and popular as a function venue, this 18th-century country house has been converted and extended to provide pleasant public areas and a modern wing of bedrooms. The spacious restaurant enjoys a good local reputation for the size of the portions offered and for being value for money.
ROOMS: 26 en suite (2 fmly) (5 GF) s £48; d £65-£85 (incl. bkfst) **LB** **FACILITIES:** Snooker ♫ **CONF:** Thtr 350 Class 250 Board 100 **PARKING:** 250 **NOTES:** ✈ **CARDS:**

LIMERICK, Co Limerick — Map 01 B3

★★★★70% Castletroy Park

Dublin Rd
☎ 061 335566 061 331117
e-mail: sales@castletroy-park.ie
Dir: *on N7(main Dublin road), 3m from Limerick city, 25mins from Shannon International Airport*
This fine modern hotel is close to the University of Limerick. Public areas combine modern comforts with very attractive décor and include the Merry Pedler pub and the fine dining McLaughlins Restaurant, which has a splendid view of the gardens and Clare Hills. Bedrooms are very well equipped to suit both leisure and business guests. There are extensive leisure and banqueting facilities.
ROOMS: 107 en suite (78 fmly) ⊗ in 79 bedrooms **FACILITIES:** STV supervised Sauna Gym Jacuzzi Running track Steam room ♫ **CONF:** BC Thtr 450 Class 270 Board 100 **SERVICES:** Lift **PARKING:** 160 **NOTES:** ✈ **CARDS:**

★★★★68% Radisson SAS

Ennis Rd
☎ 061 326666 327418
e-mail: reservations.limerick@radissonsas.com
Dir: *on N18 Ennis road, 5mins from city centre*
15mins from Shannon Airport
Situated between Limerick city and Shannon International Airport this smart new hotel has comfortable lounge areas and a choice of dining options, the contemporary-style Porters Restaurant offers fine dining while more casual fair is available in Heron's Irish Pub. Bedrooms are spacious and very well appointed. There is extensive leisure and corporate facilities.
ROOMS: 154 en suite (7 fmly) ⊗ in 70 bedrooms s €90-€120; d €110-€130 (incl. bkfst) **FACILITIES: Spa** STV supervised Sauna Solarium Gym ♫ ch fac Xmas **CONF:** BC Thtr 500 Class 250 Board 50 Del €165 **SERVICES:** Lift air con **PARKING:** 300 **NOTES:** ✈ ⊗ in restaurant **CARDS:**

★★★★65% Clarion Hotel Limerick

Steamboat Quay
☎ 061 444100 061 444101
e-mail: info@clarionhotellimerick.com
Dir: *From Shannon Airport take N18 W to city, follow Cork/Kerry exit on 1st rdbt. On crossing Shannon Bridge take 3rd exit onto Dock Rd. Hotel 1st turn right.*
The Clarion has made an imposing mark on the skyline of Limerick, for its height and oval shape. The same sleek design is to be found throughout this hotel, with contemporary styling in the bedrooms and public areas alike. Rooms vary in size and are all well appointed. Some two-bedded apartments are available for those staying longer than a few nights.
ROOMS: 123 en suite (14 fmly) ⊗ in 97 bedrooms s €115-€190; d €115-€210 **LB** **FACILITIES:** STV supervised Sauna Gym Jacuzzi Steam room **CONF:** Thtr 120 Class 70 Board 45 Del €180 **SERVICES:** Lift air con **NOTES:** ✈ ⊗ in restaurant Closed 24-25 Dec RS 26 Dec **CARDS:**

> TV dinner?
> Room service at three stars and above

L

LIMERICK, continued

★★★73% *Jurys*
Ennis Rd
JURYS DOYLE HOTELS
☎ 061 327777 📠 061 326400
e-mail: bookings@jurys.com
Dir: *at junct of Ennis Rd, O'Callaghan Strand and Sarsfield Bridge*
This hotel is located on four acres on the banks of the River Shannon, in the heart of the city and just 15 miles from Shannon Airport. Bedrooms are spacious and well appointed. Public areas include comfortable lounges, contemporary bar and restaurant, extensive conference/banqueting and leisure facilities and outdoor tennis courts.
ROOMS: 95 en suite (22 fmly) ⊗ in 16 bedrooms **FACILITIES:** STV Sauna Gym Jacuzzi Steam room Plunge pool ♫ **CONF:** Thtr 200 Class 90 Board 45 **PARKING:** 200 **NOTES:** Closed 24-27 Dec
CARDS:

★★★65% *Hotel Greenhills*
Caherdavin
☎ 061 453033 📠 061 453307
e-mail: info@greenhillgroup.com
Dir: *on N18, approx 2m from City Centre*
Situated on the outskirts of Limerick, and set amongst its own landscaped grounds, the hotel is only a short drive from Shannon International Airport. Bedrooms are attractively decorated and well appointed. There is a traditional-style bar and comfortable lounge, a new restaurant and impressive leisure and conference facilities.
ROOMS: 18 rms (13 en suite) (4 fmly) **FACILITIES:** STV Sauna Solarium Gym Jacuzzi Beauty parlour Massage ♫ **CONF:** Thtr 500 Class 200 Board 50 **PARKING:** 150 **NOTES:**
CARDS:

★★★63% Woodfield House
Ennis Rd
☎ 061 453022 📠 061 326755
e-mail: woodfieldhousehotel@eircom.net
Dir: *on outskirts of city on main Shannon road*
This intimate, family-run hotel is situated on the N18 a short distance from the city centre and within easy reach of Shannon Airport. The smart bedrooms are comfortable and well appointed. Public areas include a cosy traditional-style, bar, a patio beer garden and an attractive bistro.
ROOMS: 26 en suite (3 fmly) (5 GF) **FACILITIES:** STV **CONF:** BC Thtr 130 Class 60 Board 60 **SERVICES:** air con **PARKING:** 80 **NOTES:** Closed 24-25 Dec Civ Wed **CARDS:**

★★★60% Jurys Inn Limerick
Lower Mallow St
JURYS DOYLE HOTELS
☎ 061 207000 📠 061 400966
e-mail: info@jurysdoyle.com
Dir: *from N7 follow signs for City Centre into O'Connell St, turn off at N18 (Shannon/Galway), hotel is off O'Connell St*
Conveniently situated in the shopping and business area overlooking the River Shannon this modern Inn has a spacious lobby, cosy bar, restaurant and boardroom for meetings. The 'one price' room rate and comfortable bedrooms ensure its popularity.
ROOMS: 151 en suite (108 fmly) (10 GF) ⊗ in 79 bedrooms s €75-€80; d €75-€150 **FACILITIES:** STV **CONF:** Thtr 50 Class 25 Board 18 Del from €118 **SERVICES:** Lift **NOTES:** Closed 24-26 Dec
CARDS:

Restaurant with Rooms

Sunville Country House & Restaurant
Pallasgreen
☎ 061 384822 📠 061 384823
e-mail: enquiries@sunvillehouse.com
Situated on four acres of gardens and woodland, this elegant Georgian House has been lovingly restored. Bedrooms are individually decorated and some feature four-poster beds. There is an intimate drawing room, a library, and a dining room. The dinner menu includes local produce and organic vegetables from the walled garden in season. There is a conference room on the lower ground floor.
ROOMS: 6 rms

LISDOONVARNA, Co Clare — Map 01 B3

Restaurant with Rooms

Kincora Country House & Gallery Restaurant
☎ 065 7074300 📠 065 7074490
e-mail: kincorahotel@eircom.net
Dir: *from town centre take Doolin Rd. House on 1st T-junct 200mtrs from town*
Family owned and run Kincora House has very comfortable bedrooms all with views of the garden or countryside beyond. The restaurant (which is also an art gallery) offers fine Irish cuisine using the best local ingredients.
ROOMS: 14 en suite (3 GF) ⊗ in all bedrooms **FACILITIES:** STV Art gallery **PARKING:** 15 **NOTES:** No children 10yrs ⊗ in restaurant Closed Nov-Feb **CARDS:**

LISMORE, Co Waterford — Map 01 C2

★★66% *Ballyrafter House*
☎ 058 54002 📠 058 53050
Dir: *1km from Lismore opposite Lismore Castle*
A welcoming country house, set in its own grounds opposite Lismore Castle. Most of the bedrooms are pleasantly furnished in pine and the bar and conservatory are where guests, anglers and locals meet to discuss the day's events. The hotel has its own salmon fishing on the River Blackwater.
ROOMS: 10 en suite (1 fmly) **FACILITIES:** Fishing Riding Putt green **PARKING:** 20 **NOTES:** Closed Nov-Feb **CARDS:**

LONDONDERRY, Co Londonderry — Map 01 C5

★★★★68% Tower Hotel Derry
Off the Diamond BT48 6HL
☎ 028 7137 1000 📠 028 7137 1234
e-mail: info@thd.ie
web: www.towerhotelderry.com
Dir: *From Craigavon Bridge into city centre then take 2nd exit at end of bridge into Carlisle Rd and to Ferryquay Street for hotel straight ahead*
This stylish hotel has proved to be a big hit with tourists and corporate guests alike. Modern bedrooms are furnished with flair and style and those on the upper floors enjoy superb views of the city. Minimalist day rooms include a popular bistro, and staff in the contemporary bar provide true Irish hospitality.
ROOMS: 93 en suite (26 fmly) ⊗ in 12 bedrooms **FACILITIES:** STV Sauna Gym ♫ **CONF:** BC Thtr 250 Class 150 Board 50 Del from £90 **SERVICES:** Lift **PARKING:** 25 **NOTES:** Closed 24-27 Dec Civ Wed 300 **CARDS:**

★★★★64% City Hotel
Queens Quay BT48 7AS
☎ 028 7136 5800 🖷 028 7136 5801
e-mail: res@derry-gsh.com
Dir: *Follow city centre signs. Hotel on waterfront adjacent to the Guildhall*
Occupying a central position overlooking the River Foyle, this stylish, contemporary hotel appeals to both business and leisure guests alike. All bedrooms have excellent facilities including internet access, and the executive rooms prove a particularly good working environment. The open-plan ground floor area encourages relaxation, with the restaurant providing modern cuisine. Meeting and function facilities are extensive and there are good leisure facilities.
ROOMS: 145 en suite (16 fmly) ⊗ in 66 bedrooms s fr £67.50; d fr £90 (incl. bkfst) **LB** **FACILITIES:** Gym Jacuzzi ♫ Xmas **CONF:** BC Thtr 350 Class 150 Board 80 Del from £95 **SERVICES:** Lift air con **PARKING:** 45 **NOTES:** Closed 24 -27 Dec Civ Wed 350 **CARDS:**

★★★73%
Beech Hill Country House Hotel
32 Ardmore Rd BT47 3QP
☎ 028 7134 9279 🖷 028 7134 5366
e-mail: info@beech-hill.com
web: www.beech-hill.com
Dir: *from A6 Londonderry-Belfast take Faughan Bridge turn and continue 1m to hotel opposite Ardmore Chapel*
Dating back to 1729, Beech Hill is an impressive mansion, standing in 32 acres of glorious woodlands and gardens. Traditionally styled day rooms provide deep comfort, and ambitious cooking is served in the attractively extended dining room. The splendid bedroom wing provides spacious, well-equipped rooms in addition to the more classically designed bedrooms in the main house.
ROOMS: 17 en suite 10 annexe en suite (4 fmly) s £70-£80; d £95-£120 (incl. bkfst) **LB** **FACILITIES:** Sauna Gym Jacuzzi Country walks ch fac **CONF:** Thtr 100 Class 50 Board 30 Del from £100 **SERVICES:** Lift **PARKING:** 75 **NOTES:** ⊗ in restaurant Closed 24-25 Dec Civ Wed 80 **CARDS:**

★★★70% *Quality Hotel Davincis*
15 Culmore Rd BT48 8JB
☎ 028 7127 9111 🖷 028 7127 9222
e-mail: info@davincishotel.com
Dir: *1m from city centre along Strand Rd, adjacent to river, onto Culmore Rd, hotel on right*
Convenient for the city centre, this stylish hotel provides well-designed, spacious and well-equipped bedrooms, most with two double beds. The public areas include the popular Da Vinci's bar and restaurant where food available ranges from light snacks to innovative meals from a carte menu.
ROOMS: 67 en suite (4 fmly) (13 GF) ⊗ in 26 bedrooms **FACILITIES:** STV ♫ **CONF:** Thtr 30 Class 30 Board 30 **SERVICES:** Lift **PARKING:** 100 **NOTES:** Closed 25 Dec **CARDS:**

★★★66% White Horse
68 Clooney Rd, Campsie BT47 3PA
☎ 028 7186 0606 🖷 028 7186 0371
e-mail: info@whitehorsehotel.biz
web: www.whitehorsehotel.biz
Dir: *on A2 5km from city centre & 1km from Derry City Airport*

The bedrooms at this privately owned hotel and conference and leisure complex include full suites, family rooms and interconnecting rooms. All are spacious, modern and well equipped. These are complemented by bright, modern and spacious public areas. The extensive conference and function facilities and leisure & fitness centre are impressive.
ROOMS: 57 en suite (10 fmly) ⊗ in 14 bedrooms s £45-£80; d £55-£85 (incl. bkfst) **LB** **FACILITIES: Spa** STV Snooker Sauna Solarium Gym Jacuzzi Full health & leisure centre with beauty salon ♫ ch fac Xmas **CONF:** BC Thtr 500 Class 290 Board 120 Del from £70.30 **PARKING:** 200 **NOTES:** Civ Wed 200 **CARDS:**

Travelodge
22-24 Strand Rd BT47 2AB
☎ 08700 850 950 🖷 01287 127 1277
e-mail: ifo@thetrinityhotel.com
Dir: *approx 0.5m from Guildhall adjacent to shopping centre/cinema*
Travelodge offers good quality, good value, modern accommodation. Ideal for families, the spacious, en suite bedrooms include remote-control TV, tea and coffee-making facilities and luxury beds. Meals can be taken at the nearby family restaurant. For further details consult the Hotel Groups page.
ROOMS: 39 en suite s fr £25; d fr £25 **CONF:** Thtr 70 Class 30 Board 25

LOUGHREA, Co Galway
Map 01 B3

★★★68% *Meadow Court*
☎ 091 841051 🖷 091 842406
e-mail: meadowcourthotel@eircom.net
Meadow Court has had a very good reputation for many years for its food, and has now added comfortable and well-equipped bedrooms to complement its other facilities. It is particularly renowned for wedding receptions. Lake-fishing, golf and horse riding are all available locally.
ROOMS: 21 rms

LUCAN, Co Dublin
Map 01 D4
See also Dublin

★★★64% Lucan Spa
☎ 01 6280494 🖷 01 6280841
e-mail: info@lucanspahotel.ie
Dir: *on N4, approx 11km from city centre, approx 20mins from Dublin airport*
Set in its own grounds, the Lucan Spa is a fine Georgian house.
continued on p874

LUCAN, continued

Guests have complimentary use of Lucan Golf Course, adjacent to the hotel. A conference centre is also available.

Lucan Spa Hotel, Lucan

ROOMS: 71 rms (61 en suite) (15 fmly) ⊘ in 21 bedrooms **FACILITIES:** STV ♫ ch fac **CONF:** Thtr 600 Class 250 Board 80 **SERVICES:** Lift air con **PARKING:** 90 **NOTES:** ✗ ⊘ in restaurant Closed 25-26 Dec **CARDS:**

MACREDDIN, Co Wicklow

Map 01 D3

★★★★76% ⊛⊛ *Brooklodge at MacCreddin*

☎ 0402 36444 📠 0402 36580
e-mail: brooklodge@macreddin.ie
Dir: *N11 to Rathnew, R752 to Rathdrum, R753 to Aughrim follow signs to Macreddin Village*

The Brooklodge is a luxurious country-house hotel situated in Macreddin Village near Aughrim and is a real find, where comfort predominates among restful lounges and well-appointed bedrooms and new mezzanine suites. The award-winning Strawberry Tree Restaurant is a truly romantic setting, specialising in organic and wild food. The new Wells spa centre offers extensive treatments and leisure facilities.

ROOMS: 40 en suite (27 fmly) **FACILITIES:** STV Riding Snooker Archery Clay pigeon shooting Falconry Shiatsu Massage ♫ **CONF:** Thtr 260 Class 90 Board 40 **SERVICES:** Lift **PARKING:** 190 **CARDS:**

MACROOM, Co Cork

Map 01 B2

★★★70% ⊛ Castle

Main St
☎ 026 41074 📠 026 41505
e-mail: castlehotel@eircom.net
Dir: *on N22 midway between Cork & Killarney*

Service at this market-town hotel is excellent, with guests being made very much at home in the relaxed atmosphere. Food served in the restaurant and bar is well prepared and imaginatively presented. Bedrooms have now been redecorated and are very comfortable. There is also a fine leisure centre.

ROOMS: 60 en suite (6 fmly) s €89-€107.50; d €129-€165 (incl. bkfst) **LB** **FACILITIES: Spa** STV supervised Gym Jacuzzi Steam Room ♫ **CONF:** Thtr 200 Class 80 Board 60 Del from €110 **SERVICES:** Lift air con **PARKING:** 30 **NOTES:** ✗ ⊘ in restaurant Closed 24-28 Dec **CARDS:**

MAGHERA, Co Londonderry

Map 01 C5

★★79% ⊛⊛ Ardtara Country House

8 Gorteade Rd, Upperlands BT46 5SA
☎ 028 7964 4490 📠 028 7964 5080
e-mail: valerie@ardtara.fsbusiness.co.uk
web: www.ardtara.com
Dir: *from Maghera take A29 towards Coleraine, in 2m take B75 for Kilrea through Upperlands, pass sign 'Wm Clark & Sons' then next left*

Ardtara is a delightful, high-quality Victorian country house set in eight acres of mature gardens and woodland. The stylish public rooms include a choice of lounges and a sunroom, while the elegant dining room is perfect for enjoying the skilfully prepared cuisine. Bedrooms vary in style and size; all are richly furnished with antiques, and have open fires and well-equipped bathrooms.

ROOMS: 8 en suite (1 fmly) s £60-£100; d £100-£150 (incl. bkfst) **LB** **FACILITIES:** ✂ **CONF:** Thtr 45 Board 20 **PARKING:** 40 **NOTES:** ✗ ⊘ in restaurant Closed 25-26 Dec **CARDS:**

Town House Hotel
Country House Hotel
Travel Accommodation

MALLOW, Co Cork

Map 01 B2

Top 200 – Hotel

★★★ ⊛⊛⊛ Longueville House

☎ 022 47156 & 47306 📠 022 47459
e-mail: info@longuevillehouse.ie
Dir: *3m W of Mallow via N72 road to Killarney, right turn at Ballyclough junct, hotel entrance 200yds left*

RELAIS & CHATEAUX

This 18th-century Georgian mansion is set in a wooded estate on a 500-acre farm. The beautifully appointed bedrooms overlook the Backwater Valley. Two elegantly furnished sitting rooms feature fine examples of Italian plasterwork. William O'Callaghan's cuisine is served in the Presidents' Restaurant and newly restored Victorian Turner Conservatory; most

continued

ingredients are either raised or grown on the farm plus the fish comes from the river that runs through the estate.

ROOMS: 20 en suite (5 fmly) ⊗ in 5 bedrooms s €150-€180; d €180-€200 (incl. bkfst) LB **FACILITIES:** STV Fishing **CONF:** Thtr 50 Class 30 Board 30 Del from €295 **PARKING:** 30 **NOTES:** ⊗ in restaurant Closed 20-27 Dec RS Nov-Mar **CARDS:**

★★★65% Springfort Hall Country House Hotel

☎ 022 21278 📠 022 21557
e-mail: stay@springfort-hall.com
Dir: *on Mallow/Limerick road N20, right turn off at new Two Pot House R581, hotel 500mtrs on right sign over gate*

This 18th-century country manor is tucked away amid tranquil woodlands located just 6 kms from Mallow. There is an attractive oval dining room, drawing room and lounge bar where guests can relax. The comfortable bedrooms are in a new wing and are spacious, well appointed and command suburb country views.

ROOMS: 49 en suite (4 fmly) s €90-€103; d €150-€163 (incl. bkfst) LB **FACILITIES:** STV **CONF:** BC Thtr 300 Class 200 Board 50 Del from €130 **PARKING:** 200 **NOTES:** ⊗ in restaurant Closed 23 Dec-2 Jan Civ Wed 300 **CARDS:**

MAYNOOTH, Co Kildare — Map 01 C4

★★★75% *Moyglare Manor*

Moyglare
☎ 01 6286351 📠 01 6285405
e-mail: info@moyglaremanor.ie
Dir: *turn off N4 at Maynooth/Naas, then right to Maynooth, left at T-junct. Keep right at St Marys Church and continue 2m then left at x-roads*

Set in its own grounds in rich pasture lands, this elegant house is a haven of calm. Bedrooms are furnished in keeping with the Georgian style of the house. There are a number of peaceful lounges and a convivial cocktail bar. Cuisine is also in keeping with the feel of the house, and enjoys a good reputation.

ROOMS: 17 en suite (1 fmly) (2 GF) ⊗ in 5 bedrooms **FACILITIES:** STV **CONF:** Thtr 30 Board 20 **PARKING:** 120 **NOTES:** No children 12yrs ⊗ in restaurant Closed 24-26 Dec **CARDS:**

MIDLETON, Co Cork — Map 01 C2

★★★70% *Midleton Park Hotel & Spa*

☎ 021 4631767 📠 021 4631605
e-mail: info@midletonparkhotel.ie
Dir: *from Cork, turn off N25 hotel on right. From Waterford, turn off N25, over bridge until T-junct, turn right, hotel on right*

This hotel is located in Midleton town just off the N25. Bedrooms are spacious and attractively decorated. The comfortable public areas include a relaxing lobby lounge, The Park Café Bar where there is an interesting menu available all day and the Park Restaurant for fine dining. There are extensive banqueting, private dining rooms and leisure facilities.

ROOMS: 40 en suite (12 fmly) ⊗ in 6 bedrooms **FACILITIES:** STV **CONF:** Thtr 400 Class 200 Board 40 **SERVICES:** air con **PARKING:** 500 **NOTES:** Closed 25 Dec **CARDS:**

MONAGHAN, Co Monaghan — Map 01 C5

★★★★61% *Hillgrove*

Old Armagh Rd
☎ 047 81288 📠 047 84951
e-mail: hillgrovegm@quinn-hotels.com
Dir: *turn off N2 at Cathedral, continue for 400mtrs, on left just beyond Cathedral*

This modern hotel on the outskirts of the town offers spacious bedrooms that are well equipped and comfortable. The public areas include a split-level dining room where good food is served, and a popular local bar, serving snacks throughout the day.

ROOMS: 44 en suite (3 fmly) (9 GF) ⊗ in 7 bedrooms **FACILITIES:** STV Jacuzzi **CONF:** Thtr 1200 Class 600 Board 200 **SERVICES:** Lift air con **PARKING:** 430 **NOTES:** Closed 25 Dec **CARDS:**

MULLINGAR, Co Westmeath — Map 01 C4

Restaurant with Rooms

Crookedwood House

Crookedwood
☎ 044 72165 📠 044 72166
e-mail: info@crookedwoodhouse.com
Dir: *From Dublin take 2nd exit off Mullingar Bypass, continue to Crookedwood. At Wood Pub turn right and continue for 2km*

This beautifully restored former rectory has stunning views from its elevated site. Rooms are comfortable and well equipped. There are several relaxing lounge areas and a cocktail bar for pre-dinner drinks. Staff are particularly helpful and friendly. The restaurant has a very good reputation under the direction of chef/proprietor Noel Kenny.

ROOMS: 8 en suite **FACILITIES:** STV Basketball **SERVICES:** air con **PARKING:** 10 **NOTES:** ⊗ in restaurant Closed Xmas **CARDS:**

U Bloomfield House

Belvedere
☎ 044 40894 📠 044 43767

At the time of going to press, the star classification for this hotel was not confirmed. Please refer to the AA internet site www.theAA.com for current information.

ROOMS: 111 rms

U Mullingar Park

Dublin Rd
☎ 044 44446 📠 044 35937
e-mail: info@mullingarparkhotel.com

At the time of going to press, the star classification for this hotel was not confirmed. Please refer to the AA internet site www.theAA.com for current information.

ROOMS: 95 en suite (12 fmly) ⊗ in 28 bedrooms s €95-€130; d €150-€200 (incl. bkfst) LB **FACILITIES: Spa** STV supervised Sauna Solarium Gym Jacuzzi Aerobic studio, children's pool, hydrotherapy pool ch fac **CONF:** Thtr 1000 Class 750 Board 40 Del from €150 **SERVICES:** Lift **PARKING:** 500 **NOTES:** Closed 24-25 Dec RS 26 Dec Civ Wed 500 **CARDS:**

M

NAAS, Co Kildare

Map 01 D3

★★★★69% Killashee House

045 879277 045 887490
e-mail: reservations@killasheehouse.com
Dir: N7, then R448, hotel on left, 1.5m from town centre

This Victorian manor house, set in magnificent parkland and landscaped gardens, has been successfully converted to a hotel with spacious public areas, very comfortable bedrooms and two dining options; fine dining in Turners and the Nuns Kitchen and bar caters for casual dining.

ROOMS: 142 en suite (10 fmly) (48 GF) in 32 bedrooms s €100-€495; d €150-€495 (incl. bkfst) **LB** **FACILITIES:** STV supervised Sauna Solarium Gym Jacuzzi Archery, Biking, Clay pigeon shooting Xmas **CONF:** Thtr 1600 Class 144 Board 84 Del from €190 **SERVICES:** Lift **PARKING:** 600 **NOTES:** Closed 25-26 Dec **CARDS:**

See advert on opposite page

NAVAN, Co Meath

Map 01 C4

★★★65% Newgrange

Bridge St 046 9071 4100 046 9073 977
e-mail: info@newgrangehotel.ie

This modern hotel, in the town centre, offers comfortable lounges, bars, a restaurant, a café and extensive conference facilities. Bedrooms vary in size and are well appointed. There is a secure car park and the hotel is handy for Navan & Fairyhouse Racecourse and many golf clubs.

ROOMS: 62 en suite (41 fmly) (12 GF) in 10 bedrooms s €87.50-€105; d €124.50-€150 (incl. bkfst) **LB** **FACILITIES:** STV **CONF:** Thtr 500 Class 300 Board 300 Del from €75 **NOTES:** Closed 25 Dec **CARDS:**

★★★64% *Ardboyne Hotel*

Dublin Rd
046 902 3119 046 902 2355
e-mail: ardboyne@quinn-hotels.com
Dir: from Dublin-N3 N to Navan, hotel on left

This welcoming hotel is on the southern edge of Navan. Bedrooms are freshly decorated and many of them overlook the gardens. Public areas are smartly furnished and include a popular bar where casual food is served and a well-appointed dining room that opens for both lunch and dinner.

ROOMS: 29 en suite (25 fmly) in 10 bedrooms **FACILITIES:** STV **CONF:** Thtr 400 Class 200 Board 150 **PARKING:** 186 **NOTES:** Closed 24-26 Dec **CARDS:**

NEWBRIDGE, Co Kildare

Map 01 C3

★★★★72% Keadeen

045 431666 045 434402
e-mail: keadeen@iol.ie
Dir: M7 junct 10, right towards Newbridge, hotel on left on 1km

This family operated hotel is set in eight acres of landscaped gardens. Comfortable public areas include spacious drawing rooms, bars, an excellent leisure centre and a restaurant serving good food. Ideally located for the nearby Curragh racecourse.

ROOMS: 75 en suite (4 fmly) in 5 bedrooms s €147-€163; d €208-€305 (incl. bkfst) **LB** **FACILITIES:** STV supervised Sauna Solarium Gym Jacuzzi Aerobics studio Treatment room Massage **CONF:** Thtr 800 Class 300 Board 40 Del from €189 **SERVICES:** Lift **PARKING:** 200 **NOTES:** Closed 24 Dec-2 Jan **CARDS:**

NEWCASTLE, Co Down

Map 01 D5

★★67% *Enniskeen House*

98 Bryansford Rd BT33 0LF
028 4372 2392 028 4372 4084
e-mail: info@enniskeen-hotel.demon.co.uk
Dir: from town centre follow signs for Tollymore Forest Park, hotel 1m on left

Set in ten acres of grounds and delightful gardens, this hotel is enhanced by its thoughtful staff. Bedrooms vary but all are well equipped and many enjoy super views of the mountains and countryside. The formal dining room serves traditional cuisine and the first-floor lounge makes the most of the coastal views.

ROOMS: 12 en suite (1 fmly) in 3 bedrooms **CONF:** Thtr 60 Class 24 **SERVICES:** Lift **PARKING:** 45 **NOTES:** in restaurant Closed 12 Nov-14 Mar **CARDS:**

NEWMARKET-ON-FERGUS, Co Clare

Map 01 B3

Top 200 – Hotel

★★★★★ Dromoland Castle

061 368144 061 363355
e-mail: sales@dromoland.ie
Dir: from Shannon take N18 towards Galway, take left signed "Dromoland Interchange"

Described as a 'very large, early 18th-century, Gothic revival, castellated, irregular, multi-towered ashlar castle' Dromoland stands on a 375-acre estate and offers extensive indoor leisure and outdoor pursuits. The thoughtfully equipped bedrooms provide excellent levels of comfort. Magnificent public areas, warmed by log fires, are no less impressive. The hotel has two restaurants, the elegant fine dining Earl of Thomond, and less formal Fig Tree in the golf clubhouse. Nominated for the AA Hotel of the Year Award for the Republic of Ireland 2004-5.

ROOMS: 100 en suite (20 fmly) s €215-€397; d €215-€397 **LB** **FACILITIES:** STV supervised 18 Fishing Snooker Sauna Solarium Gym Putt green Jacuzzi Beauty clinic, Archery, Clay shooting, Mountain bikes Xmas **CONF:** BC Thtr 450 Class 220 Board 80 Del €315 **PARKING:** 120 **NOTES:** in restaurant **CARDS:**

N

NEW ROSS, Co Wexford Map 01 C3

★★★67% The Cedar Lodge Hotel & Restaurant

Carrigbyrne, Newbawn
☎ 051 428386 Fax 051 428222
e-mail: cedarlodge@eircom.net
Dir: *On N25*

Cedar Lodge nestles in a tranquil setting beneath the slopes of Carrigbyrne Forest, just a 30-minute drive from Rosslare Port. The Martin family extend warm hospitality and provide good food in the charming conservatory restaurant with its central log fire. There are comfortable lounges and bedrooms are spacious, thoughtfully appointed and decorated, and all overlook the attractive landscaped gardens.

ROOMS: 28 en suite (2 fmly) (12 GF) s €90-€150; d €140-€200 (incl. bkfst) **LB** **FACILITIES:** ♫ **CONF:** Thtr 100 Class 60 Board 60 **PARKING:** 100 **NOTES:** ✈ ⊗ in restaurant Closed 21 Dec-1 Jan **CARDS:**

NEWTOWNMOUNTKENNEDY, Co Wicklow Map 01 D3

U Druids Glen Marriott Hotel & Country Club

☎ 01 2870800 Fax 2870801
e-mail: reservations.druids@marriotthotels.com
Dir: *From Dublin take N11/H11 s'bound, through Kilmacanoque to junct for Newtownmountkennedy, turn left, follow signs for hotel*

At the time of going to press, the star classification for this hotel was not confirmed. Please refer to the AA internet site www.theAA.com for current information.

ROOMS: 148 en suite (80 fmly) ⊗ in 111 bedrooms **FACILITIES:** 36 Sauna Solarium Gym Putt green Jacuzzi ♫ **CONF:** Thtr 300 Class 220 Board 54 **SERVICES:** Lift air con **PARKING:** 350 **NOTES:** ✈ **CARDS:**

PARKNASILLA, Co Kerry Map 01 A2

★★★★75% *Great Southern*

☎ 064 45122 Fax 064 45323
e-mail: res@parknasilla-gsh.com
Dir: *on Kenmare road 3km from Sneem village*

This delightful hotel which has been in business for over a hundred years, is a popular haven of relaxation and rejuvenation for generations of Irish families. There are many spacious lounges, that together with the restaurant and many of the bedrooms, have wonderful sea views. Service is warm and friendly, underpinned by smooth professionalism.

ROOMS: 24 en suite 59 annexe en suite (6 fmly) ⊗ in 11 bedrooms **FACILITIES: Spa** STV supervised 12 Fishing Riding Snooker Sauna Putt green Jacuzzi Bike hire, Windsurfing, Clay pigeon shooting, Archery ♫ **CONF:** BC Thtr 100 Class 80 Board 20 **SERVICES:** Lift **PARKING:** 60 **NOTES:** ✈ **CARDS:**

See advert on this page

P

PORTAFERRY, Co Down Map 01 D5

★★★69% ◎ ***Portaferry***
10 The Strand BT22 1PE
☎ 028 4272 8231 📠 028 4272 8999
e-mail: info@portaferryhotel.com
web: www.portaferryhotel.com
Dir: *on Lough Shore opposite ferry terminal*
This smartly presented, popular hotel enjoys a central location almost by the ferry ramp and boasts a superb panorama of Strangford Lough. Bedrooms vary in size and style and are particularly well equipped. Day rooms include a cosy lounge and split-level dining room, whilst snacks can be enjoyed in the informal bar. Hospitality here is especially warm and staff are keen to please.
ROOMS: 14 en suite **FACILITIES:** STV **CONF:** Board 14 **PARKING:** 6 **NOTES:** Closed 24-25 Dec **CARDS:**

PORTBALLINTRAE, Co Antrim Map 01 C6

★★★70% **Bayview**
2 Bayhead Rd BT57 8RZ
☎ 028 2073 4100 📠 028 2073 4330
e-mail: info@bayviewhotelni.com
Dir: *M2 Belfast to Ballymena then A26 to Ballymena, onto B62 to Portrush, after approx 7m turn right onto B17 to Bushmills. Turn left then immediate right to Portballintrae*
This stylish hotel commands excellent views of the ocean, beach and harbour. Bedrooms are bright, modern and well equipped and include rooms for less mobile guests and for families, interconnecting rooms and non-smoking rooms. Public areas are airy and comfortable with a relaxing conservatory lounge at the front, with conferences and meeting rooms available.
ROOMS: 25 en suite (12 fmly) ⊗ in 2 bedrooms s £60-£103; d £70-£110 (incl. bkfst) **LB** **FACILITIES:** ♫ **CONF:** Thtr 40 Class 30 Board 20 **SERVICES:** Lift **PARKING:** 25 **NOTES:** **CARDS:**

P

PORTLAOISE, Co Laoise Map 01 C3

U **The Heritage Hotel**
☎ 0502 78588 📠 0502 78577
At the time of going to press, the star classification for this hotel was not confirmed. Please refer to the AA internet site www.theAA.com for current information.

PORTMARNOCK, Co Dublin Map 01 D4

Top 200 – Hotel

★★★★ ◎◎ **Portmarnock Hotel & Golf Links**
Strand Rd
☎ 01 8460611 📠 01 8462442
e-mail: sales@portmarnock.com
Dir: *Dublin Airport-N1, rdbt 1st exit, 2nd rdbt 2nd exit, next rdbt 3rd exit, T-junct turn left, over crossroads and continue, hotel is left past the Strand*
This 19th-century former home of the Jameson whiskey family is now a well run and smartly presented hotel, enjoys a superb location overlooking the sea and the PGA Championship Golf Links. Bedrooms are modern and equipped to high standard, public areas are spacious and very comfortable. The Osborne Restaurant comes highly

continued

recommended and a team of friendly staff go out of their way to welcome guests.

ROOMS: 99 en suite ⊗ in 5 bedrooms s €99-€230; d €99-€310 (incl. bkfst) **LB** **FACILITIES: Spa** STV ⛳ 18 Sauna Gym Putt green Beauty therapist Xmas **CONF:** BC Thtr 300 Class 110 Board 80 Del from €160 **SERVICES:** Lift **PARKING:** 200 **NOTES:** RS Christmas Eve/Day **CARDS:**

See advert on opposite page

PORTRUSH, Co Antrim Map 01 C6

★★★70% **The Royal Court**
233 Ballybogey Rd BT56 8NF
☎ 028 7082 2236 📠 028 7082 3176
e-mail: royalcourthotel@aol.com web: www.royalcourthotel.co.uk
Dir: *from Ballymena N on M2 to Ballymoney rdbt. Take 3rd exit to Portrush on B62. Hotel at end of road*
Located to the east of the town, this modern, comfortable hotel enjoys panoramic, coastal views of the East Strand beach, Donegal and the Scottish Islands, thanks to its high, elevated position. Bedrooms are spacious and many have balconies. Extensive menus served in the restaurant and informal bar make good use of creative, wholesome cooking.
ROOMS: 18 en suite (10 fmly) s £45-£115; d £70-£115 (incl. bkfst) **LB** **FACILITIES:** STV Xmas **CONF:** Thtr 300 Class 150 Board 50 Del from £72 **PARKING:** 200 **NOTES:** Closed 26 Dec **CARDS:**

PORTUMNA, Co Galway Map 01 B3

★★★66%
Shannon Oaks Hotel & Country Club
THE INDEPENDENTS
St Joseph Rd
☎ 090 974 1777 📠 090 974 1357
e-mail: sales@shannonoaks.ie
Dir: *on left side of St Josephs Road, on exiting Portumna*

Located in eight acres of parkland by Portumna National Park, this

continued

modern hotel offers very comfortable and spacious bedrooms and suites. The popular bar has food available most of the day, with more formal dining available in the Castlegates Restaurant. Extensive conference and leisure facilities are also on site.
ROOMS: 63 en suite **FACILITIES:** STV Sauna Solarium Gym Jacuzzi **CONF:** Thtr 600 Class 320 Board 280 **SERVICES:** Lift air con **PARKING:** 360 **NOTES:** **CARDS:**

RATHNEW, Co Wicklow Map 01 D3

★★★★69%
Tinakilly Country House & Restaurant
☎ 0404 69274 0404 67806
e-mail: reservations@tinakilly.ie
web: www.tinakilly.ie
Dir: *follow N11/M11 to Rathnew, continue on R750 towards Wicklow. Entrance to hotel is approx 500mtrs from the village on left*
This fine hospitable hotel is situated on an elevated site up a tree-lined avenue, with fine views of the Irish Sea and Broadlaugh bird sanctuary. It is full of Victorian charm, but with all the modern facilities expected of a four-star hotel today. The food served is described as country-house style, with a strong emphasis on seasonality.
ROOMS: 51 en suite **FACILITIES:** STV Gym 7 acres of gardens mapped for walking **CONF:** Thtr 65 Class 48 Board 41 **SERVICES:** Lift **PARKING:** 60 **NOTES:** in restaurant Closed 24-26 Dec
CARDS:

★★★67% ***Hunter's***

☎ 0404 40106 0404 40338
e-mail: reception@hunters.ie
Dir: *1.5km from village off N11*
A delightful hotel which is one of Ireland's oldest coaching inns. The comfortable bedrooms have wonderful views over prize-winning gardens bordering the River Varty. The restaurant has a good reputation for carefully prepared dishes, which make the best use of high quality local produce including fruit and vegetables from their own garden.
ROOMS: 16 en suite (2 fmly) (2 GF) **CONF:** Thtr 40 Class 40 Board 16 **PARKING:** 50 **NOTES:** in restaurant Closed 24-26 Dec
CARDS:

RECESS, Co Galway Map 01 A4

★★★★74% **Ballynahinch Castle**
☎ 095 31006 095 31085
e-mail: bhinch@iol.ie
Dir: *W from Galway on N59 towards Clifden. After village of Recess take Roundstone turn to the left, 4km to hotel*

Open log fires and friendly professional service are just some of the delights of staying at this castle property that originates from the 16th century. Set among 350 acres of woodland, rivers and

continued

lakes, many of the suites and rooms have stunning views, as does the award-winning restaurant.
ROOMS: 40 en suite in 4 bedrooms s fr €132; d fr €210 (incl. bkfst) **LB FACILITIES:** STV Fishing River & Lakeside walks Xmas **CONF:** Thtr 30 Class 20 Board 20 **PARKING:** 55 **NOTES:** Closed Feb & 20-26 Dec **CARDS:**

★★★77% ***Lough Inagh Lodge***
Inagh Valley
☎ 095 34706 & 34694 095 34708
e-mail: inagh@iol.ie
Dir: *after Recess take R344 towards Kylemore through Inagh valley, hotel in middle of valley*

This 19th-century former fishing lodge is a relaxing, comfortable hotel. The setting is superb, nestling in woodland, fronted by a

continued on p880

R

RECESS, continued

good fishing lake with beautiful mountain views. A choice of lounge areas is matched by very spacious, well-appointed bedrooms.
ROOMS: 12 en suite (4 GF) **FACILITIES:** STV Fishing Hill walking, Fly fishing, Cycling **CONF:** Thtr 20 Class 20 Board 20 **SERVICES:** air con **PARKING:** 16 **NOTES:** ⊗ in restaurant Closed mid Dec-mid Mar **CARDS:**

RENVYLE, Co Galway Map 01 A4

★★★70% **Renvyle House Hotel**
☎ 095 43511 095 43515
e-mail: info@renvyle.com
Dir: *N59 W of Galway towards Clifden Pass through Oughterard & Maam Cross, right at Recess, left at Kylemore, at Letterfrack turn right, hotel 5m*
This comfortable house has been operating as a hotel for over 120 years. Located on the unspoilt coast of Connemara, many leisure pursuits are available. There are spacious lounges, a library, and a range of well equipped bedrooms, but it is the relaxed friendly staff that make a visit here memorable.
ROOMS: 68 en suite (8 fmly) ⊗ in 5 bedrooms s €30-€130; d €60-€250 (incl. bkfst) **LB FACILITIES:** STV 9 Fishing Riding Snooker Putt green Clay pigeon shooting ♫ ch fac Xmas **CONF:** Thtr 200 Class 80 Board 80 **PARKING:** 60 **NOTES:** ⊗ in restaurant Closed 6 Jan-14 Feb **CARDS:**

ROSCOMMON, Co Roscommon Map 01 B4

Restaurant with Rooms

Gleesons Townhouse & Restaurant
Market Square
☎ 090 6626 954 090 6627 425
This 19th-century cut-limestone town house has been very tastefully restored. The bedrooms are decorated and furnished to a high standard. Dinner is served nightly in the Manse Restaurant and there is an extensive lunch and afternoon tea menu in the café and in the beautifully landscaped front courtyard. Conference facilities and secure car parking are available.
ROOMS: 19 rms

ROSCREA, Co Tipperary Map 01 C3

○ **Racket Hall Country Golf & Conference Hotel**
Dublin Rd
☎ 0505 21748 0505 23701
e-mail: racketh@iol.ie
ROOMS: 40 rms **NOTES:** Due to open Nov 2004

ROSSCARBERY, Co Cork Map 01 B2

★★★69% ***Celtic Ross***
☎ 023 48722 023 48723
e-mail: info@celticrosshotel.com
Dir: *take N71 out of Cork city, through Bandon towards Clonakilty. Follow signs for Skibbereen, hotel on main road*
The Celtic Ross Hotel is on the water's edge overlooking Rosscarbery Bay on the outskirts of the village. Richly textured fabrics add warmth to the polished wood of the public areas that amazingly includes a 5000-year-old Bog Yew Tree sculpture, and a choice of bars and restaurants. Bedrooms are tastefully appointed and decorated in relaxing colours; luxury suites and wheelchair accessible rooms are available.

ROOMS: 66 en suite (30 fmly) ⊗ in 10 bedrooms **FACILITIES:** STV supervised Sauna Gym Steam room Bubble pool Video rentals ♫ **CONF:** Thtr 300 Class 80 Board 40 **SERVICES:** Lift air con **PARKING:** 200 **NOTES:** ⊗ in restaurant Closed mid Jan-mid Feb **CARDS:**

ROSSLARE, Co Wexford Map 01 D2

Courtesy & Care Award
Top 200 - Hotel

★★★★ **Kelly's Resort**
☎ 053 32114 053 32222
e-mail: kellyhot@iol.ie
Dir: *10m from Wexford, turn off N25 on Rosslare/Wexford road*
Since 1895, the Kelly Family has been running this excellent hotel, where together with a dedicated team, they provide very professional and friendly service. The resort is adjacent to both the beach and Rosslare Strand. Bedrooms are thoughtfully equipped and comfortably furnished. The extensive facilities include a smart leisure club, health treatments, a children's creche and spacious gardens. La Marine Bistro offers modern cuisine and Beaches restaurant serves award-winning food. Kelly's Resort Hotel has been awarded the AA Courtesy & Care Award for the Republic of Ireland 2004-5.
ROOMS: 99 annexe en suite (15 fmly) **FACILITIES:** STV supervised Squash Snooker Sauna Solarium Gym Jacuzzi Bowls Plunge pool Badminton Crazy golf Outdoor Canadian hot tub ♫ ch fac **CONF:** Thtr 30 Class 30 Board 20 **SERVICES:** Lift **PARKING:** 99 **NOTES:** ⊗ in restaurant Closed mid Dec-late Feb **CARDS:**

★★★65% *Crosbie Cedars*

☎ 053 32124 ⎙ 053 32243
e-mail: info@crosbiecedars.iol.ie
Dir: *turn off N25 at Ashfield crossroads. Follow brown signs at cross for Rosslare village. Take 1st left, hotel on right*

This hotel is within walking distance of miles of safe, sandy beach, championship golf links, children's play areas and many other activities. The attractive foyer features a white baby grand piano, there is choice of bars - the relaxing Tavern Bar and Library lounge and Bunkers which provides entertainment at weekends. Bedrooms are well equipped, bright and spacious.
ROOMS: 34 en suite (28 fmly) (10 GF) **FACILITIES:** STV ♫
CONF: Thtr 250 Class 70 Board 70 **SERVICES:** Lift **PARKING:** 157
NOTES: Closed 24-25 Dec RS January
CARDS:

ROSSNOWLAGH, Co Donegal — Map 01 B5

★★★78% *Sand House*

MANOR HOUSE HOTELS

☎ 071 985 1777 ⎙ 071 985 2100
e-mail: info@sandhouse-hotel.ie
Dir: *on coast road from Donegal Town to Ballyshannon in the centre of Donegal Bay*

Located on Rossnowlagh Beach, famed for surfing, this hotel has now been renovated and extended. It offers well appointed bedrooms, many of which are very spacious and have sea views. Known for its hospitality, good food and service, the Sand House is an ideal base for touring the north west of Ireland
ROOMS: 55 en suite (6 fmly) ⊘ in 15 bedrooms **FACILITIES: Spa** STV Sauna Solarium Putt green Jacuzzi Mini-golf Surfing Canoeing Sailing ♫ **CONF:** Thtr 60 Class 40 Board 30 **SERVICES:** Lift
PARKING: 42 **NOTES:** ⊘ in restaurant Closed Dec & Jan
CARDS:

€ Don't forget, the Euro is now the unit of currency in the Republic of Ireland

ROUNDSTONE, Co Galway — Map 01 A4

★★72% *Eldons*

☎ 095 35933 & 35942 ⎙ 095 35871
e-mail: eldonshotel@eircom.net
Dir: *off N59 through Toombedla then left to village*
Eldons is in the main street of this picturesque village and is a welcoming family run hotel, with a very good day food business in the cosy bar. Bedrooms are comfortable and those in the annexe across the road are particularly spacious. Seafood is a speciality in Boela, the hotel restaurant.
ROOMS: 13 en suite 6 annexe en suite (2 fmly) **FACILITIES:** ♫
SERVICES: Lift **NOTES:** Closed 4 Nov-16 Mar
CARDS:

SALTHILL See Galway

SHANNON, Co Clare — Map 01 B3

★★★60% Shannon Court

Ballycasey
☎ 061 364588 ⎙ 061 364045
e-mail: stay@irishcourthotels.com
Dir: *1m from Shannon International Airport*

This friendly hotel conveniently situated just three miles from Shannon Airport and is close to Bunratty Castle. It offers contemporary styled bedrooms, the Old Lodge bar and themed restaurant and meeting rooms.
ROOMS: 54 en suite (6 fmly) ⊘ in 10 bedrooms s €39-€69; d €59-€109 **FACILITIES:** STV ♫ **SERVICES:** Lift air con **PARKING:** 154
NOTES: ⊘ in restaurant Closed 24-26 Dec
CARDS:

SKERRIES, Co Dublin — Map 01 D4

Restaurant with Rooms

Redbank House & Restaurant

THE INDEPENDENTS HOTEL ASSOCIATION

5-7 Church St ROI
☎ 01 8491005 8490439 ⎙ 01 8491598
e-mail: redbank@eircom.net
Dir: *N1 north past the airport & bypass Swords. 3m N at the end of dual carriageway at Esso station right towards Rush, Lusk & Skerries*
Adjacent to the well-known restaurant of the same name, this comfortable double-fronted period town house has two reception rooms, en suite bedrooms and a secluded garden. The restaurant is the setting for quality local produce used with an emphasis on fresh fish in imaginative cooking, served by friendly and attentive staff.
ROOMS: 7 en suite 5 annexe en suite (12 fmly) **FACILITIES:** STV
PARKING: 4 **NOTES:** Closed 24-28 Dec **CARDS:**

SKIBBEREEN, Co Cork — Map 01 B2

★★66% *Eldon*

Bridge St
☎ 028 22000 📠 028 22191
e-mail: welcome@eldon-hotel.ie
Dir: *On N71 W to Skibbereen, follow one-way system, turn right at end of Townsend St. Hotel 100yds on right*

Good company in pleasant surroundings are the aims of this family run hotel on the main street of the town. The atmosphere is casual and friendly in the popular bar with patio gardens adjoining it, with car parking at the rear.

ROOMS: 19 en suite ⊘ in 4 bedrooms **FACILITIES:** use of local leisure centre ♫ **PARKING:** 40 **NOTES:** Closed 24-27 Dec
CARDS:

SLANE, Co Meath — Map 01 D4

★★★61% *Conyngham Arms*

☎ 041 9884444 📠 041 9824205
Dir: *from N2 turn onto N51, hotel 20mtrs on left*

IRISH COUNTRY HOTELS

Situated in a picturesque village near the famous prehistoric tombs of New Grange, this hotel has very comfortable public rooms including the unique Estate Agent's Restaurant. There are attractive gardens and this is an ideal location from which to explore the area including Tara and the Boyne Valley. Bedrooms are well presented.

ROOMS: 16 en suite (4 fmly) **FACILITIES:** STV **CONF:** Thtr 150 Class 120 **PARKING:** 12 **NOTES:** ✗ **CARDS:**

SLIGO, Co Sligo — Map 01 B5

★★★71% Sligo Park

Pearse Rd
☎ 071 916 0291 📠 071 916 9556
e-mail: sligopk@leehotels.com
Dir: *on N4 1m from Sligo on Dublin Road also on Galway Rd*

Set in seven acres on the southern side of the town, this hotel is well positioned for touring the many attractions of the north-west and Yeates country. Modern facilities are a feature of the comfortable bedrooms which have been under refurbishment in recent years. A good leisure centre is also available to guests.

ROOMS: 138 en suite (5 fmly) (45 GF) ⊘ in 60 bedrooms s €70-€111; d €110-€188 **LB** **FACILITIES:** supervised Snooker Sauna Solarium Gym Jacuzzi Steam room, Plunge pool ♫ Xmas **CONF:** Thtr 520 Class 290 Board 80 Del from €123 **PARKING:** 200 **NOTES:** ✗ ⊘ in restaurant RS 24-26 & 31 Dec **CARDS:**

> Late for dinner?
> Quality Standards mean that last orders for dinner vary according to star rating and should be no earlier than:
> ★★ 7.00pm ★★★ 8.00pm ★★★★ 9.00pm
> ★★★★★ 10.00pm

★★★63% Tower

Quay St
☎ 071 914 4000 📠 071 914 6888
e-mail: towersl@iol.ie
Dir: *in town centre, next to City Hall. Follow N4 and turn off at Hughes Bridge*

Centrally located in the centre of the town, this modern hotel offers comfortable and well equipped bedrooms, there is a smart foyer lounge, popular bar serving food and a restaurant. Guests have access to a local leisure centre at reduced rates. Car parking at the rear.

ROOMS: 58 en suite ⊘ in 12 bedrooms s €55-€95; d €95-€145 (incl. bkfst) **LB** **FACILITIES:** ♫ **CONF:** Thtr 200 Class 60 Board 50 **SERVICES:** Lift air con **PARKING:** 20 **NOTES:** ✗ ⊘ in restaurant Closed 24-28 Dec **CARDS:**

SPANISH POINT, Co Clare — Map 01 B3

★★★65% *Burkes Armada*

☎ 065 7084110 📠 065 7084632
e-mail: info@burkesarmadahotel.com
Dir: *N18 from Ennis take N85 Inagh, then R460 to Miltown Malbay. Follow signs for Spanish Point*

Situated on the coastline, overlooking breaking waves and golden sands, this family run hotel is located in a natural, unspoiled environment. The public areas benefit from the stunning location, especially the contemporary restaurant. Bedrooms, many with seaviews, are well equipped and brightly decorated.

ROOMS: 61 en suite (53 fmly) **FACILITIES:** STV Gym **CONF:** Thtr 600 Class 400 Board 60 **SERVICES:** Lift **PARKING:** 175 **NOTES:** ✗
CARDS:

STRAFFAN, Co Kildare — Map 01 D4

Top 200 – Hotel

★★★★★ ◎◎◎ The Kildare Hotel & Golf Club

☎ 01 6017200 📠 01 6017298
e-mail: resortsales@kclub.ie
Dir: *from Dublin take N4, R406, hotel on right*

The Kildare Hotel and Golf Club, affectionately known at The K Club, will be the home of 2006 Ryder Cup. Two golf courses will be added to with a new spa facility to complement the truly luxurious bedrooms and suites. Public areas are opulently furnished, many of them with views of the formal gardens. Excellent cuisine is served in the elegant Byerly Turk restaurant,

continued

with a little less formal dining in Legends, the restaurant in the golf pavillion.
ROOMS: 69 en suite 10 annexe en suite (10 fmly) **FACILITIES: Spa** STV 18 Fishing Snooker Sauna Solarium Gym Putt green Jacuzzi Beauty salon Driving range Golf tuition Fishing tuition Horse riding nearby ch fac Xmas **CONF:** Thtr 160 Class 60 Board 40 Del from €365 **SERVICES:** Lift **PARKING:** 205
NOTES: in restaurant **CARDS:**

★★★76% **Barberstown Castle**
☎ 01 6288157 01 6277027
e-mail: barberstowncastle@ireland.com

With elements dating from the 13th century, the castle is now a hotel providing the very best in standards of comfort. The inviting public areas range from the original keep, which now is one of the two restaurants, to the warmth of the drawing room. Bedrooms are elegant and named after many of the extraordinary characters that have been associated with the property.
ROOMS: 58 en suite s €137.50-€150; d €220-€240 (incl. bkfst) **LB**
FACILITIES: STV Xmas **CONF:** Thtr 150 Class 120 Board 30
SERVICES: Lift **PARKING:** 200 **NOTES:** No children 12yrs in restaurant **CARDS:**

THOMASTOWN, Co Kilkenny

Map 01 C3

Top 200 – Hotel

★★★★ **Mount Juliet Conrad**
☎ 056 777 3000 056 777 3019
e-mail: info@mountjuliet.ie
Dir: *take M7 from Dublin, N9 towards Waterford then to hotel on N9 via Carlow and Gowran*
Mount Juliet Conrad is set in 1,500 acres of parkland with a Jack Nicklaus designed golf course and an equestrian centre. The elegant and spacious public areas retain much of the original architectural features including ornate plasterwork and Adam fireplaces. Bedrooms, in both the main house and

continued

the Hunters Yard annexe, are comfortable and well appointed. Fine dining is on offer at The Lady Helen, overlooking the river, and more casual dining is available in Kendels in the Hunters Yard, which also has a spa and health club.
ROOMS: 32 en suite 27 annexe en suite in 1 bedroom
FACILITIES: Spa STV 18 Fishing Riding Snooker Sauna Gym Putt green Spa Archery Cycling Clay pigeon shooting Golf tuition **CONF:** Thtr 75 Class 40 Board 20 **PARKING:** 200
NOTES: in restaurant **CARDS:**

TRALEE, Co Kerry

Map 01 A2

★★★★70% ***Ballygarry House***
Killarney Rd
☎ 066 7123322 7127630
e-mail: info@ballygarryhouse.com
Dir: *1.5km from Tralee, on N22*

Set in six acres of well tended gardens, this fine hotel has been family run for the last 50 years and has been totally renovated to a very high standard. The elegant and stylishly decorated bedrooms are spacious and relaxing and are matched by friendly professional staff. Good cuisine is served in the split-level restaurant.
ROOMS: 46 en suite (10 fmly) (6 GF) in 23 bedrooms
FACILITIES: STV ch fac **CONF:** BC **SERVICES:** Lift **PARKING:** 105
NOTES: Closed 20-26 Dec & 4-20 Jan Civ Wed 350
CARDS:

★★★69% **Meadowlands Hotel**
Oakpark
☎ 066 7180444 066 7180964
e-mail: info@meadowlands-hotel.com
Dir: *1km from Tralee town centre on N69*
This smart hotel has been extended and is within walking distance of the town centre. Bedrooms are tastefully decorated and comfortable. Johnny Frank's is the very popular pub where a wide range of food is offered throughout the day.
ROOMS: 58 en suite (1 fmly) (5 GF) in 17 bedrooms s €80-€120; d €160-€300 (incl. bkfst) **LB** **FACILITIES:** STV **CONF:** Thtr 250 Class 110 Board 30 **SERVICES:** Lift air con **PARKING:** 200 **NOTES:** Closed 24-26 Dec **CARDS:**

★★★67% **Abbey Gate**
Maine St
☎ 066 7129888 066 7129821
e-mail: info@abbeygate-hotel.com
Dir: *take N21 or N22 to town centre*
The Abbey Gate is a smart town centre hotel. The comfortable well-equipped bedrooms include some suitable for less able guests. The bar is popular with local business people and features

continued on p884

T

TRALEE, continued

music at weekends. Food is served daily in the bar or in a choice of two restaurants.
ROOMS: 100 en suite (4 fmly) s €65-€160; d €130-€170 (incl. bkfst) **LB FACILITIES:** STV ♫ Xmas **CONF:** BC Thtr 450 Class 250 Board 40 Del from €150 **SERVICES:** Lift **PARKING:** 40 **NOTES:** ✗ RS 24-26 Dec **CARDS:**

TRAMORE, Co Waterford — Map 01 C2

★★★65% Majestic

☎ 051 381761 📠 051 381766
e-mail: info@majestic-hotel.ie
Dir: *turn off N25 through Waterford onto R675 to Tramore. Hotel is on right, opposite lake*
A warm welcome awaits visitors to this long established family friendly hotel in the holiday resort of Tramore. Many of the comfortable and well-equipped bedrooms have sea views.
ROOMS: 60 en suite (4 fmly) ⊗ in all bedrooms s €70-€85; d €100-€130 (incl. bkfst) **LB FACILITIES:** STV Putt green Free access to Splashworld swimming pool & leisure club ♫ Xmas **SERVICES:** Lift **PARKING:** 10 **NOTES:** ✗ ⊗ in restaurant **CARDS:**

VIRGINIA, Co Cavan — Map 01 C4

★★66% The Park

Virginia Park
☎ 049 8546100 📠 049 8547203
e-mail: virginiapark@eircom.net
Dir: *turn off N3 in Virginia onto R194. Hotel 500yds on left*
A charming hotel, built in 1750 as the summer retreat of the Marquis of Headford. Situated overlooking Lake Ramor on a 100-acre estate, it has a 9-hole golf course, lovely mature gardens and woodland. The Park Hotel brings together generous hospitality and a relaxed leisurely pace of life.
ROOMS: 26 en suite (1 fmly) (8 GF) s €45-€65; d €90-€130 (incl. bkfst) **LB FACILITIES:** ⛳ 9 Fishing Sauna Xmas **CONF:** Thtr 70 Class 40 Board 40 Del €130 **PARKING:** 50 **NOTES:** ✗ ⊗ in restaurant **CARDS:**

WATERFORD, Co Waterford — Map 01 C2

Top 200 – Hotel

★★★★ Waterford Castle

The Island
☎ 051 878203 📠 051 879316
e-mail: info@waterfordcastle.com
Dir: *from city centre, turn onto Dunmore East Rd, continue for 1.5m, pass hospital, 0.5m left after lights, ferry at bottom of road*
This enchanting and picturesque castle dates back to Norman times and located on a 320-acre island five minutes from the mainland, is reached by chain-link ferry. The antique furnished bedrooms offer high standards of comfort. Fine dining can be enjoyed in the oak-panelled Munster Room. Its 18-hole golf course is set on beautiful parkland.
ROOMS: 19 en suite (2 fmly) **FACILITIES:** STV ⛳ 18 Putt green Clay pigeon shooting,archery(group) ♫ **CONF:** Thtr 30 Board 15 **SERVICES:** Lift **PARKING:** 50 **NOTES:** ✗ ⊗ in restaurant **CARDS:**

★★★★62% *Faithlegg House*

Faithlegg
☎ 051 382000 📠 051 382010
Faithlegg is surrounded by a championship golf course and overlooks the estuary of the River Suir. The restored house has 14 original bedrooms, with most in a modern block to the side. Comprehensive meeting facilities are provided together with a range of comfortable lounges. The leisure and treatment rooms are the perfect way to work off the excesses of the food offered in the Roseville Restaurant!
ROOMS: 82 rms

★★★72% *Athenaeum House*

Christendon, Ferrybank
☎ 051 833 999 📠 051 833 977
ROOMS: 29 rms

★★★71% Granville

The Quay
☎ 051 305555 📠 051 305566
e-mail: stay@granville-hotel.ie
Dir: *take N25 to waterfront in city centre, opposite the Clock Tower*

Centrally located on the quayside, this long established hotel has been extensively refurbished to a very high standard, while still keeping its true character. The bedrooms come in a choice of standard or executive, and are all well equipped and very comfortable. Friendliness and hospitality are hallmark of a stay here.
ROOMS: 100 en suite (5 fmly) ⊗ in 20 bedrooms s €77.50-€135; d €155-€200 (incl. bkfst) **LB FACILITIES:** STV ♫ ch fac Xmas **CONF:** Thtr 200 Class 150 Board 30 Del from €135 **SERVICES:** Lift **PARKING:** 300 **NOTES:** ✗ Closed 25-26 Dec **CARDS:**

★★★69% Tower

The Mall
☎ 051 875801 📠 051 870129
e-mail: info@thw.ie
Dir: *opposite Reginald's Tower in the centre of town, hotel at end of quay on N25 Cork road*
This long-established hotel includes two smart restaurants, a riverside bar and upgraded bedrooms. The leisure centre is about

continued

to be further developed. Good car parking is provided to the rear of the hotel.
ROOMS: 139 en suite (20 fmly) s €79-€135; d €134-€230 (incl. bkfst) **LB** **FACILITIES:** supervised Sauna Solarium Gym Jacuzzi ♫ ch fac Xmas **CONF:** BC Thtr 500 Class 250 Board 80 **SERVICES:** Lift **PARKING:** 90 **NOTES:** in restaurant Closed 24-28 Dec
CARDS:

★★★67% Dooley's
30 The Quay
☎ 051 873531 051 870262
e-mail: hotel@dooleys-hotel.ie
Dir: *on N25*
Situated on the Quay overlooking the River Suir and facing a convenient public car park. This family run hotel offers friendly and relaxed atmosphere the contemporary public areas include the New Ship Restaurant, more casual dining is available in the Dry Dock Bar. Bedrooms are comfortable and well appointed.
ROOMS: 113 en suite (3 fmly) in 75 bedrooms s €75-€129; d €80-€198 (incl. bkfst) **LB** **FACILITIES:** STV Land & water based activities ♫ **CONF:** Thtr 240 Class 150 Board 100 Del from €130 **SERVICES:** Lift **NOTES:** in restaurant Closed 25-27 Dec
CARDS:

★★★67% Waterford Manor
Killotteran, Butlerstown
☎ 051 377814 051 354545
e-mail: sales@waterfordmanorhotel.ie
Dir: *N25 from Waterford to Cork, right 2m after Waterford Crystal, left at end of road, hotel on right*

This manor house dates back to 1730 and is set in delightful landscaped and wooded grounds. The hotel provides high quality accommodation as well as extensive conference and banqueting facilities. Public areas include a charming drawing room and restaurant for intimate dining, and the Brasserie with its own bar serves carvery lunch daily.
ROOMS: 21 en suite (3 fmly) in 6 bedrooms s fr €65; d fr €120 (incl. bkfst) **LB** **FACILITIES:** STV ch fac **CONF:** BC Thtr 600 Class 300 Board 40 Del from €130 **PARKING:** 400 **NOTES:** in restaurant RS 25 Dec **CARDS:**

★★★64% Ivory's Hotel
Tramore Rd
☎ 051 358888 051 358899
e-mail: info@ivoryshotel.ie
Dir: *from city centre take N25 to Cork. After 600yds take exit to Tramore R675. Hotel on right*
This friendly, family-owned, modern hotel is well located just off the Cork road. Many of the comfortable rooms are suitable for

continued

families, and an outdoor play area is also provided. McGinty's, the popular pub carvery serves food throughout the day, and dinner is served in the Bistro.
ROOMS: 40 en suite (20 fmly) (20 GF) in 20 bedrooms s €85-€125; d €120-€180 (incl. bkfst) **LB** **FACILITIES:** STV ch fac **PARKING:** 120 **NOTES:** in restaurant Closed 24-28 Dec **CARDS:**

★★★62% Bridge Hotel
1 The Quay
☎ 051 877222 051 877229
e-mail: info@bridgehotelwaterford.com
Dir: *opposite the Waterford City Bridge on N25*
This busy hotel stands near the City Bridge, convenient for shopping, theatres and local amenities. The bedrooms vary in size and are well appointed and comfortable. Public areas include a bistro, traditional lounge bar and banqueting facilities.
ROOMS: 133 en suite (20 fmly) in 4 bedrooms s €65-€100; d €130-€170 (incl. bkfst) **LB** **FACILITIES:** STV Sauna Gym ♫ **CONF:** Thtr 400 Class 300 Board 70 **SERVICES:** Lift air con **PARKING:** 200 **NOTES:** Closed Xmas & 1st 2 wks Jan
CARDS:

★★★61% *McEniff Ard Ri Hotel*
Ferrybank
☎ 051 832111 051 832863
Dir: *on N25 1km from city centre*
In an elevated setting in 38 acres of parkland, this modern hotel enjoys spectacular views overlooking the city and harbour. Public areas are comfortable and bedrooms are spacious and well equipped. Guests can enjoy the many activities available in the extensive leisure centre.
ROOMS: 98 en suite (20 fmly) in 4 bedrooms **FACILITIES:** Sauna Solarium Gym Jacuzzi Steam room Plunge pool ♫ **CONF:** Thtr 700 Class 400 Board 100 **SERVICES:** Lift **PARKING:** 300 **NOTES:** Closed 24-27 Dec **CARDS:**

Travelodge
Travelodge
Cork Rd
☎ 08700 850 950 051 358890
Dir: *on N25, 1km from Waterford Glass Visitors Centre*
Travelodge offers good quality, good value, modern accommodation. Ideal for families, the spacious, en suite bedrooms include remote-control TV, tea and coffee-making facilities and luxury beds. Meals can be taken at the nearby family restaurant. For further details consult the Hotel Groups page.
ROOMS: 32 en suite

♫ Entertainment

WESTPORT, Co Mayo Map 01 B3

★★★73% *Hotel Westport Conference & Leisure Centre*

Newport Rd
☎ 098 25122 📠 098 26739
e-mail: reservations@hotelwestport.ie
Dir: *N5 to Westport, at end of Castlebar St turn right, 1st right, 1st left, follow road to end*

Opposite the grounds of Westport House, this hotel offers welcoming accommodation comprising a reception foyer, lounge, spacious restaurant and comfortable bedrooms including six suites. The hotel has much to offer leisure and business guests, with a swimming pool, sauna and gym, and conference and syndicate rooms.

ROOMS: 129 en suite (36 fmly) **FACILITIES:** STV Sauna Solarium Gym Jacuzzi Children's pool Jet stream Lounger pool Steam room ♫ ch fac **CONF:** Thtr 500 Class 150 Board 60 **SERVICES:** Lift **PARKING:** 220 **NOTES:** ⊗ in restaurant **CARDS:**

★★★69% The Atlantic Coast Hotel

The Quay
☎ 098 29000 📠 098 29111
e-mail: info@atlanticcoasthotel.com
Dir: *N5 follow signs into Westport then Louisburgh on R335 1m from Westport*

This distinctive hotel is in a former mill and has been renovated to a good contemporary standard. Many of the rooms have sea views, as has the award-winning restaurant on the fourth floor. The ground floor has comfortable lounge areas and a lively bar. Spa and treatment rooms have now been added to the leisure centre.

ROOMS: 85 en suite (6 fmly) ⊗ in 28 bedrooms s fr €90; d fr €140 (incl. bkfst) **FACILITIES: Spa** STV supervised Sauna Solarium Gym Treatment rooms/Hydrotherapy ♫ ch fac Xmas **CONF:** BC Thtr 180 Class 100 Board 70 Del from €157.50 **SERVICES:** Lift **PARKING:** 60 **NOTES:** ⊗ in restaurant Closed 23-27 Dec **CARDS:**

★★★65% The Wyatt

The Octagon
☎ 098 25027
e-mail: info@wyatthotel.com
Dir: *Follow one-way system in town centre. Hotel beside tall pillar monument on the Octagon*

This stylish, welcoming hotel is situated in the famous town-centre Octagon. Bedrooms are attractively decorated and well equipped. Public areas are very comfortable with open fires and a lively contemporary bar, there are two dining options, J.W's Bar food and The Wyatt Restaurant offering fine dining.

ROOMS: 53 en suite (4 GF) s fr €60; d fr €80 (incl. bkfst) **LB FACILITIES:** STV Complimentary access to leisure park 200mtrs from hotel ♫ Xmas **CONF:** BC Thtr 300 Class 200 Board 80 **SERVICES:** Lift air con **PARKING:** 20 **NOTES:** ⊗ in restaurant Closed 25-26 Dec **CARDS:**

W

★★72% The Olde Railway

The Mall
☎ 098 25166 & 25605 📠 098 25090
e-mail: railway@anu.ie
Dir: *in town centre*

Set on a tree-lined mall overlooking the Carrowbeg River, this former coaching inn has a welcoming atmosphere with blazing fires. All the bedrooms are well equipped and vary in size, with some being particularly spacious. Public areas include a cosy bar, comfortable lounge and a conservatory restaurant with access to the car park at the rear.

ROOMS: 24 en suite (2 fmly) s €65-€95; d €100-€180 (incl. bkfst) **LB FACILITIES:** Fishing & Shooting arranged ♫ **CONF:** Thtr 75 Class 100 **PARKING:** 34 **NOTES:** ⊗ in restaurant **CARDS:**

WEXFORD, Co Wexford Map 01 D3

★★★★70% Ferrycarrig

Ferrycarrig Bridge
☎ 053 20999 📠 053 20982
e-mail: ferrycarrig@ferrycarrighotel.com
Dir: *on N11 by Slaney Estuary, beside Ferrycarrig Castle*

This fine property has sweeping views of the Slaney Estuary from nearly every angle. Bedrooms are comfortable and well appointed, many of them having access to balconies. The leisure centre is particularly well equipped. The staff offer professional yet friendly service.

ROOMS: 102 en suite (10 fmly) ⊗ in 50 bedrooms s €80-€450; d €140-€450 (incl. bkfst) **LB FACILITIES:** STV Sauna Solarium Gym Jacuzzi Aerobics Beauty treatments on request Hairdresser ♫ Xmas **CONF:** Thtr 400 Class 250 Board 60 **SERVICES:** Lift **PARKING:** 235 **NOTES:** **CARDS:**

★★★73% *Talbot*

Trinity St
☎ 053 22566 📠 053 23377
e-mail: sales@talbothotel.ie
Dir: *from Rosslare, take N11 & follow the signs for Wexford, hotel on right of the Quays - 12m*

Centrally situated on the quayside, this hotel offers well-equipped bedrooms with custom-made oak furniture and attractive décor. Day rooms include a spacious foyer, comfortable lounge, and a bar with an open fireplace. The attractive restaurant serves interesting food, and there are good leisure facilities.

ROOMS: 98 en suite (12 fmly) ⊗ in 10 bedrooms **FACILITIES:** STV Sauna Solarium Gym Jacuzzi Childrens room Beauty Salon ♫ **CONF:** Thtr 450 Class 250 Board 110 **SERVICES:** Lift **PARKING:** 160 **NOTES:** Closed 24-25 Dec **CARDS:**

See advert on opposite page

★★★70% Whitford House Hotel Health & Leisure Club

New Line Rd
☎ 053 43444 📠 053 46399
e-mail: info@whitford.ie
web: www.whitford.ie
Dir: *from Rosslare follow N25 at Duncannon Road roundabout, turn right onto R733, hotel immediately left*

This is a friendly family-run hotel just 2 kilometres from the town centre and within easy reach of the Rosslare ferry. Comfortable rooms range from standard to deluxe; they are spacious and

continued

luxuriously decorated and furnished. Public areas include a choice of lounges and a popular bar where food is also served. More formal dinner is on offer in Footprints Restaurant.

ROOMS: 36 en suite (28 fmly) (18 GF) s €85-€115; d €130-€180 (incl. bkfst) **LB** **FACILITIES: Spa** STV supervised Sauna Solarium Gym Jacuzzi Childrens playground Beer garden/Adult reading room, **CONF:** Thtr 50 Class 45 Board 25 **PARKING:** 200 **NOTES:** in restaurant RS 23 Dec-2 Jan **CARDS:**

★★★65% River Bank House Hotel

☎ 053 23611 053 23342
e-mail: river@indigo.ie
Dir: *beside Wexford Bridge on R741*
Overlooking the estuary of the Slaney River, this newly renovated hotel is at the foot of the Wexford Bridge, a short distance from the town centre. Both the bar and restaurant have views of the harbour. Bedrooms are well equipped and comfortable. Impressive banqueting facilities have also been added.
ROOMS: 23 en suite (6 fmly) (7 GF) s €85-€105; d €120-€170 (incl. bkfst) **LB** **FACILITIES:** STV **CONF:** Thtr 350 Class 180 Board 48 **SERVICES:** Lift **PARKING:** 25 **NOTES:** in restaurant Closed 24-25 Dec **CARDS:**

U White's Hotel

Best Western

George St
☎ 053 22311 053 45000
e-mail: info@whiteshotel.iol.ie
Dir: *from N11 or N25 into town follow signs for Hotel*
At the time of going to press, the star classification for this hotel was not confirmed and the hotel had commenced an extensive renovations project. It is scheduled to re-open in May 2005. Please refer to the AA internet site www.theAA.com for current information.
ROOMS: 76 en suite 6 annexe en suite (1 fmly) in 16 bedrooms **FACILITIES:** STV Sauna Gym Jacuzzi Disco Bar **CONF:** Thtr 400 Class 250 Board 100 **SERVICES:** Lift **PARKING:** 100 **NOTES:** **CARDS:**

WICKLOW See Rathnew

WOODENBRIDGE, Co Wicklow

Map 01 D3

★★★64% Woodenbridge

☎ 0402 35146 0402 35573
e-mail: wbhotel@iol.ie
Dir: *between Avoca & Arklow*
Situated in the Vale of Avoca this family-run hotel is beside the Woodenbridge Golf Club. The lodge bedrooms are well equipped and spacious and enjoy the peaceful riverside setting. Public areas are comfortable, and hospitality and good food is assured.
ROOMS: 23 en suite (13 fmly) **FACILITIES:** STV **CONF:** Thtr 200 Class 200 Board 200 **PARKING:** 100 **NOTES:** in restaurant **CARDS:**

YOUGHAL, Co Cork

Map 01 C2

★★60% Devonshire Arms

Pearse Square
☎ 024 92827 024 92900
e-mail: reservations@dev.arms.ie
This 19th-century building is centrally situated with good parking to the rear. The ground floor facilities include comfortable lounges and two cosy bar areas where good food is served throughout the day.
ROOMS: 10 en suite **CONF:** Class 150 **PARKING:** 20 **NOTES:** Closed 24-31 Dec **CARDS:**

Restaurant with Rooms

Ahernes

163 North Main St
☎ 024 92424 024 93633
e-mail: ahernes@eircom.net
Dir: *rdbt on edge of town, N25. Follow signs for town centre*
In the same family for over 80 years, Ahearne's offers a very warm welcome with turf fires and a traditional atmosphere. The spacious bedrooms are well appointed to the highest standard. Seafood is a speciality of the restaurant, with menus that change daily, depending on the availability of fish. For more casual dining, a very good bar food menu is also served.
ROOMS: 13 en suite (2 fmly) (3 GF) in 3 bedrooms s €105-€110; d €140-€180 (incl. bkfst) **LB** **CONF:** Thtr 25 Class 15 Board 15 **PARKING:** 20 **NOTES:** in restaurant Closed 24-29 Dec **CARDS:**

KEY TO ATLAS

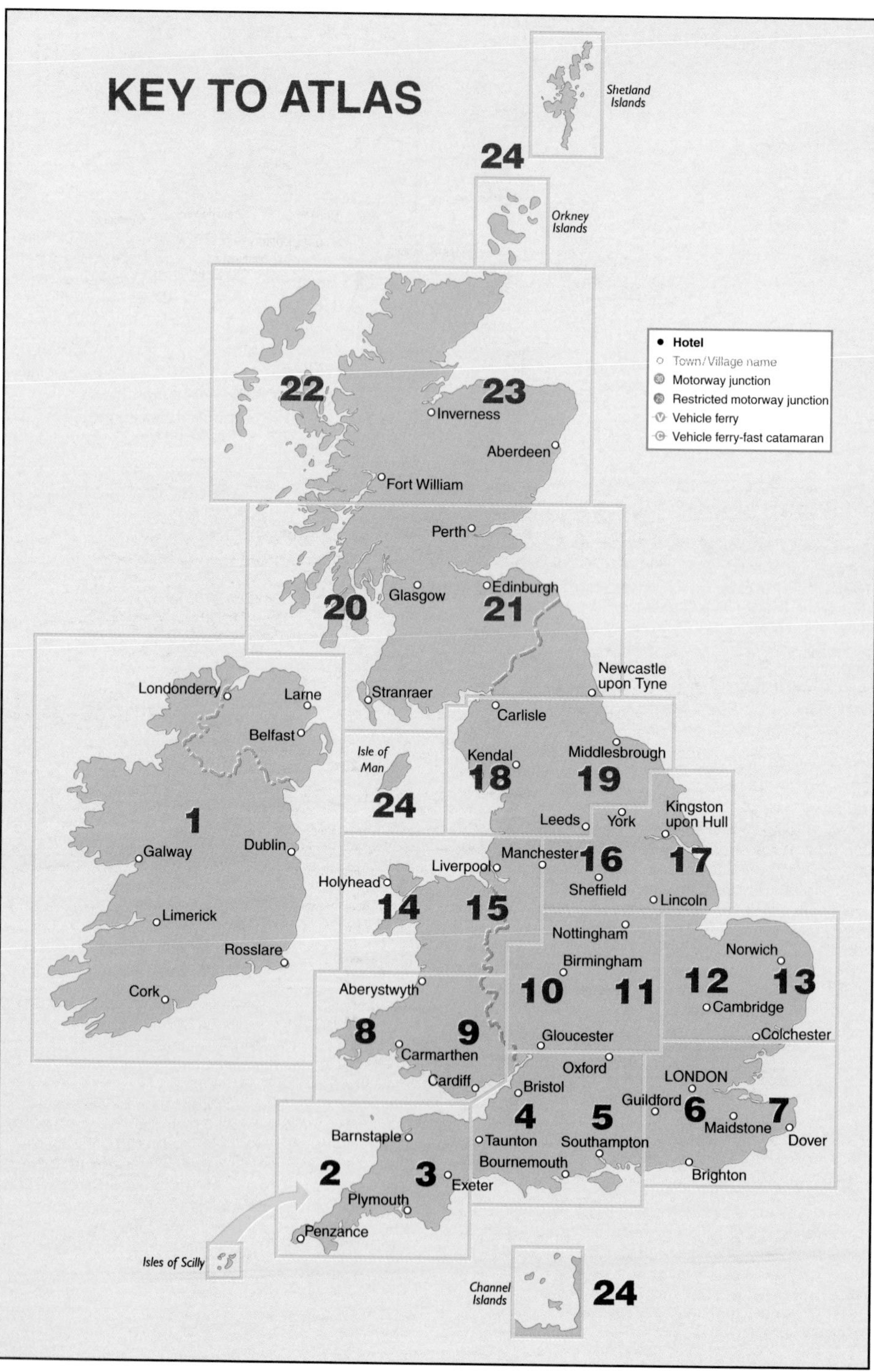

Shetland Islands
24
Orkney Islands
Hotel
Town/Village name
Motorway junction
Restricted motorway junction
Vehicle ferry
Vehicle ferry-fast catamaran
22
23
Inverness
Aberdeen
Fort William
Perth
Glasgow
Edinburgh
20
21
Newcastle upon Tyne
Londonderry
Larne
Belfast
Stranraer
Carlisle
Isle of Man
24
Kendal
18
Middlesbrough
19
1
Leeds
York
Kingston upon Hull
Galway
Dublin
Manchester
16
17
Liverpool
Holyhead
14
15
Sheffield
Lincoln
Limerick
Nottingham
Rosslare
Norwich
Birmingham
Cork
Aberystwyth
10
11
12
13
Cambridge
8
9
Gloucester
Colchester
Carmarthen
Oxford
Cardiff
Bristol
LONDON
Guildford
6
7
4
5
Maidstone
Dover
Barnstaple
Taunton
Southampton
Bournemouth
2
3
Exeter
Brighton
Plymouth
Penzance
Isles of Scilly
Channel Islands
24

1
A
B
C
D
6
5
4
3
2
1
Rathlin Island
Malin Head
Portballintrae
Ballycastle
Tory Island
Portrush
Coleraine
Dunfanaghy
Limavady
Aghadowey
Carnlough
LONDONDERRY
M2
Larne
Aran Island
Letterkenny
Maghera
Ballymena
Strabane
SPERRIN MTS
Carrickfergus
Ballybofey
Bangor
M5
NORTHERN
BELFAST
M2
Donegal
Cookstown
Newtownards
Omagh
Dungannon
Rossnowlagh
M1
Ballyshannon
IRELAND
Portaferry
Irvinestown
Portadown
Donegal Bay
Armagh
Downpatrick
Enniskillen
Newry
Newcastle
Sligo
Monaghan
MOURNE MTS
Bangor Erris
Ballina
Ballyconnell
OX MTS
Carrickmacross
Cavan
Dundalk
Achill Island
Achill Island
Foxford
Carrick-on-Shannon
M1
Boyle
Castlebar
Knock
Virginia
Drogheda
Slane
Castlerea
Kells
Bettystown
Westport
Clare Island
Longford
M1 Toll
Balbriggan
Claremorris
Navan
REPUBLIC
Skerries
Inishturk
Kilmessan
Lambay
Roscommon
Renvyle
Mullingar
Maynooth
Portmarnock
M50
Inishbofin
Tuam
Leixlip
Howth
Recess
Enfield
OF
Clifden
Straffan
DUBLIN
Cashel
Athlone
M4
Lucan
Roundstone
Oughterard
Ballinasloe
Tullamore
Kill
Killiney
Carna
GALWAY
Newbridge
M11
Kildare
Naas
Bray
IRELAND
Gorumna Island
Oranmore
Loughrea
Delgany
Blessington
Newtownmountkennedy
Galway Bay
Rathnew
Birr
SLIEVE BLOOM MTS
Glendalough
Ballyvaughan
Portumna
M7
Inishmore
Gort
Portlaoise
Macreddin
Wicklow
Doolin
Lisdoonvarna
WICKLOW MTS
Roscrea
Abbeyleix
Woodenbridge
Ennistymon
Carlow
Newmarket-on-Fergus
Nenagh
Arklow
Spanish Point
Ennis
Gorey
Bunratty
Kilkenny
Courtown Harbour
Kilkee
Shannon
Thurles
Bunclody
LIMERICK
Kilrush
Thomastown
Enniscorthy
Adare
Tipperary
Cashel
Loop Head
Cahir
Clonmel
Wexford
New Ross
GALTY MTS
Rosslare
Ballyheige
Abbeyfeale
KNOCKMEALDOWN MTS
WATERFORD
Charleville
Tralee
Castleisland
Mitchelstown
Tramore
Carnsore Point
Lismore
Dingle
Kanturk
Mallow
Great Blasket Island
Killorglin
Fermoy
Dungarvan
Killarney
Dingle Bay
BOGGERAGH MTS
Youghal
Midleton
Ardmore
Valentia Island
Blarney
Caherciveen
Macroom
Cobh
Garryvoe
Parknasilla
CORK
Kenmare
Innishannon
Ballycotton
Gougane Barra
Carrigaline
Caherdaniel
Ballylickey
Kinsale
Bantry
Clonakilty
Dursey Island
Bantry Bay
Rosscarbery
Skibbereen
Baltimore
Mizen Head
Clear Island
Hotel
Town name
0
20
40 miles
0
20
40
60 kilometres

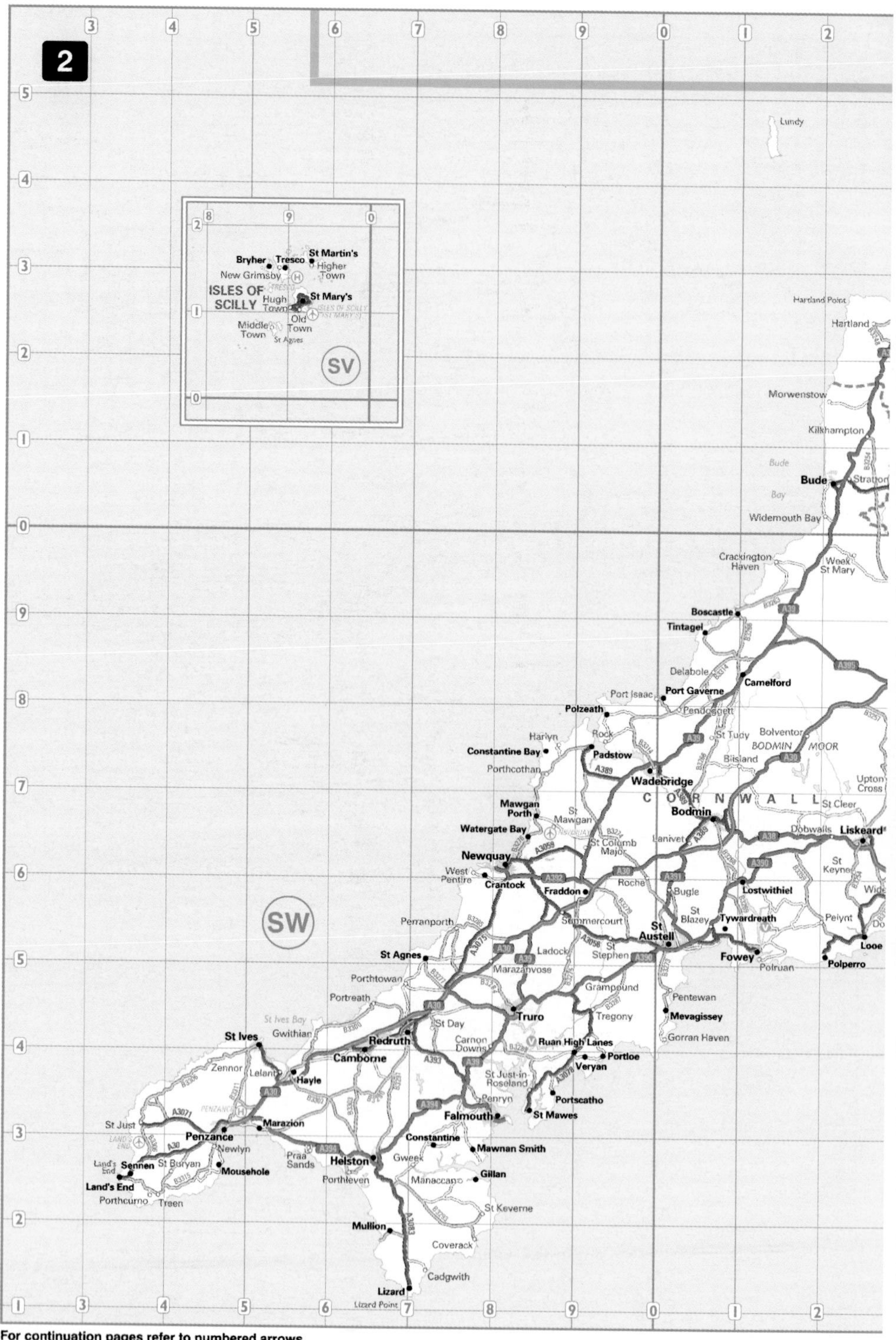

For continuation pages refer to numbered arrows

3
9
SUPER-MARE
Bridgwater Bay
Brent Knoll
Burnham-on-Sea
Martinhoe
Lynton
Lynmouth
Woody Bay
Ilfracombe
Mortehoe
Lee
Combe Martin
Woolacombe
A3123
A399
Parracombe
Brendon
Porlock Weir
Porlock
Minehead
Dunster
Blue Anchor
Watchet
Kilve
Stogursey
West Huntspill
EXMOOR FOREST
Challacombe
Wootton Courtenay
Carhampton
Sampford Brett
Holford
Williton
Nether Stowey
Cannington
Georgeham
Croyde
Saunton
Braunton
Barnstaple or Bideford Bay
Muddiford
Bratton Fleming
Simonsbath
Exford
Wheddon Cross
Bridgwater
Withypool
Brayford
Winsford
Brompton Regis
Crowcombe
Elworthy
QUANTOCK HILLS
Goathurst
North Petherton
Barnstaple
Appledore
Instow
Westward Ho!
Northam
North Molton
Dulverton
Wiveliscombe
Fitzhead
Bishops Lydeard
ST
SOM
Taunton
Lyng
North Curry
Clovelly
Horns Cross
Bideford
SS
South Molton
Parkham
Umberleigh
Exebridge
Petton
Milverton
Wellington
Taunton Deane Services
Hatch Beauchamp
Monkleigh
Great Torrington
Chittlehamholt
Bampton
Sampford Arundel
Corfe
Little Torrington
Burrington
Rackenford
Staple Fitzpaine
Beaford
Witheridge
Sampford Peverell
Culmstock
Horton
Bradworthy
Stibb Cross
Chulmleigh
Chawleigh
Hemyock
Merton
Dolton
Tiverton
Halberton
Uffculme
Milton Damerel
Eggesford
Willand
Shebbear
Lapford
Cullompton
Upottery
Chard
Chilsworthy
Black Torrington
Sheepwash
Meeth
Winkleigh
Morchard Bishop
Cheriton Fitzpaine
Bickleigh
Yarcombe
Holsworthy
Highampton
Hatherleigh
Copplestone
Silverton
Tytherleigh
Halwill Junction
Crediton
Stoke Canon
Honiton
Wilmington
Clawton
Beaworthy
D E V O N
Newton St Cyres
Tedburn St Mary
Broadclyst
Whimple
Feniton
Axminster
Shute
Ashwater
Okehampton
Ottery St Mary
Colyton
Uplyme
South Zeal
EXETER
Colyford
Rousdon
Lyme Regis
Bratton Clovelly
Whiddon Down
Crockernwell
Sourton Cross
Sourton
Dunsford
Clyst St Mary
Axmouth
Branscombe
Seaton
Beer
Bridestowe
Topsham
Woodbury
Sidmouth
Launceston
Lewdown
Chagford
Kennford
Exminster
Otterton
Lydford
Moretonhampstead
Lifton
DARTMOOR FOREST
Kenton
Budleigh Salterton
Milton Abbot
Bovey Tracey
Chudleigh
Exmouth
Postbridge
Widecombe in the Moor
Haytor Vale
Ideford
Lamerton
Mary Tavy
Chudleigh Knighton
Dawlish
Tavistock
Two Bridges
Ilsington
Bishopsteignton
Princetown
Kingsteignton
Teignmouth
Gunnislake
Gulworthy
Hexworthy
Ashburton
Shaldon
Calstock
Horrabridge
Newton Abbot
Pensilva
Holne
Maidencombe
Bere Alston
Dousland
Kingskerswell
St Mellion
Yelverton
Buckfastleigh
Ipplepen
SY
Pillaton
Bere Ferrers
Shaugh Prior
Staverton
TORQUAY
Landrake
Dartington
South Brent
Cornwood
Totnes
Paignton
Saltash
Plympton
Wrangaton
Stoke Gabriel
Tor Bay
Ivybridge
Harbertonford
Churston Ferrers
Polbathic
Dittisham
Brixham
Torpoint
PLYMOUTH
Ermington
Ugborough
Portwrinkle
Crafthole
Halwell
Kingswear
Millbrook
Heybrook Bay
Brixton
Yealmpton
Modbury
Dartmouth
Cawsand
Holbeton
Aveton Gifford
Wembury
Newton Ferrers
Stoke Fleming
Slapton
Strete
SX
Bigbury-on-Sea
Kingsbridge
Chillington
Bigbury Bay
Start Bay
Thurlestone
Torcross
Hope
Hope Cove
Malborough
Salcombe
Hallsands
Start Point
East Prawle
Hotel
Town/Village name
0
10 miles
0
10
20 kilometres

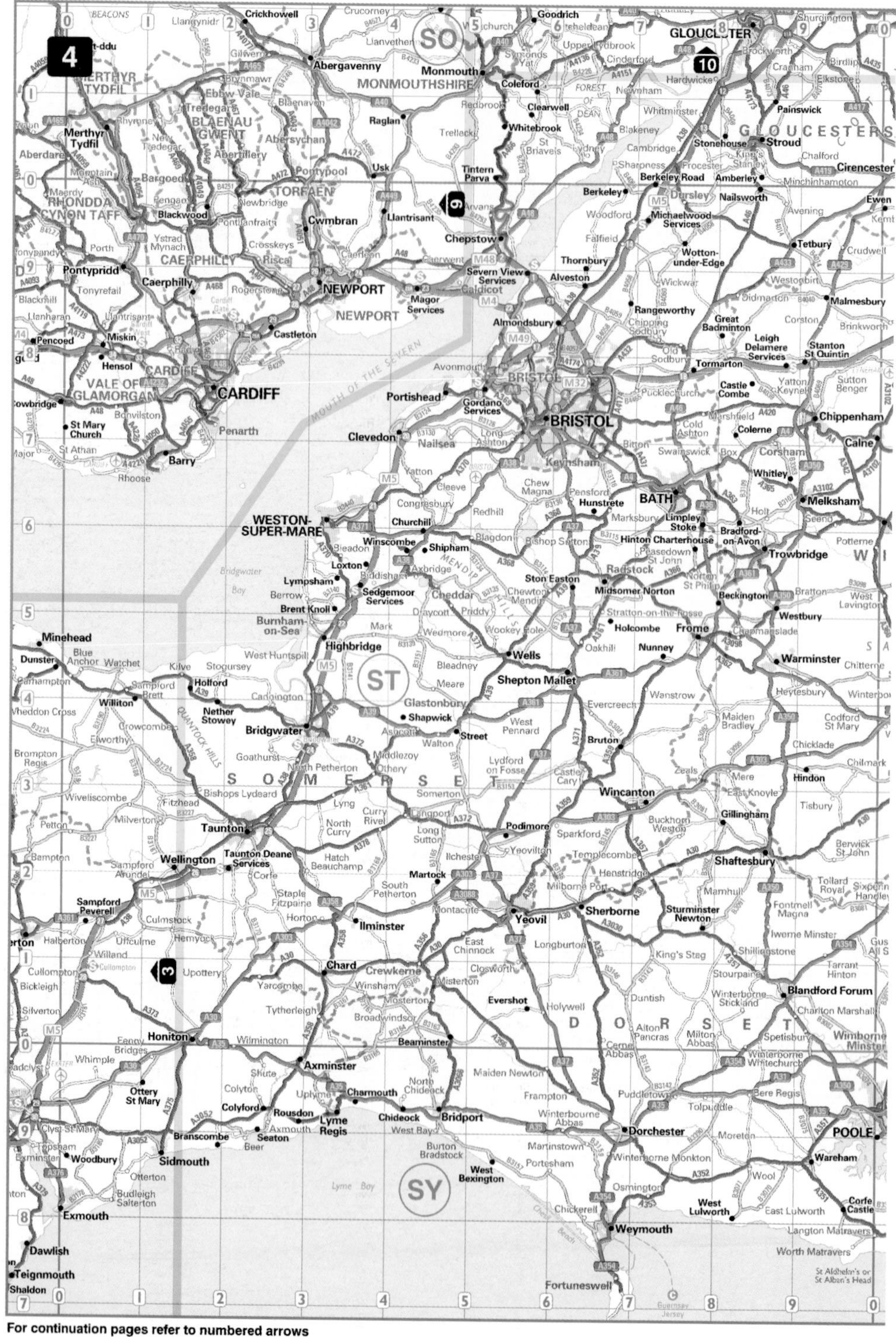

For continuation pages refer to numbered arrows

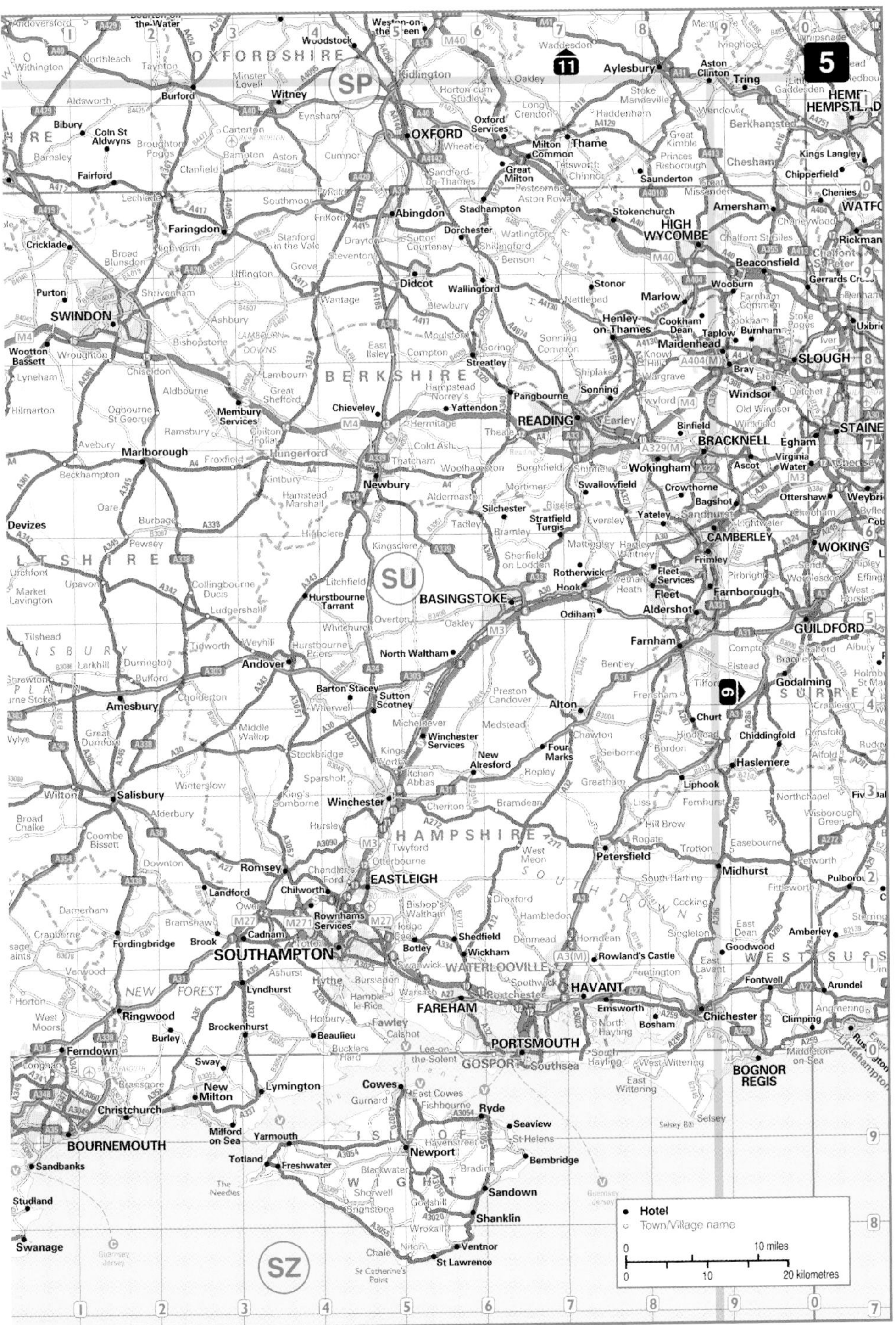
5
11
6
OXFORDSHIRE
BERKSHIRE
HAMPSHIRE
SURREY
ISLE OF WIGHT
NEW FOREST
SOUTH DOWNS
SP
SU
SZ
Woodstock
Kidlington
Witney
Burford
OXFORD
Oxford Services
Milton Common
Thame
Aylesbury
Aston Clinton
Tring
HEMEL HEMPSTEAD
Bibury
Coln St Aldwyns
Fairford
Lechlade
Abingdon
Stadhampton
Great Milton
Saunderton
Amersham
Chenies
Kings Langley
Chipperfield
Faringdon
Dorchester
Stokenchurch
HIGH WYCOMBE
Beaconsfield
Cricklade
Didcot
Wallingford
Stonor
Marlow
Wooburn
Purton
SWINDON
Henley-on-Thames
Cookham Dean
Taplow
Burnham
Maidenhead
SLOUGH
Wootton Bassett
Streatley
Bray
Windsor
Membury Services
Chieveley
Yattendon
Pangbourne
Sonning
READING
Binfield
BRACKNELL
Egham
STAINES
Marlborough
Hungerford
Newbury
Wokingham
Ascot
Virginia Water
Swallowfield
Crowthorne
Bagshot
Devizes
Silchester
Stratfield Turgis
Yateley
CAMBERLEY
WOKING
Frimley
Rotherwick
Fleet Services
Fleet
Hurstbourne Tarrant
BASINGSTOKE
Hook
Farnborough
Odiham
Aldershot
GUILDFORD
Farnham
North Waltham
Andover
Barton Stacey
Sutton Scotney
Amesbury
Alton
Godalming
Churt
Chiddingfold
Winchester Services
Four Marks
New Alresford
Haslemere
Liphook
Salisbury
Winchester
Petersfield
Midhurst
Romsey
EASTLEIGH
Pulborough
Landford
Chilworth
Rownhams Services
Cadnam
Fordingbridge
Brook
SOUTHAMPTON
Botley
Shedfield
Wickham
WATERLOOVILLE
Rowland's Castle
Amberley
Goodwood
Lyndhurst
HAVANT
Emsworth
Fontwell
Arundel
Ringwood
Burley
Brockenhurst
Beaulieu
FAREHAM
Bosham
Chichester
Climping
Ferndown
PORTSMOUTH
Sway
New Milton
Lymington
Cowes
Ryde
Seaview
BOGNOR REGIS
Christchurch
BOURNEMOUTH
Milford on Sea
Yarmouth
Newport
Bembridge
Totland
Freshwater
Sandbanks
Sandown
Studland
Shanklin
Swanage
Ventnor
St Lawrence
Hotel
Town/Village name
10 miles
20 kilometres

For continuation pages refer to numbered arrows

Earls Colne
Aldham
COLCHESTER
Ardleigh
Wix
Harwi
13
Braintree
Marks Tey
Thorpe-le-Soken
Walton on the Naze
Coggeshall
Copford Green
Wivenhoe
Elmstead Market
Weeley
Feering
Silver End
Kelvedon
Thorrington
Little Clacton
Frinton-on-Sea
Tiptree
Tolleshunt Knights
Brightlingsea
St Osyth
CLACTON-ON-SEA
Witham
TM
Hatfield Peverel
Tolleshunt D'Arcy
West Mersea
Goldhanger
Tollesbury
MSFORD
Maldon
River Blackwater
Bradwell-on-Sea
Danbury
Steeple
Cold Norton
Latchingdon
Southminster
South Woodham Ferrers
Burnham-on-Crouch
Hockley
Rayleigh
Rochford
Great Wakering
SOUTHEND-ON-SEA
Canvey Island
Grain
Sheerness
Minster
Hoo St Werburgh
Eastchurch
Leysdown-on-Sea
Isle of Sheppey
ROCHESTER
GILLINGHAM
CHATHAM
Iwade
Herne Bay
Reculver
MARGATE
Kingsgate
Broadstairs
Whitstable
Sarre
Ramsgate
Sittingbourne
Upstreet
Minster
Teynham
Faversham
Ospringe
Hersden
Brodhurst
Blean
Sturry
Fordwich
Ash
Sandwich
Maidstone Services
Boughton Street
Canterbury
Wingham
TR
Doddington
Hollingbourne
Chilham
Chartham
Bridge
Eastry
Bearsted
Lenham
Aylesham
Deal
Challock
Charing
Linton
Sutton Valence
K E N T
Kingsdown
Wye
Wingmore
Pluckley
St Margaret's at Cliffe
Headcorn
Elham
Alkham
DOVER
Smarden
Staplehurst
Ashford
Densole
Bethersden
Lyminge
CHANNEL TUNNEL TERMINAL
Hawkinge
Biddenden
High Halden
Kingsnorth
Sellindge
Channel Tunnel (Rail)
Sissinghurst
Cranbrook
Woodchurch
Lympne
FOLKESTONE
Benenden
Tenterden
Hythe
Hawkhurst
Rolvenden
Hamstreet
Wittersham
Appledore
Dymchurch
Bodiam
Brookland
Brenzett
St Mary's Bay
Northiam
New Romney
STRAIT OF DOVER
Peasmarsh
Rye
Lydd
Sedlescombe
Brede
Camber
Winchelsea
Dungeness
Westfield
Guestling Green
Fairlight
HASTINGS
Bexhill
M2
M20
A2
A20
A28
A12
A120
A133
A414
A13
A127
A130
A228
A249
A299
A28
A256
A257
A258
A251
A2070
A259
A261
A268
A21
A229
A262
A274
A255
A254
• Hotel
○ Town/Village name
0
10 miles
0
10
20 kilometres

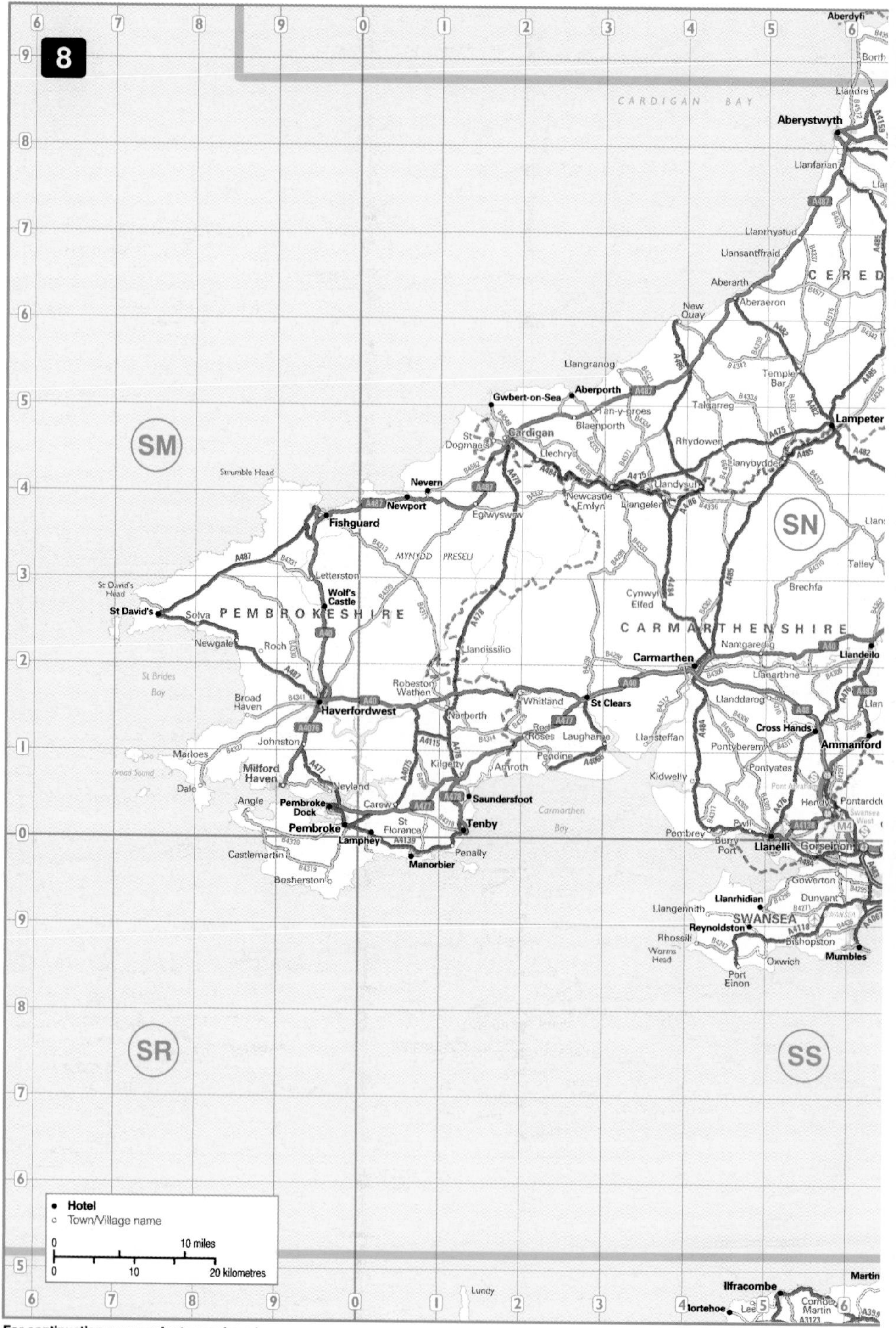

For continuation pages refer to numbered arrows

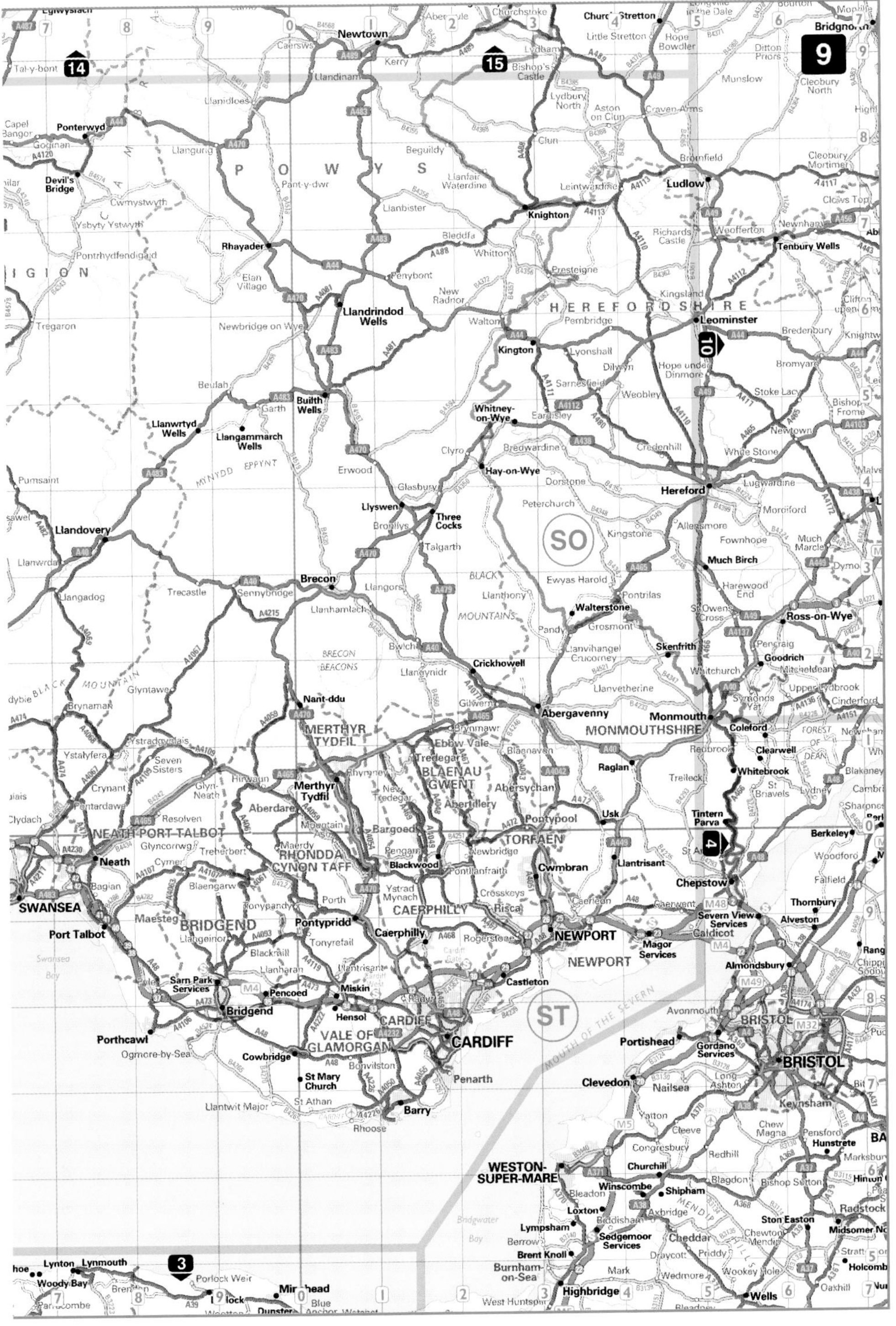

9
14
15
10
4
3
Newtown
Churchstoke
Church Stretton
Little Stretton
Hope Bowdler
Bridgnorth
Tal-y-bont
Caersws
Kerry
Bishop's Castle
Lydham
Lydbury North
Aston on Clun
Craven Arms
Ditton Priors
Munslow
Cleobury North
Llandinam
Llanidloes
Capel Bangor
Ponterwyd
Goginan
Llangurig
Devil's Bridge
Cwmystwyth
Ysbyty Ystwyth
Pontrhydfendigaid
POWYS
Pant-y-dwr
Beguildy
Llanfair Waterdine
Clun
Bromfield
Ludlow
Leintwardine
Cleobury Mortimer
Clows Top
Llanbister
Knighton
Rhayader
Bleddfa
Whitton
Richards Castle
Woofferton
Newnham
Tenbury Wells
Elan Village
Penybont
Presteigne
New Radnor
Kingsland
Tregaron
Newbridge on Wye
Llandrindod Wells
Walton
HEREFORDSHIRE
Pembridge
Leominster
Kington
Lyonshall
Dilwyn
Hope under Dinmore
Bredenbury
Bromyard
Beulah
Garth
Builth Wells
Sarnesfield
Weobley
Stoke Lacy
Bishops Frome
Llanwrtyd Wells
Llangammarch Wells
Whitney-on-Wye
Eardisley
Newtown
MYNYDD EPPYNT
Clyro
Bredwardine
Credenhill
White Stone
Pumsaint
Erwood
Hay-on-Wye
Dorstone
Hereford
Lugwardine
Glasbury
Peterchurch
Mordiford
Llyswen
Three Cocks
Bronllys
Llandovery
Allensmore
Kingstone
Fownhope
Much Marcle
Talgarth
SO
Much Birch
Dymock
Brecon
BLACK MOUNTAINS
Ewyas Harold
Harewood End
Llangadog
Trecastle
Sennybridge
Llangors
Llanthony
Pontrilas
Llanhamlach
Walterstone
St Owens Cross
Ross-on-Wye
Grosmont
Pandy
BRECON BEACONS
Bwlch
Skenfrith
Pencraig
Llanvihangel Crucorney
Crickhowell
Goodrich
Mitcheldean
Llangynidr
Whitchurch
BLACK MOUNTAIN
Glyntawe
Llanvetherine
Symonds Yat
Upper Lydbrook
Cinderford
Nant-ddu
Gilwern
Abergavenny
Monmouth
Brynamman
Coleford
MERTHYR TYDFIL
Brynmawr
MONMOUTHSHIRE
FOREST OF DEAN
Ystradgynlais
Ebbw Vale
Redbrook
Clearwell
Ystalyfera
Seven Sisters
Tredegar
Blaenavon
Raglan
Whitebrook
BLAENAU GWENT
Hirwaun
Crynant
Glyn-Neath
Merthyr Tydfil
Rhymney
New Tredegar
Abersychan
Trelleck
St Briavels
Lydney
Blakeney
Pontardawe
Aberdare
Abertillery
Resolven
Mountain Ash
Bargoed
Pontypool
Usk
Tintern Parva
Berkeley
NEATH PORT TALBOT
Maerdy
TORFAEN
Glyncorrwg
Treherbert
RHONDDA CYNON TAFF
Pengam
Newbridge
St Arvans
Woodford
Neath
Cymer
Blackwood
Pontllanfraith
Cwmbran
Llantrisant
Bagian
Blaengarw
Ystrad Mynach
Crosskeys
Chepstow
Falfield
SWANSEA
Tonypandy
Porth
CAERPHILLY
Risca
Caerleon
Caerwent
Thornbury
Maesteg
BRIDGEND
Pontypridd
Severn View Services
Alveston
Port Talbot
Llangeinor
Tonyrefail
Caerphilly
Rogerstone
NEWPORT
Magor Services
Caldicot
Swansea Bay
Blackmill
Llantrisant
Almondsbury
Sarn Park Services
Llanharan
Castleton
Pencoed
Miskin
Hensol
Bridgend
Avonmouth
ST
MOUTH OF THE SEVERN
BRISTOL
CARDIFF
VALE OF GLAMORGAN
Portishead
Gordano Services
Porthcawl
Ogmore-by-Sea
Cowbridge
Bonvilston
Clevedon
Nailsea
Long Ashton
St Mary Church
Penarth
Keynsham
Llantwit Major
St Athan
Barry
Rhoose
Yatton
Cleeve
Chew Magna
Pensford
Hunstrete
Congresbury
Redhill
WESTON-SUPER-MARE
Churchill
Marksbury
Winscombe
Blagdon
Bishop Sutton
Bleadon
Shipham
MENDIP HILLS
Loxton
Axbridge
Radstock
Lympsham
Biddisham
Ston Easton
Midsomer Norton
Sedgemoor Services
Cheddar
Chewton Mendip
Berrow
Bridgwater Bay
Brent Knoll
Draycott
Priddy
Lynton
Lynmouth
Burnham-on-Sea
Mark
Wookey Hole
Holcombe
Woody Bay
Porlock Weir
Minehead
Wedmore
Highbridge
Wells
Oakhill
Parracombe
Blue Anchor
Dunster
West Huntspill
M4
M5
M48
M49
M32
A40
A44
A49
A48
A470
A465
A483
A4120
A489
A488
A481
A4113
A4110
A4112
A4117
A438
A4103
A479
A4042
A466
A4136
A4151
A4067
A4069
A4068
A474
A4109
A4059
A4061
A4063
A4107
A4093
A4119
A4222
A4232
A4226
A4055
A4050
A4106
A473
A4229
A468
A4054
A4049
A472
A4051
A4137
A4215
A4224
A4111
A4112
A480
A4230
A4217
A4221
A371
A370
A369
A38
A368
A37
A39
A4174
A4018
A417
A432
A4201
A4137
A417
A4172
A456
A443

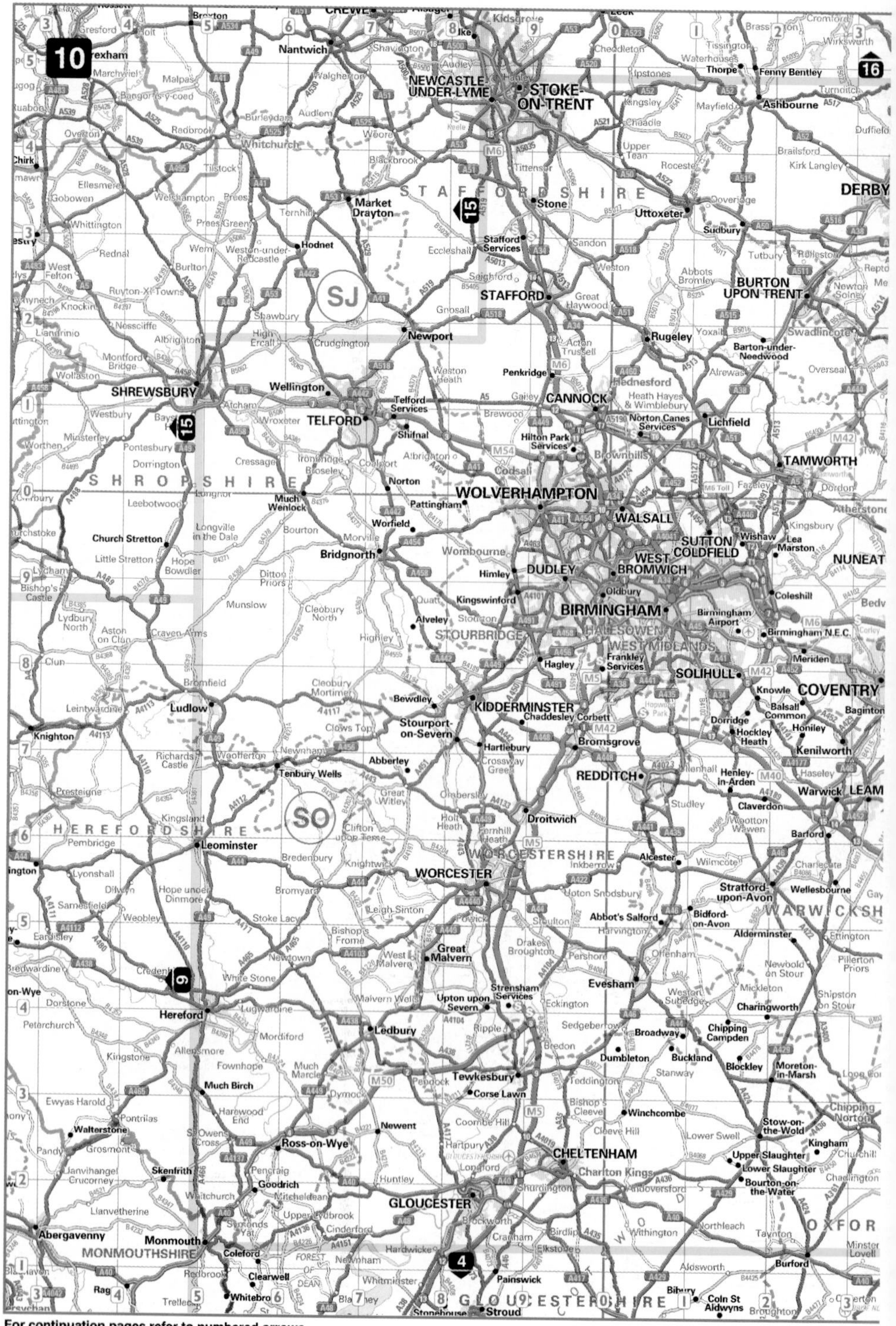

For continuation pages refer to numbered arrows

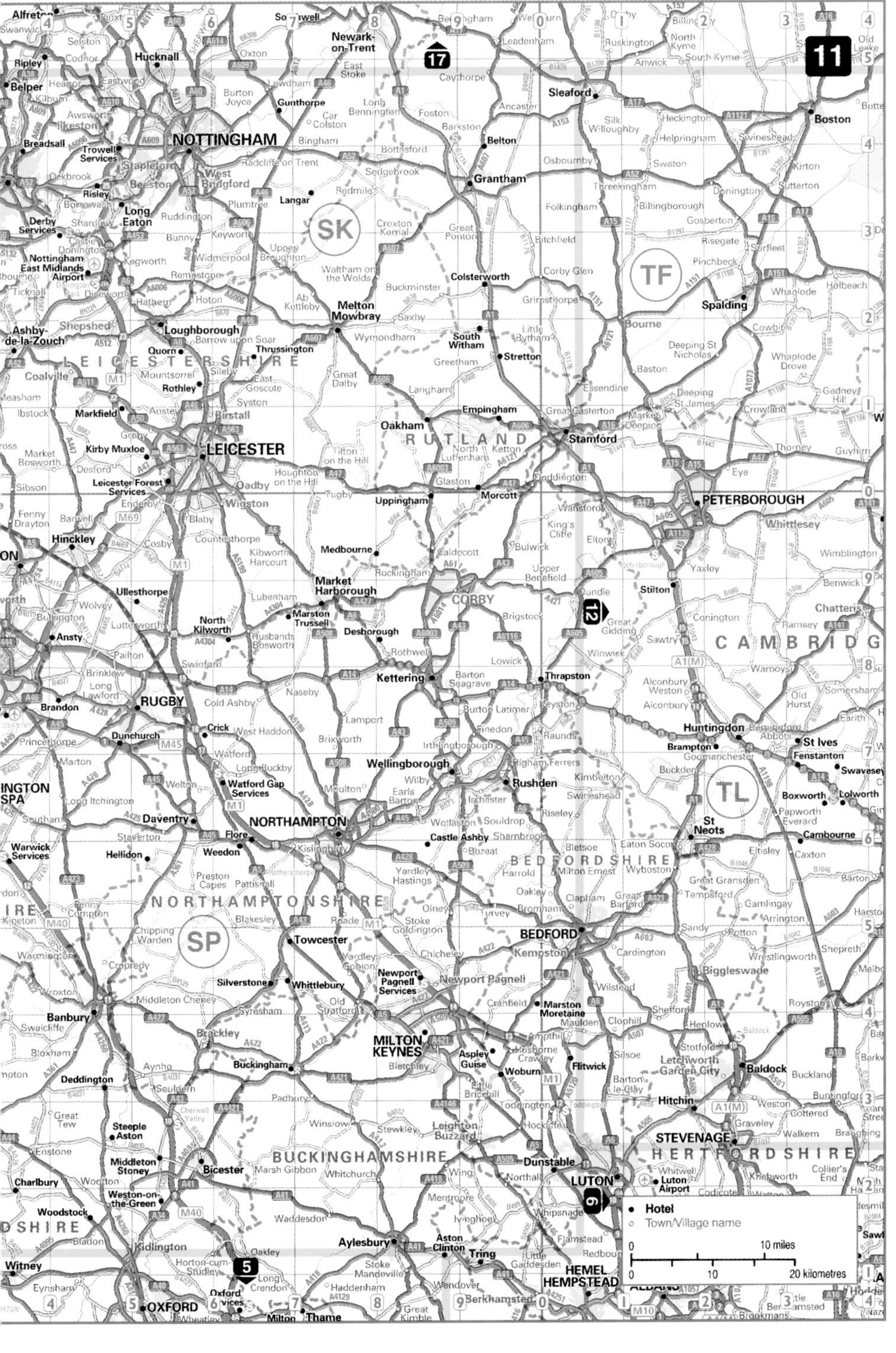
11
17
12
6
5
SK
TF
SP
TL
NOTTINGHAM
LEICESTER
NORTHAMPTON
PETERBOROUGH
MILTON KEYNES
BEDFORD
LUTON
RUGBY
CORBY
STEVENAGE
HEMEL HEMPSTEAD
OXFORD
LEICESTERSHIRE
RUTLAND
NORTHAMPTONSHIRE
BEDFORDSHIRE
BUCKINGHAMSHIRE
HERTFORDSHIRE
CAMBRIDG
Alfreton
Ripley
Belper
Hucknall
Newark-on-Trent
Sleaford
Boston
Gunthorpe
Belton
Grantham
Langar
Stapleford
West Bridgford
Trowell Services
Long Eaton
Derby Services
Nottingham East Midlands Airport
Breadsall
Risley
Colsterworth
Melton Mowbray
South Witham
Stretton
Spalding
Bourne
Loughborough
Quorn
Thrussington
Ashby-de-la-Zouch
Rothley
Markfield
Kirby Muxloe
Leicester Forest Services
Oakham
Empingham
Stamford
Uppingham
Morcott
Medbourne
Market Harborough
Hinckley
Ullesthorpe
North Kilworth
Marston Trussell
Desborough
Ansty
Kettering
Thrapston
Stilton
Huntingdon
Brampton
St Ives
Fenstanton
Swavesey
Boxworth
Lolworth
St Neots
Cambourne
Brandon
Crick
Watford Gap Services
Wellingborough
Rushden
Daventry
Flore
Weedon
Hellidon
Warwick Services
Castle Ashby
Towcester
Newport Pagnell Services
Silverstone
Whittlebury
Marston Moretaine
Banbury
Buckingham
Aspley Guise
Woburn
Flitwick
Baldock
Hitchin
Biggleswade
Deddington
Steeple Aston
Middleton Stoney
Bicester
Charlbury
Weston-on-the-Green
Woodstock
Kidlington
Witney
Aylesbury
Aston Clinton
Tring
Dunstable
Luton Airport
Thame
Hotel
Town/Village name
10 miles
20 kilometres

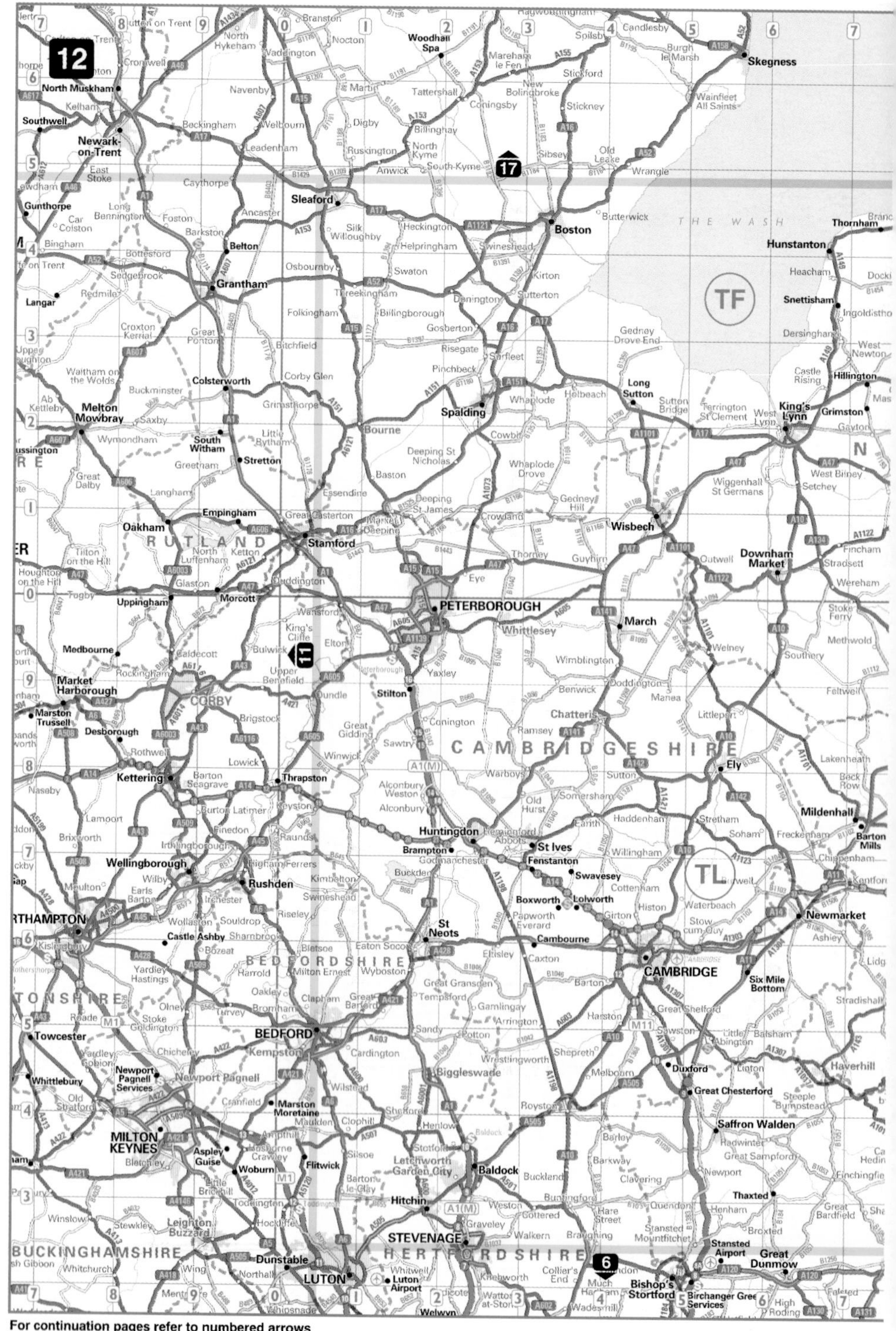

For continuation pages refer to numbered arrows

TG
TM
NORFOLK
SUFFOLK
Brancaster Staithe
Burnham Overy Staithe
Holkham
Morston
Cley next the Sea
Blakeney
Sheringham
Cromer
Titchwell
Burnham Market
Wells-next-the-sea
Stiffkey
Weybourne
West Runton
Trimingham
North Creake
Little Walsingham
Holt
Roughton
Southrepps
Mundesley
Thorpe Market
Bacton
Syderstone
Houghton St Giles
Melton Constable
Saxthorpe
North Walsham
Happisburgh
Great Bircham
Fakenham
Blickling
Aylsham
Sea Palling
East Rudham
Guist
Stalham
South Raynham
North Elmham
Reepham
Catfield
Horsey
Weasenham All Saints
Bawdeswell
Coltishall
Ludham
Castle Acre
Litcham
Beetley
Attlebridge
Wroxham
Spixworth
Horning
Rollesby
Hemsby
Ormesby St Margaret
Dereham
Taverham
Rackheath
South Walsham
Narborough
Drayton
Thorpe End
Filby
Caister-on-Sea
Honingham
Acle
Swaffham
Necton
Barnham Broom
NORWICH
Brundall
GREAT YARMOUTH
Shipdham
Cringleford
Burgh Castle
Kimberley
Hethersett
Caistor St Edmund
Belton
Hingham
Yelverton
Reedham
Watton
Wymondham
Scoulton
Brooke
Loddon
Hopton on Sea
Fritton
Northwold
Attleborough
Hales
Corton
Bunwell Street
Long Stratton
Hempnall
Haddiscoe
Mundford
Great Hockham
Ellingham
LOWESTOFT
Gillingham
New Buckenham
Bungay
Banham
Earsham
Beccles
Brandon
East Harling
Kenninghall
Tivetshall St Mary
Pulham St Mary
Homersfield
Henstead
Kessingland
Thetford
Harleston
Garboldisham
Diss
Wrentham
Elveden
Scole
Brockdish
Metfield
Redgrave
Hoxne
Honington
Botesdale
Brome
Fressingfield
Halesworth
Southwold
Stradbroke
Walberswick
Stanton
Eye
Laxfield
Bramfield
Ixworth
Dunwich
Darsham
Finningham
Peasenhall
Yoxford
Westleton
Brockford Street
Worlingworth
Bury St Edmunds
Thurston
Mendlesham
Dennington
Theberton
Framlingham
Debenham
Leiston
Horringer
Woolpit
Saxmundham
Stratford St Andrew
Stowmarket
Easton
Thorpeness
Whepstead
Snape
Helmingham
Aldeburgh
Needham Market
Wickham Market
Tunstall
Hawkedon
Hartest
Coddenham
Witnesham
Butley
Hitcham
Great Blakenham
Lavenham
Glemsford
Claydon
Bildeston
Woodbridge
Orford
Long Melford
Martlesham Heath
Clare
Hintlesham
IPSWICH
Shottisham
Stoke by Clare
Sudbury
Boxford
Hadleigh
Copdock
Nacton
Capel St Mary
Bawdsey
Great Yeldham
Stoke-by-Nayland
Shotley
East Bergholt
Holbrook
Bures
Nayland
Felixstowe
Colne Engaine
Dedham
Manningtree
Halstead
Harwich
Earls Colne
Ardleigh
Aldham
COLCHESTER
Wix
Braintree
Marks Tey
Weeley
Thorpe-le-Soken
Walton on the Naze
Coggeshall
Copford Green
Wivenhoe
Feering
Silver End
Kelvedon
Frinton-on-Sea
Hotel
Town/Village name
0
10 miles
0
10
20 kilometres

For continuation pages refer to numbered arrows

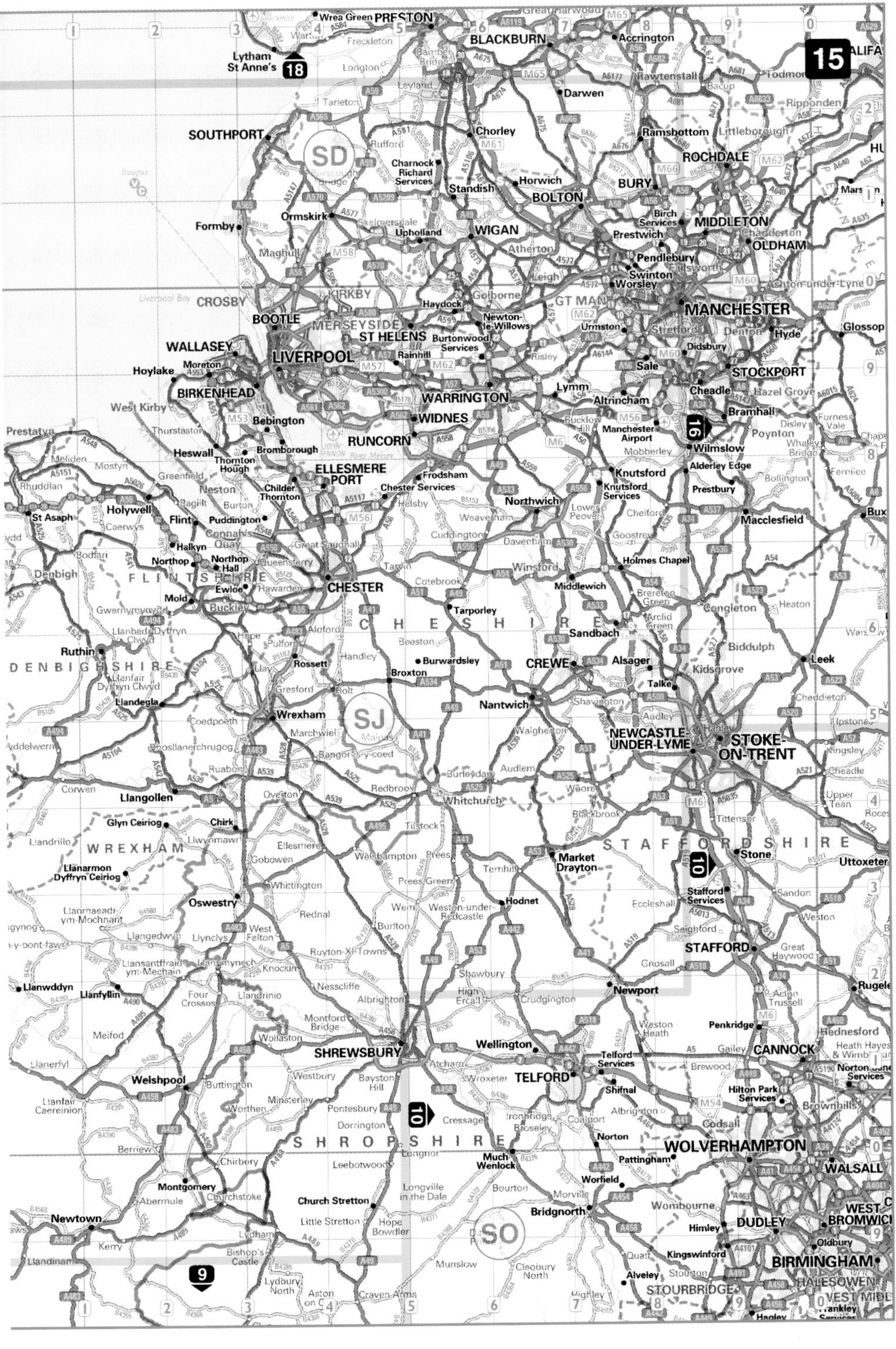

15
PRESTON
Lytham St Anne's
18
BLACKBURN
Accrington
Darwen
Rawtenstall
Bacup
Todmorden
Ripponden
Littleborough
Ramsbottom
ROCHDALE
SOUTHPORT
SD
Chorley
Charnock Richard Services
Standish
Horwich
BOLTON
BURY
Birch Services
MIDDLETON
Formby
Ormskirk
Upholland
WIGAN
Prestwich
OLDHAM
Pendlebury
Swinton
Worsley
Ashton-under-Lyne
CROSBY
KIRKBY
Haydock
Newton-le-Willows
MANCHESTER
BOOTLE
MERSEYSIDE
ST HELENS
Burtonwood Services
Urmston
Glossop
WALLASEY
LIVERPOOL
Rainhill
Didsbury
Hyde
Hoylake
Moreton
Sale
STOCKPORT
BIRKENHEAD
WARRINGTON
Lymm
Altrincham
Cheadle
Hazel Grove
West Kirby
Bebington
WIDNES
Manchester Airport
16
Bramhall
Prestatyn
RUNCORN
Poynton
Heswall
Bromborough
Wilmslow
Thornton Hough
ELLESMERE PORT
Knutsford
Alderley Edge
Frodsham
Chester Services
Knutsford Services
Prestbury
Rhuddlan
Childer Thornton
Northwich
St Asaph
Holywell
Flint
Puddington
Macclesfield
Connah's Quay
Halkyn
Northop
Northop Hall
Holmes Chapel
Denbigh
FLINTSHIRE
Ewloe
CHESTER
Middlewich
Mold
Buckley
Tarporley
Congleton
CHESHIRE
Sandbach
Ruthin
Rossett
Burwardsley
CREWE
Alsager
Leek
DENBIGHSHIRE
Broxton
Talke
Llandegla
Nantwich
Wrexham
SJ
NEWCASTLE-UNDER-LYME
STOKE-ON-TRENT
Llangollen
Whitchurch
Glyn Ceiriog
Chirk
WREXHAM
STAFFORDSHIRE
Llanarmon Dyffryn Ceiriog
Market Drayton
10
Stone
Uttoxeter
Oswestry
Hodnet
Stafford Services
STAFFORD
Llanwddyn
Llanfyllin
Newport
Rugeley
SHREWSBURY
Wellington
Penkridge
CANNOCK
Welshpool
TELFORD
Telford Services
Shifnal
Hilton Park Services
SHROPSHIRE
Much Wenlock
Norton
WOLVERHAMPTON
Pattingham
WALSALL
Montgomery
Church Stretton
Worfield
Newtown
Bridgnorth
Himley
DUDLEY
WEST BROMWICH
SO
Kingswinford
BIRMINGHAM
9
Alveley
STOURBRIDGE
HALESOWEN
Hagley

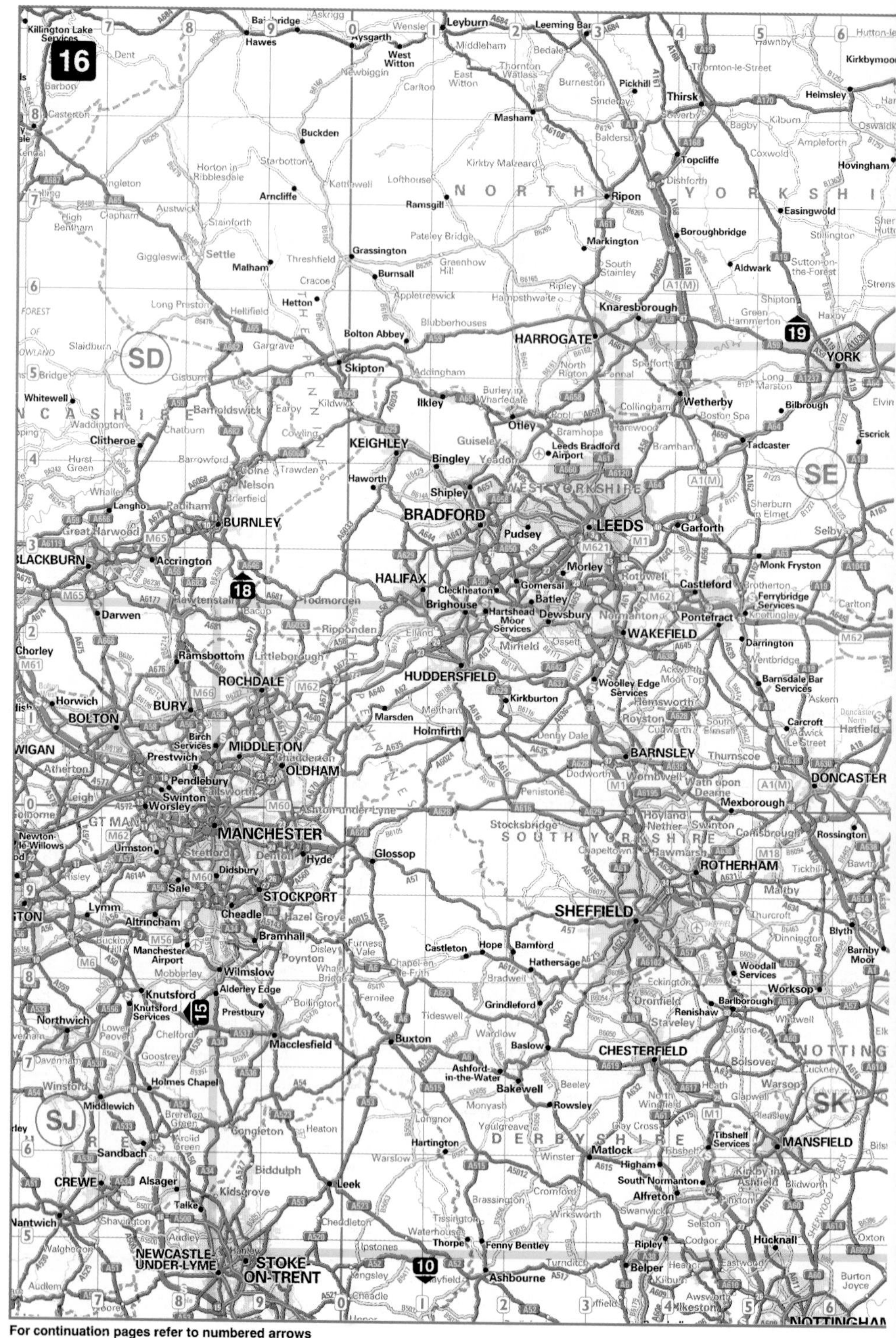

For continuation pages refer to numbered arrows

Hotel
Town/Village name
0
10 miles
0
10
20 kilometres
Lastingham
Cropton
Lockton
Hackness
Scalby
Scarborough
Wrelton
Pickering
Thornton le Dale
East Ayton
Seamer
Cayton
Ebberston
Snainton
Brompton
Flixton
Filey
Kirby Misperton
Staxton
Sherburn
Hunmanby
Reighton
Slingsby
Rillington
Bempton
Flamborough Head
Flamborough
Malton
Norton
19
North Grimston
Burton Fleming
Rudston
Carnaby
Bridlington
Langtoft
Sledmere
Kilham
Burton Agnes
Fridaythorpe
Wetwang
Driffield
Barmston
Skipsea
Stamford Bridge
North Dalton
Bainton
North Frodingham
Beeford
Atwick
Wilberfoss
EAST RIDING OF YORKSHIRE
Barmby Moor
Pocklington
Middleton on the Wolds
Brandesburton
Hornsea
Sutton upon Derwent
Leven
Goxhill
TA
Market Weighton
Shiptonthorpe
Holme upon Spalding Moor
Beverley
Aldbrough
Walkington
Bubwith
North Cave
Little Weighton
Sproatley
Cottingham
South Cave
Willerby
Howden
Newport
KINGSTON UPON HULL
Hedon
Withernsea
Elloughton
Hessle
Melton
North Ferriby
Goole
New Holland
Winteringham
Patrington
Barton-upon-Humber
Goxhill
Easington
Burton upon Stather
Winterton
Immingham Dock
River Humber
Wootton
Ulceby
Thorne
Immingham
Stallingborough
Crowle
Gunness
SCUNTHORPE
GRIMSBY
Spurn Head
Broughton
Wrawby
Cleethorpes
Althorpe
Barnetby le Wold
Belton
Brigg
Laceby
Humberston
Scawby
Waltham
Epworth
Messingham
Holton le Clay
Hibaldstow
Swallow
Caistor
Tetney
North Cotes
Blaxton
Finningley
Haxey
Scotter
Grainthorpe
Kirton in Lindsey
Ludborough
North Somercotes
Misterton
Blyton
Binbrook
Saltfleet
Gringley on the Hill
Middle Rasen
Gainsborough
Glentham
Market Rasen
Louth
Saundby
Mablethorpe
Legbourne
Lissington
Faldingworth
Ingham
Sutton on Sea
Withern
East Barkwith
Retford
Torksey
Sturton by Stow
Wragby
Scamblesby
Alford
Gamston
Saxilby
Newton on Trent
Langworth
Bilsby
Huttoft
Markham Moor
Tetford
Chapel St Leonards
Baumber
Skellingthorpe
LINCOLN
LINCOLNSHIRE
Hogsthorpe
Edlington
Tuxford
Ingoldmells
Washingborough
Bardney
Horncastle
Hagworthingham
Candlesby
Sutton on Trent
Branston
Spilsby
North Hykeham
Nocton
Woodhall Spa
Burgh le Marsh
Carlton-on-Trent
Skegness
Waddington
Mareham le Fen
Cromwell
Caunton
Stickford
TF
New Bolingbroke
Navenby
Martin
Tattershall
North Muskham
Coningsby
Wainfleet All Saints
Kelham
Stickney
Digby
Welbourn
Billinghay
Beckingham
Southwell
Newark-on-Trent
Leadenham
North Kyme
Sibsey
Old Leake
Ruskington
South Kyme
Wrangle
Anwick
East Stoke
Caythorpe
Lowdham
11
12
Sleaford
Gunthorpe
Long Bennington
Ancaster
Butterwick
THE WASH
Thornham
Car Colston
Foston
Heckington
Boston
Silk Willoughby
Hunstanton
Barkston
Helpringham
Swineshead
Bingham
Brancaster
M62
M18
M180
M181
A64
A165
A170
A1039
A169
A614
A166
A1079
A164
A1035
A1034
A163
A63
A161
A1077
A15
A18
A180
A1173
A160
A46
A631
A159
A157
A1031
A1104
A52
A1111
A158
A16
A153
A155
A1028
A57
A156
A1500
A1133
A1434
A607
A17
A6075
A616
A617
A612
A1
A620
A638
A1121
A153
B1249
B1253
B1248
B1230

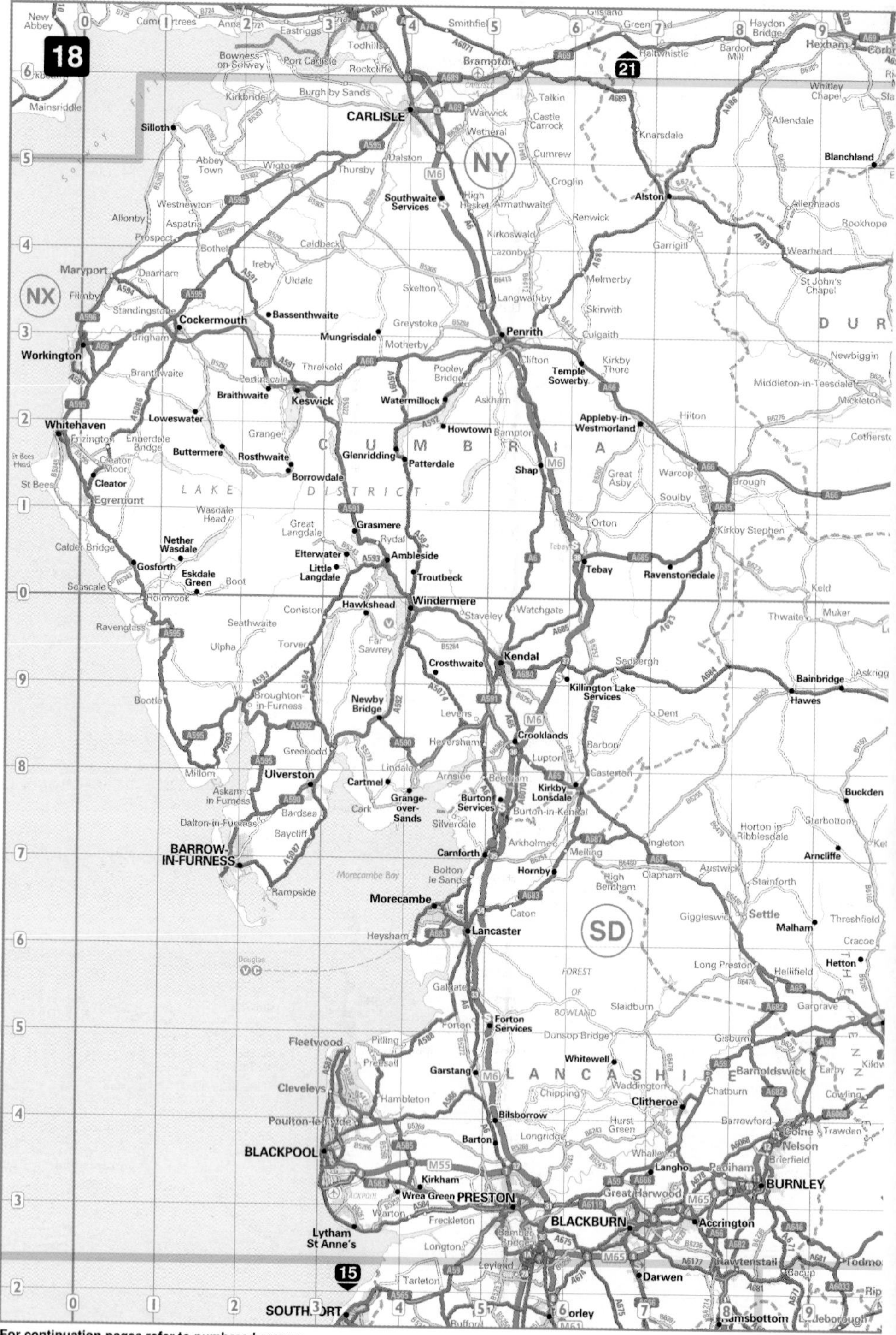

For continuation pages refer to numbered arrows

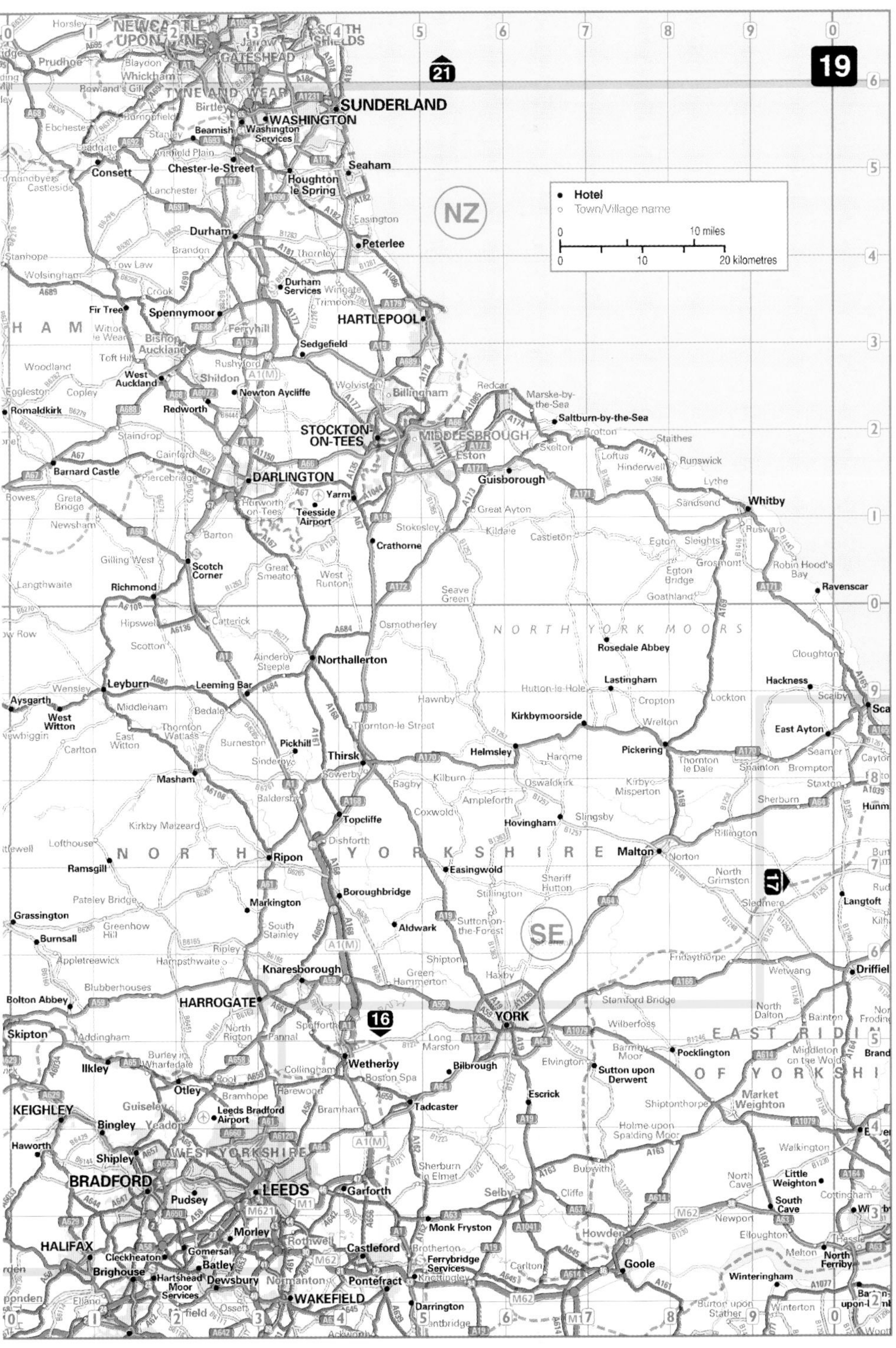
19
21
16
17
Hotel
Town/Village name
0
10 miles
0
10
20 kilometres
NZ
SE
NEWCASTLE UPON TYNE
GATESHEAD
SOUTH SHIELDS
Jarrow
TYNE AND WEAR
SUNDERLAND
WASHINGTON
Washington Services
Horsley
Prudhoe
Blaydon
Whickham
Rowland's Gill
Birtley
Burnopfield
Ebchester
Stanley
Beamish
Leadgate
Annfield Plain
Consett
Chester-le-Street
Houghton le Spring
Seaham
Castleside
Lanchester
Easington
Durham
Peterlee
Brandon
Thornley
Stanhope
Tow Law
Wolsingham
Crook
Durham Services
Wingate
Trimdon
Fir Tree
Spennymoor
HARTLEPOOL
Witton le Wear
Bishop Auckland
Ferryhill
Sedgefield
Toft Hill
Woodland
Rushyford
West Auckland
Shildon
Eggleston
Copley
Newton Aycliffe
Wolviston
Billingham
Redcar
Marske-by-the-Sea
Saltburn-by-the-Sea
Romaldkirk
Redworth
STOCKTON-ON-TEES
MIDDLESBROUGH
Brotton
Staithes
Staindrop
Gainford
Skelton
Eston
Loftus
Hinderwell
Runswick
Barnard Castle
DARLINGTON
Guisborough
Lythe
Piercebridge
Yarm
Bowes
Greta Bridge
Hurworth-on-Tees
Teesside Airport
Great Ayton
Sandsend
Whitby
Newsham
Stokesley
Kildale
Castleton
Egton
Sleights
Ruswarp
Barton
Crathorne
Grosmont
Robin Hood's Bay
Gilling West
Scotch Corner
Great Smeaton
West Rounton
Egton Bridge
Langthwaite
Richmond
Seave Green
Goathland
Ravenscar
Hipswell
Catterick
Osmotherley
NORTH YORK MOORS
Scotton
Rosedale Abbey
Ainderby Steeple
Northallerton
Cloughton
Leyburn
Wensley
Leeming Bar
Lastingham
Hackness
Aysgarth
Hutton-le-Hole
Lockton
Scalby
West Witton
Middleham
Bedale
Hawnby
Cropton
Kirkbymoorside
Wrelton
East Ayton
Thornton Watlass
Thornton-le-Street
East Witton
Carlton
Burneston
Pickhill
Thirsk
Helmsley
Harome
Pickering
Seamer
Thornton le Dale
Snainton
Brompton
Sinderby
Sowerby
Masham
Bagby
Kilburn
Oswaldkirk
Kirby Misperton
Staxton
Baldersby
Ampleton
Coxwold
Sherburn
Topcliffe
Hovingham
Slingsby
Kirkby Malzeard
Rillington
Dishforth
Lofthouse
NORTH YORKSHIRE
Ramsgill
Ripon
Malton
Norton
Easingwold
Sheriff Hutton
North Grimston
Pateley Bridge
Boroughbridge
Stillington
Langtoft
Markington
Sledmere
Grassington
South Stainley
Aldwark
Sutton-on-the-Forest
Greenhow Hill
Burnsall
Ripley
Appletreewick
Hampsthwaite
Shipton
Fridaythorpe
Driffield
Knaresborough
Green Hammerton
Haxby
Wetwang
Blubberhouses
Bolton Abbey
HARROGATE
Stamford Bridge
North Dalton
Bainton
Skipton
Addingham
North Rigton
Pannal
Spofforth
Long Marston
YORK
Wilberfoss
EAST RIDING OF YORKSHIRE
Burley in Wharfedale
Barmby Moor
Pocklington
Middleton on the Wolds
Ilkley
Collingham
Wetherby
Bilbrough
Elvington
Sutton upon Derwent
Boston Spa
Otley
Bramhope
Harewood
Escrick
Market Weighton
KEIGHLEY
Guiseley
Leeds Bradford Airport
Tadcaster
Bramham
Shiptonthorpe
Bingley
Yeadon
Holme-upon-Spalding Moor
Haworth
Shipley
WEST YORKSHIRE
Walkington
BRADFORD
Sherburn in Elmet
Bubwith
North Cave
Little Weighton
Pudsey
LEEDS
Garforth
Selby
Cliffe
South Cave
Cottingham
Newport
Monk Fryston
Morley
Ellerton
Howden
HALIFAX
Rothwell
Castleford
Brotherton
Gomersal
Cleckheaton
Batley
Ferrybridge Services
Carlton
Goole
Melton
North Ferriby
Brighouse
Hartshead Moor Services
Dewsbury
Normanton
Pontefract
Knottingley
Winteringham
WAKEFIELD
Ossett
Darrington
Burton upon Stather
Winterton
Elland
A1(M)
A19
A66
A64
A1079
M62
M621
M1

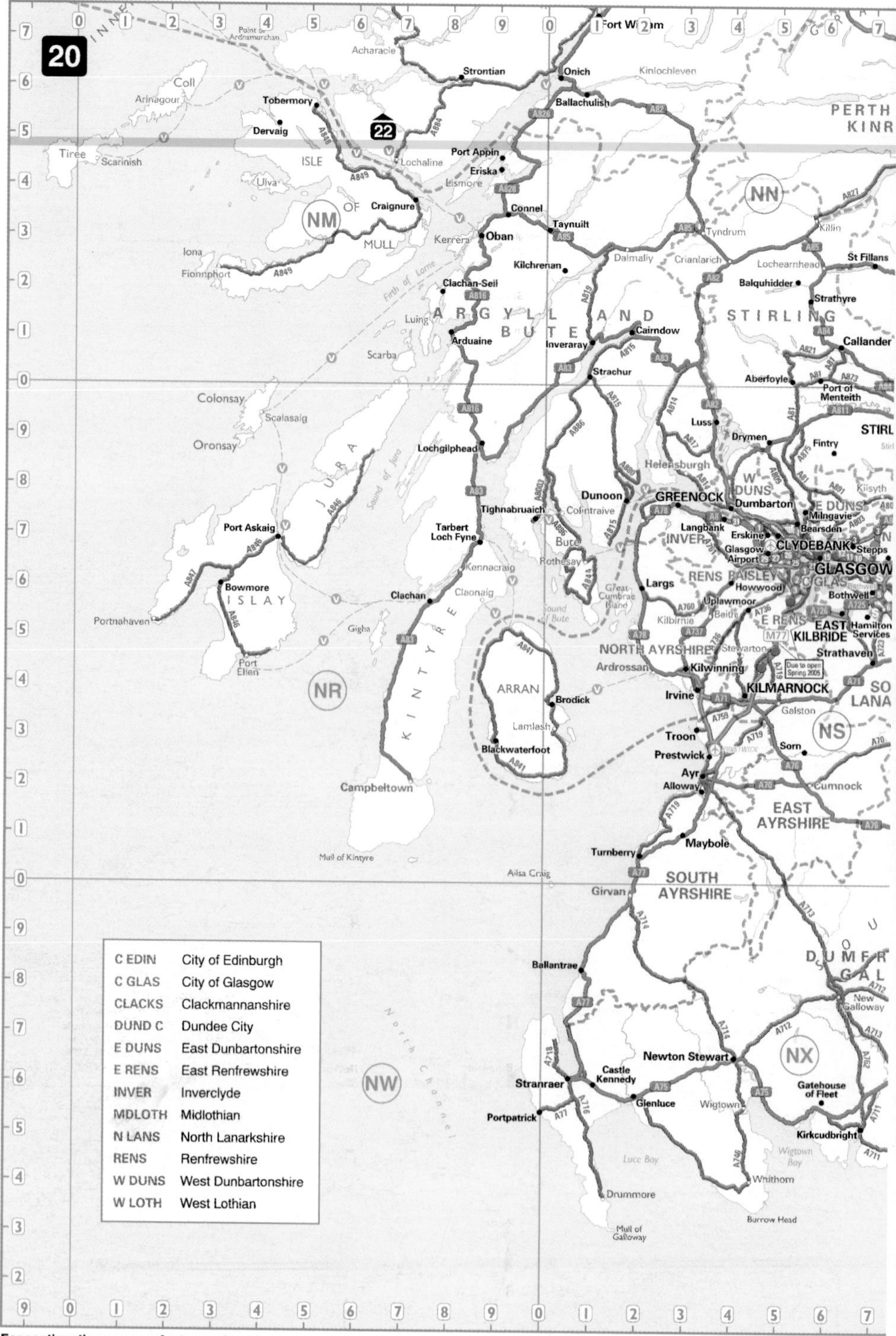

For continuation pages refer to numbered arrows

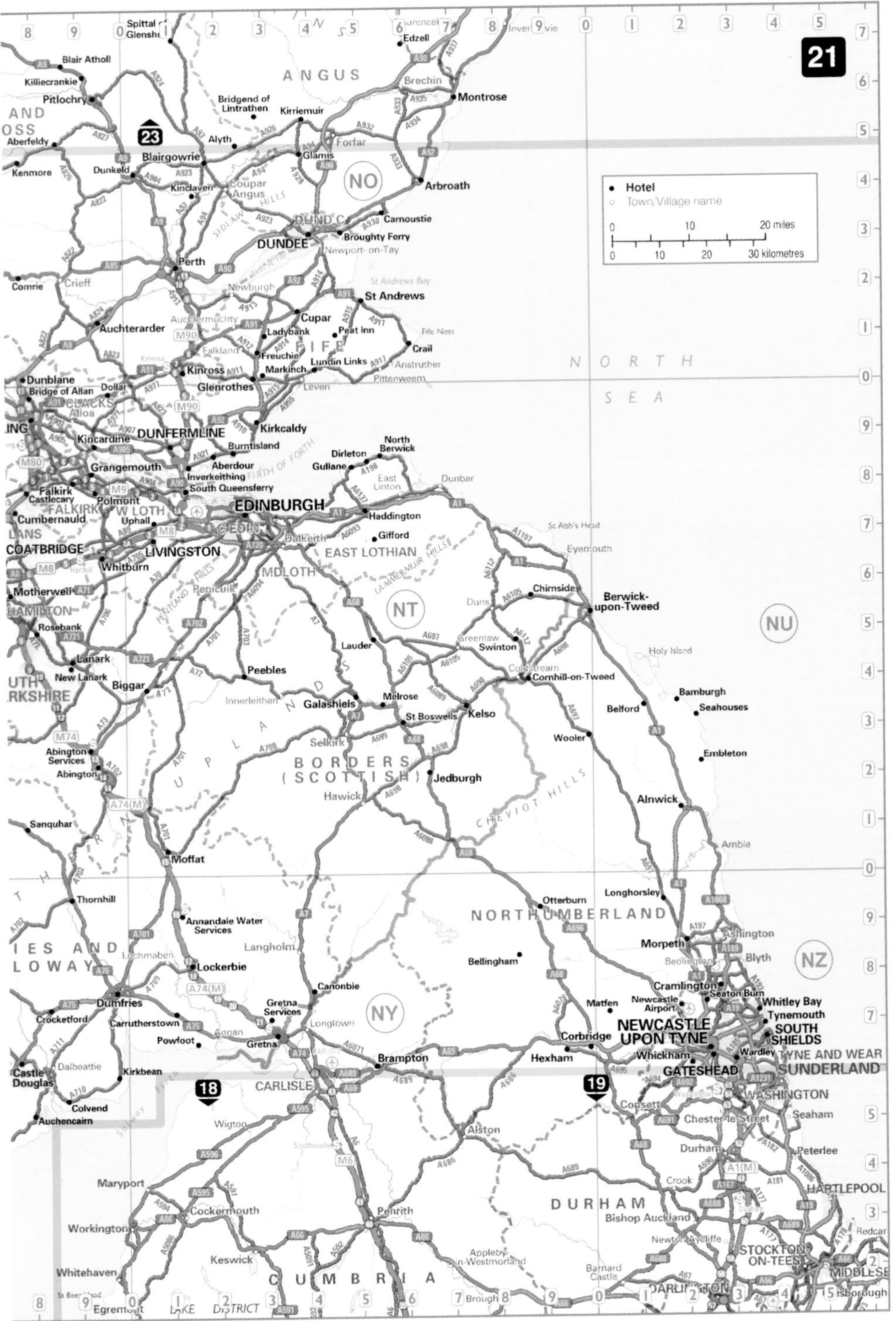

21
Hotel
Town/Village name
0 10 20 miles
0 10 20 30 kilometres
NORTH SEA
ANGUS
NO
NT
NU
NY
NZ
FIFE
EAST LOTHIAN
MIDLOTH
BORDERS (SCOTTISH)
NORTHUMBERLAND
DURHAM
CUMBRIA
CHEVIOT HILLS
LAMMERMUIR HILLS
SIDLAW HILLS
PENTLAND HILLS
FIRTH OF FORTH
LAKE DISTRICT
23
18
19
Blair Atholl
Killiecrankie
Pitlochry
Aberfeldy
Kenmore
Dunkeld
Blairgowrie
Alyth
Bridgend of Lintrathen
Kirriemuir
Edzell
Brechin
Montrose
Forfar
Glamis
Kinclaven
Coupar Angus
Arbroath
Carnoustie
DUNDEE
Broughty Ferry
Newport-on-Tay
Perth
Comrie
Crieff
Newburgh
St Andrews
Cupar
Auchterarder
Auchtermuchty
Ladybank
Peat Inn
Crail
Fife Ness
Falkland
Freuchie
Lundin Links
Anstruther
Kinross
Markinch
Pittenweem
Glenrothes
Leven
Dunblane
Bridge of Allan
Dollar
Alloa
Kirkcaldy
Kincardine
DUNFERMLINE
Burntisland
North Berwick
Dirleton
Gullane
Aberdour
Grangemouth
Inverkeithing
East Linton
Dunbar
Falkirk
Polmont
South Queensferry
EDINBURGH
Haddington
Cumbernauld
Uphall
Gifford
COATBRIDGE
LIVINGSTON
Dalkeith
St Abb's Head
Eyemouth
Whitburn
Penicuik
Chirnside
Motherwell
HAMILTON
Duns
Berwick-upon-Tweed
Rosebank
Lauder
Greenlaw
Swinton
Holy Island
Lanark
New Lanark
Peebles
Coldstream
Cornhill-on-Tweed
Biggar
Innerleithen
Galashiels
Melrose
Kelso
Bamburgh
Seahouses
Belford
St Boswells
Selkirk
Wooler
Abington Services
Abington
Embleton
Jedburgh
Hawick
Alnwick
Sanquhar
Amble
Moffat
Thornhill
Otterburn
Longhorsley
Annandale Water Services
Langholm
Morpeth
Ashington
Lochmaben
Bellingham
Bedlington
Blyth
Lockerbie
Cramlington
Seaton Burn
Canonbie
Whitley Bay
Dumfries
Gretna Services
Matfen
Newcastle Airport
Tynemouth
Crocketford
Carrutherstown
Longtown
NEWCASTLE UPON TYNE
SOUTH SHIELDS
Powfoot
Annan
Gretna
Corbridge
Whickham
Wardley
TYNE AND WEAR
Brampton
Hexham
GATESHEAD
SUNDERLAND
Dalbeattie
Castle Douglas
Kirkbean
CARLISLE
WASHINGTON
Colvend
Auchencairn
Consett
Seaham
Wigton
Alston
Chester-le-Street
Durham
Peterlee
Maryport
Crook
HARTLEPOOL
Cockermouth
Penrith
Bishop Auckland
Workington
Redcar
Newton Aycliffe
Appleby-in-Westmorland
STOCKTON-ON-TEES
Keswick
Whitehaven
Barnard Castle
DARLINGTON
MIDDLESBROUGH
Guisborough
Brough
Egremont

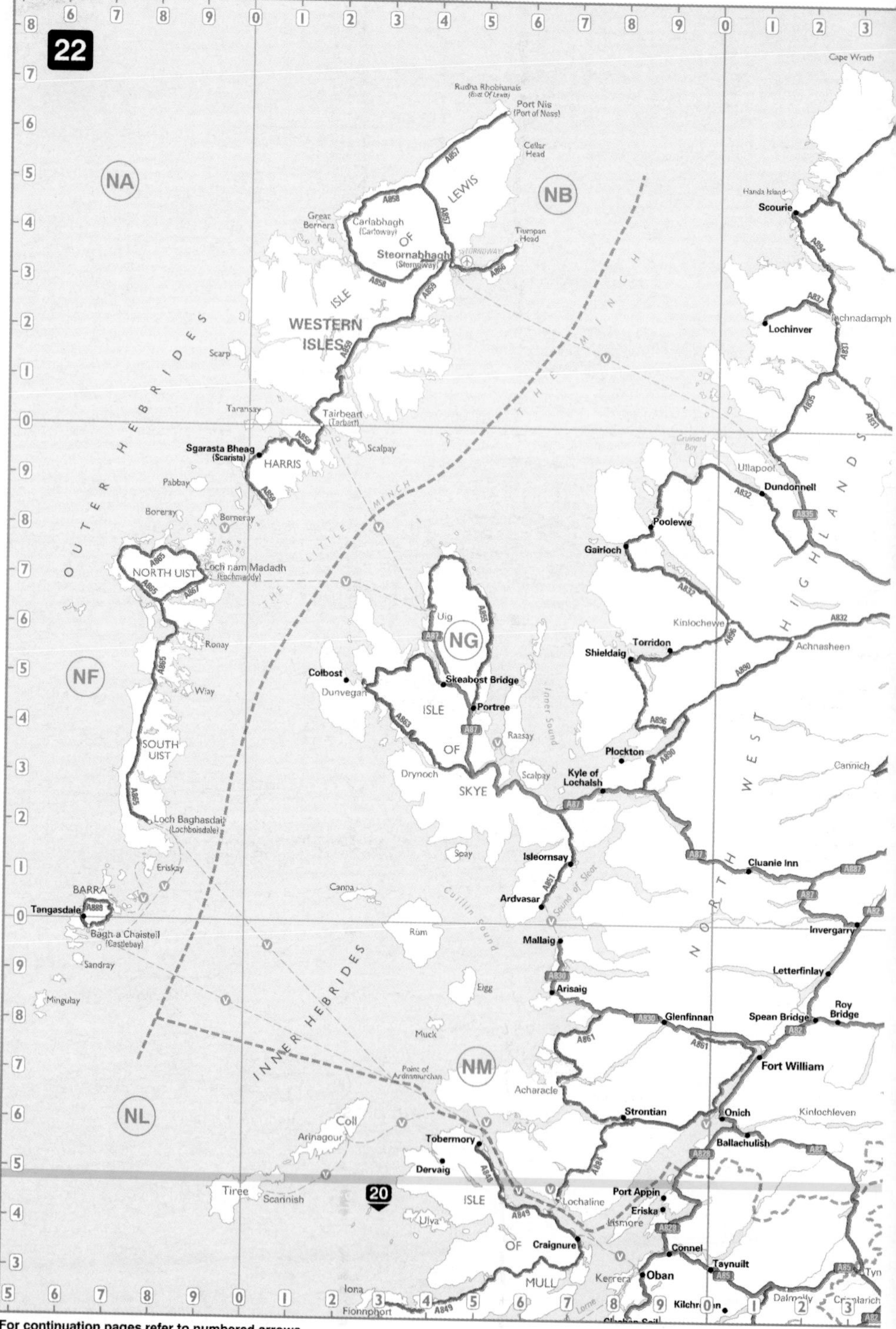

For continuation pages refer to numbered arrows

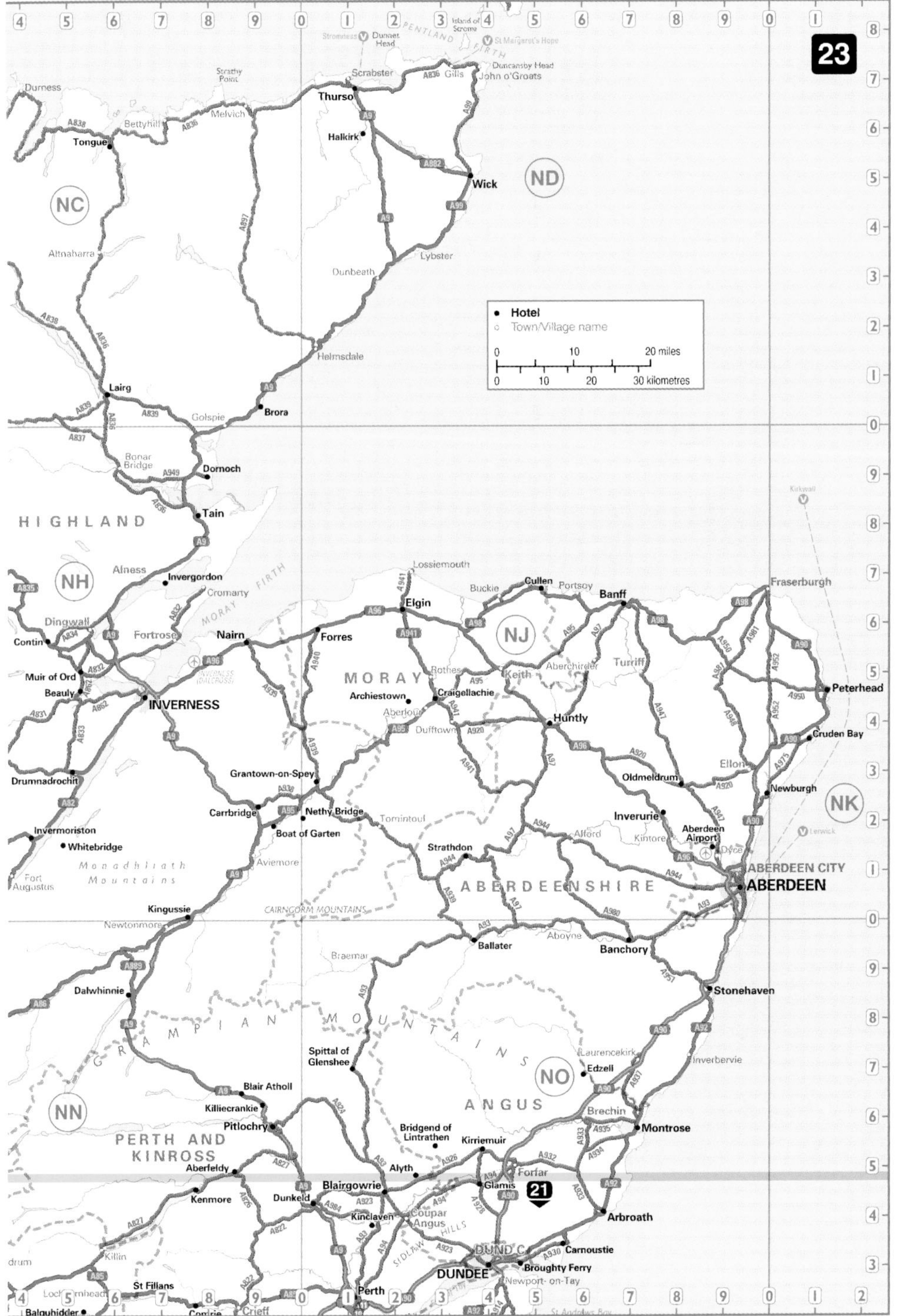

Hotel
Town/Village name
20 miles
30 kilometres
HIGHLAND
MORAY
ABERDEENSHIRE
ABERDEEN CITY
ANGUS
PERTH AND KINROSS
GRAMPIAN MOUNTAINS
CAIRNGORM MOUNTAINS
Monadhliath Mountains
MORAY FIRTH
PENTLAND FIRTH
Thurso
Halkirk
Wick
Tongue
Lairg
Brora
Dornoch
Tain
Invergordon
Nairn
Forres
Elgin
Cullen
Banff
Fraserburgh
Peterhead
Cruden Bay
Newburgh
Oldmeldrum
Inverurie
Aberdeen Airport
ABERDEEN
Huntly
Craigellachie
Archiestown
INVERNESS
Muir of Ord
Beauly
Contin
Drumnadrochit
Invermoriston
Whitebridge
Grantown-on-Spey
Carrbridge
Nethy Bridge
Boat of Garten
Kingussie
Dalwhinnie
Strathdon
Ballater
Banchory
Stonehaven
Edzell
Montrose
Spittal of Glenshee
Blair Atholl
Killiecrankie
Pitlochry
Aberfeldy
Kenmore
Dunkeld
Blairgowrie
Alyth
Bridgend of Lintrathen
Kirriemuir
Glamis
Kinclaven
Arbroath
Carnoustie
Broughty Ferry
DUNDEE
Perth
St Fillans
Balquhidder
Crieff
21

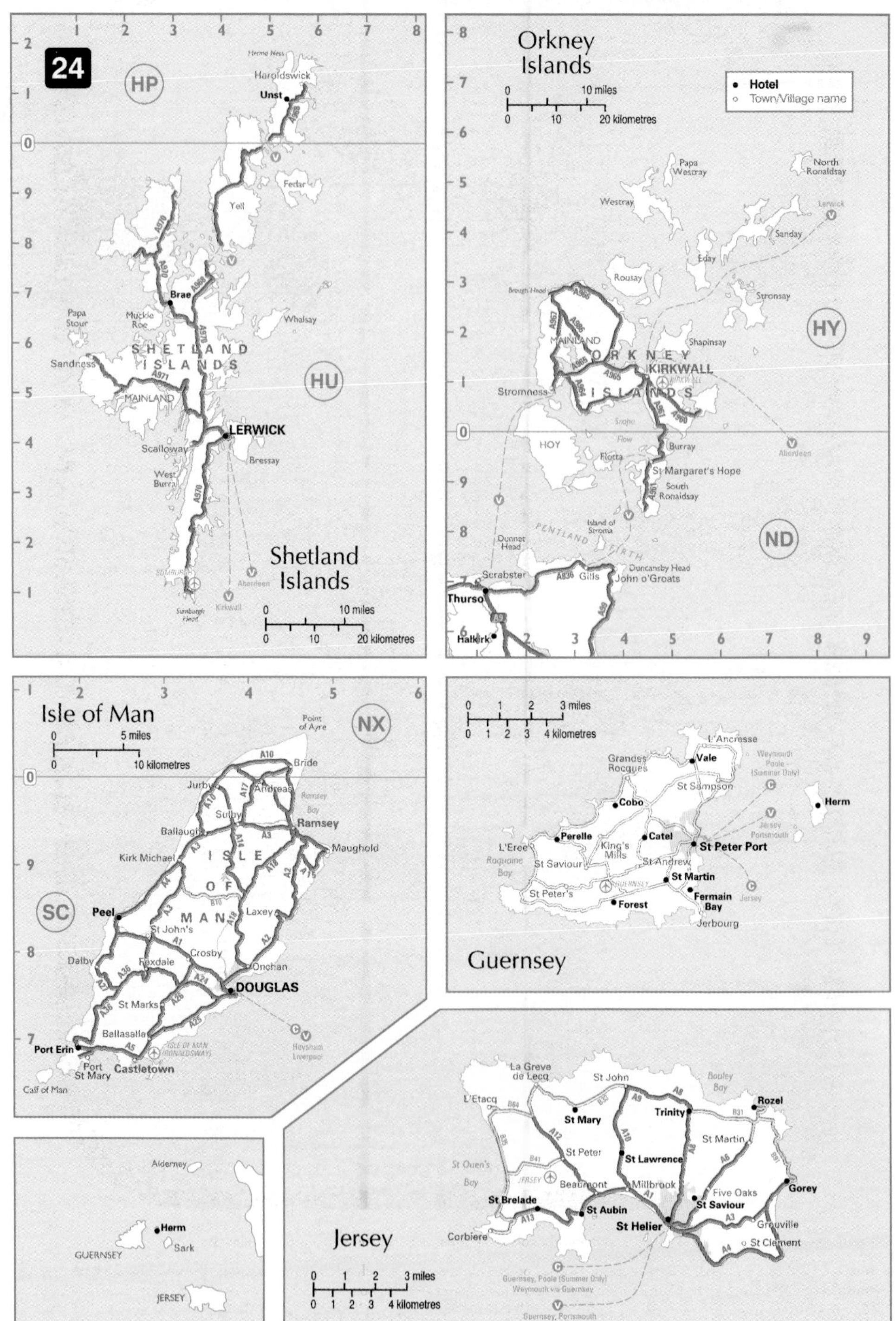
24
Shetland Islands
Orkney Islands
Isle of Man
Guernsey
Jersey
Hotel
Town/Village name
Unst
Haroldswick
Yell
Fetlar
Brae
Papa Stour
Muckle Roe
Whalsay
SHETLAND ISLANDS
Sandness
MAINLAND
LERWICK
Scalloway
Bressay
West Burra
Sumburgh Head
Kirkwall
Aberdeen
Papa Westray
North Ronaldsay
Westray
Sanday
Eday
Rousay
Stronsay
Shapinsay
ORKNEY ISLANDS
KIRKWALL
Stromness
HOY
Scapa Flow
Flotta
Burray
St Margaret's Hope
South Ronaldsay
Island of Stroma
PENTLAND FIRTH
Dunnet Head
Scrabster
Gills
John o'Groats
Duncansby Head
Thurso
Halkirk
Point of Ayre
Bride
Jurby
Andreas
Sulby
Ramsey
Ballaugh
Kirk Michael
Maughold
ISLE OF MAN
Peel
St John's
Laxey
Crosby
Dalby
Foxdale
Onchan
DOUGLAS
St Marks
Ballasalla
Port Erin
Port St Mary
Castletown
Calf of Man
Heysham
Liverpool
L'Ancresse
Vale
Grandes Rocques
St Sampson
Cobo
Herm
Perelle
Catel
L'Eree
King's Mills
St Peter Port
St Saviour
St Andrew
St Martin
St Peter's
Fermain Bay
Forest
Jerbourg
Alderney
Sark
GUERNSEY
JERSEY
La Greve de Lecq
St John
Bouley Bay
L'Etacq
St Mary
Trinity
Rozel
St Martin
St Peter
St Lawrence
St Ouen's Bay
Beaumont
Millbrook
Five Oaks
Gorey
St Brelade
St Aubin
St Saviour
St Helier
Grouville
Corbiere
St Clement
Guernsey, Poole (Summer Only)
Weymouth via Guernsey
Guernsey, Portsmouth

The Automobile Association would like to thank the following for supplying photographs for this book:

Apex City Hotel, Edinburgh 3b; Athenaeum Hotel, London 44; Beaufort Hotel, St Helier 13tr; Classic British Hotel Elstead, Bournemouth 25; Copthorne Hotel, Birmingham 42r; Crown Moran Hotel, London 4t; Exclusive Hotels: 1, 5, 9t, 16, 17, 19, 23, 45r, 46; Glenapp Castle, South Ayrshire 13 ltl; Hotel L'Horizon, St Brelade 15; The Killarney Park Hotel, Co Kerry; 13b, 24, 45l, cr; Lindeth Howe Country House Hotel, Windermere 4b; Midland Hotel, Bradford 13trt; Penmorvah Manor 22; Prestonfield, Edinburgh 13tl; Stillorgan Park Hotel, Dublin 21; Thornton Hall Hotel, Thornton Hough 43; Well House Hotel, Liskeard 42l; White Horse Hotel, Londonderry 3t; Woodlands Park 9b; The Yorkshire, Harrogate 45cl

The remaining pictures are held in the Association's own library (AA WORLD TRAVEL LIBRARY) and were taken by:Steve Day 6

Best Use of Seafood Index

The following establishments offer a wide range of seafood in their restaurants, see p.40 for more information.

ENGLAND

BERKSHIRE

CHIEVELEY	The Crab at Chieveley
MAIDENHEAD	Fredrick's Hotel
WINDSOR	Christopher Hotel

BUCKINGHAMSHIRE

AYLESBURY	Hartwell House Hotel Restaurant & Spa

CAMBRIDGESHIRE

CAMBRIDGE	Hotel Felix

CHESHIRE

ALDERLEY EDGE	Alderley Edge Hotel

CO DURHAM

ROMALDKIRK	Rose & Crown Hotel

CORNWALL & ISLES OF SCILLY

CONSTANTINE	Trengilly Wartha Inn
FALMOUTH	Greenbank Hotel
	Royal Duchy Hotel
MARAZION	Mount Haven Hotel & St Michaels Restaurant
MOUSEHOLE	Cornish Range Restaurant with Rooms
	Old Coastguard Hotel
PADSTOW	The Seafood Restaurant
PORTSCATHO	Rosevine Hotel
	Driftwood
ST MARTIN'S	St Martin's on the Isle
ST MAWES	Idle Rocks Hotel
	Rising Sun Hotel
TRURO	Alverton Manor

CUMBRIA

WINDERMERE	Lindeth Fell Country House Hotel

DEVON

ASHBURTON	Holne Chase Hotel
BRIXHAM	Quayside Hotel
EXETER	Lord Haldon Country House Hotel
	Queens Court Hotel
	St Olaves Hotel & Restaurant
GULWORTHY	The Horn of Plenty
LYNMOUTH	Rising Sun Hotel
PARKHAM	Penhaven Country House
PLYMOUTH	Langdon Court Hotel
SALCOMBE	Tides Reach Hotel
TEIGNMOUTH	Ness House Hotel
TORQUAY	Corbyn Head Hotel & Orchid Restaurant
	The Imperial
	Orestone Manor Hotel
TWO BRIDGES	Two Bridges Hotel

DORSET

BOURNEMOUTH	Chine Hotel
LYME REGIS	Alexandra Hotel
POOLE	Haven Hotel
	Mansion House Hotel
	Sandbanks Hotel

ESSEX

DEDHAM	milsoms
GREAT DUNMOW	Starr Restaurant with Rooms
HARWICH	Pier at Harwich

GLOUCESTERSHIRE

STOW-ON-THE-WOLD	Wyck Hill House Hotel
TETBURY	Calcot Manor
UPPER SLAUGHTER	Lords of the Manor

GREATER MANCHESTER

OLDHAM	Menzies Avant Hotel

HAMPSHIRE

EMSWORTH	36 on the Quay
WICKHAM	Old House Hotel & Restaurant

LINCOLNSHIRE

LINCOLN	Branston Hall Hotel
STAMFORD	The George of Stamford
WINTERINGHAM	Winteringham Fields

LONDON & GREATER LONDON

EC2	Great Eastern Hotel
SW1	The Berkeley
	Mandarin Oriental Hyde Park
	Millennium Hotel London Knightsbridge
W1	Claridge's
	The Connaught
	The Dorchester
WC1	Jurys Great Russell Street
WC2	The Savoy
HARROW WEALD	Grim's Dyke Hotel

NORFOLK

BRANCASTER STAITHE	The White Horse
BURNHAM MARKET	Hoste Arms Hotel
GRIMSTON	Congham Hall Country House Hotel
HOLKHAM	The Victoria at Holkham
SNETTISHAM	Rose & Crown
TITCHWELL	Titchwell Manor Hotel

NORTHAMPTONSHIRE

KETTERING	Kettering Park Hotel & Spa

NOTTINGHAMSHIRE

LANGAR	Langar Hall

SHROPSHIRE

LUDLOW	Dinham Hall Hotel
	Overton Grange Country House

SOMERSET

EXFORD	Crown Hotel
PORLOCK	Andrews on the Weir
SHEPTON MALLET	Charlton House & Mulberry Restaurant

SUFFOLK

ALDEBURGH	The Brudenell
LONG MELFORD	The Black Lion Hotel
LOWESTOFT	Ivy House Country Hotel
ORFORD	Crown & Castle Inn
SOUTHWOLD	The Crown
WOODBRIDGE	Seckford Hall Hotel

SUSSEX, EAST

BRIGHTON	Alias Hotel Seattle

SUSSEX, WEST

TURNERS HILL	Alexander House Hotel

TYNE & WEAR

NEWCASTLE UPON TYNE	Newcastle Marriott Hotel Gosforth Park

WARWICKSHIRE

WARWICK	Ardencote Manor Hotel, Country Club & Spa

WORCESTERSHIRE

MALVERN	The Cottage in the Wood Hotel

YORKSHIRE, NORTH

BOLTON ABBEY	The Devonshire Arms Country House
MARKINGTON	Hob Green Hotel
RAMSGILL	Yorke Arms

CHANNEL ISLANDS

GUERNSEY

COBO	Cobo Bay Hotel

SCOTLAND

ABERDEENSHIRE

NEWBURGH	Udny Arms Hotel

ARGYLL & BUTE

ERISKA	Isle of Eriska
KILCHRENAN	Taychreggan Hotel
PORT APPIN	Airds Hotel
TOBERMORY	Highland Cottage

DUMFRIES & GALLOWAY

STRANRAER	North West Castle Hotel

FIFE

ST ANDREWS	The Inn at Lathones

HIGHLAND

ISLE ORNSAY	Duisdale Country House Hotel
LOCHINVER	Inver Lodge Hotel
PORTREE	Bosville Hotel
STRONTIAN	Kilcamb Lodge Hotel

PERTH & KINROSS

DUNKELD	Kinnaird

SCOTTISH BORDERS

MELROSE	Burt's Hotel
PEEBLES	Cringletie House
	Castle Venlaw Hotel

SOUTH LANARKSHIRE

BIGGAR	Shieldhill Castle

STIRLING

DUNBLANE	Cromlix House Hotel

WESTERN ISLES

SCARISTA	Scarista House

WALES

CARDIFF

CARDIFF	Manor Parc Country Hotel & Restaurant

CEREDIGION

ABERYSTWYTH	Conrah Hotel
	Belle Vue Royal Hotel

CONWY

BETWS-Y-COED	Tan-y-Foel Country House

GWYNEDD

ABERDYFI	Penhelig Arms Hotel Restaurant

MONMOUTHSHIRE

ABERGAVENNY	Llansantffraed Court Hotel

NORTHERN IRELAND

CO DOWN

PORTAFERRY	Portaferry Hotel

CO LONDONDERRY

LONDONDERRY	Beech Hill Country House Hotel